ECONOMICS
FOR PROFESSIONAL AND BUSINESS STUDIES

R. Powell, MA., M.Sc (Econ)

Ray Powell is a lecturer in economics at Kingston College of Further Education and a Course Tutor in economics at the Open University. He is currently Chief Examiner in A-Level Economics at the Associated Examining Board and a member of the Schools Examinations and Assessment Council 18+ Committee. He is an experienced writer and educational consultant.

DP Publications Ltd
Aldine Place, 142/144 Uxbridge Road
Shepherds Bush Green
London, W12 8AA

1989

Acknowledgements

The author would like to thank the following:
THE ASSOCIATION OF ACCOUNTING TECHNICIANS (AAT)
THE CHARTERED ASSOCIATION OF CERTIFIED ACCOUNTANTS (ACCA)
THE CHARTERED INSTITUTE OF MANAGEMENT ACCOUNTANTS (CIMA)
THE INSTITUTE OF CHARTERED SECRETARIES AND ADMINISTRATORS (ICSA)
for giving permission to reproduce past examination questions.

A CIP catalogue record for this book is currently available from the British Library.

ISBN 0 905435 97 4

First published in Great Britain 1989

Printed by
The Guernsey Press Co Ltd
Braye Road, Vale
Guernsey, Channel Islands

CONTENTS

PREFACE

This manual is designed to provide full coverage of the economics syllabuses of the main professional bodies in the United Kingdom, including the ACCA, CIMA, ICSA and AAT. The manual will also prove useful for all students undertaking the first year course of an economics degree in a University, Polytechnic or College of Higher Education. Students preparing for the Institute of Bankers' examinations will find that the chapters included in the manual on money and the banking system, monetary policy, the balance of payments and exchange rates cover the syllabus for the Monetary Economics paper.

A student who conscientiously works through the manual, either by self-study or as part of a taught college course, will gain a thorough understanding of the basic principles of economics, practice in the application of these principles to current problems, and an awareness of the impact of social and technological change on business and society. The manual consists of twenty five chapters which I have chosen after a careful analysis of the syllabuses of the main professional bodies and the subject areas on which questions have been most frequently set in recent years. At the end of each chapter I have included:

- an end of chapter summary;
- self-review questions cross-referenced to appropriate sections in the chapter;
- test exercises (with answers provided at the end of Chapter 25);
- multiple choice questions (with answers also at the end of Chapter 25);
- a representative sample of examination questions drawn from a range of recent professional examination papers (with answer plans and guidance notes at the end of Chapter 25).

While writing this manual, I have tried at all times to help students to make the most of the information and skills learned in a taught college course or correspondence course, but which, sadly, many students fail to reproduce amidst the stresses and pressures of an examination. I also hope that the manual succeeds in helping students reliant on self-study to acquire the skills essential these days to do well in a modern economics examination. At all times the manual tries to explain in a clear but precise way the new developments taking place in the subject of economics, and to show how these are reflected in recent examination questions and in the answers expected by the examiners.

I wish to express my special thanks to Bob Wright of the Polytechnic of Central London, who read through the manuscript and suggested many improvements, and to my wife Christine for her encouragement and long hours spent typing the manuscript in a form fit for the printer. However, any shortcomings the book may possess are entirely my own responsibility.

Ray Powell

INTRODUCTION

The manual's aim is to help examination candidates undertaking professional examinations, or examinations at the end of the first year of a degree course, to obtain the knowledge, technique and skills, not only to be sure of passing, but also to realise what is required to achieve the highest possible grades. Professional bodies such as the ACCA and CIMA generally indicate in their published syllabuses that the standard required for a pass grade in their economics examination is equivalent to that achieved at the end of the first year of a three year economics degree course in the United Kingdom. In practice, the pass standard is probably rather lower (perhaps being more equivalent to A-level than to degree level), but it is certainly nevertheless true that to earn the highest grades, a student must display the skills and analytical ability that are required at degree level.

In general, a university first year degree course aims to give a student an idea of how economists look at the world and the techniques they use in their studies, together with a general introduction to economic theory and analysis. An important purpose of any examination is to *differentiate* and *discriminate* between candidates, so that the most able candidates score the high marks they merit, while the more limited skills and abilities of the broad mass of candidates can still be displayed and pick up the credit they deserve. Professor Roy Wilkinson of Sheffield University has identified a *pyramid of skills* which examinations in economics at this level try to test.

'Lower-level' skills of knowledge and *'factual-recall'* are at the base of the pyramid, upon which are placed in an *'incline of difficulty'* more demanding skills such as the ability to *comprehend* and *apply* economic theories in the *analysis* of an economic problem or puzzle. From the examiner's point of view, a 'good' examination question is one which both tests an important and possibly broad area of the syllabus, and also discriminates effectively between candidates in terms of their ability to handle confidently the skills of different degrees of difficulty displayed in the pyramid.

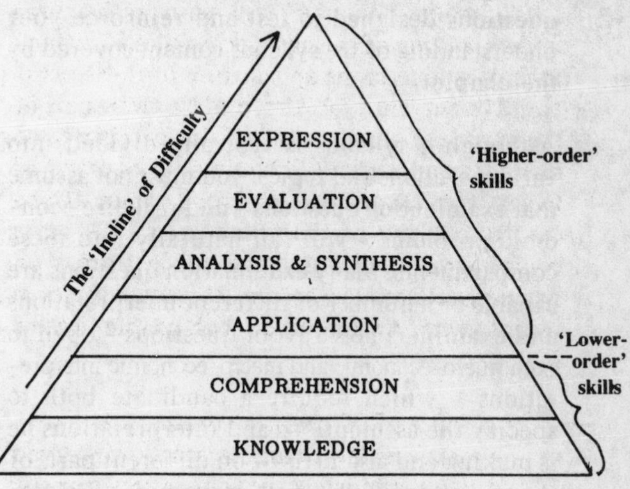

The Pyramid of Skills

The manual (and the ACCA syllabus) both follow the convention of dividing the subject broadly into two halves: **micro-economics** and **macro-economics**. **Micro-economics,** which studies the 'small' parts of the economy such as individual markets, firms and consumer behaviour, is covered first, followed by **macro-economics** in the second half of the syllabus and the manual. **Macro-economics** examines the *'large parts'* or *'aggregates'* in the economy, such as the determination of overall levels of output, employment and prices in the economy. Most teachers agree that micro-economics should be taught and studied before macro-economics is introduced, so you should organise your studies to follow the chapters in the order in which we have arranged them, thereby ensuring complete syllabus coverage. At the end of each chapter we have included

past examination questions to show how the syllabus topic has been examined in previous professional examinations. You can attempt some or all of these questions after you have completed each chapter.

Alternatively, you might prefer to leave some of the questions until you undertake your revision programme. (Answer plans and guidance notes may be found at the end of Chapter 25). At the end of each chapter we have also included **self-testing questions, exercises** and **multiple choice questions** designed to test and reinforce your understanding of the syllabus content covered by the chapter.

Although a syllabus is typically divided into various sections and topics, you must not assume that examination questions - and real-life economic problems - will fall naturally into these compartments. Many examination questions are capable of a number of different interpretations and examiners now favour questions - open to both micro-economic and macro-economic interpretations - which require a candidate both to specify the assumptions and interpretations he is making and also to draw on different parts of the syllabus if the full 'pyramid of skills' required of a good answer is to be displayed.

EXAMINATION AND REVISION TECHNIQUE

There is little doubt that essay questions in economics have become more difficult and testing over the last few years. Several years ago the examination paper included questions, and parts of questions, which tested the *'lower-order' skills* of *factual recall* and *description*. Questions answerable by factual recall can allow candidates to do well simply by 'rote-learning' pages of notes. This type of question has now fallen out of favour with examiners because it fails to discriminate between 'good' and 'bad' candidates on the basis of the ability of a good candidate to practise the *'higher-order' skills* listed in the *'pyramid of skills'*.

Once you have completed your course of study, the most daunting task still remains to be faced: to do yourself justice when presented with unseen questions amid the stresses and strains of the examination room. We shall now discuss some 'golden rules' that, if followed, should stand you in good stead and make your task rather easier, providing of course that the most useful ingredient of 'luck' is also at least a little on your side.

You can reduce the need to rely on 'luck' by preparing a properly planned revision programme. Begin your revision planning several weeks before the examination, time-tabling periods of each day when you know you can work for at least an hour - and preferably up to two or three hours - completely free of distraction. However, allow yourself a brief relaxation period every half hour or so to facilitate the absorption of what you have revised intensively in the previous period. Although you must cover the whole syllabus, concentrate on key concepts and essential economic theory rather than on descriptive fact and historical detail.

There are various methods of revision, and not all of them may suit you. It is certainly not a good idea to read through sheaves of notes or textbook chapters, or to 'rote-learn' pages of notes. Nevertheless, you must learn key concepts and definitions, though it is much more important to learn when and how to use them.

If you have studied conscientiously during your course and revised properly, once the exam is over, you will find that you have only been able to use a small fraction of your total economic knowledge. Assuming that you are able to revise in a reasonably thorough and structured way in the weeks before the examination, you must resist the temptation to work late into the night on the day preceding the examination. Answering an examination paper is a very tiring task, especially if you are to succeed in displaying the *'higher-order' skills* the questions are searching for; you need to arrive in the examination room as refreshed as possible and capable of thinking and writing clearly not just for a few minutes, but for three hours. Each year examiners are disappointed and saddened by candidates with obvious ability who start off the paper well, but who 'tail-off' towards the end of the examination through sheer tiredness rather than through a lack of knowledge.

Long-winded introductory and concluding paragraphs are probably inadvisable for many questions since they may not 'tie-in' with marks allocated on the marking scheme. Nevertheless essay questions testing *'higher-order' skills* often require a statement of the assumptions you are making when interpreting the question. Thus it is good practice to use the first paragraph both to define precisely the terms mentioned in the question and to state explicitly the assumptions you are making in your interpretation of the question. If you think that a question is open to more than one interpretation, then tell the examiner, and explain why you are choosing a particular interpretation. When many interpretations are possible, there is really no such thing as a 'single correct answer'. But try to get 'behind the question' to unravel its built-in assumptions and then use economic theory and analysis to develop a coherent line of reasoning and argument.

Every question includes at least one key instruction, calling for example for a **discussion, explanation, assessment, evaluation, comparison or a contrast.** As we have noted, very few essay questions can be answered simply by an uncritical historical account or by mere factual description. A principal purpose of an essay question in economics is to test whether you can introduce basic and relatively simple economic theory and analysis in a clear and reasoned way to cast light on a particular problem specified in the question. In this manual, we have included difficult and more advanced theories where relevant to the syllabus and to particular types of examination question, but a 'golden rule' is: *simple theories used well are always preferable to convoluted and difficult theoretical explanation obviously misunderstood by a candidate.*

Questions asking for a comparison or contrast ought not to be answered with two separate accounts. Strictly, a *'comparison'* notes points of similarity whereas a *'contrast'* draws attention to points of difference. It is also important to avoid confusing questions which ask for a discussion of *causes* with those concerned with the *economic effects* resulting from a particular event or change in the economy, or from a particular government policy. When you discuss causes or effects, always remember the central importance in market economies of the *price mechanism* and of the concept of the *margin.*

Most economic change occurs at the margin in response to movements in relative price or income, as economic agents decide that it is no longer worthwhile to engage in earlier patterns of economic behaviour. When change occurs, *small adjustments* rather than *massive structural upheaval* are the rule. And change usually takes a time to work through. A *trigger event, event A* (such as a major crop failure or a change in government policy), may directly cause *event B*, which in turn causes *event C* and so on. Usually, the immediate direct effects of A on B are easier to predict than the indirect effects that occur later and further down the 'causal chain'. The chain of events between initial cause and ultimate effect may be either *dampened* or *explosive*. With a dampened sequence, event B is smaller or milder than event A, and C is milder than B and so on. By contrast, a 'causal chain' is explosive when each succeeding event is stronger or more powerful than the preceding one. As a general rule, economic chains are likely to be dampened rather than explosive because most economic changes are ultimately 'absorbed' through relative price changes and minor adjustments at the margin. But feed-backs can complicate cause and effect. A **feed-back** occurs in a sequence of events when for example, event B feeds back to change the variable associated with the original event A. When discussing economic cause and effect, you should at all times avoid being dogmatic and remember that in economics it is often the case that 'everything depends upon everything else'.

Finally a few words about diagrams and graphs. Many, and perhaps most, economic theories can be explained using one of three methods of exposition: *a written account; a graph; or by means of algebra.* Unless a question specifies otherwise, choose the method of exposition which you can handle most confidently and with which you feel most comfortable. Algebra has the advantages of precision and brevity, but many economics students lack confidence and sufficient practice in manipulating algebraic equations. If you engage in a long or full written account of a theory or piece of analysis, by all means introduce diagrams or graphs if they appropriately add to the explanation. However, they should complement rather than simply repeat the information you are providing in written form. Candidates often draw diagrams which fail to earn any extra marks yet which waste valuable examination time. A 'golden rule' is: *if you cannot correctly remember a particular graph then leave it out.* Wrongly drawn graphs serve no purpose other than to signal in the clearest possible way that you have failed to understand properly the theory you are trying to explain.

1. Economic systems

INTRODUCTION

1. This manual is written for students studying for professional qualifications in accountancy and in related business subjects, who live in a wide variety of countries and **economic systems** throughout the world. In this introductory chapter to the manual, we ask you to think about the nature of the economy in which you live, and we also introduce you to types of economic system very different from your own country. If you live in the United Kingdom or in a similar **industrialised or developed economy**, then you are working and living in a **mixed economy**. In a mixed economy, most of the food you eat has probably been grown on a family-owned farm, either within the country or overseas, then delivered to market by a private transportation firm, and finally sold to you either by a small family-owned shop or by a supermarket chain owned privately by a large company. The same is true for most of the goods and services which you purchase in shops and stores: they have been **privately produced** and are sold to you through **the market**. But this is not true of all the goods and services consumed in a mixed economy. Much of education and health care, together with other services such as road, police and national defence are provided by the state, with **planners** rather than the market deciding how much is produced and made available. Yet a third type of provision in mixed economies is by **nationalised industries**, which are industries owned by state but selling their output at a price and through the market. Thus mixed economies are complex economic systems, containing a **mix of market and non-market provision** and **private and public ownership** of the means of producing the goods and services you eventually consume.

But not all economies are mixed economies and even if you live in a mixed economy, it has not always existed, nor will it necessarily continue to exist for ever. In this chapter, we examine how mixed economies have come into existence and where they may be going. We also survey briefly other types of economic system in the developed and developing worlds and explain how all economic systems must face up to the **problem of scarcity**, which is usually regarded as the fundamental economic problem. We shall, however, take the opportunity in this chapter to examine briefly a type of economy fundamentally different in important respects to the mixed and market economies studied in the rest of this manual. This is the **Soviet economy**, an example of a **centrally planned economy**.

WHAT IS ECONOMICS?

"Economics is the science which studies human behaviour as a relationship between ends and scarce means which have alternative uses."

> *Professor Lionel Robbins in an Essay on the Nature and Significance of Economic Science, 1932.*

"An economic system is a set of institutional arrangements whose function is to employ most efficiently scarce resources to meet the ends of society."

> *The United Nations Dictionary of the Social Science, 1964.*

2. Although economists disagree amongst themselves about many things, including how best to define their subject, by focussing attention on the **central economic problem of scarcity** and **resource allocation**, Professor Lionel Robbin's long-established definition provides perhaps the most well-known starting point for introducing and understanding what economics is about. Economics is literally the study of **economising** – the study of how human beings **make choices on what to produce, how to produce and for whom to produce**, in a world in which most of the resources are limited. Although the problem of scarcity is fundamental and common to all forms of human society, from humble tribal groupings of hunters or gatherers in the Amazonian forest, to rich national states such as the United States of America, different societies have produced different institutional frameworks and methods for allocating scarce resources among competing uses. The set of institutions within which a community decides what, how and for whom to produce is called an **'economic system'**.

THE METHOD OF ALLOCATING RESOURCES

3. Perhaps the most widely used method of defining and classifying economic systems is according to the **allocative mechanism** by which scarce resources reach the people who eventually consume or use them. Although there are a variety of ways in which wealth and purchasing power can be allocated amongst individuals, including inheritance and other types of gift, theft and luck or chance such as winning a fortune on the football pools, the two allocative mechanisms by which economic systems are defined are the **market mechanism** (or **price mechanism**) and the **command mechanism** (or **planning mechanism**). An economic system in which goods and services are purchased through the price mechanism in a system of markets is called a **market economy**, whereas one in which government officials or planners allocate economic resources to firms and other productive enterprises is called a **command economy.**

MARKET ECONOMIES

4. In a **pure market economy**, it would be the **market mechanism** (the **'price mechanism', the 'price system'** or simply **'market forces'**) that performs the central economic task of allocating scarce resources amongst competing uses. A market economy comprises a large number of markets varying in the degree to which they are separated and interrelated to each other. A **market** is a meeting of buyers and sellers in which goods or services are exchanged for other goods or services. Occasionally, the exchange is direct and is known as **barter**. More usually, however, the exchange is indirect through the **medium of money**. One good or service, such as labour, is exchanged for money which is then traded a second time for other goods or services, sometimes immediately but more usually, after a time delay. The exchange must be voluntary; if one party forces a transaction upon the other (economists call this **'force majeur'**), it is not a market transaction. While some markets exist in a particular geographical location, eg a street market and the Lloyds Insurance Market, many markets do not, though transport costs and lack of information may create barriers which separate or break up markets. In past centuries such barriers often prevented markets from operating outside the relatively small geographical areas of a single country or even a small region within a country. But in recent years, developments in modern communications which allow goods to be transported more easily and at lower cost, and in the transmission of market information via telephone and telex, have enabled many markets, especially commodity and raw material markets and markets in financial services, to become truly global or international markets functioning on a world-wide basis.

Markets are *decentralised* and *unorganised* in the sense that there is no government or central authority to decide how much is going to be traded and how much each buyer or seller in the market must trade. The three principal conditions necessary for a market to operate are:

(i) the individual buyers and sellers decide what, how, how much, where and when to trade or exchange;

(ii) they do so with reference to their self-interest and to the alternatives or opportunities open to them;

(iii) prices convey to the market participants information about self-interest and opportunities; for a market to allocate resources between different lines or activity and to co-ordinate the activities of the separate but interdependent units that make up an economy, prices must respond to the forces of supply and demand.

THE FUNCTIONS OF PRICES

5. In a market economy, prices perform two essential functions:

(i) **The signalling function.** Prices signal what is available, conveying the information which allows all the traders in the market to plan and co-ordinate their economic activities. Markets will function inefficiently, sometimes breaking down completely or leading to **'market failure'**, if prices signal wrong or misleading information.

(ii) **The incentive function.** For markets to operate in an orderly and efficient manner the buyers and sellers in the market must respond to the incentives provided by the price mechanism.

Suppose that in a particular market demand rises relative to supply, causing the market price to rise. An immediate result is that the rising price serves to limit to some extent the increase in the demand for the good or service which has now become more expensive compared to other goods, thereby creating an incentive for consumers to economise in its use. But simultaneously, the possibility of higher profits creates an incentive for firms to shift resources into producing the goods and services whose relative price has risen and to demand more resources such as labour and capital in order to increase production. In turn this may bid up wages and the price of capital, causing households and the owners of capital to switch the supply of labour and capital into industries where the prices of inputs or factors of production are rising. In this way, the changing prices of goods and services relative to each other allocate the economy's scarce resources to the consumers and firms who are willing and able to pay most for them in the pursuit of what they perceive to be their self-interest.

COMMAND ECONOMIES

6. A **complete command economy** would be an economy in which all decisions about what, how, how much, where and for whom to produce would be taken by a **central planning authority** issuing commands or directives to all the households and producers in the society. Such a system could only exist within a very rigid and probably totalitarian political framework because of the restrictions on individual decision-making that are obviously implied. In fact in much the same way that a pure market economy, in which the price mechanism alone allocates resources, is a theoretical abstraction, so no economy in the real world in which we live can properly be described as a complete or pure command economy.

It has been calculated for example that in a large economy the size of the Soviet Union, a central authority would have to issue over 200 billion orders in respect to just a single commodity if the authority were to decide exactly how much each household must consume as well as the quantity each enterprise must produce. Quite clearly, it would be completely impossible for an economy to be organised in this way. In the real world, command economies are therefore **planned economies with some household choice.** The command or planning system makes the production decisions of what, how and how much to produce, allocating resources to particular industries and productive units. But households and individual consumers are free to choose the final goods (or consumer goods) they wish to buy, subject to availability. A **central plan** may be used to allocate resources to industries and productive units which are then required to meet the output targets of the master plan. Central planners may set the prices of essential consumer goods such as meat and bread, allowing factory managers to set prices of less essential goods. Prices set by the central planners to ration goods and services which are scarce in relation to an overwhelming unfilled consumer demand are known as **shadow prices.** By seeking to ration demand in relation to supply, the prices set by the central planners resemble or 'shadow' market prices. However, market prices would provide incentives for producers to enter or leave industries, as well as incentives for housebounds to modify their consumption behaviour. The first of these incentives is lacking in a command economy, unless planners and factory managers are able to respond to the signals of scarcity by diverting more resources into the particular industry.

THE SOVIET ECONOMY

7. Because the subsequent chapters of this book are largely devoted to market and mixed economies, we shall take the opportunity in this chapter to describe how the planning mechanism operates in the largest and best known command economy in the world, the Soviet Union. As in all command economies, the economic decision makers or planners are ultimately the political authorities, the Communist Party of the Soviet Union, and the aims of the planners reflect the desired economic, social and political objectives of the Communist Party. These include a wish to prove the superiority of socialist planning over the western market economies and the possibly conflicting aims of improving living standards while maintaining a very large output of military goods and weapons.

Like other command economies, the Soviet Union is a centrally planned economy, though because of the problems involved in planning output to match consumer demands and needs, important aspects of planning are locally delegated. The key framework of Soviet planning is the **Five Year Plan**, the current one covering 1986-90 being the twelfth since the Soviet Communist Party came to power, but the key economic unit is the industrial enterprise, the equivalent of a firm in a market economy. The overall level and composition of gross industrial output in the Five Year Plan is decided by the **State Planning Committee**, known as **Gosplan.**

Between Gosplan and the 44,000 industrial enterprises which ultimately implement the plan is a hierarchy of sixty ministries each looking after a particular sector of the economy with jurisdiction over industrial associations, which are groupings of industrial enterprises in the same line of economic activity brought together for planning purposes. In the Five Year Plan, Gosplan sets targets for individual industries which the appropriate ministry divides into individual plans for its associations and enterprises. Having received the plan, the enterprises then feed back to Gosplan through the associations and ministries requests for the inputs necessary to produce their output. At this stage, any failure by Gosplan to ensure that the output plan and the input requests are consistent with each, will lead to some enterprises failing to fulfil the plan and possible shortages of vital goods and services. Because of the immense difficulties of performing this task of matching the output plan and input requests across the 44,000 enterprises in the Industrial Sector of the Soviet economy as well as across other sectors including agriculture and construction, the planners in fact concentrate on just a small number of key industrial goods such as steel and chemicals, leaving less vital industries effectively to plan themselves. Once the output plan has been decided, the supply of inputs is taken over by a second **State Committee on Material Technical Supply (Gossnab)**. Gossnab sends out instructions to each enterprise, indicating the other enterprises to approach either for the supply of inputs or for the sale of the enterprise's own output.

Complementing the Five Year Plan is an **annual plan** which follows the same pattern but which elaborates and if necessary amends the Five Year Plan provisions for that year. The annual plan instructs each enterprise on the output to be produced, its technical specifications, the inputs the enterprise can receive and sets out investment, productivity and profit targets. Although Soviet enterprises are not 'profit maximisers', in the sense that firms in western market economies are often assumed to be, financial incentives have been used since the 1960s to try to ensure the success of the plan. Bonuses are paid out of profits, so managers and workers have an incentive to ensure the profitability of the enterprise. But fulfilling the plan is probably a more important objective for Soviet enterprises than making a profit. Enterprises cannot be made bankrupt or taken-over, and workers cannot be made redundant. If losses are made, the State pays the wages, wage levels other than bonuses having been planned centrally in another section of the Five Year Plan. Besides the formidable difficulty of marrying together all the inputs and outputs of the different sectors and enterprises in the Soviet economy, a number of other problems may prevent the successful fulfilment of the Soviet plans. The timing of production is important. Ideally, enterprises should produce their output so as to be able to deliver to other enterprises at just the moment when the goods are required, but in practice production may be rushed, with quality and workmanship suffering to meet the deadline of the plan rather than the needs of customers. Further problems occur because enterprises feed misleading information to the planners. By exaggerating their input requirements and understating their true productive capacity, enterprise managers can over-fulfill their plans, thereby obtaining both praise and honour within Soviet society and financial reward. And by understating its true productivity capacity, an enterprise can lure the Soviet central planners into setting in the next plan a target which is easier to achieve and lower than the planners would have set were they in possession of correct information about the enterprise.

OWNERSHIP AND ECONOMIC SYSTEMS

8. In this chapter so far we have referred only indirectly to the **ownership of the economy**, implying that a market economy is associated with **private ownership of the means of production, distribution and exchange (private enterprise)**, while in a command economy such as the Soviet

Union, ownership rests with the state. For many purposes it is better to define economic systems in terms of ownership rather than in terms of the market and command mechanisms. This approach is particularly favoured by Marxist economists, who are interested in how economic systems have developed historically and in how one type of system has evolved into another, sometimes gradually, but sometimes through violent revolution. According to **Karl Marx**, all societies must eventually pass through six historical stages of economic development: **primitive or tribal communism; slavery; feudalism; capitalism; socialism; and communism.** For much of his working life in the middle and latter years of the 19th century, Karl Marx lived in Great Britain which, during the 18th and 19th centuries, had been the first country to industrialise and the first economy dominated by capitalism. **Capitalism** is usually defined as a system in which the means of production are privately owned by individuals (or capitalists) who employ labour to combine with the capital they own in order to produce an output for sale at a profit. Marx believed that economic systems are constantly changing and evolving. However, at any one time a particular system, such as capitalism, may dominate a country's economy or indeed the world economy because, with the prevailing state of technology and available methods of production, the system is efficient at solving the central economic problem of scarcity. Thus capitalism evolved in the United Kingdom economy in the 18th and 19th centuries, because of its superiority over earlier systems, such as feudalism, as a method of organising production in an industrialising economy.

CAPITALISM, SOCIALISM AND COMMUNISM

9. During the 19th century a powerful industrial capitalist economy came into existence in the United Kingdom, followed later in the century by a similar growth of industrial capitalism in other European countries and in the United States and Japan. Karl Marx admired the efficiency of capitalism as a method of organising production, but he believed that capitalism contained within itself important contradictions resulting from the exploitation by capitalists of workers for profit. Marx thought that these contradictions would eventually lead to the replacement of capitalism by socialism. Thus Marx regarded capitalism and the market economy with which it is usually associated as essentially a transitory stage in the development of economic society, giving way first to socialism and eventually to communism. **Socialism** is an economic system in which the means of production are socially owned by all the people, but with control usually resting in a centralised and powerful state. Modern command economies such as the Soviet Union, the Peoples Republic of China and Cuba are socialist economies which were created by people who believed in the Marxist doctrines we have just described. Following Karl Marx, the Communist Parties which rule the centrally planned socialist economies today, believe that eventually socialism will give way to **communism**, which they regard as a 'higher' form of economic system in which the all-powerful centralised state withers away as economic and political power becomes delegated to local communes. As yet however, there are few signs of this happening and most non-communists believe that it will never happen. In economic terms, the command economies of the world today are socialist rather than communist, even though economic and political power lies in the hands of the Communist Parties that rule them.

THE STAGES OF ECONOMIC GROWTH

10. Most economists who live and work in Western economies reject the Marxist historical theory we have just described, regarding it as too mechanical and deterministic. In particular, they reject the Marxist argument that capitalism and the market economy, containing the seeds of their own destruction, will inevitably be replaced by socialism and the command economy. Perhaps the best known non-Marxist theory to explain how economic societies change was put forward by the American economist, **W W Rostow**. Rostow believes that economies go through **five stages of economic development: the Traditional Society,** the **Traditional Society Preparing for 'Take-off', the 'Take-off', the Drive to Maturity,** and the **Age of High Mass-Consumption.**

(i) **The Traditional Society.** Traditional societies are very primitive and usually poor societies in which very little changes from generation to generation and in which tradition, or generally accepted customs and persistent patterns of relationship between people, govern economic life. Traditional societies face a low ceiling or limit to their total production which, because of limited available methods of production, is largely agricultural. Historically, traditional societies existed in medieval Europe and much later in other parts of the world, surviving today sometimes in tribal societies in remote areas of countries such as Brazil and India and in much of Africa.

(ii) **The Traditional Society preparing for 'Take-off'**. This is the period of history in which a traditional society prepares to develop into a more productive and advanced economy. People begin to accept that change is possible and various preconditions for successful industrial growth begin to appear. These include the establishment of an effective nation state and the emergence of enterprising men and women wishing to modernise the economy. Scope for commerce and trade appears, along with banks and other financial institutions for the mobilisation of savings into productive investment.

(iii) **The 'Take-off'**. Rostow identifies the 'Take-off' as the great watershed in the life of modern societies, when the old blocks and resistances to steady economic growth are overcome and the forces making for economic progess which had previously been limited, expand and come to dominate society. The 'Take-off' into self-sustaining growth is normally associated with **'Industrial Revolution'** or the change from a largely agricultural to an industrialised or manufacturing economy. As new industries expand, a new class of entrepreneurs or capitalists reinvest the profits received from earlier investments into new manufacturing plant and capacity. At the same time, important developments in technology are applied to improving production in both manufacturing and agriculture.

(iv) **The Drive to Maturity**. Rostow believes that the Drive to Maturity is a period lasting approximately 60 years immediately following the 'Take-off', in which modern technology and methods of production are extended across a much wider area of economic activity. During the 'Take-off' economic development focuses around a relatively narrow range of industries, for example mining and 'heavy' industries such as iron and steel, but during the drive to maturity, the range of industries is extended and technologically more complex processes are adopted. Germany, the United Kingdom, France and the United States had passed through the Drive to Maturity by 1900 or shortly after. Rostow identifies a mature economy as one 'which demonstrates the capacity to move beyond the original industries which powered its take-off and to absorb and to apply efficiently over a wide range of its resources the most advanced fruits of the (then) modern technology. The Drive to Maturity is a stage in which an economy demonstrates that it has the technological and entrepreneurial skills to produce not everything, but anything it chooses to produce'.

(v) **The Age of High Mass Consumption**. According to Rostow, the United States reached the final stage of economic development, the Age of High Mass Consumption, in the 1920s and again, following an interruption caused by the Great Depression of the 1930s, in the 1940s and 1950s. Western European countries and Japan entered the Age of High Mass Consumption in the 1950s. Rostow believes that as societies have achieved maturity in the twentieth century, two things have happened: real income per head has risen to a point where a large number of persons have gained a command over consumption which has transcended basic food, shelter and clothing; and the structure of the working force has changed in ways which have increased not only the proportion of urban to total population, but also the proportion working in offices or in skilled factory jobs - aware of and anxious to acquire the consumption fruits of a mature economy. In the Age of High Mass Consumption, continued extension of modern technology, though important, ceases to be society's overriding objective. Through the political process, Western societies have chosen to allocate increased resources to social welfare and security, the Welfare State being a sign of society's movement beyond technical maturity. But at the same time and in response to the purchasing power exercised in the market by consumers with incomes to spend, the Age of High Mass Consumption is the stage of development at which resources tend increasingly to be directed to the production of consumer durables such as automobiles and television sets and to the diffusion of services on a mass basis.

THE SECTORS OF AN ECONOMY

11. On several occasions in this chapter, we have referred to the sectors of an economy without defining precisely what we mean. A **sector** is simply a division or part of the economy. One method of dividing an economy into sectors is based on the type of economic activity or industry involved. The economy can be divided into **primary, secondary** and **tertiary** industrial sectors. The **primary sector** contains extractive industries, also known as basic industries such as agriculture, fishing, forestry and mining and quarrying. Primary industries literally extract raw materials and foodstuffs from the resources of the earth's surface. Raw materials produced by the primary sector then serve as the inputs of the secondary or manufacturing sector. **Secondary manufacturing** industries eventually convert or process raw materials into finished or final goods which satisfy consumer wants and needs. The last of the three great sectors is the **tertiary sector** which contains service industries, such as financial services, administration, transport and entertainment industries.

CAPITAL GOODS AND CONSUMER GOODS

12. For many purposes it is useful to divide the secondary or manufacturing sector into **capital goods** and **consumer goods sub-sectors. Capital goods** which are also known as **producers' goods, investment goods** and **intermediate goods**, are not bought by households for final consumption; instead they are bought by other firms as raw materials or inputs for the purposes of production. The capital goods industries, many of which are 'heavy' industries, include the iron and steel, mechanical engineering and chemical industries. As their name suggests, **consumer goods** or **final goods** are bought by persons or households for the purpose of final consumption, to satisfy wants and needs. It is wrong to think of a clear and arbitrary line separating the consumer goods industries from the capital goods industries. For example a car, the product of the automobile industry, could be a capital good or a consumer good depending on use, and it might switch from one category to the other at different times of day. When driven by a company sales representative for business purposes during the day the car is a capital good, but if used for private pleasure out of business hours, it is functioning as a consumer good. Cars, television sets, washing machines and similar goods purchased by individuals or households for ordinary consumer use are examples of **consumer durables**, consumer goods with a long average life during which they deliver a 'stream' of consumer services. In contrast, a **non-durable consumer good**, such as a packet of soap powder needs replacing after it has been used. Some consumer durable goods, especially housing, are bought for investment purposes as well as for the consumer services they deliver to the households who benefit from them. Indeed, housing is often classified as a capital good rather than as a consumer good, even though the main purchasers and users of housing are ordinary private individuals rather than businesses.

THE CHANGING SECTORS OF THE ECONOMY

13. Figure 1.1 as shown on the following page illustrates how at different stages of economic development and growth, the primary, secondary and tertiary sectors of an economy assume a different relative importance and size. In pre-industrial or traditional societies, agriculture and related activities form the largest part of the economy, which is therefore dominated by primary activity with very small secondary and tertiary sectors. Indeed, in true traditional societies, the secondary sector is restricted largely to village crafts such as shoe repairing and weaving, not yet having developed the factory or 'industrialised' production typical of the manufacturing sector in more advanced economies.

In the process of industrialisation, during Rostow's stages of 'Take-off' and the 'Drive to Maturity', the secondary or manufacturing sector grows to becomes the largest and dominant sector of the economy. During the earlier stages of industrialisation, capital goods or heavy industry are usually more important than the production of consumer goods. But as the economy matures and develops a wider range of manufacturing industries, consumer goods gradually become more important. Eventually however, the tertiary sector grows even faster than the secondary sector, becoming the largest sector in the economy during the Age of High Mass Consumption. Indeed, according to some commentators, mature industrialised economies in Western Europe and North America, including the

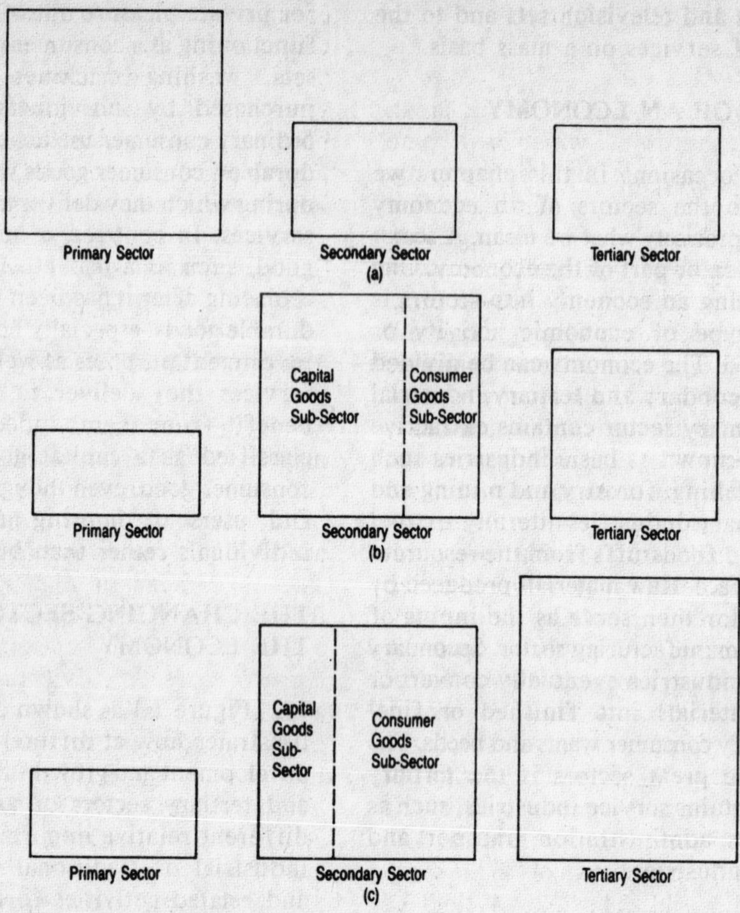

Figure 1.1: The relative sizes of the sectors of an economy at different stages of economic development:

(a) pre-industrial societies;
(b) industrialising societies;
(c) mature industrial societies.

United Kingdom, have entered a new **post-industrial** phase of development in which the secondary or manufacturing sector of the economy declines. Personal incomes remain high but the demand for consumer goods is now met by imports from **newly-industrialising countries (NICs)** entering their own 'Drives to Maturity'. The NICs are located in the Far East and other part of the developing world.

In the more successful post-industrial societies, any decline in manufacturing has usually been offset by a growth of the service sector sufficient to ensure that living standards continue to rise. Any increase in unemployment is relatively modest. But in less successful post-industrial economies, such as the United Kingdom, the decline of traditional manufacturing industries, known these days as the **de-industrialisation process**, has been rapid and great. In the United Kingdom the growth of employment in the service sector and new manufacturing industries benefitting from new technologies has failed to replace the declining employment in older industries. Total manufacturing output has stagnated or grown at a very slow rate. Thus persistently high unemployment, concentrated especially in the regions of manufacturing decline, has been perhaps the main manifestation of the de-industrialisation process and of post-industrial society.

DEVELOPED AND DEVELOPING ECONOMIES

14. Economies such as the United States, Japan and much of Western Europe, which have come through all five of Rostow's stages of economic growth and which contain large manufacturing sectors but even larger service sectors, are often referred to simply as **developed economies.** Other countries then comprise the **'developing' world**, a rather unsatisfactory and 'catch-all' label since it includes at one extreme countries of very great poverty lacking almost any form of modern development and at the other extreme **newly industrial countries (NICs)** such as Singapore and Hong Kong which have become more industrialised and urbanised than any country in the 'industrialised' or 'developed' world. Collectively, all the countries of the developing world are called the **less developed countries (LDCs).** Other labels often used to describe a country's state of development and sometimes also its political system include **'North'** and **'South'**, and the **first, second** and **third worlds.** Most of the developed industrialised economies are located in the northern part of the northern hemisphere. The countries of the **'South'** are the tropical and sub-tropical LDCs lying on the whole to the south of the developed world. The **'North'** does of course include countries such as Australia and New Zealand which are further south than any countries of the 'South' proper, but most of their population and economic development has occurred in similar non-tropical or temperate climatic zones to those of other countries in the 'North'.

The first and second worlds are part of the 'North', the **first world** comprising the developed 'western' market or capitalist economies of North America, Western Europe and Japan. The socialist and command economies of the Soviet Union and other 'Eastern Block' countries form the **second world,** which is less highly developed than the first world. Living standards are generally lower, the agricultural population is larger, there is greater reliance on 'heavy' secondary manufacturing industry and service industries are less developed than in the West. In contrast to the first and second worlds, the **third world** does not reflect a political division between West and East. The third world contains the developing economies of LDCs or the 'South', including both market and capitalist economies such as South Korea, Hong Kong and Malaysia and socialist and command economies such as the Peoples Republic of China and Cuba. While most countries of the 'South' or third world have experienced at least some significant development, there are a number of countries in which little or no development has occurred. Economists sometimes identify a **Fourth World** comprising the most backward, underdeveloped and poverty stricken countries of the South, for the most part located in Sub-Saharan Africa.

THE MIXED ECONOMY

15. A **mixed economy** as the name suggests is a mixture of different types of economic system. Figure 1.2 illustrates two ways of defining a mixed economy: in **terms of the mechanism for allocating resources** and in **terms of ownership.** The upper panel of Figure 1.2 shows a mixed economy intermediate between a market economy and a command economy, containing large market and non-market sectors, while the lower panel defines a mixed economy in terms of the large public and private sectors it contains.

THE UNITED KINGDOM ECONOMY AS A MIXED ECONOMY

16 The modern British mixed economy dates from the 1940s when a number of important industries such as coal, rail and steel were taken into public ownership by nationalisation and the provision of public sector services outside the market economy was greatly extended by the 1944 Education Act and by the creation of the National Health Service. At about the same time in the 1940s and 1950s, similar mixed economies evolved in other Western European countries, notably in Scandinavia and in the Netherlands.

THE SOCIAL MARKET ECONOMY

17 For about thirty years after the end of the Second World War, from the 1940s to the 1970s, there existed in the United Kingdom a large measure of agreement about the virtues of the mixed economy. Many economists and the major political parties believed that certain types of economic activity, particularly the production and distribution of most consumer goods and services, were best suited to private enterprise and the market economy. But there was general agreement also that some industries which are **'natural' monopolies** or **utility industries** ought to be nationalised and that important services

Figure 1.2: Alternative ways of looking at the mixed economy

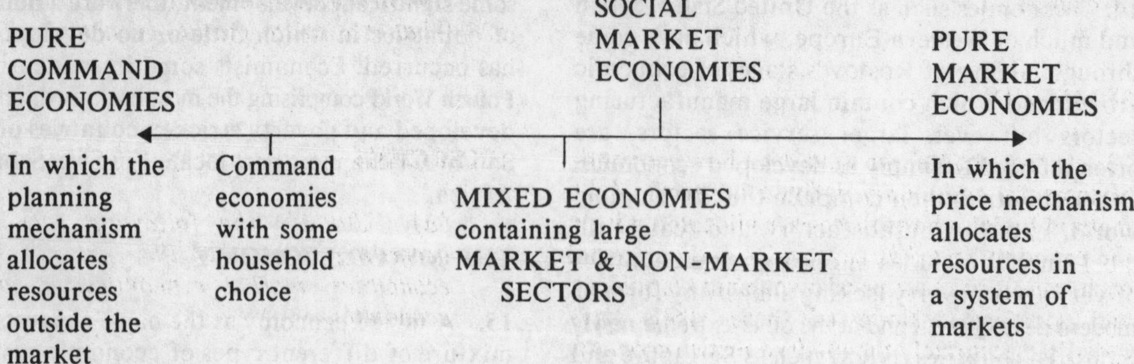

(a) The Spectrum of Economic Systems defined in terms of allocative mechanism.

(b) The Spectrum of Economic Systems defined in terms of ownership.

such as education, health care and roads should be provided by government 'outside the market' and financed through the tax system. In short a consensus existed around the belief that the mixed economy was 'about right' for Great Britain. But from the 1960s onward, a growing minority of economists and politicians began to blame the mixed economy for Britain's deteriorating economic performance relative to that of her main competitors in Western Europe and Japan. They argued that the public and non-market sectors of the economy, which they regarded as 'wealth consuming' and inefficient had become too big and that a concerted effort should be made to change fundamentally the nature of the British economy in the direction of greater private ownership and market production.

In recent years the term social **market economy** has been used by economists of a 'free-market' persuasion to describe the type of economy they would like the United Kingdom to become. A social market economy is close to being a pure market economy in which as much as possible is produced by private enterprise within a system of markets. Nevertheless, the state will still maintain a minimum economic role in two areas of economic life: in the production of goods and services which markets by their nature find it difficult to produce, eg defence and roads; and by providing a 'safety net' of welfare benefits for the groups in society such as the old, the handicapped and the long-term unemployed, who otherwise might be the victims of unregulated market forces. The process of breaking up the post-war mixed economy began in the United Kingdom in 1979 with the election of a Conservative Government firmly committed to the virtues of private enterprise, market forces and the idea of a social market economy. The two main policy instruments used to liberalise the economy are **privatisation** (the selling off of state-owned assets such as **nationalised industries** to private ownership) and **deregulation** (the removal of government red tape and bureaucracy from the operation of markets). It is currently too early to say whether the process of dismantling the mixed economy and creating a fully-fledged social market economy will be completed. By its very nature, the liberalisation of the British economy deeply divides public opinion, and political parties and voters may either support or reject at the ballot box the continuation of the process of change.

SUMMARY

18. In this chapter we have seen how economic systems are commonly defined in terms of the method by which resources are allocated within the economy (market economies and command economies), or in terms of ownership (capitalism and socialism). None of these labels have described accurately the modern British economy which has been a mixed economy containing large market and non-market sectors and large private and public sectors. The mixed economy was remarkably stable in the United Kingdom from the 1940s to the 1970s, but in recent years a process of change has begun, which may continue or be reversed, to break up the non-market sector, and to establish a social market economy. Economic systems should not be regarded as existing in a timeless vacuum; they continuously evolve. From different perspectives, Karl Marx (in the 19th century) and more recently the American W W Rostow, have emphasised the historical stages of economic growth through which economies may evolve, while most people are familiar with global divisions of economies into 'North' and 'South' and first and third worlds, based on the extent to which the countries of the world have developed or failed to develop their economies by the late 20th century.

STUDENT SELF-TESTING

1 *What is the central economic problem? (2)*
2 *What are the two main methods by which resources are allocated between competing uses? (3)*
3 *What is a market? (4)*
4 *What are the two economic functions of prices in a market economy? (5)*
5 *Define a command economy. (6)*
6 *Distinguish between capitalism and socialism. (8,9)*
7 *List Rostow's five stages of economic growth. (10)*
8 *Distinguish between the primary, secondary and tertiary sectors of an economy. (11)*
9 *Define consumer and capital goods. (12)*
10 *What are LDCs, NICs, the 'North' and the 'South'? (14)*
11 *How may a mixed economy be defined? (15)*
12 *What is a social market economy? (17)*

EXERCISES

1 *(a) Classify the following economies according to whether they are command economies, market economies or mixed economies:*

(i) Albania
(ii) Switzerland
(iii) The United Kingdom
(iv) Nigeria
(v) The United States of America
(vi) The Peoples Republic of China

(b) Could you classify the economic system of each of these countries in any other way?

MULTIPLE CHOICE QUESTIONS

1 *In a command economy, the economic problem of deciding what goods to produce is decided mainly by:*
A Relative prices
B Shadow prices
C Profit levels
D State direction

2 *The statement that 'there is no such thing as a free lunch' relates to the application of:*
A The level of public spending
B The concept of opportunity cost
C The price mechanism
D The concept of a merit good

3 *A necessary condition for a mixed economy is that there are:*
A Public and private sectors
B Primary,secondary and tertiary sectors
C Capital and consumer good sectors
D Heavy industries and light industries

4 *An advantage of a command economy is that:*
- A *The state always know what is in an individual's best interest*
- B *Social costs and benefits can be taken into account*
- C *The goods and services produced reflect the preference of consumers*
- D *Decision making is decentralised.*

5 *The essential difference between capitalism and socialism is that:*
- A *Capitalism exists in First World countries while socialism is found in Second World countries*
- B *Capitalism involves the private ownership of the means of production while socialism involves public ownership*
- C *Capitalism is a historical stage of development that always occurs before socialism*
- D *Capitalism is inevitably more efficient than socialism.*

EXAMINATION QUESTIONS

1 *(a) Outline the advantages and disadvantages of a command economy.* *(10 marks)*

(b) What justification would you advance for government intervention in a free market system? *(10 marks)*

(ACCA June 1984)

2 *(a) Explain the mixed economy approach to the allocation of scarce resources.*

(b) What factors determine the extent to which an economy is mixed?

(ACCA June 1982)

3 *The basic economic problem is not so much the amount of production from scarce resources but rather how the resulting products are distributed. You are required to:*

(a) explain the statement;

(b) show how different economies have tried to resolve the problem;

(c) consider the difficulties they face in so doing.

(CIMA November 1986)

4. *Illustrate the practical importance of the concept of opportunity cost.*

(CIMA May 1979)

Student note:

Answers to all exercises, multiple choice questions and examination questions begin on page 411.

2. The market mechanism

INTRODUCTION

1 In Chapter 1 we explained that a market economy is an economic system made up of a large number of interrelated markets, and we defined a market as a voluntary meeting of buyers and sellers for the purpose of trading or exchanging a good or service. Within a market, prices serve the important functions of:

(i) **signalling** the information which allows all the traders in the market to plan and co-ordinate their economic activities; and

(ii) **creating incentives** for buyers and sellers to behave in a manner which allows the market to operate in an orderly and efficient manner.

In this chapter, which serves as an introduction to the rest of the first half of the manual, we examine the functioning of the price mechanism in a single market within a market economy, before in subsequent chapters analysing more detailed aspects of the market mechanism such as demand and supply curves and different types of market structures.

THE GOODS MARKET AND THE FACTOR MARKET

2 Although a market economy contains a very large number of markets, many of the markets can be grouped under the heading of either the **'goods market'** or the **'factor market'**. These markets are respectively markets for **outputs**, or final goods and services (consumer goods and services), and markets for the **factors of production** or **inputs** necessary in the process of production. Household and firms operate simultaneously in both sets of markets. In the goods market, households exercise demand for consumer goods and services produced and supplied by firms. For household demand in the goods market to be an *effective demand*, ie demand backed up by an ability to pay, households must sell their labour, or possibly the services of any capital or land they own, in the factor market, where it is the firms who exercise the demand for the factor services sold by the households, as inputs into the production process.

DEMAND AND SUPPLY CURVES

3 For the rest of this chapter we shall ignore the factor market, examining instead the process of price determination within a single market in the goods market of a market economy. The essential features of such a market are shown in Figure 2.1

Figure 2.1: The market demand curve and the market supply curve

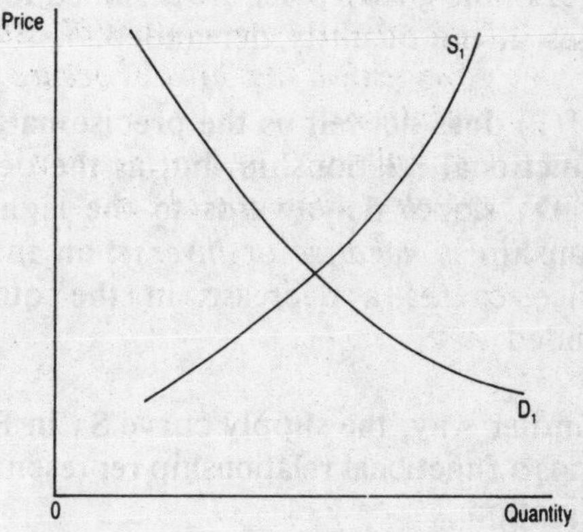

The demand curve D_1 in Figure 2.1 is a **market demand curve**, showing the quantities of the good or service which all the consumers in the market would like to purchase at different prices. In a similar way the **market supply curve** S_1 shows the quantities that all the firms in the market wish to supply at different prices. It is important not to confuse market demand and supply curves, such as those illustrated in Figure 2.1, with individual demand and supply curves. An **individual demand curve** shows how much a single consumer within the market wishes to purchase at different prices, whereas the market demand curve maps the demand decisions of all the consumers. The relationship between the two is very straightforward: to obtain the market demand curve, simply sum or add up the demand curves of each of the consumers in the market. Likewise, to obtain the **market supply curve**, add up the supply curves of each firm in the market.

FUNCTIONS

4 The market demand and supply curves illustrated in Figure 2.1 represent functional relationships. A **functional relationship** exists between two variables whenever a change in one variable, known as the *independent* variable, causes a change in a second variable, the *dependent* variable. In very general terms, we can represent the demand function illustrated in Figure 2.1 in the following equation:

$$Qd = f(P)$$

In this equation the symbol f is used to indicate that a change in the value of the independent variable shown inside the brackets will cause a change in the dependent variable on the left hand side of the equation. Thus in a **demand function,** changes in the good's price are assumed to cause changes in the quantity demanded.

Qd = f(P) does not tell us the precise nature of the functional relationship, but as the demand curve D_1 slopes downwards to the right, the relationship is *negative* or *inverse*: an increase in price causes a decrease in the quantity demanded.

In a similar way, the supply curve S_1 in Figure 2.1 maps a functional relationship represented by the equation:

$$Qs = f(P)$$

In contrast to the demand function, the **supply function** is an example of a *positive* functional relationship in which price and quantity supplied are directly related. On the diagram this results in a curve sloping upward to the right, showing that at higher prices firms are prepared to supply larger quantities of the good or service.

MARKET PLANS AND MARKET ACTION

5 Demand and supply functions are examples of **behavioural functions**; they represent theories of how human beings are assumed to behave. Households are assumed to respond to a price fall by demanding more, while firms are assumed to react by supplying less! It is also very important to understand that demand and supply functions represent how consumers and firms *intend* to behave in the market rather than how they necessarily *end up* behaving. In short, demand and supply functions represent **market plans** rather than **market action.**

A demand curve, such as D_1 in Figure 2.2 shows the quantities of a good the households would like to purchase at different prices. This is called **planned demand, intended demand,** or **ex ante demand.** Similarly, the supply curve shows how much the firms would like to supply at different prices: **planned supply, intended supply,** or **ex ante supply.**

Figure 2.2: The market mechanism and the equilibrium price

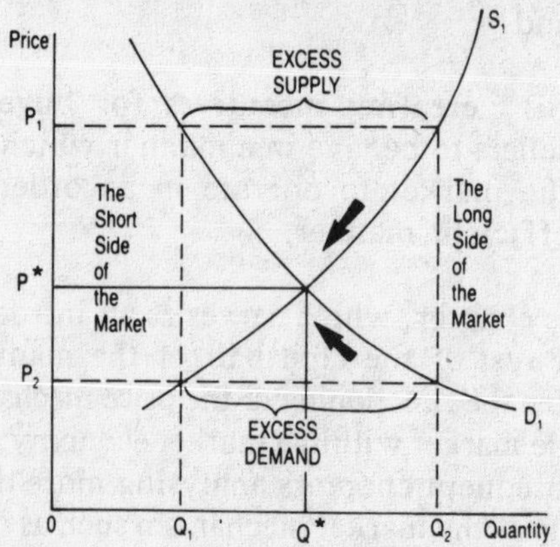

Now it is impossible at most prices for both households and firms to fulfil simultaneously their market plans. Suppose the price is P_1 in Figure 2.2. At this price firms would like to supply Q_2, but households are only willing to purchase Q_1. Planned supply is greater than planned demand, resulting in an **excess supply.**

How much will actually be traded if the price remains at P_1? The answer is Q_1. The amount bought is Q_1, the amount sold is Q_1. Now the amount bought represents **realised demand** (also known as **actual demand and ex post demand**), while the amount sold is **realised supply (actual supply** or **ex post supply).** It follows that actual demand must always equal actual supply whatever the price because the quantity bought must always equal the quantity sold. This is known as an **identity**, represented by the sign ≡ The identity sign ≡ is stronger than an ordinary sign =.

When we write:

actual demand ≡ actual supply,

the sign ≡ tells us that actual demand and actual supply are identically equal, at every possible price.

EQUILIBRIUM PRICE

6 The concepts of equilibrium and disequilibrium are of very great importance in economic theory and analysis. Essentially, equilibrium is a state of rest in which an economic agent, such as a household or firm, is able to fulfil its market plans. Conversely, a state of **disequilibrium** exists when market plans are not fulfilled or realised. In Figure 2.2, P_1 is a disequilibrium price because the firms cannot fulfil their plans at this price. As we saw in the previous section, actual demand of course equals actual supply as indeed it must. However, this is largely irrelevant; the key point is that at this price, planned supply exceeds planned demand.

We now introduce a most important assumption about economic behaviour which recurs throughout economic theory and analysis. We assume that *whenever an economic agent, such as a household or firm, fails to fulfil its market plans, it changes its market behaviour*. To explain this further, it is useful to identify two sides to the market, a **short side** and a **long side** which are illustrated in Figure 2.2. Economic agents on the short side of the market can always fulfill their market plans but those on the long side of the market cannot. When the price is P_1 the firms are on the long side of the market, wishing to sell Q_2 but only finding buyers for Q_1.

It is at this point that the market mechanism operates to get rid of the excess supply by moving the market towards an equilibrium. We assume that firms react to the stocks of unsold goods which accumulate if they try to sell at P_1 by accepting a lower price. Eventually the price falls until the amount the households wish to buy equals exactly the quantity firms are prepared to supply.

But suppose that the initial price in Figure 2.2 is P_2 rather than P_1. Firms are now on the short side and households on the long side of the market, a reversal of positions. The firms can fulfill their plans by selling exactly the amount they intend, Q_1, at the price P_2. But the households on the long side of the market cannot fulfill their plans. They wish to purchase Q_2, but unfortunately only Q_1 is available. Thus at P_2 unsatisfied or **excess demand** exists, creating an incentive for some at least of the households to offer a higher price in order to obtain the good. In this way, the households who are unable to fulfil their market plans at P_2 bid up the price to eliminate the excess demand in the market.

The equilibrium price P^* is the only price which satisfies both households and firms, who consequently have no reason to change their market plans. At P^*, planned demand equals planned supply and the market clears. In a supply and demand model of a market, we can say that

planned demand = planned supply

is the **equilibrium equation** setting out the required condition for the market to be in a state of rest. Do not confuse this equilibrium equation, or equilibrium condition, with the identity explained in the previous section:

actual demand ≡ actual supply

The identity holds true at all prices, including the equilibrium price, whereas planned demand = planned supply holds only when the market is in equilibrium.

To summarise the main conclusions of this very important section of the chapter:

Disequilibrium conditions:

(i) if planned demand < planned supply, price will fall;

(ii) if planned demand > planned supply, price will rise.

Equilibrium equation or condition:

(iii) if planned demand = planned supply, price stays the same.

Identity:

(iv) actual demand ≡ actual supply, at all prices.

CONVERGENT AND DIVERGENT EQUILIBRIUM

7 In Figure 2.2, convergence of the market mechanism towards the equilibrium price P^* is ensured by the assumptions we made abut how firms and households behave or react when unable to fulfil their market plans, given the slopes of the demand and supply curves we have drawn.

Consider however Figures 2.3 and 2.4 which contain (theoretically possible) downward-sloping supply curves. Figure 2.3 is drawn with the supply curve steeper than the demand curve, intersecting the demand curve from above. This diagram again represents a convergent equilibrium and we leave it as an exercise for the reader to work out why. However, Figure 2.4 in which the more gently sloping supply curve intersects the demand curve from below, illustrates a system in which the market mechanism fails to converge the price towards the equilibrium, instead moving it further and further away.

Figure 2.3: A downward-sloping supply curve and convergent equilibrium

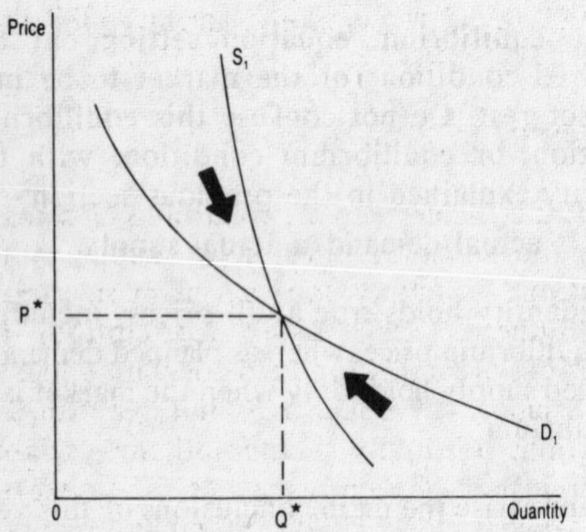

We can illustrate the divergency away from equilibrium by assuming an initial price of P_1 in Figure 2.4. The planned demand of households, Q_2, exceeds the planned supply of firms, Q_1, so excess demand exists in the market at this price. If households now react to their inability to purchase as much as they desire at P_1 by bidding up the price, the price rises further and further away from P^*. Conversely if initially excess supply exists in the market at a price such as P_2, the price falls further and further below P^* as firms reduce supply in an attempt to offload unsold stocks. If of course we assume an initial price at P^*, the equilibrium will be maintained, but any 'shock' to the system causing the price to depart from the equilibrium would trigger a movement away from P^*.

Figure 2.4: A downward-sloping supply curve and divergent equilibrium

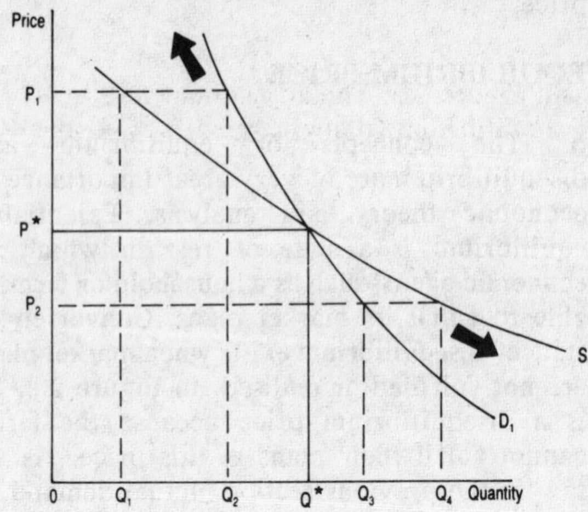

As you might expect, many markets in the real world are convergent rather than divergent showing a tendency towards stability, but there are exceptions. The foreign exchange market can under certain circumstances illustrate exactly the divergent tendencies we have just described, with the price or exchange rate at which a currency is traded tending to depart from its equilibrium or market-clearing value.

SHIFTS IN DEMAND

8 Market disequilibrium initially arises as a result of a shift in either the demand curve or the supply curve. In this section we examine **shifts in demand.**

When we draw a market demand curve to show how much of the good or service households plan to demand at various possible prices, we assume that all the other variables which may also influence planned demand are held unchanged or constant. This is known as the **ceteris paribus** assumption. Strictly, we should write the demand function shown in diagrams such as Figure 2.2 as:

$$Qd = f(P), \text{ ceteris paribus}$$

Qd = f(P) states that the planned demand, mapped as the demand curve D_1, is a function of the good's own price. Ceteris paribus means 'other things being equal'. Amongst the variables whose values are held constant or unchanged when we draw a demand curve are disposable income and tastes or fashion. Collectively, the variables other than the good's own price, whose values influence planned demand are sometimes referred to as the **conditions of demand.**

Figure 2.5: The adjustment to a new equilibrium following a shift in demand

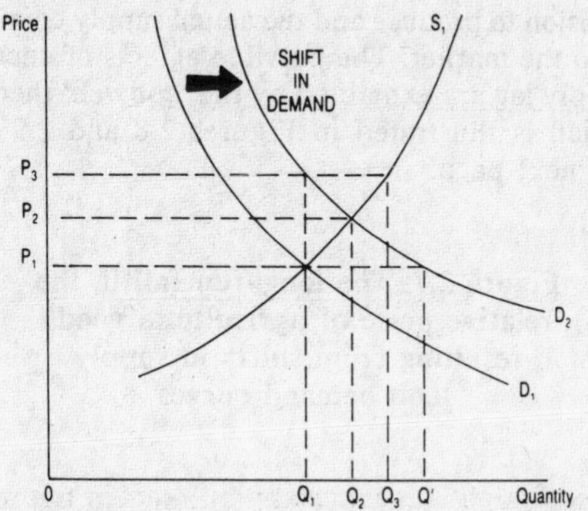

In Figure 2.5, the demand curve D_1 and the supply curve S_1 are drawn to show the initial conditions of supply and demand. The equilibrium price is P_1 and quantity Q_1 is bought and sold. Suppose now that a change in taste or fashion, perhaps caused by a successful advertising campaign, persuades households to demand more of the good at all prices. The demand curve shifts to the right (or upwards) to D_2. At the initial price of P_1, households now plan to purchase Q'. But because the supply curve is unchanged, firms still intend only to supply Q_1 at P_1, which therefore is no longer an equilibrium price. Excess demand exists in the market.

A CLOSER LOOK AT THE PROCESS OF CONVERGENCE

9 In earlier sections of this chapter we described briefly how the price mechanism converges a market towards an equilibrium. We shall now take a closer look at this process of convergence. In the immediate period following the shift in demand illustrated in Figure 2.5, firms are unable to increase the quantity they can supply beyond Q_1. This is known as the **market period** or **momentary period.** In effect, immediately following the shift in demand, the market period supply curve is a vertical line drawn through Q_1.

In the market period the price will rise to P_3 to eliminate the excess demand. At P_3, planned demand is Q_1, the maximum quantity the firms can supply immediately following the shift in demand. But beyond the market period, the supply curve S_1 shows that firms will respond to the price P_3 by being prepared to supply Q_3. When the firms are able to release Q_3 onto the market, the price will fall, since excess supply exists at P_3 and consumers will only take Q_1 at this price. If firms can reduce their supply quickly the price then falls to the new market-clearing equilibrium at P_2.

SHIFTS IN SUPPLY

10. Just as a change in the conditions of demand shifts the demand curve, so a change in the conditions of supply causes a **shift in supply.** Under the ceteris paribus assumption, the conditions of supply are held constant when we draw a supply curve such as S_1 in Figure 2.6. The conditions of supply include all the variables which influence supply except of course the good's own price which is mapped by the supply curve itself. Amongst the conditions of supply which determine the position of the supply curve are costs of production incurred by firms and taxes levied upon firms by government.

In Figure 2.6 an initial equilibrium is shown at price P_1, before conditions of supply change. Suppose that workers negotiate successfully for a wage increase which causes firms' production costs to rise. This will make the firms less willing to supply as much as previously at any price facing them, shifting the supply curve leftwards (or upwards) to S_2. The firms will now supply only Q' at the original equilibrium price P_1, and not Q_1. Excess demand therefore exists, since planned demand is still Q_1, causing the market mechanism to bid up the price to the new equilibrium at P_2.

Figure 2.6: The adjustment to a new equilibrium following a shift in supply

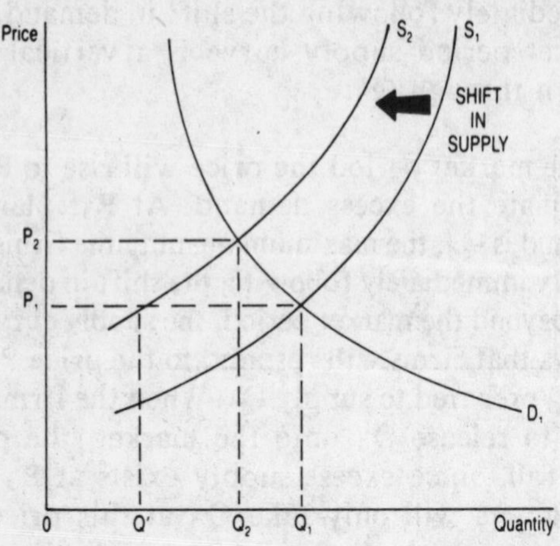

THE PROBLEM OF AGRICULTURAL PRICES

11. Throughout history, agricultural markets in foodstuffs and in primary products such as rubber have experienced two closely related problems. Firstly, there has been a long-run trend for agricultural prices to fall relative to those of manufactured goods and secondly, prices have fluctuated considerably from year to year.

The long-run trend can be explained by shifts in the demand and supply curves for agricultural products over a long period of time. In Figure 2.7 the equilibrium price for an agricultural product in an early historical period is shown at P_1. Over time both the demand and supply curves have shifted to the right as a result, for example, of increased incomes and population in the case of demand and improved methods of farming in the case of the supply curve.

For many farm products, very great increases in yields or productivity have caused the long-run shift in the supply curve to exceed the shift in demand, resulting in the fall to the lower equilibrium price, P_2, illustrated in Figure 2.7.

SHORT-RUN FLUCTUATIONS IN AGRICULTURAL PRICES

12. An important characteristic of agricultural production is a relatively long production period, compared for example with many types of manufacturing. Arable farmers make decisions to grow crops several months before the harvest, while in a similar way livestock farmers must breed animals for meat production many months before slaughter. It is possible therefore, that farmers form their market plans on how much to supply to the market on the basis of last year's price rather than on the prices current this year. Because of the length of the production period, there is a **supply lag** between the decision to produce and the actual supply coming onto the market. The possible effects of such a supply lag are explained by the **'cobweb' theory** which is illustrated in Figures 2.8 and 2.9 on the next page.

Figure 2.7: The long-run fall in the relative price of agricultural goods resulting from shifts in supply and demand curves

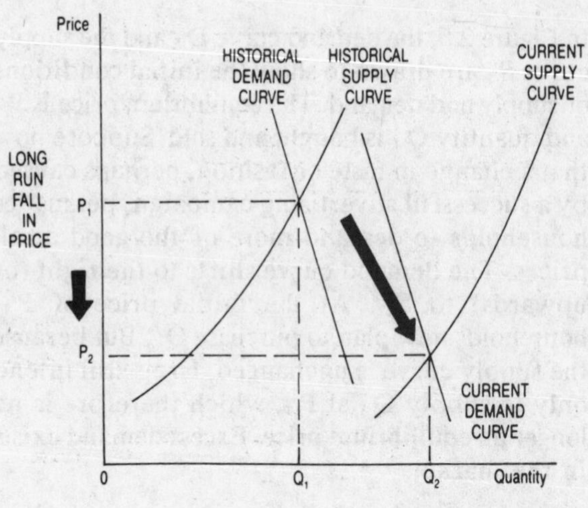

Figure 2.8 illustrates a **stable'cobweb'**, in which the market price eventually converges to an equilibrium at E, where the long-run demand and supply curves intersect. Suppose that in the market for hogs, an outbreak of swine disease reduces the number of hogs coming onto the market from Q_1 to Q_2. Within the current year (Year 1) the maximum number of pigs that can be sold on the market can be shown by a vertical line drawn through Q_2. A new price P_2, determined at point A

on this vertical line, encourages farmers to supply Q_3 onto the market in the next year (Year 2). Again a vertical line can be drawn through Q_3 to represent the maximum possible supply in Year 2. But when the supply Q_3 comes onto the market, the price drops to P_3, causing farmers to reduce the supply available in Year 3 to Q_4. Price and output then continue to oscillate in a series of decreasing fluctuations until eventually, in the absence of any further 'shock' to the market, converging to the long-run equilibrium at E.

Figure 2.8: Fluctuations from year to year in the the price of pigs in a convergent 'cobweb' model

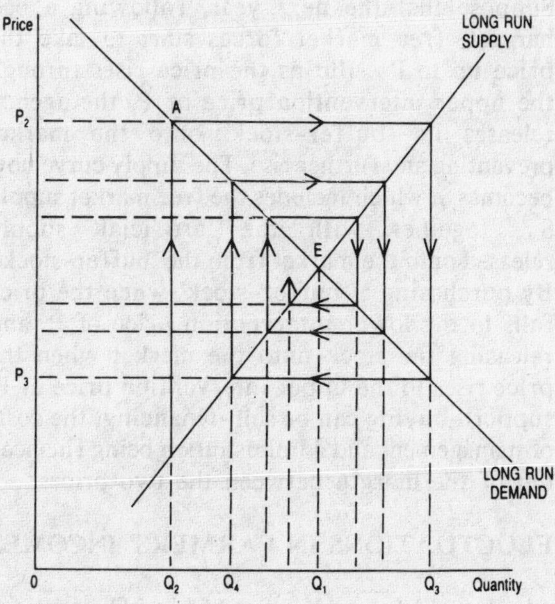

In Figure 2.8, the 'cobweb' eventually converged to the long-run equilibrium at E because the long-run demand curve was drawn with a gentler slope than the long-run supply curve. However, an **unstable 'cobweb'** in which, following the initial 'shock', the market diverges further and further away from the long-run equilibrium at E is also possible when the demand curve is drawn steeper than the supply curve. This is illustrated in Figure 2.9

Figure 2.9: Fluctuations from year to year in the price of pigs in a divergent or unstable 'cobweb' model

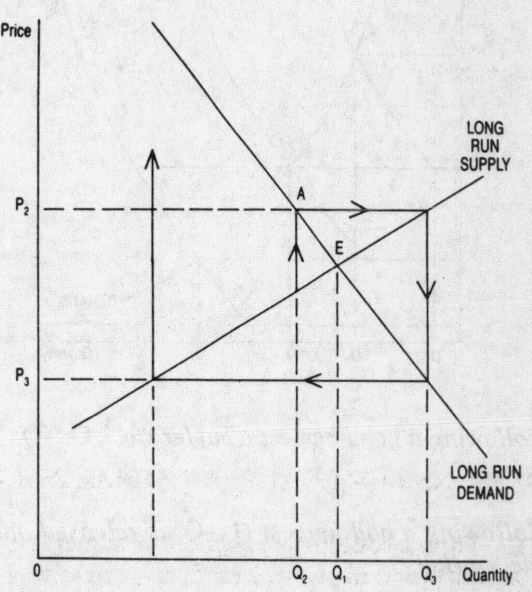

PRICE-SUPPORT POLICIES

13 Year-to-year instability in farm prices can be caused by random shifts of the short-run supply curve in response to fluctuations in the harvest. In Figure 2.10 we have drawn three short-run supply curves: a 'good harvest' supply curve S_1; a 'bad harvest' supply curve S_2; and a 'normal harvest' supply curve S_3 drawn mid-way between S_1 and S_2. Weather conditions and other factors outside the farmers' control will shift the position of the supply curve from year-to-year between the limits set by S_1 and S_2. Quite clearly, market prices will also fluctuate from year-to-year within the range P_1 to P_2.

Suppose that the government wishes to stabilise the good's price at the 'normal' year price, P_3. Following a good harvest, the government buys up the quantity Q'-Q^3 to prevent the market price falling below P_3. In the event of a bad harvest in the next year, the government will supplement supply by releasing the product onto the market from the previously accumulated stock; thereby preventing the price from rising above P_3 to P_2.

Figure 2.10: A price-support policy to stabilise price at P_3

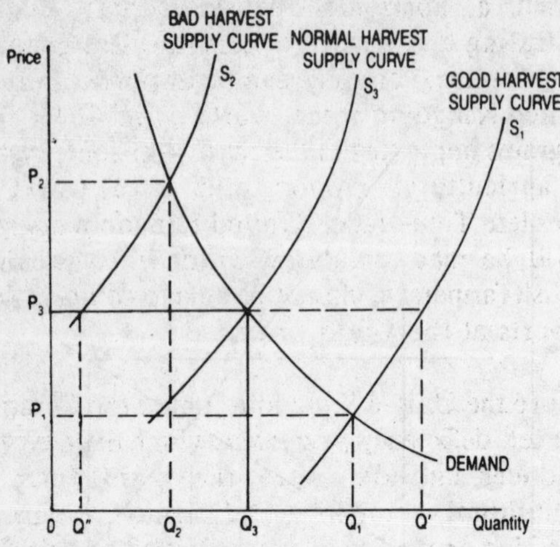

Following a good harvest a buffer stock Q'-Q_3 *is bought*

Following a bad harvest Q_3-Q" *is released onto the market*

The **support-buying policy** we have just described operates on the **'buffer-stock'** principle, in which the government or perhaps an association of producers, accumulates a buffer-stock when the harvest is good for releasing onto the market in the event of a crop failure. Instead of completely stabilising the price at P_3 in Figure 2.10, support-buying can also be used to reduce rather than to eliminate fluctuations resulting from free market forces. The government or a support-buying agency establishes **upper and lower intervention prices**, shown respectively as $\hat{P}$ and $\bar{P}$ in Figure 2.11. When the supply curve shifts to S_1 following a good harvest, the market price falls towards P_1. As the price falls through $\bar{P}$, the support-buying agency steps into the market and begins to accumulate a 'buffer-stock', thereby preventing any further fall in the price. In effect the demand curve now becomes $\bar{D}$, comprising market demand D_1, plus the 'artificial' demand of the support-buying agency.

Figure 2.11: A price-support policy with upper and lower stabilisation prices

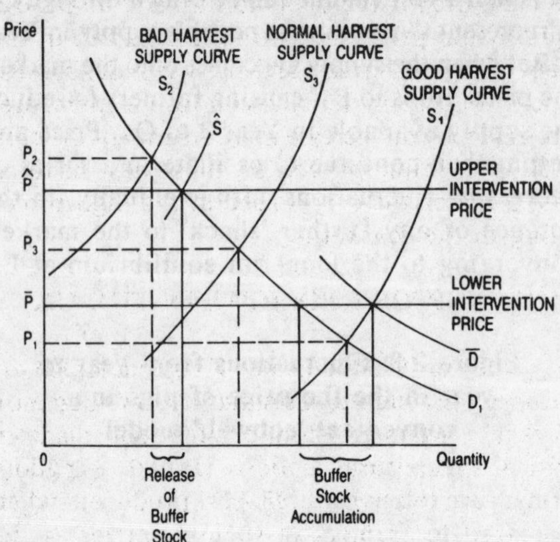

Suppose that the next year, following a bad harvest, free market forces start to take the price up to P_2. But as the price rises through the upper intervention price of $\hat{P}$, the agency releases its 'buffer-stock' onto the market preventing any further rise. The supply curve now becomes $\hat{S}$, which includes the free market supply S_1, together with the 'artificial' supply released onto the market from the 'buffer-stock'. By purchasing a 'buffer-stock' when the price falls to the lower intervention price of $\bar{P}$. and releasing the stock onto the market when the price rises to the upper intervention price of $\hat{P}$, support-buying can be self-financing, the costs of management and administration being financed out of the margin between the two prices.

FLUCTUATIONS IN FARMERS' INCOMES

14 From a farmer's point of view fluctuations in his income are more serious than fluctuations in price. In Figure 2.12(a) the demand curve has been drawn to show that a fall in price causes a rise in farm income, while a rise in price causes a fall in farm income. When the price is P_1 following a bad harvest, farmer's incomes are shown by the area OQ_1AP_1 (quantity sold x price). Following a good harvest the price falls to P_2, but farmers incomes increase to the area OQ_2BP_2.

Contrast this situation to that shown in the righthand panel of Figure 2.12. In this diagram we have drawn the demand curve so that both equilibrium price and farm incomes fall in the event of a good harvest and rise when the harvest is poor. In certain demand conditions therefore, farmers enjoy an increase in income when the crop fails, providing of course that they have at least some of the crop to sell at the high prices ruling in the market.

FARM SUPPORT POLICIES IN THE UK

15 When in 1973 the United Kingdom joined the **European Economic Community, or Common Market,** a fundamental change took place in British agricultural policy. United Kingdom farmers are relatively high-cost producers when compared to farmers in such countries as the United States, Canada and Australia, but they are efficient within the constraints imposed by the British climate and average farm size. And compared with many European farmers employed on even smaller and less mechanised farms, British farmers are relatively low-cost producers.

In Figure 2.13 on the next page, British farm costs are represented in the long-run domestic supply curve S_1. On the same diagram, we have drawn a horizontal 'world supply curve', indicating that a more or less limitless quantity of agricultural produce can be imported into the United Kingdom at the 'world price' of P_1. The diagrams imply that in the absence of some system of agricultural support and in a world of complete 'free-trade', United Kingdom demand could be met completely from imports, since British farmers would not be able to compete with imports at the world price.

Before the United Kingdom joined the Common Market, **deficiency payments, which are a type of producer subsidy,** were the main form of agricultural support. Deficiency payments provided cheap food for the British population, while ensuring the incomes of domestic farmers. Imports of food were allowed into the United Kingdom at the world price and subsidies were payed to British farmers to keep them in business. This is illustrated in Figure 2.13(a).

Figure 2.12: The effect of a fall in price on farm incomes

(a) The fall in price results in higher farm incomes.
(b) The fall in price results in reduced farm incomes.

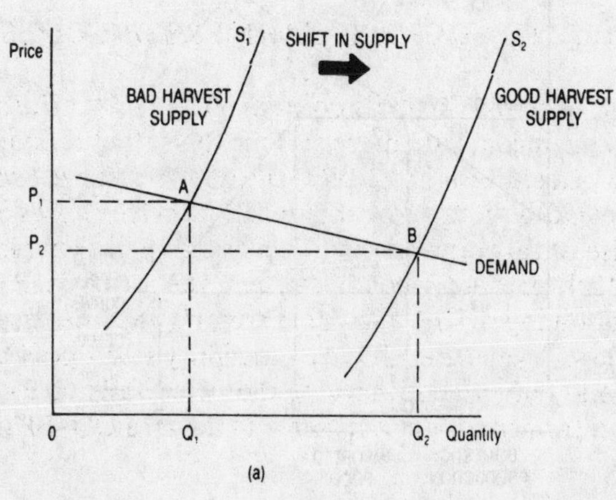

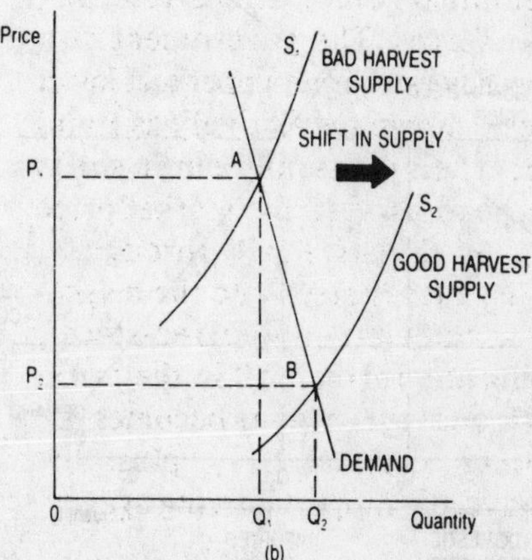

United Kingdom farmers were guaranteed a price of P_2 at which they supplied Q_2. However the domestic output Q_2 was sold to the British consumer at the world price P_1, the difference in the two prices being the deficiency payment to the farmers provided by the taxpayers. Under the deficiency payments system, the total demand Q_1 was determined at X, where the domestic demand curve intersects the world supply curve. Quantity Q_2 was domestically produced, the rest being imported.

By contrast, the **Common Agricultural Policy** of the EEC results in relatively expensive food for community consumers. The problem of cheap imports from the rest of the world is dealt with by imposing an **external tariff** or **levy** which brings the price of imported food up to the level of European costs of production. Assuming the tariff is set at P_2 in Figure 2.13 (b), the total quantity demanded reduces to Q_3 as compared to Q_1 in the deficiency payments system. The amount Q_2 will still be domestically produced, with the remainder being imported.

The external tariff levied on food imports is only part of the CAP. As indicated earlier in the chapter, the EEC also operates a support-buying policy or 'buffer-stock' with upper and lower intervention prices. A major problem in the operation of the CAP has resulted from setting the lower intervention price too high, at a level such as P_3 in Figure 2.13(b). This has encouraged an excess supply equal to AB. The price can only be sustained at P_3 if the EEC intervenes continuously to purchase the excess supply. This can be shown by shifting the demand curve to D_2 to include the amount the community purchases to maintain the price at P_3. Because lower intervention prices have been set too high, the effects of bad harvests in causing leftward shifts in the short-run supply curve have been insufficient to prevent the accumulation of grain and butter 'mountains' and wine 'lakes', which have been the logical result of the support-buying policy.

Figure 2.13

Farm support policies in the United Kingdom.
(a) before entry into the EEC
(b) after entry into the EEC.

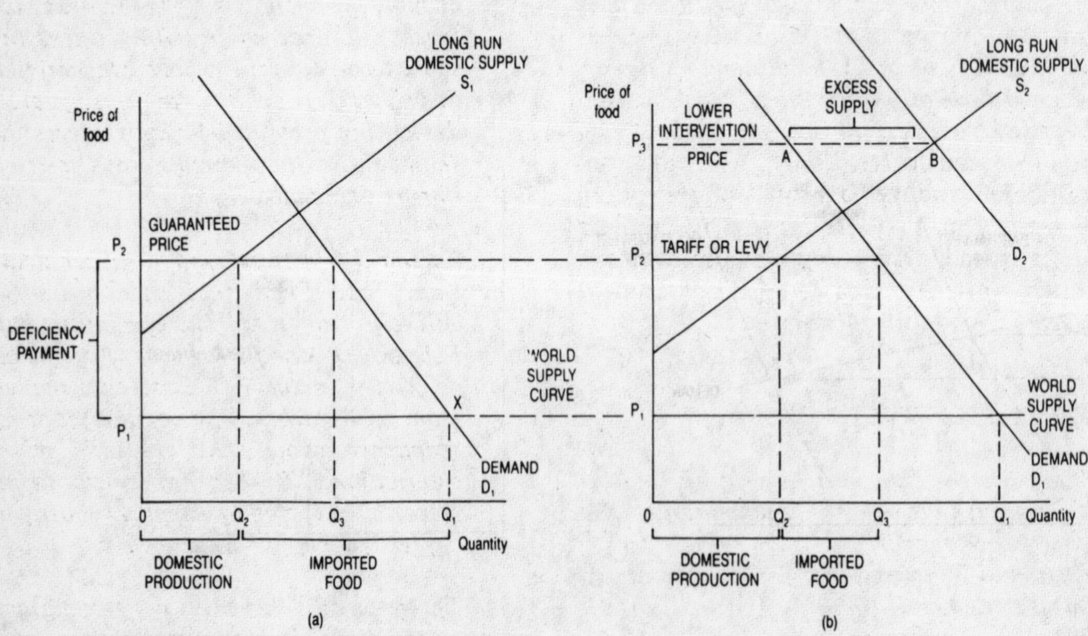

SUMMARY

16 We have examined in this chapter how the price mechanism functions to perform the central economic task of resource allocation in a single market within a market company. A market is represented by a demand curve and a supply curve, which map the market plans or intended market behaviour of households and firms. Both demand and supply curves represent functional relationships in which the market plans of the households and firms are assumed to be determined by price. However, there will be many other determinants of demand and supply, but when we draw a demand or supply curve, these are held constant under the ceteris paribus assumption. The variables other than price which influence demand or supply are known as the conditions of demand and supply. If we relax the ceteris paribus assumption and change the condition of demand or supply, the demand or supply curve will shift to a new position.

A vital economic concept introduced and explained in this chapter is the concept of equilibrium. Equilibrium can be regarded as a state of rest in which the market plans of all the economic agents we are modelling can be fulfilled. Market equilibrium occurs when planned demand = planned supply. This is an equilibrium equation. If disequilibrium exists within a market, for example following a shift in either demand or supply, the market mechanism converges the market towards equilibrium in order to relieve excess supply or excess demand. Sometimes however, market conditions may cause the price mechanism to diverge away from equilibrium. Agricultural markets in particular, may be prone to disequilibrium and random shifts of the supply curve from year-to-year, caused by climatic factors, may lead to unacceptable fluctuations in agricultural prices which require government intervention to stabilise the price.

STUDENT SELF-TESTING

1 *What are the functions of prices?* (1)
2 *Distinguish between the 'goods market' and the 'factor market'.* (2)
3 *Distinguish between individual demand and market demand.* (3)
4 *What is a function?* (4)
5 *Define planned demand and realised demand.* (5)
6 *Explain the equilibrium equation: planned demand = planned supply* (6)
7 *Briefly show how the market mechanism relieves excess demand.* (7)
8 *Why may a demand curve shift?* (8)
9 *What is the 'market period'?* (9)
10 *Why may a supply curve shift?* (10)
11 *What are the particular problems of agricultural prices?* (11)
12 *Draw a diagram to show a convergent 'cobweb'.* (12)
13 *What is a 'buffer-stock' policy?* (13)
14 *Distinguish between deficiency payments and support-buying.* (15)

EXERCISES

1 *Distinguish between:*
(a) *ex ante demand and ex post demand*
(b) *actual demand ≡ actual supply and, planned demand = planned supply*
(c) *a shift in supply and an adjustment along a supply curve.*

2 *Read the following passage which is adapted from a newspaper article, and then answer the questions at the end of the passage.*

Mounting commercial stocks of unsold rubber have been weighing down prices for many months. There are few signs that free market forces will succeed in lifting prices in the short term. Natural rubber consumption is down worldwide so far this year, the destocking prompted by high interest rates shows signs of continuing, thus restricting import demand.

Earlier this month London rubber dealers, Lewis and Peat, said that prices were unlikely to rise significantly before February or March next year when the onset of winter in the Far East cuts the yield from rubber trees. The company appeared sceptical about the ability of the International Rubber Agreement to boost prices by mopping up surplus rubber for its buffer stock.

The producers, however, are relying on the International Rubber Agreement to act as a counterbalance to the present depressing free market influences. The International

Rubber Agreement entered into force a year ago, but it is only within the past few weeks that the Pact has had funds at its disposal to finance support-buying operations. It has been reported that only some £20 million has been received so far from members, enough to buy up only 50,000 tons of rubber. Some traders argue that considerably more than this needs to be taken off the market to bring supply and demand into balance over the next few months.

(a) Use supply and demand diagrams to explain:
- *(i) How market forces depressed the price of natural rubber;*
- *(ii) Why prices were expected to rise with the onset of winter in the Far East.*

(b) (i) Explain how a buffer stock policy might raise the price of natural rubber.
- *(ii) What problems might face the International Rubber Agreement through operating the buffer stock?*

MULTIPLE CHOICE QUESTIONS

*1 Which of the following statements that refer to the price mechanism is **not** true?*
- *A Imperfect market information may prevent the market working efficiently*
- *B Trading can only take place at equilibrium prices in a market economy*
- *C A fall in the relative price of a good tends to attract consumers to buy that good instead of other goods*
- *D In a market economy consumer sovereignty is seldom complete.*

2 In a supply and demand diagram, other things remaining the same, an increase in production costs will normally shift:
- *A The demand curve to the right*
- *B The supply curve to the right*
- *C The demand curve to the left*
- *D The supply curve to the left*

3 When a minimum price is imposed on a good by the government which is above the equilibrium price:
- *A Excess supply will result*
- *B Trading will continue at the equilibrium price*
- *C A black market may occur*
- *D Firms will fulfill their market plans at this price.*

*4 In a market economy the market mechanism achieves all the following **except:***
- *A Signals changes in consumer tastes*
- *B Causes supply to respond to changes in demand*
- *C Eliminates excess supply and demand*
- *D Ensures a socially fair distribution of goods and services*

*5 The market mechanism is unsuitable as a method of allocating all the following between competing uses **except:***
- *A Private goods*
- *B Public goods*
- *C Free goods*
- *D Externalities*

EXAMINATION QUESTIONS

1 What are the arguments for and against using the price mechanism as a means of allocating scarce goods and services? Does your answer depend on the type of commodity in question? (ACCA June 1979)

2 Why do the prices of agricultural products fluctuate more than the prices of manufactured goods? (ICSA June 1985)

3 It is well established that, if left to the free market, the prices of agricultural products and hence farm incomes will fluctuate widely. Describe the methods which may be used to stabilise farm prices and incomes, indicating the advantages and disadvantages of each method. (ACCA June 1986)

4 Why may a 'black market' exist in tickets for a special event such as a football cup final? Illustrate your answer with a diagram. (CIMA May 1984)

3. Demand and consumer theory

INTRODUCTION

1. In this chapter we 'go behind' the demand curve first introduced in Chapter 2, to build up a theory of consumer behaviour which explains why consumers usually demand more of a good the lower its price.

INDIVIDUAL DEMAND AND MARKET DEMAND

2. The demand curves introduced in Chapter 2 were **market demand** curves representing the demand decisions at different prices of all the consumers or households in the market. In this chapter, we examine **individual demand**, or the demand of a single consumer within the market. Nevertheless, as explained in Chapter 2, the relationship between market demand and individual demand is straightforward: we obtain the market demand curve by adding up the demand curves of all the individual consumers in the market.

ECONOMIC MODEL-BUILDING

3. The supply and demand framework of a single market which we examined in Chapter 2 is an example of an **economic model**. This chapter is concerned with another economic model: a **model of consumer behaviour in the market**. Model-building is the most fundamental technique of analysis used by economists. Because in this and in subsequent chapters we shall be examining a large number of models which attempt to explain economic relationships, it is appropriate first to explain in some detail the important features of an economic model and the purposes to which a model might be put.

Economic theory is based on developing economic models which describe particular aspects of the economic behaviour of individuals, groups of individuals or even of the whole economy. A model which explains the behaviour of individuals or groups of individuals in the economy is called a **micro-economic model**, whereas a **macro-economic model** examines aggregate behaviour in the whole economy. Thus the model of individual consumption demand developed in this chapter, and the derivation from the model of the market demand curve, is an example of micro-economic model building, not to be confused with the macro-economic theory of the aggregate consumption demand of all the households in the economy which we study later in this manual.

A model is a small-scale replica of real-world phenomena, often, as in the case of a model aircraft or car, incorporating a number of simplifications. An economic model can be thought of as a simplification of the real world in which the essential features of an economic relationship or set of relationships are explained using diagrams, words and often algebra. Models are used by economists, firstly to understand and explain the working of the economy and secondly, to predict what might happen in the future.

A 'good' economic model simplifies reality sufficiently to allow important and often otherwise obscure, economic relationships to be studied, away from irrelevant detail or 'background noise'. The danger is that reality can be oversimplified, with the resulting model failing to reflect in a useful way the world it seeks to explain. Economic modelling involves the art of making strong assumptions about human behaviour so as to concentrate attention and analysis upon key economic relationships in a clear and tractable way, while avoiding an excessive oversimplification of the problem or relationship to be explained.

The ultimate purpose of model-building is to derive predictions about economic behaviour, such as the prediction of demand theory that demand will increase when price falls. Economic controversy often exists when models generate conflicting predictions about what will happen in a given set of circumstances. For example, a model of the labour market which predicts that the supply of labour increases as wages rise, carries the policy-making implication that a cut in income tax, being equivalent to a wage rise, creates an incentive to effort and hard work. But under alternative assumptions, the model could predict the opposite, namely that as wages rise workers prefer leisure to work and react to the tax cut by working less!

Often it may be possible to accept or dismiss a model of economic behaviour on the basis of common sense or casual observation of the world around us. But usually these days economists go further, using sophisticated statistical tests to evaluate empirically the model's predictions. 'Good' economic models or theories survive the process of empirical testing (which is part of a branch of the subject called 'econometrics'), whereas models or theories shown to be at odds with observed behaviour must be revised or discarded.

GOODS, BADS, FREE GOODS AND ECONOMIC GOODS

4. In economic theory, we use the word **'good'** as a generic term or 'catch-all' label to include all the goods which yield utility. As the name indicates, a consumer obtains utility directly from a **consumer good**, but **capital goods** yield utility indirectly via the consumer goods they help to produce.

The opposite of a 'good' is a 'bad', which is sometimes also known as a **'nuisance good'**. A 'bad' such as garbage yields only disutility and whereas people are normally prepared to pay a price to obtain quantities of a good, the opposite is true of a 'bad'; consumers are prepared to pay a price to get rid of the 'bad' or to have it taken away.

But although people are usually prepared to pay a price to obtain a good, some goods may be available free or at zero price. Strictly, there is an important difference between **'free goods'** and goods such as national defence and public health care, which are often provided by the state free to the consumer, being financed instead collectively out of general taxation. A genuine 'free good', such as air or rain water in a wet climate, is available in unlimited quantities at zero cost of production. Thus the central economic problem of scarcity does not apply to a 'free good' and there is no need to economise in its use. Figure 3.1 illustrates the demand and supply conditions for a 'free good'. The supply curve lies along the horizontal axis and the equilibrium quantity of the 'free good' consumed is equal to the amount demanded at zero price, Q^*.

Figure 3.1: Supply and demand conditions for a 'free' good; demand intersects supply at zero price

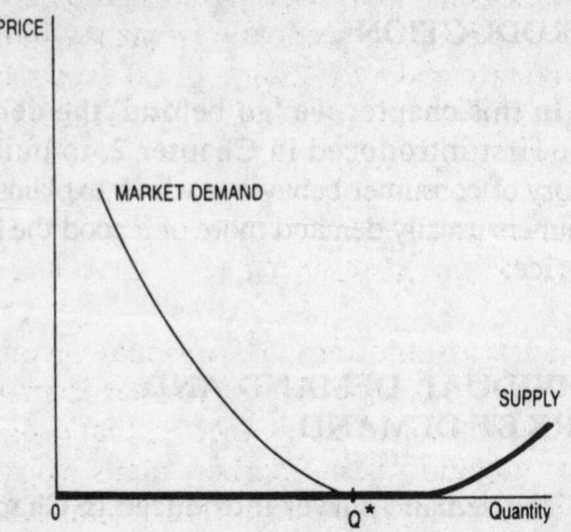

All goods other than 'free goods' are **economic goods**, including those provided at zero price by the state. Scarce resources are used up and an opportunity cost is incurred in the production of an economic good, and thus a need arises to economise in its use.

OPPORTUNITY COST

5. Whenever an economic agent makes a choice in conditions of scarcity, an opportunity cost is involved. **Opportunity cost** or **alternative** cost as it is also known, is a key economic concept, meaning much more than the money costs of production incurred by firms or the price paid by a consumer when purchasing a good or service. The opportunity cost to a consumer, resulting from the purchase of a bar of chocolate for 50 pence, might be the lost opportunity to spend the same 50 pence on the next best alternative, perhaps an icecream or a newspaper. It is important to understand that the concept of opportunity cost is not restricted just to consumer behaviour and demand theory; it occurs in many other economic contexts. For example, the opportunity cost incurred by a farmer when planting his fields with wheat, might be the sacrificed opportunity to grow the next best crop, perhaps barley. Note that the assumption of rationality implies that the 'best' alternative will always be chosen, so the opportunity cost is always the 'next best'.

THE ASSUMPTION OF RATIONAL BEHAVIOUR

6. **Perhaps the most fundamental or basic assumption underlying a large part of economic theory, especially micro-economic theory, is that**

people always attempt to act in their self-interest. From this assumption stems the economist's definition of **rationality**. Rational economic behaviour is self-interested behaviour; 'economic man' or 'economic woman' will never deliberately make a decision or take a course of action known in advance to be against self-interest.

UTILITY MAXIMISATION

7. The assumption of rational economic behaviour leads logically to a further assumption fundamental to economic theory, that economic agents decide their market plans so as to **maximise some target, objective** or **goal** believed consistent with self-interest. In demand theory, the objective function which households are assumed to wish to maximise is the utility obtained from the set of goods and services consumed. **Utility** means the usefulness or fulfilment of need which a consumer gains from consuming a good, though for many goods and services, utility can be more simply defined as the pleasure or satisfaction obtained from consumption.

MAXIMISING V MINIMISING BEHAVIOUR

8. The assumption of maximising behaviour by economic agents (consumers, workers, firms and even the government) is central to economic theory and model-building. It is worthwhile to note however, that *any maximising objective can always be restated as a minimising objective.* Thus the household's assumed objective of 'maximising the utility gained from the set of goods consumed' can be recast as 'minimising the outlay, expenditure or cost of obtaining the same combination or bundle of goods'. Whether we set up an assumed objective in maximising or minimising terms depends upon our convenience; it is perhaps more usual to investigate the maximising objective, but for some purposes a consideration of the minimising principle can shed interesting light upon economic behaviour.

MAXIMISATION SUBJECT TO CONSTRAINTS

9. If all goods were free, or if households had unlimited income, a consumer would maximise utility by obtaining all goods and services which gave him utility up to the point of satiation. **Satiation** occurs when no more utility can be gained; any further consumption will yield only **disutility** (dissatisfaction or displeasure). However because of the problem of scarcity, consumers face a number of constraints which restrict their freedom of action in the market place. The constraints are:

(i) **Limited income.** Consumers, even the very rich, do not possess an unlimited income or stock of wealth with which to purchase all the goods which could possibly yield utility. Income spent on one good cannot be spent on some other good or service.

(ii) **A given set of prices.** A consumer is seldom able by his own action to influence the market price he pays for any of the goods and services he buys; he is a **'price-taker'** and not a **'price-maker'.**

(iii) **The budget constraint.** Taken together, limited income and the set of prices faced, impose a budget constraint on the consumer's freedom of action in the market place. Assuming that all income is spent rather than saved and that stocks of wealth are not run down, a consumer can only purchase more of one good by giving up consumption of some other good or service, which therefore represents the opportunity cost of consumption.

(iv) **Fixed tastes and preferences.** We assume that a person's tastes and preferences are fixed or stable, in the short run at least. This means that if he prefers butter to margarine today, he will prefer butter tomorrow as well. A consumer is said to behave *consistently* if his preferences are stable over time.

(v) **Limited time available.** Even when goods are free, consumer choices must still be made because it is often impossible to consume more than one good at a time or to store more than a limited number of goods for future consumption.

(vi) **Limited availability of goods.** Some goods may simply be unavailable due to production bottlenecks and other causes of shortages in supply.

DIMINISHING MARGINAL UTILITY

10. We can now begin the task of deriving an individual's demand curve for a good. Following our earlier assumptions that a consumer wishes to maximise utility, but is faced with a number of constraints that limit his market action, we now assume that as he consumes more of a good within a relatively short period of time, the **total utility** derived *increases, but it does so at a decreasing or diminishing rate*. This is known as the *'law' of diminishing marginal utility*, though whether it should have the status of an economic 'law' is open to debate. Strictly, a scientific law should hold always without admitting exceptions, but quite clearly there are exceptions to the 'law' of diminishing marginal utility. It is possible that a person may experience an increasing marginal utility as the first few units of a good are consumed and in the case of an addictive good such as a narcotic drug, larger and larger quantities may be required to 'fulfill the need' of the unfortunate consumer.

THE RELATIONSHIP BETWEEN MARGINAL AND TOTAL UTILITY

11. Let us imagine a thirsty man who drinks six glasses of lemonade in a short period of time, deriving successively eight, six, four, two, zero, and minus two 'degrees of utility' from each glass consumed. This information is shown in the total and marginal utility schedules of Table 3.1, from which the total and marginal utility curves drawn in Figure 3.2 are plotted.

Table 3.1: Total and marginal utility schedules

Glasses of lemonade	Total utility (degrees of utility)	Marginal utility (degrees of utility)
0	0	
1	8	8
2	14	6
3	18	4
4	20	2
5	20	0
6	18	-2

It is important to note that the total and marginal utility schedules and likewise, the total and marginal utility curves, show exactly the same information but they show it in different ways. The **total utility schedule** and the **total utility curve** show the data *cumulatively*. For example, when drinking two glasses of lemonade, the thirsty man gains fourteen 'degrees of utility' in total. After three glasses, total utility rises to eighteen 'degrees of utility' and so on. In contrast, the **marginal utility schedule** and the **marginal utility curve** plot the same data as *separate observations*, rather than cumulatively. The last unit consumed is always the marginal unit and the utility derived from it is the **marginal utility.** So after two drinks, the second glass of lemonade is the marginal unit consumed, yielding a marginal utility of six 'degrees of utility'. But when three glasses of lemonade are consumed, the third glass becomes the marginal unit, from which the thirsty man gains a marginal utility of just four 'degrees of utility'.

In Figure 3.2, diminishing marginal utility is shown both by the *diminishing rate of increase* of the slope of the total utility curve drawn in the upper panel of the diagram and by the *negative* or *downward* slope of the marginal utility curve in the lower panel. Satiation is reached after five drinks, the fifth drink yielding zero marginal utility. Even if lemonade is free to the consumer, it would be irrational for our 'no-longer-thirsty' man to drink a sixth glass of lemonade. He would experience negative marginal utility (ie a marginal disutility), which is shown by the downward or negative slope of the total utility curve. Satiation occurs where the marginal utility curve reaches zero, becoming negative if further drinks are consumed, and at the highest point on the total utility curve.

DERIVING THE SLOPE OF THE DEMAND CURVE

12. If lemonade were available completely free, it would be rational for our thirsty man to drink exactly five glasses, consuming up to the point of satiation at which no further utility could be gained. But since lemonade is an economic good rather than a 'free good', it is reasonable to assume that he must pay for his drinks. Suppose that the price of lemonade is equal to the marginal utility gained from the fourth glass,

P_4. Now P_4 represents the opportunity cost of the fourth glass of lemonade, ie the utility which could be gained if the price of the fourth glass were spent on some other good, the next best alternative. To maximise utility, the thirsty man must drink four glasses of lemonade. It would be irrational to consume a fifth glass, since the utility he gains would now be less than the opportunity cost represented by the price P_4.

Figure 3.2: Utility curves

(a) The total utility curve
(b) The marginal utility curve

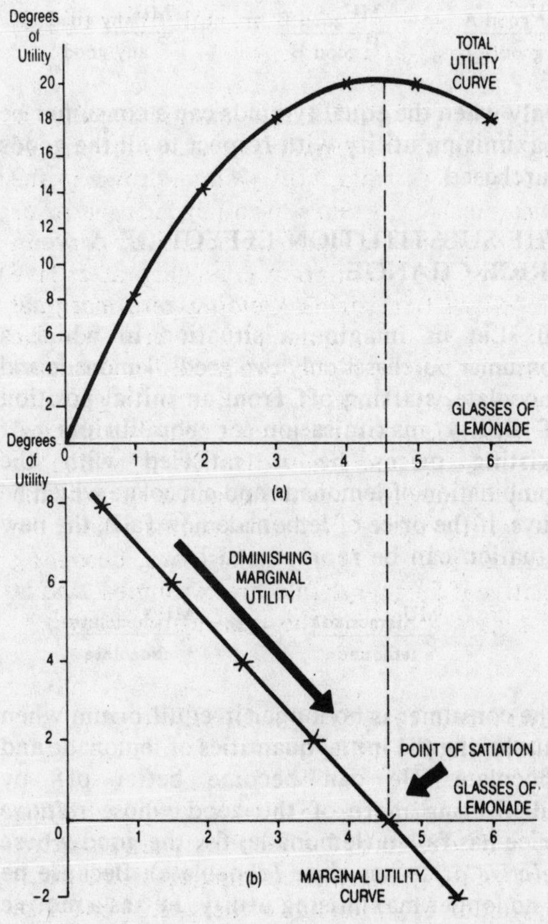

Figure 3.3: Deriving the demand curve from the marginal utility function

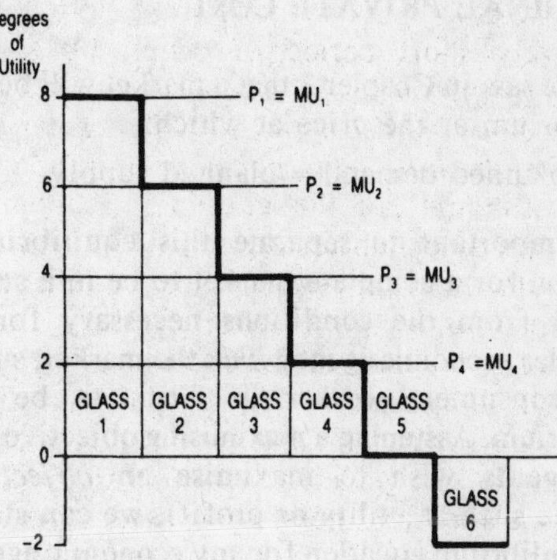

Figure 3.3 shows the price rising from P_4 successively to P_3, P_2 and P_1. The prices P_3, P_2 and P_1 equal the marginal utility derived respectively from the third, the second and the first glasses of lemonade. When the price is P_3, our thirsty man must reduce his demand to three glasses of lemonade to maximise utility in the new situation. At P_2 demand is again reduced to two drinks and so on. The higher the price, the lower the quantity demanded; we have derived the slope of the demand curve.

CONSUMER EQUILIBRIUM

13. We are now in a position to state the condition necessary for a utility maximising individual to be in **consumer equilibrium.**

Disequilibrium conditions:

(i) If when MU > P, consumption should increase to maximise utility;
(ii) and when MU < P, consumption should decrease to maximise utility

Then the equilibrium condition is:

(iii) only when MU = P should consumption remain constant.

Only when MU = P for each of the goods he demands can an individual be maximising utility over all the goods consumed. **MU = P** is therefore the **equilibrium equation for consumer equilibrium**, the necessary condition for utility maximisation.

MARGINAL PRIVATE BENEFIT AND MARGINAL PRIVATE COST

14. We saw in Chapter 2 that a market will be in equilibrium at the price at which:

planned demand = planned supply

It is important to separate this equilibrium equation for a complete market to be in a state of rest from the conditions necessary for a particular economic agent *within* the market, such as a consumer, worker or firm, to be in equilibrium. Assuming a maximising objective (ie that agents wish to maximise an *objective function* such as utility or profit), we can state the equilibrium equation for any economic agent as:

marginal private benefit = marginal private cost

To be in equilibrium with respect to any economic activity, the economic agent must undertake the activity up to the point at which the marginal benefit received by the agent (**marginal private benefit**) equals the marginal cost incurred by the agent (**marginal private cost**). If for example:

(i) MPB > MPC, more of the activity should be undertaken to maximise the objective function; or

(ii) MPB < MPC, less of the activity should be undertaken.

Therefore:

(iii) MPB = MPC represents the condition necessary for maximisation: equilibrium equation.

MU = P is a particular example of this rule, in which the marginal utility derived from the last unit consumed of a good is the consumer's marginal private benefit, while the price paid for the good is the marginal private cost incurred.

THE CONDITION OF EQUI-MARGINAL UTILITY

15. We can generalise the equilibrium equation MU = P to cover all the goods purchased by an individual. For simplicity let us assume that only two goods are in demand, lemonade and chocolate. To maximise utility, the equilibrium equation must hold for each good:

Equation 1: $MU_{lemonade} = P_{lemonade}$

Equation 2: $MU_{chocolate} = P_{chocolate}$

Dividing equation 1 by equation 2, we get:

$$\frac{MU_{lemonade}}{P_{lemonade}} = \frac{P_{lemonade}}{P_{chocolate}}$$

which can be re-arranged to become the **condition of equi-marginal utility:**

$$\frac{MU_{lemonade}}{P_{lemonade}} = \frac{MU_{chocolate}}{P_{chocolate}}$$

Generalised to cover all goods bought, the condition of equi-marginal utility is:

$$\frac{MU_{good\ A}}{P_{good\ A}} = \frac{MU_{good\ B}}{P_{good\ B}} = \ldots \frac{MU_{any\ good}}{P_{any\ good}}$$

Only when the equality holds can a consumer be maximising utility with respect to all the goods purchased.

THE SUBSTITUTION EFFECT OF A PRICE CHANGE

16. Let us imagine a situation in which a consumer purchases only two goods, lemonade and chocolate, starting off from an initial position of utility maximisation or equilibrium. At existing prices he is satisfied with the combination of lemonade and chocolate which he buys. If the price of lemonade now falls, the new situation can be represented by:

$$\frac{MU_{lemonade}}{P_{lemonade}} > \frac{MU_{chocolate}}{P_{chocolate}}$$

The consumer is no longer in equilibrium when purchasing the initial quantities of lemonade and chocolate. He can become better off by substituting more of the good whose *relative* price has fallen (lemonade) for the good whose *relative* price has risen (chocolate). Because he is no longer maximising utility, he has a motive for changing his market behaviour.

As he substitutes lemonade for chocolate, he moves 'down' his marginal utility curve for lemonade, and 'back up' his marginal utility curve for chocolate. The marginal utilities adjust until a new equilibrium is reached, when no alternative reallocation of the two goods can improve his total utility. The condition of equi-marginal utility once again holds.

THE INCOME EFFECT OF A PRICE CHANGE

17. If consumers were influenced only by the **substitution effect** of a price change, demand curves would only slope downwards, provided of course that consumers wish to maximise utility and experience diminishing marginal utility. The substitution effect operates always in the same direction, causing more to be demanded of a good whose *relative* price has fallen and less to be demanded of a good whose *relative* price has risen.

However, when we introduce the second effect of a price change, the **income effect**, matters are not quite so simple. If the price falls of one good which a consumer buys, his real income has risen and he feels better off. The nature of the resulting income effect then depends on whether the good is a **'normal' good** or an **'inferior' good**. If a consumer's expenditure on a good rises as his real income rises, then the good is normal. Conversely, the good is inferior if expenditure on the good falls when real income rises. The same good can of course be normal and inferior for different consumers and also for a single individual at different levels of real income. Suppose that the income expenditure graph, Figure 3.4, represents an individual's expenditure on a staple food such as bread at different levels of real income. At low levels of income, his expenditure on bread rises as his income rises, thus bread is a normal good. But at levels of real income above Y_1 bread becomes inferior for this consumer as he begins to substitute other more luxurious foods for bread.

Figure 3.4: An income expenditure curve for a good which becomes inferior at high level of income

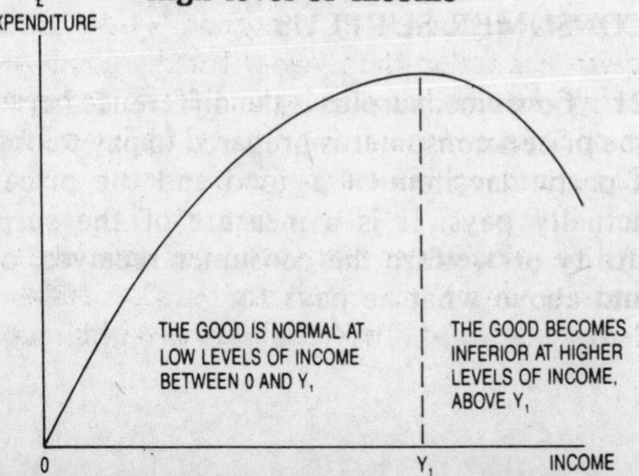

THE COMBINED SUBSTITUTION AND INCOME EFFECTS

18. Whether an individual's demand curve for a good is downward- or upward-sloping depends upon the combined substitution and income effects of a price change. Figure 3.5 illustrates the possibilities.

Figure 3.5: The arrows shows the direction of the substitution effect and the income effect resulting from a price change

TYPE OF GOOD	SUBSTITUTION EFFECT OF A PRICE CHANGE	INCOME EFFECT OF A PRICE CHANGE
(I) NORMAL GOOD	➡ (large)	➡ (small)
(II) INFERIOR GOOD	➡ (large)	⬅ (small)
(III) GIFFEN GOOD	➡ (small)	⬅ (large)

(i) A normal good: the two effects reinforce each other

(ii) Inferior good: different directions, with the substitution effect more powerful.

(iii) Giffen good: different directions, with the income effect more powerful

The demand curve for a normal good is always downward-sloping, showing that more is demanded at lower prices. This is because the substitution effect and the income effect of a price change reinforce each other. As price falls, the good is substituted for other goods which have become relatively more expensive, while at the same time more is demanded because the consumer feels better off. But in the case of inferior goods, the income effect of the price change works in the opposite direction to the substitution effect. Nevertheless for most inferior goods, the income effect is likely to be much smaller than the substitution effect because spending on a single good is likely to be only a tiny fraction of a consumer's total expenditure. Real income hardly alters when the price of a single good changes, so the income effect is very weak.

Nevertheless, there is a theoretical possibility that a good will not only be inferior, but that the income effect will be sufficiently strong to more than offset the substitution effect. This is the special case of an inferior good known as a **'Giffen' good**. The demand curve for a Giffen good slopes upward showing that as price falls, less is demanded. To be a Giffen good, a good must of course be inferior; however most inferior goods are certainly not Giffen goods. Indeed, while Giffen goods exist as a theoretical possibility, observation of the real world gives very little support to the existence of the Giffen phenomenon.

UPWARD-SLOPING DEMAND CURVES

19 There are other circumstances besides the case of the Giffen good, in which a consumer might be prepared to buy more of a good at higher rather than lower prices. These are:

(i) **Speculative demand**. A consumer might believe, for example, in the case of housing, foreign exchange, or company shares, that an increase in price indicates that the price is going to rise even higher in the future. In these circumstances, it is rational to purchase the good or financial asset in the hope that a capital gain (or speculative gain) can be realised if and when the price has indeed risen further.

(ii) **Veblen goods**. A Veblen good is a good for which the price indicates status. The higher the price, the greater the status. Therefore, amongst people motivated by 'status maximisation', people who derive a great deal of utility from status, more may be demanded at higher prices.

(iii) **Price as an indicator of quality**.. People may believe, rightly or wrongly, that price is an indicator of a good's quality; the higher the price the better the quality. If the price falls, demand may also fall if consumers become suspicious that the good's quality has deteriorated.

THE CONDITIONS OF DEMAND

20 In a previous section we explained how an increase in real income, resulting from a fall in the price of a good, influences the slope of the demand curve through an income effect. It is important to avoid confusing the income effect just described, with the effects of a change in real income which is independent of a change in the good's own price. In Chapter 2, we saw how the position of a demand curve depends upon the **conditions of demand** which include all the variables, other than the good's own price, that influence demand. If any of the conditions of demand change, the position of the demand curve will shift. A consumer's real income is one of the most important conditions of demand. If a person's real income rises as a result of a wage or salary increase, or perhaps a cut in income tax, then the demand curve of each of the goods he buys will shift. For a normal good, the demand curve will shift to the right (or upwards) and more will be demanded at every price. This is illustrated in Figure 3.6(a) on the following page. However, if the good is inferior, a rise in real income causes less to be demanded at every price and the demand curve shifts leftwards (or downwards) as shown in Figure 3.6(b).

A change in real income is only one of the possible causes of a shift in demand. In general, a change in any of the constraints facing the consumer will cause a shift in his individual demand curve, and additionally, a change in the size of the market, caused for example by population growth, can shift the market demand curve. The good's own price is not included in the conditions of demand because the demand curve itself 'maps' how demand responds to a change in price. However, a change in the price of a **substitute** or a **complementary good** will shift a demand curve. Automobiles and petrol are complementary goods. If the prices of automobiles rise significantly, the demand curve for petrol will probably shift to the left and less petrol will be demanded at all prices. Conversely, a rise in the price of a substitute for petrol such as diesel fuel, will over time cause the demand curve for petrol to shift rightwards as consumers purchase cars with petrol engines rather than cars with diesel engines.

CONSUMER SURPLUS

21 **Consumer surplus** is the difference between the price a consumer is prepared to pay to obtain a particular item of a good and the price he actually pays. It is a measure of the **surplus utility** or welfare the consumer receives, over and above what he pays for.

Figure 3.6: The effect of an increase in income

(a)

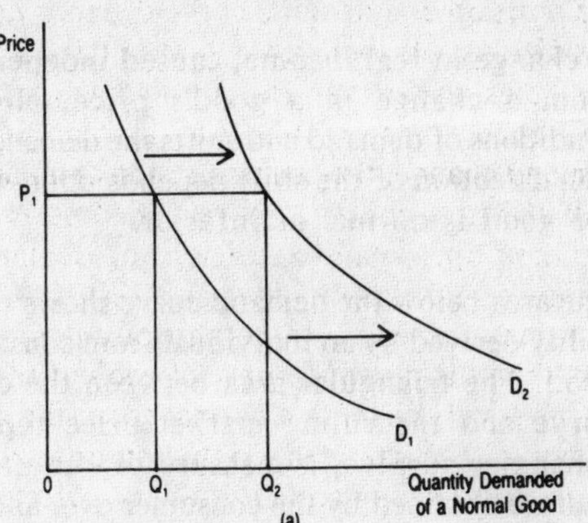

(b)

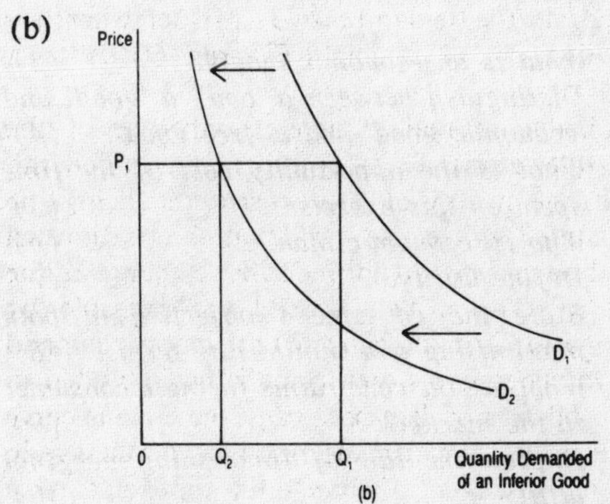

(a) Shifting the demand curve for a normal good to the right: at price P_1 demand increases from Q_1 to Q_2.

(b) Shifting the demand curve for an inferior good to the left: at price P_1 demand decreases from Q_1 to Q_2

The demand curve drawn in Figure 3.7 shows the maximum prices a particular consumer is prepared to pay for bars of chocolate: £2.00 for the first bar, £1.80 for the second bar and so on. But will the consumer need to pay these prices in order to purchase the bars of chocolate? The answer is no; by walking into a shop or supermarket, he can buy as much chocolate as he would like, at the ruling market price of 50p per bar.

For each bar of chocolate purchased, the consumer surplus gained is shown on the diagram by a vertical line drawn between the demand curve and the price actually paid, 50p. For example, he gains a consumer surplus of A B from the first bar of chocolate purchased, and C D from the second bar. The total consumer surplus gained from all the chocolate he chooses to purchase is shown by the triangle XYZ. You should note that no consumer surplus is gained from the last bar of chocolate purchased. This is the marginal bar, for which MU = P. The man is only just prepared to pay a price of 50p for this bar; if the price were to rise he would decide not to buy it.

The concept of consumer surplus can easily be extended to cover all the consumers in a market. Figure 3.8 shows market demand and supply curves, D_1 and S_1 and an initial equilibrium market price at P_1. The triangle AP_1C, which lies below the market demand curve but above the price of P_1, shows the consumer surplus gained in the market as a whole. If the supply curve now shifts upwards to S_2, causing the market price to rise to P_2, the consumer surplus triangle becomes smaller, falling to the area AP_2D.

This rather simple point is of very great significance in economic theory and policy-making. Consumer surplus can be regarded as a measure of economic welfare. Since an ultimate purpose of any economic system is to maximise economic welfare, the greater the consumer surplus, the greater the country's welfare. Anything which reduces consumer surplus, such as a rise in costs of production causing supply curves to shift upwards, represents a welfare loss.

Figure 3.7: An individual's consumer surplus shown by the shaded triangle XYZ

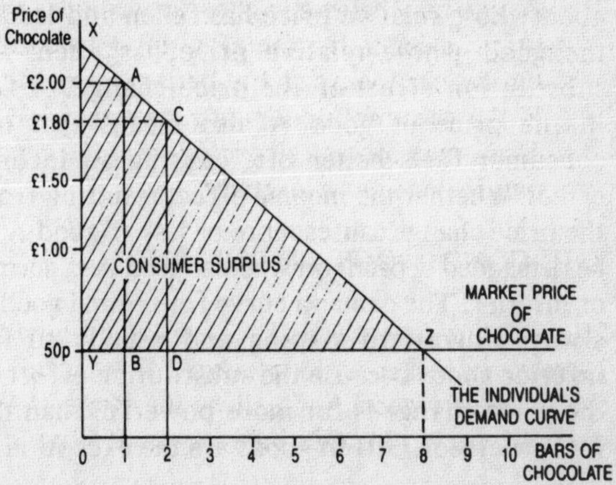

Figure 3.8: Consumer surplus and the whole market

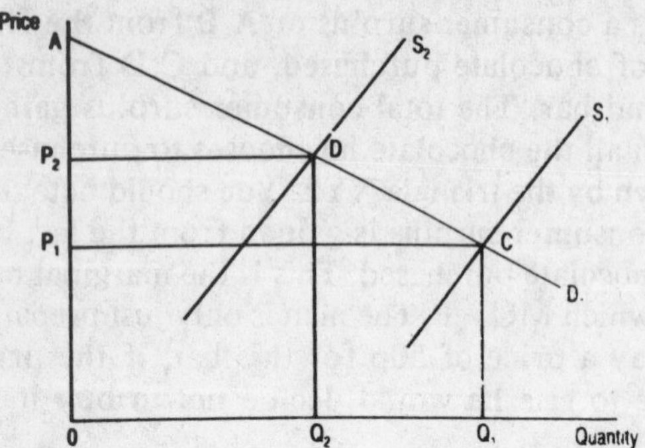

Following a shift in supply from S_1 to S_2, the consumer surplus triangle falls from AP_1C to AP_2D.

SUMMARY

22 In this chapter we have applied the economist's technique of model-building to the construction of a theory or model of individual consumer behaviour. Starting from initial assumptions of utility maximising behaviour and of diminishing marginal utility, we derived the equilibrium equation for consumer equilibrium: P = MU. Generalised to cover all goods, the equilibrium equation becomes the condition of equi-marginal utility.

$$\frac{MU_{\text{good A}}}{P_{\text{good A}}} = \frac{MU_{\text{good B}}}{P_{\text{good B}}} = \ldots \frac{MU_{\text{any good}}}{P_{\text{any good}}}$$

When for example the price of good A falls, the condition of equi-marginal utility is disturbed and the consumer no longer maximises utility. To restore equilibrium he must consume more of the good whose relative price has fallen and less of the good whose relative price has risen: the substitution effect of the price change. A fall in the price of good A also means that the consumer feels better off, causing an income effect. Whether the income effect resulting from the price change causes more or less of good A to be demanded depends on whether good A is normal or inferior. The demand curve for normal good is always downward sloping and usually so for inferior goods because the substitution effect of the price change is far more powerful than the income effect. Giffen goods are the exception to this rule; they are inferior and the income effect is more powerful than the substitution effect, resulting in an upward-sloping demand curve.

A change in real income, caused independently from a change in a good's price, alters the conditions of demand and shifts the demand curve. The direction of the shift depends upon whether the good is normal or inferior.

The area below the demand curve shows the total utility derived by an individual from consuming a good. The triangular area between the demand curve and the ruling market price represents consumer surplus, a measure of the utility or welfare obtained by the consumer over and above what he pays for.

STUDENT SELF-TESTING

1 *What is an economic model?* *(3)*
2 *Distinguish between a 'bad', a 'good' and 'economic good' and a 'free good'.* *(4)*
3 *What is the opportunity cost of the time spent on this exercise?* *(5)*
4 *Who is 'economic man'?* *(6)*
5 *Define utility.* *(7)*
6 *State the consumer's objective in both maximising and minimising terms.* *(8)*
7 *What are the constraints facing a consumer in the market?* *(9)*
8 *Explain the 'law' of diminishing marginal utility.* *(10)*
9 *What happens to total utility when marginal utility is negative?* *(11)*
10 *Why is a good's price its opportunity cost?* *(12)*
11 *What is the equation for consumer equilibrium?* *(13)*
12 *What is marginal private benefit?* *(14)*
13 *Explain the condition of equi-marginal utility.* *(15)*
14 *What is the substitution effect of a price change?* *(16)*
15 *Distinguish between an income effect and a substitution effect.* *(17)*
16 *Distinguish between a normal good, an inferior good and a Giffen good.* *(18)*
17 *List reasons why a demand curve may sometimes slope upward.* *(19)*
18 *How will a wage rise affect the demand curve for an inferior good?* *(20)*
19 *What is consumer surplus?* *(21)*

EXERCISES

1. (a) Explain briefly the conditions necessary for a consumer to be in equilibrium.

   (b) How would this equilibrium be altered by (i) a fall in the price of one good and (ii) by a fall in the general price level?

2. The table below shows the weekly utility function for three types of food for a man with a total budget of £56.

	Meat	Vegetables	Fruit
Price	£12	£8	£4
Quantity	Total utility	Total utility	Total utility
1	28	16	16
2	54	26½	28
3	78	36½	36
4	98	46	42
5	110	55	44
6	120	63½	48
7	124	71½	50
8	124	73	51

Assuming the consumer wishes to maximise utility and that he spends all his income on one or other of these three goods,

(a) If he bought only meat, when would the point of satiation be reached?
(b) If he buys all three goods, how much of each should he buy?
(c) Calculate the consumer surplus he derives from fruit when in consumer equilibrium.

MULTIPLE CHOICE QUESTIONS

1. Which of the following is not held constant when a demand schedule is drawn up?
   A The good's price
   B The price of complementary goods
   C The price of substitutes
   D The price of factors of production

2. A rise in the demand for petrol by motorists is likely to follow a rise in the price of:
   A Steel
   B Second-hand cars
   C Public transport
   D Motor insurance

3. The Law of Diminishing Marginal Utility states that the more a person consumes of a good:
   A The higher is the price he is prepared to pay
   B The smaller is his total pleasure
   C The slower is the rate of increase in his total pleasure
   D He consumes the good always up to the point of satiation

4. *Which of the following will cause the demand curve of margarine to shift to the left?*
   - A *A fall in the price of margarine*
   - B *A fall in the cost of vegetable oils*
   - C *A successful advertising campaign by butter producers*
   - D *A fall in the price of bread*

5

Good	*Quantity*	*Price*	*Marginal utility*
Y	*30*	*£36*	*12*
Z	*20*	*£90*	*?*

Assuming a household is maximising utility with respect to goods Y and Z, the marginal utility derived from Z is:

- A *10*
- B *20*
- C *30*
- D *60*

EXAMINATION QUESTIONS

1. *(a) Explain the difference between a movement along and a shift in, a demand curve.* *(8 marks)*

   (b) Demonstrate the effect on the demand for a product of:
   (i) an increase in supply; *(4 marks)*
   (ii) increased advertising; *(4 marks)*
   (iii) an increase in population. *(4 marks)*
   (ACCA December 1984)

2. *Distinguish between the income effect and the substitution effect of a decrease in the price of a product.*
   (ICSA December 1984)

3. *Why is the concept of the margin important in the study of economics?*
   (CIMA November 1979)

Appendix to Chapter 3: Indifference curves

INTRODUCTION

1. In the main body of Chapter 3, we have used the **utility approach** to demand theory to derive an individual's demand curve for lemonade. As we have seen, the utility approach requires the measurement of the utility gained by the individual from each glass of lemonade. But by their nature, 'degrees of utility' are immeasurable. For this reason, many economists prefer an alternative method of deriving a demand curve, using **indifference curve analysis**, which does not require the actual measurement of utility. The indifference curve approach to demand theory also has the advantage of showing, in a very clear way, how the substitution and income effects of a price change influences the slope of the demand curves of normal goods, inferior goods and Giffen goods.

AN INDIFFERENCE CURVE

2. Let us assume that only two goods are available for a man to purchase, lemonade and chocolate, and that he gains an equal total pleasure or satisfaction from any of the combinations of the two goods shown in Table 3.2.

Combination	*Bars of chocolate*	*Glasses of lemonade*
a	11	1
b	7	2
c	4	3
d	2	4
e	1	5

Table 3.2: Alternative combinations of lemonade and chocolate giving equal satisfaction to a consumer

These combinations or bundles of the two goods, lemonade and chocolate, which give the man the same total satisfaction are plotted on the graph drawn in Figure 3.9. A line drawn through these bundles and through any other combinations that give the same total satisfaction as a, b, c, d and e is known as an **indifference curve**. An indifference curve shows all combinations of two goods which yield the same total satisfaction to a consumer. The consumer is said to be indifferent between any two combinations represented by points on one indifference curve.

Figure 3.9: Points on an indifference curve representing combinations of chocolate and lemonade between which a particular consumer is indifferent

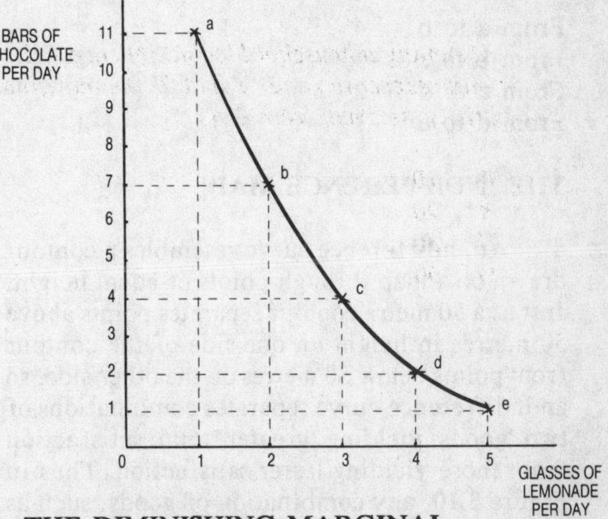

THE DIMINISHING MARGINAL RATE OF SUBSTITUTION

3. The particular slope of the indifference curve drawn in Figure 3.9, getting flatter and flatter moving down the curve, indicates a **diminishing marginal rate of substitution** of one good for another. In indifference curve theory, the assumption of a diminishing marginal rate of substitution of one good for another performs a role similar to the assumption of diminishing marginal utility in the utility approach to demand theory. A diminishing marginal rate of substitution means that if our man decides to consume more lemonade, substituting lemonade for chocolate, for each extra glass of lemonade consumed he will be less and less willing to give up chocolate. Table 3.3. illustrates the diminishing marginal rate of substitution between chocolate and lemonade. When for example our man chooses bundle b rather than bundle a, his marginal rate of substitution is -4. He is willing to sacrifice 4 bars of chocolate to gain 1 extra glass of lemonade. But moving from bundle b to bundle c he is only prepared to give up 3 bars of chocolate to obtain an extra glass of

lemonade, a marginal rate of substitution of -3. As our man gives up chocolate, the last unit sacrificed means more and more to him while the extra glass of lemonade gained means less and less. The rate at which he is prepared to give up chocolate to get more lemonade diminishes.

Table 3.3:

Movement	Change in chocolate	Change in lemonade	Marginal rate of substitution: $\frac{\Delta C}{\Delta L}$
From a to b	-4	1	-4
From b to c	-3	1	-3
From c to d	-2	1	-2
From d to e	-1	1	-1

THE INDIFFERENCE MAP

4. An indifference curve resembles a contour drawn on a map through points of equal height. Just as a 50 metre contour separates points above 50 metres in height on one side of the contour from points below 50 metres on the other side, so an indifference curve separates combinations of two goods yielding greater total satisfaction from those yielding lesser satisfaction. Thus in Figure 3.10, any combination of goods, such as bundle f, located 'beyond' or to the 'north-east' of the indifference curve gives a greater total satisfaction than any combination on the indifference curve itself. Conversely, a bundle such as g located 'inside' or to the 'south-west' of the indifference curve yields a lesser satisfaction.

Figure 3.10: Bundle f is preferred to any bundle on the indifference curve. Any bundle on the indifference curve is preferred bundle g

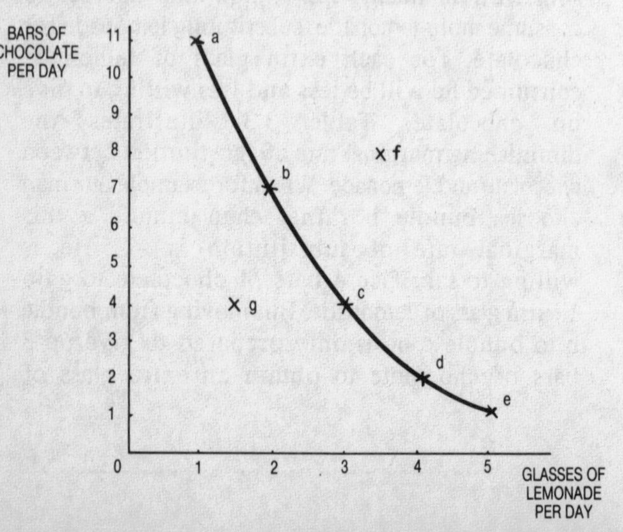

In much the same way as a geographical map normally contains a number of contours, each joining points of a particular height, so an individual's 'indifference map' can be drawn to show a set or 'family' of indifference curves, each representing bundles of two goods yielding equal satisfaction for a particular consumer. In Figure 3.11 we have drawn three indifference curves, I_1, I_2 and I_3, each representing combinations of lemonade and chocolate yielding equal satisfaction for our consumer. You should note that I_1, I_2 and I_3 are not the only indifference curves we could have drawn; they are just three selected from an infinite set.

Any combination or bundle of goods on indifference curve I_2 yields, a greater total satisfaction for our consumer than any bundle on I_1. But since curve I_2 lies 'inside' or to the 'south-west' of I_3, a combination on I_3 would be preferred to any on I_2.

THE BUDGET LINE

5. **The budget line YX drawn in Figure 3.12** shows the maximum quantities of lemonade and chocolate which our consumer can buy, given both the size of his income and the prices of the two goods. Point Y on the vertical axis of the graph shows the maximum amount of chocolate he can purchase when he spends all his income on chocolate and none on lemonade. Likewise, Point X on the horizontal axis shows the maximum number of glasses of lemonade he can buy, assuming that none of his income is spent on chocolate. Points on the budget line between X and Y, indicate the various combinations of lemonade and chocolate he can purchase when spending all his income on the two goods.

Figure 3.11: An indifference curve 'map'

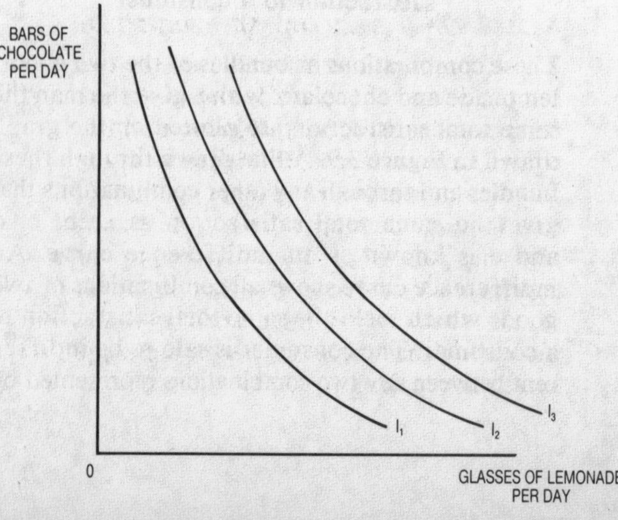

Figure 3.12: A consumer's budget line

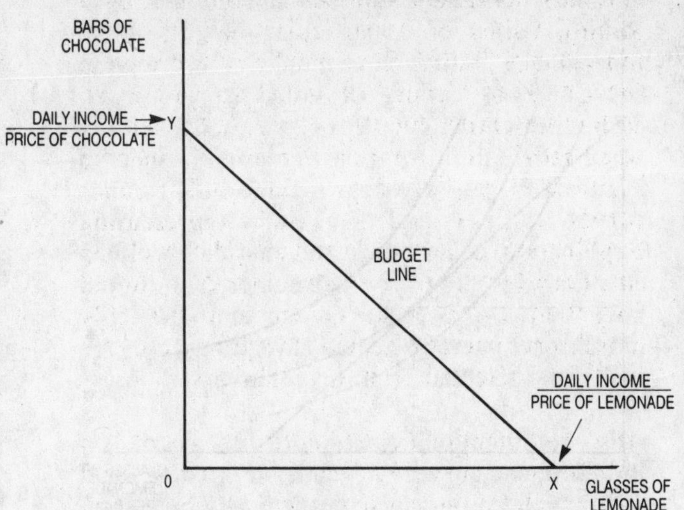

The budget line in fact represents the budget constraint facing the consumer. He cannot purchase a combination of goods 'outside' or to the 'north-east' of the budget line, unless his income increases or prices fall.

A PRICE CHANGE AND THE BUDGET LINE

6. If the price of lemonade falls but the price of chocolate remains unchanged, we must draw a new budget line YX′, illustrated in Figure 3.13. The new budget line shows that our consumer can now buy a greater quantity of lemonade, but that the maximum amount of chocolate he can purchase remains unchanged. The slope of the budget line is a measure of the *relative prices* of the two goods: the slope of the line YX reflects the original relative prices, while the slope of YX′ measures the relative prices after the fall in the price of lemonade.

A CHANGE IN INCOME AND THE BUDGET LINE

7. If our consumer's money income rises but the prices of lemonade and chocolate remain unchanged, his **real income** will of course have increased. In Figure 3.14, the increase in real income causes the budget line to shift outwards from YX to AB, allowing more of both goods to be purchased. You should note that the slopes of the two budget lines are the same, indicating that there has been no change in relative prices.

CONSUMER EQUILIBRIUM

8. To maximise utility and achieve consumer equilibrium, an individual must choose a combination of goods on the 'furthest-out' indifference curve he can reach. In general, there will be only one combination of goods, shown as bundle Z in Figure 3.15, which represents a state of consumer equilibrium. Consumer equilibrium is located where the budget line YX just touches, or is a tangent to, the 'furthest-out' attainable indifference curve I_2. Given his preference mapped by the indifference curves and the budget constraint contained in the budget line YX, our consumer maximises utility when purchasing L_2 lemonade and C_2 chocolate.

Figure 3.13: The budget line moves from YX to YX′ following a fall in the price of lemonade

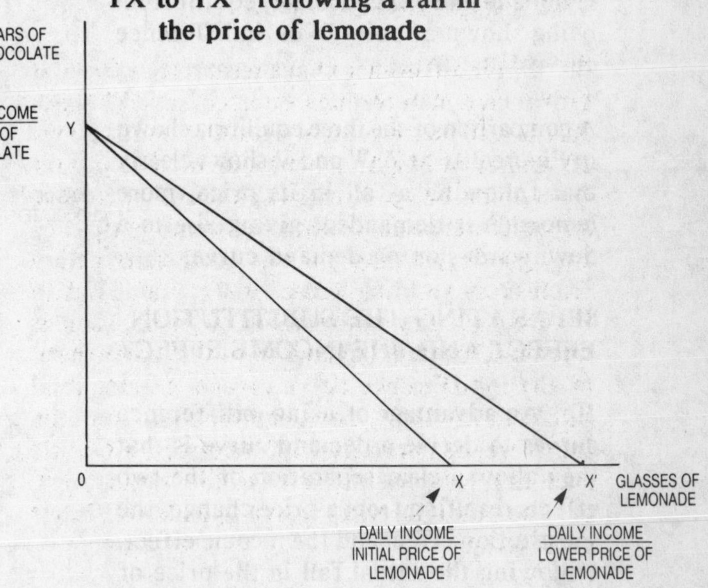

Figure 3.14: The budget line moves from YX to AB following an increase in money income, with prices remaining unchanged

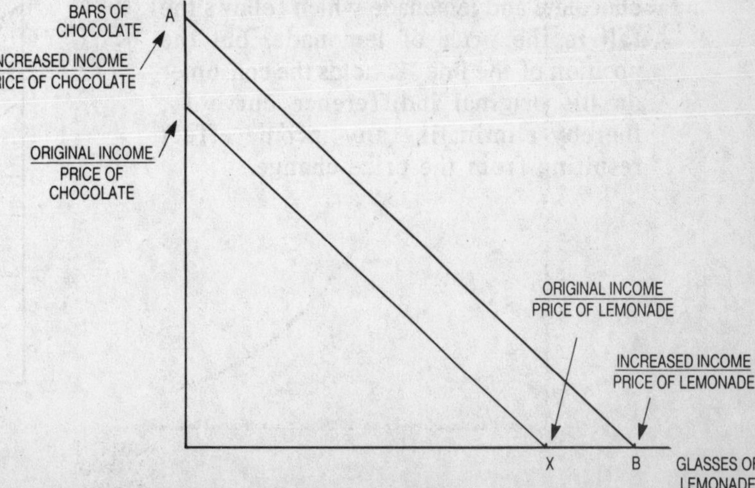

DERIVING THE DEMAND CURVE FROM THE INDIFFERENCE MAP

9. Suppose that the price of lemonade falls, causing the budget line to move to YX′ in Figure 3.16. Our consumer can now reach a 'further out' indifference curve I_3. If he continues to purchase L_2 lemonade and C_2 chocolate he will no longer be in equilibrium; to maximise utility he must now purchase L_3 lemonade and C_3 chocolate. The new equilibrium is determined at point W, where the new budget line YX′ forms a tangent to indifference curve I_3. Likewise, if the price of lemonade falls still further, causing the budget line to shift to YX", the consumer adjusts his purchases to L_4 lemonade and C_4 chocolate, equilibrium being shown at point V on indifference curve I_4.

A comparison of the three equilibria shown in Figure 3.16 at Z, W and V shows clearly that following a fall in its price, more lemonade is demanded, giving rise to a downward-sloping demand curve.

SEPARATING THE SUBSTITUTION EFFECT AND THE INCOME EFFECT

10. An advantage of using indifference curves to derive a demand curve is that they allow a clear separation of the two effects resulting from a price change, the substitution effect and the income effect. Following the initial fall in the price of lemonade which moves the budget line from YX to YX′, we can draw a new line JK with the same slope as YX′ but forming a tangent to I^2. The line JK is illustrated in Figure 3.17. The slope of the line JK reflects the new relative prices of chocolate and lemonade which follows the fall in the price of lemonade, but the position of the line JK holds the consumer on his original indifference curve I_2, thereby eliminating any income effect resulting from the price change.

Figure 3.15: Consumer equilibrium at Point Z

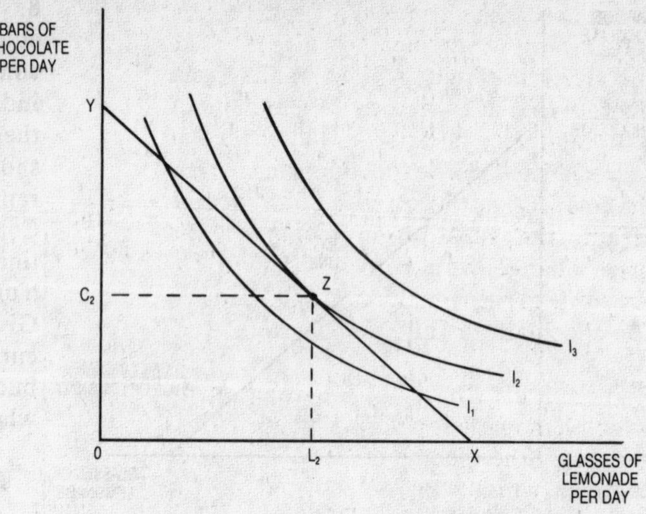

Figure 3.16: As the price of lemonade falls demand for lemonade rises from L_2 to L_4

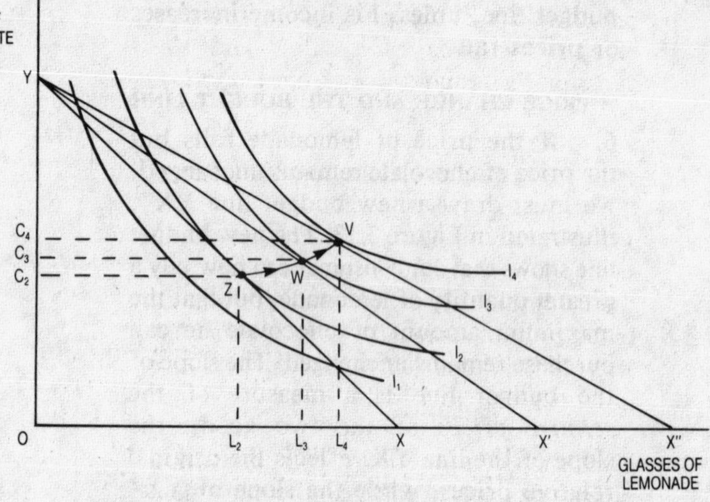

Figure 3.17: The substitution and income effects for a normal good

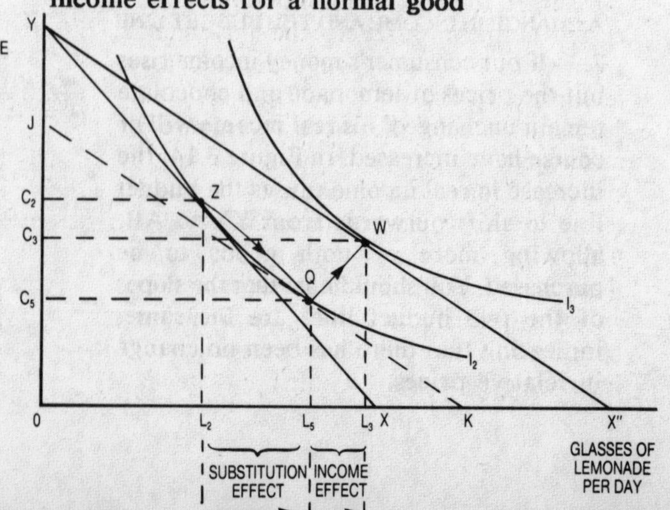

The movement from the original consumer equilibrium at Z to the new equilibrium at W can now be divided into the substitution effect and the income effect. The substitution effect, which results from the fact that at its new price lemonade is now relatively cheaper and chocolate is now relatively more expensive, is shown by the line ZQ. In the absence of an income effect, the substitution effect of the price change would cause demand for lemonade to rise from L_2 to L_5 and demand for chocolate to fall from C_2 to C_5.

Figure 3.17 illustrates a situation in which lemonade is a normal good. This is shown by the income effect of the price change, which can be isolated as the movement along the line QW. Because the consumer feels better off following the fall in the price of lemonade, the income effect causes him to increase his demand from L_5 to L_3. Combining together the substitution and the income effects resulting from the prices fall, the two effects reinforce each other and the consumer's demand rises from L_2 to L_3.

INFERIOR GOODS AND GIFFEN GOODS

11. Figures 3.18 and 3.19 show a separation of the substitution effect and the income effect which result from a fall in the price of lemonade when lemonade is an inferior good (in Figure 3.18) and a Giffen good (in Figure 3.19).

You should note that the substitution effect of the price change - the movement from Z to Q - still causes more lemonade to be demanded. However, because lemonade is assumed to be an inferior good in both cases, the income effect - the movement from Q to W - reduces the demand for lemonade. In Figure 3.18, the combined substitution and income effects would still result in a conventional downward-sloping demand curve, showing demand rising as the price of lemonade falls. This is because the income effect is too weak to offset the much more powerful substitution effect. But Figure 3.19 has been drawn to show the much more powerful income effect that would operate if lemonade was not only inferior, but sufficiently inferior to be a Giffen good.

Figure 3.18: The substitution and income effects for an inferior good

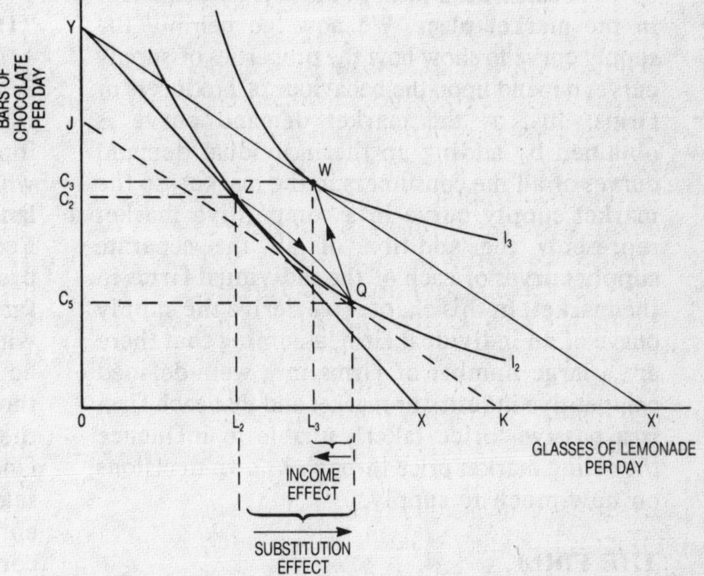

Figure 3.19: The substitution and income effects for a Giffen good

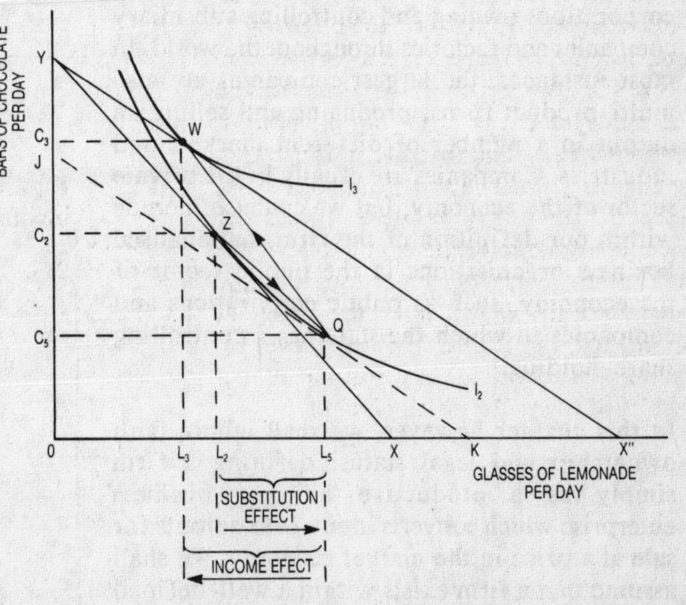

4. Supply and cost theory

INTRODUCTION

1. In Chapter 3, we 'went behind' the demand curve to construct a theory of consumer behaviour in the market place. We now 'go behind' the supply curve to show how the properties of supply curves depend upon the behaviour of producers or firms. Just as the market demand curve is obtained by adding up the individual demand curves of all the consumers in the market, so the **market supply curve** in a competitive market represents the addition of all the **separate supply curves** of each of the **individual firms** in the market. In this chapter we derive the supply curve of an individual firm, assuming that there are a large number of firms in a well-defined competitive industry or market and that each firm is a passive 'price-taker', unable to influence the ruling market price through its own decisions on how much to supply.

THE FIRM

2. In the real economy there are many different types of firm. In terms of legal organisation, firms range from very small unincorporated one-man businesses (**individual proprietorships** or **sole traders**) at one extreme, performing functions such as painting and decorating and house repairs, to massive **public companies** such as British Petroleum at the opposite end of the size spectrum. The largest public companies, including BP, are **multinational** business **corporations** owning and controlling subsidiary companies and factories throughout the world. In most instances, the largest companies are also multi-product firms, producing and selling an output in a number of different markets and industries. Companies are usually in the private sector of the economy, but we can also include within our definition of the firm, **nationalised business organisations** in the public sector of the economy, such as **public corporations** and companies in which the state has a controlling share-holding.

In this chapter however, we shall ignore both ownership and legal status, defining a firm simply as a **productive unit or business enterprise which converts inputs into outputs for sale at a price in the market economy.** We shall assume that a firm exists within a well-defined industry and the plant or plants which it operates produce a single equally well-defined product or output.

THE FACTORS OF PRODUCTION

3. **Production** is a process of converting **inputs** into **outputs** of useful goods and services. The inputs necessary for production to take place, which include the services of **labour, capital** and **land**, are known as the **factors of production.** Economists also identify a fourth factor of production, **enterprise** or the **entrepreneurial factor.** The entrepreneur is the decision maker within the firm, deciding such questions as what, how and how much to produce. In a small business, the owner is usually the entrepreneur, bearing the financial risks, but also reaping the financial rewards. However, in a large firm it is seldom possible to identify an owner-entrepreneur. Instead in modern large business corporations and nationalised industries, the entrepreneurial function tends to be split between owners, such as shareholders in private sector companies, and the salaried managers or executives whom they employ.

THE MARKET PERIOD, THE SHORT RUN AND THE LONG RUN

4. In micro-economic theory three time periods are usually defined: **the market period, the short run** and the **long run.**

(i) **The market period.** Firms are completely unable to alter supply in the **market period** or **momentary period.** For example, a street trader might arrive one morning at his stall with a truck load of strawberries which will not keep until the following day. Once at his stall, the trader is unable either to increase his available supply within the market period to meet any unexpected surge in demand, or to take the strawberries off the market for sale at a later date.

(ii) **The short run**. The **short run** is defined as a period of time in which at least one factor of production is fixed. In the short run, a firm can only increase output or supply by adding more of a

variable factor, such as labour, to the **fixed factors** of production such as capital and land. The short run is thus a time period in which a firm's ability to increase supply is constrained by its fixed capacity. We should distinguish between a firm's constrained **short-run supply curve** and its **long-run supply curve** which is unconstrained except by such factors as the prices it must pay to obtain capital and labour and the availability of technology.

(iii) **The long run**. In the long run all the factors of production are variable and a firm can increase output or supply by changing the **scale** of the factors held fixed in the short run. Only in the long run can a firm either expand the scale of its operations by moving into a bigger factory, or reduce its activities by closing down production plant. The long run is also the time period in which new firms can enter a market or industry and existing firms can leave, providing no barriers exist to prevent freedom of entry and exit.

SHORT-RUN COSTS

5 In the short run, the **total cost** of producing a particular output includes the cost of employing both the fixed and the variable factors of production. This is expressed as the identity:

$$TC \equiv TFC + TVC$$

Likewise, **average total cost** per unit can be written as:

$$ATC \equiv AFC + AVC$$

In order to explain how a firm's total costs of production vary with output, we must first examine more closely the nature of **fixed costs** and **variable costs**.

FIXED COSTS

6. **Fixed costs** of production are overheads, such as the rent of land and the maintenance costs of building which a firm must pay in the short run. Suppose, for example, that a car manufacturing company incurs overheads of £1 million a year from an assembly plant it operates. We can represent these costs both as the horizontal **total fixed cost curve** in Figure 4.1(a) and as the downward sloping **average fixed cost curve** in Figure 4.1(b). If the plant only managed to produce one automobile a year, AFC per car would be £1 million - the single car would bear all the overheads. But if the company were to increase production, average fixed costs would fall to £500,000 when two cars were produced, £333,333 when three cars were produced and so on. Average fixed costs per unit of output thus fall as output increases, as overheads are spread over a larger output.

Figure 4.1: Cost curves

(a) The total fixed cost curve
(b) The average fixed cost curve

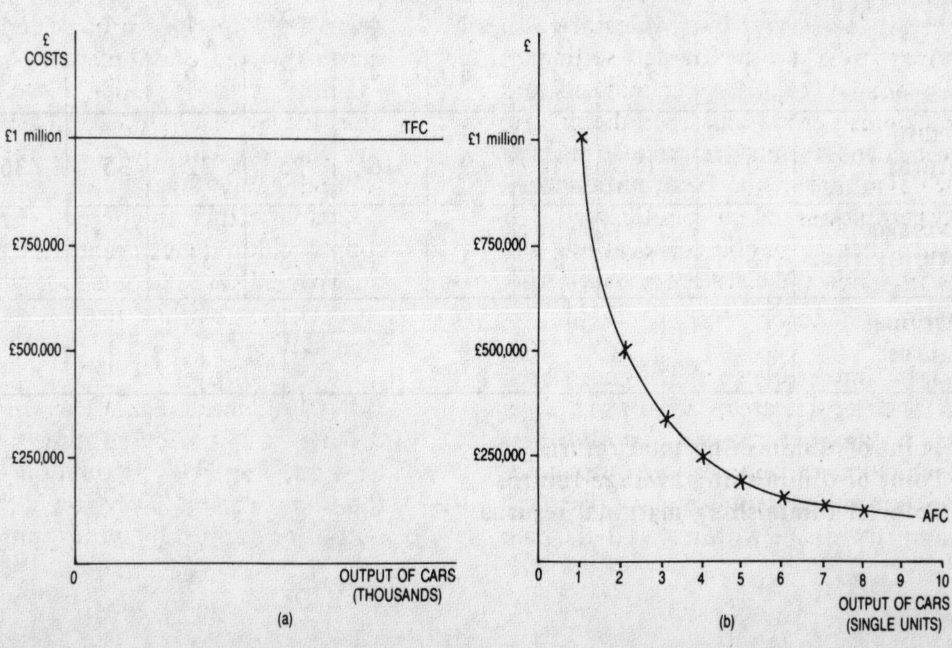

DIMINISHING RETURNS

7 Before we explain variable costs of production, we must first introduce and explain the **'law of variable proportions'**, known also as the **'law' of diminishing returns.** Let us imagine that the car firm mentioned in the previous paragraph builds luxury sports cars, employing a handful of men in a small factory building. Figure 4.2 below illustrates how the firm's output changes as the labour force grows from one man to nine men.

When just one man is employed in the otherwise empty factory, we have assumed that by performing all the many tasks involved in car production, the worker manages to build 1 car a year. If a second man is then added to the work force, total output rises to 4 cars a year and when a third worker is employed, the total increases again to 9 cars.

The additional output resulting from the employment of an extra worker represents the **marginal returns** of labour. Our example illustrates **increasing marginal returns** up to and including the fifth worker employed, as each extra worker hired raises total output by more than the previous worker. Increasing marginal returns are indeed quite likely when a firm first begins to hire labour because extra workers allow the firm to organise the workforce more efficiently. By dividing the various tasks of production amongst its growing workforce, the firm can gain from **specialisation** and the **division of labour.** Workers become better or more efficient in the particular tasks in which they specialise and the time which would be lost if workers switched between tasks is saved.

But eventually, as the firm attempts to increase output or supply in the economic short run by adding more labour to its fixed capacity, **diminishing marginal returns** to labour set in: an extra worker adds less to total output than the previous worker. In our example, the point of diminishing marginal returns is reached when 5 men are employed. A sixth worker joining the workforce raises production by only 7 cars, whereas the fifth worker had produced a marginal output of 9 cars. Diminishing marginal returns occur, not because the marginal worker joining the labour force is any less hardworking or motivated than his predecessors, but because the benefits resulting from any further specialisation and division of labour eventually become exhausted when the capital or machinery with which labour combines is fixed in supply.

Figure 4.2: Returns to a variable factor or production

Fixed capital *Variable labour*

	0	*1*	*2*	*3*	*4*	*5*	*6*	*7*	*8*	*9*
Total returns	0	1	4	9	16	25	32	35	36 *	34
Average returns	-	1	2	3	4	5	5⅓ **	5	4½	4
Marginal returns		1	3	5	7	9 ***	7	3	1	-2

* Point of diminishing total returns
** Point of diminishing average returns
*** Point of diminishing marginal returns

Figure 4.3: The relationship between total marginal and average returns

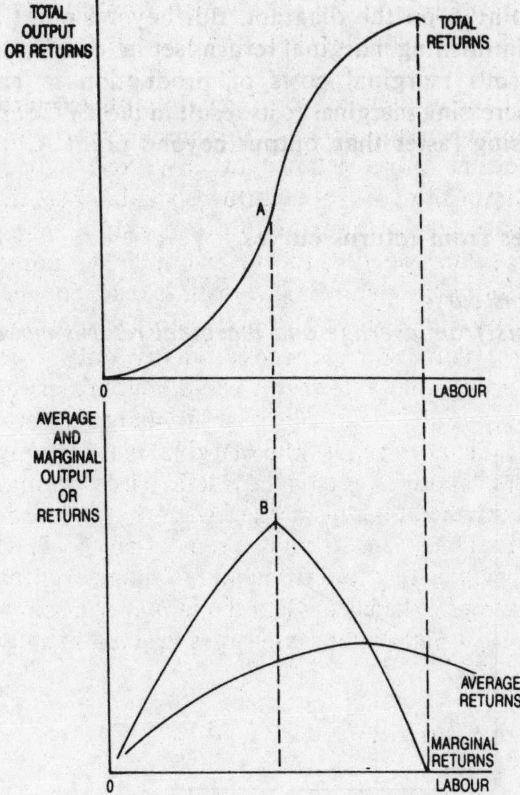

Figure 4.3 illustrates the 'law' of diminishing returns both on a **total returns curve** shown in the upper panel of the diagram and on **marginal** and **average returns curves** depicted in the lower panel. The **point of diminishing marginal returns** occurs in the upper panel at point A. Beyond point A, the total returns curve continues to rise as the labour force increases in size, but the slope of the curve becomes flatter, rising at a diminishing or decreasing rate. When the returns or output of the workforce are plotted as separate observations rather than cumulatively, in the marginal returns curve shown in the lower panel of the diagram, the point of diminishing marginal returns is indicated at point B. Increasing marginal returns are shown by the positive (or rising) slope of the marginal returns curve, while diminishing marginal returns are represented by a negative (or falling) slope.

MARGINAL RETURNS AND AVERAGE RETURNS

8. The lower panel of Figure 4.3 also distinguishes between diminishing *marginal* returns to labour and diminishing *average* returns - a source of confusion for the unwary! As we have already explained, marginal returns refer to the addition to output attributable to the last worker who joins the labour force. Average returns per worker at any size of total employment is simply the total output of all the workers divided by the number of workers employed.

The relationship between any marginal variable and the average to which it is related is:

(i) when the marginal > the average, the average rises
(ii) when the marginal < the average, the average falls
(iii) when the marginal = the average, the average is constant, neither rising nor falling

This is a universal mathematical relationship with a great many economic applications. It is vital to understand this relationship. It does not state that an average will rise when a marginal is rising, or that an average will fall when the marginal falls. The numerical example illustrated in Figure 4.2 and the returns curves drawn in Figure 4.3, clearly show that marginal returns begin to fall as soon as the point of diminishing returns is reached. Nevertheless, average returns continue to rise as long as the marginal output of any extra worker is greater than the existing average output - thereby 'pulling up' the average. The point of diminishing average returns is reached only when the whole labour force on average becomes less productive. In our numerical example diminishing average returns set in after the sixth worker, when the marginal output of 3 cars produced by the seventh worker 'pulls down' the average from $5\frac{1}{3}$ to 5 cars per worker.

VARIABLE COSTS AND AVERAGE RETURNS

9. In the upper panel of Figure 4.4 a firm's **total variable cost (TVC)** curve is illustrated alongside the total returns curve from which it is derived. When labour is the only variable factor of production employed by the firm, variable costs are simply wage costs. If the firm pays the same wage to all its workers, total wage costs will rise proportionately with the number of workers employed. However, when an extra worker adds more to total output then the previous worker, yet the wage cost of employing him remains the same, the **marginal cost (MC)** of producing an extra unit of output must fall.

Increasing marginal returns to a firm's variable factors of production thus cause the marginal costs of output to fall. In the upper panel of Figure 4.4, falling marginal costs are shown by the TVC curve rising less fast than output, up to point A on the diagram. But beyond point A, diminishing marginal returns set in, causing the firm's marginal costs of production to rise. Increasing marginal costs result in the TVC curve rising faster than output beyond point A.

Figure 4.4: Deriving cost curves from returns curves

(a) Deriving total variable costs from the total returns curve
(b) Deriving average variable costs and marginal costs from average and marginal returns curves.

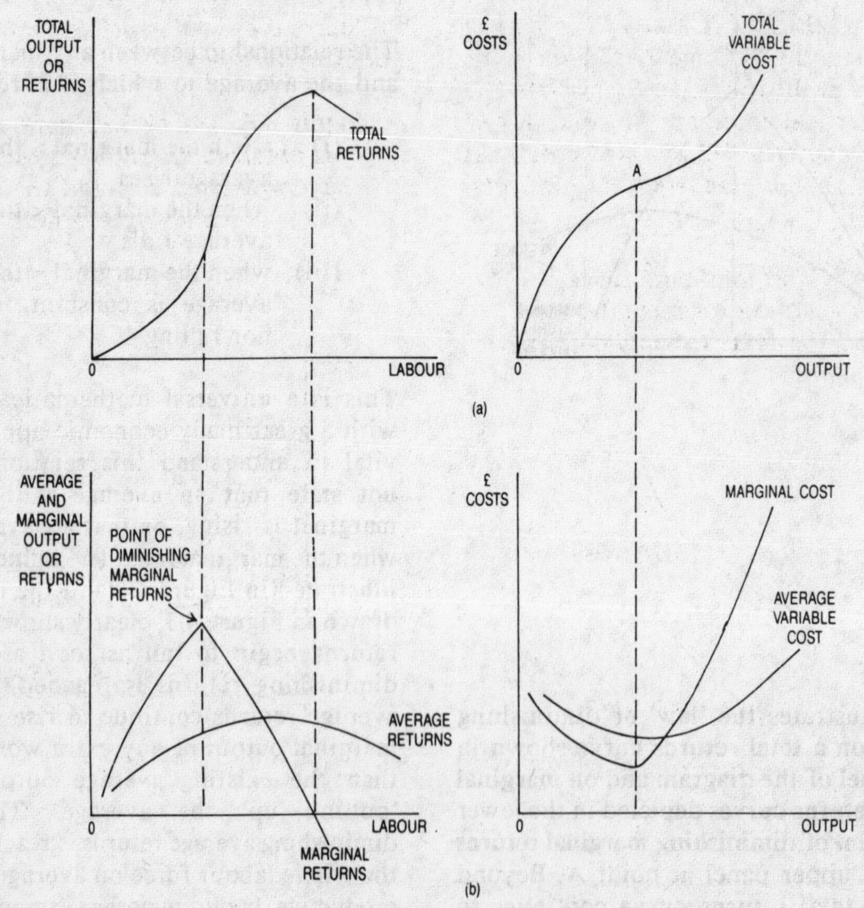

The lower panel of Figure 4.4 shows exactly the same information plotted as *separate* observations, rather than *cumulatively*, to form the firm's **marginal cost curve**. Increasing marginal returns to the variable factors of production cause the MC curve to fall, but once the point of diminishing marginal returns is reached, the MC curve rises with output.

Just as the MC curve is derived from the nature of *marginal* returns to the variable inputs, so the **average variable cost (AVC) curve** illustrated in the lower panel of Figure 4.4 is explained by *average* returns. While increasing average returns are being experienced, with the labour force on average becoming more efficient and productive, the AVC per unit of output must fall as output rises. But once diminishing average returns set in, the AVC curve begins to rise with output.

TOTAL COSTS

10. A firm's **total cost (TC)** curve is obtained by adding together the TFC and TVC curves. The resulting curve is illustrated in Figure 4.5 The *position* (or vertical intercept at point X) of the TC curve is determined by fixed costs, but variable costs explain the *slope* of the total cost curve.

Figure 4.5: The total cost curve is obtained by adding together the total fixed cost and the total variable cost curve

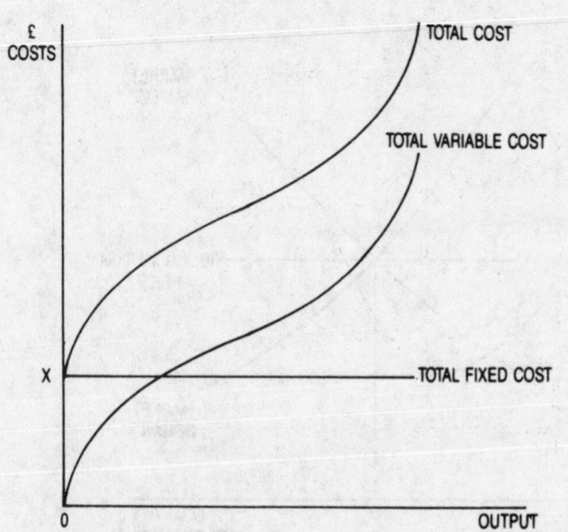

AVERAGE TOTAL COSTS

11. In the same way as a firm's TC curve is plotted by adding together the TFC and TVC curves, so its **average total cost (ATC) curve** is obtained from the addition of the AFC and AVC curves. The short-run ATC curve, illustrated in Figure 4.6 it typically U-shaped, showing that average total costs per unit of output first fall and later rise as output is increased. In the short run, average total costs must eventually rise because at high levels of output any further spreading of fixed costs becomes insufficient to offset the impact of diminishing returns upon variable costs of production.

You should note that the MC curve cuts both the AVC and the ATC curves at their lowest points. Check back to section 8 in this chapter to make sure that you know why this must be so. However, the point where the MC curve cuts the AFC curve in Figure 4.6 is of no significance because the MC curve is derived only from variable costs and not from fixed costs.

Figure 4.6: The average total cost curve is obtained by adding together the average fixed cost and the average variable cost curve

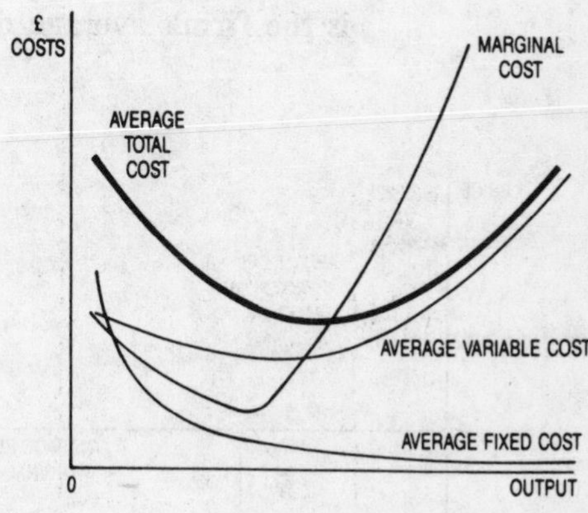

SHORT-RUN SUPPLY

12 We are now in a position to derive the short-run supply curve of a firm in a competitive industry in which the firm is a passive 'price-taker'. Whenever a firm is a passive 'price-taker', it can sell whatever output it produces at the ruling market price which is determined by supply and demand conditions in the market as a whole. The ruling market price becomes in fact the firm's **average revenue (AR) curve** and also its **marginal revenue (MR) curve**. Suppose that the ruling market price is P_1 illustrated in Figure 4.7 below. When the firm sells an output of Q_1, the average revenue received per unit of output sold is P_1. Average revenue thus equals price. If the firms now increases sales by one unit, total revenue received will rise by the amount P_1. The firm's marginal revenue received from the last unit of sales thus also equals price. In short, P = AR = MR.

We can now show that in order to maximise profits, the firm must produce the output where MR = MC. (Note we are now using MR as economic shorthand for marginal revenue and not marginal returns!)

Disequilibrium conditions are:

whenever

(i) MR > MC, the firm is sacrificing the profit it could make from an extra unit of sales. It should therefore increase output.

and whenever

(ii) MR < MC, the firm is making a loss on at least the final unit of sales. It should therefore reduce output.

Therefore when:

(iii) MR = MC, there is no incentive to increase or reduce output.

MR = MC is thus the **equilibrium equation** for a profit-maximising firm. You should note that MR = MC illustrates the general statement of the equilibrium equation for any maximising economic agent, which we explained in Chapter 3:

Marginal private benefit = marginal private cost

For any firm whose aim is to maximise profits, the marginal revenue received by the firm from the last unit of sales represents the firm's marginal private benefit, while marginal production costs are the marginal private cost incurred by the firm.

Figure 4.7: In a competitive industry in which a single firm is a passive 'price-taker' the ruling market price P_1 is the firm's average revenue and marginal revenue curve

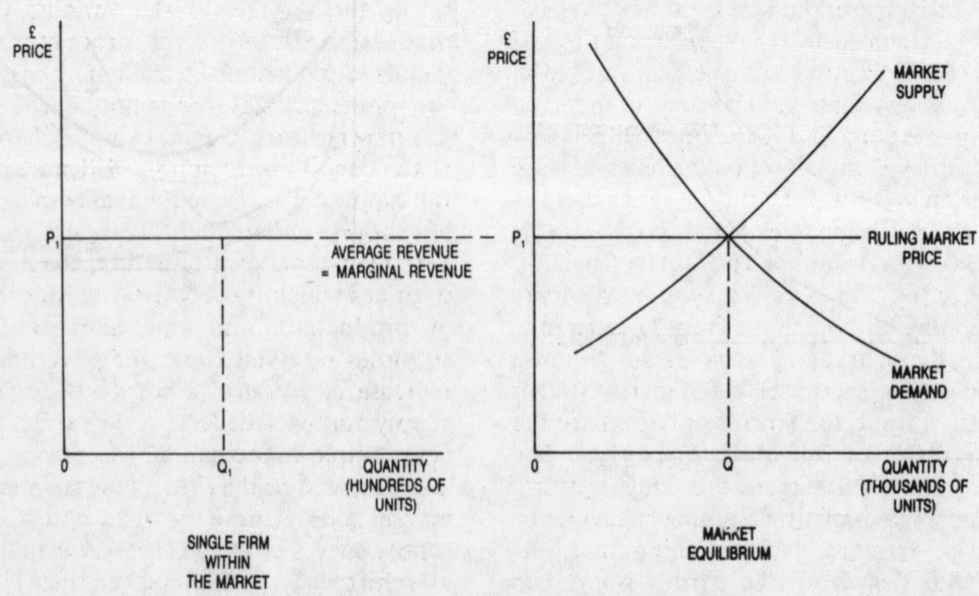

Figure 4.8: The firm's MC curve above AVC is its short-run supply curve

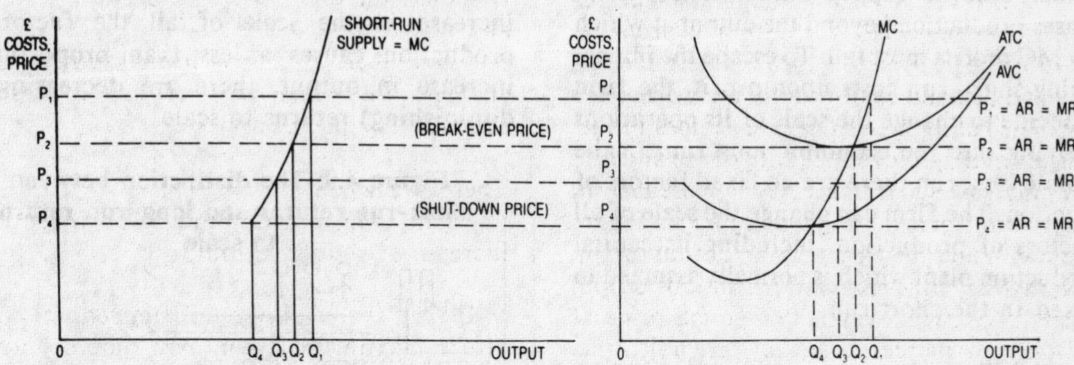

Suppose that the market-determined price facing the firm is P_1 illustrated in Figure 4.8. Using the equilibrium equation MR = MC, the firm will choose to supply quantity Q_1 onto the market, but if the price falls to P_2, it will reduce supply to Q_2. P_2 is **break-even price**, since the firm will make a loss if the price falls below the ATC curve. Nevertheless, if the price falls below P_2, the firm may continue to supply an output in the short run at least, even though it will be making a loss. As long as the price is greater than AVC, the firm will earn enough revenue to cover at least part of fixed costs. When, for example, the market price is P_3, the loss the firm makes at output Q_3 is less than the fixed costs incurred when output is zero. But if the price falls below AVC, the firm will shut down production and cease to supply an output onto the market, thereby making a loss equal to fixed costs. P_4 is therefore known as **shut-down price**. The *firm's MC curve above AVC is thus its short-run supply curve*, mapping how much the firm is prepared to supply to the market at each price. Because diminishing marginal returns cause marginal costs to rise with output, the firm is only prepared to supply a greater output if the price rises. The short-run supply curve therefore slopes upward. The assumption of profit-maximising behaviour on the part of firms and diminishing marginal returns thus 'explain' the firm's short-run supply curve in just the same way that the assumption of utility-maximising behaviour on the part of households and diminishing marginal utility 'explain' an individual's demand curve.

SHIFTS IN SUPPLY

13. In the short run, the position of a firm's MC curve or supply curve is determined by the productivity of its variable factors of production, reflected in the principle of diminishing returns, and by the money costs of hiring the services of the variable factors of production. If either the productivity of the factors of production or the money cost of hiring the inputs changes, the supply curve will shift to a new position. Generalising, a change in any of the **conditions of** supply will shift the short-run supply curve. An individual firm's conditions of supply include the productivity of its variable factors of production, the money costs or prices which must be paid to hire the factors of production, and any taxes paid to, and subsidies received from, the government. Any increase in production costs will shift a firm's supply curve to the left (or upwards), including for example an increase in wage costs, or higher taxes imposed on the firm by the government. The market supply curve obtained by adding up the supply curves of all the firms in the market, can also shift when, in the long run, new firms enter the market or existing firms leave.

THE LONG RUN AND RETURNS TO SCALE

14 When a firm increases output in the economic short run, it must eventually experience diminishing marginal returns and a rising marginal cost or supply curve. If the firm increases production beyond the output at which MR = MC profits must fall. To escape the impact of rising short-run costs upon profit, the firm may decide to change the **scale** of its operations by moving into the economic long run. In the economic long run there are no fixed factors of production. The firm can change the scale of all its factors of production, including its capital or production plant which is normally assumed to be fixed in the short run.

Figure 4.9 illustrates the important distinction between **returns to a variable factor of production**, which occur in the short run, and **returns to scale** which operate only in the economic long run. Suppose that initially a firm's fixed capital is represented by Plant Size 1. In the short run, the firm can increase production by moving along the horizontal arrow A, employing more variable factors of production such as labour. However, the only way the firm can further increase profits once the short-run profit-maximising output has been reached is to change the scale of its operations, assuming of course that the firm cannot operate its existing plant more efficiently. In the long run the firm can invest in a larger production plant, such as Plant Size 2, shown as the move along the vertical arrow X in Figure 4.9. Once Plant Size 2 is in operation, the firm is in a new short-run situation, able to increase output by moving along arrow B. But again, the impact of diminishing returns and rising short-run marginal costs upon profits, may eventually cause the firm to move once more into the long run, expanding the scale of its operations to Plant Size 3.

The 'law' of diminishing returns does not operate in the long run when a firm increases the scale of all its inputs or factors of production. Instead there are three possibilities: **increasing returns to scale; constant returns** to scale; and **decreasing returns to scale.**

(i) **Increasing returns to scale.** If an increase in the scale of all the factors of production causes a more than proportionate increase in output, there are increasing returns to scale.

(ii) **Constant returns to scale.** If an increase in the scale of all the factors of production causes a proportionate increase in output, there are constant returns to scale.

(iii) **Decreasing returns to scale.** If an increase in the scale of all the factors of production causes a less than proportionate increase in output, there are decreasing (or diminishing) returns to scale.

Figure 4.9: The distinction between short-run returns and long-run returns to scale

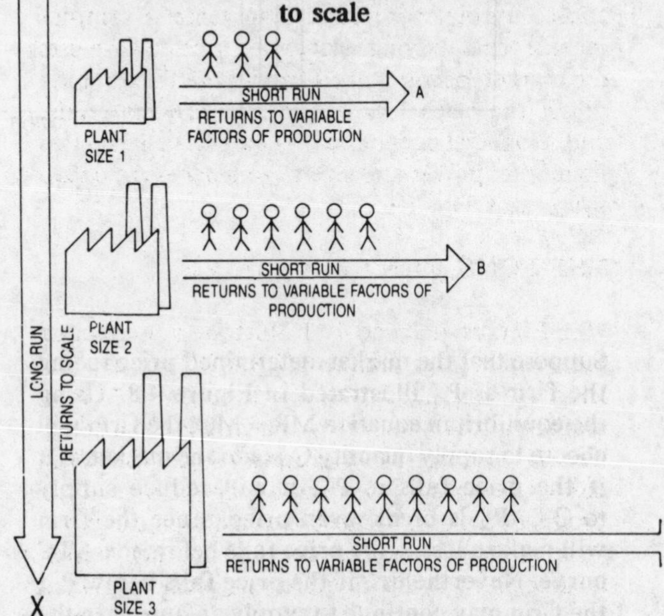

ECONOMIES AND DISECONOMIES OF SCALE

15. Just as it is important to avoid confusing short-run returns with long-run returns to scale, so **returns to scale** must be distinguished from a closely related concept: **economies and diseconomies** of scale. Returns to scale refer only to a technical relationship in production between inputs and outputs measured in physical units. For example, increasing returns to scale would occur if a doubling of a car firm's factory size and its labour force enable the firm to more than double its output of cars. You should note that there is no mention of money costs of production in this example of returns to scale.

Economies and diseconomies of scale in contrast are measured in terms of a firm's long-run average money costs of production. **Economies of scale** occur when a firm's long-run average costs of production fall as the firm increases the scale of its production plant. However, if an increase in the scale of its operations causes a firm's long-run average costs to rise, **diseconomies of scale** are said to exist.

Many economies of scale represent the translation into money costs of production of increasing returns to scale. Increasing returns to scale mean that as plant size increases, a firm can combine its inputs in a technically more efficient way. The resulting economies are called **technical economies of scale**. Increasing returns to scale therefore 'explain' technical economies of scale. However, some scale economies have causes unrelated to returns to scale. Examples include **'bulk-buying' economies**, when a firm uses the market-power gained from large size to 'bid-down' the price at which it buys raw materials, and **'financial economies'** when a large firm uses its market power and size to gain access to cheap sources of finance.

THE LONG RUN COST CURVE

16. Figures 4.10 and 4.11 illustrate a number of **long-run average total cost (LRATC) curves**. The LRATC curve shown in Figure 4.10 is a mathematical line drawn as a tangent to a set or 'family' of **short-run average total cost (SRATC) curves**, each representing a particular size of production plant. In the long run a firm can move from one short-run cost curve to another, which is associated with a different scale of fixed capacity. The shape of the LRATC curve depends upon whether economies or diseconomies of scale are experienced. Long-run costs may be falling, rising or constant.

Figure 4.10: A 'U'-shaped long-run average total cost curve showing both economies and diseconomies of scale

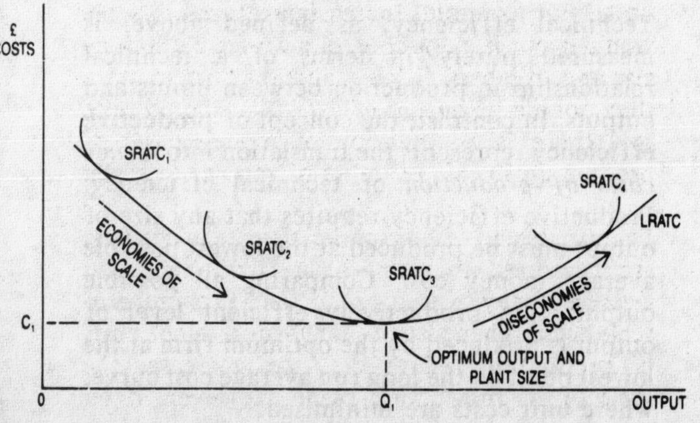

Figure 4.11: Various shapes of long run average total cost curve

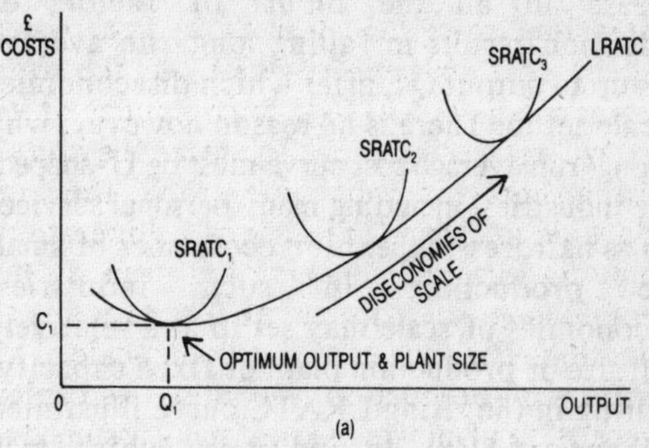

(a) An industry with economies of small scale production

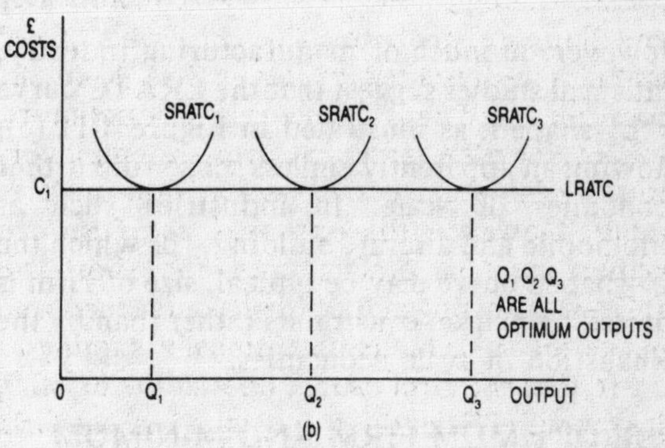

(b) An industry with neither economies nor diseconomies of scale

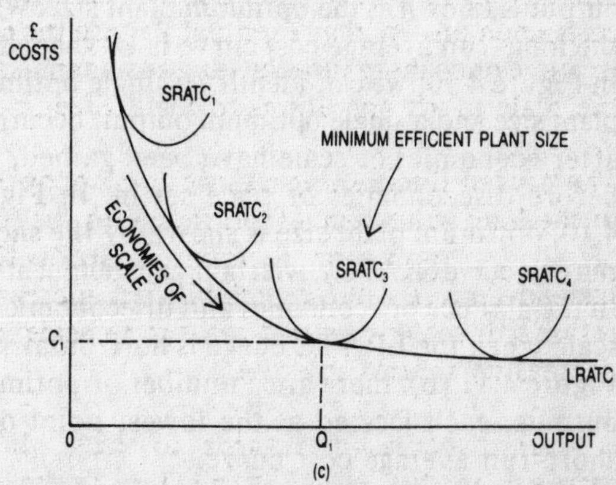

(c) The 'L'-shaped LRATC curve in an industry with economies of large scale production.

Figure 4.10 illustrates a 'U'-shaped long run average cost curve in which economies of scale are eventually followed by diseconomies. An increase in all the inputs or factors of production results in falling long-run average costs up to output Q_1, after which diseconomies of scale set in. There is no reason however, why the long-run average cost curve must be U-shaped. Some industries, including many personal services such as hairdressing, exhibit **economies of small scale production**. In such industries, diseconomies of scale may set in at a relatively small size of production plant or fixed capacity, resulting in the rising LRATC curve illustrated in Figure 4.11(a). In industries which lack significant economies or diseconomies of scale, the horizontal LRATC curve depicted in Figure 4.11(b) may be more typical, allowing firms or plants of many different sizes to exist within the same industry.

However, in much of manufacturing industry, statistical studies suggest that the LRATC curve is 'L'-shaped, as illustrated in Figure 4.11 (c), showing an apparently endless scope for further economies of scale. In industries such as automobile and aircraft building, for which the 'L'-shaped curve may be typical, size of firm is limited by market constraints rather than by the exhaustion of scale economies.

THE OPTIMUM FIRM AND MINIMUM EFFICIENT PLANT SIZE

17. For any firm, the **optimum output** is the **least-cost output**, produced at the lowest point on the firm's long-run average cost curve. The size of plant which produces the least-cost output is known as the **optimum plant size.** When the long-run average cost curve is U-shaped, as in Figure 4.10, we can identify a single optimum plant size and a single optimum output, occurring after economies of scale have been gained, but before diseconomies of scale set in. In Figure 4.10, optimum plant size is shown by the short-run cost curve $SRATC_3$, with optimum output at Q_1. In the absence of economies and diseconomies of scale when the LRATC curve is horizontal as in Figure 4.11 (b), there are a number of optimum outputs, each located at the lowest point on a short-run average cost curve.

However, when the LRATC curve is 'L'-shaped in Figure 4.11(c), there are no further substantial economies of scale to be gained after plant size 3, located where long-run average costs 'flatten out'. Plant size 3 is therefore known as **Minimum Efficient Plant Size (MEPS),** indicating the smallest size of plant that can gain all the principal available scale economies.

TECHNICAL EFFICIENCY AND PRODUCTIVE EFFICIENCY

18. For any given amount of capital and labour, a production process is **technically efficient** if it produces the largest possible output of a good from the given set of inputs. Alternatively we could say that for a particular level of output, a production process is technically efficient if it minimises the inputs of capital and labour required to produce that level of output. There will thus be a technically efficient way of producing every possible output, but the method which is technically efficient for one size of output may be inefficient at another level of output. To illustrate this, we can imagine a car which can be fitted with two different engines. With engine A the car can travel 50 miles on one gallon of petrol if driven at a constant 30 miles per hour. When fitted with engine B the car only travels 40 miles on a gallon, drive at the same speed. Under these conditions, engine A is obviously technically more efficient than engine B. But the situation could well be reversed at a different speed, with engine B travelling further on a gallon of petrol. Which engine should a potential buyer of the car regard as the technically most efficient? The answer is the engine which, on average in the conditions and range of speeds in which he wishes to drive, will deliver a mile of travel for the lowest input of petrol. Generalising, the **technically efficient level of output** for a firm is the size of output which minimises the inputs needed to produce an average unit of output.

Technical efficiency, as defined above, is measured purely in terms of a technical relationship in production between inputs and outputs. In contrast, the concept of **productive efficiency** represents the translation into *money costs of production* of technical efficiency. Productive efficiency requires that any size of output must be produced at the lowest possible average money cost. Comparing all possible outputs, the productively efficient level of output is produced by the optimum firm at the lowest point on the long run average cost curve, where unit costs are minimised.

There are occasions when technical and productive efficiency may not coincide. An example would be a technically efficient production process which requires a specific, but very expensive, raw material or energy source. Because of the high price of this input, it might be more productively efficient to employ a less technically efficient method of production which, however, uses cheaper and more widely available sources of raw materials or energy.

INTERNAL AND EXTERNAL ECONOMIES OF SCALE

19. The economies of scale referred to so far in this chapter, which cause a firm's long-run average cost curve to fall, are internal economies of scale. **Internal economies of scale** occur as a result of a firm's internal decision to increase the scale of its operations. In contrast, an **external economy of scale** is caused by factors external to the firm itself, relating to the scale of the industry or market as a whole. The average costs of individual firms within the industry fall as a direct result of an increase in the scale of the whole industry. There may be shared economies in labour-training, or the growth of the industry may cause individual firms to benefit from markets or sources of supply provided by other firms within the industry. Essentially, the economies which are *external* to individual firms within the industry are *internal* to the industry taken as a whole. If all the firms were to merge to form a single firm producing the whole of the industry output, these scale economies would become internal to the firm itself, but would remain external at a plant level between the many plants now owned by the newly-merged firm.

Likewise, scale diseconomies can be divided into internal and external diseconomies of scale. **Internal diseconomies of scale** result from a firm's internal growth, whereas **external scale diseconomies** result from the growth of the whole industry.

LONG-RUN SUPPLY

20. In previous sections of this chapter, we have explained how in a competitive industry in which all firms are assumed to be passive 'price-takers', a firm's short-run supply curve is its MC curve above AVC. We have also explained why a vertical line drawn through the output the firm is currently marketing represents the firm's market period supply curve.

Figure 4.12: Market period supply, short-run supply and long run supply of a competitive firm in an industry with no economies or diseconomies of scale

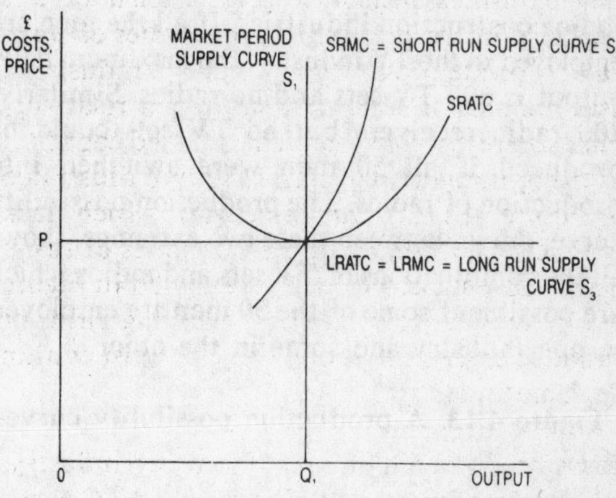

In Figure 4.12 we have drawn a **market period supply curve** S_1, and a **short-run supply curve** S_2, together with a **long-run** supply **curve** S_3. The long run supply curve S_3 illustrates the special case of a firm in an industry with constant long-run average costs. In the short run, the firm could increase output beyond Q_1 by moving up supply curve S_2. But in the long run, the firm can move along S_3 to a new size of scale of fixed capacity. In a competitive industry, and assuming an absence of economies and diseconomies of scale, S_3 will also be the long-run market supply curve, since any extra output can be supplied at the price P_1 by attracting a new firm into the market, producing at the same average cost as existing firms. The precise shape of the long-run supply curve of both the firm and the market, will depend upon whether economies or diseconomies of scale are experienced, but in general we may expect the long-run supply curve to be 'flatter' than short-run supply because firms can change their fixed capacity and, for the market as a whole, firms can enter or leave the industry,

PRODUCTION POSSIBILITY CURVES

21. A production possibility curve allows us to illustrate in a very clear way a number of the

concepts central to cost and supply theory, including the distinction between short-run returns and long-run returns to scale.

In Figure 4.13 a **production possibility curve** (or **transformation curve**) has been drawn to show the quantities of television sets or radios a labour force of 50 men could produce if employed with fixed amounts of capital in either the TV or radio construction industries. If all the men are employed in the TV industry, the maximum daily output is 600 TV sets and no radios. Similarly, 700 radio receivers but no TV sets could be produced if all 50 men were switched into production of radios. The production possibility curve, drawn between these two extremes, shows all the combinations of TV sets and radios which are possible if some of the 50 men are employed in one industry and some in the other.

Figure 4.13: A production possibility curve

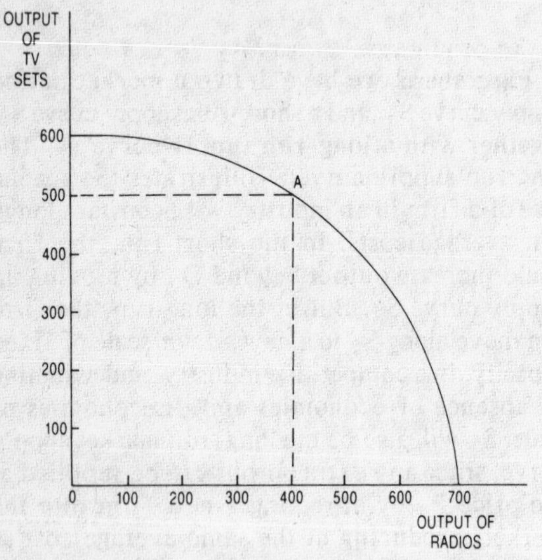

Let us suppose that point A on the production possibility curve shows a total possible output of 500 televisions and 400 radios when exactly half the labour force is employed in each industry. Now ask yourself what will happen if workers are switched from producing TV sets to produce radios (or vice versa). Whereas the first 25 workers produced a total of 500 televisions, the addition of a second 25 workers only increases output by a further 100 TV sets. Likewise, a doubling of the labour force producing radios increases output, but by less than double. Radio production would rise from 400 to 700.

We get this result because the slope of the production possibility curve in Figure 4.13 has been drawn *concave to origin*, to show **diminishing marginal returns** to labour in both industries as labour is switched from one industry to another. In contrast, the production possibility curves drawn in Figure 4.14 (a) and (b) on the following page depict respectively **increasing marginal returns** and **constant marginal returns** to labour. The production possibility curve drawn in Figure 4.14(a) is *convex to origin*, showing increasing marginal returns in both industries as workers are switched between the two industries. If however, constant marginal returns occur in both industries, when an extra worker joining either industry adds always the same marginal output as the previous worker, the straight line (or linear) production possibility curve illustrated in Figure 4.14 (b) will result.

Returns to scale can be illustrated on a production possibility diagram by shifting the position of the production possibility curve. Figure 4.15 has been drawn to show the outward shift of a production possibility curve when a firm doubles the amount of capital and labour employed, ie the firm doubles the scale of its operations. Figure 4.15(a) depicts **increasing returns to scale**: the doubling of the inputs causes the production possibility curve to shift more than proportionately outwards. **Decreasing returns to scale** are shown in Figure 4.15(b), and **constant** returns to scale in Figure 4.15(c). In Figure 4.15(b), the production possibility curve shifts outwards less than proportionately to the change in the scale of the inputs, while the outward shift in Figure 4.15(c) is exactly proportionate. In conclusion, when capital is held fixed but labour is switched between the two industries, **short-run returns** to the variable factor of production are shown by the *slope* of a production possibility curve; **long-run returns to scale** are represented by the *outward shift* of the production possibility curve to a new position.

Figure 4.14: Production possibility curves showing the effect of combining labour with fixed capital in two industries

(a) A production possibility curve showing increasing marginal returns
(b) A production possibility cost showing constant marginal returns.

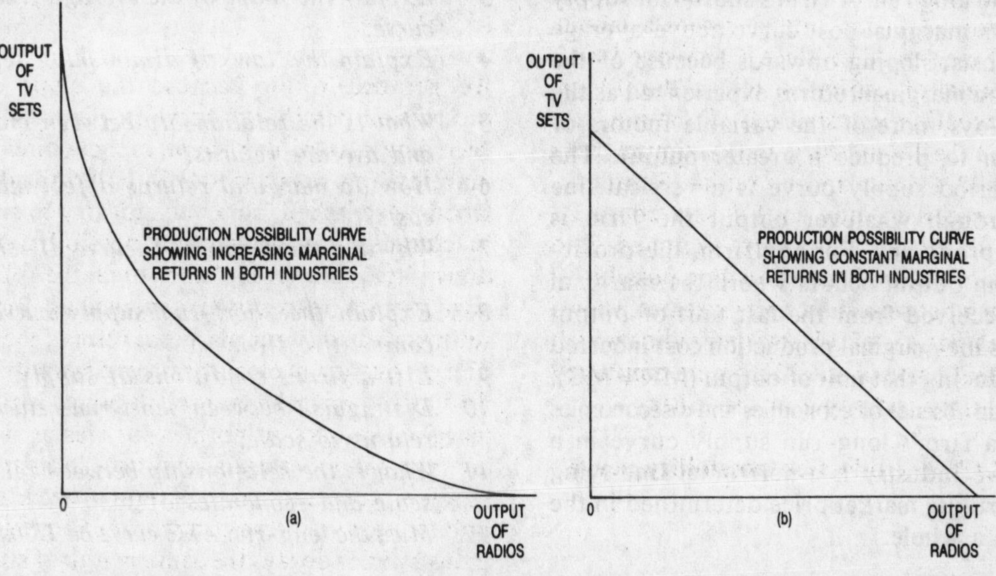

Figure 4.15: The outward shift of the production possibility curve from PP_1 to PP_2 when there are:

(a) increasing returns to scale
(b) decreasing returns to scale
(c) constant returns to scale

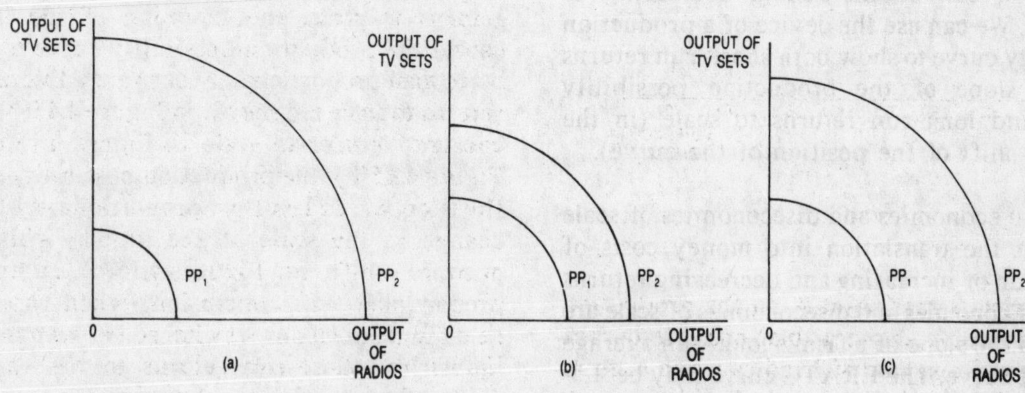

SUMMARY

22. In this chapter we have derived the supply curve of a firm in a competitive industry for three time periods: the market period, the short run and the long run. A firm's short-run supply curve is its marginal cost curve above average variable costs, sloping upwards because of the diminishing marginal returns experienced as the firm employs more of the variable factors of production to produce a greater output. The market-period supply curve is a vertical line drawn through whatever output the firm is currently producing. For any firm, the profit-maximising output occurs where the marginal revenue received from the last unit of output sold equals the marginal production cost incurred when producing that unit of output (MR = MC). Assuming an absence of economies and diseconomies of scale, a firm's long-run supply curve in a competitive industry is a horizontal line lying along the ruling market price determined in the market as a whole.

The chapter has also introduced the important distinction between short-run and long-run returns. The short-run marginal returns to a variable factor of production such as labour must eventually diminish because of the conditions in which production is taking place, namely at least one factor of production is assumed to be fixed. This principle is known as the 'law' of diminishing returns (or law of variable proportions). However, long-run returns to scale, occurring when a firm changes the scale of all its inputs, can be increasing, decreasing or constant. We can use the device of a production possibility curve to show both short-run returns (in the slope of the production possibility curve) and long-run returns to scale (in the outward shift of the position of the curve).

Technical economies and diseconomies of scale represent the translation into money costs of production of increasing and decreasing returns to scale. Economies and diseconomies of scale are shown in the slope of a firm's long-run average total cost curve. The LRATC curve may be 'L'-shaped, 'U'-shaped, or horizontal, depending on the nature of the scale economies and diseconomies experienced by the firm. However, the short-run ATC curve must be 'U'-shaped because diminishing returns inevitably cause costs to rise as a firm increases production in the economic short run.

STUDENT SELF-TESTING

1 *What are the factors of production?* (3)
2 *Distinguish between the market period, the short run and the long run.* (4)
3 *Explain the shape of the average fixed cost curve.* (6)
4 *Explain the 'law' of diminishing returns.* (7)
5 *What is the relationship between marginal and average returns?* (8)
6 *How do marginal returns affect marginal costs?* (9)
7 *Why is a short-run ATC curve 'U'-shaped?* (11)
8 *Explain the short-run supply curve of a competitive firm.* (12)
9 *List a firm's conditions of supply.* (13)
10 *Distinguish between short run returns and returns to scale.* (14)
11 *What is the relationship between returns to scale and economies of scale?* (15)
12 *Must the long-run ATC curve be 'U'-shaped?* (16)
13 *What is the optimum firm?* (17)
14 *Distinguish between technical efficiency and productive efficiency.* (18)
15 *What are external economies of scale?* (19)
16 *Explain the long-run supply curve of a firm in a competitive industry.* (20)
17 *Why is a production possibility curve likely to be 'concave to origin'?* (21)

EXERCISES

1 *The Fashionable Furniture Company manufactures cupboards, incurring fixed costs of £300 and total costs as shown in the following table:*

	Total costs			Average costs			Marginal
Output	Total	Fixed	Variable	Total	Fixed	Variable	costs
0	300	300	0	-	-	0	
1	540						
2	680						
3	750						
4	952						
5	1200						
6	1602						

(a) Complete the table.
(b) Plot the marginal and average cost curves on graph paper (plotting the marginal values midway between the average).
(c) Identify break-even price and shut-down price on your diagram.
(d) Calculate the output and the profit when the ruling market price of cupboards is £202.

2. *The marginal cost schedules of three firms are shown in the following table:*

Marginal cost £

Output	Firm A	Firm B	Firm C
0	0	0	0
1	5	10	50
2	10	20	80
3	15	30	100
4	20	40	110
5	25	50	125
6	30	60	145
7	35	70	170
8	40	80	200
9	45	90	235

Assuming that all three firms are passive 'price-takers' at the ruling market price:
(a) how much will
(i) firm A
(ii) all three firms supply at prices of £5, £10, £20, £50 and £100?
(b) If a tax of £10 per unit is imposed, how much will firm B now supply at price of £50?
(c) Are all three firms benefitting from increasing marginal returns?

MULTIPLE CHOICE QUESTIONS

1 *When a firm's average costs are less than marginal costs:*

A *An increase in output would cause average costs to fall*
B *The firm has not yet produced beyond its minimum average cost level*
C *Fixed costs must be rising*
D *An increase in output would cause average costs to rise*

2. *A firm's total fixed costs are £2,400. If at a certain output its average total costs per unit are £20 and average variable costs per unit are £14, then that level of output is:*
A *400 units*
B *600 units*
C *800 units*
D *1000 units*

3 *Diminishing returns occur in the short run when there is a reduction in:*
- A *The marginal product of the fixed factor*
- B *The average product of the variable factor*
- C *The marginal product of the variable factor*
- D *The average product of the fixed factor*

4 *In the short-run, a profit-maximising firm will cease production if revenue does not cover:*
- A *Total cost*
- B *Fixed cost*
- C *Variable cost*
- D *Average cost*

5 *If a firm's output rises by 70 per cent when it increases the employment of all its factors of production by 75 per cent, it must be operating under conditions of:*
- A *Diminishing marginal returns*
- B *Diminishing marginal utility*
- C *Diminishing returns to scale*
- D *Diminishing marginal productivity of capital*

EXAMINATION QUESTIONS

1 (*a*) *Explain what is meant by diminishing returns.* (*10 marks*)

(*b*) *How do diminishing returns relate to the shape of the firm's cost curves?* (*10 marks*)

(*ACCA June 1985*)

2 *Distinguish between the law of diminishing returns and diminishing marginal utility. Give an example of the application of each concept.*

(*ICSA June 1985*)

3 (*a*) *Explain the distinction between short-run and long-run costs of production.* (*12 marks*)

(*b*) *What will be the effect on the long-run costs of an industry and on the use of labour in the industry of:*

(*i*) *an increase in wages;*

(*ii*) *an improvement in technology?* (*8 marks*)

(*ACCA June 1984*)

4 *If there are economies of scale, why should cost curves ultimately rise?*

(*ICSA Pilot paper*)

5. Elasticity

INTRODUCTION

1. In Chapters 3 and 4 we explained why for most goods, a demand curve usually slopes downward from left to right and a supply curve normally slopes upwards. A downward-sloping demand curve shows that more of a good is demanded as its price falls, whereas an upward-sloping supply curve reflects the fact that profit-maximising firms are prepared to supply more of a good only when offered a higher price. However, the slope of a demand or supply curve is not always an accurate indicator of the extent to which households or firms respond to a price change. In this chapter we introduce and explain the concept of **price elasticity** as a measure of the responsiveness of households or firms to a change in a good's price. We also show how **elasticities of demand or supply** can be measured with respect to changes in any of the conditions of demand or supply, for example, **income elasticity of demand and cross-elasticity of demand** - before concluding the chapter by illustrating how a knowledge of various elasticities might be useful for business enterprises and for the government.

ELASTICITY AND SLOPE

2. If you examine the demand curves drawn in Figure 5.1, which show the demand for a product such as watches in two separate markets (perhaps Scotland and England), you will see that demand curve D_2 is clearly flatter than D_1. You may be tempted to conclude that of the two demand curves, gently-sloping D_2 shows a much greater market response by consumers following any change in the price of watches. Further careful inspection of the two demand curves will confirm that in one important respect this is true: when for example the price of a watch falls from £40 to £32, demand in the English market rises by 10,000 watches compared to only 2,000 in Scotland. The obvious explanation for the much greater absolute response in the English market lies in market size; many more people live in England; at all prices the English market is much bigger.

However, we must take very great care not to confuse the *absolute* response of the consumers in the two markets - indicated by the *slope* of the two demand curves - with the *proportionate* response measured by the **price elasticity of demand.** Careful inspection of Figure 5.1 shows that slope is an inaccurate indicator of proportionate response. Although the slopes of the two demand curves are clearly different, we have drawn D_1 and D_2 to show that a price fall of twenty per cent from £40 to £32, causes demand to double in both the Scottish and the English markets. Despite their different slopes D_1 and D_2 display identical elasticities whenever the price changes.

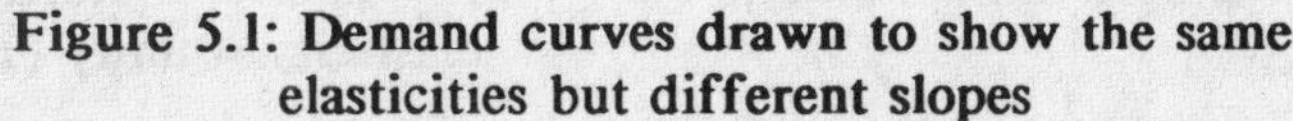

Figure 5.1: Demand curves drawn to show the same elasticities but different slopes

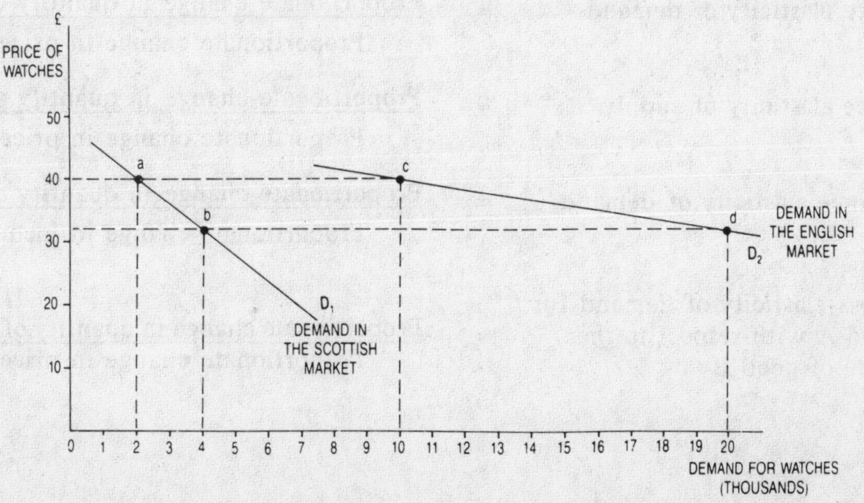

ELASTICITY AS A DESCRIPTIVE STATISTIC

3. Whenever a change in one variable causes a change in another variable, ie whenever a functional relationship exists, we can calculate an **elasticity**. Elasticity is a very useful descriptive statistic of the relationship between two variables because it is independent of the units, such as price and quantity units, in which the variables are measured. For example, a statistical study estimated that the United Kingdom income elasticity of demand for imported cars was 3.7 between 1963 and 1974. This single statistic tells us that when money income rises by one per cent, the demand for car imports is likely to increase more than proportionately, by nearly four per cent, assuming of course that the elasticity has not changed since 1974. Such information might be extremely useful, both to firms in the automobile industry, and to the government.

ESSENTIAL ELASTICITIES

4. Although in principle economists could calculate a great many elasticities, indeed one for each of the functional relationships studied, the four main elasticities of interest to economists are:

(i) **price elasticity of demand;**
(ii) **price elasticity of supply;**
(iii) **income elasticity of demand; and**
(iv) **cross-elasticity of demand.**

In each case, a simple formula can be used to calculate the elasticity:

PRICE ELASTICITY OF DEMAND

5. When a price change causes a more than proportionate change in demand, demand is said to be elastic. The elasticity statistic calculated from the formula will be greater than 1. For example, when in Figure 5.1 consumers respond to the 20% fall in the price of watches, from £40 to £32, by doubling their demand, price elasticity of demand is $\frac{+100\%}{-20\%} = -5$ or simply 5. (With downward-sloping demand curves, elasticities are always negative. However, the minus sign is frequently omitted and the elasticity statistic is written as an absolute number.)

If a price change results in a less than proportionate change in demand, demand is inelastic. The elasticity statistic will be less than 1.

A SIMPLE RULE FOR CALCULATING PRICE ELASTICITY OF DEMAND

6. As an alternative to using the formula to calculate price elasticity of demand between two points on a demand curve, we can use a simple rule:

(i) If total consumer expenditure *increases* in response to a price *fall*, demand is **elastic;**
(ii) if total consumer expenditure *decreases* in response to a price *fall*, demand is **inelastic;**
(ii) if total consumer expenditure *remains constant* in response to a price *fall*, demand is neither elastic nor inelastic - **elasticity = unity (1).**

(i) Price elasticity of demand $= \frac{\text{Proportionate change in quantity demanded}}{\text{Proportionate change in price}}$

(ii) Price elasticity of supply $= \frac{\text{Proportionate change in quantity supplied}}{\text{Proportionate change in price}}$

(iii) Income elasticity of demand $= \frac{\text{Proportionate change in quantity demanded}}{\text{Proportionate change in income}}$

(iv) Cross-elasticity of demand for good A with respect to the price of good B $= \frac{\text{Proportionate change in quantity of A demanded}}{\text{Proportionate change in price of B}}$

In Table 5.1 we have adapted the rule to cover a price rise as well as a price fall:

Table 5.1: A simple rule for calculating price elasticity of demand

Price elasticity of demand	Price	Effect on consumer expenditure
Elastic	rise fall	fall rise
Unitary	rise fall	unchanged unchanged
Inelastic	rise fall	rise fall

Figure 5.2 illustrates some possible changes in consumer expenditure which might follow a fall in price. When the price falls from P_1 to P_2 in Figure 5.2(a), total consumer expenditure increases by the shaded area n, but decreases by the area m. The area n, which shows the proportionate increase in quantity demanded, is larger than the area m, which represents the proportionate change in price. Demand is therefore elastic at all points between a and b on demand curve D_1.

However when the price falls from P_3 to P_4 on the same demand curve, the shaded area n is clearly smaller than the area m . Total consumer expenditure falls, demand is thus inelastic at all points between c and d on curve D_1.

We can now explain the misleading generalisation that a 'flat' or gently-sloping demand curve is elastic and a 'steep' curve is inelastic. Moving down a *negatively-sloping linear (straight-line)* demand curve such as D_1, price elasticity of demand falls from point to point along the curve. The gently-sloping demand curve D_2 illustrated in Figure 2.5(b) is really only the upper part of a curve which, if extended rightwards, would eventually become inelastic in its lower reaches. Similarly, the steep inelastic curve D_3 drawn in Figure 5.2(c) is the lower part of a curve which would become elastic if extended upwards. Figure 5.2(d) shows how elasticity of demand falls from infinity to zero moving down a linear demand curve. Demand is elastic (or greater than unity) at all points along the top half of the curve. Elasticity equals unity exactly half way along the curve, falling below unity and towards zero along the bottom half of the curve.

Figure 5.2: Price elasticity of demand and linear demand curves

(a) Price elasticity of demand falling moving down a linear demand curve.
(b) Demand is elastic in the upper part of a 'flat' demand curve.
(c) demand is inelastic in the lower part of a 'steep' demand curve.
(d) Elasticity at various points on a linear downward-sloping demand curve.

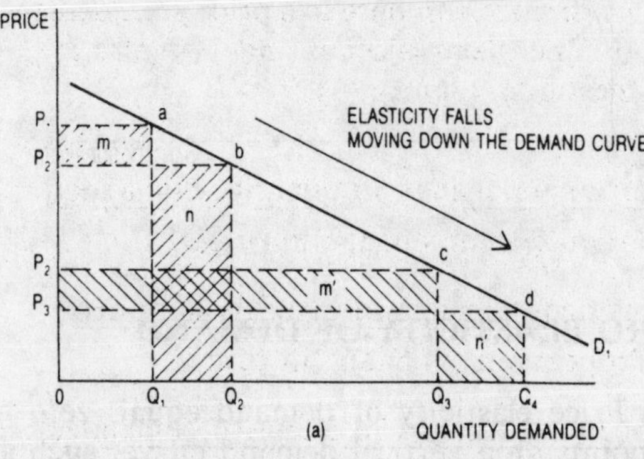

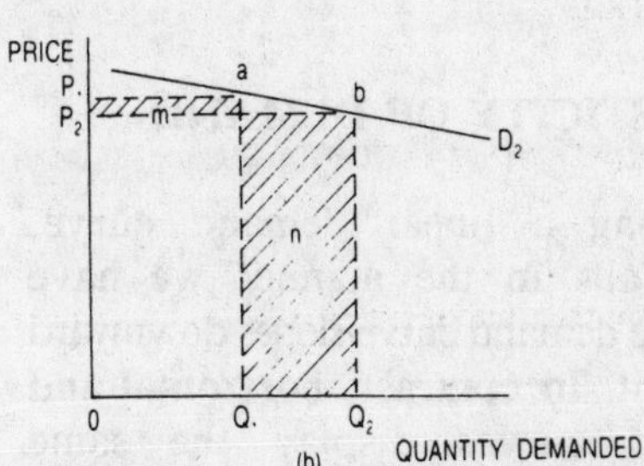

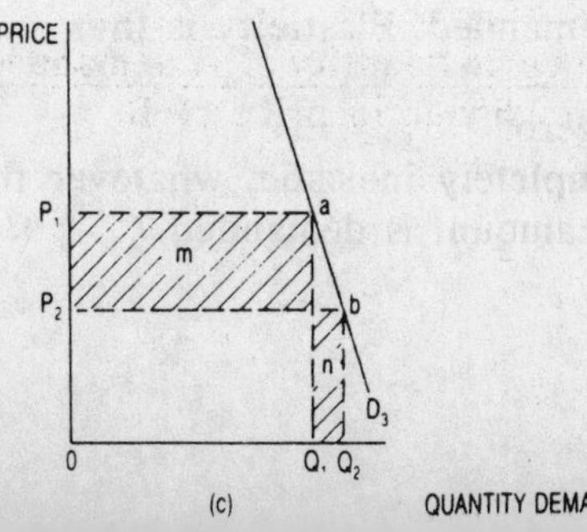

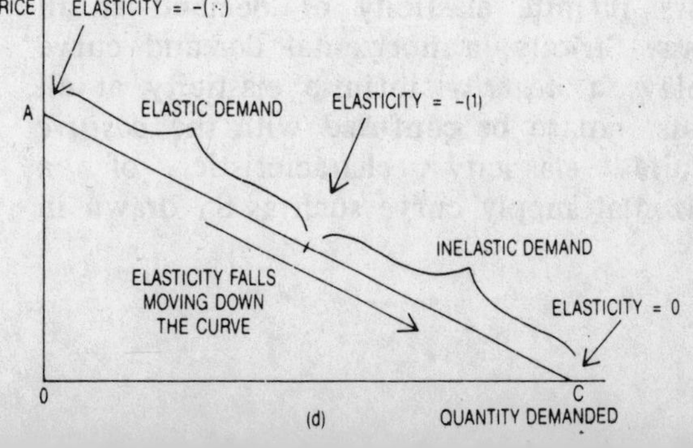

UNIT ELASTICITY OF DEMAND

7. Common sense suggests that if elasticity falls from point to point moving down a *linear* demand curve, then we require a *non-linear* curve to show the same elasticity at all points. The particular non-linear curve which shows **unit elasticity of demand** at all points is the rectangular hyperbola illustrated in Figure 5.3. Whenever the price falls, for example from P_1 to P_2, the proportionate change in quantity demanded (area n) exactly equals the proportionate change in price (area m). Thus consumer expenditure remains unchanged following a rise or fall of price.

Figure 5.3: A rectangular hyperbola showing unit elasticity of demand at all points of the demand curve

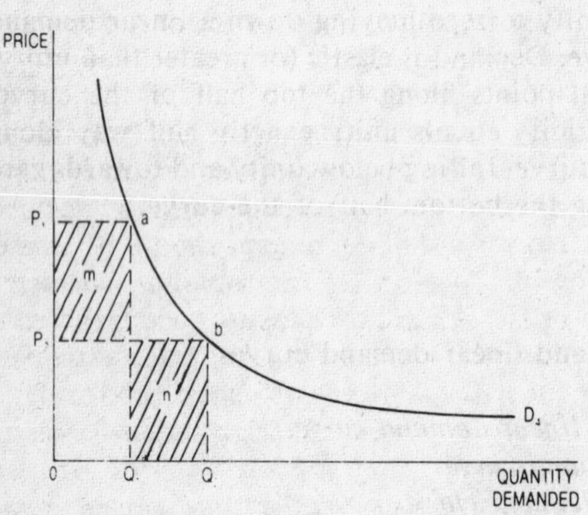

INFINITE ELASTICITY OF DEMAND

8. Moving along a linear demand curve, elasticity only falls in the manner we have described when the demand curve slopes downward from left to right. In contrast, **horizontal** and **vertical demand curves** display the same elasticity at all points on the curve. The horizontal demand curve D_5 drawn in Figure 5.4 shows **infinite elasticity of demand** at all points. Strictly, a horizontal demand curve displays a *negative* infinite elasticity at all points, not to be confused with the *positive* infinite elasticity characteristic of a horizontal supply curve such as S_1 drawn in Figure 5.5. This rather obscure mathematical point does have a special economic significance. In the case of the infinitely elastic (or **perfectly elastic**) demand curve D_5 in Figure 5.4, an infinite amount is demanded at price P_1 or below. But if the price were to rise above P_1, nothing would be demanded as consumers switch away from this good to demand other goods instead. But in the conditions of **infinitely elastic** (or **perfectly elastic**) **supply** illustrated in Figure 5.5, firms are prepared to supply an infinite amount at price P_1 or above; they would refuse to supply if the price fell below P_1.

Figure 5.4: Infinitely elastic demand

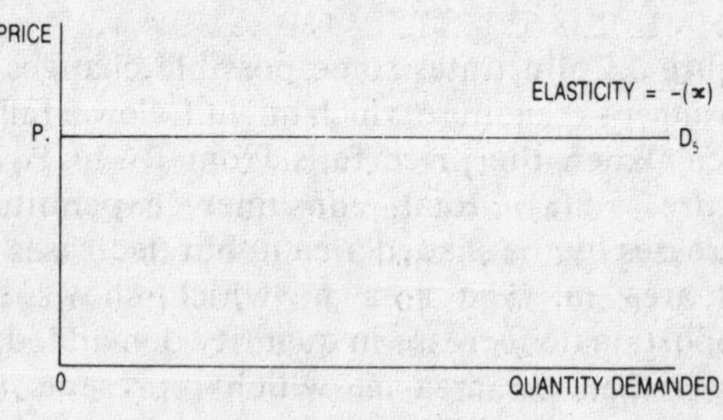

Figure 5.5: Infinitely elastic supply

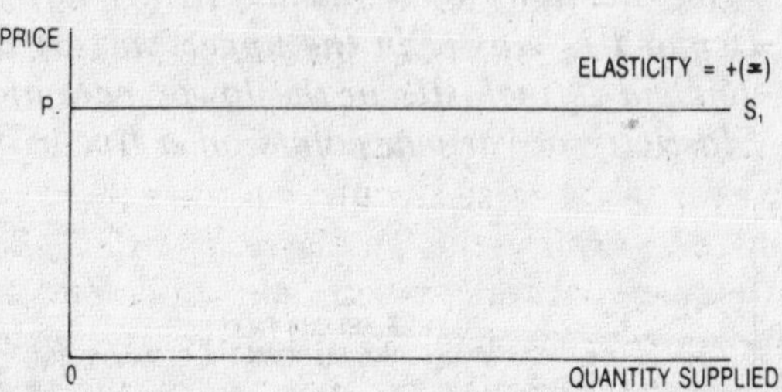

ZERO ELASTICITY OF DEMAND

9. Price elasticity of demand equals zero at all points on a vertical demand curve, such as curve D_6 drawn in Figure 5.6. When the price falls by 50% from P_1 to P_2, no change occurs in the quantity demanded. Elasticity is thus $\frac{0}{-50\%}$, or zero.
Demand is completely **inelastic**; whatever the price the same amount is demanded.

Figure 5.6: Completely inelastic demand

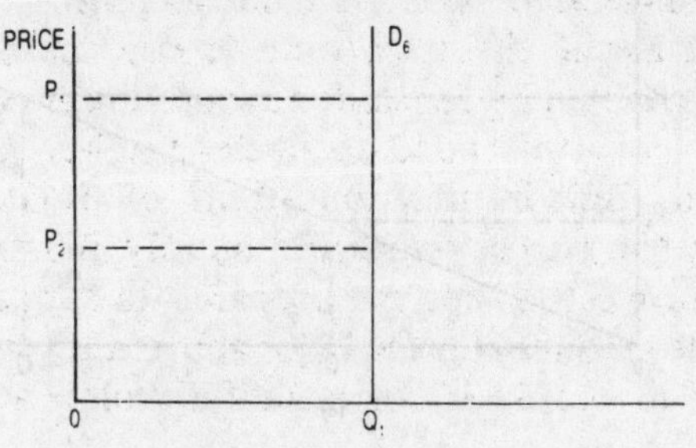

POINT ELASTICITY AND AVERAGE ELASTICITY

10. The elasticity of demand measured between any two points on a demand curve is an **average elasticity** or **arc elasticity**. Because elasticity falls from point to point moving down a negatively-sloping linear demand curve, average elasticities should be measured only for quite small changes in price.

You should also note that the average elasticity calculated for a *price fall* between any two points on a downward-sloping linear demand curve differs from the elasticity calculated between the same two points for a *price rise*. In Figure 5.1 we saw that when the price of watches falls from £40 to £32 the average elasticity between points a and b on the demand curve D_1 is -5, However the reverse calculation for a price rise from £32 to £40 yields an elasticity of -2. This discrepancy occurs when we calculate the proportionate changes in quantity and price, because the 'benchmarks' for the calculations, the initial quantities and prices, are different.

The greater the distance between any two points on the demand curve, the larger the difference in the elasticity statistics calculated respectively for a price fall and a price rise. One way round this problem is to calculate the average of the two elasticities. Averaging -5 and -2 (and forgetting the minus signs) average elasticity of demand between points a and b on demand curve D_1 in Figure 5.1 is -3.75. However, the most accurate way to calculate an elasticity is to use the mathematical technique of calculus to measure **point elasticity** of demand at a single point on the demand curve.

THE DETERMINANTS OF PRICE ELASTICITY OF DEMAND

11. (i) **Substitutability.** Substitutability is the most important determinant of price elasticity of demand. When a substitute exists for a product, consumers can respond to a price rise by switching expenditure away from the good, buying instead the substitute whose price has not risen. If a perfect substitute is available, demand for the product is likely to be highly elastic, perhaps even infinitely inelastic. Conversely, demand is usually inelastic when no substitutes are available.

(ii) **Percentage of income.** Goods or services upon which households spend a large proportion of their income tend to be in more elastic demand than small items, such as shoe polish, upon which only a fraction of income is spent.

(iii) **Necessities v luxuries.** It is sometimes said that necessities are in inelastic demand, and luxuries are in elastic demand. However, this statement should be treated with caution. If no obvious substitute exists, demand for a luxury good may well be inelastic, while at the other extreme demand for particular types of basic food stuffs is likely to elastic if other staple foods are available as substitutes. It is the existence of substitutes that really determines the elasticity, not whether the good is a luxury or necessity. Habit forming goods, to which a consumer may become addicted, also tend to be in inelastic demand, being regarded by the consumer as necessities. Tobacco is an example.

(iv) **The width of the definition.** The wider the definition of the market or product under consideration, the lower the price elasticity of demand. Thus the demand for the bread produced by a particular bakery is likely to be more elastic than the demand for bread produced by all bakeries. Quite obviously, the bread baked in other bakeries provides a number of close substitutes for the bread produced in just one bakery. And widening the market still further, the elasticity of demand for bread produced by all the bakeries will be greater than that for food as a whole.

(v) **Time**. The time period in question will also affect the elasticity of demand. For many goods and services, demand is more elastic in the long run than in the short run because it takes time to respond to a price change. For example, if the price of petrol rises relative to the price of diesel fuel, it will take time for motorists to respond because they will be 'locked-in' to their existing investment in automobiles. However, in certain circumstances, the response might be greater in the short run than in the long run. A sudden rise in the price of petrol might cause motorists to economise in its use for a few weeks before 'getting used to the price' and drifting back to their old motoring habits.

PRICE ELASTICITY OF SUPPLY

12. The mathematical properties of *upward-sloping (or positive)* supply curves are different from those of *downward-sloping (or negative)* demand curves. The important points to note are:

(i) Any linear supply curve drawn through *origin* displays **unit elasticity of supply** at all points on the curve. This is illustrated in Figure 5.7(a), where a doubling of the price causes the quantity supplied also to double.

(ii) The gently-sloping or 'flat' supply curve drawn in Figure 5.7(b) is **elastic** at all points on the curve, since a change in price always results in a more than proportionate change in supply. But the elasticity is not the same at all points on the curve. Instead the elasticity *falls* moving from point to point up the curve. Elasticity equals (+)∞ at the vertical intercept (point A), falling towards unity moving along the curve but never actually reaching unity.

(iii) Similarly, the steeply-sloping supply curve drawn in Figure 5.7(c) is **inelastic** at all points, since any price change results in a less than proportionate change in supply. Again, the elasticity varies from point to point along the curve. Price elasticity of supply is zero at the horizontal intercept (point B), *rising* towards unity moving up the curve.

Figure 5.7: Price elasticity of supply and linear supply curves

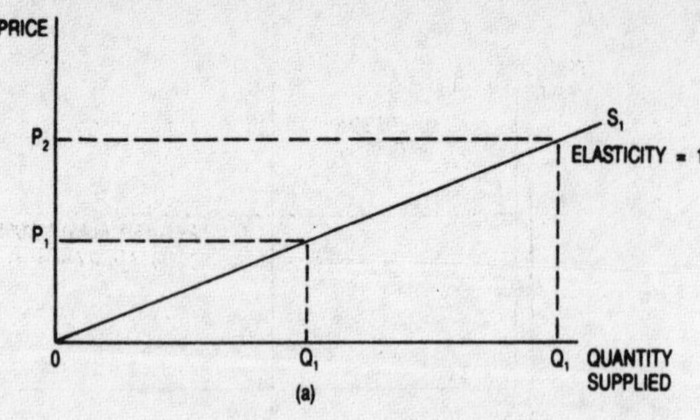

(a) Unit elasticity of supply

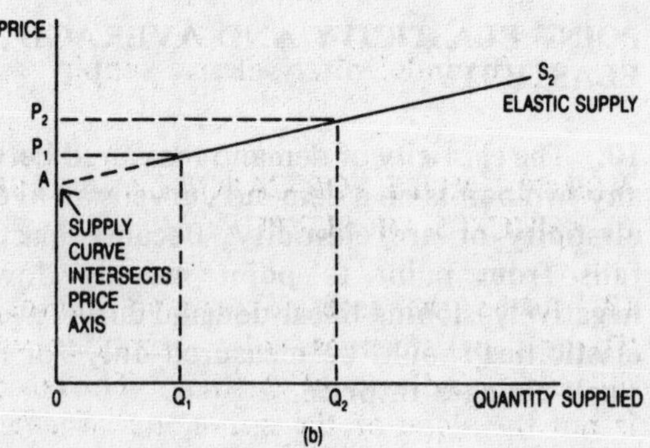

(b) Elastic supply

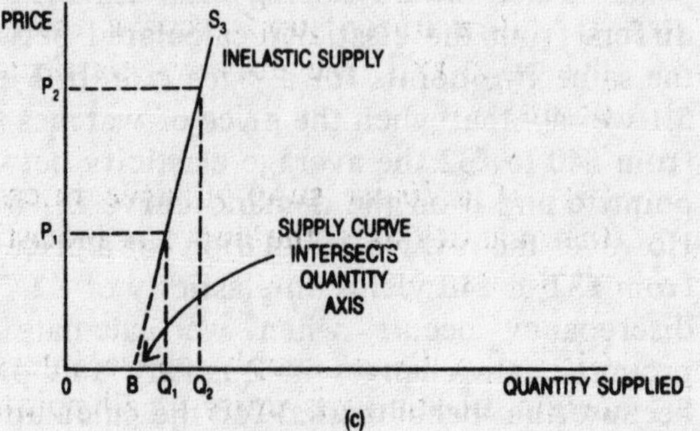

(c) Inelastic supply

Figure 5.8: Horizontal and vertical supply curves

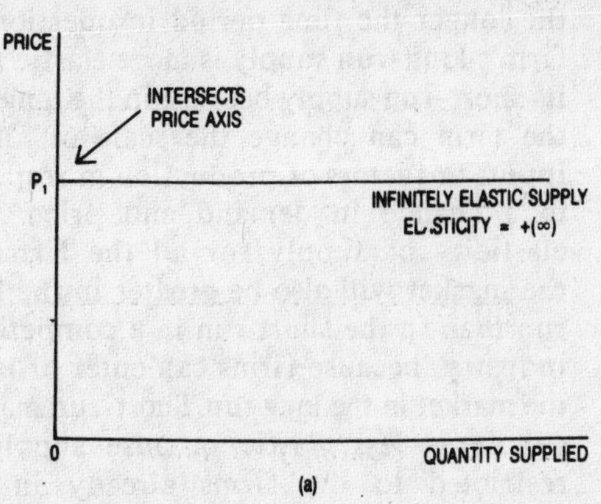

(b) Indefinitely elastic supply

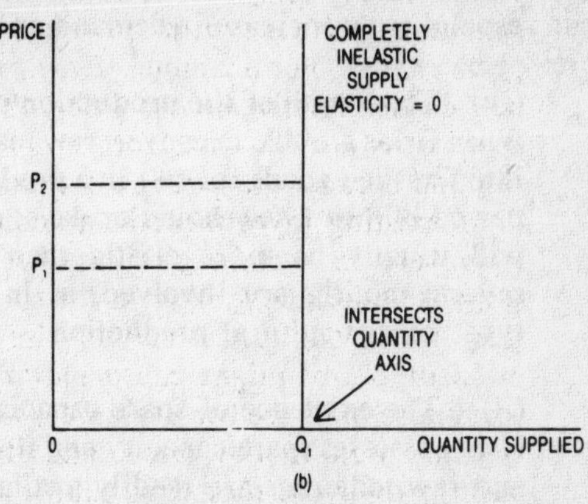

(b) Completely inelastic supply

A SIMPLE RULE FOR CALCULATING PRICE ELASTICITY OF SUPPLY

13. As in the case of demand curves, the 'flatness' or 'steepness' of a supply curve is a misleading indicator of elasticity. The key point is not the slope of the curve, but *whether the supply curve intersects the price axis or the quantity axis*. The rule is:

(i) if a linear supply curve intersects the **price axis,** the curve is **elastic** at all points;

(ii) if a *linear* supply curve intersects the **quantity axis**, the curve is **inelastic** at all points;

(iii) if a *linear* supply curve intersects **origin,** elasticity is **unity** at all points on the curve.

The **infinitely elastic** and the **completely inelastic** supply curves illustrated in Figures 5.8(a) and (b) are limiting special cases of this rule. The **horizontal supply curve** drawn in Figure 5.8(a) intersects the price axis, displaying an elasticity of (+)∞ at all points on the curve. In contrast, elasticity is zero at all points on the **vertical supply curve** depicted in Figure 5.8 (b) which intersects the quantity axis.

We can quite easily adapt the simple rule to check the elasticity at any point on an upward-sloping *non-linear* supply curve, such as S_1 illustrated in Figure 5.9. Price elasticity of supply can be checked by drawing a tangent to the point and noting the axis which the tangent intersects. At point X supply is elastic because the tangent drawn to the supply curve at X intersects the horizontal axis. Point elasticity of supply equals unity at point Y, falling to less than unity at point Z further up the curve.

Figure 5.9: Using tangents to check the elasticity at points on a non-linear supply curve

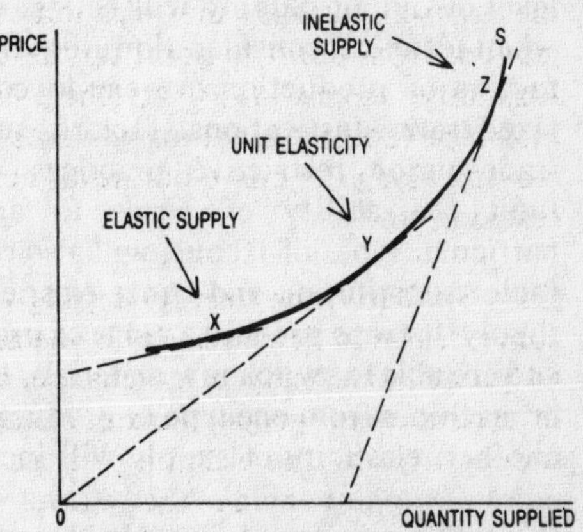

THE DETERMINANTS OF PRICE ELASTICITY OF SUPPLY

14. The factors which determine whether firms can respond to an increase in demand and price are:

(i) **The length of the production period.** When firms are able to convert raw materials into finished goods for sale in a production period of just a few hours or days, supply will usually be more elastic than when several months are involved, as in many types of agricultural production.

(ii) **The existence of spare capacity.** If a firm possesses spare capacity and if labour and raw materials are readily available, it is usually possible to increase production quickly in the short run.

(iii) **The ease of accumulating stocks.** If unsold stocks of finished goods can be stored at low cost, firms will be able to meet any sudden increase in demand from stock. They could also respond to a price fall by diverting current production into stock accumulation. The ease of accumulating stocks of raw materials or components bought from other firms will also influence elasticity of supply. Supply will tend to be elastic when firms can quickly increase production by drawing on their stocks of raw materials.

(iv) **The ease of factor substitution.** Supply will tend to be relatively elastic if firms can use different combinations of labour and capital to produce a particular level of output. Supply will be less elastic when technical considerations require that factors of production are employed in a fixed ratio. Institutional factors, such as trade union restrictive practices which limit the ability of firms to employ particular types of labour, will also reduce factor substitution and hence elasticity of supply. If firms produce a range of products and are able to switch raw materials, labour or machines from one type or production to another, elasticity of supply will increase.

(v) **The number of firms in the market.** Generally the greater the number of firms in the market, the more elastic is market or industry supply.

(vi) **Time.** If you refer back to Figure 4.12 in Chapter 4, you will see that supply is completely inelastic in the **market period** or **momentary period**, with elasticity increasing the longer the time period in question. A firm's **long-run supply** is more elastic than its **short-run supply** because in the long run the firm can change the scale of all its inputs or factors of production in response to a change in demand and price. The elasticity of supply for all the firms in the market will also be greater in the long run than in the short run in a competitive industry, because firms can enter or leave the market in the long run. Short-run market supply is less elastic because supply is restricted to the firms already in the industry.

INCOME ELASTICITY OF DEMAND

15. Income elasticity of demand - which measures how demand responds to a change in income - is always **negative** for an **inferior good** and **positive** for a **normal good**. The quantity demanded of an inferior good falls as income rises, whereas demand for a normal good rises with income. Normal goods are sometimes further subdivided into **superior goods** or **luxuries**, for which the income elasticity of demand is greater than unity and **basic goods**, with an income elasticity of less than one. Although the quantity demanded of a normal good always rises with income, it rises more than proportionately for a superior good (such as a luxury car). Conversely, demand for a basic good such as shoe polish rises at a slower rate than income.

In Chapter 3 we explained how the same good or service can be normal or inferior, both for different individuals and also for a single consumer at different levels of income. Figure 5.10 shows the **income - expenditure curve** of a single individual for bus travel. At levels of income below Y_1 he is too poor to afford bus travel. Y_1 is the threshold level of income at which he affords bus travel for the first time. From Y_1 to Y_2, bus travel functions as a superior good for our individual, his expenditure on bus travel rising faster than income. Beyond Y_2, bus travel becomes a basic good, eventually becoming an inferior good at a level of income above Y_3. Thus as income rises, the individual consumer's income elasticity of demand falls from point to point moving along the curve. Income elasticity of demand is (+)∞ at Y_1 and greater than (+)1 between Y_1 and Y_2. Elasticity equals (+)1 at Y_2, and falls to 0 at Y_3. For all levels of income above Y_3, when bus travel has become an inferior good, income elasticity of demand is negative. You should note that when bus travel is a normal good, the income expenditure curve possesses the mathematical properties of upward-sloping curves, which we explained earlier in this chapter in the context of price elasticity of supply. For levels of income at which bus travel is inferior, the income-expenditure curve displays the properties of the downward-sloping curves, discussed earlier under the heading of price elasticity of demand.

Figure 5.10: Income elasticity of demand for a good such as bus travel which switches from being normal at low income levels to becoming inferior at high income levels

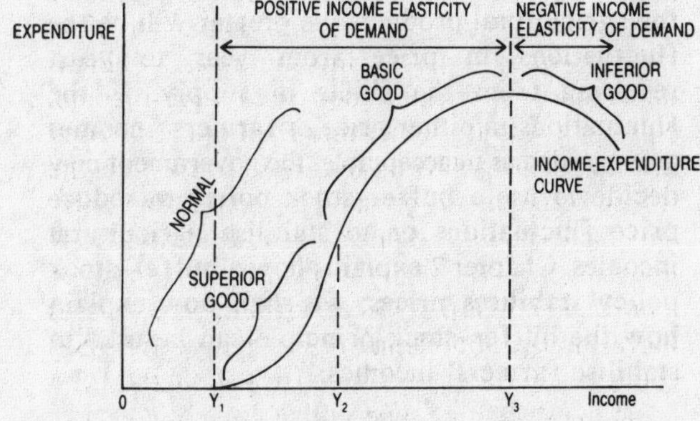

CROSS-ELASTICITY OF DEMAND

16. Cross-elasticity of demand measures the responsiveness of demand for one commodity to changes in the price of another good. The cross-elasticity of demand between two goods or services indicates the **nature of the demand relationship** between the goods. There are three possibilities: **joint demand; competing demand;** and an absence of any discernable demand relationship.

(i) **Joint demand.** Goods in joint demand are called **complementary goods.** Complementary goods always have **negative cross-elasticities,** showing that a rise in the price of one good, resulting in less being demanded of that good, then causes less to be demanded of the good in joint demand. A cross-elasticity of demand of (-) 0.2 for automobiles with respect to the price of petrol would indicate that demand for cars will fall by 2% when the price of petrol rises by 10%. This is quite a strong demand relationship. Although in principle cross-elasticity can vary between minus infinity and plus infinity, it is usual for cross-elasticities to lie within the range from (-)1 to (+)1. Cross-elasticities are typically inelastic; elastic demand relationships between two goods are rare.

(ii) **Competing demand.** The cross-elasticity of demand between two goods which are **substitutes** for each other is always **positive.** A rise in the price of one good causes demand to switch to the substitute good whose price has not risen. A cross elasticity of demand of (+)0.1 for private automobiles with respect to the price of public transport means that a 10% price rise in bus fares and other forms of public transport, causes demand for cars to rise by 1%. The closer the substitute relationship, the greater the cross-elasticity of demand, but as with goods in joint demand, cross-elasticities greater than unity are unusual.

(iii) **No discernable demand relationship.** If we select two goods at random, for example pencils and bicycles, the cross-elasticity of demand between the two goods will be zero. A rise in the price of one good will have no measurable effect upon the demand for the other good. Nevertheless, although there is no obvious demand relationship between the two goods, there is a relationship in the sense that income spent on one good cannot be spent on the other good. This is unlikely to affect the cross-elasticity of demand when both items form just a tiny fraction of a typical household's total expenditure, but the same would not be true if expenditure on the two goods occupies a large part of total spending, for example in the case of food and housing. A rise in the price of housing may reduce the demand for food, resulting in a negative cross-elasticity.

In summary, the **mathematical sign of a cross-elasticity** depends on the **nature of the demand relationship** between two goods; the **absolute size of the cross-elasticity** indicates the **strength of the relationship.**

THE IMPORTANCE OF ELASTICITY FOR FIRMS

17. In the real economy firms seldom possess perfect information about their own demand and supply curves and about the demand and supply conditions facing competitor firms in the market. In many market circumstances, a firm might find it extremely useful to estimate the elasticities of demand for its product, and also the extent to which competitor firms can or cannot respond to a change in price and demand. If a firm possesses accurate information about the likely responses of consumers and competitors to changes in price, it can estimate the probable effect upon revenue or profit, both of its own pricing and supply decisions, and also of changes in market price outside the control of the firm. For example, when a firm believes demand is elastic, it would expect a price rise to reduce total revenue, though not necessarily to reduce total profits. In contrast, when demand is inelastic, a price rise would increase total revenue. The more inelastic the demand curve facing a firm, the greater the firm's market power to raise price while suffering only a smaller proportionate loss of sales and no loss of total revenue. Conversely when demand is highly elastic, firms possess little market power to raise the price, becoming at the limit in conditions of perfectly elastic demand, passive price-takers unable to set a price above the ruling market price for fear of losing all their customers to the perfect substitutes produced by other firms.

Information about income elasticity of demand is also important for a firm's decision making. When economic growth is taking place and real incomes and living standards are rising, demand for inferior goods will fall while demand for normal goods, and especially superior goods or luxuries will rise. It is obviously in a firm's interest to diversify away from producing inferior goods for a declining market, expanding instead into the production of goods for which demand is likely to grow faster than income.

ELASTICITY AND AGRICULTURAL POLICY

18. In Chapter 2 we saw how the short-run supply curve of an agricultural product can shift from year to year up or down the demand curve for the product. The greater the elasticity of demand for the agricultural product, the greater will be the fluctuations in price from year to year, resulting from the shifts in supply. If the fluctuations in either price or farmers' incomes are regarded as unacceptable, the government may decide to use a **buffer-stock policy** to reduce price fluctuations or to stabilise agricultural incomes. Chapter 2 explains how a buffer-stock policy stabilises prices; we shall now explain how the buffer-stock principle can be used to stabilise farmers' incomes.

Figure 5.11: A buffer stock policy to stabilise farmers' incomes

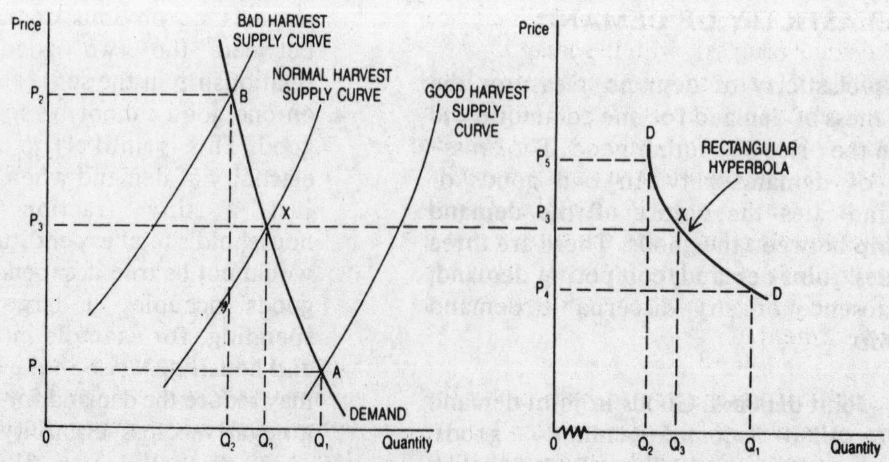

We have drawn the lefthand panel of Figure 5.11 to show both price and agricultural incomes fluctuating from year to year as the supply curve shifts leftwards and rightwards according to the state of the harvest. Following a good harvest, farmers' incomes are represented by the area OQ_1AP_1, rising to OQ_2BP_2 in the event of a bad harvest. Because the demand curve is inelastic, farmers' incomes fall when a good harvest occurs and rise following a bad harvest. You should note that the reverse would be true when demand is elastic. To stabilise farmers' incomes at the 'normal harvest' level of income OQ_3XP_3, we have drawn a rectangular hyperbola DD through X in the righthand panel of Figure 5.11. Being a rectangular hyperbola, curve DD displays a unit elasticity at all points, allowing us to read off exactly the same expenditure or farmers' incomes whatever the price. DD shows the complete range of prices at which the government must operate its buffer-stock policy to stabilise incomes.

Following a good harvest in which output Q_1 comes onto the market, the government must buy at the price P_4; farm incomes will then be exactly the same as in a normal year. Symmetrically, the government must release part of its buffer-stock onto the market at a price of P_5 to stabilise incomes when output falls to Q_2 after a bad harvest.

ELASTICITY AND TAX POLICY

19. The price elasticity of demand for a product affects both the government's total tax revenue when a tax upon expenditure is imposed upon the good, and also the pattern of consumer expenditure. In Figure 5.12 we have drawn a demand curve D_1 and a supply curve S_1 to represent demand and supply conditions before a tax is imposed upon a product. Equilibrium price and quantity are P_1 and Q_1, with the area OQ_1AP_1 showing both total consumer expenditure and the total income or revenue received by all the firms in the market. When a **flat-rate tax** (a **specific tax** or **unit tax**) is imposed by the government on each unit of the good sold by the firms, conditions of supply change and the supply curve shifts upwards to S_2. The vertical distance between S_1 and S_2 represents the tax unit levied by the government.

The firms will of course try to pass on to the consumers as much of the tax as possible by raising the price of the good. However, their ability to raise price by the full amount of the tax is limited by elasticity of demand. In Figure 5.12 we have drawn an inelastic demand curve which shows that the firms can pass on most but not all of the tax. If the firms raise the price by the full amount of the tax to P_3, an excess supply will result because at P_3 consumers are unwilling to purchase as much as the firms are prepared to supply. Market forces would reduce the price to P_2 to clear the excess supply. At the new equilibrium price of P_2, the government's total tax revenue is shown by the area $TCBP_2$. The government's tax revenue $TCBP_2$ can be divided into two parts, showing respectively the **shifted incidence** and the **unshifted incidence** of the tax. The shaded rectangle above the original pre-tax equilibrium price P_1 represents the shifted incidence of the tax. This is the part of the tax successfully passed on to the consumers as a price rise. The area of the tax rectangle below P_1 is the unshifted incidence of the tax which firms must bear themselves out of revenue.

Figure 5.12: The effect of a specific tax upon expenditure in conditions of inelastic demand

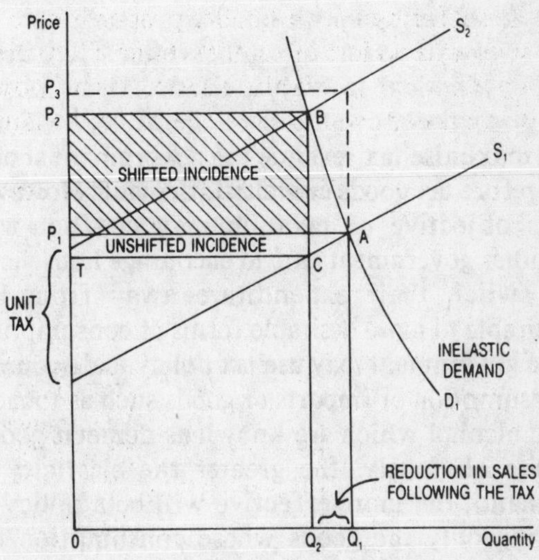

Elasticity of demand affects also the total tax revenue collected by the government, and the pattern of consumer expenditure. When demand is elastic, as in Figure 5.13, an expenditure tax causes the amount bought and sold in the new equilibrium to fall by a much greater amount than when demand is inelastic. For any size of unit tax, the government collects a larger tax revenue when demand for the taxed goods is inelastic rather than elastic.

Figure 5.13: The effect of a specific tax upon expenditure in conditions of elastic demand

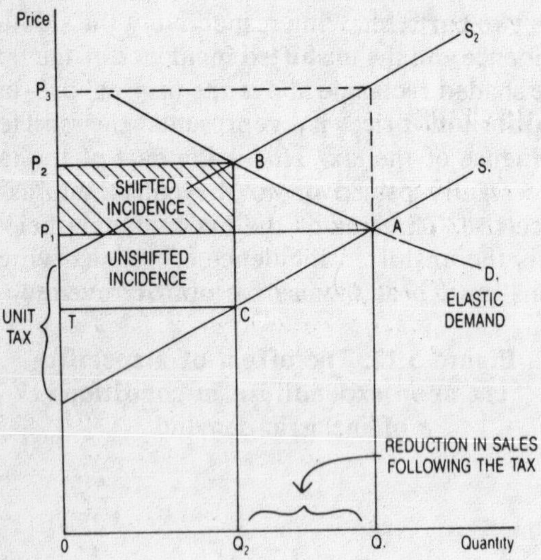

To **maximise tax revenue** the government should therefore tax goods in **inelastic demand**. However, this objective of taxation may conflict with another government aim: to encourage households to switch their expenditure away from less desirable to more desirable forms of consumption. The government may use tax policy to discourage consumption of **imports** or goods such as tobacco and alcohol which are known as **demerit goods**. Quite obviously, the greater the elasticity of demand, the more effective will be a policy of taxing only the goods whose consumption the government wishes to discourage. The tax will switch consumer demand away from the taxed goods, thereby encouraging consumption of untaxed goods. But such a policy may be ineffective if demand for imports or demerit goods is inelastic.

ELASTICITY AND THE BALANCE OF PAYMENTS

20. When the government taxes imports, the effect upon the country's balance of payments depends largely on whether the domestic demand for imports is elastic or inelastic. A tariff or import duty is most effective in improving the balance of payments (by reducing expenditure on imports) when domestic demand is price elastic. Domestic elasticity of supply is also significant. The country's inhabitants are most likely to respond to the higher price of imports by switching expenditure to domestically produced substitute goods if the nation's firms can quickly increase supply to meet the increase in demand. If domestic supply is inelastic and firms are unable to increase output, domestic price may rise, wiping out the competitive advantage over imports gained from the tariff.

In a rather similar way, elasticity may largely determine the effect of a rise or fall of the exchange rate upon the balance of payments. A fall in the exchange rate (often called a devaluation) makes imports more expensive in the domestic market and exports cheaper in overseas markets. A devaluation is likely to be most effective in improving a country's balance of payments when domestic demand for imported goods and overseas demand for the country's exports are both price elastic and when domestic supply can also quickly respond to increased domestic and overseas demand.

SUMMARY

21. Whenever one variable responds to another variable, an elasticity can be measured. Elasticity is an especially useful descriptive statistic measuring the response between two variables because it is independent of the units, such as quantity and price units, in which the variables are measured. The four main elasticities studied in micro-economic theory are price elasticity of demand, price elasticity of supply, income elasticity of demand and cross-elasticity of demand. Demand (or supply) is price elastic when a change in price induces a more than proportionate change in demand (or supply). Average elasticities can be measured between any two points on a demand or supply curve, but because the elasticity often varies from point to point on a curve, elasticities should only be measured for small changes along the curve.

Alternatively, point elasticity can be calculated at a particular point on a supply or demand curve. Price elasticity of demand is normally negative and price elasticity of supply is usually positive, but income elasticity of demand can be positive or negative depending on whether the good is normal or inferior. The cross-elasticity of demand between two goods, which measures the strength of a demand relationship between two goods is positive for substitutes and negative when the goods are in joint demand. The size of the cross-elasticity indicates the strength of the demand relationship. Information about elasticities is useful both for firms and the government. Knowledge of price elasticity of demand indicates to a firm whether a price increase will cause total sales revenue to rise or fall and informs the government of the likely effects of a sales tax upon tax revenue and the pattern of consumer expenditure. Other areas of government policy which are affected by elasticities of demand and supply include agricultural policy and the balance of payments.

STUDENTS SELF-TESTING

1 *Distinguish between elasticity and slope.* *(2)*
2 *Write out the formulas for demand and supply elasticities.* *(4)*
3 *What is meant by elastic demand?* *(5)*
4 *Write out the rule for calculating price elasticity of demand.* *(6)*
5 *What elasticity does a rectangular hyperbola display?* *(7)*
6 *Contrast infinitely elastic demand with infinitely elastic supply.* *(8)*
7 *What slope of curve shows completely inelastic demand?* *(9)*
8 *Distinguish between point elasticity and average elasticity.* *(10)*
9 *What is the most important determinant of price elasticity of demand?* *(11)*
10 *What is the elasticity of a linear supply curve rising from origin?* *(12)*
11 *Write out the rule for calculating price elasticity of supply.* *(13)*
12 *List the determinants of price elasticity of supply.* *(14)*
13 *Contrast the income elasticity of demand of normal and inferior goods.* *(15)*
14 *What can be inferred about the demand relationship between two goods with a cross-elasticity of (+)0.3?* *(16)*
15 *If demand is inelastic, what effect will a price fall have on a firm's total sales revenue?* *(17)*
16 *If demand is elastic, what effect may a good harvest have on farmers' total incomes?* *(18)*
17 *If demand is inelastic what effect might a unit sales tax have on (a) the price of the good; and (b) the quantity bought and sold?* *(19)*
18 *Explain how elasticities of demand and supply may influence the effect of a fall in the exchange rate upon the balance of payments.* *(20)*

EXERCISES

1 *The revenue received by a firm at different levels of output is shown below:*

Total production (units per day)	*Average revenue £*
1	50
2	46
3	40
4	36
5	30
6	25
7	20

Between which prices is demand (a) elastic, (b) inelastic, (c) neither elastic nor inelastic?

2 *The supply and demand schedules are shown below for a commodity on which a tax of 30 pence per unit is then imposed.*

Price before tax (pence)	*Demand (00s)*	*Supply (00s)*
50	220	400
40	240	360
30	260	320
20	280	280
10	300	240

(a) *What is the equilibrium price (i) before, and (ii) after the tax is imposed?*
(b) *How much of the tax is borne by the firms and how much is borne by the consumers?*

3 *The owner of an ice-cream stall estimates that the daily demand schedule facing him is:*

Price of ice-cream cornets (pence)	*Quantity demand*
50	*125*
45	*175*
40	*250*
35	*300*
30	*350*
25	*500*
20	*750*

(a) *What is the elasticity of demand for a price rise from 30p to 35p?*

(b) *What is the elasticity of demand for a price reduction from 45p to 40p?*

(c) *What is the elasticity of demand between 35p and 40p?*

(d) *The price of ice-cream is reduced from 20p to 15p. If elasticity equals (-)0.8, how many ice-creams will be sold at 15p?*

MULTIPLE CHOICE QUESTIONS

1 *The price elasticity of demand for fish is - 0.54 and the cross-elasticity of demand for fish with respect to the following commodities are:*

chips	*-0.31*
meat	*0.62*
sausages	*0.47*

We can predict from this information that:

A *A fall in the price of meat will lead to a rise in demand for fish*

B *A fall in the price of sausages will lead to a rise in demand for fish*

C *A fall in the price of chips will lead to a rise in demand for fish*

D *A fall in the price of fish will lead to a more than proportionate rise in demand for fish*

2 *If there is a free market in lettuces and if demand is completely inelastic, the most likely effect of a bumper crop will be:*

A *To increase the total income of lettuce growers*

B *To decrease the total income of lettuce growers*

C *To increase the price of lettuces*

D *To increase the quantity demanded*

Questions 3 and 4 are based on the following table:

Demand schedule for rice

Price per kilo ($)	*Quantity demanded per day (kilos)*
6	*1,200*
8	*960*
10	*800*
12	*600*
14	*560*
16	*490*

3 *If the price increases from $10 to $12 the demand is:*

A *Perfectly elastic*

B *Elastic*

C *Unit elastic*

D *Inelastic*

4 *Between which prices is demand neither elastic nor inelastic?*

A *$8 and $10*

B *$10 and $12*

C *$12 and $14*

D *$14 and $16*

5 *The table below contains a set of price and cross-elasticities of demand for four commodities, E, F, G and H.*

Elasticity of demand

For commodity				*With respect to price of*
H	*G*	*F*	*E*	
-0.4	*+0.6*	*+0.4*	*-1.3*	*E*
+0.8	*-0.3*	*-0.6*	*+0.5*	*F*
+0.7	*-2.7*	*-0.2*	*+0.9*	*G*
-0.1	*+0.5*	*+0.6*	*-0.3*	*H*

Which commodities are in joint demand:

A *H and E only*

B *E and F only*

C *E and F, G and E*

D *H and E, F and G*

EXAMINATION QUESTIONS

1 (a) *Define each of the following terms: price, income, and cross-elasticity of demand. Describe briefly the factors that determine each of them.* *(14 marks)*

(b) *Below is given the demand schedule for a product.*

Price (£ per unit)	*Demand (units per week)*
10	400
9	500
8	600
7	700
6	800
5	900
4	1000
3	1100

Calculate the price elasticity of demand and comment on your results when:

(i) *the price is reduced from £9 to £8 per unit.* *(3 marks)*

(ii) *the price is reduced from £5 to £4 per unit.* *(3 marks)*

(ACCA December 1985)

2 (a) *Define the price and income elasticities of demand and indicate briefly the factors which determine them.* *(10 marks)*

(b) *What are the practical uses of these two concepts?* *(10 marks)*

(ACCA June 1983)

3. *Define the concept of 'elasticity' and explain, with examples, its importance in both its demand and supply aspects.*

(CIMA November 1984)

6. Perfect competition and monopoly

INTRODUCTION

1. In Chapter 4 we examined the cost and supply conditions of a firm, without at that stage considering in detail the **market structure** in which the firm sells its output. We assumed simply that the firm exists in a competitive market, able to sell as much or as little as it pleases at a ruling market price determined in the market as a whole. In fact, we were assuming that the firm produces and sells its output within a **perfectly competitive market structure**. In this chapter we take a more detailed look at perfect competition, before examining a second type of market structure, **monopoly**. The chapter concludes by comparing the desirable and less-desirable properties of equilibrium firms in perfect competition and monopoly.

MARKET STRUCTURE AND THE THEORY OF THE FIRM

2. **Perfect competition** and **monopoly** are opposite or polar extremes which separate a spectrum of market structures known as **imperfect competition**. The main forms of market structure are illustrated and defined in Figure 6.1. Monopoly, in which a single firm produces the whole of the output of a market or industry, is the most extreme form of imperfect competition; indeed in pure form, there is no competition at all since there are no other firms to compete against. However, monopoly is best regarded as a relative rather than an absolute concept; the British Gas Corporation may be a single producer of piped gas to households and industrial customers, but it experiences competition from other sources of energy such as electricity and oil. Monopolists do therefore face competitive pressures, both from substitute products and sometimes also from 'outside' firms trying to enter the market to destroy their monopoly position.

Figure 6.1: The spectrum of market structures

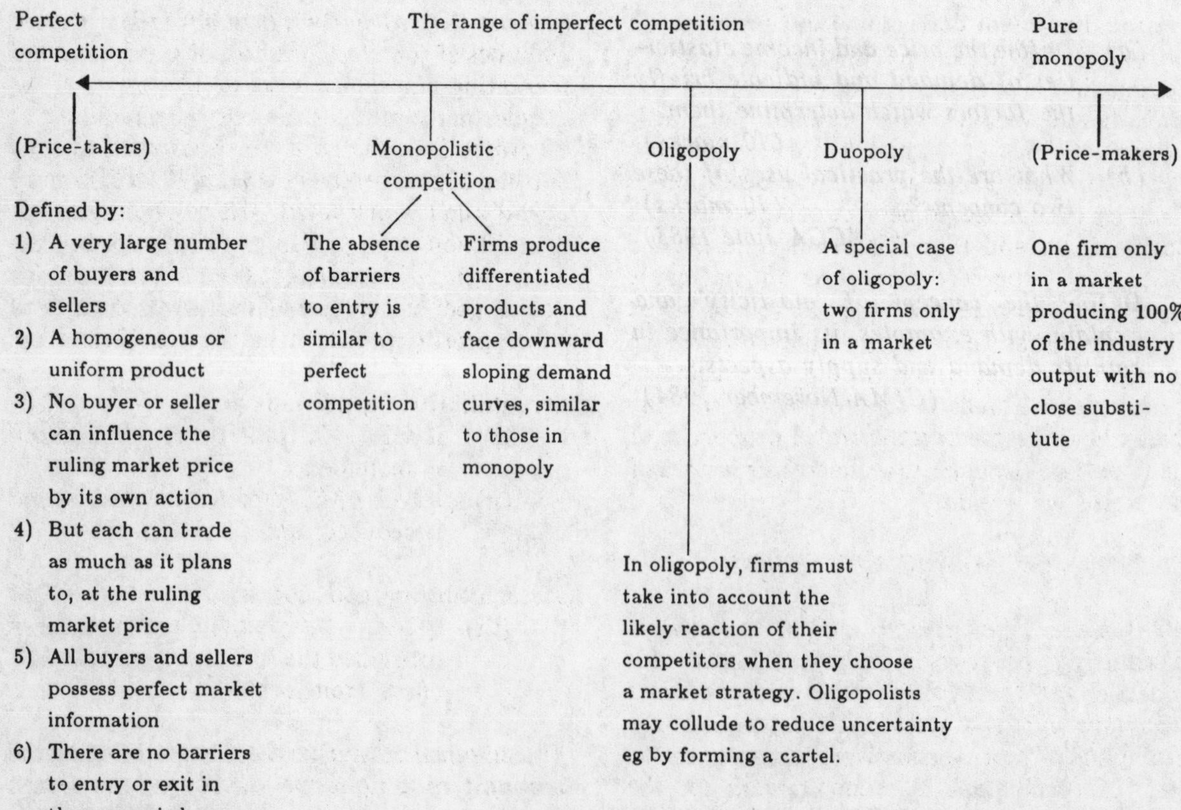

Although this chapter is restricted to perfect competition and monopoly, you should not conclude that either of these market structures is typical or representative of the real economy. Even ignoring competition from substitute products, pure monopoly is exceedingly rare; the public monopolies or nationalised industries such as the post office provide perhaps the best examples. Note however that in recent years government policy in the United Kingdom has reduced the role of the state monopolies, both by introducing competition and by transferring nationalised industries to the private sector.

At the other end of the spectrum, perfect competition is actually non-existent. Perfect competition is essentially an unreal or abstract economic model defined by the conditions we have listed in Figure 6.1. As we shall shortly see, it is not possible for any real world market to display simultaneously all the conditions necessary for perfect competition. And since any violation of the conditions of perfect competition immediately renders a market imperfectly competitive, even the most competitive markets in the real economy are examples of imperfect competition rather than perfect competition.

Despite the lack of perfect markets in the world in which we live, the theory of perfect competition is perhaps the most important and fundamental of all conventional economic theories. Critics of orthodox micro-economic theory strongly argue that undue attention is given by economists to perfect competition as a market form and that this encourages a false belief that a perfect market is an attainable 'ideal'. As you read this chapter, remember at all times that perfect competition is an unrealistic market structure, but note also that it provides a 'standard' against which we may judge the desirable or undesirable properties of the imperfectly competitive market structures of the world we live in.

PROFIT-MAXIMISING BEHAVIOUR

3. Just as the assumption of a **utility-maximising objective** on the part of **households** underlies the **theory of demand** and consumer behaviour which we studied in Chapter 3, so the assumption of **profit-maximising behaviour** on the part of **producers** is fundamental to the traditional **theory of the firm**. A firm's total profit is defined by the identity:

$$\text{total profit} \equiv \text{total revenue} - \text{total cost}$$

Assuming a profit maximising objective, the firm therefore aims to produce the level of output at which TR - TC is maximised. This represents the equilibrium condition for a profit-maximising firm, for if a firm produces and sells the output which yields the biggest possible profit, it has no incentive to change its level of output.

However, it is often more convenient to state the equilibrium condition for profit maximisation as:

$$\text{marginal revenue} = \text{marginal cost}$$

We first introduced MR = MC as the **equilibrium equation** for profit maximisation in Chapter 4, when deriving the short-run supply curve of a firm in a competitive market. MR = MC means that a firm's profits are greatest when the addition to sales revenue received from the last unit sold (**marginal revenue**) equals exactly the addition to total cost incurred from the production of the last unit of output (**marginal cost**). Imagine for example, a market gardener producing tomatoes for sale in a local market, but unable to influence the ruling market price of 50 pence per kilo. At any size of sales, average revenue is 50 pence, which also equals marginal revenue. Let us suppose that when the horticulturalist markets 300 kilos of tomatoes, the cost of producing and marketing the 300th kilo is 48 pence. If he decides not to market the kilo, he sacrifices 2p of profit. Suppose now that total costs rise by 50p and 52p respectively when a 301st kilo and a 302nd kilo are marketed. The marketing of the 302nd kilo causes profits to fall by 2p, but the 301st kilo of tomatoes leaves total profits unchanged: it represents the level of sales at which profits are exactly maximised. To sum up:

Disequilibrium conditions are:

- (i) if MR > MC; profits rise when output is increased;
- (ii) if MR < MC; profits rise when output is reduced; and

the equilibrium equation is:

- (iii) if MR = MC; profits are maximised (provided the MC curve cuts the MR curve from below).

The marginal costs incurred when producing the last unit of output are of course the firm's marginal private costs, while marginal revenue represents the marginal private benefit received from the last unit of sales. MR = MC, the equilibrium equation for a profit-maximising firm, is therefore an example of the universal equilibrium equation for any maximising economic agent which we introduced in Chapter 3:

marginal private benefit = marginal private cost

REVENUE CURVES IN PERFECT COMPETITION

4. We have already noted that perfect competition is defined by the conditions of perfect competition listed in Figure 6.1. We shall now make use of these conditions to derive the revenue curves facing a firm in a perfectly competitive market. The assumption that a perfectly competitive firm can sell as much as it plans to sell at the ruling market price, but that it cannot influence the ruling market price by its own action, means that the firm is a **'price-taker'**. The demand curve facing a perfectly competitive firm is infinitely elastic, determined by the ruling market price in the market as a whole. This horizontal demand curve or price line, which is illustrated in Figure 6.2 is also the perfectly competitive firm's **average revenue** (AR) and **marginal revenue** (MR) curve. You will notice that we have written the slogans 'no sales' and 'no sense' respectively above and below the price line P_1 drawn in Figure 6.2. 'No sales' indicates that when a firm raises its selling price above the ruling market price, determined by the interaction of market demand and supply, it loses all its customers, who desert the firm to buy the perfect substitutes produced by other firms which are available at the ruling market price. 'No sense' refers to the fact that it is irrational to sell below the price of P_1 when the firm can sell as much as it plans at the ruling price of P_1; such a course of action must reduce the firm's total profits.

We can also show the firm's revenue conditions in the **total revenue** (TR) curve illustrated in Figure 6.3 (on the next page). In perfect competition, a firm's TR curve is a straight line drawn to origin, plotted from exactly the same sales data as the marginal revenue curve. In the TR curve, the sales data is plotted *cumulatively* rather than as *separate* observations as in the MR curve. Marginal revenue is of course the addition to total revenue resulting from an extra unit of sales. Thus the TR curve is linear, rising at a constant rate or slope, when the MR curve is constant or horizontal.

NORMAL PROFIT AND ABNORMAL PROFIT

5. Before we proceed to show the profit-maximising or equilibrium firm in perfect competition, we must first explain **normal** and **abnormal profit**. The concepts of normal and abnormal (or supernormal) profit are abstract devices used in economic theory; they have nothing to do with how an accountant measures a

Figure 6.2: The perfectly competitive firm as a passive price-taker

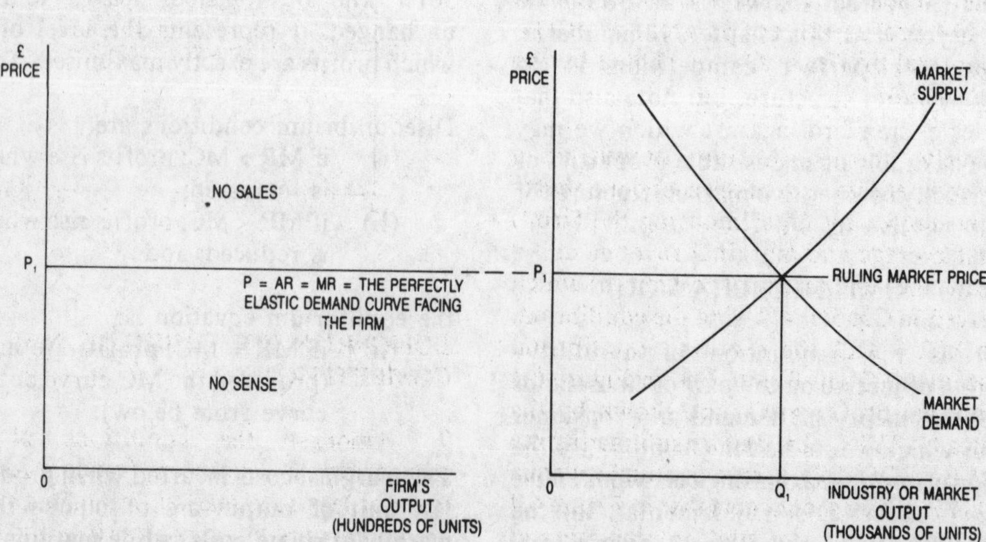

firm's profits. Normal profit is the minimum level of profit necessary to keep existing firms in production, yet being insufficient to attract new firms into the market. As such, normal profit functions as a cost of production and is included in a firm's average cost curve. Abnormal profit is any extra profit over and above normal profit.

Figure 6.3: A firm's total revenue curve in perfect competition

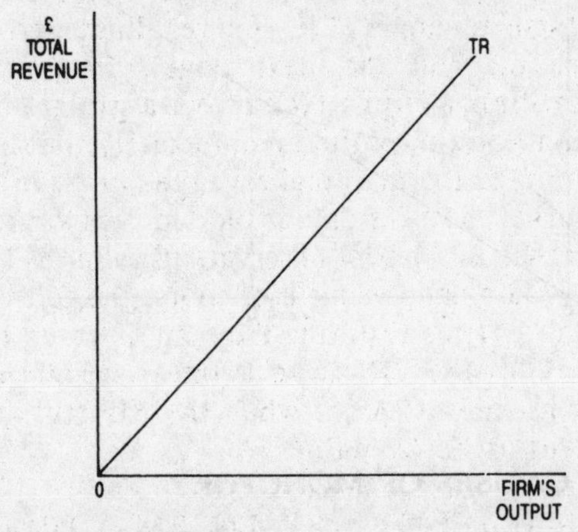

SHORT-RUN EQUILIBRIUM IN PERFECT COMPETITION

6. Figure 6.4 shows the **short-run equilibrium** output of a perfectly competitive firm in terms of the firm's total revenue and total cost curves. Since profits are maximised at the level of output at which TR - TC is maximised, equilibrium occurs at output Q_1, where the total revenue curve is furthest above the total cost curve. Other levels of output and sales are profitable - when the TR curve is above the TC curve - but profits are not as great as at Q_1. Total abnormal profits at Q_1 are shown by the *vertical line* AB.

Alternatively, the equilibrium output of a perfectly competitive firm in the economic short-run can be shown by superimposing the firm's horizontal average and marginal revenue curve upon the average and marginal cost curves which were derived in Chapter 4. Using the equilibrium equation MR = MC, the resulting equilibrium output occurs at Q_1 in Figure 6.5. In Figure 6.5 total abnormal profits at Q_1 are shown by the shaded area C_1ZYP_1, obtained by subtracting the total cost area (OQ_1ZC_1) from the total revenue area (OQ_1YP_1). You should note that in Figure 6.4 total revenue, total cost and total abnormal profit at any level of output are all shown by *vertical distances*, but in Figure 6.5 they are shown by *areas*.

Figure 6.4: Short-run equilibrium output of a perfectly competitive firm where TR - TC is maximised

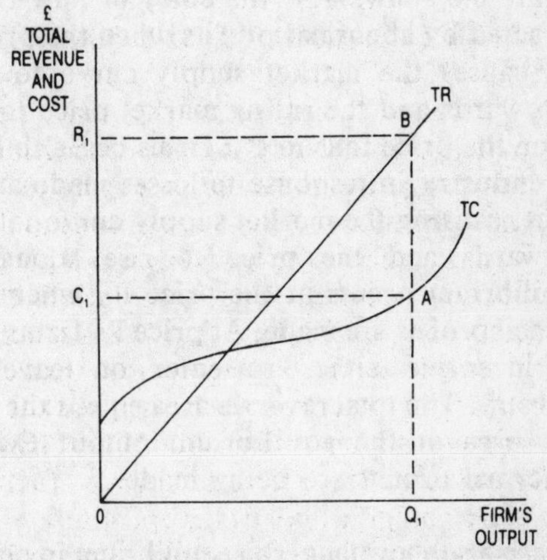

Figure 6.5: The short-run equilibrium output of a perfectly competitive firm shown by average and marginal revenue and cost curves. Equilibrium is where MR = MC

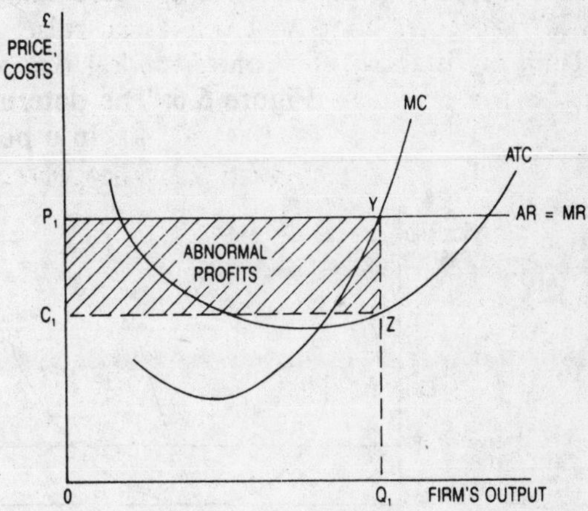

LONG-RUN EQUILIBRIUM IN PERFECT COMPETITION

7. Amongst the conditions of perfect competition is a complete freedom for firms to enter or leave the market in the long run. There are no barriers to entry or exit in the economic

long-run. In any short-run situation, the ruling market price facing all firms signals to firms whether abnormal profits, normal profits or losses can be made. Any abnormal profits made by existing firms within the market provide an incentive for new firms to enter the industry, but symmetrically, any losses made by existing firms create an incentive for firms to leave. Figure 6.6 shows how the entry of new firms, attracted by abnormal profits when the price is P_1, causes the market supply curve to shift rightwards and the ruling market price to fall. When the price falls to P_2, firms begin to leave the industry in response to losses made at this price, causing the market supply curve to shift leftwards and the price to rise. **Long-run equilibrium** occurs at the price P_3 when only normal profits are made. At price P_3 firms have no incentive either to enter or leave the industry. The total revenue area equals the total cost area at the equilibrium output Q_3; no abnormal profits are being made.

We can also show long-run equilibrium in perfect competition at the point of tangency between the total revenue and total cost curves illustrated in Figure 6.7. The falling market price, which follows the entry of new firms into the market, causes the TR curve to shift until TR equals TC at point A. Point A locates the equilibrium output Q_3, at which no abnormal profits are made.

Figure 6.7: Long-run equilibrium output of a perfectly competitive firm

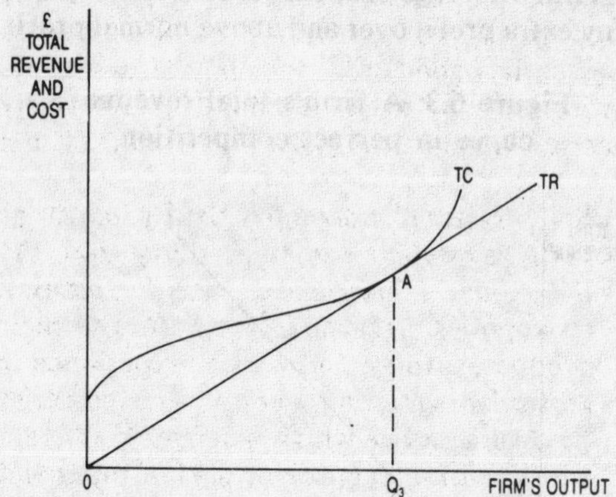

THE CAUSES OF MONOPOLY

8. Before we examine the equilibrium pricing and output conditions in a market in which there is only one firm, we shall first survey the market conditions which favour the emergence of a monopoly supplier. An effective monopoly must be able to exclude rivals from the market through

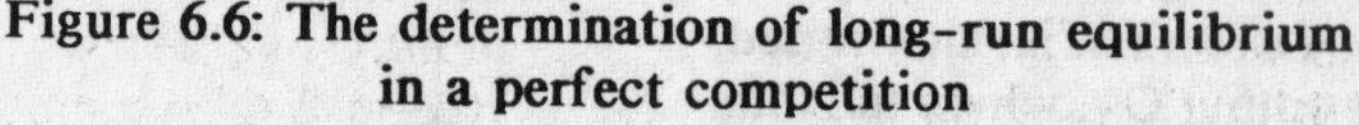

Figure 6.6: The determination of long-run equilibrium in a perfect competition

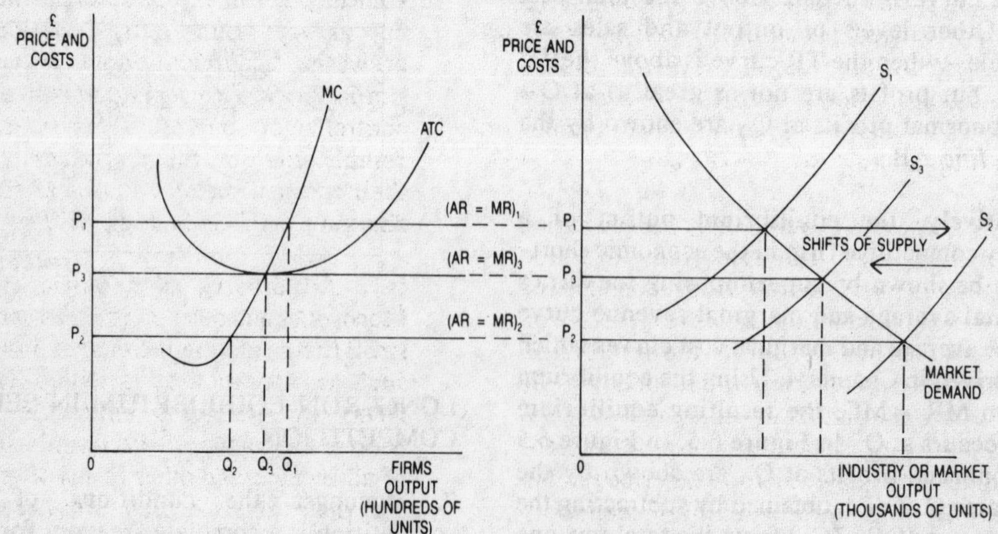

barriers to entry. However, even when a firm is a monopoly producer of a particular good or service, the monopoly position is weak if close substitutes exist produced by other firms in other industries. The closer the substitutes available, the weaker the monopoly position. A monopoly is therefore strongest when it produces an essential good for which there are no substitutes - or when demand is relatively inelastic. Amongst the causes of monopoly are:

(i) **'Natural' monopoly. Utility industries** such as water, gas, electricity and the telephone industries are **'natural' monopolies**. Because of the nature of their product, utility industries experience a particular marketing problem. The industries produce a service which is delivered through a distribution network or grid of pipes and cables into millions of separate businesses and homes. Competition in the provision of distribution grids is extremely wasteful since it requires the duplication of fixed capacity, therefore causing each supplier to incur unnecessarily high fixed costs. Utility industries tend therefore to be monopolies, but a **public policy choice** exists between **public ownership** of the utility, for example as a nationalised **industry**, and **private ownership**, possibly **subject to public regulation**. For a number of historical reasons, most of the utility industries in the United Kingdom were, until recently, public monopolies. In the 1980s, some of the utilities such as the British Gas Corporation and British Telecom have been privatised, becoming privately owned utilities. On the whole, they still remain monopolies, though subject to a certain amount of state regulation, for example Oftel regulating British Telecom.

(ii) **Economies of scale.** Many manufacturing industries, for example the aircraft-building industry, benefit from **economies of large-scale production**. However, the size of the national market limits the number of firms that can co-exist in an industry yet benefit to the full from economies of scale. Economies of scale thus help to explain 'natural' monopoly which we described in the previous paragraph; a 'natural' monopoly occurring when there is room in the market for only one firm benefitting from full economies of scale.

(iii) **Government-created monopolies.** Governments may on occasion create monopoly in industries other than utility industries or 'natural' monopolies. In the United Kingdom industries such as coal, rail and steel were nationalised in the 1940s by a Labour government and turned into state-owned monopolies. The Labour government believed that on the one hand these industries, described as the 'commanding heights of the economy' were essential for the well being and planning of the whole economy and that on the other hand state ownership was required for the industries to operate in the public interest, rather than in the narrower interest of their previous private owners. In other instances, government may deliberately create a private monopoly. Examples include the granting of a broadcasting **franchise** to a commercial TV company or a gambling franchise to a casino. Both these are examples of the state using monopoly to regulate the consumption of a good or service; in the case of the gambling franchise, regulating consumption of a **demerit good**. Finally, another example of government created monopoly is the **patent law**, which gives companies an exclusive right to exploit their inventions or innovations for a number of years.

(iv) **Control of market outlets and raw materials.** Firms may try to obtain exclusive control over market outlets in order to deny access to their competitors. Examples in the United Kingdom include oil companies buying up garages and petrol stations, and breweries acquiring public houses. In a similar way, firms may obtain exclusive control over sources of raw materials or components for their products, starving their competitors of a source of supply, or charging artificially high prices.

(v) **Advertising as a barrier to entry.** Monopolies and other large firms can prevent small firms entering the market with devices such as saturation advertising. The small firms are unable to enter the industry because they cannot afford the minimum level of advertising and other forms of promotion for their goods which are necessary to persuade retailers to stock their products. The mass-advertising, brand-imaging and other marketing strategies of large established firms effectively 'crowd-out' the newcomers from the market place.

MONOPOLY REVENUE CURVES

9. Monopoly revenue curves differ from those facing a firm in a perfectly competitive market. Because the monopoly is the industry, the **industry demand curve** and the **demand curve for monopolist's output** are identical. This means that the monopolist faces a downward-sloping demand curve, whose elasticity is determined by the nature of consumer demand for the monopolist's product. The demand curve can affect the monopolist in one of two different ways. If we regard the monopolist as a **'price-maker'**, deliberately choosing to set the price at which he sells his product, then whenever he sets the price at P_1 in Figure 6.8, the maximum quantity he can sell at this price is Q_1. If the monopolist tries to raise the price to P_2, he must accept a fall in sales to Q_2, unless of course he uses advertising or other devices to shift the demand curve rightwards.

Figure 6.8: The monopoly 'trade-off': if the monopolist sets price the demand curve determines the maximum quantity sold

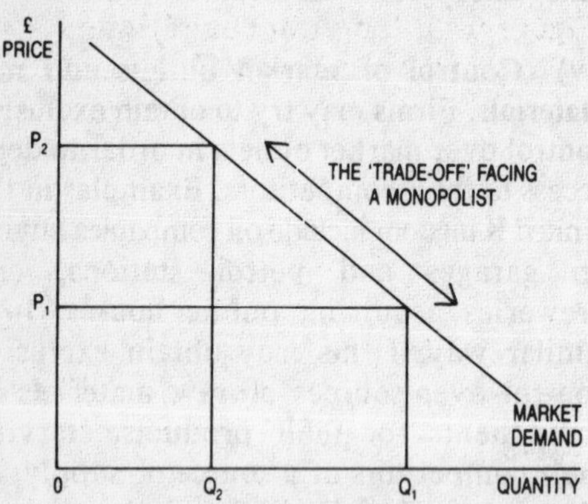

Alternatively, if the monopolist decides to act as a **'quantity-setter'**, the demand curve dictates the maximum price at which the chosen quantity can be sold. Thus the downward-sloping demand curve means that the monopolist faces a **'trade-off'**. He cannot set price and quantity independently of each other; if the monopolist acts as price-maker, the demand curve determines the maximum price he can charge at each level of output.

Because the demand curve shows the price the monopolist charges at each level of output, the **demand curve is the monopolist's average revenue curve.** Unlike perfect competition however, marginal revenue and average revenue in monopoly are not the same. In Chapter 4 we introduced the mathematical relationship between any marginal variable and the average to which it is related:

(i) if the marginal > the average, the average will rise;

(ii) if the marginal < the average, the average will fall;

(iii) of the marginal = the average, the average is constant.

If in doubt about this rule you should refer back to Chapter 4 before proceeding any further in this chapter. Make sure you understand fully the relationships between both average returns and marginal returns and average costs and marginal costs.

Since the monopolist's average revenue curve falls with output or sales, marginal revenue must be below average revenue. Figure 6.9 depicts a monopolist's AR and MR curves, with the MR curve drawn twice as steep as the AR curve. This is always the case whenever the AR curve is a straight line or linear. This mathematical property does not apply however, when the AR curve is non-linear.

Figure 6.9: Monopoly average revenue and marginal revenue curves

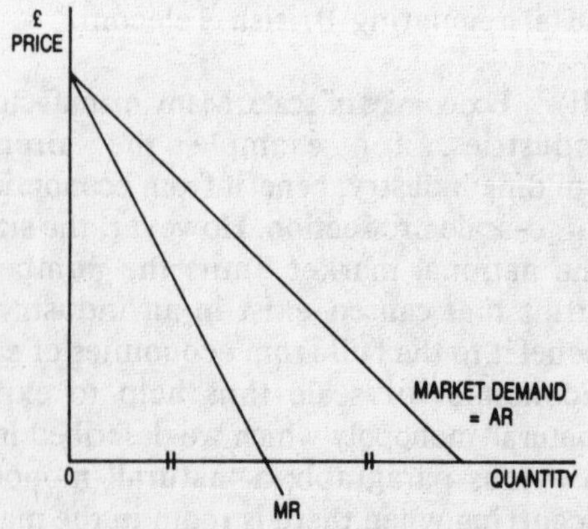

Figure 6.10: At output Q_2 monopoly marginal revenue is n - m, and is less than average revenue

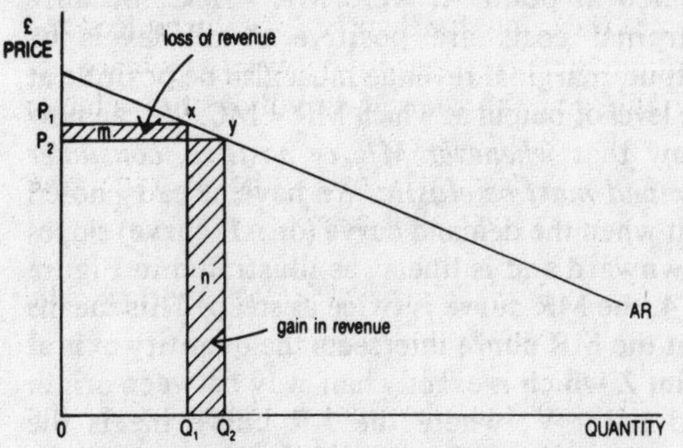

To explain further the relationship between AR and MR we can use Figure 6.10. When the monopolist produces output Q_1, the area OQ_1XP_1 represents total revenue. If output is increased by one unit to Q_2, total revenue changes to the area OQ_2YP_2. Two shaded areas m and n are drawn on Figure 6.10. The area n marked as the '*gain in revenue*' represents the extra unit sold multiplied by the new price. It also represents the average revenue per unit sold at the price of P_2. The other shaded area m shows the '*loss of revenue*' which occurs because all the units of output comprising the previous level of output Q_1 are now being sold at the lower price of P_2 rather than P_1.

Figure 6.11: Monopoly total revenue rises less fast than output and falls when marginal revenue becomes negative

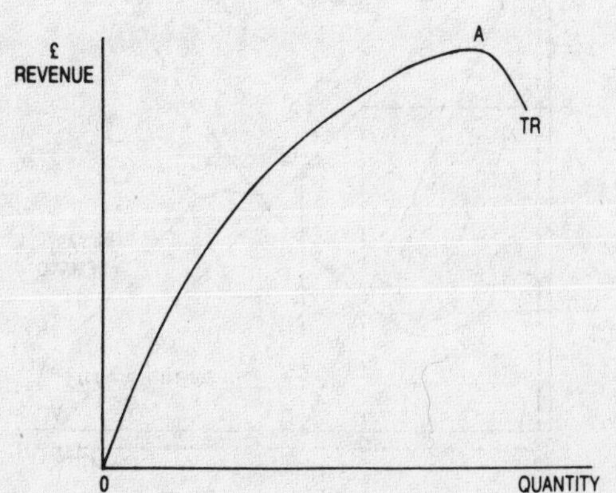

Marginal revenue at the level of output Q_2 is measured by subtracting the 'loss in revenue' (area m) from the 'gain in revenue' (area n). Because the demand curve facing the monopolist slopes downwards, there must always be a 'loss of revenue' area whenever a larger output is offered for sale; at any level of sales, MR is always therefore less than AR.

Figure 6.11 shows the **monopolist's total revenue curve**. Because marginal revenue falls as the quantity sold increases, TR rises with the total quantity sold, but rises at a decreasing rate. Total revenue begins to fall beyond point A when marginal revenue becomes negative.

MONOPOLY EQUILIBRIUM

10. Equilibrium output in a monopoly market is illustrated in Figure 6.12. As in perfect competition, the equilibrium output Q_1 is located at point A where MR = MC. It is worth repeating that providing the firm is a profit-maximiser, the equilibrium equation MR = MC applies to any firm, whatever the market structure. Avoid the temptation however, to read off the equilibrium price at point A; we must read up to point B on the average revenue curve to locate the monopolist's equilibrium price at P_1.

Figure 6.12: Monopoly equilibrium where MR = MC

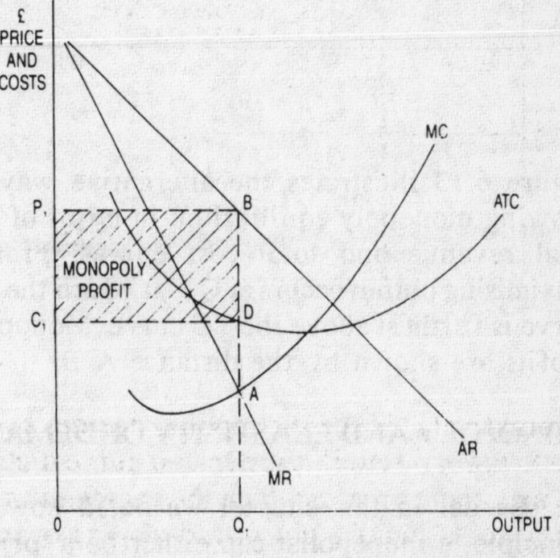

You will notice that we have labelled Figure 6.12 as **monopoly equilibrium** without distinguishing between short-run and long-run equilibrium. As in perfect competition short-run equilibrium, the monopolist makes abnormal profits, shown by the shaded area C_1DBP_1. But in monopoly, **barriers to entry** prevent new firms joining the market, attracted by the monopolist's abnormal profit. Barriers to entry thus enable the monopolist to preserve abnormal profits into the long-run, whereas in perfect competition abnormal profits are essentially temporary, being restricted to the short-run. Indeed in monopoly markets, abnormal profits are often simply called **monopoly profit**, indicating the monopolist's market power to preserve his profits by keeping competitors out.

Figure 6.13: Monopoly equilibrium where TR = TC is maximised

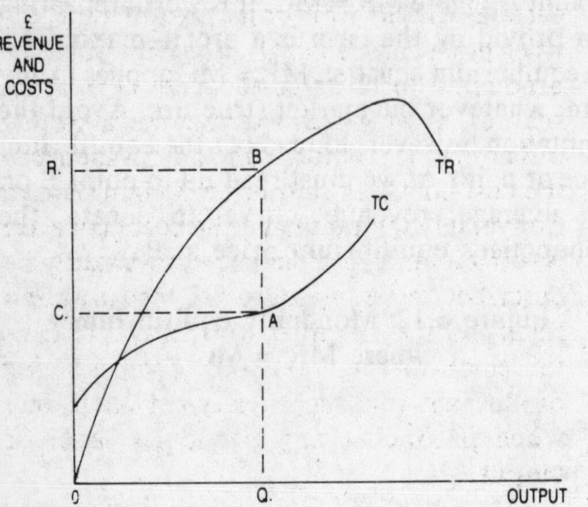

Figure 6.13 illustrates the alternative way of showing monopoly equilibrium in terms of the total revenue and total cost curves. Profit-maximising output occurs at Q_1, at which the TR curve is furthest above the TC curve. Monopoly profits are shown by the distance A B.

MONOPOLY AND ELASTICITY OF DEMAND

11. Earlier in this chapter we noted how, in principle, a monopolist can either be a 'price-maker' or a 'quantity-setter'. However, as Figure 6.12 clearly demonstrates, only at *one* combination of output and price can a monopolist succeed in maximising profits. If the monopolist chooses an output and price other than Q_1 and P_1, he will fail to maximise profits.

It is important to note that demand is *always elastic*, and *never inelastic*, at the profit-maximising level of output. Figure 6.14 shows why. The profit-maximising level of output Q_1 is located at point A, were MR = MC. Because marginal costs are positive at all levels of output, marginal revenue must also be positive at the level of output at which MR = MC. We can now show that *whenever MR is positive, consumer demand must be elastic*. We have already noted that when the demand curve (or AR curve) slopes downward and is linear, as illustrated in Figure 6.14, the MR curve is twice as steep. This means that the MR curve intersects the quantity axis at point Z which is exactly half way between origin and point V, where the AR curve meets the quantity axis. A line drawn vertically through point Z cuts the average revenue curve at point W, which is exactly half way along the AR curve. It follows therefore that the profit-maximising output Q_1, at which MR is positive, must lie below the 'top half' of the demand curve or average revenue curve. We saw in Chapter 5 that the 'top half' of a linear downward-sloping demand curve is elastic at all points. (If in doubt, refer back to section 6 Chapter 5 before proceeding any further.) Hence a profit-maximising monopolist must produce an output for which demand is elastic rather than inelastic.

Figure 6.14: Monopoly profit maximising output is always under the elastic section of the demand curve

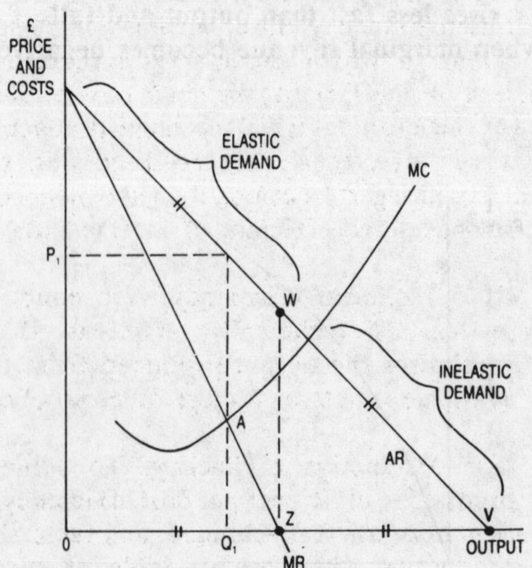

Be careful to avoid confusing the conclusion we have just reached with a commonly-made but potentially misleading generalisation about monopoly. It is often said that a monopolist's market power to exploit consumers is greatest when demand is inelastic and consumers are 'captive' in the sense that no substitutes are available. It is true that a monopolist can choose, if he wishes, to produce a level of output for which demand is inelastic. It is also true that in conditions of inelastic demand, a decision by the monopolist to cut output will result in a more than proportionate increase in total sales revenue. But the fact remains that when, for whatever reason, the monopolist produces under the inelastic section of the demand curve, he cannot be maximising profits. Profit maximisation requires elastic demand.

ECONOMIC EFFICIENCY

12. In Chapter 1 we stated that a fundamental purpose of any economic system is to achieve the highest possible state of human happiness or welfare. Within a market economy, the market structures of perfect competition, imperfect competition and monopoly, must ultimately be judged according to the extent to which they contribute to improving human happiness and well-being, remembering of course, that such a judgement will always be abstract and rather artificial because of the 'unreal' nature of perfect competition.

In order to judge the contribution of a market structure to human welfare, we must first assess the extent to which the market structure is **efficient** or **inefficient**. We shall now explain some of the meanings which economists attach to the word 'efficiency', before discussing the extent to which perfect competition and monopoly can be considered efficient or inefficient.

(i) **Technical efficiency**. A productive process is **technically efficient** if it maximises the output produced from the available inputs or factors of production.

(ii) **Productive efficiency**. To achieve **productive efficiency, or cost efficiency**, a firm must use the techniques and factors of production which are available, at lowest possible cost per unit of output. Productive efficiency is measured by the **lowest point on a firm's long-run average total cost curve**. In most instances, productive efficiency is the translation into money costs of production of technical efficiency. (For a more detailed account of technical and productive efficiency refer back to Chapter 4, section 18.)

(iii) **X-efficiency. X-efficiency** is an application of the concept of technical efficiency. Consider the short-run average total cost curve illustrated in Figure 6.15, which shows the lowest possible unit costs of producing various levels of output, given such conditions of production as the scale of the firm's fixed capacity and the prices of the factors of production. Given the cost curve, it is impossible for the firm to produce an output such as Q_1 at a level of unit costs or average costs below C_1. But if the firm combines its factors of production in a technically inefficient way, it could certainly incur unit costs greater than C_1 when producing output Q_1. The firm would be producing 'off' its cost curve, at a point such as X, at which average costs are C_2 rather than C_1. Point X and any point *above* the cost curve, is said to be X-inefficient. Conversely, all points on the cost curve are X-efficient. X-inefficiency can broadly be described as a measure of 'organisation slack', ie the extent to which a firm fails to combine its existing factors of production in a technically efficient way when producing any particular level of output.

Figure 6.15: X-inefficiency occurs when a firm produces 'off' its cost curve

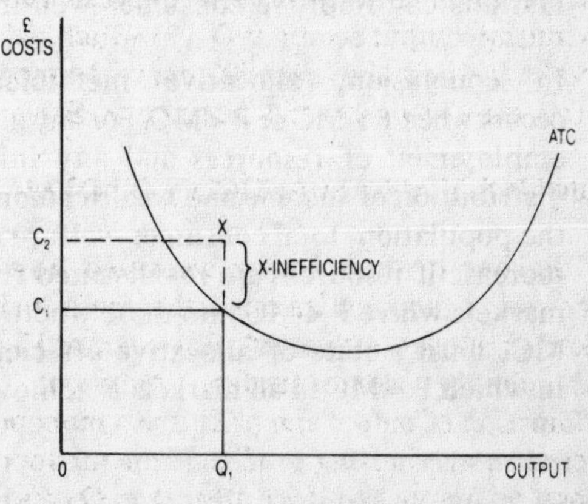

(iv) **Allocative efficiency**. This rather abstract concept is of great importance to the understanding of economic efficiency. **Allocative efficiency** occurs when P = MC in *all* the industries and markets of the economy. To explain this further, we must examine closely P and MC. The price of a good, P, is a measure of the *value in consumption* placed by buyers on the last unit consumed. P indicates the utility or welfare obtained at the margin in consumption. At the same time, MC measures the *good's opportunity cost in production*; the value of the resources which go into the production of the last unit, in their best alternative uses. Suppose that the markets within the economy divide into those in which P > MC and those in which P < MC. In the markets where P > MC, households pay a price for the last unit consumed which is greater than the cost of producing the last unit. At this price the good is *under-produced* and *under-consumed*. Conversely, in the second set of markets in which P < MC, the value (P) placed on the last unit consumed by households is less than the MC of the resources used to produce the last unit. At this price the good is *over-produced* and *over-consumed*.

Suppose now that a mechanism exists which takes resources from the second group of markets where P < MC and re-allocates these resources to the former group in which P > MC. It is possible to show that total consumer welfare or utility increases as resources are re-allocated between markets until P = MC in all markets. Beyond the point at which P = MC in all markets, no further re-allocation of resources between markets can improve consumer welfare.

In conclusion, **allocative inefficiency** occurs when P > MC or P < MC. For any given employment of resources and any initial distribution of income and wealth amongst the population, total consumer welfare can increase if resources are re-allocated from markets where P < MC into those where P > MC, until a state of **allocative efficiency** in which P = MC in all markets is achieved.

PERFECT COMPETITION AND ECONOMIC EFFICIENCY

13. Figure 6.16 illustrates the long-run equilibrium of a perfectly competitive firm. The diagram clearly shows that a perfectly competitive firm achieves both productive and allocative efficiency in the long run. The firm is productively efficient because it produces the optimum output at the lowest point on the ATC curve, and it is allocatively efficient because P = MC. (Strictly, we should qualify this conclusion by stating that the firm is allocatively efficient only if all markets in the economy are perfectly competitive and if every firm in every market is producing in long-run equilibrium where P = MC.)

Figure 6.16: Perfect competition long-run equilibrium is both productively efficient (ATC are minimised) and allocatively efficient (P = MC)

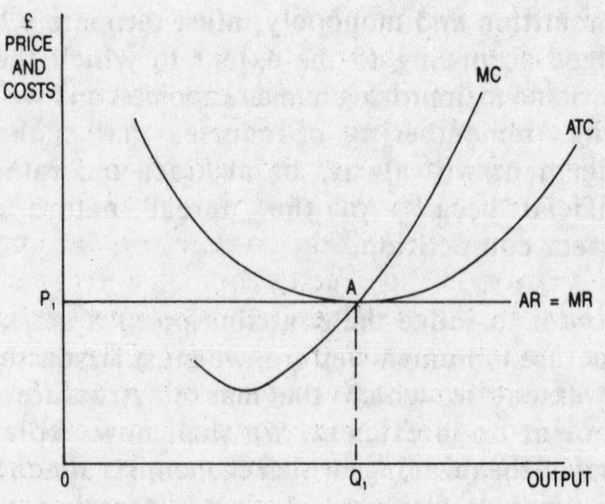

In long-run equilibrium, a perfectly competitive firm must also be X-efficient. The reason is simple. If the firm is X-inefficient, producing at a level of unit costs 'above' its ATC curve, the firm could not make normal profits in the long-run. To survive or more normal profits, the firm must take action to eliminate 'organisational slack' or X-inefficiency.

MONOPOLY AND ECONOMIC EFFICIENCY

14. In contrast to perfect competition, monopoly equilibrium is both productively and allocatively inefficient. Figure 6.12 shows that at the profit-maximising level of output Q_1, average costs are above the minimum level and P > MC. Compared to perfect competition, a *monopoly produces too low an output which it sells at too high a price*. The absence of competitive pressures, which in perfect competition serve to eliminate abnormal profit, mean that a monopoly is likely also to be X-inefficient, producing 'above' its cost curve. A monopoly can often survive perfectly happily incurring unnecessary production costs and making 'satisfactory' rather than 'maximum' profits, because the absence or weakness of competitive forces mean that there is no mechanism in monopoly to eliminate 'organisation slack'.

COMPARING PERFECT COMPETITION AND MONOPOLY

15. If we compare perfect competition equilibrium and monopoly equilibrium in the economic long-run, we can thus conclude that perfect competition is both productively and allocatively efficient whereas monopoly is neither. Monopoly is also likely to be X-inefficient. A further advantage of perfect competition relates to the concept of **consumer sovereignty**. In a perfectly competitive market economy, the goods and services produced would be those which consumers wanted. Firms and industries which produced goods other than those for which consumers are prepared to pay would not survive. However, in monopoly there is a distinct possibility of **producer sovereignty** rather than consumer sovereignty. The goods and services available for consumers to buy might be determined by the monopolist rather than by consumer preferences expressed in the market place. And even if producer sovereignty is not exercised on a 'take-it-or-leave-it' basis by a monopolist, the monopolist may still possess sufficient market power to manipulate consumer wants through such marketing devices as persuasive advertising.

For the reasons just described, perfect competition is usually regarded more desirable as a market structure than monopoly. You should note however that the 'desirable' properties of perfect competition do not result from any assumption that businessmen or entrepreneurs in competitive industries are more 'highly motivated' or public-spirited than monopolists. Indeed nothing could be further from the truth. *Economic theory assumes that everybody is motivated by self-interest and by self-interest alone.* This applies just as much to firms in competitive markets as it does to monopolies. Entrepreneurs in competitive industries would dearly like to become monopolists, both to gain an easier life and also to make bigger profits. Indeed, from a firm's point of view, 'successful' competition means eliminating competition and becoming a monopoly! But in perfect markets, market forces and the absence of barriers to entry and exit prevent this happening.

Imagine for example, a situation in which one firm in a perfectly competitive industry makes a 'technical breakthrough' that reduces production costs. For a short time the firm can make abnormal profits. But because of the assumption of perfect market information available to all firms, other firms within the market and new entrants attracted to the market can soon also enjoy the lower production costs. A new long-run equilibrium, at the lower level of costs resulting from the 'breakthrough', will soon be brought about, once again with all firms making normal profits only. Ultimately of course, consumers benefit from lower prices brought about by technical progress and the forces of competition, but it must be stressed that it is the 'hidden hand' of the market forces - and not some benign motive assumed on the part of entrepreneurs - which accounts for the 'optimality' of perfect competition as a market structure.

HOW 'COMPETITIVE' IS PERFECT COMPETITION?

16. Although perfect competition is an abstract or unreal market structure, it is interesting to speculate on the forms competition might take in a perfectly competitive market economy. The first point to note is that **price competition**, in the form of **'price wars'** or **price-cutting** by individual firms, would not take place. In perfect competition all firms are passive 'price-takers', able to sell whatever output they produce at the ruling market price determined in the market as a whole. Firms could not possibly gain sales or market share by price cutting.

Other forms of competition, involving the use of **advertising, packaging, brand-imaging** or the **provision of after-sales service to differentiate** the firm's product from those of other firms, would simply destroy the conditions of perfect competition. These are examples of precisely the forms of competition which are prevalent, together with price competition, in the imperfectly competitive markets of the real economy in which we live. So the only form of competition both available to firms and also compatible with maintaining the conditions of perfect competition would be **'cost-cutting' competition.** 'Cost-cutting' competition would occur in perfect competition because of the incentive for firms to reduce costs in order to make abnormal profits in the manner described in the previous paragraph. But the existence of 'cost-cutting' competition in a perfect market can also be questioned. Why should firms finance research into cost-cutting technical progress when they know that other firms have instant access to all market information and that any abnormal profits resulting from successful cost-cutting can only be temporary?

It is useful also to consider the nature of competition in a perfect market from the perspective of a typical consumer. The **choice** facing a consumer would be simultaneously very broad yet very narrow. The consumer would have the doubtful luxury of maximum choice in terms of the number of firms or suppliers from whom to purchase a product, yet each firm would be supplying a completely identical good or service at exactly the same price! In this sense, the range of choice in a perfectly competitive world would be extremely narrow!

MONOPOLY AND ECONOMIES OF SCALE

17. We have argued so far that perfect competition is more desirable or optimal than monopoly as a market structure because perfect competition is more economically efficient - in terms of productive efficiency, allocative efficiency and X-efficiency. Perfect competition would ensure also consumer sovereignty, whereas in monopoly there is a danger of producer sovereignty, characterised by deliberate restriction of consumer choice and output, the artificial raising of price and by manipulation of consumer wants.

However, the conclusion that *perfect competition is productively more efficient than monopoly depends on an assumption that there are no economies of scale.* When substantial economies of scale exist in an industry, and when a firm's long-run average total cost curve is L-shaped, monopoly may be productively more efficient than competition. Earlier in this chapter we described a 'natural' monopoly in which there is room in the market for only one firm benefitting from full economies of scale. Figure 6.17 illustrates such a situation. You should notice that the monopoly, producing on $SRATC_2$ is not necessarily producing the most productively efficient output on $SRATC_2$. It may produce above the lowest point on $SRATC_2$. However all points on $SRATC_2$ represent lower unit costs, and hence are productively more efficient, than any point on $SRATC_1$, which represents the cost curve of each firm if the monopoly were split up into a large number of competitive enterprises. Monopoly can therefore be justified when the benefits of economies of scale are greater than any of the disadvantages we have discussed which might result from the formation of a monopoly.

Figure 6.17: A 'natural monopoly': there is only room in the market for one firm benefitting from full economies of scale

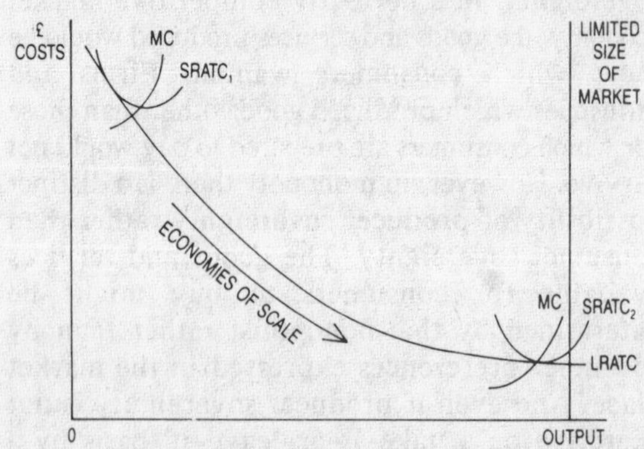

In Figure 6.18 we extend this analysis to compare monopoly with the whole of a perfectly competitive industry rather than with a single firm within a perfect market. The curve S_1 represents the supply curve of a perfectly competitive industry or the MC curve of a monopoly if all the firms merge together, in the absence of economies of scale, to form a monopoly. In conditions of perfect competition, point A locates market price P_1 and equilibrium output for the whole market, Q_1. After the merger, monopoly price (P_2) and output (Q_2) are located at point B where MR = MC. We have thus illustrated the standard case against monopoly that compared to perfect competition, output is restricted and price is raised.

But suppose that the monopoly, once formed, can begin to benefit from economies of scale. As the monopoly increases the scale of its operations, its marginal cost curve shifts to MC_2. Monopoly price and output are now determined at point C. The monopoly price P_3 is lower, and output Q_3 is higher, than those achieved in perfect competition. Of course, if the benefits of economies of scale could be combined with perfect competition an even better outcome could be achieved, P_4 Q_4 located at point D. But if the limited size of market prevents the co-existence of perfect markets and economies of scale, monopoly can be justified as a 'second-best' outcome.

Figure 6.18: The effects of economies of scale upon price and output when perfectly competitive firms merge to form a monopoly

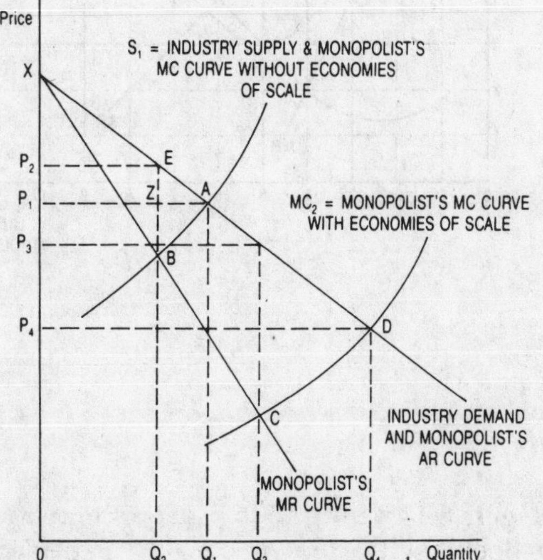

MONOPOLY AND CONSUMER SURPLUS

18. In Chapter 3 we explained how a leftward shift of the market supply curve, caused for example by an increase in production costs, results in a rise in market price. At the new higher price consumers gain less **consumer surplus** or utility over and above what they pay for, and this represents a welfare loss. If in doubt about the concept of consumer surplus, you should refer back at this stage to section 21 in Chapter 3.

When no economies of scale can be gained, the formation of a monopoly also causes a loss of consumer surplus or welfare. This is illustrated in Figure 6.18. Before the formation of the monopoly, the triangular area XP_1A shows consumer surplus obtained in a perfectly competitive market. After the firms merge to form a monopoly, consumer surplus reduces to the area XP_2E. Part of the consumer surplus has been transferred to the monopolist as monopoly profit but part, represented by the triangle EZA, is 'lost' in the sense that nobody gets it. Loss of consumer surplus or welfare is thus a further disadvantage of monopoly, though in markets where scale economies are possible, the welfare gains from economies of scale may well exceed any loss of consumer surplus.

SUMMARY

19. In this chapter we have introduced the concept of market structure, examining in detail the models of perfect competition and pure monopoly located at opposite ends of the spectrum of market forms. Pure monopoly is rare, while perfect competition is non-existent in the real economy, but both should be regarded as abstract models or bench marks by which to judge the properties of the imperfectly competitive markets of the world in which we live. The starting point for the theory of the firm is the assumption of a profit-maximising objective on the part of firms, giving rise to the concept of the equilibrium firm producing the output at which TR - TC is maximised and MR = MC. MR = MC represents the equilibrium equation of any profit-maximising firm, whatever the market structure. In perfect competition we distinguish between short-run and long-run equilibrium, noting that only in the long-run can new firms enter the industry, attracted by abnormal profits made in the short run by firms already in the market. The existence of barriers to entry in monopoly market structures, means that monopoly equilibrium is the same in the long run as in the short run, except when in the long run economies of scale enable a monopoly to move to a new, and more productively efficiently, cost curve. However, if no economies of scale are possible, a perfectly competitive market structure can be shown to be more efficient than monopoly - in terms of productive efficiency, allocative efficiency and X-efficiency. Other advantages of perfect competition include consumer sovereignty - as distinct from the producer sovereignty of the monopolist - and the greater consumer surplus or welfare generated in competitive markets because output is higher and the market price is lower than in monopoly. Again, the last conclusion depends on the assumption of an absence of economies of scale. Economies of scale therefore, provide the main advantage and justification of monopoly.

STUDENT SELF-TESTING

1 *Why is perfect competition an unreal market structure?* *(2)*
2 *What is the equilibrium equation for profit maximisation?* *(3)*
3 *Why is a perfectly competitive firm's average revenue curve horizontal?* *(4)*
4 *Distinguish between normal and abnormal profit?* *(5)*
5 *Draw a diagram to short short-run equilibrium in perfect competition.* *(6)*
6 *What happens to abnormal profit in the long-run in perfect competition?* *(7)*
7 *List the causes of monopoly.* *(8)*
8 *Explain the relationship between average revenue and marginal revenue in monopoly.* *(9)*
9 *Draw a diagram to show monopoly equilibrium.* *(10)*
10 *How does elasticity of demand affect monopoly?* *(11)*
11 *List the main types of economic efficiency.* *(12)*
12 *Is perfect competition efficient?* *(13)*
13 *Is monopoly efficient?* *(14)*
14 *What forms of competition might exist in a perfect market?* *(16)*
15 *How do economies of scale affect productive efficiency?* *(17)*
16 *How does monopoly affect consumer surplus?* *(18)*

EXERCISES

1 *A monopolist faces the cost and revenue curves illustrated in Figure 6.19.*
  - *(a) What are his profit-maximising output and price?*
  - *(b) How much profit does he make?*
  - *(c) What are his total revenue and total costs?*
  - *(d) What is the productively efficient level of output?*
  - *(e) Suppose the government orders the monopoly to set price equal to MC. What will happen to the monopolist's output, price and profits?*

Figure 6.19:

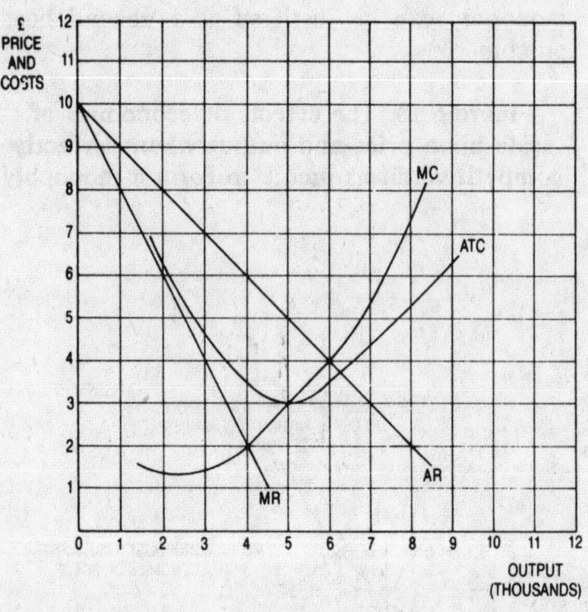

2. *In an isolated community, building sand is available in unlimited quantity from a single quarry. No production costs are involved. Demand for building sand is shown by the following schedule:*

Price (£ per ton)	*Quantity demanded per week (tons)*
100	*5*
90	*10*
80	*20*
70	*30*
60	*40*
50	*50*
40	*60*
30	*70*
20	*80*
10	*90*
0	*100*

(a) How much sand will be consumed and at what price:

(i) in the absence of a monopoly?
(ii) if the quarry becomes owned by a monopolist?

(b) How does the formation of the monopoly affect economic efficiency?

MULTIPLE CHOICE QUESTIONS

1 Which of the following is not a condition of perfect competition?
A A single market price
B A uniform product
C An inelastic demand curve for each firm
D A large number of buyers

2 In which of the following market structures would a price taker be found?
A Monopolistic competition
B Perfect competition
C Monopoly
D Oligopoly

3 Which of the following statements about a firm in long run equilibrium in perfect competition is not correct?
A Average fixed cost equals average variable cost
B Average fixed cost is falling
C Marginal cost equals marginal revenue
D Average cost equals average revenue

4 A profit-maximising monopolist will produce at the level of output at which:
A Price is greater than marginal cost
B Average revenue equals marginal revenue
C Average revenue equals marginal cost
D Total costs are minimised

5 A monopolist maximises sales revenue at the level of output at which:
A Marginal revenue equals marginal cost
B Marginal revenue equals average revenue
C Marginal revenue is zero
D Average revenue is zero

EXAMINATION QUESTIONS

1 (a) Specify the conditions necessary for the achievement of maximum profits. (12 marks)
(b) What objective beside profit maximisation might a firm pursue? (8 marks)
(ACCA June 1984)

2 'In equilibrium, profit is maximised'. 'In equilibrium profit is zero'. Explain if it is possible to reconcile these two statements in respect of the model of perfect competition.
(ICSA December 1985)

3 Outline the main characteristics of a perfectly competitive market. As these characteristics are rarely discovered in practice, to what extent does this mean that this model is irrelevant to our understanding of modern economies?
(ACCA June 1980)

4 *How does a profit-maximising monopolist decide the quantity of goods to produce and the price to be charged?*
(ICSA June 1986)

5 *Under conditions of perfect competition, a firm's price is likely to be lower and its output higher than under monopoly conditions. Explain the reasons for this.*
(ACCA December 1987)

6 *(a) Examine the case for and against monopoly.* *(12 marks)*

(b) If a monopoly was charged with operating in the public interest what price should it charge? And why?
(8 marks)
(ACCA June 1987)

7. Imperfect competition

INTRODUCTION

1. When the theory of the firm was first developed in the nineteenth century by the pioneering British economist Alfred Marshall, it was principally concerned with the nature of perfect markets. But by the early twentieth century, economists were becoming dissatisfied with perfect competition as *the* theory of the firm. Their dissatisfaction can be seen as a response to the growth of large business corporations and to the increasing tendency for markets to be dominated by a small number of large firms. Although the theoretical model of pure monopoly which we examined in Chapter 6 had been developed, what was needed was a body of economic theory to give a greater realism to the theory of the firm than that provided by the models of the two polar extremes, perfect competition and monopoly. In response to this need, theoretical models of **monopolistic competition** were created by Joan Robinson and Edward Chamberlin and a model of **oligopoly** behaviour was introduced by Paul Sweezy. In this chapter we explain these early models of imperfectly competitive market structures, which were all developed originally in the 1930s, before briefly surveying later and more sophisticated models of imperfect competition. We shall also examine particular aspects of firms' pricing behaviour in oligopoly and highly imperfect markets, before concluding the chapter with a brief look at newer or **alternative theories of the firm**, which question the realism of the profit-maximising assumption fundamental to the 'traditional' theory of the firm.

THE THEORY OF MONOPOLISTIC COMPETITION

2. In the early 1930s, the British economist Joan Robinson and an American Edward Chamberlin independently published an important new theory, **the theory of monopolistic competition**. In significant respects, monopolistic competition - as originally described by Robinson and Chamberlin - resembles both perfect competition and monopoly. As in perfect competition a large number of firms are assumed to exist in the market, but each firm produces a slightly different product. The resulting **'product differentintion'** in the market means that each firm possesses a degree of local monopoly power over its product. If a firm raises its prices slightly, it does not lose all its customers. Thus a firm faces a downward sloping demand curve as in monopoly, rather than the infinitely-elastic or horizontal demand curve of perfect competition.

Monopolistic competition resembles perfect competition in two important respects. In the first place, the monopoly power of a firm in monopolistic competition is restricted by the similar goods produced by other firms in the market. These goods provide partial but not perfect substitutes. The downward-sloping demand curve facing a firm in monopolistic competition is likely therefore to be relatively more elastic than in monopoly. Secondly, there are no barriers to entry or exit in the long run. As in perfect competition, new firms can enter the market attracted by any abnormal profits being made by existing firms, while symmetrically, any losses will encourage firms to leave the market.

EQUILIBRIUM IN MONOPOLISTIC COMPETITION

3. The absence of barriers to entry or exit is of great importance in the theory of monopolistic competition. The short-run equilibrium in monopolistic competition, which is shown in Figure 7.1, is little different from monopoly equilibrium, except that demand or average revenue is likely to be more elastic and an individual firm is producing only a small part of the market output.

Figure 7.1: Monopolistic competition short-run equilibrium

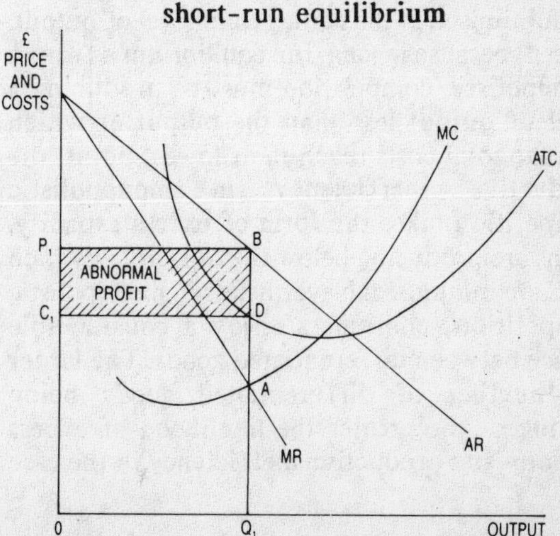

Figure 7.2 illustrates long-run equilibrium in monopolistic competition, which is achieved after the entry of new firms has competed away abnormal profits. In long-run equilibrium, firms make normal profits only. This is shown by the downward-sloping AR curve forming a tangent to the ATC curve immediately above the equilibrium output Q_1 at which MR = MC.

Figure 7.2: Monopolistic competition long-run equilibrium

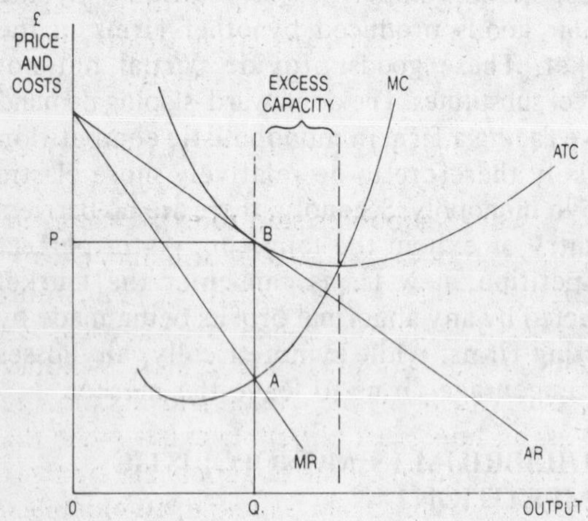

EVALUATING MONOPOLISTIC COMPETITION

4. Although the market mechanism operates in a similar way in perfect competition and monopolistic competition to eliminate abnormal profits, monopolistic competition is both **allocatively inefficient** and **productively inefficient** in comparison with perfect competition. As in monopoly, P > MC, and ATC are not minimised at the equilibrium level of output. Indeed, because in long-run equilibrium a firm in monopolistic competition must be producing a level of output less than the output at which average total costs reach their lowest point, the productive inefficiency in monopolistic competition takes the form of **excess capacity.** Firms are producing below the capacity at which ATC are minimised. Nevertheless in monopolistic competition, consumers enjoy a considerable choice between differentiated goods. The larger the number of differentiated goods being produced, the greater the likelihood of excess capacity and productive inefficiency in the case of each firm within the market. Yet at the same time, the greater is the choice available to the consumer. In recent years, important work undertaken by Kelvin Lancaster has suggested that monopolistic competition need not result in a reduction in economic efficiency. Lancaster argues that the number of differentiated products increases until the gain to the consumers in choice from adding one more product to the market exactly equals the loss resulting from having to produce less of the existing products at a higher cost. For this reason monopolistic competition does not necessarily result in economic waste. Consumers may prefer wider choice at the expense of an improvement in productive efficiency.

THE MODERN THEORY OF MONOPOLISTIC COMPETITION

5. The original theory of monopolistic competition expounded by Joan Robinson and Edward Chamberlin in the 1930s is nowadays regarded as rather unsatisfactory for two reasons. In the first place, although the theory claims to be a more realistic theory of competition in the world in which we live than the theory of perfect competition, few if any monopolistically competitive industries as described by Robinson and Chamberlin actually exist in the economy. The theory requires a large number of firms producing differentiated goods. Instead most of the competitive markets of the real economy in which a large number of differentiated products are available contain a relatively small number of firms or suppliers. Typically each firm produces a wide variety of slightly differentiated products, which compete with each other as well as with the products of the other firms in the market. In the real economy **'small group' monopolistic competition,** which is best regarded as a special case of oligopoly, is found rather than the 'large group' monopolistic competition described by Robinson and Chamberlin.

Secondly and perhaps more importantly, the original theory of monopolistic competition assumed that a differentiated good produced by a firm faces competition from all the differentiated products available as substitutes. Modern theory argues however that a good produced by a firm in monopolistic competition will face close competition from only a few of the substitute goods produced by other market members. When a new firm enters the market, its product will compete strongly with the existing products of other firms only if their **key characteristics** are very similar. The new entrant will not affect the demand curve for a good produced by an existing firm whose product is sufficiently differentiated in its most significant key characteristics from the new product. A similar argument applies to **geographical differentiation**. A new shop located in a particular part of a city will have a much greater effect on the demand for the products sold by nearby shops than on demand in more distant parts of the same city. Because products are differentiated both in their key characteristics and in a geographical sense, the modern theory of monopolistic competition rejects Chamberlin's 'large group' assumption and argues instead that we should model a market containing many firms in which a single firm faces intense competition from just 'a few among the many.'

OLIGOPOLY

6. **Oligopoly** exists when there are just a few firms in the market. However, oligopoly is better defined by **market conduct**, or the behaviour of the firms within the market, than by **market structure**. In oligopoly each of the 'small group' of firms making up the market is in a position to change price and output conditions for the whole market by its own decisions on price and output. Individual firms occupy a sufficiently important position in the market for their own decisions to have a noticeable effect on their rivals. When, for example, one firm tries to increase its profits by reducing price in order to gain an increased market share, the profit of the other firms will be reduced. Whether the price reduction increases the firm's profits clearly depends upon the likely reactions of the other firms; so when deciding whether to lower its price, the firm must make some assumption about the likely response of the other firms. Oligopoly is therefore characterised by **reactive market behaviour** and by **interdependence** between firms rather than by the independent choice of price or output which is assumed to exist in the other market structures we have examined.

MODELS OF OLIGOPOLY BEHAVIOUR

7. Because there are a very great number of possible ways in which oligopolistic firms may react to each other's marketing strategies, it is impossible to construct an all-embracing oligopoly theory. Instead, many different models of oligopoly behaviour have been developed using a variety of analytical approaches and assumptions about how the rival firms react to each other's behaviour. The more sophisticated oligopoly models are examples of **games theory**. Each oligopolist is regarded as a player in a game, choosing a strategy to win the game by attaching statistical probabilities to various possible outcomes and to the likely retaliatory strategies adopted by his rivals. Each different assumption about the likely reaction of rivals will lead to a different pricing decision by the firm itself. It is therefore very difficult to predict pricing and output behaviour under oligopoly conditions. A stable equilibrium in which each firm has no incentive to alter price or output may not exist in oligopoly.

PERFECT AND IMPERFECT OLIGOPOLY

8. **Perfect oligopoly** is said to exist when the oligopolists produce a uniform or homogeneous product. The major petrol retailing companies form a perfect oligopoly, sometimes known as the 'Seven Sisters'; an oligopoly which includes companies such as BP, Shell and Exxon. In contrast an **imperfect oligopoly** exists when the products produced by the oligopoly are by their nature differentiated, for example, automobiles.

COMPETITIVE AND COLLUSIVE OLIGOPOLY

9. **Competitive oligopoly** exists when the rival firms are *interdependent* in the sense that they must take account of the reactions of one another when forming a market strategy, but *independent* in the sense that they decide the market strategy without co-operation or collusion. The existence of uncertainty is a characteristic of competitive oligopoly; a firm can never be completely certain of how rivals will react to its marketing strategy. If the firm raises its price, will the rivals follow suite or will they hold their prices steady in the hope of gaining sales and market share?

Uncertainty can be reduced and perhaps eliminated by the rivals **co-operating** or **colluding** together to fix prices, or output, or even by allocating customers to particular members of the oligopoly. If the oligopolists collude to fix price and output in a **cartel agreement** or price ring, effectively they behave as a single monopolist. Oligopolists have an incentive to behave in this way because, by acting collectively, the firms can achieve a better outcome for all of them, in terms of joint-profit maximisation and an easier life, than by remaining a competitive oligopoly.

However, collusion or co-operative behaviour may not be good for the consumer. When oligopolists collude together to rig the market, they seldom integrate their productive plant at a technical level or engage in joint ventures in research and development. As a result technical economies of scale and cost-cutting are not achieved. Collusive oligopoly thus tends to produce the familiar disadvantages of monopoly such as restricted output, increased price, productive and allocative inefficiency, producer sovereignty and loss of consumer choice, without achieving the main benefit and ultimate justification of monopoly, economies of scale. Indeed, cartel agreements are often designed to keep the least efficient firms in business, thereby reducing the ability of the economy to adapt or rationalise its productive structure to meet changed demand or cost conditions.

For these reasons, collusive oligopolistic arrangements such as cartel agreements are normally illegal, being regarded by governments as against the public interest. However, **covert** or **illicit collusion** amongst oligopolists undoubtedly often occurs because, for the reasons we have noted, such co-operative behaviour is very much in the interest of individual firms. And on occasion governments actively promote cartel arrangements to protect employment or to try to ensure an 'orderly decline' or rationalisation of an industry such as steel which may be suffering from over-capacity in the face of international competition. On a world-wide scale, cartel agreements are also common amongst governments or producers' associations in primary-producing countries, covering commodities such as oil, tin and coffee. Because of their international nature, attempts to fix the price of primary products, by member countries accepting a quota and agreeing not to sell below the cartel price, are especially difficult to sustain. A cartel member faces a temptation to renege on the agreement, or to cheat on the other members by secretly reducing his price and 'unofficially' selling an output greater than the quota agreed by the cartel.

PRICE COMPETITION AND OTHER FORMS OF COMPETITION

10 When firms collectively agree to fix the market in conditions of collusive oligopoly, prices are of course likely to be stable. Empirical evidence suggests that prices are also very often relatively stable in competitive oligopoly. Even though no formal - or even informal - collective pricing agreement exists, firms realise that a price-war will be self-defeating for all the firms involved. They therefore may reach a tacit understanding not to indulge in aggressive price competition as a means of gaining extra profits or market share at the expense of each other. In the absence of keen price competition, oligopolistic firms are likely to undertake forms of non-price competition such as:

(i) marketing competition, including obtaining 'exclusive outlets' through which to sell their products;

(ii) the use of persuasive advertising, product-differentiation, brand-imaging and packaging;

(iii) quality competition, including the provision of after-sale service.

THE KINKED DEMAND CURVE THEORY OF OLIGOPOLY

11. The **kinked demand curve theory of oligopoly** is an early theory of oligopoly pricing behaviour, originally developed by Paul Sweezy in 1939 to explain price rigidity and the absence of price-wars in oligopolistic markets. Suppose that an oligopolist produces the output Q_1 illustrated in Figure 7.3, selling his output at price P_1. In most imperfectly competitive markets, firms do not possess accurate information about their demand and revenue curves, particularly at outputs other than those they are currently producing. This means that the demand curve DD drawn in Figure 7.3 is not necessarily the correct demand curve for the oligopolist's output; instead it represents the firm's estimation or guess of how demand will change with respect to either a price rise or a price fall. The firm expects that demand will be *relatively elastic* in response to a price rise because rivals are expected to react by keeping their prices stable in the hope of gaining

profits and market share. Conversely, the oligopolist expects his rivals to react to a price cut by decreasing their prices by an equivalent amount; he therefore expects demand to be *relatively inelastic* in response to a decision to reduce price, since he cannot hope to lure many customers away from his rivals. The oligopolist therefore expects his rivals to react assymmetrically when price is raised compared to when price is lowered. As a result, he believes his initial price and output at point A in Figure 7.3 to be at the junction of two demand curves of different elasticity, each reflecting a different assumption about how rivals are expected to react to a change in price. The oligopolist expects that sales revenue and profits may be lost whether the price is raised or cut. The best policy is to leave price unchanged.

Figure 7.3: The 'kinked' demand curve

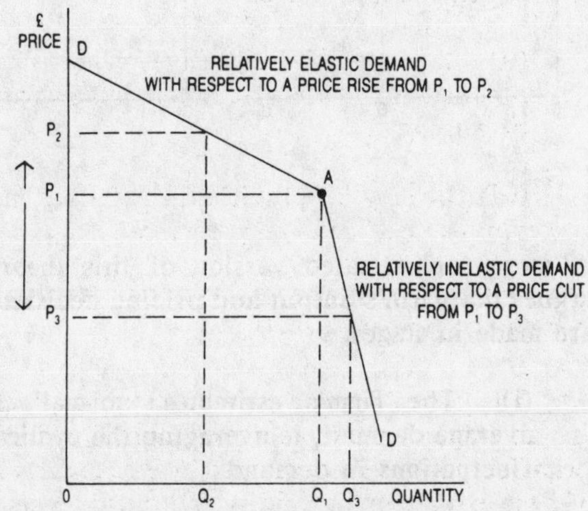

Figure 7.4 suggests a second reason why prices may tend to be stable in conditions of 'kinked' demand. A mathematical discontinuity exists along a vertical line above output Q_1, between the marginal revenue curves associated respectively with the relatively elastic and inelastic demand (or average revenue) curves. The marginal cost curve can rise or fall within the range of this discontinuity, without altering the profit-maximising output Q_1 or price P_1. If marginal costs rise above MC_1 or fall below MC_2, the profit maximising output changes and the oligopolist must set a different price to maximise profits, assuming of course that the curve DD accurately represents the correct demand curve facing the firm. But the oligopolist's selling price remains stable as long as the marginal cost curve lies between MC_1 and MC_2.

Figure 7.4: Shifts of marginal cost in conditions of kinked demand

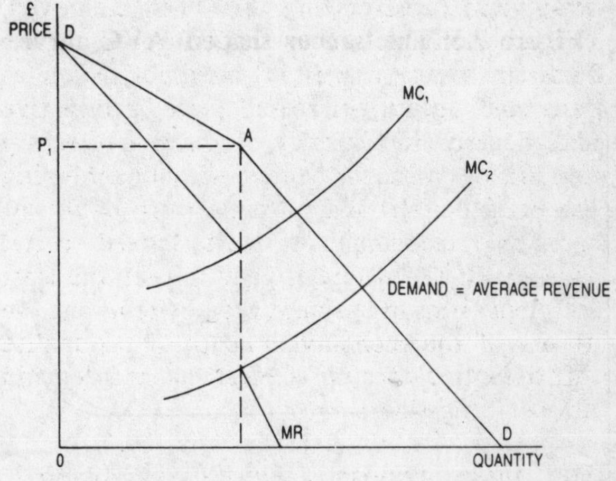

CRITICISMS OF THE KINKED DEMAND THEORY

12. Although superficially attractive as a neat and apparently plausible explanation of price stability in conditions of oligopoly, few economists now accept the 'kinked' demand theory of oligopoly pricing behaviour. It is an *incomplete* theory because it does not explain how and why a firm chooses to be at point A in the first place. Empirical evidence also gives little support to the theory. Rival firms seldom responded to price changes in the manner assumed and it would be reasonable to expect that an oligopolist would 'test the market' ie raise or lower the selling price to see if rivals reacted in the manner expected. If they did not, then surely the oligopolist would revise his estimation of the shape of the demand curve.

PRICE STABILITY: AN ALTERNATIVE EXPLANATION

13. Recent research has shown fairly conclusively that oligopoly prices tend to be

stable or sticky when demand conditions change in a predictable or cyclical way, but that oligopolists usually raise or lower prices quickly and by significant amounts, both when production costs change substantially, and when unexpected shifts in demand occur. The most plausible explanation of price stability in conditions of predictable or expected changes in demand, is provided by the theory of the **'saucer-shaped' AVC curve**, illustrated in Figure 7.5

Figure 7.5: The 'saucer-shaped' AVC curve

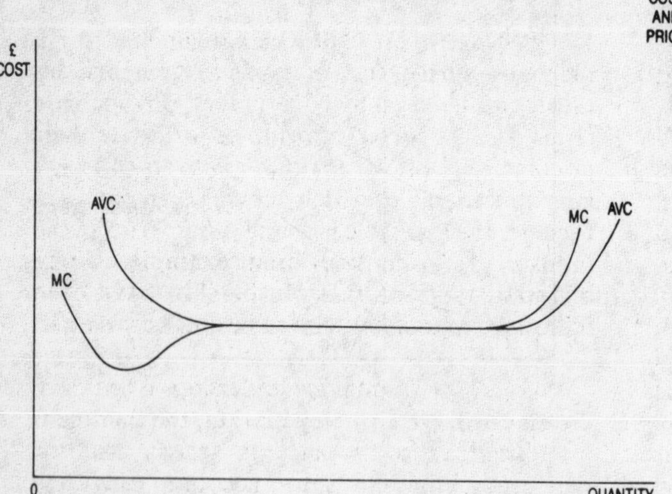

the firm meets the change in demand by varying the quantity it is prepared to supply, keeping price stable at P_1.

Figure 7.6: With price fixed at P_1 and profit mark-up P_1-C_1 short-run variations in demand from D_1 to D_2 and D_3 are met by quantity variations

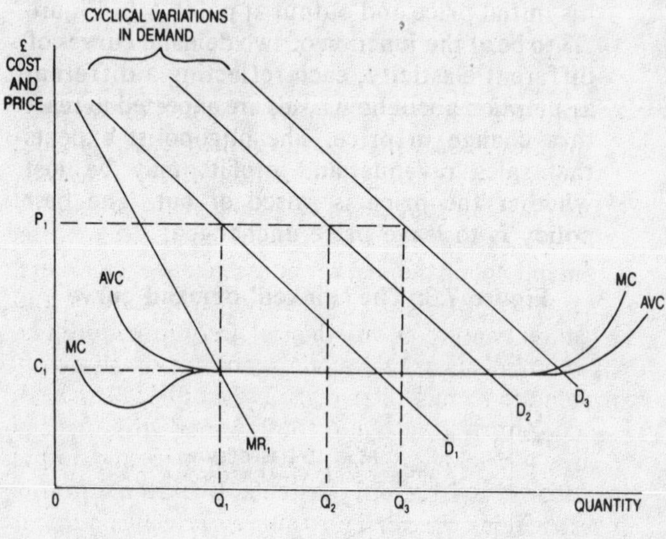

A large amount of evidence exists which indicates that firms have saucer-shaped short-run average variable cost curves. If this is the case, then marginal costs equal average costs along the flat middle section of the curve. At first sight a flat or horizontal MC curve appears to deny the law of variable proportions, since diminishing marginal returns would cause marginal costs to rise. However, the law of variable proportions (or the law of diminishing returns) stems from the assumption that a firm's fixed factors of production are *indivisible* in the short-run. Indivisibility means that a firm must use all or none of its fixed capacity; it cannot decide to use just a part of the fixed factors of production. In reality however, fixed capacity is often *divisible* - only part of available fixed capacity need be employed. If a firm decides to employ only a fraction of its fixed capacity, the firm can alter the amounts of both capital and labour it employs, yet still combine the inputs in an optimal or technically-efficient way. Marginal and average variable costs will thus be horizontal within this output range. If the demand curve now shifts as shown in Figure 7.6,

A more sophisticated version of this theory argues that firm's output and pricing decisions are made in stages:

(i) The firm's estimates 'normal' or average demand, ie averaging the cyclical fluctuations in demand.

(ii) The firm then invests in plant with a capacity capable of meeting 'normal' demand at an output at which long-run MC = MR.

(iii) The firm sets price at the profit-maximising price P_1 in Figure 7.6.

(iv) When the demand curve shifts cyclically, quantity but not price is adjusted.

Firms are likely to adjust output rather than their selling price in this way when marginal costs are constant or 'flat' at different levels of output, and when it is costly to change prices every time that demand changes. Many oligopolistic firms produce a wide range of differentiated products and publish a complicated and varied price list both for different products and for different types of customer. It would be prohibitively costly for a firm to change its price list every time there was a change in demand. However, significant changes in input costs which shift a firm's cost curves do lead to a change in the firm's selling price, as may a substantial shift in demand which the firm expects to be permanent.

COST-PLUS PRICING

14. Earlier in this chapter we noted the absence of a universal theory of equilibrium price and output determination in oligopoly markets, explaining that there can be as many oligopoly theories as there are assumptions about how the members of the market may react to each others' market strategies. Because of the abstract and unreal nature of any theory of equilibrium in an oligopoly market, modern studies of oligopoly tend to be more narrowly and empirically based, concentrating attention on how and why firms in the real economy make particular price and output decisions, or adopt particular overall marketing strategies. We shall now survey briefly a number of pricing strategies which have been observed empirically in oligopolistic and monopolistic market structures.

Surveys of business pricing practice indicate that **cost-plus pricing**, also known as **mark-up pricing** and **full-cost pricing**, is the most common pricing procedure used by firms. Price is determined by adding a standard percentage profit margin to average or unit costs:

$$P = AFC + AVC + \text{Profit margin}$$

Unless a firm knows in advance precisely the output it intends to produce, it will have to estimate its unit costs. Firms often base unit costs on **standard volumes**, which are costs associated with the level of output and capacity utilisation considered normal by a firm. If cost-plus pricing is rigidly applied, price will remain stable in the short run providing costs are stable, despite shifts in demand. Cost-plus pricing is therefore consistent with the theory of oligoply pricing which we explained in the previous section.

In practice firms do not rigidly apply cost-plus pricing. Firms producing a range of products have been observed to differentiate their profit margins on different product lines, thereby taking into account demand elasticities and competitive forces. Many firms appear to alter their mark-up in response to change business conditions. Thus it is possible to argue that although cost-plus procedures are used for price-setting, variations in profit margins which occur after firms have assessed or 'sized-up' their market mean that pricing in practice approximates to profit-maximising pricing.

PRICE LEADERSHIP

15. Because overt collusive agreements to fix the market price, such as cartel agreements, are usually made illegal by government, oligopolistic firms use less formal ways to co-ordinate their pricing decisions. An example of covert collusion is **price leadership**, which occurs when one firm becomes the **market** leader and other firms in the industry follow its pricing example. Three different types of price leadership have been identified: **dominant, collusive and barometric.**

(i) **Dominant price leadership.** When there is one large firm in a market, the dominant firm can set a price to satisfy its own needs, taking into account also the anticipated reactions of a large number of small competitors which are each too small to have a noticeable effect on price. The smaller firms in effect behave like perfect competitors, adjusting their output decisions to the 'market price' set by the dominant price leader. While the dominant firm could use its cost advantages to reduce prices and force the smaller firms out of business, fear of government intervention and knowledge that the small firms might easily re-enter the market once profit margins were restored mean that the dominant firm may tolerate the survival of the smaller firms.

(ii) **Collusive price leadership.** When several large firms together dominate the market, different firms may set the price at different times. It is usually easiest for one of the firms to set a price which its rivals will follows when:

(1) there are only a few firms;
(2) the firms produce close substitutes;
(3) the firm's cost curves are similar;

(4) there are barriers to entry; and
(5) demand is relatively inelastic.

(iii) **Barometric price leadership.** On occasion however, the price leader acts as a barometer of market conditions, indicating the various pressures on price. Within the market the barometric price leader may change over time, but is likely to be a firm monitored by the other firms because of its ability to respond to market conditions rather than because it is larger or more efficient. If, in the view of its rivals the barometric price leader makes a wrong assessment of the market, its price may not be followed and the firm may have to change its decision to keep its market share.

PRICE PARALLELISM

16. **Price parallelism** occurs when there are identical prices and price movements within an industry or market. It is worth noting that price parallelism can be caused by two completely opposite sets of circumstances. On the one hand price parallelism would occur in a very competitive market, approximating to perfect competition, as the firms adjusted to a ruling market price determined by demand and supply in the market as a whole. But on the other hand, price parallelism results from price leadership in tightly oligopolistic industries. It is generally accepted from the public interest point of view, that price leadership misallocates resources by reducing output, raising price and by restricting price flexibility.

LIMIT PRICING

17. So far both in this chapter and also in Chapter 6, we have assumed that all firms have the single objective of producing the output which maximises profits, without distinguishing between **short-run** and **long-run profit maximisation**. However, even if the assumption of a profit-maximising objective is correct, there may be a conflict or divergency between short-run and long-run profit maximisation, particularly in conditions of oligopoly. This is illustrated by a **theory of entry-deterrence in oligopoly markets** known as **'limit pricing'**. The central assumption of the 'limit pricing' theory is that existing established firms in the market set their prices taking into account the effect they may have on long-run profitability by possibly attracting new firms into the industry who would erode their monopoly power. Firms may decide to set prices which, by deterring the entry of new firms, act as a barrier to entry. Thus the established firms sacrifice the short-term maximised profits which higher prices would yield in order to maximise long-run profits, achieved through preventing or limiting the entry of new firms.

BARRIERS TO ENTRY

18. Whether a strategy of 'limit pricing' is worthwhile depends on the conditions of entry into the market. Modern oligopoly theory places considerable emphasis on the study of entry conditions and the effect of entry conditions upon the behaviour or conduct of existing firms. Entry barriers are normally classified into four divisions, categorised on the basis of height:

(i) **Easy entry.** When firms already established in the market possess no cost or other advantage over new entrants, in the long run price will be reduced by competitive pressures to the level of average costs, and abnormal profits will not be earned.

(ii) **Ineffectively impeded entry.** Some entry barriers exist which make 'limit pricing' possible, but firms can gain more from charging the short-run profit-maximising price than from 'limit pricing'.

(iii) **Effectively impeded entry.** Higher entry barriers allow firms already in the market to charge limit prices which yield larger long-run profits than would occur if short-run maximising prices were set.

(iv) **Blockaded entry.** New firms do not or cannot enter the market even when prices are set to maximise short-term profits.

PRICE DISCRIMINATION

19. We have seen that oligopolists, and indeed monopolists, often produce a range of goods and services, many of which are only slightly differentiated from other goods produced by the same firm. It is quite likely that different costs are incurred by a firm, both in production and also when marketing its differentiated brands to different customers or groups of customers. We must distinguish carefully this situation, in

which a range of prices are charged by a 'multi-product' firm, from **oligopoly** or **monopoly price discrimination,** as understood in economic theory.

Strictly, a firm engages in price discrimination only when *different* prices are charged to different customers for the *same* good or service, for reasons not based on differences in supply costs. Price discrimination normally occurs when a firm possessing a degree of monopoly power divides the market into two or more groups of customers with different elasticities of demand. Figure 7.7 depicts the demand curve of male and female customers for entrance to a night club on a particular evening. The demand curve of male customers is relatively inelastic while female demand is more elastic, indicating perhaps, that women are less enthusiastic about the prospective entertainment on offer! The horizontal addition of the individual marginal revenue curves for male and female customers gives the MR curve for all customers, which together with the MC curve determines the most profitable number of customers of both sexes to admit to the club. This is shown by Q_1 in the righthand panel of the diagram.

The nightclub maximises profit by setting separate prices for men and women customers in such a way that the MR from the last customer admitted in each sub-market is equalised and also equals MC in the market as a whole. If MR were not the same in both markets, the firm could increase profits by reallocating 'output' between the two markets. The different prices charged to male and female customers results from the difference between the elasticities of demand in the two sub-markets, with the price sensitive female customers paying less.

The conditions necessary for successful price discrimination are:

(i) It must be possible to **identify different groups** of customers or markets for the product. This is possible when customers differ in their knowledge of the market or in their ability to 'shop around'. Some customers may have special needs for a product and competition among oligopolists may vary in different parts of the market; in some geographical areas and for some products a firm may face many competitors, whereas in other parts of the market the firm may be the sole supplier.

(ii) The different groups of customers must have **different elasticities of demand.** Total profits will be maximised by charging a higher price in a market in which demand is less elastic. However, demand will never be inelastic, since this would imply that marginal revenue is negative.

(iii) The markets must be **separated** to prevent seepage. **Seepage** takes place when customers who buy at the lower price in one market resell in the other market at a price which undercuts the oligopolist's price. An example of seepage has occurred at various times when the major automobile manufacturers have charged higher prices for the same car in the United Kingdom market than in countries such as Belgium and Germany. As a result specialist car importers have set up in business buying cars in mainland Europe to resell in the British market to undercut the manufacturers' recommended prices.

Figure 7.7: Price discrimination

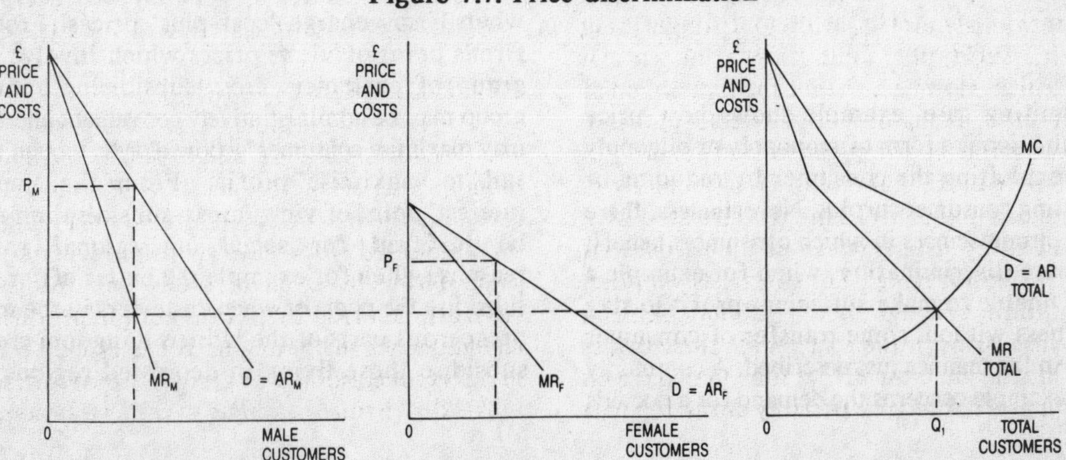

PRICE DISCRIMINATION: THE LIMITING CASE

20. Figure 7.8 illustrates an extreme or limiting case of price discrimination. This occurs when an oligopolist or monopolist 'sizes-up' and sets a price for each customer equal to the maximum he believes the individual is prepared to pay. For example customer C_1 is charged a price P_1, customer C_2 is charged P_2 and so on. In this limiting case of price discrimination, there is no market price. Instead each customer is charged a separate and perhaps unique price which transfers all the consumer surplus away from the consumer and to the firm, effectively boosting monopoly or oligopoly profit.

Figure 7.8: The limiting case of price discrimination: A monopolist or oligopolist charges each customer the maximum price the customer is prepared to pay

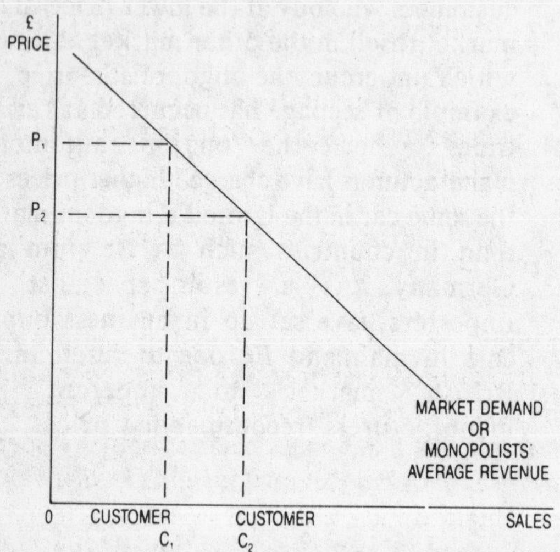

The 'limiting case' example shows how price discrimination is a form of monopoly or oligopoly abuse, exploiting the consumer by reducing or eliminating consumer surplus. Nevertheless, there may be circumstances in which consumers benefit from price discrimination, when for example a firm is unable to make sufficient profit to stay in business without some transfer of consumer surplus in the manner just described. A commonly quoted example concerns the demand for a doctor's services in an isolated small community. When charging the same price to all his patients, the doctor cannot make a large enough income to cover his opportunity cost. He is thus tempted to move to a larger city, thereby leaving the community without medical care. But if he charges each patient a price based on the individual's ability and willingness to pay, he can make sufficient income from treating the well-off to make it worthwhile to treat the poor at a lower price. In this way, everybody gets some benefit and a needed service is provided.

CROSS-SUBSIDISATION

21. It is important to avoid confusing price discrimination with **cross-subsidisation.** In our explanation of price discrimination, we assumed that marginal cost is the same for all customers supplied, but that a firm charges different prices based on the elasticity of demand of different groups of customers. In contrast, when cross-subsidisation takes place, all customers pay the same price, but the marginal cost of supplying the good varies between different groups of customers. For example, the Post Office charges the same price for all first class letters of standard weight, whether posted locally or to distant parts of the United Kingdom. For local letters the marginal cost incurred by the Post Office when delivering an extra letter is less than the price charged, but for letters delivered over a long distance, MC exceeds P. Customers posting local letters (for which $P > MC$) cross-subsidise letters mailed over greater distances (for which $P < MC$). The Post Office uses profits made on the former group to subsidise losses borne on letters posted over longer distances. But because price does not equal marginal cost, cross-subsidisation cannot result in allocative efficiency. Cross-subsidisation is particularly likely to occur when firms charge 'cost-plus' prices. From a firm's point of view, prices which involve one group of customers cross-subsidising another group may be administratively convenient and they may maximise consumer 'goodwill' even though they fail to maximise profits. From the 'public interest' point of view, cross-subsidisation may be justified for social or regional policy reasons, when for example the better off cross-subsidise the poor, or when customers in the more prosperous parts of the United Kingdom cross-subsidise those living in depressed regions.

MARGINAL COST PRICING AND OFF-PEAK PRICING

22. It is often argued that to avoid cross-subsidisation and to improve allocative efficiency, firms should charge each customer a price which reflects the marginal cost of providing the good or service consumed. This is called **marginal cost pricing**. In perfectly competitive markets, where firms are passive 'price-takers', the market mechanism ensures automatically that P = MC, providing only that firms produce the profit-maximising output. (If in doubt check back to Chapter 6 and carefully read the explanation.) However, as we have demonstrated, market pressures do not operate in this way in imperfect markets. Administrative convenience leads firms to adopt 'cost-plus' pricing and in any case, profits are maximised where P > MC.

Nevertheless, when demand varies greatly on a daily, weekly or seasonal basis, firms operating in imperfect markets may adopt a type of pricing called **off-peak pricing**, which is a special case of marginal cost pricing. Transport, energy and tourist industries provide good examples. Consider the seasonal demand for electricity illustrated in Figure 7.9 on the following page. Ask yourself what will happen if demand for electricity increases, because additional consumers have switched to electricity, in the peak winter months compared to extra demand in the off-peak summer months. The marginal cost incurred by the electricity industry when meeting any additional demand in the winter months is likely to include the cost of investing in new fixed capacity, ie it is a **long-run marginal cost**. In contrast, the marginal cost involved when meeting a surge in off-peak demand is much lower - it is the **short-run marginal cost** of additional raw materials and labour. The electricity industry can meet any increase in demand in the off-peak by using its existing fixed capacity which would otherwise lie idle. Low off-peak prices and high peak prices are therefore justified on the basis of variations in marginal cost when providing a good or service at different times of day or year. And also, by encouraging consumers to shift demand from the peak period of demand, off-peak pricing can achieve a better or more productively efficient utilisation of fixed capital throughout the day or year.

TRANSFER PRICES

23. With the growth of modern large business corporations - including **multinational corporations** operating subsidiary factories in many parts of the world - many goods and services are transferred within the firm, being 'sold' by one part of the enterprise to another. These 'sales' are co-ordinated through the firm's administrative framework rather than through the market. A British Institute of Management survey undertaken in 1971 indicated that 193 firms out of a sample of 293 firms studied had a system of inter-enterprise trading. In over a third of the sample, such transfer trading accounted for between 10 and 25 per cent of total sales. In recent years the setting of **internal transfer prices** between the subsidiaries owned by multinational corporations has attracted much attention because of the potential effects upon the economies of the countries in which the multinationals operate. In theory, multinationals might adopt a system of transfer prices to:

(i) allow their subsidiaries a degree of independence in their pricing decisions;

(ii) enable the parent company to assess accurately the performance of the subsidiaries;

(iii) ensure profit maximisation for the firm as a whole.

In practice, however, it is widely believed that multinationals set transfer prices to minimise the corporation's overall tax burden. Suppose for example that a multinational car company operates plants in the United Kingdom and Germany which exchange engines and other car components with each other. If company taxation in the United Kingdom were significantly higher than in Germany, the multinational might order its British subsidiary to sell below cost the components its supplies to the German branch of the company. Conversely, the German plant would be asked to set a high price for its 'exports' to the UK subsidiary. By manipulating transfer prices in this way, the parent company can declare profits in Germany so as to avoid company taxation in the United Kingdom. In extreme cases, multinationals may set up subsidiary plants or offices in 'off-shore' tax havens, ie countries with extremely liberal or relaxed tax regimes, which are often combined with a legal system allowing a high degree of business secrecy. Transactions undertaken between the multinational's productive subsidiaries are then diverted through the intermediary of the tax haven and transfer prices are fixed to maximise the profits taken 'off-shore' and to minimise the taxes paid in the countries where the company actually produces. As a further 'spin-off', the multinational might use the resulting 'low profitability' of its British operations as a justification for low wage increases, arguing that poor profitability results not from the system of transfer pricing adopted by the company, but from the 'low value' of the goods produced by its British labour force.

Figure 7.9: Seasonal demand and supply in the electricity supply industry in the UK

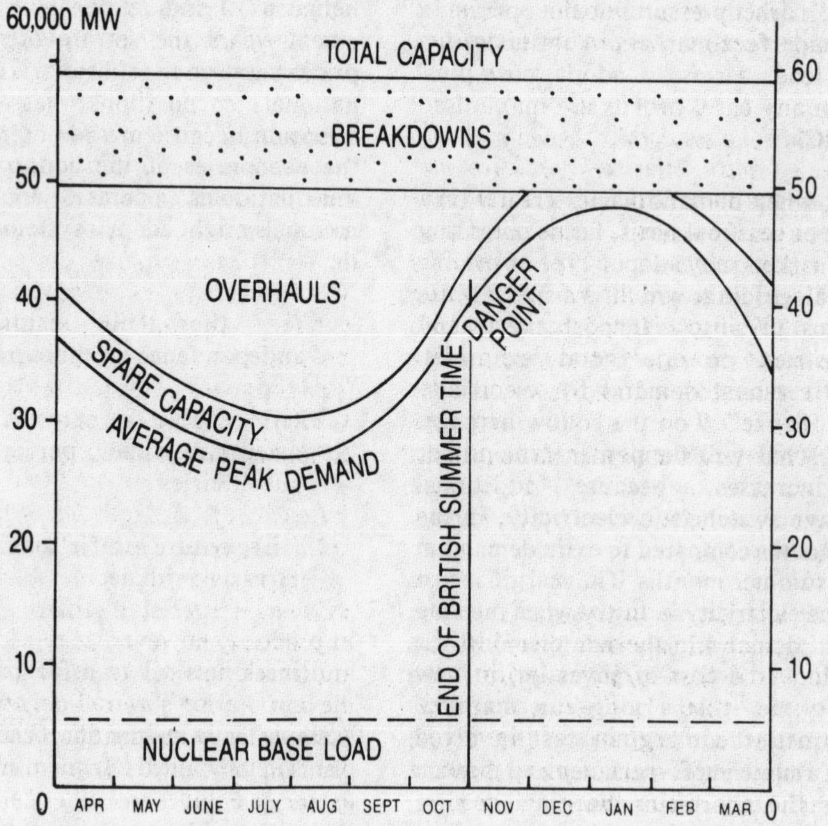

ALTERNATIVE THEORIES OF THE FIRM

24. Throughout our coverage of the theory of the firm, in this chapter and in Chapter 6 which examined perfect competition and monopoly, we have assumed that all firms share the single objective of profit maximisation. We have noted that the theories of monopoly, monopolistic competition and oligopoly were developed by economists early in the twentieth century because of a growing dissatisfaction with the theory of perfect competition as the theory of the firm. In more recent years however, particularly in the 1950s and 1960s, some economists have gone further in their attack on the 'traditional' theory of the firm by attacking the realism of the fundamental assumption of profit-maximising behaviour.

The profit-maximising assumption depends on two key premises, firstly that owners are the decision makers within a firm and secondly that the main objective of owners is higher profit. In an important study published in 1981 based on a questionnaire sent to a sample of 728 United Kingdom firms, Shipley concluded that only 15.9% of his sample could be regarded as true profit-maximisers. Nevertheless, we ought to remember that the 'traditional' theory of the firm does not seek to describe how firms maximise profits. It simply predicts what the price and output must be to maximise profits, whether by deliberate design or otherwise.

The 'newer' or alternative theories of the firm are of two types: **managerial theories** and **organisational** (or **behavioural) theories**. Both claim to be more realistic in their assumptions and hence, better at explaining the actual behaviour of firms in the real economy than the traditional profit-maximising theory of the firm.

MANAGERIAL THEORIES OF THE FIRM

25. Managerial theories of the firm share with the 'traditional' theory the assumption of a maximising objective, but argue that the target or goal to be maximised is a managerial objective rather than profit. Managerial theories, which have been popularised by Professor J.K. Galbraith in 'The New Industrial State' (1967) take as their starting point an apparent split between shareholders as owners, and managers as decision-makers, in modern large business corporations. Shareholders own companies, but they employ salaried managers or executives to make business decisions. It is argued that managers, who possess a monopoly of technical knowledge about the actual running of the company, aim to maximise managerial objectives such as sales, growth and managerial career prospects, rather than shareholders' profits.

Three main managerial theories have been developed, by Baumol (1959), Williamson (1963) and Marris (1964). Baumol argued that a manager-controlled firm has **sales maximisation** as its principal objective because the salaries and fringe benefits of top managers are related to sales revenue rather than to profits. However, a number of later studies have come to the opposite conclusion, and the evidence is generally inconclusive.

Williamson's theory is broadly similar to Baumol's and argues that a company's executives seek to maximise other objectives of **'managerial utility'** as well as sales revenue related perks. In Williamson's theory, increased sales revenue allows managers to spend more on staff levels to enhance managerial status, seniority and promotion prospects. Managers can also spend on 'discretionary' projects which are marginal to the normal operations of the firm, but which add to managerial satisfaction or utility.

Whereas both Baumol and Williamson suggested a split between shareholders' and managerial objectives, Marris argued that both groups share a common interest in **growth maximisation**. From the managers' point of view, a firm's growth increases power and status, while shareholders have a vested interested in successful growth because it increases the capital value of their wealth, as distinct from the dividend income generated by profits. Central to Marris's analysis is the **'retention ratio'**, ie company profits, 'ploughed back' into the company as a ratio of profits distributed as dividends. If the retention ratio is low, when managers distribute most of the profits, shareholders' incomes will be high and a resulting high share price may deter take-over bids. But if managers retain profits in order to maximise company growth, the share price may be low, relative to the true worth of the company's assets, thereby increasing the possibility of take-over. Marris concludes that managers therefore aim to maximise growth subject to generating just sufficient distributed profits to satisfy shareholders, so as to minimise the risk of shareholders selling out to a take-over 'raider' attracted by a low share price.

BEHAVIOURAL OR ORGANISATIONAL THEORIES OF THE FIRM

26. Managerial theories of the firm share with the 'traditional' profit-maximising theory the assumption that firms aim to maximise a single objective or goal. In contrast, organisationalists see the firm as an organisation comprising coalitions of different groups within the firm such as production managers, financial managers, production workers, research scientists, etc, each possessing a different group objective or objectives. In 1963 Cyert and March identified a **coalition** within an organisation as any group sharing a consensus on the goals it should pursue. Managers may form one coalition seeking prestige, power and high salaries, while other coalitions would include production workers wanting higher wages and improved job security and working conditions, and shareholders desiring higher profits. Differing goals or aspirations will result in group-conflict. Cyert and March argue that a firm's top managers ultimately make key decisions to resolve conflict between the different interest groups within the organisation. In order to satisfy the aspirations of as many groups within the organisation as possible, this inevitably involves compromise and the setting of minimum rather than maximum targets. Hence organisationalists have introduced the concept of **'satisficing'** to replace 'maximising', to describe how decisions are made within complex organisations.

SATISFICING VERSUS MAXIMISING

27. The concept of **satisficing** was first introduced by Simon in 1959 in an early behaviouralist theory. Simon argued that because a firm's managers are unable to locate a marginalist point such as MR = MC, in practice they set minimum acceptable levels of achievement. They satisfice rather than maximise. Minimum targets will be set for such variables as sales revenue, profit, growth, stock-holding of raw materials and so on.

The assumption of satisficing behaviour on the part of managers can, in fact, lead to conclusions remarkably similar to those of the profit-maximising or marginalist theory. This is explained by the management technique of **Management by Objectives (MBO)**. Initially managers set a limited objective and attempt to achieve it. If achieved, a new and higher objective will be set and so on. By setting achievable objectives, an initial minimal objective gives way to a series of higher targets, with the final outcome resembling a maximum target. When an objective is not achieved, managers revise downwards their 'aspiration levels' until an achievable objective has been set.

PORTFOLIO PLANNING

28. Modern research on management practice supports the organisationalist argument that no single objective is likely to be useful in explaining the actual behaviour of firms. Complex modern businesses are usually 'multi-product' firms producing a variety of products at different stages in a product 'life-cycle'. At an early stage of a product's life-cycle it requires substantial investment in product development and marketing to ensure later profitability. This investment can be financed or cross-subsidised from the cash-flow generated by profitable 'mature' products in the company's **'product portfolio'**. Firms thus attempt to balance their product portfolio so that existing profitable products provide the funds necessary to develop new products to maturity. If a firm uses the portfolio-planning approach to product development, it becomes impossible to predict its price and output decisions for a single product within its portfolio without knowledge of the relative position of that product within the company's overall portfolio.

THE THEORY OF ECONOMIC 'NATURAL' SELECTION

29. To some extent the alternative theories of the firm which we have described can be made compatible with, or synthesised into, the 'traditional' profit-maximising theory of the firm by way of the **theory of economic 'natural' selection**. There are two versions of this theory. In the older version it was assumed that firms are competitive in the **goods market**, ie the market in which they sell their output. Suppose managers within firms make pricing and output decisions for reasons other than profit maximisation. According to the theory of economic 'natural' selection, those firms which make

decisions which stray away from the profit-maximising path must inevitably incur production costs greater than the costs which would be borne under profit-maximising conditions. If the goods market is competitive, high cost firms will be competed out of existence, leaving the profit-maximisers as survivors. The fact that decision makers within firms are not deliberate or conscious profit-maximisers is irrelevant; those who behave 'as if' they are profit-maximisers will survive, the rest will not.

The weakness with the 'original' theory of economic 'natural' selection is that real world goods markets are not usually sufficiently competitive to allow this selection process to operate. The existence of barriers to entry and the weakness of competitive pressures permit inefficient high cost firms to survive. For this reason a second version of the theory of economic 'natural' selection has been developed, which argues that non-profit-maximising behaviour by firms is disciplined by competition in the **capital market** rather than by competition in the goods market. The capital market, which includes the Stock Exchange, is the financial market in which modern large business corporations raise funds to finance investment by selling shares or ownership in the business. When the managers of a firm make decisions inconsistent with profit-maximisation, the resulting low profits are likely to cause the company's share price to fall. The company then becomes vulnerable to takeover on the Stock Exchange by a new owner (or corporate raider) who believes he can manage the company's assets better and more profitably. Non-profit-maximising behaviour by firms is thus disciplined by takeover or competition in the capital market. In many cases, fear of a possible takeover, in which the successful corporate raider fires the existing company executives and installs his own team of managers, may be sufficient to stiffen the resolve of the existing managers, so that their actual decisions do not stray far from the profit-maximising path.

SUMMARY

30. In this chapter we have surveyed structures which are much more typical of markets found in the real economy in which we live than are the models of perfect competition and pure monopoly described in Chapter 6. Broadly, we have distinguished between 'large group' and 'small group' competition in imperfectly competitive markets, known respectively as monopolistic competition and oligopoly. Of the two, oligopoly is the more realistic market structure. But because there are a great many ways in which we might model the reactions of rival firms, modern oligopoly theory is more concerned with particular aspects of firms' pricing and output behaviour than with developing a general or universal theory of oligopoly. Amongst the examples of oligopoly pricing behaviour which we have briefly surveyed in this chapter are cost-plus pricing, price leadership and discriminatory pricing. To reduce uncertainty about rivals' reactions, oligopolists are also likely to engage in co-operative or collusive pricing, as for example in a cartel agreement.

The theories of monopolistic competition and oligopoly explained in this chapter are examples of profit-maximising theories. As such, they are part of the 'traditional' theory of the firm. Alternative theories of the firm, known as managerial and behavioural (or organisational) theories, question the profit-maximising assumption fundamental to the traditional theory and claim a greater realism. However, many commentators believe that the difference between the alternative and traditional theories are more apparent than real and that the alternative theories can be made consistent with the traditional theory of the firm by way of the theory of economic 'natural' selection.

STUDENT SELF-TESTING

1. *In what way is monopolistic competition similar to (a) perfect competition and (b) monopoly?* *(2)*
2. *Draw a diagram to show long-run equilibrium in monopolistic competition.* *(3)*
3. *How can monopolistic competition be justified?* *(4)*
4. *What are the weaknesses in the theory of 'large group' monopolistic competition?* *(5)*
5. *Define an oligopoly.* *(6)*
6. *Why is there no general theory of oligopoly?* *(7)*
7. *Distinguish between perfect and imperfect oligopoly.* *(8)*
8. *Why may oligopolists collude together and what forms might the collusion take?* *(9)*

9 *What forms of competition are likely in oligopoly?* (10)
10 *Why is the 'kinked' demand theory of oligopoly inadequate?* (12)
11 *What is a more plausible explanation of price stability in oligopoly?* (13)
12 *What is 'cost-plus' pricing?* (14)
13 *List the different types of price leadership.* (15)
14 *Explain price parallelism.* (16)
15 *Why may firms charge 'limit prices'?* (17)
16 *What are the necessary conditions for successful price discrimination?* (19)
17 *In what circumstances can price discrimination be justified?* (20)
18 *Why is cross-subsidisation considered inefficient?* (21)
19 *Why is marginal cost pricing considered efficient?* (22)
20 *What is a transfer price?* (23)
21 *Why may the 'traditional' theory of the firm be considered unrealistic?* (24)
22 *Name two managerial theories of the firm.* (25)
23 *Distinguish between maximising and satisficing?* (27)
24 *What is meant by economic 'natural selection'?* (29)

EXERCISES

1. *J.R. Fixit IV is president of United States Arms Suppliers Inc. By paying bribes of $10 million to government ministers in the Middle East he can be sure that they will purchase some of his weapons worth $60 million for their armed forces. His total sales to these governments depend however, on the actions of Sir Jasper Underhand, chairman of Exploitation Holdings PLC, a British producer of similar weapons who is Mr Fixit's only serious rival.*

   If Sir Jasper Underhand also bribes the ministers responsible for the arms purchases, the deal will be shared between the two suppliers. J.R. Fixit's profits will then be much less than if he alone pays bribes and gets all the business for his company. Mr Fixit thinks it a pity to have to pay out $10 million, but if he did not and Sir Jasper did, the British company would get all the business and he would make no profits at all.

   What market strategies are open to the two companies and what are the likely results of each strategy?

MULTIPLE CHOICE QUESTIONS

1 *Firms in monopolistic competition in long run equilibrium:*
A *Make super-normal profits*
B *Produce at full-capacity*
C *Produce where average revenue equals average cost*
D *Produce where average revenue equals marginal cost*

2 *A necessary condition for successful price discrimination between two groups of customers is:*
A *Costs of production must differ between the two markets*
B *Each group of customers must be free to choose which market to buy in*
C *Price elasticity of demand must be different in the two markets*
D *There must be perfect information about prices in each market*

3 *Monopolistic competition resembles:*
A *Monopoly because firms face a downward sloping demand curve*
B *Perfect competition because allocative efficiency results in the long run*
C *Oligopoly because each firm faces a 'kinked' demand curve*
D *Monopsony because there is only one buyer in the market*

4 *All the following are typical of price-setting in imperfect competition* ***except:***
A *Price leadership*
B *Parallel pricing*
C *Cost-plus pricing*
D *Price-taking*

5 *Firms are most likely to collude together:*
A *To reduce the possibility of an investigation by the Monopolies Commission*
B *To engage in joint profit maximisation*
C *To achieve economies of scale*
D *To improve the service jointly offered to consumers*

EXAMINATION QUESTIONS

1 *A firm is operating in the short-run situation in conditions of monopolistic competition.*

(a) How much will the firm produce? How much profit will the firm make? *(10 marks)*

(b) What will be the effect on the output, price and profits of the firm of each of the following changes?

(i) An increase in the rent of the factory. *(5 marks)*

(ii) A fall in the cost of raw materials. *(5 marks)*

(ACCA June 1985)

2 *Explain why the equilibrium output of a firm under monopolistic competition is less than the output where average total cost is at a minimum.*

(ICSA December 1985)

3 *(a) Define product differentation and indicate the forms which it can take.* *(6 marks)*

(b) To what extent is product differentation wasteful? *(14 marks)*

(ACCA December 1982)

4 *Why is there a tendency, in conditions of oligopoly, towards price rigidity? How may an individual oligopolist attempt to increase his share of the market?*

(CIMA November 1979)

5 *What is a 'cartel'? What are the circumstances which encourage the formation of one and what difficulties arise in maintaining its influence? Give examples in your answer.*

(ACCA June 1981)

6 *(a) In what way is freedom of entry or lack of it, likely to affect the behaviour of firms in an industry?* *(8 marks)*

(b) What factors are likely to limit the entry of firms into:

(i) soap manufacture;

(ii) motorcar manufacture;

(iii)the retail grocery trade.

(4 marks each)

(ACCA December 1985)

8. The size and growth of firms

INTRODUCTION

1. In the next three chapters we turn attention away from the rather abstract theoretical treatment of markets and firms undertaken in earlier chapters. This is the first of three chapters that examine in some detail the structure of firms and industry within the United Kingdom economy. We begin in this chapter by surveying the main types of business organisation in the UK economy, before investigating the size of firms and the ways in which business enterprises grow. The chapter concludes by examining how the relative importance of different industries has changed in recent years. Chapter 9 then considers how the growth of firms is financed, while in Chapter 10 we examine the impact of government industrial policy upon firms and the structure of industry.

THE MARKET AND NON-MARKET SECTORS OF THE ECONOMY

2. In Chapter 1 we introduced the distinction between the **market** and the **non-market sectors** of the economy. Production takes place in both sectors, but only output produced in the market sector is sold commercially at a market price for profit. The non-market sector of the economy includes all the **public sector services** such as the provision of roads, police, national defence, public health care and state education which are provided 'free' at the point of consumption (or at a token price), being financed largely or completely out of taxation. For the most part, **firms** or **business enterprises** exist only in the market sector. Organisations such as the National Health Service in the non-market sector should not be classified as business enterprises although they certainly undertake production. Nevertheless, the distinction between firms producing output for sale commercially within the market sector of the economy and other types of production and economic organisation outside the market sector is not always clear cut. On the one hand, non-market services such as the National Health Service provide contracts for market sector firms such as drug suppliers and cleaning companies, while on the other hand a part at least of the output of 'non-market' organisations such as the NHS and the BBC may be commercially marketed. Indeed, one of the thrusts of current and recent industrial policy undertaken by the Conservative Government (which we explain more fully in Chapter 10) has been to encourage public sector organisations such as the NHS and the BBC to act as business enterprises or firms and to sell commercially a part at least of the services they provide.

TYPES OF BUSINESS ENTERPRISE

3. A firm is a business enterprise engaged in production, producing its output largely or completely for sale at a market price within the market sector of the economy. A common method of classifying firms is in terms of the legal status of the enterprise. The most important types of business enterprise within the United Kingdom economy are illustrated in Figure 8.1 shown on the next page.

Figure 8.1 shows the basic division between business enterprises in the **private** and **public sectors** of the economy. The main forms of business enterprise in the private sector of the UK economy are **sole traders** (or **individual proprietors**), **partnerships**, and **private and public joint stock companies**, though other types of enterprise such as **co-operatives** and **building societies** can be important in certain specialised areas of the economy. **Public sector business enterprises** include **public corporations** (or **nationalised industries**) in the market sector of the economy and certain municipally owned trading enterprises such as local airports. Figure 8.1 also shows that the dividing line between private and public sector business enterprise is by no means clear cut. Certain businesses may be '**joint ventures**', owned in part by both the private sector and by the state. And until quite recently large business organisations such as BP and British Leyland (now the Rover Group) were '**state-majority shareholdings**', in which the state owned a controlling interest in a nominally private sector company. Effectively such companies were nationalised industries, though they have since been returned completely to the private sector in the privatisation programme of the Conservative Government.

Figure 8.1: The most important types of business enterprise in the UK economy

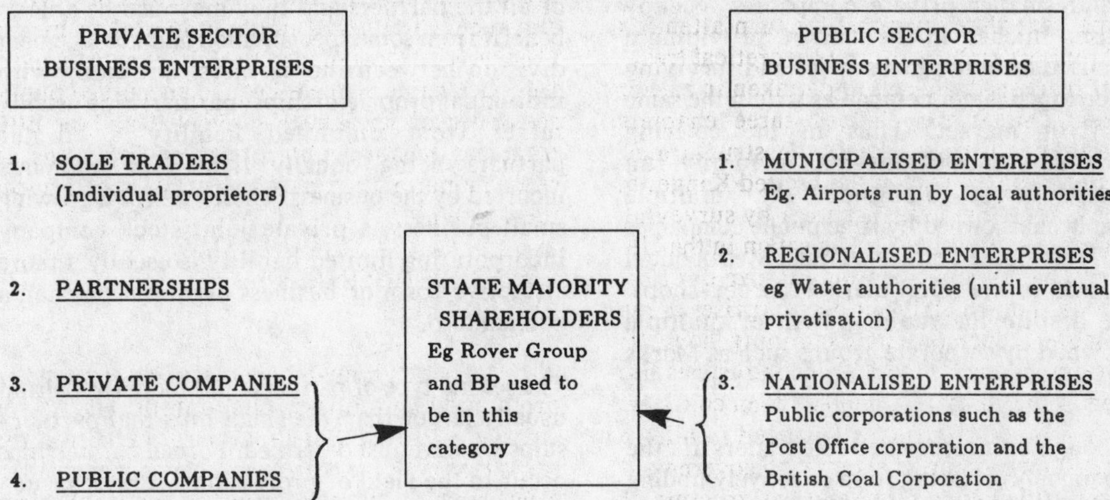

Excluding building societies and friendly societies, it has been calculated that there are between about 1.3 million and 3 million privately owned economic enterprises in the UK economy, though the precise number is not known. The lower figure (1.3 million) is calculated from the total number of businesses registered for the payment of VAT, whereas the higher figure (3 million) is taken from the official register of private and public companies at Companies House. The latter figure clearly overstates the number of companies actually trading, since many of the registered company names are either defunct or have never actively traded. By contrast the VAT figures understate the number of actively trading businesses, since many sole proprietors own businesses too small to register for VAT. Approximately 40 per cent of the businesses registered for VAT are sole traders, 25 per cent are partnerships and 35 per cent are companies.

SOLE TRADERS

4. **Sole traders, individual proprietorships** or **one man small businesses** are not so much formed, they simply happen. Suppose for example that you decide to supplement your income as a student by offering to sell a personal service to your neighbours, perhaps as a 'tax consultant'. As soon as you start trading, *de facto* you have become a sole trader, even though initially at least your business is so small and peripheral that it is hardly likely to figure in any official statistics of business enterprise. (Indeed, many sole traders like to keep things that way so as to avoid bringing their 'business activities' to the attention of the tax authorities. They are operating in the so-called **'black economy'** where transactions take place strictly for cash for the purpose of illegal tax evasion.) As a sole trader you are now literally in business on your own - even if only on a part-time basis supplementing income from other sources. You provide your own capital, take any profits as income, but you are also completely liable for any losses incurred.

According to VAT registrations, approximately 28 per cent of all sole traders are involved in *wholesaling, dealing and retailing* with 17 per cent in *building*, 15 per cent in *agriculture*, 9 per cent in *catering*, 6 per cent in *finance, property and professional services* and 5 per cent in *manufacturing*, in *road transport* and in the *motor trades*. Sole traders make up approximately 49 per cent of the total number of businesses in *road transport*, 48 per cent in *agriculture*, 46 per cent in *building*, 42 per cent in *catering*, 40 per cent in the *motor trades* and in *wholesaling, dealing and retailing*, 38 per cent in *finance, property and professional services* and just 17 per cent in *manufacturing*.

Sole traders or individual proprietors are therefore most significant in areas of economic activity that need not be capital intensive and which typically offer the customer a personal service. Very often sole traders, along with other forms of small business such as partnerships and smaller private companies, occupy specialised 'niches' in the market, providing a personalised or individual service and surviving alongside much larger companies within the same industry or market. Thus in the catering industry, thousands of one-man or family-run restaurants exist alongside the multiple restaurant chains owned by large public companies such as Trust House Forte and Grand Metropolitan Hotels, and in the retail market 'corner-shops' survive despite the rapid growth of multiple stores owned by corporate groups such as Marks and Spencer.

But although unincorporated sole traders are the most commonly occurring form of actively trading business organisation in the UK, the extremely small size of almost all of these businesses means that individual proprietorships produce only a small proportion of national output. Indeed the number of sole traders has declined in recent years, in part because individual proprietors have been driven out of business by competition from larger business organisations, but also because of the tendency for sole traders and partnerships to turn their businesses into companies to gain the advantages conferred by corporate status. Lack of capital, lack of expertise in all the aspects of running a business, lack of advice and guidance, the growth of bureaucratic overheads imposed for example by the requirement to pay VAT, together with changes in the 'way of life' such as that brought about by changing shopping patterns have also contributed to the decline of one man businesses.

PARTNERSHIPS

5. A **partnership** is formed whenever two or more people agree to undertake a business or trading activity together, instead of operating separately as sole traders. It is useful to identify two rather different kinds of partnership. On the one hand there are many **small informal partnerships**, usually with just two or three partners functioning much as if they were sole traders. Informal partnerships of this kind are to be found in industries such as retailing, catering and building, in which sole traders are also common. This is not surprising, since small informal partnership are very similar to individual proprietorships, with for the most part the same advantages and disadvantages. Partnerships do however have access to the funds or resources of all the partners and they may also be able to benefit from some specialisation and management division between the partners. But along with individual proprietorships, partnerships usually suffer from **unlimited liability** - all the partners being equally liable for any loss incurred by the business. Therefore for a growing small business, a private joint stock company incorporating limited liability is usually a more attractive form of business organisation than a partnership.

The second type of partnership is more formal and usually larger than the small informal partnerships we have just described. **Formal partnerships** occur in the field of professional services, such as architects, accountants and (before 1986) stockbrokers. A professional regulatory body may prevent the members of the profession from operating as a company, as part of the 'professional ethic' of ensuring as personalised a relationship as possible between client and professional practitioner. For many years the Stock Exchange Council prevented stockbrokers from trading as companies. However, the resulting undercapitalisation of UK stockbroking partnerships placed the firms at a severe disadvantage when competing for business with American, Japanese and European corporate giants in international capital markets. But in the **'Little Bang'** of 1986 (which preceded the more famous **'Big Bang'** which abolished the artificial division between stockbrokers and jobbers), the Stock Exchange Council amended its rules and allowed stockbroking partnerships to become companies. As a result, most of the previously independent London stockbroking firms were bought up and taken over by much larger British and foreign owned financial corporations, effectively becoming mere subsidiaries of highly-diversified multi-national financial conglomerates.

Partnerships nevertheless remain common as a form of professional business organisation. The popularity of the professional partnership probably results from the fact that, in comparison to manufacturing and retailing activities, the risk of financial failure is smaller and consequently limited liability is less essential. However, professional partnerships can be quite large, since the law allows the number of partners to exceed the limit of twenty imposed on less formal partnerships. Indeed, many professional partnerships of solicitors, accountants or architects have grown to become quite large business organisations with considerable capitalisation, specialisation and economies of scale.

COMPANIES

6. A **company** is defined as an organisation of persons contributing money to a common stock, who share in the profit or loss resulting from the employment of the common stock in a trade or business venture. The common stock is the capital of the company and the persons who contribute to the stock are the members of the company. The proportion of the capital or common stock contributed by a member is his share.

Historically, the earliest forms of business organisation were sole traders and partnerships. In the United Kingdom, the joint stock company did not become important until the development of capitalism and the spread of factory methods of production in manufacturing in the nineteenth century. Companies had first been founded in the sixteenth and seventeenth centuries when the organisation of large-scale commercial trading ventures required the separation of functions between the capital-providing employer (the capitalist) and the wage-earning employees. The earliest companies were **chartered companies**, founded by Royal Charter. However, many unchartered 'companies' were formed, but they did not constitute a legal form of organisation. Limited liability was introduced in 1662, but it was only granted to a handful of chartered companies. Right from the establishment of the first companies, dealings in their shares took place. But a massive speculative boom and crash known as the South Sea Bubble ruined many shareholders unprotected by limited liability. This led to the passing of the Bubble Act in 1720 which, by making it illegal to form a company without a charter, effectively held back the development of companies for more than a hundred years.

The next stage in the development of companies occurred during the Industrial Revolution when large sums of capital became necessary to finance the construction of canals, and later railways. By this time, companies were being formed by special Act of Parliament rather than by Royal Charter. But because it had proved extremely inconvenient for Parliament to pass a special Act to establish each of the hundreds of canal and railway companies that had been created by 1850, between 1844 and 1862, Parliament passed a series of Companies Acts which enabled a company to be set up simply by registering the company under the new legislation. Virtually all companies currently trading in the United Kingdom are private or public companies established by registration under the provisions of the various Companies Acts passed by Parliament since 1844.

LIMITED LIABILITY

7. Another important legal change which encouraged the growth of the company form of organisation was introduced by the Limited Liability Act of 1855 which enabled shareholders to gain the benefit of **limited liability.** Limited liability has proved of great significance both for the popularity of the company as a form of business organisation and in promoting the growth of large-scale methods of production. Limited liability is especially important in explaining why the owners of small business turn their enterprises into private limited companies, thus limiting the financial risk to a shareholder to the amount he has actually invested in the company. Without limited liability, only the safest and most risk-free business ventures would be able to attract the large-scale supply of funds or savings required to finance investment.

THE DISTINCTION BETWEEN PRIVATE AND PUBLIC COMPANIES

8. As we have already noted, virtually all the commercial companies actively trading in the UK today are registered companies with full limited liability, registered under the provisions of the various Companies Act which have been passed since 1844. Especially significant is the 1980 Companies Act which established the current legal distinction between **private** and **public companies.** The 1980 Companies Act completely changed the legal distinction between public and private companies as it had existed since 1908. Before 1980, the legislation defined a private company, and a public company was any company that did not fall within the legal definition of a private company. This position is now reversed. A **private company** is currently any company that does not qualify under the 1980 Companies Act to be a public company. Under the 1980 Companies Act, a **public company** is a company limited by shares (or by guarantee) which has been registered as a public company under the Companies Acts. It can invite the general public to subscribe for (ie buy) its shares or debentures (corporate bonds). A public company must have a minimum authorised and allotted share capital, currently £50,000.

All companies, private and public, must have a minimum of two members or shareholders, but there is no upper limit. This contrasts with the situation before the passing of the 1980 Companies Act, when private companies were restricted to a maximum of 50 shareholders. Also before 1980, there were legal restrictions on the transfer of shares between the members of a private company and on the freedom of individual shareholders to transfer their shares to outsiders. The 1980 Companies Act removed these restrictions, so in principle a private company can have an unlimited number of shareholders who can transfer shares freely amongst themselves. It is now also quite easy to extend the company's share capital, which enables new shareholders to inject extra capital into the company. Nevertheless, most private companies remain relatively small businesses with very few shareholders. Very often private companies have retained restrictions in their Articles of Association which limit the freedom of shareholders to transfer their shares. These restrictions allow the company's board of directors to maintain control over the company since they prevent shareholders from selling to an outsider who may wish to gain control over the company.

However, although it is now quite straightforward for a private company to extend its share capital and take on new shareholders, the essential difference between a private and public company remains: *a private company cannot advertise and offer its shares for open sale to members of the general public, whereas a public company can.*

THE MOTIVES FOR FORMING A PRIVATE COMPANY

9. We have already noted that an important motive for owners of unincorporated sole traders or partners to turn their businesses into private companies is to gain the benefit of limited liability. But for many small and risky business enterprises, the advantage of limited liability is not as great as it might at first seem. This is because any external provider of funds, such as a bank, is almost certain to require that the directors of the company - who normally own all or most of the shares in a small private company - secure any loan granted to the company with their own personal possessions. In this way limited liability is effectively bypassed by secured creditors. However, there are a number of other reasons why private companies are formed, even when the advantage of limited liability is more apparent than real. These include:

(i) **Tax avoidance**. If the owners of a small business wish to *avoid tax legally* (rather than evade tax illegally as unincorporated sole traders in the 'black economy'), there are considerable tax advantages in trading as a company.

(ii) **Separate legal identity**. A company, being an incorporated organisation, possesses a separate legal identity in its own right, independent of the people who own shares in the company. A company can operate its own bank account, enter into contracts on its own account, sue and be sued, and the company can survive without interruption as an ongoing business organisation in the event of the death of one of its owners. None of these advantages are possessed by an unincorporated sole trader.

THE MOTIVES FOR FORMING A PUBLIC COMPANY

10. Whereas there are several score thousands of private companies trading in the UK today, there are only about 8,000 actively trading public companies. Private companies are typically small and medium-sized, though there are some quite large business organisations such as the Littlewoods retailing group that have chosen to remain as private companies. The picture is complicated further by the fact that many private companies, including quite large ones, are not independently owned. Instead they are essentially subsidiary companies, wholly-owned by a 'parent' public company. For example Lever Brothers Ltd is a private company wholly-owned by Unilever PLC. In some cases the parent PLC is a mere **'holding company'**, holding ownership and control in a string of subsidiary private companies which undertake actual production and generate profits for the PLC. The PLC is the vehicle for raising capital through share issues and for maintaining overall management control over the subsidiaries, but it is not really actively trading in its own name.

A public company is usually a much larger business enterprise than a private company - though again we should note that most public companies are actually quite small and that there are only a few hundred large PLCs or 'corporate giants'. Nevertheless, there may come a time in the growth of a successful private company when it considers the advantages of '*going public*' by turning itself into a public company. By far the main reason for 'going public' is to gain access to the wider source of external funds (known as the **capital market**) that can be tapped by selling the company's extended share capital to the general public. We shall examine the role of capital market and the **Stock Exchange** in financing the growth of public companies in the next chapter.

However, as we have already noted, a public company may become vulnerable to a hostile or unwelcome takeover bid if it significantly extends its share capital. Together with the fact that a public company must incur extra costs as a result of publishing more information about itself and holding an Annual General Meeting, the vulnerability to a future takeover bid constitutes a disadvantage of 'going public'. To minimise this risk, when some public companies are formed relatively few of their shares are made available to the general public. When this is the case, the main reason for 'going public' is probably to enable the company's directors to place a market value on their shareholdings and to provide a future opportunity for the directors to convert their wealth into a more liquid form by selling their shares, should they so wish, at a favourable future share price.

SMALL BUSINESSES

11. Most **small businesses** are sole traders, partnerships and private companies, whereas the overwhelming majority of **large business** are public companies. Nevertheless the concepts of small and large businesses are less easy to define, since they do not refer to a precise legal status. When in 1971 the **Bolton Committee** reported to the government on the role of small firms in the national economy, the Committee found that there were 820,000 small firms responsible for 14 per cent of national output and 18 per cent of the net output of the private sector. The inclusion of agriculture and the professions would have increased the 1971 total to 1,250,000 enterprises employing 29 per cent of the working population. The government had recommended to the Bolton Committee that a '*small firm might be defined broadly as one with not more than 200 employees*', but the Committee decided that this definition was unsuitable for most industries. The Committee used other criteria such as turnover in distribution and the number of vehicles in road haulage, to classify small businesses. The Bolton Committee added three further criteria to the employment criterion recommended by the government in its definition of the small firm. These were that a small firm:

(i) has a relatively small share of its market;

(ii) is managed by its owners or part-owners in a personalised way;

(iii) is independent, thus excluding subsidiary firms from the definition of a small firm.

In 1979 the **Wilson Committee on the Financing of Small Firms** revised the criteria set out by the Bolton Committee, but because prices have doubled in the decade since 1979, the criteria listed below for defining small firms in particular industries are now rather out of date:

Manufacturing	: 200 employees or less
Retailing	: Annual turnover of £185,000 or less
Wholesale trades	: Annual turnover of £730,000 or less
Construction	: 25 employees or less
Mining and Quarrying	: 25 employees or less
Motor trades	: Annual turnover of £365,000 or less
Miscellaneous services	: Annual turnover of £365,000 or less
Road transport	: 5 vehicles or less
Catering	: All firms except multiples and brewery-managed public houses.

For most of the period since the Second World War, the number of small firms and their relative importance in the UK economy decreased, but in recent years there has been some recovery. By 1989 the number of new businesses registered for VAT was rising at a record rate of 1,000 a week (allowing for deregistrations). Between 1980 and 1987 the total of VAT-registered businesses had risen by 200,000 to more than 1.5 million. The number of self-employed people (less than half of whom register for VAT) rose over the same period from 2 million to 2.9 million. Nevertheless, small firms continue to be less significant in the UK than in comparable industrial countries. Per head of population, there are 1.5 times as many small firms in the USA and in West Germany, twice as many in Japan and France, and four times as many in the Netherlands.

The recent recovery of the small firm sector in the UK has been encouraged by the Conservative Government. In the next chapter we describe various financial incentives the Government has introduced to assist the growth of small firms. These reflect the Government's belief in the virtues of '*popular capitalism*' and the spread of entrepreneurship in an '*enterprise economy*', and they are also a response to a general disenchantment with the performance of large firms, particularly in the manufacturing sector. The Conservative Government believes that small firms are more effective than large firms in job creation, since they tend to be more labour intensive. It has also argued that small firms are a major source of technical inovation, and they are more cost-effective than large firms in their research and development. Many new technologies appear to suit small scale enterprise, since they are less dependent than 'older' technologies upon economies of large scale production and long production runs.

Indeed some new technologies in the field of information technology have been developed initially, not by established giants such as IBM, but by completely new **'start-up' businesses** founded by university research workers or by employees of the established large companies who decide to leave and set up on their own. In the United States, the Hewlett-Packard electronic instruments company is the classic example of a 'start-up' firms that has grown into a large business with world-wide operations, from an initial situation in which it virtually founded the industry in which it remains a leading firm.

The establishment of **worker co-operatives**, and the spread of **franchising** and **management buy-outs** have also contributed to the spread of the small firm in the UK. The **Co-operative Development Agency** and more than 70 local co-operative development agencies assist workers in setting up and running co-operatives. The rapid growth of small worker co-operatives in the early 1980s- by 1985 there were over 1,000 workers co-operatives employing over 9,000 workers - was in large part a response to the depressed state of the economy and growing unemployment. Newly laid-off workers in industries such as engineering decided to form their own co-operatives so that they could continue to work in activities in which they were skilled. At the same time, many newly-unemployed workers entered self-employment as sole traders in activities such as window-cleaning and painting and decorating, as an alternative to the dole.

Franchising has become common in the fields of retailing and catering where an individual operates his own business, but trades under the franchiser's name and sells the franchiser's products or services. The Kentucky Fried Chicken chain is an example. The individual proprietor holding a franchise typically requires about £25,000 to start up in business and then he must pay the franchiser an annual royalty payment in return for trading under the franchiser's brand name and for receiving the benefits of national advertising and a back-up service. A management buy-out occurs when a large diversified company decides to rationalise its activities by selling off the less successful parts of the company. Confident that their expertise can allow them to manage an activity better, the firm's managers and workers may offer to buy a part of the company which is being sold off, in order to run it themselves. There have been several hundred management buy-outs since 1983, the most well known being the buy-out of the National Freight Corporation, a nationalised industry that was sold to its managers and workers by the government.

THE GROWTH OF LARGE FIRMS

12. Despite the recent resurgence of the small firm sector in the United Kingdom, there is little doubt that over a longer period British industry has become increasingly dominated by large firms. Yet while large firms are proportionately more important in the United Kingdom

than in most other industrialised countries, in a world context British firms are not usually very large. And where large British companies such as ICI and the Rover Group compete in world markets, they may be substantially smaller than some of their competitors.

THE AGGREGATE CONCENTRATION RATIO

13. The growing importance of large firms in the UK economy is indicated by the **aggregate concentration ratio** which measures the share of the 100 largest firms in manufacturing output. These accounted for 16 per cent of manufacturing output in 1902, 22 per cent in 1940 and 41 per cent in 1981. The changes in the aggregate concentration ratio since 1945 indicate a substantial increase in the importance of large firms in the British economy. However, the aggregate concentration ratio has remained relatively stable at around 41 per cent since 1968, indicating that large firms have not increased their importance in manufacturing in recent years. Evidence on concentration in the service industries is less satisfactory, though retailing in general, and grocery retailing in particular, have become increasingly concentrated in a few large firms. Overall the evidence suggests that the growth in the aggregate concentration ratio has been much more rapid in the United Kingdom than in other countries, despite the relative smallness of even the largest British firms.

THE MARKET CONCENTRATION RATIO

14. A **market concentration ratio** rather than the aggregate concentration ratio is used to measure concentration within a particular industry or group of industries. For example, the **five firm concentration ratio** shows the proportion of the industry's total output produced by the five largest firms. Since 1968 the five largest firms have accounted for over 90 per cent of domestically produced manufacturing output in about a quarter of manufacturing industries. As with the aggregate concentration ratio, market concentration ratios for particular industries are higher in the UK than in the USA, France and West Germany. Market concentration ratios therefore provide further evidence of the importance of large firms in the UK economy. Nevertheless, the concentration ratio can be a misleading indicator of monopoly power in those industries in the field of manufacturing and internationally traded services where international competition in world markets leads to considerable import penetration and where foreign firms hold a considerable share of the domestic market. These industries are subject to much more competition both in the home market and in the export market than the evidence provided by the concentration ratio suggests.

PLANTS AND FIRMS

15. In micro-economic theory we often assume that a typical firm operates a single manufacturing plant to produce a specific product within a well defined industry. Though **single plant/single product firms** certainly exist, particularly amongst small businesses, large firms tend to be much more diverse. A **plant** is an individual productive unit within the firm or enterprise, such as a factory, office or shop. Many big firms operate a large number of plants producing a range of products. Such **multi-plant and multi-product firms**, often organised as holding companies owning subsidiary companies in each of the industries they operate in, are much more typical amongst big business than the single product/single plant firm. The largest business corporations are **multinational companies** owning subsidiary enterprises throughout the world. Some multinationals such as BP and ICI are British owned, with their headquarters and most of their shareholders located in the United Kingdom. However, many of the multinational corporations operating subsidiary companies and 'branch' factories in the UK are overseas-owned. The Nissan Corporation which produces cars in the north east of England and the Sony Corporation producing TV sets in South Wales are Japanese-owned multinationals which have built factories in the UK in recent years, while Ford, General Motors and IBM are examples of America multinationals that have successfully operated subsidiaries in the UK for many years. Some companies such as Unilever and Shell are also **transnationals** with ownership and control located in more than one country.

Despite the growth of large firms in the UK economy, little of the growth in manufacturing concentration is explained by increased plant size. For over fifty years, the share in manufacturing output of the 100 largest plants (as distinct from firms) has remained roughly constant at 11 per cent. Thus the explanation for increasing concentration must lie in an increase in the average number of plants owned by the largest firms rather than in a significant growth in plant size. This in turn suggests that the **external growth** of firms through take-over and merger has contributed more to the industrial dominance of large firms than the technical expansion of plant size in a process of **internal growth**.

INTERNAL ECONOMIES OF SCALE

16. As we saw in Chapter 4, **economies of scale** occur when a firm's long-run average production costs fall as output increases. We shall now examine the various sources of economies of scale and discuss their significance for UK firms. In the first place we must distinguish between **internal and external economies of scale. Internal economies of** scale ocur when a firm's long-run average costs or unit costs fall as a result of an increase in the size of the firm itself or of an increase in the size of a plant or plants operated by the firm. By contrast a firm benefits from **external economies of scale** when unit production costs fall because of the growth of the scale of the whole industry rather than of the firm itself.

PLANT-LEVEL AND FIRM-LEVEL ECONOMIES OF SCALE

17. In order to explain why firms have grown larger while the plants they operate have generally not grown significantly in size, it is useful to distinguish between those internal economies of scale that occur at the level of a single plant or establishment owned by a firm and those occurring at the level of the firm itself. In recent years, firm-level **economies of scale** have encouraged the continued growth of larger firms, but there has been much less scope for enterprises which operate large factories to enjoy further **economies of scale at the plant level.**

PLANT-LEVEL ECONOMIES OF SCALE

18. Economies of scale that occur at the level of a single plant or factory operated by a firm are largely technical economies of scale, though some management economies are also possible at plant-level.

(i) **Technical economies of scale.** These affect the size of the typical plant or establishment, rather than the overall size of the firm which may own and control several different plants. Where technical economies of scale are great, the typical plant or establishment is also large in size, whereas in industries where size provides few technical advantages and where the methods of large plants can be adopted by smaller establishments, the typical plant will usually be smaller.

The main types of technical economy of scale are:

(a) **Indivisibilities.** Many types of plant or machinery are indivisible in the sense that there is a certain minimum size below which they cannot efficiently operate. A firm requiring only a small level of output must therefore, choose between installing plant or machinery which it will be unable to use continuously, buying from an outside supplier, or using a different but less efficient method to produce the smaller required level of output.

(b) **The spreading of research and development costs.** Research and development costs associated with new products also tend to be indivisible and independent of the size of output to be produced. With large plants R and D costs can be spread over a much longer production run, reducing unit costs in the long run.

(c) **Volume economies.** These are also known as **economies of increased dimensions.** With many types of capital equipment (for example metal smelters, transport containers, storage tanks and warehouses), costs increase less rapidly than capacity. When a storage tank or boiler is doubled in dimension, its storage capacity actually increases eight fold. And since heat loss depends on the area of the container's walls (which will only have increased four fold) and not upon volume, a large smelter or boiler is technically more efficient than a small one. Volume economies are thus very important in industries such as transport, storage and warehousing, as well as in metal and chemical industries where an increase in the scale of plant provides scope for the conservation of heat and energy.

(d) **Economies of massed resources**. The operation of a number of identical machines in a large plant means that proportionately less spare parts need be kept than when fewer machines are involved. This is an application of the 'law of large numbers' since we can assume that not all the machines will develop a fault at the same time. (The massing of resources also allows for firm-level economies of scale. A multi-product multi-plant firm may benefit from the cross-fertilisation of experience and ideas between its various subsidiaries.)

(e) **Economies of vertically-linked processes**. Much manufacturing activity involves a large number of vertically related tasks and processes, from the initial purchase of raw materials, components and energy through to the completion and sale of the finished product. Within a single firm, these processes may be integrated through the linkages between the various plants owned by the firm - the output of one plant providing an input or source of component-supply for another plant further along the route to the finished product. Alternatively, the tasks or processes may be integrated within the workshops of a single large plant, enabling the plant to benefit from substantial economies of scale. The linking of processes in a single plant can lead to a saving in time, transport costs and energy, and the close physical proximity of specialist workshops within the plant may allow a subsequent stage in the production process to be sure of obtaining exactly the supplies it needs in the right quantity and technical specification at the right time.

(ii) **Managerial economies of scale**. Managerial economies of scale can be achieved both by increasing the size of an individual plant, or at the level of the firm by grouping a larger number of establishments under one management. Both methods of expansion allow for increased managerial specialisation and division of labour involving both the delegation of detail to junior managers and supervisors and also, a functional division of labour with the employment of specialist managers, for example in the fields of production, personnel and sales.

MULTI-PLANT ECONOMIES OF SCALE

19. **Multi-plant economies of scale** occur when long-run average costs fall as a result of operating more than one plant. When two or more plants are operated a firm may be able to grow larger without exhausting plant-level economies of scale. Not only may plants be duplicated, the firm can also benefit from plant specialisation and from the switching of production between plants, for example to meet seasonal or peak-load demand.

FIRM-LEVEL ECONOMIES OF SCALE

20. It is obviously in a firm's interest to benefit as much as possible from plant-level economies of scale. Firms will also try to take advantage of any scale economies associated with the growth of the enterprise that are largely independent of plant size. **Economies of scale at the firm level** arise from the firm itself being large rather than from operating a single big plant or a number of large plants. As well as covering some of the R & D economies, massed resources economies and managerial economies that we have already described, firm-level economies of scale also include:

(i) **Marketing economies**. These are of two types: **bulk-buying and bulk-marketing economies**. Large firms may be able to use their market power both to buy supplies at lower prices and also to market their products on better terms negotiated with wholesalers and retailers. It is worth noting that such bargaining advantages make a large firm more profitable, but they do not necessarily make it more efficient in a strictly economic sense. Essentially the firm gains an advantage at the expense of other firms (its suppliers or market outlets) and only if production costs fall for all the firms considered together, can we conclude that true economies have resulted. It follows therefore, that if a big firm becomes a monopoly and increases its selling price, there are no economies of scale involved, only the exploitation of a monopoly position. Nevertheless, as we noted in Chapter 6, monopolies can often benefit from scale economies that are unobtainable by smaller more competitive firms, and the possibility of achieving economies of scale is usually cited as the main justification of monopoly.

(ii) **Financial or capital-raising economies of scale**. These are similar to the bulk-buying economies we have just described, except that they relate to the 'bulk-buying' or the bulk-borrowing of funds required to finance the business's expansion. Large firms can often borrow from banks and other financial institutions at a lower rate of interest and on better terms than those available to small firms.

(iii) **Risk-bearing economies of scale**. Large firms are usually less exposed to risk than small firms, because risks can be grouped and spread. The grouping of risks is another application of the 'law of large numbers' and the massing of resources to which we have already referred. It is usually possible to predict what will happen on average over a large number of similar events with a reasonable degree of certainty, but individual events may be impossible to predict. Thus a bank can predict with some confidence the number of customers who will turn out to be bad debtors, but it is unlikely to know in advance which customers they will be. But because it knows that for each bad debt there will be many other solvent customers whose business is profitable for the bank, risks are spread and uncertainty is reduced. When the risks are dissimilar, the advantage to the firm from the grouping of risks is less predictable, but still definite. Thus large firms can spread risks by diversifying their output, their markets, their sources of supply and finance and the processes by which they manufacture their output. Such economies of diversification or risk-bearing can make the firm less vulnerable to sudden changes in demand or conditions of supply that might severely harm a smaller less-diversified business.

LEARNING EFFECTS

21. When a firm increases the scale of its plant, it is quite likely that a new technology or new methods of working an old technology will be adopted. But if the firm's workers and managers are initially unfamiliar with the new methods of production, production is likely to be inefficient. A **learning effect** occurs when managers and workers learn from experience how to operate particular technologies and methods of production more effectively. Learning effects are usually associated with a change in the scale of a firm's operations, but they can also occur as a result of reorganisation of existing capacity.

MINIMUM EFFICIENT PLANT SIZE

22. As we have explained in Chapter 4, in many industries - particularly in manufacturing - the long run average total cost curve is 'L' shaped. An 'L' shaped LRATC curve occurs when substantial plant-level economies of scale are possible up to a certain size of plant, followed by a flattening of the curve as the scope for further scale economies becomes exhausted. The size of plant at which the LRATC curve flattens is known as **Minimum Efficient Plant Size (MEPS)**. A plant smaller than MEPS is at a significant cost disadvantage, but there is little scope for further cost efficiency for establishments above MEPS. But as we have just seen, in many industries firm-level economies of scale provide greater scope for the growth of large firms than plant-level economies. In these industries, the concept of **Minimum Efficient Firm Size (MEFS)** is therefore more appropriate and useful than MEPS. Table 8.1 shows that in the automobile industry, the optimum size of a car firm (but not of plant size) is one producing two million units a year. Since only a few of the large international car manufacturers such as GMC, Ford and Nissan produce as many as 2 million automobiles from their plants scattered around the world, smaller companies such as the Rover Group in the UK are at a considerable cost disadvantage, being well below Minimum Efficient Firm Size.

Table 8.1 World-wide output of automobiles and the average cost per car

World-Wide Car Output (000s)

GMC	4,800	Lada	800
Ford	3,000	Mitsubishi	600
Toyota	2,400	Daimler-Benz	550
Nissan	2,000	Rover Group	400
Renault	2,000	Seat	400
Volkswagen	2,000	BMW	375
Peugeot-Citroen	1,500	Volvo	300
Fiat	1,500	Alfa Romero	200
Chrysler	1,000	Saab	90
Honda	900	Jaguar	40
Toyo Kogyo	850	Rolls Royce	3

Output per year	Index of average costs per car
100,000	100
250,000	83
500,000	74
1,000,000	70
2,000,000	66

THE EVIDENCE OF ECONOMIES OF SCALE IN THE UK

23. Most of the studies of economies of scale in the Uk economy have investigated plant-level economies of scale rather than firm-level economies. One of the most comprehensive studies which built on earlier work undertaken by C F Pratten at Cambridge University in the 1960s, was carried out in the late 1970s by a working party of senior British civil servants. Their report was published in a Green paper entitled '*A Review of Monopolies and Mergers Policy: a Consultative Document*', (*HMSO, 1978*). The paper looked in detail at the minimum efficient plant size in a number of industries, calculating the proportion of total UK sales of a particular product which these minimum efficient plant sizes represented.

Table 8.2 on the following page shows that in some industries such as bread, beer, commercial vehicles, oil refining and sugar refining, there is room in the UK market for a number of plants at MEPS, assuming no imports. This contrasts with other products such as turbo-generators, where MEPS exceeds the total size of the UK market. Clearly if economies of scale at the plant level are such that MEPS is over 100 per cent of the national market, a very high degree of concentration is probable. And unless a UK manufacturer such as GEC can achieve MEPS by supplementing domestic sales with exports, it is likely that the market will be dominated by imports produced from much larger plants owned by American and Japanese companies whose domestic markets are sufficiently large to allow MEPS to be attained.

EXTERNAL ECONOMIES OF SCALE

24. As we have already explained, **external economies of scale** are shared by a number of firms (or indeed by a number of industries), when the scale of production of the whole industry (or group of industries) increases. External economies are conferred on a firm not as a result of its own growth but because other firms have grown larger - though of course the firm's own growth may result in other firms receiving the benefits of external economies. Indeed, if the firms were to merge, external economies enjoyed by previously independent firms would become internal economies within the plants and subsidiaries of the combined enterprise.

Table 8.2: Some estimates of Minimum Efficient Plant Size (MEPS)

Product		*Estimates of MEPS*	*UK-produced sales of product in 1973*	*MEPS as % of UK produced sales*
Bread		30 sacks per hour	17.3m sacks	about 0.5%
Beer *	(1)	1m barrels pa	35m barrels	(1) c. 3.0%
	(2)	4.5m barrels pa		(2) c. 13.0%
	(3)	1-1.5m barrels pa		(3) 3-4.0%
	(4)	600,000 barrels pa		(4) c. 2.0%
Commercial vehicles		20 - 30,000 units pa	416,000 units	5-7.0%
Oil refining *	(1)	10m plus pa	114m tonnes	(1) 9.0%
	(2)	5m plus pa		(2) 4.0%
Sugar refined *	(1)	450-500,000	2.5m tonnes	(1) 18-20%
	(2)	190,000 plus pa		(2) 8.0%
Electric cookers		30,000 units	1.04m units	30.0%
Diesel engines		100,000 units	179,000	56.0%
Turbo generators	(1)	6,000 MW pa	c. 5,000 MW	(1) 120.0%
	(2)	8-10,000 MW pa		(2) 160-200%

* For some products more than one estimate was obtained.

(*Source: HMSO (1978) A review of monopolies and mergers policy: a consultative document*)

Thus takeover and merger can serve to internalise external economies (and diseconomies) of scale. It is also worth noting that some external economies and diseconomies are unrelated to the scale of the industry or market, and should not therefore be referred to as economies and diseconomies *of scale*. These are the external benefits and costs (positive and negative externalities) received by firms in production which we explain in detail in Chapter 11. For example, a remote farm might benefit from a road improvement constructed by the government, but this economy, though external to the farm itself, has nothing to do with the scale of the wider farming industry. As with internal scale economies, it is possible to identify a number of different types of external economy of scale. These are:

(i) **Economies of concentration**. When a number of firms in the same or related industries locate close together, they are able to gain mutual advantages through better transport facilities, the training of a pool of skilled labour and by supplying each other with sources of components and market outlets.

(ii) **Economies of information.**In a large industry it is worthwhile for specialist firms and for public bodies such as universities, to undertake research and to provide information, for example through technical and trade journals, from which all firms can benefit and share.

(iii) **Economies of disintegration**. Although firms can often benefit from the internal economies of scale that result from linking processes internally within an enlarged firm, there may be circumstances when vertically linked production processes can be provided more efficiently by independent specialist firms. An obvious example occurs in the case of indivisibilities. If a firm is too small to use continuously plant or machinery that cannot be built on a smaller scale, it makes sense to buy supplies from an independent firm which can use the plant efficiently because it supplies a number of firms within the industry.

VERTICAL GROWTH AND INTEGRATION

25. We have noted in our discussion of both internal and external economies of scale that there are various ways in which related production processes can be linked or integrated together. Within a single plant there is the obvious technical integration of related production processes carried out in separate workshops within the plant. This is an example of **vertical integration**, which refers to the linking together within a single firm of the various stages in the vertical chain of production from the initial production of raw material, energy and component supplies through to the final sale of the finished product. Besides occurring through the linkage within a single plant of related workshop activities, vertical integration also occurs at firm level when the output of one plant owned by a firm serves as the input into another plant further down the line towards the final consumer.

Such vertical integration of processes is an obvious motive for the internal growth of the firm (though, as we noted in the previous section, there may sometimes be a case for **vertical disintegration**, which occurs when a firm buys its supplies from, or markets its output through, an independent firm which can provide the service more efficiently). Vertical *internal* growth takes place when a firm invests in and builds new plant in order to extend its operations by providing its own raw materials, components or market outlets.

Vertical integration can also take place through *acquisition*. This occurs when a firm takes over or merges with a previously independent firm in order to link the existing capacity of the other firm into its operations. Vertical integration through acquisition is an example of the *external growth* of the firm.

As Figure 8.2 (shown on the following page) indicates, a firm can expand through vertical integration either backwards or forwards. **Backwards integration** occurs when a firm expands into its source of supply, either by investing in new plant which produces raw materials or components in the case of internal growth, or through take over or merger when external growth takes place. In Figure 8.2 backwards integration takes place if the car-assembly firm illustrated in the centre of the diagram decides to produce its own gear boxes, or acquires through take over a previously independent gearbox manufacturer. By contrast, **forwards integration** involves an expansion into market outlets, illustrated by the car assembly firm acquiring a chain of retail showrooms.

HORIZONTAL GROWTH AND INTEGRATION

26. As well as growing through a process of vertical expansion and integration, a firm can grow horizontally and laterally. In all three forms of growth, the firm may grow, either internally by investing in completely new productive capacity, or externally through the acquisition of other firms in a process of take over or merger. **Horizontal growth** takes place when a firm expands by building or acquiring more plants at the same stage of production in the same industry. The possibility of achieving multi-plant economies of scale is an obvious motive for horizontal growth, though a less benign motive might be to eliminate competitors so as to build up and exploit a monopoly position. A merger between two automobile manufacturing firms - shown as a movement along the horizontal arrow in Figure 8.2 - would be an example of horizontal integration. Horizontal mergers in the motor industry have included the acquisition of Audi by Volkswagen in West Germany and the Peugeot and Citroen merger in France, both of which have allowed the newly-merged companies to rationalise their production plants and product lines, and to exploit scale economies more fully.

LATERAL GROWTH AND INTEGRATION

27. **Lateral growth or integration** occurs when a firm diversifies into a completely different industry or product market. Lateral growth, which is also known as **conglomerate growth**, would occur if the car manufacturing firm shown in Figure 8.2 merged with a leisure industry firm operating cinemas and theme parks. Firms diversify in order to gain the scale economies of massed resources

Figure 8.2: Vertical, horizontal and lateral growth and integration by a motor car manufacturing company

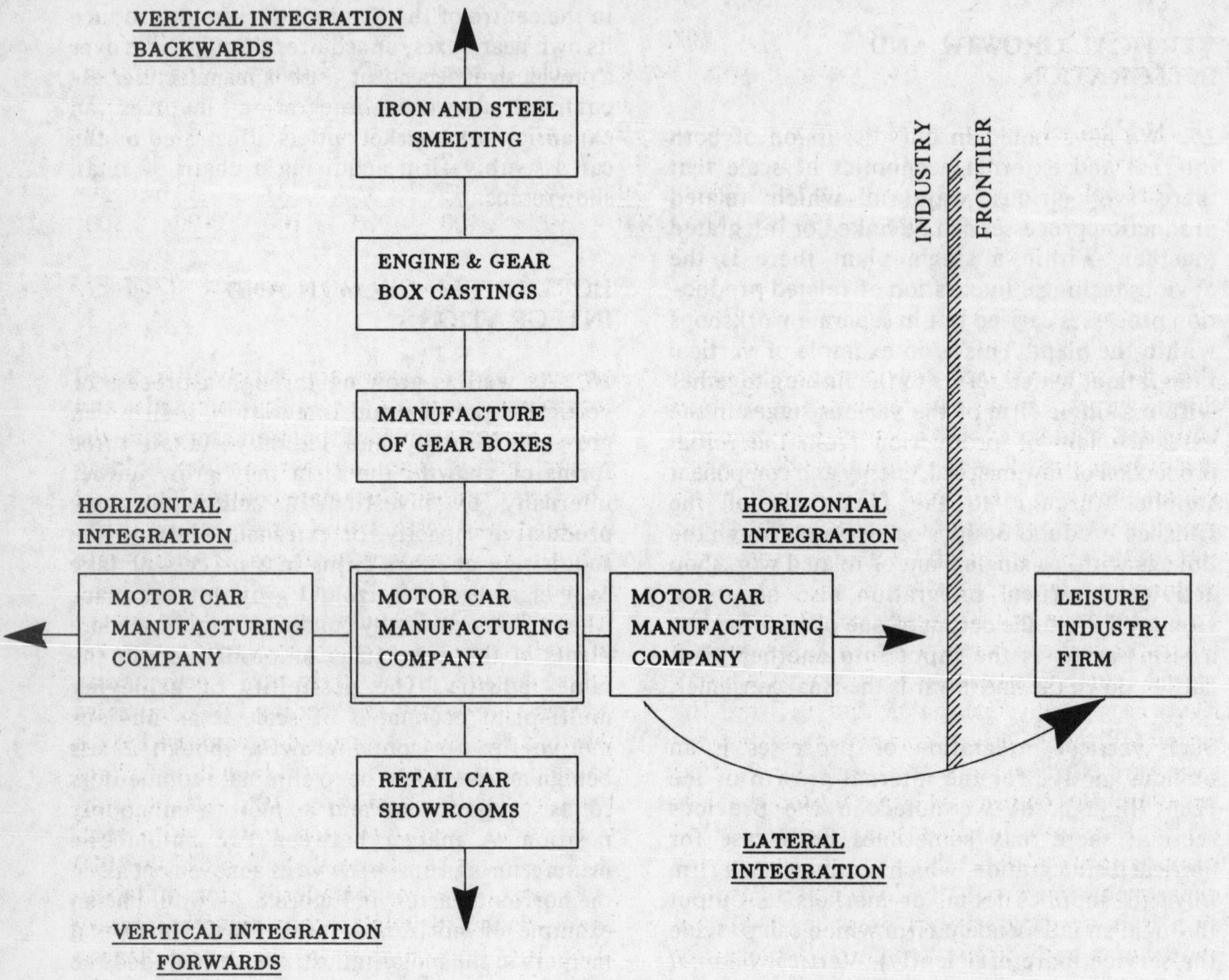

and risk-spreading which we have already described, and financial and managerial economies at the firm level may also be possible. Some lateral mergers, for example those undertaken by tobacco firms, involve the company diversifying out of a declining market into what they believe are markets with growth potential. However, managerial and organisational diseconomies might also result from the fact that the management of the diversifying company may lack expertise in the fields into which it is expanding.

STATISTICS ON MERGERS AND LARGE FIRMS

28. Many takeovers and mergers will contain elements of vertical, horizontal and lateral integration. The Office of Fair Trading has compiled a classification of mergers in the United Kingdom, which is illustrated in Table 8.3. The data indicate that most mergers are horizontal, but that a growing minority are lateral or conglomerate, perhaps because the opportunity for further horizontal amalgamation has diminished. Vertical motives for merger have not been significant.

Table 8.3: A classification of mergers in the United Kingdom

Percentages

Type	1965 No	1965 Value	1970 No	1970 Value	1974 No	1974 Value	1980 No	1980 Value	1984 No	1984 Value
Horizontal	78	75	84	70	68	65	65	68	63	79
Vertical	12	13	1	0	5	2	4	1	4	1
Lateral	10	12	15	30	27	33	31	31	33	20
	100	100	100	100	100	100	100	100	100	100

(Source: Office of Fair Trading)

Table 8.4 (shown on the following page) shows the thirty largest industrial enterprises in the United Kingdom in 1987, ranked in order of turnover or size of sales within the UK market. While most of the 'top thirty' businesses operating within the United Kingdom are UK public companies with full Stock Exchange quotations, nationalised industries such as the Electricity Council and the British Coal Corporation and the UK subsidiaries of foreign-owned multinationals such as Esso (Exxon) and the Ford Motor Company figure prominently amongst the leading firms. The largest UK owned private companies and partnerships are well outside the 'top thirty'. The largest private company is George Weston Holdings (a holding company in food manufacturing and food distribution) in fiftieth position, while the department store group, the John Lewis Partnership is in seventy seventh position. Table 8.4 shows how each of the 'top thirty' enterprises ranks in terms of capital employed, profit, number of employees and, for UK quoted public companies, their market valuation on the Stock Exchange. The main industrial activity of each business is also indicated. Some of the leading firms, for example BP, British Telecom, ICI, Sainsbury and Marks and Spencer, have grown to their present size largely as a result of internal expansion within a well defined industry or market. But others such as BAT Industries, Hanson PLC and BTR have become industrial giants through an often rapid process of takeover and merger. These firms are highly-diversified **conglomerates** whose subsidiary companies and brand names are usually better known to the general public than the less familiar holding company exercising ultimate control. It should be noted that Table 8.4 does not include banks and other financial institutions. If these were included, Barclays Bank and the National Westminster Bank would be amongst the twenty largest business organisations measured by market valuation and profit. It is also worth noting that the turnover of the leading UK companies shown in Figure 8.4 is small when compared to the leading companies in the 'world top thirty'. Thus Britain's leading company, BP, was in tenth position in the 'world top thirty' with total sales just over half those of the £64,827,000,000 turnover of the world leader, C Itoh of Japan. Shell, which is Britain's second biggest company after BP, fares higher in the world 'league table' if the sales of the Dutch arm of the transnational company are included. In 1987 Shell Transport and Trading/Royal Dutch Petroleum was the world's third largest company with total sales of £59,811,000,000. The only other British owned or part-owned business in the 'world top thirty' was another Anglo-Dutch transnational, Unilever plc/Unilever NV, which was in thirtieth position. In the 'league table' of banks and financial institutions, Barclays Bank, the largest UK bank was in thirteenth position, behind a number of Japanese banks.

Table 8.4: The thirty largest industrial enterprises in the UK in 1987, ranked by turnover

Rank	Company Name	Main activity	Turnover £million	Capital Employed £ million	Net profit before interest and tax £ million	No of employees	Equity market capital value £ million
1	British Petroleum Company	Oil industry	39,932.0	18,477.0	3,883.0	126,400	14,227.4
2	'Shell' Transport & Trading	Oil industry	23,924.0	14,579.0	2,576.0	N/A	11,335.6
3	BAT Industries	Tobacco, retailing, paper financial services	11,255.0	6,396.0	1,542.0	168,949	6,287.2
4	Imperial Chemical Industries	Petrochemicals, pharmaceuticals etc	11,123.0	6,154.0	1,574.0	127,800	7,409.8
5	Electricity Council	Electricity suppliers	11,118.6	38,777.6	803.5	131,891	Nationalised industry
6	British Telecommunications	Telecommunication services	10,185.0	12,064.0	2,661.0	235,633	15,452.1
7	British Gas	Gas suppliers etc	7,610.0	7,392.0	1,398.0	88,469	7,511.5
8	Hanson	Consumer products etc	6,682.0	4,871.0	1,041.0	88,000	5,323.8
9	Shell UK	Oil industry	6,677.0	3,685.0	1,087.0	13,636	Dutch owned
10	Grand Metropolitan	Hotel props, milk prds, brewers etc	5,705.5	3,356.5	586.1	129,436	4,313.5
11	Unilever	Food products, detergents etc	5,428.0	2,558.0	527.0	155,000	3,700.7
12	Esso UK	Oil industry	5,397.6	3,658.4	1,076.3	5,352	USA owned
13	General Electric Co	Electrical engineers	5,247.3	3,795.0	683.2	159,579	4,242.7
14	Ford Motor Co	Motor vehicles manufacturers	5,211.0	2,375.0	366.0	47,000	USA owned
15	Dalgety	International merchants	5,003.0	674.6	143.4	23,966	726.7
16	Dee Corporation	Wholesale, retail, cash & carry distn.	4,838.6	852.9	198.8	84,240	1,687.8
17	J Sainsbury	Retail distribution of food	4,791.5	1,443.6	324.4	82,607	3,381.1
18	Marks and Spencer	General store proprietors	4,577.6	2,365.9	507.6	68,450	4,573.2
19	British Coal Corporation	Coalmining	4,515.0	4,370.0	332.0	162,800	Nationalised industry
20	Allied Lyons	Brewers, vintners, hoteliers etc	4,236.1	3,174.9	551.7	78,128	3,115.4
21	BTR	Construction, energy & electrical etc	4,149.2	2,260.2	652.4	81,800	4,699.8
22	Tesco	Multiple retailing	4,119.1	1,228.6	239.8	71,262	2,244.8
23	British Aerospace	Manufacture of aircraft etc	4,075.0	2,001.0	Loss 137.0	86,800	Quotation suspended
24	Saatchi & Saatchi Company	Advertising agency	3,954.2	180.0	137.6	15,630	589.8
25	Gallaher	Tobacco, optics, pumps & Valves disbn	3,886.7	604.7	190.8	32,540	USA owned
26	British Airways	Air transportation	3,756.0	1,656.0	284.0	43,969	1,073.5
27	Post Office	Mail & parcel services etc	3,473.3	1,954.1	184.9	199,732	Nationalised industry
28	British Steel Corporation	Iron & Steel mfrs etc	3,461.0	3,638.0	2,180	56,650	Nationalised industry
29.	RTZ Corporation	Mining & industrial - metals & fuel	3,397.1	3,027.5	667.1	78,705	3,235.9
30	Bass	Brewing, drinks, pub retailing etc	3,213.4	2,828.2	3880.9	79,348	2,670.7

(Source: The Times 1.000 Top Companies 1988/1989 Edition)

THE STANDARD INDUSTRIAL CLASSIFICATION

29. In Chapter 1 we described how economic activity can be divided into primary, secondary and tertiary production. The primary sector of the economy includes extractive industries such as farming and forestry, while the secondary and tertiary sectors involve manufacturing and service industries respectively. However, the published statistics of the output of British industries are based on a much more complicated classification, known as the **Standard Industrial Classification (SIC)** which was first published in 1948. The SIC has been revised on three occasions, in 1958, 1968 and 1983, the latest revision in 1983 being undertaken to bring the SIC into line with the classification of economic activities used by the EEC. However, the SIC does not always correspond to the normal description of industries to be found in economics textbooks. The Standard Industrial Classification comprises 10 major **industrial divisions**, which are illustrated in Table 8.5. The ten basic industrial divisions are then further divided and subdivided into 60 classes, 222 groups and 334 activity headings.

Perhaps the two most important trends indicated by Table 8.5 are:

(i) **The continuing relative decline of manufacturing in UK national output.** Manufacturing now accounts for less than a quarter of national output, thus raising the question of whether Britain should still be regarded as an industrialised economy (rather than as a country which has entered the era of post-industrialism). We shall investigate the issues raised by the **de-industrialisation** of Britain when we examine government industrial policy in Chapter 10. However, it is worth noting that in many 'developing' countries such as South Korea, Taiwan and other Newly Industrialised Countries (NICs), manufacturing is now more important than in the UK.

(ii) **The growing importance of service industries.** As in most of the older industrialised economies, tertiary sector output exceeds that of manufacturing, and service industries are continuing to grow in relative importance. The growth of banking and financial services in the UK economy has been of special significance in recent years, indicating the importance and role of the City of London in the increasingly integrated world financial markets. Financial services are now the fastest growing sector in the UK economy.

Table 8.5: The Industrial Divisions of the Standard Industrial Classification and their percentage contributions to industrial output in 1977 and 1987

INDUSTRY DIVISION	1977	1987
(1) Agriculture, forestry and fishing	2.60	1.66
(2) Energy and water supply	6.78	6.81
(3) Manufacturing	29.88	24.11
(4) Construction	6.17	6.06
(5) Distribution, hotels and catering; repairs	13.42	13.80
(6) Transport	5.47	4.57
(7) Communication	2.56	2.73
(8) Banking, finance, insurance, business services and leasing	11.83	18.01
(9) Public administration, national defence and compulsory social security	7.06	7.01
(10) Education and health services	8.82	8.93
Other services	5.41	6.40

(Source: National Income Blue Book)

Table 8.5 also shows that, in comparison with similar developed economies, the United Kingdom has a relatively small agricultural sector, reflecting the shortage of agricultural land and the importance of food imports. Nevertheless, British farms are usually efficient by world standards and over-production of dairy products and cereals has sometimes occurred. General over-production within the European Community has caused the EEC to direct the eleven member countries to take surplus land out of agricultural production, thus freeing the land for other uses such as housing and leisure industries. Table 8.5 shows that the contribution of the energy industries to UK output has remained stable during the 1980s, despite the major growth in North Sea oil production during the period shown by the data. However, it must be remembered that coal production has become less important thereby offsetting to a large extent the contribution of North Sea oil and gas to national output. Finally we should note that in comparison to similar advanced western countries, defence industries are responsible for a slightly larger fraction of national output, while a rather lower proportion of national resources are devoted to the provision of education and health care.

SUMMARY

30. We started the chapter by looking at the nature of firms in the UK economy and we concluded with a brief survey of the structure of industry. Firms can be classified in a number of different ways: on the basis of legal status; into small and large businesses; or according to the industrial sector of the economy they occupy. While there are many thousands of unincorporated sole traders or individual proprietors, in terms of their contribution to national output they are less important that the much smaller number of public companies. Together with public corporations or nationalised industries and the UK subsidiaries of overseas owned multinationals, public companies form the largest business enterprises in the UK economy. All sole traders and most private companies are small businesses, while most public companies are large businesses. However, the concepts of small and large businesses are vague and imprecise. Nevertheless, there has been general recognition in the UK in recent years that small businesses have a useful role to play in making the UK economy more adaptable and responsive to change.

Large firms are of course dominant in markets and industries where there are economies of large scale production. Scale economies can be classified into external and internal economies of scale, with internal economies being further subdivided into plant-level and firm-level economies. Technical economies of scale are the most important type of plant-level economy, with marketing, financial and risk-bearing economies being significant at the firm level. But the fact that plant size has remained remarkably stable over a long period, while the overall size of the largest firm has grown, suggests that firm-level economies of scale are now more important than those occurring at the level of a single plant or establishment.

Firms can grow through either a process of internal growth, involving investment in new productive capacity, or by the external growth process of takeover and merger. Both forms of growth can be classified according to whether the expansion is vertical, horizontal or lateral, though in the case of external growth by take over, diversification or lateral growth has become increasingly common.

Many conglomerates such as BAT Industries have been formed by firms diversifying out of traditional manufacturing industries which have suffered structural decline or stagnation, into the more buoyant service sector of the economy. This reflects the fact that service industries have grown to become to most important contributors to national output, with financial services growing especially fast in recent years. Manufacturing now accounts for less than 25 per cent of UK national output, indicating perhaps that it is now appropriate to regard the UK as having entered the era of post-industrialism.

STUDENT SELF-TESTING

(1) Are firms generally in the market or non-market sector of the economy? *(2)*

(2) Give an example of a type of business in the public sector of the economy? *(3)*

(3) In what types of economic activity are sole traders common? *(4)*

(4) Why are partnerships common in professional services in the UK? *(5)*

(5) What is a company? *(6)*

(6) Explain limited liability. *(7)*

(7) Distinguish between a private and a public company? *(8)*

(8) *Why might a successful sole trader form a private company?* (9)
(9) *What are the motives for forming a public company?* (10)
(10) *How is a 'small business' defined?* (11)
(11) *What is the aggregate concentration ratio?* (13)
(12) *Explain the meaning of a five firm market concentration ratio.* (14)
(13) *Distinguish between a plant and a firm.* (15)
(14) *Distinguish between internal and external economies of scale.* (16)
(15) *Explain the difference between plant-level and firm-level economies of scale.* (17)
(16) *List the main plant-level economies of scale.* (18)
(17) *What are multi-plant economies of scale?* (19)
(18) *List the main firm-level economies of scale.* (20)
(19) *What is a learning effect?* (21)
(20) *Distinguish between MEPS and MEFS.* (22)
(21) *List the main sources of external economies of scale.* (24)
(22) *What are the advantages of vertical growth?* (25)
(23) *Distinguish between vertical, horizontal and lateral growth.* (25,26)
(24) *What is the main motive for lateral growth?* (27)
(25) *Are most mergers vertical, horizontal or lateral?* (28)
(26) *What is the Standard Industrial Classification?* (29)

EXERCISES

1. *Classify the following businesses according to their legal status:*
   (a) Littlewoods;
   (b) British Coal Corporation;
   (c) Marks & Spencer;
   (d) British Petroleum;
   (e) George Weston Holdings;
   (f) Post Office Corporation.

2. *With reference to the thirty largest businesses shown in Table 8.4:*

   (a) Identify the largest business when measured in terms of:
   (i) capital employed;
   (ii) profit;
   (iii) number of employees;
   (iv) market valuation.

   (b) Comment on the contrast between the labour intensitivity of the oil companies and the nationalised industries shown in the table.

MULTIPLE CHOICE QUESTIONS

1. *In industry X, the five largest firms produce 60 per cent of the industry's total output. In industry Y, the five largest firms produce 75 per cent of the industry's output. It can be concluded from the information that:*

   A *Firms are smaller in industry X than in industry Y*
   B *There are less economies of scale in industry X than in industry Y*
   C *Small firms have less chance of survival in industry Y than in industry X*
   D *The market concentration ratio is higher in industry Y than in industry X*

2. *Forward vertical integration occurs when a firm takes over a:*

   A *Component supplier*
   B *Competitor making the same product*
   C *Company selling its products*
   D *Company making a competing product*

3. *A fall in unit production costs resulting from the building by a firm of a larger factory is an example of:*

   A *Firm-level internal economies of scale*
   B *Plant-level internal economies of scale*
   C *Plant-level external economies of scale*
   D *The law of variable proportions*

4. *A steel making firm takes over a coal mining company. This is an example of:*

   A *A holding company being formed*
   B *Internal growth in pursuit of internal economies of scale*
   C *Horizontal integration*
   D *Vertical integration*

5. *Which of the following would be regarded as an example of horizontal integration?*

   A *A farmer buying up the neighbouring farm*
   B *A hotel group acquiring a cinema chain*
   C *A car manufacturer acquiring a chain of garages*
   D *A steel company merging with an iron mining firm.*

EXAMINATION QUESTIONS

1. *What are the major reasons for the survival of the small firm in the UK (or overseas) industrial sector? (AAT December 1988)*

2. *Examine the advantages and disadvantages of co-operatives as a form of enterprise. (CIMA November 1982)*

3. *In what ways may businesses integrate? Give reasons why they may wish to do so. (CIMA November 1984)*

4. *A firm may expand horizontally, vertically or by diversification.*

   (a) What advantages might a firm hope to gain if it were able to grow in each of these ways? (13 marks)

   (b) What disadvantages might result. (7 marks)
   (ACCA December 1982)

5. *What factors determine the size of firms in particular industries? (ACCA December 1983)*

6. *'Despite its drawbacks, the limited liability company is still the best form of private sector business organisation.' Discuss. (AAT December 1982)*

7. *The table below shows the total employment in small firms in the different sectors of industry and the percentage of total employment in each sector represented by small firms.*

Numbers employed in small firms mid-1976

Sector	*Total (000s)*	*As a percentage of total employment in the private sector*
Manufacturing	*1,549*	*22*
Distribution trades	*1,236*	*39*
Construction	*732*	*49*
Agriculture, transport and utilities	*335*	*27*
Professional and scientific services	*373*	*48*
Financial services	*231*	*20*

(Source: Bannock G (1981) The Economics of Small Firms, Basil Blackwell)

How do you account for the varying proportions of employment in small firms in the different sectors of industry? (ACCA June 1986)

9. The financing of firms

INTRODUCTION

1. In Chapter 8 we examined how a firm may grow either *internally*, by investing in new fixed capacity, hiring more workers and expanding its existing operations, or *externally* through a process of merger and takeover, which involves the integration of other previously independent firms into its activities and control. In this chapter we examine how a firm may finance the investment in new plant and productive capacity which is involved in internal growth, or the acquisition of other companies which occurs when external growth takes place.

THE MEANING OF INVESTMENT

2. It is useful to distinguish between **physical investment** and **financial investment**. In every day language, we may describe a person investing in shares on the Stock Exchange, or investing in a building society. Strictly, these are examples of *financial investment*, which involve the use of savings to purchase financial assets such as company shares or building society deposits or shares. Indeed, in every day language the words **saving** and **investment** have a similar meaning. However, the economist makes a clear distinction between saving and investment, defining *saving* simply as *income which is not spent on consumption*, including funds which simply lie idle. In contrast, to an economist *investment* means *physical investment* involving the *productive use of savings*, both in the purchase of fixed capital in the form of buildings and machinery, and also in the purchase of raw materials which are working or circulating capital. As a generalisation, *households make savings decisions* and *firms make investment decisions*, though firms simultaneously save and invest when they 'plough back' profits into the expansion of the business.

INTERNALLY AND EXTERNALLY FINANCED INVESTMENT

3. Between 60 per cent and 70 per cent of the funds used by firms in the United Kingdom economy to finance investment and growth are **internally generated funds** in the form of **'ploughed back'** or **retained profits**. When a firm finances growth from internally generated funds, it is providing its own savings out of revenue from the sale of its output. In a later section of this chapter, we shall examine both the reasons for, and the consequences of, this reliance by British firms on internally generated funds or 'ploughed back' profits. But first we shall briefly survey the alternatives to internal finance, represented by the various types of externally generated **funds**, which can be classified into **short-term, medium-term,** and **long-term sources of finance.** The main forms of external finance, which provide up to 30 per cent of the funds used by firms in the private sector of the United Kingdom economy are:

(i) Trade credit.
(ii) Borrowing from banks
(iii) Raising funds on the money markets.
(iv) Provision of finance by the government.
(v) Raising funds on the United Kingdom capital market.
(vi) Raising funds on the international money and capital markets.

THE NEED FOR DIFFERENT TYPES OF FINANCE

4. Firms need finance because of the time lag or delay which occurs between incurring costs of production and receiving revenue from the sale of output. Wages must be paid and raw materials and capital equipment must be purchased before payment is received from the sale of goods produced. The delay in the recovery of the firm's costs of production varies accordingly to the type of cost involved.

Wage and raw material costs can usually be recovered quickly, but the **cost of fixed investment** in a new factory building may take several years to recover. Efficient financing means that a firm must relate the use of its funds, as shown on the asset side of its balance sheet, to the sources of finance shown on the liability side. Investment in fixed assets must be matched against longer-term sources of funds such as shareholders' capital and long-term borrowing. In contrast, short-term assets such as investment in a stock of raw materials, which will be quickly converted into finished goods for sale, can be financed by short-term borrowing. Successful matching of assets and sources of finance improves both a firm's liquidity position and also its profitability. A firm which relied on long-term returns or cash-flows generated by investment in fixed assets to repay short-term borrowing might find itself with a severe liquidity problem, facing possible insolvency or bankruptcy. In terms of profitability, a firm must be able to adjust its sources of finance to match fluctuations in business activity. Industries subject to marked fluctuations in business activity, such as building and construction, in which a company's assets are to a large extent invested in current work in hand, tend to rely heavily on short-term sources of finance such as bank overdrafts to enable borrowing to contract when business activity contracts. If the company's assets were backed by long-term borrowing, interest charges would not contract during periods of slack economic activity, thereby harming the company's profitability. In contrast, manufacturing firms with a greater dependence on fixed assets in buildings and plant are usually more reliant on longer-term sources of finance.

SHORT-TERM FINANCE

5. (i) **Trade credit.** Trade credit, which is equivalent to an interest-free loan, refers to the practice of delaying the payment of bills for as long as possible while trying to persuade customers to settle their debts as quickly as possible in order to improve cash flow. Many businesses offer their customers a discount for quick settlement of bills, to discourage the use of extended trade credit at the firm's expense.

(ii) **Borrowing from banks.** Traditionally, British banks have lent short-term rather than long-term, to finance investment in working or circulating capital, such as the building-up of stocks of raw materials, in preference to financing fixed investment in new plant. Bank borrowing provides between 5 and 20 per cent of all the funds invested by British companies, and in most years it is the most important external source of funds. Indeed, the importance of banks as a source of finance is greater than those figures indicate, because they act as a marginal source of funds or 'safety net' upon which firms can fall back, thereby enabling firms to use their own funds and resources to the full. Firms can borrow from banks in two main ways: by **overdraft** and by **term loan**. The advantage of an overdraft is that a firm only pays interest on the daily balance outstanding. By varying the size of its overdraft in accordance with its cash flow, a firm can ensure that overdraft borrowing is a relatively cheap form of finance. The disadvantages of an overdraft relate to uncertainty; a firm may be uncertain about the exact cost of this source of finance, since the rate of interest charged varies in accordance with prevailing monetary conditions, and secondly, a firm can never be sure that its bank will continue to extend its overdraft facility indefinitely. Term loans provide a more medium-term, and occasionally long-term, source of finance, since the firm borrows a fixed sum of money over a fixed term of five or ten years, paying a rate of interest which is perhaps also fixed in advance at the time the loan is agreed.

(iii) **Raising funds on the money markets.** Firms may decide to raise short-term funds for a period of a few months on the London money markets, as an alternative to a conventional bank loan. This is especially attractive when a large sum of several million pounds is involved, because the cost to the firm will usually be slightly cheaper than a bank overdraft. The firm arranges for a bank to sell a **commercial bill** or **bill of exchange**, which is essentially an IOU which the firm and bank agree to honour in three months time. A bill carries no formal interest rate, but is sold on the money market on its day of issue at a discount price which is below its maturity value three months later. The cost to the firm which is raising finance in this way, is made up of two parts: the **discount rate** (calculated from the difference between the maturity value and the discount price of the bill), and also the fee that the firm must pay to the bank issuing the bill and accepting the risks involved. For fairly obvious reasons, the merchant banks which specialise in accepting the risk on new issues of bills sold on behalf of clients are called **acceptance** houses, while the specialised financial institutions within the UK banking system which purchase the bills at a discount price are called **discount houses.** Discount houses do not exist as separate financial institutions outside the UK, in other countries ordinary commercial banks undertake the discounting business.

MEDIUM-TERM FINANCE

6. Medium-term finance is most often used for the purchase of specific fixed plant and machinery, the expected life of which matches the sources of finance. **Hire-purchasing** and **leasing** are examples. Although hire-purchase does not strictly describe a source of funds, it most certainly is a method of finance, allowing a firm to obtain the use of machinery simply by paying a hire charge until the asset is ultimately purchased. The advantages of hire purchase include the fact that collateral is not required, since the machinery provides its own security, and there is no danger of the firm borrowing more finance than it strictly requires. Nevertheless, hire purchase suffers the disadvantage that a company is unlikely to benefit from any discounts available for a cash purchase, while at the same time the firm effectively pays a higher rate of interest than would be charged on a bank loan.

Leasing is similar to hire purchase except that the company never becomes the owner of the asset leased. There may be tax advantages in leasing capital equipment, and the fact that the leasing company usually undertakes repair and maintenance of complicated plant and machinery is a further considerable advantage.

LONG-TERM FINANCE

7. Almost all businesses must purchase or rent fixed assets such as buildings and land, and these require a long-term source of finance. The main source of long-term finance is the **capital market**. The capital market is the market for long-term loanable funds known as **debentures** or **corporate bonds**, and it also serves as a market in **company shares**. Because the capital market is essentially a market in long-term finance, it should not be confused with the money markets, which as we have already seen are markets for short-term funds. Not all firms have easy access to the capital market. In the United Kingdom, only public companies (PLCs) can generally raise funds on the main part of the capital market. Indeed, as we have seen in Chapter 8, the main reason why private companies 'go public' is to gain access to the long-term finance provided by the capital market. Other sources of long-term funds, besides those raised through the sale of shares and corporate bonds on the capital market, include:

(i) **Sale and leaseback of property.** Firms sometimes sell the freehold of property they own to financial institutions such as pension funds and insurance companies, and then lease the buildings back for long periods.

(ii) **Mortgaging property.** As an alternative to selling property assets outright, a firm may use its buildings as collateral and borrow against the security they provide.

(iii) **Specialist long-term funding institutions.** The most important of these in the UK is **'3i' (Investors in Industry)**. Set up initially in 1973 as **Finance for Industry**, '3i' incorporates the **Industrial and Commercial Finance Corporation (ICFC)** and the **Finance Corporation for Industry**, both of which were initially founded in 1945. ICFC essentially finances small and medium-sized businesses, whereas FCI provides long-term loans of ten years or more at fixed or variable interest rates to larger companies. Although large companies have access to the capital market, it can be more flexible to borrow from FCI. Another specialist institution providing a long-term source of finance is **Equity Capital for Industry (ECI)**, which was set up in 1976 by FCI and a consortium of a larger number of financial institutions such as pension funds and insurance companies. ECI provides equity or share capital for companies who might experience difficulty in raising long-term funds on the capital market proper.

(iv) **Government sources of finance.** The institutions we have just listed are all private sector sources of finance. In the UK there are also a number of public sector sources available for the long-term financing of private sector firms. Some of these are part of the government financial assistance available only to firms in the depressed parts of the United Kingdom which have been designated **Assisted Areas.** This regional aid is administered directly by a government department, the **Department of Trade and Industry (DTI).** Other government finance available mostly as venture capital to firms in new and often highly risky industries is provided via a specialist public sector agency, the **British Technology Group (BTG). Venture capital** involves the provision of funds to finance new firms in new and often 'Hi-tech', upstart industries (sometimes known as **'sunrise' industries**). In the past, private sector sources of long-term finance have often been unwilling to provide venture capital to risky new businesses in the United Kingdom. The purpose of the BTG is to provide a public sector source of venture capital. In recent years the BTG has undertaken **joint ventures** with private sector companies in which each shares risky development costs until the venture becomes sufficiently established to attract more risk-averse and conventional sources of finance. The BTG is an attractive source of venture capital for small private sector companies because the BTG invests rather than lends funds, yet it does not require a share of the profits when the venture is successful. Instead, the BTG simply asks for repayment of the amount it has invested, plus an interest payment.

Nevertheless under the Conservative Government in the 1980s, the role of government and the public sector as a source of finance and funding for private sector firms has been greatly reduced. But the gap has been filled, so far as sources of venture capital are concerned, by the growth of over one hundred **private sector venture capital funds** and also, as we shall see in later sections of this chapter, by expansion of the capital market (via the creation of an **Unlisted Securities Market**) to meet the financing needs of small growing companies.

THE CAPITAL MARKET

8. The **capital market** is not a single institution. It comprises all the institutions, including banks, insurance companies and pension funds, which are concerned with either the supply of, or the demand for, long-term funds in the form of marketable financial assets or securities.

The capital market is commonly confused with **the Stock Exchange**. The Stock Exchange is indeed a most important part of the capital market, but it is only a part, and the capital market and Stock Exchange are not interchangeable terms. To understand this, we must divide the capital market into two; into a **new issues market** or **primary market**; and into a **secondary market** on which previously issued shares and bonds can be sold second hand. The Stock Exchange is the most important part of the secondary market.

THE NEW ISSUES MARKET

9. The relationship between the primary and the secondary parts of the capital market is illustrated in Figure 9.1. The actual raising of new capital or long-term finance takes place in the primary market when public companies (in the private sector of the economy) or the government (in the public sector) decide to issue and sell new marketable securities. Companies can sell long-dated securities known as **debentures** or **corporate bonds**, or they may sell an ownership stake in the company by issuing **shares** or **equity**. The sale of corporate bonds is a form of long-term borrowing in which the company extends its debt while the purchaser of the bond becomes a creditor of the company. New issues of shares may be sold when a company 'goes public' for the first time, or when an existing public company decides to raise extra capital with a new equity issue. In the latter case, the new share issue is most often a **rights issue**, in which the company's existing shareholders are given the right to buy the new issue of shares at a discount.

New issues of shares are seldom sold directly on the Stock Exchange, though occasionally small issues of new shares may be sold by being *placed* with Stock Exchange firms for sale to the general public. Instead, the new issues market takes place by direct sale to the general public, usually arranged by merchant banks via newspaper advertisements and the use of the postal services.

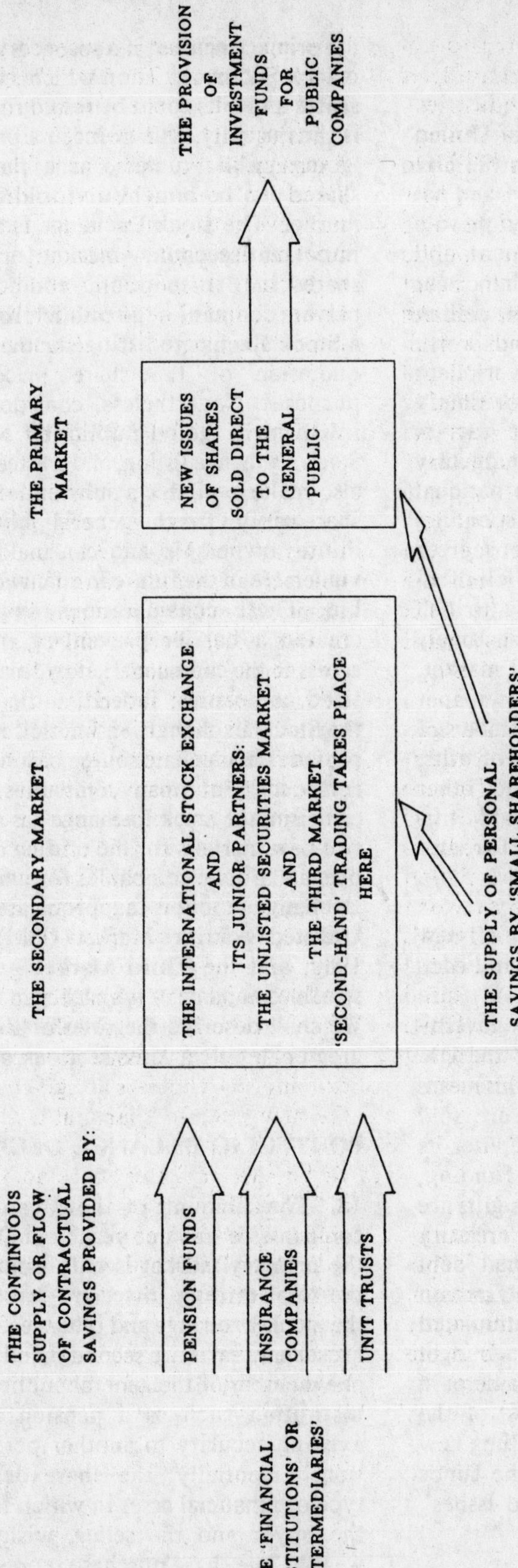

Figure 9.1: The Stock Exchange and the Wider Capital Market

THE GOVERNMENT AND THE CAPITAL MARKET

10. However, most of the new issues of United Kingdom securities sold each year on the UK capital market are government securities, and not shares or corporate bonds issued by private sector companies to finance investment and expansion. The government is the most important single operator on the capital market, selling each year new issues of government bonds worth several £billion. In the UK these government bonds are called **gilt-edged securities**, or simply **'gilts'**. Each year, the sale of new gilts is closely related to the government's budgetary position and to the need to renew the national debt. When, for example, government spending exceeds revenue from taxation and other sources by £5 billion, the resulting **budget deficit** of £5 billion has to be financed by borrowing. British governments have financed budget deficits largely through the sale of gilts on the capital market, arranging the sale in part through newspaper advertisements. But although ordinary members of the general public can buy new issues of gilts, most are sold to pension funds and other **financial institutions**, with any unsold gilts being bought by the Bank of England for later placement on the Stock Exchange.

Until recently, a significant fraction of new gilt sales financed the budget deficit, and each year the national debt increased in size approximately by the size of the current government deficit. However, since 1987/88 the UK government budget has been in **surplus**. This means that all current new issues of gilts are sold either to **renew the national debt** or to alter its composition (in a process known as **funding**, through which long-dated debt such as gilts are sold to replace short-dated debt such as Treasury bills). The need to renew the national debt results from the fact that each year a fraction of the government's historically accumulated stock of debt matures. In the event of a budget surplus, part of the maturing debt can be paid off from tax revenues. However, most of the repayment is usually made simply by selling new issues of debt such as gilts to raise the funds with which to repay the maturing 'old issues'.

THE STOCK EXCHANGE

11. Companies, and indeed the government, would find it very difficult to sell new securities on the primary market, if a secondary or secondhand market did not exist on which existing issues of shares and gilts could be resold for money. There is thus usually little point in a private company 'going public' unless, as a public company, shares can be bought and sold on a secondary market. The Stock Exchange is by far the most important secondary market for the trading of shares in British public companies, so when private companies 'go public', they usually seek a **Stock Exchange listing** for their shares and a **quotation** of the share price for trading purposes. Nevertheless, considerable costs are involved in 'going public' by obtaining a full Stock Exchange listing, and a listed company must also make available a substantial fraction of its share capital for the general public to buy. This dilutes ownership and can make the company vulnerable in the future to an unwelcome takeover bid. These considerations have in the past created a barrier preventing or discouraging access to the capital market by small and medium-sized companies. Indeed, until quite recently, the Stock Exchange was criticised for failing to provide an adequate source of long-term finance for successful small companies. To meet this criticism, the Stock Exchange has now established two new markets for the trading of shares issued by small public companies for whom a full Stock Exchange listing is inappropriate. These are the **Unlisted Securities Market (USM)**, established in 1980, and the **Third Market** - aimed at even smaller companies - which began trading in 1987. We shall describe the roles of these markets in greater detail in later sections of this chapter.

PORTFOLIO BALANCE DECISIONS

12. The amount of new capital raised by companies in any one year through new issues on the primary market is only a small fraction of the total trading in second-hand securities on the Stock Exchange and other secondary markets. Most share sales are second-hand deals in which one member of the general public (or a financial institution such as a pension fund) sells an existing security to another person or institution. Essentially, the share deal adjusts the type of financial asset in which the two parties, the buyer and the seller, wish to hold their wealth. The share purchase represents a decision to hold a dividend-earning financial asset instead of money, with the purchaser 'moving out of money' and into securities. By contrast, the person or institution selling the security makes the opposite decision - moving out of securities and 'into money'. Such decisions to alter the form in which a stock of wealth is held are called **portfolio balance decisions** or **portfolio adjustment decisions.** All of us make portfolio balance decisions often without realising it, as we go about our normal business and day-to-day activity. A decision to withdraw £20 in cash from a bank deposit is a simple example of wealth adjustment, as would be the decision made by a multinational corporation at the other end of the wealth spectrum to sell 1,000 million Deutschmarks to finance the purchase of US dollars.

THE ROLE OF THE STOCK EXCHANGE IN THE UK ECONOMY

13. As we have noted, the Stock Exchange is essentially a second-hand market on which - through the intermediary of market makers known as stock brokers - purchasers of shares who wish to 'move out of money' and into securities, arrange a trade with sellers who are making the opposite portfolio adjustment decision. We cannot emphasise too strongly that whenever second-hand shares are traded on the Stock Exchange, funds ARE NOT made available for companies to use for investment purposes. Indeed, because the Stock Exchange is simply a second-hand market, and because many of the motives for buying and selling shares are speculative, the market is often criticised for being little more than a casino in which dealers trade shares and other securities for the essentially 'short-term' motive of making quick capital gains and avoiding capital losses. Along with other financial markets in the City of London, the Stock Exchange stands accused by its detractors for being a place for the 'making of money' rather than the 'making of things'. These critics regard the Stock Exchange as a symbol of the British malaise for sacrificing the needs of the 'real economy', in which 'useful' goods and services are produced, to the needs of finance and speculation created in the City.

Nevertheless, the Stock Exchange does perform the following very important *indirect* roles in the provision of long-term capital for firms and the promotion of efficiency in the economy:

(i) As we have already explained, when a private company 'goes public', its principal objective is usually to tap a source of relatively cheap long-term finance by securing access to the capital market. But new issues of shares would attract few buyers without the existence of an efficient second-hand market upon which to resell the shares. The Stock Exchange provides such a market and ensures the success of the primary or new issues market.

(ii) Public confidence in companies listed by the Stock Exchange is increased because of the regulatory and policing roles of the Stock Exchange Council. The Council examines the financial structure and control of all quoted companies, and is prepared to suspend the quotation of a company suspected of fraud or malpractice.

(iii) The general level of share prices quoted on the Stock Exchange acts as a barometer of the general public's confidence in companies, and perhaps also of its confidence in government economic policy and the general business environment.

(iv) The Stock Exchange, together with the wider capital market, plays an important role in the restructuring of the British economy to meet changed circumstances. Because of the imperfect nature of many *product markets* or *goods markets*, industries and firms may be rather slow to respond to changed conditions of supply or demand. Market forces operating in product markets may, therefore, produce only a rather sluggish process of change to meet new conditions. But a rather more rapid process of change and adjustment may be triggered by 'market discipline' originating within the *capital market*. Highly imperfect and monopolistic goods markets are usually dominated by large public companies, whose share prices are quoted on the Stock Exchange. Bad company performance reduces profits and also the share price, making the company vulnerable to a takeover bid from a 'raider' who believes he can manage the company's assets more profitably. The process of acquisition on the capital market - or often merely the threat of an unwelcome takeover bid - provides a mechanism for the rationalisation, restructuring and modernisation of the British economy. If the Stock Exchange did not function as an efficient market in secondhand shares, an important source of market discipline and spur to change would therefore be absent from the United Kingdom economy.

THE ROLE OF THE FINANCIAL INSTITUTIONS

14. Many people falsely believe that a large proportion of the ordinary shares or equity of British public companies are owned by personal shareholders (or small shareholders), who are ordinary members of the general public. While this was once true, it has not been the case since the 1960s.

Table 9.1 below shows that private individuals now own directly well under half of all shares, whereas the financial institutions own the greater, and a growing, proportion. British banks own almost no equity because they regard shares as being too illiquid (in the sense that they might have to be sold on a falling market) for the purpose of matching bank assets against their essentially short-term deposit liabilities. Nevertheless, banks effectively control a substantial amount of equity by taking on a management role for many pension funds, and they also give portfolio advice to ordinary bank customers.

The growth of the financial institutions as major shareholders in public companies is largely explained by the growth of **contractual**, as distinct from **non-contractual**, saving. Non-contractual saving takes place when a person simply sets aside part of his income in a bank or building society deposit, or perhaps in a hoard of cash. Such non-contractual savings tend to be short term, savings being accumulated to finance intended spending in a few weeks or months time, for example at Christmas or upon a summer holiday. By contrast, contractual saving occurs when an individual makes a contract to save regularly with a financial institution such as a pension fund or an insurance company. The principal motive for entering a savings contract is usually long term, for example to finance retirement and to protect the saver's dependents against the financial problems that would result from the saver's early death. Contractual savings also allow a saver to spread risks. Instead of directly purchasing the shares of just a single company or a narrow range of companies, the saver invests indirectly in a much wider range of shares and securities by supplying his savings to a fund that gathers together the savings of a very large number of contributing individuals. The fund managers spread risks by investing all the contributions in a diverse portfolio of shares and securities.

The growing concentration of share ownership in the hands of the financial institutions which has resulted from contractual saving, is sometimes justified as being in the public interest because it represents the spread of *indirect* ownership of shares by ordinary workers - via their weekly or monthly contributions to pensions funds and life insurance schemes. But while it is true that workers receive the benefits of pension and life insurance endowments or pay-outs financed from company profits, it is the financial institutions or intermediaries - and not the workers - who possess the real ownership stake and control in the companies whose shares they have bought with employees' contributions. And the growing share ownership of the financial institutions is also an undoubted cause of imperfection in the capital market, since a relatively few financial institutions now own a large proportion of all company shares. The role of the financial institutions as shareholders has been criticised on three main grounds:

Table 9.1: The ownership of company shares (percentages)

	1963	*1975*	*1981*	*1983*
Persons and charities	56.0	39.8	30.4	27.0
Insurance companies	10.1	16.0	20.5	22.0
Pension funds	6.5	16.8	26.7	29.0
Investment trusts	11.2	10.6	6.8	6.0
Unit trusts	1.4	4.0	3.6	4.0
Banks	1.4	0.7	0.3	-
Industrial and commercial companies	5.1	2.9	5.1	5.0
Public sector	1.4	3.6	3.0	3.0
Overseas holders	6.9	5.6	3.6	4.0
	100.0	100.0	100.0	100.0

(i) The institutions have failed to act as a source of venture capital for small high risk companies, preferring instead to channel their huge volume of contractual savings into 'safe bets', eg the shares of large established 'blue chip' companies and gilts.

(ii) The financial institutions have failed to use the voting power - which the ownership of large blocks of company shares provides - to ensure good management decisions. While in principle the institutions have the voting power to encourage management teams to adopt a long-term perspective, in practice they may seldom use it in this way. Indeed, the opposite may well be true. Many company takeover bids - far from acting as a mechanism for the necessary and sensible restructuring of the economy in the manner we described in the previous section - are mounted for essentially short-term speculative motives. The role of institutional shareholders may encourage this. Company directors often control their companies only because they have the support of large institutional shareholders. In the event of an unwelcome or hostile takeover raid, institutional shareholders may sell their shares to the acquiring company, not because they believe that the 'raider' can manage the 'victim's' assets any better in the long run, but simply in order to make a short-term profit for the institution's fund. Indeed, the growth of the financial power of institutional shareholders in the UK may cause the directors and managers of the controlled companies to foresake long-term investment in research and product development, in favour of a short-term strategy to boost the company's share price so as to fend off 'unfriendly' takeover bids.

(iii) The short-term motives of the financial institutions which we have just described may be exacerbated by the '*herd*' *behaviour* they sometimes display. 'Herd' behaviour occurs when, in quick succession, the financial institutions adopt an identical view of the market, not because they all possess equal insight, but because they dare not risk not following each other. A 'herd' movement by the institutions into or out of a particular company's shares can bring about dramatic changes in the share price. In the event of a sudden and massive fall in the share price, the company may be severely destabilised and 'put into play', in the sense that its lower share price then attracts unwelcome takeover bids.

'POPULAR CAPITALISM'

15. During the 1980s the Conservative Government in the United Kingdom has attempted to reverse the trend we have just described for a growing proportion of the share capital of British public companies to be owned by financial institutions. The government has encouraged the spread of a **'popular capitalism'** based on wider personal share ownership. 'Popular capitalism' has been encouraged in two main ways:

(i) **Through the programme of privatisation.** Nationalised industries such as British Gas and British Telecom have been converted into public companies. The government has then preceded to privatise the nationalised industry by selling off at least 51 per cent of the company's equity through a floatation on the capital market. But in contrast to a conventional new issue of shares, the revenue raised has gone to the government - in return for the company's assets - and not to the privatised company itself. In the case of most of the privatisations, the government has tried to ensure that a significant fraction of the newly floated shares are bought by private shareholders rather than by the financial institutions. The government has also tried to extend share ownership in newly privatised industries to employees, both to encourage a 'responsible' work force and to increase the proportion of the country's population directly owning shares. But while in the short run the major privatisations have undoubtedly increased both the number of private shareholders and the proportion of total company shares owned by individuals, the long-term effect is likely to be smaller, perhaps failing to reverse the trend towards ever-greater institutional ownership of shares. A significant proportion of the private buyers of newly issued shares are interested only in making a quick profit by reselling their shares - usually to the financial institutions - as soon as 'second-hand' trading in the shares begins on the Stock Exchange a few days after floatation.

(ii) **Through extending tax advantages to private shareholders**. The government has introduced legislation to allow the setting up of **Personal Equity Plans (PEPs)**, which enable private shareholders to obtain considerable tax relief each year from share purchases.

THE FINANCING OF SMALL FIRMS

16. Access to the capital market has always tended to be restricted to public companies, especially those with a full Stock Exchange listing. Most small firms, being sole traders, partnerships, or private companies, must therefore rely on bank borrowing as their principal source of external finance, since they cannot raise funds by a share sale to the general public. Small businesses often complain that banks treat them less favourably than large companies when providing term loans and overdraft facilities. This view was supported by the **Wilson Committee on the Financing of Small Firms**, which published its findings in 1979. In particular, the requirement that the owner of a small business must secure a loan with personal assets, deters precisely the spirit of risk and enterprise which ought to be fostered in small companies by their limited liability status. Nevertheless, there are several reasons why banks consider that loans to small businesses are riskier than loans to large companies, requiring therefore greater security, and possibly a higher interest charge. These are:

(i) In comparison to large companies, small businesses are often much newer, lacking a successful and proven track record.

(ii) Small businesses are more likely to rely on the entrepreneurial flair of a single individual, who may be irreplaceable. While large businesses may lack this flair, banks perceive them as more solid and less risky, in part because they employ large management teams who enjoy a managerial division of labour, while simultaneously being less vulnerable to the decisions, or the departure, of one member of the management team.

(iii) Large firms are usually more diversified. If one investment or new product fails, the likelihood that others will succeed reduces the chance of insolvency. In any case, large firms are more likely to have cash reserves, or ready assets for sale, to draw upon in just such a crisis.

(iv) Large public companies are less highly *geared* than private companies and unincorporated businesses. A company's **gearing ratio** measures the business's borrowings or debt as a ratio of shareholders' funds. A high gearing ratio means that a large proportion of the company's assets are financed by borrowing rather than by shareholders' funds (shares and accumulated profits). High gearing renders a firm more vulnerable to insolvency when business is bad, because of the increased possibility that the firm may fail to generate a sufficient cash flow from sales to finance the payment of a fixed rate of interest on its outstanding debt. In contrast a lowly-geared public company, which has financed growth and long-term investment through extending its share capital rather than through borrowing, is much less vulnerable to insolvency. It can survive a recession simply by reducing or suspending the payment of dividends to share holders, though this may of course make the company more vulnerable - via a low share price - to the unwelcome attentions of a takeover raider. Small businesses are usually highly geared because they rely on borrowing and possess little equity capital. Thus when a bank considers whether to lend to a small business, it may simply regard the venture as too risky in comparison to lending to a lowly-geared large public company.

NEW SOURCES OF FINANCE FOR SMALL BUSINESSES

17. In recent years British governments have introduced a number of new measures designed to ease the problem of financing the start-up and the growth of small businesses. These measures reflect the view, accepted by all major political parties, that small businesses can play an extremely useful role in the economy by filling the gap in both output and jobs created by the decline of larger firms in older industries. And as we have seen in recent years, the Conservative Government has had a special reason for encouraging the growth of small businesses; to promote the '*popular capitalism*' and '*enterprise economy*' to which we referred in a previous section.

The three principal measures introduced in the 1980s to encourage small businesses have been **the Enterprise Allowance Scheme; the Business Expansion Scheme** and the **Small Firms Loan Guarantee Scheme.**

(1) **The Enterprise Allowance Scheme.** This scheme is designed to encourage and help unemployed workers to start up their own small businesses, usually as sole traders. Besides providing a rather limited source of finance for new businesses (£40 per week per individual assisted in 1987), by giving a weekly grant to replace unemployment benefit, the EAS creates an incentive for the unemployed to seek self-employment without suffering a financial penalty which the loss of unemployment benefit would otherwise entail.

(ii) **The Business Expansion Scheme.** The BES gives substantial tax relief to wealthy individuals who invest in small unquoted companies providing they hold on to their shares for at least five years.

(iii) **The Small Firms Loan Guarantee Scheme.** The SFLGS encourages banks to lend to small firms which possess little security. Currently, the government guarantees 70 per cent of a loan granted by a bank to a small business under the LGS, which means that if the firm fails and is unable to repay the loan, the government pays 70 per cent of the bad debt. However, banks are now required to charge a 5 per cent premium on top of their 'normal' interest rates, and this has greatly reduced the attraction of the Loan Guarantee Scheme for small firms.

THE UNLISTED SECURITIES MARKET

18. In recent years the Conservative Government has tried to develop private sources for finance for small businesses, so as to reduce the need for state funding. For the 'larger' small business, the main development has been the establishment by the Stock Exchange of the **Unlisted Securities Market (USM)** in 1980. The USM has become the most important single source of equity capital for small firms, though it remains tiny by comparison with the main market, the full Stock Exchange. The USM was established in response to the criticism made by the Wilson Committee in the late 1970s that the difficulty and expense of achieving a full Stock Exchange listing were preventing the growth of potentially successful small firms. The USM now makes it much easier and less costly for a relatively small private company to 'go public' and gain access to the capital market. The main attractions of the USM to the owners of a private company who are contemplating 'going public' are:

(i) Because USM listed companies need sell only 10 per cent of their shares to the general public (compared to 25 per cent in the case of a full Stock Exchange listing), less dilution of ownership takes place. The company is therefore less likely to become vulnerable to an 'unwelcome' takeover bid.

(ii) Only a three year trading record is necessary for a company to 'go public' on the USM, compared to five years for a full Stock Exchange listing.

(iii) A USM listing provides a means for the company's owners to place a market value on their personal wealth or stake in the company.

(iv) The floatation costs are much lower than for a full Stock Exchange listing.

Because of these advantages, the USM has been a great success since its inception in 1980. The most important function of the USM has been to provide a 'half-way-house', through which successfully growing small and medium-sized businesses such as Amstrad can pass, on their way to an eventual full Stock Exchange listing.

THE THIRD MARKET AND THE 'OVER-THE COUNTER' MARKET

19. Although the Unlisted Securities Market has been successful in assisting the growth of 'larger' small-sized companies, it was never intended to provide a forum for the public launch of really small enterprises. We have already noted in Section 7 of this chapter how specialist long-term funding institutions such as '3i' exist to provide venture capital for such small, and often high-risk businesses. Indeed, in recent years over 100 special **venture capital funds** have come into existence which can invest and inject capital into upstart small businesses. These new venture capital funds reflect the success of the USM, since the ability of new businesses to enter the USM after three years speeds up the process by which the providers of venture capital can cash in on their risks. But by no means all companies 'go public' by obtaining a listing on one of the two major markets, the USM or the full Stock Exchange. In the 1980s a small **'Over-the-Counter'(OTC) market** developed in the UK, in which shares of public companies are traded through securities firms which operate high street **'share shops'**. The OTC securities firms are completely independent of the **International Stock Exchange** which operates the London Stock Exchange, the USM, the Third Market and other security markets such as the market in traded options. But in contrast to the USA, where about 90 per cent of all company shares are now traded in OTC 'share shops' which have proliferated in American shopping centres, the OTC market in the UK is still very small. The OTC market has remained a risky and highly speculative market, dominated by the trade in the shares of small public companies which have preferred to remain unquoted so as to qualify for BES assistance. In 1987 the shares of more than 220 companies with a total capitalisation of over £660 million were traded on the OTC market (this compares to the 2,500 companies capitalised at over £1,100 billion in 1987 listed on the full Stock Exchange and more than 500 companies passing through the USM, capitalised at over £5 billion).

In 1987 the Stock Exchange decided to set its own new market, the **Third Market**, specifically designed to compete with the OTC market. The Third Market is a lightly regulated forum for the shares of small, speculative companies. However, it is a more liquid and disciplined market than the OTC market, which has suffered from a series of scandals involving the closure of some of the 20 or so licensed security dealers who previously comprised the market. The Third Market is intended to function as a junior market to both the full Stock Exchange and the USM. Entry requirements to the Third Market are very light.

'BULL' AND 'BEAR' MARKETS

20. When share prices are rising, the market is known as a **'bull market'**. Conversely, falling share prices indicate a **'bear market'**. (Specifically, a **'bull'** is a speculator who gambles on a rising share market, hoping to make a capital gain by buying shares now which can be resold later at a higher price. 'Bearish' speculation occurs on a falling market, the **'bear'** moving out of shares and into money in order to avoid a capital loss. A third type of speculation involves *'stagging'* a new issue; the **'stag'** buys the new issue at its offer price, hoping to make a capital gain by, reselling at a higher price when 'secondhand' trading starts on the Stock Exchange a few days later.)

The general level of share prices is of great importance in determining whether it is attractive both for private companies to 'go public', and also for existing public companies to make new share issues. Rising share prices mean that new issues can be sold at higher prices, so that a particular share issue will raise more capital than would be the case at a lower level of share prices. Bull markets, such as the spectacular rising share market which existed world-wide from the mid-1970s to the **stock market crash of October 1987**, tend therefore to be associated with a growing business confidence and an increase in the number of public floatations and new share issues. But besides fuelling an increase in business confidence, an extended bull market may lead eventually to a damaging state of market euphoria in which speculators believe that they face the 'one-way bet' of ever-rising share prices. The resulting massive speculative demand for shares as the market feeds off itself, causes share prices to lose touch with the real economy, ie the profitability of the companies for which the shares are merely paper claims. Eventually the bubble bursts in a stock market collapse, perhaps heralding an extended period of bearish uncertainty in which sellers outnumber buyers. In the bear market there are fewer public floatations and new issues, since lower share prices make fund raising on the capital market more expensive.

SUMMARY

21. All firms require finance for their various activities. Short-term finance is used to pay for

the purchase of raw materials (circulating or working capital) and to pay wages; long-term sources of funds are used to finance the internal or external growth of the firm via direct investment in new fixed plant, or through a process of takeover and merger. For all types of business enterprise, self-finance or the ploughing back of profits (internal finance) is by far the most important source of finance, though the ability to engage successfully in self-finance depends upon profitability.

The main external sources of finance can be divided into borrowing (or debt), and the raising of capital by share issue. Bank loans, in the form of overdrafts and term loans, provide the main source of short-term borrowing; while firms must usually gain entry to the capital market both to borrow long term (through the sale of corporate bonds) and to raise money from the general public by a sale of ordinary shares or equity. In general, for a firm to gain access to the capital market (in which the Stock Exchange is the main secondary market), the firm must be a public company. Private companies (which cannot tap the capital market to any large extent, because their shares are not on general sale) are usually more highly geared than public companies, ie the ratio of their debt to share capital is much larger. Until recently entry barriers to the capital market were a major impediment preventing or slowing the growth of potentially successful small firms which required a capital injection. To make it easier for such small companies to grow and eventually graduate to the full Stock Exchange, the Stock Exchange Council created the Unlisted Securities Market (in 1980) and the Third Market (in 1987). These new markets were established during a world-wide 'bull' market of rising share prices, which extended for over a decade until October 1987. By making capital raising through new share issue into a relatively cheap source of finance, the 'bull' market increased the importance of stock markets and public quotations during this period. However, the world-wide stock market crash of October 1987 may well have ushered in a new era of bear markets, which, by creating greater uncertainty and eroding the paper value of shareholders' wealth, may reduce business confidence and threaten a world recession. But at the time of writing (August 1989), a world recession has yet to materialise.

STUDENT SELF-TESTING

1. *Distinguish between saving and investment.* *(2)*
2. *What is meant by internally financed investment?* *(3)*
3. *Why do firms need different types of finance?* *(4)*
4. *What is the main form of short-term finance?* *(5)*
5. *What is medium-term finance used for?* *(6)*
6. *List four sources of long-term finance?* *(7)*
7. *Define the capital market.* *(8)*
8. *Distinguish between the New Issues market and the Stock Exchange.* *(9 and 11)*
9. *What is the role of the government in the capital market?* *(10)*
10. *What is a portfolio balance decision?* *(12)*
11. *What is the role of the Stock Exchange in the UK economy?* *(13)*
12. *Who owns most shares?* *(14)*
13. *What is 'popular capitalism'?* *(15)*
14. *How has the Government improved the finance of small businesses?* *(17)*
15. *Why was the Unlisted Securities Market created?* *(18)*
16. *Distinguish between the Third Market and the 'Over-The-Counter' market.* *(19)*
17. *How may a 'bear' market affect capital raising by firms?* *(20)*

EXERCISES

1. *In March 1988, the Oriental Oil Company, PLC, declared a 50 pence dividend on each of its £1 ordinary shares. At the time, the market rate of interest (and the average yield on ordinary shares quoted on the Stock Exchange) was 5%.*

   (a) *Assuming no other influence upon share prices, beyond the information already given, at what market price would Oriental's ordinary shares trade at?*

   (b) *What other factors may, in a real world situation, also influence share prices?*

MULTIPLE CHOICE QUESTIONS

1. *A public limited company declares a yearly dividend of 25p on each £1 share. Assuming that the stock market is a perfect market and that the market rate of interest is 20 per cent, the market price of the company's shares will now be:*

   A £1.00
   B £1.25
   C £2.00
   D £2.50

2. *Which of the following financial assets does not secure a loan?*

   A A corporate bond
   B An ordinary share
   C A gilt-edged security
   D A National Saving Security

3. *Which of the following is not issued by a public limited joint stock company as a way of raising capital?*

   A Debentures
   B Ordinary shares
   C Equity
   D Gilt-edged securities

4. *Mr Z owns government stock which has a nominal value of £800 yielding interest of £45 per year. If the market value of the stock falls to £600, the effective rate of interest is:*

   A 5 per cent
   B 7.5 per cent
   C 10 per cent
   D Indeterminate unless the return from other investments is known.

EXAMINATION QUESTIONS

1. (a) *What is the role of the Stock Exchange?* (6 marks)
   (b) *What do share price indices show?*
   (c) *What may determine the price of the shares of an individual company?* (7 marks)
   (CIMA November 1986)

2. *What institutions constitute the Capital Market? Explain their relative importance.*
   (CIMA November 1984)

3. *Identify and comment on the role of institutional investors, such as insurance companies, pension funds or unit trusts. How far does this role affect the functions of the entrepreneur?* (CIMA May 1983)

4. *What are the main sources of finance for private industry? How has the UK government (or overseas government) attempted to influence the provision of such finance?*
   (AAT June 1983)

5. (a) *What do you understand by the term gearing (or leverage) in relation to the financing of a company?*
   (5 marks)

   (b) *What factors would a firm be likely to take into account in determining which source of finance to utilise when expanding its business?*
   (15 marks)
   (AAT December 1981)

10. Industrial Policy

INTRODUCTION

1. In this chapter we examine the meaning of **industrial policy** and assess the effectiveness of the industrial policy implemented by the United Kingdom government in recent years. We begin the chapter by considering how governments of opposing economic and political philosophy have adopted a markedly different approach and strategy to the problems of industry. We then examine three important elements of industrial policy - **competition policy**; **private versus public ownership** of industry; and **regional policy** - before concluding the chapter with a discussion of the policy mix appropriate for tackling perhaps the most important recent industrial problem: the problem of **deindustrialisation**, or the decline of manufacturing industry.

THE BACKGROUND TO INDUSTRIAL POLICY

2. Industrial policy is part of the government's **micro-economic policy** which aims to improve the economic performance of individual economic agents, firms and industries on the **'supply-side'** of the economy. Since the 1930s, when industrial policy first began as a response to the Great Depression, all British governments have had some sort of industrial policy. However, significant changes have occurred in the nature of the policy, and also in the importance attached by different governments to industrial policy in comparison to other aspects of economic policy. The most far-reaching changes have occurred since the 1970s with the decline of **Keynesianism** as the prevailing economic orthodoxy, and the ascendancy of **monetarism** and the **neo-classical revival.**

For much of the period from 1945 until 1979, successive British governments pursued an **interventionist industrial policy**, which reflected the Keynesian view that economic problems result from a failure of market forces, and that the problems can be cured (or at least reduced) by appropriate government intervention. During the Keynesian era, industrial policy (and Keynesian economic policy in general) extended the roles of government and state planning in the economy. By contrast, the current Conservative Government's industrial policy is essentially **anti-interventionist** and based on the belief that the correct role of government is not to reduce the role of market forces, but to create the conditions in which market forces can work effectively and efficiently.

But although the Conservative Government has disbanded an interventionist industrial policy in favour of a more free-market approach, the importance attached to industrial policy in the government's overall economic strategy has increased in recent years. During the Keynesian era, industrial policy and micro-economic policy were generally subordinate and subservient to macro-economic policy. Keynesian **macro-economic policy** was aimed overwhelmingly at the **'demand-side'** of the economy, attempting to influence and control output and employment by managing the level of aggregate demand in the economy. But monetarists believe that Keynesian demand management policies led to inflation rather than to full employment and economic growth. They also believe that the almost exclusive Keynesian concern with **demand management** served to divert attention away from the 'supply-side' of the economy, where the real problems that stand in the way of increased output and employment must be tackled. It is perhaps not surprising therefore, that since the **monetarist** or **neo-classical 'counter-revolution'** of the 1970s, Keynesian 'demand-side' economic policy has been abandoned, and macro-economic policy is now generally subordinate to a **'supply-side' micro-economic policy** in which industrial policy has been elevated to a key position.

COMPETITION POLICY

3. For over forty years, since its inception in 1948, **competition policy** has formed an important part of the UK government's wider industrial policy. Competition policy is the part of industrial policy that covers **monopolies, mergers** and **restrictive trading practices**, and we shall now look at each of these in turn.

STATUTORY MONOPOLY

4. **Monopoly policy** in the UK is seldom concerned with pure monopoly - rather it attempts to regulate highly concentrated industries dominated by a few large firms. As we have seen in earlier chapters, a **pure monopoly** exists when one firm produces 100 per cent of the output in a well-defined market. But because of the existence of substitute products, monopoly is a relative rather than an absolute term. Indeed, there are few pure monopolies in the UK economy, the most complete examples being the **'natural' monoplies** in the field of **utility industries** such as gas, electricity and water provision. For policy purposes, the UK government defines monopoly in a looser way. Since 1973 a **statutory monopoly** has existed if: either one firm has at least 25 per cent of the market for the supply or acquisition of particular goods and services (a **scale monopoly**); or a number of firms, which together have a 25 per cent share, so conduct their affairs as to restrict competition (a **complex monopoly**).

THE THEORETICAL BACKGROUND TO MONOPOLY POLICY

5. In earlier chapters we have seen how economic efficiency and output are likely to be maximised, and consumer sovereignty and welfare promoted, when industries and markets are **perfectly competitive**. This provides the theoretical basis of the government's policy towards monopoly, mergers and restrictive trading practices. Compared to a perfectly competitive market, monopolies may be expected to reduce output and raise prices, and they may have less incentive to innovate. Monopolies may also exploit their producer sovereignty by manipulating consumer wants, restricting choice and by discriminating 'unfairly' between different groups of customers.

Nevertheless, as we have also seen, the argument that monopolies restrict output and raise prices assumes that monopolies and perfectly competitive firms have similar cost curves. When **economies of scale** are possible, this is unlikely to be the case. Indeed, a **'natural' monopoly** is said to exist when limited market size makes it impossible for more than one firm to benefit from full economies of scale. (In a similar way, **'natural oligopoly'** is promoted when there is only room in the market for a few firms enjoying full economies of scale.) The splitting-up of a 'natural' monopoly such as the gas industry, into a large number of competitive firms, would lead to unnecessary duplication of costly distribution networks. There is thus a strong case for these industries to continue to be organised as monopolies. The **public policy choice** is not so much between competition and monopoly; rather it is a choice between **state monopolies** run as nationalised industries, and **private monopoly** subject to severe and effective public regulation.

CARTELS AND FULLY-UNIFIED MONOPOLIES

6. We have already noted that monopolies may have less incentive to innovate than competitive industries because of the protective barriers surrounding them. Whether innovation is likely to be increased or diminished by monopoly will depend to some extent upon the reason for the creation of the monopoly. It is useful to divide monopolies into:

(a) **Cartels.** A cartel is usually regarded as the worst form of monopoly from the public interest point of view, since it is likely to exhibit most of the disadvantages of monopoly with few, if any, of the benefits. A cartel is a **price ring** which is formed when independent firms make a restrictive agreement to charge the same price, and possibly to restrict output. A cartel acts as a monopoly in the marketing of goods, but the benefits of economies of scale are unlikely to occur because the physical or technical integration of the productive capacity of the members of the cartel does not take place. Consumer choice is restricted, and cartels tend to keep inefficient firms in business while the more efficient members of the cartel make monopoly profits. In these circumstances, it is probable that the incentive to innovate by developing new products and methods of production will indeed be lacking. Cartels are thus **dynamically inefficient.**

(b) **Fully-unified monopoly.** A fully-unified or fully-integrated monopoly may result from accident rather than design. A dynamic firm grows and benefits from economies of scale, becoming a monopoly as the reward for successful competition! The monopoly position is the end result of the firm's success in innovating, reducing costs and introducing new products - all of which indicate that the firm is dynamically efficient. A fully-unified monopoly is thus likely to be the 'spin-off' of essentially 'benign' motives for growth. Once the monopoly has been established, the firm may continue to behave well, retaining its innovating habits and using its monopoly profit to finance new developments, though government regulation may be necessary to ensure continued 'good behaviour'.

THE COST-BENEFIT APPROACH OF MONOPOLY POLICY

7. Because it is recognised that monopoly can be good or bad depending upon circumstances, UK monopoly policy has always taken the essentially pragmatic view that each case of a monopoly or a trading practice that restricts competition must be judged on its merits. If the likely costs resulting from the reduction of competition exceed the benefits, monopoly should be prevented, but if the likely benefits exceed the costs, monopoly should be permitted, provided the monopoly does not abuse its position and exploit the consuming public.

THE MONOPOLIES AND MERGERS COMMISSION AND THE OFFICE FAIR TRADING

8. UK monopoly policy is implemented by the **Office of Fair Trading (OFT)** and the **Monopolies and Mergers Commission (MMC)**, which are responsible to a government ministry, the **Department of Trade and Industry (DTI)**. The OFT uses **market structure, conduct and performance indicators** to systematically scan or screen the UK economy for evidence of monopoly abuse. Concentration ratios provide evidence of monopolistic market structures, while market conduct indicators allow the OFT to monitor anti-competitive business behaviour. **Conduct indicators** include:

(i) consumer and trade complaints;
(ii) evidence of parallel pricing, price discrimination and price leadership;
(iii) evidence of merger activity; and
(iv) the ratio of advertising expenditure to sales.

The four main **performance indicators** used to measure business efficiency are:

(i) price movements;
(ii) changes in profit margins;
(iii) the ratio of capital employed to turnover; and
(iv) the return on capital employed.

When the OFT discovers evidence of statutory monopoly which, prima facie, it believes is likely to be against the public interest, the Office refers the firms involved to the MMC for further investigation. In most cases, the OFT asks the MMC to decide the relatively narrow issue of whether a particular trading practice is in the public interest and not to address the wider issue of whether the firm should be split up. The MMC interprets the public interest largely in terms of the effect upon competitiveness of the trading practices it is asked to investigate. The Commission does not possess any powers to implement or enforce its recommendations. Instead, it reports to the DTI, which may either implement some or all of the recommendations, shelve the report and do nothing, or take action completely contrary to the MMC's recommendations. For example, in 1989 the MMC recommended in its report into monopoly in the brewing industry, that the major breweries should be forced to sell off all public houses they own in excess of 2,000. However the government eventually rejected this recommendation. Usually however, the government complies with the spirit of the MMC's report. The government has quite wide powers to take action, including the power to make an order requiring that firms split up or sell off assets. But in practice, these order-making powers are seldom if ever used. It is currently usual for the government to ask the OFT to talk with the firms involved to persuade them to alter their business behaviour voluntarily. Firms may be asked to abandon any undesirable practices, and to give undertakings about their future conduct.

THE REGULATORY APPROACH OF BRITISH MONOPOLY POLICY

9. Ever since the initial establishment of the Monopolies Commission in 1948, the UK has adopted an essentially **regulatory** and **investigatory**

approach to the problem of monopoly, watching out for monopoly abuse and investigating firms or industries where abuse or inefficiency is suspected. Relatively few firms and takeover bids are actually investigated - the policy rationale apparently being that the possibility of an MMC investigation creates sufficient incentive for most large firms to behave themselves and resist the temptation to exploit their monopoly power.

ALTERNATIVE STRATEGIC APPROACHES TO MONOPOLY POLICY

10. Although the 'watchdog' investigatory/ regulatory role of the MMC which we have just described has been central to UK monopoly policy, there are a number of alternative strategic approaches that might, in principle, be used to deal with the problem of monopoly. These include:

(i) **The compulsory breaking up of all monopolies.** Some free-market economists believe that only when the economy approximates closely to the conditions of perfect competition will the advantages of a free market economy, namely economic efficiency and consumer sovereignty, be achieved. Monopoly, per se, must be regarded as bad, and can never be justified. Therefore, the adoption of an **automatic policy rule to break up existing monopolies** is suggested by this approach. However, the UK policy-makers have never adopted a 'monopoly-busting' approach, though - as we have already noted - powers do exist which allow the government to order the break-up of an established monopoly. By contrast, United States anti-trust policy does require the break-up of firms with a very large share of the American market. However, the huge size of the US market has meant that most American firms can grow to a very large size by UK standards without dominating the domestic market and running the risk of being broken up by the American courts.

(ii) **The use of price controls to restrict monopoly abuse.** Although price controls have been used by British governments at various times to restrict the freedom of UK firms to set their own prices, they have usually been a part of a prices and incomes policy designed to control inflation, rather than a part of a specific policy to control monopoly abuse. Price controls of all types have generally been abandoned in the UK in recent years, since they are anathema to a free-market monetarist government. Nevertheless, restrictions have been imposed upon newly-privatised monopolies such as British Telecom, requiring that for a number of years, price rises must be below the rate of inflation.

(iii) **Taxing monopoly profits.** As well as controlling prices directly, a government could tax monopoly profits so as to create an incentive for monopolies to reduce prices and profits. However, monopoly taxes have not been used in the UK, except on a few occasions when a tax has been imposed on the 'windfall' gain that landlords receive when the land they own is made available for property development, and when 'windfall' profits received by banks from high interest rates have been subject to a special tax.

(iv) **The public ownership of monopoly.** British Labour governments have sometimes regarded the problem of monopoly as resulting essentially from private ownership and the pursuit of private profit. At its most simplistic, this view leads to the conclusion that the problem of monopoly disappears when the firms are nationalised or taken into public ownership, since the incentive for monopoly abuse disappears as soon as the monopolies start to operate in the 'public interest'.

(v) **Privatising monopolies.** In contrast to the socialist view that the problem of monopoly stems in large part from private ownership and the profit motive, recent Conservative governments have argued that state ownership produces particular forms of abuse that would not be experienced if the industries were privately owned. These include a general inefficiency and resistance to change which stem from the belief by workers and management in the state-run monopolies that they will always be baled out by government in the event of a loss. According to the Conservative view, monopoly abuse occurs in nationalised industries, not from the pursuit of private profit, but because the industries are run in the interest of a 'feather-bedded' workforce which is protected from any form of market discipline. The Conservatives believe the privatisation of state-owned monopoly should improve efficiency and commercial performance because privatisation exposes the industry to the threat of takeover and the discipline of the capital market.

(vi) **Removal of barriers to entry.** Nevertheless it is generally agreed that privatisation alone cannot eliminate the problem of monopoly abuse, since it merely changes the nature of the problem back to private monopoly and the commercial exploitation of a monopoly position. The fact that the privatisation of the telecommunication and gas monopolies has been accompanied by the setting up of regulatory bodies such as OFTEL and OFGAS, which provide a source of regulation additional to that available from the MMC and the OFT, is a recognition of this problem.

One method of exposing monopolies - including the newly-privatised utility industries - to increased competition, is to remove artificial barriers to entry. The government can remove the protected legal monopoly status enjoyed for example, by the Post Office for letter deliveries and by bus companies, airlines and commercial TV and radio companies. Access to British Telecom's distribution network of landlines can be given to a competitor such as Mercury Communications, and private power companies can be allowed to rent the services of the national electricity distribution grid. Import competition can also be encouraged. This can be quite effective in reducing the market power of public and private monopolies producing internationally-traded goods and services, but it would be less effective in reducing the monopoly power of utility industries whose products are not generally traded internationally, and consequently are not vulnerable to import competition.

THE THEORY OF 'CONTESTABLE' MARKETS

11. In recent years, much of the theoretical debate about the best way of dealing with monopoly abuse and regulating monopoly has centred upon the need to remove barriers to market entry. This reflects the growth of an important new theory known as **the theory of 'contestable' markets**. Before the advent of this theory (and of the wider neo-classical revival of which the theory of 'contestable' markets is a part), monopoly policy and other aspects of industrial policy involved an ever-increasing extension of regulation by government into the activities of private sector firms. Increased intervention was justified by the belief that regulatory powers must be strong enough to countervail the growing power of large business organisations and make monopolies behave in a more competitive fashion. But one unforeseen result of the spread of government regulation of industry has been that the powerful established firms that the system of regulation was intended to control have often been able to use the regulatory system to their own advantage. The beneficiaries of regulation have become the regulated firms themselves, rather than consumers or outside firms attempting to gain entry to the market. This has been possible because established large firms already within the market, possess political lobbying power to influence government and the regulators, and a monopoly of much technical information relevant to their industry.

Thus, although monopoly power is supposedly contained and controlled by government regulation, large firms have to an extent 'captured' and manipulated the regulatory system by bending regulations and the regulators to their own advantage. In effect, the 'regulated' have often become the 'regulators'.

In recognition of the often counter-productive results of merely increasing the amount of government regulation of industry, the current fashion is to adopt the opposite approach: namely to reduce the amount of regulation and intervention to the minimum thought absolutely necessary. The theory of 'contestable' markets provides a strong source of theoretical support for this 'minimalist' approach to regulatory policy.

Before the advent of the theory of 'contestable' markets, monopoly was normally defined by the number of firms in the market and by the share of the leading firms, measured by a concentration ratio. The basic problem or dilemma facing the policy makers centred on how to reconcile the potential gains in productive efficiency that a monopolist's large scale of operation can allow, with the fact that lack of competitive pressure can lead to monopoly abuse and consumer exploitation. But in the theory of 'contestable' markets, monopoly is defined, not by the number of firms in the market nor by concentration ratios, but rather by the potential ease or difficulty with which new firms may enter the market. Monopoly is not regarded as a problem, even if there is only one established firm in the market, providing that an absence of barriers to entry and exit creates *the potential* for new firms to enter and contest the market. Actual competition in a market is not essential; the threat of entry by new firms is quite sufficient according to the 'contestable' market theory to ensure efficient and non-exploitive behaviour by existing firms within the market.

The theory of 'contestable' markets has had a major impact upon recent UK monopoly policy under the Conservative Government, because it implies that, providing there is adequate potential for competition, a conventional regulatory policy is superfluous. Instead of interfering with firms' pricing and output policies, the government should restrict the role of its monopoly policy to discovering which industries and markets are potentially contestable, and then developing conditions, by removing barriers to entry and exit, to ensure that contestability is possible. Appropriate policies suggested by the theory of 'contestable' markets include:

(i) **the removal of licensing** regimes for public transport and TV and radio transmissions;

(ii) **removal of controls over ownership**, such as exclusive public ownership; and

(iii) **removal of pricing controls** which act as a barrier to entry, such as those practised in the aviation industry.

MERGER POLICY

12. United Kingdom merger policy has also reflected the influence of the theory of 'contestable' markets, since a merger is only referred by the government for investigation by the MMC if the OFT has advised that, prima facie, the merger might have significant anti-competitive effects. The OFT cannot itself make merger references to the MMC, but the Office has important screening and advisory roles. The OFT keeps informed of all merger situations that might be eligible for a reference to the MMC, by picking up information from the firms themselves and from the financial press. Currently a merger is eligible for reference by the government if the merger creates a combined company with at least 25 per cent of the market, or if the assets of the company being acquired are valued at £30m or more. It is generally assumed by the government that mergers are beneficial unless it can clearly be shown that the effects are likely to be adverse. In fact very few eligible mergers are investigated, and even fewer are declared against the public interest and prohibited. Critics argue that the policy is inconsistently applied and much too weak. They believe that the stance of merger policy should be significantly changed to a presumption that mergers have adverse rather than beneficial effects, and that factors such as the 'national interest' should be considered as well as anti-competitive effects, to prevent UK-owned firms falling into foreign hands.

RESTRICTIVE TRADING PRACTICE POLICY

13. Restrictive trading practices undertaken by firms in imperfect product markets can be divided into two broad kinds: those undertaken independently by a single firm, and collective restrictive practices which involve either a written or an implied agreement among two or more firms.

(i) **Independently undertaken restrictive practices**. In the UK there is no separate legislation dealing with independently undertaken restrictive practices, for example the **decision taken by a firm to charge discriminatory prices**, the **refusal to supply a particular resale outlet**, and **'full-line forcing'**, whereby a supplier forces a distributor who wishes to sell one of his products to stock the full range of his products. Instead such practices are covered by the monopoly policy we have already described - they are considered as evidence of anti-competitive market conduct or behaviour when the OFT decides on monopoly references. As we have seen, the MMC frequently recommends in its reports that firms drop any trading practices which offend the public interest.

(ii) **Collective restrictive practices.** In contrast to independently undertaken restrictive practices, collective restrictive agreements and practices can be referred by the OFT to a court of law, the **Restrictive Practice Court (RPC).** The current legal position is that a firm must register any restrictive agreement, such as a cartel agreement, with the OFT. The OFT then automatically notifies the RPC. The restrictive agreement is presumed to be illegal unless the firm can persuade the court that the practice is in the public interest. **Eight 'gateways'** or 'escape clauses' have been permitted, which allow a firm to argue that a restrictive agreement is in the public interest. For example, an agreement can be justified on public interest grounds if its removal might cause a substantial reduction in exports. Examples of restrictive collective agreements undertaken under cartel arrangements include: **limiting the supply of goods or services; standardising contractual terms of sale; fixing a standard selling price; purchasing raw materials at an agreed price in a 'common pool'; reciprocal trading,** whereby two firms agree to purchase each other's products exclusively; and **long-term contracts** tying a distributor exclusively to a supplier's product for a long period.

THE NEED TO MODERNISE RESTRICTIVE PRACTICE LEGISLATION

14. Some economists argue that the introduction of restrictive practice legislation in the 1950s was a major cause of takeover activity in the next three decades. Firms successfully circumvented the outlawing of collusive practices such as cartel agreements by **internalising** the restrictive practice through merger! However, it is now generally agreed that the current legislative framework is less effective than it ought to be and is in need of revision. The main weaknesses in the current system are:

(i) Once a collective agreement is registered, it can continue to operate lawfully until the RPC rules whether or not the agreement is in the 'public interest'. But in practice, it can take several years for an agreement to come to court, unless the OFT pushes for an early decision.

(ii) Companies are able to avoid prosecution by skilfully drafting an agreement to take advantage of the loopholes provided by the eight 'gateways' that allow a 'public interest' defence of an agreement.

(iii) The present laws are ineffective because of concessions granted to many industrial sectors, and in particular to the professions. There are currently 43 separate exemptions, ranging from agreements concerning the marketing of eggs to long-established restrictive practices within the professions.

(iv) Although agreements that are not registered are automatically declared illegal if uncovered by the OFT, all too often they remain uncovered. This is because the OFT's powers of investigation are limited. At present OFT officials can act only when they have firm evidence that a cartel exists - evidence which is usually provided by a disgruntled ex-member of the cartel.

(v) The maximum fines that the RPC can impose upon guilty firms are much too small to act as effective deterrent to misbehaviour. The maximum fines bear no relation to the scale of cartel agreements.

THE PROPOSED CHANGES IN RESTRICTIVE PRACTICE LEGISLATION

15. In 1988 the UK government published a Green Paper outlining proposed changes to up date restrictive trading practice policy in the light of the weaknesses in the present policy which we have just discussed. The proposed changes are:

(i) **The 'public interest' defence of a collective restrictive agreement is to be abolished, to be replaced by a general prohibition of any agreements deemed by the OFT to be anti-competitive.** The OFT, and not the RPC, is intended to be the body which decides whether an agreement is anti-competitive and should be banned. This will remove the excessive legalism of the current regulatory system. But the RPC is to be retained as an appeal body, both for companies which feel that the OFT has been too harsh, and for the OFT itself. (The government has not reviewed independently-undertaken restrictive practices - as opposed to collusive agreements - and these practices can still be defended by the MMC using a 'public interest' justification.)

(ii) The practice of registering all collective agreements is to be abolished, to be replaced by the general prohibition of all anti-competitive agreements, such as **price-fixing, collusive tendering, market share agreements, advertising restrictions** and **collective refusal to supply**. The present blanket exemptions of the professions are to be abolished.

(iii) **The OFT will be given new powers of search and entry without warning, into any business in the land, to discover evidence of collusion.** The OFT will have the power to levy greatly increased fines on companies operating anti-competitive agreements, up to a maximum of 10 per cent of the total turnover of the companies involved.

In 1989 a follow-up White Paper was published, announcing the introduction of tough new legislation to outlaw cartels and anti-competitive agreements throughout business and the professions, on the lines suggested by the 1988 Green Paper. Firms found guilty of breaching the law will be liable to fines of up to £1 million.

PUBLIC OWNERSHIP AND INDUSTRIAL POLICY

16. The history of **nationalisation** in the UK extends back to the middle of the 19th century, when the Post Office was established as a civil service department. The first **public corporation** was the Port of London Authority created in 1908, while other early public corporations were the Central Electricity Board, London Passenger Transport Board and the BBC which were set up by Acts of Parliament in the 1920s. Most of the early public corporations represent what has been called *'gas and water' socialism* - the regulation through public ownership of an essential utility or service regarded as too important to be left to the vaguaries of private ownership and market forces. However, as Table 10.1 shows (overleaf), the main periods of nationalisation and extension of public ownership in the UK have occurred during the periods since the Second World War when Labour Governments have been in office. In 1929 the British Labour Party had adopted the commitment to 'common ownership of the means of production, distribution and exchange'. Although nationalisation has at times been regarded by some Labour Party supporters rather as an end in itself, socialist theoreticians have argued that increased public ownership is necessary to give the government proper control of the key industries (or **'commanding heights' of the economy**), deemed vital for the socialist planning of the economy. Socialists have also believed that nationalisation leads to improved industrial relations, and to a more equitable or fair distribution of income and wealth amongst the population. In the former case greater industrial democracy can be promoted as class conflict between capitalists and workers gives way to co-operation between workers and managers to serve the public interest. And at the same time, the abolition of private ownership and monopoly profit can allow the payment of higher real wages to the employees of nationalised industries and the charging of lower prices to consumers, both of which should improve distributional equality within society. Nevertheless, it was not originally envisaged by Labour Party politicians that nationalised industries would be subsidised and run at a loss, whether to save the industries from bankruptcy or to provide a subsidised service to the public. Indeed, the Labour Party believed that the key industries, once nationalised, would immediately begin to function more efficiently than under private ownership, thus allowing employers, consumers and taxpayers and the 'wider' public interest all to benefit.

OTHER REASONS FOR NATIONALISATION

17. Industries have therefore been nationalised in the UK for two main reasons: as an **instrument of socialist planning and control** of the economy; and as a **method of regulating the problem of monopoly** - in particular the problem of 'natural' monopoly in the utility industries. There are however other possible reasons for nationalisation, some of which have been used by supporters of public ownership as part of an ad hoc justification for keeping industries in the public sector and resisting privatisation. These include:

Table 10.1: The History of Nationalisation in the United Kingdom

19th Century	The Post Office established as a civil service department	
Pre-World War 1	1908: Port of London Authority, the first public corporation	
Inter-war	Early public corporations, the Central Electricity Board, the London Passenger Transport Board, the BBC	
1945-1950 1st Main Period of statutory Nationalisation of the 'Commanding Heights' of the Economy	1946: National Coal Board 1946: Airlines - BOAC and BEA 1947: Central Electricity Generating Board and area distribution boards 1947: Transport-British Rail and British Road Services 1948: Gas Council and area boards 1949: Iron and steel	
1951-1963 1st period of Denationalisation	Denationalisation of steel and most of BRS in the early 1950s - but Atomic Energy Authority established in 1954	
1964-1969 2nd Main Period of Statutory Nationalisation - Mostly reorganisation	1965: Reorganisation of gas industry - British Gas Corporation 1965: British Airports Authority 1967: Renationalisation of steel - British Steel Corporation 1968: National Freight Corporation 1969: Post Office Corporation	
1970-1973 Denationalisation Again	The Conservative Government sold or 'hived off' ancillary activities rather than denationalise complete industries. Nevertheless it also extended the nationalised sector by taking Rolls-Royce into public ownership in 1971 and creating two new atomic energy corporations	
1974-1978 3rd Main Period of nationalisation	STATUTORY NATIONALISATION: British Aerospace British Shipbuilders British National Oil Corporation The Ports	THROUGH A STATE HOLDING COMPANY (THE NATIONAL ENTERPRISE BOARD): The largest company owned and controlled through the State Holding Company function of the NEB was British Leyland
1979 onwards Large scale privatisation or de-nationalisation	Early privatisations: Later privatisations: Proposed privatisations:	British Aerospace, National Freight Corporation, Britoil British Telecom, British Airways, British Gas, Jaguar, Austin Rover Water, Electricity

(i) **To regulate the production of demerit goods**. Although this argument has not been applicable to the extension of the public sector in the UK, the tobacco industry has been nationalised in France and alcoholic drink industries are a state monopoly in some Scandinavian countries.

(ii) **Fiscal reasons**. Governments may be tempted to nationalise monopolies, not in order to eliminate monopoly profit and reduce prices, but simply to use monopoly profit as a source of state revenue. Again, this reason for nationalisation is especially relevant in countries where demerit goods industries such as gambling, tobacco and alcoholic drink have been taken into public ownership.

(iii) **To regulate production of merit goods and ensure public health**. This has been the main reason why much of the water industry has been publicly provided in the UK from the late 19th century onwards - though privatisation is proposed in the early 1990s. It has been argued that all the nation's citizens are entitled to the same standard of services essential for health, wherever they live in the country, and that state provision can ensure this.

(iv) **Defence and national security**. Parts of the atomic energy industry have been state-controlled because of the hazards and risks involved and for security reasons.

(v) **National prestige**. Many countries possess nationalised airlines in order to 'wave the flag'.

(vi) **The rescue of 'lame ducks' or 'hospital cases'**. In the 1970s, UK governments nationalised large private sector firms such as the Rolls-Royce aircraft engine firm and the British Leyland car company, to save jobs which were threatened by the firm's bankruptcy, and to prevent British technology from being bought up by foreign competitors.

THE PRICING AND INVESTMENT POLICIES OF NATIONALISED INDUSTRIES

18. At the time of the first major extension of the nationalised sector by a Labour government in the 1940s, little thought had been given to the details of the pricing and investment policies which state-run industries should adopt. It was generally agreed that, by their nature, most of the UK nationalised industries were capital intensive, and would therefore need much more capital investment than the average private sector firm or industry. A high rate of capital investment could also be justified in industries such as rail and coal in order to make good for years of under-investment by the previous private owners.

In terms of pricing policy, the nationalisation statutes which established the major public corporations in the 1940s were vague, simply requiring that the industries should pay their way 'taking one year with another'. Thus from the beginning, a potential conflict was created, between the commercial objective of being profitable, and the public interest duty to provide social, and often uneconomic services, for example to citizens living in remote areas.

By the 1960s, much more thought was being given to the 'correct' pricing and investment policies nationalised industries should adopt. It was suggested that the pricing policies of nationalised industries should be based on the principle of **marginal cost pricing**, while investment decisions should follow the best practice adopted in the private sector: namely to use the **discounted cash flow techniques** (which we explain in Chapter 17) to decide whether particular investment projects are worthwhile.

MARGINAL COST PRICING AND NATIONALISED INDUSTRIES

19. We have seen that many of the industries taken into public ownership in the UK have been monopolies, and that an important reason for nationalisation has been the prevention of consumer exploitation through the monopoly deliberately restricting output and raising prices. Left to itself and functioning as private profit maximiser, a nationalised industry would, of course, choose a level of output and set a price at which P > MC. But as we have explained in Chapter 6, this is **allocatively inefficient**: too little of the good or service would be produced and consumed because the price is too high. To produce the **allocatively efficient level of output**, a nationalised industry should therefore adopt marginal cost pricing, so that P = MC. By setting price equal to marginal cost, the conditions of perfect competition are approximated, while still achieving the **productive efficiency** or low average costs that economies of scale and the monopoly position of the industry allow.

THE PROBLEMS OF MARGINAL COST PRICING

20. However, there are a number of difficulties in both the theory and the application of marginal cost pricing. These include:

(i) Marginal cost pricing can be guaranteed to improve allocative efficiency *only if all other prices in the economy equal marginal costs*. Since many prices charged in the private sector do not equal the relevant marginal costs, it is therefore by no means certain that by instructing a nationalised industry to charge marginal cost prices, allocative efficiency will improve.

(ii) In any case, to ensure allocative efficiency throughout the economy, each industry - including the nationalised industries - would have to set price equal to **marginal social cost (P = MSC)** rather than just the marginal private production cost incurred by the industry itself. Thus, if the pricing decisions of a nationalised industry were to reflect the wider public interest which is measured by social costs and benefits, the value of all the external costs and benefits generated in the course of production would have to be calculated and included in the price charged by the industry. **External costs** (or **negative externalities**) would include the costs of pollution and environmental destruction, while any environmental improvement 'spun off' from production would be an example of an **external benefit** (or **positive externality**).

(iii) The question of whether price should be set equal to **short-run** or **long-run marginal cost** is significant, since the decision affects a nationalised industry's profitability. Most of the nationalised industries benefit from economies of large scale production and falling long-run average total costs (LRATC). In this situation, long-run marginal costs (LRMC) must be below LRATC. If P = LRMC, the industry inevitably makes a loss and requires a subsidy to finance the resulting deficit. But the use of taxation to finance the deficit of a nationalised industry causes fresh allocative distortions, and in any case is likely to reduce industry morale. By contrast, if an industry is instructed to set P = SRMC, profits are normally made, though the profits are of course smaller than they would be if the industry were allowed to act 'commercially' as a private profit-maximiser, producing the output at which MR = MC.

(iv) Because of **'lumpiness'** or **indivisibilities**, it may be difficult or impossible in practice to calculate the marginal cost of providing an extra unit of a good to a single consumer.

PRICING IN PRACTICE

21. Partly because of the difficulties we have just listed, the theory of marginal cost pricing has had only a very limited impact upon the actual pricing decisions of nationalised industries in the UK. This is despite the fact that in 1967 a **White Paper on Nationalised Industries** stated that marginal cost pricing would be adopted wherever possible. However, the move towards marginal cost pricing, introduced by the 1967 White Paper, was quickly submerged beneath the use by successive UK governments of nationalised industry prices as an instrument to achieve other objectives of government policy. In the 1970s, Conservative and Labour governments both used the prices charged by nationalised industry as a **counter-inflation policy instrument**. Prices were kept artificially low and the industries made large losses. More recently, this policy has been reversed. In the 1980s the Conservative Government has instructed the industries to act 'commercially', just as if they were private profit maximisers. Since the profits (or trading surpluses) of nationalised industries go to the Exchequer, this represents a form of **'implicit' taxation** - with government revenue from the profits of nationalised industries allowing the level of formal or 'official' taxation to be kept down. Many commentators also believe that the current policy of instructing nationalised industries to set profit-maximising prices and ignore any wider 'public interest' issues, represents the 'fattening up' of the industries for eventual privatisation.

PRIVATISATION

22. Following the major nationalisations of the 1940s, the next thirty years witnessed relatively little additional nationalisation. Many of the Acts of Nationalisation undertaken by Labour governments merely reorganised assets already in the public sector. But equally there was relatively little **denationalisation** or **privatisation** when Conservative governments were in office. The 1950s to the 1970s were the decades of the mixed economy, when the major political parties agreed that the mix of public and private enterprise worked and was 'right for Britain'. But with the election of a radical free-market orientated administration under Mrs Margaret Thatcher in 1979, this consensus broke down. The Conservative governments of the 1980s have set about the task of breaking up the mixed economy and replacing it with a social market economy.

This has involved an industrial policy based on the inter-related processes of **privatisation, marketisation** and **deregulation** which are illustrated in Table 10.2 (overleaf).

THE CASE FOR PRIVATISATION

23. The general case for privatisation can only be properly understood when seen as part of the revolution (or counter-revolution) in economic thinking to which we have referred earlier in this chapter. This is the neo-classical revival. Other descriptive labels which have been attached to the free-market approach of the neo-classical revival - or to particular elements of the revival - include **monetarism, New Classical economics**, the **New Right**, the **'radical right'** and **'supply-side' economics.**

In the UK and the USA, the terms **'Thatcherism'** and **'Reaganomics'** have been widely used to describe the ideology and policies of the Conservative governments of Mrs Margaret Thatcher and the Republican administrations of President Ronald Reagan. In the 1980s, both the Thatcher and the Reagan administrations enthusiastically adopted the free-market 'laissez-faire' philosophy of the neo-classical revival and the 'radical right'.

We have already noted that socialists often seem to regard nationalisation as an end in itself, apparently believing that by taking an industry into public ownership, efficiency and equity are automatically improved and the public interest served. In much the same way, many **economic 'liberals'** at the opposite end of the political and economic spectrum, seem to believe that private ownership and capitalism are always superior to public ownership, whatever the circumstances, and that the privatisation of state-run industries must inevitably improve economic performance.

Rather more specific arguments that have been used to justify the privatisation programme include:

(i) **Revenue raising.** Privatisation, or the sale of state-owned assets, provides the government with a short-term source of revenue, which in some years has reached £3-4 billion. The proposed privatisation of the electricity industry might yield as much as £25 billion. Obviously an asset cannot be sold twice, so eventually privatisation must slow down when there are no more assets left to sell.

(ii) **Reducing public spending and the PSBR.** Since 1979 the Conservative Government has aimed to reduce public spending and the **Public Sector Borrowing Requirement (PSBR).** By classifying the monies received from asset sales as '*negative expenditure*' rather than as '*revenue*', the government has been able, from an accounting point of view, to reduce the level of public spending as well as the PSBR. There are, of course, rather more concrete reasons why privatisation may cause public spending to fall, besides those related to 'creative accounting'. If the state can successfully sell loss-making industries such as the Rover Group, public spending on subsidies falls. The PSBR can also fall if private ownership returns the industries to profitability, since corporation tax revenue will be boosted.

Table 10.2: Privatisation and related industrial policies

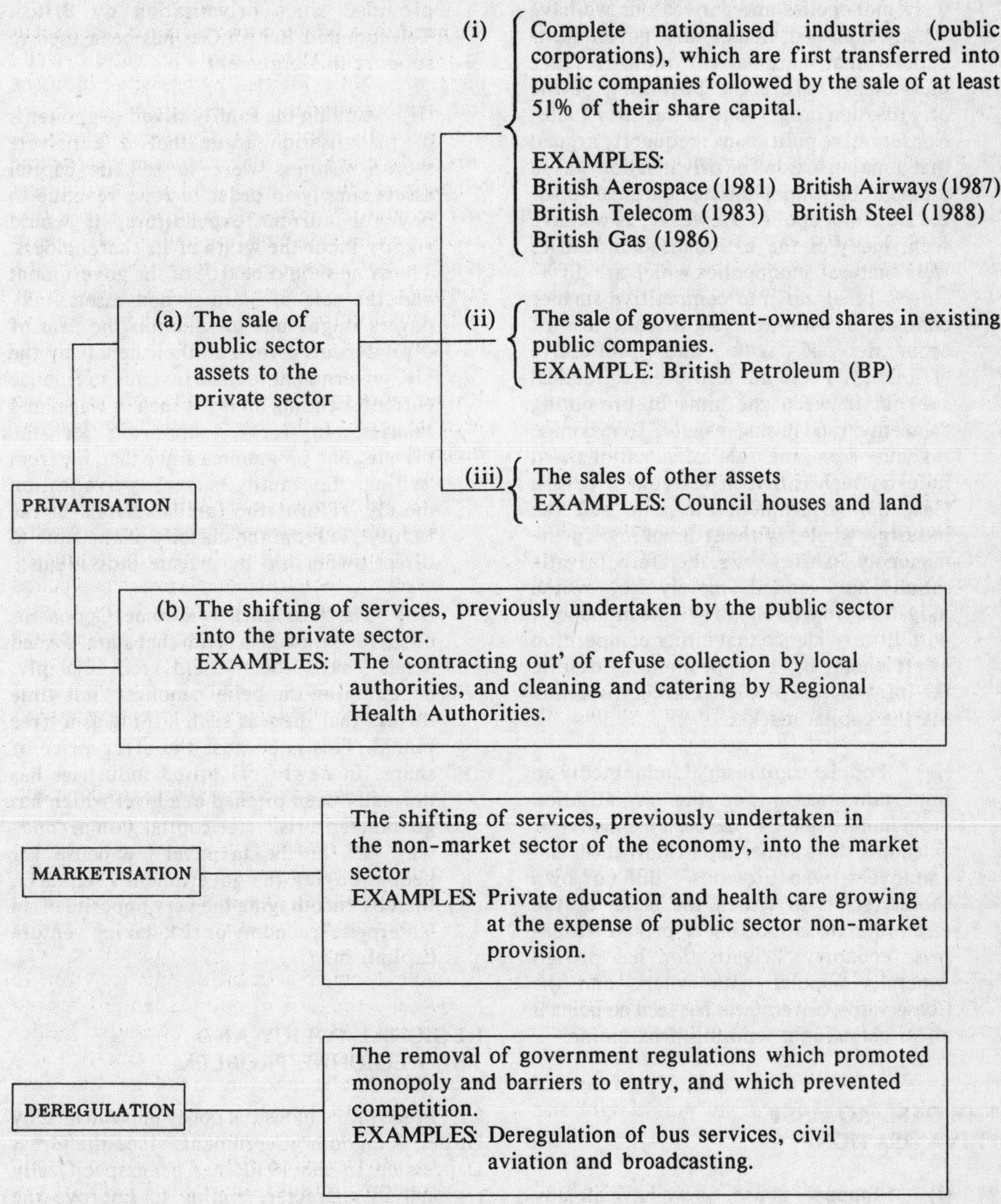

PRIVATISATION	(a) The sale of public sector assets to the private sector	(i)	Complete nationalised industries (public corporations), which are first transferred into public companies followed by the sale of at least 51% of their share capital. EXAMPLES: British Aerospace (1981), British Airways (1987), British Telecom (1983), British Steel (1988), British Gas (1986)
		(ii)	The sale of government-owned shares in existing public companies. EXAMPLE: British Petroleum (BP)
		(iii)	The sales of other assets. EXAMPLES: Council houses and land
	(b) The shifting of services, previously undertaken by the public sector into the private sector.		EXAMPLES: The 'contracting out' of refuse collection by local authorities, and cleaning and catering by Regional Health Authorities.
MARKETISATION			The shifting of services, previously undertaken in the non-market sector of the economy, into the market sector. EXAMPLES: Private education and health care growing at the expense of public sector non-market provision.
DEREGULATION			The removal of government regulations which promoted monopoly and barriers to entry, and which prevented competition. EXAMPLES: Deregulation of bus services, civil aviation and broadcasting.

(iii) **The promotion of competition and efficiency**. Most nationalised industries were monopolies and for reasons we have already explained, Conservative governments believe that nationalised industries are inefficient. Before the beginning of the privatisation programme in the early 1980s, Conservative politicians frequently argued that a major reason for privatisation was to promote competition through the break-up of the state monopolies. However, as we have seen, many of the nationalised industries were 'natural' monopolies which are difficult to break up into competitive smaller companies without a significant loss of economies of scale and productive efficiency. There has also been a practical conflict between the aims of promoting competition and raising revenue. To maximise revenue from the sale of a nationalised industry such as British Telecom or British Gas, the government chose to sell the industry whole, without breaking up the monopoly. In many cases, therefore, privatisation has tended merely to switch industries from public to private monopoly, with little evidence that either competition or efficiency has been promoted - despite the introduction of some market discipline via the capital market.

(iv) **'Popular capitalism'**. Undoubtedly an important reason for the privatisation programme in the UK has been the motive of extending share ownership to individuals and employees, who previously did not own shares, so as to widen the stake of the electorate in supporting a private enterprise economy. Privatisation has proved generally popular with voters, and the Conservative Government has seen no point at all in changing a winning programme.

THE CASE AGAINST PRIVATISATION

24. (i) **Monopoly abuse**. As we have already seen earlier in this chapter, in the context of competition policy, opponents of privatisation argue that far from promoting competition and efficiency, privatisation increases monopoly abuse by transferring socially-owned and accountable public monopolies into weakly-regulated and less-accountable private monopolies. Evidence of consumer dissatisfaction with the services provided since privatisation by British Telecom and British Gas has been used to support this argument.

(ii) **'Selling the family silver'**. Opponents of privatisation argue that if a private sector business were to sell its capital assets simply in order to raise revenue to pay for current expenditure, it would rightly incur the wrath of its shareholders. The same should be true of the government and the sale of state-owned assets: taxpayers ought not to sanction the sale of capital assets owned on their behalf by the UK government to raise revenue to finance current spending on items such as wages and salaries. In reply, supporters of the privatisation programme argue that, far from 'selling the family silver', privatisation merely 'returns the family's assets to the family', ie from the custody of the state to direct ownership by private individuals.

(iii) **The 'free lunch' syndrome**. Opponents of privatisation also claim that state-owned assets have been sold too cheaply, encouraging the belief amongst first-time buyers that there is such a thing as a 'free lunch'. This is because the offer-price of shares in newly-privatised industries has normally been pitched at a level which has guaranteed a risk-free capital gain or 'one-way bet' at the taxpayer's expense for people buying the government's sell-offs, thereby encouraging the very opposite of an 'enterprise' economy or risk-taking venture capitalism.

REGIONAL POLICY AND THE REGIONAL PROBLEM

25. Much of the industrial policy implemented by United Kingdom governments since the Great Depression in the 1930s has been specifically regional in character, aiming to improve the overall performance of the UK economy by reducing regional inequalities and by making better use of all the nation's resources wherever they happen to be located. Before we examine how regional policy has changed over the years, we shall first survey the nature of the United Kingdom regional problem.

THE EMERGENCE OF THE UK REGIONAL PROBLEM

26. Before the beginning of the Industrial Revolution in the eighteenth century, most of the British population lived in the southern half of the United Kingdom, where the best agricultural land is located. During the eighteenth and nineteenth centuries, industry and population both moved north, attracted first by water power and later by coal, which became the main source of energy used to power manufacturing industry. During the early Industrial Revolution, the main growth industries in the UK were coal mining, iron manufacture and the cotton and woollen textile industries, to which were later added the steel industry, railway building, shipbuilding and metal working, and the chemical industry. Britain thus became the first nation to industrialise, establishing an early technical lead over other countries. But the industrial structure resulting from Britain's early lead has been an important cause of recent industrial problems, including the regional problem. An industrial structure dominated by relatively small to medium-sized firms and manufacturing plants was created, which lacked the economies of scale, long production runs and up-to-date technology which were features of later industrialisation in continental Europe, the USA and Japan.

The modern British regional problem began to emerge after the First World War, when the staple industries located predominantly in northern and western Britain came under intense foreign competition, in both British and world markets. The staple industries such as coal, iron and steel, shipbuilding and textiles entered a structural decline, which became especially intense during the collapse of world trade in the Great Depression of the 1930s. During the Second World War and immediately afterwards, these older industries gained a temporary respite from the full effects of international competition. But in the 1950s, with the Japanese and German economic recoveries well under way, the British regional problem re-emerged to become an important economic and social problem which has faced all recent British governments.

THE TWO HALVES OF BRITAIN

27. In the 1960s and 1970s, the UK regional problem displayed the features illustrated in Figure 10.1 (shown on the next page). The country divided into a **'successful half'** - broadly the southern part of Britain including London and the South East, the Midlands and East Anglia - and an **'unsuccessful half'** in the north and west of the UK. The 'successful' south-eastern half of Britain is part of the **'Golden Triangle'** - a 'core' area of post-war growth in Western Europe, stretching between the English Midlands, North Germany and the Paris Basin in France. In contrast to the south-east, most of the rest of Britain is part of a **European 'periphery' region** outside the core of the 'Golden Triangle'. The European periphery is sometimes further subdivided into an **'outer'** and an **'inner' periphery**. In Britain, the **'outer periphery'** includes the older areas of 18th and 19th century industrialisation, together with the geographically remote, lowly populated and generally non-industrialised 'highlands and islands' which make up the northern and western fringe of the United Kingdom. The 'outer periphery' experienced a much slower rate of growth of output than the rest of the UK during the 1950s and 1960s. By contrast, the **'inner periphery'**, stretching in a broad belt across central Britain and including parts of the south-west, the Midlands, Lancashire and Yorkshire, achieved neither the prosperity of the 'core' nor the stagnation typical of the outer region. Instead its experience lay between these extremes.

THE CONVERGENCY APPROACH TO REGIONAL PROBLEMS

28. In large part, the modern British regional problem is a problem of mismatchment of capital and labour. The northern 'unsuccessful' half of Britain has combined a surplus of labour with a capital shortage, whereas the southern 'successful' part of Britain has been a region of plentiful capital but relative labour shortage.

In this situation, conventional market theory would predict that wage levels should rise in the south in response to the relative shortage of labour. At the same time capital should flow northwards and labour southwards, being attracted respectively by the wage differentials emerging between the two halves of Britain. Thus, by encouraging capital and labour mobility in this way, the market mechanism should ultimately lead to a process of **regional** convergence in which differences between regions are equalised, thereby causing the regional problem to disappear.

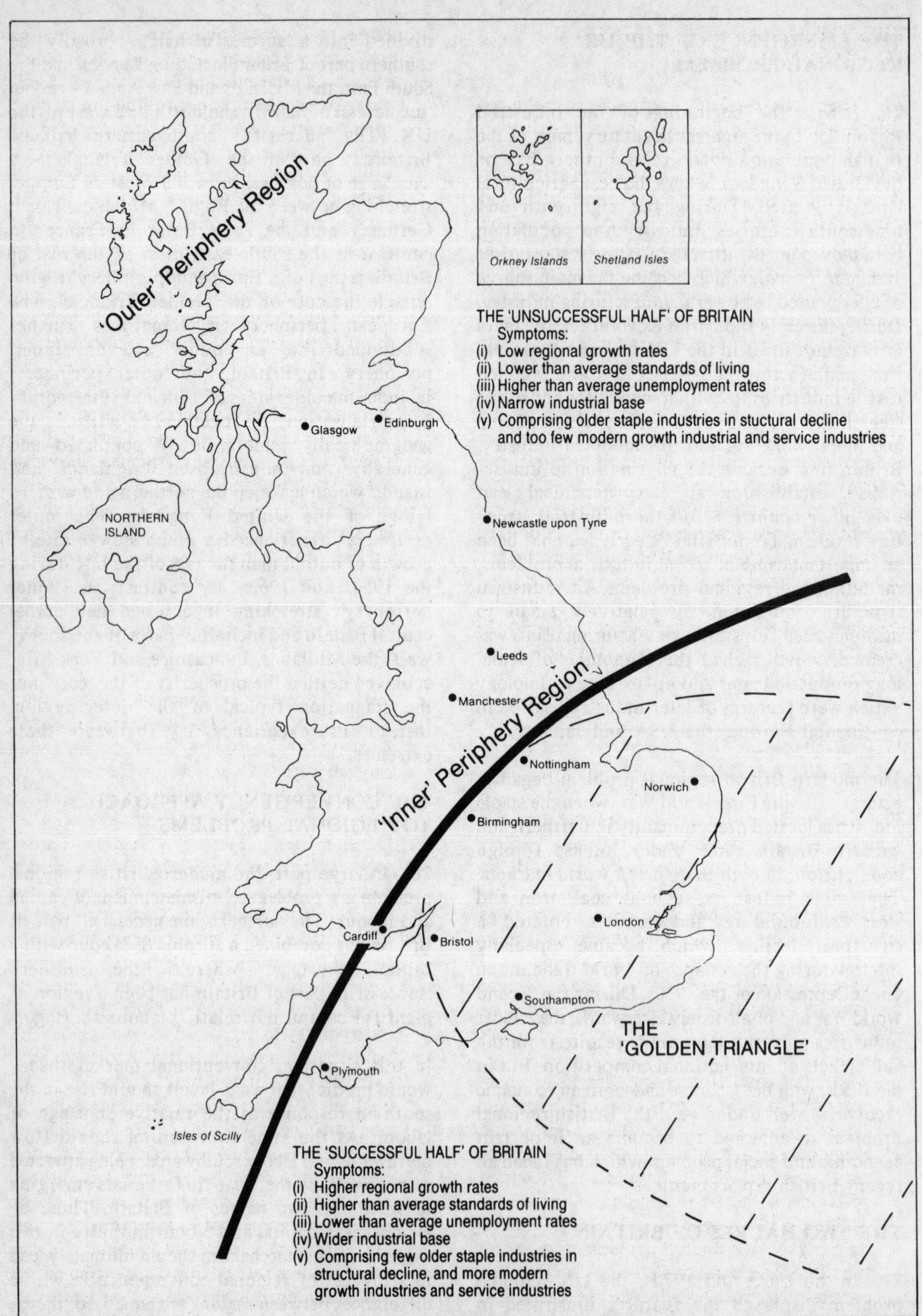
'Outer' Periphery Region
Orkney Islands
Shetland Isles
THE 'UNSUCCESSFUL HALF' OF BRITAIN
Symptoms:
(i) Low regional growth rates
(ii) Lower than average standards of living
(iii) Higher than average unemployment rates
(iv) Narrow industrial base
(v) Comprising older staple industries in stuctural decline and too few modern growth industrial and service industries
Glasgow
Edinburgh
NORTHERN ISLAND
Newcastle upon Tyne
Leeds
Manchester
'Inner' Periphery Region
Nottingham
Norwich
Birmingham
London
Cardiff
Bristol
Southampton
THE 'GOLDEN TRIANGLE'
Plymouth
Isles of Scilly
THE 'SUCCESSFUL HALF' OF BRITAIN
Symptoms:
(i) Higher regional growth rates
(ii) Higher than average standards of living
(iii) Lower than average unemployment rates
(iv) Wider industrial base
(v) Comprising few older staple industries in structural decline, and more modern growth industries and service industries

Figure 10.1

THE 'FREE-MARKET' APPROACH TO REGIONAL POLICY

29. The **'free-market' approach to regional policy**, which broadly argues the case against an interventionist regional policy, is based on the 'convergency theory' we have just described. Economists of the 'free-market' or neo-classical school believe that the market mechanism alone can solve the regional problem, and that the proper function of regional policy is simply to create the free-market environment in which the price mechanism can operate efficiently. Indeed, according to this view, an interventionist or 'active' regional policy - far from reducing regional differences - actually makes the inequalities worse because it interferes with the efficient working of the market. Free-market economists argue that, over many decades, the policies and legislation of successive British governments created inflexible markets which prevented the price mechanism from functioning properly. They blame planning controls for preventing firms choosing low-cost locations and national collective bargaining for preventing the emergence of the regional wage differentials regarded as necessary for the 'convergency' process to work.

THE 'INTERVENTIONIST' APPROACH TO REGIONAL POLICY

30. Economists who argue in favour of an **'active'** or **interventionist regional policy** reject both the 'convergency theory' and the belief that market forces alone can cure the regional problem. The case for a much more interventionalist regional and industrial policy is based upon two important arguments: (i) **regional 'divergency'**; and (ii) the argument that **social as well as private costs must be taken into account.**

(i) **Regional divergency.** Many Keynesian economists believe that market forces, far from reducing and eventually eliminating regional disparities in income, employment and standards of living, actually widen differences between regions. Although in principle low wages should attract firms to regions of high unemployment, by creating depressed regional markets they can have the opposite effect. And market forces might only be successful in pulling individual firms to depressed regions if the regions possess sufficient **external economies** attractive to modern industries. Such external economies are provided in part by government investment in infrastructure and social capital, but also by other firms supplying components, specialist services or market outlets, already located in the region. But the regional problem may exist in part, precisely because the depressed regions lack an environment of established external economies sufficient to attract inward investment by new firms. Indeed far from possessing sufficient external economies attractive to modern industry, the disadvantaged regions may contain significant **external diseconomies** which act as deterrants to incoming firms. Diseconomies resulting from remoteness from the European 'core', derelict buildings, polluted land, unsuitable transport facilities, and a labour force trained in the wrong skills and unused to modern working practices, may all counter the pull of low wages and a plentiful supply of labour, and serve to intensify rather than reduce the regional problem.

(ii) **The social cost argument.** When making an economic decision in an unregulated market economy, a firm need consider only the private costs incurred by the enterprise itself, together with the private benefits received. Thus, when choosing a suitable location for production, a firm can ignore any **externalities** received by the wider community, which may result from its private choice. But while the firm can ignore externalities, it is the government's duty to take account of external costs and benefits generated by the private locational decisions of firms, and to formulate public policy to try to maximise the welfare of the whole community rather than just the private interests of individual firms. In the absence of externalities, there is of course no public policy problem, since the social or public interest coincides with the private interests of firms. In these circumstances, and in the absence of other arguments to justify intervention, the government should refrain from interfering with market forces. But supporters of an active regional policy argue that a case for government intervention exists precisely because the location of industry generates externalities received as social costs by the wider community. These include the **costs of underutilised social capital**, for example schools and housing, in the areas of high unemployment from which workers migrate, and the costs to the community of financing unemployment benefits for the workers who remain. Further **social costs of congestion and over-utilisation of social capital** may be generated in areas such as the South-East where industry chooses to locate. By forcing or encouraging firms to locate in the depressed regions and away from the South-East, the savings in social and external costs may exceed any increase in private costs to individual firms, especially if industry is relatively 'footloose' and private costs are much the same throughout the country. In these circumstances, regional policy results in a net welfare gain to the whole community; the actual financial costs to government and taxpayers which are paid to firms as compensation for increased private costs are less than the savings in total social costs.

CAPITAL MOBILITY VERSUS LABOUR MOBILITY

31. We have already explained how the market disequilibrium of a labour surplus in one half of Britain and a relative shortage of labour in the other half can be cured either by a **greater capital mobility**, or by **greater labour mobility**. Essentially the former type of policy takes work to the workers, whereas the latter attempts to **take workers to the work**, assuming of course, that job opportunities exist in the southern 'successful' half of Britain. In principle, regional policy can be based on either approach, or indeed upon both approaches, but under successive British governments, policies to improve capital mobility have been dominant. Governments have generally accepted that a successful improvement in labour mobility sufficient to reduce regional unemployment would worsen other aspects of the regional problem. In particular, the social costs of congestion would be increased in the south, with further social costs resulting from a declining population in the north. For this reason, government employment policies have placed most emphasis on improving the *occupational* rather than the *geographical* mobility of labour. Job centres are used for labour recruitment and job advertising, training schemes for the young and retraining schemes for older workers have been established, and in recent years employment legislation has been used to reduce restrictive labour practices which prevented workers from changing occupations.

UK REGIONAL POLICY BEFORE 1984

32. For most of the period since the Second World War, British regional policy was based on the active or interventionist approach which we have already described. British regional policy has always involved **'market modification'** rather than **'market replacement'**. ie the use of policy instruments to create signals and incentives to encourage firms voluntarily to locate in the depressed regions, rather than the enforced location of investment through the command or planning mechanism. In essence, a **'carrot and stick' approach** to the regional problem was adopted. **'Carrots'** or **incentives** were offered to attract firms to the depressed regions, while at various times planning restrictions were enforced as a **'stick'** or **deterrant** to prevent location in the 'successful' southern half of Britain. The country was divided into **Assisted Areas**, in which the 'carrots' or incentives were offered to incoming firms, and the rest of Britain where planning restrictions were enforced and regional assistance was unavailable. Currently the assisted areas are called **Development Areas** and **Intermediate Areas**. The main form of regional assistance available in the assisted areas has always been financial, namely **investment grants**- **Regional Development Grants (RDGs)** - and **investment tax allowances**, together with government investment in social capital or infrastructure.

THE EFFECTIVENESS OF REGIONAL POLICY

33. There are a number of reasons why it is difficult to assess the effectiveness of regional policy. Perhaps most important is the impossibility of knowing how both the whole economy and the regions within the economy would have fared in the absence of a regional policy. Secondly, statistics on the regions have only been available since the mid-1970s, and third, the parts of Britain qualifying for regional aid

have changed over the years. A number of studies have attempted to measure the effectiveness of regional policy by estimating the number of jobs that have been created. One calculation, by Moore and Rhodes in 1977, estimated that twenty years of regional policy had created 350,000 jobs in manufacturing industries in the assisted areas. More jobs may, of course, have been created indirectly through 'multiplier' effects giving rise, for example, to employment in service industries. However, on the other side of the balance sheet, many of the apparently new jobs may not have been 'new' jobs for the economy as a whole, but simply jobs transferred from other regions.

But while it is impossible to estimate with accuracy the number of new jobs created by regional policy, it is possible to measure whether regional disparities in terms of employment and output have narrowed or widened. Generally, the best that can be claimed for the regional policy implemented by successive governments before 1984, is that regional policy measures prevented disparities from widening, but no noticeable narrowing of regional employment and output disparities took place.

THE 'CATALYTIC CRACKER SYNDROME'

34. Whatever the true effectiveness of the generally interventionist regional policy implemented in the decades before 1984, there is no doubt that it was expensive to the taxpayer in terms of the cost of each new job created. An explanation for this lies in the **'catalytic cracker syndrome'**. This refers to the spending of millions of pounds of regional aid on expensive and capital-intensive equipment, such as catalytic crackers in the oil-refining industry, with very few resulting jobs. The 'catalytic cracker syndrome' was encouraged because, prior to 1984, regional aid was channelled largely into the finance of investment by manufacturing firms in new plant and fixed capacity.

THE 'BRANCH FACTORY SYNDROME'

35. The structure of regional financial assistance available before 1984 also encouraged the **'branch factory syndrome'**. Much of the investment in new manufacturing industry in the regions which took place before 1984 established branch factories owned by large companies with headquarters and main plants outside the assisted areas. Partly because financial assistance was directed at encouraged and rewarding investment, and partly because service industries were largely excluded from receiving aid, pre-1984 regional policy did little to encourage the growth of small businesses indigenous to the regions. Successful growth of such small and often labour-intensive businesses, in service industries as well as in manufacturing, might well have created better balanced regional economies than in fact resulted from the 'branch factory syndrome'. A greater proportion of service industries could have made the regional economies less vulnerable to the changes in demand that affect heavy capital goods industries especially severely in times of recession. It is also possible that the growth of businesses indigenous to the regions might have produced a situation in which many more owners of businesses actually live within the assisted areas, with profits and higher managerial income circulating within the regional economies. Instead, regional aid largely financed the growth of branch factories owned by British and overseas multinational companies. Typically, such factories were peripheral to the main activities of the parent company, often manufacturing a narrow range of components with which to supply other factories in the multinational's wider sphere of operations. Perhaps more importantly, these branch factories tended to generate only relatively low 'production line' incomes to employees living within the assisted areas. Profits generated by the factories, together with higher managerial incomes, usually leaked out of the regional economy, being transferred to the parent company, or to shareholders and the upper echelons of management living outside the regions. But perhaps the most serious effect of the 'branch factory syndrome' occurred in the severe recession that affected the whole of British industry in the late 1970s and early 1980s. Manufacturing in general faced serious difficulties, but it was usually the outlying branch factories, located in the regions, which were the most vulnerable to closure.

RECENT CHANGES IN UNITED KINGDOM REGIONAL POLICY

36. In 1984 significant changes were introduced in British regional policy. In part these were a response to the 'catalytic cracker' and 'branch factory' syndromes we have just described, but at a more deep-seated level they represent the return to free-market principles by the Conservative Government, and a rejection of Keynesian and interventionist approaches to economic policy. Before 1984 all manufacturing firms investing in assisted areas (at the time comprising a three-tier structure of **Special Development Areas**, **Development Areas** and **Intermediate Areas)** were automatically entitled to regional development grants. Financial aid was not generally available to service industries. The main changes introduced in 1984 by the Conservative Government were:

(i) The map of assisted areas were redrawn and reduced to a two-tier structure of Development Areas and Intermediate Areas which is illustrated in Figure 10.2 (overleaf) Approximately 35 per cent of the United Kingdom population now lives within the assisted areas.

(ii) The new changes were intended to reduce the cost of regional policy to the government and to the taxpayer. Besides demoting some areas from assisted area status, the rate at which Regional Development Grants were offered to firms investing in new plant and buildings in Development Areas was reduced from 22 per cent to 15 per cent.

(iii) An element of selectivity or discretion was introduced into regional policy. Before 1984, RDGs were automatically available to manufacturing firms expanding in Development Areas and Intermediate Areas. After 1984, RDGs were available automatically at the reduced rate of 15 per cent in Development Areas, but only on new and not on replacement investment. In Development Areas, any further assistance over and above the 15 per cent RDG was made selective, while Intermediate Areas qualified for selective assistance only. Following the example of other countries in the EEC, regional policy was made selective by introducing a cost-per-job limit for the RDG of £10,000, designed to reward investment by labour-intensive firms and to avoid the 'catalytic cracker syndrome'. However, the cost-per-job limit was not applied to small firms employing less than 200 employees, in the hope that capital-intensive small firms would be couraged to grow to a viable size.

(iv) In one significant area regional policy was extended. For the first time, service industries such as advertising and data processing - but not tourism - became eligible for regional financial assistance and a new grant was created which has proved to be especially attractive to labour-intensive service industries. As an alternative to the RDG, which is available only to finance capital investment, labour-intensive firms were offered a grant of £3,000 for each new job created, provided that the total turns out to be worth more than 15 per cent of the capital cost of the project.

In 1988, automatic entitlement to RDGs was finally abolished, completing the change to a discretionary regional policy designed to encourage the growth of indigenous small businesses rather than branch factories. The assisted areas and overall cost of regional aid was left unchanged (though at about £400m compared to £700m a few years earlier).

THE EEC REGIONAL FUND

37. In some areas of economic policy, such as agricultural policy, the United Kingdom has had to adopt common EEC policies which have in effect replaced independent national policy. This is not the case with the regional policy of the European Economic Community, which essentially supplements rather than replaces each country's regional policy. Before 1975 regional assistance from the EEC was available from a number of funds such as the **EEC Social Fund** which financed the training of young workers. In 1975 a **European Regional Development Fund (ERDF)** was established to create a more unified Community regional policy. Financial assistance from the ERDF is channelled through the British government and is intended to be additional to the government's own regional aid. However, there have been criticisms that the British government has used the receipt of EEC funds as an excuse for reducing its own financial assistance to the regions. Development Areas are classified as **European Peripheral Regions** which qualify for a higher level of community assistance than other parts of Britain, designated **Central Regions**. In general, the EEC frowns upon continuous subsidies to the regions, preferring instead investment in regional infrastructure.

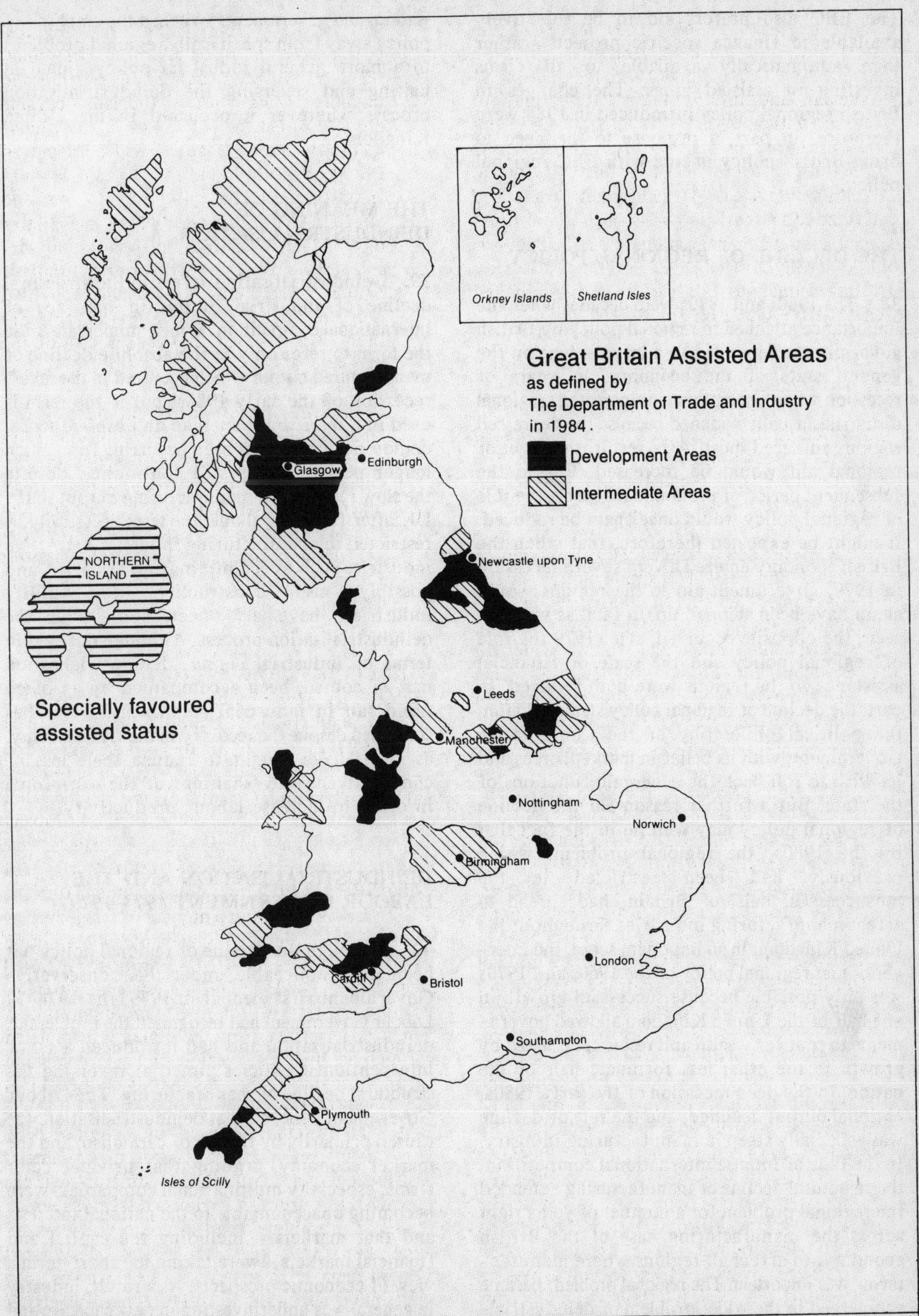
Orkney Islands
Shetland Isles
Great Britain Assisted Areas
as defined by
The Department of Trade and Industry
in 1984.
Development Areas
Intermediate Areas
NORTHERN
ISLAND
Specially favoured
assisted status
Glasgow
Edinburgh
Newcastle upon Tyne
Leeds
Manchester
Nottingham
Norwich
Birmingham
London
Cardiff
Bristol
Southampton
Plymouth
Isles of Scilly

Figure 10.2

The EEC also prefers aid to be selectively available to finance specific projects, rather than automatically available to all firms investing in assisted areas. The changes in British regional policy introduced in 1984 were therefore, in part, a response to the need to bring British policy in line with EEC regional policy.

THE DECLINE OF REGIONAL POLICY

38. The 1960s and 1970s were decades when the importance attached to regional policy by British governments depended to a large extent on the general state of the economy. In years of recession when unemployment increased, regional disparities usually widened because the depressed regions suffered most. As a result, the level of regional aid would be increased. But in the subsequent period of economic recovery, the role of regional policy would once again be reduced. It might be expected therefore, that when the British economy entered a very severe recession in 1979, government aid to the regions would again have been stepped up. In fact, as we have seen, the opposite occurred; after 1979 the role of regional policy and the scale of financial assistance to the regions were both reduced. In part, the decline of regional policy stemmed from the political philosophy of the Conservative Government, with its belief in market forces and its wish to roll back the economic functions of the state. But a further reason for the decline of regional policy may well lie in the fact that by the 1980s, the regional problem, which previously had been restricted to the 'unsuccessful half' of Britain, had spread to affect manufacturing industries throughout the United Kingdom. In an important sense, the interventionist regional policy of the 1960s and 1970s was only possible because successful growth in one half of the United Kingdom allowed governments to transfer wealth and resources created by growth to the other less fortunate half of the nation. In the deep recession of the early 1980s, national output declined, and the rate of decline was especially steep in manufacturing industry. In the face of intense international competition, the structural decline of manufacturing extended the regional problem for a number of years right across the manufacturing base of the British economy, to affect all regions where manufacturing was important. The regional problem became submerged in the wider problem of **deindustrialisation**, and governments switched the emphasis of policy away from specifically regional problems to a more general industrial policy aimed at halting and reversing the deindustrialisation process wherever it occurred in the United Kingdom.

THE MEANING OF DEINDUSTRIALISATION

39. Deindustrialisation refers to the structural decline of industrial output in the face of international competition. Some commentators use the term to refer only to the **absolute decline of manufactured output** which occurred in the severe recession of the early 1980s, but if the term is used in a *relative* rather than an *absolute* sense, deindustrialisation has been occurring for a much longer period and is still continuing, despite the slow recovery in manufacturing output in the UK after 1981. Nor should the term necessarily be restricted to manufacturing industry; extractive industries such as coalmining and fisheries, and possibly also construction and utility industries, have also been subject to the deindustrialisation process. Although defined in terms of industrial *output*, deindustrialisation has, of course, been accompanied by an often rapid fall in industrial *employment*. This has continued despite the recovery in the UK economy, as firms have sought to reduce their loss of competitiveness by 'shaking out' the work force in order to increase labour productivity.

DEINDUSTRIALISATION AND THE LABOUR GOVERNMENT 1974-1979

40. Although the decline of regional policy has been most noticeable under the Conservative Government first elected in 1979, the 1974-79 Labour Government had recognised the problem of deindustrialisation and had introduced a set of interventionist policies aimed at reversing the structural decline of manufacturing. The Labour Government believed that deindustrialisation was caused primarily by failure of capitalism and the market economy, arguing that private sector firms, especially multinational companies, were becoming unaccountable to the national interest, and that markets - including the capital and financial markets - were taking too short-term a view of economic prospects. As a result, industry in general was underinvesting in new capacity and the financial institutions were failing in their function of providing risk or venture capital to industry on a long-term basis. Between 1974 and 1979, the Labour Government introduced an **'Industrial Strategy'** which reflected this approach and which included the following interventionist measures:

(i) **Indicative planning**. In a system of indicative planning the state first indicates desired national goals to the private sector, perhaps set out in a **National Plan**, and then encourages private enterprise to cc-operate in achieving the targets or goals. In a fully developed system of indicative planning, the state may offer rewards, such as lucrative government contracts, to companies which adapt their own corporate plans to fit in with the requirements of the state's master plan, while punishing companies which do not comply by withdrawing government business from these firms.

(ii) **Planning agreements**. The Labour Government was unable to develop a fully-fledged system of indicative planning, and neither was it able to establish properly the system of planning agreements which was meant to assist indicative planning. Very often large companies set out their medium- or long-term objectives in a corporate plan, which may of course be kept secret from their competitors. The Labour Government tried to introduce a system in which the company, together with the government and trade unions representing the company's workers, would sign a tripartite planning agreement setting out agreed objectives which were in the social or national interest, and not just in the private interest of the company's shareholders.

(iii) **Extending public ownership**. The Labour Government established the **National Enterprise Board (NEB)**, which was a **state holding company** set up to take an ownership stake in private sector firms in return for providing finance. Where the Labour Government believed that indicative planning and planning agreements might fail, it was prepared to nationalise private sector companies, either by the conventional method of setting up a public corporation by an Act of Parliament, or by a 'backdoor' nationalisation, in which the NEB bought up a controlling share stake in the company.

(iv) **'Picking winners'** and **'joint ventures'**. The Labour Government hoped that the NEB would be able to identify future growth industries, or **'sunrise' industries** in which it would engage in successful 'joint ventures' by providing funds and co-operating with the private sector. In the outcome, however, most of the NEB's funds were absorbed in trying to halt or slow down the decline of the traditional **'sunset' industries** which had for so long contributed to the regional problem, and in rescuing newer **'lame duck'** or **'hospital case' industries** such as British Leyland and large engineering firms in the West Midlands which had fallen upon hard times.

DEINDUSTRIALISATION AND THE CONSERVATIVE GOVERNMENT

41. While there has been general agreement that deindustrialisation has posed serious problems for the United Kingdom economy, the policies adopted by the Conservatives since 1979 to deal with deindustrialisation have been different in almost all respects from those of the Labour Government in the 1970s. Recent Conservative policy has been based on the assumption that any problems caused by deindustrialisation, along with the regional problem, result from decades of too much rather than too little government intervention. State intervention has prevented the market mechanism from working properly, particularly in the labour market. Firms have been faced with high wage costs which, together with the crippling burden of taxation necessary to finance state intervention, have reduced international competitiveness. According to the 'radical right' philosophy adopted by recent Conservative governments, the correct way to deal with the deindustrialisation problem is to 'roll back' state intervention and to create conditions in which private enterprise and entrepreneurial initiative, operating in competitive and efficient markets, can regenerate the British economy.

The free-market 'supply-side' orientated policies adopted by recent Conservative governments to deal with the deindustrialisation problem have included (i) the **encouragement of small business**;

(ii) **tax cuts**; (iii) **abolishing labour restrictive practices and reducing the power of trade unions**; (iv) **enterprise zones**; (v) **reforming the Scottish and Welsh Development Agencies**; and (vi) **establishing Urban Development Corporations**:

(i) **Encouragement of small businesses**. The Conservatives have believed that small businesses can successfully grow, especially in **sunrise industries**, to replace declining larger firms in **'sunset'** or **'geriatric' industries** which are victims of changing demand and technology. Conservatives reject the need for the state to provide finance or to 'pick winners', preferring instead a free- market approach and reliance on the profit motive. Interventionist bodies such as the NEB have been abolished. To some extent, the Conservatives have hoped that output and employment in service industries such as tourism and leisure industries will grow to fill the gap left by the decline of manufacturing. Critics of the Conservative approach doubt whether sufficient small firms can grow to replace the large and medium-sized manufacturing firms that have disappeared. They argue that a strong manufacturing base is still essential for the overall health of the economy, both for export earnings and the reduction of import penetration, and to create a part of the economy for service industries to service.

(ii) **Tax cuts**. As part of the policy of encouraging private enterprise, small businesses and 'wealth creation', the Conservatives have cut the marginal rates of personal income tax and corporation tax paid by companies. They believe that excessive tax rates have in the past created a disincentive to effort, and that lower tax rates will encourage people to work harder.

(iii) **Abolishing labour market restrictive practices and reducing the power of trade unions**. During the 1980s, Conservative governments introduced a series of Employment Acts, which reduced the power of trade unions to undertake **industrial action** such as **strikes**, and gave workers greater freedom to decide whether or not to join a union. Government legislation also attacked **trade union restrictive practices** such as **closed shops** and similar restrictive arrangements in the professions. The general aim of the employment legislation has been to make labour markets more competitive and flexible by removing monopoly power and barriers to entry.

(iv) **Enterprise zones**. Since the Second World War, population and employment have both declined in large conurbations or built-up areas throughout the United Kingdom. Population decline has affected large cities such as London and Birmingham in the 'successful' south of the country as well as industrial cities in the northern half of Britain. This decline, which has been particularly acute in manufacturing, has reduced employment opportunities for the skilled and semi-skilled manual workers who make up a large part of the working population in industrial cities. Service industries have generally been unable to grow sufficiently to make up for the decline of manufacturing in the large cities. Inner-city decline has also contributed to the growth of a high level of public expenditure provided by local authorities in the large cities. But increased spending by local authorities in areas of urban deprivation has required higher local taxation to finance the spending. By the 1980s, Britain's inner- cities were becoming locked into a vicious spiral of decline. Falling employment led to a consequent narrowing of the local tax base, accompanied by growing demands for local public spending from a population increasingly dependent upon welfare benefits. This in turn led to an even faster rate of decline in local employment as firms went out of business or moved out of the inner-cities to escape the high taxation required to pay for the high levels of local public expenditure.

Before 1979, governments either ignored the growing **'micro-regional'problem** of the inner cities, concentrating instead on the more conventional problems of **'macro-regions'**, or they chose to deal with the problem by increasing the level of central government funding for local authorities in the affecting city centres. After 1979, the Conservatives adopted a completely different approach, reducing the level of intervention by local and central government alike, and attempting to create an environment attractive to private enterprise.

Enterprise zones were established, conceived of as areas of reduced 'red tape' and bureaucracy. Firms locating in enterprise zones, which are usually sited on previously derelict urban land in inner-cities, benefit from a ten year 'rates holiday' during which they pay no local taxation and are exempt from the need to obtain planning permission or to make redundancy payments to laid-off workers. By 1986, twenty eight enterprise zones had been established, but a number of studies have cast doubt on their effectiveness in reducing the inner-city problem. It is doubtful whether enterprise zones have attracted many completely new businesses; indeed areas of blight have tended to grow up around enterprise zones as businesses have moved into the zones from the surrounding area to benefit from the 'rates holiday'. The enterprise zones have tended to attract services industries such as retail super-stores and warehouses rather than manufacturing, creating employment for low-paid unskilled workers. Their critics argue that enterprise zones have failed to make sufficient impact upon the unemployment and social problems of inner-cities, and that they are not an appropriate base for the regeneration of areas of urban deprivation.

(v) **The Scottish and Welsh Development Agencies.** The **Scottish Development Agency (SDA)** and the **Welsh Development Agency (WDA)** were initially established in the 1970s by a Labour government as sister agencies in Scotland and Wales to the **National Enterprise Board** in England. The SDA and the WDA originally functioned as agencies through which government money was channelled to businesses investing in Scotland and Wales. Although the National Enterprise Board was abolished by the Conservatives in the early 1980s, the SDA and the WDA have been retained, but with reduced functions, using advertising and other promotional means to attract businesses to Scotland and Wales. The Agencies have been quite successful in attracting investment by American and Japanese multinational corporations, though this 'inward investment' may well have contributed to the 'branch factory' problem.

(vi) **Urban Development Corporations.** Separate from the Scottish and Welsh Development Agencies and **New Town Development Corporations** funded by central government, there have been a large number of local authority funded schemes aimed at attracting industry to particular local communities. Local authorities throughout the UK - in relatively prosperous communities such as Peterborough and Swindon as well as in depressed regions - have made use of a provision in the 1972 Local Government Act which allows municipalities to advertise to attract industry. However, much of the advertising and promotion by one local authority may simply attract business away from competing local government areas, with little effect on total industrial investment. In any case, local authority activity to attract investment has recently been bypassed by **Urban Development Corporations (UDCs)** established by central government. The Conservative Government has set up privately sponsored UDCs such as the **London Docklands Urban Development Corporation** which, like enterprise zones, are largely outside the political control of the municipalities in which they are located. Critics argue that far from decentralising power away from the state, the UDCs erode the power of local democracy in the UK and represent a further step towards the centralisation of effective power or decision making in Westminster and Whitehall.

SUMMARY

42. In this chapter we have examined competition policy, the ownership of industry, and regional policy, three elements within the industrial policy pursued by every UK government since the Second World War. For the first three decades after 1945, the industrial policy or micro-economic policy implemented by successive governments, Labour and Conservative, extended the role of the state in the market economy, yet at the same time micro-economic policy was generally less important than macro-economic policy. Under the influence of Keynesian economic theory, the management of aggregate demand at the macro-economic level dominated economic policy-making, with industrial policy and the 'supply-side' of the economy taking second place. Yet during this period of political and economic consensus around the virtue of the mixed economy, it was widely agreed that by active intervention,

a government could correct market failures such as the regional problem and the problem of monopoly abuse. There was also a considerable measure of agreement that the mix of public and private ownership created by the pre-war nationalisation of utility industries, together with nationalisation of coal and rail in the 1940s, was 'about right for Britain.'

But under the attack of monetarism and the neo-classical revival this consensus is now in disarray. The interventionist industrial policy of the Keynesian era has given way to a free-market or laissez-faire approach to economic policy, in which industrial policy and the 'supply-side' are now regarded as more important for improving the performance of the UK economy than macro-policy and the 'demand-side'. The thrust of current Conservative industrial policy has been to 'roll back' direct intervention in economic activity by the state, and to create conditions which enable markets and economic agents to function competitively and efficiently. The policies of privatisation, marketisation and deregulation have been central to this strategy. The Conservative Government has openly voiced doubts about the economic case for regional financial assistance for industry, but a regional policy has been retained perhaps more for social and electoral reasons than because the Government believes that a regional policy represents sound economics. Nevertheless, the cost to the taxpayer of financial assistance to industry has been greatly reduced, as the government has switched the stance of regional assistance away from automatic entitlement to regional aid towards a great selectivity and the creation of enterprise zones and Urban Development Corporations. At the same time, the Conservative Government's monopoly and merger policies have been strongly influenced by the 'theory of contestable markets' which suggests that it is less necessary for the state to break up a monopoly than to remove barriers to entry that would deny the potential for a market to be contested.

STUDENT SELF-TESTING

1. *Define industrial policy. (2)*
2. *What are the three main elements of competition policy? (3)*
3. *Distinguish between a scale monopoly and a complex monopoly. (4)*
4. *What is a 'natural' monopoly? (5)*
5. *Distinguish between a cartel and a fully-unified monopoly? (6)*
6. *List the possible costs and benefits of monopoly. (5 and 7)*
7. *Briefly describe the roles of the MMC and the OFT. (8 and 9)*
8. *List alternative possible approaches to the problem of monopoly. (10)*
9. *What is the theory of 'contestable' markets? (11)*
10. *How does UK merger policy operate? (12)*
11. *Distinguish between collective and non-collective restrictive practices. (13)*
12. *What have been the weaknesses in UK restrictive practice policy? (14)*
13. *What changes have been proposed in UK restrictive practice policy legislation? (15)*
14. *Briefly describe the history of nationalisation in the UK. (16)*
15. *List reasons for nationalisation. (15 and 16)*
16. *What is marginal cost pricing? (18 and 19)*
17. *Discuss the problems of marginal cost pricing. (20)*
18. *Discuss other influences upon nationalised industry pricing. (21)*
19. *What is meant by privatisation? (22)*
20. *List arguments in favour of privatisation. (23)*
21. *List arguments against privatisation. (24)*
22. *Describe the UK regional problem. (26)*
23. *Describe the 'two halves' of Britain. (27)*
24. *Explain the convergency approach to the regional problem. (28)*
25. *What is the 'free market' approach to regional policy? (29)*
26. *Explain the investment approach to regional policy. (30)*
27. *Why have governments placed emphasis on encouraging capital mobility rather than labour mobility? (31)*
28. *Summarise UK regional policy before 1984. (32)*
29. *Has UK regional policy been effective? (33)*
30. *What is the 'catalytic cracker syndrome'? (34)*

31. *What is the 'branch factory syndrome'? (35)*
32. *Describe recent changes in UK regional policy. (36)*
33. *Describe the role of the EEC Regional Development Fund. (37)*
34. *Account for the decline in the importance placed on regional policy. (38)*
35. *What is meant by deindustrialisation? (39)*
26. *Compare Labour and Conservative approaches to the problem of deindustrialisation. (40 and 41)*

EXERCISES

1. *A dispute has broken out in the UK plasterboard industry concerning allegations and counter allegations by BPB Industries, the leading UK manufacturer of plasterboard, and Iberian Trading UK, an importer of Spanish plasterboard.*

   Iberian Trading UK has convinced the European Commission to begin an investigation into BPB Industries. It was alleged that BPB has abused its dominant position in the UK market in an attempt to eliminate competition in general and Iberian Trading in particular. BPB supplies 96 per cent of the UK plasterboard market.

   The allegations included claims that BPB refused to supply, discriminated its pricing against merchants dealing with plasterboard, placed restrictions on importers and had exclusive dealings with building merchants. BPB argued that in spite of its dominant position in the UK, its plasterboard faces competition from other building materials used for internal partition walls.

   BPB Industries countered these claims by making allegations of its own. Two years ago BPB Industries complained to the EEC that Iberian Trading and a Spanish plasterboard manufacturer were dumping plasterboard in the Irish market and were now doing the same in the UK.' (Source: Financial Times 21 August 1986)

   (a) (i) Identify the trading restrictive practices allegedly undertaken by BPB Industries.

   (ii) Suggest reasons why BPB undertakes these practices.

   (b) Discuss appropriate policies for dealing with the monopoly in the plasterboard market.

2. *Variations in Regional Output 1971–83*

Index of Regional Variation in Gross Domestic Product per head (UK = 100)

		1971	1975	1979	1983
Core:	South East	111.3	112.9	115.4	119.1
	East Midlands	96.5	96.6	96.3	94.8
	East Anglia	93.8	92.2	94.2	97.1
	West Midlands	102.7	100.0	95.6	88.1
Inner periphery:	South West	94.7	90.5	93.6	95.8
	Yorks and Humberside	93.2	95.0	93.0	91.4
	North West	96.1	96.3	96.2	94.1
Outer periphery:	North	87.1	94.5	91.3	89.6
	Wales	88.4	89.6	86.4	83.8
	Scotland	93.0	96.7	95.9	96.4
	Northern Ireland	74.3	75.1	74.4	72.9

Source: Central Statistical Office

(a) Identify the richest and the poorest regions in the UK in:
(i) 1971;
(ii) 1983.

(b) Comment on the performance of the West Midlands region over the period shown by the data. What does this indicate about:
(i) the regional problem;
(ii) deindustrialisation?

MULTIPLE CHOICE QUESTIONS

1. *If the government decides that a nationalised industry, which benefits from economies of scale, should follow a policy of long-run marginal cost pricing, it is likely that:*

   A *Efficiency will improve and profits will increase*
   B *Efficiency will improve but losses will be made*
   C *The industry will be easier to privatise*
   D *The industry's monopoly power will diminish.*

2. *According to the 'theory of contestable markets', monopoly policy should:*

   A *Make sure that no firm has more than 25 per cent of the market*
   B *Eliminate barriers to market entry*
   C *Tax monopoly profits*
   D *Take monopolies into public ownership*

3. *Since 1984, all the following have increased in importance in United Kingdom regional and industrial policy EXCEPT*

   A *Enterprise zones*
   B *Selective financial assistance to firms*
   C *Automatic entitlement to regional development grants*
   D *Financial assistance available to service industries.*

4. *A monetarist economist is likely to argue that the UK regional problem can best be reduced by:*

   A *Creating conditions in which the market mechanism functions efficiently*
   B *Establishing national wage rates in the interests of social fairness*
   C *Extending the automatic entitlement to financial assistance for locating in development areas*
   D *Compulsory relocation of firms to assisted areas.*

5. *The term deindustrialisation usually refers to:*

   A *The stage of economic development reached by most Third World countries*
   B *Diseconomies of scale experienced by manufacturing industry*
   C *The UK economy before the industrial revolution*
   D *The absolute or relative decline of manufacturing industry.*

EXAMINATION QUESTIONS

1. *(a) What factors is a business likely to take into account when deciding where to locate a new plant? (12 marks)*

   (b) How successful have attempts by successive UK governments to influence such decisions been? (8 marks)
   (AAT June 1981)

2. *Discuss the economic problems of nationalisation. (AAT December 1982)*

3. *(a) What are the main factors a government might take into account when formulating anti-monopoly policy? (14 marks)*
   (b) Assess the effectiveness of the UK government's (or overseas government's) anti-monopoly policy. (6 marks)
   (AAT June 1986)

4. *Outline the case for controlling monopoly power and comment on the effectiveness of any attempts of which you are aware to limit this power.* *(CIMA December 1984)*

5. *On what basis should a nationalised industry price its product?* *(ACCA December 1984)*

6. *State enterprises have lost favour in recent years. In the USA this has resulted in deregulation and in Britain it has resulted in privatisation. With these developments in mind explain:*
   (a) the case for privatisation
   (b) the case against privatisation.
   (ACCA December 1987)

11. Market failure

INTRODUCTION

1. In Chapter 6 we explained how market forces operating in perfect markets can, in principle, achieve a long-run equilibrium which is economically efficient. We defined **economic efficiency** in terms of **productive efficiency, allocative efficiency** and **X-efficiency**. In this chapter we introduce the term **'market failure'** to describe all the circumstances in which market forces fail to achieve an economically efficient equilibrium. The main examples of market failure which we examine are **public goods, merit goods** and **demerit goods**, and **externalities**. Having examined market failures which result in market inefficiency, we shall extend the definition of market failure to cover circumstances in which market forces fail to ensure an **equitable or socially fair distribution** of resources. In particular, we shall argue that free unregulated markets are unlikely to ensure an equitable or fair distribution of income and wealth between rich and poor.

MARKET FAILURE AND PERFECT COMPETITION

2. Although **perfect competition** is used as a 'bench mark' or standard against which to judge market failure in monopoly and in other imperfectly competitive markets, market failure would be almost certain to occur in perfect competition itself, even if the conditions of perfect competition we listed in Chapter 6 were found in real world markets. This is for four main reasons:

(i) In Chapter 6 we explained that perfect competition can only achieve a state of economic efficiency *in the absence of economies of scale*. If economies of scale are possible, perfect competition may fail to achieve productive efficiency because there may not be room in the market for a large number of firms, each benefitting from full economies of scale.

(ii) *There must be no externalities present* for perfect competition to achieve an economically efficient use and allocation of resources. This point is explained in section 15 of this chapter.

(iii) *There must be markets in every single good and service* which can in principle be produced and which people would like to consume. These must include not only markets in goods and services currently available for exchange, but also **future markets**, ie markets in which buyers and sellers can make contracts to exchange goods or services at some future date. In reality, future markets exist only for a very narrow range of goods and services such as primary products and raw materials, currencies and other financial assets such as shares. Markets which do not exist, but which could in principle exist, are known as **'missing markets'**. Missing markets are an important type of market failure.

(iv) Every single market within the perfectly competitive market economy - and indeed in the whole world economy if the economy is linked through trade with the rest of the world - *must be in a state of simultaneous long-run equilibrium* to ensure economic efficiency throughout the economy.

We have just listed four highly restrictive qualifications to the argument that by 'improving' competition and making the real world approximate to the conditions of perfect competition, economic efficiency will automatically improve. However 'perfect' we make markets, some degree of market failure will always be present. This suggests an important political and economic issue. Should we allow such markets to function in a free and unregulated way, 'leaving alone' any residual market failure which will certainly be present in such markets? Or should the government intervene whenever market failure is discovered, using public policy to reduce or eliminate the failure so as to improve economic efficiency?

MARKET FAILURE, MONOPOLY AND IMPERFECT COMPETITION

3. **Monopoly** and other forms of imperfect **competition** of course provide much more obvious examples of market failure than those present in perfect markets. As Chapter 6 explained, the 'wrong' quantity is produced in monopoly, being sold at the 'wrong' price. In comparison with perfect competition (but only necessarily if we assume an absence of economies of scale) too little is produced which is sold at too high a

price and the market outcome is both allocatively and productively inefficient.

PUBLIC GOODS

4. Public goods are an example of market failure resulting from 'missing markets'; in a market economy markets may fail to provide any quantity at all of a pure public good such as national defence.

To understand this, we can compare a **public good** with a **private good**. Most goods are private goods possessing two important characteristics. The owners can **exercise private property** rights, preventing other people from using it or consuming its benefits. This property is called **excludability**. The second characteristic possessed by a private good is **diminishability**; when one person consumes it, less of the benefits are available for other people.

In contrast to the excludability and diminishability characteristics possessed by a pure private good, a pure public good exhibits the opposite characteristics of **non-excludability** and **non-diminishability**. It is these which lead to market failure.

NON-EXCLUDABILITY AND PUBLIC GOODS

5. Let us imagine a country in which national defence is not provided by the state. Instead the government decides to leave it to individual citizens or residents to purchase the defence or protection they want in the market. But markets will only provide defence if entrepreneurs can successfully charge prices for any defence services rendered. Suppose an aspiring citizen, who believes a fortune awaits him in the defence industry, establishes a company, Nuclear Defence Services Ltd, with the aim of persuading the country's residents to purchase the 'services' of nuclear missiles strategically located around the country. After estimating the money value of the defence received by each individual, Nuclear Defence Services bills each household accordingly and awaits for the payments to flow in....

But the payments may never arrive. As long as the service is provided, every household can receive its benefits without paying. It is impossible to provide the benefits of nuclear defence to those of the country's inhabitants who are prepared to pay, while excluding the benefits from those who are not prepared to pay. Withdrawing the benefits from one means withdrawing from all. Each individual therefore, faces the temptation to consume without paying, or to **'free-ride'**. If sufficient of the country's inhabitants choose to become **'free-riders'**, Nation Defence Services Ltd must make a loss. The incentive to provide the service through the market thus disappears. Assuming of course, that the majority of the country's inhabitants believe nuclear defence to be necessary (ie a 'good' rather than a 'bad') the market fails because it fails to provide a service for which there is a need.

NON-PURE PUBLIC GOODS OR QUASI-PUBLIC GOODS

6. Most public goods are **non-pure public goods** or **quasi-public goods** rather than pure public goods, because various methods could be devised to exclude free-riders. None-pure public goods include roads, TV and radio broadcasts, streetlighting and lighthouses. In principle, roads can be converted into private goods, provided for profit through the market, by constructing toll gates and by limiting points of access. In many countries motorways are provided in this way, though the state rather than private enterprise may still be responsible for providing the service through the market. Radio and TV broadcasts are public goods because anybody who purchases a radio or TV receiver can 'free-ride', receiving the programme without paying. Nevertheless, programmes can be transmitted commercially through the market, either by charging an advertiser for access to the broadcasting medium or, by transmitting the programme by cable or by satellite. In the latter case, the TV or radio programme is effectively converted into a private good, since programmes cannot be received without paying a fee to the transmitting company either for access to the cable or for a special signal decoder.

NON-DIMINISHABILITY AND PUBLIC GOODS

7. But even if non-pure public goods such as roads can be provided through the market, the second characteristic of a public good, **non-diminishability**, nevertheless creates a strong case for non-market provision. Such provision will normally be by the state (or **command mechanism**), at zero price to the consumer, being **financed collectively** out of general taxation.

Non-diminishability (or non-rivalry) means that whenever an extra individual consumes the benefits of the public good, the benefits available to other consumers are not diminished.

Non-diminishability also means that the marginal cost incurred by the provider of the public good when an extra person consumes its benefits is zero. When, for example, the population grows and more benefit from national defence, no extra missiles are required. In the same way, one more person can switch on a TV set or walk under a streetlight without either diminishing the availability of the programme or the benefits of lighting for others, or causing the provider of the service to incur extra costs.

Now we have seen from our discussion of economic efficiency earlier in this chapter and also in Chapter 6, that the **allocatively efficient** or '*correct*' quantity of any good to be produced and consumed is the quantity people choose to consume when P = MC. But we have also just seen in the case of public goods, that the MC of providing the good to an extra consumer is zero. It follows therefore, that to promote allocative efficiency, public goods must be provided at zero price so as to maximise their consumption. But assuming free-riders are excluded, private entrepreneurs are only prepared to provide goods if they can make a profit, which requires a price above zero. Market provision of public goods requires therefore, that P > MC, which, as we have seen, results in their under-production and under-consumption. There is thus a case, even when the goods can be provided through the market, for the state to provide public goods 'free', to the consumer.

PUBLIC GOODS AND GOVERNMENT GOODS

8. It is important not to confuse a **public good** with a **government good** which is any good or service provided by the government. We have just seen that public goods are normally provided by the government, usually at zero price to the consumer, but we have also noted that some public goods such as roads and TV programmes can be privately provided through the market. It is not inevitable therefore, that public goods must be provided by the government. Government goods include public goods such as defence, police and roads, but they include also another category of goods known as **merit goods**, examples of which are education and health care.

MIXED GOODS

9. Non-pure public goods or quasi-public goods are examples of **mixed goods**, which are goods having both public and private good content. Very few goods in real life are pure public or private goods. In the case of a public good such as a road, non-diminishability as well as the property of non-excludability may not be complete. We must contrast a situation when the road is heavily used, for example during the rush hour, with periods in the day or week when traffic is very light. In the off-peak period it is true that an extra motorist using the road in no way diminishes the availability of the road to other motorists, though he will marginally contribute to the road's wear and tear. Nevertheless, the marginal cost of supply is approximately zero for low levels of use. However, by contributing to congestion and delay during the rush hour, when the road is being used close to full capacity, an additional motorist does diminish the availability of the road for other road users. Marginal costs of supply are therefore significantly greater than zero for high levels of road use. In a rather similar way, private goods may have some public good content, when for example enjoyment received from an entertainment such as a football match or a theatrical show is heightened by noting the enjoyment simultaneously experienced by other members of the audience. Consumers depend on other consumers for their utility, so their consumption is not completely private. Real life therefore, displays a whole range of mixed goods of various degrees of public and private good content, with pure public goods and pure private goods representing the extremes at each end of the range.

EXTERNALITIES

10. An **externality** is a **special type of public good or public 'bad'** which is 'dumped' by those who produce it on other people who receive or consume it, whether or not they choose to. The crucial characteristic of an externality is that it is **generated and received** outside the market. Indeed, as with the public goods we have already discussed, externalities provide examples both of **'missing markets'** and of the **'free-rider' problem**. The provider of an external benefit such as a beautiful view cannot charge a market price to any 'willing free-riders' who enjoy it, while conversely, the 'unwilling free-riders' who receive or consume external costs such as

pollution and noise cannot charge a price to the polluter for the 'bad' they reluctantly consume.

Externalities can be classified in two main ways: firstly, into **external costs and benefits**; and secondly into **production externalities, consumption externalities** and **mixed externalities.**

EXTERNAL COSTS AND EXTERNAL BENEFITS

11. These are known as **negative** and **positive externalities**. A number of typical external costs and benefits are illustrated in Figure 11.1 which shows a coal-burning power station generating externalities as 'spin-offs' or by-products from its main commercial activity, namely the production of electricity for sale in the market. The negative externalities illustrated are acid rain and other forms of pollution, and the 'eyesore' provided by the power station itself and by the electricity transmission lines and pylons which carry the electricity to the market. Conversely, we have assumed that the warm water discharged by the power station provides an external benefit to the local community because it enables a larger stock of fish to breed in the nearby lake. (However, the discharged water would represent a further negative externality if it adversely disturbed local eco-systems or if it was polluted.)

PRODUCTION EXTERNALITIES AND CONSUMPTION EXTERNALITIES

12. All the externalities illustrated in Figure 11.1 are production externalities because they are generated by a business enterprise in the course of production. A **pure production externality is generated in production** and also **received in production** by other firms, either as a rise in their production costs in the case of a negative externality, or as a reduction in production costs when positive externalities are received. For example, the acid rain illustrated in Figure 11.1 stunts the growth of trees and increases the production costs of commercial forestries. Conversely, the warm water discharged by the power station leads to larger fish stocks which reduce the production costs of commercial fisheries.

Figure 11.1: Negative and positive externalities generated by a coal-burning power station

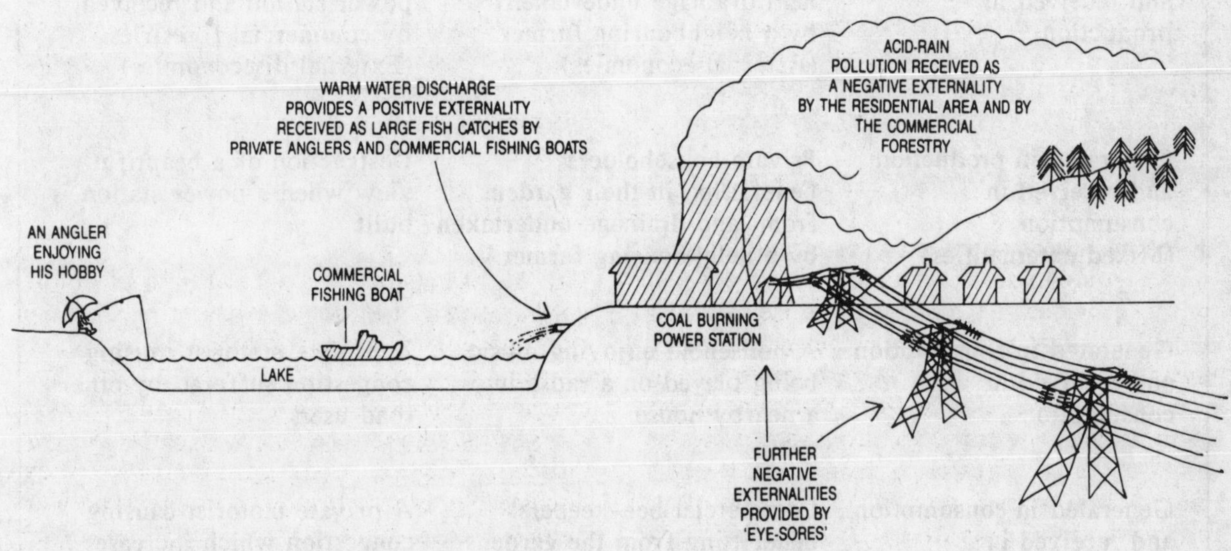

Pure consumption externalities are not illustrated in Figure 11.1, but we have included examples in Table 11.1, together with examples of **mixed externalities.** A **pure consumption externality** is **generated in the course** of **consumption** by an individual or household and **received also in consumption** by other individuals or households, either as a utility gain or a utility loss. **Mixed externalities** are of two types: those generated in production, and received as a utility gain or loss by households in the course of consumption, and those generated in consumption and received in production by firms, as either an increase or reduction in their production costs. The pollution and warm water discharged by the power station in Figure 11.1 are examples of mixed externalities when received by households in consumption, respectively as utility losses and utility gains.

EXTERNALITIES AND EXTERNAL ECONOMIES AND DISECONOMIES

13. Externalities received in production which reduce or raise the production costs of firms are **examples of external economies and diseconomies.** They may be pure production externalities generated by other firms, either in similar or in completely different industries, or they may be generated in consumption by households but received in production by firms. Examples are illustrated in Table 11.1

However, not all the external economies and diseconomies which reduce a firm's costs of production can properly be regarded as externalities. Suppose for example, that a firm successfully reduces its internal production costs and passes this benefit on to other firms by reducing the price at which it sells its products to the other firms. The availability of a cheaper source of raw materials or components is an external economy as far as the purchasing firms are concerned. But because it is an economy or benefit generated and received through the market, via the price mechanism, it does not qualify as an externality. *Externalities must be generated and received outside the market.*

Table 11.1: The different types of externality

	External benefits	*External costs*
Generated in production and received in production	A farmer benefitting from land drainage undertaken by a neighbouring farmer (External economies)	Acid rain generated by a power station and received by commercial forestries. (External diseconomies)
Generated in production and received in consumption (Mixed externalities)	Private householders benefitting in their gardens from land drainage undertaken by a neighbouring farmer	Destruction of a beautiful view when a power station is built
Generated in consumption and received in consumption	A household enjoying music being played on a radio in a nearby house	A private motorist causing congestion suffered by other road users
Generated in consumption and received in production (Mixed externalities)	Commercial bee-keepers benefitting from the gardens of private households (External economies)	A private motorist causing congestion which increases the production costs of firms (External diseconomies)

DIVERGENCIES BETWEEN PRIVATE AND SOCIAL COST AND BENEFIT

14. A central proposition of economic theory is that an economic agent in a market situation considers only the **private costs and benefits** to the agent itself of its market actions, ignoring any costs and benefits imposed on others. Households and firms seek to **maximise their private self-interest**, and not the wider **social interest** of the whole community. However, when externalities are generated, costs and benefits are inevitably imposed on others, so **private benefit maximisation no longer coincides with social benefit maximisation.**

Such a **divergency between private and social cost and benefit** is illustrated in Figure 11.2 which shows the costs and benefits occurring when a firm generates a negative production externality. Assuming no positive externalities are generated, the **marginal private benefits (MPB)** accruing to the firm from production, and the **marginal social benefits (MSB)** received by the whole community are the same. But because negative externalities such as pollution are generated in production, the **marginal social cost (MSC)** of production exceeds the **marginal private cost (MPC)** incurred by the firm. **Marginal external costs (MEC)** are the difference between MSC and MPC. At each level of output:

$$MSC \equiv MPC + MEC$$

Left to itself, the firm chooses to produce output Q_1 of the good for sale in the market, **maximising private benefit** at the level of output at which:

$$MPB = MPC$$

MSB = MSC is the **equilibrium equation for social benefit maximisation**. The level of output at which private benefit is maximised, Q_1, is greater than the level of output at which social benefit is maximised. The market fails because it results in over-production of a good when negative externalities are generated in the course of production.

Figure 11.2: Private and social costs and benefits when a negative production externality is generated

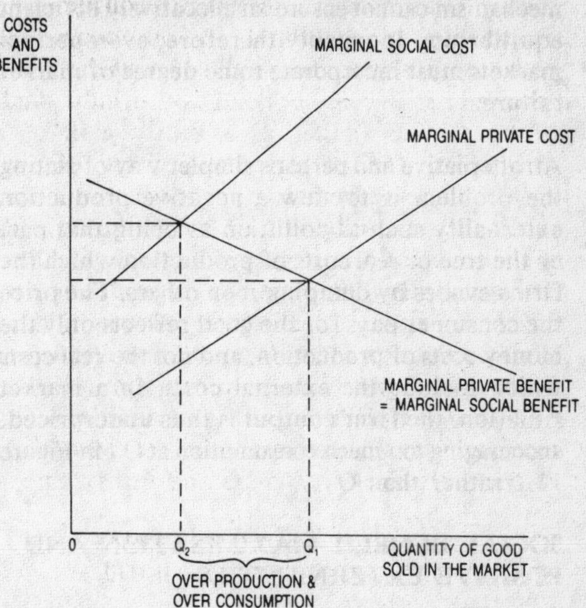

EXTERNALITIES AND ALLOCATIVE EFFICIENCY

15. We can also analyse the market failure which occurs when externalities are generated in terms of **allocative efficiency and inefficiency**. In Chapter 6 we explained how a perfectly competitive economy would achieve a state of allocative efficiency in long-run equilibrium, when P = MC in all markets. We have already noted that this conclusion holds only if:

(i) there are competitive markets for all goods and services, including future markets;

(ii) there are no economies of scale; and

(iii) all markets are simultaneously in equilibrium.

As we first stated in section 2 of this chapter, we can now add a fourth qualification: *there must be no externalities, negative or positive*. This is because long-run equilibrium occurs in a perfect market at the price at which P = MPC, which in the absence of externalities, means also that P = MSC. But if negative production externalities are generated, P < MSC when P = MPC. To achieve allocative efficiency, **price must equal the true marginal cost of production, ie the marginal social cost** and *not just the marginal* *private cost*. But in a market situation, firms can only take account of private costs and benefits, so when externalities exist, the market mechanism cannot ensure an allocatively efficient equilibrium. Inevitably therefore, even perfect markets must incorporate some degree of market failure.

An alternative and perhaps simpler way of stating the problem is to view a negative production externality such as pollution as being that part of the true or real costs of production which the firms evades by dumping it on others. The price the consumer pays for the good reflects only the **money costs** of production, and not the **real costs** which include the external costs. In a market situation, the firm's output is thus **underpriced**, encouraging too much consumption at Q_1 in Figure 11.2 rather than Q_2.

SOCIAL BENEFIT MAXIMISATION AND POSITIVE EXTERNALITIES

16. We shall now extend the analysis to cover the situation in which a firm generates only **positive externalities** in the course of production. This is illustrated in Figure 11.3. The **marginal social costs** of production are now the same as the **marginal private costs**, but the **marginal social benefits** to the whole community exceed the **marginal private benefits** to the firm. **Marginal external benefits (MEB)** are the differences between MSB and MPB. At each level of output:

$$MSB \equiv MPB + MEB$$

Pursuing **private benefit maximisation**, the firm produces an output Q_1 in Figure 11.3, which is less than the **socially optimal level** of output Q_2 at which:

$$MSB = MSC$$

Thus when positive production externalities are generated, the market fails because *too little* of the good is produced and consumed. As noted in section 11, there is a 'missing market' in the externality. When an external benefit is generated in the course of production, there is no incentive for a firm to produce the socially optimal level of output because the firm cannot charge for the by-product, the external benefit. Conversely, firms lack an incentive to produce less of a negative production externality, because no market exists in which the firm itself can be made to pay for the 'bad' dumped on others.

Figure 11.3: Private and social costs and benefits when a positive production externality is generated

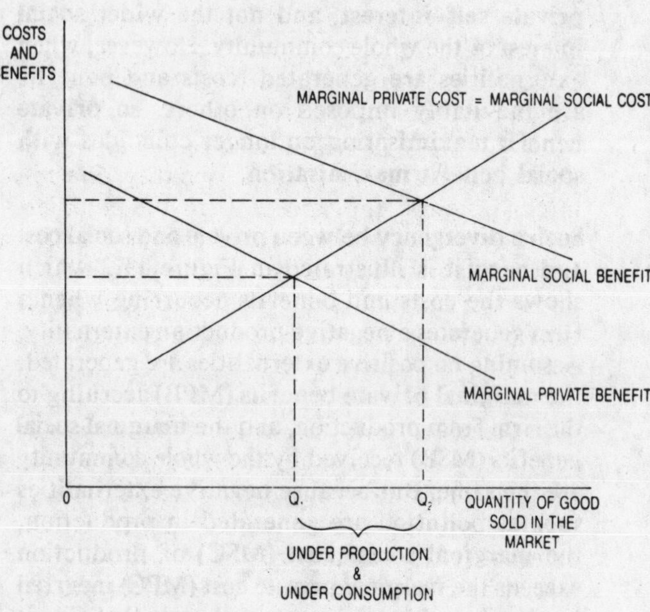

PUBLIC POLICY AND EXTERNALITIES

17. When externalities are generated in the course of the production of a good, the **public policy problem** is to ensure the '*correct*' level of production and consumption of the good, at which MSB = MSC. This can be done either by **quantity control (or regulation)** or by **taxation and subsidy**, or possibly by some combination of both methods. By introducing quantity controls or regulations, the government can influence directly the quantity of an externality a firm or household must generate. In contrast, taxation or subsidy can be used to **adjust market prices** in order to create **incentives** which are missing in the market, either for less of a negative externality of more of an external benefit to be generated.

(i) **Regulation or quantity controls**. In its most extreme form, **regulation** can be used to ban **completely, or illegalise**, the generation of negative externalities such as pollution and noise. Conversely, the generation of positive externalities may be **made compulsory**, ie it is illegal not to provide external benefits for others. Examples of the compulsory provision of external benefits include local authority bylaws or regulations requiring households and landowners to maintain their properties in good decorative order and to plant trees. In the case of external costs, it may of course be impossible to produce a good or service such as electricity in a coal-burning power station without generating at least some of a negative externality. Because illegalising the externality could have the perverse effect of preventing production of the 'good' (electricity) as well as the 'bad' (pollution), **lesser quantity controls** might be more appropriate than the complete banning of the generation of the externality. Lesser quantity controls or regulations include maximum emission limits and restrictions on the time of day or year during which the negative externality can legally be emitted.

(ii) **Taxation and subsidies**. Taxation and subsidies can, in principle, be used to correct the market failure caused by externalities, by making up for the 'missing market' in the externality. By calculating the money value of any negative externalities generated, and by imposing this on the firm as a tax - on **the principle the 'polluter must pay'** - the incentive is created, which is lacking in the market, for less of the 'bad' to be dumped on others. Essentially, the tax **'internalises the externality'**. Also, the firm now finds itself having to cover *all* its costs of production, including the cost of the negative externalities, and this will be reflected in the price charged to the consumer. If the tax is set so that the adjusted price the consumer pays equals MSC, an allocatively efficient level of production and consumption may be achieved. Nevertheless, the qualification which we made earlier still stands; we can only be certain that the firm or industry is allocatively efficient if every other market in the economy is simultaneously setting price equal to MSC, an impossible requirement. We should note also that the pollution tax, like any tax, will itself introduce new inefficiencies and distortions into the market, associated with the costs of collecting the tax and with incentives created to evade the tax illegally, for example by dumping pollution at night to escape detection.

MERIT GOODS

18. **Merit goods** and **demerit goods** provide further examples of divergency between private and social cost and benefit, and of the generation of externalities. A **merit good** such as education or health care is a good or service from which the **social benefits of consumption to the whole community exceed the private benefits to the consumer.** Whereas markets may very well fail to provide any quantity at all of a pure public good such as defence, they can certainly provide education and health care, as the existence of private fee-paying schools and hospitals clearly demonstrate. But if schools and hospitals are available only through the market at prices unadjusted by subsidy, people (especially the poor) will choose to consume too little of their services.

The tendency for merit goods to be underconsumed at market prices is illustrated in Figure 11.4 In the absence of regulation or subsidy, people choose to consume Q_1 of the merit good, maximising private benefit where MPB = MPC. However, because the social benefits of consumption exceed the private benefits, the socially optimal level of production and consumption of the merit good is Q_2, where MSB = MSC. The problem for public policy is to increase consumption from Q_1 to Q_2 and, as in the case of external benefits which Figure 11.4 closely resembles, consumption can be encouraged by regulation or subsidy. It is interesting to note that for some merit goods, for example, car seat belts and motorcycle crash helmets which are infrequently purchased by road users, the United Kingdom government uses regulation but not subsidy. Consumption is made compulsory, but road users must pay a market price for the merit good - indeed a price higher than a true cost of providing seat belts or crash helmets because the price includes value added tax. This reflects the fact that expenditure upon these merit goods is only a small part of a motorist's total expenditure, so road users can afford to pay. In contrast, other merit goods such as vaccination against contagious diseases are completely subsidised in the United Kingdom, being provided 'free', but consumption is not compulsory.

Education is a merit which is both compulsory and made available completely subsidised, at least for children between the ages of 5 and 16. Because of the expense of education, low-income families would be in an impossible situation if the law required them to send their children to school and also required them to pay. But while merit goods such as education and health care are provided by the state (in the United Kingdom) and form an important part of public spending, they can be provided through the private sector. The state may allow and, indeed encourage, the private provision of these merit goods, by paying the fees of low-income households who consume their benefits. In the United Kingdom, the assisted places scheme in private schools provides an example.

Figure 11.4: A merit good as a market failure: available at market prices unadjusted by subsidy or regulation, the merit good is underconsumed

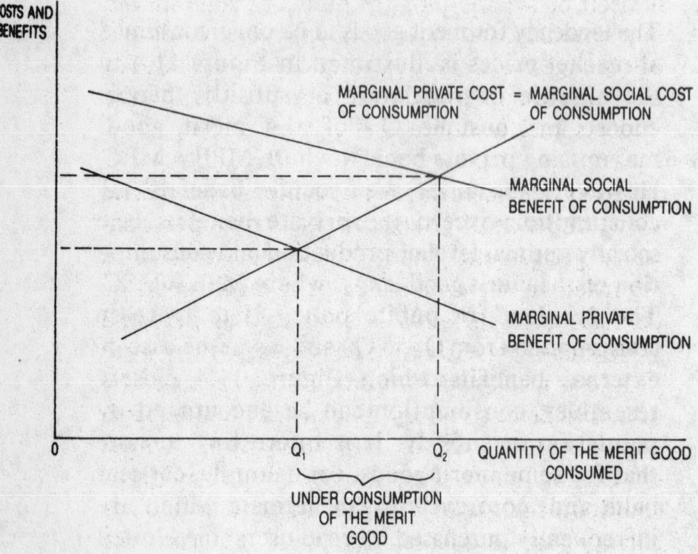

DEMERIT GOODS

19. As their name suggests, **demerit goods** are the opposite of merit goods. The social costs to the whole community which result from the consumption of a demerit good such as tobacco or alcohol exceed the private costs incurred by the consumer. The private cost can be measured by the money cost of purchasing the good, together with any health damage suffered by the person consuming the good. However, the social costs of consumption include the costs of damage and injury inflicted on other people, resulting for example from tobacco smoke and road accidents caused by drunken drivers. The social costs include also the costs imposed on other people through taxation to pay for the care of victims of tobacco and alcohol related diseases.

Thus, in the same way as the consumption of merit goods generates positive externalities for society as a whole, the consumption of demerit goods causes negative externalities to be dumped on others. As Figure 11.5 shows, too much of the demerit good is consumed. In Figure 11.5(a) the socially optimal quantity is Q_2, at which MSB = MSC, but at market prices people choose to consume Q_1, where MPB = MPC. Figure 11.5(b) shows a more extreme situation in which the social costs resulting from the consumption of the demerit good are so severe that none should be consumed. When this is the case, as in the case of 'hard' drugs such as heroin and cocaine, the state may discourage consumption by criminalising production, or consumption, or both. However, we should take care to avoid confusing a **demerit good** such as a narcotic drug with an **economic 'bad'**. A 'bad' yields only disutility or unpleasantness to the consumer, whereas a drug user certainly gains utility,at least in the short run, from his habit. Because of the addictive or habit-forming nature of the consumption of many demerit goods, attempts to maximise the social benefit by the ultimate regulation of criminalising its use are often counter-productive. The market in the demerit goods is not abolished; it is simply driven underground. Indeed the social costs of consumption in an illegal and completely unregulated market may well exceed the social costs which occur when consumption of the demerit good is legalised but closely regulated. This explains why governments often prefer to discourage or limit consumption of demerit goods by taxation and the use of regulations which stop short of an outright ban on consumption. Examples include spatial limitations on where the demerit good can legally be consumed, for example no-smoking areas and licensed premises for the sale of alcohol, and limitations on young people consuming the good, and on times of day when alcohol can legally be consumed in a public place.

Figure 11.5: A demerit good as a market failure

(a) A less severe case

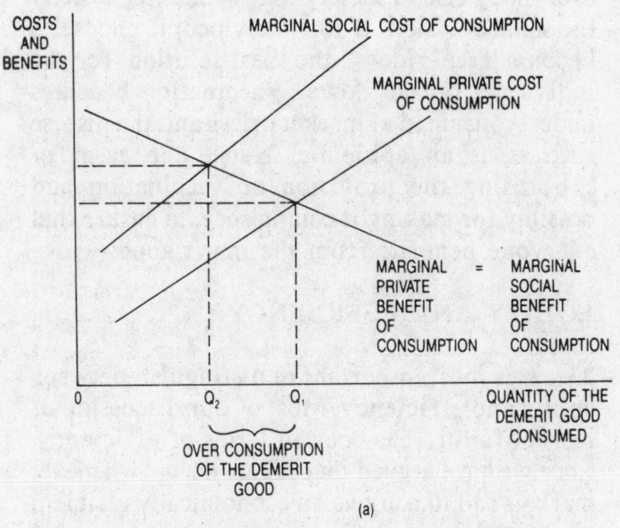

(b) A very severe case

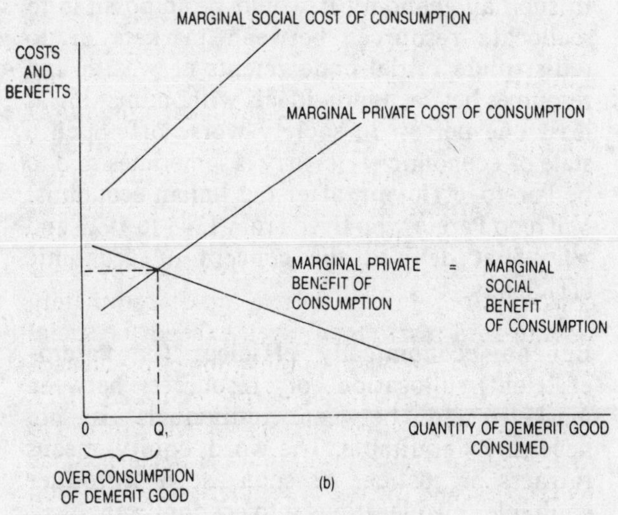

The effectiveness of a tax in discouraging consumption of a demerit good such as alcohol depends on the size of the tax and on the price elasticity of demand for the good. Because of their addictive nature, demand for demerit goods is often inelastic. This will limit the effectiveness of the tax in discouraging consumption.

VALUE JUDGEMENTS, MERIT GOODS AND DEMERIT GOODS

20. Besides generating externalities, merit goods and demerit goods possess a second important characteristic inextricably linked with value judgements. Individuals consuming merit and demerit goods may not act in their own best interest because they consider only short-term **utility maximisation** rather than **long-term utility maximisation**. A young person smoking cigarettes will regret his decisions later in life if he eventually contracts a smoking-related disease. In the case of a merit good such as education, people may choose too little early in life in the sense that later in life they may wish they had consumed more. It can be argued that an authority outside the individual, such as the state, is a better judge than the individual himself of what is good for him. The state should thus encourage the consumption of merit goods and discourage the consumption of demerit goods for the individual's own interest, as well as for the wider social interest.

Whether one agrees with this rather paternalistic view, depends of course on one's own personal value judgement! Indeed, whether a good is regarded in the first place as a merit good or demerit good depends upon a similar personal value judgement. Goods which are regarded by some people as merit goods are sometimes regarded by others as demerit goods. Examples include birth control, sterilisation and abortion, which depending on a person's ethical or religious standpoint might be regarded as good or bad for society as a whole, as well as for the individual. These examples demonstrate that the whole question of deciding whether, and to what extent, a good is a merit or demerit good, or indeed neither, depends on value judgements that are likely to vary greatly from individual to individual and between different types of society.

UNCERTAINTY AND MARKET FAILURE

21. We have mentioned already that market failure is likely to occur whenever economic agents possess less than perfect market information, or are uncertain about future market information. **Uncertainty of information** can, for example, explain why a merit good such as health care may be underconsumed if it is only available through a market. The market price of a serious operation is extremely high, involving many thousands of pounds. People seldom know in advance if they are going to be seriously ill or involved in an accident which will require the operation. In this situation, the market may fail to provide the required health care simply because when it is needed, the customer cannot afford it. A market-orientated solution is, of course, a private health insurance market, but this may fail to provide a service for the very poor and the chronically ill. It will also fail to provide the required medical care for the 'risk-takers' in society who decide not to buy insurance, as distinct from 'risk-averters' who are always the most ready customers for insurance. Public collective provision through a compulsory state insurance scheme is, therefore, another solution. You should note that both private and public insurance schemes are a response to the fact that the demand for medical care is much more predictable for a large group of people than for a single person - an application of statistical probability theory and the 'law' of large numbers.

VACCINATION AS A MERIT GOOD

22. We shall complete our coverage of merit goods and demerit goods by examining an example of a merit good which illustrates also the **'free-rider' problem**, explained earlier in this chapter in the context of public goods. Suppose that there exists a vaccination for a serious infectious disease such as smallpox which is 100 per cent certain to prevent a vaccinated person from catching the disease. The vaccination has no adverse side-effects, but if available through a market, the market price of vaccination is £25. The disease is so contagious, that if a significant proportion of the population chooses to remain unvaccinated, the disease will spread as an epidemic amongst the unvaccinated. Given all this information, we might conclude that everybody in the population, acting rationally, chooses to purchase vaccination for themselves and their children, believing that complete immunisation from the disease is well worth the price.

However, the **best possible solution from any individual's point of view** is to remain unvaccinated, providing that everyone else in society chooses to be vaccinated. In this way an individual saves £25 and 'free-rides' on the rest of the population. If everybody else is vaccinated, there is nobody from whom the disease can be caught! This will certainly be an effective solution if everybody else does choose to pay £25 for vaccination, but of course everybody else in society may be making exactly the same decision. If too many people choose to become 'free-riders', the 'best solution' for the individual breaks down. Vaccination becomes under-consumed at market prices and the disease spreads as an epidemic. Hence the case for subsidising the provision of vaccination and possibly for making it compulsory, to ensure that everyone benefits from the merit good.

EQUITY AND EFFICIENCY

23. It is most important to distinguish between **equity** and **efficiency**. Most of our discussion of market failure has been in terms of **efficiency**, since we have argued that failure occurs whenever markets fail to achieve an economically efficient use of resources, defined in terms of productive and allocative efficiency. To summarise, a market economy is economically efficient when average costs are minimised (productive efficiency) and P = MSC in every market (allocative efficiency). In such an economy it would be impossible to reallocate resources between markets or to redistribute initial endowments of wealth and resources between individuals without making at least one person in society worse off. Such a state of economic efficiency is sometimes said to be Pareto-efficient, after the Italian economist Vilfredo Pareto who lived from 1848 to 1923 and who first devised the concept of economic efficiency.

But an **economically efficient** (or **Pareto-efficient**) allocation of resources between markets and between individuals is not necessarily equitable. The word **'equity'** means fairness or justice. As soon as we introduce equitable considerations into economic analysis, we must make normative or value judgements about such matters as what is a 'socially fair' distribution of income and wealth and what goods and services people *ought* to produce and consume. You should note that we have already introduced such normative judgements into our explanation of why the market fails to provide the correct quantity of merit and demerit goods, arguing for example that people, especially the poor, will consume less of a merit good such as education than they 'ought to'.

THE DISTRIBUTION OF INCOME AND WEALTH

24. However, probably the most significant example of a market failure which results from considerations of equity rather than of economic efficiency, concerns the **fairness** or otherwise **of the distribution of income and wealth within society**. For every imaginable initial endowment of wealth and income between members of society there will be an economically efficient (or Pareto-efficient) allocation of resources between markets. But many, if not most of such Pareto-efficient allocations would be extremely inequitable. An obvious example occurs when 1 per cent of the population owns 99 per cent of the nation's wealth and receive 99 per cent of total incomes, while 99 per cent of the people own and receive only 1% in total of the economy's wealth and income. Given such an initial endowment of wealth and income, we can devise an economically efficient allocation of resources between markets, which in principle could be achieved by competitive market forces. Once achieved, it would be impossible to make one individual in society better off without making at least one other individual worse off. But this is no argument against making the 99 per cent better off by taking resources from the wealthy minority and redistributing them to the poverty-striken majority. Indeed, we can argue that in such a situation the market mechanism fails simply because it is **'value-neutral'** with regard to the social and ethical desirability or undesirability of the distribution of wealth and income within society. Extreme critics of the market argue the case for replacing markets with the command mechanism as a method of allocating resources both efficiently and equitably. However, as we saw in Chapter 1, the command mechanism can be extremely inefficient, both productively and allocatively. There is much more general agreement therefore, that instead of **replacing** the market, governments should **modify** the market so that it operates in a more equitable way, than would be the case without government intervention. **Taxing** the better-off and **re-distributing** the tax revenue as **transfers** to the less well-off is the obvious way of dealing with the failure of the market to ensure an equitable distribution of income and wealth (though we ought to note that such redistribution policies will promote new types of inefficiency and distortion within the economy).

SUMMARY

25. In this chapter we have examined four main types of market failure: public goods, externalities; merit and demerit goods; and failure resulting from the fact that market forces cannot ensure a socially fair or equitable distribution of income and wealth. We have also surveyed briefly other examples of market failure resulting from imperfect and missing markets and market information, economies of scale and from conditions of uncertainty.

Markets fail for two main reasons: inefficiency and inequity. Some examples of market failure exhibit aspects of both. For instance, the provision of merit goods and demerit goods through markets at prices unadjusted by taxation or subsidy, leads to inefficient levels of production and consumption because of divergencies between private and social costs and benefits. At the same time market provision of these goods is inequitable if it leads to poor people having too little access to merit goods such as education and health care and, perhaps too much access to a demerit good such as tobacco which may eventually prove harmful to them.

It is useful also to distinguish between complete market failure, when a market fails to provide any quantity at all of a good, and a situation in which some of a good is provided, but not the 'correct' quantity. Pure public goods such as national defence illustrate the former, whereas merit and demerit goods are examples of goods provided through the market, but in the wrong quantities. Externalities exhibit characteristics of both situations; they are examples of 'missing markets', there being no market in the externalities themselves, but they are usually generated as a 'spin-off' of market behaviour, either in production or consumption.

The public policy problem is to encourage the 'correct' levels of production and consumption of public goods, merit goods and demerit goods and of goods which when produced or consumed, generate externalities. In terms of economic efficiency, the 'correct' level is where MSB = MSC. When the price correctly reflects the marginal social benefits to the whole community, the economically efficient level of production and consumption occurs where P = MSC. In the case of public goods, which markets may fail completely to provide, direct state provision is usual with the goods made available 'free' to the consumer, being financed collectively out of general taxation. Merit goods such as health care and education are often also provided by the state in this way, though in principle markets can provide these goods. In general, the state can use regulation to try to ensure the socially optimal level of consumption of a merit or demerit good, or it can use subsidies (in the case of merit goods) and taxation (in the case of demerit goods). The purpose of the subsidy or tax is to close the divergency between private and social cost and benefit and to create the incentive, lacking at market prices, for the correct or economically efficient quantity of the good to be produced and consumed. The framework of regulation or quantity control on the one hand and taxation and subsidy on the other hand, can also be used to regulate the production and consumption of external costs and benefits.

Taxation and subsidy (in the form of transfers from rich to poor) are also appropriate for correcting the market failure resulting from unequal distributions of income and wealth. But in contrast to the other types of market failure we have described, the main concern here is to correct market failure resulting from inequity rather than to correct a Pareto-inefficient allocation of resources between markets and uses.

STUDENT SELF-TESTING

1 *When may perfect competition fail to achieve economic efficiency?* *(2)*
2 *Why is monopoly a type of market failure?* *(3)*
3 *Define a public good.* *(4)*
4 *What is a 'free-rider'?* *(5)*
5 *Distinguish between a pure and a non-pure public good.* *(6)*
6 *What is the 'correct' amount of a public good which should be provided?* *(7)*
7 *Distinguish between a public good and a government good.* *(8)*
8 *What is a mixed good?* *(9)*
9 *Define an externality.* *(10)*
10 *What is a consumption externality?* *(12)*
11 *What is the relationship between externalities and external economies and diseconomies?* *(13)*
12 *Define marginal social cost.* *(14)*
13 *How do externalities affect allocative efficiency?* *(15)*
14 *How can public policy deal with externalities?* *(17)*
15 *What is a merit good?* *(18)*
16 *Distinguish between a demerit good and a 'bad'.* *(19)*
17 *Distinguish between efficiency and equity.* *(23)*
18 *Why may the distribution of income and wealth be regarded as a market failure?* *(24)*

EXERCISES

1 *Carefully define each of the following:*
(a) a good;
(b) a bad;
(c) an economic good;
(d) a free good;
(e) a private good;
(f) a public good;
(g) a merit good.

2 *Suppose that refuse collection is available only through the market. Private enterprise companies provide a rubbish collecting service, but charge a market price of £1 for every household rubbish bin emptied. Explain why market failure might occur.*

MULTIPLE CHOICE QUESTIONS

1 *A good is defined as a public good when it is provided*
A *By the government*
B *By a public corporation*
C *To one person without diminishing the quantity available to others*
D *To everyone in the community except free-riders*

2 *The optimal output of a drug for society is the output at which*
A *Marginal private benefit equals marginal social cost*
B *Marginal social benefit equals marginal social cost*
C *Marginal social benefit exceeds marginal private benefit*
D *Marginal private cost exceeds marginal social cost*

3 *A Pareto-efficient allocation of resources in an economy occurs whenever:*
  A *Price is equated to marginal social cost in some industries*
  B *Income and wealth are distributed in a socially fair way*
  C *The existing resource allocation cannot be changed without making somebody worse off*
  D *There is full employment of resources*

4 *Merit goods are goods that:*
  A *Must be provided by the state*
  B *Are over-consumed at market price*
  C *Generate social benefits in consumption that exceed the private benefits*
  D *General negative externalities in consumption*

5 *A tax on pollution caused by motorists will*
  A *Externalise an internality*
  B *Cause zero pollution*
  C *Discourage recycling of waste products*
  D *Reduce the divergency between private and social costs.*

EXAMINATION QUESTIONS

1 *Explain how the price mechanism co-ordinates a market economy. Give details of the circumstances in which a failure of the market mechanism may occur.* (ACCA June 1975)

2 *To what extent are defence, healthcare and education, goods which require government intervention in their provision?* (ACCA June 1985)

3 (a) *Define an externality.* (4 marks)
  (b) *What effects do externalities have on the allocation of resources?* (8 marks)
  (c) *Explain briefly how the effects of externalities may be dealt with.* (8 marks)
  (ACCA June 1986)

4 *Your government is concerned with the effects of industrial pollution on the environment. Suggest some general policy guidelines.* (ACCA June 1979)

5 *Define, and explain the purpose of, cost benefit analysis. What problems would you expect to encounter in conducting an analysis?* (CIMA May 1980)

12. Distribution theory and wage determination

INTRODUCTION

1. In earlier chapters we have examined the behaviour of households and firms in markets for final goods or consumer goods - the markets which make up the **goods market** of the economy. In conducting our analysis, we generally assumed that the prices of the inputs necessary for production, or the prices of factor services were given. In this chapter, we reverse this assumption. We examine how the value of output is distributed as **factor incomes** to the owners of the inputs which are sold or hired to firms so that output can be produced. In constructing our theory, which is known both as **distribution theory**, and as **the theory of factor pricing and employment**, we shall assume that conditions and prices in the goods market are given. We shall concentrate for the most part on the determination of the levels of wages and employment within the labour market, applying the analysis as appropriate to the other factors of production and their prices. Towards the end of the chapter, we shall question whether the distribution of incomes between wages and other factor incomes such as profits, and also the distribution of wages between different groups of workers, can be explained adequately by supply and demand theory. The chapter concludes with a brief survey of alternative approaches to the distribution of incomes, examining wages and profits from institutional and sociological perspectives, for example, in terms of class conflict and the roles of the state and of trade unions.

THE FACTORS OF PRODUCTION

2. Distribution theory follows the convention, first introduced by the neo-classical economist Alfred Marshall in the nineteenth century, of dividing the inputs necessary for the production of output into four **factors of production**. These are **land, labour, capital** and **enterprise** (or the **entrepreneurial factor**), which respectively receive the factor incomes or rewards of rent, wages, interest and profit.

We must stress that this is a highly theoretical and abstract division, conforming neither to accounting conventions used in business practice, nor to the everyday use of words such as interest and rent. For example, from the standpoint of abstract economic theory, a commercial rent paid by a business or by an individual for the use of a building is partly rent (for the hire of the land on which the building is sited, and partly an interest payment on the capital tied up in the building.

THE FUNCTIONAL DISTRIBUTION OF INCOME

3. The distribution of income between the factors of production is called the **functional distribution of income**. Although the official statistics published in the National Income Accounts do not exactly match the theoretical division into wages, rent, interest and profits, they show that wages are the most important source of income in the United Kingdom, accounting for between 60 and 70 per cent of total incomes. The share of wages in total income rose slightly during the 1970s, but fell at the expense of profits during the 1980s.

Table 12.1: The functional distribution of income
(Distribution of total domestic income by percentage)

	1972	*1978*	*1984*
Income from employment	67.6	67.9	64.4
Gross trading profits and surplus of private and public enterprises, minus stock appreciation	15.4	15.2	19.3
Other income, including rent and income from self employment	17.0	16.9	16.3

Source: National Income Blue Book

THE SIZE DISTRIBUTION OF INCOME

4. The functional distribution of income should not be confused with the **size distribution of income** illustrated in Table 12.2. The size distribution of income shows, for example, the proportion of total income received by the top 20 per cent of income earners compared with other percentile groups in the population, such as the bottom 20 per cent. Table 12.2 displays both the size distribution of original income (ie income before both taxation and the receipt of transfers such as welfare benefits), and also the **size distribution of wealth** amongst different groups in the population. The data shows that both income and wealth are distributed unequally, but that the distribution of wealth is even more unequal than the distribution of income. During the 1970s, there was a slight trend for the distribution of income to become less unequal, but this trend was reversed in the 1980s with inequalities growing wider once again. Wealth is extremely unequally distributed in the United Kingdom, the top 10% of the population owning over half the nation's wealth, and the top 50% owning over 95% of wealth. The distribution has become marginally less unequal in recent years, perhaps because of the spread of house ownership and the fact that housing is the major wealth asset of a large proportion of the population. There is of course a significant link between the distribution of income and wealth.

The highest incomes received by the top 10% of income earners are made up to a large extent by dividends, interest payments and rents, which result from the ownership of shares, property, and other forms of wealth. The ownership of large wealth assets generates large incomes, a part of which are not spent on consumption but which go into the accumulation of further wealth. In contrast, most of the people in the bottom 40% of the income distribution own few wealth assets and of necessity spend on consumption most or all of any income received from the sale of their labour services. They have few opportunities to accumulate wealth.

THE LORENZ CURVE

5. **The Lorenz curve** is a statistical measure of the degree of equality or inequality in the size distribution of income, which can be used to compare distributions both between countries and between different periods of time. A Lorenz curve, examples of which are illustrated in Figure 12.1, normally has the numbers of income units on the horizontal axis marked off in cumulative percentages from 0 per cent to 100 per cent. The vertical axis, which is drawn to the same length, shows shares in total income again marked in cumulative percentages.

Table 12.2: The size distributions of income and wealth

Distribution of original income
(Income before tax and receipt of benefits)

Income received by: Population:		*1976*	*1981*	*1983*
Top	20%	44.4	46.4	48.0
Next	21-40%	26.2	26.9	27.2
Next	41-60%	18.8	18.0	17.7
Next	61-80%	9.4	8.1	6.7
Bottom	20%	0.8	0.6	0.3

Distribution of marketable wealth

owned by: Population		*1976*	*1981*	*1983*
Top	1%	24	22	20
Next	2-10%	36	34	34
Next	11-25%	24	24	24
Next	26-59%	11	16	18
Bottom	50%	5	4	4

Source: Social Trends

Figure 12.1: Lorenz curves which show the degree of inequality in the size distribution of income

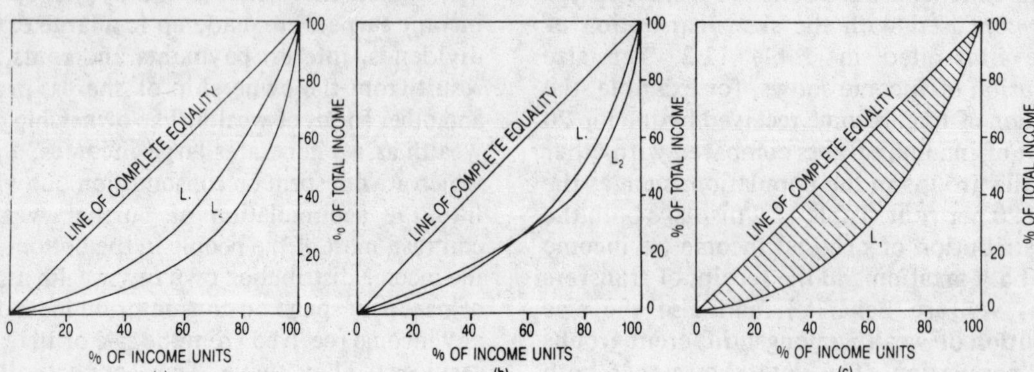

If incomes were distributed equally, the Lorenz curve would be the diagonal line drawn in Figure 12.1 showing for example that 20 per cent of income units receive 20 per cent of incomes, 40 per cent receive 40 per cent, and so on. In contrast, a state of complete inequality in which a single income unit received all the economy's income, would be represented by a Lorenz curve following first the horizontal axis and then the vertical axis. Within these two limiting cases, the nearer a Lorenz curve is to the diagonal, the more equal is the distribution of income.

We can draw a number of Lorenz curves on the same diagram to compare equality between various distributions of income. In Figure 12.1(a) Lorenz curve L_1, which is drawn nearer to the diagonal at all points between 0 and 100 than Lorenz curve L_2, shows unambiguously a more equal distribution of income. But when Lorenz curves intersect, as in Figure 12.1(b), it is not immediately clear which curve shows the greater degree of equality. However, a statistical measure exists called a **Gini coefficient**, which in terms of Figure 12.1(c) measures the shaded area between the diagonal line of complete equality and the relevant Lorenz curve. The larger the shaded area, the higher the Gini coefficient and the greater the degree of inequality. The Gini coefficient is normally expressed as a percentage, with complete inequality represented by 100 per cent. For industrial capitalist countries in Western Europe and North America, Gini coefficients are in the range 30-45 per cent, with lower values representing a greater equality calculated for Eastern European socialist countries.

DISTRIBUTION THEORY AND PRICE THEORY

6. Distribution theory is really just the price theory which we studied in earlier chapters in the goods market of an economy, now viewed from the 'other side', operating in the factor market. As Figure 12.2 clearly indicates, households and firms function simultaneously in both sets of markets, but their roles are reversed. Whereas firms are the source of supply in the goods market, in the factor market firms exercise demand for factor services supplied by households. The incomes received by the households from the sale and supply of factor services contribute of course in large measure to the household's ability to demand the output supplied by the firms in the goods market. Indeed the relationship between households and firms in the two markets is essentially circular. In the goods market, output flows from firms to households in return for money revenues. In the factor market the money revenues received enable the firms to purchase factor services supplied by the households. The circle is complete when households spend this income on the goods produced by the firms.

Figure 12.2: Households and firms are operating simultaneously in two sets of markets, but their roles are reversed in the goods and factor markets

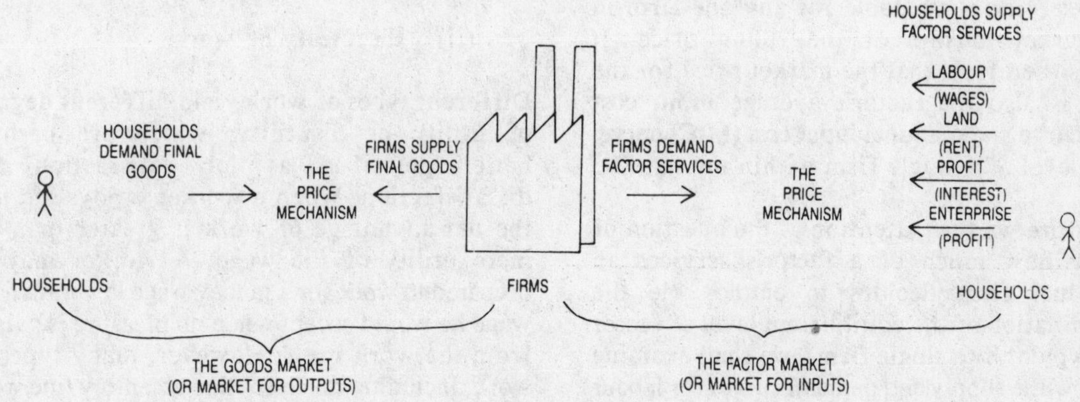

Being a part of traditional neo-classical price theory, distribution theory explains the determination of equilibrium prices and levels of employment of factors of production solely in terms of market forces or supply and demand. However, as in the goods markets, equilibrium price and level of employment of a factor depend upon **market structure** ie the extent to which the factor market is competitive or monopolistic. We shall follow normal convention by assuming initially that factor markets are perfectly competitive, comprising a large number of buyers and sellers, each unable to influence the ruling market price and operating in conditions of perfect market information. The other conditions of perfect competition which we first described in the context of the goods market in Chapter 6 also apply. Having examined the determination of the equilibrium market price of a factor of production and the equilibrium level of its employment both in the market as a whole and at the level of a single firm within the market, we shall relax the assumptions of perfect competition and examine less competitive market structures. We should however instil a word of caution. Real life factor markets, especially the labour market, are often highly imperfect. Thus the model of a perfectly competitive factor market should be regarded very much as the exception to the rule, rather than as the rule. As with the study of price theory in the goods market, the 'neo-classical' theory of distribution can be criticised for treating real life as a 'special case' or aberration from the norm of perfect competition, whereas the reverse is much more true. Imperfect factor markets are the norm, and we should perhaps regard perfect competition merely as a rarified and unrealistic limiting case or theoretical possibility.

A PERFECTLY COMPETITIVE LABOUR MARKET

7. We saw in Chapter 6 that when a firm is perfectly competitive in the goods market (or market for output), it can sell as much as it wants to at the ruling market price, which can be viewed also both as the perfectly elastic demand curve facing the firm and as the firm's average and marginal revenue curve. Essentially the firm is a passive 'price-taker' at the ruling price determined in the market as a whole, choosing the quantity to produce but not price. A very similar situation exists when a firm is perfectly competitive in a factor market such as the labour market, except that now the firm can buy as much labour as it wants at the ruling market wage. The firm could, of course, pay a higher wage, but there is no need to, since as many workers as the firm plans to employ are available at the ruling wage. Conversely, a firm offering a wage below the market wage would find no workers since, from labour's point of view, all employers are perfect substitutes. Why work for a firm paying below the market wage when work is available from employers offering the market wage?

As we have just noted, in a perfectly competitive goods market the perfectly elastic demand curve facing each firm is the firm's AR and MR curve.

By contrast in a perfectly competitive factor market (or market for inputs), the ruling market price of a factor of production serves as the **perfectly elastic supply curve facing a single firm in the market**. An infinite supply of the factor service is available for any one firm in the market to hire at the ruling price. It follows therefore, that the market price for the factor is also the factor's **average input cost (AIC) curve** and **marginal input cost (MIC) curve**, at the level of a single firm within the market.

But before we turn attention to the question of exactly how much of a factor's services an individual firm decides to employ (ie the determination of the equilibrium level of factor employment by a single firm), we shall examine first how the supply and demand curves for labour are determined in the market as a whole.

THE SUPPLY OF LABOUR

8. The **market supply curve of a factor of production** such as labour is obtained simply by adding together the **individual supply curves** of all the workers in the particular labour market. We must therefore derive the supply curve of labour of a single worker, showing how much labour he plans to supply at different wage-rates. We do this by invoking exactly the same maximising principles and assumptions which we have used in earlier chapters to determine supply and demand curves in the goods market for a commodity such as chocolate. The **assumptions of profit-maximising behaviour by firms** and **utility maximisation by households** are as fundamental and crucial to the neo-classical theory of distribution as they are to the rest of price theory. Firms are assumed to demand the services of factors of production only if profits can be increased by their employment. Likewise, we assume that households supply more labour, or hire out the capital or land they own, only if by so doing, they increase total household utility. An individual's supply curve of labour derives from exactly the same utility maximising assumption which underlies the theory of consumer demand in the goods market, which we studied in Chapter 3.

NET ADVANTAGE

9. The utility which a worker derives from the supply of his labour can be divided into two parts, which taken together are called **net advantage**. A worker's net advantage includes:

(i) the **utility of the wage** (or strictly the utility of the goods and services bought with the money wage) and

(ii) the **utility of work**.

Different types of work yield different degrees of utility or disutility, which are perhaps better described as job satisfaction and dissatisfaction. When a worker enjoys his job, the net advantage of work is greater than the mere utility of the wage. A worker may be prepared to work for a money wage lower than the wage he would accept when no pleasure is gained from the work itself. However, many types of work, including much routine assembly line work in factories and heavy manual labour, are unpleasant, yielding only job dissatisfaction. In these circumstances, the supply curve of labour reflects the fact that the hourly wage rate must provide some compensation for the unpleasantness of the work involved.

THE UPWARD-SLOPING SUPPLY CURVE OF LABOUR

10. For the sake of simplicity, we shall assume that work itself yields neither job satisfaction nor dissatisfaction, so that a worker's net advantage equals the utility of the wage. We must now consider the **opportunity** cost involved whenever an individual decides to work. Essentially, **a worker chooses between work and leisure**, which are substitutes for each other. When deciding to supply an extra 'man-hour' of labour time, he is choosing also an hour less of leisure time. The choice is influenced not only by the wage rate, but also by the fact that both the money wage (or strictly the goods the wage buys) and leisure respond to the **law of diminishing marginal utility**. When more labour is supplied at a particular wage rate, the extra income yields less and less extra utility. At the same time, each extra hour of leisure sacrificed results in an increasing utility loss. To maximise utility, labour must be supplied up to the point at which:

MU of the wage = MU of leisure

This is another example of an **equilibrium equation**. The marginal utility of the wage represents the **marginal private benefit** received by a worker from the last unit of labour time supplied, while the marginal utility of the substitute, leisure, is the **marginal cost** incurred by working. When the MU of the wage = MU of leisure, a worker is in equilibrium in the sense that he has no incentive to supply more labour time at the existing wage rate, providing his utility functions for goods and leisure are unchanged. A higher wage would be needed to encourage him to supply voluntarily more labour beyond this point; hence the upward-sloping supply curve of labour shown in Figure 12.3.

Figure 12.3: The upward-sloping supply curve of labour showing the higher the wage rate, the more labour time is supplied

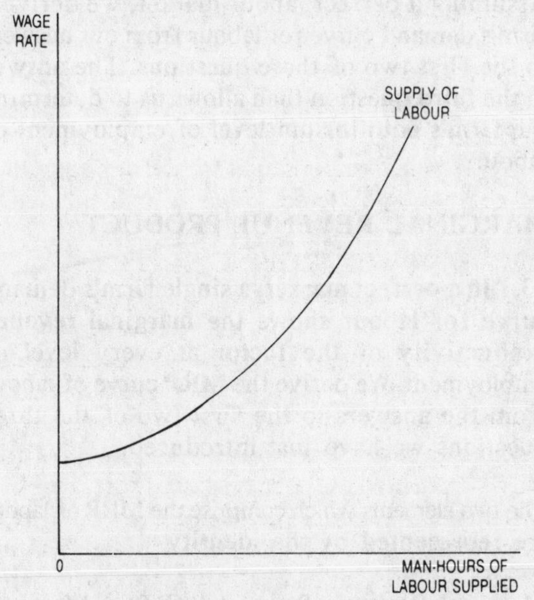

THE BACKWARD-BENDING SUPPLY CURVE OF LABOUR

11. It is not inevitable, however, for a worker's supply curve of labour to be upward-sloping, as illustrated in Figure 12.3. Under some circumstances the supply curve may be **backward-bending** or **perverse**, showing that as the wage rises, less labour is supplied. This is illustrated in Figure 12.4 in which the supply curve is drawn 'normal' for only part of its length. There are two ways of explaining the possibility that beyond the wage rate W_1 in Figure 12.4, a worker will choose to work for fewer hours. On the one hand we can continue to assume a utility maximising objective, but explain the supply curve in terms of the **substitution effect** and the **income effect** resulting from an increase in the wage rate. As the wage rate rises, leisure time in effect becomes more expensive compared to the goods the money wage can buy. Up to the wage rate W_1, the **substitution effect of any wage increase** exceeds the income effect and the worker chooses more work and less leisure. **The income effect of a wage rise** results from the fact that for most people leisure is a normal good and not an inferior good. As income rises so does the demand for leisure. Beyond the wage rate W_1 the income effect of a wage rise becomes more powerful than the substitution effect. A worker chooses to work fewer hours so as to enjoy more leisure. Total money income may not of course fall. Given freedom of choice, a worker may, for example, decide to work 40 hours a week when the wage rate is £3 an hour, for a weekly income of £120. When the wage rate rises to £4, he may respond by working for only 35 hours, yet his weekly income has risen to £140.

An alternative, though not fundamentally different, approach to the backward-bending supply curve is to assume that a workers aspires **to a target standard of living** in terms of the goods and services the money wage can buy. When the money wage rate rises, a worker can meet his target or fulfill his aspirations by working fewer hours, choosing more leisure time rather than more material goods and services. Workers are especially likely to behave in this way when the work itself is highly unpleasant, as perhaps in the coal mining industry, yielding negative job satisfaction.

Figure 12.4: The backward-bending or perverse supply curve or labour showing beyond W_1 that at higher wage rates less labour time is supplied

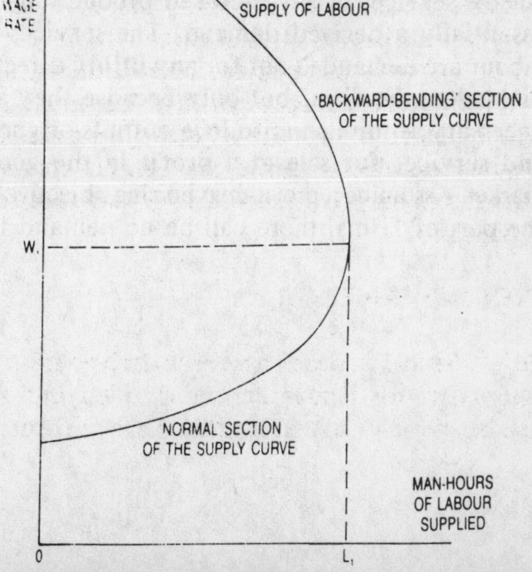

Whether an individual's supply curve of labour is upward-sloping as in Figure 12.3 or backward-bending as depicted in Figure 12.4 is very important for tax policy. An increase in the rate of income tax is equivalent to a fall in the wage rate. If the supply curve of labour is upward-sloping, a rise in income tax causes less labour to be supplied, acting as a disincentive to effort. If however, the supply curve is backward-bending, a rise in income tax results in more man-hours of labour being supplied, since a worker must now work longer to maintain his material standard of living. The tax increase has an incentive effect on effort, though it may of course, create an even greater incentive for law-breaking through illegal tax evasion.

Whatever the shape of an individual's supply curve of labour, it is however likely that the market supply curve of labour is upward-sloping. This is because more workers are likely to enter the labour market in response to a wage rise, attracted both from other labour markets and from unemployment.

THE DEMAND CURVE FOR LABOUR IN A PERFECT LABOUR MARKET

12. Just as the market supply curve of labour is the sum of the supply curves of all the individual workers in the labour market, so the **market demand curve for labour** is obtained by adding together **each firm's demand curve for labour** at different wages. In a perfectly competitive labour market, a **single firm's demand curve for labour** is the factor's **marginal revenue product (MRP)** curve.

To explain this we must first emphasise that a firm's demand for labour - or indeed its demand for the services of any factor of production - is essentially a **derived demand**. The services of labour are demanded not for any utility directly yielded to the firm, but only because they are necessary as inputs to produce outputs of goods and services for sale at a profit in the goods market. Assuming a profit-maximising objective on the part of firms, there can be no demand for factor services in the long run unless firms sell the outputs produced for at least a normal profit in the goods market.

Broadly, a firm must ask three questions when deciding whether it is worthwhile to employ or demand the services of an extra unit of a factor of production. It must ask by how much will:

(i) total output rise?

(ii) total revenue rise when the extra output is sold in the goods market? and

(iii) total costs rise as a result of paying the factor of production?

Assuming a perfect labour market, we derive a firm's demand curve for labour from our answers to the first two of these questions. The answer to the third question then allows us to determine the firm's equilibrium level of employment of labour.

MARGINAL REVENUE PRODUCT

13. In a perfect market, a single firm's demand curve for labour shows the **marginal revenue productivity** of the factor at every level of employment. We derive the **MRP curve** of labour from the answers to the first two of the three questions we have just introduced.

The two elements which comprise the MRP of labour are represented by the identity:

Marginal Revenue Product (MRP) ≡ Marginal Physical Product (MPP) x Marginal Revenue (MR)

The **marginal physical product (MPP)** of labour, which measures the amount by which a firm's total output rises when an extra worker is employed, is simply the **marginal returns of labour**, which we explained in Chapter 4. Assuming **diminishing marginal returns** as labour is combined with fixed quantities of land and capital, the MPP curve drawn in Figure 12.5(a) falls as additional workers are employed.

Figure 12.5: Deriving the MRP curve by multiplying the MPP of labour [in figure (a)] by the MR resulting from its sale in the goods market [figure (b)]

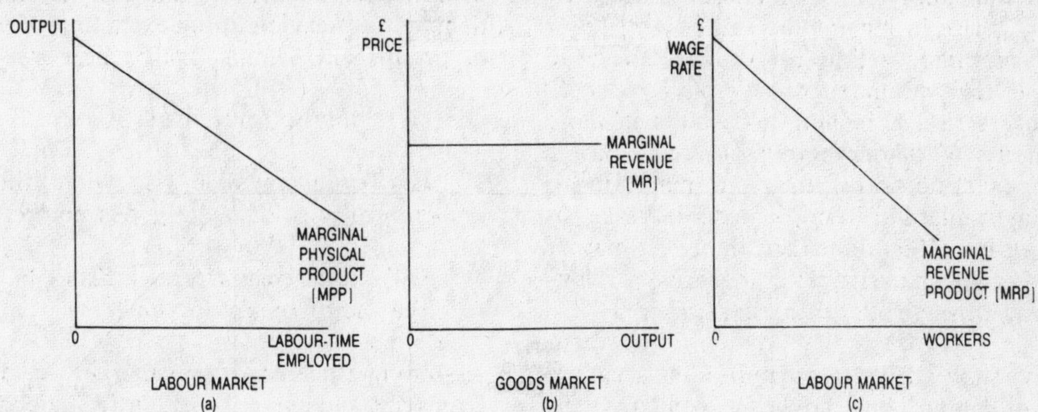

(a) Labour market *(b) Goods market* *(c) Labour market*

To find the money value of the MPP of labour, we multiply MPP by the addition to the firm's total revenue resulting from the sale of the extra output in the goods market. In other words, we multiply MPP by **marginal revenue**. If the goods market is perfectly competitive, MR is identical to the goods price or average revenue. The MRP curve of labour shown in Figure 12.5 (c) is thus obtained by multiplying the MPP of labour by the horizontal MR curve drawn in Figure 12.5 (b). In this example, the diminishing marginal revenue productivity of labour is explained solely by the diminishing marginal physical product ie by the law of diminishing returns. If however, the firm sells its output in an imperfect product market marginal revenue product of labour declines even faster, since the marginal revenue the firm obtains from selling an extra worker's output falls as output is increased.

THE EQUILIBRIUM WAGE AND LEVEL OF EMPLOYMENT IN A PERFECT LABOUR MARKET

14. We are now in a position to show the determination of the equilibrium wage and level of employment in the whole labour market, and also the determination of equilibrium employment or demand for labour at the level of a single firm within the market. These are shown in Figure 12.6.

The equilibrium wage and equilibrium employment for the whole labour market are shown in the left hand panel of Figure 12.6, at the intersection of the market demand curve for labour and the market supply curve of labour. We have already explained that the market supply curve of labour is obtained by adding up the individual supply curves of all the workers in the market at different possible wages. In a similar way, we add up the demand curves for labour of all the firms in the market to obtain the market demand curve for labour. Since each firm's demand for labour is shown by its MRP curve, the **market demand curve for labour** is the sum of the MRP curves. The equilibrium wage W* and equilibrium employment L* in the whole labour market are determined in Figure 12.6 at the intersection of the market supply curve of labour and the market demand curve for labour.

We can now show in the righthand panel of Figure 12.6 how the ruling market wage W* affects individual firms within the market. An individual firm is a price-taker at the ruling wage, which as we saw earlier, is both the perfectly elastic supply curve of labour facing the firm and the average and marginal input cost curve (AIC and MIC). The firm can employ as much labour as it wishes at the ruling market wage, but it cannot influence the ruling wage by its own actions. To maximise profits when its product is sold in the output market an individual firm must employ labour up to the point at which:

$$MRP = MIC$$

Figure 12.6: The determination of the equilibrium wage and level of employment in a perfectly competitive labour market, and the determination of the equilibrium level of employment of a single firm within the market

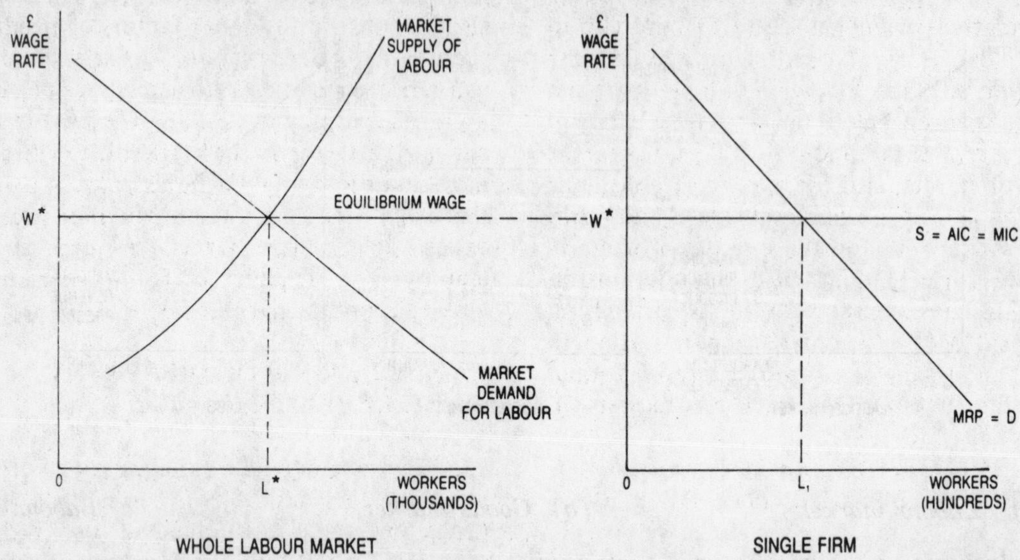

You should note that MRP = MIC is another example of an **equilibrium equation.** The MRP of labour is the **marginal private benefit** received by the firm from the output of an extra worker. Likewise, marginal input cost (MIC) is the **money cost** incurred by the firm when employing an additional worker. In a perfectly competitive labour market, MIC = W, therefore in perfect competition, the equilibrium equation becomes:

MRP = W

In Figure 12.6, the firm's equilibrium level of employment at which MRP = W is L_1. If the firm goes beyond the level of employment at which MRP = W and hires a worker who adds more to total cost than to total revenue, profits must fall. Conversely, if the employer decides to limit the size of the workforce at a point at which the MRP of the last worker is greater than the wage, the firm is sacrificing potential profits. In summary:

Disequilibrium conditions are:

(i) If MRP > W, profit maximisation requires increased employment;

(ii) If MRP < W, profit maximisation requires decreased employment;

the equilibrium equation is:

(iii) If MRP = W, profits can be maximised in the product market.

THE CONDITION OF EQUI-MARGINAL RETURNS

15. We can generalise the equilibrium equation MRP = W for the employment of labour in a perfectly competitive factor market to cover any factor of production or input. In competitive markets, where the price of each factor equals its marginal input cost, profit maximisation requires that the factor is employed until:

MRP = factor price

For all factors taken together, the equilibrium equation becomes:

(See separate sheet - this will have to be stuck on later

$$\frac{\text{MRP of labour}}{\text{wage rate}} = \frac{\text{MRP of land}}{\text{rent}} = \frac{\text{MRP of capital}}{\text{rate of interest}}$$

The condition of **equi-marginal returns** neatly illustrates when it is in a firm's interest to substitute one factor of production for another. When the equality holds for any given set of factor prices and technical conditions of production and supply, the firm must be producing at the lowest possible total cost of production for that level of output. If factor prices or productivity change, the equality is disturbed, requiring the firm to substitute factors of production in order to continue producing at the lowest possible cost. For example, an increase in the wage rate creates an incentive for the firm to substitute the other factors of production whose relative prices have fallen, for labour whose relative price has risen. To maximise profits, the firm must continue factor substitution until the condition of equi-marginal returns is restored. (Note the similarity between this analysis of the demand by a firm for factor services or inputs, and the theory of consumer demand explained in Chapter 3. The relationship between **MRP = W** and the **condition of equi-marginal returns** is identical to the relationship between the consumer equilibrium equation for a single good **MU = P** and its generalisation to cover all goods, the **condition of equi-marginal utility**. If in doubt check back to Chapter 3.)

THE SUBSTITUTION EFFECT AND THE OUTPUT EFFECT

16. An increase in the price of one factor of production will have both a **substitution effect** and an **output effect**. The **substitution effect**, which we have just described, requires a firm to produce a given output using a technique of production which employs more of the factors whose relative prices have fallen and less of a factor whose relative price has risen. But an increase in the price of a factor of production also raises the production costs of output, shifting the firm's TC and MC curves upwards. Since we have supposed no reason for the firm's marginal revenue curve to alter, the firm's profit-maximising output must fall. This is the **output effect** resulting from an increased factor price. The output effect tends to reduce the quantity demanded of all factors and not just the demand for the factor whose price has risen. The output effect is largest where demand for the firm's output is highly elastic.

WAGE EQUALISATION IN A PERFECTLY COMPETITIVE MARKET ECONOMY

17. Assuming perfect competition in all markets, including labour markets, market forces will tend to produce an **equalisation of wages** throughout the economy, reducing differences in wage rates paid for different types of labour and in different industries. The explanation of this is extremely simple. If, in any labour market or any industry, wages are higher than in other markets, incentives exist for firms to reduce their demand for labour and for workers to increase their supply of labour. Employers can economise by employing other types of labour, for example semi-skilled rather than skilled workers, and also by substituting other factors of production such as capital for labour. At the same time, workers are attracted between labour markets by high relative wages, shifting the labour supply curve rightwards in the market into which they move, thus bringing down the wage. In principle, the wage rate falls until no further incentives exists either for firms to change their employment of labour or for workers to shift between labour markets.

EXPLANATIONS OF DIFFERENT WAGE LEVELS

18. The most obvious explanation of different wage levels, despite the equalising market process we have just described, lies in the fact that **real life labour markets are imperfectly competitive**, characterised by imperfect market information and by barriers and sources of friction which prevent or restrict movement between markets. We shall examine some of the causes of labour immobility in the next section. However, even within the rarified and abstract assumptions of perfect competition, we might expect certain wage differentials to exist at any point of time. This is for two main reasons:

(i) **Different jobs have different non-monetary characteristics.** We have already explained how the 'net advantage' of any type of work includes job satisfaction or dissatisfaction as well as the utility of the wage. Other things being equal, a worker must be paid a higher wage to compensate for any relative unpleasantness in the job. We can define an **equalising wage differential** as the payment which must be made to compensate a worker for the different non-monetary characteristics of jobs, so that there is no incentive to switch between jobs and between labour markets.

(ii) **Disequilibrium trading.** It is reasonable to assume that an economy is subject to constant change, involving the development both of new goods and services and of improved methods of production or technical progress, and subject also to changing patterns of demand. In response to such ongoing change, markets, including factor markets, are characterised therefore by disequilibrium rather than by equilibrium. This means that although market forces tend to equalise wages and other factor prices across competitive markets, at any point of time disparities exist which reflect the disequilibrium conditions existent at that time.

THE IMMOBILITY OF LABOUR

19. Like the product or goods market which we have examined in earlier chapters, **real life factor markets are imperfectly rather than perfectly competitive**. This is especially true of the labour market. In this section we explain how the **occupational and geographical immobility of labour** contribute to imperfect labour markets, before in the next sections going on to examine imperfect market structures resulting from a single employer in the labour market and from a trade union as a monopoly supplier of labour.

(i) **Occupational immobility of labour** occurs when workers are prevented by either natural or man-made barriers from moving between different types of jobs. Workers are obviously not homogeneous or uniform, so **differences in natural ability may prevent or restrict movement between** jobs. Some types of work require an **innate ability**. such as physical strength or perfect eyesight, which prevent a worker immediately switching between labour markets. Examples of **man-made barriers** include membership qualifications imposed by professional bodies such as accountancy associations, and **trade union restrictive practices** such as **pre-entry closed shops**, which restrict employment to those already belonging to the union. Various forms of racial, religious and sexual discrimination are also man-made causes of occupational immobility of labour.

(ii) **Geographical immobility of labour** occurs when a worker is prevented by such factors as ignorance of job opportunities, family and cultural ties and the financial costs of moving or travel, from filling a job vacancy located at a distance from his present place of residence or work. Perhaps the most significant cause of geographical immobility within the United Kingdom in recent years has been the state of the housing market, which itself reflects imperfections in other factor markets. Low paid and unemployed workers in the northern half of Britain have been prevented from filling job vacancies in the more prosperous South-East of England because the prices of owner-occupied housing have soared out of reach and because of the lack of available housing to rent in either the private or the public sector. At the same time, workers living in their own houses in the South-East have been reluctant to apply for jobs elsewhere in the country for fear that they could never again afford to move back to the South-East.

IMPERFECT MARKET STRUCTURE

20. We shall now turn attention to imperfect **factor market structures**, investigating three departures from the model of a perfectly competitive labour market which we examined earlier in this chapter. These are:

(i) a **monopsony** labour market;

(ii) the effect of introducing a trade **union as a monopoly supplier of labour into a perfectly competitive labour market**; and

(iii) the effect of introducing a trade **union as a monopoly supplier of labour into a monopsony labour market**.

MONOPSONY LABOUR MARKETS

21. Monopsony means a single buyer, just as monopoly means a single seller. A monopsony labour market is therefore, a market in which there is **only one firm** or employer available to hire the services of all the workers in the labour market. For the time being, we shall assume that there are a large number of workers in the labour market and that they each act independently and have not formed a trade union.

In terms of economic analysis, a monopsony labour market is very similar to the monopoly goods market which we studied in Chapter 6. In much the same way that the market demand curve facing a monopoly supplier of a good is also the monopolist's average revenue curve, so in a monopsony labour market, the **market supply curve of labour** is the **firm's average input cost (AIC) curve**. The curve shows how much labour is supplied at different wage rates, the wage rate being the average input cost to the firm of employing the number of workers who are supplying their services.

You should note that the supply curve or AIC curve shows the wage which must be paid to all workers at each size of employed labour force, to persuade the workers to supply their services. However, the AIC curve is *not* the **marginal input cost (MIC) curve of labour** in a monopsony labour market. At any size of total employment, the firm must raise the wage rate to attract extra workers, paying the higher wage to all its workers. The MIC of an extra worker includes the total amount by which the wage bill rises, and not just the wage paid to the additional worker hired. The MIC curve of labour which is illustrated in Figure 12.7 is thus *above* the AIC or supply curve (just as in the goods market, a monopolist's AR curve is above its MR curve).

The equilibrium wage and the equilibrium level of employment in a monopsony labour market are shown in Figure 12.8. As in a perfectly competitive labour market, **the firm's equilibrium level of employment** is determined where MRP = MIC, at point A in Figure 12.8. However, the equilibrium wage is below A and less than the MRP of labour, being determined at point B on the supply curve of labour. Although the employer could pay a wage determined at A and equal to the MRP of labour without incurring a loss on the last worker employed, he has no need to. He can employ all the workers he requires by paying the wage W_1, determined at point B. Indeed, if the firm pays a wage higher than W_1, it must incur unnecessary production costs, and it cannot therefore be maximising profits. Thus profit maximisation in the goods market requires a wage no higher than W_1 in the labour market! (Once again, note the similarity of the proceeding analysis with the theory of monopoly in the goods market. As we saw in Chapter 6, Figure 6.12, the monopolist could reduce price below P_1 and still make profits, but such action would of course, fail to maximise profits.)

Figure 12.7: The relationship between AIC MIC in a monopsony labour market

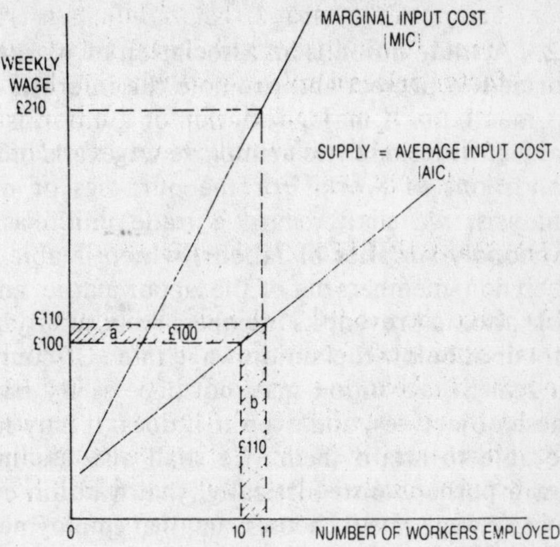

To persuade an eleventh worker to supply his labour, the firm must increase the wage from £100 to £110. All eleven workers are now paid £110, which is the AIC, shown by the shaded area (b). However, the MIC is larger than the AIC. The MIC is not only the £110 paid to the eleventh worker; it includes also the wage increase paid to the other ten workers. This is shown by the shaded area (a), which amounts to £100. MIC is thus (a) + (b), or £210 when eleven workers are employed.

Figure 12.8: Equilibrium wage and level of employment in a monopsony labour market

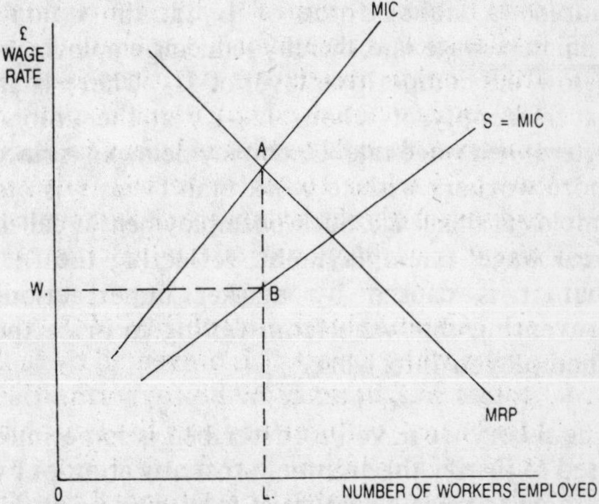

THE EFFECT OF INTRODUCING A TRADE UNION INTO A PERFECTLY COMPETITIVE LABOUR MARKET

22. A **trade union** is an association of workers formed to protect and promote the interests of its members. A major function of a union is to bargain with employers to improve wages and other conditions of work. For the purposes of our analysis, we shall regard a trade union as a **monopoly supplier of labour**, which is able to keep non-members out of the labour market and, able also, to prevent its members from supplying labour at below the 'union wage rate'. Of course in real life, a union may not necessarily have these objectives, and even if it does, it may not be able to attain them. We shall also assume, again perhaps unrealistically, that a union can fix any wage rate it chooses, and that employment is then determined by the amount of labour employers will hire at this wage.

The possible effects resulting from the formation of a union in a previously competitive labour market are shown in Figure 12.9. In the absence of a union, the competitive wage is W_1, and the supply of labour is shown by the curve S_1. When the trade union succeeds in raising the minimum wage to W_2, the **supply curve of labour** becomes in effect the line W_2XS_1. Supply is perfectly elastic at the trade union's minimum wage up to a labour force of L_3, but the curve S_1 shows the supply of labour for any level of employment above L_3. Beyond L_3 firms would have to offer a higher wage in order to attract a greater supply of labour. However, firms are only prepared to employ a labour force of L_2 at the union's minimum wage rate, thereby reducing employment below the competitive level of L_1. There is an excess supply of labour L_3-L_2 at the union-determined wage rate. Unemployment exists since more workers wish to work than firms wish to employ at this wage. Such unemployment is called **'real wage' unemployment,** reflecting the fact that it is caused by market imperfections preventing the wage from falling to price the unemployed into work.

The theory we have just described is sometimes used to justify the argument that any attempt by a union to raise wages must *inevitably* be at the expense of jobs, and that if unions were really interested in reducing unemployment, they would accept wage cuts. However, such conclusions are not inevitable. In the first place we have assumed that the conditions of demand for labour are unchanged, which is very often an unrealistic assumption to make. By agreeing to accept technical progress by working with new capital equipment and new methods of organising work, and by improving the skills of their members, for example through training, a union may be able to ensure - with the co-operation of management - that the MRP curve of labour shifts rightwards. In these circumstances, increased productivity creates scope for both increased wages and increased employment Likewise, both wages and employment may rise when a union negotiates for higher wages in an expanding market, since increased demand for outputs creates increased demand for inputs. Indeed, rising real wages throughout the economy are likely to increase the aggregate demand for the output of all firms producing consumer goods because wages are the most important source of consumption expenditure in the economy.

Figure 12.9: The effect of introducing a trade union into a perfectly competitive labour market

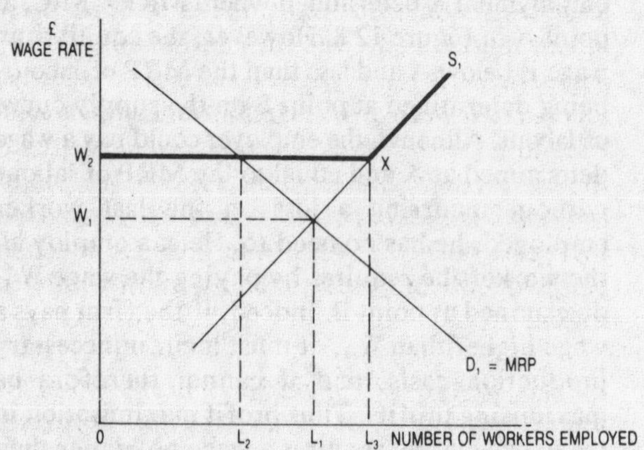

THE EFFECT OF INTRODUCING A TRADE UNION INTO A MONOPSONISTIC LABOUR FORCE

23. We can also show that the assertion that unions raise wages at the expense of jobs is heavily dependent on the assumption of a perfectly competitive labour market. If a trade union is formed as a monopoly supplier of labour in a market where a single employer is a monopsony buyer of labour, then, in principle at least, the union can increase both the wage rate and employment, without the need for the MRP

curve to shirt rightwards. Such a situation is illustrated in Figure 12.10. As in Figure 12.8 the competitive supply of labour in the absence of a union would result in an equilibrium wage of W_1 and equilibrium employment at L_1. We shall now suppose that a union is formed which fixes the wage rate at W_2. The **supply curve of labour** is now the line W_2XS_1, for exactly the same reasons as in Figure 12.9. W_2XS_1 is also the **average input cost curve,** but it is *not* the **marginal input cost curve** in a monopsonistic labour market. Instead, the MIC curve is the line W_2XZV. We explain this in the following way. As long as the labour force is below L_2, the marginal input cost of employing an extra worker is the same as the union determined wage or AIC of employing labour. But when a larger labour force than L_2 is employed the wage must rise in order to persuade additional workers to supply labour. Because all workers must be paid the higher wage, the MIC of employing an extra worker is now above the supply curve or AIC curve. Between the horizontal section of the MIC curve for levels of employment below L_2, and the competitive section of the curve ZV, is a vertical line or discontinuity, XZ. We saw in Figure 12.8 how, in the absence of a union, the equilibrium wage in a monopsony labour market is W_1 and the equilibrium level of employment is L_1. Figure 12.10 shows that at the union-fixed wage of W_2, **equilibrium employment** rises to L_2 - the level of employment at which the MRP curve intersects the vertical section of the MIC curve between X and Z. The union increases both the wage rate and the level of employment compared to the situation without a union.

Indeed, we can use Figure 12.10 to show that the union, providing it possesses the necessary bargaining power, can increase the wage beyond W_2 and still increase employment. Wage rates can be increased along with employment up to levels shown at point Y, at which the wage is W_3 and employment is maximised at L_3. If the union increases wages beyond W_3, some of the extra employment is lost. Any attempt to increase the wage rate beyond W_4, shown at point A, can be achieved only by reducing employment below L_1, which was the equilibrium level of employment before the union was formed.

In Figure 12.10 the shaded area between W_1 and W_4 is called the **zone of bargaining,** reflecting the fact that in an imperfect labour market a union may sometimes 'trade-off' between higher wage rates and higher employment levels, without having to accept a reduction in employment below L_1. The zone of bargaining represents '**monopsony profit**' (the exact equivalent of monopoly profit in the goods market) which by bargaining, can be diverted away from the employer to increase the wage rate and employment.

Figure 12.10: The effect of introducing a trade union into a monopsonistic labour market

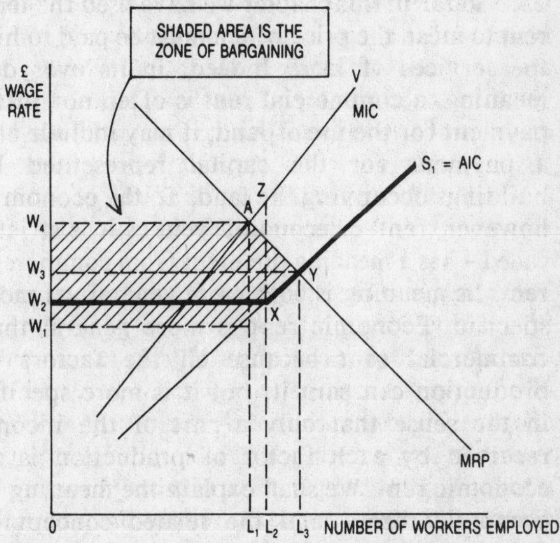

SOME FURTHER ASPECTS OF TRADE UNION ACTIVITY

24. In real life, trade unions sometimes possess sufficient power through the threat of strikes and the disruption of the continuous-flow production processes on which much industry depends, to persuade employers to sacrifice profit-maximisation for the sake of securing at least some profit from uninterrupted production. When this happens, both the wage and the level of employment are determined at a point 'off' the MRP curve. For example, a union may force firms to incur avoidable costs by employing more workers than are strictly necessary; hence firms sacrifice potential profits at the union-fixed wage in order to secure industrial peace. But in this situation, are firms really sacrificing profits? The answer depends on whether we are considering **short-run** or **long-run profits.** By giving in to the union's demands and sacrificing **short-term profits,** firms may ensure **long-run profit maximisation** in conditions of industrial

peace. However, this conclusion depends on the assumption that the employers must 'live with' the union and are unable to break the union's power. This is not always the case. Employers may decide to sacrifice short-term profits to an even greater extent in an all-out industrial dispute, hoping that by destroying the union or its power, conditions can be created for long-run profit maximisation in a union-free labour market.

ECONOMIC RENT AND TRANSFER EARNINGS

25. So far in this chapter we have used the term **rent** to mean the price which must be paid to hire the services of land. Indeed, in its everyday meaning, a **commercial rent** is often not just a payment for the use of land; it may include also a payment for the capital represented by buildings occupying the land. To the economist however, rent-or **economic rent** as it is strictly called - has a meaning different from commercial rent. Its meaning is both more general yet more specific. Economic rent is more general than commercial rent because all the factors of production can earn it, but it is more specific in the sense that only a part of the income received by each factor of production is an economic rent. We shall explain the meaning of economic rent - and the related concept of **transfer earnings** - in the context of the labour market, but the analysis can easily be applied to the other factors of production.

Figure 12.11: Economic rent and transfer earnings

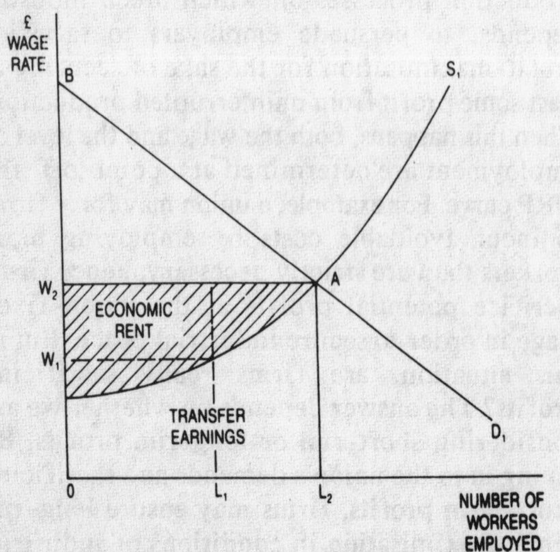

Figure 12.11 illustrates the demand and supply conditions for labour in a competitive labour market. At any wage rate, we may identify a **marginal worker** who is just prepared to supply his labour services at that wage, but who would *transfer out* of the labour market at a lower wage rate. For example, at a level of employment of L_1, the marginal worker will offer his services at a wage of W_1, but would refuse to supply labour at a lower wage rate. The wage W_1 thus represents this worker's **supply price** or **transfer earnings**, and the supply curve S_1 shows the supply price or transfer earnings of each of the workers in the labour market. But is a worker paid a wage equal to his supply price? The answer is usually no. In a competitive market, all the workers are paid the same wage rate, the **equilibrium wage** W_2, which exceeds the supply price or transfer earnings of all but the marginal worker, at the equilibrium level of employment, L_2. Apart from the marginal worker whose wage is his transfer earnings, each worker earns an **economic rent** equal to the difference between what he is paid and his supply price or transfer earnings. For example, a student with a Saturday job who might be prepared to work for a wage of £2 per hour, may in fact receive a wage of £3.50 per hour. In these circumstances, his economic rent is £1.50, while his transfer earnings are £2. This example illustrates that economic rent is essentially a **surplus**, while transfer earnings measure a factor's **opportunity cost.** Taking all the workers in the labour market together, their collective economic rent is shown in Figure 12.11 by the shaded area above the supply curve, while their transfer earnings are shown by the area below the supply curve.

ECONOMIC RENT AND NORMAL PROFIT

26. In Figure 12.11 the triangle W_2AB represents the labour force's contribution to the entrepreneurial profits made by the firm. It is the difference between the value of the total **product of labour** (the area OL_2AB), and the employers' **total wage cost** of employing labour. Entrepreneurial profit is essentially a *residual*, being the difference between the value of the total product of the factor inputs, and the total input cost paid to the factors for their services. Entrepreneurial profit can itself be divided into economic rent and transfer earnings. **Normal profit** is the **entrepreneur's transfer earnings**, since a firm will transfer out of a market if normal profit is not earned. **Abnormal**

or **supernormal profit**, which is earned over and above normal profit, thus becomes the **'economic rent of enterprise'**.

ELASTICITY OF SUPPLY AND ECONOMIC RENT

27. A quick glance at Figure 12.11 will show that the relative importance of economic rent and transfer earnings in the firms' total wage bill depends on the **elasticity of supply of labour**. The more elastic the supply of labour, the smaller is the proportion of the total wage bill made up of economic rent and the larger is the proportion comprising transfer earnings. The extreme limiting case, where all the wage bill forms transfer earnings, is illustrated in Figure 12.12 (a), in which the supply curve of labour is perfectly elastic. Figure 12.12 (b) shows the opposite limiting case when the supply of labour remains fixed and no workers transfer out of the labour market. All the wage bill is therefore economic rent, transfer earnings being zero. When the supply curve of labour is unit-elastic, as in Figure 12.12 (c), exactly half the wage bill is economic rent and half is transfer earnings.

REMOVAL OF ECONOMIC RENT

28. We have already noted that economic rent is a 'surplus' received by a factor of production over and above the minimum payment necessary to keep it in its present use. An important aspect of this is that removal of economic rent will not reduce the supply of the factor. A large part of the income received by highly-paid workers who possess specialised talents which are in short supply, can be regarded as economic rent, as can the income received by landlords from land owned in highly profitable locations which cannot easily be converted to alternative profitable uses. A government could, in principle, tax away the economic rent of any factor of production in inelastic supply, without affecting the supply of resources to the whole economy.

A rather different example of the removal of economic rent is very similar to the model of a **price discriminating monopolist or oligopolist** which we studied in Chapter 7. We saw in Chapter 7, how by charging each customer in the goods market a price equal to the maximum the customer is prepared to pay, a firm can transfer **consumer surplus** away from the consumers to increase monopoly profit. In much the same way, a monopsony employer of labour would increase profits if he could engage successfully in wage **discrimination** in the labour market. This would involve paying each worker his supply price or transfer earnings instead of paying each worker the same wage rate. Successful wage discrimination effectively transfers **economic rent** away from the workers to boost the employer's profits.

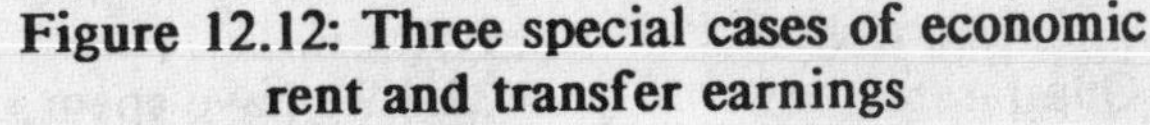

Figure 12.12: Three special cases of economic rent and transfer earnings

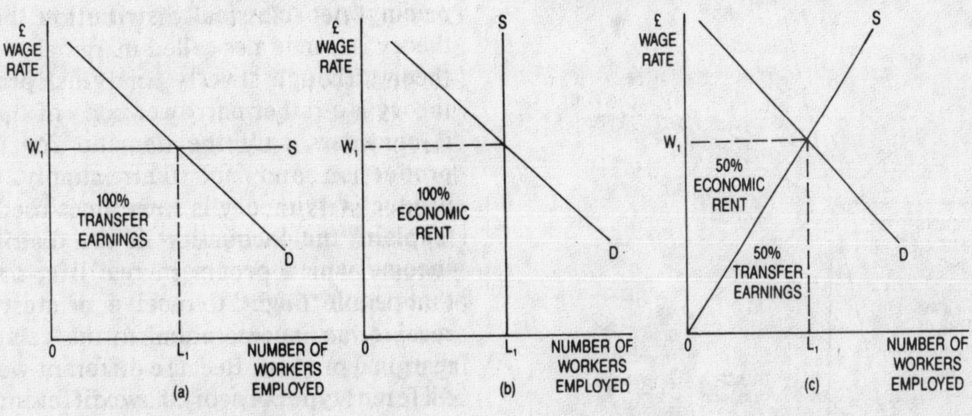

(a) Perfectly elastic supply *(b) Completely inelastic supply* *(c) Unit elasticity of supply*

QUASI-RENT

29. The concept of **quasi-rent** is closely related to economic rent. The short-run supply of a factor of production is likely to be less elastic than the long-run curve. This means that a factor which will eventually transfer to an alternative use in the long run, in response to a fall in its factor price, may not be transferred in the short run. The part of its earnings, which is *economic rent in the short run*, but *transfer earnings in the long run*, is called a quasi-rent. In Figure 12.13, quasi-rent is shown by the part of the total wage cost of employing the labour force L_1, between the short run and the long-run supply curves of labour.

THE DETERMINANTS OF THE ELASTICITY OF SUPPLY OF LABOUR

30. The supply of unskilled labour is usually more elastic than the supply of a particular type of skilled labour, since the training period of unskilled labour is usually very short, and any innate abilities required are less likely to be restricted to a small proportion of the total population. Indeed all the factors promoting the occupational and geographical immobility of labour, which we have already described, also tend to reduce the elasticity of supply of labour. Amongst other influences upon the elasticity of supply of labour are the time periods in question and the existence of unemployed labour.

Figure 12.13: Quasi-rent

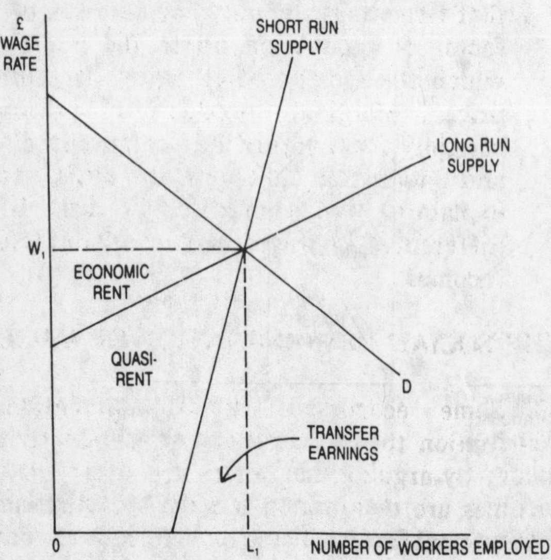

THE DETERMINANTS OF THE ELASTICITY OF DEMAND FOR LABOUR

31. If the wage rate increases, but nothing else which affects the demand for labour changes, by how much will employment fall? The answer clearly depends upon firms' elasticity of demand for labour, or more strictly, upon the **elasticity of derived demand for labour** since, as we have seen, the demand for labour is ultimately derived from the demand exercised by consumers in the goods market for the output the firms are producing. In general, the derived demand for a particular type of labour will be relatively inelastic if:

(i) the relevant wage costs form only a small part of total production costs - this is known as the **'importance of being unimportant'**;

(ii) the demand for the final product is inelastic;

(iii) it is difficult to substitute other factors of production for labour, or other types of labour for the particular type in question;

(iv) the shorter the time period in question, since it usually takes some time for firms to adjust to higher wages.

CRITICISMS OF NEO-CLASSICAL DISTRIBUTION THEORY

32. We have spent most of this chapter so far, explaining and exploring particular aspects of the standard micro-economic theory of factor pricing: **neo-classical distribution theory**. The theory is sometimes called **marginal productivity theory,** though strictly, marginal productivity theory is a rather narrower body of theory since it considers only the demand for factors of production and not their supply. Marginal productivity theory is sometimes used either to 'explain' the **inequality in the distribution of income** which occurs in real life, or to argue that people 'ought' to receive, or must expect to receive, an income equal to the value of their marginal product. Because different workers and different types of work have different marginal products, high wages and factor incomes can be explained in the theory by high marginal products, while low-wage industries are those in which the marginal productivity of labour is low.

Indeed, in the past it has been claimed that marginal productivity theory has ethical implications. An early proponent of the theory, **J.B. Clark,** argued in 1899 that the well paid receive a 'just wage' because their marginal productivity is high whereas the low paid 'deserve' the relative poverty resulting from low productivity. Clark believed that in the long run, human intervention could not alter the returns to productive economic agents. Whether or not one agrees with such 'normative' interpretations of marginal productivity theory, there are a number of serious problems in explaining the distribution of incomes and the demand for factor services in terms of the theory. The problems are:

(i) At a fundamental level, marginal productivity theory is sometimes criticised as a **circular theory**. According to the theory, the demand for a factor depends upon the value of what is produced; this in turn depends upon the effective demand of consumers exercised in the goods market; finally consumers' effective demand for goods depends on the distribution of income. Hence the explanation of the distribution of income depends ultimately on the initial distribution of income. To give the theory an explanatory power, an initial distribution of income must be assumed, and this initial distribution cannot, of course, be explained by the theory.

(ii) The theory can only explain incomes and levels of employment in perfectly competitive factor markets. We have seen that in imperfect factor markets, such as where there is a monopsony buyer of labour, a factor is not paid an equilibrium price equal to the value of its marginal product. Since factor markets in real life are often highly imperfect, and in disequilibrium rather than equilibrium, marginal productivity theory is of limited value in explaining the actual distribution of wages and other factor incomes.

(iii) The theory predicts that firms respond to a fall in the wage rate by employing more labour. However, this prediction depends on the **ceteris paribus assumption**, ie the assumption that conditions are held constant in other parts of the economy. Relaxing the ceteris paribus assumption, a fall in wages in one part of the economy may reduce the aggregate demand for goods and services throughout the economy (for example because profits rise at the expense of wages, and people who receive profits save a larger fraction of their income). The resulting decrease in aggregate demand can then cause the demand curve for labour in each labour market to shift inwards. In these circumstances, a cut in the wage rate leads to less rather than more labour being demanded.

(iv) The theory assumes that the marginal productivity of labour can be separated from the marginal productivity of capital, ie that it is possible and realistic to isolate the marginal product of labour by measuring changes in total output occurring when more labour is added to a fixed quantity of capital. But is is often more realistic to regard capital and labour as *complementary* rather than as *substitutes*. To increase output, a firm must employ more labour and more capital in a *relatively fixed ratio.* When this is the case, the concept of a factor's marginal product, which can be measured separate from the contribution of other factors of production, is almost meaningless.

Marginal productivity theory should therefore be regarded as a rather frail and limited theory, which interpreted properly, predicts little more than that, in conditions of perfect competition, a *necessary condition for profit maximisation in the output market* (or goods market) is that firms must employ the services of a factor of production up to the point at which the factor's MRP equals its input price. Marginal productivity theory certainly does not provide a comprehensive and universal theoretical basis for explaining and predicting real life differences in wages and in other factor incomes.

THE 'SOCIAL' DETERMINATION OF WAGES

33. Some economists attack conventional distribution theory and marginal productivity theory by arguing that wages and other factor incomes are determined largely by **social and institutional factors**. These include conventional attitudes within society to differentials between

the wages received by different groups of workers, skilled and unskilled, young and old, male and female etc, and between wages and other types of income such as profits, and also the role of power conferred on different groups through the political and legal system.

However the conventional marginal productivity approach and the social and institutional approach to wage determination are not necessarily incompatible. If a group of workers wants to raise its wages above the equilibrium level determined by supply and demand, it may only be able to do so in the long run by taking steps to influence the demand and supply schedules for the type of labour involved, eg by restrictive practices to limit the flow of new entrants, or in the case of state employees such as nurses, by persuading the government to employ more nurses, thereby shifting the demand curve for nurses to the right. Nevertheless, in this interpretation, the social and institutional factors which influence the demand and supply curves for labour are as important in determining wages and relative factor incomes as the position and shape of the curves themselves.

REASONS WHY WOMEN EARN LESS THAN MEN

34. Women account for about 45 per cent of employment in the United Kingdom, but on average, females in full-time employment earned 74 per cent of male hourly pay in 1985. There are two main reasons why women earn less than men:

(i) Women work predominantly in low-paid industries and occupations.

(ii) Within many occupational groups, women are paid less than men. This is often because women are under-represented in the higher-paid posts within an occupation, rather than because women are paid less for doing the same job.

Discrimination against women in labour markets may, of course, contribute to both these sets of circumstances. In addition, women are disproportionately represented in industries where the average size of firm and plant is small. These industries tend to pay lower wages and offer fewer promotional prospects than large firms and large industries. Also these industries are seldom unionised. Indeed, within all industries, women workers are less unionised than men. This relates to another reason why women earn less than men; on average their attachment to the labour force is weaker. Each year of work experience raises the pay of both men and women by an average 3 per cent. Yet when women leave the labour force, usually to look after young children, their potential pay falls by 3 per cent for each year involved. If, for example, a man and woman enter employment with equal potential and after 8 years the woman leaves the work force for a further 8 years in order to raise a family, she may re-enter the labour force 16 years in pay terms behind the man - as if she is starting work 16 years after the man. The higher labour turnover of women also imposes costs on the employer, for example, the costs of training replacement workers. Employers may therefore have less incentive to train female workers. Similarly, women may have less incentive to spend time and money on their own education and training if they expect the benefits received will be less than the costs incurred.

CLASS CONFLICT AND THE SHARES OF WAGES AND PROFITS

35. Marxist economists view completely differently the processes within society which determine how the value of output is distributed as wages and profits, compared to the neo-classical theory of distribution which has dominated orthodox or non-Marxist thinking. Marxists argue that the forces which determine how the value of output is distributed between wages and profits can be explained only in terms of the laws of motion of **capitalism** as an economic system. They argue that in a capitalist economic system, there are two opposing classes in conflict with each other: a **class of capitalists** who own the means of production and a **class of workers** who are employed by them. The laws of motion of capitalism centre around the need of capitalists for a continuing accumulation of more and more capital. Yet capital can only accumulate if the labour-power supplied by workers and bought by the capitalists, produces a larger output than is paid for in wages. Marxists call this **surplus value**. Surplus value represents the unpaid labour-time that the worker is forced to work for the capitalist. According to Marxists, the extraction of surplus value inevitably involves the **exploitation of labour** by capitalists. Without exploitation there is no capitalism; every capitalist must exploit his workers to obtain surplus value in order to accumulate yet more capital. The extraction of surplus value is the driving force of production and capitalism. Two forms of exploitation are possible, involving the *absolute* and the *relative* extraction of surplus value. **Absolute extraction** means making labour work harder at a given wage, for example by increasing the speed of an assembly line. However **relative extraction** of surplus value occurs not by making workers work longer or harder, or for lower pay, but by raising productivity by **capital widening and deepening**, ie investing in more and better machines. Marxists argue that such relative exploitation of labour in modern capitalist economies has dominated the absolute exploitation of labour, allowing workers' wages and conditions to improve so long as the productivity of labour has increased even more.

Marxists believe that what they see as the contradictory nature of capitalist society inevitably produces crises which interrupt production and the accumulation of capital. In each crisis, barriers to the further accumulation of capital are revealed which have to be overcome before accumulation can resume. For example, during the boom before a crisis, rising real wages may cause the rate of profit to fall and encroach upon surplus value. Accumulation then slackens, the industrial cycle moves into crisis, unemployment grows and real wages fall. But the crisis allows capitalists to undertake major structural changes which the ordinary workings of the market would not allow. Production is reorganised, new machines are introduced, and accumulation starts again with lower real wages and a reduced labour force.

INSTITUTIONAL METHODS OF PAY DETERMINATION

36. We shall conclude the chapter by surveying briefly various institutional aspects of wage and pay determination in the United Kingdom:

(i) **Collective bargaining.** In 1984 there were over 11 million trade union members in the United Kingdom, or nearly half of the labour force (including registered unemployed). Trade union membership fell rapidly in the early 1980s, by about 17 per cent from a figure of 13.3 million in 1979. The fall, which has continued since 1984 though at a slower rate, may in part be a response to the Conservative Government's legislation reducing the power of trade unions, but it largely reflects the decline of employment in manufacturing industry where union membership is strongest. The pay of most but not all union members is determined by collective bargaining. The main function of trade unions is to bargain collectively on behalf of their members to determine rates of pay and other conditions of employment, ranging from pensions, holidays and disputes procedures, to conditions of work within a particular work place. There are many different forms of collective bargaining, which reflect the varied structure of industries and labour markets and also, the haphazard way in which both unions and employers' associations have developed their present-day structure. In one industry there may be a single trade union representing all the employed workers which bargains either with a single employer, or perhaps with all the firms in the industry organised as an employer's association. In other industries, separate unions representing specific groups of skilled and unskilled workers may jointly bargain with the employer or employers, or they may bargain separately and perhaps in competition with each other.

We can also distinguish between **national collective bargaining** and various forms of **local collective bargaining**, for example at **regional, plant and shop-floor level.** National bargaining may determine **basic or minimum agreed wage rates** in an industry, while local bargaining determines any payments such as **bonuses** paid over and above the nationally agreed minimum and **piece-work rates.** At various times when free collective bargaining has been restricted and distorted by a government's **Incomes Policy**, there has been a tendency for more and more of total earnings to be locally negotiated, so that the basic wage forms a declining proportion of total earnings. This is known as **wage drift**, which occurs partly because a formal incomes policy may fail to detect and police a locally negotiated pay deal specific to a particular piece of work passing through a factory.

(ii) **Individual negotiation.** This generally takes place in the non-unionised parts of the economy. Two contrasting types of worker most usually determine their pay by individual negotiation. At the one extreme are **highly-paid executives, managers and consultants** offering specialist professional services. At the other extreme, **unorganised low-paid workers**, especially those who are casually employed in industries such as tourism and agriculture, negotiate individually with a prospective employer. In these circumstances however, when the weight of bargaining power often lies with employers who offer wages on a 'take it or leave it' basis, the method of pay determination may more accurately represent **employer determination** rather than individual negotiation.

(iii) **State determination.** In most industries where the state or public authority is the employer, trade unions are recognised and wages are determined by collective bargaining. However, there are exceptions, such as the armed forces, the police and more recently civil servants employed in jobs relating to national security, where normal trade union activity is not allowed. In these industries, pay is effectively determined by the state, sometimes with the aid of a review body which advises the government on pay awards, usually on the basis of comparability with other groups of workers in either the private or public sectors.

For most of the period since 1945, successive governments have believed in the need to use the powers of the state to protect low-paid workers in industries such as catering and agriculture where trade unions are ineffective and difficult to organise. **Wages councils** have been established in these industries to determine minimum rates of pay. Wages councils represent a selective form of **minimum pay legislation. In many European countries, a minimum legal wage** has been established covering all industries. In the United Kingdom, Conservative governments have, in recent years, opposed the introduction of a minimum legal wage, believing that its main effect would be to increase unemployment. Indeed, the powers of wages councils have been restricted in the 1980s. However, the Labour Party and the trade union movement are both committed to pressing for the introduction of a national minimum wage, arguing that evidence from other European countries suggests that the benefits in terms of social fairness exceed any costs involved.

A national minimum wage would constraint or restrict free collective bargaining by imposing a *lower limit* or *floor* below which bargaining could not legally take place. At various times in recent history, particularly during the 1960s and 1970s, government intervention in wage determination has had the opposite effect, namely by imposing an *upper limit* or *ceiling* constraining bargaining. This has been when a formal or **statutory incomes policy** has been in operation. Trade unions have often been suspicious of incomes policies which they believe may undermine the central bargaining function of a union. The main purpose of incomes policies has been to attack the causes of cost-push inflation which are closely related to the nature of wage bargaining in the UK. Governments have also justified incomes policies as a method of ensuring a fairer distribution of income than that achieved by market forces and collective bargaining.

A further function of the state in the process of pay and wage determination relates to **arbitration and conciliation**. In the process of collective bargaining, a trade union may demand a pay rise greater than the increase the employer is at first prepared to pay. Essentially, bargaining is a process in which each party modifies its offer or claim, perhaps to the accompaniment of threats, until agreement is reached. For example, a union may threaten a **strike** or other forms of **'industrial action'** such as a work-to-rule, whereas an employer's threats can include **redundancy** and **'lock-outs'**. However, it must be stressed that the vast majority of pay agreements which are eventually signed, are reached without a breakdown in the bargaining process and without an industrial dispute. Nevertheless, on occasion agreement cannot be reached; bargaining breaks down and a dispute occurs or is threatened. Many collective agreements contain negotiating procedures which both unions and employers agree to follow when breakdown occurs, to speed the process to eventual agreement without a harmful dispute. The procedural arrangements commonly specify the stage in the breakdown of bargaining at which outside conciliators or arbitrators should be brought in to assist both sides reach agreement. Since 1975, an official government sponsored conciliation service has existed, the **Advisory Conciliation and Arbitration Service (ACAS)**, which if both sides agree, is available to try and settle a dispute.

SUMMARY

37. In this chapter we have examined price theory from 'the other side', operating in the factor market, which is the market for inputs into the production process, rather than in the goods market or market for consumer goods and services. As in the goods market, wages and other factor prices are assumed to be determined by supply and demand, as are equilibrium levels of factor employment. Distribution theory shares also with other aspects of neo-classical theory the assumptions of maximising objectives and behaviour on the part of households and firms. However, compared to the goods market, their roles are reversed in the factor market, households being the suppliers of factor services and firms the source of demand. We have seen that the demand for factors of production is essentially a derived demand, inputs being demanded not in themselves, but for their contribution to entrepreneurial profit and ultimately because the goods they produce are demanded by consumers.

In a perfectly competitive factor market, the equilibrium factor price and level of employment are determined by market forces in the market as a whole. In a perfect labour market for example, each firm is just a passive 'price-taker' at the ruling market wage, choosing how much labour to employ but having no influence over the wage.

Equilibrium in perfect factor markets requires that each factor of production is employed up to the point at which its MRP equals the factor price. This central proposition of marginal productivity theory is sometimes used to justify arguments that wage rises must inevitably be at the expense of jobs and that the 'market contains its own morality', eg the well paid deserve their relatively high reward because they are productive while conversely, the lowly paid deserve their station in life because of their lack of productivity. We have suggested however, that arguments and conclusions like these should be treated with caution, depending as they do on assumptions of perfect markets, equilibrium trading and unchanged conditions of supply and demand (the ceteris paribus assumption). It is also theoretically invalid to build ethical judgements into the operation of the market mechanism; market forces are essentially 'value neutral' with regard to the social fairness and equity of the outcome they achieve.

Indeed, we have shown how, in condition of expanding demand in the goods market or increasing labour productivity, both wages and employment can, in principle, be increased. Additionally, there may be scope for increasing both wages and employment in monopsony labour markets where a single firm is the only employer of labour. Equilibrium in a monopsony labour market is achieved at the level of employment at which MRP = MIC, but unlike perfect competition, MRP does not equal the wage.

We have argued that while a study of supply and demand must inevitably be a central and necessary part of any explanation of relative incomes and factor rewards, abstract supply and demand analysis does not provide a complete or sufficient explanation. For a more complete theory of distribution, we must include a role for social, political and institutional factors in determining and shifting the positions of the supply and demand curves for factors of production, and we must examine the process of decision making in real life, for example in terms of the institutional arrangements such as collective bargaining through which the wages of a significant proportion of the working population are determined.

STUDENT SELF-TESTING

1 *List the four factors of production.* *(2)*
2 *Distinguish between the functional distribution and the size distribution of income.* *(3 and 4)*
3 *How may inequalities in the distribution of income be measured?* *(5)*
4 *Compare the roles of households in the factor market and in the goods market.* *(6)*
5 *Distinguish between AIC and MIC.* *(7)*
6 *What is the fundamental assumption underlying the supply curve of labour?* *(8)*
7 *When may a worker's net advantage be less than the utility of the wage?* *(9)*
8 *What is the equilibrium equation for the amount of labour supplied by a single worker?* *(10)*

9 *Why may a worker's supply curve of labour bend backwards?* *(11)*

10 *List the three questions relevant to the demand for labour of a single firm.* *(12)*

11 *What is marginal revenue product (MRP)?* *(13)*

12 *What is the equilibrium equation for a firm's level of employment:*
(i) for any profit-maximising firm;
(ii) for a firm in a perfectly competitive labour market? *(14)*

13 *Explain the condition of equi-marginal returns.* *(15)*

14 *Distinguish between the substitution effect and the output effect of a wage rise.* *(16)*

15 *List two reasons for differences in wages.* *(18)*

16 *Distinguish between the occupational and the geographical immobility of labour.* *(19)*

17 *How is the equilibrium wage determined in a monopsony labour market?* *(21)*

18 *How may a trade union affect equilibrium employment and the wage in:*
(i) a perfectly competitive labour market; *(22)*
(ii) a monopsony labour market? *(23)*

19 *Distinguish between economic rent and transfer earnings.* *(25)*

20 *How may an entrepreneur earn economic rent?* *(26)*

21 *How does elasticity of supply affect economic rent?* *(27)*

22 *Describe two circumstances in which economic rent may be removed.* *(28)*

23 *What is quasi-rent?* *(29)*

24 *List the determinants of the elasticity of supply of labour.* *(30)*

25 *List the determinants of the elasticity of demand for labour.* *(31)*

26 *Briefly describe two criticisms of the neo-classical theory of distribution.* *(32)*

27 *Describe some of the social determinants of wages.* *(33)*

28 *Why are women often paid less than men?* *(34)*

29 *How do Marxists approach the determination of wages and profits?* *(35)*

30 *What is collective bargaining?* *(36)*

EXERCISES

1. *Two factors or production, capital and labour, are combined by a firm to make fountain pens, the capital being fixed in the short run. The firm's total hourly output is:*

Workers employed	*Fountain pens produced*	*MPP of labour*
1	*10*	
2	*18*	
3	*24*	
4	*28*	
5	*30*	
6	*31*	

(a) Complete the MPP of labour schedule.

(b) Assume the firm is perfectly competitive in both the goods market and the labour market. How many men will it employ if the hourly wage rate is £10 per hour and the price of a fountain pen is £5?

(b) The worker's trade union raises the wage to £20 per hour? What will happen to employment, assuming other conditions in the labour and goods market remain unchanged?

MULTIPLE CHOICE QUESTIONS

1 *When a worker earns more than the wage just sufficient to keep him in his job, the excess income is called:*
A An opportunity cost
B An economic rent
C Transfer earnings
D Surplus value

2 *In Figure 12.14, given that all other factors of production are fixed, the most profitable number of workers for the firm to employ is:*

A OW
B OX
C OY
D OZ

Figure 12.14

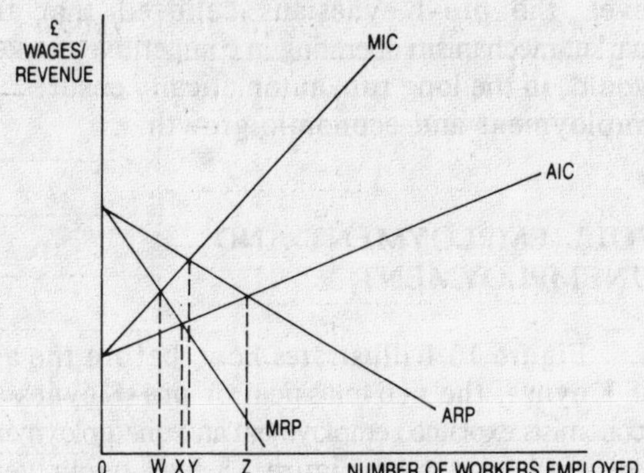

3 *An employer with a labour force of 5 men, each paid at the rate of £30 per day, raises the wage rate by £3 per day to attract one more worker. If other costs remain constant, the marginal input cost of employing the additional worker is:*

A £3
B £33
C £48
D £18

4 *A pop star earns £2,000 a week. He would be prepared to remain an entertainer even if his earnings fell to £200 per week. £1,800 therefore, represents his:*

A *Quasi-rent*
B *Transfer payment*
C *Overtime pay*
D *Economic rent*

5 *The amount of quasi-rent earned by a factor will be determined by the:*

A *Short and long run elasticities of supply of the factor*
B *Short run elasticity of supply of the factor*
C *Long run elasticity of demand for the factor*
D *Short and long run elasticities of demand for the factor.*

EXAMINATION QUESTIONS

1 *What role do the rewards to factors of production play:*
(a) *in the operation of the market economy;* *(12 marks)*
(b) *within the firm?* *(8 marks)*
(ACCA December 1986)

2 (a) *Define and show the differences between transfer earnings, economic rent and quasi-rent.* *(10 marks)*
(b) *What role do the rewards to factors of production play in the operation of the market economy.* *(10 marks)*
(ACCA December 1985)

3 *'Rent is a scarcity payment'. What does this statement mean? Give examples of economic rent accruing to different factors of production.* *(ACCA December 1980)*

4 (a) *Distinguish between economic and commercial rent.* *(6 marks)*
(b) *Analyse the consequences of a government imposing controls on the level of rents for private accommodation.* *(14 marks)*
(ACCA December 1983)

5 *A firm sells a product in a very competitive market. The manufacture of the product involves the simple assembly of bought-out components by unskilled labour, the cost of which amounts to 70% of total manufacturing costs.*

What are likely to be the elasticity of demand for the services of:
(a) *the factory manager?* *(10 marks)*
(b) *the assembly worker?* *(10 marks)*
(ACCA December 1986)

6. *Why are the earnings of women in many occupations less than those of men?*
(CIMA May 1987)

7. *Examine the contention that wages are determined by trade unions these days and not by the conditions of supply and demand.*
(AAT December 1982)

13. The growth of modern macro-economics

INTRODUCTION

1. In earlier chapters we have investigated questions such as 'What determines the price of bread'? and 'How many workers might an employer wish to hire'?. Questions such as these are the subject to **micro-economics** - the part of economics concerned with economic behaviour in the individual markets that make up the economy.

We now switch attention away from the 'little bits' of the economy towards such questions as 'What determines the average price level?' and 'How do we explain the overall levels of employment and unemployment in the economy?' These are the concern of **macro-economics**, the part of economics that attempts to explain 'How the whole economy works'. Macro-economics examines **the aggregates** rather than the 'little bits': the aggregate levels of output, income, prices, employment and unemployment, and the trade flows that make up the balance of payments.

In this chapter we explain how modern macro-economics has its origins in the **Keynesian revolution** of the 1920s and 1930s and how it developed during the **Keynesian era** which lasted from World War II until the **monetarist counter-revolution** of the 1970s and 1980s. We shall conclude by taking an introductory look at the conflicts and controversies that separate Keynesians and monetarists today and which dominate current macro-economic discussion.

EARLY MACRO-ECONOMICS AND JOHN MAYNARD KEYNES

2. The term macro-economics is a fairly recent addition to economic vocabulary. Before the 1970s, macro-economics was associated largely with the work of John Maynard Keynes, who lived from 1883 to 1946. In the 1920s and 1930s, Keynes had changed the nature of economic science by creating modern macro-economics. Indeed, until the advent of monetarism in the late 1960s and the 1970s, macro-economics and Keynesian economics were much the same thing, growing out of Keynes's great and influential book, *'The General Theory of Employment Interest and Money'*, published in 1936. Before Keynes, most economists belonged to a school of thought known as the **'neo-classical school'**, referred to by Keynes as **'the classicals'**. Neo-classical or pre-Keynesian economists were concerned largely with micro-economics and the functioning of individual markets within the economy. At the macro-economic level, the pre-Keynesians believed that the market mechanism operating in competitive markets would, in the long run, automatically ensure full employment and economic growth.

FULL EMPLOYMENT AND UNEMPLOYMENT

3. Figure 13.1 illustrates how, before the age of Keynes, the neo-classical or pre-Keynesian economists explained employment and unemployment. You will recognise Figure 13.1 as being very similar to Figure 12.6 in Chapter 12, which shows how wages are determined within a single labour market. Indeed, we can use this similarity to introduce a very significant point about economics before Keynes: essentially it explained macro-economic phenomena such as the aggregate levels of employment and unemployment by invoking micro-economic theories.

Figure 13.1: The 'classical' theory of employment and unemployment

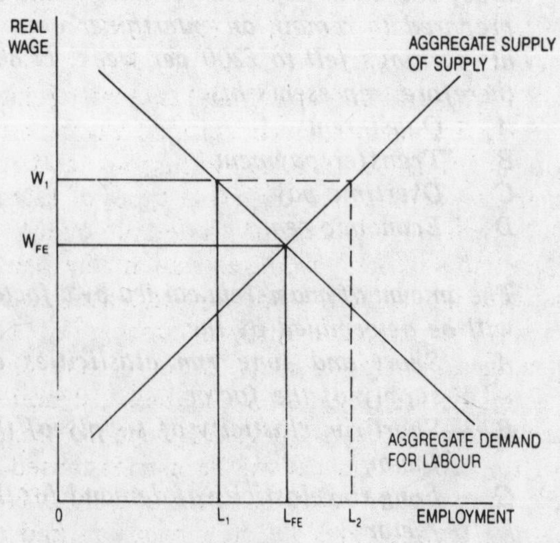

Full employment is determined in Figure 13.1 where the aggregate demand for labour equals the aggregate supply, at the wage W_{FE}. It is worth noting that **full employment** does not necessarily mean that every single member of the working population is in work. Rather it means a situation in which the number of people wishing to work at the going market wage equals the number of workers that employers wish to hire at this wage. But even this definition needs qualifying, since in a dynamic economy, change is constantly taking place with some industries declining and others growing. As new products are developed and demand and cost conditions change, firms demand more of some labour skills while the demand for other types of labour declines. Economists use the term **frictional** and **structural unemployment** to describe the resulting unemployment.

FRICTIONAL UNEMPLOYMENT

4. **Frictional unemployment**, which is also known as **transitional unemployment**, is essentially 'between jobs' unemployment. It is caused by **geographical** and **occupational immobility of labour** which prevent workers who are layed off from immediately filling job vacancies. Family ties, ignorance about vacancies in other parts of the country and above all the cost of moving and difficulties of obtaining housing are responsible for the geographical immobility of labour, while the need for training and the effects of restrictive practices and discrimination in labour markets are amongst the causes of occupational immobility.

STRUCTURAL UNEMPLOYMENT

5. **Structural unemployment** is closely related to frictional unemployment since both result from the changing nature of industries and the changing demand for different types of labour. But whereas frictional unemployment is essentially temporary, occurring in the period between jobs and on the assumption that a vacancy exists for the unemployed worker to fill, structural unemployment is more severe. In contrast to frictional unemployment, structural unemployment results from a decline in the demand for the products of certain industries caused by changing cost or demand conditions, the effects of new technologies and new products and the emergence of similar but more efficient competitors in other countries.

THE 'NATURAL' RATE OF UNEMPLOYMENT

6. Economists have always accepted that there will be some frictional and structural unemployment in the economy, but many have argued that the more competitive and adaptable the economy is, then the lower will be this 'minimum level' of unemployment. To the pre-Keynesians, this minimum level of frictional and structural unemployment represented full employment. In more recent years, modern monetarists have revived the idea, calling this minimum level of unemployment **the 'natural' rate of unemployment.**

'CLASSICAL' UNEMPLOYMENT

7. We can use Figure 13.1 to show how the pre-Keynesians explained any unemployment above the 'natural' rate of unemployment. Indeed in recent years this old pre-Keynesian theory has been revived as an important part of **the monetarist explanation of unemployment**. According to Figure 13.1 any unemployment above the 'natural' rate is caused by wages being too high - by workers pricing themselves out of jobs. Suppose the wage is W_1. At this wage, employers wish to hire L_1 workers, but a greater number of workers equal to L_2 wish to supply their labour at this wage. In this 'classical' or neo-classical theory, unemployment represents an excess supply of labour at the going wage rate.

THE MARKET MECHANISM AND 'CLASSICAL' UNEMPLOYMENT

8. The pre-Keynesians believed that, as long as the labour market was competitive, 'classical' unemployment could only be temporary. Market forces operating in the labour market would cure the problem. Wages would be bid down in response to the excess supply of labour until the number of workers willing to work equalled the number that firms wished to hire. At the wage of W_{FE} in Figure 13.1, employment is L_{FE}, with unemployment reduced to the 'natural' rate, or the minimum level of frictional and structural unemployment consistent with cultural, institutional and structural conditions in the economy.

UNEMPLOYMENT IN THE 1920s AND 1930s

9. In the 1920s large-scale persistent unemployment occurred in the United Kingdom, preceding the spread of unemployment world-wide in the Great Depression of the 1930s. Much of

British unemployment in the 1920s was probably structural, resulting from the lack of competitiveness and decline of nineteenth century staple industries such as shipbuilding and textiles. But the pre-Keynesians blamed a substantial part of the unemployment on excessively high wages. However, according to their own theory, such 'classical' unemployment ought to have been only temporary - the market mechanism should have reduced wages and priced the unemployed into jobs again. When this did not happen, the pre-Keynesians reacted, not by blaming the theory, but by arguing that institutional factors in the real world and particularly the actions of trade unions, were responsible for preventing the market mechanism from operating. In short, they blamed trade unions for preventing wage cuts. Responsibility for unemployment lay with the workers in work and their trade unions, who by refusing to accept lower wages, prevented the unemployed from pricing themselves into jobs.

KEYNES AND THE 'CLASSICAL' THEORY OF UNEMPLOYMENT

10. Keynes did not reject completely the 'classical' theory; he accepted that high wages could cause unemployment and that under certain circumstances, cuts in wages would create employment. But whereas the economists of his day blamed the real world and not the theory for persistent large-scale unemployment, Keynes started from the opposite premise: *if a theory inadequately explains the real world, do not blame the real world, instead improve or replace the theory*! Hence, in his 'General Theory' published in 1936, Keynes set out what he clearly thought was a 'better and more general' theory to explain the determination of output and employment in the economy than that offered by the 'classical' theory. *From Keynes's 'General Theory' was developed modern macro-economics.*

THE MONEY WAGE AND THE REAL WAGE

11. So far in this chapter we have discussed the 'wage level' and 'wage cuts' without distinguishing between the **money wage (or nominal wage)** and **the real wage. Money** or **nominal wages** are simply the money income that workers are paid, for example, £200 per week. In contrast, a worker's **real wage** is the purchasing power of his money wage, its command over goods and services. The relationship between the money wage and the real wage is expressed in the following identity:

$$\text{Real wage} \equiv \frac{\text{Money wage}}{\text{Price level}}$$

Strictly, the demand curves for labour illustrated in Figure 12.6 should be specified in terms of the real wage rather than the money wage, showing that only when real wages fall will firms employ more workers. But in a monetary economy in which firms pay their workers in money rather than in goods or services, the only wage that a firm can cut is the money wage. For real wages to fall following a cut in money wages, prices must either remain unchanged or fall by a smaller percentage than money wages. Keynes doubted whether this would occur. He argued that if the labour market is sufficiently competitive for employers to be able to cut money wages, the goods market will be sufficiently competitive for prices to fall also. A fall in money wages will induce an equal proportionate fall in prices, leaving the real wage and hence the level of unemployment unchanged. Reductions in money wages may be insufficient to price the unemployed into jobs.

THE FALLACY OF COMPOSITION

12. Keynes went on to argue that even if real wages fall, the neo-classical theory of unemployment suffers from a fundamental defect known as a **fallacy of composition**. A fallacy of composition occurs when what is true at the individual or micro-economic level becomes untrue at the aggregate or macro-economic level. If an individual employer or indeed, all the firms in a particular industry, cuts wages in a single labour market within the economy, more workers will be hired. This is because at the micro-economic level we can invoke the ceteris paribus assumption of holding constant all the other influences upon the demand for labour. In particular, we can assume that the cut in wages has no effect upon the state of aggregate demand in the economy because the firm or industry is only a tiny part of the whole economy. This assumption which is reasonable when studying a single labour market, becomes unreasonable when examining the effects of a cut in real wages in all the labour markets in the economy. At the macro-level, we can no longer invoke the ceteris paribus assumption. Wages are the most important source of aggregate demand in the economy. If real wages are cut throughout the economy, then aggregate demand may fall and firms find that they cannot sell the output they produce. Far from reducing unemployment, the wage cuts may increase it. We have already noted that for real wages to fall following a cut in money wages, the price level must either remain unchanged or fall by a smaller proportion. The immediate effect of this will be to raise profits at the expense of wages. Now people who receive profits as their main source of income, are usually both better off and save a bigger fraction of their income than people who rely on wages. If this is the case, a cut in real wages and the resulting increase in profits can reduce the level of consumption spending in the economy. Too much saving and too little spending can create a condition of deficient demand in the economy.

DEMAND - DEFICIENT UNEMPLOYMENT AND SAY'S LAW

13. Keynes argued that a major cause of persistent large-scale unemployment in the United Kingdom economy in the 1920s and 1930s lay in the existence of **deficient demand**. The question of whether deficient demand can exist in an economy as a long-term phenomenon is a very important source of controversy between economists. The neo-classical or pre-Keynesian economists refused to believe that deficient demand can exist in the economy for any length of time. They argued that any temporary lack of aggregate demand or spending in the economy would quickly be eliminated by the self-regulating nature of market forces. To explain this, we must introduce **Say's Law**, named after an early 19th century French economist, Jean-Baptiste Say. In popular form, Say's Law states that 'supply creates its own demand'. Whenever an output, or supply, is produced, factor incomes such as wages and profits are generated which are just sufficient, if spent, to purchase the output at the existing price level, thereby creating a demand for the output produced. Stated thus, there is nothing controversial about Say's Law; it is really just an identity that is true by definition. The controversial and critical issue concerns whether the potential demand or incomes generated will actually be spent on the output produced. The pre-Keynesians believed that the incomes are spent and that Say's Law holds; Keynes argued that under some circumstances the incomes are not spent, Say's Law breaks down and unemployment is caused by the resulting deficient demand.

THE PRE-KEYNESIANS AND SAY'S LAW

14. To explain the differences between Keynes and his predecessors over Say's Law and deficient demand, it is useful to introduce the two principal functions of money in a monetary economy: the **medium of exchange** and the **store of value** functions. The pre-Keynesians believed that money functions mainly as a medium of exchange, that people hold money in order to finance transactions, literally they hold money so as to buy things: the **transactions motive** for holding money. They believed that because money earns no interest, it is irrational for people to hold money as an idle store of value. Thus in a monetary economy, workers, who are paid in money and not in kind, will quickly spend their money incomes or, if they save, lend their incomes in return for interest for others to spend. Under these circumstances, all money incomes are quickly spent, Say's Law holds and aggregate demand is just sufficient to purchase the output produced.

KEYNES AND SAY'S LAW

15. Unlike his predecessors, Keynes drew attention to the store of value function of money and to the fact that people may want to hold money as a **passive wealth asset**. Keynes believed that in a monetary economy people may decide to save by holding part of their money incomes as an idle store of value, despite the fact that no interest is earned. If money incomes are stored as idle savings and not lent to other people and firms to spend, aggregate demand in the economy will be insufficient to purchase the output produced. Herein, according to Keynes, lies the explanation of how deficient demand can initially occur in the economy. Saving, regarded as a virtue at the individual level, can become a vice at the aggregate level if people save too much of their income and spend too little. This is known as the **paradox of thrift**. And if real wages are cut in the 'mistaken' belief that too high real wages and not deficient demand are the true underlying cause of unemployment, then, according to Keynes, unemployment might be made worse rather than better.

THE KEYNESIAN REVOLUTION

16. Following the publication by Keynes of his 'General Theory' in 1936, **the theory of aggregate demand** gradually became the new orthodoxy in economics, for the next generation replacing the domination of neo-classical thinking. However, for the first few years after 1936, the influence of the 'General Theory' was largely restricted to converting many of Keynes's fellow academic economists to his way of thinking and there was much less influence upon governments and upon government policy. Nevertheless, policies of public spending adopted in the early 1930s in the American New Deal and by the Nazi regime in Germany, were certainly Keynesian in their effect, though hardly inspired by Keynes's writing. In the United Kingdom, Keynes' theories had minimal influence upon government policy during the 1930s and it is wrong to link Keynes with the rather slow but 'natural' recovery from the Great Depression. But during the Second World War, Keynesian policies were adopted by the war-time coalition government in the United Kingdom, firstly to prevent excess demand from causing inflation and then towards the end of the war in the preparation for peace. In 1944, a famous **White Paper on Employment Policy**, inspired by Keynes but largely written by **Lord Beveridge**, effectively committed the next generation of post-war governments to the management of aggregate demand, and the attainment of full employment - defined by Beveridge as 3% of the labour force unemployed - became for the first time an objective of government economic policy. For the next thirty years Keynesianism became the new orthodoxy, though Keynes, who died in 1946, did not live to experience the era in which his followers, the Keynesians, put into operation the demand management policies based on the theory he had developed in the 1930s.

KEYNESIAN DEFICIT FINANCING

17. If unemployment is caused by excessive saving and by deficient demand, it follows that the correct policy solution is to inject just enough demand back into the economy to counter the leakage of demand through saving. To understand this further, it is useful to divide the economy into the four large sectors of demand depicted in Figure 13.2.

Each sector can be a source of either **injections** or **leakages of demand.** The **personal sector** or **households** is the source of **consumption demand** (C),but any household **saving** (S) represents a leakage of demand. **Investment spending (I)** by

Figure 13.2: Sources of injections and leakages of aggregate demand in the economy

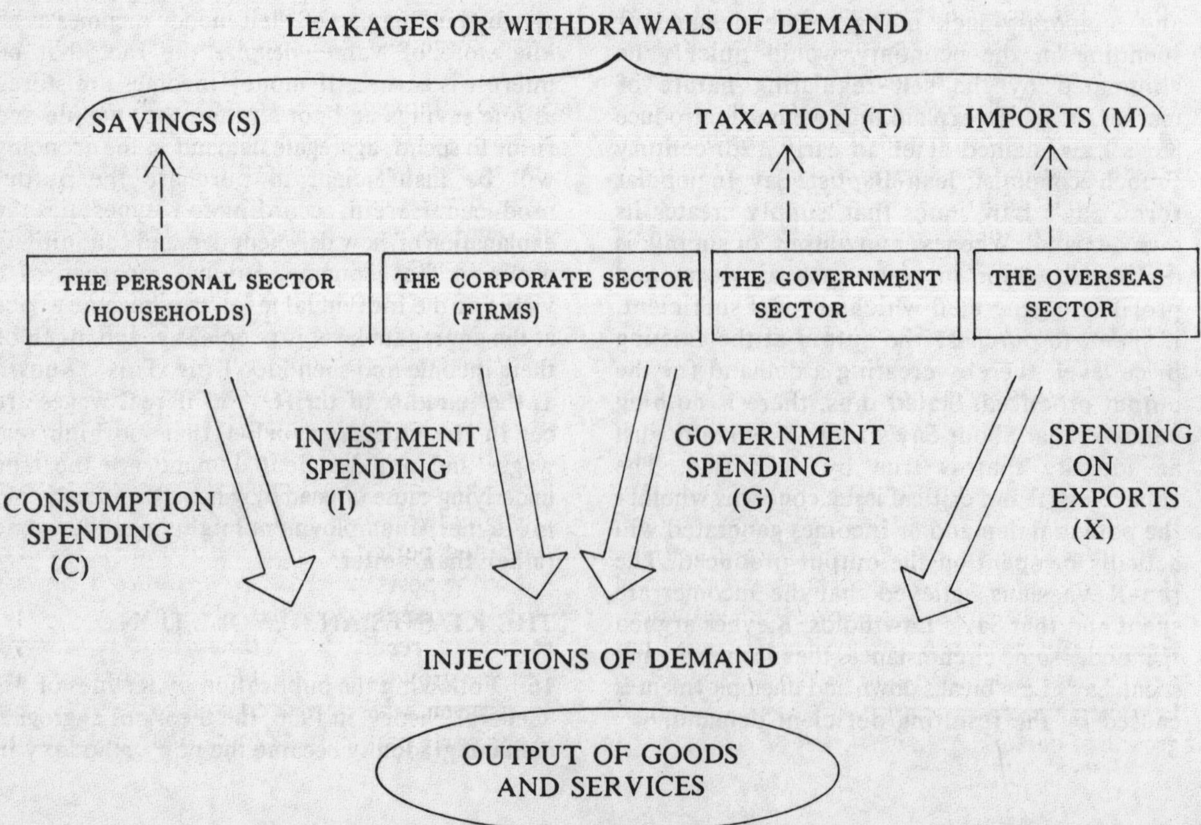

firms in the **corporate** sector is an injection of demand. The **government sector** and the **overseas sectors** are sources of injections - **government spending** (G) and **export demand** (X) - and of leakages, **taxation** (T) and **import demand** (M). Suppose that within the private sector, household saving exceeds the investment by firms (S > I). Keynes argued that in these circumstances an attempt by the government to balance its budget (G = T) would result in deficient demand in the economy unless of course the excess savings of the households were matched by an excess of export demand over imports in the overseas sector. Keynes's predecessors, the neo-classical economists, believed that governments had a moral duty to indulge in the **financial orthodoxy** or **sound finance of a balanced budget**. In contrast, Keynes believed that when saving by households exceeds the investment spending of firms, the government should deliberately **deficit finance**, running a **budget deficit** (G > T) exactly equal to the excess of saving over investment. Via the **borrowing requirement** with which the budget deficit is financed, the government borrows the excess savings of the private sector, which it spends itself, thereby injecting demand back into the economy and preventing the emergence of deficient demand.

THE KEYNESIAN ERA

20. The **Keynesian era** began at the end of the Second World War when governments started to use demand management policies to achieve the objective of full employment. The era ended in the 1970s with the advent of monetarism. In the intervening thirty years governments in many industrial countries, including the United Kingdom, used **fiscal policy** and **monetary policy to manage demand.**

For most of the Keynesian era, demand management policies were used in the following way in the United Kingdom. When unemployment was judged to be excessive, the government would expand demand either by increasing the budget deficit as a part of fiscal policy or by an expansionary monetary policy, or through a combination of both methods. Once full employment was reached, it was believed that any further stimulation of demand would cause prices to rise in a **demand-pull inflation**, since in the short run at least output could not rise to meet the increase in demand. In practice however, the main constraint upon a continued growth of demand, output and employment in the 1950s and 1960s was the **balance of payments** rather than inflation. An expansion of consumer demand usually increased the demand for imports and caused a serious deterioration in the balance of payments. The government then had to reverse its demand management policy to deal with the resulting sterling crisis. A contractionary or deflationary policy of increased taxation and public spending cuts would be implemented, usually supplemented with a tightening of monetary policy. The reduction of demand would decrease the demand for imports and improve the balance of payments, but the growth of output would also slow down and unemployment would increase until the government felt able to expand demand and reflate the economy again. Macro-economic policy in the Keynesian era thus became dominated by the management of demand and by **'stop-go'** - the popular name given to the successive periods of **deflation** and **reflation** characteristic of the Keynesian years.

THE DECLINE OF KEYNESIANISM

21. In 1944 Beveridge defined full employment as being consistent with 3% of the working population unemployed. However, in the light of the then recent history of the Great Depression, Beveridge doubted whether governments would be able to reduce unemployment to 3%. Nevertheless in the outcome, the Keynesian governments of the 1950s and 1960s succeeded in performing much better, reducing unemployment to an average of about 2% of the working population or about 500,000. Indeed, for some periods during the Keynesian era, unemployment actually fell to as low as 1%. The Keynesian economic policy of demand management, involving the '*fine-tuning*' of aggregate demand to a level consistent with full employment but without excessive inflation, appeared to be working, though as we have noted, a continuing expansion of demand was constrained by recurrent balance of payments crises. This was a period of continuous economic growth - literally a 'post-war boom' - and although the annual growth rate of about 2% was low by the standards of economic 'miracle' countries such as Japan and West Germany, it was the longest ever sustained period of growth in British history. But as the post-war boom proceeded, the periods of 'stop' lengthened and the periods of 'go' shortened, resulting in a decline the economy's average growth rate. At the same time, the rate of inflation, which averaged well under 5% a year in the early part of the Keynesian era, began to

creep up, rising towards 10% during the late 1960s and accelerating towards 20% in the early 1970s. As a result of these unfortunate trends, opponents of Keynesianism became more confident in their criticism of Keynesian theories and policies, arguing that Keynesian demand management could achieve full employment only through injecting greater and greater doses of inflation into the economy. Moreover, once achieved, full employment was becoming less and less sustainable. Any expansion of demand seemed to bring about an acceleration of inflation or a balance of payments crisis much more quickly than previously, requiring a reduction of demand almost before the reflation had got off the ground.

THE CRISIS IN KEYNESIAN ECONOMICS

22. *'We used to think that you could spend your way out of a recession and increase employment by cutting taxes and boosting government spending. I tell you in all candour that that option no longer exists and that in so far as it ever did exist it worked by injecting bigger doses of inflation into the economy followed by higher levels of unemployment as the next step ... that is the history of the past twenty years.* (Extract from a speech made by Prime Minister James Callaghan at the Labour Party Conference, 28 September 1976)

By the mid 1970s Keynesianism was is disarray. Keynesian theory had been relatively invulnerable to serious attack as long as Keynesian economic management performed reasonably well when measured against the **five principal objectives of economic policy**:

(i) full employment;
(ii) growth;
(iii) a socially acceptable distribution of income and wealth;
(iv) control of inflation; and
(v) a satisfactory balance of payments.

But just as a generation earlier Keynesianism had become the prevailing orthodoxy when neo-classical economics appeared to fail to deal satisfactorily with the inter-war problem of unemployment, so Keynesianism itself became vulnerable to attack when there was a simultaneous failure to achieve any of the primary policy objectives in the mid-1970s. The **'stagflation'** or **'slumpflation'** of stagnant or declining output and growing unemployment combined with accelerating inflation, together with social conflict over the distribution of income and a deteriorating balance of payments, signalled the end of the Keynesian era.

THE MONETARIST COUNTER-REVOLUTION

Extract from a Daily Express editorial, August 19th 1977:

WE ARE ALL MONETARISTS NOW

From time to time a revolution in political ideas takes place. The trouble is that the process is so slow and so subtle that hardly anybody notices until it has happened.

But if you can spot the thing immediately it is worth noting and discussing.

In the end the country, indeed the world, is governed by ideas and hardly anything else. In the management of the British economy for the last 20 years or so the prevailing idea has been a doctrine called 'Keynesianism'.

Now most of us get a bit impatient when people start going on about various 'isms'. But this particular 'ism' matters to you.

If you have the misfortune to be out of work, if you are a housewife appalled by the constantly rising cost of living you are angry when you look at your wage-packet or salary cheque and see how much has gone in tax, then you ought to know that all this is a product not of chance or of the stars but of an idea.

The big-spending high-taxing governments we have had have largely created the inflation, unemployment and falling living standards that you now suffer. They did what they did because they thought Keynes was the Great Economist and this was what he advised.

What has happened is that, through unpleasant experience, Keynesianism has been discredited. Callaghan and Healey are now talking a quite different language. It is the old language of controlling the money supply, trying to hold back public spending, balancing the budget.

If you think this is just common sense, then you are right. The Daily Express has been calling for it for years. We are not always wrong. And of course this is excellent news for Britain.

23. The decade of the 1970s witnessed the decline of Keynesianism and the ascendency of monetarism. It is useful to distinguish between a **'narrow'** and a **'wider'** meaning of **monetarism**, a term first introduced in the USA by Professor Karl Brunner in 1968. In a strictly 'narrow' sense, a monetarist is a person who believes that the immediate cause of all inflation lies in a prior increase, permitted by governments, of the money supply. But in a 'wider' sense, monetarism is the modern label attached to the revival into a **'New Classical' body of theory** of the 'old' neo-classical or 'classical' theories that predated Keynes. Monetarism is essentially the economics of a self-adjusting or self-regulating private enterprise market economy subject to minimal government intervention and regulation. **The monetarist** or **'New Classical' counter-revolution** represents a return to the 'old' economics which Keynes opposed in the 1920s and 1930s.

THE REVIVAL OF OLD THEORIES

24. The beginning of the monetarist counter-revolution can be dated in 1956 when Professor Milton Friedman of the University of Chicago revived the 'old' pre-Keynesian theory of inflation, **the quantity theory of money**. Broadly, the quantity theory argues that the quantity of money in the economy determines the price level and the rate of inflation. The revival of the quantity theory underpinned the later growth of monetarism and Milton Friedman went on to become the leading theoretician of the monetarist counter-revolution and the most forceful advocate of monetarist economic policy.

EARLY MONETARISM

25. Monetarism made great advances in the early 1970s, 'capturing' from the Keynesians influential citadels in the departments of economics in many universities, especially in the USA. Though for a time monetarism failed to displace Keynesianism as the dominant influence upon the British and American governments, many bankers and especially the International Monetary Fund (IMF) became converts. The conversion of the IMF to monetarism was particularly significant. When in 1976 the United Kingdom faced a very serious balance of payments crisis, the IMF forced the Labour Government to sign a Declaration of Intent which effectively committed the UK to adopting monetarist economic policies as the condition for securing a loan. However, the Labour Government remained then - as the Labour Party still is today - predominantly Keynesian. The Labour Government did not really believe in the monetarist policies it was forced to adopt - largely the monetary 'targetry' of announcing target rates of growth for the money supply and for government borrowing. Essentially, this early period of monetarism from 1976 to 1979 in the UK was a period of **superficial** or **cosmetic monetarism** imposed on the government from outside. It did not represent the conversion of the government of the day to monetarist theories and ways of thinking.

MONETARISM IN THE EARLY 1980s

26. 'Cosmetic' monetarism gave way to a more deep-seated monetarism in the United Kingdom with the election in 1979 of a Conservative government firmly committed to monetarist theories and policies. The election of the Reagan administration in the USA in 1980 marks a similar transition from Keynesianism to monetarism in that country. Under both administrations the short-term discretionary demand management characteristic of the Keynesian years was completely abandoned and economic policies were set in motion to try to reduce, rather than extend, the economic role of the state. In the early part of the Keynesian era, macro-economic policy had meant demand management. The Keynesians had apparently assumed that when unemployed resources exist in the economy, supply would automatically adjust to meet any increase in demand. Under the Keynesians, Say's Law was reversed: demand created its own supply! However, under monetarism, economic policy switched from the **'demand-side'** to the 'supply-side' of the economy. The Keynesian emphasis on macro-economics and on **short-term management of aggregate demand** gave way in the early 1980s to a much more **medium-term** and **'micro-economic'** policy aimed at improving the supply-side or structure of the economy. In response to the growing problems evident in the British economy, many Keynesians (often now called **post-Keynesians** or **neo-Keynesians**) have also become converts to supply-side economics, but there is a striking contrast between the approaches of the post-Keynesians and of the monetarists to the supply-side or structure of the economy. Whereas the post-Keynesians recommend an increase in government interventionism - in such forms as state finance, an extension of planning and the

use of selective import controls - to make up for what they see as the failure of the market to induce the necessary structural changes on the supply-side of the economy, the monetarists have adopted a completely opposite approach. Under monetarism an attempt has been made to 'roll back the state', to abandon the mixed economy of the Keynesian years and by a process of deregulation and privatisation and the freeing of markets, to turn the British economy into a **social market economy** in which private enterprise operating in a system of competitive markets, and not the state, is responsible for inducing the necessary structural change in the economy.

THE CURRENT 'NEW CLASSICAL' ECONOMICS

27. Before the 1980s, monetarism, unlike Keynesianism, lacked a track record; it could not be judged by results because monetarist policies had not been implemented on a sufficient scale. However, during the 'monetarist experiment' of the 1980s, empirical evidence has cast great doubt upon the central tenet of monetarism that an increase in the money supply will inevitably cause inflation. In the United Kingdom for example, the growth in the money supply measured by M3 consistently outstripped the growth in prices. Perhaps as a result of their reduced faith in 'narrow' monetarism, many economists of a free-market persuasion have quietly dropped the label of monetarism, preferring to be known as **'New Classical' economists**, embracing the 'wider' rather than the 'narrower' aspects of monetarism which we noted earlier in section 23 of this chapter. To many economists, the 'New Classical' economics represents a form of **post-monetarism**.

SUMMARY

28. In this chapter we have traced a brief history of macro-economic theory and policy from its origins in the Keynesian Revolution of the 1930s to the recent return to dominance of the older neo-classical or 'classical' orthodoxy in its modern guise as monetarism. Until the monetarist counter-revolution of the 1970s, macro-economics and Keynesianism were largely interchangeable terms. Macro-economic theory was predominantly a theory of the 'demand-side' of the economy, and Keynesian economic policy was dominated by the macro-economic and essentially short-term management of demand. Under monetarism or the New Classical economics - a more embracing label for the views of many members of the monetarist school - a short-term discretionary demand management has been abandoned in favour of a more medium term policy aimed at improving the supply-side of the economy. Monetarism has also reversed the trend evident under Keynesianism of extending the economic role of the state and of government. Instead, by a process of deregulation, privatisation, and the freeing of markets, a deliberate attempt has been made by the monetarists to 'roll back the state', to abandon the post-war consensus around a Keynesian mixed economy and to establish a new consensus around the supposed virtues of a social market economy.

STUDENT SELF-TESTING

1 Distinguish between macro-economics and micro-economics. (1)
2 What is meant by neo-classical economics? (2)
3 What is meant by full employment? (3)
4 What may cause the geographical and occupational immobility of labour? (4)
5 Distinguish between frictional and structural unemployment. (5)
6 What is meant by the 'natural' rate of unemployment? (6)
7 What is the relationship between wage rates and 'classical' unemployment? (7 to 10)
8 Distinguish between the money wage and the real wage. (11)
9 What is a fallacy of composition? (12)
10 Explain Say's Law. (13)
11 Relate Say's Law to demand-deficient unemployment. (15)
12 What is deficit financing? (17)
13 Briefly explain Keynesian demand management? (20)
14 What are the objectives of macro-economic policy? (22)
15 What is monetarism? (23 to 26)
16 Distinguish between monetarism and 'New Classical' economics. (27)

EXERCISES

1 Calculate:
(a) The real wage increase when inflation is 6% and money wages increase by 4%.
(b) The budget deficit when government spending is £140 billion while tax revenues and other sources of government income are £150 billion.

MULTIPLE CHOICE QUESTIONS

1 *'Classical' economists believe that long-term unemployment can be caused by all the following except:*
- A *Excessive real wages*
- B *Geographical immobility of labour*
- C *Deficient aggregate demand*
- D *Barriers between labour markets*

2 *Macro-economics studies the determination of:*
- A *Relative prices of goods and services*
- B *Equilibrium prices of individual goods*
- C *Equilibrium levels of employment of different types of labour*
- D *The average price level in the economy*

3 *Monetarism can be defined as the school of economic thought that:*
- A *Studies the monetary and banking system within the economy*
- B *Explains inflation in terms of an increase in the stock of money*
- C *Studies aggregate money demand in the economy*
- D *Identifies deficient aggregate demand as a major cause of unemployment*

4 *A worker's real wage is:*
- A *Paid in cash rather than through a bank credit transfer*
- B *The rate of growth of inflation minus the rate of growth of the money wage*
- C *Paid in goods rather than in money*
- D *The purchasing power of the money wage*

5 *Say's Law states:*
- A *Demand creates its own supply*
- B *In equilibrium demand equals supply*
- C *The amount actually demanded in the economy equals the amount actually supplied*
- D *Supply creates its own demand*

EXAMINATION QUESTIONS

1 (a) *Outline the causes of unemployment.* *(10 marks)*

(b) *What policies can be used to cure unemployment?* *(10 marks)*

(ACCA December 1984)

2 *Economists since the time of Keynes's general theory have been taught that the way to combat unemployment is to increase public spending. Why, faced with high and rising unemployment, are many Western governments attempting to cut public expenditure?*

(ACCA December 1980)

3. (a) *Why did Keynes believe that governments should control the level of aggregate demand in the economy?*

(b) *How did he suggest this control should be achieved?*

(c) *Explain briefly why the techniques he advocated are considered to be less important now.*

(AAT December 1981)

4. *Explain the economic reasons for the British Government's switch from the Keynesian interventionist policies of the 1950s and 1960s to Friedman style monetarist policies.*

(AAT December 1980)

14. Consumption and saving

INTRODUCTION

1. In Chapter 13 we explained how modern macro-economics developed out of the Keynesian revolution in the 1920s and 1930s and how Keynes believed that a large part of the unemployment in the United Kingdom between the two World Wars was caused by deficient demand. In this chapter, we introduce and explain various theories of aggregate consumption and saving and discuss whether deficient demand may occur in the economy because of a tendency for households to spend too little and to save too much of their income.

CONSUMPTION AND SAVING

2. In macro-economic theory, **consumption** is defined as the spending by all the households in the economy upon goods and services produced within the economy. Aggregate consumption does not include household expenditure upon imports which are part of the goods and services produced in other countries. Nor does it include spending by firms upon goods and services, which economists define as **investment**. Indeed, great care must be taken in understanding the use made by economists of the terms consumption, saving and investment. The relation between consumption and saving is expressed in the following *identity*:

$$Y \equiv C + S$$

If we assume a closed economy, pretending there are no exports or import, this identity states that at any level of income (Y) consumption and saving must equal income because of the way that economists define the two terms. By rewriting the identity as:

$$S \equiv Y - C$$

we arrive at the economist's definition of saving in a closed economy: **saving** is income not spent on consumption. It is vital to understand that economists make a clear separation between saving and investment, even though in everyday language the two terms are often used interchangeably. To an economist, saving is income not consumed; investment is the spending on goods and services by firms. As a general rule, households make saving decisions and only firms make investment decisions. There are however, exceptions to this rule. When a firm makes a decision to 'plough back' profits rather than to distribute them as income to the owners of the business, the firm is simultaneously saving and investing. But if the firm simply stores the profits as a 'cash reserve' - usually on deposit in a bank - it is only saving.

PLANNED AND REALISED CONSUMPTION AND SAVING

3. In Chapter 2 the extremely important distinction between *ex ante* and *ex post* variables in economics was introduced and explained. Before proceeding with reading this section, it is advisable to refer back and thoroughly read section 5 of Chapter 2.

Normally when an economist refers to aggregate consumption, he means the **planned, intended** or **ex ante consumption** of *all* the households in the economy. Similarly, **saving** means **ex ante saving.** It is vital to be quite sure of the difference between **ex ante consumption and saving on the one hand** and, on the other hand, **ex post, realised,** or **actual consumption and saving.** To illustrate the difference, consider a student who receives an income of £20 in a particular week and who wishes to spend all the income on clothes.

Planned or ex ante consumption = £20
Planned or ex ante saving = £0

Suppose that the student finds to his regret when he arrives at the shops that the clothes he wished to buy are unavailable. As a result he saves his income, at least for the time being, even though, ex ante, he had wished to spend it.

Thus:

Actual or ex post consumption = £0
Actual or ex post saving = £20

This imaginary example clearly shows that *planned and realised consumption (or saving) may not be the same.* Ex post consumption equals ex ante consumption only when members of a household *fulfill* or *realise* their consumption plans. But under certain circumstances, when for example goods are unavailable, the members of the household may not be able to consume as much as they wished, in which case the households ends up saving more than originally intended.

THE PROPENSITIES TO CONSUME AND SAVE

4. Suppose in the example illustrated in the last section, the student changes his plans, intending now to spend £16 of his £20 income on consumption. In the absence of spending on imports, consumption and saving must add up to equal income; his planned saving is therefore £4. Economists use the terms **the propensity to consume** and **the propensity to save** to measure planned or ex ante consumption and saving as a ratio of income. At any level of income (Y):

(a) **The average propensity to consume (APC)** is total planned consumption as a ratio of income:

$$APC \equiv \frac{C \text{ (ex ante)}}{Y}$$

(b) **The average propensity to save (APS)** is total planned saving as a ratio of income:

$$APS \equiv \frac{S \text{ (ex ante)}}{Y}$$

When income changes by ΔY:

(c) **The marginal propensity to consume (MPC)** is the change in planned consumption (ΔC) as a ratio of the change in income (ΔY):

$$MPC \equiv \frac{\Delta C \text{ (ex ante)}}{\Delta Y}$$

(d) **The marginal propensity to save (MPS)** is the change in planned saving (ΔS) as a ratio of the change in income (ΔY):

$$MPS \equiv \frac{\Delta S \text{ (ex ante)}}{\Delta Y}$$

When income is £20, the student's average propensity to consume = 0.8 and his average propensity to save = 0.2, *the average propensities to consume and save always summing to unity*:

$$1 \equiv APC + APS$$

Suppose now that income rises by £2, out of which the student intends to spend £1.20 on consumption and to save 80p. His marginal propensity to consume is now 0.6 and his marginal propensity to save is 0.4. *Again the two propensities must sum to unity:*

$$1 \equiv MPC + MPS$$

Calculate the new average propensities to consume and save at the new level of income of £22. You will note that when the MPC is below the APC, the APC falls as income rises.

THE PERSONAL SAVINGS RATIO

5. It is rather difficult for economists to measure the propensities to consume and to save because they are *ex ante* - statements of how much people wish to consume and to save at different levels of income. Because of the difficulty of measurement, the **personal savings ratio** is often used as an approximate indicator of the average propensity to save. The personal savings ratio is an *ex post* measure of actual household saving as a ratio of total personal disposal income. **Disposable income (Yd)** is the net income that households have available to spend after paying income taxes and after the receipt of government transfers such as unemployment pay and child benefit.

$$\text{Personal saving ratio} \equiv \frac{S \text{ (ex post)}}{Yd}$$

Figure 14.1: The personal savings ratio in the United Kingdom

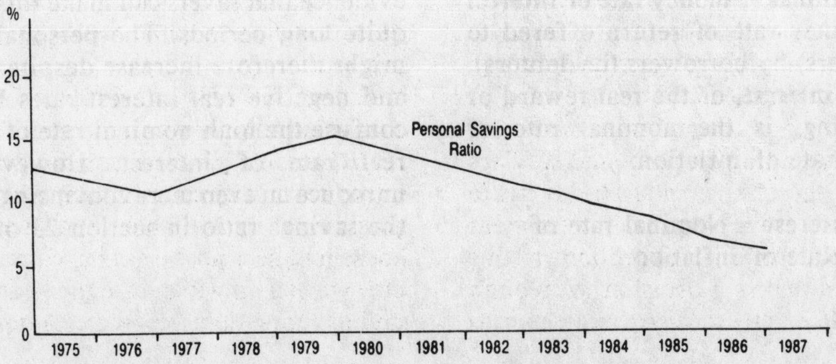

Changes in the personal saving ratio in the 1970s and the 1980s are illustrated in Figure 14.1. Savings were relatively stable during the 1960s, being less than 10% of disposable income, but the savings ratio almost doubled during years of rapid inflation in the 1970s and around 1980. When the rate of inflation fell in the early 1980s, the savings ratio also decreased, falling to less than 5% in 1988.

CONSUMPTION, SAVING AND THE RATE OF INTEREST

6. Before Keynes, economists gave little attention to explaining how the level of aggregate consumption spending is determined in the economy. They simply assumed, following **Say's Law**, that 'supply creates its own demand'. We can however identify the **'classical' theory of saving**. Before Keynes, it was widely accepted that the main determinant of the level of aggregate saving in the economy is the real rate of interest. The rate of interest rewards savers for sacrificing current consumption, and the higher the real rate of interest, the greater is the real reward. Accordingly, at any particular level of income, the amount saved will increase as the real rate of interest rises. In short, the pre-Keynesians believed that saving is a positive function of the real rate of interest. If saving is a positive function of the real rate of interest, consumption must be a negative function of the real interest rate. (From the identity $Y \equiv C + S$, $C \equiv Y - S$ at every level of income.) Therefore the higher the real rate of interest, the less people plan to consume at any particular level of income.

NOMINAL AND REAL INTEREST RATES

7. To understand macro-economic theory properly, it is necessary to understand the difference between **nominal** and **real economic variables**. The rate of interest provides a good example. The **nominal** or **money rate of interest** refers to the money rate of return offered to savers (or creditors) by borrowers (or debtors). The **real rate of interest,** or the real reward or return on lending, is the nominal rate of interest less the rate of inflation:

Real rate of interest ≡ Nominal rate of interest - Rate of inflation

Whenever inflation occurs, the real rate of interest will be lower than the nominal rate. Real rates of interest are negative whenever the rate of inflation is higher than nominal interest rates. In these circumstances, the real value of savings is eroded by inflation at a faster rate than it is added to by money interest payments.

THER PERSONAL SAVINGS RATIO IN THE 1970s AND 1980s

8. If aggregate saving is a positive function of the real rate of interest, as the pre-Keynesians evidently believed, the personal savings ratio ought to have fallen in the second half of the 1970s and around 1980 when real rates of interest were negative. Figure 14.2 on the following page shows this did not happen. Changes in the nominal rate of interest and in the rate of inflation are illustrated in the upper panel of Figure 14.2 and from these changes, the real rate of interest is derived. The changes in the personal savings ratio shown in Figure 14.1 are then reproduced in the lower panel of Figure 14.2.

The evidence illustrated in Figure 14.2 suggests that the real rate of interest is not an important influence upon aggregate saving and consumption decisions, and that we must look elsewhere for a possible explanation of changes in the savings ratio. Aggregate consumption and saving may be relatively inelastic with respect to changes in the real rate of interest.

MONEY ILLUSION

9. Figure 14.2 does however illustrate a fairly strong positive correlation between the personal savings ratio and nominal interest rates. In times of inflation savers suffer from **money illusion** when they believe, falsely, that the nominal rate of interest earned by their savings is also the real rate. There is considerable evidence that savers can make this confusion for quite long periods. The personal savings ratio might therefore increase despite high inflation and negative real interest rates because savers confuse the high nominal rate offered with the real rate of interest. However, we shall introduce an even more convincing explanation of the savings ratio in section 23 of this chapter.

Figure 14.2: The savings ratio, interest rates and inflation in the United Kingdom

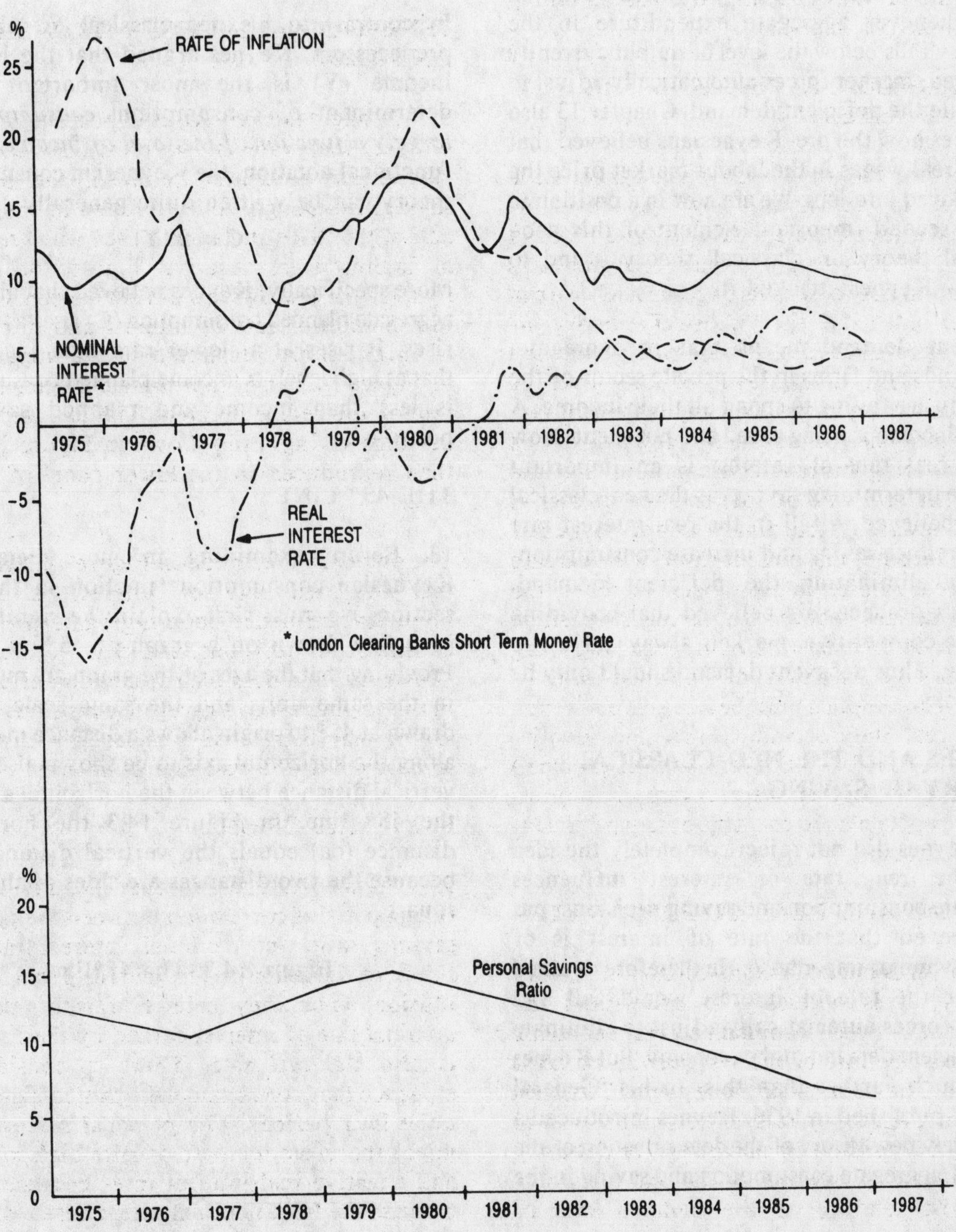

THE RATE OF INTEREST, SAVING AND DEFICIENT DEMAND

10. In Chapter 13 we explained how the neo-classical school of economists who preceded Keynes rejected the idea of **demand-deficient unemployment**, except as an essentially temporary phenomenon. Instead the pre-Keynesians believed that whenever aggregate expenditure in the economy falls below the level of output currently produced, market forces automatically adjust to eliminate the deficient demand. Chapter 13 also describes how the pre-Keynesians believed that falling real wages in the labour market price the unemployed into jobs. We are now in a position to state a second important element of this neo-classical theory or 'classical' theory - and to see how Keynes attacked it.

Deficient demand means that in aggregate, households and firms in the private sector of the economy are failing to spend all their income. A part of income is being saved and not spent. Now if the real rate of interest is an important variable determining saving, as the neo-classical school believed, a fall in the real interest rate should reduce saving and increase consumption, thereby eliminating the deficient demand. Keynes's predecessors believed that providing they are competitive, markets always adjust in this way. Thus deficient demand should only be temporary.

KEYNES AND THE NEO-CLASSICAL THEORY OF SAVING

11. Keynes did not reject completely the idea that the real rate of interest influences aggregate consumption and saving decisions, but he believed that the rate of interest is of relatively minor importance. He therefore doubted whether the rate of interest would fall and market forces automatically adjust to eliminate any deficient demand in the economy. But Keynes went much further than this. In his 'General Theory' published in 1936, Keynes introduced a completely new theory of the determination of the levels of aggregate consumption and saving in the economy.

THE KEYNESIAN CONSUMPTION FUNCTION

12. In his 'General Theory', Keynes explained his theory of aggregate consumption in the following way:

"The fundamental psychological law, upon which we are entitled to depend with great confidence ....., is that men are disposed, as a rule and on average, to increase their consumption as their income increases, but not by as much as the increase in their income."

In contrast to his neo-classical or 'classical' predecessors, Keynes argued that the level of income (Y) is the most important single determinant of consumption: *consumption is largely a function of the level of income*. Using functional notation, the Keynesian consumption theory can be written quite generally as:

$$C = f(Y)$$

More specifically, Keynes believed that although aggregate planned consumption (C) rises as income rises, it rises at a slower rate than income so that at high levels of income planned consumption is less than income and planned saving is positive.

THE 45° LINE

13. Before examining in more detail the Keynesian consumption function in the next section, we must first explain the significance of a line drawn on a graph at 45° to origin. Providing that the axes of the graph are measured in the same units and the same scale, a line drawn at 45° to origin allows a distance measured along the horizontal axis to be shown also as the vertical distance between the horizontal axis and the 45° line. In Figure 14.3 the horizontal distance (oa) equals the vertical distance (ab) because the two distances are sides of the same square.

Figure 14.3: The 45°line

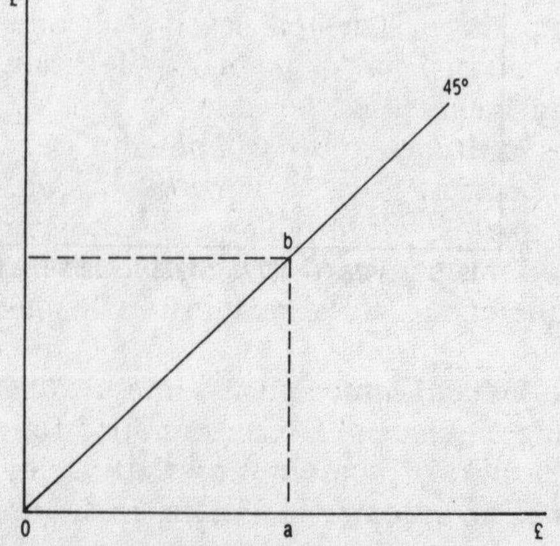

AUTONOMOUS CONSUMPTION AND INCOME-INDUCED CONSUMPTION

Figure 14.4: A linear Keynesian consumption function, showing autonomous and income-induced consumption

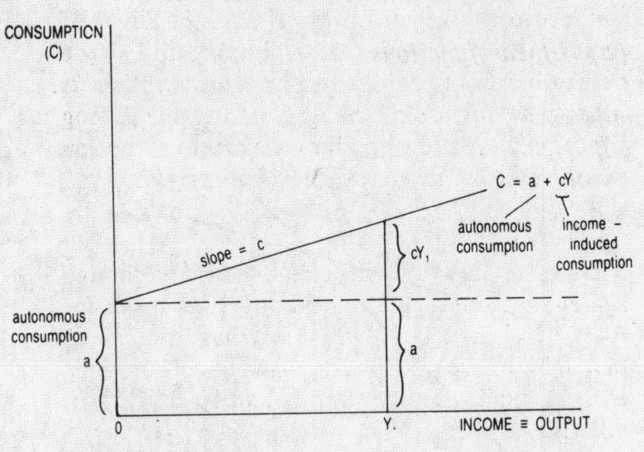

14. Figure 14.4 illustrates the essential features of the Keynesian consumption function, showing that total planned consumption (C) comprises two elements: **autonomous consumption** and **income-induced consumption.** The consumption function in Figure 14.4 which is drawn as a straight line (a *linear consumption function*), can be expressed as the linear equation:

$$C = a + cY$$

in which (a) represents autonomous consumption and (cY) represents income-induced consumption.

Autonomous consumption (a) is the part of total consumption constant at all levels of income. The value of autonomous consumption is determined by such influences as the rate of interest and peoples' attitudes to thrift. For example, if the rate of interest falls, or if people become less thrifty at all levels of income, the consumption function shifts upwards (by an amount Δa), but the slope of the curve remains unchanged.

Income-induced consumption is measured by (cY), (c) being the slope of the consumption function. It is the part of consumption that varies with the level of income. In Figure 14.4, income-induced consumption equals cY_1 when the level of income is Y_1.

THE CONSUMPTION FUNCTION AND THE PROPENSITY TO CONSUME

Figure 14.5: The propensities to consume and a linear consumption function

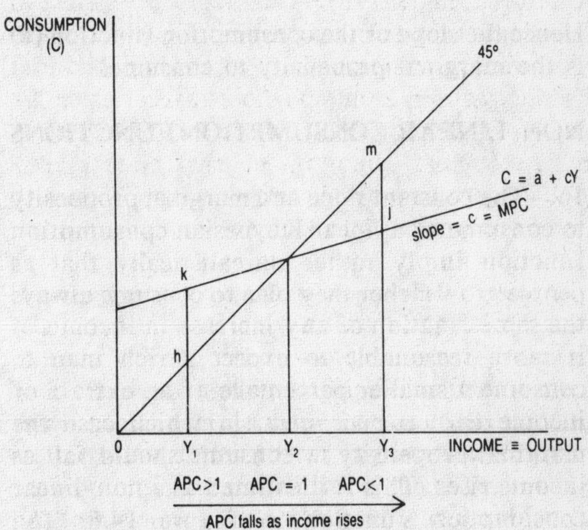

15. Figure 14.5 brings together a Keynesian consumption function and the 45° line. A level of income such as Y_1 can be shown by the vertical line Y_1h drawn between Y_1 and the 45° line. The line Y_1k measures planned consumption at this level of income. Clearly, at a level of income such as Y_1, at which the consumption function is above the 45° line, planned consumption is greater than income and the average propensity to consume is greater than unity (APC > 1). If in doubt refer back at this stage to the earlier section of this chapter on the propensity to consume and save. Remember

$$APC \equiv \frac{C\ (\text{ex ante})}{Y}$$

and

$$MPC \equiv \frac{\Delta C\ (\text{ex ante})}{\Delta Y}$$

You will notice that as income rises, the average propensity to consume falls to unity at Y_2, the level of income at which the consumption function crosses the 45° line, before falling below unity at all higher levels of income where the consumption function lies below the 45° line. But although the average propensity to consume falls as income rises in Figure 14.5, the marginal propensity to consume remains constant. This is because *the marginal propensity to consume is the slope of the consumption function* and a linear consumption function has a constant slope at all levels of income. For any change in income, ΔY, consumption changes by $c\Delta Y$:

$$\Delta C = c\Delta Y$$

and thus

$$\frac{\Delta C}{\Delta Y} = c$$

Hence the slope of the consumption function (c) is the marginal propensity to consume!

NON-LINEAR CONSUMPTION FUNCTIONS

16. The constant slope and marginal propensity to consume of a linear Keynesian consumption function imply rather unrealistically that as people grow richer they plan to consume always the same fraction of any increase in income. It is more reasonable to expect a rich man to consume a smaller percentage of an extra £ of income than a poor man, in which case the marginal propensity to consume should fall as income rises. This is illustrated as a non-linear consumption function in Figure 14.6. The consumption function is drawn rising with income, but as income rises, the consumption function becomes flatter and the marginal propensity to consume falls.

Figure 14.6: A non-linear Keynesian consumption function

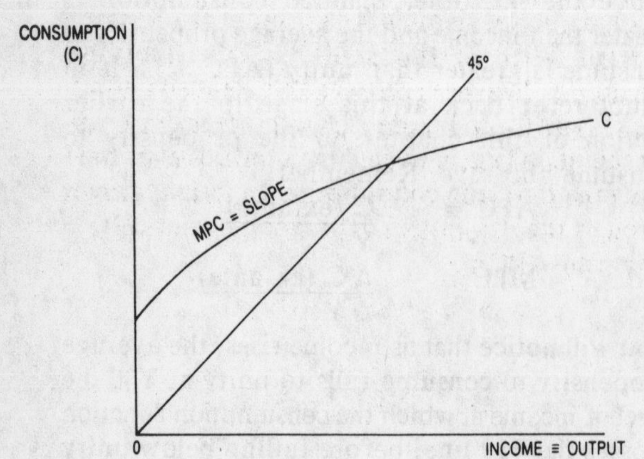

DERIVING THE SAVING FUNCTION

17. Figure 14.7 shows how a savings function can be derived from a Keynesian consumption function by subtracting planned consumption from income at every level of income.

Figure 14.7: Deriving a saving function from a consumption function

(a) Linear functions

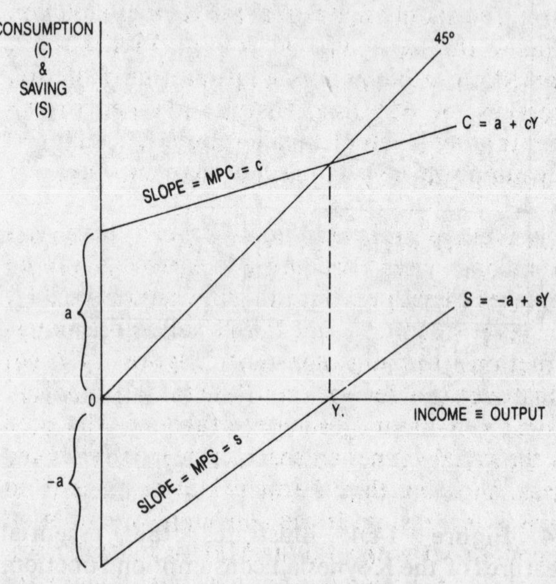

(b) Non-linear functions

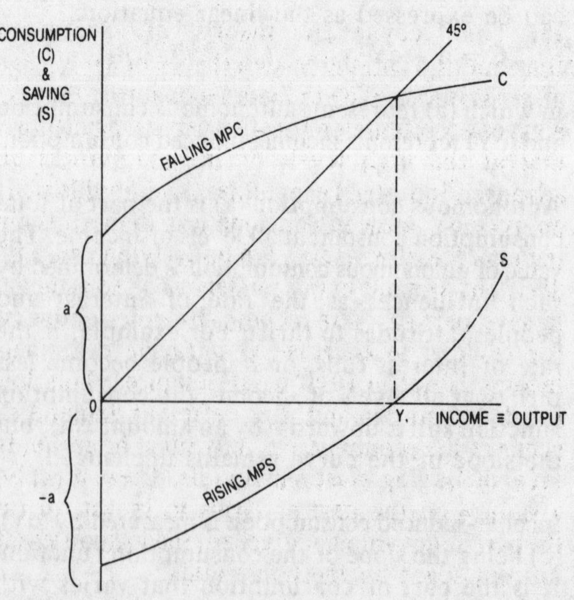

The equation of the linear savings function illustrated in Figure 14.7 (a) is:

$$S = -a + sY$$

The term (-a) represents **autonomous (negative) saving** or **dissaving**, while (s), the slope of the savings function, is the **marginal propensity to save**. At levels of income below Y_1, households plan to dissave by borrowing or running down previously accumulated stocks of saving to finance consumption plans which exceed income. Y_1 is the level of income at which planned consumption equals income and planned saving is zero. You should notice that the savings function crosses the zero axis at Y_1 in Figure 14.7, immediately below the consumption function crossing the 45° line. Positive planned saving occurs at all levels of income above Y_1, planned consumption now being less than income.

The average propensity to save (APS) thus rises as income rises, becoming positive as saving replaces dissaving, but the marginal propensity to save (MPS) or the slope of the savings functions remains constant. Figure 14.7 (b) illustrates the derivation of the saving function from a non-linear consumption function. The slope of the savings function becomes steeper as income rises, showing that the marginal propensity to save is increasing. If the consumption function is non-linear with a falling MPC as income rises, the saving function must also be non-linear with a rising MPS.

THE IMPORTANCE OF THE KEYNESIAN CONSUMPTION FUNCTION

18. The Keynesian theory of aggregate consumption and the related theory of saving are of great importance in macro-economic theory. Keynes's consumption function carries the message that at the high levels of income typical of advanced industrial economies, households will, on average, wish to consume less than all their income. Keynes located the underlying cause of deficient demand in this tendency for households to save part of their income. But the tendency for savings to increase at a faster rate than income is not in itself a sufficient explanation for deficient demand. For deficient demand to occur in the economy, not only must households save, the saving must remain idle. There must be a failure on the part of firms to invest, or on the part of government to spend, the income saved but not spent by the households.

SHORT-RUN AND LONG-RUN CONSUMPTION FUNCTIONS

19. As might be expected, economists have on many occasions measured consumption and savings decisions in order to 'test' the Keynesian consumption theory that consumption rises with income, but at a slower rate. Broadly, such empirical tests can be divided into **cross-sectional** and **time-series** studies. A **cross-sectional** test of the Keynesian consumption theory examines the incomes of the poor, the middle-income groups and the well-off at a particular point in time, for example measuring each group's consumption and savings decisions in a single year. In contrast, a **time-series** study measures how aggregate consumption and saving of all income groups taken together vary with income over the extended period of a number of years.

In general, cross-sectional studies of different income groups support the Keynesian consumption hypothesis, as do time-series studies made over the relatively short period of a single business cycle. However, time-series studies undertaken over extended periods much longer than the four to five years of a single business cycle do not support the Keynesian theory. Instead, extended time-series studies show aggregate consumption rising proportionately with income, rather than declining as a proportion of income as Keynes had predicted.

The Keynesian consumption function should therefore be regarded essentially as a **short-run consumption function**, reflecting short-term fluctuations in household income. In the long-run, consumption increases in proportion with income, being depicted in Figure 14.8 as an upward shift in the short-run consumption function as incomes rise over an extended period. C_1, C_2 and C_3 in Figure 14.8, represent short-run consumption functions shifting upwards over time along the **long-run consumption function**, drawn through the origin, for which long-run MPC = long-run APC.

Figure 14.8: Long-run and short-run consumption functions

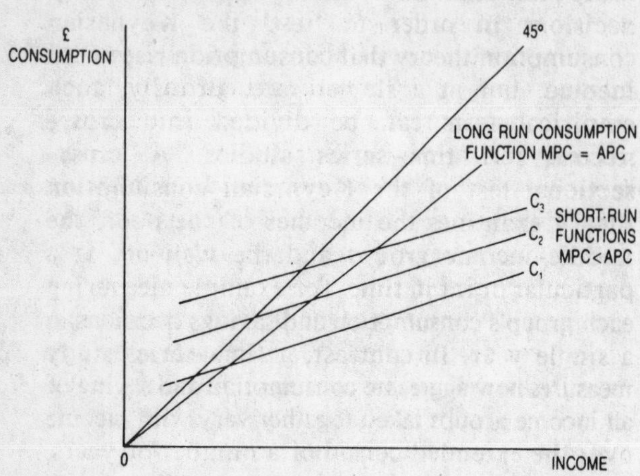

ALTERNATIVE THEORIES OF CONSUMPTION

20. The Keynesian consumption theory which, as we have just explained, should be regarded as a short-run theory of aggregate consumption, is sometimes known as the **absolute income consumption theory** because it assumes that the most important influence on consumption is the *absolute* level of current income. Later generations of economists have explained the upward shift we have noted in the short-run consumption function, by arguing that the level of income in a particular year has much less influence upon an individual's planned consumption than some notion of his *expected* income over a much longer time period, perhaps even over a lifetime. Two rather similar theories have been developed to explain aggregate consumption in terms of income over a long period: Milton Friedman's **Permanent Income Consumption Theory** and Franco Modigliani's **Life-Cycle Consumption Theory.**

THE PERMANENT INCOME CONSUMPTION THEORY

21. The permanent income consumption theory developed by Milton Friedman and the life-cycle theory both have a basic foundation in the micro-economic theory of consumer choice. They begin from the assumption that rational consumers aim to maximise utility over an expected lifetime by allocating a stream of life-time earnings to an optimal life-time pattern of consumption.

Milton Friedman distinguished between **permanent** income, or expected income over a long time period, and **transitory** income which is a 'windfall' income in a particular year, unlikely to be received in other years. Friedman argued that consumption plans are stable in terms of permanent income, but that they may be unstable in terms of income in a particular year which is likely to be 'distorted' by windfall receipt - or loss - of transitory income.

THE LIFE-CYCLE CONSUMPTION THEORY

22. In most important respects, the life-cycle theory, which is illustrated in Figure 14.9 is similar to the permanent income theory.

Figure 14.9: The Life-cycle consumption theory: How a life-cycle income stream is distributed between consumption and savings

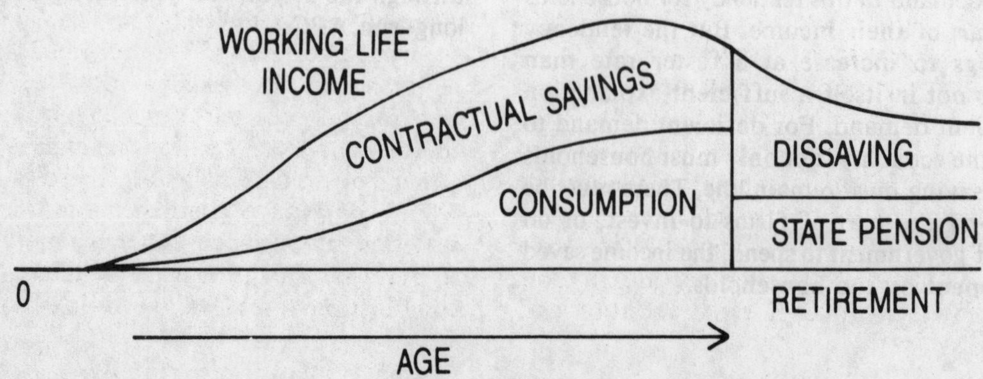

In order to understand the life-cycle theory, it is useful to distinguish between two different types of saving: **contractual (or non-discretionary) saving** and **non-contractual (or discretionary) saving.**

(a) **Contractual saving.** Many people save especially early on in their working lives to finance house purchase, and throughout their working lives to finance retirement. Usually such savings are contractual, taking the form of life insurance premiums and contributions to pension funds, building societies and other financial institutions. Saving takes place regularly over a number of years, to be followed in later years by dissaving when a house is purchased or upon retirement.

(b) **Non-contractual saving.** In contrast to contractual saving, which takes place over a number of years, non-contractual or discretionary savings are much more transitory. Examples include 'one-off' decisions to save in order to finance a summer holiday or the purchase of Christmas presents. Typically, saving in one part of the year is followed a few weeks or months later by dissaving to finance a major item of consumption. Thus over a number of months or a single year, discretionary saving 'nets out' and becomes close to zero.

Most savings are therefore contractual or non-discretionary, planned by households on the basis of a long-term view of life-time or permanent income and of likely spending plans over the remaining length of an expected life-cycle. Regular contractual savings contributed to pension schemes and to the purchase of life insurance policies are unlikely to alter very much if yearly income temporarily fluctuates, partly because later in life it becomes considerably more expensive to purchase new life insurance.

THE LIFE-CYCLE THEORY AND THE PERSONAL SAVINGS RATIO

23. The life-cycle theory of consumption and saving provides perhaps the best explanation for the changes in the personal savings ratio illustrated in Figures 14.1 and 14.2. We have already noted in an earlier section of this chapter how at a time of rapid inflation and sometimes negative real interest rates in the 1970s and around 1980, saving increased as a ratio of personal disposable income. To their dismay, households may have discovered that inflation had eroded the real value of savings accumulated over the earlier years of working life. In these circumstances it was rational to take out new contractual savings in order to 'top-up' or restore the real value of accumulated saving. Only by saving in this way could households hope to finance retirement in real terms as previously planned. Greater uncertainty about the future, itself caused by rapid inflation, may also have caused the savings ratio to rise. A high rate of inflation, fluctuating considerably from year to year, is likely to cause people to save for precautionary reasons. Thus despite low or even negative real interest rates, the savings ratio increased during the 1970s.

The life-cycle theory also explains why the savings ratio fell after about 1981, even though real rates of interest became very high by historical standards. Because inflation had ceased to erode the value of accumulated stocks of saving, households no longer needed to take out extra contractual saving. At the same time, uncertainty about future inflation may have diminished, providing a second explanation for the decrease in savings. Finally, the inflation of the 1970s and especially the inflation of house prices, may have contributed to the later fall in the savings ratio. When a house is first bought, the purchaser usually borrows a large fraction of the sum needed on a mortgage. During periods of rapid inflation, the value of the house rises, but the mortgage does not. As a result, house owners become much wealthier. When households realise this, they may decide to capitalise a fraction of their wealth, converting part of their wealth from illiquid bricks and mortar into money, with the intention of spending the money on consumption. This is what has happened in the United Kingdom in the 1980s. Some houseowners simply increased their borrowing, or dissaved, using the value of their houses as security. In effect such households 'geared-up' or increased the 'gearing ratio' of debts or borrowing to capital or wealth, just as a firm increases its gearing ratio whenever it borrows. Other households, believing that house prices would continue to rise faster than the average inflation rate, decided to borrow more in order to purchase a more expensive house. So, for a combination of reasons, the savings ratio fell in the early 1980s as houseowners decided to borrow more in order to finance a higher level of consumption.

OTHER INFLUENCES UPON CONSUMPTION AND SAVING

24. (a) **Wealth.** The *stock* of personal wealth, as well as the *flow* of income, influences consumption decisions. In the Keynesian consumption function, wealth is one of the determinants of autonomous consumption and the position of the consumption function. An increase in wealth shifts the consumption function upwards, increasing consumption at all levels of income, while a decrease in wealth reduces consumption. When in October 1987, the world-wide stock market crash reduced the value of most shares by a third, many commentators feared that shareholders would cut consumption and increase saving in order to restore the eroded value of their personal wealth. If this had happened, the 'wealth effect' of the stock market crash might have reduced consumption world-wide and ushered in a new world depression. At the time of writing - in April 1989 - this has not happened, perhaps because governments of leading industrial countries have learned the lesson of the much earlier stock exchange crash in 1929. Governments reacted to the 1929 crash by tightening monetary policy, which unfortunately reinforced the effects of the crash and reduced consumption still further. By contrast, immediately following the 1987 crash, interest rates were cut and monetary policy was relaxed with the specific aim of offsetting the effects of the crash on consumption - and avoiding a world recession.

(b) **Expectations of future inflation.** The effects on consumption and saving of expectations about the future rate of inflation are rather unpredictable. On the one hand, as described in the previous section, uncertainty about future inflation may encourage precautionary saving. But on the other hand, households may decide to bring forward consumption decisions by spending now on consumer durables such as cars or TV sets, thereby avoiding expected future price increases. And, as we also saw in the previous section, there is even more reason to borrow to finance the purchase of goods such as houses whose value appreciates and which serve as a hedge against inflation.

(c) **The availability of credit.** We have already noted that the rate of interest affects autonomous consumption and the position of the Keynesian consumption function. Other aspects of monetary policy, such as controls on bank lending and hire-purchase controls have a similar effect. If credit is easily and cheaply available, consumption is likely to increase at all levels of income as people supplement current income by borrowing on credit created by the banking system in order to finance consumption. Conversely a tight monetary policy will shift the consumption function downwards.

(d) **The distribution of income.** We have already explained how the marginal propensity to consume is likely to be greater at low rather than high levels of income. At any overall level of aggregate income, a redistribution of income from rich to poor is therefore likely to increase consumption and to reduce saving.

SUMMARY

25. We have examined in this chapter various theories which explain the determination of the aggregate level of consumption in the economy. Consumption is of vital importance in the economy, accounting for over half of national expenditure. In explaining consumption, the principal distinction to be made is between the neo-classical or 'classical' theory that saving and hence consumption decisions, are determined primarily by the rate of interest, and the Keynesian view that the level of income is the dominant influence. The former theory supports the view that the market mechanism, working through the rate of interest, will automatically rid the economy of any deficient demand that may temporarily come into existence. Conversely, the Keynesian consumption function is an extremely important element in the wider Keynesian argument, to be developed in the next chapter, that deficient demand can be permanent and that an economy, left to itself, may settle into an under-fully employed equilibrium.

We have concluded the chapter with an examination of short-run and long-run influences upon aggregate consumption and saving, and a brief survey of alternative theories of the consumption function, which include the permanent income consumption theory and the life-cycle consumption theory.

STUDENT SELF-TESTING

1 *Distinguish between consumption, saving and investment.* (2)
2 *What is meant by ex ante consumption?* (3)
3 *Distinguish between the average and marginal propensities to consume and save.* (4)
4 *What is the personal savings ratio?* (5)
5 *What is the 'classical' theory of saving?* (6)
6 *Define the real rate of interest.* (7)
7 *What is 'money illusion'?* (9)
8 *Express the Keynesian consumption function as an equation.* (12 to 14)
9 *What is the mathematical significance of a 45° line?* (13)
10 *Distinguish between the autonomous consumption and income-induced consumption.* (14)
11 *What does the slope of the consumption function represent?* (15)
12 *Derive a savings function from* $C = a + cY$. (17)
13 *What are meant by cross-sectional and time-series data on consumption?* (19)
14 *Distinguish between permanent income and transitory income.* (21)
15 *Briefly describe the life-cycle theory of consumption.* (22)
16 *List other influences upon consumption.* (24)

EXERCISES

1 *The following tables shows planned consumption at various levels of income.*

Income	Planned consumption	Planned saving
0	500	
1000	1400	
2000	2300	
3000	3200	
4000	4100	
5000	5000	
6000	5900	
7000	6800	
8000	7700	
9000	8600	
10000	9500	

(a) Complete the table to show planned saving at each level of income.

(b) What is the equation of the consumption function shown by the table?

(c) Calculate:
(i) autonomous consumption;
(ii) the marginal propensity to consume;
(iii) the average propensity to save at income levels of 1000, 5000 and 7000.

2 *(a) Plot on a graph the following consumption function:*

$$C = 1000 + 0.4Y$$

(b) Derive the equation of the saving function.

(c) Plot the savings function on the same graph.

(d) Calculate the level of income at which half of income is consumed and half is saved.

MULTIPLE CHOICE QUESTIONS

1 *If a government wishes to stimulate consumption, which one of the following measures is likely to be most effective?*

A *An increase in regional aid to industry*
B *An increase in old age pensions*
C *A decrease in the higher rates of income tax*
D *A decrease in personal tax allowances*

2 *An increase in the personal savings ratio when real rates of interest are negative is best explained by:*

A *Money illusion*
B *The life-cycle theory of consumption and saving*
C *The Keynesian theory of aggregate consumption and saving*
D *The liquidity preference theory*

3 *The marginal propensity to consume measures the relation between a change in:*

A *Actual consumption and changes in income*
B *Planned consumption and changes in income*
C *Consumption and changes in saving*
D *Aggregate money demand and changes in income*

4 **Figure 14.10**

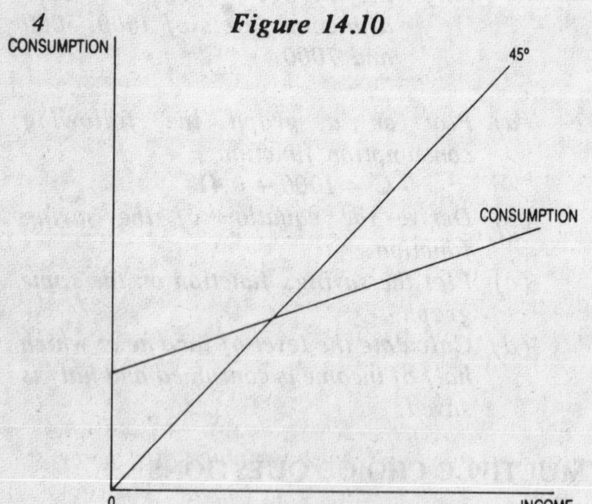

In the diagram above, the average propensity to consume is:

A *Constant at all levels of income*
B *Rising with income*
C *Falling with income*
D *Less than the marginal propensity to consume at all levels of income*

5 *Given the average propensity to consume, total savings in the economy depend upon:*

A *The marginal propensity to save*
B *Changes in the rate of interest*
C *The level of national income*
D *Wealth*

EXAMINATION QUESTIONS

1 *What factors are likely to determine the aggregate level of consumption spending in an economy?* *(20 marks)*
(ACCA December 1984)

2 *What is meant by the 'paradox of thrift' in times of unemployment? What measures can a government take to deal with this problem in time of recession?*
(ACCA December 1976)

3 *(a) Define and explain the marginal and average propensities to save. (6 marks)*

(b) Demonstrate the consequences of an increase in the flow of savings in an economy. *(14 marks)*
(ACCA June 1984)

4\. *(a) What are the main factors which influence the proportion of national income which is saved?*

(b) How important are changes in this proportion for economic policy.
(AAT June 1980)

15. National income and expenditure

INTRODUCTION

1. In Chapters 13 and 14 we have mentioned an important division separating economists into two schools of thought with regard to the nature of the macro-economic processes operating within the economy. On one side of the division is the **neo-classical** or **'classical' tradition** which, with the growth of **monetarism**, has experienced a revival in the 1970s and 1980s. Opposing the monetarists and the **'New Classical' school** are the **Keynesian** economists who claim to have inherited the mantle of the influential English economist, **John Maynard Keynes**. The Keynesian tradition descends from the publication in 1936 of Keynes's 'General Theory' an event which marked the beginning of modern macro-economics. The major controversial issue separating economists of the two schools concerns whether a market economy will, if left to itself, automatically adjust to achieve full employment. Keynesians reject the idea of an automatic adjustment process, believing that without government management, an unregulated market economy can quite easily settle into an under-full employment equilibrium, in which persistent unemployment is caused by deficient demand. In contrast, members of the 'New Classical' school - including many monetarists - argue that providing markets are competitive, market forces alone will adjust automatically to a full employment equilibrium. In this chapter we begin to explain in greater detail the issues involved, introducing within a **Keynesian model of the economy**, the important concept of **equilibrium national income**.

NATIONAL INCOME, WEALTH AND CAPITAL

2. Figure 15.1 illustrates the very important relationships and distinctions between national **income, wealth** and **capital**. National **wealth** comprises all the physical assets or things that have value, owned by the nation's residents. The national **capital stock** is the part of national wealth capable of producing more wealth. It includes all the capital goods and raw materials owned by the country's residents as well as social capital such as roads, hospitals and schools, but it excludes consumer goods which are a part of national wealth but not national capital. All capital is wealth, but the reverse is untrue: not all wealth is capital. However, wealth and capital are examples of economic *stocks* and are thus distinguished from income which is a *flow*. **National income** is the *flow* of new wealth resulting from the productive use of the national capital *stock*. Being part of a continuous flow, national income is measured per time period, monthly, quarterly, or more usually yearly.

Figure 15.1: The flow of national income

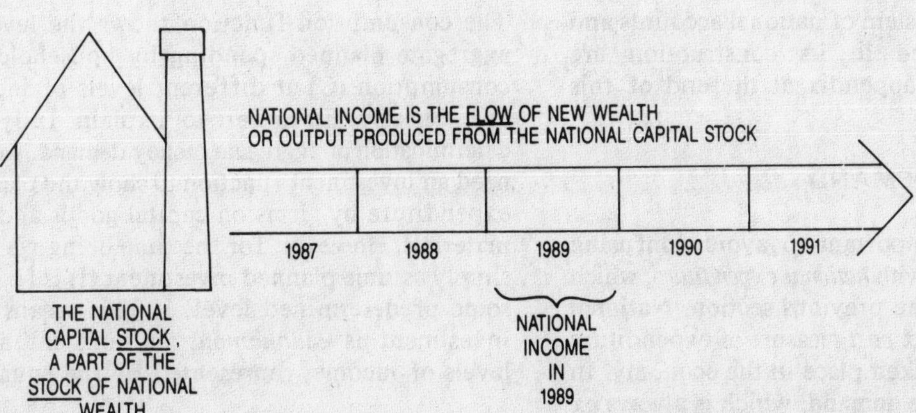

NATIONAL INCOME NATIONAL PRODUCT AND NATIONAL EXPENDITURE

3. Three different methods can be used to measure national income or the flow of new wealth produced by an economy. They are:

(a) **The product method**. The money value of all the goods and services, or output, produced in the economy are added together. The final total is called **national product**, which we shall represent by the symbol Q.

(b) **The income method**. The money values of the incomes received by factors of production employed in producing the output are added together. This is **national income**, represented by Y.

(c) **The expenditure method**. The money values of all spending upon output are added up. The total is **national expenditure**, shown by the symbol E.

Since these are simply three methods of measuring the same thing, namely the *flow of new wealth or output produced*, national income, product and expenditure must be identical! This can be expressed as the accounting identity:

national income ≡ national product ≡ national expenditure

or:

$$Y \equiv Q \equiv E$$

This identity is always *ex-post*, measuring a flow of new wealth or output as it is produced or after it has been produced. $Y \equiv Q \equiv E$ is the most fundamental of all the identities in the system of national income accounts, which are published officially by the government in a 'Blue Book' a few months after the end of the year to which they apply. The system of national accounts and problems involved in its construction are explained in the appendix at the end of this chapter.

AGGREGATE DEMAND

4. It is most important to avoid confusing *aggregate demand* with *national expenditure*, which we explained in the previous section. **National expenditure** is an *ex post* measure of expenditure that has already taken place in the economy. In contrast, **aggregate demand**, which is always *ex ante*, is a measure of *planned* or *intended* expenditure upon goods and services within the economy. Ex post, national expenditure must always equal national income and national product because they measure the same flow of new output or wealth produced in the economy, but it *does not follow* that planned expenditure in the economy - aggregate demand - must equal national income or output. Indeed, the purpose of this chapter is to explain the very special condition that must exist for planned expenditure to equal income or output, a situation known as equilibrium national income.

AGGREGATE DEMAND IN A TWO SECTOR COMPANY

5. Total aggregate demand in the economy comprises the planned or intended demand of all the households and firms within the economy, together with the demand exercised by government and overseas sectors. But for the time being we shall simplify by assuming a **closed economy without a government sector**. We are pretending that households and firms alone make up the economy, there being no government or foreign trade. However, we shall assume a monetary economy in which money is used as a means of payment. Demand is therefore expressed in money units such as £s and pence. The term **aggregate money demand (AMD)** is used to describe the *nominal* aggregate demand or planned expenditure measured in money units. In a two sector economy, aggregate money demand is represented by the ex ante identity:

$$AMD \equiv C + I$$

We shall now reintroduce the Keynesian consumption function which was explained in some detail in Chapter 14:

$$C = a + cY$$

The consumption function shows the level of aggregate planned spending by households on consumption (C) at different levels of income (Y). Strictly, in order to explain fully the determination of aggregate money demand, we also need an investment function to show the planned expenditure by firms on capital goods and raw materials. However, for the time being we shall simply assume planned investment (I) is fixed at some predetermined level, $\bar{I}$. This means that investment is *autonomous* or constant at all levels of income, represented by the equation:

$$I = \bar{I}$$

(the 'bar' sign above I is economic shorthand for a constant)

Using the identity AMD ≡ C + I we now add together the consumption function (a + cY) and autonomous investment ($\bar{I}$) to obtain the aggregate money demand function:

$$AMD = a + cY + \bar{I}$$

Figure 15.2: The aggregate demand function in a two sector economy

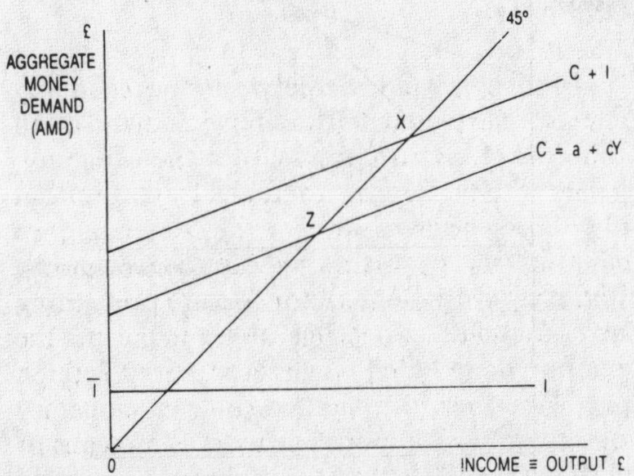

Figure 15.2 illustrates the construction of the AMD function from its component parts C and I. We have also included in the diagram a 45° line, the significance of which was explained in Chapter 14. When interpreting the diagram, it is important to avoid confusing points z and x on the 45° line. Point z locates the level of income at which the consumption function (C) crosses the 45° line. You will remember from Chapter 14 that at this level of income households plan to consume all, and save none of their income, thus APC = 1 and APS = 0. In contrast, point x where the AMD function crosses the 45° lines, locates **equilibrium national income.**

EQUILIBRIUM NATIONAL INCOME

6. Suppose that the level of nominal or money national income or output currently being produced in the economy is Y_1, illustrated in Figure 15.3. By making use of the property of the 45° line, we can show the level of income Y_1 as the vertical line Y_1a. At this level of income, planned expenditure (Y_1b) exceeds the level of income or output available (Y_1a). Insufficient real output is being produced at the current price level to meet the aggregate money demand. Firms could react to this situation in one of three ways. In the immediate period, firms might be able to meet the level of demand by *destocking*, running down stocks of previously accumulated unsold goods. Clearly, the ability of firms to meet demand in this way is limited by the size of any previously accumulated stocks or inventories. Indeed, the depletion of stocks may itself create an incentive for firms to consider one of the other ways of meeting the excess demand, by increasing real output, or by raising prices. Either way, nominal income or money national income, Y, will rise. Y_1 therefore is a *disequilibrium* level of national income.

Figure 15.3: Equilibrium national income in a two sector economy

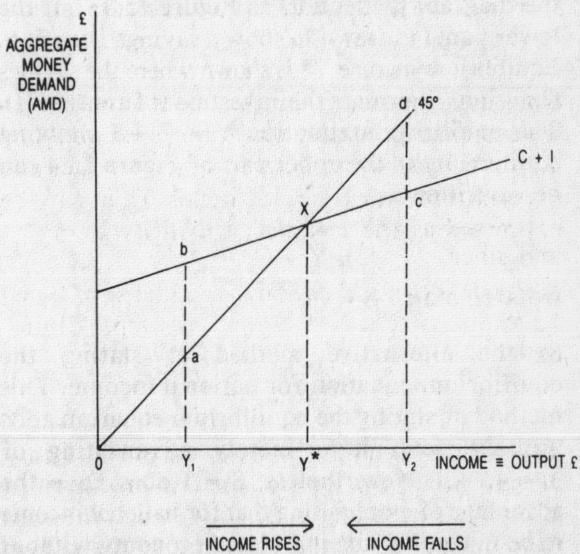

By using very similar reasoning, we can show that levels of income such as Y_2 also represent disequilibrium in the goods market. When income is Y_2, planned expenditure (AMD) is less than the income or output available at the current price level. Firms are unable to sell all their current output and an amount equal to cd accumulates as unsold stocks. Firms may react to this *unintended stock accumulation* by reducing real output or prices. Nominal income Y thus falls, therefore Y_2 is not an equilibrium level of income. Thus:

Disequilibrium conditions apply:

if, when $Y < C + I$, Y tends to rise
and when $Y > C + I$, Y tends to fall

it follows that only when
Y = C + I, will Y remain unchanged.

Y = C + I is the **equilibrium equation** or condition for the goods market of the economy to be in a state of rest or equilibrium. In Figure 15.3 equilibrium income or output is shown at Y*, where the AMD function crosses the 45° line at point x. Only at Y* are the market plans of households and firms fulfilled and consistent with each other. At any other level of nominal income or output, the unintended accumulation or running down of stocks will create an incentive for firms to change Y by changing either real output or prices, or possibly both output and prices.

SAVING AND INVESTMENT

7. Figure 15.4 illustrates an alternative way of showing equilibrium income. The upper panel of the diagram is identical to Figure 15.3, but the lower panel is drawn to show a savings function. Equilibrium income Y* is shown where the savings function (S) crosses the investment function (I). The equilibrium equation Y = C + I showing equilibrium in the upper part of Figure 15.4 can be rewritten as:

Y - C = I

and since S ≡ Y - C

we arrive at: S = I

as the alternative method of stating the equilibrium equation for national income. This method of stating the equilibrium equation adds nothing new; it is merely a rewriting of Y = C + I. Nevertheless, S = I does have the advantage of emphasising that for national income to be in equilibrium in a closed economy without a government sector (ie an economy comprising households and firms only), *planned saving decisions of households must equal the planned investment decisions of firms.*

THE CIRCULAR FLOW OF INCOME

8. The **saving = investment** method of showing the equilibrium equation for national income is also illustrated in the **circular flow diagram** in Figure 15.5 on the following page. The solid lines in the diagram show the *real flows* occurring in the economy between households and firms. Households supply labour and other factor services or inputs, in exchange for real goods and services or outputs. But in a monetary economy, real flows shown by the sold lines will generate *money flows* of income and expenditure shown by the broken lines.

Figure 15.4: The two ways of showing equilibrium national income in a two sector economy

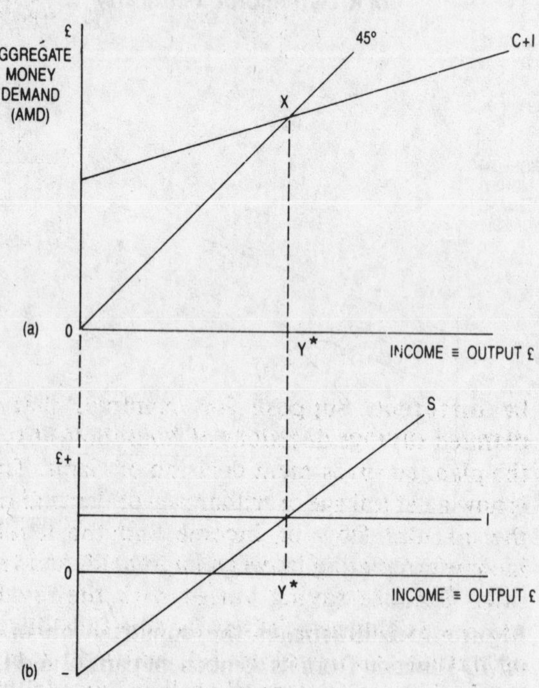

(a) Y = C + I
(b) S = I

If households consume all the income they receive, the circular flow of income is complete; the level of income circulating between households and firms represents an equilibrium. But if households plan to save part of the income received, the circular flow is broken. In Figure 15.5 saving is represented as a *leakage* or *withdrawal* of demand from the circular flow of income, whereas investment spending by firms is shown as an *injection* of demand. Because households and firms make saving and investment decisions for different reasons, it is likely that at any particular level of income, the levels of planned saving and investment will also

Figure 15.5: Withdrawals and injections of demand and the circular flow of income in a two sector economy

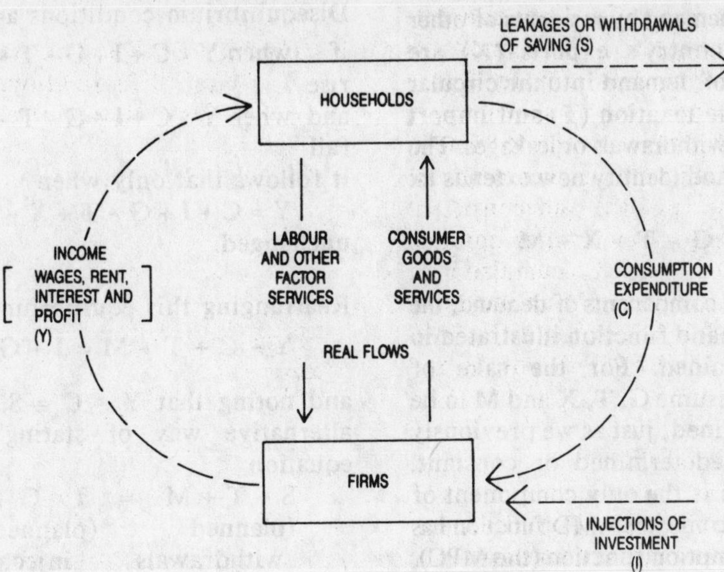

be different. Suppose for example, that the planned savings decisions of households exceed the planned investment decision of firms. There is now a net leakage or withdrawal of demand from the circular flow of income and the level of income circulating between households and firms falls. Because saving varies with the level of income, saving also falls as income falls. Income or output continues to fall until at a lower level of income, planned savings have fallen to equal planned investment. Conversely, at an initial level of income circulating between households and firms at which planned investment exceeds planning saving, there is a net injection of demand into the circular flow of income. Income rises until a sufficient level of planned saving is generated to equal the investment plans of firms. In summary:

Disequilibrium conditions apply
if when $S > I$, income falls
and when $S < I$, income rises
it follows that only when $S = I$, income remains unchanged. $S = I$ is thus the equilibrium equation or condition for equilibrium national income in a two sector model of the economy.

THE TWO SECTOR MODEL: A SUMMARY

9. The essential features of the two sector model of the goods market of an economy can be summarised in three equations:

$C = a + cY$: the consumption function
$I = \bar{I}$: autonomous investment
$Y = C + I$: the equilibrium equation

$C = a + cY$ is a behavioural equation or function, embodying assumptions about how households make consumption decisions. $I = \bar{I}$ indicates that the level of investment is assumed to be predetermined or constant. Finally $Y = C + I$ is the key equation in the model, stating the condition necessary for the level of income to be in a state of rest or equilibrium. It is most important to avoid confusing the equilibrium equation $Y = C + I$, with accounting identities such as $Y \equiv C + S$ and $AMD \equiv C + I$. Although apparently very similar, their meanings are completely different. Accounting identities, which simply define relationships between economic variables, always holds true whatever the level of income. But the equilibrium equation $Y = C + I$, or its alternative version $S = I$ only hold at the particular level of income at which planned expenditure within the economy exactly equals the income or output available.

A FOUR SECTOR MODEL

10. It is obviously rather artificial to assume an economy made up only of households and firms.

We shall now extend the model to four sectors, by introducing the government sector and the overseas or foreign trade sector. Government spending (G) and the demand by residents of other countries for the country's exports (X) are additional injections of demand into the circular flow of income, while taxation (T) and import demand (M) are extra withdrawals or leakages. The aggregate money demand identity now extends to:

$$AMD \equiv C + I + G - T + X - M$$

By adding together the components of demand, the aggregate money demand function illustrated in Figure 15.6 is obtained. For the sake of simplicity, we shall assume G, T, X and M to be autonomously determined, just as we previously assumed I to be predetermined or constant. Because consumption is the only component of demand to vary with income, the AMD function has the *slope* of the consumption function (the MPC), but its *position* is determined by adding I, G and X to, and subtracting T and M from, the consumption function.

Figure 15.6: Aggregate money demand and equilibrium national income in a four sector model of the economy

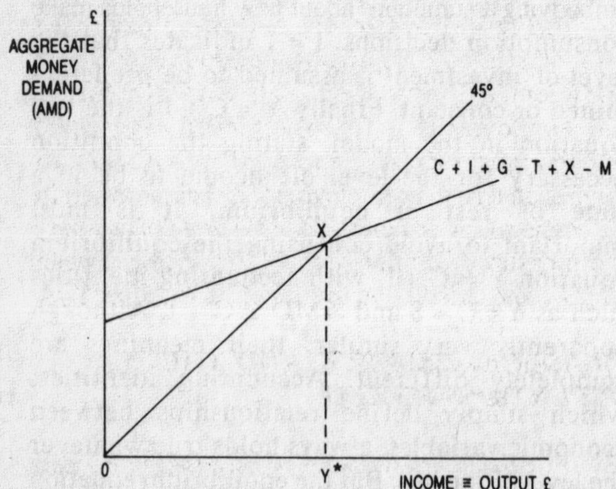

By using reasoning identical to that described for the two sector model:

Disequilibrium conditions apply:

if when $Y < C + I + G - T + X - M$, Y tends to rise

and when $Y > C + I + G - T + X - M$, Y tends to fall

it follows that only when

$Y = C + I + G - T + X - M$, does Y remain unchanged.

Rearranging this equilibrium equation as:

$$Y - C + T + M = I + G + X$$

and noting that $Y - C \equiv S$, we arrive at the alternative way of stating the equilibrium equation:

S + T + M	=	I + G + X
(planned withdrawals or leakages)		(planned injections)

This alternative way of showing equilibrium income in a four sector model of the goods market of an economy is illustrated in Figure 15.7 and Figure 15.8.

Figure 15.7: The alternative way of showing equilibrium national income in a four sector model of the economy

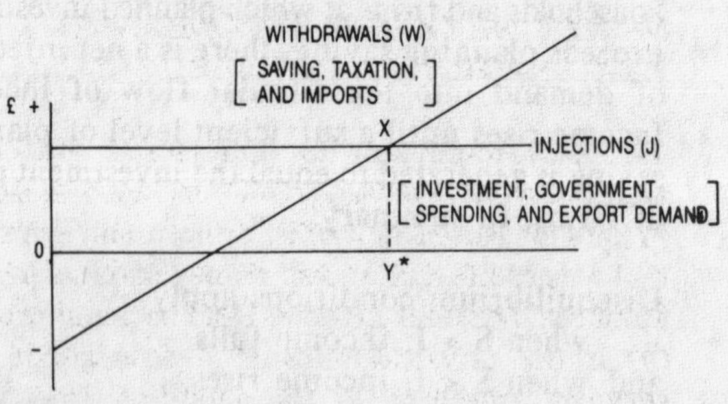

Figure 15.8: Withdrawals and injections of demand and the circular flow of income in a four sector model of the economy

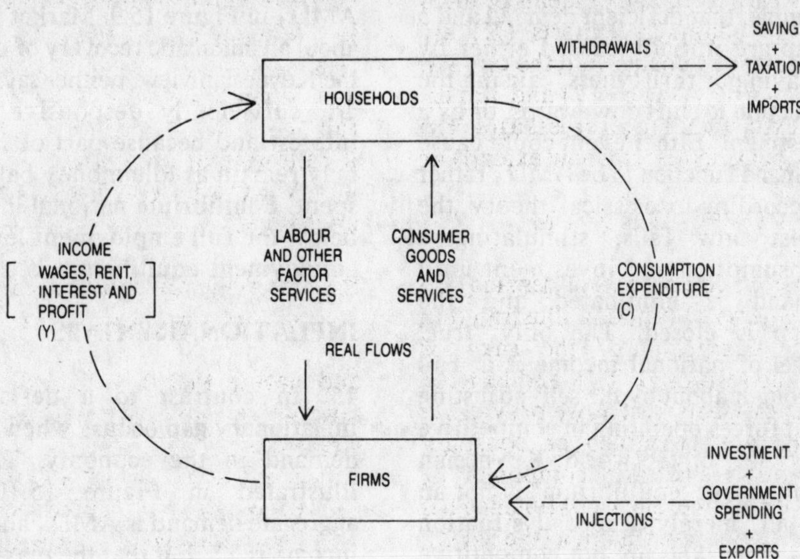

Equilibrium occurs in Figure 15.7 at the level of income Y*, where the **withdrawals function (W)** crosses the **injections function (J)**. Figure 15.8 shows that the circular flow of income is complete, and thereby in equilibrium, only when leakages or withdrawals of demand out of the circular flow equal injections of demand into the circular flow. At any other level of income, income will either rise or fall until planned leakages or withdrawals of demand equal the planned injections.

MONEY NATIONAL INCOME AND REAL NATIONAL INCOME

11. It is important to understand that both aggregate money demand (AMD) and national income (Y) are measured in money or nominal terms and that we need to distinguish **money national income** from **real national income**. Real national income (y) is the physical output of new goods and services produced in the economy in a year. Nominal or money national income (Y) measures this real income or output at the current price level (P). The relationship between nominal and real income is expressed in the identity:

$$Y \equiv Py$$

Thus nominal national income (Y) can rise either if output increases, usually causing employment to increase as well, or if the price level rises and inflation takes place.

EQUILIBRIUM INCOME AND FULL EMPLOYMENT INCOME

12. We shall now assume that the equilibrium level of nominal income Y*, produced when aggregate demand is AMD_1, is insufficient to employ fully the working population, and that at Y_{FE} in Figure 15.9 (on the following page) the level of real income or output produced is just sufficient to bring about full employment. If full employment is to be achieved, aggregate demand must increase from AMD_1 to AMD_2. In Keynesian terms, unemployment is being caused in the economy by **deficient demand** or a **deflationary gap** measured, by the vertical distance between AMD_1 and AMD_2 at the level of income Y_{FE}.

'CLASSICAL THEORY' AND THE DEFLATIONARY GAP

13. For deficient demand to be eliminated and the deflationary gap to be closed, the aggregate demand function must shift upwards from AMD_1 to AMD_2. In principle, an upward shift of *any* of the components of aggregate demand can close the gap and bring about an equilibrium level of income at full employment. Keynes' predecessors, the neo-**classical school**, believed that providing the economy is sufficiently competitive, market forces automatically eliminate deficient demand and close a deflationary gap, which can therefore

only exist as a temporary phenomenon in the economy. Many **modern monetarists** and **'New Classical' economists** share this view. Let us assume, for example, that deficient demand and a deflationary gap are initially caused either by an increase of saving or thriftyness, causing the consumption function to shift downwards, or by a collapse in investment. Either event could cause the aggregate demand function to be AMD_1 rather than AMD_2. According to 'classical' theory, the rate of interest now falls, stimulating a recovery of consumption and investment until deficient demand is eliminated and the deflationary gap is closed. The only 'true' equilibrium level of national income is at full employment, brought about by the self-adjusting nature of market forces operating in competitive markets. In this view of the world, Keynesian under-full employment 'equilibrium' is not an equilibrium at all, merely a special situation that only occurs if markets are not competitive enough to allow the self-regulating process of the market mechanism to work.

Figure 15.9: Deflationary gaps and deficient demand

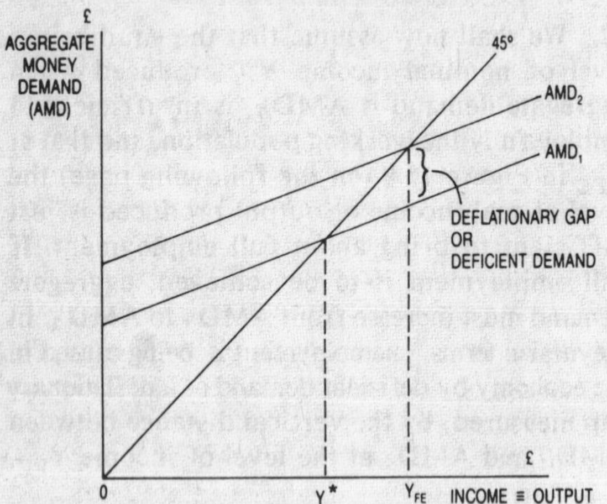

KEYNESIANS AND THE DEFLATIONARY GAP

14. In contrast to the neo-classical or 'classical' tradition more recently revived in modern monetarism, **Keynesians** reject the view that a market economy automatically adjusts to equilibrium at full employment. We have already discussed the controversy in Chapter 13 in terms of Say's Law, that 'supply creates its own demand', a proposition accepted by the neo-classical school but rejected by Keynes. Keynesians have traditionally believed that under certain circumstances deficient demand can come into existence on a more or less permanent basis, with aggregate demand settling at a level such as AMD_1 in Figure 15.9. Market forces fail to bring about an automatic recovery of demand because, in the Keynesian view, neither saving nor investment are sufficiently responsive to the rate of interest and because part of household savings may remain as idle money balances and are not spent. Equilibrium national income may remain below the full employment level; an **under-full employment equilibrium** is a real possibility.

INFLATIONARY GAPS

15. In contrast to a deflationary gap, an **inflationary gap** occurs when there is too much demand in the economy. This possibility is illustrated in Figure 15.10. Suppose that aggregate demand is AMD_1 and that equilibrium income is Y*, but that the maximum level of real output which the economy is capable of producing at current prices is at a lower level of nominal income, Y_{FE}. Because beyond Y_{FE} there are no idle resources or unemployed labour that can quickly be brought into production, an equilibrium level of income such as Y* can only be attained if the price level rises. Excess demand pulls up prices in a **demand-pull inflation**! It follows that for equilibrium income to occur at full employment and without inflation, aggregate demand must be reduced to AMD_2. The vertical distance between AMD_1 and AMD_2 at Y_{FE} is called an inflationary gap, measuring the extent of excess demand at full employment in the economy.

Figure 15.10: Inflationary gaps and excess demand

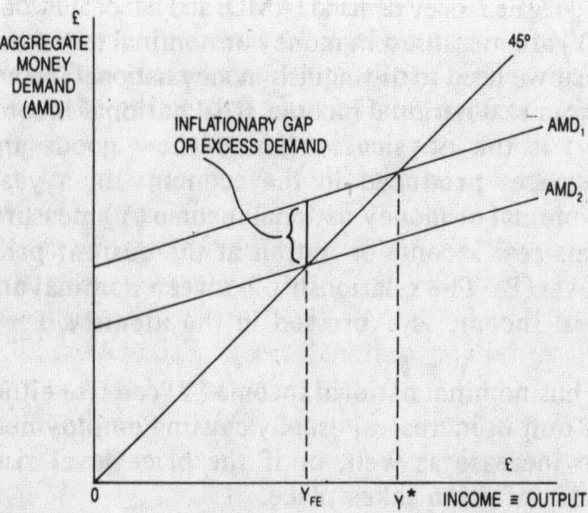

GOVERNMENT POLICY AND DEFLATIONARY AND INFLATIONARY GAPS

16. Just as an upward shift of any component of aggregate demand can close a deflationary gap, so a downward shift can, in principle, close an inflationary gap. The critical question concerns whether market forces alone can close a deflationary or inflationary gap, or whether the government should intervene to manage demand. If, as the New Classical school believe, market forces tend automatically in a competitive market economy to eliminate deficient or excess demand, the main function of government is 'to set markets free', or to create the competitive conditions in which the self-regulating properties of the market mechanism can operate. The correct government policy is one of 'disengaging' the state from the economy, and reduced government intervention. In contrast, Keynesians, who generally reject this self-equilibrating view of markets and the price mechanism, have traditionally argued that government intervention is needed in the form of policies to manage the level of aggregate demand, to close deflationary and inflationary gaps and to bring about equilibrium at full employment.

Figure 15.11: An increase in government spending from G_1 to G_2 raises the AMD function and closes a deflationary gap

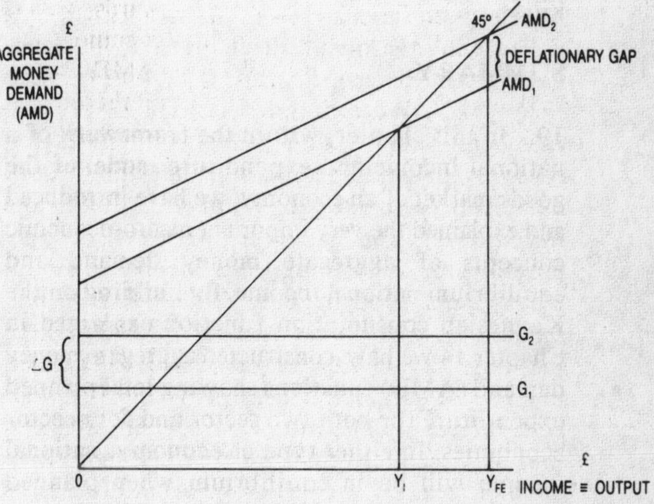

DEMAND MANAGEMENT AND FISCAL AND MONETARY POLICIES

17. In principle, both **fiscal** and **monetary policy** can be used to manage the level of aggregate money demand in the economy and indeed, during the Keynesian era both policies were used in the United Kingdom. An expansionary **monetary policy** can stimulate demand, for example by reducing interest rates or by making credit available or easier to obtain. These policies would cause the consumption function and the investment function to shift upwards, thereby increasing aggregate demand in the economy. Conversely, a tight monetary policy would have the opposite effect of depressing demand. Traditionally however, Keynesians have usually favoured **fiscal policy** as an instrument for managing demand. This has a more direct effect on aggregate demand because the government can by its own policy shift the government spending function or the tax function. For example, an increase in government spending shown by ΔG in Figure 15.11, directly shifts the AMD function upwards from AMD_1 to AMD_2 and closes the deflationary gap.

MONETARISM AND DEMAND MANAGEMENT

18. For many years from the 1950s to the 1970s, a discretionary fiscal policy, which used deliberate changes in government spending, taxation, and the budget deficit to manage the level of aggregate money demand in the economy, occupied a central place in Keynesian economic management of the economy. Changes in taxation and government spending and sometimes changes in monetary policy were used to *'fine tune'* the level of aggregate demand in the economy to try to achieve full employment and economic growth, but without excessive inflation or a balance of payments crisis. Under monetarism however, the use of fiscal policy or monetary policy to manage demand was abandoned in the late 1970s and during the 1980s. Monetarists believe that any expansion of aggregate money demand will cause inflation rather than a growth in real output or income, whatever the level of unemployment in the economy. This is not to say that monetarists dismiss the use of fiscal policy or monetary policy in the management of the economy. A popular belief is that monetarists advocate the use of monetary policy rather than fiscal policy to manage demand because they believe it is more powerful, effective and predictable. This is untrue. Monetarist governments most certainly possess and implement fiscal policies and monetary policies, but neither is used, under strict monetarism, to manage the level of aggregate demand in the economy. In theory, monetarists and New Classical economists reject short-term demand-management policies of all kinds.

SUMMARY

19. In this chapter, within the framework of a national income and expenditure model of the goods market of an economy, we have introduced and explained the very important macro-economic concepts of aggregate money demand and equilibrium national income. By building on the Keynesian consumption function explained in Chapter 14 we have constructed aggregate money demand (AMD) functions showing total planned expenditure for both two sector and four sector economies. In either type of economy, national income will be in equilibrium when planned expenditure equals income (Y = AMD), but, according to Keynesians, the equilibrium level of income may not be the same as full employment income. Keynesians believe that under certain circumstances either too little or too much demand may occur in the economy. In the former case, a deflationary gap exists causing demand-deficient unemployment, while in the opposite circumstances of an inflationary gap and over-full employment, excess demand pulls up prices in a demand-pull inflation. Traditionally, Keynesians have argued that governments should use macro-economic policy, especially fiscal policy, to manage the level of aggregate demand so as to eliminate deflationary and inflationary gaps and bring about equilibrium at full employment. However, monetarists, inheriting the old neo-classical or 'classical' view of the self-regulating nature of market forces, reject these Keynesian arguments, believing that left to itself, a competitive market economy will automatically adjust to equilibrium at full employment.

STUDENT SELF-TESTING

1. *Distinguish between income, wealth and capital.* *(2)*
2. *Describe briefly the methods of measuring national income.* *(3)*
3. *Distinguish between national expenditure and aggregate demand.* *(4)*
4. *What are the two ways of stating the equilibrium equation for equilibrium national income in a two sector economy?* *(6-9)*
5. *What is meant by the circular flow of income?* *(8)*
6. *What are injections and leakages of demand in a four sector economy?* *(10)*
7. *Distinguish between nominal and real national income.* *(11)*
8. *What is a deflationary gap?* *(12)*
9. *Briefly contrast Keynesian and monetarist views on deflationary and inflationary gaps.* *(14-17)*
10. *What is meant by demand management?* *(17-18)*

EXERCISES

1 *You are given the following information on an economy:*

	£million
Consumers' expenditure	*30,100*
Gross trading profits of companies	*5,400*
Gross domestic fixed capital formation	*13,200*
Public authorities' current expenditure on goods and services	*12,600*
Exports of goods and services	*10,700*
Value of physical increase in stocks and work in progress	*– 800*
Taxes on expenditure	*7,300*
Imports of goods and services	*12,200*
Net property income from abroad	*+ 650*
Subsidies	*1,300*
Capital consumption	*4,700*

(a) Calculate:

(i) national income

(ii) gross national product

(iii) gross domestic product at market prices

(iv) gross domestic product at factor cost

(b) To what extent might these national accounts give an accurate measure of the level of economic activity in the country?

2 *In a closed economy, investment spending is £620 million, government expenditure is £400 million, income tax is 30 pence in the £ and consumption spending is 70 per cent of disposable income.*

(a) Calculate:
(i) the equilibrium level of national income;
(ii) the size of the government budget deficit or surplus at the equilibrium level of income.

(b) Income tax is cut to 25 per cent in the £. Calculate:
(i) the new equilibrium level of income;
(ii) the new budget deficit or surplus at the equilibrium level of income.

MULTIPLE CHOICE QUESTIONS

1. *Gross national product at market prices minus gross national product at factor cost equals:*
A *Net property income from abroad*
B *Indirect taxation less subsidies*
C *Depreciation*
D *Exports less imports*

2. *The following figures are from a country's national income accounts for a particular year:*

	£million
Consumers' expenditure	*400*
Fixed capital formation	*120*
Net addition to stocks during the year	*20*
Government current expenditure	*140*
Exports of goods and services	*120*
Imports of goods and services	*100*
Property income received from abroad	*20*
Property income paid abroad	*40*
Taxes on expenditure	*60*
Food and housing subsidies	*20*
Capital consumption	*40*

The country's national income is:
A *£600 million*
B *£640 million*
C *£660 million*
D *£700 million*

3. *Gross national product figures may not be accurate indicators of the welfare of a country's inhabitants because:*
A *GNP figures include transfers such as social security benefits*
B *GNP figures do not include all the non-marketable goods and services enjoyed by the country's inhabitants*
C *GNP figures do include incomes earned on assets located abroad*
D *GNP figures show the real rather than the nominal value of output*

4. *The following data relates to a closed economy with no government activity:*

Income	*Consumption expenditure*
£m	*£m*
4,000	*3,000*
5,000	*3,510*
6,000	*3,910*
7,000	*4,200*
8,000	*4,400*

For the equilibrium level of national income to be £7,000m, investment must be:
£m
A *1,200*
B *2,000*
C *2,800*
D *3,600*

5. *In the United Kingdom economy, an increase in aggregate money demand may be brought about by:*
A *The monetary authorities selling securities in open market operations*
B *An increase in the standard rate of income tax*
C *An increase in personal tax allowances*
D *An increase in interest rates*

6 *Which of the following represents an injection into the circular flow of income?*
A *Interest paid abroad to owners of capital invested in the UK*
B *Savings deposited in building societies*
C *Current expenditure of nationalised industries*
D *National insurance contributions received by the government*

EXAMINATION QUESTIONS

1. *(a) What is meant by national income?* *(8 marks)*

   (b) What are the main problems involved in its calculation? *(12 marks)*

   (AAT June 1987)

2. *(a) Explain what is meant by equilibrium when referring to the general level of output and employment.* *(10 marks)*

   (b) What will be the effect on output and employment of each of the following changes?

   (i) an increase in investment *(5 marks)*

   (ii) an increase in imports. *(5 marks)*

   (ACCA June 1985)

3. *(a) What is the difference between the cost of living and the standard of living?* *(6 marks)*

   (b) What are the differences of measuring changes in the standard of living? *(14 marks)*

   (ACCA December 1985)

4. *'Savings and investment will always tend to equality, but the point of equality will not necessarily be the point of full employment. This is the essence of the Keynesian revolution.' Explain and make clear the main features of the Keynesian analysis.*

   (CIMA November 1979)

5. *Explain three different approaches to the measurement of National Income? What is the relationship between National Income and Gross Domestic Product at market prices?*

   (ICSA December 1984)

Appendix to Chapter 15: The systems of national income accounts

INTRODUCTION

1. The implementation of modern macro-economic policy requires that governments possess accurate information on what is being produced and on the composition and level of income and expenditure in the economy. During Keynes's lifetime in the first half of the twentieth century, there was a distinct lack of such information. The growth, in the post-war era, of a **system of national income** accounts developed directly out of the need of governments when pursuing policies of Keynesian demand management, to have comprehensive and up-to-date statistics on national income, output and expenditure, in order to intervene successfully in the economy. The principal function of the national income accounts is to **provide the basic data for economic policy-making**, particularly at the macro-economic level, and for **economic forecasting**.

THE NATIONAL INCOME BLUE BOOK

2. We have already explained in the main body of this chapter how the flow of goods and services produced by a country's capital stock within a year can be measured as either:

(i) **the value of the output itself (national product)**, or
(ii) **the value of factor incomes received** from the production of the output (**national income**), or
(ii) **the value of expenditure** upon the flow of goods and services (**national expenditure**).

Since these are simply three methods of measuring the same flow of output of goods and services, they must be identical. Hence: **national income ≡ national product ≡ national expenditure.** Each year the Central Statistical Office in the United Kingdom publishes the United Kingdom's national income accounts in a **National Income and Expenditure Blue Book**. Although the Blue Book contains a large number of tables of various degrees of aggregation and disaggregation, the three basic tables from which all the rest are developed, represent the three methods we have just described for measuring national income. We shall now investigate the three methods in turn, starting with the income method.

THE INCOME METHOD OF MEASURING NATIONAL INCOME

3. An estimate of British national income in 1987, based on the measurement of factor incomes, is shown in Table 15.1, taken from the 1988 National Income and Expenditure Blue Book.

Table 15.1: National income shown by category of income 1987

		£m
1	Income from employment	226,343
2	Income from self-employment	32,959
3	Gross trading profits of companies	65,596
4	Gross trading surplus of public corporations	6,623
5	Gross trading surplus of general government enterprises	-177
6	Rent	24,798
7	Imputed charge for consumption of non-traded capital	3,235
8	Total domestic income	359,377
9	*Less stock appreciation*	-4,858
10	Gross domestic product at factor cost (income based)	354,519
11	Statistical discrepancy	-2,282
12	Gross domestic product at factor cost (average extimate)	352,237
13	Net property income from abroad	5,523
14	Gross national product at factor cost	357,760
15	*Less capital consumption*	-48,238
16	National income	309,522

Table 15.1 introduces an important distinction between **national** and **domestic income (and product). Total domestic income**, shown in row 8 is obtained by adding the various **factor incomes** in row 1-7. Total domestic income is then converted into **gross domestic product** in row 10 by subtracting **stock appreciation**, which occurs when firms purchase stocks of raw materials or components that rise in value before being converted into the goods or services sold by the firms. Stock appreciation must be deducted from

firms' profits recorded in the national income statistics because it results from inflation and is not a reward to a factor of production. The **statistical adjustment** in row 11 is made to convert GDP measured from factor incomes into GDP measured in terms of expenditure upon output, which is shown in Table 15.3. Although conceptually national income must equal national product and expenditure, mistakes inevitably occur in data collection so that the three methods of measurement do not yield exactly identical totals. A statistical adjustment must be made to each of the tables to ensure that the totals are the same.

Gross domestic product (GDP) at factor cost in rows 10 and 12 measures the incomes received and the outputs produced by factors of production actually employed within the United Kingdom economy, or within United Kingdom national boundaries. GDP is *not* the same as gross **national product (GNP)** because part of domestically generated incomes flows overseas to foreign owners of companies operating in the United Kingdom, and to residents of other countries who own shares in British companies. Similarly, United Kingdom residents receive dividend incomes and profits remitted on assets they own abroad. GDP (in row 12) is thus converted into GNP (in row 14) by adding the **net property income from abroad**, which results from such profit and dividend flows. A positive figure for net property income from abroad indicates that UK residents receive more profits from assets owned in other countries than overseas residents receive from the assets they own in the United Kingdom.

Finally, the estimate for **national income** in row 16 is obtained by deducting **capital consumption** or **depreciation** from gross national product. You should note that in the British national accounts, national income is always presented net of depreciation, whereas national product is presented as gross national product (GNP) and as net national product (NNP), before and after depreciation is subtracted. Thus as accounting identities:

national income ≡ net national product

and GNP - depreciation ≡ national income

THE DANGER OF DOUBLE COUNTING

4. Income, as measured in Table 15.1, is a payment for productive services rendered by the factors of production. Transfer payments such as unemployment pay, welfare benefits and pensions must be excluded from the measurement of national income since they are simply a transfer, via taxation and government spending, from one group of people to another, without the recipients adding to production. If such transfers were wrongly added to the national income total, the error of double counting would occur, leading to an over-estimate of national income.

THE ARBITRARY NATURE OF NATIONAL INCOME STATISTICS

5. Nevertheless, the national income statistics are based on a number of rather arbitrary judgements on what is and is not 'productive work'. In any economy a certain amount of production takes place in **the non-monetised economy**, without money incomes being received for production undertaken. The non-monetised economy is, of course, most significant in developing economies, but within developed economies such as the United Kingdom, housework and 'do-it-yourself' home improvement take place within the non-monetised economy. Any measurement of national income must therefore, either estimate or ignore the value of production undertaken in the non-monetised economy. The United Kingdom accounts can be criticised for estimating the value of some but not all the production taking place in the non-monetised sector of the economy. Thus **imputed rents** are estimated for the 'housing services' received by owner-occupiers from the houses they live in, equal to the rent which would be paid if the house-owners were tenants of the same properties. But house-keeping allowances paid within households, are not estimated, implying that housework - most of which is undertaken by women - is unproductive! An anomoly which results from such arbitrary judgements is that national income appears to fall whenever a man marries his housekeeper or paints his own house where previously he employed a decorator.

NATIONAL INCOME AND THE 'HIDDEN' ECONOMY

6. Official statistics tend to underestimate the actual volume of economic activity that occurs, not only because various activities occurring in the non-monetised economy are ignored, but also because illegal activities are omitted. This is because of the existence of the so-called **'hidden'** or **underground economy,**

sometimes popularly known as the **'black' economy**. The 'hidden' economy refers to all the economic transactions conducted in cash which are not recorded in the national income figures because of tax evasion. In 1979, the Chairman of the Inland Revenue Board estimated that economic activity taking place in the 'hidden' economy accounted for 7.5 per cent of national income, but the Central Statistical Office estimated the much lower figure of 3.5 per cent in 1980. The gap between the GDP total obtained by the income and expenditure methods of measurement can be used to approximate the size of the 'hidden' economy.

THE OUTPUT METHOD OF MEASURING NATIONAL INCOME

7. The **output method** involves adding up the money values of all the goods and services produced in the economy. As with the income method there is a danger of double counting which can be avoided in one of two ways. Only the **money values of final goods and services** sold to consumers must be totalled, or alternatively we can measure the **'value added'** by all industries, including producers of raw materials and other capital goods, at each stage of production. Table 15.2 illustrates the output method of measuring national income for 1987, showing the calculation of GDP at factor cost by totalling the value added by groups of industries and services. You should notice that stock appreciation has already been deducted from the figures, but that the a statistical adjustment is again made to convert the value of domestic output in row 15 to GDP at factor cost in row 17. As with the income method illustrated in Table 15.1, GDP can be converted into national income, firstly by adding net property income from abroad to obtain the figure for GNP, and then by subtracting depreciation or capital consumption.

Table 15.2 illustrates also the distinction between **GNP (and GDP) at market prices** and **GNP (and GDP) at factor cost. Market prices,** which are the actual prices consumers and firms pay for the goods and services purchased, *over-estimate* national income when they include indirect taxes such as value added tax (VAT) and excise duties, but *under-estimate* national income to the extent that they include subsidies paid to firms. **National income aggregates at market prices** must be converted to **factor cost** by **subtracting indirect taxes** and **adding subsidies.** The distinction between GNP at market prices and at factor cost, and other important national income aggregates, are summarised in Figure 15.12.

Figure 15.12: The national income aggregates in 1987

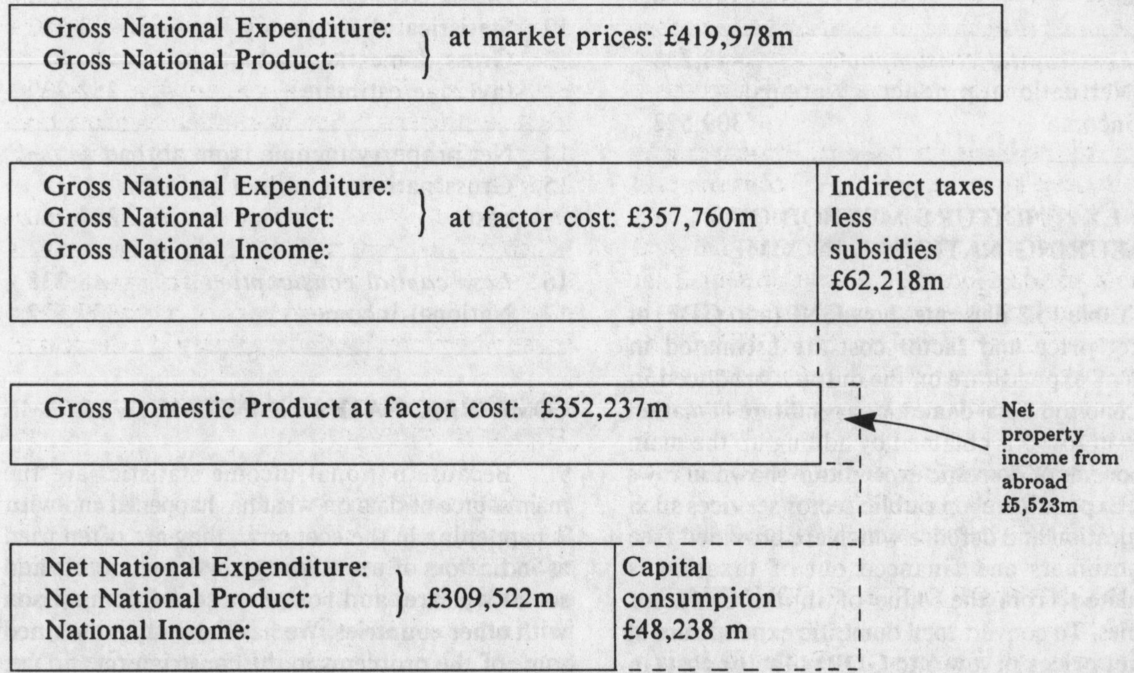

Table 15.2 Gross and net national product for the United Kingdom 1987

		£m
1	Agriculture, forestry and fishing	5,901
2	Energy and water supply	24,184
3	Manufacturing	85,552
4	Construction	21,524
5	Distribution, hotels and catering, repairs	48,963
6	Transport	16,227
7	Communication	9,688
8	Banking, finance, insurance, business services and leasing	63,903
9	Ownership of dwellings	20,180
10	Public administration, national defence and compulsory social security	24,895
11	Education and health services	31,681
12	Other services	22,366
13	Total	375,064
14	Adjustment for financial services	-20,545
15	Gross domestic product at factor cost (income based)	354,519
16	Statistical discrepancy	-2,282
17	Gross domestic product at factor cost (average estimate)	352,237
18	Net property income from abroad	5,523
19	Gross national product at factor cost	357,760
20	*Less capital consumption*	-48,238
21	Net national product ≡ National income	309,522

THE EXPENDITURE METHOD OF MEASURING NATIONAL INCOME

8. Table 15.3 illustrates how GNP (and GDP) at market price and factor cost are estimated in terms of expenditure on the outputs produced in the economy. **Total domestic expenditure** at market prices in row 5 is obtained by adding up the **main components of domestic expenditure** shown in rows 1-4. **'Expenditure' on public sector services** such as education and defence which are provided free to consumers and financed out of taxation is calculated from the value of inputs or factor incomes. To convert **total domestic expenditure at market prices** in row 5 to **GDP at factor cost** (in row 11), not only must indirect taxes be deducted and subsidies added, but a deduction must also be made for **domestic expenditure on imports** (row 8). Similarly, the **value of exports (row 6)** must be **added**, because it represents expenditure on a part of United Kingdom domestic output.

Table 15.3: National expenditure for the United Kingdom 1987

		£m
1	Consumers' expenditure	258,431
2	General government final consumption	85,772
	of which: central government	51,689
	local authorities	34,083
3	Gross domestic fixed capital formation	70,767
4	Value of physical increase in stocks and work in progress	627
5	Total domestic expenditure	415,597
6	Exports	107,506
7	Total final expenditure	523,103
8	*Less imports*	-112,030
9	Gross domestic product at market prices (expenditure based)	411,073
10	FACTOR COST ADJUSTMENT:	
	less taxes on expenditure	-67,980
	plus subsidies	5,762
11	Gross domestic product at factor cost	348,855
12	Statistical discrepancy	3,382
13	Gross domestic product (average estimate)	352,237
14	Net property income from abroad	5,523
15	Gross national product at factor cost	357,760
16	*Less capital consumption*	-48,238
17	National income	309,522

COMPARING NATIONAL INCOME OVER TIME

9. Because national income statistics are the main source of data on what has happened and what is happening in the economy, they are often used as **indicators of economic growth, economic and social welfare,** and for purposes of **comparison with other countries.** We have already mentioned some of the problems in the construction and use of national income statistics, and in particular, the likelihood that the statistics under-estimate the true level of economic activity because the non-monetised economy is under represented and because activity undertaken illegally in the 'hidden' economy is omitted. We shall now survey briefly a number of other problems involved in the interpretation of national income statistics.

An obvious problem faced when comparing national income statistics over a number of years is the **need to make allowances for changes in prices or inflation. Money national income** figures must be converted to **'real' figures** if we are to make valid comparisons over time. This is done by converting the figures expressed in the **current prices** of each year into the **constant prices** of a single representative year. An **index number**, such as the **Retail Price Index**, used to deflate GNP to constant prices is known as a GNP deflator. National output figures deflated in this way into the prices of a single year are presented in the national income tables **at constant factor cost.**

To see how living standards change over time we must look at **real per capita GNP** figures, which are real GNP divided by the number of people living in the country. Rising real GNP per capita gives a general indication that living standards are rising, but it may of course, conceal great and sometimes growing **disparities in income distribution**. This is especially significant in developing countries where the income distribution is typically extremely unequal and where only a small fraction of the population may benefit materially from economic growth.

The **quality of goods** is also likely to change for the better or worse over time, presenting a particularly difficult problem in the construction and interpretation of national income figures. This is true also of services; deteriorating services such as public transport and health care may actually cause GNP to rise even though welfare and real living standards decline. More generally, national income statistics cannot measure **intangibles** which change over time and which affect the general quality of life and level of welfare in a country. Intangibles such as the **value people place on leisure time** and living close to work, and externalities, including both external costs and benefits generated from the production of national income, escape measurement. In so far as externalities are measured in the national accounts, what is in effect a **welfare loss** may be shown as an increase in national output, *falsely* indicating **an apparent welfare gain**. For example, the stresses and strains of producing an ever higher national output may not only lead to a loss of leisure time; it may make people ill more often. They will regard both loss of leisure and poorer health as a welfare loss. However, as far as the national accounts are concerned, this will show up as extra production and as extra consumption of health care, indicating only a welfare gain.

COMPARING NATIONAL INCOME BETWEEN COUNTRIES

10. We have already mentioned how comparisons of GNP per head between countries are misleading if the **relative importance of the non-monetised economy is greatly different**. Related to this are **differences in the degree of statistical sophistication in the collection of data**, particularly between developed and developing countries, and a lack of international uniformity in methods of classifying and categorising the national accounts. Further problems occur when making comparisons if **different commodities are consumed**. For example, expenditure on fuel, clothing and building materials is likely to be greater in developed countries with cold climates than in much warmer developing economies, but we must take care not to deduce from this single fact that greater expenditure, for example on home heating, indicates higher real income and living standards.

A common method of comparing GNP per capita in different countries is to convert the GNP figures for each country into a common currency such as the US dollar. However, this calculation suffers from the assumption that the exchange rates between local currencies and the $ are correctly valued in the sense that a dollar's worth of output in one country becomes immediately and accurately comparable with a dollar's worth of output in any other country. This can never be so. Exchange rates can only correctly reflect the values of **internationally traded goods** such as automobiles or internationally traded food stuffs and raw materials. The purchasing power of a currency over domestically produced goods and services, which do not enter into international trade or compete domestically with imports, may be completely different from the currency's purchasing power over imported goods. Exchange rate changes only reflect the price changes of internationally traded goods, and in so far that there is a much wider gap in developing countries than in developed countries between the price changes of internationally traded and non-traded goods, GNP figures measured in US dollars tend to underestimate real levels of income and output in developing economies. The correct solution to this problem is to establish **'real' exchange rates** which take into account differences in the internal price levels in non-traded goods and in consumption patterns.

16. The multiplier

INTRODUCTION

1. In Chapter 15, we explained how when **aggregate money demand (AMD)** in the economy is greater (or less) than the level of **money national income** or output that is being produced, the level of money national income will rise (or fall) until an equilibrium is reached at which AMD equals the available output. In this chapter, we investigate in more detail a very important aspect of the adjustment process to the new equilibrium level of national income: **the national income multiplier**.

THE MULTIPLIER RELATIONSHIP

2. A **multiplier** exists whenever a change in one variable induces or causes *multiple* and *successive* stages of change in a second variable. Each succeeding stage of change is usually smaller than the previous one so that the total change induced in the multiplier process comes effectively to an end when further stages of change approach zero. We can calculate the value of a multiplier by dividing the total change induced in the second variable by the size of the initial change in the first variable. For example; a multiplier of 8 tells us that an increase in the first variable will cause successive stages of change in the second variable which are eight times greater in total than the initial 'triggering' change.

THE NATIONAL INCOME MULTIPLIER AND THE MONEY MULTIPLIER

3. In macro-economic theory, we examine *two* very important multipliers, the **national income multiplier** and the **money multiplier**, both of which have great significance for economic policy. The money multiplier, which is significant in the analysis of monetary policy, measures the relationship between a change in the supply of notes and coins or cash to the banking system and the resulting change in total bank deposits in the economy. In this chapter however, we are concerned with the **national income multiplier** which measures the relationship between a **change in aggregate demand** in the economy and the **resulting change in the equilibrium level of national income.** As a broad generalisation, the size and stability of the *money multiplier* influences the power and effectiveness of *monetary policy*, whereas the size of the *national income multiplier* is significant - as we shall shortly explain - for the power and effectiveness of the government's *fiscal policy*.

THE NATIONAL INCOME MULTIPLIER AND THE KEYNESIAN REVOLUTION

4. The national income multiplier has become a vital part of Keynesian economic theory. The multiplier concept was first developed in 1931 by R.F. Kahn, a colleague and former pupil of Keynes at Cambridge. In its early days, the multiplier theory was essentially an **employment multiplier** showing how a change in public sector investment, for example in road building, might trigger a subsequent multiple growth in employment. Keynes made use of Kahn's employment multiplier for the first time in 1933 when discussing the effects of an increase in government spending of £500, a sum which he assumed to be just sufficient to employ one man for one year in road construction. Keynes wrote: *'If the new expenditure is additional and not merely in substitution for other expenditure, the increase of employment does not stop there. The additional wages and other incomes paid out are spent on additional purchases, which in turn lead to further employment .... the newly employed who supply the increased purchases of those employed on the new capital works will, in their turn, spend more, thus adding to the employment of others and so on'*.

By 1936, when Keynes's 'General Theory' was published, the multiplier had become a central part of Keynes's explanation of how unemployment might be caused by deficient aggregate demand. In the 'General Theory', Keynes explained the **investment multiplier**, which suggests how a collapse in investment and business confidence might cause a multiple contraction in output, leading in turn to large scale unemployment. Keynes then went on to argue that the **government spending multiplier** might be used to reverse the process. In terms of the national income/ expenditure model of the economy, which we explained in Chapter 15, an increase in public spending which is unaccompanied by an increase in taxation has an expansionary multiplier effect identical to that resulting from an autonomous increase in investment.

Indeed, it is now recognised that *a change in any of the components of aggregate money demand* can induce multiple stages of change in the level of money national income or output. The national income multiplier should be regarded as a generic term, covering the multiplier effects arising from a change in any of the components of aggregate demand. We can recognise the **autonomous consumption multiplier**, the **investment multiplier**, the **government spending multiplier** and various **tax and foreign trade multipliers** as examples of specific national income multipliers. The government spending multiplier and the investment multiplier are the most frequently encountered national income multipliers.

THE MULTIPLIER AS A DYNAMIC PROCESS

5. The multiplier process is essentially a *dynamic process* which takes place over a considerable period of time. In order to illustrate the dynamic multiplier process, we shall assume for convenience that all the components of aggregate demand are **autonomous** (*predetermined* or *constant*), with the exception of consumption which varies with income. We shall also assume that the **marginal propensity to consume (MPC)**, is 0.9 for all households at all levels of income. This of course means that the **marginal propensity to save (MPS)** must be 0.1. Saving is thus the only *income-induced leakage* or *withdrawal* of demand in our economy, and whenever income increases by £10, consumption spending increases by £9 and £1 is saved. Finally, we shall assume that a margin of spare capacity and unemployed labour exists in the economy which the government wishes to reduce.

According to Keynesian theory, the government can increase real income and output, and reduce unemployment, by deliberate deficit financing. **Deficit financing** occurs when the government increases public sector expenditure so that government spending exceeds income from taxes and other sources of revenue. The government could, for example, increase unemployment pay, welfare benefits and other *transfer incomes*, or transfers to industry such as regional aid. Alternatively, the government might invest in public works or *social capital*, for example in hospital building or road construction. Figure 16.1 illustrates an increase in public spending of £1 billion, spent for example on the renewal of sewage systems or on a similar urban infrastructure regeneration programme.

Figure 16.1: The multiplier process when the marginal propensity to consume is 0.9, saving being the only income-induced leakage of demand

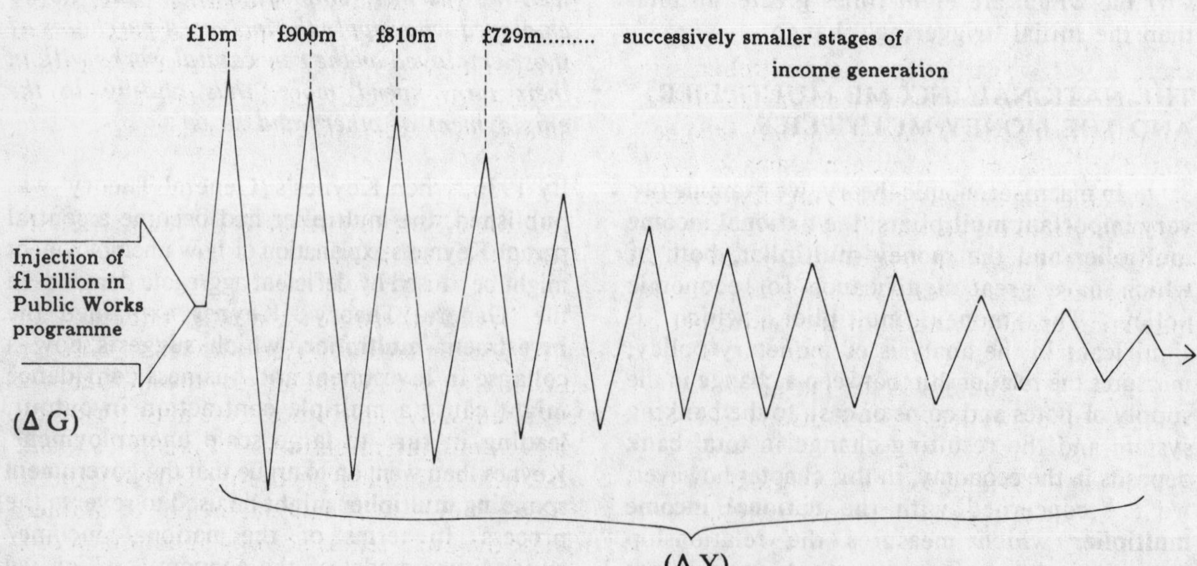

We shall assume that the increase in public spending is received as income by building workers who, like everybody in the economy, spend ninety pence of every pound of income on consumption. Since we are assuming that imports and taxation are constant at every level of income, this means that at the second stage, £900 million of the £1 billion income initially received by the building workers is spent within the economy on consumer goods and services, with the remaining £100 million leaking into unspent savings. At the next and third stage, people employed in the consumer goods industries spend 0.9 of the £900 million incomes received at the second stage of income generation. Further stages of income generation then occur, with each successive stage being 0.9 of the previous stage. Each stage is smaller than the preceding stage to the extent that part of income leaks into savings. Assuming that nothing else changes in the time taken for the process to work through the economy, the eventual increase in income resulting from the initial injection of government spending is the sum of all the stages of income generation. The sum of the successive stages is, of course, greater than, or a *multiple of*, the initial increase in government spending which triggered the multiplier process. Indeed, the value of the government spending multiplier

equals: $\dfrac{\text{change in income}}{\text{initial change in government spending}}$

or $k = \dfrac{\Delta Y}{\Delta G}$

where k is the **symbol for the multiplier** - in this example, the **government spending multiplier**. Providing that consumption is the only income-related component of aggregate demand (with saving thus being the only income-induced leakage of demand from the circular flow of income), the value of the multiplier *depends on the values of the marginal propensities to consume and save*. In this example, the formula for the multiplier is:

$k = \dfrac{1}{1-c}$ where c is the marginal propensity to consume (MPC)

or $k = \dfrac{1}{s}$ where s is the marginal propensity to save (MPS)

The formula reflects the fact that at each succeeding stage of the dynamic multiplier process, a fraction of income, determined by the MPS, leaks into saving and is not available for consumption at the next stage of income generation. The larger the MPC (and the smaller the MPS), the larger is the value of the multiplier. In our example, the value of the multiplier is 10

(ie $\dfrac{1}{1 - 0.9}$)

indicating that an initial increase in government spending of £1 billion, financed by a budget deficit, will subsequently increase money national income by £10 billion in total.

THE MULTIPLIER PROCESS AND DISEQUILIBRIUM IN THE ECONOMY

6. It is important to realise that because the multiplier is a *dynamic process* taking months, if not years, to work through its total stages, the economy is seldom, if ever, going to reach a state of equilibrium. Instead, the economy will be in a permanent state of **disequilibrium**. The multiplier does not involve an instantaneous adjustment from one equilibrium level of national income to another. Not only does the adjustment process take time; it is also likely that the economy will experience the 'outside shock' of an autonomous change in one or other of the components of aggregate demand while the process is working through. Such a 'demand shock' will trigger a further multiplier process before the first one is completed! Thus it is useful to think of the economy as *tending towards an equilibrium* as the multiplier process works through its stages, without ever reaching a state of equilibrium because of the renewed impact of 'outside' or 'exogenous' demand shocks.

THE MULTIPLIER AND THE 'KEYNESIAN CROSS' DIAGRAM

7. We can illustrate the multiplier process on a **'Keynesian cross' diagram** similar to those we used in Chapter 15. But because the multiplier is essentially a dynamic process, we must treat with caution our interpretation of Figures 16.2 and 16.3 which illustrate the change from one *static* equilibrium level of national income to another. These diagrams tell us nothing about the nature and length of the adjustment process itself.

Figure 16.2: When the MPC is relatively large (0.6), the size of the multiplier (ΔY/ΔG) is also large

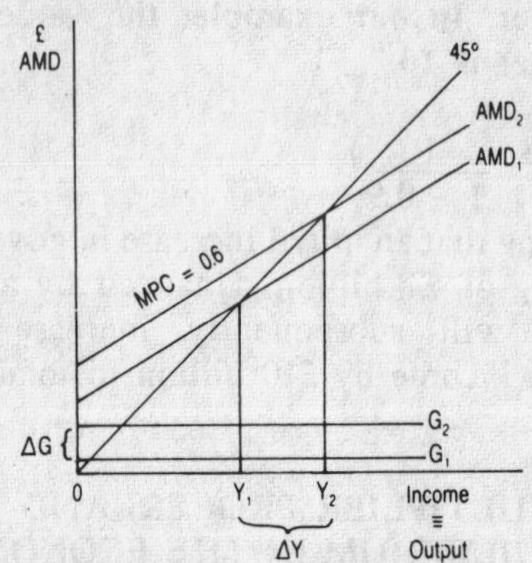

Figure 16.3: When the MPC is relatively small (0.2), the size of the multiplier (ΔY/ΔG) is close to unity

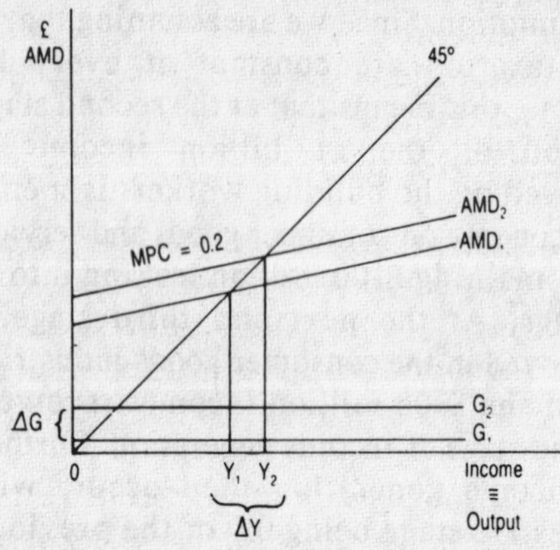

Following an increase in government spending, from G_1 to G_2 (shown by ΔG), the AMD function shifts upwards from AMD_1 to AMD_2, causing the equilibrium level of national income to rise from Y_1 to Y_2 or by ΔY. The multiplier is shown by $\frac{\Delta Y}{\Delta G}$. Since we have assumed that saving is the only income-induced leakage or withdrawal of demand from the flow of income, the slope of the AMD function depends upon the value of the MPC. In Figure 16.2 we have drawn an AMD function with a slope of 0.6, dipicting an MPC also of 0.6. The multiplier is therefore $\frac{1}{1 - 0.6}$,or 2.5, so that ΔY is two and a half times greater than the initial change in government spending, ΔG. But we should emphasise again that a comparison of the equilibrium levels of income reveals nothing about the dynamic adjustment process from Y_1 to Y_2. In Figure 16.3, we have drawn the AMD function with a slope of only 0.2, showing therefore, an MPC also equal to 0.2. The multiplier is now smaller, equal to 1.25, and the increase in income induced by the initial change in government spending is therefore also correspondingly smaller.

DERIVING THE MULTIPLIER

8. In the next four sections we shall use algebra to **derive the formula for the multiplier**. If you find the algebra forbidding, you can ignore the step-by-step algebraic derivation of each of the four multipliers we shall examine. Nevertheless, it is important to know the multiplier formula presented at the end of each of the sections. However, it is our belief that you are more likely to remember a multiplier formula if you understand how the formula has been derived. So try and persevere with the algebra; you will find that the algebra in sections 10, 11 and 12 is similar to section 9 in method.

DERIVING THE SIMPLE MULTIPLIER

9. So far in this chapter, the multiplier we have been using is the **simple multiplier**:

$$k = \frac{1}{1 - c} \quad \text{or } k = \frac{1}{s}$$

We shall now explain how the multiplier is derived. We shall begin by writing out in a *set of equations* the **income/expenditure model** of the **goods market** of an economy. The first six equations represent the various **components of aggregate demand**, whereas equation (vii) is the **equilibrium equation** for the goods market. The important point to note is that when deriving the simple multiplier, we are treating all the components of demand-with the significant exception of consumption - as constants: $I = \bar{I}$, $G = \bar{G}$, etc.

(i) $C = a + cY$, where c is the MPC; : the consumption function
(ii) $I = \bar{I}$: the investment
(iii) $G = \bar{G}$: government spending
(iv) $T = \bar{T}$: taxation
(v) $X = \bar{X}$: exports
(vi) $M = \bar{M}$: imports
(vii) $Y = C + I + G - T + X - M$: the equilibrium equation

In order to derive the formula for the multiplier, we shall now subject the seven equations of the model - known as the **structural equations of the model** - to some algebraic manipulation:

(a) substitution
(b) gathering terms
(c) factorising

(a) **Substitution:** This involves substituting the *components of demand* - equations (i) to (vi) - into the *equilibrium equation* (equation vii). We get:

(viii) $Y = a + cY + \overline{I} + \overline{G} - \overline{T} + \overline{X} - \overline{M}$

(b) **Gathering terms:** Now let us gather all the *income-related terms* on the left hand side of equation (viii), so as to leave all the *autonomous components of demand* on the right-hand side. We get:

(ix) $Y - cY = a + \overline{I} + \overline{G} - \overline{T} + \overline{X} - \overline{M}$

(c) **Factorising:** Income (Y) is the *common term* on the left hand side of equation (ix). Factorising, we get:

(x) $Y(1 - c) = a + \overline{I} + \overline{G} - \overline{T} + \overline{X} - \overline{M}$

Finally, we can derive the multiplier by dividing both sides of equation (x) by (1 - c). We get:

(xi) $Y = \frac{1}{1 - c}(a + I + G - T - X - M)$

where

$\frac{1}{1 - c}$ is the multiplier

Equation (xi) is known as the **reduced form version of the equilibrium equation**, reflecting the fact that the seven structural equations of the model have reduced to a single equation.

We obtain this formula for the multiplier because of the assumption, when setting up equations (i) to (vi), that saving alone of the leakages or withdrawals of demand varies with the level of income, ie saving is the only income-induced leakage of demand.

If we now assume that government spending increases by ΔG, or private sector investment rises by ΔI, then the resulting change in the equilibrium level of income ΔY is represented by:

(xii) $\Delta Y = \frac{1}{1 - c}(\Delta G)$,

in the case of an increase in government spending; and by:

(xiii) $\Delta Y = \frac{1}{1 - c}(\Delta I)$

when investment changes.

DERIVING THE TAX MULTIPLIER

10. In the model we have just described, $\frac{1}{1 - c}$ or $\frac{1}{s}$ is the formula for the multiplier when either **autonomous consumption, investment, government spending** or **exports** change. But when the level of either **taxation** or **imports** increases, the multiplier is *negative*, and income falls by ΔT or ΔM x the multiplier. Thus:

$\Delta Y = \frac{-1}{1 - c}(\Delta T)$: the tax multiplier

and $\Delta Y = \frac{-1}{1 - c}(\Delta M)$: the import multiplier

So far we have assumed that households make their consumption decisions out of **pre-tax income** rather than out of **post-tax disposable income.** We shall now see how the tax multiplier changes when the consumption function is:

$C = a + c(Y - T)$,

reflecting the fact that *post-tax disposable income* **Yd** (or Y - T), rather than *pre-tax income* determines consumption decisions. Once again, we begin the process of deriving the multiplier by writing out the structural equations of the model:

(i) $C = a + c(Y - T)$
(ii) $I = \overline{I}$
(iii) $G = \overline{G}$
(iv) $T = \overline{T}$
(v) $X = \overline{X}$
(vi) $M = \overline{M}$
(vii) $Y = C + I + G + X - M$

You should note that taxation is missing from the equilibrium equation: $Y = C + I + G + X - M$. However, T will enter the equilibrium equation when we substitute the consumption function $C = a + c(Y - T)$ into equation (vii). First however, we must substitute the tax equation (iv) into the consumption function. The consumption function now becomes:

(i′) $C = a + c(Y - \overline{T})$
or $C = a + cY - c\overline{T}$

The next stage is to **substitute** equations (i′) (ii) (iii) (v) and (vi) into the equilibrium equation to get:

(viii) $Y = a + cY - c\overline{T} + \overline{I} + \overline{G} + \overline{X} - \overline{M}$

Then **gathering terms:**
(xi) $Y - cY = a - c\overline{T} + \overline{I} + \overline{G} + \overline{X} - \overline{M}$

Factorising:
(x) $Y(1 - c) = a - c\overline{T} + \overline{I} + \overline{G} + \overline{X} - \overline{M}$

And dividing by (1 - c):

(xi) $Y = \frac{1}{1 - c}(a - c\overline{T} + \overline{I} + \overline{G} + \overline{X} - \overline{M})$

Suppose now that taxation increases by ΔT. The resulting change in income, ΔY, is represented by:
(xii) $\Delta Y = \frac{1}{1 - c}(-c\ \Delta T)$

which can be written as:

$$\Delta Y = \frac{-c}{1 - c}(\Delta T)$$

In equation (xii), the formula for the **tax multiplier** is $\frac{-c}{1 - c}$
(though the formulae for the other multipliers remain as $\frac{1}{1 - c}$
and $\frac{-1}{1 - c}$ in the case of imports).

Not only is the tax multiplier negative, but since the value of c (the MPC) is less than unity, the *absolute* value of the tax multiplier in this model (ignoring the + or - sign) is always less than the value of the government spending multiplier $\frac{1}{1 - c}$. When for example the MPC is 0.9, the government spending multiplier $\frac{1}{1 - c}$ is 10 and the tax multiplier $\frac{-c}{1 - c}$ is -9. As an exercise, you might calculate the size of the two multipliers for other values of the MPC. Whatever the chosen value of the MPC, you will find that the absolute size of the government spending multiplier always equals to the tax multiplier plus 1.

Thus a tax increase generates a smaller multiplier effect than a similar increase in government spending. This is explained by the fact that disposable income initially falls by an amount equal to the size of the tax increase, but since part of disposable income is saved anyway, the tax increase does not cause consumption spending to fall by the full amount of the change in taxation. In the initial stage of the multiplier process, the fall in consumption spending induced by the increase in taxation is -cΔT rather than -ΔT. Summing all the succeeding stages of the multiplier, the total change in spending and income is

$$\frac{-c}{1 - c}(\Delta T)$$

rather than $\frac{-1}{1 - c}(\Delta T)$

DERIVING THE BALANCED BUDGET MULTIPLIER

11. Suppose that government spending and taxation are increased by equal amounts, so that ΔG = ΔT. Continuing with our assumption that consumption decisions are made out of post-tax disposable income, the combined government spending and tax multipliers can be shown as:

(i) $\Delta Y = \left[\frac{1}{1 - c}\right]\Delta G + \left[\frac{-c}{1 - c}\right]\Delta T$

Since ΔG = ΔT, we can write equation (i) as:

(ii) $\Delta Y = \left[\left(\frac{1}{1 - c}\right) + \left(\frac{-c}{1 - c}\right)\right]\Delta G$

or
(iii) $\Delta Y = \left[\frac{1 - c}{1 - c}\right]\Delta G$

The expression $\frac{1 - c}{1 - c}$ is known as the **balanced budget multiplier**, which must be 1. If you find the algebra difficult, you can note from the previous section that when, for example, the MPC is 0.9, the government spending multiplier is 10 and the tax multiplier is -9. The balanced budget multiplier, which is simply the sum of the two multipliers, is 10 + (-9) = 1!

The balanced budget multiplier has a very important implication for economic policy. We shall assume that a government is using fiscal policy in a 'traditional Keynesian' way, to manage the level of aggregate demand in the economy in order to expand or reflate the level of national income. (We shall note some 'monetarist' objections to this assumption later in the chapter.) If the government increases public spending by £5 billion, but leaves taxation unchanged (financing the spending via a **budget deficit** and borrowing), national income will increase by £5 billion x the government spending multiplier. When the government spending multiplier is 10, ΔY = £50 billion. But if the increase in public spending is financed by raising taxation rather than through a budget deficit, the resulting increase in national income will be restricted to £5 billion x the balanced budget multiplier, ie £5bn x 1 = £5bn. Therefore, to maximise the expansionary effect of an increase in public spending, the government should **deficit finance** rather than aim to balance the budget.

DERIVING A MORE COMPLICATED MULTIPLIER

12. We shall now drop the simplifying assumption that taxation and imports are *autonomous* or *constant* at all levels of income. The tax and import equations are now:

$$T = tY$$

and $M = mY$

where t is the **marginal tax rate** (and tY represents a **proportionate** income tax) and m is the **marginal propensity to import**. Thus in this model, all three leakages or withdrawals of demand - *savings, taxation* and *imports* - vary with income or are *income-induced*:

(i) $C = a + cY$
(ii) $I = \bar{I}$
(iii) $G = \bar{G}$
(iv) $T = tY$
(v) $X - \bar{X}$
(vi) $M = mY$
(vii) $Y = C + I + G - T + X - M$

Since we have reverted to our original consumption function, $C = a + cY$, in which pre-tax income determines consumption, we can derive the formula for the multiplier by going through exactly the same stages of *substitution, gathering terms* and *factorising* which we used for deriving the simple multiplier in section 9.

Thus:
by substituting equations (i) to (vi) into equation (vii) we get:

(xiii) $Y = a + cY + \bar{I} + \bar{G} - tY + \bar{X} - mY$

and gathering terms:

(ix) $Y - cY + tY + mY = a + \bar{I} + \bar{G} + \bar{X}$

then factorising:

(x) $Y(1 - c + t + m) = a + \bar{I} + \bar{G} + \bar{X}$

and finally dividing by $(1 - c + t + m)$

(xi) $Y = \dfrac{1}{1 - c + t + m}(a + \bar{I} + \bar{G} + \bar{X})$

For this model the multiplier is:

$$\frac{1}{1 - c + t + m}$$

And because (1-c) equals the marginal propensity to save, the multiplier can be written as:

$$k = \frac{1}{s + t + m}$$

THE FORMULA FOR THE MULTIPLIER: SOME CONCLUSIONS

13. The most important conclusion to draw from our derivation of the multiplier is that the multiplier formula depends upon the assumptions made when specifying the nature of aggregate money demand in the economy. Different assumptions yield different multipliers. However, in general terms, the formula for the multiplier is:

$$k = \frac{1}{\text{marginal change in net income-induced leakages of demand}}$$

When saving is the only income-induced leakage of demand - taxation and imports being treated as autonomous or constants - the multiplier is:

$$k = \frac{1}{s}$$

But when levels of taxation and imports are determined by the level of income, the multiplier is: $\dfrac{1}{s + t + m}$

The introduction of other assumptions about aggregate demand complicates the multiplier still further. When consumption decisions are made out of post-tax disposable income, the tax multiplier becomes:

$$k = \frac{-c}{1 - c}$$

rather than

$$k = \frac{-1}{1 - c}$$

The tax multiplier $\frac{-c}{1-c}$ occurs of course only in a model in which taxation and imports are assumed to be autonomous. We shall leave it as an exercise for the reader to derive the multiplier in a model which combines the assumptions that consumption is determined by post-tax disposable income and that taxation and income are determined by income. The consumption function is:

$$C = a + c(Y - T)$$

and the tax and import equations are:

$$T = tY$$

and $M = mY$

If you correctly go through the algebraic stages used in the preceding sections, you will find that the relevant formula for the multiplier, given these assumptions, is:

$$k = \frac{1}{s + ct + m}$$

THE MULTIPLIER AND KEYNESIAN DEMAND MANAGEMENT

14. During the Keynesian era, from the 1940s to the 1970s, governments in industrialised mixed economies - and especially governments in the United Kingdom - based their macro-economic policy around the **management of aggregate demand.** To achieve full employment, the Keynesians expanded aggregate demand, but sometimes too much demand 'overheated' the economy. Excess demand pulled up the price level in a **demand-pull inflation,** or pulled imports into the country and caused a balance of payments crisis. In these circumstances, the Keynesians were forced to reverse the thrust of fiscal policy, cutting public spending or raising taxes to take demand out of the economy. Essentially, the Keynesians used fiscal policy, supplemented at times by monetary policy, to 'fine-tune' the level of aggregate demand in the economy to stabilise the fluctuations in the business cycle, and to try to achieve the macro-economic objectives of full-employment and economic growth without excessive inflation or an unsustainable deterioration in the balance of payments.

When using a **discretionary fiscal policy** to manage the level of aggregate demand in the economy, the size of the government spending multiplier is significant. The larger the government spending multiplier, the smaller is the increase in public spending that is needed to bring about a required increase in national income. Similarly, the greater the size of the tax multiplier, the smaller is the required tax cut. It follows therefore, that if the government spending and tax multipliers are large, and that if most of the change in money income induced by a change in the budget deficit is in real output rather than in prices, then fiscal policy used as a demand management instrument might be an effective way of controlling the economy.

THE MULTIPLIER IN THE UK ECONOMY

15. But as we have already explained, a high marginal propensity to import and a high marginal tax rate both serve to reduce the size of the multiplier. In the United Kingdom, the marginal tax rate is relatively high - at least 0.4 when taxes such as National Insurance contributions and expenditure taxes are added to income tax - and the British economy is relatively small and open to trade. Thus the marginal propensity to import is also quite high. Given the multiplier as $\frac{1}{s+t+m}$, and s = 0.15, t = 0.4 and m = 0.35, the value of the multiplier is $\frac{1}{0.9}$ or 1.1. This example shows that the value of the government spending multiplier in the UK economy is quite small. We must therefore modify the conclusion reached in the preceding section about the effectiveness of fiscal policy for managing demand. Because a significant fraction of the income received from an increase in government spending leaks into taxation and imports as well as into savings, the main effect of an expansionary fiscal policy may be to pull imports into the economy - even when there is substantial unemployment - with relatively little increase in domestic output and reduction in unemployment.

MONETARISTS AND THE MULTIPLIER

16. The multiplier measures the relationship between a change in aggregate demand and the resulting change in the equilibrium value of money national income. But **money national income** (or **nominal national income**) can grow if either **real output** of the **price level** rises, since:

money income ≡ price level *x* real income

or $Y \equiv Py$.

Keynesians have believed that, providing there is unemployed labour and spare capacity in the economy, the main effect of an increase in aggregate demand falls upon *real output* rather than on *prices*. In other words, Keynesians have argued that an expansionary fiscal policy reflates the 'real economy', boosting living standards and creating jobs, and only begins to inflate the price level as full employment is approached and excess demand appears.

In contrast to the 'traditional' Keynesian view we have just described, monetarist and 'New Classical' economists believe that the main effect of any increase in demand - resulting from either an expansionary fiscal policy or an expansionary monetary policy - falls upon prices rather than real output. Thus the effect is *inflationary* rather than *reflationary*, even when unemployment is quite high. The size of the government spending multiplier may, of course, be quite large with respect to money or nominal national income. But because prices rather than real output rises, the size of the multiplier is close to zero when measured in real terms. Monetarists conclude therefore, that demand management and expansionary fiscal and monetary policies are completely inappropriate and irresponsible government policies.

THE MONETARY EFFECTS OF AN INCREASE IN GOVERNMENT SPENDING

17. We have already explained how an increase in government spending will have a larger multiplier effect upon money national income if it is financed by a budget deficit (ie by keeping taxation unchanged) than when financed by an increase in taxation. But during the Keynesian era, Keynesian economists seemed to ignore any monetary side-effects that might result from the method of financing the resulting budget deficit. In contrast to the traditional Keynesian view, monetarists have placed considerable emphasis on the monetary effects of an expansionary fiscal policy. These effects depend upon the type of borrowing used to finance the budget deficit. Broadly, there are two possibilities: the government can finance its budget deficit using methods of borrowing which either:

(i) **increase the money supply** and possibly **cause inflation**; or
(ii) **raise interest rates** and **'crowd-out' the private sector.**

THE BUDGET DEFICIT, THE MONEY SUPPLY AND INFLATION

18. As we shall explain in greater detail in later chapters, most monetarists believe that an expansionary fiscal policy increases the money supply and causes inflation whenever the budget deficit is financed by borrowing from the banking system. The private sector banking system creates bank deposits when it lends to the government and the new money created recirculates to the general public when spent by the government. And when the general public spend this extra money, excess demand pulls up the price level.

THE BUDGET DEFICIT AND 'CROWDING-OUT'

19. As an alternative to financing a budget deficit by borrowing from the banking system (and thereby expanding the money supply), the government can borrow by selling gilt-edged securities and National Savings securities to the general public. But although such methods of borrowing do not expand the money supply, monetarists argue that they 'crowd-out' the private sector by causing investment by firms to fall. Suppose for example, that the government increases public spending by £10 billion, financing the resulting budget deficit with a sale of new gilt-edged securities. In order to persuade the general public to buy the extra debt, the guaranteed annual interest rate offered on new issues of gilts must be raised. But this in turn raises interest rates generally and 'crowds-out' or displaces private sector investment by making it more expensive for firms to borrow or raise funds on the capital market through new issues of corporate bonds and shares. As a result the size of the government spending multiplier with respect to real output is likely to be close to zero, rendering fiscal policy ineffective as a method of stimulating levels of activity and employment in the economy.

FINANCIAL 'CROWDING-OUT' AND RESOURCE 'CROWDING-OUT'

20. The process we have just described, in which the government competes with private sector businesses for the supply of household savings and funds, is known as **financial 'crowding-out'**. By contrast, **resource 'crowding-out'** is a more general term which relates to the fundamental economic problem of scarcity. Resource 'crowding-

out' simply means that real resources such as land capital and labour cannot be employed simultaneously in both the private and public sectors. Therefore, the opportunity cost of employing more resources in the public sector inevitably involves the sacrificed opportunity to use the same resources in private employment. However, as we shall see in the next section, this definition implicitly assumes full employment of all resources. When spare capacity and unemployed labour exist in the economy, it is more correct to describe the opportunity cost of increased government spending in terms of the foregone opportunity for resources to remain idle.

MONETARIST 'CROWDING-OUT' VERSUS KEYNESIAN 'CROWDING-IN'

21. Thus, while Keynesians accept the monetarist argument that 'crowding-out' can occur when the economy is at full-employment and full-capacity, they dispute whether 'crowding-out' takes place when the economy is well below full employment. Indeed, in these circumstances, Keynesians argue that an increase in public spending financed by a budget deficit will stimulate or **'crowd-in'** the private sector, via the multiplier process which we have described in this chapter. This is because an increase in public spending, such as a public-works road building programme, involves orders or contracts placed by the government for the output of private sector construction firms who, through their own subsequent spending in the succeeding stages of the multiplier process, generate further business for the private sector.

We can illustrate the dispute over 'crowding-out' and 'crowding-in' on a **production possibility diagram**. Figure 16.4 depicts the economy's production possibility frontier in terms of the maximum levels of output that can be produced with various combinations of public and private sector spending and output. Assuming the economy is initially at a position such as A (on the economy's production possibility frontier, and therefore at full employment), an increase in public sector spending from Pu_1 to Pu_2 'crowds-out' or displaces private sector spending, which falls from Pr_1 to Pr_2. The multiplier effect with respect to real output is therefore close to zero. Indeed, 'extreme' monetarists argue that the multiplier may even be negative because an increase in public sector spending causes the production possibility frontier to shift inwards, resulting in falling output. According to 'extreme' monetarists, this occurs because 'unproductive' or 'wealth-consuming' public sector spending 'crowds-out' or displaces 'wealth-producing' private sector spending. (In the extreme, this argument is rather absurd since it implies that all private sector spending, eg gambling is 'wealth-producing', while all public sector spending, eg on roads or hospitals is 'wealth-consuming' or unproductive.)

Figure 16.4: Monetarist 'Crowding-out' and Keynesian 'Crowding-in' illustrated on a production possibility diagram

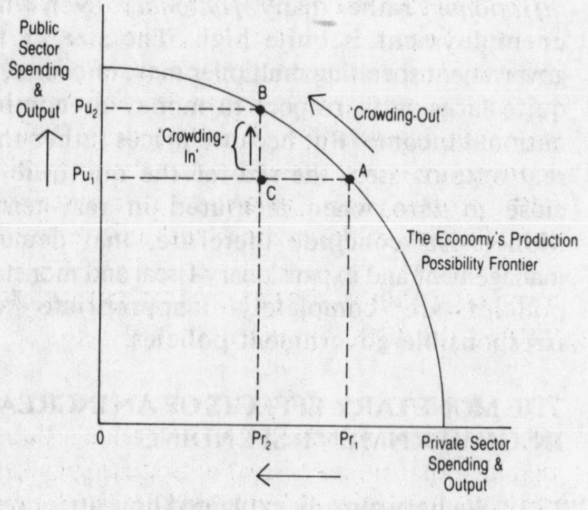

While Keynesians agree that 'crowding-out' can occur if initially the economy is at a point such as A, they argue that because the actual position of the economy is likely to be inside its production possibility frontier at a point such as C, 'crowding-out' will not take place. An increase in public sector spending which is sufficient, via the multiplier process, to move the economy from C to the production possibility frontier, merely takes up the slack productive potential of the economy, stimulating or 'crowding-in' the private sector through the generation of new business orders and employment.

In principle, therefore, the issue of whether an increase in public sector spending 'crowds-out' or 'crowds-in' the private sector, ought to depend upon whether the economy is initially on its production possibility frontier - at a position such as A - or inside the frontier, eg at C. Keynesians often argue that the size of unemployment indicates whether or not the economy is on or inside the production possibility frontier, and that with UK unemployment close to three million through most of the 1980s, the British economy has been well within its frontier. Monetarists reply by arguing that unemployment figures provide a misleading indicator of whether the economy is on its production possibility frontier - the correct indicator is the existence of spare capacity or idle factories and assembly lines that could quickly and *competitively* be brought into production to meet any increase in demand. Many monetarists argue that even though large-scale unemployment exists in the UK, the economy has nevertheless been on its production possibility frontier because of a lack of competitive spare capacity in the manufacturing sector. In these circumstances, any increase in public sector spending intended to stimulate or reflate the economy, triggers instead either the 'crowding-out' process, or inflation, or possibly a combination of 'crowding-out' and inflation.

THE MULTIPLIER EFFECTS OF DIFFERENT TYPES OF FISCAL POLICY

22. For the sake of convenience, we shall begin this section by accepting the Keynesian argument that an expansionary fiscal policy can generate a positive multiplier effect upon real output when there is spare capacity in the economy. However, the size of the resulting multiplier is likely to vary, depending upon the nature of the fiscal expansion. We have already seen that the taxation multiplier is likely to be smaller than the government spending multiplier, and that an increase in public spending will therefore, have a larger expansionary effect than a tax cut of similar size.

Different types of taxation and public spending can also lead to different multipliers. The multiplier effect resulting from tax cuts directed at the poor will generally be larger than when tax cuts benefit the rich. Because both the MPS and the marginal propensity to import rise with income, the rich spend a smaller fraction of any increase in disposable income upon consumption. It follows therefore, that fiscal policy can be used to expand demand even when the overall burden of taxation and level of public expenditure remain unchanged. By taxing the rich more heavily and reducing taxes paid by the poor, aggregate consumption spending can be boosted. A similar effect can be achieved by directing public spending towards the lower-paid, for example through welfare benefits and other transfer incomes claimed largely by the poor. However, any stimulation to the economy resulting from shifting the structure of taxation and transfers might, of course, be countered by adverse 'supply-side' effects which reduce incentives to work amongst rich and poor alike. High marginal tax rates might reduce effort and entrepreneurial ability supplied by the better-off, while the poor might choose to receive benefits rather than to work.

In conditions of high unemployment and severely deficient demand, increased government spending on public works might be more effective than transfers. In a depressed economy, spending on public works, such as road building, has the following advantages:

(i) Public works can be directed to regions of especially high local unemployment.
(ii) Lasting social capital is provided, which improves the economic infrastructure and creates external economies and an environment attractive to private investment.
(iii) Construction schemes employ relatively large numbers of unskilled and semi-skilled manual workers and as a result, the government is seen to be 'doing something about unemployment'.
(iv) Public works are seldom 'import-intensive' since they create a demand for domestically produced building materials. Since less of the initial government spending 'leaks' into the imports, the multiplier is correspondingly larger.

However, in Keynesian terms, spending on transfers and tax adjustments are probably more suited to 'fine-tuning' the level of aggregate demand in an economy closer to full employment. In contrast to public works which are slow to start and difficult to change once started, tax rates can be adjusted relatively easily to meet changed circumstances.

AUTOMATIC STABILISERS

23. Often it is impractical to reduce rates of

unemployment pay and welfare benefits, if only because the poor naturally resent any downward adjustment in their already low standards of living. So instead of using income tax rates and transfer incomes as instruments of discretionary Keynesian demand management, it is perhaps more appropriate to focus on their role as **automatic stabilisers** which dampen or reduce the multiplier effects resulting from any change in aggregate demand within the economy. Following a sudden fall in aggregate demand (caused perhaps by a 'monetarist' government cutting public expenditure so as to reduce the budget deficit), national income begins to fall, declining by the initial fall in demand x the multiplier. But as national income falls and unemployment rises, 'demand-led' public spending on unemployment pay and welfare benefits also rises. And if the income tax system is progressive, the government's tax revenues fall faster than national income. In this way, increased public spending on transfers and declining tax revenues effectively inject demand back into the economy, thereby stabilising or lessening the deflationary impact of the initial fall in aggregate demand, and reducing the overall size of the multiplier. Indeed, it is even possible for the budget deficit to be greater in size at the end of the process than at the beginning, as the Conservative Government discovered when public expenditure was cut in the early 1980s.

Automatic stabilisers also operate in the opposite direction to dampen the expansionary effects of an increase in aggregate demand. As incomes and employment rise, the take-up of 'means tested' welfare benefits and unemployment pay automatically falls, while at the same time tax revenues rise faster than income. Again, the size of the multiplier is reduced.

It is widely agreed that automatic stabilisers such as progressive taxation and transfer incomes have contributed to milder business cycles. Before 1939, business cycles - or trade cycles as they were then known - were much more volatile, displaying greater fluctuations between boom and slump, than in the years since the Second World War. Keynesians have sometimes claimed that the relatively mild modern business cycle is evidence of the success of Keynesian demand management policies in stabilising cyclical fluctuations. But the business cycle has been relatively mild not only in the UK, but also in countries such as West Germany where a Keynesian policy of discretionary demand management was never implemented. This suggests that automatic stabilisers such as progressive taxation and the 'safety net' provided by welfare benefits for the poor - both of which occurred widely in western industrialised economies after 1945 - have been more significant in reducing cyclical fluctuations than Keynesian management of aggregate demand.

Yet the most severe recession of the last fifty years occurred in the early 1980s when monetarist policies were being pursued in the United Kingdom and in other western economies. Indeed, immediately after its election in 1979, the Conservative Government in the UK abandoned counter-cyclical demand management and implemented severely deflationary monetary and fiscal policies which took no account of any perceived need to stabilise the business cycle. As a result, the subsequent recession started earlier in the UK and cut deeper than in other developed western countries. In the light of this 'blood-letting' experience, the British government has now 'modified its monetarism', adopting a more pragmatic approach and seemingly being prepared to relax fiscal and monetary policy to offset - rather than reinforce - the 'natural' fluctuations of the business cycle.

SUMMARY

24. In this chapter we have investigated the national income multiplier, and we have briefly surveyed the implications of the multiplier for fiscal policy, under both Keynesian and monetarist assumptions. In nominal terms, the national income multiplier measures the relationship between a change in aggregate money demand in the economy and the resulting change in the equilibrium level of money national income. But stated in real terms, the multiplier measures the relationship between a change in aggregate demand and real output in the economy. This distinction is important, because it leads on to the question of whether an expansion of aggregate demand reflates real output and employment in the economy, or simply inflates the price level through a process of demand-pull inflation.

The larger the size of the multiplier in terms of real output, the more powerful and effective is fiscal policy as a method of controlling the economy through the management of aggregate demand. Until recently at least, many Keynesians believed the multiplier to be sufficiently large and predictable for demand management, based on a discretionary fiscal policy, to be an effective instrument of government macro-economic policy. But the effectiveness of the multiplier depends not only on whether real output is stimulated rather than prices; it also depends on leakages of demand at each stage of the multiplier process. In a simple Keynesian model in which the multiplier is

$$\frac{1}{1-c} \text{ or } \frac{1}{s},$$

the size of the multiplier can be quite high, implying that fiscal policy can be a powerful demand management tool. But in a more complicated (and realistic) model in which part of any increase in income is paid to the government in taxes or is spent on imports, the value of the multiplier

$$\frac{1}{s + t + m} \text{ or } \frac{1}{s + ct + m} \text{ is much smaller.}$$

We should thus conclude that in a relatively small economy such as the UK, which is open to trade and in which effective tax rates are quite high in total, an expansionary fiscal policy is not likely to have a powerful effect on real output.

The 'real output' government spending multiplier is also likely to be small if 'crowding-out' takes place. Many monetarists believe that increased government spending displaces or 'crowds-out' the private sector, except possibly in an extremely depressed economy. In reply, Keynesians have argued that 'crowding-out' only occurs in a fully-employed economy, and that when there is a margin of spare capacity in the economy an increase in public spending 'crowds-in' or stimulates the private sector, via the government spending multiplier. But whether or not Keynesian or monetarist fiscal policies are pursued, progressive taxation and transfers tend in modern economies to act as automatic stabilisers, dampening or reducing the multiplier effects which result from a demand 'shock' hitting the economy.

STUDENT SELF-TESTING

1. *Define a multiplier.* *(2)*
2. *Distinguish between the national income multiplier and the money multiplier.* *(3)*
3. *Distinguish between an investment multiplier and an employment multiplier.* *(4)*
4. *Explain the stages of the multiplier process.* *(5)*
5. *Why is the economy likely to be in disequilibrium?* *(6)*
6. *Derive the formula for the government spending multiplier, under varying sets of assumptions about the components of aggregate demand.* *(9, 12)*
7. *Derive the tax multiplier.* *(10)*
8. *Derive the balanced budget multiplier.* *(11)*
9. *Why has the multiplier concept been important for Keynesian economic policy?* *(14)*
10. *Why is the value of the multiplier small in the UK economy?* *(15)*
11. *What views have monetarists on the size of the government spending multiplier?* *(16)*
12. *Summarise the possible monetary effects of an increase in government spending.* *(17)*
13. *Why may the budget deficit be inflationary?* *(18)*
14. *What is 'crowding-out'?* *(19)*
15. *Distinguish between 'financial crowding-out' and 'resource crowding-out'.* *(20)*
16. *Why do monetarists believe 'crowding-out' occurs even in an economy with substantial unemployment?* *(21)*
17. *Why may an increase in transfer incomes to the poor have a larger multiplier effect than tax cuts for the rich?* *(22)*
18. *What is an automatic stabiliser?* *(23)*

+

EXERCISES

1. *In an economy:*
   Consumption = 0.8 disposal income
   Investment = £520 million
   Government spending = £800 million
   Taxation = 0.5 Income
   Exports = 600
   Imports = 0.2 Income

   (a) Calculate the equilibrium level of national income.
   (b) The government wishes to increase national income by £1,200 million to reduce unemployment. By how much must government spending rise to achieve this?
   (c) What are the formula and value of the government spending multiplier?
   (d) What is the effect of the increase in government spending upon:
   (i) the government's budget;
   (ii) the balance of payments.

MULTIPLE CHOICE QUESTIONS

1. *In the following, Y = income, C = consumption, S = Saving and c is the marginal propensity to consume. Assuming no foreign trade or government sector, given investment, a multiplier of 2.5 and C = 100 + cY.*
   Then:
   A S = 100 + 0.6Y
   B C = 100 + 0.6Y
   C S = 100 + 0.4Y
   D C = 100 + 0.4Y

2. *In an economy national income is £100,000 and in equilibrium government spending is £30,000 million. When income increases by £100, £20 is saved, £10 is taken in taxes, and £10 is spent on imports. To increase national income to £120,000 million, the government would need to increase public spending to:*
   A £32,000 million
   B £34,000 million
   C £36,000 million
   D £38,000 million

3. *In a closed economy with no foreign trade, the marginal propensity to consume is 0.8, and the average propensity to consume is 0.9. The value of the multiplier is:*
   A 1.7
   B 0.2
   C 5
   D 10

4. *If the marginal propensity to consume is 0.75 in a fully employed closed economy in which taxes are unrelated to the level of income, an increase in government expenditure of £2,000 million will increase national income by:*
   A £0
   B £150 million
   C £8,000 million
   D £15,000 million

5. *According to monetarists, public sector spending 'crowds-out' private sector investment as a result of a rise in:*
   A The money supply
   B Aggregate money demand
   C Interest rates
   D The multiplier

EXAMINATION QUESTIONS

1. *(a) Explain the operation of the investment multiplier in a closed economy without government.* *(10 marks)*
   (b) If foreign trade and government are introduced what effect does this have on the multiplier? *(10 marks)*
   (ACCA December 1986)

2. *(a) To what extent is the investment multiplier of use to governments?* *(10 marks)*
   (b) Explain the multiplier process. *(3 marks)*
   (c) How is the size of the multiplier determined? *(7 marks)*
   (AAT December 1987)

3. *Using the multiplier concept analyse and explain the effect on the national income and the balance of payments of (a) an independent extra increase in government expenditure; and (b) an independent extra increase in the level of exports.*
(ACCA December 1976)

4. *'In an economy with no government and no international trade, the value of the multiplier is given by the reciprocal of the marginal propensity to save.' Explain this statement and briefly indicate how the value of the multiplier is affected by the introduction of a government sector and international trade.*
(ACCA December 1980)

17. Investment

INTRODUCTION

1. In Chapter 12, where we developed the theory of the aggregate demand in the economy, we assumed, as a simplification, that investment is fixed at some constant level. In this chapter we drop the **assumption that** investment is **autonomous**, and introduce various theories to explain the determination of the level of investment in the economy. After constructing a **micro-economic theory of how a single profit-maximising firm makes investment decisions**, we introduce two macro-economic theories of investment; the **marginal efficiency of investment theory** and the **accelerator theory**. This chapter concludes by bringing together the **accelerator** and the **multiplier** to explain **business cycles** in the economy.

THE MEANING OF INVESTMENT

2. In everyday speech, 'investment' is often used to describe a situation in which a person 'invests' in stocks or shares, paintings or antiques. However, to an economist **investment** must involve the **purchase** - usually by firms - **of real resources** which add to the economy's capital stock and productive potential. Since 'investments' in second-hand shares, or in most works of art, involve merely the transfer of ownership of existing assets from one person to another, and not the production of new productive assets, they should not be regarded as investment in the economist's meaning of the word.

STOCKS AND FLOWS

3. Investment can be of two types: (i) **investment in fixed capital**, such as new factories or plant and social **capital** such as roads or publicly-owned hospitals, and (ii) **inventory investment** in stocks of raw materials or variable capital. It is important to realise that capital is a **'stock'** concept, but investment is a **'flow'**. We can measure the **national capital stock** at any particular point of time. It represents the total of all the nation's **capital goods**, of all types, which are still in existence and capable of production. In contrast, we measure the flow of investment over a period, usually a year. A country's **gross investment** includes two parts: **replacement investment** (or **depreciation**) which simply maintains the size of the existing capital stock by replacing worn-out capital and **net investment** which adds to the capital stock, thereby increasing productive potential. We can think of a country's net investment essentially as the engine of economic growth. The *flow* of net investment therefore, equals the *change* in the capital *stock*; or

$$I \text{ net} \equiv \Delta K$$

where K is the symbol of the capital stock.

INVESTMENT AND THE NATIONAL ACCOUNTS

4. In the United Kingdom National Accounts investment is measured in two ways. **Gross fixed investment** is measured in the National Expenditure tables as **gross domestic fixed capital formation (GDFCF)**, which is defined as 'expenditure on fixed assets either for replacing or adding to the stock of existing fixed assets.' **Inventory investment** is measured as the **'value of physical increase in stocks and work in progress'**. In 1985, investment in fixed capital, as measured by GDFCF, was about 14 per cent of total expenditure in the economy, while inventory investment was negative (at -0.2 per cent), showing that firms were running down rather than adding to their stocks or inventories of raw materials. It is worth noting, however, that in any one year, the total *stock* or inventory of raw materials and finished goods which firms possess, or have invested in, is a much larger percentage of national output - about 40 per cent - and that current inventory investment simply adds to, or when negative subtracts from, the total existing stock of inventories. We should also note that at around 14 per cent of national output and expenditure, **total investment** is a much smaller - but more volatile - component of aggregate demand that **consumption expenditure**. which in 1985 accounted for approximately 50 per cent of the total.

The measurement of investment, as defined by the National Accounts, is also restricted largely to investment by firms and by the government. If a household purchases a 'consumer durable' such as a computer or word-processor, it is classified in the National Accounts as consumption expenditure.

The same expenditure by a firm would be classified as investment. When for tax purposes, a householder becomes self-employed, the same expenditure becomes investment rather than consumption! It would perhaps be more accurate to classify all household expenditure on consumer durables as investment, since they are effectively capital assets delivering a stream of useful services throughout their life. (Expenditure by households on new dwellings is, indeed, classified in the National Accounts as investment.)

In the UK, the components of gross domestic fixed capital formation have changed significantly in recent years. **Public sector investment** in fixed capital by the government and nationalised industries has fallen from over 50 per cent of GDFCF in the late 1960s to just 26 per cent in 1984. The fall has been especially great in the 1980s, reflecting the policy of the Conservative government to reduce the size of the public sector. In terms of type of production, **investment in the manufacturing sector** has been much more volatile than investment overall, becoming negative in the 1980s during a period of **deindustrialisation** when UK manufacturing industries were in absolute decline.

A MICRO-ECONOMIC THEORY OF INVESTMENT

5. A sound **macro-economic theory** which attempts to explain how economic agents behave at the aggregate level, should always be based firmly in the **micro-economic theory of how an individual economic agent behaves**. Thus, the theories of aggregate consumption, which we examined in Chapter 14, take as their starting point the micro-economic theory of household demand or consumption behaviour. In just the same way, we must develop our macro-economic theory of firms' investment behaviour from the micro-theory of the investment decisions of a single firm.

MARGINAL PRODUCTIVITY THEORY

6. In Chapter 12 we saw how, in competitive factor markets, a profit-maximising firm's demand for the services of a factor of production depends upon (i) the productivity of the factor and (ii) the price or cost of hiring the factor. We developed this theory with respect to the demand for labour and the wage, but the theory can also be applied to a firm's demand for capital, and hence to investment. Assuming competitive factor markets and a profit-maximising objective, the theory states that a firm will invest in new capital up to the point at which the marginal revenue productivity (MRP) of capital equals the cost of capital (the rate of interest).

THE RELATIVE PRICES OF CAPITAL AND LABOUR

7. We also saw in Chapter 12 how the equilibrium quantities of all the factors of production employed by a firm depend upon their relative prices. In equilibrium, the condition of equi-marginal returns must hold:

$$\frac{\text{MRP labour}}{\text{Wage rate}} = \frac{\text{MRP capital}}{\text{Rate of interest}}$$

If technology allows a firm to **substitute** one factor of production for another, then **changes in their relative prices** will influence the demand for capital, or investment. For example, a fall in the rate of interest makes capital relatively cheaper to employ than labour. If firms expect this to be permanent, the cheaper cost of borrowing will encourage them to adopt more capital-intensive methods of production, demanding more capital and less labour, ie engaging in factor substitution.

EXPECTED FUTURE PRODUCTIVITY

8. However a businessman's demand for fixed capital goods is rather different from his demand for most types of labour. When a firm considers employing an extra manual worker, the firm will probably be interested only in the current productivity of the worker, and not in the worker's likely production several years ahead. With fixed capital it is different. If the investment takes several months or even years to complete, it will not begin to yield a profit or return until well into the future. It is then quite likely that the firm will expect the investment to have an economic life lasting several years into the future.

It is therefore insufficient to state that a profit-maximising firm will invest in new capital up to the point where the *current* marginal product of capital equals the rate of interest. We must modify the businessman's decision rule to take into account the fact that the returns on a new investment are **future returns**, which are produced over the useful economic life of the investment. As a generalisation, we can state that to maximise profits, a firm will invest in a new capital asset if:

The rate of return per period expected over the life of the investment	>	the expected rate of interest per cent per period which must be paid on borrowed funds to finance the investment

Although a businessman may know the initial fixed cost of the investment and the current cost of borrowing or rate of interest, he cannot know with complete certainty either the length of the asset's useful economic life or the details of the net returns or **income stream** which will be produced in each year of the investment's life. Instead, he must guess or forecast them, knowing that an investment's **economic life** may be much shorter than its **technical life**. The development of a competing new technology, or changes in the price of labour or energy, may render a machine **productively inefficient** long before it actually wears out.

Likewise, an estimate of the size and shape of the expected income stream is fraught with uncertainty; not only must the physical product or returns of the investment be calculated for each year in the asset's expected economic life, so also must the prices at which the output is sold and the running costs of the investment, including the prices of other inputs such as labour and raw materials.

DISCOUNTING THE FUTURE

9. Suppose that a firm is considering an investment whose details are shown in Figure 17.1. The initial investment which costs £100,000, takes one year to complete (Year 0). The investment then has an expected economic life of ten years (Year 1 to Year 10). The **expected net returns in each year** - the investment's **expected income stream** - are also shown in the diagram. The investment is expected to earn most of its returns early in the ten year period, and we have assumed no scrap or second-hand value at the end of ten years and no disposal costs.

Figure 17.1: The initial cost and the expected future income stream of an investment in a fixed capital asset

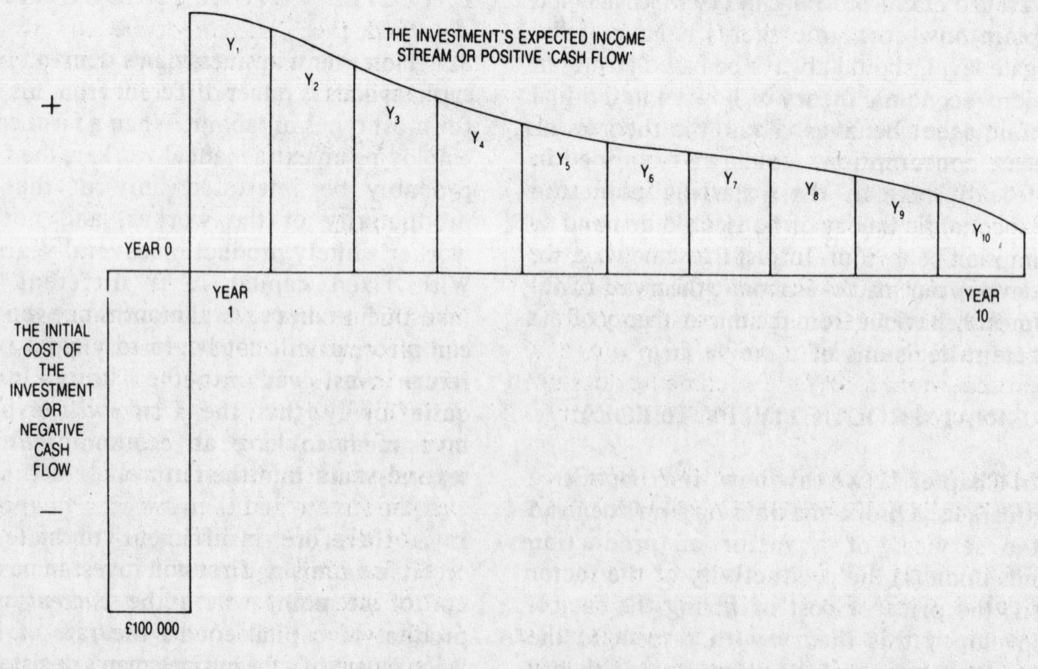

In deciding whether the investment in a fixed capital asset is worthwhile, the firm might calculate what the £100,000 could become if 'invested', for example, in government bonds for the ten year period. It could then forecast the capital asset's expected income in Year 1 and estimate what this would become if reinvested to earn the expected rate of interest over the remaining nine years of the investment's expected life. Similar estimates would also be made to calculate what the income expected in Year 2 would become, reinvested over eight years, Year 3's income reinvested over seven years and so on. The investment in the capital asset would be worthwhile, according to this test, if the eventual total income, including reinvested income, yielded by the capital asset exceeds what £100,000 would become, invested in government bonds over the same ten year period (allowing perhaps for a risk premium on the 'riskier' investment in fixed capital).

But instead of *adding* on the rate of interest over the ten year period in the manner we have just described, the firm could decide whether the investment in the fixed capital asset is worthwhile, by undertaking the *opposite* process: by **discounting the future.** When discounting the future, the firm's decision rule is:

Invest in all projects for which the **discounted present** value of the expected income stream	>	the initial known cost of the capital asset.

As before, the firm estimates the capital asset's expected returns for each year of the investment's expected life. But when **discounting** the expected future income stream, *instead of adding on* the **rate of interest** to calculate the reinvested value of the income at the end of the asset's life, the businessman *must subtract* **a discount rate,** to calculate **the value to him now (the present value or PV)** of income he does not expect to receive until some time in the future.

THE DISCOUNTED CASH FLOW (DCF) TECHNIQUE OF INVESTMENT APPRAISAL

10. Discounting the future is the basis of the **Discounted Cash Flow (DCF)** technique of investment appraisal. If a firm is to maximise the profits resulting from investment, the year in which an asset's income or net returns are received is crucial. £1,000 received next year is worth less than the same amount received now, even if we assume a zero rate of inflation. To be worth the same, any monies received next year must be equal to those received this year plus the rate of interest. It follows that income received early in the life of a capital asset is worth more than a similar income received later.

With the DCF method of investment appraisal, the income expected in each year of the investment's life is discounted the appropriate number of times. The formula for calculating the discounted present value of income received at the end of one year ahead is:

$$PV = \frac{Y_1}{(1 + r)}$$

Y_1 is the income expected at the end of Year 1, and r is a **test rate of discount,** chosen for example on the basis of either current or expected rates of interest.

In a similar way, the formula for calculating the PV of income expected at the end of Year 2 is:

$$PV = \frac{Y_2}{(1 + r)^2}$$

and income at the end of Year 3:

$$PV = \frac{Y_3}{(1 + r)^3}$$

and so on.

To find the discounted present value of a complete income stream, we simply sum these expressions:

THE DCF FORMULA :

$$PV = \frac{Y_1}{(1+r)} + \frac{Y_2}{(1+r)^2} + \frac{Y_3}{(1+r)^3} + ... + \frac{Y_n}{(1+r)^n}$$

The DCF technique of investment appraisal 'picks up' information about the size, shape and length of an investment's expected income stream (or cash flow), together with information about the cost of borrowing or rate of interest. The businessman or decision maker estimates the income stream and then chooses an appropriate rate of discount at which to conduct the DCF test. The chosen discount rate can reflect the rate of interest that would be paid to borrow the funds which finance the cost of the project. Alternatively, if the firm already possesses its own internally-accumulated funds, the discount rate may be chosen on the basis of what the firm thinks it could earn if it lent the funds, for example by purchasing government bonds, instead of investing them itself in a capital asset. If the PV of the expected income stream is greater than the known initial cost of the investment, the firm can expect to 'do better' by investing in its own capital project than by lending out the equivalent funds to earn the going rate of interest. And assuming a particular chosen discount rate, the firm should invest in all capital projects which yield a PV greater than the initial cost of each investment.

THE INTERNAL RATE OF RETURN

11. We shall now explain a most important link between the **micro-economic theory** of how a single firm makes investment decisions, which we have just described, and the **macro-economic theory** of aggregate investment which we shall develop in the next section. As a first step, we must compare the **DCF formula**, which we explained in the previous section, with a second way of stating the discounting principle: the **internal rate of return formula.**

(i) THE DCF FORMULA:

$$PV = \frac{Y_1}{(1+r)} + \frac{Y_2}{(1+r)^2} + \frac{Y_3}{(1+r)^3} + \ldots + \frac{Y_n}{(1+r)^n} \quad ($$

(ii) THE INTERNAL RATE OF RETURN FORMULA :

$$\text{Initial cost of investment} = \frac{Y_1}{(1+i)} + \frac{Y_2}{(1+i)^2} + \frac{Y_3}{(1+i)^3} + \ldots + \frac{Y_n}{(1+i)^n}$$

In the DCF formula, r is the **test rate of discount** chosen by a businessman to calculate the PV of an expected future income stream. The correct value of r to choose depends on the rate of interest or cost of borrowing. For each investment project a businessman is considering, different values of r would yield a different PV. An investment project judged as just worthwhile when tested against a 9 per cent discount rate would fail a 10 per cent discount test.

Alternatively, in equation (ii), we can calculate directly the **rate of return**, i, which a businessman expects to earn over the life of an asset when he makes the investment. This is known as **the investment's internal rate of return.** For each investment, the internal rate of return is the *unique* rate of discount which makes the present value of the expected income stream exactly equal the asset's initial cost.

THE MARGINAL EFFICIENCY OF INVESTMENT

12. We are now in a position to introduce the first of the two macro-economic theories of investment which we shall consider: the **marginal efficiency of investment (MEI) theory.** This theory is also known as the **marginal efficiency of capital (MEC) theory.** At any point of time, there will be thousands, if not millions of potential investment projects not yet undertaken in the economy. Each project will have its own internal rate of return, i , based on a calculation of its expected future income stream and the initial cost of the investment. If the internal rate of return is calculated for each and every possible capital project available to all the business enterprises in the economy, we can, in principle, **rank the investments in descending order** of expected future yields or IRR. The resulting curve is known as the **marginal efficiency of investment function,** which is illustrated in Figure 17.2

Figure 17.2: By ranking potential investment projects in descending order of IRR, the marginal efficiency of investment function is derived

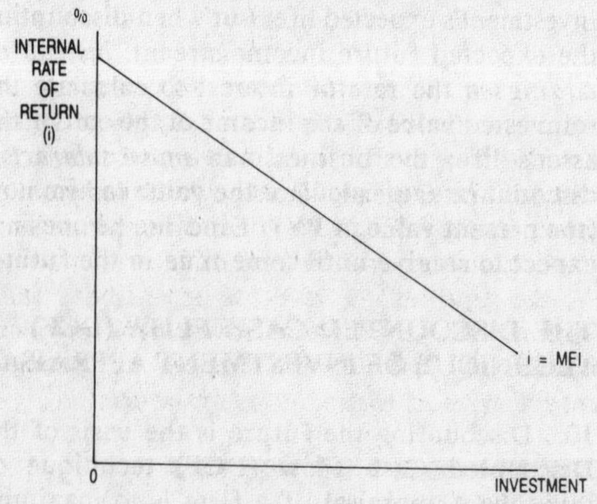

THE DETERMINATION OF THE AGGREGATE LEVEL OF INVESTMENT

13. The theory of the marginal efficiency of investment was first developed in 1936 by **Keynes** in his **'General Theory'** to explain the determination of the aggregate level of investment in the economy. Keynes assumed that the cost of borrowing or rate of interest, r, is determined in the money markets by forces outside the control of businessmen. Taking the rate of interest as given at r_1, the equilibrium level of aggregate investment is determined in Figure 17.3 at the point where the marginal efficiency of capital equals the cost of borrowing, ie where i = r.

Figure 17.3: The determination of the equilibrium level of aggregate investment in the MEI theory of investment

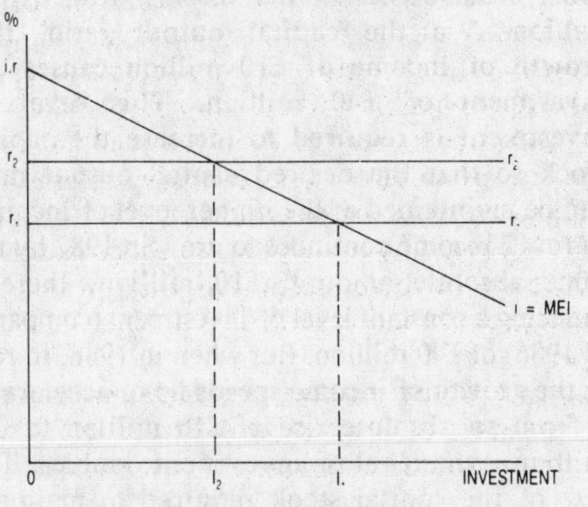

In Figure 17.3, the **rate of interest** r_1 represents the **perfectly elastic supply of funds** assumed to be available to finance investment. By contrast, the **aggregate demand** for investment is shown by the MEI curve. If conditions in money markets change and the rate of interest rises to r_2, the equilibrium level of investment falls from I_1 to I_2. Potential investment projects considered just worthwhile at r_1 become unprofitable at higher rates of interest.

THE STABILITY OF THE MEI FUNCTION

14. Early in this chapter we stated that investment is a much more volatile or unstable component of aggregate demand in the economy than aggregate consumption expenditure. We can now begin to explain why. The *position* of the MEI curve (*as distinct from its slope*) is determined by businessmen's expectations of an unknown and possibly uncertain future. In his 'General Theory', Keynes referred to the **'animal spirits'** of businessmen as a most important determinant of the level of aggregate investment in the economy. If 'animal spirits' are high, ie if business confidence improves, businessmen will immediately revise upwards their expectations of future profits and income streams yielded by the investments they are considering. This means that for each prospective investment project in the economy, its internal rate of return improves and for the economy as a whole the MEI curve shifts outwards. In Figure 17.4 the aggregate level of investment increases from I_1 to I_2, when the MEI function shifts outwards from MEI_1 to MEI_2.

Figure 17.4: Shifts of the MEI function in response to changing moods of business optimisim and pessimism

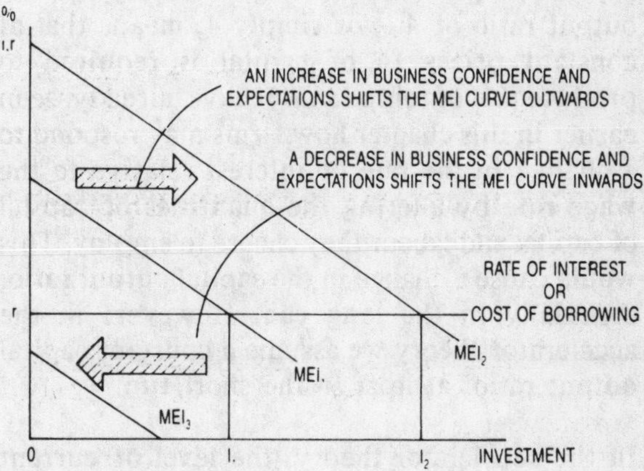

But the opposite is true when a collapse of business confidence or 'animal spirits' occurs. Firms revise downwards the expected return of each project and the MEI curve shifts inwards. In Figure 17.4 we have illustrated a situation in which the MEI curve shifts inwards to such an extent, from MEI_1 to MEI_3, that even if the rate of interest falls to zero, investment fails to recover to its previous level. This reflects

Keynes's view that in a depressed economy (such as the 1930s when Keynes was writing the 'General Theory') business pessimism will cause the cancellation of investment projects because even at very low costs of borrowing, businessmen believe that the future is so bleak that almost all investments will be unprofitable. Keynes considered businessmen to be extremely jittery about the future, and that the resulting sudden changes in business confidence are responsible for erratic shifts of the MEI curve which causes the volatile nature of aggregate investment.

THE ACCELERATOR THEORY

15. We shall now consider a second and very different explanation of the determination of the aggregate level of investment in the economy: the **accelerator theory**. In contrast to the MEI theory, which as we have seen is based very firmly on the micro-economic foundations of how a profit-maximising firm makes investment decisions, the accelerator theory stems from the rather simple assumption that **firms wish to keep a relatively fixed ratio between the output they are currently producing and their existing stock of fixed capital assets**. This is called the **capital output ratio**. For example, a capital output ratio of 4:1, or simply 4, means that at constant prices £4 of capital is required to produce £1 of output. We have already seen earlier in this chapter how firms may respond to a change in the rate of interest relative to the wage rate by altering the quantities of capital of capital and labour they choose to employ. This would cause a change in the capital output ratio, especially in the long run. However, in the accelerator theory we assume a constant capital output ratio, at least in the short run.

In the accelerator theory, the level of current net investment in fixed capital depends on the change in income or output in the previous year:

$$I = v(\Delta Y)$$

$$\text{or} \quad I_t = v(Y_t - Y_{t-1})$$

where I_t is net investment this year, Y_t is current national income, Y_{t-1} is national income last year and v is the capital output ratio. The **capital output ratio,** v, is also known as the **accelerator coefficient**, or simply as the **accelerator.** Gross investment equals net investment plus any replacement investment to make good capital worn out in the course of production last year. Thus:

$$I\ \text{gross}_t = v(Y_t - Y_{t-1}) + I\ \text{replacement}_t$$

To illustrate the accelerator principle, we shall assume that no replacement investment is needed and that the average capital output ratio in the economy is 4.

Let us consider the following numerical example:

Year	*Net Investment*		*Current income*		*Last years income*
t	I_t				
t = 1986:	£40m	=	4(£100m	-	£90m)
t = 1987:	£40m	=	4(£110m	-	£100m)
t = 1988:	£80m	=	4(£130m	-	£110m)
t = 1989	£40m	=	4(£140m	-	£130m)

You should note that in each of the four years shown in this example national income grows. Between 1985 (which is year t - 1 in row 1) and 1986, we have assumed that income grows by £10 million. Via the capital output ratio, this growth of income of £10 million causes net investment of £40 million. This level of investment is required to increase the capital stock so that the desired capital output ratio can be maintained at the higher level of income. In row 2 income continues to grow in 1987 by the same absolute amount, £10 million, thereby inducing a constant level of investment (compared to 1986) of £40 million. But when in 1988, in row 3, the **growth of income speeds up or accelerates** - from an absolute rise of £10 million to £20 million - the level of investment doubles. The size of the capital stock required to maintain the capital output ratio is £80 million larger in 1988 than in 1987. Finally, we have assumed in row 4 that the growth of income falls back again to £10 million in 1989. Although income is still growing, net investment now declines back to its previous level of £40 million.

This very simple illustration shows how the accelerator theory derives its name. It is the **rate of growth of income and output** rather than **the fact that output is growing**, that determines whether investment is **growing, falling,** or at a **constant level.** According to the acceleration principle:

(i) if income is **growing by a constant amount** each year, **net investment is constant;**

(ii) if the **rate of growth of income accelerates, net investment increases;** and
(iii) if the **rate of growth of income decelerates, net investment declines.**

Thus relatively slight changes in the rate of growth of income or output can cause quite large absolute rises and falls in investment as firms adjust their capital stocks to the required level. The acceleration principle therefore provides a second explanation of why investment in capital goods is a more volatile or unstable component of aggregate demand than consumption.

WEAKNESSES OF THE ACCELERATOR THEORY

16. (i) **The accelerator theory is too mechanical.** It assumes that all firms react to increased demand for their output in the same way. Some firms may wait to see if the higher level of demand is maintained, whilst others may order more plant and machinery than is immediately required.

(ii) This **implies that there is no spare capacity in existence.** If firms already possess excess capacity left over from a previous boom in demand, they can increase output by utilising this spare capacity, without the need to invest in additional fixed capital.

(iii) Demand may increase at a time when the capital goods industries are themselves at full capacity and unable to meet a higher level of investment demand. The price of capital goods is likely to rise, creating an incentive for firms to economise in the use of capital. The capital output ratio will therefore alter.

MULTIPLIER-ACCELERATOR INTERACTION

17. By bringing together the multiplier theory (which we explained in Chapter 16) and the accelerator theory of investment, it is possible to construct a **dynamic macro-economic theory** which models changes in income and output through time. Writing the **investment multiplier relationship** as:

$$\Delta Y = k\,(\Delta I)$$

and the **accelerator relationship** as

$$I = v\,(\Delta Y)$$

where k is the **investment multiplier** and v is the **accelerator**, we can bring the two together in a **multiplier-accelerator dynamic model** of the goods market. In essence:

$$\underbrace{\Delta I \rightarrow k \rightarrow \Delta Y}_{\text{multiplier}} \underbrace{\rightarrow v \rightarrow}_{\text{accelerator}} \underbrace{\Delta I \rightarrow k \rightarrow \Delta Y \ldots}_{\text{multiplier and so on}}$$

An initial multiplier effect, triggered by some event increasing investment (or indeed by some other event leading to an increase in aggregate demand) causes income to rise which then in turn induces, via the accelerator, a 'feed-back' to investment leading to a further multiplier effect, and so on. Continuing multiplier-accelerator interaction allows us to plot the dynamic growth path of the economy. An interesting feature of the multiplier-accelerator model is that different values of the multiplier, k, and the accelerator, v, can lead to different changes of the growth path of income. The various possibilities are illustrated in Figure 17.5 (on the following page) which shows that certain values of k and v can lead to **cyclical** changes in income. Indeed, multiplier-accelerator interactions provide a method of explaining the **business cycles** which are a feature of most modern economies. In Figure 17.6 (on the following page) we have illustrated the main features of the modern 'short' business cycle, which usually lasts a period of about 4 or 5 years, though in the past the cycle has lasted up to about 10 years.

AN OVERALL VIEW OF INVESTMENT

18. Perhaps the best approach to explaining investment is to accept that no one single theory can completely explain why businessmen invest in certain capital projects and not in others. Using functional notation, we could write a theory of investment which combines the **acceleration principle,** the **cost of borrowing** and the **role of business expectation** as:

$$I_t = f(\Delta Y, r, MEI)$$

where ΔY represents the **change in income,** r is the **rate of interest** and MEI is the **marginal efficiency of investment,** which incorporates the role of **business expectations** as an explanatory variable. Other determinants of investment might include the **relative prices of capital and labour** (which we have already discussed), the **nature of**

technical progress, the adequacy of financial institutions in the supply of investment funds and the impact of government policies and activities upon investment by the private sector.

Figure 17.5: Multiplier-accelerator interaction. Different values of the multiplier and accelerator leads to different growth paths of output in dynamic mathematical models of the economy

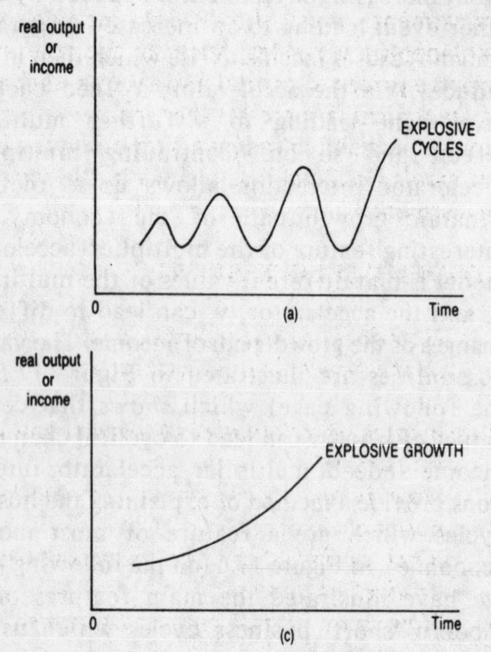

Figure 17.6: The phases of the 'short' business cycle which usually lasts about 4 or 5 years.

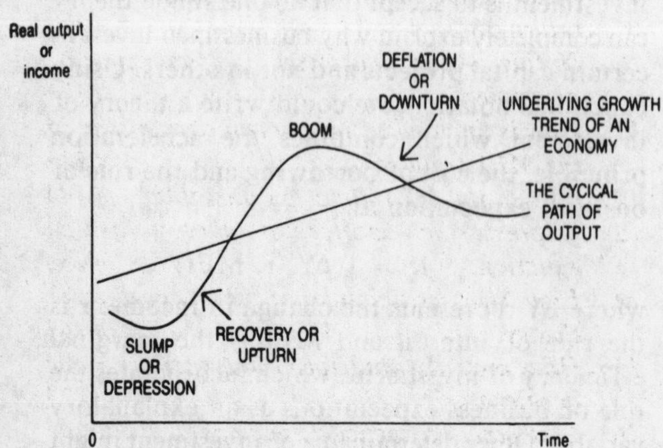

'CROWDING-OUT' AND 'STOP-GO'

19. As we have seen in previous chapters, macro-economic policy during the Keynesian era largely involved the use of a discretionary fiscal policy to manage the level of aggregate demand in the economy. According to monetarists, this resulted in **'stop-go'** - the **'go'** being the period of rapid growth of output induced by an expansion of demand, with the **'stop'** being caused by the subsequent deflation of demand. Monetarists argue that Keynesian economic management had two undesirable effects upon private sector investment. In the first place, 'stop-go' created an uncertain business climate which affected business confidence adversely, discouraging investment. Firms learned from bitter experience that if they began investment projects during periods of growth, the investment might be rendered unprofitable by dampened demand when it came 'on-stream' during the subsequent recession. Monetarists argue that governments should resist the temptation to manage the level of aggregate demand. Instead the correct aim of government should be to provide stable medium-term policies in order to create a steady and profitable business climate in which firms adopt a long 'time horizon' and are encouraged to invest in capital projects which take several years to mature and deliver their income. Secondly, monetarists believe that the general level of government expenditure in the Keynesian era deterred private sector investment through the **'crowding-out' process**. You should refer back to sections 19 to 21 of Chapter 16 for a discussion of whether government spending 'crowds-out', or 'crowds-in' and stimulates, investment by the private sector.

SUMMARY

20. A firm's demand for new capital equipment (or investment) is different from its demand for most types of labour, because it must consider the future productivity or yield of the investment over the life of the capital asset, rather than just the current productivity. To decide whether an investment is worthwhile, a businessman can use the discounting principle to discount the investment's expected future income stream. This gives rise to the Discounted Cash Flow technique of investment appraisal. An important macro-economic theory of investment, the marginal efficiency of investment (MEI) theory, has its origins in the micro-economic theory of how an individual firm uses the discounting principle to make investment decisions. In the MEI theory, we calculate each potential investment's internal rate of return (IRR), the rate of discount which measures the capital asset's expected future productivity. By ranking each potential project's IRR in descending order, the Keynesian investment function, the MEI schedule is obtained. In the MEI theory, the expected return on investment - itself heavily dependent on the state of business confidence - and the cost of borrowing or rate of interest are the main determinants of investment. However, the MEI theory does not pretend to be a complete or wide-ranging theory of aggregate investment. Another influential macro-economic theory of investment is provided by the acceleration principle, which stems from the assumption that firms wish to maintain a fixed capital output ratio. The MEI theory and the accelerator theory both suggest that firms' demand for new capital goods is likely to be more volatile or unstable than the demand for consumer goods and output in general. Although the accelerator theory is heavily dependent on some rather over-simple assumptions, the acceleration principle has been used frequently by economists for forecasting purposes and for the construction of dynamic macro-models of the economy, such as the multiplier-accelerator model of business cycles. A universal or more complete theory of investment must however, include other explanatory variables, such as the role of the relative prices of capital and labour, the nature of technical progress, the influence of the government and the adequacy or otherwise of the country's financial institutions in the supply of investment funds.

STUDENT SELF-TESTING

1 *How does (a) an economist and (b) the 'man in the street' define investment?* (2)
2 *What is the relationship between capital and investment?* (3)
3 *How is investment measured in the UK national accounts?* (4)
4 *What is meant by the marginal revenue product of capital?* (6)
5 *How may a rise in wage rates affect investment?* (7)
6 *Why does a firm's demand for fixed capital differ from its demand for labour?* (8)
7 *Distinguish between an interest rate and a discount rate.* (9)
8 *State the Discounted Cash Flow formula.* (10)
9 *What is an investment's internal rate of return?* (11)
10 *Define the marginal efficiency of investment.* (12)
11 *How is the level of investment determined in the MEI theory?* (13)
12 *Why is the MEI function unstable?* (14)
13 *Express the accelerator theory as an equation.* (15)
14 *List two criticisms of the accelerator theory.* (16)
15 *How may the multiplier interact with the accelerator?* (17)
16 *List other influences upon investment.* (18)
17 *What is meant by 'crowding-out'?* (19)

EXERCISES

1 *At the beginning of 1987, a firm possessed 50 machines, which it purchased at a rate of 10 per year during the previous 5 years. Each machine which lasts 5 years and then needs replacing, produces 25 units of output per year. Demand for the firm's output is:*

Year	*Demand*
1986	*1250*
1987	*1500*
1988	*2500*
1989	*3000*
1990	*3000*
1991	*2500*

(a) *Calculate:*
(i) each firm's net investment in each year between 1987–1991;

(ii) each firm's gross investment in each year between 1987–1991.

(b) *Comment on the changes in investment over the period.*

(c) *What theory of investment does the example illustrate?*

2

Year	*Number of units demanded*	*Number of machines purchased*
1	*1800*	*60*
2	*3600*	*60*
3	*5400*	*60*
4	*5580*	*66*
5	*5940*	*72*
6	*5940*	*?*

The table shows how the level of gross investment undertaken by a small engineering firm beginning production in year 1 is determined by the level of demand. Machines must be replaced after 3 years. How many machines will be purchased in year 6?
A *30*
B *60*
C *66*
D *72*

3 *What do economists mean by 'fixed capital'?*
A *Stocks or inventories of raw materials*
B *The corporate bonds secured on a company's fixed assets*
C *The plant machines and energy used in production*
D *Factory and office buildings and equipment used in the production process.*

4 *If capital consumption is greater than gross investment:*
A *Gross investment must be negative*
B *Gross investment must be declining*
C *Net investment is negative*
D *Replacement investment is rising*

5 *A businessman calculates that an investment project will earn an internal rate of return of 8 per cent. The cost of borrowing is 6 per cent, so he decides the investment is worthwhile.*

This is the basis of the:
A *Accelerator principle*
B *Marginal propensity to invest*
C *Marginal efficiency of investment theory*
D *Multiplier principle*

MUTLIPLE CHOICE QUESTIONS

1 *The cash flows shown in the table below are generated by four investment projects (A, B, C or D) available to a firm. Given that any income generated by an investment can be reinvested at the current interest rate, which is the most profitable investment project for the firm?*

CASH FLOWS £

	Project:			
	A	*B*	*C*	*D*
Year 1	*0*	*40*	*10*	*160*
Year 2	*0*	*40*	*40*	*30*
Year 3	*10*	*40*	*100*	*10*
Year 4	*30*	*40*	*40*	*0*
Year 5	*160*	*40*	*10*	*0*

EXAMINATION QUESTIONS

1 (a) *How important is the rate of interest as a determinant of the level of investment by firms?*

(b) *What effects will increased investment have on the general level of economic activity?*

(ACCA June 1982)

2 *Distinguish between the 'multiplier' and the 'accelerator'. How do they interact in the determination of national income?*

(ACCA June 1979)

3 *Explain why the volume of aggregate capital investment in the private sector of the economy fluctuates more than the volume of aggregate private consumption.*

(ACCA June 1977)

4 (a) *What are business cycles?*

(8 marks)

(b) *Why do business cycles take place?*

(12 marks)

(ACCA December 1987)

5. *What is the accelerator principle? Why is it relevant to investment decisions.*

(ICSA December 1984)

6. *What, according to the Keynesian analysis, are the determinants of investment?*

(CIMA May 1988)

18. Taxation, government spending and fiscal policy

INTRODUCTION

1. This chapter investigates the three elements of **public finance**:

(i) **government spending;**

(ii) **taxation and the other** sources of **revenue** which finance public spending; and

(iii) the resulting **budget deficit** or **surplus** which occurs whenever government expenditure does not exactly equal revenue.

We start the chapter with an introductory survey of these public finance aggregates before examining their role in the government's **fiscal policy**. We then explain how fiscal policy has changed in the United Kingdom in recent years as Keynesianism has given way to monetarism and to 'supply-side' economics. After discussing the economic implications of budget deficits and surpluses, the chapter concludes by relating the **borrowing requirement** through which a deficit is financed to the **national debt,** which is the stock of past borrowing or accumulated debt that the government still owes.

PUBLIC EXPENDITURE

2. The public sector of the United Kingdom economy can be divided into three parts: **central government; local government;** and **nationalised industries**. However, the measurement of public expenditure is usually restricted largely to spending by central and local government, though in the UK spending on net investment in new capital by nationalised industries is also included. Most of the spending by nationalised industries is excluded from the definition of public spending on the grounds that it is financed by revenue raised from the sale of the industries' output and is not dependent on finance from the taxpayer. Spending by central and local government taken together is known as **general government expenditure**. Table 18.1 shows the totals of general government expenditure in the United Kingdom for each year since 1982, together with the planned totals until 1991 announced in the government's 1988 White Paper on Public Expenditure.

Perhaps more significant than the absolute totals of public expenditure, is the ratio of public expenditure to national income or output, which indicates the share of the nation's resources taken by the government. Figure 18.1 (on the following page) shows how general government expenditure has changed as a ratio of gross domestic product in the UK over a period of nearly ninety years.

Apart from the periods from 1914 to 1918 and from 1939 to 1945 which saw very rapid, but temporary, increases in government spending to pay for the First and Second World Wars, the twentieth century has witnessed a steady but relatively slow increase in government expenditure from around 10 per cent to over 40 per cent of GDP, reaching 46.75 per cent in 1982-83. Indeed, the ratio continued to rise in the early 1980s, despite the election in 1979 of a monetarist Conservative Government committed to reducing the share of both public spending and taxation in national output. One explanation of this apparent paradox lies in the role of **unemployment pay and welfare benefits** as **automatic stabilisers** - a role which we explained in Chapter 16. When the Conservative Government cut public spending on goods and services such as hospitals and schools, the immediate effect was to deflate the economy (via the *multiplier process*), reducing output and unemployment. But as real incomes fell and unemployment increased, demand-led public spending on transfer incomes to the poor and the unemployed also increased. This in turn then led to public expenditure rising as a proportion of GDP (and also the taxation required to finance it), although this was, of course, the complete opposite of the Conservative Government's intentions. More recently, UK national output has recovered strongly from the depths of the recession experienced in the early 1980s, a recession which was partly caused by the public spending cuts we have just described. Growing national output has allowed the Government to plan for real increases in public expenditure on goods and services, while at the same time

Table 18.1 General government spending totals in the UK 1982–1991 £m (real terms at 1986–87 prices)

	What happened					*Estimate*	*What is planned*		
	1982/83	1983/84	1984/85	1985/86	1986/87	1987/88	1988/89	1989/90	1990/91
General Government Expenditure	158,044	159,826	164,044	162,983	164,839	165,000	168,000	171,300	174,000

Source: 1988 White Paper on Public Expenditure

Figure 18.1: Expenditure by central and local government (General Government Expenditure) in the UK, as a percentage of gross domestic product (GDP) 1890–1986

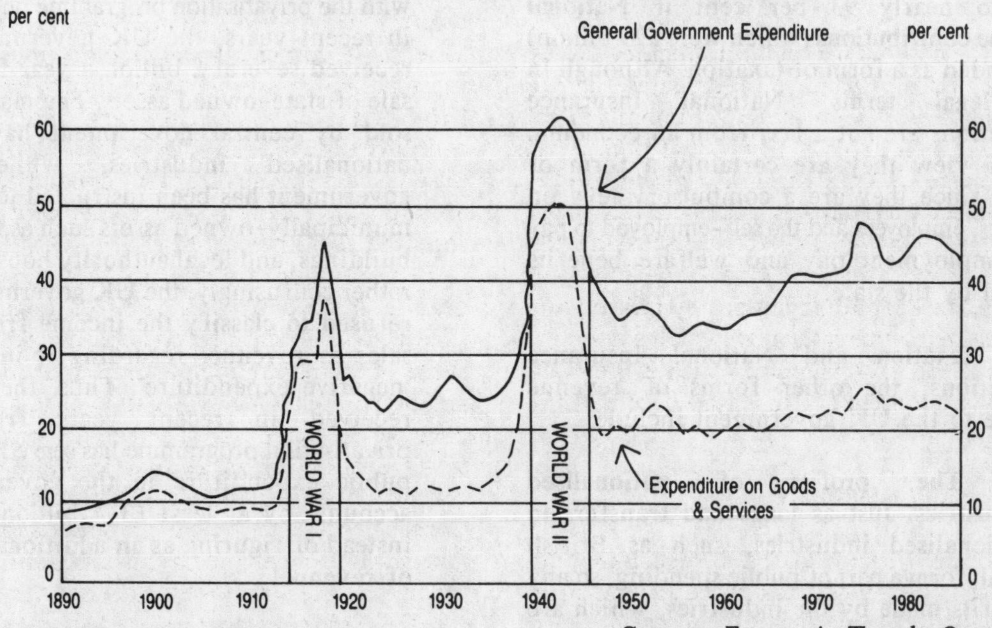

Source: Economic Trends October 1987

reducing public spending's share of national output back towards, and perhaps below, 40 per cent. At the time of the publication of the 1989 Public Spending White Paper, it was expected that economic growth would cause public spending to fall from 39.75 per cent of national output to 38.75 per cent in 1991–92, the lowest share since 1966–67.

The ratio of total government expenditure to GDP is an accurate measure of the share of the nation's total financial resources under the command of the government, but because a large part of government expenditure is upon transfers – such as the unemployment pay and welfare benefits we have just described – it is a misleading indicator of the share of national output produced by government itself. Transfers do not involve a claim by the government on national output, or a diversion of resources by the government away from the private sector. Rather government expenditure on transfers merely redistributes income and spending power from one part of the private sector to another – from taxpayers to recipients of state benefits and pensions. When transfers are excluded, then – as Figure 18.1 shows – government spending falls from over 40 per cent of GDP to between only 20 and 30 per cent. This figure is a more accurate measure of the share of national output directly commanded by the state - and thus unavailable for use in the private sector - to produce the hospitals, roads and other goods and services which government collectively provides and finances for the most part out of taxation.

SOURCES OF REVENUE

3. **Taxation** is of course the principal source of government revenue in almost all types of economy. In the financial year 1987-88, the total receipts from taxation collected by central and local government in the UK amounted to £132 billion, out of a total government revenue of £174 billion. Thus taxation accounted for approximately 76 per cent of total revenue, rising to nearly 93 per cent if **National Insurance contributions** (which were £29 billion) are included as a form of taxation. Although in strict legal terms, National Insurance contributions are not a tax, from an economic point of view they are certainly a form of taxation since they are a compulsory levy on employers, employees and the self-employed to pay for unemployment pay and welfare benefits provided by the state.

Besides taxation and National Insurance contributions, the other forms of revenue available to the UK government include:

(i) **The profits of nationalised industries.** Just as loans and transfers to nationalised industries, such as British Coal, form a part of public spending, so any profits made by the industries, which are called **trading surpluses** are paid to the state which owns the industries. During the 1980s, the more profitable nationalised industries in the United Kingdom were *de-nationalised* or *privatised*, so the revenue available from nationalised industries' trading surpluses became much smaller. The industries which remain in the nationalised sector are generally either less profitable or loss-making and thus a drain on public funds rather than a source of government revenue.

(ii) **Interest and dividend income.** The UK government receives interest on loans granted to individuals, firms and nationalised industries within the domestic economy and also on international loans to foreign governments. Dividend income paid on state-owned shareholdings in private enterprise companies is another source of income. The government still holds up to 49 per cent of the share capital of many of the previously nationalised industries which have been privatised. In recent years dividends on these shareholdings have become a significant source of revenue, though it is the government's long-run intention to reduce this source of income by selling off all state-owned shares to the private sector.

(iii) **Income from the sale of state-owned assets.** Before the 1980s income from the sale of assets was an insignificant source of government revenue in the UK. However, with the privatisation programme undertaken in recent years, the UK government has received several £ billion a year from the sale of state-owned assets. The main assets sold by central government have been nationalised industries, while local government has been instructed to sell off municipally-owned assets such as land and buildings, and local authority housing. But rather confusingly, the UK government has refused to classify the income from asset sales as revenue, regarding it instead as 'negative expenditure'. Thus, the income received in recent years from the privatisation programme has served to lower public expenditure in the government's accounts by at least £3-4 billion a year, instead of figuring as an additional source of revenue!

(iv) **Income from the sale of government services.** In the UK, central government receives a small amount of revenue from the sale of services, provided for example by Her Majesty's Stationery Office (HMSO), which sells government publications such as the National Income Blue Book and government white papers. In a similar way, local government raises revenue by charging for admission to public swimming baths and leisure centres and by operating municipal bus services. Quite clearly, a 'trade-off' exists between *selling assets* and *selling services* produced by the assets. Asset sales, such as those undertaken in the privatisation programme, represent a 'once-and-for-all' source of revenue, since once sold to the private sector an asset is no longer available as a source of government income. In recent years, the Conservative Government in the UK has generally preferred to sell assets rather than the services provided by the assets, though it has certainly explored ways of raising revenue by marketing and selling services which were previously financed completely out of taxation and provided 'free' to the user. Thus public hospitals operated by the National Health Service have been encouraged to generate revenue by charging a price for some services they provide, eg by accepting more private patients and by allowing private hospitals to use their specialised services for a fee. Eventually, public hospitals may charge prices for the meals and other 'hotel services' at present provided free to patients.

(v) **Rents**. Central government raises a small amount of revenue by leasing government-owned buildings and land to the private sector. Health authorities are now encouraged to raise money by leasing out sites within public hospitals to commercial activities like banks and insurance companies. Local government within the UK receives a substantial source of income from council house rents.

BUDGET DEFICITS, SURPLUSES AND BALANCED BUDGETS

4. A **budget deficit** occurs whenever government spending exceeds revenue from taxation and from the other sources which we listed in the previous section. Conversely, a **budget surplus** results when government revenue exceeds expenditure. A third possibility is a balanced budget. Using the symbols G for government spending and T for taxation and other sources of revenue, the three possibilities are:

$G = T$: balanced budget
$G > T$: budget deficit
$G < T$: budget surplus

We can measure the budget deficit (or surplus) for *central government alone*, or for *central and local government taken together*, in which case it is known as the **general government budget deficit (or surplus).**

Before the Keynesian revolution of the 1930s, British governments usually aimed for the *'sound finance'* or *'financial orthodoxy'* of a balanced budget, believing budget deficits to be morally bad and destructive of confidence. Nevertheless, involuntary but usually small budget deficits did occur which had to be financed by borrowing. However, as we have seen in Chapters 13, 14 and 15, deliberate **deficit financing** became an integral part of government macro-economic policy in general, and fiscal policy in particular, during the Keynesian decades of the 1950s, 1960s and 1970s. In these years, Keynesian-inspired governments deliberately used the budget deficit to inject spending power or demand into the economy to achieve full employment and to stabilise the business cycle. But in recent years under monetarism and 'New Classical' thinking, deliberate deficit financing has once again been rejected and there has been a return to the belief in the virtues of the *fiscal neutrality* of a balanced budget.

THE PUBLIC SECTOR BORROWING REQUIREMENT

5. It is important not to confuse the *elimination* of a budget deficit with the *financing* of a deficit. A budget deficit can be eliminated by cutting public spending or by raising taxation, both of which can balance the budget or move it into surplus. But assuming the deficit persists, it must be financed by borrowing. The borrowing which finances the central government budget deficit is known as the **central government borrowing requirement (CGBR).** But central government is only one part of the public sector, which also includes local government and nationalised industries. The PSBR is thus made up of three components: the **borrowing of central government (CGBR), local authorities (LABR)**, which together form the **general government borrowing requirement (GGBR)**, and **public corporations (PCBR)** or:

$$PSBR \equiv CGBR + LABR + PCBR$$

The PSBR (or strictly the CGBR) is thus 'the other side of the coin' to the budget deficit. Whenever there is a budget deficit there will be a *positive* borrowing requirement. By contrast, a budget surplus means that the government can use the excess of revenue over expenditure to repay previous borrowing. In this situation, the **Public Sector Debt Repayment (PSDR)**, which is associated with a *negative* borrowing requirement, is perhaps a more appropriate measure of the government's net borrowing position than the PSBR.

RECENT CHANGES IN THE UK PSBR

6. During most of the years of Keynesian deficit financing, the PSBR was positive and growing both in absolute terms and as a percentage of national output or GDP. By contrast, in recent years under monetarism, the PSBR has fallen from nearly £10 billion in 1979/80 (or approximately 5.25 per cent of GDP) to £3.4 billion in 1986/87 (0.75 per cent of GDP). Indeed in 1987/88 buoyant tax revenues and the proceeds of privatisations caused the budget to move into surplus, with the PSBR becoming negative at £3.5 billion. In his budget speech in March 1988, the Chancellor of the Exchequer, Mr Nigel Lawson, announced a planned budget surplus in 1988/89, after which he thought a balanced budget would become the norm, providing of course, that policies of 'sound finance' and fiscal neutrality continue to be pursued. However in the outcome, the budget surplus (and PSDR) in 1988/89 turned out to be larger than planned, the PSDR being £14 billion or 3 per cent of GDP. In his 1989 budget, the Chancellor planned a further budget surplus and national debt repayment of £14 billion for 1989/90 but with the long-term objective of gradual return to a balanced budget.

THE NATIONAL DEBT

7. The **budget deficit** and the **borrowing requirement**, which are examples of economic *flows* (and which are essentially the difference between the two much larger flows of expenditure and revenue), must not be confused with the national debt, which is a *stock* concept. The national debt is a rather misleading term. It is *not* the debt of the whole of the nation, or even of the whole of the public sector and it is largely unrelated to the balance of payments deficit with which it is sometimes confused. Rather, the national debt is simply the *total stock of central government debt* - the borrowing which has accumulated over the years and which the government has not yet paid back. We can trace the origins of the United Kingdom national debt back to 1694 when special privileges were granted to the Bank of England in return for lending to the state. Over the next three centuries, the national debt steadily increased, rising each year by the size of the current budget deficit or CGBR. The fastest growth occurred during wartime - particularly during the First and Second World Wars - but in more recent times rapid growth also occurred during the three decades of Keynesian deficit financing from the 1950s to the 1970s. But whereas a budget deficit and a positive CGBR increase the size of the national debt, a budget surplus and the accompanying negative CGBR allow debt repayment to take place, resulting therefore in a reduction in the stock of accumulated national debt. In March 1987, after many years of budget deficits, the United Kingdom national debt reached a peak at £185,751 million, having risen from £142,909 million in 1984. A small fall in the national debt was then achieved in 1987/8 - the budget surplus of approximately £3.5 billion allowing the government to pay off part of the maturing debt. The much larger budget surplus achieved since 1987/8 has allowed more of the national debt to be repayed.

TYPES OF TAXATION

8. A tax, which is a compulsory levy charged by government or by a public authority to pay for its expenditure, can be classified in a number of ways:

(i) **According to who levies the tax**. In the UK most taxes (89.5 per cent in 1986) are levied by central government, with local government taxation - currently the local rate - accounting in 1986 for the remaining 10.5 per cent of taxation levied by government. In addition, non-governmental public authorities such as water authorities levy a water rate to finance the services they provide to households.

(ii) **According to what is taxed**. Figure 18.2 on the next page illustrates the relative importance in the UK in 1988/9 of the three main categories of **taxation on income, expenditure and capital**, as a proportion of all sources of general government revenue. Taxes on income were expected to raise 32 per cent of total revenue, with this figure rising to 49 per cent if national insurance and other social security contributions are included. Taxes on expenditure (including the local rate) were expected to raise a further 34 per cent of government revenue, but capital taxes are insignificant, raising only 3 per cent of revenue in the UK.

Personal income tax is the most important tax on income in the UK, though **corporation tax** (a tax on company income or profits) and **employees' National Insurance contributions (NIC)** are other examples. The Inland Revenue is the department of the civil service responsible for collecting taxes on income and capital (though NIC are collected by the Department of Health and Social Security), while the Board of Customs and Excise collects taxes on expenditure levied by central government. Expenditure taxes can usefully be divided into **ad valorem** or **percentage** taxes such as **value-added tax (VAT)** and **specific taxes (unit** or **'lump sum' taxes)** which include the **excise duties on alcohol, tobacco and petrol**. A specific tax such as motor vehicle tax is levied on each car on the road regardless of its price or value. A Rolls Royce thus bears the same motor vehicle tax as a mini. In Figure 18.2, the main tax levied by local government in the UK, the **local rate**, has been classified as an expenditure tax. The local rate can also be classified as a capital tax, since it is levied on the capital value of property. However, the local rate on residential property, but not the business rate - is due to disappear around 1990, being replaced by a **community charge** or **poll tax** levied on each adult resident in a local authority area. A poll tax, which is a tax 'on being a human being', was last levied in the UK in the 14th century, causing social unrest and a peasants revolt which led to the hasty withdrawal of the tax. It remains to be seen whether the new poll tax will have similar consequences.

(iii) **Direct and indirect taxation.** These concepts are often used interchangeably with taxes on income and expenditure, though it is not strictly true that a tax on spending *must* be an indirect tax. Income tax is a direct tax because the person who receives and benefits from the income is liable to pay the tax. By contrast, most taxes on spending are indirect taxes since the seller of the good, and not the purchaser who benefits from its consumption, is liable to pay the tax. Nevertheless, the purchaser indirectly pays some or all of the tax when the seller passes on the **incidence of the tax** through a price rise.

Figure 15.2: The relative importance of taxes upon income, expenditure and capital, and social security contributions in general government revenue in the United Kingdom, 1988/89

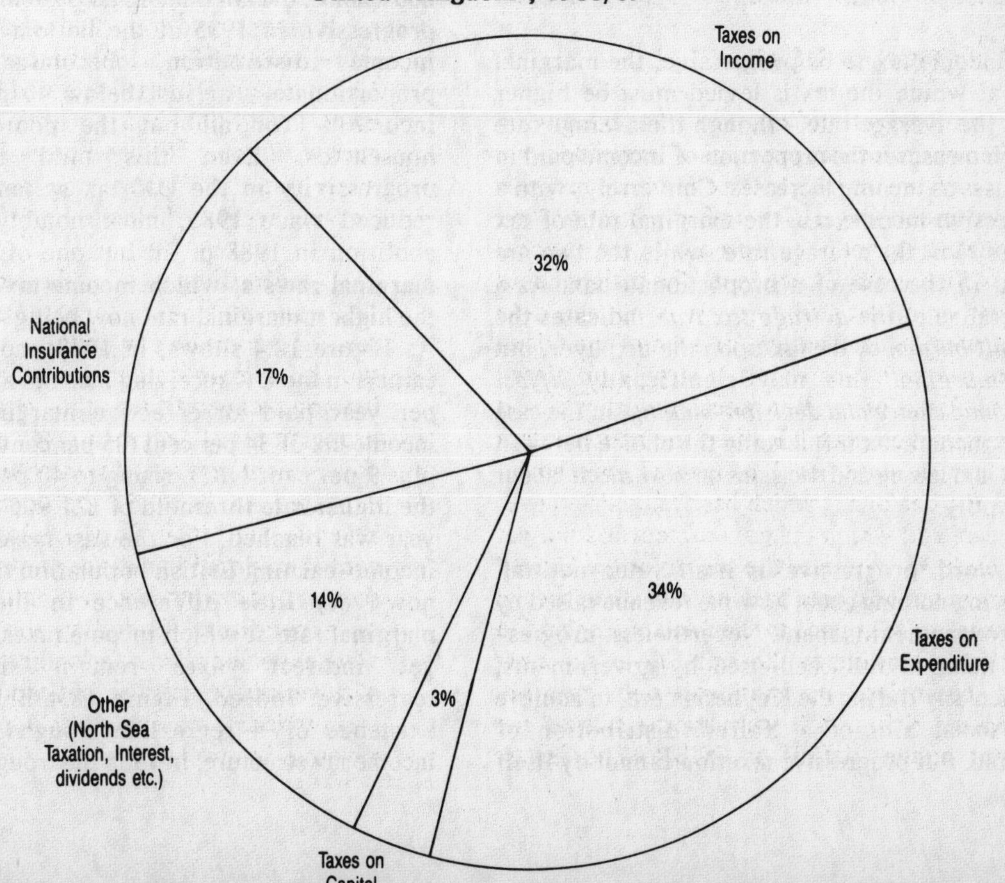

PROGRESSIVE, REGRESSIVE AND PROPORTIONATE TAXATION

9. In a **progressive tax system** the proportion of a person's income paid in tax increases as income rises, while in a **regressive tax system**, the proportion paid in tax falls. A tax is **proportionate** if exactly the same proportion of income is paid in tax at all levels of income.

Progressivity can be defined for a single tax or for the tax system as a whole. For single taxes such as income tax or inheritance tax, we can identify whether the tax is progressive, regressive or proportionate by examining the relationship between the **average rate** at which the tax is levied and the **marginal rate**.

The average rate of tax

$$\equiv \frac{\text{total tax paid}}{\text{total income}}$$

$$\text{or ART} \equiv \frac{T}{Y}$$

whereas, the marginal rate of tax

$$\equiv \frac{\Delta \text{ change in tax paid}}{\Delta \text{ change in income}}$$

$$\text{or MRT} \equiv \frac{\Delta T}{\Delta Y}$$

For income tax to be progressive, the marginal rate at which the tax is levied must be higher than the average rate - though the average rate which measures the proportion of income paid in tax rises as income increases. Conversely, with a regressive income tax, the marginal rate of tax is less than the average rate, while the two are equal in the case of a proportionate tax. As a general rule, the *average tax rate* indicates the *overall burden* of the tax upon the taxpayer, but the *marginal rate* may significantly *affect economic choice and decision-making*, in the case of an income tax influencing the choice between work and leisure and decisions on how much labour to supply.

The word 'progressive' is itself value-neutral, implying nothing about how the revenue raised by the government is spent. Nevertheless, progressive taxation has been used by governments, particularly during the Keynesian era, to achieve the social aim of a 'fairer' distribution of income. But progressive taxation cannot by itself redistribute income - a policy of transfers in the government's public expenditure programme is required for this. Progressive taxation used on its own merely reduces post-tax income differentials compared to pre-tax differentials.

HOW PROGRESSIVE IS THE UK TAX SYSTEM?

10. It is often assumed that the UK tax system is very progressive, being used by governments to reduce inequalities in income and wealth. In fact, wealth taxation (or capital taxation) is almost non-existent in the UK, so inequalities in the distribution of wealth have hardly been affected by the tax system. Figure 18.3 (see following page) shows that in 1985 direct taxes in the UK, which for the most part are income taxes, were progressive - though we should note that social security contributions (National Insurance contributions) are not included in Figure 18.3

The progressivity of UK income taxes is considerably reduced when National Insurance contributions are included, because NIC become significantly regressive on higher incomes above about £300 a week. And because indirect taxes - mostly expenditure taxes - are regressive, taking a declining proportion of the income of rich households, overall the UK tax system was mildly progressive in 1985 at the bottom end of the income distribution, becoming roughly proportionate - at just below 40 per cent of income - for all but the poorest British households. Even this mild degree of progressivity in the UK tax system has been reduced since 1985, most notably with the abolition in 1988 of all but one of the higher marginal rates at which income tax is levied - the highest marginal rate now being 40 per cent. As Figure 18.4 shows, in 1988, most income-earners in the UK receiving incomes above £5,460 per year paid an effective marginal rate of income tax of 34 per cent (25 per cent income tax plus 9 per cent NIC), rising to 40 per cent once the higher rate threshold of £21,905 income per year was reached. For the vast majority of the income-earning British population there is thus now very little difference in the effective marginal rate at which income taxes are levied, yet indirect taxes remain significantly regressive. Indeed, Figure 18.4 illustrates the existence of a regressive trough within the income tax structure. In 1988 the trough extended between incomes of £15,860 at which 9 per cent NIC ceased to be paid on any extra income, and £21,905 at which the higher 40 per cent rate of income tax was levied. Within the trough, the effective marginal rate of taxation fell from 34 per cent to 25 per cent.

Figure 18.3: Indirect and direct taxation as a per cent of gross household income for quintile groups of households in the UK, 1985

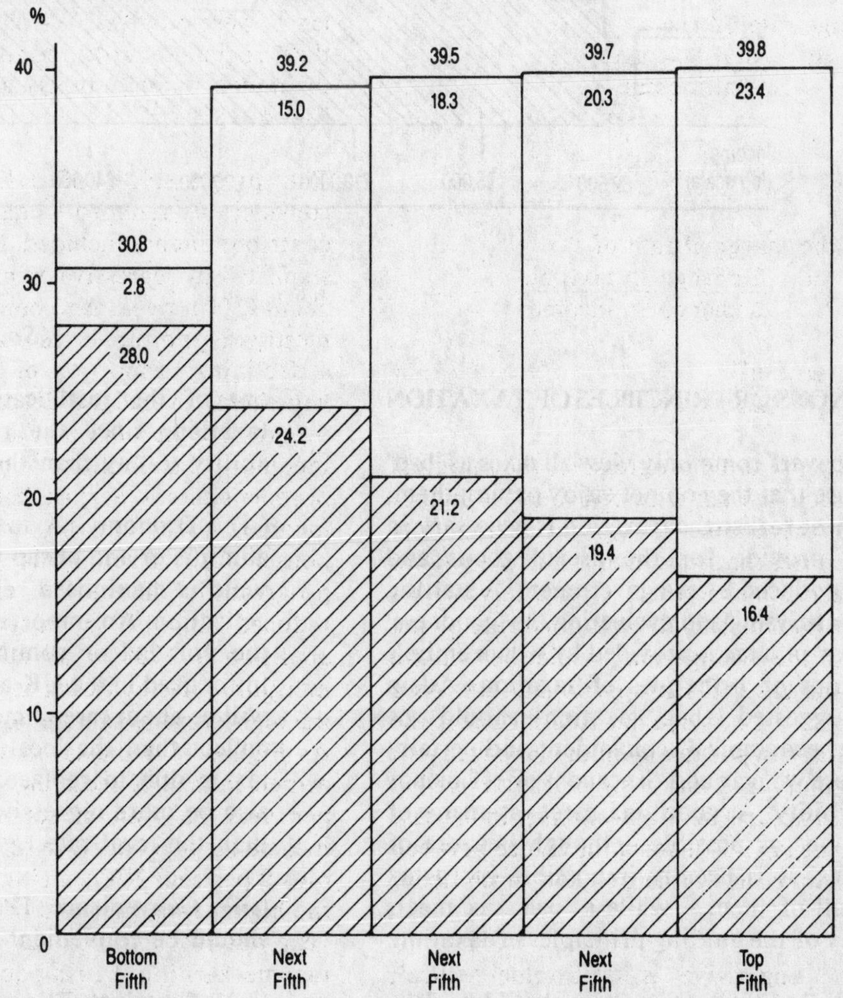

Source: Economic Trends July 1987

Figure 18.4: The effective marginal rate of taxes upon personal income at different levels of income in the UK in 1988

Tax rates for a single person on each extra £ of earnings (income tax plus NICs)

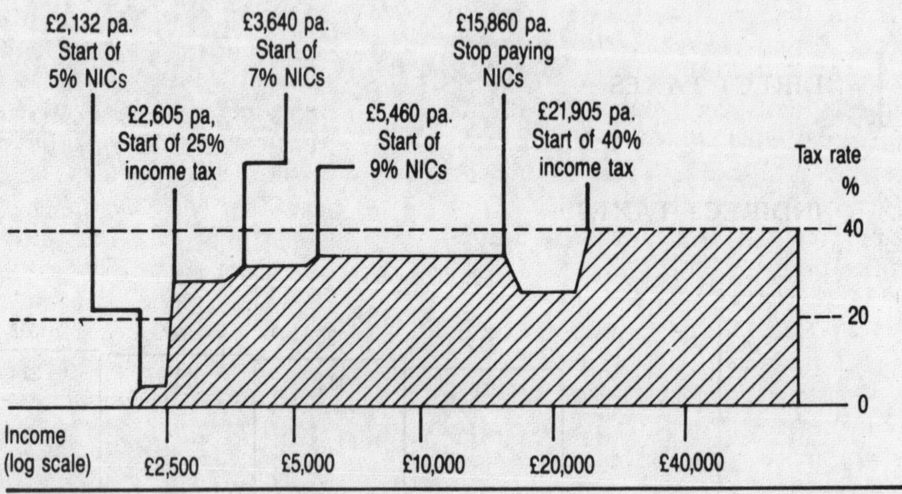

(Source: The Guardian)

THE CANONS OR PRINCIPLES OF TAXATION

11. Taxpayers commonly view all taxes as 'bad' in the sense that they do not enjoy paying them, though most realise that taxation is necessary in order to provide for the useful goods and services produced by the government. A starting point for analysing and evaluating the 'goodness' or 'badness' of a tax is provided by Adam Smith's four **canons** or **principles of taxation**. Adam Smith suggested that taxation should be **equitable, economical, convenient and certain,** and to these we may add the canons of **efficiency** and **flexibility**. A 'good' tax meets as many of these canons as possible - though because of 'trade-offs' it is usually impossible for a tax to meet all of them - while a 'bad' tax meets few if any of the guiding principles of taxation.

(i) **Equity.** A tax system should be fair, though of course there may be different and possibly conflicting interpretations of what is fair or equitable. Specifically, a particular tax should be based on the taxpayer's **ability to pay**. This principle is one of the justifications of progressive taxation, since the rich have a greater ability to pay than the poor.

(ii) **Economy.** A tax should be easy to administer and cheap to collect so that the yield is maximised relative to the cost of collection. An important argument against the poll tax or community charge to be introduced in the UK around 1990, is that it will be about three times more expensive to collect than the local rate which the poll tax is due to replace. (The poll tax will also be more regressive and less equitable than the local rate.)

(iii) **Convenience.** The method of payment should be convenient to the taxpayer.

(iv) **Certainty.** The taxpayer should know *what, when, where* and *how* to pay, in such a manner that tax evasion is difficult. (**Tax evasion** is the illegal failure to pay a lawful tax, whereas **tax avoidance** involves the arrangement of personal or business affairs within the law to minimise tax liability.)

(v) **Efficiency**. A tax should achieve its intended aim or aims with **minimum undesired distortion or side-effects**. If, for example, the cut in the top marginal rate of taxation in the UK from 60 per cent to 40 per cent, which was designed to increase incentives and in the long run to increase total tax revenue, instead results in the rich choosing to spend more time on leisure activities, the tax change will be inefficient. Since it is almost always impossible to avoid all the undesirable side-effects and distortions resulting from taxation, the tax system should aim to minimise them.

(vi) **Flexibility**. If the tax system is used as a means of economic management then, in order to meet new circumstances, the tax structure and the rates at which individual taxes are levied must be capable of easy alteration.

THE AIMS OF TAXATION AND PUBLIC SPENDING

12. The aims of taxation should not be confused with the *principles* or *canons* of taxation, although an aim is, of course, to arrange the tax system in accordance with the principles of taxation. We shall also see in the next sections of this chapter how the aims of both taxation and public spending depend upon the underlying philosophy and ideology of the government in power - differing significantly for example, between Keynesianism and monetarism. We may divide the aims or objectives of taxation (and of public spending) into three main categories: **allocation; distribution** and **economic management**.

(i) **Allocation**. The allocative function of taxation and public spending relates largely to the goods and services directly provided to final users by the government. The goods and services collectively provided by government and financed partly or completely out of taxation fall into two categories: **public goods** such as defence, police and roads, and **merit goods**, for example education and public health care. Essentially, the government provides public goods and merit goods to *correct the allocative deficiencies of the market mechanism* and you should refer back at this stage to a more detailed coverage of these '*market failures*' and the reason for government provision of public goods and merit goods in Chapter 11. Other examples of market failure include monopoly and externalities. Taxation can be used to deter monopoly by removing the 'windfall gain' accruing to a monopolist as a result of barriers to entry and inelastic supply. It can also be used to discourage and reduce the generation of negative externalities on the principle 'the polluter must pay', while public spending can at the same time subsidise and encourage the provision of external benefits or positive externalities. These are examples of taxation (and public spending) being used to *close divergencies between private and social cost and benefit* and to improve allocative efficiency within the economy - though as we have already noted, taxation itself inevitably introduces new distortions and inefficiencies into the economic system.

(ii) **Distribution**. As we saw in Chapter 12, the price mechanism is completely 'value-neutral' with regard to the equity or social fairness of the distributions of income and wealth that result from the free play of market forces in a market economy. If the government decides that the distribution of income - and possibly also the distribution of wealth - resulting from free market forces is undesirable, it can use taxation and transfers in its public spending programme to modify these distributions and reduce the market failure. Before 1979, British governments of all political complexions used progressive taxation and a policy of transfers of income to the less well-off in a deliberate attempt - albeit with limited success - to reduce inequalities in the distribution of income. They also extended the provision of merit goods such as free state education and health care, in order to improve the 'social wage' of lower-income groups. (The **'social wage'** is the part of a worker's standard of living received as goods and services provided at zero price by the state, being financed collectively out of taxation.) But since 1979, the Conservative Government in the UK has deliberately changed the structure of both taxation and public spending to widen rather than reduce the inequalities in the distributions of income and wealth. The reasons for this important change in policy will be explored later in this chapter, but fundamentally they relate to the conflict between two of the canons of taxation: equity and efficiency. The Conservative Government believes that the pattern of taxation and public spending which is *efficient* in terms of maximising the growth of the country's wealth or economic cake is one in which *greater inequalities* give both rich and poor a greater incentive to work and enterprise. According to the Conservatives, the use of progressive taxation and transfers to the poor in pursuit of a greater social fairness or equity has destroyed the incentive for the better-off to work harder and engage in entrepreneurial risk, while the ease of obtaining welfare benefits and the level at which they are available has created a **'dependency culture'** in which the poor rationally choose unemployment and state benefits in preference to wages and work. The logic of this view is that to make everyone, including the poor, ultimately better off, the poor must first be made worse off! Increased inequalities are necessary to produce the conditions in which a growing 'economic cake' can, in the long run, allow everyone to be better off in absolute terms - thought the poor will still remain relatively worse off compared to the rich.

(iii) **Economic management**. Taxation, public spending and the budget deficit or surplus provide the government with a range of *policy instruments* - known collectively as **fiscal policy instruments** - which the government can use in its overall management of the economy in pursuit of whatever are its economic objectives. In the next sections of this chapter, we shall now turn our attention to fiscal policy, drawing attention to the differences between **Keynesian** and **monetarist fiscal policy**, and between the **macro-economic** and **micro-economic** elements of fiscal policy.

THE MEANING OF FISCAL POLICY

13. **Fiscal policy** is the part of a government's overall economic policy which aims to achieve the government's economic objectives through the use of the **fiscal instruments** of **taxation, public spending** and the **budget deficit or surplus.** As an economic term, fiscal policy is often associated with Keynesian economic theory and policy, largely because Keynes was influential in advocating the abandonment of the 'fiscal neutrality' of 'sound finance' and balanced budgets, and the adoption of an active fiscal policy as the most important single instrument of government economic management. But it is misleading to associate fiscal policy exclusively with Keynesianism. These days, the **Keynesian fiscal policy** based on the *management of aggregate demand* which was implemented in the UK in the three decades before 1979, has been superseded by a very different **'monetarist' fiscal policy**. But before we explain the instruments and the objectives of modern 'supply-side' or monetarist fiscal policy, we shall first survey the essentially *'demand-side'* fiscal policy pursued by Keynesian governments in the years before 1979.

KEYNESIAN FISCAL POLICY

14. During the Keynesian era, fiscal policy took on a meaning more narrow and specific than the rather general definition given at the beginning of the previous section. In the Keynesian era, fiscal policy came to mean the use of the **overall levels of public spending,** taxation and the **budget deficit** to **manage the level of aggregate money demand (AMD)** in the economy, so as to achieve **full employment** and **stabilise the business cycle**. Because we have already explained important aspects of Keynesian fiscal policy in earlier chapters (Chapters 13, 15 and 16) we shall present here only a brief summary. The Keynesian fiscal policy which was implemented with varying degrees of success in the decades before 1979 included the following main elements:

(i) A belief that, left to itself, an unregulated market economy results in unnecessarily low economic growth, high unemployment and volatile business cycles.

(ii) Because of a lack of aggregate money demand - illustrated by a **deflationary gap** diagram and caused by a tendency for the private sector to save too much and invest too little - the economy can settle into an **'under-full employment equilibrium'** characterised by **demand-deficient unemployment.**

(iii) But by deliberate **deficit financing**, the government can - through using fiscal policy as a demand management instrument - inject demand and spending power into the economy to eliminate deficient demand and achieve full employment.

(iv) Once having achieved full employment, the government can then use fiscal policy in a discretionary way (ie changing tax rates and levels of public spending to meet new circumstances) to **'fine-tune'** the level of **aggregate demand**. For much of the Keynesian era, the Keynesians believed that fiscal policy could achieve full employment and stabilise the business cycle, while avoiding an unacceptable increase in the rate of inflation.

(v) During the Keynesian era, the overall 'stance' of fiscal policy - and indeed of economic policy in general - was orientated towards the **'demand-side'** of the economy. The more **'micro-economic elements of fiscal policy'**, such as transfers to industry in the government's regional policy, were of course aimed at improving economic performance on the **'supply-side'** of the economy, but on the whole 'micro-economic' or 'supply-side' fiscal policy was treated as subordinate to the macro-economic management of aggregate demand and to the assumption that output would respond to demand stimulation. The Keynesians did not use fiscal policy in the 'supply-side' manner we shall shortly describe. The 'supply-side' elements of Keynesian fiscal policy were generally interventionist, extending rather than reducing the state's role in the market economy.

MONETARIST FISCAL POLICY

15. Whereas in the Keynesian era fiscal policy played a central role in the UK in the creation of a mixed economy based on the political consensus that the British economy should contain a mix of market and non-market economic activity and public and private ownership, the **'monetarist' fiscal policy** pursued in the years since 1979 is completely different. It should be viewed as part of an overall monetarist and 'New Classical' attempt to break up the mixed economy by increasing the role of markets and of private sector economic activity and by reducing the economic role of the state.

The main elements of the fiscal policy implemented by the Conservative Government in the United Kingdom since 1979 have included:

(i) **The rejection of the use of taxation and public spending as discretionary instruments of demand management.** Under monetarist influence, the Government believes that a policy of stimulating or reflating aggregate demand to achieve growth and full employment is, in the long run, at best ineffective, and at worst damaging. Monetarists argue that any growth of output and employment resulting from an expansionary fiscal policy is essentially short-lived and that in the long term, the main effect is to produce inflation which ultimately destroys the conditions necessary for satisfactory market performance and 'wealth creation'.

(ii) The **adoption of a medium-term policy 'rule'** (in place of short-term discretionary fiscal changes) **to reduce public spending, taxation and government borrowing as proportions of national output**. Besides wishing to reduce what they see as the inflationary effects of 'big government spending', the monetarists believe that the increased high levels of government spending, taxation and borrowing of the Keynesian era led to the **'crowding-out'** of the private sector. As we have already explained in Chapter 16, **'resource crowding-out'** might occur if the government uses productive resources in its public spending programme which could otherwise be employed in private sector production. **'Financial crowding-out'** relates to how public spending is financed through borrowing - an increased PSBR causing interest rates to rise, which increases the cost of investment finance for the private sector. The 'extreme' version of the 'crowding-out' theory assumes that resources which would otherwise be employed productively in 'wealth creation' in the private sector are instead diverted, by Keynesian fiscal policy, into 'unproductive' or 'wealth-consuming' public sector use. This then increases the tax burden imposed on the market sector of the economy, which in turn serves to reduce the efficiency of businesses and their competitiveness in markets exposed to international competition.

(iii) The **subordination of the 'macro-economic' elements of fiscal policy** which were dominant during the Keynesian era **to a more 'micro-economic' fiscal policy** combining an overall reduction in the levels of taxation and public spending with the creation of incentives aimed at improving economic performance on the **'supply-side'** of the economy.

(iv) As well as being subordinated to a more 'micro-economic' and 'supply-side' orientated fiscal policy, the **macro-economic elements of fiscal policy** have also been **subordinated under monetarism to the needs of monetary policy.** Fundamental to monetarism is the belief that the levels of public spending and the PSBR must be used as a policy instrument to achieve control over growth of the money supply. Control over public spending and the PSBR is regarded by monetarists as a pre-condition for successful control of the money supply.

THE MONETARY EFFECTS OF THE PSBR

16. In the Keynesian era, economists often ignored any possible **monetary side-effects** caused by an expansionary fiscal policy. By contrast, monetarists reject the use of fiscal policy to manage the level of aggregate demand and they subordinate fiscal policy to the needs of monetary policy precisely because they believe the **monetary effects of fiscal expansion** to be harmful. Essentially, the monetary effects of an expansionary fiscal policy result from the **method of financing the budget deficit and the PSBR.** Broadly, there are four possible ways of financing the PSBR, which are shown in the following **PSBR financing identity**:

		New Currency Issue		Borrowing from the Private Sector Banking System		Borrowing from the Non-Bank Private Sector		Borrowing Overseas
PSBR	≡	New Currency Issue	+	Borrowing from the Private Sector Banking System	+	Borrowing from the Non-Bank Private Sector	+	Borrowing Overseas

To finance the PSBR, the government can borrow either from the banking system (including from its own bank the Bank of England, in the case of new currency issue), from private residents (the non-bank general public or private sector), or from overseas. Monetarists believe that each method of borrowing gives rise to harmful and undesirable consequences. If the funds are borrowed from the general public, competition for funds results in the 'financial crowding-out' process we have already described. Overseas borrowing eventually leads to a drain of national resources in interest payments, while borrowing from the banking system increases the money supply and (according to monetarists) is inflationary. It is not surprising therefore, that since monetarists believe that each method of financing the PSBR gives rise to undesirable monetary consequences, they consider reduction of the PSBR to be an important objective of fiscal policy.

THE PSBR AND THE MONEY SUPPLY

17. Of the four methods of financing the PSBR, **new currency issue** and **borrowing from the private sector banking system increase the money supply,** but **borrowing overseas** and **from the non-bank private sector** do not - though as we have seen borrowing from the general public can result in undesirable 'crowding-out'. We shall now examine each of these methods of financing the PSBR in greater detail.

(i) **The issue of new currency.** The government can finance the PSBR by borrowing directly from the **central bank,** which in the UK is the **Bank of England.** The government borrows by selling its own securities (gilts) to the Bank of England in return for an increase in the note issue which enters into circulation when spent by the government in its public spending programme. Eventually, a part of the increased note issue in circulation is deposited in the commercial banking system, which then uses the cash to expand deposits lent to customers. In this way the **money supply (cash and bank deposits) increases.**

(ii) **Government borrowing from the Private Sector Banking System.** The same effect will take place if the government finances its increased expenditure by borrowing directly from the commercial banks rather than from its 'own' bank, the Bank of England. The government can borrow from the private sector banking system either by selling

long-dated debt (gilts) to the banks, or **short-dated debt (Treasury bills)**. In either case the money supply expands because bank deposits (which are part of the money supply) are created by the banks and lent to the government - the bank deposits recirculating to the general public when spent by the government. Additionally, Treasury bill sales to the banking system can increase the money supply because like cash they increase the banks' liquidity, allowing further bank lending to the private sector to take place.

(iii) **Borrowing from the non-bank private sector (or general public)**. In contrast to new currency issue and borrowing from the banking system, government spending which is financed by borrowing from the non-bank private sector is generally *neutral* in its effects on the money supply. Bank deposits owned by the general public are simply lent to the government in return for gilts and National Savings Securities, with the result that the government - and not the general public - spend the bank deposits. No new bank deposits are created in this process, so the money supply remains more or less unchanged.

(iv) **Overseas borrowing**. Around 1975 there was a large budget deficit (and PSBR) in the United Kingdom at a time when the balance of payments was also substantially in deficit. In these circumstances, the UK government was able to finance both the **budget deficit** (the **internal deficit**) and the **balance of payments deficit** (the **external deficit**) by borrowing overseas. The effect on the money supply was generally neutral because the government was simply borrowing - and recirculating back into the domestic economy - sterling which had flowed into overseas ownership in payment for goods and services imported by British residents. More recently, the American federal budget deficit and America's external balance of payments deficit have been financed in much the same way, through the sale of US government debt overseas.

'MONETARIST' FISCAL POLICY AND 'SUPPLY-SIDE ECONOMICS'

18. The term **'supply-side economics'** first came into prominence in the USA to describe the economic policies which Ronald Reagan promised in his successful campaign for the American Presidency in 1980. The term was then applied to describe the underlying ideology and the dominant thrust of the policies adopted by other 'free market' orientated governments - including of course, the Conservative administration of Mrs Thatcher in the UK. In terms of basic economic philosophy, supply-side economics is closely linked to the emergence of the 'radical right' and the growth out of a more narrow 'monetarism' of the 'New Classical' economics which we described in Chapter 13. Professor Arthur Laffer, a prominent American 'supply-sider' and adviser to President Reagan has described supply-side economics as *'providing a framework of analysis which relies on personal and private incentives. When incentives change, people's behaviour changes in response. People are attracted towards positive incentives and repelled by the negative. The role of government in such a framework is carried out by the ability of government to alter incentives and thereby, affect society's behaviour*.' The fiscal elements of 'supply-side' economics are essentially micro-economic. They centre on a reduction in the overall levels of taxation and public spending - as the state reduces its role and disengages from the market economy - combined with a deliberate policy of setting tax rates and reducing the availability of welfare benefits so as to create incentives for the supply of labour and entrepreneurship.

THE LAFFER CURVE

19. Supply-side theory depends crucially upon the assumption that the supply curve of labour is 'upward-sloping' and not 'backward-bending', and that increases in income tax create disincentives for the further supply of labour. (You should refer back to Chapter 12 at this stage for an explanation of the supply curve of labour.) Many studies have been made of whether higher taxes do indeed result in less labour being supplied. Some of the studies indicate a slight disincentive effect for certain groups when income tax rates are increased, but others show no discernable relationship. Nevertheless, 'extreme' supply-siders continue to argue that high rates of income tax and the overall burden of income tax

upon taxpayers create disincentives which eventually, as taxation increases, diminish national income and cause total tax revenue to decline. This can be illustrated by a **'Laffer curve'**, which we have drawn in Figure 18.5. The Laffer curve shows the government's total tax revenue as the average tax rate increases from 0 to 100 per cent. Tax revenue is of course zero when the tax rate is 0 per cent, and it is assumed also to be zero at an average tax rate of 100 per cent - there being no incentive to produce output other than for subsistence if any extra output is completely taxed away. In between these limiting rates of 0 and 100 per cent, the Laffer curve shows tax revenue first rising and then falling as the average rate of taxation is increased. Tax revenue reaches its maximum at the highest point on the Laffer curve, after which any further increase in the average tax rate becomes counterproductive as total tax revenue falls.

Various attempts have been made to estimate a Laffer curve for the United Kingdom and for other countries. In 1979, the 'monetarist' London Business School estimated a Laffer curve for the United Kingdom based on a 'composite tax rate' covering income taxes, social security contributions and indirect taxes. The LBS calculated that at a composite tax rate of around 45 per cent the Laffer curve flattens out, and that tax revenue is maximised at a tax rate of around 60 per cent, with any higher tax rate resulting in a rapid fall in overall tax revenue.

Figure 18.5: The Laffer Curve

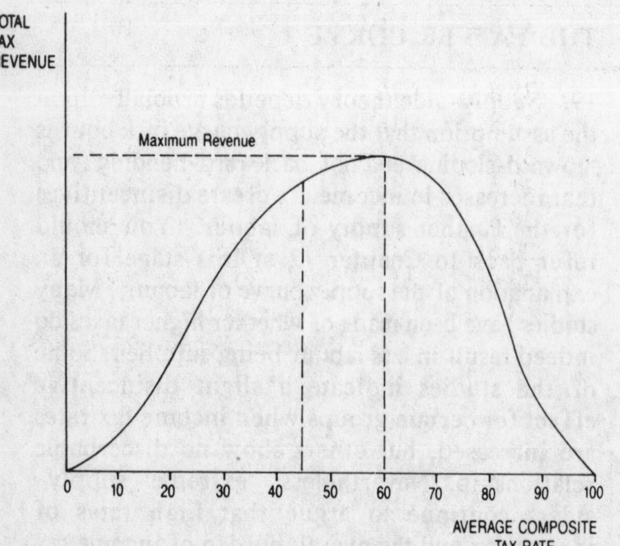

IS BRITAIN OVER-TAXED?

20. But since the average composite rate of taxation in the UK has never been higher than 45 per cent, the LBS estimate of the Laffer curve gives at best only weak support for the view that Britain is 'over-taxed' - in the sense that a further tax rise will reduce total tax revenue. Nevertheless, the Conservative Government has justified cuts in the higher rates of income tax on the grounds that Britain is 'over-taxed' and lower tax rates improve incentives. Whether a country is considered to be over-taxed depends, of course, on the view taken on the correct role of government in the economy. Goods and services provided by the state have to be financed. Economists who believe that the role of government should include the 'free' provision of public goods and merit goods, and the use of transfers financed by taxation to rearrange the distribution of income, inevitably therefore justify a larger burden of taxation than the 'free market' or 'supply-side' economists of a monetarist or 'New Classical' persuasion, who favour the provision of as much as possible through the market and a 'minimalist' role for the state.

Another way of approaching the question of 'over-taxation' is to compare the burden of taxation in the UK with that in similar industrialised economies. It is often assumed that the tax burden is higher in Britain than in other developed countries. But just how highly has the UK economy been taxed compared to other countries and what is the current position?

Table 18.2 shows the share of GNP taken as taxes and social security contributions by the government in seventeen industrialised and developed economies. The figures are for 1975 and 1985 and the countries are ranked in their 1985 positions in the tax 'league table'.

The table shows that taxation has increased as a percentage of national output in all industrial economies and that, compared to the other countries, Britain is neither heavily nor lowly taxed, being in a 'mid-league' position in both 1975 and 1985. Indeed by 1985, the change from Keynesian to monetarist economic policies appeared to have had little impact on Britain's position in the tax league compared to a decade before. It is also worth noting that a country's relative position in the tax 'league table' indicates little about its economic success as measured by current living standards and growth of GNP. Although 'more successful' countries such as Switzerland and Japan are taxed at significantly lower rates than the UK, the more heavily taxed Scandinavian countries have also achieved high living standards and - until recently - better growth rates than the UK.

Tables 18.3, 18.4 and 18.5 show Britain's position in the 'league table' when **direct taxes, indirect taxes and social security contributions** are separated. In terms of **direct taxation upon households**, Table 18.3 is of particular interest, showing Britain again in a 'mid-league' position but with the share of direct taxation in total tax receipts falling from 39 per cent in 1975 to 28 per cent a decade later. This is mirrored in Table 18.4 by the increase in **indirect taxes** from 36 per cent to 41 per cent over the decade, indicating a significant shift in the structure of British taxation away from direct taxation and towards indirect taxation. Compared to similar countries, Britain is now high in the 'league table' of countries relying on indirect taxation, but relatively low in terms of direct taxation. And, as Table 18.5 shows, the United Kingdom is also quite low in the 'league table' depicting the share of total government revenue collected from **social security contributions**. In 1985, only 18 per cent of total revenues were derived from social security contributions, compared to a figure as high as 45 per cent in the Netherlands and 44 per cent in France (where a large part of social security contributions are made by employers rather than by employees).

Table 18.2: Total taxes and social security contributions as a percentage of GNP at factor cost and ranking

	1975	*Ranking*	*1985*	*Ranking*
Denmark	47.8	4	61.2	1
Sweden	49.0	2	58.5	2
Norway	54.2	1	57.9	3
France	42.4	8	52.5	4
Belgium	44.6	6	51.2	5
Austria	45.7	5	50.2	6
Netherlands	48.8	3	49.9	7
German Federal Republic	44.5	7	45.9	8
Italy	30.8	13	44.9	9
United Kingdom	40.0	9	44.1	10
Finland	38.6	10	41.9	11
Greece	27.5	16	37.8	12
Canada	35.8	11	37.2	13
Australia	31.4	12	35.7	14
Switzerland	30.4	14	31.6	15
USA	29.6	15	30.8	16
Japan	24.0	17	30.4	17

Source: Economic Trends

Table 18.3: Percentage of total taxes and social security contributions derived from direct taxes on households

	1975	*Ranking*	*1985*	*Ranking*
Australia	44	2	45	1
Finland	42	3	42	2
Switzerland	42	3	40	3
Sweden	46	1	39	4
USA	34	6	37	5
Canada	34	6	36	6
Belgium	33	8	35	7
Austria	25	12	29	8
UK	39	5	28	9
German Federal Republic	27	11	25	10
Japan	22	13	24	11
Netherlands	28	10	21	12
Norway	29	9	21	12
France	14	14	15	14
Greece	11	15	13	15

Source: Economic Trends

Table 18.4: Percentage of total taxes and social security contributions derived from indirect taxes

	1975	*Ranking*	*1985*	*Ranking*
Greece	57	1	48	1
Australia	43	3	46	2
UK	36	8	41	3
Finland	35	9	39	4
Canada	40	4	39	4
Austria	44	2	39	4
Denmark	38	6	37	7
Norway	38	6	37	7
France	39	5	35	9
Sweden	32	10	33	10
Federal Republic of Germany	32	10	29	11
USA	32	10	29	11
Italy	32	10	28	13
Japan	29	14	28	13
Netherlands	25	16	27	15
Belgium	28	15	25	16
Switzerland	22	17	22	17

Source: Economic Trends

Table 18.5: Percentage of total taxes and social security contributions derived from social security contributions

	1975	*Ranking*	*1985*	*Ranking*
Netherlands	40	3	45	1
France	41	2	44	2
German Federal Republic	38	4	39	3
Greece	27	9	34	4
Italy	45	1	34	4
Belgium	31	5	32	6
Switzerland	28	6	31	7
Japan	28	6	29	8
Austria	26	10	28	9
Sweden	19	12	25	10
USA	21	11	25	10
Norway	28	6	23	12
UK	18	13	18	13
Finland	17	14	15	14
Canada	11	15	14	15
Denmark	1	16	4	16
Australia	0	17	0	17

Source: Economic Trends

Thus compared to similar industrialised countries, it does not seem that Britain is overtaxed, either in terms of the percentage of national output taken by the government in taxation, or in terms of the shares of direct taxation and social security contributions in total tax revenue. However, as we noted earlier in this chapter, the marginal rates at which income taxes are levied may be more significant in their effects upon economic performance and incentives than the overall burden of taxation. Before 1979, the highest marginal rate of income tax in the UK was 83 per cent, a figure which rose to 98 per cent on investment (or 'unearned') income. Because the Conservative Government believed that such a high rate of tax has serious disincentive and distortive effects, the top marginal tax rate was cut to 60 per cent in 1979 and the surcharge on investment income was abolished. But by 1988 the Government was arguing that the highest marginal rates in other industrialised economies had been reduced to levels significantly below the 60 per cent rate charged on higher incomes in the UK. The government therefore decided to abolish higher rates altogether, except for the 40 per cent rate which is now the highest marginal rate. The standard rate of income tax was also cut in the 1988 budget to 25 per cent, and the Chancellor stated that eventually he hoped to cut the standard rate to 20 per cent.

We shall conclude this section with a brief look at **corporate taxation**, since it might be argued that high rates of company taxation reduce economic performance and encourage businesses to migrate to countries with more benign corporate tax regimes.

Table 18.6 shows that in 1985 company taxation (mostly corporation tax) amounted to 13 per cent of total revenue in the United Kingdom, placing the UK in fourth position in the corporate 'league table'. Compared to the position a decade earlier, this represents an increase from 7 per cent (and seventh position), apparently indicating a rise in company taxation under monetarism and the Conservative Government - the very opposite of what the 'supply-siders' wish to achieve! However, first impressions are misleading in this case since the increase is partly explained by the recovery of company profits in the 1980s from a position of very low profitability and losses experienced in the

1970s. Indeed 'supply-side' theory predicts that lower rates will generate higher total tax revenues. Revenues from North Sea oil taxation - which increased rapidly over the decade - are also included in the company taxation measured in Table 18.6 - providing a further explanation for the rise in company taxation from 7 to 13 per cent of total tax revenue. We should also note that the table over-represents the true position of the UK in the company tax 'league table' because social security contributions paid by firms are not included in the table. In many countries, for example France, companies must pay much higher social security contributions on each worker employed than in Britain. This increases the true burden of company taxation in these countries.

FISCAL DRAG

21. **Fiscal drag** occurs in a progressive income tax system when the government fails to raise tax thresholds (or personal tax allowances) to keep pace with inflation. Figure 18.6(a) illustrates an income pyramid (showing the rich at the top of the pyramid and the poor at the bottom), with the **tax threshold** fixed at an income of £2,000. In this example, a person with an income of £1,900 who is just below the threshold, pays no income tax. Now suppose that both prices and all money incomes exactly double. In the absence of taxation, real incomes would be unchanged, with households no better off and no worse off. But if the government fails to increase personal tax allowances in line with inflation (ie to raise the tax threshold to £4,000), our individual whose money income is now £3,800 will be liable for tax on £1,800 of his income and thus, worse off in real terms. Figure 18.6 (b) shows this process of fiscal drag, in which inflation drags low-paid workers across the basic tax threshold and into the tax net. In a similar way, higher-paid workers might be dragged deeper into the tax net, possibly into higher tax bands where they will pay at steeper marginal tax rates.

Table 18.6: Percentage of total taxes and social security contributions derived from direct taxes

	1975	*Ranking*	*1985*	*Ranking*
Norway	5	10	19	1
Japan	20	1	19	1
Canada	15	2	14	3
UK	7	7	13	4
Australia	12	3	9	5
USA	12	3	8	6
Netherlands	8	5	7	7
Belgium	8	5	7	7
German Federal Republic	4	13	5	9
France	6	9	5	9
Switzerland	7	7	5	9
Austria	5	10	4	12
Finland	5	10	4	12
Greece	4	13	3	14
Sweden	3	15	3	14

Source: Economic Trends

Figure 18.6: The process of fiscal drag.
In Figure (b) all incomes have doubled compared to Figure (a), but so have all prices. The tax threshold has not been adjusted, remaining at £2,000. Thus a person earning £1,900 in Figure (a) is dragged into the tax net when his income doubles in Figure (b), even though his pre-tax real income is unchanged

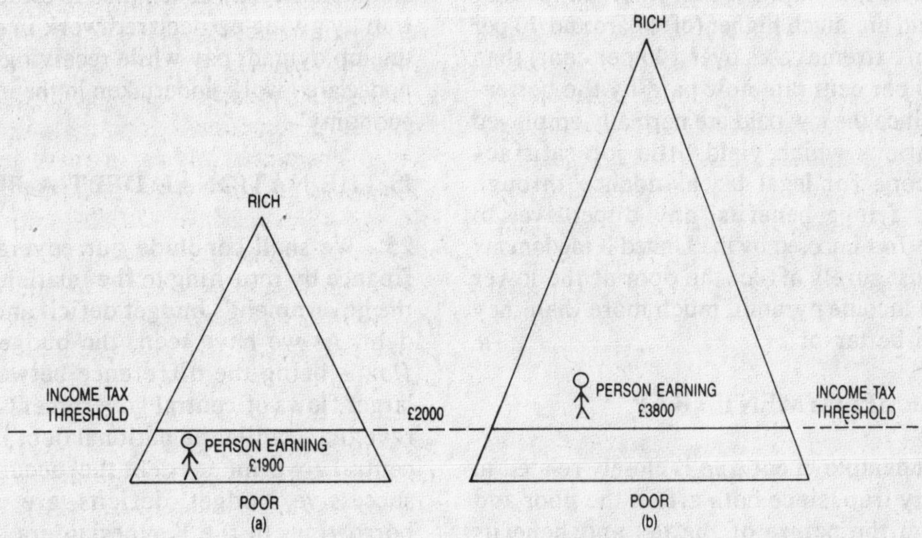

FISCAL BOOST

22. When fiscal drag occurs, the government's total revenue from income tax rises faster than the rate of inflation even though tax rates and the basic structure of taxation have not been changed. This is because more people are dragged into the income tax net, paying a growing proportion of their income in tax. But simultaneously another process may be having an almost opposite effect. In times of inflation, the real value of *specific duties* (but not *ad valorem taxes* such as VAT) falls if the government fails to raise the duties in line with inflation. This process is known as **fiscal boost**.

The simultaneous occurrence of fiscal drag and fiscal boost in times of rapid inflation can explain a shift in the structure of taxation away from taxes upon expenditure and towards taxation upon income. Such a shift occurred in the United Kingdom economy in the 1970s when income tax thresholds and specific expenditure taxes were not raised at the same rate as inflation. Since 1979, the Conservative Government has pursued a deliberate policy of raising income tax thresholds by more than the rate of inflation, so as to shift the structure of taxation towards expenditure once again. Though in part this is simply a decision to reverse the process of fiscal drag which was rife during the 1970s, it also reflects the Government's 'supply-side' belief that income taxes have a more harmful effect upon incentives and that people ought to be as free as possible to choose to spend or not to spend their incomes.

THE POVERTY TRAP

23. The fiscal drag that occurred in the UK economy in the 1970s was an important cause of the emergence of a phenomenon known as the **poverty trap**. The immediate cause of the poverty trap is the **overlap** - which is illustrated in Figure 18.7 - **between the income tax threshold** (the level of income at which income tax starts to be paid) and **the means-tested welfare benefits ceiling** (the level of income at which means-tested transfer incomes cease to be paid). When welfare benefits are **means-tested**, a person's right to claim the benefit is reduced and eventually disappears completely, as income rises. A low-paid worker caught within this zone of overlap not only pays income tax and National Insurance contributions on each extra pound earned; he also loses part or all of his right to claim benefits. Thus low-paid workers and their families whose income falls within this zone of overlap have become trapped in relative poverty since any increase in their pay results in little

or no increase - and in extreme cases a fall - in their disposable income. The **effective marginal rate of taxation** of workers in poorly-paid occupations is therefore very high indeed when the loss of means-tested benefits is added to deductions through income tax and NIC. When calculated in this way, the marginal tax rates of the low paid are much higher (often around 70 per cent and in extreme cases over 100 per cent) than the top 40 per cent rate now paid by the better-off. And since the low paid are normally employed in occupations which yield little job satisfaction or scope for legal tax avoidance through perks and fringe benefits, any discentives to work and effort imposed by the United Kingdom tax system must surely affect the poor at the lower end of the income pyramid much more than they affect the better-off.

THE UNEMPLOYMENT TRAP

24. **The unemployment trap** is closely related to the poverty trap, since both affect the poor and result from the nature of the tax and benefits systems. But whereas the poverty trap affects low-paid workers *in employment*, the poor in the unemployment trap are *out of work* - at least in terms of officially declared employment. The unemployment trap contains 'un-waged' social security claimants who 'choose' unemployment to paid work, in the sense that they are 'better-off' out of work living on benefits than in low-paid jobs paying income tax and NIC and losing some or all of their right to claim means-tested benefits. One link between the poverty trap and the unemployment trap is the **'black economy'** - the hidden or informal economy in which people work, usually for cash payments, while failing to declare income and often fraudulently claiming social security benefits. Low-paid workers in employment may be tempted to escape the poverty trap by giving up declared work in order to claim unemployment pay while receiving income from undeclared work undertaken in the informal 'black economy'.

IS THE NATIONAL DEBT A BURDEN?

25. We shall conclude our coverage of public finance by returning to the relationship between the government's budget deficit and the national debt. As we have seen, the budget deficit is a *flow* - being the difference between the much larger flows of central government spending and revenue - while the national debt is the *stock* of central government debt that accumulates when successive budget deficits are financed by borrowing. In the Keynesian era, when almost continuous deficit financing led to a steadily accumulating national debt in the UK, the reduction of the overall size of the national debt was not a fiscal policy objective. By contrast, in recent years - and related to the Conservative Government's aim of reducing the levels of both public expenditure and the PSBR as proportions of national output - national debt reduction has become part of the overall aim of its 'monetarist' fiscal policy.

Figure 18.7: The poverty trap

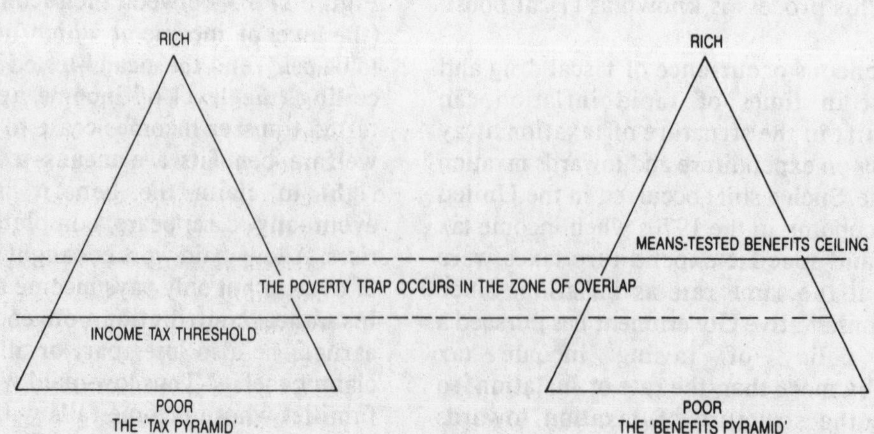

The question of whether fiscal policy should aim to reduce the absolute size of the national debt relates closely to whether the national debt is a burden - both on the government and its freedom to pursue the economic policy of its choice, and upon the nation as a whole. We shall now look at some of the ways in which the UK national debt may or may not represent a burden to the government and to the nation:

(i) **The Nominal Debt and the Real Debt.** It is important to avoid confusing the **nominal** or **absolute** size of the national debt with the **'real' national debt.** In so far as the national debt imposes a burden upon the government - and indirectly upon the nation as taxpayers who must finance interest payments on the debt - it is the 'real' debt that is significant. The nominal national debt (which as we have seen has grown steadily over the years except when there has been a budget surplus) is simply the accumulated money value of all central government debt. In contrast, the 'real' national debt is measured by the nominal debt as a proportion or ratio of GDP or national output. Thus:

$$\text{Real national debt} \equiv \frac{\text{Nominal national debt}}{\text{GDP at market prices}}$$

Figure 18.8: The United Kingdom 'real' national debt - The 'nominal' national debt at end March each year as a ratio of GDP at market prices for each year

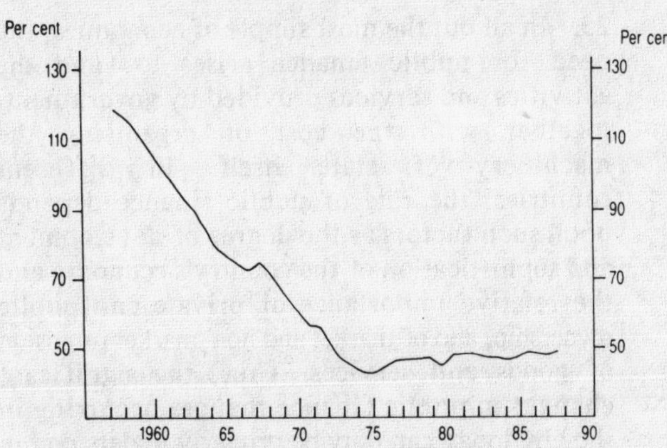

Figure 18.8 shows how the real value of the national debt has fallen in the United Kingdom from over 100 per cent of GDP in 1960 to under 50 per cent in the 1970s and 1980s. This fall has occurred despite the fact that the nominal value of the debt has (until recently) risen. In the 1950s and 1960s the fall in the 'real' national debt could be explained by economic growth. The economy grew in real terms faster than the rate at which successive budget deficits added to the nominal national debt, thereby reducing in real terms the 'overhang' of debt accumulated during the Second World War. But since the 1950s - and especially in the 1970s - inflation and not economic growth has been the most important single cause of the falling real value of the UK national debt. If the rate of inflation is greater than the rate at which the CGBR adds to the national debt, the money value of the debt as a proportion of money GDP usually falls. And if the rate of inflation is greater than the nominal interest rate the government pays to debt-holders, the government gains and debt-holders lose. This is essentially an example of inflation redistributing wealth from lenders (holders of the national debt) to borrowers (the government), thereby reducing the real burden of the debt to the government.

(ii) **The Servicing Burden.** But although inflation has reduced the real value of the national debt, it has probably contributed to an increased cost of servicing the national debt. The cost **of servicing the national debt** - represented by interest payments to debt holders - is not really a burden upon the nation taken as a whole, providing the debt is held internally by people living in the country. When the debt is internally held, servicing costs - apart from management costs - are really just a **transfer from taxpayers** (whose taxes are higher than they would be in the absence of debt interest payments) **to debt-holders** who have lent to the government. But when - in times of inflation - savers or debt-holders begin to realise that they have lost out by lending their savings at negative real interest rates, the government may experience considerable difficulty in persuading the general public to buy new debt, at least at current interest rates. The government will have to raise interest rates both to finance the current CGBR and also to replace existing debt as it matures. (This is called **renewing the national debt.**

Each year part of the national debt matures and, unless there is a budget surplus, the government must sell new debt in order to raise the funds with which to repay maturing debt.) In the 1980s the cost of servicing the UK national debt has been quite high, even though the real debt is now less than 50 per cent of GDP. Savers have learned the lesson of the rapid inflation and negative real interest rates experienced in the 1970s and now seem reluctant to lend to the government unless nominal rates of interest are well above the rate of inflation, thus ensuring an attractive real return on their savings. And the high real interest rates caused by the government's need to sell debt then leads to the 'crowding-out' process we have already described.

(iii) **Constraints upon Economic Policy**. The national debt is a burden, or more accurately a **'constraint'**, if a large national debt and the accompanying servicing or interest costs limit the government's freedom of action in other important aspects of economic policy. In the Keynesian era the UK government's monetary policy was often determined by the need to secure conditions in which new debt could easily be sold and in which servicing costs would not be too high. Monetary policy was thus 'unavailable' for securing other possible policy objectives.

(iv) **The Externally-held Debt.** In so far as the national debt is held externally by residents of other countries, it can represent a burden since part of current income and output must flow overseas as interest payments. This may reduce living standards within the country, and large quantities of externally-held debt can also constrain domestic economic policy, since policies unpopular with overseas debt-holders may trigger the mass selling of both the externally-held debt and then the country's currency. A foreign exchange crisis could then ensue. However, the externally-held debt should not be regarded as a significant burden on the United Kingdom, since less than 4 per cent of the national debt is currently owned overseas. Unfortunately, the same is not true for many developing countries because external holdings of government debt form a major part of the Third World debt problem.

(v) **The 'Deadweight Debt' and the 'Reproductive Debt'**. There are many ways of classifying a country's national debt, for example into the **internally-held** debt and the **externally-held debt** and into the **floating debt (short-term debt)** such as Treasury bills) and the **funded debt** (long-**term debt** such as gilts). These should not be confused with the **'deadweight' debt** and the **'reproductive' debt**. Suppose that the government sells gilts and uses the revenues to build a motorway or some other **capital project**. Although the government is borrowing for a period of many years, the resulting *liability* is matched by a *wealth-producing asset*, the motorway. This type of **'reproductive' borrowing** is not a burden on future generations, since interest payments on the debt are in essence 'paid for' out of the motorway's contributions to future national output. In contrast, any long-term borrowing used to finance **current spending**, for example on wars, can be regarded as a burden on future generations whose taxes will be required to pay interest on the **deadweight spending** indulged in by the government today. A large part of the United Kingdom national debt is a deadweight debt incurred to pay for past wars. Since the deadweight debt does not cover any real asset, interest payments are a burden on the current generation of taxpayers.

SUMMARY

25. In all but the most simple of economies, the need for public finance arises to fund the activities and services provided by government, together with the cost of organising the machinery of state itself. In different countries, the role of public finance depends upon such factors as the degree of development and sophistication of the country's economy and the relative importance of private and public ownership, and of market and non-market provision of goods and services. Thus, the significant changes in public finance that are occurring in the UK today can only be properly understood in the context of the break-up of the post-1945 political consensus which centred around the idea that Keynesian economic policy and the mixed economy were 'right' for Britain. In recent years, not only has the structure of public

finance changed in the UK – the overall nature of the Government's fiscal policy has become fundamentally different as Keynesianism and the management of aggregate demand have given way to monetarism and to 'supply-side' economics.

STUDENT SELF-TESTING

1. *What are the three main elements of public finance?* *(1)*
2. *Why is spending by nationalised industries not usually included in the measure of public expenditure?* *(2)*
3. *List the main sources of revenue which finance public expenditure.* *(3)*
4. *What is meant by 'fiscal neutrality'?* *(4)*
5. *Relate the PSBR to the budget deficit.* *(5)*
6. *How has the PSBR changed in recent years?* *(6)*
7. *Relate the PSBR to the national debt.* *(7)*
8. *Distinguish between:*
   (i) direct and indirect taxation;
   (ii) income and expenditure taxes. *(8)*
9. *Distinguish between a progressive and a regressive tax.* *(9)*
10. *List the canons or principles of taxation.* *(11)*
11. *Distinguish between the allocative and the distributional aims of taxation.* *(12)*
12. *Define fiscal policy.* *(13)*
13. *How was fiscal policy mainly used in the Keynesian era?* *(14)*
14. *Why do monetarists reject a discretionary fiscal policy which aims to manage aggregate demand?* *(15)*
15. *List the four ways of financing the PSBR.* *(16)*
16. *Explain why borrowing from the banking system increases the money supply.* *(17)*
17. *Define 'supply-side' economics.* *(18)*
18. *Explain the Laffer curve.* *(19)*
19. *Is Britain over-taxed compared to similar countries?* *(20)*
20. *What is fiscal drag?* *(21)*
21. *Distinguish between fiscal drag and fiscal boost.* *(22)*
22. *Explain the causes of the poverty trap.* *(23)*
23. *Relate the unemployment trap to the 'black economy'.* *(24)*
24. *Explain what has happened to the real national debt in recent years.* *(25)*

EXERCISES

1. *Three years after the present Government reduced the highest rate of income tax to 60 per cent, there are still 120,000 families today who are subject to a marginal tax rate of more than 80 per cent. However, they are not the rich, but the poor.*

   They are families with children where the working head earns between £47 and £87 a week, that is as little as only a quarter to a half of the current national average wage. Yet liability to income tax at 30 per cent and national insurance contributions at $8\frac{3}{4}$ per cent, plus the loss of 50p of family income supplement for each extra £1 earned, cripple such families with poverty surtax.

   Their position is even worse if rent and rate rebates are added in. As a result, the Department of Health and Social Security estimates from the evidence of its Family Expenditure Survey, that there are more than 250,000 poor families subject to a marginal rate in excess of 50 per cent (not reach at the top end of the income scale till the £19,000 – £23,500 bracket). Within these 250,000 there are even 50,000 poor families subject to a marginal rate in excess of 100 per cent, ie each extra pound they earn makes them actually worse off than before. These extraordinary consequences flow from a tax structure which has become distorted out of all recognition as a result of decades of incremental adjustment at successive annual budgets.

   (Michael Meacher: Labour Party Spokesman on Social Security, 4th August 1982)

   (a) What is the problem to which Mr Michael Meacher is referring?

   (b) Explain the causes of the problem.

   (c) How could the problem be reduced or eliminated?

2. COMPOSITION OF THE UNITED KINGDOM NATIONAL DEBT
(£m at 31 March, percentages of totals in brackets)

	1970	*1974*	*1978*	*1982*	*1987*
Treasury bills and other floating debt	4,989 (15.1%)	6,339 (15.8%)	12,703 (16.1%)	5,778 (4.9%)	9,487 (5.2%)
Gilt-edged securities and other marketable securities	19,720 (59.6%)	26,747 (66.7%)	51,300 (64.9%)	91,025 (77.2%)	136,509 (73.4%)
National savings securities	3,558 (10.8%)	4,075 (10.1%)	5,828 (7.4%)	14,990 (12.7%)	26,578 (14.3%)
Externally held debt	4,115 (12.4%)	2,735 (6.8%)	7,777 (9.8%)	4,198 (3.5%)	5,915 (3.2%)
Other debt	697 (2.1%)	229 (0.6%)	1,475 (1.8%)	1,968 (1.7%)	7,262 (3.9%)
Total national debt	33,079	40,125	79,083	117,959	185,751
Gross national product at market prices	51,661	84,529	165,493	270,657	414,228
	1969/70	*1973/74*	*1977/78*	*1981/82*	*1986/87*
Cost of servicing the National Debt, including management and interest costs	1,458	2,341	5,929	11,205	17,579

Source: Financial Statistics

(a) Explain the changes in the composition of the national debt over the period 1970/1987.
(b) Does the data indicate that the national debt is a burden?

MULTIPLE CHOICE QUESTIONS

1 The incidence of a tax refers to:
- *A Who eventually bears the burden of tax*
- *B A principle or canon of taxation*
- *B Whether a tax is direct or indirect*
- *D Whether the tax is continuously or periodically levied*

2. When, during a period of inflation, income tax revenue rises faster than national income, this illustrates:
- *A The unemployment trap*
- *B The poverty trap*
- *C Fiscal boost*
- *D Fiscal drag*

3. *Income (£) Amount of tax deducted (£)*

Income (£)	*A*	*B*	*C*	*D*
4,000	*1,000*	*1,000*	*1,000*	*0*
8,000	*2,000*	*1,000*	*2,000*	*2,000*
16,000	*4,000*	*1,000*	*4,060*	*8,000*

Which of the above tax structures is progressive at all the levels of income illustrated?

4. *Causes of the poverty trap include the:*
   - A *Income tax threshold being set lower than the benefits ceiling*
   - B *Existence of the 'black economy'*
   - C *Process of fiscal boost*
   - D *Regressive nature of income tax*

5. *Which of the following **cannot** be described as fiscal policy?*
   - A *A change in income tax aimed at altering the distribution of income*
   - B *A planned reduction in the budget deficit aimed at reducing government borrowing*
   - C *A reduction in interest rates which has the side-effect of reducing the cost of servicing the national debt*
   - D *An increase in government regional aid to industry.*

EXAMINATION QUESTIONS

1 (a) *Outline the functions of taxation.* *(12 marks)*

(b) *What are the possible disadvantages of a progressive income tax system?* *(8 marks)*

(ACCA December 1984)

2 *Describe the principles on which an efficient modern system of taxation should be based.* *(CIMA November 1987)*

3. *What are the likely economic effects of a general increase in direct taxation?* *(CIMA May 1988)*

4. *Explain the work, organisation and power of the UK (or overseas) Treasury.* *(AAT June 1983)*

5 (a) *Distinguish between the Public Sector Borrowing Requirements and the National Debt.* *(6 marks)*

(b) *Why has so much importance recently been attached to the Public Sector Borrowing Requirement?* *(14 marks)*

(ACCA June 1986)

6 (a) *Define the National Debt. (5 marks)*

(b) *To what extent does the National Debt form a burden on society?* *(15 marks)*

(ACCA December 1984)

19. Money and the banking system

INTRODUCTION

1. The economy we live in is a **monetary economy** in which most of the goods and services produced are traded or exchanged via the intermediary of money. In this chapter, we examine the **nature** and **functions of money** in a modern monetary economy, before going on to explain how most modern money takes the form of **bank deposits** which are created by the private enterprise banking system.

THE FUNCTIONS OF MONEY

2. Money is best defined by the **three principal functions** it performs in the economy. These are:

(i) **A medium of exchange.** Money must be acceptable for the purpose of settling transactions and the payment of debts.
(ii) **A store of value or wealth.** It must be possible for a person to store his personal wealth in the form of money, so that he can transfer his purchasing power into the future.
(iii) **A unit of account.** Money is the unit in which the prices of other goods are quoted and in which accounts are kept.

In addition, a **fourth function** of money is usually identified, as a **standard of deferred payment.** This means that people may make a contract or an agreement now to exchange goods or settle a debt in the future, agreeing now in monetary units the payment to be settled in the future.

BARTER

3. In a developed market economy, nearly all the exchanges involved in distributing the goods and services produced in the 'real economy' require the use of money as a medium of exchange. In a very simple or primitive economy, such as a tribal village economy, exchange could be based on **barter**. However barter is inefficient and impractical in a more complex economic system. Successful barter requires a **'double coincidence of wants'**, which means that a person wishing to trade a TV set for a refrigerator must not only establish contact with someone with equal but opposite wants, ie an individual possessing a refrigerator who wishes to exchange it for a TV set; they must also agree that the TV set and refrigerator are of equal value. Barter is *inefficient* because the time and energy wasted in searching the market in order to establish the double coincidence of wants results in unnecessary **search costs** or **transaction costs.** The search or transactions costs associated with barter would indeed promote a much greater inefficiency - they would **prevent the development of specialisation, the division of labour** and the **large scale production** which provide the foundation for the productive efficiency and range of consumer choice available in a modern monetary economy.

THE HISTORICAL DEVELOPMENT OF MONEY

4. Since early historical times when money first superseded the use of barter as a medium of exchange, three main forms of money have existed. These are:

(i) commodity money;
(ii) representative money; and
(iii) token money;

which are illustrated in Figure 19.1, (see next page).

COMMODITY MONEY

5. To function as money, an asset must be **both an acceptable medium of exchange and a possible store of value.** Early forms of money were commodities with an *intrinsic* value of their own, ie they yielded utility or consumer services to their owners. Commodities such as cattle which served as money could be slaughtered and eaten if their owners no longer wanted to keep them as money; while other commodities such as beads, shells and dogs' teeth, which have also functioned as money, could be used for decorative purposes while being 'stored' as wealth. Gradually, the precious metals, gold and silver, replaced other forms of commodity money because they possessed, to a greater degree, the **desirable characteristics** necessary for a commodity to function as money: relative **scarcity, uniformity, durability, portability** and **divisibility,** all of which contribute to confidence in money and to its **acceptability.**

Figure 19.1: The historical development of money

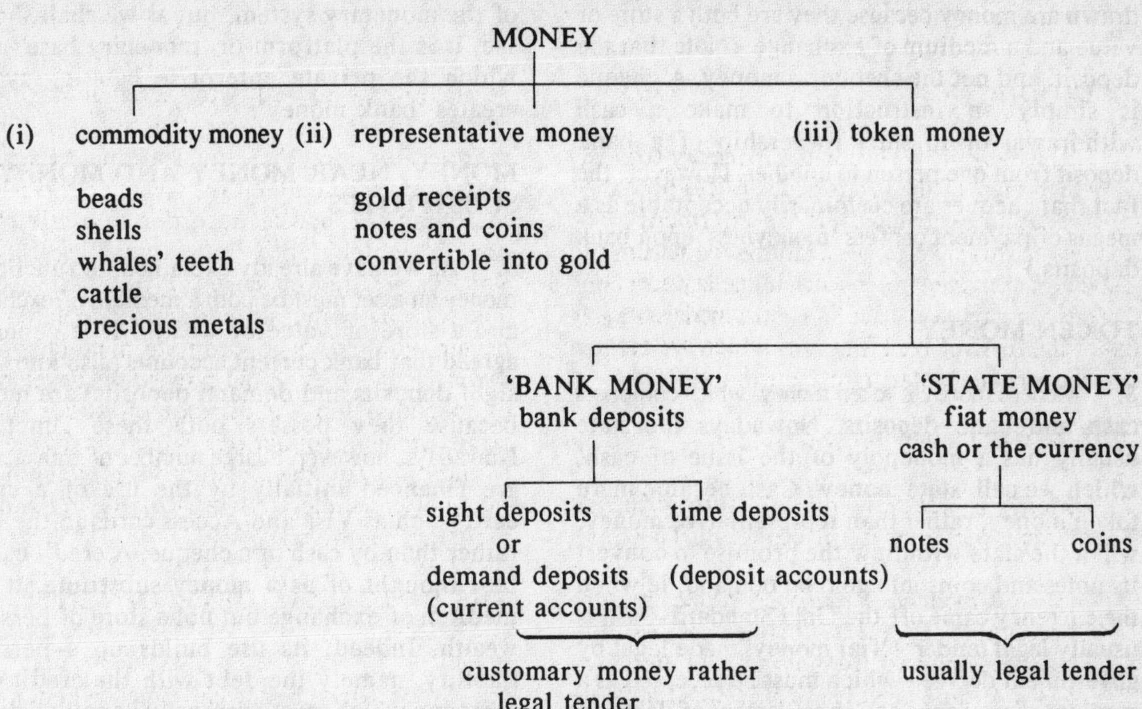

REPRESENTATIVE MONEY

6. Nevertheless, because gold and silver are vulnerable to theft and difficult to store safely, it became the custom in European countries a few hundred years ago, for individuals to deposit their precious metals with goldsmiths for safekeeping. The next step in the development of money was for the goldsmiths to develop into **banks**,and the **gold receipts** which they issued to depositors of gold became **bank-notes** or **paper money**. The notes were acceptable as a means of payment because they could be exchanged for gold on demand. Early banknotes were **representative money** issued by privately-owned banks. Although worthless in themselves, these pieces of paper could function as money because people were willing to accept them, knowing that they represented ownership of gold which has an intrinsic value.

THE DEVELOPMENT OF BANK DEPOSITS

7. In the 19th century, banks discovered that they could increase their profits by issuing notes to customers requesting loans, which meant that the banks' note issue grew to exceed the gold deposits they held. Prudent banking requires that a bank keeps sufficient **reserve assets** (in this case gold) to meet all likely calls by customers on the **bank's liabilities**. In the early 19th century, greedy banks were tempted, in pursuit of profit, to over-extend their note issue, meaning that they possessed insufficient gold to meet the demands of customers who wished to convert bank notes (the banks' liabilities) into gold. Imprudent over-extension of the note issue thus led to bank crashes, which periodically occurred when banks could not meet demands by the public to convert notes into gold. As a direct result of these bank crashes in the United Kingdom, the **1844 Bank Charter Act** largely removed the right of British banks to issue their own notes. The Bank Charter Act encouraged a new monetary development, the creation of **deposit money**. Instead of issuing its own notes to a customer requesting a loan, a modern bank makes a ledger or book-keeping entry crediting the customer's account with a bank deposit. Bank deposits are obviously a store of wealth or value, and chequing-deposits are also a medium of exchange, since the use of cheque allows payment to be made by shifting ownership of the deposit.

Thus bank deposits upon which cheques can be drawn are money because they are both a store of value and a medium of exchange. (Note that the deposit, and not the cheque, is money. A cheque is simply an instruction to make a cash withdrawal or to shift ownership of a bank deposit from one person to another. However, the fact that cheques are customarily acceptable as a means of payment confers **'moneyness'** upon bank deposits.)

TOKEN MONEY

8. Modern money is **token money**, which comprises **cash and bank deposits**. Nowadays the state usually has a monopoly of the issue of cash, which we call **'state money'**. Cash became mere token money, rather than representative money, when the state withdrew the promise to convert its notes and coins into gold on demand, ie when the currency came off the **Gold Standard**. Cash is usually **legal tender - 'fiat money'** made legal by government decree - which must be accepted as a medium of exchange and in settlement of debts. In contrast, **bank deposits** in the private enterprise banking system - **'bank money'** - are customary money rather than legal tender. They are token money which is generally accepted because of peoples' confidence in the banks and in the monetary system. In the United Kingdom, the use of cheque guarantee cards adds to the acceptability of bank deposits as a medium of exchange, since banks guarantee in advance to honour a payment by cheque up to a certain value, currently £50 per transaction. Bank deposits make up by far the largest part of modern money, between about two-thirds and 90 per cent depending on how money is defined. These days, cash or 'state money' is just the 'small change' of the monetary system, but as we shall shortly see, it is the platform or **'monetary base'** upon which the private enterprise banking system creates 'bank money'.

MONEY, NEAR MONEY AND MONEY SUBSTITUTES

9. As we have already explained, to function as money an asset must be both a medium of exchange and a store of value or wealth. It is generally agreed that **bank current accounts** (also known as **sight deposits** and **demand deposits**) are money because they possess both these functions. Nowadays, however, a large number of transactions are financed initially by the use of a **credit card** (such as Visa and Access cards in the UK) rather than by cash or a cheque. A credit card is best thought of as a **money substitute.** It is a medium of exchange but not a store of personal wealth. Indeed, its use builds up a personal liability, namely the debt with the credit card company which must eventually be settled with a cash or cheque transaction.

Whereas a money substitute such as a credit card is a medium of exchange but not a store of value, the reverse is true of **near money.** A number of financial assets such as building society deposits are usually regarded as near monies rather than as money. A building society deposit is certainly a store of value or wealth, but it cannot function directly as a medium of exchange unless the building society grants a cheque facility, allowing cheques to be drawn on the deposit.

In summary:

NEAR MONEY	*MONEY*	*MONEY SUBSTITUTES*
store of value but insufficiently liquid to be a medium of exchange	medium of exchange and store of value cash and bank deposits	medium of exchange but not a store of value
Eg Building Society deposits, National Savings securities		Eg credit cards and charge cards

THE PROBLEM OF DEFINING THE MONEY SUPPLY

10. Before the 1970s - during the **Keynesian era** - little attention was given to the precise definition of the money supply or stock of money in the economy. This reflected the Keynesian view that 'money did not matter' in the macro-economic management of the economy. But under **monetarism**, which began to supersede Keynesianism as the prevailing orthodoxy in the 1970s, money does matter, control of the money supply becoming an important part of monetarist economic management in general and monetary policy in particular. During the 1970s and 1980s, monetarists devoted considerable attention to the problem of precisely which assets to include and exclude when defining the money supply or stock of money. A significant problem which has faced the monetarists has become known as **'Goodhart's Law'**, named after Charles Goodhart who was a Bank of England official in the 1970s. Goodhart's Law states that the more successful a monetarist government appears to be in controlling the rate of growth of the financial assets which it defines as the money supply, the more likely it is that other financial assets, regarded previously as near monies outside the existing definition and system of control, will take on the function of a medium of exchange and become money. Goodhart's Law has the significant implication for monetarism that, by its nature, money is a 'will-o'-the wisp' that cannot be controlled. Essentially, **'money is as money does'**. Any attempt at controlling the growth of the money supply is likely to be cosmetic. The authorities may succeed in controlling what they define as money, but other financial assets will have become money.

DEFINITIONS OF THE MONEY SUPPLY

11. Goodhart's Law helps to explain why the **monetary authorities** in the United Kingdom - the **Bank of England** and the **Treasury** - have commonly used more than one definition of the money supply. The various definitions of money supply currently used by the Bank of England are illustrated in Figure 19.2 (see following page).

Until fairly recently, the two main measures of the money supply were **M1** and **M3**. The '*narrower*' definition of the money supply, **M1**, concentrated on the '*medium of exchange*' function of money, including only those financial assets - cash plus bank sight deposits - which could directly function as a means of payment. However, wealthy individuals and most companies will normally hold interest-earning **deposit accounts** or **time deposits** alongside their current accounts or sight deposits. Should time deposits be included in the definition of money? Time deposits do not function directly as a medium of exchange. Unlike a sight deposit, a time deposit cannot be shifted by cheque. But to compete with other financial institutions such as buildings societies, the banks have allowed their time deposits to become increasingly more liquid. Thus a customer may keep a low balance in a sight deposit, upon which cheques can be drawn, intending when a large payment is due to be made to shift part of his time deposit into the current account. Bank customers certainly treat their time deposits as money, a practice encouraged by the banks to attract business away from building societies and National Savings. Thus, time deposits are included in the '*wider*' definition of money, **M3**. M3, sometimes known as '*broad money*' includes bank deposits which are stores of value, but which can quickly and without capital loss be converted into a medium of exchange.

M3 AND M3c

12. One of the most important reasons why, under monetarism, the monetary authorities wish to define and to control the money supply, is because they believe that the size of the stock of money available to spend in the economy is a major determinant of the price level and the rate of inflation. In the United Kingdom however, only bank deposits denominated in sterling are likely to be spent within the economy. Because foreign currency bank deposits held in the United Kingdom banking system are unlikely to be used as a medium of exchange in the UK economy, they will have little or no effect upon either domestic economic activity or the domestic price level. For this reason, only *sterling* bank deposits are included in **the measure of broad money, M3**. Foreign currency deposits held in United Kingdom banks are however included in the measure, **M3c**. (Before the most recent revision by the Bank of England of definitions of the money supply in May 1987, M3 and M3c were known respectively as **Sterling M3** and **M3**. The monetary label M3 has thus significantly changed its meaning.)

Figure 19.2: The measures of money, (as revised May 1987)

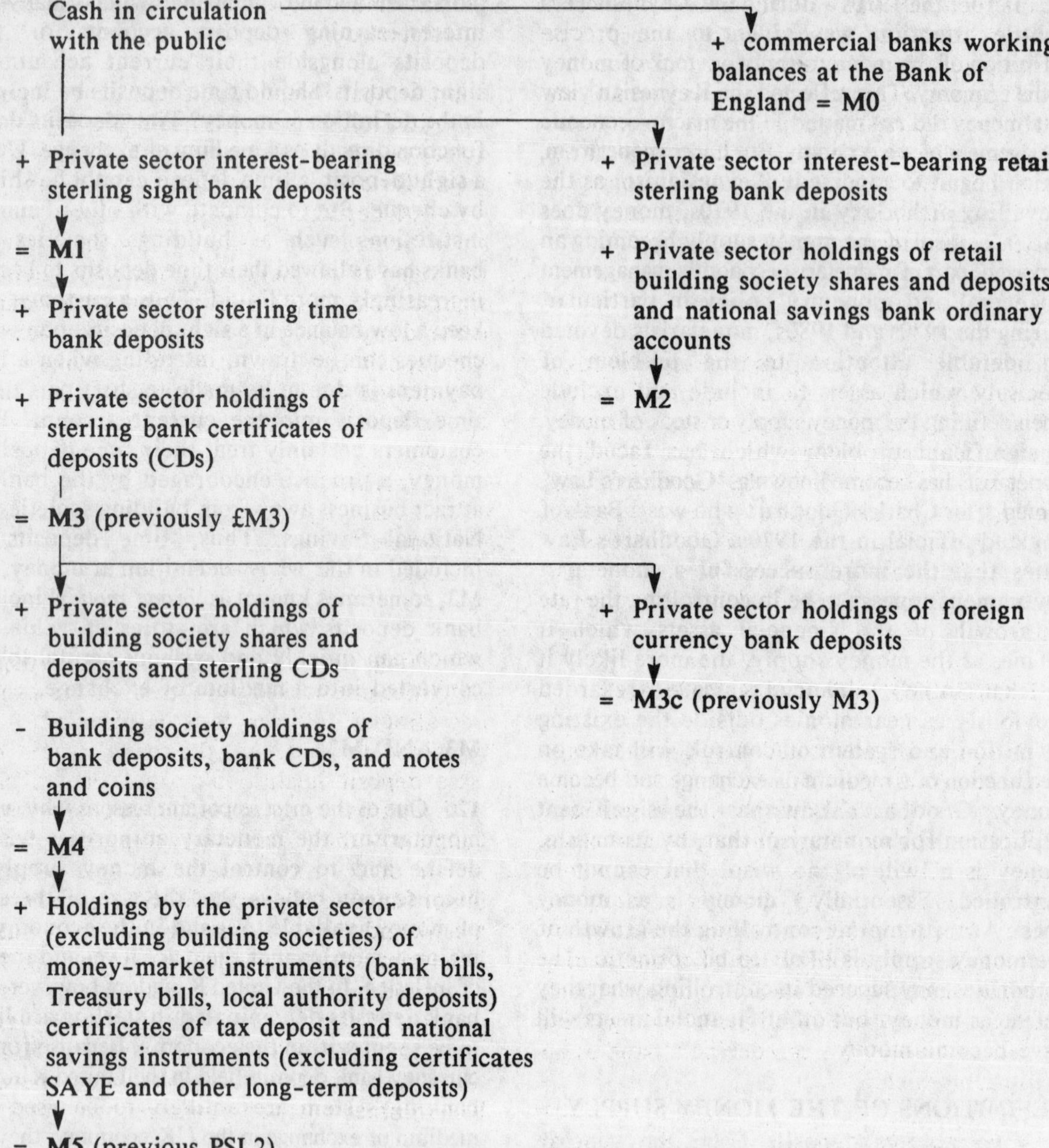

RETAIL AND WHOLESALE BANK DEPOSITS

13. Both M1 and M3 include bank deposits, but exclude deposits held by the general public in **non-bank financial institutions** such as **building societies**. However, there is no logical reason why only time deposits held in banks, but not building society deposits which are very similar, should be regarded as money. Perhaps the most accurate measures of money currently used in the UK are now **M2** and **M4**. The definition of M2 is based upon the distinction between retail and **wholesale deposits**, whether held in banks or in non-bank financial institutions - or **'near' banks** - such as building societies. Retail deposits are liquid - or relatively liquid - deposits held by the general public which are likely to be spent. They include a wide range of building society deposits. In contrast, wholesale deposits are normally owned by banks and financial institutions themselves, and held in other banks and financial institutions. They reflect the

asset portfolio management decisions of banks and other financial institutions and have relatively little effect upon the retail spending decisions of the general public. Therefore wholesale deposits, and any other deposits which are unlikely quickly to be translated into spending power, should be excluded from measures of the money supply designed primarily to monitor 'retail' conditions. This is the logic behind the creation of M2, which includes retail deposits in all financial institutions, but excludes wholesale and long-term deposits.

M0

14. Although M1 - cash plus bank sight deposits - has conventionally been regarded as the definition of 'narrow' money, an even narrower measure, **M0,** was created by the United Kingdon monetary authorities in 1983. M0 comprises largely cash in circulation with the general public. It is a measure of the **'monetary base'** - the part of the total money stock over which the monetary authorities can, in principle, exercise a monopoly control

THE CREATION OF BANK DEPOSITS

15. We have already noted that bank deposits form the largest part of the stock of money whichever way the money supply is measured. Bank deposits are the main form of money because banks possess the ability to create new deposits where none previously existed. In this section, we shall explain the process of deposit creation by assuming a highly **simplified model of the banking system** in which there is just *one* commercial bank which has a *monopoly* of all bank dealings with the general public. We can define a **bank** as an institution which:

(i) **accepts deposits** from the general public that can be transferred by cheque; and

(ii) **creates deposits** for the general public when it makes **advances** or **bank loans.** (These can be either **overdrafts** or **term loans**).

We shall further assume that the bank aims to maximise profits, but that profits are ultimately constrained by the bank's need to conduct itself prudently, ie by its need to hold a percentage of bank assets in cash to meet any likely demand by customers to convert deposits into cash. We shall assume that the bank chooses to operate a 10 per cent **cash ratio,** which means that cash held by the bank must not fall below 10 per cent of total customers' deposits.

Suppose that a member of the general public deposits £1,000 cash in the bank. The bank has in effect 'purchased' the cash from the customer, in return for crediting the customer's account with a £1,000 deposit. The cash is the *bank's asset*, since it can use the cash how it wishes, whereas the deposit is the *bank's liability*. Being a sight deposit, the bank is liable to honour on demand any request by the customer to re-convert the deposit back into cash, ie to make a cash withdrawal. £1,000 thus figures both as a liability and as an asset in the bank's balance sheet:

Liabilities		*Assets*	
Customers' deposits:	£1,000	Cash:	£1,000

As things stand, all the bank's deposit liabilities are backed with cash, ie the bank is operating a 100 per cent cash ratio. If this remained the position, the 'bank' would be a **'safe-deposit institution'** rather than a bank. Although banks do indeed have a safe-deposit function - they guard valuables, for a fee, on behalf of their customers - it is a relatively minor function. The essential difference between a bank and a safe-deposit institution is that the latter simply guards valuables (including cash) deposited by customers, whereas a bank accepts deposits of cash from one group of customers in order to 'make the cash go to work' for the bank through the creation of completely new deposits lent to other customers who require credit.

Operating on a 10 per cent cash ratio, the bank can increase profits by granting loans of £9,000 for every £1,000 of cash deposited in the bank. On the **assets side** of the bank's balance sheet, this will be shown as an advance of £9,000 - whether the loan is granted through an overdraft facility or as a term loan for a definite term of years does not matter. But since the bank must honour any cheques which are drawn on the advance up to the value of £9,000, **deposit liabilities,** shown on the left-hand side of the balance sheet, will have increased by exactly the same amount as interest-earning assets.

Liabilities		*Assets*	
Initial deposits:	£1,000	Cash:	£1,000
Created deposits	£9,000	Advances to customers	£9,000
Total liabilities:	£10,000	Total assets	£10,000

The fact that both the assets side and the liabilities side of the balance sheet increase by equal amounts is a point of some significance. During the Keynesian era in the United Kingdom, monetary policy was often operated, together with fiscal policy, to influence the level of **aggregate money demand (AMD)** in the economy. An expansion of bank loans or credit would stimulate aggregate demand, whereas a restriction of lending or credit would depress AMD. The Keynesians were interested in the right-hand side of the balance sheet since they were concerned with the effect of an increase in bank lending or credit upon aggregate demand. An expansion of bank loans or credit would stimulate aggregate demand, whereas a restriction of lending or credit would depress AMD. The left-hand side of the balance sheet was given much less attention by the Keynesians, largely because in Keynesian theory the absolute size of the stock of money and its rate of growth were held at the time to be of little consequence. However, in recent years under monetarism, this emphasis has been reversed. Monetarists are interested in the left-hand side of the balance sheet because the liabilities of the private enterprise banking system (bank deposits) are the largest component of the money supply. Thus control of the growth of bank deposits is an essential pre-requisite for achieving the central objective of monetarist economic policy in the fight against inflation: control of the growth of the money supply. Nevertheless, it remains true that a change in the cash or reserve assets deposited in the banking system will change both assets and liabilities by equal amounts, and for many purposes it does not really matter which side of the balance sheet we examine.

In our simple model of credit and deposit creation, deposits will be expanded whether the bank expands advances or purchases interest-earning securities such as bonds from the general public. Suppose the bank creates £7,000 of advances for customers requesting loans, and uses the rest of its credit-creating facility to purchase £2,000 of bonds. The bank pays for the bonds with a cheque for £2,000 drawn on itself, which increases customers' deposits by £2,000 when the cheque is paid into the account of the person who sold the bonds to the bank. The spectrum of assets owned by the bank would now be different from the previous position, but total assets - and the deposit liabilities which represent the creation of money - are the same.

DEPOSIT AND CREDIT CREATION IN A MULTI-BANK SYSTEM

16. The model of credit or deposit creation which we have just described is based on the simplifying assumption of a **monopoly bank**, ie a single bank representing the whole of the banking system. In principle, a monopoly bank can create deposits to the full extent that its cash ratio allows in a single step or stage, eg £9,000 deposits created from an initial deposit of £1,000 cash, assuming the constraint of a 10% cash ratio. This is because with a monopoly bank, there is no danger that customers who have been granted loans will draw cheques on their deposits payable to customers of other banks. Nevertheless, there could be a **cash drain** from the banking system, which might occur for example if customers to whom advances have been made decide to keep a constant proportion of their money in the form of cash. A cash drain would limit the bank's ability to create deposits to a figure somewhat below that illustrated in our example.

When we drop the simplification of a monopoly bank, and assume a **multi-bank system** similar to that in the United Kingdom, the general conclusions of our simple model still hold. If the increase in cash deposits is spread over all the banks, deposits can expand to £10,000 provided that every bank in the system is prepared to create deposits to the full extent the cash ratio allows. But if only one bank is willing to expand deposits to the full, it will begin to face demands for cash which it cannot meet. This will happen when the bank's customers draw cheques on their deposits which are paid into the accounts of the customers of the banks which have refused to expand credit. When the cheques are cleared, the bank which has expanded deposits must pay cash to the other banks, equal to the shift of deposits between the banks. To avoid this possibility, the bank must restrict the extent to which it is prepared to expand deposits. However, if all banks are prepared to expand credit to the full, payments to customers of other banks will largely cancel out. The banking system as a whole can expand deposits to £10,000, though some banks may gain business at the expense of others.

THE MONEY MULTIPLIER

17. The central principle of credit creation or deposit creation is that the banking system as a whole can create an expansion in bank deposits (and thus the money supply) which is a **multiple** of the liquid assets or reserve assets held by the banks. Because, in our simple model, cash is the only reserve asset held to fractionally back the banking system's deposit liabilities, the ability of the banks to create credit and new bank deposits is dependent on the cash ratio. The **money multiplier** (also known as the **credit multiplier** and as the **bank multiplier**) measures the maximum expansion of bank deposits (or **'low-powered' money**) which is possible for a given increase in cash (or **'high-powered' money**) deposited in the banking system. Assuming that there is no cash drain and that cash is the banks' only reserve asset or liquid asset:

$$\text{the money multiplier} = \frac{1}{\text{cash ratio.}}$$

With a cash ratio of 10 per cent, the money multiplier is 10, which as we have seen, means that total bank deposits can extend to ten times the size of an initial deposit of cash into the banking system.

As we shall shortly see, banks in fact possess **reserve assets** or **liquid assets** other than just cash. In the event of a withdrawal of deposits by customers, these reserve assets can quickly be turned into cash without capital loss to meet likely demands for cash. It is useful, therefore, to write the formula for the money multiplier more generally as:

$$\text{the money multiplier} = \frac{1}{\text{liquid assets ratio}}$$

$$\text{or} \quad \frac{1}{\text{reserve assets ratio.}}$$

THE BANKING SYSTEM IN THE UNITED KINGDOM

18. So far in this chapter, we have defined a bank rather loosely as an institution which both accepts deposits from the general public and which creates deposits, for example when it makes loans or advances. Until 1979, there were no legal restrictions in the UK to prevent any institution calling itself a 'bank'. Officially, however, the **UK banking sector** comprised all the listed banks which recognised a uniform reserve ratio, together with the banking department of the Bank of England (the country's **central bank**), and the institutions which make up the **London Discount Market**. This situation was regularised when the **1979 Banking Act** introduced restrictions on banks that are authorised to operate in the UK by establishing a **two-tier system of 'recognised banks' and 'licensed deposit-taking institutions'**. Shortly afterwards, in November 1981, the Bank of England defined a new **monetary sector** which amalgamated the old banking sector with a number of other related financial institutions. Since 1979, it has been an offence to take deposits unless authorised to do so by the Bank of England. The authorised listed banks operating in the UK are divided into three main groups: **British banks, overseas banks and consortium banks.** There has been recent rapid growth in the operations in the UK of overseas banks and consortium banks and also of the more specialised British banks. In response to this growth, banking regulations which only applied to the UK clearing banks have been applied to all listed banks. However, because the British banking system now exists within a global financial system in which business is mobile and in which the major centres such as London, Tokyo and New York are in fierce competition with each other, the UK monetary authorities have, on the whole, relaxed rather than increased the degree of control and regulation exercised on banks and other financial institutions operating within the UK. They gave done this to allow British banks to compete in world-wide markets and to attract overseas and consortium banks into the London financial markets. A **consortium bank** is a bank which is owned by a group of other banks, including at least one overseas bank, but no one bank owns more than 50 per cent of the share capital.

THE UK CLEARING BANKS

19. All banks with the exception of the central bank are **commercial banks** in the sense that their ultimate objective is to make a profit for their owners. The **clearing banks** and in particular the **London clearing banks** are the most important commercial banks in the UK, with the sight and time deposits which they accept and create forming the most important part of the supply of money. The clearing banks are **general purpose banks**, most of whose business is **retail banking** with the individuals and firms which make up the general public. But because retail banking business in sterling within the UK has been growing more slowly than both large-scale wholesale lending of deposits between banks in what is known as the 'inter-bank' market and also overseas lending of sterling in the **'Euro-currency market'**, merchant banks which specialise in wholesale and international banking business have tended to grow at a faster rate than the UK clearers. **Merchant banks** are based in the City of London, where most of their work is located operating in wholesale and international money markets and in the other financial services they offer. Because they are not involved in extensive retail business with the general public (and with the clearing of cheques which gives the clearing banks their name), the merchant banks do not possess large networks of branches spread across the country. As a result, the merchant banks do not incur the considerable overhead costs suffered by the clearing banks from maintaining their expensive branch networks.

THE LONDON DISCOUNT MARKET

20. The eleven **discount houses** which are members of the **London Discount Market Association** play a special role within the UK financial system, a role which is not exactly paralleled in other countries where discount houses do not exist. In other countries, clearing banks and other banks perform the functions undertaken by the discount houses within the UK. The function of the discount houses is to supply both private sector commercial firms and also the government with a cheap source of short-term finance, as an alternative to a conventional bank loan. They do this through **bill finance**. There are two main types of bills: **commercial bills (or bills of exchange)**, which are issued by merchant banks to raise funds for private sector firms, and **Treasury bills** which are sold by the Bank of England on behalf of the government. A bill is a **short-dated financial asset** or security, which matures three months (91 days) after it was first issued. Unlike a long-dated security such as a bond, for which a guaranteed fixed interest rate is paid, a bill does not earn a formal rate of interest. Instead it is sold on its day of issue at a **discount price** ie a price below its face value or maturity value, to a **discount house.** By buying the bill, the discount house is in effect lending funds to the firm responsible for its issue, or to the government. The discount house thus earns the **bill discount rate,** which is the difference between the discount price paid for the bill on the day of issue and the maturity value to be obtained when the bill is redeemed 91 days later. Before a commercial bill - but not a Treasury bill - is sold to a discount house, it first needs **accepting**. To convert a bill into a marketable security, it is sold under the name of a bank - usually a merchant bank - rather than in the name of the firm which is raising finance through the sale of a bill. In return for a fee paid by the firm, the merchant bank accepts all the financial risks involved. Accepting the risks on bills (as an **acceptance house**), is one of the specialist financial services performed by merchant banks.

THE CLEARING BANKS AND THE DISCOUNT MARKET

21. Earlier in this chapter we used a simple model of the banking system - in which banks possessed just three assets, cash, bonds and advances - to explain the principle of credit or deposit creation. In order to explain the relationships within the UK monetary system between the clearing banks and the discount houses, we must first introduce a rather more detailed version of the assets side of the balance sheet of a clearing bank:

Table 19.1: The asset structure of a UK clearing bank

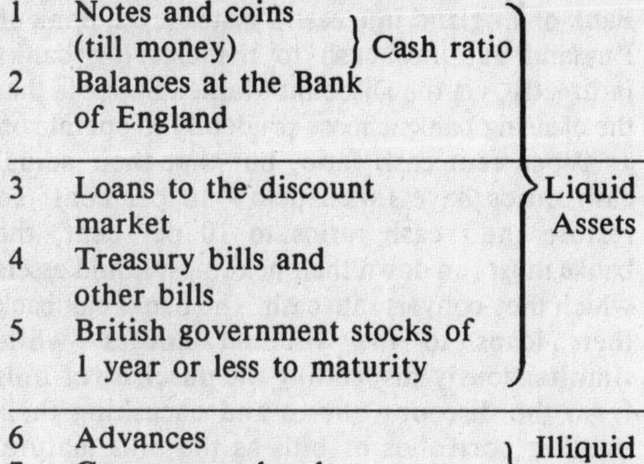

	Asset		
1	Notes and coins (till money)	Cash ratio	
2	Balances at the Bank of England		
3	Loans to the discount market		Liquid Assets
4	Treasury bills and other bills		
5	British government stocks of 1 year or less to maturity		
6	Advances	Illiquid assets	
7	Government bonds (investments)		

In arranging its structure of assets, a bank faces a **'trade-off' between liquidity and profitability**. Because **illiquid assets** (advances to the general public in the form of overdrafts and term loans and investments in government bonds or gilts) are the most profitable of a bank's assets, it will expand these as much as possible, subject to the constraint imposed by its need to maintain cash and liquid asset ratios. In the event of a loss of deposits to other banks or a cash drain to the general public, a bank must be able to convert some at least of its profitable or interest-earning assets into cash. (Note that item 2 in the balance sheet, **balances at the Bank of England**, is part of the cash ratio. Just as members of the general public choose to deposit spare cash in the clearing banks, so the clearing banks in their turn deposit any cash they possess surplus to their day-to-day needs in the Bank of England. At any time the clearing banks can replenish their notes and coins or till money by withdrawing cash from their balances at the Bank of England.)

To replenish their overall cash ratio however, the clearing banks must convert some of their liquid assets into cash. Banks come to possess liquid assets, which they keep precisely for this purpose of replenishing their cash ratios, as a direct result of their special relationship with the discount houses in the **Discount Market**. Each week, the discount houses borrow millions of pounds from the clearing banks in order to finance their discounting business. To be profitable the discount houses must borrow funds at a rate of interest lower than the bill discount rate which they earn through the use of the borrowed funds. The clearing banks charge a very low rate of interest on their **loans to the Discount Market** (item 3 in the balance sheet), but in return they can demand very early repayment. Loans to the Discount Market comprise **money at call**, which must be repaid on call (the next day) if requested, and **money at short notice** for which 7 to 14 days notice of repayment is granted.

Although discount houses can hold on to bills until the bills mature 91 days after their initial purchase, in practice many bills are resold to the clearing banks before maturity. This accounts for item 4 in the clearing banks' balance sheets.

By purchasing bills as they approach maturity rather than as new issues, the clearing banks can build up **portfolios of bills** which can be converted into cash as they mature, if the banks need to restore their cash ratios. Commercial bills and Treasury bills provide the banks with a highly liquid asset. Item 5, **government stocks with one year of less to maturity** is essentially similar. If the banks are ever in a situation in which they need to restore their cash ratios, they can either encash their securities as they mature or sell them to the general public, suffering only a small capital loss because the securities are so close to maturity.

THE BANK OF ENGLAND

22. **The Bank of England**, which is the United Kingdom's **central bank**, is technically a nationalised industry, owned and ultimately controlled by the government. It is organised in two departments, the **Issue Department** responsible for note issue and the **Banking Department** which conducts the Bank of England's banking business. The most important, or '*wider*', function of the Bank of England is to implement the government's monetary policy. We shall examine this aspect of the Bank of England's activities in the next chapter. In this section, we shall describe the '*narrower*' or specific banking functions of the Bank of England. The Bank of England is:

(i) **banker to the clearing banks and other banks in the monetary sector**. As we have already seen, the clearing banks deposit any 'spare' cash they possess into their balances at the Bank of

England. These working balances allow the banks to settle indebtedness between themselves by shifting the ownership of a balance or deposit from one bank to another;

(ii) **banker to the government**. The Bank of England keeps the government's principal bank accounts, receiving tax and other revenue and making payments with respect to government expenditure. The bank also manages the national debt on behalf of the government, selling new issues and redeeming maturing Treasury bills and gilts;

(iii) **holder of the country's stock of gold and foreign currency reserves**. The Bank of England manages the nation's foreign exchange reserves, implementing the government's exchange rate and balance of payments policy and any exchange control regulations which are in force;

(iv) **banker to other countries**. The Bank of England acts as banker to those overseas countries that wish to hold their foreign currency reserves in sterling on deposit in London;

(v) **General banking supervisor**. The Bank of England decides who can operate as a bank or licensed deposit taker and the ways in which banks must operate to protect depositors. Recent banking legislation and a growing need to oversee the orderly integration of UK banks into the world financial system have greatly expanded this function, though as we have already explained, international financial competition has caused the Bank of England to relinquish regulations which would reduce the competitive ability of British-based banks in the new global market.

THE BANK OF ENGLAND AND THE DISCOUNT MARKET

23. Traditionally, the Bank of England has functioned as **'lender of last resort'** to the UK banking system, being prepared to supply cash in order to maintain confidence and liquidity, so as to prevent bank failures. But the Bank of England does not supply cash directly to the clearing banks when they need to restore their cash ratios (as distinct from altering the composition of their cash ratios by converting balances at the Bank of England into cash). Instead, the Bank of England supplies cash to the clearing banks indirectly, via the Discount Market. Suppose that the clearing banks choose prudently to operate on a 10 per cent cash ratio, but that their actual cash ratios have fallen below 10 per cent. To restore their cash ratios to 10 per cent, the banks must run down their next most liquid assets which they convert into cash. The banks call back their loans to the discount houses, while simultaneously suspending the purchase of bills from the discount houses and encashing their existing portfolios of bills as the bills mature. In effect, this passes the cash shortage on to the discount houses, who must find the cash to repay the money at call and the money at short notice which they have borrowed from the clearing banks. The discount houses obtain the cash to repay the clearing banks by 'going to the Bank of England', ie they sells bills to the Bank of England at **the Bank of England's lending rate** or **discount rate** (which used to be called **Bank Rate** and later **Minimum Lending Rate**). Thus, by always being prepared to supply cash in return for bills to the clearing banks via the Discount Market, - but at a rate of interest or discount of the Bank's own choosing - the Bank of England acts as 'lending of last resort' to the banking system.

THE DEMAND FOR MONEY

24. Earlier in this chapter we discussed in some detail the problem of how to define the **money supply**, but so far we have made no mention of the **demand for money**. As we saw in Chapter 3, the demand by the general public to hold most commodities is explained by utility theory and the underlying assumption of a utility-maximising objective. We cannot however, explain the general public's demand to hold money in terms of the utility yielded by money itself, since modern token money has no intrinsic value. Instead, it is usual to identify three reasons or motives to explain the demand for money. These are shown in Table 19.2.

Table 19.2: The three demands for money

THE DEMAND FOR 'ACTIVE' MONEY BALANCES	(i) **The transactions demand** for money is explained by the general public's need to hold money balances to finance **planned expenditure** in the near future	THESE STEM FROM THE MEDIUM OF EXCHANGE FUNCTION OF MONEY
	(ii) **The precautionary demand** for money is explained by the need to hold money balances to finance **unplanned** expenditure eg for an unexpected car repair	
THE DEMAND FOR 'PASSIVE' OR 'IDLE' MONEY BALANCES	(iii) **The speculative demand** for money is explained by peoples' decisions to hold their personal wealth in the form of money, rather than in interest-earning alternatives to money, ie non-money financial assets.	STEMS FROM THE STORE OF VALUE FUNCTION OF MONEY

THE TRANSACTIONS DEMAND FOR MONEY

25. Members of the general public will normally wish to hold money balances for the essentially 'active' purpose of financing planned expenditure which they intend to undertake in the near future. This is called the **'transactions motive'** for holding money balances. The transactions demand for money depends upon:

(i) **real income**. At higher real incomes, total planned real consumption expenditure is greater, so people need larger transactions money balances to finance their planned expenditure.

(ii) **the price level**. At higher prices, larger nominal transactions balances are required to finance the same level of real expenditure;

(iii) **financial innovation**. The development of near monies which can be converted quickly and at zero cost into money reduces the need to hold transactions and precautionary money balances. The growing use of money substitutes such as credit cards has a similar effect.

(iv) **institutional factors**. Figure 19.3 illustrates an institutional change which has tended to increase the size of the transactions balances which people hold. Suppose a worker is paid a weekly wage of £200 and that:

(a) his only motive for holding money is the transactions motive;

(b) he spends the £200 at an even rate through the week. His transactions money balances can be shown by the solid line, conveying a 'dog-tooth' effect, in Figure 19.3. At the beginning of the week, the worker's transactions balance is £200, falling to zero at the end of the week, immediately before the next receipt of pay. On average, therefore, the transactions balance is £100. If, however, the method of paying wages is changed, so that the worker is paid £800 every 28 days instead of £200 weekly, the resulting transactions balances are shown by the broken line in Figure 19.3. Average transactions balances have risen from £100 to £400. An increase in the length of time between pay days thus tends to increase the transactions money balances which people hold.

Figure 19.3: The effect of length the time between pay days upon the transactions demand for money

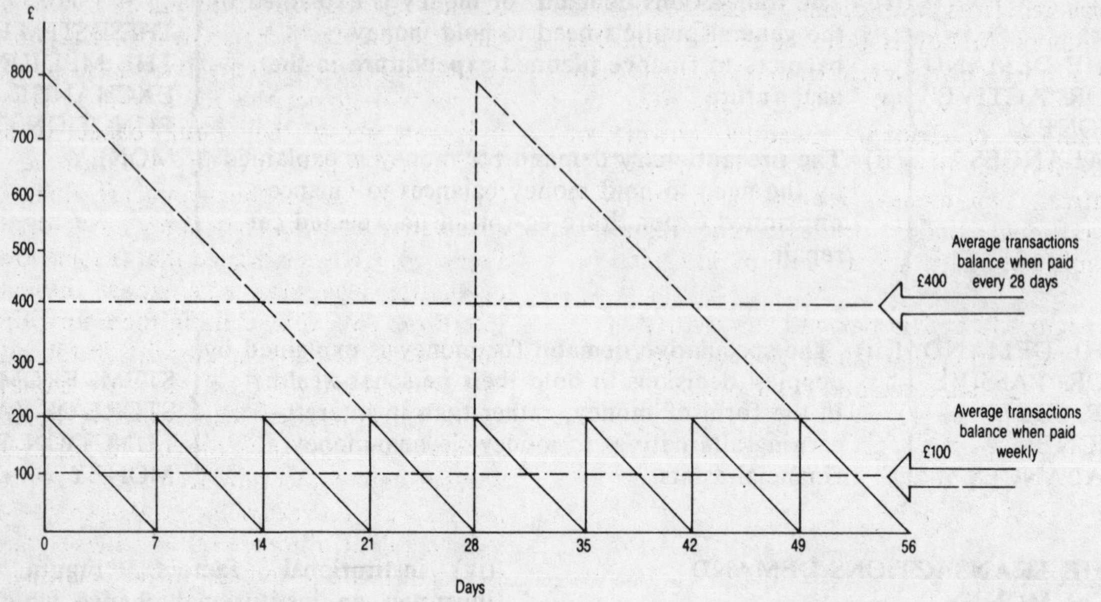

THE PRECAUTIONARY DEMAND FOR MONEY

26. The **precautionary demand for money** is broadly similar to the transactions demand, except that it relates to the need to hold money balances in order to finance *unplanned* transactions, resulting for example from unexpected ill-health or a washing machine breaking down. The existence of near monies and credit cards may reduce the need for precautionary money balances.

THE SPECULATIVE DEMAND FOR FOR MONEY

27. The transactions and precautionary demands for money are assumed to be unaffected by the rate of interest. In Figure 19.4, we have added together the transactions and precautionary demands for money - to form the **demand for 'active' money balances** - which we have depicted as a vertical line plotted against the rate of interest. If real income, the price level or institutional factors change, the curve will shift position, but it will remain a vertical line, or **interest-inelastic.**

Figure 19.4: The demand for 'active' money balances (transactions and precautionary money balances)

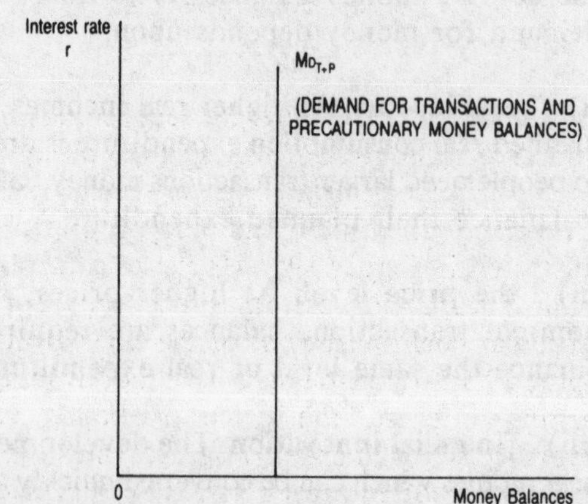

However, in the 'General Theory', Keynes argued the existence of a third, **speculative** motive for holding money balances in which **changes and expected changes in the rate of interest** became a crucial influence over people's demand to hold money. The speculative demand for money, which is illustrated in Figure 19.5 is sometimes called **the demand to hold passive or idle money balances**

as a **wealth asset** or **store of value**. It contrasts with the essentially *active* nature of the transactions and precautionary demands for money which stem from the medium of exchange function of money. Money is just one of the financial assets in which an individual may decide to store his personal wealth. Money possesses the advantage of instant spending power, or liquidity, but it earns little or no interest. In contrast, **non-money financial assets** such as **government bonds** or **gilts** are relatively illiquid, but earn a fixed rate of interest.

Figure 19.5: The demand for passive or idle money balances (speculative of asset demand for money)

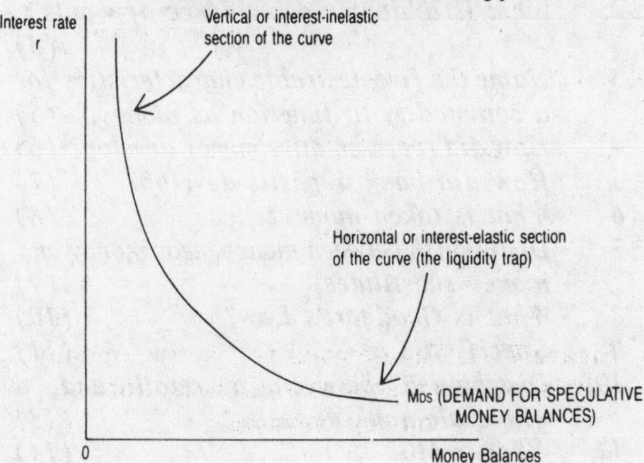

At higher rates of interest it becomes more attractive to hold bonds as wealth, rather than money. Thus the demand for passive money balances is *inversely related* to the rate of interest, as illustrated in Figure 19.5. However, speculation about future interest rates accounts for the particular non-linear slope of the curve drawn in Figure 19.5. Although bonds have the advantage of earning interest, the price of bonds varies inversely with market interest rates. If the market rate of interest rises, then the price of second-hand bonds must fall in order to convert their fixed interest payment into the new market interest rate. Now because falling bond prices inevitably mean that existing bond holders suffer *capital losses*, it is in their interest to guess correctly future changes in the rate of interest. If they *expect, or speculate*, that interest rates will rise, they should sell bonds now and hold their wealth in money so as to avoid the capital losses that would result from holding bonds. Conversely, if interest rates are expected to fall, people should move out of money now and purchase bonds so as to benefit from future *capital gains* when bond prices rise.

Keynes believed that there will be a value of the rate of interest which people regard as 'normal'; if the current rate is below the 'normal' rate people will expect the actual rate to rise, and if it were above, they would expect it to fall. This part of Keynes's theory explains the upper (vertical) and lower (horizontal) sections of the speculative demand for money curve drawn in Figure 19.5. Keynes argued that at some low rate of interest everyone will expect the rate of interest to rise, thus making them unwilling to hold bonds. For any further fall in the interest rate below this level, the demand for money will be perfectly elastic. The resulting horizontal section of the speculative demand for money curve Keynes called the **liquidity trap**. In a rather similar way, Keynes believed that there will be some high rate of interest at which everyone will expect the rate of interest to fall, making them unwilling to hold money as a passive wealth asset. For any further rise in the interest rate above this level, there will be no further movement out of money and into bonds; hence the speculative demand for money curve will be vertical or interest-inelastic.

THE LIQUIDITY PREFERENCE CURVE

28. In Figure 19.6, by **summing the transactions, precautionary, and speculative demands for money**, we obtain the **overall demand for money curve**, described by Keynes as the **liquidity preference curve**. Liquidity preference simply describes the fact that at lower interest rates, people prefer liquidity, or to hold their wealth in the form of money rather than bonds. While the *slope* of the demand for money curve is explained by the speculative demand for money, (and by liquidity preference), its *position* is determined by the transactions and precautionary demands. An increase in the demand for 'active' money balances, resulting for example, from an increase in real income, causes the M_D curve to shift rightwards. This is known as an **increase in liquidity preference**, showing that people wish to hold larger money balances at all interest rates.

THE MONETARIST THEORY OF THE DEMAND FOR MONEY

29. In the liquidity preference theory, developed by Keynes in the 1930s, the demand to

hold money balances is determined by the relative attraction of money and government bonds as wealth assets. Twenty years later in the 1950s, the American economist **Milton Friedman** made significant further developments to the theory, which form the basis to **current monetarist theories of the demand for money and of inflation** (the **modern quantity theory of money**). Friedman argued that there are many more influences upon peoples' demand to hold money as a wealth asset, besides current and expected interest rates on government bonds. Friedman's theory is essentially a theory of the demand for real money balances (M_D/P) rather than nominal money balances (M_D). He sees the real demand for money as being determined by total wealth (which is the sum of human and non-human wealth), the expected rate of return on various forms of wealth, the ratio of human wealth to non-human wealth and society's tastes and preferences. Perhaps the most significant difference between the Keynesian liquidity preference theory and Milton Friedman's theory of the demand for money is that *in the Keynesian theory money and bonds are close substitutes*, whereas *in Friedman's theory money is a substitute for all other assets, financial and real*. In the Keynesian theory, the demand for money is *interest-elastic* because wealth holders are assumed to react to changes in interest rates by altering their holdings of bonds and money only. By contrast, in the monetarist theory, wealth holders react to changes in interest rates by altering the composition of a much wider wealth portfolio in which money is just one asset. Friedman believed that changes in interest rates have *little effect* on the general public's demand to hold money, ie that the demand for money is *interest-inelastic*.

Figure 19.6: The demand for money or liquidity preference curve
[$MD_T + MD_P + MD_S \equiv MD(L)$]

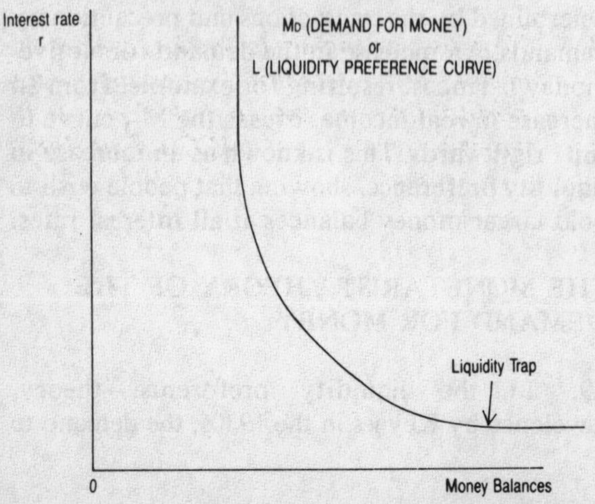

SUMMARY

30. We started this chapter by examining the nature of money and conditions which affect its supply, and completed the chapter by surveying the theory of the demand for money. Between discussing the supply of, and demand for, money, we explained how, through the credit or deposit creating process, banks are responsible for creating the larger part of modern money and we examined some institutional aspects of the United Kingdom banking system.

STUDENT SELF-TESTING

1 *List the four functions of money.* *(2)*
2 *What is a 'double coincidence of wants'?* *(3)*
3 *Name the five desirable characteristics for a commodity to function as money.* *(5)*
4 *How did representative money develop?* *(6)*
5 *How did bank deposits develop?* *(7)*
6 *What is token money?* *(8)*
7 *Distinguish between money, near money and money substitutes.* *(9)*
8 *What is Goodhart's Law?* *(10)*
9 *Specify M3.* *(11)*
10 *Distinguish between a retail and a wholesale bank deposit.* *(13)*
11 *What is M0?* *(14)*
12 *Define a bank.* *(15)*
13 *What is a cash drain?* *(15-16)*
14 *What is the money multiplier?* *(17)*
15 *List the main types of banks in the UK.* *(18)*
16 *Distinguish between a clearing bank and a merchant bank.* *(19)*
17 *What is a commercial bill?* *(20)*
18 *What is the role of the clearing banks in the discount market?* *(21)*
19 *List the functions of the Bank of England.* *(22)*
20 *Explain the 'lender of the last resort' function.* *(23)*
21 *List the three main motives for demanding money.* *(24)*
22 *What are the determinants of the transactions demand for money.* *(25)*
23 *Explain the precautionary demand for money.* *(26)*
24 *What is liquidity preference?* *(27)*
25 *What is meant by an increase in liquidity preference?* *(28)*
26 *What are real money balances?* *(29)*

EXERCISES

1 *The Barcwest and Midlloyd Bank is the only bank in the country. Initially, its balance sheet is:*

Liabilities		*Assets*	
Customers' deposits:	*£1,000*	*Cash:*	*£80*
		Treasury bills:	*£320*
		Advances:	*£600*
Total liabilities:	*£1,000*	*Total assets:*	*£1,000*

(a) *What is the bank's cash ratio?*
(b) *What is the bank's liquid asset ratio?*

A customer deposits a further £200 of cash into the bank.

(c) *What is the bank's cash ratio immediately after the deposit?*
(d) *Assuming a return to the initial cash ratio, by how much can the bank expand total deposits?*

MULTIPLE CHOICE QUESTIONS

1 *Assuming that a banking system keeps 8 per cent of its deposits in cash and lends out the remainder in the form of advances to customers, an initial deposit of £100 can lead to an increase in bank deposits of:*
A *£800*
B *£700*
C *£1,250*
D *£1,150*

2 *The money supply, when defined as M3, includes:*
A *Cash only*
B *Cash and current accounts only*
C *Cash, current accounts and deposit accounts*
D *Current accounts and deposit accounts only.*

3 *Which of the following assets held by a clearing bank should not be regarded as a reserve asset?*
A *British government securities (with under 1 year to maturity)*
B *Advances*
C *Loans to the discount market*
D *Bills*

Questions 4 - 6 relate to the following:
A *Balances at the Bank of England*
B *Advances*
C *Treasury bills*
D *Money at short notice*

Which of the above:

4 *is the most liquid of a clearing bank's assets?*

5 *represents the bank's lending to the Discount Market?*

6 *represents the bank's lending to the government?*

EXAMINATION QUESTIONS

1 (a) *Define money and indicate its functions.* *(6 marks)*

(b) *Examine the monetarist view that an increase in the supply of money above the rate of increase of real output will lead to rising prices.* *(14 marks)*
(ACCA June 1987)

2 *What are the functions of the Bank of England?* *(CIMA May 1987)*

3 *How does a commercial bank reconcile the need for security, liquidity and profitability in the distribution of its assets?* *(ACCA June 1985)*

4 *What is the relationship between the aims of a commercial bank and the types of asset which it holds?* *(ACCA June 1982)*

5. (a) *Why are there so many rates of interest in a developed economy?* *(15 marks)*

(b) *Describe how these different rates of interest are illustrated by the opearations of a commerical bank?* *(10 marks)*
(IOB April 1987)

6. (a) *Explain the three Keynesian reasons for holding money.* *(12 marks)*

(b) *Illustrate the relationship between the rate of interest and the demand for money.* *(4 marks)*

(c) *In what way does the Keynesian demand for money differ from saving?* *(4 marks)*
(AAT June 1988)

7 *Explain the liquidity preference theory of interest rate determination.* *(ACCA June 1987)*

20. Monetary policy

INTRODUCTION

1. This is the second of two chapters devoted to the study of the role of money in a monetary economy. In Chapter 19, we explained the nature and functions both of money and of the banking system in a modern economy, and we examined in some detail the supply of money and the demand for money. We begin this chapter by explaining the **meaning of monetary policy** and by identifying **policy objectives** and the **policy instruments** through which monetary policy is implemented. We shall then describe the fundamental changes in monetary policy which have occurred in the UK during the last thirty years, as **Keynesian monetary policy** has given way to **monetarism**. The chapter concludes with a brief survey of alternative strategies which a monetarist government might adopt to control the money supply, together with an explanation of the actual strategy adopted by the United Kingdom government and an assessment of its success.

THE MEANING OF MONETARY POLICY

2. All governments have a variety of economic objectives, such as full employment, economic growth and low inflation, which contribute towards, or are necessary to achieve, the **ultimate economic objective** of increased welfare and living standards. A number of different types of economic policy can be used to achieve these objectives, including monetary policy and fiscal policy. In Chapter 18 we defined **fiscal policy** as any deliberate action undertaken by the government to achieve its economic objectives using the *fiscal* instruments of taxation, government spending and the budget deficit. In much the same way, we can define **monetary policy** in terms of deliberate action undertaken to achieve the government's objectives using *monetary* instruments, such as controls over bank lending and the rate of interest. Monetary policy is implemented by the country's **monetary authorities: the finance ministry and the central bank**. In the UK, these are **the Treasury** and the **Bank of England**. The direction and broad objectives of monetary policy are decided upon jointly by the Treasury and the Bank of England, with the Treasury, in principle, having the final say because it is a government department. The Bank of England then implements the details of monetary policy, and in practice it possesses a considerable amount of independence in determining the nature and direction of monetary policy. Although technically subordinate to the Treasury, the Bank of England operates in the knowledge that the Treasury is unlikely to enter into open conflict with the Bank, because of the damaging effects on confidence which would probably result.

THE OBJECTIVES AND INSTRUMENTS OF MONETARY POLICY

3. Monetary policy can be an extremely complicated subject. To assist your understanding of the complex and often confusing issues involved, we shall analyse monetary policy in terms of the **objectives** and **instruments** of monetary policy which are illustrated in Figure 20.1 (see following page).

As a simplification, we shall assume that an **ultimate objective** of monetary policy is to control inflation, in order to create the conditions in which the **'true' ultimate objective** of policy, improved economic welfare, can be attained. (We should note, however, that control of inflation has not always been the principal objective of monetary policy. In a later section of this chapter, we explain how the objectives of monetary policy have changed. Nevertheless, in recent years in the UK, a 'monetarist' monetary policy has been pursued, with the general aim of controlling inflation.)

Monetarists believe that inflation is caused by a prior increase in the stock of money (or money supply), and that to control inflation the growth of the money supply must first be controlled. In **'monetarist' monetary policy, the money supply** (or more strictly **the rate of growth of the money stock**), therefore became an important **intermediate objective** or target. But it is impossible to control the money supply directly. In order to 'hit' an intermediate target specified in terms of the money supply, the authorities must first aim to control an **immediate** or **operative target** of monetary policy, such as **the rate of interest** or the **liquid assets** possessed by the banking

Figure 20.1: The objectives and instruments of monetary policy

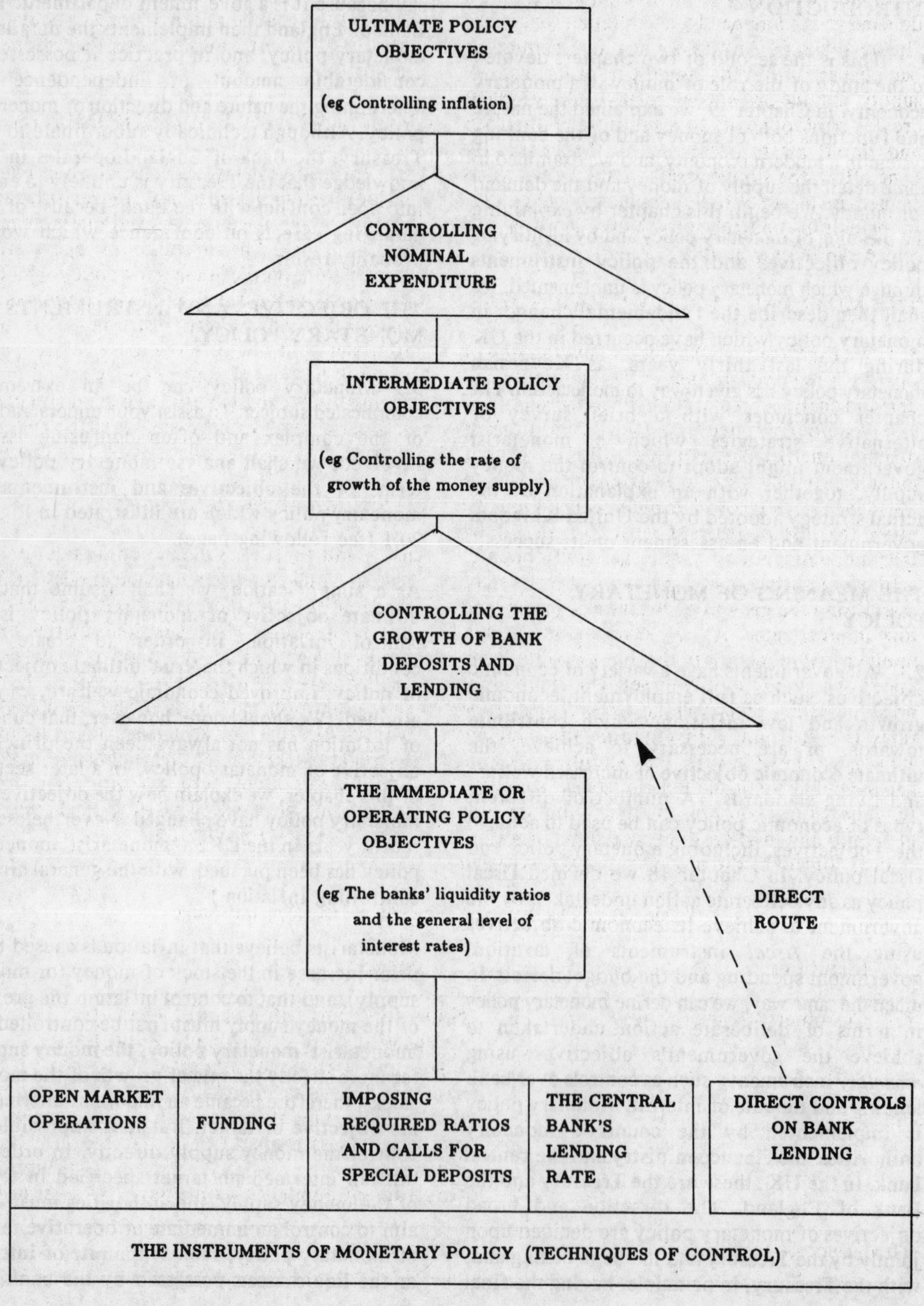

system. As we shall explain in greater depth later in this chapter, by acting on the rate of interest as an immediate target of monetary policy, the authorities hope to control the stock of money by influencing the general public's demand to hold money balances rather than other financial assets. And as we saw in Chapter 19, bank deposits form the largest part of the money-supply, and the private enterprise banking system creates bank deposits to a multiple of the cash and liquid assets possessed by the banks. By controlling the liquid assets of the banks as an immediate target of policy, monetary policy can, in principle, control total bank deposits and hence the money supply.

THE MONETARY POLICY 'TRADE-OFF'

4. We explained in Chapter 19 how the *rate of interest is the price of money*. Simple supply and demand analysis predicts that when the supply of any commodity is decreased with conditions of demand unchanged, its price will rise. Thus if monetary policy aims to restrict the growth of the money stock below demand at current interest rates, the rate of interest must rise. It follows that monetary policy cannot generally hope to achieve simultaneously the twin objectives of **restraining the growth of the money supply** and **low interest rates**. As we have already noted, 'monetarist' monetary policy has generally been aimed at a money supply target. The monetarists must therefore, accept whatever level of interest rates is consistent with attaining their money supply targets, given the stability of the general public's demand to hold money. However, in the Keynesian era monetary policy was generally aimed at an interest rate target rather than at control of the money supply. Keynesian monetary policy allowed the money supply to expand or contract to whatever level was consistent with achieving the interest rate target. Essentially, the money supply was allowed to fluctuate to *finance* or *accommodate* the money balances the general public wished to hold at the rate of interest chosen by the monetary authorities.

MONETARY POLICY INSTRUMENTS

5. In the following sections we shall explain various **policy instruments**, or **techniques of control**, which the monetary authorities can use to try to 'hit' one or other of operative or immediate targets of monetary policy which we described in section 3. It is important to realise that not all the instruments or techniques of control will necessarily be used; some of the techniques of control which found favour during the Keynesian era have been rejected as unsuitable under monetarism. We shall explain the reasons why in later sections of this chapter.

OPEN MARKET OPERATIONS

6. Traditionally, a main technique of control used in United Kingdom monetary policy has been through **open market operations** - a policy of buying or selling government securities by the Bank of England on the open market, ie the **capital market**. With the aid of Table 20.1 which shows in simplified form a bank's balance sheet, we shall describe how open market operations can be used to influence the clearing banks' cash and liquid assets ratios, with the aim of indirectly influencing the banking system's total credit and deposit creating ability.

Table 20.1: The balance sheet of a UK clearing bank

Liabilities		Assets		
1. Customers' deposits	1	Notes and coins (till money)	Cash Ratio	Liquid Assets
	2	Balances at Bank of England		
	3	Loans to the Discount Market		
	4	Treasury bills and other bills		
	5	British Government stocks with one year or less to maturity		
	6	Advances		Illiquid Assets
	7	Government bonds (Investments)		
Total Deposit Liabilities		Total Assets		

In principle, a sale of **government securities (gilts)** to the general public should lead, via the money multiplier, to a multiple contraction of credit and total assets (shown on the right hand side of the bank's balance sheet), and to an equal fall in total deposits (shown on the left hand side). **Contractionary open market operations** proceeds through the following stages:

(i) The Bank of England sells gilts to the general public, who purchase the securities with cheques drawn on their deposits in the clearing banks.

(ii) When the cheques are paid into the Bank of England, the balance sheets of the clearing banks will show an equal fall in customers' deposits, on the liabilities side and balances at the Bank of England on the assets side.

(iii) Because customers' deposits have fallen, contractionary open market operations have reduced the money supply. There may, however, be a **secondary and much larger** fall in the money supply if banks now have to take action to reduce total bank deposits in order to restore their cash ratios. In the UK banking system, the clearing banks restore their cash ratios by recalling loans to the discount market (item 3 in the balance sheet) and by cashing bills as they mature (item 4). In effect, this passes the cash squeeze on to the discount houses, who obtain the cash to repay the banks by selling bills to the Bank of England. This is part of the Bank of England's **lender of last resort** function, which we described in Chapter 19. The Bank of England has traditionally been prepared to supply cash to the banking system, via the discount market, so as to prevent bank crashes and to maintain liquidity and confidence. But although the clearing banks restore their cash ratios with cash supplied in this way by the Bank of England, they do so by running down their holdings of other liquid assets.

(iv) The ratio of liquid assets to total deposits will now have fallen. If the banks were initially operating close to their desired ratio of liquid assets to total deposits, they must now reduce lending (shown on the assets side of the balance sheet) and total deposits (on the liabilities side) to restore their liquid assets ratios. Thus in practice, a clearing bank's **liquid assets ratio** (or **reserve assets ratio**) tends to be a more important fulcrum for control in the operation of monetary policy than its cash ratio. Given the money multiplier as:

$$\frac{1}{\text{liquid asset ratio}}$$

in principle total bank deposits will fall or contract by the size of the initial fall in liquid assets x the money multiplier.

EXPANSIONARY OPEN MARKET OPERATIONS

7. The Bank of England can, of course, use open market operations *to expand*, rather than *to contract*, total bank lending and deposits. In this case, the central bank buys securities from the general public, paying for the gilts with cheques drawn on itself. When the cheques are paid into the general public's deposits in the clearing banks, the money supply rises directly and the clearing banks find that their cash ratios are higher than the level necessary for prudent banking. In pursuit of profit, the banks may then expand total lending and deposits until constrained once again by their cash and liquid assets ratios. In this way, a secondary and larger rise in the money supply takes place, which is a multiple of the initial increase.

THE EFFECTIVENESS OF OPEN MARKET OPERATIONS

8. The initial change in bank deposits and in the money supply which is caused by open market operations may not always be followed by a secondary and larger change in total bank deposits. In the case of expansionary open market operations, banks may only succeed in expanding total deposits if there is a general demand by credit-worthy customers for bank loans, or if there are assets available such as bills and gilts which the banks can profitably purchase. And if the banks possess a 'cushion' of liquid assets, over and above their desired liquid assets ratio, contractionary open market operations may not induce a secondary stage of deposit reduction. In this situation, banks can simply run down the 'cushion', without having to reduce loans to the general public until the 'cushion' has been eliminated. If the banks

possess a substantial cushion of 'spare' liquid assets over and above their minimum prudential ratios, open market operations on a massive scale might be needed to have a significant effect upon total bank lending and the money supply.

OPEN MARKET OPERATIONS AND THE RATE OF INTEREST

9. At this point, we should note that open market operations may have a much greater effect on **interest rates** than on total bank deposits and the money supply. In the case of contractionary open market operations, a sale of government securities by the central bank of sufficient size to induce a secondary fall in bank deposits, would almost certainly 'flood' the capital market, causing gilt prices to fall and interest rates to rise. The main purpose of contractionary open market operations may well be to raise interest rates, especially if the authorities wish to reduce the demand for bank credit. But we should also note that, in the United Kingdom, the sale of government securities by the Bank of England has on many occasions been undertaken, not with the attempted **discretionary control** of **bank deposits** and **interest rates** in mind, but to **finance** and **manage the national debt** and to sell new debt to **finance the current budget deficit and PSBR**. Usually, the Bank of England must sell new debt so as to renew the national debt as it matures. And when there is a budget deficit caused by government expenditure exceeding income, new debt must also be sold to finance the resulting borrowing requirement. The sale of government securities by the Bank of England has often reflected the needs of national debt and PSBR management, rather than the control by open market operations of bank lending and the money supply.

OPEN MARKET OPERATIONS IN THE DISCOUNT MARKET

10. As well as engaging in open market operations which affect **long-term interest rates** in the **gilts market**, the Bank of England can influence **short-term interest rates** by selling and buying **bills** in the **discount market**. Open market operations in the discount market do not affect the size of a bank's overall liquid assets ratio, but by changing the proportions of cash and bills held by the bank, they change the composition of the liquid assets ratio.

FUNDING

11. We have already noted that the government borrows for two different though related reasons. These are:

(i) **To renew the national debt.** Each year part of the national debt matures and must be repaid. Usually the government simply sells new debt to raise the funds with which to pay off the maturing debt. (An exception occurs when there is a **budget surplus**, in which case tax revenues are used to redeem maturing debt, thereby reducing the size of the national debt.)

(ii) **To finance the current budget deficit and borrowing requirement**. When spending by the government (and indeed by the whole of the public sector) exceeds tax revenue and income from other sources, the resulting budget deficit must be financed by borrowing. The government sells new debt, which adds to the national debt, to **finance the CGBR** (while extra debt sold by the whole of the public sector **finances the PSBR**).

Funding is a process by which the government sells *long-dated debt* (gilts and National Savings securities) rather than *short-dated* or *floating debt* (Treasury bills). Successful funding of the national debt means that the general public buy illiquid securities, paid for with cheques drawn on clearing bank deposits. This reduces the supply of bills available to the banking system and it causes a fall in the general public's deposits in the clearing banks which has an effect identical to the contractionary open market operations we have already described.

FUNDING THE PSBR

12. The government **funds the PSBR** when it sells gilts and National Savings securities rather than bills to finance the public sector's *current* borrowing requirement. We have just noted that funding the *existing stock* of national debt has a contractionary effect upon bank lending and the money supply because it reduces both bank deposits in the private sector banking system, and the liquid assets or bills available for the banks to purchase. However, when the government funds the PSBR, the effect on the money supply is better described as *neutral* rather than *contractionary*. This is because the government is borrowing to finance the *flow of current expenditure*, and not just simply to *alter the composition of an existing stock of debt*. The government borrows bank deposits from the general public, but these then recirculate back to the general public when the government spends the funds borrowed. If, as a result, total deposits in the banking system remain unchanged, there is no effect upon the money supply.

THE 'FULL-FUND' RULE AND 'OVER-FUNDING' THE PSBR

13. In recent years the UK government has followed a **'full-fund' rule**, based on the principle that if the government puts money into the economy by spending more than it receives, it must take the same amount out again by funding:

THE 'FULL-FUND' RULE

The authorities will seek to fund the net total of:

(i) maturing debt;
(ii) PSBR/PSDR;
(iii) Any underlying changes in foreign exchange reserves;

by selling long-dated date, eg gilts outside the banking system, usually to the general public

'Over-funding' takes place when the total of long-dated debt sold is more than required by this rule. **'Under-funding'** is when the total of funding is less than required by the rule. 'Over-funding' alters the composition of the national debt in the manner described in Section 11 and has a contractionary effect upon the money supply. In the early 1980s, until 1985, the authorities pursued a policy of systematic 'over-funding'. More gilts were sold than were needed for a full fund and the net proceeds were used to purchase commercial bills so as to reduce liquidity in the banking system. But systematic 'over-funding' led to the Bank of England acquiring a commercial bill 'mountain' that set up undesirable distortions in the financial system. As a result, 'over-funding' as a method of achieving control over monetary growth was abandoned in 1985.

'Over-funding' can take place whether there is a PSBR or a PSDR. In today's circumstances of a budget surplus and PSDR, a policy of 'over-funding' would involve the authorities choosing to use the budget surplus to acquire more commercial bills from the banking system instead of using the surplus to redeem debt. However, the government has decided to use the budget surplus and PSDR to reduce the size of the national debt rather than to use 'over-funding' as a policy of monetary control. The government's stated policy is *'the neutral one of full-funding, avoiding inflationary forms of financing but not seeking to use 'over-funding' to offset the growth of liquidity resulting from the operation of market forces in the private sector... When the Government wishes to tighten or loosen monetary policy, it will do so by adjusting short-term interest rates.' (Treasury Economic Progress Report: February 1989).*

IMPOSING REQUIRED RESERVE RATIOS UPON THE BANKS

14. Open market operations and 'over-funding' (or funding the National Debt) are examples of techniques of monetary control which seek to influence the credit and deposit creating abilities of the commercial banks by *acting on the supply* of cash and liquid assets available to the banks. In principle, both open market operations and over-funding can engineer a multiple contraction of total bank lending and deposits because, as a part of normal banking practice, the commercial banks choose to keep **prudent cash and liquid assets ratios**. But instead of leaving the clearing banks free to decide their own prudent ratios, the monetary authorities have sometimes imposed **required reserve asset ratios** upon the banks. When left to themselves, the banks might, for example, choose to operate on a liquid assets ratio of 20 per cent. But if the central bank imposes a required ratio of 30 per cent, the commercial banks must undertake a multiple contraction of bank deposits until liquid assets equal the required ratio, unless of course the banks are able to purchase extra liquid assets from the general public by offering bank deposits in exchange. In order to bring about a further reduction in lending and bank deposits, the central bank could simply **raise the required reserve assets ratio**. Conversely, the authorities could reduce the ratio if they wished to encourage an expansion in lending and deposits.

For many decades until 1981, the United Kingdom monetary authorities did indeed impose required cash and liquid assets upon the British clearing banks, though in recent years, for reasons we shall shortly explain, required ratios have been largely abandoned. However, the UK authorities have never engaged in a policy of raising or lowering the required ratios from year to year in order to contract or expand total bank lending. Instead, the authorities operated **special deposits policy**, which had an effect similar to the raising or lowering of a required reserve ratio.

As a part of normal banking practice, the UK clearing banks keep **working or operational balances at the Bank of England** (item 2 in the balance sheets), which form part of their cash ratios. In the 1960s and 1970s the Bank of England frequently called for special deposits, equal for example to 2 per cent of the clearing banks' deposit liabilities. Immediately upon the call for special deposits, part of the banks' operational balances at the Bank of England became frozen or completely illiquid, ceasing therefrom, to be a part of the cash ratio. The effect was equivalent to raising a required cash ratio by 2 per cent. Similarly, the release of special deposits was equivalent to reducing the required cash ratio. There have been no calls for special deposits in the UK in the 1980s.

Required reserve ratios were abandoned by the Bank of England in 1981, and there is little sense in calling for special deposits in the absence of required ratios imposed on the banking system. Indeed, even when required ratios were imposed, calls for special deposits were probably more effective as a 'tax' upon the banking system than as a serious constraint upon the banks' lending and deposit creating ability. Although the Bank of England usually paid money market rates of interest on all special deposits, a call for special deposits 'taxed' the banking system because it prevented the banks from using more profitably the funds that became tied up at the Bank of England.

DIRECT CONTROLS ON BANK LENDING

15. As we have just seen, the imposition of required reserve asset ratios and calls for special deposits are forms of control imposed on the commercial banks which limit the banks' freedom to act commercially and in their self-interest. However, the monetary authorities can, if they wish, impose a form of control that interferes much more severely and directly in the banks' freedom to make their own commercial decisions. Such controls are known as **direct controls**, which are two types: **quantitative** and **qualitative.**

(i) **Quantitative controls.** These involve imposing *maximum limits* or *ceilings* upon the amount that banks can lend, or upon the rate at which banks can expand total deposits.

(ii) **Qualitative controls.** These are **'directional' controls** which instruct or possibly 'persuade' banks to lend only to certain types of customers, eg business customers requiring credit to finance investment or exports might be given a high priority, with consumer credit being relegated to a much lower position in the 'queue' for advances. **Selective higher purchase controls** represent another form of directional control.

Direct controls on bank lending were widely used as a technique of monetary control in the United Kingdom in the 1960s and 1970s. However, for reasons which we shall explain shortly, direct controls on lending, together with required ratios, have been abandoned in the 1980s.

CONTROL VIA INTEREST RATES

16. All the techniques of monetary control which we have so far described operate on the ability of the clearing banks to *supply* credit and to create bank deposits - though by causing security prices to rise or fall, open market operations and funding affect interest rates also. The final technique of control we shall consider attempts to influence the supply of credit and bank deposits through an *indirect* route, by acting on the general public's *demand* for bank loans. Whereas the direct controls on bank lending which we described in the previous section *ration the quantity or supply* of credit available, by raising or lowering interest rates, the monetary authorities can seek to *ration demand via price.*

As well as using open market operations to raise or lower interest rates, the Bank of England has another instrument at its disposal: the **discount rate** or **lending rate** at which it undertakes the **lender of last resort function** of supplying cash to the banking system through the discount market. Changes in the Bank of England's lending rate affect interest rates in two ways. In the first place, a change in the lending rate usually has an immediate effect upon the **bill discount rate** at which the discount houses conduct business with the clearing banks, and thence upon other short-term interest rates. The bill discount rate is normally a fraction of a per cent below the Bank of England's lending rate - if it were higher then the clearing banks might find that there were no bills on offer, since the discount houses could obtain a better price by selling their bills to the Bank of England instead! It follows therefore, that the Bank of England can force the bill discount rate down by reducing its own lending rate. Secondly, changes in the Bank of England's lending rate tend to act as a *psychological signal* to financial institutions and markets that the Bank of England wants interest rates to move in a particular direction.

THE TECHNIQUES OF MONETARY CONTROL: A SUMMARY

17. If monetary policy is used to control the growth of the money supply, the monetary authorities face the problem that bank deposits, the main component of the money supply, are a *liability of the private enterprise banking system*, and are not directly under the authorities' control. This means that the authorities must seek to control other variables, such as the cash supplied to the banking system, gilt and bill sales, and the central bank's own lending rate, which are used as instruments of policy in pursuit of operative targets such as the banks' liquidity ratios and the general level and structure of interest rates. One or other of these operative or immediate targets of monetary policy must be attained if the authorities are to exercise any semblance of control over the money supply.

Most of the instruments of monetary policy which we have described act largely on the ability of the banking system to *supply* credit and bank deposits. The exception is the central bank's lending rate and to some extent also open market sales of gilts and bills, which act on the *demand* for credit or bank loans, via price.

We can also identify three general ways in which the central bank can try to make the private enterprise banking system behave in the way it wishes. The central bank can:

(i) operate on instruments directly under the authorities' control, such as the supply of cash, and gilt and bill sales, hoping to influence total bank deposits and credit as banks adjust their balance sheets to attain liquidity ratios, prudently chosen by the banks themselves, acting in their own self-interest;

(ii) impose controls, such as required reserve ratios and quantitative and qualitative controls on bank lending, which artificially constrain the banking system's ability to act commercially;

(iii) use 'moral persuasion' to encourage the banks to operate in line with the central bank's wishes. In the UK moral persuasion exercised by the Bank of England, or the Governor's 'nods and winks', has usually had a significant effect upon the banking system's behaviour, though it must be remembered that such 'persuasion' always carries the veiled threat of more direct action if the private enterprise banks were ever to ignore the Governor's 'polite requests'.

MONETARY POLICY DURING THE KEYNESIAN ERA

18. Both the **objectives** and the **instruments** of UK monetary policy have changed significantly in recent decades. In large part this reflects the change since 1970 from a **broadly Keynesian monetary policy** to a **'monetarist' monetary policy**. We shall now describe the main elements of the monetary policy implemented in the United Kingdom during the Keynesian era, before in the concluding sections of this chapter going on to survey and assess the monetarist strategy adopted in the 1980s.

For most of the period from 1945 until the 1970s, British monetary policy, under both Conservative and Labour governments, could be described as **Keynesian**. So far in this chapter, we have assumed that control of the money supply is an important intermediate objective of monetary policy and that the rate of interest is one of the policy instruments available for 'targeting' at the money supply objective. While this has certainly been true under monetarism, during the Keynesian era the roles were reversed: the **rate of interest** was the **objective of policy** and the Keynesians were prepared to allow the **money supply** to expand or contract, to accommodate whatever rate of interest target that the authorities had in mind. For the Keynesians, 'money did not matter' in the macro-economic management of the economy. Inflation was not a serious problem in the UK during most of the Keynesian era and control of inflation was ranked fairly low in the Keynesian order of economic priorities. And because the Keynesians did not locate the cause of inflation in the growth of the money supply, control of the money supply was not a part of Keynesian monetary policy.

In 'traditional' Keynesian theory, monetary policy affects the 'real economy' through changes in the rate of interest influencing businessmen's investment decisions, via the **marginal efficiency of investment**. (If in doubt about this, refer back to Chapter 17.) By lowering or raising interest rates, aggregate money demand (AMD) can be managed, causing an increase or decrease in the equilibrium level of national income. Along with fiscal policy, monetary policy was used by the Keynesians to manage aggregate demand, in pursuit of the objectives of full employment and stable growth. Although the Keynesians ignored the effects of monetary policy upon the money supply, they placed considerable emphasis on the **need to control credit and bank lending** as a part of the overall **management of aggregate demand**. Required reserve asset ratios and direct controls on bank lending were introduced which restricted the commercial freedom of the banks to expand their asset portfolios through consumer lending. And unlike modern monetarists, the Keynesians usually regarded monetary policy and fiscal policy as independent policy instruments, ignoring, for example, the effects on the money supply resulting from an expansionary fiscal policy and budget deficit.

KEYNESIANS AND NATIONAL DEBT MANAGEMENT

19. However, it is over simple to conclude that the Keynesians used monetary policy *solely* to manage the level of aggregate demand in the UK. For much of the Keynesian era, monetary policy was assigned to other objectives, particularly **national debt management**. Being the largest borrower in the economy, the government stands to benefit most from low interest rates, which reduce the cost of servicing the national debt. During the Keynesian period, an overriding aim of monetary policy was the procurement of **orderly financial markets** in which the governments could sell new debt - gilts and Treasury bills - at favourable prices, both to renew the national debt and to finance the current public sector borrowing requirement.

MONETARY POLICY AND THE BALANCE OF PAYMENTS

20. During the Keynesian era, the UK balance of payments was usually in deficit, with imports exceeding exports. On several occasions this persistent trade or current account deficit developed into a full-blown sterling crisis, as owners of sterling, on deposit in the UK banking system and in British government securities, sold pounds and took their funds out of the UK. In these circumstances, the interest rate target of Keynesian monetary policy was switched away from the '*normal*' objective of low and stable interest rates and national debt management to a **'crisis' objective** of **high interest rates to protect the exchange rate**. High interest rates would stem the capital outflow and attract funds back into the UK. (Indeed, despite the benefits of North Sea Oil revenues, which transformed the UK balance of payments in the 1980s, monetary policy in the monetarist era has continued to face similar problems. On occasion, the monetarists have had to subordinate the domestic money objective of controlling the money supply to the external objective of supporting the exchange rate, when for example in January 1985, the Bank of England significantly raised its lending rate to stem a 'run on the pound'.)

MONETARY POLICY UNDER THE MONETARISTS

21. In the 1980s, UK monetary policy displayed the following **'monetarist'** characteristics:

(i) As we have already explained, an important monetarist objective has been the control of inflation. Because monetarists believe that inflation is caused by an excess supply of money, control of the rate of growth of the money supply has become the main intermediate objective of monetary policy in the UK, replacing the other aims which we have described in the context of Keynesian monetary policy.

(ii) Most monetarists believe that monetary policy can have a greater expansionary or contractionary effect upon aggregate money demand and nominal national income than fiscal policy. However, this *does not mean* that monetarists wish to use monetary policy in the 'traditional' Keynesian manner, as a **short-term** or **discretionary instrument** of **demand management**. Instead, the monetarists have used monetary policy (and indeed, macro-economic policy in general) as a **medium-term policy for influencing and stabilising the wider economic environment**, in order to create conditions in which markets and private enterprise may function properly.

THE MEDIUM TERM FINANCIAL STRATEGY

22. In the United Kingdom, the framework within which monetary policy has been conducted in recent years has been the **Medium Term Financial Strategy (MTFS)**, adopted by the Conservative Government in its 1980 budget. Initially, the MTFS was based almost exclusively on the monetarist or 'New Classical' belief, that a firm announcement of a money supply target for a medium-term period stretching several years ahead would itself bring down the rate of inflation, through its effect on expectations of future inflation. According to the Conservative Government, the MTFS 'plots the path for bringing inflation down through a **steady reduction in the rate of growth of the money supply secured by the necessary fiscal policies**'. The objective of the MTFS has been to bring about a gradual reduction in the growth of money GDP (or the nominal value of domestic output), in the belief that this will result in lower inflation, whilst leaving the growth of real GDP unaffected. Central to the strategy has been the announcement of medium-term targets for the growth of the money supply, designed to 'talk-down' the rate of inflation by causing workers and firms to reduce their inflationary expectations. If people believe that a 'tough' government means business in reducing inflation, they will immediately begin to behave in a less-inflationary way, which in itself will reduce inflation!

THE SUCCESS OF THE MEDIUM TERM FINANCIAL STRATEGY

23. During the 1980s the main measure of money targeted in the MTFS has been **M3** (which before 1987 was known as **Sterling M3**). However, the government's record in 'hitting' its M3 target has been extremely poor. Throughout the 1980s M3 grew at a rate generally well above the target rate of growth set out in the MTFS. Yet according to the monetarists' own philosophy, a failure to 'hit' a pre-announced target might be expected to affect expectations adversely and - even worse- it would then be rational for workers and firms to conclude that the government had lost control over the economy!

But instead of the failure to 'hit' the M3 target leading to inflation accelerating out of control (as the above argument would indicate), average price rises in the UK fell to below 5 per cent - a rate of inflation not experienced in the UK since the 1960s. Can we conclude therefore, that the 'monetarist experiment' in the UK and the MTFS have been a success? Keynesians say 'not so'. They argue that the statistical evidence destroys the central tenet of monetarism, namely the prediction that an increase in the money supply will be followed, after a lag, by a similar increase in the price level. According to Keynesians, the Conservative Government's apparent success in bringing inflation down has had very little to do with monetarist theory and much more to do with an 'old-fashioned' severe deflation of aggregate demand in the early 1980s, combined with the Government's 'luck' in benefitting from external events such as the worldwide fall in energy and raw material prices which occurred in the 1980s. Falling commodity prices significantly reduced domestic production costs and inflationary pressure, just as rising prices of oil and other primary products had contributed to inflation in the 1970s.

Monetarists (as we might expect) argue that the MTFS has been a success, the 'proof' being the lower inflation rate (until 1988 at least) and the improved business environment claimed by the monetarists. However, any success is probably due more to the fiscal policy elements of the MTFS (which we described in Chapter 18), than with the ability of monetary policy to 'hit' a money supply target. Some monetarists have excused the lack of correlation between M3 and the inflation rate by arguing that M3 has 'misbehaved' for purely 'technical reasons', and that we really need not rely on an observed relationship between any particular measure of money - such as M3 - and the price level for the central monetarist argument still to be correct. In some years, the Conservative Government responded to M3's 'misbehaviour' by 'moving the goal posts', ie by raising the M3 target for the next year, while still claiming that the MTFS framework was necessary for the control of inflation. Finally, the government largely **abandoned the formal announcement of targets** for measures of money such as M3, which have been relegated from their earlier role in the MTFS as objectives or targets of policy. Instead M3, M0 and the other monetary aggregates have tended to become mere **indicators** of the 'tightness' or 'looseness' of monetary policy, which are monitored along with other monetary indicators - the value of money GDP and the exchange rate - to assess whether the MTFS is 'on course'.

THE ABANDONMENT OF REQUIRED RATIOS AND DIRECT CONTROLS

24. On several occasions in this chapter we have mentioned how, under monetarism, monetary policy has been used primarily to control the growth of the money supply. Yet in achieving (or failing to achieve!) this control, the monetarists have rejected and largely abandoned the use of required reserve ratios, calls for special deposits and direct controls on bank lending. How do we explain this paradox? The answer is really quite simple. Most monetarists belong to the 'classical' or 'free-market' school of economic thought, which regards markets as inherently stable and efficient and government interventionism as destabilising, distortive and inefficient. Monetarists apply this view of the world to monetary policy as well as to other aspects of economic theory and policymaking. Thus, although monetarists wish to achieve control over monetary growth, they reject as unsuitable the more interventionist techniques of monetary control which constrain artificially the commercial freedom of the private enterprise banks to act in their own best interest in the market economy.

DISINTERMEDIATION

25. Disintermediation is an example of a distortion or inefficiency caused by direct controls on bank lending. In the 1960s, UK monetary policy (which was then basically Keynesian) relied heavily upon the more interventionist forms of control which we have described: required reserve ratios, calls for special deposits and quite stringent qualitative and quantitative controls on bank lending. These controls discouraged competition amongst the clearing banks, and the search for new business by the banks. But the controls encouraged other financial institutions to become banks by developing banking business in competition with the high street clearing banks. At that time, the finance houses and the other financial institutions which developed into **'fringe' banks** or **'secondary' banks**, were not subject to the interventionist controls imposed on the **'primary' banks** by the Bank of England as a part of monetary policy. This competitive advantage allowed the 'fringe' banks to 'cream' banking business away from the clearers who were subject to restrictive controls. This process is called **distintermediation** - when only part of the banking system is controlled, banking business disintermediates away from the banks subject to the restrictions, towards those that are not. When quantitative and qualitative controls on bank lending were removed in the UK in the 1970s, much banking business **'reintermediated'** back to the primary banks. The clearing banks' 'financial economies of scale' enabled them to charge lower interest rates than the secondary banks, and their branch networks allowed easy access.

Disintermediation has also had an international dimension, which has been especially significant for the UK since 1979 when the British Government abolished **foreign exchange controls**. In the conditions of free movement of funds between countries which have existed since 1979, banking business would simply disintermediate overseas if the Bank of England imposed controls on UK banking operations that limited their commercial freedom and raised their costs. This is perhaps the main reason why the Bank of England has largely abandoned required reserve ratios. The monetary authorities now believe that all banks operating within the UK must be free to choose their own liquidity ratios if they are to compete on an equal footing in what has become a truly international and global market for banking services. Thus, while the Bank of England has tightened up and **extended its supervisory** role over all banks and financial institutions, domestic and overseas-owned, operating within the UK, at the same time it has **abandoned direct**

intervention in commercial banking activities undertaken by the banks.

CONTROL OF THE MONEY SUPPLY

26. We shall conclude this chapter by examining **three broad strategic approaches** to controlling the money supply which the authorities can adopt, given the fact they have rejected the use of direct controls on bank lending, for the reasons we have just described. The three broad strategies of monetary control are:

(i) **monetary base control;**
(ii) controlling monetary growth by **'PSBR control';**
(iii) controlling monetary growth via **the rate of interest.**

MONETARY BASE CONTROL

27. In the 1970s many 'academic' monetarists such as Professor Milton Friedman, then of the University of Chicago, argued that once 'monetarist' governments were elected in countries such as the United Kingdom and the USA, they should pursue control of the money supply by adopting a strict policy of **monetary base control**. The basic principle of monetary base control is quite simple. The state (or the monetary authorities) can in principle exercise monopoly control over **the supply of cash** or **'high-powered' money** which forms the **monetary base**. By reducing the supply of cash to the banking system (using techniques such as open market operations and funding), the authorities can engineer a multiple contraction in **the part of the money supply which they do not themselves issue, namely bank deposits**. Required reserve ratios need not be imposed on the banks. The banks can be left to choose their own liquidity ratios as a part of normal prudent banking practice. But for monetary base control to have a *predictable* effect upon the total money supply, **the money multiplier must be fairly stable**, ie it is assumed that the commercial banks will not react to a cash squeeze simply by altering their ratios, leaving total bank deposits unchanged.

To be effective, a system of monetary base control would require **the abandonment by the central bank of its lender of last resort function.** Normally, when the Bank of England squeezes cash through contractionary open market operations or funding, it immediately gives the cash back to the banking system via the discount market, in its role as lender of last resort. In a strict system of monetary base control, this practice would cease. Once cash was squeezed, it would not be re-supplied by the authorities, and the banks would have no option but to reduce total deposits in order to restore their ratios.

THE BANK OF ENGLAND AND MONETARY BASE CONTROL

28. Although many 'academic' monetarists continue to argue that **'true' monetarism** requires that the authorities adopt and pursue a system of monetary base control, the Bank of England has refused to base monetary policy upon such a system. The Bank of England - and most other central banks - reject monetary base control for essentially pragmatic reasons, arguing that the costs would exceed the benefits.

A strictly enforced system of monetary base control, in which the authorities effectively squeezed the supply of cash, might have the following disadvantages:

(i) As we have already noted, to have predictable effects upon the total money supply, the money multiplier must be stable, or at least itself predictable. It is quite likely that **the money multiplier is insufficiently stable** for a system of monetary base control to be effective.

(ii) Strict monetary base control would almost certainly be accompanied by **much higher and more volatile interest rates,** than have been normal in the past. High interest rates might have undesirable side-effects, discouraging business investment, leading to an over-valued exchange rate and raising the cost of servicing the national debt. The effect of strict monetary base control upon interest rates is illustrated in Figure 20.2. Figure 20.2(a) illustrates an essentially Keynesian monetary policy in which the authorities aim at an interest rate target $\bar{r}$. Following an increased demand by the public to hold cash, the authorities increase the supply of cash from H_1 to H_2, so as to maintain the interest rate at $\bar{r}$. In contrast, Figure 20.2(b), depicts a system of monetary base control. The authorities choose a target supply of cash or high-powered money that is completely inelastic with respect to the rate of interest. In Figure 20.2(b), the supply of cash is shown by a vertical line; if the general public's demand for cash increases from D_1 to D_2, successful control of the monetary base must mean that the rate of interest is allowed to rise from r_1 to r_2.

(iii) Monetary base control might **clash irreconcilably with the Bank of England's supervisory role over the banking system** and with the need to maintain confidence both in the system and in individual financial institutions. As we have already explained, adopting strict monetary base control would mean that the Bank of England would abandon most if not all of its lender of last resort function, since it would refuse to supply cash to rescue financial institutions with liquidity problems. In these circumstances, there would surely be an increase in the number of financial crashes, accompanied possibly by a general loss of confidence in the banking system.

PSBR CONTROL

29. Having rejected the move to a system of monetary base control, the UK monetary authorities attempted to control monetary growth in the 1980s with a rather pragmatic '*belt and braces' mixture* of **PSBR control**, combined with **interest rate policy**. PSBR control illustrates how, under monetarism, **fiscal policy** (at the macro-economic level) is **subordinated** to the **needs of monetary policy**. Essentially, PSBR control involves two different, though related, elements of policy:

(i) **The reduction of the PSBR (and of public expenditure) as proportions of GDP**, so that the need for new government borrowing is reduced. As we have explained in Chapter 18, PSBR reduction has been so successful that the budget was in surplus and the PSBR negative by 1988.

(ii) **Funding the PSBR** by selling gilts rather than Treasury bills, so that the government extends its borrowing with methods that do not expand the money supply. Indeed, from 1979 to 1985, the Bank of England deliberately **'over-funded'** the PSBR, ie it sold more gilts than were needed to finance the current borrowing requirement, so that the excess gilts 'mopped up' or contracted total private sector bank deposits. However, this 'over-funding' caused cash shortages in the banking system, which the Bank of England met by purchasing huge quantities of commercial bills from the discount market. Because of problems caused by the Bank's resulting 'bill mountain', the Bank of England ceased its policy of deliberate 'over-funding' in 1985.

Figure 20.2: The contrast between Keynesian and 'pure' monetarist monetary policy

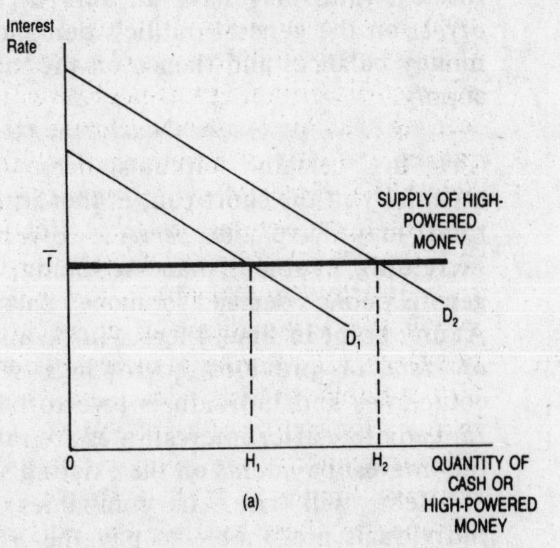

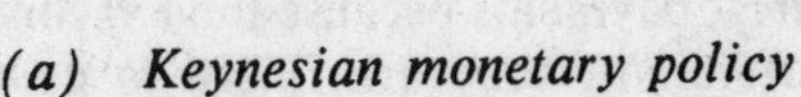
(a) Keynesian monetary policy

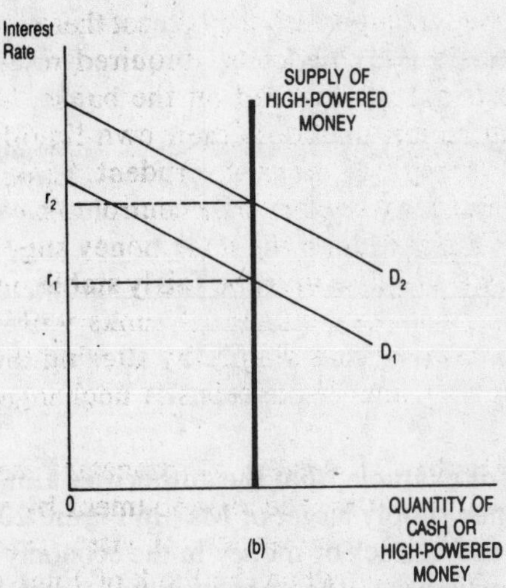

(b) A system of monetary base control

CONTROLLING MONETARY GROWTH VIA THE RATE OF INTEREST

30. Since the Bank of England abandoned its deliberate policy of 'over-funding' the PSBR in 1985, 'practical monetarism' in the UK has relied almost exclusively upon the rate of interest as a policy instrument for achieving control over the money supply. The result has not been very successful. We have already noted how operating monetary policy so that the rate of interest determines the money supply, and not vice versa, involves a reversal of the 'traditional' roles assumed in many elementary textbooks. Instead of the money **supply** being used as an **exogenous policy instrument** to determine an **endogenous rate of interest objective, the rate of interest has been used as the policy instrument with the money supply becoming the policy** objective. Thus **the money supply is treated as endogenous** within the money market illustrated in Figure 20.3, its equilibrium value being determined by 'sliding' **the exogenous policy instrument, the rate** of **interest,** up or down the general public's demand curve for money balances.

Figure 20.3: 'Sliding' the rate of interest along the demand for money function to achieve a money supply target

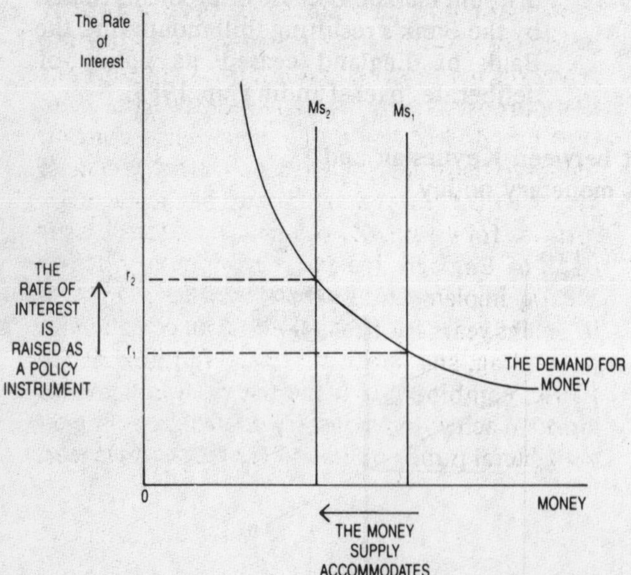

Suppose for example, that the authorities aim to 'hit' a money supply target of Ms_2 in Figure 20.3 when the actual stock of money in the economy is Ms_1. In principle, the money supply can be reduced to Ms_2 by raising the rate of interest from r_1 to r_2. At the higher rate of interest, the general public will wish to hold smaller money balances for transactions purposes and as a store of wealth, and the money supply should passively adapt or accommodate to equal the size of money balances people wish to hold. As we explained earlier in this chapter, if implemented in this way, monetary policy seeks to achieve its money supply target by using the price of money to ration the general public's demand for money balances.

However, controlling the money supply by raising or lowering interest rates involves a number of problems which help to explain the authorities' poor performance in the 1980s in 'hitting' their M3 targets. The problems include:

(i) As with a system of monetary base control, the Bank of England and the government may not wish to see interest rates rising to the extent that might be necessary to achieve effective control over the money supply.

(ii) If the demand curve for money (the liquidity preference curve) is *inelastic* with respect to the rate of interest, substantial changes in the rate of interest may have *little effect* on the general public's demand for money balances and thence on the money supply.

(iii) If the demand curve for money is *unstable* (ie shifting its position, for example because the velocity of circulation of money is changing), an increase in interest rates may have an *unpredictable effect* on the general public's demand for money balances and thence on the money supply.

(iv) In certain circumstances, and especially in the short run, higher interest rates may have the *perverse effect* of increasing, rather than reducing, the general public's demand for money balances. At any point in time, there will be a *stock of debt* or previous borrowings which companies and individuals owe to banks. Immediately after interest rates are raised, the interest payments on the existing stock of debt will rise. If companies and individuals are unable to pay the higher interest payments because their incomes are insufficient, they are likely to go to the banks to ask to borrow more simply to finance their existing debt! This is called **'distress lending'.** When 'distress lending' occurs, bank lending rises following an increase in interest rates and hence, the money supply also grows. On a global scale, Third World developing countries are often in a rather similar position. When interest rates rise they may be unable to pay the interest on funds borrowed from the First World banking system. In these circumstances, they either renege on their debts, or negotiate a rescheduling of the interest payments, or ask to borrow more to allow them to make the interest payments!)

(v) Although the Bank of England may use its lending rate and open market operations in the gilt and bill markets to influence interest rates, the authorities may not have complete control over interest rates.

SUMMARY

31. In this chapter we have surveyed both the 'narrow' policy instruments and the 'broad' strategies that a country's monetary authorities may implement in pursuit of the objectives of monetary policy. We have defined monetary policy as the part of the government's overall economic policy which attempts to achieve the government's objectives using monetary instruments. A range of operating instruments or techniques or control are available to the authorities, such as open market operations, funding, raising or lowering the central bank's lending rate, and imposing required reserve ratios and direct controls on the banking system. We can divide these techniques of control into:

(i) the instruments which reduce or increase the supply of cash or liquid assets to the banking system; aiming thereby to influence how the banks behave commercially and in the pursuit of their self-interest;

(ii) direct controls and required reserve ratios which artificially constrain the bank's freedom to act commercially; and

(iii) the use of 'moral' persuasion.

The use of interest rates as a policy instruments does not fall into any of these three categories since it aims to influence the *demand* by bank customers for credit, rather than to act on the banking system's ability to *supply* credit.

Since 1970, the favoured instruments of monetary policy have changed in the United Kingdom, as a broadly Keynesian monetary policy has given way to monetarism. Direct controls and required ratios have been abandoned, recent monetary policy having relied instead on instruments such as funding and interest rate changes, which influence respectively the banking systems commercial ability to supply credit and the general public's willingness to demand credit.

At the same time, both the objectives and the overall strategy of monetary policy have changed. In the Keynesian era, management of aggregate demand and the national debt were important objectives of monetary policy, occasionally over-ridden by the need to use monetary policy to stem a capital outflow to protect the exchange rate in the event of a balance of payments crisis. Although this 'crisis' objective of monetary policy has occasionally surfaced since Keynesianism gave way to monetarism, by far the most important intermediate objective of 'monetarist' monetary policy has been control of the rate of growth of the money supply. Give the rejection by monetarists of direct controls for this purpose, three broad strategies have been considered for achieving monetary control. Monetary base control has been the method most favoured by 'pure' monetarists, but it has been rejected for essentially pragmatic reasons by the Bank of England. Instead, the monetary policy actually implemented by the authorities in the UK in recent years has been based on an eclectic mix of funding, and until 1985 'over-funding' of the PSBR, combined with the use of interest rates aimed at achieving monetary control by acting on the general public's demand for money balances.

STUDENT SELF-TESTING

1. *Define monetary policy.* (2)
2. *Distinguish between an intermediate and an operational objective of monetary policy.* (3)
3. *What is the monetary policy 'trade-off'?* (4)
4. *List the stages of 'contractionary' open market operations.* (6)
5. *What is the aim of 'expansionary' open market operations.* (7)
6. *Why may open market operations be ineffective?* (8)
7. *What happens to the rate of interest when 'contractionary' open market operations are undertaken?* (9)
8. *What does the Bank of England sell when undertaking open market operations in the discount market?* (10)
9. *How is the National Debt funded?* (11)
10. *What is meant by funding the PSBR?* (12)
11. *What was special deposits policy?* (14)
12. *Distinguish between quantitative and qualitative controls.* (15)
13. *How may interest rates affect total bank deposits?* (16)
14. *List the three ways in which monetary policy can influence bank deposits.* (17)
15. *What were the objectives of monetary policy during the Keynesian era?* (18)
16. *Why may National Debt management be an important policy objective?* (19)
17. *How may the balance of payments affect the objectives of monetary policy?* (20)
18. *What is the principal objective of 'monetarist' monetary policy?* (21)
19. *In what sense is 'monetarist' monetary policy a medium-term policy?* (22)
20. *Assess the effectiveness of the Medium Term Financial Strategy.* (23)
21. *Why have monetarists abandoned required ratios and direct controls?* (24)
22. *What is disintermediation?* (25)
23. *List the three broad methods of controlling the money supply.* (26)
24. *Explain monetary base control.* (27)
25. *Why has the Bank of England rejected monetary base control?* (28)
26. *How may PSBR control reduce the money supply?* (29)
27. *Is the money supply exogenous or endogenous?* (30)

EXERCISES

1 *Structure of UK interest rates February 1988*

Interest rate	*% premium*
Bank base rates	*9.0*
Bank personal loan rate	*19.5*
Bank credit card rate	*23.5*
Store credit card rate	*32.5*
Bank deposit account rate (net)	*5.0*
Building society mortgage rate	*10.5*
Building society personal loan rate	*19.5*
Building society share deposit rate (net)	*4.0*
Treasury bill rate (3 months)	*8.9*
UK long gilts	*9.36*

(a) *What is meant by the 'structure' of interest rates?*

(b) *Explain why there are so many different interest rates.*

MULTIPLE CHOICE QUESTIONS

1 *In order to reduce total bank deposits, a central bank pursues open market operations. The following stages then occur:*

1 *The commercial banks reduce deposits by a multiple if their reserve assets ratio is at a minimum.*
2 *The central bank sells bonds*
3 *The central bank receives cheques from the general public in payment for the bonds*
4 *The reserve assets ratios of the commercial banks fall*

In what order do these stages occur?

A *1, 2, 3, 4*
B *4, 3, 2, 1*
C *2, 3, 4, 1*
D *2, 3, 1, 4*

2 *If the Bank of England decides to reduce the rate of growth of the money supply, it will:*
A Sell Treasury bills
B Reduce its lending rate
C Sell gilt-edged securities to the general public
D Replace gilts with Treasury bills in the national debt.

3 *Other things being equal, a fall in the foreign exchange rate of the UK pound could be the result of a decrease in:*
A The UK money supply
B UK interest rates
C Foreign interest rates
D UK bank lending

4 *Central government funding of the national debt can achieve all the following except:*
A A reduction in the supply of liquid assets to the banking system
B A lengthening of the average maturity of the national debt
C A reduction in total bank lending
D A reduction in gilt sales relative to Treasury bill sales

5 *Bank deposits will increase as a result of an increase in:*
A A required reserve ratio imposed on the banks
B The proportion of wealth the public wish to hold as cash
C Treasury bill sales to the banking system
D The banks' prudent liquidity ratios.

EXAMINATION QUESTIONS

1 (a) *Outline the different techniques available to the monetary authorities for controlling the money supply.* *(15 marks)*
(b) *Discuss the techniques for controlling the money supply which have been used in the UK during the 1980s.* *(8 marks)*
(IOB April 1987)

2 *What determines the general level of interest rates?*
(ACCA June 1983)

3 *What effects will an increase in rates of interest be likely to have on the level of economic activity?* *(20 marks)*
(ACCA December 1985)

21. Unemployment and inflation

INTRODUCTION

1. In recent years large scale **unemployment** and **inflation** have been arguably the most serious economic problems facing governments throughout the world. Accelerating and highly variable rates of inflation caused acute problems in almost every developing and developed country in the non-Communist world in the 1970s. Although the rate of inflation fell considerably in developed economies during the 1980s, fears of a return to rapid inflation persist and have continued to influence economic behaviour and government policy, while unacceptably high inflation rates continue in many countries of the developing world. Indeed by the late 1980s, the UK inflation rate was rising again, perhaps justifying these fears. But while the problem of inflation has lessened in countries such as the United Kingdom, large scale unemployment grew in the early 1980s and has persisted at high levels in recent years. In this chapter we shall examine the causes of unemployment and inflation and we shall investigate the policies recommended by **Keynesian** and **monetarist economists** for reducing and possibly eliminating these twin evils.

THE CAUSES OF UNEMPLOYMENT

2. In the following sections we briefly survey the main types of unemployment which economists have identified. We must realise however, that there is considerable disagreement amongst economists about the significance and even the existence of some of the types of unemployment which we list.

It would be especially useful, before proceeding with this chapter, to review Chapter 13 in which we explained the general approach of economists of different schools of thought to the causes of unemployment and inflation. From a Keynesian perspective of employment, an important distinction is made between the concepts of **voluntary** and **involuntary unemployment**. Keynesians explain at least a part of mass unemployment in terms of deficient aggregate demand, which is outside the influence and control of workers. In this sense, demand-deficient unemployment is involuntary. But economists of the 'classical' school, who include most modern monetarists, reject the possibility of demand-deficient unemployment, except possibly as a temporary phenomenon which is soon corrected by market forces, providing only that markets are sufficiently competitive. For a monetarist or 'New Classical' economist, much of modern unemployment is voluntary, explained by workers *choosing* higher wages and fewer jobs.

FRICTIONAL UNEMPLOYMENT (OR TRANSITIONAL UNEMPLOYMENT)

3. We first came across **frictional unemployment** (and the closely related type of unemployment known as **structural unemployment**) in our introduction to macro-economics in Chapter 13. Frictional unemployment, as its name suggests, results from frictions in the labour market which create a time-lag during which a worker is unemployed when he moves from one job to another. Our definition of frictional unemployment assumes that a job vacancy exists and that a friction in the job market, caused by either the **geographical** or the **occupational immobility of labour**, prevents an unemployed worker from filling the vacancy. It follows therefore, that the number of unfilled job vacancies which exist can be used as a measure of the level of frictional unemployment in the economy.

CASUAL AND SEASONAL UNEMPLOYMENT

4. **Casual unemployment** is a special case of frictional unemployment, which occurs when workers are laid-off on a short-term basis in trades such as tourism, agriculture, catering and building. When casual unemployment results from regular fluctuations in weather conditions or demand, it is called seasonal unemployment.

STRUCTURAL UNEMPLOYMENT

5. **Structural unemployment** results from the structural decline of industries, unable to compete or adapt in the face of either changing demand and new products, or the emergence of more efficient competitors in other countries. The growth of international competition has been a particularly important cause of structural unemployment. During the post-war era, structural unemployment in the UK was regionally concent-

rated in areas where '19th century staple industries' such as textiles and shipbuilding were suffering structural decline. Thus structural unemployment was largely regional. Such regional unemployment caused by the decline of **'sunset' industries** was more than offset by the growth of employment elsewhere in the UK in **'sunrise' industries** which took the place of the declining industries. However, in the severe recession of the early 1980s, structural unemployment affected almost all regions in the UK as the **deindustrialisation** process spread right across the manufacturing base. Structural unemployment became a major cause of large scale unemployment in the 1980s.

TECHNOLOGICAL UNEMPLOYMENT

6. **Technological unemployment** can be regarded as a special case of structural unemployment which results from the successful growth of new industries using labour-saving technology such as automation. In contrast to **mechanisation** which has usually increased the overall demand for labour, **automation** involves machines (such as robots) rather than men, operating other machines. Whereas the growth of mechanised industry increases employment, automation of production can lead to the shedding of labour even when industry output is expanding.

'CLASSICAL' UNEMPLOYMENT OR REAL WAGE UNEMPLOYMENT

7. We saw in Chapter 13 how **pre-Keynesian** or **'classical' economists** believed that large scale unemployment in the 1920s and 1930s was caused by an excessively high level of **real wages** in labour markets which were insufficiently competitive for market forces to eliminate the problem. In recent years the view that a large part of modern unemployment in the UK, especially youth unemployment, has been caused by too high a level of real wages has been revived by **monetarist** and **'New Classical' economists.**

KEYNESIAN OR DEMAND-DEFICIENT UNEMPLOYMENT

8. We discussed the possibility of this type of unemployment in some depth in Chapter 13. Keynes - but not his opponents - believed that **deficient aggregate demand** was a major cause of persistent mass unemployment between the wars. Economists generally agree that temporary unemployment (called **cyclical unemployment**) may be caused by a lack of demand in the downswing of the business cycle. However, Keynes went further, arguing that the economy could settle into an under-full employment equilibrium caused by a continuing lack of effective aggregate demand.

RESIDUAL UNEMPLOYMENT

9. This is a 'catch-all' category covering any other cause of unemployment. **Residual unemployment** includes the **unemployable** and the **'workshy'**. It is now recognised in the UK that long-term unemployment in itself may make a worker unemployable when job-skills and work habits are eroded and when employers perceive that workers with more recent job experience present fewer risks. The existence of the 'workshy' represents a form of **voluntary unemployment**. In recent years an **'unemployment trap'** has been identified in the United Kingdom. Lowly-skilled workers become trapped in unemployment when they are better-off living off state benefits than in a poorly-paid job paying tax and National Insurance contributions. In these circumstances it is rational to choose unemployment.

SEARCH THEORIES OF UNEMPLOYMENT

10. The existence of the 'workshy' and of the 'unemployment trap' is closely related to an explanation of frictional unemployment in terms of **search theory**. Suppose that a worker earning £300 a week in a skilled occupation loses his job. Few vacancies exist in his occupation, but unskilled vacancies are freely available paying £100 a week. To start with at least, the worker is likely to choose to remain unemployed rather than to fill the lower-paid vacancy because (i) the wage and perhaps also the conditions of work and status associated with the job *do not meet his aspirations* and (ii) he is uncertain whether better-paid and higher status vacancies exist which he does not know about. Accordingly, the voluntary unemployment the worker chooses is essentially a search period spent scanning the labour market for a job which meets his aspirations. The worker's unemployment will end either when he finds a vacancy which meets his initial aspirations, or when he has reduced his aspirations sufficiently to accept a low-paid vacancy he knew existed all along.

The longer the search an unemployed worker is

prepared to undertake, the greater will be the size of frictional unemployment in the economy. As an unemployed worker runs down his stock of savings, the threat of poverty creates incentives both to search the job market more vigorously, and also to reduce personal aspirations. But the existence of a **state 'safety net' of unemployment pay, redundancy payments** and **welfare benefits** might increase frictional unemployment by allowing an unemployed worker to finance a longer voluntary search period. 'New Classical' and monetarist economists generally recommend the reduction of the real value of welfare benefits for the unemployed, to create incentives for workers to reduce aspirations more quickly and hence to shorten search periods. Cutting the real value of welfare benefits also serves to widen the gap between disposable income in and out of work, thereby reducing or eliminating the 'unemployment trap'.

The weakness of the search theory lies in the assumption that unfilled vacancies exist. Although the search theory of unemployment may explain *some* of the growth of unemployment in the UK in the 1970s and 1980s, it cannot explain *all* unemployment, especially in the parts of the country where industries have collapsed. Nevertheless, the search theory carries the political implication that reductions in welfare benefits will 'cure' unemployment. However, the growth of structural unemployment resulting from the deindustrialisation of manufacturing industry has probably been the most important single cause of the massive growth in unemployment from one million to three million which occurred in the UK in the early 1980s.

POLICIES TO REDUCE UNEMPLOYMENT

11. The appropriate policy to reduce unemployment obviously depends on identifying correctly the underlying cause of unemployment. If, for example, unemployment is incorrectly diagnosed in terms of demand deficiency, when the 'true' cause is structural, a policy of fiscal or monetary expansion to stimulate aggregate demand will be ineffective and inappropriate. Indeed, reflation of demand in such circumstances is likely to produce excess demand which then pulls up the price level in a demand-pull inflation, with no lasting beneficial effects upon employment.

It is now widely agreed, by neo-Keynesians as well as by monetarists, that the cause of most modern unemployment in countries such as the UK, lies on the **'supply-side' of the economy** - rather than on the **'demand-side'**. There is major controversy and disagreement however, on the appropriate policies to improve 'supply-side' performance so as to achieve a significant reduction in unemployment. Monetarists and 'New Classical' economists argue that poor 'supply-side' performance is the long-term result of decades of Keynesian interventionism in the economy, from the 1940s to the 1970s. The way to cut frictional, structural and 'real wage' unemployment is to reduce rather than extend the economic role of the state. By setting markets free, encouraging competition and fostering private enterprise and the 'entrepreneurial spirit', an 'enterprise culture' can be created in which the price mechanism and not the government, will deliver economic growth and reduce unemployment. According to this view, the correct role of government is merely to create the conditions, eg through maintaining the rule of law and social order, in which the market mechanism and private enterprise can function properly.

Economists of the Keynesian school (and also Marxist and socialist economists) disagree. They believe that **unemployment represents a massive market failure** which can only be cured by interventionist policies to modify the market and make it function better. Socialists and Marxists generally go further, arguing the case for the command or planning mechanism to replace the market. Thus policies of public ownership (or increased nationalisation) and import controls have been recommended by socialists to reduce unemployment, together with the adoption of powers by the state to direct savings into investment in domestic manufacturing industry to aid the 'reindustrialisation' of Britain. However, in terms of influencing government policy in the UK, such advice has fallen on deaf ears, since the Conservative Governments in office throughout the 1980s have wholeheartedly endorsed the monetarist or 'New Classical' approach, dismantling rather than extending state intervention in the economy.

THE MEANING OF INFLATION

12. **Inflation** is defined as a **continuing or persistent tendency for the price level to rise. Deflation** is the opposite, namely a persistent

tendency for the price level to fall. However, because the overall price level has seldom, if ever, fallen in western industrialised countries since the 1930s, the term deflation is usually used in a rather looser way to describe a reduction in aggregate demand and levels of economic activity, output and employment. A **deflationary policy** (also known as a **disinflationary policy**) refers to a deliberate reduction of aggregate demand, using fiscal or monetary policy. Likewise, **reflation** refers to an increase in economic activity and output, and a **reflationary policy** stimulates aggregate demand. Very often, inflation is reflation 'gone wrong', stimulating the price level rather than real output and activity. In the next sections we shall survey particular types of inflation that have been identified, before discussing the extent to which inflation is an economic problem.

SUPPRESSED INFLATION

13. Although inflation involves the *tendency* for prices to rise, it is not inevitable that the price level will actually rise. Tough controls on prices and wage levels introduced by strong governments may prevent the price level from rising without however, eliminating the underlying inflationary process. The Soviet Government has often claimed zero inflation in the USSR, but there has certainly been evidence of excess demand and inflationary pressure in the Soviet economy. But because 'official' prices are administered, the suppression of price rises through the command mechanism has diverted the inflationary process into quantity shortages, queues, waiting-lists and black markets.

CREEPING INFLATION

14. During the 1950s and 1960s, western industrialised countries experienced an inflation rate that was fairly stable from year to year, averaging less than 5 per cent. However, the inflation rate in the UK gradually crept up during the early part of the Keynesian era, developing into a strato-inflation in the 1970s, which as we shall shortly see, contributed to the crisis in Keynesian economics and the monetarist counter-revolution.

STRATO-INFLATION

15. In many developing countries, particularly in Latin America, **strato-inflation** has been more typical than **creeping inflation**. In a strato-inflation the inflation rate ranges from about 10 per cent to several hundred per cent without ever completely spiralling into a **hyper-inflation**. For a few years the United Kingdom experienced a relatively mild strato-inflation in the 1970s and early 1980s, which like all strato-inflations varied considerably from year to year and proved difficult to anticipate correctly. In more recent years, UK inflation has fallen back to a rate more typical of a creeping inflation. Indeed by the late 1980s the inflation rate was again creeping upwards towards 10 per cent.

HYPER-INFLATION

16. When in the 1970s, inflation in the UK and in some other industrialised economies developed from a creeping inflation into a low strato-inflation, many people feared that it would grow into a **hyper-inflation**. The famous German inflation of 1923 was a hyper-inflation, in which the inflation rate accelerated to several hundred per cent per day. Similar, but less publicised hyper-inflations occurred in other countries in central and eastern Europe in the years following both the World Wars. However, accelerating hyper-inflations are usually short-lived and unsustainable, unlike a strato-inflation which can persist for many years. Hyper-inflations usually occur in a political crisis when a weak government loses control of the economy and turns to printing money to pay its debts. Whereas the functions of money as a medium of exchange, store of value and unit of account are eroded and perform less efficiently in a strato-inflation, these functions completely break down in a full hyper-inflation. Normal economic activity in turn breaks down, which deepens the political crisis. Out of the political and economic crisis may emerge a new government which is able to rebase the currency and end the hyper-inflation.

STAGFLATION

17. The incidence of accelerating and relatively high rates of inflation combined with growing unemployment in the UK in the 1970s and early 1980s led economists to coin the word **'stagflation'**. Stagflation or **'slumpflation'** combines stagnation in output and economic activity with price inflation. The emergence of stagflation seemed to make conventional Keynesian demand management policies inappropriate and politically damaging as a means of controlling unemployment and inflation, contributing to the ascendency of monetarist and 'New Classical' theory and policy over Keynesianism in the 1980s.

THE COSTS AND BENEFITS OF INFLATION

18. Everybody agrees that inflation can have serious adverse effects or costs. However, the seriousness of the adverse effects depends on whether inflation is **anticipated** or **unanticipated**. If inflation could be anticipated with complete certainty, it would pose few problems. Households and firms would simply build the expected rate of inflation into their economic decisions which would not be distorted by wrong guesses. When inflation is relatively low, with little variation from year to year, it is relatively easy to anticipate more or less fully next year's inflation rate. Indeed, during the creeping inflation of the 1950s and 1960s, it was often argued that a mild amount of inflation yields benefits which exceed the costs. Creeping inflation became associated with growing markets, healthy profits and a general climate of business optimism. This attitude helps to explain why control of inflation was a relatively minor policy objective during most of the Keynesian era. Indeed, in recent years Keynesian economists have again argued that a low rate of inflation - and not absolute price stability or zero inflation - should be accepted as a necessary side-effect or cost of expansionary policies to reduce unemployment. Monetarist and 'New Classical' economists disagree, believing instead that inflation must be 'bled from the system' to produce the conditions in which the private sector and not the government, can produce growing output and employment.

Economists of all schools are in general agreement that the costs of a strato-inflation exceed its benefits. It is very difficult for people fully to anticipate a strato-inflation as the actual inflation rate tends to vary substantially from year to year. The adverse effects are much more severe than in a creeping inflation, creating distortions which may completely destabilise normal economic activity. The main adverse effects or costs of inflation are:

(i) **Distributional effects**. Weaker social groups in society such as pensioners on fixed incomes lose, while other in strong bargaining positions gain. **Indexing** of pensions and welfare benefits can reduce the unfairness in income distributions caused by inflation. In the absence of indexation, inflation may draw the lowly paid into the tax net through the process of fiscal drag, which we explained in Chapter 18.

A second important distributional effect occurs between borrowers and lenders. In times of rapid inflation, real rates of interest are often negative. (Negative real interest rates occur when the rate of inflation exceeds the nominal interest rate offered to savers, thereby eroding the real value of the stock of savings.) Thus lenders are really paying borrowers for the doubtful privilege of lending to them! In these circumstances, inflation acts as a hidden tax redistributing income and wealth from lenders or creditors to borrowers or debtors. In the UK the main borrowers who have benefited from the redistributive effects of inflation are house buyers and the government. For house buyers, inflation has eroded the real value of the amount borrowed (the mortgage), while ensuring that the value of property asset rises, often faster than the average rate of inflation on all goods. For the UK government, rapid inflation in the 1970s eroded the real value of accumulated government borrowings, the national debt.

(ii) **The distortion of normal economic behaviour**. Inflation can distort consumer behaviour by causing households to bring forward purchases and hoard if they expect the rate of inflation to accelerate. However, during the rapid inflation of the 1970s, the personal savings ratio rose, indicating that households actually reduced rather than increased consumption, choosing to save a bigger fraction of their income. You should refer back to Chapter 14 for an explanation of the changes in the personal savings ratio and consumption during the 1970s and 1980s.

In a rather similar way, inflation distorts the behaviour of firms and imposes costs upon them. Uncertainty about future inflation, production costs and profits makes long-term planning difficult. In these conditions, firms may be tempted to divert funds out of productive investment in fixed capital or long-term projects into activities such as commodity hoarding and speculation. Profit margins can be squeezed severely in a cost-inflation and firms may try to avoid this by hoping to make capital gains on property, land and currency speculation, rather than by using their funds in actual production.

(iii) **The breakdown in the function of money**. In a severe strato-inflation, money becomes less useful and efficient as a medium of exchange and store of value. Although more money is needed to finance transactions at higher prices, this is countered by the disadvantage of holding money which is falling in value. Rapidly changing prices will also erode money's functions as a unit of account and standard of deferred payment. In a hyper-inflation, the use of money may completely break down, leading to its replacement with much less efficient barter. This imposes extra costs on most transactions.

THE THEORIES OF INFLATION

19. Table 21.1 (on the following page) provides a summary of the historical development of the major theories of inflation, which we shall examined in more detail in the subsequent sections of this chapter.

THE 'OLD' QUANTITY THEORY OF MONEY

20. The Quantity Theory of Money is the oldest theory of inflation, dating back at least to the 18th century. For two centuries until the 1930s, when it went out of fashion with the Keynesian revolution, the Quantity Theory was *the* theory of inflation. However, Milton Friedman's revival of the Quantity Theory in 'modern' form in the 1950s is usually regarded as marking the beginning of the **monetarist counter-revolution**. Nowadays, the Quantity Theory once again occupies a central place in debate and controversy about the causes of inflation. All versions of the Quantity Theory, old and new, form a *special case of demand inflation*, in which rising prices are caused by excess demand. In the Quantity Theory the source of excess demand is located in *monetary* rather than *real forces*, in an excess supply of money created or condoned by the government. At its simplest, the Quantity Theory is sometimes stated as 'too much money chasing too few goods'. The starting point for developing the theory is the **Fisher equation of exchange**, devised by an American economist Irving Fisher early in the twentieth century:

$$MV \equiv PT$$

In the Fisher equation, **the money supply (M)** multiplied by the number of times money changes hands (**V, the velocity of circulation of money**) equals the **price level (P)** times the **total number of transactions (T)**. T measures all transactions involving goods and services in the economy, including second-hand transactions. Another formulation of the equation of exchange devised by economists at Cambridge University - also early in the twentieth century - specifies the equation in terms of transactions involving *current* real income or output produced in the economy, omitting *second-hand* transactions. In the **Cambridge equation**, V represents the income velocity of circulation of money:

$$MV \equiv Pq$$

The Cambridge version of the equation of exchange forms the basis of a **theory of the demand for money**, which anticipated the 'modern' Quantity Theory of Money which we shall describe in a later section of this chapter. We can rewrite the Cambridge equation as:

$$M_D = kPq$$

in which k is the reciprocal of the income velocity of circulation of money (1/V). For the money market to be in equilibrium, the supply of money must equal the demand for money, ie $M_S = M_D$. Substituting the Cambridge equation into $M_S = M_D$:

$$M_S = kPq$$

The Cambridge economists who developed the Cambridge equation believed that with k (or the velocity of circulation) and real output (q) constant, an increase in the money supply requires the price level P to rise in order to maintain equilibrium in the money market. The exact mechanism through which this was assumed to occur is called the **cash balance mechanism.** If initially the money market is in equilibrium, an increase in the money supply creates a situation in which $M_S > M_D$, ie there is now an excess supply of money in the economy. Assuming that people wish to hold money balances only as a medium of exchange and not as an idle wealth

Table 21.1: The theories of inflation

1 18th Century to the 1930s: **The 'Old' Quantity Theory of Money**

2 1930s: Keynes's General Theory explains deflation in terms of deficient aggregate demand

3 1940s: Keynes develops his General Theory to explain how, in conditions of full employment, excess demand can pull up the price level in a **Demand-Pull inflation**

4 1950s/1960s: Many Keynesians switch to the **Cost-Push** or **Structuralist Theory of Inflation**

5 1950s/1960s: Keynesian **demand-pull** v **cost-push** debate conducted with the aid of the **Phillips Curve.**

6 1950s: The early Monetarist Theory of Inflation: Milton Friedman's Revival of the Quantity Theory of Money (the **'Modern' Quantity Theory)**

7 1968: The incorporation of the role of expectations into the inflationary process in the Monetarist Theory of Inflation: the role of Adaptive Expectations in Milton Friedman's **Theory of the 'Expectations - Augmented Phillips Curve'**

8 1970s: The apparent breakdown of the Phillips Relationship.

9 1970s/1980s: The incorporation of the role of **Rational Expectations** into the inflationary process: the **'New Classical'** School

10 The current controversy: **Cost-Push or Structural explanations of inflation,** eg post-Keynesian or neo-Keynesian explanations v **Monetarist and 'New Classical' explanations.**

asset (ie for transactions purposes only), they will spend their excess money holdings, thereby pulling up the price level. The price level continues to rise until the transactions demand for money equals the supply of money once again and all excess money holdings have been eliminated.

KEYNESIAN ATTACKS UPON THE QUANITY THEORY

21. We can use the Quantity Theory to illustrate the very important difference between an **identity** and a **theory**. The equation of exchange, in itself, is a mere identity or truism, indicating little more than that the amount spent in the economy always equals the amount bought. To convert the equation of exchange from an identity into the Quantity Theory we have had to impose the following assumptions upon the relationship:

(a) that the price level is determined by the money supply, and not vice versa; or

$$P = f\ (M_S);\ \text{and}$$

(b) that the velocity of circulation V and real income or output q are relatively constant.

We shall now examine how Keynesians attack the Quantity Theory by attacking these key assumptions:

(i) In an '*extreme*' attack upon the Quantity Theory, the Keynesian economist Lord Kaldor argued that the functional relationship between the money supply and the price level is specified completely the wrong way round. Instead of changes in the money supply causing changes in the price level, the 'true' relationship is the opposite, ie changes in the price level cause the money supply to change! This is sometimes known as **'reverse causation'**. In this interpretation, inflation is caused by 'cost-push' institutional factors (which we shall shortly explain) in the real economy. The money supply then *passively adapts* or *accommodates* to finance the level of transactions desired by the general public at the new higher price level.

Keynesians agree with what they consider to be the rather trivial point that an increase in the money supply is needed to finance an inflation and allow it to continue, but they reject the view that an increase in the money supply is *the cause* of inflation. They also argue that if a 'monetarist' government tightly restricts the growth of money to try to stem an inflation, the main effects might be that the current level of transactions cannot be financed, so real activity will fall, resulting in higher unemployment. Another possibility is that near monies will simply begin to function as money, rendering ineffective the government's apparent 'success' in achieving monetary control.

(ii) **'Lesser'** Keynesian attacks upon the Quantity Theory (which are 'lesser' in the sense that, for convenience, they accept the functional relationship running from the money supply to nominal income Pq), question whether V and q can be regarded as constant. Even if the assumption that changes in the money supply can cause changes in the price level is correct, the influence will be small if an increase in the supply of money is 'absorbed' in a lower velocity of circulation, V, rather than an increase in the price level. Much of the debate between Keynesians and monetarists about the Quantity Theory centres on the issue of whether V is constant. Recent evidence from the 1980s suggests that the velocity has not been constant, slowing down in response to an increase in the money supply. However, monetarists have now changed the grounds of their argument, requiring that V should be *relatively stable* and *predictable* rather than *constant*, for the Quantity Theory to hold. This dispute extends to the cash balance transmission mechanism which we have described. In the 'modern' Quantity Theory, monetarists believe that the demand for money is a stable function of the level of money income or nominal income, money being required for transactions purposes rather than as a passive wealth asset. As we have noted, if the money supply increases, people simply spend their excess money holdings on all the assets which are available, including goods, and not just on financial assets. By contrast, in the theory of the speculative demand for money which we explained in Chapter 19, Keynes assumed that an increased supply of money will be spent largely on financial assets such as bonds, with no effect on the price level for goods.

Even if it is accepted that the velocity of circulation is sufficiently constant and that the demand for money is a stable function of nominal income, Keynesians have a further line of attack upon the Quantity Theory. An increase of the money supply may increase real income q rather than the price level P, particularly if there is substantial spare capacity and unemployment in the economy.

Professor Milton Friedman, the leading exponent of 'early' versions of monetarism has agreed that monetary expansion can increase real output, but he argues that the effect is short-lived and that the main long-term effect is on the price level. But 'New Classical' monetarists reject even this limited possibility, arguing that since output and employment are always at or near their equilibrium levels, output cannot respond to a demand stimulation.

(iii) Lastly, Keynesians attack the Quantity Theory by appealing to the empirical evidence. Whereas statistical data from countries such as the USA and UK appeared to support the Quantity Theory in the 1970s, Keynesians believe that this is no longer the case. They argue that the monetarists 'fiddled' the evidence, deliberately designing their statistical (or econometric) tests so that they would support the Quantity Theory. And they argue that the growth in the 1980s of the main measure of the money supply, M3 (previously known as **Sterling M3**), far exceeded the growth of the price level, destroying in the process the empirical validity of the Quantity Theory. Monetarists retort that measures of the money supply such as M3 are always inaccurate and that the Quantity Theory is still supported by the general correlation between monetary expansion and movements in nominal national income.

THE KEYNESIANS DEMAND-PULL THEORY OF INFLATION

22. At the beginning of the Second World War Keynes adapted his theory of how deficient demand

in a deflated or depressed economy can cause unemployment to explain how **excess demand** can cause inflation in a fully employed economy. The theory can be illustrated in terms of the **inflationary gap** diagram shown in Figure 21.1.

Figure 21.1: The Keynesian demand-pull theory of inflation, illustrated with an inflationary gap diagram

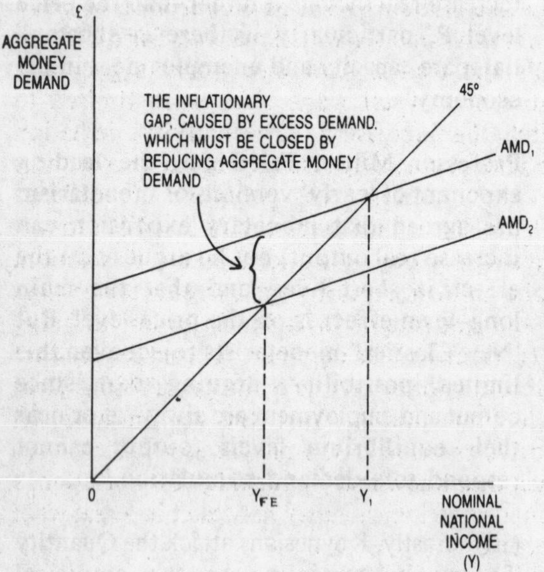

In Figure 21.1 nominal income (or money income), and not real income, is shown on the horizontal axis. Y_{FE} is the level of nominal income at which real income or output is maximised, given the productive capacity available and given the current price level. In the short run, nominal income can only increase beyond Y_{FE} if the price level rises. If the level of aggregate money demand in the economy is AMD_1, the price level will be pulled up by excess demand to achieve an equilibrium level of nominal income at Y_1. Thus a sustained reduction in aggregate demand to AMD_2 is necessary to close the inflationary gap so as to eliminate excess demand and achieve full employment without inflation.

In contrast to the Quantity Theory of Money which treats inflation essentially as a **monetary phenomenon**, the Keynesian demand-pull theory locates the engine of inflation firmly in the 'real' economy. In the Keynesian theory, excess demand occurs when the combined claims on output of households, firms, the government and the overseas sector are greater than the real output that can be produced. Inflation is explained by the **'real forces'** which determine how people behave. However, the Keynesian demand-pull theory and the Quantity Theory may not be as different as they appear at first sight. In both theories, the ultimate cause of inflation may lie with the government. In the Quantity Theory of Money, the government's budget deficit and borrowing requirement can cause the monetary expansion which creates and sustains an inflation. In the Keynesian demand-pull theory, the budget deficit may also be the source of excess demand for real output, though it is worth noting that the excess demand could also have other causes, such as excess consumption demand by households. Nevertheless, a high level of consumer demand can also be linked to the role of government. In the UK economy of the Keynesian era, in which governments pursued full employment, people behaved in an inflationary way both as workers and as voters. As workers, they could bargain for money wage increases in excess of any productivity increase without the fear of unemployment, while in the political arena they could add to the pressure of demand by voting for increased public spending and budget deficits.

COST-PUSH OR STRUCTURALIST THEORIES OF INFLATION

23. During the Keynesian era, creeping inflation continued even when there was no evidence of excess demand in the ecomony. Towards the end of the 1950s and during the 1960s and 1970s this caused many Keynesians to switch away from the demand-pull theory of inflation to a 'new' theory: **the cost-push** or **structuralist theory of inflation**. Cost theories of inflation locate the cause of inflation in structural and institutional conditions on the 'supply-side' of the economy, particularly in the **labour** market and the **wage bargaining process**. Most cost-push theories are essentially **'wage-push' theories**, though other variants include **'profits-push'** and **'import-cost push'** theories.

Cost-push theories argue that **the growth of monopoly power** in both the labour market and the goods market is responsible for inflation. In labour markets, growing trade union strength in the Keynesian era enabled trade unions to bargain for money wage increases in excess of any rise in labour productivity. Monopoly firms were prepared to pay these wage increases partly because of the costs of disrupting production and partly because they believed that they could pass on the increasing costs as price rises when they sold the output in the goods market. Cost-push theories usually assume that in the labour market wages are determined through the process of **collective bargaining**, while in the goods market prices are formed by a **'cost-plus' pricing rule** in which monopolistic firms add a standard profit margin to their costs when setting prices. Thus **trade union militancy** or **'pushfulness'** and perhaps **'big business'** are blamed for inflation. The question then arises as to why trade union militancy and power grew in the Keynesian era. As in the demand-pull theory of inflation, the 'guarantee' of full employment by the state and the provision of a 'safety net' of labour protection legislation and welfare benefits may have sustained the inflationary process - in the cost-push theory by creating the conditions in which trade unions could successfully be more militant.

A SIMPLE MODEL OF COST-PUSH INFLATION

24. We shall now construct a model of cost-push inflation which illustrates the roles of **pay relativities** and **different rates of productivity growth** in the inflationary process. We begin by assuming two productivity sectors in the economy, one with a high rate of growth of labour productivity, eg 6 per cent a year and the other with a zero rate. It is reasonable to suppose that firms in the 'high-productivity' sector are willing to grant money wage increases of 6 per cent but that they would resist paying any higher wage increases. Providing wage increases do not exceed 6 per cent, cost inflation does not occur in this sector. But we now assume that workers in the 'zero productivity' sector bargain with their employers to maintain comparability or to restore differentials relative to less skilled workers. They therefore try to obtain at least the same percentage wage increase as workers in the 'high productivity' sector. If a 6 per cent wage increase is granted to all workers, cost inflation will be generated as firms in the 'zero productivity' sector pass on the increased wage costs to consumers as price increases.

The inflationary process then continues through a combination of a **wage-price 'spiral'** and **'leap-frogging'**. A wage-price **'spiral'** is unleashed as workers in both sectors realise that their real wage increase has been eroded by price inflation and attempt to restore the increase through further wage claims. 'Leap-frogging' refers to the fact that when one group of workers improves its relative position in the pay 'league table', other groups will lodge retaliatory wage claims in order to restore their relative position or even to improve upon it.

In contrast to monetarists, who often treat the labour market as one large aggregated and relatively competitive market, neo-Keynesians view the labour market as a collection of non-competitive and separated markets for different skills and trades. Although workers generally realise that if *all* wage rises were limited to match the increase in productivity, inflation need not occur, they also appreciate that what is in the interest of workers considered collectively is not necessarily in the interest of a single group of workers taken in isolation. If one union accepts a wage increase lower than the current rate of inflation in order 'to bring inflation down', its members will suffer if other unions do not behave in a similar fashion. Thus each trade union must try to preserve its relative position in the pay 'league table', even when they know that by fuelling cost-inflation, a money wage increase may not result in a real wage increase.

THE PHILLIPS CURVE

25. Thirty years ago, Keynesians could be divided into **'demand-pull'** and **'cost-push' schools** in terms of the views held by members of each school on the causes of inflation. After 1958, the debate between 'demand-pull' and 'cost-push' Keynesians was conducted with the aid of a recently discovered statistical relationship, the **Phillips curve**, which is illustrated in Figure 21.2

Figure 21.2: The Phillips curve

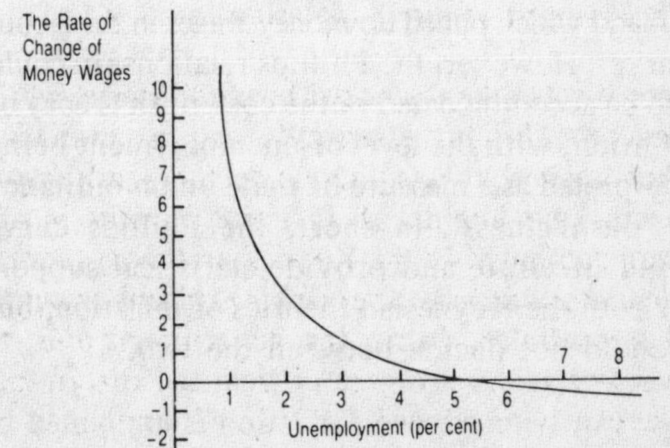

On the evidence of statistical data from the United Kingdom over a period extending from the 1860s to the 1950s, A W Phillips suggested that a stable but non-linear relationship exists between the rate of change of wages (**the rate of wage inflation**) and the **percentage of the labour force unemployed**. Taking the rate of growth of labour productivity into account, Phillips estimated that in the UK an unemployment level of about 2.5 per cent was compatible with zero inflation or price stability and that an unemployment level of 5.5 per cent would lead to stable money wages. In the years after 1958, Keynesian economists grasped on the supposed stability of the Phillips curve over a long period to argue that it provided statistical support for the existence of a '*trade-off*' between the policy objectives of price stability and reducing unemployment. On the basis of the Phillips relationship, Keynesian economists advised governments of the opportunity cost in terms of inflation of achieving any desired unemployment target. When offering this advice, the non-linearity of the Phillips curve was significant. As Figure 21.2 shows, a reduction in unemployment from 2 per cent to 1 per cent involves a much greater cost in terms of wage inflation than a reduction from 3 per cent to 2 per cent. Indeed, the Phillips curve seemed to justify the view held by many Keynesians in the United Kingdom in the 1950s and 1960s that an unemployment rate of about 1½ per cent represented full employment; any lower level of unemployment would indicate an **'over-heated economy'** and **'over-full' employment**, associated with an excessive cost in terms of inflation.

It is important to realise that the Phillips curve itself is *not* a theory of inflation. Initially, the Phillips curve was used by 'demand-pull' Keynesians, including A W Phillips himself, to illustrate how the rate of inflation varies with the amount of excess demand in the economy. In the demand-pull theory, the level of unemployment was used as an indicator of excess demand which pulled up money wages in the labour market. However, the Phillips relationship could also be accommodated in the cost-push theory of inflation, with the level of unemployment being interpreted as a measure of trade union militancy or 'pushfulness'. In short, the Phillips curve could illustrate and provide statistical support for both the Keynesian theories of inflation, but it could not decide between the two.

MONETARIST THEORIES OF INFLATION

26. It is possible to identify three stages in the development of modern monetarist theories of inflation. These are:

(i) **The revival** in 1956 by Milton Friedman **of the Quantity Theory of Money;**

(ii) The development, also by Milton Friedman, of **the theory of the 'expectations – augmented Phillips curve': ('Gradualist' Monetarism)**

iii) The incorporation of the **theory of rational expectations** into the explanation of the inflationary process: **('New Classical' Monetarism)**

Stages two and three of the monetarist theory relate to the apparent breakdown of the Phillips relationship which we have just described. But before we examine the 'fall of the Phillips curve'. we shall first take a brief look at the 'modern' Quantity Theory of Money.

THE 'MODERN' QUANTITY THEORY OF MONEY

27. We noted earlier, in the context of the 'old' Quantity Theory, how the Cambridge version of the equation of exchange concentrates on the factors that determine the demand for money. When Milton Friedman revived the Quantity Theory in 1956, he continued the process of turning it into a theory of the demand for money. In section 29 of Chapter 19, we explained how Milton Friedman's theory of the demand for money differs from earlier Keynesian theory. Essentially, Friedman argued that the general public's demand for money to hold as an asset is a stable function of a relatively small number of variables, and that the velocity of circulation of money V, though not constant, is stable. A simplified version of Friedman's theory of the demand for money can be written as:

$$M_D = f(q, P, i)$$

where:

q is real national income or output

P is the price level

and i is the average real rate of return on all non-money assets, including bonds, shares and consumer durables.

If q and P rise, the demand for money increases because larger money balances are required for transactions purposes. If i rises, the demand for money falls because other assets become more attractive than money as stores of wealth. When the money supply rises (by ΔM_s), the demand for money must also rise (so that $\Delta M_D = M_S$), in order to maintain equilibrium in the money market. This requires a change in either q, P or i, if ΔM_D is to equal ΔM_S. Friedman believed that in the short run, either real income (q) or the return on substitutes for money (i) could adjust. However, he argued that in the long run - after about two years - real income is at its equilibrium value which is fixed by real forces in the economy and the rate of return on non-monetary assets has little influence. Therefore, the price level must rise so as to increase the transactions demand for money and bring about a situation in which the demand to hold money balances increases to match the initial increase in the money supply.

THE BREAKDOWN OF THE PHILLIPS RELATIONSHIP

28. During the 1970s, the Phillips relationship appeared to break down in the United Kingdom economy (and in many other countries as well), as **accelerating inflation** and **growing unemployment** occurred together. Out of **stagflation** and the breakdown of the Phillips relationship, developed the second and third stages in the monetarist explanation of inflation, in which **theories on the role of expectations in the inflationary process** were tacked on to the Quantity Theory of Money. First, in 1968 Milton Friedman developed the **theory of the 'expectations-augmented Phillips curve'**, while in the 1970s and 1980s the **'New Classical' school** of monetarists explained inflation in terms of **the theory of rational expectations.**

THE THEORY OF THE 'EXPECTATIONS-AUGMENTED PHILLIPS CURVE'

29. When, in 1968, Milton Friedman introduced the **theory of 'the expectations-augmented Phillips curve'**, he predicted the breakdown of the Phillips relationship a few years before it actually happened. He argued that the Keynesian theories explaining the Phillips curve were based on a misunderstanding of the relationship between inflation and unemployment. According to Friedman, the Keynesian theories wrongly took into account only the *current* rate of inflation as it affects workers and firms, and ignored the important influence of the *expected* rate of inflation. Milton Friedman believed that a stable relationship between inflation and unemployment, allowing a long-term trade-off, had never existed. Instead, the *apparent* relationship identified by A W Phillips was at best *short-term* and *unstable*. Friedman's theory suggests that the only 'true' **long-term relationship between unemployment and inflation** lies along a vertical line, on which trade-offs are not possible, running through the **'natural' rate of unemployment** or the **'non-accelerating inflation rate of unemployment' (NAIRU).** This vertical line, illustrated in Figure 21.3, is sometimes called the **'long-run Phillips curve'.**

The theory of the 'expectations-augmented Phillips curve' brings together two important theories supported by modern monetarists:

(i) the **'classical' theory of the labour market;** and

(ii) **a theory of the role of expectations** in the inflationary process.

Figure 21.3: 'Short-run' and 'long-run' Phillips curves in the theory of the 'expectations-augmented Phillips curve'

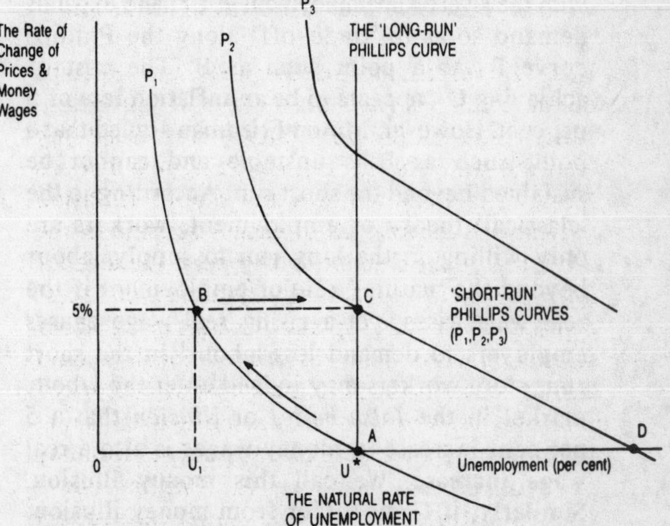

As we have seen, both earlier in this chapter and also in Chapter 13, in the **'classical' or 'real wage' theory of employment**, the **'natural' levels of employment and unemployment** are determined in the labour market at the equilibrium real wage at which workers voluntarily supply exactly the amount of labour that firms voluntarily employ. Because monetarists, and 'classical' economists in general, do not recognise demand-deficient unemployment, it follows that, at the 'natural' rate, unemployment is composed largely of frictional and structural unemployment. In Figure 21.3, the 'natural' rate of unemployment, determined in the labour market, is assumed to be U*.

We now introduce the role of expectations into the inflationary process. So as to keep the analysis as simple as possible, we shall assume that the rate of growth of labour productivity is zero, and that therefore the rate of increase of prices (ie **price inflation**) equals the rate of increase of wages (ie **wage inflation**). Suppose that the economy is initially at point A illustrated in Figure 21.3. Unemployment is at the 'natural' rate U*, and the rates of increase of both money wages and prices are zero and stable. We now assume that economic agents form their expectations of future inflation in the *next* period on the basis of the *current* rate of inflation. Thus at point A, workers expect the future rate of inflation also to be zero.

But suppose that the government is dissatisfied with the level of unemployment at U*, and expands demand so as to 'trade-off' along the Phillips curve P_1 to a point such as B. The cost of achieving U_1 appears to be an inflation rate of 5 per cent. However, Milton Friedman argued that a point such as B is unstable and cannot be sustained beyond the short run. According to the 'classical' theory of employment, workers are only willing in the long run to supply labour beyond the 'natural' rate of employment if the real wage rises, yet a rising real wage causes employers to demand less labour! In the short run, more workers may indeed enter the labour market in the *false belief* or *illusion* that a 5 per cent increase in money wages is also a real wage increase. We call this **money illusion**. Similarly, if firms suffer from money illusion, falsely believing that revenues are rising faster than labour costs, they may employ more labour. But to sustain an increase in employment beyond the 'natural' rate, workers and employers must suffer permanent money illusion in equal but opposite directions!

Friedman believed that workers and employers soon '*see through their money illusion*' and realise that they have confused money quantities with real quantities. Employment can only be sustained above its 'natural' level if inflation continuously accelerates to keep workers' expectations of inflation, formed in the previous time period, consistently below the actual rate to which inflation has risen. As workers continuously adjusts their expectations of future inflation to the rising actual rate and bargain for ever higher money wages so as to restore the real wage necessary to reduce unemployment below U*, the short-run Phillips curve *shifts outward* from P_1 to P_2 and so on. In Friedman's analysis, there is a separate 'short-run Phillips curve' for each expected rate of inflation. 'Further out' short-run Phillips curves such as P_2 and P_3 are associated with higher expected rates of future inflation, while the short-run Phillips curve would shift inwards if the expected rate of inflation falls.

Milton Friedman argued that *in the long run* unemployment can be kept below its 'natural' rate at U* only if the government allows the inflation rate to accelerate through a continuing monetary expansion. However, even in these circumstances, the inflation will eventually accelerate into a hyper-inflation which, in the resulting breakdown of economic activity, will cause unemployment ultimately to rise above its 'natural' rate.

Monetarists therefore believe that any attempt to reduce unemployment below the 'natural' rate is foolhardy and irresponsible, in the short-run accelerating inflation, while in the long-run perversely increasing unemployment above its 'natural' rate to an unnecessarily high level. But suppose that the government realises its 'mistake' in expanding the economy to a position such as B, which is below the 'natural' level of unemployment, and attempts to take corrective action. By refusing to allow the money supply to grow by more than 5 per cent per year (ie by *refusing to finance or accommodate* an accelerating inflation) the government may hope to stabilise inflation at 5 per cent. Workers and employers will now see through their earlier money illusion, and employment will return to the 'natural' rate.

In Friedman's theory, unemployment above the 'natural' rate is necessary if inflation is to return to zero. Unemployment must rise above the 'natural' rate in order to 'bleed' the economy of expectations of inflation built up when unemployment was below the 'natural' rate. Just as inflation accelerates whenever unemployment is below its 'natural' rate, so it decelerates when it is above the 'natural' rate. This is explained in each case by workers and employers gradually adapting their expectations of inflation to the actual rate. *Above* the 'natural' rate of unemployment actual inflation is always below the rate people were expecting, so economic agents revise their expectations downwards. The economy can only return to zero inflation and unemployment at the 'natural' rate (at point A) when the expected rate of inflation has fallen to zero.

THE THEORY OF RATIONAL EXPECTATIONS

30. Milton Friedman's 'expectations-augmented Phillips curve' is based on the **theory of adaptive expectations**, in which economic agents such as workers and firms form expectations of what will happen in the *future* only on the basis of what *has happened* in the *recent past*. However, in recent years, **'New Classical' economists** have rejected the theory of adaptive expectations in favour of an *alternative theory* of how expectations are formed: the **theory of rational expectations.** To illustrate the difference between the two theories, consider the situation of a gambler at a race meeting deciding whether to place a bet on a horse in the next race. One horse in the race came fourth three races ago, improving to third place two races ago and second place in its last race. In accordance with **the theory of adaptive expectations**, our gambler may decide to place his bet on this horse, believing it is now due for a win. But gambling on the basis of past form alone could be less successful than a *strategy that makes use of every single piece of relevant and up-to-date information available*, including of course past form. Information about the jockey riding the horse, and about such other relevant matters as the other horses and their jockeys, the length of the race and the state of the track, together perhaps with 'inside information' provided by a stable lad, would provide additional information and the basis for a more 'rational' gambling decision.

And just as it is irrational to gamble on the basis of limited information when much more up-to-date and relevant information is also available, 'New Classical' economists argue that it is unrealistic to assume that a *rational economic agent*, acting in its self-interest, will form expectations of *future* inflation only on the basis of *past* or *experienced* inflation. If economic agents on average correctly forecast the results of events taking place in the economy now, it is in their self-interest quickly to modify their economic behaviour in line with expectations based on the most up-to-date information available.

The incorporation of the theory of rational expectations into the explanation of the inflationary process thus represents the third and most recent stage in the development of monetarist theories of inflation. The 'New Classical' theory continues to accept the **Friedmanite concept of the 'natural' rate of unemployment**, which as we have noted is really a much older idea, pre-dating Friedman's theory of the 'expectations-augmented Phillips curve', and descending directly from the 'classical' tradition. But whereas Milton Friedman believed that governments can 'trade-off' along a Phillips curve and reduce unemployment below the 'natural' rate in the short run at least, the theory of rational expectations leads to the rejection of this possibility. According to the 'New Classical' school, money illusion does not occur even for a short period because it is in the interests of workers and employers to realise instantly any mistakes they have made when forming expectations and to 'see through' any attempt by an 'irresponsible' government to reflate the economy. 'New Classical' economists believe that if the government expands demand in order to stimulate output and employment, this is *fully anticipated* by private economic agents. Workers and firms modify their behaviour to offset or neutralise the effects intended by the government, so the expansion of demand has no effect upon real activity and employment, even in the short run.

An important difference between the adaptive and rational expectations versions of monetarism centres on the length of time unemployment *above* the 'natural' rate must be suffered as the cost or penalty of 'irresponsible' reflation of demand to reduce unemployment *below* the 'natural' rate. In the Friedmanite theory, the economy must experience a lengthy period of deflation and unemployment above the 'natural' rate to 'bleed' the system gradually of inflationary expectations built up during the period of fiscal or monetary expansionism. By contrast, the New Classical school argue that if workers and employers realise that a monetarist government, in possession of the correct (ie monetarist) 'model of how the economy works' announces that it will pursue firmly monetarist policies to bring the rate of inflation down at all costs, it is in their interest to modify their expectations immediately upon receiving this information. By believing that the government means business in reducing the money supply and the rate of inflation, workers and firms immediately build a lower expected rate of inflation into their wage-bargaining and price-setting behaviour. In this way, the New Classical school argue that inflation can be reduced relatively painlessly and without a lengthy period of unemployment above the 'natural' level. Such New Classical thinking lay behind the **Medium Term Financial Strategy (MTFS)** introduced by the Conservative Government in the UK in 1980 and deployed with varying degrees of success during most of the 1980s. You should refer back to Chapter 20 for further details of the MTFS and its role in UK monetary policy.

REDUCING THE 'NATURAL' RATE OF UNEMPLOYMENT

31. For modern monetarists and 'New Classical' economists, the 'natural' rate of unemployment represents **'full employment'** or equilibrium in the labour market. Nevertheless, considerable unemployment may exist at the 'natural' rate, explained largely by frictional, structural and technological causes. Indeed, with high levels of registered unemployment in the United Kingdom in recent years, monetarists have claimed that employment has been at its 'natural' rate and that the growth in unemployment from around 1 million to 3 million in the early 1980s could be explained by an increase in the 'natural' rate, together with some 'classical' unemployment caused by real wages being too high.

It is vital to understand that while **monetarists reject demand management policies** involving either fiscal or monetary expansionism aimed at reducing unemployment below its 'natural' rate, they support fully the use of **policies which reduce the 'natural' rate itself**. In terms of Figure 21.3, such policies would shift the vertical 'long-term' Phillips curve leftwards. New Classical economists believe that **'supply-side policies'** should be used to improve the structure of individual industries and markets so as to reduce the 'natural' rate of unemployment. But unlike neo-Keynesians who recommend supply-side policies which increase government intervention in the market economy, 'New Classical' or monetarist supply-side policy aims to *reduce* rather than *expand* the role of the state. As we noted earlier, appropriate policies (for a New Classical economist) include tax and public expenditure cuts, both to reduce the burden of taxation on the private sector and to create incentives to individuals and firms, and all micro-economic policies which might make individual markets more competitive, efficient and adaptable to change.

SUMMARY

32. In this chapter we have examined two of the most significant economic problems of recent years, unemployment and inflation. After explaining the possible causes and types of unemployment, including frictional, structural, 'real-wage' and demand-deficient unemployment, we introduced various theories of inflation, examined from a historical perspective. Then, by bringing the theories of unemployment and inflation together, we have shown how, in the first half of the Keynesian era in the 1950s and early 1960s, Keynesians explained both unemployment and inflation in terms of aggregate demand. In Keynesian theory, a lack of demand in the economy causes a deflationary gap to emerge and demand-deficient unemployment, while excess demand, illustrated with an inflationary gap, pulls up the price levels in a demand-pull inflation. In terms of economic policy, Keynesians believed that a 'trade-off' exists, illustrated by the Phillips curve, between the policy objectives of full employment and controlling inflation. In later years, many Keynesians abandoned the demand-pull theory of inflation in favour of the cost-push or structuralist theory, explaining the Phillips curve trade-off in terms of trade union militancy and structural conditions in the economy, rather than in terms of excess demand.

However, the earlier debate between demand-pull and cost-push Keynesians has now been superseded by the growth of monetarist and 'New Classical' theories of employment and inflation. The monetarist or New Classical 'counter-revolution' has involved the revival of pre-Keynesian explanations of unemployment and the rejection of both the concept of demand-deficient unemployment and demand management as a policy appropriate for reducing unemployment. By introducing the concept of the 'natural' rate of unemployment, the monetarists have revived the old 'classical' belief that the economy will tend 'naturally' towards equilibrium levels of output and employment at full employment. Uncompetitive markets and inefficiencies, including those caused by too much government intervention, will increase the 'natural' rate of unemployment, while too high 'real wages' largely explain any unemployment over and above the 'natural' rate. In terms of inflation theory, we may identify three stages in the development of monetarist or New Classical theory. Early monetarist theory centred exclusively on the revival of the oldest theory of inflation, the Quantity Theory of Money, which explains inflation purely as a monetary phenomenon, unrelated to the 'real economy'. However, later developments in the monetarist theory of inflation have tacked on to the Quantity Theory explanations of the role of expectations in the inflationary process. The theory of the 'expectations-augmented Phillips curve' represents the second Friedmanite or 'Gradualist' stage of monetarist inflation theory, while the third and latest stage incorporates the 'New Classical' theory of rational expectations. It is worth noting that in both the 'adaptive expectations' and the 'rational expectations' versions of monetarist inflationary theory, inflation is no longer treated as being purely a monetary phenomenon. Instead, the behaviour of workers and firms in the real economy, determined significantly by their expectations of future inflation and reactions to current and past inflation, form an important part of the inflation process.

STUDENT SELF-TESTING

1 *State the Keynesian and 'classical' attitudes to voluntary and involuntary unemployment.* (2)
2 *What causes frictional unemployment?* (3)
3 *Define casual unemployment.* (4)
4 *What is structural unemployment?* (5)
5 *Distinguish between structural unemployment and technological unemployment.* (6)
6 *Explain classical unemployment.* (7)
7 *What is another name for Keynesian unemployment?* (8)
8 *Who are the residually unemployed?* (9)
9 *Relate search theories to frictional unemployment.* (10)
10 *Why is it important to identify correctly the cause of unemployment?* (11)
11 *Define inflation.* (12)
12 *How is inflation suppressed in the Soviet Union?* (13)
13 *Distinguish between creeping inflation and strato-inflation.* (14, 15)
14 *Why is hyper-inflation usually short lived?* (16)
15 *What is meant by stagflation?* (17)
16 *List four costs of inflation.* (18)
17 *List three theories of inflation.* (19)
18 *Explain the equation of exchange.* (20)
19 *List three ways in which Keynesians attack the quantity theory.* (21)
20 *Draw an inflationary gap diagram to illustrate the demand-pull theory.* (22)
21 *Briefly explain cost-push inflation.* (23)
22 *What is (a) a 'wage-price spiral' and (b) 'leap-frogging'?* (24)
23 *What is the 'Phillips relationship'?* (25)
24 *List the three stages in the development of the monetarist theory of inflation.* (26)
25 *Explain the 'modern' quantity theory of money.* (27)
26 *When did the Phillips curve break down?* (28)
27 *Explain the 'natural' rate of unemployment.* (29)
28 *Distinguish between the theory of adaptive expectations and the theory of rational expectations.* (30)
29 *How may the 'natural' rate of unemployment be reduced?* (31)

EXERCISES

1

	UK inflation rate (%)	Unemployment in the UK (% of total labour force)
1978	8.6	5.9
1979	13.4	5.0
1980	17.8	6.4
1981	12.0	9.8
1982	8.6	11.3
1983	4.5	12.5
1984	5.0	11.7
1985	6.1	11.2
1986	3.4	11.1
1987	4.2	10.5

(a) Suggest reasons for the changes in (i) inflation and (ii) unemployment over the period shown by the data.

(b) Does the data indicate that a 'trade-off-exists between inflation and unemployment?

MULTIPLE CHOICE QUESTIONS

1 The 'natural' rate of unemployment can be reduced by:
A Expansionary monetary policy
B Expansionary fiscal policy
C Incomes policy
D Policies which improve competition in the labour market.

2 In an economy with full employment, which of the following policies would be most suitable for controlling inflation?
A Import controls
B Increasing exports
C Increasing tax rates
D Increasing personal tax allowances

3 According to Keynesian theory, which of the following policies would be most suitable for reducing unemployment?

A Reflation of demand and revaluation of the exchange rate
B Reflation of demand and devaluation of the exchange rate
C Deflation of demand and revaluation of the exchange rate
D Deflation of demand and devaluation of the exchange rate

4 The equation of exchange MV = PT is:
A A theory of inflation
B The equilibrium equation for national income
C An identity which is true by definition
D Relevant only for a barter company

5 Which of the following is a possible cause of cost-push inflation?
A Increased demand for the country's exports
B Increased trade union militancy
C Increased bank lending
D An increased public sector borrowing requirement.

EXAMINATION QUESTIONS

1 To what extent is technological change likely to increase or decrease levels of employment?
(ACCA December 1986)

2 (a) Outline the causes of unemployment. (10 marks)
(b) What policies can be used to cure unemployment? (10 marks)
(ACCA December 1984)

3 (a) What different forms may unemployment take? (10 marks)
(b) Why do unemployment rates vary within the UK? (10 marks)
(AAT June 1980)

4 Explain the relationships which may exist between inflation and unemployment.
(ACCA June 1983)

5 What are the assumptions and predictions of the quantity theory of money?
(ICSA June 1985)

6 'The view that inflation is a case of too much money chasing too few goods should be thought of as a hypothesis rather than a definition.' Discuss.
(ACCA June 1980)

7 Why is it important that governments should keep inflation under control?
(AAT December 1988)

22. Keynesian and monetarist instruments and objectives

INTRODUCTION

1. In this chapter we bring together many of the themes and strands of argument which have been developed in the chapters since our initial survey of macro-economic schools of thought in Chapter 13. In Chapter 21, we saw how it has proved difficult for governments to achieve two of the most important goals of economic policy: full employment and price stability. We shall now conclude our coverage of macro-economies in the domestic economy, by presenting a more general overview of **Keynesian** and **monetarist economic goals** or **objectives.** We shall continue to develop the **instruments and objectives approach** to economic policy which we have used on occasion in previous chapters, explaining how different **policy instruments,** for example fiscal and monetary policy, are used by economists of the two schools to try to achieve their **desired objectives.**

THE AIMS OR GOALS OF MACRO-ECONOMIC POLICY

2. At the risk of over-simplification, it is useful to conceive of macro-economic policy as a problem of assigning separate policy instruments to particular objectives or goals. Since the Second World War, governments in industrial mixed economies such as the UK have faced the same broad range of objectives, namely to:

(i) create and maintain **full employment;**

(ii) achieve **economic growth** and **improved living standards;**

(iii) achieve a **fair** or **acceptable distribution of income and wealth,** between both regions and different income groups in society;

(iv) to **control or limit inflation,** or to achieve some measure of **price stability;**

(v) to attain a **satisfactory balance of payments,** usually defined as the avoidance of an external deficit which might create an exchange rate crisis.

The order in which we have listed these objectives is by no means accidental. There is general agreement amongst economists of all schools, monetarist as well as Keynesian, that objectives (i) to (iii) are the **ultimate objectives** of economic policy - though there is considerable disagreement both on the nature of full employment and social fairness, and on how to attain them. By contrast, objectives (iv) and (v) are **intermediate objectives** or possibly **constraints** in the sense that an unsatisfactory performance in controlling inflation or the balance of payments can prevent the attainment of one or other of the ultimate policy objectives.

THE INSTRUMENTS OF ECONOMIC POLICY

3. At a general level, we can divide the **instruments of economic policy** into monetary policy, **fiscal** policy and the **use of direct controls** which constrain or limit the freedom of market forces and of economic agents, such as firms or workers, to behave and make decisions in the way they would otherwise wish.

Incomes policy is an example of a policy based on direct controls. In Chapter 18 we defined fiscal **policy** as economic policy to achieve the government's economic objectives using fiscal **instruments** such as **government spending, taxation** and the **budget deficit.** Likewise, Chapter 20 defined **monetary policy** in terms of monetary **instruments** such as the **money supply,** the **rate of interest** and **controls over bank lending.** It is often appropriate to disaggregate broad labels such as fiscal policy and monetary policy and look in a more detailed fashion at specific policy instruments such as changes in particular taxes and types of government spending (in fiscal policy), changes in interest rates (as a monetary policy instrument) and the use of the exchange rate as a macro-policy instrument. As a generalisation, in the Keynesian era policy instruments of all kinds were used at the macro-level to influence in a **discretionary** way, to manage **aggregate demand** or the **'demand-side' of the economy**. Under monetarism, the reverse is true, policy being aimed largely if not exclusively, at **improving 'supply-side' performance**. Monetary policy is the exception, being targeted in a non-discretionary way at controlling the overall growth of the level of nominal expenditure in the economy, in order to control inflation.

KEYNESIANISM

4. We shall now review briefly the meaning of **Keynesianism** and **monetarism**, though you should refer back to Chapter 13 for a more detailed discussion of the origins of the two schools of thought. **Keynesianism** is a label attached to the theories and policies of those economists who claim to have inherited the mantle of the great English economist, **J M Keynes**. After Keynes's death in 1946, Keynesianism became associated with an **increased level of government intervention** in the economy, especially through budget deficits and fiscal policy, to 'fine-tune' or manage aggregate demand in an attempt to achieve the best possible performance in terms of the five objectives of policy we listed earlier. However it is important to realise that neither Keynesianism nor monetarism should be regarded as monolithic structures, and that each is a broad label encompassing a wide range of differing viewpoints. In the United Kingdom, a distinction is sometimes drawn between **'Old School'** and **'New School' Keynesians.** As we explained in Chapter 13, a crisis occurred in Keynesian economics in the 1960s and 1970s when traditional Keynesian demand management policies failed to secure full employment, economic growth and price stability. This led to a breakaway by a group of **'New School' Keynesian economists**, the **Cambridge Economic Policy Group (CEPG)**, centred in the Department of Applied Economics at Cambridge University. Traditionally, Cambridge University - Keynes's own university - has always been the academic centre of Keynesianism. The older generation of Keynesians are sometimes known as **'Old School' Keynesians**, whereas the younger members of the CEPG form the **'New School'**. Paradoxically, the New School shares with monetarism a distrust of **short-term demand management** via the traditional Old School instrument of discretionary fiscal policy. Like monetarists, New School Keynesians have advocated a more **medium-term economic policy** to replace demand management. However, unlike the monetarists, members of the New School have generally played down the importance of monetary policy in general and control of the money supply in particular, retaining instead the essentially Keynesian belief in the need for extended government intervention in the economy through incomes policy, the direction of investment funds into industry by the state, and possibly import controls. **'New School' Keynesians**, who are sometimes labelled as **neo-Keynesian** or **post-Keynesian**, also share with monetarists an emphasis on 'supply-side'-rather than 'demand-side'-economic policy, though unlike the monetarists they locate the causes of inflation in cost-push or structural factors, rather than in excess demand.

MONETARISM

5. As we noted in Chapter 13, **monetarism** takes its name from the belief held by all monetarists that inflation is explained by the Quantity Theory of Money; according to monetarists all inflation, at least in a closed economy, is caused by a prior expansion of the money supply. In fact, monetarism means rather more than this, extending to encompass a large part of the **pre-Keynesian** or **'classical'** view of how the economy works. As with Keynesianism, a number of different 'brands' or 'varieties' of monetarism can be identified. Perhaps the most significant distinction is between **Friedmanite** or **'Gradualist' monetarism** and **'rational expectations' monetarism,** known also as the **'New Classical' school of monetarism**. We explained this distinction in the previous chapter. In brief, **Friedmanite monetarists**, following Milton Friedman, accept that when using demand management policies, 'trade-offs' are possible in the short run between reducing unemployment and achieving control of inflation. However, no 'trade-off' is possible in the long run, except at the cost of an ever-accelerating inflation. In contrast, the **'New Classical' school of monetarists** reject the idea of a 'trade-off' even in the short run, thereby also completely rejecting the effectiveness of Keynesian demand management policies. Both schools of monetarism have incorporated theories of the role of expectations of future inflation into their explanations of the cause of current inflation, but their models of the formation of inflationary expectations are different. Friedmanite monetarism is based on the **theory of adaptive expectations**, whereas 'New Classical' monetarism

incorporates the **rational expectations** model. Both of these are treated more fully in Chapter 21.

Indeed, as we explained briefly in Chapter 13, many members of the New Classical school no longer label themselves as monetarist. In part this may be a response to the fact that empirical evidence in the 1980s arguably has thrown considerable doubt both on the central tenet of monetarism that all inflation is caused by a previous monetary expansion and on the belief that control of the money supply is all that is needed to control inflation. Perhaps it is more accurate to regard the New Classical school less as a 'variety' of monetarism than as a revival of 19th century 'classical' economic liberalism wedded to the modern theory of rational expectations which we explained in Chapter 21. Nevertheless, members of the New Classical school are monetarists in the sense that they recommend that economic policy should aim simply to provide conditions which, in the longer run, will enable the economy to grow at its 'natural' rate, and that these conditions include ensuring that the money stock expands steadily at a rate consistent with the 'natural' rate of growth of real output and a stable rate of price inflation.

SOME FUNDAMENTAL ISSUES OF DISPUTE BETWEEN KEYNESIANS AND MONETARISTS

6. Before we examine in detail policy differences between Keynesians and monetarists, we shall first survey briefly some rather more deep-seated differences in the views held by the two schools on the fundamental nature of the economy and how it works. We shall examine (i) the **separation of 'real' and monetary forces** in the economy and (ii) the **stability of market forces**.

THE SEPARATION OF 'REAL' AND 'MONETARY' FORCES

7. Many monetarists seem to accept the old pre-Keynesian or 'classical' view (known as the **Classical Dichotomy**) that *real* and *monetary* forces in the economy are separate. They believe that an increase in the money supply will, via the Quantity Theory of Money, cause the price level to rise, leaving unaffected the equilibrium values of relative prices and equilibrium levels of output and employment. This view, which is rejected by Keynesians, implies that a policy of monetary expansion, resulting from either an expansionary monetary policy or an expansionary fiscal policy, will in the long run increase prices but not output and employment. Friedmanite monetarists accept that in the short run (a period of up to five or ten years according to Milton Friedman) monetary changes can primarily affect output, but New Classical monetarists reject the possibility of even a short-run stimulation of output and reduction in unemployment.

THE STABILITY OF MARKET FORCES

8. Most monetarists regard a market economy as a calm and orderly place in which the price mechanism, working through the incentives signalled by price changes in competitive markets, achieves a more optimal and efficient outcome than could result from a policy of government intervention. They believe that risk-taking businessmen or entrepreneurs, who will lose or gain through the correctness of their decisions in the market place, 'know better' what to produce than civil servants and planners employed by the government on risk-free salaries with secured pensions. Providing only that markets are sufficiently competitive, what is produced is ultimately determined by consumer sovereignty, with consumers knowing better than governments what is good for them. According to this philosophy, the correct function of government is to reduce to a minimum its economic activities and interference with private economic agents. Thus government should be restricted to a 'nightwatchman' role, maintaining law and order, providing public goods and offering other minor corrections when markets fail, and generally ensuring a suitable environment in which 'wealth creating' entrepreneurship can function in competitive markets subject to minimum regulation.

This philosophy of the correct role of markets and of government leads most monetarists to reject **discretionary intervention** in the economy by the government as a means of achieving goals such as reduced unemployment. Monetarists believe that at best such intervention will be ineffective, at worst it will be damaging, destabilising and inefficient. Instead, monetarists prefer that governments should adopt, if necessary, by law, **fixed** or **automatic policy rules**. To ensure against the use of a discretionary fiscal policy to manage demand, and also to assist the 'hitting' of a money supply target, monetarists have recommended that **fiscal policy** should be based on a **fiscal rule to balance the budget**, or perhaps to **reduce the deficit or PSBR to a fixed proportion of GDP**. **Monetary policy** should, in turn, be based on a **monetary rule** to expand the money supply in line with the growth of real GDP in order to control inflation.

Finally, monetarists have at times recommended an **exchange rate rule**, though as we shall see in a later section of this chapter, an important distinction can be made between monetarists who recommend a **'floating exchange rate' rule** and those who believe in the virtues of a **'fixed exchange rate' rule.**

THE KEYNESIAN VIEW ON THE STABILITY OF MARKET FORCES

9. In contrast to the monetarist view we have just described, Keynesians believe that unregulated markets may function in an unstable and erratic way. In particular, Keynesians stress:

(i) the imperfect nature of generally uncompetitive markets, characterised by the growth of producer sovereignty and monopoly power;

(ii) the importance of uncertainty about the future and the lack of correct market information as potentially destabilising forces;

(iii) the likelihood of breakdown of the money linkages between markets. In monetary economies - as distinct from economies based on barter - money is used as a means of payment or medium of exchange for market transactions. The linkage between markets may fail if workers receiving money incomes from the sale of their labour in the labour market decide to hold their income as idle money balances, instead of immediately purchasing goods and services in the goods market. According to Keynesians, this causes the breakdown of Say's Law that 'supply creates its own demand'. The resulting excess savings become the cause of deficient demand and the involuntary unemployment of labour and other resources.

DISPUTES BETWEEN MONETARISTS AND KEYNESIANS: A SUMMARY

10. In summary therefore, monetarists emphasise the *optimal* aspects of a *competitive market economy* in a state of general and fully employed equilibrium, and the role in achieving such an equilibrium of private economic agents reacting to the price signals provided by the market in conditions of near-perfect market information. They believe that in competitive markets *flexible prices*, which readily adjust upwards or down, *quickly move* to clear a disequilibrium. In contrast, Keynesians emphasise the *inflexible or 'sticky' nature of prices and particularly wages*. For a Keynesian, a market economy is characterised by *disequilibrium* rather than by *equilibrium* and is subject to random 'shocks' or autonomous changes, which by triggering destabilising multiplier effects, hold no guarantee of a smooth and orderly adjustment towards a full employment equilibrium. But by managing the level of aggregate demand, the government can 'know better' than unregulated market forces. Deliberate government intervention can anticipate and counter the destabilising forces existent in the market economy, achieving a better outcome than could be achieved in an economy subject to market forces alone. Thus, while monetarists lay great stress on what they see as the essentially stabilising properties of the price mechanism and market forces, regarding government intervention as inefficient and destabilising, Keynesians adopt the opposite view. They justify discretionary government intervention on the grounds that it stabilises an otherwise inherently unstable market economy.

AN INSTRUMENTS AND OBJECTIVES APPROACH TO ECONOMIC POLICY

11. In order to explain the main differences and disputes between Keynesians and monetarists with regard to specific economic policies, such as the use of fiscal policy and monetary policy, we shall adopt an **instruments and objectives approach**. First we identify the **principal objectives or goals** that the policy makers wish to achieve. We then see how each school of thought assigns a **specific types of economic policy** to achieve a **particular objective**. According to the 'instruments and objectives' approach to economic policy, successful management of the economy requires a government to have as many policy instruments as there are

objectives, with a separate instrument assigned to each objective. The decision of which policy instrument or type of policy to assign to each objective is called an **assignment rule**. As we shall see, monetarist and Keynesian assignment rules have differed significantly, and Keynesian economic policy in particular has suffered from the problem of insufficient policy instruments to meet desired objectives.

KEYNESIAN INSTRUMENTS AND OBJECTIVES

12. In the earlier part of the Keynesian era, before about 1967, Keynesian economic policy in the United Kingdom relied on *just one principal policy instrument* - **fiscal policy** which was used for the discretionary management of aggregate demand. At the time, demand management was used to achieve **three potentially conflicting policy objectives: full employment; control of inflation** and a **satisfactory balance of payments** (and the protection of a fixed exchange rate). This led to a frequent switching of fiscal policy between objectives, depending upon which objective was considered most important at the time. In order to create full employment and growth, the Keynesians used tax cuts and increased public spending to expand demand. However, an expansion of demand increased imports, and excess demand pulled up prices. Eventually rising imports would cause a balance of payments crisis which, together with an unacceptable rise in the inflation rate, led to a reversal of policy with fiscal policy being used to deflate demand in order to protect the exchange rate and reduce inflation. Thus Keynesianism became associated with **'trade-offs' between policy objectives** (as illustrated by the **Phillips relationship** which we explained in Chapter 21) and with the **'stop-go' management of aggregate demand**.

THE KEYNESIANS AND MONETARY POLICY

13. In the Keynesian era **discretionary fiscal policy** was used as the principal demand management policy instrument, partly because the Keynesians believed it was more powerful and effective for this purpose than monetary policy and partly because monetary policy was in the main assigned to another objective: national debt management. But, as we explained in Chapter 20, the **role of monetary policy** in the Keynesian era was never very clear. At times monetary policy was used along with fiscal policy to manage demand and also as a means of protecting the exchange rate in the recurrent balance of payments crises that affected the UK at the time. To deflate aggregate demand, open market operations would be used in a contractionary way and interest rates would be raised. Higher interest rates also served to protect the exchange rate by attracting capital flows into the country.

KEYNESIANS AND THE EXCHANGE RATE

14. The role of the **sterling exchange** rate during the Keynesian era illustrates an important feature of the 'instruments and objectives' approach to economic policy. Under certain circumstances, an *instrument* of economic policy can switch roles, becoming instead a policy *objective*. Equally, what was previously a target or goal in its own right can becomes an instrument or a means of attaining some other objective of economic policy. And thirdly, an instrument or objective which the policy makers judge to have performed unsatisfactorily, may be relegated to the 'less demanding' role of being simply an **'economic indicator'** - signalling to the government whether its policy is 'on course'.

Early in the Keynesian era - from the 1940s to about 1966/72 - successive British governments were committed to **preserving a fixed exchange rate**. The exchange rate was therefore an *objective* rather than an *instrument* of policy. As we noted in the previous section, demand management policies were used to deflate demand in order to support the exchange rate. But in the latter part of the Keynesian era, many Keynesians came to the conclusion that if 'stop-go' was to be avoided, a separate policy instrument must be assigned to each objective or goal of policy. Demand management policies - especially fiscal policy - were assigned to achieve the objectives of full employment and growth, and the Keynesians began to use the exchange rate as a policy instrument assigned to the objective of supporting the balance of payments. In short, after 1967, the Keynesians abandoned their previous belief in the virtues of fixed exchange rates, being prepared instead to devalue the exchange rate or to allow it to float, so as to prevent a deteriorating balance of payments position.

KEYNESIANS AND INCOMES POLICY

15. As well as requiring an *extra* policy instrument, namely the exchange rate, to assign to the balance of payment objective, the Keynesians began to realise that discretionary fiscal policy or demand management alone was unable to secure *both* full employment *and* price stability. As a result, Keynesians of the cost-push school recommended the introduction of an **incomes policy** as the appropriate instrument to reduce inflation. The saw an incomes policy as a form of direct control over market forces. However, many economists dispute the idea that an incomes policy should be regarded as a well-defined policy instrument. They regard an incomes policy as an extremely loose label for a variety of *statutory* and *voluntary, short-term* and more *medium-term* policies for the *freezing, restraining* or *planned growth* of wages, incomes and sometimes prices as well. In principle, incomes policies can vary from ad hoc hastily thought out emergency measures, usually of short duration in response to a panic or crisis, to a much longer-term forward planning of the growth of incomes based on some consensus of social fairness.

KEYNESIAN ASSIGNMENT RULES A SUMMARY

16. During the Keynesian era, and particularly during the period leading up to the crisis in Keynesian economics in the mid-1970s - when there was a failure to achieve any of the standard objectives of macro-policy - the Keynesians searched for an ever-wider range of policy instruments with which to conduct the management of the UK economy.

Indeed, a leading Keynesian, GDN Worswick, compared Keynesian economic policy to a game of musical chairs in which the policy makers were always one policy instrument short. As soon as a 'new' instrument was invented, such as incomes policy, a new problem would emerge, such as the breakdown of law and order and social cohesion, for which the government would lack an appropriate policy instrument.

(1) ***The Keynesian Assignment Rule in the UK during the early part of the Keynesian era (1940s/1960s)***

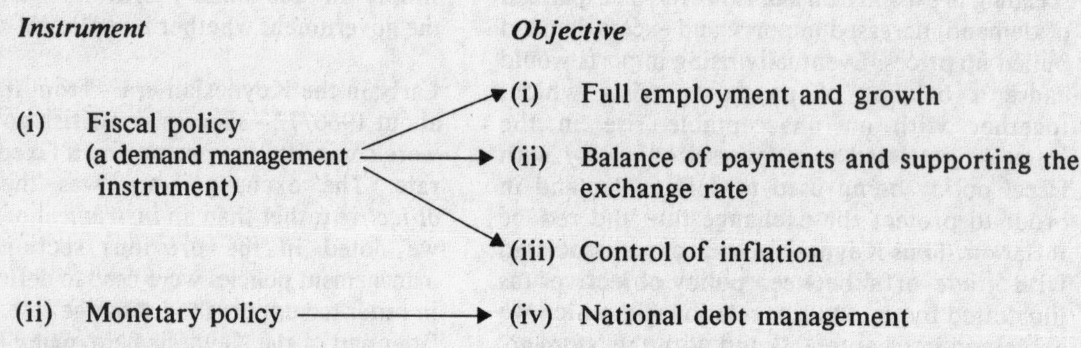

(2) ***The Keynesian Assignment Rule in the UK during the later part of the Keynesian era (late 1960s; 1970s)***

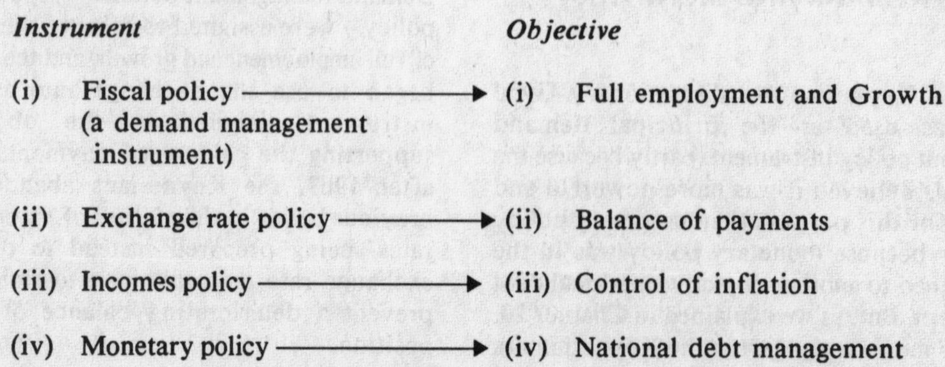

MONETARIST INSTRUMENTS AND OBJECTIVES

17.	Instrument		Objective
(i)	Fiscal policy	→	(i) The creation of 'supply-side' incentives (at the micro-level) and PSBR control (at the macro-level)
(ii)	'Market forces' (a freely-floating exchange rate)	→	(ii) Balance of payments
(iii)	'Market forces'	→	(iii) Full employment
(iv)	Monetary policy	→	(iv) Control of inflation

Some commentators argue that the 'instruments and objectives' framework is inappropriate for the analysis of monetarist economic policy because monetarists generally wish to *reduce rather than extend* government intervention in the market economy. However, if we consider **'market forces'** themselves as a policy instrument (or perhaps more appropriately as an 'anti-policy' in the sense that relying on market forces represents a policy of disengagement or non-intervention), the **monetarists' assignment rule** is shown above.

Alternatively, we can order or 'rank' the objectives and instruments of monetarist policy in the following way:

(i) **Improved economic welfare** is the **ultimate objective** of monetarist economic policy. But unlike Keynesians, most monetarists believe that only private enterprise, and not the government, can deliver the full employment, economic growth and higher living standards that increase the nation's welfare. For monetarists, the correct function of government is to create the market conditions in which the private sector can ensure the growth of output and employment.

(ii) But before market forces can work properly, **price stability** must first be achieved. Thus monetarists believe **control of inflation** to be the most important **intermediate objective** of macro-economic policy. (Critics sometimes argue that, under monetarism, control of inflation has become the *ultimate* policy objective, but monetarists say that this misrepresents their views - control of inflation is a *means to an end*, but *not an end itself*.)

(iii) Central to monetarism is the **Quantity Theory of Money and the belief that inflation is caused by an excessive rate of growth of the money supply** *or stock of money in the economy*. Therefore, control of the rate of growth of the money supply is also a necessary *intermediate* (or *immediate*) objective of policy. Nevertheless, for reasons which we explained in Chapters 19 and 20, control of the money supply may be difficult to achieve. Some monetarists therefore, believe that measures of the money supply such as M4 should be regarded as general *indicators* of the 'tightness' of monetary policy rather than as instruments or intermediate objectives of policy. In recent years monetarists have argued that monetary policy should be operated to monitor a number of **indicators of monetary growth,** including the **exchange rate** and the **money value or nominal value of GDP**. And if a target for monetary growth is needed, it should be expressed in terms of the exchange rate or money GDP, rather than as a measure of the money stock such as M4. Nevertheless, monetarists of the New Classical or 'rational expectations' school have believed that the announcement of money supply targets which the government firmly intends to hit can bring inflation down, by influencing expectations favourably. However, as we explained in Chapter 20, failure to hit an announced target might of course have an adverse effect upon expectations of future inflation.

(iv) Monetary policy and fiscal policy are *interdependent* and monetary policy cannot be separated from the government's fiscal stance. At the root of the monetarism implemented by recent UK governments, is the belief that the **levels of both public spending** and the **budget deficit** (and hence the **PSBR**) must be used as policy instruments to achieve control over monetary growth. Besides aiding the 'fight against inflation', monetarists argue that a tight fiscal stance and the reduction of both public spending and the PSBR as proportions of GDP, also reduce what they see as undesirable **'crowding-out'** in the economy, by freeing a greater volume of resources for use and employment in the private sector.

MONETARISTS AND THE EXCHANGE RATE

18. It is worth repeating and emphasising that 'practical monetarism' involves the rejection of *discretionary economic management in general*, and *short-term demand management in particular*, and the adoption of much more *medium-term automatic policy rules*. But while many monetarists are generally agreed on the need for monetary policy and fiscal policy rules, there is much less agreement amongst monetarists on the appropriate exchange rate rule to adopt.

Monetarists who have studied the inflationary process on a world-wide basis under a system of fixed exchange rates are known as **international monetarists** or **global monetarists**. In such a system, the **world inflation rate** is determined by the **rate of growth of the world money supply**. For a relatively small economy open to world trade, such as the United Kingdom, the **domestic rate of inflation** becomes **determined by the world rate of inflation**, with the domestic money supply responding *endogenously* to *'accommodate' or finance* the rate of inflation 'imported' from the rest of the world. Instead of changes in the domestic money supply causing inflation, in the theory of global monetarism or fixed exchange rate monetarism **the 'imported' rate of inflation causes changes in the domestic money supply**. The direction of causation between money and the price level at the level of an individual small country is thus completely the opposite of the 'traditional' theory of monetarism developed originally by Milton Friedman as appropriate either for a closed economy or for a system of floating exchange rates. Nevertheless, in the fixed exchange rate theory, the rate of world inflation is still caused by world monetary growth.

In the 1960s and 1970s, the monetarist 'counter-revolution' accompanied a growing disenchantment amongst economists with fixed exchange rates and the emergence of a consensus in favour of a floating exchange rate system, in which market forces alone determine the exchange rate. However in recent years, many economists - monetarist and Keynesian - have changed their minds once again and now recommend a return to a relatively fixed system of exchange rates. Monetarists are probably fairly evenly divided between those who favour a freely floating exchange rate regime and those who argue for a return either to a managed system or to a rigidly fixed system.

A 'freely floating' exchange rate system is consistent with the belief held by most monetarists that market forces, and not the government, should determine as far as possible the level of economic activity within the economy. As with other forms of government intervention, 'floating exchange rate' monetarists believe that any attempt by government to manage the exchange rate is liable to create inefficiencies and distortions, and that in the long run it will in any case be unable to defy market forces. Additionally, a floating exchange rate has the advantage - at least in theory - of isolating a country from international inflationary pressure. With a fixed exchange rate, a country may 'import' inflation from the rest of the world as happened in the 1960s when the USA expanded its domestic economy and built up a huge balance of payments deficit with the rest of the world. The Americans managed to persuade other countries to maintain their fixed exchange rates against the dollar and to accept US dollars in payment for American imports from the rest of the world. As a result, dollars flowed out of the USA and into the economies of other countries, greatly swelling domestic demand in the rest of the world. In the monetarist explanation, this process added greatly to world monetary growth and was responsible for an international acceleration of inflation in later years. Suppose instead, that other exchange rates freely floated against the dollar. In these circumstances, other countries would not have imported the dollars created by the American monetary authorities and the American payments deficit would simply have caused the exchange rate of the dollar to fall until the US deficit had been eliminated.

The recent change of opinion back in favour of fixed exchange rates is largely explained by the experience of floating exchange rates in the 1970s and 1980s. Many economists, of all schools of thought, now accept that a freely floating exchange rate may in fact contribute to the inflationary process, and that a fixed rate acts as a *source of discipline* which reduces, rather than increases, inflationary pressures. When, for example, trade unions bargain for wage increases of 8 per cent and the average rate of growth of productivity is only 3 per cent, then the domestic price level is likely to rise, unless of course increased real costs are absorbed as reduced profits. However in a regime of freely floating exchange rates, international competitiveness need not be affected adversely since the exchange rate simply falls to maintain the initial price of domestically produced goods relative to imports. But the inflationary process need not stop there. Trade unions may respond to the rising money price of imports caused by the falling exchange rate, by demanding even higher money wages to restore the eroded gain in their real wage. This causes a further rise in prices which in turn causes the exchange rate to fall and so on. The process continues in a **cumulative vicious inflationary spiral**, accompanied by a **plummeting exchange rate**.

In a fixed exchange rate system, this cannot happen. Inflationary cost-push behaviour by domestic workers and businesses which raises wages and prices at a faster rate in other countries is simply 'disciplined' by a loss of competitiveness and by the resulting threat of unemployment and bankruptcy.

MONETARISM AND INCOMES POLICY

19. Most monetarists reject the use of a **formal incomes policy**, which they regard as another example of unnecessary and inefficient government intervention in the market economy. For monetarists, incomes policies are undesirable because they distort and interfere with the market mechanism, preventing prices from performing their *signalling* and *incentive* functions. According to this view, the net effect of incomes policies is to make the economy resistant to change and less competitive. In the long run, the 'natural' rate of unemployment rises and inflation may also be increased. But although monetarists reject a *formal* and especially a *statutory*, incomes policy, they certainly have a **'policy towards incomes'**, or an *informal* incomes policy. The monetarists' 'incomes policy' is essentially a 'supply-side' policy aimed at improving the competitiveness of the labour market. We can identify four distinct aspects of the monetarist 'policy towards incomes'. These are:

(i) the reduction of trade union monopoly power over the supply of labour;

(ii) the removal of labour restrictive practices in labour markets;

(iii) the education of workers in the 'reality of the market place'; and

(iv) the direct imposition of wage restraint in the public sector where the state is the employer.

MONETARISM AND 'SUPPLY-SIDE' ECONOMIC POLICY

20. The informal incomes policy which we have just described is an example of **'supply-side' economic policy**. We can define 'supply-side' economic policy as the set of government policies which aim to change the underlying structure of the economy and improve the economic performance of markets and industries, and also of individual workers and firms within markets. 'Supply-side' policies are, for the most part, *micro-economic* rather than *macro-economic*, since they aim to improve general economic performance by acting on the motivation and efficiency of individual economic agents within the economy. Most monetarists place considerably emphasis on the need for suitable (free market) supply-side policies, believing that they are much more significant in the long run than macro-policy in changing the nature of the economy towards the sort of **social market economy** the monetarists would like to see. Under monetarism, **'supply-side' economics** has gained an ascendancy over the **'demand-side' economics** that prevailed during the Keynesian era, and **macro-economic policy** has to a large extent become subordinate to **micro-economic policy**. Monetarists of the New Classical school believe that while the economy is always close to its **'natural' levels of output and employment,**

these 'natural' levels can be unnecessarily low because of distortions which reduce both an individual's willingness to supply labour and a firm's willingness to supply goods. The appropriate micro-policies are therefore those which remove these distortions, and improve 'supply-side' incentives within the economy. In the Keynesian era, micro-economic policy - along with macro-policy - usually *extended* rather than *reduced* government interventionism in markets, in such fields as **regional policy, competition policy** (or **anti-monopoly policy**), **labour market policy**, and in the government's general **industrial policy**. By contrast, monetarist governments have pursued a policy of 'rolling back' the functions of the state and reducing the level of government intervention in the economy. New Classical monetarists advocate cuts in tax and welfare benefits in order to create incentives to work and to supply entrepreneurial flair. In the short run such policies may widen inequalities in the distribution of income and wealth but New Classical economists justify this by arguing that to *reduce poverty in the long run, inequalities must be widened in the short run*, so as to generate incentives necessary for the wealth creation that can eventually serve to reduce poverty. Critics of the New Classical School reply by arguing that these policies are socially unjust since they involve 'wealth incentives' for the already well-off and 'poverty incentives' for the already poor.

PRIVATISATION, MARKETISATION AND DEREGULATION

21. Three rather more general aspects of the 'supply-side' policy recommended by monetarist and New Classical economists and introduced in the United Kingdom in recent years are **privatisation, marketisation and deregulation**:

(i) **Privatisation:** The privatisation programme has involved the **selling of state owned assets** such as nationalised industries and public sector housing (council housing) to the private sector and the **contracting out** of work previously undertaken in the public sector to private sector firms, eg hospital cleaning.

(ii) **Marketisation:** The opening up of as many economic activities as possible to the 'discipline' of market forces and the price mechanism, even when these activities continue to be provided by the state. Consumers receive goods and services after paying a price and exercising choice, rather than through collective provision financed from general taxation.

(iii) **Deregulation:** The removal of 'unnecessary' bureaucratic regulations and 'red tape' which interfere with individual decision making and choice, and which restrict competition.

KEYNESIANS, MONETARISTS AND THE NATURE OF AGGREGATE SUPPLY

22. We shall conclude our survey of Keynesianism and monetarism by contrasting Keynesian and monetarist theories of **aggregate supply** (as distinct from their more micro-economic views on the nature of the 'supply-side' of the economy which includes attitudes to privatisation, marketisation and deregulation). In Figure 22.1 we show aggregate demand for and aggregate supply of real output as functions of the price level. We have drawn a **downward-sloping aggregate demand curve**, showing the aggregate demand for real output as a negative function of the price level. This is explained by a **wealth effect** or **real balance effect**. If the price level falls, peoples' nominal money balances become worth more, ie they can purchase more goods. **Real money balances** are therefore greater. This increases the demand for real output and it may also cause the rate of interest to fall, which further stimulates consumption and investment spending.

However, our main interest in Figure 22.1 is the curve showing the **aggregate supply of real output**. We have drawn three possibilities, each of which carries an important implication for economic policy:

(a) **The 'inverted L-shaped' Keynesian aggregate supply function:** Figure 22.1 (a) illustrates the 'traditional' but simplistic Keynesian view that an expansion of demand will *reflate* real output rather than *inflate* prices, providing there is unemployment and spare capacity in the economy. Following an expansion of aggregate demand, which shifts the aggregate demand function from AD_1 to AD_2, real output increases from y_1 to y_2 but the price level does not change. In this diagram aggregate demand affects real output rather than prices because the **supply of real output is assumed to be perfectly elastic** with respect to an increase in demand. In effect, Say's Law is reversed: instead of 'supply creating its own demand', demand is assumed to 'create its own supply'. But once full employment is reached at the level of real output y_3, any further increase in aggregate demand (eg to AD_3) causes prices and not output to rise.

(b) **The 'extreme' monetarist or New Classical aggregate supply function:** If Figure 22.1 (a) represents 'extreme' and a rather crude version of Keynesianism, Figure 22.1 (b) illustrates 'extreme' or simplistic monetarism. Here we have drawn a vertical monetarist or New Classical aggregate supply function, determined at the level of real output consistent with the 'natural' rate of unemployment in the labour market. Because output and employment are assumed to be at their 'natural' or equilibrium levels, any expansion of aggregate demand, for example from AD_1 to AD_2, causes the price level to rise with no effect at all upon the levels of real output and employment.

(c) **An 'intermediate' aggregate supply function:** Many economists adopt a position somewhere between the two extremes we have just described. This intermediate position, which represents perhaps an area of agreement between 'moderate' Keynesians and monetarists, is depicted in Figure 22.1 (c). We have drawn the aggregate supply curve as an upward-sloping function of the price level, becoming steeper at higher levels of real output. An expansion of aggregate demand which shifts the AD function along the upward-sloping section of the AS curve, eg from AD_1 to AD_2, results both in increased output and inflation. At low levels of output where the AS curve is nearly horizontal, the main effect is upon real output, but as full employment is approached, the inflationary effect upon the price level becomes dominant.

Figure 22.1: The aggregate demand and supply model

The effect of an expansion of aggregate demand for real output with:
(a) an 'inverted L-shaped' Keynesian aggregate supply function;
(b) a vertical New Classical or monetarist aggregate supply function;
(c) an upward-sloping aggregate supply function.

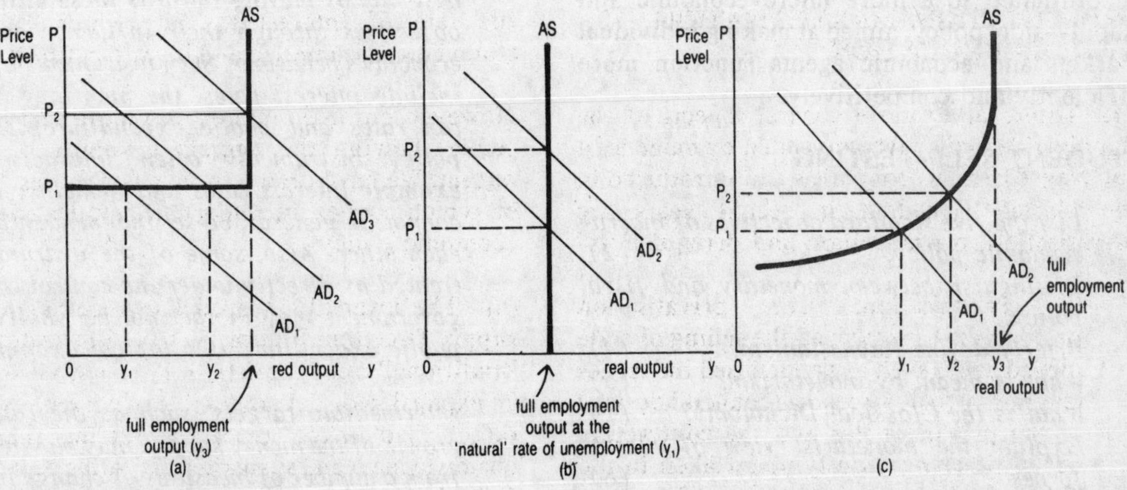

SUMMARY

23. In this chapter we have introduced an 'instruments and objectives' approach to explain how the two dominant economic schools of thought in recent times (in western mixed economies) have attempted to translate abstract theory into practical economic policy. The Keynesian approach to economic policy reflects the belief held by most Keynesians that an unregulated market economy is inherently unstable and government interventionism can produce a better outcome than market forces alone. Monetarists generally support the opposite view. Thus, while Keynesian economic policy, which was implemented by successive British governments from the 1940s to the 1970s, involved an on-going search for 'extra' policy instruments or types of economic policy to assign to newly-identified objectives, the broadly monetarist economic policy of the 1980s has in some senses been an 'anti-policy' in which Keynesian policy instruments such as incomes policy have been abandoned. Under monetarism, the interventionist policies favoured by the Keynesians have to a large extent been replaced by the use of 'market forces' as a policy instrument. And whereas in the Keynesian era government economic policy (at least in the UK) was both macro-economic and 'demand-side' orientated, under monetarism and the influence of the New Classical School, macro-economic and 'demand-side' economic policy have been subordinated to a more micro-economic and 'supply-side' policy, aimed at making individual markets and economic agents function more efficiently and competitively.

STUDENT SELF-TESTING

1 *List the five standard objectives of macro-economic policy.* (2)
2 *Distinguish between monetary and fiscal policy.* (3)
3 *Briefly define Keynesianism.* (4)
4 *What is meant by monetarism?* (5)
5 *What is the Classical Dichotomy?* (7)
6 *Explain the monetarist view of market forces.* (8)
7 *Explain the Keynesian view of market forces.* (9)
8 *Distinguish between a policy instrument and a policy objective.* (11)
9 *What was the most important policy instrument in the early part of the Keynesian era?* (12)
10 *What was the role of monetary policy in the Keynesian era?* (13)
11 *Has the exchange rate been an instrument or an objective of economic policy?* (14)
12 *What is an incomes policy?* (15)
13 *Explain how the Keynesian assignment rule changed.* (16)
14 *List the monetarist assignment rule.* (17)
15 *What is 'global' monetarism?* (18)
16 *Do monetarists have an incomes policy?* (19)
17 *What is meant by 'supply-side' policy?* (20)
18 *Distinguish between privatisation, marketisation and deregulation.* (21)
19 *Draw diagrams to show Keynesian and monetarist aggregate supply curves.* (22)

EXERCISES

1 *Read the following passage and then answer the questions:*

Instruments and objectives

Any government will have a set of ultimate targets or objectives. The true ultimate target of economic policy would be some broad notion of economic welfare. Instruments of economic policy are chosen by governments as being, in their opinion, the best way of moving towards these ultimate objectives through their influence on the economy's behaviour. Such instruments might include interest rates, the monetary base, tax rates and public expenditure. These policy instruments often interact; for example interest rates and monetary base cannot, in general, be set independently of each other. Also, some of the instruments treated as directly under the control of the government may in fact not be wholly so, public expenditure is a topical example.

Intermediate targets, such as the rate of growth of the money supply, may be selected from a number of measures of change in the economy, not because they are of themselves of intrinsic concern or because they are directly controllable, but because they are thought to provide a link between a policy instrument, eg interest rates and an ultimate target, eg price stability.

Two virtues claimed for intermediate targets are that they influence expectations and that meeting them enhances the credibility of the government's policy. But intermediate targets do of course, have the corresponding vices if targets are not met, influencing expectations the wrong way and undermining the credibility of the government's policy. Credibility of government policy is a precondition for policy announcements to have any desired effects of expectations.

(Adapted from the House of Commons Third Report from the Treasury and Civil Service Committee, Session 1980-81, Volume 1 (1981) H.M.S.O)

(a) Distinguish between ultimate and intermediate targets of economic policy.

(b) What is the ultimate objective of economic policy specified in the passage?

(c) Explain how the announcement of targets can influence expectations favourably. What is the possible disadvantage?

MULTIPLE CHOICE QUESTIONS

1 *According to monetarists, the 'natural' rate of unemployment can be reduced by:*
- *A Stimulating aggregate demand*
- *B 'Supply-side' economic policies*
- *C Increasing the PSBR as a proportion of GDP*
- *D Increased welfare payments for the unemployed*

2 *Monetarists believe that public sector investment 'crowds-out' private sector investment as a result of a rise in the:*
- *A Value of the multiplier*
- *B Value of the accelerator*
- *C Rate of interest*
- *D Money supply*

3 *In Keynesian theory, which of the following sets of policies would be most suitable for a government seeking to reduce the level of unemployment?*
- *A Devalue, reduce taxes and increase government expenditure*
- *B Devalue, increase taxes and increase interest rates*
- *C Revalue, reduce taxes and increase government expenditure*
- *D Revalue, increase taxes and increase interest rates*

4 *Important differences between Keynesian and monetarists include their views on all the following except:*
- *A The causes of inflation*
- *B The role of government*
- *C The existence of 'crowding-out'*
- *D The need for some 'supply- side' policies.*

EXAMINATION QUESTIONS

1 *Set out the major economic objectives of the United Kingdom government.*
(AAT June 1982)

2 *(a) What is meant by 'supply side' policies? (8 marks)*
(b) Why has there been so much emphasis on such policies in recent years? (12 marks)
(ACCA December 1985)

3 *(a) Under what circumstances would you expect prices and incomes policy to be an effective method of controlling inflation? (10 marks)*

(b) What problems have arisen with the implementation of such policies in practice? (10 marks)
(AAT June 1981)

4 *What part do you think a prices and incomes policy could play in reducing inflation?*
(ACCA December 1982)

5 (a) *Why are a stable price level and full employment regarded as being desirable objectives of government policy?*
(6 marks)

(b) *Why have governments in recent years generally not succeeded in attaining these objectives simultaneously?*
(14 marks)
(ACCA December 1986)

6 *What is 'economic growth' and how may it best be achieved in a developed industrial country?*
(CIMA November 1987)

23. Trade

INTRODUCTION

1. In previous chapters we have examined the nature and the functioning of economic processes within a single economy - and in particular within the British economy - without devoting much attention to economic relations between countries. We now describe and explain the reasons for the **international specialisation of production** between countries and the resulting **trade** or **exchange** of goods and services that takes place. After describing and explaining **patterns of world trade**, past and present, we examine the case for tariffs or import duties and other forms of **protectionism** and we assess the **costs and benefits of protectionism**. The chapter concludes with a brief survey of **free trade areas** and **customs unions**, considering whether such **trading blocs** promote or hinder the development of world trade.

SPECIALISATION AND THE DIVISION OF LABOUR

2. Over two hundred years ago, the great classical economist, Adam Smith, first explained how, within a single production unit or firm (he took the example of a pin factory), output could be increased if workers specialised at different tasks in the manufacturing process. Smith had established one of the most fundamental of all economic principles: the **benefits of specialisation or the division of labour**. According to Adam Smith, there are three main reasons why a factory's total output can be increased if workers perform specialised tasks rather than if each worker attempts all the tasks himself. These are:

(i) a worker will not need to switch between tasks so time will be saved;

(ii) more and better machinery or capital can be employed (we now call this **capital widening** and **capital deepening**); and

(iii) practice makes a worker more efficient or productive at the task he is doing - though this latter advantage can easily become a disadvantage involving 'deskilling' and the creation of boredom and alienation among workers.

The principle of the division of labour explains not only specialisation between workers within a factory; it can be extended to explain the specialisation between productive units, plants or factories within a firm, specialisation between separate firms and lastly, geographical specialisation both internally within a country and between countries: the **international specialisation** which is the subject of this chapter.

ABSOLUTE ADVANTAGE

3. The benefits of the division of labour suggest that if each of the world's countries with its own endowment both of natural or 'God-given' resources such as soil, climate and minerals, and of 'man-made' resources such as capital, know-how and labour skills, specialises in 'what it does best', total world output or production can be increased compared to a situation without specialisation. In economic terms, being 'better at ' producing a good or service means that a country can produce a particular output of the good at the lowest cost in terms of resources used (factors of production or inputs); in the language of Chapter 4, the country is **technically** and **productively** efficient in producing the good. We can say that if a country is 'best at' producing a good or service, it possesses an **absolute advantage** in the good's production, whereas if it is not the best at producing it, the country has an **absolute disadvantage**.

THE PRINCIPLE OF COMPARATIVE ADVANTAGE

4. **Absolute advantage** must not be confused with the rather more subtle concept of **comparative advantage**. To introduce and illustrate this most important economic principle, we shall construct a highly simplified model of the 'world' economy, by assuming just two countries Atlantis and Pacifica, each with just two units of resource (for example man-years of labour) that can produce just two commodities, guns or butter.

Each unit of resource, or indeed a fraction of each unit, can be switched from one industry to another if so desired in each country. Suppose in each country the **production possibilities** are that one unit of resource can produce:

In Atlantis: 4 guns or 2 tons of butter
In Pacifica: 1 gun or 1 ton of butter

Quite clearly, Atlantis is best at, or has an *absolute advantage* in, producing both guns and butter, but it only possesses a *comparative advantage* in gun production. This is because comparative advantage is measured in terms of **opportunity cost**, or of what a country gives up when it increases output of one industry by one unit. The country which gives up least when increasing output of a commodity by one unit possesses the comparative advantage in that good. Ask yourself how many guns would Atlantis have to stop producing or give up in order to increase its butter output by one ton. The answer is two guns, but Pacifica would only have to give up one gun to produce an extra ton of butter. Thus Pacifica possesses a comparative advantage in butter production even though it has an absolute disadvantage in both products.

When one country possesses an absolute advantage in both industries, as in the example above, its comparative advantage will always lie in producing the good in which its absolute advantage is greatest. Similarly, the country that is worst at both activities will possess a comparative advantage in the industry in which its absolute disadvantage is least. But can we use our example to show that total world production will be greater if each country specialises in the activity in which it has a comparative advantage, compared to when each country devotes exactly half its resources to each industry? We can, but only if we specify rather carefully the degree of specialisation undertaken in each country. Suppose for example that no specialisation occurs and each country devotes one unit of resource to each industry. Total world production will be:

5 guns and 3 tons of butter

But now suppose that each country completely specialises in producing the good in which it possesses a comparative advantage. In this case, world production becomes:

8 guns and 2 tons of butter

It is important to note that while production of one good (guns) has risen, production of the other (butter) has fallen. Since we are not comparing like with like, this does not necessarily represent a net gain in output. Suppose finally however, that Pacifica completely specialises, but that Atlantis - the country with the absolute advantage in both goods - devotes just enough resource (half a unit) to 'top up' world production of butter to 3 tons. This would allow Atlantis to *partially specialise*, directing 1½ units of resource into gun production and producing 6 guns. Total world production will now be:

6 guns and 3 tons of butter

Since at least as much butter and more guns are now produced compared to the earlier 'self-sufficient' situation, quite clearly specialisation in accordance with the principle of comparative advantage has led to an increased output.

THE ASSUMPTIONS UNDERLYING THE PRINCIPLE OF COMPARATIVE ADVANTAGE

5. To show that definite benefits are likely to result from specialisation and trade in accordance with the principle of comparative advantage, a number of rather strong assumptions have to be made. The case for trade - and hence the case against import controls and other forms of protectionism - is thus heavily dependent upon the realism of these assumptions. Equally, the case against trade and the case in favour of import controls - which we shall develop shortly - can be based on questioning the realism of the assumptions underlying the principle of comparative advantage. The assumptions include:

(i) **Each country's endowment of factors of production, including capital and labour is assumed to be fixed.** Capital and labour are treated as being immobile between countries, though they are capable of being switched between industries within a country. Finished goods, but not factors of production or inputs, are assumed to be mobile between countries.

(ii) **The principle of comparative advantage assumes constant returns to scale.** One unit of resource is assumed to produce 4 guns or 2 tons of butter in Atlantis whether it is the first unit of resource employed or the millioneth unit. But in the real world,

increasing returns to scale or **decreasing returns to scale** are both possible. In a world of increasing returns, the more a country specialises in a particular industry, the more efficient it becomes, thereby increasing its comparative advantage. But if decreasing returns to scale occur, specialisation erodes efficiency and destroys the initial comparative advantage. In agriculture, over-specialisation can result in monoculture, in which the growing of a single cash crop for export may lead to soil erosion, vulnerability to pests and falling agricultural yields in the future.

(iii) Over-specialisation may also cause a country to become particularly **vulnerable to sudden changes in demand or to changes in the cost and availability of imported raw materials or energy.** Changes in costs and new inventions and technical progress can eliminate a country's comparative advantage. The principle of comparative advantage implicitly assumes relatively stable demand and cost conditions. The greater the uncertainty about the future, the weaker the case for complete specialisation. Indeed, if a country is self-sufficient in all important respects, it is effectively neutralised against the danger of importing recession and unemployment from the rest of the world if international demand collapses.

COMPARATIVE ADVANTAGE AND THE PATTERN OF WORLD TRADE

6. When over two centuries ago Adam Smith first explained the advantages of the division of labour, and a few years later in the early 19th century another distinguished classical economist, David Ricardo, developed Adam Smith's ideas into the principle of comparative advantage, they were not just interested in abstract theory. Instead, like most great economists they wished to change society for the better by influencing the politicians and thinking people of their day. Smith and Ricardo believed in the virtues of a competitive market economy and industrial capitalism. Ricardo in particular believed that a single country such as the United Kingdom and indeed, the whole world economy, could only reach their full productive potential, maximising output, welfare and living standards, if the market economy was truly international; each country specialising in what it did best and trading the output surplus to its needs in a world free of **tariffs** and other forms of **protectionism.**

To many people living in industrial countries during the 19th century and the first half of the 20th century, it must have seemed almost 'natural' that the earliest countries to industrialise, such as Britain, had done so because they possessed a comparative advantage in manufacturing. It probably seemed equally natural that a pattern of world trade should have developed in which industrialised countries in what is now called **the 'North'** exported manufactured goods in exchange for foodstuffs and raw materials produced by countries whose comparative advantage lay in the production of primary products - in modern parlance the countries of the **'South'** or **Third World.**

THE HECKSCHER-OHLIN THEORY

7. In the 1930s two Swedish economists, Heckscher and Ohlin constructed a theory to explain the 'North/South' exchange of manufactured goods for primary products in terms of **factor endowments.** The **Heckscher-Ohlin** theory is really an extension of the principle of comparative advantage, arguing that if a country possesses a lot of capital relative to labour it will industrialise and export capital-intensive manufactured goods, but if capital is scarce relative to labour, a country will specialise in and export labour-intensive primary products.

THE DEPENDENCY THEORY

8. There are however, two serious problems in explaining the pattern of world trade in terms of the Heckscher-Ohlin theory. In the first place, in the simple form outlined above, the theory is rather circular, since industrialisation partly creates the factor endowment used to explain why a country initially industrialises! In recent years, the Heckscher-Ohlin explanation of the pattern of world trade has been attacked in a **dependency theory** of trade and development. The dependency theory argues that Third World countries possess little capital because the system of world trade and payments has been organised by developed industrial economies to their own advantage. The **terms of trade** - the ratio of a country's export prices to its import prices - have as a general rule moved in favour of industrialised countries and against primary producers. This means that by exporting the same amount of manufactured goods to the Third World, a developed economy can import a greater quantity of raw materials or foodstuffs in exchange. From a Third World country's point of view, it must export more in order to buy the same quantity of capital goods or energy vital for development! Globally, the movement of the terms of trade in favour of developed nations, has raised levels of income and standards of living in the richer countries at the expense of Third and Fourth Worlds - the one exception, for a time at least in the 1970s and early 1980s, being the oil producing non-industrial countries who benefited from substantial increases in the price of oil. Economists of the dependency school further argue that the transfer of wealth and resources to the richer countries is also promoted by a flow of profits and dividends to multinational corporations with headquarters in North America, Western Europe and Japan from their subsidiaries in the developing world, and by a flow of interest payments to western banks on loans originally made to finance development; indeed flows of dividends and interest payments from 'South' to 'North' may well exceed aid flows in the opposite direction.

THE PATTERN OF WORLD TRADE

9. The second objection to the Heckscher-Ohlin explanation of world trade can be illustrated from Figure 23.1 (on following page) showing world trade totals and directions of flow in 1984 and from Table 23.1 which shows the pattern of the United Kingdom's trade in 1986.

Table 23.1: Analysis of United Kingdom visible trade by area, 1986

	Exports %	*Imports* %
EEC	*48.0*	*51.8*
Other Western Europe	*9.6*	*13.8*
North America	*16.7*	*11.8*
Other developed (including Japan)	*5.0*	*8.0*
Oil exporting developing	*7.6*	*2.3*
Other developing	*10.6*	*10.0*
Centrally planned economies	*2.5*	*2.3*

Source: Department of Trade and Industry

Figure 23.1 shows quite strikingly how most of the trade of the developed industrial economies is between themselves and how only a relatively small amount is with the developing world. In 1984, the industrialised market economies dominated world exports and indirectly provided a market for a further 19%. Only 16% of trade took place with no involvement by an advanced capitalist country. Trade between the advanced industrial economies amounted to 47% of world trade, being nearly two thirds greater in total value than their trade with all the countries of the developing world and nearly two and a half times greater if the oil exporting developing countries are excluded.

The impression presented by Figure 23.1, that the actual pattern of world trade in recent years has been quite different from the '19th century' North/South exchange of manufactured goods for primary products, is reinforced by the analysis of United Kingdom visible trade shown in Table 23.1. In 1986, nearly 80% of British exports were sold to other industrial or developed countries, while an even greater 85% of imports were from these countries. Within this total, a growing proportion of British trade takes place with other European countries and especially with members of the **customs union** or **common market** to which the UK belongs, the **European Economic Community (EEC).**

Neither Figure 23.1 nor Table 23.1 show the breakdown of world trade into manufactured goods and primary products. A study by Batchelor, Major and Morgan in 1980 shows that in 1977 the industrial market economies exported $150 billion of manufactures to the developing world. Perhaps surprisingly, countries in the 'South' sold more manufactured goods to the 'North' ($40.5 billion worth) than to each other ($21.8 billion), an indication of the growth amongst the developing countries of **Newly Industrialising Countries (NICs)**, such as Taiwan, Hong Kong, Singapore and South Korea. The exports of manufactured goods from the 'non-industrial' developing world were of course much smaller than their exports of primary products ($177 billion to 'the North' and $54 billion to each other), but perhaps most significantly, the exports of primary products from the industrial economies to the developing world at $117 billion were as much as two-thirds as large as the exports of foodstuffs and raw materials to the 'industrial' countries from the 'primary producers', a ratio that would become

Figure 23.1: World trade flows 1984

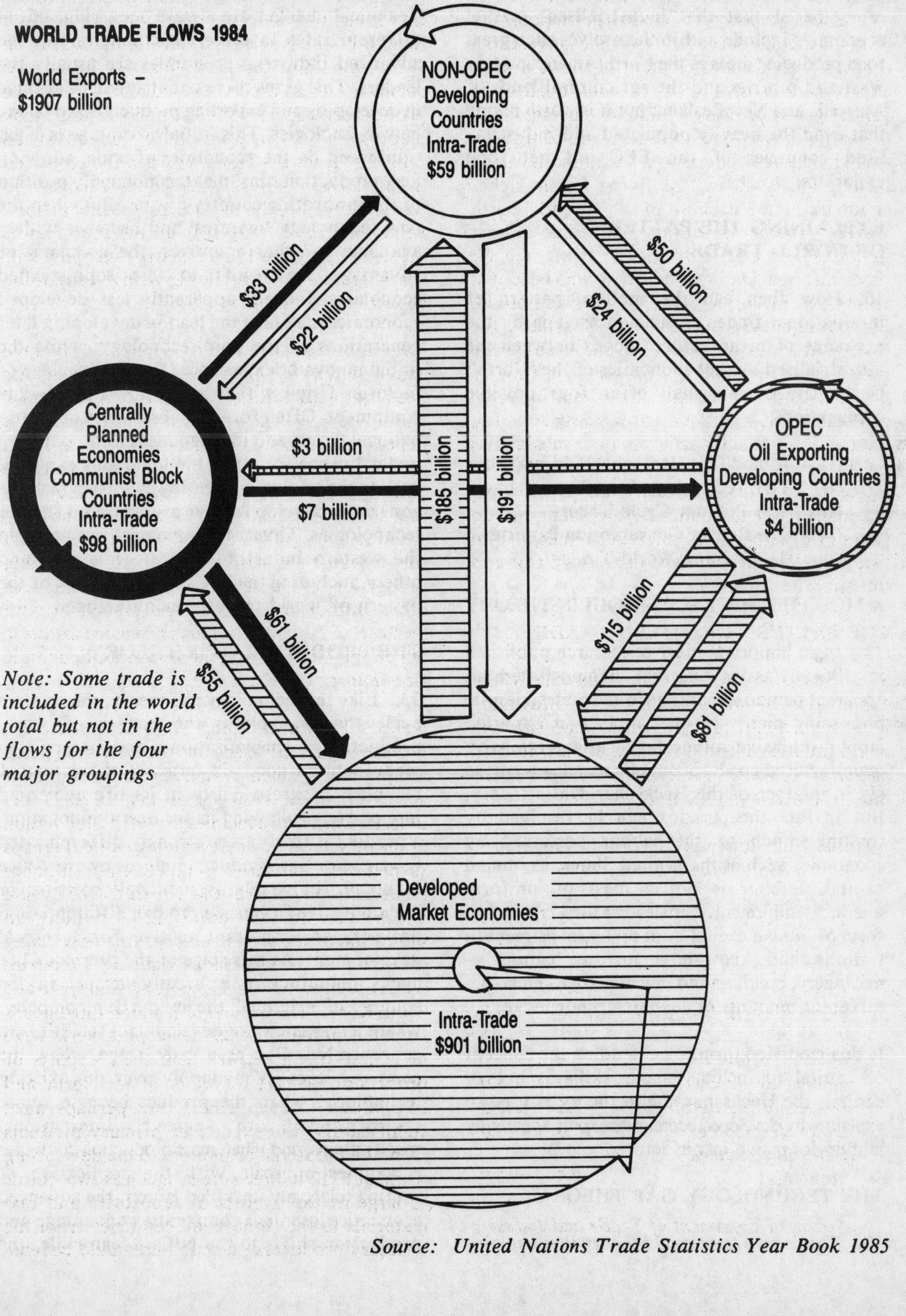

WORLD TRADE FLOWS 1984

World Exports – $1907 billion

NON-OPEC Developing Countries Intra-Trade $59 billion

Centrally Planned Economies Communist Block Countries Intra-Trade $98 billion

OPEC Oil Exporting Developing Countries Intra-Trade $4 billion

Developed Market Economies Intra-Trade $901 billion

$33 billion

$22 billion

$50 billion

$24 billion

$3 billion

$7 billion

$185 billion

$191 billion

$61 billion

$55 billion

$115 billion

$81 billion

Note: Some trade is included in the world total but not in the flows for the four major groupings

Source: United Nations Trade Statistics Year Book 1985

even more equal if trade in oil were excluded. This figure becomes less surprising when it is remembered that the 'industrialised' market economies include within themselves such great food producing areas as the North American Mid-West and prairies and the agricultural lands of Australia and New Zealand, but it is worth noting that even the heavily populated and industrialised countries of the EEC are net food exporters.

EXPLAINING THE PATTERN OF WORLD TRADE

10. How then can the modern pattern of international trade, dominated as it is by the exchange of manufactured goods between the industrialised market economies of the 'North', be explained? We shall offer four possible explanations:

(i) A modified Heckscher-Ohlin Theory
(ii) The Technology Gap Theory
(iii) The Product Cycle Theory
(iv) The Role of Consumption Patterns in determining World Trade

A MODIFIED HECKSCHER-OHLIN THEORY

11. In an important piece of research published in 1968, Wassily Leontief demonstrated an apparent paradox, that the United States, despite possessing plenty of capital, in fact exported labour-intensive rather than capital-intensive manufactured goods. Leontief's paradox seems to fly in the face of the Heckscher-Ohlin theory. But in fact the paradox can be resolved by treating much of the labour possessed by economies such as the United States, as **human capital**. Labour is not a mass of uniform uneducated humanity; instead skilled labour is a form of human capital built up by **investment** in training and know-how just as 'capital' - machinery, buildings and raw materials - embodies different amounts of technical knowledge.

If this modified form, by extending the concept of capital to include labour skills as human capital, the Heckscher-Ohlin theory is used to explain why developed economies export apparently labour-intensive manufactured goods.

THE TECHNOLOGY GAP THEORY

12. This is an example of a theory that explains the growth and the pattern of world trade in terms of the nature of **technical progress**. Technical changes are always occurring, but at different rates in different countries and the advanced industrial economies are usually the leaders. This gives these countries an advantage in developing and exporting products based on the new technologies. This initial advantage is often reinforced by the **economies of scale**, allowing long production runs, that the monopoly position of the innovating country creates. But when the new technology 'matures' and becomes widely available to other countries, the comparative advantage may shift to less sophisticated economies. Indeed, apparently less-developed economies may take the lead in developing later generations of the new technology, while the initial innovator experiences the disadvantage of factories fitted with what is now out-of-date equipment. Often foreign subsidiaries of multinational firms, and independent firms operating under licence, produce the good and export it back to the original pioneering country which has gone on to develop further products and further technologies. Thus a **technological gap** between the western industrial market economies and others, including the NICs explains much of the pattern of world trade in manufactures.

THE PRODUCT CYCLE THEORY

13. Like the technology gap theory, the product cycle theory explains the pattern of world production, specialisation and trade in manufactured goods in terms of the nature of technical progress. Early in its **life cycle** and immediately following its successful innovation, a product is likely to be strongly differentiated from competing products. Indeed, by creating a highly profitable relative monopoly position for the innovative firm, such product differentiation provides an important motive for technical development. At this stage of the product's life cycle, manufacture is usually located in the country of origin of the innovative company, where its research and development facilities are concentrated. But at a later stage when the company loses its monopoly over the existing technology, when the product becomes more standardised with agreed international specifications, and when mass production combines economies of scale with the application of routine relatively unskilled labour, the advanced economies lose their comparative advantage and production shifts to the NICs. Meanwhile, the innovative firms in the advanced industrial countries attempt to maintain their lead by further technical progress and product development, while at the same time owning branch factories or subsidiaries in the NICs in which they manufacture for export back to the developed world the 'older' products well into their life cycles.

THE ROLE OF CONSUMPTION PATTERNS IN DETERMINING WORLD TRADE

14. The theories discussed so far in this chapter explain a country's comparative advantage and the patterns of world trade solely in terms of **supply conditions** in different countries. We have said very little about **demand**, except perhaps implicitly to assume that for a country to specialise and trade, demand must exist in other countries.

An alternative approach is to examine patterns of income, tastes and consumption, or **demand conditions** in the world's most important trading countries, to explain why so much of international trade involves the exchange of essentially rather similar manufactured goods between already industrialised economies. It can be argued that a country's comparative advantage often lies in producing goods related to its inhabitants' domestic tastes. Close contact with the needs of the domestic market makes a country's firms efficient at meeting domestic demand and very often the inhabitants of other industrial countries with similar incomes, possess similar demand. Trade therefore takes place between countries with similar tastes and incomes. At the same time, high income consumers value choice and product differentiation. A pattern of trade thus develops between industrialised countries in which a very wide range of differentiated manufactured consumer goods is made available to all - for example automobiles or television sets. A single country could seldom provide its consumers with the desired variety, so international trade extends the range of choice.

PROTECTIONISM

15. Figure 23.2 shows how international trade in both manufactured goods and primary products grew from 1900 to 1977. The graphs show that most of the growth in world trade, in both manufactured goods and primary products, has taken place since 1945 and especially since the widespread removal or reduction of **tariffs** and other forms of **import control** that took place in the 1950s and 1960s.

Indeed, in earlier years in the 1930s at a time of growing protectionism, world trade actually fell. However, it is difficult to be sure whether the decline of trade was caused by protectionism or whether both were caused by a third event, the decline of production and consumption levels in the Great Depression of the 1930s. Probably all three events interacted together, just as the rapid growth of trade in the post-1945 years should be viewed as a *response* to as well as a *cause* of the growth of world output in boom conditions.

Figure 23.2: The growth of world trade measured in real terms in the twentieth century

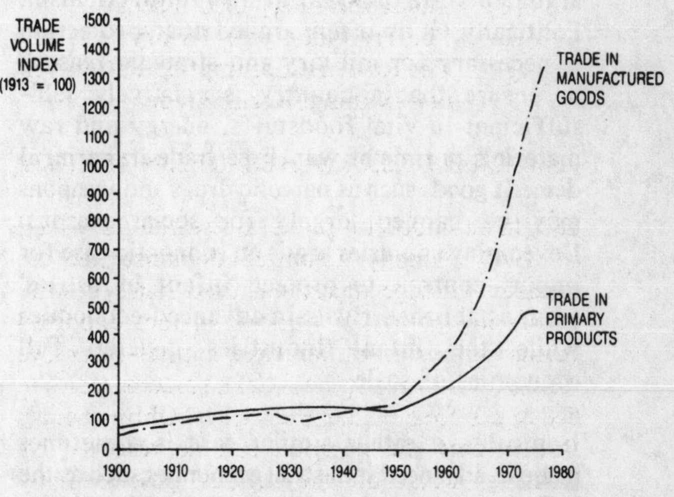

More recently however, there has once again been a worldwide trend towards protectionism, though taking the form of **'non-tariff' barriers** such as 'voluntary' export restrictions and administr-ative procedures and technical standards to hinder imports, rather than the traditional form of tariffs or **import** duties, and **quotas** or quantity controls. Just as in the 1930s, the growth of protection is probably both a cause of and a response to the slow down of economic growth in many of the countries of the developed and developing worlds. The covert nature of modern protectionism is largely explained by the fact that many trading countries are signatories of the **General Agreement on Tariffs and Trade**

(GATT), the forum for liberalising world trade which covers 122 countries. GATT provides a system of rules governing world trade based on non-discrimination which prevent member nations from introducing the traditional forms of import control that discriminate against particular countries. For much of the post-1945 era, GATT has been directly responsible for the freeing of world trade in a series of **'rounds'** of **multilateral tariff reductions**, culminating in the **'Tokyo round'** negotiated between 1973 and 1979. The Tokyo round covered more than tariffs; it extended the reduction of import controls to technical barriers to trade, government procurement and action against dumping. But in the recent world economic climate, many non-tariff barriers have proliferated, representing a creeping protectionism.

THE CASE FOR IMPORT CONTROLS

16. A number of political, social and economic arguments are used to justify protectionism. Politically, it is often argued that protection is necessary for military and strategic reasons to ensure that a country is relatively self-sufficient in vital foodstuffs, energy and raw materials in time of war. Free trade in harmful **demerit goods** such as narcotic drugs and weapons may be banned largely for social reasons. Developing countries argue an economic case for import controls to protect **'infant industries'** from established rivals in advanced economies while the infant industries develop full economies of scale.

Ironically, a rather similar case is sometimes made in advanced industrial economies such as the UK to protect **'sunset' or 'geriatric' industries** in the older industrial regions from the competition of precisely these infant industries in developing countries. Both arguments are really special cases of a more general argument in favour of protectionism: that import controls are justified, at least on a temporary basis to minimise the social and economic costs of the painful adjustment process as the structure of an economy alters in response to either changing demand or to changing technology and comparative advantage. In recent years many Keynesians have advocated the selective use of import controls in the macro-economic management of the economy. They regard import controls as a potentially effective **supply-side** policy instrument, to be used either in place of or in addition to traditional **demand-side** Keynesian policies, to prevent unnecessary **deindustrialisation** and to allow orderly rather than disruptive structural change in the manufacturing base of the economy.

Structural, frictional and regional unemployment are of course some of the major costs of economic change. A simple model of comparative advantage such as the one described earlier in this chapter, assumes that factors of production are both immobile between countries and instantly switchable between industries. Protectionism is sometimes justified on the basis that neither of these assumptions is true in the world in which we live. On this basis, trade unions argue that import controls are necessary to prevent multi-national firms shifting their capital to the low wage conditions of developing countries and exporting their output back to the countries from which the capital was moved. They further argue the case for employing labour, however inefficiently, in protected industries rather than allowing labour to suffer the greatest inefficiency of all: mass unemployment.

THE COSTS AND BENEFITS OF PROTECTIONISM

17. We have of course explained the case against protectionism in the earlier parts of this chapter, arguing that if countries specialise according to their comparative advantage, all countries can become better off. In 1985, the **Organisation for Economic Co-operation and Development (OECD)** published a detailed report on the **Costs and Benefits of Protection**, surveying a wide range of empirical evidence on import controls. The main conclusions of the OECD report were:

(i) although tariffs have been reduced under GATT on a world wide scale, there has been a significant growth of non-tariff protectionism;

(ii) a small but growing number of industries are protected by non-tariff barriers;

(iii) trade barriers have distorted trade patterns and reduced total trade;

(iv) quantity controls have resulted in higher prices;

(v) while in the short term protection saves jobs to the extent of about 2 to 3 per cent in the protected industries, in the long run the effect is smaller because capital is substituted for labour;

(vi) the effect on employment is further lessened by jobs lost in non-protected industries, for example in response to a higher exchange rate;

(vii) some industries have used protection to achieve structural adjustment, but most have not;

(viii) protection by the developed countries harms the developing world, it worsens their debt problems by restricting their access to export markets.

FREE TRADE AREAS AND CUSTOMS UNIONS

18. Both **free trade areas** and **customs unions** are examples of **trading blocs** and **multilaterial trading agreements**. For many years before entering the **European Economic Community** in 1973, the United Kingdom belonged to two free trade areas, the **European Free Trade Association (EFTA)** and the **Commonwealth** which operated a system of trade preference between members. Membership of a free trade area requires a country to reduce or eliminate tariffs against other members while being free to choose its own tariffs against non-members. Consequently, a country can belong to two or more free trade areas simultaneously.

Like a free trade area, the rules of a customs union require the abolition of internal tariffs between members, but unlike in a free trade area, all members must adopt a **common external tariff** aimed against the rest of the world. Membership of a customs union is not usually compatible with continued membership of a free trade area; thus the UK left EFTA and the Commonwealth ceased to function as a trading area on entry to the EEC.

The EEC is of course rather more than just a customs union or common market. It embodies certain aspects of a full **economic union** including some **common economic policies**, notably the **agricultural and fisheries policies**, a **European Monetary System (EMS)** and certain political institutions transcending the national institutions of member states, pointing to an eventual possible **political union**.

Customs unions and to a lesser extent free trade areas, occupy a rather enigmatic position regarding trade liberalisation and protection. On the one hand they promote free trade between members, but conversely they certainly distort and in the case of customs unions, perhaps reduce trade between member countries and the rest of the world. The extent to which a customs union is *'outward-looking'* and *'trade-liberalising'* or *'inward-looking'* and *protectionist* depends most obviously upon the size and range of its common external tariff and, in the case of the EEC, upon its attitude to and treatment of the developing world.

SUMMARY

19. The general case for specialisation and trade stems from the proposition that regions or countries can attain levels of production, consumption and welfare which are beyond the production possibility frontier open to them in a world without trade. The immobility of some factors of production and the production possibility open to each country are different. Some countries can produce goods or services which the factor endowment of other countries does not allow them to produce. In this situation, there is a clear case for countries to trade any surplus production exceeding their own needs.

However, even when factor endowments allow countries to produce the same products, gains can still be realised from international specialisation if countries specialise in the activities in which they possess a comparative advantage. Comparative advantage should not be confused with absolute advantage. A country possesses an absolute advantage over other countries when it produces a good or service with the smallest input of factors of production. In contrast, comparative advantage is indicated by relative efficiency rather than by absolute efficiency. A country may suffer an absolute disadvantage in the production of a commodity, yet it can still possess a comparative advantage. Comparative advantage is measured in terms of opportunity cost, or what a country gives up, in order to increase production of a good or service.

In the nineteenth century, a 'North/South' pattern of world trade emerged in which industrialising countries, such as the United Kingdom, traded manufactured goods for food and raw materials produced in tropical countries and in 'New World' agricultural countries such as Australia and New Zealand. 'North/South' exchange of manufactured goods for primary products can be explained by the Heckscher-Ohlin theory of factor endowments and also by the dependency theory, which argues that the pattern of world trade has been organised by the developed world to its own advantage.

In the twentieth century however, the pattern of world trade has changed, becoming dominated by 'North/North' exchange in which the industrialised countries of the 'First World' trade manufactured goods and services with each other. Various theories have been proposed to explain the current pattern of world trade, including a modified Heckscher-Ohlin theory, a technology gap theory and a product cycle theory.

Not only has there been a change in the pattern of world trade in the twentieth century, there has also been a very great expansion in the quantity of goods and services traded. Most of the growth in world trade occurred in the decades after 1945, during which import duties and other forms of protectionism were lowered or removed. Nevertheless, under certain conditions, import controls can be justified, especially as temporary or selective measures to help a country adjust to new circumstances. Whether trading blocs such as free trade areas and customs unions should be regarded as 'trade-liberalising' or 'trade-protecting' depends on whether the extent to which they open up trade between members exceeds any reduction in world trade caused by tariff barriers introduced against the rest of the world.

STUDENT SELF-TESTING

1. *List three advantages of the division of labour.* *(2)*
2. *Define absolute advantage.* *(3)*
3. *Distinguish between absolute advantage and comparative advantage.* *(4)*
4. *What are the assumptions of the principle of comparative advantage?* *(5)*
5. *How did the pattern of world trade develop in the nineteenth century?* *(6)*
6. *What is the Heckscher-Ohlin theory?* *(7)*
7. *What are the terms of trade?* *(8)*
8. *Briefly describe the present day pattern of world trade.* *(9)*
9. *Why does the United States export labour-intensive goods?* *(11)*
10. *How may technology gaps explain the pattern of trade?* *(12)*
11. *What is a product cycle?* *(14)*
12. *What is GATT?* *(15)*
13. *List three reasons for import controls.* *(16)*
14. *Distinguish between a free trade area and a customs union.* *(18)*

EXERCISES

1 *The following table relates to the output per worker in two countries and for two products iron and coffee:*

	Iron	*Coffee*
Country A	*40*	*60*
Country B	*20*	*40*

(a) *In which commodity does each country possess a comparative advantage?*

(b) (i) *Assuming ten workers in each country, calculate total output if five workers in each country are employed in each industry.*

(ii) *Devise a system of specialisation which increases output.*

MULTIPLE CHOICE QUESTIONS

1 *There are two countries which produce only two goods. Figure 23.3 shows the production possibility curves of the two countries. There is perfect mobility of factors of production within the two countries, but none between them.*

Figure 23.3

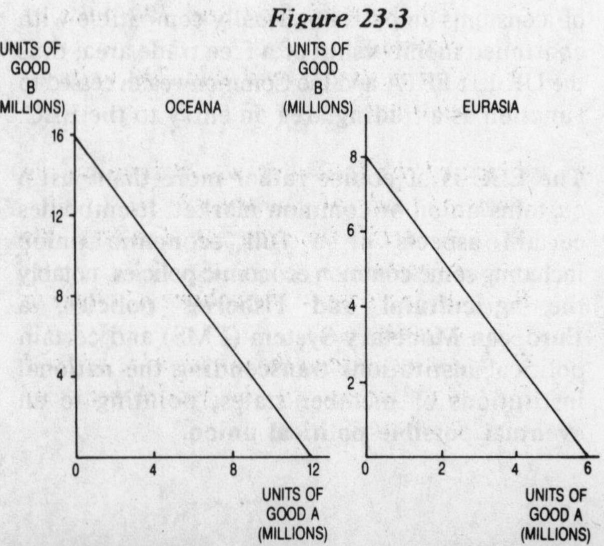

In these circumstances:

A Oceana will specialise in A and Eurasia in B

B No trade will occur because Oceana is more efficient in both goods

C No trade will occur because neither country has an incentive to trade

D The diagrams provide insufficient information to allow us to say which good each country should specialise in.

2 *The General Agreement on Tariffs and Trade aims to:*

A Provide a forum in which countries can agree to impose tariffs

B Increase the number of trading blocs

C Eliminate quotas and reduce tariffs

D Impose trade sanctions on non-member countries.

Questions 3 and 4 refer to the following information:

In a simple model of world trade there are two countries A and B and two commodities, food and clothing. When each country divides its resources equally between the two products, they produce:

	Food (units)	*Clothing (units)*
Country A	*300*	*200*
Country B	*400*	*100*

3 *Assuming constant returns to scale, if each country specialises in producing the commodity in which it possesses a comparative advantage, total output will increase by:*

A 100 units of food

B 200 units of food and 100 units of clothing

C 100 units of food and 100 units of clothing

D 100 units of food and 200 units of clothing

4 *Which of the following would improve the terms of trade of country A?*

A A tariff imposed on Country B's exports

B An increase in the volume of clothing exports

C An increase in the world price of food

D An increase in the world price of clothing.

5 *Protectionism can be justified as a means of increasing total world welfare by the argument that:*

A The country's inhabitants will gain at the expense of foreigners

B By reducing demand for imports, a tariff protects the country's real wealth

C A tariff is necessary to eliminate cost advantages possessed by other countries

D There are some commodities in which a country may possess a long-term comparative advantage which can only be developed at first behind a tariff barrier.

6 *A country's Terms of Trade for a number of years are shown by the following index:*

	Terms of Trade Index (1986 = 100)
1983	*90*
1984	*100*
1985	*95*
1986	*100*
1988	*120*
1988	*115*

Over the period shown by the data, the country's terms of trade:

A Improved by 25 per cent

B Deterioriated by 5 per cent

C Improved by 15 per cent

D Improved by about 28 per cent.

EXAMINATION QUESTIONS

1 *Give a brief account of the principle of comparative advantage, stating clearly the assumptions you are making.*

Does your reasoning lead to the conclusion that economists should support a policy of free trade in all circumstances?

(ACCA June 1980)

2 *Many developing countries have specialised historically in the production of primary commodities. In view of their comparative and absolute advantage in this field, this may seem reasonable; if so how can you justify, on economic grounds, attempts by these countries to industrialise?*
(ACCA June 1979)

3 *Demonstrate that international trade can lead to the production of greater amounts of both commodities when one country is more efficient at producing both of them.*
(CIMA June 1985)

4. *Argue the case for protection by tariffs in international trade.*
(AAT June 1987)

5. *Explain the following:*

(a) *invisible trade;* *(8 marks)*
(b) *the terms of trade;* *(8 marks)*
(c) *briefly explain the link, if any, between the two expressions.* *(4 marks)*

(AAT December 1988)

24. The balance of payments

INTRODUCTION

1. In Chapter 23 we explained how the existence of **barriers to trade** such as tariffs and import controls can prevent two countries from trading together, even though they would both benefit from international exchange. In this chapter, we investigate how **payment difficulties** may create further barriers to trade. We examine the structure of a country's **balance of payments**, and the various policies the government might use to reduce or eliminate **balance of payments disequilibrium**.

THE BALANCE OF PAYMENTS ACCOUNTS

2. The balance of payments is the part of a country's National Accounts which measures all the **currency flows** into and out of the economy within a particular time period, usually a year. Whenever international trade takes place between countries, payment must eventually be made in a currency, or other means of payment, which is acceptable to the country from whom the goods and services have been purchased. Since the balance of payments is an official record collected by a government, the presentation of the currency flows depends on how the government decides to group and classify all the different items of payment. Until recently, the United Kingdom government divided the balance of payments into three main categories:

(1) Current account
(2) Investment and other capital flows
(3) Official financing

In 1987 the official United Kingdom balance of payments were presented in a new and different way. Although the current account remains, investment and other capital flows, and official financing no longer now appear in the main balance of payments tables. Nevertheless, because their economic meaning is very clear and allows us a most ready way of understanding the nature of the flows which make up the balance of payments, we shall explain the 'old presentation' of the current account, capital flows and official financing, before we describe the new UK presentation of the balance of payments introduced in 1987.

THE CURRENT ACCOUNT

3. **The balance of payments on current account** measures the flow of expenditure on **goods** and **services**, broadly indicating the country's income gained and lost from **trade**. The current account is usually regarded as the most important part of the balance of payments because it reflects the economy's international competitiveness and the extent to which it is living within its means. If receipts from exports are less than payments for imports, there is a current account **deficit**, whereas if receipts exceed payments there is of course, a **surplus**. The current balance is obtained simply by adding together the **balance of visible trade** and the **balance of invisible trade** which we shall now examine in turn.

THE BALANCE OF VISIBLE TRADE

4. Visible trade is perhaps the most important single item in the balance of payments, yet is the simplest to define. The **visible balance of trade** measures the value of **goods** exported minus the value of goods imported, expressed in the country's own currency. The visible balance is also known as the **balance of trade**. This is a rather misleading term since it implies (falsely) that invisible trade is also included. The balance of trade refers only to trade in goods and not services.

THE BALANCE OF INVISIBLE TRADE

5. **The balance of invisible trade** is sometimes defined as the value of **services** exported minus the value of services imported. Examples of service earnings which contribute to UK invisible exports include:

(a) a large part of the earnings of the City of London eg financial services, insurance and brokerage services. These form a major contribution to both the invisible balance and the whole current account;

(b) spending in the UK by foreign tourists;

(c) the overseas earnings of British aviation and shipping services.

However, not all invisible exports and imports are strictly services. Amongst other items included in the UK invisible account are:

(a) gifts of money sent by overseas residents to UK residents;

(b) expenditure by overseas governments on embassies in the UK and by the US government on military bases in the UK;

(c) **net property income from abroad.** When British residents own capital assets overseas, eg, shares in overseas companies, each year they will normally receive dividends paid on the company's profits. At the same time profits will flow out of the country to the overseas owners of assets in the UK, eg Japanese or American multinational companies operating in the UK. Net property income from abroad is the difference between the inward and outward profit flows. In recent years, as we explain shortly in the context of capital flows, net property income from abroad has been a major contributor to the UK current account.

(d) Since 1973, the UK has been a net contributor to the European Economic Community's budget. Britain's net contribution to the EEC budget has become an important invisible import.

(e) Various types of aid to developing countries are also classified in the invisible account.

CAPITAL FLOWS

6. An **outward capital flow** takes place when a country's residents purchase capital assets located in another country. Conversely there is an **inward capital** flow when people resident in the rest of the world purchase capital assets within the country. Net **capital flows** are the difference between these inward and outward capital movements. A positive net outward capital flow which continues over a period of years means that the country's residents (both individuals and companies) are acquiring overseas capital assets greater in total than the country's own assets being bought by the rest of the world. When the UK abolished foreign exchange controls in 1979, British residents became very large net exporters of capital, presumably because they believed that investment abroad would be more profitable than investment within the UK. This positive net flow of capital out of the UK during the 1980s has led to Britain becoming the second largest owner of external capital assets in the world - Japan being the leader. In contrast, the USA is now a 'debtor' nation, ie assets owned in the US by other countries currently exceed those owned by America in the rest of the world.

LONG-TERM CAPITAL FLOWS

7. In order to understand properly the importance of capital flows in the balance of payments, we shall distinguish between **long-term** and **short-term** capital flows. A long-term capital flow occurs when residents of one country purchase or invest in productive resources located in another country. Such investment can be either direct investment or portfolio investment. Real or **direct investment** occurs when, for example, a United Kingdom owned multinational company buys or creates a foreign subsidiary, perhaps when ICI establishes a chemical factory in a developing country. In contrast, portfolio investment is less direct. **Portfolio investment** takes place when British residents purchase shares of overseas companies and the securities issued by foreign governments. Following the 'internationalisation' of securities markets in recent years, which has made it much easier for individuals living in the developed world to purchase shares in any company they wish, there has been a great increase in portfolio investment on a truly global scale. Individuals now buy shares, either directly or through the intermediary of institutions such as insurance companies and unit trusts, in companies whose shares were only previously available on the capital market of the company's country of origin.

SHORT-TERM CAPITAL FLOWS

8. Long-term capital flows can be explained in terms of the principle of comparative advantage, which we investigated in Chapter 23. Essentially, people decide to invest in economic activities and industries located in countries to which the comparative advantage has moved. Since changes in comparative advantage usually take place slowly, long-term capital flows are relatively stable and predictable. The same is not true of **short-term capital flows**. Short term capital movements are sometimes known as **'hot money'** flows. In contrast to long-term capital movements, 'hot money' flows are largely speculative. These flows occur because the owners of funds, who include companies and banks as well as wealthy private individuals, believe that they can make a quick speculative profit or capital gain by moving funds out of one currency and into another. If speculators believe that one currency is going to rise in value while the value of another currency is going to fall (via movements of the exchange rate), it makes sense to move funds out of bank deposits or government securities denominated in the currency whose value is expected to fall. The speculator should sell the currency involved, purchasing instead the currency which he expects to rise, prior to placing his funds in a bank deposit or government securities denominated in that currency. A 'hot money' movement may also be triggered by international differences in interest rates, as funds flow into countries where interest rates are temporarily high. International crises, such as the outbreak of a Middle East War can also cause funds to be moved into 'safe havens' such as gold and into currencies of countries regarded as politically stable.

If the world-wide pool of 'hot money' was relatively small, there would be few problems. However, for the reasons which we explain in the next section, short-term capital flows have become extremely large in recent years. As a result, speculative movements of funds have become self-fulfilling. This is because a large-scale movement of funds out of one currency and into another, causes an excess supply of the former currency and an excess demand for the latter at existing exchange rates. This then, in turn, causes the exchange rate of the first currency to fall and the exchange rate of the second currency to rise to relieve the excess supply and demand. In this way, the movement of speculative funds produces exactly the change in exchange rates necessary to give the owners of capital the speculative gain they were expecting in the first place! By flowing into - and just as quickly out of - currencies, 'hot money' movements can destablise a country's exchange rate, balance of payments and also, its domestic economy. Indeed, huge speculative flows between currencies such as the US $ and the £, which occupy a central place in the finance of international trade, have on occasion tended to destablise large parts of the world economy and the whole of the international monetary system.

EURODOLLARS

9. 'Hot money' is the name given to the pool of 'footloose' hard currencies owned privately, usually outside any exchange controls enforced by the currency's country of origin. Perhaps the most important single cause of the growth of 'hot money' flows lies in the emergence of the Eurodollar market after 1957.

A Eurodollar is a US dollar owned outside the USA, and lent or deposited short-term rather than long-term. The growth of the pool of Eurodollars is related directly to the US balance of payments deficit. Because of its central role in the world economy, the USA has been able - unlike most other countries - to finance a large balance of payments deficit by paying for imports in its own currency. Pools of dollars owned outside the USA have thus accumulated as a direct result of a continuing US trade deficit. Other Eurodollars have originated from capital investment overseas by American firms, and from the growth of overseas bank deposits owned by American residents. Indeed, the early growth of the Eurodollar market was caused by restrictions imposed by the US monetary authorities upon the domestic American banking system. American residents found that they could evade the domestic monetary restrictions by depositing dollars in overseas bank accounts, often in the subsidiaries of US owned banks, rather than in deposits held in the USA. The overseas banks would then relend the Eurodollars deposited with them to whoever wished to borrow dollars to finance trade, investment or speculation.

From its origins in the late 1950s and 1960s, the Eurodollar market grew rapidly in the 1970s and 1980s, greatly aided by the injection of **'petrodollars'** after the oil crisis in the 1970s. A 'petrodollar' is a dollar originally received by an oil producing country in payment for oil exports which must be paid for in dollars. Following the massive increases in the price of crude oil which occurred in the 1970s, OPEC countries accumulated large balance of payments surpluses matched by growing deficits in oil-consuming industrial countries. The OPEC countries deposited a large proportion of their oil revenues in the European banking system, thus adding to the pool of footloose money. Today, the Eurodollar market is perhaps better called the **Eurocurrency market**, reflecting the fact that although the dollar is still the most important currency deposited and 'lent on' in the European banking system, other currencies such as the Deutschmark and sterling are also involved. International banks, operating largely through European financial centres of which London is the most important, have developed a growing and thriving business in the short-term borrowing and lending of Eurocurrencies, outside the exchange controls which may exist in the country of origin.

OFFICIAL FINANCING

10. Visible and invisible trade, and long-term capital flows are sometimes known as the **autonomous** or **spontaneous** part of the balance of payments. This means that they are 'real' flows which result from decisions by individuals and firms to buy goods and services or to invest in capital assets. If imports and capital flows out of the country exceed exports and inward capital flows, there will be a **deficit** in the autonomous part of the balance of payments. But like any balance-sheet, the balance of payments must exactly balance in the sense that all the items included in the balance-sheet must sum to zero. It follows therefore, that a deficit in the autonomous part of the balance of payments must be matched by equal **accommodating** flows elsewhere in the balance-sheet which **finance** the deficit. **Official financing** takes place if the country's central bank runs down **official reserves** of gold or hard currencies to finance the deficit, or undertakes official borrowing to supplement the reserves, borrowing for example from foreign central banks or from the International Monetary Fund. Conversely, a balance of payments **surplus** in the autonomous flows might be financed by accumulating official reserves or by early repayment of official borrowing previously undertaken.

THE PRESENTATION OF THE UK BALANCE OF PAYMENTS

11. It is now realised that the separation of the balance of payments into **spontaneous** or **autonomous** items comprising the current account and capital flows, and into an **accommodating** official financing section is rather artificial. In recent years, the United Kingdom authorities have allowed a current account surplus or deficit to be financed not so much by official financing, involving a change in reserves, as by private sector capital flows which were previously regarded as autonomous. Indeed, capital flows have been actively encouraged as an alternative to official financing. Foreign exchange controls were abolished in 1979 so as to encourage a long-term capital outflow and build-up of assets overseas. In the early 1980s, the resulting capital outflows financed a surplus in the current account created - for a few years - by oil exports. Interest rates have on occasion been raised or lowered to engineer 'hot money' or short-term capital flows.

In large part, the decision to play down official financing and to rely on capital flows to finance the current account reflects the fact that since 1972 the UK exchange rate has **floated. In a fixed exchange rate regime**, the authorities must use official reserves to finance a current account deficit or surplus in order to prevent the exchange rate falling below, or rising above, the rate at which the authorities have fixed it. But in a floating exchange rate regime, market forces and not the authorities, determine the exchange rate. It is no longer necessary therefore, to use official reserves to influence the exchange rate and to finance a current account surplus or deficit.

Table 24.1: The United Kingdom balance of payments 1987

		£m
Current account		
	Visibles	- 10,162
	Invisibles	+ 7,475
A	Current balance	- 2,687
UK EXTERNAL ASSETS AND LIABILITIES		
	Transactions in assets	- 76,186
	Transaction in liabilities	+ 73,869
B	Net transactions	- 2,317
C	Balancing item	+ 5,004
	A + B + C	0

Table 24.1 illustrates the way in which the UK balance of payments figures are now presented. The new system of presentation, introduced for the first time in 1987 for the 1986 balance of payments, replaces the old division of items into current account, investment and other capital

flows and official financing. The current account remains unchanged, but the distinction between capital flows and official financing has been dropped. This reflects the fact, which we have already noted, that in recent years capital flows rather than changes in reserves have financed a current account surplus or deficit. In the new presentation, capital flows and official financing have been replaced with a new **'transactions section'** in the balance of payments, comprising all private, public and 'official' movements of capital funds. In Table 24.1, **'transactions in assets'** measure the outward flow of funds (capital flows and official financing), while **'transactions in liabilities'** represent the inward flow. (Note that the assets purchased by the rest of the world in the UK become the United Kingdom's liabilities!)

Finally, we may note a rather strange feature of the new presentation of the balance of payments. As we have already explained, the new presentation reflects the fact that official financing through the use of reserves became much less important after 1972 when the exchange rate was floated. Yet by 1987 when the new system of presenting the balance of payments was introduced, many commentators believed that the £ would soon join a system of fixed exchange rates: the **European Monetary System (EMS)**. Indeed, by 1987 the £'s exchange rate was already 'shadowing' EMS exchange rates. Thus, just when the United Kingdom's exchange rate was beginning once again to behave like a fixed exchange rate, the British authorities introduced a new presentation of the balance of payments more appropriate to a floating exchange rate system!

THE BALANCE ITEM

12. Because of the imperfect nature of data collection, the official estimate of the balance of payments will never be completely accurate. For this reason a **'balancing item'**, similar to the statistical discrepancy in the National Income Accounts, must be added or subtracted as the last item of the balance of payments to make the balance-sheet sum to zero. In the years following the first publication of the UK balance of payments, the statistics are continuously revised. A very large balancing item on first publication - as illustrated in Table 24.1 - means that the statistics must be interpreted with caution. Over subsequent years it is usual for the published figures for both the current account and capital flows to change and for the balancing item to become smaller, as it is gradually 'allocated' to a 'real' flow in the balance of payments. It is possible therefore, that a current account deficit apparent when the statistics are first published can be transformed into a surplus on later publication and vice versa.

RECENT CHANGES IN THE UK CURRENT ACCOUNT

13. Because the current account is the most important part of the balance of payments, reflecting the country's trading competitiveness with the rest of the world, we shall examine in some detail recent changes in the structure of the major UK trading flows. For most of the 20th century, the UK current account has displayed a deficit on the balance of visible trade and a surplus on the invisible balance. This can be explained by the emergence of competing industrial countries which have reduced or eliminated the UK's advantage in many manufacturing industries whilst Britain has built up a comparative advantage in services, particularly in financial services. Whether the overall current account is in deficit or surplus in any single year has depended on whether the invisible surplus has been sufficient to offset the visible deficit.

In recent years however, some important structural changes have occurred in the United Kingdom current account. These are:

(a) North Sea oil revenues have made a significant contribution to the balance of trade, both through import-saving and oil exports. From the mid-1970s and reaching a peak in the mid-1980s, North Sea revenues transformed the current account from deficit to surplus, though a deficit has now returned.

(b) However, the contribution of North Sea oil disguised the continuing deterioration of the balance of non-oil visible trade, caused by a growing propensity to import and the uncompetitiveness of British manufactured goods. It is thus useful to divide the visible balance into a **balance of trade in manufactured goods** and **non-manufactures**, as well as into the **balance of trade in oil** and the **non-oil balance**. From the 18th century until the 1980s the UK balance of trade in manufactured goods remained in surplus, reflecting the United Kingdom's importance as a manufacturing economy. Around 1982 however, imports of manufactured goods began to exceed exports, moving the balance of trade in manufactures into deficit for the first time since before the Industrial Revolution. This partly reflects the **deindustrialisation** process whereby large parts of UK manufacturing industry went into structural decline in the 1970s and early 1980s. Although deindustrialisation has now apparently reversed, with manufacturing output showing a recovery, the deficit in the trade in manufactured goods has not been reversed. We can relate the growing deficit in a manufacturing trade to the oil trade surplus. Essentially they reflect the fact that North Sea oil revenues have been used to finance, not investment in the re-equipment of the UK's manufacturing base, but short-term standards of living through the import of consumer goods.

(c) Invisible exports now account for more than half of the United Kingdom's export credits, rising from 38.5 per cent in 1970 to 51.9 per cent in 1984. Likewise, invisible imports have also grown in relative importance, accounting for 48.7 per cent of total imports in 1984. The growth of invisible exports and imports, in both absolute and relative importance, reflects the changing pattern of world trade in which the world's richest countries increasingly trade specialised services with each other. The rapid growth of the UK's invisible exports also reflects the importance of dividend income, or net property income from abroad. As we have already noted, UK residents and companies invested large amounts of capital overseas following the abolition of exchange controls in 1979. These investments are now remitting profits which are nearly sufficient to offset the fall in oil revenues in the visible balance which occurred when the price of crude oil dramatically fell by 50 per cent in 1985 and 1986. And after a difficult period in the early 1980s when it appeared that the invisible earnings of the City of London might decline under the growth of competition from other financial centres such as Tokyo and New York, there has been a spectacular recovery in the City's earnings, particularly after the reorganisation of many financial services which followed the 'Big Bang' in 1986.

BALANCE OF PAYMENTS EQUILIBRIUM AND DISEQUILIBRIUM

14. Although in an accounting sense the balance of payments must always balance, the country's payments may not be in a state of equilibrium. **Balance of payments equilibrium** or **(external equilibrium)** occurs when desired spontaneous or **autonomous trade and capital flows** into and out of the country are equal over a number of years. Alternatively, we may define equilibrium in a rather narrower sense, referring only to the current account. The balance of payments is in equilibrium when the current account more or less balances over a period of years. Balance of payments equilibrium is perfectly compatible with occurrence of **short-term** deficits and surpluses. But **fundamental disequilibrium** exists when there is a persistent tendency for payments for imports to be greater or less than corresponding payments for exports over a period of years.

THE PROBLEM OF A CURRENT ACCOUNT DEFICIT

15. While a short-run deficit or surplus on current account does not pose a problem, a persistent imbalance indicates a fundamental disequilibrium. However, the nature of any resulting problem depends upon the **size** and **cause** of the deficit or surplus and also, upon the type of **exchange rate regime.** The larger the deficit the greater the problem is likely to be. The problem is also likely to be serious if the deficit is caused by the uncompetitiveness of the country's industries. Although in the short run, a deficit allows a country's residents to enjoy living standards boosted by imports and thus higher than would be possible from the consumption of the country's output alone, in the long run the decline of the country's industries in the face of international competition will lower living standards.

A balance of payments deficit is usually considered more of a problem in a regime of **fixed exchange rates** than when the exchange rate is **freely floating.** The immediate cause of a deficit usually lies in the fact that exports are too expensive in overseas markets, while imports are too cheap at home. Obviously there are more deep-seated causes of over-priced exports and under-priced imports, relating for example to domestic wage costs compared to those in other countries. However, in a floating exchange rate regime, the external price of the currency - the exchange rate - simply responds to market forces and falls, thereby restoring export competitiveness and curing the balance of payments disequilibrium. In contrast, when the exchange rate is fixed, overvaluation of the exchange rate may occur, which cannot be cured by market forces because in a fixed system, the exchange rate is not allowed to respond to market forces. In the absence of inward capital flows financing the resulting persistent payments deficit, the country will simply lose official reserves. Official reserves are of course limited, so a country cannot go on financing a deficit for ever. Eventually therefore in a fixed exchange rate system, a country must take action to try to reduce or eliminate a persistent payments deficit.

POLICIES TO CURE A BALANCE OF PAYMENT DEFICIT

16. We shall now describe the three policy measures which a government can use to try to cure a persistent deficit caused by an overvalued exchange rate. These are **deflation, import controls**, and **devaluation** of a fixed exchange rate (or a **managed** or **'dirty' downward float** of the exchange rate).

(a) **Deflation. Fiscal policy** or **monetary policy** can be used to deflate the level of aggregate demand in the economy. Deflation is an **expenditure-reducing policy** which cures a deficit by reducing the demand for imports. Because of the unused capacity in domestic industry which it creates (resulting from the fall in demand for domestic output as well as for imports), deflation may also encourage firms to seek export orders so that they make use of their spare capacity. However, many economists argue that this is less likely, because a sound and expanding home market is necessary for a successful export drive, since exports are usually less profitable than domestic sales. In addition to its expenditure-reducing effect, a deflation of demand can also have a subsidiary **expenditure-switching** effect upon the balance of payments. The depression of demand may cause the domestic inflation rate to fall relative to that in competitor countries, thereby increasing the price competitiveness of exports and reducing the competitiveness of imports. Residents of other countries may then switch their demand towards the country's exports, while its own residents switch away from imports, preferring instead to buy domestically-produced substitutes.

However, deflation can involve severe domestic costs, since in modern economies **output** and **employment** tend to fall rather than the **price level**. For this reason, governments may prefer to use the *expenditure-switching* policies of import controls and devaluation, as alternatives to *expenditure-reducing* deflation.

(b) **Import controls**. Import controls have an immediate expenditure-switching effect upon the balance of payments. **Embargoes** and **quotas** directly prevent or reduce expenditure on imports, while **import duties** or **tariffs** discourage expenditure by raising the price of imports. However, import controls are not aimed at the underlying cause of disequilibrium - the uncompetitiveness of a country's goods and services - and they are likely to cause retaliation, with an undesirable decrease in specialisation and world trade. In any case, import controls may be 'unavailable' to many countries as a policy alternative, because of their membership of a trading body such as GATT which discourages the use of quotas and tariffs.

(c) **Devaluation (or a downward 'managed' float)**. The 'unavailability' of import controls, has meant that the real choice facing countries such as the UK, has been between deflation and devaluation. **Devaluation** of a fixed exchange rate, or a **'managed'** or **'dirty' downward float**, is mainly expenditure-switching in its effect. Payments disequilibrium is cured in a manner essentially similar to the freely-floating adjustment mechanism we have already briefly described. By increasing the price of imports relative to the price of exports, a successful devaluation or managed float switches domestic demand away from imports and towards home-produced goods. Similarly, overseas demand for the country's exports increases in response to the fall in their price. (A 'managed' or 'dirty' float occurs when the exchange rate is 'officially' freely-floating, but the country's monetary authorities 'unofficially' intervene and use reserves to support the exchange rate in foreign exchange markets, so that it becomes semi-fixed. By temporarily reducing their support, the authorities can engineer or 'manage' a downward float of the exchange rate, equivalent to a formal devaluation in a fixed exchange rate regime.)

THE MARSHALL-LERNER CONDITION

17. The effectiveness of a devaluation (and of any expenditure-switching policy) in reducing a payment deficit depends upon the **price elasticities** of demand for exports and imports. It is easy to show that when the demands for exports and imports are both highly price elastic, a devaluation can improve the balance of payments. This is illustrated in Figure 24.1

Figure 24.1: The effect of a devaluation of fall in the exchange rate upon the demand for imports and exports when demand for imports and exports are both elastic

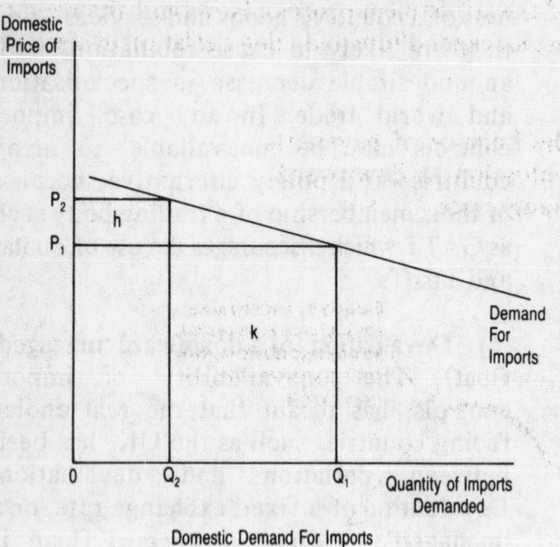

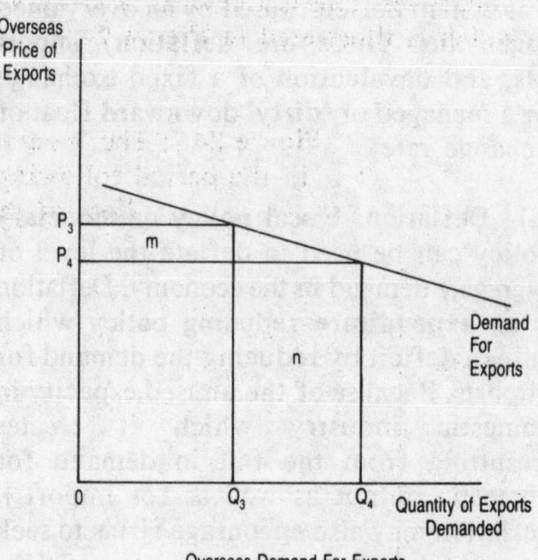

Following a devaluation, the domestic price of imports rises from P_1 to P_2, while the overseas price of exports falls from P_3 to P_4. Overseas residents are likely to spend more on the country's exports following a fall in their relative price, while the country's residents will spend less on imports. When demands are elastic - as illustrated in Figure 24.1 - total domestic expenditure on imports falls by the area k-h, while overseas expenditure on exports rises by the area n-m. The balance of payments improves by (k-h) + (n-m).

However, it is rather more difficult to see what will happen to the balance of payments if the demands are less elastic. Fortunately, the **Marshall-Lerner condition** provides a simple rule we can use to assess whether a change in the exchange rate can reduce a balance of payments disequilibrium. The Marshall-Lerner condition states that when the **sum of the export and import price elasticities is greater than unity,** a fall in the exchange rate can reduce a deficit (and a rise in the exchange rate can reduce a surplus). If however the export and import elasticities are both highly inelastic, summing to less than unity, a fall in the exchange rate might have the perverse effect of worsening a deficit (and a revaluation might increase a surplus).

EXPENDITURE-REDUCING VERSUS EXPENDITURE-SWITCHING POLICIES

18. The Marshall-Lerner condition is a **necessary condition** but not a **sufficient condition** for a fall in the exchange rate to reduce a payments deficit. For a devaluation or downward float to be successful, domestic supply must be able to respond to meet the surge in demand brought about by the fall in the exchange rate. Spare capacity is thus needed so that supply may be increased to meet the switching of overseas and domestic demand away from foreign produced goods and towards the home-produced substitutes. We should therefore regard **expenditure-reducing deflation** and **expenditure-switching devaluation** as complementary policies rather than as substitutes in the task of reducing a payments disequilibrium. Deflation alone may be unnecessarily costly in terms of lost domestic employment and output, yet it may still be necessary to provide the spare capacity and conditions in which a falling exchange rate can successfully cure a payments deficit.

THE J-CURVE

19. Even if the Marshall-Lerner condition is met and spare capacity exists in the economy, a country's firms may still be unable *immediately* to increase supply following a fall in the exchange rate. Indeed, the Marshall-Lerner condition may not in fact be met in the immediate period because elasticities of demand are lower in the short run than in the long run. In these circumstances, the balance of payments may worsen before it improves. This is known as the **J-curve effect,** which is illustrated in Figure 24.2.

The initial worsening in the balance of payments which follows the fall in the exchange rate may, of course, reduce confidence in the effectiveness of changing the exchange rate as an appropriate method of tackling a payments imbalance. Falling confidence may then in turn cause capital outflows which destabilise both the balance of payments and the exchange rate. The J-curve effect thus reduces the attractiveness of exchange rate adjustment as an instrument to correct payments disequilibrium. And even when the benefits of a falling exchange rate are realised, they may be short-lived. The increased price competitiveness produced by the devaluation is likely to be eroded away as increased import prices raise the country's inflation rate.

THE ABSORPTION APPROACH TO THE BALANCE OF PAYMENTS

20. The Marshall-Lerner condition and the J-curve illustrate what is sometimes called the **elasticities approach** to the balance of payments which emphasises the expenditure-switching nature of the adjustment process. However, the need to use an expenditure-reducing deflation of demand

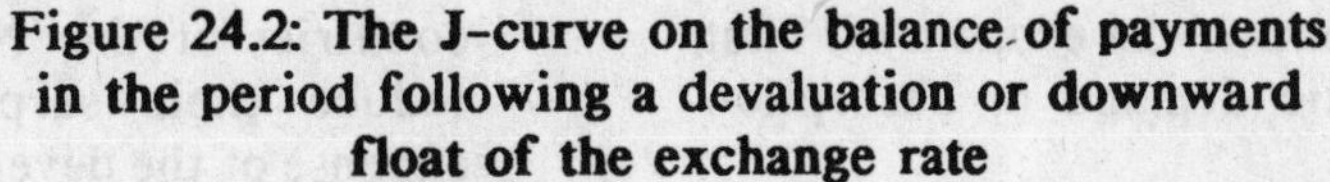

Figure 24.2: The J-curve on the balance of payments in the period following a devaluation or downward float of the exchange rate

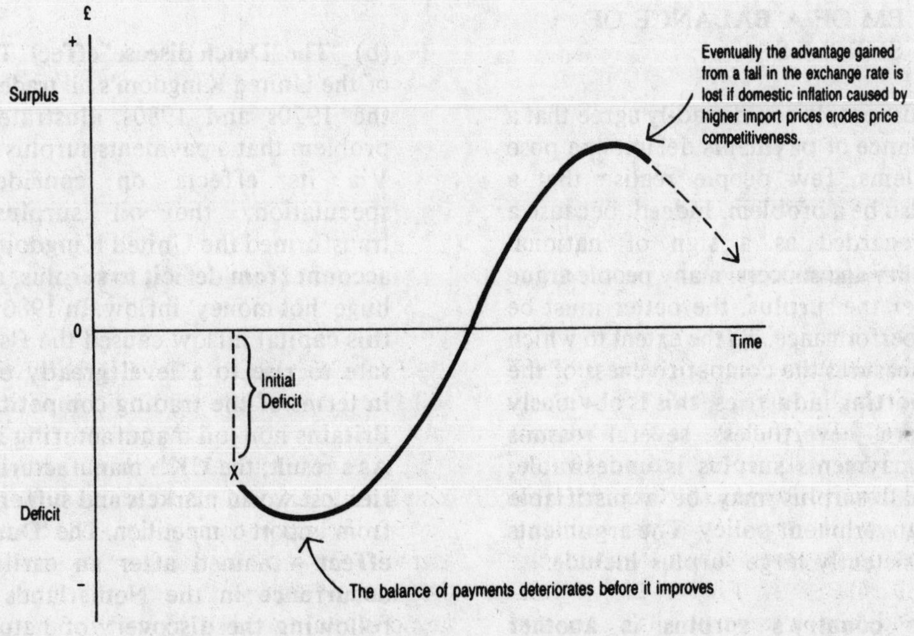

to prepare for a fall in the exchange rate reflects the **absorption approach** to the balance of payments. The absorption approach examines the balance of payments from a Keynesian perspective in terms of aggregate demand absorbing, or being insufficient to absorb, the economy's domestic output. The equilibrium equation for national income in a Keynesian income-expenditure model of the economy can be written as:

$$Y = C + I + G + X - M$$

Rewriting the equation, we can get:

$$X - M = Y - (C + I + G)$$

This indicates that the balance of payments (X - M) will be in deficit if the economy *absorbs* or consumes more goods and services than it produces, ie if (C + I + G), which represents domestic absorption, exceed the level of national output (Y). In this approach, the balance of payments equals national output minus national absorption. If spare capacity and unemployed labour exist, an expenditure-switching lowering of the exchange rate can reduce a payments deficit without having to reduce the domestic level of demand or absorption, but if all resources are fully employed, Y cannot increase. In this situation, a devaluation can only improve the balance of payments if the economy is first deflated and domestic demand or absorption reduced.

THE PROBLEM OF A BALANCE OF PAYMENTS SURPLUS

21. While most people could readily agree that a persistent balance of payments deficit can pose serious problems, few people realise that a surplus can also be a problem. Indeed, because a surplus is regarded as a sign of national economic virility and success, many people argue that the bigger the surplus, the better must be the country's performance. To the extent to which the surplus measures the competitiveness of the country's exporting industries, this is obviously true. There are, nevertheless, several reasons why a large payments surplus is undesirable, though a small surplus may be a justifiable objective of government policy. The arguments against a persistently large surplus include:

(a) **One country's surplus is another country's deficit**. Because the balance of payments must balance for the world as a whole, it is impossible for all countries to run surpluses simultaneously. Unless countries with persistently large surpluses agree to take action to reduce their surpluses, deficit countries will not be able to reduce their deficits. As a consequence and in desperation, deficit countries may then be forced to resort to import controls from which all countries, including the surplus countries, eventually suffer. In the extreme, a world recession could be triggered by a collapse of world trade. In the 1970s, the main problem was posed by the surpluses of the oil-producing countries, though in the 1980s the oil surpluses have largely disappeared. Perhaps more serious currently, is the Japanese payments surplus, which is matched by an American trade deficit. On several occasions the US government has faced pressure from American manufacturing and labour interests to introduce import controls and other forms of protectionism. If introduced, American protectionism would undoubtedly harm world trade. We should also note the problems posed for **the non-oil exporting developing countries** who almost without exception, suffer chronic deficits. This imbalance cannot be reduced without the industrialised countries of the **'North'** taking action to reduce their surpluses, gained at the expense of the developing economies of the **'South'**.

(b) **The 'Dutch disease' effect**. The growth of the United Kingdom's oil trade surplus in the 1970s and 1980s illustrates another problem that a payments surplus can cause. Via its effects on confidence and speculation, the oil surplus, which transformed the United Kingdom's current account from deficit to surplus, attracted a huge 'hot money' inflow. In 1980 and 1981, this capital inflow caused the £'s exchange rate to rise to a level greatly overvalued in terms of the trading competitiveness of Britains non-oil manufacturing industries. As a result, the UK's manufacturing industries lost world markets and suffered acutely from import competition. The **'Dutch disease' effect** - named after an earlier similar occurrence in the Netherlands economy following the discovery of natural gas in northern Holland - was arguably a major cause of the **deindustrialisation** of the UK economy in the early 1980s and the growth of unemployment in the UK from 1 million to over 3 million. Overall, the effect of the oil trade surplus on the 'real' economy - via the exchange rate - caused much of the benefit of North Sea oil revenues to be 'lost' in financing imports and the upkeep of the unemployed.

(c) **A balance of payments surplus is inflationary**. It is often not realised that a balance of payments surplus can be an important cause of domestic inflation. The tendency for a balance of payments surplus to be inflationary (and for a deficit to be deflationary) can be explained both in Keynesian and in monetarist terms.

(i) **The Keynesian explanation**. This is an extension to the absorption approach to the balance of payments which we have already explained. Essentially a balance of payments surplus in an **injection** of aggregate demand into the circular flow of income, which, via a multiplier effect, will increase the equilibrium level of **nominal** or **money** national income. To a Keynesian, the effect is likely to be **reflationary** if there are unemployed resources in the economy, but inflationary if there is no spare capacity. (Conversely, a deficit represents a **leakage** or **withdrawal** of demand which deflates the equilibrium level of income.)

(ii) **The monetarist explanation**. If the exchange rate is held fixed in an open economy, the domestic money supply is affected by the balance of payments; a surplus tends to increase the money supply while a deficit reduces the money supply.

When there is a balance of payments surplus, the country's currency is in short supply on foreign exchange markets, causing the exchange rate to rise. To prevent the exchange rate rising, the authorities must sell their own currency and buy other currencies which are then added to the country's official reserves. But because more of the country's currency has been issued, the money supply must have increased. If the increased supply of money is then spent on the country's exports or invested in the purchase of the country's capital assets, the domestic price level may be bid up, causing inflation.

POLICIES TO CURE A BALANCE OF PAYMENTS SURPLUS

22. The policies available to a government for reducing a balance of payments surplus are simply the opposite of the policies of deflation, import controls and devaluation appropriate for correcting a payments deficit. To reduce or eliminate a surplus, a government can either **reflate** demand, thereby increasing a country's demand for imports; it can liberalise trade by **removing import controls**; or it can **revalue** the country's exchange rate. In recent years there have been frequent calls for Japan and for other successful industrialised countries with large payments surpluses, to expand or reflate their domestic economies and to remove any forms of protectionism, including informal limits on imports, so as to help redress the global payments imbalance between the developed and developing worlds. As we have already noted, a large payments surplus either places pressure on a country to revalue a fixed exchange rate, or it will directly cause a floating exchange rate to rise. In either circumstance, an upward movement of the exchange rate will only reduce a surplus providing the Marshall-Lerner condition is met. There may also be a **'reverse J-curve'** effect immediately following the revaluation, when the payments surplus gets bigger before it begins to get smaller.

SUMMARY

23. In this chapter we have examined the currency flows into and out of a country which comprise the balance of payments, before in the next chapter we examine exchange rates in greater detail. The most important part of a country's balance of payments is the current account, which reflects the country's trading competitiveness. The current account divides into the balance of trade, which shows exports and imports of visibles or goods, and the invisible balance, which includes mostly services and dividend flows. Capital flows make up the second part of a country's balance of payments. Traditionally, the current account and capital flows have been

regarded as spontaneous or autonomous, with any surplus or deficit on current and capital account, taken together, being financed or accommodated by a compensating flow in the third part of the balance of payments: official financing. However, because it is now realised that capital flows, particularly short-term speculative 'hot money' flows, can to a large extent finance the current account, the distinction between capital flows and official financing has been dropped from the official presentation of the UK balance of payments statistics.

Although in a strict accounting sense, the balance of payments must always exactly balance, this must not be confused with balance of payments equilibrium. Equilibrium occurs if the current account more or less balances over a period of years; conversely a persistent deficit or surplus indicates disequilibrium. To reduce a persistent deficit, a government may deflate domestic demand, impose import controls, or devalue (if the exchange rate is fixed, or allow market forces to float the exchange rate downwards). The appropriate policies to reduce a surplus are reflation, the relaxing of import controls and revaluation or an upward float. Deflation and reflation are respectively expenditure-reducing and expenditure-expanding, whereas the imposition and withdrawal of import controls and devaluation and revaluation are expenditure-switching policies.

In recent years there have been important changes in the UK balance of payments. Most significantly, the balance of trade in manufactured goods has moved from surplus into deficit, thus reversing an historical trend established since the UK became an industrialised economy. The deterioration of the balance of trade in manufactures was to some extent disguised by a large surplus in the balance of trade in oil following the development of the North Sea oil fields in the 1970s. However, North Sea oil's contribution to the UK balance of payments has passed its peak, pointing to serious problems for the UK which may emerge when North Sea oil eventually runs dry. Nevertheless, the outlook may not be too gloomy, since the oil revenues have been used to finance capital flows which have built up large UK owned holdings of assets overseas. These will continue to yield a dividend income after North Sea oil production has diminished, thereby filling the hole left in the current account by the decline of oil revenue.

STUDENT SELF-TESTING

1 *What items are included in the UK current account?* *(3)*
2 *Define the balance of trade.* *(4)*
3 *List various items in the invisible account.* *(5)*
4 *What is a long-term capital flow?* *(7)*
5 *Why do short-term capital flows take place?* *(8)*
6 *What is a Eurodollar?* *(9)*
7 *How may the balance of payments be officially financed?* *(10)*
8 *Describe the changes in the presentation of the UK balance of payments which were introduced in 1986/87.* *(11)*
9 *What is the purpose of the balancing item?* *(12)*
10 *What has happened to the UK balance of trade in manufactured goods in recent years?* *(13)*
11 *Explain the meaning of balance of payments disequilibrium.* *(14)*
12 *Why is a current account deficit a problem?* *(15)*
13 *List the policies to reduce a payments deficit.* *(16)*
14 *Explain the Marshall-Lerner condition.* *(17)*
15 *What is an expenditure-switching policy?* *(18)*
16 *Explain the J-curve.* *(19)*
17 *What is meant by national absorption?* *(20)*
18 *How may a payments surplus pose problems?* *(21)*
19 *How may a surplus be reduced?* *(22)*

EXERCISES

1. *Selected items from the UK balance of payments*

	1979	1981	1983
			£m
Balance of trade in manufactured goods	*+1,965*	*+2,905*	*-2,119*
Balance of trade in oil	*-731*	*+3,112*	*+7,001*
Balance of visible trade	*-3,449*	*+3,008*	*- 500*
Balance of invisible trade	*+2,796*	*+3,539*	*+2,549*
Balance of payments on current account	*-653*	*+6,547*	*+2,049*
Investment and other capital transactions	*+2,307*	*-7,209*	*-2,044*

(a) Describe and account for the main changes in the UK balance of payments over the period 1979 to 1983.

(b) What relationships may exist between the current account and capital flows?

MULTIPLE CHOICE QUESTIONS

1 Selected UK balance of payments statistics 1986

	£m
Visible balance	*-8,254*
Invisible balance	*+7,154*
Net transactions	*-5,758*
Balancing item	*+6,858*

From these figures it is possible to conclude that in 1986 there was a:
A A current account deficit
B Balance of payments disequilibrium
C Favourable balance of trade
D Fall in official reserves

2 A balance of payments surplus may cause:
A Employment and the money supply to rise
B The money supply to fall
C Employment to rise and the money supply to fall
D Employment and the money supply to fall.

3 A capital inflow in the balance of payments will cause:
A The current account to move into surplus
B The exchange rate to rise
C Dividend payments to flow into the country
D An accommodating hot money outflow.

4 A country's invisible exports include all the following EXCEPT:
A Money spent abroad by the country's residents on tourism
B Dividend flows into the country
C Gifts of money received by residents from relations living overseas
D Spending by the US government on military bases located within the UK.

5 In a freely floating exchange rate regime, the government will:
A Use official reserves to finance a balance of payments deficit
B Issue more money to finance a balance of payments surplus
C Not need to maintain official reserves
D Allow market forces to determine the exchange rate within a strictly limited band.

EXAMINATION QUESTIONS

1 (a) What is meant by a balance of payments deficit? (10 marks)

(b) How might a government eliminate such a deficit? (10 marks)
(AAT December 1987)

2 If the balance of payments must balance why then do we have deficits or surpluses on the balance of payments?
(ACCA December 1983)

3 *In the last few years the national debt of the US has reached a record level whilst at the same time some of the developing countries, such as Mexico, have run up huge external debts.*

(a) Explain the difference between national debt and external debt. (4 marks)

(b) Compare and contrast the problems of a developed country, such as the USA, which has a large national debt, with the problems of a developing country, such as Mexico, which has a large external debt. (16 marks)

(ACCA December 1987)

25. Exchange rates

INTRODUCTION

1. In Chapter 24 we examined the structure of a country's balance of payments, emphasising how the mechanism for curing a persistent deficit or surplus depends to a large extent upon the nature of the country's exchange rate regime. In this chapter, we investigate in greater detail the mechanisms through which **freely floating** and **fixed exchange rates** might restore a balance of payments equilibrium, before describing the various **managed exchange rates** that have existed in the modern world economy. We shall conclude the chapter by examining the roles of the **International Monetary Fund (IMF)** and the **European Monetary System (EMS)**, which have provided the institutional framework within which managed exchange rates have operated.

DIFFERENT MEASURES OF THE EXCHANGE RATE

2. **Exchange rates** and a **foreign exchange market** exist because different countries use different currencies to pay for **internal** trade. A currency's exchange rate is simply its **external** price, expressed in terms of another currency such as the US dollar, or gold, or indeed in terms of an artificial unit such as a weighted average of a sample or 'basket' of leading trading currencies. In this chapter we shall assume that we are explaining the exchange rate of the pound sterling, expressing the £'s exchange rate in terms of the US dollar. It is worth noting, however, that the convention of quoting exchange rates in terms of the US dollar is of fairly recent origin. Before 1914 most exchange rates were expressed in terms of gold and only after 1945 did the dollar become the near universally accepted standard by which the external values of other currencies were measured. But in recent years the dollar has become much less stable, and consequently the US currency has become less useful as a fulcrum or standard against which to measure the value of other currencies. In the UK the **Sterling Index** has now replaced the dollar as the official measure of the exchange rate. The Sterling Index does not measure the £'s external value against a particular currency. Rather it is a trade-weighted average of the £'s exchange rate against about 16 leading trading currencies, calculated to reflect the importance of each currency in international trade. On 18th May 1988, the Sterling Index was 78.3 compared to its 1975 index of 100. This means that over the years since 1975 when the Sterling Index was first created, the sterling exchange rate had depreciated or lost 21.7 per cent of its value when measured against the exchange rates of Britain's most important trading partners.

THE THEORY OF A FREELY FLOATING EXCHANGE RATE

3. In a regime of **freely floating** (or **'cleanly') floating** exchange rates, the external value of a country's currency is determined on foreign exchange markets by the forces of demand and supply alone. Later in this chapter we shall see that in recent years capital flows and speculation have been extremely significant in influencing the supply of and demand for a currency and hence its exchange rate. However, we shall first simplify and assume that a currency is demanded on foreign exchanges only for the payment of trade and that trade flows alone determine exchange rates. We shall assume also that any holdings of foreign currencies surplus to the immediate requirement of paying for trade are straightway sold on the foreign exchange market.

On foreign exchange markets, the pound sterling is demanded by residents of other countries who require pounds for purchasing British exports priced in sterling. Now, the lower the exchange rate of the pound, the more competitive become British exports when priced in foreign currencies. Therefore, at lower exchange rates, the volume of exports increases, leading to greater overseas demand for pounds to finance their purchase. The result is the **downward-sloping curve for pounds** illustrated in Figure 25.1

Whereas exports generate a demand for pounds on foreign exchange markets to finance the purchase by foreigners of British produced goods and services, imports generate a supply of pounds. This is because UK residents must supply or sell sterling in order to purchase the foreign currencies needed to pay for the goods and services demanded as imports. At lower exchange rates, the competitiveness of imports in the UK domestic market is reduced, when these imports are priced in sterling. As a result, fewer imports are demanded as the exchange rate falls, so less sterling is supplied to pay for them. Conversely a rising exchange rate would require more sterling to be supplied. The result is the **upward-sloping supply curve of sterling** depicted in Figure 25.1

Figure 25.1: Exchange rate adjustment in a system of freely floating exchange rates

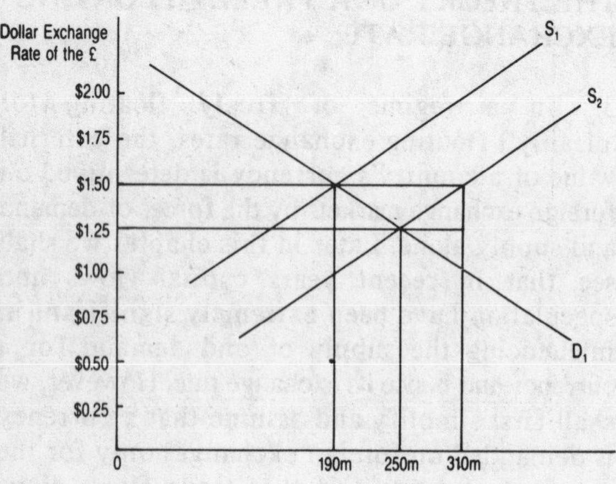

Quantity of £s sterling traded on foreign exchange markets

With a demand curve for sterling D_1 and a supply curve of sterling at S_1, the exchange rate illustrated in Figure 25.1 is initially £1 = $1.50. This is the **equilibrium exchange rate** at which the demand for and supply of pounds are equal. And because we are assuming that exports and imports are the only items in the country's balance of payments, the balance of payments is also in equilibrium, the value of exports (paid for in sterling) equalling the value of imports (paid for in foreign currencies) at the equilibrium exchange rate. Because we are ignoring any complications introduced by capital flows, *exchange rate equilibrium implies balance of payments equilibrium* on the current account and vice versa. The two concepts are really just different sides of the same coin: exchange rate equilibrium is stated in terms of **price**, whereas balance of payments equilibrium reflects quantities of currency flowing into and out of the country. If the balance of payments is in equilibrium, there should be no pressure on the exchange rate to rise or fall.

We shall now suppose that some event or 'shock' disturbs the initial equilibrium, for example an increase in the quality of foreign produced goods, which increases planned imports at all existing prices expressed in sterling. As a result, British residents demand more foreign exchange in order to purchase imports, so the supply curve of sterling in Figure 25.1 shifts rightwards to S_2. (Remember, when more foreign currencies are demanded, more sterling must be supplied.) In the new situation, $1.50 is no longer an equilibrium exchange rate, since at this exchange rate overseas residents accumulate sterling holdings of £310m whereas they only require £190m to pay for their own purchases of British exports. The market mechanism now operates to restore equilibrium, for both the exchange rate and the balance of payments. Overseas residents sell their excess holdings of sterling accumulated at the exchange rate of £1.50 and this sale depresses or depreciates the exchange rate. The falling exchange rate increases the price competitiveness of British exports while reducing the competitiveness of imports. The adjustment process will continue until the new equilibrium exchange rate of $1.25 is reached. Conversely, if the initial equilibrium was disturbed by an event such as the increased production of financial services by the City of London, which would move the balance of payments into surplus, the exchange rate would rise or appreciate until the excess demand for sterling is eliminated and a new equilibrium is achieved at a higher exchange rate.

THE MARSHALL-LERNER CONDITION AND EXCHANGE RATE STABILITY

4. The convergent adjustment mechanism illustrated in Figure 25.1 which moves the exchange rate to a stable equilibrium is only ensured by our assumption that the demand for imports is price elastic. If demand for imports is inelastic, more sterling will be needed at lower exchange rates to pay for imports. This is because the fall in the quantity of imports as the exchange rate depreciates is insufficient to offset the effects of the higher sterling price of each unit of imports. The result is a downward-sloping supply curve of sterling,

showing more sterling supplied as the exchange rate falls. The market-clearing or equilibrium exchange rate will still be determined where the demand and supply curves intersect, but the equilibrium need not always be stable. The **stability condition** for a convergent exchange rate mechanism is provided by the **Marshall-Lerner criterion** which we introduced and explained in Chapter 24. Provided that the sum of the export and import elasticities of demand exceeds unity, there will be a tendency to move towards a stable equilibrium exchange rate following an initial disturbance, even though the demand for imports may be inelastic.

THE THEORY OF A FIXED EXCHANGE RATE

5. In the theory of a freely floating exchange rate system, the currency's **external** value rises or falls to eliminate a balance of payments surplus or deficit. We have assumed that the domestic level of economic activity **within the country**, and the **internal price level** are little affected during the adjustment process, except perhaps to the extent that changing import prices affect domestic prices. In contrast, in a regime of fixed exchange rates, the currency's external value remains unchanged while the **internal price level**, or possibly the **level of domestic economic activity and output**, adjust to eliminate balance of payments disequilibrium. We can approach the adjustment process from either a Keynesian or a monetarist perspective.

THE KEYNESIAN APPROACH TO BALANCE OF PAYMENTS ADJUSTMENT IN A SYSTEM OF FIXED EXCHANGE RATES

6. The Keynesian approach to the adjustment process in a system of fixed exchange rates is closely related to the **absorption approach** to the balance of payments which we described in Chapter 24. We can begin by assuming that the level of **aggregate money demand** in the economy is $(C + I + G + X - M)_1$ in Figure 25.2 and that the balance of payments is in equilibrium, ie X = M. The equilibrium level of national income is Y_1.

If imports now increase by ΔM, perhaps because UK residents believe that the quality of foreign-produced goods has improved, the balance of payments will move into deficit, with X < M. But because the increase in imports is a **leakage** or **withdrawal** of demand from the circular flow of income, the AMD function shifts downwards to $(C + I + G + X - M)_2$. This triggers a negative **multiplier effect**, causing the equilibrium level of income to fall to Y_2. If we now assume that the level of imports are partly determined by the level of income, via the **marginal propensity to import**, imports will fall by mΔY (m being the marginal propensity to import).

Figure 25.2: Eliminating a balance of payments deficit in a fixed exchange rate regime

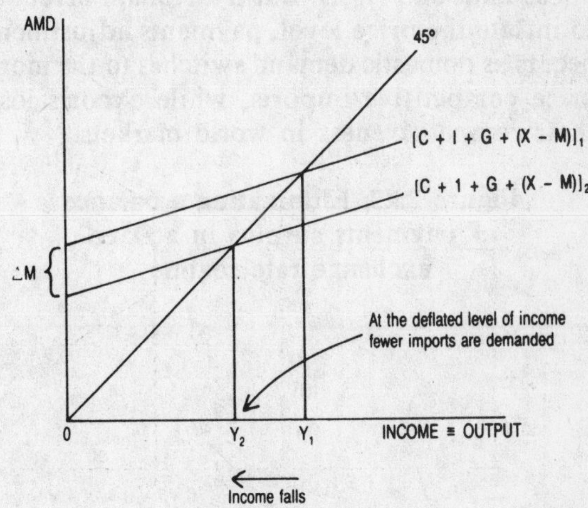

The Keynesian adjustment process we have just described illustrates how a balance of payments deficit is inherently **deflationary**. The leakage of demand represented by the deficit deflates the level of money **national income** (or **nominal national income**) within the economy. But **nominal** income can fall, either because the **price level** falls, or because the level of **real output** or **income** falls. If the domestic price level falls, exports become more price competitive in overseas markets whereas imports become more expensive. Assuming the Marshall-Lerner condition holds, the resulting adjustment process which eliminates the payments deficit is essentially **expenditure-switching**. In contrast, if the main effect of the deflation of demand falls not on the domestic price level but on the level of real economic activity within the country, the adjustment process is of a largely **expenditure-reducing** nature. At lower levels of real income, output and employment, fewer imports are demanded.

Conversely, when an increase in exports or a fall

in imports moves the balance of payments into surplus, the adjustment mechanism is simply the opposite of the process we have just described. In Figure 25.3, we have assumed that an increase in exports, shown as ΔX, shifts the AMD function upwards. Being an injection of demand into the flow of income the surplus has a **reflationary** or **inflationary** effect upon the level of income and output, depending on whether real activity or prices are stimulated. Either way, nominal income rises from Y_1 to Y_2. If the real level of economic activity is reflated or stimulated, more imports will be 'absorbed' into the economy to meet the increased real demand being exercised by households and firms. But if the main effect is to inflate the price level, payments adjustment occurs as domestic demand switches to the more price competitive imports, while exports lose their competitiveness in world markets.

Figure 25.3: Eliminating a balance of payments surplus in a fixed exchange rate regime

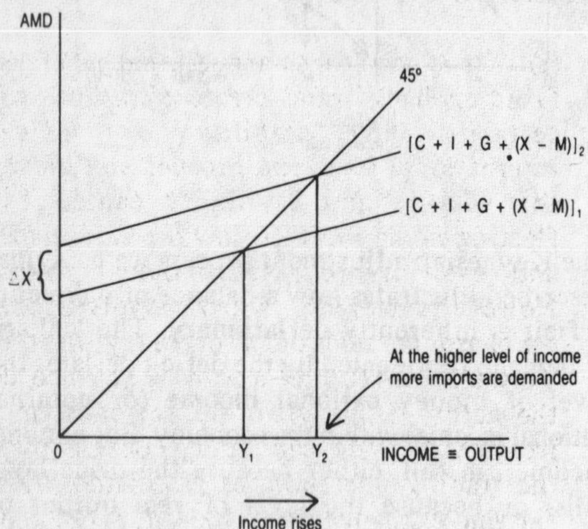

THE MONETARIST APPROACH TO BALANCE OF PAYMENTS ADJUSTMENT IN A SYSTEM OF FIXED EXCHANGE RATES

7. The monetarist explanation of the adjustment mechanism which restores equilibrium in a fixed exchange rate system is similar to the Keynesian approach to the extent that a **deficit** is **eliminated by deflation**, and a **surplus is reduced by reflation or inflation**. However, monetarists emphasise the linkages between the balance of payments and the domestic money supply in the adjustment process. This contrasts with the Keynesian emphasis on the role of the linkages between changes in aggregate demand, the national income multiplier and a resulting increased or decreased absorption of imports. As we explained in Chapter 24, a balance of payments surplus leads to a shortage of the country's currency on foreign exchange markets. When the exchange rate is fixed, the country's monetary authorities must then supply more of their own currency onto the foreign exchange market and buy other currencies which accumulate as reserves, in order to keep the currency's market price at the fixed exchange rate. This is called **exchange equalisation**. The country's money supply thus expands as new currency is issued to stabilise the exchange rate. According to monetarists, the increased money supply inflates the domestic price level, improving the price competitiveness of imports while reducing the competitiveness of exports. Conversely, a payments deficit leads to a fall in the domestic money supply because the monetary authorities must sell reserves and buy back their own currency to prevent the exchange rate from falling. The resulting monetary contraction as currency is taken out of circulation depresses or deflates the domestic economy, thereby increasing the relative competitiveness of exports.

THE ADVANTAGES OF FLOATING EXCHANGE RATES

8. (i) In a system of freely floating exchange rates, the **external price** of the currency (the exchange rate) moves up or down to correct a payments imbalance. In theory, the exchange rate should never be over- or under-valued for very long. In the event of an overvalued or 'too-high' exchange rate causing export uncompetitiveness and a payments deficit, market forces should quickly adjust towards an equilibrium exchange rate which also achieves equilibrium in the balance of payments, assuming of course that the Marshall-Lerner condition holds. Similarly, undervaluation should be quickly corrected by an upward movement of the exchange rate.

(ii) If the world's resources are to be efficiently allocated between competing uses, exchange rates must be correctly valued. For efficient resource allocation in a constantly changing world, market prices must accurately reflect the shifts in demand

and in comparative advantage that result from technical progress and events such as discoveries of new mineral resources. In principle, a freely floating exchange rate should respond and adjust to slow changes in demand and comparative advantage whereas a fixed exchange rate may become gradually over-or under-valued as demand or comparative advantage move either against or in favour of a country's industries.

(iii) It is sometimes argued that when the exchange rate is freely floating, balance of payments surpluses and deficits cease to be a policy problem for the government and a constraint holding back the pursuit of the domestic economic objectives of full employment and growth. Governments can simply allow market forces to 'look after' the balance of payments while they concentrate on domestic economic policy. And if, in the pursuit of the domestic objectives of full employment and growth, the inflation rate rises out of line with other countries, the exchange rate should simply fall to restore competitiveness. (This is the **purchasing power parity theory**, which states that when a country's inflation rate is 10 per cent higher than its main competitors, its exchange rate will fall by 10 per cent to compensate exactly for the higher inflation rate.) By contrast, in a fixed exchange rate system, a country with an overvalued exchange rate may effectively 'import unemployment' from the rest of the world as a result of its deteriorating competitiveness and because it must deflate the domestic economy in order to correct the payment deficit.

(iv) In much the same way, a 'responsible' country with a lower than average inflation rate should benefit from a floating exchange rate because the exchange rate insulates the country from 'importing inflation' from the rest of the world. We can explain this in two ways. If inflation rates are higher in the rest of the world, a fixed exchange rate causes a country to 'import' inflation through the rising price of imported goods and services. Alternatively, excess demand in countries with large payments deficits causes the inflationary pressure within the country to be 'exported' to surplus countries. The deficit countries avoid the full inflationary consequences of excess demand generated within their economies, since the excess demand is 'spent' bidding up the price level in the surplus countries whose goods are exported to the deficit country.

(v) With a floating exchange rate, a country's monetary policy (and also its fiscal policy) can in principle be completely independent of external conditions and influences. There is no need to keep official reserves to support the exchange rate or to finance a payments deficit. In the event of a deficit, the exchange rate simply falls to correct the disequilibrium without any drain on the reserves. The country's domestic money supply is therefore unaffected by a change in official reserves, and interest rate policy is not determined by the need to protect the exchange rate.

THE DISADVANTAGES OF FLOATING EXCHANGE RATES

9. (i) It is sometimes argued that whereas fixed exchange rates create conditions of certainty and stability in which international trade can prosper and grow, the volatity and instability caused by floating exchange rates slow the growth of, and even destroy, international trade. However, **hedging**, which involves the purchase or sale of a currency in the **'forward' market** three months in advance of the actual delivery of the currency and payment of trade, can reduce considerably the trading uncertainties associated with floating exchange rates. Indeed, fixed and managed exchanged rates may also cause uncertainty, especially when a currency is obviously overvalued and a devaluation is expected.

(ii) The argument that a freely floating exchange rate can never be over- or under-valued for very long depends crucially upon the assumption that currencies are bought and sold on foreign exchange markets only to finance trade and that **speculation** and **capital flows** have no influence upon exchange rates. This assumption is quite simply at odds with reality. More than ninety per cent of the currency transactions taking place on foreign exchange markets relate to capital flows and to the decisions of individuals, business corporations, financial institutions and even of governments, to switch their wealth portfolios between different currencies. Trade flows typically have very little to do with the day-to-day demand for and supply of currencies on foreign exchange markets. Exchange rates have therefore become extremely vulnerable to speculative capital movements into or out of a particular currency, which are just as likely as any fixed exchange rate to lead to the over- or under-valuation of the currency, and a failure to reflect correctly the trading competitiveness of the country's industries.

Nevertheless the growth of currency speculation in the modern era may be related less to floating exchange rates than to the growth of the **pool of footloose 'hot money'** which we described in Chapter 24. It can also be argued that there is more scope for speculators to 'win' at the expense of governments when exchange rates are fixed than in a freely floating system. In a fixed system, a speculator faces the 'one-way option' of selling currency to the central bank defending the currency. If successful, the speculator forces a devaluation and realises a capital gain when he buys back the currency at a lower rate following the devaluation. If unsuccessful and failing to force a devaluation, the speculator will only make a small loss since he can buy back the currency at or near the original price. By contrast, in a freely floating system, a speculator wishing to sell must find another private individual - possibly also a speculator - wishing to buy. In the subsequent trading, the speculator who guesses future currency prices correctly will gain at the expense of the one who guesses wrongly. If successful speculators correctly sell when the exchange rate is overvalued and buy when it is undervalued, their activities can stabilise rather than destabilise the market, smoothing out rather than reinforcing temporary fluctuations.

However, when there is a massive and perhaps irrational 'herd' movement of speculative funds into a currency for reasons completely unrelated to the competitiveness of the 'real economy' of the country in question, the main effect of speculation is undoubtedly harmful. Hot money flows 'sloshing' into and out of currencies have, in recent years, threatened to destabilise not only the exchange rates and balance of payments of the individual countries affected, but also their domestic economies and even the world system of trade and payments. During 1984 and the early part of 1985, there were substantial hot money flows out of currencies such as sterling and into the dollar, taking the exchange rate of the pound down almost to £1 = $1. The capital flows were completely unrelated to the underlying trade competitiveness of the UK and the USA - the United Kingdom's current account was in approximate balance, whereas the United States had a massive trading deficit! The immediate effect was, of course, to overvalue the dollar and to reduce still further the competitiveness of American exports, promoting exactly the conditions for an eventual loss of confidence in the US economy and a 'bounce-back' by speculators out of the dollar in 1987 and 1988. Exchange rate movements such as these often have very little to do with the state of the 'real economy' and the trading competitiveness of the countries whose currencies are involved. Much modern exchange rate fluctuation is caused by essentially speculative hot money movements, which are in part irrational, but in part also a rational response - at least in the short run - to interest rate differences between countries and to expectations that exchange rates might rise or fall.

(iii) We noted earlier in this chapter that fixed exchange rates have been blamed for the 'export' of inflation from deficit countries to surplus countries. However, a counter-argument, which we explained in Chapter 21, is that floating exchange rates cause inflation and that fixed exchange rates exhibit a deflationary bias which reduces inflation. We can explain this deflationary bias in the following way. When a country's inflation rate exceeds that of its trading competitors, its balance of payments will move into severe deficit. But the resulting uncompetitiveness of the country's exports and import penetration will then **'discipline'** any domestic 'cost-push' causes of the inflation, via the increased unemployment and bankruptcies which the uncompetitiveness causes. At the same time, the loss of reserves which results from official intervention to support the fixed exchange rate puts pressure on the deficit country to deflate its domestic economy in order to cure the imbalance. This creates a deflationary bias, since with fixed exchange rates, there is no effective symmetrical pressure placed on surplus countries to reflate their economies to cure their imbalances.

By contrast, a floating exchange rate system lacks an equivalent source of discipline to make deficit countries reduce their domestic inflation rates. (Indeed, as we argued earlier, the lack of such discipline can be regarded as a virtue of floating exchange rates, because its absence allows a country to pursue the domestic objective of full employment and growth unconstrained by the necessity of supporting the exchange rate and the payments position.) However, the experience of floating exchange rates in the 1970s illustrates the dangers of pursuing domestic objectives irrespective of their effects on the exchange rate. Firstly, a **vicious circle** or **cumulative spiral** may be unleashed of **ever faster inflation** and **exchange rate depreciation**. This may occur if rising import prices caused by a falling exchange rate, then in their turn fuel an acceleration in domestic inflation, via their effect on food and raw material prices and the wage claims made by unions. An increased rate of domestic inflation will then erode the export competitiveness won by the initial depreciation of the exchange rate, which therefore requires a further fall in the exchange rate to recover the lost advantage - and so on! The resulting downward spiral can eventually destablise large parts of the domestic economy and prevent full employment and growth from being achieved.

Secondly, in a world untrammelled by the need of deficit countries to deflate their domestic economies to protect their payments position, there is a danger of a large number of countries simultaneously expanding demand. This may create worldwide excess demand and fuel inflation on a global scale. This is what happened after exchange rates were floated in 1972, creating the conditions for rapidly rising prices, especially of oil and other primary commodities, during the 1970s. In individual countries, the resulting inflation often appeared to be of a cost-push nature, related to the cost of oil and raw materials. However, the true cause lay deeper in the excess demand created by the effects of simultaneous expansion and floating exchange rates in a world in which world supply could not be increased, in the short run at least, to meet the surge in demand.

THE ADVANTAGES AND DISADVANTAGES OF FIXED EXCHANGE RATES

10. Because the advantages and disadvantages of fixed exchange rates are closely but oppositely related to those of floating rates, we shall include only a brief summary. The main **advantages of fixed exchange rates** are:

(a) certainty and stability;
(b) the anti-inflationary 'discipline' imposed on a country's domestic economic management and upon the behaviour of its workers and firms.

In contrast, the principal **disadvantages of fixed exchange rates** include:

(a) uncertainty may actually be increased;
(b) a currency may remain over- or under-valued , in which case;
(c) a deficit country will suffer severe deflationary costs of lost output and unemployment whereas a surplus country will 'import' inflation;
(d) resources which could be used more productively elsewhere are tied up in official reserves.

MANAGED EXCHANGE RATES

11. Since the Second World War, exchange rates have never been rigidly fixed and seldom have they freely or 'cleanly' floated. Instead, the exchange rates of the world's principal currencies have to a greater or lesser extent been **managed**. An exchange rate is managed when the country's central bank actively intervenes on foreign exchange markets, buying and selling

reserves and its own currency, to influence the movement of the exchange rate in a particular direction. By managing the exchange rate, a country's monetary authorities hope to achieve **the stability and certainty associated with fixed exchange rates** combined with a **floating exchange rate's ability to avoid over- and under-valuation** by responding to market forces. But critics of managed exchange rates have argued that, instead of combining the advantages of both fixed and floating exchange rates with the disadvantages of neither, in practice exchange rate management has too often achieved the opposite: the disadvantages of uncertainty and instability combined with the ineffective and wasteful use of official reserves in frequent fruitless attempts by governments to stem speculative 'hot money' flows into or out of currencies.

Since 1945 exchange rates have been managed in a number of different ways, some of which have been closer to a freely floating system, while others have been much more similar to a rigidly fixed regime. The three principal systems of managed exchange rates have been:

(i) **The Bretton Woods system**, which lasted from 1947 to 1972;

(ii) **'Managed' floating** (or **'dirty' floating**), from 1972 to the present day;

(iii) **The European Monetary System (EMS)**, from 1979 to the present day.

THE BACKGROUND TO MANAGED EXCHANGE RATES

12. During the 1920s, world exchange rates were at times fixed (under a system known as the **Gold Standard**, in which exchange rates were pegged against gold), while during the 1930s, most exchange rates freely floated. Neither system worked very well, the Gold Standard was too rigid and the freely floating system was too unstable or volatile. Indeed, both systems were blamed for contributing in part to the **Great Depression** of the 1930s. The rigid Gold Standard system forced countries with currencies overvalued against gold into domestic policies of deflation which led to high unemployment. Then, following the collapse of the Gold Standard in 1931, attempts to gain a comparative advantage at other countries' expense by floating the exchange rate, together with 'begger-my-neighbour' protectionism, contributed to the deepening of the Great Depression.

THE BRETTON WOODS SYSTEM

13. Perhaps in reaction to the failure of both the Gold Standard and floating exchange rates in the 1920s and 1930s, during the Second World War the United States and United Kingdom began to discuss the creation of a post-war system of managed exchange rates designed to be more flexible than the Gold Standard, but more stable than the floating exchange rates of the 1930s. The new system was agreed at the **Bretton Woods Conference**, held in the small American mountain resort of Bretton Woods in 1944, but the system did not come into full operation until 1947. **Lord Keynes** was the principal British architect of the new system and of the **International Monetary Fund (IMF)**, which was set up to supervise and police the new post-war system of managed exchange rates. But since the USA was providing the main financial support for the new arrangements in which the dollar occupied a central role, the Bretton Woods exchange rate system and the IMF strongly reflected American views on how to tackle world trade and payments problems. As we shall see later, when we examine the International Monetary Fund in more detail, if Keynes had had his way, a much stronger international monetary institution would have been established.

To understand the Bretton Woods System, we must realise that it had much more in common with fixed exchange rates and the Gold Standard, than with freely floating exchange rates. The Gold Standard had failed for two main reasons:

(i) a shortage of gold for the finance of payments deficits; and

(ii) the lack of an adequate adjustment mechanism to correct a 'wrongly' valued currency.

To overcome the former problem, the US dollar replaced gold as the central standard or 'pivot currency' of the new system. Supplemented by gold, which still remained (as it does today) a major reserve asset and source of liquidity, the dollar became the key currency in the Bretton Woods System. Indeed, because the dollar remained (until 1971) on the Gold Standard, the 'new' system was essentially a **gold exchange standard** in which other currencies' exchange rates were fixed, via the dollar, against gold.

FIXED PEGS

14. The second problem - the lack of a suitable adjustment mechanism - which had contributed to the abandonment of the Gold Standard, was tackled in the Bretton Woods System through the creation of a **zone of flexibility** around a **fixed peg** (or **adjustable peg**) exchange rate. Market forces were free to determine the day-to-day exchange rate of a currency between a **ceiling** and **floor** which bounded the zone of flexibility 1 per cent each side of an agreed par value or 'peg'. If the balance of payments moved into surplus, the resulting excess demand for the country's currency would cause market forces to bid the exchange rate up above the peg, moving it towards the ceiling. In a similar but opposite way, the exchange rate would be depressed towards the floor in the event of a payments deficit. Each member country of the IMF agreed to intervene in the foreign exchange market to keep its currency's exchange rate within the prescribed zone of flexibility. This was achieved through exchange equalisation. When an exchange rate rose and threatened to move through the ceiling, IMF rules required that the country's central bank should intervene by artificially increasing the supply of its currency on the foreign exchange market. By selling its own currency and purchasing reserves, the exchange rate could be kept below the ceiling and within the zone of flexibility. Conversely, the central bank was required to sell reserves and buy its own currency to prevent market forces from depressing the xchange rate through the floor.

A persistent payments surplus or deficit would, of course, be associated with an equally persistent tendency for the exchange rate to leave the zone of flexibility. This would indicate a **fundamental disequilibrium** in the balance of payments and a 'wrongly' valued exchange rate. To deal with this problem, IMF rules allowed a country to adjust the par value of its exchange rate with a formal **revaluation** in the case of a surplus, and a **devaluation** in the case of a deficit.

THE BREAKDOWN OF BRETTON WOODS

15. In this way, it was hoped that member countries of the IMF would benefit from a **'managed flexibility'** yielded by the Bretton Woods System. But in the 1960s and early 1970s, the fixed peg system increasingly displayed signs of **'managed inflexibility'**. The Bretton Woods System suffered from the same rigidity as the Gold Standard. The IMF interpreted its own rules in such a severe way that devaluation became effectively ruled out, except as a last resort and sign of weakness, for countries suffering from persistent payments deficits. The IMF placed pressure on deficit countries to deflate their domestic economies, but deflation could not be successful without a simultaneous pressure on surplus countries to reflate - and generally this pressure was lacking.

A number of factors eventually caused the Bretton Woods System finally to collapse in 1971/72. In the first place, it is always exceedingly difficult to maintain relatively fixed exchange rates if inflation rates differ widely between countries and especially if the inflation rate in deficit countries is markedly higher than in surplus countries. The Bretton Woods System worked best in the 1950s when inflation rates in the developed world were very similar. Strains on the system began to occur in the 1960s when higher inflation rates in deficit countries started to erode their export competitiveness, contributing to the worsening of the payments deficits. As a result, pressures began to mount in deficit countries for a freeing of the exchange rate from the harsh requirement imposed by the IMF, that a deficit should be cured by domestic deflation and not by devaluation. However, the Bretton Woods System finally collapsed because of another weakness - the contradictory role of the US dollar in the system. As we have already noted, the dollar was the 'key currency' in the Bretton Woods System - the standard or fulcrum against which all other countries fixed their exchange rates. At the same time, the dollar provided the main source international liquidity in the system, as a supplement to gold. But the dollar was transmitted into the ownership of other countries, in sufficient quantities to allow it to provide a source of international liquidity, via the mechanism of a large United States payments deficit. US imports greatly exceeded exports and the difference was paid in dollars. To serve as a 'key currency', the dollar needed to be **hard**, but the American payments deficit which allowed the dollar to become a major source of liquidity in the Bretton Woods System **softened** the currency, making it less desirable and acceptable both as a reserve asset and as a means of international payment or liquidity. By the late 1960s, dollars held outside the USA far exceeded American gold reserves. Being the pivot currency of the Bretton Woods System, it was impossible to devalue the dollar against other currencies in order to restore American trading competitiveness and to stem the speculative runs which were taking place against the dollar. The dollar could only be devalued against gold, and when in 1971 a series of dollar crises finally caused the dollar to be taken off the Gold Standard and allowed to float, the Bretton Woods System had lost its pivot. The system immediately collapsed.

'DIRTY' FLOATING

16. Whereas the Bretton Woods System of managed exchange rates resembled fixed exchange rates rather than freely floating exchange rates, the reverse is true of 'dirty' floating. **'Dirty'** or **'managed' floating** occurs when the exchange rate is 'officially' floating in the sense that a country's monetary authorities announce that market forces are determining the exchange rate, though in fact the authorities intervene 'unofficially' behind the scenes to buy or sell their own currency in order to influence the exchange rate. At one extreme, such intervention can be regarded simply as a **smoothing operation** in a regime of clean or freely floating exchange rates, but when the intervention is designed to secure an **'unofficial' exchange rate target** it is better described as **'dirty' floating**. Since the breakdown of the Bretton Woods System in 1971/72, the currencies of many of the world's trading countries have floated in this way, though there have been short-lived periods when governments have withdrawn their intervention and allowed their currencies to float freely.

THE UK EXPERIENCE OF 'DIRTY' FLOATING

17. The British experience of 'dirty' floating since 1972 has exhibited four distinct phases:

(i) **1972–1977.** During the initial period of 'dirty' floating, the United Kingdom current account was in deficit and North Sea oil revenues had not yet transformed the balance of payments. In these circumstances, market forces aided by massive speculative 'hot money' movements out of sterling caused the exchange rate to fall. Indeed, sterling's fall was in line with the predictions of the purchasing power parity theory, since inflation in Britain was higher than in other industrial countries. However, the British government considered the £'s depreciation to be excessive and intervened (unsuccessfully in the 1975 and 1976 sterling crises) to try to prevent the exchange rate falling below an unofficial target or floor selected by the government. In each case, the intervention was unsuccessful, the government abandoning its 'unofficial' target and allowing the exchange rate to continue its downward float.

(ii) **1977–1981.** In the 1970s North Sea oil revenues began to transform the UK current account, turning a persistent deficit into a surplus. Indeed, for a period sterling was regarded by speculators as a 'petro-currency', made additionally attractive as a haven for 'hot money' by the UK's relative political stability. As speculative funds moved into the pound, the sterling exchange rate was forced up. In an attempt to halt the rise - in order to maintain the competitiveness of British exports - the authorities began to sell sterling and purchase reserves. Again the intervention was largely unsuccessful. To have an effect on the exchange rate, large amounts of sterling had to be issued, which after 1979 increased the UK money supply at a rate unacceptable to the now monetarist Conservative Government. The authorities resolved the conflict between attempting to halt the exchange rate's appreciation and maintaining domestic monetary control by abandoning control of the exchange rate. The pound then floated upwards, becoming severely overvalued against the US dollar at $2.40 early in 1981.

(iii) **1981–1985.** Thus for a time the pound freely floated, the monetarist Conservative Government having announced that in its view 'markets know best' and that any attempt by government to interfere with market forces was doomed to failure. Soon, however, speculative flows turned against sterling and moved in favour of the dollar, culminating in January 1985 in a massive speculative run against the £ which carried the exchange rate down to an all time historical 'low' of approximately £1 = $1.

(iv) **1985 onwards**. In January 1985 the pound was as clearly undervalued as it had been overvalued four years earlier. Perhaps in reaction to this obvious failure of markets to 'know best', the Conservative Government abandoned its earlier policy of **'benign neglect'** and began once again to intervene actively in the foreign exchange market to influence the sterling exchange rate.

Since 1985, the UK government seems to have adopted an 'unofficial' target for sterling which 'shadows' the currencies of the **European Monetary System (EMS)**. Many commentators believe that this may be in preparation for an eventual full entry of the pound to the system of fixed exchange rates operated by the EMS. Further evidence of the 'U'-turn undertaken by the Conservative Government away from floating exchange rates has been provided by the policy of seven leading industrial nations including the UK - known as the **Group of Seven, or G7** - to intervene collectively in foreign exchange markets to support the US dollar. However, managed intervention by G7 has not always been successful in the face of severe speculative flows into and out of the dollar. There are always great difficulties in persuading independent nations to take effective concerted action to manage the world's exchange rates by defending vulnerable currencies against 'hot money' movements.

In the late 1980s, a 'high' exchange rate has also been used by the UK government as perhaps the main instrument in its counter-inflation policy. The Conservative Government has hoped that a high exchange rate will act as a discipline against domestic inflationary pressure.

THE EUROPEAN MONETARY SYSTEM

18. The **European Monetary System (EMS)**, which began operations in 1979, is both a revival of the **fixed peg** exchange rate system (which we examined earlier in the context of the Bretton Woods System), and a **'joint float'** of the EEC currencies against the currencies of the rest of the world. The currencies of the EMS members are fixed against each other, but with rather wider zones of flexibility than under the old Bretton Woods System, via a specially created artificial standard or measure, the **European Currency Unit (ECU)**. Inside the 'joint float', currencies can move within the relatively wide and overlapping zones of flexibility. And because the EMS rules allow for periodic readjustments or realignments of the zones of flexibility against the ECU, and require action by both surplus and deficit nations to keep the currencies within the permitted bands, the EMS is designed to be considerably more flexible or less rigid than the now defunct Bretton Woods System.

THE UK AND THE EMS

19. Initially, the United Kingdom decided to remain outside the EMS, at least as a full member committed to the EMS exchange rate arrangements, but this decision contradicts the spirit if not the rules of the EEC membership. With erratically floating exchange rates, it was difficult to implement the common economic policies of the EEC, such as the Common Agricultural Policy. The members of the EEC established the EMS so that the Common Market might function better. For the United Kingdom therefore, the costs and benefits of joining the EMS ought to be closely associated with the costs and benefits of developing the common economic policies of the EEC.

We have already noted that in recent years the sterling exchange rate has been managed so as to 'shadow' movements of EEC currencies, particularly the Deutschmark. If the UK does eventually become a full member of the EMS, a major benefit should be the ability to draw on the help of other members to deter destabilising 'hot money' movements into and out of sterling. Britain might also benefit if a successfully established EMS eventually develops the ECU into a new source of world liquidity additional to the dollar which is capable of taking pressure off the reserve role of the dollar.

However, the UK might also suffer the disadvantages of any system of relatively fixed exchange rates. The EMS has tended to become a 'Deutschmark area' in which the West German mark is the key currency. In the 'joint float' a strong DM tends to pull up the fixed values of the other currencies, leading to overvaluation against the rest of the world. Although the zones of flexibility are designed to prevent this happening, great pressure could still be placed on weaker EMS currencies, particularly if member countries experience divergent inflation rates. In Britain's case, the domestic costs of lost output and higher unemployment resulting from the deflationary policies necessary to reduce the inflation rate is regarded by some economists as too high a cost to merit full entry to the EMS. Lastly, the role of sterling as a reserve currency and source of international liquidity might create problems. The volume of sterling owned outside the UK and the attraction of London as a centre for 'hot money' operators have caused greater fluctuations in the sterling exchange rate than in most other European exchange rates. This might place even greater pressure on the UK government to deflate the British economy in order to keep the sterling exchange rate steady against the EMS currencies.

THE INTERNATIONAL MONETARY FUND

20. In earlier chapters we have explained how, in the years following the Second World War, Keynesian economic policies were adopted **within** countries to pursue the objectives of growth and full employment through an extension of government intervention in the domestic economy. Keynesian economic policies were a response to the Great Depression and to the large-scale unemployment of the inter-war years. In part, however, the Great Depression had been caused, and certainly made worse, by the collapse of world trade which followed the breakdown of the Gold Standard system in 1931. Perhaps it is not surprising therefore, that the 1940s were also the decade in which interventionism was extended to the management of exchange rates, through the creation of the **International Money Fund (IMF).**

The principal objective of the IMF has been to promote a growing and freer system of world trade and payments. To achieve this general objective, the original Articles of Agreement of the International Monetary Fund specified that the IMF should:

(i) promote international monetary co-operation;

(ii) promote stable exchange rates, maintain orderly exchange arrangements and avoid competitive exchange depreciation;

(iii) encourage full convertibility between currencies and an ending of exchange controls;

(iv) lend its resources to countries to enable them to correct payments imbalances without resorting to harmful restrictions on trade;

(v) shorten periods of disequilibrium in the balance of payments of member countries.

Certainly, over the forty year period since the establishment of the IMF, objectives (i) and (iii) have been achieved, at least among the richer members of the IMF, though not for most developing country members. However, the influence of the IMF upon the stability of exchange rates has diminished rather than increased and it is debatable whether the activities of the IMF have had much effect upon the length of periods of payments imbalance or upon the ease with which payments deficits can be cured.

The three main **roles** adopted by the IMF have been:

(i) an **advisory role** as a consultant giving expert advice to members.

(ii) **'policing' the Bretton Woods System of exchange rates**, until the system broke down in 1971/72. In recent years the IMF has tried, rather ineffectively, to produce orderly conditions in a world of 'dirty' floating. In recent years the IMF's policing role has been directed less at regulating exchange rates, than at limiting the freedom of deficit countries, who wish to borrow from the Fund, to pursue the domestic economic policies of their choice. Although initially established to reflect Keynesian ideas of economic management, the IMF is now generally monetarist in both aim and action. As a result, countries are usually required to adopt 'sound' monetarist policies as a condition for the extension of IMF credit. Developing countries in particular, have been severely hit by the deflationary policies forced on them as a condition of IMF loans.

(iii) **a banking role**. In 1944 the Bretton Woods Agreement hoped to promote the orderly development of world trade by ensuring an adequate supply of **international liquidity** to tide deficit countries over temporary payments difficulties. The dollar provided the main source of **primary liquidity**, but its own weakening eventually contributed to the downfall of the Bretton Woods exchange rates. To supplement the primary liquidity provided by the dollar, specially created **IMF reserves** were intended to supply a source of **secondary liquidity**. Initially, when the IMF was first set up, each member paid a **quota** (75 per cent in its own currency and 25 per cent in gold) into an IMF 'basket' or pool of currency reserves which were then available for member countries to draw upon when experiencing a payment deficit. In the event of a temporary payments deficit, the first part of a country's drawing entitlement is automatic, but beyond a certain limit the IMF can impose conditions upon a further loan. At regular intervals since 1944, the size of quotas and the IMF's overall reserves have been increased.

Other methods of lending, additional to IMF currency reserves, have also been created. These include (i) the creation of **stand-by credits** in the 1950s; (ii) **currency swaps** and the **General Agreement to Borrow (GAB)** in 1962, under which ten leading industrial members, the **Group of Ten (G10)**, agreed to support each other's currencies through a supplementary IMF pool; and (iii) the **Special Drawings Rights (SDR)** scheme initially established in 1970.

SDRs illustrate an important aspect of the Fund's banking function. The Bretton Woods Agreement which set up the IMF was really a compromise between the radical and ambitious **Keynes Plan** put forward by the UK, and the much more conservative **White Plan** advocated by the USA. Keynes wished the new institution to be a **world 'super bank'** issuing a **world trading currency (bancor)** which Keynes hoped would replace gold and national currencies in financing world trade. If the Keynes plan had been adopted, the IMF might have been able to increase the supply of world liquidity without having to use national currencies such as the dollar. But because world trade grew faster in the 1950s and 1960s than the supply of IMF reserves, the burden of financing world trade fell upon the dollar, imposing the strains upon the currency which led eventually in 1971/72 to the collapse of the Bretton Woods System of exchange rates.

Before the creation of SDRs, the Fund's lending ability was restricted by the size of IMF currency reserves deposited by members. The IMF could only lend what it possessed, and many currencies in its reserves were too 'soft' to be acceptable for trade. With the creation of SDRs or **'paper gold'**, the IMF developed a role rather similar to a domestic bank within a country - for the first time the Fund could expand its lending ability beyond the size of the currencies deposited with it by members. SDRs are essentially **book-keeping units of account** allocated by the IMF to each member country. In principle, the allocation of SDRs can be expanded to keep pace with the growth of world trade. However, the usefulness of SDRs depends upon their acceptability and SDRs have never been very acceptable. Because many countries lack trust in SDRs, their creation has not really solved the problem of world liquidity. They regard SDRs as artificial man-made assets, far inferior to gold, the asset which has proved its value as a means of payment over thousands of years.

SUMMARY

21. In this chapter we have examined three types of exchange rate regime - freely floating, fixed and managed - and we have seen how the international monetary system has developed over the years. In many ways, the current situation resembles the position in the 1940s, when disenchantment with the instability of floating exchange rates led to the creation of the IMF, and the relatively rigid Bretton Woods system of managed exchange rates. Following the experience of freely floating exchange rates in the 1970s and 1980s, managed exchange rates have once again returned to favour. Supporters of managed and relatively fixed exchange rates argue that their stability represents a form of 'public good' shared by all, which, by reducing uncertainty, is conducive to the efficient use of the world's resources and to the growth of output and trade. Secondly, relatively fixed exchange rates impose 'rules of the game' which act as a source of external discipline on policy makers and economic agents within countries. By imposing discipline,

the exchange rate reduces inflation within countries, both by directly discouraging inflationary wage and price rises and also, less directly by lowering inflationary expectations.

In 1989, the system of world exchange rates can be summarised as follows. There are three basic currencies, the dollar, the Deutschmark and the yen, widely used as reserve currencies and as sources of international liquidity. One hundred and twenty eight other currencies are either formally pegged (or more usually informally linked) to one or other of the three key currencies, the EEC currencies (except sterling) being pegged to the DM via the arrangements of the European Monetary System. Although sterling does not participate fully in the EMS exchange rate mechanism, the sterling exchange rate has been 'shadowing' EMS exchange rates on an ad hoc basis. Although most other currencies are essentially 'satellite' currencies to either the dollar, the DM or the yen, sterling, the French franc and the Swiss franc also perform relatively minor roles as reserve assets and as pegs for a limited number of other currencies - in the case of the UK and France, these being ex-colonial countries with strong political and economic ties with the former Imperial 'mother' country.

STUDENT SELF-TESTING

1 *List three ways in which a country's exchange rate can be measured.* (2)

2 *Using a supply and demand diagram, show the determination of a freely-floating exchange rate.* (3)

3 *What is the condition for exchange rate stability?* (4)

4 *How is adjustment achieved in a fixed exchange rate system?* (5)

5 *Illustrate the adjustment process in a fixed exchange rate system, using a Keynesian 45° line diagram.* (6)

6 *What happens to the money supply in the event of a balance of payments surplus when the exchange rate is fixed?* (7)

7 *List the advantages of a floating exchange rate.* (8)

8 *List the disadvantages of a floating exchange rate.* (9)

9 *How may a fixed exchange rate discipline inflationary behaviour?* (9,10)

10 *List three types of of managed exchange rate.* (12)

11 *What was the key currency in the Bretton Woods system?* (13)

12 *How did the fixed peg principle function in the Bretton Wood system?* (14)

13 *Why did the Bretton Wood System break down?* (15)

14 *Distinguish between the 'dirty' and 'clean' floating.* (16)

15 *Briefly describe the four phases of 'dirty' floating by the UK.* (17)

16 *What is the key currency in the European Monetary System?* (18)

17 *What roles has the International Monetary Fund pursued?* (19)

EXERCISES

1. (a) *Explain the meaning of the Sterling Index shown in Figure 25.4*

   (b) *Why is the sterling index considered to be a better measure of the United Kingdom's exchange rate and competit-iveness than the dollar exchnge rate?*

   (c) *Suggest reasons for the changes in the United Kingdom's exchange rate shown in Figure 22.4.*

Figure 25.4: Sterling exchange rates

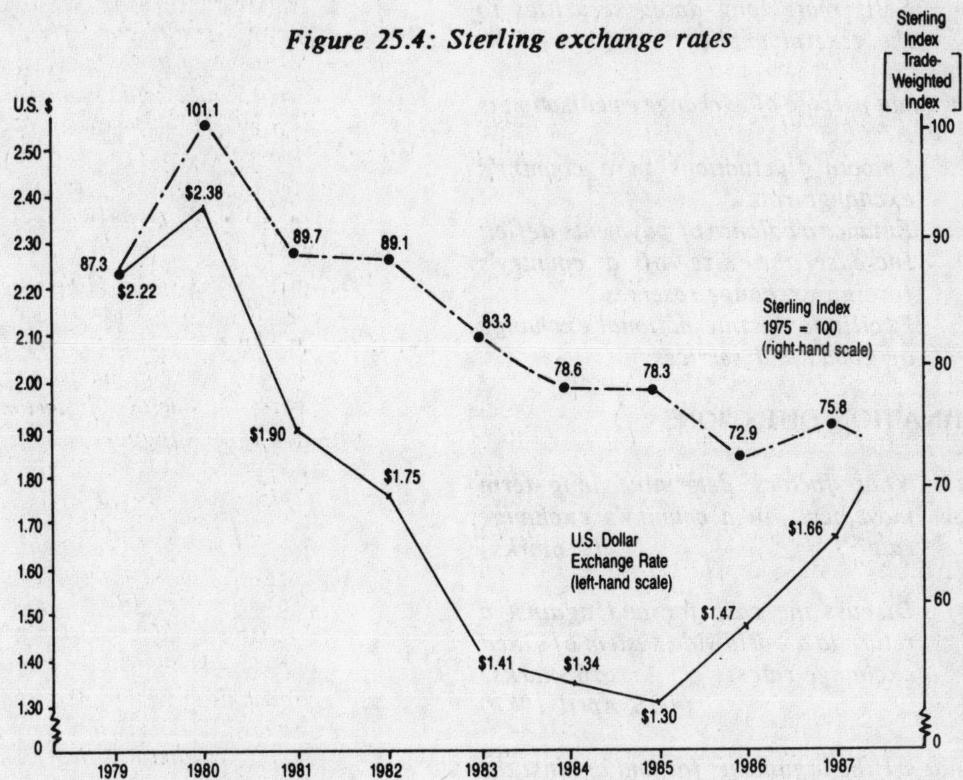

MULTIPLE CHOICE QUESTIONS

1 *Other things being equal, which of the following is* **unlikely** *to lead to a fall in the exchange rate of the UK pound?*
- A *A fall in UK interest rates*
- B *The Bank of England selling sterling for foreign currencies*
- C *A fall in the UK inflation rate*
- D *A 'hot money', move into the US dollar*

2 *Devaluation of a fixed exchange rate, or a downward float,* **must** *have the effect of:*
- A *Improving the terms of trade*
- B *Improving the balance of trade*
- C *Worsening the terms of trade*
- D *Worsening the balance of trade*

3 *Which of the following is most likely to occur if a country experiences a rate of wage inflation higher than the rest of the world, and a rising exchange rate caused by an inward 'hot money' flow?*
- A *An increase in domestic fixed capital formation*
- B *An increase in unemployment*
- C *An increase in exports*
- D *An increase in company profits*

4 *In a system of fixed exchange rates, a balance of payments surplus will cause a country's money supply to rise unless the central bank:*
- A *Imposes exchange controls which limit the outflow of capital*
- B *Imposes import controls*
- C *Sells its own currency and buys reserves*
- D *Sells more long-dated securities to the general public*

5 *The main purpose of exchange equalisation is to:*
- A *Smooth fluctuations in a country's exchange rate*
- B *Finance a balance of payments deficit*
- C *Increase the size of a country's foreign exchange reserves*
- D *Facilitate the international exchange of goods and services*

EXAMINATION QUESTIONS

1 (a) *What factors determine long-term movements in a country's exchange rate?* *(9 marks)*

(b) *Discuss the case for and against a return to a worldwide system of fixed exchange rates.* *(16 marks)*

(IOB April 1987)

2 *What are the arguments for and against the adopting of*
(a) *floating; and*
(b) *fixed rates of exchange.* *(20 marks)*

(ACCA June 1987)

3 (a) *What factors determine exchange rates?*
(b) *At certain times a country's currency may be strong. At others it may be weak. Outline the problems which both these situations pose to governments.*

(ACCA June 1982)

4 *What are the main functions of the International Monetary Fund now that most countries have adopted managed floating exchange rates and the members of the Organisation of Petroleum Exporting Countries have persistent balance of payments surpluses.*

(ACCA December 1978)

5. (a) *Describe the nature and purpose of exchange controls.* *(8 marks)*

(b) *What are the advantages and disadvantages of these controls?* *(12 marks)*

(CIMA May 1987)

Answers to end of chapter exercises and questions

ANSWERS TO QUESTIONS IN CHAPTER 1

EXERCISES

1 *(a)* *(i)* *command*

(ii) *market*

(iii) *mixed, becoming more of a market economy*

(iv) *market*

(v) *mixed*

(vi) *command.*

(b) *On the basis of degree of development: developing, industrialised economies, etc; First World Third World, etc; North/South divisions.*

MULTIPLE CHOICE QUESTIONS

1 *D*
2 *B*
3 *A*
4 *B*
5 *B*

EXAMINATION QUESTIONS

Q1 *(a)* *It is useful to start off an answer to this question with a definition of a command economy. In contrast to a market economy which is characterised by private property and individual decentralised decision-making, a command economy is characterised by socialised ownership and the centralised decision-making undertaken by planners, who are usually part of the machinery of a centralised state. Although you can mention the political implications of a command economy in relation to personal freedoms etc, the question is implicitly about economic advantages and disadvantages. It is worth making the point that in an abstract model the centralised planning of the command mechanism can produce exactly the same allocation of goods and services as could be achieved in a perfectly competitive market economy, but the command economies of the real world are very different. Because of the logistic impossibility of implementing a full command economy, real world command economies, such as the Soviet Union, are 'command economies with some household choice'. Remember also to discuss to whom the advantages and disadvantages may accrue. Advantages to the state may not necessarily result in advantages to a lot of individuals.*

(b) *The main justification for government intervention in a free market system is to correct 'market failure', while ensuring that the market mechanism is left free to continue to provide 'private goods' in competitive markets. The main 'market failures', which we discuss in detail in Chapter 11, including failure to provide public goods; underprovision of merit goods and positive externalities; over-provision of demerit goods and negative externalities; monopoly and produce sovereignty; 'missing markets'; 'short-termism v long-termism'; inequitable distributions of income and wealth; and unemployment and wasted resources.*

ANSWER PLAN

(a) *(i)* *Define a command economy.*

(ii) *List and briefly discuss possible advantages, eg maximisation of social benefit rather than private benefit; ability to take a 'long-term' viewpoint; avoidance of the exploitative features of private enterprise, etc.*

(ii) List and briefly discuss possible disadvantages, eg bureaucratic costs; lack of consumer sovereignty; reduction of individual freedoms, etc.

(b) (i) Justify government intervention in terms of correcting 'market failure' and thus improving upon the market in terms of improved efficiency and equity.

(ii) Illustrate with examples, eg the need to provide public goods; the need to alter the distribution of income etc.

Q2 *(a) In principle a mixed economy contains a mix of both market and non-market provision of goods and services, and private and public ownership. It is a pragmatic response to the fact that many, if not most, goods and services, can be classified as private goods which the market is good at providing, but there are a number of market failures (which we listed in the context of Question 1 where there is a case for state and non-market provision).*

(b) The extent to which an economy is mixed depends in part upon historical factors and (in a democracy) on what people have voted for at the ballot box. Marxists argue that a mixed economy is really just a capitalist economy in which the state has taken over some economic functions in order to create conditions in which capitalism can continue to produce profitability. Other economists argue an opposite case - that the taxation needed to finance public sector non-market provision of goods and services in a market economy creates a burden upon the market sector. This latter view lies behind the deliberate attack upon the mixed economy in the UK in recent years - increasing market and private sector provision, and reducing non-market and public sector economic activity.

ANSWER PLAN

(a) (i) Define a mixed economy.

(ii) Explain it as a compromise between market (and private enterprise) provision of goods and services on the one hand and non-market (and public enterprise) provision on the other hand.

(iii) Illustrate in terms of what markets are good at (eg the provision of private goods in competitive markets), and bad at (eg dealing with 'market failure').

(b) (i) Explain the development of a political consensus around the virtues of a mixed economy in countries such as the UK after 1945.

(ii) Explain the reasons for the breakdown of this consensus and the shift of the system (or the alteration of the mix) towards a social market economy.

Q3 ANSWER PLAN

(a) (i) State the basic economic problem and divide it into the three problems of what, how and for whom to produce.

(ii) Explain that the statement in the question assumes that the third of these issues is the most important, ie the 'cut of the cake' is more important than the 'size of the cake'.

(b) (i) However, there may be a conflict between distributing 'the cake' and ensuring the growth of a large enough 'cake' to achieve satisfactory living standards for all. This is the conf-

lict between equity and efficiency. An equitable distribution may reduce the growth rate, for example through its effect on incentives.

(ii) *A pure market economy (the USA is an approximation) ignores questions of equity and distribution and leaves everything to market forces. A command economy such as the USSR uses the planning mechanism to achieve a more equitable distribution, perhaps achieved at the expense of efficiency and growth. A mixed economy, eg the UK in the 1970s, uses progressive taxation and public spending transfers to modify the market distribution of income.*

(c) *Discuss the problems of each, eg inequality as a 'market failure' in a pure market economy; destruction of personal incentives in a command economy or in a mixed economy with a highly progressive tax system.*

Q4 *Although we have not explicitly mentioned the concept in Chapter 1, an* opportunity cost *arises whenever a choice has to be made in conditions of scarcity. The use of a resource for one purpose precludes its use in any other way. Income received by a business could be spent on extra machinery or capital goods, or on hiring extra labour, but a single unit of income could not be spent simultaneously on both. If a firm spends all its income on capital goods, then the opportunity cost is the sacrificed opportunity to spend the same income on some alternative, such as hiring more labour. The choice involves a sacrifice or cost - an opportunity cost or alternative cost. And since we assume that rational economic agents always act in their best interest, the opportunity cost of any decision rationally undertaken must, therefore, be the next best alternative foregone.*

The concept of opportunity cost is of great value in economic analysis. Every decision taken in conditions of scarcity involves an opportunity cost, whether taken by individuals, businesses or governments. This is obviously the case when monetary expenditure is involved, but an opportunity cost also exists when goods or resources are available free, if only because time and possibly storage capacity are scarce. Thus the decision to watch a television programme involves an opportunity cost, for example the sacrificed opportunity to spend half an hour reading a book. In this example time is scarce. When a purchase price is involved, the price paid can often be used as a measure of the opportunity cost. If for example a newspaper is bought for 50 pence, the same 50 pence cannot be spent on other goods or services. 50 pence is thus the opportunity cost of purchasing the newspaper. But although opportunity cost can often be measured in this way in monetary units, the concept of opportunity cost tends to be used in abstract analysis in economic theory, and is not a term used by accountants. Nevertheless, it is highly practical to consider the opportunity cost of business decisions. Imagine a firm which owns a stock of raw materials purchased by the firm several months ago for £10 million. The firm is considering whether to accept a manufacturing contract which would use up the stock of raw materials. If the firm rejects the contract it would have to sell the raw materials for £4 million. The opportunity cost of using the stockpile of raw materials on the contract is therefore £4 million and not the £10 million stock value recorded in the company's accounts. £4 million is the value of the sacrifice made if the contract is accepted.

ANSWER PLAN

(i) *Define precisely the concept of opportunity cost.*

(ii) *Relate opportunity cost to choice in*

conditions of scarcity.

(*iii*) *Explain, with examples, how decisions made by individuals, businesses and governments all involve as an opportunity cost.*

(*iv*) *Give examples of the practical importance of the concept, eg the cost to society, involving the sacrificed opportunity to have more and better hospitals, if the government decides to purchase more nuclear weapons.*

ANSWERS TO QUESTIONS IN CHAPTER 2

EXERCISES

1 (*a*) *Ex ante demand is intended or planned demand. Ex post demand is actual, fulfilled or realised demand. A demand curve always show ex ante or planned demand at various possible prices.*

(*b*) *Actual demand ≡ actual supply is an identify, indicating that the amount bought (actual or ex post demand) must always equal or be identical to the amount sold (actual or ex post supply).*

(*c*) *A shift in supply occurs when one of the variables influencing supply - other than the good's own price - changes. A new supply curve must be drawn. By contrast when the good's own price changes - in response to a shift in demand - an adjustment takes place along the supply curve as firms decide how much they are willing to supply at the new price.*

2 (*a*) (*i*) *The price of natural rubber was depressed by the demand curve for natural rubber shifting leftwards. This was caused by rubber-using industries running down their stocks of previously bought rubber. The destocking of rubber was a response to higher interest rates. The interest rate is the opportunity cost of holding a stock - the funds tied up in the stock of stored rubber could instead earn the rate of interest.*

(*ii*) *Climatic conditions would increase the yield of rubber trees, thereby shifting the supply of natural rubber rightwards.*

(*b*) (*i*) *Free market forces tend to reduce the market price of natural rubber when, for example, an increase in the number of rubber producers shifts the supply curve rightwards. By purchasing buffer stock, the International Rubber Agreement can create extra demand for rubber - effectively shifting the demand curve rightwards - which prevents the price from falling.*

(*ii*) *If the supply curve of rubber shifts permanently rightwards, the members of the IRA might find themselves permanently intervening to purchase a buffer stock, never being able to release part of the buffer stock onto the market to depress a price rise. Besides encountering problems of storage, the IRA would then face the problem of how to finance the cost of purchasing huge quantities of rubber. Individual members of the IRA might renege on the agreement, perhaps causing its collapse.*

MULTIPLE CHOICE QUESTIONS

1 *B*
2 *D*
3 *A*
4 *D*
5 *A*

EXAMINATION QUESTIONS

Q1 *The use of the price mechanism does not presuppose any particular institutional set-up; in principle it can be applied - perhaps through shadow pricing - to socialist and command economies as well as to market and capitalist economies. You might begin with a brief statement of the signalling and incentive functions of prices in a market economy, going on then to describe how in a competitive economy the market mechanism results in goods being produced which consumers want - the idea of consumer sovereignty. Other advantages of the price mechanism result from its decentralised nature - cost of bureaucracy and state administration are largely eliminated when the price mechanism operates in a market economy - and also from the productive and allocative efficiency it achieves in a competitive economy. The disadvantages of the price mechanism include the under-provision of public goods and merit goods and the over-provision of demerit goods. Obviously therefore, there is a case against the provision of these goods through the price mechanism alone. Alternative provision, for example through public spending financed from taxation, or through prices modified by taxation or subsidy, is more appropriate for public goods, merit goods and demerit goods. But the price mechanism provides probably the most efficient mechanism for allocating most goods and services to final users.*

ANSWER PLAN

(i) *Briefly describe the price mechanism.*

(ii) *Explain the signalling and incentive functions of prices.*

(iii) *List and briefly explain the advantages of the price mechanism.*

(iv) *Explain the circumstances when the price mechanism fails to operate properly, eg monopoly.*

(v) *Some goods such as public goods and merit goods are under-provided by the price mechanism.*

(vi) *Others, called demerit goods, are over-provided.*

(vii) *But the provision of 'private goods' is usually best left to the market.*

Q2 *The explanation of fluctuating agricultural prices is given in sections 11 and 12 of Chapter 2, to which you should now refer. It is often argued that the prices of manufactured goods fluctuate much less than agricultural prices because of the nature of the production process in manufacturing. Output or supply can be adjusted to demand more easily and at less cost than is possible with many agricultural products. Manufacturers can hold stocks both of raw materials and also of finished goods, whereas many agricultural products are perishable and difficult to store. Agricultural production is also characterised by thousands of small producers - for many products scattered world wide. Oligopoly and monopoly are notable by their absence in agricultural markets - though producers' cartels may attempt to create a similar producer sovereignty. Generally, agricultural producers are passive 'price takers' who - unlike - multi-national manufacturing companies - are unable to manage markets and set selling prices. It would be worthwhile, however, to include brief details of any exceptions to the rule - examples of processed foods produced by large 'agri-business' companies compared to 'manufactured' products such as petrol whose prices have fluctuated considerably in recent years.*

ANSWER PLAN

(i) *Distinguish long-term trends in agri-*

cultural prices from year-to-year fluctuations in price.

(ii) *Explain short-term fluctuations in terms of shifts in supply - caused for example by good and bad harvests, along a demand curve that may be relatively inelastic.*

(iii) *Explain fluctuations caused by supply lags, eg the 'cobweb' theory.*

(iv) *Discuss other causes of fluctuations, eg the effects of large numbers of scattered producers, unable to control the market.*

(v) *Explain why many manufactured products exhibit less price fluctuation, eg the ease of stocking raw materials and finished goods; short production periods; producer sovereignty, etc.*

(vi) *Briefly note that there may be exceptions to the rule.*

Q3 *We have already discussed possible causes of fluctuations in agricultural prices in the context of Question 2. Two methods of stabilising prices are through a 'buffer stock' scheme involving support-buying and through a 'deficiency payments' scheme. Both of these are described in detail in Chapter 2. Do note however, that intervention prices (used in a buffer scheme) which stabilise agricultural prices may not necessarily stabilise farmers' incomes.*

ANSWER PLAN

(i) *Show how agricultural prices may fluctuate when year-to-year (or short-run) supply curves shift up or down the demand curve.*

(ii) *Describe how a buffer-stock scheme can be used to stabilise prices.*

(iii) *Consumers may benefit from stability, but prices may be higher (in some years) than they would be otherwise.*

(iv) *There will also be a burden on taxpayers who finance the scheme.*

(v) *Price stability may be at the expense of increased instability of farmers' incomes.*

(vi) *Discuss other disadvantages of a buffer stock policy - eg overproduction.*

(vii) *Describe how a buffer stock policy can stabilise farmers' incomes rather than product prices. Discuss possible advantages and disadvantages.*

(viii) *Describe a deficiency payments system (as operated in the UK before 1973). Both prices and farmers' incomes can be stabilised, but it may be expensive for the taxpayer.*

Q4 ANSWER PLAN

'Black markets', or secondary markets, may be legal or illegal. Illegal 'black markets' occur when the government outlaws the trade in a good or service, eg demerit goods such as harmful drugs, or the slavery market. However, 'black markets' in cup final or concert tickets are normally perfectly legal. They result from an inelastic supply of tickets in conditions in which the official supplier of the tickets (eg the Football Association in the UK) sets its selling price or supply price below the free market price. The resulting effect is similar to when the government imposes a maximum legal price at which trading can take place, setting the maximum price below the free market equilibrium price. The effect is shown in the diagram on the next page.

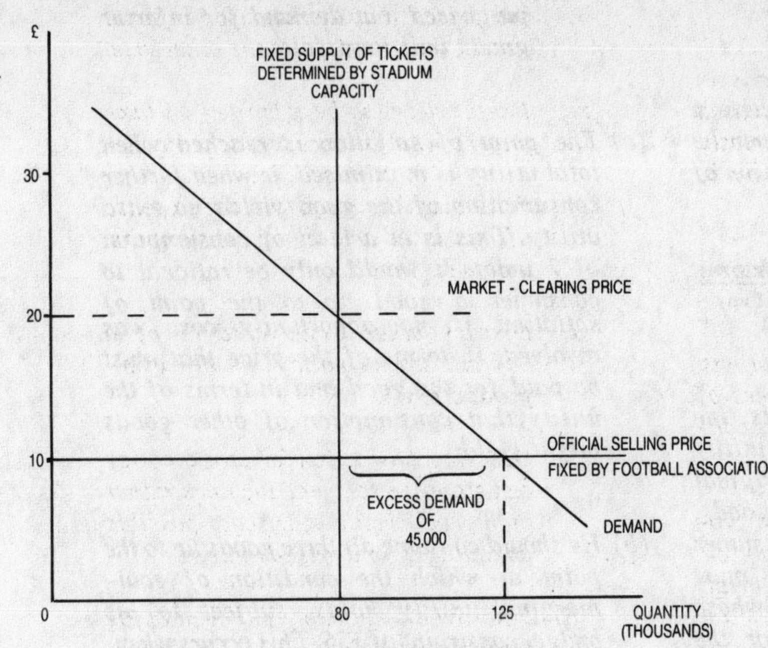

Figure 2.14: The emergence of a 'black market' for cup final tickets

The supply curve of tickets is the vertical line drawn through the capacity of the stadium, assumed to be 80,000. The demand curve shows how many tickets are demanded at each price (for simplicity we are assuming that all seats in the stadium are of the same comfort and that the game can be watched equally well from any part of the stadium). If the tickets were auctioned by the Football Association before the match, a free market price of £20 per ticket would result, with no excess supply or demand in the market. But instead of auctioning the tickets, the Football Association fixes the selling price at £10 per ticket and then proceeds to sell the tickets at this price. The tickets might be sold on a 'first come first served' basis, or a system of allocation to soccer fans through the football clubs might be used. Either way excess demand of 45,000 exists at the fixed price of £10, since 125,000 people wish to purchase tickets at this price.

At the price of £10 per ticket, 80,000 football fans are 'lucky' in the sense that they succeed in purchasing a ticket at this price. But 45,000 have been 'unlucky' - wishing to buy a ticket but failing to purchase one because of deficient supply. This creates the incentive for a 'black market' to emerge. A 'black market' is a meeting of some of the 'lucky' 80,000 who are prepared to re-sell their tickets at a price higher than £10 and those of the 'unlucky' 45,000 who are prepared to pay a price higher than £10. Ticket touts or spivs act as intermediaries between buyers and sellers in the 'black market' and tickets may also be advertised for sale in newspapers. However, 'black markets' are frequently characterised by imperfect market information and by a number of different prices existing in different parts of the market.

ANSWER PLAN

(i) Briefly explain the meaning of a 'black market'.

(ii) Explain how the incentive for a 'black market' to come into existence is created by holding the official price of tickets below the market-clearing price.

(iii) Illustrate this on a diagram.

(iv) Explain how the 'black market' deals with the excess demand for tickets.

(v) Briefly mention typical characteristics of 'black markets': informational problems; the role of 'middlemen' or ticket touts, etc.

ANSWERS TO QUESTIONS IN CHAPTER 3

EXERCISES

1(a) *Assuming a utility maximising objective, a consumer will be in equilibrium when he spends his income so that the condition of equi-marginal utility holds:*

$$\frac{\text{MU good A}}{\text{Price of good A}} = \frac{\text{MU good B}}{\text{Price of good B}} = \ldots \frac{\text{MU any good}}{\text{Price of any good}}$$

(b) (i) *If the price of good A falls, the condition of equi-marginal utility will no longer hold at the original levels of consumption of all goods. To return to a state of consumer equilibrium, our consumer must substitute more of good A (whose relative price has fallen) for the other goods, whose relative prices (though not their absolute prices) have correspondingly risen. However, there will also be an income effect operating, the nature of which depends on whether good A is a normal good or an inferior good. The consumer's real income increases as a result of the price fall and, feeling better off, he demands less of the inferior good. For most inferior goods, the income effect of the price change is not sufficiently strong to offset the substitution effect. However, there is an 'extreme' possibility that good A is a Giffen good. A Giffen good is not only inferior - the income effect of the price change is stronger than the substitution effect. Demand will fall for good A following a price fall if good A is a Giffen good.*

(ii) *A fall in the general level leaves relative prices unchanged but increases the consumer's real income. In the new equilibrium increased quantities of normal goods will be purchased, but demand for inferior goods will have fallen.*

2(a) *The point of satiation is reached when total utility is maximised, ie when further consumption of the good yields no extra utility. This is at a level of consumption of 7 units. It would only be rational to consumer a good up to the point of satiation if no opportunity cost was involved, in terms of the price that must be paid for the good and in terms of the utility that consumption of other goods might yield.*

(b) *He should consume all three goods up to the point at which the condition of equi-marginal utility holds, subject to his budget constraint of £56. This occurs when:*

$$\frac{\text{MUm(24)}}{\text{Price m(£12)}} = \frac{\text{MUv(16)}}{\text{Price v(£8)}} = \frac{\text{MUf(8)}}{\text{Price f(£4)}}$$

He should consume:

(i) *3 units of meat, spending £36 in total and deriving a marginal utility of 24.*

(ii) *1 unit of vegetables, spending £8, and deriving a marginal utility of 16.*

(iii) *3 units of fruit, spending £12, and deriving a marginal utility of 8.*

(c) *In equilibrium, consuming 3 units of fruit, his total utility derived from fruit is 36 units of utility. In equilibrium P = MU so, measured in utility units, the price equals 8 units of utility. Total expenditure measured in utility units is therefore (3 x 8) = 24 units of utility. Consumer surplus which is total utility - expenditure is therefore (36 - 24) = 12 units of utility.*

MULTIPLE CHOICE QUESTIONS

1 *A*
2 *C*
3 *C*
4 *C*
5 *C*

EXAMINATION QUESTIONS

Q1 ANSWER PLAN

(a) *A demand curve maps out how much consumers plan to demand at various possible prices. If price changes (in response to a shift in supply) an adjustment occurs along the demand curve as the consumer responds to the price change. The movement along the demand curve is sometimes known as an extension or contraction of demand. If any of the conditions of demand change, for example income or tastes, the demand curve shifts leftwards (a decrease in demand) or rightwards (an increase in demand).*

(b) *(i)* *An increase in supply (or rightward shift in supply) leads to a rightwards adjustment or movement along the demand curve. More will be demanded at a lower price, providing the demand curve slopes downwards in a conventional manner.*

(ii) *Increased advertising is likely to influence consumers' tastes favourably, causing the demand curve to shift rightwards (an increase in demand). In equilibrium, the price and quantity bought and sold will both rise, assuming a conventional upward-sloping supply curve.*

(iii) *An increase in population is likely to have the same effect as an increase in advertising, though it may take much longer for the effect to occur. An increase in population means that there are more consumers in the market, causing the market demand curve to shift rightwards. The size of the shift will depend in part upon the nature of the good and upon whether population growth is caused by an increase in the birth rate, longer life expectancy or through migration. For example, an increase in the birth rate will have a significant effect upon the demand for prams, but no effect on the demand for walking sticks.*

Q2 *This question can be answered with or without indifference curve analysis. The answer plan is based on indifference curve analysis.*

ANSWER PLAN

(i) *State clearly that both effects relate to an individual's demand for a good, assuming a utility maximising objective.*

(ii) *Show an initial position of consumer equilibrium on an indifference curve 'map' similar to Figure 3.15.*

(iii) *With a diagram similar to Figure 3.16 show how demand for a normal good increases following a fall in its price.*

(iv) *Show, with the aid of a diagram similar to Figure 3.17 how the response can be divided into a substitution effect and an income effect. Explain how the two effects reinforce each other.*

(v) *Show the two effects in the case of an inferior good. Use a diagram similar to Figure 3.18.*

(vi) *Finally, repeat for a Giffen good, using a diagram similar to Figure*

3.19. Explain how in the case of an inferior good, the two effects operate in opposite directions. In the case of a Giffen good, the (perverse) income effects is more powerful, causing less of the good to be demanded following a fall in its price.

Q3 *Orthodox or conventional economic theory (which is sometimes called 'neo-classical' economic theory) centres on the study of* optimisation. *This is the study of economic agents (households, firms and sometimes the government) attempting to maximise or optimise an assumed objective (utility, profit or social welfare). Essentially a private economic agent is assumed to maximise private benefit or self-interest, while the government maximises social welfare or the public interest. In the case of a household or firm, utility or profit is maximised by consuming or demanding a good (in the case of a household) or producing and selling a good (in the case of a firm) up to the point at which:*

marginal private benefit = marginal private cost.

For household demand this is:

marginal utility = price.

For a firm's supply it is:

marginal revenue = marginal cost.

These are just two examples of optimisation or equilibrium conditions which must hold if a household or firm is to succeed in maximising or achieving its assumed objective. In a rather similar way, the public interest or social welfare is maximised when a good is produced and consumed up to the point at which:

marginal social benefit = marginal social cost.

Marginalist conditions such as these therefore occupy a central place in neo-classical theory and analysis. They are especially important in micro-economic analysis, while concepts such as the marginal propensities to consume, save and import, and the marginal tax rate are quite significant in macro-economic analysis.

ANSWER PLAN

(i) *Clearly explain the meaning of 'the margin'.*

(ii) *Illustrate with two or three examples, eg the marginal product or returns of labour, marginal utility, marginal cost etc.*

(iii) *Relate the concept to the assumed optimising or maximising objectives of economic agents.*

(iv) *Illustrate in terms of two or three marginalist conditions, eg MR = MC, MU = P etc.*

(v) *Relate briefly to the 'laws' of diminishing marginal utility and diminishing marginal returns.*

(vi) *Perhaps give a few macro-economic examples of the application of the concept, eg the marginal propensity to save related to the multiplier.*

ANSWERS TO QUESTIONS IN CHAPTER 4

EXERCISES

1 *(a)*

	Total costs			*Average costs*			*Marginal*
Output	*Total*	*Fixed*	*Variable*	*Total*	*Fixed*	*Variable*	*costs*
0	*300*	*300*	*0*	*-*	*-*	*0*	
							240
1	*540*	*300*	*240*	*540*	*300*	*240*	
							140
2	*680*	*300*	*380*	*340*	*150*	*190*	
							70
3	*750*	*300*	*450*	*250*	*100*	*150*	
							202
4	*952*	*300*	*652*	*238*	*75*	*163*	
							248
5	*1,200*	*300*	*900*	*240*	*60*	*180*	
							402
6	*1,602*	*300*	*1,302*	*267*	*50*	*217*	

(b) Break-even even price occurs at the lowest point on the average total cost curve: £238 Shut-down price occurs at the lowest point on the average variable cost curve: £150

(c) Assuming that the Fashionable Furniture Company produces in a perfectly competitive industry, price = MR = £202. The profit maximising output occurs where MR = MC = £202. This is at a level of output of four cupboards. Total revenue is £808; but total cost is £952. The firm would thus make a loss of £144 at this price, but since the variable costs are covered, it should produce the four cupboards - at least in the short run. In the long run the firm should shut down.

2(a) If the firms are passive price-takers, price equals marginal revenue. At each price, each firm should produce the output at which MC = Price.

(i) Firm A
£5 (1 unit)
£10 (2 units)
£20 (4 units)
£50 (answer indeterminate)
£100 (answer indeterminate)

(ii) Firm B
£5 (zero)
£10 (1 unit)
£20 (2 units)
£50 (5 units)
£100 (answer indeterminate)

(iii) Firm C
£5 (zero)
£10 (zero)
£20 (zero)
£50 (1 unit)
£100 (3 units)

(b) If a tax of £10 is imposed. Firm B will now be prepared to supply at a price of £50 the quantity previously supplied at £40: 40 units of output, whereas without the tax it would supply 50 units.

(c) Since marginal costs are rising for each firm, each firm is suffering from diminishing marginal returns as it increases output.

MULTIPLE CHOICE QUESTIONS

1 *D*
2 *A*
3 *C*
4 *C*
5 *C*

EXAMINATION QUESTIONS

Q1 *(a)* *Diminishing returns usually refers to the economic short run, when some of a firm's factors of production (usually capital) are fixed. In the short run a firm can only increase output by adding more of its variable factors of production (eg labour) to the fixed factors. Although increasing marginal returns to labour may be experienced at first, eventually diminishing marginal returns will set in. This occurs when an extra unit of labour adds less to total output than the previous worker who joined the labour force. In the long run, a firm may experience diminishing (or decreasing) returns to scale. However, this is not inevitable - increasing returns to scale and constant returns to scale are other possibilities.*

(b) *Short-run returns influence short-run cost curves, whereas returns to scale influence long-run cost curves. Increasing marginal returns to variable factors of production cause short-run marginal costs to fall, whereas diminishing marginal returns cause marginal costs to rise. Likewise, diminishing average returns to the variable factors of production cause average variable costs to rise. In the long run, if a firm experience diminishing returns to scale, long-run average costs are likely to rise.*

ANSWER PLAN

(a) *(i)* *Distinguish between the short run and the long run.*

(ii) *Explain the law of diminishing marginal returns in the short run.*

(iii) *Relate diminishing marginal returns to diminishing average returns.*

(iv) *Explain diminishing returns to scale in the long run.*

(b) *(i)* *Relate diminishing marginal returns to the firm's short-run marginal cost curve.*

(ii) *Relate diminishing average returns to the firm's short-run average variable cost curve.*

(iii) *Relate diminishing returns to scale to the firm's long-run average cost curve.*

Q2 *The law of diminishing marginal returns plays a similar role in production theory and the derivation of short-run supply curves that the law of diminishing marginal utility plays in consumer theory and the derivation of demand curves. Students often confuse the two laws and use the law of diminishing returns to 'explain' the 'downward-slopingness' of demands curve, or the law of diminishing utility to 'explain' the 'upward-slopingness' of a supply curve. Unfortunately, an examiner can award you no credit for such a fundamental theoretical mistake.*

ANSWER PLAN

(i) *State the law of diminishing marginal returns.*

(ii) *Briefly illustrate the law with a diagram or simple numerical example.*

(iii) *State the law of diminishing marginal utility.*

(iv) *Briefly illustrate the law with a diagram or simple numerical example.*

(v) *Apply the law of diminishing returns, eg in the derivation of the MC curve and supply curve in perfect competition, or in the derivation of the demand curve for labour in perfect competition.*

(vi) *Apply the law of diminishing marginal utility in the derivation of a demand curve.*

Q3 *(a)* *Short-run costs accrue when the firm increases production when at least one of its inputs or factors of production is fixed. You must carefully show the nature of short-run marginal, average and total costs, giving particular emphasis to the 'U'-shaped short-run average cost curve. Long-run cost curves relate to the situation when none of the factors of production are fixed. Show how the long-run average cost curve indicates whether economies or diseconomies of scale are occurring and relate the LRATC curve to returns to scale.*

(b) *Assuming labour cannot be replaced by capital, an increase in wages increases a firm's production costs in both the short run and the long run, though the effect will be smaller to the extent to which the firm can substitute capital for labour. An improvement of technology, which usually favours more capital-intensive methods of production, will shift the firm's long-run cost curves downwards.*

ANSWER PLAN

(a) (i) *Explain how short-run costs occur when at least one factor of production is fixed.*

(ii) *Briefly explain short-run marginal, average and total costs.*

(iii) *Illustrate short-run average costs with a 'U'-shaped cost curve.*

(iv) *Explain how in the long run all the factors of production can be varied.*

(v) *Show how the LRATC curve can display various possible shapes.*

(b) (i) *Show how increased wages raise the firm's production costs, though in the long run there may be scope for replacing labour with more capital intensive methods of production.*

(ii) *Explain how technological improvement reduces long-run production costs.*

Q4 *To answer this question you can draw on the reasons given in Chapter 8 for the growth and survival of small firms, though you must also relate your answer to the theoretical treatment of economies of scale presented in Chapter 4. The central points to make in your answer are that many industries do not exhibit economies of scale and that even when they occur there may be specialised 'niches' in the market for small firms.*

is 1/7 and the proportionate rise in price is 1/6. Elasticity is 1/7 ÷ 1/6, which is 0.86. Note that we would obtain a different figure when calculating the elasticity for a price fall from 35 pence to 30 pence.

(b) *3/7 ÷ 1/9, which is 3.86. Again, the elasticity statistic would be different for a price rise from 40 pence to 45 pence.*

(c) *For this question, we must calculate the elasticity both for a price rise from 35 pence to 40 pence and for a price fall from 40 pence to 35 pence and then take an average.*

For a price rise:
elasticity equals 1/6 ÷ 1/7, which is 1.17

For a price fall:
elasticity equals 1/5 ÷ 1/8, which is 1.6
Averaging, the elasticity is 1.38.

(d) *The proportionate fall in price is a quarter.*

$$(-)0.8 = \frac{\text{proportionate change in quantity demanded}}{(-)0.25}$$

The proportionate change in quantity demanded is thus:

(-)0.8 x (-)0.25 = 0.2

The quantity now demanded is
750 + (0.2 x 750) which is 900

Since the amount bought equals the quantity sold, 900 ice creams will be sold.

MULTIPLE CHOICE QUESTIONS

1 C
2 B
3 D
4 D
5 D

EXAMINATION QUESTIONS

Q1 ANSWER PLAN

(a) (i) *Price elasticity of demand measures the responsiveness of demand to a change in the good's price.*

(ii) *List and explain briefly how the availability of substitutes, the importance of expenditure upon the good in consumers' total budget, the definition of the market and the time period involved all determine price elasticity of demand.*

(iii) *Income elasticity of demand measures the responsiveness of demand to a change in consumers' income.*

(iv) *Cross-elasticity of demand measures the responsiveness of demand for one good to a change in the price of another good.*

(vi) *The existence and strength of a joint demand or a substitute relationship determine the cross-elasticity of demand.*

(b) (i) *Price elasticity is 1/5 ÷ 1/9, which is 1.8. Demand is therefore elastic, this means that a 1 per cent fall in price causes demand to increase by 1.8 per cent (remember the elasticity is really - 1.8).*

(ii) *Price elasticity is 1/9 ÷ 1/5, which is 0.55. Demand is therefore inelastic. A 1 per cent fall in price, now causes demand to increase by only 0.55 of 1 per cent. The two calculations show that price elasticity of demand falls at lower prices as we move down the demand schedule.*

Q2 (a) *See Question 1 for guidance on this part of the question.*

(b) In real life firms are seldom likely to calculate elasticities of demand for their products, but nevertheless, market research techniques often involve collecting information of interest and use to a firm which relates to the elasticity concept. Firms usually wish to know what is likely to happen to consumer demand is they change the price of an established product. Likewise, a firm must judge consumer demand when deciding the launch price for a new product. As we have explained in Chapter 5, knowledge of price elasticity of demand is also important to forecasters and policy makers when deciding upon tax policies, agricultural support policies and policies towards the balance of payments and exchange rates. Income elasticity of demand indicates which products are going to benefit from expanding markets and which are going to decline, when national income is growing and people are becoming better off.

ANSWER PLAN

(a) (i) Define price elasticity of demand.

(ii) List and briefly explain the factors determining price elasticity of demand.

(iii) Define income elasticity of demand.

(iv) List and briefly explain the factors determining income elasticity of demand, taking care to relate the concept to normal and inferior goods.

(b) (i) Discuss: practical for whom? – firms, policy makers, forecasters etc.

(ii) Explain the sense in which price elasticity of demand is of interest to
(a) firms;
(b) policy makers and the government.

(iii) Repeat, for income elasticity of demand.

Q3 ANSWER PLAN

(i) Explain how elasticity measures responsiveness.

(ii) Briefly define, with the aid of elasticity formulae, the principal elasticities of interest to economists: price elasticity of demand; price elasticity of supply; income elasticity of demand; and cross-elasticity of demand.

(iii) Illustrate the meaning of a particular elasticity, eg a price elasticity of demand of (–)2 means that a 10 per cent increase in price may be expected to cause a fall in demand of 20 per cent.

(iv) Explain the importance of price elasticity of demand for analysing:
(a) whether a firm can shift the incidence of a tax onto consumers as a price rise;
(b) whether a devaluation could reduce a balance of payments deficit etc.

(v) Explain the importance of price elasticity of supply for analysing:
(a) the distribution of wage income between economic rent and transfer earnings;
(b) whether domestically-produced output can increase to respond to the price incentive resulting from a devaluation.

ANSWERS TO QUESTION IN CHAPTER 6

EXERCISES

1 (a) *Output 4,000 units; price £6*

(b) *Profit = Total revenue - Total cost*
Profit = £24,000 - £14,000
Profit = £10,000

(c) *£24,000 and £14,000*

(d) *5,000 units of output*

(e) *Output rises to 6,000 units*
Price falls to £4
Total revenue is £24,000
Total cost is now £21,000
Total profit has therefore fallen to £3,000.

2(a) (i) *Sand is a free good, so the island's inhabitants will consume the quantity demanded at zero price: 100 tons.*

(ii) *A monopolist can exercise private property rights and charge a price by restricting supply to below 100 tons. The monopolist's profit-maximising output is where MC = MR. Since MC is zero, profit-maximising output is therefore, where MR is zero, or where TR is maximised. Calculate a total revenue (TR) schedule by multiplying quantity demanded by price at each price. TR is maximised at a level of sales of 50 tons at which total revenue is £2,500. Price is £50 per ton.*

(b) *The allocatively efficient level of production and consumption occurs where P = MC. Since MC are zero, allocative efficiency requires that sand is provided free, with 100 tons being consumed. The monopolist is restricting output and raising price so that P > MC. This is allocatively inefficient - too little is being consumed.*

MULTIPLE CHOICE QUESTIONS

1 C
2 B
3 A
4 A
5 C

EXAMINATION QUESTIONS

Q1 (a) *You must explain that a firm maximises profit at the level of output at which (TR - TC) is maximised, and where MR = MC (providing MC are rising and cutting MR from below). This applies in all market structures, perfect competition, monopoly and imperfect competition, but you should illustrate your answer with at least one example.*

(b) *To answer this part of the question, you should draw on the coverage undertaken in Chapter 7 of 'alternative' theories of the firm. Managerial theories of the firm assume objectives such as sales and growth maximisation and the maximisation of 'managerial' objectives. Behavioural theories replace maximising objectives with the concept of 'satisficing'. You might also include an ad hoc list of possible objectives, such as the desire for a 'quiet life', service to the community, good labour relations etc.*

ANSWER PLAN

(a) (i) *Define profits.*

(ii) *Explain how profits are maximised at the level of output at which (TR - TC) are maximised.*

(iii) *Explain the marginalist rule: MR = MC.*

(iv) Illustrate from at least one market structure, eg perfect competition.

(b) (i) List and discuss 'managerial' objectives.

(ii) Explain possible 'satisficing' objectives.

(iii) Discuss possible objectives particularly relevant to small businesses.

Q2 *The key to understanding this question is the distinction between normal and abnormal profit (above-normal or supernormal profit). Economic theory conventionally assumes that all firms in all market structures - monopoly and imperfect competition as well as perfect competition - aim to make the biggest possible profit. However, any abnormal profit made by firms already established in the industry serves to attract new firms into the market. Given the absence of barriers to entry in a perfectly competitive market, the entry of new firms brings down the ruling market price and market forces compete away the abnormal profits of the established firms. Nevertheless in long run competitive equilibrium, the surviving firms continue to make normal profits, which are analytically treated as a cost of production. Zero abnormal profits are made in long-run equilibrium in a perfectly competitive market.*

ANSWER PLAN

(i) Explain the profit maximising objective of all firms.

(ii) Show on a diagram, perfect competition short-run equilibrium, with abnormal profits being made.

(iii) Explain how the absence of barriers to entry allows new firms to enter the market.

(iv) Show on a diagram, perfect competition long-run equilibrium.

(v) Reconcile the statement by applying the distinction between abnormal and normal profits.

Q3 *You must explain the six conditions or characteristics of perfect competition which are listed in Figure 6.1 of Chapter 6. Then explain that the model of perfect competition is unrealistic because it is impossible for all the characteristics to occur simultaneously. For example, perfect market information is almost impossible and products will almost always be slightly differentiated. Although the assumptions of the model are unrealistic, it may nevertheless provide a useful benchmark or 'yardstick' for assessing the properties of real world market structures - for example in terms of productive and allocative efficiency, consumer sovereignty etc.*

ANSWER PLAN

(i) Define perfect competition in terms of its conditions or characteristics.

(ii) Briefly explain each of the characteristics.

(iii) Discuss the lack of realism of perfect competition.

(iv) Discuss the role of the model of perfect competition as a standard by which to assess the imperfectly competitive market structures of the real world.

(v) State the case against this argument: perfect competition represents a false 'ideal'.

Q4 *(a) You must develop the standard argument that, compared to perfect com-*

petition, monopoly restricts output and raises price and is less efficient in terms of both allocative efficiency and productive efficiency. In addition, monopoly may restrict consumer choice and stifle the development of cost-cutting techniques of production and new product development.

(b) *In Chapter 6 we have developed at length the argument that monopoly can be justified in industries where substantial economies of scale - and resulting gains in productive efficiency - can only be achieved if the market is restricted to only one firm. This is the 'natural' monopoly argument and it is especially powerful in the case of utility industries. Monopolies are also sometimes justified to control production and consumption of demerit goods such as armaments; to 'countervail' the market power of foreign-based multinational firms; and to provide sufficient monopoly profits to finance research and development. This latter argument was first advanced by the Austrian economist Joseph Schumpeter who believed that monopolies - far from stifling technological progress and product development - could provide an engine of growth in the economy.*

We can distinguish between 'cartels', as examples of 'bad' or malign monopoly, and 'fully-unified' monopolies as examples of potentially 'good' or benign monopoly. A cartel is a price ring, usually formed to protect inefficient firms and to exploit the consumer. By contrast, a fully-unified monopoly may simply be a dynamic firm which, through successful growth and the pursuit of economies of scale, has become dominant in an industry. Although, in principle, the firm might begin to exploit its monopoly position, this was not a significant motive which led to the growth of its monopoly power and the monopoly can be justified provided it 'behaves itself'.

ANSWER PLAN

(a) (i) *With the aid of graphs, show how a monopoly restricts output and raises price compared to perfect competition.*

(ii) *Extend the analysis in terms of productive and allocative inefficiency.*

(iii) *Briefly mention any other arguments against monopoly, eg loss of consumer sovereignty.*

(b) (i) *State firmly that economies of scale provide the main case for monopoly.*

(ii) *Illustrate in terms of a 'natural' monopoly such as a utility industry.*

(iii) *Explain other possible advantages of monopoly, eg the ability to finance research and development.*

(iv) *Make the point that a 'fully-unified' monopoly is more likely to achieve these advantages than a 'cartel'.*

Q5 ANSWER PLAN

(i) *Draw two diagrams to show perfect competition short-run equilibrium and monopoly equilibrium.*

(ii) *Briefly explain why they represent equilibrium. (You do* **not** *need to explain the derivation of the curves in the diagram).*

(iii) *Draw a diagram to show perfect competition long-run equilibrium.*

(iv) Explain how market forces and the absence of barriers to entry, bring about the long-run equilibrium.

(v) Explain that barriers to entry prevent the competing away of abnormal profits in monopoly.

(vi) Draw a diagram similar to Figure 6.18 in Chapter 6. Explain that in the absence of economies of scale, industry output is greater and price is lower in perfect competition than in monopoly - in long-run equilibrium.

Q6 *(a) Part (a) of this question is similar to Question 4 and a similar answer plan is appropriate. But because there are two halves to this question, develop your answer in less detail than Question 5.*

(b) Left to themselves, profit-maximising monopolies product the output where MR = MC, but as we have seen this is both productively inefficient (average costs are not minimised) and allocatively inefficient (P > MC). It is sometimes argued that to operate in the public interest, monopolies should be ordered to adopt marginal cost pricing, ie to set price equal to marginal cost. It is generally agreed that if P = MC, allocative efficiency will be achieved, leading to a more efficient use of society's resources. If you refer back to Figure 6.19, you will notice that the profit-maximising output for the monopolist is 4,000 and the profit maximising price is £6. If the monopolist adopts marginal cost pricing, output increases to 6,000 and price falls to £4. Consumers benefit from the greater output available and the lower price. The monopolist still makes some abnormal profit (in Figure 6.19 it is £3,000), though the profit is less than at the profit-maximising level of output.

Of course, the public interest might be interpreted in other ways. There may be a case for setting price equal to ATC, so that the monopolist makes no abnormal profit, or for prices in which one group of customers (for example, the rich) subsidise another group (the poor). This is a case for cross-subsidisation.

ANSWER PLAN

(a) See answer plan for Question 4.

(b) (i) If the public interest is interpreted in terms of allocative efficiency, the monopolist should adopt marginal cost pricing.

(ii) Explain how this will improve allocative efficiency.

(ii) Explain how the interpretations of the public interest could lead to other pricing policies, eg average cost pricing; cross-subsidisation.

ANSWERS TO QUESTIONS IN CHAPTER 7

EXERCISES

1 *This question illustrates the most important feature of competitive oligopoly (or in this case duopoly): when choosing a price and output strategy, each firm needs to take account of the likely reactions of the other firms. There are three possible strategies available to each of the duopolists:*

(a) Pay the bribe, while the other firm does not bribe. Outcome:

(i) for the firm that pays the bribe: $50 million

(ii) for the firm that does not bribe: nothing.

(b) Both pay the bribe. Outcome: Each firm gains $25 million.

(c) A collusive agreement between the two companies, in which the companies agree not to bribe and to share the business between themselves. Outcome: Each firm gains $30 million.

For each firm the best possible outcome is (a), but this involves the worst possible outcome for the other firm. If each firm believes that in a competitive situation, the other firm will offer a bribe, the two firms can improve upon the competitive outcome - outcome (b) - by colluding together and engaging in joint profit maximisation - outcome (c). There is always the possibility however, that one of the firms will 'cheat' on the agreement and secretly bribe the government ministers! A collusive agreement can never completely get rid of uncertainty.

MULTIPLE CHOICE QUESTIONS

1 C
2 C
3 A
4 D
5 B

EXAMINATION QUESTIONS

Q1 ANSWER PLAN

(a) (i) *Draw a diagram, similar to Figure 7.1 in Chapter 7 to show monopolistic competition short-run equilibrium.*

(ii) *Explain that as in any market structure, the profit-maximising output is determined where MR= MC.*

(iii) *Explain how in the short run, the firm can be making abnormal profits, shown by the profits rectangle in the diagram.*

(b) (i) *An increase in rent will increase the firm's fixed costs, which in turn shifts the ATC curve (but not the MC curve) upwards. Profit-maximising price and output will stay the same, but the upward shift of the ATC curve reduces abnormal profits.*

(ii) *An increase in raw materials costs increases the firm's variable costs, which raises both the ATC and the MC curve. The effect is to reduce the profit-maximising level of output, which in turn means that the firm can charge a higher price. However, abnormal profits will be smaller than they were before marginal costs increased.*

Q2 ANSWER PLAN

(i) *Describe the characteristics of monopolistic competition as a market structure.*

(ii) *Draw a diagram to illustrate monopolistic competition long-run equilibrium.*

(iii) *Explain that the profit-maximising level of output (at which MC = MR which is immediately below the point of tangency between AR and ATC) must be at a level of output less than the output where ATC are minimised).*

Q3 *Your answer to part (b) of this question should be similar to the suggested answer for Question 2(b). You should answer part (a) by describing some of the ways in which firms can differentiate their products and by explaining why firms can differentiate their products and why firms may wish to* *introduce differentiation. Products may be differentiated by physical differences such as fashion, design and quality; by marketing devices such as packaging and advertising and by such features as the offer of an after-sales service. The main reason suggested by traditional economic theory for differentiation is to make the demand curve for the product less elastic. In the absence of product differentiation, the firm faces a perfectly elastic demand curve for its product. Product differentiation introduces an element of local monopoly, and allows the firm to increase the price without losing all its customers.*

ANSWER PLAN

(a) (i) *Define production differentiation in terms of a firm deliberately making its product different in one or more ways from competitors' products.*

(ii) *Explain that product differentiation is likely in monopolistic competition and oligopoly.*

(iii) *Besides shifting the demand curve for the firm's product rightwards, the aim is to make demand less elastic, thereby introducing an element of relative monopoly power.*

(iv) *Briefly describe various of the forms that product differentiation can take.*

(b) *Your answer plan to this part of the question should be similar to Question 2(b).*

Q4 *If you base your answer around the theory of the 'kinked' demand curve facing an oligopolist, it is wise to indicate the weaknesses of this theory as an explanation of price rigidity in conditions of oligopoly. The evidence indicates that oligopoly prices are stable in the face of temporary fluctuations in demand, but that oligopolists do in fact change their selling price when production costs increase. The theory of the 'saucer-shaped' AVC curve offers a rather better theory of observed pricing decisions by oligopolists.*

Price-cutting might, of course, increase an individual oligopolist's share of the market in conditions of 'perfect oligopoly', when the products of each of the firms are very close substitutes. However, market share is unlikely to increase if price-cutting causes instant retaliation. Oligopolists are perhaps much more likely to use forms of non-price competition aimed at increasing the differentiation of their products from the goods produced by other firms. Advertising, packaging, design, brand-imaging and the offer of an after-sales service might all be used, together with the acquisition of 'exclusive outlets' for retail sales.

ANSWER PLAN

(i) *Briefly explain the meaning of oligopoly.*

(ii) *Explain how the 'kinked' demand curve theory accounts for price rigidity.*

(iii) *Briefly point out the weaknesses of this explanation.*

(iv) *Describe how the theory of the 'saucer-shaped' AVC curve offers a more convincing explanation.*

(v) *Explain how price-cutting may lead to retaliation and thus be counter-productive as a method of expanding market share.*

(vi) *Briefly describe various methods of increasing the firm's monopoly power through product product differentiation, obtaining exclusive outlets such as petrol stations etc.*

Q5 *A cartel is a price ring formed when members of an oligopolistic industry collude together to agree a single price. They may also artificially restrict output, possibly even 'allocating' customers to particular members of the cartel. International cartels are also possible when producers in various countries - and often their governments - form an agreement to raise the price and restrict output. Cartels are often regarded as the worst form of monopoly, since they artificially restrict competition, raise price and encourage inefficiency, often without any of the benefits associated with monopoly such as economies of scale. Competitive oligopolists may wish to form a cartel to gain an easy life and to increase their monopoly power. Cartel agreements also reduce the uncertainty facing individual firms in a competitive oligopoly. Within countries such as the UK, cartel agreements are usually illegal, so the absence of hostile government policy is obviously a necessary condition for the successful formation of a cartel. Nevertheless, cartel agreements are sometimes justified as being in the public interest in order to protect an industry from unacceptable free market fluctuations in demand or supply, or to create conditions in which rationalisation and the orderly decline of an industry can be achieved.*

The difficulties which arise in maintaining the influence of a cartel include:

(i) Undercutting by firms which are not members of the cartel.

(ii) The emergence of new products competing with the cartel's product.

(iii) Government policy to break up the cartel.

(iv) Individual members of the cartel 'cheating' by exceeding their quotas and secretly selling below the agreed price.

ANSWER PLAN

(i) Define a cartel and describe its key characteristics.

(ii) Give at least one example of a domestic cartel (eg BBC and ITV in the UK) and an international cartel (OPEC; the European steel cartel etc).

(iii) List and briefly explain why firms may wish to form a cartel, eg to reduce uncertainty; to increase profits; to aid rationalisation of an industry.

(iv) Briefly explain government attitudes to cartels.

(v) Suggest other reasons, besides government hostility, which explain why a cartel may collapse. The difficulties facing OPEC provide a good example.

Q6 *(a) In the traditional theory of the firm, firms in all market structures are assumed to produce the level of output at which MR = MC and set a price dictated by the demand curve facing the firm. Barriers to entry do not affect this central proposition of the theory of the firm, but they do affect the shape and position of the demand curve and the ability of the firm in the long run to make abnormal profits. You should explain this with reference to at least two market structures: perfect competition, monopolistic competition, oligopoly, or monopoly. Firms may also wish to erect or increase barriers to entry so as to increase their monopoly power and abnormal profits.*

(b) For this part of the question you could discuss the barriers to entry in the three industries in terms of

the framework discussed in Chapter 7 of:

(i) easy entry;
(ii) ineffectively impeded entry;
(iii) effectively impeded entry; and
(iv) blockaded entry.

ANSWER PLAN

(a) (i) Explain that barriers to entry exist in all market structures in the short run.

(ii) But in the long run there is freedom of entry into perfectly competitive markets and into monopolistic competition.

(iii) Explain how this competes away abnormal profits. If any firm reduces its costs and increases its profits, freedom of entry results in the demand curve for the firm's output shifting downward, competing away the profits again.

(iv) However, firms have an incentive to create barriers to entry to prevent this happening. The existence of barriers to entry increase a firm's monopoly power.

(b) (i) Heavy advertising is used as a barrier to entry by soap and detergent manufacturers. A newcomer would face great difficulty in persuading retailers to stock his product.

(ii) The significant economies of large scale production achieved by the major automobile manufacturers, together with their exclusive retail outlets, provide the main barrier to entry in the motor car industry.

(iii) Economies of bulk-buying and heavy investment in the largest and most favourably located retail sites, prevent small grocery shops from expanding and competing effectively with the major supermarket chains.

ANSWERS TO QUESTIONS IN CHAPTER 8

EXERCISES

1 (a) Private company
(b) Public corporation
(c) Public company
(d) Public company
(e) Private company
(f) Public corporation

2(a) (i) Electricity Council
(ii) British Petroleum
(iii) British Telecommunications
(iv) British Telecommunications

2(b) The oil industry is an example of a particularly capital-intensive industry. Large amounts of fixed capital are needed, but because many of the refining processes are highly automated, a relatively small number of production workers are required. By contrast, the nationalised industries are generally more labour-intensive. This is especially true of the Post Office Corporation, since it is almost impossible to automate the delivery of mail to millions of homes and places of work. And until recently at least, the nationalised industries have been protected from competition, experiencing therefore less incentive to reduce costs by shedding labour.

MULTIPLE CHOICE QUESTIONS

1 D
2 C
3 B
4 D
5 A

EXAMINATION QUESTIONS

Q1 *You should start your answer by defining a small firm, though indicate that a range of definitions is possible. Then list and briefly describe the possible reasons for the survival (and growth) of small firms, stating which you believe are the most important reasons. Where relevant, quote real world examples and evidence. Chapter 9, which covers the financing of small firms, provides supplementary information. The term 'industrial sector' specified in the question is rather vague; it might refer just to manufacturing, but according to the Standard Industrial Classification, a broader interpretation is possible.*

ANSWER PLAN

(i) Define a small firm, giving applications to specific industries suggested by the Wilson Committee. Explain how you are interpreting 'industrial sector'.

(ii) Explain that the existence of diseconomies of scale (or economies of small-scale production) provide an important explanation for the survival of small firms. Illustrate with an appropriate LRATC curve and state any relevant examples, eg the provision of personalised services.

(iii) Explain individual choice: many business owners may prefer to keep their enterprises small or they may lack the entrepreneurial flair to pursue a successful growth strategy.

(iv) Discuss constraints preventing successful growth: limited market size, capital raising difficulties etc.

(v) Today's upstart-firms in 'sunrise' industries may simply be in the early stages of growth, becoming eventually tomorrow's established corporate giants.

(vi) Relate the survival of small firms to external economies of scale: large firms may benefit from 'buying in' specialised services or components from small suppliers.

(vii) This relates closely to the fact that small firms can often survive by occupying specialist 'niches' in the market.

Q2 *The word 'co-operative' comes from the verb 'to co-operate' which means to join together in an activity. Co-operatives differ from most companies in that their main aim may be to give useful and meaningful employment to their members, rather than to make as much profit as possible for shareholders. There are two main types of co-operatives in the UK: producer co-operatives and consumer or retail co-operatives. Producer co-operatives are enterprises owned by some or all of the workers in the business. The co-operative is likely to be a company in which the workers own the shares. The workers thus provide the capital and they have to find some way of making decisions. They may appoint managers to whom such decision making is delegated, or the members of the co-operative may make decisions jointly, for example through voting. The members of the co-operative also have to decide how to distribute any profits amongst themselves.*

The main advantage of a producer co-operative is the lack of a conflict of interest between producer and owner - between employee and shareholder. Industrial relations should therefore be good. Most co-operatives also have the advantage of limited liability and co-operatives are also likely to be engaged in more socially worthwhile types of production than an ordinary company.

The disadvantages of co-operatives include (i) difficulty of raising sufficient capital; (ii) the members of the co-operative may lack management expertise and sufficient business ruthlessness. In the UK consumer co-operatives have declined rapidly in recent years squeezed by competition from large retailing PLCs and by the flexibility of family-owned retail outlets in which the owners are prepared to work for very long hours.

Q3 *This is a straightforward question testing your understanding of vertical, horizontal and lateral integration and the application of these concepts to the processes of the internal and external growth of firms. You must clearly state possible reasons or motives specific to each type of integration, while clearly relating your discussion to the underlying assumed objective of the firm, such as profit maximisation, managerial utility maximisation, a 'quiet life' etc.*

ANSWER PLAN

(i) Explain that integration relates to the expansion or growth of a business and the technical relationship within the business between the different activities undertaken by the business.

(ii) Describe, with examples, vertical, horizontal and lateral integration.

(iii) Explain how each can take place through internal growth or through external growth (acquisition via takeover and merger).

(iv) Clearly state that the most universal or deep-seated reason for each of the types of integration is the belief by the firm that it is consistent with the firm's ultimate business objective, eg profit maximisation.

(v) Suggest motives for backwards vertical integration, eg to secure sources of supply.

(vi) Suggest motives for forwards vertical integration, eg to secure market outlets.

(vii) Suggest motives for horizontal integration, eg to obtain economies of scale.

(viii) Suggest motives to lateral integration, eg diversification.

(ix) Discuss other motives that might be relevant to more than one type of integration, eg asset-stripping motive; the pursuit of monopoly power etc.

(x) Perhaps indicate that some reasons for integration, while in the private interest of the firm, may conflict with the social interest, eg the monopoly motive.

Q4 *Your answer plan should be similar to that for Question 3, except that you should devote a third of your answer to discussing the disadvantages of the different types of integration. Clearly distinguish between the disadvantages to the firm (eg diversification into an industry in which the expanding firm lacks managerial expertise) and disadvantages to the general public (eg restricted output and higher prices resulting from the exploitation of a monopoly position).*

Q5 *The question asks you to consider particular industries and you will be penalised if you write too generalised an account, without reference to specific industries. You should illustrate your answer with accurate and relevant examples, drawn from at least three industries, preferably chosen because of their different characteristics.*

ANSWER PLAN

(i) *Explain briefly that a firm is an organisation or enterprise active in the market economy, producing an output of goods or services for sale commercially. Firms can vary from single plant/single product businesses in a well-defined industry to multi-plant/multi-product firms active in a range of industries.*

(ii) *Distinguish between optimum plant size (and MEPS) and optimum firm size (and MEFS). These relate to the existence of plant-level economies of scale and firm-level economies of scale.*

(iii) *Choosing an industry dominated by small firms, eg a personal service dependent on market location such as hairdressing, explain how economies of small-scale production at both the plant and firm levels give small firms an advantage.*

(iv) *At the other extreme, an industry such as aircraft building is dominated by just a few very large firms (world wide) because of the very large Minimum Efficient Plant Size (MEPS).*

(v) *Other industries, such as grocery retailing, may contain firms ranging in size from small corner shops to major supermarket chains benefitting from significant scale economies. The existence of specialist 'niches' in the market may explain this diversity. The absence of significant scale economies and diseconomies can also contribute to diversity in firm size.*

Q6 You must discuss 'best for whom': the owners of the business, customers, employees or the wider social interest? You can agree or disagree with the assertion in the question, or you could adopt an 'it all depends on the circumstances' approach. But whichever approach you adopt, you must direct your answer at the set question and argue a reasoned case.

ANSWER PLAN

(i) *Explain clearly the meaning of 'limited liability company', distinguishing between private and public companies and fully explaining limited liability.*

(ii) *Explain particular advantages to the owner of the private limited liability company, eg the benefits of limited liability itself; separate legal identity; continuity of existence; tax advantages. You should explain that these benefits may not exist for unincorporated businesses, hence the advantage of a small or medium sized business being organised as a private company.*

(iii) *Public limited companies have the further major advantage of access to the capital market. In terms of the national interest, limited companies, especially public companies, provide an organisational means for channelling savings to finance risky but worthwhile entrepreneurial activity that might not take place in the absence of the company form of organisation.*

(iv) *Discuss possible advantages, eg customers and creditors can lose if a company becomes insolvent; the interests of shareholders may override the interest of employees; public companies may become vulnerable to takeover activity harmful to the interest of the company and the wider social interest etc.*

(v) *Suggest circumstances in which other forms of business organisation may be deemed preferable, eg partnerships in the provision of professional services, co-operatives in the interests of the workforce; friendly societies such as building societies in the interests of the customer using the service provided.*

(vi) *Round off your answer with a definite conclusion addressed at the assertion in the question.*

Q7 *The varying importance of employment in small firms in the different industries shown in the data, in general reflects the relative importance of small firms in each of the industrial sectors. To answer the question well, you must apply economic concepts such as economies of scale (a 'supply-side' influence) and the size of the market and the existence of specialist 'niches' in the market ('demand-side' influences) to each of the industries shown in the data. The scope for economies of scale and the mass-marketing of products favours large rather than small firms in manufacturing, and financial services are also dominated by the large financial institutions such as banks and the major insurance companies benefitting from scale economies. By contrast, the distributive trades and construction industries exhibit a coexistence between large retail store groups and building companies on one hand, and small corner shops and jobbing builders catering for local retail needs and small building works. Agriculture, transport and utilities have been grouped together in the data. However, there is much diversity in the firm size in these industries. Agricultural production is dominated by thousands of relatively small producers - even the largest farm is small as a business unit. The land-extensive nature of agricultural production, the historical pattern of land ownership and the lack of significant production economies of scale have all contributed to the importance of the small firm in agriculture. In transport, the importance of small firms varies, being least in railways and aviation, but relatively great in road transport where large freight hauliers have few advantages. Utilities such as gas, water and electricity are 'natural' monopolies or oligopolies, in which small firms would suffer a very severe cost disadvantage.*

ANSWER PLAN

(i) *State clearly that the varying proportions of employment in different industrial sectors results from the varying importance of small firms themselves in these sectors.*

(ii) *Briefly state what you mean by a 'small firm'.*

(iii) *Make the general point that both 'demand-side' factors (such as market size) and 'supply-side' factors (such as scope for economies of scale, barriers to entry etc) will influence the relative importance of small firms in each industrial sector.*

(iv) *With explicit reference to the data, discuss specific factors contributing to the relative importance or unimportance of small firms in each of the industrial sectors included in the question.*

ANSWERS TO QUESTION IN CHAPTER 9

EXERCISES

1(*a*) *We can use the following formula to calculate the share's market price:*

$$\frac{\text{Dividend}}{\text{Market price}} = \text{rate of interest}$$

Thus:

$$\frac{50p}{\text{Market price}} = 5 \text{ per cent}$$

The market price which converts the 50 pence dividend into a yield of 5 per cent is 1,000 pence, ie £10.

(b) *Amongst the factors that influence share prices are: expectations of future announcements by companies about dividends, profitability, new product developments, rights issues and corporate bond issues; rumours about takeover activity; government policy; and the general state of business and shareholder confidence.*

MULTIPLE CHOICE QUESTIONS

1 B
2 B
3 D
4 B

EXAMINATION QUESTIONS

Q1 ANSWER PLAN

(a) (i) *State clearly that the Stock Exchange is part of the wider capital market.*

(ii) *Explain the role of the Stock Exchange as a 'second-hand' or secondary market.*

(iii) *Relate the Stock Exchange to the primary or new issues market.*

(iv) *Explain how the Stock Exchange ensures public confidence in quoted public companies and aids the process of structural change in the UK economy.*

(b) (i) *Clearly distinguish a share price index from the daily quoted market price of a particular company's shares. Give examples, eg the Stock Exchange Index of 30 leading industrial shares and the Financial Times/ Stock Exchange 100 Share Index ('FOOTSIE').*

(ii) *Explain how each share index shows changes in the average daily market price of the representative sample of shares measured by the index.*

(iii) *Long-term changes (taking place over several years) reflect changes in the competitiveness and profitability of the companies represented in the index and serve as indicators of the health and well-being of the whole economy. More short-term movements can reflect rapidly changing market sentiment, the influence of speculation and takeover activity and confidence in the government.*

(c) (i) *Trends in share prices in general (explained above) obviously affect particular share prices.*

(ii) *Other factors specific to a particular company which will influence that company's share price include: statements about the company by directors or external commentators; changes or rumoured changes in the company's profits; announcements or rumours about an impending takeover bid etc.*

Q2 (i) *Explain that the capital market is the market for long-term funds, in which the government and public companies (in the private sector of the economy) raise funds by borrowing (through bond sales) and public companies raise funds also by selling new issues of shares.*

(ii) *Clearly distinguish between the new issues market and the Stock Exchange which functions as a 'second-hand' or secondary market.*

(iii) *Explain the role of the Stock Exchange in some detail (see answer plan for Question 1).*

(iv) *Briefly explain the relative importance of other secondary markets: the Unlisted Securities Market (USM); the Third Market; the 'over-the-counter' market (OTC).*

(v) *Explain the role of financial intermediaries such as pension funds and insurance companies and assess their relative importance in the capital market.*

Q3 (i) *Explain that institutional investors act as 'financial intermediaries' between the general public on the one hand (and the supply of personal savings) and the capital market on the other hand - and 'behind' the capital market), the government and companies towards whom the supply of personal savings is ultimately channelled, where new issues of bonds and shares are sold.*

(ii) *Explain the 'narrow' function of pension funds and insurance companies in investing the accumulated contractual savings of contributors in a portfolio or fund of financial assets such as bonds and shares whose yield will eventually finance the payment of pensions and life insurance endowments. Explain how risks are spread and how fund managers may 'trade-off' between the capital growth of the fund's portfolio and dividend and interest income.*

(iii) *Explain the 'wider' function of the institutions as the owners of the larger part of the shares of quoted public companies.*

(iv) *Explain the advantages and disadvantages of the ownership of companies by the institutions (compared to the direct ownership of shares by individuals).*

(v) *Define the entrepreneurial function in terms of decision-making and financial risk-taking. The growth of large firms leads to a split in the entrepreneurial function between salaried managers and shareholders, irrespective of whether the shareholders are personal shareholders or institutional shareholders.*

(vi) *But institutional shareholders often have the power to influence company decisions and they can decide the outcome of takeover battles.*

(vii) *Discuss whether the power of the institutions as the effective owners of companies is good or bad in terms of entrepreneurial decision-making by boards of directors and by the managers they employ, eg are the institutions too interested in short-term profits or capital growth at the expense of the long-term development of a company, its products and its markets?*

ANSWERS TO QUESTIONS IN CHAPTER 10

EXERCISES

1(*a*) (*i*) *BPB Industries, it is alleged, has refused to supply dealers with its plasterboard products, unless the dealers agree to sell BPB products exclusively. Alternatively, or additionally, it is alleged that BPB has engaged in a form of price discrimination, charging higher prices to dealers stocking imported plasterboard.*

(ii) The main reason for the restrictive practices is to reduce competition by erecting an artificial barrier to market entry, so as to achieve monopoly profit and possibly to secure a 'quiet life'.

(b) The government, or one of its agencies such as the Office of Fair Trading or the Restrictive Practices Court, could declare the practices illegal (if appropriate legislation exists). In the current legislative situation in the UK, the OFT would be most likely to refer the plasterboard industry to the Monopolies Commission, asking the Commission to investigate the structure, conduct and performance of BPB, which constitutes a scale monopoly. The MMC would eventually report, indicating whether in its view the practices undertaken by BPB are anti-competitive and against the public interest. The MMC would probably recommend that the OFT enters into discussion with BPB, to obtain voluntary assurances that the company will desist from such practices.

2*(a) (i) Richest region: South East; poorest region: Northern Ireland.*

(ii) Richest region: South East; poorest region: Northern Ireland.

(b) In 1971, the West Midlands was the second most prosperous region in the United Kingdom, the only region apart from the South East with a per capita income above the national average. But by 1983, per capita income in the West Midlands had fallen to a level well below the national average and to a position third from bottom in the national 'league table'. This indicates that the 'regional problem' had spread to a previously successful growth area, a fact reinforced by the designation of the West Midlands as an Assisted Area in 1984. Indeed, in the 1980s the West Midlands became a victim of earlier regional policy which had prevented the location of new manufacturing plants in the West Midlands, forcing them instead to areas such as Scotland and the North. As a result, the manufacturing base in the West Midlands became too narrowly centred on the car industry and related engineering industries.

Although these industries had been growth industries or 'sunrise' industries in earlier decades, by the late 1970s they too were entering a structural decline largely caused by a loss of international competitiveness. Perhaps more than any other region in the UK, the West Midlands suffered from the deindustrialisation process which was particularly intense in the severe recession of the early 1980s.

MULTIPLE CHOICE QUESTIONS

1 B
2 B
3 C
4 A
5 D

EXAMINATION QUESTIONS

Q1 ANSWER PLAN

(a) (i) State that as well as deciding what, when, how, for whom and how much to produce, a firm must choose where to produce.

(ii) Assuming a profit-maximising objective, this means that it must choose the location at which the total costs of producing the desired level of output are likely to be minimised.

(iii) State and explain the factors influencing a firm's level of production costs: the costs of raw materials and energy; labour costs; marketing and transport costs etc; the existence or

absence of external economies of scale in different locations.

(iv) *Cost-minimisation requires that a 'bulk-reducing' industry such as metal smelting be located near to its source of raw materials, or possibly energy, or with access to good bulk transportation. By contrast, 'bulk-adding' industries and industries supplying personal services to a geographically-spread population, tend to be market located.*

(v) *Industries which are highly 'specifically-located' have relatively little choice over location, eg coal mining can only be located where coal geologically occurs. But many industries are 'footloose' in the sense that there is a wider choice of possible locations which differ little in terms of likely production costs. In general, improvements in transport and greater flexibility in energy sources have loosened locational constraints and made a wide range of locations possible.*

(vi) *If a firm suspects that the optimal location might change or if it is a 'satisficer' rather than a 'maximiser', perhaps cushioned by monopoly profits and protected by barriers to entry, then it might not of course wish to choose the profit-maximising location.*

(b) (i) *Describe the 'carrot and stick' approach adopted by British governments in regional policy to influence locational decisions.*

(ii) *Assess the effectiveness of 'carrots', such as financial assistance.*

(iii) *Assess the effectiveness of 'sticks', such as planning controls.*

(iv) *Assess the overall effectiveness, in both the short run and the long run, of British regional policy as it has affected locational decisions. Note that recent Conservative governments have generally reduced their attempts to influence industrial locational decisions in the belief that businessmen motivated by profit 'know better' than planners and politicians.*

Q2 ANSWER PLAN

(i) *Briefly explain the meaning of nationalisation.*

(ii) *Some nationalised industries have been 'natural' monopolies, eg utility industries such as water and electricity. Explain the problem of lack of competition and monopoly exploitation and discuss whether the social ownership involved in nationalisation adds to or reduces the problem of potential monopoly abuse compared to private ownership of the monopoly.*

(iii) *Other industries have been nationalised which face problems of lack of competitiveness and structural decline. Discuss whether nationalisation aids or hinders the rationalisation of these industries to meet changed circumstances.*

(iv) *Discuss other problems of operating in the social interest rather than as simple profit-maximisers, eg the problems resulting from the provision of uneconomic services.*

(v) *Discuss other specific problems involving pricing, investment, financing, 'featherbedding' of the workforce, public accountability etc.*

Q3 ANSWER PLAN

(a) (i) Define a monopoly, distinguishing between pure monopoly and a relatively monopolistic industry.

(ii) The government must decide whether to judge monopoly on the grounds of market structure, conduct, or performance, or upon some combination of all three.

(iii) Costs and benefits must be taken into account. Costs include loss of productive and allocative efficiency, restriction of consumer choice and loss of consumer sovereignty. Benefits include possible dynamic efficiency and productive efficiency resulting from economies of scale.

(iv) The government can also consider different methods of dealing with monopoly abuse: breaking-up existing monopolies; prohibiting mergers that would create a monopoly; regulating monopolies; taxing monopoly profits; public ownership; privatising state monopolies; removing barriers to entry etc.

(b) (i) Briefly describe the main elements of the UK government's current policy towards monopoly (privatising state monopolies; removing barriers to entry etc).

(ii) Argue whether you believe that it effectively reduces or eliminates monopoly abuse and exploitation. Justify your argument. Use up-to-date examples where relevant.

Q4 *Your answer plan to this question should be broadly similar to that for Question 3. The question asks explicitly for a discussion of the case against control. However, you might argue that the case for controlling monopoly depends upon the circumstances of each separate example of monopoly, and that a pragmatic or 'cost-benefit' policy stance towards monopoly may be justified.*

Q5 ANSWER PLAN

(i) Briefly define a nationalised industry as an industry or firm owned by the state.

(ii) If the government decides that a nationalised industry should make decisions 'as if' it was a private sector company, then the industry should decide its prices just like any well-run private sector firm, eg in pursuit of an objective such as profit maximisation. But because of the impracticability of the marginalist rule (setting MR = MC), some form of 'cost-plus' pricing is likely to be adopted.

(iii) 'Cost-plus' pricing is likely to involve cross-subsidisation. While this may be justified for reasons of administrative convenience and upon social and regional grounds, cross-subsidy is allocative efficiency, the government might instruct nationalised industries to adopt marginal cost pricing (setting P = MC).

(iv) If the nationalised industry is instructed to take the social interest into account, loss-making prices subsidised by the government might be justified. Loss-making prices might be justified for distributional reasons, to provide cheap services to the poor. In the 1970s, the prices of nationalised industries were kept artificially low, as a counter-inflation instrument.

Q6 ANSWER PLAN

(a) (i) Briefly define privatisation.

(ii) Argue the case for privatising state-owned monopolies.

(iii) Privatisation is sometimes justified because it reduces the size of an 'overgrown' state sector, allowing public spending and borrowing to be reduced, preventing 'crowding-out' etc.

(iv) It also results in a short-term boost to government revenues.

(v) Explain the wider ideological case in terms of dismantling the mixed economy, freeing markets, encouraging 'popular capitalism' and an 'enterprise economy'.

(vi) By encouraging more people to own shares and by privatising public sector housing, a Conservative government can build up political support and reduce the risk of being voted out of office.

(b) (i) The government loses direct control over important sections of the economy.

(ii) State owned monopolies may merely be replaced by privately-owned monopolies, exploiting the consumer by restricting output and raising prices. There may be little or no benefit in terms of increased competition.

(iii) When profitable nationalised industries are sold off, an on-going source of government revenue is sacrificed for a once and for all lump sum.

(iv) The 'selling the family silver' argument - it is bad economics to sell capital assets to finance current revenue needs.

ANSWERS TO QUESTIONS IN CHAPTER 11

EXERCISES

1 (a) A good yields utility, directly in the case of a consumer good, and indirectly via the intermediary of the goods it allows to be produced, in the case of a capital good.

(b) A 'bad' is the opposite of a good, yielding disutility to the consumer. 'Bads' are also known as 'nuisance goods'.

(c) The fundamental economic problem of scarcity applies to economic goods; people have to 'economise' in their use.

(d) The problem of scarcity does not apply; free goods are available in limitless quantity at zero cost of production.

(e) The private owner of a private good can exercise private property rights and prevent people from benefitting from the good. Private goods are defined by the twin characteristics of excludability and diminishability.

(f) The private owner or provider of a public good such as defence cannot exercise private property rights and prevent people from benefitting who do not pay. Public goods are defined by the twin characteristics of non-excludability and non-diminishability.

(g) A merit good is a good or service for which the social benefits of consumption to the whole community exceed the private benefits to the consumer. The long-term benefits to the consu-

mer may also exceed the short-term benefits.

2 *Refuse is an example of an economic 'bad'. Since disutility is gained from 'consuming' refuse, people may be prepared, in principle, to pay for the refuse to be taken away. However, they may not need to pay, since in a market situation, they can 'free-ride' by dumping their rubbish in the road or in other peoples' gardens. If too many people become free-riders, the commercial incentive to provide the service of refuse collection through the market disappears. A service - for which there is a need - fails to be provided because private entrepreneurs cannot make a profit from its provision. Even if the service is provided commercially, it may be under-consumed if a significant number of people instead choose to free-ride and dump their rubbish. Refuse is therefore a 'public bad'.*

MULTIPLE CHOICE QUESTIONS

1 *C*
2 *B*
3 *C*
4 *C*
5 *D*

EXAMINATION QUESTIONS

Q1 *You should answer the first part of the question by explaining how the signalling and incentive functions of prices lead to households and firms making the decisions on how much of a good to consume and produce and on how much of a factor service to supply and demand, in pursuit of private benefit maximisation. Market failure occurs whenever the resulting allocation of economic resources achieved through the price mechanism is judged as inefficient or inequitable. The principal examples of market failure include: monopoly and imperfect competition; the failure to benefit from economies of scale; missing markets, including future markets and markets in public goods and externalities; wasted resources, including unemployment; under-provision of merit goods and over-provision of demerit goods and an inequitable or unfair distribution of income and wealth. You will not, of course, be able to explain all of these in detail. Nevertheless, it is useful to show the examiner that you understand how wide-ranging is the concept of 'market failure' before discussing two or three examples in some detail.*

ANSWER PLAN

(i) *Explain the signalling and incentive functions of prices.*

(ii) *Explain how in a competitive market economy, the 'hidden hand' of the market creates incentives for households and firms to alter their decision-making in pursuit of utility and profit, producing an eventual outcome that may be judged optimal in terms of productive and allocate efficiency.*

(iii) *But whenever such optimality is not achieved, market failure is said to occur.*

(iv) *Markets may fail on grounds of inefficiency or inequity.*

(v) *List details of examples of each type of failure.*

(vi) *Explain at least two examples in greater detail, eg public goods and an inequitable distribution of income.*

Q2 *Defence, health care and education are goods which are usually provided through* *government spending at zero price to the consumer, being financed collectively out of general taxation. They are provided because the market either fails completely to provide them (defence) or under-provides (health care and education). Defence is an example of a public good whereas health care and education are merit goods. You must draw on the information in Chapter 11 to explain fully why markets fail to provide or under-provide these goods and why there is a case for government provision. Develop the argument that direct government provision is not inevitable, especially in the case of merit goods. The government can allow private hospitals and schools to exist, overcoming the problem of under-provision and consumption in a market situation by subsidising or paying in part or in full the fees of the poor.*

ANSWER PLAN

(i) *Explain that defence is a public good which, because of the property of non-excludability, may fail to be provided by markets.*

(ii) *Even if provided by markets, the property of non-diminishability means that it will be under-provided.*

(iii) *Alternative provision is therefore required. Direct provision through state spending at zero price to the consumer is the most common situation.*

(iv) *Explain that health care and education are merit goods which markets can provide, but which markets are likely to under-provide.*

(v) *There is a case for subsidising provision of merit goods so as to encourage consumption. Illustrate on a diagram similar to Figure 11.4.*

(vi) *Argue the case for and against direct state provision or state subsidy of private sector provision.*

Q3 (a) *You must firmly state the key characteristic of an externality, namely that it is the 'spin-off' from an economic agent's main activity, generated and received 'outside the market'. Do not confuse externalities received by firms (which are a form of production economy or diseconomy) with other external economies and diseconomies received through the market. As we have explained in Chapter 8, externalities can be classified in terms of positive and negative externalities (external benefits and costs), and into production externalities, consumption externalities and mixed externalities. But since this part of the question carries only 4 marks, do not over-elaborate.*

(b) *You must explain how externalities result in a misallocation of resources since divergencies occur between private and social cost and benefit. In the case of external benefits, the marginal social benefits resulting from the generation of the externality exceed the marginal private benefits, but the market mechanism takes no account of this. With external costs, the market fails to take account of the fact that the marginal social costs generated exceed the marginal private costs.*

(c) *Externalities can be dealt with either through taxation and subsidy on the one hand, or through regulation or quantity control. We discuss the use of taxation and regulation to limit the generation of negative externalities in the context of Question 4 below. With positive exter-*

nalities, or external benefits, the policy problem is to encourage their generation so as to maximise the social benefit. The households or firms who generate the externalities can be subsidised, so as to create the incentive to generate more. Alternatively, generation can be made compulsory - the symmetrical opposite form of regulation to illegalising the generation of an external cost.

ANSWER PLAN

(a) (i) *Define an externality in term of its essential characteristics.*
(ii) *Illustrate with examples.*

(b) (i) *Show carefully how the generation of externalities leads to a misallocation of resources.*
(ii) *Illustrate with diagrams similar to Figures 8.2 and 8.3.*

(c) (i) *Describe how taxation can be used to deal with external costs.*
(ii) *Describe how regulation can be used to deal with external costs.*
(iii) *Describe how subsidy can be used to deal with external benefits.*
(iv) *Describe how regulations can be used to deal with external benefits.*

Q4 *You must explain that industrial pollution is a negative externality which does not figure in the money costs of production incurred by firms. If in the market situation P = MPC, then it follows that P < MSC whenever negative production externalities such as pollution are generated. Too much of the firms' industrial product is produced and consumed since part of the true or real costs of production is not reflected in the price, being dumped on others. As we have explained in Chapter 8, the public policy problem is to close the resulting divergency between private and social marginal costs. The government can calculate the monetary value of the external cost and impose it as a tax upon the polluters, or - and this is more common in real life - the government can use regulation or quantity controls to restrict pollution by law. Ordering the polluter to compensate the unwilling 'consumers' of pollution is another possibility.*

ANSWER PLAN

(i) *Explain how pollution is a negative externality.*

(ii) *With a diagram similar to Figure 8.2 show how the marginal social costs of production exceed the marginal private costs or production.*

(iii) *Explain that at market prices, overproduction occurs, and the public policy problem is to ensure the socially optimal level of production (of the good the firms are producing).*

(iv) *This can be done through taxation or regulation, or through a combination of the two.*

(v) *Explain how each policy would operate and briefly discuss the advantages and disadvantages of each policy option. Include real world examples.*

Q5 *Cost benefit analysis (CBA) is a technique for evaluating all the costs and benefits of any economic action or decision, ie the social costs and benefits to the whole community and not just the private costs and benefits accruing to the economic agent undertaking the action. CBA is most often used by governments to help decide whether to invest in a major public project such as a motorway, an airport, or a major investment by a nationalised industry. However, there is no reason in principle why a pri-*

vate sector investment such as the Channel Tunnel, or indeed any action by a private economic agent or by the government (eg a tax change), cannot be examined by CBA.

CBA is really an extension of the discounted cash flow (DCF) technique of investment appraisal which is explained in Chapter 17. Using DCF, a firm attempts to calculate all the private costs and benefits occurring in the future as a result of an investment or decision undertaken now. The central problem is guessing and putting money values to an unknown and uncertain future. But CBA is even more difficult because many of the social costs and benefits resulting in the future from an action undertaken now take the form of externalities that are difficult to quantify. How does one put a monetary value to the saving of a human life resulting from fewer accidents on a proposed motorway? What is the social cost of the destruction of a beautiful view? It is extremely difficult to decide on all the likely costs and benefits, to 'draw the line' on which to include and exclude, to put monetary values to all the chosen costs and benefits accruing immediately with those which will only be received in the distant future.

Critics of CBA argue that it is 'pseudo-scientific' - value judgements and arbitrary decisions disguised as objectivity. CBA is also criticised as being a costly waste of time and money and as a method whereby politicians distance themselves from, and induce delay in, unpopular decisions, deflecting the wrath of local communities away from themselves and onto the 'impartial experts' undertaking the CBA. Nevertheless, supporters of CBA argue that for all its defects it remains the best method of appraising public investment decisions because all the likely costs and benefits are exposed to public discussion.

ANSWER PLAN

(i) *Explain that CBA is a technique of appraisal, similar to DCF in discounting a future stream of costs and benefits, but including all the costs and benefits, external as well as private.*

(ii) *Discuss the problems of deciding which costs and benefits to include; choosing money values; choosing an appropriate discount rate etc.*

(iii) *Assess whether CBA is worthwhile.*

ANSWER TO QUESTIONS IN CHAPTER 12

EXERCISES

1 *(a)*

Workers employed	*MPP of labour*
1	*10*
2	*8*
3	*6*
4	*4*
5	*2*
6	*1*

(b) *The firm will employ labour up to the point at which MRP = W, MRP = MPP x £5, so the firm will employ labour up to the point at which the MRP of the last worker employed equals £10. This occurs when 5 workers are employed.*

(c) *The firm will reduce employment to four workers.*

MULTIPLE CHOICE QUESTIONS

1 *B*
2 *A*
3 *C*
4 *D*
5 *A*

EXAMINATION QUESTIONS

Q1 *This question requires you to apply your knowledge of the role of the price mechanism in the market economy to the factor market or the market for inputs. Take care to balance your answer between the two parts of the question.*

ANSWER PLAN

(a) (i) Briefly explain the factor prices: wages, rent, interest and profit.

(ii) Describe the signalling function of factor prices in the market economy.

(iii) With the use of an example, perhaps wages in the labour market, show how factor prices create incentives both for firms and for workers to make choices respectively in terms of profit and 'net advantage' maximisation.

(iv) Discuss the 'equalising tendency' of market forces in a competitive economy.

(b) (i) Explain how the relative prices of capital, labour etc, influence the choice of the method of production and how much of each factor to employ. The condition of equi-marginal returns is relevant here.

(ii) Explain how abnormal profit or the economic rent of enterprise encourages firms to shift between different markets and industries.

Q2 ANSWER PLAN

(a) (i) Draw a diagram to show the supply and demand for a factor service such as labour.

(ii) Explain how the part of the factor's income above the supply curve is the factor's economic rent, while the income below the supply curve is the factor's transfer earnings. Carefully define both terms.

(iii) Explain, possibly with extra diagrams, how the proportions of the factor's income which are economic rent and transfer earnings depend upon the elasticity of supply of the factor service.

(iv) Show how elasticity of supply can vary between the short run and the long run.

(v) Explain that in these circumstances we can identify a quasi-rent (rent in the short run but transfer earnings in the long run).

(b) Your answer plan to (b) should be similar to the plan for Question 1(a).

Q3 *In this question 'rent' means 'economic rent' rather than just the reward to a factor of production, land. The term originated in the early 19th century when the English classical economist David Ricardo constructed a model to explain how landlords could command an income merely because they owned a scarce resource, agricultural land, and even though the landlords contributed no effort themselves to the productive process. Ricardo argued that landlords' income is a rent resulting from the scarcity of the resource they own, given the landlords' ability to exercise private property rights over their land. In later years the term became applied to the earnings of any factor of production that results from its scarcity.*

ANSWER PLAN

(i) Carefully distinguish between rent as

the factor reward of land alone and 'rent' as an economic rent.

(*ii*) *Show how if a factor is in completely inelastic supply all its income is an economic rent and none of the income is transfer earnings. This is the context in which the term originated.*

(*iii*) *As a factor becomes less and less scarce, its supply curve becomes more elastic and the proportion of the income which is economic rent becomes less. With an infinite supply of the factor there is no economic rent. Illustrate this on a series of diagrams drawn with supply curves of differing elasticity.*

(*iv*) *Give examples drawn from at least two factors of production.*

Q4 (*a*) *This part of the question requires a brief distinction. A commercial rent is a market rent charged for use of land, including usually a charge for the use of any buildings (or fixed capital) occupying the land. Part of the commercial rent will be an economic rent, but part will be transfer earnings. As we have indicated in the context of Questions 2 and 3, an economic rent can be earned by all the factors of production and is a more abstract theoretical term rather than a separate monetary payment.*

(*b*) *This is a variation of 'maximum price legislation'. If rent controls are set lower than commercial or free market rents, shortages of housing in the rented sector will result, or excess demand. This may lead to queues or waiting lists for rented accommodation, and possibly illegal payments in a form of 'black market'. If the controlled rents are set below individual landlords' opportunity cost or transfer earnings, landlords may take their houses out of the rented housing sector and convert them to an alternative use. For example, the houses might be sold for owner-occupancy. Three decades of rent controls have had this effect in the UK housing market.*

ANSWER PLAN

(*a*) (*i*) *Carefully distinguish between commercial rent and economic rent, emphasising that all factors can earn an economic rent.*

(*ii*) *Illustrate economic rent on a diagram and note that a commercial rent is usually in part transfer earnings.*

(*b*) (*i*) *Draw a supply and demand diagram to show the free market commercial rent of housing.*

(*ii*) *Show an imposed maximum rent, set below the free market commercial rent of housing.*

(*iii*) *Explain how excess demand and a rented housing shortage will then result.*

(*iv*) *Waiting lists and various rationing devices, together with a 'black market' will now emerge.*

(*v*) *Explain how housing will be converted to alternative use.*

Q5 *The elasticity of demand for a particular type of labour depends on the following five influences:*

(*i*) *The technical possibility of substituting alternative factors of production for labour.*

(*ii*) *the technical possibility of substi-*

tuting alternative types of labour for a specific type of labour.

(iii) The elasticity of supply of alternative factors and types of labour.

(iv) The proportion of labour costs to total costs.

(v) The elasticity of demand for the final product.

The elasticity of demand for a factory manager may be low because other factors of production or types of labour cannot be substituted for him. However, there may be a supply of alternative factory managers available, currently employed by other firms or listed at job agencies. Although he is possibly well paid, the total cost of employing the factory manager is probably only a small part of total costs. The situation is probably very different for individual assembly workers. In their case, all the determinants of the elasticity of demand for labour may well contribute to an elastic demand, especially in the long run.

ANSWER PLAN

(i) Define elasticity of demand for labour.

(ii) List and briefly explain the determinants of the elasticity of demand for labour.

(iii) Apply the list to a discussion of the elasticity of demand for the firm's factory manager.

(iv) Apply the list to a discussion of the elasticity of demand for the firm's assembly workers. Make sure you relate your answer to the information given in the question, which suggests that individual assembly workers are easily substitutable.

Q6 *To answer this question you should draw on section 34 of Chapter 12, clearly stating that women work predominantly in low-paid industries and occupations and that within many occupational groups, women are paid less than men.*

ANSWER PLAN

(i) Introduce the possibility that women may be paid less than men because they are less productive, but state firmly that if this is the case, it may result from the fact that female workers have less access to training and skills than male workers.

(ii) Underlying lower pay for women is the fact that:
(a) women are mostly in low-paid industries and occupations;
(b) within a particular occupation, fewer women occupy the better-paid posts.

(iii) Introduce possible explanations:
(a) discrimination by employers and male workers against women;
(b) fewer women are trade union members and unions tend to be weak in occupations with largely female employment;
(c) the effects of weaker female attachment to the labour force and career disruption for family reasons;
(d) the reasons why employers might be reluctant to invest in the training of women;
(e) the effects of social conditioning reducing women's aspirations.

Q7 *In the 1970s many people argued that British trade unions had become so powerful that they could effectively 'buck the market' and determine wage levels. More recently however, trade union power has been considerably weakened in the UK, as a res-*

ult of legislation, higher levels of unemployment and increased international competition. Because wage rates are often agreed through institutional arrangements such as collective bargaining, it may seem that trade unions and not market forces determine wages. But in industries subject to competition from imports or substitute products, or where capital can easily be substituted for labour, in the long run trade unions possess little ability to achieve levels of wages higher than those indicated by supply and demand. Nevertheless, as the theory of the monopsony labour market shows, by creating a monopoly of labour to countervail the monopsony bargaining power of the employer, trade unions may succeed in raising wages at the expense of the employer's profits in less competitive labour markets.

ANSWER PLAN

(i) *Briefly explain that the wages of many workers in trade unions are determined by collective bargaining between the union and employers, which on first sight may appear to have replaced market forces in determining wage levels.*

(ii) *But even when unions have successfully raised wages, they have done so by altering the conditions of supply and demand rather than by abolishing market forces. For example, unions may be able to shift the position and elasticity of the supply curve of labour, or prevent employers substituting capital for labour.*

(iii) *Illustrate with the model of a monopsony demand for labour, how a trade union may be able to raise wages at the employer's expense by altering the position of the supply curve of labour.*

(iv) *Argue that in competitive industries, unions are unlikely to be able to sustain wage levels and levels of employment in the long run that are higher than those indicated by market forces.*

Q8 *This question is subtly different from Question 7 because it requires a discussion of the factors that influence the power of a union to persuade employers to increase the wage rate. Obviously the likely effects of a wage rise upon employment is one of the factors the union must consider, but other relevant considerations include the ability to persuade all the workers in the labour market to join the trade union.*

ANSWER PLAN

(i) *Draw a diagram to show the effect of introducing a trade union into a perfectly competitive labour market.*

(ii) *Explain that the weight that the union attaches to the employment consequences of a real wage increase will influence the vigour with which it pursues a wage claim.*

(iii) *The higher the real wage rise, and the greater the elasticity of demand for labour, the greater will be the unemployment consequences.*

(iv) *The union can increase its bargaining power by achieving a monopoly supply over all labour. Explain that if some workers are not members of the union, the power of the union is weakened.*

(v) *Following a wage increase, the union must be able to prevent non-members from undercutting the wage if the wage increase is to be maintained.*

(vi) *Extend the analysis to a monopsony*

labour market. Explain how in principle, a union should be able to increase wages in this type of market structure without a loss of employment, but ultimately it depends on the bargaining power of the union and the employer.

Q9 *The effect of introducing a national minimum wage is very similar to the effect of a trade union determining the wage. Thus use diagrams similar to Figures 12.9 and 12.10 to show the effect of setting a minimum legal wage in perfectly competitive and monopsony markets. In perfectly competitive labour markets, the main effect of setting a minimum wage above the free market or market-clearing wage might be to increase unemployment. Firms would choose to employ fewer workers, responding to the higher relative price of labour by substituting capital for labour. A 'black market' in labour might also result, in which workers were illegally employed below the minimum wage. Firms might move their factories abroad to countries where labour is cheaper.*

These conclusions assume that a national minimum wage has no effect upon the state of aggregate demand for output in the economy. Under certain assumptions, a minimum wage might stimulate consumption spending and shift the aggregate demand for labour rightwards as firms need more labour to meet the demand for output.

Finally, we must not ignore the effects of a national minimum wage upon the distribution of income. In principle, a minimum wage which increases the income of workers in low-paid jobs should reduce inequalities in the distribution of income. However, this effect would be countered if a significant number of low-paid workers lost their jobs and became unemployed.

ANSWER PLAN

(i) *Draw a diagram to show the effect of setting a national minimum wage in a perfectly competitive labour market.*

(ii) *Explain that increased unemployment is the most likely result.*

(iii) *Though if increased consumption spending boosts aggregate demand, the demand curve curve for labour might shift rightwards.*

(iv) *A 'black market' in the labour might also result.*

(v) *Draw a diagram to show the effect of setting a national minimum wage in a monopsony labour market.*

(vi) *Explain that in this market structure, employment might increase.*

(vii) *Discuss possible effects upon the distribution of income.*

ANSWERS TO QUESTIONS IN CHAPTER 13

EXERCISES

1 (a) *The real wage increase is negative: (-2) per cent.*

(b) *The budget deficit is negative, ie the budget is in surplus, the size of the surplus being £10 billion.*

MULTIPLE CHOICE QUESTIONS

1 *C*
2 *D*
3 *B*
4 *D*
5 *D*

EXAMINATION QUESTIONS

Q1 (a) *Besides listing and briefly describing all the types of unemployment, a good answer should give some indication of what are the most important causes of unemployment in the world today. Chapter 13 covers 'real wage' (or 'classical') unemployment, frictional unemployment, structural unemployment and demand-deficient (or Keynesian) unemployment, but you should refer to Chapter 21 for a more comprehensive listing.*

(b) *When answering this part of the question, you must relate policies to causes. For example, expansionary fiscal policy or monetary policy which might be appropriate if unemployment is caused by demand-deficiency, would be completely inappropriate if unemployment has other causes. It is important to identify correctly the cause of unemployment so as to match the appropriate policy remedy to the cause. Give plenty of examples.*

ANSWER PLAN

(a) (i) *Briefly list the types of unemployment.*

(ii) *Discuss the causes of each type of unemployment you have listed, taking care to concentrate on the main types: frictional, structural, 'classical' and 'demand deficient'.*

(b) (i) *Briefly explain appropriate policies, to cure or reduce each type of unemployment that you have listed.*

(ii) *Indicate important differences of opinion between, for example, Keynesians and monetarists.*

(iii) *Emphasise that it is important to match policies with causes.*

Q2 *This question relates to whether 'demand-deficiency' is an important cause of modern unemployment. In the early 1980s, unemployment was close to 3 million, a similar figure to the total unemployed in the Great Depression in the 1930s. In 1936, Keynes argued in his 'General Theory' that much, if not all, the persistent unemployment of his day was caused by demand-deficiency and that the government should deliberately run a budget deficit so as to inject spending power into the economy. But even if Keynes was correct in his diagnosis of the cause of unemployment in the 1930s, it does not necessarily follow that today's large scale unemployment has a similar cause. You must explain why monetarist and 'New Classical' economists reject the possibility of demand-deficient unemployment and why they suggest that unemployment has other causes. You should also explain how monetarists believe that Keynesian demand management has contributed to modern unemployment, through the long-term effect of higher taxation and interest rates reducing the competitiveness of the private and market sectors of the economy. Explain also, how they believe that inflation and 'crowding-out' are the main long-term effects of increased government spending. Western governments have attempted to cut public expenditure because they have been strongly influenced by monetarist and 'New Classical' thinking. Note also that increased public spending and budget deficits in the 1960s and 1970s had at best only a short-term effect on real output and employment, giving support to the monetarist argument that the main effects related to inflation and the 'crowding-out' process.*

ANSWER PLAN

(i) *Briefly explain why Keynes believed*

that deficient demand is an important cause of large scale and persistent unemployment.

(ii) Briefly explain how Keynes recommended deliberate deficit planning as the appropriate cure.

(iii) Keynesian demand management policies were implemented in the three decades after 1945 and to begin with they were very successful.

(iv) But gradually demand management policies became less successful in securing full employment and their main effect appeared to be inflation.

(v) Relate to the 'crisis in Keynesian economics' and to the monetarist 'counter-revolution'.

(vi) Explain why monetarists reject demand management and increased public spending.

(vii) Briefly explain the types of economic policy that monetarists believe are more appropriate for reducing unemployment.

Q3 ANSWER PLAN

(a) (i) Explain how Keynes believed that Say's Law can break down, leading to the paradox of thrift and excess savings in the economy.

(ii) Illustrate the resulting under-full employment equilibrium on a deflationary gap diagram.

(b) (i) State how Keynes believed that both fiscal policy and monetary policy can be used to manage aggregate demand.

(ii) Explain how Keynes thought monetary policy would be less effective in a depressed economy (interest rates would have little effect in stimulating expenditure).

(iii) Explain how government spending, taxation and the budget deficit can be used in Keynesian fiscal policy to close a deflationary gap.

(c) (i) Explain how monetarists believe that reflation of aggregate demand leads ultimately only to inflation and/or 'crowding-out', with only a short-term boost to output and employment.

Q4 This question covers much of the ground of Questions 2 and 3, but it is perhaps worth noting that the economic policies pursued by successive Conservative governments in the UK since 1979 have not always been completely supported by the 'high priest' of monetarism, Milton Friedman. Friedman has recommended that governments adopt a policy of strict monetarism in which the growth of the money supply is tightly contained by the government establishing a rigid control over the supply of cash to the economy. 'Purist' monetarists have argued that the monetary policy implemented by the Thatcher governments has been an extremely watered-down and pragmatic version of monetarism. It is also worth noting that aspects of a 'wider' monetarism (relating to the pursuit of free market 'supply-side' policies) have gained an ascendency in UK government in recent years over a 'narrow' or strict monetarism defined simply in terms of policies to secure control over monetary growth.

ANSWER PLAN

(i) Briefly explain the meaning of Keynesian interventionist policies.

(ii) Describe how they appeared successful in the early part of the Keynesian era.

(iii) *But eventually they became associated, particularly by monetarists, with causing inflation and 'crowding-out'.*

(iv) *Briefly explain what is meant by 'Friedman style monetarist policies'.*

(v) *Describe how the UK Labour government was forced to adopt aspects of monetarist policy in 1976 and how a Conservative government was elected under Mrs Thatcher in 1979, committed to monetarist policies.*

(vi) *If you have time, briefly note that Milton Friedman has not completely supported the 'monetarism' of the Thatcher governments, arguing that it is insufficiently pure.*

ANSWERS TO QUESTIONS IN CHAPTER 14

EXERCISES

1 (a)

Income	Planned saving
0	-500
1,000	-400
2,000	-300
3,000	-200
4,000	-100
5,000	0
6,000	+100
7,000	+200
8,000	+300
9,000	+400
10,000	+500

(b) $Y = 500 + 0.9Y$

(c) (i) 500
(ii) 0.9
(iii) (-0.4); zero; 0.03 (approx)

2. (a) *With the vertical axis labelled consumption and the horizontal axis labelled income, you should draw a positive-sloping linear consumption function for which (i) the vertical intercept is 1,000 and (ii) the slope is 0.4.*

(b) $S = -1{,}000 + 0.6Y$

(c) *The savings function should be a positive-sloping linear line with a vertical intercept of (-1,000) and a slope of 0.6.*

(d) $Y = 10{,}000$

MULTIPLE CHOICE QUESTIONS

1 B
2 B
3 B
4 C
5 C

EXAMINATION QUESTIONS

Q1 *A good answer should survey a number of the possible influences upon aggregate consumption spending which we have covered in Chapter 14: the rate of interest; current income; expected life-cycle income; wealth; expected inflation; the availability of credit; and the distribution of income. However, the main body of the answer should be devoted to explaining the role of current income as the explanatory variable in the Keynesian consumption function. Carefully distinguish between autonomous consumption and income-induced consumption and consider also the weaknesses of the Keynesian theory.*

ANSWER PLAN

(i) *Explain the meaning of aggregate planned consumption.*

(ii) *State the Keynesian theory of aggre-*

gate consumption.

(iii) Illustrate the theory on a 45° line diagram and carefully distinguish between autonomous and income-induced consumption.

(iv) Describe (briefly) how the Keynesian theory is really a theory of short-run consumption behaviour and not a long-run theory.

(v) Introduce the life-cycle consumption theory to explain the role of expected income in determining long-run consumption behaviour.

(vi) Briefly comment on other possible influences upon consumption behaviour, eg the rate of interest; wealth; peoples' attitudes to thrift etc.

Q2 *The paradox of thrift relates to the possibility that saving, which at the individual level is regarded as a virtue, might become a 'vice' at the aggregate level if the whole community saves too much of its income. Saving alone does not cause the paradox; a problem only occurs if the community's savings are not spent but simply lie idle. The question therefore requires a consideration of Say's Law (that 'supply creates its own demand'). According to the 'classical' (or pre-Keynesian) tradition, any excess supply of savings in the economy will quickly be eliminated via falling interest rates which serve to discourage saving and encourage investment spending by firms. But Keynes argued that Say's Law can break down, producing the paradox of thrift and a depressed level of economy activity within the economy. Keynesians argue that the breakdown of Say's Law and the paradox of thrift justify the government taking measures in a depressed economy through deficit financing. 'Extreme' New Classical economists and monetarists would disagree, arguing that the correct policy is to create conditions in which market forces - including the role of the rate of interest - operate effectively. Nevertheless more 'moderate' monetarists accept that in an extremely depressed economy, there is a limited role for counter-cyclical deficit financing.*

ANSWER PLAN

(i) Briefly state the paradox of thrift.

(ii) Introduce Say's Law.

(iii) If Say's Law holds the paradox is denied. Explain the role of the rate of interest in eliminating an excess supply of savings.

(iv) If Say's Law breaks down, the paradox occurs.

(v) Relate the existence of the paradox to Keynesian versus 'classical' controversies.

(vi) Describe the Keynesian argument that government deficit financing is justified to inject spending into the economy.

(vii) Explain that many monetarists reject this argument, except possibly in an extremely depressed economy.

Q3 *(a) You should define precisely the marginal and average propensities to save, illustrating your answer both with a numerical example and with the aid of a savings function drawn on a 45° line diagram.*

(b) To answer this part of the question you must draw on Chapter 12. Savings is a leakage from the circular flow of income. Assuming an initial equilibrium level of national income at

which planned injections equals planned withdrawals: $(I + G + X = S + T + M)$, an increase in the flow of savings out of the circular flow will reduce or deflate the level of income until once again injections equal withdrawals at a new lower level of income. The consequences depend upon the size of the resulting fall in income. If the economy initially contained excess demand - as illustrated by an 'inflationary gap' diagram - the main effect may simply be to reduce inflation, leaving output and employment relatively unaffected. But if the economy was initially below full employment and displaying no evidence of excess demand, the level of real output would be deflated and (according to Keynesians) large scale demand-deficient unemployment might occur.

ANSWER PLAN

(a) (i) *Define the marginal propensity to save as:*

$$MPS \equiv \frac{\Delta S}{\Delta Y}$$

(ii) *Define the average propensity to save as:*

$$APS \equiv \frac{S}{Y}$$

(iii) *With the aid of a numerical example show how a change in the MPS affects the APS.*

(iv) *Illustrate the MPS and the APS in terms of the Keynesian savings function.*

(b) (i) *Explain how savings represents a withdrawal of income from the circular flow of income.*

(ii) *Illustrate, either on a 45° line diagram, or with a circular flow diagram.*

(iii) *Explain how an increase in autonomous savings leads to a negative multiplier effect.*

(iv) *Show how the equilibrium level of income falls.*

(v) *Discuss possible effects on the levels of prices, output and employment.*

Q4 *A useful starting point for part (a) of this answer is the identity: $Y \equiv C + S$, rearranged as $S \equiv Y - C$. This tells us that the determinants of saving are exactly the same as the determinants of consumption, since saving is simply income which is not spent on consumption. You should therefore base your answer upon exactly the same factors or determinants as are relevant for Question 1, though discussed in terms of savings rather than consumption. A large part - but not all - of your answer should be devoted to the Keynesian savings function and the related concepts of autonomous savings (or dissaving), income-induced saving and the average propensity to save.*

The answer to part (b) should consider the effects of an increased propensity to save at higher levels of income, the possibility of Say's Law breaking down and demand-deficient unemployment or Keynesian unemployment resulting. Traditionally, Keynesians have considered this to be a serious possibility, whereas monetarist and 'classical' economists have not.

ANSWER PLAN

(a) (i) *Briefly define saving as income which is not spent on consumption.*

(ii) Introduce the Keynesian saving (and consumption) functions.

(iii) Explain that in the Keynesian theory the proportion of income saved increases as income rises.

(iv) Briefly describe other influences upon the proportion of income saved besides the level of income itself, eg the rate of interest, expected life-cycle income; wealth; the efficiency and availability of financial intermediaries etc.

(b) (i) Discuss the significance of the Keynesian theory that the proportion of income saved rises with income. Relate this to the paradox of thrift, the emergence of deficient demand and Keynesian unemployment.

(ii) Introduce the monetarist or 'classical' argument that the rate of interest equates saving and investment decisions and prevents the emergence of deficient demand except as an essentially temporary phenomenon. According to this view, an increase in the proportion of income saved is not a likely cause of problems.

(iii) If you have time, relate the fall in the personal savings ratio in the 1980s in the UK to the rapid growth of consumption spending as a cause of inflation.

ANSWERS TO QUESTIONS IN CHAPTER 15

EXERCISES

1 *(a) These questions are based on the national expenditure method of calculating the value of national income and other national income aggregates. See the appendix at the end of Chapter 15 for further details.*

(i) £48,950 million
(ii) £53,650 million
(iii) £59,000 million
(iv) £53,000 million

(b) National income and expenditure figures are probably a more accurate indicator of economic activity than of economic welfare. Nevertheless, they are only estimates of expenditure in the economy and will be inaccurate to the extent that they over-estimate or under-estimate the real economic activity taking place in the economy. Some goods and services produced and consumed in the non-monetised economy have an imputed measure included in the national expenditure estimates, but others - for example housework - are missed out altogether. These figures are presented in highly aggregated form - obviously they would need disaggregating further to present a more detailed picture of economic activity in different industries.

2(a) *(i) The equilibrium equation is:*

$Y = c(Y - tY) + I + G$
or $Y = 0.7(Y-0.37Y) + £620m + £400m$
or $Y = 0.49Y + £1{,}020m$
Thus $0.51Y = £1{,}020m$
and $Y = £2{,}000m$

(ii) The budget is represented by
$T - G$
or $tY - G$
or $0.3(£2{,}000m) - £400m$
or $£600m - £400m$
There is a budget surplus of £200 billion.

(b) (i) $Y = 0.7(Y - 0.25Y) + £1{,}020m$
or $Y + 0.527Y + £1{,}020m$
Thus $Y = £1{,}247.37m$

(ii) The budget is now

0.25 (£2,147.37m) - £400m
= £536.84m - £400m
There is thus a reduced budget surplus of £136.84 million.

MULTIPLE CHOICE QUESTIONS

1 *B*
2 *A*
3 *B*
4 *C*
5 *C*
6 *C*

EXAMINATION QUESTIONS

Q1 ANSWER PLAN

(a) (i) *Define national income as the flow of new income or output produced from assets owned by a country's residents in the course of a year.*

(ii) *Briefly explain the three ways of measuring national income: in terms of the value of output (national product); incomes received (national income); and expenditure upon output (national expenditure).*

(b) (i) *Illustrating your answer from one or more of the three methods of measuring national income, explain at least* three *problems of calculation:*
(a) *deciding which goods and services to include;*
(b) *avoiding double counting;*
(c) *inadequate information;*
(d) *how to deal with quality changes etc.*

Q2 (a) This is a straightforward question on equilibrium national income. When answering this type of question, it is best to avoid unnecessary repetition, ie it is not necessary to explain equilibrium in a 'two-sector model' and then to proceed through exactly the same stages of derivation in detail in a 'four-sector' model. Instead, clearly spell out the simplifying assumptions you are making and then proceed to show that you thoroughly understand that equilibrium in the goods market occurs when planned expenditure equals the output that is available. You can show the equilibrium diagrammatically, algebraically, or in words, though probably the use of a 45° *line diagram is most helpful. Indicate also, the alternative way of showing equilibrium in terms of planned injections of demand into the circular flow of income equalling planned withdrawals. Equilibrium income may not however coincide with full employment income. With the aid of deflationary and inflationary gap diagrams you must show how equilibrium in the good market may not coincide with equilibrium in the labour market, ie full employment.*

(b) *To answer this question you should first read about the multiplier in Chapter 16. Investment is an injection into the circular flow of income. An increase in investment shifts the AMD function upwards, causing the equilibrium level of income to rise - conversely imports are a withdrawal or leakage of demand. An increase in imports causes the AMD function to shift downwards, leading to a fall in the equilibrium level of income.*

ANSWER PLAN

(a) (i) *Explain equilibrium as a state of rest in which all the economic agents whose behaviour is being modelled can fulfil their market plans.*

(ii) *With the aid of a 45° line diagram, explain equilibrium national income (equilibrium in the goods market) occurring when $Y = C + I + G - T + X - M$ (4 sector model).*

(iii) *Briefly explain the alternative method of showing equilibrium: $I + G + X = S + T + M$.*

(iv) *Explain that equilibrium in the labour market occurs at full employment.*

(v) *With the aid of a deflationary gap diagram and an inflationary gap diagram explain that equilibrium national income may not coincide with full employment income.*

(b) (i) *Show the positive multiplier effect resulting from an increase in investment. Illustrate on a 45° line diagram.*

(ii) *Show the negative multiplier effect resulting from an increase in imports. Illustrate on a 45° line diagram.*

Q3 (a) *The standard of living refers to the general level of economic welfare attained either by the population as a whole, or by a single individual or household. The standard of living includes the utility obtained from:*

(i) *Goods and services bought in the market economy.*

(ii) *Goods and services provided 'free' by the state, either as public goods or merit goods.*

(iii) *Positive externalities received 'outside the market'. (Conversely, negative externalities which yield disutility reduce the standard of living.)*

(iv) *Other intangibles such as the value placed by individuals on leisure and on family and friends etc.*

The cost of living refers to the monetary cost of obtaining the goods and services bought in the market economy, though some measures of the cost of living might include a measure of the cost of providing health care and education etc through the state.

(b) *The simplest way of measuring changes in the standard of living is to compare GNP figures per capita over a number of years. There are two main problems involved:*

(i) *The measure of the change in the standard of living is only as accurate as the estimate of the GNP figures. We have already noted in the context of Question 1 the problems involved in measuring national income.*

(ii) *GNP figures at best measures only the part of people's standard of living resulting from economic activity in the market economy and from goods and services produced by the state. The impact of externalities upon the standard of living and other 'intangibles' is not reflected by the GNP figures. Consider, for example, a situation in which higher real incomes and the increased ownership of automobiles lead to increased traffic congestion. This in turn causes motorists to waste more time sitting in traffic jams and to spend more money on petrol and motor maintenance.*

The latter will be measured in the national income tables as increased expenditure by consumers and firms, implying a welfare gain! But of course, this increased expenditure really represents a welfare loss caused by the unwelcome receipt of a negative externality. Motorists would be better off without the congestion, though their expenditure on motoring might correspondingly fall.

ANSWER PLAN

(a) (i) *Carefully define the standard of living, clearly indicating its components.*

(ii) *Define the cost of living in terms of the monetary expenditure required to purchase the goods and services bought in the market economy.*

(iii) *Emphasise that the standard of living includes components not measured by the cost of living, eg leisure time and 'quality of life' factors.*

(b) (i) *Explain the difficulties in accurately measuring GNP per capita as a measure of standards of living.*

(ii) *Explain how in any case GNP per capita will be an inaccurate measure of the standard of living because it fails to measure the contribution of externalities and other intangibles to the standard of living. Give examples.*

Q4 *Strictly, planned savings and planned investment only tend to equality in a two-sector model of the economy, for which the equilibrium equation is: planned saving = planned investment. In a four sector economy (comprising the government and overseas sectors as well as households and firms), it is more true to say that S + T + M tend to equality with I + G + X (ie in equilibrium, planned withdrawals = planned injections). Nevertheless, the essence of the question is that Keynesian analysis centres upon the possibility (or likelihood?) that households will plan to save more of their incomes than firms wish to borrow to finance investment. The resulting excess supply of savings causes income and output to fall via a downward multiplier process, with S and I being equated at an under-full employment level of income.*

ANSWER PLAN

(i) *State firmly that you are going to answer the question in terms of a 'two sector' Keynesian income-expenditure model.*

(ii) *Illustrate the model in terms of a deflationary gap diagram, in which S = I at an equilibrium level of income below full employment.*

(iii) *Explain that, in Keynesian terms, this is caused by deficient aggregate demand in the economy.*

(iv) *Contrast the Keynesian and 'classical' models, drawing attention to the fact that in the 'classical' model the rate of interest equates S and I, whereas in the Keynesian model, the level of income or output changes to bring about equilibrium.*

(v) *Emphasise that this is of critical importance, since in the 'classical' model, equilibrium should occur at full employment, whereas in the Keynesian model an under-full employment equilibrium at a depressed level of income and output is a possibility.*

Q5 *ANSWER PLAN*

(i) The answer plan to the first part of this question can be the same as for part (a) of Question 1.

(ii) Explain that in the UK National Accounts, the term national income is used more specifically, being equal to net national product at factor cost.

(iii) Explain that to convert GDP at market prices into NNP at factor cost:

(a) depreciation must be subtracted;
(b) net property income from abroad must be added;
(c) indirect taxes must be subtracted, but subsidies added.

ANSWERS TO QUESTIONS IN CHAPTER 16

EXERCISES

1(a) *The equilibrium (in reduced form) is:*

$$Y = \frac{1}{x + ct + m}(I + G + X)$$

Thus

$$Y = \frac{1}{(0.2)+(0.4)+(0.2)}(£1{,}920m)$$

$$Y = (1.25) \times (£1{,}920m)$$

$$Y = £2{,}400 \text{ million}$$

(b) Since the multiplier is 1.25 and

$$G = \frac{\Delta Y}{1.25}$$

$$G = \frac{£1{,}200m}{1.25}$$

$$G = £960 \text{ million}$$

(c) The formula for the government spending multiplier is:

$$\frac{1}{s + ct + m}$$

Its value is: 1.25.

(d) (i) The government's budget (T - G) initially is:

0.5 (£2,400m) - £800m

which is

£1,200m - £800m
or a surplus of £400 million

After the increase in government spending and the resulting increase in income, the budget becomes:

0.5 (£3,600m) - £1,760m
or £1,800m - £1,760m

Thus the budget surplus falls to £40 million.

In the new equilibrium, the balance of payments becomes:

£600m - £90.2 x £3,600m) or
£600m - £720m
which is a deficit of £120 million.

(ii) The balance of payments (X - M) initially is:
£600m - (0.2 x £2,400m) or
£600m - £480m
which is a surplus of £120 million.

The expansion of demand has pulled more imports into the economy, causing the balance of payments to move into deficit.

MULTIPLE CHOICE QUESTIONS

1 B
2 D
3 C
4 C
5 C

EXAMINATION QUESTIONS

Q1 (a) *It is insufficient just to state the multiplier formula. You must explain the multiplier as a dynamic process using an example similar to the one introduced in section 5 of Chapter 16 illustrated in Figure 16.1. In this example, savings is the only leakage of demand from the circular flow of income at each stage of the multiplier process, so the investment multiplier is:*

$$\frac{1}{s}$$

where s is the marginal propensity to save.

(b) *Assuming that imports and taxation are in part income-induced and not autonomous, the formula for the multiplier becomes:*

$$\frac{1}{s + t + m} \text{ or}$$

$$\frac{1}{s + ct + m}$$

if consumption decisions are made out of post-tax disposable income. At each stage of the income generation process, part of current income leaks into taxation and imports, as well as into savings, and thus is not available for spending in the next round of income generation.

ANSWER PLAN

(a) (i) *Define the investment multiplier.*

(ii) *Illustrate the process on a diagram similar to Figure 16.1.*

(iii) *Explain how the size of the multiplier depends upon the marginal propensity to save only.*

(b) (i) *Explain that taxation and imports will now cause further leakages of demand at each stage of the multiplier process.*

(ii) *Explain how this affects the formula for the multiplier and reduces the size of the multiplier.*

Q2 ANSWER PLAN

(a) (i) *Define the investment multiplier.*

(ii) *Explain that the investment multiplier is not* directly *useful to governments, since private sector investment is not a policy instrument available to the government. Perhaps briefly contrast this with government spending and taxation.*

(iii) *Nevertheless, if the government wishes to forecast the likely effects upon the economy of an announcement by the CBI that investment is picking up or collapsing, knowledge of the size of the investment multiplier is important.*

(iv) *Such knowledge is probably more important for a Keynesian government than for a monetarist government. A Keynesian government is much more likely to wish to use fiscal policy to counter the effects of a change in private sector expenditure, in order to stabilise and manage the level of aggregate demand.*

(b) (i) *Illustrate with a diagram or numerical example the dynamic nature of the multiplier process.*

(c) (i) *Explain how income-induced leakages of aggregate demand determine the size of the multiplier.*

(ii) *Illustrate with a numerical example.*

(iii) *If you have time, explain that the multiplier effect in terms of real output may differ from the effect in terms of nominal output or money income.*

Q3 ANSWER PLAN

(a) (i) *Explain the multiplier concept.*

(ii) *Show that the government spending multiplier is represented by:*

$$\Delta Y = k\Delta G$$

(iii) *Briefly discuss the determinants of the value of k.*

(iv) *Explain how the larger the size of both* ΔG *and k, the greater will be the effect upon equilibrium income* (ΔY).

(v) *Given the balance of payments as* ($X - M$) *and assuming that exports are autonomous and that the import function is* $M = mY$, *imports will increase by* $m\Delta Y$. *Since exports are assumed not to change, the effect is to reduce an initial balance of payments surplus, or to increase the size of an initial payments deficit.*

(b) (i) *An increase in exports of* ΔX *improves the balance of payments.*

(ii) *It also causes a multiplier effect similar to that caused by the government spending multiplier.*

(iii) *This in turn, via the increase in income, causes imports to rise which cause the balance of payments to deteriorate.*

Q4 ANSWER PLAN

(i) *Draw a diagram similar to Figure 13.1.*

(ii) *Show how an initial increase in income, caused by an increase in aggregate demand, causes further stages of income generation with each stage being smaller than the previous stage.*

(iii) *Explain how income leaking into savings at each stage of the multiplier process causes each stage to be smaller than the last one.*

(iv) *The relative size of each stage thus depends upon the marginal propensity to save. (Don't forget to define the MPS.) The formula for the multiplier is:* $\frac{1}{s}$

(v) *Illustrate the multiplier on a 45° line diagram.*

(vi) *Show how when additional income-induced leakages of demand are introduced into the model (a marginal tax rate and a marginal propensity to import), the multiplier becomes*

$$\frac{1}{s + t + m} \text{ or possibly}$$

$$\frac{1}{s + ct + m}.$$

ANSWERS TO QUESTIONS IN CHAPTER 17

EXERCISES

1(a)

Year	*(i) Net Investment*	*(ii) Gross Investment*
1987	*5 machines*	*15 machines*
1988	*20 machines*	*30 machines*
1989	*10 machines*	*20 machines*
1990	*0 machines*	*10 machines*
1991	*-10 machines*	*0 machines*

(b) In 1992 the 15 machines purchased in 1987 will need replacing. If demand for the firm's output continues to fall net investment will be negative, so gross investment will be less than 15 machines. If demand for the firm's output is constant at 2,500, net investment will be zero and gross investment will equal replacement investment (15 machines). If demand begins to grow again, net investment will be positive, so gross investment will exceed 15 machines.

(c) The accelerator theory.

MULTIPLE CHOICE QUESTIONS

1 *D*
2 *B*
3 *D*
4 *C*
5 *C*

EXAMINATION QUESTIONS

Q1 *(a) You should base your answer around the marginal efficiency of investment (MEI) theory. According to this theory, investment is determined by the expected future returns of potential investment projects, together with the cost of borrowing (the rate of interest). Even when firms do not need to borrow, the rate of interest still influences investment because the rate of interest represents the opportunity cost of investment, ie what the firm could earn from lending its funds rather than investing the funds in a capital project. Having briefly explained the MEI theory, show with the aid of a diagram how the interest-elasticity of the MEI curve reflects the importance of the rate of interest. If the MEI curve is interest-inelastic, the rate of interest is less important than other determinants of investment. Suggest what these other determinants might be and also discuss why businessmen may not be responsive to the rate of interest.*

(b) Base your answer around the investment multiplier. The larger the investment multiplier and the larger also the initial increase in investment, the greater will be the impact upon nominal income. Discuss (briefly) the role of leakages of demand in determining the size of the investment multiplier and discuss also, whether the multiplier effect results in real output and employment (economic activity) being stimulated, or simply results in inflation. Note also that increased investment adds to the country's production potential, shifting the economy's production possibility frontier outwards and contributing, in the long run, to economic growth and international competitiveness.

ANSWER PLAN

(a) (i) Carefully define investment, distinguishing between fixed investment and inventory investment.

(ii) Explain the MEI theory.

(iii) Show how the importance of the rate of interest as a determinant of investment depends upon the slope (and elasticity) of the MEI curve.

(iv) Develop the Keynesian argument that the state of business confidence may be more important than the rate of interest as a determinant of investment.

(v) Discuss briefly other possible influences upon investment, eg role of technical progress.

(b) (i) Explain the investment multiplier.

(ii) Discuss the short-term effects on economic activity resulting from the investment multiplier.

(iii) Discuss more long-term changes resulting from the effects upon economic growth, the competitiveness of the capital stock, multiplier-accelerator interactions etc.

Q2 *The multiplier measures the change in the equilibrium level of national income resulting from an initial change in aggregate demand. We can identify separate multipliers for each of the components of aggregate demand, eg the government spending multiplier and the import multiplier. However, for the purpose of this question concentrate upon the investment multiplier:*

$$\Delta Y = k(\Delta I)$$

Whereas the investment multiplier represents a functional relationship running from a change in investment to a change in income, in the accelerator relationship the direction of causation is reversed:

$$I = v(\Delta Y)$$

You must explain how the nature of each relationship depends in part upon the two coefficients k and v. The multiplier coefficient k is 'demand-determined' by leakages of demand from the circular flow of income, where v, the capital-output ratio, is 'supply-side' determined. Having explained each concept clearly and distinguished between the two, you must then show how the multiplier interacts with the accelerator to model the 'dynamic' movement through time of income and output. This is the basis of 'growth models' of the economy and the interaction can also produce business cycles.

ANSWER PLAN

(i) Define the multiplier.

(ii) Define the accelerator.

(iii) Explain the determinants of the multiplier and accelerator coefficients (k and v).

(iv) Explain how the functional relationship between I and Y is reversed in the accelerator theory compared to the investment multiplier theory.

(v) Show how the two relationships can be brought together.

(vi) Explain how interactions between the multiplier and the accelerator may model the growth (and decline) of income and output over time.

(vii) Briefly explain that business cycles may result.

Q3 *You should answer this question in terms of the marginal efficiency of investment (MEI) theory and the accelerator theory, both of which suggest (in different ways) why investment is likely to be volatile. In the MEI theory, sudden changes in business con-*

fidence and expectations cause the MEI curve to be unstable, resulting in fluctuations in investment. In the accelerator theory, relatively small chances in the rate of growth of output and demand can induce large rises and falls in the absolute level of investment. Don't however devote all your answer to investment. A balanced answer will include some mention of why consumption may be relatively stable. You might explain this in terms of the predictions of the permanent income consumption theory or the life-cycle consumption theory (see Chapter 14).

ANSWER PLAN

(i) *Carefully distinguish between aggregate investment and consumption and, perhaps briefly note their relative importance in aggregate expenditure.*

(ii) *Explain volatile investment in terms of the MEI theory and the role of business confidence and expectations.*

(iii) *Explain volatile investment in terms of the accelerator theory.*

(iv) *Explain stable consumption in terms of the permanent income consumption theory or the life-cycle consumption theory.*

Q4 *(a)* *The term 'business cycle' is a relatively new label for a phenomenon previously know as the 'trade cycle'. It refers to the fact that over a number of years economic activity displays a cyclical tendency to rise and fall around its long-term trend, which in western industrialised countries, has generally been a long-term upward growth path. At various times, economists have identified cycles in economic activity ranging in length from a cycle as short as 52 months, to 'long cycles' (also known as Kondratieff cycles after the Russian scientist who identified them in the 1920s), each lasting about 50 or 60 years. However, the modern business cycle or 'short cycle' is normally held to be about 4 or 5 years in length, marked by the four phases illustrated in Figure 17.6: slump or depression; recovery or upturn; boom; and deflation or downturn.*

(b) *There is no generally agreed theory on the cause of business cycle. In Chapter 17 we have considered one theory in some depth: the mathematical 'multiplier-accelerator' theory which models the cyclical growth of income or output in terms of interactions between the multiplier and the accelerator. But business cycles have been 'explained' in terms of such diverse causes as sun-spot activity affecting agricultural harvests and psychological swings in business mood between pessimism and optimism. Milton Friedman, a leading monetarist, has explained the business cycle in terms of monetary expansion followed by bank crashes and monetary contraction. Marxists argue that the downturn in a business cycle is a necessary part of the restructuring process whereby capitalism attempts to ensure its survival as an economic system through restoring the rate of profit. Political scientists relate the economic cycle to the need by modern democratic governments to appeal to the electorate for reelection every 4 or 5 years, 'buying' votes by engineering a pre-election boom. This is known as the 'political business cycle'. In short, there are many and diverse explanations of the business cycle, each of which may contain an element of truth, but none of which finds wide acceptance amongst economists in general as a uni-*

versally applicable theory of cyclical activity.

ANSWER PLAN

(a) (i) *Describe the modern business cycle as an observed feature of economic activity in the world economy.*

(ii) *Illustrate the four phases of the cycle on a diagram similar to Figure 17.6 and carefully distinguish the actual path of output from the underlying trend or growth path.*

(iii) *Briefly note that cycles of different length have sometimes been identified, eg 'long-waves' or 'Kondratieff cycles', but that the modern 'short' business cycle is usually held to be about 4 or 5 years in length.*

(b) (i) *Develop* **one** *explanation of business cycles in some depth, eg the 'multiplier-accelerator' theory, but point out its limitations (eg values of v and k that are not empirically observed are necessary to produce regular cycles in the mathematical model).*

(ii) *Briefly suggest other theories and suggest causes, eg sunspots; monetary expansion and contraction; Marxist theory; the theory of the 'political business cycle'.*

(iii) *Conclude by emphasising that there is no generally agreed theory of business cycle.*

Q5 ANSWER PLAN

(i) *State that the accelerator principle is a theory of investment.*

(ii) *It centres on the proposition that firms desire to keep a fixed ratio between their capital stock and their current flow of output. If demand for output is growing, firms must invest in additional capital goods to maintain this ratio.*

(iii) *Illustrate with a numerical example, drawing attention to the fact that when the rate of growth of output accelerates, an absolute increase in investment is induced.*

(iv) *Argue that the acceleration principle is probably of little direct relevance in explaining the decision making process undertaken by firms when they make investment decisions. Firms are much more likely to be influenced by expected profit, the cost of borrowing, the availability of new types of capital goods etc, none of which are relevant to the acceleration principle.*

(v) *Nevertheless, the acceleration principle provides an explanation of the volatility or instability of investment and forms the basis of the investment equation in macro-economic model building and forecasting.*

Q6 *The theory of investment which Keynes introduced in his 'General Theory' in 1936 is the marginal efficiency of investment theory (or marginal efficiency of capital theory). In the MEI theory, the main determinants of investment are businessmens' expectations of the future productivity of investment (embodied in the internal rate of return of each investment), and the cost of borrowing or rate of interest. In much Keynesian analysis, the resulting MEI curve or investment function is interest inelastic, indicating that investment is not very responsive to changes in the rate of interest. The state of business confidence (or 'animal spirits') is regarded as much more important, causing the MEI function to* *shift leftwards or rightwards as businesses change their expectations about an unknown and uncertain future. Keynes believed that the resulting volatility of investment contributes to the instability of aggregate demand in a market economy, justifying the use of fiscal policy to stabilise demand the business cycle.*

ANSWER PLAN

(i) *State firmly that the MEI theory is the Keynesian theory of investment.*

(ii) *Explain the theory, drawing attention to the roles of the state of business expectations and the rate of interest as determinants of investment.*

(iii) *Discuss the importance of the rate of interest, according to Keynesians.*

(iv) *Discuss the role of expectations and the state of business confidence.*

(v) *If you have time, indicate that modern Keynesians accept that there are other determinants of investment besides those modelled in the MEI theory, eg the acceleration principle, the state of technical progress etc.*

ANSWERS TO QUESTIONS IN CHAPTER 18

EXERCISES

1 (a) *The poverty trap.*

(b) *The poverty trap is caused by the existence of a zone of overlap between the income tax threshold and the means-tested welfare benefits ceiling. A low-paid worker caught in this zone of overlap, finds himself little (if any) better-off following an increase in his income, since he will pay income tax and National Insurance contributions and lose some or all of his ability to claim means-tested benefits. The zone of overlap is itself caused by the progressive nature of income tax and the means-tested nature of welfare benefits. Fiscal drag has made the overlap worse by reducing the income tax threshold in real terms, moving it down the income pyramid.*

(c) *The poverty trap can be reduced or eliminated by any policy which reduces or eliminates the zone of overlap between the income tax threshold and the benefits ceiling. Raising the income tax threshold in real terms so that the low paid pay no tax is one possibility. The abolition of means-tested benefits and their replacement with universal benefits would also abolish the zone of overlap. Finally, the benefits system could be merged into the tax structure in a negative income tax scheme.*

2 (a) *The main change is the increase in the importance of the fixed or long-term debt (gilts and National Saving securities) from 70.4% of the national debt in 1970 to 87.7% in 1987. At the same time, floating or short-term debt fell from 15.1% to 5.2% of the total. The other major change is the fall in the externally-held debt as a proportion of the total.*

(b) *The key statistics here are ratio of national debt to GNP, and the cost of servicing the national debt as a ratio of GNP. The national debt as a ratio of GNP (the 'real' debt) fell from 64% in 1970 to 43.6% in 1982, though it then slightly increased during the 1980s to 44.8% in 1987. Thus in so far as the burden of the debt is measured by the 'real' debt, the burden fell. The proportional importance of the externally-held debt, which is another indicator of the burden of the debt, also fell. However, servicing costs as a ratio of GNP rose from 2.8% in 1970 to 4.2% in 1987, indicating an increasing burden upon the government and taxpayers (but not upon the nation as a whole) of interest payments.*

MULTIPLE CHOICE QUESTIONS

1 A
2 D
3 D
4 A
5 C

EXAMINATION QUESTIONS

Q1 (a) This is a question about the aims or objectives of taxation, rather than the canons or principles of taxation. Nevertheless, one function of taxation is to accord as much as possible with the principles of taxation. However, you should structure your answer in the main around the allocative, distributive and economic management objectives of taxation which are described in Chapter 18.

(b) The main disadvantages of a progressive income tax relate to incentives and disincentives. If the supply curve of labour is upward-sloping, the higher marginal rates at which a progressive income tax is levied have a disincentive effect on effort. Hourly-paid workers may be discouraged from working overtime while highly paid workers such as doctors, may join a 'brain-drain' leaving the country to live in a more benign tax regime. At the same time a steeply progressive income tax may create an incentive for tax avoidance and tax evasion, workers in the latter case failing to declare income earned in the 'black' economy.

A further disadvantage of a progressive income tax relates to the emergence of the poverty trap which we have discussed in the context of Exercise 1 above.

ANSWER PLAN

(a) (i) Define taxation.

(ii) State that a function of taxation is to meet as many of the principles or canons of taxation as possible. Briefly list these.

(iii) Discuss the allocative functions of taxation (in terms of improving resource allocation).

(iv) Discuss the distributive functions of taxation (in terms of achieving a 'desirable' distribution of income and wealth).

(v) discuss the use of taxation for economic management, eg should it be used for demand management?

(b) (i) Define a progressive income tax.

(ii) Discuss the disincentive effects of the tax. Relate your answer to assumptions about the slope of the supply curve of labour. Introduce the Laffer curve.

(iii) Explain how progressive income tax may contribute to the poverty trap and to the unemployment trap.

(iv) However, the seriousness of the possible disadvantages depend upon the structure of the tax and the marginal and average rates at which it is

levied. The disadvantages will not be serious with a mildly progressive tax and they may of course be exceeded by the advantages or benefits of the tax.

Q2 *This is a straightforward question about the principles of taxation: equity; economy; convenience; certainty; efficiency; and flexibility. You should structure your answer around a discussion of each of these in turn, taking care to relate the principle to the economy as it is now. For example, the need in the late 1980s to reform the system of local authority taxation can be considered in terms of the principles of equity, economy and efficiency.*

ANSWER PLAN

(i) *Clearly state that you are going to discuss each of the principles or canons of taxation in turn.*

(ii) *Briefly list the principles of taxation.*

(iii) *Devote a paragraph to a discussion of each principle. Discuss equity, economy and efficiency in greatest depth. Illustrate, where appropriate, from recent or proposed reforms to the UK tax system (or to the tax system of any other country).*

Q3 *Since the question does not specify whether the increase in direct taxation represents an increase in the total burden of taxation or merely a shift of the burden away from indirect taxation, it would be wise to state both possibilities. And clearly also, the effects will differ according to whether there is a small or a massive general increase in direct taxation. The main form of direct increase in taxation is income tax and the effects of an increase in personal income tax depends largely upon the shape of an individual's supply curve of labour. If the supply curve of labour is upward-sloping, an increase in direct taxation has a disincentive effect. But in the case of a 'backward-bending' supply curve of labour, more labour would be supplied as workers were forced to work longer in order to maintain their living standards.*

ANSWER PLAN

(i) *Define a direct tax, stating that income tax is the main example of a direct tax.*

(ii) *State that the effects will differ according to whether or not the general burden of taxation is increased and according to the relative size of the increase in direct taxation.*

(iii) *Argue that the nature of the effects of an increase in income tax depend on the shape of the supply curve of labour. Discuss incentive and disincentive effects, analysed in terms of upward-sloping and 'backward-bending' supply curves of labour.*

(iv) *Discuss related effects, such as tax avoidance and evasion, the 'black' economy, the effect of lowering tax thresholds upon the poverty trap etc.*

Q4 *In the United Kingdom, the Treasury is the government's finance ministry. The Treasury is probably the most important single government department or ministry, since it has ultimate control of the budgets of all the main spending departments, such as Health, Social Security, Defence and Education. Together with the Bank of England, the Treasury constitutes the country's 'monetary authorities', and it stands at the heart of the economic policy-making process, ultimately responsible for mone-*

tary policy and exchange rate policy as well as fiscal policy. But although it is the most powerful government department, the Treasury is also the smallest, with just 350 senior officials in effect running the whole of British economic policy. The five main specific tasks of the Treasury are:

(i) General management of the economy. *This involves responding to signals such as changes in the money supply and working in close co-operation with the Bank of England to raise or lower interest rates, influence the foreign exchange market and manage the national debt.*

(ii) Participation in international economic management, *for example with bodies such as the EEC and the IMF, or less formal or official groupings such as the 'Group of Seven' leading western industrial countries within the IMF.*

(iii) The annual budget-making process.

(iv) The control of public expenditure.

(v) Management of the civil service.

The Budgetary process begins in the autumn with the so-called 'Budget starters' which are technical changes in tax law required by EEC directives or requested by the Inland Revenue or Customs and Excise. In January and early February, various interest groups or pressure groups such as the CBI and cigarette manufacturers lobby the Chancellor of the Exchequer to plead their cases. But as the budget day in mid-March approaches, the Chancellor (who is the senior Treasury minister) ceases contact with the outside world and goes 'into purdah'. The momentum within the Treasury increases as at this late stage the final form of the Budget takes shape. The Cabinet is consulted about the broad shape of the Budget but has little real influence over the Treasury. On Budget Day in mid-March the Chancellor announces changes in tax codes and any proposed legislation required for more major reform to the tax structure. In the weeks that follow, the Finance Bill passes through Parliament, putting into legislative form the changes in tax rates announced in the Budget. On Budget Day, the Chancellor also publishes his Financial Statement or 'Red Book', presenting his views on the state of the UK economy, its performance in the past year and the prospects for the future. Since 1980, this has involved the publication of the Medium Term Financial Strategy (MTFS) which has provided the formal framework within which the Chancellor's 'monetarist' fiscal and monetary policies have been pursued.

Strictly, the budgetary process we have just described, involves only the revenue side of the 'fiscal equation' and not the question of the level and pattern of public expenditure. But while the budgetary process is taking place, the annual public expenditure 'round' of negotiation between the Treasury and spending ministries is also under way. Essentially, the Treasury's job is to say 'no' to increases in public expenditure, while traditionally each spending department seeks to defend its existing programmes and perhaps to expand and add to them. The battle between the Treasury and the spending departments takes place during the summer months, with the Chief Secretary to the Treasury playing a crucial role - in effect as Minister for Public Expenditure. Once general agreement has been reached by the Cabinet (usually in July) about the overall level of public expenditure, the Chief Secretary enters into bilateral negotiations with individual departments about their spending totals. Any differences that cannot be resolved then go to the 'Star Chamber' - a Cabinet committee largely made up of non-spending ministers. The results of the negotiations are announced in November in the Autumn

Statement to Parliament *presented by the Chancellor. This is followed in January or February with the publication of the Government's* White Paper on Public Expenditure *which sets out the Government's medium-term plans for expenditure in broad terms three or four years ahead, as well as spending details for individual ministries for the next financial year. Though subject to much less 'media hype' than the Budget, the White Paper effectively sets the parameters on the public spending side of the 'fiscal equation', which limit the Chancellor's freedom of manoeuvre to reduce tax rates in his Budget a month or so later.*

ANSWER PLAN

(i) Explain that the Treasury in the UK is the country's finance ministry.

(ii) Briefly describe its organisation in terms of a senior minister (the Chancellor of the Exchequer), a Chief Secretary, junior ministers and civil servants.

(iii) List the five functions of the Treasury.

(iv) Discuss its broad function in overall management of the economy.

(v) Discuss the budgetary function.

(vi) Discuss the control of public expenditure.

(vii) Assess the power of the Treasury over other government ministries and over the economy in general.

Q5 *(a) The national debt is a stock whereas the PSBR is a flow. Strictly, it is the national debt and the central government borrowing requirement (CGBR) which are linked since the national debt is the accumulated stock of past central government borrowing and the CGBR is the flow of current new central government borrowing that adds to the stock. But since the CGBR is the major part and 'prime mover' within the PSBR, the national debt and the PSBR are related, though less closely than the national debt and the CGBR.*

(b) The growth in the importance attached to the PSBR closely parallels the growing dominance in the 1970s and early 1980s of monetarist and 'classical' theory over Keynesian theory. You must explain why monetarists attach importance to the PSBR because they believe its growth has two undesirable consequences: 'crowding-out' and monetary growth which itself causes inflation. Explain these in some detail and critically assess whether they are indeed caused by PSBR growth. Given that both these consequences of PSBR growth are undesirable, they explain why control of PSBR growth - and the attainment of a balanced budget - are important aims of monetarist economic policy.

ANSWER PLAN

(a) (i) Define the PSBR as a flow (distinguishing it from the CGBR).

(ii) Define the national debt as a stock.

(iii) Explain the linkage between the two.

(b) (i) Relate PSBR growth to the 'Keynesian v monetarist' controversy.

(ii) State the Keynesians attached little importance to PSBR growth.

(iii) But monetarists attach importance to PSBR growth because they believe it

causes both 'crowding-out' and inflation (via monetary growth).

(iv) *Therefore PSBR control (and reduction) is an important part of monetarist fiscal policy.*

Q6 ANSWER PLAN

(a) (i) *Define the national debt as the accumulated stock of central government borrowing.*

(ii) *Briefly explain its components, eg fixed and floating debt; dead-weight and reproductive debt; domestically-held and externally-held debt.*

(b) (i) *In so far that the debt is externally-held it consititutes a burden, but interest payments on domestically-held debt are simply an internal transfer.*

(ii) *Deadweight debt (but not reproductive debt) is a burden.*

(iii) *Servicing costs may also represent a burden.*

(iv) *A large debt may also constrain or limit the government's freedom of choice in its macro-economic policy.*

(v) *But the best measure of the extent to which the debt may constitute a burden is the 'real' debt. Explain how the 'real debt' (ie the nominal debt as a ratio of national output at market prices) may be falling even though the nominal debt is rising.*

ANSWERS TO QUESTIONS IN CHAPTER 19

EXERCISES

1 (a) *8 per cent*
(b) *40 per cent*
(c) *28 per cent*
(d) *£2,500.*

MULTIPLE CHOICE QUESTIONS

1 *D*
2 *C*
3 *B*
4 *A*
5 *D*
6 *C*

EXAMINATION QUESTIONS

Q1 (a) *As Question 2 indicates, money is sometimes defined as 'anything generally acceptable in payment of debt'. However, this is too narrow a definition since it concentrates only on the medium of exchange function of money. A credit card would increasingly meet this definition in countries such as the UK and USA, but a credit card is a money substitute rather than money. This is because it does not fulfil the other condition necessary for an asset to function as money: the function of a store of value or wealth. The other two functions of money are as a unit of account and standard of deferred payment.*

(b) *To answer this part of the question properly, you must first read Chapter 18 which covers the Quantity Theory of Money and the monetarist theory of inflation. You must briefly explain the theory and then discuss the assumptions necessary for the Quantity Theory to hold. Mention briefly how Keynesians attack the theory by attacking these assumptions and perhaps also, discuss whether the Quantity Theory stands up to empirical evidence.*

ANSWER PLAN

(a) (i) *State that money is defined by its two principal functions: medium of exchange and unit of account.*

(ii) *Contrast 'money' with 'near monies' and 'money substitutes'.*

(iii) *List and briefly explain the other functions of money as a unit of account and a standard of deferred payment.*

(b) (i) *Explain that the monetarist theory of inflation is based upon the Quantity Theory of Money.*

(ii) *Explain the theory, drawing attention to its key assumptions.*

(iii) *Briefly describe how Keynesians attack the theory.*

(iv) *Discuss whether the empirical evidence supports the Quantity Theory.*

Q2 ANSWER PLAN

(i) *State that the Bank of England is the United Kingdom's central bank.*

(ii) *List the 'narrow' or specific functions of the Bank of England: responsibility for note issue; bankers' bank; the government's bank; management of the country's foreign exchange reserves; supervisor and regulator of the banking and financial systems; lender of last resort to the banking system.*

(iii) *Briefly describe each of the functions listed.*

(iv) *Explain that the 'wider' and most important function of the Bank of England is to implement the government's monetary policy.*

(v) *Briefly explain some of the techniques of control through which monetary policy is implemented, eg open market operations; the Bank of England's lending rate.*

Q3 *This is a question which tests your ability to show how a commercial bank arranges the assets side of its balance sheet so as to 'trade-off' between profitability and liquidity. Certain of a bank's assets are secure either in the sense that the government guarantees to redeem Treasury bills and gilts on maturity, or because the bank itself secures a loan or advance to a customer against the collateral of other assets owned by the debtor, eg property.*

ANSWER PLAN

(i) *Define a commercial bank as a profit-making institution whose main business is (a) to accept deposits from the general public, (b) to create deposits when making advances or loans to the general public.*

(ii) *Set out a commercial bank's balance sheet.*

(iii) *Explain how the bank's ability to be both profitable and solvent is constrained by the need to keep a cash ratio and a liquid assets ratio. Explain how the bank organises its assets so as to trade-off liquidity against profitability.*

(iv) *Explain how the bank can minimise the risks of default or bad debts by securing its loans.*

Q4 *This question is testing exactly the same topic as Question 3, illustrating how* *slightly different wording can 'disguise' a 'standard question'. The answer plan for Question 3 is relevant for this question also.*

Q5 *For your answer to part (a) of this question, see the suggested solution to Exercise 1, Chapter 20. The structure of interest rates displayed in the numerical example in this Exercise also indicates how you might approach part (b). In recent years all the United Kingdom clearing banks have announced a base rate, usually chosen with reference to the Bank of England's lending rate and the general level of short-term interest rates in money markets. The clearing banks then set the various interest rates they charge on overdraft and term loans a fixed percentage above their base rates, while rates of interest offered to attract deposits from the general public are normally set below base rate. The general structure of a clearing bank's interest rates reflect all the influences upon interest rates listed in the context of part (a) of the question. Thus credit card interest rates are normally the highest since users of credit cards are prepared to pay a higher interest rate because of the convenience that 'borrowing on plastic' offers. The interest charged by banks on term loans is higher than overdraft rates, because a bank can demand repayment of an overdraft immediately. However, mortgage rates charged by banks are usually lower, because the loan is secured and because economies of large-scale borrowing are involved.*

ANSWER PLAN

(a) (i) *Briefly define a rate of interest.*

(ii) *List and briefly explain the determinants of different interest rates: the differential between borrowing and lending; risk; security; time; convenience; creditworthiness; economies of scale; the impact of monetary policy; barriers between markets.*

(b) (i) *Introduce examples of rates of interest charged to borrowers and paid to depositers by commercial banks.*

(ii) *Explain how each of these illustrates the influence of the factors listed in your answer to (a).*

Q6 ANSWER PLAN

(a) (i) *List the three motives specified by Keynes for holding or demanding money: the transactions, precautionary and speculative motives.*

(ii) *With the aid of diagrams, explain each in some detail.*

(b) (i) *Draw a diagram to show the demand for money curve (the liquidity preference curve). Show how the demand for money increases moving down the curve at lower rates of interest.*

(ii) *But the extent depends upon the interest elasticity of the demand for money. Traditionally, Keynesians have assumed that the demand for money is interest elastic. As the rate of interest falls, the demand for money increases more than proportionately. By contrast monetarists assume the demand for money is interest inelastic. As the rate of interest falls, the demand for money increases less than proportionately.*

(c) (i) *Define savings as income not consumed.*

(ii) *Explain how savings can be held in the form of money, eg cash and bank deposits, or in non-money financial assets such as shares and government bonds.*

Q7 *Liquidity preference theory is the name given to the theory of the demand for money developed by Keynes in his 'General Theory' published in 1936. In particular, Keynes emphasised the existence of a speculative motive for wishing to hold money as a passive wealth asset or store of value in order to avoid capital losses and to realise capital gains resulting from expected movements in the rate of interest and bond prices. The Keynesian demand for money curve - with its slope reflecting the speculative motive for holding money balances - is also known as the liquidity preference curve. You must explain this curve, concentrating in particular upon the speculative demand for money and show how the equilibrium rate of interest and stock of money in the economy are determined where the liquidity preference curve intersects the supply of money curve.*

ANSWER PLAN

(i) *State the liquidity preference theory is the Keynesian theory of the demand for money.*

(ii) *List the transaction, precautionary and speculative motives identified by Keynes for holding money balances.*

(iii) *Briefly explain the transactions and precautionary motives.*

(iv) *Explain at some length the speculative motive, explaining how the demand to hold money as a passive store of value involves a portfolio balance decision or choice between the liquidity of money and the illiquidity of bonds. Also explain the role of speculation in this choice.*

(v) *Show that when the supply curve of money is introduced, the equilibrium rate of interest and stock of money are determined in the money market.*

ANSWER TO QUESTIONS IN CHAPTER 20

EXERCISES

1(a) The structure of interest rates refers to the fact that there are many different interest rates for different types of loan and financial asset, and for different lengths of loan or maturity of financial asset.

(b) The most important influences upon interest rates include:

(i) ***The differential between borrowing and lending.*** *Financial institutions or intermediaries such as banks and building societies charge customers a higher rate of interest for a loan than the rate they offer to savers to attract deposits. The differential is an important part of the intermediary's profit.*

(ii) ***Risk.*** *The greater the risk involved to the lender, the higher the rate of interest.*

(iii) ***Security.*** *When borrowers offer collateral, such as property, to secure a loan (as in the case of mortgages), the risk to the lender is considerably lower, so the interest rate is lower.*

(iv) ***Time.*** *Generally, the longer the time period of a loan the greater the risk, so the higher the rate of interest. Term loans fixed for long periods 'tie up' the lenders funds (they are illiquid) and thus are not available for the lender to use. In these circumstances, the rate of interest charged is higher.*

(v) ***Convenience.*** *Credit card users are prepared to pay very high rates of interest for the convenience the credit card provides.*

(vi) ***Credit-worthiness.*** *Credit-worthy customers with good repayment 'track records' can usually obtain cheaper loans.*

(vii) ***Economies of scale.*** *Lower interest rates may be offered on very large loans because the administrative costs 'per unit' of the loan are considerably reduced.*

(viii) ***Monetary policy.*** *Some interest rates such as the Bank of England's lending rate are determined as a part of monetary policy.*

(ix) ***Separation of markets and disequilibrium.*** *At any point of time, separated financial markets will be adjusting to changed market circumstances and will be in a state of disequilibrium.*

MULTIPLE CHOICE QUESTIONS

1 *C*
2 *C*
3 *B*
4 *D*
5 *C*

EXAMINATION QUESTIONS

Q1 *In Chapter 20 we have drawn attention to the distinction between the broad strategy of monetary policy and the more specific or narrow techniques of monetary control pursued within the wider selected strategy. This question is explicitly about the narrower techniques of control such as open market operations, funding and alterations to the Bank of England's lending rate, but nevertheless, it would show depth of understanding to relate these to the overall strategy of monetary control employed. This is especially appropriate for part (b) of the question, with the UK authorities deciding against the implementation of a system of monetary base control, falling back instead on an increased reliance on interest rate manipulation as the principal technique of monetary control employed.*

ANSWER PLAN

(a) (i) *Briefly define money, indicating that most of the stock of money takes the form of bank deposits.*

(ii) *Explain that to control the money supply, the ability of the banking system to create deposits must be controlled.*

(iii) *List specific techniques of control: open market operations; funding; imposing and manipulating required reserve asset ratios; direct controls on bank lending; raising or lowering the Bank of England's lending rate.*

(iv) *Explain briefly how each method works in principle.*

(b) (i) *Explain that the authorities have rejected the introduction of a system of monetary base control, through which the money supply would be influenced via control of the supply of cash to the banking system.*

(ii) *Funding and PSBR control were significant in the early 1980s, but explain that a policy of deliberate 'over-funding' of the PSBR has been abandoned.*

(iii) *Explain that monetary policy relied increasingly during the 1980s upon the rate of interest as an instrument to achieve control over the supply of money by influencing the public's demand for money.*

(iv) *Mention also the abandonment of*

required reserve ratios in 1981 and the suspension of MLR and its replacement with the Bank of England's less formal lending rate in 1982.

Q2 *The conventional approach to this question would be to explain the determination of the equilibrium rate of interest in a supply and demand framework within the money market. The demand for money curve is the liquidity preference curve which was examined in Chapter 19. The money supply is then assumed to be exogenously determined by the monetary authorities as a part of monetary policy, using techniques of control such as open market operations. By shifting the supply of money up or down the liquidity preference curve, the general level of interest rates is determined, though of course, there will be quite a complicated structure of interest rates around the 'general level' reflecting such factors as risk, time and borrowing economies of scale. As we explain in Chapter 20, this conventional approach to interest rate determination assumes that the money supply is exogenous and that the rate of interest is exogenously determined within the supply and demand framework. This approach can be questioned. The rate of interest can be regarded as the exogenous policy instrument, determined as a party of monetary policy by the authorities, with the money supply viewed as passively adapting to accommodate or finance desired transactions at the rate of interest determined by the authorities.*

ANSWER PLAN

(i) *Define the rate of interest as the price of borrowed money.*

(ii) *In liquidity preference theory the rate of interest is determined within the money market at the intersection of the demand curve for money and the supply curve of money.*

(iii) *Explain how the money supply is regarded as exogenous, and how the rate of interest is endogenously determined within the supply and demand framework.*

(iv) *'Real world' interest rates will reflect the structure of interest around the 'general level'.*

(v) *Introduce the possibility that we should reverse our assumptions about the exogeneity and endogeneity respectively of the money supply and the rate of interest.*

Q3 *You should start your answer by defining the rate of interest and then structure your answer to cover the effect of the rate of interest upon investment, consumption, savings and the balance of payments. In Keynesian analysis, the main effect of the rate of interest upon economic activity or the 'real economy' occurs via its effect on business investment through the marginal efficiency of investment theory. A change in investment (or in any component of aggregate demand affected by the rate of interest) then affects nominal income via the multiplier. Briefly discuss whether prices would fall, or real income and employment. Also discuss the interest-elasticity or responsiveness of business investment to the rate of interest. Household consumption and savings decisions may also respond to the rate of interest, though there is considerable evidence that the availability of credit rather than its price is the main factor here. Finally, trace the linkages from high domestic interest rates via capital flows in the balance of payments and an appreciating exchange rate to reduced economic activity at home resulting from uncompetitiveness.*

ANSWER PLAN

(i) *Define the rate of interest, distinguishing the real rate from the nominal rate.*

(ii) *Discuss the effects of a rise in the real rate upon business investment and then trace the multiplier effect upon equilibrium income.*

(iii) *Discuss whether household consumption and savings decisions are affected by the rate of interest.*

(iv) *Explain the linkages between domestic interest rates, capital flows in the balance of payments, the exchange rate and domestic competitiveness.*

ANSWERS TO QUESTIONS IN CHAPTER 21

EXERCISES

1(a) *(i)* *In the years immediately before the decade shown in the data, the UK inflation rate had developed into a strato-inflation, peaking at about 26 per cent in 1975/76. An incomes policy imposed by the Labour Government from 1975 to 1979 then brought the rate of inflation down, without necessarily eliminating the underlying inflationary pressures. Thus the rate of inflation accelerated once again after 1979, when the monetarist Conservative Government elected in 1979 abandoned the incomes policy it inherited from the Labour administration. Monetarists explain the acceleration of inflation in terms of excess monetary growth and expectations of inflation built up during the Keynesian years. Keynesians explained it in terms of trade union militancy, rising commodity prices and other cost-push factors, including the abandonment of the incomes policy. Likewise monetarists explain the falling inflation rate after 1981 in terms of the success of the Medium Term Financial Strategy and other aspects of monetarist policy involving tight monetary control and the reduction of inflationary expectations. Keynesian argue that monetarism, per se, had little to do with the fall in inflation, which is better explained by the impact of falling world commodity prices and the generally deflationary stance of government policy.*

(ii) *As the rate of inflation diminished, so the level of unemployment increased. Explain this in terms of the growth of frictional unemployment (and the unemployment trap) technological unemployment and structural unemployment, which itself is related to the effects of the high exchange rate of the £ upon the competitiveness of UK industries in the early 1980s. Debate also the contribution of the government's deflationary policies and tight monetary and fiscal stances to unemployment. By 1987 employment was growing as the UK economy recovered, though the growth of the working population, as a large number of 18 year olds entered the labour force, meant that the unemployment rate fell only slowly. Most of the growth in employment was in service industries since manufacturing employment continued to decline.*

(b) *According to the data, inflation was greatest when unemployment was lowest and vice versa. Therefore, the data does appear to be consistent with the existence of a 'trade-off' between inflation and unemployment. However, the level of unemployment was higher in all years shown in the data than in had been in the 1950s and 1960s, indicating that the 'trade-off' (represented by the Phillips relationship) had shifted outwards. But we must be very careful about inferring the existence of any sort of relationship from such a small amount of statistical information.*

MULTIPLE CHOICE QUESTIONS

1 *D*
2 *C*
3 *B*
4 *C*
5 *B*

EXAMINATION QUESTIONS

Q1 *Technological change simply means changed methods of combining capital and labour in the process of production. We usually assume that 'technical progress' is taking place, ie that more advanced forms of capital and production processes are being used. When defining 'technical progress', we must distinguish between '**invention**' and '**innovation**'. Invention results from pure scientific research, whereas innovation refers to the application of inventions by firms in the process of production. Technical change usually involves the adoption of methods of production that are more capital-intensive, ie employing more capital and less labour. However, we must distinguish between '**capital-widening**' and '**capital-deepening**'. Capital-widening occurs when more capital per worker is employed, whereas capital-deepening involves a qualitative improvement in the capital combined with each worker, ie better capital. The adoption of more capital-intensive methods of production inevitably means that the same total amount of output can be produced with less labour. Thus if output remains the same after the adoption of the new technology, unemployment must result, both in terms of the overall size of labour force employed and also because different types of skilled or unskilled labour are likely to be needed for working the new technology. But by simultaneously reducing real costs of production while increasing real incomes, technical change can serve to shift society's production possibility curve outwards and increase the level of demand for the product of the industries benefitting from the technical progress. A balanced answer must therefore indicate clearly that technical change can be both job-destroying and job-creating. For any one country such as the United Kingdom, the overall effect will depend in part on whether domestic industries are able to gain a lead in the new technology and export successfully in world markets, in which case any unemployment will be 'exported' to other countries. Conversely, if other countries take the lead in the new technology, domestic unemployment is likely to be high as the country's industries are rendered uncompetitive. Finally, a good answer should display some knowledge of the nature of recent technical progress. It would be useful to compare **automation** with **mechanisation**. Both involve an increase in capital-intensitivity and the use of assembly line production techniques and long production runs that are associated with economies of scale. But whereas **mechanisation** involves men operating machines, thereby creating employment opportunities for unskilled and semi-skilled manual labour, **automation** leads to machines operating other machines and the wholesale shedding process. It also leads to a situation in which manufacturing generally takes place in much smaller factories, employing just a few hundred workers at most. This contrasts with the huge factories employing several thousand workers that were more typical of the age of mechanisation in the early twentieth century.*

ANSWER PLAN

(i) *Define technical change, noting that it usually also involves technical progress.*

(ii) Distinguish between 'capital-widening' and 'capital-deepening' technical change.

(iii) Explain that if output remains unchanged, a move towards capital-intensitivity means that less labour is needed in production. Unemployment is therefore likely.

(iv) Technical change also creates a demand for different skills. Workers with the wrong skills will become unemployed.

(v) But if demand for output increases, the overall demand for labour may also increase, especially in the long run.

(vi) Distinguish between mechanisation and automation and assess their effects on employment.

(vii) Distinguish between the effects of new technology within one country such as the UK and the world-wide effects upon employment.

Q2 ANSWER PLAN

(a) (i) List the various possible causes of unemployment (frictional, structural, 'real wage', demand-deficiency etc).

(ii) Briefly, explain the causes of each type you have listed. Give most emphasis to frictional, structural, 'real-wage' and 'demand-deficient' causes of unemployment.

(b) (i) Suggest appropriate policies to reduce each of the causes you have listed, giving most emphasis to the principal causes listed above.

(ii) Explain that it is vital to 'match' policies with causes, since a misdiagnosis of the true causes of unemployment might render the policy 'cure' ineffective.

Q3 ANSWER PLAN

(a) (i) List the main types or forms of unemployment: 'real wage'; frictional'; structural; technological demand-deficiency etc.

(ii) Briefly explain each type listed.

(b) (i) State that this part of the question requires an explanation of differing regional unemployment rates in the UK.

(ii) Explain that unemployment rates are much higher in the remoter regions and in the older industrial regions and lowest in the south-east.

(iii) Discuss the extent to which frictional unemployment contributes to regional unemployment, eg through the geographical and occupational immobility of labour.

(iv) Discuss the extent to which structural unemployment (eg via the deindustrialisation process) contributes to regional unemployment.

(v) Discuss whether government policies have contributed to regional unemployment, eg by preventing the market mechanism from operating; via the effects of 'stop-go' policies on regional economic performance etc.

Q4 *This is a question about the Phillips curve, and the 'expectations-augmented Phillips curve'. You should draw on sections 25, 28, 29 and 30 of Chapter 21 to answer this question.*

(i) *Draw a diagram to show a Phillips curve.*

(ii) *Describe how the Phillips curve purported to show an observed relationship or 'trade-off' between employment and wage-inflation.*

(iii) *Briefly explain the trade-off in terms of the Keynesian demand-pull theory of inflation.*

(iv) *Then explain the trade-off in terms of the Keynesian cost-push theory of inflation.*

(v) *Note that the Keynesians believed the Phillips relationship to be stable, but that the relationship appeared to break down in the 1970s when accelerating inflation and growing unemployment occurred together.*

(vi) *Explain the breakdown in terms of the 'expectations-augmented Phillips curve'. Explain that in this theory, unemployment can be reduced below its 'natural' rate in the short run, but only at the cost of accelerating inflation.*

(vii) *Note the New Classical or rational expectations argument that it is impossible to reduce unemployment below its 'natural' rate.*

Q5 ANSWER PLAN

(i) *State clearly that the Quantity Theory of Money is a theory of inflation, which explains a rising price level in terms of a prior increase in the supply or stock of money in the economy.*

(ii) *The theory predicts that an increase in the supply of money, created or condoned by the government, will pull up the price level in a demand-pull inflation, possibly after a lag of one to two years.*

(iii) *Explain how the Quantity Theory is developed out of the 'equation of exchange': $MV \equiv Pq$. The necessary assumptions to convert the identity into the Quantity Theory are:*

(a) *the functional relationship $P = f(Ms)$; the assumption of a constant velocity of circulation of money;*

(b) *the assumption that real output is at its equilibrium level.*

(iv) *Briefly note that the Quantity Theory can be attacked by attacking these assumptions.*

(v) *Explain the 'transmission mechanism' whereby an increase in the money supply pulls up the price level, possibly introducing Milton Friedman's 'Modern Quantity Theory'.*

Q6 *The quotation in the question is not a definition of inflation since it begs the question of the cause of inflation. Indeed, the quotation is a popular and simple statement of the Quantity Theory of Money. And as we have seen in sections 20 and 21 of Chapter 21 - and in the context of Question 5 - by no means all economists are agreed that the Quantity Theory offers an adequate explanation of inflation.*

ANSWER PLAN

(i) *Define a hypothesis, eg a supposition made as the basis for reasoning, as a starting point for developing a theory.*

(ii) *As such, the quotation which is the starting point for developing the*

Quantity Theory of Money, represents a hypothesis rather than a definition.

(iii) *It is inadequate as a definition of inflation because it begs the question of the cause of inflation, ie it assumes the price level is pulled up by excess monetary demand.*

(iv) *Present what you feel is a clear, precise definition of inflation.*

(v) *Explain that your definition of inflation is consistent with other theoretical explanations, eg cost-push explanations, besides the Quantity Theory explanation.*

Q7 *This is a slightly disguised question about the costs and benefits of inflation which are thoroughly covered in section 18 of Chapter 21. If the benefits of inflation ever exceed the costs (perhaps in a low creeping inflation) then it might be argued that a policy of completely eliminating inflation would be unwise. Nevertheless in these circumstances, the rate of inflation would presumably be under control and a government could argue that a policy of preventing the rate of inflation creeping upwards into a strato-inflation is a justifiable aim of policy.*

ANSWER PLAN

(i) *Define inflation.*

(ii) *Argue that governments should aim to reduce the rate of inflation if the costs of the current inflation rate exceed the benefits.*

(iii) *Argue that the government might be justified in containing, but not necessarily further reducing, a low rate of inflation on the ground that the cost of any further reduction would exceed the benefits.*

(iv) *Explain the adverse effects or costs of inflation that might result from allowing inflation to rise out of control: distributional effects; disincentive effects; effects upon output; effects upon international competitiveness etc.*

(v) *Show clearly that these effects are most severe, the higher and more variable is the rate of inflation - in large part because of the difficulty in anticipating inflation. Inflation distorts and may eventually destroy, normal economic activity.*

ANSWERS TO QUESTIONS IN CHAPTER 22

EXERCISES

1 (a) *As the passage indicates, the* ***'true' ultimate target*** *of economic policy is improved economic welfare, defined generally in terms of increased standards of living. We can think of full (or relatively full) employment, economic growth and a socially acceptable distribution of income and wealth as constituting vital elements of any general definition of economic welfare. Control of inflation and a satisfactory balance of payments should, perhaps, be regarded as* ***'high-level' intermediate objectives*** *rather than as integral parts of the ultimate objective itself. A satisfactory balance of payments and performance in terms of controlling inflation, are pre-requisites or conditions which must be achieved before any general increase in economic welfare can be attained. And below the 'high-level' intermediate targets such as control of inflation, are the* ***'lower-level' intermediate targets***

specified in the passage such as control of the money supply.

(b) *Some broad notion of economic welfare.*

(c) *Monetarist economists believe that expectations of future inflation function as an important explanatory variable causing current inflation. If people believe inflation is going to be high, they will begin to behave in an inflationary way in their wage-bargaining and price-setting behaviour. The result will be self-fulfilling, producing exactly the high inflation people were expecting. But if a strong 'monetarist' government announces firmly that it is going to bring inflation down - setting a 'tight' monetary target which it announces it will aim to 'hit' - even at the sacrifice of other aims of policy - then (according to monetarists) people will immediately revise downwards their expectations of future inflation and begin to behave in a less inflationary way. In this way, the government can 'talk down' the rate of inflation. This line of reasoning (which reflects the theory of rational expectations) strongly influenced the Conservative Government in the UK when it was first elected in 1979, and provided the basis of its Medium Term Financial Strategy. The disadvantage of such a strategy - according to its own logic - is that if the government fails to hit its pre-announced target, it would be rational for people to conclude that the government has lost control of the economy. In these circumstances, they might revise upwards their expectations of inflation and begin to behave in an even more inflationary way!*

MULTIPLE CHOICE QUESTIONS

1 *B*
2 *C*
3 *A*
4 *D*

EXAMINATION QUESTIONS

Q1 *Rather than restricting your answer to a 'shopping-list' description of the standard objectives of macro-economic policy, you should show that you understand how the priority attached to each objective has changed during the years in which Keynesianism gave way to monetarism as the prevailing economic orthodoxy. Thus control of inflation has been elevated to a prime position, with the objective of full employment being relegated to a more subordinate position. It would also display an analytical sophistication if you could distinguish between* ultimate, intermediate *and* immediate *policy objectives and explain how a policy* objective *may in effect become an* instrument *of policy (or vice versa) eg the exchange rate. Also, show an awareness of the existence of 'trade-offs' between objectives.*

ANSWER PLAN

(i) *List the five standard objectives of macro-policy: full-employment; growth; an equitable distribution of income; control of inflation; and a satisfactory balance of payments.*

(ii) *Briefly describe each.*

(iii) *Indicate possible 'trade-offs' between objectives, eg between full employment and control of inflation.*

(iv) *Explain how the 'ranking' of the objectives has changed under monetarism.*

(v) *Indicate that the objectives may be classified in terms of their 'ultimate', 'intermediate' or 'immediate' status; and that an 'immediate' or 'intermediate' objective of policy, eg control of the money supply becomes an instrument to achieve a more 'ultimate' objective such as control of inflation.*

Q2 (a) *Sections 20, 21 and 22 of Chapter 22 are relevant for this question and also sections 18 and 19 of Chapter 18. Supply-side policies are economic policies which are aimed at improving economic performance by individual economic agents in the industries and markets that make up the economy. Supply-side policy is micro-economic in its impact rather than macro-economic. It is useful to distinguish between Keynesian and monetarist supply-side policy. Keynesian supply-side policy as implemented in the UK in the 1960s and 1970s tended to be interventionist and was generally subordinated to the management of aggregate demand in Keynesian macro-economic policy. Indeed, the term 'supply-side' economic policy did not come into prominence until the monetarist counter-revolution in the late 1970s and the 1980s when monetarists criticised Keynesian economic policy for being both too interventionist and too 'demand-side' orientated. Under monetarism, supply-side policy aims to reduce the 'natural' level of unemployment in the economy by increasing the equilibrium level of output. This is to be achieved by 'setting markets free' through tax cuts aimed at increasing incentives and through policies of privatisation, marketisation and deregulation.*

(b) *The reason for the emphasis on supply-side policies in recent years relates to the apparent failure of Keynesian 'demand-side' policies in the 1970s and the resulting growing dominance of the monetarist and New Classical schools of thought over Keynesianism. Even Keynesians are now agreed on the need for an emphasis upon supply-side policy, though as we have noted, Keynesian supply-side policy tends to be interventionist.*

ANSWER PLAN

(a) (i) *Briefly define supply-side policy.*

(ii) *Distinguish monetarist supply-side policy from Keynesian supply-side policy.*

(iii) *Identify the main elements of monetarist supply-side policy; its anti-interventionist emphasis; tax cuts to create incentives; privatisation; marketisation; deregulation.*

(b) (i) *Explain that the growth of supply-side policy relates to the apparent failure of Keynesian 'demand-side' policies, the monetarist counter-revolution and the influence of New Classical economies. Relate it to the Laffer curve.*

(ii) *Discuss the extent to which Keynesians have also been converted to supply-side policies.*

Q3 *To answer this question you need to define what you understand by a 'prices and incomes policy'. Over the years, 'incomes policy' has been a label for a wide variety of statutory and voluntary, short-term and long-term policies for the freezing, restraint, or 'planned growth' of wages and other types of income. On occasion, a 'prices policy' has also been implemented, though more usually the policy has applied* *to incomes only, degenerating as often as not into a 'wages policy' because of the difficulties of controlling other types of income, eg dividends and capital gains.*

During the 1960s and 1970s, Keynesian economists of the 'cost-push school' recommended the use of a prices and incomes policy instrument appropriate for controlling inflation. It had become increasingly clear that, on its own, discretionary fiscal policy or demand management was unable to secure both full employment and price stability. However, a statutory prices and incomes policy which imposes limits or ceilings on price and wage rises represents a severe form of intervention in the market economy. Monetarist and New Classical economists completely oppose such a formal policy arguing that the costs it imposes on the economy (in terms of distortions and inefficiencies) far exceed any benefits. They argue that the policy suppresses the symptom of inflation (rising prices) without dealing with the underlying inflationary pressures. When eventually the policy breaks down - perhaps as a result of social discontent and trade union militancy - a 'catching up' period occurs when wages and prices rise at an extremely fast rate to make good the loss of wages and profits that occurred during the period the policy was implemented. But although monetarist reject formal or statutory 'prices and incomes policies', this is not to say that monetarists and New Classical economists have no 'policy towards incomes'. Monetarists believe that market forces will only achieve an equilibrium at a minimum level of unemployment providing that all markets, including the labour market, are sufficiently competitive. Thus a 'monetarist incomes policy' involves the adoption of a set of policies which have the general aim of making the labour market more competitive, essentially 'educating workers about the reality of the market place'. And while monetarists reject a statutory income policy that directly prevents the free working of market forces, they nevertheless favour the imposition of wage restraint in the public sector where the state is the employer and the announcement of the rate of wage increases in the economy as a whole that is compatible with the government's inflation rate target.

ANSWER PLAN

(a) (i) Briefly explain the meaning of a prices and incomes policy.

(ii) The most favourable circumstances for the policy's success are when:

(a) inflation is caused only by cost-push factors and not by excess demand;

(b) there is political support for the policy throughout the community and the policy continues to be regarded as fair;

(c) there is a strong government;

(d) the policy is quickly seen to be effective in reducing inflationary expectations, causing workers and firms to behave in a less inflationary way.

(b) (i) Make the general point that problems arise when any of the circumstances outlined above are not met.

(ii) Explain that prices and incomes policies are most successful as short-run measures to deal with a crisis and that the longer a formal and rigid policy is imposed, the greater the distortions and sense of unfairness it creates, contributing to the policy's eventual failure.

(iii) Evidence from the 1960s and 1970s suggests that apparently successful

incomes policies were followed by a 'catching up' period after price and income controls had been removed.

(iv) Fewer problems might occur with informal and non-statutory incomes policies, eg in a policy of voluntary restraint, or with a system which allows firms complete freedom to set prices and wages, but penalises through the tax system those firms judged guilty of excessive price or wage rises.

Q4 ANSWER PLAN

(i) Explain what is meant by a prices and incomes policy.

(ii) Explain that an incomes policy is favoured by 'cost-push Keynesians' as an extra policy instrument with which to control inflation. They believe it can effectively constrain inflationary pressures caused by wage bargaining and price-setting procedures.

(iii) Discuss whether prices and incomes policies were effective in controlling inflation in the UK in the 1960s and 1970s.

(iv) Explain why monetarists reject the use of a formal or statutory incomes policy.

(v) Nevertheless, monetarists certainly have an informal 'policy towards incomes' and a more formal policy in the public sector.

Q5 ANSWER PLAN

(a) (i) Explain that the ultimate objective of economic policy is improved economic welfare for all the people. Full employment is an important element of this overall objective, since unemployment means reduced living standards and welfare for those affected.

(ii) Explain that while price stability is not directly related to economic welfare, an accelerating rate of inflation may prevent the sustained attainment of the full employment, growth and distributional aims of economic policy. Control of inflation may be regarded as a necessary condition - or intermediate objective - to be attained before the ultimate policy objective can be achieved.

(b) (i) Describe how a 'trade-off' has appeared to exist between the two policy objectives.

(ii) Briefly explain the trade-off in terms of the demand-pull and cost-push theories of inflation and illustrate it in terms of the Phillips curve.

(iii) Introduce the concept of the 'natural' rate of unemployment and briefly explain that monetarists believe that unemployment cannot be reduced below the 'natural' rate without accelerating the rate of inflation.

(iv) Discuss whether or not policies such as an incomes policy or various supply-side policies might allow the two objectives to be achieved.

Q6 *The first part of this question is straightforward, but there are a number of different ways of approaching the second part of the question. There are two main ways of measuring economic growth. One method is by measuring the growth of real national income, eg growth of GNP at constant factor cost. To give an accurate indication of the growth of living standards, the growth of real national income* *per head of population should perhaps be measured. Secondly, growth can be measured by the growth of the economy's production potential, assuming that the existing production potential is fully employed and working at capacity.*

A possible approach to the second part of the question is to contrast the views taken by economists of different and opposing schools of thought. Thus monetarist and New Classical economists generally argue that self-interest and the profit motive operating in a capitalist market economy subject to a minimal level of state intervention and regulation are necessary to procure rapid and sustained economic growth. By contrast, Keynesian economists point to the tendency of unregulated market economies to suffer periods of under-utilisation and slow growth of capacity during downswings in the business cycle. They argue that greater or lesser amounts of government intervention are necessary to stabilise the cycle and to improve the underlying growth trend. The 'laissez-faire' economists reply with the argument that counter-cyclical demand management policies have generally appeared to reduce rather than improve the underlying growth trend. The views of socialist and Marxist economists might also be mentioned, particularly their belief that much of the growth achieved in capitalist market economies has involved the production of socially unnecessary goods and services. However, the growth record of centrally planned Eastern Bloc countries is hardly impressive in terms of the growth of living standards and consumption levels enjoyed by their populations.

Alternatively (or additionally) a rather narrower approach to the question could be adopted, concentrating on such factors as technical progress, the availability of natural resources and investment in human and non-human forms of capital. The interaction of the demand and supply sides of the economy is worth mentioning, namely that for the growth process to be sustained there must be sufficient aggregate demand on the 'demand-side' of the economy to absorb the increased levels of real output that growth of the 'supply-side' is capable of producing. The Keynesian critique of an unregulated economy centres on the proposition that slumps are caused and growth unnecessarily sacrificed, by failure of the 'demand-side' to absorb the growth of output produced by the 'supply-side'.

ANSWER PLAN

(i) *Explain how economic growth can be defined in terms either of an increase in real national income (per capita), or in terms of an increase in the economy's productive potential.*

(ii) *Discuss whether unregulated market forces, or a measure of government intervention in market forces and planning, will best achieve economic growth in a developed industrial country.*

(iii) *Discuss the role of such factors as the nature of technical progress and the rate of investment in the growth process.*

(iv) *Discuss the role of aggregate demand as well as supply-side factors in the growth process.*

Q7 *The answer to this question depends upon the type of unemployment and also upon whether a Keynesian or monetarist approach to the question is adopted. A Keynesian might argue that if the unemployment is caused by deficient demand, then both an increase in government expenditure and a tax cut might be effective in reducing unemployment because both will increase the level of aggregate demand in the economy.*

However, as we saw in Chapter 13, the government spending multiplier is likely to be larger than the tax multiplier, so the increase in public expenditure will probably be more effective.

But a monetarist would approach the question from a completely different perspective, denying the existence of deficient demand as a significant cause of unemployment. Monetarists believe that registered unemployment can be reduced by creating incentives for firms to demand and workers to supply more labour. Cuts in taxes imposed on both firms and workers can create the appropriate incentives and increase employment. Essentially therefore, monetarists place emphasis on the 'supply-side' effects of tax cuts while believing that an increase in public spending would merely 'crowd-out' the private sector without increasing the equilibrium levels of output and employment in the economy.

ANSWER PLAN

(i) *Explain that in traditional Keynesian analysis, unemployment is assumed to result from deficient demand. In Keynesian theory, any policy to increase aggregate demand can reduce unemployment.*

(ii) *Both an increase in government spending or a tax cut would increase aggregate demand. However, the increase in government spending is likely to have the more powerful expansionary effect because the size of the multiplier is larger.*

(iii) *But monetarist theory argues that the main effect of any expansion of public spending is either inflationary or involves 'crowding-out'.*

(iv) *Monetarists would favour the tax cut policy - but for completely different reasons. In monetarist theory, tax cuts create incentives and lead to higher levels of employment for 'supply-side' reasons.*

ANSWERS TO QUESTIONS IN CHAPTER 23

EXERCISES

1(a) *Although Country A possesses an absolute advantage in both iron and coffee, its comparative advantage is restricted to iron production. Country A is 100 per cent more efficient at producing iron, but only 50 per cent more efficient at coffee production. Country B has a comparative advantage in coffee production.*

(b) (i)

	Iron	Coffee
Country A	*200*	*300*
Country B	*100*	*200*
Total production	*300*	*500*

(ii) *If each country specialises completely in the industry in which it possesses a comparative advantage, Country A will produce 400 units of iron and Country B will produce 400 units of coffee. There is thus a gain in iron production compared to the situation without specialisation. We can devise a system of specialisation which increases output of both products by allowing Country B to specialise completely in coffee production and by arranging for two workers in Country A to produce coffee and eight workers to produce iron:*

	Iron	Coffee
Country A	*320*	*120*
Country B	-	*400*
Total prod'n	*320*	*520*

Compared to the situation without specialisation, there is a gain of 20 units of iron and 20 units of coffee.

MULTIPLE CHOICE QUESTIONS

1 *C*
2 *C*
3 *C*
4 *D*
5 *D*
6 *D*

EXAMINATION QUESTIONS

Q1 *You should answer this question by drawing on the following sections of Chapter 23:*

(a) section 4 for an account of the principle of comparative advantage;

(b) section 5 for a discussion of the underlying assumptions; and

(c) sections 15, 16 and 17 fo a discussion of when import controls may be justified as an interference with free trade.

Since the question does not indicate the mark totals for each part of the question, you should assume that each part of the question carries half the total marks and structure your answer accordingly.

ANSWER PLAN

(i) State clearly that the principle of comparative advantage shows that gains in total output can result if two countries (or regions within a country) specialise in activities in which each possesses a comparative advantage.

(ii) Define the concept of comparative advantage, taking care to distinguish it from absolute advantage.

(iii) Construct a simple numerical example to illustrate the principle, and use the example to show the gains from specialisation.

(iv) List and briefly discuss the underlying assumptions, eg constant returns to scale; full employment in both countries; factor immobility between countries etc.

(v) List and briefly discuss the case for import controls, eg 'infant industry' argument; protection against 'unfair' dumping etc.

(vi) Assess the extent to which these arguments justify an interference in free trade.

Q2 *The question deliberately builds in the assumption that developing countries possess a comparative and absolute advantage in the production of primary commodities. This is indeed true for agricultural commodities such as rubber and coffee that can only be produced in the tropical climatic zones in which many developing countries are located. However, highly urbanised island NICs such as Hong Kong and Singapore certainly do not possess a comparative advantage in primary production. You can tackle the question by arguing that the dependency theory of world trade offers an alternative explanation to comparative advantage to explain why ex-colonial and developing countries have traditionally specialised in the production of primary commodities. Then go on to introduce the product-cycle and technology gap theories to explain why much recent industrialisation has taken place in the NICs. Indeed, these theories are not inconsistent with the theory of comparative advantage, since they indicate that for many types of industrial production, comparative and absolute advantage has shifted to the developing world where manufacturing costs are lower.*

ANSWER PLAN

(i) Briefly explain absolute and comparative advantage.

(ii) Note that in the 19th century and the early 20th century a 'North/South' pattern of trade developed in which developed countries specialised in manufactured goods and less-developed countries specialised in primary production.

(iii) Discuss the extent to which the less-developed countries possess both an absolute and a comparative advantage in primary production.

(iv) However, the dependency theory provides an alternative explanation of the pattern of 'North/South' specialisation.

(v) Argue the case for industrialisation shifting to the previously less-developed countries:

(a) comparative advantage may have shifted;

(b) the product-cycle theory;

(c) the technology gap theory;

(d) manufacturing may also be necessary to increase employment within developing countries and to raise living standards, since manufacturing has more scope for productivity growth than other forms of economic activity.

Q3 *If two countries completely specialise in the activity in which each possesses a comparative advantage (when one country possesses an absolute advantage in both products), then more of one product but less of the other will result. However, as section 4 of Chapter 23 explains, it is possible to ensure 'at least as much of one product and more of the other' by devising a system of less than complete specialisation. The only exception is when the comparative cost ratios (and the opportunity cost ratios) are the same in both countries. In these circumstances specialisation always results in a fall in the output of one product.*

ANSWER PLAN

(i) State that the question assumes that one country has an absolute advantage in both products.

(ii) Devise a numerical example to illustrate this, taking care to make sure that the opportunity cost ratios differ.

(iii) Introduce and briefly explain, the concept of comparative advantage.

(iv) Show the outputs of both goods with complete specialisation.

(v) Devise a system of partial specialisation that shows that more of both goods can be produced.

(vi) If you have time, explain that differing opportunity cost ratios are necessary to obtain this result.

Q4 ANSWER PLAN

(i) Briefly explain the meaning of a tariff.

(ii) State that the underlying case for tariffs depends on the fact that in the real world, the conditions may not hold whereby output and welfare gains result from the complete freeing of trade:

(a) resources might be unemployed and idle;

(b) it may be impossible to switch resources quickly and without cost from one use to another, in response to changing comparative advantage.

(iii) Explain particular economic arguments in favour of tariffs:

(a) to allow the build up of 'infant industries';

(b) to allow the orderly decline of 'geriatric industries';

(c) it is better to employ resources inefficiently, than not to employ them at all;

(d) to counter unfair trading practices undertaken by other countries;

(e) to prevent the country becoming over-specialised and vulnerable to a sudden change in world demand.

(iv) Mention the existence of non-economic arguments in favour of tariffs, eg military and strategic arguments.

(v) Round off your answer by indicating that, while the question calls for an argument in support of tariffs, there are also many arguments against protectionism and that on balance the case against may be stronger than the case for.

Q5 ANSWER PLAN

(a) (i) Explain that invisible trade refers largely to trade in services, as distinct from visible trade in goods.

(ii) Briefly mention that other currency flows, besides those resulting from trade, are included in the invisible balance of trade, eg profit or dividend flows between countries and gifts.

(b) (i) Define the terms of trade as average export prices as a ratio of average import prices.

(ii) Explain the meaning and briefly suggest the causes of favourable and unfavourable movements in the terms of trade.

(c) (i) Explain that if the price of invisible exports rises faster than the price of invisible imports, the terms of trade will improve, assuming no change in the average prices of visible exports and imports.

(ii) Conversely, if the price of invisible exports rises at a slower rate than the price of invisible imports, the terms of trade will deteriorate.

ANSWERS TO QUESTIONS IN CHAPTER 24

EXERCISES

1(a) The balance of payments on current account moved from a small deficit of £653 million in 1979 to a surplus in the early 1980s, though the surplus fell from £6,547 million in 1981 to £2,049 in 1983 - heralding the move back into deficit in the later part of the 1980s. The main reason for the move into surplus was the contribution of North Sea oil to the current account.In 1979 before North Sea oil came fully on stream, Britain was still a net importer of oil. But by 1983 the oil account was contributing over £7 billion to the current account as a result of oil exports and import saving. However, North Sea oil's contribution to the balance of payments was used in part to finance a massive increase in the imports of manufactured goods. The balance of trade in manufactured goods moved into deficit in 1983 after being in surplus for two centuries. The invisible balance remained in steady surplus between 1979 and 1983, indicating the export competitiveness of service industries, especially financial services. Net capital inflows into the UK of £2,307 million in 1979 turned into a capital outflow of £7,209 million in 1981, though the outflow fell to £2,044 million in 1983. The volatility of capital flows is probably explained by 'hot money' movements. In the late 1970s, short-term capital (hot money) flowed into the £, but in the early 1980s the flow was reversed. The abolition of foreign exchange controls in 1979 probably also contributed to a long-term capital outflow of direct and portfolio investment in the 1980s.

(b) *In 1979 the current account deficit was financed by a capital account surplus whereas in 1981 and 1983 the position was reversed - current account surpluses being financed by capital outflows. One link between the current account and the capital account is provided by 'net property income from abroad'. While this item is not explicitly shown in the data, it is an important part of the invisible balance of trade in the current account. Capital outflows which build up the stock of capital assets owned by the nation's residents abroad contribute to a net property income inflow (in the form of profit remittances) in future years. This contributed to a growth in invisible exports later in the 1980s. The 'Dutch disease' effect provided another link between the capital account and the current account - via the exchange rate. When North Sea oil came on stream in the late 1970s, owners of 'hot money' began to view the pound as a 'petro-currency'. Capital flows into the pound caused the sterling exchange rate to rise, which in turn caused manufactured goods produced in the UK to become uncompetitive in world markets. This helps account for the deterioriation in the balance of trade in manufacturers shown in the data.*

MULTIPLE CHOICE QUESTIONS

1 A
2 A
3 B
4 A
5 C

EXAMINATION QUESTIONS

Q1 *A balance of payments deficit is normally taken to refer to the current account alone, especially since the new method of presentation of the UK balance of payments statistics introduced in 1987 merged together private sector capital flows and official financing. You must show clearly that the current account includes the balance of visible trade and the balance of invisible trade, and that invisibles may be in surplus (for example) while visibles and the overall current account are in deficit. Distinguish also between a persistent deficit which indicates balance of payments disequilibrium and a small and temporary deficit which does not usually pose problems. In the second part of your answer, it is important that you do not confuse eliminating a deficit with financing a deficit. Adopt the framework of* expenditure-reducing *versus* expenditure-switching *policies, and relate your answer to explicit assumptions about the exchange rate regime.*

ANSWER PLAN

(a) (i) *Explain the meaning of a balance of payments deficit on current account.*

(ii) *Illustrate with a numerical example, either hypothetical or from recent UK experience (or the experience of any other country).*

(iii) Mention the possibility of a capital account deficit, though indicate that such a deficit is no longer explicitly shown in the UK balance of payments accounts.

(b) *(i) List the three policy options: deflation; devaluation; direct controls.*

(ii) Briefly explain each, comparing them in terms of their expenditure-reducing or expenditure-switching operation.

(iii) Discuss whether they should be regarded as policy substitutes or as complementary policies, eg introduce the J-curve effect.

(iv) Explain that the 'availability' of policy options depends in part upon international agreements, eg membership of GATT prohibits an extension of protectionism, and the exchange rate regime in operation.

Q2 *You must explain that like any balance sheet, the balance of payments must always balance in the sense that all the items in the balance sheet must sum to zero. But nested within the overall balance, individual items and sets of items may be in surplus or deficit. A surplus or deficit normally refers to the current account only – the part of the balance of payments which reflects the economy's trading competitiveness in world markets. Since the current account measures the 'real' flows of goods and services into and out of any economy, surpluses or deficits are explained by whatever causes these real flows to occur. You must explain the various influences upon the trading competitiveness of a country's industries, concentrating in particular upon price competitiveness (itself affected by the exchange rate) and quality competitiveness. Other influences upon the current account include the extent to which a country is dependent on external supplies of raw materials, foodstuffs and energy and the various determinants of comparative advantage and elasticities of supply and demand.*

ANSWER PLAN

(i) Explain how in an accounting sense the balance of payments always balances.

(ii) But within the overall balance there may be surpluses or deficits in the current account.

(iii) Distinguish between 'balance' and 'equilibrium' in the balance of payments.

(iv) List and briefly describe various causes of current account deficit, eg loss of comparative advantage; overvalued exchange rate etc.

(v) List and briefly describe various causes of current account surplus, eg overseas demand for the country's exports is price inelastic; undervalued exchange rates etc.

Q3 (a) *A country's national debt is strictly the debt of the central government. Part of this may be externally held by residents of other countries, including overseas banks which have lent to the government. However, a country's external debt also includes overseas lending to private sector individuals and companies within the country.*

(b) *To answer this part of the question, you should first refer back to section 25 of Chapter 18 which explains how the national debt in a developed country may pose problems. These pro-*

blems also exist for the government of a developing country which has a large national debt. However, the problems are far worse if a large part of the national debt is externally held and if there is also a large externally-held private sector debt. Interest and debt repayments must normally be made in a hard currency such as the US dollar. If a developing country possesses a trade surplus on current account, then it can generate the hard currency earnings to finance interest and debt repayment. However, most developing countries have chronic current account deficits and are unable to earn the dollars necessary to service and repay the external debt. Very often they have to borrow more simply to pay interest on previous borrowing! In these circumstances, their exchange rates are likely to 'soften' still further, which increases the cost in dollars of making the interest payments and repaying the debt. Finally, the IMF and First World banks are likely to require Third World governments to impose severely deflationary domestic economic policies as a condition for renewing existing loans and providing new credit.

ANSWER PLAN

(a) (i) Define the national debt as government debt. Note that part of it may be externally held.

(ii) Explain that a country's external debt also includes private sector debt externally held.

(b) (i) Explain how a large national debt can pose problems for a developed country: servicing costs; 'deadweight' costs; constraints on domestic economic policy etc.

(ii) Explain that these problems also exist for developing countries, but that they are usually far worse.

(iii) Relate the externally held debt to the balance of payments.

(iv) Explain that overseas creditors such as the IMF and First World banks may interfere in the country's domestic policy.

ANSWERS TO QUESTIONS IN CHAPTER 25

EXERCISES

1(a) The Sterling Index is a trade-weighted measure of the pound's exchange rate, expressing the exchange rate as an index number. Instead of being measured against a single currency such as the US dollar or the West German Deutschmark, the Sterling Index measures the pound's value against a 'basket' of about 16 leading currencies, each given a 'weight' reflecting the importance of their trade with Britain. It is sometimes known as the 'effective exchange rate' of the pound.

(b) The dollar exchange rate is a good indicator of the competitiveness of Britain's traded goods and services in America, but only a small part of the United Kingdom's trade is with the USA and other 'dollar area' countries. Because the Sterling Index measures the pound's exchange rate against the currencies of 16 nations with whom Britain trades - including of course the USA - it is a better indicator of trading competitiveness with all of the United Kingdom's major trading partners.

(c) Capital flows - especially speculative 'hot money' movements provide the main explanation for changes in the dollar exchange rate of the pound. In 1979 and 1981, speculative funds flowed out of the dollar and into the pound - which at the time was

regarded as a 'petrocurrency'. After 1981 however, hot money movements reversed, flowing into the dollar and out of the pound. The pound's dollar exchange rate reached an 'all-time low' in January 1985 - trading for a time at around $1 to £1 - before increased UK interest rates and changing market sentiment reversed the direction of hot money flows. It was not the dollar's turn to experience a currency crisis as international speculators moved out of the dollar and into other currencies, including the pound.

Speculative flows are less significant in determining the Sterling Index, though they still have some impact. The main reason for the long term depreciation of the Sterling Index is the higher inflation rate and declining export competitiveness of the UK compared to her main trading competitors. The decline is more or less in line with the predictions of the purchasing power parity theory which is explained in section 8 of Chapter 25.

MULTIPLE CHOICE QUESTIONS

1 C
2 C
3 B
4 D
5 A

EXAMINATION QUESTIONS

Q1 *The question requires you to discuss the long-term (rather than the short-term) influences upon a country's exchange rate. There are many factors which cause dramatic 'short-term' movements in exchange rates, but which generally have little effect upon long-term movements taking place over several years. Short-term influences include strikes, political uncertainty, interest rate changes and other causes of 'hot money' movements or short-term capital flows. By all means briefly mention these, but do not allow yourself to be deflected away from addressing the issue of long-term movements. Explain how supply and demand determine the equilibrium exchange rate and that the exchange rate will rise or fall over time as the conditions of supply and demand change. The long-term supply and demand curves for the country's currency reflect the international demand for the country's exports and the domestic demand for imports. If a country's main industries become less efficient over a number of years, the demand curve for the country's currency will shift leftwards and the supply curve will shift rightwards. These movements are a response to the fact that demand for the country's exports falls, while domestic demand switches away from home-produced goods towards increasingly attractive imports. As a result, a long-term fall in the country's exchange rate takes place in order to restore price competitiveness and reduce the payments imbalance. Underlying such long-term falls (and rises) in exchange rates are losses (and gains) of comparative advantage resulting from factors such as the discovery or exhaustion of natural resources, new technologies and changes in the relative costs of labour. Long-term differences in domestic inflation rates are also responsible for changes over time in a currency's nominal exchange rate. For example, a country experiencing an inflation rate 5 per cent higher than the average of its trading partners and competitors, would expect to suffer a 5 per cent fall in its nominal exchange rate to restore the competitiveness and real purchasing power of its exports. However such changes in* nominal *exchange rates leave unaffected the* real *exchange rate (at which a unit of export exchanges for a unit of imports).*

Your answer to part (b) can start with a straightforward coverage of the advantages and disadvantages of fixed exchange rates. However, it would be appropriate to include some discussion of the political difficulties of organising and maintaining the institutional arrangements of a system of fixed exchange rates, mentioning perhaps how such difficulties have contributed to the breakdown of previous fixed exchange rate systems, such as the Bretton Woods System.

ANSWER PLAN

(a) (i) *Define an exchange rate.*

(ii) *Mention the existence of short-term determinants, such as 'hot money' flows, but don't elaborate.*

(iii) *State that such influences have little effect on long-term changes.*

(iv) *Show the determination of the exchange rate on a supply and demand diagram.*

(v) *Explain how long-term changes result from shifts in the supply or demand curve.*

(vi) *Explain how these reflect changing comparative advantage.*

(vii) *Mention how differences in inflation rates contribute to changes in the nominal exchange rate.*

(b) (i) *Explain the advantages of fixed exchange rates:*

(a) *certainty and stability;*
(b) *anti-inflationary 'discipline'.*

(ii) *Explain the disadvantages of fixed exchange rates:*

(a) *uncertainty may sometimes be increased;*

(b) *permanent incorrect valuation;*

(c) *deflationary bias and restriction of domestic economic policy options.*

(iii) *Discuss political and institutional problems, eg the success of a fixed exchange system has depended in the past upon the political power and hegemony of a dominant country - the UK in the 19th century Gold Standard System, the USA in the Bretton Woods System; West Germany in the European Monetary System.*

(iv) *Reach a balanced conclusion for or against fixed exchange rates.*

Q2 *You should draw on sections 8, 9 and 10 of Chapter 25 to answer this question. It is important to balance your answer, though it is well worth stressing that the advantages of fixed exchange rates (for example) are simply the obverse of the disadvantages of floating exchange rates.*

ANSWER PLAN

(i) *Very briefly explain how the exchange rate is determined in a regime of cleanly floating exchange rates.*

(ii) *Explain the main advantages of floating exchange rates that:*

(a) *the government does not need to intervene to correct a payments imbalance - market forces should automatically correct a balance of payments deficit or surplus;*

(b) *resources do not need to be tied up in official reserves;*

(c) *the currency should never be overvalued or undervalued for very long.*

(iii) *Explain the disadvantages of floating exchange rates that:*

(a) capital flows and speculation may lead to overvalued or undervalued exchange rates in terms of trading competitiveness and current account imbalance;

(b) floating exchange rates fail to 'discipline' domestic causes of cost-push inflation;

(c) highly volatile exchange rate movements may disrupt international trade.

(iv) *Explain the advantages and disadvantages of fixed exchange rates as the obverse of the arguments listed above.*

Q3 (a) *See Question 1 for guidance on this part of the question.*

(b) *A 'strong' currency is one which is greatly in demand and for which market forces are tending to raise or 'harden' the exchange rate. Conversely a 'weak' currency is one for which there is an excess supply on foreign exchange markets, which tends to lower or 'soften' the exchange rate. If the strength of a currency results from the success of the country's economy and particularly from the export competitiveness of its industries, a strong currency should not, in principle, pose problems for the country's government. The strengthening or hardening of the currency should be viewed simply as part of the adjustment mechanism in a floating exchange rate system through which balance of payments equilibrium is restored. But if the country's government does not wish to see the exchange rate harden further, it may decide to engage in exchange equilisation to supply its own currency and purchase reserves on foreign exchange markets. At the same time it may have to reduce domestic interest rates to deter any inward capital movements that are raising the exchange rate. Both these measures will tend to increase the country's money supply, which may run counter to the government's domestic monetary policy, particularly if monetarist policies are being pursued. But if the government instead decides to abandon equilisation and to allow the exchange rate to 'find its own level', any continuing inward capital flows may lead to an overvalued exchange rate that prices the country's industries out of both world and domestic markets. And while a 'weakening' currency is - in a similar way - part of the automatic adjustment mechanism that restores competitiveness when there is a current account deficit, a softening currency is often interpreted as a sign of national failure and weak government. It may also trigger a 'hot money' flow out of the currency which lowers the exchange rate for below the level necessary to restore trading competitiveness and increases the feeling of national helplessness. By raising the price of imports and by removing the 'discipline' provided by a strong exchange rate to domestic cost-push inflationary pressures, a falling exchange rate can lead to an accelerating downward-spiral of external depreciation of the exchange rate and internal depreciation of the price level (ie inflation).*

ANSWER PLAN

(a) See part (a) of Question 1 for your answer plan to this part of the question.

(b) (i) Explain what is meant by a 'strong' and a 'weak' currency.

(ii) Explain how in principle a strong currency is not a source of problems to a successful country with a balance of payments surplus.

(iii) But if demand for the country's exports is inelastic, a strengthening currency may perversely increase a balance of payments surplus rather than reduce it.

(iv) Explain why the 'strength' may pose problems if it is caused by hot money inflows.

(v) Explain how a strengthening currency may conflict with domestic monetary policy, particularly for a 'monetarist' government.

(vi) Explain how, in principle, a weakening currency is not a source of problems if the exchange rate was previously overvalued and there was a balance of payments deficit.

(vii) But if the Marshall-Lerner condition is not met, a weakening currency may perversely make the payments deficit worse.

(viii) A weakening currency may also be interpreted as a sign of national failure.

(ix) It may trigger a capital outflow that further weakens the currency, and it may directly contribute to domestic inflation.

Q4 *The question implicitly refers to the fact that before 1971/72, an important function of the IMF was the policing of the managed exchange rate regime known as the Bretton Woods System. Although following the final breakdown of the Bretton Woods System in 1972 this function no longer exists, you should base your answer around a careful description of the advisory role, and especially the banking role, of the IMF which are explained in section 19 of Chapter 22.*

At the time this question was set (in 1978), the quadrupling of crude oil prices which occurred in the first oil crisis of 1973/74 had caused the balance of payments of the OPEC countries to move into strong surplus. This resulted for the fact that in the short run - a period of a few years - the demand for oil of the rest of the world was price inelastic. For a time therefore, a major problem facing the IMF centred around the need to recycle the oil revenues by creating some mechanism through which the OPEC payments surpluses could be lent to the oil importers - particularly to the non-oil producing developing countries - to allow them to continue to finance the import of oil. In more recent years however, this problem has largely resolved itself, though the non-oil producing developing countries still face considerable problems in financing all imports, including oil. The world price of crude oil has at times fallen considerably and there has often been a surplus rather than a shortage of crude oil in the world market. Many members of OPEC have considerable balance of payments problems themselves. A growing fraction of total world oil production is now produced by non-OPEC countries such as the UK, Norway, the USA and Canada.

ANSWER PLAN

(i) Briefly explain that in the 1940s the IMF was created to police the Bretton Woods System of managed exchange rates.

(ii) This system broke down in 1971/72.

(iii) But the advisory and banking functions of the IMF survived the breakdown of the Bretton Woods System.

(iv) The IMF has taken on the function of encouraging international co-operation in a world of 'dirty' floating.

(v) Explain that in the late 1970s and early 1980s the main problem involved the recycling of oil revenues to prevent a breakdown of world trade and to maintain international liquidity.

(vi) The most deep-seated problem facing the IMF is the problem of the chronic current account deficits of the non-oil producing developing countries, and their outstanding debts to the IMF and to First World countries.

Q5 Exchange controls limit, and sometimes completely restrict, the freedom of individuals and firms to buy and sell currencies and to move currencies in and out of a country. Exchange controls function as a form of import control, whose purpose is to reduce a balance of payments deficit or to prevent a deficit growing larger. Exchange controls are therefore likely to be imposed by countries - particularly developing countries - with serious or potentially serious payments deficits. In these circumstances, the country's own currency is likely to be 'soft' and unacceptable to other countries in payment for imports. As a result the deficit country's ability to pay for imports is limited by its hard currency reserves and by the extent to which export earnings add to these reserves. In order to ensure that scarce hard currencies are used only to purchase imports which the government deems essential, controls may be imposed which force exporters to sell hard currency earnings to the central bank and also ration the supply of hard currency sold by the central bank to importers. Sometimes a dual system of exchange rates is operated through which luxury consumer goods can still be imported, but only with hard currency bought at a much less favourable price form the central bank.

Exchange controls - used as a form of import control to protect the balance of payments - are usually 'assymetrical' in the sense that restrictions are placed on the outflow, but not the inflow of currencies. Indeed, exports may be artificially subsidised and foreign tourists visiting the country may be allowed to buy the local currency at an especially favourable rate so as to boost visible and invisible export earnings. On occasion however, some countries have imposed restrictions on currencies coming into the country in order to 'protect' national residents from exposure to free-spending tourists. Also, it may be made illegal for foreign tourists to sell hard currencies to private citizens within the country - instead they can sell only at the officially agreed exchange rate to the central bank.

Destabilising speculative capital flows or 'hot money' movements between countries may provide a further reason for exchange controls. However, most major western industrialised countries have removed (rather than reintroduced) foreign exchange controls in recent years, despite the potential for the destabilisation of their economies from any resulting capital movements.

The disadvantages of foreign exchange controls relate closely to the disadvantages of import controls; they can promote inefficiency and distort trade so that specialisation does not take place in accordance with the principle of comparative advantage. As a result, the world's productive potential fails to be realised, leading ulimately to a welfare loss. And like all controls, exchange controls divert human energy and ability into the essentially wasteful pursuit of finding ways round the controls - for example through smuggling, bribery, corruption and the emergence of 'black markets'.

ANSWER PLAN

(a) (i) *Explain that exchange controls limit or restrict the freedom to buy or sell currencies and the freedom to move currencies between countries.*

(ii) *Describe their purpose to restrict imports, reduce payments deficits and conserve scarce reserves.*

(b) (i) *Besides acting as a form of import control, exchange controls may discourage destabilising 'hot money' movements, and deflect domestic savings into internal investment within the country and away from overseas investment opportunities.*

(ii) *Exchange controls have the disadvantage of any form of import control, by preventing specialisation in accordance with the principle of comparative advantage.*

(iii) *They may also lead to smuggling, bribery, 'black markets' and other distortions.*

(iv) *They may discourage inward investment by overseas companies, and inhibit the development of a country's financial markets.*

(v) *Reach a balanced conclusion, eg exchange controls might be justified in developing countries, but not in more advanced economies.*

Questions without answers

Chapter 1: Economic systems

1 *How efficient is the Price Mechanism as a system for the allocating of resources in a developed economy? (CIMA)*

2 *Illustrate the practical importance of the concept of opportunity cost. (CIMA)*

3 *In most developed countries employment in primary and secondary industries is contracting whilst tertiary or service employment is increasing.*

(a) How would you account for these changes in employment?

(b) Should the governments of developed countries try to limit these trends? (ACCA)

4 *Outline the main features of a free market economy and discuss its advantages and disadvantages. (AEB)*

5 *Describe the main features of a command economy and assess its advantages and disadvantages. (AEB)*

Chapter 2: The market mechanism

1 *Why do the prices of agricultural products fluctuate more than the prices of manufactured goods? (ICSA)*

2 *'If price rises, demand will fall.' 'If demand rises prices will rise.'*

(a) Explain these two statements.
(b) Illustrate these two statements. (AAT)

3 *Explain the role of prices in the allocation of scarce resources in a mixed capitalist economy. (AAT)*

4 *What would you expect to be the economic consequences of the imposition by the government of a maximum price for, say, private rented accommodation. (AAT)*

5 *(a) Explain briefly the difference between:*
(i) increases in supply and extensions in supply;
(ii) decreases in supply and contractions in supply.

(b) Explain the effect of the following changes on the demand for chocolate:
(i) a fall in the price of chocolate;
(ii) a health campaign which claims that chocolate makes you fat;
(iii) a rise in the price of chocolate substitutes;
(iv) a fall in consumers' income';
(v) an increase in the wages of chocolate workers.
(ACCA December 1987)

Chapter 3: Demand and consumer theory

1 *How does a consumer with a fixed income, all of which he spends, react to a fall in the price of one commodity? (ICSA)*

2 *(i) What are the main factors which influence the quantity of a good demanded?*

(ii) How is the equilibrium price and quantity of a good determined?

(iii) Show, using diagrams what happens to the equilibrium price of a good when consumers' incomes rise if:

(a) the supply curve is perfectly price elastic;

(b) the supply curve is perfectly price inelastic;

(c) the supply curve has unit elasticity. (AAT)

3 *(a) 'Alterations in the demand for a commodity caused by changes in its price are measured on the same demand schedule.' Explain this statement.*

(b) *What factors, other than the price of the commodity, might cause changes in its demand? How would these changes be *shown on a demand schedule diagram? (CIMA)*

Chapter 4: Supply and cost theory

1 (a) *What are the main factors which influence the quantity of a good supplied?*

(b) *How is the equilibrium price and quantity of a good determined? (AAT)*

2 *What basic concepts are illustrated by a 'production possibility' or 'transformation' curve? (CIMA)*

3 *Show the importance to the economist of the distinction between fixed cost and variable cost in: (a) the short run; and (b) the long run. (CIMA)*

4 *If there are economies of scale, why do we still have small firms? (ICSA)*

5 *What are the main factors which determine the optimum size of a firm in the long run?*

Chapter 5: Elasticity

1 *What is the difference between the price elasticity of demand and the income elasticity of demand for a product? What determines the two elasticities. (ICSA)*

2 *Explain, illustrate as appropriate and give examples of the usefulness of:*
(a) *price elasticity of demand;*
(b) *income elasticity of demand;*
(c) *cross elasticity of demand. (AAT)*

3 *Explain why it is that, in economically advanced countries, food stuffs have a low price elasticity of demand and a low income elasticity of demand. (ACCA)*

Chapter 6: Perfect competition and monopoly

1 *How should a profit maximising monopolist fix the price of his product?*

2 *Contrast the profit maximising equilibrium of:*
(a) *perfect competition; and*
(b) *pure monopoly.*

Illustrate your answers highlighting the price and output equilibrium of the marginal cost = marginal revenue rule. (AAT)

3 (a) *Define profits, distinguishing between normal and above-normal profits. (10 marks)*

(b) *What role do profits play in the operation of the market economy. (10 marks) (ACCA)*

4 *Why will a firm which is making excess or super-normal profits in conditions of perfect competition maintain or change its short-run cost curve in the long run? (ICSA)*

5 (a) *Why is monopoly regarded as being undesirable? (10 marks)*

(b) *What possible advantages may monopoly have? (10 marks) (ACCA)*

6 *Discuss the barriers which might be encountered when an industrial company enters a new market. (CIMA)*

Chapter 7: Imperfect competition

1 *Explain why at any level of output there always exists some system of discriminatory prices that will provide a higher total revenue than will any single price. (ICSA)*

2 *To what extent is the theory of the firm assumption of the maximisation of profit a realistic business goal? (AAT)*

3 (a) *Explain the short and long-run equilibrium positions of a firm operating in conditions of monopolistic competition. (10 marks)*

(b) *To what extent does monopolistic competition involve waste? (ACCA)*

4 Why is there said to be a divorcee of ownership from control in many companies? What implications does this have for the operation of these companies? (AAT)

5 Many organisations employ the cost plus percentage method of pricing. Examine the limitations of this method. (AAT)

6 Why can it be argued that many companies no longer pursue maximum profit as their only objective? (AAT)

7 (a) In many industries consisting of a few firms the prices at which all firms sell their products tend to be the same. Why does this happen? (10 marks)

(b) What forms of competition are likely to occur in such situations? (ACCA)

Chapter 8: The size and growth of firms

1 The economic value of small firms is such as to justify the Government's policy of encouragement and assistance. Discuss. (CIMA)

2 You are required to distinguish between a cartel, a merger, and a holding company, describing the main characteristics of each. (CIMA)

3 Traditionally, companies engaged in the retail trade have tended to be small, but this tendency has been reversed in the last 25 years. Why has this change occurred? (CIMA)

4 Why might a manufacturing company decide to change its geographical location? (CIMA)

5 What difficulties may arise in large scale production and why, in spite of these problems, is there a continuing trend to large scale enterprise? (CIMA)

6 What factors might lead to the emergence of each of the following types of company?

(Illustrate your answer with reference to companies with which you are familiar.)

(a) A horizontally integrated company.
(b) A vertically integrated company.
(c) A multinational company.

(AAT)

Chapter 9: The financing of firms

1 (a) What economic services are provided by a stock exchange?

(b) Why do share prices fluctuate? (CIMA)

2 Consider the relative merits of the various sources of finance for an industrial company. What criteria would the company take into account when deciding on any particular method of raising capital? (CIMA)

3 Why is there said to be a 'divorce of ownership from control' in many British companies?

What implications does this have for the operation of these companies? (AAT)

4 Explain what is meant by the capital market, and how it can provide finance for organisations. (AAT)

5 What are the main features which distinguish the operation of a public corporation from a joint stock company? (AAT)

Chapter 10: Industrial policy

1 (a) What are the causes of regional imbalance in the level of unemployment?

(b) How might this imbalance be alleviated? (CIMA)

2 What are the dangers of monopoly power and how may a government attempt to curb such power? (CIMA)

3 (a) What are the main factors the government is likely to take into account when formulating its policy towards monopoly and mergers?

(b) Briefly assess the effectiveness of the UK government's anti-monopoly policy. (AAT)

4 *What are the main features of the regional problem in the UK?*

How have successive governments attempted to deal with these problems since the Second World War? *(AAT)*

5 *What are the main economic reasons for taking an industry into public ownership? Use one of the nationalised industries in the UK to illustrate your answer.* *(AAT)*

Chapter 11: Market failure

1 *Suppose that the government of a mixed economy wishes to discourage consumption of petrol. What are the advantages and disadvantages of alternative methods of achieving this objective?* *(ACCA)*

2 *What is meant by market failure and how may it be caused? Illustrating your answer with two examples, discuss whether governments can correct market failure.* *(AEB)*

3 *What are the advantages and disadvantages of state provision of education?* *(AEB)*

4 *Distinguish between social and private costs. Examine the problems that arise if there is a divergence between social and private costs.* *(AEB)*

5 *What are public goods? Explain the case for government provision of public goods in order to improve the allocation of scarce resources.* *(AEB)*

6 *Discuss the economic arguments for and against the imposition of high taxes to deter cigarette smoking.* *(AEB)*

7 *Describe briefly what are externalities. How and why might taxes and subsidies be used to regulate externalities?* *(AEB)*

Chapter 12: Distribution theory and wage determination

1 *Under what conditions may the trade unions involved in a particular industry succeed in raising the real wages of their members:*
(a) in the short run;
(b) in the long run? *(ICSA)*

2 *Explain why a firm will substitute one factor for another factor as long as the marginal product of the one factor per penny of expenditure on it is greater than the marginal product of the other factor per penny expended on it?* *(ICSA)*

3 *Identify and discuss the factors which influence the supply of labour and the efficiency of labour in your own country.* *(CIMA)*

4 *'A fair day's pay for a fair day's work.' How far has this statement a basis in the economic theory of wage determination?* *(CIMA)*

5 *Why do women in many occupations still earn less than men?* *(CIMA)*

6 *What factors determine the relative pay of a surgeon and a road sweeper?* *(20 marks)* *(ACCA)*

7 *What are likely to be the effects on employment in an industry if trade union action results in wages being raised?* *(20 marks)* *(ACCA)*

8 *What factors are likely to determine the ability of a trade union to gain large wage increases for its members?* *(ACCA)*

9 *It is often argued that a national minimum wage should be set. Critically assess the possible affects of so doing.* *(ACCA)*

Chapter 13: The growth of modern macro-economics

1 *Explain the monetarist view of an economy. What problems are likely to arise in the implementation of monetarist policy?* *(CIMA)*

2 *Assess the monetarist view that the economy is inherently self-regulating and that an active stabilisation policy is both unnecessary and undesirable.* *(AEB)*

Chapter 14: Consumption and saving

1 *What are autonomous consumption and income-induced consumption? Explain and discuss the determination of aggregate consumption.* (AEB)

2 *'Aggregate consumption is mainly a function of the level of income.' Discuss.* (AEB)

3 *Examine the concepts of income that are relevant to consumption theory.* (AEB)

Chapter 15: National income and expenditure

1 *Explain why there is no reason to assume that the full employment level of national income will be the same as the equilibrium level of national income.* (ICSA)

2 *Explain how a deflationary gap can occur in an economy if savings always equals investment.* (ICSA)

3 (a) *What is meant by national income?*
(b) *What are the main problems involved in its calculation?* (AAT)

4 *If the rate of interest rises we would expect savings to rise and investment to fall. If savings must equal investment, how can this be?* (ICSA)

5 *Explain what is meant by 'injections' and 'withdrawals' from the circular flow of income. Analyse the effect of (a) increased government spending and (b) a government tax cut.* (ACCA)

Chapter 16: The multiplier

1 *What is the Keynesian mutliplier? What is its importance for economic policy making?* (AAT)

2 (a) *What conditions must hold for national income to be in equilibrium?*

(b) *What will be the effect on the equilibrium level of income of an increase in investment?*

(c) *The equilibrium level of income is £100. Investment increases by £20. What will be the new equilibrium level of income assuming that the marginal propensity to consume is 0.8?* (ACCA)

3 *Explain the differences between the multiplier and the accelerator.* (ICSA)

4 *Explain carefully what is meant by the multiplier. Show how the multiplier concept can be extended from a closed economy with no government sector to an open economy with a government sector.* (AEB)

Chapter 17: Investment

1 *Discuss whether the rate of interest is the most important determinant of investment expenditure by firms.* (ICSA)

2 *How does an increase in the level of investment affect the level of income and how does an increase in the level of income affect the level of investment?* (ICSA)

3 *Explain what is meant by the capital market and how it can provide finance for organisations?* (AAT)

4 *What are the main sources of finance for private industry? How has the UK government (or overseas government) attempted to influence the provision of such finance?* (AAT)

5 *What is meant by 'investment'? What factors influence the level of investment by the private and public sectors of the economy?* (AAT)

6 (a) *What are the main functions of the stock exchange?*
(b) *What factors determine the general level of share prices on the stock exchange.* (AAT)

Chapter 18: Taxation government, spending and fiscal policy

1 *What are the relative advantages and disadvantages of regressive, proportional and progressive forms of taxation?* (ICSA)

2 *What effects will the imposition of income tax have on the level of wages and the level of employment?* (ICSA)

3 *If indirect taxes are imposed on consumer goods, who effectively bears the burden or pays the tax?* (ICSA)

4 (a) *Define a subsidy and show diagrammatically the effect of a subsidy on price and output.*

(b) *For what reason may some goods be taxed and the production of other goods subsidised?* (ACCA)

Chapter 19: Money and the banking system

1 (a) *Explain the services traditionally undertaken by the commercial banks (UK or overseas).*

(b) *What new services have the banks offered more recently?*

(c) *How might a bank create credit?*

(d) *Are there are limits to the credit creation process?* (AAT)

2 *Why will people hold more or less money if the rate of interest rises?* (ICSA)

3 (a) *Explain the role of the commercial banks in the creation of money.*

(b) *What are the implications of this role for the control of the money supply by the central bank?* (AAT)

4 *To what extent is the pursuit of profit by the commercial banking sector constrained by the need to maintain liquidity?* (AAT)

5 *'It is more difficult to define money, than to control its supply.'* (ICSA)

6 *Show how commercial banks create bank deposits by making advances to their customers. What is the significance of their cash and liquidity ratios (in the United Kingdom their eligible reserve asset ratios) in this process?* (ACCA)

7 *'Money is anything generally acceptable in payment of a debt.' What are the problems with this definition? How is the money stock measured in government statistics?* (ACCA)

Chapter 20: Monetary policy

1 *Why should a government control the supply of money?* (ICSA)

2 (a) *What is money?*
(b) *What are the main methods available to Central Banks for control of the money supply?* (AAT)

3 *Outline the functions of the Bank of England and explain the mechanism by which it controls credit in the banking system.* (CIMA)

4 *Why do monetarists believe that public expenditure and the public sector borrowing requirements should be used as policy instruments to achieve control over the rate of growth of the money supply?* (AEB)

5 (a) *How may a government seek to control the supply of money?*

(b) *How effective are the methods of control likely to be?* (ACCA)

Chapter 21: Unemployment and inflation

1 *Why is inflation generally regarded as an economic problem?* (ACCA)

2 *An increase in aggregate demand will reduce unemployment. A reduction in aggregate demand will reduce inflation. Assess the validity of these Keynesian statements for a country faced with high unemployment and high inflation simultaneously.* (AAT)

3 *Does an increase in the supply of money affect the level of employment or the level of prices?* (ICSA)

4 *To what extent is the simultaneous achievement of reasonably full employment and reasonably stable prices possible in a modern industrial economy?* (AAT)

5 *How is an increase in the supply of money likely to affect the general level of prices?* (ACCA)

6 *'The postwar commitment to high employment has led to high unemployment?' Do you agree? Give the arguments for and against.* (ACCA)

7 *Distinguish between cyclical and technological unemployment. What is the significance of this distinction for government economic policies?* (CIMA)

Chapter 22: Keynesian and monetarist instruments and objectives

1 (a) *What are the objectives of macro-economic policy?*

(b) *What conflicts arise when a government endeavours to obtain these objectives simultaneously?* (ACCA)

2 *Compare and contrast 'Keynesian' and 'Monetarist' views on the determinants of the demand for money. What implications have these differences for economic policy?* (ACCA)

3 (a) *Identify the main objectives of government economic policy.*

(b) *What is meant by 'indicative planning' and how can this be used to achieve these objectives?* (CIMA)

4 *Contrast the Neo-Keynesian theory with that of the monetarist school as propounded by Friedman. What practical problems arise in the implementation of monetary policy?* (CIMA)

5 *Assess the relative merits of alternative macro-economic policy instruments available to a government seeking to reduce the level of unemployment.* (AEB)

6 (a) *Why is economic growth considered a desirable economic objective?*

(b) *For what reasons might economic growth be thought to be undesirable?* (ACCA)

Chapter 23: Trade

1 *Explain why the gains from specialisation and trade depend on the pattern of comparative, not absolute, advantage?* (ICSA)

2 *Argue the case for protection by tariffs in international trade.* (AAT)

3 *What are the assumptions and predictions of the theory of comparative costs between countries?* (ICSA)

4 (a) *Show how, in theory, free trade leads to an increase in economic welfare.*

(b) *What, if any, is the economic case for tariffs and import controls?* (ACCA)

5 *Who will gain and who will lose if a country imposes restrictions on its imports in order to protect certain of its industries?* (ACCA)

6 *One consequence of the world recession has been a renewed call by some writers for a period of 'protectionism' in respect of their own economies. With this in mind, explain:*

(a) *the case for protectionism;*
(b) *the case against protectionism.* (ACCA)

7 *Explain the practical advantages of multi-lateral international trade to the participating countries.* (CIMA)

8 *Examine the economic arguments for and against custom unions.* (AEB)

Chapter 24: The balance of payments

1 *Examine the courses of action open to a country faced with a deficit on its balance of payments.* *(ACCA)*

2 *Why can a balance of payment deficit not be allowed to persist? What policies are available for eliminating a balance of payments deficit under a system of fixed exchange rates?* *(AAT)*

3 *A balance of payments must, by definition, balance. What then is meant by:*
(a) a favourable; and
(b) an unfavourable;
balance of payments? Why may each be significant? *(CIMA)*

4 *What effect does a fall in the domestic rate of interest have on a country's balance of payments?* *(ICSA)*

Chapter 25: Exchange rates

1 *How do variable exchange rates help in dealing with balance of payments imbalances?* *(ICSA)*

2 *How does a depreciation of the rate of exchange of its currency affect a country's balance of trade?* *(ICSA)*

3 *What are the main advantages for the organisation of freely fluctuating foreign exchange rates?* *(AAT)*

4 *(a) Distinguish between fixed and floating exchange rates.*

(b) What are likely to be the most important determinants of the exchange rate for the pound sterling in the early 1980's?
(AAT)

5 *(a) What factors determine exchange rates?* *(12 marks)*
(b) How do you account for the high price of the UK $ in relation to other currencies in 1984 and 1985? *(8 marks)*
(ACCA)

INDEX

Note to students:
References are to **Chapter** and Section

THE LAW AND POLICY OF THE

World Trade Organization

Text, Cases and Materials

Since the publication of its first edition, this textbook has been the prime choice of teachers and students alike, due to its clear and detailed explanation of the basic principles of the multilateral trading system and the law of the World Trade Organization (WTO). The fourth edition continues to explore the institutional and substantive law of the WTO. It has been updated to incorporate all new developments in the WTO's ever-growing body of case law. Moreover, each chapter now includes a 'Further Readings' section to encourage and facilitate research and discussion on the topics addressed. As in previous editions, each chapter also features a summary to reinforce learning. Questions, assignments and exercises on WTO law and policy are contained in an online supplement, updated regularly and available on the website of Cambridge University Press (www.cambridge.org/VanDenBossche&Zdouc). The questions and assignments allow students to assess their understanding while the exercises, reflecting real-life trade problems, challenge students (as well as practitioners) and enable them to hone their analytical skills. This textbook is an essential tool for all WTO law students and will also serve as a practitioner's introductory guide to the WTO.

Peter Van den Bossche has been a Member of the Appellate Body of the WTO since 2009 and served as its Chair in 2015. He is Director of Studies and Professor of International Economic Law at World Trade Institute of the University of Bern, Switzerland. He is a visiting professor at the College of Europe, Bruges, Belgium; Maastricht University, the Netherlands; the University of Barcelona, Spain; and the Universidad San Francisco de Quito, Ecuador. From 1997 to 2001, he was counsellor at the Appellate Body Secretariat, and in 2001 served as Acting Director of the Secretariat. In the early 1990s, he worked as référendaire at the European Court of Justice. He studied law at the University of Antwerp (Lic. jur.), the University of Michigan (LLM) and the European University Institute, Florence (PhD).

Werner Zdouc has been Director of the WTO Appellate Body Secretariat since 2006. He obtained a law degree from the University of Graz in Austria and then went on to earn an LLM from the University of Michigan and a PhD from the University of St Gallen in Switzerland. Dr Zdouc joined the WTO Legal Affairs Division in 1995 and the Appellate Body Secretariat in 2001. In 2008 to 2009, he chaired the WTO Joint Advisory Committee to the Director-General. He has been a lecturer and visiting professor at Vienna Economic University, the Universities of St Gallen, Zurich, Barcelona, Seoul, and Shanghai and the Geneva Graduate Institute. From 1987 to 1989, he worked for governmental and non-governmental development aid organisations in Austria and Latin America.

THE LAW AND POLICY OF THE

World Trade Organization

Text, Cases and Materials

Peter Van den Bossche

Werner Zdouc

CAMBRIDGE
UNIVERSITY PRESS

University Printing House, Cambridge CB2 8BS, United Kingdom

One Liberty Plaza, 20th Floor, New York, NY 10006, USA

477 Williamstown Road, Port Melbourne, VIC 3207, Australia

4843/24, 2nd Floor, Ansari Road, Daryaganj, Delhi – 110002, India

79 Anson Road, #06–04/06, Singapore 079906

Cambridge University Press is part of the University of Cambridge.

It furthers the University's mission by disseminating knowledge in the pursuit of education, learning, and research at the highest international levels of excellence.

www.cambridge.org
Information on this title: www.cambridge.org/9781107157989
DOI: 10.1017/9781316662496

First published 2017

Printed in the United Kingdom by TJ International Ltd. Padstow Cornwall

A catalogue record for this publication is available from the British Library.

Library of Congress Cataloging-in-Publication Data
Names: Bossche, Peter van den, author. | Zdouc, Werner.
Title: The law and policy of the World Trade Organization : text, cases and materials / Peter Van den Bossche Universitat Bern, Switzerland; Werner Zdouc Graduate Institute of International Studies, Geneva.
Description: Cambridge, United Kingdom ; New York, NY, USA : Cambridge University Press, 2017. | Includes bibliographical references and index.
Identifiers: LCCN 2017012384 | ISBN 9781107157989 (alk. paper)
Subjects: LCSH: World Trade Organization. | Foreign trade regulation. | Tariff – Law and legislation. | LCGFT: Casebooks.
Classification: LCC K4610 .B67 2017 | DDC 343.08/70261–dc23
LC record available at https://lccn.loc.gov/2017012384

ISBN 978-1-107-15798-9 Hardback
ISBN 978-1-316-61052-7 Paperback

Additional resources for this publication at www.cambridge.org/VanDenBossche&Zdouc

CONTENTS

FIGURES

PREFACE

Four years have passed since the publication of the third edition of this book. These four years were marked by the demise of the Doha Round negotiations, challenges to the WTO dispute settlement system, a further proliferation of regional trade agreements and growing hostility towards economic globalisation and international trade. The fourth edition of this book has been updated and revised to reflect the developments in WTO law and policy up to 31 October 2016. This fourth edition has also been restructured with the intention to make it user-friendlier for both students and practitioners. For the first time, this edition includes at the end of each chapter a 'Further Readings' section. Also, this edition is accompanied by an on-line supplement, containing questions, assignments and exercises, which will be regularly updated and may assist students (and practitioners) to further their understanding of WTO law and policy.

I was very lucky to find, once again, Werner Zdouc willing to share the burden of updating, revising and restructuring this book, and act as a co-author of the fourth edition. Werner focused primarily on Chapters 11 (Dumping) and 12 (Subsidies). However, we both reviewed and sign for all chapters. This book reflects the current state of WTO law. We do not express any opinion on how issues not yet adjudicated should be decided or, more broadly, how WTO law should develop in the future. Where we quote or refer to various and often divergent statements of negotiators, academics or other eminent experts, we do so in order to give the reader a full picture of open debates. It is evident that the description of the current state of WTO law contained in this book is to be attributed to the authors in their private capacity and does not represent the views of the Appellate Body or the WTO.

As was the case with the previous editions, this fourth edition benefited from the advice, comments and suggestions of many. Werner and I would like to thank in particular Parika Ganeriwal for her invaluable research and editorial work on this edition. We also owe thanks to Iveta Alexovicová, Miguel Burnier da Silveira, Kaarlo Castren, Svetlana Chobanova, Louis-Philippe Coulombe,

Sidonie Descheemaker, Victoria Donaldson, Ilaria Espa, Octavio Fernandez, Mateo Ferrero, Camille Flechet, Carlo Gamberale, Shashank Kumar, Maria Kotsi, Kholofelo Kugler, Lauro Locks, Tamal Mandal, Hugo Cahueñas Muñoz, Gabrielle Marceau, Jesse Nicol, Fernando Pierola, Rodrigo Polanco, Iryna Polovets, Denise Prévost, Ricardo Ramírez, Roy Santana, Andreas Sennekamp, Kelly Shang, Maarten Smeets, Tommaso Soave, Marisol Gonzálcz Vallej, Hannu Wager, Rhian Wood, and Xiaolu Zhu. Of course, none of those mentioned above bear any responsibility for any error or omission in this book. Any such error or omission remains the responsibility of the authors. Werner and I are grateful to Marta Walkowiak, Commissioning Editor, Law Textbooks, at Cambridge University Press and her colleagues, in particular Martin Barr, Rachel Cox, Caitlin Lisle, and Dominic Stock, for their unfailing and well-organised assistance in matters large and small. We are also grateful to Finola O'Sullivan, Executive Publisher, Law, at Cambridge University Press for her continued support for this book.

The royalties from previous editions of this book were used to provide financial assistance to students and scholars from developing countries. The royalties from the fourth edition will be used for the same purpose.

PETER VAN DEN BOSSCHE

ABBREVIATIONS

ACP	African, Caribbean and Pacific
ACWL	Advisory Centre on WTO Law
AFTA	Association of Southeast Asian Nations Free Trade Area
AMS	aggregate measurement of support
ASEAN	Association of Southeast Asian Nations
Anti-dumping Agreement	Agreement on Implementation of Article VI of the General Agreement on Tariffs and Trade 1994
BCI	business confidential information
Berne Convention	Berne Convention for the Protection of Literary and Artistic Works of 1971
BoP	balance of payments
BoP Committee	Committee on Balance-of-Payments Restrictions
CARICOM	Common Market of the Caribbean
CIF	cost, insurance and freight
Code of Good Practice	Code of Good Practice for the Preparation, Adoption and Application of Standards
COMESA	Common Market of Eastern and Southern Africa
CITES	Convention on International Trade in Endangered Species
CRTA	Committee on Regional Trade Agreements
CTD	Committee on Trade and Development
CTE	Committee on Trade and Environment
CTG	Council for Trade in Goods
CTS	Council for Trade in Services
Customs Valuation Agreement	Agreement on the Implementation of Article VII of the GATT 1994
DSB	Dispute Settlement Body
DSU	Understanding on Rules and Procedures Governing the Settlement of Disputes
EC	European Communities or European Community
ECJ	European Court of Justice
EGA	Environmental Goods Agreement

EIF	Enhanced Integrated Framework for Least-Developed Countries
Enabling Clause	Decision of the GATT Contracting Parties of 28 November 1979 on Differential and More Favourable Treatment, Reciprocity and Fuller Participation of Developing Countries
ETP	Eastern Tropical Pacific
EU	European Union
FAO	Food and Agricultural Organization
FOB	free on board
GATS	General Agreement on Trade in Services
GATT	General Agreement on Tariffs and Trade
GDP	gross domestic product
GIs	geographical indications
Goods Schedule	Schedule of Concessions
GSP	Generalised System of Preferences
GVCs	global value chains
Harmonized System	*see* HS
HS	Harmonized System [International Convention on the Harmonized Commodity Description and Coding System]
HSBI	highly sensitive business information
ICC	International Chamber of Commerce
ICJ	International Court of Justice
IMF	International Monetary Fund
Import Licensing Agreement	Agreement on Import Licensing Procedures
ILC	International Law Commission
IP	intellectual property
IPIC Treaty	Treaty on Intellectual Property in respect of Integrated Circuits of 1989
ITA	Agreement on Trade in Information Technology Products
ITLOS	International Tribunal on the Law of the Sea
LDC	least-developed country
MERCOSUR	Southern Common Market
MFN	most-favoured nation
NAFTA	North American Free Trade Agreement
NAMA	Non-Agricultural Market Access
NGO	non-governmental organisation
NPR–PPMs	non-product-related processes and production methods
ODA	official development assistance
OECD	Organisation for Economic Co-operation and Development

OIE	World Organisation for Animal Health
OIO	Office of Internal Oversight
Paris Convention	Paris Convention for the Protection of Industrial Property of 1967
PLS	progressive learning strategy
PPM	process and production method
PTAs	preferential trade agreements
QRs	quantitative restrictions
Rome Convention	International Convention for the Protection of Performers, Producers of Phonograms and Broadcasting Organizations of 1961
Rules of Conduct	Rules of Conduct for the Understanding on Rules and Procedures Governing the Settlement of Disputes
RTA	regional trade agreement
S&D treatment	special and differential treatment
SADC	Southern African Development Community
SCM Agreement	Agreement on Subsidies and Countervailing Measures
SCM Committee	Committee on Subsidies and Countervailing Measures
Services Schedule	Schedule of Specific Commitments
SDGs	Sustainable Development Goals
SG&A	selling, general and administrative [cost]
SPS	sanitary and phytosanitary
SPS Agreement	Agreement on the Application of Sanitary and Phytosanitary Measures
SPS Committee	Committee on Sanitary and Phytosanitary Measures
SMEs	small and medium-size enterprises
SSG	special safeguards
STDF	Standards and Trade Development Facility
TBT	technical barriers to trade
TBT Agreement	Agreement on Technical Barriers to Trade
TBT Committee	Committee on Technical Barriers to Trade
TFA	Agreement on Trade Facilitation
TiSA	Trade in Services Agreement
TiVA	trade in value-added
TNC	Trade Negotiations Committee
TPP	Trans-Pacific Partnership
TPRB	Trade Policy Review Body
TPRM	Trade Policy Review Mechanism
TRIPS Agreement	Agreement on Trade-Related Aspects of Intellectual Property Rights
TRIPS Council	Council for Trade-Related Aspects of Intellectual Property Rights

TTIP	Transatlantic Trade and Investment Partnership
T-T methodology	transaction-to-transaction comparison methodology
UN	United Nations
UNCTAD	United Nations Conference on Trade and Development
UN CPC	United Nations Central Product Classification
Understanding on BoP Provisions	Understanding on the Balance of Payments Provisions of the GATT 1994
US	United States of America
VAT	value-added tax
VCLT	Vienna Convention on the Law of Treaties
VERs	voluntary export restraints
WCO	World Customs Organization
WHO	World Health Organization
WIPO	World Intellectual Property Organisation
W-T methodology	weighted-average-to-transaction comparison methodology
WTO	World Trade Organization
WTO Agreement	Marrakesh Agreement Establishing the World Trade Organization
W-W methodology	weighted-average-to-weighted-average comparison methodology

TABLE OF WTO CASES

The year in brackets following the short name of the case refers to the year in which the panel or Appellate Body report in that case was adopted by the DSB. Where awards or decisions by arbitrators under Articles 21.3(c), 22.6 or 25 of the DSU are concerned, the year in brackets refers to the year in which these awards or decisions were circulated.

Short title	Full case title
Argentina – Ceramic Tiles (2001)	*Argentina – Definitive Anti-Dumping Measures on Imports of Ceramic Floor Tiles from Italy*, WT/DS189.
Argentina – Financial Services (2016)	*Argentina – Measures Relating to Trade in Goods and Services*, WT/DS453.
Argentina – Footwear (EC) (2000)	*Argentina – Safeguard Measures on Imports of Footwear*, WT/DS121.
Argentina – Hides and Leather (2001)	*Argentina – Measures Affecting the Export of Bovine Hides and Import of Finished Leather*, WT/DS155 and Corr.1.
Argentina – Hides and Leather (Article 21.3(c)) (2001)	*Argentina – Measures Affecting the Export of Bovine Hides and Import of Finished Leather – Arbitration under Article 21.3(c) of the DSU*, WT/DS155.
Argentina – Import Measures (2015)	*Argentina – Measures Affecting the Importation of Goods*, WT/DS438.
Argentina – Poultry AntiDumping Duties (2003)	*Argentina – Definitive Anti-Dumping Duties on Poultry from Brazil*, WT/DS241.
Argentina – Preserved Peaches (2003)	*Argentina – Definitive Safeguard Measure on Imports of Preserved Peaches*, WT/DS238.

Short title	Full case title
Argentina – Textiles and Apparel (1998)	*Argentina – Measures Affecting Imports of Footwear, Textiles, Apparel and Other Items*, WT/DS56 and Corr.1.
Australia – Apples (2010)	*Australia – Measures Affecting the Importation of Apples from New Zealand*, WT/DS367.
Australia – Automotive Leather II (1999)	*Australia – Subsidies Provided to Producers and Exporters of Automotive Leather*, WT/DS126.
Australia – Automotive Leather II (Article 21.5 – US) (2000)	*Australia – Subsidies Provided to Producers and Exporters of Automotive Leather – Recourse to Article 21.5 of the DSU by the United States*, WT/DS126 and Corr.1.
Australia – Salmon (1998)	*Australia – Measures Affecting Importation of Salmon*, WT/DS18.
Australia – Salmon (Article 21.3(c)) (1999)	*Australia – Measures Affecting Importation of Salmon – Arbitration under Article 21.3(c) of the DSU*, WT/DS18/9.
Australia – Salmon (Article 21.5 – Canada) (2000)	*Australia – Measures Affecting Importation of Salmon – Recourse to Article 21.5 of the DSU by Canada*, WT/DS18.
Brazil – Aircraft (1999)	*Brazil – Export Financing Programme for Aircraft*, WT/DS46.
Brazil – Aircraft (Article 21.5 – Canada) (2000)	*Brazil – Export Financing Programme for Aircraft – Recourse by Canada to Article 21.5 of the DSU*, WT/DS46.
Brazil – Aircraft (Article 21.5 – Canada II) (2001)	*Brazil – Export Financing Programme for Aircraft – Second Recourse by Canada to Article 21.5 of the DSU*, WT/DS46.
Brazil – Aircraft (Article 22.6 – Brazil) (2000)	*Brazil – Export Financing Programme for Aircraft – Recourse to Arbitration by Brazil under Article 22.6 of the DSU and Article 4.11 of the SCM Agreement*, WT/DS46.
Brazil – Desiccated Coconut (1997)	*Brazil – Measures Affecting Desiccated Coconut*, WT/DS22.
Brazil – Retreaded Tyres (2007)	*Brazil – Measures Affecting Imports of Retreaded Tyres*, WT/DS332.

Short title	Full case title
Brazil – Retreaded Tyres (Article 21.3(c)) (2008)	*Brazil – Measures Affecting Imports of Retreaded Tyres – Arbitration under Article 21.3(c) of the DSU*, WT/DS332.
Canada – Aircraft (1999)	*Canada – Measures Affecting the Export of Civilian Aircraft*, WT/DS70.
Canada – Aircraft (Article 21.5 – Brazil) (2000)	*Canada – Measures Affecting the Export of Civilian Aircraft – Recourse by Brazil to Article 21.5 of the DSU*, WT/DS70.
Canada – Aircraft Credits and Guarantees (2002)	*Canada – Export Credits and Loan Guarantees for Regional Aircraft*, WT/DS222 and Corr.1.
Canada – Aircraft Credits and Guarantees (Article 22.6 – Canada) (2003)	*Canada – Export Credits and Loan Guarantees for Regional Aircraft – Recourse to Arbitration by Canada under Article 22.6 of the DSU and Article 4.11 of the SCM Agreement*, WT/DS222.
Canada – Autos (2000)	*Canada – Certain Measures Affecting the Automotive Industry*, WT/DS139.
Canada – Autos (Article 21.3(c)) (2000)	*Canada – Certain Measures Affecting the Automotive Industry – Arbitration under Article 21.3(c) of the DSU*, WT/DS139, WT/DS142.
Canada – Continued Suspension (2008)	*Canada – Continued Suspension of Obligations in the EC – Hormones Dispute*, WT/DS321.
Canada – Dairy (1999)	*Canada – Measures Affecting the Importation of Milk and the Exportation of Dairy Products*, WT/DS103, WT/DS113, and Corr.1.
Canada – Dairy (Article 21.5 – New Zealand and US) (2001)	*Canada – Measures Affecting the Importation of Milk and the Exportation of Dairy Products – Recourse to Article 21.5 of the DSU by New Zealand and the United States*, WT/DS103, WT/DS113.
Canada – Dairy (Article 21.5 – New Zealand and US II) (2003)	*Canada – Measures Affecting the Importation of Milk and the Exportation of Dairy Products – Second Recourse to Article 21.5 of the DSU by New Zealand and the United States*, WT/DS103, WT/DS113.
Canada – Patent Term (2000)	*Canada – Term of Patent Protection*, WT/DS170.

Short title	Full case title
Canada – Patent Term (Article 21.3(c)) (2001)	*Canada – Term of Patent Protection – Arbitration under Article 21.3(c) of the DSU*, WT/DS170/10.
Canada – Periodicals (1997)	*Canada – Certain Measures Concerning Periodicals*, WT/DS31.
Canada – Pharmaceutical Patents (2000)	*Canada – Patent Protection of Pharmaceutical Products*, WT/DS114.
Canada – Pharmaceutical Patents (Article 21.3(c)) (2000)	*Canada – Patent Protection of Pharmaceutical Products – Arbitration under Article 21.3(c) of the DSU*, WT/DS114/13.
Canada – Renewable Energy / Canada – Feed-in Tariff Program (2013)	*Canada – Certain Measures Affecting the Renewable Energy Generation Sector / Canada – Measures Relating to the Feed-in Tariff Program*, WT/DS412 / WT/DS426.
Canada – Wheat Exports and Grain Imports (2004)	*Canada – Measures Relating to Exports of Wheat and Treatment of Imported Grain*, WT/DS276.
Chile – Alcoholic Beverages (2000)	*Chile – Taxes on Alcoholic Beverages*, WT/DS87, WT/DS110.
Chile – Alcoholic Beverages (Article 21.3(c)) (2000)	*Chile – Taxes on Alcoholic Beverages – Arbitration under Article 21.3(c) of the DSU*, WT/DS87/15, WT/DS110/14.
Chile – Price Band System (2002)	*Chile – Price Band System and Safeguard Measures Relating to Certain Agricultural Products*, WT/DS207.
Chile – Price Band System (Article 21.3(c)) (2003)	*Chile – Price Band System and Safeguard Measures Relating to Certain Agricultural Products – Arbitration under Article 21.3(c) of the DSU*, WT/DS207/13.
Chile – Price Band System (Article 21.5 – Argentina) (2007)	*Chile – Price Band System and Safeguard Measures Relating to Certain Agricultural Products – Recourse to Article 21.5 of the DSU by Argentina*, WT/DS207.
China – Auto Parts (2009)	*China – Measures Affecting Imports of Automobile Parts*, WT/DS339 / WT/DS340 / WT/DS342.
China – Autos (US) (2014)	*China – Anti-Dumping and Countervailing Duties on Certain Automobiles from the United States*, WT/DS440 and Add.1.
China – Broiler Products (2013)	*China – Anti-Dumping and Countervailing Duty Measures on Broiler Products from the United States*, WT/DS427 and Add.1.

Short title	Full case title
China – Electronic Payment Services (2012)	*China – Certain Measures Affecting Electronic Payment Services*, WT/DS413.
China – GOES (2012)	*China – Countervailing and Anti-Dumping Duties on Grain Oriented Flat-Rolled Electrical Steel from the United States*, WT/DS414.
China – GOES (Article 21.3(c)) (2013)	*China – Countervailing and Anti-Dumping Duties on Grain Oriented Flat-Rolled Electrical Steel from the United States – Arbitration under Article 21.3(c) of the Understanding on Rules and Procedures Governing the Settlement of Disputes*, WT/DS414/12.
China – GOES (Article 21.5 – US) (2015)	*China – Countervailing and Anti-Dumping Duties on Grain Oriented Flat-Rolled Electrical Steel from the United States – Recourse to Article 21.5 of the DSU by the United States*, WT/DS414.
China – HP-SSST (EU) / China – HP-SSST (Japan) (2015)	*China – Measures Imposing Anti-Dumping Duties on High-Performance Stainless Steel Seamless Tubes ('HP-SSST') from Japan / China – Measures Imposing Anti-Dumping Duties on High-Performance Stainless Steel Seamless Tubes ('HP-SSST') from the European Union*, WT/DS454 and Add.1 / WT/DS460.
China – Intellectual Property Rights (2009)	*China – Measures Affecting the Protection and Enforcement of Intellectual Property Rights*, WT/DS362.
China – Publications and Audiovisual Products (2010)	*China – Measures Affecting Trading Rights and Distribution Services for Certain Publications and Audiovisual Entertainment Products*, WT/DS363.
China – Rare Earths (2014)	*China – Measures Related to the Exportation of Rare Earths, Tungsten, and Molybdenum*, WT/DS431 / WT/DS432 / WT/DS433.
China – Raw Materials (2012)	*China – Measures Related to the Exportation of Various Raw Materials*, WT/DS394 / WT/DS395 / WT/DS398.
China – X-Ray Equipment (2013)	*China – Definitive Anti-Dumping Duties on X-Ray Security Inspection Equipment from the European Union*, WT/DS425 and Add.1.
Colombia – Ports of Entry (2009)	*Colombia – Indicative Prices and Restrictions on Ports of Entry*, WT/DS366 and Corr.1.

Short title	Full case title
Colombia – Ports of Entry (Article 21.3(c)) (2009)	*Colombia – Indicative Prices and Restrictions on Ports of Entry – Arbitration under Article 21.3(c) of the DSU*, WT/DS366/13.
Colombia – Textiles (2016)	*Colombia – Measures Relating to the Importation of Textiles, Apparel and Footwear*, WT/DS461 and Add.1.
Dominican Republic – Import and Sale of Cigarettes (2005)	*Dominican Republic – Measures Affecting the Importation and Internal Sale of Cigarettes*, WT/DS302.
Dominican Republic – Import and Sale of Cigarettes (Article 21.3(c)) (2005)	*Dominican Republic – Measures Affecting the Importation and Internal Sale of Cigarettes – Arbitration under Article 21.3(c) of the DSU*, WT/DS302/17.
Dominican Republic – Safeguard Measures (2012)	*Dominican Republic – Safeguard Measures on Imports of Polypropylene Bags and Tubular Fabric*, WT/DS415, WT/DS416, WT/DS417, WT/DS418, and Add.1.
EC – The ACP–EC Partnership Agreement (2005)	*European Communities – The ACP–EC Partnership Agreement – Recourse to Arbitration Pursuant to the Decision of 14 November 2001*, WT/L/616.
EC – The ACP–EC Partnership Agreement II (2005)	*European Communities – The ACP–EC Partnership Agreement – Second Recourse to Arbitration Pursuant to the Decision of 14 November 2001*, WT/L/625.
EC – Approval and Marketing of Biotech Products (2006)	*European Communities – Measures Affecting the Approval and Marketing of Biotech Products*, WT/DS291.
EC – Asbestos (2001)	*European Communities – Measures Affecting Asbestos and Asbestos-Containing Products*, WT/DS135.
EC – Bananas III (1997)	*European Communities – Regime for the Importation, Sale and Distribution of Bananas*, WT/DS27.
EC – Bananas III (Ecuador) (1997)	*European Communities – Regime for the Importation, Sale and Distribution of Bananas, Complaint by Ecuador*, WT/DS27.
EC – Bananas III (Guatemala and Honduras) (1997)	*European Communities – Regime for the Importation, Sale and Distribution of Bananas, Complaint by Guatemala and Honduras*, WT/DS27.
EC – Bananas III (Mexico) (1997)	*European Communities – Regime for the Importation, Sale and Distribution of Bananas, Complaint by Mexico*, WT/DS27.

Short title	Full case title
EC – Bananas III (US) (1997)	*European Communities – Regime for the Importation, Sale and Distribution of Bananas, Complaint by the United States*, WT/DS27.
EC – Bananas III (Article 21.3(c)) (1998)	*European Communities – Regime for the Importation, Sale and Distribution of Bananas – Arbitration under Article 21.3(c) of the DSU*, WT/DS27/15.
EC – Bananas III (Article 21.5 – EC) (1999)	*European Communities – Regime for the Importation, Sale and Distribution of Bananas – Recourse to Article 21.5 of the DSU by the European Communities*, WT/DS27.
EC – Bananas III (Article 21.5 – Ecuador) (1999)	*European Communities – Regime for the Importation, Sale and Distribution of Bananas – Recourse to Article 21.5 of the DSU by Ecuador*, WT/DS27.
EC – Bananas III (Article 21.5 – US) (2008)	*European Communities – Regime for the Importation, Sale and Distribution of Bananas – Second Recourse to Article 21.5 of the DSU by United States*, WT/DS27.
EC – Bananas III (Article 21.5 – Ecuador II) (2008)	*European Communities – Regime for the Importation, Sale and Distribution of Bananas – Second Recourse to Article 21.5 of the DSU by Ecuador*, WT/DS27.
EC – Bananas III (Ecuador) (Article 22.6 – EC) (2000)	*European Communities – Regime for the Importation, Sale and Distribution of Bananas – Recourse to Arbitration by the European Communities under Article 22.6 of the DSU*, WT/DS27.
EC – Bananas III (US) (Article 22.6 – EC) (1999)	*European Communities – Regime for the Importation, Sale and Distribution of Bananas – Recourse to Arbitration by the European Communities under Article 22.6 of the DSU.*
EC – Bed Linen (2001)	*European Communities – Anti-Dumping Duties on Imports of Cotton-Type Bed Linen from India*, WT/DS141.
EC – Bed Linen (Article 21.5 – India) (2003)	*European Communities – Anti-Dumping Duties on Imports of Cotton-Type Bed Linen from India – Recourse to Article 21.5 of the DSU by India*, WT/DS141.
EC – Butter (1999)	*European Communities – Measures Affecting Butter Products*, WT/DS72 (unadopted).

Short title	Full case title
EC – Chicken Cuts (2005)	*European Communities – Customs Classification of Frozen Boneless Chicken Cuts*, WT/DS269, WT/DS286 and Corr.1.
EC – Chicken Cuts (Brazil) (2005)	*European Communities – Customs Classification of Frozen Boneless Chicken Cuts, Complaint by Brazil*, WT/DS269.
EC – Chicken Cuts (Thailand) (2005)	*European Communities – Customs Classification of Frozen Boneless Chicken Cuts, Complaint by Thailand*, WT/DS286.
EC – Chicken Cuts (Article 21.3(c)) (2006)	*European Communities – Customs Classification of Frozen Boneless Chicken Cuts – Arbitration under Article 21.3(c) of the DSU*, WT/DS269/13, WT/DS286/15.
EC – Commercial Vessels (2005)	*European Communities – Measures Affecting Trade in Commercial Vessels*, WT/DS301.
EC – Computer Equipment (1998)	*European Communities – Customs Classification of Certain Computer Equipment*, WT/DS62, WT/DS67, WT/DS68.
EC – Countervailing Measures on DRAM Chips (2005)	*European Communities – Countervailing Measures on Dynamic Random Access Memory Chips from Korea*, WT/DS299.
EC – Export Subsidies on Sugar (2005)	*European Communities – Export Subsidies on Sugar*, WT/DS265, WT/DS266, WT/DS283.
EC – Export Subsidies on Sugar (Australia) (2005)	*European Communities – Export Subsidies on Sugar, Complaint by Australia*, WT/DS265.
EC – Export Subsidies on Sugar (Brazil) (2005)	*European Communities – Export Subsidies on Sugar, Complaint by Brazil*, WT/DS266.
EC – Export Subsidies on Sugar (Thailand) (2005)	*European Communities – Export Subsidies on Sugar, Complaint by Thailand*, WT/DS283.
EC – Export Subsidies on Sugar (Article 21.3(c)) (2005)	*European Communities – Export Subsidies on Sugar – Arbitration under Article 21.3(c) of the DSU*, WT/DS265/33, WT/DS266/33, WT/DS283/14.
EC – Fasteners (China) (2011)	*European Communities – Definitive Anti-Dumping Measures on Certain Iron or Steel Fasteners from China*, WT/DS397.

Short title	Full case title
EC – Fasteners (China) (Article 21.5 – China) (2016)	*European Communities – Definitive Anti-Dumping Measures on Certain Iron or Steel Fasteners from China – Recourse to Article 21.5 of the DSU by China*, WT/DS397.
EC – Hormones (1998)	*EC Measures Concerning Meat and Meat Products (Hormones)*, WT/DS26, WT/DS48.
EC – Hormones (Canada) (1998)	*EC Measures Concerning Meat and Meat Products (Hormones), Complaint by Canada*, WT/DS48.
EC – Hormones (US) (1998)	*EC Measures Concerning Meat and Meat Products (Hormones), Complaint by the United States*, WT/DS26.
EC – Hormones (Article 21.3(c)) (1998)	*EC Measures Concerning Meat and Meat Products (Hormones) – Arbitration under Article 21.3(c) of the DSU*, WT/DS26/15, WT/DS48/13.
EC – Hormones (Canada) (Article 22.6 – EC) (1999)	*European Communities – Measures Concerning Meat and Meat Products (Hormones), Original Complaint by Canada – Recourse to Arbitration by the European Communities under Article 22.6 of the DSU*, WT/DS48.
EC – Hormones (US) (Article 22.6 – EC) (1999)	*European Communities – Measures Concerning Meat and Meat Products (Hormones), Original Complaint by the United States – Recourse to Arbitration by the European Communities under Article 22.6 of the DSU*, WT/DS26.
EC – IT Products (2010)	*European Communities and its member States – Tariff Treatment of Certain Information Technology Products*, WT/DS375 / WT/DS376/ WT/DS377.
EC – Poultry (1998)	*European Communities – Measures Affecting the Importation of Certain Poultry Products*, WT/DS69.
EC – Salmon (Norway) (2008)	*European Communities – Anti-Dumping Measure on Farmed Salmon from Norway*, WT/DS337 and Corr.1.
EC – Sardines (2002)	*European Communities – Trade Description of Sardines*, WT/DS231.
EC – Scallops (Canada) (1996)	*European Communities – Trade Description of Scallops – Request by Canada*, WT/DS7 (unadopted).
EC – Scallops (Peru and Chile) (1996)	*European Communities – Trade Description of Scallops – Requests by Peru and Chile*, WT/DS12, WT/DS14 (unadopted).

Short title	Full case title
EC – Seal Products (2014)	*European Communities – Measures Prohibiting the Importation and Marketing of Seal Products*, WT/DS400 / WT/DS401.
EC – Selected Customs Matters (2006)	*European Communities – Selected Customs Matters*, WT/DS315.
EC – Tariff Preferences (2004)	*European Communities – Conditions for the Granting of Tariff Preferences to Developing Countries*, WT/DS246.
EC – Tariff Preferences (Article 21.3(c)) (2004)	*European Communities – Conditions for the Granting of Tariff Preferences to Developing Countries – Arbitration under Article 21.3(c) of the DSU*, WT/DS246/14.
EC – Trademarks and Geographical Indications (Australia) (2005)	*European Communities – Protection of Trademarks and Geographical Indications for Agricultural Products and Foodstuffs, Complaint by Australia*, WT/DS290.
EC – Trademarks and Geographical Indications (US) (2005)	*European Communities – Protection of Trademarks and Geographical Indications for Agricultural Products and Foodstuffs, Complaint by the United States*, WT/DS174.
EC – Tube or Pipe Fittings (2003)	*European Communities – Anti-Dumping Duties on Malleable Cast Iron Tube or Pipe Fittings from Brazil*, WT/DS219.
EC and certain member States – Large Civil Aircraft (2011)	*European Communities and Certain Member States – Measures Affecting Trade in Large Civil Aircraft*, WT/DS316.
EC and certain member States – Large Civil Aircraft (Article 21.5 – US)	*European Communities and Certain Member States – Measures Affecting Trade in Large Civil Aircraft – Recourse to Article 21.5 of the DSU by the United States*, WT/DS316 and Add.1 [appeal pending].
Egypt – Steel Rebar (2002)	*Egypt – Definitive Anti-Dumping Measures on Steel Rebar from Turkey*, WT/DS211.
EU – Biodiesel (Argentina) (2016)	*European Union – Anti-Dumping Measures on Biodiesel from Argentina*, WT/DS473 and Add.1.
EU – Footwear (China) (2012)	*European Union – Anti-Dumping Measures on Certain Footwear from China*, WT/DS405.

Short title	Full case title
Guatemala – Cement I (1998)	*Guatemala – Anti-Dumping Investigation Regarding Portland Cement from Mexico*, WT/DS60.
Guatemala – Cement II (2000)	*Guatemala – Definitive Anti-Dumping Measures on Grey Portland Cement from Mexico*, WT/DS156.
India – Additional Import Duties (2008)	*India – Additional and Extra-Additional Duties on Imports from the United States*, WT/DS360.
India – Agricultural Products (2015)	*India – Measures Concerning the Importation of Certain Agricultural Products*, WT/DS430.
India – Autos (2002)	*India – Measures Affecting the Automotive Sector*, WT/DS146, WT/DS175.
India – Patents (EC) (1998)	*India – Patent Protection for Pharmaceutical and Agricultural Chemical Products, Complaint by the European Communities and their member States*, WT/DS79.
India – Patents (US) (1998)	*India – Patent Protection for Pharmaceutical and Agricultural Chemical Products*, WT/DS50.
India – Quantitative Restrictions (1999)	*India – Quantitative Restrictions on Imports of Agricultural, Textile and Industrial Products*, WT/DS90.
India – Solar Cells (2016)	*India – Certain Measures Relating to Solar Cells and Solar Modules*, WT/DS456.
Indonesia – Autos (1998)	*Indonesia – Certain Measures Affecting the Automobile Industry*, WT/DS54, WT/DS55, WT/DS59, WT/DS64, Corr.1, Corr.2, Corr.3 and Corr.4.
Indonesia – Autos (Article 21.3(c)) (1998)	*Indonesia – Certain Measures Affecting the Automobile Industry – Arbitration under Article 21.3(c) of the DSU*, WT/DS54/15, WT/DS55/14, WT/DS59/13, WT/DS64/12.
Japan – Agricultural Products II (1999)	*Japan – Measures Affecting Agricultural Products*, WT/DS76.
Japan – Alcoholic Beverages II (1996)	*Japan – Taxes on Alcoholic Beverages*, WT/DS8, WT/DS10, WT/DS11.
Japan – Alcoholic Beverages II (Article 21.3(c)) (1997)	*Japan – Taxes on Alcoholic Beverages – Arbitration under Article 21.3(c) of the DSU*, WT/DS8/15, WT/DS10/15, WT/DS11/13.

Short title	Full case title
Japan – Apples (2003)	*Japan – Measures Affecting the Importation of Apples*, WT/DS245.
Japan – Apples (Article 21.5 – US) (2005)	*Japan – Measures Affecting the Importation of Apples – Recourse to Article 21.5 of the DSU by the United States*, WT/DS245.
Japan – DRAMs (Korea) (2007)	*Japan – Countervailing Duties on Dynamic Random Access Memories from Korea*, WT/DS336 and Corr.1.
Japan – DRAMs (Korea) (Article 21.3(c)) (2008)	*Japan – Countervailing Duties on Dynamic Random Access Memories from Korea – Arbitration under Article 21.3(c) of the DSU*, WT/DS336
Japan – Film (1998)	*Japan – Measures Affecting Consumer Photographic Film and Paper*, WT/DS44.
Japan – Quotas on Laver (2006)	*Japan – Import Quotas on Dried Laver and Seasoned Laver*, WT/DS323 (unadopted).
Korea – Alcoholic Beverages (1999)	*Korea – Taxes on Alcoholic Beverages*, WT/DS75, WT/DS84.
Korea – Alcoholic Beverages (Article 21.3(c)) (1999)	*Korea – Taxes on Alcoholic Beverages – Arbitration under Article 21.3(c) of the DSU*, WT/DS75/16, WT/DS84/14.
Korea – Bovine Meat (Canada) (2012)	*Korea – Measures Affecting the Importation of Bovine Meat and Meat Products from Canada*, WT/DS391 (unadopted).
Korea – Certain Paper (2005)	*Korea – Anti-Dumping Duties on Imports of Certain Paper from Indonesia*, WT/DS312.
Korea – Certain Paper (Article 21.5 – Indonesia) (2007)	*Korea – Anti-Dumping Duties on Imports of Certain Paper from Indonesia – Recourse to Article 21.5 of the DSU by Indonesia*, WT/DS312.
Korea – Commercial Vessels (2005)	*Korea – Measures Affecting Trade in Commercial Vessels*, WT/DS273.
Korea – Dairy (2000)	*Korea – Definitive Safeguard Measure on Imports of Certain Dairy Products*, WT/DS98.
Korea – Procurement (2000)	*Korea – Measures Affecting Government Procurement*, WT/DS163.
Korea – Various Measures on Beef (2001)	*Korea – Measures Affecting Imports of Fresh, Chilled and Frozen Beef*, WT/DS161, WT/DS169.

Short title	Full case title
Mexico – Anti-Dumping Measures on Rice (2005)	*Mexico – Definitive Anti-Dumping Measures on Beef and Rice, Complaint with Respect to Rice*, WT/DS295.
Mexico – Corn Syrup (2000)	*Mexico – Anti-Dumping Investigation of High Fructose Corn Syrup (HFCS) from the United States*, WT/DS132.
Mexico – Corn Syrup (Article 21.5 – US) (2001)	*Mexico – Anti-Dumping Investigation of High Fructose Corn Syrup (HFCS) from the United States – Recourse to Article 21.5 of the DSU by the United States*, WT/DS132.
Mexico – Olive Oil (2008)	*Mexico – Definitive Countervailing Measures on Olive Oil from the European Communities*, WT/DS341.
Mexico – Steel Pipes and Tubes (2007)	*Mexico – Anti-Dumping Duties on Steel Pipes and Tubes from Guatemala*, WT/DS331.
Mexico – Taxes on Soft Drinks (2006)	*Mexico – Tax Measures on Soft Drinks and Other Beverages*, WT/DS308.
Mexico – Telecoms (2004)	*Mexico – Measures Affecting Telecommunications Services*, WT/DS204.
Peru – Agricultural Products (2015)	*Peru – Additional Duty on Imports of Certain Agricultural Products*, WT/DS457.
Peru – Agricultural Products (Article 21.3(c)) (2015)	*Peru – Additional Duty on Imports of Certain Agricultural Products – Arbitration under Article 21.3(c) of the DSU*, WT/DS457/15.
Philippines – Distilled Spirits (2012)	*Philippines – Taxes on Distilled Spirits*, WT/DS396, WT/DS403.
Russia – Pigs (EU)	*Russian Federation – Measures on the Importation of Live Pigs, Pork and Other Pig Products from the European Union*, WT/DS475, (appeal pending).
Russia – Tariff Treatment (2016)	*Russia – Tariff Treatment of Certain Agricultural and Manufacturing Products*, WT/DS485, Corr.1, Corr.2, and Add.1.
Thailand – Cigarettes (Philippines) (2011)	*Thailand – Customs and Fiscal Measures on Cigarettes from the Philippines*, WT/DS371.
Thailand – H-Beams (2001)	*Thailand – Anti-Dumping Duties on Angles, Shapes and Sections of Iron or Non-Alloy Steel and H-Beams from Poland*, WT/DS122.

Short title	Full case title
Turkey – Rice (2007)	*Turkey – Measures Affecting the Importation of Rice*, WT/DS334.
Turkey – Textiles (1999)	*Turkey – Restrictions on Imports of Textile and Clothing Products*, WT/DS34.
Ukraine – Passenger Cars (2015)	*Ukraine – Definitive Safeguard Measures on Certain Passenger Cars*, WT/DS468 and Add.1.
US – 1916 Act (2000)	*United States – Anti-Dumping Act of 1916*, WT/DS136, WT/DS162.
US – 1916 Act (Article 21.3(c)) (2001)	*United States – Anti-Dumping Act of 1916 – Arbitration under Article 21.3(c) of the DSU*, WT/DS136/11, WT/DS162/14.
US – 1916 Act (EC) (Article 22.6 – US) (2004)	*United States – Anti-Dumping Act of 1916, Original Complaint by the European Communities – Recourse to Arbitration by the United States under Article 22.6 of the DSU*, WT/DS136.
US – Animals (2015)	*United States – Measures Affecting the Importation of Animals, Meat and Other Animal Products from Argentina*, WT/DS447 and Add.1.
US – Anti-Dumping and Countervailing Duties (China) (2011)	*United States – Definitive Anti-Dumping and Countervailing Duties on Certain Products from China*, WT/DS379.
US – Anti-Dumping Measures on Oil Country Tubular Goods (2005)	*United States – Anti-Dumping Measures on Oil Country Tubular Goods (OCTG) from Mexico*, WT/DS282.
US – Anti-Dumping Measures on PET Bags (2010)	*United States – Anti-Dumping Measures on Polyethylene Retail Carrier Bags from Thailand*, WT/DS383.
US – Carbon Steel (2002)	*United States – Countervailing Duties on Certain Corrosion-Resistant Carbon Steel Flat Products from Germany*, WT/DS213 and Corr.1.
US – Carbon Steel (India) (2014)	*United States – Countervailing Measures on Certain Hot-Rolled Carbon Steel Flat Products from India*, WT/DS436.
US – Certain EC Products (2001)	*United States – Import Measures on Certain Products from the European Communities*, WT/DS165.

Short title	Full case title
US – Clove Cigarettes (2012)	*United States – Measures Affecting the Production and Sale of Clove Cigarettes*, WT/DS406.
US – Continued Suspension (2008)	*United States – Continued Suspension of Obligations in the EC – Hormones Dispute*, WT/DS320.
US – Continued Zeroing (2009)	*United States – Continued Existence and Application of Zeroing Methodology*, WT/DS350.
US – COOL (2012)	*United States – Certain Country of Origin Labelling (COOL) Requirements*, WT/DS384 / WT/DS386.
US – COOL (Article 21.3(c)) (2012)	*United States – Certain Country of Origin Labelling (COOL) Requirements – Arbitration under Article 21.3(c) of the DSU*, WT/DS384/24, WT/DS386/23.
US – COOL (Article 21.5 – Canada and Mexico) (2015)	*United States – Certain Country of Origin Labelling (COOL) Requirements – Recourse to Article 21.5 of the DSU by Canada and Mexico*, WT/DS384 / WT/DS386.
US – COOL (Article 22.6 – United States) (2015)	*United States – Certain Country of Origin Labelling (COOL) Requirements – Recourse to Article 22.6 of the DSU by the United States*, WT/DS384 and Add.1 / WT/DS386 and Add.1.
US – Corrosion-Resistant Steel Sunset Review (2004)	*United States – Sunset Review of Anti-Dumping Duties on Corrosion-Resistant Carbon Steel Flat Products from Japan*, WT/DS244.
US – Cotton Yarn (2001)	*United States – Transitional Safeguard Measure on Combed Cotton Yarn from Pakistan*, WT/DS192.
US – Countervailing and Anti-Dumping Measures (China) (2014)	*United States – Countervailing and Anti-Dumping Measures on Certain Products from China*, WT/DS449 and Corr.1.
US – Countervailing Duty Investigation on DRAMS (2005)	*United States – Countervailing Duty Investigation on Dynamic Random Access Memory Semiconductors (DRAMS) from Korea*, WT/DS296.
US – Countervailing Measures (China) (2015)	*United States – Countervailing Duty Measures on Certain Products from China*, WT/DS437.
US – Countervailing Measures (China) (Article 21.3(c)) (2015)	*United States – Countervailing Duty Measures on Certain Products from China – Arbitration under Article 21.3(c) of the DSU*, WT/DS437/16.
US – Countervailing Measures on Certain EC Products (2003)	*United States – Countervailing Measures Concerning Certain Products from the European Communities*, WT/DS212.

Short title	Full case title
US – Countervailing Measures on Certain EC Products (Article 21.5 – EC) (2005)	*United States – Countervailing Measures Concerning Certain Products from the European Communities – Recourse to Article 21.5 of the DSU by the European Communities*, WT/DS212.
US – Customs Bond Directive (2008)	*United States – Customs Bond Directive for Merchandise Subject to Anti-Dumping/Countervailing Duties*, WT/DS345.
US – DRAMS (1999)	*United States – Anti-Dumping Duty on Dynamic Random Access Memory Semiconductors (DRAMS) of One Megabit or Above from Korea*, WT/DS99.
US – DRAMS (Article 21.5 – Korea) (2000)	*United States – Anti-Dumping Duty on Dynamic Random Access Memory Semiconductors (DRAMS) of One Megabit or Above from Korea – Recourse to Article 21.5 of the DSU by Korea*, WT/DS99 (unadopted).
US – Export Restraints (2001)	*United States – Measures Treating Exports Restraints as Subsidies*, WT/DS194 and Corr.2.
US – FSC (2000)	*United States – Tax Treatment for 'Foreign Sales Corporations'*, WT/DS108.
US – FSC (Article 21.5 – EC) (2002)	*United States – Tax Treatment for 'Foreign Sales Corporations' – Recourse to Article 21.5 of the DSU by the European Communities*, WT/DS108.
US – FSC (Article 21.5 – EC II) (2006)	*United States – Tax Treatment for 'Foreign Sales Corporations' – Second Recourse to Article 21.5 of the DSU by the European Communities*, WT/DS108.
US – FSC (Article 22.6 – US) (2002)	*United States – Tax Treatment for 'Foreign Sales Corporations' – Recourse to Arbitration by the United States under Article 22.6 of the DSU and Article 4.11 of the SCM Agreement*, WT/DS108.
US – Gambling (2005)	*United States – Measures Affecting the Cross-Border Supply of Gambling and Betting Services*, WT/DS285.
US – Gambling (Article 21.3(c)) (2005)	*United States – Measures Affecting the Cross-Border Supply of Gambling and Betting Services – Arbitration under Article 21.3(c) of the DSU*, WT/DS285.
US – Gambling (Article 21.5 – Antigua and Barbuda) (2007)	*United States – Measures Affecting the Cross-Border Supply of Gambling and Betting Services – Recourse to Article 21.5 of the DSU by Antigua and Barbuda*, WT/DS285.

Short title	Full case title
US – Gambling (Article 22.6 – US) (2007)	*United States – Measures Affecting the Cross-Border Supply of Gambling and Betting Services – Recourse to Arbitration by the United States under Article 22.6 of the DSU*, WT/DS285.
US – Gasoline (1996)	*United States – Standards for Reformulated and Conventional Gasoline*, WT/DS2.
US – Hot-Rolled Steel (2001)	*United States – Anti-Dumping Measures on Certain Hot-Rolled Steel Products from Japan*, WT/DS184.
US – Hot-Rolled Steel (Article 21.3(c)) (2002)	*United States – Anti-Dumping Measures on Certain Hot-Rolled Steel Products from Japan – Arbitration under Article 21.3(c) of the DSU*, WT/DS184/13.
US – Lamb (2001)	*United States – Safeguard Measures on Imports of Fresh, Chilled or Frozen Lamb Meat from New Zealand and Australia*, WT/DS177, WT/DS178.
US – Large Civil Aircraft (2nd complaint) (2012)	*United States – Measures Affecting Trade in Large Civil Aircraft (Second Complaint)*, WT/DS353.
US – Lead and Bismuth II (2000)	*United States – Imposition of Countervailing Duties on Certain Hot-Rolled Lead and Bismuth Carbon Steel Products Originating in the United Kingdom*, WT/DS138.
US – Line Pipe (2002)	*United States – Definitive Safeguard Measures on Imports of Circular Welded Carbon Quality Line Pipe from Korea*, WT/DS202.
US – Line Pipe (Article 21.3(c)) (2002)	*United States – Definitive Safeguard Measures on Imports of Circular Welded Carbon Quality Line Pipe from Korea – Arbitration under Article 21.3(c) of the DSU*, WT/DS202/17.
US – Malt Beverages (1992)	*US – Measures Affecting Alcoholic and Malt Beverages, DS23/R -39S/206.*
US – Offset Act (Byrd Amendment) (2003)	*United States – Continued Dumping and Subsidy Offset Act of 2000*, WT/DS217, WT/DS234.
US – Offset Act (Byrd Amendment) (Article 21.3(c)) (2003)	*United States – Continued Dumping and Subsidy Offset Act of 2000 – Arbitration under Article 21.3(c) of the DSU*, WT/DS217/14, WT/DS234/22.
US – Offset Act (Byrd Amendment) (Brazil) (Article 22.6 – US) (2004)	*United States – Continued Dumping and Subsidy Offset Act of 2000, Original Complaint by Brazil – Recourse to Arbitration by the United States under Article 22.6 of the DSU*, WT/DS217.

Short title	Full case title
US – Offset Act (Byrd Amendment) (Canada) (Article 22.6 – US) (2004)	*United States – Continued Dumping and Subsidy Offset Act of 2000, Original Complaint by Canada – Recourse to Arbitration by the United States under Article 22.6 of the DSU*, WT/DS234.
US – Offset Act (Byrd Amendment) (Chile) (Article 22.6 – US) (2004)	*United States – Continued Dumping and Subsidy Offset Act of 2000, Original Complaint by Chile – Recourse to Arbitration by the United States under Article 22.6 of the DSU*, WT/DS217.
US – Offset Act (Byrd Amendment) (EC) (Article 22.6 – US) (2004)	*United States – Continued Dumping and Subsidy Offset Act of 2000, Original Complaint by the European Communities – Recourse to Arbitration by the United States under Article 22.6 of the DSU*, WT/DS217.
US – Offset Act (Byrd Amendment) (India) (Article 22.6 – US) (2004)	*United States – Continued Dumping and Subsidy Offset Act of 2000, Original Complaint by India – Recourse to Arbitration by the United States under Article 22.6 of the DSU*, WT/DS217.
US – Offset Act (Byrd Amendment) (Japan) (Article 22.6 – US) (2004)	*United States – Continued Dumping and Subsidy Offset Act of 2000, Original Complaint by Japan – Recourse to Arbitration by the United States under Article 22.6 of the DSU*, WT/DS217.
US – Offset Act (Byrd Amendment) (Korea) (Article 22.6 – US) (2004)	*United States – Continued Dumping and Subsidy Offset Act of 2000, Original Complaint by Korea – Recourse to Arbitration by the United States under Article 22.6 of the DSU*, WT/DS217.
US – Offset Act (Byrd Amendment) (Mexico) (Article 22.6 – US) (2004)	*United States – Continued Dumping and Subsidy Offset Act of 2000, Original Complaint by Mexico – Recourse to Arbitration by the United States under Article 22.6 of the DSU*, WT/DS234.
US – Oil Country Tubular Goods Sunset Reviews (2004)	*United States – Sunset Reviews of Anti-Dumping Measures on Oil Country Tubular Goods from Argentina*, WT/DS268.
US – Oil Country Tubular Goods Sunset Reviews (Article 21.3(c)) (2005)	*United States – Sunset Reviews of Anti-Dumping Measures on Oil Country Tubular Goods from Argentina – Arbitration under Article 21.3(c) of the DSU*, WT/DS268.
US – Oil Country Tubular Goods Sunset Reviews (Article 21.5 – Argentina) (2007)	*United States – Sunset Reviews of Anti-Dumping Measures on Oil Country Tubular Goods from Argentina – Recourse to Article 21.5 of the DSU by Argentina*, WT/DS268.

Short title	Full case title
US – Orange Juice (Brazil) (2011)	*United States – Anti-Dumping Administrative Reviews and Other Measures Related to Imports of Certain Orange Juice from Brazil*, WT/DS382.
US – Poultry (China) (2010)	*United States – Certain Measures Affecting Imports of Poultry from China*, WT/DS392.
US – Section 110(5) Copyright Act (2000)	*United States – Section 110(5) of the US Copyright Act*, WT/DS160.
US – Section 110(5) Copyright Act (Article 21.3(c)) (2001)	*United States – Section 110(5) of the US Copyright Act – Arbitration under Article 21.3(c) of the DSU*, WT/DS160/12.
US – Section 110(5) Copyright Act (Article 25) (2001)	*United States – Section 110(5) of the US Copyright Act – Recourse to Arbitration under Article 25 of the DSU*, WT/DS160.
US – Section 129(c) (1) URAA (2002)	*United States – Section 129(c) (1) of the Uruguay Round Agreements Act*, WT/DS221.
US – Section 211 Appropriations Act (2002)	*United States – Section 211 Omnibus Appropriations Act of 1998*, WT/DS176.
US – Section 301 Trade Act (2000)	*United States – Sections 301–310 of the Trade Act of 1974*, WT/DS152.
US – Shrimp (1998)	*United States – Import Prohibition of Certain Shrimp and Shrimp Products*, WT/DS58.
US – Shrimp (Article 21.5 – Malaysia) (2001)	*United States – Import Prohibition of Certain Shrimp and Shrimp Products – Recourse to Article 21.5 of the DSU by Malaysia*, WT/DS58.
US – Shrimp (Ecuador) (2007)	*United States – Anti-Dumping Measure on Shrimp from Ecuador*, WT/DS335.
US – Shrimp (Thailand) / US – Customs Bond Directive (2008)	*United States – Measures Relating to Shrimp from Thailand / United States – Customs Bond Directive for Merchandise Subject to Anti-Dumping/Countervailing Duties*, WT/DS343 / WT/DS345.
US – Shrimp (Thailand) (2008)	*United States – Measures Relating to Shrimp from Thailand*, WT/DS343.
US – Shrimp (Viet Nam) (2011)	*United States – Anti-Dumping Measures on Certain Shrimp from Viet Nam*, WT/DS404.

Short title	Full case title
US – Shrimp II (Viet Nam) (2015)	*United States – Anti-Dumping Measures on Certain Shrimp from Viet Nam*, WT/DS429, and Corr.1
US – Shrimp II (Viet Nam) (Article 21.3(c)) (2015)	*United States – Anti-Dumping Measures on Certain Shrimp from Viet Nam – Arbitration under Article 21.3(c) of the DSU*, WT/DS429/12.
US – Shrimp and Sawblades (2012)	*United States – Anti-Dumping Measures on Certain Shrimp and Diamond Sawblades from China*, WT/DS422 and Add.1.
US – Softwood Lumber III (2002)	*United States – Preliminary Determinations with Respect to Certain Softwood Lumber from Canada*, WT/DS236.
US – Softwood Lumber IV (2004)	*United States – Final Countervailing Duty Determination with Respect to Certain Softwood Lumber from Canada*, WT/DS257.
US – Softwood Lumber IV (Article 21.5 – Canada) (2006)	*United States – Final Countervailing Duty Determination with Respect to Certain Softwood Lumber from Canada – Recourse by Canada to Article 21.5 of the DSU*, WT/DS257.
US – Softwood Lumber V (2004)	*United States – Final Dumping Determination on Softwood Lumber from Canada*, WT/DS264.
US – Softwood Lumber V (Article 21.3(c)) (2004)	*United States – Final Dumping Determination on Softwood Lumber from Canada – Arbitration under Article 21.3(c) of the DSU*, WT/DS264/13.
US – Softwood Lumber V (Article 21.5 – Canada) (2006)	*United States – Final Dumping Determination on Softwood Lumber from Canada – Recourse to Article 21.5 of the DSU by Canada*, WT/DS264.
US – Softwood Lumber VI (2004)	*United States – Investigation of the International Trade Commission in Softwood Lumber from Canada*, WT/DS277.
US – Softwood Lumber VI (Article 21.5 – Canada) (2006)	*United States – Investigation of the International Trade Commission in Softwood Lumber from Canada – Recourse to Article 21.5 of the DSU by Canada*, and Corr.1, WT/DS277.
US – Stainless Steel (Korea) (2001)	*United States – Anti-Dumping Measures on Stainless Steel Plate in Coils and Stainless Steel Sheet and Strip from Korea*, WT/DS179.

Short title	Full case title
US – Stainless Steel (Mexico) (2008)	*United States – Final Anti-Dumping Measures on Stainless Steel from Mexico*, WT/DS344.
US – Stainless Steel (Mexico) (Article 21.3(c)) (2008)	*United States – Final Anti-Dumping Measures on Stainless Steel from Mexico – Arbitration under Article 21.3(c) of the DSU*, WT/DS344.
US – Stainless Steel (Mexico) (Article 21.5 – Mexico) (2013)	*United States – Final Anti-Dumping Measures on Stainless Steel From Mexico – Recourse to Article 21.5 of the DSU by Mexico*, WT/DS344, (unadopted).
US – Steel Plate (2002)	*United States – Anti-Dumping and Countervailing Measures on Steel Plate from India*, WT/DS206 and Corr.1.
US – Steel Safeguards (2003)	*United States – Definitive Safeguard Measures on Imports of Certain Steel Products*, WT/DS248, WT/DS249, WT/DS251, WT/DS252, WT/DS253, WT/DS254, WT/DS258, WT/DS259.
US – Textiles Rules of Origin (2003)	*United States – Rules of Origin for Textiles and Apparel Products*, WT/DS243 and Corr.1.
US – Tuna II (Mexico) (2012)	*United States – Measures Concerning the Importation, Marketing and Sale of Tuna and Tuna Products*, WT/DS381.
US – Tuna II (Mexico) (Article 21.5) (2015)	*United States – Measures Concerning the Importation, Marketing and Sale of Tuna and Tuna Products – Recourse to Article 21.5 of the DSU by Mexico*, WT/DS381 and Add.1.
US – Tyres (China) (2011)	*United States – Measures Affecting Imports of Certain Passenger Vehicle and Light Truck Tyres from China*, WT/DS399.
US – Underwear (1997)	*United States – Restrictions on Imports of Cotton and Man-made Fibre Underwear*, WT/DS24.
US – Upland Cotton (2005)	*United States – Subsidies on Upland Cotton*, WT/DS267.
US – Upland Cotton (Article 21.5 – Brazil) (2008)	*United States – Subsidies on Upland Cotton – Recourse to Article 21.5 of the DSU by Brazil*, WT/DS267.
US – Upland Cotton (Article 22.6 – US I) (2009)	*United States – Subsidies on Upland Cotton – Recourse to Arbitration by the United States under Article 22.6 of the DSU and Article 4.11 of the SCM Agreement*, WT/DS267.

Short title	Full case title
US – Upland Cotton (Article 22.6 – US II) (2009)	*United States – Subsidies on Upland Cotton – Recourse to Arbitration by the United States under Article 22.6 of the DSU and Article 7.10 of the SCM Agreement*, WT/DS267 and Corr.1.
US – Washing Machines (2016)	*United States – Anti-Dumping and Countervailing Measures on Large Residential Washers from Korea*, WT/DS464 and Add.1.
US – Wheat Gluten (2001)	*United States – Definitive Safeguard Measures on Imports of Wheat Gluten from the European Communities*, WT/DS166.
US – Wool Shirts and Blouses (1997)	*United States – Measure Affecting Imports of Woven Wool Shirts and Blouses from India*, WT/DS33 Corr.1.
US – Zeroing (EC) (2006)	*United States – Laws, Regulations and Methodology for Calculating Dumping Margins ('Zeroing')*, WT/DS294 and Corr.1.
US – Zeroing (EC) (Article 21.5 – EC) (2009)	*United States – Laws, Regulations and Methodology for Calculating Dumping Margins ('Zeroing') – Recourse to Article 21.5 of the DSU by the European Communities*, WT/DS294 and Corr.1.
US – Zeroing (Japan) (2007)	*United States – Measures Relating to Zeroing and Sunset Reviews*, WT/DS322.
US – Zeroing (Japan) (Article 21.3(c)) (2007)	*United States – Measures Relating to Zeroing and Sunset Reviews – Arbitration under Article 21.3(c) of the DSU*, WT/DS322/21.
US – Zeroing (Japan) (Article 21.5 – Japan) (2009)	*United States – Measures Relating to Zeroing and Sunset Reviews – Recourse to Article 21.5 of the DSU by Japan*, WT/DS322.
US – Zeroing (Korea) (2011)	*United States – Use of Zeroing in Anti-Dumping Measures Involving Products from Korea*, WT/DS402.

TABLE OF GATT CASES

The year in brackets following the short name of the case refers to the year in which the GATT panel or working party report in that case was adopted. Where unadopted reports are concerned, the year in brackets refers to the year in which these reports were circulated.

Short title	Full case title
Australia – Ammonium Sulphate (1950)	Working Party Report, *The Australian Subsidy on Ammonium Sulphate*, GATT/CP.4/39.
Belgium – Family Allowances (allocations familiales) (1952)	GATT Panel Report, *Belgian Family Allowances*, G/32.
Border Tax Adjustments (1970)	Working Party Report, *Border Tax Adjustments*, L/3464.
Canada – FIRA (1984)	GATT Panel Report, *Canada – Administration of the Foreign Investment Review Act*, L/5504.
Canada – Herring and Salmon (1988)	GATT Panel Report, *Canada – Measures Affecting Exports of Unprocessed Herring and Salmon*, L/6268.
Canada – Provincial Liquor Boards (US) (1992)	GATT Panel Report, *Canada – Import, Distribution and Sale of Certain Alcoholic Drinks by Provincial Marketing Agencies*, DS17/R.
EEC – Animal Feed Proteins (1978)	GATT Panel Report, *EEC – Measures on Animal Feed Proteins*, L/4599.
EEC – Apples (Chile I) (1980)	GATT Panel Report, *EEC Restrictions on Imports of Apples from Chile*, L/5047.
EEC – Bananas II (1994)	GATT Panel Report, *EEC – Import Regime for Bananas*, DS38/R (unadopted).

Short title	Full case title
EEC – Cotton Yarn (1995)	GATT Panel Report, *European Economic Community – Imposition of Anti-Dumping Duties on Imports of Cotton Yarn from Brazil*, ADP/137.
EEC – Dessert Apples (1989)	GATT Panel Report, *European Economic Community – Restrictions on Imports of Dessert Apples – Complaint by Chile*, L/6491.
EEC – Import Restrictions (1983)	GATT Panel Report, *EEC – Quantitative Restrictions Against Imports of Certain Products from Hong Kong*, L/5511.
EEC – Imports of Beef (1981)	GATT Panel Report, *European Economic Community – Imports of Beef from Canada*, L/5099.
EEC – Minimum Import Prices (1978)	GATT Panel Report, *EEC – Programme of Minimum Import Prices, Licences and Surety Deposits for Certain Processed Fruits and Vegetables*, L/4687.
EEC – Oilseeds I (1990)	GATT Panel Report, *European Economic Community – Payments and Subsidies Paid to Processors and Producers of Oilseeds and Related Animal-Feed Proteins*, L/6627.
EEC – Parts and Components (1990)	GATT Panel Report, *European Economic Community – Regulation on Imports of Parts and Components*, L/6657.
Italy – Agricultural Machinery (1958)	GATT Panel Report, *Italian Discrimination Against Imported Agricultural Machinery*, L/833.
Japan – Alcoholic Beverages I (1987)	GATT Panel Report, *Japan – Customs Duties, Taxes and Labelling Practices on Imported Wines and Alcoholic Beverages*, L/6216.
Japan – Leather (US II) (1984)	GATT Panel Report, *Panel on Japanese Measures on Imports of Leather*, L/5623.
Japan – Semi-Conductors (1988)	GATT Panel Report, *Japan – Trade in Semi-Conductors*, L/6309.
Japan – SPF Dimension Lumber (1989)	GATT Panel Report, *Canada/Japan – Tariff on Imports of Spruce, Pine, Fir (SPF) Dimension Lumber*, L/6470.
Korea – Beef (Australia) (1989)	GATT Panel Report, *Republic of Korea – Restrictions on Imports of Beef – Complaint by Australia*, L/6504.

Short title	Full case title
Spain – Unroasted Coffee (1981)	GATT Panel Report, *Spain – Tariff Treatment of Unroasted Coffee*, L/5135.
Thailand – Cigarettes (1990)	GATT Panel Report, *Thailand – Restrictions on Importation of and Internal Taxes on Cigarettes*, DS10/R.
US – Canadian Tuna (1982)	GATT Panel Report, *United States – Prohibition of Imports of Tuna and Tuna Products from Canada*, L/5198.
US – Customs User Fee (1988)	GATT Panel Report, *United States – Customs User Fee*, L/6264.
US – Export Restrictions (Czechoslovakia) (1949)	Contracting Parties Decision, *Article XXI – United States Exports Restrictions.*
US – Fur Felt Hats (1951)	*Report on the Withdrawal by the United States of a Tariff Concession under Article XIX of the General Agreement on Tariffs and Trade*, GATT/CP/106.
US – Malt Beverages (1992)	GATT Panel Report, *United States – Measures Affecting Alcoholic and Malt Beverages*, DS23/R.
US – MFN Footwear (1992)	GATT Panel Report, *United States – Denial of Most-Favoured-Nation Treatment as to Non-Rubber Footwear from Brazil*, DS18/R.
US – Nicaraguan Trade (1986)	GATT Panel Report, *United States – Trade Measures Affecting Nicaragua*, L/6053 (unadopted).
US – Norwegian Salmon AD (1994)	GATT Panel Report, *Imposition of Anti-Dumping Duties on Imports of Fresh and Chilled Atlantic Salmon from Norway*, ADP/87.
US – Section 337 Tariff Act (1989)	GATT Panel Report, *United States Section 337 of the Tariff Act of 1930*, L/6439.
US – Spring Assemblies (1983)	GATT Panel Report, *United States – Imports of Certain Automotive Spring Assemblies*, L/5333.
US – Sugar (1989)	GATT Panel Report, *United States Restrictions on Imports of Sugar*, L/6514.
US – Sugar Quota (1984)	GATT Panel Report, *United States – Imports of Sugar from Nicaragua*, L/5607.

Short title	Full case title
US – Superfund (1987)	GATT Panel Report, *United States – Taxes on Petroleum and Certain Imported Substances*, L/6175.
US – Taxes on Automobiles (1994)	GATT Panel Report, *United States – Taxes on Automobiles*, DS31/R (unadopted).
US – Tobacco (1994)	GATT Panel Report, *United States – Measures Affecting the Importation, Internal Sale and Use of Tobacco*, DS44/R.
US – Tuna (Mexico) (1991)	GATT Panel Report, *United States – Restrictions on* Imports of Tuna, DS21/R.

1

International Trade and the Law of the WTO

CONTENTS

1 INTRODUCTION

On 25 September 2015, after years of intergovernmental negotiations and consultations with civil society and other stakeholders, the 193 Member States of the United Nations unanimously adopted Resolution 70/1, *Transforming our World: the 2030 Agenda for Sustainable Development.*[1] In the preamble to this Resolution, the UN Member States declared:

1 United Nations, Resolution adopted by the General Assembly on 25 September 2015, A/RES/70/1, *Transforming our world: the 2030 Agenda for Sustainable Development.*

> We are resolved to free the human race from the tyranny of poverty and want and to heal and secure our planet. We are determined to take the bold and transformative steps which are urgently needed to shift the world on to a sustainable and resilient path. As we embark on this collective journey, we pledge that no one will be left behind.[2]

Resolution 70/1 sets out a fifteen-year plan to end poverty and hunger, fight inequality and injustice, and protect our planet. This plan, the 2030 Agenda, provides for seventeen Sustainable Development Goals (SDGs), which are indivisible and balance the three dimensions of sustainable development: the economic, social and environmental.[3] The SDGs build on the Millennium Development Goals, adopted by the UN General Assembly in September 2000, and 'seek to address their unfinished business'.[4] While significant progress was made with regard to a number of Millennium Development Goals, with hundreds of millions of people emerging from poverty since 2000, billions of people continue to live in poverty and 'are denied a life of dignity'.[5] Also, there are rising inequalities within and among countries.[6] While many developing countries in Asia have made significant progress in terms of economic development and poverty reduction, most of the least-developed countries have been much less successful.[7] Also, within most countries, both developing and developed, the income gap between the rich and the rest of the population has grown markedly.[8] In its *Global Risks 2014* report, the World Economic Forum identified severe income inequality as the global risk that is most likely to manifest itself over the next ten years.[9] Such income inequality entrenches corruption and injustice, gives rise to xenophobic nationalism and religious fundamentalism, fosters political instability and leads to violence and economic destruction.

Reflecting the magnitude and nature of the challenges to be addressed, the SDGs 'go far beyond' the Millennium Development Goals.[10] As Resolution 70/1 states:

> Alongside continuing development priorities such as poverty eradication, health, education and food security and nutrition, it sets out a wide range of economic, social and environmental objectives. It also promises more peaceful and inclusive societies. It also, crucially, defines means of implementation.[11]

To achieve the SDGs by 2030, action in many different fields is needed. One of the defining features of today's world is economic globalisation and the associated

2 *Ibid.*, Preamble. 3 *Ibid.*, 14. These seventeen SDGs are further specified in 169 associated targets.
4 *Ibid.*, para. 2.
5 *Ibid.*, paras. 14 and 16. Note in 1990, 37.1 per cent of the global population (i.e. 1.95 billion people) lived in extreme poverty; in 2015 that number was down to 9.6 per cent (i.e. 702 million people). See World Bank, *Global Monitoring Report 2015/2016*, Figure 0.1.
6 United Nations, Resolution adopted by the General Assembly on 25 September 2015, A/RES/70/1, *Transforming our world: the 2030 Agenda for Sustainable Development*, para. 14.
7 See World Bank, *Global Monitoring Report 2014/15*, 22, and United Nations, *The Millennium Development Goals Report 2015*, 23.
8 See http://inequality.org/income-inequality. 9 See World Economic Forum, *Global Risks 2014*, 13.
10 United Nations, *Transforming our world: the 2030 Agenda for Sustainable Development*, para. 17.
11 *Ibid.*

high levels of international trade. The question therefore arises whether economic globalisation, in general, and international trade, in particular, can contribute to the achievement of the SDGs or whether, to the contrary, they are more likely to aggravate poverty and hunger in many developing countries and the ever-growing gap between the richest and poorest of the world.

With regard to six SDGs, Resolution 70/1 explicitly refers to the role international trade can and should play in the realisation of these goals,[12] and paragraph 68 of the resolution states:

> International trade is an engine for inclusive economic growth and poverty reduction, and contributes to the promotion of sustainable development. We will continue to promote a universal, rules-based, open, transparent, predictable, inclusive, non-discriminatory and equitable multilateral trading system under the World Trade Organization, as well as meaningful trade liberalization.[13]

This chapter deals in turn with: (1) economic globalisation and international trade; (2) the law of the WTO; (3) the sources of WTO law; and (4) WTO law in context, i.e. its relationship with other international law and national law.

2 ECONOMIC GLOBALISATION AND INTERNATIONAL TRADE

'Economic globalisation' has been a popular buzzword for many years now. Politicians, government officials, businesspeople, trade unionists, environmentalists, church leaders, public health experts, third-world activists, economists and lawyers all speak of 'economic globalisation'. This section deals with economic globalisation and international trade. It discusses: (1) the concept of 'economic globalisation' and the emergence of the global economy; (2) whether economic globalisation, the emergence of the global economy and, in particular, international trade, is a blessing or a curse; (3) what are the arguments for free trade and the arguments for restrictions on trade; and (4) whether international trade can be to the benefit of all.

2.1 Emergence of the Global Economy

Over the past three decades and as a result of the process of economic globalisation, a *global* economy has been emerging, gradually replacing the patchwork of national economies. This subsection discusses in turn: (1) the concept of 'economic globalisation'; (2) the forces driving economic globalisation and creating the global economy; (3) facts and figures on international trade and

12 These are SDG 2, 3, 8, 10, 14 and 17. See *ibid.*, 16, 17, 20, 21, 24 and 27.
13 On the role of trade in reducing poverty, see World Bank, *Global Monitoring Report 2015/16*, 20–1.

foreign direct investment; and (4) the changing nature of international trade in the global economy.

2.1.1 The Concept of 'Economic Globalisation'

The concepts of 'globalisation', and, in particular, 'economic globalisation', have been used by many to describe one of the defining features of the world in which we live. But what do these terms mean? Joseph Stiglitz, former Chief Economist of the World Bank and winner of the Nobel Prize for Economics in 2001, described the concept of globalisation in his 2002 book, *Globalization and Its Discontents*, as:

> the closer integration of the countries and peoples of the world which has been brought about by the enormous reduction of costs of transportation and communication, and the breaking down of artificial barriers to the flow of goods, services, capital, knowledge, and (to a lesser extent) people across borders.[14]

In *The Lexus and the Olive Tree: Understanding Globalisation*, Thomas Friedman, the award-winning journalist of the *New York Times*, defined 'globalisation' as follows:

> [I]t is the inexorable integration of markets, nation-states and technologies to a degree never witnessed before – in a way that is enabling individuals, corporations and nation-states to reach around the world farther, faster, deeper and cheaper than ever before, and in a way that is enabling the world to reach into individuals, corporations and nation-states farther, faster, deeper and cheaper than ever before.[15]

Economic globalisation is a multifaceted phenomenon. In essence, however, economic globalisation is the gradual integration of national economies into one borderless global economy. It encompasses both (free) international trade and (unrestricted) foreign direct investment. Economic globalisation affects people everywhere in many aspects of their daily lives. It affects their jobs, their food, their health, their education and their leisure time. Innumerable examples of how economic globalisation affects each of us could be given, ranging from the clothes we wear, the cars we drive, the movies we watch, the bananas we eat, the coffee we drink, the insurance policies we buy, the university education we get, to the smart phones we so rely on. However, to give but one example, consider the following story which featured in the *Financial Times* in August 2003, but which illustrates today's reality of economic globalisation even better than it did a decade ago:

> Clutching her side in pain, the woman with suspected appendicitis who was rushed to a hospital on the outskirts of Philadelphia last week had little time to ponder how dependent her life had become on the relentless forces of globalisation. Within minutes of her arrival at the Crozer-Chester Medical Center, the recommendation on whether to operate was being made

14 J. Stiglitz, *Globalization and Its Discontents* (Penguin, 2002), 9.

15 T. Friedman, *The Lexus and the Olive Tree: Understanding Globalisation*, 2nd edn (First Anchor Books, 2000), 9.

> by a doctor reading her computer-aided tomography (CAT) scan from a computer screen 5,800 miles away in the Middle East. Jonathan Schlakman, a Harvard-trained radiologist based in Jerusalem, is one of a new breed of skilled professionals proving that geographic distance is no obstacle to outsourcing even the highest paid jobs to overseas locations ... At present, only 35 patients' scans are transmitted each day from US emergency rooms to Dr Schlakman's small team of doctors in Israel. But with senior radiologists costing up to $300,000 a year to hire in the US and many emergency cases arriving at night, the use of medical expertise based in a different time zone and earning less than half US rates is almost certain to rise. 'It's much more expensive to use night staff in the US because they need time off the following day', says Dr Schlakman.[16]

While economic globalisation is often presented as a new phenomenon, it is worth noting that today's global economic integration is not unprecedented. During the fifty years preceding the First World War, there were also large cross-border flows of goods and capital and more economic integration than now.[17]

If one looks at the ratio of trade to GDP, Britain and France are only slightly more open to trade today than they were in 1913, while Japan is less open now than it was then.[18] However, this earlier period of economic globalisation ended abruptly in 1914 and was followed by one of the darkest periods in the history of humankind.

While today's process of economic globalisation is strong and was, at least until recently, gathering ever more strength,[19] the extent of global economic integration already achieved can be, and frequently is, exaggerated. International trade should normally force high-cost domestic producers to lower their prices and bring the prices of products and services between different countries closer together. However, large divergences in prices persist. This may be due to, *inter alia*, differences in transport costs, taxes and the efficiency of distribution networks. But this is also due to the continued existence of significant barriers to trade. Furthermore, while goods, services and capital move across borders with greater ease, restrictions on the free movement of workers, i.e. restrictions on economic migration, remain multiple and rigorous.

2.1.2 Forces Driving Economic Globalisation

It is commonly argued that economic globalisation has been driven by two main forces. The first, *technology*, makes globalisation feasible; the second, the *liberalisation* of trade and foreign direct investment, makes it happen.[20] Due to technological innovations resulting in a dramatic fall in transport, communication and computing costs, the natural barriers of time and space that separate

16 D. Roberts, E. Luce and K. Merchant, 'Service Industries Go Global', *Financial Times*, 20 August 2003.
17 Also, the Roman Empire (27 BC–476 AD) and the Chinese Song dynasty (960–1279) can be seen as (early) examples of economic globalisation.
18 'One World?', *The Economist*, 18 October 1997.
19 On the recent trend in economic globalisation, see below, pp. 6–11.
20 See also M. Wolf, 'Global Opportunities', *Financial Times*, 6 May 1997.

national economies have been coming down. As noted by Thomas Friedman in his 2005 book, *The World Is Flat: A Brief History of the Globalized World in the Twenty-First Century*:

> Clearly, it is now possible for more people than ever to collaborate and compete in real time with more other people on more different kinds of work from more different corners of the planet and on more equal footing than at any previous time in the history of the world – using computers, e-mail, networks, teleconferencing, and dynamic new software.[21]

The second driving force of economic globalisation has been the liberalisation of international trade and foreign direct investment. Since the late 1940s, most developed countries have gradually but significantly lowered barriers to foreign trade and investment. Over the last thirty years, the liberalisation of trade and investment has become a worldwide trend, including in developing countries, although liberalisation proceeds at different rates in different parts of the world. In his book, *Has Globalization Gone Too Far?*, Dani Rodrik, of the John F. Kennedy School of Government at Harvard University, observed with regard to this second driving force of globalisation:

> Globalization is not occurring in a vacuum. It is part of a broader trend that we may call marketization. Receding government, deregulation, and the shrinking of social obligations are the domestic counterparts of the intertwining of national economies. Globalization could not have advanced this far without these complementary forces.[22]

While the then US President Bill Clinton stated at the 1998 WTO Ministerial Conference in Geneva that '[g]lobalization is not a policy choice – it is a fact',[23] Lord Jordan, former General Secretary of the International Confederation of Free Trades Unions, wrote in December 2000 that globalisation 'is not an unstoppable force of nature, but is shaped by those who set the rules'.[24]

2.1.3 Economic Globalisation Today

While some politicians and opinion-makers claim otherwise, the process of economic globalisation is not irreversible. Lionel Barber, editor of the *Financial Times*, noted in 2004:

> For all its merits, globalization must never be taken for granted. The continued integration of the world economy depends on support not only from rich beneficiaries in the west but increasingly from the still disadvantaged in Africa, India, and Latin America. Cultural barriers also pose increasingly powerful obstacles to globalization. The rise of Islamic fundamentalism offers an alternative vision of society, one which will appeal to all those left behind in countries with exploding populations and persistent high unemployment among young people.[25]

21 T. Friedman, *The World Is Flat: A Brief History of the Globalized World in the Twenty-First Century* (Farrar, Straus & Giroux, 2005), 8.
22 D. Rodrik, *Has Globalization Gone Too Far?* (Institute for International Economics, 1997), 85.
23 See www.wto.org/english/thewto_e/minist_e/min99_e/english/book_e/stak_e_3.htm.
24 B. Jordan, 'Yes to Globalization, But Protect the Poor', *International Herald Tribune*, 21 December 2000.
25 L. Barber, 'A Symposium of Views: Is Continued Globalisation of the World Economy Inevitable?', *International Economy*, summer 2004, 70.

In 2016, David Lipton, First Deputy Managing Director of the IMF, observed:

> During the years since the global financial crisis, the future of globalization has darkened. Global growth has slowed, along with international trade. For many, vulnerability and insecurity have become more salient than the gains from interconnectedness, as those linkages have brought market volatility, powerful spillovers, and dislocations. Politics have soured. Whether justified or not, much of the resentment is focused on globalization.[26]

As further discussed below, the growth of international trade has been sluggish in recent years when compared with the growth before the global economic crisis of 2008–9.[27] The ratio of international trade to global GDP has in recent years not increased, but has remained constant or decreased marginally.[28] As the ratio of international trade to global GDP is often considered as a good measurement of economic globalisation,[29] this trend may be an indication that the process of economic globalisation has (at least temporarily) stopped. However, in its 2016 report *Digital Globalization: The New Era of Global Flows*, the McKinsey Global Institute noted in this regard:

> Many observers point to this trend as evidence that globalization has stopped. We have a different view: globalization has instead entered a new era defined by data flows that transmit information, ideas, and innovation. Digital platforms create more efficient and transparent global markets in which far-flung buyers and sellers find each other with a few clicks. The near-zero marginal costs of digital communications and transactions open new possibilities for conducting business across borders on a massive scale ... While global flows of trade and finance have lost momentum, the volume of data being transmitted across borders has surged, creating an intricate web that connects countries, companies, and individuals.[30]

In an address delivered at the World Trade Symposium in June 2016, WTO Director-General Roberto Azevêdo also argued that 'globalisation has not stopped'.[31] Azevêdo noted in this regard that while the growth of international trade is lower than before, the share of trade in components has not declined. This is indicative of the spread of global production chains, which is 'a defining feature of the globalization phenomenon'.[32]

2.1.4 Facts and Figures on International Trade and Foreign Direct Investment

In 1948, world merchandise exports, i.e. exports of goods, amounted to US$58 billion per year. In 2015, world merchandise exports amounted to US$16.5 trillion.[33] World exports of commercial services, marginal in 1948, amounted in

26 David Lipton, 'Can Globalization Still Deliver?', Stavros Niarchos Lecture, 24 May 2016, Peterson Institute for International Economics, at www.imf.org/external/np/speeches/2016/052416a.htm.

27 See below, p. 8. 28 See below, p. 8.

29 The trade-to-GDP ratio indicates the dependence of domestic producers on foreign demand (exports) and of domestic consumers and producers on foreign supply (imports), relative to the country's economic size (GDP). The trade-to-GDP ratio is a basic indicator of openness to foreign trade and economic integration. See http://data.worldbank.org/news/new-data-visualizers-for-trade-data.

30 McKinsey Global Institute, *Digital Globalization: The New Era of Global Flows*, Executive Summary, March 2016, 9–10.

31 R. Azevêdo, 'Trade and Globalisation in the 21st Century: the Path to Greater Inclusion', speech delivered at the World Trade Symposium, London, 7 June 2016, at www.wto.org/english/news_e/spra_e/spra126_e.htm.

32 *Ibid.*

33 See WTO Statistics Database, at http://stat.wto.org. In 1968, 1988 and 2008, world merchandise exports amounted to US$242 billion, US$2.9 trillion and US$15.2 trillion respectively. See *ibid.*

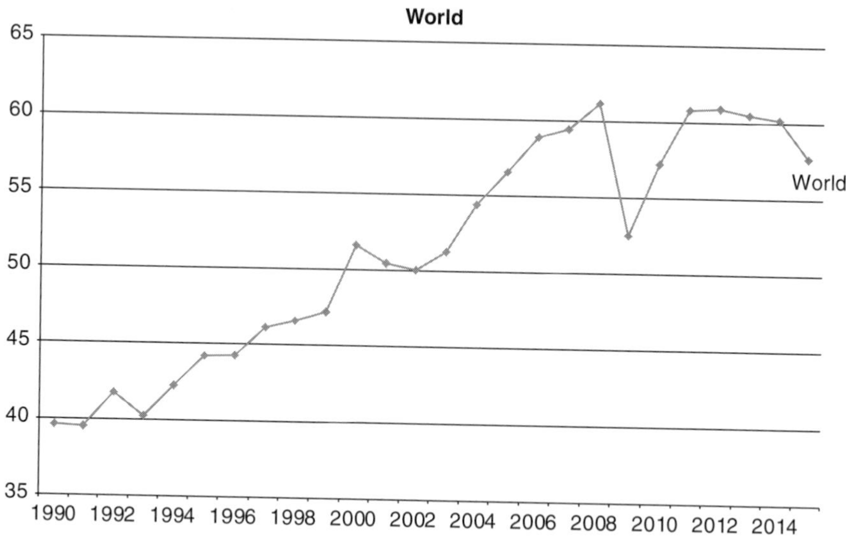

Figure 1.1 Ratio of global trade in merchandise and commercial services to global GDP (1990–2015)

2015 to US$4.75 trillion.[34] Especially during the period from 2002 to 2008 world merchandise exports and exports of commercial services boomed. In 2009, at the height of the global economic crisis, world merchandise exports shrunk by 22.3 per cent in value terms (the sharpest decline since the Second World War), but in 2010 grew again by 21.8 per cent and in 2011 by 19.8 per cent.[35] In recent years, however, world merchandise exports have grown between a mere 0.25 and 2.4 per cent in value terms; and, in 2015, fell by 13.2 per cent.[36] Exports of commercial services shrunk by 10.8 per cent in value terms at the height of the global economic crisis in 2009, but grew again by 8.7 per cent in 2010 and 13.2 per cent in 2011.[37] In 2015, the exports of commercial services declined 6.1 per cent in value terms.[38]

As shown by Figure 1.1, over the past two decades, before the crisis year of 2009, the ratio of global trade to GDP increased significantly, indicating the extent of economic globalisation in these years. As is also shown, in 2010, this trend of economic globalisation picked up again. The ratio of global trade to GDP increased from 39 per cent in 1990 to an all-time high of 61.1 per cent in 2008, plummeting to 52.5 per cent in 2009, increasing to 60.8 per cent in 2011 and remaining almost constant from 2012–14 and then dropping to 57.0 in 2015.[39]

34 See *ibid.* In 1995 and 2005, world exports of commercial services amounted to US$1.2 trillion and US$2.5 trillion respectively. See *ibid.*

35 Calculated on the basis of data found in the WTO Statistical Database, at http://stat.wto.org. In volume terms, world merchandise exports fell in 2009 by 12 per cent. In the last thirty years, the volume of world merchandise exports fell only on one other occasion, namely in 2001 by 0.2 per cent. See *ibid.*

36 See *ibid.* 37 Calculated on the basis of data found in the WTO Statistical Database, at http://stat.wto.org.

38 See *ibid.* 39 See http://data.worldbank.org/indicator/NE.TRD.GNFS.ZS?end=2015&start=1990.

The degree of economic globalisation, when measured as the ratio of trade to GDP, varies from country to country, but has, until 2015, increased in all major trading nations over the past two decades.[40]

Country	1990	2015
Bangladesh	19	42
Brazil	15	27
Canada	50	65
China	30	41
EU (including intra-EU trade)	51	83
India	15	49
Indonesia	49	42
Mexico	38	73
Russian Federation	36	51
South Africa	43	63
South Korea	53	85
United States	20	28

Figure 1.2 Ratio of trade in merchandise and commercial services to GDP for selected countries (1990–2015)[41]

As shown by the data in Figure 1.2, the economies of many countries are to a large and increased degree dependent on trade. This is true for developed as well as developing countries. Note the extent to which, for example China (from 30 to 41 per cent), India (from 15 to 49 per cent), Bangladesh (from 19 to 42 per cent) and Mexico (from 38 to 73 per cent) have 'globalised' over the past two decades. It is interesting, and perhaps surprising to some, that least-developed countries are more 'globalised' than OECD countries. Brazil and the United States have the least 'globalised' economies of all major trading nations. South Korea has the most 'globalised' economy of all major trading nations. Note that the data on the EU include trade between EU Member States, i.e. intra-EU trade. When one considers only EU trade with non-EU countries, the ratio of trade to GDP for the EU was 33.9 per cent.[42]

It is not only the value and volume of world trade and the ratio of trade to GDP that have changed significantly over the years. The share of world trade of various countries and regions of the world also changed significantly.

Overall, the share of world trade of developed countries has in recent years dropped from 80 per cent in 1995 to 54 per cent in 2014, while the share of

40 For a world map of trade-to-GDP ratios, see www.wto.org/english/res_e/statis_e/statis_maps_e.htm.
41 See *ibid*. For India, the data relate to the year 2014. 42 See *ibid*.

developing countries has increased from 20 per cent in 1995 to 44 per cent in 2014.[43] Remarkable is the decline of the share of North America (the United States, Canada and Mexico) from 28.1 per cent in 1948 to 13.5 in 2014, and the modest increase of the share of Western Europe (primarily the European Union) from 35.1 per cent in 1948 to 36.8 per cent in 2014 (down from 45.9 per cent in 2003).[44] Equally remarkable are the steep decline of the shares of South and Central America (down from 11.3 per cent to 3.8 per cent) and Africa (down from 7.3 per cent to 3 per cent) and the significant increase of Asia's share (up from 14 per cent to 32 per cent).[45] The share of the least-developed countries increased in recent years from 0.5 to 1 per cent (although note that it stood at 1.7 per cent in 1970).

Further, the composition of the trade of developing countries has also undergone a change. While many developing countries remain dependent on their exports of primary commodities, the share of manufactured goods has been growing. Since the early 1990s, there has been a boom in high-technology exports, with countries such as China, India and Mexico emerging as major suppliers of cutting-edge technologies, as well as labour-intensive goods. The data referred to above clearly indicate that there is, with regard to trade in merchandise and commercial services, a 'redistribution of the geopolitical deck of cards on a global scale'.[46]

The leading exporters of merchandise in 2015 were: China (17.4 per cent), the European Union (15.2 per cent), the United States (11.5 per cent), Japan (4.8 per cent) and Korea (4.0 per cent).[47] The leading importers of merchandise were: the United States (17.3 per cent), the European Union (14.4 per cent), China (12.6 per cent), Japan (4.9 per cent) and Hong Kong, China (4.2 per cent).[48] The leading exporters of commercial services in 2015 were: the European Union (24.9 per cent), the United States (18.8 per cent), China (7.8 per cent), Japan (4.3 per cent) and India (4.2 per cent).[49] The leading importers of commercial services were: the European Union (20.2 per cent), the United States (12.9 per cent), China (12.9 per cent), Japan (4.8 per cent), Singapore (3.9 per cent) and India (3.4 per cent).[50]

43 See *WTO International Trade Statistics 2015*, 35. 44 *Ibid.*, table 1.5 45 *Ibid.*

46 See Pascal Lamy in his welcome address to the participants in the WTO's Public Forum, 24 September 2012, at: www.wto.org/english/news_e/sppl_e/sppl244_e.htm.

47 See WTO, *World Trade Statistical Review 2016*, table A7. Note that this ranking is on the basis of world merchandise trade excluding intra-EU trade. Also, note that Hong Kong, China was the sixth biggest exporter of merchandise (3.9 per cent) (before Canada (3.1 per cent), Mexico (2.9 per cent), Singapore (2.7 per cent), and the Russian Federation (2.6 per cent)); and that India was the thirteenth (2.0 per cent) and Brazil the eighteenth biggest exporter of merchandise (1.5 per cent).

48 See *ibid.* Note that India was the ninth (2.9 per cent), the Russian Federation the seventeenth (1.5 per cent) and Brazil the eighteenth biggest importer of merchandise (1.3 per cent).

49 See *ibid.*, table A9. Note that this ranking is on the basis of world trade in commercial services excluding intra-EU trade. Note also that Singapore was the sixth biggest exporter of commercial services (3.8 per cent) before Switzerland (2.9 per cent), Hong Kong, China (2.8 per cent), Korea (2.6 per cent) and Canada (2.1 per cent). The Russian Federation was the thirteenth (1.4 per cent), Brazil the twentieth (0.9 per cent) biggest exporter of commercial services.

50 See *ibid.* Note that the Russian Federation was the tenth (2.4 per cent) and Brazil the twelfth biggest importer of commercial services (1.9 per cent).

As noted above, next to international trade, the second important aspect of economic globalisation is foreign direct investment (FDI). This book does not deal with FDI, but it should be noted that inflows of FDI have – similarly to international trade flows – increased notably over the past decades. In 1990, global FDI inflows amounted to US$207 billion. In its *World Investment Report 2016*, the United Nations Conference on Trade and Development (UNCTAD) reported that, in 2015, global FDI inflows amounted to US$1.76 trillion, the highest level since the financial crisis of 2008–9.[51] FDI inflows to developing countries reached the historical high level of US$765 billion.[52] While the trend of the ratio of international trade to global GDP may, as discussed above, be an indication that the process of economic globalisation has (at least temporarily) stopped, the trend of FDI would rather indicate the opposite. In 2015, FDI inflows to developed countries accounted for 55 per cent of global FDI, up from 41 per cent in 2014.[53] FDI outflows from developed economies accounted for 72 per cent of global FDI outflows in 2015, up from 61 per cent in 2014. By contrast, FDI outflows declined in most developing and transition regions, China being an exception. China's outward FDI rose in 2015 from $123 billion to $128 billion, as a result of which it held its position as the third largest investor in the world.[54]

2.1.5 Changing Nature of International Trade in the Global Economy

For many centuries, trade was mostly about raw materials or finished products from country A being exported to country B for use or consumption in the latter country. However, as has been noted by economists and policy-makers alike, the nature of trade is changing. Trade in the globalised economy of today is increasingly trade in tasks and in value-added. Trade is increasingly trade in intermediate products. Ever more trade now takes place in international supply chains, also often referred to as global value chains (GVCs). Technological innovations, resulting in much lower transportation and communication costs, as well as the emergence of a 'rules-based', more secure and predictable trading environment (i.e. the prime focus of this book), have allowed companies to fragment, or unbundle, production across many countries. Today, products are often not produced in a single location or by a single company. Many companies no longer produce products in their entirety but focus on the production of components

51 See UNCTAD, *World Investment Report 2016*, 1. Note that a surge in cross-border mergers and acquisitions to $721 billion, from $432 billion in 2014, was the principal factor behind the global rebound. In 2009, global FDI inflows plummeted to US$1.2 trillion but in 2011 already global FDI inflows had gone up to US$1.5 trillion again, exceeding the pre-crisis average, albeit still some 23 per cent below the 2007 peak. UNCTAD forecasts that over the medium term, FDI flows are projected to resume growth in 2017 and to surpass $1.8 trillion in 2018.

52 See *ibid.*, 2. 53 *Ibid.*, 1. In 2015, the United States became the largest FDI recipient in the world. See *ibid.*, 4.

54 See *ibid.*, 3 and 5.

or related services. They do so in function of their comparative advantage. Ever more products are 'the end result of a highly coordinated series of steps carried out in many countries around the world by many people with many different skills'.[55] Rather than 'Made in China', 'Made in Australia' or 'Made in Mexico', many products are now 'Made in the World'. Karel De Gucht, the then European Commissioner for Trade, noted in April 2012:

> Most of you will be familiar with the example of the Nokia smartphone. It is listed as being made in China, but in reality 54% of its value comes from tasks that are carried out in Europe. Key components are produced in other parts of Asia and only the assembly itself actually happens in China.[56]

While many may think of the Boeing 787 Dreamliner as a product 'Made in the USA', the components that make up this aircraft 'come from more than 40 suppliers based in over 130 sites around the world'.[57]

Trade in value-added, or trade in GVCs, is not a totally new phenomenon. To some extent, it has always existed. However, in recent years it has rapidly increased in importance, breadth and depth. Trade in intermediate products increased from just under US$4 trillion in 2004 to about US$7.5 trillion in 2014.[58] This development has been described as the 'most important development in the world economy since the beginnings of globalization'.[59] In a 2016 report *Decent Work in Global Supply Chains*, the International Labour Organization (ILO) outlined the key factors resulting in the proliferation of GVCs as follows:

> First, the development of telecommunications, financial services and information technologies, which have enabled real-time coordination and logistics of fragmented production in various parts of the globe. Second, improvements in infrastructure, logistics and transport services have enabled more reliable and speedy delivery of inputs and final goods and have reduced their cost. Third, trade agreements have played a role in facilitating and reducing the costs of trade, including through tariff reduction, harmonization of institutional frameworks and liberalization of services under the General Agreement on Tariffs and Trade and subsequently the World Trade Organization (WTO) as well as bilateral and plurilateral trade agreements. Lastly, the emergence of China and India, and their participation in global supply chains, has doubled the supply of labour to the global economy.[60]

55 *Ibid.*

56 Karel De Gucht, 'Trading in Value and Europe's Economic Future', High-Level Conference on 'Competitiveness, Trade, Environment and Jobs in Europe: Insights from the New World Input Output Database (WIOD)', 16 April 2012, at http://europa.eu/rapid/press-release_SPEECH-12-264_en.htm.

57 Azevêdo, 'Trade and Globalisation in the 21st Century'.

58 UNCTAD, *Key Statistics and Trends in International Trade 2015*, 17.

59 World Trade Organization, *World Trade Report 2013*, 269 referring to Richard E. Baldwin, 'Global supply chains: Why they emerged, why they matter, and where they are going', London Centre for Economic Policy Research, CEPR Discussion Paper No. 9103.

60 International Labour Organization, *Decent Work in Global Supply Chains*, Report IV, International Labour Conference, 105th Session, 2016, 5.

For developing countries, the unbundling of production has made it possible to industrialize by joining the GVCs. In the words of WTO Director-General Roberto Azevêdo:

> The logic is that it is easier to develop the skills and infrastructure needed to make one part of an engine than it is to build the whole aircraft.[61]

In a 2015 paper *Participation of Developing Countries in Global Value Chains*, the OECD noted that:

> Many developing countries are increasingly involved in GVCs, and that this participation tends to bring about economic benefits in terms of enhanced productivity, sophistication and diversification of exports.[62]

The country in which companies prefer to outsource production is, apart from geography, largely determined by factors such as the state of the transport and telecommunication infrastructure, the level of technical and professional skills of the workforce, the effective protection of intellectual property, the ease of customs formalities, the prevalence of the rule of law and the absence of endemic corruption. Due to the abundance of cheap, unskilled labour, developing countries typically complete the low value-added, unskilled labour-intensive tasks while developed countries complete the high value-added, skill- and capital-intensive tasks.[63] To move up the global value chain from low value-added tasks to high value-added tasks, countries must pursue policies aimed at upgrading the factors referred to above.[64]

In 2013, the WTO and the OECD jointly launched the Trade in Value-Added (TiVA) database, which takes into account value added by each country in the production of goods and services consumed worldwide.[65] The trade data available through the TiVA database give us three important insights into today's international trade.[66] First, these trade data clearly show the importance of trade in services. While trade in services represents about 20 per cent of total trade, its share doubles when one considers its contribution to the value-added that is traded internationally. Second, the TiVA data highlight the importance of trade in intermediate products and the significance of such trade in improving the competitiveness of the exports. Today, trade in intermediate products accounts for more than half of global merchandise exports; and the average

61 R. Azevêdo 'The importance of the WTO in value-chain development for countries like Colombia' delivered at the Universidad Sergio Arboleda Colombia, 19 May 2016, at www.wto.org/english/news_e/spra_e/spra123_e.htm.
62 OECD, *Participation of Developing Countries in Global Value Chains*, Summary Paper, 2015, 1.
63 World Trade Organization, *World Trade Report 2013*, 144 and 234.
64 See UNCTAD, *Tracing the Value Added in Global Value Chains: Product-Level Case Studies in China*, 2015, 14.
65 The 2015 edition of the TiVA database included sixty-one economies covering OECD, EU28, G20, most East and South-East Asian economies and a selection of South American countries.
66 See Pascal Lamy, Round Table Discussion 'New Steps in Measuring Trade in Value Added' at the OECD, Paris, 16 January 2013, at www.wto.org/english/news_e/sppl_e/sppl261_e.htm.

import content of exported goods is 40 per cent. Therefore, in order for exported goods to be competitive on the world market, manufacturers need access to the cheap imported inputs. Third, the TiVA data, which reflect imports and exports measured according to their true national content, permit, and indeed require, a redefinition of bilateral trade balances. Such a redefinition results, for example, in a significant reduction of the politically sensitive trade deficit that many countries have with China.

The changing nature of international trade cannot but affect – certainly in the longer term – the way in which governments think about trade and trade policy.[67] The acute realisation that cheap imports are the lifeblood of competitive exports is perhaps one of the reasons – next to the strength of the multilateral trading system – why countries did not, as history would expect them to do, react to the 2008–9 global economic crisis with a barrage of restrictions on trade.[68] Participation in global value chains is also closely linked with unilateral tariff reductions.[69] Further, global value chains have resulted in negotiated tariff reductions in the WTO,[70] and also at the regional/bilateral level.[71] In order to facilitate smooth operation of value chains, there has been an increased demand for deep forms of integration covering more than just preferential tariffs.[72] As noted in the *World Trade Report, 2013*:

> Countries intensively involved in supply chain trade may find it increasingly difficult to rely on broad GATT/WTO principles alone to address their trade-related problems, and may turn to more narrowly focused PTAs to achieve the deep and customized bargains they need ... With parts and components crossing multiple borders and the cost of imports increasingly determining export competitiveness – anti-protectionist tendencies have dominated. Regulatory cooperation has intensified, leading to deeper integration at the regional level.[73]

2.2 A Blessing or a Curse?

All around the world people feel the effects of economic globalisation and international trade, but these effects are not felt by all in an even or equitable way. In the 1990s and early 2000s, the large and often violent street demonstrations that rocked Seattle, Prague, Montreal, Cancún, Washington, Hong Kong, Geneva, Genoa, Zurich and other cities around the world gave expression to many people's dissatisfaction with, and rejection of, economic globalisation and international trade. While such demonstrations seem to be – at least for now – a thing

67 See e.g. Global Agenda Council on the Global Trade System, *The Shifting Geography of Global Value Chains: Implications for Developing Countries and Trade Policy* (World Economic Forum, 2012).
68 See also below, pp. 104–5. 69 World Trade Organization, *World Trade Report 2013*, 269 and 271.
70 See e.g. Ministerial Conference, *Ministerial Declaration of 16 December 2015 on the Expansion of Trade in Information Technology Products*, WT/MIN(15)/25, dated 16 December 2015, wherein certain WTO Members agreed on the elimination of customs duties on 201 information technology products valued at over US$1.3 trillion per year. See below p. 430.
71 World Trade Organization, *World Trade Report 2013*, 272. 72 *Ibid.* 73 *Ibid.*, 270 and 292.

of the past, the debate on the benefits and dangers of economic globalisation and international trade is, in these times of global crises (economic, financial, environmental and food), more relevant than ever. In recent years, there has been in many countries a notable rise in anti-globalisation and anti-trade rhetoric by populist, as well as some mainstream, politicians. In the 2016 US presidential elections, the candidates of the Democratic as well as the Republican Party took anti-trade positions in an obvious attempt to appeal to the working-class voters. The Republican presidential candidate, Donald Trump, proposed *inter alia* to terminate the North American Free Trade Agreement (NAFTA) with Canada and Mexico and to impose a 45 per cent customs duty on imports from China in the United States. As noted by Kenneth Rogoff, Professor of Economics and Public Policy at Harvard University, the latter proposal 'appeals to many Americans who believe that China is getting rich from unfair trade practices'.[74] In what was labelled as a major economic policy speech in Detroit on 8 August 2016, Donald Trump argued that the United States must fight globalisation and trade deals which he believes have led to the demise of manufacturing and blue-collar jobs. In terms which make one wonder whether autarchy is at the core of his proposed economic policy, he stated:

> American cars will travel the roads, American planes will connect our cities, and American ships will patrol the seas. American steel will send new skyscrapers soaring. We will put new American metal into the spine of this nation. It will be American hands that rebuild this country, and it will be American energy – mined from American sources – that powers this country. It will be American workers who are hired to do the job. Americanism, not globalism, will be our new credo.[75]

In the same speech, and seemingly unconcerned by what might be seen as a contradictory statement, Trump stated:

> Trade has big benefits, and I am in favor of trade. But I want great trade deals for our country that create more jobs and higher wages for American workers. Isolation is not an option, only great and well-crafted trade deals are.[76]

While electoral campaign speeches must not be given more importance than they deserve, such statements by the presidential candidate of one of the two main political parties of the United States is a clear sign of the times.

74 K. Rogoff, 'Anti-Trade America?', *Project Syndicate*, 7 April 2016, at www.project-syndicate.org/commentary/us-presidential-campaign-protectionist-rhetoric-by-kenneth-rogoff-2016-04?barrier=true. Rogoff observed that 'for all its extraordinary success in recent decades, China remains a developing country where a significant share of the population live at a level of poverty that would be unimaginable by Western standards'. See *ibid.* Also, according to the McKinsey Global Institute, only around 700,000 of the 6 million manufacturing jobs lost in the United States between 2000 and 2010 went to China. Most manufacturing jobs were lost because of technological innovation (and in particular the introduction of high-tech robots) and the decrease in consumer demand during the 2008–9 global economic crisis. See R. Foroohar, 'Is China Stealing U.S. Jobs?', *Time*, 11 April 2016, 40. However, a study by David Autor and others from the Massachusetts Institute of Technology (MIT) estimated that rising Chinese imports from 1999 to 2011 costs up to 2.4 million American jobs. See E. Porter, 'On Trade, Voters May Have a Point', *International New York Times*, 16 March 2016, 14.

75 See http://time.com/4443382/donald-trump-economic-speech-detroit-transcript. 76 *Ibid.*

According to a 2015 survey of public opinion on economic globalisation in the European Union, 57 per cent of Europeans agreed that globalisation is an opportunity for economic growth, while 28 per cent disagreed with this statement.[77] Not surprisingly, the better educated, high-skilled respondents agreed more often with the statement than did the lower educated, low-skilled respondents. Equally unsurprising, northern Europeans (and in particular the Danes, Swedes and Dutch) significantly more often agreed with the statement than southern Europeans (and in particular the French and Greeks).[78] While in the European Union and most other countries, the majority of people are not *opposed* to economic globalisation and international trade, there is widespread concern and considerable anxiety about the harmful effect that economic globalisation and international trade may have: (1) on jobs and wages (affected by delocalisation and outsourcing, or the threat thereof); (2) on the global ecosystem as well as the local environment (by promoting unsustainable patterns of production and consumption); (3) on world poverty and hunger (in the face of growing income disparity between the rich and the poor); (4) on the economic development of developing countries (by obliging these countries to open their markets too far too fast, and not protecting or promoting their export opportunities); (5) on social, labour, health and safety regulation (as a result of regulatory competition resulting in a 'race to the bottom'); (6) on the livelihood of hundreds of millions of small farmers (endangered by the importation of cheap agricultural produce); (7) on cultural identity and diversity (threatened by the rise of a global Anglo-Saxon popular monoculture); and (8) on national sovereignty and the democratic process (under threat from international organisations promulgating rules for the global economy beyond the control of individual States).

Radical proponents of economic globalisation and international trade tend to present globalisation and trade as a panacea for many of the world's problems. These cheerleaders of globalisation usually show little sympathy for, or understanding of, the concerns referred to above.[79] On the contrary, opponents often see economic globalisation and international trade as malignant forces that destroy the livelihood of millions of workers and exacerbate income inequality, social injustice, environmental degradation and cultural homogenisation. They campaign for the replacement of the current 'unfair and oppressive trade system' with a 'new, socially just and sustainable trading framework'. It is unfortunate that the debate on economic globalisation and international trade

77 European Commission, Standard Eurobarometer 83, *Public Opinion in the European Union*, Report, spring 2015, 149, at http://ec.europa.eu/public_opinion/archives/eb/eb83/eb83_publ_en.pdf. Of the 56 per cent agreeing with this statement, 12 per cent totally agreed and 44 per cent tended to agree. Of the 27 per cent disagreeing, 7 per cent totally disagreed and 20 per cent tended to disagree. Note that 17 per cent expressed no opinion.

78 See *ibid.*, 149 and 150.

79 The term 'globalisation's cheerleaders' was used by Dani Rodrik in a 2007 contribution to the *Financial Times*, in which he argued that not the 'protesters on the streets', but these 'cheerleaders' in government or at elite universities in North America and Europe presented the greater menace to globalisation. See D. Rodrik, 'The Cheerleaders' Threat to Global Trade', *Financial Times*, 26 March 2007.

is often emotionally charged and thus not constructive. Oxfam noted in its 2002 study, *Rigged Rules and Double Standards: Trade, Globalization, and the Fight Against Poverty*, the following:

Current debates about trade are dominated by ritualistic exchanges between two camps: the 'globaphiles' and the 'globaphobes'. 'Globaphiles' argue that trade is already making globalisation work for the poor. Their prescription for the future is 'more of the same'. 'Globaphobes' turn this world-view on its head. They argue that trade is inherently bad for the poor. Participation in trade, so the argument runs, inevitably leads to more poverty and inequality. The corollary of this view is 'the less trade the better'. The anti-globalisation movement deserves credit. It has raised profoundly important questions about social justice – and it has forced the failures of globalisation on to the political agenda. However, the war of words between trade optimists and trade pessimists that accompanies virtually every international meeting is counter-productive. Both world views fly in the face of the evidence – and neither offers any hope for the future.[80]

Oxfam's characterisation of the debate on economic globalisation and international trade in 2002 – unfortunately – still rings true today. While not sharing the extreme positions of anti-globalists and being careful 'not to make the mistake of attributing to globalisation the blemishes of other faces',[81] many observers and scholars recognise both the benefits *and* the dangers of economic globalisation and international trade. In his 2002 book, *Globalization and Its Discontents*, Joseph Stiglitz wrote:

Opening up to international trade has helped many countries grow far more quickly than they would otherwise have done. International trade helps economic development when a country's exports drive its economic growth. Export-led growth was the centrepiece of the industrial policy that enriched much of Asia and left millions of people there far better off. Because of globalization many people in the world now live longer than before and their standard of living is far better. People in the West may regard low-paying jobs at Nike as exploitation, but for many people in the developing world, working in a factory is a far better option than staying down on the farm and growing rice. Globalization has reduced the sense of isolation felt in much of the developing world and has given many people in the developing countries access to knowledge well beyond the reach of even the wealthiest in any country a century ago ... Even when there are negative sides to globalization, there are often benefits. Opening up the Jamaican milk market to US imports in 1992 may have hurt local dairy farmers but it also meant poor children could get milk more cheaply. New foreign firms may hurt protected state-owned enterprises but they can also lead to the introduction of new technologies, access to new markets, and the creation of new industries.[82]

Stiglitz commented that those who vilify globalisation too often overlook its benefits.[83] However, Stiglitz also pointed out:

[T]he proponents of globalization have been, if anything, even more unbalanced. To them, globalization (which typically is associated with accepting triumphant capitalism, American style) *is* progress; developing countries must accept it, if they are to grow and to fight

80 Oxfam, *Rigged Rules and Double Standards: Trade, Globalization, and the Fight Against Poverty* (2002), Summary of Chapter 1, at www.maketradefair.org.

81 J. Bhagwati, 'Globalization in Your Face', *Foreign Affairs*, July/August 2000, 137.

82 Stiglitz, *Globalization and Its Discontents*, 4–5. 83 *Ibid.*, 5.

poverty effectively. But to many in the developing world, globalization has not brought the promised economic benefits.[84]

Elsewhere, Stiglitz wrote about the problems and dangers of economic globalisation and international trade:

We should be frank. Trade liberalization, conducted in the wrong way, too fast, in the absence of adequate safety nets, with insufficient reciprocity and assistance on the part of developed countries, can contribute to an increase in poverty ... Complete openness can expose a country to greater risk from external shocks. Poor countries may find it particularly hard to buffer these shocks and to bear the costs they incur, and they typically have weak safety nets, or none at all, to protect the poor. These shocks, resulting essentially from contagion associated with globalization, integration and interdependence can affect workers and employers in the developed world. It must be said, however, that highly industrialized countries are able to deal with these shocks a lot better through re-employment and through other safety nets.[85]

In 2006, Stiglitz further reflected on the dark side of globalisation as follows:

There were once hopes that globalisation would benefit all, both in advanced industrial countries and the developing world. Today, the downside of globalisation is increasingly apparent. Not only do good things go more easily across borders, so do bad; including terrorism ... What is remarkable about globalisation is the disparity between the promise and the reality. Globalisation seems to have unified so much of the world against it, perhaps because there appear to be so many losers and so few winners ... Growing inequality in the advanced industrial countries was a long predicted but seldom advertised consequence: full economic integration implies the equalisation of unskilled wages throughout the world. Although this has not (yet) happened, the downward pressure on those at the bottom is evident. Unfettered globalisation actually has the potential to make many people in advanced industrial countries worse off, even if economic growth increases.[86]

On the positive *and* negative aspects of economic globalisation, Pascal Lamy, the then WTO Director-General, made the following remarks in August 2007:

Globalization has enabled individuals, corporations and nation-states to influence actions and events around the world – faster, deeper and cheaper than ever before – and equally to derive benefits for them. Trade opening and the vanishing of many walls have the potential for expanding freedom, empowerment, democracy, innovation, social and cultural exchanges, while offering outstanding opportunities for dialogue and understanding. This is the good side of globalization. But the global nature of an increasing number of worrisome phenomena – the scarcity of energy resources, the deterioration of the environment, the migratory movements provoked by insecurity, poverty and political instability or even financial markets volatility, as we have seen in recent weeks – are also by-products of globalization. Indeed, it can be argued that in some instances, globalization has reinforced the strong economies and weakened those that were already weak.[87]

84 *Ibid.*

85 J. Stiglitz, 'Addressing Developing Country Priorities and Needs in the Millennium Round', in R. Porter and P. Sauvé (eds.), *Seattle, the WTO and the Future of the Multilateral Trading System* (Harvard University Press, 2000), 53–5.

86 J. Stiglitz, 'We Have Become Rich Countries of Poor People', *Financial Times*, 7 September 2006.

87 P. Lamy, 'Trends and Issues Facing Global Trade', speech delivered in Kuala Lumpur, Malaysia, 17 August 2007, at www.wto.org/english/news_e/sppl_e/sppl65_e.htm. On the positive and negative effects of economic globalisation and international trade on growth, employment and (in)equality in developing countries as well as developed countries, see also the 2011 study by the International Labour Office (ILO) and the WTO, *Making Globalization Socially Sustainable*, edited by Marc Bacchetta and Marion Jansen (ILO/WTO, 2011).

As UN Secretary-General Ban Ki-moon said at the 2014 WTO Public Forum *Why Trade Matters to Everyone*:

> The question is not whether trade matters, but how we can make trade a better driver of equitable, sustainable development. How can we make trade the foundation of a life of dignity for all? ... International trade is an essential component of an integrated effort to end poverty, ensure food security and promote economic growth. An ounce of trade can be worth a pound of aid ... Trade can – and should – benefit everyone. That is why the international community needs to avoid protectionism ... If managed well, international trade can be a key driver of sustainable development.[88]

WTO Director-General Roberto Azevêdo, at his keynote address delivered at the 2016 World Trade Symposium in London stated:

> We have to acknowledge that, in many constituencies, trade is not perceived so positively. First, we must rectify the perception that imports make jobs disappear. Actually, the vast majority of jobs are lost because of new technologies and increased productivity. Second, we must recognize that while the benefits of trade are spread across the economy, the effects of increased competition can hit specific communities hard. We need to put more focus on how governments can mitigate those impacts. Third, trade is sometimes seen as only favouring the big companies. This is obviously not true – however, it is true that trading internationally is much more costly and difficult for small enterprises. We need to respond to that, particularly as SMEs are huge job creators – around 90% of the workforce in many countries.[89] All these points indicate that we need to promote a well-informed debate, not one based on rhetoric and unsubstantiated assertion ... If we allow this uncritical approach to prosper, trade will indeed become the culprit of all economic afflictions.

2.3 Free Trade versus Restricted Trade

For as long as people have traded across borders, the benefits and drawbacks of trade have been debated. This subsection discusses in turn: (1) the arguments for free trade; and (2) the arguments for restrictions on trade.

2.3.1 Arguments for Free Trade

Most economists agree that countries can benefit from international trade. In 1776, Adam Smith wrote in his classic book, *The Wealth of Nations*:

> It is the maxim of every prudent master of a family, never to attempt to make at home what it will cost him more to make than to buy. The tailor does not attempt to make his own shoes, but he buys them from the shoemaker. The shoemaker does not attempt to make his own clothes, but employs a tailor. The farmer attempts to make neither the one nor the other, but employs those different artificers. All of them find it for their interest to employ their whole industry in a way in which they have some advantage over their neighbours, and to purchase with a part of its produce, or what is the same thing, with the price of a part of it, whatever else they have occasion for.

88 Secretary-General's remarks at the WTO Public Forum, 1 October 2014, at www.un.org/sg/statements/index.asp?nid=8076.

89 Azevêdo, 'Trade and Globalisation in the 21st Century'.

What is prudence in the conduct of every private family, can scarce be folly in that of a great kingdom. If a foreign country can supply us with a commodity cheaper than we ourselves can make it, better buy it of them with some part of the produce of our own industry, employed in a way in which we have some advantage. The general industry of the country ... will not thereby be diminished, no more than the above-mentioned artificers; but only left to find out the way in which it can be employed with the greatest advantage. It is certainly not employed to the greatest advantage, when it is thus directed towards an object which it can buy cheaper than it can make.[90]

Adam Smith's lucid and compelling argument for specialisation and international trade was further built upon by David Ricardo, who, in his 1817 book, *The Principles of Political Economy and Taxation*, developed the theory of 'comparative advantage'. This theory is still the predominant explanation for why countries, even the poorest, can and do benefit from international trade.

What did the classical economist David Ricardo (1772–1823) mean when he coined the term *comparative advantage*? Suppose country A is better than country B at making automobiles, and country B is better than country A at making bread. It is obvious (the academics would say 'trivial') that both would benefit if A specialized in automobiles, B specialized in bread and they traded their products. That is a case of *absolute* advantage. But what if a country is bad at making everything? Will trade drive all producers out of business? The answer, according to Ricardo, is no. The reason is the principle of comparative advantage, arguably the single most powerful insight in economics. According to the principle of comparative advantage, countries A and B still stand to benefit from trading with each other even if A is better than B at making everything, both automobiles and bread. If A is much more superior at making automobiles and only slightly superior at making bread, then A should still invest resources in what it does best – producing automobiles – and export the product to B. B should still invest in what it does best – making bread – and export that product to A, even if it is not as efficient as A. Both would still benefit from the trade. A country does not have to be best at anything to gain from trade. That is *comparative* advantage. The theory is one of the most widely accepted among economists. It is also one of the most misunderstood among non-economists because it is confused with *absolute* advantage. It is often claimed, for example, that some countries have no comparative advantage in anything. That is virtually impossible. Think about it ...[91]

The Ricardo model is of course a vast simplification, in that it is built on two products and two countries only and assumes constant costs and constant prices. Many of the complexities of the modern economy are not taken into account in this model. Economists in the twentieth century have endeavoured to refine and build on the classic Ricardo model. While pushing the analysis further, the refined models, such as the Heckscher–Ohlin model,[92] have confirmed the basic

90 A. Smith, *An Inquiry into the Nature and Causes of the Wealth of Nations* (1776), edited by E. Cannan (University of Chicago Press, 1976), Volume 1, 478–9.

91 WTO Secretariat, *Trading into the Future*, 2nd revised edn (WTO, 2001), 9.

92 The Heckscher–Ohlin model is a general equilibrium mathematical model of international trade. It builds on David Ricardo's theory of comparative advantage by predicting patterns of commerce and production based on the factor endowments of a trading region. The model essentially says that countries will export products that use their abundant and cheap factor(s) of production and import products that use the countries' scarce factor(s). See M. Blaug, *The Methodology of Economics, or, How Economists Explain* (Cambridge University Press, 1992), 286.

conclusions drawn from the Ricardo model concerning the theory of comparative advantage and the gains from trade via specialisation.[93]

While the theory of comparative advantage has won approval from most economists since the early nineteenth century and continues to win approval,[94] Jagdish Bhagwati, professor of economics and law at Columbia University, observed in *Free Trade Today* that it has only infrequently carried credibility with the populace at large. In search of an explanation, he noted that, when asked which proposition in the social science was the most counterintuitive yet compelling, Paul Samuelson, the 1970 winner of the Nobel Prize for Economics, chose the theory of comparative advantage.[95] According to Samuelson, there is essentially only one – but one very powerful – argument for free trade:

> Free trade promotes a mutually profitable division of labor, greatly enhances the potential real national product for all nations, and makes possible higher standards of living all over the globe.[96]

In a 2015 report on *The Economic Benefits of U.S. Trade*, the Executive Office of the President of United States noted that expansion in trade has allowed efficient use of production units such as labour and capital, raising overall productivity, promoting economic growth and development.[97] The report, summing up the classic gains from trade as 'enhanced productivity, increased innovative activity, and lower prices on and greater variety of goods and services for consumers and producers', states in particular that:

> Evidence for the United States suggests that, in manufacturing, average wages in exporting firms and industries are up to 18 percent higher than average wages in non-exporting firms and industries.
>
> In addition, international trade helps U.S. households' budgets go further ... Trade also offers a much greater diversity of consumption opportunities, from year-round fresh fruit to affordable clothing. This increase in variety provides U.S. consumers with value equivalent to 2.6 percent of gross domestic product (GDP). According to other estimates, the reduction in U.S. tariffs since World War II contributed an additional 7.3 percent to U.S. GDP, or approximately $1.3 trillion in 2014. Distributed equally, that translates into an additional over $10,000 in income per American household.[98]

93 Note, however, as Jagdish Bhagwati does, that: 'The case of free trade rests on the extension to an open economy of the case for market-determined allocation of resources. If market prices reflect "true" or social costs, then clearly Adam Smith's invisible hand can be trusted to guide us to efficiency; and free trade can correspondingly be shown to be the optimal way to choose trade (and associated domestic production). But if markets do not work well, or are absent or incomplete, then the invisible hand may point in the wrong direction: free trade cannot then be asserted to be the best policy.' See J. Bhagwati, *Free Trade Today* (Princeton University Press, 2002), 12.

94 For a dissenting, neo-Marxist view from legal scholars, see M. H. Davis and D. Neacsu, 'Legitimacy, Globally: The Incoherence of Free Trade Practice, Global Economics and Their Governing Principles of Political Economy', *Kansas City Law Review*, 2001, 733–90.

95 See Bhagwati, *Free Trade Today*, 5.

96 P. Samuelson, *Economics*, 10th edn (McGraw-Hill, 1976), 692.

97 Report by the Executive Office of the President of United States, *The Economic Benefits of U.S. Trade*, May 2015, 5 at www.whitehouse.gov/sites/default/files/docs/cea_trade_report_final_non-embargoed_v2.pdf.

98 *Ibid.*, 5.

Michael Froman, the then US Trade Representative, wrote in 2015:

> According to one recent study, American consumers in the lowest decile of income distribution owe more than half of their purchasing power to international trade. By contrast, Americans in the top decile gain only 3 percent in purchasing power through the benefits of trade.
>
> Remaining barriers also disproportionately harm America's poorest. For example, tariffs on luxury leather shoes are 8.5 percent, while tariffs on basic sneakers can reach 48 percent. Likewise, tariffs on acrylic sweaters are twice as high as those on wool sweaters and eight times the tariff on cashmere sweaters. Eliminating tariffs like these helps all consumers, but helps low-income consumers the most.[99]

Also, in the context of the European Union, a study published in 2014 by the European Commission noted with regard to benefits from free trade:

> Trade liberalisation creates additional opportunities for innovation and stronger productivity growth. Trade and investment flows spread new ideas and innovation, new technologies and the best research, leading to improvements in the products and services that people and companies use. Experience in EU countries shows that a 1% increase in the openness of the economy results in a 0.6% rise in labour productivity the following year.
>
> Benefits from trade include lower prices and greater choice for consumers, as imported food, consumer goods and components for products manufactured in Europe become cheaper.[100]

On the question of whether free trade indeed leads to greater economic growth, Jagdish Bhagwati observed that:

> those who assert that free trade will also lead necessarily to greater growth *either* are ignorant of the finer nuances of theory and the vast literature to the contrary on the subject at hand *or* are nonetheless basing their argument on a different premise: that is, that the preponderant evidence on the issue (in the postwar period) suggests that freer trade tends to lead to greater growth after all.[101]

A 2001 study by the World Bank showed that the developing countries that increased their integration into the world economy in the 1980s and 1990s achieved higher growth in incomes, longer life expectancy and better schooling. Many of these countries, including China and India, have adopted domestic policies and institutions that have enabled people to take advantage of global markets and have thus sharply increased the share of trade in their GDP.[102] These countries have been catching up with the rich ones – their annual growth rates increased from 1 per cent in the 1960s to 5 per cent in the 1990s. In 2015, China and India achieved an economic growth of 6.9 and 7.6 per cent respectively.[103] However, not all developing countries have integrated successfully into the global economy, and not all sections of the population in both developed

99 Michael Froman, 'Getting Trade Right', *Democracy*, issue 38, Fall 2015.
100 European Commission, *The European Union Explained: Trade*, 2014, 5.
101 Bhagwati, *Free Trade Today*, 42. 102 See above, pp. 9–10.
103 See http://data.worldbank.org/indicator/NY.GDP.MKTP.KD.ZG. Even in 2009, at the height of the global economic crisis, China and India still had an economic growth of 7.2 and 9.2 per cent respectively, while the OECD countries had a negative growth of 3.5 per cent. See *ibid*.

and developing countries have benefited from international trade. As a 2000 WTO study, *Trade, Income Disparity and Poverty*, on the relationship between international trade and poverty concluded, the evidence seems to indicate that trade liberalisation is *generally* a positive contributor to poverty alleviation. It allows people to exploit their productive potential, assists economic growth, curtails arbitrary policy interventions and helps to insulate against shocks in the domestic economy. The study warned, however, that most trade reforms will create some losers (some even in the long run). Poverty may be exacerbated temporarily, but the appropriate policy response in those cases is to alleviate the hardship and facilitate adjustments rather than abandon the reform process.[104] A 2003 WTO study, *Adjusting to Trade Liberalization*, concluded that adjustment costs are typically smaller, and sometimes much smaller, than the gains from trade.[105] Also, governments can identify individuals and groups that are likely to suffer from the adjustment process, and they can develop policies to alleviate the burden on those adversely affected.[106]

In its 2002 study, *Rigged Rules and Double Standards: Trade, Globalization, and the Fight Against Poverty*, Oxfam stated:

> History makes a mockery of the claim that trade cannot work for the poor. Participation in world trade has figured prominently in many of the most successful cases of poverty reduction – and, compared with aid, it has far more potential to benefit the poor.[107]

Recognising and elaborating on the significant role played by trade in reducing poverty, the joint WTO–World Bank study published in 2015 notes:

> Opening up to trade increases a country's GDP because it allows each country to use its resources more efficiently by specializing in the production of the goods and services that it can produce more cheaply, while importing the others. Trade also affects long-term growth since it gives access to more advanced technological inputs available in the global market and because it enhances the incentives to innovate. Trade contributes directly to poverty reduction by opening up new employment opportunities, for example for agricultural producers, with the expansion of export sectors, and by bringing about structural changes in the economy that increase employment of low-skilled, poor workers in the informal sector. Trade also provides better access to external markets for the goods that the poor produce.[108]

Few will question that international trade has the *potential* to make a significant contribution to economic growth and poverty reduction. However, it is definitely not a 'magic bullet for achieving development'.[109] As discussed below, more is needed to achieve sustained economic growth and widespread poverty reduction.[110]

104 See D. Ben-David, H. Nordström and A. Winters, *Trade, Income Disparity and Poverty*, Special Studies Series (WTO, 2000), 6.

105 See M. Bacchetta and M. Jansen, *Adjusting to Trade Liberalization: The Role of Policy, Institutions and WTO Disciplines*, Special Studies Series (WTO, 2003), 6.

106 *Ibid.* 107 Oxfam, *Rigged Rules and Double Standards*, Summary of Chapter 2.

108 World Trade Organization and the World Bank Group, *The Role of Trade in Ending Poverty*, 2015, 7.

109 See Justice C. Nwobike, 'The Emerging Trade Regime under the Cotonou Partnership Agreement: Its Human Rights Implications', *Journal of World Trade*, 2006, 292.

110 See below, pp. 29–33.

International trade not only has the potential to bring economic benefits, but may also bring considerable non-economic gains. International trade intensifies cross-border contacts and exchange of ideas, which may contribute to better mutual understanding. In a free-trading world, other countries and their people are more readily seen as business partners, less as enemies. As Baron de Montesquieu wrote in 1748 in *De l'Esprit des Lois*:

> Peace is the natural effect of trade. Two nations who traffic with each other become reciprocally dependent; for if one has an interest in buying, the other has an interest in selling; and thus their union is founded on their mutual necessities.[111]

A country restricting trade directly inflicts economic hardship upon exporting countries. Therefore, trade protectionism is a festering source of conflict. It is often stated that, 'if goods do not cross frontiers, soldiers will'.[112] International trade can make an important contribution to peaceful and constructive international relations. Just two weeks after the terrorist attacks of 11 September 2001 on the World Trade Center in New York and on the Pentagon in Washington, DC, Robert Zoellick, the then US Trade Representative, made the following simple but profound statement about the importance of continued openness in trade:

> Let me be clear where I stand: Erecting new barriers and closing old borders will not help the impoverished. It will not feed hundreds of millions struggling for subsistence. It will not liberate the persecuted. It will not improve the environment in developing countries or reverse the spread of AIDS. It will not help the railway orphans I visited in India. It will not improve the livelihoods of the union members I met in Latin America. It will not aid the committed Indonesians I visited who are trying to build a functioning, tolerant democracy in the largest Muslim nation in the world.[113]

Two months after the attacks of 11 September 2001, the WTO Members agreed to start the Doha Round, a new round of negotiations on the further liberalisation of international trade.[114] According to former WTO Director-General Pascal Lamy, the rationale behind this decision was simple: '[T]errorism is about increasing instability; global trade rules are about promoting stability.'[115]

Apart from peaceful relations between nations, open international trade may also promote democracy. In *Free Trade Today*, Jagdish Bhagwati observed:

> One could argue this proposition by a syllogism: openness to the benefits of trade brings prosperity that, in turn, creates or expands the middle class that then seeks the end of

111 C. de Montesquieu, *De l'Esprit des Lois*, original version available online at http://classiques.uqac.ca/classiques/montesquieu/de_esprit_des_lois/de_esprit_des_lois_tdm.html. An English translation by Thomas Nugent is available at www.constitution.org/cm/sol.htm.

112 P. Lamy, 'Managing Global Security: The Strategic Importance of Global Trade', speech to the International Institute for Strategic Studies, in Geneva on 8 September 2007, at www.wto.org/english/news_e/sppl_e/sppl66_e.htm.

113 As reported by the then WTO Director-General Mike Moore in a speech to the Foreign Affairs Commission of the French Assemblée Nationale in October 2001, available at www.wto.org.

114 On the Doha Round, see below, pp. 93–100.

115 P. Lamy, 'Managing Global Security: The Strategic Importance of Global Trade', Speech to the International Institute for Strategic Studies, in Geneva on 8 September 2007, at www.wto.org/english/news_e/sppl_e/sppl66_e.htm.

authoritarianism. This would fit well with the experience in South Korea, for instance. It was also the argument that changed a lot of minds when the issue of China's entry into the WTO came up in the US Congress recently.[116]

2.3.2 Arguments for Restrictions on Trade

While most economists advise that governments should – in the interest of their country as a whole and that of the world at large – pursue policies aimed at promoting international trade and exchange goods and services on the basis of their comparative advantage, political decision-makers do not necessarily heed this advice. In fact, governments frequently intervene in international trade by adopting trade-restrictive measures. Why do governments restrict international trade? In light of the economic and other benefits of free trade, discussed above, what are the arguments for restrictions on trade?

Governments have multiple, often overlapping, reasons for restricting trade. Governments take trade-restrictive measures for example: (1) to protect a domestic industry and jobs threatened by import competition; (2) to assist the establishment of a new industry; (3) to support a domestic industry to establish itself on the world market; (4) to generate government revenue in the form of customs duties; (5) to protect national security and ensure self-sufficiency; and (6) to protect and promote non-economic societal values and interests, such as public morals, public health, a sustainable environment, human rights, minimum labour standards, consumer safety, and cultural identity and diversity.

An often-cited reason for governments to restrict trade is the *protection of a domestic industry*, and employment in that industry, from competition arising from imported products, foreign services or service suppliers. As noted in the 2003 WTO study *Adjusting to Trade Liberalization*:

> In the United States, for instance, 45,000 steelworkers have lost their jobs since 1997 and 30 per cent of the country's steel making capacity has filed for bankruptcy since 1998, while steel imports were on the rise. In Mozambique liberalization of trade in cashew nuts resulted in 8,500 of 10,000 cashew processing workers losing their jobs.[117]

When a domestic industry is in crisis and jobs are lost, the political decision-makers may well 'scramble for shelter' by adopting protectionist measures.[118] This may happen even when the decision-makers are well aware that such measures are by no means the best response to the crisis in the industry concerned. While the import competition would probably benefit most of their constituents (through lower prices, better quality and/or more choice), import competition is likely to hurt a small group of their constituents significantly (through lower salaries or job losses). If this small group is vocal and well organised, as it often is,

116 Bhagwati, *Free Trade Today*, 43–4.

117 M. Bacchetta and M. Jansen, *Adjusting to Trade Liberalization: The Role of Policy, Institutions and WTO Disciplines*, Special Studies Series (WTO, 2003), 6.

118 'Survey World Trade', *The Economist*, 3 October 1998, 3.

it will put a great deal of pressure on the (elected) decision-makers to take protectionist measures for the benefit of the few and to the detriment of the many. In such a situation, protectionism can constitute 'good' politics.[119] The *public choice theory* explains that, when the majority of the voters are unconcerned with the (*per capita* small) losses they suffer, the vote-maximising political decision-makers will ignore the interests of the many, and support the interests of the vocal and well-organised few.[120] The then WTO Director-General Pascal Lamy called in 2007 for recognition of the fact that the politics of trade suffer from an 'inbuilt asymmetry'. He noted:

> [T]hose who benefit from gains in purchasing power stemming from trade opening are millions, but they are little aware of the source of their gains. Those who suffer from trade opening are thousands who can easily identify the source of their pain. For politicians, such an asymmetry is difficult to cope with and too often the easy way out is to treat foreigners as scapegoats, which we know is one of the safest old tricks of domestic politics.[121]

However, as discussed above, trade protectionist measures to protect the interests of some eventually leave everyone worse off. Joseph Stiglitz, reflecting on his own experience as Chair of the Council of Economic Advisors in the Clinton Administration, observed in this respect:

> One might have thought that each country would promote liberalization in those sectors where it had most to gain from a societal perspective; and similarly, that it would be most willing to give up protectionism in those sectors where protection was costing the most. But political logic prevails over economic logic: after all, if economic logic dominated, countries would engage in trade liberalization on their own. High levels of protection are usually indicative of strong political forces, and these higher barriers may be the last to give way ... The political force behind the resistance to free trade is a simple one: Although the country as a whole may be better off under free trade, some special interests will actually be worse off. And although policy could in principle rectify this situation (by using redistribution to make everybody better off), in actuality, the required compensations are seldom paid.[122]

A second reason for governments to restrict trade is their wish to assist the establishment of a new industry, i.e. to offer *infant industry protection*. The argument for infant industry protection was made by Alexander Hamilton in 1791, Friedrich List in 1841 and John Stuart Mill in 1848, and has been invoked many times since. In the nineteenth century, the infant manufacturing industries of the United States and Germany were protected against import competition on the basis of this argument. Today, this argument may be of particular relevance to developing countries, which may find that, while they have a potential comparative advantage in certain industries, new producers in these countries

119 B. Hoekman and M. Kostecki, *The Political Economy of the World Trading System: The WTO and Beyond*, 2nd edn (Oxford University Press, 2001), 22.

120 On the role of international trade law in 'helping' national decision-makers to make the 'right' decision, i.e. a decision in the best interest of the country as a whole, see below, p. 28. On measures taken to protect an industry (and jobs) threatened by import competition, see also below, p. 27.

121 Lamy, 'Trends and Issues Facing Global Trade'.

122 Stiglitz, 'Addressing Developing Country Priorities and Needs in the Millennium Round', 51–3.

cannot yet compete with established producers in the developed countries. By means of a customs duty or import restriction, temporary protection is then given to the national producers to allow them to become strong enough to compete with well-established producers.[123] The infant industry argument for protectionist measures has some appeal and validity. However, protecting the new producers from import competition does not necessarily remedy the problems that caused the new producers to be uncompetitive. Furthermore, the success of an infant industry policy crucially depends on a correct diagnosis of which industries could over time become competitive. It is often very difficult for governments to identify, in an objective manner and free from pressure from special interest groups, the new industries that merit protection. Moreover, in practice, the protection, which is by nature intended to be temporary, frequently becomes permanent. When it becomes clear that the protected national industry will never 'grow up' and will always be unable to face import competition, it is often politically difficult to remove the protection in place.[124]

A third reason for governments to take trade-restrictive measures is to support a domestic industry to establish itself on the world market. This *strategic trade policy* argument for restrictions on trade is relatively new. In an industry with economies of scale, a country may, by imposing a tariff or quantitative restriction and thus reserving the domestic market for a domestic firm, allow that firm to cut its costs and undercut foreign competitors in other markets. This may work in an industry where economies of scale are sufficiently large that there is only room for very few profitable companies in the world market. Economists reckon that this might be the case for civil aircraft, semiconductors and cars.[125] The aim of government intervention is to ensure that the domestic rather than a foreign company establishes itself on the world market and thus contributes to the national economic welfare. However, as Paul Krugman noted:

> Strategic trade policy aimed at securing excess returns for domestic firms and support for industries that are believed to yield national benefits are both beggar-thy-neighbour policies and raise income at the expense of other countries. A country that attempts to use such policies will probably provoke retaliation. In many (though not all) cases, a trade war between two interventionist governments will leave both countries worse off than if a hands-off approach were adopted by both.[126]

This does not mean that such policies will not be pursued, because, as Krugman also pointed out:

> [g]overnments do not necessarily act in the national interest, especially when making detailed microeconomic interventions. Instead, they are influenced by interest group pressures. The kinds of interventions that new trade theory suggests can raise national income will typically

123 See below, p. 423 (with regard to customs duties) and pp. 480–1 (with regard to import restrictions).

124 A. Deardorff and R. Stern, 'Current Issues in US Trade Policies: An Overview', in R. Stern (ed.), *US Trade Policies in a Changing World Economy* (Massachusetts Institute of Technology Press, 1987), 39–40.

125 'Survey World Trade', *The Economist*, 3 October 1998, 6.

126 P. Krugman, 'Is Free Trade Passé?', *Journal of Economic Perspectives*, 1987, 141.

raise the welfare of small, fortunate groups by large amounts, while imposing costs on larger, more diffuse groups. The result, as with any microeconomic policy, can easily be that excessive or misguided intervention takes place because the beneficiaries have more knowledge and influence than the losers.[127]

A fourth reason for governments to adopt trade-restrictive measures, and, in particular, customs duties, has always been, and still is, to *generate revenue for government*.[128] Taxing trade is an easy way to collect revenue. While taxation of trade for revenue is no longer significant for developed countries, for many developing-country governments customs duties remain a significant source of revenue.[129]

A fifth reason for governments to restrict trade is to protect *national security* and/or ensure *self-sufficiency*. The steel industry, as well as farmers, can, for example, be heard to argue that their presence and prosperity is essential to the national security of the country. The basic argument is that a country should be able to rely on its domestic industries and farmers to meet its basic needs for vital material and food, because it will be impossible to rely – in times of crisis and conflict – on imports from other countries. Alan Sykes noted in this respect that the probability of this type of crisis seems small, and that, if such crisis nevertheless were to arise, it may well be possible to reopen or rebuild productive facilities quickly enough to satisfy essential needs.[130] For Sykes, arguments for trade-restrictive measures to protect national security and ensure self-sufficiency rarely hold up to careful scrutiny.[131] Sykes argued that:

stockpiling during peacetime may well be a superior alternative to the protection of domestic capacity. Where the item in question is not perishable, a nation might be better off by buying up a supply of vital material at low prices in an open trading system than to burden itself over time with the high prices attendant on protectionism as a hedge against armed conflict. The funds tied up in a stockpile have some opportunity cost to be sure, but this cost can easily be smaller than the costs of excluding efficient foreign suppliers from the domestic market.[132]

A sixth and ever more prevalent reason for governments to restrict trade is the *protection and promotion of non-economic societal values and interests*, such as public morals, public health, a sustainable environment, human rights, minimum labour standards, consumer safety, and cultural identity and diversity. Measures taken to protect and/or promote these societal values and interests may, intentionally or not, restrict trade in products or services. However, the protection and promotion of these values and interests are core tasks of government, and, in many instances, trade-restrictive measures may

127 *Ibid.* 128 See below, pp. 422–3. 129 *Ibid.*

130 See J. Jackson, W. Davey and A. Sykes, *Legal Problems of International Economic Relations*, 4th edn (Westgroup, 2002), 20–1.

131 *Ibid.* 132 *Ibid.*

not only be legitimate, but also necessary. In other instances, such measures are, however, mere fronts for protectionist measures intended to shield domestic producers from import competition. Domestic producers adversely affected by import competition are generally well aware that trade-restrictive measures are more likely to get adopted if justifications other than protection from import competition are invoked. Protectionism can take on very sophisticated guises.[133]

Note that in 2016 the world is confronted with a rising tide of protectionism. In its June 2016 *Report on G20 Trade Measures*, the WTO found that in the period from October 2015 to May 2016, the G20 economies imposed an average of twenty-one new trade-restrictive measures per month, which was the highest monthly average registered since the 2008–9 global economic crisis when the WTO began its monitoring exercise.[134] WTO Director-General Roberto Azevêdo, expressing concerns over these findings, commented:

> These trade-restrictive measures, combined with a notable rise in anti-trade rhetoric, could have a further chilling effect on trade flows, with knock-on effects for economic growth and job creation. If we are serious about addressing slow economic growth then we need to get trade moving again, not put up barriers between economies. The G20 economies have made a commitment to lead in this endeavour as the world's largest traders. I urge them to act on this commitment.[135]

2.4 International Trade to the Benefit of All?

As discussed in the previous section, governments may in certain situations have good reasons to restrict trade. This will be the case, in particular, when trade-restrictive measures are necessary to protect and/or promote important societal values and interests. However, there is a broad consensus that governments are well advised to adopt free trade policies. As explained above, international trade has the potential of contributing to economic development and lifting people out of poverty.[136] It has realised this potential – albeit to varying degrees – in many countries; over the past two decades, this has been the case, in particular, in Asia. However, at the same time, it is undisputed that not all countries, and within countries not all sections of the population, have benefited from international trade. In fact, many people have been left behind or are now – because of international trade – worse off than they were before. At the WTO Ministerial

133 See below, p. 885.

134 World Trade Organization, *Report on G20 Trade Measures (Mid-October 2015 to Mid-May 2016)*, 21 June 2016, 2, at www.wto.org/english/news_e/news16_e/g20_wto_report_june16_e.pdf. Since 2009, G20 countries imposed a total of 1,583 trade-restrictive measures, and only a quarter of these measures have been removed. See *ibid*. The G20 economies comprise Argentina, Australia, Brazil, Canada, China, France, Germany, India, Indonesia, Italy, Republic of Korea, Japan, Mexico, the Russian Federation, Saudi Arabia, South Africa, Turkey, the United Kingdom and the United States, as well as the European Union.

135 See www.wto.org/english/news_e/news16_e/trdev_21jun16_e.htm.

136 See above, pp. 2 and 23.

Conference in Cancún in September 2003, the then UN Secretary-General Kofi Annan noted, not without a measure of frustration:

> The reality of the international trading system today does not match the rhetoric (of improving the quality of life). Instead of open markets, there are too many barriers that stunt, stifle and starve. Instead of fair competition, there are subsidies by rich countries that tilt the playing field against the poor. And instead of global rules negotiated by all, in the interest of all, and adhered to by all, there is too much closed-door decision-making, too much protection of special interests, and too many broken promises.[137]

In its 2002 study, *Rigged Rules and Double Standards: Trade, Globalization, and the Fight Against Poverty*, Oxfam noted that, just as in any national economy, economic integration in the global economy can be a source of shared prosperity and poverty reduction, or a source of increasing inequality and exclusion. Oxfam stated:

> Managed well, the international trading system can lift millions out of poverty. Managed badly, it will leave whole economies even more marginalised. The same is true at a national level. Good governance can make trade work in the interests of the poor. Bad governance can make it work against them.[138]

In a speech to the G-20 Finance Ministers and Central Bank Governors in November 2001, James Wolfensohn, then President of the World Bank, analysed the challenge to make economic globalisation and international trade to work to the benefit of all. This analysis still holds true today. Wolfensohn first observed:

> In my view, with the improvements in both technology and policies that we have seen over recent decades, some form of globalization is with us to stay. But the kind of globalization is not yet certain: it can be either a *globalization of development and poverty reduction* – such as we have begun to see in recent decades, although this trend still cannot be taken for granted – or a *globalization of conflict, poverty, disease, and inequality*. What can we do to tip the scales decisively toward the right kind of globalization?[139]

To ensure that economic globalisation and international trade contribute to economic development, equity and the well-being of all people, Wolfensohn advocated the following four-point agenda for action: (1) good governance at the national level; (2) a further reduction of trade barriers; (3) more development aid; and (4) better international cooperation and global governance of economic globalisation and international trade. First, with regard to *good governance* at the national level, Wolfensohn stated:

> [D]eveloping countries must continue the move toward *better policies, investment climate, and governance*. Despite progress in macroeconomic management and openness, there

137 See www.wto.mvs.com/mino3_webcast_e.htm/archives. 138 *Ibid.*

139 'Responding to the Challenges of Globalization', Remarks to the G-20 Finance Ministers and Central Bank Governors by James D. Wolfensohn, President, World Bank Group, Ottawa, 17 November 2001, at www.worldbank.org/html/extdr/extme/jdwsp111701.htm.

remain many domestic barriers to integration. Many countries have fallen short in creating an investment climate for productivity, growth, entrepreneurship, and jobs. These domestic barriers include inadequate transport infrastructure, poor governance, bureaucratic harassment of small businesses, a lack of electric power, an unskilled workforce ... And countries also need to make possible the participation of poor people in growth, through support for targeted education, health, social protection, and their involvement in key decisions that shape their lives. Poor people need much greater voice.[140]

Second, with regard to the *further reduction of trade barriers*, Wolfensohn noted that:

all countries – developed and developing – must *reduce trade barriers* and give developing countries a better chance in world markets ... Rich countries must increase market access for the exports of developing countries, through both multilateral negotiations and unilateral action, to increase the payoffs to developing-country policy and institutional reforms.[141]

Third, with regard to the *increase in development aid*, Wolfensohn recommended that:

developed countries must *increase development aid*, but allocate it better and cut down the burden its implementation can impose ... The evidence from the Bank's research is that well-directed aid, combined with strong reform efforts, can greatly reduce poverty. If we are serious about ensuring a beneficial globalization and meeting multilateral development goals we have all signed up to, we must double ODA [overseas development aid] from its current level of about $50 billion a year.[142]

Fourth, with regard to *better international cooperation* and *global governance* of economic globalisation and international trade, Wolfensohn stated that:

we must *act as a global community* where it really matters. Effective globalization requires institutions of global governance, and multilateral action to confront global problems and provide global public goods. This means confronting terrorism, internationalized crime, and money laundering, as we are doing in response to September 11th. But it also means that as a community, we need to address longer-term needs, by: combating communicable diseases like AIDS and malaria; *building an equitable global trading system*; promoting financial stability to prevent deep and sudden crises; and safeguarding the natural resources and environment on which so many poor people depend for their livelihoods. As we do all this, we must bring poor countries into the decision-making of this global community.[143]

In the same vein, the then WTO Director-General Pascal Lamy noted in 2007 when addressing the question of how to ensure that economic globalisation and international trade benefits all, that this question has two sides:

A first one is how to ensure trade benefits are shared more fairly among nations. The second side is how to ensure a better distribution of the benefits stemming from trade within a nation.

140 *Ibid.* 141 *Ibid.* 142 *Ibid.* 143 *Ibid.* Emphasis added.

On the action that needs to be taken at the *international level* (the 'first side' of the question), Lamy stated:

> I believe two elements are fundamental: fairer multilateral trade rules and building of trade capacity in developing countries. One primary objective of the ongoing WTO negotiations under the Doha Development Agenda is precisely to address the remaining imbalances in the WTO rules against developing countries, whether in agriculture or in areas such as textiles or footwear ... But negotiating a fairer playing field, difficult as it is, will not be enough. New trade opportunities do not automatically convert into growth and development. The international community also has a responsibility to make sure poorer countries have the capacity to trade and make full use of the market access opportunities provided to them, through more and better focused Aid for Trade.

On the action that needs to be taken at the *national level* (the 'second side' of the question), Lamy observed that:

> [t]rade opening can and does translate into greater growth and poverty alleviation, but this is neither automatic [nor] immediate. Trade opening must be accompanied by a solid domestic agenda to spur on growth and cushion adjustment costs. Appropriate tax policies, competition policy, investment in quality education, social safety nets and innovation fostering healthy environments must all be part of the mix needed for trade to translate into real benefits for the people. In this respect, trade policy cannot be isolated from domestic macroeconomic, social or structural policies. The same trade policy will result in different outcomes depending on the quality of economic policies, and this is true across the board, whether you look at the US, Europe, Japan, or at Vietnam, Cambodia, Kenya or Paraguay.[144]

On the action, both at the national and international level, that needs to be taken to ensure that international trade promotes, rather than hurts, economic growth, employment and equality in developing countries as well as developed countries, refer also to the 2011 study by the International Labour Office and the WTO, *Making Globalization Socially Sustainable*.[145]

Just as Wolfensohn and Lamy have done, Peter Sutherland, former GATT and WTO Director-General and later Chair of BP Amoco and Goldman Sachs International, has also emphasised that more is needed than international trade and economic openness to eradicate poverty and inequality. He already noted in a 1997 contribution to the *International Herald Tribune* that:

> There are those who oppose redistribution policies in principle, whether in the domestic or the international context. This is wrong. It is morally wrong, it is pragmatically wrong, and we ought not be ashamed to say so. I have been personally and deeply committed to promoting the market system through my entire career. Yet it is quite obvious to me that the market will never provide all of the answers to the problems of poverty and inequality. The fact is that there are those who will not be able to develop their economies simply because market access has been provided. I do not believe that we in the global community will

144 Lamy, 'Trends and Issues Facing Global Trade'.

145 *Making Globalization Socially Sustainable*, co-publication by the International Labour Office and the Secretariat of the World Trade Organization, edited by Mac Bacchetta and Marion Jansen (ILO/WTO, 2011).

adequately live up to our responsibility if we have done no more than provide the poorest people and the poorest countries with an opportunity to succeed. We must also provide them with a foundation from which they have a reasonable chance of seizing that opportunity – decent health care, primary education, basic infrastructure.[146]

It is clear that international trade and economic openness are necessary but not sufficient conditions for economic development and prosperity. The simple spread of markets will not eliminate poverty. A global economy and more international trade will not automatically lead to rising prosperity for all countries and for all people. In fact, without the international and national action referred to above, international trade will not bring prosperity to all, but, on the contrary, is likely to result in more income inequality, social injustice, environmental degradation and cultural homogenisation.

3 THE LAW OF THE WTO

As discussed above, international trade can make a significant contribution to economic development and prosperity in developed as well as developing countries. However, for this potential to be realised, there must be: good governance at the national level; a further reduction of trade barriers; more development aid; and better international cooperation and global governance of economic globalisation and international trade. This book on the law and the policy of the World Trade Organization (WTO) touches upon the national and international action required in each of these four areas, but deals primarily with the requirement of global governance of international trade. Nobel Peace Prize winner, Muhammad Yunus, founder of the Grameen Bank for the Poor, stated the following in his Nobel Lecture in December 2006:

I support globalization and believe it can bring more benefits to the poor than its alternative. But it must be the right kind of globalization. To me, globalization is like a hundred-lane highway criss-crossing the world. If it is a free-for-all highway, its lanes will be taken over by the giant trucks from powerful economies. Bangladeshi rickshaw will be thrown off the highway. In order to have a win–win globalization we must have traffic rules, traffic police, and traffic authority for this global highway. Rule of 'strongest takes it all' must be replaced by rules that ensure that the poorest have a place and piece of the action, without being elbowed out by the strong.[147]

This section deals with: (1) the international rules on international trade; and (2) the basic rules of WTO law.

146 P. Sutherland, 'Beyond the Market, a Different Kind of Equity', *International Herald Tribune*, 20 February 1997.

147 Muhammad Yunus, Nobel Lecture, Oslo, 10 December 2006, available at http://nobelprize.org/nobel_prizes/peace/laureates/2006/yunus-lecture-en.html.

3.1 International Rules on International Trade

This subsection on the international rules on international trade discusses: (1) the need for international rules; and (2) international economic law and WTO law.

3.1.1 Need for International Rules

Peter Sutherland wrote in 1997:

> [T]he greatest economic challenge facing the world is the *need to create an international system* that not only maximizes global growth but also achieves a greater measure of equity, a system that both integrates emerging powers and assists currently marginalized countries in their efforts to participate in worldwide economic expansion ... The most important means available to secure peace and prosperity into the future is to *develop effective multilateral approaches and institutions.*[148]

The multilateral approaches and institutions to which Sutherland referred may embrace many structures and take many forms but, as John Jackson noted:

> it is very clear that law and legal norms play the most important part of the institutions which are essential to make markets work. The notion that 'rule of law' (ambiguous as that phrase is) or a *rule-based or rule-oriented system* of human institutions is essential to a beneficial operation of markets, is a constantly recurring theme in many writings.[149]

Among the writings to which Jackson referred, note those of Ronald Coase, who in 1960 had already concluded that:

> it is evident that, for their operation, markets ... require the establishment of legal rules governing the rights and duties of those carrying out transactions ... *To realize all the gains of trade* ... there has to be a legal system and political order.[150]

But what exactly is the role of legal rules and, in particular, international legal rules in international trade? How do international trade rules allow countries to realise the gains of international trade?

There are basically four related reasons why there is a need for international trade rules. First, countries must be restrained from adopting trade-restrictive measures, and this both in their own interest and in the interest of the world economy.[151] International trade rules *restrain countries from taking trade-restrictive measures.* As noted above, national policy-makers may come under considerable pressure from influential interest groups to adopt trade-restrictive measures in order to protect domestic industries from import competition or to enhance their ability to compete abroad. Such measures may benefit the specific, short-term interests of the groups advocating them, but they seldom benefit

148 Sutherland, 'Beyond the Market, a Different Kind of Equity'. Emphasis added.

149 J. Jackson, 'Global Economics and International Economic Law', *Journal of International Economic Law*, 1998, 5 (reproduced by permission of Oxford University Press). Emphasis added.

150 R. Coase, *The Firm, the Market and the Law* (reprint of 1960 article), Chapter 5, as quoted by Jackson, *ibid.*, 4. Emphasis added.

151 Note, however, that, as discussed throughout this book, there are many instances in which trade-restrictive measures are legitimate, and even called for, to promote or protect important societal values and interests. See e.g. below, pp. 28, 35, 42, and 544–617.

the larger economic interests of the country adopting them.[152] As Ernst-Ulrich Petersmann observed:

> Governments know very well ... that by 'tying their hands to the mast' (like Ulysses when he approached the island of the Sirenes), reciprocal international pre-commitments help them to resist the siren-like temptations from 'rent-seeking' interest groups at home.[153]

In other words, international trade rules are the *shield* behind which a government with the interests of its people in mind can seek protection against the onslaught of politically powerful special interest groups calling for trade-restrictive measures. International trade rules are often referred to by governments when they refuse to give in to demands for trade protectionism. In this way, international trade rules play a very important role in international trade policy. Moreover, countries also realise that, if they take trade-restrictive measures, other countries will do so too. This may lead to an escalation of trade-restrictive measures, a disastrous move for international trade and for global economic welfare. International trade rules help to avoid such escalation.

A second and closely related reason why international trade rules are necessary is the need of traders for a degree of *security and predictability*. Traders operating, or intending to operate, in a country that is bound by international legal rules will be better able to predict how that country will act in the future on matters affecting their operations in that country. The predictability and security resulting from international trade rules will encourage trade and will thus contribute to economic welfare. As John Jackson wrote, international trade rules:

> may provide the only predictability or stability to a potential ... trade-development situation. Without such predictability or stability, trade ... flows might be even more risky and therefore more inhibited than otherwise ... To put it another way, the policies which tend to reduce some risks, lower the 'risk premium' required by entrepreneurs to enter into international transactions. This should result in a general increase in the efficiency of various economic activities, contributing to greater welfare for everyone.[154]

A third reason why international trade rules are necessary is that, as a result of the greatly increased levels of trade in goods and services, the *protection and promotion of important societal values and interests* such as public health, a sustainable environment, consumer safety, cultural identity and minimum labour standards is no longer a purely national matter. Attempts to ensure the protection and promotion of these values and interests at the national level alone are doomed to be ineffective and futile. For example, in this age of mass global air travel, an epidemic of an infectious disease, such as SARS or avian flu, cannot be addressed effectively by countries just acting on their own. In the same vein, in a world in which financial products are traded globally and with lightning speed,

152 See above, p. 27. On the optimal tariff argument and the strategic trade policy argument, see above, p. 28.
153 E. U. Petersmann, *The GATT/WTO Dispute Settlement System: International Law, International Organizations and Dispute Settlement* (Kluwer Law International, 1997), 36–7.
154 Jackson, 'Global Economics and International Economic Law', 5–6.

national regulation of these products was found to be terribly inadequate and at the source of the 2008–9 global economic crisis. Also, there is general recognition that global warming is unlikely to be addressed in an effective manner by unilateral measures of individual countries. In addition to being ineffective and futile, national measures to address these and other global challenges and risks may well have damaging effects on both the national and global economy. Even when such national measures do not directly or expressly restrict trade, the mere fact that such measures differ from country to country may act as a significant constraint on trade. International trade rules are needed to ensure that countries maintain only those national measures that are necessary for (or at the very least related to) the protection of key societal values and interests.[155] International trade rules may also introduce a degree of harmonisation of domestic regulatory measures and thus promote an effective, international protection of these societal values and interests.[156]

A fourth and final reason why international trade rules are necessary is the need to achieve a *greater measure of equity* in international economic relations. As Father Lacordaire stated in one of his renowned 1835 sermons at the Notre Dame in Paris:

> Entre le fort et le faible, entre le riche et le pauvre ... c'est la liberté qui opprime et la loi qui affranchit.[157]

Without international trade rules, binding and enforceable on rich as well as poor countries, and rules recognising the special needs of developing countries, many countries are not able to integrate fully in the world trading system and derive an equitable share of the gains of international trade.

However, for international legal rules to play these multiple roles, such rules have, of course, to be observed. It is clear that international trade rules are not always followed. Yet, while both the media and academia inevitably pay more attention to instances of breach, it should be stressed that international trade rules are generally well observed. Countries realise that they cannot expect other countries to observe the rules if they do not do so themselves. The desire to be able to depend on other countries' compliance with the rules leads many countries to observe the rules even though this might be politically inconvenient in a given situation.[158]

All countries and their people benefit from the existence of rules on international trade which make the trading environment more predictable and stable.

155 For a discussion on the protection of key societal values and interests, see below, pp. 544–623, 630–68 and 671–94.

156 See below, pp. 883–932, 935–90, and 944–1054.

157 Translation: 'Between the strong and the weak, between the rich and the poor ... it is freedom which oppresses and the law which sets free.' Abbé Jean-Baptiste Lacordaire (1802–61) was a French Catholic priest, journalist and political activist.

158 See L. Henkin, *How Nations Behave*, 2nd edn (1979), as referred to in Jackson, 'Global Economics and International Economic Law', 5.

However, provided the rules take into account their specific interests and needs and leave sufficient 'policy space' to pursue economic development, developing countries, with generally limited economic and political power, should benefit even more from the existence of rules on international trade. The weaker countries are likely to suffer most where the law of the jungle reigns. They are more likely to thrive in a *rules-based*, rather than a power-based, international trading system.

3.1.2 International Economic Law and WTO Law

The legal rules governing trade relations between countries are part of international economic law. International economic law is a very broad field of international law. With regard to 'international economic law', John Jackson noted that:

> [it] is not by any means a new phenomenon although the phrase may be considered relatively new. International law has always had considerable 'economic content', as manifested by international economic institutions and by the international law jurisprudence throughout the centuries devoted to various economic subjects including trade, investment, commerce, and navigation (FCN treaties). In addition, activities of the League of Nations, as well as, more currently, the United Nations, have had a very substantial economic institutional dimension.[159]

Jackson once suggested that 90 per cent of international law work relates in fact to international economic law in one form or another. He also observed that international economic law does not enjoy as much glamour or media attention as work on armed conflicts and human rights seems to do.[160]

International economic law can be defined, broadly, as covering all those international rules pertaining to economic transactions and relations, as well as those pertaining to governmental regulation of economic matters. As such, international economic law includes international rules on trade in goods and services, economic development, intellectual property rights, foreign direct investment, international finance and monetary matters, commodities, food, health, transport, communications, natural resources, private commercial transactions, nuclear energy, etc. International rules on trade in goods and services, i.e. international trade law, constitute the 'hard core' of international economic law. International trade law consists of, on the one hand, numerous bilateral or regional trade agreements and, on the other hand, multilateral trade agreements. Examples of bilateral and regional trade agreements are manifold. The *North American Free Trade Agreement* (NAFTA) and the *MERCOSUR Agreement* are typical examples of regional trade agreements. The *Trade Agreement between the United States and Israel* and the *Agreement on Trade in Wine between the*

159 J. Jackson, 'International Economic Law: Complexity and Puzzles', *Journal of International Economic Law*, 2007, 3.

160 J. Jackson, 'International Economic Law: Reflections on the "Boilerroom" of International Relations', *American University Journal of International Law and Policy*, 1995, 596.

European Community and Australia are examples of bilateral trade agreements. The number of multilateral trade agreements is more limited. This group includes, for example, the 1983 *International Convention on the Harmonized Commodity Description and Coding System*, as amended (the '*HS Convention*')[161] and the 1973 *International Convention on the Simplification and Harmonization of Customs Procedures*, as amended (the '*Kyoto Convention*').[162] The most important and broadest of all multilateral trade agreements is the 1994 *Marrakesh Agreement Establishing the World Trade Organization*, commonly referred to as the *WTO Agreement*. It is the law of this Agreement which is the subject matter of this book.

3.2 Basic Rules of WTO Law

The law of the WTO is a complex set of rules dealing with trade in goods and services and the protection of intellectual property rights. WTO law addresses a broad spectrum of issues, ranging from tariffs, import quotas and customs formalities to compulsory licensing, food safety regulations and national security measures. However, five groups of basic rules can be distinguished: (1) rules of non-discrimination; (2) rules on market access; (3) rules on unfair trade; (4) rules on the conflict between trade liberalisation and other societal values and interests; and (5) institutional and procedural rules, including those relating to WTO decision-making, trade policy review and dispute settlement. These substantive, institutional and procedural rules of WTO law make up what is commonly referred to as the *multilateral trading system*. Referring to this system, Peter Sutherland and others wrote the following in 2001:

> The multilateral trading system, with the World Trade Organization (WTO) at its centre, is the most important tool of global economic management and development we possess.[163]

Martin Wolf of the *Financial Times* noted in 2001:

> The multilateral trading system at the beginning of the twenty-first century is the most remarkable achievement in institutionalized global economic cooperation that there has ever been.[164]

The following sections of this chapter briefly review the basic rules constituting the multilateral trading system. These rules will be discussed in greater detail in subsequent chapters of this book.

161 See www.wcoomd.org/~/media/WCO/Public/Global/PDF/Topics/Nomenclature/Instruments%20and%20Tools/HS%20Nomenclature%202012/NG0163B1.ashx?db=web. See also below, p. 450.

162 See www.wcoomd.org/en/topics/facilitation/instrument-and-tools/conventions/pf_revised_kyoto_conv/kyoto_new.aspx.

163 P. Sutherland, J. Sewell and D. Weiner, 'Challenges Facing the WTO and Policies to Address Global Governance', in G. Sampson (ed.), *The Role of the World Trade Organization in Global Governance* (United Nations University Press, 2001), 81.

164 M. Wolf, 'What the World Needs from the Multilateral Trading System', *ibid*, 182.

3.2.1 Rules of Non-Discrimination

There are two basic rules of non-discrimination in WTO law: (1) the most-favoured-nation (MFN) treatment obligation; and (2) the national treatment obligation.

The *MFN treatment obligation* requires a WTO Member that grants certain favourable treatment to any given country to grant that same favourable treatment to all other WTO Members. A WTO Member is not allowed to discriminate *between* and *among* its trading partners by, for example, giving the products imported from some countries more favourable treatment with respect to market access than the treatment it accords to the 'like' products of other Members.[165] Despite many exceptions and deviations from this obligation, the MFN treatment obligation is arguably the single most important rule in WTO law.[166] Without this rule, the multilateral trading system could and would not exist. Chapter 4 examines in detail this rule as it applies to trade in goods and services.[167]

The *national treatment obligation* requires a WTO Member to treat foreign products, services and service suppliers no less favourably than it treats 'like' domestic products, services and service suppliers. Where the national treatment obligation applies, foreign products, for example, should, once they have crossed the border and entered the domestic market, not be subject to less favourable taxation or regulation than 'like' domestic products. Pursuant to the national treatment obligation, a WTO Member is not allowed to discriminate *against* foreign products, services and service suppliers. The national treatment obligation is an important rule in WTO law which has given rise to many trade disputes. For trade in goods, the national treatment obligation has *general* application to all measures affecting trade in goods.[168] By contrast, for trade in services, the national treatment obligation does not have such general application. It applies only to the extent that a WTO Member has explicitly committed itself to grant 'national treatment' in respect of specific services sectors.[169] Such commitments to give 'national treatment' are made in a Member's Schedule of Specific Commitments on Services, i.e. its Services Schedule. Chapter 5 discusses in detail the national treatment obligation as it applies to trade in goods and services.[170]

3.2.2 Rules on Market Access

WTO law contains four groups of rules regarding market access: (1) rules on *customs duties* (i.e. tariffs); (2) rules on *other duties and financial charges*; (3) rules on *quantitative restrictions*; and (4) rules on *other non-tariff barriers*. These 'other non-tariff barriers' to trade are a very broad, residual category of measures,

165 See Article I of the GATT 1994.
166 On the 'exceptions', see e.g. Chapter 8, at pp. 544–623. On the 'deviations', see in particular Chapter 10, at pp. 671–94.
167 See below, pp. 305–39. 168 See Article III of the GATT 1994. 169 See Article XVII of the GATS.
170 See below, pp. 399–412.

actions or omissions of Members, including, *inter alia*: the lack of transparency regarding the applicable trade laws, regulations and procedures; the unfair and arbitrary application of trade measures; technical barriers to trade; sanitary and phytosanitary measures; customs formalities and procedures; government procurement laws and practices; and the lack of effective protection of intellectual property rights.

Under WTO law, the imposition of customs duties is not prohibited. In fact, customs duties are a legitimate trade policy instrument, and WTO Members impose customs duties on many products. However, WTO law calls upon WTO Members to negotiate mutually beneficial reductions of customs duties.[171] These negotiations result in tariff concessions or bindings, set out in a Member's Schedule of Concessions, i.e. its Goods Schedule. On products for which a tariff concession or binding exists, the customs duties imposed may no longer exceed the maximum level of duty agreed to.[172] Chapter 6 examines the rules applicable to customs duties.[173] It also discusses the rules on other duties and financial charges.[174]

While customs duties are a legitimate trade policy instrument (provided they do not exceed the maximum level agreed to), quantitative restrictions on trade in goods are, as a general rule, forbidden under WTO law.[175] Unless one of many exceptions apply, WTO Members are not allowed to ban the importation or exportation of goods or to subject them to quotas. With respect to trade in services, quantitative restrictions are only prohibited in services sectors for which specific market-access commitments have been undertaken.[176] These market-access commitments, and their scope, are set out in a Member's Services Schedule. Chapter 7 examines the rules applicable to quantitative restrictions on trade in goods and services.[177]

Among 'other non-tariff barriers', the lack of transparency of national trade regulations definitely stands out as a major barrier to international trade. Uncertainty and confusion regarding the trade regulations applicable in other countries has a chilling effect on trade. Likewise, the arbitrary application of national trade regulations also discourages traders and hampers trade. Transparency and the fair application of trade regulations are therefore part of the basic rules on market access examined in Chapter 7.[178] Non-tariff barriers to trade, such as customs formalities and government procurement practices, are, for many products and in many countries, more important barriers to trade than customs duties or quantitative restrictions. Chapter 7 also deals

171 See Article XXVIII *bis* of the GATT 1994. 172 See Article II of the GATT 1994.
173 See below, pp. 417–22. 174 See below, pp. 461–6. 175 See Article XI of the GATT 1994.
176 Article XVI of the GATS. To be precise, the prohibition of Article XVI of the GATS applies to 'market access barriers' as defined in Article XVI:2. All but one category of 'market access barriers' are quantitative restrictions. See below, pp. 518–20.
177 See below, pp. 482–92; 520–1. 178 See below, pp. 499–510; 534–5.

with the rules on many of these non-tariff barriers.[179] As mentioned above, 'other non-tariff barriers' to trade can also take the form of technical barriers to trade, sanitary and phytosanitary measures, and the lack of effective protection of intellectual property rights. Due to their importance and detailed nature, the rules on these 'other non-tariff barriers' are discussed, separately, in Chapters 13, 14 and 15 respectively.[180] Note that the rules on technical barriers to trade, the rules on sanitary and phytosanitary measures, and the rules ensuring a minimum level of protection and enforcement of intellectual property rights have in common that they go far beyond the usual trade liberalisation rules and venture into 'behind-the-border' regulation to a greater extent than any other WTO rules. In addition to imposing the usual WTO disciplines, these rules harmonise, or promote the harmonisation of, national regulation around international standards.

3.2.3 Rules on Unfair Trade

WTO law, at present, does not provide for general rules on unfair trade practices, but it does have detailed rules that relate to specific forms of 'unfair' trade. These rules deal with dumping and subsidised trade.

Dumping, i.e. bringing a product onto the market of another country at a price less than the normal value of that product, is 'condemned' but not prohibited under WTO law. However, when dumping causes or threatens to cause material injury to the domestic industry of a Member producing a 'like' product, WTO law allows that Member to impose anti-dumping duties on the dumped products in order to offset the dumping.[181] The rules on the imposition of these anti-dumping duties are examined in Chapter 11.

Subsidies, i.e. financial contributions by governments or public bodies that confer a benefit, are subject to an intricate set of rules.[182] Some subsidies, such as export and import substitution subsidies, are, as a rule, prohibited. Other subsidies are not prohibited, but when they cause adverse effects to the interests of other Members, the subsidising Member should withdraw the subsidy or take appropriate steps to remove the adverse effects. If the subsidising Member fails to do so, countermeasures commensurate with the degree and nature of the adverse effect may be authorised.[183] If a prohibited or other subsidy causes or threatens to cause material injury to the domestic industry of a Member producing a 'like' product, that Member is authorised to impose countervailing duties on the subsidised products to offset the subsidisation. Subsidies relating

179 See below, pp. 498–540. 180 See below, pp. 883–932, 935–90 and 933–1054.
181 See Article VI of the GATT 1994 and the *Anti-Dumping Agreement*.
182 See Articles VI and XVI of the GATT 1994 and the *Agreement on Subsidies and Countervailing Measures* (the '*SCM Agreement*').
183 See Article 7.9 of the *SCM Agreement*.

to agricultural products are subject to special (and overall more lenient) rules.[184] The rules applicable to subsidies and countervailing duties are examined in Chapter 12.

3.2.4 Rules on the Conflict Between Trade Liberalisation and Other Societal Values and Interests

The Appellate Body in *China – Raw Materials (2012)* stated:[185]

> we understand the *WTO Agreement, as a whole*, to reflect the balance struck by WTO Members between trade and non-trade-related concerns.

Therefore, apart from the basic rules referred to above, WTO law also provides for rules that address the conflict between trade liberalisation and other societal values and interests and that allow to strike the intended balance. These rules, which are commonly referred to as 'exceptions', allow WTO Members to deviate – under specific conditions – from basic WTO rules in order to take account of economic and non-economic values and interests that compete or conflict with free trade. The *non-economic* values and interests include the protection of the environment, public health, public morals, national treasures and national security. The relevant rules can be found in, for example, Articles XX and XXI of the GATT 1994 and Articles XIV and XIV *bis* of the GATS. The *economic* interests include: the protection of a domestic industry from serious injury inflicted by an unexpected and sharp surge in imports; the safeguarding of the balance of payments; and the pursuit of regional economic integration. The relevant rules can be found in, for example, Articles XII, XIX and XXIV of the GATT 1994, Articles V, X and XII of the GATS and the *Agreement on Safeguards*. The WTO rules allowing Members to take into account economic or non-economic values and interests that may conflict with free trade are examined in detail in Chapters 8, 9 and 10.[186]

Recognising the need for positive efforts designed to ensure that developing-country Members, and especially the least-developed countries among them, are integrated into the multilateral trading system, WTO law includes many provisions granting a degree of special and differential treatment to developing-country Members.[187] These provisions attempt to take the special needs of developing countries into account. In many areas, they provide for fewer obligations or differing rules for developing countries as well as for technical assistance. The rules on the special and differential treatment of developing-country Members are discussed throughout this book.[188]

184 Articles 6–11 of the *Agreement on Agriculture*.
185 Appellate Body Report, *China – Raw Materials (2012)*, para. 306.
186 See below, pp. 544–623, 630–68 and 671–94.
187 For example, Article XVIII and Part IV of the GATT 1994 as well as the Enabling Clause. See below, pp. 423–8 and 687–8.
188 See e.g. below, pp. 292–4, 687–92, 763–5, 866–7 and 1051–3.

3.2.5 Institutional and Procedural Rules

All basic rules referred to above are substantive rules. However, the multilateral trading system also includes, and depends on, institutional and procedural rules relating to WTO decision-making, trade policy review and dispute settlement. The rules regarding the institutions and procedures for the formulation and implementation of trade rules are discussed in detail in Chapter 2. The rules and procedures regarding the settlement of trade disputes are dealt with in Chapter 3.

4 SOURCES OF WTO LAW

WTO law is, by international law standards, a wide-ranging and complex body of law. This section reviews various sources of WTO law. Not all sources of WTO law reviewed below are of the same nature or are on the same legal footing. Some sources provide for specific legal rights and obligations for WTO Members that can be enforced through WTO dispute settlement. Many other sources, reviewed below, do *not* in and of themselves provide for specific, enforceable rights or obligations. They nevertheless assist in 'clarifying' or 'defining' the law that applies between WTO Members on WTO matters.

The principal source of WTO law is the *Marrakesh Agreement Establishing the World Trade Organization*, concluded on 15 April 1994 and in force since 1 January 1995. This section first discusses in some detail this principal source of WTO law. Subsequently, other sources of WTO law are discussed.

4.1 The *Marrakesh Agreement Establishing the World Trade Organization*

The *Marrakesh Agreement Establishing the World Trade Organization* (the '*WTO Agreement*') is the most ambitious and far-reaching international trade agreement ever concluded.[189] It consists of a short basic agreement (of sixteen articles) and numerous other agreements included in the annexes to this basic agreement.[190] On the relationship between this basic agreement and the agreements in the annexes as well as on the binding nature of the latter agreements, Article II of the *WTO Agreement* states:

> 2. The agreements and associated legal instruments included in Annexes 1, 2 and 3 (hereinafter referred to as 'Multilateral Trade Agreements') are integral parts of this Agreement, binding on all Members.

189 The official version of the *WTO Agreement* and its Annexes is published by the WTO and Cambridge University Press as *The Results of the Uruguay Round of Multilateral Trade Negotiations: The Legal Texts*. The *WTO Agreement* and its Annexes are also available on the WTO website at www.wto.org/english/docs_e/legal_e/legal_e.htm.

190 Article XVI of the *WTO Agreement* indicates that this Agreement is equally authentic in its English, French and Spanish version. This is of particular relevance for the interpretation of the provisions of the *WTO Agreement*.

> 3. The agreements and associated legal instruments included in Annex 4 (hereinafter referred to as 'Plurilateral Trade Agreements') are also part of this Agreement for those Members that have accepted them, and are binding on those Members. The Plurilateral Trade Agreements do not create either obligations or rights for Members that have not accepted them.

While the *WTO Agreement* consists of many agreements, the Appellate Body in one of the first cases before it, *Brazil – Desiccated Coconut (1997)*, stressed that the *WTO Agreement* had been accepted by WTO Members as a 'single undertaking'.[191] All multilateral WTO agreements apply equally and are equally binding on all WTO Members. The provisions of these agreements represent 'an *inseparable package* of rights and disciplines which have to be considered in conjunction'.[192] The *WTO Agreement* is thus a single treaty. However, it should be noted that the agreements making up the *WTO Agreement* were negotiated in multiple separate committees, which operated quite independently and without much coordination. Only towards the end of the Uruguay Round were some efforts made at coordinating and harmonising the texts of the various agreements. At that stage, however, the negotiators – for fear of seeing disagreement re-emerge – were often unwilling to change the agreed texts, and some 'inconsistencies' or 'tensions' between the texts remained. Note that Article XVI:3 of the *WTO Agreement* provides:

> In the event of a conflict between a provision of this Agreement and a provision of any of the Multilateral Trade Agreements, the provision of this Agreement shall prevail to the extent of the conflict.[193]

Most of the substantive WTO law is found in the agreements contained in Annex 1. This Annex consists of three parts. Annex 1A currently contains thirteen multilateral agreements on trade in goods; Annex 1B contains the *General Agreement on Trade in Services* (the 'GATS'); and Annex 1C the *Agreement on Trade-Related Aspects of Intellectual Property Rights* (the '*TRIPS Agreement*').[194] The most important of the thirteen multilateral agreements on trade in goods, contained in Annex 1A, is the *General Agreement on Tariffs and Trade 1994* (the 'GATT 1994'). The plurilateral agreements in Annex 4 also contain provisions of substantive law but they are – as set out in Article II:3 of the *WTO Agreement*, quoted above – only binding upon those WTO Members that are a party to these agreements. Annexes 2 and 3 cover, respectively, the *Understanding on Rules and Procedures for the Settlement of Disputes* (the 'DSU') and the *Trade Policy Review Mechanism* (the 'TPRM'), and contain procedural provisions. The next subsections give a brief description of the agreements annexed to the *WTO*

191 See Appellate Body Report, *Brazil – Desiccated Coconut (1997)*, 177.

192 See Appellate Body Report, *Argentina – Footwear (EC) (2000)*, para. 81.

193 On the concept of a 'conflict', see e.g. below, p. 48.

194 Note that the *Agreement on Textiles and Clothing*, which was one of the original thirteen multilateral agreements on trade in goods annexed to the *WTO Agreement*, is since 1 January 2005 no longer in force. See below, pp. 139–40. Note also that pursuant to the Protocol of Amendment adopted by the General Council on 27 November 2014, the *Agreement on Trade Facilitation* has been added to the agreements contained in Annex 1A. The latter agreement is, however, not yet in force. See also below, p. 152.

Agreement and of which they are an integral part. For a more in-depth discussion of the substantive, institutional and procedural provisions of these agreements, see Chapters 3 to 15. Chapter 2 discusses in detail the *WTO Agreement* to which these agreements are annexed.

4.1.1 General Agreement on Tariffs and Trade 1994

The GATT 1994 sets out the basic rules for trade in goods. This agreement is, however, somewhat unusual in its appearance and structure. Paragraph 1 of the introductory text of the GATT 1994 states:

> The General Agreement on Tariffs and Trade 1994 ('GATT 1994') shall consist of:
>
> a. the provisions in the General Agreement on Tariffs and Trade, dated 30 October 1947 ...
> b. the provisions of the legal instruments set forth below that have entered into force under the GATT 1947 before the date of entry into force of the WTO Agreement ...
> c. the Understandings set forth below ... and
> d. the Marrakesh Protocol to GATT 1994.

The GATT 1994 would obviously have been a less confusing and more user-friendly legal instrument if the negotiators had drafted a *new* text reflecting the basic rules on trade in goods as agreed during the Uruguay Round. However, as paragraph 1(a) of the introductory text of the GATT 1994, quoted above, shows, the Uruguay Round negotiators chose to *incorporate by reference* the provisions of the GATT 1947 into the GATT 1994.[195] By doing so, they were able to limit the debate on the provisions of the GATT 1994. If the negotiators had opted for a *new* text reflecting the basic rules on trade in goods, it would not have been possible to keep a lid on the many contentious issues relating to the interpretation and application of GATT provisions.[196] The current arrangement obliges one to consult: (1) the provisions of the GATT 1947; (2) the provisions of relevant GATT 1947 legal instruments, such as decisions taken by the GATT Contracting Parties between 1948 and 1994; and (3) the Understandings agreed upon during the Uruguay Round, in order to know what the GATT 1994 rules on trade in goods are. The negotiators were obviously aware that this arrangement might lead to some confusion, especially with regard to the continued relevance of the GATT 1947. They therefore felt the need to state explicitly in Article II:4 of the *WTO Agreement* that:

> [t]he General Agreement on Tariffs and Trade 1994 as specified in Annex 1A (hereinafter referred to as 'GATT 1994') is legally distinct from the General Agreement on Tariffs and Trade, dated 30 October 1947. [hereinafter referred to as 'GATT 1947']

195 Together with the provisions of the GATT 1947, the provisions of the legal instruments that have entered into force under the GATT 1947, referred to in paragraph 1(b) of the introductory text of the GATT 1994, are incorporated into the GATT 1994.

196 It was understood among the negotiators that these issues concerning the interpretation and application of GATT 1947 provisions could and would be addressed through dispute settlement under the *WTO Agreement*. Only a few contentious GATT issues were addressed and resolved during the Uruguay Round negotiations. See the Understandings listed in paragraph 1(c) of the introductory text of the GATT 1994 and included in this instrument.

It should be stressed that the GATT 1947 is, in fact, no longer in force. It was terminated in 1996. However, as explained, its provisions have been incorporated by reference in the GATT 1994.[197]

The GATT 1994 contains rules on: most-favoured-nation treatment (Article I);[198] tariff concessions (Article II);[199] national treatment on internal taxation and regulation (Article III);[200] anti-dumping and countervailing duties (Article VI);[201] valuation for customs purposes (Article VII);[202] customs fees and formalities (Article VIII);[203] marks of origin (Article IX);[204] the publication and administration of trade regulations (Article X);[205] quantitative restrictions (Article XI);[206] restrictions to safeguard the balance of payments (Article XII);[207] administration of quantitative restrictions (Article XIII);[208] exchange arrangements (Article XV);[209] subsidies (Article XVI);[210] State trading enterprises (Article XVII);[211] governmental assistance to economic development (Article XVIII);[212] safeguard measures (Article XIX);[213] general exceptions (Article XX);[214] security exceptions (Article XXI);[215] dispute settlement (Articles XXII and XXIII);[216] regional economic integration (Article XXIV);[217] modification of tariff schedules (Article XXVIII) and tariff negotiations (Article XXVIII *bis*);[218] and trade and development (Articles XXXVI to XXXVIII).[219] A number of these provisions have been amended by one of the Understandings, listed in paragraph 1(c) of the introductory text of the GATT 1994 and contained in the GATT 1994. Note, for example, the *Understanding on the Interpretation of Article II:1(b) of the General Agreement on Tariffs and Trade 1994*;[220] and the *Understanding on the Interpretation of Article XXIV of the General Agreement on Tariffs and Trade 1994*.[221] Finally, note the *Marrakesh Protocol*, which is an important part of the GATT 1994. This Protocol contains the national Schedules of Concessions, i.e. the Goods Schedules, of all WTO Members. In these Schedules, the commitments to eliminate or reduce customs duties applicable to trade in goods are recorded.[222] The Protocol is over 25,000 pages long, and is a key instrument for traders and trade officials.

4.1.2 Other Multilateral Agreements on Trade in Goods

In addition to the GATT 1994, Annex 1A to the *WTO Agreement* contains a number of other multilateral agreements on trade in goods. These agreements

197 To facilitate the necessary reference to the provisions of the GATT 1947 – and for that reason only – the official WTO *Legal Texts* include the complete text of the GATT 1947. The inclusion of this text should *not* be seen as an indication of the continued application of the GATT 1947.

198 See below, p. 307. 199 See below, pp. 467–9. 200 See below, pp. 342–4. 201 See below, pp. 699–702.

202 See below, pp. 454–7. 203 See below, pp. 467–9. 204 See below, pp. 492–8.

205 See below, pp. 499–510.

206 See below, pp. 428–8. 207 See below, p. 659. 208 See below, pp. 492–8. 209 See below, p. 516.

210 See below, p. 773. 211 See below, p. 516. 212 See below, p. 661. 213 See below, pp. 631–4.

214 See below, pp. 546–604. 215 See below, pp. 618–23. 216 See below, pp. 233–5.

217 See below, pp. 679–88.

218 See below, p. 424. 219 See below, p. 426. 220 See below, pp. 424–6. 221 See below, pp. 464–5.

222 See below, p. 69.

include: (1) the *Agreement on Agriculture*, which requires the use of tariffs instead of quotas or other quantitative restrictions, imposes minimum market access requirements and provides for specific rules on domestic support and export subsidies in the agricultural sector;[223] (2) the *Agreement on the Application of Sanitary and Phytosanitary Measures* (the '*SPS Agreement*'), which regulates the use by WTO Members of measures adopted to ensure food safety and protect the life and health of humans, animals and plants from pests and diseases;[224] (3) the *Agreement on Textiles and Clothing*, which provided for the gradual elimination by 1 January 2005 of quotas on textiles and clothing (and is no longer in force);[225] (4) the *Agreement on Technical Barriers to Trade* (the '*TBT Agreement*'), which regulates the use by WTO Members of technical regulations, standards and procedures to test conformity with these regulations and standards;[226] (5) the *Agreement on Trade-Related Investment Measures* (the '*TRIMS Agreement*'), which provides that WTO Members' regulations dealing with foreign investments must respect the obligations in Article III (national treatment obligation) and Article XI (prohibition on quantitative restrictions) of the GATT 1994;[227] (6) the *Agreement on Implementation of Article VI of the General Agreement on Tariffs and Trade 1994* (the '*Anti-Dumping Agreement*'), which provides for detailed rules on the use of anti-dumping measures;[228] (7) the *Agreement on Implementation of Article VII of the General Agreement on Tariffs and Trade 1994* (the '*Customs Valuation Agreement*'), which sets out in detail the rules to be used by national customs authorities for valuing goods for customs purposes;[229] (8) the *Agreement on Preshipment Inspection*, which regulates activities relating to the verification of the quality, the quantity, the price and/or the customs classification of goods to be exported;[230] (9) the *Agreement on Rules of Origin*, which provides for negotiations aimed at the harmonisation of non-preferential rules of origin, sets out disciplines to govern the application of these rules of origin, both during and after the negotiations on harmonisation, and sets out disciplines applicable to preferential rules of origin;[231] (10) the *Agreement on Import Licensing Procedures*, which sets out rules on the use of import licensing procedures;[232] (11) the *Agreement on Subsidies and Countervailing Measures* (the '*SCM Agreement*'), which provides for detailed rules on subsidies and the use of countervailing measures;[233] and (12) the *Agreement on Safeguards*, which provides for detailed rules on the use of safeguard measures and prohibits the use of voluntary export restraints.[234]

223 See below, pp. 489–91, 655–7 and 867–9. 224 See below, p. 936. 225 See below, p. 140.
226 See below, pp. 885–9. 227 See below, pp. 381 and 482–8. 228 See below, pp. 699–701.
229 See below, pp. 454–7. 230 See below, pp. 514–16. 231 See below, pp. 458–61.
232 See below, pp. 496–8. 233 See below, pp. 698–9. 234 See below, pp. 631–4.

The WTO Members adopted on 27 November 2014, the Protocol of Amendment to insert the *Agreement of Trade Facilitation* into Annex 1A of the *WTO Agreement.*[235] This agreement was agreed on at the Bali Ministerial Conference in December 2013 and will enter into force once two-thirds of the WTO Members complete their domestic ratification process.[236]

Most of the multilateral agreements on trade in goods provide for rules that are more detailed than, and sometimes possibly in conflict with, the rules contained in the GATT 1994. The Interpretative Note to Annex 1A addresses the relationship between the GATT 1994 and the other multilateral agreements on trade in goods. It states:

> In the event of conflict between a provision of the General Agreement on Tariffs and Trade 1994 and a provision of another agreement in Annex 1A to the Agreement Establishing the World Trade Organization (referred to in the agreements in Annex 1A as the 'WTO Agreement'), the provision of the other agreement shall prevail to the extent of the conflict.

However, it is only where a provision of the GATT 1994 and a provision of another multilateral agreement on trade in goods are *in conflict* that the provision of the latter will prevail. Provisions are in conflict where adherence to the one provision will necessarily lead to a violation of the other provision and the provisions cannot, therefore, be read as complementing each other.[237] While it is undisputed that a conflict exists when one provision *requires* what another provision *prohibits*, international lawyers tend to disagree on whether such a conflict may exist where one provision expressly *permits* what another provision *prohibits*.

If there is no conflict, both the GATT 1994 and the other relevant multilateral agreement on trade in goods apply. In *Argentina – Footwear (EC) (2000)*, the Appellate Body ruled with regard to the relationship between, and the application of, the safeguard provision of the GATT 1994 (Article XIX) and the *Agreement on Safeguards* that:

> [t]he GATT 1994 and the *Agreement on Safeguards* are *both* Multilateral Agreements on Trade in Goods contained in Annex 1A of the *WTO Agreement*, and, as such, are *both* 'integral parts' of the same treaty, the *WTO Agreement*, that are 'binding on all Members'. Therefore, the provisions of Article XIX of the GATT 1994 *and* the provisions of the *Agreement on Safeguards* are *all* provisions of one treaty, the *WTO Agreement*. They entered into force as part of that treaty at the same time. They apply equally and are equally binding on all WTO Members. And, as these provisions relate to the same thing, namely the application by

235 General Council, Decision of 27 November 2014, *Protocol Amending the Marrakesh Agreement Establishing the World Trade Organization*, WT/L/940, dated 28 November 2014, incorporating in Annex IA the *Agreement on Trade Facilitation*, Ministerial Decision of 7 December 2013, WT/MIN(13)/36 – WT/L/911, dated 11 December 2013. See below, pp. 511–12.

236 As of October 2016, ninety-four WTO Members have notified the WTO of their acceptance of the Protocol of Amendment. See www.tfafacility.org/ratifications.

237 Note that in international law, there is a strong presumption against conflict, as it can be assumed that countries will not undertake conflicting obligations.

Members of safeguard measures, the Panel was correct in saying that 'Article XIX of GATT and the Safeguards Agreement must *a fortiori* be read as representing an *inseparable package* of rights and disciplines which have to be considered in conjunction'.[238]

4.1.3 General Agreement on Trade in Services

The *General Agreement on Trade in Services* (the 'GATS') is the first ever multilateral agreement on trade in services. The GATS establishes a regulatory framework within which WTO Members can undertake and implement commitments for the liberalisation of trade in services. The GATS covers measures of Members affecting trade in services.[239] Trade in services is defined in Article I:2 of the GATS as the supply of a service: (1) from the territory of one Member into the territory of any other Member (cross-border supply); (2) in the territory of one Member to a service consumer of any other Member (consumption abroad); (3) by a service supplier of one Member, through a commercial presence in the territory of any other Member (supply through a commercial presence); and (4) by a service supplier of one Member, through the presence of natural persons of a Member in the territory of any other Member (supply through the presence of natural persons).[240] 'Services' includes any service in any sector except services supplied in the exercise of governmental authority.[241] The supply of services includes the production, distribution, marketing, sale and delivery of a service.[242] It is clear from the third mode of supply (i.e. supply through a commercial presence) that the GATS also covers measures relating to foreign investment by suppliers of services.

The GATS contains provisions on: most-favoured-nation treatment (Article II);[243] transparency (Article III);[244] increasing participation of developing countries (Article IV);[245] economic integration (Article V);[246] domestic regulation (Article VI);[247] recognition (Article VII);[248] emergency safeguard measures (Article X);[249] payments and transfers (Article XI);[250] restrictions to safeguard the balance of payments (Article XII);[251] government procurement (Article XIII);[252] general exceptions (Article XIV);[253] security exceptions (Article XIV *bis*);[254] subsidies (Article XV);[255] market access (Article XVI);[256] national treatment (Article XVII);[257] negotiation and schedules of specific commitments (Articles XIX to XXI);[258] dispute settlement (Articles XXII and XXIII);[259] and institutional issues (Articles XXIV to XXVI).[260] Attached to the GATS are a number of annexes, including the Annex on Article

238 Appellate Body Report, *Argentina – Footwear (EC) (2000)*, para. 81. On the context in which this finding was made and its practical implications, see below, pp. 632–3.
239 See Article I:1 of the GATS. See also below, p. 327.
240 See Article I:2(a)–(d) of the GATS. See also below, p. 330.
241 See Article I:3(b) of the GATS. See also below, pp. 328–9.
242 See Article XXVIII(b) of the GATS. See also below, p. 534.
243 See below, pp. 523–7. 244 See below, p. 534. 245 See below, p. 688. 246 See below, p. 92.
247 See below, pp. 536–7. 248 See below, p. 338. 249 See below, p. 658. 250 See below, p. 540.
251 See below, pp. 658–68. 252 See below, pp. 537–8. 253 See below, pp. 605–18. 254 See below, p. 623.
255 See below, pp. 91–101. 256 See below, pp. 518–20. 257 See below, pp. 399–42.
258 See below, pp. 521–2. 259 See below, p. 179. 260 See below, pp. 134–5.

II Exemptions,[261] the Annex on Movement of Natural Persons Supplying Services under the Agreement,[262] and the Annexes on Financial Services.[263] The Schedules of Specific Commitments, i.e. Services Schedules, of all WTO Members concerning their market access and national treatment commitments are also attached to the GATS and form an integral part thereof.[264]

On the relationship between the GATS and the GATT 1994, and in particular the question whether they are mutually exclusive agreements, the Appellate Body ruled in *EC – Bananas III (1997)*:

> The GATS was not intended to deal with the same subject-matter as the GATT 1994. The GATS was intended to deal with a subject-matter not covered by the GATT 1994, that is, with trade in services ... Given the respective scope of application of the two agreements, they may or may not overlap, depending on the nature of the measures at issue. Certain measures could be found to fall exclusively within the scope of the GATT 1994, when they affect trade in goods as goods. Certain measures could be found to fall exclusively within the scope of the GATS, when they affect the supply of services as services. There is yet a third category of measures that could be found to fall within the scope of both the GATT 1994 and the GATS. These are measures that involve a service relating to a particular good or a service supplied in conjunction with a particular good. In all such cases in this third category, the measure in question could be scrutinized under both the GATT 1994 and the GATS. However, while the same measure could be scrutinized under both agreements, the specific aspects of that measure examined under each agreement could be different. Under the GATT 1994, the focus is on how the measure affects the goods involved. Under the GATS, the focus is on how the measure affects the supply of the service or the service suppliers involved. Whether a certain measure affecting the supply of a service related to a particular good is scrutinized under the GATT 1994 or the GATS, or both, is a matter that can only be determined on a case-by-case basis.[265]

A measure restricting trade in bananas may thus be challenged under both the GATT 1994 (to the extent that it affects trade in bananas) and under the GATS (to the extent that it affects the supply of a service, such as wholesale trading in bananas).

4.1.4 Agreement on Trade-Related Aspects of Intellectual Property Rights

The *Agreement on Trade-Related Aspects of Intellectual Property Rights* (the '*TRIPS Agreement*') is not an agreement concerning trade as such or trade measures in the strict sense of the word. However, the value of many goods and services, particularly those traded by developed countries, is largely determined by the idea, the design or the invention they incorporate. If the value of such goods and services is not protected against the unauthorised use of the incorporated ideas, designs or inventions (for example, if a patented medicine produced by

261 See below, pp. 331–2. 262 See below, pp. 532–3. 263 See below, p. 617.

264 See Article XX of the GATS. The Final Act also contains an Understanding on Commitments in Financial Services that is not part of the *WTO Agreement* but which was the basis for post-1995 negotiations on the further liberalisation of trade in financial services. See below, p. 525.

265 Appellate Body Report, *EC – Bananas III (1997)*, para. 221.

a pharmaceutical company of Member A is produced without authorisation as a generic medicine in Member B),[266] trade in these products or services will be affected. For that reason, developed-country Members sought and obtained the inclusion in the *WTO Agreement* of an agreement specifying minimum standards of protection of intellectual property rights and requiring the effective enforcement of these rights. The *TRIPS Agreement* covers seven types of intellectual property: (1) copyright and related rights (Articles 9–14);[267] (2) trademarks (Articles 15–21);[268] (3) geographical indications (Articles 22–24);[269] (4) industrial designs (Articles 25–26); (5) patents (Articles 27–34);[270] (6) layout designs (topographies) of integrated circuits (Articles 35–38); and (7) undisclosed information, including trade secrets (Article 39). With regard to these types of intellectual property, the *TRIPS Agreement* provides for minimum standards of protection.

Furthermore, the *TRIPS Agreement* requires WTO Members to ensure that enforcement procedures and remedies are available to permit effective action against any act of infringement of the intellectual property rights referred to above, including civil and administrative procedures and remedies, provisional measures and criminal procedures (Articles 41–61).[271] Pursuant to Articles 3 and 4 of the *TRIPS Agreement*, each WTO Member must accord other WTO Members national treatment and most-favoured-nation treatment, subject to a number of exceptions.[272] The *TRIPS Agreement* frequently refers to, and incorporates by reference, provisions of other intellectual property agreements, such as the *Paris Convention for the Protection of Industrial Property (1967)*, the *Berne Convention for the Protection of Literary and Artistic Works (1971)*, the *Rome Convention for the Protection of Performers, Producers of Phonograms and Broadcasting Organizations (1961)* and the *Washington Treaty on Intellectual Property in Respect of Integrated Circuits (1989)*, making provisions of these agreements applicable to all WTO Members.[273]

4.1.5 Understanding on Rules and Procedures for the Settlement of Disputes

The *Understanding on Rules and Procedures for the Settlement of Disputes*, commonly referred to as the *Dispute Settlement Understanding* or DSU, is arguably the single most important achievement of the Uruguay Round negotiations.[274] The WTO dispute settlement system applies to all disputes between WTO

266 For a further discussion on the issue of patent protection of medicines, see below, pp. 1039–42.
267 See below, pp. 1021–9.
268 See below, pp. 1013–21. 269 See below, pp. 1029–33. 270 See below, pp. 1033–42.
271 See below, pp. 1042–7. 272 See below, pp. 1003–11.
273 e.g. Article 2.1 of the *TRIPS Agreement* (with regard to the *Paris Convention*); and Article 9 of the *TRIPS Agreement* (with regard to the *Berne Convention*). See below, p. 1002.
274 See below, pp. 167–8.

Members arising under the WTO agreements. In 1997, Renato Ruggiero, then Director-General of the WTO, referred to the dispute settlement system provided for by the DSU as:

> in many ways the central pillar of the multilateral trading system and the WTO's most individual contribution to the stability of the global economy.[275]

Building on almost fifty years of experience with settling trade disputes in the context of the GATT 1947, the DSU sets out a dispute settlement system, characterised by compulsory jurisdiction, short time frames, an appellate review process and an enforcement mechanism.[276] The DSU provides for rules: on the coverage and scope of the dispute settlement system, its administration, its objectives and its operation (Articles 1–3);[277] on mandatory pre-litigation consultations (Article 4);[278] on good offices, conciliation and mediation (Article 5);[279] on the panel process (Articles 6–16 and 18–20)[280] on the appellate review process (Articles 17–20);[281] on compliance and enforcement (Articles 21–22);[282] on banning unilateral action (Article 23);[283] on least-developed-country Members (Article 24);[284] on arbitration as an alternative means of dispute settlement (Article 25);[285] on non-violation and situation complaints (Article 26);[286] and on the role of the WTO Secretariat (Article 27).[287] Attached to the DSU are appendices on: the WTO agreements covered by the DSU (Appendix 1);[288] on special or additional rules and procedures on dispute settlement contained in WTO agreements (Appendix 2);[289] on the working procedures of panels (Appendix 3);[290] and on expert review groups (Appendix 4).[291]

4.1.6 Trade Policy Review Mechanism

It is very important for WTO Members, their companies and citizens involved in trade to be informed as fully as possible about trade regulations and policies of other WTO Members. To that end, many of the WTO agreements referred to above provide for an obligation on WTO Members to inform or notify the WTO of new trade regulations, measures or policies or changes to existing ones.[292] In addition, the WTO conducts regular reviews of individual Members' trade policies. The procedural rules for these reviews are set out in Annex 3 on the *Trade Policy Review Mechanism*.[293]

275 As reported in WTO, *Trading into the Future*, 2nd revised edn (WTO, 2001), 38.
276 For a full discussion of the WTO dispute settlement system, see below, pp. 164–294.
277 See below, pp. 167, 209, 224. 278 See below, pp. 268–70.
279 See below, p. 187. 280 See below, pp. 285–92.
281 See below, pp. 278–85. 282 See below, pp. 285–92.
283 See below, p. 169. 284 See below, pp. 292–3. 285 See below, pp. 297–8.
286 See below, pp. 180–1 287 See below. pp. 219–20. 288 See below, p. 170.
289 See below, p. 931. 290 See below, pp. 271–8. 291 See below, p. 230.
292 See e.g. below, pp. 646 and 926. 293 See below, pp. 102–4.

4.1.7 Plurilateral Agreements

All agreements in Annexes 1 to 3 are binding on all WTO Members. Membership of the WTO is conditional upon the acceptance of these 'multilateral agreements'. In contrast, Annex 4 contains two agreements, referred to as 'plurilateral agreements', which are only binding on those WTO Members that are a party to these agreements.[294] The first plurilateral agreement is the *Agreement on Trade in Civil Aircraft*. This is, in fact, an agreement concluded during the 1979 Tokyo Round of trade negotiations. Attempts during the Uruguay Round to negotiate a new agreement failed. The *Agreement on Trade in Civil Aircraft*, which is of particular interest to the United States and the European Communities: (1) provides for duty-free trade in civil aircraft and parts thereof; (2) prohibits quotas and other trade restrictions on civil aircraft; and (3) addresses the issue of government support to aircraft manufacturers. Disputes relating to this agreement *cannot* be brought to the WTO settlement system for resolution. The second plurilateral agreement is the *Agreement on Government Procurement*, as revised in 2014.[295] Under GATT 1994 and GATS rules, WTO Members are free to discriminate in favour of domestic products, services and service suppliers in the context of government procurement.[296] This is an important exception to the national treatment obligations of Article III of the GATT 1994 and Article XVII of the GATS.[297] Under the terms of the *Agreement on Government Procurement*, the parties have agreed to accord national treatment in respect of government procurement above certain thresholds by designated government entities.[298] The Agreement also obliges parties to make procurement opportunities public, and to provide for a procedure allowing unsuccessful bidders to challenge a procurement award. Disputes under the *Agreement on Government Procurement* can be, and have already been, brought to the WTO dispute settlement system for resolution.[299]

4.1.8 Protocols of Accession

Since 1995, thirty-six protocols of accession have been adopted, one for each new WTO Member. As explicitly stated in these protocols of accession, they are an integral part of the *WTO Agreement*. Paragraph 1.2, second sentence, of China's Accession Protocol, for example, states:

> This Protocol, which shall include the commitments referred to in paragraph 342 of the Working Party Report, shall be an integral part of the WTO Agreement.

294 When the *WTO Agreement* entered into force on 1 January 1995, Annex 4 included four plurilateral agreements. However, two of those agreements – the *International Dairy Agreement* and the *International Bovine Meat Agreement* – were terminated at the end of 1997.

295 The revised WTO *Agreement on Government Procurement* (GPA) came into force on 6 April 2014, two years from the date on which the Protocol amending the Agreement was adopted in March 2012.

296 See below, pp. 512–14.

297 See Article III:8(a) of the GATT 1994 and Article XIII of the GATS. See also below, pp. 347–50.

298 See below, pp. 512–13. 299 e.g. Panel Report, *Korea – Procurement (2000)*. See below, p. 60.

The precise legal status of accession protocols has been the subject of discussion among WTO Members. This discussion arose in the context of the question of whether provisions providing for exceptions, such as Article XX of the GATT 1994, could be invoked to justify measures that are inconsistent with obligations under an accession protocol.[300] In *China – Rare Earths (2014)*, China argued that to the extent that a provision of an accession protocol would be an integral part of the GATT 1994, Article XX thereof would be available to justify measures that are inconsistent with that provision. The Appellate Body disagreed. Upholding the panel's finding, it ruled in *China – Rare Earths (2014)*:

> In our view, Paragraph 1.2 of China's Accession Protocol serves to build a bridge between the package of Protocol provisions and the package of existing rights and obligations under the WTO legal framework. Nonetheless, neither obligations nor rights may be automatically transposed from one part of this legal framework into another. The fact that Paragraph 1.2 builds such a bridge is only the starting point, and does not in itself answer the questions of whether there is an objective link between *an individual provision* in China's Accession Protocol and existing obligations under the Marrakesh Agreement and the Multilateral Trade Agreements, and whether China may rely on an exception provided for in those agreements to justify a breach of such Protocol.[301]

4.1.9 Ministerial Decisions and Declarations

Finally, note the twenty-seven Ministerial Decisions and Declarations, which together with the *WTO Agreement* form the Final Act adopted in Marrakesh in April 1994 at the end of the Uruguay Round negotiations. These Ministerial Decisions and Declarations include, for example, the *Decision on Measures in Favour of Least-Developed Countries*,[302] the *Declaration on the Contribution of the World Trade Organization to Achieving Greater Coherence in Global Economic Policymaking*[303] and the *Decision on the Application and Review of the Understanding on Rules and Procedures Governing the Settlement of Disputes*.[304] These Ministerial Decisions and Declarations do not generate specific rights and obligations for WTO Members, which can be enforced through WTO dispute settlement.

4.2 Other Sources of WTO Law

The *WTO Agreement*, with its multiple annexes, is undisputedly the *principal* source of WTO law. However, this Agreement is not the only source of WTO law. As indicated above, there are also other sources of WTO law. But note, however,

300 See below, pp. 427–3.

301 Appellate Body Reports, *China – Rare Earths (2014)*, para. 5.74. For a detailed discussion on the availability of Article XX of the GATT 1994 to justify measures inconsistent with a provision of China's Accession Protocol, see below, pp. 427–3.

302 See www.wto.org/english/docs_e/legal_e/legal_e.htm. 303 See *ibid.*, and below, p. 105. 304 See *ibid.*

that these other sources are *not* of the same nature or on the same legal footing as the WTO agreements discussed above. The WTO agreements (with the exception of the *Trade Policy Review Mechanism* and the *Agreement on Trade in Civil Aircraft*) provide for specific legal rights and obligations for WTO Members that can be enforced through WTO dispute settlement. *Most* of the other sources reviewed below do *not* in and of themselves provide for specific, *enforceable* rights or obligations. They do, however, assist in 'clarifying' or 'defining' the law that applies between WTO Members on WTO matters. This subsection discusses in turn: (1) dispute settlement reports; (2) acts of WTO bodies; (3) agreements concluded in the context of the WTO; (4) customary international law; (5) general principles of law; (6) other international agreements; (7) subsequent practice of WTO Members; (8) the negotiating history of WTO agreements; and (9) teachings of the most highly qualified publicists.

4.2.1 Dispute Settlement Reports

Reports of WTO panels and the Appellate Body are the most important source of clarifications and interpretations of WTO law. In addition, reports of GATT 1947 panels are also relevant. In principle, adopted panel and Appellate Body reports are only binding on the parties to a particular dispute.[305] However, in *Japan – Alcoholic Beverages II (1996)* the Appellate Body held with regard to prior GATT panel reports:

> Adopted panel reports are an important part of the GATT *acquis*. They are often considered by subsequent panels. They create legitimate expectations among WTO Members, and, therefore, should be taken into account where they are relevant to any dispute.[306]

In adopting this approach, the Appellate Body was clearly inspired by the practice of the International Court of Justice. Article 59 of the *Statute of the International Court of Justice* provides that the decisions of the Court have no binding force except between the parties and in respect of the particular case. However, as the Appellate Body noted:

> [t]his has not inhibited the development by that Court (and its predecessor) of a body of case law in which considerable reliance on the value of previous decisions is readily discernible.[307]

Referring to its reasoning in *Japan – Alcoholic Beverages II (1996)*, the Appellate Body stated in *US – Shrimp (Article 21.5 – Malaysia) (2001)*:

> This reasoning applies to adopted Appellate Body Reports as well. Thus, in taking into account the reasoning in an adopted Appellate Body Report – a Report, moreover, that was

305 On the adoption of panel and Appellate Body reports, see below, pp. 210–11. With respect to *unadopted* reports, see Panel Report, *Japan – Alcoholic Beverages II (1996)*, para. 6.10. See also Panel Report, *EU – Footwear (China) (2012)*, para. 7.83.

306 Appellate Body Report, *Japan – Alcoholic Beverages II* (1996) 108.

307 *Ibid.*, fn. 30.

directly relevant to the Panel's disposition of the issues before it – the Panel did not err. The Panel was correct in using our findings as a tool for its own reasoning.[308]

In *US – Oil Country Tubular Goods Sunset Reviews (2005)*, the Appellate Body stated that:

following the Appellate Body's conclusions in earlier disputes is not only appropriate, but is what would be expected from panels, especially where the issues are the same.[309]

The issue of the role of precedent in WTO dispute settlement was critical in *US – Stainless Steel (Mexico) (2008)*. At issue was the Appellate Body's case law – fiercely contested by the United States – on the WTO consistency of the zeroing methodology to calculate a dumping margin.[310] The panel in *US – Stainless Steel (Mexico) (2008)* found that it was not, 'strictly speaking, bound by previous Appellate Body or panel decisions that have addressed the same issue'. The panel noted that the Appellate Body had stated in earlier cases that panels were 'expected' to take into account relevant adopted reports. The panel stated that it had done so, but that, after careful consideration of these reports, it decided that it had 'no option but to respectfully disagree with the line of reasoning developed by the Appellate Body regarding the WTO consistency of simple zeroing in periodic reviews'.[311] Because it fundamentally disagreed with the Appellate Body's interpretation of the relevant WTO provision, and agreed with the different interpretation advocated by the United States in this and prior cases, the panel 'felt compelled to depart' from the Appellate Body's well-established case law.[312] In its report in this case, the Appellate Body stated that it was 'deeply concerned' about the panel's decision to depart from the Appellate Body's well-established case law as the panel's approach had 'serious implications for the proper functioning of the WTO dispute settlement system'.[313] The Appellate Body stated:

It is well settled that Appellate Body reports are not binding, except with respect to resolving the particular dispute between the parties. This, however, does not mean that subsequent panels are free to disregard the legal interpretations and the *ratio decidendi* contained in previous Appellate Body reports that have been adopted by the DSB.[314]

The Appellate Body recalled in this respect its rulings in *Japan – Alcoholic Beverages II (1996)* and *US – Oil Country Tubular Goods Sunset Reviews (2005)*, both quoted above, and furthermore stated that:

[d]ispute settlement practice demonstrates that WTO Members attach significance to reasoning provided in previous panel and Appellate Body reports. Adopted panel and Appellate Body reports are often cited by parties in support of legal arguments in dispute settlement

308 Appellate Body Report, *US – Shrimp (Article 21.5 – Malaysia) (2001)*, para. 109.
309 Appellate Body Report, *US – Oil Country Tubular Goods Sunset Reviews (2005)*, para. 188.
310 On the zeroing methodology to calculate a dumping margin, see below, pp. 712–20.
311 See Panel Report, *US – Stainless Steel (Mexico) (2008)*, para. 7.106. 312 See *ibid.*
313 Appellate Body Report, *US – Stainless Steel (Mexico) (2008)*, para. 162. 314 *Ibid.*, para. 158.

proceedings, and are relied upon by panels and the Appellate Body in subsequent disputes ... Thus, the legal interpretation embodied in adopted panel and Appellate Body reports becomes part and parcel of the *acquis* of the WTO dispute settlement system.[315]

In other words, whereas the *application* of a provision may be regarded as confined to the context of the case in which it takes place, the relevance of *clarification* contained in adopted Appellate Body reports is not limited to the application of a particular provision in a specific case.[316] Most importantly, the Appellate Body found that:

[e]nsuring 'security and predictability' in the dispute settlement system, as contemplated in Article 3.2 of the DSU, implies that, *absent cogent reasons*, an adjudicatory body will resolve the same legal question in the same way in a subsequent case.[317]

According to the Appellate Body, 'consistency and stability in the interpretation' of rights and obligations of Members under the covered agreements is 'essential to promote "security and predictability" in the dispute settlement system, and to ensure the "prompt settlement" of disputes'.[318] The panel's failure to follow previously adopted Appellate Body reports addressing the same issues 'undermines the development of a coherent and predictable body of jurisprudence clarifying Members' rights and obligations under the covered agreements as contemplated under the DSU'.[319]

A few months after the adoption of the Appellate Body report in *US – Stainless Steel (Mexico) (2008)*, the panel in *US – Continued Zeroing (2009)*, while expressing doubts regarding the correctness of the Appellate Body's relevant case law but recognising that this case law was well established, stated:

[W]e consider that providing prompt resolution to this dispute in this manner will best serve the multiple goals of the DSU, and, on balance, is furthered by following the Appellate Body's adopted findings in this case.[320]

The panel in *US – Continued Zeroing (2009)* thus concluded that the United States acted inconsistently with the *Anti-Dumping Agreement* and the GATT 1994 by applying the zeroing methodology in periodic reviews. The United States appealed this finding of inconsistency, but – not surprisingly – the Appellate Body upheld the panel's finding. In a concurring opinion, one of the members of the division of the Appellate Body hearing the appeal in *US – Continued Zeroing (2009)*, stated as follows:

In matters of adjudication, there must be an end to every great debate. The Appellate Body exists to clarify the meaning of the covered agreements. On the question of zeroing it has

315 *Ibid.*, para. 160. The Appellate Body also observed that, 'when enacting or modifying laws and national regulations pertaining to international trade matters, WTO Members take into account the legal interpretation of the covered agreements developed in adopted panel and Appellate Body reports'. See *ibid.*

316 See *ibid.*, para. 161. 317 *Ibid.*, para. 160. Emphasis added. 318 *Ibid.* 319 *Ibid.*, para. 161.

320 Panel Report, *US – Continued Zeroing (2009)*, para. 7.182.

spoken definitively. Its decisions have been adopted by the DSB. The membership of the WTO is entitled to rely upon these outcomes.[321]

As discussed above, the Appellate Body ruled in *US – Stainless Steel (Mexico) (2008)* that, *absent cogent reasons*, an adjudicatory body will resolve the same legal question in the same way in a subsequent case.[322] To date, the Appellate Body has not yet defined the concept of 'cogent reasons'. The panel in *China – Rare Earths (2014)* stated, however, that it 'may be understood as referring generally to a high threshold'.[323] The panel in *US – Countervailing and Anti-Dumping Measures (China) (2014)* ruled on 'cogent reasons' the following:

> In our view, bearing in mind the Appellate Body's particular function in the WTO dispute settlement system, reasons that could support but would not compel a different interpretative result to the one ultimately adopted by the Appellate Body would not rise to the level of 'cogent' reasons. To our minds, 'cogent' reasons, i.e. reasons that could in appropriate cases justify a panel in adopting a different interpretation, would encompass, inter alia: (i) a multilateral interpretation of a provision of the covered agreements under Article IX:2 of the WTO Agreement that departs from a prior Appellate Body interpretation; (ii) a demonstration that a prior Appellate Body interpretation proved to be unworkable in a particular set of circumstances falling within the scope of the relevant obligation at issue; (iii) a demonstration that the Appellate Body's prior interpretation leads to a conflict with another provision of a covered agreement that was not raised before the Appellate Body; or (iv) a demonstration that the Appellate Body's interpretation was based on a factually incorrect premise.[324]

4.2.2 Acts of WTO Bodies

Acts of WTO bodies, such as authoritative interpretations under Article IX:2 of the *WTO Agreement* and waivers under Article IX:3 of the *WTO Agreement*, are clearly a source of WTO law which give rise to rights and obligations for WTO Members that can be enforced through the dispute settlement system.[325] In this regard, consider, for example, the ruling of the Appellate Body in *EC – Bananas III (1997)* on the European Communities' invocation of the Lomé Waiver as a justification for its breach of the MFN treatment obligations of Articles I:1 and XIII of the GATT 1994.[326]

Other acts of WTO bodies are also sources of WTO law and must be taken into account by panels and the Appellate Body. They are a part of WTO law. However, the Appellate Body has not yet ruled explicitly on whether such acts of WTO bodies provide for rights and obligations which can be enforced through the dispute settlement system.[327] In *US – Clove Cigarettes (2012)*, the issue arose whether paragraph 5.2 of the *Doha Ministerial Decision on Implementation-Related*

321 Appellate Body Report, *US – Continued Zeroing (2009)*, para. 312.

322 Appellate Body Report, *US – Stainless Steel (Mexico) (2008)*, para. 160. Emphasis added.

323 Panel Report, *China – Rare Earths (2014)*, paras. 7.59–7.61.

324 Panel Report, *US – Countervailing and Anti-Dumping Measures (China) (2014)*, para. 7.317. On the multilateral interpretation of a provision under Article IX:2 of the *WTO Agreement*, see below, p. 58.

325 For a discussion of authoritative interpretations and waivers, see below, pp. 149 and 150.

326 See Appellate Body Report, *EC – Bananas III (1997)*, para. 183. On Article I:1 and XIII of the GATT 1994, see below, pp. 307–21 and 540, respectively.

327 For a discussion on the scope of the jurisdiction of the WTO dispute settlement system, see below, pp. 168–79.

Issues and Concerns, which defined the term 'reasonable interval' in Article 2.12 of the *TBT Agreement* as meaning in most cases a period of at least six months, could be relied on by the complainant in that case.[328] After ruling that paragraph 5.2 of the Decision was not an authoritative interpretation under Article IX:2 of the *WTO Agreement* (because it was not adopted in conformity with the procedure set out in that provision),[329] the Appellate Body ruled with regard to paragraph 5.2 that:

> a decision adopted by Members, *other than* a decision adopted pursuant to Article IX:2 of the *WTO Agreement*, may constitute a 'subsequent agreement' on the interpretation of a provision of a covered agreement under Article 31(3)(a) of the *Vienna Convention*.[330]

Therefore, to the extent that an act of a WTO body is a 'subsequent agreement' between Members on the interpretation (or application) of a WTO provision, panels and the Appellate Body *must*, pursuant to Article 31.3(a) of the *Vienna Convention on the Law of Treaties*, take into account such an act when interpreting that provision.[331]

In *US – Tuna II (Mexico) (2012)*, the same issue arose but now with regard to a decision of a technical committee, the TBT Committee.[332] The Appellate Body ruled with regard to the TBT Committee *Decision on Principles for the Development of International Standards, Guides and Recommendations with Relation to Articles 2, 5, and Annex 3 to the Agreement* that:

> the TBT Committee Decision can be considered as a 'subsequent agreement' within the meaning of Article 31(3)(a) of the *Vienna Convention*. The extent to which this Decision will inform the interpretation and application of a term or provision of the *TBT Agreement* in a specific case, however, will depend on the degree to which it 'bears specifically' on the interpretation and application of the respective term or provision.[333]

4.2.3 Agreements Concluded in the Framework of the WTO

As discussed in more detail in Chapter 2, WTO Members have over the past twenty years negotiated and concluded, in the framework of the WTO: (1) multilateral agreements providing further market access commitments for specific services and service suppliers, such as the 1995 *Second Protocol to the General Agreement on Trade in Services*;[334] (2) plurilateral agreements providing for the elimination of customs duties and other duties and charges on information technology products, such as the 2015 *Agreement on Expansion in Trade in Information Technology Products (ITA-II)*;[335] (3) a multilateral agreement on trade facilitation, namely the 2013 *Agreement on Trade Facilitation*;[336] and (4)

328 On Article 2.12 of the *TBT Agreement*, see below, pp. 927–8. 329 See below, p. 148.
330 Appellate Body Report, *US – Clove Cigarettes (2012)*, para. 260.
331 On Article 31.3(a) of the *Vienna Convention*, see below, pp. 196–7.
332 With regard to the legal status of a decision of the SPS Committee, namely, the Decision on Equivalence (see below, p. 974), see Panel Report, *US – Poultry (China) (2010)*, para. 7.136.
333 Appellate Body Report, *US – Tuna II (Mexico) (2012)*, para. 372. 334 See below, p. 92.
335 See below, p. 430. 336 See below, pp. 511–12.

thirty-six protocols of accession.[337] All these agreements are an integral part of the *WTO Agreement* and the rights and obligations provided therein are enforceable in WTO dispute settlement.

As also discussed in more detail in Chapter 2, WTO Members are currently engaged in the negotiations of two plurilateral agreements: the *Trade in Services Agreement* (TiSA) and the *Environmental Goods Agreement* (EGA).[338] Note, however, that the negotiations on the TiSA are not taking place in the framework of the WTO. The negotiations on the EGA take place within the framework of the WTO but it is currently not clear whether EGA rights and obligations will be enforceable in WTO dispute settlement.[339]

4.2.4 Customary International Law

Article 3.2, second sentence, of the DSU provides:

> The Members recognize that [the WTO dispute settlement system] serves to preserve the rights and obligations of Members under the covered agreements, and to clarify the existing provisions of those agreements *in accordance with customary rules of interpretation of public international law.*[340]

The DSU thus explicitly refers to customary international law on treaty interpretation and makes this law applicable in the context of the WTO. The status in WTO law of other rules of customary international law is less clear. In *Korea – Procurement (2000)*, the panel went so far as to hold that customary international law applies:

> to the extent that the WTO treaty agreements do not 'contract out' from it.[341]

Customary international law is part of general international law and the rules of general international law are, in principle, binding on all States. Each new State, as well as each new treaty, is automatically born into it. This, however, does not answer the question whether any such customary international law could be the basis for claims or defences, or, in other words, would be enforceable in WTO dispute settlement. This question is further discussed below.[342]

In addition to the rules of customary international law on treaty interpretation, explicitly referred to in Article 3.2 of the DSU, the Appellate Body and panels have referred to and applied other rules of customary international law. The Appellate Body has made reference to and/or applied customary rules on dispute settlement and, in particular, on standing,[343] representation by private counsel,[344] the burden of proof,[345] and the treatment of municipal law.[346] In addition, panels have referred to and/or applied customary rules on State responsibility and, in particular, rules

337 See above, p. 53. 338 See below, p. 101 339 See below, p. 101.
340 Emphasis added. See also below, pp. 190–3.
341 Panel Report, *Korea – Procurement (2000)*, para. 7.96. This panel report was not appealed.
342 See below, p. 77. 343 See e.g. Appellate Body Report, *EC – Bananas III (1997)*, para. 133.
344 See *ibid.*, para. 10. See also below, pp. 259–60.
345 See e.g. Appellate Body Report, *US – Wool Shirts and Blouses (1997)*, 14. See also below, pp. 179–85.
346 See e.g. Appellate Body Report, *India – Patents (US) (1998)*, para. 65.

on countermeasures[347] and attribution.[348] The customary rules on State responsibility and, in particular, rules on compensation of harm caused by unlawful acts, are often referred to as rules that do not apply between WTO Members because WTO law, and in particular the DSU, provides for a *lex specialis*.[349]

4.2.5 General Principles of Law

Like customary international law, general principles of law are part of general international law. As noted in the previous section, rules of general international law are, in principle, binding on all States. Both panels and the Appellate Body have referred to and used general principles of law as a basis for their rulings or in support of their reasoning. In *US – Shrimp (1998)*, the Appellate Body noted with regard to the principle of good faith:

> The chapeau of Article XX is, in fact, but one expression of the principle of good faith. This principle, at once a general principle of law and a general principle of international law, controls the exercise of rights by states. One application of this general principle, the application widely known as the doctrine of *abus de droit*, prohibits the abusive exercise of a state's rights and enjoins that whenever the assertion of a right 'impinges on the field covered by [a] treaty obligation, it must be exercised *bona fide*, that is to say, reasonably'. An abusive exercise by a Member of its own treaty right thus results in a breach of the treaty rights of the other Members and, as well, a violation of the treaty obligation of the Member so acting.[350]

The principle of due process,[351] the principle of proportionality,[352] the principle of judicial economy,[353] the principle of non-retroactivity[354] and the interpretative principles of effectiveness,[355] of *in dubio mitius*[356] and of *ejusdem generis*[357] have also been applied by panels and the Appellate Body in numerous reports.

347 See e.g. Decision by the Arbitrators, *Brazil – Aircraft (Article 22.6 – Brazil) (2002)*, para. 3.44 and fn. 46 and 48.

348 See e.g. Panel Report, *Canada – Dairy (1999)*, para. 7.77 and fn. 427; and Panel Report, *Turkey – Textiles (1999)*, para. 9.33.

349 See below, pp. 208–9. Note that Article 55 of the International Law Commission's *Articles on Responsibility of States for Internationally Wrongful Acts*, entitled 'Lex specialis', provides that '[t]hese articles do not apply where and to the extent that the conditions for the existence of an internationally wrongful act or the content or implementation of the international responsibility of a State are governed by special rules of international law'.

350 Appellate Body Report, *US – Shrimp (1998)*, para. 158. See also Appellate Body Report, *US – FSC (2000)*, para. 166.

351 See e.g. Appellate Body Report, *US – Shrimp (1998)*, para. 182; Appellate Body Report, *Chile – Price Band System (2002)* para. 144 See also below, pp. 264–5.

352 See e.g. Appellate Body Report, *US – Shrimp (1998)*, para. 141. See also Appellate Body Report, *US – Cotton Yarn (2001)*, para. 120.

353 See e.g. Appellate Body Report, *US – Wool Shirts and Blouses (1998)*, 17–20; Appellate Body Report, *Australia – Salmon (1998)*, paras. 219–26; Appellate Body Report, *US – Tuna II (Mexico) (2012)*, para. 403; and Appellate Body Report, *Argentina – Import Measures (2015)*, paras. 5.185–5.195.

354 See Appellate Body Report, *Brazil – Desiccated Coconut (1997)*, 179; Appellate Body Report, *EC – Bananas III (1997)*, para. 235; Appellate Body Report, *Canada – Patent Term (2000)*, paras. 71–4; and Appellate Body Report, *EC – Aircraft (2011)*, para. 672.

355 See Appellate Body Report, *US – Gasoline (1996)*, 16; Appellate Body Report, *Korea – Dairy (2000)*, para. 81; and Appellate Body Report, *India – Agricultural Products (2015)*, para. 5.24.

356 See e.g. Appellate Body Report, *EC – Hormones (1998)*, fn. 154. Note that, in *China – Publications and Audiovisual Products (2010)*, the Appellate Body discussed, but did not apply, the principle of *in dubio mitius*. See Appellate Body Report, *China – Publications and Audiovisual Products (2010)*, para. 411. See also below, pp. 190–9.

357 See Appellate Body Report, *US – Large Civil Aircraft (2nd complaint) (2012)*, para. 615; and Appellate Body Reports, *US – COOL (2012)*, para. 444.

4.2.6 Other International Agreements

Other international agreements can also be relevant as sources of WTO law. This is definitely the case when these agreements are incorporated or referred to specifically in a WTO agreement. As mentioned above, the *TRIPS Agreement* incorporates a number of provisions of other intellectual property agreements, such as the *Paris Convention (1967)* and the *Berne Convention (1971)*, thus making provisions of these agreements part of WTO law, applicable to all WTO Members and enforceable through WTO dispute settlement. The *SCM Agreement* refers to the *OECD Arrangement on Guidelines for Officially Supported Export Credits.*[358]

Whether, and, if so, to what extent, other international agreements *not* referred to in a WTO agreement can be a source of WTO law, is a controversial issue. This issue is of particular relevance to multilateral environmental agreements (MEAs) and International Labour Organization (ILO) conventions on minimum labour standards. It is broadly accepted that these other international agreements may play a role in the interpretation of WTO legal provisions. Please refer to the discussion in Chapter 3 on the relevance of other international agreements under Article 31 of the *Vienna Convention* in the interpretation of WTO agreements. It suffices to note here that, in *US – Shrimp (1998)*, the Appellate Body made use of principles laid down in multilateral environmental agreements such as the *United Nations Convention on the Law of the Sea*, the *Convention on Biological Diversity* and the *Convention on the Conservation of Migratory Species of Wild Animals* (CITES) to interpret Article XX(g) of the GATT 1994.[359]

However, it is contested whether these other international agreements (i.e. international agreements to which WTO agreements do not explicitly refer) can be a source of WTO law in the sense that they provide rights and obligations for Members that can be invoked as a basis for claims or defences in WTO dispute settlement. As discussed below, Joost Pauwelyn has argued in this respect that WTO Members cannot base a claim before a WTO panel on the violation of rights and obligations set out in a non-WTO agreement. However, in his opinion, WTO Members that are parties to a particular non-WTO agreement can invoke in a WTO dispute between them the rules of that agreement as a defence against a claim of violation of WTO rules.[360] This position is, however, quite controversial. Other WTO scholars do not agree that rules of non-WTO agreements can be invoked before a panel or the Appellate Body as a defence.[361] In *Mexico – Soft Drinks (2006)*, the Appellate Body held that it saw:

> no basis in the DSU for panels and the Appellate Body to adjudicate non-WTO disputes. Article 3.2 of the DSU states that the WTO dispute settlement system 'serves to preserve the

358 See Annex I(k) to the *SCM Agreement*. Grants by governments of export credits that meet the requirements of this Arrangement are not considered an export subsidy prohibited under the *SCM Agreement*.

359 See below, pp. 229–30.

360 See J. Pauwelyn, *Conflict of Norms in Public International Law: How WTO Law Relates to Other Norms of International Law* (Cambridge University Press, 2003), 473 and 491.

361 See below, pp. 67–8.

> rights and obligations of Members under the *covered agreements*, and to clarify the existing provisions of *those agreements*'. Accepting Mexico's interpretation would imply that the WTO dispute settlement system could be used to determine rights and obligations outside the covered agreements.[362]

The Appellate Body stated that adjudication of disputes under non-WTO agreements 'is not the function of panels and the Appellate Body as intended by the DSU'.[363]

The issue of the status of non-WTO agreements in WTO law was raised again in *Peru – Agricultural Products (2015)*. In that case, Guatemala challenged the WTO consistency of the imposition by Peru of additional duties on imports of a number of agricultural products. These additional duties were determined using a mechanism known as the 'Price Range System' (PRS). According to Guatemala, these additional duties resulting from the PRS were inconsistent with Article 4.2 of the *Agreement on Agriculture* and Article II:1(b) of the *GATT 1994*. In its defence, Peru *inter alia* argued that the provisions of the Free Trade Agreement (FTA) between Peru and Guatemala allowed it to maintain a WTO-inconsistent PRS. Peru referred in this regard to Article 41 of the *Vienna Convention on the Law of Treaties*, which concerns agreements modifying multilateral treaties between certain parties only and which states in relevant part:

> 1. Two or more of the parties to a multilateral treaty may conclude an agreement to modify the treaty as between themselves alone if:
>   (a) the possibility of such a modification is provided for by the treaty; or
>   (b) the modification in question is not prohibited by the treaty and:
>   (i) does not affect the enjoyment by the other parties of their rights under the treaty or the performance of their obligations;
>   (ii) does not relate to a provision, derogation from which is incompatible with the effective execution of the object and purpose of the treaty as a whole.

The Appellate Body found that it was 'not convinced that such alleged modification as between the FTA parties would be subject to Article 41 of the Vienna Convention'.[364] The Appellate Body noted that:

> the WTO agreements contain specific provisions addressing amendments, waivers, or exceptions for regional trade agreements, which prevail over the general provisions of the Vienna Convention, such as Article 41.[365]

According to the Appellate Body, this is particularly true in the case of free trade agreements because Article XXIV and the Enabling Clause of the GATT 1994 and Article V of the GATS specifically allow for the derogation from certain WTO disciplines in free trade agreements, *but* only when the conditions set out

362 Appellate Body Report, *Mexico – Soft Drinks (2006)*, para. 56. Emphasis added. On the underlying legal issue (the applicability of Article XX(d) of the GATT 1994, invoked by Mexico as a defence) and the context in which this statement was made (whether Mexico's measure claimed to have been taken in response to the alleged breach by the United States of its obligations under the NAFTA could be justified under Article XX(d)), see below, pp. 564–73.
363 Appellate Body Report, *Mexico – Soft Drinks (2006)*, para. 78.
364 Appellate Body Report, *Peru – Agricultural Products (2015)*, para. 5111. 365 *Ibid.*, para. 5.112.

in these provisions are fulfilled.[366] Free trade agreements concluded between WTO Members modify the WTO rights and obligations of these Members, and are, in this sense, a source of WTO law, only when the conditions set out in these provisions are fulfilled.

4.2.7 Subsequent Practice of WTO Members

As discussed in Chapter 3, 'subsequent practice' within the meaning of Article 31.3(b) of the *Vienna Convention* must, pursuant to this provision, be taken into account in the interpretation of the rights and obligations set out in the *WTO Agreement*.[367] Therefore, 'subsequent practice' of the WTO, WTO bodies or WTO Members must be considered to be a source of WTO law. An isolated act, however, is generally not sufficient to establish subsequent practice.[368] In *Japan – Alcoholic Beverages II (1996)*, the Appellate Body stated that 'subsequent practice' within the meaning of Article 31.3(b) must be:

> a 'concordant, common and consistent' sequence of acts or pronouncements which is sufficient to establish a discernible pattern implying the agreement of the parties regarding its interpretation.[369]

4.2.8 Negotiating History of WTO Agreements

Pursuant to Article 32 of the *Vienna Convention*, the negotiating history of an agreement may serve as a supplementary means of interpretation. However, as noted in Chapter 3, there is no formally recorded negotiating history of the WTO agreements, and WTO panels and the Appellate Body have given limited weight to various country-specific and often conflicting negotiating proposals and very little importance to the often contradictory and self-serving *personal* recollections of negotiators.[370] Note that the negotiating history of the GATT 1947 and the 1948 *Havana Charter on an International Trade Organization* have been of some use in the interpretation of the provisions of the GATT 1994.[371]

4.2.9 Teachings of Publicists

Finally, pursuant to Article 38.1 of the *Statute of the International Court of Justice*, the 'teachings of the most highly qualified publicists' are subsidiary means for the determination of rules of international law. WTO panels and the Appellate Body occasionally cite the writings of scholars in support of their reasoning where they found them persuasive.[372]

366 See *ibid.*, paras. 5.112–5.116. 367 See below, pp. 193–7. 368 See *ibid.*

369 Appellate Body Report, *Japan – Alcoholic Beverages II (1996)*, 106–7. See also Appellate Body Report, *Chile – Price Band System (2002)*, paras. 213–14 and 272; Appellate Body Report, *US – Gambling (2005)*, paras. 192–3; and Appellate Body Report, *EC – Chicken Cuts (2005)*, paras. 259, 265–6 and 271–3.

370 See below, pp. 197–8.

371 See e.g. in Panel Report, *US – Countervailing and Anti-Dumping Measures (China) (2014)*, paras. 7.286–90 (regarding the interpretation of Article X:3(b) of the GATT 1994).

372 See e.g. Appellate Body Report, *US – Wool Shirts and Blouses (1998)*, fn. 15 and 16 (on burden of proof). The scholarly writings cited by panels and the Appellate Body often concern general issues of international law or specific legal problems under relevant national law, rather than scholarly writings on WTO law.

5 WTO LAW IN CONTEXT

Earlier in this chapter, WTO law was described as a significant component of international economic law, which itself is an important part of public international law. However, the relationship between WTO law and *international law* deserves to be explored further. Likewise, the relationship between WTO law and *national law* also raises questions that need to be addressed.

5.1 WTO Law and International Law

This section on WTO law and international law deals in turn with: (1) the position of WTO law in international law; and (2) conflicts between WTO agreements and other international agreements.

5.1.1 WTO Law as an Integral Part of International Law

In the past, most handbooks on international law and general courses on this topic gave little or no attention to international trade law. International law commonly excluded the regulation of international trade from its purview. In his 1996 Hague Lecture, Donald McRae noted:

> International trade law and international economic law were not of concern to international lawyers; trade and economic law were not central to the way international lawyers defined their discipline ... Particular social traditions may have played some role in this. In some countries the idea of commerce, of buying and selling, or of economic matters generally, was not viewed with favour. The professions of medicine and law were respectable; those engaged in business did not have the same social status. This, no doubt, helped fashion the attitudes of international lawyers to international trade law and international economic law ... The field of trade law, and that of economic matters generally, are seen as closely intertwined with the field of economics which is perceived as presenting a barrier to those without formal training in that discipline. In his extremely insightful work, *International Law in a Divided World*, Professor Cassese, who does recognize the significance of international economic relations to the study of international law, and devotes a full chapter to it, nevertheless states that 'international economic relations are usually the hunting ground of a few specialists, who often jealously hold for themselves the key to this abstruse admixture of law and economics'.[373]

However, in the current era of globalisation, economic issues and problems have moved to the front lines of international relations and international law. In a later article, McRae described the work of the WTO as the 'new frontier' of international law.[374] The importance of international economic law and international trade law is now broadly recognised among international lawyers.

373 D. McRae, *The Contribution of International Trade Law to the Development of International Law*, Academy of International Law, *Recueil des Cours*, Volume 260, 1996, 114–15.

374 D. McRae, 'The WTO in International Law: Tradition Continued or New Frontier?', *Journal of International Economic Law*, 2000, 30 and 41.

It should be noted that, in the past, international trade lawyers were also quite ambivalent with regard to the relationship between international trade law and international law. Many considered international trade law to be a self-contained system of international law.[375] This position has been discredited. International trade law, and in particular WTO law, is now generally considered to be an integral part of international law.

A genuine turning point in the relationship between international law and international trade law was the Appellate Body Report in *US – Gasoline (1996)*. In this report, its very first, the Appellate Body ruled that Article 3.2 of the DSU, which directs panels and the Appellate Body to interpret the WTO agreements according to the 'customary rules of interpretation of public international law', reflects:

> a measure of recognition that the *General Agreement* is not to be read in clinical isolation from public international law.[376]

The discussion above of the sources of WTO law shows that WTO law is *not* a closed, self-contained system, isolated from the rest of international law.

5.1.2 Conflicts Between WTO Agreements and Other Agreements

It may happen that the rights and obligations of WTO Members under the WTO agreements are in conflict with their rights and obligations under other international agreements.[377] A classic example of such a conflict is the situation in which a multilateral environmental agreement (an MEA) obliges the parties to that agreement to impose quantitative restrictions on trade in certain products whereas the GATT 1994 prohibits such restrictions. Pascal Lamy has pointed out in this regard:

> The WTO, its treaty provisions and their interpretation, confirms the absence of any hierarchy between WTO norms and those norms developed in other forums: WTO norms do not supersede or trump other international norms.[378]

First, it should be noted that WTO rules should, if possible, be interpreted in such a way that they do not conflict with other rules of international law. As Gabrielle Marceau noted:

> [p]anels and the Appellate Body have the obligation to interpret the WTO provisions taking into account all relevant rules of international law applicable to the relations between the WTO Members. One of those rules is the general principle against conflicting interpretation

375 As reported by P. J. Kuijper, 'The Law of GATT as a Special Field of International Law: Ignorance, Further Refinement or Self-Contained System of International Law?', *Netherlands Yearbook of International Law*, 1994, 257.

376 Appellate Body Report, *US – Gasoline (1996)*, 16.

377 As mentioned above, while it is undisputed that a conflict exists when one provision *requires* what another provision *prohibits*, international lawyers tend to disagree on whether such a conflict may exist where one provision expressly *permits* what another provision *prohibits*. See above, p. 44.

378 P. Lamy, 'The Place of the WTO and Its Law in the International Legal Order', *European Journal of International Law*, 2007, 978.

(Article 31.3(c) together with 30 of the Vienna Convention). Therefore, in most cases the proper interpretation of the relevant WTO provisions – themselves often drafted in terms of specific prohibitions leaving open a series of WTO compatible alternative measures – should lead to a reading of the WTO provisions so as to avoid conflict with other treaty provisions.[379]

While there will undoubtedly be many instances in which an adjudicator can interpret WTO rules and non-WTO rules so as to avoid conflict, in some instances this will not be possible. As already briefly mentioned above, some scholars, and, in particular, Joost Pauwelyn, have taken a controversial view on the conflict of WTO rules with non-WTO rules.[380] Central to Pauwelyn's view is that most WTO obligations are essentially reciprocal in nature.[381] Reciprocal obligations are obligations from which parties to a multilateral treaty may deviate, as long as such deviation does not infringe the rights of third parties. Pauwelyn explains his view on the conflict between WTO rules and non-WTO rules as follows:

In the event of conflict involving WTO provisions, WTO provisions may not always prevail, including before a WTO panel. The trade obligations in the WTO treaty are of the 'reciprocal type'. They are not of an 'integral nature'. Hence, WTO provisions can be deviated from as between a limited number of WTO members only, as long as this deviation does not breach third party rights. Affecting the economic interests of other WTO members does not amount to breaching their WTO rights. Recognizing that WTO obligations are of a reciprocal nature allows for the taking into account of the diversity of needs and interests of different WTO members. It shows that in most cases of conflict between, for example, human rights and environmental conventions (generally setting out obligations of an 'integral type'), on the one hand, and WTO obligations (of the 'reciprocal' type), on the other, the WTO provisions will have to give way.[382]

Pauwelyn is of the view that, in case of conflict, rules of MEAs or other international agreements, such as human rights treaties or ILO conventions, may thus often prevail over rules of WTO law. However, Pauwelyn added:

the fact that non-WTO norms may ... prevail over the WTO treaty, even as before a WTO panel, does not mean that WTO panels must judicially enforce compliance with these non-WTO rules. Non-WTO rules may be part of the applicable law before a WTO panel, and hence offer, in particular, a valid legal defence against claims of WTO breach. However, they cannot form the basis of legal claims, the jurisdiction of WTO panels being limited to claims under WTO covered agreements only.[383]

This particular view of the relationship between WTO rules and conflicting rules of other international agreements is not shared by other WTO scholars. On the

379 G. Marceau, 'Conflicts of Norms and Conflicts of Jurisdictions: The Relationship Between the WTO Agreement and MEAs and Other Treaties', *Journal of World Trade*, 2001, 1129.

380 See above, p. 62.

381 Pauwelyn regards *reciprocal* obligations as a 'promise ... made towards each and every state individually' whereas he views *integral* obligations as a 'promise ... towards the collectivity of all state parties taken together'. See Pauwelyn, *Conflict of Norms in Public International Law*, 476.

382 *Ibid.*, 491. 383 *Ibid.*

contrary, Gabrielle Marceau has argued that WTO panels confronted with a conflict between a WTO rule and a non-WTO rule may perhaps have alternative courses of action to deal with the conflict, but that:

> [a]ny of these courses of action would be possible only to the extent that the conclusions reached by the panels do not constitute an amendment of the WTO, or do not add to or diminish the rights and obligations of WTO Members or do not affect the rights of third WTO Members.[384]

As Marceau noted, and as discussed in Chapter 3, it is prohibited for panels and the Appellate Body to 'add to or diminish the rights and obligations' of WTO Members, as provided for in the WTO agreements.[385] If panels or the Appellate Body were to allow a respondent to invoke a non-WTO rule in defence against a claim of violation of WTO law, would they then not, in fact, 'add to or diminish the rights and obligations' of WTO Members? As discussed above, in *Mexico – Soft Drinks (2006)*, the Appellate Body saw 'no basis in the DSU for panels and the Appellate Body to adjudicate non-WTO disputes'.[386] Note, however, that Martti Koskenniemi stated in this regard that although a tribunal may have jurisdiction only with regard to a specific instrument or instruments:

> it must always *interpret* and *apply* that instrument in its relationship to its normative environment – that is to say 'other' international law.[387]

As discussed above, in *Peru – Agricultural Products (2015)*, Peru invoked the provisions of a non-WTO agreement, namely its Free Trade Agreement with Guatemala, to defend the measure challenged by Guatemala.[388] According to Peru, Article 41 of the *Vienna Convention on the Law of Treaties* allows parties to a multilateral treaty to modify their obligations as between themselves. The Appellate Body was 'not convinced'.[389] It noted that:

> the WTO agreements contain specific provisions addressing amendments, waivers, or exceptions for regional trade agreements, which prevail over the general provisions of the Vienna Convention, such as Article 41.[390]

While the Appellate Body's finding in *Peru – Agricultural Products (2015)* specifically concerned regional trade agreements, the question arises whether its statement quoted above is also of relevance to other types of non-WTO agreements.

384 G. Marceau, 'Conflicts of Norms and Conflicts of Jurisdictions: The Relationship Between the WTO Agreement and MEAs and Other Treaties', *Journal of World Trade*, 2001, 1130.
385 See below, pp. 190–3.
386 Appellate Body Report, *Mexico – Soft Drinks (2006)*, para. 56.
387 M. Koskenniemi, *Report of the ILC Study Group, Fragmentation of International Law: Difficulties Arising from the Diversification and Expansion of International Law*. Doc.A/CN.4/L.682 and Add.1. and Corr.1, 2 May 2006, para. 423.
388 See above, p. 63. 389 Appellate Body Report, *Peru – Agricultural Products (2015)*, para. 5.111.
390 *Ibid.*, para. 5.112.

5.2 WTO Law and National Law

There are two aspects of the relationship between WTO law and national law that need to be examined: (1) the place of national law in WTO law; and (2) the place of WTO law in the domestic legal order.

5.2.1 National Law in WTO Law

With regard to the place of national law in WTO law, Article XVI:4 of the *WTO Agreement* states:

> Each Member shall ensure the conformity of its laws, regulations and administrative procedures with its obligations as provided in the annexed Agreements.

It is a general rule of international law, reflected in Article 27 of the *Vienna Convention on the Law of Treaties*, that:

> [a] party may not invoke the provisions of its internal law as justification for its failure to perform a treaty.

In *Brazil – Aircraft (Article 21.5 – Canada) (2000)*, the Appellate Body observed:

> We note Brazil's argument before the Article 21.5 Panel that Brazil has a contractual obligation under domestic law to issue PROEX bonds pursuant to commitments that have already been made, and that Brazil could be liable for damages for breach of contract under Brazilian law if it failed to respect its contractual obligations. In response to a question from us at the oral hearing, however, Brazil conceded that *a WTO Member's domestic law does not excuse that Member from fulfilling its international obligations.*[391]

Note, however, that, with regard to measures and actions by regional and local governments and authorities, Article XXIV:12 of the GATT 1994 provides:

> Each Member shall take such reasonable measures as may be available to it to ensure observance of the provisions of this Agreement by the regional and local governments and authorities within its territories.[392]

It follows that WTO Members are obliged to enforce compliance with the obligations under the GATT 1994 by regional and local governments and authorities *only* to the extent that they – i.e. the Members – dispose of the necessary constitutional powers to do so.[393] However, when in *EC – Selected Customs Matters (2006)* the European Union invoked Article XXIV:12 as a limitation of its obligation to administer its customs laws in 'a uniform ... manner' as required under Article X:3(a) of the GATT 1994, the panel found that:

391 Appellate Body Report, *Brazil – Aircraft (Article 21.5 – Canada) (2000)*, para. 46. Emphasis added.
392 See also the *Understanding on the Interpretation of Article XXIV of the General Agreement on Tariffs and Trade 1994*, para. 13.
393 T. Cottier and K. Schefer, 'The Relationship Between World Trade Organization Law, National Law and Regional Law', *Journal of International Economic Law*, 1998, 85–6. See also Panel Report, *US – Alcoholic and Malt Beverages*, paras. 5.79–5.80.

Article XXIV:12 of the GATT 1994 cannot be relied upon to attenuate nor to derogate from the provisions of the GATT 1994 (including Article X:3(a) of the GATT 1994), to which Article XXIV:12 of the GATT 1994 refers.[394]

Also note that – as discussed in Chapter 3 – Article 22.9 of the DSU states:

The dispute settlement provisions of the covered agreements may be invoked in respect of measures affecting their observance taken by regional or local governments or authorities within the territory of a Member. When the DSB has ruled that a provision of a covered agreement has not been observed, the responsible Member shall take such reasonable measures as may be available to it to ensure its observance. The provisions of the covered agreements and this Understanding relating to compensation and suspension of concessions or other obligations apply in cases where it has not been possible to secure such observance.[395]

The 1994 *Understanding on the Interpretation of Article XXIV of the GATT 1994* provides for a similar provision.[396] Note that the panel in *Brazil – Retreaded Tyres (2007)* found that the measures of Rio Grande do Sul, a state of the Federative Republic of Brazil, were attributable to Brazil as a WTO Member.[397] The panel also found in that case that the Brazilian government was ultimately responsible for ensuring that its constituent states respected Brazil's obligations under the WTO.[398]

With respect to the question of how panels and the Appellate Body should handle national law, the Appellate Body held in *India – Patents (US) (1998)* that, in public international law, an international tribunal may treat municipal law in several ways. Municipal law may serve as evidence of facts and may provide evidence of State practice. Municipal law may also constitute evidence of compliance or non-compliance with international obligations. The Appellate Body found support for this position in the ruling of the Permanent Court of International Justice in *Certain German Interests in Polish Upper Silesia*, in which the Court had observed:

It might be asked whether a difficulty does not arise from the fact that the Court would have to deal with the Polish law of July 14th, 1920. This, however, does not appear to be the case. From the standpoint of International Law and of the Court which is its organ, municipal laws are merely facts which express the will and constitute the activities of States, in the same manner as do legal decisions and administrative measures. The Court is certainly not *called upon to interpret* the Polish law as such; but there is nothing to prevent the Court's giving judgment on *the question whether or not*, in applying that law, *Poland is acting in conformity with its obligations* towards Germany under the Geneva Convention.[399]

394 Panel Report, *EC – Selected Customs Matters*, para. 7.144. See also Panel Report, *Canada – Gold Coins*, paras. 58–72; and Panel Report, *Canada – Provincial Liquor Boards (US) (1992)*, paras. 4.34–4.37.

395 See below, p. 178.

396 See *Understanding on the Interpretation of Article XXIV of the General Agreement on Tariffs and Trade 1994*, para. 14, last sentence.

397 See Panel Report, *Brazil – Retreaded Tyres (2007)*, para. 7.400.

398 See *ibid.*, para. 7.406. 399 [1926] PCIJ Rep., Series A, No. 7, 19. Emphasis added.

In *India – Patents (US) (1998)*, the Appellate Body thus concluded:

> It is clear that an examination of the relevant aspects of Indian municipal law ... is essential to determining whether India has complied with its obligations under Article 70.8(a). There was simply no way for the Panel to make this determination without engaging in an examination of Indian law. But, as in the *Certain German Interests in Polish Upper Silesia* case ... before the Permanent Court of International Justice, in this case, the Panel was not interpreting Indian law 'as such'; rather, the Panel was examining Indian law solely for the purpose of determining whether India had met its obligations under the *TRIPS Agreement*.[400]

Panels and the Appellate Body have been required in numerous disputes to ascertain the meaning of municipal law in order to determine whether the measure at issue was WTO-consistent. The Appellate Body ruled in *US – Hot-Rolled Steel (2001)* that:

> [a]lthough it is not the role of panels or the Appellate Body to interpret a Member's domestic legislation as such, it is permissible, indeed essential, to conduct a detailed examination of that legislation in assessing its consistency with WTO law.[401]

As to what needs to be examined in order to ascertain the meaning of municipal law, the Appellate Body ruled in *US – Carbon Steel (2002)* that in some cases the examination of the text of the relevant law on its face may suffice, while in other cases the examination would include:

> evidence of the consistent application of such laws, the pronouncements of domestic courts on the meaning of such laws, the opinions of legal experts and the writings of recognized scholars.[402]

In *US – Countervailing and Anti-Dumping Measures (2014)*, the Appellate Body stated:

> We consider that, in ascertaining the meaning of municipal law, a panel should undertake a holistic assessment of all relevant elements, starting with the text of the law and including, but not limited to, relevant practices of administering agencies.[403]

5.2.2 WTO Law in National Law

With respect to the role of WTO law in the national legal order, it should first be observed that, where a provision of national law allows different interpretations, this provision should, whenever possible, be interpreted in a manner that avoids any conflict with WTO law. In the United States, the European Union and elsewhere, national courts have adopted this doctrine of *treaty-consistent*

400 Appellate Body Reports, *India – Patents (US) (1998)*, para. 66. See also Appellate Body Report, *US – Section 211 Appropriations Act (2002)*, paras. 104–5; Appellate Body Report, *US – Carbon Steel (2002)*, para. 157; Appellate Body Report, *China – Auto Parts (2008)*, paras. 224–5; and Appellate Body Report, *China – Publications and Audiovisual Products (2009)*, paras. 177–8 and 187.

401 Appellate Body Report, *US – Hot-Rolled Steel (2001)*, para. 200.

402 Appellate Body Report, *US – Carbon Steel (2002)*, para. 157.

403 Appellate Body Report, *US – Countervailing and Anti-Dumping Measures (China) (2014)*, para. 4.101. See also Appellate Body Report, *US –Shrimp II (2015)*, para. 4.32.

interpretation. The European Court of Justice (ECJ) stated in 1996 in *Commission* v. *Germany (International Dairy Arrangement)* with regard to the GATT 1947:

> When the wording of secondary EC legislation is open to more than one interpretation, preference should be given as far as possible to the interpretation which renders the provision consistent with the Treaty ... Similarly, the primacy of international agreements concluded by the Community over the provisions of secondary Community legislation means that such provisions must, so far as is possible, be interpreted in a manner consistent with those agreements.[404]

The ECJ confirmed the doctrine of treaty-consistent interpretation of national/EC law with regard to the *WTO Agreement* in its judgments in *Hermès* (1998) and *Schieving-Nijstad* (2001).[405] The United States Supreme Court held already in 1804 in *Murray* v. *The Charming Betsy*:

> It has also been observed that an act of Congress ought never to be construed to violate the law of nations if any other possible construction remains.[406]

If a conflict between a provision of national law and a WTO law provision cannot be avoided through treaty-consistent interpretation, the question arises as to whether the provision of WTO law can be invoked before the national court to challenge the legality and validity of the provision of national law. Could a German importer of bananas challenge the EC's import regime for bananas in court on the basis that this regime was inconsistent with, for example, Articles I and XIII of the GATT 1994? Can a US beef exporter challenge the EU import ban on hormone-treated meat on the basis that this ban is inconsistent with the provisions of the *SPS Agreement*? Can a Brazilian steel exporter challenge an anti-dumping duty imposed by India on its hot-rolled steel before an Indian court on the basis that this duty is inconsistent with the provisions of the *Anti-Dumping Agreement*? This is the issue of the 'direct effect' of provisions of WTO law.[407] It is clear that, if provisions of WTO law were to have direct effect and could be invoked to challenge the legality of national measures, this would significantly increase the enforceability and effectiveness of these provisions, non-compliance with which could and would then be sanctioned by domestic courts.

There is a fierce academic debate on whether provisions of WTO law should be granted direct effect. On that debate, Cottier and Schefer wrote:

> Among the scholars writing on the topic of direct effect of international trade agreements, there are three that stand out as the main proponents of the two schools of thought on the

404 Judgment of the Court of 10 September 1996, *Commission of the European Communities* v. *Federal Republic of Germany (International Dairy Arrangement)*, Case C-61/94, EU:C:1996:313, para. 52.

405 See Judgment of the Court of 13 September 2001, *Schieving-Nijstad vof and Others* v. *Robert Groeneveld*, Case C-89/99, [2001] ECR I-5851; and Judgment of the Court of 15 June 1998, *Hermès International and FHT Marketing Choice BV*, Case 53/96, [1998] ECR I-3603.

406 *Murray* v. *The Charming Betsy*, 6 US (2 Cranch) 64 (1804).

407 In many jurisdictions, the issue of direct effect, i.e. the issue of direct invocability, is to be distinguished from the issue of direct applicability, i.e. the issue of whether a national act of transformation is necessary for an international agreement to become part of national law. On the latter issue, it should be noted that WTO law is directly applicable in the EU legal order. It became part of EU law without any act of transformation.

issue: Jan Tumlir and Ernst Ulrich Petersmann advocating direct effect and John H. Jackson for the critics of direct effect. A fourth author, Piet Eeckhout, has set out what we call an 'intermediate position' on the issue.[408]

With respect to the arguments of the advocates of direct effect of WTO rules, Cottier and Schefer noted:

> The late Jan Tumlir, whose main thesis supporting direct effect is followed by Ernst Ulrich Petersmann, looks at the direct effect of trade treaties as a weapon against inherently protectionist tendencies in domestic law systems. Tumlir and Petersmann set forth the idea of 'constitutionalizing' international trade principles, elevating the rights of an individual to trade freely with foreigners to the level of a fundamental right. To prevent the erosion of a state's sovereignty, Tumlir suggests granting individuals the right to invoke treaty provisions in front of their domestic courts. Allowing for standing in this way would be available to those citizens harmed by protectionist national policies put into effect by other national interest groups. Thus, direct effect widely defined 'helps to correct the asymmetries in the political process' ... Pleading for keeping the possibility of judicial review open to individuals, Jacques Bourgeois put it quite bluntly: 'Quite simply, what is in the end the use of making law, also international law, designed to protect private parties, if these private parties cannot rely on it?'[409]

For the advocates of direct effect of WTO rules, it is a necessary and effective 'weapon' against national governments that encroach on the right to trade freely with foreigners, a right these advocates consider to be a fundamental right.

John Jackson, and along with him many others, objected to the direct effect of WTO rules. Central to his position against the direct effect of WTO rules is that it might be dangerous for democracy and that it conflicts with the legitimate wish of legislatures to adapt international treaty language to their respective domestic legal systems. Cottier and Schefer noted:

> John Jackson ... basically supports US trade policies of denying direct effect due to the imbalances in the institutional balance of government it would cause domestically ... He does ... find the idea of granting standing and allowing for an international treaty to be superior to federal legislation (let alone the constitution) to be dangerous to the idea of democracy and democratic representation of individuals ... While Jackson acknowledges that governments have an obligation to abide by international commitments they undertake, direct effect is not necessary to ensure this. The stronger reasons for denying direct effect are what Jackson calls 'functional arguments'. These arguments include the fact that '[s]ome constitutions provide for very little democratic participation in the treaty-making process; for example, by giving no formal role to Parliaments or structuring the government so that control over foreign relations is held by certain elites'. There are also legitimate desires of legislatures to adapt international treaty language to their respective domestic legal systems (such as translating the obligations into the native language, using local terms for legal principles, or further explaining certain provisions). And, some governments may want the opportunity to implement the obligations in a national legislative process because '[...] the legislature desires to preserve the *option to breach* the treaty in its method of application'. Even such uses of the separate implementation process are legitimate in Professor Jackson's mind because 'some

408 T. Cottier and K. Schefer, 'The Relationship Between World Trade Organization Law, National Law and Regional Law', *Journal of International Economic Law*, 1998, 93.

409 *Ibid.*, 93–5.

> breaches may be "minor" and therefore *preferable to the alternative of refusing to join the treaty altogether*.[410]

An intermediate position in this debate on the direct effect of WTO law has been taken by Piet Eeckhout. Eeckhout opposes direct effect of WTO law, but concedes that, if a case has been specifically decided by the WTO dispute settlement system, domestic effect should be given to this decision. According to Eeckhout:

> [t]he reasons for not granting direct effect – whether it is the agreement's flexibility, or the division of powers between the legislature and the judiciary, or the respect for appropriate dispute settlement forums – cease to be valid where a violation is established.[411]

The *WTO Agreement* could have specified what effect its provisions are to have in the domestic legal order of WTO Members. However, it did not do so. Therefore, although each Member must fully execute the commitments that it has undertaken, it is free to determine the legal means appropriate for attaining that end in its domestic legal system. At present, most WTO Members, including the European Union, the United States, China, India, Japan, South Africa and Canada, refuse to give 'direct effect' to WTO law.[412] Only a few WTO Members give 'direct effect' to WTO law.[413] The European Court of Justice (ECJ) addressed the issue of whether it could review the legality of Community law in the light of WTO law in its judgment of 23 November 1999 in *Portugal* v. *Council*. As the ECJ did not want to deprive: (1) the European Union of the possibility for temporary non-compliance with WTO law provided for in Article 22 of the DSU (the temporary non-compliance argument);[414] and (2) the legislative or executive organs of the Union of the scope for manoeuvre with respect to compliance enjoyed by their counterparts in the Union's trading partners (the non-reciprocity argument),[415] it concluded:

> having regard to their nature and structure, the WTO agreements are not in principle among the rules in the light of which the Court is to review the legality of measures adopted by the Community institutions.[416]

In support of the conclusion reached, the ECJ noted that this interpretation corresponded to what was stated in the Preamble to the Council Decision of 22

410 *Ibid.*, 97–8.

411 P. Eeckhout, 'The Domestic Legal Status of the WTO Agreements: Interconnecting Legal Systems', *Common Market Law Review*, 1997, 53.

412 For an overview of whether specific WTO Members give direct effect to WTO law in their domestic legal order, see C. George and S. Orava (eds.), *A WTO Guide for Global Business* (Cameron May, 2002), 398.

413 See above, fn. 411.

414 See Judgment of the Court of 23 November 1999, *Portuguese Republic* v. *Council of the European Union*, Case C-149/96, [1999] ECR I-8395, para. 40. With respect to this possibility for temporary non-compliance with WTO law, see below, pp. 125–6.

415 See Judgment of the Court of 23 November 1999, *Portuguese Republic* v. *Council of the European Union*, Case C-149/96, [1999] ECR I-8395, para. 46.

416 *Ibid.*, para. 47. These arguments were reiterated in Judgment of the Court of 1 March 2005, *Van Parys* v. *Belgisch Interventie- en Restitutiebureau*, Case C-377/02, [2005] ECR I-1465; and Judgment of the Court of First Instance of 3 February 2005, *Chiquita* v. *Commission*, Case T-19/01. These arguments have been criticised by e.g. Advocate General Ruiz-Jarabo Colomer in his Opinion of 23 January 2007 in *Merck Genéricos-Produtos Farmacêuticos Lda* v. *Merck & Co. Inc. and Merck Sharp & Dohme Lda*, Case C-431/05, paras. 81–6.

December 1994 on the conclusion of the *WTO Agreement*. In the Preamble to this Decision, the Council of Ministers of the European Union stated that:

> [b]y its nature, the Agreement Establishing the World Trade Organization, including the Annexes thereto, is not susceptible to being directly invoked in Community or Member State courts.[417]

In its judgment of 14 December 2000 in *Dior* v. *TUK*, the ECJ confirmed its reasoning in *Portugal* v. *Council* and concluded that private persons cannot invoke WTO law before the courts by virtue of Community law.[418] As an exception to the general rule, the ECJ does, however, grant direct effect to provisions of the *WTO Agreement* when the European Union intended to implement a particular obligation assumed in the context of the WTO, *or* where the EU measure refers expressly to the precise provisions of the WTO agreements.[419] Note that, in the 2003 *Biret* v. *Council* cases, the ECJ left open the possibility for an action for damages against the European Union, in a situation in which an EU measure, which was found to be WTO-inconsistent, caused harm after the end of the reasonable period of time for withdrawal or modification of the WTO-inconsistent measure.[420] However, this possibility was excluded by the Court of First Instance (CFI) in the 2005 *Chiquita Brands* case.[421]

It is interesting to note that the domestic courts of several Member States of the European Union have accepted the direct effect of provisions of the *TRIPS Agreement*.[422] In 2013, however, the issue of whether Article 27 of the *TRIPS Agreement* has direct effect arose in *Daiichi Sankyo* v. *DEMO* as part of a larger

417 Council Decision 94/800/EC of 22 December 1994 concerning the conclusion on behalf of the European Community, as regards matters within its competence, of the agreements reached in the Uruguay Round multilateral negotiations, OJ 1994, L336, 1. Note that the European Commission and the Council of Ministers were in agreement on the issue of 'direct effect' of WTO law. The text adopted by the Council had been proposed by the European Commission.

418 See Judgment of the Court of 14 December 2000, *Parfums Christian Dior SA* v. *TUK Consultancy BV and Assco Gerüste GmbH* and *Rob van Dijk* v. *Wilhelm Layher GmbH & Co. KG and Layher BV*, Joined Cases C-300/98 and C-392/98, [2000] ECR I-11307, paras. 42–4.

419 In its judgment of 22 June 1989 in *Fediol* v. *Commission*, Case 70/87, [1989] ECR 1781, and its judgment of 7 May 1991 in *Nakajima* v. *Council*, Case 69/89, [1991] ECR I-2069, the ECJ gave direct effect to provisions of the GATT 1947 in these circumstances. The ECJ applied its *Fediol/Nakajima* case law to the provisions of the *WTO Agreement* in its judgment of 9 January 2003 in *Petrotub* v. *Council*, Case C-76/00 [2003] ECR I-79, para. 54. That these are the only two exceptions, even in situations where the WTO's Dispute Settlement Body has adopted a report finding the legislation at issue inconsistent with WTO law, was confirmed by the ECJ in its judgment of 1 March 2005 in *Van Parys* v. *Belgisch Interventie- en Restitutiebureau*, Case C-377/02, [2005] ECR I-1465, paras. 39–40 and 52. See also *Commission* v. *Rusal Armenal*, Case C21/14 P, paras. 41–50 wherein the ECJ in its judgment of 16 July 2015 held that the provision of the basic regulation cannot be considered to be a measure intended to ensure the implementation in the EU legal order of a particular obligation assumed in the context of the WTO due to absence of a co-relation between the basic regulation (which laid down rules applicable to imports from non-market economy WTO member countries) and the rules set forth in Article 2 of the *WTO Anti-Dumping Agreement* (which does not contain any specific rules directed to such category of countries).

420 See Judgment of the Court of 30 September 2003, *Biret International SA* v. *Council of the European Union*, Case C-93/02, [2003] ECR I-10497; and Judgment of the Court of 30 September 2003, *Etablissements Biret et Cie SA* v. *Council of the European Union*, Case C-94/02, [2003] ECR I-10565.

421 Judgment of the Court of First Instance of 3 February 2005, *Chiquita* v. *Commission*, Case T-19/01, paras. 156–70. See in this regard P. J. Kuijper, in G. Sacerdotti, A. Yanovich and J. Bohanes (eds.), *The WTO at Ten: The Contribution of the Dispute Settlement System* (Cambridge University Press, 2006), 277–8.

422 For Germany, see e.g. Bundesgerichtshof, Urteil vom 25.2.1999 – I ZR 118/96 – *Kopienversanddienst*; OLG München. For Ireland, see e.g. *Allen & Hanbury and Another, Controller of Patents, Designs and Trademarks* (1997); for the Netherlands, see e.g. Rb. 's-Gravenhage 1 April 1998 (kortgeding), BIE 2001, 119–22 Mistral/ Tiki – 45(1).

issue as to whether, after the entry into force of the *Treaty of Lisbon* in 2009, Article 27 of the *TRIPS Agreement* still falls – within a field for which the Member States have competence.[423] The ECJ answered the larger issue in the negative, agreeing with the European Commission that the rules on patentable subject matter in Article 27 of the *TRIPS Agreement* now fall within the field of the common commercial policy, in which the European Union has exclusive competence.[424] The ECJ, however, did not rule on the sub-issue of direct effect of Article 27 of the *TRIPS Agreement*.[425] In his Opinion in this case, Advocate General G. Cruz Villalón did address the issue of direct effect of Article 27 of the *TRIPS Agreement*, and, based on the content of Article 27, concluded that it does not have direct effect.[426]

With regard to the domestic law effect of WTO law in the United States, the *Restatement (Third) of Foreign Relations Law of the United States* provides:

> Since generally the United States is obligated to comply with a treaty as soon as it comes into force for the United States, compliance is facilitated and expedited if the treaty is self-executing ... Therefore, if the Executive Branch has not requested implementing legislation and Congress has not enacted such legislation, there is a strong presumption that the treaty has been considered self-executing by the political branches, and *should be considered self-executing by the courts*.[427]

In the United States, trade treaties have historically been granted direct effect in court.[428] As has been the case with a number of other recent trade agreements,[429] the approval of the *WTO Agreement* was made conditional upon the inclusion of a provision in the implementing legislation, explicitly denying direct effect to the Agreement.[430] As David Leebron noted:

> Although Congress specifically approved the agreements, it simultaneously provided 'no provision of any of the Uruguay Round Agreements, nor the application of any such provision to any person or circumstances, that is inconsistent with any law of the United States shall have effect'. Furthermore, Congress mandated that no person other than the United States 'shall have any cause of action or defence under any of the Uruguay Round Agreements' or challenge 'any action or inaction ... of the United States, any state, or any political subdivision of a state on the ground that such action or inaction is inconsistent' with one of those agreements. In short, the Uruguay Agreements themselves are unlikely to be directly applied in any proceedings other than a proceeding brought by the United States for the purpose of enforcing obligations under the agreements.[431]

423 See Judgment of the Court of 18 July 2013, *Daiichi Sankyo* v. *DEMO*, Case C-414/11, para. 40. Note also that in September 2016, the European Court of Justice held its hearing for *Opinion 2/15*, which regards the competence of the European Union to conclude a free-trade agreement with Singapore. *Opinion 2/15* will further delineate the scope of the European Union's exclusive competence in the field of trade policy.

424 See *ibid*., paras. 60 and 51.

425 See *ibid*., para. 62.

426 See Opinion in Case C-414/11, para. 104. Also see *ibid*., paras. 85, 89, 100–3.

427 *Restatement (Third) of Foreign Relations Law of the United States*, para. 111, Reporters' Notes, reproduced in B. Carter and P. Trimble, *International Law* (Little, Brown and Co., 1991), 151. Emphasis added.

428 See T. Cottier and K. Schefer, 'The Relationship Between World Trade Organization Law, National Law and Regional Law', *Journal of International Economic Law*, 1998, 107.

429 See e.g. the *North American Free Trade Agreement* (NAFTA), 17 December 1992.

430 See Uruguay Round Agreements Act of 1994, 19 USC §3512, Pub. L. No. 104–305 (1996), para. 102(c).

431 D. Leebron, 'Implementation of the Uruguay Round Results in the United States', in J. Jackson and A. Sykes (eds.), *Implementing the Uruguay Round* (Oxford University Press, 1997), 212.

Likewise, India denies direct effect to WTO law. Indian courts will not consider the consistency of any domestic statute vis-à-vis WTO law, as they are constitutionally barred from striking down domestic law on grounds of violation of international law. The issue of direct effect on WTO law in Indian courts arose in 2007 before the Madras High Court in *Novartis* v. *Union of India*.[432] At issue in *Novartis* v. *Union of India* was the decision of the Indian authorities to deny – on the basis of Section 3(d) of the Indian Patent Act – the pharmaceutical multinational Novartis a patent on Glivec, a cancer medicine, thereby allowing the production of cheap generic copies. Before the Madras High Court, Novartis challenged, *inter alia*, the consistency of Section 3(d) of the Indian Patent Act with the relevant provisions of the *TRIPS Agreement*. The Madras High Court held that, as the WTO provides a comprehensive mechanism for the settlement of disputes in the DSU, any disputes under WTO law are properly litigated through this mechanism.[433]

6 SUMMARY

Economic globalisation and, in particular, international trade can make a significant contribution to economic development and prosperity in developed as well as developing countries. International trade has realised this potential – albeit to varying degrees – in many countries. Over the past decades, this has been the case particularly in Asia. It is, however, undisputed that not all countries, and within countries not all sections of the population, have benefited from international trade. For the potential of international trade to be realised, there must be: (1) good governance at the national level; (2) a further reduction of trade barriers; (3) more development aid; and (4) better international cooperation and global governance of economic globalisation and international trade. More international trade will not automatically lead to rising prosperity for all countries and for all people. In fact, without national and international action in the four areas referred to above, international trade will not bring prosperity to all; on the contrary, it is likely to result in more income inequality, social injustice, environmental degradation and cultural homogenisation.

International rules on trade are necessary for four related reasons: (1) to restrain countries from taking trade-restrictive measures, and this both in their own interest and in the interest of the world economy; (2) to give traders and investors a degree of security and predictability regarding the trade policies of

432 See Judgment of the Madras High Court, dated 6 August 2007, published in *Madras Law Journal*, 2007, 1153, also available at http://judis.nic.in/chennai/qrydisp.asp?tfnm=11121.

433 The Madras High Court also refused to exercise its discretion to grant declaratory relief as it would serve no useful purpose to the petitioner.

other countries; (3) to allow for the effective protection and promotion of important societal values and interests (such as public health, a sustainable environment, consumer safety, cultural identity and minimum labour standards), while at the same time ensuring that countries maintain only those measures that are necessary for (or at the very least related to) the protection of these values and interests; and (4) to achieve a greater measure of equity in international economic relations.

WTO law, which is the core of international economic law, provides for rules on international trade. There are five groups of basic rules of WTO law: (1) the rules of non-discrimination; (2) the rules on market access; (3) the rules on unfair trade; (4) the rules on the conflict between trade liberalisation and other societal values and interests; and (5) institutional and procedural rules. The principal source of WTO law is the *WTO Agreement*, in force since 1 January 1995. The *WTO Agreement* is a short agreement (of sixteen articles) establishing the World Trade Organization, but it contains, in its annexes, a significant number of agreements with substantive and/or procedural provisions, such as the GATT 1994, the GATS, the *TRIPS Agreement* and the DSU. However, the *WTO Agreement* is not the only source of WTO law. There are also other sources of WTO law, although these other sources are neither of the same nature nor on the same legal footing as the WTO agreements discussed above. The WTO agreements (with the exception of two) provide for specific legal rights and obligations for WTO Members that can be enforced through WTO dispute settlement. *Most* of the other sources do *not* in and of themselves provide for specific, *enforceable* rights or obligations. They do, however, assist in 'clarifying' or 'defining' the law that applies between WTO Members on WTO matters. These other sources of WTO law include: (1) dispute settlement reports; (2) acts of WTO bodies; (3) agreements concluded in the framework of the WTO; (4) customary international law; (5) general principles of law; (6) other international agreements; (7) subsequent practice of WTO Members; (8) the negotiating history of WTO agreements; and (9) teachings of the most highly qualified publicists.

While for many years international trade law was not part of the mainstream of international law, WTO law is now firmly established as an integral part of public international law. However, the relationship between WTO rules and other, conflicting rules of public international law, such as rules of multilateral environmental agreements (MEAs), is controversial. A generally accepted view on this relationship is yet to emerge. With regard to the relationship between WTO law and the national law of WTO Members, it is undisputed that WTO Members must ensure that their respective national laws are consistent with WTO law. Note also that, while some WTO scholars forcefully plead for the granting of direct effect to WTO law in the domestic legal order of WTO Members, in most WTO Members a breach of WTO law cannot be challenged in domestic courts.

FURTHER READINGS

R. Howse, 'The World Trade Organization 20 Years On: Global Governance by Judiciary', *European Journal of International Law*, 2016, 27(1), 1–77.

E.-U. Petersmann, 'From Fragmentation to Constitutionalization of International Economic Law: Comments on Schneiderman's Constitutionalism', *European Yearbook of International Economic Law*, 2016, 46–66.

M. Matsushita, 'Implementing International Trade Agreements in Domestic Jurisdictions', *Journal of International Economic Law*, 2016, 0, 1–4.

L. Boisson de Chazournes, 'WTO and Non-Trade Issues: Inside/Outside WTO', *Journal of International Economic Law*, 2016, 19, 379–81.

F. Altemöller, 'A Future for Multilateralism? New Regionalism, Counter-Multilateralism and Perspectives for the World Trade System after the Bali Ministerial Conference', *Global Trade and Customs Journal*, 2015, 10(1), 42.

J. Hallaert, 'Importing Growth: The Critical Role of Imports in a Trade-Led Growth Strategy', *Journal of World Trade*, 2015, 49(1), 49–84.

J. Lopez-Gonzalez, P. Kowalski and P. Achard, 'Trade, Global Value Chains and Wage-Income Inequality', OECD Trade Policy Papers No. 182, 2015, OECD Publishing, Paris.

S. Priyadarshi and T. Biswas, 'The Role of Trade-Led Economic Growth in Fostering Development: Lessons for the Post-2015 Development Agenda', WTO Working Paper ERSD-2014–10, July 2014, World Trade Organization.

A. L. Cortez and M. Arda, 'Global Trade Rules for Supporting Development in the Post-2015 Era', CDP Background Paper No. 19 ST/ESA/2014/CDP/19, September 2014, Department of Economic and Social Affairs, United Nations.

L. Fontagné, J. Fouré and A. Keck, 'Simulating World Trade in the Decades Ahead: Driving Forces and Policy Implications', WTO Working Paper ERSD-2014–05, April 2014, World Trade Organization.

D. Dixit, 'Agricultural Value Chains and Food Security', *Journal of World Trade*, 2014, 48(5), 967–82.

E. N. Hannah, 'The Quest for Accountable Governance: Embedded NGOs and Demand Driven Advocacy in the International Trade Regime', *Journal of World Trade*, 2014, 48(3), 457–80.

K. Heydon, 'Plurilateral Agreements and Global Trade Governance: A Lesson from the OECD', *Journal of World Trade*, 2014, 48(5), 1039–56.

R. Banga, 'Measuring Value in Global Value Chains', Background Paper No. RVC-8, May 2013, UNCTAD.

P. C. Mavroidis, 'Free Lunches? WTO as Public Good, and the WTO's View of Public Goods', *European Journal of International Law*, 2012, 23(3), 731–42.

2 The World Trade Organization

CONTENTS

1 INTRODUCTION

The World Trade Organization was established and became operational on 1 January 1995. It is the youngest of all major international intergovernmental organisations and yet it is possibly – in spite of the challenges it currently faces – one of the most influential in these times of economic globalisation. As Marco Bronckers stated in 2001, it has 'the *potential* to become a key pillar of global governance'.[1] The WTO is also one of the most criticised international organisations.[2] In the late 1990s, it was referred to as '*un gouvernement mondial dans l'ombre*'.[3] Civil society opponents of the WTO considered it to be 'pathologically secretive, conspiratorial and unaccountable to sovereign States and their electorate'.[4] In these early years of the WTO, developing-country Members considered the WTO to be a 'rich men's club' and objected to their marginalisation in WTO negotiations and decision-making. While parts of civil society remain highly suspicious of the WTO, and the participation of many developing-country Members in WTO negotiations and decision-making can certainly still be improved, the criticism directed at the WTO is now primarily of a different nature. In recent years, developed- and developing-country Members alike have become disenchanted with the WTO for its apparent inability to bring long-running negotiations on further trade liberalisation to a successful close and to agree on new rules addressing the challenges international trade is facing in the twenty-first century.

As discussed in Chapter 1, in March 2013 WTO Director-General Pascal Lamy compared the multilateral trading system to a computer, and noted that, while the 'hardware' of the system was sufficient, the 'software' was in need of an upgrade.[5] This chapter deals with both the 'hardware' and some of the 'software' of the multilateral trading system. It discusses the distinctive features of the WTO as the principal intergovernmental organisation for international trade and successively addresses: (1) the origins of the WTO; (2) the mandate of the WTO, i.e. its objectives and functions; (3) the membership and institutional structure of the WTO; and (4) decision-making in the WTO.

2 THE ORIGINS OF THE WTO

The origins of the WTO lie in the *General Agreement on Tariffs and Trade* of 1947, now commonly referred to as the 'GATT 1947' but for almost five decades just referred to as the 'GATT'. The study of these origins is relevant because the decisions, procedures and customary practices of the GATT 1947 still guide the WTO in its actions. Article XVI:1 of the *WTO Agreement* states:

> Except as otherwise provided under this Agreement or the Multilateral Trade Agreements, the WTO shall be guided by the decisions, procedures and customary practices followed by the Contracting Parties to GATT 1947 and the bodies established in the framework of GATT 1947.

1 M. Bronckers, 'More Power to the WTO?', *Journal of International Economic Law*, 2001, 41 (reproduced by permission of Oxford University Press). Emphasis added.
2 See below, fn. 4 on p. 82.
3 M. Khoh, 'Un gouvernement mondial dans l'ombre', *Le Monde Diplomatique*, May 1997. Translation: 'A lurking world government'.
4 G. de Jonquières, 'Prime Target for Protests: WTO Ministerial Conference', *Financial Times*, 24 September 1999.
5 See Pascal Lamy, 'Changing Landscape of International Trade', www.wto.org/english/news_e/sppl_e/sppl271_e.htm.

This section will discuss: (1) the genesis of the GATT and its operation as the *de facto* international organisation for international trade until the end of 1994; and (2) the GATT Uruguay Round of Multilateral Trade Negotiations (1986–94) and the emergence of the WTO, operational as of 1 January 1995.

2.1 The General Agreement on Tariffs and Trade of 1947

For almost five decades, the GATT was the *de facto* international organisation for international trade. This subsection deals with: (1) the genesis of the GATT and the stillbirth of the International Trade Organization (ITO); and (2) the success and failure of the GATT as *de facto* international trade organisation.

2.1.1 The GATT 1947 and the International Trade Organization

The history of the GATT begins in December 1945 when the United States invited its wartime allies to enter into negotiations to conclude a multilateral agreement for the reciprocal reduction of tariffs on trade in goods. These multilateral tariff negotiations took place in the context of a more ambitious project on international trade. At the proposal of the United States, the newly established United Nations Economic and Social Council adopted a resolution, in February 1946, calling for a conference to draft a charter for an 'International Trade Organization'.[6] At the 1944 Bretton Woods Conference, where the International Monetary Fund (IMF) and the International Bank for Reconstruction and Development (the 'World Bank') were established, the problems of trade had not been taken up as such, but the Conference did recognise the need for a comparable international institution for trade to complement the IMF and the World Bank.[7] A Preparatory Committee was established in February 1946 and met for the first time in London in October 1946 to work on the charter of an international organisation for trade on the basis of a proposal by the United States. The work continued from April to November 1947 in Geneva. As John Jackson explained:

> The 1947 Geneva meeting was actually an elaborate conference in three major parts. One part was devoted to continuing the preparation of a charter for a major international trade institution, the ITO. A second part was devoted to the negotiation of a multilateral agreement to reduce tariffs reciprocally. A third part concentrated on drafting the 'general clauses' of obligations relating to the tariff obligations. These two latter parts together would constitute the General Agreement on Tariffs and Trade. The 'general clauses' of the draft GATT imposed obligations on nations to refrain from a variety of trade-impeding measures.[8]

The negotiations on the GATT advanced well in Geneva, and by October 1947 the negotiators had reached an agreement. The negotiations on the ITO, however,

6 1 UN ECOSOC Res. 13, UN Doc. E/22 (1946). For an overview of the negotiations of the GATT 1947 and the ITO with references to official documents, see *Analytical Index: Guide to GATT Law and Practice* (WTO, 1995), 3–6.
7 See J. Jackson, *The World Trade Organization: Constitution and Jurisprudence* (Royal Institute of International Affairs, 1998), 15–16.
8 *Ibid.*, 16.

were more difficult and it was clear, towards the end of the 1947 Geneva meeting, that the *ITO Charter* would not be finished before 1948. Although the GATT was intended to be attached to the *ITO Charter*, many negotiators felt that it was not possible to wait until the *ITO Charter* was finished to bring the GATT into force. According to Jackson, there were two main reasons for this:

> First, although the tariff concessions were still secret, the negotiators knew that the content of the concessions would begin to be known. World trade patterns could thus be seriously disrupted if a prolonged delay occurred before the tariff concessions came into force. Second, the US negotiators were acting under the authority of the US trade legislation which had been renewed in 1945 ... But the 1945 Act expired in mid-1948. Thus, there was a strong motivation on the part of the United States to bring the GATT into force before this Act expired.[9]

It was therefore decided to bring the provisions of the GATT into force immediately. However, this created a new problem. Under the provisions of their constitutional law, some countries could not agree to certain obligations of the GATT (and, in particular, those obligations that might require changes to national legislation) without submitting this agreement to their parliaments. Since they anticipated the need to submit the final draft of the *ITO Charter* to their parliaments in late 1948 or the following year, they feared that 'to spend the political effort required to get the GATT through the legislature might jeopardise the later effort to get the ITO passed'.[10] Therefore, they preferred to take the *ITO Charter* and the GATT to their legislatures as one package.

To resolve this problem, on 30 October 1947, eight of the twenty-three countries that had negotiated the GATT 1947 signed the 'Protocol of Provisional Application of the General Agreement on Tariffs and Trade' (PPA). Pursuant to this Protocol, these Contracting Parties undertook *to apply provisionally as from 1 January 1948* Parts I and III of the GATT 1947 in full, and Part II 'to the fullest extent not inconsistent with existing legislation'.[11] Part II contained most of the substantive provisions, the application of which could require the modification of national legislation and thus the involvement of the legislature. The other fifteen of the original twenty-three Contracting Parties also soon agreed to the provisional application of the GATT 1947 through the PPA. According to the PPA, a GATT Contracting Party was entitled to maintain any provision of its legislation, which was inconsistent with a GATT Part II obligation. The PPA thus provided for an 'existing legislation exception', also referred to as 'grandfather rights'. This was quite 'convenient' and explains why the GATT 1947 itself was never adopted by the Contracting Parties. Until 1996, the provisions of the GATT 1947 were applied through the PPA of 30 October 1947.

9 *Ibid.*, 17–18. 10 *Ibid.*, 18.

11 GATT BISD, Volume IV, 77. Part I of the GATT 1947 contained the MFN obligation and the obligation regarding tariff concessions, and Part III procedural provisions.

In March 1948, the negotiations on the *ITO Charter* were successfully completed in Havana. The Charter provided for the establishment of the ITO, and set out basic rules and disciplines for international trade and other international economic matters. However, the *ITO Charter* never entered into force. While the United States had been the initiator of, and driving force behind, the negotiations on the *ITO Charter*, the United States Congress could not agree to approve it. In 1951, President Truman eventually decided that he would no longer seek congressional approval of the *ITO Charter*. Since no country was interested in establishing an international organisation for trade of which the United States, the world's leading economy and trading nation, would not be a member, the ITO was 'stillborn'. As the ITO was intended to complete the Bretton Woods structure of international economic institutions, its demise left a significant gap in that structure.

2.1.2 The GATT as a *de facto* International Organisation for Trade

In the absence of an international organisation for trade, countries gradually turned, from the early 1950s onwards, to the only existing multilateral 'institution' for trade, the GATT 1947, to handle problems concerning their trade relations.[12] Although the GATT was conceived as a multilateral *agreement* for the reduction of tariffs, and *not* an international *organisation*, it would successfully 'transform' itself – in a pragmatic and incremental manner – into a *de facto* international organisation. The 'institutional' provisions in the GATT 1947 were scant.[13] However, over the years, the GATT generated – through experimentation and trial and error – some fairly elaborate procedures for conducting its business.

The GATT was very successful in reducing tariffs on trade in goods, in particular on industrial goods from developed countries. In eight rounds of negotiations between 1947 and 1994,[14] the average level of tariffs imposed by developed countries on industrial products was brought down from over 40 per cent to less than 4 per cent.[15] The first five rounds of negotiations (Geneva (1947), Annecy (1949), Torquay (1951), Geneva (1956) and Dillon (1960–1)) focused on the reduction of tariffs. As from the Kennedy Round (1964–7) onwards, however, the negotiations would increasingly focus on non-tariff barriers (which were becoming a more serious barrier to trade than tariffs). With respect to the reduction of non-tariff barriers, the GATT was notably less successful than it was

12 A second and more modest attempt in 1955 to establish an 'Organization for Trade Cooperation' also failed because the US Congress was again unwilling to give its approval.

13 See Article XXV of the GATT 1947, entitled 'Joint Action by the Contracting Parties'.

14 The first of these rounds of negotiations, in 1947, led to the agreement of the GATT 1947 itself. See above, pp. 82–3.

15 See World Bank, *World Development Report 1987*, 134–35. See also below, pp. 84–8. Note that in a December 2015 VOX column, entitled 'The Urban Legend: Pre-GATT Tariffs of 40%', Chad Bown and Douglas Irwin suggested that the average tariffs in 1947 were around 22 per cent, rather than 40 per cent. See http://voxeu.org/article/myth-40-pre-gatt-tariffs.

with the reduction of tariffs. Negotiations on the reduction of non-tariff barriers were much more complex and, therefore, required, *inter alia*, a more 'sophisticated' institutional framework than that of the GATT. The Kennedy Round produced very few results on non-tariff barriers. The Tokyo Round (1973–9) produced better results; however, a number of the agreements decided upon clearly showed a lack of real consensus among the negotiators and proved to be difficult to implement. Moreover, the Tokyo Round agreements were plurilateral, rather than multilateral, in nature and did not bind many Contracting Parties.[16] In the early 1980s, it was clear that a new round of trade negotiations would be necessary. As Jackson noted:

> the world was becoming increasingly complex and interdependent, and it was becoming more and more obvious that the GATT rules were not satisfactorily providing the measure of discipline that was needed to prevent tensions and damaging national activity.[17]

The United States and a few other countries were in favour of a new round of negotiations with a very broad agenda including novel subjects such as trade in services and the protection of intellectual property rights. Other countries objected to such a broad agenda or were opposed to the starting of a round altogether. However, in September 1986, at Punta del Este, Uruguay, the GATT Contracting Parties eventually agreed to the start of a new round.

2.2 Uruguay Round of Multilateral Trade Negotiations

The 1986 Punta del Este Ministerial Declaration contained a very broad and ambitious mandate for negotiations. According to this Declaration, the Uruguay Round negotiations would cover, *inter alia*, trade in goods (including trade in agricultural products and trade in textiles), as well as – for the first time in history – trade in services. The establishment of a new international organisation for trade was not, however, among the Uruguay Round's initial objectives. The Punta del Este Ministerial Declaration explicitly recognised the need for institutional reforms in the GATT system but the ambitions were limited in this respect. The institutional issues for negotiation identified in the Punta del Este Declaration focused on: regular monitoring of trade policies and practices of Contracting Parties; improving the overall effectiveness and decision-making of the GATT; and strengthening the GATT's relationship with the IMF and the World Bank to achieve greater coherence in global economic policy-making.[18]

During the first years of the Uruguay Round negotiations, major progress was made with respect to all of the institutional issues identified in the Punta

16 On the distinction between multilateral and plurilateral agreements, see above, pp. 43–53. Note that the agreements concluded at the end of the Tokyo Round are commonly also referred to as 'codes'.
17 Jackson, *The World Trade Organization*, 24.
18 *Ministerial Declaration on the Uruguay Round*, GATT MIN.DEC, dated 20 September 1986, Part I, Section E, 'Functioning of the GATT System'.

del Este Ministerial Declaration. In December 1988, at the Montreal Ministerial Mid-Term Review Conference, it was decided in principle to implement, on a provisional basis, a trade policy review mechanism to improve adherence to GATT rules.[19] This Mid-Term Review also resulted in an agreement attempting to create greater cooperation between the GATT, the IMF and the World Bank. In April 1989, it was agreed that, in order to improve the functioning of the GATT, the Contracting Parties would meet at least once every two years at ministerial level.[20] At the time, however, the establishment of a new international trade organisation was not discussed. It was only in February 1990 that the then Italian Trade Minister, Renato Ruggiero (later the second Director-General of the WTO) floated the idea of establishing a new international organisation for trade. A few months later, in April 1990, Canada formally proposed the establishment of what it called a 'World Trade Organization', a fully-fledged international organisation which was to administer the different multilateral instruments related to international trade. Along the same lines, in July 1990, the European Community submitted a proposal calling for the establishment of a 'Multilateral Trade Organization'. The European Community argued that the GATT needed a sound institutional framework 'to ensure the effective implementation of the results of the Uruguay Round'.[21]

The reactions of the United States and most developing countries to these proposals were anything but enthusiastic.[22] In 1990, there was still little support for a major institutional overhaul.[23] Fear of supranationalism, the reluctance of major trading nations to give in to voting equality and the traditional worry of national leaders about 'tying their hands' were thought to inhibit the possibility of reconstructing the GATT into an international organisation for trade.[24] The December 1990 Brussels Draft Final Act, discussed at what was initially planned to be the closing conference of the Uruguay Round, did not contain an agreement with regard to a new international organisation for trade.[25] Albeit for very different reasons, this conference was a total failure, and the Uruguay Round was subsequently suspended.[26] In April 1991, however, the negotiations were

19 In April 1989, the Contracting Parties formally established the Trade Policy Review Mechanism.

20 See T. Stewart, *The GATT Uruguay Round* (Kluwer Law and Taxation, 1993), 1928.

21 See *Communication from the European Community*, GATT Doc. No. MTN.GNG/NG14/W/42, dated 9 July 1990, 2.

22 Many developing countries were hostile to the idea of an international trade organisation, *unless* this organisation was situated within the framework of the United Nations, such as the United Nations Conference on Trade and Development (UNCTAD).

23 J. Jackson, 'Strengthening the International Legal Framework of the GATT–MTN System: Reform Proposals for the New GATT Round 1991', in E. U. Petersmann and M. Hilf (eds.), *The New GATT Round of Multilateral Trade Negotiations: Legal and Economic Problems* (Kluwer, 1991), 17, 21 and 22. See also P. VerLoren van Themaat, *ibid.*, 29: 'It is highly unlikely that the world's government leaders would be willing, at this point in history, to even start serious discussions about such a new institution.'

24 See J. Jackson, 'Strengthening the International Legal Framework of the GATT–MTN System: Reform Proposals for the New GATT Round 1991', *ibid.*, 21.

25 *Draft Final Act Embodying the Results of the Uruguay Round of Multilateral Trade Negotiations*, GATT Doc. MTN.TNC/W/35/Rev.1, dated 3 December 1990.

26 The negotiations broke down because of the fundamental disagreement between the European Community and the United States on the issue of agricultural subsidies.

taken up again, and, in November 1991, the European Community, Canada and Mexico tabled a joint proposal for an international trade organisation. This joint proposal served as the basis for further negotiations, which resulted, in December 1991, in the draft *Agreement Establishing the Multilateral Trade Organization.* The latter agreement was part of the 1991 Draft Final Act, commonly referred to as the Dunkel Draft, after the then Director-General of the GATT.[27]

For the reasons already referred to above, the United States remained opposed to the establishment of a multilateral trade organisation and campaigned against the idea throughout 1992. However, by early 1993 most other participants in the Round were prepared to agree to the establishment of a multilateral trade organisation. This isolation of the United States perhaps explains the turnabout in its position during 1993 when the new Clinton Administration dropped its outspoken opposition of the United States to a new international trade organisation. Nevertheless, uncertainty about US support for such a new international organisation persisted until the last days of the Round.[28] The United States formally agreed to the establishment of the new organisation on 15 December 1993. To the surprise of many, however, the United States demanded a change of name as a condition for giving its consent. The United States suggested that the name of the new organisation should be the 'World Trade Organization' as had originally been proposed by Canada. The proponents of an international trade organisation had opted for 'Multilateral Trade Organization', as was proposed by the European Community, in the hope that this rather technical, and therefore less menacing, name would appease the United States and others opposed to an international organisation perceived as a threat to national sovereignty. Reportedly, the United States did not want to give the European Community the satisfaction of having given the new organisation its name, and further considered that an organisation with such a tongue-twisting and unappealing name as the 'Multilateral Trade Organization' would have a hard time winning the hearts and minds of the American people.[29] The *Agreement Establishing the World Trade Organization*, commonly referred to as the *WTO Agreement*, was signed in Marrakesh in April 1994, and entered into force on 1 January 1995.[30] A perceptive observer noted:

> Those who constructed the WTO are proud of having created what has been described as the greatest ever achievement in institutionalized global economic cooperation.[31]

27 *Draft Final Act Embodying the Results of the Uruguay Round of Multilateral Trade Negotiations*, GATT Doc. MTN.TNC/W/FA, dated 20 December 1991.

28 Withholding its consent to a new international trade organisation proved a useful bargaining chip in negotiations with the European Community. See *Financial Times*, 16 December 1993, 5.

29 See *ibid.* Note that the World Trade Organization and the World Tourism Organization concluded an agreement on the use of the abbreviation 'WTO'. To avoid confusion, the World Trade Organization agreed to use a distinct logo and avoid using the abbreviation in the context of tourism. See GATT Doc. MTN. TNC/W/146, 3. The World Tourism Organization is now commonly referred to as the UNWTO.

30 Note that, after the entry into force of the *WTO Agreement* and the establishment of the WTO on 1 January 1995, the WTO and the GATT 1947 existed side by side for one year. The GATT 1947 was terminated only at the end of 1995.

31 G. Sampson, 'Overview', in Sampson (ed.), *The Role of the World Trade Organization in Global Governance*, 5.

The Sutherland Report on *The Future of the WTO* noted:

The creation of the World Trade Organization (WTO) in 1995 was the most dramatic advance in multilateralism since the inspired period of institution building of the late 1940s.[32]

3 MANDATE OF THE WTO

The WTO was formally established and became operational on 1 January 1995 when the *WTO Agreement* entered into force. Pursuant to the *WTO Agreement*, the WTO has a broad and ambitious mandate. This section examines two main aspects of this mandate, namely: (1) the objectives of the WTO; and (2) the functions of the WTO.

3.1 Objectives of the WTO

The reasons for establishing the WTO and the policy objectives of this international organisation are set out in the Preamble to the *WTO Agreement*. According to the Preamble, the Parties to the *WTO Agreement* agreed to the terms of this agreement and the establishment of the WTO:

Recognizing that their relations in the field of trade and economic endeavour should be conducted with a view to raising standards of living, ensuring full employment and a large and steadily growing volume of real income and effective demand, and expanding the production of and trade in goods and services, while allowing for the optimal use of the world's resources in accordance with the objective of sustainable development, seeking both to protect and preserve the environment and to enhance the means for doing so in a manner consistent with their respective needs and concerns at different levels of economic development,

Recognizing further that there is need for positive efforts designed to ensure that developing countries, and especially the least developed among them, secure a share in the growth in international trade commensurate with the needs of their economic development.

The ultimate objectives of the WTO are thus: (1) the increase in standards of living; (2) the attainment of full employment; (3) the growth of real income and effective demand; and (4) the expansion of production of, and trade in, goods and services. However, it is clear from the Preamble that in pursuing these objectives the WTO must take into account the need for preservation of the environment and the needs of developing countries. The Preamble stresses the importance of *sustainable* economic development, i.e. economic development taking account of environmental as well as social concerns. The Preamble also stresses the importance of the *integration* of developing countries, and in

32 Report by the Consultative Board to the Director-General Supachai Panitchpakdi, *The Future of the WTO: Addressing Institutional Challenges in the New Millennium* (the 'Sutherland Report') (WTO, 2004), para. 1.

particular least-developed countries, in the world trading system. The latter aspects were absent from the Preamble to the GATT 1947.

The statements in the Preamble on the objectives of the WTO are not without legal significance. In *US – Shrimp (1998)*, the Appellate Body stated:

> [The language of the Preamble to the *WTO Agreement*] demonstrates a recognition by WTO negotiators that optimal use of the world's resources should be made in accordance with the objective of sustainable development. As this preambular language reflects the intentions of negotiators of the *WTO Agreement*, we believe it must *add colour, texture and shading to our interpretation of the agreements* annexed to the *WTO Agreement*, in this case, the GATT 1994. We have already observed that Article XX(g) of the GATT 1994 is appropriately read with the perspective embodied in the above preamble.[33]

The preambular statements of the objectives of the WTO contradict the contention that the WTO is only about trade liberalisation without regard for the sustainability of economic development, environmental degradation and global poverty. The panel in *China – Rare Earths (2014)* agreed with China, the respondent in this case, that an interpretation of the WTO agreements that 'resulted in sovereign States being legally prevented from taking measures that are necessary to protect the environment or human, animal or plant life or health would likely be inconsistent with the object and purpose of the WTO Agreement'.[34]

The Preamble to the *WTO Agreement* also states how the objectives referred to are to be achieved:

> *Being desirous* of contributing to these objectives by entering into reciprocal and mutually advantageous arrangements directed to the substantial reduction of tariffs and other barriers to trade and to the elimination of discriminatory treatment in international trade relations.

According to the Preamble to the *WTO Agreement*, the two main instruments, or means, to achieve the objectives of the WTO are: (1) the reduction of tariff barriers and other barriers to trade; and (2) the elimination of discriminatory treatment in international trade relations. The reduction of trade barriers and elimination of discrimination were also the two main instruments of the GATT 1947, but the *WTO Agreement* aims at constituting, as the Preamble states in its fourth recital, the basis of an integrated, *more* viable and *more* durable multilateral trading system.

In the Doha Ministerial Declaration of 14 November 2001, the WTO Members stated, with regard to the objectives of the WTO and its instruments for achieving these objectives:

> International trade can play a major role in the promotion of economic development and the alleviation of poverty. We recognize the need for all our peoples to benefit from the increased opportunities and welfare gains that the multilateral trading system generates. The majority of WTO Members are developing countries. We seek to place their needs and

33 Appellate Body Report, *US – Shrimp (1998)*, para. 153. Emphasis added. For the interpretation of Article XX(g) of the GATT 1994, in light of the Preamble to the *WTO Agreement*, see below, pp. 89–90.

34 Panel Report, *China – Rare Earths (2014)*, para. 7.114.

> interests at the heart of the Work Programme adopted in this Declaration. Recalling the Preamble to the Marrakesh Agreement, we shall continue to make positive efforts designed to *ensure that developing countries*, and especially the least-developed among them, *secure a share in the growth of world trade* commensurate with the needs of their economic development ...
>
> We strongly reaffirm our commitment to the objective of *sustainable development*, as stated in the Preamble to the Marrakesh Agreement. We are convinced that the aims of upholding and safeguarding an open and non-discriminatory multilateral trading system, and acting for the protection of the environment and the promotion of sustainable development, can and must be mutually supportive.[35]

3.2 Functions of the WTO

In the broadest of terms, the primary function of the WTO is to:

> provide the common institutional framework for the conduct of trade relations among its Members in matters related to the agreements and associated legal instruments included in the Annexes to [the WTO] Agreement.[36]

More specifically, the WTO has been assigned six widely defined functions. Article III of the *WTO Agreement* states:

> 1. The WTO shall *facilitate the implementation*, administration and operation, and further the objectives, of this Agreement and of the Multilateral Trade Agreements, and shall also provide the framework for the implementation, administration and operation of the Plurilateral Trade Agreements.
> 2. The WTO shall provide the *forum for negotiations* among its Members concerning their multilateral trade relations in matters dealt with under the agreements in the Annexes to this Agreement. The WTO may also provide a forum for further negotiations among its Members concerning their multilateral trade relations, and a framework for the implementation of the results of such negotiations, as may be decided by the Ministerial Conference.
> 3. The WTO shall administer the Understanding on Rules and Procedures Governing the *Settlement of Disputes* (hereinafter referred to as the 'Dispute Settlement Understanding' or 'DSU') in Annex 2 to this Agreement.
> 4. The WTO shall administer the *Trade Policy Review Mechanism* (hereinafter referred to as the 'TPRM') provided for in Annex 3 to this Agreement.
> 5. With a view to achieving greater coherence in global economic policy-making, the WTO shall *cooperate*, as appropriate, with the International Monetary Fund and with the International Bank for Reconstruction and Development and its affiliated agencies.[37]

In addition to the five functions of the WTO explicitly referred to in Article III of the *WTO Agreement*, technical assistance to developing-country Members, to allow the latter to integrate into the world trading system, is, undisputedly, also an important sixth function of the WTO.[38]

35 Ministerial Conference, *Doha Ministerial Declaration*, WT/MIN(01)/DEC/1, dated 20 November 2001, paras. 2 and 6. Emphasis added.

36 Article II:1 of the *WTO Agreement*.

37 Emphasis added.

38 See Ministerial Conference, *Doha Ministerial Declaration*, WT/MIN(01)/DEC/1, dated 20 November 2001, para. 38. See also below, p. 90.

This section will examine the following functions of the WTO: (1) the facilitation of the implementation of the WTO agreements; (2) negotiations on new trade rules; (3) the settlement of disputes; (4) trade policy review; (5) cooperation with other organisations; and (6) technical assistance to developing countries.

3.2.1 Facilitation of the Implementation of the WTO Agreements

According to Article III of the *WTO Agreement*, the first function of the WTO is to facilitate the implementation, administration and operation of the *WTO Agreement* and the multilateral and plurilateral agreements annexed to it.[39] The WTO is also entrusted with the task of furthering the objectives of these agreements. For two concrete examples of what this function of 'facilitating' and 'furthering' entails, refer to the work of the WTO Committee on Sanitary and Phytosanitary Measures (the 'SPS Committee') and the work of the WTO Committee on Safeguards.[40] Article 12, paragraph 2, of the *SPS Agreement* states that the SPS Committee shall, *inter alia*:

> encourage and facilitate *ad hoc* consultations or negotiations among Members on specific sanitary or phytosanitary issues. The Committee shall encourage the use of international standards, guidelines or recommendations by all Members and, in this regard, shall sponsor technical consultation and study with the objective of increasing coordination and integration between international and national systems and approaches for approving the use of food additives or for establishing tolerances for contaminants in foods, beverages or feedstuffs.

Pursuant to Article 13 of the *Agreement on Safeguards*, the tasks of the Committee on Safeguards include:

> (a) to monitor, and report annually to the Council for Trade in Goods on, the general implementation of this Agreement and make recommendations towards its improvement;
> (b) to find, upon request of an affected Member, whether or not the procedural requirements of this Agreement have been complied with in connection with a safeguard measure, and report its findings to the Council for Trade in Goods;
> (c) to assist Members, if they so request, in their consultations under the provisions of this Agreement.

This function of facilitating the implementation, administration and operation of the WTO agreements and furthering the objectives of these agreements is an essential function of the WTO. It involves most of its bodies and takes up much of their time.[41]

3.2.2 Negotiations on New Trade Rules

A second function of the WTO is to provide a forum for negotiations among WTO Members on new trade rules. The WTO provides 'the' forum for negotiations on

39 For an overview of these agreements, see above, pp. 43–53.

40 For a further discussion of these and other examples, see below, pp. 646 (Committee on Safeguards), 759 (Anti-Dumping Committee), 865 (Subsidies Committee), 930 (TBT Committee), and 983 (SPS Committee).

41 For a discussion on these WTO bodies, see below, pp. 58–9.

matters already covered by the WTO, and the WTO is 'a' forum among others with regard to negotiations on matters not yet addressed. To date, WTO Members have negotiated and concluded, in the framework of the WTO, trade agreements providing, *inter alia*, for: (1) further market access commitments for specific services and service suppliers (on financial services,[42] on basic telecommunications services,[43] and on the movement of natural persons);[44] (2) the liberalisation of trade in information technology products;[45] (3) the amendment of the *TRIPS Agreement* regarding the rules on compulsory licensing to ensure access for developing countries to pharmaceutical products;[46] (4) the amendment of the *Agreement on Government Procurement* which expands the coverage of and disciplines under this Agreement;[47] (5) the facilitation of the flow of goods across borders by expediting their movement, release and clearance (i.e. the *Trade Facilitation Agreement*);[48] and (6) the accession of thirty six countries to the WTO.[49] Furthermore, negotiations within the WTO have resulted in a number of decisions by WTO bodies, such as the 2001 Ministerial Decision on implementation-related issues and concerns,[50] the 2011 Decision of the SPS Committee on SPS-related private standards,[51] and the 2015 Decision of the Ministerial Conference on the elimination of agricultural export subsidies.[52]

42 See *Second Protocol to the General Agreement on Trade in Services*, S/L/11, dated 24 July 1995; and *Fifth Protocol to the General Agreement on Trade in Services*, S/L/45, dated 3 December 1997.

43 See *Fourth Protocol to the General Agreement on Trade in Services*, S/L/20, dated 30 April 1996.

44 See *Third Protocol to the General Agreement on Trade in Services*, S/L/12, dated 24 July 1995.

45 See *Agreement on Trade in Information Technology Products (ITA)*, in *Ministerial Declaration on Trade in Information Technology Products*, adopted on 13 December 1996 and entered into force on 1 July 1997. The ITA was agreed at the close of the Singapore Ministerial Conference in December 1996. The ITA provided for the elimination of customs duties and other duties and charges on information technology products by the year 2000 on an MFN basis. The implementation of the ITA was contingent on approximately 90 per cent of world trade in information technology products being covered by the ITA. On 26 March 1997, that criterion was met. From 29 Members originally, the number of participants increased to 82, representing 97 per cent of world trade in information technology products. In June 2012, 33 WTO Members (which eventually increased to 54) initiated an informal process towards negotiations for the expansion/updating of the product coverage of the ITA. In December 2015, at the Ministerial Conference in Nairobi, Members representing major exporters of IT products, agreed on the timetable (2016–19) for eliminating tariffs on 201 IT products, previously not covered and valued at over US$1.3 trillion per year. See Ministerial Conference, *Ministerial Declaration of 16 December 2015 on the Expansion of Trade in Information Technology Products*, WT/MIN(15)/25, dated 16 December 2015. See below, p. 430.

46 See *Protocol Amending the TRIPS Agreement*, WT/L/641, dated 8 December 2005. As of October 2016, 105 Members have submitted their instruments of acceptance for the Protocol (this figure includes the EU Member States). The Protocol will enter into force once two-third Members, formally accept it. See below, pp. 150 and 1040–1.

47 See *Protocol Amending the Agreement on Government Procurement*, GPA/113, dated 2 April 2012. The revised *Agreement on Government Procurement* came into force on 6 April 2014, once the Protocol amending the Agreement was accepted by two-third of the Parties to the Agreement. See below, pp. 512–14 and 537–8.

48 See Ministerial Conference, *Ministerial Declaration of 7 December 2013 on the Agreement on Trade Facilitation*, WT/MIN(13)/36, dated 11 December 2013. The WTO adopted on 27 November 2014 a *Protocol of Amendment* to insert the new Agreement in Annex 1A of the *WTO Agreement*. See below, p. 98.

49 On accession protocols, such as the *Protocol on the Accession of the People's Republic of China*, see below, pp. 53–4.

50 See Ministerial Conference, *Decision of 14 November on Implementation-Related Issues and Concerns*, WT/MIN(01)/17, dated 20 November 2001. See also below, pp. 148–9.

51 See Committee on Sanitary and Phytosanitary Measures, *Decision of the Committee on Actions regarding SPS-Related Private Standards*, G/SPS/55, dated 6 April 2011.

52 See Ministerial Conference, *Decision of 19 December 2015 on Export Competition*, WT/MIN(15)/45, dated 21 December 2015. See also below, p. 872.

Before the establishment of the WTO, multilateral trade negotiations under the GATT were primarily conducted in specially convened, 'time-limited' rounds of negotiations covering a wide range of issues.[53] The WTO provides for a *permanent* forum for negotiations in which each trade matter can be negotiated separately and on its own merits. It was initially thought that consequently there would no longer be need for specially convened rounds of negotiations. However, soon after the establishment of the WTO, its Members considered that, to negotiate successfully on further trade liberalisation at the multilateral level, they needed the political momentum, and the opportunity for package deals, brought by the old GATT-type round of negotiations. Therefore, WTO Members decided at the Doha Ministerial Conference in November 2001 to start such a round of multilateral trade negotiations.[54] This round is commonly referred to as the 'Doha Round'.[55] Pursuant to the Doha Ministerial Declaration, the Doha Round negotiations should have been concluded no later than 1 January 2005. However, this and subsequent deadlines were not met. As discussed below, after the 2015 Nairobi Ministerial Conference the current status of the Doha Round negotiations is not clear.[56]

The Doha Ministerial Declaration provided for an ambitious agenda for negotiations. These negotiations include matters on which WTO Members had already agreed in the *WTO Agreement* to continue negotiations, such as: (1) trade in agricultural products;[57] and (2) trade in services.[58] In fact, negotiations on these matters had already started in early 2000. Furthermore, the Doha Round negotiations included negotiations on: (1) problems of developing-country Members with the implementation of the existing WTO agreements (the so-called 'implementation issues'); (2) market access for non-agricultural products (NAMA); (3) TRIPS issues such as access for developing countries to essential medicines and the protection of geographical indications; (4) rules relating to dumping, subsidies and regional trade agreements; (5) dispute settlement; and (6) special and differential treatment for developing-country Members and least-developed-country Members.[59] The stated ambition of the Doha Round negotiations was to place economic development and poverty alleviation at the heart of the multilateral trading system.[60]

53 See above, pp. 84–5.

54 Note that the WTO Members already tried, but dismally failed, to start such round of multilateral trade negotiations at the ill-fated Seattle Ministerial Conference in November–December 1999. Note also that the willingness of WTO Members to agree to the launch of the Doha Round in November 2001 was related to the need for the international community to express its faith in international cooperation and negotiations after the terrorist attacks on the United States of 11 September 2001.

55 In the Doha Ministerial Declaration, the WTO Members stressed their 'commitment to the WTO as the unique forum for global trade rule-making and liberalization'. See Ministerial Conference, *Doha Ministerial Declaration*, WT/MIN(01)/DEC/1, dated 20 November 2001, para. 4.

56 See below, p. 99. 57 See Article 20 of the *Agreement on Agriculture*.

58 See Article XIX of the GATS.

59 For a complete list of the matters on the agenda of the Doha Round, see Ministerial Conference, *Doha Ministerial Declaration*, WT/MIN(01)/DEC/1, dated 20 November 2001.

60 See *ibid.*, para. 2.

In view of the many distinct matters on the agenda of the Doha Round negotiations, it is important to note that the Doha Ministerial Declaration stated that 'the conduct, conclusion and entry into force of the outcome of the negotiations shall be treated as parts of a single undertaking'.[61] Under this 'single undertaking' approach to the negotiations, there is no agreement on anything until there is an agreement on everything.[62]

Some WTO Members, and in particular the then European Communities, wanted an even broader agenda for the Doha Round. They also wanted the WTO to start negotiations on, for example, the relationship between trade and investment, the relationship between trade and competition law and the relationship between trade and core labour standards. There was, however, strong opposition, especially among developing-country Members, to the inclusion of some or all of these matters on the agenda of the Round. At the Doha Ministerial Conference, WTO Members decided that there would be no negotiations, within the context of the WTO, on the relationship between trade and core labour standards.[63] However, with respect to what is commonly referred to as the 'Singapore issues'[64] – namely: (1) the relationship between trade and investment; (2) the relationship between trade and competition law; (3) transparency in government procurement; and (4) trade facilitation[65] – the WTO Members decided in Doha that negotiations would start after they had agreed, by 'explicit consensus', on the modalities of these negotiations.[66] This agreement on the modalities of the negotiations on the Singapore issues was to be reached at the next session of the Ministerial Conference in Cancún in September 2003. However, at this session, no such agreement was reached. Developing-country Members were unwilling to consent to the request of the European Communities and others to start negotiations on the Singapore issues. Moreover, at the Cancún Ministerial Conference, it became clear that little progress had been achieved on most of the issues on which Members had been negotiating since the start of the negotiations in February 2002. As was the case during the Uruguay Round negotiations, agricultural subsidies and market access for agricultural products were again the most contentious issues

61 *Ibid.*, para. 47. The only subject matter exempted from the 'single undertaking' approach are the negotiations on the improvements to and clarifications of the *Dispute Settlement Understanding*. See *ibid*. See also below, pp. 96–7.

62 Note, however, that para. 47 of the Doha Ministerial Declaration provides room for deviation from the 'single undertaking' approach when it states: 'However, agreements reached at an early stage may be implemented on a provisional or a definitive basis.' See *ibid.*

63 WTO Members took 'note of work under way in the International Labour Organization (ILO) on the social dimension of globalization'. See Ministerial Conference, *Doha Ministerial Declaration*, WT/MIN(01)/DEC/1, dated 20 November 2001, para. 8.

64 At the Singapore Ministerial Conference in December 1996, these issues were first identified as possible issues for further negotiations within the WTO.

65 On 'trade facilitation', see below, pp. 511–12.

66 Note that the concept of 'explicit consensus' was a *novum* in WTO law. See below, p. 146, fn. 383.

on the negotiating table.[67] The Cancún Ministerial Conference turned out to be a dismal failure, with nothing agreed upon.[68]

The deadlock in the negotiations after the Cancún Ministerial Conference was only overcome during the summer of 2004 when, following weeks of intense discussions, a new Doha Work Programme was adopted by the General Council on 1 August 2004.[69] In its Decision of 1 August, the General Council called on all Members 'to redouble their efforts towards the conclusion of a balanced overall outcome of the Doha Development Agenda'.[70] A key element of the Decision of the General Council was to not start negotiations on the Singapore issues, save and except the issue of trade facilitation.[71] The 'redoubling of efforts' did not, however, yield the results hoped for. At the Hong Kong Ministerial Conference in December 2005, an agreement was reached on the elimination of agricultural export subsidies by 2013.[72] This was in itself a significant achievement but of little value if no agreement was also reached on all other major issues on the negotiating table, such as market access for agricultural products, domestic support for agricultural production, market access for non-agricultural products (NAMA), and the liberalisation of trade in services. With regard to these other issues, Members were unfortunately only able to agree to disagree and to put forward the summer of 2006 as a new deadline for an agreement on the broad lines of an overall deal on NAMA. When that deadline was missed, the then WTO Director-General Lamy decided at the end of July 2006 to suspend the negotiations. In February 2007, the negotiations were resumed. In the summer of 2008, a breakthrough in the negotiations seemed within reach but failed to materialise. The mini-ministerial meeting in July 2008 in Geneva failed over the inability to reach agreement on a special safeguard mechanism (SSM) for the protection of poor farmers in developing-country Members. However, Ambassador Servansing from Mauritius, the Coordinator and Chief Negotiator of the ACP Group in Geneva, noted:

> The SSM was only the immediate trigger that precipitated the failure. The real causes were more fundamental ... The underlying reason was the growing development deficit that slowly crept into the negotiations and emptied the development ambition of the DDA [Doha Development Agenda] mandate. There was a clear feeling among the developing countries that the imbalances that the DDA was meant to correct were not being addressed and the

67 See below, p. 86, fn. 26.

68 Note that, in the run-up to the Cancún Ministerial Conference, the General Council of the WTO did reach an agreement on the waiver to the *TRIPS Agreement* enabling the import by developing countries of generic medicines produced under compulsory licences. See General Council, *Decision on the Implementation of Paragraph 6 of the Doha Declaration on TRIPS and Public Health*, WT/L/540, dated 1 September 2003. See further below, p. 131, fn. 292.

69 See General Council, *Doha Work Programme Decision adopted by the General Council on 1 August 2004*, WT/L/579, dated 2 August 2004.

70 *Ibid.*, para. 3. 71 See below, pp. 94–5.

72 See Ministerial Conference, *Hong Kong Ministerial Declaration*, WT/MIN(05)/DEC, dated 22 December 2005, para. 6. The elimination of export subsidies by 2013 was an important concession on the part of the European Communities.

> outcome was being skewed more in their disfavour. While in agriculture, higher ambition, which served a developmental objective, was being consistently diluted through multiple flexibilities for developed countries, in NAMA the developmental concerns of protecting industrial development and employment in developing countries were being denied by a predatory mercantilist approach of seeking higher market access in developing countries.[73]

For a detailed and technical account of the negotiations, refer to the regular reports of the Chair of the Trade Negotiations Committee to the General Council, which are an excellent, and sobering, public source of information.[74] Many reasons have been advanced to explain why the Doha Round negotiations have been so difficult, including: (1) the increase in the WTO membership and its diversity, and the emergence of developing-country Members as full participants in the negotiations;[75] (2) the difficulties arising from the fact that not only the decision on the ultimate result of the negotiations, but also decisions on all intermediate steps in the negotiations, must be adopted by consensus;[76] (3) the fact that the decision to launch the Doha Round was ill-prepared and not based on a consensus regarding necessary economic reforms;[77] (4) the fact that the 'easy' steps in the process of trade liberalisation have all been taken in previous negotiations and that what is now 'left' includes primarily trade barriers or distortions fiercely defended by strong domestic interests; (5) the ambitious agenda of the negotiations and the 'single undertaking' approach;[78] (6) the fact that Members are unwilling to agree to new rights and obligations formulated in ambiguous wording (a technique much used in other international negotiations to overcome deadlock) because such ambiguously worded rights and obligations may later be 'clarified' in the context of the WTO's binding dispute settlement system in a manner inconsistent with their interests;[79] and finally (7) a general questioning of economic globalisation and a reduced enthusiasm for further trade liberalisation, in particular since the outbreak of the global economic and financial crisis in the summer of 2007.

In April 2011, the then Director-General Lamy, in his capacity as Chair of the Trade Negotiations Committee,[80] presented to the Members the so-called 'Easter Package', a document reflecting the work done so far.[81] For the first time since the start of the negotiations almost ten years earlier, Members had 'the opportunity to consider the entire Doha package in all market access and regulatory

73 Shree B. C. Servansing, 'Non-Agricultural Market Access (NAMA) – Balancing Development and Ambition', in P. Mehta, A. Kaushik and R. Kaukab (eds.), *Reflections from the Frontline: Developing Country Negotiators in the WTO* (CUTS International, 2012), 88–9.

74 See, for example, General Council, *Minutes of Meeting of 31 July 2008*, WT/GC/M/115, dated 10 October 2008.

75 See below, pp. 146–8. 76 See below, p. 108.

77 As discussed above, the launch of the Doha Round has been seen as a 'political response' by the international community to the terrorist attacks on the United States of 11 September 2001. See above, pp. 24–5.

78 See above, p. 94. 79 See below, pp. 190–9. 80 See below, p. 433, fn. 78.

81 The 'Easter Package' consisted of documents of the chairs of the negotiating committees on the work done by their committee, as well as an accompanying report by Pascal Lamy. See www.wto.org/english/tratop_e/dda_e/chair_texts11_e/chair_texts11_e.htm.

areas'.[82] This document showed that in many areas progress had been made, but it also made clear that Members had still to come to an agreement on many core issues, in particular on NAMA. The issue of market access for industrial products, a 'classic mercantilist issue' which had been 'the bread and butter' of the negotiations since the start, divided Members as no other issue.[83] Chapter 6 discusses this issue in greater detail.[84] The then Director-General Lamy reported to the Members that it appeared that the 'political gap' which separated Members was 'not bridgeable' at that time.[85] The Members, concurring with Lamy's assessment, subsequently made an effort to agree by the next Ministerial Conference in December 2011, on a smaller 'package' of issues. These issues related primarily to issues of particular interest to the least-developed-country Members (such as duty-free and quota-free market access and associated rules of origin; cotton subsidies; and a waiver of the GATS MFN treatment obligation). However, such narrow focus was not acceptable to all Members. Lamy thus presented a non-exhaustive list of other issues, such as trade facilitation, export competition and fisheries subsidies ('LDC plus' issues), which could be part of the smaller package to be agreed on by December 2011. In July 2011 it was clear, however, that Members would not be able to agree on an 'LDC plus' package.

The Doha Round negotiations were in a deep crisis. Even an intermediate agreement on a smaller package of issues, a so-called 'Doha Lite', was not possible. Members did, however, express their willingness to continue with the Doha Round negotiations. As reflected in the Chair's Concluding Statement, Members recognised:

> [the] need to more fully explore different negotiating approaches while respecting the principles of transparency and inclusiveness.[86]

Members declared themselves willing to abandon the 'single undertaking' approach.[87] They agreed to advance negotiations on issues where progress could be achieved with the aim of reaping an 'early harvest', i.e. concluding provisional or definitive agreements *before* the full conclusion of the single undertaking.[88] Half a year later, in July 2012, the then WTO Director-General, Pascal Lamy reported to the General Council as follows:

> [P]rogress and activity have been mixed, to use diplomatic language ... [W]e have to recognize that prolonged and dogmatic discussions about whether or not to deliver on everything or a few things or nothing at all have not and will not take us very far. The only thing we know is that an 'all' or 'nothing' does not work. A 'my way or the highway' is the best way to ensure paralysis ... [T]he guidance from Ministers is clear ... [U]ltimately the ball lies

82 See *WTO Annual Report 2012*, 22.

83 See Opening Remarks of Director-General Pascal Lamy at the informal TNC meeting of 29 April 2011, www.wto.org/english/news_e/news11_e/tnc_dg_infstat_29apr11_e.htm.

84 See below, pp. 415–74. 85 See *WTO Annual Report 2012*, 22. 86 *Ibid.*

87 While the emphasis since the start of the Doha Round had always been on the 'single undertaking' approach, note that the 2001 Doha Ministerial Declaration itself provided room for deviation from this approach. As discussed above, para. 47 of the Declaration states: 'However, agreements reached at an early stage may be implemented on a provisional or a definitive basis.' See above, p. 94, fn. 61.

88 See *ibid.*

in your court. You, the negotiators, have to achieve the needed substantive and balanced progress across all areas of our negotiations that you all say you desire.[89]

However, this call on Geneva-based negotiators to show flexibility and creativity should not be misunderstood as implying that the impasse in the negotiations is mainly due to disagreement on technical trade issues. The impasse is primarily political and must be addressed at the (highest) political level.[90]

After many years of setbacks and lack of progress, the WTO was finally able to reach agreement on a few issues on the agenda of the Doha Round negotiations at the Bali Ministerial Conference in December 2013. This agreement on what is referred to as the 'Bali Package' concerned in the first place trade facilitation,[91] but also a number of issues relating to agriculture (in particular the issue of public stockholding for food security purposes),[92] and issues relating to development and least-developed countries.[93]

In the Bali Ministerial Declaration, WTO Members welcomed the Bali Package as 'an important stepping stone towards the completion of the Doha Round'.[94] The Ministerial Conference instructed the Trade Negotiations Committee to prepare by the end of 2014 a clearly defined work programme on the remaining issues of the Doha Development Agenda.[95] While the agreement on the Bali Package gave a much-needed boost to the morale of the WTO, and the agreement on trade facilitation is important in its own right, it must be acknowledged that most of the work in the context of the Doha Round negotiations remained to be done. In the two years following the Bali Ministerial Conference, very little further progress was made. WTO Members even failed to agree on the work programme called for in Bali.[96] Not surprisingly, the expectations for the Nairobi Ministerial Conference, in December 2015, were thus very low. Nevertheless, the WTO succeeded in taking a number of decisions in Nairobi, most importantly the decision on the elimination of agricultural export subsidies.[97] Other decisions,

89 Report by the Chairman of the Trade Negotiations Committee to the General Council on 25 July 2012, www.wto.org/english/news_e/news12_e/gc_rpt_25jul12_e.htm.

90 See also Pascal Lamy, 'Strengthening the Multilateral Trading System', speech delivered at the Singapore Schuman Lecture Series of the European Chamber of Commerce in Singapore on 21 September 2012.

91 See *Agreement on Trade Facilitation*, Ministerial Declaration of 7 December 2013, WT/MIN(13)/36-WT/L/911, dated 11 December 2013. See below, pp. 511–12.

92 See Ministerial Conference, *Ministerial Decision of 7 December 2013 on Public Stockholding for Food Security Purposes*, WT/MIN(13)/38 – WT/L/913, dated 11 December 2013. See below, p. 434.

93 See *Ministerial Decision on Preferential Rules of Origin for Least Developed Countries*, WT/MIN(13)/42 or WT/L/917; *Ministerial Decision on Operationalization of the Waiver Concerning Preferential Treatment to Services and Service Suppliers of Least Developed Countries*, WT/MIN(13)/43 or WT/L/918; *Ministerial Decision on Duty-Free and Quota-Free Market Access for Least Developed Countries*, WT/MIN(13)/44 or WT/L/919; and *Ministerial Decision on Monitoring Mechanism on Special and Differential Treatment, Ministerial Decision*, WT/MIN(13)/45 or WT/L/920. See below, p. 458.

94 See Ministerial Conference, *Bali Ministerial Declaration*, adopted on 7 December 2013, WT/MIN(13)/DEC, dated 11 December 2013, para 1.10.

95 See *ibid.*, para. 1.11.

96 Due to a disagreement between India and the United States on what exactly had been agreed in Bali on public stockholding for food security purposes, progress on any issue was blocked and WTO Members *inter alia* failed to adopt the amendment protocol to insert the TFA into Annex 1A of the WTO Agreement by 31 July 2014, the deadline set in Bali. The amendment protocol was eventually only adopted on 27 November 2014 after the disagreement on the public stockholding issue was overcome.

97 See Ministerial Conference, *Ministerial Decision of 19 December 2015 on Export Competition*, WT/MIN(15)/45, WT/L/980, dated 21 December 2015. See also below, p. 872.

which formed part of the 'Nairobi Package', concerned other agricultural issues[98] and issues pertaining to least-developed countries.[99] WTO Members also agreed on the elimination of customs duties on 201 information technology products valued at over US$1.3 trillion per year.[100]

On the future of the Doha Round negotiations, WTO Members agreed to disagree at the Ministerial Conference in Nairobi. Consequently, there is much confusion and uncertainty regarding the current status of the negotiations. The Nairobi Ministerial Declaration states:

> We recognize that many Members reaffirm the Doha Development Agenda, and the Declarations and Decisions adopted at Doha and at the Ministerial Conferences held since then, and reaffirm their full commitment to conclude the DDA on that basis. Other Members do not reaffirm the Doha mandates, as they believe new approaches are necessary to achieve meaningful outcomes in multilateral negotiations. Members have different views on how to address the negotiations. We acknowledge the strong legal structure of this Organization.
>
> Nevertheless, there remains a strong commitment of all Members to advance negotiations on the remaining Doha issues. This includes advancing work in all three pillars of agriculture, namely domestic support, market access and export competition, as well as non-agriculture market access, services, development, TRIPS and rules. Work on all the Ministerial Decisions adopted in Part II of this Declaration will remain an important element of our future agenda.[101]

The Nairobi Ministerial Declaration highlights the dichotomy of views among WTO Members with regard to the Doha Round negotiations. For the first time since its launch in 2001, WTO Members could not agree on reaffirming the negotiating mandate, with the United States particularly adamant that a different approach is needed if negotiations are to deliver a successful outcome.[102] At the same time, however, the Declaration also explicitly recognises the continued 'strong commitment of all Members' to advance negotiations on the remaining Doha issues.

98 See *Ministerial Decision on the Special Safeguard Mechanism (SSM) for Developing Countries*, WT/MIN(15)/43 – WT/L/978 (it was agreed that developing-country Members 'will have the right to have recourse to a special safeguard mechanism', as had already been envisaged in the 2005 *Hong Kong Ministerial Declaration*, and that negotiations to this end would continue; *Ministerial Decision on Public Stockholding for Food Security Purposes*, WT/MIN(15)/44 – WT/L/979 (it was agreed that 'Members shall engage constructively to negotiate and make all concerted efforts to agree and adopt a permanent solution') and *Ministerial Decision on Cotton*, WT/MIN(15)/46 – WT/L/981 (regarding the reduction in trade distorting domestic subsidies for cotton production and improvement in market access for least-developed countries).

99 See *Ministerial Decision on Preferential Rules of Origin for Least Developed Countries*, WT/MIN(15)/47 – WT/L/917/Add.1; and *Ministerial Decision on Implementation of Preferential Treatment in Favour of Services and Service Suppliers of Least Developed Countries and Increasing LDC Participation in Services Trade*, WT/MIN(15)/48 – WT/L/982; see below, p. 338.

100 See Ministerial Conference, *Ministerial Declaration of 16 December 2015 on the Expansion of Trade in Information Technology Products*, WT/MIN(15)/25, dated 16 December 2015. See below, p. 430.

101 See Ministerial Conference, *Nairobi Ministerial Declaration*, adopted on 19 December 2015, WT/MIN(15)/DEC, dated 21 December 2015, paras. 30 and 31.

102 See 'WTO Members Eye New Negotiating Landscape', *Bridges Weekly*, 20(6), 18 February 2016, 7.

At the February 2016 meeting of the General Council, WTO Director-General Roberto Azevêdo observed with regard to the future of negotiations within the WTO on Doha Round issues as well as other issues, the following:

> There is no consensus about how to address the [Doha Development Agenda]. Nonetheless, in Nairobi, all members gave a 'strong commitment' to advancing negotiations on the remaining Doha issues. It is important to underline this point, even though members do not currently have a shared view on how it should be achieved.
>
> Turning to [non-Doha] issues, again members were not of a common view. But it was clear that some want to discuss issues outside the [Doha Development Agenda]. It is not clear yet how that conversation would take place, but there is a clear understanding that if there's a desire to launch multilateral negotiations that would have to happen with the agreement of all members.[103]

It is most uncertain whether or not the Doha Round negotiations will proceed in any meaningful manner. It takes two to tango, and a number of Members have become tired of this particular dance. Generally speaking, there are a number of factors that have made, and would continue to make, the successful conclusion of the Doha Round negotiations a major challenge. First, there is the ever-increasing number of negotiations on regional trade agreements, which have diverted, and would continue to divert, political attention and negotiating resources away from the Doha Round negotiations.[104] Second, the agenda of the Doha Round, agreed upon fifteen years ago, may have become in view of the rapidly changing reality of international trade, outdated, i.e. insufficiently focused on more pressing problems faced by the multilateral trading system today (such as e-commerce, export restrictions and trade-related energy and investment issues).[105] Finally, the rapidly increasing importance of emerging economies in the global economy, their growing assertiveness within the WTO, and the divergence of their interests (with those of developed countries but also *inter se*) make the successful conclusion of multilateral trade negotiations, such as the Doha Round negotiations, an ever more formidable challenge. However, contrary to some alarmist commentary in the media, the breakdown of the Doha Round negotiations does not herald the imminent demise of the WTO. As discussed above and below, the WTO fulfils, besides the function of negotiating new trade rules, also other important functions, and does so quite successfully.[106] Nevertheless, failure to update and add to the current WTO rules in order to keep these rules adapted to the ever-changing reality of international trade and the needs of WTO Members will, over time, weaken the rules-based multilateral trading system and result in a 'creeping return of the law of the jungle'.[107]

103 *Report of the Chairman of the Trade Negotiations Committee*, 24 February 2016. See www.wto.org/english/news_e/news16_e/gc_rpt_24feb16_e.htm. 104 See below, p. 673.

105 On the rapidly changing reality of international trade, see Chapter 1, at pp. 6–14.

106 See above, p. 90. Note also that the WTO had a number of negotiating successes. See above, p. 92.

107 See Opening Remarks of Director-General Pascal Lamy at the informal TNC meeting of 29 April 2011, www.wto.org/english/news_e/news11_e/tnc_dg_infstat_29apr11_e.htm.

A possible indication of things to come are the current talks among a group of twenty-three developed- and developing-country Members on a Trade in Services Agreement (TiSA), a plurilateral agreement on an ambitious liberalisation of trade in services, building upon but going beyond the existing GATS.[108] Together, the WTO Members participating in the TiSA negotiations account for 70 per cent of world trade in services.[109] Tellingly, this group of Members, referred to as the 'Real Good Friends of Services' (RGF), includes the European Union and the United States but not Brazil, China or India. The latter Members have warned of the consequences for the multilateral trading system of adopting a plurilateral approach to negotiations on trade liberalisation in reaction to the impasse in the Doha Round negotiations.[110] Note that TiSA negotiations take place outside the framework of the WTO and are conducted without the involvement or support of the WTO Secretariat. Another recent plurilateral initiative – outside the Doha Round negotiations but within the framework of the WTO – are the negotiations on the *Environmental Goods Agreement (EGA)* involving seventeen WTO Members.[111] The EGA aims to remove barriers to trade in environmental or 'green' goods that are crucial for environmental protection and climate change mitigation.[112] The EGA is being envisioned as an open plurilateral agreement, with tariff reductions being extended to all WTO members, consistent with the most-favoured nation treatment obligation.[113]

At a meeting of all WTO Members on 30 September 2016, Director-General Roberto Azevêdo urged Members to deepen discussions to advance negotiating work. Referring to the G20 Summit in Hangzhou and the UN General Assembly meeting in New York, he stated:

> In all of my recent meetings, I have sensed a growing interest in our work, especially as the past two WTO Ministerial Conferences have shown our ability to deliver multilateral results. I have been encouraged by the calls I have heard to strengthen the WTO, resist protectionism and increase co-operation on trade issues ... It is therefore important that we deepen our discussions about what members want to achieve between now and the 11th Ministerial Conference [at the end of 2017]. I think we have made some progress in the first half of the year – and we need to keep up the momentum in all areas, including the long-standing issues.[114]

108 See http://ec.europa.eu/trade/policy/in-focus/tisa. 109 See *ibid.*

110 See *Bridges Weekly Trade News Digest*, 4 April 2012, 11 July 2012, 26 September 2012 and 12 December 2012. Other Members involved include Australia, Canada, Chile, Colombia, Costa Rica, Hong Kong China, Iceland, Israel, Japan, Liechtenstein, Mauritius, Mexico, New Zealand, Norway, Pakistan, Panama, Peru, South Korea, Switzerland, Chinese Taipei and Turkey.

111 The participating WTO Members include Australia, Canada, China, Costa Rica, Chinese Taipei, the European Union, Hong Kong (China), Japan, Korea, New Zealand, Norway, Switzerland, Singapore, United States, Israel, Turkey and Iceland. Note that WTO Members also sought to reach agreement on an EGA in the context of the Doha Round negotiations. The failure of this multilateral effort triggered plurilateral negotiations.

112 The list of 'green goods' comprises fifty-four goods including, for example, catalytic converters, air filters, recycling machinery and solar panels.

113 See http://trade.ec.europa.eu/doclib/press/index.cfm?id=1116. Note that also the *Information Technology Agreement II* (ITA II), which was, as discussed above, agreed upon at the 2015 Nairobi Ministerial Conference, is a plurilateral agreement, which is applied on a most-favoured-nation basis. On the most-favoured-nation treatment obligation, see pp. 305–39.

114 See www.wto.org/english/news_e/news16_e/hod_30sep16_e.htm.

3.2.3 Dispute Settlement

A third and very important function of the WTO is the administration of the WTO dispute settlement system. As stated in Article 3.2 of the *Dispute Settlement Understanding*:

> The dispute settlement system of the WTO is a central element in providing security and predictability to the multilateral trading system.

The prompt settlement of disputes under the WTO agreements is essential for the effective functioning of the WTO and for maintaining a proper balance between the rights and obligations of Members.[115] The WTO dispute settlement system serves: (1) to preserve the rights and obligations of Members under the WTO agreements; and (2) to clarify the existing provisions of those agreements.[116] However, the dispute settlement system is explicitly proscribed from adding to or diminishing the rights and obligations provided in the WTO agreements.[117]

The WTO dispute settlement system, referred to as the 'jewel in the crown' of the WTO, has been operational for twenty-one years now, and has arguably been the most prolific of all State-to-State dispute settlement systems in that period. Since 1 January 1995, 513 disputes have been brought to the WTO for resolution.[118] Some of these disputes, involving, for example, national legislation on public health or environmental protection, were politically sensitive and have attracted considerable attention from the media.[119] With its compulsory jurisdiction, its strict time frames, the possibility of appellate review and a detailed mechanism to ensure compliance with recommendations and rulings, the WTO dispute settlement system is unique among international dispute settlement systems. Chapter 3 examines in detail the basic principles, institutions and procedures of the WTO dispute settlement system.[120]

3.2.4 Trade Policy Review

A fourth function of the WTO is the administration of the Trade Policy Review Mechanism (TPRM).[121] The TPRM provides for the regular *collective* appreciation and evaluation of the full range of *individual* Members' trade policies and practices and their impact on the functioning of the multilateral trading system.[122] The purpose of the TPRM is: (1) to achieve greater transparency in, and

115 See Article 3.3 of the DSU. 116 See Article 3.2, second sentence, of the DSU.
117 See Article 3.2, last sentence, of the DSU.
118 i.e. the number of requests for consultations notified to the DSB up to 1 October 2016 (not including requests for consultations in the context of Article 21.5 compliance proceedings). See www.worldtradelaw.net/databases/searchcomplaints.php.
119 Other disputes, such as those concerning the methodologies used by domestic trade remedy authorities (see e.g. below, pp. 716–20) are also, at least in some Members, politically very sensitive, albeit they do not attract much attention in the non-specialised media.
120 See below, pp. 164–300.
121 See Annex 3 to the *WTO Agreement*, entitled 'Trade Policy Review Mechanism'.
122 See Trade Policy Review Mechanism, para. A(i).

understanding of, the trade policies and practices of Members; and (2) to contribute to improved compliance by all Members with their WTO obligations.[123]

Under the TPRM, the trade policies and practices of all Members are subject to *periodic review*. The frequency of review is determined by reference to each Member's share of world trade in a recent representative period.[124] The four largest trading entities, i.e. the European Union, the United States, Japan and China, are subject to review every two years. The next sixteen are reviewed every four years. Other Members are reviewed every six years, except that for least-developed-country Members a longer period may be fixed.[125] In 2015, the Trade Policy Review Body (TPRB) carried out twenty reviews.[126]

Trade policy reviews are carried out by the TPRB[127] on the basis of two reports: a report supplied by the Member under review, in which the Member describes the trade policy and practices it pursues; and a report, drawn up by the WTO Secretariat, based on the information available to it and that provided by the Member under review.[128] These reports, together with the concluding remarks by the TPRB Chair and the minutes of the meeting of the TPRB, are published shortly after the review and are a valuable source of information on a WTO Member's trade policy. The reports and the minutes of the TPRB are searchable by country and available on the WTO website as WT/TPR documents.

It is important to note that the TPRM is not intended to serve as a basis for the enforcement of specific obligations under the WTO agreements or for dispute settlement procedures.[129] However, by *publicly* deploring inconsistencies with WTO law of a Member's trade policy or practices, the TPRM intends to 'shame' Members into compliance and to support domestic opposition to trade policy and practices inconsistent with WTO law. Likewise, by *publicly* praising WTO-consistent trade policies, the TPRM bolsters, both internationally and domestically, support for such policies. By way of example, note the remarks made by the TPRB Chair at the conclusion of the trade policy review of Bangladesh in 2006. In these concluding remarks, the TPRB Chair stated:

> Members commended Bangladesh's efforts to ensure steady growth of GDP through prudent macroeconomic policies and reforms in certain areas, despite endogenous and exogenous challenges. While noting efforts to improve governance, certain Members encouraged Bangladesh to increase its capacity for revenue collection and move away from dependence on tariffs and other border charges as a main source of revenue. Some Members considered that there was room for progress in implementing privatization plans.

123 See above pp. 7–11. 124 See *ibid.*, para. C(ii).

125 Exceptionally, in the event of changes in a Member's trade policies or practices that may have a significant impact on its trading partners, the Member concerned may be requested by the TPRB, after consultation, to bring forward its next review. See *ibid.*

126 See www.wto.org/english/tratop_e/tpr_e/tp_rep_e.htm#chronologically.

127 See below, pp. 132–4.

128 The two reports cover all aspects of the Member's trade policy broadly speaking, including its domestic laws and regulations; the institutional framework; bilateral, regional and other preferential agreements; the wider economic needs; and the external environment.

129 See Trade Policy Review Mechanism, para. A(i).

Members congratulated Bangladesh on its increased Foreign Direct Investment inflows during the period under review and encouraged further improvements in the foreign investment framework. Members noted that Bangladesh's comprehensive poverty reduction strategy had led to an improvement of certain social indicators, including the share of people living below the poverty line. Trade and trade policy measures were an integral part of these efforts.[130]

Trade policy reviews of developing-country Members also give an opportunity to identify the needs of these countries in terms of technical and other assistance. The remarks of the TPRB Chair at the conclusion of the trade policy review of Pakistan in 2002 are also noteworthy:

Purely as an aside, and as much a comment on the review process as on this Review, I was struck by [Pakistan's] Secretary Beg's remarks that questions had given his delegation food for considerable thought and that sources of information had been found of which he was unaware. This goes to the heart of our work: not only do we learn a lot about the Member, but often the Member learns a lot about itself.[131]

Post review, TPR follow-up workshops may be organised to help developing countries discuss and disseminate the results of their trade policy reviews in their capitals, and to convince national stakeholders of the need to address concerns expressed by other WTO Members about their trade regimes.[132] These workshops have enhanced the benefits of the TPR exercise for developing countries, particularly the least-developed countries.[133]

Apart from carrying out individual trade policy reviews, the TPRB also undertakes an *annual overview* of developments in the international trading environment, which have an impact on the multilateral trading system. To assist the TPRB with this review, the Director-General presents an *annual report* setting out the major activities of the WTO and highlighting significant policy issues affecting the trading system.

In the context of the global financial and economic crisis, the then WTO Director-General Pascal Lamy in February 2009 took the initiative to report regularly to the TPRB on developments in trade as a result of the crisis. At the request of the G-20 leaders, the WTO Secretariat, together with the OECD and UNCTAD Secretariats, also prepares regular reports on trade and investment measures taken by the G-20 countries in the face of the crisis.[134] Chapter 1 refers to the findings of these reports.[135]

130 Trade Policy Review Body – Review of Bangladesh – TPRB's Evaluation, PRESS/TPRB/269, dated 13 and 15 September 2006.

131 Trade Policy Review Body – Review of Pakistan – TPRB's Evaluation, PRESS/TPRB/187, dated 25 January 2002.

132 In 2015, a regional follow-up workshop was organised for the Organization of Eastern Caribbean States (Antigua and Barbuda, Dominica, Grenada, Saint Kitts and Nevis, Saint Lucia, and Saint Vincent and the Grenadines). National follow-up workshops were organised for Myanmar, the Dominican Republic and Pakistan. One envisaged for Madagascar was postponed to 2016 at the country's request. See *WTO Annual Report 2016*, 88.

133 The demand for TPR follow-up workshops has increased from two in 2014 to four in 2015. See *ibid*.

134 The first such report is dated 14 September 2009 and is, as are later reports, available on the WTO website. In 2015, the WTO published two such reports. *WTO Annual Report 2016*, 147.

135 See above, pp. 11–14.

3.2.5 Cooperation with Other Organisations

Article III:5 of the *WTO Agreement* refers specifically to cooperation with the IMF and the World Bank. Such cooperation is mandated by the need for greater coherence in global economic policy-making. The 'linkages' between the different aspects of global economic policy (financial, monetary and trade) require that the international institutions with responsibilities in these areas follow coherent and mutually supportive policies.[136] The WTO has concluded agreements with both the IMF and the World Bank to give form to the cooperation required by Article III:5 of the *WTO Agreement.*[137] These agreements provide for consultations and the exchange of information between the WTO Secretariat and the staff of the IMF and the World Bank. The WTO, the IMF and the World Bank now cooperate quite closely on a day-to-day basis, in particular in the area of technical assistance to developing countries. Along with three other international organisations,[138] the IMF, the World Bank and the WTO participate actively in the Enhanced Integrated Framework for Trade-Related Technical Assistance (EIF) to help the least-developed countries expand their exports.[139] Furthermore, the IMF and the World Bank have observer status in the WTO, and the WTO attends the meetings of the IMF and the World Bank. Officials of the three organisations meet regularly to discuss issues of global economic policy coherence.[140]

Pursuant to Article V:1 of the *WTO Agreement*, the WTO is also to cooperate with other international organisations. Article V, which is entitled 'Relations with Other Organizations', states in its first paragraph:

> The General Council shall make appropriate arrangements for effective cooperation with other intergovernmental organizations that have responsibilities related to those of the WTO.

The WTO has made cooperation arrangements with, *inter alia*, the World Intellectual Property Organization (WIPO)[141] and the United Nations Conference on Trade and Development (UNCTAD).[142] In these and other international

136 See also *Declaration on the Contribution of the World Trade Organization to Achieving Greater Coherence in Global Economic Policymaking*, Final Act Embodying the Results of the Uruguay Round of Multilateral Trade Negotiations, para. 5.

137 See *Agreement between the International Monetary Fund and the World Trade Organization*, contained in Annex I to WT/GC/W/43, dated 4 November 1996; and the *Agreement between the International Bank for Reconstruction and Development and the International Development Association and the World Trade Organization*, contained in Annex II to WT/GC/W/43, dated 4 November 1996.

138 UNCTAD, the ITC and the UNDP. 139 See below, p. 112.

140 In June 2015, together with the IMF and the World Bank, the WTO hosted a two-day workshop on international trade in Geneva. Experts from the three institutions presented research and exchanged views on current international trade issues, including the links between trade and growth, global value chains, services trade, trade finance, and trade and other policy links. See *WTO Annual Report 2016*, 146. Further, the World Bank and WTO jointly published a study entitled 'The Role of Trade in Ending Poverty' in 2015.

141 In October 2015, the WTO held a joint technical symposium with the WHO and WIPO entitled 'Public Health, Intellectual Property, and TRIPS at 20: Innovation and Access to Medicines', which looked at access to, and innovation in, medical technologies. See *WTO Annual Report 2016*, 146.

142 In October 2015, the heads of the WTO and UNCTAD signed a declaration to strengthen their collaboration, to provide training and technical assistance to developing and least-developed countries. The declaration commits them to work together to harness trade as a tool for development and poverty alleviation. See *WTO Annual Report 2016*, 144.

organisations the WTO has observer status. The WTO and UNCTAD also cooperate in a joint venture, the International Trade Centre (ITC).[143] The ITC works with developing countries and economies in transition to set up effective trade promotion programmes to expand export opportunities with the aim of fostering sustainable development. It focuses on supporting the 'internationalisation' of small and medium-sized enterprises (SMEs).[144]

The WTO also works in close cooperation with the Organisation for Economic Co-operation and Development (OECD) in publishing joint reports and maintaining a joint database on trade.[145]

Recently, post conclusion of the Trade Facilitation Agreement, several international organisations, including the OECD, UNCTAD, the ITC, the World Bank and the World Customs Organization (WCO), have pledged to assist WTO Members in implementing their commitments under the aforesaid Agreement.[146]

The WTO Director-General participates in the meetings of the United Nations Chief Executives Board (CEB), a body consisting of the heads of UN organisations.[147] The objective of the CEB is to enhance international cooperation on global issues, such as, currently, the international response to the global economic crisis. The WTO is also represented on the United Nations High-Level Task Force (HLTF) on the Global Food Security Crisis, which was established by the CEB in April 2008, following the rise in global food prices and the subsequent crisis triggered by it.[148]

In addition, the WTO Secretariat has concluded a large number of so-called Memoranda of Understanding (MOUs) with other international secretariats. These MOUs provide mainly for technical assistance from the WTO to these other secretariats or the geographical regions in which they work. In September 2003, for example, the then WTO Director-General, Supachai Panitchpakdi, and the Secretary-General of the ACP Group, Jean-Robert Goulongana, signed an MOU committing both organisations to cooperate more closely to provide training, technical assistance and support to negotiators of the ACP Member States in the Doha Round.[149]

143 The WTO collaborates with ITC and UNCTAD *inter alia* in the annual publication of the *World Tariff Profiles*.
144 See www.intracen.org/itc/about/how-itc-works.
145 The OECD and the WTO cooperate in the Trade in Value-Added (TIVA) database, launched in January 2013. The 2015 edition covers sixty-one economies and thirty-four manufacturing and services sectors. Further, they have also developed a set of trade facilitation indicators (TFIs), the 2015 update of this interactive web tool covers 152 countries. The TFIs identify areas for action and help to assess the potential impact of trade facilitation reforms so that governments can prioritise action and mobilise technical assistance. See *WTO Annual Report 2016*, 145.
146 See *WTO Annual Report 2015*, 41.
147 The CEB comprises executive heads of UN agencies, funds and programmes as well as the executive heads of the Bretton Woods institutions (IMF and World Bank) and the WTO. It is chaired by the UN Secretary-General. See *WTO Annual Report 2016*, 144.
148 Since January 2013, the HLTF has focused on the zero hunger challenge (ZHC) as its central theme. Launched at the 2012 UN Conference on Sustainable Development (Rio+20), the ZHC is working towards a hunger-free world.
149 The ACP (African, Caribbean and Pacific) Group comprises seventy-nine members, forty of which are least-developed countries, most of them from Africa. The objective of the ACP Group is to contribute to the economic development and social progress of its Member States.

Almost 140 international intergovernmental organisations have been granted formal or *ad hoc* observer status with WTO councils and committees.[150] Likewise, the WTO participates in the work of many international organisations. In all, the WTO Secretariat maintains working relations with almost 200 international organisations active in areas of interest to the WTO.

Apart from cooperating with international intergovernmental organisations, the WTO also cooperates with non-governmental organisations (NGOs). Article V:2 of the *WTO Agreement* states:

> The General Council may make appropriate arrangements for consultation and cooperation with non-governmental organizations concerned with matters related to those of the WTO.

On 18 July 1996, the General Council thus adopted a set of guidelines clarifying the framework for relations with civil society in general and NGOs in particular.[151] In these guidelines, the General Council explicitly recognised 'the role NGOs can play to increase the awareness of the public in respect of WTO activities'.[152] However, the General Council was equally clear that NGOs could not, and should not, be *directly* involved in the work of the WTO. A very modest 'breakthrough' of sorts in the relationship between the WTO and civil society was realised in the context of the Singapore Ministerial Conference in December 1996, when NGOs were invited to attend the plenary meetings of the Ministerial Conference.[153] However, the 108 NGOs that attended did not have observer status; they were only passive auditors, and were not allowed to make any statements. Not surprisingly, this degree of involvement did not satisfy civil society, and their dissatisfaction expressed itself in publications and in public debates as well as in large and rowdy demonstrations. The expression of this dissatisfaction reached its apex on the streets of Seattle during the 1999 Ministerial Conference in that American city. Overnight, the global public became familiar with the WTO through images of violent protest against it. In the year following the Seattle debacle, the General Council held informal but intensive consultations on the issue of the involvement of civil society in the work of the WTO.[154] From these consultations, it was clear that no Member wished to undermine the intergovernmental character of the WTO. Moreover, most, if not all, Members were of the opinion that the dialogue with civil society is first and foremost a responsibility for Member governments and should take place at the national level. However, the positions of Members differed significantly on whether civil society, and in particular NGOs, can and should play a greater role in the work of the WTO. On the one hand, the position championed by many of the industrialised Members was (and is) that the

150 See www.wto.org/english/thewto_e/coher_e/coher_e.htm.

151 *Guidelines for Arrangements on Relations with Non-Governmental Organizations*, Decision adopted by the General Council on 18 July 1996, WT/L/162, dated 23 July 1996.

152 *Ibid.*

153 Moreover, an NGO centre with facilities for organising gatherings and workshops was set up alongside the official conference centre.

154 This issue is also referred to as the 'external transparency' issue. See also below, fn. 154, p. 430.

involvement of NGOs in the work of the WTO should be a 'two-way street'. The involvement of NGOs should be a 'give and take' relationship; it involves not only informing NGOs about the work and activities of the WTO but also being informed by NGOs on issues of relevance to the WTO. On the other hand, the position of many developing-country Members was (and is) that the relationship between the WTO and NGOs can only be a 'one-way street'. Treading on (very) thin ice, the then WTO Director-General, Mike Moore, noted in March 2002 with regard to the role of NGOs in the WTO:

> The WTO will always remain an inter-governmental organization, because ultimately it is always our member Governments and Parliaments that must ratify any agreements we conclude. We need to encourage better-focused and more constructive inputs from civil society. *They should be given a voice, but not a vote.*[155]

Many Members would not agree to give NGOs 'a voice' in the WTO. The debate on the desirability of the involvement of NGOs in the work of the WTO is a complex one, with both arguments in favour and arguments against such greater involvement. There are four main *arguments in favour* of greater NGO involvement. First, NGO participation will enhance the WTO decision-making process because NGOs have a wealth of specialised knowledge, resources and analytical capacity that governments do not necessarily have. Second, public confidence in the WTO will increase when NGOs have the opportunity to be heard and to observe the decision-making process. Third, transnational interests and concerns may not be adequately represented by any national government. By allowing NGO involvement in WTO discussions, the WTO would hear about these interests and concerns. Fourth, hearing NGOs at the WTO can compensate for the fact that NGOs are not always and everywhere heard at the national level. There are equally four main *arguments against* greater involvement of NGOs in the work of the WTO. First, NGO involvement may lead the decision-making process to be captured by special interests. Second, many NGOs are neither accountable to an electorate nor representative in a general way, and may thus lack legitimacy. NGOs typically advocate relatively narrow interests. Third, WTO decision-making, with its consensus requirement, is already very difficult. NGO involvement will make negotiations and decision-making even more difficult. Fourth, since developed-country NGOs are usually better organised and funded than developing-country NGOs, greater NGO involvement would introduce another element of asymmetry in WTO negotiations. Note that most developing-country Members object to greater involvement of NGOs in the WTO because they view many NGOs, and in particular NGOs focusing on environmental or labour issues, as inimical to their interests.[156]

155 M. Moore, 'How Trade Liberalization Impacts on Employment', speech to the International Labour Organization, 18 March 2002. Emphasis added.

156 With regard to developing-country NGOs focusing on environmental and labour issues, it has been alleged that the source of funding of these NGOs is not always transparent and may come from developed-country Members.

Since Seattle, the WTO's relationship with civil society has much improved, and this not as a result of a major institutional reform but as a result of a number of concrete, pragmatic initiatives by the WTO Secretariat.[157] Today, 'cooperation' with civil society essentially focuses on: (1) symposia or public fora;[158] (2) regular briefings for NGOs on the work of WTO bodies and trade topics of specific interest;[159] (3) the dissemination to WTO Members and the general public of NGO position papers and studies;[160] (4) organising regional workshops for NGOs;[161] and (5) the setting up of a NGO centre during ministerial conferences to facilitate the lobbying work of NGOs in the margin of these meetings.[162] The WTO also collaborates with certain NGOs to deliver technical assistance.[163]

One of the most successful outreach activities of the WTO is the annual WTO Public Forum. First organised in 2001, the Public Forum 'has become one of the most important meeting grounds for dialogue' between the WTO and civil society.[164] The WTO Public Forum attracts each year over 1,500 participants, including not only NGO representatives, but also government officials, business representatives, academics, students, officials of other international organisations, parliamentarians, lawyers and journalists from countries worldwide.[165] Under the title 'Inclusive Trade', the 2016 Public Forum discussed and assessed – over three days – the role of SMEs in international trade, how new technologies transform international trade, and how women can participate more fully in international trade.[166]

The improved and timely access to WTO documents has also contributed to the improvement of the relationship between the WTO and civil society. In the Doha Ministerial Declaration of November 2001, Members stated:

> [W]e are committed to making the WTO's operations more transparent, including through more effective and prompt dissemination of information, and to improve dialogue with the public.[167]

157 Note also that the mobilisation of civil society against economic globalisation has weakened in force (see above, p. 80); and that the WTO's weakness as a global rule-maker, apparent from its failure to reach agreement in the context of the Doha Development Round negotiations, has made it a much less appealing target for protest. Some would say that civil society has lost interest in the WTO.

158 On the 2016 WTO Public Forum, see below, p. 109.

159 In 2014, the WTO Secretariat undertook ten NGO briefings. Since 2000, the WTO Secretariat organised 230 NGO briefings. See *WTO Annual Report 2015*, 128.

160 In 2015 NGOs submitted seventeen position papers and studies to the WTO Secretariat. See *WTO Annual Report 2016*, 139.

161 In 2015, the WTO organised three regional workshops for NGOs: in Nairobi, Kenya (also attended by Kenyan Members of Parliament); in Cape Town, South Africa (in collaboration with the Friedrich Ebert Stiftung (FES)); and in Senegal (in collaboration with Organisation Internationale de la Francophonie). See *WTO Annual Report 2016*, 138.

162 At the Nairobi Ministerial Conference, 232 NGOs from 49 countries were accredited. See *ibid.*, 138.

163 Note, in this regard, for example, the collaboration with the International Centre for Trade and Sustainable Development (ICTSD) on technical assistance relating to WTO dispute settlement, and in particular the Specialized Training Course on WTO Litigation, organised in April–May 2012. This course also involved the Advisory Centre on WTO Law (ACWL).

164 See *WTO Annual Report 2012*, 126.

165 See www.wto.org/english/forums_e/public_forum_e/public_forum_e.htm. 166 See *ibid.*

167 Ministerial Conference, *Doha Ministerial Declaration*, WT/MIN(01)/DEC/1, dated 20 November 2001, para. 10.

In May 2002, WTO Members agreed, after years of discussion, to accelerate the de-restriction of official WTO documents. Pursuant to the Decision of the General Council of 14 May 2002 on *Procedures for the Circulation and De-restriction of WTO Documents*, most WTO documents are now immediately available to the public and those documents that are initially restricted are de-restricted sooner.[168]

At the February 2016 meeting of the General Council, WTO Director-General Roberto Azevêdo reported:

> Over recent weeks I have also been in touch with the private sector – and with civil society more broadly. Again, these exchanges have been positive. Several parties expressed their interest in having a deeper, more interactive dialogue about WTO work with other stakeholders. I have been approached by some – in particular the ICC and B20 – to facilitate such a dialogue amongst them and others here in Geneva.[169]

In response to this request of the International Chamber of Commerce (ICC) and the B20 group of leading independent business associations from G20 economies, the WTO organised on 30 May 2016 its first Trade Dialogues event, bringing together over sixty business leaders from developed as well as developing countries to discuss the challenges and opportunities they face in conducting trade operations and to discuss how the WTO can help in dealing with them.[170]

3.2.6 Technical Assistance to Developing Countries

The functions of the WTO listed in Article III of the *WTO Agreement* do not explicitly include technical assistance to developing-country Members. Yet this is, in practice, an important function of the WTO. Of course, it could be argued that this function is implied in the other functions discussed above, in particular the function of facilitating the implementation, administration and operation, and of furthering the objectives, of the *WTO Agreement*. However, in view of its importance, it deserves to be mentioned separately.

In order to exercise their rights and obligations under the *WTO Agreement*, to reap the benefits of their membership of the WTO and to participate fully and effectively in trade negotiations, most developing-country Members need to have more expertise and resources in the area of trade law and policy. This is recognised in many WTO agreements, including the *SPS Agreement*, the *TBT Agreement*, the *TRIPS Agreement*, the *Customs Valuation Agreement* and the *Dispute Settlement Understanding*, which all specifically provide for technical assistance to developing-country Members. This technical assistance may take the form of bilateral assistance, given by other Members, or multilateral assistance, given by, *inter alia*, the WTO.

168 See General Council, *Procedures for the Circulation and De-restriction of WTO Documents*, WT/L/452, dated 16 May 2002.

169 See www.wto.org/english/news_e/news16_e/gc_rpt_24feb16_e.htm.

170 See www.wto.org/english/news_e/news16_e/bus_30may16_e.htm.

In the Doha Ministerial Declaration of November 2001, the Ministerial Conference declared that:

> technical cooperation and capacity building are core elements of the development dimension of the multilateral trading system.[171]

As an essential element of the Doha Development Agenda, the WTO embarked in 2002 on a programme of greatly enhanced support for developing countries in the form of trade-related technical assistance and training.[172] Under the current Biennial Technical Assistance and Training Plan 2016–17, the WTO budget for trade-related technical assistance and training amounts to CHF 19 million (Swiss francs) for 2016 and 2017.[173] Much of this funding does not come out of the regular WTO budget but out of the Doha Development Agenda Global Trust Fund, commonly referred to as the Global Trust Fund.[174] The Global Trust Fund is a fund to which Members make *voluntary* contributions. During most of the previous decade, funding available for WTO technical assistance activities grew rapidly due to generous contributions by WTO Members. However, as a result of budget austerity measures by Member governments in the wake of the global economic crisis, the voluntary contributions have decreased dramatically in the last few years.[175] The WTO has, however, done much with relatively little and declining funding.

The WTO's technical assistance and training activities come in many different forms and sizes. In 2015, the WTO organised 321 different activities, either in Geneva or around the world. The technical assistance and training activities undertaken by the WTO include: (1) e-learning courses, the first level of the Progressive Learning Strategy (PLS);[176] (2) regional trade policy courses and seminars for intermediate level training;[177] (3) advanced trade policy courses and seminars held in Geneva;[178] (4) technical support missions to specific developing-country

171 Ministerial Conference, *Doha Ministerial Declaration*, WT/MIN(01)/DEC/1, dated 20 November 2001, para. 38.

172 For an overview, see M. Smeets, 'Trade Capacity Building in the WTO: Main Achievements Since Doha and Key Challenges', *Journal of World Trade*, 47(5), 2013, 1047–90.

173 See Biennial Technical Assistance and Training Plan 2016–17, WT/COMTD/W/211, dated 30 October 2015.

174 See *ibid.*, para 151.

175 There has been a progressive decrease in the contributions from an annual average of CHF 19 million between 2005 and 2009 down to less than CHF 8 million in 2014. See *ibid.*, para 153.

176 There were twenty-four certified online courses on a dedicated e-platform accessible from the WTO website. Note that successful participation in these e-learning courses is a prerequisite for eligibility to apply for the trade policy courses mentioned under points (2) and (3) of this list. In 2015, a total of 7,523 participants from 145 countries enrolled in these e-learning courses. See *WTO Annual Report 2016*, 134.

177 Regional activities held in 2015 comprised eight-week regional trade policy courses, held for generalists in seven regions (English-speaking Africa; French-speaking Africa; Asia and the Pacific; the Caribbean; Latin America; Arab and Middle East countries; and Central and Eastern Europe and Central Asia) and courses for specialists such as a workshop on SPS measures and TBT for English-speaking Africa held in Kenya; a regional workshop on intellectual property and public health for French-speaking Africa, held in Côte d'Ivoire; a seminar on the Government Procurement Agreement for Central and Eastern Europe and Central Asia and the Caucasus, held at the Joint Vienna Institute; a seminar on agriculture for Arab and Middle East countries, held in the UAE; and the 3rd Singapore–WTO Policy Dialogue on the world trading system. See *WTO Annual Report 2016*, 132.

178 In 2015, three Geneva-based advanced trade policy courses, each lasting eight weeks, were held for generalists. Advanced courses were run on various subjects, including dispute settlement, TRIPS, regional trade agreements, SPS issues, trade in services and trade policy analysis. See *ibid.*

Members;[179] (5) the 'WTO reference centres' in developing countries;[180] (6) support for teaching and research on the WTO and international trade;[181] (7) the 'Geneva Week';[182] and (8) internship programmes for government officials.[183]

The Institute for Training and Technical Cooperation (ITTC), established within the WTO Secretariat in 2003 coordinates these technical assistance and training activities. The ITTC implements a biennial technical assistance and training plan (TA Plan), adopted by the WTO Committee on Trade and Development, in which all WTO Members are represented.[184]

In recent years, trade-related official development assistance (ODA) has amounted to about US$25–30 billion a year.[185] The technical assistance and training activities of the WTO – in this larger context very modest – are part of the broader spectrum of bilateral, regional and multilateral efforts to enhance trade. Note that at the Hong Kong Ministerial Conference in December 2005, the WTO launched the Aid for Trade initiative, which concerns all ODA specifically targeted at assisting developing countries, particularly least-developed countries, in developing trade-related skills and infrastructure.[186] In the context of the Aid for Trade initiative, the WTO's role is to: (1) ensure that the many national, regional and international donors and organisations understand the *trade-related* needs of developing countries and least-developed countries; (2) encourage them to meet those needs; (3) facilitate and coordinate the efforts made in this respect by different donors and organisations; (4) support improved ways of monitoring and evaluating Aid for Trade; and (5) encourage mainstreaming of trade into national development strategies. In 2007, the WTO organised the First Global Review of Aid for Trade, a two-day meeting attended by donor governments,

179 Such technical missions are undertaken at the request of the developing-country Member concerned to: (i) assist developing-country Members on specific tasks related to the implementation of obligations under the WTO agreements (such as the adoption of trade legislation or notifications); and/or (ii) provide support to mainstream trade into national plans for economic development. An example being, TPR follow-up workshops, for details see above, p. 104.

180 In 2015, nine new WTO reference centres were established: seven in Africa (Chad, Lesotho, Cameroon, Democratic Republic of the Congo, Equatorial Guinea, Guinea and Uganda); one in the Middle East (Lebanese Republic); and one in Central Asia (Kyrgyz Republic). See *WTO Annual Report 2016*, 134.

181 This support is provided through: (1) the WTO Chairs Programme, which is now in its second phase (launched in May 2014) and encompasses twenty-one universities in developing-country Members and least-developed-country Members; and (2) the Academic Support Programme, which supports academic institutions from developing-country and least-developed-country Members outside the scope of the WTO Chairs Programme. See *WTO Annual Report 2016*, 163.

182 The 'Geneva Week' is a special week-long event which brings to Geneva representatives of developing-country Members without a permanent representation (see below, p. 129) to brief them on recent developments at the WTO. From 23 to 27 November 2015, the WTO organised the 31st 'Geneva Week'. See www.wto.org/english/tratop_e/devel_e/genwk31_e.htm.

183 The Netherlands Trainee Programme (NTP), the Mission Internship Programme (MIP), the Regional Coordinator Internship Programme (RCI) and the Accession Internship Programme give priority to applicants from Africa and LDCs, small and vulnerable economies, and countries in the process of acceding to the WTO. In 2015, seventeen interns completed the MIP, fourteen the NTP and nine each the RCI and the Accession Internship Programme. See *WTO Annual Report 2016*, 134.

184 See below, p. 111. For the current biennial technical assistance and training plan, see WT/COMTD/W/211, dated 30 October 2015.

185 See Aid for Trade Factsheet, www.wto.org/english/tratop_e/devel_e/a4t_e/a4t_factsheet_e.htm.

186 See Ministerial Declaration adopted on 18 December 2005 at the Hong Kong Ministerial Conference (6th MC), WT/MIN(05)/DEC, dated 22 December 2005, para. 57.

other international organisations, civil society and the private sector, to assess critically the success of the Aid for Trade initiative. The Fifth Global Review, which took place in July 2015, was based on the theme 'Reducing Trade Costs for Inclusive, Sustainable Growth' and focused on how high trade costs can negatively affect the ability of developing countries, and in particular least-developed countries, to fully benefit from the market access opportunities of the multilateral trading system.[187]

The main mechanism through which least-developed countries access Aid for Trade resources is the Enhanced Integrated Framework for Least-Developed Countries (EIF).[188] The WTO is one of the six partner agencies of the EIF, along with the IMF, the World Bank, UNCTAD, UNDP and the ITC. The EIF Executive Secretariat is housed at the WTO.[189] Presently, the EIF is in its second phase (2016–22)[190] and aims at: (1) a strengthened role of trade in policies to reduce poverty; (2) an increase in productive capacity and presence in international markets of least-developed countries; and (3) the adoption by least-developed countries of fully sustainable trade policies and the development of their institutional capacity.[191]

4 MEMBERSHIP AND INSTITUTIONAL STRUCTURE

The *institutional structure* of the WTO differs little from that of many other intergovernmental international organisations. By contrast, its *membership* has features that are uncommon among these organisations. Below, both the WTO's membership and its institutional structure will be discussed in turn.

4.1 Membership of the WTO

With 164 Members,[192] representing approximately 99.5 per cent of the world population and 98 per cent of world trade, the WTO is a universal organisation.[193]

187 The three-day meeting attracted over 1,500 delegates to its 18 plenary sessions and 28 side events. See *WTO Annual Report 2016*, 124.

188 In the first phase of EIF (2009–15), 141 projects totalling US$140.690 million across 51 countries were delivered. Of these projects, 105 supported trade and development capacity while 36 projects aimed to help countries address supply-side constraints and increase their ability to trade. See *WTO Annual Report 2016*, 129.

189 Note in this context also the *Standards and Trade Development Facility*. See below, p. 990.

190 Fifteen donor countries have pledged US$90 million for Phase Two of the EIF (Australia, Denmark, Estonia, the European Union, Finland, France, Germany, Korea, Luxembourg, Norway, the Netherlands, Saudi Arabia, Sweden, Switzerland and the United Kingdom). The support was confirmed at the Pledging Conference in Nairobi on 14 December 2015, the eve of the WTO's Ministerial Conference. Phase Two commenced on 1 January 2016. See *WTO Annual Report 2016*, 128.

191 See EIF Website, www.enhancedif.org/en/eif-phase-2. The role of the EIF in achieving sustainable development is recognised in the United Nations 2030 Agenda for Sustainable Development – the Sustainable Development Goals (SDGs), specifically SDG8, adopted by the UN General Assembly on 25 September 2015. See above, p. 2.

192 Afghanistan joined the WTO as its 164th Member on 29 July 2016.

193 The world trade figure is based on *WTO Annual Report 2015*; and world population figure is based on data available on the website of the World Bank and the WTO.

This section will consecutively deal with: (1) the current membership of the WTO; (2) accession to the WTO; (3) special and differential treatment; (4) waivers and opt-outs; and (5) withdrawal, suspension and expulsion.

4.1.1 Current Membership

The composition of the current membership of the WTO is very diverse as well as confusing. It includes States but also separate customs territories; it includes all developed countries but also most developing countries; it includes the European Union but also all EU Member States; and it features multiple, often overlapping, groups, coalitions and alliances pursuing different goals.

First, the WTO membership does not include only States. Separate customs territories possessing full autonomy in the conduct of their external commercial relations and in the other matters covered by the *WTO Agreement* can also be WTO Members.[194] There are currently three WTO Members which are not States but separate customs territories: Hong Kong, China (commonly referred to as Hong Kong), Macau, China (commonly referred to as Macau) and Chinese Taipei (which joined the WTO as the Separate Customs Territory of Taiwan, Penghu, Kinmen and Matsu).[195]

Second, three-quarters of the 164 Members of the WTO are developing countries. There is no WTO definition of the concept of 'developing country'.[196] The status of 'developing-country Member' is based, to a large extent, on self-selection. Members announce whether they consider themselves 'developing' countries.[197] As discussed throughout this book, developing-country Members benefit from special and differential treatment under many of the WTO agreements and may receive WTO technical assistance.[198] Other Members can, and occasionally do, challenge the decision of a Member to claim developing-country member status and to make use of special and differential treatment provisions available to developing countries. For some Members, such as China, the status of 'developing-country Member' was part of the accession negotiations.[199]

The group of WTO developing-country Members is very diverse in its composition. This group includes: continent-sized countries and minuscule island States;

194 See Article XII:1 of the *WTO Agreement*. The Explanatory Notes attached to the *WTO Agreement* stipulate that the 'terms "country" or "countries" as used in this Agreement and the Multilateral Trade Agreements are to be understood to include any separate customs territory Member of the WTO'.

195 On the European Union, see below, pp. 115–16.

196 Note, however, that Article XVIII:1 of the GATT 1994 (Governmental Assistance to Economic Development) refers to: 'those [Members] the economies of which can only support low standards of living and are in the early stages of development'. Furthermore, Article XXXVI of the GATT 1994 (under Part IV, Trade and Development), reminding the Members of the objectives and principles of the Agreement, refers to lower standards of living, lower export earnings and a less diversified economy in relation to 'less developed [Members]'.

197 Note that, in the context of the national Generalized Systems of Preferences (GSP), adopted under the Enabling Clause of the GATT 1994 (see below, p. 322), it is, on the contrary, the preference-giving Member that decides which countries qualify for the preferential tariff treatment.

198 See e.g. below, pp. 687, 692, 763, 866 and 980.

199 See Report of the Working Party on the Accession of China, WT/ACC/CHN/49, dated 1 October 2001, paras. 8 and 9. Para. 9 of the Report of the Working Party noted 'the pragmatic approach taken in China's case in a few areas'. For example, China conceded that it would not seek to invoke Articles 27.8, 27.9 and 27.13 of the *SCM Agreement*, but reserved the right to benefit from Articles 27.10, 27.11, 27.12 and 27.15. See *ibid.*, para. 171.

fast-growing, export-oriented emerging economies and quasi-autarkic countries; agricultural-products-exporting countries and net-food-importing countries; mineral-rich countries and countries less endowed by nature; and democratic, well-governed countries and totalitarian, corruption-riddled countries.

The group of WTO developing-country Members includes: upper-middle income countries, such as Brazil, China, South Africa, Ecuador, Tonga and Saint Lucia; lower-middle income countries, such as Bangladesh, India, Pakistan, Nigeria, Kenya, Egypt and Ghana; and low-income countries, such as Cambodia, Haiti, Mali and Nepal.[200] As discussed in Chapter 1 as well as later in this chapter, over the last decade, developing-country Members, and in particular the emerging economies among them, have played an ever more important role in the WTO, not so much because of their numbers but because of their increasing importance in the global economy.[201]

Among the low-income country Members, there are currently thirty-six least-developed countries.[202] Least-developed-country Members constitute one-fifth of the WTO membership. The WTO recognises as least-developed countries those countries which have been designated as such by the United Nations.[203] As discussed throughout this book, least-developed-country Members benefit from *additional* special and differential treatment.[204] By far the most populous of the least-developed-country Members is Bangladesh.[205] The group of least-developed-country Members includes many African countries, such as Angola, Mozambique and Niger, and a few Asian countries, such as Cambodia, Laos and Myanmar.

A third aspect of the diverse and confusing nature of the current WTO membership is the status of the European Union and its twenty-eight Member States. Article XI:1 of the *WTO Agreement* explicitly provides for the WTO membership of the 'European Communities', now referred to as the 'European Union'.[206] At the

200 For this classification of countries as upper-middle income (GNI per capita of US$4,126 to US$12,735), lower-middle income (GNI per capita of US$1,046 to US$4,125) and low income (GNI per capita of US$1,045 or lower), see http://data.worldbank.org/about/country-and-lending-groups. On Bangladesh, see below, p. 115, fn. 205.

201 See above, pp. 7–11, and below, pp. 152–6. On the question whether 'emerging economies' should still benefit from special and differential treatment linked to the status of developing-country Member, see below, pp. 687–8.

202 See for the complete list of LDC Members www.wto.org/english/thewto_e/whatis_e/tif_e/org7_e.htm.

203 The United Nations designates forty-eight countries as least-developed. See UNCTAD, *The Least Developed Countries Report 2015*, UNCTAD/LDC/2015. Note that the share of world trade of the least-developed countries is 1.1 per cent of the total. See also above, pp. 9–10.

204 See above, p. 124.

205 Note that while Bangladesh is now ranked by the World Bank among the lower-middle income countries (see http://data.worldbank.org/country/bangladesh), the UN still lists it among the least-developed countries (see www.un.org/en/development/desa/policy/cdp/cdp_ldcs_countryfacts.shtml).

206 On 29 November 2009, the World Trade Organization received a Verbal Note (WT/L/779) from the Council of the European Union and the Commission of the European Communities stating that, by virtue of the *Treaty of Lisbon amending the Treaty on European Union and the Treaty establishing the European Community* (done at Lisbon, 13 December 2007), as of 1 December 2009, the 'European Union' replaces and succeeds the 'European Community'. On 13 July 2010, the World Trade Organization received a second Verbal Note (WT/Let/679) from the Council of the European Union confirming that, with effect from 1 December 2009, the European Union replaced the European Community and assumed all the rights and obligations of the European Community in respect of all WTO agreements. Note that the Verbal Notes refer to the 'European Community' rather than the 'European Communities', the term used in Article XI:1 of the *WTO Agreement*. In *EC and certain member States – Large Civil Aircraft (2011)*, the Appellate Body stated that it 'understand[s] the reference in the Verbal Notes to the "European Community" to be a reference to the "European Communities"'. See Appellate Body Report, *EC and certain member States – Large Civil Aircraft (2011)*, fn. 1.

same time, all EU Member States are also WTO Members. This 'dual' membership reflects the division of competence between the European Union and its Member States in the various policy areas covered by the *WTO Agreement*.[207] However, it is important to note the following. First, both the European Union and all EU Member States are *full* Members of the WTO and that all rights and obligations of the *WTO Agreement* apply equally to all of them. Second, in practice, it is the European Commission that will act and speak for the European Union *and* all EU Member States in WTO meetings and negotiations.[208]

A fourth aspect of the diverse and confusing nature of the current WTO membership is that the membership features multiple, often overlapping, groups, coalitions and alliances pursuing different goals.[209] The developing-country Members, the least-developed-country Members, and the European Union and its Member States are not the only distinguishable groups within the WTO membership. Other formal or informal groups and alliances exist in the WTO. Some of these groups have been formed to defend common interests and advance common positions; they coordinate (or try to coordinate) positions and, when appropriate, speak in unison. This category of groups includes the Association of South East Asian Nations (ASEAN), the Group of Latin America and Caribbean Countries (GRULAC) and the African, Caribbean and Pacific Group (ACP). However, the North American Free Trade Agreement (NAFTA) and the Southern Common Market (MERCOSUR), while constituting significant efforts at regional economic integration, have not, or have hardly ever, spoken with one voice within the WTO. A well-known and quite effective alliance of a different kind was the Cairns group of nineteen agricultural-products-exporting developed and developing countries, including Canada, Australia, Brazil and Indonesia. This group was set up in the mid 1980s to campaign for agricultural trade liberalisation and was an important force in negotiations on trade in agricultural products. However, at the Cancún Ministerial Conference in September 2003, the Cairns group seemed to have all but disappeared. In the run-up to, and at, the Cancún Ministerial Conference, a new influential group of developing countries, including China, India, Indonesia, Brazil, Egypt, Argentina and South Africa,

207 See Opinion 1/94 of the European Court of Justice of 15 November 1994 regarding the competence of the then European Communities (now European Union) to conclude international agreements concerning services and the protection of intellectual property, *European Court Reports* 1994 I-05267. Note, however, the subsequent adoption of the Treaty of Lisbon (which entered into force on 1 December 2009) and the evolution in the ECJ's case law in favour of the exclusive competence of the European Union. See in particular the Judgment of the Court of 22 October 2013, *European Commission* v. *Council of the European Union*, Case C-137/12, overruling Opinion 1/94 regarding competence of the European Union to conclude international agreements concerning services, *European Court Reports* 2013, 675. Note also that in September 2016, the ECJ held its hearing for *Opinion 2/15*, which regards the competence of the European Union to conclude a free-trade agreement with Singapore. *Opinion 2/15* will further delineate the scope of the European Union's exclusive competence in the field of trade policy.

208 This is not the case for matters relating to the WTO budget. In particular, in the Budget Committee, the EU Member States, and not the European Commission, are active. On the contributions by the European Union and its Member States to the WTO budget, see below, pp. 157–8.

209 For a list of, and a map showing geographically, the groupings, coalitions and alliances of WTO Members, see www.wto.org/english/tratop_e/dda_e/negotiating_groups_maps_e.htm.

emerged. This group, commonly referred to as the 'G-20',[210] forcefully demanded the dismantling of the trade-distorting and protectionist agricultural policies of the European Union, the United States and other industrialised countries.[211]

Also in Cancún, a new group known as the ACP/LDC/AU alliance, but also referred to as the 'G-90', emerged as the 'representative' of the interests of the poorest countries.[212] Among the many other 'common interest' groups, coalitions and alliances, note the 'Cotton Four' or 'C-4', a group of four West African cotton-producing Members, campaigning against the 'unfair' practices of the United States and the European Union affecting trade in cotton.[213] As discussed below, 'common interest' groups, coalitions and alliances play an important role in helping developing-country Members to overcome, or at least mitigate, their lack of resources and expertise, and to participate more effectively in WTO negotiations and decision-making.

Other groups have been formed to allow for discussion in small(er) groups of Members, to agree on new initiatives, to break deadlocks and to achieve compromises. The best-known example of such a group was the 'Quad', which during the Uruguay Round and in the early years of the WTO was the group of the then four largest trading entities, i.e. the European Communities, the United States, Japan and Canada. The Quad was at the core of all negotiations. However, the Quad has now been replaced by a new group of key WTO Members, the G-5, consisting of the European Union, the United States, India, Brazil and China.[214] As already noted above, without agreement among these key Members, progress within the WTO on the further liberalisation and/or regulation of trade is not feasible. This shift in political power within the WTO reflects the growing importance of China, India and Brazil in the world economy.[215]

210 Note that, *outside* the WTO, the 'G-20' commonly refers to a different group of countries, consisting of the major (developed as well as developing) economies, which as a group account for more than 80 per cent of the gross world product, 80 per cent of world trade and two-thirds of the world's population. This group has met regularly since 2008 to discuss international (economic) issues.

211 The G-20 includes countries from Africa (Egypt, Nigeria, South Africa, Tanzania and Zimbabwe), from Asia (China, India, Indonesia, Pakistan, Philippines and Thailand) and from Latin America (Argentina, Bolivia, Brazil, Chile, Cuba, Ecuador, Guatemala, Mexico, Paraguay, Peru, Uruguay and Venezuela). Contrary to what the term 'G-20' seems to imply, the *number* of countries that are members of the G-20 has in fact varied over time.

212 This group is made up of the ACP countries, the least-developed countries and the countries of the African Union.

213 Note further the following 'common interest' groups: G-10 (regarding non-trade concerns in agriculture); G-33 ('Friends of Special Products' in agriculture); NAMA-11 (regarding limits on market opening for industrial products); Small, Vulnerable Economies (SVEs); Friends of Fish (FoFs); Friends of Anti-Dumping Negotiations (FANs); Friends of Ambition (NAMA); Paragraph 6 Countries; Tropical Products; W52 Sponsors (TRIPS); and Low Income Economies in Transition.

214 Next to the G-5, also the G-7, consisting of the G-5 plus Japan and Australia, has played a role since the demise of the Quad in efforts to agree on new initiatives, to break deadlocks and to achieve compromises. This was the case, for example, during the intense Doha Round negotiations in July 2008. Note that, *outside* the WTO, the 'G-7' refers to a different group of countries, namely, the group of the major developed economies, which have met regularly since 1975 to discuss international (economic) issues. Finally, note that the term 'G-5' is occasionally (and confusingly) also used to refer to the group of the five major emerging economies (Brazil, China, India, Mexico and South Africa).

215 See above, p. 10.

Finally, note that, in addition to Members, the WTO also has twenty Observer Governments. With the exception of the Holy See, these Observer Governments must start accession negotiations within five years of becoming an Observer. Intergovernmental international organisations, such as the UN, the IMF, the World Bank, UNCTAD, the FAO, WIPO and the OECD, also have permanent Observer status. Other international organisations have Observer status in the WTO bodies that deal in particular with the matters within their mandate. As such, the Joint FAO/WHO Codex Alimentarius Commission has Observer status in the WTO SPS Committee; and the Convention on International Trade in Endangered Species (CITES) has Observer status in the WTO Committee on Trade and Environment.[216]

4.1.2 Accession

Becoming a Member of the WTO is not an easy matter. This subsection discusses the accession process and looks at some past accessions and ongoing accession negotiations.

The *WTO Agreement* initially provided for two ways of becoming a WTO Member. The first, 'original membership', was provided for in Article XI:1 of the *WTO Agreement*, and allowed Contracting Parties to the GATT 1947 (and the European Communities) to join the WTO by: (1) accepting the terms of the *WTO Agreement* and the Multilateral Trade Agreements; and (2) making concessions and commitments for both trade in goods and services (embodied in national goods and services schedules respectively). This way of becoming a WTO Member was only available at the time of establishment of the WTO.[217] Of the 164 WTO Members, 123 are 'original Members' in that they became Members pursuant to Article XI:1 of the *WTO Agreement*.[218]

The second way of becoming a WTO Member is through accession, and this way is open indefinitely. The procedure for accession is set out in Article XII of the *WTO Agreement*. To become a WTO Member through accession, a State or customs territory has to negotiate the terms of accession with the current Members. The applicant for membership must in principle always accept the terms of the *WTO Agreement* and all Multilateral Trade Agreements. This is not up for negotiation.[219] The accession negotiations focus on: (1) whether the

216 For an exhaustive list of all international organisations having Observer status in the WTO or in one or more WTO bodies, see www.wto.org/english/thewto_e/igo_obs_e.htm.

217 The term 'original membership' is a misnomer. It suggests that there are two sorts of membership with different rights and obligations. This is not the case. In principle, all Members have the same membership rights and obligations. The term 'original membership' is used merely to distinguish between the different ways of acquiring membership. It must be noted, however, that, in the context of WTO accession negotiations, applicants for membership have in certain cases been forced to accept 'WTO-plus' obligations and/or 'WTO-minus' rights. See below, p. 122.

218 Yugoslavia and Syria are the only GATT Contracting Parties which did not become a WTO Member in this way.

219 However, there may be negotiations on whether the applicant for membership should be allowed a transitional period for compliance with specific obligations.

legislation and practices of the applicant for membership are WTO-consistent, and, if not, what needs to be done to make them so; and (2) the market access concessions (for trade in goods) and commitments (for trade in services) the applicant for membership has to make. With regard to the latter, it could be said that the price of the 'ticket of admission' is negotiated. When a State or customs territory accedes to the WTO, it instantly benefits from all the efforts that WTO Members have undertaken in the past to reduce barriers to trade and increase market access. In return for the access to the markets of current Members that a new Member will obtain, that new Member will itself have to open up its market to the current Members. The extent of the market access concessions and commitments that an applicant for membership will be expected to make, or in other words the price of the 'ticket of admission' that it will be expected to pay, will depend to a large extent on its level of economic development.

Generally speaking, there are four phases in the accession process. In the first phase – the 'tell-us-about-yourself' phase[220] – the State or customs territory applying for membership has to report on all aspects of its trade and economic policies that are relevant to the obligations under the WTO agreements, and has to submit a memorandum on these policies to the WTO. A WTO working party, established especially to deal with the request for accession and composed of all (interested) WTO Members, will, on the basis of this 'memorandum on the foreign trade regime' and additional information supplied later, examine with care the WTO consistency of the relevant legislation and practices of the applicant for membership.

When the working party has made satisfactory progress with its examination of the trade and economic policies of the applicant for membership, the second phase is initiated. In this phase – the 'work-out-with-us-individually-what-you-have-to-offer' phase – individual Members and the applicant for membership start bilateral negotiations on market access. Since different Members obviously have different export interests, these negotiations cannot but be bilateral. However, the new Member's market access concessions and commitments, made in any of the bilateral negotiations, will eventually apply equally to all WTO Members as a result of the MFN treatment obligation.[221] These bilateral market access negotiations can be very difficult.

When the working party has fully completed its examination of the WTO consistency of relevant legislation and practices of the applicant *and* individual Members and the applicant for membership have successfully concluded their bilateral market access negotiations, the third phase of the accession process can start. In this phase – the 'let-us-draft-membership-terms' phase – the working party finalises the terms of accession which are set out in: (1) a working party report; (2) a draft 'protocol of accession'; and (3) the draft 'goods schedule' and

220 For the name given to this and the other phases, see the WTO website, www.wto.org.

221 On the MFN treatment obligation, see below, pp. 305–40.

'services schedule', which list all of the market access concessions and commitments of the applicant for membership. This package is submitted to the Ministerial Conference or the General Council.

In the fourth and final phase of the accession process – the 'decision' phase – the Ministerial Conference or the General Council decides, in practice by consensus, on the application for membership.[222] In case of a positive decision, the candidate for membership accedes to the WTO thirty days after it has deposited its instrument of ratification of the protocol of accession. Note that protocols of accession become integral parts of the *WTO Agreement* and are enforceable in dispute settlement.[223]

Even when no major problems are encountered, accession negotiations typically take much time. The shortest accession negotiation to date was that of Kyrgyzstan, lasting two years and ten months. The accession negotiations with Algeria have been going on since 1987.[224] The delays in completing accession negotiations have been severely criticised. However, this situation is not only the result of hard bargaining on the part of WTO Members or political factors. It is also a result of the tardy supply of information by the applicant and the slow pace at which it makes the necessary amendments to its legislation and practices.[225] It can take years to draft, approve and apply the new legislation required for accession to the WTO. As noted by the Minister of Industry and Commerce of Laos at the conclusion of Laos' accession negotiations in September 2012:

> We ... underestimated the difficult negotiations we would have to undergo at the internal front. Quite frankly, trying to convince our trading partners of the position of Lao PDR only to go home, and to convince our internal partners of the justification of the reforms requested, was one of our most difficult and hard tasks.[226]

In recent years Montenegro (2012), Samoa (2012), Russia (2012), Vanuatu (2012), Laos (2013), Tajikistan (2013), Yemen (2014), Seychelles (2015), Kazakhstan (2015), Liberia (2016) and Afghanistan (2016) joined the WTO. Russia was the last major country to join the WTO. On 16 December 2011, the Ministerial Conference adopted the Protocol on the Accession of the Russian Federation, and Russia subsequently became a Member of the WTO on 22 August 2012.[227] While quite different from the accession negotiations with China, discussed

222 On decision-making within the WTO, see below, pp. 145–6.

223 See above, p. 54. The terms of accession are set out in the Protocol of Accession *and* the accompanying working party report. The commitments set out in the working party report, and incorporated in the Protocol by cross-reference, are binding and enforceable. See Panel Reports, *China – Raw Materials (2012)*, paras. 7.112 and 7.114.

224 Algeria originally applied to become a Contracting Party to the GATT 1947 (as it then was).

225 Least-developed countries, in particular, often lack the administrative capacity to conduct the complex negotiations and to draft and apply the necessary changes in national legislation and practices. On General Council guidelines to facilitate the accession of least-developed countries to the WTO (adopted in 2002 and 2012), see below, pp. 121–2.

226 See *Bridges Weekly*, 3 October 2012.

227 Note that, at the time of the adoption of the Russian Accession Protocol, the United States invoked the 'non-application' clause of Article XIII of the *WTO Agreement* with regard to Russia, and Russia invoked this clause against the United States. See below, p. 127.

below,[228] the accession negotiations with Russia were also fraught with disagreements and obstacles.[229] They took eighteen years to complete. In order to join the WTO, Russia had to bring 300 legal acts into conformity with WTO law and had to make substantial market access concessions and commitments.[230] However, according to Russia's Minister of Economic Development, the benefits of accession are expected to be numerous, and include: (1) 'improved quality of goods'; (2) 'a signal to investors of a better business climate'; and (3) 'having access to the WTO's dispute settlement system'.[231]

Initiated in July 2011, the WTO's Least Developed Countries and Accessions Programme (also known as the 'China Programme'),[232] aims to facilitate accession of least-developed countries to the WTO and support their integration into the global economy by strengthening their participation in WTO activities. The China Programme provides financing to support (1) WTO accessions internships;[233] (2) WTO accessions round table meetings;[234] (3) participation of least-developed countries in WTO meetings; (4) South–South dialogue on least-developed countries and development; and (5) Trade Policy Review follow-up workshops for least-developed countries.[235]

As of October 2016, there are nineteen States negotiating their accession to the WTO, including Algeria, Iran, Iraq, Serbia and six least-developed countries.[236] On 25 July 2012, the General Council approved, at the recommendation of the Sub-Committee on Least-Developed Countries, new guidelines to facilitate and speed up accession negotiations with least-developed countries.[237] Of particular interest is that the General Council's Decision sets out concrete guidelines

228 See below, pp. 42–3. Unlike Russia's main exports (oil, gas and minerals), China's main exports (manufactured products) competed with, and constituted a threat to, products of the then WTO Members.

229 The last obstacle to overcome was the opposition of neighbouring WTO Member Georgia to Russia's accession. In 2008, Russia and Georgia fought a brief war over South Ossetia, a disputed border area. A last-minute deal brokered by Switzerland ensured that Georgia did not block the consensus on Russia's accession. On decision-making on accession, see below, pp. 146–7.

230 See WT/L/839, dated 17 December 2011, containing the Decision of the Ministerial Conference of 16 December 2011, with, in an annex, Russia's Protocol of Accession. See also the Report of the Working Party on the Accession of Russia, WT/ACC/RUS/70, dated 17 November 2011.

231 'After Eighteen Year "Marathon", Russia Crosses WTO Finish Line', *Bridges Daily Update*, 17 December 2011.

232 The programme was launched under the WTO Aid for Trade initiative and the funds are contributed by China. In 2015, the government of China pledged to contribute US$500,000 to the programme. See www.wto.org/english/news_e/pres15_e/pr742_e.htm.

233 The accessions internship programme aims to help young professionals from least-developed countries and developing countries to increase their understanding of the WTO and of trade law, international economics and international relations in general. Under this programme five intern positions are available at the WTO on an annual basis. See www.wto.org/english/thewto_e/acc_e/acc_internship_e.htm.

234 In 2015, two round tables were held, the first in Dushanbe, Tajikistan in June, and the second in Nairobi, Kenya, in December. *WTO Annual Report 2016*, 27.

235 In 2015, three TPR follow-up workshops were organised. See above p. 104.

236 See www.wto.org/english/thewto_e/minist_e/mc10_e/briefing_notes_e/brief_accessions_e.htm.

237 This Decision, which is set out in document WT/COMTD/LDC/21, dated 6 July 2012, strengthens the General Council Decision of 10 December 2002 on the facilitation and acceleration of the negotiations for the accession of LDCs to the WTO, contained in document WT/L/508, dated 20 January 2003. Note that, since 1995, nine least-developed countries (Cambodia (2004), Nepal (2004), Cape Verde (2008), Samoa (2012), Vanuatu (2012), Laos (2013), Yemen (2014), Liberia (2016) and Afghanistan (2016)) acceded to the WTO pursuant to Article XII of the *WTO Agreement*. As of October 2016, six least-developed countries were in the process of negotiating their accession to the WTO.

for Members on how to apply 'restraint' when seeking concessions and commitments from least-developed countries applying for membership.

The most difficult and most important accession negotiations ever conducted were those with the People's Republic of China. In 1947, China was one of the original signatories of the GATT, but, after the revolution in 1949, the Chinese nationalist government in Chinese Taipei announced that China would leave the GATT system. The Government of the People's Republic of China in Beijing never recognised this withdrawal decision and, in 1986, it notified the GATT of its wish to resume its status as a GATT Contracting Party. The GATT Contracting Parties considered, however, that China would have to negotiate its re-accession. In 1987, a GATT Working Party on the Accession of China was established, and in 1995 this Working Party was converted into a WTO Working Party. The accession negotiations with China eventually took almost fifteen years and resulted in a legal text of some 900 pages. On 10 November 2001, in Doha, the Ministerial Conference approved by consensus the Protocol on the Accession of the People's Republic of China.[238] On 11 December 2001, China formally became a Member of the WTO.

In order to join the WTO, China agreed to: (1) important market access concessions and commitments; (2) some, as they have been called, 'WTO-plus' obligations and 'WTO-minus' rights; and (3) more generally, offer a more predictable environment for trade and foreign investment in accordance with WTO rules. While China reserves the right of exclusive State trading for products such as cereals, tobacco, fuels and minerals, and maintains some restrictions on transportation and distribution of goods inside the country, many of the restrictions on foreign companies were to be eliminated or considerably eased after a three-year phase-out period. During a twelve-year period starting from the date of accession, a special transitional safeguard mechanism applied. This mechanism allowed other WTO Members to restrict – more easily than under the normal rules on safeguard measures – imports of products of Chinese origin that cause or threaten to cause market disruption to their domestic producers.[239] China is also bound under its Protocol of Accession not to impose export duties on most of its exports, while most WTO Members are not subject to such obligation.[240] On the other hand, measures adversely affecting imports from China in a manner inconsistent with WTO obligations, are phased out, or otherwise dealt with, by the Members maintaining such measures in accordance with mutually agreed terms and timetables specified in an annex to the Protocol of Accession.[241]

238 See WT/L/432, dated 23 November 2001, containing the Decision of the Ministerial Conference of 10 November 2001, with, in Annex, the Protocol on the Accession of the People's Republic of China. See also the Report of the Working Party on the Accession of China, WT/ACC/CHN/49, dated 1 October 2001.

239 See below, pp. 657–8. Note in this regard the *US – Tyres (China) (2011)* dispute.

240 See below, pp. 427–3. Note in this regard the *China – Raw Materials (2012)* dispute.

241 See 'WTO Successfully Concludes Negotiations on China's Entry', WTO Press/243, dated 17 September 2001.

4.1.3 Special and Differential Treatment

As discussed above, many WTO Members are developing countries and thirty-six of them are least-developed countries.[242] Their level of economic development and, with a few exceptions, their participation in international trade are obviously not at par with those developed-country Members. As explicitly stated in the Preamble to the *WTO Agreement*, there is:

> need for positive efforts designed to ensure that developing countries, and especially the least developed among them, secure a share in the growth in international trade commensurate with the needs of their economic development.

The 'positive efforts' undertaken by the WTO in favour of developing countries, take many forms. Almost all WTO agreements have provisions providing for 'special and differential treatment' for developing-country Members to facilitate their integration into the world trading system and to promote their economic development. These 'special and differential treatment' provisions can be subdivided into five categories: (1) provisions aimed at increasing the trade opportunities of developing-country Members; (2) provisions under which WTO developed-country Members should safeguard the interests of developing-country Members; (3) provisions allowing for flexibility of commitments, of action, and use of policy instruments; (4) provisions on transitional time periods; and (5) provisions on technical assistance. In many cases, *additional* special and differential treatment is provided for least-developed-country Members. Therefore, with regard to membership rights and obligations, not all Members are equal. For good reason, there are at least three different categories of Members: developed-country Members, developing-country Members, and least-developed-country Members.[243]

A detailed overview of all WTO 'special and differential treatment' provisions, agreement by agreement, can be found in the 2001 Note by the WTO Secretariat on *Implementation of Special and Differential Treatment Provisions in WTO Agreements and Decisions*.[244] In this book, the 'special and differential treatment' provisions are discussed in the context of the rules to which they relate. For example, Chapter 6 entitled 'Tariff barriers' discusses Article XXXVI:8 of the GATT 1994, which provides that, in tariff negotiations with developed-country Members, developing-country Members are expected to 'reciprocate' only to the extent that is consistent with their development, financial and trade needs.[245]

242 See above, p. 150.

243 In addition, there may be Members, which, as a result of the terms of their Protocol of Accession, are subject to 'WTO plus' obligations and 'WTO-minus' rights. See below, p. 472.

244 See Committee on Trade and Development, *Implementation of Special and Differential Treatment Provisions in WTO Agreements and Decisions*, Note by the WTO Secretariat, WT/COMTD/W/77/Rev.1, dated 21 September 2001, para. 3. See also the addenda to this Note and, in particular, Addendum 4, WT/COMTD/W/77/Rev.1/Add.4, dated 7 February 2002.

245 See below, pp. 426–8.

Note that many 'special and differential treatment' provisions are couched in hortatory language, or at most entail 'best endeavour' obligation.[246] Not surprisingly, developing-country Members have therefore expressed serious concerns regarding the effectiveness of these provisions to address the problems they face. It was therefore agreed that, as part of the Doha Round negotiations, all 'special and differential treatment' provisions shall be reviewed 'with a view of strengthening them and making them more precise, effective and operational'.[247]

Developed-country Members have, however, insisted on the need to differentiate among developing-country Members between, on the one hand, 'emerging economies', of which the GDP in some cases equals or even surpasses the GDP of some EU Member States, and, on the other hand, other developing-country Members still in need of special and differential treatment. Not surprisingly, emerging economies have shown little enthusiasm for such differentiation. Disagreement on who still 'deserves' special and differential treatment is one of the causes for the impasse in the Doha Round negotiations, discussed above.[248]

Of particular interest is the new approach towards special and differential treatment adopted by the recently concluded *Trade Facilitation Agreement* (TFA).[249] The special and differential treatment provisions of the TFA enable developing-country and least-developed-country Members to self-designate the implementation periods of their commitments under the TFA and identify their technical assistance needs.[250] This Member-specific approach grants discretion to developing-country and least-developed-country Members to determine when and how they implement their TFA commitments, without any further negotiation or consultation with other Members.[251] Nora Neufeld noted with regard to this new approach towards special and differential treatment:

> S&D treatment in most WTO Agreements focuses on transition periods. While grace periods are still foreseen in the TF mandate, they are but one part of a much more comprehensive flexibilities package, crucially complemented by the introduction of a conditional link between the existence of implementation capacity and requirements to undertake a commitment. This novel concept was further expanded by determining that developing and

246 See, for example, Article 15 of the *Anti-Dumping Agreement*, discussed below, pp. 763–5; or Article 10.1 of the *SPS Agreement*, discussed below, pp. 980–3.
247 See Doha Ministerial Declaration, para. 44.
248 See above, pp. 91–101. 249 See above, p. 124, and below, pp. 511–12.
250 Under the TFA, developing-country and least-developed-country Members are required to categorise each provision of the TFA, into Category A (provisions that the Member will implement by the time the TFA enters into force (or in the case of a least-developed-country Member within one year after entry into force)); Category B (provisions that the Member will implement after a transitional period following the entry into force of the TFA); or Category C (provisions that the member will implement on a date after a transitional period following the entry into force of the TFA and requiring assistance and support for capacity building). They must notify other WTO Members of these categorisations in accordance with specific timelines outlined in the TFA.
251 See Ben Czapnik, 'The Unique Features of Trade Facilitation Agreement: A Revolutionary New Approach to Multilateral Negotiations or the Exception Which Proves the Rule?', *Journal of International Economic Law*, 2015, 1–22.

least-developed countries would not be obliged to implement aspects of a TF Agreement when required support for infrastructure was not forthcoming.[252]

This new approach constitutes an important departure from the traditional practice of the WTO of granting special and differential treatment based on whether a country belongs to the group of developing-country or least-developed-country Members. Under this new approach, the granting of special and differential treatment is based on the individual situation of a Member. It is, in other words, 'a tailor-made, rather than one-size-fits all approach'.[253]

4.1.4 Waivers and Opt-Outs

Article XVI:4 of the *WTO Agreement* provides that:

> Each Member shall ensure the conformity of its laws, regulations and administrative procedures with its obligations as provided in the annexed Agreements.[254]

However, when a Member finds it difficult, if not impossible, to meet an obligation under one of the WTO agreements, that Member can request the WTO to waive the 'problematic' obligation. Pursuant to Article IX:3 of the *WTO Agreement*, 'exceptional circumstances' may justify such a waiver.[255] The decision of the Ministerial Conference (or the General Council) granting the waiver shall state the exceptional circumstances, the terms and conditions governing the application of the waiver and the date on which the waiver shall be terminated.[256] In 2015, the General Council granted seven waivers. There were in total fourteen waivers in force in 2015.[257]

As is provided in Article IX:4 of the *WTO Agreement*, any waiver granted for a period of more than one year is reviewed annually. The General Council examines whether the exceptional circumstances justifying the waiver still exist and whether the terms and conditions attached to the waiver have been met. On the basis of this annual review, the waiver may be extended, modified or terminated.

One of the most important waivers, which was in force from 2001 to 2007, was a waiver of the MFN treatment obligation of Article I:1 of the GATT 1994, granted to the then European Communities, with respect to preferential tariff treatment given to products of African, Caribbean and Pacific countries under the terms of the Cotonou *ACP–EC Partnership Agreement*. Similar waivers,

252 Nora Neufeld, 'The Long Winding Road: How Members Finally Reached a Trade Facilitation Agreement', WTO, Staff Working Paper ERSD-2014–06, 7 April 2014, 8.

253 *Ibid.*

254 With regard to reservations to the provisions of the WTO agreements, note that Article XVI:5 of the *WTO Agreement* provides that no reservations may be made in respect of provisions of the *WTO Agreement*, and reservations in respect of any of the provisions of the Multilateral Trade Agreements may only be made to the extent provided for in those Agreements. See e.g. Article 15.1 of the *TBT Agreement*, which states that no reservations may be entered without the consent of the other Members.

255 Note that, for waivers of GATT 1994 obligations, provisions of the *Understanding in Respect of Waivers of Obligations under the General Agreement on Tariffs and Trade 1994* also apply.

256 Article IX:4 of the *WTO Agreement*. As discussed below, decisions on waivers are, in practice, always taken by consensus. See below, pp. 125–8.

257 See WT/GC/W/713, dated 19 January 2016.

currently in force, are: (1) the waiver granted to the European Union allowing it to grant preferential tariff treatment to countries of the Western Balkans to 'promote economic expansion and recovery';[258] and (2) the waiver granted to the United States allowing it to provide duty-free treatment to products from sub-Saharan African countries under the African Growth and Opportunity Act (AGOA) to 'alleviate poverty and promote stability and sustainable economic development in sub-Saharan Africa'.[259]

A well-known waiver is the waiver granted to Members producing, under a compulsory licence, essential medicines for HIV, malaria and other life-threatening diseases for export to eligible least-developed countries.[260] Under this waiver, the obligations under Article 31(f) and (h) of the *TRIPS Agreement* are waived to give least-developed-countries access to these essential medicines.[261] Another waiver worth noting is the waiver granted to a large group of Members to allow these Members to take domestic measures under the Kimberley Process aimed at banning trade in conflict diamonds, also referred to as 'blood diamonds'.[262] Under this waiver, the obligations under Articles I, XI and XIII of the GATT 1994 are waived.[263] Another waiver, which has received significant attention of late, is the LDC services waiver, allowing WTO Members to grant preferential treatment to services and service suppliers from least-developed-country Members and eliminate market access limitations. Under this waiver, the obligations under paragraph 1 of Article II of the GATS are waived.[264]

In 2015, the General Council renewed the waiver granted to LDC Members from obligations under paragraphs 8 and 9 of Article 70 of the TRIPS Agreement, until 1 January 2033 or the date when the Member ceases to be a least-developed country.[265]

In *EC – Bananas III (1997)*, the then European Communities argued that the Lomé Waiver, which waived the provisions of Article I:1 of the GATT 1994, should be interpreted to waive also the provisions of Article XIII of the GATT

258 See General Council Decision of 30 November 2011, WT/L/836, dated 5 December 2011. This waiver will expire on 31 December 2016.

259 See General Council Decision of 27 May 2009, WT/L/754, dated 29 May 2009. The General Council extended the waiver, upon request by the United States until 30 September 2025. General Council Decision of 30 November 2015, WT/L/970, dated 2 December 2015.

260 See General Council Decision of 30 August 2003, WT/L/540, dated 2 September 2003. This waiver will terminate for each Member on the date on which an amendment to the *TRIPS Agreement* replacing its provisions takes effect for that Member. See below, p. 1040.

261 See below, pp. 1039–40.

262 See General Council Decision of 15 December 2006, WT/L/676, dated 19 December 2006. This waiver was granted to Australia, Botswana, Brazil, Canada, Croatia, India, Israel, Japan, Korea, Mauritius, Mexico, Norway, the Philippines, Sierra Leone, Chinese Taipei, Thailand, the United Arab Emirates, the United States and Venezuela, and any other Member that has notified the CTG since December 2006 that it wishes to be covered by this waiver. This waiver was extended (until 31 December 2018) by the General Council at its meeting of 11 December 2012.

263 On these GATT 1994 obligations, see below, pp. 307–39 and 482–500.

264 Adopted at the WTO Eighth Ministerial Conference in Geneva in 2011 (WT/L/847), the waiver was originally granted for fifteen years, to 2026, but was extended at the Tenth Ministerial Conference, Nairobi until 2030 (WT/L/982). See www.wto.org/english/news_e/news15_e/serv_05feb15_e.htm.

265 See General Council Decision of 30 November 2015, WT/L/971, dated 2 December 2015.

1994. In that case, the panel accepted this argument to the extent that 'the scope of Article XIII:1 is identical with that of Article I'.[266] The Appellate Body reversed this finding, and noted, with regard to the nature and the interpretation of waivers, the following:

> Although the WTO Agreement does not provide any specific rules on the interpretation of waivers, Article IX of the WTO Agreement and the Understanding in Respect of Waivers of Obligations under the General Agreement on Tariffs and Trade 1994, which provide requirements for granting and renewing waivers, stress the exceptional nature of waivers and subject waivers to strict disciplines. Thus, waivers should be interpreted with great care.[267]

In addition to the possibility to waive obligations under the WTO agreements, the *WTO Agreement* also provides for an 'opt-out' possibility. For political or other reasons (including economic reasons), a Member may not want the WTO rules to apply to its trade relations with another Member. Article XIII of the *WTO Agreement*, entitled 'Non-Application of Multilateral Trade Agreements between Particular Members', states in its first paragraph:

> This Agreement and the Multilateral Trade Agreements in Annexes 1 and 2 shall not apply as between any Member and any other Member if either of the Members, at the time either becomes a Member, does not consent to such application.

It is thus possible for a Member to prevent WTO rules from applying to its trade relations with another Member. However, the 'non-application' or 'opt-out' clause has to be invoked at the time that this Member, or the other, joins the WTO. The 'opt-out' clause cannot be invoked at any later time. The decision to opt out must be notified to the Ministerial Conference (or the General Council) before the latter decides on the accession. In practice, the importance of the 'non-application' clause under the *WTO Agreement* has been limited. Since 1995, this clause has been invoked twelve times (including nine times by the United States)[268] but only three of these invocations are currently still in force.[269] In December 2011, the United States invoked the 'non-application' clause when the Protocol on the Accession of the Russian Federation was adopted and the US Congress had not yet adopted legislation allowing for Russia to be granted MFN status.[270] Russia reciprocated by also invoking Article XIII against the United States.

266 Panel Report, *EC – Bananas III*, para. 7.107.

267 Appellate Body Report, *EC – Bananas III (1997)*, para. 185.

268 See *WTO Analytical Index 2012*, Volume 1, 57. The United States invoked the 'non-application' clause of Article XIII:1 of the *WTO Agreement* with respect to Armenia, Georgia, Kyrgyzstan, Moldova, Mongolia, Romania and Vietnam. Since the publication of the *WTO Analytical Index 2012*, the United States has further invoked the 'non-application' clause with respect to Russia and Tajikistan.

269 As of June 2015, still in force are the invocations of the opt-out clause of Turkey against Armenia (WT/L/501, dated 29 November 2002) of El Salvador against China (WT/L/429, dated 5 November 2001) and of United States against Tajikistan (WT/L/871, dated 7 December 2012).

270 Some Members of Congress objected to granting Russia MFN status, or, as it is now referred to in US law, 'permanent normal trade relations' status because of concerns regarding specific trade issues (such as Russia's use of SPS measures to restrict imports of US-produced meat and weak enforcement of intellectual property rights) and/or concerns regarding human rights and foreign policy issues. See W. H. Cooper, *Permanent Normal Trade Relations (PNTR) Status for Russia and US–Russian Economic Ties*, Congressional Research Service Report for Congress, 15 June 2012.

In December 2012, the US Congress adopted the necessary legislation and Russia was granted MFN status.[271] The United States subsequently revoked its invocation of the 'non-application' clause against Russia and so did Russia vis-à-vis the United States.[272]

4.1.5 Withdrawal, Suspension and Expulsion

Article XV:1 of the *WTO Agreement* states:

> Any Member may withdraw from this Agreement. Such withdrawal shall apply both to this Agreement and the Multilateral Trade Agreements and shall take effect upon the expiration of six months from the date on which written notice of withdrawal is received by the Director-General of the WTO.

WTO Members may thus, at any time, unilaterally withdraw from the WTO. A withdrawal only takes effect, however, upon the expiration of six months from the notification of the decision to withdraw.[273] Note that, when a Member withdraws from the WTO, it cannot remain a party to any of the Multilateral Trade Agreements. Withdrawal is thus an 'all or nothing' option. There is no such thing as a WTO *à la carte*.[274] To date, no Member has ever withdrawn from the WTO. A group of Caribbean banana-producing countries, very disappointed with the outcome of the *EC – Bananas III (1997)* dispute, reportedly 'threatened' at one point to withdraw from the WTO but did not do so.

The *WTO Agreement* does – except in one specific situation – not provide for the suspension or expulsion of a Member.[275] There is no procedure to suspend or exclude from the WTO Members that systematically breach their obligations under the WTO agreements.[276] There are also no rules or procedures for the suspension or expulsion of Members that are guilty of gross violations of human rights or acts of aggression.

4.2 Institutional Structure of the WTO

To carry out the functions and tasks entrusted to the WTO, the *WTO Agreement* provides for manifold bodies. The basic institutional structure of the WTO is set out in Article IV of the *WTO Agreement*, and is shown in Figure 2.1. Subordinate committees and working groups have been added to this structure by later decisions.

271 See W. H. Cooper, *Permanent Normal Trade Relations (PNTR) Status for Russia and US – Russian Economic Ties*, Congressional Research Service Report for Congress, 17 December 2012.

272 In December 2012, the United States also revoked its invocation of the 'non-application' clause against Moldova. See *ibid*.

273 The notification to withdraw is made to the WTO Director-General.

274 Except, of course, with regard to the (currently two) plurilateral agreements. See above, p. 53.

275 Note that the expulsion of a Member is provided for in case of the non-acceptance of certain amendments to the WTO agreements. See below, p. 151.

276 Note, however, the possibility for the DSB to authorise under Article 22.6 of the DSU the suspension of concessions or other obligations with respect to a Member that fails to comply with dispute settlement decisions. See below, pp. 289–91.

Date	Time	Meeting
1	10:00	Council for Trade Related Aspects of Intellectual Property Rights
2	10:00	Council for Trade Related Aspects of Intellectual Property Rights
3	10:00	Preparatory Committee on Trade Facilitation
9–10	10:00	Committee on Agriculture
9–10	10:00	Committee on Technical Barriers to Trade
15+17	10:00	Trade Policy Review Body – Turkey
16–17	10:00	Committee on Sanitary and Phytosanitary Measures
21+23	10:00	Trade Policy Review Body – Maldives
22	10:00	Council for Trade in Goods
23	10:00	Dispute Settlement Body
25		Good Friday (WTO non-working day)
28		Easter Monday (WTO non-working day)

Figure 2.1 WTO organisation chart

At present, the WTO has a total of thirty-five standing bodies and about thirty *ad hoc* bodies.[277] Many of these WTO bodies meet on a regular basis, making for a heavy workload for WTO diplomats. In 2012, WTO bodies held nearly 500 formal and informal meetings. For many developing-country Members, with only a small, and sometimes no, permanent representation in Geneva, this workload is a daunting challenge.[278] The schedule of meetings at the WTO is posted on the WTO website. Consider the schedule of meetings in March 2016, as shown in Figure 2.2.

The institutional structure of the WTO includes, at the highest level, the Ministerial Conference, at a second level, the General Council, the Dispute Settlement Body (DSB) and the Trade Policy Review Body (TPRB) and, at lower levels, specialised councils, committees, working groups and working parties. Furthermore, and not reflected in the organisational chart shown in Figure 2.1, the institutional structure of the WTO includes judicial and other non-political bodies, as well as the WTO Secretariat. This subsection examines in turn these various elements of the institutional structure of the WTO. In addition, this subsection also briefly discusses political bodies lacking the formal institutional structure of the WTO.

277 Most of these *ad hoc* bodies are working groups on accession. This group of *ad hoc* bodies also includes the bodies especially established for the Doha Round negotiations. See below, pp. 134–6.

278 Most WTO Members have a 'permanent representation', also referred to as a 'permanent mission', in Geneva. This is, however, often a 'permanent representation' to *all* Geneva-based international organisations, which means that the limited human and other resources are spread (thinly) over a great number of meetings and activities. A number of developed-country as well as developing-country Members have a separate 'permanent representation' to the WTO. This is the case, for example, for Brazil, China, India, the European Union, Honduras, Japan, Malaysia, the Philippines and the United States. The meetings of WTO bodies are usually attended by diplomats from the permanent representation, but often government officials specialising in a specific subject matter are flown in from the capital to attend important meetings in Geneva and present their governments' views. This is obviously, however, not an option for many developing-country Members. Furthermore, there are about thirty developing-country Members that do not have a permanent representation in Geneva. See above, p. 112, fn. 182.

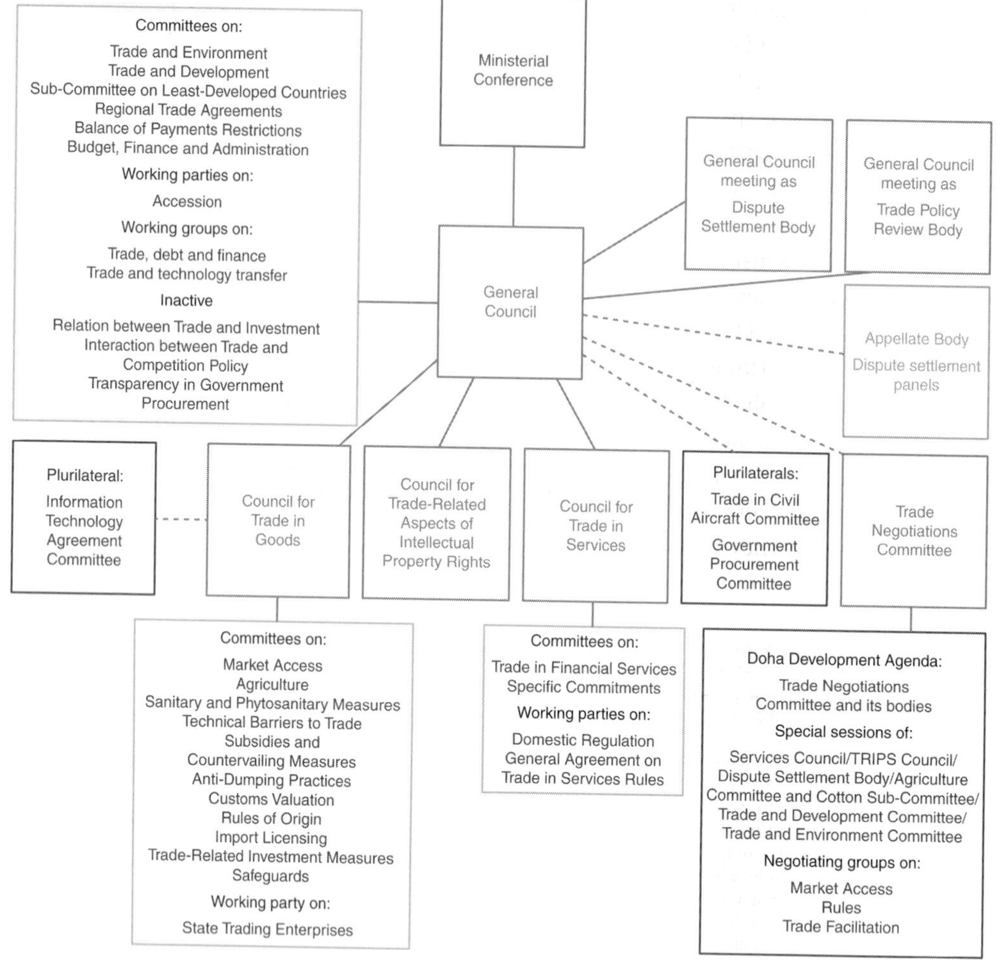

Figure 2.2 Programme of WTO meetings in March 2016

4.2.1 Ministerial Conference

Article IV:1 of the *WTO Agreement* states:

There shall be a Ministerial Conference composed of representatives of all the Members, which shall meet at least once every two years. The Ministerial Conference shall carry out the functions of the WTO and take actions necessary to this effect. The Ministerial Conference shall have the authority to take decisions on all matters under any of the Multilateral Trade Agreements, if so requested by a Member, in accordance with the specific requirements for decision-making in this Agreement and in the relevant Multilateral Trade Agreement.

The Ministerial Conference is the 'supreme' body of the WTO. It is composed of minister-level representatives from *all* Members and has decision-making powers on *all* matters under *any* of the multilateral WTO agreements.[279] Decisions by the Ministerial Conference are binding on Members.[280] In addition to this very broad decision-making power, the Ministerial Conference has been explicitly granted a number of specific powers, such as: (1) adopting authoritative interpretations of the WTO agreements;[281] (2) granting waivers;[282] (3) adopting amendments;[283] (4) making decisions on accession;[284] (5) appointing the Director-General;[285] and (6) adopting staff regulations.[286]

The Ministerial Conference is not often in session. Since 1995, there have only been ten sessions of the Ministerial Conference, each lasting a few days only: Singapore (1996),[287] Geneva (1998),[288] Seattle (1999),[289] Doha (2001),[290] Cancún (2003),[291] Hong Kong (2005),[292] Geneva (2009),[293] Geneva (2011),[294] Bali (2013)[295] and Nairobi (2015).[296] The next session of the Ministerial Conference will be held in Buenos Aires in December 2017. Sessions of the Ministerial Conference are major media events and focus the minds of the political leaders of WTO Members on the current challenges to, and the future of, the multilateral trading system. They offer a much-needed opportunity to give political leadership and guidance to the WTO and its actions.[297]

279 For the Rules of Procedure for the Ministerial Conference, see WT/L/161, dated 25 July 1996.

280 However, whether these decisions can be enforced through WTO dispute settlement is another matter dealt with below, p. 194.

281 Article IX:2 of the *WTO Agreement*. See below, pp. 148–51.

282 Article IX:3 of the *WTO Agreement*. See below, pp. 148–51.

283 Article X of the *WTO Agreement*. See below, pp. 148–51.

284 Article XII of the *WTO Agreement*. See below, pp. 118–22.

285 Article VI:2 of the *WTO Agreement*.

286 Article VI:3 of the *WTO Agreement*. See below, pp. 688–9. Note also that, pursuant to Article XII:5(b) and XII:6 of the GATS, the Ministerial Conference also has the power to establish certain procedures in connection with balance-of-payments restrictions. Pursuant to Article 64.3 of the *TRIPS Agreement*, the Ministerial Conference has the power to extend the provisions relating to non-violation and situation complaints to the *TRIPS Agreement* (see below, p. 1050).

287 For the Ministerial Declarations adopted on 13 December 1996 at the Singapore Ministerial Conference (1st MC), see WT/MIN(96)/DEC, dated 18 December 1996, and WT/MIN(96)/16, dated 13 December 1996.

288 For the Ministerial Declarations adopted on 20 May 1998 at the Geneva Ministerial Conference (2nd MC), see WT/MIN(98)/DEC/1, dated 25 May 1998, and WT/MIN(98)/DEC/2, dated 25 May 1998.

289 No Ministerial Declaration was adopted at the Seattle Ministerial Conference in November/December 1999 (3rd MC).

290 For the Ministerial Declarations and Decisions adopted on 14 November 2001 at the Doha Ministerial Conference (4th MC), see WT/MIN(01)/DEC/1, dated 20 November 2001, WT/MIN(01)/DEC/2, dated 20 November 2001, WT/MIN(01)/15, dated 14 November 2001, WT/MIN(01)/16, dated 14 November 2001, and WT/MIN(01)/17, dated 20 November 2001.

291 No Ministerial Declaration was adopted at the Cancún Ministerial Conference in September 2003 (5th MC). However, the Ministerial Conference did issue on 14 September 2003 a Ministerial Statement. See WT/MIN(03)/20, dated 23 September 2003.

292 For the Ministerial Declaration adopted on 18 December 2005 at the Hong Kong Ministerial Conference (6th MC), see WT/MIN(05)/DEC, dated 22 December 2005.

293 No Ministerial Declaration was adopted at the Geneva Ministerial Conference in November 2009 (7th MC).

294 No Ministerial Declaration was adopted at the Geneva Ministerial Conference in December 2011 (8th MC). For the Ministerial Decisions adopted at this session on 17 December 2011, see WT/L/842–848, dated 19 December 2011. For the Chair's Concluding Statement on 17 December 2011, see WT/MIN(11)/11, dated 11 December 2011.

295 For the Ministerial Declaration adopted on 7 December 2013 at the Bali Ministerial Conference (9th MC), see WT/MIN(13)/DEC, dated 11 December 2013.

296 For the Ministerial Declaration adopted on 19 December 2015 at Nairobi Ministerial Conference (10th MC), see WT/MIN(15)/DEC, dated 21 November 2015.

297 Note, however, that there was no Ministerial Conference in 2007, as it was not considered useful to have a session at that time due to the lack of progress in the Doha Round negotiations.

4.2.2 General Council, DSB and TPRB

Article IV:2 of the *WTO Agreement* states:

> There shall be a General Council composed of representatives of all the Members, which shall meet as appropriate. In the intervals between meetings of the Ministerial Conference, its functions shall be conducted by the General Council. The General Council shall also carry out the functions assigned to it by this Agreement. The General Council shall establish its rules of procedure and approve the rules of procedure for the Committees provided for in paragraph 7.

The General Council is composed of ambassador-level diplomats and meets at least every two months.[298] All WTO Members are represented in the General Council. As with all other WTO bodies, except the Ministerial Conference, the General Council meets on the premises of the WTO in Geneva. Each year, the General Council elects its Chair from among its members.[299] The Chair of the General Council holds the highest elected office within the WTO. In February 2016, the General Council elected Harald Neple, Norway's Ambassador and Permanent Representative to the WTO, as its Chair for 2016.[300]

General Council

3–4 October 2016
Proposed agenda

1. Report by the Chairman of the Trade Negotiation Committee
2. Implementation of the Bali and Nairobi Outcomes – Statement by the Chairman
3. Work Programme on small economies – Report by the Chairman of the dedicated session of the Committee on Trade and Development
4. Eleventh Session of the Ministerial Conference – Date and Venue – Statement by the Chairman
5. Appointment of Officers to WTO Bodies – Negotiating Group on Market Access, Council for Trade In Services Special Session and Preparatory Committee on Trade Facilitation – Statement by the Chairman
6. Committee on Budget, Finance and Administration – Report of Meeting of September 2016 (WT/BFA/156)
7. WTO Pension Plan Management Board – Election of Chairperson – Statement by the Chairman

...Other Business

Figure 2.3 Proposed agenda for the meeting of the General Council of 3–4 October 2016

298 For the Rules of Procedure of the General Council, see WT/L/161, dated 25 July 1996.
299 The Chair of the General Council alternates between ambassadors from developed-country and developing-country Members.
300 The list of the 2016 chairs of all WTO bodies can be found on the WTO website.

The General Council is responsible for the continuing, 'day-to-day' management of the WTO and its many activities. In between sessions of the Ministerial Conference, the General Council exercises the full powers of the Ministerial Conference. In addition, the General Council also carries out some functions specifically assigned to it. The General Council is responsible for adopting the annual budget and the financial regulations[301] and for making appropriate arrangements for effective cooperation with international organisations and NGOs.[302] By way of example of the matters dealt with by the General Council, consider the proposed agenda for the meeting of the General Council of 3–4 October 2016, set out in Figure 2.3.

Rule 37 of the *Rules of Procedure for the Meetings of the General Council* states:

> The meeting of the General Council shall ordinarily be held in private. It may be decided that a particular meeting or meetings should be held in public.

In practice, the General Council always meets behind closed doors. After the meeting, the Chair may issue a *communiqué* to the press.[303] The Chair and/or the Director-General, assisted by the WTO spokesperson, usually hold a press conference after the meeting. The minutes of a meeting of the General Council (as are the minutes of meetings of all WTO bodies except the TPRB) are 'restricted' documents, i.e. not available to the public, until they are 'de-restricted' under the rules on the de-restriction of official documents.[304] The lack of transparency and openness of the General Council and other WTO bodies compares unfavourably with many UN bodies.[305]

The functions specifically assigned to the General Council also cover dispute settlement and trade policy review. Article IV:3 and 4 of the *WTO Agreement* state respectively:

> 3. The General Council shall convene as appropriate to discharge the responsibilities of the Dispute Settlement Body provided for in the Dispute Settlement Understanding. The Dispute Settlement Body may have its own chairman and shall establish such rules of procedure as it deems necessary for the fulfilment of those responsibilities.
>
> 4. The General Council shall convene as appropriate to discharge the responsibilities of the Trade Policy Review Body provided for in the TPRM. The Trade Policy Review Body may have its own chairman and shall establish such rules of procedure as it deems necessary for the fulfilment of those responsibilities.

The General Council, the DSB and the TPRB are, in fact, the same body. The DSB and the TPRB are the *alter ego* of the General Council; they are two emanations of the General Council. When the General Council administers the WTO dispute settlement system, it convenes and acts as the DSB. When the General Council administers the WTO trade policy review mechanism, it convenes and acts as the

301 Article VII:3 of the *WTO Agreement*. See also below, p. 151.
302 Article V:1 and 2 of the *WTO Agreement*. See also above, pp. 105–10.
303 See Rule 38 of the Rules of Procedure for the Meetings of the General Council, WT/L/161, dated 25 July 1996.
304 General Council, Decision on *Procedures for the Circulation and Derestriction of WTO Documents*, WT/L/452, dated 16 May 2002.
305 Note, however, that the transparency and openness of these UN bodies may be deceptive.

TPRB. To date, the DSB and the TPRB have always had a different Chair from the General Council,[306] and both the DSB and the TPRB have developed their own Rules of Procedure, which take account of the special features of their work.[307]

The DSB has a regular meeting once a month, but, in between, additional meetings (called 'special meetings') may be requested by WTO Members in order to enable them to exercise their rights within specified time frames as provided for in the DSU.[308] In 2015, for example, the DSB met in total seventeen times.[309]

4.2.3 Specialised Councils, Committees, Working Groups and Working Parties

At the level below the General Council, the DSB and the TPRB, there are three so-called specialised councils provided for in Article IV:5 of the *WTO Agreement*: the Council for Trade in Goods (CTG),[310] the Council for Trade in Services (CTS)[311] and the Council for TRIPS.[312] These specialised councils assist the General Council and operate under its general guidance. The CTG, CTS and TRIPS Council oversee, respectively, the functioning of the WTO agreements on trade in goods, the GATS and the *TRIPS Agreement*. These specialised councils carry out the functions assigned to them by the *WTO Agreement*,[313] by their respective agreements[314] and by the General Council. Overall, however, few specific powers have been entrusted to the specialised councils, and their general power to *oversee* the functioning of relevant agreements does not explicitly include the power to take any decision. An often-cited example of an instance in which a WTO body went beyond its powers relates to the CTS and, in particular the CTS's decision to extend the deadline for the entry into force of the result of negotiations on emergency safeguard measures in the field of services. Article X:1 of the GATS sets this deadline explicitly at 'not later than three years from the date of entry

306 Note, however, that it is an established practice that the Chair of the DSB in year *n* becomes the Chair of the General Council in year *n* + 1. In line with this practice, Ambassador Jonathan Fried from Canada who was DSB Chair in 2013, was General Council Chair in 2014; Ambassador Fernando De Mateo from Mexico, who was DSB Chair in 2014, was General Council Chair in 2015; and Ambassador Harald Neple from Norway, who was DSB Chair in 2015, is the General Council Chair in 2016.

307 For the Rules of Procedure for the TPRB, see Trade Policy Review Body, *Rules of Procedure for Meetings of the Trade Policy Review Body*, WT/TPR/6/Rev.1, dated 10 October 2005. For the Rules of Procedure for the DSB, see below, p. 211, fn. 261. Note that the TPRB and the DSB follow, *mutatis mutandis* and with certain deviations, the Rules of Procedure for the General Council (WT/L/160).

308 See below, p. 211.

309 *DSB Annual Report 2015*, WT/DSB/67, dated 19 November 2015.

310 For the Rules of Procedure for the CTG, see WTL/79, dated 7 August 1995.

311 For the Rules of Procedure for the CTS, see S/L/15, dated 19 October 1995.

312 For the Rules of Procedure for the Council for TRIPS, see IP/C/1, dated 28 September 1995.

313 See Article IX:2 of the *WTO Agreement* which provides that the Ministerial Conference and the General Council may only exercise their authority to adopt authoritative interpretations of the multilateral trade agreements of Annex 1 on the basis of a recommendation from the specialised council overseeing the functioning of the agreement at issue. See below, pp. 148–51. The specialised councils also play a role in the procedure for the adoption of waivers and the amendment procedure. See Article IX:3(b) and Article X:1 of the *WTO Agreement*. See below, pp. 148–51.

314 The GATS explicitly empowers the CTS to develop disciplines on domestic regulation, and to establish rules and procedures for the rectification and modification of services schedules. See Articles VI:4 and XXI:5 of the GATS. The *TRIPS Agreement* empowers the TRIPS Council to extend, upon a duly motivated request, the ten-year transition period for the implementation of the *TRIPS Agreement* granted to the least-developed-country Members. See Article 66.1 of the *TRIPS Agreement*.

into force of the *WTO Agreement*', i.e. on 1 January 1998. This treaty-mandated deadline was extended five times by the CTS even though the CTS did not have any apparent legal mandate to do so.[315] The political need to extend the deadline prevailed over any jurisdictional concern.

The specialised councils meet as necessary. In 2015, for example, the CTG met three times in formal session[316] and the CTS met five times.[317] Furthermore, these specialised councils also met informally. All WTO Members are represented in these specialised councils, although some Members, in particular developing-country Members, may find it difficult to attend all meetings.

In addition to the three specialised councils, there are numerous committees and working parties that assist the Ministerial Conference and the General Council in carrying out their functions. The committees include the Committee on Trade and Environment (CTE), which was established by the 1994 Ministerial Decision on Trade and Environment, adopted in Marrakesh on 14 April 1994. Another important committee is the Committee on Trade and Development (CTD), which is explicitly provided for in Article IV:7 of the *WTO Agreement* and was established by the General Council in 1995.[318] In 1996, the General Council also established the Committee on Regional Trade Agreements (CRTA).[319] Furthermore, all but one of the multilateral agreements on trade in goods provide for a committee to carry out certain functions relating to the implementation of the particular agreement.[320] All of these committees are under the authority of, and report to, the CTG. In practice, however, they tend to be relatively independent, arguably due to the technical nature of their work. Note, by way of example, the SCM Committee. Article 24.1 of the *SCM Agreement* states:

> There is hereby established a Committee on Subsidies and Countervailing Measures composed of representatives from each of the Members. The Committee shall elect its own Chairman and shall meet not less than twice a year and otherwise as envisaged by relevant provisions of this Agreement at the request of any Member. The Committee shall carry out responsibilities as assigned to it under this Agreement or by the Members and it shall afford Members the opportunity of consulting on any matter relating to the operation of the Agreement or the furtherance of its objectives. The WTO Secretariat shall act as the secretariat to the Committee.[321]

315 The most recent extension was decided on in March 2004, and on that occasion the CTS decided to extend the deadline for an indefinite period. See Decision of the Council for Trade in Services, adopted on 15 March 2004, S/L/159, dated 17 March 2004.

316 See, *Report (2015) of the Council for Trade in Goods*, G/L/1140, dated 19 November 2015. In addition, the CTG met once in informal session.

317 See, *Annual Report of the Council for Trade in Services to the General Council (2015)*, S/C/48, dated 2 November 2015. In addition, the CTS met twice in informal session (see WTO website).

318 At the same meeting of the General Council on 31 January 1995, at which the Committee on Trade and Development, the Committee on Balance-of-Payment Restrictions and the Committee on the Budget, Finance and Administration were established (see WT/GC/M/1, dated 28 February 1995).

319 See WT/GC/M/10, dated 6 March 1996, para. 11.

320 The exception is the *Agreement on Preshipment Inspection*. However, the CTG established a Committee on Preshipment Inspection.

321 The powers of the Committee on Anti-Dumping (AD) Practices, the Committee on Customs Valuation (CV) and the Committee on Technical Barriers to Trade (TBT) are worded in similar terms.

Note that, under Article 27.4 of the *SCM Agreement*, the SCM Committee has the power to determine whether a request by a developing-country Member to extend the special transitional period for the maintenance of export subsidies is justified.[322] Such specific decision-making powers to add to, or diminish, the obligations of certain Members are, however, quite exceptional.[323]

Furthermore, Article IV:6 of the *WTO Agreement* provides that the specialised councils may also establish subsidiary bodies as required. For example, the CTS created the Working Party on Professional Services. A number of committees also have this power to establish subordinate bodies where necessary.[324]

Subsidiary bodies set up to study and report on a particular issue are usually referred to as 'working parties' or 'working groups'.[325] In 2015, there were nineteen working parties on the accession of would-be Members.[326]

When a working party, a committee or a specialised council is called upon to take a decision but is unable to do so, the applicable Rules of Procedure commonly require the matter to be referred to a higher body if a Member so requests.

The Plurilateral Agreements, i.e. the *Agreement on Trade in Civil Aircraft* and the *Agreement on Government Procurement*, provide for a Committee on Trade in Civil Aircraft and a Committee on Government Procurement respectively. These bodies carry out the functions assigned to them under those agreements. They operate within the institutional framework of the WTO, keeping the General Council informed of their activities on a regular basis.[327]

4.2.4 Trade Negotiations Committee

The Doha Round negotiations are conducted in the Trade Negotiations Committee (TNC) and its subordinate negotiating bodies.[328] The TNC was established at the Doha Ministerial Conference in November 2001.[329] This body supervises the overall conduct of the negotiations under the authority of the General Council. The TNC reports on the progress of the negotiations to each regular meeting of the General Council. The 'detailed' negotiations take place either in special sessions of standing WTO bodies or in specially created negotiating groups. At its first meeting in 2002, the TNC established two such new negotiating groups, one on market access and one on rules; later the TNC also established a

322 Furthermore, Article 29.4 of the *SCM Agreement* gives the SCM Committee the power to allow Members in the process of transformation into a market economy to derogate from their notified programmes and measures and their timeframes. See also below, p. 866, fn. 527.

323 Another example is the power given to the TBT Committee under Article 12.8 of the *TBT Agreement* relating to granting exceptions from TBT obligations to developing-country Members. See also below, pp. 928–9.

324 See e.g. Article 13.2 of the *TBT Agreement*.

325 See, for example, the Working Group on Trade, Debt and Finance, and the Working Party on State Trading Enterprises.

326 *WTO Accessions, 2015 Annual Report by Director General*, WT/GC/174, dated 16 November 2015, para. 115. Note that some of these working parties were 'inactive and dormant'. See *ibid.*

327 See Article IV:8 of the *WTO Agreement*.

328 On the current state of the Doha Round negotiations, see above, pp. 98–101.

329 See Ministerial Conference, *Doha Ministerial Declaration*, WT/MIN(01)/DEC/1, dated 20 November 2001, para. 46.

negotiating group on trade facilitation. Most of the negotiations, however, take place in special sessions of standing WTO bodies (such as the Dispute Settlement Body, the Council for Trade in Services and the Committee on Agriculture). The TNC and its negotiating bodies consist of all the WTO Members and all countries negotiating accession to the WTO.[330] On 1 February 2002, the TNC decided that the WTO Director-General would *ex officio* chair the TNC. The TNC is the only political WTO body chaired by a WTO official, rather than an ambassador or senior diplomat of a Member.[331] In 2015, the TNC met twice in formal sessions and once in an informal session.[332] The TNC did not meet in 2016.

4.2.5 Political Bodies Lacking in the Formal Institutional Structure

While the WTO's institutional structure is in many respects similar to that of other intergovernmental organisations, it does not have, unlike, for example, the United Nations, the IMF and the World Bank, an 'executive body' consisting of the most important Members and a selection of other Members. In the aforementioned organisations, an executive body facilitates decision-making by concentrating discussions in a smaller but representative group of members, or by taking certain decisions for the whole membership. Also, unlike intergovernmental organisations such as the OECD and the ILO, the WTO does not have any permanent body in which stakeholders other than governments are represented.

As noted above, all political WTO bodies comprise all 164 WTO Members. However, it is clear that it is impossible to negotiate effectively with such a large number, or even with the lower number that is likely to turn up for meetings. Over the years, informal 'solutions', such as 'green room meetings', have been developed to address, or at least mitigate, this problem. These informal 'solutions', and in particular green room meetings, are discussed later in this chapter.[333] However, as noted above, the WTO institutional structure does not currently provide for a formal solution to this problem in the form of an 'executive body'. There have been a few proposals to create such an executive body to facilitate decision-making within the WTO. The 2004 Sutherland Report, *The Future of the WTO*, for example, recommended that the informal 'mini-ministerials' should be replaced by a permanent 'senior level consultative body'.[334] In order for this body to be effective, its membership should not exceed thirty Members. While most seats might be filled on a 'rotating basis', taking into account different criteria, such as 'geographical areas, regional trading arrangements or mixed

330 Note, however, that decisions on agreements, that would result from the negotiations, are taken by WTO Members only.

331 Note that the choice of the WTO Director-General as Chair of the TNC is controversial among WTO Members.

332 Some of the negotiating bodies met much more. For example, the Special Session of the Dispute Settlement Body met three times in informal session and the Negotiating Group on Market Access met four times in informal session.

333 See below, pp. 152–6.

334 See the Sutherland Report, para. 323. This 'senior level consultative body' would be similar to the Consultative Group of 18 (CG-18), a body which operated in the GATT for many years.

constituencies', the permanent presence of certain Members would be a 'must', given the significance of their trade flows.[335] However, this and similar proposals have not received much support from WTO Members.[336] Disagreement on its composition is likely to be the major stumbling block for the establishment of a formal, permanent 'executive body'.

In addition to an 'executive body', the WTO also does not have any permanent consultative body in which representatives of national parliaments or NGOs are represented. As is the case in other international organisations, such a body could serve as a forum for 'dialogue' between the WTO and civil society. In 2001, Pascal Lamy, the then European Trade Commissioner, proposed the establishment of a WTO Parliamentary Consultative Assembly.[337] While there seems to be little support among Members for the establishment of such an assembly, it should be noted that, in recent years, contacts with national parliamentarians have been greatly enhanced through regular visits to capitals by the WTO Director-General and through various seminars and briefings with the Inter-Parliamentary Union and, *inter alia*, the European Parliament and the US Congress.[338] Since 2003, the Inter-Parliamentary Union (IPU) and the European Parliament have organised a number of sessions of the Parliamentary Conference on the WTO. Since 2011, these sessions have been organised annually at the WTO headquarters and have been attended by several hundred parliamentarians.[339]

As discussed above, it has been argued that 'outside voices', such as expert NGOs, can provide valuable advice to Members.[340] The WTO could obtain such advice through permanent consultative bodies of individuals and/or NGOs reflecting a broad range of views and interests. However, suggestions to establish such consultative bodies have received little support from Members to date. In 2003, Supachai Panitchpakdi, the then WTO Director-General, established on his own initiative two advisory bodies: the Informal NGO Advisory Body, made up of eleven high-level representatives from NGOs, and the Informal Business Advisory Body, which comprised fourteen captains of industry from developed as well as developing-country Members. Both bodies were to advise the WTO Director-General, channel the positions of civil society and global business on trade issues to the WTO, and ultimately aim at facilitating mutual

335 *Ibid.*, para. 325.

336 See, for example, General Council, *Minutes of Meeting*, WT/GC/M/91, dated 26 January 2005, 20.

337 See speech given in Berlin on 26 November 2001.

338 In 2015, the WTO organised two regional workshops for parliamentarians from Asia and from the Indian Ocean Commission and the East African Community. Further, the IMF invited the WTO Secretariat to contribute to two regional meetings organised for parliamentarians from the Arab and Central and Eastern European & Central Asian Countries (CEECAC). See *WTO Annual Report 2016*, 143.

339 The Parliamentary Conference on the WTO, in its 2015 session, expressed strong support for the multilateral trading system. Parliamentarians from around the world called for prompt ratification of the Trade Facilitation Agreement, redoubling efforts to conclude the Doha Round and finding a permanent solution to the issue of public stockholding for food security purposes. See *WTO Annual Report 2016*, p. 142. The theme of the 2016 session of the Parliamentary Conference was 'What future for the WTO?'. See www.ipu.org/splz-e/trade16.htm.

340 See above, pp. 106–10.

understanding. However, this initiative died a silent death. In April 2012, the then WTO Director-General Pascal Lamy established the Panel on Defining the Future of Trade, a twelve-member panel comprising representatives from the business community, such as the President and CEO of a Brazilian aircraft manufacturer, representatives of civil society, such as the Secretary-General of the International Trade Union Confederation, and former politicians, such as the former President of Botswana. The panel examined and analysed the challenges to opening of global trade in the twenty-first century, and published a report with its findings in April 2013.[341]

In response to a request of the International Chamber of Commerce (ICC) and the B20 group of leading independent business associations from G20 economies, the WTO organised in May 2016 a first Trade Dialogues event. As discussed above, this event brought together over sixty business leaders from developed as well as developing countries to discuss the challenges and opportunities they face in conducting trade operations and to discuss how the WTO can help in dealing with them.[342] Similar events may be organised in the future and the Trade Dialogues may thus become an informal feature of the WTO's institutional structure.

4.2.6 Judicial, Quasi-Judicial and Other Non-Political Bodies

All the WTO bodies discussed above are political in nature. The WTO also has a number of judicial, quasi-judicial and other non-political bodies. The most prominent among the judicial and quasi-judicial bodies are the standing Appellate Body and the *ad hoc* dispute settlement panels respectively. These bodies are discussed in detail in Chapter 3.[343]

The WTO also has other non-political bodies. An example of such a body is the Permanent Group of Experts (PGE) provided for under the *SCM Agreement*. The PGE consists of five independent persons with a high level of expertise in the fields of subsidies and trade relations. The members of the PGE are appointed by the SCM Committee. The PGE may be requested to assist a dispute settlement panel in determining whether a subsidy is a prohibited subsidy.[344] The PGE may also be requested by the SCM Committee for an advisory opinion on the existence and nature of any subsidy.[345] Furthermore, a WTO Member may request the PGE for a confidential advisory opinion on the nature of any subsidy proposed to be introduced or currently maintained by that Member.[346] Reportedly, to date no use has yet been made of the PGE.

Until 1 January 2005, a prime example of a non-political body was the Textile Monitoring Body (TMB), provided for in the *Agreement on Textiles and Clothing*.

341 To access the report, see www.wto.org/english/thewto_e/dg_e/dft_panel_e/future_of_trade_report_e.pdf.
342 See above, p. 110. See www.wto.org/english/news_e/news16_e/bus_30may16_e.htm.
343 See below, pp. 209–45. 344 See Articles 4.5 and 24.3 of the *SCM Agreement*.
345 See *ibid.*, Article 24.3. 346 See *ibid.*, Article 24.4.

The TMB was to examine all relevant measures taken by Members and assess their consistency with the *Agreement on Textiles and Clothing.* The eleven members of the TMB were appointed by Members designated by the CTG but were to discharge their functions in an independent and impartial manner (not as the representative of a WTO Member). As discussed in Chapter 1, the *Agreement on Textiles and Clothing* ceased to be in force on 1 January 2005 and, as of that date, the TMB also ceased to exist.[347]

4.2.7 WTO Secretariat

The WTO Secretariat is based in Geneva at the Centre William Rappard (CWR), beautifully situated by the Lac Léman.[348] The Secretariat has regular staff of 634 persons.[349] This makes it undoubtedly one of the smallest secretariats of any of the major international organisations. However, as Hoekman and Kostecki observed:

> The small size of the secretariat is somewhat misleading ... [T]he WTO is a network-based organization. The WTO secretariat and the national delegates in Geneva work in close cooperation with numerous civil servants in their respective capitals. The total size of the network is impossible to determine, but certainly spans at least 5,000 people.[350]

As discussed below, the Secretariat's prime function is to keep the 'WTO network' operating smoothly.[351]

The WTO Secretariat is headed by a Director-General, who is appointed by the Ministerial Conference.[352] The Ministerial Conference adopts regulations setting out the powers, duties, conditions of service and the term of office of the Director-General.[353] In the brief history of the WTO, the appointment of the Director-General has often been a contentious matter.[354] In particular, the process of appointing a successor for Renato Ruggiero,[355] the WTO's second Director-General, was particularly divisive. After a year of discussions, WTO Members finally agreed in July 1999 to an unprecedented term-sharing arrangement under which Mike Moore, of New Zealand,[356] was appointed as

347 See above, p. 47. See also below, p. 491.

348 Note that the WTO does not have any offices outside Geneva.

349 See www.wto.org/english/thewto_e/secre_e/intro_e.htm.

350 Hoekman and Kostecki, *The Political Economy of the World Trading System*, 55.

351 See below, pp. 104–45. 352 See Article VI:1 and 2 of the *WTO Agreement*.

353 See Article VI:2 of the *WTO Agreement*.

354 To date, the following persons have served as WTO Director-General: Peter Sutherland from Ireland (January 1995–April 1995); Renato Ruggiero of Italy (May 1995–April 1999); Mike Moore of New Zealand (September 1999–August 2002); Supachai Panitchpakdi of Thailand (September 2002–August 2005); Pascal Lamy of France (September 2005–August 2013); and Roberto Azevêdo of Brazil (September 2013–present).

355 Renato Ruggiero of Italy was Italy's Trade Minister during the Uruguay Round. He has been credited for being the first senior government official to propose the establishment of an international organisation for trade to replace the GATT. He also held posts in private companies such as the car manufacturer Fiat and the energy firm ENI. After leaving the WTO, Ruggiero briefly served as Italy's Foreign Minister.

356 Mike Moore, a former printer, social worker and trade union researcher, was the youngest Member of Parliament ever elected in New Zealand. In the 1980s, he served six years as New Zealand's Minister of Overseas Trade and Marketing, and was New Zealand's Prime Minister for a brief period in 1990.

Director-General for a term of three years beginning on 1 September 1999, and Supachai Panitchpakdi, of Thailand,[357] was appointed for a three-year term beginning on 1 September 2002. Mr Pascal Lamy, of France,[358] served as Director General from September 2005 to August 2013.[359] The current Director-General, Roberto Azevêdo, of Brazil,[360] took office for a four-year term on 1 September 2013.

Chastised by the bruising experience of the 1998–9 appointment process, discussed above, the General Council adopted in December 2002 new procedures for the appointment of a Director-General.[361] Under these new procedures, the appointment process shall start nine months prior to the expiry of the term of an incumbent Director-General. The various steps of the process are carefully set out. The process shall be conducted by the Chair of the General Council, assisted by the Chairs of the Dispute Settlement Body and the Trade Policy Review Body acting as facilitators. Only WTO Members may nominate candidates.[362] While the Sutherland Report found these procedures to be steps in the right direction, it stated that it:

> would favour the abandonment of the agreement that permits WTO Members to make nominations only of their own nationals or that candidates must have the backing of their own governments. Indeed, there would be more logic in disallowing such national nominations completely. Any tendency towards alternating between developing and developed countries and any regional sequencing should be avoided. By the same token we would favour reducing the intensity of candidate 'campaigns'. A further option requiring that an initial independent search for appropriate candidates be carried out may be worth further examination.[363]

The overriding objective of Members is to reach a decision on the appointment of a Director-General by consensus. However, note that the new procedures explicitly state:

> If, after having carried out all the procedures set out above, it has not been possible for the General Council to take a decision by consensus by the deadline provided for the appointment, Members should consider the possibility of recourse to a vote as a last resort by

357 Supachai Panitchpakdi held a range of senior government positions in Thailand and was in charge of Thailand's participation in the final stages of the Uruguay Round negotiations. At the time of his appointment to the post of WTO Director-General, Supachai served as Thailand's Deputy Prime Minister and Minister of Commerce. After leaving the WTO, Supachai was appointed Secretary-General of UNCTAD.

358 Pascal Lamy served as the EU Trade Commissioner for five years until shortly before his appointment as WTO Director-General. Lamy began his career in the French civil service, served as Chief of Staff to Jacques Delors, President of the European Commission, and later was CEO of the bank Crédit Lyonnais.

359 Pascal Lamy was reappointed for a second four-year term beginning September 2009.

360 Prior to being appointed as the sixth Director-General, Ambassador Roberto Carvalho de Azevêdo, a Brazilian career diplomat, served as the Permanent Representative of Brazil to the WTO and other international economic organisations in Geneva since 2008.

361 See General Council, *Decision on the Procedures for the Appointment of Directors-General*, adopted 10 December 2002, WT/L/509, dated 20 January 2003.

362 According to the General Council Decision of 10 December 2002, a candidate for the post of WTO Director-General should have extensive experience in international relations, encompassing economic, trade and/or political experience; a firm commitment to the work and objectives of the WTO; proven leadership and managerial ability; and demonstrable communication skills.

363 Para. 352.

a procedure to be determined at that time. Recourse to a vote for the appointment of a Director-General shall be understood to be an exceptional departure from the customary practice of decision-making by consensus, and shall not establish any precedent for such recourse in respect of any future decisions in the WTO.[364]

The present Director-General, Roberto Azevêdo, was selected and appointed by the General Council, from a pool of nine candidates, nominated by their respective governments.[365] In January 2013, each of these candidates made a presentation to the General Council on their vision for the WTO, followed by a question-and-answer session. Subsequently, the candidates engaged in intensive campaigning in support of their candidacy.[366] Eventually, on 8 May 2013, the General Council appointed, by consensus, Roberto Azevêdo as the sixth WTO Director-General.

With regard to the role of the Director-General and the WTO Secretariat, it is important to note that the Members of the WTO set the policy agenda and take all policy decisions. Neither the Director-General nor the WTO Secretariat has any autonomous policy decision-making powers. The Director-General and the WTO Secretariat act primarily as an 'honest broker' in, or a 'facilitator' of, the decision-making processes within the WTO. They are not expected to act as initiators of proposals for action or reform. In such a seemingly modest role, the Director-General and the WTO Secretariat can, however, make an important contribution to the building of consensus among Members on a specific agreement or decision. As noted above, the Director-General serves *ex officio* as Chair of the Trade Negotiations Committee, which oversees the Doha Round negotiations.[367] Speaking about his role as Director-General and the role of the WTO Secretariat, Supachai Panitchpakdi noted in January 2003:

As you know the WTO is, if I may use the cliché, a 'member-driven' organization. In the negotiations, Member governments negotiate directly with each other. As Chairman of the TNC, I shall be doing my utmost to keep all Members on board, facilitate their discussions, mediate in their problems and consult with all. And the WTO Secretariat, through its technical assistance work programme, is working hard to help developing and least-developed-country Members prepare effectively for the negotiations. But we cannot make any decisions on behalf of Members, we cannot unplug blockages when Members' positions are intractable and we cannot force consensus. It is Members who have the very difficult responsibility of developing policy positions, negotiating concessions and deciding how far they are able to go in any given area.[368]

The main duties of the WTO Secretariat are: (1) to provide technical, secretarial and professional support for the many WTO bodies (including the writing of the

364 See General Council, *Decision on the Procedures for the Appointment of Directors-General*, adopted 10 December 2002, WT/L/509, dated 20 January 2003, para. 21. On decision-making in the WTO, see below, pp. 145–56.

365 Mr Taeho Bark (Republic of Korea), Mr Herminio Blanco (Mexico), Mr Roberto Carvalho de Azevêdo (Brazil), Ms Anabel González (Costa Rica), Mr Tim Groser (New Zealand), Mr Ahmad Thougan Hindawi (Jordan), Ms Amina C. Mohamed (Kenya), Mr Alan John Kwadwo Kyerematen (Ghana) and Ms Mari Elka Pangestu (Indonesia).

366 After their presentation to the General Council, each of the candidates held a press conference, which was webcasted and can be viewed at http://gaia.world-television.com/wto/2013/dgsel_webcast_e.htm.

367 See above, p. 134.

368 See Supachai Panitchpakdi, 'Build Up: The Road to Mexico', speech on 8 January 2003 at Plenary Session XI of the Partnership Summit 2003 in Hyderabad.

minutes of the meetings of these bodies; and the organisation of the biennial sessions of the Ministerial Conference); (2) to provide technical assistance to developing-country Members; (3) to monitor and analyse developments in world trade; (4) to advise governments of countries wishing to become Members of the WTO; and (5) to provide information to the public and the media. As discussed in Chapter 3, the WTO Secretariat also provides administrative support and legal assistance for WTO dispute settlement panels.[369]

Developing-country Members have been apprehensive regarding the role of the WTO Secretariat and the Director-General of the WTO in negotiations and debates on policy matters. In 2002, in a joint communication, addressing, *inter alia*, the issue of the role of the Secretariat and the Director-General at sessions of the Ministerial Conference, fifteen developing-country Members, led by India, stated:

> The Secretariat and the Director-General of the WTO ... should assume a neutral/impartial and objective role. They shall not express views explicitly or otherwise on the specific issues being discussed in the Ministerial Conference.[370]

The Sutherland Report recommended, however, that the Director-General and the WTO Secretariat take on a greater, more proactive role. The Report stated:

> The WTO needs a convincing and persistent institutional voice of its own. If Members are not prepared to defend and promote the principles they subscribe to, then the Secretariat must be free to do so ... Further, a clearer – though always careful – lead on policy issues should be emerging from the Secretariat. Members should not be afraid of asking the Secretariat to provide policy analysis.[371]

With regard to the status of the Director-General and WTO staff as *independent* and *impartial* international officials, Article VI:4 of the *WTO Agreement* states:

> The responsibilities of the Director-General and of the staff of the Secretariat shall be exclusively international in character. In the discharge of their duties, the Director-General and the staff of the Secretariat shall not seek or accept instructions from any government or any other authority external to the WTO. They shall refrain from any action which might adversely reflect on their position as international officials. The Members of the WTO shall respect the international character of the responsibilities of the Director-General and of the staff of the Secretariat and shall not seek to influence them in the discharge of their duties.

As noted above, the WTO Secretariat is headed by the WTO Director-General. The Director-General is assisted by four Deputy Directors-General (DDGs), also political appointees serving for a limited period of time. They are appointed by the Director-General – in consultation with WTO Members – and form, together with the Director-General, the senior management of the WTO Secretariat. Currently, Yonov Frederick Agah (of Nigeria), Karl Brauner (of Germany), David Shark (of the United States) and Yi Xiaozhun (of China) serve as DDGs under Roberto Azevêdo.

369 See below, pp. 219–20. Note that the Appellate Body has its own Secretariat, which is separate from and independent of the WTO Secretariat, but which shares the same facilities and makes use of the general support services of the WTO Secretariat (translation, library, etc.). See below, p. 237.

370 Communication from Cuba, Dominican Republic, Egypt, Honduras, India, Indonesia, Jamaica, Kenya, Malaysia, Mauritius, Pakistan, Sri Lanka, Tanzania, Uganda and Zimbabwe, *Preparatory Process in Geneva and Negotiating Procedure at the Ministerial Conferences*, WT/GC/W/471, dated 24 April 2002, para. (i).

371 Sutherland Report, paras. 361 and 366.

The number of DDGs has been the subject of discussions in the General Council.[372] While it is argued that there could be fewer than four, having four DDGs makes it possible for the main regions of the world to be represented in senior management.

The WTO Secretariat is organised into divisions with a functional role (e.g. the Rules Division, the Services Division and the Market Access Division), divisions with an information and liaison role (e.g. the Information and Media Relations Division) and divisions with a supporting role (e.g. the Administration and General Services Division and the Language Services and Documentation Division). Divisions are normally headed by a Director, who reports to one of the WTO's four DDGs or directly to the Director-General. In addition to the Divisions, the WTO Secretariat also includes the Institute for Training and Technical Cooperation (ITTC), which was established in 2003 to ensure a coherent and coordinated approach to capacity-building and technical assistance. Figure 2.4 shows the organisation of the WTO Secretariat.

The Director-General appoints the staff and determines their duties and conditions of service in accordance with the Staff Regulations adopted by the Ministerial Conference.[373]

Eighty different nationalities are represented in the staff of the WTO Secretariat.[374] Nationals of France, the United Kingdom, Spain, Switzerland, the United States and Canada are best represented among the staff.[375] The representation of developing-country nationals in the staff is growing but remains a matter of concern.[376] There are no formal or informal national or regional quotas for WTO Secretariat officials.[377] Still, ensuring the broadest possible diversification of the WTO Secretariat is an important objective of the WTO's recruitment policy. Most of the professional staff are lawyers or economists. The working languages within the WTO Secretariat are English, French and Spanish, with English being the language most frequently used.

The WTO Secretariat has an internship programme for graduate students and young professionals who wish to gain practical experience and deeper knowledge of the activities of the WTO. Only a limited number of internships are available. The eligibility requirements, as well as the terms and conditions of the internship and the application procedure, are set out on the WTO website.

372 See statement by Ambassador Ali Mchumo, Chair of the General Council, at the meeting on 6 October 1999, WT/GC/27, dated 12 October 1999.

373 See Article VI:3 of the *WTO Agreement*. According to the *Staff Regulations*, the paramount objective in the determination of conditions of service is to secure staff members of the highest standards of competence, efficiency and integrity and to meet the requirements of the WTO taking into account the needs and aspirations of the staff members. The Director-General has established and administers *Staff Rules*. The *Staff Rules* implement the provisions of the *Staff Regulations*. The Director-General furthermore issues staff administrative memoranda in elaboration of the *Staff Rules*.

374 See *WTO Annual Report 2016*, p. 168.

375 See *ibid.*, pp. 172–3. There are 171 from France, 54 from the United Kingdom, 41 from Spain, 33 from the United States, 31 from Switzerland and 22 from Canada.

376 There are 68 officials from South and Central America, 57 from Asia and 38 from Africa. Respectively 12, 14 and 12 staff are from Brazil, China and India. See *ibid.*

377 Vacancies are the subject of open competition. The final selection of professional staff is done on the basis of a written exam and an interview. The recruitment process is highly competitive. All vacancy notices are posted on the WTO website.

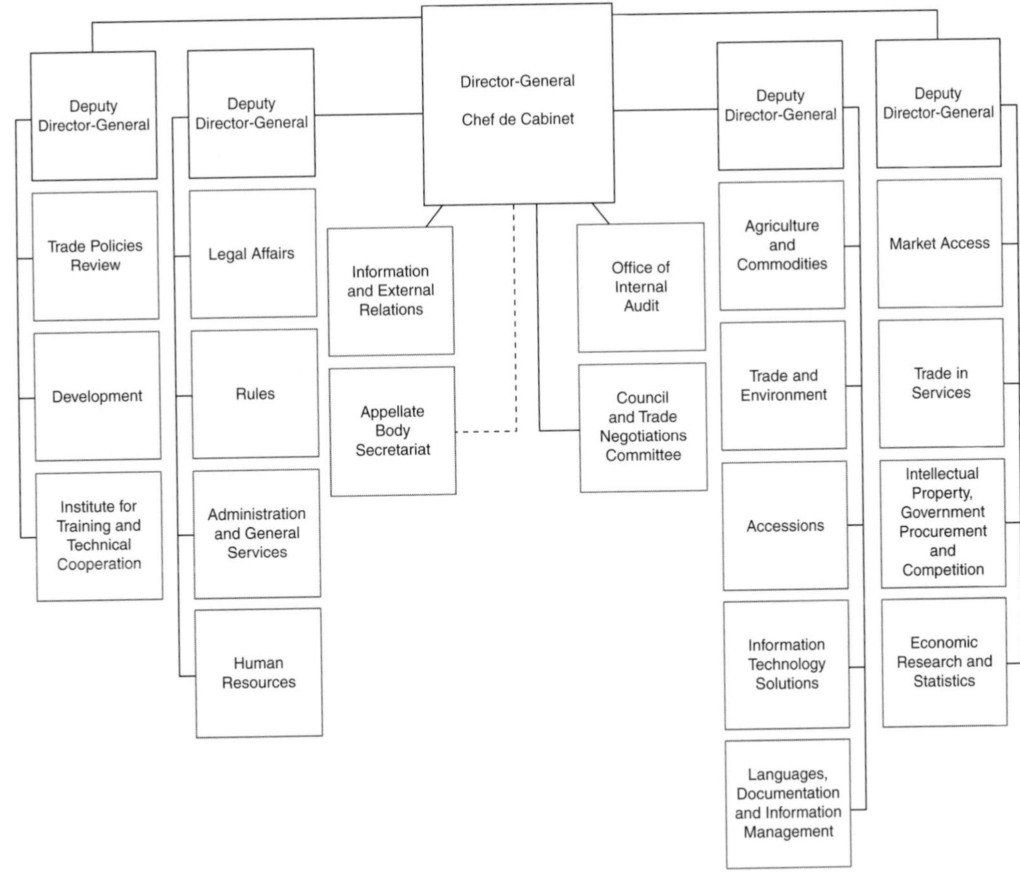

Figure 2.4 WTO Secretariat organisation chart

5 DECISION-MAKING IN THE WTO

The WTO decision-making process has been criticised for being undemocratic, non-transparent and accountable to no one. A decade ago, in 2003, War on Want, a British NGO fighting poverty in developing countries, noted:

> From formulating the agenda to reaching a decision, the process is dominated by the most powerful and richest countries. As such, negotiations at the WTO are fertile ground for horse-trading that inevitably favour those with greatest financial and political might. To keep on top of the massive agenda at the WTO, rich countries, such as US, EU, Japan and Canada, have large teams of well-resourced specialists in Geneva. Half of the poorest countries in the WTO cannot even afford one.[378]

This section examines WTO decision-making in theory and in practice, and will, by discussing participation in WTO decision-making, allow the careful reader to

378 Excerpt from *5th Ministerial: Free Trade on Trial*, available at www.waronwant.org.

assess to what extent the criticism by War on Want and others was valid in 2003 and is still valid in 2016.

5.1 WTO Decision-Making in Theory

The standard decision-making procedure for WTO bodies is set out in Article IX:1 of the *WTO Agreement*, which states:

> The WTO shall continue the practice of decision-making by consensus followed under GATT 1947. Except as otherwise provided, where a decision cannot be arrived at by consensus, the matter at issue shall be decided by voting. At meetings of the Ministerial Conference and the General Council, each Member of the WTO shall have one vote ... Decisions of the Ministerial Conference and the General Council shall be taken by a majority of the votes cast, unless otherwise provided in this Agreement or in the relevant Multilateral Trade Agreement.[379]

However, Article 2.4 of the DSU and Articles VII:3, IX:2, IX:3, X and XII:2 of the *WTO Agreement* provide for special decision-making procedures. This subsection first deals with the standard decision-making procedure and subsequently with the special procedures. Keep in mind that what is explained in this section is WTO decision-making *in theory*. WTO decision-making *in practice* is discussed in the next section.[380]

5.1.1 Standard Procedure

Pursuant to Article IX:1 of the *WTO Agreement*, Members first try to take decisions *by consensus*. Footnote 1 to Article IX defines consensus decision-making by WTO bodies as follows:

> The body concerned shall be deemed to have decided by consensus on a matter submitted for its consideration, if no Member, present at the meeting when the decision is taken, *formally* objects to the proposed decision.[381]

In other words, unless a Member *explicitly* objects to the proposed decision, that decision is taken.[382] No voting takes place.[383] Decision-making by

379 The Rules of Procedure of the various WTO bodies set out the quorum requirement. For example, Rule 16 of the *Rules of Procedure for the Meetings of the General Council* states: 'A simple majority of the Members shall constitute a quorum.' Most WTO bodies have the same quorum requirement. In practice, the quorum is not checked.

380 See below, pp. 151–6. 381 Emphasis added.

382 Note that the Doha Ministerial Declaration of November 2001 introduced the concept of 'explicit consensus' (for decisions on the inclusion of 'Singapore issues' in the agenda of the Doha Development Round). See above, p. 94. It is not clear what is meant by 'explicit consensus'. The inclusion of this concept in the Doha Ministerial Declaration was, however, a condition of India and other developing-country Members agreeing to the Declaration. At the close of the Doha Ministerial Conference, the Conference Chair, the Qatari Finance, Economy and Trade Minister Youssef Hussain Kamal, stated that 'his understanding of the requirement of "explicit consensus" was that it would give each member the right to take a position on modalities that would prevent negotiations from proceeding after the next Ministerial Conference until that member is prepared to join in an explicit consensus'. If this is indeed the meaning of the concept of 'explicit consensus', the question arises whether an 'explicit' consensus differs from a 'normal' consensus.

383 In decision-making by consensus, unlike in decision-making by unanimity, no voting takes place.

consensus gives all Members *veto power*.[384] John Jackson noted, however, in this respect:

> the practice ... is that some countries that have difficulty with a particular decision will nevertheless remain silent out of deference to countries with a substantially higher stake in the pragmatic economic consequences of a decision.[385]

Decision-making by consensus involves a degree of deference to economic power. It is 'only' when important national, economic or other interests are at stake that a WTO Member would consider blocking the consensus.[386]

As Hoekman and Kostecki noted, decision-making by consensus is a useful device to ensure that only decisions which have a good chance of being implemented are adopted because the decisions adopted are all decisions to which there was no major opposition. However, Hoekman and Kostecki also observed that, as further discussed below,[387] decision-making by consensus:

> reinforces conservative tendencies in the system. Proposals for change can be adopted only if unopposed, creating the potential for paralysis.[388]

If consensus cannot be achieved, Article IX:1, second sentence, of the *WTO Agreement* provides for voting. For a decision to be adopted, it must have a simple majority of the votes cast. Pursuant to Article IX:1, third sentence, each Member has one vote.[389] However, there is one exception to this rule. Article IX:1, fourth sentence, states:

> Where the European Communities exercise their right to vote, they shall have a number of votes equal to the number of their member States which are Members of the WTO.

In a footnote to this sentence, it is further explained that the total number of votes of the European Communities, now referred to as the European Union, *and* the EU Member States shall in no case exceed the number of the EU Member States. It is thus clear that either the European Union *or* the EU Member States (each individually) will participate in a vote. Who participates in a vote is not a matter of WTO law but of EU constitutional law. For reasons relating to the practice of WTO decision-making, discussed below, the fact that the European Union currently has twenty-eight votes and the United States, China and India only one, does not have much, if any, impact on the political decision-making processes at the WTO.[390]

384 As noted in the Sutherland Report, however, the definition of consensus favours Members that can afford to be present at all meetings, since absence does not defeat a consensus. See Sutherland Report, para. 282.
385 Jackson, *The World Trade Organization*, 46.
386 See *ibid.* 387 See above, p. 140, fn. 351.
388 Hoekman and Kostecki, *Political Economy of the World Trading System*, 57.
389 Compare this with decision-making and voting in the IMF or the World Bank. In the IMF, for example, each member country is assigned a quota, based on its relative position in the world economy. This quota largely determines a member's voting power in IMF decision-making.
390 See below, pp. 145–56.

As already discussed above, it should be pointed out that, as a rule, the European Commission speaks for the European Union *and* the EU Member States at meetings of WTO bodies, even if those bodies deal with matters that are not within the exclusive competence of the European Union.[391] Delegates from the EU Member States attend the meetings but do not speak. The EU Member States speak (and vote, if a vote is called) only with regard to budgetary, finance and administrative matters.[392] Furthermore, the Ministers of the EU Member States make short formal statements at the biennial sessions of the Ministerial Conference.

5.1.2 Special Procedures

In addition to the standard decision-making procedure, provided for in Article IX:1 of the *WTO Agreement* and discussed in the previous subsection, the *WTO Agreement* sets out a number of decision-making procedures which deviate from the standard procedure. This subsection briefly discusses these special procedures.[393]

With regard to decision-making by the DSB, Article 2.4 of the DSU states that the DSB shall take decisions by consensus. As discussed in detail in Chapter 3, the DSB takes certain decisions, such as the decisions on the establishment of a panel, on the adoption of dispute settlement reports, or on the authorisation of retaliation measures, by *negative consensus*.[394] Other decisions, such as the appointment of Members of the Appellate Body, are taken by a *positive consensus*.[395]

With regard to authoritative interpretations of provisions of the *WTO Agreement* and the multilateral agreements of Annex 1, 2 and 3, Article IX:2 of the *WTO Agreement* states that the Ministerial Conference and the General Council shall have the *exclusive authority* to adopt such interpretations,[396] and that the decision to adopt an authoritative interpretation shall be taken by a *three-quarter majority* of the Members.[397] To date, the WTO has not made any *explicit* use of the possibility to adopt 'authoritative interpretations'. The Doha Ministerial Decision on *Implementation-Related Issues and Concerns* contains a number of provisions which are obviously interpretations of provisions of the WTO agreements. However, in its Preamble, the Decision does not explicitly

391 See Article 207 of the *Treaty on the Functioning of the European Union*, Official Journal, C 83, 30 March 2010.

392 Note that the EU Member States, and not the European Union, contribute to the WTO budget. See below, pp. 158–9.

393 Note that not all special decision-making procedures are discussed below. Not discussed is, for example, Article 12.1 of the *SPS Agreement*, pursuant to which the SPS Committee always takes its decisions by consensus.

394 See below, pp. 207–8. 395 See below, p. 210.

396 On the difference between 'authoritative interpretations' of provisions of WTO agreements by the Ministerial Conference and the General Council, on the one hand, and 'clarification' of those provisions by panels and the Appellate Body, see above, p. 180, fn. 314 and below, pp. 190–9.

397 Recall that, in the case of an interpretation of a multilateral trade agreement in Annex 1, the Ministerial Conference and the General Council shall adopt an authoritative interpretation on the basis of a recommendation by the Council overseeing the functioning of that Agreement. See above, fn. 314, p. 180.

refer to Article IX:2 of the *WTO Agreement* and at least some of these interpretations were adopted without a recommendation of the relevant specialised council.[398] Note that the Appellate Body ruled in *US – Clove Cigarettes (2012)* that paragraph 5.2 of this Decision – which defines the term 'reasonable interval' in Article 2.12 of the *TBT Agreement* was at least six months[399] – was not an authoritative interpretation because it was not based on a recommendation of the Council on Trade in Goods.[400] The Appellate Body emphasised that:

> the recommendation from the relevant Council is an *essential element* of Article IX:2, which constitutes the legal basis upon which the Ministerial Conference or the General Council exercise their authority to adopt interpretations of the *WTO Agreement*.[401]

With regard to decisions on the accession of new Members, Article XII:2 of the *WTO Agreement* provides that such decisions are taken by the Ministerial Conference (or the General Council) by a *two-thirds majority* of the Members. However, on 15 November 1995, the General Council agreed that, for decisions on accession, it will first seek to reach *consensus*.[402] Only when a decision cannot be arrived at by consensus shall the matter be decided by a two-thirds majority vote.[403] To date, only the 1995 decision on the accession of Ecuador was taken by majority vote.

With regard to decisions to waive an obligation imposed on a Member, Article IX:3 of the *WTO Agreement* distinguishes between waivers of obligations under the *WTO Agreement* and waivers of obligations under the multilateral trade agreements of Annex 1. Decisions on waivers of the first type require consensus and, if consensus cannot be reached within a time period not exceeding ninety days, a *three-quarters majority* of the Members.[404] Decisions on waivers of the more common, second type require a *three-quarters majority* of the Members.[405] However, on 15 November 1995, the General Council decided that – in spite of Article IX:3 – it would also with regard to this second type of waivers first seek to reach *consensus*.[406] Only when a decision cannot be arrived at by consensus shall the matter be decided by a three-quarters majority.

With regard to decisions on amendments of the *WTO Agreement* and the multilateral agreements of Annexes 1, 2, and 3, Article X of the *WTO Agreement* sets out a complex regime. In general terms, the amendment procedure is as

398 See above, fn. 314, p. 180.
399 On Article 2.12 of the *TBT Agreement*, see below, pp. 927–9.
400 See Appellate Body Report, *US – Clove Cigarettes (2012)*, para. 255.
401 *Ibid.*, para. 254. Emphasis added.
402 See Statement by the Chairman, as agreed by the General Council on 15 November 1995, *on Decision-Making Procedures under Articles IX and XII of the WTO Agreement*, WT/L/93, dated 24 November 1995, first paragraph.
403 *Ibid.*
404 See Article IX:3(a) and the chapeau of Article IX:3 of the *WTO Agreement*.
405 See the chapeau of Article IX:3 of the *WTO Agreement*. Note that a request for a waiver concerning the multilateral agreements of Annex 1 shall be submitted initially to the relevant specialised council for consideration during a time period which shall not exceed ninety days. See Article IX:3(b) of the *WTO Agreement*.
406 See General Council Decision of 15 November 1995 on *Decision-Making Procedures under Articles IX and XII of the WTO Agreement*, WT/L/93, dated 24 November 1995, first paragraph.

follows. Individual Members or one of the three specialised councils (the CTG, CTS and the TRIPS Council)[407] initiate the amendment procedure by submitting an amendment proposal to the Ministerial Conference or the General Council. In a first period of at least ninety days, the Ministerial Conference or the General Council tries to reach *consensus* on the proposal for amendment. If consensus cannot be reached, the Ministerial Conference or the General Council will resort to voting. To be adopted, the proposal for amendment requires a *two-thirds majority* of the Members. Once adopted by consensus or by a two-thirds majority, the amendment is forthwith submitted to the Members for acceptance in accordance with their national constitutional requirements and procedures. An amendment shall take effect for the Members that have accepted the amendment upon acceptance by two-thirds of the Members.[408] As a rule, the amendment is effective only in respect of those Members that have accepted it.[409] However, Article X:2 lists a number of fundamental provisions (concerning the MFN treatment obligation under the GATT 1994, the GATS and the *TRIPS Agreement*, the GATT 1994 tariff schedules and WTO decision-making and amendment) which have to be accepted by all Members before they can take effect. Moreover, a decision to amend the DSU must be made by consensus, and amendments to the DSU take effect for all Members upon approval by the Ministerial Conference. Amendments to the DSU are not submitted to the Members for acceptance.[410] Article X:4 also provides that amendments that do not alter the rights and obligations of the Members take effect for *all* Members upon acceptance by *two-thirds* of the Members. Finally, Article X:3 states in pertinent part:

> The Ministerial Conference may decide by a three-fourths majority of the Members that any amendment made effective under this paragraph is of such a nature that any Member which has not accepted it within a period specified by the Ministerial Conference in each case shall be free to withdraw from the WTO or to remain a Member with the consent of the Ministerial Conference.

While conveyed in diplomatic language, this means, in effect, that a Member that refuses to accept certain amendments may be expelled from the WTO.[411] The actual importance of this provision, however, seems limited. Note that this power also existed under the GATT 1947 but was never used.[412] It is likely that this will also be the case in the WTO.

The first amendment to the WTO agreements was adopted by the General Council in December 2005 and concerned an amendment to the *TRIPS Agreement*.[413] Pursuant to the amendment decision, an Article 31 *bis* is inserted

407 See above, pp. 134–6.

408 See Article X:3 of the *WTO Agreement*. See, however, Article X:4 of the *WTO Agreement*, discussed below, with regard to amendments that do not alter the rights and obligations of Members.

409 See *ibid.* 410 See *ibid.*, Article X:8. 411 See above, p. 128, fn. 276.

412 See *Analytical Index: Guide to GATT Law and Practice*, 6th edn (GATT, 1994), 934.

413 General Council, *Decision of 6 December 2005 on the Amendment of the TRIPS Agreement*, WT/L/641, dated 8 December 2005.

after Article 31 of the *TRIPS Agreement* and an Annex to the *TRIPS Agreement* is inserted after Article 73 thereof. As discussed in Chapter 15, the amendment concerns a relaxation of the obligations of Members when they export to certain eligible developing countries pharmaceutical products produced under a compulsory licence.[414] Pursuant to Article X:3 of the *WTO Agreement*, this amendment will take effect when two-thirds of the Members have accepted the amendment in accordance with their national constitutional requirements and procedures. As of October 2016, 105 Members had notified their acceptance of the amendment.[415] Therefore, this amendment, agreed on in December 2005, has yet to take effect.

Most recently, the WTO agreements were amended by adding to Annex 1A of the *WTO Agreement*, the *Agreement on Trade Facilitation* (TFA). The latter Agreement was agreed at the Bali Ministerial Conference in December 2013 and the Protocol of Amendment was adopted on 27 November 2014.[416] As of October 2016, ninety-four Members had notified their acceptance of the protocol.[417]

Finally, with regard to decisions on the annual budget and financial regulations, Article VII:3 of the *WTO Agreement* provides that the General Council adopts the annual budget and the financial regulations by a *two-thirds majority* of the votes cast but comprising more than half of the Members of the WTO.

5.2 WTO Decision-Making in Practice

Although the *WTO Agreement* provides for the possibility to take decisions by voting, it is very exceptional for bodies to vote. In practice, WTO decisions are taken by consensus. In 1999, when discussion on the selection of a new Director-General came to a deadlock, some developing countries suggested that the decision on the new Director-General should be taken by vote (as provided for in Article IX:1 of the *WTO Agreement*). However, this suggestion was not well received, in particular by the developed countries, which argued that this was 'contrary to the way things were done in the WTO'.[418] Jackson wrote in 1998:

> [T]he spirit and practice of the GATT has always been to try to accommodate through consensus negotiation procedures the views of as many countries as possible, but certainly to

414 See below, pp. 1038–41.

415 See www.wto.org/english/tratop_e/trips_e/amendment_e.htm. Note that the European Union notified its acceptance and did so also on behalf of the twenty-seven EU Member States (note that Croatia was not a member of the European Union at that time).

416 *Agreement on Trade Facilitation*, Ministerial Decision of 7 December 2013, WT/MIN(13)/36 – WT/L/911, dated 11 December 2013. See below, pp. 511–12.

417 See www.wto.org/english/tratop_e/tradfa_e/tradfa_agreeacc_e.htm. Note that the European Union notified its acceptance and did so also on behalf of the twenty-eight EU Member States.

418 Note, however, that the *Decision on the Procedures for the Appointment of Directors-General*, adopted in 2002, states that: 'Members should consider the possibility of recourse to a vote as a last resort by a procedure to be determined at that time.' See General Council, *Decision on the Procedures for the Appointment of Directors-General*, adopted 10 December 2002, WT/L/509, dated 20 January 2003, para. 21. See also above, pp. 146–51.

give weight to the views of countries that have power in the trading system. This is not likely to change.[419]

In a speech in February 2000 at UNCTAD X in Bangkok, a few weeks after the failure of the Seattle Ministerial Conference, Mike Moore, the then WTO Director-General, stated:

> [T]he consensus principle which is at the heart of the WTO system – and which is a fundamental democratic guarantee – is not negotiable.[420]

It cannot be disputed that decisions taken by consensus have more 'democratic legitimacy' than decisions taken by majority vote. At the same time, it should be noted that the consensus requirement does, of course, make decision-making in the WTO difficult and susceptible to paralysis. According to the Sutherland Report, there is definitely 'a larger sense of legitimacy' for decisions adopted by consensus.[421] The Sutherland Report noted, however, that:

> [a]s the number of Members grows larger and larger (now 148, perhaps going to 170 and more), it becomes harder and harder to implement needed measures that require decisions, even when there is a vast majority of the Members that desire a measure. The consensus requirement can result in the majority's will being blocked by even one country. If the measure involved a fundamental change, such difficulty would probably be worthwhile, as adding a measure of 'constitutional stability' to the organization. But often there are non-fundamental measures at stake, some of which are just fine-tuning to keep the rules abreast of changing economic and other circumstances.[422]

The Sutherland Report recommended that:

> WTO Members give serious further study to the problems associated with achieving consensus in light of possible distinctions that could be made for certain types of decisions, such as purely procedural issues.[423]

The Sutherland Report also recommended that:

> WTO Members to cause the General Council to adopt a Declaration that a Member considering blocking a measure which otherwise has very broad consensus support shall only block such consensus if it declares in writing, with reasons included, that the matter is one of vital national interest to it.[424]

5.3 Participation in WTO Decision-Making

As discussed above, in practice the WTO takes decisions by consensus. As such, the WTO seems to ensure the participation of all Members, including

419 Jackson, *World Trading System*, 2nd edn, 73.
420 M. Moore, 'Back on Track for Trade and Development', keynote address at UNCTAD X, Bangkok, 16 February 2000.
421 Para. 282.
422 *Ibid.*, para. 283. As noted by the Sutherland Report, observers of WTO decision-making sometimes contend that consensus decision-making is not a problem, as they do not observe many instances in which consensus is blocked. However, it should be noted that 'almost all potential decisions are prepared informally in advance and usually do not move to a formal proposition in a decision-making body if they are not ripe for consensus'. See *ibid.*, para. 285.
423 *Ibid.*, para. 288. 424 *Ibid.*, para. 289.

developing-country Members. However, it is obviously neither possible nor practical to involve directly all 164 Members in negotiations aimed at reaching agreement on controversial issues. It is likely that such broad participation would make these negotiations ineffective. Over the years, mechanisms have, therefore, been developed to facilitate negotiations and decision-making in the WTO. The best-known and most frequently used of these mechanisms is the 'green room meeting'.[425] Green room meetings bring together the major powers in the WTO (which obviously include the European Union, the United States, China, Brazil and India) *and* a select number of other Members, which either are the coordinator/representative of a larger group of Members (such as, for example, the least-developed-country Members) or have a particular interest in the subject matter under discussion.[426] In recent years, these green room meetings have become more open and inclusive, with rising active participation of developing-country Members.

In green room meetings, ministers, ambassadors or senior officials of the twenty or so Members invited meet under the chairship of the WTO Director-General or the chair of a WTO council or committee to explore possible approaches to the key issues under discussion and to reach, if possible, a preliminary agreement. Such preliminary agreement is then subsequently presented to the rest of the WTO membership for adoption. As noted above, this mechanism was much criticised at the ill-fated Seattle Ministerial Conference.[427] Peter Sutherland wrote in this respect:

> Ironically, in Seattle, WTO Director-General Mike Moore and US Trade Representative Charlene Barshefsky, the co-chairs of the Ministerial Meeting, made a concerted, good-faith effort to broaden the participation of delegations in the negotiations. They divided the Ministerial agenda into several sections, created working groups for each, and invited all delegations to participate in all the working groups. Their goal was to keep Green Rooms to a minimum. But developing country delegations, in particular, had difficulty covering all of the working groups, and as the Ministerial week proceeded and agreements remained elusive, the temptation to pull together smaller groups of countries for harder bargaining – Green Rooms, in other words – understandably grew. In communiqués released towards the end of the week, large groupings of African and Latin American countries denounced what they described as the Ministerial's exclusive and non-democratic negotiating structure.[428]

In the first half of 2000, after the debacle of the Seattle Ministerial Conference in November and December 1999, Members conducted intensive consultations

425 See above, pp. 152–6. Other mechanisms are 'mini-ministerials', ambassadorial group meetings (AGMs) and 'heads of delegation meetings' (HODs). These mechanisms are not discussed in this book.

426 While green room meetings are frequently held in the conference room of the WTO Director-General, the term 'green room' does not refer to a specific location. In fact, green room meetings can be, and are, held anywhere. The term 'green room' has its origins in British theatre and refers to the space where actors would wait when they were not required on stage. However, an alternative and more colourful explanation for the use of the term 'green room' is that the conference room of the GATT Director-General, where the first green room meetings were held, had green wallpaper. While this conference room has fortunately been redecorated since, the term 'green room' stuck.

427 See above, p. 93, fn. 54.

428 P. Sutherland, J. Sewell and D. Weiner, 'Challenges Facing the WTO and Policies to Address Global Governance', in Sampson (ed.), *Role of the World Trade Organization in Global Governance*, 87–8.

on the issue of the effective participation of developing countries in WTO decision-making.[429] These consultations, however, did not result in any reform of the WTO's institutional structure or its decision-making process. In fact, the consultations indicated that Members thought that there was no need for such reform. At the General Council meeting of 17–19 July 2000, the Chair of the General Council summarised the outcome of the consultations as follows:

> First, within the framework of the WTO Agreement it seemed that Members generally did not see the need for any major institutional reform which could alter the basic character of the WTO as a Member-driven organization and its decision-making process. There was also a strong commitment of the Members to reaffirm the existing practice of taking decisions by consensus. Second, Members seemed to recognize that interactive open-ended informal consultation meetings played an important role in facilitating consensus decision-making. As a complement to, but in no way a replacement of this open-ended consultation process, consultations might also take place with individual Members or groups of Members.[430]

While the consultations of 2000 did not result in any reform of the WTO's decision-making process, they did, however, serve to 'clear the air' and rebuild a degree of confidence in the process after the Seattle debacle. In order to ensure that negotiations conducted by only a select group of Members, such as green room meetings, contribute to the achievement of genuine consensus among all Members, it was recognised that there was a need: (1) to inform all Members that such negotiations conducted by a select group of Members were taking place; (2) to allow all interested Members to make their views known in such negotiations; (3) not to make any assumptions on the representation of Members by other Members in such negotiations; and (4) to report back promptly on the results of the negotiations to all Members.[431] The consultations of 2000 also made clear that the WTO needed: (1) to schedule its meetings carefully so as to avoid overlapping meetings as much as possible; and (2) to ensure prompt and efficient dissemination of information and documents to Members, and, in particular, to non-resident Members and Members with small missions. Since 2000, improvements along these lines have been made to the WTO decision-making process. The success of the Doha Ministerial Conference and the launch of the Doha Round at the end of 2001 may be considered as an early result of improvements made. Note, however, that these improvements fell short of the expectations of some Members and that the discussion on how to improve the WTO's decision-making process continued in 2002 and thereafter.[432]

429 As a sort of shorthand, this issue was also referred to as the 'internal transparency' issue. The 'internal transparency' issue was distinguished from the 'external transparency' issue, which related to the involvement of civil society in WTO decision-making. See above, p. 107, fn. 154.

430 General Council, *Minutes of Meeting*, WT/GC/M/57, dated 14 September 2000, para. 134.

431 See *ibid.*

432 See General Council, *Minutes of Meetings*, WT/GC/M/73, dated 11 March 2002; WT/GC/M/74, dated 1 July 2002; WT/GC/M/75, dated 27 September 2002; and WT/GC/M/77, dated 13 February 2002. See also Communication from Cuba, Dominican Republic, Egypt, Honduras, India, Indonesia, Jamaica, Kenya, Malaysia, Mauritius, Pakistan, Sri Lanka, Tanzania, Uganda and Zimbabwe, *Preparatory Process in Geneva and Negotiating Procedure at the Ministerial Conferences*, WT/GC/W/471, dated 24 April 2002.

With regard to negotiations and decision-making, the main challenge for the WTO and its 164 Members is to strike an appropriate *balance* between inclusiveness, transparency and efficiency. To date, green room meetings (as they have evolved over time) are the WTO's best effort to strike such balance. Disparities in economic and political power will of course always affect, if not determine, the weight of Members in the WTO negotiations and decision-making. No institutional mechanism can ever totally 'undo' these differences. However, in recent years, the WTO is definitely no longer the 'rich men's club' that the GATT, its predecessor, was, or that the WTO in its early years arguably also was. As discussed in Chapter 1 and noted earlier in this chapter, over the last decade, developing-country Members, and in particular the emerging economies among them, have played an ever more important role in the WTO because of their increasing importance in the global economy.[433] The Coordinator and Chief Negotiator of the ACP Group in Geneva, Ambassador Servansing from Mauritius,[434] wrote in 2012, referring to the crucial NAMA negotiations in the context of the Doha Round, that:

> the dominant role of developed countries in determining the contours of a deal for the rest is no longer on the cards.[435]

Also in 2012, Ambassador Bhatia from India,[436] wrote:

> At the heart of the present impasse in the [Doha Round] negotiations are the changes in the political economy of the organisation since the conclusion of the Uruguay Round. In previous Rounds under the aegis of the GATT, developed countries played a pre-eminent role in agenda setting as well as in shaping the final outcomes. Developing countries while active in varying degrees were not always sufficiently well organized to translate their interests and concerns in key areas into negotiated outcomes. However, the Doha Round has witnessed unprecedented engagement of developing countries, both in their individual capacity, as well as through their various coalitions.[437]

As noted above, three developing-country Members, Brazil, China and India, are now part of the very select group of Members, whose consent is necessary to get anything done within the WTO.[438] A larger group of emerging economies among the developing-country Members, including Argentina, Chile, Indonesia, Malaysia, Mexico, Pakistan, Peru, Philippines, Thailand and Turkey, have in recent years – acting on their own, but more commonly as part of a group, coalition or alliance – significantly gained in influence in WTO negotiations and

433 See above, pp. 22–4 and 115–18.

434 Ambassador Shree B. C. Servansing is the Permanent Representative of Mauritius to the United Nations and other international organisations in Geneva. Since October 2014, Ambassador Servansing is a Member of the WTO Appellate Body. See below, p. 235.

435 Shree B. C. Servansing, 'Non-Agricultural Market Access (NAMA) – Balancing Development and Ambition', in Mehta, Kaushik and Kaukab (eds.), *Reflections from the Frontline*, 94.

436 Ambassador Ujal Singh Bhatia was the Permanent Representative of India to the WTO from 2004 to 2010. Since December 2011, Ambassador Bhatia is a Member of the WTO Appellate Body. See below, p. 235.

437 Ujal S. Bhatia, 'G20 – Combining Substance with Solidarity and Leadership', in Mehta, Kaushik and Kaukab (eds.), *Reflections from the Frontline*, 239.

438 See above, p. 155.

decision-making. Many other developing-country Members, including of course the least-developed-country Members, still lack in resources and expertise to participate effectively in WTO negotiations and decision-making.[439] Nevertheless, these Members have increasingly been able to make their voice heard and their concerns considered in WTO negotiations and decision-making. This has been the result of: (1) trade-related technical assistance and training, discussed above;[440] and (2) the systematic coordination of positions and the pooling of resources and expertise in groups, coalitions and alliances of developing-country Members with common interests, also discussed above.[441] Overall, developing-country Members are now participating in WTO negotiations and decision-making in a much more active and effective manner than ever before. However, as already suggested above, there is a drawback to this welcome development.[442] The active and effective participation of a greater number of Members with very different economic and trade interests has inevitably made WTO negotiations and decision-making also more difficult than ever before.

6 OTHER ISSUES

The final section on 'other issues' addresses briefly issues relating to the legal status of the WTO under international law and issues relating to the WTO budget.

6.1 Legal Status of the WTO

Pursuant to Article VIII of the *WTO Agreement*, the WTO has legal personality, and shall be accorded by each of its Members such legal capacity as well as such privileges and immunities as may be necessary for the exercise of its functions.[443] The privileges and immunities to be accorded by a Member to the WTO, its officials, and the representatives of its Members shall be similar to the privileges and immunities stipulated in the 1947 United Nations *Convention on the Privileges and Immunities of the Specialised Agencies*.[444] Article III, Section 4, of this Convention stipulates that:

439 In addition to the relative lack of experienced trade negotiators, two particular problems faced by many of these developing-country Members are: (1) the lack of effective coordination between ministries and government agencies; and (2) the lack of a structured, i.e. institutionalised, dialogue with domestic stakeholders. These problems often result in a situation in which a Member does not have a clear picture of its offensive and defensive interests in specific negotiations.

440 See above, pp. 110–13. 441 See above, pp. 114–18. 442 See above, p. 100.

443 See Article VIII:1 and 2 of the *WTO Agreement*. With regard to the privileges and immunities of WTO staff and the representatives of the WTO Members, see Article VIII:3 of the *WTO Agreement*: 'The officials of the WTO and the representatives of the Members shall similarly be accorded by each of its Members such privileges and immunities as are necessary for the independent exercise of their functions in connection with the WTO.'

444 Article VIII:4 of the *WTO Agreement*.

> The specialized agencies ... shall enjoy immunity from every form of legal process except in so far as in any particular case they have expressly waived their immunity.

The privileges and immunities which Switzerland accords to the WTO, its officials and the representatives of WTO Members are set out in detail in the 1995 *WTO Headquarters Agreement* concluded between the WTO and Switzerland.[445]

It deserves to be mentioned that the WTO is *not* part of the UN 'family'. It is a fully independent international organisation with its own particular 'corporate' culture. John Jackson noted, with regard to the question of the 'specialised-agency-of-the-UN' status for the WTO, that this question:

> was explicitly considered and explicitly rejected by the WTO members, possibly because of the skepticism of some members about the UN budgetary and personnel policies and their alleged inefficiencies.[446]

However, this 'separateness' does not preclude that the WTO maintains a close working relationship with many UN organisations and agencies.[447]

6.2 WTO Budget

The total WTO budget for 2016 amounted to CHF 197 million (Swiss francs).[448] In comparison with the annual budget of other international organisations or some NGOs, the WTO's annual budget is quite modest. In 2001, the then WTO Director-General, Mike Moore, noted that the World Wildlife Fund had three times the resources of the WTO.[449] The modest budget of the WTO reflects the small size of the Secretariat and the relatively limited scope of the WTO's activities outside Geneva. Peter Sutherland has, however, criticised the limited size of the WTO budget:

> Lacking either the courage of their own convictions or confidence in their ability to prevail over domestic opposition, the chief financial backers of the WTO have failed to provide adequate funding for a WTO Secretariat (by far the smallest of all the major multilateral institutions) that is already overburdened by technical assistance demands as well as dispute settlement cases and new accessions.[450]

Pursuant to Article VII:1 of the *WTO Agreement*, the WTO Director-General presents a budget proposal to the Committee on Budget, Finance and Administration, which will review the proposal and make recommendations thereon to the General Council. As discussed above, Article VII:3 of the *WTO Agreement* provides that

445 For the *WTO Headquarters Agreement*, see WT/GC/1 and Add.1.

446 *World Trade Organization*, 52. 447 See above, pp. 105–10.

448 See *WTO Annual Report 2016*, 175. Of these CHF197 million, CHF189.7 million is for the WTO Secretariat, and CHF 7.4 million is for the Appellate Body and its Secretariat. Of the total budget of CHF197 million, CHF131 million, or 66 per cent, was for staff costs. In recent years, there has been no growth in the WTO budget. In earlier years, the WTO budget was gradually increased. In 2003 and 2008, the WTO budget amounted to CHF154.9 million and CHF184.8 million respectively.

449 Reported by F. Lewis, 'The Anti-Globalization Spoilers Are Going Global', *International Herald Tribune*, 6 July 2001.

450 P. Sutherland, J. Sewell and D. Weiner, 'Challenges Facing the WTO and Policies to Address Global Governance', in Sampson (ed.), *Role of the World Trade Organization in Global Governance*, 82.

the General Council adopt the budget by a *two-thirds majority* of the votes cast but comprising more than half of the Members of the WTO. However, in practice, the budget is adopted by consensus.

With respect to the financial contributions to be made by Members to the budget of the WTO, the WTO *Financial Regulations*, as last amended by the General Council in May 2007, set out: (1) the scale of contributions apportioning the expenses of the WTO among its Members; and (2) the measures to be taken in respect of Members in arrears.[451] Pursuant to Article VII:4 of the *WTO Agreement*, each Member shall promptly contribute to the WTO its share in the expenses of the WTO in accordance with the *Financial Regulations*.[452]

As provided for in the *Financial Regulations*, the contribution of a Member to the WTO budget is established on the basis of that Member's international trade (imports plus exports) in relation to the total international trade of all WTO Members.[453] In other words, a Member's contribution is based on that Member's share in international trade. Members of which the share in the total international trade of all WTO Members is less than 0.015 per cent make a minimum contribution to the budget of 0.015 per cent.[454] The European Union does not contribute to the WTO budget. The twenty-eight EU Member States contribute to the WTO budget, and their contribution is by far the largest. This is because, in calculating the contribution of the EU Member States, not only trade between the EU with other WTO Members but also trade between the EU Member States, is taken into account. Together, the EU Member States contributed, in 2016 34.7 per cent of the WTO budget; the United States 11.2 per cent; China 9.1 per cent; Japan 4.3 per cent; Canada 2.6 per cent; Korea 3.0 per cent; Hong Kong 2.6 per cent; Singapore 2.4 per cent; India 2.2 per cent; Mexico 1.7 per cent; Chinese Taipei 1.5 per cent; Australia 1.4 per cent; Brazil 1.3 per cent; Saudi Arabia 1.2 per cent; Malaysia 1.1 per cent; Indonesia 0.9 per cent; Norway 0.8 per cent; and South Africa 0.5 per cent.[455]

In addition to the annual budget, the WTO also manages a number of trust funds, which have been contributed to by Members. Trust funds such as the Doha Development Agenda Global Trust Fund are used in support of special activities for technical assistance and training meant to enable least-developed and developing countries to make better use of the WTO and draw greater benefit from the multilateral trading system.

451 For the currently applicable *Financial Regulations of the World Trade Organization*, see WT/L/156/Rev.2, dated 21 May 2007. For the currently applicable detailed *Financial Rules of the World Trade Organization*, see WT/L/157/Rev.1, dated 21 May 2007.

452 Note that, in addition to the contributions made by Members, the WTO has miscellaneous income from contributions made by Observer countries and the sale of publications.

453 See Regulation 12.2 of the *Financial Regulations of the World Trade Organization*.

454 See *ibid.*, Regulation 12.7. 455 See *WTO Annual Report 2016*, 176–7.

In March 2008, the Office of Internal Audit (OIA) was established to undertake the independent examination and evaluation of the WTO's financial and budgetary control systems and processes, with the aim of ensuring that the contributions by Members to the WTO budget are used 'efficiently and effectively to obtain the best value for money'.[456] Based on the recommendations of the external auditor and the strategic review, the Office of Internal Oversight (OIO) was established, in November 2015, to provide for an independent and objective assessment of management practices, expenses, budgetary control and allegations of misconduct in all its forms.[457] The OIO took over the functions formerly exercised by the OIA.

The WTO accounts are also subject to external audits.[458] The main findings of the 2013 Audit Report were:

> The WTO has presented financial statements rectified in one essential respect compared to those of 2012, in order to ensure consistency with the IPSAS: application of the standards relating to long-term employee benefits (pensions and after-service health insurance). However, these financial statements are not yet in conformity with the IPSAS as regards the International Trade Centre (ITC), a 'jointly controlled entity' of the WTO and the UN.
>
> Our recommendations are to remedy this situation and to make minor improvements to the accounting methods for some operations and the presentation of the notes to the financial statements. The notes should indicate the changes in accounting methods and explain the main developments in the accounts compared to the previous financial year.[459]

The five external auditors conducting the 2013 audit certified that the accounts for the financial year 2013 'present fairly the financial position of the WTO as at 31 December 2013'.[460]

7 SUMMARY

The WTO is a young international organisation with a long history. The origins of the WTO lie in the GATT 1947, which for almost fifty years was – after the 'stillbirth' of the ITO – the *de facto* international organisation for trade. While the GATT was successful with respect to the reduction of tariffs, effectively addressing the problems of international trade in goods and services in the era of economic globalisation would require a more 'sophisticated' institutional framework. The Uruguay Round negotiations resulted, in December 1993, in an

456 Regulation 41(d) of the *Financial Regulations of the World Trade Organization*, WT/L/156/Rev.2, dated 21 May 2007, provides the relevant legal basis.

457 *WTO Annual Report 2016*, p. 174.

458 See Regulations 46 and 47 of the *Financial Regulations of the World Trade Organization*, WT/L/156/Rev.2, dated 21 May 2007.

459 *Letter of Final Observations on the Financial Statements for the Financial Year Ended 31 December 2013 and Performance Audit*, WT/BFA/W/335, dated 8 September 2014, 5.

460 *Ibid.*, 20.

agreement on the establishment of the World Trade Organization, which was subsequently signed in Marrakesh, Morocco, in April 1994. The WTO has been operational since 1 January 1995.

Pursuant to the Preamble to the *WTO Agreement*, the ultimate objectives of the WTO are: (1) the increase of standards of living; (2) the attainment of full employment; (3) the growth of real income and effective demand; and (4) the expansion of production of, and trade in, goods and services. However, it is clear from the Preamble that, in pursuing these objectives, the WTO must take into account the need for sustainable development and the needs of developing countries. The two main instruments, or means, to achieve the objectives of the WTO are: (1) the reduction of trade barriers; and (2) the elimination of discrimination. The primary function of the WTO is to provide the common institutional framework for the conduct of trade relations among its Members. More specifically, the WTO has been assigned six widely defined functions: (1) to facilitate the implementation, administration and operation of the WTO agreements; (2) to be a forum for negotiations on new trade rules; (3) to settle trade disputes between its Members; (4) to review the trade policies of its Members; (5) to cooperate with other international organisations and non-governmental organisations; and (6) to give technical assistance to developing-country Members to allow them to integrate into the world trading system and reap the benefits of international trade.

Since the accession of China in December 2001 and even more so with the accession of Russia in 2012, the WTO is a universal organisation. Its 164 Members account for almost all international trade. Three out of every four WTO Members are developing countries. It is noteworthy that not only States but also autonomous customs territories can be, and are, Members of the WTO. Equally noteworthy is that both the European Union *and* all EU Member States are Members of the WTO. Accession to the WTO is a difficult process, since applicants for membership have to: (1) negotiate an 'entrance ticket' of market access concessions and commitments; and (2) bring their national legislation and practices into conformity with the WTO agreements. With regard to membership rights and obligations, not all Members are equal. For good reason, there are at least three different categories of Members: developed-country Members, developing-country Members; and least-developed-country Members. The latter two categories benefit from some degree of 'special and differential treatment' under most of the WTO agreements. All WTO Members can, and do, in exceptional circumstances obtain temporary waivers of WTO obligations. They can also, but have not done so to date, withdraw from the WTO. With one insignificant exception, the *WTO Agreement* does not provide for the possibility to expel Members from the WTO.

The WTO has a complex institutional structure which includes: (1) at the *highest* level, the Ministerial Conference, which is in session only for a few days every two years; (2) at a *second* level, the General Council, which exercises the powers of the Ministerial Conference in between its sessions; and the Dispute Settlement Body (DSB) and the Trade Policy Review Body (TPRB), which are both emanations of the General Council; and (3) at *lower* levels, specialised councils and manifold committees, working parties and working groups. The current Doha Round negotiations are conducted in special sessions of existing WTO bodies and in two specially created, negotiating groups. The conduct of these negotiations is supervised by the Trade Negotiations Committee (TNC), which regularly reports to the General Council. Furthermore, the institutional structure of the WTO includes judicial, quasi-judicial and other non-political bodies as well as the WTO Secretariat, headed by the WTO Director-General. The WTO is a 'Member-driven' organisation. The Members – and not the Director-General or the WTO Secretariat – set the agenda, make proposals and take decisions. The Director-General and the WTO Secretariat act primarily as an 'honest broker' in, or a 'facilitator' of, the political decision-making processes in the WTO. In such a seemingly modest role, the Director-General and the WTO Secretariat can, however, make an important contribution to the building of consensus among Members on a specific agreement or decision. Unlike other international organisations, the WTO does not have a permanent body through which the 'dialogue' between the WTO and civil society can take place. Furthermore, all WTO bodies (except for the non-political bodies) comprise all 164 Members of the WTO. The WTO does not have an executive body, comprising only core WTO Members, to facilitate negotiations and decision-making. However, it is obviously neither possible nor practical to involve directly all 164 Members in negotiations aimed at reaching agreement on controversial issues. Over the years, mechanisms have, therefore, been developed to facilitate negotiations and decision-making in the WTO. The best-known and most frequently used of these mechanisms is the 'green room meeting'. Since the ill-fated Seattle Ministerial Conference in 1999, a number of practical improvements have been made to the 'green room meetings' to ensure that negotiations taking place between the select number of Members invited to attend the 'green room meeting', contribute to the achievement of genuine consensus among all Members.

With respect to decision-making by WTO bodies, one must distinguish between WTO decision-making in theory and decision-making in practice. The *WTO Agreement* provides for a standard decision-making procedure, which applies as the default procedure, and a number of special procedures for specific decisions. *In theory*, WTO Members, under the standard and most of the special procedures, take decisions by consensus, and, if that is not possible, by majority voting. In the latter case, every Member has one vote, except the European Union, which has as many votes as there are EU Member States (currently twenty-eight). *In practice*, however, the WTO very seldom resorts to voting. WTO decisions are made almost exclusively by consensus. Decision-making by consensus is at the heart of the WTO system and is regarded as a fundamental democratic guarantee. However, the consensus requirement renders decision-making by the WTO difficult and susceptible to paralysis.

In recent years, the WTO is definitely no longer the 'rich men's club' that the GATT, its predecessor, was, or that the WTO in its early years arguably also was. Three developing-country Members, Brazil, China and India, are now part of the very select group of Members, whose consent is necessary to get anything done within the WTO. A larger group of emerging economies among the developing-country Members, have in recent years – acting on their own, but more commonly as part of a group, coalition or alliance – significantly gained in influence in WTO negotiations and decision-making. Many other developing-country Members, including of course the least-developed-country Members, still lack in resources and expertise to participate effectively in WTO negotiations and decision-making. Nevertheless, these Members have increasingly been able to make their voice heard and their concerns considered in WTO negotiations and decision-making. This has been the result of: (1) trade-related technical assistance and training; and (2) the systematic coordination of positions and the pooling of resources and expertise in groups, coalitions and alliances of developing-country Members with common interests. However, the active and effective participation of a greater number of Members with very different economic and trade interests has inevitably made WTO negotiations and decision-making more difficult than ever before.

FURTHER READINGS

R. Lanz, M. Roberts and S. Taal, 'Reducing Trade Costs in LDCs: The Role of Aid for Trade', WTO Working Paper ERSD-2016-05, July 2016, World Trade Organization.

I. Feichtner, 'Subsidiarity in the World Trade Organization: The Promise of Waivers', *Law and Contemporary Problems*, 2016, 79, 75–97.

J. Y. Qin, 'Mind the Gap: Navigating between the WTO Agreement and Its Accession Protocols', Wayne State University Law School Research Paper No. 2016-05, February 2016.

D. Bièvre, A. Poletti, M. Hanegraaff and J. Beyers, 'International Institutions and Interest Mobilization: The WTO and Lobbying in EU and US Trade Policy', *Journal of World Trade*, 2016, 50(2), 289–312.

R. Adlung, 'The Trade in Services Agreement (TiSA) and Its Compatibility with GATS: An Assessment Based on Current Evidence', *World Trade Review*, October 2015, 14(4), 617–41.

B. Hoekman and P. C. Mavroidis, 'Regulatory Spillovers and the Trading System: From Coherence to Co-operation', E-15 Task Force on Regulatory Systems Coherence, Overview Paper, April 2015, International Centre for Trade and Sustainable Development and World Economic Forum.

K. Bagwell, C. P. Bown and R. W. Staiger, 'Is the WTO Passé?', Policy Research Working Paper 7304, World Bank Group, June 2015.

R. Wolfe, 'First Diagnose, Then Treat: What Ails the Doha Round?', *World Trade Review*, January 2015, 14(1), 7–28.

K. Bagwell, R.W. Staiger and A. Yurukoglu, 'Multilateral Trade Bargaining: A First Peek at the GATT Bargaining Records', NBER Working Paper No. 21488, August 2015.

Y. Decreux and L. Fontagné, 'What Next for Multilateral Trade Talks? Quantifying the Role of Negotiation Modalities', *World Trade Review*, 2015, 14(1), 29–43.

J. Hallaert, 'The Aid for Trade Initiative: A WTO Attempt at Coherence', Robert Schuman Centre for Advanced Studies Research Paper No. 2015/06, October 2015, European University Institute.

T. Cottier, 'International Economic Law in Transition from Trade Liberalization to Trade Regulation', *Journal of International Economic Law*, 2014, 17, 671–7.

M. Wu, 'Why Developing Countries Won't Negotiate: The Case of the WTO Environmental Goods Agreement,' *Trade Law and Development*, 2014, 6(1), 93–176.

M. Matsushita, 'A View on Future Roles of the WTO: Should There Be More Soft Law in the WTO', *Journal of International Economic Law*, 2014, 17(3), 701–15.

E.-U. Petersmann, 'Multilevel Governance Problems of the World Trading System Beyond the WTO Conference at Bali 2013', *Journal of International Economic Law*, 2014, 17, 233–70.

J. Chaisse and M. Matsushita, 'Maintaining the WTO's Supremacy in the International Trade Order: A Proposal to Refine and Revise the Role of the Trade Policy Review Mechanism', *Journal of International Economic Law*, 2013, 16(1), 9–36.

M. Smeets, 'Trade Capacity Building in the WTO: Main Achievements since Doha and Key Challenges', *Journal of World Trade*, 2013, 47(5), 1047–90.

R. Wolfe, 'Letting the Sun Shine in at the WTO: How Transparency Brings the Trading System to Life', WTO Staff Working Paper ERSD-2013-03, March 2013, World Trade Organization.

P. N. Pedersen, 'The Case for Creating a Working Party on the Functioning of the WTO', WTO Staff Working Paper ERSD-2011-16, October 2011, World Trade Organization.

3 WTO Dispute Settlement

CONTENTS

1 INTRODUCTION

As discussed in Chapter 1, the WTO agreements provide for many wide-ranging and broadly formulated rules concerning international trade in goods, trade in services and trade-related aspects of intellectual property rights.[1] In view of the importance of their impact, economic and otherwise, it is not surprising that WTO Members do not always agree on the correct interpretation and application of these rules. In fact, Members frequently argue about whether or not a particular law or practice constitutes a violation of a right or obligation provided for in a WTO agreement. The WTO has a remarkable system to settle disputes between WTO Members concerning their rights and obligations under the WTO agreements. As mentioned in Chapter 2, dispute settlement is one of the core functions of the WTO.[2]

The WTO dispute settlement system has been operational for more than two decades now. In that period, it has arguably been the most prolific of all international State-to-State dispute settlement systems. Between 1 January 1995 and 1 October 2016, a total of 566 disputes were brought to the WTO for resolution.[3] In more than one-fifth of these disputes, the parties were able to reach an amicable solution through consultations, or the dispute was otherwise resolved without recourse to adjudication. In other disputes, parties have resorted to adjudication. Between 1 January 1995 and 1 October 2016, such adjudication resulted in 202 reports of dispute settlement panels and 127 reports of the Appellate Body.[4] During the same period, the International Court of Justice (ICJ) in The Hague rendered 65 judgments and 5 advisory opinions, and the International Tribunal for the Law of the Sea (ITLOS) in Hamburg rendered 12 judgments and 2 advisory opinions and issued orders in another 11 cases.[5] Also in comparison to its 'predecessor', the GATT dispute settlement system, the WTO dispute settlement system has obviously been very active. During the forty-seven years that the GATT dispute settlement system was operational (from 1948 to 1994), only 132 GATT dispute settlement reports were issued.[6] Most importantly, however, in more than eight out of ten disputes in which the respondent had to withdraw (or modify) a WTO-inconsistent measure, it has done so.[7]

The WTO dispute settlement system has been used by developed-country Members and developing-country Members alike.[8] Developing-country Members have frequently used the WTO dispute settlement system to challenge

1 See above, pp. 38–44. 2 See above, p. 90.

3 i.e. the number of requests for consultations notified to the DSB until 1 October 2016 (this figure includes Article 21.5 'compliance' complaints). See http://worldtradelaw.net/databases/basicfigures.php.

4 See http://worldtradelaw.net/databases/basicfigures.php.

5 See www.icj-cij.org and www.itlos.org.

6 See www.worldtradelaw.net/reports/gattpanels/gattpanels.asp. This number includes some chair's rulings and decisions by the Contracting Parties in the late 1940s.

7 Moreover, in most cases it did so in a timely manner.

8 The most active user of the system has been the United States, closely followed by the European Union. The system has, however, also been used 'against' the United States more often than against any other Member, the European Union being a distant second in this respect. For statistics on complainants and respondents in WTO dispute settlement, see www.worldtradelaw.net.

the WTO consistency of measures of developed-country Members as well as of other developing-country Members.[9] In the WTO, might is not necessarily right. Particularly noteworthy is the successful use of the dispute settlement system by small, sometimes very small, developing-country Members against the largest among the developed-country Members.[10]

A number of disputes brought to the WTO dispute settlement system have triggered considerable controversy and public debate and have attracted much media attention. This has been the case, e.g., for disputes on national legislation for the protection of public health, the environment, public morals, or other core national interests, such as the *EC – Hormones (1998)* dispute on the European Union's import ban on meat from cattle treated with growth hormones (complaints by the United States and Canada);[11] the *US – Shrimp (1998)* dispute on the US import ban on shrimp harvested with nets that kill sea turtles (complaints by India, Malaysia, Pakistan and Thailand);[12] the *Brazil – Retreaded Tyres (2007)* dispute on a Brazilian ban on the import of retreaded tyres for environmental reasons (complaint by the European Union);[13] the *EC – Approval and Marketing of Biotech Products (2006)* dispute on measures affecting the approval and marketing of genetically modified products in the European Union (complaint by the United States, Canada and Argentina); the *US – Clove Cigarettes (2012)* dispute concerning a tobacco-control measure taken by the United States that prohibits cigarettes with 'characterizing flavours' other than tobacco or menthol (complaint by Indonesia); the *US – Tuna II (Mexico) (2012)* dispute and the compliance dispute in the same matter *US – Tuna II (Mexico) (Article 21.5)* (*2015*) concerning US regulation on the use of the dolphin-safe label on tuna cans; the *Canada – Feed-In Tariff/Renewable Energy (2013)* dispute (complaints by the European Union and Japan) and the *India – Solar Cells (2016)* dispute (complaints by the European Union, Japan and the United States), both disputes concerning measures relating to renewable energy generation; the *China – Rare Earths (2014)* dispute regarding Chinese export duties and export restrictions on minerals that are vital to many modern technologies (complaints by the European Union, Japan and the United States); the *EU – Seal Products (2014)* dispute regarding European animal welfare measures (complaints by Canada and Norway); the *Argentina – Financial Services (2016)* dispute concerning Argentina's financial, taxation and foreign exchange measures to combat tax evasion (complaint by Panama); the *Colombia – Textiles (2016)* dispute regarding measures taken to combat money laundering (complaint by Guatemala).[14] Other highly 'sensitive' disputes include the *EC and*

9 The most active users of the system among developing-country Members have been Brazil, India, Argentina, Thailand, Chile and China. See www.wto.org/english/tratop_e/dispu_e/dispu_e.htm.

10 e.g. the disputes between Costa Rica and the US *(US – Underwear (1997))*; and Antigua and Barbuda and the United States, *US – Gambling (2005)*. See below, pp. 205–6.

11 See below, p. 297. 12 See below, pp. 228 and 261.

13 See below, pp. 558–64.

14 Also, the *EC – Bananas III (1997)* dispute on the European Communities' preferential import regime for bananas was, for many years, headline news (complaints by Ecuador, Guatemala, Honduras, Mexico and the United States).

certain member States – Large Civil Aircraft (2011) ('Airbus') and *US – Large Civil Aircraft (2nd complaint) (2012) ('Boeing')* disputes concerning subsidies to Airbus and Boeing respectively (complaints by the United States and the European Union respectively) and the respective compliance proceedings.[15] The latter two disputes were undoubtedly the biggest and most complex original disputes and compliance proceedings handled by the WTO dispute settlement system to date. Many trade remedy disputes, and in particular disputes over 'zeroing',[16] or disputes involving so-called 'non-market economy' countries also caused much commotion, although perhaps more among the industries or companies directly affected (and their interest groups and lawyers) than among the general public.

The WTO dispute settlement system, which has been in operation since 1 January 1995, was not established out of the blue. It is not an entirely novel system. On the contrary, this system is based on, and has taken on board, almost fifty years of experience in the resolution of trade disputes in the context of the GATT 1947. Article 3.1 of the DSU states:

> Members affirm their adherence to the principles for the management of disputes heretofore applied under Articles XXII and XXIII of GATT 1947 and the rules and procedures as further elaborated and modified herein.

The GATT 1947 contained only two brief provisions on dispute settlement (Articles XXII and XXIII), which neither explicitly referred to 'dispute settlement' nor provided for detailed procedures to handle disputes. However, the GATT Contracting Parties 'transformed', in a highly pragmatic manner over a period of five decades, what was initially a rudimentary, power-based system for settling disputes through diplomatic negotiations into an elaborate, rules-based system for settling disputes through adjudication. While for decades quite successful in resolving disputes to the satisfaction of the parties,[17] the GATT dispute settlement had some serious shortcomings which became ever more acute in the course of the 1980s. The most important shortcoming related to the fact that the findings and conclusions of the panels of experts adjudicating disputes only became legally binding when adopted *by consensus* by the GATT Council. The responding party could thus prevent any unfavourable conclusions from becoming legally binding upon it. As discussed in this chapter, the WTO dispute settlement system, negotiated during the Uruguay Round and provided for in the *Understanding on Rules and Procedures for the Settlement of Disputes*, commonly referred to as the *Dispute Settlement Understanding* (DSU), remedied this and a number of other shortcomings of the GATT dispute settlement system.[18] The DSU is generally considered to be one of the most important achievements of the Uruguay Round negotiations.[19]

15 On compliance proceedings, see below, pp. 285–91.
16 On the 'zeroing' methodology, i.e. a methodology to calculate anti-dumping margins, see below, pp. 712–20.
17 On the GATT dispute settlement system, see R. E. Hudec, D. L. M. Kennedy and M. Sgarbossa, 'A Statistical Profile of GATT Dispute Settlement Cases: 1948–1989', *Minnesota Journal of Global Trade*, 1993, 285–7.
18 As discussed in Chapter 1, the DSU is attached to the *WTO Agreement* as Annex 2 thereto. See above, p. 90.
19 On the Uruguay Round negotiations, see above, p. 94.

It is not the ambition of this chapter to give a detailed account of the evolution and current operation of the WTO dispute settlement system, the manifold relevant provisions in the WTO agreements and the impressive body of case law on those provisions. The relevant section in the WTO Analytical Index together with its supplement runs over 400 pages. This chapter will also not address the many proposals for the improvement of the WTO dispute settlement which have been tabled by Members over the last twelve years in the context of the DSU reform negotiations.[20] Instead, this chapter focuses on the basics of WTO dispute settlement and addresses in turn: (1) the jurisdiction of the WTO dispute settlement system; (2) access to WTO dispute settlement; (3) the key features of WTO dispute settlement; (4) the institutions of WTO dispute settlement; (5) the process of WTO dispute settlement; and (6) developing-country Members and WTO dispute settlement.

2 JURISDICTION OF THE WTO DISPUTE SETTLEMENT SYSTEM

The WTO dispute settlement system stands out by virtue of the nature as well as the scope of its jurisdiction. This section examines these two aspects – nature and scope – of the jurisdiction of the WTO dispute settlement system in turn.

2.1 Nature of the Jurisdiction

Unlike the jurisdiction of other important State-to-State dispute settlement mechanisms, such as the International Court of Justice or the International Tribunal for the Law of the Sea, the jurisdiction of the WTO dispute settlement system is: (1) compulsory; (2) exclusive; and (3) only contentious (i.e. it does not provide for advisory opinions).

2.1.1 Compulsory Jurisdiction

The jurisdiction of the WTO dispute settlement system is compulsory in nature. A responding Member has, as a matter of law, no choice but to accept the jurisdiction of the WTO dispute settlement system. Note that Article 6.1 of the DSU states:

> *If* the complaining party *so requests*, a *panel* shall *be established* at the latest at the DSB meeting following that at which the request first appears as an item on the DSB's agenda, unless at that meeting the DSB decides by consensus not to establish a panel.[21]

Unlike in other international dispute settlement systems, there is no need for the parties to a dispute, arising under the covered agreements, to accept, in a specific declaration or agreement, the jurisdiction of the WTO dispute settlement system

20 For a general overview of the DSU reform negotiations, see below, p. 294. 21 Emphasis added.

to adjudicate the dispute. Membership of the WTO constitutes consent to, and acceptance of, the jurisdiction of the WTO dispute settlement system.

2.1.2 Exclusive Jurisdiction

The jurisdiction of the WTO dispute settlement system is also exclusive. Article 23.1 of the DSU states:

> When Members seek the redress of a violation of obligations or other nullification or impairment of benefits under the covered agreements or an impediment to the attainment of any objective of the covered agreements, they shall have recourse to, and abide by, the rules and procedures of this Understanding.

Pursuant to this provision, a complaining Member is obliged to bring any dispute arising under the covered agreements to the WTO dispute settlement system to the exclusion of any other system.[22] Article 23.1 of the DSU both ensures the exclusivity of the WTO vis-à-vis other international fora *and* protects the multilateral system from unilateral conduct.[23] As Article 23.2(a) of the DSU provides, Members are prohibited from making a determination to the effect that a violation has occurred, that benefits have been nullified or impaired, or that the attainment of any objective of the covered agreements has been impeded, *except* through recourse to dispute settlement in accordance with the rules and procedures of the DSU.[24]

2.1.3 Contentious Jurisdiction

Unlike the International Court of Justice or the International Tribunal for the Law of the Sea, the WTO dispute settlement system has only contentious jurisdiction, and it does not render advisory opinions.

Pursuant to Article 3.2 of the DSU, the WTO dispute settlement system is called upon to clarify WTO law only in the context of a dispute.[25]

2.2 Scope of the Jurisdiction

This section on the scope of the jurisdiction of the WTO dispute settlement system deals with two separate but obviously closely related questions, namely: (1) which *disputes* are subject to WTO dispute settlement?; and (2) which *measures* can be subject to WTO dispute settlement?

22 See Panel Report, *US – Section 301 Trade Act (2000)*, para. 7.43. On the concept of 'covered agreement', see below, p. 247.

23 See Panel Report, *EC – Commercial Vessels (2005)*, para. 7.193. On the multilateral nature of WTO dispute settlement, see below, pp. 188–9.

24 Note, however, the DSU provides for several, different methods to resolve disputes. See below, p. 187.

25 See Appellate Body Report, *US – Wool Shirts and Blouses (1997)*, 340. See also below, p. 192. Note, however, that the panel in *EC – Bananas III (Article 21.5 – EC) (1999)* considered it did have jurisdiction in spite of the fact that there were no respondents in this case. The panel ruled against the European Communities and the report was never put on the agenda of the DSB for adoption and remained unadopted.

2.2.1 Disputes Subject to WTO Dispute Settlement

Article 1.1 of the DSU states, in relevant part:

> The rules and procedures of this Understanding shall apply to disputes brought pursuant to the consultation and dispute settlement provisions of the agreements listed in Appendix 1 to this Understanding (referred to in this Understanding as the 'covered agreements').

The WTO dispute settlement system thus has jurisdiction *ratione materiae* over disputes between WTO Members arising under the 'covered agreements'. The covered agreements, referred to in Appendix 1 to the DSU, include the *WTO Agreement*, the GATT 1994 and all other multilateral agreements on trade in goods, the GATS, the *TRIPS Agreement*, the DSU and the plurilateral *Agreement on Government Procurement*.[26] It is clear that the scope of jurisdiction of the WTO dispute settlement system is very broad as it ranges from disputes over measures regarding customs duties, disputes regarding sanitary measures, disputes regarding subsidies, disputes regarding measures affecting market access for services, to disputes regarding intellectual property rights enforcement measures.

2.2.2 Measures Subject to WTO Dispute Settlement

While the DSU refers in many of its provisions to the 'measure' or 'measures' that can be subject to WTO dispute settlement, it does, however, not define this term.[27] In *US – Corrosion-Resistant Steel Sunset Review (2004)*, the Appellate Body ruled that:

> [i]n principle, any act or omission attributable to a WTO Member can be a measure of that Member for purposes of dispute settlement proceedings.[28]

However, this general statement leaves a number of questions regarding the precise scope of the measures that can be challenged in WTO dispute settlement proceedings unanswered. The following paragraphs focus on those types of measure that have raised complex questions as to whether they can be subject to WTO dispute settlement, namely: (1) action or conduct by private parties attributable to a Member; (2) measures that expire or are withdrawn during the proceedings and are thus no longer in force; (3) legislation as such (as opposed to the actual application of this legislation in specific instances); (4) discretionary legislation (as opposed to mandatory legislation); (5) unwritten norms or rules of Members, including practices or policies which are not set out in law; (6) ongoing conduct by Members and concerted, systematic action or practice

26 Only two WTO agreements are not 'covered agreements': the *Trade Policy Review Mechanism* and the plurilateral *Agreement on Trade in Civil Aircraft*. Regarding the *Agreement on Trade Facilitation*, note that Article 18.5 thereof provides: 'Developing Members shall not be subject to *Dispute Settlement Understanding* (DSU) proceedings after the notification of inability to implement relevant provisions until the first Committee meeting after it receives the recommendation of the Expert Group.'

27 The term 'measure(s)' appears over twenty-five times in the DSU.

28 Appellate Body Report, *US – Corrosion-Resistant Steel Sunset Review (2004)*, para. 81.

of Members; (7) measures composed of several different instruments; and (8) measures by regional and local authorities.

The question whether *action or conduct by private parties*, the first type of measure mentioned above, can be subject to WTO dispute settlement arises because the WTO agreements, as is traditionally the case with international agreements, bind the States that are party to them, not private parties. The panel in *Japan – Film (1998)* ruled in this respect:

> [P]ast GATT cases demonstrate that the fact that an action is taken by private parties does not rule out the possibility that it may be deemed to be governmental if there is sufficient government involvement with it. It is difficult to establish bright-line rules in this regard, however. Thus, that possibility will need to be examined on a case-by-case basis.[29]

Each case will have to be examined on its facts to determine whether the level of *government involvement* in the actions of private parties is such that these actions can be properly attributed to a Member. Note in this regard Article 8 of the *Articles on Responsibility of States for Internationally Wrongful Acts* of the International Law Commission (ILC), which states:

> The conduct of a person or group of persons shall be considered an act of a State under international law if the person or group of persons is in fact acting on the instructions of, or under the direction or control of, that State in carrying out the conduct.[30]

Any measure, including action or conduct by private parties, which can be properly attributed to a WTO Member, can be challenged in WTO dispute settlement proceedings. The second type of measure, referred to above and which can be subject to WTO dispute settlement, are *measures which expire or are withdrawn during the proceedings*, and are thus no longer in force.[31] As the Appellate Body noted in *China – Raw Materials (2012)*, the DSU does not specifically address whether a WTO panel may or may not make findings and recommendations with respect to such measures. Panels have made findings on expired measures in some cases and declined to do so in others, depending on the particularities of the disputes before them.[32] While a measure that has expired or has been withdrawn can be subject to WTO dispute settlement, it is clear that a panel or

29 Panel Report, *Japan – Film (1998)*, para. 10.56. Note that the panel in this case found that the United States, the complainant, had failed to demonstrate that there was sufficient level of governmental involvement or incentives so that the private acts could be attributed to Japan. See Panel Report, *Japan – Film (1998)*, paras. 2.7–2.10, 10.56, 10.402–10.404. See also GATT Panel Report, *Japan – Semi-Conductors (1988)*, para. 117; and GATT Panel Report, *EEC – Restrictions on Imports of Dessert Apples (1989)*, para. 12.9.

30 Article 8, *Articles on Responsibility of States for Internationally Wrongful Acts 2001*, Annex to General Assembly Resolution 56/83 of 12 December 2001. See also Article 5 of the *Articles* regarding persons or entities, which are not an organ of the State but which are empowered by law to exercise elements of governmental authority. Note in this respect Article I:3(a)(ii) of the GATS regarding measures 'taken by non-governmental bodies', see below, p. 328; and the concepts of 'public body' and 'private body' under Article 1.1 of the *SCM Agreement*, see below, pp. 783–5.

31 Note that to be subject to WTO dispute settlement, the measure at issue must be in force at the time the panel is established. See below, p. 213.

32 See Appellate Body Reports, *China – Raw Materials (2012)*, para. 263. See in this regard also Appellate Body Report, *US – Upland Cotton (2005)*, para. 262, on measures which are no longer in force but still affect the operation of a covered agreement.

the Appellate Body cannot recommend with regard to such measure its withdrawal.[33] As the Appellate Body noted in *China – Raw Materials (2012)*, a recommendation made with respect to such measure is 'prospective in nature in the sense that it has an effect on, or consequences for, a WTO Member's implementation obligations that arise after the adoption of a panel and/or Appellate Body report by the DSB'.[34]

The third type of measure, referred to above and which can be subject to WTO dispute settlement, concerns *legislation as such*.[35] It is clear that the WTO consistency of the actual application of national legislation, i.e. legislation as applied in specific instances, can be challenged in WTO dispute settlement proceedings. However, can national legislation as such, i.e. independently from its application in specific instances, be challenged in WTO dispute settlement proceedings?[36]

In *US – 1916 Act (2000)*, the Appellate Body noted that a number of WTO panels have – following a GATT practice in this respect – dealt with dispute settlement claims brought against a Member on the basis of its legislation *as such*, independently of the application of that legislation in specific instances.[37] As already noted above, in *US – Corrosion-Resistant Steel Sunset Review (2004)*, the Appellate Body stated that 'any act or omission attributable to a WTO Member can be a measure of that Member for purposes of dispute settlement proceedings'.[38] The Appellate Body noted in particular that, in addition to acts applying legislation in a specific instance, also 'acts setting forth rules or norms that are intended to have general and prospective application' can be the subject of WTO dispute settlement.[39] According to the Appellate Body, this is so because the disciplines of the WTO and its dispute settlement system 'are intended to protect not only existing trade but also the security and predictability needed to conduct future trade'.[40] The Appellate Body also pointed out that, if legislation could not be challenged as such, but only in the instances of its application, this would lead to a multiplicity of litigation.[41] Allowing claims against legislation as such thus 'serves the purpose of preventing future disputes by allowing the root of WTO-inconsistent behaviour to be eliminated'.[42] The Appellate Body did,

33 See *ibid.*, para. 272.
34 Appellate Body Reports, *China – Raw Materials (2012)*, para. 260.
35 While 'legislation as such' is referred to as a category of 'atypical' measures, it should be emphasised that 'legislation as such' is frequently subject to WTO dispute settlement.
36 Note that, as discussed below at p. 172, 'legislation as applied' and 'legislation as such' do not exhaustively define the types of measures that are susceptible to challenge in WTO dispute settlement.
37 See Appellate Body Report, *US – 1916 Act (2000)*, para. 60. See, e.g. panel reports in *Japan – Alcoholic Beverages II (1996); Canada – Periodicals (1997); EC – Hormones (1998); Korea – Alcoholic Beverages (1999); Chile – Alcoholic Beverages (2000); United States – FSC (2000)*; and *United States – Section 110(5) Copyright Act (2000)*. With regard to the GATT practice referred to, see the GATT panel reports in *US – Superfund (1987); US – Section 337 (1989); Thailand – Cigarettes (1990)*; and *US – Malt Beverages (1992)*.
38 Appellate Body Report, *US – Corrosion-Resistant Steel Sunset Review (2004)*, para. 81.
39 *Ibid.*, para. 82.
40 *Ibid.* 41 *Ibid.* 42 *Ibid.*

however, emphasise, in *US – Oil Country Tubular Goods Sunset Reviews (2004)*, the *seriousness* of 'as such' claims, stating:

> In essence, complaining parties bringing 'as such' challenges seek to prevent Members *ex ante* from engaging in certain conduct. The implications of such challenges are obviously more far-reaching than 'as applied' claims.[43]

In view of the seriousness of 'as such' claims of inconsistency, a complainant should be 'especially diligent in setting out [such claims] as clearly as possible'.[44] Such diligence is even more called for when the measure at issue does not concern legislation, but an unwritten measure, which, if it set forth a rule or norm of general and prospective application, may, under current case law, be challenged 'as such'.[45]

The fourth type of measure, referred to above and which can be subject to WTO dispute settlement, concerns *discretionary legislation*, i.e. legislation that leaves authorities leeway as to what action (WTO-consistent or WTO-inconsistent) to take (whereas mandatory legislation does not leave such leeway). The Appellate Body in *US – 1916 Act (2000)* noted that, in *examining* claims relating to legislation 'as such':

> panels developed the concept that mandatory and discretionary legislation should be distinguished from each other, reasoning that only legislation that mandates a violation of GATT obligations can be found as such to be inconsistent with those obligations.[46]

The discussion on the relevance of the distinction between mandatory and discretionary legislation has been marred by confusion. As clearly stated by the Appellate Body in *US – Corrosion-Resistant Steel Sunset Review (2004)*, the mandatory or discretionary nature of legislation is 'relevant, *if at all*, only as part of the panel's assessment of whether the measure is, as such, inconsistent with particular obligations'.[47] In the same report, the Appellate Body observed that 'the import of the "mandatory/discretionary distinction" may vary from case to case', and cautioned 'against the application of this distinction in a mechanistic fashion'.[48] The discretionary nature of a measure is not, in and of itself, determinative of the question of WTO consistency.[49] However, the discretionary nature of a measure may inform whether the measure is capable of operating in a WTO consistent manner, or whether it is 'necessarily inconsistent with a Member's WTO obligations'.[50]

43 Appellate Body Report, *US – Oil Country Tubular Goods Sunset Reviews (2004)*, para. 172.

44 *Ibid.*, para. 173.

45 See Appellate Body Report, *US – Zeroing (EC) (2006)*, paras. 196–8.

46 Appellate Body Report, *US – 1916 Act (2000)*, para. 60. In a footnote, the Appellate Body referred to the panel reports in *US – Superfund (1987)*; *US – Section 337 (1989)*; *Thailand – Cigarettes (1990)*; and *US – Malt Beverages (1992)*.

47 Appellate Body Report, *US – Corrosion-Resistant Steel Sunset Review (2004)*, para. 89. Emphasis added.

48 *Ibid.*, para. 93. Moreover, note that the 'discretionary' nature of legislation does not merely depend on the characterisation under municipal law but requires an objective examination by WTO adjudicators of the nature and character of the legislation concerned.

49 See *ibid.*, paras. 87–9.

50 See *ibid.*, para. 172.

In *EU – Biodiesel (2016)*, the Appellate Body observed that there is no basis, either in the practice of the GATT and the WTO generally or in the provisions of the *Anti-Dumping Agreement*, for finding that only certain types of measures (such as mandatory legislation) can be challenged 'as such'. Allowing measures to be the subject of dispute settlement proceedings, whether or not they are of a mandatory character, is consistent with the comprehensive nature of the right of Members, enshrined in Article 3.2 of the DSU, to resort to dispute settlement to preserve their rights and obligations under the covered agreements.[51] Referring to its earlier report in *US – Carbon Steel (2002)*, the Appellate Body ruled in *EU – Biodiesel (2016)* that a complainant challenging the WTO consistency of a discretionary measure must demonstrate:

> either that the measure at issue mandated the investigating authority to act inconsistently with the relevant provision of WTO law, or that such law 'restrict[ed] in a material way' the authority's discretion to make a determination consistent with WTO law.[52]

The Appellate Body emphasised that precisely what is required to establish that a measure is inconsistent 'as such' will vary, depending on the particular circumstances of each case, including the nature of the measure and the WTO obligations at issue.[53]

The fifth type of measure, referred to above and which can be subject to WTO dispute settlement, are *unwritten norms or rules*, i.e. rules and norms that are not expressed in the form of a 'written' document. This type of measure concerns, e.g., practices or policies of Members, which are not set out in law.[54] The Appellate Body first addressed the question whether an unwritten 'norm of rule' of Members can be challenged in WTO dispute settlement proceedings in *US – Zeroing (EC) (2006)*. In that case, the United States argued on appeal that the panel had erred in finding that the zeroing methodology, which was not expressed in writing, was a measure that can be challenged, as such, in dispute settlement proceedings. The Appellate Body ruled that the determination whether a measure can be challenged in WTO dispute settlement proceedings 'must be based on the "content and substance" of the alleged measure, and "not merely on its form"'.[55] Accordingly, the Appellate Body found that:

> the mere fact that a 'rule or norm' is not expressed in the form of a written instrument, is not determinative of the issue of whether it can be challenged, as such, in dispute settlement proceedings.[56]

51 See Appellate Body Report, *EU – Biodiesel (2016)*, para. 6.228, referring to Appellate Body Report, *US – Corrosion-Resistant Steel Sunset Review (2004)*, para. 89.

52 Appellate Body Report, *EU – Biodiesel (2016)*, para. 6.229, referring to Appellate Body Report, *US – Carbon Steel (2002)*, para. 162.

53 See *ibid.*, para. 6.230.

54 Already in 2003, the Appellate Body ruled in *US – Countervailing Measures on Certain EC Products (2003)* that the US 'administrative practice' at issue, which was not prescribed by US law, could be a measure subject to dispute settlement. See Appellate Body, *US – Countervailing Measures on Certain EC Products (2003)*, para. 151.

55 Appellate Body Report, *US – Zeroing (EC) (2006)*, para. 192, referring to Appellate Body Report, *US – Corrosion-Resistant Steel Sunset Review (2004)*, para. 87.

56 Appellate Body Report, *US – Zeroing (EC) (2006)*, para. 192.

Based on its review of the DSU and the *Anti-Dumping Agreement*, the agreement at issue in this case, the Appellate Body saw:

> no basis to conclude that 'rules or norms' can be challenged, as such, only if they are expressed in the form of a written instrument.[57]

However, the Appellate Body cautioned panels that they:

> must not lightly assume the existence of a 'rule or norm' constituting a measure of general and prospective application, especially when it is not expressed in the form of a written document.[58]

The Appellate Body ruled that, when bringing a challenge against such an unwritten rule or norm, a complaining party must clearly establish: (1) that the rule or norm is attributable to the responding Member; (2) the precise content of the rule or norm; and (3) that the rule or norm does have general and prospective application.[59] The Appellate Body emphasised that 'it is only if the complaining party meets this high threshold, and puts forward sufficient evidence with respect to each of these elements', that a panel can find that an unwritten rule or norm may be challenged, as such.[60] The evidence referred to may include proof of the systematic application of the unwritten rule or norm.[61] In *US – Countervailing Measures (China) (2015)*, the panel ruled that the 'rebuttable presumption' policy of the United States Department of Commerce at issue, which was not set out in US law, could be challenged 'as such', after it had found that: (1) the policy had normative value and was therefore a 'rule or norm'; (2) the policy was attributable to the United States; (3) the precise content of the policy was clear; (4) the policy seemed to have general and prospective application; and (5) the policy had been applied consistently for a considerable period of time.[62]

As the Appellate Body recalled in *Argentina – Import Measures (2015)*, the distinction between rules or norms of general and prospective application and their individual applications does not define exhaustively the types of measure that are subject to WTO dispute settlement.[63] The Appellate Body found that when tasked with assessing a challenge against an unwritten measure, a panel is not always required to apply rigid legal standards or criteria that are based on the 'as such' or the 'as applied' nature of the challenge.[64] Rather, the specific measure challenged and how it is described or characterised by a complainant will determine the kind of evidence a complainant is required to submit and

57 See *ibid.*, para. 193. 58 *Ibid.*, para. 196.

59 See *ibid.*, para. 198. See, however, *EC and certain member States – Large Civil Aircraft (2011)*, para. 794.

60 *Ibid.*, para. 198.

61 See *ibid.* Applying its test to the facts in *US – Zeroing (EC) (2006)*, the Appellate Body thus concluded that the zeroing methodology was an unwritten 'rule or norm' that could be challenged in WTO dispute settlement proceedings. See *ibid.*, para. 205. On zeroing, see below, pp. 712–20

62 See Panel Report, *US – Countervailing and Anti-Dumping Measures (China) (2014)*, paras. 7.111–7.119.

63 See Appellate Body Report, *Argentina – Import Measures (2015)*, para 5.109. See earlier in e.g. Appellate Body Reports, *US – Continued Zeroing (2009)*, paras. 179–81.

64 See above, p. 172.

the elements that it must prove in order to establish the existence of the measure challenged. A complainant seeking to prove the existence of an unwritten measure will invariably be required to prove the attribution of that measure to a Member and its precise content. Depending on the specific measure challenged and how it is described or characterized by a complainant, however, other elements may need to be proven.[65]

The sixth type of measure, referred to above and which can be subject to WTO dispute settlement, concerns '*ongoing conduct*', or concerted, systematic action or practice of Members.[66] In *US – Continued Zeroing (2009)*, the question arose whether 'the continued use of the zeroing methodology in successive proceedings in which duties resulting from ... 18 anti-dumping duty orders are maintained, constitute "measures" that can be challenged in WTO dispute settlement'.[67] The Appellate Body agreed with the complainant, the European Union, that this continued use did indeed constitute 'measures' that can be challenged in WTO dispute settlement.[68] The Appellate Body saw no reason to exclude 'ongoing conduct' that consists of the use of the zeroing methodology from challenge in WTO dispute settlement.[69]

In light of the Appellate Body's analysis in *US – Continued Zeroing (2009)*, the United States argued in *EC and certain member States – Large Civil Aircraft (2011)* that what it referred to as the 'launch aid programme', i.e. the 'systematic and coordinated' provision of launch aid by France, Germany, Spain and the United Kingdom for the development of various models of Airbus large civil aircraft was 'ongoing conduct', and, as such, a measure subject to challenge in WTO dispute settlement proceedings.[70] The Appellate Body in that case did not exclude, as a general proposition:

> the possibility that concerted action or practice could be susceptible to challenge in WTO dispute settlement.[71]

The Appellate Body added that it did not consider that a complainant would necessarily be required to demonstrate the existence of a rule or norm of general and prospective application in order to show that such concerted action or practice exists.[72]

65 See Appellate Body Report, *Argentina – Import Measures (2015)*, para. 5.110.
66 'Ongoing conduct' is conduct that is currently taking place and is *likely* to continue in the future. See Panel Report, *US – Orange Juice (Brazil) (2011)*, para. 7.176.
67 Appellate Body Report, *US – Continued Zeroing (2009)*, para. 185. On the 'zeroing methodology', see below, pp. 712–20.
68 See *ibid*., para. 185. 69 See *ibid*., para. 181.
70 See Appellate Body Report, *EC and certain member States – Large Civil Aircraft (2011)*, para. 475.
71 *Ibid*., para. 794.
72 *Ibid*. Note, however, the Appellate Body found in *EC and certain member States – Large Civil Aircraft (2011)* that the alleged 'launch aid programme' was not within the panel's terms of reference. The Appellate Body therefore did not consider the arguments regarding the alleged 'launch aid programme'. See *ibid*., paras. 795–6, and below, p. 214.

Another example of a systematic action or practice challenged in WTO dispute settlement was the *de facto* moratorium on the approval of biotech products at issue in *EC – Approval and Marketing of Biotech Products (2006)*. While the European Union denied the existence of this measure, the panel concluded, on the basis of extensive evidence showing repeated and consistent blocking or delays in the approval process *and* indirect evidence of a concerted policy, that the EU applied a *de facto* moratorium.[73] Note that the panel did not rule on whether the moratorium was a rule or norm of general and prospective application.

The seventh type of measure, referred to above and which can be subject to WTO dispute settlement, are measures composed of several different instruments. When a measure comprises multiple composite elements or instruments which are each allegedly WTO-inconsistent, the question may arise whether in WTO dispute settlement a complainant must challenge each of the elements or instruments of this measure individually or whether it can challenge the measure as a whole, i.e. as a single, complex, overarching measure. The Appellate Body explained in *Argentina – Import Measures (2015)* that a complainant challenging a single measure composed of several different instruments will normally need to provide evidence of how the different components operate together as part of a single measure and how a single measure exists as distinct from its components.[74] The Appellate Body noted that in deciding whether to treat composite elements of a measure as multiple measures or as a single measure, the panel in *US – COOL (2012)* considered the following factors:

> (i) the manner in which the complainant presented its claim(s) in respect of the concerned instruments; (ii) the respondent's position; and (iii) the legal status of the requirements or instrument(s), including the operation of, and the relationship between, the requirements or instruments, namely whether a certain requirement or instrument has autonomous status.[75]

In *Argentina – Import Measures (2015)*, the Appellate Body came to the conclusion that the panel correctly established the existence of the single 'TRRs measure, composed of several interlinked individual TRRs and exhibiting several characteristics, *in particular its systematic and continued application*'.[76] The last type of measure, referred to above and which can be subject to WTO dispute settlement, are *measures by regional or local authorities*. It is clear that measures by the central government of Members can be challenged in

73 See Panel Report, *EC – Approval and Marketing of Biotech Products (2006)*, para. 7.1272. The evidence included press releases, fact sheets and statements of the European Commission, and statements of EU Commissioners and EU Member State officials.

74 Appellate Body Report, *Argentina – Import Measures (2015)*, para. 5.108 and fn. 451, referring Panel Report, *US – COOL (2011)*, para. 7.50. See also Panel Report, *US – Export Restraints (2001)*, para. 8.8.

75 Panel Report, *US – COOL (2011)*, para. 7.50.

76 Appellate Body Report, *Argentina – Import Measures (2015)*, para. 5.204. Emphasis added. 'TRRs' stands for trade-related requirements and the 'TRRs measure' is an unwritten measure consisting of one or more TRRs. See *ibid.*, para. 1.2.

WTO dispute settlement proceedings and it is undisputed that the central government includes all branches of government (legislative, executive and judicial).[77] However, do the 'acts of all its departments of government' to which the Appellate Body refers include acts of regional or local authorities? This question may be of particular relevance to Members with a federal system of government under which the federal government may have little control over measures taken by subfederal levels of government. As discussed in Chapter 1, Article 22.9 of the DSU states:

> The dispute settlement provisions of the covered agreements may be invoked in respect of measures affecting their observance taken by regional or local governments or authorities within the territory of a Member. When the DSB has ruled that a provision of a covered agreement has not been observed, the responsible Member shall take such reasonable measures as may be available to it to ensure its observance. The provisions of the covered agreements and this Understanding relating to compensation and suspension of concessions or other obligations apply in cases where it has not been possible to secure such observance.[78]

This appears to give a clear answer to the question whether measures by regional or local authorities can be challenged in WTO dispute settlement proceedings. Even in situations in which the central government lacks the authority under its constitution to 'control' regional or local authorities, measures by these regional or local authorities can be subject to WTO dispute settlement. Dispute settlement proceedings against such measures can be brought against the Member concerned.[79]

A final remark may be made on measures adopted or maintained by Member States of the European Union. As discussed in Chapter 2, both the European Union and all its twenty-eight Member States are WTO Members. Measures by EU Member States can, and have been, challenged in dispute settlement proceedings brought: (1) against the EU Member State concerned;[80] (2) against the European Union and the EU Member State(s) concerned;[81] or (3) against the European Union alone.[82] In all disputes involving measures of EU Member States, it was always the European Union which made the submissions and defended the EU Member State measure(s) concerned.[83]

77 In *US – Shrimp (1998)*, the Appellate Body ruled that a WTO Member 'bears responsibility for acts of all its departments of government, including its judiciary'. Appellate Body Report, *US – Shrimp (1998)*, para. 173, referring in footnote to Appellate Body Report, *US – Gasoline (1996)*, 28.

78 See also *Understanding on the Interpretation of Article XXIV of the General Agreement on Tariffs and Trade 1994*, para. 14, last sentence, and above, p. 70.

79 Note that, unlike under the GATT 1994, under the GATS, measures by regional or local authorities are explicitly found to be attributable to the Member concerned. Article I:3(a)(i) of the GATS explicitly defines 'measures by Members' as 'measures by central, regional or local authorities'. Compare with Article XXIV:12 of the GATT 1994.

80 See e.g. *Belgium – Administration of Measures Establishing Customs Duties for Rice* (DS 210), concerning measures imposed by Belgium. In this dispute, a mutually agreed solution was notified to the DSB by the United States and the European Commission.

81 See e.g. *EC and certain member States – Large Civil Aircraft (2011)*, concerning measures by Germany, France, Spain and the United Kingdom, and the EU.

82 See e.g. *EC – Asbestos (2001)*, concerning measures imposed by France.

83 See Panel Report, *EC and certain member States – Large Civil Aircraft (2011)*, fn. 2047.

3 ACCESS TO THE WTO DISPUTE SETTLEMENT SYSTEM

It is clear and undisputed that access to the WTO dispute settlement system is limited to Members of the WTO. The Appellate Body ruled in *US – Shrimp (1998)*:

> It may be well to stress at the outset that access to the dispute settlement process of the WTO is limited to Members of the WTO. This access is not available, under the *WTO Agreement* and the covered agreements as they currently exist, to individuals or international organizations, whether governmental or non-governmental.[84]

The WTO dispute settlement system is a *government-to-government* dispute settlement system for disputes concerning rights and obligations of WTO Members. Only WTO Members can have recourse to WTO dispute settlement; only they are entitled to initiate proceedings against breaches of WTO law by other WTO Members. The WTO Secretariat cannot prosecute breaches of WTO law on its own motion nor are other international organisations, non-governmental organisations, industry associations, companies or individuals entitled to do so. While it is clear that only Members have access to the WTO dispute settlement system, the question arises whether WTO membership alone suffices to allow recourse to WTO dispute settlement or whether Members must have a specific trade or legal interest in having recourse.

3.1 Right of Recourse to WTO Dispute Settlement

Each covered agreement contains one or more consultation and dispute settlement provisions. These provisions set out when a Member can have recourse to WTO dispute settlement. For the GATT 1994, the relevant provisions are Articles XXII and XXIII. Of particular importance is Article XXIII:1 of the GATT 1994, which states:

> If any Member should consider that any benefit accruing to it directly or indirectly under this Agreement is being nullified or impaired or that the attainment of any objective of the Agreement is being impeded as the result of
>
> (a) the failure of another Member to carry out its obligations under this Agreement, or
> (b) the application by another Member of any measure, whether or not it conflicts with the provisions of this Agreement, or
> (c) the existence of any other situation,
>
> the Member may, with a view to the satisfactory adjustment of the matter, make written representations or proposals to the other Member or Members which it considers to be concerned.[85]

84 Appellate Body Report, *US – Shrimp (1998)*, para. 101.
85 Note that there is no need to exhaust local remedies before having recourse to WTO dispute settlement.

The consultation and dispute settlement provisions of most other covered agreements incorporate, by reference, Articles XXII and XXIII of the GATT 1994. For example, Article 11.1 of the *SPS Agreement*, entitled 'Consultations and Dispute Settlement', states:

> The provisions of Articles XXII and XXIII of GATT 1994 as elaborated and applied by the Dispute Settlement Understanding shall apply to consultations and the settlement of disputes under this Agreement, except as otherwise specifically provided herein.

With regard to a Member's right to have recourse to WTO dispute settlement, the Appellate Body held in *India – Quantitative Restrictions (1999)*:

> This dispute was brought pursuant to, *inter alia*, Article XXIII of the GATT 1994 ... The United States considers that a benefit accruing to it under the GATT 1994 was nullified or impaired as a result of India's alleged failure to carry out its obligations regarding balance-of-payments restrictions under Article XVIII:B of the GATT 1994. Therefore, the United States was entitled to have recourse to the dispute settlement procedures of Article XXIII with regard to this dispute.[86]

As was the case in *India – Quantitative Restrictions (1999)*, the nullification or impairment of a benefit (or the impeding of the realisation of an objective) may, and most often will, be the result of a violation of an obligation prescribed by a covered agreement (see Article XXIII:1(a)). Nullification or impairment may, however, also be the result of 'the application by another Member of any measure, whether or not it conflicts with the provisions' of a covered agreement (see Article XXIII:1(b) and Article 26.1 of the DSU). Nullification or impairment may also be the result of 'the existence of any other situation' (see Article XXIII:1(c) and Article 26.2 of the DSU). Unlike other international dispute settlement systems, the WTO system thus provides for three types of complaint: (1) 'violation' complaints; (2) 'non-violation' complaints; and (3) 'situation' complaints.[87] In the case of a 'non-violation' complaint or a 'situation' complaint, the complainant must demonstrate that there is nullification or impairment of a benefit or that the achievement of an objective is impeded.[88] The panel in *Japan – Film (1998)* stated with regard to non-violation claims that it must be demonstrated: (1) that the imported products at issue are subject to and *benefiting from* a relevant market access concession; (2) that the *competitive position* of the imported products is being upset (i.e. 'nullified or impaired'); and (3) that the competitive position is being upset by (i.e. 'as the result of') the application of a *measure not reasonably anticipated*.[89]

86 Appellate Body Report, *India – Quantitative Restrictions (1999)*, para. 84.

87 Note, however, that, pursuant to Article XXIII:3 of the GATS, situation complaints cannot be raised in disputes arising under the GATS; and that, pursuant to Article 64.2 and 3 of the *TRIPS Agreement* and successive ministerial decisions, non-violation complaints and situation complaints are *currently* not possible in disputes arising under the *TRIPS Agreement*. See below, p. 1050.

88 On the idea underlying non-violation complaints, see Appellate Body Report, *EC – Asbestos (2001)*, para. 185. See also Panel Report, *EEC – Oilseeds I (1990)*, para. 144.

89 See Panel Report, *Japan – Film (1998)*, para. 10.82. With regard to what a complainant must show in a non-violation complaint, see also *ibid.*, para. 9.5. See also Panel Report, *EC – Asbestos (2001)*, para. 8.288; Appellate Body Report, *EC – Asbestos (2001)*, paras. 38 and 185–6; and Panel Reports, *US – COOL (Article 21.5 – Canada and Mexico) (2015)*, paras. 7.673–7.716.

Unlike in the case of a 'non-violation' complaint, in the case of a 'violation' complaint, there is no need for the complainant to show nullification or impairment of a benefit. There is a *presumption* of nullification or impairment when the complainant demonstrates the existence of the violation.[90] In only a few cases to date has the respondent argued that the alleged violation of WTO law did not nullify or impair benefits accruing to the complainant. In no case has the respondent been successful in rebutting the presumption of nullification or impairment.[91] It has been suggested that this presumption of nullification or impairment is in fact not rebuttable.[92]

Violation complaints are by far the most common type of complaint. To date, there have been only a dozen disputes in which a non-violation complaint was filed.[93] Note that the Appellate Body stated in *EC – Asbestos (2001)* that:

> the ['non-violation' nullification or impairment] remedy ... 'should be approached with caution and should remain an exceptional remedy'.[94]

The reason for this caution is obvious. As the panel in *Japan – Film (1998)* noted:

> Members negotiate the rules that they agree to follow and only exceptionally would expect to be challenged for actions not in contravention of those rules.[95]

None of the non-violation complaints brought to the WTO to date have been successful.[96] Moreover, there has never been any adjudication of situation complaints.[97] The difference between the WTO system and other international dispute settlement systems with regard to causes of action is, therefore, of little practical significance.

In *EC – Bananas III (1997)*, the Appellate Body held:

> [W]e believe that a Member has broad discretion in deciding whether to bring a case against another Member under the DSU. The language of Article XXIII:1 of the GATT 1994 and of Article 3.7 of the DSU suggests, furthermore, that a Member is expected to be largely self-regulating in deciding whether any such action would be 'fruitful'.[98]

90 See Article 3.8 of the DSU.

91 See, e.g., Appellate Body Report, *EC – Export Subsidies on Sugar (2005)*, para. 298.

92 Note that the panel in *EC – Bananas III (1997)* expressed doubts whether this presumption could be rebutted. See Panel Report, *EC – Bananas III (1997)*, para. 7.398.

93 Note that Article 26.1 of the DSU provides for some special procedural rules applicable to non-violation complaints. For a list of disputes in which a non-violation complaint was made (up to June 2015), see *WTO Analytical Index together with its supplement*. For two recent examples of non-violation complaints, see Panel Reports, *EU – Seal Products (2014)*, paras. 7.666–7.683; and Panel Reports, *US – COOL (Article 21.5 – Canada and Mexico) (2015)*, para. 7.673–716.

94 Appellate Body Report, *EC – Asbestos (2001)*, para. 186. This was reiterated by the panel in *US – Offset Act (Byrd Amendment) (2003)* with regard to non-violation complaints under the *SCM Agreement*. See Panel Report, *US – Offset Act (Byrd Amendment) (2003)*, para. 7.125.

95 Panel Report, *Japan – Film (1998)*, para. 10.36. See also Appellate Body Report, *EC – Asbestos (2001)*, para. 186.

96 Note, however, that, in all disputes in which there was a non-violation complaint, violation complaints were also raised. These violation complaints were usually successful and subsequently the panel usually exercised judicial economy with regard to the non-violation complaint. See e.g. Panel Reports, *EU – Seal Products (2014)*, paras. 7.666–7.683.

97 See GATT Analytical Index (WTO, 1995), 668–91. Pursuant to Article 26.2 of the DSU, the procedural rules of the Decision of 12 April 1989, and not the rules of the DSU, apply to situation complaints. As a result, reports addressing a situation complaint would have to be adopted by the DSB with positive consensus, rather than by reverse consensus.

98 Appellate Body Report, *EC – Bananas III (1997)*, para. 135. The Appellate Body also noted in *EC – Bananas III (1997)* that the DSU neither explicitly stated nor implied that a Member must have a 'legal interest' to have recourse to WTO dispute settlement. See *ibid.*, para. 132.

In *EC – Export Subsidies on Sugar (2005)*, the Appellate Body ruled that Articles 3.7 and 3.10 of the DSU are 'among the few provisions that expressly limit the right of Members to bring an action'.[99] The first sentence of Article 3.7 of the DSU states:

> Before bringing a case, a Member shall exercise its judgement as to whether action under these procedures would be fruitful.

The last clause of Article 3.10 of the DSU states:

> if a dispute arises, all Members will engage in these procedures in good faith in an effort to resolve the dispute.

In *EC – Bananas III (1997)* the Appellate Body explicitly agreed with the statement of the panel that:

> with the increased interdependence of the global economy ... Members have a greater stake in enforcing WTO rules than in the past since any deviation from the negotiated balance of rights and obligations is more likely than ever to affect them, directly or indirectly.[100]

Note that, in *EC – Bananas III (1997)*, the Appellate Body decided that the United States could bring a claim under the GATT 1994 despite the fact that the United States does not export bananas. In coming to this decision, the Appellate Body considered the fact that the United States is a producer and a potential exporter of bananas, the effects of the EC banana regime on the US internal market for bananas and the fact that the US claims under the GATS and the GATT 1994 were inextricably interwoven.

In *Mexico – Corn Syrup (Article 21.5 – US) (2001)*, the Appellate Body ruled with respect to the role of panels in assessing a Member's decision to have recourse to WTO dispute settlement:

> Given the 'largely self-regulating' nature of the requirement in the first sentence of Article 3.7, panels and the Appellate Body must presume, whenever a Member submits a request for establishment of a panel, that such Member does so in good faith, having duly exercised its judgement as to whether recourse to that panel would be 'fruitful'. Article 3.7 neither requires nor authorizes a panel to look behind that Member's decision and to question its exercise of judgement.[101]

Note, however, that, although a Member's decision to have recourse to WTO dispute settlement is largely beyond judicial review, it is apparent from the 'success rate' of complainants in WTO dispute settlement that Members do duly exercise their judgement as to whether recourse to WTO dispute settlement will be '*fruitful*'. To date, panels and/or the Appellate Body have agreed with the complainant in approximately 90 per cent of disputes brought before them that the respondent acted inconsistently with WTO law.[102]

99 Appellate Body Report, *EC – Export Subsidies on Sugar (2005)*, para.

100 *Ibid.*, para. 136. Here the Appellate Body referred to Panel Reports, *EC – Bananas III (1997)*, para. 7.50.

101 Appellate Body Report, *Mexico – Corn Syrup (Article 21.5 – US) (2001)*, para. 74. The Appellate Body referred to its earlier finding, quoted above, in *EC – Bananas III (1997)*, para. 135.

102 See http://worldtradelaw.net/databases/violationcount.php. The percentage figure takes into account only adopted disputes.

As to the question of whether WTO Members can relinquish their right under the DSU to have recourse to WTO dispute settlement, the Appellate Body held in *EC – Bananas III (Article 21.5 – Ecuador II)/EC – Bananas III (Article 21.5 – US) (2008)* that such 'relinquishment of rights granted by the DSU could not be lightly assumed'.[103] A Member must have clearly agreed, either explicitly or by necessary implication, to such relinquishment. In *Peru – Agricultural Products (2015)*, the question arose whether, in challenging Peru's price range system, Guatemala had acted contrary to good faith under Articles 3.7 and 3.10 of the DSU on account of the alleged relinquishment of its right to challenge the price range system before the WTO dispute settlement mechanism.[104] Peru was of the view that Guatemala had *explicitly* waived its right to bring a case with respect to Peru's price range system when it agreed in the free-trade agreement negotiated between the two countries that Peru may maintain its price range system.[105] The Appellate Body noted that, while Article 3.7 of the DSU acknowledges that parties may enter into a mutually agreed solution, Members cannot relinquish their rights and obligations under the DSU beyond the settlement of specific disputes.[106] In this respect, the Appellate Body recalled that Article 23 of the DSU mandates that '[w]hen Members seek the redress of a violations of obligations or other nullification or impairment of benefits under the covered agreements [...] they shall have recourse to, and abide by, the rules and procedures of this Understanding'. The Appellate Body concluded that Guatemala had not acted contrary to its good faith obligations under Articles 3.7 and 3.10 when it initiated proceedings to challenge the WTO consistency of Peru's price range system.[107]

3.2 Access of Members other than the Parties

In addition to the complainant and, albeit not by its own choice, the respondent, other Members may also have access to WTO dispute settlement proceedings. As discussed in more detail below, if consultations are conducted pursuant to Article XXII of the GATT 1994 (rather than Article XXIII) thereof, any Member, which has a 'substantial trade interest' in the consultations, can be allowed to join, i.e. to participate, in these consultations.[108] More importantly, any Member, having a 'substantial interest' in a matter before a panel and having notified its interest in a timely manner to the DSB, may be a third party in the panel proceedings;[109] and any Member, who was a third party in the panel proceedings,

103 Appellate Body Report, *EC – Bananas III (Article 21.5 – Ecuador II)/EC – Bananas III (Article 21.5 – US) (2008)*, para. 217.
104 Guatemala claimed that Peru's price range system was inconsistent with Article 4.2 of the *Agreement on Agriculture* and Article II:1(b) of the GATT 1994. See below, p. 463.
105 Appellate Body Report, *Peru – Agricultural Products (2015)*, para. 5.19.
106 *Ibid.*, fn. 106 to para. 5.26. 107 *Ibid.*, para. 5.28.
108 See Article 4.11 of the DSU. For a further discussion of the right to join consultations, see below, p. 269.
109 See Article 10 of the DSU. On the rights of third parties in panel proceedings, see below, p. 275.

may be a third participant in the Appellate Body proceedings.[110] In recent years, the number of third parties participating in panel and appellate review proceedings has increased significantly.[111] Third parties and third participants have a *right* to be heard by the panel and the Appellate Body respectively.[112] While only Members having a 'substantial interest' in the matter before the panel may become third parties, it is very rare for parties to challenge the third party status of a Member claiming to have such an interest.

3.3 Indirect Access to the WTO Dispute Settlement System

As discussed above, only WTO Members have access to the WTO dispute settlement system. Companies, industry associations or NGOs cannot have recourse to WTO dispute settlement, nor can they join consultations or be a third party or third participant in panel or Appellate Body proceedings. Yet, it would be incorrect to state that companies, industry associations and NGOs are not 'involved' in WTO dispute settlement. It is undisputed that most of the disputes brought to the WTO dispute settlement system are brought by Members *at the instigation of* a company or industry association. Companies and industry associations are the 'driving force' behind the initiation of dispute settlement proceedings in most cases. In fact, it is hard to identify cases in which this was not so. Moreover, companies or industry associations will not only lobby governments to bring dispute settlement cases to the WTO, they (and their law firms) will often also play an important, 'behind-the-scenes' role in planning the legal strategy and drafting the submissions. It could be argued that companies and industry associations have an 'indirect' access to the WTO dispute settlement system and make abundant use of this 'indirect' access. The legal system of some WTO Members explicitly provides for the possibility for companies and industry associations to bring a violation of WTO obligations, by another WTO Member, to the attention of their government and to 'induce' their government to start WTO dispute settlement proceedings against that Member. In EU law, this possibility is provided for under the Trade Barriers Regulation;[113] in US law, under Section 301 of the 1974 Trade Act;[114] and, in Chinese law, under the Investigation Rules of Foreign Trade Barriers.[115] In many other Members, the process of lobbying the government to bring WTO cases has not been regulated and institutionalised in

110 See Article 17.4 of the DSU. On the rights of third participants in Appellate Body proceedings, see below, p. 237.

111 In *China – Rare Earths (2014)*, there were eighteen third parties/third participants in the panel and appellate proceedings.

112 On the rights of third parties and third participants, see below, pp. 216 and 237.

113 Council Regulation (EC) No. 3286/94 on Community procedures for the exercise of rights under international trade rules, in particular those established under the WTO, OJ 1994, L349, 71, as amended by Council Regulation (EC) No. 356/95, OJ 1995, L41, 3.

114 Section 301(a)(1) of the Trade Act 1974, 19 USC 2411(a)(1).

115 Investigation Rules of Foreign Trade Barriers, entered into force on 1 March 2005. The English translation of these rules is available on the official website of the Ministry of Commerce of China.

the same manner, but the process is no less present. In addition to this 'indirect' access, it should also be noted that, according to the Appellate Body, companies and industry associations as well as NGOs can be 'involved' in panel and Appellate Body proceedings as an *amicus curiae*. This controversial case law is discussed later in this chapter.[116]

4 KEY FEATURES OF WTO DISPUTE SETTLEMENT

The prime object and purpose of the WTO dispute settlement system is the *prompt settlement of disputes* between WTO Members concerning their respective rights and obligations under WTO law, and to provide *security and predictability* to the multilateral trading system. As stated in Article 3.3 of the DSU, the prompt settlement of disputes is:

> essential to the effective functioning of the WTO and the maintenance of a proper balance between the rights and obligations of Members.[117]

Article 3.2 of the DSU states:

> The dispute settlement system of the WTO is a central element in providing security and predictability to the multilateral trading system. The Members recognize that it serves to preserve the rights and obligations of Members under the covered agreements, and to clarify the existing provisions of those agreements.

According to the panel in *US – Section 301 Trade Act (2000)*, the WTO dispute settlement system is one of the *most important instruments* of the WTO in protecting the security and predictability of the multilateral trading system.[118] As discussed in Chapter 1 in the context of the sources of WTO law and the role of 'precedent' in WTO dispute settlement, the Appellate Body ruled in *US – Stainless Steel (Mexico) (2008)* that ensuring security and predictability, as contemplated in Article 3.2 of the DSU, implies that, absent cogent reasons, an adjudicatory body will resolve the same legal question in the same way in a subsequent case.[119]

The importance of WTO dispute settlement to the multilateral trading system is uncontested, and the frequent and successful recourse to WTO dispute settlement to date confirms and reinforces this importance.[120] This section describes key features of WTO dispute settlement, which, in addition to the compulsory and exclusive jurisdiction of the WTO dispute settlement system, discussed above, and the process of WTO dispute settlement, discussed below, contribute

116 On *amicus curiae* briefs, see below, pp. 260–4.
117 The Appellate Body referred to this principle of 'prompt settlement of disputes' in, e.g. Appellate Body Report, *US – Upland Cotton (Article 21.5 – Brazil) (2008)*, para. 246; and in Appellate Body Report, *US – Zeroing (Japan) (Article 21.5 – Japan) (2009)*, para. 122.
118 See Panel Report, *US – Section 301 Trade Act*, para. 7.75.
119 See Appellate Body Report, *US – Stainless Steel (Mexico) (2008)*, para. 160.
120 See above, p. 165, and also below, p. 294.

to, if not explain, the importance and success of WTO dispute settlement to date. Some of these features set apart the WTO dispute settlement system from other international dispute settlement mechanisms.[121] This section discusses in turn: (1) the single, comprehensive and integrated nature of the WTO dispute settlement system; (2) the methods of WTO dispute settlement; (3) the multilateral nature of WTO dispute settlement; (4) the preference for mutually acceptable solutions; (5) the mandate to clarify WTO provisions; and (6) remedies for breach of WTO law. Other key features, such as the short time frames, confidentiality and transparency, and appellate review, are discussed separately in subsequent sections of this chapter.

4.1 Single, Comprehensive and Integrated System

The DSU provides for a single dispute settlement system applicable to disputes arising under any of the covered agreements.[122] This is different from the pre-WTO situation when each of the GATT agreements had its own dispute settlement system and the jurisdiction of each of these systems was limited to disputes arising under a specific agreement. While the DSU now provides for a single WTO dispute settlement system, some of the covered agreements provide for some special and additional rules and procedures 'designed to deal with the particularities of dispute settlement relating to obligations arising under a specific covered agreement'.[123] Pursuant to Article 1.2 of the DSU, these special or additional rules and procedures *prevail* over the DSU rules and procedures to the extent that there is a 'difference' between them. The Appellate Body in *Guatemala – Cement I (1998)* ruled in this regard:

> [I]f there is no 'difference', then the rules and procedures of the DSU apply *together with* the special or additional provisions of the covered agreement. In our view, it is only where the provisions of the DSU and the special or additional rules and procedures of a covered agreement *cannot* be read as *complementing* each other that the special or additional provisions are to *prevail*.[124]

The special and additional rules and procedures of a particular covered agreement combine with the generally applicable rules and procedures of the DSU 'to form a comprehensive, integrated dispute settlement system for the *WTO Agreement*'.[125]

121 With regard to the compulsory jurisdiction, see above, p. 168. With regard to e.g. remedies, appellate review and timeframes, see below, pp. 199–209 (remedies), 278–85 (appellate review), 285–92 (timeframes), respectively.

122 See Appellate Body Report, *Guatemala – Cement I (1998)*, para. 64.

123 *Ibid.*, para. 66.

124 *Ibid.*, para. 65. The Appellate Body further noted that: 'A special or additional provision should only be found to *prevail* over a provision of the DSU in a situation where adherence to the one provision will lead to a violation of the other provision, that is, in the case of a *conflict* between them.' See *ibid.* See also Appellate Body Report, *US – Hot-Rolled Steel (2001)*, paras. 55 and 62, and below, p. 760, with regard to Article 17.6 of the *Anti-Dumping Agreement*.

125 Appellate Body Report, *Guatemala – Cement I (1998)*, para. 66.

4.2 Different Methods of Dispute Settlement

The WTO dispute settlement system provides for several dispute settlement methods. In addition to *consultations*, i.e. negotiations, between the parties, provided for in Article 4 of the DSU, and *adjudication* by a panel and the Appellate Body, provided for in Articles 6 to 20 of the DSU, which are by far the methods most frequently used and the methods focused on in this chapter, the WTO dispute settlement system also provides for other dispute settlement methods, and in particular: arbitration; and good offices, conciliation and mediation. Pursuant to Article 25 of the DSU, parties to a dispute arising under a covered agreement may decide to resort to *arbitration* as an alternative means of binding dispute settlement, rather than have the dispute adjudicated by a panel and the Appellate Body.[126] When parties opt for arbitration, they must agree on the procedural rules that will apply to the arbitration process; and they must explicitly agree to abide by the arbitration award.[127] Arbitration awards need to be consistent with WTO law,[128] and must be notified to the DSB where any Member may raise any point relating thereto.[129] To date, Members have resorted only once to arbitration under Article 25 of the DSU.[130] The DSU also provides for arbitration in Articles 21.3(c) and 22.6. As discussed below, these arbitration procedures concern specific issues that may arise in the *context* of a dispute, such as the determination of the reasonable period of time for implementation (Article 21.3(c) of the DSU) and the appropriate level of retaliation (Article 22.6 of the DSU).[131] Members frequently resort to arbitration under Article 21.3(c) or 22.6. As mentioned above, the DSU also provides for *good offices, conciliation* and *mediation* as methods of dispute settlement. These dispute settlement methods are provided for in Article 5 of the DSU. Their use may be requested at any time by any party to a dispute. They may begin at any time and be terminated at any time.[132] Their use requires the agreement of all parties to the dispute.[133] Proceedings involving good offices, conciliation and mediation are confidential, and without prejudice to the rights of either party in any further proceedings under the DSU.[134] Pursuant to Article 5.6 of the DSU, the WTO Director-General may, acting in an *ex officio* capacity, offer good offices, conciliation or mediation with a view to assisting Members to settle a dispute.[135]

126 Article 25.1 of the DSU refers to 'expeditious' arbitration, suggesting that this dispute settlement method will be quicker and more efficient than adjudication pursuant to Articles 6 to 20 of the DSU.

127 See Articles 25.2 and 25.3 of the DSU.

128 See Article 3.5 of the DSU. 129 See Article 25.3 of the DSU.

130 In 2001, the United States and the European Communities resorted to arbitration under Article 25 to resolve a dispute on the appropriate level of compensation due by the United States after it failed to comply with the panel report in *US – Section 110(5) Copyright Act (2000)*. See Award of the Arbitrators, *US – Section 110(5) Copyright Act (Article 25) (2001)*, Recourse to Arbitration under Article 25 of the DSU, WT/DS160/ARB25/1, dated 9 November 2001. See below, p. 298.

131 See below, pp. 289–91. 132 See Article 5.3 of the DSU.

133 See Article 5.1 of the DSU. 134 See Article 5.2 of the DSU.

135 In July 2001, the Director-General reminded Members of his availability to help settle disputes through good offices, mediation or conciliation. See Communication from the Director-General, *Article 5 of the Dispute Settlement Understanding*, WT/DSB/25, dated 17 July 2001.

However, similar to arbitration under Article 25 of the DSU, Members have made little use of these dispute settlement methods.[136]

4.3 Multilateral Dispute Settlement

The object and purpose of the WTO dispute settlement system is for Members to settle disputes with other Members through the *multilateral* procedures of the DSU, rather than through *unilateral* action. Article 23.1 of the DSU states:

> When Members seek the redress of a violation of obligations or other nullification or impairment of benefits under the covered agreements or an impediment to the attainment of any objective of the covered agreements, they shall have recourse to, and abide by, the rules and procedures of this Understanding.

According to the Appellate Body in *US – Certain EC Products (2001)*, Article 23.1 of the DSU imposes a general obligation to redress a violation of WTO law through the multilateral DSU procedures, and not through unilateral action.[137] Pursuant to Article 23.2 of the DSU, WTO Members may not make a *unilateral* determination that a violation of WTO law has occurred and may not take retaliation measures *unilaterally* in the case of a violation of WTO law.[138] It has been argued that concerns regarding unilateral action taken by the United States against what it considered to be violations of GATT law were the driving force behind the Uruguay Round negotiations on dispute settlement, which eventually resulted in the DSU. During the 1980s, the United States increasingly took unilateral action against purported GATT violations by other countries. The United States did so under Section 301 of the Trade Act of 1974, and, with the adoption of the Trade and Competitiveness Act of 1988, the United States considerably expanded its ability to take such unilateral action. Many other countries considered this unilateral action to be a form of 'vigilante justice' and demanded that the United States cease to act unilaterally against purported

136 To date there has been no reported instance of the use of the dispute settlement methods referred to in Article 5 of the DSU. See *WTO Analytical Index (2012)*, Volume II, 1555–6 together with the supplement (until June 2015). However, note the successful mediation of Deputy Director-General Rufus Yerxa in 2002 in a dispute between the European Communities and the Philippines and Thailand on the tariff treatment of canned tuna (see Communication from the Director-General, *Request for Mediation by the Philippines, Thailand and the European Communities*, WT/GC/66, dated 16 October 2002; WT/GC/66/Add.1, dated 23 December 2002; and Joint Communication from the European Communities, Thailand and the Philippines, *Request for Mediation by the Philippines, Thailand and the European Communities*, WT/GC/71, dated 1 August 2003).

137 Appellate Body Report, *US – Certain EC Products (2001)*, para. 111. The panel in this case noted that unilateral action is contrary to the essence of the multilateral trading system because such action threatens the system's stability and predictability. See Panel Report, *US – Certain EC Products (2001)*, para. 6.14.

138 The panel in *EC – Commercial Vessels (2005)* held that the obligation to have recourse to the DSU when Members seek the redress of a violation covers *any act of a Member* in response to what it considers to be a violation of a WTO obligation. See Panel Report, *EC – Commercial Vessels (2005)*, para. 7.207. Note, however, that the Appellate Body found in *US/Canada – Continued Suspension (2008)* that statements made in the DSB regarding the WTO consistency of measures of other Members are 'generally diplomatic or political in nature' and 'do not have the legal status of a definitive determination in themselves'. See Appellate Body Report, *US/Canada – Continued Suspension (2008)*, para. 398.

violations of GATT law. The United States, however, argued that the existing GATT dispute settlement system was too weak to protect US trade interests effectively.[139] In this way, agreement was eventually reached on the current WTO dispute settlement system. It is unlikely that, without, on the one hand, the frustration of the United States with the GATT dispute settlement system and, on the other hand, the concerns of other GATT Contracting Parties about US unilateralism in international trade disputes, the Uruguay Round negotiators would ever have been able to agree on a dispute settlement system as far-reaching, innovative and effective as the current WTO system.

While unilateralism remains a concern, in recent years, it is the proliferation of free-trade agreements containing their own dispute settlement mechanisms that have been considered as a threat to the multilateral WTO dispute settlement. To date, there is, however, no empirical support for that proposition that WTO Members have recourse to dispute settlement systems under free trade agreements rather than to the WTO dispute settlement system.[140]

4.4 Preference for Mutually Acceptable Solutions

Article 3.7 of the DSU states, in relevant part:

> The aim of the dispute settlement mechanism is to secure a positive solution to a dispute. A solution mutually acceptable to the parties to a dispute and consistent with the covered agreements is clearly to be preferred.

The DSU thus expresses a clear preference for solutions mutually acceptable to the parties reached through negotiations, rather than solutions resulting from adjudication. In other words, the DSU prefers parties *not* to go to court, but to settle their dispute amicably out of court. Accordingly, each dispute settlement process must start with consultations (or an attempt to have consultations) between the parties to the dispute.[141] To resolve disputes through consultations is obviously cheaper and more satisfactory for the long-term trade relations with the other party to the dispute than adjudication by a panel. Note, however, that any mutually agreed solution reached through consultations needs to be consistent with WTO law,[142] and must be notified to the DSB, where any Member may raise any point relating thereto.[143] For a further discussion on consultations and mutually agreed solutions, refer to section 6.2 of this chapter on the process of WTO dispute settlement.[144]

139 This weakness was primarily the result of the requirement that panel reports had to be adopted by consensus to become legally binding.

140 C. Chase, A. Yanovich, J. Crawford and P. Ugaz, 'Mapping of Dispute Settlements Mechanisms in Regional Trade Agreements: Innovative or Variations on a Theme?', Staff Working Paper ERSD-2013-07, World Trade Organization. Consider in this regard also the implications of the Appellate Body's ruling in *Peru – Agricultural Products (2015)*, discussed above, p. 183.

141 On consultations, see also below, section 6.2 of this chapter.

142 See Articles 3.5 and 3.7 of the DSU.

143 See Article 3.6 of the DSU.

144 See below, pp. 266–71.

4.5 Mandate to Clarify WTO Provisions

Article 3.2, second sentence, of the DSU states that the WTO dispute settlement system serves not only 'to preserve the rights and obligations of Members under the covered agreements', but also 'to clarify the existing provisions of those agreements'. This subsection discusses in turn: (1) the scope and nature of this mandate to clarify, i.e. to interpret, the provisions of the covered agreements; (2) the general rule of interpretation set out in Article 31 of the *Vienna Convention on the Law of Treaties*; and (3) supplementary means of interpretation set out in Article 32 of the *Vienna Convention.*

4.5.1 Scope and Nature of the Mandate to Clarify

As stated above, Article 3.2, second sentence, of the DSU mandates the WTO dispute settlement system with the task of clarification of the existing provisions of the covered agreements. As more than twenty years of WTO dispute settlement have shown, many provisions of the covered agreements are a masterpiece of 'constructive ambiguity'.[145] There is, therefore, much need for clarification in particular dispute settlement proceedings. However, the scope and nature of this clarification mandate is circumscribed. Article 3.2, third sentence, provides:

> Recommendations and rulings of the DSB cannot add to or diminish the rights and obligations provided in the covered agreements.

In the same vein, Article 19.2 of the DSU states:

> In accordance with paragraph 2 of Article 3, in their findings and recommendations, the panel and Appellate Body cannot add to or diminish the rights and obligations provided in the covered agreements.

While allowing the WTO dispute settlement system to clarify WTO law, Articles 3.2 and 19.2 explicitly preclude the system from adding to or diminishing the rights and obligations of Members. The DSU thus explicitly cautions against 'judicial activism'. WTO panels and the Appellate Body are not to take on the role of 'legislator'.[146] Furthermore, as noted in Chapter 2, pursuant to Article IX:2 of the *WTO Agreement*, it is the exclusive competence of the Ministerial Conference and the General Council to adopt 'authoritative' interpretations of the provisions of the *WTO Agreement* and the Multilateral Trade Agreements.[147] Article 3.9 of the

145 It is often such 'constructive ambiguity' that allowed negotiators to conclude the negotiations and agree on the provisions of an agreement.

146 WTO Members losing a dispute sometimes raise accusations of judicial activism. For example, United States Trade Representative Ron Kirk reacted to some adverse findings in the Appellate Body report in *US – Anti-Dumping and Countervailing Duties (China) (2011)* as follows: 'I am deeply troubled by this report. It appears to be a clear case of overreaching by the Appellate Body. We are reviewing the findings closely in order to understand fully their implications.' See www.ustr.gov/about-us/press-office/press-releases/2011/march/ustr-statement-regarding-wto-appellate-body-report-c.

147 For a discussion on Article IX:2 of the *WTO Agreement*, see above, p. 149.

DSU stipulates that the provisions of the DSU are without prejudice to the rights of Members to seek such 'authoritative' interpretation. In *US – Certain EC Products (2001)*, the Appellate Body held:

> Determining what the rules and procedures of the DSU *ought to be* is not our responsibility nor the responsibility of panels; it is clearly the responsibility solely of the Members of the WTO.[148]

Note that, in *Chile – Alcoholic Beverages (2000)*, Chile argued before the Appellate Body that the panel had acted inconsistently with Articles 3.2 and 19.2 of the DSU as it had added to the rights and obligations of Members. The Appellate Body found, however that:

> [w]e have difficulty in envisaging circumstances in which a panel could add to the rights and obligations of a Member of the WTO if its conclusions reflected a correct interpretation and application of provisions of the covered agreements.[149]

As the Appellate Body explained in *US – Stainless Steel (Mexico) (2008)*:

> Clarification, as envisaged in Article 3.2 of the DSU, elucidates the scope and meaning of the provisions of the covered agreements in accordance with customary rules of interpretation of public international law. While the application of a provision may be regarded as confined to the context in which it takes place, the relevance of clarification contained in adopted Appellate Body reports is not limited to the application of a particular provision in a specific case.[150]

For panels and the Appellate Body to stay within their mandate to clarify existing provisions, it is therefore important that they interpret and apply the provisions concerned correctly. Article 3.2 of the DSU explicitly states in this respect that the dispute settlement system serves:

> to clarify the existing provisions of [the covered] agreements *in accordance with customary rules of interpretation of public international law*.[151]

A correct interpretation of a WTO provision is thus an interpretation in accordance with customary rules of interpretation of public international law. In its very first report, the report in *US – Gasoline (1996)*, the Appellate Body noted with regard to the general rule of interpretation in Article 31 of the *Vienna Convention*:

> Th[is] 'general rule of interpretation' [set out in Article 31(1) of the *Vienna Convention on the Law of Treaties*] has attained the status of a rule of customary or general international law. As such, it forms part of the 'customary rules of interpretation of public international law' which the Appellate Body has been directed, by Article 3(2) of the *DSU*, to apply in seeking to clarify the provisions of the [WTO agreements].[152]

148 Appellate Body Report, *US – Certain EC Products (2001)*, para. 92. Emphasis added.

149 Appellate Body Report, *Chile – Alcoholic Beverages (2000)*, para. 79.

150 Appellate Body Report, *US – Stainless Steel (2008)*, para. 161.

151 Emphasis added. Note that it is uncommon for the statute or constituent document of an international court or tribunal to set out how the court or tribunal is to interpret the relevant treaty.

152 Appellate Body Report, *US – Gasoline (1996)*, 15–16.

In its second report, the report in *Japan – Alcoholic Beverages II (1996)*, the Appellate Body added:

> There can be no doubt that Article 32 of the *Vienna Convention*, dealing with the role of supplementary means of interpretation, has also attained the same status [of a rule of customary international law].[153]

In accordance with Articles 31 and 32 of the *Vienna Convention on the Law of Treaties*, panels and the Appellate Body interpret provisions of the covered agreements in accordance with the ordinary meaning of the words of the provision in their context and in light of the object and purpose of the agreement involved; and, if necessary and appropriate, they have recourse to supplementary means of interpretation. While the mandate of panels and the Appellate Body to clarify the provisions of the covered agreements is – as discussed above – limited by Articles 3.2 and 19.2 of the DSU and 'judicial activism' is not condoned, note that the Appellate Body held in *Japan – Alcoholic Beverages II (1996)* with regard to the degree of 'flexibility' and 'interpretability' of the covered agreements that:

> WTO rules are reliable, comprehensible and enforceable. WTO rules are not so rigid or so inflexible as not to leave room for reasoned judgements in confronting the endless and ever-changing ebb and flow of real facts in real cases in the real world. They will serve the multilateral trading system best if they are interpreted with that in mind. In that way, we will achieve the 'security and predictability' sought for the multilateral trading system by the Members of the WTO through the establishment of the dispute settlement system.[154]

As the Appellate Body's interpretation of the term 'exhaustible natural resources' of Article XX(g) of the GATT 1994 in *US – Shrimp (1998)* demonstrated, the meaning of a term may evolve over time.[155] An 'evolutionary' interpretation of terms and provisions of WTO law is not excluded.

With regard to one of the more controversial interpretations of the Appellate Body, namely, the interpretation of the relevant provisions of the *Anti-Dumping Agreement* which led the Appellate Body to rule that the United States' zeroing methodology is WTO-inconsistent,[156] one of the Members of the Appellate Body in *US – Continued Zeroing (2009)* stated in a concurring opinion:

> The interpretation of the covered agreements requires scrupulous adherence to the disciplines of the customary rules of interpretation of public international law ... Just as the interpreter of a treaty strives for coherence, there is an inevitable recognition that a treaty bears the imprint of many hands. And what is left behind is a text, sometimes negotiated

153 Appellate Body Report, *Japan – Alcoholic Beverages II (1996)*, 104. The rule also reflected in Article 33 of the *Vienna Convention* has been used by panels and the Appellate Body in the interpretation of provisions of WTO agreements. See e.g. Appellate Body Report, *US – Anti-Dumping and Countervailing Duties (China) (2011)*, paras. 330–2; and Appellate Body Report, *US – Countervailing and Anti-Dumping Measures (China) (2014)*, paras. 4.76–4.77. Other customary rules or principles of interpretation which panels and/or the Appellate Body have already had recourse to (or at least discussed) are the *in dubio mitius* rule (see *EC – Hormones (1998)* and *China – Publications and Audiovisual Products (2010)*) and the *ejusdem generis* rule (see *US – COOL (2012)* and *US – Large Civil Aircraft (2nd complaint) (2012)*).

154 Appellate Body Report, *Japan – Alcoholic Beverages II (1996)*, 122–3.

155 For a discussion of this interpretation of the term 'exhaustible natural resources', see below, pp. 575–8.

156 On the zeroing methodology to calculate a dumping margin, see below, pp. 712–20.

to a point where an agreement to regulate a matter could only be reached on the basis of constructive ambiguity, carrying both the hopes and fears of the parties. Interpretation is an endeavour to discern order, notwithstanding these infirmities, without adding to or diminishing the rights and obligations of the parties.[157]

4.5.2 Article 31 of the *Vienna Convention*

Article 31 of the *Vienna Convention on the Law of Treaties*, entitled 'General Rule of Interpretation', states in its first paragraph:

> A treaty shall be interpreted in good faith in accordance with the ordinary meaning to be given to the terms of the treaty in their context and in the light of its object and purpose.

The panel in *US – Section 301 Trade Act (2000)* stressed that the elements of Article 31 of the *Vienna Convention* – text, context and object and purpose – constitute 'one holistic rule of interpretation', and not 'a sequence of separate tests to be applied in a hierarchical order'.[158] To determine the ordinary meaning of a term, it makes sense to start with the dictionary meaning of that term but, as the Appellate Body noted more than once, a term often has several dictionary meanings and dictionary meanings thus leave many interpretative questions open.[159] The ordinary meaning of a term can often not be determined outside the context in which the term is used and without consideration of the object and purpose of the agreement at issue.[160]

In *Japan – Alcoholic Beverages II (1996)*, the Appellate Body stated:

> Article 31 of the *Vienna Convention* provides that the words of the treaty form the foundation for the interpretive process: 'interpretation must be based above all upon the text of the treaty'. The provisions of the treaty are to be given their ordinary meaning in their context. The object and purpose of the treaty are also to be taken into account in determining the meaning of its provisions.[161]

The duty of an interpreter is to examine the words of the treaty to determine the *common* intentions of the parties to the treaty.[162]

One of the corollaries of the 'general rule of interpretation' of Article 31 of the *Vienna Convention* is that interpretation must give meaning and effect to *all* the terms of a treaty (i.e. the interpretative principle of effectiveness). An interpreter is not free to adopt a reading that would result in reducing whole clauses or

157 Appellate Body Report, *US – Continued Zeroing (2009)*, para. 306.

158 *Ibid.* See also Appellate Body Report, *China – Publications and Audiovisual Products (2010)*, para. 176, where the Appellate Body stated that interpretation under Article 31 of the *Vienna Convention* is 'ultimately a holistic exercise that should not be mechanically subdivided into rigid components'.

159 See Appellate Body Report, *Canada – Aircraft (1999)*, para. 153; and Appellate Body Report, *EC – Asbestos (2001)*, para. 92.

160 On the concept of 'ordinary meaning', see also Appellate Body Report, *EC – Chicken Cuts (2005)*, paras. 170–87.

161 Appellate Body Report, *Japan – Alcoholic Beverages II (1996)*, 104.

162 See e.g. Appellate Body Report, *India – Patents (US) (1998)*, para. 45; and Appellate Body Report, *EC – Computer Equipment (1998)*, para. 84. Note that, in both these cases, the Appellate Body rejected the relevance of the 'legitimate expectations' of *one of the parties* in the interpretation of the meaning of the provision at issue.

paragraphs of a treaty to redundancy or inutility.[163] Furthermore, the Appellate Body in *EC – Hormones (1998)* cautioned interpreters as follows:

> The fundamental rule of treaty interpretation requires a treaty interpreter to read and interpret the words actually used by the agreement under examination, and not words the interpreter may feel should have been used.[164]

As stated above, the words used must be interpreted in their context. In fact, the ordinary meaning of the words used can often only be determined when considered in their context. As Article 31.2 of the *Vienna Convention* states, the relevant context includes, in addition to the rest of the text of the agreement, the preamble and annexes, also: (1) any agreement relating to the treaty which was made between all the parties in connection with the conclusion of the treaty (see Article 31.2(a)); and (2) any instrument which was made by one or more parties in connection with the conclusion of the treaty and accepted by the other parties as an instrument related to the treaty (see Article 31.2(b)). In *EC – Chicken Cuts (2005)*, the Appellate Body found that the Harmonized Commodity Description and Coding System, commonly referred to as the 'Harmonized System' and discussed in Chapter 6,[165] serves as 'context' within the meaning of Article 31.2(a) of the *Vienna Convention* for the purpose of interpreting the WTO agreements.[166] The Appellate Body referred to the 'close link' between the Harmonized System and the WTO and the 'broad consensus' among Members to use the Harmonized System.[167]

Pursuant to Article 31.3 of the *Vienna Convention*, a treaty interpreter must take into account together with the context: (1) any subsequent agreement between the parties regarding the interpretation of the treaty or the application of its provisions (see Article 31.3(a)); (2) any subsequent practice in the application of the treaty which establishes the agreement of the parties regarding its interpretation (see Article 31.3(b)); and (3) any relevant rules of international law applicable in the relations between the parties (see Article 31.3(c)). It is important to note the mandatory nature of Article 31.3. As the wording of its chapeau ('[t]here shall be taken into account') indicates, Article 31.3 mandates a treaty interpreter to take into account subsequent agreements, subsequent practice and relevant rules of international law; it does not merely give a treaty interpreter the option of doing so.[168]

163 See Appellate Body Report, *US – Gasoline (1996)*, 21. See also e.g. *Canada – Dairy (1999)*, para. 135.

164 Appellate Body Report, *EC – Hormones (1998)*, para. 181. See also Appellate Body Report, *India – Patents (US) (1998)*, para. 45, regarding the importation into a treaty of 'words that are not there' or 'concepts that were not intended'.

165 See below, pp. 451–3.

166 See Appellate Body Report, *EC – Chicken Cuts (2005)*, paras. 197–9. Note, however, that, in *US – Gambling (2005)*, the Appellate Body ruled that the panel in that case erred in categorising document W/120 and the 1993 Scheduling Guidelines as 'agreements' within the meaning of Article 31.2(a) of the *Vienna Convention*. See Appellate Body Report, *US – Gambling (2005)*, paras. 175–6.

167 See Appellate Body Report, *EC – Chicken Cuts (2005)*, paras. 197–9.

168 See Panel Reports, *EC – Approval and Marketing of Biotech Products (2006)*, para. 7.69. While the panel made this observation on the mandatory nature in particular with regard to Article 31.3(c), the same reasoning applies to the other paragraphs of Article 31.3.

With regard to *subsequent agreements* within the meaning of Article 31.3(a), note that the Appellate Body considered in *US – Clove Cigarettes (2012)* that a decision by the Ministerial Conference, namely, the *Doha Ministerial Decision on Implementation-Related Issues and Concerns*, and in particular paragraph 5.2 thereof, constituted a subsequent agreement between the parties, within the meaning of Article 31.3(a).[169]

With regard to *subsequent practice* within the meaning of Article 31.3(b), the Appellate Body stated in *Japan – Alcoholic Beverages II (1996)*:

> [I]n international law, the essence of subsequent practice in interpreting a treaty has been recognized as a 'concordant, common and consistent' sequence of acts or pronouncements which is sufficient to establish a discernible pattern implying the agreement of the parties regarding its interpretation. An isolated act is generally not sufficient to establish subsequent practice; it is a sequence of acts establishing the agreement of the parties that is relevant.[170]

With regard to *relevant rules of international law* within the meaning of Article 31.3(c), the panel in *EC – Approval and Marketing of Biotech Products (2006)* noted:

> Textually, this reference [to relevant rules of international law] seems sufficiently broad to encompass all generally accepted sources of public international law, that is to say, (i) international conventions (treaties), (ii) international custom (customary international law), and (iii) the recognized general principles of law. In our view, there can be no doubt that treaties and customary rules of international law are 'rules of international law' within the meaning of Article 31(3)(c).[171]

Earlier, the Appellate Body had already held in *US – Shrimp (1998)* that general principles of international law are 'rules of international law' within the meaning of Article 31.3(c).[172] However, the panel in *EC – Approval and Marketing of Biotech Products (2006)* pointed out that Article 31.3(c) of the *Vienna Convention* contains an important limitation, namely, that only those rules of international law 'applicable in the relations between the parties' are to be taken into account. It held 'the parties' to mean those States that have consented to be bound by the treaty being interpreted (i.e. *all* WTO Members).[173] The panel's finding that 'rules of international law' within the meaning of Article 31.3(c) do not include treaties signed by only some WTO Members has been criticised by some international law scholars, who observed that it is unlikely that the *WTO Agreement* and other multilateral treaties have 'a precise congruence' in membership.[174] Note,

169 See Appellate Body Report, *US – Clove Cigarettes (2012)*, para. 268. With regard to the question whether a TBT Committee decision could be considered to be a 'subsequent agreement', see Appellate Body Report, *US – Tuna II (Mexico) (2012)*, para. 372. See also above, p. 59, and below, p. 197.

170 Appellate Body Report, *Japan – Alcoholic Beverages II (1996)*, 105–6 and Panel Report, *US – FSC (2000)*, para. 7.75; Panel Report, *Canada – Patent Term (2000)*, para. 5.5 and para. 6.89, fn. 48; and Appellate Body Report, *Chile – Price Band System (2002)*, para. 272.

171 Panel Reports, *EC – Approval and Marketing of Biotech Products (2006)*, para. 7.67.

172 See Appellate Body Report, *US – Shrimp (1998)*, para. 158.

173 Panel Reports, *EC – Approval and Marketing of Biotech Products (2006)*, para. 7.68.

174 See International Law Commission, 58th Session, *Fragmentation of International Law: Difficulties Arising from the Diversification and Expansion of International Law*, Report of the Study Group of the International Law Commission, finalised by Martti Koskenniemi, A/CN.4/L.682, 13 April 2006, para. 471.

however, that the panel in *EC – Approval and Marketing of Biotech Products (2006)* did not rule that a treaty interpreter may not take into account treaties to which not all WTO Members are a party, but that a treaty interpreter is not required to do so.[175] In *EC and certain member States – Large Civil Aircraft (2011)*, the Appellate Body ruled that an interpretation of 'the parties' in Article 31.3(c) should be guided by the Appellate Body's statement in *EC – Computer Equipment (1998)* that 'the purpose of treaty interpretation is to establish the common intention of the parties to the treaty'. This suggests that one must exercise caution in drawing from an international agreement to which not all WTO Members are party.[176] However, the Appellate Body also recognised in *EC and certain member States – Large Civil Aircraft (2011)* that:

> a proper interpretation of the term 'the parties' must also take account of the fact that Article 31(3)(c) of the Vienna Convention is considered an expression of the 'principle of systemic integration' which, in the words of the International Law Commission, seeks to ensure that 'international obligations are interpreted by reference to their normative environment' in a manner that gives 'coherence and meaningfulness' to the process of legal interpretation.[177]

The Appellate Body therefore concluded in *EC and certain member States – Large Civil Aircraft (2011)* that:

> [i]n a multilateral context such as the WTO, when recourse is had to a non-WTO rule for the purposes of interpreting provisions of the WTO agreements, a delicate balance must be struck between, on the one hand, taking due account of an individual WTO Member's international obligations and, on the other hand, ensuring a consistent and harmonious approach to the interpretation of WTO law among all WTO Members.[178]

While the Appellate Body did not rule on the meaning of the term 'parties' in Article 31(3)(a) and (c) of the *Vienna Convention* in *Peru – Agricultural Products (2015)*, it expressed reservations as to whether certain provisions of the free trade agreement between Guatemala and Peru could be relied upon pursuant to Article 31(3) in establishing the *common* intention of WTO Members underlying the WTO provisions at issue in that dispute. The Appellate Body cautioned that such an approach would suggest that WTO provisions can be interpreted differently, depending on the Members to which they apply and depending on their rights and obligations under an free trade agreement to which they are parties.[179]

The Appellate Body recalled its rulings in *US – Anti-Dumping and Countervailing Duties (China) (2011)* and *EC and certain member States – Large Civil Aircraft (2011)*, that in order to be 'relevant' for purposes of interpretation, rules of international law within the meaning of Article 31(3)(c) of the

175 Panel Reports, *EC – Approval and Marketing of Biotech Products (2006)*, paras. 7.92–7.93. Note that, in *EC – Approval and Marketing of Biotech Products (2006)*, not even all parties to the dispute, let alone all WTO Members, were parties to the non-WTO agreements which the panel considered in its interpretative exercise.

176 See Appellate Body Report, *EC and certain member States – Large Civil Aircraft (2011)*, para. 845.

177 *Ibid.* 178 *Ibid.* 179 Appellate Body Report, *Peru – Agricultural Products (2015)*, para. 5.106.

Vienna Convention must concern the same subject matter as the treaty terms being interpreted.[180] The Appellate Body also recalled that it had held in previous disputes that agreements 'regarding the interpretation of the treaty or the application of its provisions' within the meaning of Article 31(3)(a) of the *Vienna Convention* are 'agreements bearing specifically upon the interpretation of a treaty'.[181] Therefore, the Appellate Body did *not* consider 'regarding the interpretation' of the WTO provisions at issue that, certain provisions of the Guatemala–Peru free-trade agreement and certain ILC Articles on State Responsibility[182] are 'relevant' rules of international law within the meaning of Article 31(3)(c), and that the free-trade agreement is a subsequent agreement, within the meaning of Article 31(3)(a) of the *Vienna Convention.*[183]

Finally, as discussed above, interpretation pursuant to Article 31 requires a treaty interpreter to consider the terms used 'in the light of the object and purpose' of the treaty. In *EC – Chicken Cuts (2005)*, the Appellate Body emphasised that the starting point for ascertaining 'object and purpose' is the treaty itself, *in its entirety*, but that Article 31.1 did not exclude taking into account the object and purpose of particular treaty provisions, if doing so assists the interpreter in determining the treaty's object and purpose on the whole.[184] The Appellate Body did not consider it necessary 'to divorce a treaty's object and purpose from the object and purpose of specific treaty provisions, or *vice versa*'.[185] The Appellate Body stated:

> To the extent that one can speak of the 'object and purpose of a treaty provision', it will be informed by, and will be in consonance with, the object and purpose of the entire treaty of which it is but a component.[186]

4.5.3 Article 32 of the *Vienna Convention*

Article 32 of the *Vienna Convention*, entitled 'Supplementary Means of Interpretation', states:

> Recourse may be had to supplementary means of interpretation, including the preparatory work of the treaty and the circumstances of its conclusion, in order to confirm the meaning resulting from the application of article 31, or to determine the meaning when the interpretation according to article 31:
>
> a. leaves the meaning ambiguous or obscure; or
> b. leads to a result which is manifestly absurd or unreasonable.

180 *Ibid.*, para. 5.101 (referring to Appellate Body Reports, *US – Anti-Dumping and Countervailing Duties (China) (2011)*, para. 308; and *EC and certain member States – Large Civil Aircraft (2011)*, para. 846).

181 Appellate Body Report, *Peru – Agricultural Products (2015)*, para. 5.101 (referring to Appellate Body Reports, *EC – Bananas III (Article 21.5 – Ecuador II / Article 21.5 – US) (2008)*, para. 390; *US – Clove Cigarettes (2012)*, para. 266; and *US – Tuna II (Mexico) (2012)*, para. 372).

182 Articles 20 and 45 of the ILC's *Articles on Responsibility of States for Internationally Wrongful Acts.*

183 The provisions at issue were Article 4.2 of the *Agreement on Agriculture* and Article II:1(b) of the GATT 1994.

184 See Appellate Body Report, *EC – Chicken Cuts (2005)*, para. 238.

185 *Ibid.* 186 *Ibid.*

As the Appellate Body observed in *EC – Computer Equipment (1998)*, the application of the general rule of interpretation set out in Article 31 of the *Vienna Convention*, and discussed above, will usually allow a treaty interpreter to establish the meaning of a term. However, if that is not the case, Article 32 of the *Vienna Convention* allows a treaty interpreter to have recourse to supplementary means of interpretation, including the preparatory work of the treaty and the circumstances of its conclusion.[187] A treaty interpreter may also have recourse to Article 32 in order to confirm, i.e. further support, the interpretation resulting from the application of the general rule of interpretation of Article 31. Article 32 of the *Vienna Convention* does not provide an exhaustive list of sources. In *China – Publications and Audiovisual Products (2010)*, the Appellate Body stressed that:

> an interpreter has a certain flexibility in considering relevant supplementary means in a given case so as to assist in ascertaining the common intentions of the parties.[188]

With regard to the 'preparatory work of the treaty', commonly also referred to as the 'negotiating history' of a treaty, it must be noted that there exists no officially recorded negotiating history of the WTO agreements (unlike for the GATT 1947 and the 1948 *Havana Charter for an International Trade Organization*).[189] It is, therefore, not surprising that panels and the Appellate Body have made little use of the 'preparatory work of the treaty' in their interpretative efforts.[190] Panels and the Appellate Body have given limited weight to various country-specific and often conflicting negotiating proposals and very little importance to the often contradictory and self-serving personal recollections of negotiators.[191] With regard to 'the circumstances of [the] conclusion' of a treaty, the Appellate Body considered in *EC – Computer Equipment (1998)*, that Article 32 of the *Vienna Convention* permits, in appropriate cases, the examination of the historical background against which the treaty was negotiated. In this case, the Appellate Body considered that the tariff classification practice in the European Communities during the Uruguay Round was part of 'the circumstances of [the] conclusion' of the *WTO Agreement* and could therefore be used as a supplementary means of interpretation within the meaning of Article 32 of the *Vienna Convention*.[192]

187 Appellate Body Report, *EC – Computer Equipment (1998)*, para. 86. See also Appellate Body Report, *Canada – Dairy (1999)*, para. 138.

188 Appellate Body Report, *China – Publications and Audiovisual Products (2010)*, para. 283. See also Appellate Body Report, *EC – Chicken Cuts (2005)*, para. 283.

189 In *India – Quantitative Restrictions (1999)*, the Appellate Body explicitly noted 'the absence of a record of the negotiations' on the 1994 WTO Understanding at issue in that case. See Appellate Body Report, *India – Quantitative Restrictions (1999)*, para. 94.

190 The Appellate Body referred to the negotiating history of the provision at issue in *Canada – Periodicals (1997)*. However, the negotiating history referred to was the negotiating history of the *Havana Charter*. See Appellate Body Report, *Canada – Periodicals (1997)*, 34.

191 See, e.g., Appellate Body Report, *US – Line Pipe (2002)*, para. 175. Note, however, that the panel in *US – Large Civil Aircraft (2nd complaint) (2012)* did attach some significance to the negotiating history. Panel Report, *US – Large Civil Aircraft (2nd complaint) (2012)*, paras. 7.963–7.964. On the use of 'negotiating history', see also Panel Report, *US – Countervailing and Anti-Dumping Measures (2014)*, paras. 7.286–7.290.

192 See Appellate Body Report, *EC – Computer Equipment (1998)*, para. 92. See also Appellate Body Report, *EC – Poultry (1998)*, para. 83; Appellate Body Report, *Canada – Dairy (1999)*, para. 139; and Appellate Body Report, *US – Gambling (2005)*, para. 196.

4.6 Remedies for Breach

The DSU provides for three types of remedy for breach of WTO law: one final remedy, namely, the withdrawal (or modification) of the WTO-inconsistent measure; and two temporary remedies which can be applied pending the withdrawal (or modification) of the WTO-inconsistent measure, namely, compensation *and* suspension of concessions or other obligations (commonly referred to as 'retaliation'). The DSU makes clear that compensation and/or the suspension of concessions or other obligations are *not* alternative remedies, which Members may want to apply *instead of* withdrawing (or modifying) the WTO-inconsistent measure. Article 22.1 of the DSU explicitly states:

> Compensation and the suspension of concessions or other obligations are *temporary measures* available in the event that the recommendations and rulings are not implemented within a reasonable period of time. However, neither compensation nor the suspension of concessions or other obligations is preferred to full implementation of a recommendation to bring a measure into conformity with the covered agreements.[193]

This subsection discusses in turn the final remedy and the two temporary remedies for breach of WTO law. It also briefly examines whether other types of remedy may be available.

4.6.1 Withdrawal of the WTO-Inconsistent Measure

Article 3.7, fourth sentence, of the DSU states:

> In the absence of a mutually agreed solution, the first objective of the dispute settlement mechanism is usually to secure the withdrawal of the measures concerned if these are found to be inconsistent with the provisions of any of the covered agreements.

Furthermore, Article 3.7, fifth sentence, suggests that the withdrawal of the WTO-inconsistent measure should normally be 'immediate'.[194] Article 19.1 of the DSU provides:

> Where a panel or the Appellate Body concludes that a measure is inconsistent with a covered agreement, it shall recommend that the Member concerned bring the measure into conformity with that agreement.

Such a recommendation, once adopted by the DSB, is legally binding on the Member concerned.[195] With regard to recommendations and rulings adopted by the DSB, Article 21.1 of the DSU provides that:

> *Prompt* compliance with recommendations or rulings of the DSB is essential in order to ensure effective resolution of disputes to the benefit of all Members.[196]

193 Emphasis added.

194 As discussed below, Article 3.7 provides: 'The provision of compensation should be resorted to only if the *immediate* withdrawal of the measure is impracticable.' Emphasis added.

195 On the adoption of recommendations and rulings of panel reports, see below, pp. 277–8.

196 Emphasis added.

It is pertinent to note two observations with regard to the obligations set out in Articles 3.7 and 21.1 of the DSU. First, while Article 3.7 of the DSU refers to the withdrawal of the measure found to be WTO-inconsistent, the withdrawal or the modification of the WTO-inconsistent aspects or elements of such a measure usually suffices to bring the measure into conformity with WTO law pursuant to the recommendations or rulings of the DSB.[197] Second, while prompt or immediate compliance with the DSB recommendations and rulings, i.e. prompt or immediate withdrawal or modification of the WTO-inconsistent measure, is essential to the effective functioning of the WTO and is the primary obligation, Article 21.3 of the DSU provides that if it is impracticable to comply immediately with the recommendations and rulings, and this may often be the case, the Member concerned has a reasonable period of time in which to do so. The 'reasonable period of time for implementation' may be: (1) agreed on by the parties to the dispute; or (2) determined through binding arbitration at the request of either party.[198] In most cases – in particular in recent years – the parties to the dispute succeed in agreeing on what constitutes a 'reasonable period of time for implementation'.[199] The period agreed on by the parties ranges from two months and seven days (*Dominican Republic – Bag and Fabric Safeguards (2012)*) to twenty-four months (*Dominican Republic – Import and Sales of Cigarettes (2005)*).[200] In twenty-nine cases to date, the 'reasonable period of time for implementation' was decided through binding arbitration under Article 21.3(c) of the DSU.[201] The latter provision states:

> In such arbitration, a guideline for the arbitrator should be that the reasonable period of time to implement panel or Appellate Body recommendations should not exceed 15 months from the date of adoption of a panel or Appellate Body report. However, that time may be shorter or longer, depending upon the particular circumstances.

Since the Article 21.3(c) arbitration in *EC – Hormones (1998)*, it is generally accepted and clearly reflected in practice, that the fifteen-month period mentioned in Article 21.3(c) of the DSU is a mere guideline for the arbitrator and that it is neither an '*outer* limit' nor, of course, *a floor* or '*inner* limit' for a 'reasonable period of time for implementation'.[202] In *EC – Hormones (1998)*, the arbitrator ruled that the 'reasonable period of time for implementation', as determined under Article 21.3(c), should be:

> the shortest period possible within the legal system of the Member to implement the recommendations and rulings of the DSB.[203]

197 While it is appropriate for panels and the Appellate Body to rule on the WTO consistency of measures that are no longer in force (see above, p. 171), it is not 'appropriate' for them to recommend that a measure that is no longer in force be brought into conformity. See Appellate Body Report, *Dominican Republic – Import and Sale of Cigarettes (2005)*, para. 129.

198 See Article 21.3(b) and (c) of the DSU. See also below, pp. 285–6.

199 In 83 cases to date, the parties were able to agree under Article 21.3(b) on the reasonable period of time for implementation. See www.worldtradelaw.net/databases/implementationprovision.php.

200 See *ibid.*

201 See *ibid.* On the appointment of an Article 21.3(c) arbitrator and the Article 21.3(c) arbitration proceeding, see below, pp. 285–6.

202 See e.g. Award of the Arbitrator, *US – Hot-Rolled Steel (Article 21.3 (c)) (2002)*, para. 25.

203 Award of the Arbitrator, *EC – Hormones (Article 21.3 (c)) (1998)*, para. 26.

While this has become the core rule in establishing the reasonable period of time for implementation, the arbitrator in *US – Gambling (2005)* stated:

> In my view, the determination of the 'shortest period possible for implementation' can, and must, also take due account of the two principles that are expressly mentioned in Article 21 of the DSU, namely reasonableness and the need for prompt compliance. Moreover, as differences in previous awards involving legislative implementation by the United States have shown, and as the text of Article 21.3(c) prescribes, each arbitrator must take account of 'particular circumstances' relevant to the case at hand.[204]

Moreover, as the arbitrator in *Korea – Alcoholic Beverages (1999)* ruled, a Member is not required to utilise extraordinary legislative procedures, rather than the normal procedure, in order to shorten the period of implementation.[205] In *EC – Hormones (1998)*, the arbitrator also noted that, when implementation does not require changes in legislation but can be effected by administrative means, the reasonable period of time 'should be considerably less than 15 months'.[206] In *Canada – Pharmaceutical Patents (2000)*, the arbitrator listed a number of other 'particular circumstances' that can influence what the shortest period possible for implementation may be within the legal system of the implementing Member. Apart from the means of implementation (legislative or administrative), this arbitrator referred to the complexity of the proposed implementation[207] and the legally binding, as opposed to the discretionary, nature of the component steps in the process leading to implementation.[208] The domestic political or economic situation in the Member concerned is not relevant in determining the 'reasonable period of time for implementation'.[209] The absence of a political majority to adopt implementing measures or economic hardship resulting from implementation, e.g., are not taken into consideration by the arbitrator in determining the 'reasonable period of time for implementation'.[210] The implementing Member bears the burden of proof that the period of time it seeks is a *reasonable* period of time within the meaning of Article 21.3 of the DSU.[211]

204 Award of the Arbitrator, *US – Gambling (Article 21.3(c)) (2005)*, para. 44.

205 See Award of the Arbitrator, *Korea – Alcoholic Beverages (Article 21.3(c)) (1999)*, para. 42. In *Canada – Autos (2000)*, the arbitrator held that the question whether a Member could take 'extraordinary action' to bring about compliance was not even relevant to the determination of the reasonable period of time. See Award of the Arbitrator, *Canada – Autos (Article 21.3(c)) (2000)*, para. 53.

206 See Award of the Arbitrator, *EC – Hormones (Article 21.3(c)) (1998)*, para. 25. See also e.g. Award of the Arbitrator, *EC – Chicken Cuts (Article 21.3(c)) (2006)*, para. 67.

207 Note that the complexity of the proposed implementation must be a 'particular circumstance'. On this ground, a number of arbitrators have refused to accept the 'complexity' argument made by the respondent. See e.g. Award of the Arbitrator, *US – Offset Act (Byrd Amendment) (Article 21.3(c)) (2003)*, paras. 60–1; and Award of the Arbitrator, *EC – Export Subsidies on Sugar (Article 21.3(c)) (2005)*, para. 88.

208 See Award of the Arbitrator, *Canada – Pharmaceutical Patents (Article 21.3(c)) (2000)*, paras. 48–52.

209 With regard to developing-country Members, see, however, Article 21.2 of the DSU, discussed below, p. 202.

210 Note, however, that the arbitrator in *Chile – Price Band System (2002)* considered that the unique role and *impact* of the Price Band System on Chilean society was a relevant factor in his determination of the reasonable period of time for implementation. See Award of the Arbitrator, *Chile – Price Band System (Article 21.3(c)) (2003)*, para. 48.

211 See Award of the Arbitrator, *US – Countervailing Measures (2015)*, para. 3.7; and Award of the Arbitrator, *EC – Export Subsidies on Sugar (Article 21.3(c)) (2005)*, para. 59. The original complainant may be expected to point at the economic harm suffered by its exporters. However, the arbitrator in *US – Offset Act (Byrd Amendment) (Article 21.3(c)) (2003)* explicitly stated that such harm did not, and could not, impact on what the reasonable period of time for implementation was. See Award of the Arbitrator, *US – Offset Act (Byrd Amendment) (Article 21.3(c)) (2003)*, para. 79.

Article 21.2 of the DSU requires that, in determining the 'reasonable period of time for implementation', particular attention should be paid to matters affecting the interests of developing-country Members.[212] On that legal basis, the arbitrator in *Indonesia – Autos (1998)* ruled:

> Indonesia is not only a developing country; it is a developing country that is currently in a dire economic and financial situation. Indonesia itself states that its economy is 'near collapse'. In these very particular circumstances, I consider it appropriate to give full weight to matters affecting the interests of Indonesia as a developing country pursuant to the provisions of Article 21.2 of the DSU. I, therefore, conclude that an additional period of six months over and above the six-month period required for the completion of Indonesia's domestic rule-making process constitutes a reasonable period of time for implementation of the recommendations and rulings of the DSB in this case.[213]

It is clear that the mere fact that either of the parties to a dispute is a developing-country Member does not *ipso facto* affect the determination of the period of time for implementation unless such party is able to substantiate why the otherwise normal period for implementation should cause it hardship.[214]

Finally, it should be emphasised that the mandate of an Article 21.3(c) arbitrator relates to determining the 'reasonable period of time for implementation'.[215] As the arbitrator in *US – COOL (2012)* stated:

> Like previous arbitrators, I consider that my mandate relates to the *time* by when the implementing Member must achieve compliance, not to the *manner* in which that Member achieves compliance ... Yet, *when* a Member must comply cannot be determined in isolation from the means used for implementation. In order 'to determine *when* a Member must comply, it may be necessary to consider *how* a Member proposes to do so'. Thus, the means of implementation that are available to the Member concerned, and that this Member intends to use, are relevant for a determination under Article 21.3(c).

The arbitrator in *US – Countervailing Measures (China) (2015)*, referring to earlier awards, recalled that the implementing Member has a measure of discretion in choosing the means of implementation that it deems most appropriate.[216] However, the implementing Member does not have an unfettered right to choose any method of implementation. Rather, the arbitrator:

> must consider, in particular, 'whether the implementing action falls within the range of permissible actions that can be taken in order to implement the DSB's recommendations and rulings'.[217]

212 Note that Article 21.2 directs an arbitrator to pay attention to matters affecting the interests of *both* complaining and implementing developing-country Members. See Award of the Arbitrator, *EC – Export Subsidies on Sugar (Article 21.3(c)) (2005)*, para. 99.

213 Award of the Arbitrator, *Indonesia – Autos (Article 21.3(c)) (1998)*, para. 24. However, note that 'criteria' for the determination of 'the reasonable period of time' are not 'qualitatively' different for developed and for developing-country Members. See Award of the Arbitrator, *Chile – Alcoholic Beverages (Article 21.3(c)) (2000)*, para. 45.

214 See e.g. Award of the Arbitrator, *US – Offset Act (Byrd Amendment) (Article 21.3(c)) (2003)*, para. 81; and Award of the Arbitrator, *EC – Tariff Preferences (Article 21.3(c)) (2004)*, para. 59.

215 See Award of the Arbitrator, *Korea – Alcoholic Beverages (Article 21.3(c)) (1999)*, para. 45.

216 See Award of the Arbitrator, *US – Countervailing Measures (Article 21.3(c)) (2015)*, para. 3.3.

217 *Ibid.* See also Award of the Arbitrator, *US – COOL (Article 21.3(c)) (2012)*, para. 69.

The means of implementation chosen must be apt in form, nature and content to effect compliance and should otherwise be consistent with the covered agreements.[218]

It is also worthwhile to note that the means of implementation is a relevant consideration for determining the reasonable period of time.[219] However, at the same time, there are certain limitations on the mandate of the arbitrator under Article 21.3(c). In particular, it is not for the arbitrator to determine the consistency of the measure taken to comply with the covered agreements. Rather, if this question is raised, it is to be answered by a compliance panel pursuant to Article 21.5 of the DSU.[220]

To date, the 'reasonable period of time for implementation' determined through arbitration ranges between six months (in *Canada – Pharmaceutical Patents (2000)*) and fifteen months and one week (in *EC – Bananas III (1997)*).[221] The average time granted for implementation as a 'reasonable period' under Article 21.3 arbitrations to date is just under twelve months.[222] Members should make good use of the time following an adverse ruling to bring about compliance as the obligation to implement starts at the moment of the adoption of the report by the DSB, and *not* at the moment of the arbitrator's award setting the reasonable period of time.

Note that, in nine out of ten disputes in which the responding party had to bring its challenged measure or legislation into conformity with WTO law, it has done so. In almost all cases, therefore, the responding party implements the recommendations and rulings adopted by the DSB. The media and academia tend to focus on disputes in which there is no, or only partial, implementation, as was, or is, the case in, e.g., *EC – Bananas III (1997), EC – Hormones (1998), US – FSC (2000), US – Hot-Rolled Steel (2001), US – Offset Act (Byrd Amendment) (2003), EC – Approval and Marketing of Biotech Products (2006), US – Zeroing (EC) (2006)* and *US – Upland Cotton (2008).*[223] However, the overall record of compliance with the recommendations and rulings adopted by the DSB is quite positive and encouraging. One can conclude on the basis of this record of compliance that the WTO dispute settlement system 'works'.

As discussed in detail below, any disagreement as to (1) the existence of measures taken to comply with the recommendations and rulings or (2) the

218 See *ibid.* See also Award of the Arbitrator, *China – GOES (Article 21.3(c))*, para 3.2; and Award of the Arbitrator, *Colombia – Ports of Entry (Article 21.3(c))*, para. 64.

219 See Award of the Arbitrator, *Japan – DRAMs (Korea) (Article 21.3(c)) (2008)*, para. 26; and Award of the Arbitrator, *China – GOES (Article 21.3(c)) (2013)*, para. 3.2.

220 See Award of the Arbitrator, *US – Countervailing Measures (Article 21.3(c)) (2015)*, para. 3.4.

221 See Award of the Arbitrator, *Canada – Pharmaceutical Patents (Article 21.3(c)) (2000)*, paras. 62–4; and Award of the Arbitrator, *EC – Bananas III (Article 21.3(c)) (1998)*, paras. 18–20.

222 See www.worldtradelaw.net/databases/implementaverage.php.

223 In some of these cases, the DSB's recommendations and rulings have been implemented, but *US – Section 110(5) Copyright Act (2000), US – Hot-Rolled Steel (2001), US – Section 211 Appropriations Act (2002)* and *EC – Approval and Marketing of Biotech Products (2006)* are examples of non-compliance many years after the end of the reasonable period of time for implementation. These cases remain under DSB surveillance.

WTO consistency of these measures, shall be settled through proceedings which are provided for in Article 21.5 of the DSU (therefore commonly referred to as Article 21.5 'compliance' proceedings which are discussed in detail below).[224]

4.6.2 Compensation

As noted above, only the withdrawal (or modification) of the WTO-inconsistent measure constitutes a final remedy for breach of WTO law.[225] However, if a Member has not withdrawn or modified the WTO-inconsistent measure by the end of the 'reasonable period of time for implementation', the DSU provides for the possibility of recourse to *temporary* remedies, namely: (1) compensation; or (2) suspension of concessions or other obligations, commonly referred to as 'retaliation'. This subsection briefly deals with the less important – and hardly used – of the two temporary remedies, namely, compensation. Compensation within the meaning of Article 22 of the DSU is: (1) voluntary, i.e. the complainant is free to accept or reject compensation; and (2) forward looking, i.e. the compensation concerns only the nullification or impairment (i.e. the harm) that will be suffered in the future. Compensation must be consistent with the covered agreements and must therefore, *inter alia*, be granted on an MFN treatment basis.[226] To date, parties have been able to agree on compensation in very few cases. In *Japan – Alcoholic Beverages II (1996)*, the parties agreed on compensation which took the form of temporary, additional market access concessions for certain products of export interest to the original complainants.

4.6.3 Retaliation

As is explicitly stated in Article 3.7 of the DSU, the suspension of concessions or other obligations, commonly referred to as 'retaliation', is a measure of 'last resort'. When the 'reasonable period of time for implementation' has expired and the parties have not been able to agree on compensation, the original complaining party may request authorisation from the DSB to retaliate against the offending party by suspending concessions or other obligations with respect to that offending party. Since the DSB decides on such a request by reverse consensus, the granting of authorisation is quasi-automatic.[227] To date, requests for authorisation to retaliate were filed in forty requests in twenty-three cases.[228] Note, however, that these requests were often not further pursued.[229]

With regard to the concessions or other obligations that may be suspended, Article 22.3 of the DSU provides that: (1) the complaining party should first seek to suspend concessions or other obligations with respect to the same sector(s) as

224 See below, pp. 287–9. 225 See above, p. 200. 226 On MFN treatment, see below, p. 307.
227 See below, pp. 210, 216, 272 and 289–90.
228 See www.worldtradelaw.net/databases/retaliationrequests.php. In cases with multiple complainants, there may be multiple requests. See e.g. *US – Offset Act (Byrd Amendment) (2003)* in which there were eight separate requests for authorisation.
229 See below, p. 206.

that in which a violation was found; (2) if that is not practicable or effective, the complaining party may seek to suspend concessions or other obligations in other sectors under the same agreement; and (3) if also that is not practicable or effective, and circumstances are serious enough, the complaining party may seek to suspend concessions or other obligations under another covered agreement.[230] In other words, if the violation of WTO law concerns an obligation regarding trade in goods, or regarding trade in financial services, or regarding the protection of patents, suspension of concessions or other obligations should first be sought in the *same* sector. If this is not 'practicable' or 'effective', then suspension may be sought in another sector or under another agreement. The latter is known as 'cross-retaliation'. To date, cross-retaliation has been requested, and authorised, only a few times. In *EC – Bananas III (1997)*, Ecuador requested, and the DSB authorised, retaliation under an agreement (the *TRIPS Agreement*) other than the agreements under which WTO inconsistencies were found in that dispute (the GATT 1994 and the GATS).[231] With regard to the level of retaliation, Article 22.4 of the DSU provides:

> The level of the suspension of concessions or other obligations authorized by the DSB shall be equivalent to the level of the nullification or impairment.

While the purpose of retaliation measures is to induce compliance, the arbitrators in *EC – Bananas III (US) (Article 22.6 – EC) (1999)* found that nothing in Article 22 of the DSU could be read as a justification for retaliation measures 'of a *punitive* nature'.[232] The DSB can only authorise retaliation measures *equivalent* to the level of nullification or impairment. Determining the level of the nullification or impairment resulting from the WTO-inconsistent measure(s) may, however, be a difficult and contentious exercise. Pursuant to Article 22.6 of the DSU, disputes between the parties on the level of nullification or impairment, and thus on the appropriate level of retaliation, are to be resolved through arbitration by the original panel.[233]

To date, Article 22.6 arbitrators have determined the appropriate level of retaliation in ten cases.[234] Typically, the Article 22.6 arbitrators determine the appropriate level of retaliation, to be (considerably) lower than the level of retaliation requested. An extreme example of this was *US – Gambling (2005)* in which Antigua and Barbuda requested retaliation in the amount of US$3,443 million per year, and the Article 22.6 arbitrators set the appropriate level of retaliation at US$21 million per year.[235] The level of retaliation requested has ranged from less than €1.3 million per

230 For definitions of, e.g., the concept of 'sectors', and further rules, see Article 22.3(d)–(g) of the DSU.

231 See Dispute Settlement Body, *Minutes of Meeting held on 18 May 2000*, WT/DSB/M/80, dated 26 June 2000, paras. 48–58.

232 Decision by the Arbitrators, *EC – Bananas III (US) (Article 22.6 – EC) (1999)*, para. 6.3.

233 On the procedural aspects of these Article 22.6 arbitration proceedings, see below, p. 290.

234 See www.worldtradelaw.net/databases/suspensionawards.php.

235 See www.worldtradelaw.net/databases/retaliationrequests.php and www.worldtradelaw.net/databases/suspensionawards.php.

year in *US – Section 110(5) Copyright Act (2000)* to US$12 billion per year in *US – Large Civil Aircraft (2nd complaint) (2012)*.[236] In recent arbitrations under Article 22.6 of the DSU, the level of retaliation in *US – COOL (2015)* was set for Canada at C$1,055 million annually, and for Mexico at US$228 million annually.[237]

To date, the DSB has authorised retaliation measures in ten cases.[238] However, in only four of these cases did the complaining parties actually suspend concessions or other obligations.[239] Retaliation often takes the form of a drastic *increase* in the customs duties (e.g. an increase up to 100 per cent *ad valorem*) on selected products of export interest to the offending party. In *US – FSC (2000)*, however, the European Communities opted for retaliation measures on selected products consisting of an additional customs duty of 5 per cent, increased each month by 1 per cent up to a maximum of 17 per cent. Retaliation can also take the form of the suspension of 'obligations' rather than the suspension of tariff 'concessions'. For example, retaliation can consist of the non-protection of the intellectual property rights of products originating in the offending party.[240] It is clear that retaliation puts economic and political pressure on the offending party to comply with the recommendations and rulings. The producers of the products or services hit by the retaliation – typically not the beneficiaries of the WTO-inconsistent measure – will lobby energetically for the withdrawal or modification of the WTO-inconsistent measure. By strategically selecting the products, or services or IPRs of the offending party hit by the retaliation, the complaining party can maximise the economic pain inflicted and the political commotion generated.

Retaliation measures are by nature *trade destructive* and the complaining party imposing these measures is also negatively affected by them. In particular, for developing-country Members, applying retaliation measures is often not a genuine option. In *EC – Bananas III (1997)*, Ecuador was authorised to (cross-)retaliate for an amount of US$201.6 million per year but found it impossible to make use

236 Note that the request in *US – Section 110(5) Copyright Act (2000)* was not further pursued; and that the request in *US – Large Civil Aircraft (2nd complaint) (2012)* is pending.

237 Decisions of the Arbitrator, *US – COOL (Article 21.5 – Canada and Mexico (2015))*, para. 7.1.

238 The DSB authorised retaliatory measures in *EC – Bananas III (1997)* (US); *EC – Bananas (Ecuador)*; *EC – Hormones (1998)* (US and Canada); *Brazil – Aircraft (1999)* (Canada); *US – FSC (2000)* (EC); *Canada – Aircraft Credits and Guarantees (2002)* (Brazil); *US – Offset Act (Byrd Amendment) (2003)* (Brazil, Canada, Chile, EC, India, Japan, Korea and Mexico); *US – Upland Cotton (2005)* (Brazil); *US – Gambling (2005)*; and *US – COOL (Article 21.5 – Canada and Mexico (2015)*. See www.worldtradelaw.net/databases/suspensionawards.php. Note that, in *US – Section 110(5) Copyright Act (2000)*, the original complainant, the European Union, has not (to date) pursued its request for authorisation to retaliate. Also in *US – Gambling (2005)*, the original complainant, Antigua and Barbuda, did for many years not pursue its request for authorisation. However, at the DSB meeting of 28 January 2013, Antigua and Barbuda requested the DSB to authorise retaliation measures against the United States, and the DSB did so.

239 This was the case in *EC – Bananas III (1997)* (retaliation by the United States for an amount of US$191.4 million per year), in *EC – Hormones (1998)* (retaliation by the United States and Canada for an amount of US$116.8 million and C$11.3 million per year respectively), in *US – FSC (2000)* (retaliation by the European Communities for an amount of US$4,043 million per year) and in *US – Offset Act (Byrd Amendment) (2003)* (retaliation by the European Communities, Canada and Japan for an amount of US$27.8 million, US$11.2 million and US$52.1 million, respectively per year).

240 Such retaliation was authorised, e.g. in *EC – Bananas III (1997)* (retaliation by Ecuador against the European Communities); and in *US – Upland Cotton (2005)* (retaliation by Brazil against the United States). In neither case, however, was this retaliation actually put into effect.

of this possibility without causing severe harm to its own economy. This and later cases, especially cases involving developing-country complainants, have given rise to doubts as to the effectiveness of retaliation as a (temporary) remedy for breach of WTO law. However, in *EC – Bananas III (1997)* and in *US – FSC (2000)*, the retaliation measures imposed by the United States on the European Communities and imposed by the European Communities on the United States respectively, have arguably led to some degree of compliance with the recommendations and rulings in those disputes.[241]

It is debated whether a Member authorised to retaliate may periodically (e.g. every six months) rotate, i.e. change, the products or services on which the retaliation measures are applied. This issue, commonly referred to as the 'carousel retaliation', arose because US legislation foresees a periodic shift in the focus of retaliation measures to maximise their impact. It appears that rotation of the products or services on which the retaliation measures are applied would 'inflict' harm on a wider section of producers and exporters of the Member concerned and thus add to the pressure on that Member to comply with WTO law. It has been argued, however, that a periodic rotation in the products and services 'hit' by the retaliation measure cannot be allowed since it would result in retaliation measures going beyond the level of nullification or impairment caused.

4.6.4 Other Remedies

Under customary international law, a breach of an international obligation leads to responsibility entailing certain legal consequences. The first legal consequence of international responsibility is the obligation to cease the illegal conduct.[242] According to the International Law Commission's *Articles on Responsibility of States for Internationally Wrongful Acts*, the injured State is furthermore entitled to claim 'full reparation' in the form of: (1) restitution in kind; (2) compensation; (3) satisfaction; and (4) assurances and guarantees of non-repetition.[243] Restitution in kind means that the wrongdoing State has to re-establish the situation that existed before the illegal act was committed.[244] If damage is not made good by restitution, the State responsible for the internationally wrongful act is under an obligation to compensate for the damage caused by this act.[245] Compensation covers any economically assessable damage suffered by the injured State and may include interest, and also, under certain circumstances, lost profits.[246] The DSU does not contain a rule providing for the compensation

241 Note that, in both cases, the implementing measures taken 'under pressure' from retaliation were later challenged and found to be WTO-inconsistent. See *US – FSC (Article 21.5 – EC II) (2006)*; and *EC – Bananas III (Article 21.5 – Ecuador II)/EC – Bananas III (Article 21.5 – US) (2008)*. However, in both disputes, eventually, the WTO-inconsistent measures were withdrawn or modified to the satisfaction of the complainants.

242 See Article 30 of the *Articles on Responsibility of States for Internationally Wrongful Acts 2001*, in *Yearbook of the International Law Commission*, 2001, Volume II (Part Two). Text reproduced as it appears in the annex to General Assembly resolution 56/83 of 12 December 2001, and corrected by document A/56/49(Vol.I)/Corr.4.

243 See *ibid.*, Article 34. 244 See *ibid.*, Article 35.

245 See *ibid.*, Article 36(a). 246 See *ibid.*, Article 36(b).

of damage suffered.[247] However, the question is whether the rules of customary international law on State responsibility, as reflected in the International Law Commission's *Articles on Responsibility of States for Internationally Wrongful Acts*, apply to breaches of WTO law. Are the only possible remedies for breach of WTO law the remedies explicitly provided for in the provisions of the DSU quoted and discussed above? Or, in the absence of a specific rule in the DSU excluding compensation of damage suffered, is the customary international law rule on compensation applicable? Note that Article 55 of the *Articles on Responsibility of States for Internationally Wrongful Acts*, entitled 'Lex Specialis', states:

> These articles do not apply where and to the extent that the conditions for the existence of an internationally wrongful act or the content or implementation of the international responsibility of a State are governed by special rules of international law.

By providing a detailed set of rules regarding the legal consequences of a breach of WTO law, the DSU has contracted out of customary international law on State responsibility. The customary international law rule on compensation for damage suffered therefore does not apply.[248] This issue is part of the larger issue of the relationship between WTO law and other international law, discussed in Chapter 1.[249]

While controversial, in very specific circumstances, repayment of sums illegally received could constitute a remedy for breach of WTO law. Article 4.7 of the *SCM Agreement* states that, if a measure is found to be a prohibited subsidy, the panel shall recommend that the subsidising Member withdraw the subsidy without delay. As discussed in Chapter 12, the panel in *Australia – Automotive Leather II (Article 21.5 – US) (2000)* concluded that, in the circumstances of that case, repayment is necessary in order to 'withdraw' the prohibited subsidies found to exist.[250] However, the panel's ruling in *Australia – Automotive Leather (Article 21.5 – US) (2000)* that, at least with regard to prohibited subsidies, the DSU not only provides for a 'prospective' but also for a 'retrospective' remedy was criticised by many WTO Members, including *both* parties to this dispute.[251]

Also note that following the Article 22.6 arbitration in *US – Upland Cotton (Article 21.5 – Brazil) (2008)*, the United States and Brazil reached in October 2014 an agreement to settle their dispute over US subsidies to cotton producers. Under this agreement, the United States set new limits on its export credit programme for cotton and made a one-time payment of US$300 million to the Brazilian cotton industry, while Brazil dropped the case against the United States pending at the WTO, gave up its right to impose retaliation measures which the

247 Compensation under Article 22 of the DSU concerns only damages suffered after the reasonable period of time for implementation. See above, p. 204.

248 See also above, p. 61. 249 See above, pp. 60–1.

250 See Panel Report, *Australia – Automotive Leather II (Article 21.5 – US) (2000)*, para. 6.48.

251 The panel report was not appealed because the parties to this dispute, the United States and Australia, had agreed at the outset of the Article 21.5 'compliance' proceeding not to appeal the panel report.

DSB had authorized in 2009 and agreed to a 'peace clause' under which it will not challenge the US cotton subsidy programmes until September 2018, and not challenge the US export credit programme as long as the United States does not exceed the new limits set.

5 INSTITUTIONS OF WTO DISPUTE SETTLEMENT

Among the institutions involved in WTO dispute settlement, one can distinguish between *political institutions*, such as the Dispute Settlement Body, and *judicial-type institutions*, such as the *ad hoc* dispute settlement panels and the standing Appellate Body. While the WTO has entrusted the adjudication of disputes to panels and the Appellate Body, the Dispute Settlement Body continues to play an active role in the WTO dispute settlement system. Other institutions as well as persons also contribute to the functioning of this system. This section deals in turn with: (1) the Dispute Settlement Body; (2) panels; and (3) the Appellate Body. In conclusion, this section also briefly discusses the other institutions, bodies and persons involved in WTO dispute settlement.

5.1 Dispute Settlement Body

As already noted in Chapter 2, the Dispute Settlement Body, commonly referred to as the DSB, is an emanation, or an alter ego, of the WTO's General Council.[252] Article IV:3 of the *WTO Agreement* states, in the relevant part:

> The General Council shall convene as appropriate to discharge the responsibilities of the Dispute Settlement Body provided for in the Dispute Settlement Understanding. The Dispute Settlement Body may have its own chairman and shall establish such rules of procedure as it deems necessary for the fulfilment of those responsibilities.

When the General Council administers the WTO dispute settlement system, it convenes and acts as the DSB. Like the General Council, the DSB is composed of diplomats representing all WTO Members.[253] With respect to the functions of the DSB, Article 2.1 of the DSU broadly defines these functions as the *administration* of the dispute settlement system and then specifies them by stating:

> Accordingly, the DSB shall have the authority to establish panels, adopt panel and Appellate Body reports, maintain surveillance of implementation of rulings and recommendations, and authorize suspension of concessions and other obligations under the covered agreements.

252 See above, p. 132.
253 See Article IV:2 of the *WTO Agreement*. Where the DSB administers the dispute settlement provisions of a WTO plurilateral trade agreement, only those WTO Members that are parties to that agreement may participate in the decisions or actions taken by the DSB with respect to that dispute. See Article 2.1 of the DSU.

However, the administration of the dispute settlement system is not limited to these functions. It also includes, e.g., the appointment of the Members of the Appellate Body,[254] and the adoption of the rules of conduct for WTO dispute settlement.[255] Article 2.4 of the DSU stipulates that, where the DSU provides for the DSB to take a decision, such a decision is always taken by consensus.[256] It is important to note, however, that, for some key decisions, such as: (1) the decision on the establishment of panels; (2) the adoption of panel and Appellate Body reports; and (3) the authorisation of suspension of concession and other obligations, the consensus requirement is in fact a 'reverse' or 'negative' consensus requirement.[257] With respect to the DSB's decision to adopt an Appellate Body report, e.g., Article 17.14 of the DSU states, in relevant part:

> An Appellate Body report shall be adopted by the DSB ... unless the DSB decides by consensus not to adopt the Appellate Body report within 30 days following its circulation to the Members.

The 'reverse' consensus requirement means that the DSB is deemed to have taken a decision unless there is a consensus among WTO Members *not* to take that decision. Since there will usually be at least one Member with a strong interest in the establishment of a panel, it is unlikely that there will be a consensus in the DSB *not* to adopt the panel and/or Appellate Body reports or the authorisation to suspend concessions.[258] As a result, decision-making by the DSB on these matters is, for all practical purposes, automatic and a matter of course. Furthermore, it should be noted that the DSU provides for time limits within which decisions on these matters must be taken.[259] The DSB meets as often as necessary to carry out its functions within the time frames provided in the DSU. In practice, the DSB holds one regular meeting per month and, in addition, special meetings when the need for a meeting arises. In 2016, the DSB met twenty times.[260] By way of example, consider the agenda of the DSB meeting of 26 September 2016, as shown in Figure 3.1.

Meetings of the DSB are always held in Geneva, usually last around two hours and are well attended. With minor deviations regarding Observers (Chapter IV) and the Chair (Chapter V), the Rules of Procedure for the General Council apply

254 See below, p. 235. 255 See below, p. 214.

256 Footnote 1 to the DSU states: 'The DSB shall be deemed to have decided by consensus on a matter submitted for its consideration, if no Member, present at the meeting of the DSB when the decision is taken, formally objects to the proposed decision.' On decision-making by consensus, see also above, pp. 152–6.

257 See Articles 6.1, 16.4, 17.14 and 22.6 of the DSU. Other decisions of the DSB, such as the appointment of the Members of the Appellate Body, are taken by 'normal' consensus. Note, however, that, with regard to the 'decision' to initiate the information-gathering procedure under Annex V to the *SCM Agreement*, the Appellate Body ruled that paragraph 2 of Annex V imposes 'an obligation on the DSB to initiate an Annex V procedure upon request', and that such DSB action 'occurs automatically when there is a request for initiation of an Annex V procedure and the DSB establishes a panel'. See Appellate Body Report, *US – Large Civil Aircraft (2nd complaint) (2012)*, para. 531.

258 Note, however, that, in very exceptional circumstances, it is possible that no Member puts the adoption of the report on the agenda of the DSB and that the report therefore remains unadopted. This happened with the Panel Report, *EC – Bananas III (Article 21.5 – EC)*, circulated on 12 April 1999.

259 e.g., the decision to adopt an Appellate Body report shall be taken within thirty days following its circulation to the Members (see Article 17.14 of the DSU). If there is no meeting of the DSB scheduled during this period, such a meeting shall be held for this purpose (see fn. 8 to the DSU).

260 This includes two informal meetings held in September and October 2016.

PROPOSED AGENDA

1. **SURVEILLANCE OF IMPLEMENTATION OF RECOMMENDATIONS ADOPTED BY THE DSB**

   A. UNITED STATES – ANTI-DUMPING MEASURES ON CERTAIN HOT-ROLLED STEEL PRODUCTS FROM JAPAN: STATUS REPORT BY THE UNITED STATES (WT/DS184/15/ADD.164)

   B. UNITED STATES – SECTION 110(5) OF THE US COPYRIGHT ACT: STATUS REPORT BY THE UNITED STATES (WT/DS160/24/ADD.139)

   C. EUROPEAN COMMUNITIES – MEASURES AFFECTING THE APPROVAL AND MARKETING OF BIOTECH PRODUCTS: STATUS REPORT BY THE EUROPEAN UNION (WT/DS291/37/ADD.102)

2. **UNITED STATES – CONTINUED DUMPING AND SUBSIDY OFFSET ACT OF 2000: IMPLEMENTATION OF THE RECOMMENDATIONS ADOPTED BY THE DSB**

   A. STATEMENTS BY THE EUROPEAN UNION AND JAPAN

3. **CHINA – CERTAIN MEASURES AFFECTING ELECTRONIC PAYMENT SERVICES**

   A. STATEMENT BY THE UNITED STATES

4. **UNITED STATES – COUNTERVAILING MEASURES ON CERTAIN HOT-ROLLED CARBON STEEL FLAT PRODUCTS FROM INDIA**

   A. STATEMENT BY INDIA

5. **INDIA – MEASURES CONCERNING THE IMPORTATION OF CERTAIN AGRICULTURAL PRODUCTS**

   A. STATEMENT BY THE UNITED STATES

6. **COLOMBIA – MEASURES CONCERNING IMPORTED SPIRITS**

   A. REQUEST FOR THE ESTABLISHMENT OF A PANEL BY THE EUROPEAN UNION (WT/DS502/6)

7. **RUSSIAN FEDERATION – MEASURES ON THE IMPORTATION OF LIVE PIGS, PORK AND OTHER PIG PRODUCTS FROM THE EUROPEAN UNION**

   A. REPORT OF THE PANEL (WT/DS475/R AND WT/DS475/R/ADD.1)

8. **RUSSIA – TARIFF TREATMENT OF CERTAIN AGRICULTURAL AND MANUFACTURING PRODUCTS**

   A. REPORT OF THE PANEL (WT/DS485/R; WT/DS485/R/CORR.1; WT/ DS485/R/CORR.2 AND WT/DS485/R/ADD.1)

9. **UNITED STATES – ANTI-DUMPING AND COUNTERVAILING MEASURES ON LARGE RESIDENTIAL WASHERS FROM KOREA**

   A. REPORT OF THE APPELLATE BODY (WT/DS464/AB/R AND WT/DS464/AB/R/ADD. 1) AND REPORT OF THE PANEL (WT/DS464/R AND WT/DS464/R/ADD.1)

10. **APPELLATE BODY MATTERS**

OTHER BUSINESS

Figure 3.1 Agenda of the DSB meeting of 26 September 2016

to the meetings of the DSB.[261] In 2016, Ambassador Xavier Carim of South Africa served as Chair of the DSB.

Given that the DSB takes the core dispute settlement decisions referred to above by reverse consensus, the DSB's impact on, and influence over, consultations and

261 See WT/Air/4068, dated 18 January 2013.

adjudication by panels and the Appellate Body in specific disputes is very limited. The involvement of the DSB is largely a legacy of the past when, under the GATT 1947 trade dispute settlement was more diplomatic and political than judicial in nature.[262] Nevertheless, the involvement of the DSB in each major step of a dispute fulfils three useful purposes: (1) it keeps all WTO Members directly informed of WTO dispute settlement; (2) it ensures multilateral surveillance of the implementation of the DSB recommendations and rulings, thereby exerting pressure on the offending party to comply; and (3) it gives WTO Members a designated political forum in which issues arising from the use of the dispute settlement system can be debated.

5.2 Panels

The actual adjudication of disputes brought to the WTO is carried out, at the first-instance level, by *ad hoc* dispute settlement panels. This section discusses: (1) the establishment of panels; (2) the composition of panels; (3) the mandate of panels; and (4) panel reports.

5.2.1 Establishment of Panels

WTO dispute settlement panels are not standing bodies. They are *ad hoc* bodies established for the purpose of adjudicating a particular dispute and are dissolved once they have accomplished this task. According to Article 11 of the DSU the function of a panel is 'to assist the DSB in discharging its responsibilities'. The complainant requests the DSB to establish a panel. Such a 'request for the establishment of a panel', also referred to as a 'panel request', serves two essential purposes: (1) it defines the scope of the dispute and delimits the jurisdiction of the panel;[263] and (2) it serves the due process objective of notifying the respondent and third parties of the nature of the complainant's case.[264] The panel request is thus a document of critical importance in WTO dispute settlement.

Pursuant to Article 6.2 of the DSU, the panel request must be made in writing and must: (1) indicate *whether* consultations were held;[265] (2) identify the *specific* measures at issue; and (3) provide a brief summary of the legal basis of the complaint, i.e. of the claim(s) of WTO inconsistency, *sufficient* to present

262 See above, p. 167.

263 Note that, in the exceptional situation in which the parties agree to special terms of reference for the panel, the panel request does not define the scope of the dispute. On the jurisdiction of panels, i.e. their terms of reference, see below, section 5.2.3.

264 See Appellate Body Report, *EC and certain member States – Large Civil Aircraft (2011)*, paras. 639 and 786. See also e.g. Appellate Body Report, *US – Countervailing and Anti-Dumping Measures (China) (2014)*, para. 4.6; Appellate Body Report *EC – Chicken Cuts (2005)*, para. 155; Appellate Body Report, *US – Carbon Steel (2002)*, para. 126; and Appellate Body Report, *EC – Bananas III (1997)*, para. 142. Note that 'this due process objective is not constitutive of, but rather follows from, the proper establishment of a panel's jurisdiction'. See Appellate Body Report, *EC and certain member States – Large Civil Aircraft (2011)*, para. 640. See also Appellate Body Reports, *China – Raw Materials (2012)*, para. 233; and Appellate Body Report, *US – Countervailing and Anti-Dumping Measures (China) (2014)*, para. 4.7. For a finding that a panel request is inconsistent with Article 6.2 of the DSU, it is, therefore not required to show that the ability of the respondent was prejudiced by the 'vagueness' of the panel request. Even when the respondent was not prejudiced, the panel request may be found lacking.

265 On the relationship between the request for consultations and the panel request, see below, p. 267.

the problem clearly.[266] In light of the critical importance of the panel request, in particular for defining the scope of the dispute and delimiting the jurisdiction of the panel, it is not surprising that in many WTO disputes the question arises whether the panel request meets the second and third requirement of Article 6.2.

In *US – Countervailing and Anti-Dumping Measures (China) (2014)*, the Appellate Body, summarising its prior case law, stated that for a panel request to fulfil its functions of establishing a panel's jurisdiction and safeguard due process:

> a panel must determine whether the panel request is 'sufficiently clear' or 'sufficiently precise' on the basis of an 'objective examination' and careful scrutiny of the panel request, read as a whole, and in the light of the exact language used therein. Moreover, a panel must determine compliance with Article 6.2 'on the face' of the panel request as it existed at the time of filing.[267]

Note that the complainant's subsequent submissions and statements during the panel proceedings cannot 'cure' any defects in the panel request.[268] However, these submissions and statements can be consulted to the extent that they may confirm or clarify the meaning of the words used in the panel request.[269] Also, in considering the sufficiency of a panel request, a panel may take into account the 'attendant circumstances'.[270] A relevant attendant circumstance could be the fact that the WTO provision referred to in the panel request establishes not one single, but multiple obligations.[271] The consideration of attendant circumstances should, however, never go beyond the text and context of the panel request, because Article 6.2 required that the panel request must be examined 'on its face'.[272]

With regard to the question whether the 'specific measure at issue' was sufficiently identified in the panel request, the panel in *Canada – Wheat Exports and Grain Imports (2004)*, the panel noted that:

> the fact that a panel request does not specify by name, date of adoption, etc. the relevant law, regulation or other legal instrument to which a claim relates does not necessarily render the panel request inconsistent with Article 6.2, provided that the panel request contains sufficient information that effectively identifies the precise measures at issue.[273]

It should also be noted that, as the Appellate Body ruled in *EC – Chicken Cuts (2005)*, in order to be included in a panel's terms of reference, a measure must be *in existence* at the time of the establishment of the panel.[274]

266 Article 6.2 of the DSU. Note that Article 6.2 of the DSU also applies to requests for the establishment of a panel under Article 21.5 of the DSU, but it needs to be interpreted in the light thereof, and, as a result, its requirements need to be adapted to compliance proceedings. See Appellate Body Report, *US – FSC (Article 21.5 – EC II) (2006)*, paras. 52–69.

267 Appellate Body Report, *US – Countervailing and Anti-Dumping Measures (China) (2014)*, para. 4.7, referring in footnotes to relevant earlier Appellate Body reports.

268 See *ibid.* 269 See *ibid.*

270 See Appellate Body Report, *US – Carbon Steel (2002)*, paras. 128–33.

271 See Appellate Body Report, *Korea – Dairy (2000)*, para. 124.

272 See Appellate Body Report, *US – Countervailing and Anti-Dumping Measures (China) (2014)*, para. 4.43.

273 Panel Reports, *Canada – Wheat Exports and Grain Imports (2004)*, para. 6.10.

274 See Appellate Body Report, *EC – Chicken Cuts (2005)*, para. 156. For a particular 'exception' to this rule, i.e. when a subsequent measure does not change 'the essence of' the previous measure. See below, p. 221. See Appellate Body Report, *Chile – Price Band System (2002)*, para. 144.

In *EC and certain member States – Large Civil Aircraft (2011)*, the Appellate Body ruled with regard to the question whether the complainant, the United States, had sufficiently identified a French research and technology development (R&TD) funding measure in the panel request, that:

> [this] may ... depend on the extent to which that measure is specified in the public domain. We do not understand Article 6.2 to impose a standard that renders it more difficult to challenge a measure simply because information in the public domain concerning that measure is of a general character.[275]

Also, in *EC and certain member States – Large Civil Aircraft (2011)*, the Appellate Body considered that while it was uncontested that numerous references in the United States' panel request could be read as referring to individual provisions of Launch Aid/Member State Financing (LA/MSF), the same references could not 'be read simultaneously to refer to a *distinct* measure, consisting of an unwritten LA/MSF Programme'.[276] The Appellate Body thus found that the alleged LA/MSF Programme was not within the panel's jurisdiction 'because it was not identified in the request for the establishment of a panel, as required by Article 6.2 of the DSU'.[277] Note that the European Union did *not* raise before the Appellate Body the issue of whether the alleged LA/MSF Programme was within the jurisdiction of the panel. However, as the Appellate Body ruled in *US – Carbon Steel (2002)*, 'certain issues going to the jurisdiction of a panel are so fundamental that they may be considered at any stage in a proceedings'.[278] In *EC and certain member States – Large Civil Aircraft (2011)*, the Appellate Body deemed it necessary to consider this issue on its own motion.[279]

With regard to the requirement that the panel request must 'provide a brief summary of the legal basis of the complaint sufficient to present the problem clearly', the Appellate Body noted that the DSU demands only a *brief* summary of the legal basis of the complaint, i.e. a *brief* summary of the claim(s) of WTO inconsistency.[280] The summary must, however, be one 'sufficient to present the problem clearly'.[281] All the claims, but *not* the arguments,[282] must be specified sufficiently in the panel request.[283]

In order for a panel request to 'present the problem clearly', it must 'plainly connect the challenged measure(s) with the provision(s) of the covered agreements

275 Appellate Body Report, *EC and certain member States – Large Civil Aircraft (2011)*, para. 641.

276 *Ibid.*, para. 790. 277 *Ibid.*, para. 795.

278 Appellate Body Report, *US – Carbon Steel (2002)*, para. 123.

279 Appellate Body Report, *EC and certain member States – Large Civil Aircraft (2011)*, para. 791.

280 See Appellate Body Report, *Korea – Dairy (2000)*, para. 120.

281 *Ibid.*

282 The *arguments* are set out and progressively clarified in the written submissions to the panel and at the panel meetings.

283 See Appellate Body Report, *EC – Bananas III (1997)*, para. 143. Note that the Appellate Body ruled in *EC – Tariff Preferences (2004)* that in the particular circumstances of that case 'a complaining party challenging a measure taken pursuant to the Enabling Clause must allege more than mere inconsistency with Article I:1 of the GATT 1994, for to do only that would not convey the "legal basis of the complaint sufficient to present the problem clearly"'. See Appellate Body Report, *EC – Tariff Preferences (2004)*, para. 110.

claimed to have been infringed'.[284] In its brief summary of the legal basis of the complaint, a panel request:

> aims to explain succinctly *how* or *why* the measure at issue is considered by the complaining Member to be violating the WTO obligation in question.[285]

Note, however, a brief summary of the legal basis of the complaint is to be distinguished from arguments in support of a particular claim. A panel request must set out the claims, not the arguments.[286]

In *EC – Bananas III (1997)*, the Appellate Body found that, in view of the particular circumstances of that case, the listing of the articles of the agreements alleged to have been breached satisfied the minimum requirement of Article 6.2 of the DSU.[287] In *Korea – Dairy (2000)*, however, the Appellate Body noted that, where the articles listed establish not one single, distinct obligation but, rather, multiple obligations, the listing of articles of an agreement, in and of itself, *may* fall short of the standard of Article 6.2 of the DSU.[288] The Appellate Body held that the question of whether the mere listing of the articles suffices must be examined on a case-by-case basis.

In *US – Countervailing and Anti-Dumping Measures (China) (2014)*, the complainant, China, had made in its panel request only a general reference to Articles 10, 19 and 32 of the *SCM Agreement*, whereas its principal claim of inconsistency with the *SCM Agreement* concerned specifically Article 19.3 thereof. The respondent, the United States, argued before the panel that by making only a reference to the relevant articles of the *SCM Agreement* in general (rather than to specific provisions in the relevant articles), China failed to 'provide a brief summary of the legal basis of the complaint sufficient to present the problem clearly'. The panel disagreed with the United States and ruled that China's panel request was not inconsistent with Article 6.2 of the DSU. On appeal, the Appellate Body, upholding the panel's finding, ruled that:

> the references to Articles 10, 19, and 32 of the SCM Agreement, read in the context of the *narrative explanation*, allow for the identification of the relevant claims – Articles 10, 19.3, and 32.1 – relating to the measure at issue in this dispute.[289]

284 See Appellate Body Report, *US – Oil Country Tubular Goods Sunset Review (2005)*, para. 162. See also, e.g., Appellate Body Report, *US – Countervailing and Anti-Dumping Measures (China) (2014)*, para. 4.9. The panel request must make it clear which claim of WTO inconsistency pertained to which particular measure identified in the panel request, i.e. it must 'plainly connect' particular claims to particular measures. See Appellate Body Report, *China – Raw Materials (2012)*, para. 226.

285 Appellate Body Report, *EC – Selected Customs Matters (2006)*, para. 130. See also, e.g., Appellate Body Report, *US – Countervailing and Anti-Dumping Measures (China) (2014)*, para. 4.9.

286 See Appellate Body Report, *Korea – Dairy (2000)*, para. 139, referring to Appellate Body Report, *EC – Bananas III (1998)*, para. 141. See also, Appellate Body Report, *US – Countervailing and Anti-Dumping Measures (China) (2014)*, para. 4.8. The *arguments* are set out and progressively clarified in the written submissions to the panel and at the panel meetings. They are, together with the supporting evidence, put forth by a party in order to prove its claim(s).

287 See Appellate Body Report, *EC – Bananas III (1997)*, para. 141.

288 See Appellate Body Report, *Korea – Dairy (2000)*, para. 124. See also, Appellate Body Report, *US – Countervailing and Anti-Dumping Measures (China) (2014)*, para. 4.9.

289 Appellate Body Report, *US – Countervailing and Anti-Dumping Duties (China) (2014)*, para. 4.45. Emphasis added.

Specifically, the Appellate Body considered that the narrative in the panel request, and in particular the reference to and explanation of 'double remedies', allowed the identification of Article 19.3 as the relevant obligation.[290] However, the Appellate Body cautioned future complainants when it stated:

> A challenge to a panel request under Article 6.2 may be avoided by specifying the particular paragraph of a treaty provision containing more than one obligation, and making a plain connection between the measure at issue and the legal claim sufficient to present the problem clearly.[291]

A panel request is addressed to the Chair of the DSB. It is subsequently circulated to all WTO Members, and posted on the WTO website, as a WT/DS document. If the complaining party so requests, a meeting of the DSB for the purpose of establishing a panel shall be convened within fifteen days of the request.[292] The panel is established *at the latest* at the second DSB meeting at which the panel request is discussed. At this meeting, the panel is established *unless* the DSB decides by consensus *not* to establish a panel ('reverse consensus'). Since it is very unlikely that the Member requesting the panel will object, the establishment of a panel by the DSB is, for all practical purposes 'automatic'. A panel can be, and occasionally is, established at the first DSB meeting at which the panel request is considered.[293] At this meeting, the establishment of the panel requires a 'normal consensus' decision of the DSB. The panel can thus only be established at the first DSB meeting if the respondent does not object to its establishment. Often, however, the respondent objects to the panel's establishment at the first DSB meeting, arguing that it 'hopes' and 'believes' that a mutually agreed solution to the dispute can still be found.

The decision of the DSB on the establishment of a panel is usually preceded by short statements by the parties to the dispute setting forth their respective positions. Decisions to establish a panel very seldom give rise to much debate within the DSB. A practice has evolved whereby, immediately after the DSB's decision to establish the panel, other Members may, at the DSB meeting itself, notify their interest in the dispute and reserve their third party rights; or, alternatively, they may do so in writing within ten days as of the DSB meeting.[294]

290 See *ibid.*, paras. 4.45 and 4.52. On 'double remedies' and Article 19.3 of the *SCM Agreement*, see below, p. 861.
291 *Ibid.*, para. 4.46.
292 Note, however, that, as for all WTO meetings, Members must be given at least ten days' advance notice of the meeting. See fn. 5 to Article 6.1 of the DSU.
293 See e.g. in *Australia – Plain Packaging*, with regard to the request of Cuba and Indonesia to establish a panel. Note, however, that a panel had already been established on the same matter at the request of Ukraine and that the DSB was at the same time considering for the second time the panel request of Honduras and Dominican Republic relating also to the same matter.
294 In *EC – Export Subsidies on Sugar (2005)*, Kenya (twenty-eight days) and Côte d'Ivoire (sixty-eight days) made a request to participate as third parties long after the establishment of the panel (but before the panel was composed). While the parties objected to the participation of these two Members, the panel allowed them to take part in the panel proceedings as third parties. See Panel Report, *EC – Export Subsidies on Sugar (2005)*, para. 2.4. Also in cases where the third party request was made *after* the composition of the panel, panels have accepted this request. See e.g. Panel Report, *Turkey – Rice (2007)*, para. 6.9. In the latter case, the third party request was made 151 days after the establishment of the panel.

Where more than one Member requests the establishment of a panel related to the same matter, Article 9.1 of the DSU states that:

> a single panel may be established to examine these complaints taking into account the rights of all Members concerned. A single panel *should* be established to examine such complaints *whenever feasible*.[295]

In cases in which it is not possible to establish a single panel to examine complaints relating to the same matter, Article 9.3 of the DSU requires that – to the extent possible – the same persons shall serve as panellists on each of the separate panels and that the timetable for the panel process in such disputes shall be harmonised. This was done, e.g., in *EC – Hormones (1998)* and *US – 1916 Act (2000)*.[296]

The DSU does not deal with the situation in which a Member files a second panel request on the same matter. A Member may do this in order to clarify and/or extend the scope of its first panel request. This situation has arisen in, e.g., *Canada – Wheat Exports and Grain Imports (2004)* and *US – Large Civil Aircraft (2nd complaint) (2012)*, and was addressed differently in these disputes.[297]

5.2.2 Composition of Panels

As set forth in Article 8.5 of the DSU, panels are normally composed of three persons. The parties to the dispute can agree, within ten days from the establishment of the panel, to a panel composed of five panellists. However, to date, this has never occurred in WTO dispute settlement. Pursuant to Article 8.1 of the DSU, panels must be composed of well-qualified governmental and/or non-governmental individuals. By way of guidance, the Article 8.1 indicates that these individuals can be:

> persons who have served on or presented a case to a panel, served as a representative of a Member or of a contracting party to GATT 1947 or as a representative to the Council or Committee of any covered agreement or its predecessor agreement, or in the Secretariat, taught or published on international trade law or policy, or served as a senior trade policy official of a Member.

Article 8.2 of the DSU stipulates that panellists should be selected with a view to ensuring their independence, providing a sufficiently diverse background and

295 e.g., in *US – Steel Safeguards (2003)*, the DSB at first established multiple panels to hear and decide similar complaints by the European Communities, Japan, Korea, China, Switzerland, Norway, New Zealand and Brazil. Subsequently, the United States and the complainants reached an agreement on the establishment of a single panel, under Article 9.1, to hear the matter at issue.

296 See Panel Report, *EC – Hormones (US) (1998)*; Panel Report, *EC – Hormones (Canada) (1998)*; Panel Report, *US – 1916 Act (EC) (2000)*; and Panel Report, *US – 1916 Act (Japan) (2000)*. In *Canada – Wheat Exports and Grain Imports (2004)*, it was decided that the panellists that composed the panel established pursuant to the first panel request would also compose the panel established pursuant to the second panel request, and that the proceedings of both panels would be harmonised pursuant to Article 9.3 of the DSU.

297 In *US – Large Civil Aircraft (2nd complaint) (2012)*, a second panel was established pursuant to the second panel request. Subsequently, the first panel, which had a different composition, from the second panel, was rendered inactive.

a wide spectrum of experience. Nationals of Members that are parties or third parties to the dispute shall not serve on a panel concerned with that dispute unless the parties to the dispute agree otherwise.[298] While this is not common, parties have in some cases agreed on a panellist who is a national of one of the parties.[299] When a dispute occurs between a developing-country Member and a developed-country Member, the panel shall, if the developing-country Member so requests, include at least one panellist from a developing-country Member.[300] To date, panellists have been predominantly current or retired government trade officials or Geneva-based diplomats with a background in law, although academics and trade law practitioners have also served on panels.[301] The DSU explicitly provides, that panellists shall serve in their individual capacities and not as government representatives. Members shall therefore not give panellists any instructions nor seek to influence them with regard to matters before a panel.[302] Once a panel is established by the DSB, the parties to the dispute will try to reach an agreement on the composition of the panel. The WTO Secretariat shall propose nominations for the panel to the parties to the dispute. The DSU requires the parties to the dispute not to oppose the Secretariat's nominations except for compelling reasons.[303] However, in practice, parties often reject these nominations initially proposed by the WTO Secretariat without much justification, except that they consider that a proposed panellist may hold views that are not in line with the argument(s) they wish to advance. In practice, the composition of the panel is often a difficult and contentious process. If the parties are unable to agree on the composition of the panel within twenty days of its establishment by the DSB, either party *may* request the Director-General of the WTO to determine the composition of the panel.[304] Within ten days of such a request, the Director-General shall – after consulting the parties to the dispute and the Chair of the DSB and of the relevant WTO council or committee – appoint the panellists whom he considers most appropriate. In recent years, the Director-General has determined the composition of most panels.[305]

To assist in the selection of panellists, the WTO Secretariat maintains a list of governmental and non-governmental individuals possessing the required

298 See Article 8.3 of the DSU.

299 e.g., of a dispute in which the parties agreed on the appointment of nationals, see *US – Zeroing (EC) (2006)*, a dispute between the European Communities and the United States. The panel in this dispute included William Davey from the United States and Hans-Friedrich Beseler from Germany.

300 See Article 8.10 of the DSU.

301 For a list of all persons who served as panellists to date and the panels on which they served, see www.worldtradelaw.net/dsc/database/panelistcases.asp. Note that many panellists serve more than once as panellist.

302 See Article 8.9 of the DSU. 303 See Article 8.6 of the DSU.

304 See Article 8.7 of the DSU. Often, however, parties will allow more time to reach an agreement on the composition of a panel instead of requesting the Director-General to decide on the composition. If neither party pushes for the composition of the panel, the panel may remain 'in limbo' indefinitely.

305 In 2013, 2014 and 2015, 75 per cent, 92 per cent and 62.5 per cent respectively of the panels were composed by the Director-General. It may be the case that parties can agree on one or two, but not on all three, panellists. In such case, the Director-General will appoint all three panellists, although it is likely that the panel will include the panellists on which the parties agreed.

qualifications to serve as panellists.[306] Members periodically suggest names of individuals for inclusion on this list, and those names are added to the list upon approval by the DSB. However, this list is merely *indicative* and individuals not included in this list may be selected as panellists. In fact, most first-time panellists were not on the list at the time of their selection.

When hearing and deciding a WTO dispute, panellists are subject to the *Rules of Conduct for the Understanding on Rules and Procedures Governing the Settlement of Disputes* (the '*Rules of Conduct*').[307] To preserve the integrity and impartiality of the WTO dispute settlement system, the *Rules of Conduct* require that panellists:

> shall be independent and impartial, shall avoid direct or indirect conflicts of interest and shall respect the confidentiality of proceedings.[308]

To ensure compliance with the *Rules of Conduct*, panellists must disclose:

> the existence or development of any interest, relationship or matter that the person could reasonably be expected to know and that is likely to affect, or give rise to justifiable doubts as to, that person's independence or impartiality.[309]

This disclosure obligation includes information on financial, professional and other active interests as well as considered statements of personal opinion on issues relevant to the dispute and employment or family interests.[310] Parties may request the disqualification of a panellist on the ground of *material* violation of the obligations of independence, impartiality, confidentiality or the avoidance of direct or indirect conflicts of interest.[311] The evidence of such material violation is provided to the Chair of the DSB, who will, in consultation with the Director-General of the WTO and the chairs of the relevant WTO bodies, decide whether a material violation has occurred. If it has, the panellist is replaced. To date, no panellist has ever been found to have committed a material violation of the *Rules of Conduct*, and thus disqualified. However, very exceptionally, a panellist has resigned from the panel, at his or her own initiative, after a party raised concerns about a possible conflict of interest.[312]

Panels are assisted by the WTO Secretariat. Pursuant to Article 27.1 of the DSU, the WTO Secretariat has the responsibility of assisting panels, especially

306 See Article 8.4 of the DSU. For the most recent consolidated list, see WT/DSB/44/Rev.35, dated 27 September 2016.

307 WT/DSB/RC/1, dated 11 December 1996. As discussed below, these *Rules of Conduct* also apply to Appellate Body Members (see below, p. 235), arbitrators (see below, p. 246) and the support staff (see below, pp. 220 and 237).

308 Para. II(1) of the *Rules of Conduct*.

309 Para. III(1) of the *Rules of Conduct*. This information shall be disclosed to the Chair of the DSB for consideration by the parties to the dispute. See para. VI(4)(a) of the *Rules of Conduct*. Panellists are subject to this disclosure obligation prior to as well as after the confirmation of their appointment as panellist. See paras. VI(4)(a) and (5).

310 See Annex 2 to the *Rules of Conduct*. 311 See para. VIII of the *Rules of Conduct*.

312 e.g., in *Russia – Pigs (2016)*, upon composition of the panel by the Director-General, on two occasions, two different panellists tendered their resignation. Also in *Turkey – Textiles (1999)*, Robert Hudec resigned from the panel within three weeks of its composition. See Panel Report, *Turkey – Textiles (1999)*, para. 1.6, and WT/DS34/4, dated 23 July 1998.

on the legal, historical and procedural aspects of the matters dealt with, and of providing secretarial and technical support. The Legal Affairs Division and the Rules Division are the main divisions of the WTO Secretariat that assist dispute settlement panels. Generally speaking, panels considering cases related to anti-dumping, countervailing and safeguard measures and State trading are assisted by staff from the Rules Division. Panels considering all other cases are assisted by the Legal Affairs Division and sometimes by other divisions of the WTO Secretariat. For example, a panel in an SPS dispute will be assisted by the Legal Affairs Division, but usually experts from the relevant 'operational division', e.g., the Agriculture and Commodities Division will also assist the panel. Officials of the WTO Secretariat assigned to assist panels are also subject to the *Rules of Conduct* and bound by the obligations of independence, impartiality, confidentiality and the avoidance of direct or indirect conflicts of interest.[313]

5.2.3 Mandate of Panels

As stated above, at the first-instance level, the adjudication of disputes is carried out by panels. This subsection deals with the various aspects of the mandate of panels, i.e. the scope and nature of the task(s) entrusted to panels. It will discuss in turn: (1) the terms of reference of a panel; (2) the standard of review to be applied by panels; (3) the exercise of judicial economy; (4) acts *ultra petita*; and (5) the use of experts by panels.

First, with regard to the *terms of reference of a panel*, Article 7.1 of the DSU states that, unless the parties agree otherwise within twenty days from the establishment of the panel, a panel is given the following *standard* terms of reference:

> To examine in the light of the relevant provisions in (name of the covered agreement(s) cited by the parties to the dispute), the *matter referred to the DSB* by (name of party) *in document* ... and make such findings as will assist the DSB in making the recommendations or in giving the rulings provided for in that/those agreement(s).[314]

The 'matter referred to the DSB' consists of two elements: (1) the specific measure(s) at issue; and (2) the legal basis of the complaint, i.e. the claims of WTO inconsistency.[315] The 'document' referred to in these standard terms of reference is the panel request. Hence, a specific measure and a claim of WTO inconsistency regarding that measure fall within the panel's terms of reference, i.e. within the jurisdiction of the panel, only if they are identified, with sufficient precision in the panel request. A panel is *bound* by its terms of reference.[316] It follows that the complainant cannot, in the course of the panel proceedings, put new measures or new claims before the panel. Note, however, that a complainant may decide in the course of the panel proceedings not to pursue its case with regard to certain measures and/or claims, which fall within the terms of reference of the

313 See above, p. 219. 314 Emphasis added.
315 See Appellate Body Report, *Guatemala – Cement I (1998)*, paras. 72 and 76.
316 See *ibid.*, para. 93.

panel. The complainant may always reduce the scope of the dispute and it is not uncommon for a complainant to do so.[317]

Unlike in the early years of WTO dispute settlement, in recent years respondents frequently request the panel at the outset of the proceedings to make a preliminary ruling on the scope of the panel's terms of reference, i.e. its jurisdiction.[318]

Within twenty days of the establishment of the panel, the parties to the dispute *can* agree on *special* terms of reference for the panel, i.e. terms of reference that are not determined by the complainant's panel request.[319] However, it very rarely occurs that parties agree on *special* terms of reference.[320] If no agreement on *special* terms of reference is reached within twenty days of the establishment of the panel, the panel shall have *standard* terms of reference, determined – as explained above – by the complainant's panel request.

Note that the panel in *Colombia – Textiles (2016)*, referring to the Appellate Body's ruling in *Chile – Price Band System (2002)*, found:

> a panel's terms of reference may include 'amendments' to the measures described in the panel request as long as the terms of reference are broad enough and the amendments do not change the essence of the original measures.[321]

In *Colombia – Textiles (2016)*, Colombia amended, after the panel had been established and composed, the measure at issue identified in the panel request of Panama, the complainant. In its first panel submission, Panama challenged the GATT consistency of this amended measure at issue. The panel considered that the amended measure was closely related to the measure identified in the panel request and maintained its essence and nature, and thus concluded that the amended measure fell within its terms of reference.[322]

Another question that deserves to be mentioned with respect to a panel's terms of reference, is whether a panel *can* decline to exercise jurisdiction which it has according to its terms of reference. With regard to this question, the Appellate Body held in *Mexico – Taxes on Soft Drinks (2006)*:

> A decision by a panel to decline to exercise validly established jurisdiction would seem to 'diminish' the right of a complaining Member to 'seek the redress of a violation of obligations' within the meaning of Article 23 of the DSU, and to bring a dispute pursuant to Article 3.3 of the DSU. This would not be consistent with a panel's obligations under Articles 3.2 and 19.2 of the DSU. We see no reason, therefore, to disagree with the Panel's

317 See Appellate Body Report, *Japan – Apples (2003)*, para. 136.

318 See e.g. *EU – Biodiesel (2016)*; *US – Washing Machines (2016)*; *Argentina – Financial Services (2016)*; and *EC – Fasteners (Article 21.5) (2016)*.

319 See Article 7.1 of the DSU.

320 See e.g. Panel Report, *Brazil – Desiccated Coconut (1997)*, para. 9. Note that this is the only example mentioned in the *WTO Analytical Index (2012)*, Volume II, 1622–3.

321 Panel Report, *Colombia – Textiles (2016)*, para. 7.35, referring to Appellate Body Report, *Chile – Price Band System (2002)*, para. 139. A panel may also consider whether it is necessary to take account of amendments to the measure in order to secure a positive solution to the dispute. See *ibid.*, referring to Panel Reports, *EC – IT Products (2010)*, para. 7.139.

322 See Panel Report, *Colombia – Textiles (2016)*, paras. 7.38–7.40.

statement that a WTO panel 'would seem ... not to be in a position to choose freely whether or not to exercise its jurisdiction'.[323]

With regard to the *standard of review*, i.e. the nature and intensity of the review that panels must undertake when they examine the WTO consistency of the measure at issue in a dispute, Article 11 of the DSU stipulates:

The function of panels is to assist the DSB in discharging its responsibilities under this Understanding and the covered agreements. Accordingly, a panel should make an objective assessment of the matter before it, including an objective assessment of the facts of the case and the applicability of and conformity with the relevant covered agreements, and make such other findings as will assist the DSB in making the recommendations or in giving the rulings provided for in the covered agreements.[324]

In *EC – Hormones (1998)*, the Appellate Body noted that Article 11 of the DSU:

articulates with great succinctness but with sufficient clarity the appropriate standard of review for panels in respect of both the ascertainment of facts and the legal characterization of such facts under the relevant agreements.[325]

With regard to the ascertainment of facts, i.e. *fact-finding*, panels have 'to make an objective assessment of the facts'. With regard to the legal characterisation of such facts under the relevant agreement, i.e. the *assessment of WTO consistency*, Article 11 imposes the same standard on panels, namely, 'to make an objective assessment' of the applicability of and conformity with the relevant covered agreement.[326]

In *US – COOL (2012)*, the Appellate Body summarised its case law on Article 11 of the DSU as follows:[327]

a panel is required to 'consider all the evidence presented to it, assess its credibility, determine its weight, and ensure that its factual findings have a proper basis in that evidence'. It must further provide in its report 'reasoned and adequate explanations and coherent reasoning' to support its findings. Within these parameters, 'it is generally within the discretion of the [p]anel to decide which evidence it chooses to utilize in making findings'. Although a panel must consider evidence before it in its totality, and 'evaluate the relevance and probative force' of all of the evidence, a panel is not required 'to discuss, in its report, each and every piece of evidence' put before it, or 'to accord to factual evidence of the parties the same meaning and weight as do the parties'.

323 Appellate Body Report, *Mexico – Taxes on Soft Drinks (2006)*, para. 53. For a further discussion, see Chapter 10, on regional trade agreements, at p. 671.

324 Note that Article 11 of the DSU states that 'a panel *should* make an objective assessment of the matter'. Emphasis added. In *Canada – Aircraft (1999)*, the Appellate Body noted in this respect, be it in a different context, that, 'although the word "should" is often used colloquially to imply an exhortation, or to state a preference, it is not always used in those ways. It can also be used "to express a duty [or] obligation"'. It is in this way that the word 'should' is used in Article 11 of the DSU. See Appellate Body Report, *Canada – Aircraft (1999)*, para. 187.

325 Appellate Body Report, *EC – Hormones (1998)*, para. 116. See also Panel Report, *US – Underwear (1997)*, paras. 7.10, 7.12 and 7.13; and Panel Report, *US – Wool Shirts and Blouses (1997)*, paras. 7.16 and 7.17.

326 See Appellate Body Report, *Chile – Price Band System (2002)*, para. 172; and Appellate Body Report, *Dominican Republic – Import and Sale of Cigarettes (2005)*, para. 105.

327 Appellate Body Reports, *US – COOL (2012)*, para. 299.

Not every error committed by a panel in the appreciation of the evidence will amount to a violation of Article 11 of the DSU. As the Appellate Body recalled in *US – COOL (2012)*, it will not 'interfere lightly' with a panel's factual findings, and will find that a panel failed to comply with its duties under Article 11 of the DSU only if it is satisfied that the panel has exceeded its authority as the initial trier of the facts. When a participant claims that a panel 'ignored' or 'disregarded' a particular piece of evidence, the mere fact that a panel did not explicitly refer to that evidence in its reasoning does not suffice to demonstrate that the panel acted inconsistently with Article 11.[328] As the Appellate Body stated in *US – COOL (2012)*, to claim with success that the panel acted inconsistently with Article 11:

> a participant must explain why such evidence is so material to its case that the panel's failure explicitly to address and rely upon it casts doubt on the objectivity of the panel's factual assessment.[329]

While claims that a panel failed 'to make an objective assessment of the matter before it' are often unsuccessful, the number of such claims has grown incessantly over the years. In most appeals today, there is at least one, and often many more, such claims. In *China – Rare Earths (2014)* the Appellate Body cautioned appellants in this respect as follows:

> we wish to encourage appellants to consider carefully when and to what extent to challenge a panel's assessment of a matter pursuant to Article 11, bearing in mind that an allegation of violation of Article 11 is a very serious allegation. This is in keeping with the objective of the prompt settlement of disputes, and the requirement in Article 3.7 of the DSU that Members exercise judgement in deciding whether action under the WTO dispute settlement procedures would be fruitful.[330]

With regard to the panel's task of carrying out an objective assessment of the matter before it, as required under Article 11 of the DSU, the panel in *US – Stainless Steel (Mexico) (2008)* expressed, in the context of the divisive debate on the role of precedent in WTO dispute settlement, the view that the concern over the preservation of a consistent line of case law should not override this central task of the panel under Article 11 of the DSU. The panel noted that, in two previous cases, the Appellate Body had reversed decisions of panels that found a particular practice of zeroing to be WTO-consistent and that its own reasoning was very similar to that of those two panels. Nonetheless, referring to the obligation under Article 11 of the DSU to carry out an objective examination of the matter, that panel 'felt compelled to depart' from the Appellate Body's approach.[331] The Appellate Body reversed the panel's finding. It noted that it is 'well settled that Appellate Body reports are not binding, except with respect to

328 See *ibid.* 329 *Ibid.*, para. 300.

330 Appellate Body Report, *China – Rare Earths (2014)*, para. 5.228.

331 See Panel Report, *US – Stainless Steel (Mexico) (2008)*, paras. 7.105–7.106. On the debate on the role of precedent in WTO dispute settlement, see above, pp. 56–8.

resolving the particular dispute between the parties'.[332] However, this 'does not mean that subsequent panels are free to disregard the legal interpretations and the *ratio decidendi* contained in previous Appellate Body reports that have been adopted by the DSB'.[333] It found that the general provisions of Article 3 of the DSU, and in particular paragraph 2 thereof, inform the obligation under Article 11 of the DSU for panels to carry out an objective examination of the matter.[334] Paragraph 2 of Article 3 provides that '[t]he dispute settlement system of the WTO is a central element in providing security and predictability to the multilateral trading system'.[335] The Appellate Body clarified that, in the hierarchical structure of the dispute settlement system, panels and the Appellate Body have distinct roles to play, and stated that ensuring 'security and predictability' in the dispute settlement system, as contemplated in Article 3.2 of the DSU, implies that, absent cogent reasons, an adjudicatory body will resolve the same legal question in the same way in a subsequent case. The Appellate Body concluded that the panel's failure to follow previously adopted Appellate Body reports addressing the same issues undermines the development of a coherent and predictable body of jurisprudence clarifying Members' rights and obligations under the covered agreements.[336] It added that dispute settlement practice demonstrates that 'WTO Members attach significance to reasoning provided in previous panel and Appellate Body reports. Adopted panel and Appellate Body reports are often cited by parties in support of legal arguments in dispute settlement proceedings, and are relied upon by panels and the Appellate Body in subsequent disputes'.[337] As the Appellate Body stated in *US – Stainless Steel (Mexico) (2008)*:

> [T]he legal interpretation embodied in adopted panel and Appellate Body reports becomes part and parcel of the *acquis* of the WTO dispute settlement system.[338]

In other words, whereas the *application* of a provision may be regarded as confined to the context of the case in which it takes place, the relevance of *clarification* contained in adopted Appellate Body reports is not limited to the application of a particular provision in a specific case.[339]

The Appellate Body has not yet defined the concept of 'cogent reasons'. The panel in *China – Rare Earths (2014)* considered that this concept of 'cogent reasons' may be understood as referring generally to a high threshold.[340] The panel in *US – Countervailing and Anti-Dumping Measures (China) (2014)* considered

332 See Appellate Body Report, *Japan – Alcoholic Beverages II (1996)*, 106–8. See also Appellate Body Report, *US – Softwood Lumber V (2004)*, paras. 109–12; and Appellate Body Report, *US – Shrimp (Article 21.5 – Malaysia) (2001)*, para. 109. While Appellate Body reports adopted by the DSB shall be accepted unconditionally by the parties to the dispute, it is the exclusive authority of the Ministerial Conference and the General Council to adopt, pursuant to Article IX:2 of the *WTO Agreement*, interpretations that are binding upon the WTO membership.

333 Appellate Body Report, *US – Stainless Steel (Mexico) (2008)*, para. 158.

334 See *ibid.*, para. 157. 335 See above, p. 35.

336 See Appellate Body Report, *US – Stainless Steel (Mexico) (2008)*, para. 161.

337 *Ibid.*, para. 160. 338 *Ibid.*

339 See *ibid.*, para. 161. 340 See Panel Report, *China – Rare Earths (2014)*, para. 7.61.

that the concept of 'cogent reasons' could encompass, *inter alia*: (1) a multilateral interpretation of a provision of the covered agreements under Article IX:2 of the WTO Agreement that departs from a prior Appellate Body interpretation; (2) a demonstration that a prior Appellate Body interpretation proved to be unworkable in a particular set of circumstances falling within the scope of the relevant obligation at issue; (3) a demonstration that the Appellate Body's prior interpretation leads to a conflict with another provision of a covered agreement that was not raised before the Appellate Body; and (4) a demonstration that the Appellate Body's interpretation was based on a factually incorrect premise.[341]

With regard to the standard of review for panels, three more observations should be made. First, Article 11 of the DSU sets forth the appropriate standard of review for panels in disputes under all but one of the covered agreements. Only for disputes under the *Anti-Dumping Agreement* is there a 'special' standard of review, which is set out in Article 17.6 of the *Anti-Dumping Agreement* and which is discussed in Chapter 11.[342] Second, as the Appellate Body found in *US – Lamb (2001)*, the appropriate standard is neither a '*de novo* review' of the facts nor 'total deference' to the determinations of national authorities. However, in particular when national authorities are the first trier of facts, a degree of deference is due to the factual determinations by national authorities.[343] In *US – Countervailing Duty Investigation on DRAMS (2005)*, the Appellate Body stated that the 'objective assessment' to be made by a panel when it reviews a national authority's determination in a countervailing duty investigation is to be informed by an examination of whether the national authority provided a reasoned and adequate explanation as to: (1) how the evidence on the record supported its factual findings; and (2) how those factual findings supported the overall determination.[344] A panel cannot substitute its judgement for that of the investigation authority.[345] Third, while uncommon, it has happened that the respondent did not make any argument to contest the complainant's claims of inconsistency. It is important to note that in such cases the panel must also make an objective assessment of the matter as required by Article 11 of the DSU, and it must assess whether the complainant made a *prima facie* case.[346]

As indicated above, this section on the mandate of panels also covers, apart from the terms of reference of and the standard of review for panels, the exercise of judicial economy by panels, the issue of panels acting *ultra petita* and the use of experts by panels.

With regard to the exercise of *judicial economy*, note that complainants often assert with regard to one and the same measure numerous violations under various

341 See Panel Report, *US – Countervailing and Anti-Dumping Measures (China) (2014)*, paras. 7.369–7.370.
342 See below, p. 760. 343 See Appellate Body Report, *US – Lamb (2001)*, paras. 106–7.
344 See Appellate Body Report, *US – Countervailing Duty Investigation DRAMS (2005)*, para. 186.
345 See *ibid.*, para. 187. For a more detailed discussion of the standard of review in cases in which national authorities are the first trier of facts, see Chapters 11, 12 and 14 at pp. 760–3, 854–5 and 987–9 respectively
346 See e.g. Panel Report, *US – Shrimp (Ecuador) (2007)*, paras. 7.1–7.11; and Panel Report, *China – Publications and Audiovisual Products (2010)*, para. 7.942.

agreements. It is well-established case law that panels are not required to examine each and every one of the legal claims that a complainant makes. In *US – Wool Shirts and Blouses (1997)*, the Appellate Body had already ruled that panels:

> need only address those claims which must be addressed in order to resolve the matter in issue in the dispute.[347]

In *Argentina – Import Measures (2015)*, the Appellate Body explained that the principle of judicial economy 'allows a panel to refrain from making multiple findings that the same measure is *inconsistent* with various provisions when a single, or a certain number of findings of inconsistency, would suffice to resolve the dispute'.[348] Thus, panels need address only those claims 'which must be addressed in order to resolve the matter in issue in the dispute',[349] and panels 'may refrain from ruling on every claim as long as it does not lead to a "partial resolution of the matter"'.[350] However, the Appellate Body has cautioned panels that:

> '[t]o provide only a partial resolution of the matter at issue would be false judicial economy', and that '[a] panel has to address those claims on which a finding is necessary in order to enable the DSB to make sufficiently precise recommendations and rulings so as to allow for prompt compliance by a Member with those recommendations and rulings "in order to ensure effective resolution of disputes to the benefit of all Members"'.[351]

For another example of false judicial economy, refer to *US – Export Subsidies on Sugar (2005)*, in which the panel, after finding that the export subsidies at issue were inconsistent with the *Agreement on Agriculture*, exercised judicial economy with regard to the claim of inconsistency with the *SCM Agreement*. The Appellate Body held that this was false judicial economy because the remedies under the *SCM Agreement* would be different and more specific than those under the *Agreement on Agriculture*.[352] In *US – Tuna II (Mexico) (2012)*, the Appellate Body ruled that a panel that engages in 'false judicial economy' acts inconsistently with its obligations under Article 11 of the DSU, and in particular a panel's obligation to 'make such other findings as will assist the DSB in making recommendations or giving the rulings provided for in the covered agreements'.[353]

347 Appellate Body Report, *US – Wool Shirts and Blouses (1997)*, 340. See also Appellate Body Report, *Australia – Salmon (1998)*, para. 224. However, as the Appellate Body observed in *Canada – Autos (2000)*, para. 117: 'for purposes of transparency and fairness to the parties, a panel should, however, in all cases, address expressly those claims which it declines to examine and rule upon for reasons of judicial economy. Silence does not suffice for these purposes.'

348 Appellate Body Report, *Argentina – Import Measures (2015)*, para. 5.190, referring to Appellate Body Report, *Canada – Wheat Exports and Grain Imports*, para. 133.

349 See *ibid.*, referring to Appellate Body Report, *US – Wool Shirts and Blouses (1997)*, 19 and Appellate Body Report, *US – Tuna II (Mexico) (2012)*, para. 403.

350 See Appellate Body Report, *Argentina – Import Measures (2015)*, para. 5.190, referring to Appellate Body Report, *US – Upland Cotton (2005)*, para. 732; and Appellate Body Report, *US – Tuna II (Mexico) (2012)*, para. 404.

351 Appellate Body Report, *Argentina – Import Measures (2015)*, para. 5.190, referring to Appellate Body Report, *Australia – Salmon (1998)*, para. 223.

352 See Appellate Body Report, *US – Export Subsidies on Sugar (2005)*, paras. 334–5.

353 See Appellate Body Report, *US – Tuna II (Mexico) (2012)*, para. 405. In, *US – Tuna II (Mexico) (2012)*, the panel engaged 'in false judicial economy', inconsistently with Article 11 of the DSU, regarding Mexico's claim under Article III:4 of the GATT 1994, after it had found that the measure at issue was *not* inconsistent with Article 2.1 of the *TBT Agreement*.

Panels frequently exercise judicial economy with regard to claims before them. However, in some instances, panels may decide to continue their legal analysis and to make factual findings beyond those that are strictly necessary to resolve the dispute because this 'may assist the Appellate Body should it later be called upon to complete the analysis'.[354]

Since panels may exercise judicial economy with regard to *claims*, it is not surprising that they may also exercise judicial economy with regard to *arguments* made by a party with regard to a claim. As long as it is clear in a panel report that a panel has reasonably considered a claim, the fact that a particular *argument* relating to that claim is not addressed does not amount to an inconsistency with Article 11 of the DSU.[355]

In *EC – Fasteners (China) (2011)*, the Appellate Body rejected China's contention that the panel erred by not addressing one of its main arguments concerning a claim. The Appellate Body found that:

> a panel has the discretion 'to address only those arguments it deems necessary to resolve a particular claim' and 'the fact that a particular argument relating to that claim is not specifically addressed in the "Findings" section of a panel report will not, in and of itself, lead to the conclusion that that panel has failed to make the "objective assessment of the matter before it" required by Article 11 of the DSU'.[356]

With regard to the issue of panels acting *ultra petita*, i.e. making a finding on a claim that does not fall within its terms of reference, the Appellate Body found in *Chile – Price Band System (2002)* that a panel acting *ultra petita* does not make an objective assessment of *the matter before it*, and thus acts inconsistently with Article 11 of the DSU.[357] However, if the panel's finding relates to a *claim* which does fall within its terms of reference, it is not restricted to considering only those *legal arguments* made by the parties to the dispute. The Appellate Body ruled in *EC – Hormones (1998)* that:

> Panels are inhibited from addressing legal claims falling outside their terms of reference. However, nothing in the DSU limits the faculty of a panel freely to use arguments submitted by any of the parties – or to develop its own legal reasoning – to support its own findings and conclusions on the matter under its consideration.[358]

A panel, which uses legal arguments or reasoning that have not been submitted or developed by any of the parties to the dispute, does not act *ultra petita*. Panels

354 Appellate Body Report, *US – Gambling (2005)*, para. 344. On the 'completing of the legal analysis' by the Appellate Body, see below, pp. 244–5.

355 See Appellate Body Report, *EC – Poultry (1998)*, para. 135. See also Appellate Body Report, *Dominican Republic – Import and Sale of Cigarettes (2005)*, para. 125.

356 Appellate Body Report, *EC – Fasteners (China) (2011)*, para. 511.

357 See Appellate Body Report, *Chile – Price Band System (2002)*, para. 173. In *Chile – Price Band System (2002)*, the panel made findings regarding Article II:1(b), second sentence of the GATT 1994, while Argentina, the complainant, had not made any claim of inconsistency with that provision.

358 Appellate Body Report, *EC – Hormones (1998)*, para. 156. See also Appellate Body Reports, *Canada – Renewable Energy/Canada – Feed-in Tariff Program (2013)*, para. 5.215; and Panel Report, *Australia – Automotive Leather II (Article 21.5 – US) (2000)*, para. 6.19.

are restricted to the claims falling within their terms of reference but they are not restricted to the legal arguments and reasoning submitted or developed by the parties.[359]

Finally, with regard to the use of experts by panels, note that disputes brought to panels for adjudication often involve complex factual, technical and scientific issues. These issues frequently play a central role in WTO dispute settlement proceedings. Article 13 of the DSU gives a panel the authority to seek information and technical advice from any individual or body, which it deems appropriate.[360] Panels may consult experts to obtain their opinion on certain aspects of the matter under consideration. As the Appellate Body ruled in *Argentina – Textiles and Apparel (1998)*, '[t]his is a grant of discretionary authority'.[361] In *US – Shrimp (1998)*, the Appellate Body further stated:

> [A] panel ... has the authority to *accept or reject* any information or advice which it may have sought and received, or to *make some other appropriate disposition* thereof. It is particularly within the province and the authority of a panel to determine the *need for information and advice* in a specific case, to ascertain the *acceptability* and *relevancy* of information or advice received, and to decide *what weight to ascribe to that information or advice* or to conclude that no weight at all should be given to what has been received.[362]

This authority is 'indispensably necessary' to enable a panel to discharge its duty under Article 11 of the DSU to 'make an objective assessment of the matter before it'.[363] Note that, while the authority under Article 13 to seek information is 'discretionary', failure by the panel to seek information necessary to make an objective assessment of the facts may, as discussed above, amount to a violation of Article 11 of the DSU.[364]

To date, panels have consulted experts in, e.g., *EC – Hormones (1998)*, *EC – Asbestos (2001)*, *EC – Approval and Marketing of Biotech Products (2006)*, *US/Canada – Continued Suspension (2008)*, *Australia – Apples (2010)*, *India – Agricultural Products (2015)* and *Russia – Pigs (2016)* which were all disputes involving complex scientific issues. In these cases, the panels typically selected the experts in consultation with the parties; presented the experts with a list of questions to which each expert individually responded in writing; and finally

359 See *Appellate Body Report, EC – Hormones (1998)*. However, when a panel rules on a claim in the absence of evidence and supporting arguments, it acts inconsistently with its obligations under Article 11 of the DSU.

360 In addition to Article 13 of the DSU, panels have either the right or the obligation to consult experts under a number of other covered agreements: see Article XV:2 of the GATT 1994; Article 11.2 of the *SPS Agreement* (see below, p. 986); Articles 14.2 and 14.3 of the *TBT Agreement* (see below, p. 931); Articles 19.3 and 19.4 of, and Annex II to, the *Agreement on Customs Valuation*; and Articles 4.5 and 24.3 of the *SCM Agreement* (see below, pp. 809 and 866).

361 Appellate Body Report, *Argentina – Textiles and Apparel (1998)*, para. 84. This case concerned the question whether the panel was obliged to consult the IMF with regard to Argentina's imposition of import surcharges. The Appellate Body noted that the only provision that *requires* consultation of the IMF is Article XV:2 of the GATT (dealing with problems of monetary reserves, balances of payments or foreign exchange arrangements).

362 Appellate Body Report, *US – Shrimp (1998)*, para. 104.

363 *Ibid.*, para. 106. See also Appellate Body Report, *US – Continued Zeroing (2009)*, para. 347.

364 See Appellate Body Report, *US – Large Civil Aircraft (2nd complaint) (2012)*, para. 1145.

called a special meeting with the experts at which the panel's questions as well as other questions were discussed with the panellists and the parties.[365] Note that experts consulted by the panel are subject to the Rules of Conduct and must therefore be independent and impartial, avoid conflicts of interest, and respect the confidentiality of the proceedings.[366] In *US/Canada – Continued Suspension (2008)*, the Appellate Body – while recognising the difficulty in selecting experts who have the required level of expertise and are acceptable to the parties – found that the institutional affiliation of two of the panel experts 'was likely to affect or give justifiable doubts as to their independence or impartiality', given that studies made by their institution were at the heart of the controversy between the parties.[367] The Appellate Body thus concluded that the panel had infringed the due process rights of the European Communities in this case.

Under Article 13 of the DSU, a panel may not only consult individual experts and scientists; it may also consult specialised international organisations.[368] For example, in *EC – Approval and Marketing of Biotech Products (2006)*, the panel sought information from the Secretariat of the Convention on Biological Diversity, the Codex Alimentarius Commission, the Food and Agriculture Organization, the International Plant Protection Convention, the International Organization for Epizootics, the UN Environment Programme and the World Health Organization.[369] In *EC – Chicken Cuts (2005)* and *China – Auto Parts (2009)*, the panel sought information from the World Customs Organization.[370] In *Dominican Republic – Import and Sale of Cigarettes (2005)*, the panel consulted with the International Monetary Fund;[371] and, in *EC – Trademarks and Geographical Indications (2005)*, the panel requested from the World Intellectual Property Organization 'assistance in the form of any factual information available to it relevant to the interpretation of certain provisions of the *Paris Convention for the Protection of Industrial Property*'.[372]

Apart from consulting individual experts and international organisations, a panel can, with respect to a factual issue concerning a scientific or other technical matter, request a report in writing from an expert review group.[373] Rules for the establishment of such a group and its procedures are set forth in Appendix 4 to the DSU. Expert review groups are under the authority of the panel and report

365 Panel reports usually include in annex the expert's written responses and a transcript of the discussion at their meeting with the panel.

366 See above, p. 219.

367 See Appellate Body Report, *US/Canada – Continued Suspension (2008)*, paras. 480–1.

368 Such consultations of specialised international organisations are also possible under the other legal bases for consultations listed in fn. 360 above. For a list of proceedings in which information was sought from other international organisations, see *WTO Analytical Index (2012)*, Volume II, 1715.

369 See Panel Reports, *EC – Approval and Marketing of Biotech Products (2006)*, paras. 7.19 and 7.31–7.32.

370 See Panel Report, *EC – Chicken Cuts (2005)*, paras. 7.52–7.53 (complaint by Brazil) and paras. 7.52–7.53 (complaint by Thailand).

371 See Panel Report, *Dominican Republic – Import and Sale of Cigarettes (2005)*, paras. 1.8 and 7.138–7.154.

372 Panel Reports, *EC – Trademarks and Geographical Indications (2005)*, paras. 2.16–2.18 (complaint by Australia) and paras. 2.16–2.18 (complaint by the US).

373 See Article 13.2 of the DSU.

to the panel. The panel decides their terms of reference. The report of an expert review group is advisory only; it does not bind the panel. To date, panels have made no use of this possibility to request an advisory report from an expert review group. Panels have preferred to seek information from experts directly and on an individual basis.[374]

It should be noted that, while a panel has broad authority to consult experts to help it to understand and evaluate the evidence submitted and the arguments made by the parties, a panel may not – with the help of its experts – make the case for one or the other party. In *Japan – Agricultural Products II (1999)*, the Appellate Body held:

> Article 13 of the DSU and Article 11.2 of the *SPS Agreement* suggest that panels have a significant investigative authority. However, this authority cannot be used by a panel to rule in favour of a complaining party which has not established a *prima facie* case of inconsistency based on specific legal claims asserted by it. A panel is entitled to seek information and advice from experts and from any other relevant source it chooses, pursuant to Article 13 of the DSU and, in an SPS case, Article 11.2 of the *SPS Agreement*, to *help it to understand and evaluate the evidence* submitted and the arguments made by the parties, but not to make the case for a complaining party.[375]

The possible and permissible role of panel experts under Article 13.2 of the DSU was further clarified in *Australia – Apples (2010)* when the Appellate Body ruled:

> Experts may assist a panel in assessing the level of risk associated with SPS measures and potential alternative measures, but whether or not an alternative measure's level of risk achieves a Member's appropriate level of protection is a question of legal characterization, the answer to which will determine the consistency or inconsistency of a Member's measure with its obligation under Article 5.6. Answering this question is not a task that can be delegated to scientific experts.[376]

In other words, panels cannot delegate to their scientific experts the core questions and issues that determine whether or not there has been a breach of a WTO obligation.

5.2.4 Required Content of Panel Reports

Article 12.7 of the DSU requires that a panel submits its findings to the DSB in the form of a written report, and that this report sets out: (1) the findings of fact; (2) the applicability of relevant provisions; and (3) the basic rationale behind any findings and recommendations that it makes.[377] In *Mexico – Corn Syrup (Article 21.5 – US)*

374 The DSU leaves it to the discretion of a panel to determine whether the establishment of an expert review group is necessary or appropriate. See Appellate Body Report, *EC – Hormones (1998)*, para. 147.

375 Appellate Body Report, *Japan – Agricultural Products II (1999)*, para. 129. Emphasis added. See further Appellate Body Report, *Japan – Apples (2003)*, para. 158 where the Appellate Body further clarified that that a panel may also use the evidence of its experts to assist it in assessing the allegations of the responding Member.

376 Appellate Body Report, *Australia – Apples (2010)*, para. 384.

377 Note the special requirements for panel reports in cases where parties have reached a mutually acceptable solution during the panel proceedings (see Article 12.7 of the DSU). See e.g. Panel Report, *Japan – Quotas on Laver*.

(2001), the Appellate Body stated that Article 12.7 sets a 'minimum standard' for the basic rationale with which panels must support their findings and recommendations.[378] The Appellate Body explained further:

> In our view, the duty of panels under Article 12.7 of the DSU to provide a 'basic rationale' reflects and conforms with the principles of fundamental fairness and due process that underlie and inform the provisions of the DSU. In particular, in cases where a Member has been found to have acted inconsistently with its obligations under the covered agreements, that Member is entitled to know the reasons for such finding as a matter of due process. In addition, the requirement to set out a 'basic rationale' in the panel report assists such Member to understand the nature of its obligations and to make informed decisions about: (i) what must be done in order to implement the eventual rulings and recommendations made by the DSB; and (ii) whether and what to appeal. Article 12.7 also furthers the objectives, expressed in Article 3.2 of the DSU, of promoting security and predictability in the multilateral trading system and of clarifying the existing provisions of the covered agreements, because the requirement to provide 'basic' reasons contributes to other WTO Members' understanding of the nature and scope of the rights and obligations in the covered agreements.[379]

In a few cases to date, parties have challenged a panel report before the Appellate Body for lack of a basic rationale behind the panel's findings and recommendations.[380]

In *Chile – Price Band System (Article 21.5 – Argentina) (2007)*, the Appellate Body curtly observed that:

> [t]he mere fact that Chile disagrees with the substance of [the Panel's] reasoning cannot suffice to establish a violation of Article 12.7.[381]

The Appellate Body also stated that the requirement to set out a basic rationale behind any findings or recommendations means that the explanations and reasons provided by the panel must suffice 'to disclose the essential, or fundamental, justification for those findings and recommendations'.[382] Panels do not need to 'expound at length on the reasons for their findings or recommendations'.[383]

In a dispute involving a developing-country Member, the panel report must explicitly indicate how the panel has taken account of any special or differential treatment provision that the developing-country Member has invoked before the panel. In *India – Quantitative Restrictions (1999)*, the panel specifically referred to this requirement and noted:

> In this instance, we have noted that Article XVIII:B as a whole, on which our analysis throughout this section is based, embodies the principle of special and differential treatment in relation to measures taken for balance-of-payments purposes. This entire part G therefore

378 See Appellate Body Report, *Mexico – Corn Syrup (Article 21.5 – US) (2001)*, para. 106.
379 *Ibid.*, para. 107.
380 See e.g., Appellate Body Report, *Argentina – Footwear (EC) (2000)*, para. 149.
381 Appellate Body Report, *Chile – Price Band System (Article 21.5 – Argentina) (2007)*, para. 247. See also Appellate Body Report, *US – Steel Safeguards (2003)*, para. 507.
382 Appellate Body Report, *Chile – Price Band System (Article 21.5 – Argentina) (2007)*, para. 243
383 *Ibid.* Appellate Body Report, *Mexico – Corn Syrup (Article 21.5 – US) (2001)*, para. 106.

reflects our consideration of relevant provisions on special and differential treatment, as does Section VII of our report (suggestions for implementation).[384]

Where a panel concludes that a Member's measure is inconsistent with a covered agreement, it shall recommend that the Member concerned bring that measure into conformity with that agreement.[385] The recommendations and rulings of a panel are *not* legally binding by themselves. They become legally binding only when they are adopted by the DSB and thus have become the recommendations and rulings of the DSB.[386] In addition to making recommendations and rulings, the panel may suggest ways in which the Member concerned could implement those recommendations.[387] These suggestions are not legally binding on the Member concerned (even after the report is adopted).[388] However, because the panel making the suggestions might later be called upon to assess the sufficiency of the implementation of the recommendations, such suggestions are likely to have a certain impact.[389] To date, few panels (*EC – Bananas III (Ecuador) (1999)* or *Mexico – Steel Pipes and Tubes (2007))* have made use of this authority to make suggestions regarding implementation of their recommendations.[390] In fact, panels often refuse to make such suggestions. The panel in *EC – Tariff Preferences (2004)* explained its refusal as follows:

[I]n light of the fact that there is more than one way that the European Communities could bring its measures into conformity with its obligations under GATT 1994 and the fact that the European Communities has requested a waiver which is still pending, the Panel does not consider it appropriate to make any particular suggestions to the European Communities as to how the European Communities should bring its inconsistent measures into conformity with its obligations under GATT 1994.[391]

However, in *EC – Export Subsidies on Sugar (2005)*, in light of the concerns expressed by developing-country third parties with regard to their preferential access to the EC market for their sugar exports, the panel in that case suggested that:

[i]n bringing its exports of sugar into conformity with its obligations under Article 3.3 and 8 of the *Agreement on Agriculture*, the European Communities consider measures to bring its production of sugar more in line with domestic consumption whilst respecting its international commitments with respect to imports, including its commitments to developing countries.[392]

384 Panel Report, *India – Quantitative Restrictions (1999)*, para. 5.157.
385 See Article 19.1 of the DSU.
386 On the adoption of panel reports, below, pp. 277–8.
387 See Article 19.1 of the DSU.
388 On the legal effect of suggestions, see Appellate Body Report, *EC – Bananas III (Ecuador) (Article 21.5 – Ecuador II)/EC – Bananas III (US) (Article 21.5 – US) (2008)*, paras. 321–6.
389 See below, section 4.6.1.
390 See e.g. Panel Report, *EC – Bananas III (Ecuador) (1999)*, paras. 6.154–6.159. Panel Report, *Mexico – Steel Pipes and Tubes (2007)*, paras. 8.12–8.13.
391 Panel Report, *EC – Tariff Preferences (2004)*, para. 8.3.
392 Panel Report, *EC – Export Subsidies on Sugar (2005)*, para. 8.7.

Pursuant to Article 14.3 of the DSU, panellists can express a separate opinion in the panel report, be it dissenting or concurring. However, if they do, they must do so anonymously. To date, there have only been thirteen panel reports setting out a separate opinion of one of the panellists.[393]

In cases in which the DSB decides to establish one panel to hear complaints of several Members,[394] any party may, pursuant to Article 9.2 of the DSU, request a separate report from the panel. As such, the panel in *United States – Steel Safeguards (2003)* decided 'to issue its Reports in the form of one document constituting eight Panel Reports' with a common cover page and a common descriptive part.[395] Panel reports are always circulated to WTO Members, and made available to the public, in English, French and Spanish. Reports are not circulated until all three language versions are available. Most reports are written in English and then translated into French and Spanish. However, there have been a few panel reports written in Spanish,[396] and one written in French.[397] Panel reports often are several hundred pages long. The longest reports to date were *EC – Approval and Marketing of Biotech Products (2006)* (1,087 pages) and *EC and certain member States – Large Civil Aircraft (2011)* (1,044 pages).

5.3 The Appellate Body

Article 17.1 of the DSU provides for the establishment of a standing Appellate Body to hear appeals from reports of panels. The DSB established the Appellate Body in February 1995.[398] The WTO dispute settlement system is one of very few international dispute settlement mechanisms that provide for appellate review and has an appellate court. In 2003, Claus-Dieter Ehlermann referred to the Appellate Body as the 'World Trade Court'.[399] This section discusses: (1) the membership and structure of the Appellate Body; (2) the scope of appellate review; (3) the mandate of the Appellate Body; and (4) the requirements for Appellate Body reports.

393 See *WTO Analytical Index (2012)*, Volume II, 1720; and *Supplement to Analytical Index* (June 2015). Four of those separate opinions were referred to as 'dissenting opinions'. See e.g. Panel Report, *US – Tuna II*, para. 146ff.; Panel Report, *Canada – Feed-in Tariff Programme (2012)*, paras. 9.1–9.3; Panel Report, *US – Countervailing and Anti-Dumping Measures (China) (2014)*, paras. 7.212–7.241; Panel Reports, *China – Rare Earths (2014)*, paras. 7.118–7.138; and *US – Tuna II (Mexico) (Article 21.5) (2015)*, paras. 7.264–7.283, 7.606–7.607

394 See above, section 5.2.1.

395 Separate panel reports were also issued as a single document in, e.g., *EC – Approval and Marketing of Biotech Products (2006)*; *Philippines – Distilled Spirits (2012)*; and *EC – Seal Products (2014)*. Separate panel reports were issued in different documents in, e.g., *EC – Trademarks and Geographical Indications (2005)* and *EC – Bananas III (1997)*.

396 See e.g. Panel Report, *Peru – Agricultural Products (2015)*; Panel Report, *Argentina – Financial Services (2015)*.

397 See e.g. Panel Report, *EC – Asbestos (2001)*.

398 See Recommendations by the Preparatory Committee for the WTO approved by the Dispute Settlement Body on 10 February 1995, *Establishment of the Appellate Body*, WT/DSB/1, dated 19 June 1995.

399 See C.-D. Ehlermann, 'Six Years on the Bench of the World Trade Court: Personal Experiences as a Member of the Appellate Body of the World Trade Organization', *Journal of World Trade*, 2003, 605.

5.3.1 Membership and Structure of the Appellate Body

Unlike panels, the Appellate Body is a permanent international tribunal.[400] The Appellate Body is composed of seven judges referred to as 'Members' of the Appellate Body.[401] With respect to the required qualifications of Members of the Appellate Body, Article 17.3 of the DSU states in relevant part:

> The Appellate Body shall comprise persons of recognized authority, with demonstrated expertise in law, international trade and the subject-matter of the covered agreements generally. They shall be unaffiliated with any government.

It is understood that the expertise of Appellate Body Members should be of a type that allows them to resolve 'issues of law covered in the panel report and legal interpretations developed by the panel'.[402] While the overriding concern is to provide highly qualified Members for the Appellate Body,[403] Article 17.3 also requires that:

> [t]he Appellate Body membership shall be broadly representative of membership in the WTO.

Therefore, factors such as different geographical areas, levels of development and legal systems are taken into account.[404] In its *Decision Establishing the Appellate Body*, the DSB stated:

> The success of the WTO will depend greatly on the proper composition of the Appellate Body, and persons of the highest calibre should serve on it.[405]

In October 2016, the composition of the Appellate Body was as follows: Mr Ujal Singh Bhatia (India), Mr Thomas R. Graham (United States), Mr Ricardo Ramírez-Hernández (Mexico), Mr Shree Baboo Chekitan Servansing (Mauritius), and Mr Peter Van den Bossche (European Union).[406] Two positions on the Appellate Body were vacant.[407] Appellate Body Members are not required to reside permanently in Geneva and most do not. However, Article 17.3 of the DSU requires that they 'be available at all times and on short notice'.[408] Article 17.2 of the

400 See Article 17.1 of the DSU.

401 Note that from December 2013 to October 2014, the Appellate Body had six rather than seven Members due to the fact that the WTO Members could not agree on a successor to Mr David Unterhalter (South Africa), whose second term as an Appellate Body Member expired in December 2013. In October 2016, the Appellate Body had only five Members because WTO Members could not agree on a successor for Ms Yuejiao Zhang when she completed her second term and Members could not agree on the reappointment of Mr Seung Wha Chang for a second term.

402 Recommendations by the Preparatory Committee for the WTO approved by the Dispute Settlement Body on 10 February 1995, *Establishment of the Appellate Body*, 10 February 1995, WT/DSB/1, dated 19 June 1995, para. 5.

403 See *ibid.*, para. 6. 404 See *ibid.* 405 *Ibid.*, para. 4.

406 For biographical information on the current and former Members of the Appellate Body and their respective terms of office, see www.wto.org/english/tratop_e/dispu_e/ab_members_descrp_e.htm.

407 See above, p. 234, fn. 401.

408 Note that Appellate Body Members have 'part-time' appointments. This arrangement reflects the expectation on the part of WTO Members, in 1995, that the Appellate Body would not be so 'busy' as to justify a full-time employment arrangement. In fact, in most years, the workload of the Appellate Body has been such that it was difficult, and at times impossible, for Appellate Body Members to pursue other professional activities.

DSU states with respect to the appointment of Appellate Body Members and their term of office:

> The DSB shall appoint persons to serve on the Appellate Body for a four-year term, and each person may be reappointed once.

The Members of the Appellate Body thus serve a term of four years, which can be renewed once. Pursuant to Article 2.4 of the DSU, the DSB takes the decision on the appointment and reappointment of Appellate Body Members by consensus. It takes this decision on the recommendation of a Selection Committee, composed of the Chairs of the General Council, the DSB, the Council for Trade in Goods, the Council for Trade in Services, and the TRIPS Council and the WTO Director-General. The Selection Committee selects among candidates nominated by WTO Members. Note that in the context of the appointment processes in 2016, the Selection Committee interviewed seven candidates in April 2016 and two candidates in October 2016; it conducted individual consultations with fifty-one delegations in May and November 2016 before it formulated its recommendation. The DSB appointed Zhao Hong (China) and Hyon Chong Kim (Korea) as of 1 December 2016.

As already noted, Appellate Body Members shall not be affiliated with any government.[409] They must exercise their office without accepting or seeking instructions from any international, governmental or non-governmental organisation or any private source.[410] During their term of office, Members must not accept any employment, nor pursue any professional activity that is inconsistent with their duties and responsibilities.[411] The Members of the Appellate Body are *mutatis mutandis* subject to the same *Rules of Conduct* as those applicable to panellists, discussed above.[412] Under these Rules, Appellate Body Members:

> shall be independent and impartial, shall avoid direct or indirect conflicts of interest and shall respect the confidentiality of proceedings.[413]

They may not participate in the consideration of any appeal that would create a direct or indirect conflict of interests.[414] Parties can request the disqualification of an Appellate Body Member on the ground of a material violation of the obligations of the *Rules of Conduct*. It is, however, for the Appellate Body itself, and not for the Chair of the DSB (as is the case for panellists), to decide whether a material violation has occurred and, if so, to take appropriate action.[415]

As to the institutional structure of the Appellate Body, note first of all that the Appellate Body does not hear or decide appeals *en banc*. It hears and

409 See Article 17.3 of the DSU. 410 See Rule 2(3) of the *Working Procedures*.

411 See Rule 2(2) of the *Working Procedures*. 412 See above, p. 219.

413 Para. II(1) of the *Rules of Conduct*.

414 With regard to the disclosure obligation applicable to Appellate Body Members, see para. III(1), and para. VI(4)(b) and (5) of the *Rules of Conduct*.

415 See para. VIII(14)–(17) of the *Rules of Conduct*.

decides appeals in divisions of three Members.[416] Pursuant to Rule 6(2) of the *Working Procedures for Appellate Review*, commonly referred to as the *Working Procedures*, the Members constituting the division hearing and deciding a particular appeal are selected on the basis of *rotation*, taking into account the principles of random selection and unpredictability and opportunity for all Members to serve, regardless of their nationality. Unlike in the process for panellist selection, the nationality of Appellate Body Members is irrelevant. Appellate Body Members can, and will, sit in cases to which their countries of origin are party. The Members of a division select their presiding Member.[417] Pursuant to Rule 7(2) of the *Working Procedures*, the responsibilities of the presiding Member shall include: (1) coordinating the overall conduct of the appeal proceeding; (2) chairing all oral hearings and meetings related to that appeal; and (3) coordinating the drafting of the appellate report.

All decisions relating to an appeal are taken by the division assigned to that appeal. However, to ensure consistency and coherence in its case law and to draw on the individual and collective expertise of all seven Members, the division responsible for deciding an appeal exchanges views with the other Members on the issues raised by the appeal.[418] This exchange of views, which may take two to three days (or longer), is held before the division has come to any definitive views on the issues arising in the appeal.[419] While it is for the Appellate Body Members on the division to decide on the issues arising in the appeal and they are free not to take into account any 'advice' by other Members, the exchange of views, and the importance given to it, has undoubtedly contributed to the quality and consistency of the Appellate Body's case law and the limited number of separate opinions.[420]

A division makes every effort to take its decision on the appeal by consensus. However, if a decision cannot be reached by consensus, the *Working Procedures* provide that the matter at issue be decided by majority vote.[421] Pursuant to Article 17.11 of the DSU, individual Members may express separate opinions in the report, but these opinions (whether concurring or dissenting) must be anonymous. Separate opinions are rare in Appellate Body reports. To date, in only eight Appellate Body reports has an Appellate Body Member expressed an individual opinion.[422]

In addition to their meetings to exchange views on each appeal, all Appellate Body Members also convene on a regular basis to discuss matters of policy,

416 See Article 17.1 of the DSU and Rule 6(1) of the *Working Procedures*.
417 See Rule 7(1) of the *Working Procedures*.
418 See Rule 4(3) of the *Working Procedures*. Each Member therefore receives all documents filed in an appeal.
419 See also below, pp. 283–4.
420 On separate opinions, see e.g. above, p. 233, and below, p. 719, fn. 105, p. 873, fn. 554, and p. 893, fn. 43.
421 See Rule 3(2) of the *Working Procedures*.
422 For separate opinion(s) see, e.g., the Appellate Body reports in *EC and certain member States – Large Civil Aircraft (2011)*, *US – Washing Machines (2016)*, paras. 5.191ff. and *India – Solar Cells (2016)*, paras. 5.156ff.

practice and procedure.[423] If the Appellate Body is called upon to take a decision, it will try to do so by consensus. However, if it fails to reach a consensus, the decision will be taken by majority vote.

Each year the Appellate Body Members elect a chair from among themselves.[424] In 2016, Mr Thomas Graham served as the Chairperson of the Appellate Body. Rule 5(3) of the *Working Procedures* states that the Chair shall be responsible for the overall direction of the Appellate Body business. His or her responsibilities shall include: (1) the supervision of the internal functioning of the Appellate Body; and (2) any such other duties as the Members may agree to entrust to him/her.

The Appellate Body has its own secretariat, which is separate from and independent of the WTO Secretariat.[425] The Appellate Body Secretariat provides the Appellate Body with legal and administrative support.[426] The *Rules of Conduct* and their requirements of independence, impartiality and confidentiality apply to the staff of the Appellate Body Secretariat.[427] The Appellate Body Secretariat has its offices in the Centre William Rappard, the lakeside premises of the WTO Secretariat in Geneva. All meetings of the Appellate Body or of divisions of the Appellate Body, as well as the oral hearings in appeals, are also held on these premises.

5.3.2 Scope of Appellate Review

As stated above, appellate review of panel reports is entrusted to the Appellate Body. This subsection deals with the scope of this review, and focuses on the following two questions: (1) who can appeal; and (2) what can be appealed.

First, with regard to the question who can appeal, Article 17.4 states in clear terms:

> Only parties to the dispute, not third parties, may appeal a panel report.

However, while third parties or other WTO Members cannot appeal a panel report, third parties, i.e. WTO Members, which have notified the DSB of a substantial interest in the dispute at the time of the establishment of the panel,[428] can participate in the Appellate Body proceedings.[429] Members which were not third parties in the panel proceedings, cannot participate in Appellate Body proceedings.[430]

423 See Rule 4 of the *Working Procedures.*
424 See Rule 5(1) of the *Working Procedures.* While the term of office of the chair is one year, the Appellate Body may exceptionally decide to extend the term of office for an additional period of up to one year.
425 See Recommendations by the Preparatory Committee for the WTO approved by the Dispute Settlement Body on 10 February 1995, *Establishment of the Appellate Body*, 10 February 1995, WT/DSB/1, dated 19 June 1995, para. 17.
426 Article 17.7 of the DSU. As of 31 December 2015, the Appellate Body Secretariat consisted of a director, seventeen staff lawyers, one administrative assistant and four support staff.
427 See above, p. 219. 428 See above, p. 216.
429 On the participants' rights in Appellate Body proceedings, see below, p. 238.
430 Note, however, that these Members may submit an *amicus curiae* brief. See below, pp. 260–4.

In Appellate Body proceedings, the parties are referred to as 'participants'. The participant that appeals a panel report is called the 'appellant', while the participant responding to an appeal is called the 'appellee'. Once one of the participants has appealed certain aspects of a panel report, it is not uncommon for other participants to 'cross-appeal' other aspects of the report.[431] A participant cross-appealing is known as an 'other appellant'. Third parties choosing to participate in the Appellate Body proceedings are referred to as 'third participants'.

Second, with regard to the question what can be appealed, Article 17.6 of the DSU states:

> An appeal shall be limited to issues of law covered in the panel report and legal interpretations developed by the panel.

In *EC – Hormones (1998)*, the Appellate Body found that factual findings of panels are, in principle, excluded from the scope of appellate review. The Appellate Body stated:

> Under Article 17.6 of the DSU, appellate review is limited to appeals on questions of law covered in a panel report and legal interpretations developed by the panel. Findings of fact, as distinguished from legal interpretations or legal conclusions, by a panel are, in principle, not subject to review by the Appellate Body.[432]

In many cases, the characterisation of findings as findings on issues of fact, rather than on issues of law or legal interpretations, is fairly straightforward. In *EC – Hormones (1998)*, the Appellate Body noted that:

> [t]he determination of whether or not a certain event did occur in time and space is typically a question of fact.[433]

In that dispute, the Appellate Body found that the panel's findings regarding whether or not international standards had been adopted by the Codex Alimentarius Commission were findings on issues of fact and were, therefore, not subject to appellate review. In other cases, the task of distinguishing between findings on issues of fact and findings on issues of law can be a complex exercise. The Appellate Body has made it clear, however, that findings involving the application of a legal rule to a specific fact or a set of facts are findings on issues of law and thus fall within the scope of appellate review. As stated in *EC – Hormones (1998)*:

> [t]he consistency or inconsistency of a given fact or set of facts with the requirements of a given treaty provision is ... a legal characterization issue. It is a legal question.[434]

431 See below, p. 280.

432 Appellate Body Report, *EC – Hormones (1998)*, para. 132. See also Appellate Body Report, *EC – Bananas III (1997)*, para. 239.

433 Appellate Body Report, *EC – Hormones (1998)*, para. 132.

434 *Ibid.* Considerable reliance has been placed by later decisions on this proposition. Note that in *EC – Seal Products (2014)*, the Appellate Body held that a panel's identification of the policy objective pursued by a measure is a matter of legal characterisation and thus subject to appellate review under Article 17.6 of the DSU. See Appellate Body Reports, *EC – Seal Products (2014)*, para. 5.144.

The Appellate Body had used similar reasoning in *Canada – Periodicals (1997)* to explain why the panel's determination of 'like products', for the purposes of Article III:2 of the GATT 1994, was subject to appellate review:

> The determination of whether imported and domestic products are 'like products' is a process by which legal rules have to be applied to facts.[435]

In *EC – Seal Products (2014)* the Appellate Body held that a panel's identification of the policy objective pursued by a measure is a matter of legal characterisation and thus subject to appellate review under Article 17.6 of the DSU.[436]

With regard to the question whether panel findings on the meaning of municipal law fall within the scope of appellate review the Appellate Body ruled in *US – Section 211 Appropriations Act (2002)* that:

> a panel may examine the municipal law of a WTO Member for the purpose of determining whether that Member has complied with its obligations under the *WTO Agreement*. Such an assessment is a legal characterization by a panel. And, therefore, a panel's assessment of municipal law as to its consistency with WTO obligations is subject to appellate review under Article 17.6 of the DSU.[437]

Therefore, the scope and content of the municipal law of a Member, as determined by a panel, for the purpose of ascertaining the Member's compliance with WTO obligations, is a question of law, which the Appellate Body can review.[438]

Referring to its report in *US – Carbon Steel (2002)*, the Appellate Body ruled in *US – Countervailing and Anti-Dumping Measures (China) (2014)* with regard to the elements that a panel and eventually the Appellate Body would need to examine to ascertain the meaning of municipal law that:

> Whereas in some cases the text of the relevant legislation may suffice to clarify the scope and meaning of the relevant legal instruments, in other cases the complainant will also need to support its understanding of the scope and meaning of such legal instruments with 'evidence of the consistent application of such laws, the pronouncements of domestic courts on the meaning of such laws, the opinions of legal experts and the writings of recognized scholars'.[439]

The Appellate Body further clarified in *US – Countervailing and Anti-Dumping Measures (China) (2014)* that:

> Although factual aspects may be involved in the individuation of the text and of some associated circumstances, an assessment of the meaning of a text of municipal law for purposes of determining whether it complies with a provision of the covered agreements is

435 Appellate Body Report, *Canada – Periodicals (1997)*, 468.

436 See Appellate Body Reports, *EC – Seal Products (2014)*, para. 5.144.

437 Appellate Body Report, *US – Section 211 Appropriations Act (2002)*, paras. 105–6. See also, e.g., Appellate Body Report, *India – Patents (US) (1998)*, para. 68; and Appellate Body Report, *China – Auto Parts (2009)*, para. 225.

438 See Appellate Body Report, *US – Section 211 Appropriations Act (2002)*, paras. 105–6, relying on Appellate Body Report, *India – Patents (US) (1998)*, paras. 65–6 and 68. See also Appellate Body Report, *US – Countervailing and Anti-Dumping Measures (China) (2014)*, paras. 4.98–4.102.

439 Appellate Body Report, *US – Countervailing and Anti-Dumping Measures (China) (2014)*, para. 4.100, referring to Appellate Body Report, *US – Carbon Steel (2002)*, para. 157.

a legal characterization. Similarly, whether or when a domestic court ruling has been rendered and finalized, or what a writing by a recognized scholar contains, may involve factual aspects. However, the examination of the legal interpretation given by a domestic court or by a domestic administering agency as to the meaning of municipal law with respect to the measure being reviewed for consistency with the covered agreements may be a legal characterization.[440]

As the Appellate Body summed up in *EU – Biodiesel (2016)* that:

a panel's assessment of municipal law for the purpose of determining its consistency with WTO obligations is subject to appellate review under Article 17.6 of the DSU. Just as it is necessary for the panel to seek a detailed understanding of the municipal law at issue, so too is it necessary for the Appellate Body to review the panel's examination of that municipal law.[441]

In brief, pursuant to Article 17.6 of the DSU, the Appellate Body can review a panel's interpretation of WTO provisions as well as the panel's application of these provisions to the facts in the case at hand. However, there is more. As explained below, the Appellate Body can also review whether a panel has made an objective assessment of the facts as a panel is required to do under Article 11 of the DSU.[442] As a panel's factual determinations are, in principle, not subject to appellate review, a panel's weighing and assessment of evidence before it is also, in principle, not subject to appellate review.[443] In *EC – Hormones (1998)*, the Appellate Body found:

Determination of the credibility and weight properly to be ascribed to (that is, the appreciation of) a given piece of evidence is part and parcel of the fact finding process and is, in principle, left to the discretion of a panel as the trier of facts.[444]

In *Korea – Alcoholic Beverages (1999)*, in which Korea sought to cast doubt on certain studies relied on by the panel in that case, the Appellate Body stated:

The Panel's examination and weighing of the evidence submitted fall, in principle, within the scope of the Panel's discretion as the trier of facts and, accordingly, outside the scope of appellate review[445] ... We *cannot second-guess* the Panel in appreciating either the evidentiary value of such studies or the consequences, if any, of alleged defects in those studies. Similarly, it is not for us to review the relative weight ascribed to evidence on such matters as marketing studies.[446]

Panels thus have wide-ranging discretion in the consideration and weight they give to the evidence before them.[447] However, a panel's discretion in the

440 *Ibid.*, para. 4.101.

441 Appellate Body Report, *EU – Biodiesel (2016)*, para. 6.155 (referring to Appellate Body Report, *India – Patents (US) (1998)*, para. 68); and Appellate Body Report, *US – Section 211 Appropriations Act (2002)*, para. 105.

442 On a panel's obligations under Article 11 of the DSU, see above, pp. 222–7.

443 Appellate Body Report, *US – Offset Act (Byrd Amendment) (2003)*, para. 220.

444 Appellate Body Report, *EC – Hormones (1998)*, para. 132.

445 This is true, for instance, with respect to the panel's treatment of the Dodwell Study, the Sofres Report and the Nielsen Study.

446 Appellate Body Report, *Korea – Alcoholic Beverages (1999)*, para. 161. Emphasis added.

447 See also e.g. Appellate Body Report, *Australia – Salmon (1998)*, para. 261; Appellate Body Report, *India – Quantitative Restrictions (1999)*, para. 143; and Appellate Body Report, *Korea – Dairy (2000)*, para. 137.

consideration and weight it gives to evidence is *not* unlimited.[448] A panel's factual determinations must be consistent with Article 11 of the DSU, i.e. consistent with the standard of review the panel must apply.[449] As noted by the Appellate Body in *EC – Hormones (1998)*:

> Whether or not a panel has made an objective assessment of the facts before it, as required by Article 11 of the DSU, is also a legal question which, if properly raised on appeal, would fall within the scope of appellate review.[450]

Therefore, a factual finding may be subject to appellate review when the appellant alleges that this finding was not reached in a manner consistent with the requirements of Article 11 of the DSU, which were discussed in some detail above.[451]

In a number of appeals to date, the appellant claimed with regard to specific findings that the panel erred in its application of the law to the facts *as well as* in its duty to make an objective assessment of the facts under Article 11 of the DSU.[452] While both claims of error are within the appellate jurisdiction of the Appellate Body under Article 17.6 of the DSU, it is important to determine which claim of error is properly made with regard to specific findings. This is so because the threshold for a finding that a panel erred in its duty to make an objective assessment of the facts is much higher than the threshold for a finding that the panel erred in its application of the law to the facts. In *China – GOES (2012)*, the Appellate Body observed the following in this respect:

> In most cases ... the issue raised by a particular claim 'will either be one of application of the law to the facts or an issue of the objective assessment of facts, and not both'. The Appellate Body has found that allegations implicating a panel's appreciation of facts and evidence fall under Article 11 of the DSU. By contrast, '[t]he consistency or inconsistency of a given fact or set of facts with the requirements of a given treaty provision is ... a legal characterization issue' and is therefore a legal question.[453]

With regard to the question whether the Appellate Body may consider 'new facts' on appeal, the Appellate Body held in *US – Offset Act (Byrd Amendment) (2003)* that it had no authority to do so, even if these new facts are contained in

448 See Appellate Body Report, *Korea – Alcoholic Beverages (1999)*, para. 162.

449 See above, pp. 222–7.

450 Appellate Body Report, *EC – Hormones (1998)*, para. 132. See also e.g. Appellate Body Report, *Korea – Alcoholic Beverages (1999)*, para. 162.

451 See above, pp. 222–7.

452 As the Appellate Body explained in *EC and certain member States – Large Civil Aircraft (2011)*, a failure to make a claim under Article 11 of the DSU on an issue that the Appellate Body determines to concern a factual assessment (rather than the application of the law to the facts) may have serious consequences for the appellant. Therefore, an appellant may 'feel safer putting forward both a claim that the Panel erred in the application of the law to the facts *and* a claim that the panel failed to make an objective assessment of the facts under Article 11 of the DSU'. See Appellate Body Report, *EC and certain member States – Large Civil Aircraft (2011)*, para. 872.

453 Appellate Body Report, *China – GOES (2012)*, para. 183. See also Appellate Body Report, *EC and certain member States – Large Civil Aircraft (2011)*, para. 872.

documents that are 'available on the public record'.[454] In *US – Softwood Lumber V (2004)*, Canada asked that the United States be requested to submit certain documents to the Appellate Body. The Appellate Body declined to do so, stating that:

> the materials at issue constituted new factual evidence and, therefore, pursuant to Article 17.6 of the DSU, fell outside the scope of the appeal.[455]

However, data need not be presented to the Appellate Body in *precisely* the same manner as before the panel. If the data presented on appeal can be clearly traced to the data in the panel record and the way in which such data has been converted can be readily understood, the evidence presented on appeal will not amount to 'new evidence', excluded by Article 17.6.[456]

With regard to 'new arguments' (as opposed to 'new facts'), the Appellate Body held in *Canada – Aircraft (1999)* that 'new arguments' on appeal cannot be rejected 'simply because they are new'. However, the Appellate Body recognised that Article 17.6 of the DSU forecloses the possibility for the Appellate Body to decide on a new argument that would involve reviewing new facts.[457]

The Appellate Body had occasion in *EC – Poultry (1998)* to note that Article 17.6, read together with Article 17.13, discussed below, precludes from appellate review comments[458] or statements[459] by the panel (as opposed to legal findings and conclusions). However, in recent years the Appellate Body does not seem to have taken an overly restrictive approach as to what can be appealed. Based on Article 17.12 of the DSU, discussed below, the Appellate Body has repeatedly addressed panel statements that do not constitute legal findings or conclusions.[460]

Finally, note that during the first years of the WTO dispute settlement system, all panel reports were appealed. To date, by average, 68 per cent of the circulated panel reports have been appealed.[461] This high rate of appeal is not necessarily a reflection of the quality of the panel reports but rather of the fact that appealing

454 See Appellate Body Report, *US – Offset Act (Byrd Amendment) (2003)*, paras. 221–2. Note, however, that a new fact in a document that is publicly available may *in principle* be considered on appeal if the document is expressly referred to in the measure in question and its contents were discussed before the panel. The other party may have to establish prejudice in entertaining such a document so as to render it inadmissible before the Appellate Body. See Appellate Body Report, *Chile – Price Band System (2002)*, para. 13.

455 Appellate Body Report, *US – Softwood Lumber V (2004)*, para. 9.

456 See Appellate Body Report, *Chile – Price Band System (2002)*, para. 13. See also e.g. Appellate Body Report, *EC – Export Subsidies on Sugar (2005)*, para. 242.

457 See Appellate Body Report, *Canada – Aircraft (1999)*, para. 211. See also e.g. Appellate Body Report, *US – FSC (2000)*, para. 103.

458 See Appellate Body Report, *EC – Poultry (1998)*, para. 107.

459 See Appellate Body Report, *US – Wool Shirts and Blouses (1997)*, 338.

460 See Appellate Body Reports, *China – Raw Materials (2010)*, para. 390. The panel statement at issue regarded the requirements under Article XX(g) of the GATT 1994. This statement was not a legal finding or conclusion, but the Appellate Body nevertheless addressed the claim of error raised by China since the statement concerned pertained to a core element of the panel's interpretation of Article XX(g) and could have created confusion in later disputes if left unaddressed by the Appellate Body. See also Appellate Body Report, *EC and certain member States – Large Civil Aircraft (2011)*, paras. 930–4.

461 See www.worldtradelaw.net/databases/appealcount.php. In 2016, the rate of appeal had risen to 88 per cent.

an unfavourable panel report is a rational decision for a losing party to take. As discussed above, in most disputes the panel finds against the respondent, at least in respect of part of the complainant's claims. Often the respondent will consider that it has little to lose by appealing.[462] On the contrary, an appeal – even if eventually unsuccessful – will allow a party, found to have acted inconsistently with WTO law, to delay the moment at which it has to bring its legislation or policy into consistency by usually three months. An appeal will also demonstrate to domestic constituencies that a Member has exhausted *all* legal means available to avert what may be economically painful and/or politically sensitive changes to national legislation or policies.

5.3.3 Mandate of the Appellate Body

The mandate of the Appellate Body is set out in Articles 17.12 and 17.13 of the DSU. Article 17.12 states:

> The Appellate Body shall address each of the issues raised in accordance with paragraph 6 during the appellate proceeding.

Article 17.13 states:

> The Appellate Body may uphold, modify or reverse the legal findings and conclusions of the panel.

With regard to Article 17.12 of the DSU, it should be noted that the Appellate Body has repeatedly ruled that this provision does not preclude it from exercising judicial economy.[463] Underlying this position may be the reasoning that expressly exercising judicial economy with regard to an issue (as opposed to remaining silent on that issue) is considered to amount to 'addressing' the issue.

When the Appellate Body agrees with both the panel's reasoning and the conclusion regarding the WTO consistency of a measure, it *upholds* the relevant findings. When the Appellate Body agrees with the conclusion but not with the reasoning leading to that conclusion, it *modifies* the relevant findings. If the Appellate Body disagrees with the conclusion regarding the WTO consistency of a measure, it *reverses* the relevant findings. In practice, however, the distinction between 'upholding' and 'modifying' is not always as clear-cut as suggested above, and the Appellate Body may 'uphold' a panel finding even though it amends or supplements the panel's reasoning leading to this finding.[464]

When the Appellate Body upholds all findings appealed, it upholds the panel report *as a whole*. In very few panel reports appealed the Appellate Body found

462 However, when a respondent fears that after the Appellate Body has considered the issues that may be raised on appeal, it might find itself 'worse off', it is likely to decide not to appeal an adverse panel report. An example of such panel reports may be *US – Section 301 Trade Act (2000)*.

463 See e.g. Appellate Body Report, *US – Upland Cotton (2005)*, paras. 761–2.

464 See e.g. Appellate Body Report, *US – Hot-Rolled Steel (2001)*, paras. 90 and 158; and Appellate Body Report, *US – Lamb (2001)*, para. 188.

such fundamental error that it could not but reverse the whole report.[465] In most appeals, the results of the appellate review were mixed. Some of the findings appealed were upheld, some modified and/or reversed. The panel report as a whole therefore was modified.

Although Article 17.13 of the DSU allows the Appellate Body only to uphold, modify or reverse the panel's findings appealed, the Appellate Body has, in a number of cases, gone beyond that mandate and has, explicitly or implicitly, 'completed the legal analysis'. The need for 'completing the legal analysis' may arise when a dispute could potentially remain unresolved due to the Appellate Body's disposition of a claim on appeal. For example, if the panel report is appealed and the Appellate Body reverses the panel's findings of inconsistency with WTO provisions A and B, the question arises as to what the Appellate Body can do with regard to the claims of inconsistency with WTO provision C, which the panel, in its exercise of judicial economy, did not address. The question of whether the Appellate Body can complete the legal analysis also arises in cases in which a panel concludes that a provision or provisions of WTO law (e.g. the *TBT Agreement*, as was the case in *EC – Asbestos (2001)*) is not applicable in the case at hand but in which, on appeal of this finding of inapplicability, the Appellate Body comes to the opposite conclusion.

In many domestic judicial systems, the appeals court would in similar situations 'remand' the case to the court of first instance. However, the DSU does not provide the Appellate Body with the authority to remand a dispute to the panel. In the absence of a remand authority, the Appellate Body is left with two options: (1) either to leave the dispute unresolved; or (2) to go on to 'complete the legal analysis'. In *Canada – Periodicals (1997)*, the Appellate Body stated:

> We believe the Appellate Body *can, and should*, complete the analysis of Article III:2 of the GATT 1994 in this case by examining the measure with reference to its consistency with the second sentence of Article III:2, *provided that there is a sufficient basis in the Panel Report to allow us to do so*.[466]

In the circumstances of that case, the Appellate Body considered that it would be 'remiss in not completing the analysis of Article III:2'.[467] The Appellate Body would be 'remiss in not completing the analysis' because the prompt settlement of disputes is a fundamental objective of the WTO dispute settlement system.

However, the Appellate Body has 'completed the legal analysis' only in cases in which there were sufficient factual findings in the panel report or undisputed

465 For examples of panel reports reversed, see e.g. the reports in *Guatemala – Cement I (1998)* and *Canada – Dairy (Article 21.5 – New Zealand and US) (2001)*.

466 Appellate Body Report, *Canada – Periodicals (1997)*, 469. Emphasis added. 467 *Ibid.*

facts in the panel record to enable it to carry out the legal analysis.[468] In practice, the Appellate Body has often found it impossible to 'complete the legal analysis' due to insufficient factual findings in the panel report or a lack of undisputed facts in the panel record.[469] In addition, the Appellate Body has declined to complete the legal analysis because of the novel character of the claims, which the panel did not address.[470] The absence of full exploration of the issues before the panel or in the course of the Appellate Body proceedings has also been a reason for the Appellate Body not to complete the legal analysis.[471] In such situations, the Appellate Body would not complete the legal analysis out of consideration for parties' due process rights.[472] The Appellate Body will also decline to complete the legal analysis when a panel is thought to have improperly excluded evidence, or erred in its assessment of evidence, and the Appellate Body would have to examine the evidence in order to complete the legal analysis.[473] Finally, the Appellate Body will not complete the legal analysis if the completion is not necessary to resolve the dispute.[474]

5.4 Other Entities Involved in WTO Dispute Settlement

Apart from the DSB, panels and the Appellate Body, there are a number of other institutions, bodies and persons involved in the WTO's efforts to resolve disputes between its Members, including: (1) the Chair of the DSB;[475] (2) the WTO Director-General;[476] (3) arbitrators under Articles 21.3, 22.6 and 25 of the DSU;[477] (4) experts under Articles 13.1 and 13.2 of the DSU, Article 11.2 of the *SPS Agreement* and

468 See Appellate Body Report, *Australia – Salmon (1998)*, para. 118. See also Appellate Body Report, *EC and certain member States – Large Civil Aircraft (2011)*, paras. 1174–8. 'Undisputed' or 'uncontested' facts are facts put forward by one party and not disputed/contested by the other party, or facts in which both parties rely in their argumentation. Note that the Appellate Body has also completed the legal analysis on the basis of facts that the losing party submitted and, therefore, admitted. See e.g. Appellate Body Report, *US – Large Civil Aircraft (2nd Complaint) (2012)*, paras. 662 and 741.

469 See e.g. Appellate Body Report, *US – Zeroing (EC) (2006)*, paras. 228 and 243; Appellate Body Report, *EC and certain member States – Large Civil Aircraft (2011)*, paras. 1143–7; Appellate Body Reports, *US – COOL (2012)*, para. 481; and Appellate Body Report, *US – Countervailing and Anti-Dumping Measures (China) (2014)*, paras. 4.182–4.183.

470 See Appellate Body Report, *EC – Asbestos (2001)*, para. 82. Claims are 'novel' when they concern issues, which have not yet been dealt with in the WTO case law, as was the case in *EC – Asbestos (2001)* with regard to the obligations under Articles 2.1, 2.2, 2.4 and 2.8 of the *TBT Agreement*; or in *EC – Seal Products (2014)* with regard to the term 'related processes and production methods' under Annex 1.1 of the *TBT Agreement*.

471 See Appellate Body Reports, *Canada – Renewable Energy / Canada – Feed-in Tariff Program (2013)*, para. 5.224 (referring to Appellate Body Report, *EC – Export Subsidies on Sugar (2005)*, para. 339, fn. 573).

472 See *ibid.*

473 See Appellate Body Report, *US – Countervailing Duty Investigation on DRAMs (2005)*, paras. 196–7.

474 See e.g. Appellate Body Report, *US – Steel Safeguards (2003)*, paras. 430–1.

475 See e.g. above, pp. 216, 218 and 219, and below, pp. 270 and 279.

476 See e.g. above, pp. 187 and 218 and below, pp. 279 and 286.

477 See e.g. above, p. 187 and below, p. 286.

Article 14 of the *TBT Agreement*;[478] (5) Expert Review Groups under Article 13.2 of and Appendix 4 to the DSU;[479] (6) Technical Expert Groups under Article 14.3 of and Annex 2 to the *TBT Agreement*;[480] (7) the Permanent Group of Experts under Article 4.5 of the *SCM Agreement*;[481] and (8) the Facilitator under Annex V.4 to the *SCM Agreement* on information gathering.[482] The institutions, bodies or persons listed above, such as arbitrators, experts and expert groups, which directly participate in panel or Appellate Body proceedings, are subject to the *Rules of Conduct*, discussed earlier.[483]

6 PROCESS OF WTO DISPUTE SETTLEMENT

Having discussed in previous sections the jurisdiction, the object and purpose, and the structure, role and operation of the institutions of WTO dispute settlement, this section finally focuses on the process of WTO dispute settlement. The WTO dispute settlement process may – and often does – entail four major steps: (1) consultations; (2) panel proceedings; (3) Appellate Body proceedings; and (4) implementation and enforcement. As already indicated above, the process always starts with *consultations*, or at least an attempt by the complainant to involve the respondent in consultations, to resolve the dispute amicably. If that is not possible, the complainant can refer the dispute to a panel for adjudication. The *panel proceedings* will result in a panel report. This report can be appealed to the Appellate Body. The *appellate review proceedings* will result in an Appellate Body report upholding, modifying or reversing the panel report. The panel report, or, in the case of an appeal, the Appellate Body report *and* the panel report, will be adopted by the Dispute Settlement Body. After the adoption of the reports, the respondent, if found to be in breach of WTO law, will have to implement the recommendations and rulings adopted by the DSB. This *implementation and enforcement* of the adopted recommendations and rulings constitute the last major step in the WTO dispute settlement process.

Figure 3.2, a flowchart prepared by the WTO Secretariat, reflects the four major steps, adding some additional detail, which is discussed below. It is, however, not the ambition of this section to inform the reader in detail of the multiple

478 See e.g. above, p. 228, and below, pp. 274, 986 and 931–2.
479 See below, p. 229.
480 See below, p. 931. 481 See below, p. 809.
482 See e.g. above, p. 210, fn. 257.
483 See para. IV(1) of the *Rules of Conduct*.

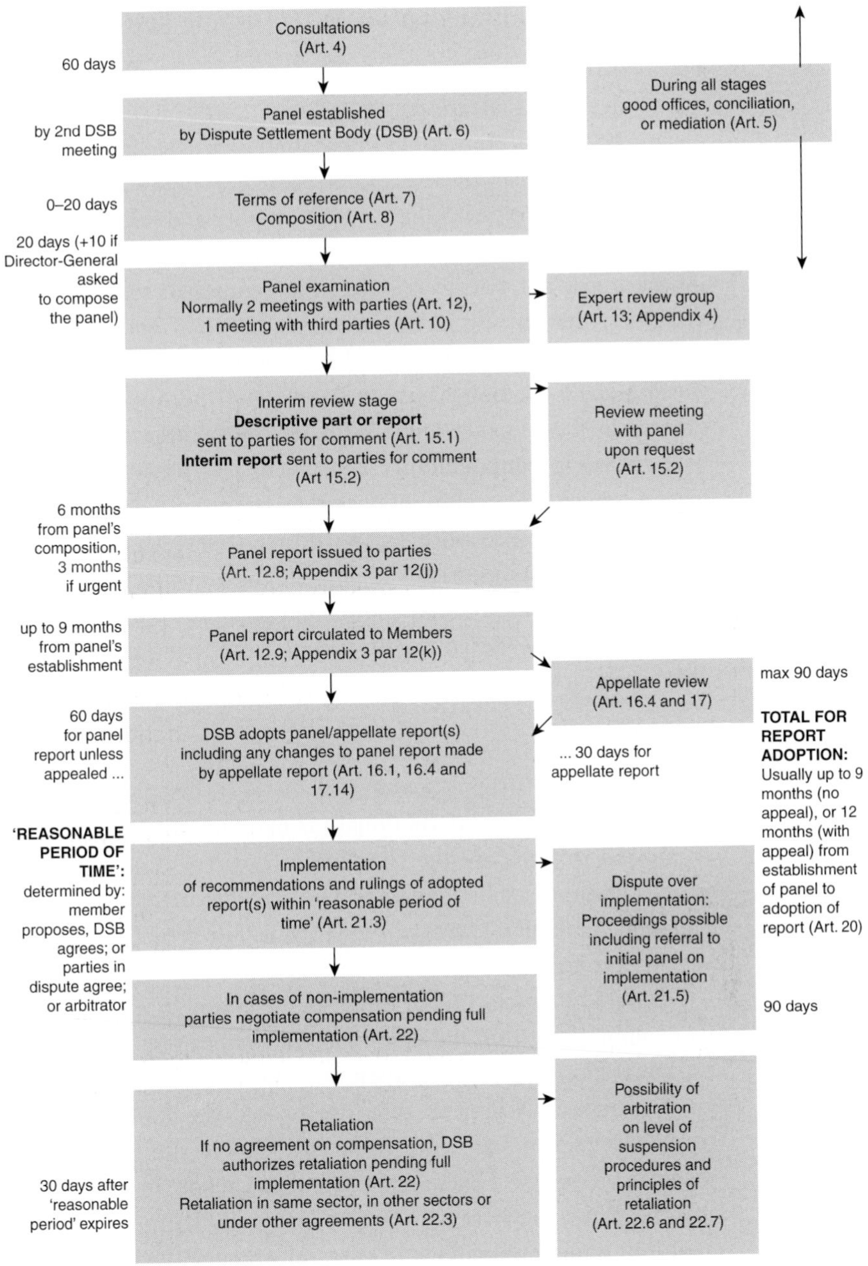

60 days

Consultations (Art. 4)

↓

by 2nd DSB meeting

Panel established by Dispute Settlement Body (DSB) (Art. 6)

↓

0–20 days

Terms of reference (Art. 7)
Composition (Art. 8)

↓

20 days (+10 if Director-General asked to compose the panel)

Panel examination
Normally 2 meetings with parties (Art. 12),
1 meeting with third parties (Art. 10)
→ Expert review group (Art. 13; Appendix 4)

↓

Interim review stage
Descriptive part or report sent to parties for comment (Art. 15.1)
Interim report sent to parties for comment (Art 15.2)
→ Review meeting with panel upon request (Art. 15.2)

↓

6 months from panel's composition, 3 months if urgent

Panel report issued to parties (Art. 12.8; Appendix 3 par 12(j))

↓

up to 9 months from panel's establishment

Panel report circulated to Members (Art. 12.9; Appendix 3 par 12(k))
→ Appellate review (Art. 16.4 and 17) — max 90 days

↓

60 days for panel report unless appealed ... / ... 30 days for appellate report

DSB adopts panel/appellate report(s) including any changes to panel report made by appellate report (Art. 16.1, 16.4 and 17.14)

TOTAL FOR REPORT ADOPTION: Usually up to 9 months (no appeal), or 12 months (with appeal) from establishment of panel to adoption of report (Art. 20)

↓

'REASONABLE PERIOD OF TIME': determined by: member proposes, DSB agrees; or parties in dispute agree; or arbitrator

Implementation of recommendations and rulings of adopted report(s) within 'reasonable period of time' (Art. 21.3)
→ Dispute over implementation: Proceedings possible including referral to initial panel on implementation (Art. 21.5) — 90 days

↓

In cases of non-implementation parties negotiate compensation pending full implementation (Art. 22)

↓

30 days after 'reasonable period' expires

Retaliation
If no agreement on compensation, DSB authorizes retaliation pending full implementation (Art. 22)
Retaliation in same sector, in other sectors or under other agreements (Art. 22.3)
→ Possibility of arbitration on level of suspension procedures and principles of retaliation (Art. 22.6 and 22.7)

During all stages good offices, conciliation, or mediation (Art. 5)

Figure 3.2 Flowchart of the WTO dispute settlement process

procedural provisions of WTO dispute settlement. Rather, this section will first include six general observations on the WTO dispute settlement process, and, then, in a broad manner, deal in turn with each of the major steps in the WTO dispute settlement process, as listed above.

6.1 General Observations on the WTO Dispute Settlement Process

The WTO dispute settlement process has many noteworthy features, but there are six features that are particularly so, partly because they distinguish WTO dispute settlement from other international dispute settlement mechanisms. This subsection discusses these features, namely: (1) the short time frame for each of the steps in the process; (2) the confidentiality and resulting lack of transparency of the process; (3) the burden of proof in WTO dispute settlement proceedings; (4) the important role of private legal counsel in representing parties in WTO dispute settlement; (5) the controversial issue of *amicus curiae* briefs; and (6) the obligation on Members to act in good faith in WTO dispute settlement proceedings, and the obligation on panels and the Appellate Body to ensure due process in these proceedings. With regard to these features, and in particular with regard to confidentiality and the role of private legal counsel, there has been a remarkable evolution since the initiation of the WTO dispute settlement system in 1995. Also, with regard to time frames and confidentiality, there has been – and continues to be – a marked tension between theory and practice, i.e. between the world of legal requirements and noble ambitions on the one hand, and the world of limited resources and short-term political convenience on the other hand.

6.1.1 Time frame

One of the most striking features of the WTO dispute settlement process when compared with other international (or national) dispute settlement mechanisms or judicial systems are the short time frames within which, in particular, the panel and Appellate Body proceedings must be completed. Also, the consultation and implementation stages of the WTO dispute settlement process are subject to (strict) time frames.[484]

Pursuant to Article 12.8 of the DSU, the period in which a panel must conduct its examination, from the date that the composition and terms of reference of the panel have been agreed upon until the date the final report is issued to the parties, shall, as a general rule, not exceed six months.[485] However, as stated in Article 12.9 of the DSU, in no case should the period from the establishment of the panel to the circulation of the report to the Members exceed nine months.[486] Even shorter time frames (generally half of the standard time frame) apply for panel proceedings in cases of urgency (including disputes relating to

484 On the time frames for consultation and implementation stages, see below, pp. 268 and 287, respectively.

485 When a panel considers that it cannot issue its report within six months, it shall inform the DSB in writing of the reasons for the delay, together with an estimate of the period within which it will issue its report.

486 See Article 12.9 of the DSU. When compared to the time frame of Article 12.8, the time frame of Article 12.9 starts earlier (the establishment of the panel precedes its composition) and finishes later (the panel report is first issued to the parties and later circulated). See also below, pp. 249–50.

perishable goods) and with respect to disputes regarding subsidies under the *SCM Agreement*.[487] Also, the Article 21.5 compliance panel proceedings are subject to a shorter time frame than the standard panel proceedings.[488]

In practice, however, the panel proceedings often exceed the standard time frames of six and nine months. On average, a panel process – from the establishment of the panel until the circulation of the panel report – lasts 484 days, or approximately sixteen months.[489] The reasons for exceeding the DSU time frames include: the complexity of the case; the need to consult experts; the availability of experts; problems with scheduling meetings; and the time taken to translate the report. The longest panel proceedings to date have been those in *US – Large Civil Aircraft (2nd complaint) (2012)*, which lasted for 61 months; and in *EC and certain member States – Large Civil Aircraft (2011)*, which lasted for 59.2 months.[490] In both *EC – Approval and Marketing of Biotech Products (2006)* and *US/Canada – Continued Suspension (2008)*, it took the panel, respectively, 37 months to complete the panel proceedings.[491]

With regard to the time frame for Appellate Body proceedings, Article 17.5 of the DSU provides that, as a general rule, the proceedings shall not exceed sixty days from the date a party to the dispute formally notifies its decision to appeal to the date the Appellate Body circulates its report.[492] As Article 17.5 explicitly states, 'in no case shall the proceedings exceed ninety days'.[493] As for panel proceedings, even shorter time frames (generally half of the standard time frames) apply for Appellate Body proceedings in cases of urgency (including disputes relating to perishable goods) and with respect to disputes regarding subsidies under the *SCM Agreement*.[494]

In practice, the Appellate Body has, in almost all cases, taken more than sixty days to complete the appellate review.[495] However, until 2011, the Appellate Body has been able to complete the appellate review proceedings in ninety days in the vast majority of cases.[496] The longest Appellate Body proceedings to date have been those in *US – Large Civil Aircraft (2nd complaint) (2012)*, which

487 See Article 12.8 of the DSU and Article 4 of the *SCM Agreement*. See below, pp. 808–10.

488 On the Article 21.5 compliance panel proceedings, see below, p. 287. According to Article 21.5 of the DSU, such proceedings *should not* take more than ninety days.

489 See www.worldtradelaw.net/databases/paneltiming.php. This is the average length of original, as opposed to Article 21.5 compliance panel proceedings. See below, p. 287.

490 See *ibid*. 491 See *ibid*.

492 When the Appellate Body believes that it cannot render its report within sixty days, it shall inform the DSB in writing of the reasons for the delay together with an estimate of the period within which it will submit its report.

493 Note that Article 12.9 of the DSU, with regard to the time frame for panel proceedings, uses the word 'should', rather than 'shall'. This implies more 'flexibility' for panels than for the Appellate Body with regard to the timeframes set out in Articles 12.9 and 17.5 of the DSU respectively.

494 See Article 17.5 of the DSU and Article 4 of the *SCM Agreement*.

495 During the first years of its operation, the Appellate Body succeeded a few times in completing appellate review proceedings within the sixty-day time frame. See e.g. *Japan – Alcoholic Beverages (1996)* and *Canada – Aircraft (Article 21.5 – Brazil) (2000)*. It has not done the same since May 2000.

496 Before 2011, the Appellate Body took longer than 90 days to complete its proceedings in e.g. *EC – Hormones (1998)* (114 days), *EC – Asbestos (2001)* (140 days), *US – Upland Cotton (2005)* (136 days) and *EC – Export Subsidies on Sugar (2005)* (105 days).

lasted for 346 days; and in *EC and certain member States – Large Civil Aircraft (2011)*, which lasted for 301 days.[497] Recall that the panel proceedings in these cases lasted 1,868 days and 1,806 days, respectively.[498] While the Appellate Body aspires to complete its proceedings in a particular appeal in ninety days, since 2011, this has often not been possible. By way of example, note that in *US – Tuna II (Mexico) (2012)*, which took 117 days rather than ninety days, the Chair of the Appellate Body informed the Chair of the DSB on 20 March 2012 as follows:

> The Appellate Body will not be able to circulate its Report within 90 days. This is due in part to the size of this appeal, including the number and complexity of the issues raised by the participants. It is also due to the large caseload that the Appellate Body was, and is, facing, and scheduling constraints resulting therefrom.[499]

To date, Appellate Body proceedings have taken on average 101 days, rather than the ninety days allowed for under Article 17.5 of the DSU.[500]

Some Members, and in particular the United States and Japan, have repeatedly criticised the Appellate Body for exceeding the ninety-day time frame without the express consent of the parties. At the DSB meeting of 23 July 2012, a number of WTO Members made comments on the Appellate Body's circulation of reports beyond the ninety-day time limit set forth in Article 17.5 of the DSU.[501] Almost all Members recognised that, while in the great majority of cases the Appellate Body has respected the ninety-day time limit, the workload faced by the Appellate Body, compounded by the increasing complexity of the issues raised, makes it impossible for the Appellate Body to meet the ninety-day deadline in some cases. However, Members disagreed on two issues, namely: (1) whether the ninety-day time limit set out in Article 17.5 was a rigid one that must be enforced in all circumstances; and (2) what actions the Appellate Body should take when circulation of reports within the ninety-day time limit was not possible.

Note that no other international court or tribunal operates with similarly short time frames as WTO panels and the Appellate do. These time limits, and in particular the time limits for appellate review, have been criticised as excessively short and demanding for both the parties to the dispute and the Appellate Body. It is, however, of great importance that the dispute settlement process is short and comes to a determination regarding the WTO consistency of the measure at issue quickly because, as discussed above, the WTO dispute settlement system does not provide for compensation of harm caused

497 See www.worldtradelaw.net/dsc/database/abtiming.asp.

498 See above, p. 249.

499 See Communication from the Appellate Body, *US – Tuna II (Mexico)*, WT/DS381/12, dated 22 March 2012.

500 See www.worldtradelaw.net/databases/abtiming.php. However, if the 2011–12 aircraft subsidies cases are not included in the calculation of the average time taken, the average time for Appellate Body proceedings is very close to ninety days.

501 Dispute Settlement Body, *Minutes of Meeting held on 23 July 2012*, WT/DSB/M/320, dated 28 September 2012, paras. 97–109.

by the measure at issue during the time that the dispute settlement process is running.[502]

6.1.2 Confidentiality and Transparency

The second feature of the WTO dispute settlement process is its confidentiality and resulting lack of transparency. The DSU provides that consultations, panel proceedings and Appellate Body proceedings shall be 'confidential'.[503] This confidentiality requirement relates to: (1) the written submissions of parties, third parties, participants and third participants; (2) the meetings of panels with the parties and hearings of the Appellate Body; and (3) to some extent, the reports of panels. The confidentiality of the WTO dispute settlement process is considered indispensable by some Members and companies, while the lack of transparency necessarily resulting from this confidentiality has been criticised by other Members and civil society.

First, with regard to the written submissions of parties and third parties, Article 18.2 of the DSU states that 'written submissions to the panel or the Appellate Body shall be treated as confidential'.[504] Parties may only make their *own* submissions available to the public.[505] While a few Members do so in a consistent manner (see e.g. the United States and the European Union), most Members choose to keep their submissions confidential.[506] The DSU provides that a party to a dispute must, upon request of any WTO Member, provide a non-confidential summary of the information contained in its submissions that could be disclosed to the public.[507] However, this provision does not provide for a deadline by which such a non-confidential summary must be made available. In the few instances in which WTO Members requested such a summary, it was usually made available too late to be of any practical relevance. Also, note that the confidentiality of the written submissions is in any case limited in time, since panel reports and Appellate Body reports (since 2014) contain in annexes executive summaries of the parties' and third parties' submissions (prepared by the parties themselves).

In WTO dispute settlement, access to and/or knowledge of sensitive and confidential business information may be indispensable for parties to make their case, and for panels and the Appellate Body to decide, on the WTO consistency of the measure at issue. Recognising that parties, and more specifically the companies concerned, have a legitimate interest in protecting such information submitted

502 See above, p. 208.

503 See Article 4.6 of the DSU (with regard to consultations), Appendix 3 to the DSU (with regard to panel proceedings) and Article 17.10 of the DSU (with regard to Appellate Body proceedings).

504 See Articles 18.2 and 17.10, and Appendix 3, para. 3, of the DSU.

505 See in this respect also Panel Report, *Argentina – Poultry Anti-Dumping Duties (2003)*, paras. 7.13–7.16.

506 As Article 18.2, first sentence, of the DSU explicitly states, a party can of course not keep its submissions confidential from the other party or parties to the dispute. Any submission filed with, and more broadly any evidence or information given to, the panel must be shared with the other party. This also follows from Article 18.1 of the DSU, which prohibits *ex parte* communications between the panel and one of the parties.

507 See Article 18.2 of the DSU.

to a panel, the panels in *Canada – Aircraft (1999)* and *Brazil – Aircraft (1999)* adopted special procedures governing business confidential information (BCI) that go beyond the protection afforded by Article 18.2 of the DSU.[508] Whether panels consider the adoption of special procedures for the protection of BCI appropriate, however, varies from case to case.[509] The party that has concerns about the protection of BCI must request the panel to adopt special procedures to handle such information, and explain to the panel the nature of the information it seeks to protect and justify the insufficiency of the standard confidentiality requirements.[510]

With regard to the confidentiality of Appellate Body proceedings, the Appellate Body ruled in *Canada – Aircraft (1999)*, after carefully considering all the requirements already provided for in the DSU to protect the confidentiality of Appellate Body proceedings, that:

> we do not consider that it is necessary, under all the circumstances of this case, to adopt *additional* procedures for the protection of business confidential information in these appellate proceedings.[511]

The Appellate Body considered the protection offered by the confidentiality requirements of Articles 17.10 and 18.2 of the DSU more than sufficient. However, a decade later, in *EC and certain member States – Large Civil Aircraft (2011)* and in *United States – Large Civil Aircraft (2012)*, the Appellate Body took a different approach and provided for detailed additional procedures for the protection of BCI and highly sensitive business information (HSBI).[512] By way of example, note that, to protect HSBI, the additional procedures required that:

> [a]ll HSBI shall be stored in a combination safe in a designated secure location on the premises of the Appellate Body Secretariat. Any computer in that room shall be a stand-alone computer, that is, not connected to a network. Appellate Body Members and assigned Appellate Body Secretariat staff may view HSBI only in the designated secure location referred to above. HSBI shall not be removed from this location, except as provided in paragraph (x) or in the form of handwritten notes that may be used only on the Appellate Body Secretariat's premises and shall be destroyed once no longer in use.[513]

508 See Panel Report, *Canada – Aircraft (1999)*, Annex 1; and Panel Report, *Brazil – Aircraft (1999)*, Annex 1. Under the Procedures Governing Business Confidential Information adopted by the panel in *Canada – Aircraft (1999)*, the BCI was to be stored in a safe in a locked room at the premises of the relevant Geneva missions, with restrictions imposed on access; and was to be returned or destroyed after completion of the panel proceedings. Note that, in spite of these procedures, Canada refused to submit certain confidential business information because the procedures did not, according to Canada, provide the requisite level of protection. On the consequences of such a refusal to submit information requested by the panel, see below, p. 274.

509 For a list of panel proceedings in which parties requested BCI protection and the action taken by the panel see *WTO Analytical Index (2012)*, Volume II, 1763–4 together with the Supplement (up to June 2015).

510 See Panel Report, *Canada – Dairy (Article 21.5 – New Zealand and United States) (2001)*, paras. 2.20–2.21.

511 Appellate Body Report, *Canada – Aircraft (1999)*, para. 147. See also Appellate Body Report, *Brazil – Aircraft (1999)*, para. 125.

512 For a full exposition of these detailed additional procedures, refer to the Appellate Body's Procedural Ruling and Additional Procedures to Protect Sensitive Information of 10 August 2010. See Appellate Body Report, *EC and certain member States – Large Civil Aircraft (2011)*, Annex III.

513 See *ibid.*, para. 28(ix).

Second, with regard to the confidentiality of panel meetings and Appellate Body hearings, paragraph 2 of Appendix 3 of the DSU provides that the meetings of the panel with the parties 'take place behind closed doors'; and Article 17.10 of the DSU states that the proceedings of the Appellate Body, and thus also the Appellate Body hearings, are 'confidential'. As a rule, nobody, except the parties themselves and the officials of the WTO Secretariat assisting the panel, is allowed to attend all meetings of the panel with the parties. Third parties are usually invited to attend only one session of the first substantive panel meeting.[514] The 2004 Sutherland Report noted in this respect that:

> the degree of confidentiality of the current dispute settlement proceedings can be seen as damaging to the WTO as an institution.[515]

The Report therefore recommended that, as a matter of course, the panel meetings and Appellate Body hearings should generally be open to the public.[516] Certain WTO Members share this view, as evidenced by their requests for opening of panel meetings and Appellate Body hearings to public observation in disputes in which those Members were parties. At the request of the parties, the panel in *US/Canada – Continued Suspension (2008)*, complaint by the European Communities, authorised in September and October 2006 the real-time closed-circuit television broadcast of its meetings with experts and the parties to a separate viewing room at WTO Headquarters in Geneva.[517] In July 2007, the panel in *EC and certain member States – Large Civil Aircraft (2011)* was more cautious (because of concerns regarding the protection of BCI) and merely allowed its second meeting with the parties to be video-taped and broadcast in an edited version two days later in Geneva.[518] In November 2007, the panel in *EC – Bananas III (Article 21.5 – US) (2008)* decided to allow the delegates of WTO Members and members of the general public to observe the panel's meeting with the parties from the public gallery above the meeting room. As only a limited number of places was available, prior registration with either party in this dispute, the United States or the European Communities, was required to secure a seat.[519] Note that, in *Brazil – Retreaded Tyres (2007)*, the Centre for International Environmental Law (CIEL) requested the panel to allow the webcasting of the first meeting of the panel with the parties. After consultations with the parties, Brazil and the European Communities, and in light of the views expressed by them, the panel informed CIEL that its meetings with the parties would be held in closed sessions in accordance with the working procedures

514 See below, p. 275.

515 Sutherland Report, para. 261 (emphasis omitted). 516 See *ibid.*, para. 262.

517 The 200 places reserved for the public were allocated on a first-come-first-served basis upon receipt of the completed application form. However, despite the frequent calls by civil society for increased transparency of dispute settlement proceedings, few attended the meetings of the panel. See Communication from the Chair of the Panels, *US/Canada – Continued Suspension*, WT/DS320/8, WT/DS321/8, dated 2 August 2005.

518 The delayed broadcasting allowed the parties and the panel to verify that no BCI would be inadvertently disclosed in showing the videotape. See also e.g. in *US – Large Civil Aircraft (2nd complaint) (2012)*.

519 See Panel Report, *EC – Bananas III (Article 21.5 – US) (2008)*, para. 1.11.

adopted by the panel at the beginning of the proceedings.[520] The legal basis for the panel to allow public observation of its meetings is to be found in Article 12.1 of the DSU. As discussed below, Article 12.1 provides that panels shall follow the *Working Procedures* in Appendix 3 unless the panel decides otherwise after consulting the parties to the dispute. Paragraph 2 of the *Working Procedures* in Appendix 3 provides that: 'The panel shall meet in closed session.' Pursuant to Article 12.1, however, panels can deviate from this rule and open up the panel meetings to the public.

The legal basis for allowing public observation of Appellate Body hearings was less obvious. The question whether the Appellate Body could allow public observation of its hearings first arose in *US/Canada – Continued Suspension (2008)*, when all participants (the European Communities, the United States and Canada) requested the Appellate Body to allow public observation of the hearing in this case.[521] However, some of the third participants in this case, namely, Brazil, China, India and Mexico, objected to the request to allow public observation.[522] They pointed out that Article 17.10 of the DSU explicitly states that:

> [t]he proceedings of the Appellate Body shall be confidential.

According to these third participants, the confidentiality requirement in Article 17.10 is absolute and permits no derogation. The Appellate Body disagreed. According to the Appellate Body, Article 17.10 must be read in context, particularly in relation to Article 18.2 of the DSU. The second sentence of Article 18.2 expressly provides that '[n]othing in this Understanding shall preclude a party to a dispute from disclosing statements of its own positions to the public'. Thus, under Article 18.2, second sentence, the parties may decide to forgo confidentiality protection in respect of their statements of position.[523] The Appellate Body observed that notices of appeal as well as Appellate Body reports are disclosed to the public, and that the latter contain summaries of the participants' and third participants' written and oral submissions and frequently quote directly from them. Clearly, in practice, the confidentiality requirement in Article 17.10 has its limits; confidentiality under the DSU is 'relative and time-bound'.[524] According to the Appellate Body:

> The requirement that the proceedings of the Appellate Body are confidential affords protection to these separate relationships and is intended to safeguard the interests of the participants and third participants and the adjudicative function of the Appellate Body, so as to foster the system of dispute settlement under conditions of fairness, impartiality, independence and integrity ... The question is thus whether the request of the participants to forego confidentiality protection satisfies the requirements of fairness and integrity that

520 See Panel Report, *Brazil – Retreaded Tyres (2007)*, para. 1.9.

521 See Appellate Body Report, *US/Canada – Continued Suspension (2008)*, Annex IV, para. 1. Annex IV contains the Procedural Ruling of 10 July 2008 to allow public observation of the oral hearing.

522 *Ibid.*, para. 1. Note that other third participants, namely, Australia, Chinese Taipei, New Zealand and Norway, supported the request to allow public observation of the Appellate Body oral hearing. See *ibid.*

523 See *ibid.*, para. 4. The Appellate Body further referred to Article 18.2, third and fourth sentences, for contextual support for the view that the confidentiality rule in Article 17.10 is not absolute. See *ibid.*

524 See *ibid.*, para. 5.

are the essential attributes of the appellate process and define the relationship between the Appellate Body and the participants.[525]

The Appellate Body subsequently noted that the DSU does not specifically provide for an oral hearing at the appellate stage. The oral hearing was instituted by the Appellate Body in its *Working Procedures*, which were drawn up pursuant to Article 17.9 of the DSU, and the conduct and organisation of the oral hearing 'falls within the authority of the Appellate Body (*compétence de la compétence*) pursuant to Rule 27 of the *Working Procedures*'.[526] The Appellate Body thus concluded that it holds:

> the power to exercise control over the conduct of the oral hearing, including authorizing the lifting of confidentiality at the joint request of the participants as long as this does not adversely affect the rights and interests of the third participants or the integrity of the appellate process.[527]

The Appellate Body authorised public observation of its oral hearing in *US/Canada – Continued Suspension (2008)* by means of real-time closed-circuit television broadcast to a separate viewing room at WTO Headquarters in Geneva.[528] To safeguard the rights of confidentiality of the third participants, which did not agree to public observation, the transmission was turned off during statements made by those third participants. To date, the Appellate Body has allowed public observation of its hearings either through real time or delayed closed-circuit television broadcast to a separate viewing room in all cases in which the participants requested public observation to be allowed.[529]

Third, with regard to the confidentiality of panel reports, note that the interim report of the panel and the final panel report, as long as it has merely been issued to the parties to the dispute, are confidential.[530] The final panel report only becomes a public document when it is circulated to all WTO Members. In reality, however, the interim report, and even more so the final report issued to the parties, are frequently 'leaked' to the media. In *US – Gambling (2005)*, the panel regretted the breach of the duty of confidentiality by the parties, and stated that 'disregard for the confidentiality requirement contained in the DSU affects the

525 *Ibid.*, para. 6. 526 *Ibid.*, para. 7.

527 *Ibid.* The Appellate Body emphasised that authorising the participants' request to forgo confidentiality did not affect the rights of third participants to preserve the confidentiality of their communications with the Appellate Body. See *ibid.*

528 See *ibid.*, para. 11.

529 This was the case e.g. in *US/Canada – Continued Suspension (2008)*; *Australia – Apples (2010)*; *EC and certain member States – Large Civil Aircraft (2011)*; *US – COOL (2012)*; *Canada – Renewable Energy (2013)*; and *EC – Seal Products (2014)*. In cases involving BCI, the broadcast was delayed. See e.g. *EC and certain member States – Large Civil Aircraft (2011)*. Note that, in *US – COOL (2012)*, the Appellate Body allowed public observation of its hearing at the request of two of the three participants in this case, namely, the European Union and the United States, and the fact that the other participant, Mexico, did not object to public observation in the case at hand. Mexico did, however, maintain its objection in principle to opening up the hearings of the Appellate Body to the public.

530 On interim review and the interim report, and the issuance of panel reports to the parties, see below, pp. 276–7.

credibility and integrity of the WTO dispute settlement process, of the WTO and of WTO Members and is, therefore, unacceptable'.[531] Note that there is no interim review of Appellate Body reports, and that Appellate Body reports are issued to the parties and circulated to all WTO Members at the same time and are as of that moment a public document.[532] Unlike for panel reports, the problem of 'leaking' Appellate Body reports does not therefore present itself.

6.1.3 Burden of Proof

The DSU does not contain any specific rules concerning the burden of proof in WTO dispute settlement proceedings. However, in *US – Wool Shirts and Blouses (1997)*, the Appellate Body noted:

> [W]e find it difficult, indeed, to see how any system of judicial settlement could work if it incorporated the proposition that the mere assertion of a claim might amount to proof. It is, thus, hardly surprising that various international tribunals, including the International Court of Justice, have generally and consistently accepted and applied the rule that the party who asserts a fact, whether the claimant or the respondent, is responsible for providing proof thereof. Also, it is a generally accepted canon of evidence in civil law, common law and, in fact, most jurisdictions, that the burden of proof rests upon the party, whether complaining or defending, who asserts the affirmative of a particular claim or defence. If that party adduces evidence sufficient to raise a presumption that what is claimed is true, the burden then shifts to the other party, who will fail unless it adduces sufficient evidence to rebut the presumption.[533]

This basic rule on burden of proof identified by the Appellate Body in *US – Wool Shirts and Blouses (1997)* has since been consistently applied by panels, the Appellate Body and arbitrators.[534] Precisely how much and precisely what kind of evidence is required to establish such a presumption 'will necessarily vary from measure to measure, provision to provision, and case to case'.[535]

In *EC – Hormones (1998)*, the Appellate Body further clarified the burden of proof in WTO dispute settlement proceedings, and stated with respect to disputes under the *SPS Agreement*:

> The initial burden lies on the complaining party, which must establish a *prima facie* case of inconsistency with a particular provision of the *SPS Agreement* on the part of the defending

531 Panel Report, *US – Gambling (2005)*, paras. 5.3–5.13. Another infamous example of leaked interim panel reports were the reports in *EC – Approval and Marketing of Biotech Products (2006)*.

532 See below, pp. 276–7.

533 Appellate Body Report, *US – Wool Shirts and Blouses (1997)*, 335. Note that, in *Japan – Apples (2003)*, the Appellate Body stated: 'It is important to distinguish, on the one hand, the principle that the complainant must establish a *prima facie* case of inconsistency with a provision of a covered agreement from, on the other hand, the principle that the party that asserts a fact is responsible for providing proof thereof. In fact, the two principles are distinct.' See Appellate Body Report, *Japan – Apples (2003)*, para. 157.

534 Note, however, that in *EC – Tariff Preferences (2004)* the Appellate Body ruled that: '[a]lthough a responding party must defend the consistency of its preference scheme with the conditions of the Enabling Clause and must prove such consistency, a *complaining* party has to define the parameters within which the *responding* party must make that defence'. See Appellate Body Report, *EC – Tariff Preferences (2004)*, para. 114. Note also that while the responding party must show that an otherwise GATT- or GATS-inconsistent measure is necessary for e.g. the protection of the life or health of humans under Article XX(b) of the GATT 1994 or Article XIV(b) of the GATS, it is for the complaining party to identify possible alternative measures to the otherwise inconsistent measure. See below, p. 563.

535 Appellate Body Report, *US – Wool Shirts and Blouses* (1997), 335.

party, or more precisely, of its SPS measure or measures complained about. When that *prima facie* case is made, the burden of proof moves to the defending party, which must in turn counter or refute the claimed inconsistency.

... It is also well to remember that a *prima facie* case is one which, in the absence of effective refutation by the defending party, requires a panel, as a matter of law, to rule in favour of the complaining party presenting the *prima facie* case.[536]

With regard to the concept of a '*prima facie* case', the Appellate Body further stated in *US – Gambling (2005)*:

A *prima facie* case must be based on 'evidence *and* legal argument' put forward by the complaining party in relation to each of the elements of the claim. A complaining party may not simply submit evidence and expect the panel to divine from it a claim of WTO-inconsistency. Nor may a complaining party simply allege facts without relating them to its legal arguments.

... The evidence and arguments underlying a *prima facie* case, therefore, must be sufficient to identify the challenged measure and its basic import, identify the relevant WTO provision and obligation contained therein, and explain the basis for the claimed inconsistency of the measure with that provision.[537]

The above should not be understood as imposing a requirement on panels to make an explicit ruling on whether the complainant has established a *prima facie* case of violation *before* they may proceed to examine the respondent's defence and evidence.[538] The jurisprudence of the Appellate Body regarding the rules on burden of proof is well summarised by the panel in *US – Section 301 Trade Act (2000)*, where it is stated:

In accordance with this jurisprudence, both parties agreed that it is for the EC, as the complaining party, to present arguments and evidence sufficient to establish a *prima facie* case in respect of the various elements of its claims regarding the inconsistency of Sections 301–310 with US obligations under the WTO. Once the EC has done so, it is for the US to rebut that *prima facie* case. Since, in this case, both parties have submitted extensive facts and arguments in respect of the EC claims, our task will essentially be to balance all evidence on record and decide whether the EC, as party bearing the original burden of proof, has convinced us of the validity of its claims. In case of uncertainty, i.e. in case all the evidence and arguments remain in equipoise, we have to give the benefit of the doubt to the US as defending party.[539]

As stated by the panel in *US – Section 301 Trade Act (2000)*, the task of a panel is essentially to *balance all evidence* on record and decide whether the party bearing the original, i.e. the ultimate, burden of proof has convinced it of the validity of its claims. Moreover, the panel in the same case made an important observation that the rules on burden of proof are relevant with respect to issues of fact but not with respect to issues of legal interpretation. The panel noted that:

536 Appellate Body Report, *EC – Hormones (1998)*, paras. 98 and 104.

537 Appellate Body Report, *US – Gambling (2005)*, paras. 140–1. See also e.g. Appellate Body Report, *Canada – Wheat Exports and Grain Imports (2004)*, para. 191.

538 See Appellate Body Report, *Korea – Dairy (2000)*, para. 145. See also e.g. Appellate Body Report, *Thailand – H-Beams (2001)*, para. 134.

539 Panel Report, *US – Section 301 Trade Act (2000)*, para. 7.14.

when it comes to deciding on the correct interpretation of the covered agreements a panel will be aided by the arguments of the parties but not bound by them; its decisions on such matters must be in accord with the rules of treaty interpretation applicable to the WTO.[540]

With regard to the burden of establishing the correct legal interpretation of provisions of the covered agreements, the Appellate Body further clarified in *EC – Tariff Preferences (2004)*:

Consistent with the principle of *jura novit curia*, it is not the responsibility of the European Communities to provide us with the legal interpretation to be given to a particular provision in the Enabling Clause; instead, the burden of the European Communities is to adduce sufficient evidence to substantiate its assertion that the Drug Arrangements comply with the requirements of the Enabling Clause.[541]

Thus, the burden of establishing what the applicable rule of WTO law is, and how that rule must be interpreted, is not on the parties but on the panel and the Appellate Body.

With regard to the kind of evidence a complainant must produce, the Appellate Body found in *US – Carbon Steel (2002)* as follows:

[A] responding Member's law will be treated as WTO-consistent until proven otherwise. The party asserting that another party's municipal law, as such, is inconsistent with relevant treaty obligations bears the burden of introducing evidence as to the scope and meaning of such law to substantiate that assertion. Such evidence will typically be produced in the form of the text of the relevant legislation or legal instruments, which may be supported, as appropriate, by evidence of the consistent application of such laws, the pronouncements of domestic courts on the meaning of such laws, the opinions of legal experts and the writings of recognized scholars. The nature and extent of the evidence required to satisfy the burden of proof will vary from case to case.[542]

Finally, note that the panel in *EC – Approval and Marketing of Biotech Products (2006)* addressed the question of when a provision should be characterised as an *exception* to another provision, and when it should instead be characterised as a *right creating an exemption* from the scope of application of another provision.[543] Referring to the findings of the Appellate Body in *EC – Tariff Preferences (2004)*,[544] the panel in *EC – Approval and Marketing of Biotech Products (2006)* found that a provision can be characterised as a right (rather than as an exception) in relation to another provision if the relationship between them is one:

where one provision permits, in certain circumstances, behaviour that would otherwise be inconsistent with an obligation in another provision, [where] one of the two provisions refers to the other provision, [and] where one of the provisions suggests that the obligation is not applicable to the said measure.[545]

540 *Ibid.*, paras. 7.15 and 7.16.
541 Appellate Body Report, *EC – Tariff Preferences (2004)*, para. 105.
542 Appellate Body Report, *US – Carbon Steel (2002)*, para. 157.
543 See Panel Reports, *EC – Approval and Marketing of Biotech Products (2006)*, para. 7.2985.
544 See Appellate Body Report, *EC – Tariff Preferences (2004)*, para. 88.
545 Panel Reports, *EC – Approval and Marketing of Biotech Products (2006)*, para. 7.2985.

Otherwise, the permissive provision is characterised as an exception or defence. The panel in *EC – Approval and Marketing of Biotech Products (2006)* subsequently addressed the implications for the burden of proof regarding a provision embodying a right rather than an exception. According to the panel, in cases where the complainant claims a violation of a provision embodying a *right creating an exemption* from the scope of application of another provision, it is incumbent on the complainant, and not the respondent, to prove that the challenged measure is also inconsistent with at least one of the requirements of the provision creating the exemption. As the panel stated:

> If such non-compliance is demonstrated, then, and only then, does the relevant obligation ... apply to the challenged ... measure.[546]

Note that in *Canada – FIT/Renewable Energy (2014)*, the Appellate Body characterised Article III:8(a) of the GATT 1994 as 'a derogation limiting the scope of the national treatment obligation and it is not a justification for measures that would otherwise be inconsistent with that obligation', but subsequently stated:

> At the same time, we note that the characterization of the provision as a derogation does not pre-determine the question as to which party bears the burden of proof with regard to the requirements stipulated in the provision.[547]

6.1.4 Role of Private Legal Counsel

The DSU does not explicitly address the issue of representation of the parties before panels or the Appellate Body. In *EC – Bananas III (1997)*, the issue arose whether private legal counsel, i.e. legal counsel not in government employ, may represent a party or third party in WTO dispute settlement proceedings. The United States objected to the presence at the panel meeting of a private legal counsel acting on behalf of a third party to the case, Saint Lucia, a tiny Caribbean banana-producing island State with a very significant interest in the outcome of the case. The panel ruled, in line with the established practice in GATT dispute settlement, that only government officials could represent parties and third parties. However, when this issue arose again in the Appellate Body proceedings in this case, the Appellate Body took a very different approach from the panel. The Appellate Body noted that nothing in the *WTO Agreement* or the DSU, or in customary international law or the prevailing practice of international tribunals, prevents a WTO Member from determining the composition of its own delegation in WTO dispute settlement proceedings.[548] The Appellate

546 *Ibid.*, para. 7.2976.

547 Appellate Body Report, *FIT-Renewable Energy (2014)*, para. 5.56. The Appellate Body recalled that, in *China – Raw Materials (2012)*, the Appellate Body already distinguished between 'exceptions' (such as the general exception of Article XX) and limitations of the scope of an obligation (such as Article XI:2(a)). See Appellate Body Reports, *China – Raw Materials (2012)*, para. 334.

548 See Appellate Body Report, *EC – Bananas III (1997)*, para. 10.

Body thus ruled that a party can decide that private legal counsel forms part of its delegation and will represent it in Appellate Body proceedings. As a result, the Appellate Body allowed Saint Lucia to be represented by private legal counsel. The Appellate Body noted in its ruling:

> that representation by counsel of a government's own choice may well be a matter of particular significance – especially for developing-country Members – to enable them to participate fully in dispute settlement proceedings.[549]

While the ruling of the Appellate Body concerned the proceedings before this body, the reasoning of this ruling is equally relevant for panel proceedings. This was confirmed in the panel report in *Indonesia – Autos (1998)*, adopted one year after the Appellate Body report in *EC – Bananas III (1997)*.

At present, private legal counsel is involved in almost all panel and Appellate Body proceedings, and act on behalf of WTO Members in these proceedings.[550] A question which arises as a result of this involvement is which, if any, rules of conduct apply to private legal counsel active in WTO dispute settlement.[551] It is useful to make two observations in this regard. First, the Member, for which private legal counsel acts, is responsible for compliance by the counsel with the relevant rules of the DSU (such as the confidentiality requirement), as counsel is part of the delegation of that Member. Second, while private legal counsel will usually be subject to the rules of conduct of his or her bar association or professional organisation, it may be argued that there is need for specific rules of conduct for private legal counsel acting in WTO dispute settlement proceedings.

6.1.5 Amicus Curiae Briefs

As discussed above, the WTO dispute settlement system is a government-to-government dispute settlement system for disputes concerning the rights and obligations of WTO Members. Individuals, companies, industry associations, labour unions, international organisations and NGOs have no direct access to the WTO dispute settlement system.[552] They cannot bring claims of violation of WTO rights or obligations. Moreover, under the current rules, they do not have the *right* to be heard in the proceedings. However, under Appellate Body case law, panels and the Appellate Body have the authority to accept and consider written briefs submitted by individuals, companies or organisations.[553] The acceptance by panels and the Appellate Body of these briefs, which are commonly referred

549 Appellate Body Report, *EC – Bananas III (1997)*, para. 12.

550 Note that private legal counsel is usually also already involved in the consultations.

551 See in this regard e.g. Appellate Body Report, *Thailand – H-Beams (2001)*, paras. 62–78. In this case, Hogan & Hartson LLP withdrew as Poland's legal counsel after Thailand's appellant submission had been 'leaked' and the Appellate Body had instituted an investigation into this breach of the confidentiality of the Appellate Body proceedings. See also Panel Report, *EC – Tariff Preferences (2004)*, paras. 7.3–7.10. In that case, the European Communities objected to the 'joint representation' by the Advisory Centre on WTO Law (ACWL) of both India, the complainant, and Paraguay, a third party.

552 On 'indirect' access to the WTO dispute settlement system, see above, p. 184.

553 Note that panels and the Appellate Body also have the authority to accept and consider briefs submitted by Members which are not parties or third parties. See above, pp. 237–8.

to as *amicus curiae* briefs ('friend of the court' briefs), has been controversial and criticised by most WTO Members.

With respect to the authority of *panels* to accept and consider *amicus curiae* briefs, the Appellate Body noted in *US – Shrimp (1998)*, first, the *comprehensive* nature of the authority of a panel – under Article 13 of the DSU – to 'seek' information and technical advice from 'any individual or body' it may consider appropriate, or from 'any relevant source'.[554] Second, the Appellate Body considered it also pertinent to note that Article 12 of the DSU authorises panels to develop their own working procedures, which should provide *sufficient flexibility* so as to *ensure high-quality panel reports* while *not unduly delaying the panel process*.[555] The Appellate Body found that:

> [t]he thrust of Articles 12 and 13, taken together, is that the DSU accords to a panel ... ample and extensive authority to undertake and to control the process by which it informs itself both of the relevant facts of the dispute and of the legal norms and principles applicable to such facts.[556]

According to the Appellate Body, that 'authority, and the breadth thereof, is indispensably necessary' to enable a panel to make an objective assessment of the matter before it, as it is required to do pursuant to Article 11 of the DSU.[557] On the basis of Articles 11–13 of the DSU, the Appellate Body thus came to the conclusion in *US – Shrimp (1998)* that panels have the authority to accept and consider *amicus curiae* briefs. To date, several panels have accepted and considered *amicus curiae* briefs.[558] This was the case, e.g., in *US – Tuna II (Mexico) (2012)*. The panel in this case considered the information contained in the *amicus curiae* brief submitted by Humane Society International and American University's Washington College of Law.[559] The panel noted that where it considered the information in the *amicus curiae* submission relevant, it 'sought the views of the parties in accordance with the requirements of due process'.[560] The panel added that it deemed it appropriate to refer to this information in its findings to the extent that one of the parties had cited or referred to the brief during the panel proceedings.[561] In many other disputes, however, panels refused to accept or consider *amicus curiae* briefs submitted to them.[562]

With respect to the authority of the Appellate Body to accept and consider *amicus curiae* briefs submitted in Appellate Body proceedings, the Appellate Body noted in *US – Lead and Bismuth II (2000)* that, pursuant to Article 17.9

554 See Appellate Body Report, *US – Shrimp (1998)*, para. 104. On Article 13 of the DSU, see (above) p. 230, (below) p. 274.

555 See *ibid.*, para. 105. On Article 12 of the DSU, see below, p. 271. 556 *Ibid.*, para. 106.

557 See *ibid.* On Article 11 of the DSU, see above, pp. 240–1.

558 For a list of *amicus curiae* briefs *received* by panels, see *WTO Analytical Index (2012)*, Volume II, 1712–13 together with the Supplement (up to June 2015), 70.

559 See Panel Report, *US – Tuna II (Mexico) (2012)*, para. 7.9.

560 *Ibid.* 561 See *ibid.*

562 See, e.g. Panel Report, *EC – Bed Linen (2001)*, para. 6.1, fn. 10; Panel Reports, *EC – Export Subsidies on Sugar (2005)*, paras. 2.20 and 7.76–7.85; Panel Reports, *EC – Approval and Marketing of Biotech Products (2006)*, paras. 7.10–7.11; and Panel Report, *US – Zeroing (EC) (2006)*, para. 1.7.

of the DSU and Rule 16(1) of the *Working Procedures for Appellate Review*, it has broad authority to adopt procedural rules which do not conflict with any rules and procedures in the DSU or the covered agreements.[563] On that basis, the Appellate Body concluded that:

> as long as we act consistently with the provisions of the DSU and the covered agreements, we have the legal authority to decide whether or not to accept and consider any information that we believe is pertinent and useful in an appeal.[564]

In *US – Lead and Bismuth II (2000)*, the Appellate Body did not find it necessary to take the two *amicus curiae* briefs filed into account in rendering its decision.[565]

In October 2000, the Appellate Body division hearing the appeal in *EC – Asbestos (2001)* adopted an Additional Procedure to deal with *amicus curiae* briefs which the division expected to receive in great numbers in that dispute.[566] This Additional Procedure set out substantive and procedural requirements to be met by any person or entity, other than a party or a third party to this dispute, wishing to file a written brief with the Appellate Body. The Additional Procedure provided, for a requirement to apply for leave to file, and for a maximum page limit (twenty) on the *amicus curiae* briefs that were allowed to be filed. In the *EC – Asbestos (2001)* appeal, the Appellate Body received eleven applications for leave to file an *amicus curiae* brief, but decided to deny all applications for failure to comply sufficiently with the substantive requirements for filing an *amicus curiae* brief. While, in the end, the Appellate Body did not allow any *amicus curiae* brief to be filed, many WTO Members heavily criticised the Appellate Body's adoption of the Additional Procedure and its apparent willingness to accept and consider *amicus curiae* briefs where certain requirements are fulfilled. On 20 November 2000, a special meeting of the General Council was convened to discuss this issue. The discussion at this meeting reflected the deep division between the vast majority of WTO Members opposing the Appellate Body's case law on this issue and the United States, which fully supported this case law. At the end of this tumultuous meeting, the Chair of the General Council concluded that he believed that there had been a large sentiment, expressed by almost all delegations, that there was a need to put clear rules in place for *amicus curiae* briefs, and he called for further consultations on the content of such rules. The Chair finally also stated:

563 Appellate Body Report, *US – Lead and Bismuth II (2000)*, para. 39.

564 *Ibid.* Note that the Appellate Body indicated in *EC – Sardines (2002)* that it would refuse to accept and consider *amicus curiae* briefs if this would interfere with the 'fair, prompt and effective resolution of trade disputes'. This could arise, e.g. if an *amicus curiae* brief were to be submitted at a very late stage in the appellate proceedings, with the result that accepting the brief would impose an undue burden on participants. See Appellate Body Report, *EC – Sardines (2002)*, para. 167.

565 See Appellate Body Report, *US – Lead and Bismuth II (2000)*, para. 42.

566 See Appellate Body Report, *EC – Asbestos (2001)*, paras. 51–2. The Additional Procedure was adopted pursuant to Rule 16(1) of the *Working Procedures for Appellate Review*. See below, p. 278.

> [I]n light of the views expressed and in the absence of clear rules, he believed that the Appellate Body should exercise extreme caution in future cases until Members had considered what rules were needed.[567]

There are two main reasons for the antagonism of many Members at that time, especially developing-country Members, against *amicus curiae* briefs. First, Members feared that the need to consider and react to *amicus curiae* briefs would take up scarce legal resources and will further bend the WTO dispute settlement proceedings in favour of Members with more legal resources at their disposal. Second, developing-country Members in particular believed that the most vocal and best-funded NGOs (such as Greenpeace, WWF and labour unions) often took positions that are considered 'unfriendly' to the interests and policies of developing-country Members. However, in recent years it has become clear that this is not (or no longer) necessarily the case.[568]

To date, WTO Members have been unable to adopt any clear rules on *amicus curiae* briefs.[569] The Appellate Body has repeatedly confirmed its case law on its authority (and that of panels) to accept and consider *amicus curiae* briefs. To date, a total of sixty-three *amicus curiae* briefs have been submitted in eighteen Appellate Body proceedings.[570] However, in no proceeding thus far did the Appellate Body consider it useful to consider *amicus curiae* briefs submitted to it.

The *amicus curiae* brief filed by Morocco in the appellate proceedings in *EC – Sardines (2002)* is of particular interest. Morocco, which had not reserved third party rights in this dispute, was the first WTO Member to file an *amicus curiae* brief. Peru, the complainant in *EC – Sardines (2002)*, argued that the Appellate Body should not accept or consider this brief. In considering the issue, the Appellate Body first recalled its case law on *amicus curiae* briefs and then noted:

> We have been urged by the parties to this dispute not to treat Members less favourably than non-Members with regard to participation as *amicus curiae*. We agree. We have not. And we will not. As we have already determined that we have the authority to receive an *amicus curiae* brief from a private individual or an organization, *a fortiori* we are entitled to accept such a brief from a WTO Member, provided there is no prohibition on doing so in the DSU. We find no such prohibition.[571]

The Appellate Body therefore concluded that it was entitled to accept the *amicus curiae* brief submitted by Morocco, and consider it.[572] Having concluded

567 General Council, *Minutes of Meeting held on 22 November 2000*, WT/GC/M/60, dated 23 January 2001, para. 120.

568 Consider e.g. the position taken by NGOs on the *TRIPS Agreement* and access to essential medicines (see below, pp. 1039–40) or on subsidies on agricultural exports (see below, pp. 869–74).

569 Members have made proposals both for the prohibition (e.g. India; and the Africa Group) and for admittance of *amicus curiae* briefs (e.g. the European Union) in the context of DSU review negotiations.

570 Most recently, *amicus curiae* briefs were submitted in *EC – Seal Products (2014)*; and *Canada – Energy / Feed-In Tariff Program (2013)*. See Supplement to the Analytical Index (up to June 2015), 70.

571 Appellate Body Report, *EC – Sardines (2002)*, para. 164.

572 See *ibid.*, para. 167. The quote cited by the Appellate Body comes from Appellate Body Report, *US – FSC (2000)*, para. 166.

that it had the authority to accept the *amicus curiae* brief filed by Morocco, the Appellate Body then considered whether this brief could assist it in this appeal. Morocco's *amicus curiae* brief provided mainly factual information, which is, in view of the mandate of the Appellate Body under Article 17.6 of the DSU, no longer pertinent in Appellate Body proceedings.[573] Morocco also put forward arguments relating to legal issues.[574] However, the Appellate Body decided not to make findings on these specific issues and, therefore, Morocco's arguments on these issues did not assist the Appellate Body in this appeal.[575]

6.1.6 Good Faith and Due Process

Finally, it is important to make a few observations regarding: (1) the obligation on Members to use WTO dispute settlement proceedings in good faith; and (2) the obligation on panels and the Appellate Body to ensure due process in WTO dispute settlement proceedings.

Article 3.10 of the DSU provides that the use of the dispute settlement procedures 'should not be intended or considered as contentious acts' and that all Members must 'engage in these procedures in good faith in an effort to resolve the dispute'.[576] Article 3.10 obliges Members to participate in dispute settlement proceedings in good faith.[577] Engaging in dispute settlement *in good faith*, i.e. with the genuine intention to see the dispute resolved, is part of the object and purpose of the WTO dispute settlement system.[578] In *US – FSC (2000)*, the Appellate Body found that the United States had failed to act in good faith, by failing to bring procedural deficiencies 'seasonably and promptly' to the attention of the complainant and the panel, so that corrections, if needed, could have been made.[579] In *Argentina – Poultry Anti-Dumping Duties (2003)*, Argentina argued that Brazil failed to act in good faith by first challenging Argentina's anti-dumping measure before a MERCOSUR Ad Hoc Tribunal and then, having lost that case, challenging the same measure in WTO dispute settlement proceedings.[580] The panel, referring to the findings of the Appellate Body in *US – Offset Act (Byrd Amendment) (2003)*, held:

573 See Appellate Body Report, *EC – Sardines (2002)*, para. 169. On the mandate of the Appellate Body under Article 17.6 of the DSU, see above, pp. 243–5.

574 Morocco's brief contained arguments relating to Article 2.1 of the *TBT Agreement* and the GATT 1994.

575 See Appellate Body Report, *EC – Sardines (2002)*, para. 314.

576 Note that Article 4.3 of the DSU also refers to 'good faith', where it requires that the respondent enter into consultations in 'good faith'.

577 See Appellate Body Report, *US – Lamb (2001)*, para. 115; and Appellate Body Report, *EC – Sardines (2002)*, para. 140.

578 On the relationship between 'good faith' and 'estoppel', see Panel Report, *EC and certain member States – Large Civil Aircraft (2011)*, para. 7.101, where it is stated that the good faith obligation of Article 3.10 of the DSU can reasonably be analysed 'in the light of the general international law principle of estoppel'. See also Appellate Body Report, *EC – Export Subsidies on Sugar (2005)*, para. 312, where the Appellate Body stated that 'even assuming *arguendo* that the principle of estoppel could apply in the WTO, its application would fall within [the] narrow parameters set out in' Articles 3.7 and 3.10 of the DSU.

579 See Appellate Body Report, *US – FSC (2000)*, para. 165–6.

580 See also above, p. 116.

> [W]e consider that two conditions must be satisfied before a Member may be found to have failed to act in good faith. First, the Member must have violated a substantive provision of the WTO agreements. Second, there must be something 'more than mere violation'.[581]

As Argentina had not argued that Brazil had violated any substantive provision of the WTO agreements in bringing its case, the first requirement was not met, and the panel did not find a violation of the principle of good faith.[582]

In *EC – Bananas III (Article 21.5 – Ecuador II)/ EC – Bananas III (Article 21.5 – US) (2008)*, the Appellate Body held that if a Member has not clearly agreed that it would not initiate WTO dispute settlement proceedings with respect to a certain measure, initiating such proceedings 'cannot be regarded as failing to act in good faith'.[583]

In *Peru – Agricultural Products (2015)*, Peru argued that Guatemala, the complainant, had not initiated dispute settlement proceedings in that case in good faith because, according to Peru, the measure challenged by Guatemala had been accepted by it under the Peru–Guatemala Free Trade Agreement (an agreement which had not yet entered into force). The panel found no evidence that Guatemala had initiated proceedings in this case in a manner contrary to its good faith obligations.[584] On appeal, the Appellate Body upheld this finding by the panel. The Appellate Body ruled that Guatemala could not be considered to have acted contrary to its good faith obligation under the DSU since there was no clear stipulation of a relinquishment by Guatemala of its right to have resource to the WTO dispute settlement system.[585]

With regard to the obligation for panels and the Appellate Body to ensure *due process* in WTO dispute settlement proceedings, the Appellate Body ruled in *Chile – Price Band System (2002)*, that due process is an obligation inherent to the WTO dispute settlement system.[586] According to the Appellate Body in *US/Canada – Continued Suspension (2008)* the protection of due process is an essential feature of a rules-based system of adjudication, such as that established under the DSU.[587] In *Thailand – Cigarettes (Philippines) (2011)*, the Appellate Body ruled that:

> [d]ue process is a fundamental principle of WTO dispute settlement. It informs and finds reflection in the provisions of the DSU.[588]

581 Panel Report, *Argentina – Poultry Anti-Dumping Duties (2003)*, para. 7.36. See also Appellate Body Report, *US – Offset Act (Byrd Amendment) (2003)*, para. 298.
582 See Panel Report, *Argentina – Poultry Anti-Dumping Duties (2003)*, para. 7.36.
583 Appellate Body Report, *EC – Bananas III (Article 21.5 – Ecuador II)/ EC – Bananas III (Article 21.5 – US) (2008)*, para. 228.
584 See Panel Report, *Peru – Agricultural Products (2015)*, para. 7.96.
585 See Appellate Body Report, *Peru – Agricultural Products (2015)*, para. 5.28. See also above, p. 183.
586 See Appellate Body Report, *Chile – Price Band System (2002)*, para. 176.
587 See Appellate Body Report, *US/Canada – Continued Suspension (2008)*, para. 433.
588 Appellate Body Report, *Thailand – Cigarettes (Philippines) (2011)*, para. 147.

The principle of due process guarantees that proceedings are conducted 'with fairness and impartiality, and that one party is not unfairly disadvantaged with respect to other parties in a dispute'.[589] The due process obligation requires panels and the Appellate Body to afford parties an adequate opportunity to pursue their claims, make out their defences, and establish the facts in the context of proceedings conducted in a balanced and orderly manner, according to established rules.[590] In the interest of 'due process', parties should also bring alleged procedural deficiencies to the attention of a panel or the Appellate Body at the earliest possible opportunity.[591]

6.2 Consultations

As noted above, the DSU expresses a clear preference for resolving disputes amicably rather than through adjudication.[592] To that end, WTO dispute settlement proceedings always start with consultations (or, at least, an attempt to have consultations) between the parties to the dispute.[593] In *Mexico – Corn Syrup (Article 21.5 – US) (2001)*, the Appellate Body stressed the importance of consultations in WTO dispute settlement as follows:

> Through consultations, parties exchange information, assess the strengths and weaknesses of their respective cases, narrow the scope of the differences between them and, in many cases, reach a mutually agreed solution in accordance with the explicit preference expressed in Article 3.7 of the DSU. Moreover, even where no such agreed solution is reached, consultations provide the parties an opportunity to define and delimit the scope of the dispute between them. Clearly, consultations afford many benefits to complaining and responding parties, as well as to third parties and to the dispute settlement system as a whole.[594]

As already noted, the resolution of disputes through consultations is obviously more cost-effective and more satisfactory for the long-term trade relations with the other party to the dispute than adjudication by a panel.[595] Consultations enable the disputing parties to understand better the factual situation and the legal claims in respect of the dispute. Such understanding may allow them to resolve the matter without further proceedings and, if not, will at least allow a party to learn more about the facts and the legal arguments that the other party is likely to use when the dispute goes to adjudication. In this way, the consultations *can* serve as an informal pretrial discovery mechanism. Their primary object and purpose, however, is to settle the dispute amicably.

This subsection discusses the following issues that arise with respect to consultations, namely: (1) their initiation; (2) their conduct; and (3) their outcome.

589 Appellate Body Report, *US/Canada – Continued Suspension (2008)*, para. 433.
590 See Appellate Body Report, *Thailand – Cigarettes (Philippines) (2011)*, para. 147.
591 See Appellate Body Report, *US – Carbon Steel (2002)*, para. 123. See also e.g. Appellate Body Report, *Canada – Wheat Exports and Grain Imports (2004)*, para. 205.
592 See above, p. 189.
593 See Article 4 of the DSU. Note in particular Article 4.5 but also Articles 4.3 and 4.7 of the DSU.
594 Appellate Body Report, *Mexico – Corn Syrup (Article 21.5 – US) (2001)*, para. 54.
595 See above, p. 189.

6.2.1 Initiation of Consultations

Any WTO Member considering that a benefit accruing to it under the *WTO Agreement* is being impaired or nullified by measures taken by another WTO Member may request consultations with that other Member.[596] WTO Members are required to accord sympathetic consideration to, and afford adequate opportunity for, consultations.[597] Consultations can be requested pursuant to *either* Article XXII of the GATT 1994 (or the corresponding provision in other covered agreements), *or* Article XXIII of the GATT 1994 (or the corresponding provision in other covered agreements). The Member requesting consultations is free to choose either type of consultations. As discussed below, this choice affects the conduct of the consultations.[598]

A request for consultations, giving the reasons for the request, must be submitted in writing and must: (1) identify the measure at issue; and (2) give an indication of the legal basis for the complaint.[599] The request for consultations circumscribes the scope of the dispute.[600] All requests for consultations are to be notified to the DSB by the Member requesting consultations.[601] Requests for consultations are made public on the WTO website as a WT/DS document.

With respect to the relationship between the request for consultations and the later panel request,[602] the Appellate Body noted, in *Brazil – Aircraft (1999)*, that Articles 4 and 6 of the DSU do *not* require a *precise and exact identity* between the specific measures and claims of WTO inconsistency that were the subject of consultations and the specific measures and claims of WTO inconsistency that were identified in the panel request. What is important is that the essence of the challenged measures and claims has not changed.[603] It is to be expected that the identification of challenged measures and the formulation of the claims in the panel request is shaped and influenced by the consultation process. As the Appellate Body found in *Mexico – Anti-Dumping Measures on Rice (2005)*, 'consultations may lead to the reformulation of a complaint, since a complaining party may learn of additional information or get a better understanding of the operation of a challenged measure'.[604]

Note that, in *US – Certain EC Products (2001)*, the Appellate Body found that, while a specific measure was explicitly referred to in the panel request, it was not referred to in the request for consultations, and for that reason was not

596 On access to WTO dispute settlement, see above, pp. 179–85.
597 See Article 4.2 of the DSU. 598 See below, pp. 268–70.
599 See Article 4.4 of the DSU.
600 See Appellate Body Report, *Mexico – Corn Syrup (Article 21.5 – US) (2001)*, para. 54.
601 See Article 4.4 of the DSU.
602 On the request for the establishment of a panel, see above, pp. 212–17.
603 See Appellate Body Report, *Brazil – Aircraft (1999)*, para. 132. See e.g. also Appellate Body Report, *US – Zeroing (Japan) (2007)*, paras. 89–96 (with regard to the challenged measures); Appellate Body Report, *Mexico – Anti-Dumping Measures on Rice (2005)*, para. 138 (with regard to the claims of WTO inconsistency made); and Appellate Body Reports, *Argentina – Import Measures (2015)*, paras. 5.10–5.13.
604 Appellate Body Report, *Mexico – Anti-Dumping Measures on Rice (2005)*, para. 138.

properly before the panel.[605] The Appellate Body ruled in *US – Upland Cotton (2005)* that measures or claims not listed in the consultation request cannot be added to the panel request, and can therefore not be within the panel's jurisdiction.[606] In the same case, the Appellate Body also ruled that the scope of the consultations is determined by the request for consultations, rather than by what actually happened, i.e. what actually was discussed, during the consultations.[607]

6.2.2 Conduct of Consultations

Parties have broad discretion with regard to the manner in which consultations are to be conducted. The DSU provides few rules on the conduct of consultations. The consultation process essentially is meant to resolve a dispute by diplomatic means. In *India – Patents (US) (1998)*, the Appellate Body noted:

> All parties engaged in dispute settlement under the DSU must be fully forthcoming *from the very beginning* both as to the claims involved in a dispute and as to the facts relating to those claims. Claims must be stated clearly. Facts must be disclosed freely. This must be so in consultations as well as in the more formal setting of panel proceedings. In fact, the demands of *due process* that are implicit in the DSU make this especially necessary during consultations. For the claims that are made and the facts that are established during consultations do much to shape the substance and the scope of subsequent panel proceedings.[608]

Unless otherwise agreed, the Member to which a request for consultations is made must *reply* to the request within ten days of the date of its receipt, and enter into consultations within a period of no more than thirty days after the date of receipt of the request.[609] If the Member does not respond within ten days after the date of receipt of the request, or does not enter into consultations within a period of no more than thirty days (or a period otherwise mutually agreed), then the Member that requested the consultations may proceed directly to request the establishment of a panel. As the Appellate Body noted in *Mexico – Corn Syrup (Article 21.5 – US) (2001)*, in such a case the respondent, by its own conduct, relinquishes the potential benefits that could be derived from consultations.[610]

While the request for consultations is notified to the DSB and posted on the WTO website, Article 4.6 of the DSU stipulates that the consultations themselves shall be confidential. However, the requirement of confidentiality does not mean that information acquired during consultations may not be used during panel proceedings between the same parties on the same matter. It means that the information acquired may not be disclosed to anyone not involved in the consultations.[611] In addition to stipulating that the consultations shall be confidential,

605 See Appellate Body Report, *US – Certain EC Products (2001)*, paras. 69–82.
606 See Appellate Body Report, *US – Upland Cotton (2005)*, paras. 284–5. See Panel Report, *US – Countervailing Measures (China) (2014)*, paras. 7.23–7.29.
607 See Appellate Body Report, *US – Upland Cotton (2005)* paras. 286–7.
608 Appellate Body Report, *India – Patents (US) (1998)*, para. 94. Emphasis added.
609 See Article 4.3 of the DSU. For the deadlines applicable in cases of urgency, see Article 4.8 of the DSU.
610 See Appellate Body Report, *Mexico – Corn Syrup (Article 21.5 – US) (2001)*, para. 59.
611 See e.g. Panel Report, *Korea – Alcoholic Beverages (1999)*, para. 10.23.

Article 4.6 of the DSU also states that the consultations shall be 'without prejudice to the rights of any Member in any further proceedings'. Therefore, evidence pertaining to settlement offers made during the consultations is 'of no legal consequence to the later stages' of WTO dispute settlement proceedings. On this basis, the panel in *US – Underwear (1997)* refused to consider as evidence the settlement proposals made by the United States during consultations, which had been submitted to it by Costa Rica.

As noted above, a Member can request consultations pursuant to *either* Article XXII (or corresponding provisions) *or* Article XXIII of the GATT 1994 (or corresponding provisions).[612] Members are free to choose between either type of consultations. With regard to the conduct of the consultations, there is, however, a significant difference between these types of consultations. Only in the context of consultations pursuant to Article XXII (or corresponding provisions) can a Member other than the consulting Members be allowed to participate in the consultations.[613] A Member that considers that it has a 'substantial trade interest' may notify the consulting Members and the DSB of such interest within ten days after the date of the circulation of the request for consultations.[614] Provided that the respondent to the dispute agrees that the claim of substantial trade interest is well founded, this Member shall join in the consultations. If consultations are instead conducted pursuant to Article XXIII (or corresponding provisions), it is not possible for other Members to join in the consultations.

Generally, consultations are held in Geneva and involve Geneva-based diplomats as well as capital-based trade officials and private lawyers of the parties to the dispute (and Members allowed to join the consultations).[615] The WTO Secretariat is neither present at, nor in any other way associated with, the consultations. As the Appellate Body noted in *US – Upland Cotton (2005)*:

> There is no public record of what actually transpires during consultations and parties will often disagree about what, precisely, was discussed.[616]

Occasionally, respondents have argued that the consultations held had not been adequate or meaningful or that the complainant had not engaged in consultations in good faith.[617] The panel in *Korea – Alcoholic Beverages (1999)* ruled in this respect that it was not for panels to assess the 'adequacy' of consultations.[618] Consultations are a matter reserved for the parties. What takes place in these

612 See above, pp. 179–80. 613 See above, p. 183.

614 See Article 4.11 of the DSU.

615 Note, however, that the consultations between the European Union and the Philippines in *Philippines – Distilled Spirits (2012)* were held in Manila. See Panel Reports, *Philippines – Distilled Spirits (2012)*, para. 1.2.

616 Appellate Body Report, *US – Upland Cotton (2005)*, para. 287.

617 See the requirements in Articles 3.10 and 4.2 of the DSU. Note also Article 4.10 of the DSU, which provides that during consultations Members 'should' give special attention to the particular problems and interests of developing-country Members.

618 See Panel Report, *Korea – Alcoholic Beverages (1999)*, para. 10.19. See also e.g. *US – Poultry (China) (2010)*, para. 7.35.

consultations is not the concern of panels. Panels may only ascertain whether consultations were held or at least were requested.[619] Note, however, that, if a respondent raises in a timely manner the lack of a request for consultations or the lack of consultations, a panel would have to conclude that it has no authority to hear and decide the dispute.[620]

6.2.3 Outcome of Consultations

If consultations are successful and lead to a mutually agreed solution to the dispute, this solution must be notified to the DSB.[621] Any Member may raise any point relating to this notified solution at meetings of the DSB.[622] Note that mutually agreed solutions must be consistent with WTO law.[623] As discussed above, consultations have frequently been successful in resolving disputes.[624]

If consultations between the parties fail to settle the dispute within sixty days of the receipt of the request for consultations, the complainant may request the DSB to establish a panel to adjudicate the dispute.[625] In many cases, however, the complainant will not, immediately upon the expiration of the sixty-day period, request the establishment of a panel but will allow for more time to settle the dispute through consultations.

For consultations involving a measure taken by a developing-country Member, Article 12.10 of the DSU explicitly provides that the parties may agree to extend the sixty-day period. If, after the sixty-day period has elapsed, the consulting parties cannot agree that the consultations have concluded, the Chair of the DSB shall decide, after consultation with the parties, whether to extend this period and, if so, for how long.

Consultations between the parties with the aim of settling the dispute can, and do, continue *during* the panel proceedings. Article 11 of the DSU provides that panels should consult the parties to the dispute regularly and give them an adequate opportunity to develop a mutually satisfactory solution.[626] There have been a number of disputes in which a mutually agreed solution was reached

619 See Panel Reports, *EC – Bananas III (1997)*, para. 7.19.

620 The lack of prior consultations is, however, not a defect that a panel must examine on its own motion. See Appellate Body Report, *Mexico – Corn Syrup (Article 21.5 – US) (2001)*, para. 64.

621 See Article 3.6 of the DSU. For a list of all mutually agreed solutions notified to the DSB, see *WTO Analytical Index (2012)*, Volume II, 1530–1 together with the Supplement (up to June 2015).

622 See *ibid.* 623 See Article 3.5 of the DSU.

624 See above, p. 189.

625 The complainant may also request a panel *during* the sixty-day period if the consulting parties jointly consider that consultations have failed to settle the dispute. See Article 4.7 of the DSU. Another possible situation is that the respondent does not object, explicitly and in a timely manner, to the failure of the complainant to request or engage in consultations. In such situation, the respondent may be deemed to have consented to the lack of consultations. See Appellate Body Report, *Mexico – Corn Syrup (Article 21.5 – US) (2001)*, para. 63.

626 See Article 11 of the DSU. Note that in *Peru – Agricultural Products (2015)*, the panel explicitly reminded the parties of its readiness to consult with them and give them adequate opportunity to develop a mutually satisfactory solution. See Panel Report, *Peru – Agricultural Products (2015)*, para. 1.12.

while the dispute was already before a panel.[627] In such a case, Article 12.7 of the DSU provides that the panel report 'shall be confined to a brief description of the case and to reporting that a solution has been reached'.

6.3 Panel Proceedings

As noted above, when consultations are unsuccessful,[628] the complainant may decide to advance to the next stage of the process of WTO dispute settlement, namely, the panel proceedings. The basic rules governing panel proceedings are set out in Article 12 of the DSU. Article 12.1 of the DSU directs a panel to follow the *Working Procedures* contained in Appendix 3 to the DSU, while at the same time authorising a panel to do otherwise after consulting the parties to the dispute. While Article 12.1 of the DSU merely requires that the panel 'consult' the parties, panels are often hesitant to deviate from the *Working Procedures* contained in Appendix 3 without the 'consent' of the parties. Moreover, panels usually agree to requests on procedural issues tabled by the parties jointly. In *EC – Hormones (1998)*, the Appellate Body noted that panels enjoy:

> a margin of discretion to deal, always in accordance with due process, with specific situations that may arise in a particular case.[629]

In *India – Patents (US) (1998)*, however, the Appellate Body cautioned panels as follows:

> Although panels enjoy some discretion in establishing their own working procedures, this discretion does not extend to modifying the substantive provisions of the DSU. To be sure, Article 12.1 of the DSU says: 'Panels shall follow the Working Procedures in Appendix 3 unless the panel decides otherwise after consulting the parties to the dispute.' Yet that is *all* that it says. Nothing in the DSU gives a panel the authority either to disregard or to modify other explicit provisions of the DSU.[630]

Article 12.2 of the DSU requires that panel procedures provide sufficient flexibility so as to ensure high-quality panel reports while not unduly delaying the panel process. Since the *Working Procedures* contained in Appendix 3 to the DSU are rudimentary, most panels now find it useful, if not necessary, to adopt more detailed *ad hoc* working procedures.[631] As the Appellate Body stated in *Thailand – Cigarettes (Philippines) (2011)*:

627 See e.g. *EC – Scallops* (complaints by Canada, Peru and Chile (1996)); *EC – Butter* (complaint by New Zealand ((1996)) *US – DRAMs (Article 21.5 – Korea)* (complaint by Korea (2006)); and *Japan – Quotas on Laver* (complaint by Korea (2006)).

628 For the exceptional situation in which the complainant can request the establishment of a panel without having had consultations with the respondent, see above, p. 212.

629 Appellate Body Report, *EC – Hormones (1998)*, para. 152, fn. 138.

630 Appellate Body Report, *India – Patents (US) (1998)*, para. 92. In this case, the Appellate Body reversed a decision by the panel that it would consider all claims made prior to the end of the first substantive meeting. All parties had agreed with this panel decision.

631 For an example of such *ad hoc* panel working procedures, see Panel Report, *US – Carbon Steel (India) (2014)*, Annex A-1. While these working procedures are *ad hoc*, they often include many *standardised* provisions.

> Panel working procedures should both embody and reinforce due process ... As the Appellate Body has previously observed, the use by panels of detailed standardized working procedures promotes fairness and the protection of due process.[632]

Generally speaking, the parties to a dispute enjoy a high degree of discretion to argue before panels in the manner they deem appropriate. This discretion, however, does not detract from their obligation under the DSU to engage in dispute settlement proceedings 'in good faith in an effort to resolve the dispute'.[633] Both the complaining and the responding parties must comply with the requirements of the DSU in good faith. In *US – FSC (2000)*, the Appellate Body held:

> By good faith compliance, complaining Members accord to the responding Members the full measure of protection and opportunity to defend, contemplated by the letter and spirit of the procedural rules. The same principle of good faith requires that responding Members seasonably and promptly bring claimed procedural deficiencies to the attention of the complaining Member, and to the DSB or the Panel, so that corrections, if needed, can be made to resolve disputes. The procedural rules of WTO dispute settlement are designed to promote, not the development of litigation techniques, but simply the fair, prompt and effective resolution of trade disputes.[634]

This subsection discusses the following issues which arise with respect to panel proceedings: (1) the initiation of panel proceedings; (2) the written submissions and panel meetings; (3) panel deliberations and interim review; and (4) the adoption or appeal of panel reports.

6.3.1 Initiation of Panel Proceedings

As discussed above, when consultations are unsuccessful, the complainant may request the establishment of a panel.[635] The DSB usually establishes the panel by reverse consensus at the second meeting at which it discusses the panel request.[636] Subsequently, the parties agree on the composition of the panel or, if they fail to do so, the WTO Director-General decides on the composition of the panel.[637] Once composed, the panel will – whenever possible within a week of its composition – fix the timetable for its work on the basis of the 'proposed timetable for panel work' set out in Appendix 3 to the DSU.[638] At that time the panel may also decide on detailed *ad hoc* working procedures.[639] Before deciding on the timetable and *ad hoc* working procedures, the panel

632 Appellate Body Report, *Thailand – Cigarettes (Philippines) (2011)*, para. 148. On 'due process' in WTO dispute settlement, see above, pp. 264–6.

633 Article 3.10 of the DSU.

634 Appellate Body Report, *US – FSC (2000)*, para. 166. See also Appellate Body Report, *US – Lamb (2001)*, para. 115.

635 See above, pp. 212–17. 636 See above, p. 216. 637 See above, pp. 217–19.

638 See Article 12.3 of the DSU. The timetable includes precise deadlines for written submissions by the parties, which the parties must respect (see Article 12.5 of the DSU). In determining the timetable, the panel must provide sufficient time for the parties to prepare their submissions (see Article 12.4 of the DSU). It is not uncommon for this timetable to be modified in the course of the panel proceedings. See e.g. Panel Report, *US – Countervailing Measures (China) (2015)*, para. 1.7.

639 See above, p. 271.

will consult with the parties at what is commonly referred to as the 'organisational meeting'.[640]

Note with regard to the decision on the timetable for the panel proceedings that Article 12.10 of the DSU provides that:

> in examining a complaint against a developing country Member, the panel shall accord sufficient time for the developing country Member to prepare and present its argumentation.[641]

Note that, pursuant to Article 12.12 of the DSU, the panel may, at the request of the complaining party, at any time during the panel proceedings, suspend its work for a maximum period of twelve months. While not common, this does happen occasionally.[642] The authority of the panel lapses if the work of the panel is suspended for more than twelve months.[643]

6.3.2 Written Submissions and Panel Meetings

Each of the parties to a dispute submits two written submissions to the panel: (1) a 'first written submission'; and (2) a 'rebuttal submission'. In their first written submissions, the parties present the facts of the case as they see them and their arguments relating to the alleged inconsistencies with WTO law.[644] In their rebuttal submissions, they reply to the argument and evidence submitted by the other party.[645] As the Appellate Body ruled in *US – Shrimp (1998)*, the parties have a *legal right* to make the above-mentioned submissions to the panel, and the panel in turn is *obliged in law* to accept and give due consideration to these submissions.[646]

After the first written submissions of the parties have been filed, the panel holds its first substantive meeting with the parties.[647] At this meeting, the panel first asks the complainant to present its case, and then gives the respondent the opportunity to react to the case brought against it.[648] The panel holds a second substantive meeting with the parties after the rebuttal submissions have been filed.[649] While not mandatory, panel meetings are always held on the premises of the WTO Secretariat

640 See Articles 12.3 and 12.5 of the DSU.

641 See e.g. Panel Report, *India – Solar Cells (2016)*, para. 1.7, fn. 6.

642 See e.g. Panel Report, *EC – Butter (1999)*, para. 12.

643 See e.g. *India – Wines and Spirits* (complaint by the EC); and *Australia – Tobacco Plain Packaging* (complaint by Ukraine). Note that it is for the complainant to request the panel to resume its work.

644 Note that, even if the complainant fails to include any arguments on certain claims in its first written submission, these claims, if properly identified in the panel request, remain within the terms of reference of the panel. See Appellate Body Report, *EC – Bananas III (1997)*, paras. 145–7.

645 The first written submission of the complainant is usually filed two to three weeks in advance of the first written submission of the respondent. The rebuttal submissions are filed simultaneously. See Article 12.6 of, and para. 12 of Appendix 3 to, the DSU. On the 'late' submission of evidence, see below, p. 274.

646 See Appellate Body Report, *US – Shrimp (1998)*, para. 101. This is also the case for submissions by third parties but not for submissions by any other Member or person (*amicus curiae* briefs). See above, pp. 260–4.

647 See para. 4 of Appendix 3 to the DSU.

648 See para. 5 of Appendix 3 to the DSU.

649 Additional meetings with the parties may be scheduled if required: see para. 12 of Appendix 3 to the DSU. In practice, however, very few panels have had additional meetings with the parties.

in Geneva. A panel meeting may take one or more days. While initially far less formal and less 'court-like' than the oral hearings of the Appellate Body, WTO panel meetings have become increasingly formal in recent years.[650] All *ex parte* communications with the panel, on matters under consideration, are explicitly proscribed.[651] As already discussed, until 2006 panels always met in closed session with only the delegations of the parties present. In recent years, however, panel meetings with the parties are open to public observation if the parties so agree and the panel so rules.[652]

The panel may, at any time, put questions to the parties and ask them for explanations either in the course of a meeting or in writing.[653] The DSU provides panels with discretionary authority to request and obtain information from *any* Member, including *a fortiori* a Member, which is a party to the dispute before the panel.[654] The parties are under an *obligation* to provide the panel with the information or the documents that the panel requests. Article 13.1 of the DSU states, in relevant part:

> A Member *should* respond promptly and fully to any request by a panel for such information as the panel considers necessary and appropriate.[655]

In *Canada – Aircraft (1999)*, the Appellate Body ruled that the word 'should' in Article 13.1 is used in a normative sense.[656] As held by the Appellate Body in this case, it is within the discretion of panels to draw adverse inferences from the fact that a party has refused to provide information requested by the panel. However, the Appellate Body stressed that panels must draw inferences on the basis of all the facts of record (and not only the refusal to provide information).[657]

The DSU does not establish precise rules or deadlines for the submission of evidence by a party to the dispute. In *Argentina – Textiles and Apparel (1998)*, the panel allowed the United States to submit certain evidence two days before the second substantive meeting. Argentina appealed the panel's decision to admit this evidence. The Appellate Body rejected the appeal by noting that neither Article 11 of the DSU nor the *Working Procedures* set out in Appendix 3 thereof establish time limits for the submission of evidence to a panel.[658] The Appellate Body

650 See below, pp. 278–81.

651 See Article 18.1 of the DSU. See e.g. Panel Report, *Turkey – Rice (2007)*, para. 7.100; and Panel Report, *Korea – Certain Paper (2005)*, paras. 7.13–7.18.

652 See above, p. 254.

653 See para. 8 of Appendix 3 to the DSU. During panel meetings, parties may also question each other. This does not happen during hearings of the Appellate Body.

654 See Article 13.1 of the DSU. On the discretionary nature of this authority to request information, see e.g. Appellate Body Report, *EC – Bed Linen (Article 21.5 – India) (2003)*, paras. 165–7; and Panel Report, *EC – Selected Customs Matters (2006)*, paras. 7.77–7.83.

655 Emphasis added.

656 See Appellate Body Report, *Canada – Aircraft (1999)*, para. 187.

657 See *ibid.*, paras. 204–5; and Appellate Body Report, *US – Wheat Gluten (2001)*, paras. 173–6. In *US – Upland Cotton (2005)*, the United States responded in part to the request of the panel to provide certain information and also argued that other information could not be provided. The panel ultimately, based on all of the information before it, determined that it was not necessary to draw adverse inferences in respect of information allegedly not submitted by the United States. See Panel Report, *US – Upland Cotton (2005)*, paras. 7.20–7.42 and 7.609–7.633. See also Panel Report, *Canada – Aircraft Credits and Guarantees (2002)*, paras. 7.379–7.386.

658 See Appellate Body Report, *Argentina – Textiles and Apparel (1998)*, para. 79. See also Panel Report, *Canada – Aircraft (1999)*, paras. 9.75–9.78.

acknowledged that the DSU clearly contemplates two distinct stages in panel proceedings: a first stage during which the parties should set out their case in chief, including a full presentation of the facts on the basis of submission of supporting evidence; and a second stage which is generally designed to permit 'rebuttals' by each party of the arguments and evidence submitted by the other party.[659] Nevertheless, unless specific deadlines for the submission of evidence are set out in the *ad hoc* working procedures of the panel, parties can submit new evidence as late as the second substantive meeting with the panel.[660] The panel must, of course, always be careful to observe due process, which, *inter alia*, entails providing the parties with adequate opportunity to respond to the evidence submitted.[661] Most panels now have *ad hoc* working procedures that set out precise deadlines for the submission of evidence. These *ad hoc* working procedures commonly require that each party shall submit all factual evidence to the panel no later than during the first substantive meeting. As an exception to this rule, evidence necessary for purposes of rebuttal, answers to questions or comments on answers may be accepted at a later point in time upon a showing of good cause and provided that the other party is accorded a period of time for comment. As the Appellate Body noted in *Thailand – Cigarettes (Philippines) (2010)*, 'due process is a fundamental principle of WTO dispute settlement' and 'due process may be of particular concern in cases where a party raises new facts at a late stage of the panel proceedings'.[662] In *China – Rare Earths (2014)*, the panel rejected evidence submitted by the complainants after the second substantive meeting because the evidence 'could have been submitted earlier and in a manner consistent with due process'.[663]

Finally, as discussed above, any WTO Member having a substantial interest in a matter before a panel and having notified its interest in a timely manner to the DSB shall have an opportunity to be heard by the panel and to make written submissions to the panel.[664] These third parties to the dispute are invited by the panel to present their views during a special session of the first substantive meeting.[665] Their written submissions to the panel are shared with the parties to the dispute.[666] Third parties,

659 See Appellate Body Report, *Argentina – Textiles and Apparel (1998)*, para. 79. See also Panel Report, *Korea – Commercial Vessels (2005)*, paras. 7.277–7.279.

660 In *EC – Selected Customs Matters (2006)*, the Appellate Body upheld the panel's decision to exclude evidence contained in exhibits provided by the European Communities at the interim review stage. The Appellate Body noted that 'the interim review stage is not an appropriate time to introduce new evidence'. See Appellate Body Report, *EC – Selected Customs Matters (2006)*, paras. 248, 250 and 259. See also Panel Reports, *EC – Approval and Marketing of Biotech Products (2006)*, paras. 6.134 and 6.162–6.164. However, note that the panel in *US – Anti-Dumping Measures on Oil Country Tubular Goods (2005)* saw 'no harm' in accepting a letter from the United States drawing the panel's attention to the Appellate Body Report in *US – Gambling (2005)*, circulated after the interim report was issued. See Panel Reports, *US – Anti-Dumping Measures on Oil Country Tubular Goods (2005)*, paras. 6.24–6.25.

661 Appellate Body Report, *Argentina – Textiles and Apparel (1998)*, paras. 80–1; and Appellate Body Report, *Australia – Salmon (1998)*, para. 272.

662 Appellate Body Report, *Thailand – Cigarettes (Philippines) (2010)*, para. 149.

663 See Panel Report, *China – Rare Earths (2014)*, paras. 7.27–7.28.

664 See Article 10.2 of the DSU. See also above, p. 237.

665 See Article 10.2 of, and para. 6 of Appendix 3 to, the DSU.

666 Article 10.2 of the DSU. These submissions are reflected in, or attached to, the panel report.

however, only receive the first written submissions of the parties.[667] It is clear from the above that the rights of third parties to participate in the panel proceedings are, as a rule, somewhat limited. In a number of cases, however, third parties have sought and sometimes obtained enhanced third party rights. In *EC – Bananas III (1997)*, third party developing-country Members that had a major interest in the outcome of this case, were allowed to attend the entire first and second substantive meetings of the panel with the parties, as well as to make statements at both meetings. Third parties were also granted enhanced third party rights in, e.g., *EC – Hormones (1998)*, *EC – Tariff Preferences (2004)*, *EC – Export Subsidies on Sugar (2005)* and *US – COOL (Article 21.5) (2015)*.[668] Note that the grant of enhanced third party rights is within 'the sound discretion' of the panel, although '[s]uch discretionary authority is, of course, not unlimited and is circumscribed, e.g., by the requirements of due process'.[669] Third parties were refused enhanced third party rights in, e.g., *EC and certain member States – Large Civil Aircraft (2011)* and *China – Rare Earths (2014)*.[670]

In *China – Rare Earths (2014)*, the panel declined Canada's request for enhanced third party rights because Canada failed to show that its legal, systemic and/or economic interests distinguished Canada from the other third parties in this dispute. Moreover, the panel considered that granting the third parties in this dispute extended third party rights would seriously impede the prompt settlement of the dispute and create undue additional burden for the parties. Finally, the panel also took note of the fact that the four parties to the dispute unanimously objected to Canada's request.[671]

6.3.3 Panel Deliberations and Interim Review

As provided for in Article 14 of the DSU, panel deliberations are confidential.[672] The reports of panels are drafted without the presence of the parties to the dispute; they are drafted in light of the information provided and the statements made during the proceedings.[673]

667 See Article 10.3 of the DSU.

668 In *EC – Hormones (1998)*, enhanced third party rights were granted because the third parties in the two disputes were complainants in a parallel panel procedure concerning the same EC measure, to be dealt with by the same panellists. See Panel Report, *EC – Hormones (US) (1998)*, para. 8.15; and Panel Report, *EC – Hormones (Canada) (1998)*, paras. 8.12–8.20 (upheld by the Appellate Body: see Appellate Body Report, *EC – Hormones (1998)*, paras. 150–4). In *EC – Tariff Preferences (2004)*, eleven of the eighteen third parties had requested enhanced third party rights. The panel decided to grant additional rights to *all* third parties. See Panel Report, *EC – Tariff Preferences (2004)*, Annex A, para. 7. See also Panel Reports, *EC – Export Subsidies on Sugar (2005)*, paras. 2.5–2.9, and Panel Reports, *US – COOL (Article 21.5) (2015)*, para. 1.16.

669 Appellate Body Report, *US – 1916 Act (2000)*, paras. 149 and 150. In this case, the Appellate Body upheld the panel's decision not to grant enhanced third party rights. Note that in e.g. *US – Countervailing Measures (China) (2015)*, para. 6.3, the United States argued that the opposition of the parties to a request for enhanced third party rights 'serves as an independent and sufficient basis for such a request to be rejected'. The United States thus disagreed that it is within the discretion of the panel to grant enhanced third party rights.

670 See Panel Report, *EC and certain member States – Large Civil Aircraft (2011)*, para. 7.167; and Panel Report, *China – Rare Earths (2014)*, paras. 7.9–7.10.

671 See Panel Report, *China – Rare Earths (2014)*, paras. 7.9–7.10. See also e.g. Panel Reports, *Argentina – Import Restrictions (2015)*, para. 1.24.

672 See Article 14.1 of the DSU. 673 See Article 14.2 of the DSU.

Having completed a draft of the descriptive (i.e. facts and argument) sections of its report, the panel issues, pursuant to Article 15 of the DSU, this draft to the parties for their comments.[674] Following the expiration of the time period for comments, the panel subsequently issues an interim report to the parties, including both the descriptive sections and the panel's findings and conclusions.[675] A party may submit written comments on the interim report and request the panel to review particular aspects of the report. The parties are given an opportunity to comment on each other's comments on the interim report in writing. At the request of a party, the panel may hold a further meeting with the parties on the issues identified in the written comments.[676] Parties have rarely requested such an interim review meeting with the panel.[677] Instead, parties have responded in writing on each other's interim review comments. The final panel report must include a summary and discussion of the arguments made at the interim review stage.[678]

The comments made by the parties at the interim review stage frequently give rise to corrections of technical errors or unclear drafting. However, panels seldom changed the conclusions reached in their reports in any substantive way as a result of the comments made by parties, although it should be noted that there have been some panels that have done so.[679] To safeguard the 'ability' of the panel to alter the conclusions reached in its interim report in light of comments made by parties, it is important that this report remains confidential. A panel will be 'disinclined' to make substantive changes to its report if the latter is already in the public domain. Disregard for the confidentiality of the interim report is therefore a matter of systemic concern. In *EC – Approval and Marketing of Biotech Products (2006)*, the panel sharply criticised two NGOs, Friends of the Earth Europe and the Institute of Agriculture and Trade Policy, for having posted the interim report on their websites.[680] It is clear that the interim report in this case was leaked in order to bring political pressure to bear on the panel during the interim review process. Interim review is an unusual feature in judicial or quasi-judicial dispute settlement proceedings.[681]

6.3.4 Adoption or Appeal of Panel Reports

The final panel report is first *issued* to the parties to the dispute, and some weeks later, once the report has been translated into all three working languages of the

674 See Article 15.1 of the DSU. 675 See Article 15.2 of the DSU.

676 See *ibid.*

677 Note that there was an interim review meeting in *Thailand – Cigarettes (Philippines) (2011)*. See Panel Report, *Thailand – Cigarettes (Philippines) (2011)*, para. 6.1.

678 See Article 15.3 of the DSU. If no comments are received from any party within the comment period, the interim report shall be considered the final panel report. See Article 15.3 of the DSU.

679 See e.g. Panel Reports, *EC – Approval and Marketing of Biotech Products (2006)*, para. 8.18 (with regard to the US complaint) and para. 8.36 (with regard to the Canadian complaint); Panel Report, *Korea – Certain Paper (2005)*, paras. 6.3–6.5 and 7.106–7.112; and Panel Report, *US – Carbon Steel (2002)*, paras. 7.24 and 8.120–8.145.

680 See Panel Reports, *EC – Approval and Marketing of Biotech Products (2006)*, para. 7.696.

681 See also Communication from the Chair of the Panel, *EC – Approval and Marketing of Biotech Products (2006)*, WT/DS291/32, WT/DS292/26 and WT/DS293/26, dated 29 September 2006, para. 2.

WTO, it is *circulated* to the general WTO membership. Once circulated to WTO Members, the panel report is an unrestricted document available to the public. On the day of its circulation, a panel report is posted on the WTO's website as a WT/DS document.[682]

According to Article 16.4 of the DSU, within sixty days after the date of circulation of the panel report to the Members, the report is adopted at a DSB meeting unless: (1) a party to the dispute formally notifies the DSB of its decision to appeal; or (2) the DSB decides by consensus not to adopt the report. Note that, in some cases, the parties reached a procedural agreement to request the DSB to extend the sixty-day deadline for the adoption or appeal of the panel report.[683] Typically, these requests have been made, and the DSB has granted such requests, to manage workload and scheduling difficulties at the stage of the appellate review proceedings.

If a panel report is appealed, it is not discussed by the DSB until the appellate review proceedings are completed and the Appellate Body report – together with the panel report – comes before the DSB for adoption. When the DSB does consider and debate a panel report, the parties to the dispute, as well as all other Members, have the right to comment on the report. All views expressed shall be fully recorded in the minutes of the DSB meeting.[684] In order to provide sufficient time for the Members to review panel reports, the reports shall not be considered for adoption by the DSB until twenty days after they have been circulated.

As the Appellate Body noted in *EC – Bed Linen (Article 21.5 – India) (2003)*, a panel report that is adopted by the DSB must be treated by the parties to a particular dispute 'as a final resolution to that dispute'.[685]

6.4 Appellate Body Proceedings

Almost seven out of ten panel reports circulated to date were appealed to the Appellate Body. In contrast to panels, the Appellate Body has detailed standard working procedures set out in the *Working Procedures for Appellate Review* (the '*Working Procedures*').[686] Pursuant to Article 17.9 of the DSU, the Appellate Body has the authority to draw up these *Working Procedures* itself, in consultation with

682 Panel reports are also included in the official *Dispute Settlement Reports of the World Trade Organization*, published by Cambridge University Press. See www.cambridge.org/gb/knowledge/series/series_display/item3937379/?site_locale=en_GB.

683 See e.g. in *EC – Export Subsidies on Sugar (2005)*; *Brazil – Retreaded Tyres (2007)*; *US – Anti-Dumping and Countervailing Duties (China) (2011)*; *US – Clove Cigarettes* (2011); *US – Tuna II (2011)*; *US – COOL (2012)*; and *India – Agricultural Products (2015)*.

684 See Articles 16.1 and 16.3 of the DSU.

685 See Appellate Body Report, *EC – Bed Linen (Article 21.5 – India) (2003)*, para. 95.

686 *Working Procedures for Appellate Review*, WT/AB/WP/6, dated 16 August 2010. This is a consolidated, revised version of the original *Working Procedures for Appellate Review*, WT/AB/WP/1, dated 15 February 1996.

the Chair of the DSB and the WTO Director-General. In addition, where a procedural question arises that is not covered by the *Working Procedures*, the division hearing the appeal may, 'in the interest of fairness and orderly procedure in the conduct of the appeal', adopt an appropriate procedure for the purpose of that appeal.[687] The Additional Procedure adopted in the context of *EC – Asbestos (2001)* in respect of the filing of *amicus curiae* briefs, discussed above, is arguably the best-known example of the use of this authority.[688] More recently, the Appellate Body divisions in *EC and certain member States – Large Civil Aircraft (2011)* and *US – Large Civil Aircraft (2nd complaint) (2012)* adopted, *inter alia*, Additional Procedures for the protection of business confidential information (BCI) and highly sensitive business information (HSBI) submitted by the parties in these disputes.[689]

This subsection discusses the following key aspects of the appellate review proceedings and issues that arise with respect to these proceedings: (1) the initiation of appellate review proceedings; (2) written submissions and the oral hearing; (3) the exchange of views and deliberations; and (4) the adoption of the Appellate Body report.

6.4.1 Initiation of Appellate Review Proceedings

Pursuant to Rule 20(1) of the *Working Procedures*, appellate review proceedings commence with a party's notification in writing to the DSB of its decision to appeal *and* the simultaneous filing of a notice of appeal with the Appellate Body. The notice of appeal must adequately identify the findings or legal interpretations of the panel that are being appealed as erroneous. To this end, Rule 20(2)(d) of the *Working Procedures* requires that a notice of appeal include: (1) identification of the alleged errors made by the panel; (2) a list of the legal provision(s) of the covered agreements that the panel is alleged to have erred in interpreting or applying; and (3) an indicative list of the paragraphs of the panel report containing the alleged errors.[690]

The notice of appeal delineates the Appellate Body's terms of reference in a specific appeal.[691] It is important that all claims made on appeal are *expressly* and *sufficiently* identified in the notice of appeal.[692]

687 Rule 16(1) of the *Working Procedures*. Such procedure must, however, be consistent with the DSU, the other covered agreements and the *Working Procedures*.

688 See above, p. 262. 689 See above, p. 252.

690 The latter list is without prejudice to the ability of the appellant to refer to other paragraphs of the panel report in the context of its appeal. See Rule 20(2)(d)(iii) of the *Working Procedures*. Note that in *China – Rare Earths (2014)*, the Appellate Body denied the request by China to reject the US notice of appeal on the grounds that it did not constitute a proper notice of appeal due to its 'conditional' nature. The Appellate Body ruled that the notice of appeal conformed to the requirements set out in Rule 20 of the *Working Procedures*. See Appellate Body Report, *China – Rare Earths (2014)*, para. 1.31.

691 As further discussed below, since the 2010 amendment of the *Working Procedures*, the notice of appeal and the appellant submission are filed on the same day, and the notice of appeal has thus lost the function it had before 2010 of giving 'advance' notice of the appellant's claims of error. However, the notice of appeal still fulfils the important task of setting out, in brief and clearly, what the appeal is about, and delineating the Appellate Body's terms of reference in a specific appeal.

692 See Appellate Body Report, *US – Upland Cotton (2005)*, para. 495.

With regard to the issue of a panel's jurisdiction, however, the Appellate Body held in *US – Offset Act (Byrd Amendment) (2003)* that this issue is so fundamental that it is appropriate to consider claims that a panel has exceeded its jurisdiction even if such claims were not raised in the notice of appeal.[693] In the interest of due process, it would of course be preferable for the appellant to raise such an important issue, as the panel's jurisdiction, in the notice of appeal.

A party can appeal a panel report as soon as the report is circulated to WTO Members, and it can do so as long as the report has not yet been adopted by the DSB. In practice, parties usually appeal shortly before the meeting of the DSB that would consider the adoption of the panel report.

Upon the commencement of an appeal, the Appellate Body division responsible for deciding the appeal draws up an appropriate working schedule guided by the time periods stipulated in the *Working Procedures*.[694] The working schedule sets forth precise dates for the filing of documents.[695] This working schedule will be communicated to the parties within one or two days after the filing of the appeal.[696] In exceptional circumstances, where strict adherence to a time period would result in manifest unfairness, a party or third party to the dispute may request modification of the working schedule for the appeal. This possibility is provided for in Rule 16(2) of the *Working Procedures* and has been used occasionally.[697]

If the other party to the dispute decides to 'cross appeal' pursuant to Rule 23 of the *Working Procedures*, it must file a 'notice of other appeal' within five days of the first notice.[698] The notice of other appeal must meet the same requirements as the first notice.[699] Once the other appeal has been filed, the composition of the division hearing the appeal is disclosed to the participants and third participants.

A party to a dispute may not only initiate an appeal, it may – pursuant to Rule 30(1) of the *Working Procedures* – also withdraw that appeal at any stage of the process. Such a withdrawal leads normally to the termination of the appellate review. This was the case in *India – Autos (2002)*, where the Appellate Body issued, subsequent to the withdrawal, a brief report on the procedural history and the reason for not having completed its work, namely India's withdrawal

693 See Appellate Body Report, *US – Offset Act (Byrd Amendment) (2003)*, para. 208.

694 See Rule 26(1) of the *Working Procedures*. 695 See Rule 26(2) of the *Working Procedures*.

696 Note that the date for the oral hearing may be communicated later.

697 The Appellate Body has agreed to modify its working schedule in instances where a Member has a deadline for written submission or a hearing in another WTO dispute, very close to the initial date set for filing of submissions (see Appellate Body Report, *Chile – Price Band System (Article 21.5 – Argentina) (2007)*, para. 11); where lead counsel for a party had prior commitments (see Appellate Body Report, *US – Softwood Lumber VI (Article 21.5 – Canada) (2006)*, para. 13); and where suspected bioterrorist attacks prevent internal consultations in legislative circles of a Member (see Appellate Body Report, *US – FSC (Article 21.5 – EC) (2002)*, para. 8). Note that in *EC – Seal Products (2014)*, the Appellate Body decided at the joint request of the parties to postpone the oral hearing by two weeks due to certain logistical difficulties faced by the parties in securing reasonable hotel accommodation in Geneva on the dates on which the hearing was originally scheduled. See Appellate Body Reports, *EC – Seal Products (2014)*, para. 1.14 and Annex 5.

698 On 'cross appeals', see above, p. 238.

699 See Rule 23(2) of the *Working Procedures*.

of its appeal.[700] However, in some cases, parties withdrew their appeal in order to refile it or submit a new one. This happened, in *EC – Sardines (2002)*. In this case, Peru contended that the appeal of the European Communities was insufficiently clear. In response, the European Communities withdrew its appeal and filed a more detailed one. The Appellate Body rejected Peru's claim that the withdrawal of the European Communities' appeal was invalid and clarified that there was no indication in Rule 30 that the right of withdrawal only encompasses unconditional withdrawal.[701] Conditions are allowed as long as they do not undermine the fair, prompt and effective resolution of the dispute and as long as the disputing party involved acts in good faith.[702] Note that Rule 23 *bis* of the *Working Procedures* set out detailed rules for the amendment of a notice of appeal or notice of other appeal. Upon a request of the appellant or other appellant the division may authorise the amendment of a notice, taking into account the time frame for appellate review and the interests of fairness and orderly procedure.

Finally, note that in *China – Rare Earths (2014)*, the appeal filed by the United States in DS431 on 8 April 2014 was filed simultaneously with the appeal by China of the panel report in a different dispute, namely, *US – Countervailing and Anti-Dumping Measures (China) (2014)*. For the first time, appeals in different disputes were filed simultaneously. Normally the Appellate Body attributes appeal numbers sequentially based on the date and time of the filing of the notice of appeal. Since the notices were filed simultaneously, the Appellate Body could not resort to this practice. However, before the composition of the divisions in either appeal could be established, an appeal number had to be assigned to each appeal. To resolve this exceptional situation, on 11 April 2014, a random draw was held at the Appellate Body Secretariat, in the presence of the parties of both cases. As a result of this draw, the appeal by the United States in *China – Rare Earths* (DS431) was assigned appeal number AB-2014-3, and the appeal by China in *US – Countervailing and Anti-Dumping Measures (China)* (DS449) was assigned appeal number AB-2014-4.[703]

6.4.2 Written Submissions and the Oral Hearing

On the same day as the filing of the notice of appeal, the appellant must file a written submission.[704] This written submission sets out a precise statement

700 See Appellate Body Report, *India – Autos (2002)*, paras. 14–18.

701 See Appellate Body Report, *EC – Sardines (2002)*, para. 141.

702 See *ibid*. This technique of withdrawal and refiling of the notice of appeal has also been used in order to resolve workload and scheduling problems the Appellate Body is faced with. The Appellate Body allows an appellant to attach conditions to the withdrawal of its notice of appeal, saving its right to file a replacement notice. In *US – Line Pipe (2002)* and *US – FSC (2000)*, the Appellate Body division and the appellees had prior knowledge of, and agreed to, the United States' reservation that it would file a new notice of appeal on withdrawing its initial notice under Rule 30(1). See Appellate Body Report, *US – Line Pipe (2002)*, para. 13; and Appellate Body Report, *US – FSC (2000)*, para. 4.

703 See Appellate Body Reports, *China – Rare Earths (2014)*, paras. 1.27–1.29.

704 See Rule 21(1) of the *Working Procedures*.

of the grounds of appeal, including the specific allegations of legal errors in the panel report, and the legal arguments in support of these allegations.[705] The parties to the dispute that have filed a notice of other appeal must file an other appellant's submission on the same day as the filing of the notice of other appeal.[706] Within eighteen days of the filing of the notice of appeal, any party that wishes to respond to allegations of legal errors by the panel, whether raised in the submission of the original appellant or in the submission(s) of other appellants, may file an appellee's submission.[707] The appellee's submission(s) set(s) out a precise statement of the grounds for opposing the specific allegations of legal errors raised in the (other) appellant's submission(s) and includes legal arguments in support thereof.[708] Third participants' submissions have to be filed within twenty-one days from the filing of the notice of appeal.[709] Should a participant or a third participant fail to file a submission within the required time periods, the division, after hearing the views of the participants, issues such order, including dismissal of the appeal, as it deems appropriate.[710]

The division responsible for deciding the appeal holds an oral hearing. According to the *Working Procedures*, the oral hearing should, as a general rule, be held between thirty and forty-five days after the notice of appeal is filed.[711] The purpose of the oral hearing is to provide participants with an opportunity to present and argue their case before the division, in order to clarify the legal issues in the appeal. At the hearing, the appellant(s), appellee(s) and third participants first make brief opening statements on the core legal issues raised in the appeal.[712] After the oral presentations, the participants answer detailed questions posed by Appellate Body Members serving on the division regarding the issues raised in the appeal. At the end of the oral hearing, the participants are given the opportunity to make a brief concluding statement. In recent years, the oral hearing has usually been completed in two to three days. In complex cases, however, the oral hearing may take (much) longer. In *EC and certain member States – Large Civil Aircraft (2011)* and *US – Large Civil Aircraft (2nd complaint) (2012)*, the oral

705 See Rule 21(2) of the *Working Procedures*. The submission also sets out the nature of the decision or ruling sought. Pursuant to the Appellate Body communication on 'Executive Summaries of Written Submissions in Appellate Proceedings' and 'Guidelines in Respect of Executive Summaries of Written Submissions in Appellate Proceedings' (WT/AB/23, 11 March 2015), the appellant must also file an executive summary of its submission. This requirement also applies to all other submissions filed in appellate review proceedings. These executive summaries are annexed to the Appellate Body report.

706 See Rule 23(3) of the *Working Procedures*.

707 See Rules 22(1) and 23(4) of the *Working Procedures*.

708 See Rules 22(2) and 23(4) of the *Working Procedures*.

709 A third participant that does not wish to file a written submission may notify the Secretariat that it intends to appear at the oral hearing and whether it intends to make an oral statement. See Rules 24(1), 24(2) and 24(4) of the *Working Procedures*.

710 See Rule 29 of the *Working Procedures* ('Failure to Appear'). To date, there has been no need for such an order. Note also that Rule 18(5) provides for a procedure for parties and third parties to request authorisation to correct clerical errors (such as 'typographical mistakes, errors of grammar, or words or numbers placed in the wrong order') in the documents submitted.

711 See Rule 27(1) of the *Working Procedures*.

712 See Rule 27(3) of the *Working Procedures*. Any third participant may also make an oral presentation and may be questioned at the oral hearing. See below, pp. 283–4.

hearings took nine days and eight days, respectively. In both these disputes, the oral hearing took place in two sessions, each covering different issues.[713]

At any time during the appellate review proceedings, the division may address questions to, or request additional memoranda from, any participant or third participant and specify the time periods by which written responses or memoranda shall be received.[714] Any such questions, responses or memoranda are made available simultaneously to the other participants and third participants in the appeal who are then given an opportunity to respond.[715]

Throughout the proceedings, the participants and third participants are precluded from having *ex parte* communications with the Appellate Body in respect of matters concerning the appeal. Neither a division nor any of its Members may meet with or contact a participant or third participant in the absence of the other participants and third participants.[716]

As discussed above, the rights of third parties in panel proceedings are limited.[717] Normally, third parties only attend, and are heard at, a special session of the first substantive meeting of the panel, and receive the first written submissions of the parties only. Third participants, i.e. third parties participating in Appellate Body proceedings, have more comprehensive rights. In appellate review proceedings, third participants receive all submissions of the participants and have a right to file a written submission themselves, within twenty-one days of the filing of the notice of appeal, containing the grounds and legal arguments in support of their position.[718] A third participant has the right to participate in the oral hearing when: (1) it has filed a written submission; or (2) it has notified the Appellate Body Secretariat of its intention to participate in the oral hearing within twenty-one days of the notice of appeal.[719] A third party that has neither filed a written submission nor notified its intention to participate in the oral hearing within twenty-one days may, at the discretion of the division and taking into account the requirements of due process, still be allowed to participate in the oral hearing.[720]

6.4.3 Exchange of Views and Deliberations

As noted above, the division responsible for deciding an appeal will exchange views on issues raised by the appeal with the other Members of the Appellate

713 See Appellate Body Report, *EC and certain member States – Large Civil Aircraft (2011)*, paras. 19 and 26; and Appellate Body Report, *US – Large Civil Aircraft (2nd complaint) (2012)*, para. 32.

714 See Rule 28(1) of the *Working Procedures*.

715 See Rule 28(2) of the *Working Procedures*. See also e.g. Appellate Body Report, *US – Section 211 Appropriations Act (2002)*, para. 13.

716 See Article 18.1 of the DSU and Rule 19(1) of the *Working Procedures*. Also, a Member of the Appellate Body who is not assigned to the division hearing the appeal shall not discuss any aspect of the subject matter of the appeal with any participant or third participant. See Rule 19(3) of the *Working Procedures*.

717 See above, p. 276.

718 See Rule 24(1) of the *Working Procedures*.

719 See Rule 27(3) of the *Working Procedures*. Third participants are encouraged to file written submissions to facilitate their positions being taken into account. See Rule 24(3) of the *Working Procedures*.

720 See Rule 27(3)(b) and (c) of the *Working Procedures*.

Body, before finalising its report.[721] The exchange of views puts into practice the principle of collegiality set out in the *Working Procedures*.[722] Depending on the number and complexity of the issues under discussion, this process usually takes place over two or more days, after the division has had its first deliberations on the issues raised by the appeal.[723]

Following the exchange of views, the division continues its deliberations and drafts the report. While initially Appellate Body reports were short (and lacked paragraph numbering), over the years the reports became much longer, due to: (1) the increased number of panel findings and legal interpretations developed by panels that are appealed; and (2) the increased complexity of the appeals. The longest report to date, the report in *EC and certain member States – Large Civil Aircraft (2011)*, is 645 pages long.

6.4.4 Adoption of Appellate Body Reports

When the report is finalised, the three Members of the division sign it. The report is then translated into all three official languages of the WTO.[724] After translation, the report is circulated to the WTO Members as an unrestricted document available to the public. The Appellate Body report is posted on the WTO website as a WT/DS document. Appellate Body reports are also included in the official *Dispute Settlement Reports of the World Trade Organization*.[725]

Within thirty days following circulation of the Appellate Body report, the Appellate Body report *and* the panel report as upheld, modified or reversed by the Appellate Body are adopted by the DSB *unless* the DSB decides by consensus not to adopt the reports.[726] As stated in Article 17.14 of the DSU:

> The adopted Appellate Body report must be accepted unconditionally by the parties to the dispute.

The adoption procedure is, however, without prejudice to the right of Members to express their views on an Appellate Body report.[727] WTO Members often take full advantage of this opportunity to comment on the reports at the meeting of the DSB at which they are adopted. Generally, the winning party briefly praises the Appellate Body (and the panel) while the losing party is more critical. In recent years, participants and third participants tend to make more substantive comments on the findings and reasoning contained in the reports and on

721 See above, p. 236. 722 See Rule 4 of the *Working Procedures*.

723 On the importance of the exchange of views, see above, p. 236.

724 In all appellate review proceedings to date, English has been the working language of the Appellate Body, and the Appellate Body reports were all drafted in English and then translated into French and Spanish. In a few appellate review proceedings, participants or third participants filed submissions or made oral statements in French or Spanish. When requested, interpretation is provided at the oral hearing.

725 Appellate Body reports are also included in the official *Dispute Settlement Reports of the World Trade Organization*, published by Cambridge University Press. See www.cambridge.org/gb/knowledge/series/series_display/item3937379/?site_locale=en_GB.

726 See Article 17.14 of the DSU. On the reverse consensus requirement, see above, p. 210.

727 See Article 17.14, last sentence, of the DSU.

systemic implications of the rulings for future cases. The views of WTO Members on Appellate Body reports (and panel reports) are fully recorded in the minutes of the DSB meeting.

As the Appellate Body noted in *US – Shrimp (Article 21.5 – Malaysia) (2001)*, an Appellate Body report that is adopted by the DSB must be treated by the parties to a particular dispute 'as a final resolution to that dispute'.[728]

6.5 Implementation and Enforcement

If a panel and/or the Appellate Body concludes that the responding Member acted inconsistently with its obligations under one or more of the covered agreements, the process of WTO dispute settlement reaches its final stage, namely the stage of the implementation and enforcement of the recommendations and rulings of the panel and/or the Appellate Body, as adopted by the DSB. Within thirty days of the adoption of the panel and/or Appellate Body report, the Member concerned must inform the DSB of its intentions in respect of the implementation of the recommendations and rulings.[729] This subsection discusses the following procedural issues, which arise with respect to the implementation and enforcement of recommendations and rulings: (1) arbitration on the 'reasonable period of time for implementation'; (2) the surveillance of implementation by the DSB; (3) disagreement on implementation; and (4) arbitration on, and authorisation of, suspension of concessions or other obligations.

6.5.1 Arbitration on the 'Reasonable Period of Time for Implementation'

As discussed above, prompt or immediate compliance with the recommendations and rulings of the panel and/or the Appellate Body, as adopted by the DSB, is essential for the effective functioning of the WTO and the primary obligation of the Member concerned.[730] Prompt or immediate compliance with the recommendations and rulings means prompt or immediate withdrawal or modification of the WTO-inconsistent measure. However, if it is 'impracticable' to comply with the recommendations and rulings immediately – and this may often be the case – the Member concerned has, pursuant to Article 21.3 of the DSU, a reasonable period of time in which to do so.[731]

As discussed above, in most cases to date, the parties reach agreement on the 'reasonable period of time for implementation' as foreseen under Article 21.3(b) of the DSU.[732] However, if no agreement can be reached within forty-five days of the adoption of the recommendations and rulings, the original complainant can refer the matter to arbitration under Article 21.3(c) of the DSU. The parties may agree on an arbitrator, and, if they cannot do so within ten days, either party may

728 See Appellate Body Report, *US – Shrimp (Article 21.5 – Malaysia) (2001)*, para. 97.
729 See Article 21.3 of the DSU. 730 See above, p. 200.
731 See Article 21.3(a), (b) and (c) of the DSU. 732 See above p. 200.

request the Director-General of the WTO to appoint an arbitrator.[733] The Director-General will consult the parties on criteria for selection and appoint an arbitrator within further ten days. The DSU does not provide for any rule or guideline as to the professional or other requirements persons should meet to serve as an Article 21.3(c) arbitrator. However, a practice has developed that present or former Members of the Appellate Body serve as Article 21.3(c) arbitrators.[734] They do so not as Members of the Appellate Body but in a personal capacity.

While not set out in the DSU, the arbitration proceedings involve the sequential filing of written submissions and an oral hearing. The DSU does require that the arbitration proceedings do not exceed ninety days commencing on the date of the adoption of the panel and Appellate Body reports by the DSB. Often this requirement is not realistic.[735] Then, with the agreement of the parties – this time line is commonly set aside. The arbitration award indicating the 'reasonable period of time for implementation' is issued to the parties and circulated to all WTO Members. Note that, unlike panel or Appellate Body reports, an Article 21.3(c) arbitration award is *not* adopted by the DSB. An arbitration award is posted as a WT/DS document on the WTO website.

6.5.2 Surveillance of Implementation by the DSB

During the 'reasonable period of time for implementation', the DSB keeps the implementation of adopted recommendations and rulings under surveillance.[736] At any time following adoption of the recommendations and rulings, any WTO Member may raise the issue of implementation at the DSB. Pursuant to Article 21.6 of the DSU, starting six months after establishment of the reasonable period of time, the issue of implementation is placed on the agenda of each DSB meeting. At least ten days prior to such a DSB meeting, the Member concerned must provide the DSB with a status report on its progress in the implementation of the recommendations or rulings.[737] Note that, pursuant to Article 22.8 of the DSU, the DSB shall 'continue to keep under surveillance the implementation of adopted recommendations or rulings' also after the reasonable period of time has expired and this for as long as there is no implementation. For example, at the DSB meeting of 26 September 2016, the United States presented its status report on its implementation of the recommendations and rulings in two cases: *US – Section 110(5) Copyright Act (2000)*; and *US – Hot-Rolled Steel (2001)*.[738]

733 To date, the parties have been able to agree on the Article 21.3(c) arbitrator in most cases.

734 Note that in *US – Shrimp II (Vietnam) (2015)* the parties agreed on the chairman of the panel as an Article 21.3(c) arbitrator.

735 This is of course especially so when the arbitration is initiated later than ninety days as of the adoption of the underlying panel and Appellate Body reports.

736 See Article 21.6 of the DSU.

737 See *ibid*. The status reports under Article 21.6 of the DSU are posted on the WTO website as WT/DS documents. For the debate on these reports, see the minutes of the relevant DSB meeting (WT/DSB/M/ ...).

738 Status Report by the United States in: *US – Section 110(5) Copyright Act (2000)*, WT/DS160/24/Add.139, dated 16 September 2016; and *US – Hot-Rolled Steel (2001)* WT/DS184/15/Add.164, dated 16 September 2016.

6.5.3 Disagreement on Implementation

Before the expiry of the reasonable period of time, the respondent must withdraw or modify the measure that was found to be WTO-inconsistent. In other words, the respondent must take the appropriate measures to comply with the recommendations and rulings adopted by the DSB in a WTO-consistent manner. It is, however, not uncommon for the original complainant and respondent to disagree on whether any implementing measure is taken or whether the implementing measure taken is fully WTO-consistent. Article 21.5 of the DSU provides that such disagreement as to the existence, or consistency with WTO law, of implementing measures shall be decided:

> through recourse to these dispute settlement procedures, including wherever possible resort to the original panel.

It is now generally accepted that recourse to 'these dispute settlement procedures' means recourse to the procedures set out in Articles 4 to 20 of the DSU.[739] The normal procedures discussed in previous sections apply with a few deviations. The most notable of these deviations is that Article 21.5 requires that the panel circulate its report within ninety days after the date of the referral of the matter to it.[740] However, this time frame is not realistic, as is demonstrated by the fact that the average duration of Article 21.5 compliance proceedings is now 282 days, i.e. more than double the time allowed.[741]

The issue of which measures fall within the scope of jurisdiction of a 'compliance' panel, or, in other words, when a measure is a 'measure taken to comply with the recommendations and rulings', was addressed by the Appellate Body in *US – Softwood Lumber IV (Article 21.5 – Canada) (2005)*. The Appellate Body noted that the limits on the claims that can be raised in Article 21.5 proceedings 'should not allow circumvention by Members by allowing them to comply through one measure, while, at the same time, negating compliance through another'.[742] According to the Appellate Body, for a new measure to be a 'measure taken to comply with the recommendations and rulings' within the meaning of Article 21.5 of the DSU, there have to be 'sufficiently close links' in terms of nature, content and timing between the original measure and the new measure so that the latter can be characterised as 'taken to comply' with the recommendations and rulings concerning the original measure.[743] Also

739 It is still disputed by some WTO Members that 'these procedures' also include consultations pursuant to Article 4 of the DSU. Note that in *US – COOL (Article 21.5 – Canada and Mexico) (2015)*, Canada and Mexico, the complainants, and the United States, the respondent, agreed that it was not required that consultations be held before requesting the establishment of an Article 21.5 compliance panel. See Panel Reports, *US – COOL (Article 21.5 – Canada and Mexico) (2015)*, para. 1.2.

740 For the timeframe of the standard panel proceedings, see above, p. 248. Another notable deviation is that the complainant and respondent will each file only one submission to the panel and the panel will have only one meeting with the parties. See Panel Reports, *US – COOL (Article 21.5 – Canada and Mexico) (2015)*, para. 1.9.

741 See www.worldtradelaw.net/databases/paneltiming1.php.

742 Appellate Body Report, *US – Softwood Lumber IV (Article 21.5 – Canada) (2005)*, para. 72.

743 See Appellate Body Report, *Canada – Aircraft (Article 21.5 – Brazil) (2000)*, para. 36.

note that, as the Appellate Body ruled in *Canada – Aircraft (Article 21.5 – Brazil) (2000)*:

> in carrying out its review under Article 21.5 of the DSU, a panel is not confined to examining the 'measures taken to comply' from the perspective of the claims, arguments and factual circumstances that related to the measure that was the subject of the original proceedings. Although these may have some relevance in proceedings under Article 21.5 of the DSU, Article 21.5 proceedings involve, in principle, not the original measure, but rather a new and different measure which was not before the original panel.[744]

If an Article 21.5 panel were restricted to examining the new measure from the perspective of the claims, arguments and factual circumstances that related to the original measure, the effectiveness of an Article 21.5 review would be seriously undermined because an Article 21.5 panel would then be unable to examine fully the 'consistency with a covered agreement of the measures taken to comply', as required by Article 21.5 of the DSU.[745] The Appellate Body accordingly ruled in *Canada – Aircraft (Article 21.5 – Brazil) (2000)* that the panel was not merely mandated to review if the revised subsidy programme of Canada had dropped the WTO-inconsistent aspects that the original dispute pertained to, but was also mandated to consider Brazil's new claim that the revised programme was inconsistent with Article 3.1(a) of the *SCM Agreement*. Inconsistency with Article 3.1(a) of the *SCM Agreement* had not been claimed before the original panel but this did not prevent the Article 21.5 panel from examining this claim. In *EC – Bed Linen (Article 21.5 – India) (2003)*, the Appellate Body found that:

> *new* claims, arguments, and factual circumstances different from those raised in the original proceedings [may be raised], because a 'measure taken to comply' may be *inconsistent* with WTO obligations *in ways different* from the original measure ... [A]n Article 21.5 panel could not properly carry out its mandate to assess whether a 'measure taken to comply' is *fully consistent* with WTO obligations if it were precluded from examining claims additional to, and different from, the claims raised in the original proceedings.[746]

The panel in *US – COOL (Article 21.5– Canada and Mexico) (2015)* found that the scope of jurisdiction of an Article 21.5 compliance panel may also include non-violation claims under Article XXIII:1(b) of the GATT 1994.[747] On appeal, given that the Appellate Body upheld the violation findings, the conditions for these appeals were not fulfilled.[748] Therefore, the Appellate Body was not required nor inclined to rule on these non-violation claims under Article XXIII:1(b) of the GATT 1994.

In a number of Article 21.5 compliance proceedings to date, the concern was raised that these proceedings would be used by the respondent to relitigate the WTO consistency of a measure already found to be WTO-inconsistent in the original proceedings.

744 *Ibid.*, para. 41. 745 See *ibid.*

746 Appellate Body Report, *EC – Bed Linen (Article 21.5 – India) (2003)*, para. 79.

747 See Panel Reports, *US – COOL (21.5 – Canada and Mexico) (2015)*, para. 7.663.

748 Appellate Body Reports, *US – COOL (Article 21.5 – Canada and Mexico) (2015)*, paras. 5.381–5.384.

In *EC – Fasteners (Article 21.5) (2016)* the Appellate Body summarised its prior case law on the scope of the jurisdiction of Article 21.5 compliance panels as follows:

> we recall that, in *EC – Bed Linen (Article 21.5 – India)*, the Appellate Body stated that a complainant should not be allowed to raise claims in compliance proceedings that were already raised and dismissed in the original proceedings in respect of a component of the implementation measure that is the same as in the original measure. However, in subsequent disputes, the Appellate Body clarified that the same claim with respect to an unchanged element of the measure can be re-litigated in Article 21.5 proceedings if, in the original proceedings, the matter was not resolved because, for instance, the Appellate Body was not able to complete the analysis.[749]

To date, Members have initiated fifty-six Article 21.5 'compliance' proceedings;[750] and thirty-three Article 21.5 panel reports and twenty-three Article 21.5 Appellate Body reports have been circulated.[751] In most Article 21.5 procedures thus far, the original panellist served on the compliance panel.[752]

Like 'original' panel and Appellate Body reports, Article 21.5 'compliance' panel and Appellate Body reports become legally binding on the parties only after adoption by the DSB. The DSB adopts these reports by reverse consensus within thirty days after circulation.

An important difference between the recommendations and rulings of 'original' reports and Article 21.5 'compliance' reports is that the respondent does not benefit from another reasonable period of time to implement the recommendations and rulings of Article 21.5 reports. Immediately after the adoption of these report(s), the complainant can request authorisation from the DSB to suspend the application of concessions or other obligations to the respondent.

6.5.4 Compensation or Retaliation

If the respondent fails to implement the recommendations and rulings correctly within the reasonable period of time agreed by the parties or determined by an arbitrator, the respondent shall, if so requested by the complainant, enter into negotiations with the latter party in order to come to an agreement on mutually acceptable compensation.[753] If satisfactory compensation is not agreed upon within twenty days of the expiry of the reasonable period of time, the complainant may request authorisation from the DSB to suspend the application to the respondent of concessions or other obligations under the covered agreements.[754] In other words, it may seek authorisation to retaliate. The DSB must decide on

749 Appellate Body Report, *EC – Fasteners (Article 21.5) (2016)*, para. 5.15, referring to Appellate Body Report, *EC – Bed Linen (Article 21.5 – India) (2003)*, paras. 96 and 98.

750 See www.worldtradelaw.net/databases/searchcomplaintscompliance.php.

751 See www.worldtradelaw.net/databases/art215reports.php.

752 Note, however, that in e.g., *US – Softwood Lumber IV (Article 21.5 – Canada) (2005)* and *Chile – Price Band System (Article 21.5 – Argentina) (2007)* certain panellists of the original panel were replaced because they had the nationality of third parties in the Article 21.5 proceedings.

753 See Article 22.2 of the DSU. On compensation under Article 22, see above, p. 204.

754 See *ibid.*

the authorisation to retaliate within thirty days of the expiry of the reasonable period of time.[755] As discussed above, the DSB decides on the authorisation to retaliate by reverse consensus; therefore, the authorisation is, for all practical purposes, automatic.[756]

However, if the non-complying Member objects to the level of suspension proposed, or claims that the principles and procedures for suspension set out in Article 22.3 of the DSU have not been followed,[757] the matter may be referred to arbitration before the DSB takes a decision.[758] This arbitration under Article 22.6 of the DSU is carried out by the original panel, if the same members are available, or by an arbitrator appointed by the Director-General.[759] The arbitration must be completed within sixty days of expiry of the reasonable period of time,[760] and a second arbitration or appeal is not permitted.[761] The DSB is informed promptly of the decision of the arbitrator and grants, upon request by the responding party, by reverse consensus, the requested authorisation to suspend concessions or other obligations to the extent that the request is consistent with the decision of the arbitrators.[762] Decisions by the arbitrators under Article 22.6 of the DSU are circulated to WTO Members, and posted on the WTO website as WT/DS documents.

Finally, there are two issues with regard to the decision-making on retaliation that are currently not, or not adequately, dealt with in the DSU and have, therefore, given rise to considerable controversy, namely: (1) the 'sequencing issue'; and (2) the 'post-retaliation issue'.

With regard to the 'sequencing issue', recall that if the respondent fails to implement the recommendations and rulings within the 'reasonable period of time' and agreement on compensation cannot be reached, the complainant may request the DSB authorisation to retaliate.[763] However, it is clear that such retaliation is *only* called for when the respondent has failed to take a WTO-consistent implementing measure. As also discussed above, the complainant and the respondent may disagree on whether such implementing measure exists or whether it is WTO-consistent. To resolve such disagreements, the DSU provides for the Article 21.5 procedure. However, due to 'sloppy' drafting of the DSU, there is a conflict between the time frame for this Article 21.5 procedure and the time frame within which authorisation for the suspension of concessions and other obligations must be requested and obtained from the DSB. Pursuant to Article 22.6, the authorisation for retaliation must be granted by the DSB within thirty days of the expiry of the reasonable period of time. It is clear that it is not possible to obtain authorisation for retaliation within thirty days, in

755 See *ibid.* 756 See above, p. 204. 757 See above, pp. 204–5.

758 See Article 22.6 of the DSU. On the appropriate level of suspension and on the principles and procedures of suspension, see above, pp. 204–5.

759 See *ibid.* 760 See *ibid.* In practice, this time frame has proved to be unrealistic.

761 See Article 22.7 of the DSU.

762 See *ibid.* Note that the Decision of the Arbitrators under Article 22.6 is notified to the DSB but is not adopted by it.

763 See above, p. 204.

cases where the complainant must first submit the disagreement on implementation to an Article 21.5 'compliance' panel that 'should' take ninety days. In *EC – Bananas III (1997)*, this inconsistency led in 1999 to a serious institutional crisis in which the United States insisted on its right to obtain authorisation for retaliation and the European Communities asserted that an Article 21.5 'compliance' panel first had to establish that the implementing measures taken by the European Communities were not WTO-consistent. Eventually, a pragmatic compromise was found to defuse the crisis. However, the problem of the relationship between these two procedures (referred to as the 'sequencing issue') remains, and a change to the DSU is required to resolve the problem. In the meantime, parties commonly agree, on an *ad hoc* basis, that the procedure of examining the WTO consistency of the implementing measures will need to be completed before the authorisation for retaliation measures may be granted.[764]

With regard to the 'post-retaliation issue', note that the DSU currently does not provide for a procedure for the withdrawal or termination of the authorisation to retaliate. The lack of such procedure is of course not a problem when the complainant is satisfied that the respondent has withdrawn the WTO-inconsistent measure. A problem arises, however, when the complainant is not satisfied that the respondent has withdrawn or adequately modified the WTO-inconsistent measure and thus maintains the retaliation measure. This situation arose in *EC – Hormones (1998)*, and led the European Communities to initiate new dispute settlement proceedings against the United States' and Canada's retaliation measures in an effort to secure their lifting. In *US/Canada – Continued Suspension (2008)*, the Appellate Body held:

> both the suspending Member and the implementing Member share the responsibility to ensure that the application of the suspension of concessions is 'temporary' ... Where, as in this dispute, an implementing measure is taken and Members disagree as to whether this measure achieves substantive compliance, both Members have a duty to engage in WTO dispute settlement in order to establish whether the conditions in Article 22.8 have been met and whether, as a consequence, the suspension of concessions must be terminated. Once substantive compliance has been confirmed through WTO dispute settlement procedures, the authorization to suspend concessions lapses by operation of law (*ipso jure*).[765]

The Appellate Body recommended that the DSB request Canada, the United States and the European Communities:

> to initiate Article 21.5 proceedings without delay in order to resolve their disagreement as to whether the European Communities has removed the measure found to be inconsistent in *EC – Hormones* and whether the application of the suspension of concessions by the United States remains legally valid.[766]

764 See e.g. Understanding between the European Union and the United States Regarding Procedures under Articles 21 and 22 of the DSU, *European Communities and certain member States – Large Civil Aircraft (2011)*, WT/DS316/21, dated 17 January 2012.

765 Appellate Body Report, *US/Canada – Continued Suspension (2008)*, para. 310.

766 See *ibid.*, para. 737.

7 DEVELOPING-COUNTRY MEMBERS AND WTO DISPUTE SETTLEMENT

As noted above, developing-country Members have made much use of the WTO dispute settlement system. In many years since 2000, developing-country Members, as a group, have brought more disputes to the WTO than developed-country Members. To date, Brazil (twenty-nine complaints), Mexico (twenty-three complaints), India (twenty-three complaints), Argentina (twenty complaints), Thailand (thirteen complaints), China (thirteen complaints) and Chile (ten complaints) are among the biggest users of the system.

Developing-country Members have used the WTO dispute settlement system to bring cases against the economic superpowers and have done so successfully. *US – Underwear*, a complaint by Costa Rica, and even more so *US – Gambling (2005)*, a complaint by Antigua and Barbuda, are well-known examples of successful 'David versus Goliath' use of the system. Developing-country Members have also used the system against other developing-country Members. Examples of such use of the system are *Turkey – Textiles (1999)*, a complaint by India; *Chile – Price Band System (2002)*, a complaint by Argentina; *Thailand – Cigarettes (Philippines) (2011)*, a complaint by the Philippines; and *Dominican Republic – Safeguard Measures (2012)*, complaints by Costa Rica, El Salvador, Guatemala and Honduras; and *Argentina – Financial Services (2016)*, complaint by Panama. To date, least-developed-country Members have used the WTO dispute settlement system only once.[767] The WTO dispute settlement system has never been used *against* least-developed-country Members. Note in this respect that Article 24.1 of the DSU requires Members to 'exercise due restraint' in using the WTO dispute settlement system in disputes involving a least-developed-country Member. The DSU contains in addition a number of other provisions providing for special treatment or consideration for developing-country Members involved in WTO dispute settlement. This section examines these provisions. It also discusses the legal assistance available to developing-country Members involved in WTO dispute settlement.

7.1 Special Rules for Developing-Country Members

The DSU recognises the difficulties developing-country Members may encounter when they are involved in WTO dispute settlement. Therefore, the DSU contains some special rules for developing-country Members. Such special DSU rules are

767 Request for Consultations by Bangladesh, *India – Anti-Dumping Measure on Batteries from Bangladesh*, WT/DS306/1, dated 2 February 2004. See Notification of Mutually Satisfactory Solution, *India – Anti-Dumping Measure on Batteries from Bangladesh*, WT/DS306/3, dated 23 February 2006.

found in Article 3.12 (regarding the application of the 1966 Decision),[768] Article 4.10 (regarding consultations), Article 8.10 (regarding the composition of panels), Article 12.10 (regarding consultations and the time to prepare and present arguments), Article 12.11 (regarding the content of panel reports), Article 21.2 (regarding implementation of adopted recommendations and rulings), Article 21.7 (regarding the DSB surveillance of the implementation of adopted recommendations or rulings), Article 24 (regarding least-developed countries) and Article 27 (on the assistance of the WTO Secretariat). Most of these special rules for developing countries are discussed above.[769] The special rules, for the most part, have been of limited significance to date.

7.2 Legal Assistance for Developing-Country Members

Many developing-country Members do not have the specialised 'in-house' legal expertise to participate in the most effective manner in WTO dispute settlement. However, as discussed above, WTO Members can be assisted and represented by private legal counsel in WTO dispute settlement proceedings.[770]

However, assistance and representation by private legal counsel has its costs, and these costs may be quite burdensome for developing-country Members. Other forms of assistance are needed to: (1) lower further the threshold for developing-country Members, and, in particular, low-income-country and least-developed-country Members, to bring complaints against other Members; or (2) support developing-country Members against whom complaints are brought by other Members. The WTO Secretariat assists all Members in respect of dispute settlement when they so request. However, the DSU recognises that there may be a need to provide additional legal advice and assistance to developing-country Members.[771] To meet this additional need, Article 27.2 of the DSU requires that the WTO Secretariat make qualified legal experts available to help any developing-country Member that so requests.[772] The extent to which the Secretariat can assist developing-country Members is, however, limited by the

768 Decision of 5 April 1966 on Procedures under Article XXIII of the GATT, BISD 14S/18. Article 3.12 of the DSU allows a developing-country Member that brings a complaint against a developed-country Member to invoke the provisions of the Decision of 5 April 1966 of the GATT Contracting Parties. These provisions may be invoked as an 'alternative' to the provisions contained in Articles 4, 5, 6 and 12 of the DSU. To date, the provisions of the 1966 Decision have been 'invoked' only once, on 21 March 2007, in a complaint brought by Colombia against the European Communities' new 'tariff-only' regime for bananas applied from 1 January 2006. See Request for Consultations by Colombia, *European Communities – Regime for the Importation of Bananas*, WT/DS361/1. The reason for the lack of enthusiasm for the provisions of the 1966 Decision is undoubtedly that the DSU provisions afford developing-country complaining parties treatment at least as favourable as, if not more favourable than, the treatment afforded by the 1966 Decision.

769 See e.g. above, pp. 202, 218, 270 and 292. 770 See above, p. 259.

771 See Article 27.2 of the DSU.

772 For this purpose, the Institute for Training and Technical Cooperation, a division of the WTO Secretariat, presently employs two independent consultants on a permanent part-time basis. See *WTO Analytical Index (2012)*, Volume II, 1884.

requirement that the Secretariat's experts give assistance in a manner 'ensuring the continued impartiality of the Secretariat'.[773]

Effective legal assistance for developing-country Members in dispute settlement proceedings is given by the Geneva-based ACWL. The ACWL is an inter-governmental organisation, fully independent from the WTO, which functions essentially as a law firm specialising in WTO law, providing legal services and training – at low or no cost – to thirty-three developing-country and economy-in-transition members of the ACWL and *all* forty-two least-developed countries. The ACWL provides support at all stages of WTO dispute settlement proceedings at discounted rates. The ACWL currently has forty-four members: eleven developed countries and thirty-three developing countries and economies-in-transition.[774] The services of the ACWL are at present available to a total of seventy-five countries. On the occasion of the official opening of the ACWL on 5 October 2001, Mike Moore, then WTO Director-General, said:

> The International Court of Justice has a small fund out of which costs of legal assistance can be paid for countries who need such help. But today marks the first time a true legal aid centre has been established within the international legal system, with a view to combating the unequal possibilities of access to international justice as between States.[775]

Since its establishment, the ACWL has become a major player in WTO dispute settlement. During the period from 2001 to 2015, the ACWL provided support in almost fifty WTO dispute settlement proceedings.[776] In addition, the ACWL provides free-of-charge legal advice on substantive and procedural aspects of WTO law.[777] Finally, the ACWL also offers training courses and seminars on WTO law and policy and provides for the Secondment Programme for Trade Lawyers, under which government lawyers from least-developed countries and developing-country ACWL members join the staff of the ACWL for a period of nine months.[778]

8 CHALLENGES TO WTO DISPUTE SETTLEMENT

In 1996, the then WTO Director-General Renato Ruggiero referred to the WTO dispute settlement system as 'the jewel in the crown of the WTO'. While obviously not perfect, the WTO dispute settlement system has by and large lived up to, if not surpassed, Ruggiero's high expectations. The frequent use by a significant number of developed- as well as developing-country Members to

773 Article 27.2, final sentence, of the DSU.
774 See www.acwl.ch/members/Introduction.html.
775 Inauguration of the ACWL: Speech delivered by Director-General of the WTO, 5 October 2001, at www.acwl.ch/e/news/milestone_0004.html.
776 See www.acwl.ch/WTO_disputes.html. 777 See www.acwl.ch/legal_advice/legal_advice.html.
778 See www.acwl.ch/e/training/training.html.

resolve often politically sensitive issues, and the high degree of compliance with the recommendations and rulings, testify to the success of the WTO dispute settlement system.

The WTO dispute settlement system makes an important contribution to the objective that within the WTO 'right prevails over might'. As the legendary Julio Lacarte Muró, the first Chair of the Appellate Body, remarked, the system works to the advantage of all Members, but it especially gives security to developing-country Members that have often, in the past, lacked the political or economic clout to enforce their rights and to protect their interests.[779]

While there exists much satisfaction with the performance of the WTO dispute settlement system, there have been negotiations on its further improvement ever since 1998.[780] The proposals for improvement tabled and discussed since the start of these negotiations are many and wide-ranging.[781] A few of these proposals suggest quite radical reforms to the system, such as the EU proposals for the replacement of the *ad hoc* panels with a permanent panel body or a roster of permanent panellists (these proposals are currently no longer actively considered); and the US proposals for more Member control over WTO dispute settlement, and in particular over panel and Appellate Body reports (these proposals to curtail the WTO dispute settlement system are still being considered but enjoy very limited support). Most proposals for improvement are, however, more technical in nature, although they may touch on politically sensitive issues. Examples of such proposals are: (1) time frames and time-saving by, e.g., halving the time for mandatory consultations, and establishing panels by reverse consensus at the *first* DSB meeting; (2) improved conditions for Members seeking to join consultations; (3) the notification of mutually agreed solutions; (4) the facilitation of panel composition; (5) the extension of third party rights; (6) the protection of business confidential information; (7) the issue of *amicus curiae* briefs; (8) enhanced transparency through opening panel meetings and Appellate Body hearings to the public; (9) the suspension of panel proceedings; (10) the introduction of remand in Appellate Body proceedings; (11) the 'sequencing' issue; (12) the 'post-retaliation' issue; (13) the promotion of prompt and effective compliance by strengthening the remedies available for breach of WTO law, including collective retaliation and monetary compensation; and (14) the strengthening of special and differential treatment for developing-country Members.

779 See J. Lacarte and P. Gappah, 'Developing Countries and the WTO Legal and Dispute Settlement System', *Journal of International Economic Law*, 2000, 400. Ambassador Lacarte Muró served as the Deputy Executive Secretary of the GATT in 1947–8, and as Permanent Representative of Uruguay to the GATT in the 1960s, 1980s and early 1990s. He was the Chair of the Uruguay Round committee that negotiated the DSU.

780 As agreed at the time of the adoption of the *WTO Agreement*, the WTO Members first reviewed the DSU in 1998 and 1999.

781 All publicly available documents relating to the DSU reform negotiations can be found on the WTO website as TN/DS documents.

To date, Members have not been able to reach agreement on the reform of the DSU.

However, the problem of the WTO dispute settlement system in the years to come may not be its shortcomings and Members' inability to address these shortcomings. Its problem will rather be its success, discussed throughout this chapter. This success has created an unwelcome institutional imbalance in the WTO between its 'judicial' branch and its political, 'rule-making' branch. As discussed in Chapter 2, the WTO has not been very successful in negotiating new and/or improved rules for the multilateral trading system.[782] Confronted with the ineffectiveness of the political branch of the WTO, WTO Members may be ever more tempted to use the dispute settlement system to bring about new or improved rules to address the manifold problems confronting the multilateral trading system. Already in 2001, Claude Barfield of the Washington-based American Enterprise Institute suggested that the WTO dispute settlement system is 'substantively and politically unsustainable'. Barfield suggested that governments may only continue to obey its rulings if its powers are curbed.[783] While strongly disagreeing with Barfield's prescription, others have also warned against excessive reliance by WTO Members on adjudication, instead of seeking political agreement on new rules, to resolve problems arising in trade relations.[784]

9 SUMMARY

The WTO has a remarkable system to settle disputes between its Members concerning their rights and obligations under the WTO agreements. This system is based on the dispute settlement system of the GATT. The latter system evolved between the late 1940s and the early 1990s from a system that was primarily a power-based system of dispute settlement through diplomatic negotiations, into a rules-based system of dispute settlement through adjudication. The WTO dispute settlement system, one of the most significant achievements of the Uruguay Round, is a further step in that process of progressive 'judicialisation' of the settlement of international trade disputes. Since January 1995, the WTO dispute settlement system has been widely used and its 'output', in terms of the number of dispute settlement reports, has been remarkable. Both developed- and developing-country Members have frequently used the system to resolve their trade disputes, and these disputes have concerned a very broad range of matters under WTO law.

782 See also above, p. 81.

783 See C. Barfield, *Free Trade, Sovereignty, Democracy: The Future of the World Trade Organization* (American Enterprise Institute Press, 2001), 1–68.

784 See C.-D. Ehlermann, *Some Personal Experiences as Member of the Appellate Body of the WTO*, Policy Papers, RSC No. 02/9 (European University Institute, 2002), 14.

The jurisdiction of the WTO dispute settlement system is compulsory, exclusive and contentious in nature. Furthermore, it is very broad in scope. It covers disputes arising under the *WTO Agreement*, the DSU, all multilateral agreements and one plurilateral agreement on trade in goods, the GATS and the *TRIPS Agreement* (commonly referred to as the covered agreements). In principle, any act or omission attributable to a WTO Member can be a measure that is subject to WTO dispute settlement. Measures that can be subject to WTO dispute settlement include: (1) action or conduct by private parties attributable to a Member; (2) measures that expire or are withdrawn during the proceedings and are thus no longer in force; (3) legislation as such (as opposed to the actual application of this legislation in specific instances); (4) discretionary legislation (as opposed to mandatory legislation); (5) unwritten norms or rules of Members, including practices or policies which are not set out in law; (6) ongoing conduct by Members and concerted, systematic action or practice of Members; (7) measures composed of several different instruments; and (8) measures by regional and local authorities. Access to the WTO dispute settlement system is limited to WTO Members. A WTO Member can have recourse to the system when it claims that a benefit accruing to it under one of the covered agreements is being nullified or impaired. A complainant will almost always argue that the respondent violated a provision of WTO law and file a violation complaint. If the violation is shown, there is a presumption of nullification or impairment of a benefit. Alternatively, a complainant can file a non-violation complaint (seldom done) or situation complaint (never done). NGOs, industry associations, companies or individuals have no direct access to the WTO dispute settlement system. However, it should be noted that most disputes are brought to the WTO for resolution at the instigation of companies and industry associations (i.e. indirect access).

The prime object and purpose of the WTO dispute settlement system is the prompt settlement of disputes between WTO Members and to provide security and predictability to the multilateral trading system. WTO dispute settlement has six key features, which in addition to the compulsory and exclusive jurisdiction of the WTO dispute settlement system and the process of WTO dispute settlement contribute to, if not explain, the importance and success of WTO dispute settlement to date. Some of these features set apart the WTO dispute settlement system from other international dispute settlement mechanisms. *First*, the WTO dispute settlement system is a single, comprehensive and integrated dispute settlement system. The rules of the DSU apply to all disputes arising under the covered agreements while some of these covered agreements provide for some special and additional rules and procedures 'designed to deal with the particularities of dispute settlement relating to obligations arising under a specific covered agreement'. *Second*, the DSU provides for several methods to settle disputes between WTO Members: consultations or negotiations (Article 4 of the DSU); adjudication by panels and the Appellate Body (Articles 6–20 of the

DSU); arbitration (Articles 21.3(c), 22.6 and 25 of the DSU); and good offices, conciliation and mediation (Article 5 of the DSU). Of these methods, arbitration under Article 25 and good offices, conciliation and mediation under Article 5 have only played a marginal role; in almost all WTO disputes, Members had recourse to consultations, and, if those were unsuccessful, adjudication. *Third*, pursuant to Article 23 of the DSU, Members must settle disputes with other Members over compliance with WTO obligations through the *multilateral* procedures of the DSU, rather than through *unilateral* action. Concerns regarding unilateral action taken by the United States against what it considered to be violations of GATT law were the driving force behind the Uruguay Round negotiations on dispute settlement, which eventually resulted in the DSU. *Fourth*, the WTO dispute settlement system prefers Members to resolve a dispute through consultations, resulting in a mutually acceptable solution, rather than through adjudication. In other words, the DSU prefers parties *not* to go to court, but to settle their dispute amicably out of court. *Fifth*, pursuant to Article 3.2, second sentence, of the DSU, the WTO dispute settlement system serves not only 'to preserve the rights and obligations of Members under the covered agreements', but also 'to clarify the existing provisions of those agreements'. The scope and nature of this clarification mandate is, however, circumscribed by Article 3.2, third sentence, and Article 19.2 of the DSU, which explicitly preclude the system from adding to or diminishing the rights and obligations of Members. The DSU does not condone judicial activism. For panels and the Appellate Body to stay within their mandate to clarify existing provisions and not stray into judicial activism, it is therefore important that they interpret and apply the provisions concerned correctly, i.e. in accordance with customary rules of interpretation of international law, as codified in Articles 31 and 32 of the *Vienna Convention on the Law of Treaties*. Pursuant to Articles 31 and 32, panels and the Appellate Body interpret provisions of the covered agreements in accordance with the ordinary meaning of the words of the provision in their context and in light of the object and purpose of the agreement involved; and, if necessary and appropriate, they have recourse to supplementary means of interpretation. *Sixth*, the DSU provides for three types of remedy for breach of WTO law: one final remedy, namely, the withdrawal (or modification) of the WTO-inconsistent measure; and two temporary remedies which can be applied awaiting the withdrawal (or modification) of the WTO-inconsistent measure, namely, compensation *and* suspension of concessions or other obligations (commonly referred to as 'retaliation'). A measure which was found to be WTO-inconsistent must be withdrawn immediately or, if that is impracticable, within a 'reasonable period of time'. In more than four out of five disputes, the offending party withdraws (or modifies) the WTO-inconsistent measure by the end of the 'reasonable period of time'. However, when the offending party fails to do so, and the parties were subsequently unable to agree on compensation for the harm that will result from the lack of compliance, the original complaining party may request authorisation from the DSB to retaliate against the offending party by suspending concessions or other obligations with respect to that offending party. Retaliation, often in the form of a drastic increase in the customs duties on strategically selected products, puts economic and political pressure on the offending party to withdraw (or modify) its WTO-inconsistent measure(s). Subject to certain conditions, the retaliation may take the form of the suspension of obligations under agreements other than those with regard to which a violation was found in the underlying dispute (i.e. cross-retaliation). To date, Members applied retaliation measures in four cases, while the number of disputes in which the DSB authorised Members to do so was significantly higher. The effectiveness and/or appropriateness of retaliation – which is by definition trade destructive – as a temporary remedy for breach of WTO law is the subject of debate.

Among the institutions involved in WTO dispute settlement one must distinguish between a political institution, the Dispute Settlement Body (DSB), and two independent, judicial-type institutions, the dispute settlement panels and the Appellate Body. The DSB, which is composed of all WTO Members, administers the dispute settlement system. It has the authority to establish panels, adopt panel and Appellate Body reports, and authorise retaliation in case of non-compliance. It takes decisions on these important matters by *reverse consensus*. As a result, the DSB decisions on these matters are quasi-automatic.

The actual adjudication of disputes brought to the WTO is done, at the first-instance level, by dispute settlement panels and, at the appellate level, by the Appellate Body. Panels are *ad hoc* bodies established for the purpose of adjudicating a particular dispute and are dissolved once they have accomplished this task. A panel is established by the DSB at the request of the complainant. At the latest at the second DSB meeting at which the panel request is discussed, the panel is established by reverse consensus. The parties decide on the composition of the panel by mutual accord. However, if they fail to do so within twenty days after the establishment of the panel, either party can ask the Director-General of the WTO to appoint the panellists. As a rule, panels are composed of three well-qualified governmental and/or non-governmental individuals, who are not nationals of the parties or third parties to the dispute. Pursuant to the *Rules of Conduct* for WTO dispute settlement, panellists must be independent and impartial, avoid direct and indirect conflicts of interest and respect the confidentiality of proceedings. Almost all panels have standard terms of reference, which refer back to the complainant's request to establish a panel. Hence, a claim and/or measure falls within the panel's terms of reference, i.e. within its jurisdiction, only if that claim or measure is identified in the panel request. The standard of review of panels, as set forth in Article 11 of the DSU, is 'to make an objective assessment of the matter'. Pursuant to Article 11 of the DSU, a panel, as a trier of facts: (1) must base its findings on a sufficient evidentiary basis on the record;

(2) may not apply a double standard of proof; (3) must treat evidence in an 'even-handed' manner; (4) must consider evidence before it in its totality (which includes consideration of submitted evidence in relation to other evidence); and (5) should not disregard evidence that is relevant to the case of one of the parties. Panels may exercise judicial economy; they need only address (but at the same time are required to address at least) those claims which must be addressed in order to resolve the matter at issue in the dispute. A panel report must, at a minimum, set out the findings of fact, the applicability of relevant provisions and the basic rationale behind any findings and recommendations it makes. Where a panel concludes that a Member's measure is inconsistent with WTO law, it shall recommend that the Member concerned bring that measure into conformity with WTO law. The recommendations and rulings of the panel become legally binding when they are adopted – by reverse consensus – by the DSB.

The Appellate Body is a standing, i.e. permanent, international tribunal of seven individuals of recognised authority, appointed by the DSB for a term of four years (renewable once). Pursuant to the *Rules of Conduct* for WTO dispute settlement, Members of the Appellate Body must be independent and impartial, avoid direct and indirect conflicts of interest and respect the confidentiality of proceedings. The composition of the Appellate Body shall be broadly representative of WTO membership. The Appellate Body hears and decides appeals in divisions of three of its Members. Only parties to the dispute can appeal a panel report. An appeal is limited to issues of law covered in the panel report and legal interpretations developed by the panel. Issues of fact cannot be appealed. However, the treatment of the facts or evidence by a panel may raise the question of whether the panel has made an objective assessment of the facts as required under Article 11 of the DSU. This is a legal issue and can therefore be examined by the Appellate Body. The Appellate Body may uphold, modify or reverse the legal findings and conclusions of the panel that were appealed. On occasion, the Appellate Body has also – in the absence of the authority to remand a case to the panel – felt compelled to 'complete the legal analysis' on issues not addressed by the panel. It has done so in order to provide a prompt resolution of the dispute.

The WTO dispute settlement process may – and often does – entail four major steps: (1) consultations; (2) panel proceedings; (3) Appellate Body proceedings; and (4) implementation and enforcement. The four-step WTO dispute settlement process has six features that are particularly noteworthy, partly because they distinguish WTO dispute settlement – in both positive and negative ways – from other international dispute settlement mechanisms. These six features are: (1) the short time frame for each of the steps in the process; (2) the confidentiality and resulting lack of transparency of the process; (3) the burden of proof in WTO dispute settlement proceedings, which is on the party that asserts the affirmative of a particular claim or defence; (4) the important role of private legal counsel in representing parties in WTO dispute settlement; (5) the acceptance and consideration by panels and the Appellate Body of *amicus curiae* briefs; and (6) the obligation on Members to act in good faith in WTO dispute settlement proceedings, and the obligation on panels and the Appellate Body to ensure due process in these proceedings.

The WTO dispute settlement process always begins with consultations (or, at least, an attempt to have consultations) between the parties to the dispute. The consultations enable the disputing parties to understand better the factual situation and the legal claims in respect of the dispute. Parties have broad discretion regarding the manner in which consultations are to be conducted. The consultation process essentially tries to resolve a dispute by diplomatic means and has frequently been successful in resolving disputes. However, if consultations do not resolve the dispute within sixty days after the request for consultations, the complainant may request the DSB to establish a panel.

The basic rules governing panel proceedings are set out in Article 12 of the DSU. Article 12.1 of the DSU directs a panel to follow the *Working Procedures* contained in Appendix 3 to the DSU, but at the same time authorises a panel to do otherwise. A panel will – whenever possible within one week of its composition – fix the timetable for its work and decide on detailed *ad hoc* working procedures. Each party to a dispute normally submits two written submissions to the panel: a 'first written submission' and a 'rebuttal submission'. During the proceedings, the panel will meet with the parties twice, first after the filing of the 'first written submissions' and then after the filing of the 'rebuttal submissions'. Unless specific deadlines for the submission of evidence are set out in the *ad hoc* working procedures of the panel (which is often the case now), parties can submit new evidence as late as the second meeting with the panel. The panel must of course always be careful to ensure due process. Panels have the discretionary authority to seek information and technical advice from any source including experts, in order to help them to understand and evaluate the evidence submitted and the arguments made by the parties. The parties are under an obligation to provide the panel with the information or the documents that the panel requests at any time during the proceedings. The rights of third parties to participate in the panel proceedings are limited but have been, in some cases, extended. Panels submit their draft reports to the parties for comment in a so-called 'interim review'. After this interim review, the panel finalises the report, issues it to the parties and eventually – when the report is available in the three official languages of the WTO – circulates the report to all Members, at which time it is also made public. Panel proceedings in theory should not exceed nine months, but in practice panel proceedings take, on average, fifteen months. Within sixty days of its circulation, a panel report is either adopted by the DSB by negative consensus or appealed to the Appellate Body.

In contrast to panels, the Appellate Body has detailed standard working procedures set out in the *Working Procedures for Appellate Review*. Appellate review proceedings are initiated by a notice of appeal. A party to the dispute other than the original appellant may also appeal alleged legal errors in the panel report by filing a notice of other appeal. The appellant's and other appellant's submissions are filed at the same time as the notice of appeal or the notice of other appeal. The appellee's submission(s) and the third participants' submissions are due within, respectively, eighteen and twenty-one days after the date of the notice of appeal. In each appellate review proceedings there is usually one hearing. Compared to panel proceedings, third parties have broader rights to participate in Appellate Body proceedings. After the oral hearing and before finalising its report, the division responsible for deciding an appeal will always exchange views on the issues raised by the appeal with the Members of the Appellate Body not serving on the division. When the report is available in the three official languages of the WTO, it is circulated to all WTO Members and made public. Article 17.5 of the DSU requires that Appellate review proceedings not exceed ninety days, and, in most cases, the Appellate Body has been able to complete its review within that very short time frame. Within thirty days of its circulation, the Appellate Body report, together with the panel report, as upheld, modified or reversed by the Appellate Body, is adopted by the DSB by reverse consensus.

Recommendations and rulings of panels and/or the Appellate Body, as adopted by the DSB, must be implemented immediately or within a 'reasonable period of time'. Often the parties are able to agree on the duration of that period, but, if they cannot, the 'reasonable period of time' can – at the request of either party – be determined through binding arbitration (under Article 21.3(c) of the DSU). During the 'reasonable period of time for implementation', the DSB keeps the implementation of adopted recommendations and rulings under surveillance. If by the end of the reasonable period there is disagreement as to the existence or the WTO consistency of the implementing measures, this dispute is resolved in Article 21.5 compliance proceedings. If the offending party is found to have failed to implement the recommendations and rulings within the 'reasonable period of time' and agreement on compensation cannot be reached, the complainant may request authorisation from the DSB to retaliate against the offending party. A practice has developed under which the parties agree to resort first to an Article 21.5 'compliance' proceeding before obtaining authorisation from the DSB to retaliate (i.e. the sequencing issue). Under the Article 21.5 'compliance' proceeding, disagreement as to the existence or consistency with WTO law of implementing measures shall be decided through recourse to the DSU dispute settlement procedures, including, wherever possible, resort to the original panel. If the respondent did indeed fail to implement, the DSB can at the request of the complainant, authorise retaliation measures by reverse consensus. If the non-complying Member objects to the level of suspension proposed or claims that the principles and procedures for suspension have not been followed, the matter may be referred to arbitration (under Article 22.6 of the DSU) before the DSB takes a decision on the retaliation.

In recognition of the difficulties developing-country Members may encounter when they are involved in WTO dispute settlement, the DSU contains some special rules for developing-country Members. Most of these rules are, however, of limited significance. Effective legal assistance to developing-country Members in dispute settlement proceedings is given by the Geneva-based ACWL, which is established as an independent, international organisation that offers legal advice and representation to its developing-country Members and to least-developed countries.

The WTO system for resolving trade disputes between WTO Members has been a remarkable success in many respects. However, the current system can undoubtedly be further improved. In the context of the Doha Round, WTO Members are currently negotiating on proposals for the clarification and amendment of the DSU. The main challenge to the WTO dispute settlement system is, however, not its further improvement but the dangerous imbalance between the WTO's efficient judicial arm and its far less effective political negotiating arm.

FURTHER READINGS

R. Howse, 'The World Trade Organization 20 Years On: Global Governance by Judiciary', *European Journal of International Law*, 2016, 27(1), 1–77.

P. C. Mavroidis, 'Dispute Settlement in the WTO: Mind Over Matter', Robert Schuman Centre for Advanced Studies, EUI Working Paper RSCAS 2016/04, January 2016, European University Institute.

J. R. Ram, 'Pitching Outside the DSU: Preliminary Rulings in WTO Dispute Settlement', *Journal of World Trade*, 2016, 50(3), 369–89.

A. Wolff, 'The WTO Appellate Body at 30: Exploring the Limits of WTO Dispute Settlement in the Next Decade', E15Initiative, ICTSD and World Economic Forum, May 2016.

C. P. Bown and K. M. Reynolds, 'Trade Agreements and Enforcement: Evidence from WTO Dispute Settlement', Policy Research Working Paper 7242, April 2015, World Bank.

J. Eckhardt and D. Bièvre, 'Boomerangs over Lac Léman: Transnational Lobbying and Foreign Venue Shopping in WTO Dispute Settlement', *World Trade Review*, July 2015, 14(3), 507–30.

L. Xiaoling and C. Yusong, 'Constraints of the WTO Compensation Mechanism and Implications from Recent Practice', *Journal of World Trade*, 2015, 49(4), 643–64.

N. Meagher, 'Regulatory Convergence and Dispute Settlement in the WTO', *Journal of International Trade Law and Policy*, 2015, 14(3), 157–62.

W. Alschner, 'Amicable Settlements of WTO Disputes: Bilateral Solutions in a Multilateral System', *World Trade Review*, 2014, 13(1), 65–102.

L. Bartels, 'Jurisdiction and Applicable Law in the WTO', Paper No. 59/2014, Legal Studies Research Paper Series, 2014, University of Cambridge.

W. J. Davey, 'The WTO and Rules-Based Dispute Settlement: Historical Evolution, Operational Success, and Future Challenges', *Journal of International Economic Law*, 2014, 17, 679–700.

L. Johns and K. J. Pelc, 'Who Gets to Be in the Room? Manipulating Participation in WTO Disputes', *International Organization*, 2014, 68(3), 663–99.

M. Bronckers and F. Baetens, 'Reconsidering Financial Remedies in WTO Dispute Settlement', *Journal of International Economic Law*, 2013, 16(2), 281–311.

C. Chase, A. Yanovich, J. Crawford and P. Ugaz, 'Mapping of Dispute Settlements Mechanisms in Regional Trade Agreements: Innovative or Variations on a Theme?', Staff Working Paper ERSD-2013-07, World Trade Organization.

A. Dukgeun, L. Jihong and P. Jee-Hyeong, 'Understanding Non-Litigated Disputes in the WTO Dispute Settlement System', *Journal of World Trade*, 2013, 47(5), 985–1012.

G. Marceau, A. Izaguerri and V. Lanovoy, 'The WTO's Influence on Other Dispute Settlement Mechanisms: A Lighthouse in the Storm of Fragmentation', *Journal of World Trade*, 2013, 47(3), 481–574.

R. W. Staiger and A. O. Sykes, 'Non-Violations', *Journal of International Economic Law*, 2013, 16, 741–75.

G. Vidigal, 'Re-assessing WTO Remedies: The Prospective and the Retrospective', *Journal of International Economic Law*, 2013, 16(3), 505–34.

J. Bohanes and F. Garza, 'Going Beyond Stereotypes: Participation of Developing Countries in WTO Dispute Settlement, Trade', *Law and Development*, 2012, 4(1), 45–124.

S. Hariharan, 'Standard of Review and Burden of Proof in WTO Jurisprudence', *Journal of World Investment and Trade*, 2012, 13(5), 795–811.

G. Marceau and M. Hurley, 'Transparency and Public Participation: A Report Card on WTO Transparency Mechanisms', *Trade Law and Development*, 2012, 4(1), 19–44.

G. Marceau and J. K. Hawkins, 'Experts in WTO Dispute Settlement', *Journal of International Dispute Settlement*, 2012, 3(3), 493–507.

J. Pauwelyn, 'Appeal without Remand: A Design Flaw in the WTO Dispute Settlement and How to Fix It', ICTSD Project on Dispute Settlement, Issue Paper No. 1, June 2007, International Centre for Trade and Sustainable Development.

Most-Favoured-Nation Treatment

CONTENTS

1 INTRODUCTION

As discussed in Chapter 1, discrimination in matters relating to trade breeds resentment and poisons the economic and political relations between countries.[1] Moreover, discrimination makes scant economic sense as, generally speaking, it distorts the market in favour of goods and services that are more expensive and/or of lower quality. Non-discrimination is, therefore, a key concept in WTO law and policy. The importance of eliminating discrimination is highlighted in

1 See above, pp. 23–4.

the Preamble to the *WTO Agreement*, where the 'elimination of discriminatory treatment in international trade relations' is identified as one of the two main means by which the objectives of the WTO may be attained.[2]

As stated in Chapter 1, there are two main non-discrimination obligations under WTO law: the most-favoured-nation (MFN) treatment obligation and the national treatment obligation.[3] In simple terms, an MFN treatment obligation relates to whether a country favours some countries over others. An MFN treatment obligation prohibits a country from discriminating *between* and *among* other countries. A national treatment obligation relates to whether a country favours itself over other countries. A national treatment obligation prohibits a country from discriminating *against* other countries. The national treatment obligation under WTO law will be discussed in the next chapter; the MFN treatment obligation under WTO law is the topic of this chapter. This MFN treatment obligation applies to trade in goods as well as trade in services. The key provision dealing with the MFN treatment obligation for measures affecting trade in goods is Article I:1 of the GATT 1994. The key provision dealing with the MFN treatment obligation for measures affecting trade in services is Article II:1 of the GATS. This chapter discusses these MFN treatment obligations in turn.[4]

With regard to the MFN treatment obligation under Article I:1 of the GATT 1994, the questions that may arise include the following:

(1) Can Richland, a WTO Member, impose a 10 per cent *ad valorem* customs duty on beer from Newland, also a WTO Member, while imposing a 5 per cent *ad valorem* customs duty on beer from Oldland, another WTO Member?
(2) Can Richland impose a 10 per cent domestic sales tax on soft drinks from Newland while imposing a 5 per cent domestic sales tax on mineral water from Oldland?
(3) Can Richland impose on soft drinks a labelling requirement to indicate the sugar content while not imposing such a requirement on fruit juice?

With regard to the MFN treatment obligation under Article II:1 of the GATS, the following questions may arise:

(1) Can Richland allow doctors from Newland to practise medicine in its territory but bar doctors from Oldland from doing so?
(2) Can Richland impose strict qualification requirements on nannies from Oldland while leaving the qualifications of domestic workers from Newland largely unregulated?
(3) Can Richland impose a 20 per cent domestic tax on English-language courses, while exempting French-language courses from domestic taxation?

2 See above, p. 88. 3 See above, p. 39.

4 As discussed in Chapter 15, Article 4 of the *TRIPS Agreement* provides for an MFN treatment obligation with regard to intellectual property rights. See below, pp. 993–1056.

2 MOST-FAVOURED-NATION TREATMENT UNDER THE GATT 1994

Article I of the GATT 1994, entitled 'General Most-Favoured-Nation Treatment', states in paragraph 1:

> With respect to customs duties and charges of any kind imposed on or in connection with importation or exportation or imposed on the international transfer of payments for imports or exports, and with respect to the method of levying such duties and charges, and with respect to all rules and formalities in connection with importation and exportation, and with respect to all matters referred to in paragraphs 2 and 4 of Article III, any advantage, favour, privilege or immunity granted by any [Member] to any product originating in or destined for any other country shall be accorded immediately and unconditionally to the like product originating in or destined for the territories of all other [Members].[5]

The GATT 1994 contains a number of other provisions requiring MFN or MFN-like treatment, such as: Article III:7 (regarding local content requirements); Article V (regarding freedom of transit); Article IX:1 (regarding marks of origin); Article XIII:1 (regarding the non-discriminatory administration of quantitative restrictions); and Article XVII (regarding State trading enterprises). Article XX of the GATT 1994, and in particular the chapeau of this 'general exceptions' provision, also contains an MFN-like obligation.[6] The very existence of these MFN-type clauses demonstrates the pervasive character of the MFN principle of non-discrimination.[7] Other multilateral agreements on trade in goods such as the *TBT Agreement*, the *SPS Agreement*, the *Agreement on Rules of Origin*, the *Agreement on Import Licensing Procedures* and the *Agreement on Trade Facilitation* likewise require MFN treatment.[8] However, this section is only concerned with the MFN treatment obligation set out in Article I:1 of the GATT 1994.

2.1 Nature of the MFN Treatment Obligation of Article I:1 of the GATT 1994

As the Appellate Body observed in *EC – Tariff Preferences (2004)*, it is well settled that the MFN treatment obligation set out in Article I:1 of the GATT 1994 is a 'cornerstone of the GATT' and 'one of the pillars of the WTO trading system'.[9] The importance of the MFN treatment obligation to the multilateral trading system is undisputed.[10] However, as discussed in Chapter 10, in the last fifteen years

5 Paragraphs 2, 3 and 4 of Article I of the GATT 1994 deal with so-called colonial preferences and allow the continuation of such preferences, albeit within certain limits. While important and controversial when the GATT 1947 was negotiated, these colonial preferences are now of very little significance and will therefore not be discussed.

6 See below, pp. 593–603. 7 See Appellate Body Report, *Canada – Autos (2000)*, para. 82.

8 See below, pp. 883–934 (TBT), 935–92 (SPS), 457–61 (ROOs) and 496–8 (Import licensing). In the *Agreement on Trade Facilitation*, see e.g. Articles 1.1.1, 3.9(d), 4.3, 5.1(d), 5.3.2, 7.4.2, 7.7.2(b)(i).

9 Appellate Body Report, *EC – Tariff Preferences (2004)*, para. 101 (quoting Appellate Body Report, *Canada – Autos (2000)*, para. 69).

10 In *US – Section 211 Appropriations Act (2002)*, para. 297, the Appellate Body stated that 'most-favoured-nation treatment in Article I of the GATT 1994 has been both central and essential to assuring the success of a global rules-based system for trade in goods'.

there has been a proliferation of customs unions, free-trade agreements and other arrangements, which provide for preferential, i.e. discriminatory, treatment in trade relations between WTO Members.[11] Considering this proliferation, the 2004 Sutherland Report on *The Future of the WTO* arrived, not without some pathos, at the following conclusion:

> [N]early five decades after the founding of the GATT, MFN is no longer the rule; it is almost the exception. Certainly, much trade between the major economies is still conducted on an MFN basis. However, what has been termed the 'spaghetti bowl' of customs unions, common markets, regional and bilateral free trade areas, preferences and an endless assortment of miscellaneous trade deals has almost reached the point where MFN treatment is exceptional treatment.[12]

As discussed in Chapter 10, the situation may not be as dramatic as suggested in the Sutherland Report.[13] While MFN treatment is in practice perhaps less prevalent than one might expect of 'one of the pillars of the WTO trading system', it undoubtedly is, and remains, a principal obligation for WTO Members.

As the Appellate Body stated in *Canada – Autos (2000)*, Article I:1 of the GATT 1994 prohibits discrimination *between* like products *originating in*, or destined for, different countries.[14] In other words, Article I:1 prohibits WTO Member Richland from giving products from WTO Member Newland treatment less favourable than the treatment it gives to like products from any other WTO Member or other country. Also, Article I:1 prohibits Richland from giving products destined for Newland treatment less favourable than the treatment it gives to like products *destined for* any other WTO Member or other country. The principal purpose of the MFN treatment obligation of Article I:1 is to ensure all WTO Members *equality of opportunity* to import from, or to export to, other WTO Members (or any other country). In *EC – Bananas III (1997)*, the Appellate Body stated, with respect to WTO non-discrimination obligations (such as the obligation set out in Article I:1):

> The essence of the non-discrimination obligations is that like products should be treated equally, irrespective of their origin. As no participant disputes that all bananas are like products, the non-discrimination provisions apply to *all* imports of bananas, irrespective of whether and how a Member categorizes or subdivides these imports for administrative or other reasons.[15]

In *EC – Bananas III (1997)*, the measure at issue was the import regime for bananas of the European Communities under which bananas from Latin American countries ('dollar bananas') were treated less favourably than bananas from, broadly speaking, former European colonies ('ACP bananas').

11 See below, pp. 671–92. 12 The Sutherland Report, para. 60. 13 See below, p. 673.
14 See Appellate Body Report, *Canada – Autos (2000)*, para. 84.
15 Appellate Body Report, *EC – Bananas III (1997)*, para. 190.

In *EC – Seal Products (2014)*, the Appellate Body again emphasised that the fundamental purpose of Article I:1 is:

> to preserve the equality of competitive opportunities for like imported products from all Members.[16]

Article I:1 of the GATT 1994 covers not only 'in law', or *de jure*, discrimination but also 'in fact', or *de facto*, discrimination. In other words, Article I:1 applies not only to 'origin-based' measures (which are discriminatory by definition), but also to measures which, on their face, appear 'origin-neutral' but are *in fact* discriminatory. A measure may be said to discriminate in law (or *de jure*) in a case in which it is clear from reading the text of the law, regulation or policy that it treats the product from one WTO Member less favourably than the like product from another WTO Member or country. For example, if Richland imposed a customs duty of 10 per cent *ad valorem* on chocolate from Newland while imposing a customs duty of 20 per cent *ad valorem* on chocolate from other WTO Members, the imposition of the 20 per cent customs duty on other WTO Members constitutes 'in law' or *de jure* discrimination. However, if the measure at issue does not appear on its face to discriminate against particular WTO Members, it may still constitute 'in fact' or *de facto* discrimination if, on reviewing all the facts relating to the application of the measure, it becomes clear that it treats, in practice or in fact, the product from one WTO Member less favourably than the like product from another WTO Member or country. For example, if Richland imposes a customs duty of 10 per cent *ad valorem* on chocolate made with milk from cows that spent at least six months per year at an altitude of more than 1,500 metres, while imposing a customs duty of 20 per cent *ad valorem* on chocolate made with other milk, the imposition of the 20 per cent customs duty may well constitute 'in fact' or *de facto* discrimination. This would be so if, in fact, in Newland, cows spent at least six months per year at an altitude of more than 1,500 metres, while the highest point in Oldland, a major chocolate producer and exporter, is 300 metres above sea level.[17] The panel in *Canada – Pharmaceutical Patents (2000)* noted that:

> *de facto* discrimination is a general term describing the legal conclusion that an ostensibly neutral measure transgresses a non-discrimination norm because its actual effect is to impose differentially disadvantageous consequences on certain parties, and because those differential effects are found to be wrong or unjustifiable.[18]

While instances of *de jure* discrimination still occur, ever more sophisticated legislators and/or regulators of WTO Members are more likely to adopt measures that constitute *de facto* discrimination.

16 Appellate Body Reports, *EC – Seal Products (2014)*, para. 5.87.

17 It is assumed here that chocolate made with milk from highland cows is 'like' chocolate made with milk from lowland cows. For the discussion on the concept of 'likeness', see below, pp. 316–19.

18 Panel Report, *Canada – Pharmaceutical Patents (2000)*, para. 7.101. Note that *Canada – Pharmaceutical Patents* concerned the national treatment obligation under Article III:4 of the GATT and not the MFN treatment obligation under Article I:1 thereof. However, this does not affect the relevance of the panel statement quoted.

In *Canada – Autos (2000)*, the Appellate Body rejected, as the panel had done, Canada's argument that Article I:1 does not apply to measures which appear, on their face, to be 'origin-neutral' vis-à-vis like products.[19] According to the Appellate Body, measures which appear, on their face, to be 'origin-neutral' can still give certain countries more opportunity to trade than others and can, therefore, be in violation of the non-discrimination obligation of Article I:1. The measure at issue in *Canada – Autos (2000)* was a customs duty exemption accorded by Canada to imports of motor vehicles by certain manufacturers.[20] Formally speaking, there were no restrictions on the origin of the motor vehicles that were eligible for this exemption. In practice, however, the manufacturers imported only their own make of motor vehicle and those of related companies. As a result, only motor vehicles originating in a small number of countries benefited *de facto* from the exemption.

Previously, the panel in *EEC – Imports of Beef (1981)* found that EC regulations, making the suspension of an import levy on beef conditional on the production of a certificate of authenticity, were inconsistent with the MFN treatment obligation of Article I:1 of the GATT 1947 after it was established that the only certifying agency authorised to produce a certificate of authenticity was an agency in the United States.[21] While on its face the EC regulations at issue applied in the same way to all imported beef, irrespective of its origin, it is clear that these regulations *de facto* discriminated against beef from Canada, the complainant in that case.

In *EC – Seal Products (2014)*, the panel noted that while virtually all Greenlandic seal products were likely to qualify under the IC exception for access to the EU market, the vast majority of seal products from Canada and Norway did not meet the IC requirements for access to the EU market. Therefore, in terms of its design, structure, and expected operation, the EU Seal Regime, the measure at issue, detrimentally affected the conditions of competition for Canadian and Norwegian seal products as compared to seal products originating in Greenland. The panel thus concluded that the measure at issue, although origin-neutral on its face, was *de facto* inconsistent with Article I:1.[22]

The panel in *US – Tuna II (Mexico) (Article 21.5) (2015)* noted in the context of Article I:1 of the GATT 1994 that:

> where a condition attached to an advantage is found to detrimentally modify the competitive opportunities of imported like products, the fact that that the disadvantaged Member could modify its practices so as to conform to the condition in question in no way changes the fact that the condition has upset the competitive equality that Article I:1 protects ... Article I:1 of the GATT 1994, like Article 2.1 of the TBT Agreement, is concerned with the

19 See Appellate Body Report, *Canada – Autos (2000)*, para. 78.

20 This exemption was granted to car manufacturers when their production of motor vehicles in Canada reached a minimum amount of Canadian value added (CVA) and a certain production-to-sales ratio in Canada.

21 See Panel Report, *EEC – Imports of Beef (1981)*, paras. 4.2 and 4.3.

22 See Appellate Body Reports, *EC – Seal Products (2014)*, para. 5.95.

conditions of competition as they exist, and not as they might exist if the Member whose like products have suffered a detrimental impact were to somehow modify its practices.[23]

2.2 MFN Treatment Test of Article I:1 of the GATT 1994

Article I:1 of the GATT 1994 sets out a four-tier test of consistency with the MFN treatment obligation. There are four questions which must be answered to determine whether or not a measure affecting trade in goods is consistent with the MFN treatment obligation of Article I:1, namely:

- whether the measure at issue is a measure covered by Article I:1;
- whether that measure grants an '*advantage*';
- whether the products concerned are '*like products*'; and
- whether the advantage at issue is *accorded 'immediately and unconditionally'* to all like products concerned, irrespective of their origin or destination.[24]

Below, each element of this four-tier test of consistency will be discussed in turn.

To date, WTO Members have been found to have acted inconsistently with the MFN treatment obligation of Article I:1 of the GATT 1994 in thirteen disputes.[25]

2.2.1 Measures Covered by Article I:1

The MFN treatment obligation of Article I:1 of the GATT 1994 concerns 'any advantage, favour, privilege or immunity' granted by any Member to any product originating in, or destined for, any other country with respect to: (1) customs duties; (2) charges of any kind imposed *on* or *in connection with* importation or exportation (e.g. import surcharges, export duties, customs fees or quality inspection fees); (3) charges imposed on the international transfer of payments for imports or exports; (4) the method of levying such duties and charges, such as the method of assessing the base value on which the duty or charge is levied; (5) all rules and formalities in connection with importation and exportation; (6) internal taxes or other internal charges (i.e. the matters referred to in Article III:2 of the GATT 1994); and (7) laws, regulations and requirements affecting internal

23 Panel Report, *US – Tuna II (Mexico) (Article 21.5) (2015)*, paras. 7.443 and 7.445. Note that the Appellate Body reversed the panel's findings due to failure by the panel to conduct a holistic assessment of how the various labelling conditions, taken together, adversely affect the conditions of competition for Mexican tuna products in the US Market as compared to like US and other tuna products. See Appellate Body Report, *US – Tuna II (Mexico) (Art 21.5) (2015)*, para. 7.280.

24 See e.g. Appellate Body Reports, *EC – Seal Products (2014)*, para. 5.57. Note that the panel in *Indonesia – Autos (1998)* set out a three-tier, rather than a four-tier, test of consistency with the MFN treatment obligation. Under the panel's test, the first and second questions were merged. See Panel Report, *Indonesia – Autos (1998)*, para. 14.138.

25 See *EC – Bananas III (1997); Indonesia – Autos (1998); EC – Bananas III (Article 21.5 – Ecuador) (1999); Canada – Autos (2000); US – Certain EC Products (2001); EC – Tariff Preferences (2004); EC – Bananas III (Article 21.5 – Ecuador II) (2008); EC – Bananas III (Article 21.5 – US) (2008); Colombia – Ports of Entry (2009); US – Poultry (China) (2010); EU – Footwear (China) (2012); EC – Seal Products (2014)*; and *US – Tuna II (Mexico) (Article 21.5) (2015)*.

sale, offering for sale, purchase, transportation, distribution or use of any product (i.e. the matters referred to in Article III:4 of the GATT 1994).

In brief, the MFN treatment obligation of Article I:1 covers both border measures and internal measures. The *border measures* include, in particular, customs duties, other charges on imports and exports, import and export prohibitions and quotas, tariff quotas, import licences and customs formalities. The *internal measures* include, in particular, internal taxes on products and internal regulations affecting the sale, distribution or use of products. Generally, there has been little debate about the kind of measures covered by Article I:1. Both panels and the Appellate Body have recognised that Article I:1 covers a broad range of measures.

In *Argentina – Financial Services (2016)*, the panel looked into the meaning of the term 'rules and formalities in connection with exportation' and noted that for a measure to be considered a rule 'in connection with exportation', there must be a certain association, link or logical relationship between the measure and the exports.[26] The panel cautioned, however, that the broad interpretation:

> adopted by that panel does not mean that any measure that has a hypothetical or remote connection with importation or exportation can be considered to be covered by Article I:1 of the GATT 1994.[27]

In the past, there has been some debate on the applicability of Article I:1 to safeguard measures, anti-dumping duties and countervailing duties. With regard to safeguard measures, the *Agreement on Safeguards* makes it clear that the MFN treatment obligation normally applies to safeguard measures. Article 2.2 of the *Agreement on Safeguards* states:

> Safeguard measures shall be applied to a product being imported irrespective of its source.

However, as further discussed in Chapter 9, the *Agreement on Safeguards* does allow, under certain conditions, the discriminatory use of safeguard measures.[28] With regard to countervailing duties, the panel in *US – MFN Footwear (1992)* found:

> the *rules and formalities* applicable to countervailing duties, including those applicable to the revocation of countervailing duty orders, are rules and formalities imposed in connection with importation, within the meaning of Article I:1.[29]

In principle, countervailing duties as well as anti-dumping duties fall within the scope of the MFN treatment obligation of Article I:1. Article 9.2 of the *Anti-Dumping Agreement* provides:

> When an anti-dumping duty is imposed in respect of any product, such anti-dumping duty shall be collected in the appropriate amounts in each case, on a *non-discriminatory basis* on imports of such product from all sources found to be dumped and causing injury.[30]

26 See Panel Report, *Argentina – Financial Services (2015)*, para 7.984.
27 See *ibid.*, para 7.995. 28 See below, pp. 630–58.
29 Panel Report, *US – MFN Footwear (1992)*, para. 6.8. 30 Emphasis added.

Article 19.3 of the *SCM Agreement* contains a very similar provision. As further discussed in Chapters 11 and 12, where the relevant facts concerning dumping or subsidisation of products of different origins are the same, anti-dumping duties or countervailing duties should be applied without discrimination.[31] However, it should be noted that the relevant facts concerning dumping or subsidisation of products from different origins will more often than not differ from one country of origin to another country of origin.

While Article I:1 of the GATT 1994 covers a broad range of measures, the panel in *EC – Commercial Vessels (2005)* made it clear that the scope of application of Article I:1 is not unlimited. This dispute concerned EC subsidies to support the building of commercial vessels in the European Union. Korea claimed that these subsidies were inconsistent with Article I:1. As noted above, Article I:1 applies to 'all matters referred to in paragraphs 2 and 4 of Article III'. According to Korea, the subsidies at issue were measures within the meaning of Article III:4 and therefore covered by Article I:1. Having found that the EC subsidies at issue were covered by Article III:8(b) and that Article III:4 therefore did *not* apply,[32] the panel turned to the question whether the subsidies were consequently outside the scope of the MFN obligation in Article I:1. In replying to this question, the panel stated:

> [T]he phrase 'matters referred to in ... ' in Article I:1 refers to the subject-matter of those provisions in terms of their substantive legal content. Understood in this sense, it is clear to us that the 'matters referred to in paragraphs 2 and 4 of Article III' cannot be interpreted without regard to limitations that may exist regarding the scope of the substantive obligations provided for in these paragraphs. If ... a particular measure is not subject to the obligations of Article III, that measure in our view does not form part of the 'matters referred to' in Articles III:2 and 4. Thus, since Article III:8(b) provides that Article III 'shall not prevent the payment of subsidies exclusively to domestic producers', such subsidies are not part of the subject-matter of Article III:4 and cannot be covered by the expression 'matters referred to in paragraphs 2 and 4 of Article III' in Article I:1.[33]

To the extent that measures covered by Article III:8(b) (i.e. subsidies to domestic producers) fall outside the scope of application of Article III:2 and 4, these measures also fall outside the scope of application of Article I:1. The same logic would seem to apply to laws, regulations and requirements governing government procurement, which – as discussed below – are excluded from the scope of application of Article III:4 pursuant to Article III:8(a).[34]

31 See below, pp. 750–1.
32 Panel Report, *EC – Commercial Vessels (2005)*, para. 7.75. On Article III:8(b) of the GATT 1994, see below, p. 313.
33 *Ibid.*, para. 7.83.
34 See below, pp. 347–50. Note, however, that Article III:1(b) of the plurilateral *Agreement on Government Procurement* imposes on those WTO Members which are a party to this Agreement an MFN treatment obligation with regard to laws, regulations and requirements governing government procurement. On measures regarding government procurement and the plurilateral *Agreement on Government Procurement*, see below, pp. 512–14 and 537–8.

Finally, note that, pursuant to Article XXIV:3(a) of the GATT 1994, a measure that grants an advantage to adjacent countries in order to facilitate frontier traffic, is not subject to the MFN treatment obligation of Article I:1.

2.2.2 Measure Granting an 'Advantage'

The second element of the test of consistency with the MFN treatment obligation of Article I:1 of the GATT 1994 relates to the question of whether the measure at issue grants an '*advantage*'. The text of Article I:1 of the GATT 1994 refers to 'any advantage, favour, privilege or immunity granted by any [Member]'. In light of the use of the word 'any', it is not surprising that the term 'advantage' has been given a broad meaning in the case law.[35] The panel in *EC – Bananas III (1997)* considered that a measure granting an 'advantage' within the meaning of Article I:1 is a measure that creates 'more favourable competitive opportunities' or affects the commercial relationship between products of different origins.[36] The Appellate Body held in this case:

> [T]he Panel found that the procedural and administrative requirements of the activity function rules for importing third-country and non-traditional ACP bananas differ from, and go significantly beyond, those required for importing traditional ACP bananas. This is a factual finding. Also, a broad definition has been given to the term 'advantage' in Article I:1 of the GATT 1994 by the panel in [*US – MFN Footwear (1992)*] ... For these reasons, we agree with the Panel that the activity function rules are an 'advantage' granted to bananas imported from traditional ACP States, and not to bananas imported from other Members, within the meaning of Article I:1.[37]

In *Canada – Autos (2000)*, the Appellate Body further clarified the meaning of the term 'advantage' and thus the scope of the MFN treatment obligation by ruling:

> Article I:1 requires that '*any advantage*, favour, privilege or immunity granted by any Member to *any product* originating in or destined for any other country shall be accorded immediately and unconditionally to the like product originating in or destined for the territories of *all other Members*.' [emphasis added] The words of Article I:1 refer not to *some* advantages granted 'with respect to' the subjects that fall within the defined scope of the Article, but to '*any advantage*'; not to *some* products, but to '*any product*'; and not to like

35 See Panel Report, *Belgium – Family Allowances (allocations familiales) (1952)*, para. 3; Panel Report, *US – Customs User Fee (1988)*, para. 122; Panel Report, *US – MFN Footwear (1992)*, para. 6.9; and Panel Report, *Colombia – Ports of Entry (2009)*, paras. 7.340 and 7.345. Note, however, that the panel in *US – Anti-Dumping and Countervailing Duties (China) (2011)* found that China had failed to establish the existence of an 'advantage' within the meaning of Article I:1, and therefore rejected China's claim of inconsistency with the MFN treatment obligation of Article I:1. See Panel Report, *US – Anti-Dumping and Countervailing Duties (2011)*, paras. 14.150–14.182.

36 See Panel Report, *EC – Bananas III (Guatemala and Honduras) (1997)*, para. 7.239. See also Panel Report, *Colombia – Ports of Entry (2009)*, para. 7.341; and Panel Report, *US – Poultry (China) (2010)*, para. 7.415. The panel in *US – Poultry (China) (2010)* found that, when a measure creates market access opportunities and affects the commercial relationship between products of different origins, that measure grants an 'advantage' within the meaning of Article I:1 of the GATT 1994. See Panel Report, *US – Poultry (China) (2010)*, para. 7.417. At issue in this case was the opportunity to export poultry products to the United States. This opportunity was considered to be a 'very favourable market opportunity and not having such an opportunity would mean a serious competitive disadvantage'. See *ibid.*, para. 7.416.

37 Appellate Body Report, *EC – Bananas III (1997)*, para. 206.

> products from *some* other Members, but to like products originating in or destined for '*all other*' Members.[38]

In other words, the term 'advantage' in Article I:1 refers to *any* advantage granted by a Member to *any* like product from or for another country.[39]

By way of example, note that the panel in *Colombia – Ports of Entry (2009)* found that Colombian customs regulations on the importation of textiles, apparel and footwear required importers of goods arriving from Panama to submit import declarations in advance, and, accordingly, to pay customs duties and taxes in advance, while importers of goods from other countries were not required to file import declarations in advance. On this basis, the panel concluded that the Colombian customs regulations granted an advantage within the meaning of Article I:1 of the GATT 1994 to the goods from countries other than Panama.[40]

In *US – Tuna II (Mexico) (2012)* and *US – Tuna II (Mexico) (Article 21.5) (2015)*, the panels found and the participants on appeal acknowledged that access to the dolphin-safe label constituted an 'advantage' on the United States market for tuna products by virtue of that label's significant commercial value.[41]

The question has arisen whether a Member could offset less advantageous treatment of a product under certain circumstances with more advantageous treatment of that product under other circumstances and thus avoid inconsistency with Article I:1. In line with earlier case law concerning Article III:4, the panel in *US – MFN Footwear (1992)* categorically rejected such possibility and ruled that Article I:1 does not permit 'balancing' less advantageous treatment with more advantageous treatment.[42] The panel noted that:

> [i]f such a balancing were accepted, it would entitle a contracting party to derogate from the most-favoured-nation obligation in one case, in respect of one contracting party, on the ground that it accords more favourable treatment in some other case in respect of another contracting party. In the view of the Panel, such an interpretation of the most-favoured-nation obligation of Article I:1 would defeat the very purpose underlying the unconditionality of that obligation.[43]

38 Appellate Body Report, *Canada – Autos (2000)*, para. 79. See also Appellate Body Reports, *EC – Seal Products (2014)*, para. 5.86.

39 Note that the MFN treatment obligation of Article I:1 of the GATT 1994 clearly concerns not only advantages granted to other WTO Members, but also advantages granted to non-WTO Members. However, now that the membership of the WTO is nearly universal and trade between WTO Members comprises 97 per cent of all international trade, this particular aspect of the MFN treatment obligation is now of little significance.

40 See Panel Report, *Colombia – Ports of Entry (2009)*, para. 7.352.

41 See Panel Report, *US – Tuna II (Mexico) (2012)*, paras. 7.289 and 7.291; Panel Report, *US – Tuna II (Mexico) (Article 21.5) (2015)*, para. 7.424; and Appellate Body Report, *US – Tuna II (Mexico) (Article 21.5) (2015)*, para. 7.236.

42 See Panel Report, *US – MFN Footwear (1992)*, para. 6.10. The panel in *US – Section 337 Tariff Act (1989)* rejected a similar 'balancing' argument in the context of the national treatment obligation in Article III:4. See Panel Report, *US – Section 337 Tariff Act (1989)*, para. 5.14.

43 Panel Report, *US – MFN Footwear (1992)*, para. 6.10. See also Panel Report, *EC – Bananas III (Ecuador) (1997)*, para. 7.239.

2.2.3 'Like Products'

The third element of the test of consistency with the MFN treatment obligation of Article I:1 of the GATT 1994 relates to the question of whether the products at issue are '*like products*'. Article I:1 concerns any product originating in or destined for any other country and requires that an advantage granted to such products shall be accorded to 'like products' originating in or destined for the territories of all other Members. It is only between 'like products' that the MFN treatment obligation applies and discrimination within the meaning of Article I:1 of the GATT 1994 is prohibited. Products that are not 'like' may be treated differently; different treatment of products that are not 'like' will not constitute discrimination within the meaning of Article I:1. For the application of the MFN treatment obligation of Article I:1, it is therefore important to be able to determine whether, for example, a sports utility vehicle (SUV) is 'like' a family car; orange juice is 'like' tomato juice; a laptop is 'like' a tablet computer; pork is 'like' beef; or whisky is 'like' brandy within the meaning of Article I:1.

The concept of 'like products' is used not only in Article I:1 but also in Articles II:2(a), III:2, III:4, VI:1(a), IX:1, XI:2(c), XIII:1, XVI:4 and XIX:1 of the GATT 1994. Nevertheless, the concept of 'like products' is not defined in the GATT 1994.[44] In its examination of the concept of 'like products' under Article III:4, the Appellate Body in *EC – Asbestos (2001)* considered that the dictionary meaning of 'like' suggests that 'like products' are products that share a number of identical or similar characteristics.[45] However, as the Appellate Body already noted in *Canada – Aircraft (1999)*, 'dictionary meanings leave many interpretive questions open'.[46] With regard to the concept of 'like products', there are three questions of interpretation that need to be resolved: (1) which characteristics or qualities are important in assessing 'likeness'; (2) to what degree or extent must products share qualities or characteristics in order to be 'like products'; and (3) from whose perspective 'likeness' should be judged.[47]

It is generally accepted that the concept of 'like products' has a different scope or 'width' in the different contexts in which it is used. In *Japan – Alcoholic Beverages II (1996)*, the Appellate Body illustrated the possible differences in the scope of the concept of 'like products' in different provisions of the *WTO Agreement* by evoking the image of an accordion:

> The accordion of 'likeness' stretches and squeezes in different places as different provisions of the *WTO Agreement* are applied. The width of the accordion in any one of those places

44 Note that the concept of 'like product' is also used in the *Anti-Dumping Agreement*, the *SCM Agreement* the *Agreement on Safeguards* and the *TBT Agreement*, and that this concept is defined in the first two of these agreements. See below, pp. 696–765 (Anti-Dumping), 769–817 (SCM), 630–68 (Safeguards) and 883–932 (TBT).

45 See Appellate Body Report, *EC – Asbestos (2001)*, para. 91. The reference to 'similar' as a synonym of 'like' also echoes the language of the French version of Article III:4, '*produits similaires*', and the Spanish version, '*productos similares*'. See *ibid*. On the Appellate Body's analysis of the concept of 'like products' in *EC – Asbestos (2001)*, see below, pp. 357–8.

46 Appellate Body Report, *Canada – Aircraft (1999)*, para. 153. See also Appellate Body Report, *EC – Asbestos (2001)*, para. 92.

47 See Appellate Body Report, *EC – Asbestos (2001)*, para. 92.

must be determined by the particular provision in which the term 'like' is encountered as well as by the context and the circumstances that prevail in any given case to which that provision may apply.[48]

In other words, products such as orange juice and tomato juice may be 'like' under one provision of the GATT 1994 and not 'like' under another provision.

The meaning of the phrase 'like products' in Article I:1 was addressed in a few GATT working party and panel reports.[49] In *Spain – Unroasted Coffee (1981)*, the panel had to decide whether various types of unroasted coffee ('Colombian mild', 'other mild', 'unwashed Arabica', 'Robusta' and 'other') were 'like products' within the meaning of Article I:1. Spain did not apply customs duties to 'Colombian mild' and 'other mild', while it imposed a 7 per cent customs duty on the other three types of unroasted coffee. Brazil, which exported mainly 'unwashed Arabica', claimed that the Spanish tariff regime was inconsistent with Article I:1. In examining whether the various types of unroasted coffee were 'like products' to which the MFN treatment obligation applied, the panel considered: (1) the physical characteristics of the products;[50] (2) their end use; and (3) tariff regimes of other Members. The panel found that:

unroasted coffee was mainly, if not exclusively, sold in the form of blends, combining various types of coffee, and that coffee in its end-use, was universally regarded as a well-defined and single product intended for drinking.[51]

The panel also found that:

no other contracting party applied its tariff régime in respect of unroasted, non-decaffeinated coffee in such a way that different types of coffee were subject to different tariff rates.[52]

On the basis of these findings, the panel in *Spain – Unroasted Coffee (1981)* concluded that the different types of unroasted coffee should be considered to be 'like products' within the meaning of Article I:1.[53]

In addition to the physical characteristics of the products, their end use and the tariff regimes of other Members (the criteria used by the panel in *Spain – Unroasted Coffee (1981)*), a WTO panel examining whether products are 'like'

48 Appellate Body Report, *Japan – Alcoholic Beverages II (1996)*, 114.

49 See e.g. Working Party Report, *Australian Subsidy on Ammonium Sulphate (1950)*, para. 8; and Panel Report, *EEC – Animal Feed Proteins (1978)*, para. 4.2. See also Panel Report, *Japan – SPF Dimension Lumber (1989)*, paras. 5.13 and 5.14.

50 These physical characteristics included the organoleptic properties (i.e. the taste, smell, aroma, etc.) of the different types of coffee. The panel found that the differences between the different kinds of coffee in organoleptic properties (differences mainly resulting from geographical factors, cultivation methods, the processing of the beans and the genetic factor) were not sufficient to consider the different types of coffee not to be 'like products'. See Panel Report, *Spain – Unroasted Coffee (1981)*, para. 4.6.

51 *Ibid.*, para. 4.7. 52 *Ibid.*, para. 4.8.

53 See *ibid.*, paras. 4.6–4.9. In *EEC – Animal Feed Proteins (1978)*, the panel decided, on the basis of such factors as 'the number of products and tariff items carrying different duty rates and tariff bindings, the varying protein contents and the different vegetable, animal and synthetic origins of the protein products', that the various protein products at issue could not be considered as 'like products' within the meaning of Articles I and III of the GATT 1947. See Panel Report, *EEC – Animal Feed Proteins (1978)*, para. 4.2. It has been suggested that some GATT panels, and in particular the panel in *Japan – SPF Dimension Lumber (1989)*, considered tariff classification as the dominant criterion to establish 'likeness' within the meaning of Article I:1. See Panel Report, *Japan – SPF Dimension Lumber (1989)*, para. 5.13.

within the meaning of Article I:1 would now definitely also consider consumers' tastes and habits as well as any other relevant criterion. Since the case law on 'likeness' within the meaning of Article I:1 of the GATT 1994 is limited, the more extensive case law on 'likeness' within the meaning of Article III of the GATT 1994, discussed in Chapter 5, should be considered carefully, even though one should be cautious regarding a wholesale transfer of this case law.[54] In the context of Article III:2, first sentence, and Article III:4 of the GATT 1994, the Appellate Body found that the determination of whether products are 'like products' is, fundamentally, 'a determination about the nature and extent of a competitive relationship between and among products'.[55] To make such a determination, a panel examines on a case-by-case basis *all* relevant criteria or factors, including: (1) the products' properties, nature and quality, i.e. their physical characteristics; (2) the products' end uses (i.e. the extent to which products are capable of performing the same, or similar, functions); (3) consumers' tastes and habits, also referred to as consumers' perceptions and behaviour, in respect of the products (i.e. the extent to which consumers are willing to use the products to perform these functions or the extent to which consumers perceive products to be substitutable); and (4) the products' tariff classification. It is reasonable to expect that this case law regarding Article III will inform the interpretation of the concept of 'like products' in Article I:1. Future case law will clarify whether the concept of 'like products' in Article I:1 has as narrow a scope as the concept of 'like products' in Article III:2, first sentence; as broad a scope as the concept of 'like products' in Article III:4; or a scope that lies somewhere in between. In other words, future case law will tell whether the accordion of 'likeness' stretches or squeezes in Article I:1 of the GATT 1994.[56]

In *EC – Seal Products (2014)*, the Appellate Body held with regard to Articles I:1 and Article III:4 of GATT 1994 that:

> notwithstanding their textual differences, both of these provisions are concerned with 'prohibiting discriminatory measures' and ensuring 'equality of competitive opportunities' between products that are in a competitive relationship.[57]

It is much debated whether, under current WTO law, a product's process and production method (PPM) is relevant in determining whether products are 'like' if the PPM by which a product is made does *not* affect the physical characteristics of the product. The traditional view is that such non-product-related processes and production methods (NPR–PPMs) are not relevant. Consequently, products produced in an environmentally unfriendly manner cannot be treated less favourably than products produced in an environmentally friendly manner

54 On the meaning of 'like products' in Article III of the GATT 1994, see below, pp. 350–1 and 354–63.

55 Appellate Body Report, *EC – Asbestos (2001)*, para. 99. See also Appellate Body Reports, *Philippines – Distilled Spirits (2012)*, para. 170.

56 The question arises whether the case law since *Japan – SPF Dimension Lumber (1989)* suggests that the accordion of 'likeness' stretches *and* squeezes in Article I:1, depending on the measure at issue (e.g. customs duties *versus* internal taxation or regulation).

57 See Appellate Body Reports, *EC – Seal Products (2014)*, para 5.82.

on the sole basis of the difference in NPR–PPMs. Note, however, in this respect, the discussion on the concept of 'likeness' in Article III:4 in the context of the *EC – Asbestos (2001)* dispute.[58]

While the determination of whether products are 'like' is often a significant challenge, note that the panels in *Colombia – Ports of Entry (2009)* and *US – Poultry (China) (2010)* – inspired by panel reports in disputes concerning Article III of the GATT 1994[59] – sidestepped the issue of 'likeness' and proceeded on the *assumption* that there are 'like' products concerned.[60] To date the Appellate Body has not ruled on this approach for determining 'likeness' under Article I:1 of the GATT 1994. However, as discussed below, the Appellate Body has upheld the origin-base presumption of likeness in the context of Articles II:1 and XVII of the GATS,[61] while also acknowledging the application of this presumption by various panels in disputes under Articles I:1, III:2 and III:4 of the GATT 1994.[62]

2.2.4 Advantage Accorded 'Immediately and Unconditionally'

The fourth and final element of the test of consistency with the MFN treatment obligation of Article I:1 relates to the question of whether the advantage granted by the measure at issue is accorded 'immediately and unconditionally' to all like products irrespective of their origin or destination. Article I:1 of the GATT 1994 requires that any advantage granted by a WTO Member to imports from, or exports to, any country must be granted 'immediately and unconditionally' to imports from, or exports to, all other WTO Members.

There is little debate on the meaning of the requirement to accord an advantage 'immediately' to all like products. 'Immediately' means 'without delay, at once, instantly'. No time should lapse between granting an advantage to a product and according that advantage to all like products.

More problematic has been the meaning of the requirement to accord an advantage 'unconditionally'.[63] In *EC – Seal Products (2014)*, the Appellate Body clarified this requirement as follows:

> as Article I:1 is concerned, fundamentally, with protecting expectations of equal competitive opportunities for like imported products from all Members, it does not follow that Article I:1 prohibits a Member from attaching any conditions to the granting of an 'advantage' within

58 See below, pp. 381–90.

59 See Panel Report, *Colombia – Ports of Entry (2009)*, para. 7.357; and Panel Report, *US – Poultry (China) (2010)*, paras. 7.431–7.432. Both panels referred to Panel Report, *Indonesia – Autos (1998)*, para. 14.113; and Appellate Body Report, *Canada – Periodicals (1997)*, 466.

60 See *Colombia – Ports of Entry (2009)*, para. 7.357; and *US – Poultry (China) (2010)*, paras. 7.431–7.432.

61 See Appellate Body Report, *Argentina – Financial Services (2016)*, paras. 6.32 and 6.38, discussed below, pp. 405–12.

62 With regard to Article I:1 of the GATT 1994, see Panel Reports, *Colombia – Ports of Entry (2009)*, paras. 7.355–7.356; *US – Poultry (China) (2010)*, paras. 7.424–7.432. With regard to Articles III:2 and III:4, see below, pp. 351–76 and 376–99.

63 See in this respect, on the one hand Panel Report, *Indonesia – Autos (1998)*, para. 14.143–4; Panel Report, *Canada – Autos (2000)*, para. 10.29; *Colombia – Ports of Entry (2009)*, paras. 7.362–7.366; and in *US – Poultry (China) (2010)*, paras. 7.437–7.440, but on the other hand Panel Report, *EC – Tariff Preferences (2004)*, para. 7.59.

the meaning of Article I:1. Instead, it prohibits those conditions that have a detrimental impact on the competitive opportunities for like imported products from any Member.[64]

In *US – Tuna II (Mexico) (Article 21.5) (2015)*, the Appellate Body while adjudicating on the consistency of the US amended dolphin-safe labelling measure with Articles I:1 and III:4 of the GATT 1994, referred to its observations in *EC – Seal Products (2014)* and noted that the inquiry to be conducted in the dispute at hand under both Articles I:1 and III:4 of GATT 1994 must focus on the question as to:

> whether the amended tuna measure modifies the conditions of competition in the US market to the detriment of Mexican tuna products vis-à-vis US tuna products or tuna products imported from any other country.[65]

Note that in *EC – Seal Products (2014)*, the European Union argued that Article I:1 does not prohibit measures which have a detrimental impact on competitive opportunities for like imported products *if* that detrimental impact stems exclusively from a legitimate regulatory distinction. According to the European Union the legal standard for the MFN-treatment obligation under Article 2.1 of the *TBT Agreement*, which was articulated by the Appellate Body in 2012 and is discussed in Chapter 13, applies equally to claims under Article I:1 of the GATT 1994.[66] The Appellate Body disagreed with the European Union and upheld the panel's finding that legal standard for the non-discrimination obligations under Article 2.1 of the *TBT Agreement* does not apply equally to claims under Article I:1 of the GATT 1994.[67] In *US – Tuna II (Mexico) (Article 21.5) (2015)*, the Appellate Body reiterated its observations in *EC – Seal Products (2014)* and further stated:

> unlike in Article 2.1 of the TBT Agreement, the most-favoured nation obligation in Article I:1 is not expressed in terms of 'treatment no less favourable', but rather through an obligation to extend any 'advantage' granted by a Member to any product originating in or destined for any other country 'immediately and unconditionally' to the 'like product' originating in or destined for all other countries.[68]

The Appellate Body added and emphasised, however, that:

> These differences notwithstanding, important parallels exist between the non-discrimination provisions contained in Article 2.1 of the TBT Agreement and Articles I:1 and III:4 of the GATT 1994. Accordingly, in assessing whether a measure affects competitive conditions under Article I:1 and/or Article III:4 of the GATT 1994, it may be reasonable for a panel to rely on any relevant findings it made in examining that measure's detrimental impact under Article 2.1 of the TBT Agreement.[69]

By way of conclusion, a comment may be made on two uncontroversial but important aspects of the MFN treatment obligation of Article I:1 of the GATT

64 Appellate Body Reports, *EC – Seal Products (2014)*, para. 5.88.
65 See Appellate Body Report, *US – Tuna II (Mexico) (Article 21.5) (2015)*, para. 7.338.
66 See pp. 883–932.
67 See Appellate Body Reports, *EC – Seal Products (2014)*, para. 5.94. For a discussion of the main arguments made by the European Union and their rejection by the Appellate Body, see *ibid.*, paras. 5.84–5.93 and 5.118–5.129.
68 See Appellate Body Report, *US – Tuna II (Mexico) (Article 21.5) (2015)*, para. 7.277.
69 See *ibid.*, para. 7.278.

1994. A complainant has to show neither any *actual trade effects* nor the *discriminatory intent* of the measure at issue to be successful in claiming inconsistency with the MFN treatment obligation of Article I:1. Note in this respect that: (i) the Appellate Body in *EC – Seal Products (2014)*, ruled that Article I is 'concerned, fundamentally, with prohibiting discriminatory measures by requiring ... equality of competitive opportunities for like imported products from all Members' and for that reason, Article I does not 'require a demonstration of the *actual* trade effects of a specific measure';[70] and (ii) the panel in *EC – Bananas III (1997)* found that it is the mere fact of creating *more favourable competitive opportunities* for some WTO Members only that triggers the inconsistency with the MFN treatment obligation of Article I:1 of the GATT 1994.[71]

2.3 Most-Favoured-Nation Treatment Obligation and the Enabling Clause of the GATT 1994

An important exception to the MFN treatment obligation of Article I:1 of the GATT 1994, and arguably the most significant special and differential treatment provision in WTO law, is the 1979 GATT Decision on Differential and More Favourable Treatment, Reciprocity and Fuller Participation of Developing Countries, commonly referred to as the 'Enabling Clause'.[72] The Enabling Clause, which is now an integral part of the GATT 1994,[73] states, in paragraph 1:

> Notwithstanding the provisions of Article I of the General Agreement, [Members] may accord differential and more favourable treatment to developing countries, without according such treatment to other [Members].

2.3.1 Preferential Tariff Treatment for Developing Countries under the Enabling Clause

Paragraph 2(a) of the Enabling Clause provides that the differential and more favourable treatment referred to in paragraph 1 includes:

> Preferential tariff treatment accorded by [developed-country Members] to products originating in developing countries in accordance with the Generalized System of Preferences ...[74]

70 Appellate Body Reports, *EC – Seal Products (2014)*, para. 5.82. Emphasis added. See also *ibid.*, para. 5.87.

71 See Panel Report, *EC – Bananas III (Mexico) (1997)*, para. 7.239.

72 GATT Document L/4903, dated 28 November 1979, BISD 26S/203. The Enabling Clause was adopted by the GATT Contracting Parties in the context of the Tokyo Round of Multilateral Trade Negotiations. Note that the Enabling Clause replaced, and expanded, a 1971 *Waiver Decision on the Generalized System of Preferences*, GATT Document L/3545, dated 25 June 1971, BISD 18S/24. This Waiver Decision was in turn adopted to give effect to the *Agreed Conclusions* of the UNCTAD Special Committee on Preferences, adopted in 1970. These *Agreed Conclusions* recognised in para. I:2 that preferential tariff treatment accorded under a generalised scheme of preferences was key for developing countries '(a) to increase their export earnings; (b) to promote their industrialization; and (c) to accelerate their rates of economic growth'.

73 The Enabling Clause is one of the 'other decisions of the CONTRACTING PARTIES' within the meaning of para. 1(b)(iv) of Annex 1A incorporating the GATT 1994 into the *WTO Agreement*. See Appellate Body Report, *EC – Tariff Preferences (2004)*, para. 90 and fn. 192.

74 The footnote in the original reads: 'As described in the Decision of the Contracting Parties of 25 June 1971, relating to the establishment of "generalized, non-reciprocal and non-discriminatory preferences beneficial to the developing countries" (BISD 18S/24).'

As the Appellate Body ruled in *EC – Tariff Preferences (2004)*, the Enabling Clause operates as an 'exception' to Article I:1 of the GATT 1994.[75] Paragraph 1 of the Enabling Clause explicitly exempts Members from complying with the obligation contained in Article I:1 for the purposes of providing differential and more favourable treatment to developing countries.[76] The Enabling Clause authorises developed-country Members to grant enhanced market access to products from developing countries extending beyond the access granted to like products from developed countries.[77] The Enabling Clause thus permits Members to provide 'differential and more favourable treatment' to developing countries in spite of the MFN treatment obligation of Article I:1, which normally requires that such treatment be extended to all Members 'immediately and unconditionally'. What is more, WTO Members are *not merely allowed* to deviate from Article I:1 in the pursuit of 'differential and more favourable treatment' for developing countries; they are *encouraged* to do so.[78] Note that most developed-country Members grant preferential tariff treatment to imports from developing countries under their respective Generalised System of Preferences (GSP) schemes. The Enabling Clause plays a vital role in promoting trade as a means of stimulating economic growth and development.[79]

Before the Enabling Clause can successfully be invoked, certain conditions must be fulfilled. The deviation from the MFN obligation of Article I:1 is allowed only when, and to the extent that, the conditions set out in paragraphs 3 and 4 of the Enabling Clause are met. Paragraph 3 sets out the following substantive conditions:

Any differential and more favourable treatment provided under this clause:

a. shall be designed to facilitate and promote the trade of developing countries and not to raise barriers to or create undue difficulties for the trade of any other [Members];
b. shall not constitute an impediment to the reduction or elimination of tariffs and other restrictions to trade on a most-favoured-nation basis;
c. shall in the case of such treatment accorded by [developed-country Members] to developing countries be designed and, if necessary, modified, to respond positively to the development, financial and trade needs of developing countries.

75 See Appellate Body Report, *EC – Tariff Preferences (2004)*, para. 99. On this point, the Appellate Body upheld the finding of the panel; see Panel Report, *EC – Tariff Preferences (2004)*, para. 7.53. The European Communities argued in *EC – Tariff Preferences (2004)* that the Enabling Clause, reflecting the fundamental objective of assisting developing-country Members, is not an exception to Article I:1 of the GATT 1994 but exists 'side-by-side and on an equal level' with Article I:1. The Appellate Body disagreed and ruled that: 'characterising the Enabling Clause as an exception, in our view, does not undermine the importance of the Enabling Clause within the overall framework of the covered agreements and as a "positive effort" to enhance economic development of developing-country Members. Nor does it "discourag[e]" developed countries from adopting measures in favour of developing countries under the Enabling Clause.' Appellate Body Report, *EC – Tariff Preferences (2004)*, para. 95.

76 See *ibid.*, para. 90. 77 See *ibid.*, para. 106. 78 See *ibid.*, para. 111.

79 See *ibid.*, para. 106. Note, however, that the Sutherland Report is very critical of the functioning of the GSP in practice. See *ibid.*, paras. 88–102.

Paragraph 4 sets out the procedural conditions for the introduction, modification and withdrawal of a preferential measure for developing countries. Pursuant to paragraph 4, Members granting preferential tariff treatment to developing countries must notify the WTO and afford adequate opportunity for prompt consultations at the request of any interested Member with respect to any difficulty or matter that may arise.

2.3.2 Additional Preferential Tariff Treatment under the Enabling Clause

In *EC – Tariff Preferences (2004)*, the question arose as to whether the European Communities could grant *additional* preferential tariff treatment to certain developing countries to the exclusion of others. Council Regulation (EC) No. 2501/2001 of 10 December 2001, the EC's former Generalised System of Preferences Regulation,[80] provided for five preferential tariff 'arrangements', namely: (1) the 'General Arrangements'; (2) special incentive arrangements for the protection of labour rights; (3) special incentive arrangements for the protection of the environment; (4) special arrangements for least-developed countries; and (5) special arrangements to combat drug production and trafficking. The General Arrangements, which provide for tariff preferences for all developing countries, and the special arrangements for least-developed countries, were, and still are, not problematic. Both arrangements were, and are, justified under the Enabling Clause: the General Arrangements under paragraph 2(a), discussed above; and the special arrangements for least-developed countries under paragraph 2(d).

The latter provision states that the Enabling Clause also covers:

> [s]pecial treatment of the least developed among the developing countries in the context of any general or specific measures in favour of developing countries.

However, questions as to GATT consistency arose with regard to the other preferential arrangements, i.e. the special incentive arrangements for the protection of labour rights, the special incentive arrangements for the protection of the environment and the special arrangements to combat drug production and trafficking. Only some developing countries were beneficiaries of these special arrangements. For example, preferences under the special incentive arrangements for the protection of labour rights and the special incentive arrangements for the protection of the environment were restricted to those countries that were 'determined by the European Communities to comply with certain labour [or] environmental policy standards', respectively. Preferences under the special arrangements to combat drug production and trafficking (the 'Drug Arrangements') were provided only to eleven Latin American countries and Pakistan.[81]

80 *Official Journal of the European Union*, 2001, L346, 1.

81 See Appellate Body Report, *EC – Tariff Preferences (2004)*, para. 3. Preferences under the Drug Arrangements were provided to Bolivia, Colombia, Costa Rica, Ecuador, El Salvador, Guatemala, Honduras, Nicaragua, Pakistan, Panama, Peru and Venezuela.

While India, the complainant in *EC – Tariff Preferences (2004)*, challenged, in its panel request, the WTO consistency of the Drug Arrangements as well as the special incentive arrangements for the protection of labour rights and the environment, it later decided to limit its complaint to the Drug Arrangements. Accordingly, the *EC – Tariff Preferences (2004)* dispute, and the rulings in this case, only concerned the WTO consistency of the Drug Arrangements. However, it is clear that the rulings in this case may also be of relevance to other special arrangements.

The main substantive issue disputed between India and the European Communities in *EC – Tariff Preferences (2004)* was whether the Drug Arrangements were consistent with paragraph 2(a) of the Enabling Clause, and, in particular, the requirement of non-discrimination in footnote 3 thereto, quoted above.[82] With regard to paragraph 2(a) and its footnote, the panel in *EC – Tariff Preferences (2004)* found that:

> the clear intention of the negotiators was to provide GSP equally to all developing countries and to eliminate all differentiation in preferential treatment to developing countries.[83]

As the Drug Arrangements did not provide identical tariff preferences to *all* developing countries, the panel concluded that the Drug Arrangements were inconsistent with paragraph 2(a) of the Enabling Clause and, in particular, the requirement of non-discrimination in footnote 3 thereto.[84] According to the panel, the term 'non-discriminatory' in footnote 3 requires that identical tariff preferences under GSP schemes be provided to all developing countries without differentiation.[85]

On appeal, the Appellate Body reversed this finding.[86] After a careful examination of the text and context of footnote 3 to paragraph 2(a) of the Enabling Clause, and the object and purpose of the *WTO Agreement* and the Enabling Clause, the Appellate Body came to the conclusion that:

> the term 'non-discriminatory' in footnote 3 does not prohibit developed-country Members from granting different tariffs to products originating in different GSP beneficiaries, provided that such differential tariff treatment meets the remaining conditions in the Enabling Clause. In granting such differential tariff treatment, however, preference-granting countries are required, by virtue of the term 'non-discriminatory', to ensure that identical treatment is available to all similarly situated GSP beneficiaries, that is, to all GSP beneficiaries that have the 'development, financial and trade needs' to which the treatment in question is intended to respond.[87]

In other words, a developed-country Member may grant additional preferential tariff treatment to some, and not to other, developing-country Members, as long

82 The requirement of non-discrimination is derived from the words 'non-discriminatory preferences' in fn. 3. See above, p. 321, fn. 74.
83 Panel Report, *EC – Tariff Preferences (2004)*, para. 7.144.
84 See *ibid.*, para. 7.177. 85 See *ibid.*, paras. 7.161 and 7.176.
86 See Appellate Body Report, *EC – Tariff Preferences (2004)*, para. 174.
87 See *ibid.*, para. 173.

as additional preferential tariff treatment is available to all *similarly situated* developing-country Members. *Similarly situated* developing-country Members are all those that have the development, financial and trade needs to which additional preferential tariff treatment is intended to respond. The determination of whether developing-country Members are similarly situated must be based on objective criteria. With respect to the Drug Arrangements of the European Communities, however, the Appellate Body found in *EC – Tariff Preferences (2004)* that these arrangements provided for a *closed* list of twelve identified beneficiaries and contained no criteria or standards to provide a basis for distinguishing developing-country Members which are beneficiaries under the Drug Arrangements from other developing-country Members.[88] The Appellate Body therefore upheld – albeit for very different reasons – the panel's conclusion that the European Communities 'failed to demonstrate that the Drug Arrangements are justified under paragraph 2(a) of the Enabling Clause'.[89]

3 MOST-FAVOURED-NATION TREATMENT UNDER THE GATS

As mentioned above, the MFN treatment obligation is also one of the basic provisions of the GATS. This section examines: (1) the nature of the MFN treatment obligation provided for in Article II:1 of the GATS; and (2) the test of consistency with Article II:1.

3.1 Nature of the MFN Treatment Obligation of Article II:1 of the GATS

Article II:1 of the GATS states as follows:

> With respect to any measure covered by this Agreement, each Member shall accord immediately and unconditionally to services and service suppliers of any other Member treatment no less favourable than that it accords to like services and service suppliers of any other country.

88 See *ibid.*, paras. 187 and 188.

89 *Ibid.*, para. 189. On 27 June 2005, the EC adopted Council Regulation (EC) No. 980/2005, replacing Council Regulation (EC) No. 221/2003 and establishing a new scheme of preferential tariff arrangements. The preferential tariff arrangements were reduced from five to three: (1) the 'General Arrangements'; (2) the 'special incentive arrangement for sustainable development and good governance' (GSP+); (3) the 'Everything But Arms' (EBA) arrangement. While the 'General Arrangements' provided tariff preferences for all developing countries, the GSP+ was available only to developing countries that have ratified and implemented a number of international conventions set out in Annex 3 to the Regulation. The GSP+ system replaced the Drug Arrangements (and the special incentive arrangements referred to above) so as to comply with the Appellate Body's ruling in *EC – Tariff Preferences (2004)*. It applied to 'vulnerable' countries meeting a set of objective criteria set out in Articles 9 and 10 of the Regulation. Note that the following countries are eligible for GSP+: Bolivia, Colombia, Costa Rica, Ecuador, El Salvador, Georgia, Guatemala, Honduras, Moldova, Mongolia, Nicaragua, Panama, Peru, Sri Lanka and Venezuela. Finally, the EBA arrangement extends duty-free and quota-free market access to least-developed countries, save for arms and ammunition. The Regulation applied from 1 January 2006 until 31 December 2008, but the GSP+ provisions were already applied from 1 July 2005. See WTO Secretariat, *Trade Policy Review Report – European Communities*, WT/TPR/S/177, dated 22 January 2007, 35–6.

Article II:1 prohibits discrimination *between* like services and service suppliers from different countries. In other words, Article II:1 prohibits WTO Member Richland from giving services and service suppliers from WTO Member Newland treatment less favourable than the treatment it gives to like services and service suppliers from any other WTO Members or other country. The principal purpose of the MFN treatment obligation of Article II:1 of the GATS is to ensure all WTO Members *equality of opportunity* to supply like services, regardless of the origin of the services and service suppliers.

Article II:1 is supplemented by a number of other MFN or MFN-like provisions found elsewhere in the GATS. These provisions include: Article VII (regarding recognition of education or experience obtained); Article VIII (regarding monopolies and exclusive service suppliers); Article X (regarding future rules on emergency safeguard measures); Article XII (regarding balance of payments measures); and Article XXI (regarding the modification of schedules).[90] Article XIV of the GATS, and in particular the chapeau of this 'general exceptions' provision, also contains an MFN-like obligation.[91]

The Appellate Body in *EC – Bananas III (1997)* found that the MFN treatment obligation of Article II:1 of the GATS applies both to *de jure* and to *de facto* discrimination.[92] The Appellate Body came to this conclusion in spite of the fact that Article II of the GATS, unlike Article XVII thereof, does not explicitly state that it applies to *de facto* discrimination.[93] The European Communities had argued in this case that, if the negotiators of the GATS had wanted Article II:1 to cover also *de facto* discrimination, they would have explicitly said so. The Appellate Body disagreed and ruled:

> [t]he obligation imposed by Article II is unqualified. The ordinary meaning of this provision does not exclude *de facto* discrimination. Moreover, if Article II was not applicable to *de facto* discrimination, it would not be difficult – and, indeed, it would be a good deal easier in the case of trade in services, than in the case of trade in goods – to devise discriminatory measures aimed at circumventing the basic purpose of that Article.[94]

An example of *de jure* discrimination inconsistent with Article II:1 would be a regulation of WTO Member Richland on content quota for TV broadcasting that gives TV series produced in Spain (such as *Amar en tiempos revueltos*)[95] preference over TV series produced in other WTO Members (such as *Friends*). Such a measure discriminates explicitly on the basis of the origin of the service and therefore constitutes *de jure* discrimination. An example of *de facto*

90 See also Article 5(a) of the GATS *Annex on Telecommunications* and the Preamble to the GATS *Understanding on Commitments in Financial Services*.

91 See below, pp. 615–17.

92 With respect to the concepts of *de jure* and *de facto* discrimination, see above, pp. 309–10.

93 See below, p. 335.

94 Appellate Body Report, *EC – Bananas III (1997)*, para. 233. See also Appellate Body Report, *Argentina – Financial Services (2016)*, para. 6.105.

95 Translation: 'To love in troubled times'.

discrimination inconsistent with Article II:1 may be a regulation of Richland on content quota for TV broadcasting that gives TV series with a storyline based on historical events (such as *Amar en tiempos revueltos*) preference over TV series with a storyline based on silly everyday events of life (such as *Friends*). Although this measure does not distinguish between the services on the basis of national origin, it may *de facto* offer less favourable treatment to some WTO Members than to others because they do not, or are less likely to, make TV series with a storyline based on historical events.[96]

3.2 MFN Treatment Test of Article II:1 of the GATS

As the Appellate Body found in *Canada – Autos (2000)*, the wording of Article II:1 of the GATS suggests that the test of consistency with the MFN treatment obligation of this provision proceeds in *three* steps.[97] There are three questions which need to be answered to determine whether or not a measure is consistent with the MFN treatment obligation of Article II:1 of the GATS, namely:

- whether the measure at issue falls *within the scope of application* of *Article II:1* of the GATS;
- whether the services and service suppliers concerned are '*like*'; and
- whether like services and service suppliers are accorded *treatment no less favourable.*

Below, each element of this three-tier test of consistency will be discussed in turn.[98]

To date, WTO Members have been found to have acted inconsistently with the MFN treatment obligation of Article II:1 of the GATS in three disputes.[99]

3.2.1 Measure Covered by Article II:1

The first element of the test of consistency with the MFN treatment obligation of Article II:1 of the GATS is whether the measure at issue is covered by, i.e. falls within the scope of application of, Article II:1 of the GATS. To answer this question, one must assess whether the measure at issue is a measure to which the GATS applies. However, some measures to which the GATS applies are exempted from the MFN treatment obligation of Article II:1. One must, therefore, also always assess whether the measure at issue is not one of the measures exempted from the MFN treatment obligation.

96 It is assumed here that TV series with a storyline based on historical events *and* TV series with a storyline based on silly everyday events of life are 'like' services. For the discussion on the concept of 'likeness' of services and services suppliers under Article II:2 of the GATS, see below, pp. 332–5.

97 See Appellate Body Report, *Canada – Autos (2000)*, paras. 170–1. See also Panel Report, *Argentina – Financial Services (2015)*, para 7.149.

98 See below, pp. 327–38.

99 See *EC – Bananas III (1997)*; *EC – Bananas III (Article 21.5 – Ecuador) (1999)*; and *EC – Bananas III (US) (Article 22.6 – EC) (1999)*. There was no finding of inconsistency in *Canada – Autos (2000)*; and *Argentina – Financial Services (2016)*. In each of these cases the Appellate Body reversed the panel's finding of inconsistency.

Article I:1 of the GATS states with regard to the measures to which the obligations of the GATS apply that:

> [t]his Agreement applies to measures by Members affecting trade in services. Therefore, for the GATS to apply to a measure, that measure must be: (1) a measure by a Member; and (2) a measure affecting trade in services.

A 'measure by a Member' is a very broad concept. Article XXVIII(a) of the GATS defines a 'measure' for the purposes of the GATS to be:

> any measure by a Member, whether in the form of a law, regulation, rule, procedure, decision, administrative action, or any other form.

Article I:3(a) of the GATS further clarifies that 'measures by Members' means measures taken by central, regional or local governments and authorities.[100] Measures taken by non-governmental bodies are also 'measures by Members' when they are taken in the exercise of powers delegated by central, regional or local governments or authorities.[101] For example, in many WTO Members, the government has delegated the regulation of the legal or medical profession to the relevant professional association and, consequently, a measure taken by such association in the exercise of this delegated authority is considered to fall within the scope of 'measures by Members' within the meaning of Article II:1 of the GATS. In brief, a 'measure by a Member' within the meaning of Article II:1 can therefore be a national parliamentary law as well as municipal decrees or rules adopted by professional associations.

With regard to the concept of 'measures affecting trade in services', note that Article XXVIII(c) of the GATS gives a number of examples of such measures, including measures in respect of the purchase, payment or use of a service and measures in respect of the access to services which are required to be offered to the public generally. The concept of a 'measure affecting trade in services' was clarified by the Appellate Body in *Canada – Autos (2000)*. The measure at issue in that case was an import duty exemption accorded by Canada to imports of motor vehicles by certain manufacturers. The complainants, the European Communities and Japan, argued that this measure was inconsistent with Article II:1 of the GATS as it accorded 'less favourable treatment' to certain Members' services and service suppliers than to those of other Members. The panel found that the import duty exemption was indeed inconsistent with Article II:1 of the GATS. In addition to appealing this finding, Canada challenged, as a threshold matter, the panel's finding that the measure at issue fell within the scope of application of Article II:1 of the GATS. According to Canada, the measure at issue was not a measure 'affecting trade in services'. The Appellate Body stated that two key issues must be examined in order to determine whether a measure is

100 See also above, pp. 176–7. 101 See *ibid*.

one 'affecting trade in services', namely: (1) whether there is 'trade in services' in the sense of Article I:2; and (2) whether the measure at issue 'affects' such trade in services within the meaning of Article I:1.[102]

With respect to the question of whether there is 'trade in services', note that the GATS does not define what a 'service' is. Article I:3(b) of the GATS, however, states that the term 'services' includes:

any service in any sector except services supplied in the exercise of governmental authority.

'Services supplied in the exercise of governmental authority' are defined in Article I:3(c) of the GATS as any services which are supplied neither on a commercial basis nor in competition with one or more service suppliers. It is clear that what are 'services supplied in the exercise of governmental authority' differ from WTO Member to WTO Member. For most WTO Members, police protection and penitentiary services are 'services supplied in the exercise of governmental authority'. However, for a growing number of WTO Members, services that were traditionally considered to be 'services supplied in the exercise of governmental authority', such as primary healthcare, basic education, mail delivery, rail transport and garbage disposal, have in recent years been subject to privatisation, and, consequently, measures affecting such services now fall within the scope of application of the GATS.[103] Services which the government offers on a commercial basis and/or in competition with one or more (private) service suppliers are not 'services supplied in the exercise of governmental authority' and, therefore, 'services' within the meaning of Article I:3(b).

While the GATS does not define 'services', Article I:2 thereof defines 'trade in services' as 'the supply of a service' in any one of four listed 'modes of supply'. Article I:2 states:

For the purpose of this Agreement, trade in services is defined as the supply of a service:

(a) from the territory of one Member into the territory of any other Member;
(b) in the territory of one Member to the service consumer of any other Member;
(c) by a service supplier of one Member, through commercial presence in the territory of any other Member;
(d) by a service supplier of one Member, through presence of natural persons of a Member in the territory of any other Member.

These four modes of supply of services are commonly referred to as:

- 'cross border supply' (mode 1), such as legal advice given by a lawyer in Richland to a client in Newland;

102 Appellate Body Report, *Canada – Autos (2000)*, para. 155. Note that the Appellate Body eventually reversed the panel's conclusion that the import duty exemption was inconsistent with the requirements of Article II:1 of the GATS. However, it did so, not because it came to the conclusion that Canada acted consistently with its MFN treatment obligation, but because the panel failed to substantiate its conclusion that the import duty exemption was inconsistent with Article II:1 of the GATS. See *ibid.*, paras. 182–3.

103 Note also that many measures affecting services in the air transport sector do not fall within the scope of application of the GATS. See GATS *Annex on Air Transport Services*, para. 2.

- 'consumption abroad' (mode 2), such as medical treatment given by a doctor in Richland to a patient from Newland who comes to Richland for treatment;
- 'commercial presence' (mode 3), such as financial services supplied in Newland by a bank from Richland through a branch office established in Newland;[104] and
- 'presence of natural persons' (mode 4), such as the programming services supplied in Newland by a computer programmer from Richland, who travels to Newland to supply such services.

Furthermore, Article XXVIII(b) makes clear that the 'supply of a service' includes not only the sale of a service, but also its production, distribution, marketing and delivery.

Clearly, the concept of 'trade in services' within the meaning of Article I:1 is very broad. The panel in *Mexico – Telecoms (2004)* clarified the meaning of two of the modes of supply, namely, 'cross-border supply' and 'commercial presence'. The question in *Mexico – Telecoms (2004)* was whether telecommunication services, provided by a United States service provider to consumers in Mexico without operating or being present in Mexico, could be considered services supplied 'cross-border' within the meaning of Article I:2(a) of the GATS. The panel found that Article I:2(a) does not require the presence of the supplier in the territory of the country where the service is provided.[105] With regard to 'commercial presence' within the meaning of Article I:2(c), the panel stated:

> The definition of services supplied through a commercial presence makes explicit the location of the service supplier. It provides that a service supplier has a commercial presence – any type of business or professional establishment – *in the territory* of any other Member. The definition is silent with respect to any other territorial requirement (as in cross-border supply under mode 1) or nationality of the service consumer (as in consumption abroad under mode 2). Supply of a service through commercial presence would therefore not exclude a service that originates in the territory in which a commercial presence is established (such as Mexico), but is delivered into the territory of any other Member (such as the United States).[106]

With regard to the question of whether the measure at issue *affects* trade in services within the meaning of Article I:1, the Appellate Body clarified the term 'affecting' in *EC – Bananas III (1997)* as follows:

> In our view, the use of the term 'affecting' reflects the intent of the drafters to give a broad reach to the GATS. The ordinary meaning of the word 'affecting' implies a measure that has 'an effect on', which indicates a broad scope of application. This interpretation is further reinforced by the conclusions of previous panels that the term 'affecting' in the context of Article III of the GATT is wider in scope than such terms as 'regulating' or 'governing'.[107]

104 Note that, pursuant to Article XXVIII(d) of the GATS, 'commercial presence' means any type of business or professional establishment, including through the constitution, acquisition or maintenance of a juridical person, or the creation or maintenance of a branch or a representative office, within the territory of a Member for the purpose of supplying a service.

105 The panel noted that the words of Article I:2(a) do not address the service supplier or specify where the services supplier must operate, or be present in some way, much less imply any degree of presence of the supplier in the territory into which the service is supplied. See Panel Report, *Mexico – Telecoms (2004)*, para. 7.30.

106 *Ibid.*, para. 7.375.

107 Appellate Body Report, *EC – Bananas III (1997)*, para. 220.

For a measure to affect trade in services, the measure need not regulate or govern the trade in, i.e. the supply of, services. A measure is covered by the GATS if it *affects* trade in services, even though the measure may regulate other matters, such as trade in goods.[108] A measure affects trade in services when the measure bears upon 'the conditions of competition in supply of a service'.[109]

In brief, the concept of 'measures by Members affecting trade in services' is, in all respects, a concept with a broad meaning.[110] Consequently, the scope of measures to which the MFN treatment obligation applies is likewise broad.

As noted above, to answer the question whether the measure at issue is covered by Article II:1, it does not suffice to determine whether that measure is a measure to which the GATS applies. It must also be established whether or not the measure at issue is exempted from the MFN treatment obligation of Article II:1 of the GATS. Unlike the GATT 1994, the GATS allows Members *to exempt* measures from the MFN treatment obligation. Article II:2 of the GATS provides:

> A Member may maintain a measure inconsistent with paragraph 1 provided that such a measure is listed in, and meets the conditions of, the Annex on Article II Exemptions.

Members could list measures in the Annex on Article II Exemptions *until* the date of entry into force of the *WTO Agreement*. For original Members, this meant until 1 January 1995.[111] About two-thirds of WTO Members have listed MFN exemptions. In total, Members have listed over 400 exempted measures. The exempted measures often concern maritime transport, audiovisual, financial and business services, bilateral investment treaties and measures regarding the presence of natural persons. The list of exempted measures that a particular Member has included in the Annex on Article II Exemptions can be found – and easily consulted – on the WTO website.[112] Note, by way of example, that the European Union included in its list of exempted measures:

> Measures granting the benefit of any support programmes (such as Action Plan for Advanced Television Services, MEDIA or EURIMAGES) to audiovisual works, and suppliers of such works, meeting certain European origin criteria.[113]

108 See Panel Reports, *EC – Bananas III (1997)*, para. 7.285.

109 See *ibid.*, para. 7.281. Regarding the question whether measures adopted by regional and local governments and authorities can 'affect the supply of a service', see Panel Report, *US – Gambling (2005)*, para. 6.252. With regard to the function of the term 'affecting' in the context of Article I:1 of the GATS, see Appellate Body Report, *US – FSC (Article 21.5 – EC) (2002)*, para. 209.

110 Note that pursuant to the GATS *Annex on Movement of Natural Persons Supplying Services under the Agreement*, measures regarding citizenship, residence or employment on a permanent basis do not fall within the scope of application of the GATS in spite of the fact that such measures are likely affect mode 4 trade in services.

111 For WTO Members that have acceded to the WTO pursuant to Article XII of the *WTO Agreement* after 1 January 1995, exemptions from the MFN treatment obligation of Article II:1 of the GATS were part of their accession negotiations and needed to be agreed on before accession. After the *WTO Agreement* has entered into force for a particular Member, that Member can only exempt a measure from the application of the MFN obligation under Article II:1 by obtaining a waiver from the MFN obligation pursuant to Article IX:3 of the *WTO Agreement* (see paragraph 2 of the Annex on Article II Exemptions). On waivers, see above, pp. 125–8.

112 See www.wto.org.

113 See European Communities and Their Member States, *Final List of Article II (MFN) Exemptions*, GATS/EL/31, 15 April 1994.

This allows the European Union to give support to, for example, Canadian film-makers, while denying such support to US filmmakers.

Paragraph 6 of the Annex on Article II Exemptions states that, in principle, the exemptions should not exceed ten years. Therefore, one might have expected that most, if not all, exemptions under Article II:2 would have come to an end by 1 January 2005.[114] However, this did not happen. Relying on the language of paragraph 6 (which states that 'in principle' exemptions 'should not' exceed ten years), many Members continue to apply the exemptions they listed in the Annex on Article II Exemptions.

Pursuant to paragraph 3 of the Annex on Article II Exemptions, all exemptions granted for a period of more than five years are reviewed by the Council for Trade in Services. As stated in paragraph 4 of the Annex, the Council examines whether the conditions that created the need for the exemption still prevail. If the Council concludes that these conditions are no longer present, the Member concerned would arguably be obliged to accord MFN treatment in respect of the measure previously exempted from this obligation. Perhaps not surprisingly,[115] the reviews that took place in 2000, 2004–5 and 2010–11 did not result in any finding that a listed exemption was no longer justified.[116] As observed by Hong Kong, China, during the 2010–11 review, 'most, if not all, MFN exemptions that had been listed, persisted'.[117]

Finally, note that, pursuant to Article II:3 of the GATS, a measure that grants advantages to adjacent countries in order to facilitate trade in services between contiguous frontier zones is not subject to the MFN treatment obligation of Article II:1. For Article II:3 to apply, it is required, however, that the services concerned are both locally produced and consumed. An example of such services would be taxi services between Geneva and 'la France voisine' (i.e. neighbouring France).

3.2.2 'Like Services and Service Suppliers'

Once it has been established that the measure at issue is covered by Article II:1 of the GATS, the second element of the three-tier test of consistency with the MFN treatment obligation of Article II:1 of the GATS comes into play. Namely, it must be determined whether the services and services suppliers concerned are 'like services and like service suppliers'. It is only between 'like services and service suppliers' that the MFN treatment obligation applies and that discrimination within the meaning of Article II:1 of the GATS is prohibited. Services and service suppliers that are not 'like' may be treated differently; different

114 This is so at least for original Members. For Members that acceded to the WTO pursuant to Article XII of the *WTO Agreement*, the date on which the ten-year period expires will be later than 1 January 2005.

115 Note that, in practice, the Council on Trade in Services makes its decisions by consensus, and a finding that an exemption is no longer justified would thus require the consent of the Member that listed the exemption. On WTO decision-making, see above, pp. 145–56.

116 See S/C/M/44, dated 21 June 2000; S/C/M/76, dated 4 February 2005; S/C/M/78, dated 17 May 2005; S/C/M/79, dated 16 August 2005; and S/C/M/105, dated 6 June 2011. The next review will take place in the second half of 2016. See S/C/M/126, dated 19 April 2016.

117 See S/C/M/105, dated 6 June 2011, para. 31.

treatment of services and service suppliers that are not 'like' will not constitute discrimination within the meaning of Article II:1. For the application of the MFN treatment obligation of Article II:1, it is therefore important to be able to determine whether, for example, movie actors are 'like' stage actors, whether the distribution of books is 'like' the distribution of e-books; whether doctors with a German medical degree are 'like' doctors with a Chinese medical degree; whether Internet gambling is 'like' casino gambling; and whether a 500-partner law firm is 'like' a sole legal practitioner.

With regard to the determination of 'likeness' of services and service suppliers under Article II:1 of the GATS, the Appellate Body noted in *Argentina – Financial Services (2016)*:

> While Article II:1 refers to 'treatment no less favourable', we note that Article II:3 refers to 'advantages'. An 'advantage' is '[t]he fact or state of being in a better position with respect to another'. Being in a better position as compared to another is closely related to the concept of competition. This suggests that, also in the context of Article II of the GATS, the determination of 'likeness' of services and service suppliers must focus on the competitive relationship of the services and service suppliers at issue.[118]

The Appellate Body further stated that the 'likeness' of services and service suppliers under Article II:1 of the GATS can only be determined on a case-by-case basis, taking into account the specific circumstances of the particular case.

In reply to the question whether in determining 'likeness' under Article II:1 of the GATS a panel has to examine, and make findings on, the 'likeness' of both the services and the service suppliers concerned, the Appellate Body clarified in *Argentina – Financial Services (2016)*:

> In our view, the reference to 'services and service suppliers' indicates that considerations relating to both the service and the service supplier are relevant for determining 'likeness' under Articles II:1 and XVII:1 of the GATS. The assessment of likeness of services should not be undertaken in isolation from considerations relating to the service suppliers, and, conversely, the assessment of likeness of service suppliers should not be undertaken in isolation from considerations relating to the likeness of the services they provide. We see the phrase 'like services and service suppliers' as an integrated element for the likeness analysis under Articles II:1 and XVII:1, respectively. Accordingly, separate findings with respect to the 'likeness' of services, on the one hand, and the 'likeness' of service suppliers, on the other hand, are not required ... In any event, in a holistic analysis of 'likeness', considerations relating to both the service and the service supplier will be relevant, albeit to varying degrees, depending on the circumstances of each case.[119]

Further, the Appellate Body also provided guidance on how a panel should proceed to determine 'likeness' of services and service suppliers in the particular context of Article II:1 of the GATS. It noted:

> We consider that the analysis of 'likeness' serves the same purpose in the context of both trade in goods and trade in services, namely, to determine whether the products or services and service suppliers, respectively, are in a competitive relationship with each other. Thus,

118 See Appellate Body Report, *Argentina – Financial Services (2016)*, para. 6.29.

119 See *ibid.*, para. 6.29.   120 See *ibid.*, para. 6.31.

> to the extent that the criteria for assessing 'likeness' traditionally employed as analytical tools in the context of trade in goods are relevant for assessing the competitive relationship of services and service suppliers, these criteria may be employed also in assessing 'likeness' in the context of trade in services, provided that they are adapted as appropriate to account for the specific characteristics of trade in services.[120]

As noted previously, the term 'services' is not defined in the GATS, but Article I:3(c) states that 'services' includes 'any service in any sector except services supplied in the exercise of governmental authority'. The term 'service supplier' is defined in the GATS. Article XXVIII(g) provides that a 'service supplier' is 'any person who supplies a service', including natural and legal persons as well as service suppliers providing their services through forms of commercial presence, such as a branch or a representative office.

The panels in *EC – Bananas III (1997)* and *Canada – Autos (2000)* found that, to the extent that service suppliers provide 'like services', they are 'like service suppliers'.[121] However, the question arises whether this is always the case, or whether, for example, the size of the service suppliers, their assets and the nature and extent of their expertise must also be taken into account when deciding whether service suppliers providing 'like services' are 'like service suppliers'.[122] In *Argentina – Financial Services (2016)*, the Appellate Body clarified that the following could be relevant for determining 'likeness' under the GATS: (1) characteristics of services and service suppliers; (2) consumers' preferences in respect of services and service suppliers; and (3) tariff classification and description of services under, for instance, the UN Central Product Classification (CPC).[123] As in the context of trade in goods, however, these criteria for analysing 'likeness' of services and service suppliers are 'simply analytical tools to assist in the task of examining the relevant evidence'.[124] They are neither a treaty-mandated nor a closed list of criteria.[125]

While the Appellate Body suggested that the criteria employed for assessing likeness in the context of trade in goods are also suitable in case of trade in services, it noted that 'what is being compared for *likeness* is different in the context of trade in goods and trade in services'. Where Articles II:1 and XVII:1 of the GATS refer to 'like services and service suppliers', Articles I:1, III:2, and III:4 of the GATT 1994, refer to 'like products' only and do not include a reference to 'like producers'.[126] Further, as defined in Article I:2 of GATS, different modes of supply exist only in trade in services and not in trade in goods, and, accordingly, the analysis of 'likeness' of services and service suppliers may require additional considerations of whether or how this analysis is affected by the mode(s) of service supply.[127]

121 See Panel Report, *EC – Bananas III (1997)*, para. 7.322; and Panel Report, *Canada – Autos (2000)*, para. 10.248.
122 See in this regard the statement regarding 'likeness' under Article XVII:1 of the GATS made by the panel in *China – Electronic Payment Services (2012)*, para. 7.705.
123 Appellate Body Report, *Argentina – Financial Services (2016)*, para. 6.32.
124 See *ibid*. See also Appellate Body Report, *EC – Asbestos*, para. 102, discussed below, pp. 357–63.
125 See Appellate Body Report, *Argentina – Financial Services (2016)*, para. 6.32.
126 See *ibid*., para. 6.27. 127 *Ibid*., para. 6.33.

With regard to the presumption of likeness in the context of trade in services, the Appellate Body ruled in *Argentina – Financial Services (2016)* that such presumption can be validly made only in cases where a measure provides for a distinction based *exclusively* on origin.[128] In such cases the complainant is not required to establish 'likeness' on the basis of the relevant criteria as discussed above.[129] However, the Appellate Body cautioned that the scope of this presumption under the GATS is more limited than it is under the GATT 1994, and involves greater complexity.

3.2.3 Treatment No Less Favourable

The third and final element of the test of consistency with the MFN treatment obligation of Article II:1 of the GATS relates to the treatment accorded to 'like services and service suppliers'. A WTO Member must accord, immediately and unconditionally, to services and service suppliers of any given WTO Member 'treatment no less favourable' than the treatment it accords to 'like services and service suppliers' of any other country. Article II of the GATS does not provide any guidance as to the meaning of the concept of 'treatment no less favourable'. However, as discussed below, Article XVII of the GATS on the national treatment obligation contains guidance on the meaning of the concept of 'treatment no less favourable'.[130] Article XVII:3 states:

> Formally identical or formally different treatment shall be considered to be less favourable if it modifies the conditions of competition in favour of services or service suppliers of the Member compared to the like services or service suppliers of any other Member.

In the context of Article XVII, a measure thus accords 'less favourable treatment' if it *modifies* the *conditions of competition* in favour of the domestic service or service supplier. As the Appellate Body cautioned in *EC – Bananas III (1997)*, it should not be assumed that, in interpreting Article II:1, and in particular the concept of 'treatment no less favourable', the guidance of Article XVII equally applies to Article II:1. However, as noted above, the Appellate Body has already concluded that the concept of 'treatment no less favourable' in Article II:1 and Article XVII of the GATS should be interpreted to include both *de facto* as well as *de jure* discrimination although only Article XVII states so explicitly.[131] Moreover, note that the panel in *EC – Bananas III (Article 21.5 – Ecuador) (1999)* found that the EC import licensing measures were inconsistent with the

128 In *Argentina – Financial Services (2016)*, the panel found that the differing treatment of services and service suppliers from cooperative countries as opposed to services and service suppliers from non-cooperative countries inherent in the eight measures at issue was origin-related and that the services and service suppliers of cooperative and non-cooperative countries could therefore be presumed to be 'like'. The Appellate Body, however, disagreed with the panel's finding of 'likeness' because the panel did not find that the measures at issue made a distinction based *exclusively* on origin. See Appellate Body Report, *Argentina – Financial Services (2016)*, paras. 6.60–6.61 and 6.70.

129 See *ibid.*, paras. 6.38–6.41.

130 See below, pp. 408–12.

131 See Appellate Body Report, *EC – Bananas III (1997)*, para. 234. See also Appellate Body Report, *Argentina – Financial Services (2016)*, para. 6.105.

MFN treatment obligation of Article II:1, because Ecuador, the complainant, had shown that:

> its service suppliers do not have opportunities to obtain access to import licences on terms equal to those enjoyed by service suppliers of EC/ACP origin under the revised regime and carried on from the previous regime.[132]

Note also that the Appellate Body stated in *EC – Bananas III (1997)* that it saw no specific authority in Article II:1 of the GATS for the proposition, advanced by the European Communities, that the 'aims and effects' of a measure are relevant in determining whether that measure is inconsistent with the MFN treatment obligation of Article II:1.[133] The Appellate Body rejected the EC's argument that its licensing procedure, one of the measures at issue, was not inconsistent with Article II:1 because this measure 'pursued entirely legitimate policies' and 'was not inherently discriminatory in design or effect'.[134]

In *Argentina – Financial Services (2016)*, Argentina, the respondent, argued that Panama had not established a *prima facie* case that services and service suppliers of non-cooperative countries receive less favourable treatment, since Panama enjoys cooperative country status and thus receives the most-favoured-nation treatment.[135] According to Argentina, the treatment of services and service suppliers of the complainant should be compared with the treatment accorded to 'the services and service suppliers that are the subject of the complaint', whether domestic (in the case of claims under Article XVII of the GATS) or of another origin (in the case of claims under Article II of the GATS).[136] Panama contended that Articles II and XVII refer to the treatment accorded to 'any other Member'.[137] The panel ruled that: 'determining the existence of less favourable treatment does not necessarily imply comparing the treatment given to services and service suppliers of the complaining Member'.[138] The panel concluded that: 'the submission of claims under Article II:1 of the GATS does not require that the alleged less favourable treatment that is the subject of the complaint must refer to the complainant party in this dispute, i.e. Panama'.[139]

The panel further considered that, like under Article 2.1 of the *TBT Agreement*, regulatory aspects, and in particular the regulatory framework in which service suppliers operate and services are offered, must be taken into account to determine whether a measure accords treatment less favourable under Article II:1 of the GATS. In coming to this conclusion, the panel placed much importance on the fact that the GATS refers to both services and

132 Panel Report, *EC – Bananas III (Article 21.5 – Ecuador) (1999)*, para. 6.133.
133 See Appellate Body Report, *EC – Bananas III (1997)*, para. 241. The Appellate Body came to the same finding regarding the national treatment obligation of Article XVII:1 of the GATS. See below, p. 410.
134 Appellate Body Report, *EC – Bananas III (1997)*, para. 240.
135 See Panel Report, *Argentina – Financial Services (2016)*, para. 7.189.
136 See *ibid.*, para. 7.190. 137 See *ibid.*, para. 7.191. 138 *See ibid.*, para. 7.192.
139 See *ibid.*, para. 7.196. 140 See *ibid.*, para. 7.232.

service suppliers (while the GATT 1994 refers only to products (and not to producers)).[140]

The Appellate Body disagreed and reversed this finding of the panel. The Appellate Body observed that the GATS provides certain flexibilities to Members when they undertake their GATS commitments and qualify their obligations by exceptions or other derogations contained in the GATS and its annexes. The Appellate Body referred in this regard to Article XX of the GATS, pursuant to which a Member may limit its market access and national treatment commitments to the service sectors or subsectors, and to the modes of supply, that it wishes to liberalise and inscribe in its Services Schedule.[141] The Appellate Body also referred to the general and security exceptions from obligations under Article XIV and Article XV *bis* of the GATS, discussed in Chapter 8, and deviations from obligations provided for in various annexes to GATS, such as paragraph 2(a) of the *Annex on Financial Services*, also discussed in Chapter 8.[142] The Appellate Body stated in *Argentina – Financial Services (2016)*:

> Through these flexibilities and exceptions, the GATS seeks to strike a balance between a Member's obligations assumed under the Agreement and that Member's right to pursue national policy objective ... Where a measure is inconsistent with the non-discrimination provisions, regulatory aspects or concerns that could potentially justify such a measure are more appropriately addressed in the context of the relevant exceptions. Addressing them in the context of the non-discrimination provisions would upset the existing balance under the GATS.[143]

The Appellate Body thus ruled that the legal standard of 'treatment no less favourable' in Articles II:1 and XVII involves an assessment of whether the measure modifies the conditions of competition in favour of the services or service suppliers of any other Member.[144] The Appellate Body specifically noted that:

> this legal standard does not contemplate a separate step of analysis regarding whether the 'regulatory aspects' relating to service suppliers could 'convert[]' the measure's detrimental impact on the conditions of competition into 'treatment no less favourable'.[145]

However, this does not mean that the 'regulatory aspects' are totally irrelevant in the assessment of whether the measure at issue accords 'treatment no less favourable'. As the Appellate Body stated in *Argentina – Financial Services (2016)*:

> Such assessment must begin with a careful scrutiny of the measure, including consideration of the design, structure and expected operation of the measure at issue. In such assessment, to the extent that evidence relating to the regulatory aspects has a bearing on conditions of competition, it might be taken into account, subject to the particular circumstances of a

141 See Appellate Body Report, *Argentina – Financial Services (2016)*, para. 6.112.

142 See *ibid.*, paras. 6.113–6.114. 143 See *ibid.*, para. 6.115. 144 See *ibid.*, para. 6.111.

145 *Ibid.* The Appellate Body referred here to the panel's finding in para. 7.514 of the Panel Report.

case, and as an integral part of a panel's analysis of whether the measure at issue modifies the conditions of competition to the detriment of like services or service suppliers of any other Member.[146]

3.3 Deviations from the Most-Favoured-Nation Treatment Obligation under the GATS

Two deviations from the MFN treatment obligation under Article II:1 of the GATS must be briefly mentioned as part of this chapter, namely: (1) the 'LDC services waiver'; and (2) Article VII of the GATS regarding recognition of diplomas and certificates.

First, the GATS does not have an equivalent of the Enabling Clause of the GATT 1994, discussed above.[147] However, the Ministerial Conference in Geneva in December 2011 adopted the 'LDC services waiver', which was subsequently 'operationalized' at the Bali Ministerial Conference in 2013 and extended in time at the Nairobi Ministerial Conference in 2015.[148] Under this temporary waiver, the obligations under Article II:1 of the GATS are waived, allowing WTO Members to grant preferential treatment to services and service suppliers from least-developed-country Members.[149] The preferential treatment covered by the 'LDC services waiver' takes the form of, for example, waiving fees for business and employment visas for services suppliers from least-developed countries, and extending the duration of their authorised stay in the markets of preference granting Members.[150]

Second, pursuant to Article VII of the GATS, entitled 'Recognition', a Member may recognise the education or experience obtained, requirements met or licences or certificates granted in a particular country. Such recognition may be based upon an agreement or arrangements with the country concerned or may be accorded autonomously. In either case, such recognition, when it benefits the services or service suppliers of one or some WTO Members but not the like services or service suppliers of other WTO Members, will be consistent with the MFN treatment obligation if it meets the requirements of Article VII. Article VII:2, first

146 See *ibid.*, para. 6.127. 147 See section 2.3 above.

148 See Geneva Ministerial Conference, *Preferential Treatment to Services and Service Suppliers of Least Developed Countries*, Decision of 17 December 2011, WT/L/847, dated 19 December 2011; Bali Ministerial Conference, *Operationalization of the Waiver Concerning Preferential Treatment to Services and Service Suppliers of Least-Developed Countries*, Decision of 7 December 2013, WT/MIN(13)/43, WT/L/918, dated 11 December 2013; and Nairobi Ministerial Conference, *Implementation of Preferential Treatment in favour of Services and Service Suppliers of Least Developed Countries and Increasing LDC Participation in Services Trade*, Decision of 19 December 2015, WT/MIN(15)/48, WT/L/847, dated 21 December 2015.

149 The waiver was originally granted for fifteen years, to 2026, but was extended at the Nairobi Ministerial Conference to 2030. At the meeting of the Council for Trade in Services, held on 18 March 2016, the Chairman took note of notifications from twenty-three WTO Members in respect of the LDC services waiver. See Note by the Secretariat, *Report of the Meeting Held on 18 March 2016*, Council for Trade in Services, S/C/M/126 dated 19 April 2016, para. 3.3.

150 See *ibid.*

sentence, requires a WTO Member, which has negotiated a recognition agreement or arrangement with another Member, to afford 'adequate opportunity' for other interested Members to negotiate their accession to such an agreement or arrangement or to negotiate a comparable one with it. Article VII:2, second sentence, provides that a WTO Member, which accords recognition autonomously, must afford 'adequate opportunity' for any other Member to demonstrate that education, experience, licences or certifications obtained or requirements met in that other Member's territory should be recognised. Moreover, Article VII:3 states:

> A Member shall not accord recognition in a manner which would constitute a means of discrimination between countries in the application of its standards or criteria for the authorization, licensing or certification of services suppliers, or a disguised restriction on trade in services.

Recognition under Article VII is further discussed in Chapter 7.[151]

4 SUMMARY

There are two main rules of non-discrimination in WTO law: the most-favoured-nation (MFN) treatment obligation, discussed in this chapter, and the national treatment obligation, discussed in the next chapter. In simple terms, an MFN treatment obligation relates to whether a country favours some countries over others. An MFN treatment obligation prohibits a country from discriminating *between* other countries. The MFN treatment obligation under WTO law applies to trade in goods as well as trade in services. The key provision that deals with the MFN treatment obligation for measures affecting trade in goods is Article I:1 of the GATT 1994. The key provision that deals with the MFN treatment obligation for measures affecting trade in services is Article II:1 of the GATS.

Article I:1 of the GATT 1994 prohibits discrimination *between* like products originating in, or destined for, different countries. The principal purpose of the MFN treatment obligation of Article I:1 is to ensure all WTO Members *equality of opportunity* to import from, or to export to, other WTO Members. The MFN treatment obligation of Article I:1 prohibits *de jure* as well as *de facto* discrimination. There are four questions which must be answered to determine whether or not a measure affecting trade in goods is consistent with the MFN treatment obligation of Article I:1, namely: (1) whether the measure at issue is a measure covered by Article I:1; (2) whether that measure grants an '*advantage*'; (3) whether the products concerned are '*like products*'; and (4) whether the advantage at issue is *accorded 'immediately and unconditionally*' to all like products concerned irrespective of their origin or destination. An important exception to the MFN treatment obligation of Article I:1 of the GATT 1994 and arguably the most significant special and differential

151 See below, p. 539.

treatment provision in WTO law is the Enabling Clause of the GATT 1994. The Enabling Clause allows, under certain conditions, developed-country Members to grant preferential tariff treatment to imports from developing countries. This exception therefore allows Members to deviate from the basic MFN treatment obligation of Article I:1 of the GATT 1994 to promote the economic development of developing-country Members. Under specific conditions, the Enabling Clause also allows developed-country Members to grant additional preferential tariff treatment to some developing countries to the exclusion of others.

Article II:1 of the GATS prohibits discrimination *between* like services and service suppliers from different countries. The principal purpose of the MFN treatment obligation of Article II:1 is to ensure all WTO Members *equality of opportunity* to supply like services. The MFN treatment obligation of Article II:1 prohibits *de jure* as well as *de facto* discrimination. There are three questions which must be answered to determine whether or not a measure is consistent with the MFN treatment obligation of Article II:1 of the GATS, namely: (1) whether the measure at issue is covered by Article II:1; (2) whether the services and service suppliers concerned are '*like*'; and (3) whether like services and service suppliers are accorded *treatment no less favourable.*

FURTHER READINGS

B. Hoekman and P. C. Mavroidis, 'MFN Clubs and Scheduling Additional Commitments in the GATT: Learning from the GATS', Robert Schuman Centre for Advanced Studies Research Paper No. RSCAS 2016/06, January 2016.

A. M. Johnston and M. J. Trebilcock, 'Fragmentation in International Trade Law: Insights from the Global Investment Regime', *World Trade Review*, 2013, 12(4), 621–52.

J. Gowa and R. Hicks, 'The Most-Favored Nation rule in principle and practice: discrimination in the GATT', *Review of International Organizations*, 2012, 7, 247–66.

D. McRae, 'MFN in the GATT and the WTO', *Asian Journal of WTO & International Health Law and Policy*, 2012, 7(1), 1–24.

R. Adlung and A. Carzaniga, 'MFN exemptions under the General Agreement on Trade in Services: grandfathers striving for immortality?', *Journal of International Economic Law*, 2009, 12(2), 357–92.

L. Ehring, 'De Facto Discrimination in WTO Law: National and Most-Favoured-Nation Treatment – or Equal Treatment', *Journal of World Trade*, 2002, 36(5), 921–77.

5 National Treatment

CONTENTS

1 INTRODUCTION

As stated in Chapter 1, there are two main non-discrimination obligations under WTO law: the most-favoured-nation (MFN) treatment obligation, discussed in the previous chapter, and the national treatment obligation, which is discussed in this chapter. In simple terms, a national treatment obligation relates to whether a country favours itself over other countries. A national treatment obligation prohibits a country to discriminate *against* other countries. The national treatment obligation under WTO law applies – albeit not in the same manner – to trade in goods as well as trade in services. The key provisions dealing with the national treatment obligation for measures affecting trade in goods are Articles III:2 and III:4 of the GATT 1994. The key provision dealing with the national treatment obligation for measures affecting trade in services is Article XVII:1 of the GATS. In this chapter, we will discuss these national treatment obligations in turn.[1]

Discrimination *against* foreign products, services or service suppliers, as compared to like domestic products, services or service suppliers, occurs frequently. There is often widespread popular support for such discrimination. To many, it is only normal that their government accords treatment more favourable to domestic products, services or service suppliers than it accords to products, services or service suppliers of foreign origin. However, for the reasons already set out in Chapters 1 and 4, discrimination is clearly ill advised from an international relations perspective and makes scant sense from an economic perspective.[2] Therefore, WTO law seeks to eliminate discrimination *against* foreign products, services and service suppliers. It succeeds in doing so to varying degrees.

With regard to the national treatment obligation under Article III of the GATT 1994, the questions that may arise include the following: (1) Can Richland, a WTO Member, impose a 10 per cent sales tax on beer imported from Newland, also a WTO Member, while imposing a 5 per cent sales tax on domestic beer? (2) Can Richland impose a 10 per cent sales tax on soft drinks imported from Newland while imposing a 5 per cent sales tax on domestic mineral water? (3) Can Richland impose on soft drinks a labelling requirement to indicate the sugar content while not imposing such a requirement on fruit juice?

With regard to the national treatment obligation under Article XVII of the GATS, the following questions may arise: (1) Can Richland bar all foreign doctors from practising medicine in its territory? (2) Can Richland impose strict qualification requirements on nannies from Oldland while leaving the qualifications of domestic workers from Richland itself largely unregulated? (3) Can Richland, a country with a large French-speaking minority, impose a 20 per cent tax on language courses, while exempting French-language courses from taxation?

2 NATIONAL TREATMENT UNDER THE GATT 1994

Article III of the GATT 1994, entitled 'National Treatment on Internal Taxation and Regulation', states, in relevant part:

> 1. The [Members] recognize that internal taxes and other internal charges, and laws, regulations and requirements affecting the internal sale, offering for sale, purchase,

1 As discussed in Chapter 15, the *TRIPS Agreement* also provides for a national treatment obligation. See below, pp. 1003–9.

2 See above, pp. 39 and 305–39.

transportation, distribution or use of products, and internal quantitative regulations requiring the mixture, processing or use of products in specified amounts or proportions, should not be applied to imported or domestic products so as to afford protection to domestic production.

2. The products of the territory of any [Member] imported into the territory of any other [Member] shall not be subject, directly or indirectly, to internal taxes or other internal charges of any kind in excess of those applied, directly or indirectly, to like domestic products. Moreover, no [Member] shall otherwise apply internal taxes or other internal charges to imported or domestic products in a manner contrary to the principles set forth in paragraph 1.
3. ...
4. The products of the territory of any [Member] imported into the territory of any other [Member] shall be accorded treatment no less favourable than that accorded to like products of national origin in respect of all laws, regulations and requirements affecting their internal sale, offering for sale, purchase, transportation, distribution or use.

Other paragraphs of Article III deal with the application (or non-application) of the national treatment obligations to particular kinds of measures, such as: local content requirements (paragraph 5);[3] government procurement (paragraph 8(a)); subsidies to domestic producers (paragraph 8(b)); internal maximum price control measures (paragraph 9);[4] and screen quotas for cinematograph films (i.e. movies) (paragraph 10).[5] Of particular interest are paragraphs 8(a) and 8(b) of Article III, which are therefore discussed in some details in this chapter.[6]

The paragraphs of Article III, quoted or referred to above, should always be read together with the Note *Ad* Article III contained in Annex I, entitled 'Notes and Supplementary Provisions', of the GATT 1994. As discussed below, this is important in particular with regard to the obligation under Article III:2, second sentence.[7]

Note that Article XX of the GATT 1994 as well as other multilateral agreements on trade in goods, such as the *TBT Agreement*, the *SPS Agreement* and the *Agreement on Trade-Related Investment Measures*, also provide for a national treatment obligation.[8] However, this section is only concerned with the national treatment obligation set out in Article III of the GATT 1994.

3 A local content requirement is an internal quantitative regulation, which requires that a specified share of the components of a product is supplied from domestic sources. Pursuant to Article III:5 of the GATT 1994 local content requirements are prohibited.

4 Article III:9 of the GATT 1994 requires Members 'to take account of' the interests of exporting Members when adopting internal maximum price control measures with a view to avoiding as much as possible the prejudicial effects of such measures on imported products.

5 Article III:10 of the GATT 1994 allows for internal quantitative restrictions relating to exposed cinematograph films which are inconsistent with the national treatment obligations under Article III, provided that such measures meet the requirements of Article IV of the GATT 1994.

6 See below, pp. 347–50.

7 See below, p. 365. The Note *Ad* Article III also clarifies the scope of the measures (internal measures *versus* border measures) to which Article III applies. See below, p. 346.

8 See below, pp. 899–912, 950–1 and 1003–9.

2.1 Nature of the National Treatment Obligation of Article III of the GATT 1994

This subsection on the nature of the national treatment obligation of Article III of the GATT 1994 deals with: (1) the object and purpose of this obligation; (2) three issues relating to the scope of this obligation (namely, the issue of *de jure* and *de facto* discrimination, the issue of internal *versus* border measures; and the issue of the application of the non-discrimination obligation to government procurement and subsidies to domestic producers); and (3) the structure of Article III.

2.1.1 The Object and Purpose of the National Treatment Obligation

As noted above, Article III of the GATT 1994 prohibits discrimination *against* imported products. Generally speaking, it prohibits Members from treating imported products less favourably than like domestic products once the imported product has entered the domestic market, i.e. once it has been cleared through customs.

In *Japan – Alcoholic Beverages II (1996)*, the Appellate Body stated with respect to the purpose of the national treatment obligation of Article III of the GATT 1994:

> The broad and fundamental purpose of Article III is to avoid protectionism in the application of internal tax and regulatory measures. More specifically, the purpose of Article III 'is to ensure that internal measures "not be applied to imported or domestic products so as to afford protection to domestic production"'. Toward this end, Article III obliges Members of the WTO to provide equality of competitive conditions for imported products in relation to domestic products.[9]

In *Korea – Alcoholic Beverages (1999)*, the Appellate Body identified the objectives of Article III of the GATT 1994 as 'avoiding protectionism, requiring equality of competitive conditions and protecting expectations of equal competitive relationships'.[10] In *EC – Asbestos (2001)*, the Appellate Body stated that the purpose of Article III is:

> to prevent Members from applying internal taxes and regulations in a manner which affects the competitive relationship, in the marketplace, between the domestic and imported products involved, 'so as to afford protection to domestic production'.[11]

As Article III not merely requires equality of competitive conditions between imported and domestic products, but also protects 'the *expectations* of equal competitive relationships', the actual trade effects of the measure at issue are

9 Appellate Body Report, *Japan – Alcoholic Beverages II (1996)*, 109. In the footnotes to this paragraph, the Appellate Body refers to the following panel reports: Panel Report, *US – Section 337 Tariff Act (1989)*, para. 5.10; Panel Report, *US – Superfund (1987)*, para. 5.1.9; and Panel Report, *Italy – Agricultural Machinery (1958)*, para. 11.

10 Appellate Body Report, *Korea – Alcoholic Beverages (1999)*, para. 120. See also Appellate Body Report, *Canada – Periodicals (1997)*, 464.

11 Appellate Body Report, *EC – Asbestos (2001)*, para. 98.

not dispositive of the consistency with Article III. A measure can be found to be inconsistent with Article III even when the effect of the measure on the volume of imports is insignificant or even non-existent.[12] In *EC – Seal Products (2014)*, the Appellate Body ruled that Article III of the GATT 1994 is 'concerned, fundamentally, with prohibiting discriminatory measures by requiring ... equality of competitive *opportunities* for imported products and like domestic products' and that, for that reason, Article III does not 'require a demonstration of the *actual* trade effects of a specific measure'.[13]

Panels and scholars have affirmed that one of the main purposes of Article III of the GATT 1994 is to guarantee that internal measures of WTO Members do not undermine their commitments on tariffs under Article II of the GATT 1994.[14] Note, however, that the Appellate Body stressed in *Japan – Alcoholic Beverages II (1996)* that the purpose of Article III of the GATT 1994 is broader. The Appellate Body stated:

> The sheltering scope of Article III is not limited to products that are the subject of tariff concessions under Article II. The Article III national treatment obligation is a *general prohibition* on the use of internal taxes and other internal regulatory measures so as to afford protection to domestic production. This obligation clearly extends also to products not bound under Article II.[15]

In brief, the national treatment obligation of Article III of the GATT 1994 is an obligation of *general application* that applies both to measures affecting products with regard to which Members have made tariff concessions and to measures affecting products with regard to which Members have not done so.[16]

2.1.2 *De jure* and *de facto* Discrimination

Article III of the GATT 1994 covers not only 'in law' or *de jure* discrimination; it also covers 'in fact' or *de facto* discrimination. The concepts of *de jure* and *de facto* discrimination were discussed at length in the previous chapter.[17] An example of a *de jure* discriminatory measure to which the national treatment obligation of Article III has been applied is the measure at issue in *Korea – Various Measures on Beef (2001)*.[18] In that case, the disputed measure was an 'origin-based' dual retail distribution system for the sale of beef. Under this system, *imported* beef was to be sold in specialist stores selling only imported beef or in separate sections of supermarkets. An example of a *de facto* discriminatory

12 See Appellate Body Report, *Japan – Alcoholic Beverages II (1996)*, 109, referring in footnote to Panel Report, *US – Superfund (1987)*, para. 5.1.9. In the same paragraph, the Appellate Body even stated that the actual trade effects were 'irrelevant'.

13 Appellate Body Reports, *EC – Seal Products (2014)*, para. 5.82. Emphasis added.

14 See e.g. Panel Report, *Japan – Alcoholic Beverages II (1996)*, para. 6.13. With regard to the commitments on tariffs under Article II of the GATT, see below, p. 436.

15 Appellate Body Report, *Japan – Alcoholic Beverages II (1996)*, 16. Emphasis added.

16 Note the difference with the national treatment obligation of Article XVII:1 of the GATS. See below, p. 399.

17 See above, pp. 345–6. 18 See below, p. 390.

measure to which the national treatment obligation of Article III has been applied is the measure at issue in *Japan – Alcoholic Beverages II (1996)*.[19] In that case, the disputed measure was tax legislation that provided for higher taxes on, for example, whisky, brandy and vodka (whether domestic or imported) than on shochu (whether domestic or imported). On its face, this Japanese tax legislation was 'origin-neutral'. However, in fact, it discriminated against imported alcoholic beverages.[20]

2.1.3 Internal Measures versus Border Measures

Article III of the GATT 1994 applies only to internal measures, not to border measures. It is therefore important to determine whether a measure is an internal or a border measure. When the measure is applied to imported products at the time or point of importation, it is not always easy to distinguish an internal measure from a border measure. The Note *Ad* Article III clarifies:

> Any internal tax or other internal charge, or any law, regulation or requirement of the kind referred to in paragraph 1 which applies to an imported product and to the like domestic product and is collected or enforced in the case of the imported product at the time or point of importation, is nevertheless to be regarded as an internal tax or other internal charge, or a law, regulation or requirement of the kind referred to in paragraph 1, and is accordingly subject to the provisions of Article III.

It follows that, if the importation of a product is barred at the border because that product fails, for example, to meet a public health or consumer safety requirement that applies also to domestic products, the consistency of this import ban with the GATT is to be examined under Article III.[21] However, the Note *Ad* Article III, quoted above, leaves it unclear whether Article XI could also apply to such a measure. In *India – Autos (2002)*, the panel noted on the relationship between Article III and Article XI of the GATT 1994 that:

> it ... cannot be excluded *a priori* that different aspects of a measure may affect the competitive opportunities of imports in different ways, making them fall within the scope either of Article III (where competitive opportunities on the domestic market are affected) or of Article XI (where the opportunities for importation itself, i.e. entering the market, are affected), or even that there may be, in perhaps exceptional circumstances, a potential for overlap between the two provisions, as was suggested in the case of state trading.[22]

The panel in *India – Autos (2002)* further considered that:

> [t]he fact that the measure applies only to imported products need not [be], in itself, an obstacle to its falling within the purview of Article III. For example, an internal tax, or a product standard conditioning the sale of the imported but not of the like domestic product, could nonetheless 'affect' the conditions of the imported product on the market and could be a source of less favorable treatment. Similarly, the fact that a requirement is imposed as

19 See below, p. 354. 20 See further below, pp. 357, 358 and 367.
21 See Panel Report, *Canada – FIRA (1984)*, para. 5.14.
22 Panel Report, *India – Autos (2002)*, para. 7.224.

a condition on importation is not necessarily in itself an obstacle to its falling within the scope of Article III:4.[23]

As discussed below, in *China – Auto Parts (2009)*, the question whether the measures concerned were subject to Article III (applicable to internal measures) or Article II (applicable to border measures) was a threshold issue in that case.[24]

2.1.4 Government Procurement and Subsidies to Domestic Producers

In determining the scope of application of the national treatment obligation of Article III of the GATT 1994, paragraphs 8(a) and 8(b) thereof are of particular interest. Article III:8(a) states:

> The provisions of this Article shall not apply to laws, regulations or requirements governing the procurement by governmental agencies of products purchased for governmental purposes and not with a view to commercial resale or with a view to use in the production of goods for commercial sale.

In *Canada – Renewable Energy / Feed-In Tariff Program (2013)*, the Canadian Province of Ontario bought green electricity from the electricity generators at a guaranteed and favourable price if those generators had *inter alia* purchased part of their solar panels and windmills from local suppliers in Ontario. The European Union and Japan challenged the domestic content requirements at issue as inconsistent with Article III:4 of the GATT 1994. Canada argued that since the domestic content requirements were a condition for the purchase of the green electricity by the Province of Ontario, the domestic content requirements were, pursuant to Article III:8(a), not subject to Article III:4. The panel agreed with Canada. The Appellate Body, however, reversed the panel. On the basis of the use in the opening clause of Article III:8(a) of the term 'apply' in the negative, the Appellate Body first ruled with regard to the nature of this provision that it is:

> a derogation limiting the scope of the national treatment obligation and it is not a justification for measures that would otherwise be inconsistent with that obligation.[25]

Measures governing government procurement are excluded from the scope of the national treatment obligation under Article III, provided that these measures meet the requirements set out in Article III:8(a). In *Canada – Renewable Energy / Feed-In Tariff Program (2013)*, the Appellate Body identified and clarified the five requirements of Article III:8(a) as follows. *First*, Article III:8(a) requires an 'articulated connection' between the measure (i.e. the law, regulation

23 *Ibid.*, para. 7.306. The panel applied this finding subsequently to the 'indigenisation' condition, at issue in this case. See *ibid.*, paras. 7.307–7.317.
24 See below, p. 352.
25 Appellate Body Reports, *Canada – Renewable Energy / Feed-In Tariff Program (2013)*, para. 5.56. See also *ibid.*, para. 5.74; The Appellate Body noted that 'the characterization of the provision as a derogation does not predetermine the question as to which party bears the burden of proof with regard to the requirements stipulated in the provision'. See *ibid.*, para. 5.56.

or requirement) and the procurement, in the sense that 'the act of procurement is undertaken within a binding structure of laws, regulations, or requirements'.[26] The Appellate Body found with regard to the term 'procurement' that this term refers to 'the process of obtaining products, rather than as referring to an acquisition itself'.[27] *Second*, the procurement must be by a 'governmental agency', i.e. 'an entity acting for or on behalf of government and performing governmental functions within the competences conferred on it'.[28] *Third*, the 'products purchased' referred to in Article III:8(a) must be in a competitive relationship with the products of foreign origin that are being discriminated under Article III.[29] As the Appellate Body explained, the derogation of Article III:8(a) must be understood in relation to the obligations stipulated in Article III, and Article III:8(a) 'thus concerns, in the first instance, the product that is subject to the discrimination'.[30] *Fourth*, the 'products purchased' must be purchased for '*governmental purposes*'. According to the Appellate Body, this is the case when the products purchased are 'consumed by the government' or are 'provided by government to recipients in the discharge of its public functions'.[31] As Article III:8(a) refers to purchases '*for*' governmental purposes, the Appellate Body ruled that there must be 'a *rational relationship* between the product and the governmental function being discharged'.[32] *Fifth*, the purchase may not be 'with a view to commercial resale or with a view to use in the production of goods for commercial sale'. According to the Appellate Body, a 'commercial resale' is a resale made at 'arm's length between a willing seller and a willing buyer', which would normally, but not necessarily, be a resale for profit.[33] Applying these five requirements to the measure at issue in *Canada – Renewable Energy / Feed-In Tariff Program (2013)*, the Appellate Body concluded that Article III:8(a) did not apply because the imported product being discriminated against (i.e. the solar panels and the windmills) were not in a competitive relationship with the product purchased by the government (i.e. the green electricity).[34]

In *India – Solar Cells (2016)*, the respondent, India, invoked Article III:8(a) to argue that the national treatment obligation of Article III:4 of the GATT did not apply to the domestic content requirements imposed on solar power generators. Under the National Solar Mission of the Government of India, government agencies bought electricity from solar power generators under long-term contracts at a guaranteed price on the condition that the solar power generators used Indian,

26 *Ibid.*, para. 5.58. 27 *Ibid.*, para. 5.59. 28 *Ibid.*, para. 5.61.
29 See *ibid.*, paras. 5.63 and 5.74. See also Appellate Body Report, *India – Solar Cells (2016)*, para. 5.21.
30 Appellate Body Reports, *Canada – Renewable Energy / Feed-In Tariff Program (2013)*, para. 5.63.
31 *Ibid.*, para. 5.68.
32 *Ibid.* Emphasis added.
33 See *ibid.*, para. 5.71. The Appellate Body explained that whether a resale is 'commercial' 'must be assessed having regard to the entire transaction', both from the seller's and the buyer's perspective. On the clause 'not ... with a view to use in the production of goods for commercial sale', see *ibid.*, paras. 5.72–5.73.
34 See *ibid.*, para. 5.79.

rather than imported, solar cells and modules. The panel in this case was not persuaded that the domestic content requirement measures at issue were 'distinguishable in any relevant respect' from the measures examined by the Appellate Body in *Canada – Renewable Energy / Canada Feed-in Tariff Program (2013)*.[35] On the basis of the Appellate Body's interpretation and application of Article III:8(a) in *Canada – Renewable Energy / Canada Feed-in Tariff Program (2013)*, discussed above, the panel in *India – Solar Cells (2016)* found that the discrimination relating to solar cells and modules under the domestic content requirement measures is not covered by the derogation of Article III:8(a) of the GATT 1994.[36] As in *Canada – Renewable Energy / Canada Feed-in Tariff Program (2013)*, the product discriminated against (i.e. solar cells and modules) was not in a competitive relationship with the products purchased (i.e. electricity). On appeal, India argued that the test of 'competitive relationship' between the product discriminated against and the product purchased 'is not a single inflexible rule to be applied in all circumstances for consideration under Article III'.[37] According to India the Appellate Body left room in *Canada – Renewable Energy / Canada Feed-in Tariff Program (2013)* for an alternative test to determine the applicability of Article III:8(a).[38] The Appellate Body disagreed. Referring to its ruling in *Canada – Renewable Energy / Canada Feed-in Tariff Program (2013)*, the Appellate Body held:

> since 'the derogation of Article III:8(a) must be understood in relation to the obligations stipulated in Article III', the product of foreign origin must be either 'like' or 'directly competitive [with] or substitutable' for, i.e. in a 'competitive relationship' with, the product purchased'. We do not consider that the scope of a derogation can extend beyond the scope of the obligation from which derogation is sought.[39]

The Appellate Body concluded that:

> Under Article III:8(a), the product purchased by way of procurement must necessarily be ... in a 'competitive relationship' with – the foreign product subject to discrimination.[40]

35 See Panel Report, *India – Solar Cells (2016)*, para. 7.135.

36 See *ibid.*, para. 7.135.

37 See Appellate Body Report, *India – Solar Cells (2016)*, para. 5.19 (quoting from India's appellant submission, paras. 4 and 9).

38 India recalled that the Appellate Body explicitly noted in *Canada – Renewable Energy / Feed-in Tariff Program (2013)* that '[w]hether the derogation in Article III:8(a) can extend also to discrimination [relating to inputs and processes of production used in respect of products purchased by way of procurement] is a matter we do not decide in this case'. See Appellate Body Reports, *Canada – Renewable Energy / Feed-in Tariff Program (2013)*, fn. 523, para. 5.73.

39 Appellate Body Report, *India – Solar Cells (2016)*, para. 5.22 (quoting from Appellate Body Reports, *Canada – Renewable Energy / Canada Feed-in Tariff Program (2013)*, para. 5.74).

40 *Ibid.*, para. 5.40. The Appellate Body noted that while a consideration of inputs and processes of production of the product purchased may *inform* the question of whether that product is in a competitive relationship with the product being discriminated against, it does not *displace* the competitive relationship standard. See *ibid.* The Appellate Body also noted that 'conditions imposed in the context of government procurement relating to inputs and processes of production of products purchased, such as conditions regarding "the environmental profile or the environmental attributes that a particular product may incorporate ... could legitimately form part of the requirements of the product purchased that are closely related to the subject matter of the contract." Such conditions may thus be relevant to the analysis under Article III:8(a) insofar as they can be said to be "governing" the relevant procurement process.' See *ibid.*, fn. 101, para. 5.24 (referring to fn. 499, para. 5.63 of Appellate Body Reports, *Canada – Renewable Energy / Canada Feed-in Tariff Program (2013)*).

While the national treatment obligation of Article III of the GATT 1994 does not apply to measures governing government procurement that meet the requirements of Article III:8(a) discussed above, such measures may nevertheless be subject to a national treatment obligation. It deserves to be recalled that Article III:1(a) of the plurilateral *Agreement on Government Procurement* imposes on those WTO Members, which are a party to this Agreement, a national treatment obligation.[41]

Apart from paragraph 8(a), paragraph 8(b) of Article III of the GATT 1994 also deserves attention. Pursuant to paragraph 8(b), the national treatment obligation of Article III 'shall not prevent' the payment of subsidies exclusively to domestic producers. Note that the panel in *Italy – Agricultural Machinery (1958)* already gave in the early days of the GATT 1947 a narrow interpretation to this provision. If paragraph 8(b) were to be interpreted broadly, any discrimination against imports could be qualified as a subsidy to domestic producers and thus render the discipline of Article III meaningless. The panel in *US – Malt Beverages (1992)* therefore found that the term 'payment of subsidies' in paragraph 8(b) refers only to direct subsidies involving a payment, not to other subsidies, such as tax credits or tax reductions.[42]

2.1.5 Articles III:1, III:2 and III:4

As stated above, and as explicitly noted by the Appellate Body in *Japan – Alcoholic Beverages II (1996)*, Article III:1 of the GATT 1994 articulates a general principle that internal measures should not be applied so as to afford protection to domestic production. According to the Appellate Body in *Japan – Alcoholic Beverages II (1996)*:

> This general principle informs the rest of Article III. The purpose of Article III:1 is to establish this general principle as a guide to understanding and interpreting the specific obligations contained in Article III:2 and in the other paragraphs of Article III, while respecting, and not diminishing in any way, the meaning of the words actually used in the texts of those other paragraphs.[43]

The general principle that internal measures should not be applied so as to afford protection to domestic production is elaborated in Article III:2 with regard to internal taxation and in Article III:4 with regard to internal regulation.[44] In Article III:2, two non-discrimination obligations can be distinguished: one obligation is set out in the first sentence of Article III:2, relating to internal taxation

41 See above, p. 347, and below, p. 381.

42 See Panel Report, *US – Malt Beverages (1992)*, para. 5.8. On Article III:8(b), see also Appellate Body Report, *Canada – Periodicals (1997)*, 32–5; and Panel Report, *EC – Commercial Vessels (2005)*, paras. 7.55–7.75. Note also that, while the payment of a subsidy to domestic producers escapes the disciplines of Article III of the GATT 1994, the disciplines of the *SCM Agreement* may well apply. See below, p. 807.

43 Appellate Body Report, *Japan – Alcoholic Beverages II (1996)*, 111. See also Appellate Body Report, *EC – Asbestos (2001)*, para. 93.

44 As the Appellate Body noted in *Canada – Renewable Energy / Feed-In Tariff Program (2013)*, para. 5.55 (referring to the Appellate Body Report, *EC – Asbestos (2001)*, para. 93), other paragraphs of Article III constitute 'specific expressions' of the overarching, general principle set out in Article III:1.

of 'like products'; and the other obligation is set out in the second sentence of Article III:2, relating to internal taxation of 'directly competitive or substitutable products'. The subsections below discuss in turn the national treatment tests for internal taxation (on like products and on directly competitive or substitutable products) under Article III:2, first and second sentence; and for internal regulation under Article III:4.

2.2 National Treatment Test for Internal Taxation on Like Products

Article III:2, first sentence, of the GATT 1994 states:

> The products of the territory of any [Member] imported into the territory of any other [Member] shall not be subject, directly or indirectly, to internal taxes or other internal charges of any kind in excess of those applied, directly or indirectly, to like domestic products.

In *Canada – Periodicals (1997)*, the Appellate Body found:

> there are two questions which need to be answered to determine whether there is a violation of Article III:2 of the GATT 1994: (a) whether imported and domestic products are like products; and (b) whether the imported products are taxed in excess of the domestic products. If the answers to both questions are affirmative, there is a violation of Article III:2, first sentence.[45]

However, before addressing the questions set out by the Appellate Body in *Canada – Periodicals (1997)*, it has to be determined whether the measure at issue is an 'internal tax or other internal charge of any kind' within the meaning of Article III:2, first sentence. In *China – Auto Parts (2009)*, the Appellate Body referred to this question as a 'threshold issue'.[46] This question constitutes in fact a third tier or element of the test under Article III:2, first sentence, which must be addressed first.

The three-tier test of consistency of internal taxation with Article III:2, first sentence, requires the examination of:

- whether the measure at issue is an *internal tax or other internal charge* on products;
- whether the imported and domestic products are *like products*; and
- whether the imported products are *taxed in excess* of the domestic products.

Recall that Article III:1 of the GATT 1994 provides that internal taxation must not be applied so as to afford protection to domestic production. However, according to the Appellate Body in *Japan – Alcoholic Beverages II (1996)*, the presence of a protective application need not be established separately from the *specific* requirements of Article III:2, first sentence.[47] Whenever imported

45 Appellate Body Report, *Canada – Periodicals (1997)*, 468.
46 See Appellate Body Reports, *China – Auto Parts (2009)*, para. 181.
47 See Appellate Body Report, *Japan – Alcoholic Beverages II (1996)*, 111–12.

products from one Member are subject to taxes in excess of those applied to like domestic products in another Member, this is deemed to 'afford protection to domestic production' within the meaning of Article III:1.[48]

Below, each element of the three-tier test of consistency will be discussed in turn.

To date, WTO Members have been found to have acted inconsistently with Article III:2, first sentence, of the GATT 1994 in ten disputes.[49]

2.2.1 'Internal Taxes ... '

Article III:2, first sentence, of the GATT 1994 concerns 'internal taxes and other charges of any kind' which are applied 'directly or indirectly' on products. Examples of such internal taxes or other internal charges on products are value added taxes (VAT), sales taxes and excise duties.[50] Income taxes are not covered by Article III:2, first sentence, since they are not internal taxes or other internal charges on *products*.[51] Likewise, customs duties or other border charges are not covered since they are not *internal* taxes or other *internal* charges on products. In *China – Auto Parts (2009)*, the panel had to determine whether the charges at issue in that case were an 'internal charge' (as argued by the complainants) or a 'customs duty' (as argued by China). With the exception of one particular charge, the panel found that the charges were an 'internal charge', and thus concluded that the national treatment obligation of Article III:2, first sentence, applied.[52] In addressing this issue, the Appellate Body noted that 'the time at which a charge is collected or paid is not decisive' when determining whether a charge is an internal charge or a border charge (such as a customs duty).[53] In other words, it is not because a charge is paid at the time of importation that it is a customs duty or other border charge within the meaning of Article II:1, and not an internal charge within the meaning of Article III:2. According to the Appellate Body, what is important for the applicability of Article III:2 is that:

> the *obligation* to pay a charge must accrue due to an internal event, such as the distribution, sale, use or transportation of the imported product.[54]

48 See also Panel Report, *Argentina – Hides and Leather (2001)*, para. 11.137.

49 See *Japan – Alcoholic Beverages II (1996), Canada – Periodicals (1997), Indonesia – Autos (1998), Argentina – Hides and Leather (2001), Dominican Republic – Import and Sale of Cigarettes (2005), Mexico – Taxes on Soft Drinks (2006), China – Auto Parts (2009), Colombia – Ports of Entry (2009), Thailand – Cigarettes (Philippines) (2011)* and *Philippines – Distilled Spirits (2012)*.

50 With regard to 'other [internal] charges', the panel in *Argentina – Hides and Leather (2001)* noted that the term 'charge' denotes, *inter alia*, a 'pecuniary burden' and a 'liability to pay money laid on a person', and concluded that two of the measures at issue, while not taxes in their own right, were tax measures within the meaning of Article III:2 because they imposed a 'pecuniary burden' and created 'a liability to pay money'. See Panel Report, *Argentina – Hides and Leather (2001)*, para. 11.143.

51 With regard to taxes on *income*, note that an income tax regulation can be considered to be an internal regulation and thus to fall within the scope of Article III:4 of the GATT 1994, discussed below, pp. 376–99. See also Panel Report, *US – FSC (Article 21.5 – EC) (2002)*, para. 8.145. With regard to taxes on *services* and the applicability of Article III:2, first sentence, see Panel Report, *Mexico – Taxes on Soft Drinks (2006)*, para. 8.152.

52 See Panel Reports, *China – Auto Parts (2009)*, para. 7.212.

53 See Appellate Body Reports, *China – Auto Parts (2009)*, para. 162.

54 *Ibid.*

A determination of whether a particular measure falls within the scope of Article III:2 of the GATT 1994 must be made in the light of the characteristics of the measure and the circumstances of the case. The Appellate Body observed that in many cases this is 'a straightforward exercise', but that in other cases a panel may face a 'more complex' challenge.[55] Note, in particular, that neither the way in which a measure is characterised in a Member's domestic law nor the intent of a Member's legislator is dispositive of the characterisation of such measure under WTO law as an internal tax or a border charge.[56]

Subject to Article III:2, first sentence, are 'internal taxes and other charges of any kind' which are applied 'directly or indirectly' on products. The words 'applied *directly or indirectly*' on products should be understood to mean 'applied *on or in connection with* products'. According to the panel in *Japan – Alcoholic Beverages I (1987)*, the term 'indirect taxation' refers to taxes imposed on the raw materials used in the product during the various stages of its production.[57] The panel in *Mexico – Taxes on Soft Drinks (2006)* found that non-cane sugar sweeteners were 'indirectly' subject to the soft drink tax when they were used in the production of soft drinks.[58] Indirect taxation may also refer to a tax on the production process.

In *US – Tobacco (1994)*, the panel examined the question of whether financial penalty provisions for the enforcement of a domestic content requirement for tobacco could be qualified as 'internal taxes or other charges of any kind' within the meaning of Article III:2, first sentence, of the GATT 1994. The panel found that a financial penalty provision for the enforcement of a domestic law is not an 'internal tax or charge of any kind'.[59] Such a penalty provision is an internal regulation within the meaning of Article III:4 of the GATT 1994, as discussed below.[60]

Also, the panel in *EEC – Animal Feed Proteins (1978)* did not consider a security deposit to be a fiscal measure within the meaning of Article III:2, although this deposit accrued to the EEC when the buyers of vegetable proteins failed to fulfil the obligation to purchase milk powder. The panel considered the security deposit, including any associated cost, to be only an enforcement mechanism for the purchase requirement and, as such, its GATT consistency should be examined, together with the purchase requirement, under Article III:4.[61]

55 See *ibid.*, para. 171. See in this context also *India – Additional Import Duties (2008)*, in which the panel agreed with the parties that the measures at issue were border charges within the meaning of Article II:1, and not internal charges within the meaning of Article III:2. See Appellate Body Report, *India – Additional Import Duties (2008)*, fn. 304 to para. 153.

56 See Appellate Body Reports, *China – Auto Parts (2009)*, para. 178.

57 See Panel Report, *Japan – Alcoholic Beverages I (1987)*, para. 5.8.

58 See Panel Report, *Mexico – Taxes on Soft Drinks (2006)*, para. 8.45. The panel in *Mexico – Taxes on Soft Drinks (2006)* also found that, while on its face the distribution tax is a tax on the provision of certain services, in the circumstances of this case it is also a tax applied *indirectly* on soft drinks and syrups. See Panel Report, *Mexico – Taxes on Soft Drinks (2006)*, para. 8.152.

59 See Panel Report, *US – Tobacco (1994)*, para. 80.

60 See below, pp. 376–99.

61 See Panel Report, *EEC – Animal Feed Proteins (1978)*, para. 4.4.

The issue of border tax adjustment must also be mentioned in this context. Border tax adjustments are:

> any fiscal measures which put into effect, in whole or in part, the destination principle (i.e. which enable exported products to be relieved of some or all of the tax charged in the exporting country in respect of similar domestic products sold to consumers on the home market and which enable imported products sold to consumers to be charged with some or all of the tax charged in the importing country in respect of similar domestic products).[62]

Such a fiscal measure involving the imposition of taxes by the importing country is obviously a fiscal measure which falls within the scope of application of Article III:2.[63]

Finally, with regard to 'tax administration' and 'tax collection' measures, the panel in *Argentina – Hides and Leather (2001)* rejected the contention of Argentina that such measures do not fall under Article III:2. The panel stated:

> We agree that Members are free, within the outer bounds defined by such provisions as Article III:2, to administer and collect internal taxes as they see fit. However, if, as here, such 'tax administration' measures take the form of an internal charge and are applied to products, those measures must, in our view, be in conformity with Article III:2.[64]

In *US – Malt Beverages (1992)*, the panel considered a measure preventing imported products from being sold in a manner that would enable them to avoid taxation, to be a measure within the scope of Article III:2, first sentence, because it assigned a higher tax rate to the imported products.[65] The Appellate Body ruled in *Thailand – Cigarettes (Philippines) (2011)* that:

> even if a measure at issue consisted solely of administrative requirements, we do not exclude the possibility that such requirements may have a bearing on the respective tax burdens on imported and like domestic products, and may therefore be subject to Article III:2.[66]

2.2.2 'Like Products'

The second element of the test of consistency with the national treatment obligation of Article III:2, first sentence, of the GATT 1994 relates to the question of whether the products at issue are '*like products*'. It is only between 'like' imported and domestic products that the national treatment obligation applies and discrimination within the meaning of Article III:2, first sentence, may occur. Imported and domestic products that are not 'like' may be treated differently; different treatment of such 'unlike' products will not constitute discrimination within the meaning of Article III:2, first sentence. For the application of the national treatment obligation of Article III:2, first sentence, it is therefore

62 Working Party Report, *Border Tax Adjustments (1970)*, BISD 18S/97, 25.
63 See *ibid.*, para. 14.
64 Panel Report, *Argentina – Hides and Leather (2001)*, para. 11.144. The panel argued that excluding 'tax administration' measures from the scope of Article III:2 would 'create a potential for abuse and circumvention of the obligations contained in Article III:2'. See *ibid.*
65 See Panel Report, *US – Malt Beverages (1992)*, paras. 5.21–5.22.
66 Appellate Body Report, *Thailand – Cigarettes (Philippines) (2011)*, fn. 144 to para. 114.

important to be able to determine whether, for example, a sports utility vehicle (SUV) is 'like' a family car; orange juice is 'like' tomato juice; a laptop is 'like' a tablet computer; pork is 'like' beef; or whisky is 'like' brandy within the meaning of Article III:2, first sentence.

Just as the concept of 'like products' in Article I:1 of the GATT 1994, the concept of 'like products' in Article III:2, first sentence, is not defined in the GATT 1994. There are, however, a number of GATT and WTO dispute settlement reports that shed light on the meaning of the concept of 'like products' in Article III:2, first sentence, of the GATT 1994.

Under the Japanese tax system at issue in *Japan – Alcoholic Beverages II (1996)*, the internal tax imposed on domestic shochu was the same as that imposed on imported shochu; the higher tax imposed on imported vodka was also imposed on domestic vodka. Identical products (not considering brand differences) were thus taxed identically. However, the question in that case was whether shochu and vodka should be considered to be 'like products'. If shochu and vodka were 'like products', vodka could not be taxed in excess of shochu. As already discussed above in the context of 'likeness' under Article I:1 of the GATT 1994, the Appellate Body in *Japan – Alcoholic Beverages II (1996)* stated:

> The concept of 'likeness' is a relative one that evokes the image of an accordion. The accordion of 'likeness' stretches and squeezes in different places as different provisions of the *WTO Agreement* are applied. The width of the accordion in any one of those places must be determined by the particular provision in which the term 'like' is encountered as well as by the context and the circumstances that prevail in any given case to which that provision may apply.[67]

With respect to 'like products' in Article III:2, first sentence, the Appellate Body in *Japan – Alcoholic Beverages II (1996)* ruled that the 'accordion of "likeness" is meant to be narrowly squeezed'.[68] According to the Appellate Body, the concept of 'like products' in Article III:2, first sentence, should be construed narrowly because of the existence of the concept of 'directly competitive or substitutable products' used in the second sentence of Article III:2.[69] If 'like products' in Article III:2, first sentence, were to be given a broad meaning, the scope of this concept would be identical, or at least largely overlap, with the concept of 'directly competitive or substitutable products' in Article III:2, second sentence, and thus render Article III:2, second sentence, redundant. Such interpretation would be inconsistent with the interpretative principle of effectiveness, as discussed in Chapter 3.[70] To give meaning to the concept of 'directly competitive or substitutable products' in Article III:2, second sentence, the concept of 'like products' in Article III:2, first sentence, must be construed narrowly.

67 Appellate Body Report, *Japan – Alcoholic Beverages II (1996)*, 114.
68 *Ibid.*
69 *Ibid.*, 112–13. See also Appellate Body Report, *EC – Asbestos (2001)*, paras. 94–5.
70 See above, p. 193.

In *Japan – Alcoholic Beverages II (1996)*, the Appellate Body expressly agreed with the basic approach for determining 'likeness' set out in the working party report in *Border Tax Adjustments (1970)*.[71] In this report, a working party established by the GATT Council in 1968 found with regard to the term 'like' that:

> the interpretation of the term should be examined on a case-by-case basis ... Some criteria were suggested for determining, on a case-by-case basis, whether a product is 'similar': the product's end-uses in a given market; consumers' tastes and habits, which change from country to country; the product's properties, nature and quality.[72]

This basic approach was followed in almost all post-1970 GATT panel reports involving a GATT provision in which the concept of 'like products' was used.[73] According to the Appellate Body in *Japan – Alcoholic Beverages II (1996)*, this approach should be helpful in identifying on a case-by-case basis the range of 'like products' that falls within the limits of Article III:2, first sentence, of the GATT 1994. However, the Appellate Body added:

> In applying the criteria cited in [the working party report in] *Border Tax Adjustments* to the facts of any particular case, and in considering other criteria that may also be relevant in certain cases, panels can only apply their best judgement in determining whether in fact products are 'like'. This will always involve an unavoidable element of individual, discretionary judgement.[74]

In *Japan – Alcoholic Beverages II (1996)*, the Appellate Body called upon panels to consider, in addition to the *Border Tax Adjustments* criteria, also 'other criteria that may be relevant'.[75] One of such criteria considered by panels and the Appellate Body has been the tariff classification of the products at issue.[76] The Appellate Body acknowledged in *Japan – Alcoholic Beverages II (1996)* that classification under the same Harmonized System tariff heading or subheading can provide a 'useful basis for confirming "likeness" in products'.[77] However, this is only so if the tariff heading is sufficiently detailed.[78] 'Other criteria that may

71 The working party considered the concept of 'like' or 'similar' products as used throughout the GATT.

72 Working Party Report, *Border Tax Adjustments (1970)*, BISD 18S/97, para. 18.

73 See e.g. GATT working party or panel reports in *Australia – Ammonium Sulphate (1950)*, *EEC – Animal Feed Proteins (1978)*, *Spain – Unroasted Coffee (1981)*, *Japan – Alcoholic Beverages I (1987)* and *US – Superfund (1987)*.

74 Appellate Body Report, *Japan – Alcoholic Beverages II (1996)*, 113–14. The Appellate Body disagreed with the panel's observation in para. 6.22 of the panel report that distinguishing between 'like products' and 'directly competitive or substitutable products' under Article III:2 is 'an arbitrary decision'. According to the Appellate Body, it is 'a discretionary decision that must be made in considering the various characteristics of products in individual cases'. Appellate Body Report, *Japan – Alcoholic Beverages II (1996)*, 114.

75 See above in the quote from Appellate Body Report, *Japan – Alcoholic Beverages II (1996)*, 113–14.

76 Note that the tariff classification of the products concerned by other countries was a criterion considered by the panel in *Spain – Unroasted Coffee (1981)*. See above, p. 193. See most recently in Panel Report, *Thailand – Cigarettes (Philippines) (2011)*, para. 7.433; Panel Reports, *Philippines – Distilled Spirits (2012)*, para. 7.63; and Appellate Body Reports, *Philippines – Distilled Spirits (2012)*, para. 161.

77 Appellate Body Report, *Japan – Alcoholic Beverages II (1996)*, 116. See also Appellate Body Reports, *Philippines – Distilled Spirits (2012)*, para. 161.

78 See Appellate Body Reports, *Philippines – Distilled Spirits (2012)*, para. 161.

be relevant' have also included internal regulations, or the internal regulatory framework or regime, applicable to the products at issue.[79] Regulations, or the regulatory framework or regime, applicable to the products at issue may indicate that consumers perceive the products as having similar or distinct characteristics.[80] Also, the price level of the products at issue and the expendable income of the population has been considered a criterion that may be relevant in deciding on whether products are 'like' within the meaning of Article III:2, first sentence, of the GATT 1994.[81]

Note that the Appellate Body ruled in *Canada – Periodicals (1997)*:

> As Article III:2, first sentence, normally requires a comparison between imported products and like domestic products, and as there were no imports of split-run editions of periodicals because of the import prohibition in Tariff Code 9958 ... *hypothetical imports* of split-run periodicals have to be considered.[82]

The Appellate Body thus provides for a 'hypothetical like products' analysis in cases where there are no imports because of, for example, an import prohibition.[83]

The current state of the law regarding the determination of 'likeness' under Article III:2, first sentence, of the GATT 1994 is best reflected in the Appellate Body reports in *Philippines – Distilled Spirits (2012)*. Taking as a given that the concept of 'like products' in Article III:2, first sentence, should be construed narrowly for the reasons set out above, the Appellate Body ruled in this case, as it had already done in *EC – Asbestos (2001)* with regard to the concept of 'like products' in Article III:4,[84] that:

> the determination of 'likeness' under Article III:2, first sentence, of the GATT 1994 is, fundamentally, a determination about the nature and extent of a competitive relationship between and among products.[85]

79 See Panel Report, *Thailand – Cigarettes (Philippines) (2011)*, para. 7.441; and Panel Reports, *Philippines – Distilled Spirits (2012)*, paras. 7.72–7.73. In the Panel Report, *Thailand – Cigarettes (Philippines) (2011)*, para. 7.442, the panel noted that imported and domestic product were subject to the same types of tax and to the same domestic regulation on advertising, marketing, distribution, labelling and health. In the Panel Reports, *Philippines – Distilled Spirits (2012)*, paras. 7.72 and 7.84, the panel noted that local ordinances against drunk driving and the domestic regulation on distilled spirits do not distinguish between imported and domestic spirit, nor between spirits made from designated materials and those made from other materials. See also Appellate Body Reports, *Philippines – Distilled Spirits (2012)*, paras. 118 and 169, although it is unclear whether the relevant statements of the Appellate Body stand for the proposition that the regulatory framework of the responding Member, in itself, may be an additional criterion for determining 'likeness' *or* merely for the proposition that the analysis of likeness must focus on the competitive relationship in the market of the responding Member and that the competitive relationship in other markets is irrelevant.

80 See Appellate Body Reports, *Philippines – Distilled Spirits (2012)*, para. 167.

81 See Panel Report, *Thailand – Cigarettes (Philippines) (2011)*, para. 7.428; and Panel Reports, *Philippines – Distilled Spirits (2012)*, para. 7.59.

82 Appellate Body Report, *Canada – Periodicals (1997)*, 466. Emphasis added.

83 See also Panel Report, *Indonesia – Autos (1998)*, para. 14.113; and Panel Report, *Colombia – Ports of Entry (2009)*, para. 7.356. Note that the 'hypothetical like products approach' has also been applied in another context. See below, pp. 363 and 389.

84 See below, p. 382.

85 See Appellate Body Reports, *Philippines – Distilled Spirits (2012)*, para. 170.

To make such a determination, a panel examines on a case-by-case basis all relevant criteria, including: (1) the products' properties, nature and quality, i.e. their physical characteristics; (2) the products' end uses (i.e. the extent to which products are capable of performing the same, or similar, functions); (3) consumers' tastes and habits, also referred to as consumers' perceptions and behaviour, in respect of the products (i.e. the extent to which consumers are willing to use the products to perform these functions or the extent to which consumers perceive products to be substitutable); and (4) the products' tariff classification.[86] With regard to these criteria, the Appellate Body observed that they are not exhaustive and also not treaty text, but rather:

> tools available to panels for organizing and assessing the evidence relating to the competitive relationship between and among the products ...[87]

The adoption of a particular framework to examine the evidence regarding the 'likeness' of products does not dissolve the duty or the need to examine, in each case, *all* of the pertinent evidence.

Also, while the criteria referred to above are 'distinct', they are not mutually exclusive.[88] Certain evidence may well fall, and can be examined, under more than one criterion.[89] As to the relative importance of each of these criteria, the Appellate Body noted that:

> while in the determination of 'likeness' a panel may logically start from the physical characteristics of the products, none of the criteria a panel considers necessarily has an overarching role in the determination of 'likeness' under Article III:2 of the GATT 1994.[90]

As the Appellate Body explained, products that have very similar physical characteristics may not be 'like', within the meaning of Article III:2 of the GATT 1994, if their competitiveness or substitutability is low, while products that present physical differences may still be considered 'like' if such physical differences have a limited impact on the competitive relationship among the products.[91]

86 See *ibid.*, para. 118. On other possible criteria, see below, pp. 369–70.

87 Appellate Body Reports, *Philippines – Distilled Spirits (2012)*, para. 131. In its report in *EC – Asbestos (2001)*, the Appellate Body had already made this observation in the context of the 'likeness' analysis under Article III:4 of the GATT 1994. See below, p. 382.

88 See Appellate Body Reports, *Philippines – Distilled Spirits (2012)*, para. 131. On the distinctiveness of the criteria, see Appellate Body Report, *EC – Asbestos (2001)*, para. 111. See below, p. 382.

89 See Appellate Body Reports, *Philippines – Distilled Spirits (2012)*, para. 131. The evidence at issue in *Philippines – Distilled Spirits (2012)* concerned the perceptibility of differences in physical characteristics. Such evidence can be examined both under the 'physical characteristics' criterion and under the criterion of 'consumers' tastes and habits'. Note that, in *EC – Asbestos (2001)*, the Appellate Body considered health risks under the 'physical characteristics' criterion as well as under the criterion of 'consumers' tastes and habits'. See Appellate Body Report, *EC – Asbestos (2001)*, paras. 114 and 120.

90 Appellate Body Reports, *Philippines – Distilled Spirits (2012)*, para. 119. Note, however, that the Appellate Body in *EC – Asbestos (2001)*, para. 117, stated that evidence with regard to end uses and consumers' tastes and habits is 'of particular importance under Article III, precisely because that provision is concerned with competitive relationships in the marketplace'.

91 See Appellate Body Reports, *Philippines – Distilled Spirits (2012)*, para. 120.

In *Japan – Alcoholic Beverages II (1996)*, shochu and vodka were found to be 'like products' within the meaning of Article III:2, first sentence.[92] In *Korea – Alcoholic Beverages (1999)*, however, soju and vodka were not found to be 'like products'.[93] In *Mexico – Taxes on Soft Drinks (2006)*, soft drinks sweetened with beet sugar or high fructose corn syrup (HFCS) and soft drinks sweetened with cane sugar were considered to be 'like products' within the meaning of Article III:2, first sentence.[94] In the same case, beet sugar and cane sugar were also considered to be 'like products' but cane sugar and HFCS were not.[95] In *Philippines – Distilled Spirits (2012)*, distilled spirits of a specific type (such as whisky and brandy) made from designated raw materials (and in particular sugar cane) and distilled spirits of the same type made from other raw materials (cereals for whisky and grapes for brandy) were found to be 'like products' within the meaning of Article III:2, first sentence.[96] In the latter case, the Appellate Body found that:

> as long as the differences among the products, including a difference in the raw material base, leave fundamentally unchanged the competitive relationship among the final products, the existence of these differences does not prevent a finding of 'likeness' if, by considering all factors, the panel is able to come to the conclusion that the competitive relationship among the products is such as to justify a finding of 'likeness' under Article III:2.[97]

While examining the concept of 'directly competitive or substitutable products' within the meaning of Article III:2, second sentence, of the GATT 1994, the Appellate Body in *Canada – Periodicals (1997)* as well as in *Korea – Alcoholic Beverages (1999)* observed that products that are perfectly substitutable would be 'like products' within the meaning of Article III:2, first sentence.[98] However, the Appellate Body in *Philippines – Distilled Spirits (2012)* noted in this regard:

> We do not understand the statements by the Appellate Body in *Canada – Periodicals* and in *Korea – Alcoholic Beverages* to mean that *only* products that are perfectly substitutable

92 See Panel Report, *Japan – Alcoholic Beverages II (1996)*, para. 6.23, referring to the panel report in *Japan –Alcoholic Beverages I (1987)*. The panel found that shochu and vodka were 'like products' because 'they were both white/clean spirits, made of similar raw materials, and the end-uses were virtually identical'. The panel also found that the traditional Japanese consumer habits with regard to shochu provided no reason for not considering vodka to be a 'like product'. The panel found that shochu and a number of other alcoholic beverages were not 'like products' because of the 'substantial noticeable differences' in physical characteristics such as the use of additives (for liqueurs and gin), the use of ingredients (for rum) and appearance (for whisky and brandy). As discussed below, the panel would, however, find shochu and these other alcoholic beverages 'directly competitive or substitutable' within the meaning of Article III:2, second sentence. See below, p. 367.

93 See Panel Report, *Korea – Alcoholic Beverages (1999)*, para. 10.104. These products were, however, considered to be directly competitive or substitutable within the meaning of the second sentence of Article III:2. See below, p. 367.

94 See Panel Report, *Mexico – Taxes on Soft Drinks (2006)*, para. 8.136.

95 See *ibid.*, paras. 8.36 and 8.78. Cane sugar and HFCS were, however, considered to be directly competitive or substitutable within the meaning of the second sentence of Article III:2. See below, p. 395.

96 See Appellate Body Reports, *Philippines – Distilled Spirits (2012)*, para. 172.

97 *Ibid.*, para. 125.

98 In *Canada – Periodicals (1997)*, the Appellate Body stated: 'A case of perfect substitutability would fall within Article III:2, first sentence, while we are examining the broader prohibition of the second sentence.' Appellate Body Report, *Canada – Periodicals (1997)*, 473. See also Appellate Body Report, *Korea – Alcoholic Beverages (1999)*, para. 118.

> can fall within the scope of Article III:2, first sentence. This would be too narrow an interpretation and would reduce the scope of the first sentence essentially to identical products. Rather, we consider that, under the first sentence, products that are close to being perfectly substitutable can be 'like products', whereas products that compete to a lesser degree would fall within the scope of the second sentence.[99]

According to the panel in *Dominican Republic – Import and Sale of Cigarettes (2005)*, the actual price at which products are sold on the market of the importing country is a criterion – in addition to the criteria already discussed above – to be considered when determining whether products are 'like' within the meaning of Article III:2, first sentence.[100] Also, the panel in *Philippines – Distilled Spirits (2012)* recognised the relevance of the price of products in the determination of whether products are 'like'.[101] In this case, the Philippines contended that imported 'non-sugar-based' spirits were priced regularly above PHP150 per bottle, that only 1.8 per cent of its population could afford these imported distilled spirits, and that the imported 'non-sugar-based' spirits and the much cheaper domestic 'sugar-based' spirits were, therefore, not in competition, i.e. were not 'like products'. The panel considered price and expendable income to be a relevant criterion for determining 'likeness', but came to the conclusion that, while a large proportion of the Philippine population had indeed a limited ability to purchase distilled spirits beyond certain price levels, the Philippine market was *not* divided into two segments (namely, high-priced imported spirits *and* low-priced domestic spirits).[102] In *Thailand – Cigarettes (Philippines) (2011)*, the panel found that it was not required that 'all' imported cigarettes and 'all' domestic cigarettes were like, and it limited its examination to whether the imported and domestic cigarettes 'within particular price segments' were 'like'.[103]

In *US – Malt Beverages (1992)*, the panel held that legislation giving special tax exemptions to products of small firms (whether domestic or foreign) would constitute discrimination against imports from a larger foreign firm and therefore infringe Article III because its products would be treated less favourably than the like products of a small domestic firm.[104] According to the panel in *US – Malt Beverages (1992)*, the fact that products were produced by small, artisanal *or* large, industrial firms (i.e. a process and production method (PPM) of the products concerned) was irrelevant in the determination of their 'likeness'. While there has been no further attempt in dispute settlement cases to refer to PPMs in the determination of 'likeness' in Article III:2, first sentence, it is not

99 Appellate Body Reports, *Philippines – Distilled Spirits (2012)*, para. 149.

100 See Panel Report, *Dominican Republic – Import and Sale of Cigarettes (2005)*, paras. 7.333–7.336. Note, however, that a price difference between the imported and the domestic product may be a consequence of discriminatory discrimination.

101 See Panel Reports, *Philippines – Distilled Spirits (2012)*, para. 7.59.

102 See *ibid.* On the basis of the evidence before it, the panel found that there were in fact lower-priced imported 'non-sugar-based' spirits that competed with domestic 'sugar-based' spirits, as well as high-priced domestic 'sugar-based' spirits that competed with imported 'non-sugar-based' spirits. See *ibid.*

103 Panel Report, *Thailand – Cigarettes (Philippines) (2011)*, para. 7.428. This finding was not appealed.

104 See Panel Report, *US – Malt Beverages (1992)*, para. 5.19.

clear whether this 1992 panel statement on the irrelevance of PPMs reflects the current state of the law.[105]

The panel in *US – Malt Beverages (1992)* also considered, however, with regard to the determination of 'likeness' that:

> the like product determination under Article III:2 also should have regard to the purpose of the Article ... The purpose ... is ... not to prevent contracting parties from using their fiscal and regulatory powers for purposes other than to afford protection to domestic production. Specifically, the purpose of Article III is not to prevent contracting parties from differentiating between different product categories for policy purposes unrelated to the protection of domestic production ... Consequently, in determining whether two products subject to different treatment are like products, it is necessary to consider whether such product differentiation is being made 'so as to afford protection to domestic production'.[106]

The panel found domestic wine containing a particular local variety of grape to be 'like' imported wine not containing this variety of grape after considering that the purpose of differentiating between the wines was to afford protection to the local production of wine. The panel noted that the United States did not advance any alternative policy objective for the differentiation. According to the panel, the reason for the product differentiation was to be considered when deciding on the 'likeness' of products. The panel in *US – Malt Beverages (1992)* thus for the first time referred to a 'regulatory intent' approach, more commonly referred to as an 'aim-and-effect' approach, to the determination of 'likeness' of products.

In a dispute concerning, *inter alia*, special tax levels for luxury vehicles, *US – Taxes on Automobiles (1994)*, the panel elaborated on the 'aim-and-effect' approach to determining 'likeness'.[107] The United States imposed a retail excise tax on cars with prices above US$30,000 and the panel had to determine whether cars with prices above and below US$30,000 were 'like products'. The complainant in this dispute, the European Community, argued before the panel that 'likeness' should be determined on the basis of criteria such as the end use of the products, their physical characteristics and tariff classification. The United States contended that the key factor in determining 'likeness' should be whether the measure was applied 'so as to afford protection to domestic industry'. The panel reasoned that the determination of 'likeness' would, in all but the most straightforward cases, have to include an examination of the *aims and effects* of the particular tax measure. According to the panel in *US – Taxes on Automobiles (1994)*, 'likeness' should be examined in terms of whether the less favourable treatment was based on a regulatory distinction made so as to afford protection to domestic production. *In casu*, the panel decided that the luxury tax was not implemented to afford protection to the domestic production of cars and that,

105 For a discussion on the relevance of PPMs in the determination of 'likeness' in Article III:4, see below, p. 388.
106 Panel Report, *US – Malt Beverages (1992)*, paras. 5.24–5.25.
107 Panel Report, *US – Taxes on Automobiles (1994)*, para. 5.10.

therefore, cars above and below US$30,000 could not, for the purpose of the luxury tax, be considered as 'like products' under Article III:2, first sentence.[108]

The 'aim-and-effect' test for determining 'likeness', i.e. determining 'likeness' by considering whether the regulatory distinction between the products at issue has a bona fide *aim* or whether it creates a protectionist *effect*, was, however, explicitly rejected in 1996 by the panel in *Japan – Alcoholic Beverages II (1996)*. The panel found as follows:

> the proposed aim-and-effect test is not consistent with the wording of Article III:2, first sentence. The Panel recalled that the basis of the aim-and-effect test is found in the words 'so as to afford protection' contained in Article III:1. The Panel further recalled that Article III:2, first sentence, contains no reference to those words. Moreover, the adoption of the aim-and-effect test would have important repercussions on the burden of proof imposed on the complainant. The Panel noted in this respect that the complainants, according to the aim-and-effect test, have the burden of showing not only the effect of a particular measure, which is in principle discernible, but also its aim, which sometimes can be indiscernible. The Panel also noted that very often there is a multiplicity of aims that are sought through enactment of legislation and it would be a difficult exercise to determine which aim or aims should be determinative for applying the aim-and-effect test.[109]

In further support of its rejection of the aim-and-effect test in determining 'likeness' in the context of Article III:2 of the GATT 1994, the panel in *Japan – Alcoholic Beverages II (1996)* also noted:

> the list of exceptions contained in Article XX of GATT 1994 could become redundant or useless because the aim-and-effect test does not contain a definitive list of grounds justifying departure from the obligations that are otherwise incorporated in Article III ... [I]n principle, a WTO Member could, for example, invoke protection of health in the context of invoking the aim-and-effect test. The Panel noted that if this were the case, then the standard of proof established in Article XX would effectively be circumvented. WTO Members would not have to prove that a health measure is 'necessary' to achieve its health objective. Moreover, proponents of the aim-and-effect test even shift the burden of proof, arguing that it would be up to the complainant to produce a *prima facie* case that a measure has both the aim and effect of affording protection to domestic production and, once the complainant has demonstrated that this is the case, only then would the defending party have to present evidence to rebut the claim.[110]

The Appellate Body in *Japan – Alcoholic Beverages II (1996)* implicitly affirmed the panel's rejection of the 'aim-and-effect' (or 'regulatory intent') approach to determining whether products are 'like'.[111]

Finally, while the determination of whether products are 'like' within the meaning of Article III:2, first sentence, may often be quite problematic, there have been disputes concerning Article III:2, first sentence, in which panels have

108 Note that the panel report in *US – Taxes on Automobiles (1994)* was never adopted by the GATT Contracting Parties.

109 Panel Report, *Japan – Alcoholic Beverages II (1996)*, para. 6.16.

110 *Ibid.*, para. 6.17. For a detailed discussion of Article XX of the GATT 1994 and the conditions it imposes for the justification of an otherwise GATT-inconsistent measure, see below, pp. 544–623.

111 The Appellate Body stated: 'With these modifications to the legal reasoning in the Panel Report, we affirm the legal conclusions and the findings of the Panel with respect to "like products" in all other respects.' Appellate Body Report, *Japan – Alcoholic Beverages II (1996)*, 115.

sidestepped the 'likeness' issue and have proceeded on the *presumption* that there are 'like' products.[112] The panels in these disputes have assumed that there are 'like' products when the measure at issue distinguishes between products solely on the basis of their origin. The panel in *Indonesia – Autos (1998)* stated:

> Under the Indonesian car programmes the distinction between the products for tax purposes is based on such factors as the nationality of the producer or the origin of the parts and components contained in the product ... In our view, such an origin-based distinction in respect of internal taxes suffices in itself to violate Article III:2, without the need to demonstrate the existence of actually traded *like* products.[113]

The panel in *Colombia – Ports of Entry (2009)* stated:

> where a WTO Member imposes an origin-based distinction with respect to internal taxes, imported and domestic products may be considered as like products, and a case-by-case determination of 'likeness' between the foreign and domestic would be unnecessary.[114]

To date the Appellate Body has not ruled on this approach for determining 'likeness' under Article III:2 of the GATT 1994.[115] However, as discussed above and below, the Appellate Body has upheld the origin-base presumption of likeness in the context of Articles II:1 and XVII of the GATS.[116]

2.2.3 Taxes 'in Excess of'

The third and last element of the test of consistency with the national treatment obligation of Article III:2, first sentence, of the GATT 1994 relates to the question of whether the imported products are *taxed in excess* of the domestic products. Pursuant to Article III:2, first sentence, internal taxes on imported products should not be 'in excess of' the internal taxes applied to 'like' domestic products. In *Japan – Alcoholic Beverages II (1996)*, the Appellate Body established a strict benchmark for the 'in excess of' requirement. The Appellate Body ruled that the prohibition of discriminatory taxes in Article III:2, first sentence, is not qualified by a *de minimis* standard. According to the Appellate Body, 'even the smallest amount of "excess" is too much'.[117]

112 See also above, pp. 316–19 (regarding 'likeness' under Article I:1 of the GATT 1994) and below, pp. 351–65 (regarding 'likeness' under Article III:4).

113 Panel Report, *Indonesia – Autos (1998)*, para. 14.113. Emphasis added.

114 Panel Report, *Colombia – Ports of Entry (2009)*, para. 7.182. See also Appellate Body Report, *Canada – Periodicals (1997)*, 466; and Panel Report, *Indonesia – Autos (1998)*, para. 14.113. The panel in *Colombia – Ports of Entry (2009)* noted that both the Appellate Body and panels have previously recognised the possibility of the existence of hypothetical like products.

115 The presumption of likeness was applied by panels with respect to Article III:2 in *Argentina – Hides and Leather (2000); and China-Auto Parts (2008)*. See Panel Reports, *Argentina – Hides and Leather (2000)*, para. 11.168; and Panel Reports, *China – Auto Parts (2008)*, para. 7.216.

116 See above, pp. 333–7 and below, p. 405. See Appellate Body Report, *Argentina – Financial Services (2016)*, paras. 6.32 and 6.38.

117 Appellate Body Report, *Japan – Alcoholic Beverages II (1996)*, 27–8. With respect to the absence of a *de minimis* standard, note that the panel in *US – Superfund (1987)* already ruled that, although the rate of tax applied to the imported petroleum was merely 3.5 cents per barrel higher than the rate applied to the like domestic petroleum, the US tax on petroleum was inconsistent with Article III:2, first sentence. See Panel Report, *US – Superfund (1987)*, para. 5.1.1. In *Argentina – Hides and Leather (2001)*, the panel rejected Argentina's argument that the tax burden differential between imported and domestic products was *de minimis* because it would only exist for a thirty-day period. See Panel Report, *Argentina – Hides and Leather (2001)*, para. 11.245. See also Panel Report, *Colombia – Ports of Entry (2009)*, para. 7.195; and Panel Report, *China – Auto Parts (2009)*, para. 7.221.

Furthermore, the prohibition of discriminatory taxes in Article III:2, first sentence, is not conditional on a 'trade effects test'. As discussed above, the Appellate Body stated in *Japan – Alcoholic Beverages II (1996)*:

> it is irrelevant that the 'trade effects' of the tax differential between imported and domestic products, as reflected in the volumes of imports, are insignificant or even non-existent; Article III *protects expectations* not of any particular trade volume but rather *of the equal competitive relationship* between imported and domestic products.[118]

In *Argentina – Hides and Leather (2001)*, the panel emphasised that Article III:2, first sentence, requires a comparison of *actual tax burdens* rather than merely of nominal tax rates. The panel ruled:

> Article III:2, first sentence, is not concerned with taxes or charges as such or the policy purposes Members pursue with them, but with their economic impact on the competitive opportunities of imported and like domestic products. It follows, in our view, that what must be compared are the tax burdens imposed on the taxed products.[119]

The panel noted that, if Article III:2, first sentence, would not require a comparison of actual tax burdens, Members could easily evade the prohibition on tax discrimination by, for example, using different methods of computing tax bases for imported and domestic products resulting in a greater actual tax burden for imported products.[120]

In *Thailand – Cigarettes (Philippines) (2011)*, the tax measure at issue imposed the same nominal value added tax (VAT) rate, 7 per cent *ad valorem*, on domestic as well as imported cigarettes. However, resellers of domestic cigarettes incurred no VAT liability while resellers of imported cigarettes did incur VAT liability, and this liability was not offset automatically.[121] Resellers of imported cigarettes had to satisfy certain administrative requirements in order for the VAT paid to be offset against the VAT due. The Appellate Body 'agree[d] with the Panel that Thailand subjects imported cigarettes to internal taxes in excess of those applied to like domestic cigarettes, within the meaning of Article III:2, first sentence, of the GATT 1994'.[122]

A Member which applies higher taxes on imported products in some situations but 'balances' this by applying lower taxes on the imported products in other situations also acts inconsistently with the national treatment obligation of Article III:2, first sentence. The panel in *Argentina – Hides and Leather (2001)* ruled:

> Article III:2, first sentence, is applicable to each individual import transaction. It does not permit Members to balance more favourable tax treatment of imported products in some instances against less favourable tax treatment of imported products in other instances.[123]

118 Appellate Body Report, *Japan – Alcoholic Beverages II (1996)*, 110. Emphasis added.

119 Panel Report, *Argentina – Hides and Leather (2001)*, para. 11.182.

120 See *ibid.*, para. 11.183. See already Panel Report, *Japan – Alcoholic Beverages I (1987)*, para. 5.8. See also Panel Report, *Colombia – Ports of Entry (2009)*, paras. 7.188–7.196.

121 In respect of sales of domestic cigarettes, only Thailand Tobacco Monopoly (TTM), the only manufacturer of cigarettes in Thailand, was subject to VAT.

122 Appellate Body Report, *Thailand – Cigarettes (Philippines) (2011)*, para. 116.

123 Panel Report, *Argentina – Hides and Leather (2001)*, para. 11.260.

2.3 National Treatment Test for Internal Taxation on Directly Competitive or Substitutable Products

The second sentence of Article III:2 of the GATT 1994 states:

> Moreover, no [Member] shall otherwise apply internal taxes or other internal charges to imported or domestic products in a manner contrary to the principles set forth in paragraph 1.

As discussed above, the relevant leading principle set forth in paragraph 1 of Article III is that internal taxes and other internal charges:

> should not be applied to imported or domestic products so as to afford protection to domestic production.

Furthermore, the Note *Ad* Article III provides with respect to Article III:2:

> A tax conforming to the requirements of the first sentence of paragraph 2 would be considered to be inconsistent with the provisions of the second sentence only in cases where competition was involved between, on the one hand, the taxed product and, on the other hand, a directly competitive or substitutable product which was not similarly taxed.

The relationship between the first and the second sentence of Article III:2 was addressed by the Appellate Body in *Canada – Periodicals (1997)*, a dispute concerning, *inter alia*, a Canadian excise tax on magazines. The Appellate Body considered that, if an internal tax on products is found to be consistent with Article III:2, first sentence, there is a need to examine further whether the measure is consistent with Article III:2, second sentence.[124] As the Appellate Body stated in *Japan – Alcoholic Beverages II (1996)* and again in *Canada – Periodicals (1997)*, Article III:2, second sentence, contemplates a 'broader category of products' than Article III:2, first sentence.[125] With regard to this broader category of products, it sets out a different test of consistency.[126] In *Japan – Alcoholic Beverages II (1996)*, the Appellate Body stated:

> three separate issues must be addressed to determine whether an internal tax measure is inconsistent with Article III:2, second sentence. These three issues are whether:
>
> 1. the imported products and the domestic products are 'directly competitive or substitutable products' which are in competition with each other;
> 2. the directly competitive or substitutable imported and domestic products are 'not similarly taxed'; and
> 3. the dissimilar taxation of the directly competitive or substitutable imported [and] domestic products is 'applied ... so as to afford protection to domestic production'.[127]

However, before this test of consistency of internal taxation with Article III:2, second sentence, of the GATT 1994 can be applied, it must be established that

124 See Appellate Body Report, *Canada – Periodicals (1997)*, 468.

125 See *ibid.*, 470. See also Appellate Body Report, *Japan – Alcoholic Beverages II (1996)*, 112.

126 See also Appellate Body Reports, *Philippines – Distilled Spirits (2012)*, para. 190.

127 Appellate Body Report, *Japan – Alcoholic Beverages II (1996)*, 116. See also Appellate Body Report, *Canada –Periodicals (1997)*, 470; Appellate Body Report, *Chile – Alcoholic Beverages (2000)*, para. 47; and Appellate Body Reports, *Philippines – Distilled Spirits (2012)*, para. 190.

the measure at issue is an 'internal tax or other internal charge' within the meaning of Article III:2, second sentence.

Therefore, the four-tier test of consistency of internal taxation with Article III:2, second sentence, requires the examination of:

- whether the measure at issue is an *internal tax or other internal charge* on products;
- whether the imported and domestic products are *directly competitive or substitutable*;
- whether the imported and domestic products are *dissimilarly taxed*; and
- whether the dissimilar taxation is applied so as to afford protection to domestic production.

Below, each element of this four-tier test of consistency will be discussed in turn.[128]

To date, WTO Members have been found to have acted inconsistently with Article III:2, second sentence, of the GATT 1994 in seven disputes.[129]

2.3.1 'Internal Taxes ...'

As is the case with Article III:2, first sentence, Article III:2, second sentence, of the GATT 1994 is also concerned with 'internal taxes or other internal charges' which are applied directly or indirectly on products. For a discussion on the meaning and scope of these concepts, recall the discussion above in the subsection dealing with Article III:2, first sentence.[130] With regard to this constituent element of the national treatment test, there is no difference between the first and the second sentences of Article III:2.

2.3.2 'Directly Competitive or Substitutable Products'

The second element of the test of consistency with the national treatment obligation of Article III:2, second sentence, of the GATT 1994 relates to the question of whether the imported and domestic products concerned are 'directly competitive or substitutable products'. The national treatment obligation of Article III:2, second sentence, of the GATT 1994 applies to 'directly competitive or substitutable products'. As with the concept of 'like products' discussed above, the concept of 'directly competitive or substitutable products' is not defined in the GATT 1994. However, the relevant case law to date provides us with a number of examples of products that panels and/or the Appellate Body have found to be 'directly competitive or substitutable' on the market of a particular Member. In *Canada – Periodicals (1997)*, the 'directly competitive or substitutable products'

128 See below, pp. 366–73.

129 See *Japan – Alcoholic Beverages II (1996)*; *Canada – Periodicals (1997)*; *Indonesia – Autos (1998)*; *Korea – Alcoholic Beverages (1999)*; *Chile – Alcoholic Beverages (2000)*; *Mexico – Taxes on Soft Drinks (2006)*; and *Philippines – Distilled Spirits (2012)*.

130 See above, pp. 360–3.

were the imported split-run periodicals and domestic non-split-run periodicals at issue in that case.[131] In *Japan – Alcoholic Beverages II (1996)* and *Korea – Alcoholic Beverages (1999)*, the traditional local alcoholic beverages, shochu and soju respectively, were found to be 'directly competitive or substitutable' with imported 'Western-style' liquors, such as whisky, vodka, brandy, cognac, rum, gin and liqueurs.[132] In *Chile – Alcoholic Beverages (2000)*, the domestically produced pisco was considered 'directly competitive or substitutable' with imported distilled spirits, such as whisky, brandy and cognac.[133] In *Mexico – Taxes on Soft Drinks (2006)*, the 'directly competitive or substitutable products' were the domestic cane sugar and imported high fructose corn syrup.[134] Most recently, in *Philippines – Distilled Spirits (2012)*, domestic distilled spirits from designated raw materials (and in particular sugar cane) were found to be 'directly competitive or substitutable' with imported distilled spirits from other raw materials (such as cereals, grapes).[135]

In *Canada – Periodicals (1997)*, the Appellate Body ruled that, to be 'directly competitive or substitutable' within the meaning of Article III:2, second sentence, contrary to what Canada had argued, products do not have to be perfectly substitutable. The Appellate Body noted:

> A case of perfect substitutability would fall within Article III:2, first sentence, while we are examining the broader prohibition of the second sentence.[136]

With regard to the relationship between the concept of 'like products' of Article III:2, first sentence, and the concept of 'directly competitive or substitutable products' of Article III:2, second sentence, the Appellate Body stated in *Korea – Alcoholic Beverages (1999)*:

> 'Like' products are a subset of directly competitive or substitutable products: all like products are, by definition, directly competitive or substitutable products, whereas not all

131 See Appellate Body Report, *Canada – Periodicals (1997)*, 474. A split-run periodical is a periodical with different editions distributed in different countries, in which part of the editorial material is the same or substantially the same as editorial material that appears in other editions but in which advertisements differ (as they are focused on the local market of a specific edition). The Appellate Body found split-run and non-split-run periodicals to be directly competitive or substitutable products insofar as they are part of the same segment of the Canadian market for periodicals.

132 See Panel Report, *Japan – Alcoholic Beverages II (1996)*, para. 6.32 ('whisky, brandy, gin, genever, rum, and liqueurs', para. 6.28); and Panel Report, *Korea – Alcoholic Beverages (1999)*, para. 10.98 ('vodka, whiskies, rum, gin, brandies, cognac, liqueurs, tequila and ad-mixtures', para. 10.57). Recall that, in *Japan – Alcoholic Beverages (1996)*, shochu and vodka were found to be 'like products' under Article III:2, first sentence. See above, p. 355.

133 See Panel Report, *Chile – Alcoholic Beverages (2000)*, para. 7.83.

134 See Panel Report, *Mexico – Taxes on Soft Drinks (2006)*, para. 8.78. Recall that, in this case, the domestic cane sugar and the imported beet sugar were found to be 'like products' under Article III:2, first sentence. Also, the domestic soft drinks sweetened with cane sugar and imported soft drinks sweetened with beet sugar or HFCS were found to be 'like products'. See above, p. 359.

135 See Appellate Body Reports, *Philippines – Distilled Spirits (2012)*, para. 242. Recall that, in this case, distilled spirits of a specific type (such as whisky and brandy) made from designated raw materials (and, in particular, sugar cane) and distilled spirits of the same type made from other raw materials (cereals for whisky and grapes for brandy) were found to be 'like products'. See above, p. 359.

136 Appellate Body Report, *Canada – Periodicals (1997)*, 473. As to the implications of this statement for the scope of the concept of 'like products', see above, pp. 350–9.

'directly competitive or substitutable' products are 'like'. The notion of like products must be construed narrowly but the category of directly competitive or substitutable products is broader.[137]

As to the meaning of the concept of 'directly competitive or substitutable products', the Appellate Body further stated in *Korea – Alcoholic Beverages (1999)* that products are 'competitive' or 'substitutable' when:

they are interchangeable or if they offer, as the Panel noted, 'alternative ways of satisfying a particular need or taste'.[138]

The words 'competitive' or 'substitutable' are qualified by the word 'directly'. In the context of Article III:2, second sentence, the word 'directly' suggests a 'degree of proximity' in the competitive relationship between the domestic and the imported products.[139] According to the Appellate Body in *Philippines – Distilled Spirits (2012)*, the requisite degree of competition is met where the imported and domestic products are characterised by a high, but imperfect, degree of substitutability.[140]

In *Korea – Alcoholic Beverages (1999)*, the Appellate Body further clarified the concept of 'directly competitive or substitutable products' by noting that:

Competition in the market place is a dynamic, evolving process. Accordingly, the wording of the term 'directly competitive or substitutable' implies that the competitive relationship between products is *not* to be analyzed *exclusively* by reference to *current* consumer preferences.[141]

According to the Appellate Body, the word '*substitutable*' indicates that:

the requisite relationship *may* exist between products that are not, at a given moment, considered by consumers to be substitutes but which are, nonetheless, *capable* of being substituted for one another.[142]

In assessing whether products are 'directly competitive or substitutable', a panel must thus consider not only extant demand (or current competition) but also latent demand (or potential competition). As the Appellate Body noted in *Korea – Alcoholic Beverages (1999)*, particularly in a market where there are barriers to trade or to competition, there may well be latent demand.[143] In *Philippines – Distilled Spirits (2012)*, the Appellate Body held that:

137 Appellate Body Report, *Korea – Alcoholic Beverages (1999)*, para. 118. In a footnote, the Appellate Body referred to the Appellate Body Report, *Japan – Alcoholic Beverages II (1996)*, and Appellate Body Report, *Canada – Periodicals (1997)*.

138 *Ibid.*, para. 115. 139 *Ibid.*, para. 116.

140 See Appellate Body Reports, *Philippines – Distilled Spirits (2012)*, para. 205. In a footnote, the Appellate Body refers to Appellate Body Report, *Korea – Alcoholic Beverages (1999)*, para. 118; Appellate Body Report, *Canada – Periodicals (1997)*, 473; and Appellate Body Report, *US – Cotton Yarn (2001)*, fn. 68 to para. 97.

141 Appellate Body Report, *Korea – Alcoholic Beverages (1999)*, para. 114.

142 *Ibid.* 143 See *ibid.*, para. 115.

instances of *current* substitution are likely to *underestimate* latent demand for imported spirits as a result of distortive effects introduced by the excise tax at issue.[144]

The tax measure at issue as well as (current and prior) other protectionist taxation, import restrictions and regulatory measures can have the effect of creating, and even freezing, consumer preferences for domestic products.[145] It is thus highly relevant to examine latent demand. The competitive relationship between products is clearly not to be analysed by reference to *current* consumer preferences only.[146]

In justification of its position that when determining whether products are 'directly competitive or substitutable' a panel should also consider *latent* demand, and thus *potential* competition, the Appellate Body stated in *Korea – Alcoholic Beverages (1999)*:

> In view of the objectives of avoiding protectionism, requiring equality of competitive conditions and protecting expectations of equal competitive relationships, we decline to take a static view of the term 'directly competitive or substitutable'. The object and purpose of Article III confirms that the scope of the term 'directly competitive or substitutable' cannot be limited to situations where consumers *already* regard products as alternatives. If reliance could be placed only on current instances of substitution, the object and purpose of Article III:2 could be defeated by the protective taxation that the provision aims to prohibit.[147]

In brief, products are considered to be 'directly competitive or substitutable' when they are interchangeable or when they offer alternative ways of satisfying a particular need or taste. In examining whether products are 'directly competitive or substitutable', an analysis of *latent* as well as *extant* demand is required since 'competition in the marketplace is a dynamic, evolving process' and the object and purpose of Article III is, fundamentally, 'protecting expectations of equal competitive relationships'.[148]

With respect to the criteria to be taken into account in establishing whether products are 'directly competitive or substitutable' within the meaning of

144 Appellate Body Reports, *Philippines – Distilled Spirits (2012)*, para. 226.

145 See Appellate Body Report, *Korea – Alcoholic Beverages (1999)*, para. 120 (quoting Panel Report, *Japan – Alcoholic Beverages II (1996)*, para. 6.28); and Appellate Body Reports, *Philippines – Distilled Spirits (2012)*, para. 226. The Appellate Body noted in *Korea – Alcoholic Beverages (1999)* and again in *Philippines – Distilled Spirits (2012)* that current demand for products is a function of actual retail prices, which could be distorted by the tax measure at issue *and* other related effects, such as higher distribution costs, lower volumes and economies of scale (see paras. 122–3 and para. 221 respectively). For these reasons, the Appellate Body did not agree with the Philippines that an analysis of potential competition is limited to an assessment of whether competition would otherwise occur if the challenged taxation were not in place. According to the Appellate Body, such a 'but for' test reflects an overly restrictive interpretation of the term 'directly competitive or substitutable' products, one which assumes that internal taxation is the *only* factor restricting potential substitutability. See Appellate Body Reports, *Philippines – Distilled Spirits (2012)*, para. 227.

146 As the Appellate Body noted in *Philippines – Distilled Spirits (2012)*, it follows from this that for products to be 'directly competitive or substitutable', Article III:2, second sentence, does not require – contrary to what was argued by the Philippines in this case – '*identity* in the "nature and frequency" of the consumer's purchasing behaviour'. If that were the case, the competitive relationship between the imported and domestic products in a given market would only be assessed with reference to *current* consumer preferences. See Appellate Body Reports, *Philippines – Distilled Spirits (2012)*, paras. 217–18.

147 Appellate Body Report, *Korea – Alcoholic Beverages (1999)*, para. 120.

148 *Ibid.*, paras. 114–20.

Article III:2, second sentence, the Appellate Body agreed with the panel in *Japan – Alcoholic Beverages II (1996)* that, in addition to the products' physical characteristics, end use and tariff classification, a panel needs to look at the 'market place'.[149] The Appellate Body held:

> The GATT 1994 is a commercial agreement, and the WTO is concerned, after all, with markets. It does not seem inappropriate to look at competition in the relevant markets as one among a number of means of identifying the broader category of products that might be described as 'directly competitive or substitutable'.[150]
>
> Nor does it seem inappropriate to examine elasticity of substitution as one means of examining those relevant markets.[151]

The Appellate Body thus considered an examination of the cross-price elasticity of demand in the relevant market, as a means of establishing whether products are 'directly competitive or substitutable' in that market. However, in *Korea – Alcoholic Beverages (1999)*, the Appellate Body was careful to stress that cross-price elasticity of demand for products is not the decisive criterion in determining whether these products are 'directly competitive or substitutable'. The Appellate Body agreed with the panel's emphasis on the 'quality' or 'nature' of competition rather than the 'quantitative overlap of competition'. The Appellate Body shared the panel's reluctance to rely unduly on quantitative analyses of the competitive relationship. In the Appellate Body's view, an approach that focused solely on the quantitative overlap of competition would, in essence, make cross-price elasticity the decisive criterion in determining whether products are 'directly competitive or substitutable'.[152] Making cross-price elasticity the decisive criterion would likely result in underestimating latent demand and potential competition between the products at issue and, therefore, result in an incomplete, i.e. wrong, assessment of whether these products are 'directly competitive or substitutable' within the meaning of Article III:2, second sentence.

In *Philippines – Distilled Spirits (2012)*, the panel came to the conclusion that the products at issue – distilled spirits made from designated raw materials (and in particular sugar cane) and distilled spirits made from other raw materials (such as cereals, grapes) – were 'directly competitive or substitutable' by considering the following criteria: (1) the competitive relationship between the products at issue in the Philippines' market; (2) the products' channels of distribution; (3) their physical characteristics; (4) their end uses and marketing; (5) their tariff classification; and (6) internal regulations regarding these products.[153]

149 See Appellate Body Report *Japan – Alcoholic Beverages II (1996)*, 117. 150 *Ibid.* 151 *Ibid.*
152 See Appellate Body Report, *Korea – Alcoholic Beverages (1999)*, para. 134.
153 See Appellate Body Reports, *Philippines – Distilled Spirits (2012)*, para. 198. On appeal, the Philippines challenged only the panel's assessment of the competitive relationship between the products concerned in the Philippine market. See *ibid.*, para. 199.

With regard to the first of these criteria, namely, the competitive relationship between the products at issue, the Appellate Body found on appeal that:

the Panel did not err in its assessment of the competitive relationship between the imported and domestic distilled spirits at issue in the Philippine market. In our view, studies showing a significant degree of substitutability in the Philippine market between imported and domestic distilled spirits, as well as instances of price competition and evidence of actual and potential competition between imported and domestic distilled spirits in the Philippine market, sufficiently support the Panel's conclusion that there is 'a direct competitive relationship [in the Philippines] between domestic and imported distilled spirits, made from different raw materials'.[154]

Subsequently, the Appellate Body concluded:

This factor, combined with the other elements upon which the Panel relied, such as overlap in the channels of distribution, and similarities in the products' physical characteristics, end-uses, and marketing, sufficiently supports the Panel's finding that all imported and domestic distilled spirits at issue are 'directly competitive or substitutable' within the meaning of Article III:2, second sentence, of the GATT 1994.[155]

Note that, with regard to the relevance of 'price' in the determination of whether products are 'directly competitive or substitutable', the Appellate Body noted in *Philippines – Distilled Spirits (2012)* that:

price is very relevant in assessing whether imported and domestic products stand in a sufficiently direct competitive relationship in a given market. This is because evidence of price competition indicates that the imported product exercises competitive constraints on the domestic product, and *vice versa*. In this respect, we agree with the Philippines that evidence of major price differentials could demonstrate that the imported and domestic products are in completely separate markets.[156]

However, the panel in *Philippines – Distilled Spirits (2012)* made a factual finding that there was overlap in the prices of imported and domestic distilled spirits in the Philippines, and that such overlap was not 'exceptional' but rather occurred for both high- and low-priced products.[157] This factual finding was not challenged on appeal.[158]

In establishing whether products are 'directly competitive or substitutable' in the market of the responding Member, the market situation in *other* Members may be relevant and can be taken into consideration. In *Korea – Alcoholic Beverages (1999)*, the Appellate Body stated:

It is, of course, true that the 'directly competitive or substitutable' relationship must be present in the market at issue, in this case, the Korean market. It is also true that consumer responsiveness to products may vary from country to country. This does not, however,

154 *Ibid.*, para. 242. 155 *Ibid.* 156 *Ibid.*, para. 215.
157 See Panel Reports, *Philippines – Distilled Spirits (2012)*, para. 7.118.
158 Appellate Body Reports, *Philippines – Distilled Spirits (2012)*, para. 214. The Philippines argued instead that existing price overlaps do not show a sufficiently direct degree of competition.

preclude consideration of consumer behaviour in a country other than the one at issue. It seems to us that evidence from other markets may be pertinent to the examination of the market at issue, particularly when demand on that market has been influenced by regulatory barriers to trade or to competition.[159]

The Appellate Body emphasised that obviously not every other market will be relevant to the market at issue. However, if another market has characteristics similar to the market at issue, then evidence of consumer demand in that other market may be of some relevance to the market at issue.[160]

The question has arisen as to whether, in examining whether products are 'directly competitive or substitutable', it is necessary to scrutinise products on an item-by-item basis or whether it is permitted to group products together for the purpose of this examination. In *Korea – Alcoholic Beverages (1999)*, the panel compared soju (the domestic Korean liquor at issue in this case) with imported liquor products (vodka, whisky, rum, gin, brandy, cognac, liqueurs, tequila and ad-mixtures) on a group basis, rather than on an item-by-item basis. Korea appealed the panel's 'grouping' of products, but the Appellate Body rejected this appeal.[161] The Appellate Body first noted that the question whether, and to what extent, products can be grouped is a matter to be decided on a case-by-case basis, and that, in this case, the panel decided to group the imported products at issue on the basis that, 'on balance, all of the imported products specifically identified by the complainants have sufficient common characteristics, end-uses and channels of distribution and prices'.[162] The Appellate Body then observed that the panel's subsequent analysis of the physical characteristics, end uses, channels of distribution and prices of the imported products confirmed the correctness of its decision to group the products for analytical purposes. The Appellate Body also observed that, where appropriate, the panel did take account of individual product characteristics.[163]

In *Philippines – Distilled Spirits (2012)*, the Philippines argued on appeal that the panel incorrectly found direct competition between the imported and domestic distilled spirits at issue on the basis of a 'narrow segment' of the population having 'access' to imported distilled spirits. The Philippines contended that Article III:2, second sentence, requires that competition be assessed in relation to the market that is most representative of the 'market as a whole'. The Appellate Body considered that:

the Panel was correct in concluding that Article III of the GATT 1994 'does not protect just *some* instances or *most* instances, but rather, it protects *all* instances of direct competition'.[164]

159 Appellate Body Report, *Korea – Alcoholic Beverages (1999)*, para. 137. 160 See *ibid.*, para. 137.

161 See *ibid.*, para. 144. According to the Appellate Body, 'grouping' is an *analytical tool* to minimise repetition when examining the competitive relationship between a large number of differing products. Some grouping is almost always necessary in cases arising under Article III:2, second sentence. See Appellate Body Report, *Korea – Alcoholic Beverages (1999)*, para. 142.

162 See *ibid.*, para. 143, quoting from para. 10.60 of the panel report.

163 See *ibid.*, para. 144.

164 Appellate Body Reports, *Philippines – Distilled Spirits (2012)*, para. 221, referring to Panel Report, *Chile –Alcoholic Beverages (2000)*, para. 7.43.

And that:

> it was reasonable for the Panel to conclude that actual competition in a segment of the market *further supports* its conclusion that imported and domestic distilled spirits are capable of being substituted in the Philippines.[165]

2.3.3 Dissimilar Taxation

The third element of the test of consistency with the national treatment obligation of Article III:2, second sentence, of the GATT 1994 relates to the question of whether the products at issue are 'not similarly taxed', i.e. whether they are dissimilarly taxed. If imported products and directly competitive or substitutable domestic products are 'similarly taxed', there is no inconsistency with Article III:2, second sentence. While under Article III:2, first sentence, even the slightest tax differential leads to the conclusion that the internal tax imposed on imported products is GATT-inconsistent, under Article III:2, second sentence, the tax differential has to be more than *de minimis* to support a conclusion that the internal tax imposed on imported products is GATT-inconsistent. In *Japan – Alcoholic Beverages II (1996)*, the Appellate Body explained:

> To interpret 'in excess of' and 'not similarly taxed' identically would deny any distinction between the first and second sentences of Article III:2. Thus, in any given case, there may be some amount of taxation on imported products that may well be 'in excess of' the tax on domestic 'like products' but may not be so much as to compel a conclusion that 'directly competitive or substitutable' imported and domestic products are 'not similarly taxed' for the purposes of the *Ad* Article to Article III:2, second sentence.[166]

Whether any particular differential amount of taxation is *de minimis* or not, or, in other words, whether products are 'similarly taxed' or not, must be determined on a case-by-case basis.[167] Note that the Appellate Body found in *Canada – Periodicals (1997)* that the amount of the tax differential was 'far above the *de minimis* threshold', considering that the amount was 'sufficient to prevent the production and sale of split-run periodicals in Canada'.[168] In *Philippines – Distilled Spirits (2012)*, the imported distilled spirits were taxed ten to forty times more than the domestic distilled spirits. Not surprisingly, the panel in that case found that the products at issue were 'not taxed similarly'.[169]

165 Appellate Body Reports, *Philippines – Distilled Spirits (2012)*, para. 222. Emphasis added.
166 Appellate Body Report, *Japan – Alcoholic Beverages II (1996)*, 118. On the *de minimis* standard, see also Appellate Body Report, *Canada – Periodicals (1997)*, 474; Panel Report, *Indonesia – Autos (1998)*, para. 14.116; and Appellate Body Report, *Chile – Alcoholic Beverages (2000)*, para. 49.
167 See Appellate Body Report, *Japan – Alcoholic Beverages II (1996)*, 118.
168 Appellate Body Report, *Canada – Periodicals (1997)*, 474.
169 See Panel Reports, *Philippines – Distilled Spirits (2012)*, para. 7.154.

Note that there is also 'dissimilar taxation' when only *some* of the imported products are not taxed similarly. The Appellate Body stated in *Canada – Periodicals (1997)* that:

> dissimilar taxation of even *some* imported products as compared to directly competitive or substitutable domestic products is inconsistent with the provisions of the second sentence of Article III:2.[170]

2.3.4 'So as to Afford Protection to Domestic Production'

The fourth and last element of the test of consistency with the national treatment obligation of Article III:2, second sentence, of the GATT 1994 relates to the question of whether dissimilar taxation is applied 'so as to afford protection to domestic production'.

This fourth element of the consistency test must be distinguished from the third element of the test, discussed above, namely, whether there is dissimilar taxation. In *Japan – Alcoholic Beverages II (1996)*, the Appellate Body noted:

> [T]he Panel erred in blurring the distinction between [the issue of whether the products at issue were 'not similarly taxed'] and the entirely separate issue of whether the tax measure in question was applied 'so as to afford protection'. Again, these are separate issues that must be addressed individually.[171]

It must be stressed that WTO Members are allowed to apply dissimilar taxes on directly competitive or substitutable products as long as these taxes are not applied so as to afford protection to domestic production. As to how to establish whether a tax measure was applied so as to afford protection to domestic production, the Appellate Body noted in *Japan – Alcoholic Beverages II (1996)*:

> As in [the GATT panel report on *Japan – Alcoholic Beverages I (1987)*], we believe that an examination in any case of whether dissimilar taxation has been applied so as to afford protection requires a comprehensive and objective analysis of the structure and application of the measure in question on domestic as compared to imported products. We believe it is possible to examine objectively the underlying criteria used in a particular tax measure, its structure, and its overall application to ascertain whether it is applied in a way that affords protection to domestic products.
>
> Although it is true that the aim of a measure may not be easily ascertained, nevertheless its protective application can most often be discerned from the design, the architecture, and the revealing structure of a measure.[172]

170 Appellate Body Report, *Canada – Periodicals (1997)*, 474. Emphasis added. To support this conclusion, the Appellate Body referred to the panel in *US – Section 337 Tariff Act (1989)* concerning treatment less favourable under Article III:4 of the GATT. See Panel Report, *US – Section 337 Tariff Act (1989)*, para. 5.14.

171 Appellate Body Report, *Japan – Alcoholic Beverages II (1996)*, 119.

172 *Ibid.*, 120.

Thus, to determine whether the application of a tax measure affords protection to domestic production, a panel must examine the design, the architecture, the structure and the overall application of the measure.[173] For example, if the tax measure operates in such a way that the lower tax bracket covers primarily domestic production, whereas the higher tax bracket embraces primarily imported products, the implication is that the tax measure is applied so as to afford protection to domestic production. More difficult is the situation that arose in *Chile – Alcoholic Beverages (2000)*, where 75 per cent of the domestically produced products fell in the lower tax bracket and 95 per cent of the imported products fell in the higher tax bracket, *but* at the same time the majority of the products falling in that higher tax bracket were domestically produced products.[174] The Appellate Body noted that this did not exclude that the tax measure was inconsistent with Article III:2, second sentence, of the GATT 1994. The Appellate Body pointed out that Article III:2, second sentence:

> provides for equality of competitive conditions of *all* directly competitive or substitutable imported products, in relation to domestic products, and not simply, as Chile argues, those imported products within a particular [tax bracket].[175]

As the Appellate Body acknowledged in *Japan – Alcoholic Beverages II (1996)*, the very magnitude of the tax differential may be evidence of the protective application of a tax measure. Most often, however, other factors will also be considered.[176] As the Appellate Body found in *Korea – Alcoholic Beverages (1999)*, the protective application of dissimilar taxation can only be determined 'on a case-by-case basis, taking account of all relevant facts'.[177]

In *Korea – Alcoholic Beverages (1999)*, Korea argued that a finding that an internal tax measure affords protection 'must be supported by proof that the tax difference has some identifiable trade effect'.[178] However, the Appellate Body curtly rejected this argument, pointing out that 'Article III is not concerned with trade volumes' and that thus a complaining party did not have 'to prove that tax measures are capable of producing any particular trade effect'.[179]

With regard to the relevance of the intent of the legislator or regulator, the Appellate Body in *Japan – Alcoholic Beverages II (1996)* noted:

> [Whether a tax measure is applied so as to afford protection to domestic production] is not an issue of intent. It is not necessary for a panel to sort through the many reasons legislators

173 The *subjective intent* of the legislator or regulator is irrelevant (see below, p. 376). What needs to be examined and identified are the tax measure's 'objectives or purposes as revealed or objectified in the measure itself'. See Appellate Body Report, *Chile – Alcoholic Beverages (2000)*, para. 71.

174 See Panel Report, *Chile – Alcoholic Beverages (2000)*, para. 7.158.

175 Appellate Body Report, *Chile – Alcoholic Beverages (2000)*, para. 67. See also Appellate Body Reports, *Philippines – Distilled Spirits (2012)*, para. 221; and see above, p. 376.

176 Note that, in *Korea – Alcoholic Beverages (1999)*, *Chile – Alcoholic Beverages (2000)* and *Philippines – Distilled Spirits (2012)*, both the tax differential (in all three cases quite substantial) *and* the design, architecture and structure of the tax measure at issue were examined. See Appellate Body Report, *Korea – Alcoholic Beverages (1999)*, para. 150; Appellate Body Report, *Chile – Alcoholic Beverages (2000)*, para. 71; and Appellate Body Reports, *Philippines – Distilled Spirits (2012)*, para. 255.

177 Appellate Body Report, *Korea – Alcoholic Beverages (1999)*, para. 137.

178 *Ibid.*, para. 153. 179 *Ibid.*

and regulators often have for what they do and weigh the relative significance of those reasons to establish legislative or regulatory intent. If the measure is applied to imported or domestic products so as to afford protection to domestic production, then it does not matter that there may not have been any desire to engage in protectionism in the minds of the legislators or the regulators who imposed the measure. It is irrelevant that protectionism was not an intended objective if the particular tax measure in question is nevertheless, to echo Article III:1, '*applied* to imported or domestic products so as to afford protection to domestic production'. This is an issue of how the measure in question is *applied.*[180]

The *intent* of the legislator or regulator is irrelevant. As the Appellate Body stated in *Chile – Alcoholic Beverages (2000)*:

We called for examination of the design, architecture and structure of a tax measure precisely to permit identification of a measure's objectives or purposes as revealed or objectified in the measure itself.[181]

In *Chile – Alcoholic Beverages (2000)*, Chile argued that the internal taxation on alcoholic beverages at issue in that case was aimed at, among other things, reducing the consumption of alcoholic beverages with higher alcohol content. The Appellate Body held that the mere statement of such or other objectives pursued by Chile did not constitute effective rebuttal on the part of Chile of the alleged protective application of the internal taxation on alcoholic beverages.[182]

Note, however, that, in *Canada – Periodicals (1997)*, the Appellate Body did seem to attach at least some importance to statements of representatives of the Canadian Government about the policy objectives of the tax measure at issue.[183]

2.4 National Treatment Test for Internal Regulation

The national treatment obligation under Article III of the GATT 1994 does not only concern internal taxation dealt with in Article III:2. Article III also concerns internal regulation, dealt with primarily in Article III:4. Article III:4 states, in relevant part:

The products of the territory of any [Member] imported into the territory of any other [Member] shall be accorded treatment no less favourable than that accorded to like products of national origin in respect of all laws, regulations and requirements affecting their internal sale, offering for sale, purchase, transportation, distribution or use.

In *Korea – Various Measures on Beef (2001)*, the Appellate Body stated:

For a violation of Article III:4 to be established, three elements must be satisfied: that the imported and domestic products at issue are 'like products'; that the measure at issue

180 Appellate Body Report, *Japan – Alcoholic Beverages II (1996)*, 119.

181 Appellate Body Report, *Chile – Alcoholic Beverages (2000)*, para. 71.

182 See *ibid.* The Chilean tax system had two levels of taxation on alcoholic beverages (27 per cent *ad valorem* and 47 per cent *ad valorem*) separated by only 4 degrees of alcohol content.

183 See Appellate Body Report, *Canada – Periodicals (1997)*, 475–6. *In casu*, these statements of Canadian officials confirmed that the tax measure was indeed applied so as to afford protection to domestic production.

is a 'law, regulation, or requirement affecting their internal sale, offering for sale, purchase, transportation, distribution, or use'; and that the imported products are accorded 'less favourable' treatment than that accorded to like domestic products.[184]

In other words, the three-tier test of consistency of internal regulation with Article III:4 requires the examination of:

- whether the measure at issue is a *law, regulation or requirement* covered by Article III:4;
- whether the imported and domestic products are *like products*; and
- whether the imported products are accorded *less favourable treatment.*

Unlike Article III:2, second sentence, Article III:4 does *not* specifically refer to Article III:1 of the GATT 1994. Therefore, while Article III:1 has 'particular contextual significance in interpreting Article III:4, as it sets forth the "general principle" pursued by that provision',[185] a determination of whether there has been a violation of Article III:4 does *not* require a separate consideration of whether a measure 'afford[s] protection to domestic production'.[186] The test of consistency with Article III:4 of the GATT 1994 thus has three, rather than four, elements.

Below, each element of this three-tier test of consistency will be discussed in turn.

To date, WTO Members have been found to have acted inconsistently with Article III:4 of the GATT 1994, in twenty-two disputes.[187]

2.4.1 'Laws, Regulations and Requirements Affecting ...'

Article III:4 of the GATT 1994, concerns 'all laws, regulations and requirements affecting [the] internal sale, offering for sale, purchase, transportation, distribution or use [of products]'. Broadly speaking, the national treatment obligation of Article III:4 applies to domestic regulations affecting the sale and use of products. In *EC – Bananas III (1998)* the Appellate Body defined the term 'affecting' as 'having an effect on'.[188] Forty years earlier, the panel in *Italy – Agricultural Machinery (1958)* already ruled that:

> The selection of the word 'affecting' would imply, in the opinion of the Panel, that the drafters of the Article intended to cover in paragraph 4 not only laws and regulations which

184 Appellate Body Report, *Korea – Various Measures on Beef (2001)*, para. 133.

185 Appellate Body Report, *EC – Asbestos (2001)*, para. 93.

186 Appellate Body Report, *EC – Bananas III (1997)*, para. 216.

187 See *US – Gasoline (1996); Canada – Periodicals (1997); EC – Bananas III (1997); Korea – Various Measures on Beef (2001); US – FSC (Article 21.5 – EC) (2002); India – Autos (2002); Canada – Wheat Exports and Grain Imports (2004); EC – Trade Marks and Geographical Indications (2005); Dominican Republic – Import and Sale of Cigarettes (2005); Mexico – Taxes on Soft Drinks (2006); EC – Approval and Marketing of Biotech Products (2006); Turkey – Rice (2007); Brazil – Retreaded Tyres (2007); China – Auto Parts (2009); China – Publications and Audiovisual Products (2010); Thailand – Cigarettes (Philippines) (2011); Canada – Renewable Energy / Feed-In Tariff Program (2013); EC – Seal Products (2014); Argentina – Import Measures (2015); US – COOL (Article 21.5 – Canada and Mexico) (2015); US –Tuna II (Mexico) (Article 21.5) (2015)*; and *India – Solar Cells (2016)*. No inconsistency with Article III:4 was found in *Japan – Film (1998); EC – Poultry (1998); Canada –Autos (2000)*; and *EC – Asbestos (2001)*.

188 See Appellate Body Report, *EC – Bananas III (1998)*, para. 220.

directly governed the conditions of sale or purchase but also any laws or regulations which might adversely modify the conditions of competition between the domestic and imported products on the internal market.[189]

The panel thus interpreted the scope of application of Article III:4 broadly as including all measures that may modify the conditions of competition in the market. In *US – FSC (Article 21.5 – EC) (2002)*, the Appellate Body affirmed this broad interpretation of the word 'affecting'.[190]

The panel in *US – Section 337 Tariff Act (1989)* addressed the issue of whether only substantive laws, regulations and requirements *or* also procedural laws, regulations and requirements can be regarded as 'affecting' the internal sale of imported goods. Referring back to the paragraph from *Italy – Agricultural Machinery (1958)* quoted above, the panel found that such *procedural* measures are also covered by Article III:4, as otherwise circumvention of the national treatment obligation would be easy.[191]

According to GATT and WTO case law, Article III:4 applies, *inter alia*, to: (1) minimum price requirements applicable to domestic and imported beer;[192] (2) the requirement that imported beer and wine be sold only through in-State wholesalers or other middlemen;[193] (3) a ban on cigarette advertising;[194] (4) trade-related investment measures;[195] (5) requirements that imported cigarettes cannot leave the bonded warehouse unless the tax stamps are affixed to each cigarette packet in the presence of a tax inspector;[196] (6) regulation resulting in higher railway transportation costs for imported grain;[197] (7) regulation prohibiting storage of grain of foreign origin in grain elevators containing domestic grain;[198] (8) a requirement to purchase paddy rice from domestic producers to obtain the right to import rice at reduced tariff levels;[199] (9) an obligation to dispose of ten used tyres as a prerequisite for the importation of one retreaded tyre;[200] (10) regulation requiring that all imported newspapers and periodicals be distributed through only one particular distribution channel;[201] (11) regulation subjecting imported sound recordings intended for electronic distribution

189 Panel Report, *Italy – Agricultural Machinery (1958)*, para. 12.

190 See Appellate Body Report, *US – FSC (Article 21.5 – EC) (2002)*, para. 210. Moreover, as the panel in *India – Autos (2002)* stated, and the Appellate Body affirmed in *China – Auto Parts (2009)*, the fact that a measure is not primarily aimed at *regulating* the sale, offering for sale, purchase, transportation, distribution and use of the products at issue 'is not an obstacle to its "affecting" them'. See Appellate Body Reports, *China – Auto Parts (2009)*, para. 194.

191 See Panel Report, *US – Section 337 Tariff Act (1989)*, para. 5.10.

192 See Panel Report, *Canada – Provincial Liquor Boards (US) (1992)*, para. 5.30.

193 See Panel Report, *US – Malt Beverages (1992)*, para. 5.32.

194 See Panel Report, *Thailand – Cigarettes (1990)*, para. 78.

195 See Panel Report, *Canada – FIRA (1984)*, paras. 5.12 and 6.1.

196 See Panel Report, *Dominican Republic – Import and Sale of Cigarettes (2005)*, paras. 7.170–7.171.

197 See Panel Reports, *Canada – Wheat Exports and Grain Imports (2004)*, paras. 6.331–6.332.

198 See *ibid.*, para. 6.262.

199 See Panel Report, *Turkey – Rice (2007)*, para. 7.219.

200 See Panel Report, *Brazil – Retreaded Tyres (2007)*, para. 7.433.

201 See Panel Report, *China – Publications and Audiovisual Products (2010)*, para. 7.1513.

to content review regimes;[202] and (12) VAT-related administrative requirements imposed on resellers of imported cigarettes.[203] It is clear from this *illustrative* list of 'laws, regulations and requirements ... ' within the meaning of Article III:4 that the scope of this concept is very broad. Panels and the Appellate Body have drawn the outer limits of this concept generously.

In *EC – Bananas III (1997)*, the Appellate Body agreed with the panel that Article III:4 of the GATT 1994 was applicable to the EC requirements at issue. This was contested by the European Communities on the ground that import licensing was a border measure and not an internal measure within the scope of Article III:4. However, the Appellate Body ruled with regard to the EC requirements at issue, which concerned the *distribution* of banana import licences among eligible operators *within* the European Union, that:

> [t]hese rules go far beyond the mere import licence requirements needed to administer the tariff quota ... These rules are intended, among other things, to cross-subsidize distributors of EC (and ACP) bananas and to ensure that EC banana ripeners obtain a share of the quota rents. As such, these rules affect 'the internal sale, offering for sale, purchase ...' within the meaning of Article III:4, and therefore fall within the scope of this provision.[204]

In *Canada – Autos (2000)*, the panel held that a measure can be considered to be a measure affecting, i.e. having an effect on, the internal sale or use of imported products even if it is not shown that *under the current circumstances* the measure has an impact on the decisions of private parties to buy imported products. The panel noted:

> The word 'affecting' in Article III:4 of the GATT has been interpreted to cover not only laws and regulations which directly govern the conditions of sale or purchase but also any laws or regulations which *might* adversely modify the conditions of competition between domestic and imported products.[205]

While, to date, most cases involving Article III:4 concerned *generally applicable* 'laws' and 'regulations', i.e. measures that apply across the board, Article III:4 also covers 'requirements' which may apply to *isolated cases only*.[206] The panel in *Canada – FIRA (1984)* noted:

> The Panel could not subscribe to the Canadian view that the word 'requirements' in Article III:4 should be interpreted as 'mandatory rules applying across-the-board' because this latter concept was already more aptly covered by the term 'regulations' and the authors of this provision must have had something different in mind when adding the word 'requirements'. The Panel also considered that, in judging whether a measure is contrary to obligations

202 See *ibid.*, para. 7.1595.

203 See Panel Report. *Thailand– Cigarettes (Philippines) (2011)*, para. 7.665.

204 Appellate Body Report, *EC – Bananas III (1997)*, para. 211.

205 Panel Report, *Canada – Autos (2000)*, para. 10.80. Emphasis added. This follows from the fact that, to show inconsistency with Article III:4, it is not necessary to establish that the measure at issue has *actual* adverse trade effects. See below, p. 375.

206 See Panel Report, *Canada – FIRA (1984)*, para. 5.5. See also Panel Report, *India – Autos (2002)*, paras. 7.189–7.191; and Panel Reports, *China – Auto Parts (2009)*, paras. 7.241 and 7.243.

under Article III:4, it is not relevant whether it applies across-the-board or only in isolated cases. Any interpretation which would exclude case-by-case action would, in the view of the Panel, defeat the purposes of Article III:4.[207]

The question has arisen whether a 'requirement' within the meaning of Article III:4 necessarily needs to be a government-imposed requirement, or whether a (voluntary) action by a private party can constitute a 'requirement' to which Article III:4 applies.[208] In *Canada – Autos (2000)*, the panel examined commitments by Canadian car manufacturers to increase the value added to cars in their Canadian plants. These commitments were communicated in letters addressed to the Canadian government. The panel characterised these commitments as 'requirements' subject to Article III:4. According to the panel, (voluntary) private action can be a 'requirement' within the meaning of Article III:4 if, and only if, there is such a *nexus*, i.e. a close link, between that action and the action of a government, that the government must be held responsible for that private action.[209] Such nexus may exist, for example, when a Member makes the grant of an advantage (such as an exemption from customs duties) conditional upon the private action concerned.[210] Note that the panel in *China – Publications and Audiovisual Products (2010)* found with regard to one of the measures at issue in that case, namely, the distribution duopoly for films, that the United States, the complainant, had not established that the distribution duopoly was attributable to China and that, therefore, the consistency of this measure with Article III:4 could not be challenged in WTO dispute settlement.[211]

The panel in *Argentina – Import Measures (2015)* concluded that the measure at issue, i.e. the trade-related requirements (TRRs) measure, by requiring economic operators to achieve a certain level of local content in order for them to obtain certain advantages such as soft loans or tax advantages, constitutes a 'requirement' within the meaning of Article III:4 of the GATT 1994.[212]

207 Panel Report, *Canada – FIRA (1984)*, para. 5.5. The measures at issue in *Canada – FIRA (1984)* were written undertakings by investors to purchase goods of Canadian origin in preference to imported goods or in specified amounts or proportions, or to purchase goods from Canadian sources.

208 On the general question whether actions by private parties can be challenged in WTO dispute settlement, see Panel Reports, *China – Auto Parts (2009)*, paras. 7.242–7.243.

209 See Panel Report, *Canada – Autos (2000)*, para. 10.107. See also Panel Report, *Canada – Periodicals (1997)*, paras. 5.33–5.36; Panel Report, *India – Autos (2002)*, paras. 7.177–7.194; and Panel Report, *Turkey – Rice (2007)*, paras. 7.217–7.226. For older case law, see *Canada – FIRA (1984)*, para. 5.4; and Panel Report, *EEC – Parts and Components (1990)*, para. 5.21.

210 See Panel Report, *Canada – Autos (2000)*, para. 10.106.

211 See Panel Report, *China – Publications and Audiovisual Products (2010)*, paras. 7.1693–7.1694. Note also the Appellate Body's statement in *Korea – Various Measures on Beef (2001)* that dual distribution systems are not measures within the scope of Article III:4 when they are 'solely the result of private entrepreneurs acting on their own calculation of comparative costs and benefits of differentiated distribution systems' (para. 149). See also above, p. 345.

212 Panel Reports, *Argentina – Import Measures (2015)*, para. 6.280. See also Panel Report, *India – Solar Cells (2016)*, para. 7.88.

While Article III:2 concerns internal taxation and Article III:4 internal regulation, the panel in *Mexico – Taxes on Soft Drinks (2006)* found that:

> the soft drink tax, the distribution tax and the bookkeeping requirements may be considered as measures that affect the internal use in Mexico of non-cane sugar sweeteners, such as beet sugar and [high fructose corn syrup], within the meaning of Article III:4 of the GATT 1994.[213]

Taxes can thus be measures subject to Article III:4. Note that, in *China – Auto Parts (2009)*, the same legal provisions of Chinese law were found to be inconsistent with both Article III:2 and Article III:4.[214]

The *Agreement on Trade-Related Investment Measures* (the *TRIMs Agreement*) contains an illustrative list of trade-related investment measures that are inconsistent with Article III:4.[215] This illustrative list includes measures that require the purchase or use by an enterprise of products of domestic origin; or require that an enterprise's purchases or use of imported products be limited to an amount related to the volume or value of local products that it exports. As the panel in *India – Solar Cells (2016)* found:

> measures falling under paragraph 1(a) of the TRIMs Illustrative List are necessarily inconsistent with Article III:4 of the GATT 1994, thus obviating the need for separate and additional examination of the legal elements of Article III:4 of the GATT 1994.[216]

As discussed above, Article III:8(a) of the GATT 1994 explicitly excludes laws, regulations or requirements governing government procurement from the non-discrimination obligation of Article III, provided that the measures meet the requirements set out in that provision.[217] Moreover, note that Article III:8(b) states that the national treatment obligation of Article III 'shall not prevent' the payment of subsidies exclusively to domestic producers.[218]

2.4.2 'Like Products'

The second element of the test of consistency with the national treatment obligation of Article III:4 of the GATT 1994, relates to the question of whether the imported and domestic products concerned are 'like'. As with Articles I:1 and III:2, first sentence, both discussed above, the non-discrimination obligation of Article III:4 only applies to 'like products'. Therefore, it is also important for the application of the national treatment obligation of Article III:4 to be able to determine whether, for example, a sports utility vehicle (SUV) is 'like' a family car; orange juice is 'like' tomato juice; a laptop is 'like' a tablet computer; pork

213 Panel Report, *Mexico – Taxes on Soft Drinks (2006)*, para. 8.113.
214 Appellate Body Reports, *China – Auto Parts (2009)*, paras. 183 and 197.
215 See Article 2.2 of, and the Annex to, the *TRIMs Agreement*.
216 See Panel Report, *India – Solar Cells (2016)*, para. 7.54. See also, *ibid.*, para. 7.73.
217 See above, p. 313.
218 See above, p. 313.

is 'like' beef; or whisky is 'like' brandy. As discussed above, the answer to these questions may be different in the context of Article III:4 of the GATT 1994 than in the context of other non-discrimination provisions of the GATT 1994.[219] The answer may also be different from the market of one WTO Member to the market of another WTO Member. Products that are 'like' in Richland are not necessarily 'like' in Newland.

The Appellate Body considered the meaning of the concept of 'like products' in Article III:4 in *EC – Asbestos (2001)*. In its report in that case, the Appellate Body first noted that the concept of 'like products' was also used in Article III:2, first sentence, and that, in *Japan – Alcoholic Beverages II (1996)*, it had held that the scope of 'like products' was to be construed 'narrowly' in that provision.[220] The Appellate Body then examined whether this interpretation of 'like products' in Article III:2 could be taken to suggest a similarly narrow reading of 'like products' in Article III:4, since both provisions form part of the same Article. The Appellate Body recalled its considerations in *Japan – Alcoholic Beverages II (1996)* that led it to conclude in that case that the concept of 'like products' in Article III:2, first sentence, must be construed narrowly,[221] and observed:

> In construing Article III:4, the same interpretive considerations do not arise, because the 'general principle' articulated in Article III:1 is expressed in Article III:4, not through two distinct obligations, as in the two sentences in Article III:2, but instead through a single obligation that applies solely to 'like products'. Therefore, the harmony that we have attributed to the two sentences of Article III:2 need not and, indeed, cannot be replicated in interpreting Article III:4. Thus, we conclude that, given the textual difference between Articles III:2 and III:4, the 'accordion' of 'likeness' stretches in a different way in Article III:4.[222]

Having distinguished the concept of 'like products' in Article III:4 from the concept in Article III:2, first sentence, the Appellate Body then proceeded to examine the meaning of this concept in Article III:4. It first recalled that, in *Japan – Alcoholic Beverages II (1996)*, it had ruled that the broad and fundamental purpose of Article III is to avoid protectionism in the application of internal tax and regulatory measures.[223] As is explicitly stated in Article III:1, the purpose of Article III is to ensure that internal measures 'not be applied to imported and domestic products so as to afford protection to domestic production'. To this end, Article III obliges WTO Members to provide equality of competitive conditions for imported products in relation to domestic products.[224] This 'general principle' is not explicitly invoked in Article III:4. Nevertheless, it does 'inform' that provision.[225] The Appellate Body in *EC – Asbestos (2001)* thus reasoned that

219 On the 'accordion of likeness', see above, pp. 316–17.

220 Appellate Body Report, *EC – Asbestos (2001)*, para. 93. The Appellate Body referred to Appellate Body Report, *Japan – Alcoholic Beverages II (1996)*, 112 and 113, and to Appellate Body Report, *Canada – Periodicals (1997)*, 473. See above, p. 357.

221 Appellate Body Report, *EC – Asbestos (2001)*, para. 95. For the Appellate Body's considerations in *Japan – Alcoholic Beverages II (1996)*, see above, p. 356.

222 Appellate Body Report, *EC – Asbestos (2001)*, para. 96. 223 See above, p. 344.

224 See Appellate Body Report, *Japan – Alcoholic Beverages II (1996)*, 109–10. 225 *Ibid.*, 111.

the term 'like product' in Article III:4 must be interpreted to give proper scope and meaning to the anti-protectionism principle of Article III:1.[226] It is clear that an internal regulation can *only* afford protection to domestic production if the internal regulation addresses domestic and imported products that are in a competitive relationship. In the absence of a competitive relationship between the domestic and imported products, internal regulation cannot be applied to these products so as to afford protection to domestic production. The Appellate Body thus came to the following conclusion with respect to the meaning of 'like products' in Article III:4:

> [A] determination of 'likeness' under Article III:4 is, fundamentally, a determination about the nature and extent of a competitive relationship between and among products.[227]

Note that the Appellate Body referred to both the nature *and* the extent of a competitive relationship between and among products. A mere economic analysis of the cross-price elasticity of demand for the products at issue will not suffice to determine whether these products are 'like'. 'Likeness' is a matter of judgment – qualitatively as well as quantitatively.

Having concluded that the determination of 'likeness' is a determination of the nature and extent of a competitive relationship between and among the products at issue, the Appellate Body subsequently noted in *EC – Asbestos (2001)* that it is mindful that there is a spectrum of degrees of 'competitiveness' of products in the marketplace, and that it is difficult, if not impossible, in the abstract, to indicate precisely where on this spectrum the word 'like' in Article III:4 of the GATT 1994 falls.[228] The Appellate Body found, however, that:

> [i]n view of [the] different language [of Articles III:2 and III:4], and although we need not rule, and do not rule, on the precise product scope of Article III:4, we do conclude that the product scope of Article III:4, although broader than the *first* sentence of Article III:2, is certainly *not* broader than the *combined* product scope of the *two* sentences of Article III:2 of the GATT 1994.[229]

Moreover, the Appellate Body found that the product scope of Article III:4 and that of Article III:2, first *and* second sentence, cannot be significantly different.[230] As pointed out by the Appellate Body, there is no sharp distinction between fiscal measures covered by Article III:2, and regulatory measures, covered by Article III:4. Both forms of measure can often be used to achieve the same

226 See Appellate Body Report, *EC – Asbestos (2001)*, para. 98.

227 *Ibid.*, para. 99. As discussed above, in *Philippines – Distilled Spirits (2011)*, the Appellate Body ruled that the same basic test applies to determine whether products are 'like' within the meaning of Article III:2, first sentence, of the GATT 1994. See above, p. 357. As discussed below, in *US – Clove Cigarettes (2012)*, the Appellate Body ruled that this test also applies to determine whether products are 'like' within the meaning of Article 2.1 of the *TBT Agreement*. See below, p. 386.

228 Appellate Body Report, *EC – Asbestos (2001)*, para. 99.

229 *Ibid.* The panel in *Mexico – Taxes on Soft Drinks (2006)* therefore concluded that, as it had found cane sugar and beet sugar to be 'like' under Article III:2, first sentence, these products could also be considered 'like' under Article III:4. See Panel Report, *Mexico – Taxes on Soft Drinks (2006)*, para. 8.105.

230 See Appellate Body Report, *EC – Asbestos (2001)*, para. 99.

ends. Therefore, 'it would be incongruous' if, due to significant difference in the product scope of these two provisions, Members were prevented from using one form of measure (fiscal measures) to protect domestic production of certain products, but were able to use another form of measure (regulatory measures) to achieve the same ends. According to the Appellate Body, '[t]his would frustrate a consistent application of the "general principle" in Article III:1'.[231]

Having reached a conclusion on the meaning and the scope of the concept of 'like products' under Article III:4, the Appellate Body turned in *EC – Asbestos (2001)* to the question of *how* one should determine whether products are 'like' within the meaning of Article III:4. The Appellate Body first noted:

> As in Article III:2, in this determination, '[n]o one approach ... will be appropriate for all cases'. Rather, an assessment utilizing 'an unavoidable element of individual, discretionary judgement' has to be made on a case-by-case basis.[232]

The Appellate Body then recalled that, in analysing 'likeness', panels and the Appellate Body itself had followed, and further developed, the approach outlined in the working party report in *Border Tax Adjustments (1970)*.[233] According to the Appellate Body, this approach has, essentially, consisted of employing four general criteria in analysing 'likeness': (i) the properties, nature and quality of the products; (ii) the end uses of the products; (iii) consumers' tastes and habits – also referred to as consumers' perceptions and behaviour – in respect of the products; and (iv) the tariff classification of the products.[234] These four criteria comprise four categories of 'characteristics' that the products involved might share: (i) the physical properties of the products; (ii) the extent to which the products are capable of serving the same or similar end uses; (iii) the extent to which consumers perceive and treat the products as alternative means of performing particular functions in order to satisfy a particular want or demand; and (iv) the international classification of the products for tariff purposes.[235] The Appellate Body hastened to add, however, that, while these general criteria, or groupings of potentially shared characteristics, provide a framework for analysing the 'likeness' of particular products, they are 'simply tools to assist in the task of sorting and examining the relevant evidence'.[236] The Appellate

231 *Ibid.* The panel in *Mexico – Taxes on Soft Drinks (2006)* therefore concluded that cane sugar and high fructose corn syrup (HFCS), which were considered 'directly competitive or substitutable' within the meaning of Article III:2, second sentence, were in a close competitive relationship and could thus be considered 'like' products within the meaning of Article III:4. See Panel Report, *Mexico – Taxes on Soft Drinks (2006)*, para. 8.106.

232 Appellate Body Report, *EC – Asbestos (2001)*, para. 101.

233 See *ibid.* In a footnote to para. 101, the Appellate Body referred to Appellate Body Report, *Japan – Alcoholic Beverages II (1996)*, 113. It also referred to Panel Report, *US – Gasoline (1996)*, para. 6.8, where the approach set out in the working party report in *Border Tax Adjustments (1970)* was adopted in a dispute concerning Article III:4 of the GATT 1994.

234 See Appellate Body Report, *EC – Asbestos (2001)*, para. 101. The Appellate Body noted in a footnote to para. 101 that the fourth criterion, tariff classification, was not mentioned in the working party report in *Border Tax Adjustments (1970)*, but was included by subsequent panels (see e.g. Panel Report, *EEC – Animal Feed Proteins (1978)*, para. 4.2; and Panel Report, *Japan – Alcoholic Beverages I (1987)*, para. 5.6).

235 See Appellate Body Report, *EC – Asbestos (2001)*, para. 101. 236 See *ibid.*, para. 102.

Body stressed that these criteria are 'neither a treaty-mandated nor a closed list of criteria that will determine the legal characterisation of products'.[237] In each case, *all* pertinent evidence, whether related to one of these criteria or not, must be examined and considered by panels to determine whether products are – or could be – in a competitive relationship in the marketplace, i.e. are 'like'.[238] The Appellate Body also found:

> When all the relevant evidence has been examined, panels must determine whether that evidence, *as a whole*, indicates that the products in question are 'like' in terms of the legal provision at issue.[239]

It follows that, in and of itself, evidence under one of the criteria cannot be determinative of the 'likeness' of products. A panel always has to examine the totality of the relevant evidence.

In *EC – Asbestos (2001)*, the Appellate Body was highly critical of the manner in which the panel examined the 'likeness' of the products at issue in that case, namely, chrysotile asbestos fibres and cement-based products containing chrysotile asbestos fibres on the one hand *and* PCG fibres and cement-based products containing PCG fibres on the other hand.[240] The Appellate Body criticised the panel for not examining each of the criteria set forth in the working party report in *Border Tax Adjustments (1970)*[241] and for not examining these criteria separately.[242] The Appellate Body also disagreed with the panel's refusal to consider the health risks posed by asbestos in the determination of 'likeness', stating that panels must evaluate *all* of the relevant evidence.[243] According to the Appellate Body, the carcinogenic or toxic nature of chrysotile asbestos fibres constitutes a defining aspect of the physical properties of those fibres and must therefore be considered when determining 'likeness' under Article III:4.[244] According to the Appellate Body, 'evidence relating to health risks may be relevant in assessing the *competitive relationship in the marketplace* between allegedly "like" products'.[245] The Appellate Body also noted that consumers' tastes and habits regarding asbestos fibres or PCG fibres are very likely to be shaped by the health risks associated with a product which is known to be highly carcinogenic

237 See *ibid.* 238 See *ibid.*, para. 103.
239 *Ibid.* Emphasis added.
240 *Ibid.*, para. 109. PCG fibres are PVA, cellulose and glass fibres.
241 The panel declined to examine the third criterion (consumers' tastes and habits) and dismissed the fourth criterion (tariff classification) as non-decisive. With respect to consumers' tastes and habits, for example, the Appellate Body was very critical of the panel for declining to examine this criterion because, as the panel stated, 'this criterion would not provide clear results'. See Appellate Body Report, *EC – Asbestos (2001)*, paras. 120–2.
242 In the course of the examination of the first criterion (the properties, nature and quality of the products), the panel relied on the second criterion (end use) to come to the 'conclusion' that the products were like.
243 Appellate Body Report, *EC – Asbestos (2001)*, para. 113. 244 See *ibid.*, para. 114.
245 *Ibid.*, para. 115. According to the Appellate Body, considering evidence relating to the health risks associated with a product, under Article III:4, does not nullify the effect of Article XX(b) of the GATT 1994. For a discussion on Article XX of the GATT 1994, see below, pp. 546–604. The fact that an interpretation of Article III:4 taking into account health risks, implies a less frequent recourse to Article XX(b) does not deprive the exception in Article XX(b) of effectiveness. On the rules of treaty interpretation and effectiveness, see above, p. 193.

(as asbestos fibres are).[246] While the Appellate Body in *EC – Asbestos (2001)* did not consider regulatory concerns, such as the health risks, to be a separate, additional criterion for the determination of 'likeness', such concerns may still be quite relevant in that determination. As the Appellate Body further clarified in *US – Clove Cigarettes (2012)*:

> in concluding that the determination of likeness should not be based on the regulatory purposes of technical regulations, we are not suggesting that the regulatory concerns underlying technical regulations may not play a role in the determination of whether or not products are like. In this respect, we recall that, in *EC – Asbestos*, the Appellate Body found that regulatory concerns and considerations may play a role in applying certain of the 'likeness' criteria (that is, physical characteristics and consumer preferences) and, thus, in the determination of likeness under Article III:4 of the GATT 1994.[247]

With regard to the second and third criteria set out in the working party report in *Border Tax Adjustments (1970)*, i.e. end uses and consumers' tastes and habits, the Appellate Body found in *EC – Asbestos (2001)*:

> Evidence of this type is of particular importance under Article III of the GATT 1994, precisely because that provision is concerned with competitive relationships in the marketplace. If there is – or could be – *no* competitive relationship between products, a Member cannot intervene, through internal taxation or regulation, to protect domestic production. Thus, evidence about the extent to which products can serve the same end-uses, and the extent to which consumers are – or would be – willing to choose one product instead of another to perform those end-uses, is highly relevant evidence in assessing the 'likeness' of those products under Article III:4 of the GATT 1994.[248]

According to the Appellate Body in *EC – Asbestos (2001)*, evidence relating to end uses and consumers' tastes and habits is *especially* important in cases where the evidence relating to properties establishes that the products at issue are physically quite different. In such cases, in order to overcome this indication that products are *not* 'like', a higher burden is placed on complaining Members to establish that, despite the pronounced physical differences, there is a competitive relationship between the products such that *all* of the evidence, taken together, demonstrates that the products are 'like' under Article III:4.[249]

With respect to end uses, the Appellate Body further found that, while it is certainly relevant that products have similar end uses for a 'small number of ... applications', a panel must also consider the other, *different* end uses of products. It is only by forming a complete picture of the various (similar as well as different) end uses of a product that a panel can assess the significance of the fact that products share a limited number of end uses.[250]

246 See *ibid.*, para. 122.

247 Appellate Body Report, *US – Clove Cigarettes (2012)*, para. 117. Note that this ruling by the Appellate Body concerned the concept of 'likeness' in the context of the national treatment obligation of Article 2.1 of the *TBT Agreement*. See below, p. 900.

248 Appellate Body Report, *EC – Asbestos (2001)*, para. 117.

249 See *ibid.*, paras. 117–18.

250 See *ibid.*, para. 119.

In general, the Appellate Body confirmed in *EC – Asbestos (2001)* the prior case law by upholding the market-based, economic interpretation of the concept of 'likeness' (and thus confirmed the marketplace approach to determining 'likeness').[251] At the same time, however, the Appellate Body 'remedied' the narrow scope given to the concept of 'likeness' in prior case law by allowing non-economic interests and values, such as health, to be considered in the determination of 'likeness'.

After reversing the panel's findings, in *EC – Asbestos (2001)*, on the 'likeness' of chrysotile asbestos fibres and PCG fibres, the Appellate Body itself examined the 'likeness' of these products and came to the conclusion that the evidence was certainly far from sufficient to satisfy the complainant's burden of proving that chrysotile asbestos fibres are 'like' PCG fibres under Article III:4. The Appellate Body considered that the evidence tended rather to suggest that these products are not 'like products'.[252]

Two additional observations on the determination of 'likeness' under Article III:4 of the GATT 1994 are called for: one observation regarding the 'regulatory intent' or 'aim-and-effect' approach discussed above in the context of Article III:2, first sentence, of the GATT 1994;[253] and one observation regarding the relevance of processes and production methods (PPMs) discussed above in the context of Article I of the GATT 1994.[254] With regard to the former, note that in *US – Malt Beverages (1992)*, the panel considered the regulatory intent (or aim) of the measure in determining whether low alcohol beer and high alcohol beer were 'like products' within the meaning of Article III:4. In this regard, the panel recalled its earlier statement on like product determinations under Article III:2, first sentence,[255] and held that:

> in the context of Article III, it is essential that such determinations be made not only in the light of such criteria as the products' physical characteristics, but also in the light of the purpose of Article III, which is to ensure that internal taxes and regulations 'not be applied to imported or domestic products so as to afford protection to domestic production'.[256]

The panel noted that, on the basis of their 'physical characteristics', low and high alcohol beers were 'similar'. However, in order to determine whether low and high alcohol beers were 'like products' under Article III:4 of the GATT 1994, the panel considered that it had to examine whether the purpose of the distinction

251 Note, however, that, in a separate 'concurring' opinion, one of the Appellate Body Members on the division in *EC – Asbestos (2001)* considered that 'the necessity or appropriateness of adopting a "fundamentally" economic interpretation of the "likeness" of products under Article III:4 of the GATT 1994 does not appear to me to be free from substantial doubts'. See *ibid.*, para. 154. According to that Appellate Body member, it is difficult to imagine what evidence relating to economic competitive relationships as reflected in end uses and consumers' tastes and habits could outweigh the undisputed deadly nature of chrysotile asbestos fibres, compared with PCG fibres. See *ibid.*, para. 152.

252 See *ibid.*, para. 141. Also, with regard to the products containing asbestos and PCG fibres, the Appellate Body concluded that Canada had not satisfied the burden of proof that these products were 'like'. See *ibid.*, para. 147.

253 See above, p. 361. 254 See above, p. 319. 255 See above, p. 360.

256 Panel Report, *US – Malt Beverages (1992)*, para. 5.71.

between low and high alcohol beers was 'to afford protection to domestic production'. The panel noted that the United States argued that the distinction was made to encourage the consumption of low rather than high alcohol beer. The panel eventually concluded that the purpose of the regulatory distinction was not to afford protection to domestic production and that low and high alcoholic beers were, therefore, not 'like products'.[257]

For reasons discussed above, this 'regulatory intent' or 'aim-and-effect' approach to the determination of 'likeness' has been discredited and abandoned by WTO panels and the Appellate Body.[258] A first indication that WTO panels would not follow this approach was given in *US – Gasoline (1996)*, in which the panel found that chemically identical imported and domestic gasoline were 'like products' because 'chemically identical imported and domestic gasoline by definition have exactly the same physical characteristics, end-uses, tariff classification, and are perfectly substitutable'.[259] The intent or the aim of the regulatory distinction made was not given any consideration in determining 'likeness'. Shortly after *US – Gasoline (1996)*, the 'regulatory intent' or 'aim-and-effect' approach to the determination of 'likeness' was explicitly rejected in *Japan – Alcoholic Beverages II (1996)*.[260]

With regard to the processes and production methods, which do not affect the characteristics or properties of the products concerned (NPR–PPMs), note that the panel in *US – Tuna (Mexico) (1991)* found that differences in NPR–PPMs are not relevant in determining 'likeness'. The panel stated:

> Article III:4 calls for a comparison of the treatment of imported tuna *as a product* with that of domestic tuna *as a product*. Regulations governing the taking of dolphins incidental to the taking of tuna could not possibly affect tuna as a product.[261]

Thus, whether tuna was fished in a dolphin-friendly manner or not (i.e. an NPR–PPM) was, according to the panel in *US – Tuna (Mexico) (1991)*, of no relevance in determining whether the imported tuna was 'like' the domestic tuna. However, as reflected above, the concept of 'likeness' has evolved since *US – Tuna (Mexico) (1991)*.[262] The question of whether NPR–PPMs may be of relevance in the determination of 'likeness' now requires a more nuanced answer than that given by the panel in *US – Tuna (Mexico) (1991)*.[263] It should be noted that NPR–PPMs may have an impact on consumers' perceptions and behaviour, and thus on the nature and the extent of the competitive relationship between products. If the consumers in a particular market shun carpets made by children,

257 See *ibid.*, paras. 5.25–5.26 and 5.71–5.76. 258 See above, pp. 361–5.
259 Panel Report, *US – Gasoline (1996)*, para. 6.9. 260 See above, pp. 361 and 362.
261 Panel Report, *US – Tuna (Mexico) (1991)*, para. 5.15. Note that this report was never adopted.
262 See above, p. 381.
263 As discussed in Chapter 13, the issue of 'likeness' of tuna fished in a dolphin-friendly manner and tuna fished otherwise re-emerged in *US – Tuna II (Mexico) (2012)*, albeit not under Article III:4, but under Article 2.1 of the *TBT Agreement*. See below, pp. 901–3.

a situation may arise in which there is in fact no (or only a weak) competitive relationship between these carpets and carpets made by adults. In light of the nature and the extent of the competitive relationship between them, carpets made by children and carpets made by adults could in such a situation be found to be not 'like'. While this differs from market to market, an increasing number of consumers are interested in, and sensitive to, the labour, environmental and other conditions under which products are produced. However, more often, consumers are, in their choice between products, primarily guided by the price and quality of the products, rather than the conditions under which these products were produced.

Finally, it should be noted that, while the 'likeness' of products is often a controversial issue in disputes concerning Article III:4 of the GATT 1994, there have been a number of disputes in which panels have sidestepped the 'likeness' issue and have proceeded on the *assumption* that there are 'like' products.[264] The panels in these disputes have assumed that there are 'like' products when the measure at issue distinguishes between products solely on the basis of their origin. In *Canada – Wheat Exports and Grain Imports (2004)*, for example, the measures at issue provided either for requirements applicable *only* to imported grain[265] or benefits granted *only* to domestic grain.[266] 'Likeness' was therefore considered not to be an issue in *Canada – Wheat Exports and Grain Imports (2004)*.[267]

The panel in *China – Publications and Audiovisual Products (2010)* stated the view that:

> when origin is the sole criterion distinguishing the products, it is sufficient for purposes of satisfying the 'like product' requirement for a complaining party to demonstrate that there *can or will be* domestic and imported products that are 'like'.[268]

However, in disputes concerning measures that are, on their face, 'origin-neutral', such as *EC – Asbestos (2001)*, the 'likeness' of the products concerned is usually at the core of the dispute.[269] Note that, in *EC – Asbestos (2001)*, the Appellate Body stated not without a touch of despair regarding the 'likeness' analysis in the context of disputes concerning measures that are, on their face, 'origin-neutral':

> There will be few situations where the evidence on the 'likeness' of products will lend itself to 'clear results'. In many cases, the evidence will give conflicting indications, possibly within each of the four criteria.[270]

264 See also above, pp. 316–19 (regarding 'likeness' under Article I:1 of the GATT 1994), and pp. 354–63 (regarding 'likeness' under Article III:2, first sentence).
265 See Panel Reports, *Canada – Wheat Exports and Grain Imports (2004)*, para. 6.165.
266 See *ibid.*, paras. 6.262 and 6.331–6.332.
267 See *ibid.*, paras. 6.164, 6.264 and 6.333.
268 Panel Report, *China – Publications and Audiovisual Products (2010)*, para. 7.1446. Emphasis added. This approach to likeness has also been referred to as the 'hypothetical like products approach'. See above, pp. 357–63.
269 See above, p. 346. 270 Appellate Body Report, *EC – Asbestos (2001)*, para. 120.

The panel in *US – COOL (Article 21.5 – Canada and Mexico) (2015)*, in analysing the likeness of the products at issue in the amended COOL measure noted that 'the products at issue can be distinguished solely on the basis on origin' and thereby concluded that the products at issue were like products within the meaning of Article III: 4 of the GATT 1994.[271]

2.4.3 'Treatment No Less Favourable'

The third and last element of the test of consistency with the national treatment obligation of Article III:4 relates to the question of whether the measure at issue accords 'treatment no less favourable'. The fact that a measure distinguishes between 'like products' does not suffice to conclude that this measure is inconsistent with Article III:4.[272] As the Appellate Body noted in *EC – Asbestos (2001)*:

> A complaining Member must still establish that the measure accords to the group of 'like' *imported* products 'less favourable treatment' than it accords to the group of 'like' *domestic* products.[273]

The panel in *US – Section 337 Tariff Act (1989)* interpreted 'treatment no less favourable' as requiring 'effective equality of opportunities'.[274] In later GATT and WTO reports, panels and the Appellate Body have consistently interpreted 'treatment no less favourable' in the same way.[275] In *US – Gasoline (1996)*, a dispute concerning legislation designed to prevent and control air pollution, the panel recalled the ruling in *US – Section 337 Tariff Act (1989)* that the words 'treatment no less favourable' in Article III:4 call for effective equality of competitive opportunities for imported products, and then found:

> since ... imported gasoline was effectively prevented from benefiting from as favourable sales conditions as were afforded domestic gasoline ... imported gasoline was treated less favourably than domestic gasoline.[276]

In *Korea – Various Measures on Beef (2001)*, a dispute concerning a dual retail distribution system for the sale of beef under which *imported* beef was, *inter alia*, to be sold in specialised stores selling only imported beef or in separate sections of supermarkets, the panel ruled that 'any regulatory distinction that is based exclusively on criteria relating to the nationality or the origin of the products is incompatible with [Article III:4 of the GATT 1994]'.[277] The Appellate Body disagreed with the panel and reversed this ruling. According to the Appellate Body, the formal difference in treatment between domestic and imported products is neither necessary nor sufficient for a violation of Article III:4. Formally

271 Panel Reports, *US – COOL (Article 21.5 – Canada and Mexico) (2015)*, paras. 7.633–7.634. See also Panel Reports, *Argentina – Import Measures (2015)*, para. 6.275; and Panel Report, *India – Solar Cells (2016)*, para. 7.83.
272 See below, p. 391.
273 Appellate Body Report, *EC – Asbestos (2001)*, para. 100.
274 Panel Report, *US – Section 337 Tariff Act (1989)*, para. 5.11.
275 For the GATT panel reports, see e.g. Panel Report, *Canada – Provincial Liquor Boards (US) (1992)*, paras. 5.12–5.14 and 5.30–5.31; and Panel Report, *US – Malt Beverages (1992)*, para. 5.30.
276 Panel Report, *US – Gasoline (1996)*, para. 6.10. See also e.g. Panel Reports, *EC – Bananas III (1997)*, paras. 7.179–7.180; and Panel Report, *Japan – Film (1997)*, para. 10.379.
277 Panel Report, *Korea – Various Measures on Beef (2001)*, para. 627.

different treatment of imported products does not necessarily constitute less favourable treatment while the absence of formal difference in treatment does not necessarily mean that there is no less favourable treatment.[278] The Appellate Body stated in *Korea – Various Measures on Beef (2001)*:

We observe ... that Article III:4 requires only that a measure accord treatment to imported products that is 'no less favourable' than that accorded to like domestic products. A measure that provides treatment to imported products that is *different* from that accorded to like domestic products is not necessarily inconsistent with Article III:4, as long as the treatment provided by the measure is no 'less favourable'. According 'treatment no less favourable' means, as we have previously said, according *conditions of competition* no less favourable to the imported product than to the like domestic product.[279]

As the Appellate Body noted in *EC – Asbestos (2001)*, a Member may draw distinctions between products which have been found to be 'like', without, for this reason alone, according to the group of imported products 'less favourable treatment' than that accorded to the group of 'like' domestic products.[280] The Appellate Body's interpretation of 'treatment no less favourable' focuses on the *conditions of competition* between imported and domestic like products and, as a result, a measure according formally *different* treatment to imported products does not *per se*, that is, necessarily, violate Article III:4.[281] In *Korea – Various Measures on Beef (2001)*, the Appellate Body concluded:

A formal difference in treatment between imported and like domestic products is thus neither necessary, nor sufficient, to show a violation of Article III:4. Whether or not imported products are treated 'less favourably' than like domestic products should be assessed instead by examining whether a measure modifies the *conditions of competition* in the relevant market to the detriment of imported products.[282]

Under current case law, a measure gives rise to 'treatment less favourable' inconsistent with Article III:4 when it modifies the conditions of competition in the relevant market to the detriment of the imported products. In *Dominican Republic – Import and Sale of Cigarettes (2005)*, for example, the panel found with respect to the tax stamp to be affixed to all cigarette packets marketed in the Dominican Republic that:

although the tax stamp requirement is applied in a formally equal manner to domestic and imported cigarettes, it does modify the conditions of competition in the marketplace to the detriment of imports. The tax stamp requirement imposes additional processes and costs on imported products. It also leads to imported cigarettes being presented to final consumers in a less appealing manner.[283]

278 See also Panel Report, *US – Section 337 Tariff Act (1989)*, para. 5.11; and Panel Report, *US – Gasoline (1996)*, para. 6.25.

279 Appellate Body Report, *Korea – Various Measures on Beef (2001)*, para. 135.

280 See Appellate Body Report, *EC – Asbestos (2001)*, para. 100.

281 See Appellate Body Report, *Korea – Various Measures on Beef (2001)*, para. 136. See also, for example, Panel Report, *US – Section 337 Tariff Act (1989)*, para. 5.11; and Panel Report, *India – Autos (2002)*, para. 7.199.

282 Appellate Body Report, *Korea – Various Measures on Beef (2001)*, para. 137.

283 Panel Report, *Dominican Republic – Import and Sale of Cigarettes (2005)*, para. 7.196. The panel noted that the Dominican Republic could have chosen to apply the tax stamp requirement in a different manner to imported products than on domestic products, to ensure that the treatment accorded to them is *de facto* not less favourable. See *ibid.*, para. 7.197.

As already noted above, the Appellate Body ruled in *EC – Asbestos (2001)* that for a measure to be inconsistent with Article III:4 that measure must accord:

> to the group of 'like' *imported* products 'less favourable treatment' than it accords to the group of 'like' *domestic* products.[284]

When establishing whether there is 'treatment less favourable', what is to be compared is the treatment given to the *group* of imported products as a whole and the treatment given to the *group* of like domestic products as a whole.[285] However, this does not mean that for there to be 'treatment less favourable', every single product in the group of imported products must be given treatment less favourable compared to every single product in the group of like domestic products. A measure, which does not accord treatment less favourable to *some* products in the group of imported products, may still be found to accord 'treatment less favourable' to the whole *group* of imported products.

The panel in *US – Gasoline (1996)* ruled that under Article III:4 of the GATT 1994, as under Articles I:1 and III:2,[286] balancing *less* favourable treatment to some imported products with *more* favourable treatment to other imported products does not save a measure from a finding of inconsistency. In *US – Gasoline (1996)*, the panel rejected the US contention that the regulation at issue was not inconsistent with Article III:4 because it treated imported products and domestic products 'equally overall'.[287] The panel noted that:

> the argument that on average the treatment provided was equivalent amounted to arguing that *less* favourable treatment in one instance could be *offset* provided that there was correspondingly *more* favourable treatment in another. This amounted to claiming that less favourable treatment of particular imported products in some instances would be balanced by more favourable treatment of particular products in others.[288]

The panel rejected this argument, recalling that the panel in *US – Section 337 Tariff Act (1989)* had already held that:

> the 'no less favourable' treatment requirement of Article III:4 has to be understood as applicable to each individual case of imported products. The Panel rejected any notion of balancing more favourable treatment of some imported products against less favourable treatment of other imported products. If this notion were accepted, it would entitle a [Member] to derogate from the no less favourable treatment obligation in one case, or indeed in respect of one [Member], on the ground that it accords more favourable treatment in some other case, or to another [Member]. Such an interpretation would lead to great uncertainty about the conditions of competition between imported and domestic products and thus defeat the purposes of Article III.[289]

284 Appellate Body Report, *EC – Asbestos (2001)*, para. 100.
285 See *ibid.* 286 See above, pp. 314–15 and pp. 363–4.
287 See Panel Report, *US – Gasoline (1996)*, para. 6.14.
288 *Ibid.* The panel referred to Panel Report, *US – Section 337 Tariff Act (1989)*, para. 5.14.
289 Panel Report, *US – Section 337 Tariff Act (1989)*, para. 5.14. See in this context also Appellate Body Report, *Thailand – Cigarettes (Philippines) (2011)*, para. 139.

In brief, under Article III:4, as under Articles I:1 and III:2,[290] balancing *less* favourable treatment to some imported products with *more* favourable treatment to other imported products does not save a measure from a finding of inconsistency.

In *Canada – Wheat Exports and Grain Imports (2004)*, the panel stated that the measures at issue (i.e. a prohibition on depositing foreign grain in Canadian grain elevators unless specifically authorised; the granting of a standing mixing authorisation for Eastern Canadian grain only; and the application of a revenue cap for rail transportation of Western Canadian grain only) would appear to be inconsistent with Article III:4 of the GATT 1994 because imported grain is treated less favourably than like domestic grain.[291] The panel recognised that there may be legitimate reasons for Canada to treat domestic grain and 'like' imported grain differently, for example because the latter has not been subjected to the Canadian quality assurance system, which imposes certain restrictions and conditions on Canadian grain, including with respect to production.[292] However, it was not clear to the panel how the arguments put forward by Canada to justify the difference in treatment between domestic grain and 'like' imported grain could support the conclusion that the measure at issue treated imported grain 'no less favourably' than 'like' domestic grain. The panel, therefore, confirmed its provisional conclusion that the authorisation requirement for foreign grain to enter grain elevators is, as such, inconsistent with Article III:4 of the GATT 1994.[293] Moreover, the panel also made clear that a *de minimis* impact of the measure does not prevent it from finding that the measure treated imported products less favourably. In a footnote, the panel noted that neither the text of Article III:4 nor GATT/WTO case law indicates that there is a *de minimis* exception to the 'no less favourable treatment' requirement in Article III:4.[294]

As the Appellate Body found in *US – FSC (Article 21.5 – EC) (2002)*, and reaffirmed in *Thailand – Cigarettes (Philippines) (2011)*, an examination of whether a measure involves less favourable treatment 'need not be based on the actual effects of the contested measure in the marketplace'.[295] The fact that no 'actual effects' of the measure in the market are required means that 'potential effects' of the measure may suffice as a basis for a finding that a measure involves 'less favourable treatment'. Above, it has been explained why this is so.[296] The panels

290 See above, p. 315 and pp. 363–4.

291 See Panel Reports, *Canada – Wheat Exports and Grain Imports (2004)*, paras. 6.187, 6.290 and 6.352.

292 See *ibid.*, para. 6.209.

293 See *ibid.*, para. 6.214. Similar findings were made with regard to Canada's defences relating to the advantage of standing mixing authorisation it granted to Eastern Canadian grain only and relating to the revenue cap on rail transportation of Western Canadian grain. See *ibid.*, paras. 6.297 and 6.359.

294 See *ibid.*, fn. 281 to para. 6.190.

295 Appellate Body Report, *US – FSC (Article 21.5 – EC) (2002)*, para. 215; and Appellate Body Report, *Thailand – Cigarettes (Philippines) (2011)*, para. 135. Of course, nothing *prevents* a panel from considering evidence relating to actual effects of the contested measure in the market place. See *ibid.*, para. 129.

296 See above, pp. 344–5.

in *India – Autos (2002)* and *China – Publications and Audiovisual Products (2010)* considered that, for a measure to afford 'less favourable treatment' to imported products, it is required that this measure 'is more than likely'[297] or 'may reasonably be expected'[298] to modify adversely the conditions of competition. The Appellate Body in *Thailand – Cigarettes (Philippines) (2011)*, however, found that an analysis of 'less favourable treatment' should not be anchored in an assessment of the degree of likelihood that an adverse impact on competitive conditions will materialise. The Appellate Body ruled:

> Rather, an analysis under Article III:4 must begin with careful scrutiny of the measure, including consideration of the design, structure, and expected operation of the measure at issue. Such scrutiny may well involve – but does not require – an assessment of the contested measure in the light of evidence regarding the actual effects of that measure in the market.[299]

It is clear that measures imposing an additional administrative burden or hurdle on imported products may modify the competitive conditions of such products in the marketplace, and may thus be found to accord 'treatment less favourable'. The panel in *US – Section 337 Tariff Act (1989)* found that the fact that patent infringement claims regarding *imported* products could be brought in the US International Trade Commission (USITC), in a federal district court, or in both fora, while patent infringement claims regarding *domestic* products could only be brought in a federal district court, constituted less favourable treatment for the imported products.[300] In *Thailand – Cigarettes (Philippines) (2011)*, however, the Appellate Body added a cautionary note in this respect:

> [W]here a Member's legal system applies a single regulatory regime to both imported and like domestic products, with the sole difference being that an additional requirement is imposed only on imported products, the existence of this additional requirement may provide a significant indication that imported products are treated less favourably. Because, however, the examination of whether imported products are treated less favourably 'cannot rest on simple assertion', close scrutiny of the measure at issue will normally require further identification or elaboration of its implications for the conditions of competition in order properly to support a finding of less favourable treatment under Article III:4 of the GATT 1994.[301]

In other words, the mere existence of an additional requirement on imported products does *not automatically* lead to the conclusion that imported products are accorded 'treatment less favourable'.

Finally, note that, in *Korea – Various Measures on Beef (2001)*, the Appellate Body found that a measure, which does *not legally require* certain treatment of

297 Panel Report, *India – Autos (2002)*, para. 7.201.
298 Panel Report, *China – Publications and Audiovisual Products (2010)*, para. 7.1471.
299 Appellate Body Report, *Thailand – Cigarettes (Philippines) (2011)*, para. 134.
300 See Panel Report, *US – Section 337 Tariff Act (1989)*, para. 5.18.
301 Appellate Body Report, *Thailand – Cigarettes (Philippines) (2011)*, para. 130. Note that the Appellate Body in this case indicated that 'the Panel might have made further inquiry into the issue', but found that 'the Panel's analysis was sufficient to support its finding that the additional administrative requirements modify the conditions of competition to the detriment of imported cigarettes'. See *ibid.*, para. 138.

imports, may still be considered to accord 'treatment less favourable'. This may be so when such measure creates incentives for market participants to behave in certain ways, and thereby has the 'practical effect' of treating imported products less favourably.[302] Following this line of reasoning, the panel in *Mexico – Taxes on Soft Drinks (2006)* found with respect to the tax exemptions at issue in that case:

> The challenged measures create an economic incentive for producers to use cane sugar as a sweetener in the production of soft drinks and syrups, instead of other non-cane sugar sweeteners such as beet sugar or HFCS ... These measures do not legally impede producers from using non-cane sugar sweeteners ... However, they significantly modify the conditions of competition between cane sugar, on the one hand, and non-cane sugar sweeteners, such as beet sugar or HFCS, on the other.[303]

However, it has been argued by some that the Appellate Body ruled in *Dominican Republic – Import and Sale of Cigarettes (2005)* that panels, in examining whether a measure accords treatment less favourable, should inquire further whether 'the detrimental effect is unrelated to the foreign origin of the product'.[304] The relevant measure in *Dominican Republic – Import and Sale of Cigarettes (2005)* was a requirement that importers and domestic producers post a bond of 5 million Dominican pesos (RD$). Honduras argued that the requirement to post a bond of RD$5 million accorded 'less favourable treatment' to imported cigarettes because, as the sales of domestic cigarettes are greater than those of imported cigarettes on the Dominican Republic market, the per unit cost of the bond requirement for imported cigarettes is higher than for domestic products.[305] The panel in *Dominican Republic – Import and Sale of Cigarettes (2005)* found that Honduras had failed to establish that the measure at issue accorded less favourable treatment to imported cigarettes.[306] On appeal, the Appellate Body upheld the panel's finding.[307] In its report, the Appellate Body stated, *inter alia*, that:

> the existence of a detrimental effect on a given imported product resulting from a measure does not necessarily imply that this measure accords less favourable treatment to imports if the detrimental effect is explained by factors or circumstances unrelated to the foreign origin of the product, such as the market share of the importer in this case.[308]

In *US – Clove Cigarettes (2012)*, the Appellate Body recognised that this statement, 'when read in isolation, could be viewed as suggesting that further inquiry

302 See Appellate Body Report, *Korea – Various Measures on Beef (2001)*, para. 144–5. See also Appellate Body Reports, *China – Auto (2009)*, paras. 195 and 196; and Appellate Body Reports, *US – COOL (2012)*, para. 288. For a detailed discussion of *US – COOL (2012)*, see below, p. 892.

303 Panel Report, *Mexico – Taxes on Soft Drinks (2006)*, para. 8.117. 'HFCS' stands for 'high fructose corn syrup'.

304 See e.g. United States' appellant's submission in *US – Clove Cigarettes (2012)*, para. 101, referred to in Appellate Body Report, *US – Clove Cigarettes (2012)*, fn. 372 to para. 179. See also Panel Report, *EC – Approval and Marketing of Biotech Products (2006)*, para. 7.2514.

305 See Appellate Body Report, *Dominican Republic – Import and Sale of Cigarettes (2005)*, para. 96.

306 See Panel Report, *Dominican Republic – Import and Sale of Cigarettes (2005)*, paras. 7.311 and 7.316.

307 See Appellate Body Report, *Dominican Republic – Import and Sale of Cigarettes (2005)*, para. 96.

308 *Ibid.*

into the rationale for the detrimental impact is necessary'.[309] The Appellate Body noted, however, that it rejected Honduras' claim under Article III:4 because 'the difference between the per-unit costs of the bond requirement alleged by Honduras is explained by the fact that the importer of Honduran cigarettes has a smaller market share than two domestic producers'.[310] Thus, in *Dominican Republic – Import and Sale of Cigarettes (2005)*, the Appellate Body merely held that the higher *per unit* costs of the bond requirement for imported cigarettes did not conclusively demonstrate less favourable treatment, because such costs were not attributable to the specific measure at issue but, rather, were a function of sales volumes. The Appellate Body noted that it had already ruled in *Thailand – Cigarettes (Philippines) (2011)* that to support a finding of 'treatment less favourable' under Article III:4 of the GATT 1994:

> there must be in every case a genuine relationship between the measure at issue and its adverse impact on competitive opportunities for imported versus like domestic products.[311]

Thus, a finding of 'treatment less favourable' does not require that the detrimental impact of the measure on the conditions of competition is related to the foreign origin of the products, but does require that there is a *genuine relationship* between the measure and the detrimental impact. In other words, if a genuine relationship between the measure and the detrimental impact exists, i.e. if the detrimental impact can be attributed genuinely to the measure, the measure may be found to accord 'treatment less favourable' even if the detrimental impact can be explained by factors or circumstances that are unrelated to the foreign origin of the product.[312]

In *EC – Seal Products (2014)*, the Appellate Body summarised the case law on the term 'treatment no less favourable' under Article III:4 as follows:

> The meaning of the term 'treatment no less favourable' in Article III:4 has been considered by panels and the Appellate Body in prior disputes. As a result, the following propositions are well established. First, the term 'treatment no less favourable' requires effective equality of opportunities for imported products to compete with like domestic products. Second, a formal difference in treatment between imported and domestic like products is neither necessary, nor sufficient, to establish that imported products are accorded less favourable treatment than that accorded to like domestic products. Third, because Article III:4 is concerned with ensuring effective equality of competitive opportunities for imported products, a determination of whether imported products are treated less favourably than like domestic products involves an assessment of the implications of the contested measure for the equality of competitive conditions between imported and like domestic products. If the outcome of this assessment is that the measure has a detrimental impact on the conditions of competition for like imported products, then such detrimental impact will amount to treatment that is 'less favourable' within the meaning of Article III:4. Finally, for a measure to be found to modify the conditions of competition in the relevant market to the detriment of

309 Appellate Body Report, *US – Clove Cigarettes (2012)*, fn. 372 to para. 179. For a discussion on *US – Clove Cigarettes (2012)*, see below, pp. 899–912.

310 *Ibid.* 311 Appellate Body Report, *Thailand – Cigarettes (Philippines) (2011)*, para. 134.

312 See also Appellate Body Reports, *US – COOL (Article 21.5) (2015)*, para. 5.358.

imported products, there must be a 'genuine relationship' between the measure at issue and the adverse impact on competitive opportunities for imported products.[313]

In *EC – Seal Products (2014)* the question arose as to whether for the purposes of establishing a violation of Article III:4 of the GATT 1994, a finding that a measure has a detrimental impact on competitive opportunities for imported products, compared to like domestic products, is dispositive.[314] The European Union, the respondent in that case, argued that it was not and that a panel must conduct an *additional inquiry* into whether the detrimental impact on competitive opportunities for like imported products stems exclusively from a legitimate regulatory distinction.[315] As discussed in Chapter 13, such additional inquiry is required for establishing a violation of the non-discrimination obligations under Article 2.1 of the *TBT Agreement*.[316] In the European Union's view, the legal standard for the non-discrimination obligations under Article 2.1 of the *TBT Agreement* applied equally to claims under Article III:4 of the GATT 1994.[317] Both the panel and the Appellate Body disagreed with the European Union. The Appellate Body observed in this respect:

> The fact that, under the GATT 1994, a Member's right to regulate is accommodated under Article XX, weighs heavily against an interpretation of Articles I:1 and III:4 that requires an examination of whether the detrimental impact of a measure on competitive opportunities for like imported products stems exclusively from a legitimate regulatory distinction.[318]

In other words, the 'treatment no less favourable' requirement under Article III:4 of the GATT 1994 does not require any examination of whether the detrimental impact of a measure on competitive opportunities for like imported products stems exclusively from a legitimate regulatory distinction.[319]

The Appellate Body subsequently addressed the argument of the European Union that under such interpretation of Article III:4 of the GATT 1994, a measure could be considered non-discriminatory under the *TBT Agreement*, but still violate the GATT 1994, since the list of possible legitimate objectives that may factor into an analysis under Article 2.1 of the *TBT Agreement* is open, in contrast to the closed list of objectives enumerated under Article XX of the GATT 1994.[320] According to the European Union, this would 'render

313 Appellate Body Reports, *EC – Seal Products (2014)*, para. 5.101 (footnotes omitted).

314 Appellate Body Reports, *EC – Seal Products (2014)*, para. 5.100.

315 *Ibid.* 316 See above, p. 910.

317 See Appellate Body Reports, *EC – Seal Products (2014)*, para. 5.100. On the European Union's argument, see *ibid.*, paras. 5.102–5.103 and 5.106.

318 *Ibid.*, para. 5.125.

319 See *ibid.*, 5.116–5.117; See also Panel Reports, *US – COOL (Article 21.5 – Canada and Mexico) (2015)*, para. 7.624, Appellate Body Report, *US – Tuna II (Mexico) (Article 21.5) (2015)*, para. 7.277.

320 Appellate Body Reports, *EC – Seal Products (2014)*, para. 5.118. For a detailed discussion of Article XX of the GATT 1994 and the policy objectives enumerated therein, as well as a discussion of the legitimate objectives under Article 2.1 of the *TBT Agreement*, refer to Chapter 8 (see below, pp. 546–605) and Chapter 13 (see below, pp. 883–925) respectively.

Article 2.1 of the *TBT Agreement* irrelevant' as complainants would have a strong incentive not to invoke Article 2.1 of the *TBT Agreement*, and, instead, would bring claims under the GATT 1994, even if the measure at issue qualified as a technical regulation. On the basis of a detailed review of its case law on Article 2.1 of the *TBT Agreement*, which is discussed in Chapter 13, the Appellate Body disagreed with the European Union that its interpretation of Article III:4 of the GATT 1994 would render Article 2.1 of the *TBT Agreement* irrelevant.[321] The Appellate Body recalled its finding in *US – Clove Cigarettes (2012)* that under the *TBT Agreement*, the balance between the desire to avoid creating unnecessary obstacles to international trade (under the fifth recital) and the recognition of Members' right to regulate (under the sixth recital) is not, in principle, different from the balance set out in the GATT 1994, where obligations such as national treatment in Article III are qualified by the general exceptions provision of Article XX of the GATT 1994.[322] The Appellate Body also observed that the European Union had not pointed to any concrete examples of a legitimate objective that could factor into an analysis under Article 2.1 of the *TBT Agreement*, but would not fall within the scope of Article XX of the GATT 1994.[323] Finally, the Appellate Body noted that:

> our interpretation of the legal standards under Articles I:1 and III:4 of the GATT 1994, and Article 2.1 of the TBT Agreement, is based on the text of those provisions, as understood in their context, and in the light of the object and purpose of the agreements in which they appear, as is our mandate. If there is a perceived imbalance in the existing rights and obligations under the TBT Agreement and the GATT 1994, the authority rests with the Members of the WTO to address that imbalance.[324]

GATT and WTO panels and the Appellate Body have found a wide variety of measures to be inconsistent with the national treatment obligation of Article III:4. In addition to the reasoning discussed above, the following reasoning by GATT panels is also noteworthy and further illustrates the broad scope of the national treatment obligation of Article III:4. With respect to minimum price requirements, the panel in *Canada – Provincial Liquor Boards (US) (1992)* ruled that:

> minimum prices applied equally to imported and domestic beer did not necessarily accord equal conditions of competition to imported and domestic beer. Whenever they prevented imported beer from being supplied at a price below that of domestic beer, they accorded in fact treatment to imported beer less favourable than that accorded to domestic beer: when they were set at the level at which domestic brewers supplied beer – as was presently the case in New Brunswick and Newfoundland – they did not change the competitive opportunities accorded to domestic beer but did affect the competitive opportunities of imported beer which could otherwise be supplied below the minimum price.[325]

321 See Appellate Body Reports, *EC – Seal Products (2014)*, para. 5.126.
322 Appellate Body Reports, *EC – Seal Products (2014)*, para. 5.127.
323 *Ibid.*, para. 5.128. 324 *Ibid.*, para. 5.129.
325 Panel Report, *Canada – Provincial Liquor Boards (US) (1992)*, para. 5.30.

With respect to a general ban on cigarette advertising, the panel in *Thailand – Cigarettes (1990)* noted:

> It might be argued that such a general ban on all cigarette advertising would create unequal competitive opportunities between the existing Thai supplier of cigarettes and new, foreign suppliers and was therefore contrary to Article III:4.[326]

The panel in *US – Malt Beverages (1992)* found with regard to regulations concerning internal transportation that:

> the requirement for imported beer and wine to be transported by common carrier, whereas domestic in-state beer and wine is not so required, may result in additional charges to transport these imported products and therefore prevent imported products from competing on an equal footing with domestic like products.[327]

3 NATIONAL TREATMENT UNDER THE GATS

Article XVII of the GATS, which is entitled 'National Treatment', states, in paragraph 1:

> In the sectors inscribed in its Schedule, and subject to any conditions and qualifications set out therein, each Member shall accord to services and service suppliers of any other Member, in respect of all measures affecting the supply of services, treatment no less favourable than that it accords to its own like services and service suppliers.

This section first explores the nature of the national treatment obligation of Article XVII:1 of the GATS and then discusses the test of consistency with this obligation.[328]

3.1 Nature of the National Treatment Obligation of Article XVII:1 of the GATS

The national treatment obligation of Article XVII:1 of the GATS is different from the national treatment obligation of Article III of the GATT 1994. As discussed above, save and except the exclusions provided for in Article III:8, the national treatment obligation of Article III of the GATT 1994 has *general* application to all measures affecting trade in goods.[329] On the contrary, the national treatment obligation for trade in services of Article XVII:1 of the GATS does not have such general application; it does not apply to all measures affecting trade in

326 Panel Report, *Thailand – Cigarettes (1990)*, para. 78. Note that such a general ban on cigarette advertising was not the measure at issue in this case but a suggested alternative measure of which the panel considered the GATT-consistency.

327 Panel Report, *US – Malt Beverages (1992)*, para. 5.50.

328 On the relationship between the national treatment obligation of Article XVII:1 of the GATS and the market access obligation of Article XVI:1 of the GATS, see below, pp. 528–9.

329 See above, pp. 344–5.

services. The national treatment obligation *only* applies to a measure affecting trade in services *to the extent* that a WTO Member has explicitly committed itself to grant 'national treatment' in respect of the specific services sector concerned. Such commitments are set out in a Member's 'Schedule of Specific Commitments', also referred to as its 'Services Schedule'. These commitments to grant national treatment are often made subject to certain conditions, qualifications and limitations, which are also set out in the Schedule. A Member can, for example, grant national treatment in a specific services sector only with respect to certain modes of supply (such as cross-border supply) and not others (such as commercial presence).[330] Typical national treatment limitations included in Services Schedules relate to: (1) nationality or residence requirements for service suppliers; (2) requirements to invest a certain amount of assets in local currency; (3) restrictions on the purchase of land by foreign service suppliers; (4) special subsidy or tax privileges granted only to domestic service suppliers; and (5) differential capital requirements and special operational limits applying only to operations of foreign service suppliers.[331]

Note, by way of example, the national treatment column of the Services Schedule of the European Union and its Member States with respect to higher education services, as included in Figure 5.1. It appears from this Schedule that the European Union and its Member States agreed to accord national treatment to higher education services supplied in mode 1 ('cross-border supply') (with a qualification by Italy), mode 2 ('consumption abroad') and mode 3 ('commercial presence'). However, no commitment to accord national treatment is made with regard to mode 4 ('presence of natural persons'), except commitments made for all services sectors (see 'horizontal commitments').[332]

To determine the scope of the national treatment obligation of a Member, or to determine whether, in respect of a specific services sector, a Member must grant national treatment to services and service suppliers of other Members, it is necessary to examine the commitments, conditions, qualifications and limitations set out in the Member's Schedule very carefully. The Services Schedules of Members can be found on the WTO website.[333]

Generally speaking, many Members, especially developing-country Members, have made national treatment commitments with regard to a limited number of services sectors only, and when commitments are made, they are often accompanied by extensive limitations. Negotiations on more ambitious national treatment commitments are an important element of the ongoing negotiations on trade in services in the context of the Doha Round.

330 On the modes of supply of services, see above, pp. 329–30.
331 See WTO Secretariat, *Market Access: Unfinished Business*, Special Series Studies 6 (WTO, 2001), 103.
332 On 'horizontal commitments', see below, p. 526.
333 See www.wto.org/english/tratop_e/serv_e/serv_commitments_e.htm. For an explanation on how to 'read' Services Schedules, see below, pp. 525–32.

Sector or subsector	Limitations on market access	Limitations on national treatment
C. Higher Education Services (CPC 923)	5. PRIVATELY FUNDED EDUCATION SERVICES	
	1) F: Condition of nationality. However, third country nationals can have authorization from competent authorities to establish and direct an education institution and to teach.	1) I: Condition of nationality for service providers to be authorised to issue state recognised diplomas.
	2) None	2) None
	3) E, I: Needs test for opening of private universities authorised to issue recognised diplomas or degrees; producers involves an advice of the Parliament. GR: Unbound for education institutions granting recognised State diplomas.	3) None
	4) Unbound except as indicated in the horizontal section and subject to the following specific limitations: DK: Condition of nationality for professors. F: Condition of nationality. However, third country nationals may obtain authorization from competent authorities to establish and direct an education institution and to teach. I: Condition of nationality for service providers to be authorised to issue state recognised diplomas.	

Figure 5.1 Excerpt from the Services Schedule of the European Union and its Member States

As all other non-discrimination obligations in both the GATT 1994 and the GATS, also the national treatment obligation of Article XVII:1 of the GATS covers both *de jure* and *de facto* discrimination.[334] In fact, unlike for other non-discrimination obligations, for the national treatment obligation under the GATS, the treaty text clearly indicates that *de facto* discrimination is covered by this obligation. As discussed further below, Article XVII:3 states:

> *Formally identical* or formally different *treatment* shall be considered to be less favourable if it modifies the conditions of competition in favour of services or service suppliers of the Member compared to like services or service suppliers of any other Member.[335]

The 2001 *Scheduling Guidelines* give the following example of a *de facto* discriminatory measure:

> A measure [which] stipulates that prior residency is required for the issuing of a licence to supply a service.[336]

With regard to this measure, the *Scheduling Guidelines* note:

> Although the measure does not formally distinguish service suppliers on the basis of national origin, it *de facto* offers less favourable treatment to foreign service suppliers because they

334 See e.g. Panel Report, *EC – Bananas III (Article 21.5 – Ecuador) (1999)*, para. 6.126; and Decision by the Arbitrators, *EC – Bananas III (US) (Article 22.6 – EC) (1999)*, paras. 5.89–5.95.

335 Emphasis added.

336 *Guidelines for the Scheduling of Specific Commitments under the General Agreement on Trade in Services*, adopted by the Council for Trade in Services on 23 March 2001, S/L/92, dated 28 March 2001, 6.

are less likely to be able to meet a prior residency requirement than like service suppliers of national origin.[337]

The panel in *China – Electronic Payment Services (2012)* deduced from Article XVII:3 that the objective of the national treatment obligation of Article XVII:1 is 'to ensure equal competitive opportunities for like services [and like service suppliers] of other Members'.[338]

3.2 National Treatment Test of Article XVII:1 of the GATS

In its analysis of the consistency of the EC licensing regime for the importation of bananas with the national treatment obligation under Article XVII:1 of the GATS, the panel in *EC – Bananas III (1997)* noted:

> In order to establish a breach of the national treatment obligation of Article XVII, three elements need to be demonstrated: (i) the EC has undertaken a commitment in a relevant sector and mode of supply; (ii) the EC has adopted or applied a measure affecting the supply of services in that sector and/or mode of supply; and (iii) the measure accords to service suppliers of any other Member treatment less favourable than that it accords to the EC's own like service suppliers.[339]

The panels in *China – Publications and Audiovisual Products (2010)* and *China – Electronic Payment Services (2012)* structured their analysis of the consistency with Article XVII:1 of the measures at issue in these cases along the same broad lines.[340]

Article XVII:1 of the GATS thus sets out a four-tier test of consistency with the national treatment obligation thereof. This test of consistency requires the examination of:

- whether, and to what extent, a *national treatment commitment* was made in respect of the relevant services sector and relevant mode of supply;
- whether the measure at issue is *a measure by a Member affecting trade in services*, i.e. a measure to which the GATS applies;
- whether the foreign and domestic services and service suppliers are '*like services* and *service suppliers*'; and
- whether the foreign services and service suppliers are accorded '*treatment no less favourable*'.

Below, each element of this four-tier test of consistency will be discussed in turn.[341]

To date, WTO Members have been found to have acted inconsistently with the national treatment obligation of Article XVII:1 of the GATS in six disputes.[342]

337 *Ibid.* 338 Panel Report, *China – Electronic Payment Services (2012)*, para. 7.700.

339 Panel Reports, *EC – Bananas III (1997)*, para. 7.314. See also Panel Report, *EC – Bananas III (Article 21.5 – Ecuador) (1999)*, para. 6.100.

340 See, for example, Panel Report, *China – Publications and Audiovisual Products (2010)*, paras. 7.942ff.

341 See below, pp. 403–4, 404–5, 405–8 and 408–12.

342 See *EC – Bananas III (1997)*; *EC – Bananas III (Article 21.5 – Ecuador) (1999)*; *EC – Bananas III (US) (Article 22.6 – EC) (1999)*; *Canada – Autos (2000)*; *China – Publications and Audiovisual Products (2010)*; and *China – Electronic Payment Services (2012)*. In *Argentina – Financial Services (2016)*, the Appellate Body reversed the panel's findings of consistency, but was unable to complete the legal analysis.

3.2.1 National Treatment Commitment

As explained above, the national treatment obligation of Article XVII:1 of the GATS does not apply generally to all trade in services. The national treatment obligation applies only to the extent that a WTO Member has explicitly committed itself to grant 'national treatment' in respect of a specific services sector.[343] In applying Article XVII:1, panels must therefore first examine the responding Member's Services Schedule to establish whether, and to what extent, that Member has made a national treatment commitment with respect to the services sector at issue in the dispute.

In *China – Publications and Audiovisual Products (2010)*, the issue arose as to whether China had made a national treatment commitment with respect to the distribution of sound recordings through electronic means. China argued that the entry 'Sound recording distribution services' under the heading 'Audiovisual Services' (sector 2.D) in China's Services Schedule, with regard to which it had made a national treatment commitment, does *not* extend to the distribution of sound recordings through electronic means. According to China, the entry at issue covers only the distribution of sound recordings in physical form, for example, music embedded on compact discs (CDs). This dispute thus called for an interpretation of China's Services Schedule and in particular the meaning and scope of the entry 'Sound recording distribution services'. After interpreting this entry in accordance with Articles 31 and 32 of the *Vienna Convention on the Law of Treaties*, the panel concluded that China's commitment in the entry 'Sound recording distribution services' covers both physical distribution as well as the electronic distribution of sound recordings.[344] The Appellate Body upheld the panel's finding. After reviewing the panel's reasoning, the Appellate Body concluded that the panel did not err in its consideration of dictionary definitions of the terms 'sound recording' and 'distribution'.[345] Furthermore, the Appellate Body was persuaded that, on balance, the analysis of a number of contextual elements (such as China's Services Schedule, provisions of the GATS, and the Services Schedules of other Members) supported the interpretation of China's commitment on 'Sound recording distribution services' as including the electronic distribution of sound recordings.[346] With regard to the object and purpose of the GATS, the Appellate Body noted that it did not consider that the principle of progressive liberalisation – a core purpose of the GATS – lends support to an interpretation that would constrain the scope and coverage of specific commitments that have already been undertaken by Members.[347] More generally, the Appellate Body considered in *China – Publications and Audiovisual Products (2010)* that the terms used in China's Services Schedule ('sound recording' and

343 On the concept of 'services sectors', see below, pp 525–32. A list of the services sectors is contained in GATT Secretariat, *Note by the Secretariat, Services Sectoral Classification List*, MTN.GNS/W/120, dated 10 July 1991. A Member's national treatment commitments are set out in its Services Schedule. See below, pp. 525–32.

344 See Panel Report, *China – Publications and Audiovisual Products (2010)*, para. 7.1265.

345 See Appellate Body Report, *China – Publications and Audiovisual Products (2010)*, para. 357.

346 See *ibid.*, para. 387.

347 See *ibid.*, para. 394.

'distribution') are 'sufficiently generic that what they apply to may change over time'.[348] Even more generally, the Appellate Body noted in this respect that the Services Schedules, like the GATS itself and all WTO agreements, constitute 'multilateral treaties with continuing obligations that WTO Members entered into for an indefinite period of time'.[349] The Appellate Body further stated that:

> interpreting the terms of GATS specific commitments based on the notion that the ordinary meaning to be attributed to those terms can only be the meaning that they had at the time the Schedule was concluded would mean that very similar or identically worded commitments could be given different meanings, content, and coverage depending on the date of their adoption or the date of a Member's accession to the treaty. Such interpretation would undermine the predictability, security, and clarity of GATS specific commitments.[350]

3.2.2 'Measures by Members Affecting Trade in Services'

The second element of the test of consistency with the national treatment obligation of Article XVII:1 of the GATS relates to the question of whether the measure at issue is a measure by a Member affecting trade in services, i.e. a measure to which the GATS applies. As discussed above in the context of the MFN treatment obligation of Article II:1 of the GATS, the concept of a 'measure by a Member' is broad, including not only measures of central government or authorities but also measures of regional and local governments and authorities as well as – in specific circumstances – measures of non-governmental bodies.[351]

The concept of a 'measure affecting trade in services' has been clarified by the Appellate Body in *Canada – Autos (2000)*, where it stated that two key issues must be examined to determine whether a measure is one 'affecting trade in services', namely, first, whether there is 'trade in services' in the sense of Article I:2, and, second, whether the measure at issue 'affects' such trade in services within the meaning of Article I:1.[352] Recall, with respect to the first question, the broad scope of the concept of 'trade in services', including all services except services supplied in the exercise of governmental authority. Trade in services includes services supplied in any of the four distinct modes of supply (cross-border supply, consumption abroad, commercial presence and the presence of natural persons).[353] With respect to the second question, recall that, for a measure to 'affect' trade in services, this measure need not regulate or govern the trade in, i.e. the supply of, services. A measure affects trade in services when the measure bears 'upon the conditions of competition in supply of a service'.[354] The panel in *China – Publications and Audiovisual Products (2010)* noted in the context of its assessment of the prohibition on wholesale

348 *Ibid.*, para. 396. 349 *Ibid.* 350 *Ibid.*, para. 397. 351 See above, p. 313.
352 See Appellate Body Report, *Canada – Autos (2000)*, para. 155. See above, p. 328.
353 See above, p. 400. 354 See above, p. 401.

trading of reading materials that the term 'affecting' is wider in scope than 'regulating' or 'governing', and thus concluded that the measures at issue 'affect' the supply of reading materials distribution services for the purpose of Article XVII:1.[355]

3.2.3 'Like Services and Service Suppliers'

The third element of the test of consistency with the national treatment obligation of Article XVII:1 of the GATS relates to the question of whether the foreign and domestic services and service suppliers are 'like services and service suppliers'. It is only between 'like services and service suppliers' that the national treatment obligation applies and that discrimination within the meaning of Article XVII:1 of the GATS may occur. Services and service suppliers that are not 'like' may be treated differently; different treatment of services and service suppliers that are not 'like' will not constitute discrimination within the meaning of Article XVII:1 of the GATS. For the application of the national treatment obligation of Article XVII:1, it is therefore important to be able to determine whether, for example, movie actors are 'like' stage actors, whether the distribution of books is 'like' the distribution of e-books; whether doctors with a foreign medical degree are 'like' doctors with a domestic medical degree; whether Internet gambling is 'like' casino gambling; and whether a 500-partner law firm is 'like' a sole practitioner.

As already noted in Chapter 4, the GATS does not define the terms 'like services and service suppliers'. However, there is useful case law regarding the meaning of the terms 'like services and service suppliers'.

In *Argentina – Financial Services (2016)* the Appellate Body clarified that reference to 'services and service suppliers' indicates that considerations relating to both the service and service supplier are relevant for determining 'likeness' under Articles II:1 and XVII:1 of the GATS.[356] It noted:

> The assessment of likeness of services should not be undertaken in isolation from considerations relating to the service suppliers, and, conversely, the assessment of likeness of service suppliers should not be undertaken in isolation from considerations relating to the likeness of the services they provide. We see the phrase 'like services and service suppliers' as an integrated element for the likeness analysis under Articles II:1 and XVII:1, respectively. Accordingly, separate findings with respect to the 'likeness' of services, on the one hand, and the 'likeness' of service suppliers, on the other hand, are not required.[357]

Referring to the considerable body of case law on 'likeness' in the context of Article III of the GATT 1994,[358] the panel in *China – Electronic Payment Services (2012)* first observed that it did not assume that 'without further analysis, [it] may simply transpose' to trade in services the criteria or analytical framework used to determine 'likeness' in the context of Article III of the GATT 1994.[359] The

355 See Panel Report, *China – Publications and Audiovisual Products (2010)*, para. 7.971.
356 See Appellate Body Report, *Argentina – Financial Services (2016)*, para. 6.29.
357 *Ibid.* 358 See above, pp. 354–63.
359 See Panel Report, *China – Electronic Payment Services (2012)*, para. 7.698.

panel noted that there are 'important dissimilarities' between the two areas of trade, such as the intangible nature of services, their supply through four different modes, and possible differences in how trade in services is conducted and regulated.[360] The determination of 'likeness' in the context of Article XVII:1 of the GATS undoubtedly raises even more difficult conceptual problems than the determination of 'likeness' in the context of Article III of the GATT 1994.

The panel in *China – Electronic Payment Services (2012)* observed that the dictionary defines 'like' as:

> [h]aving the same characteristics or qualities as some other person or thing; of approximately identical shape, size, etc., with something else; similar.[361]

According to the panel, this range of meanings suggests that:

> for services to be considered 'like', they need not necessarily be exactly the same, and that in view of the references to 'approximately' and 'similar', services could qualify as 'like' if they are essentially or generally the same.[362]

The panel further noted that the dictionary definition of 'like' made clear that something or someone is 'like' *in some respect*, such as – in the terms of the definition – the 'shape, size, etc.' of a thing or person. To determine in what respect services need to be essentially the same for them to be 'like', the panel subsequently turned to consider the context of the term 'like services', and, in particular, Article XVII:3 of the GATS. As discussed below, Article XVII:3 clarifies the 'treatment no less favourable' requirement of Article XVII:1 and states that a Member is deemed to provide less favourable treatment if it 'modifies the conditions of competition in favour of services ... of [that] Member compared to like services ... of any other Member'.[363] According to the panel, this suggests that:

> like services are services that are in a competitive relationship with each other (or would be if they were allowed to be supplied in a particular market).[364]

The panel argued that this is so because:

> only if the foreign and domestic services in question are in such a competitive relationship can a measure of a Member modify the conditions of competition in favour of one or other of these services.[365]

Consistent with the approach to 'likeness' under Article III of the GATT 1994, the panel in *China – Electronic Payment Services (2012)* ruled that any determination of 'likeness' under Article XVII:1 of the GATS should 'take into account the particular circumstances of each case', or, in other words, 'should be made on a case-by-case basis'.[366] Also consistent with the approach to 'likeness' under

360 See *ibid.* 361 Panel Report, *China – Electronic Payment Services (2012)*, para. 7.699.
362 *Ibid.* 363 See below, pp. 408–9.
364 Panel Report, *China – Electronic Payment Services (2012)*, para. 7.700. 365 *Ibid.*
366 *Ibid.*, para. 7.701. For the relevant case law under Article III of the GATT 1994, see above, p. 402 and p. 406.

Article III of the GATT 1994, the panel held that a determination of 'likeness' under Article XVII:1 of the GATS:

> should be based on arguments and evidence that pertain to the competitive relationship of the services being compared.[367]

Moreover, such determination of 'likeness':

> must be made on the basis of the evidence as a whole.[368]

According to the panel in *China – Electronic Payment Services (2012)*, services are 'like' for the purposes of Article XVII:1 if:

> it is determined that the services in question in a particular case are essentially or generally the same in competitive terms.[369]

In *Argentina – Financial Services (2016)* the Appellate Body clarified that 'the analysis of "likeness" serves the same purpose in the context of both trade in goods and trade in services, namely, to determine whether the products or services and service suppliers, respectively, are in a competitive relationship with each other'.[370] It noted:

> Thus, to the extent that the criteria for assessing 'likeness' traditionally employed as analytical tools in the context of trade in goods are relevant for assessing the competitive relationship of services and service suppliers, these criteria may be employed also in assessing 'likeness' in the context of trade in services, provided that they are adapted as appropriate to account for the specific characteristics of trade in services.[371]

Further, in *Argentina – Financial Services (2016)*, the Appellate Body thus clarified that the following could be relevant for determining 'likeness' under the GATS: (1) characteristics of services and service suppliers; (2) consumers' preferences in respect of services and service suppliers; and (3) tariff classification and description of services under, for instance, the UN Central Product Classification (CPC).[372] As in the context of trade in goods, however, these criteria for analysing 'likeness' of services and service suppliers are 'simply analytical tools to assist in the task of examining the relevant evidence'.[373] They are neither a treaty-mandated nor a closed list of criteria.[374]

While the Appellate Body suggested that the criteria employed for assessing likeness in the context of trade in goods are also suitable in case of trade in services, it noted that 'what is being compared for *likeness* is different in the context of trade in goods and trade in services'. Where Articles II:1 and XVII:1 of the GATS refer to 'like services and service suppliers', Articles I:1, III:2 and

367 *Ibid.*, para. 7.702. For the relevant case law under Article III of the GATT 1994, see above, p. 402 and p. 406.
368 *Ibid.* 369 *Ibid.*
370 Appellate Body Report, *Argentina – Financial Services (2016)*, para. 6.31.
371 *Ibid.* 372 See *ibid.*, para. 6.32.
373 See *ibid.* See also Appellate Body Report, *EC – Asbestos*, para. 102, discussed below, p. 560.
374 See Appellate Body Report, *Argentina – Financial Services (2016)*, para. 6.32.

III:4 of the GATT 1994, refer to 'like products' only and do not include a reference to 'like producers'.[375] Further, as defined in Article I:2 of the GATS, different modes of supply exist only in trade in services and not in trade in goods, and, accordingly, the analysis of 'likeness' of services and service suppliers may require additional considerations of whether or how this analysis is affected by the mode(s) of service supply.[376]

In *Argentina – Financial Services (2016)*, the panel found – on the basis of its understanding of the Appellate Body's rulings in *EC – Asbestos (2001)* and *US – Clove Cigarettes (2012)*[377] that regulatory concerns, and in particular the possibility of Argentine authorities to have access to tax information on foreign service suppliers 'may be considered to be an "other factor" to be taken into account in [the] likeness analysis, provided that it is reflected in the competitive relationship'.[378] On appeal, the Appellate Body disagreed with the panel and found that regulatory concern is not to be assessed as an 'other factor' or additional criterion for determining 'likeness'.[379] The Appellate Body did recognise, however, that evidence with regard to the possibility of Argentine authorities to have access to tax information on foreign service suppliers might be a relevant consideration relating to the competitive relationship between services and service suppliers, in particular with respect to the characteristics of the services and service suppliers as well as with regard to consumer preferences regarding these services and service suppliers.[380]

With regard to the origin-based presumption of likeness, the Appellate Body in *Argentina – Financial Services (2016)* stated:

> In our view, where a measure provides for a distinction based exclusively on origin, there will or can be services and service suppliers that are the same in all respects except for origin and, accordingly, 'likeness' can be presumed and the complainant is not required to establish 'likeness' on the basis of the relevant criteria set out above.[381]

However, the Appellate Body did caution that in comparison to trade in goods, the scope of origin-based presumption under the GATS would be more limited and establishing 'likeness' based on presumption may often involve greater complexity in trade in services for the reasons explained above in the context of establishing 'likeness' of services and service suppliers.[382]

3.2.4 'Treatment No Less Favourable'

The fourth and final element of the test of consistency with the national treatment obligation of Article XVII:1 of the GATS relates to the question of whether the foreign services and service suppliers are accorded treatment no less favourable

375 *Ibid.*, para. 6.27. 376 *Ibid.*, para. 6.33. 377 See above, p. 398.
378 Panel Report, *Argentina – Financial Services (2016)*, para. 7.179.
379 Appellate Body Report, *Argentina – Financial Services (2016)*, para. 6.106. 380 See *ibid.*, para. 6.64.
381 *Ibid.*, para. 6.38. See also Panel Report, *China – Publications and Audiovisual Products (2010)*, para. 7.975.
382 Appellate Body Report, *Argentina – Financial Services (2016)*, para. 6.38.

than 'like' domestic services and service suppliers. Paragraphs 2 and 3 of Article XVII:1 of the GATS clarify the requirement of 'treatment no less favourable' set out in paragraph 1 by stating:

2. A Member may meet the requirement of paragraph 1 by according to services and service suppliers of any other Member, either formally identical treatment or formally different treatment to that it accords to its own like services and service suppliers.
3. Formally identical or formally different treatment shall be considered to be less favourable if it modifies the conditions of competition in favour of services or service suppliers of the Member compared to like services or service suppliers of any other Member.

It follows that a Member that gives formally identical treatment to foreign and domestic services and service suppliers may nevertheless be in breach of the national treatment obligation. This happens if that Member, by giving formally identical treatment, modifies the conditions of competition in favour of the domestic services or service suppliers. Also, a Member that gives formally *different* treatment to foreign and domestic services or service suppliers does not act in breach of the national treatment obligation if that Member, by giving formally *different* treatment, does not modify the conditions of competition in favour of the domestic services and service suppliers. The latter would obviously be the case if the different treatment would be in favour of the foreign services or service suppliers but it may also be that a formally different treatment has no impact on the conditions of competition. As the panel in *China – Electronic Payment Services (2012)* noted:

subject to all other Article XVII conditions being fulfilled, formally identical or different treatment of service suppliers of another Member constitutes a breach of Article XVII:1 if and only if such treatment modifies the conditions of competition to their detriment.[383]

Note that the panel in this case proceeded with its examination of this fourth and last element of the national treatment test of Article XVII:1 of the GATS in two steps. First, it analysed whether, and, if so, how, the measures at issue provided for different treatment between domestic services and service suppliers and 'like' services and service suppliers of other Members. Second, it examined whether any different treatment amounts to less favourable treatment.[384] *In casu*, the panel found that there was such different treatment;[385] and that this different treatment amounted to less favourable treatment.[386]

As discussed above, for the national treatment obligation of Article XVII:1 of the GATS (unlike for other non-discrimination obligations), the treaty text itself, and in particular Article XVII:3, clearly indicates that *de facto* discrimination is covered by this national treatment obligation.[387] Recall that the panel

383 Panel Report, *China – Publications and Audiovisual Products (2010)*, para. 7.687.
384 See *ibid.*, para. 7.689. 385 See *ibid.*, paras. 7.709, 7.722 and 7.733.
386 See *ibid.*, paras. 7.712, 7.714, 7.725 and 7.736. 387 See above, p. 401.

in *EC – Bananas III (Article 21.5 – Ecuador) (1999)* and the arbitrators in *EC – Bananas III (Article 22.6 – US) (1999)* found that certain measures under the revised EC banana import regime accorded to foreign service suppliers, and in particular service suppliers of Ecuador and the United States, *de facto* less favourable conditions of competition than to 'like' EC service suppliers.[388]

In *China – Publications and Audiovisual Products (2010)*, the panel found in the context of its assessment of the prohibition on wholesale trading of reading materials that:

> [s]ince the measures at issue have the effect of prohibiting foreign service suppliers from wholesaling imported reading materials, while like Chinese suppliers are permitted to do so, these measures clearly modif[y] the conditions of competition to the detriment of the foreign service supplier and thus constitutes 'less favourable treatment' in terms of Article XVII.[389]

As discussed above in the context of the MFN treatment obligation under Article II:1 of the GATS, the panel in *Argentina – Financial Services (2016)* found with regard to the national treatment obligation under Article XVII:1 of the GATS that:

> like Article II of the GATS, Article XVII of the GATS refers not only to 'like services' but also to 'like service suppliers'. For the reasons explained above in connection with our analysis of 'treatment no less favourable' under Article II of the GATS, we understand that the reference to service suppliers may also lead the interpreter, depending on the specific circumstances of each dispute, to take other aspects into account when interpreting 'treatment no less favourable' in the context of Article XVII, for example, the relevant regulatory aspects concerning service suppliers which have an impact on the conditions of competition. Consideration of these regulatory aspects could, depending on the case, mean that certain regulatory distinctions between service suppliers established by a Member do not necessarily constitute 'treatment less favourable' within the meaning of Article XVII of the GATS.[390]

The Appellate Body in *Argentina – Financial Services (2016)* reversed the panel's interpretation of the concept of 'treatment no less favourable' and found instead that the legal standard of 'treatment no less favourable' in Articles II:1 and XVII of the GATS 'focuses on a measure's modification of the conditions of competition, and does not contemplate a separate and additional inquiry into the regulatory objective of, or the regulatory concerns underlying, the contested measure'.[391] The Appellate Body supported this interpretation of the legal standard by referring to the structure of the GATS stating:

> Under this structure, Members can utilize certain flexibilities, available to them uniquely under the GATS, when undertaking their GATS commitments, and their obligations are qualified by exceptions or other derogations contained in the GATS and its Annexes. More specifically, pursuant to Article XX of the GATS, a Member may undertake specific market access commitments and national treatment obligations only in service sectors or subsectors,

388 See Panel Report, *EC – Bananas III (Article 21.5 – Ecuador) (1999)*, para. 6.126; and Decision by the Arbitrators, *EC – Bananas III (US) (Article 22.6 – EC) (1999)*, paras. 5.89–5.95. The measures at issue concerned the criteria for acquiring 'newcomer' status under the revised EC licensing procedures.

389 Panel Report, *China – Publications and Audiovisual Products (2010)*, para. 7.996.

390 Panel Report, *Argentina – Financial Services (2016)*, para. 7.493.

391 See Appellate Body Report, *Argentina – Financial Services (2016)*, para. 6.106.

and only with respect to the modes of supply that it wishes to liberalize and inscribe in its Schedule of GATS Commitments ... Furthermore, the GATS sets out general exceptions and security exceptions from obligations under that Agreement in the same manner as does the GATT 1994. In particular, both Article XIV of the GATS and Article XX of the GATT 1994 affirm the right of Members to pursue various regulatory objectives identified in the paragraphs of these provisions even if, in doing so, Members act inconsistently with obligations set out in other provisions of the respective Agreements ... In addition, the various Annexes to the GATS also contain mechanisms that could allow for certain deviations from a Member's obligations, such as paragraph 2(a) of the Annex on Financial Services.[392]

The Appellate Body in *Argentina – Financial Services (2016)* observed that 'it is through these flexibilities and exceptions, that the GATS seeks to strike a balance between a Member's obligations assumed under this agreement and the Member's right to pursue national policy objectives'.[393] The Appellate Body specifically stated that:

This balance, too, reinforces the established legal standard for 'treatment no less favourable' under the non-discrimination provisions of the GATS, that is, whether a measure modifies the conditions of competition to the detriment of like services or service suppliers of any other Member. Where a measure is inconsistent with the non-discrimination provisions, regulatory aspects or concerns that could potentially justify such a measure are more appropriately addressed in the context of the relevant exceptions. Addressing them in the context of the non-discrimination provisions would upset the existing balance under the GATS.[394]

However, this does not mean that the 'regulatory aspects' are totally irrelevant in the assessment of whether the measure at issue accords 'treatment no less favourable'. As the Appellate Body stated in *Argentina – Financial Services (2016)*:

[S]uch assessment must begin with a careful scrutiny of the measure, including consideration of the design, structure and expected operation of the measure at issue. In such assessment, to the extent that evidence relating to the regulatory aspects has a bearing on conditions of competition, it might be taken into account, subject to the particular circumstances of a case, and as an integral part of a panel's analysis of whether *the measure at issue* modifies the conditions of competition to the detriment of like services or service suppliers of any other Member.[395]

Finally, note with respect to *inherent* competitive disadvantages resulting from the fact that the service or service supplier is foreign and not domestic, footnote 10 to Article XVII:1 states:

Specific commitments assumed under this Article shall not be construed to require any Member to compensate for any inherent competitive disadvantages which result from the foreign character of the relevant services or service suppliers.

The 'foreign character' that gives rise to 'inherent competitive disadvantages' is related to, for example, language barriers, cultural differences, or the physical distance between the service suppliers and the service consumers.[396]

392 *Ibid.*, paras. 6.112–6.113. 393 *Ibid.*, para. 6.114.

394 *Ibid.*, para. 6.115. 395 *Ibid.*, para. 6.127.

396 Note that with regard to the latter, the panel noted in *Canada – Autos (2000)* that the supply of some repair and maintenance services on machinery and equipment through modes 1 and 2 might not have been technically feasible for foreign suppliers, as they require the physical presence of the supplier. See Panel Report, *Canada – Autos (2000)*, para. 10.301.

The panel in *Canada – Autos (2000)*, however, stressed the limited scope of this provision as follows:

> Footnote 10 to Article XVII only exempts Members from having to compensate for disadvantages due to the foreign character in the application of the national treatment provision; it does not provide cover for actions which might modify the conditions of competition against services or service suppliers which are already disadvantaged due to their foreign character.[397]

The Appellate Body in *Argentina – Financial Services (2016)* clarified that footnote 10 by referring to 'inherent competitive disadvantages which result from the foreign character' of the relevant services and service suppliers makes clear that 'such disadvantages must be "inherent" to the services and service suppliers owing to their foreign character, and must not be caused by the measure affecting trade in services adopted by the importing Member' and noted:

> The 'inherent competitive disadvantages' within the meaning of footnote 10 do not include, and should not mask, the detrimental impact that is genuinely attributable to the contested measure, such as what the Panel found in this dispute.[398]

4 SUMMARY

There are two main non-discrimination obligations under WTO law: the most-favoured-nation (MFN) treatment obligation, discussed in the previous chapter, and the national treatment obligation, which is discussed in this chapter. In simple terms, a national treatment obligation relates to whether a country favours itself over other countries. A national treatment obligation prohibits a country to discriminate *against* other countries. The national treatment obligation under WTO law applies – albeit not in the same manner – to trade in goods as well as trade in services. The key provision that deals with the national treatment obligation for measures affecting trade in goods is Article III of the GATT 1994. The key provision that deals with the national treatment obligation for measures affecting trade in services is Article XVII:1 of the GATS.

The principal purpose of the national treatment obligation of Article III of the GATT 1994 is to *avoid protectionism* in the application of internal tax and regulatory measures. As is explicitly stated in Article III:1, the purpose of Article III is to ensure that internal measures 'not be applied to imported and domestic products so as to afford protection to domestic production'. To this end, Article III obliges WTO Members to provide *equality of competitive opportunities* for imported products in relation to domestic products. Article III protects the

397 *Ibid.*, para. 10.300.
398 Appellate Body Report, *Argentina – Financial Services (2016)*, para. 6.146.

expectations of an equal competitive relationship between imported and domestic products.

The test of consistency of internal taxation with the national treatment obligation of Article III:2, first sentence, of the GATT 1994 requires the examination of: (1) whether the measure at issue is an *internal tax or other internal charge* on products; (2) whether the imported and domestic products are *like products*; and (3) whether the imported products are *taxed in excess* of the domestic products.

Article III:2, second sentence, also concerns national treatment with respect to internal taxation, but it contemplates a 'broader category of products' than Article III:2, first sentence. It applies to 'directly competitive or substitutable products'. Article III:2, second sentence, of the GATT 1994 sets out a different test of consistency, which requires the examination of: (1) whether the measure at issue is an *internal tax or other internal charge* on products; (2) whether the imported and domestic products are *directly competitive or substitutable*; (3) whether these products are *dissimilarly taxed*; and (4) whether the dissimilar taxation is applied *so as to afford protection to domestic production.*

The national treatment obligation of Article III of the GATT 1994 concerns not only internal taxation, but also internal regulation. The national treatment obligation for internal regulation is set out in Article III:4. To determine whether a measure is consistent with the national treatment obligation of Article III:4 of the GATT 1994, there is a three-tier test which requires the examination of: (1) whether the measure at issue is a law, regulation or requirement covered by Article III:4; (2) whether the imported and domestic products are 'like products'; and (3) whether the imported products are accorded 'treatment no less favourable'.

The national treatment obligation with respect to measures affecting trade in services is set out in Article XVII:1 of the GATS. The national treatment obligation of Article XVII:1 is different from the national treatment obligation of Article III of the GATT 1994. While the national treatment obligation of Article III of the GATT 1994 has general application to all measures affecting trade in goods, the national treatment obligation of Article XVII:1 of the GATS *only* applies to a measure affecting trade in services *to the extent* that a WTO Member has explicitly committed itself to grant 'national treatment' in respect of the specific services sector concerned. Such commitments are set out in a Member's Services Schedule. Often these commitments are subject to conditions and qualifications limiting the scope of the commitment. To determine whether a measure is consistent with the national treatment obligation of Article XVII:1 of the GATS, there is a four-tier test, which requires the examination of: (1) whether, and to what extent, a *national treatment commitment* was made in respect of the relevant services sector; (2) whether the measure at issue is a *measure by a Member affecting trade in services*; (3) whether the foreign and domestic services or service suppliers are '*like services and service suppliers*';

and (4) whether the foreign services and service suppliers are granted '*treatment no less favourable*'.

Generally speaking, internal measures (whether taxation or regulation) are inconsistent with the national treatment obligations under the GATT 1994 and the GATS when they modify the conditions of competition in the relevant market to the detriment of the imported products, foreign services and service suppliers.

FURTHER READINGS

E. Lydgate, 'Sorting Out Mixed Messages under the WTO National Treatment Principle: A Proposed Approach', *World Trade Review*, 2016, 15, 423–50.

W. Zhou, 'Rethinking National Treatment and the Role of Regulatory Purpose: Lessons from the "Theory of Distortions and Welfare"', *Manchester Journal of International Economic Law*, July 2015, 12(3), 243–69.

M. Du, '"Treatment No Less Favorable" and the Future of National Treatment Obligation in GATT Article III:4 after EC–Seal Products', *World Trade Review*, June 2015, 1–25.

F. Roessler, 'The Scope of Regulatory Autonomy of WTO Members Under Article III:4 of the GATT: A Critical Analysis of the Jurisprudence of the WTO Appellate Body', RSCAS Policy Paper 2015/04, European University Institute.

B. Natens and D. Geraets, 'Modification of the Conditions of Competition for Goods and Services: Has "Treatment No Less Favourable" Lost Its Meaning?', Working Paper No. 142, July 2014, Leuven Centre for Global Governance Studies.

D. Neven and J. P. Trachtman, 'Philippines – Taxes on Distilled Spirits: Like Products and Market Definition', *World Trade Review*, April 2013, 12(2), 297–326.

J. Flett, 'WTO Space for National Regulation: Requiem for a Diagonal Vector Test', *Journal of International Economic Law*, 2013, 16(1), 37–90.

6 Tariff Barriers

CONTENTS

1 INTRODUCTION

There can be no international trade without access to the domestic markets of other countries, and it is essential for traders in goods and services that this access is secure and predictable. Therefore, rules on market access are at the core of WTO law. Market access for goods and services from other countries may be impeded or restricted in many different ways, but two main categories of barriers to market access can be distinguished: (1) tariff barriers; and (2) non-tariff barriers. The category of tariff barriers primarily includes customs duties, but also other duties and charges on imports (and exports). Tariff barriers are particularly relevant for trade in goods; they are of marginal importance for trade in services. The category of non-tariff barriers is a residual category that includes quantitative restrictions (such as quotas) and 'other non-tariff barriers' (such as lack of transparency of trade regulation, unfair and arbitrary application of trade regulation, customs formalities, technical barriers to trade, sanitary and phytosanitary measures, and government procurement practices). These 'other non-tariff barriers' undoubtedly constitute the largest and most diverse subcategory of non-tariff barriers. Unlike tariff barriers, non-tariff barriers significantly affect both trade in goods and trade in services.

As set out in the Preamble to the *WTO Agreement*, WTO Members pursue the objectives of higher standards of living, full employment, growth and economic development by:

> entering into reciprocal and mutually advantageous arrangements directed to the substantial reduction of tariffs and other barriers to trade.

The substantial reduction of tariff and non-tariff barriers to trade is, together with the elimination of discrimination, the key instrument of the WTO to achieve its overall objectives.[1] As discussed in Chapter 1, few economists and trade policy-makers dispute that further trade liberalisation *can* make a significant contribution to the economic development of countries.[2] The possible annual increase in global GDP resulting from the ongoing Doha Round negotiations on the reduction of customs duties is conservatively estimated to be US$63 billion.[3] Significantly, developing-country Members are expected to benefit more than developed-country Members from a successful conclusion of these tariff negotiations.[4]

As already noted in Chapter 1, some barriers to market access, such as quantitative restrictions on trade in goods, are prohibited, while other barriers, such as customs duties, are allowed in principle and are only limited to the extent of a Member's specific agreement. Thus, different rules apply to different forms of barriers. This difference in rules reflects a difference in the negative effects they have on trade and on the economy.[5] The rules on non-tariff barriers will

1 See above, pp. 88–90. 2 See above, p. 24.

3 See Gary Clyde Hufbauer, Jeffrey J. Schott and Woan Foong Wong, 'Figuring out the Doha Round', *Policy Analysis in International Economics*, No. 91 (Peterson Institute for International Economics, 2010), 35. On the Doha Round negotiations on the reduction of customs duties on non-agricultural products (the NAMA negotiations), see below, pp. 428–36.

4 See *ibid.*, 640 According to this study, the overall Doha Round package would result for the developing-country Members in a 1.3 per cent gain in GDP, while for developed-country Members the package would result in a 0.3 per cent gain.

5 See below, p. 419.

be examined in the next chapter. The rules on tariff barriers are discussed in this chapter, which, first, deals with rules on customs duties on imports, second, with rules on other duties and charges on imports, and, third, with customs duties and other duties and charges on exports. Since tariff barriers are not imposed on trade in services, this chapter only addresses tariff barriers on trade in goods.[6]

2 CUSTOMS DUTIES ON IMPORTS

A very common and widely used barrier to market access for goods are customs duties, also referred to as tariffs, on imports. This section discusses: (1) the definition and types of customs duties on imports; (2) the purpose of customs duties on imports; (3) customs duties as a lawful instrument of protection; (4) negotiations on the reduction of customs duties; (5) tariff concessions and Schedules of Concessions; (6) protection of tariff concessions; (7) modification or withdrawal of tariff concessions; and (8) the imposition of customs duties on imports.

2.1 Definition and Types

The term 'customs duty' is not defined in the GATT 1994 or in any of the other multilateral agreements on trade in goods. Moreover, these agreements use not only the term 'customs duty' but also the term 'tariff' (equally undefined), and they use these terms as synonyms. The GATT 1994 and the other multilateral agreements on trade in goods also do not set out the different types of customs duties. However, for the reasons explained below, it is important to define what a customs duty is, as well as to distinguish between the various types of customs duties. This subsection addresses the definition and types of customs duties on imports in turn.

2.1.1 Definition of a Customs Duty on Imports

Generally speaking, a customs duty or tariff on imports is a financial charge or tax on imported goods, due because of their importation. Market access for the

6 Note, however, that tariff barriers imposed on trade in goods may relate to goods which contain services outputs, embedded in digital form, for example a DVD containing audiovisual material or software, professional advice, *or* embedded in a non-digital form, for example in a book containing professional advice. The notion of a 'tariff barrier' on trade in services has also arisen in cases where there is *no embedding* of a service output in a good. The prime example is the so-called 'bit tax', which could theoretically be imposed 'at the border' on electronic communications containing services outputs, or 'digital products'. In 1998, Members agreed to maintain the practice not to impose customs duties on electronic transmissions. This and later 'moratorium' decisions reflect the concern of Members regarding such tariff barriers. For the currently applicable 'moratorium' decision, see Ministerial Conference, Decision of 19 December 2015, *Work Programme on Electronic Commerce*, WT/MIN(15)/42 – WT/L/977, dated 21 December 2015.

goods concerned is conditional upon the payment of the customs duty. In *EC – Poultry (1998)*, the Appellate Body held that:

> it is upon entry of a product into the customs territory, but before the product enters the domestic market, that the *obligation* to pay customs duties ... accrues.[7]

As discussed in Chapter 5, the panel in *China – Auto Parts (2009)* had to determine whether the charges at issue in that case were 'internal charges' (as argued by the complainants) or 'customs duties' (as argued by China).[8] With the exception of one particular charge, the panel found that the charges were not 'customs duties' but 'internal charges'.[9] In addressing this issue, the Appellate Body noted that 'the time at which a charge is collected or paid is not decisive' in determining whether a charge is a customs duty or an internal charge.[10] Customs duties may be collected after the moment of importation, and internal charges may be collected at the moment of importation.[11] What is important in determining whether a charge is a border charge (such as a customs duty) or an internal charge is whether the *obligation* to pay that charge accrues due to the importation or to an internal event (such as the distribution, sale, use or transportation of the imported product).[12] For a charge to constitute a customs duty, the *obligation* to pay it must accrue at the moment and by virtue of or on importation.[13] A determination of whether a particular charge is a customs duty or an internal charge must be made in light of the characteristics of the measure and the circumstances of the case. As noted in Chapter 5, the Appellate Body observed that in many cases this is 'a straightforward exercise', but that in other cases a panel may face a 'more complex' challenge.[14] However, neither the way in which a measure is characterised in a Member's domestic law nor the intent of a Member's legislator is dispositive of the characterisation of such measure under WTO law as a customs duty or internal charge.[15]

7 Appellate Body Report, *EC – Poultry (1998)*, para. 145. Emphasis added.
8 See above, p. 352.
9 See Panel Reports, *China – Auto Parts (2009)*, para. 7.212. Since they were internal charges, they were subject to the national treatment obligation of Article III:2, first sentence. See above, p. 352.
10 See Appellate Body Reports, *China – Auto Parts (2009)*, para. 162.
11 See Note *Ad* Article III of the GATT 1994, as discussed in Chapter 5. See above, p. 346.
12 See Appellate Body Reports, *China – Auto Parts (2009)*, para. 162. See also Panel Reports, *China – Auto Parts (2009)*, paras. 7.128–7.129.
13 See Appellate Body Reports, *China – Auto Parts (2009)*, para. 158. With regard to the difference between a 'customs duty' and 'other duties and charges on imports', see below, p. 462.
14 See Appellate Body Reports, *China – Auto Parts (2009)*, para. 171. See in this context also *India – Additional Import Duties (2008)*, in which the panel agreed with the parties that the measures at issue were border charges within the meaning of Article II, and not internal charges within the meaning of Article III:2. See Appellate Body Report, *India – Additional Import Duties (2008)*, fn. 304 to para. 153.
15 See Appellate Body Reports, *China – Auto Parts (2009)*, para. 178. Note that the 1973 *Kyoto International Convention on the Simplification and Harmonization of Customs Procedures*, to which many WTO Members are a party, defines 'customs duties' as 'the duties laid down in the Customs tariff to which goods are liable on entering ... the Customs territory'. Therefore, according to the *Kyoto Convention*, but contrary to the ruling of the Appellate Body in *China – Auto Parts (2009)*, a duty is a customs duty because a country characterises it as such by including it in its national customs tariff. See *International Convention on the Simplification and Harmonization of Customs Procedures* (as amended), done at Kyoto, 18 May 1973, General Annex, Chapter 2, E8./F11.

2.1.2 Types of Customs Duties

Customs duties are either *ad valorem* or non-*ad valorem*. An *ad valorem* customs duty on a good is an amount based on the value of that good. It is a percentage of the value of the imported good, for example a 15 per cent *ad valorem* duty on computers. In that case, the duty on a computer worth €1,000 will be €150. Non-*ad valorem* customs duties (or NAV duties) can be specific, compound, mixed or 'other' customs duties.[16] A specific customs duty on a good is an amount based on a unit of quantity such as weight (kg), length (m), area (m^2), volume (m^3 or l) or numbers (pieces, pairs, dozens, or packs) of that good, for example a duty of €100 per hectolitre of vegetable oil or a duty of €3,000 on each car. A compound customs duty is a duty comprising an *ad valorem* duty to which a specific duty is added or, less frequently, subtracted, for example a customs duty on wool of 10 per cent *ad valorem* and €50 per tonne.[17] In that case, the duty on three tonnes of wool worth €1,000 per tonne will be €450. A mixed customs duty is a duty that can be either an *ad valorem* duty or a specific duty, subject to an upper and/or a lower limit, for example a customs duty on shirts of 10 per cent *ad valorem* or €4 per shirt, whichever duty is the higher. Finally, 'other' non-*ad valorem* customs duties, also referred to as technical customs duties, are duties determined by technical factors often related to the content, composition or nature of the goods concerned.[18]

Ad valorem customs duties are by far the most common type of customs duties.[19] They are preferable to non-*ad valorem* duties for several reasons. First, *ad valorem* duties are more transparent than non-*ad valorem* duties. The protectionist impact and the negative effect on prices for consumers are easier to assess for *ad valorem* duties than for non-*ad valorem* duties. The lack of transparency of non-*ad valorem* duties makes it easier for special interest groups to obtain government support for high levels of protection.[20] Second, by definition, *ad valorem* customs duties are index-linked. In times of inflation, the government's tariff revenue will keep up with price increases and the level of protection will remain the same. By contrast, non-*ad valorem* duties will constantly have to be changed to maintain the same real tariff revenue or maintain the same level of protection. Third, non-*ad valorem* duties 'punish' efficiency, because the cheaper like products are subject to a higher duty in *ad valorem* terms. Overall, with respect to industrial products, non-*ad valorem* duties

16 See Negotiating Group on Market Access, Note by the Secretariat, *Incidence of Non-Ad Valorem Tariffs in Members' Tariff Schedules and Possible Approaches to the Estimation of Ad Valorem Equivalents*, TN/MA/S/10/Rev.1, dated 18 July 2005, para. 3.

17 e.g. the measure at issue in *Colombia – Textiles (2016)* was a compound tariff, with an *ad valorem* component of 10 per cent and a specific component of US$1.75/pair, US$3/kg, US$5/kg or US$5/pair depending on the product concerned and its declared f.o.b. price, Appellate Body Reports, *Colombia – Textiles (2016)*, para. 1.3.

18 See Negotiating Group on Market Access, Note by the Secretariat, *Incidence of Non-Ad Valorem Tariffs in Members' Tariff Schedules and Possible Approaches to the Estimation of Ad Valorem Equivalents*, para. 3.

19 See *ibid.*, paras. 5–6.

20 See WTO Secretariat, Market Access: Unfinished Business, Special Studies Series 6 (WTO, 2001), 9.

are unusual.[21] With respect to agricultural products, however, non-*ad valorem* duties, and in particular compound duties, are still common.[22]

Ad valorem or non-*ad valorem* duties can be MFN duties, preferential duties or neither of the two. *MFN duties* are the 'standard' customs duties applicable to all other WTO Members in compliance with the non-discrimination MFN treatment obligation of Article I:1 of the GATT 1994.[23] *Preferential duties* are customs duties applied to specific countries pursuant to conventional or autonomous arrangements under which products from these countries are subject to duties lower than MFN duties.[24] For example, the customs duties applied by the European Union and sixteen Caribbean countries on each other's products under the terms of the *CARIFORUM–EC Economic Partnership Agreement* are conventional preferential duties.[25] The customs duties applied by the European Union on products from developing countries under the EU's Generalised System of Preferences (GSP) are autonomous preferential duties.[26] Finally, there are customs duties that are neither MFN duties nor preferential duties. These are the duties applicable to goods from countries which are not WTO Members and do not benefit from MFN treatment.[27] However, since the number of countries that are not Members of the WTO is now very small and their share in world trade is negligible, the latter category of customs duties is therefore of limited importance.

2.1.3 National Customs Tariff

As stated above, the terms 'customs duty' and 'tariff' are used as synonyms in the multilateral agreements on trade in goods. However, the term 'tariff' has a second meaning, different from 'customs duty'. A 'tariff', or 'customs tariff', is also a structured list of product descriptions and their corresponding customs duty. The customs duties or tariffs, which are due on importation, are set out in a country's customs tariff.[28] Most national customs tariffs now follow or reflect

21 For only five Members, more than 5 per cent of their tariff lines for industrial products are bound in non-*ad valorem* terms. Only Switzerland uses non-*ad valorem* terms for all its non-zero duties. See TN/MA/S/10/Rev.1, dated 18 July 2005, para. 5. Note that the General Council, in its Decision of 1 August 2004 on the Doha Work Programme, decided that 'all non-*ad valorem* duties [on non-agricultural products] shall be converted to *ad valorem* equivalents on the basis of a methodology to be determined' (WT/L/579, dated 2 August 2004, Annex B, para. 5).

22 WTO Secretariat, *Market Access: Unfinished Business*, Special Studies Series 6 (WTO, 2001), 46 and 47. That is the case, for example, for the European Union and the United States.

23 See above, p. 321.

24 The existence of preferential duties makes it important to determine the country of origin of products. On rules of origin, see below, pp. 457–61.

25 See *CARIFORUM–EC Economic Partnership Agreement*, signed on 15 October 2008. Under this Agreement, goods from the CARIFORUM countries may be imported into the European Union free of customs duties.

26 See above, p. 322.

27 Note that non-WTO Members may benefit from MFN treatment under the terms of bilateral or regional trade agreements.

28 The 'national' customs tariff of the European Union is referred to as the Common Customs Tariff. See Council Regulation (EEC) No. 2658/87 of 23 July 1987 on the tariff and statistical nomenclature and on the Common Customs Tariff, OJ 1987, L256, 7 September 1987. Every year, the European Commission adopts a Regulation reproducing a complete version of the Common Customs Tariff, taking into account Council and Commission amendments of that year. The Regulation is published in the *Official Journal of the European Communities* no later than 31 October. It applies from 1 January of the following year.

Tariff item	Description of goods	Unit	Rate of duty	
			Standard	Preferential areas
1801 00 00	COCOA BEANS, WHOLE OR BROKEN, RAW OR ROASTED	kg.	30%	–
1802 00 00	COCOA SHELLS, HUSKS, SKINS AND OTHER COCOA WASTE	kg.	30%	–
1803	COCOA PASTE, WHETHER OR NOT DEFATTED			
1803 10 00	– Not defatted	kg.	30%	–
1803 20 00	– Wholly or partly defatted	kg.	30%	–
1804 00 00	COCOA BUTTER, FAT AND OIL	kg.	30%	–
1805 00 00	COCOA POWDER, NOT CONTAINING ADDED SUGAR OR OTHER SWEETENING MATTER	kg.	30%	–
1806	CHOCOLATE AND OTHER FOOD PREPARATIONS CONTAINING COCOA			
1806 10 00	Cocoa powder, containing added sugar or other sweetening matter	kg.	30%	–
1806 20 00	Other preparations in blocks, slabs or bars weighing more than 2 kg. or in liquid, paste, powder, granular or other bulk form in containers or immediate packings, of a content exceeding 2 kg.	kg.	30%	–
	– Other, in blocks, slabs or bars:			
1806 31 00	– Filled	kg.	30%	–
1806 32 00	– Not Filled	kg.	30%	–
1806 90	– Other:			
1806 90 10	– Chocolate and chocolate products	kg.	30%	–
1806 90 20	– Sugar confectionery containing cocoa	kg.	30%	–
1806 90 30	– Spreads containing cocoa	kg.	30%	–
1806 90 40	– Preparations containing cocoa for making beverages	kg.	30%	–
1806 90 90	– Other	kg.	30%	–

Figure 6.1 Excerpt from the customs tariff of India, 2015–16

the structure set out in the Harmonized Commodity Description and Coding System, usually referred to as the 'Harmonized System' or 'HS' discussed in detail later in this chapter.[29]

Figure 6.1, an excerpt from the customs tariff of India, shows that the MFN customs duties on cocoa are 30 per cent *ad valorem*. India's customs duties on some goods are even higher than 30 per cent, while on other goods they are lower. The customs duty on, for example, tariff item 1704 10 00 ('Chewing gum ...') is 45 per cent *ad valorem* and the customs duty on tariff item 8703 21 10 ('Vehicles principally designed for the transport of more than seven persons,

29 See below, pp. 451–3.

including the driver') is 125 per cent *ad valorem*. The customs duty on tariff item 2501 00 10 ('Common salt ...') is 10 per cent *ad valorem*. As discussed below, average customs duties imposed by developing-country Members are, generally speaking, considerably higher than those of developed-country Members.[30]

Many WTO Members have an online database of the customs duties they apply. The website of the World Customs Organization gives easy access to many of these databases, including the TARIC database of the European Union.[31] However, information on customs duties is perhaps most conveniently obtained via the WTO's Tariff Analysis Online (for registered users only) or, for less sophisticated searches, via the Tariff Download Facility (for all users).[32] Also quite useful and presenting data in an easily accessible and graphic way is the International Trade and Market Access interactive tool, launched by the WTO Secretariat in November 2012.[33]

2.2 Purpose of Customs Duties on Imports

Customs duties or tariffs on imports serve two main purposes. First, customs duties are a source of revenue for governments. In fact, it is one of the oldest ways for a government to collect revenue.[34] This purpose is now less important for industrialised countries with a well-developed system of direct and indirect taxation. For many developing countries, however, customs duties are an important source of government revenue. In comparison with income taxes and sales taxes, customs duties are easy to collect. Imports are relatively easy to monitor and the collection of customs duties can be concentrated in a few points of entry. Second, customs duties are used to protect and/or promote domestic industries. The customs duties imposed on imported products make the 'like' domestic products relatively cheaper, giving them a price advantage and thus some degree of protection from import competition. Developing countries are likely to use customs duties to protect infant industries (and thus as an instrument of economic

30 See below, pp. 423–4. However, note also that while India reduced its overall applied rate between 2001/2 and 2006/7 from 32.3 per cent to 15.8 per cent, and between 2006/7 and 2010/11 from 15.1 per cent to 12 per cent, there was a marginal increase from 12 per cent in 2010–11 to 13 per cent in 2014–15. See WTO Secretariat, *Trade Policy Review Report – India, Revision*, WT/TPR/S/182/Rev.1, dated 24 July 2007, vii, para. 2; WTO Secretariat, *Trade Policy Review Report – India, Revision*, WT/TPR/S/249/Rev.1 dated 20 October 2011, para. 12; and WTO Secretariat, *Trade Policy Review Report – India, Revision*, WT/TPR/S/313/Rev.1, dated 14 September 2015, para. 13.

31 See www.wcoomd.org. For the TARIC database, see http://ec.europa.eu/taxation_customs/dds2/taric/taric_consultation.jsp.

32 See www.wto.org/english/tratop_e/tariffs_e/tariff_data_e.htm. The information on customs duties in Tariff Analysis Online (http://tariffanalysis.wto.org) and the Tariff Download Facility (http://tariffdata.wto.org) is drawn from the WTO's Integrated Database (IDB), which is fed with the information that Members annually supply on the customs duties they apply. Anybody can register as a user of Tariff Analysis Online, but only WTO Members have access to import statistics beyond six digits.

33 See www.wto.org/english/res_e/statis_e/statis_e.htm.

34 There is historical evidence of the imposition of customs duties in the ancient Egyptian, Indian and Chinese civilisations. See H. Asakura, *World History of the Customs and Tariffs* (World Customs Organization, 2003), 19–105.

development policy), while developed countries use them more often to protect industries in decline.[35]

2.3 Customs Duties as a Lawful Instrument of Protection

In principle, WTO Members are free to impose customs duties on imported products. WTO law, and in particular the GATT 1994, does not prohibit the imposition of customs duties on imports.[36] This is in sharp contrast to the general prohibition on quantitative restrictions, discussed in Chapter 7.[37] In *India – Additional Import Duties (2008)*, the Appellate Body stated:

> Tariffs are legitimate instruments to accomplish certain trade policy or other objectives such as to generate fiscal revenue. Indeed, under the GATT 1994, they are the preferred trade policy instrument, whereas quantitative restrictions are in principle prohibited. Irrespective of the underlying objective, tariffs are permissible.[38]

Customs duties, unlike quantitative restrictions, represent an instrument of protection against imports generally allowed by the GATT 1994.[39]

2.4 Negotiations on the Reduction of Customs Duties

While WTO law does not prohibit customs duties, it does recognise that customs duties constitute an obstacle to trade. Article XXVIII *bis* of the GATT 1994, therefore, calls upon WTO Members to negotiate the reduction of customs duties. This article provides, in relevant part:

> [T]hus negotiations on a reciprocal and mutually advantageous basis, directed to the substantial reduction of the general level of tariffs and other charges on imports and exports and in particular to the reduction of such high tariffs as discourage the importation even of minimum quantities, and conducted with due regard to the objectives of this Agreement and the varying needs of individual [Members], are of great importance to the expansion of international trade. The [Members] may therefore sponsor such negotiations from time to time.

Note that Article XXXVII:1 of the GATT 1994 calls upon developed-country Members to accord, in the interest of the economic development of developing-country Members:

> high priority to the reduction and elimination of barriers to products currently or potentially of particular export interest to [developing-country Members].[40]

35 Note in addition that customs duties can also be used to promote a *rational* allocation of scarce foreign exchange (by imposing low duties on capital goods (e.g. industrial machinery) and high duties on luxury goods (e.g. SUVs or perfumes)).
36 Note, however, that Article V:3 of the GATT 1994 does prohibit customs duties on goods *in transit*.
37 See below, pp. 478–540.
38 Appellate Body Report, *India – Additional Import Duties (2008)*, para. 159.
39 The reasons behind the GATT's preference for customs duties are discussed below, p. 488.
40 Note, however, that Article XXXVII qualifies its call to give high priority to the reduction and elimination of barriers with the words 'except when compelling reasons ... make it impossible'.

Implementation period	Round covered	Weighted tariff reduction
1948	Geneva (1947)	−26
1949	Annecy (1949)	−3
1952	Torquay (1950–1)	−4
1956–8	Geneva (1955–6)	−3
1962–4	Dillon Round (1961–2)	−4
1968–72	Kennedy Round (1964–7)	−38
1980–7	Tokyo Round (1973–9)	−33
1995–9	Uruguay Round (1986–94)	−38

Figure 6.2 Sixty years of GATT/WTO tariff reductions

2.4.1 Success of Past Tariff Negotiations

Under the GATT 1947, negotiations on the reduction of customs duties, commonly and in short referred to as tariff negotiations, took place primarily in the context of eight successive 'Rounds' of trade negotiations. In fact, the first five of these Rounds (Geneva, Annecy, Torquay, Geneva and Dillon) were exclusively dedicated to the negotiation on the reduction of tariffs. The sixth, seventh and eighth Rounds (Kennedy, Tokyo and Uruguay) had an increasingly broader agenda, although the negotiation of tariff reductions remained an important element on the agenda of these Rounds. The eight GATT Rounds of trade negotiations were very successful in reducing customs duties. In the late 1940s, the average duty on industrial products imposed by developed countries was about 40 per cent *ad valorem*.[41] As a result of the eight GATT Rounds, the average duty of developed-country Members on industrial products is now below 3.8 per cent *ad valorem*.[42] Figure 6.2 sets out the tariff reductions achieved by the GATT/WTO over the past sixty years.

2.4.2 Importance of Customs Duties as Trade Barriers

Economists often consider a customs duty below 5 per cent *ad valorem* to be a nuisance rather than a barrier to trade. Nevertheless, customs duties remain a significant barrier in international trade for several reasons. First, most developing-country Members still impose relatively high customs duties. Many of them have a simple average duty ranging between 10 and 15 per cent *ad valorem*.[43]

41 See World Bank, *World Development Report 1987*, 134–5. Note that in a December 2015 VOX column, entitled 'The Urban Legend: Pre-GATT Tariffs of 40%', Chad Bown and Douglas Irwin suggested that the average tariffs in 1947 were around 22 per cent, rather than 40 per cent. See http://voxeu.org/article/myth-40-pre-gatt-tariffs.

42 See 'Tariffs: More Bindings and Closer to Zero' in *Understanding the WTO: The Agreements*, at www.wto.org/english/thewto_e/whatis_e/tif_e/agrm2_e.htm.

43 The simple average duties referred to in this paragraph are simple average applied MFN duties on all products (agricultural and non-agricultural). See WTO/ITC/UNCTAD, *World Tariff Profiles 2015*, available at www.wto.org/english/res_e/booksp_e/tariff_profiles15_e.pdf.

The simple average duty of Argentina is 13.6 per cent, of Bangladesh 13.9 per cent, of Brazil 13.5 per cent, China 9.6 per cent, India 13.5 per cent, Mexico 7.5 per cent, Nigeria 11.9 per cent and Pakistan 13.4 per cent.[44] In comparison, the simple average applied MFN duty of Japan is 4.2 per cent, the European Union 5.3 per cent, Canada 4.2 per cent, United States 3.5 per cent, and Hong Kong, China 0 per cent.[45] Second, developed-country Members as well as developing-country Members still have high, to very high, duties on specific groups of 'sensitive' industrial and agricultural products.[46] With respect to industrial products, these so-called 'tariff peaks' are quite common for textiles and clothing, leather and, to a lesser extent, transport equipment.[47] With respect to agricultural products, under the *WTO Agreement on Agriculture*, all non-tariff barriers to trade have been eliminated and substituted by customs duties at often very high levels.[48] Third, in very competitive markets and in trade between neighbouring countries, a very low duty may still constitute a barrier.

In addition, customs duties may also impede the economic development of developing-country Members to the extent that duties increase with the level of processing that products have undergone. The duties on processed and semi-processed products are often higher than the duties on non-processed products and raw materials. This phenomenon is referred to as 'tariff escalation'. Tariff escalation discourages manufacturing or processing in countries where those non-processed products or raw materials are produced, often developing countries.[49] The customs duties of Canada and Australia increase at each production stage. US customs duties increase significantly only between raw materials and semi-processed products. The same holds true for the customs duties of Japan. On average, the customs duties of the European Union appear to de-escalate, i.e. they are higher on raw materials than on semi-processed or processed products.[50] However, this is not always the case. As a clear example

44 See *ibid.* 45 See *ibid.*

46 See *ibid.* For example, the average duty imposed by the European Union on products in the product group 'dairy products' is 42.1 per cent; on products in the product group 'sugars and confectionary' 25.2 per cent; and on products in the product group 'clothing' 11.4 per cent. The average duty imposed by India on products in the product group 'tea and coffee' is 56.3 per cent; on products in the product group 'beverages and tobacco' 69.1 per cent; on products in the product group 'sugars and confectionery' 35.9 per cent; and on products in the product group 'fish and fish products' 29.9 per cent. The average duty imposed by Brazil on products in the product group 'clothing' is 34.9 per cent; on products in the product group 'textiles' 23.3 per cent; and on products in the product group 'transport equipment' 18.6 per cent.

47 Tariff peaks are tariffs that exceed a selected reference level. The OECD distinguishes between 'national peaks' and 'international peaks'. 'National peaks' are tariffs which are three times or more than the national mean tariff. 'International peaks' are tariffs of 15 per cent or more. See WTO Secretariat, *Market Access: Unfinished Business*, Special Studies Series 6 (WTO, 2001), 12.

48 See below, p. 489.

49 Note that Article XXXVII:1 of the GATT 1994 calls upon developed-country Members to accord 'high priority to the reduction and elimination of barriers to products currently or potentially of particular export interest to [developing-country Members], including customs duties and other restrictions *which differentiate unreasonably between such products in their primary and in their processed forms*' (emphasis added). See, in this respect, however, also p. 423, fn. 40.

50 See WTO Secretariat, *Market Access: Unfinished Business*, Special Studies Series 6 (WTO, 2001), 12 and 13, and Table II.3.

of tariff escalation, consider that the MFN duty applied by the European Union on cotton is zero per cent; on cotton yarn between 4 and 5 per cent; on woven fabric of cotton 8 per cent; and on men's or boy's shirts of cotton 12 per cent.[51]

2.4.3 Basic Rules Governing Tariff Negotiations

As noted above, Article XXVIII *bis* of the GATT 1994 calls for negotiations on the reduction of customs duties, in short tariff negotiations, on a 'reciprocal and mutually advantageous basis'. Furthermore, as discussed in Chapter 4, Article I:1 of the GATT 1994 requires that with respect to customs duties any advantage granted by any Member to any product originating in any other country shall be accorded immediately and unconditionally to the like product originating in all other Members.[52] The basic principles and rules governing tariff negotiations are thus: (1) the principle of reciprocity and mutual advantage; and (2) the most-favoured-nation (MFN) treatment obligation.

The principle of reciprocity and mutual advantage, as applied in tariff negotiations, entails that, when a Member requests another Member to reduce its customs duties on certain products, it must be ready to reduce its own customs duties on products which the other Member exports, or wishes to export. For tariff negotiations to succeed, the tariff reductions requested must be considered to be of equivalent value to the tariff reductions offered. There is no agreed method to establish or measure reciprocity. Each Member determines for itself whether the economic value of the tariff reductions received is equal to the value of the tariff reductions granted. Although some Members apply rather sophisticated economic methods to measure reciprocity, in general the methods applied are basic. The final assessment of the 'acceptability' of the outcome of tariff negotiations is primarily political in nature.[53]

The principle of reciprocity does not apply, at least not to its full extent, to tariff negotiations between developed- and developing-country Members. Article XXXVI:8 of Part IV ('Trade and Development') of the GATT 1994 provides:

> [Developed-country Members] do not expect reciprocity for commitments made by them in trade negotiations to reduce or remove tariffs and other barriers to the trade of [developing-country Members].

This provision is further elaborated in the 1979 Tokyo Round Decision on Differential and More Favourable Treatment, Reciprocity and Fuller Participation of Developing Countries, commonly referred to as the Enabling Clause, which provides, in paragraph 5:

> [Developed-country Members] shall ... not seek, neither shall [developing-country Members] be required to make, concessions that are inconsistent with the latter's development, financial and trade needs.

51 See http://web.ita.doc.gov/tacgi/OverSeasNew.nsf/alldata/Italy#Tariffs.

52 See above, p. 311.

53 Note that the principle of reciprocity applies not only to tariff negotiations adopting a product-by-product approach but also to tariff negotiations adopting a formula approach (be it a linear reduction approach or a non-linear reduction approach) or a sectoral approach. See below, p. 428.

In tariff negotiations between developed- and developing-country Members, the principle of *relative* reciprocity applies. In tariff negotiations with developed-country Members, developing-country Members are expected to 'reciprocate' only to the extent consistent with their development, financial and trade needs. With respect to least-developed-country Members, paragraph 6 of the Enabling Clause furthermore instructs developed-country Members to exercise the 'utmost restraint' in seeking any concessions for commitments made by them to reduce or remove tariffs.

Note, however, that paragraph 7 of the Enabling Clause states, in pertinent part:

> [Developing-country Members] expect that their capacity to make contributions or negotiated concessions ... would improve with the progressive development of their economies and improvement in their trade situation and they would accordingly expect to participate more fully in the framework of rights and obligations under the General Agreement.

Because of the principle of relative reciprocity, few developing-country Members agreed to any reductions of their customs duties up to and including the Tokyo Round. Before the Uruguay Round, tariff negotiations were, in practice, primarily conducted between developed-country Members. This changed in the Uruguay Round when almost all developing-country Members got involved in the tariff reduction negotiations, albeit that the reductions agreed to were – in accordance with the principle of relative reciprocity – smaller than the reductions agreed to by developed-country Members. The increased willingness of developing-country Members to participate actively in tariff reduction negotiations during the Uruguay Round can be attributed to two factors. First, a number of developing-country Members had made significant progress in their economic development. Second, a fundamental change had occurred in the trade policy of many developing-country Members. In the 1980s, many developing-country Members moved away from protectionist trade policies to more open and liberal trade policies.[54]

As noted above, tariff negotiations are governed not only by the principle of reciprocity (full or relative) but also by the MFN treatment obligation set out in Article I:1 of the GATT 1994. Any tariff reduction a Member grants to any country as the result of tariff negotiations with that country must be granted to all other Members, immediately and unconditionally. This considerably complicates tariff negotiations. Member A, interested in exporting product *a* to Member B, will request Member B to reduce its customs duties on product *a*. In return for such a reduction, Member A will offer Member B, interested in exporting product *b* to Member A, a reduction of its customs duties on product *b*. As a result of the MFN treatment obligation, the tariff reductions to which Members A and B agree would also benefit all other Members. However, Members A and B will be hesitant to give other Members the benefit of the tariff reductions 'without

54 See *Business Guide to the World Trading System*, 2nd edn (International Trade Centre/Commonwealth Secretariat, 1999), 59.

getting something in return'. Member A is therefore likely to put a hold on the agreement to reduce the customs duty on product *b* until it has been able 'to get something in return' from, for example, Member C which also exports product *b* to Member A and would thus also benefit from the reduction of the customs duty on product *b*. Likewise, Member B will be hesitant to reduce the customs duty on product *a* as long as Member D, which also has an interest in exporting product *a* to Member B, has not given Member B 'something in return' for this reduction. In tariff negotiations, Members may try to benefit from tariff reductions agreed between other Members without giving anything in return. If their export interests are small, they are likely to succeed and will therefore be 'free-riders'. The free-rider problem can be mitigated by opting for an approach to tariff negotiations other than the product-by-product approach described above. Other approaches to tariff negotiations include the formula approach (be it the linear reduction approach or the non-linear reduction approach) and the sectoral approach, all discussed below.[55]

2.4.4 Organisation of Tariff Negotiations

Tariff negotiations can be organised in different ways. As Article XXVIII *bis* of the GATT 1994 provides, tariff negotiations may be carried out: (1) on a selective product-by-product basis; or (2) by the application of such multilateral procedures as may be accepted by the Members concerned. Negotiators may thus opt for different tariff reduction approaches or methodologies, also referred to in WTO-speak as 'modalities'.[56]

During the first GATT Rounds (up to and including the 1961–2 Dillon Round), negotiators opted for a *product-by-product approach* to tariff negotiations. Under this approach, each of the participants in the tariff negotiations submits first its request list and then its offer list, identifying respectively the products with regard to which it is seeking and is willing to make tariff reductions. The negotiations take place between the principal suppliers and importers of each product. However, the product-by-product approach has one major disadvantage. For practical reasons, the number of products that can be subject to this kind of tariff negotiation is necessarily limited, and the product coverage of the tariff reductions that can be achieved is thus 'restricted'.

The product-by-product approach to tariff negotiations is still used, in bilateral or plurilateral negotiations outside a Round, both for Article XXVIII renegotiations and for tariff negotiations in the context of the accession of new Members to the WTO. However, since the 1963–7 Kennedy Round, the product-by-product

55 In fact, as discussed in the next section of this chapter, the increasing complexity of multilateral (as opposed to bilateral) tariff negotiations has led to the abandonment of the product-by-product approach to multilateral tariff negotiations. Note, however, that the principle of reciprocity (full or relative) and the MFN treatment obligation continue to be the underlying principles governing the negotiations.

56 For a detailed discussion of the different approaches to tariff negotiations, see Patrick Low and Roy Santana, 'Trade Liberalization in Manufactures: What Is Left After the Doha Round?', *Journal of International Trade and Diplomacy*, November 2008.

approach has no longer been used as the main approach in multilateral tariff negotiations. Multilateral tariff negotiations have been primarily conducted on the basis of a *formula approach*. Under the formula approach, tariff reductions that are derived from the application of a mathematical formula, result in either a linear reduction (linear reduction approach) or a non-linear reduction (non-linear reduction approach). These 'formula approach' negotiations always involve: (1) the selection of an appropriate formula; and (2) the identification of products to which the formula will not apply. With respect to the latter products, the tariff negotiations may be conducted on a product-by-product basis. For the Kennedy Round tariff negotiations, a *linear reduction approach* to tariff negotiations was adopted. While successful, this linear reduction approach also presented problems. Contracting Parties with low average customs duties argued that it was not reasonable to expect them to cut these duties by the same percentage as Contracting Parties with high customs duties. It is clear that a 50 per cent reduction of a customs duty of 40 per cent still leaves a 20 per cent customs duty in place, i.e. a significant degree of protection from import competition. However, a 50 per cent reduction of a customs duty of 10 per cent leaves only a 5 per cent customs duty. To mitigate this problem, the negotiators in the Tokyo Round (1973–9) applied a *non-linear reduction approach*, often referred to as the 'Swiss formula', which requires larger cuts of higher customs duties than of lower customs duties.

In the Uruguay Round tariff negotiations (1986–94), the negotiators applied different approaches, or modalities, to reduce agricultural and non-agricultural customs duties. Customs duties on agricultural products were reduced using the 'Uruguay Round formula', whereby developed-country Members eventually had to reduce customs duties on a simple average basis by 36 per cent, with a minimum reduction of 15 per cent for each tariff line.[57] Developing-country Members were required to do two-thirds of that effort.[58] With regard to the reduction of customs duties on non-agricultural products, the negotiators were never able to agree on the specific approach to apply to the tariff negotiations. In 1990, they did agree, however, on the result to be achieved, namely, an overall tariff reduction of at least 33 per cent. Each participant in the negotiations was free to determine the manner in which it would reach that reduction target.[59] Different participants applied different approaches. While some participants, and in particular Canada, the European Union and Japan, applied a formula to produce their initial offers, others, and in particular the United States, engaged in

57 These modalities for the tariff negotiations on non-agricultural products, which were set out in the so-called 'Dunkel text' of 1991, were never accepted by the Uruguay Round participants (see GATT document MTN.GNG/MA/W/24). However, in 1992, the participants proceeded to table comprehensive draft schedules which were in line with these modalities.

58 i.e. reduce customs duties on a simple average by 24 per cent, with a minimum reduction of 10 per cent for each tariff line.

59 See Negotiating Group on Market Access, Note by the Secretariat, *Sector Specific Discussions and Negotiations on Goods in the GATT and WTO*, TN/MA/S/13, dated 24 January 2005.

product-by-product negotiations. Subsequently, in 1993, Canada, the European Union, Japan and the United States announced they had reached an agreement on a number of elements they considered necessary for a final agreement on a global and balanced package, which included the large-scale use of the *sectoral approach* to tariff negotiations. The sectoral approach is an approach in which negotiators aim at reducing or eliminating tariffs in a specific sector (such as the chemical products, pharmaceuticals, construction equipment, medical equipment and beer sectors).[60]

Between the end of the Uruguay Round and the start of the current Doha Round, a group of WTO Members agreed to eliminate all customs duties on information technology products (i.e. computers, telecommunications equipment, semiconductors, etc.). At the Singapore Ministerial Conference in 1996, twenty-nine Members adopted the *Ministerial Declaration on Trade in Information Technology Products* and thus agreed to the *Agreement on Trade in Information Technology Products* (ITA) attached to the Ministerial Declaration.[61] The ITA provided for participants to eliminate duties completely on information technology products by 1 January 2000. The ITA entered into force in 1997 when forty Members, accounting for more than 90 per cent of world trade in information technology products covered by the ITA, had adopted the Agreement. At present, eighty-two Members, accounting for approximately 97 per cent of world trade in the information technology products covered by the ITA, have adopted the Agreement.[62] In 2013 the trade in information technology products covered by the ITA was valued at an estimated US$1.6 trillion and accounts today for approximately 10 per cent of global merchandise exports.[63] In June 2012, 33 WTO Members (which eventually increased to 54) initiated an informal process towards negotiations for expansion of product coverage under the ITA. At the Nairobi Ministerial Conference in December 2015, over 50 Members representing major exporters of IT products, adopted the *Ministerial Declaration on the Expansion in Trade in Information Technology Products* (ITA II) and agreed on the timetable for eliminating tariffs on 201 IT products, previously not covered and valued at over US$1.3 trillion per year.[64] All 164 WTO Members will benefit from ITA II as they will all enjoy, as a result of the MFN treatment obligation under Article I:1 of GATT 1994, duty-free market access to the markets of the Members eliminating tariffs on these products.[65]

60 See *ibid.*

61 Ministerial Conference, *Singapore Ministerial Declaration on Trade in Information Technology Products*, WT/MIN(96)/16, dated 13 December 1996.

62 See www.wto.org/english/tratop_e/inftec_e/inftec_e.htm.

63 See www.wto.org/english/tratop_e/inftec_e/itaintro_e.htm.

64 See Ministerial Conference, *Nairobi Ministerial Declaration on the Expansion of Trade in Information Technology Products*, WT/MIN(15)/25, dated 16 December 2015. The declaration established that the first set of tariff cuts are to be implemented by 1 July 2016 and the second set no later than 1 July 2017, with successive reductions taking place by 1 July 2018 and effective elimination no later than 1 July 2019.

65 On the MFN treatment obligation under Article I:1 of the GATT 1994, see above, pp. 307–25.

The Doha Ministerial Declaration of November 2001, in which the WTO Members agreed to start the Doha Round, provided little guidance with respect to the approach to be taken to the Doha Round tariff negotiations on non-agricultural products. However, the level of ambition of these tariff negotiations was clearly high. The Doha Ministerial Declaration states, in relevant part:

> We agree to negotiations which shall aim, *by modalities to be agreed*, to reduce or as appropriate eliminate tariffs, including the reduction or elimination of tariff peaks, high tariffs, and tariff escalation, as well as non-tariff barriers, in particular on products of export interest to developing countries. Product coverage shall be comprehensive and without *a priori* exclusions. The negotiations shall take fully into account the special needs and interests of developing and least-developed country participants, including through less than full reciprocity in reduction commitments.[66]

The approach to be taken to these tariff negotiations – negotiations commonly referred to as negotiations on non-agricultural market access or NAMA negotiations – was further 'clarified' by the General Council in its Decision of 1 August 2004. In this Decision, the General Council stated:

> We recognize that a *formula approach* is key to reducing tariffs, and reducing or eliminating tariff peaks, high tariffs, and tariff escalation. We agree that the Negotiating Group should continue its work on a non-linear formula applied on a line-by-line basis which shall take fully into account the special needs and interests of developing and least-developed country participants, including through less than full reciprocity in reduction commitments.
>
> We recognize that a *sectoral tariff component*, aiming at elimination or harmonization is another key element to achieving the objectives of paragraph 16 of the Doha Ministerial Declaration with regard to the reduction or elimination of tariffs, in particular on products of export interest to developing countries.[67]

At the subsequent Ministerial Conference in Hong Kong in December 2005, Members were unable to agree on the specific approach to (or, in WTO-speak, the modalities of) the NAMA negotiations.[68] After the Hong Kong Ministerial Conference, the positions of developed-country and developing-country Members in the NAMA negotiations became increasingly polarised. Developed-country Members wanted developing-country Members, and in particular emerging economies, to agree to a much greater reduction of tariff bindings than the latter were willing to accept.[69] Against this background, Ambassador Don Stephenson, the Chair of the Negotiating Group on Non-Agricultural Market Access (NAMA),

66 Ministerial Conference, *Doha Ministerial Declaration*, WT/MIN(1)/DEC/1, dated 20 November 2001, para. 16. Emphasis added.

67 See General Council, *Doha Work Programme, Framework for Establishing Modalities in Market Access for Non-Agricultural Products*, WT/L/579, dated 2 August 2004, Annex B, paras. 4 and 7. Emphasis added. See paras. 5–6 and 8–13 for further details on the 'initial elements' for future work on the modalities for the Doha Round tariff negotiations.

68 Ministerial Conference, *Hong Kong Ministerial Declaration*, WT/MIN(05)/DEC, dated 22 December 2005, 4–5. However, Members were able – four years after the start of the Doha Round – to frame better the agenda of the NAMA negotiations.

69 The European Union and the United States needed more market access for non-agricultural goods to balance the liberalisation of trade in agricultural goods requested by developing-country Members.

proposed in July 2007 the first 'NAMA Draft Modalities' with regard to the tariff negotiations on non-agricultural products.[70] The Chair proposed to conduct the tariff reduction negotiations primarily on the basis of a *non-linear reduction approach*, commonly referred to as the 'Swiss formula'. As explained above, the 'Swiss formula' requires larger cuts of higher customs duties than of lower customs duties. According to the 'Swiss formula', which applies on a line-by-line basis, the tariff reductions will be calculated as follows:

$$t_1 = \frac{(a\,or\,b) \times t_0}{(a\,or\,b) + t_0}$$

where:

t_1 is the final bound rate of duty
t_0 is the base rate of duty
a is the coefficient for developed Members, and is in the range 8–9
b is the coefficient for developing Members, and is in the range 19–23.[71] Note that the 'Swiss formula' provides for different coefficients for developed- and developing-country Members.[72] Least-developed-country Members would not be required to undertake tariff reduction commitments.

The Chair's July 2007 proposals for tariff negotiations on non-agricultural products were not received with much enthusiasm. Many developing-country Members had grave concerns regarding the 'Swiss formula' as well as other issues, which they considered were not satisfactorily addressed, such as the issue of preference erosion and the issue of sectoral tariff elimination. They considered that the specific interests of developing countries were not sufficiently taken into account. The *Financial Times* reported on the reaction of developing-country Members to the Chair's proposals, as follows:

> Serious opposition emerged ... to new proposals to cut manufacturing tariffs in the troubled Doha round of trade talks, with a group of developing countries saying the draft agreement was unacceptable. The group, led by South Africa and including Argentina and Venezuela, wants to continue protecting its industry against imports ... Mr Stephenson's [Canadian Ambassador] paper, released this week ... suggested a ceiling of 19–23 per cent for developing country industrial tariffs. The group wanted a ceiling of more than 30 per cent.[73]

70 Negotiating Group on Market Access, *Draft NAMA Modalities*, JOB(07)/126, dated 17 July 2007. This draft was revised by the Chair in February 2008. See Negotiating Group on Market Access, *Draft Modalities for Non-Agricultural Market Access*, TN/MA/W/103, dated 8 February 2008.

71 Negotiating Group on Market Access, *Draft NAMA Modalities*, JOB(07)/126, dated 17 July 2007, para. 5.

72 As an exception, the Chair proposed that developing-country Members with a binding coverage of non-agricultural tariff lines of less than 35 per cent would be exempted from making tariff reductions through the formula. Instead, they would be expected to bind 90 per cent of non-agricultural tariff lines at an average level that does not exceed the overall average of bound tariffs for all developing countries after full implementation of current concessions (28.5 per cent). The developing countries concerned are Cameroon, Congo, Côte d'Ivoire, Cuba, Ghana, Kenya, Macao, Mauritius, Nigeria, Sri Lanka, Suriname and Zimbabwe. See *ibid.*, para. 8.

73 See A. Beattie, 'Attack on Doha Talks Plan to Cut Tariffs', *Financial Times*, 25 July 2007.

Developed-country Members were also dissatisfied with the Chair's proposals, as the proposals were not, in their opinion, sufficiently ambitious in reducing customs duties.[74] The Chair's proposals triggered intense negotiations, which made meaningful progress by providing, for example, for more flexible modalities for certain categories of developing-country Members.[75] However, these negotiations eventually ended in failure at the mini-ministerial meeting in Geneva in July 2008.[76]

As discussed in Chapter 2, in April 2011, the then WTO Director-General Pascal Lamy presented to the Members the so-called 'Easter Package', a document reflecting the work done in the Doha Round negotiations so far.[77] This document showed that in many areas progress had been made, but it also made clear that Members had still to come to an agreement on many core issues, in particular on NAMA. The issue of market access for industrial products, a 'classic mercantilist issue' which had been 'the bread and butter' of the negotiations since the start, divided Members as no other issue.[78] Developed-country Members demanded, in particular from emerging economies, a substantial and meaningful 'Swiss-formula' cut in tariff bindings, combined with tariff elimination in important sectors. Emerging economies considered that these demands would: (1) lower their tariff bindings to a point where their policy space would be greatly reduced; and (2) have huge adverse impacts – especially as a result of sectoral tariff elimination – on their industrial development prospects. The Members subsequently made an effort to agree by the next Ministerial Conference in December 2011, on a smaller 'package' of issues relating primarily to issues of particular interest to the least-developed-country Members (an LDC package), including duty-free and quota-free market access and associated rules of origin. However, such narrow focus was not acceptable to all Members and agreement was subsequently sought on a somewhat extended package of issues, including for example trade facilitation and export competition (an 'LDC plus' package).[79]

Ambassador Servansing from Mauritius, the Coordinator and Chief Negotiator of the ACP Group in Geneva, noted in 2012:

It could be said that the NAMA negotiations ultimately floundered on the conflict between market access mercantilism on the one hand and development concerns on the other. But,

74 This was so, in particular, because developing-country Members would in fact only be required to cut 'water' (i.e. the difference between the bound and the applied duties) and would, therefore, fail to create new market access opportunities. On 'water', see below, p. 446. Moreover, developed-country Members considered that emerging economies should join a number of sectoral tariff elimination initiatives.

75 A 'sliding scale' with five options was established for developing-country Members applying the formula. Moreover, separate and more flexible modalities were established for 'small, vulnerable economies' (SVEs), 'Members with low binding coverage', and 'recently acceded Members' (RAMs).

76 See above, p. 95. 77 See above, p. 96.

78 See Opening Remarks of Director-General Pascal Lamy at the informal TNC meeting of 29 April 2011, www.wto.org/english/news_e/news11_e/tnc_dg_infstat_29apr11_e.htm. As Lamy noted, trade negotiators have haggled over market access for industrial products for more than sixty years and they were eventually always able to find a compromise, 'using a mix of imagination, determination and spirit of compromise'. It was, therefore 'deeply disappointing that no ground for compromise has been found on the issue of industrial tariffs yet'. See *ibid.*

79 See above, p. 97.

this failure in large measure also shows the complexity of finding a new balance in global economic governance in today's globalised world.[80]

At the Bali Ministerial Conference in December 2013, there was hardly any progress in the negotiations on the NAMA front, and in 2014, the disagreement on the Bali decision on public stockholding for food security purposes virtually paralysed work in almost all aspects of the Doha Round, including NAMA.[81] Despite regular meetings in 2015, with the aim of drawing up a work programme and achieve progress in the negotiations before the Nairobi Ministerial Conference in December 2015, not much could be achieved.[82] The stalemate partly stemmed from the difficulty some WTO members had with the 2008 draft modalities of NAMA (commonly referred to as 'Rev. 3'), and in particular the Swiss Formula.[83] In his July 2015 report to the Trade Negotiations Committee, Ambassador Remigi Winzap, the Chair of the Negotiating Group on Market Access, observed:

> In my view, Members should further engage in a more numbers-based discussion on a non-prejudicial basis. It is hard to define ambition in abstract terms, and difficult to make an honest assessment of what one can do when one does not know what one can get. Possibly the best way forward is to work backwards from acceptable results.[84]

Further, in May 2016 at a meeting with the heads of delegations, Ambassador Winzap described the main challenge in NAMA as follows:

> How to build convergence in a situation where, on the one hand, Members' appetite to pursue NAMA negotiations in the WTO varies greatly and, on the other hand, no negotiated outcome may probably be reached in other areas without a result in NAMA?[85]

In the context of the Doha Round, Members are, in addition to tariff negotiations on non-agricultural products, also engaged in tariff negotiations on agricultural products. Reflecting the dissatisfaction of some countries with the result reached in the Uruguay Round regarding agricultural trade, Article 20 of the *Agreement on Agriculture* provided, as part of the so-called 'built-in agenda', for the restart of negotiations on agricultural trade, including tariff negotiations on agricultural products, by the end of 1999. The need for further negotiations on agricultural tariff reductions was particularly 'acute' since the Uruguay Round 'tariffication exercise' (discussed in Chapter 7) resulted in many (prohibitively) high tariff

80 See Shree B. C. Servansing, 'Non-Agricultural Market Access (NAMA) – Balancing Development and Ambition', in Mehta, Kaushik and Kaukab (eds.), *Reflections from the Frontline*, 94.

81 See *WTO Annual Report 2015*, 33.

82 See *WTO Annual Report 2016*, 36.

83 See *ibid.* The NAMA draft modalities Rev.3 (TN/MA/W/103/Rev.3) foresee the Swiss Formula to reduce tariffs of developed and more advanced developing Members ('formula-applying Members'). The discussion is affected by the fact that some formula-applying Members do not have a mandate to move away from the Swiss Formula, while for others using a Swiss Formula is not doable.

84 Negotiating Group on Market Access, *Report by the Chairman, Ambassador Remigi Winzap to the Trade Negotiations Committee*, TN/MA/27, dated 30 July 2015, para 3.1.

85 Meeting of 9 May 2016, Negotiating Group on Market Access, *Oral Report by the Chairman, Ambassador Remigi Winzap, to the Heads of Delegations*, TN/MA/30, dated 10 May 2016.

bindings.[86] Pursuant to paragraph 13 of the Doha Ministerial Declaration of November 2001, these negotiations were made a core part of the agenda of the Doha Round negotiations. As in the NAMA negotiations, discussed above, in the agricultural tariff negotiations the major challenge is to agree on the approach to be taken to the tariff reduction. Since the early years of the Doha Round negotiations, Members are discussing a tiered formula approach to the agricultural tariff negotiations. Under this approach, developed countries would reduce their customs duties on agricultural products in equal annual instalments over a number of years in accordance with a formula that provides for larger reductions in the higher tiers of customs duties. For example, duties in the tier from 21 to 50 per cent would be reduced by x per cent, while duties in the tier from 51 to 75 per cent would be reduced by $x + y$ per cent. In addition, developed-country Members would have to achieve a minimum average cut of their customs duties on agricultural products. Developing-country Members would also have to reduce their customs duties on agricultural products but would have to do so over a longer period in accordance with a tiered formula similar to the formula for developed-country Members but which provides for relatively smaller reductions in each tier. Also, developing-country Members would have to achieve a minimum average cut of their customs duties on agricultural products but this minimum average cut would be smaller than for developed-country Members. Small, vulnerable economies (SVEs) and recently acceded Members (RAMs) would be allowed to reduce their customs duties on agricultural products by a smaller amount than other developing-country Members. While various proposals have been worked out in excruciating technical detail,[87] final agreement on the tiered formula to be applied in the agricultural tariff negotiations has not been reached to date.

Recent discussions have also focused on alternative approaches to the reduction of tariffs on agricultural products.[88] The Chair of the Negotiating Group on Agriculture identified in July 2015 three types of tariff reduction approaches: the tiered formula approach (discussed above); an approach targeting a reduction in average bound tariffs – the so-called 'cut to the average' approach; and an average tariff cut approach. With regard to the two latter (alternative) approaches, the Chairman stated:

> The fundamental challenge, once again, relates to the differences of views among key participants on their respective contributions to any outcome and what they stand to get in return. The point has also been registered very strongly from a range of Members that while they may accept that the level of ambition achievable in current circumstances may

86 On the tariffication exercise, see below, p. 490.

87 See, for example, Negotiating Group on Agriculture, *Report by the Chairman, H. E. Mr David Walker, to the Trade Negotiations Committee*, TN/AG/26, dated 21 April 2011, which contains in an annex the Revised Draft Modalities for Agriculture, TN/AG/W/4/Rev.4, dated 6 December 2008.

88 See Negotiating Group on Agriculture, *Report by the Chairman, H. E. Mr John Adank, to the Trade Negotiations Committee*, TN/AG/30 dated 30 July 2015, para. 1.8.

be less than that envisaged in the 2008 draft modalities, in order for a deal to be politically viable it must be of substantive value when compared to the status quo. Finding this optimal level, and being able to present it in a balanced way that respects the interests of all Members, therefore remains the key challenge if we are to reach closure here.[89]

Before agreeing on any tariff reduction approach, Members will want to address numerous related concerns, such as the designation and treatment of 'sensitive products', the designation and treatment of 'special products', tariff escalation, tariff simplification, tariff quotas, cotton market access and the special safeguard mechanism (SSM), as well as broader issues such as domestic support.[90]

2.5 Tariff Concessions and Schedules of Concessions

The results of tariff negotiations are referred to as 'tariff concessions' or 'tariff bindings'. This subsection discusses the concept of 'tariff concessions' or 'tariff bindings', and explains where they can be found and how they are to be interpreted.

2.5.1 Tariff Concessions or Tariff Bindings

A tariff concession, or a tariff binding, is a commitment not to raise the customs duty on a certain product above an agreed level. As a result of the Uruguay Round tariff negotiations, almost all customs duties imposed by developed-country Members are now 'bound', i.e. are subject to a maximum level.[91] Most Latin American developing-country Members have bound all customs duties.[92] However, for Asian and African developing-country Members the situation is more varied. While Members such as Indonesia and South Africa have bound more than 95 per cent of their customs duties, India and Thailand have bound about 75 per cent; Hong Kong, China, 45.9 per cent; Zimbabwe, 22.2 per cent; Bangladesh, 15.5 per cent; and Cameroon, 13.3 per cent.[93]

2.5.2 Schedules of Concessions

The tariff concessions or bindings of a Member are set out in that Member's Schedule of Concessions (also referred to as a Goods Schedule). Each Member of the WTO has a schedule, except when the Member is part of a customs union, in which case the Member has a common schedule with the other members of the customs union.[94] The Schedules of Concessions resulting from the Uruguay Round negotiations are all annexed to the *Marrakesh Protocol* to the GATT 1994.

89 *Ibid.*, para 1.10. 90 On agricultural domestic support, see below, p. 874.

91 For both the European Union and the United States, the binding coverage is 100 per cent. See WTO/ITC/UNCTAD, *World Tariff Profiles 2015*, available at www.wto.org/english/res_e/booksp_e/tariff_profiles15_e.pdf.

92 Note that many Latin American Members apply a 'uniform ceiling binding', i.e. they have bound their customs duties to a single maximum level. For Chile, for example, this uniform maximum level is 25 per cent.

93 See WTO/ITC/UNCTAD, *World Tariff Profiles 2015*. Note that these percentages are not weighted according to trade volume or value. With regard to Hong Kong, China, note also that, while a high percentage of customs duties is unbound, the applied duties are zero.

94 e.g. the twenty-eight Member States of the European Union do not have their 'own' individual schedule. Their common schedule is the Schedule of the European Communities, now the European Union.

Pursuant to Article II:7 of the GATT 1994, the Schedules of Members are an integral part of the GATT 1994. The Schedules are available on the WTO website.[95] Information on tariff bindings can also be obtained via Tariff Analysis Online or, for less sophisticated searches, via the Tariff Download Facility.[96] Also the International Trade and Market Access interactive tool is quite useful.[97]

Each Schedule of Concessions contains four parts. The most important part, Part I, sets out the MFN concessions with respect to agricultural products and non-agricultural products. Furthermore, a Schedule sets out preferential concessions (Part II), concessions on non-tariff measures (Part III) and specific commitments on domestic support and export subsidies on agricultural products (Part IV). Figure 6.3 sets out an excerpt from Chapter 18 of the Schedule of Concessions of the European Union.

It is not possible for Members to agree in their Schedules to treatment that is inconsistent with the basic GATT obligations. In *EC – Bananas III (1997)*, the Appellate Body addressed the question of whether the allocation of tariff quotas agreed to and inscribed in the EC's Schedule was inconsistent with Article XIII of the GATT 1994. The Appellate Body referred first to the report of the panel in *US – Sugar (1989)*, which stated, *inter alia*:

> Article II permits contracting parties to incorporate into their Schedules acts yielding rights under the General Agreement but not acts diminishing obligations under that Agreement.[98]

Subsequently, the Appellate Body ruled in *EC – Bananas III (1997)*:

> This principle is equally valid for the market access concessions and commitments for agricultural products contained in the Schedules annexed to the GATT 1994. The ordinary meaning of the term 'concessions' suggests that a Member may yield rights and grant benefits, but it cannot diminish its obligations.[99]

Most Schedules are structured according to the Harmonized Commodity Description and Coding System ('Harmonized System' (or HS)), discussed below. Although the format is not identical in all cases, they generally contain the following information for each product subject to tariff concessions: (1) HS tariff item number; (2) description of the product; (3) base rate of duty; (4) bound rate of duty; (5) initial negotiating rights (INR);[100] (6) other duties and charges;[101] and (7) for agricultural products only, special safeguards.[102]

95 See www.wto.org/english/tratop_e/schedules_e/goods_schedules_table_e.htm.
96 See www.wto.org/english/tratop_e/tariffs_e/tariff_data_e.htm. The information on tariff bindings in Tariff Analysis Online and the Tariff Download Facility is based on the WTO's Consolidated Tariff Schedules (CTS) database. As discussed above, Tariff Analysis Online and the Tariff Download Facility also contain information on the applied duties. That information is drawn from the WTO's Integrated Database (IDB), which is fed with the information that Members annually supply on the duties they apply.
97 See www.wto.org/english/res_e/statis_e/statis_e.htm.
98 GATT Panel Report, *US – Sugar (1989)*, para. 5.2.
99 Appellate Body Report, *EC – Bananas III (1997)*, para. 154. The Appellate Body confirmed this ruling in Appellate Body Report, *EC – Poultry (1998)*, para. 98.
100 See below, p. 447. 101 See below, p. 461.
102 See below, p. 655. Since the Schedules are structured according to the Harmonized System, the periodic amendments to the Harmonized System to take account of changes in technology and patterns in international trade will give rise to changes in the Schedules.

SCHEDULE LXXX – EUROPEAN COMMUNITIES

PART I – MOST-FAVOURED-NATION TARIFF

SECTION I – Agricultural Products

SECTION I – A Tariffs

Tariff item number	Description of products	Base rate of duty			Bound rate of duty		Implementation period from/to	Special safeguard	Initial negotiating right	Other duties and charges	Comments
		Ad valorem (%)	Other	U/B/C	Ad valorem (%)	Other					
1	2	3			4		5	6	7	8	9
1802.00.00	Cocoa shells, husks, skins and other cocoa waste	3.0			0.0						
1803	Cocoa pastes, whether or not defatted:										
1803.10.00	– Not defatted	15.0			9.6						
1803.20.00	– Wholly or partly defatted	15.0			9.6						
1804.00.00	Cocoa butter, fat and oil	12.0			7.7						
1805.00.00	Cocoa powder, not containing added sugar or other sweetening matter	16.0			8.0						
1806	Chocolate and other food preparations containing cocoa:										
1806.10	– Cocoa powder, containing added sugar or other sweetening matter:										
1806.10.10	– Containing no more or less than 5% by weight of sucrose (including invert sugar expressed as sucrose) or isoglucose expressed as sucrose	10.0			8.0						
	– Containing 5% or more but less than 65% by weight of sucrose (including invert sugar expressed as sucrose) or isoglucose expressed as sucrose	10.0	+ 315 ECU/T		8.0	+ 252 ECU/T					

1806.10.30	– Containing 65 % or more but less than 80 % by weight of sucrose (including invert sugar expressed as sucrose) or isoglucose expressed as sucrose	10.0	+ 393 ECU/T	8.0	+ 314 ECU/T	
1806.10.90	– Containing 80 % or more by weight of sucrose (including invert sugar expressed as sucrose) or isoglucose expressed as sucrose	10.0	+ 524 ECU/T	8.0	+ 419 ECU/T	
1806.20	– Other preparations in block slabs or bars weighing more than 2 kg or in liquid, paste, powder, granular or other bulk form in containers or immediate packings, of a content exceeding 2 kg:					
1806.20.70	– Chocolate milk crumb, containing a combined weight of less than 25% of cocoa butter and milkfat and containing less than 18% by weight of cocoa butter	22.3	*	15.4	*	* see annex 1
1806.20.80	– Other	12.0	* MAX 27% + AD S/Z	8.3	* MAX 18.7% + AD S/Z	* see annex 1
	– Other, in blocks, slabs or bars:					
1806.31.00	– Filled	12.0	* MAX 27% + AD S/Z	8.3	* MAX 18.7% + AD S/Z	* see annex 1
1806.32.50	– Not filled	12.0	* MAX 27% + AD S/Z	8.3	* MAX 18.7% + AD S/Z	* see annex 1
1806.90.49	– Other	12.0	* MAX 27% + AD S/Z	8.3	* MAX 18.7% + AD S/Z	* see annex 1

Figure 6.3 Excerpt from the EU Goods Schedule

Note that the Schedules of the major trading entities such as the European Union and the United States, which have made tariff concessions on virtually all products, are lengthy and detailed. The file containing the Schedule of the European Union on the WTO's website is 759KB in size. By contrast, the Schedules of many developing-country Members are general and short. The files containing the Schedules of Botswana and the Dominican Republic are only 12 and 13KB respectively.[103]

2.5.3 Interpretation of Tariff Schedules and Concessions

Since the tariff schedules are an integral part of the GATT 1994 pursuant to Article II:7 thereof, they are part of a 'covered agreement' under the DSU.[104] Article 3.2 of the DSU therefore applies to the interpretation of tariff schedules and the concessions set out therein. As discussed in Chapter 3, Article 3.2 of the DSU provides that the provisions of the covered agreements are to be clarified in accordance with customary rules of interpretation of public international law, which have been codified in Articles 31 and 32 of the *Vienna Convention on the Law of Treaties*.[105] In *EC – Computer Equipment (1998)*, at issue was a dispute between the United States and the European Communities on whether the EC's tariff concessions regarding automatic data-processing equipment applied to local area network (LAN) computer equipment.[106] The panel based its interpretation of the EC's tariff concessions on the 'legitimate expectations' of the exporting Member, *in casu*, the United States. On appeal, the Appellate Body rejected this approach to the interpretation of tariff concessions, ruling as follows:

> The purpose of treaty interpretation under Article 31 of the *Vienna Convention* is to ascertain the *common* intentions of the parties. These *common* intentions cannot be ascertained on the basis of the subjective and unilaterally determined 'expectations' of *one* of the parties to a treaty. Tariff concessions provided for in a Member's Schedule – the interpretation of which is at issue here – are reciprocal and result from a mutually advantageous negotiation between importing and exporting Members. A Schedule is made an integral part of the GATT 1994 by Article II:7 of the GATT 1994. Therefore, the concessions provided for in that Schedule are part of the terms of the treaty. As such, the only rules which may be applied in interpreting the meaning of a concession are the general rules of treaty interpretation set out in the Vienna Convention.[107]

103 See www.wto.org/english/tratop_e/schedules_e/goods_schedules_e.htm.

104 On the concept of 'covered agreement', see above, p. 297. 105 See above, pp. 193–8.

106 In the context of the Uruguay Round tariff negotiations, the European Communities agreed to a tariff binding for automatic data processing equipment of 4.9 per cent (to be reduced to 2.5 per cent for some products or duty-free for others). According to the United States, during and shortly after the Uruguay Round, the European Communities classified LAN computer equipment as automatic data processing equipment. Later, however, it started classifying LAN computer equipment as telecommunications equipment, a product category subject to generally higher duties, in the range of 4.6–7.5 per cent (to be reduced to 3–3.6 per cent).

107 Appellate Body Report, *EC – Computer Equipment (1998)*, para. 84.

The Appellate Body furthermore noted with respect to the lack of clarity of tariff concessions and tariff schedules:

Tariff negotiations are a process of reciprocal demands and concessions, of 'give and take'. It is only normal that importing Members define their offers (and their ensuing obligations) in terms which suit their needs. On the other hand, exporting Members have to ensure that their corresponding rights are described in such a manner in the Schedules of importing Members that their export interests, as agreed in the negotiations, are guaranteed ... [T]he fact that Members' Schedules are an integral part of the GATT 1994 indicates that, while each Schedule represents the tariff commitments made by *one* Member, they represent a common agreement among *all* Members.

For the reasons stated above, we conclude that the Panel erred in finding that 'the United States was not required to clarify the scope of the European Communities' tariff concessions on LAN equipment'. We consider that any clarification of the scope of tariff concessions that may be required during the negotiations is a task for *all* interested parties.[108]

Note that, at the very end of the Uruguay Round, a special arrangement was made to allow the negotiators to check and control, through consultations with their negotiating partners, the scope of tariff concessions agreed to. This 'process of verification' took place from 15 February to 25 March 1994.[109]

As discussed above, most schedules are structured according to the Harmonized System. The Uruguay Round tariff negotiations were held on the basis of the Harmonized System's nomenclature; requests for, and offers of, concessions were normally made in terms of this nomenclature. In *EC – Chicken Cuts (2005)*, the Appellate Body stated that:

[these] circumstances confirm that, prior to, during, as well as after the Uruguay Round negotiations, there was broad consensus among the GATT Contracting Parties *to use* the Harmonized System as the basis for their WTO Schedules, notably with respect to agricultural products. In our view, this consensus constitutes an 'agreement' between WTO Members 'relating to' the WTO Agreement that was 'made in connection with the conclusion of' that Agreement, within the meaning of Article 31(2)(a) of the Vienna Convention. As such, this agreement is 'context' under Article 31(2)(a) for the purpose of interpreting the WTO agreements, of which the EC Schedule is an integral part.[110]

The Appellate Body thus considered that the Harmonized System is relevant for purposes of interpreting tariff commitments in the Members' Schedules.[111] The Appellate Body also considered that Chapter Notes and Explanatory Notes to the Harmonized System could also be relevant for interpretation purposes.[112]

108 *Ibid.*, paras. 109 and 110. 109 See MTN.TNC/W/131, dated 21 January 1994.

110 Appellate Body Report, *EC – Chicken Cuts (2005)*, para. 199. See also Appellate Body Reports, *China – Auto Parts (2009)*, para. 149. Already in *EC – Computer Equipment (1998)*, the Appellate Body expressed surprise that in that case neither the European Communities nor the United States argued before the panel that the Harmonized System and its Explanatory Notes were relevant in the interpretation of the EC's Goods Schedule. See Appellate Body Report, *EC – Computer Equipment (1998)*, para. 89.

111 See Appellate Body Report, *EC – Chicken Cuts (2005)*, para. 199. Note that the panel in *EC – IT Products (2010)* stated that it does not follow from the Appellate Body's case law that the Harmonized System will necessarily be relevant in interpreting *all* tariff concessions, including tariff concessions that are not based on the Harmonized System. See Panel Reports, *EC – IT Products (2010)*, para. 7.443.

112 See Appellate Body Report, *EC – Chicken Cuts (2005)*, paras. 219–29.

Finally, note that the consistent classification practice at the time of the tariff negotiations is also relevant to the interpretation of tariff concessions.[113] As the Appellate Body noted in *EC – Computer Equipment (1998)*, the classification practice during the Uruguay Round is part of 'the circumstances of [the] conclusion' of the *WTO Agreement*. Therefore, this practice may be used as a supplementary means of interpretation within the meaning of Article 32 of the *Vienna Convention*.[114]

2.6 Protection of Tariff Concessions

As noted above, under WTO law customs duties are not prohibited. It was envisaged, however, that customs duties would be 'bound' and then progressively reduced through rounds of negotiations. WTO rules on customs duties relate primarily to the protection of tariff concessions agreed to in the context of tariff negotiations. The basic rules are set out in Article II:1 of the GATT 1994.

2.6.1 Articles II:1(a) and II:1(b), First Sentence, of the GATT 1994

Article II:1 of the GATT 1994 states:

> a. Each [Member] shall accord to the commerce of the other [Members] treatment no less favourable than that provided for in the appropriate Part of the appropriate Schedule annexed to this Agreement.
>
> b. The products described in Part I of the Schedule relating to any [Member], which are the products of territories of other [Members], shall, on their importation into the territory to which the Schedule relates, and subject to the terms, conditions or qualifications set forth in that Schedule, be exempt from ordinary customs duties in excess of those set forth and provided therein.

Article II:1(a) provides that Members shall accord to the commerce of other Members, that is, in any case the products imported from other Members, *treatment no less favourable* than that provided for in their Schedule.[115] Article II:1(b), first sentence, provides that products described in Part I of the Schedule of any Member shall, on importation, be *exempt from ordinary customs duties in excess of* those set out in the Schedule. This means that products may not be subjected to customs duties above the tariff concessions or bindings.[116] With respect to the relationship between Article II:1(a) and Article II:1(b), first sentence, the Appellate Body noted in *Argentina – Textiles and Apparel (1998)*:

> Paragraph (a) of Article II:1 contains a general prohibition against according treatment less favourable to imports than that provided for in a Member's Schedule. Paragraph

113 On tariff classification, see above, p. 384.

114 See above, pp. 197–8. See also Appellate Body Report, *EC – Computer Equipment (1998)*, paras. 92 and 95. Note that, while the prior classification practice of only *one* of the parties may be relevant, it is clearly of more limited value than the practice of all parties. See *ibid.*, para. 93.

115 The question whether the concept of the 'commerce of other [Members]' refers not only to the imports from other Members but also to the exports to other Members, has not yet been addressed in WTO dispute settlement.

116 For the most recent application of, and findings of inconsistency with, Article II:1(b), first sentence, of the GATT 1994, see Panel Report, *Russia – Tariff Treatment (2016)*, para. 8.1.

(b) prohibits a specific kind of practice that will always be inconsistent with paragraph (a): that is, the application of ordinary customs duties in excess of those provided for in the Schedule.[117]

The requirement of Article II:1(b), first sentence, that a Member may not impose customs duties *in excess of* the duties set out in its Schedule was at issue in *Argentina – Textiles and Apparel (1998)*. In its Schedule, Argentina has bound its customs duties on textiles and apparel to 35 per cent *ad valorem*. In practice, however, these products were subject to the higher of *either* a 35 per cent *ad valorem* duty *or* a minimum specific import duty (the so-called 'DIEM'). The panel found the DIEM to be inconsistent with Argentina's obligations under Article II:1(b) of the GATT 1994 for two reasons: (1) because Argentina applied a different *type* of import duty (a specific duty) than that set out in its Schedule (an *ad valorem* duty); and (2) because the DIEM would, in certain cases, be in excess of the binding of 35 per cent *ad valorem*. On appeal, the Appellate Body agreed with the panel that the DIEM was inconsistent with Argentina's obligations under Article II:1(b), but it modified the panel's reasoning. The Appellate Body first noted:

The principal obligation in the first sentence of Article II:1(b) ... requires a Member to refrain from imposing ordinary customs duties *in excess of* those provided for in that Member's Schedule. However, the text of Article II:1(b), first sentence, does not address whether applying a *type* of duty different from the *type* provided for in a Member's Schedule is inconsistent, in itself, with that provision.[118]

According to the Appellate Body, the application of a type of duty different from the type provided for in a Member's Schedule is only inconsistent with Article II:1(b) *to the extent that* it results in customs duties being imposed in excess of those set forth in that Member's Schedule.[119]

As Article II:1(b), first sentence, explicitly states, the obligation to exempt products from customs duties in excess of those set forth in the Schedule is

117 Appellate Body Report, *Argentina – Textiles and Apparel (1998)*, para. 45. See also Panel Report, *Colombia – Textiles (2016)*, para. 7.84. A finding of inconsistency with Article II:1(b), first sentence, of the GATT 1994, may therefore lead a panel to conclude, without the need for further analysis, that the measure at issue is also inconsistent with Article II:1(a) of the GATT 1994.

118 Appellate Body Report, *Argentina – Textiles and Apparel (1998)*, para. 46.

119 See *ibid.*, para. 55. On this basis, the Appellate Body found the DIEM regime inconsistent with Article II:1(b), first sentence, of the GATT 1994. In *Colombia – Textiles (2016)*, the panel found, as upheld by the Appellate Body, that the compound duty at issue exceeded the bound level (expressed in *ad valorem* terms) established in its Schedule and was therefore inconsistent with Article II:1(b), first sentence, of the GATT 1994. See Panel Report, *Colombia – Textiles (2016)*, paras. 7.189 and 7.193–7.194; and Appellate Body Report, *Colombia – Textiles (2016)*, para. 5.44. On how to assess whether a specific or compound duty exceeds the level bound expressed in *ad valorem* terms, see Appellate Body Report, *Argentina – Textiles and Apparel (1998)*, paras. 50ff.; and Panel Report, *Colombia – Textiles (2016)*, paras. 7.145ff. Note also that the Appellate Body indicated in *Argentina – Textiles and Apparel (1998)* that it is possible for a Member to provide for a legislative ceiling or cap on the level of specific or compound duties applied which would ensure that the duties applied do not exceed the bound level. See Appellate Body, *Argentina – Textiles and Apparel (1998)*, para. 54. See also Panel Report, *Colombia – Textiles (2016)*, paras. 7.182–7.186. In neither *Argentina – Textiles and Apparel (1998)* nor *Colombia – Textiles (2016)* the measure at issue was considered to provide for such legislative ceiling or cap.

'subject to the terms, conditions or qualifications set forth in that Schedule'. In *Canada – Dairy (1999)*, the Appellate Body ruled in this respect:

> In our view, the ordinary meaning of the phrase 'subject to' is that such concessions are without prejudice to and are *subordinated to*, and are, therefore, *qualified by*, any 'terms, conditions or qualifications' inscribed in a Member's Schedule ... A strong presumption arises that the language which is inscribed in a Member's Schedule under the heading, 'Other Terms and Conditions', has some *qualifying* or *limiting* effect on the substantive content or scope of the concession or commitment.[120]

Some of the disputes under Article II:1(a) and (b), first sentence, of the GATT 1994 do not directly stem from duties or charges imposed in excess of those contained in the Schedules of Concessions. In *EC – Chicken Cuts (2005)*, the European Communities did not deviate from the customs duties as contained in its Schedule of Concessions. It did, however, reclassify a certain type of chicken meat, namely, frozen boneless chicken cuts impregnated with salt, under a different tariff heading (heading 02.07 'Meat and edible offal, of the poultry of heading No. 0105, fresh, chilled or frozen').[121] Under that particular tariff heading, the customs duty imposed was higher than under the heading that applied according to the complainants in the case (heading 02.10 'Meat and edible meat offal, salted, in brine, dried, smoked; edible flours and meals of meat or meat offal'). As in *EC – Computer Equipment (1998)*, discussed above, the outcome of the *EC – Chicken Cuts (2005)* dispute depended on the interpretation of the tariff headings, and, in this case more specifically, on the interpretation of the term 'salted'. According to the European Communities, the key element under heading 02.10 was preservation and therefore the term 'salted' implied that the meat should be impregnated with salt sufficient to ensure long-term preservation. The complainants, Thailand and Brazil, contended that 'salted' did not imply long-term preservation and that the salted chicken cuts at issue thus fell within heading 02.10. Both the panel and the Appellate Body came to the conclusion that 'salted' did not imply long-term preservation in any way and that therefore the chicken cuts did fall under the

120 Appellate Body Report, *Canada – Dairy (1999)*, para. 134. At issue in *Canada – Dairy (1999)* was a tariff quota for fluid milk of 64,500 tonnes included in Canada's Schedule. In the column 'Other Terms and Conditions' of Canada's Schedule, it states that 'this quantity [64,500 tonnes] represents the estimated annual cross-border purchases imported by Canadian consumers'. In practice, Canada restricted imports under the 64,500 tonnes tariff quota to dairy products for the personal use of the importer and his household not exceeding C$20 in value for each importation. The United States contested that the restriction of access to imports for personal use not exceeding C$20 in value constituted a violation of Article II:1(b) of the GATT 1994. The panel agreed with the United States. The panel found that the 'condition' in Canada's Schedule is *descriptive* and does not establish restrictions on access to the tariff quota for fluid milk. The Appellate Body disagreed with the panel that the 'condition' was merely descriptive, and concluded that the limitation of cross-border purchases to 'Canadian consumers' referred to in Canada's Schedule justifies Canada's effective limitation of access to the tariff quota to imports for 'personal use'. However, the Appellate Body found that the C$20 value limitation was not contained in Canada's Schedule. See *ibid.*, para. 143.

121 See Panel Report, *EC – Chicken Cuts (2005)*, paras. 7.46–7.47.

more favourable tariff heading 02.10.[122] The European Communities had thus acted inconsistently with Article II:1(a) and (b) by wrongly classifying the chicken cuts, which resulted in treatment less favourable than that provided for in its Schedule.[123] To date, WTO Members have been found to have acted inconsistently with the obligations under Articles II:1(a) and II:1(b), first sentence, of the GATT 1994 in ten disputes[124]

In *Colombia – Textiles (2016)*, the respondent, Colombia, considered imports of textiles, apparel and footwear at a price below certain thresholds to be 'illicit trade' because there is a very high chance that such imports at below-threshold prices are being used to launder money. Colombia argued before the panel that the obligations of Articles II:1(a) and II:1(b), first sentence, are not applicable to 'illicit trade'. For Colombia, the term 'commerce' in Article II:1(a) and the term 'importation' in Article II:1(b) do not cover 'illicit trade'. The panel in *Colombia – Textiles (2016)* did not pronounce on whether 'illicit trade' is covered by the obligations under Article II:1.[125] On appeal, however, the Appellate Body found that the scope of the term 'commerce' in Article II:1(a) and the term 'importation' in Article II:1(b) is not qualified in respect of the nature or type of 'commerce' or 'imports' in a manner that excludes what Colombia considers to be illicit trade.[126] The Appellate Body concluded:

> we do not see that the text of Article II:1(a) and (b) of the GATT 1994 excludes what Colombia classifies as illicit trade. Moreover, the context provided in Articles II:2 and VII:2 of the GATT 1994 and the Customs Valuation Agreement supports our view that the scope of Article II:1(a) and (b) of the GATT 1994 is not limited in the manner suggested by Colombia.[127]

122 This conclusion was reached by applying the customary rules of interpretation of public international law, as codified in Articles 31 and 32 of the *Vienna Convention on the Law on Treaties*. Note, however, that the Appellate Body reversed the panel's conclusion that: 'the European Communities' practice of classifying, between 1996 and 2002, the products at issue under heading 02.10 of the EC Schedule "amounts to subsequent practice" within the meaning of Article 31.3(b) of the Vienna Convention'. See Appellate Body Report, *EC – Chicken Cuts (2005)*, para. 276.

123 See *ibid.*, paras. 346, 347(b)(i)–(iii) and 347 (c)(i)–(iii).

124 See *Argentina – Textiles and Apparel (1998); Canada – Dairy (1999); Korea – Various Measures on Beef (2001); EC – Chicken Cuts (2005); EC – Bananas III (Article 21.5 – Ecuador II)/EC – Bananas III (Article 21.5 – US) (2008); China – Auto Parts (2009); US – Zeroing (Japan – Article 21.5 – Japan) (2009); EC – IT Products (2010); Colombia – Textiles (2016)*; and *Russia – Tariff Treatment (2016)*. Note that, in *EC – Computer Equipment (1998)*, the Appellate Body reversed the panel's finding of inconsistency for the reasons discussed above, and did not complete the legal analysis.

125 The Panel considered it was not necessary for it to interpret Article II:1 of the GATT 1994 and determine whether 'illicit trade' fell within the scope of application of this provision, because the compound tariff was not structured or designed to apply 'solely to operations which have been classified as "illicit trade"'. See Panel Report, *Colombia – Textiles (2016)*, para. 7.106. On appeal, the Appellate Body noted that the compound tariff applies, or could apply, to some illicit trade, and that therefore the panel was required to address the interpretative issue pertaining to the scope of Article II:1 of the GATT 1994. See Appellate Body Report, *Colombia – Textiles (2016)*, para. 5.27. The Panel's failure to do so constituted a violation of its obligation under Article 11 of the DSU to make an objective assessment of the matter, including an objective assessment of the applicability of the relevant covered agreements. See *ibid.*, para. 5.28.

126 See Appellate Body Report, *Colombia – Textiles (2016)*, paras. 5.34–5.35.

127 *Ibid.*, para. 5.45. 128 *Ibid.*, para. 5.45.

Note that, having reached this conclusion, the Appellate Body stated:

> we wish to remark that our analysis set out above should not be understood to suggest that Members cannot adopt measures seeking to combat money laundering. This, however, cannot be achieved through interpreting Article II:1 of the GATT 1994 in a manner excluding from the scope of that provision what a Member considers to be illicit trade. A Member's right to adopt and pursue measures seeking to address concerns relating to money laundering can be appropriately preserved when justified, for example, in accordance with the general exceptions contained in Article XX of the GATT 1994.[128]

2.6.2 Tariff Concessions and Customs Duties Actually Applied

Note the difference between tariff concessions or bindings and the customs duties actually applied. As the Appellate Body observed in *Argentina – Textiles and Apparel (1998)*:

> A tariff binding in a Member's Schedule provides an upper limit on the amount of duty that may be imposed, and a Member is permitted to impose a duty that is less than that provided for in its Schedule.[129]

For many Members, tariff bindings for industrial products are considerably higher than the customs duties actually applied to these products. This means that the customs duties applied are significantly lower than the maximum levels agreed upon. This is in particular the case for developing-country Members. Figure 6.4 shows simple average tariff bindings and applied duties of selected Members. For example, the simple average tariff binding of India is 48.5 per cent, while its simple average applied duty is 13.5 per cent. Likewise, the simple average tariff binding of Brazil is 31.4 per cent, while its simple average applied duty is 13.5 per cent. In WTO-speak, the difference between the tariff binding and the applied duty is referred to as 'water' or 'binding overhang'. The presence of 'water' reflects a unilateral lowering of tariff barriers and thus allows for better market access. In this respect, 'water' is very welcome. However, 'water' also gives the importing Members concerned ample opportunity to increase the applied duties. Importing Members have the discretion to increase the applied duty to the level of the tariff binding. Therefore, when there is a lot of 'water', i.e. when the difference between the tariff bindings and the applied duties is large, exporting Members and traders have much less security and predictability with respect to the level of duties that will actually be applied on their products. However, as is clear in the Doha Round tariff negotiations,[130] Members, and in particular developing-country Members, are often hesitant to agree to lower bindings and to give up their 'water', even when their applied duties have for years been much lower than their bindings. Agreeing to lower bindings means giving up economic and fiscal policy space.

129 Appellate Body Report, *Argentina – Textiles and Apparel (1998)*, para. 46.
130 See above, pp. 93–9.

	Bound rate	MFN applied rate
Argentina	31.8	13.6
Brazil	31.4	13.5
Burundi	67.1	12.8
China	10	9.6
European Union	5.0	5.3
India	48.5	13.5
Japan	4.6	4.2
Kuwait	97.8	4.7
Malaysia	22.2	6.1
Nigeria	118.3	11.9
United States	3.5	3.5

Figure 6.4 Tariff rates: bound and applied[131]

2.7 Modification or Withdrawal of Tariff Concessions

As discussed above, Members may not apply customs duties above the tariff concessions or bindings agreed to in tariff negotiations and reflected in their Schedules. However, the GATT 1994 provides a procedure for the modification or withdrawal of agreed tariff concessions. Article XXVIII:1 of the GATT 1994 states, in pertinent part:

> [A Member] ... may, by negotiation and agreement ... modify or withdraw a concession included in the appropriate schedule annexed to this Agreement.

The negotiations on the modification or withdrawal of tariff concessions are to be conducted with: (1) the Members that hold so-called 'Initial Negotiating Rights' (INRs); and (2) any other Member that has a 'principal supplying interest'. In addition, consultations should be held with Members having a 'substantial interest'. The Members holding INRs are those Members with which the concession was bilaterally negotiated, initially. As mentioned above, INRs are commonly, though not always, specified in the Schedule of the Member granting the concession, but can also be determined on the basis of the negotiation records. Due to the approach to tariff negotiations adopted during the Uruguay Round,[132] many tariff concessions did not result from bilateral negotiations and thus INRs are much less common in respect of concessions agreed during the

131 See *World Tariff Profiles 2015*, available at www.wto.org/english/res_e/booksp_e/tariff_profiles15_e.pdf.
132 See above, pp. 428–36.

Uruguay Round. It was therefore agreed in the *Understanding on Article XXVIII* that:

Any Member having a principal supplying interest ... in a concession which is modified or withdrawn shall be accorded an initial negotiating right.[133]

A Member has a 'principal supplying interest' if, as provided in Note *Ad* Article XXVIII, paragraph 1.4:

that [Member] has had, over a reasonable period of time prior to the negotiations, a larger share in the market of the applicant [Member] than a Member with which the concession was initially negotiated or would ... have had such a share in the absence of discriminatory quantitative restrictions maintained by the applicant [Member].

The *Understanding on Article XXVIII*, paragraph 1, further elaborates on the concept of 'principal supplying interest' as follows:

[T]he Member which has the highest ratio of exports affected by the concession (i.e. exports of the product to the market of the Member modifying or withdrawing the concession) to its total exports shall be deemed to have a principal supplying interest if it does not already have an initial negotiating right or a principal supplying interest as provided for in paragraph 1 of Article XXVIII.

Pursuant to Article XXVIII, the *negotiations* on the modification or withdrawal of a tariff concession are to be conducted only with the Members holding INRs or those having a principal supplying interest. However, the Member wishing to modify or withdraw a tariff concession must *consult* any other Member that has a substantial interest in such concession.[134] The Note *Ad* Article XXVIII, paragraph 1.7, states:

The expression 'substantial interest' is not capable of a precise definition and accordingly may present difficulties ... It is, however, intended to be construed to cover only those [Members] which have, or in the absence of discriminatory quantitative restrictions affecting their exports could reasonably be expected to have, a significant share in the market of the [Member] seeking to modify or withdraw the concession.

A 'significant share', required to claim a 'substantial interest', has generally been considered to be 10 per cent of the market of the Member seeking to modify or withdraw a tariff concession.

With respect to the objective of the negotiations and agreement on the modification or withdrawal of tariff concessions, Article XXVIII:2 provides:

In such negotiations and agreement ... the [Members] concerned shall endeavour to maintain a general level of reciprocal and mutually advantageous concessions not less favourable to trade than that provided for in this Agreement prior to such negotiations.

When a tariff concession is modified or withdrawn, compensation in the form of new concessions needs to be granted to maintain a general level of concessions not less favourable to trade.[135]

133 *Understanding on the Interpretation of Article XXVIII of the GATT 1994*, para. 7.

134 See Article XXVIII:1 of the GATT 1994. The Ministerial Conference determines which Members have a 'substantial interest'. See *ibid.*

135 See Award of the Arbitrator, *EC–ACP Partnership Agreement – Recourse to Arbitration Pursuant to the Decision of 14 November 2001.*

It follows from the above that the modification or withdrawal of a tariff binding is based on the principle of renegotiation and compensation. However, if the negotiations fail to lead to an agreement, Article XXVIII:3(a) provides, in relevant part, that:

> [T]he [Member] which proposes to modify or withdraw the concession shall, nevertheless, be free to do so.

In that case, any Member holding an INR, any Member having a principal supplying interest *and* any Member having a substantial interest shall be free to withdraw substantially equivalent concessions.[136]

In 2012, Ukraine requested – less than four years after its accession to the WTO – the renegotiation of its tariff bindings on 371 tariff lines. Both the size and the timing of this request for renegotiation alarmed many Members. In support of its request for renegotiation, Ukraine argued that, on joining the WTO in 2008, it agreed on very low tariff bindings 'with the expectation that the ongoing Doha Round talks would lead to additional liberalisation among other WTO members with more protected economies'.[137] As such additional liberalisation has clearly not been realised, Ukraine argued that 'today's reality [now] makes the adjustment necessary'.[138] However, in light of the negative reaction of many WTO Members to its request for renegotiation, Ukraine announced at the General Council meeting of 21 October 2014 that it no longer sought to renegotiate its tariff bindings.

Finally, note that Article XVIII:7 of the GATT 1994 allows developing-country Members to *modify or withdraw a tariff concession* in order to promote the establishment of a particular industry.[139] However, the developing-country Member concerned must enter into negotiations with the Members primarily affected by the modification or withdrawal of the tariff concession in order to come to an agreement on compensatory adjustment.[140] If no agreement is reached, it is for the General Council to decide whether the compensatory adjustment offered is adequate. Where the General Council considers the compensation to be adequate, the developing-country Member is then free to modify or withdraw the tariff concession provided that, at the same time, it gives effect to the compensatory adjustment. Should the General Council find the compensation offered to be inadequate, but also that every reasonable effort was made to offer adequate compensation, the developing-country Member may proceed with the modification or withdrawal of the tariff concession.[141] Any other Member affected by the modification or withdrawal is then free to modify or withdraw substantially equivalent concessions with regard to the developing-country Member concerned.[142] Under the GATT 1947, the GATT Council was generous in allowing developing-country Members to modify or withdraw tariff concessions without

136 See Article XXVIII:3 of the GATT 1994.
137 See *Bridges Weekly Trade News Digest*, 17 October 2012. 138 See *ibid.*
139 For a discussion of the 'infant industry' argument for trade-restrictive measures, see above, p. 27.
140 See Article XVIII:7(a) of the GATT 1994. 141 See Article XVIII:7(b) of the GATT 1994.
142 See *ibid.*

requiring any compensatory adjustment. The contribution of the exception under Article XVIII:7 to the economic development of developing countries has been limited. In fact, the infant-industry-protection exception under Article XVIII:7 has not been invoked by any developing-country Member since the entry into force of the *WTO Agreement* in 1995.[143]

2.8 Imposition of Customs Duties on Imports

In addition to rules for the protection of tariff concessions, WTO law also provides for rules on the manner in which customs duties must be imposed. The imposition of customs duties may require three determinations to be made: (1) the determination of the proper classification of the imported good, which allows customs authorities to determine which duty to levy; (2) the determination of the customs value of the imported good; and (3) the determination of the origin of the imported good.

The need for these determinations follows from the fact that customs duties differ from good to good (customs classification); are usually *ad valorem* duties and thus calculated on the basis of the value of the products concerned (customs valuation); and may differ depending on the exporting country (determination of origin).

2.8.1 Customs Classification

As illustrated above when discussing *EC – Computer Equipment (1998)* and *EC – Chicken Cuts (2005)*, the imposition of customs duties requires the determination of the proper customs classification of the imported good.[144] WTO law does not *specifically* address the issue of customs classification. In *Spain – Unroasted Coffee (1981)*, the panel ruled that:

> there was no obligation under the GATT to follow any particular system for classifying goods, and that a contracting party had the right to introduce in its customs tariff new positions or sub-positions as appropriate.[145]

However, in classifying products for customs purposes, Members have of course to consider their general obligations under the WTO agreements, such as the MFN treatment obligation. As discussed in Chapter 4, the panel in *Spain – Unroasted Coffee (1981)* ruled that:

> whatever the classification adopted, Article I:1 required that the same tariff treatment be applied to 'like products'.[146]

143 Committee on Trade and Development, *Implementation of Special and Differential Treatment Provisions in WTO Agreements and Decisions*, Note by the WTO Secretariat, WT/COMTD/W/196, dated 14 June 2013, 7.

144 See above, pp. 444 and 445.

145 Panel Report, *Spain – Unroasted Coffee (1981)*, para. 4.4.

146 *Ibid.*; and Panel Report, *Japan – SPF Dimension Lumber (1989)*, para. 5.9.

Specific rules on classification can be found in the *International Convention on the Harmonized Commodity Description and Coding System* (the '*HS Convention*'), which entered into force on 1 January 1988 and to which most WTO Members are a party.[147] The Harmonized Commodity Description and Coding System, commonly referred to as the 'Harmonized System' or 'HS', is an *international commodity classification system*, developed under the auspices of the Brussels-based Customs Cooperation Council (CCC), known today as the World Customs Organization (WCO).[148] As of 1 January 2016, 207 countries, territories or customs or economic unions are applying the Harmonized System.[149]

The Harmonized System consists of 21 sections covering 97 chapters, 1,241 headings and over 5,000 commodity groups. The sections and chapters are:

- Section I (Chapters 1–5, live animals and animal products);
- Section II (Chapters 6–14, vegetable products);
- Section III (Chapter 15, animal or vegetable fats and oils);
- Section IV (Chapters 16–24, prepared foodstuffs, beverages and spirits, tobacco);
- Section V (Chapters 25–7, mineral products);
- Section VI (Chapters 28–38, chemical products);
- Section VII (Chapters 39–40, plastics and rubber);
- Section VIII (Chapters 41–3, leather and travel goods);
- Section IX (Chapters 44–6, wood, charcoal, cork);
- Section X (Chapters 47–9, wood pulp, paper and paperboard articles);
- Section XI (Chapters 50–63, textiles and textile products);
- Section XII (Chapters 64–7, footwear, umbrellas, artificial flowers);
- Section XIII (Chapters 68–70, stone, cement, ceramic, glass);
- Section XIV (Chapter 71, pearls, precious metals);
- Section XV (Chapters 72–83, base metals);
- Section XVI (Chapters 84–5, electrical machinery);
- Section XVII (Chapters 86–9, vehicles, aircraft, vessels);
- Section XVIII (Chapters 90–2, optical instruments, clocks and watches, musical instruments);
- Section XIX (Chapter 93, arms and ammunition);
- Section XX (Chapters 94–6, furniture, toys, miscellaneous manufactured articles); and
- Section XXI (Chapter 97, works of art, antiques).[150]

147 *International Convention on the Harmonized Commodity Description and Coding System*, Brussels, 14 June 1983, as amended by the Protocol of Amendment of 24 June 1986, available at www.wcoomd.org/home_wco_topics_hsoverviewboxes_hsconvention.htm.

148 The Harmonized System was developed not only for customs classification purposes, but also for the collection of trade statistics and for use in the context of various types of transactions in international trade (such as insurance and transport).

149 See www.wco.org. The *HS Convention* has 154 Contracting Parties (including the European Union and all EU Member States).

150 Chapters 98 and 99 are reserved for special use by Contracting Parties. Most Members do not use these chapters.

In the Harmonized System, each commodity group has a six-digit HS code.[151] For example, the HS Code for 'Electric trains, including tracks, signals and other accessories therefor; reduced-size (scale) model assembly kits' is 9503 30. Of this code, the first two digits refer to the Chapter, in this case Chapter 95 ('Toys, games and sport requisites; parts and accessories thereof'), while the first four digits refer to the heading, in this case Heading 95.03 ('Tricycles, scooters, pedal cars and similar wheeled toys; dolls' carriages; dolls; other toys; reduced-size (scale) models and similar recreational models working or not; puzzles of all kinds').

To keep the Harmonized System up to date, to include new products (resulting from new technologies) and to take account of new developments in international trade, the Harmonized System is revised every four to six years.[152]

To allow for a systematic and uniform classification of goods, the Harmonized System not only provides for a structured list of commodity descriptions and related numerical codes, but also compromises: (1) Chapter, Heading and Subheading Notes; and (2) General Rules for the Interpretation of the Harmonized System. The Chapter, Heading and Subheading Notes, which precede the chapters of the Harmonized System are the most important source for determining classification in case of doubt. The General Rules for the Interpretation of the Harmonized System, set out in an annex to the *HS Convention*, provide that the classification of goods shall be governed, *inter alia*, by the following principles: (1) incomplete or unfinished goods are classified as finished goods (in the event that they do not have their own line) when the goods already have the essential character of the complete or finished goods;[153] (2) when goods are, *prima facie*, classifiable under two or more headings, classification shall be effected as follows: (a) the heading which provides the most specific description shall be preferred to headings providing a more general description;[154] (b) when goods cannot be classified as provided under (a), mixtures, composite goods consisting of different materials or made up of different components, and goods put up in sets for retail sale, shall be classified as if they consisted of the material or component which gives them their essential character;[155] and (c) when goods cannot be classified as provided under (a) or (b), they shall be classified under the heading which occurs last in numerical order among those which equally merit consideration;[156] and (3) goods which cannot be classified in accordance with the above rules shall be classified under the heading appropriate to the goods to which they are most akin, i.e. with which they bear most likeness.[157]

151 Note, however, that, pursuant to Article 3.3 of the *HS Convention*, parties to the Convention can, and do, use more than six-digit codes. Article 3.3 of the *HS Convention*. See, for example, Figures 6.1 and 6.3, at p. 421 and pp. 438–9, respectively.

152 See Article 16 of the *HS Convention*. To date, there have been revisions in 1992, 1996, 2002, 2007 and 2012. The next revision is to take place in 2017.

153 See General Rules for the Interpretation of the Harmonized System, para. 2(a).

154 *Ibid.*, para. 3(a). 155 *Ibid.*, para. 3(b).

156 *Ibid.*, para. 3(c). 157 *Ibid.*, para. 4.

In addition to the Chapter, Heading and Subheading Notes and the General Rules for the Interpretation of the Harmonized System, the Explanatory Notes and Classification Opinions are also of importance. As stated in Article 8.2 of the *HS Convention*, the Explanatory Notes and Classification Opinions serve to secure uniformity in the interpretation and application of the Harmonized System. The Explanatory Notes are commentaries on the Harmonized System finalised by the WCO Harmonized System Committee (HSC) and adopted by the WCO Council, while the Classification Opinions are decisions taken by the WCO's HSC on the classification of specific products.[158]

WTO Members are not obliged under the GATT 1994 to adopt the Harmonized System.[159] However, as already noted, most WTO Members are a party to the *HS Convention*. Article 3.1(a) of this Convention provides, in relevant part, that a party to the *HS Convention*:

> undertakes that, in respect of its customs tariff and statistical nomenclatures:
> i. it shall use all the headings and subheadings of the Harmonized System without addition or modification, together with their related numerical codes;
> ii. it shall apply the General Rules for the Interpretation of the Harmonized System and all the Section, Chapter and Subheading Notes, and shall not modify the scope of the Sections, Chapters, headings or subheadings of the Harmonized System; and
> iii. it shall follow the numerical sequence of the Harmonized System.

Consequently, most WTO Members use the Harmonized System, its Section, Chapter and Subheading Notes and its General Rules for the Interpretation in their national customs tariffs and for the customs classification of goods. Although the Harmonized System is not a WTO agreement, as discussed above, the Appellate Body ruled in *EC – Chicken Cuts (2005)* and confirmed in *China – Auto Parts (2009)* that the Harmonized System is relevant for the interpretation of WTO Schedules and the tariff bindings contained therein.[160]

Disputes between the importer and the relevant customs authorities on proper classification are resolved by national courts or tribunals.[161] Parties to the *HS Convention* may bring a dispute to the WCO for settlement under Article 10 thereof.[162]

158 They are published in four volumes in English and French but are also available on CD-ROM and online, as part of a database giving the HS classification of more than 200,000 goods. Information about all HS publications can be found at www.publications.wcoomd.org.

159 Note, however, that the WTO *Agreement on Agriculture*, when defining its product scope, does refer to the Harmonized System, and in particular to HS Chapters 1 to 24. See Article 2 of and Annex 1 to the *Agreement on Agriculture*.

160 See above, p. 441.

161 Article X of the GATT 1994 concerns the access to national courts and tribunals. See below, p. 499.

162 Pursuant to Article 10 of the *HS Convention*, any dispute between Contracting Parties concerning the interpretation or application of the Convention shall, so far as possible, be settled by negotiation. Any dispute, which is not so settled shall be referred to the HS Committee. If the HS Committee is unable to settle the dispute, it shall refer the matter to the WCO Council. The parties to the dispute may agree in advance to accept the recommendations of the HS Committee or the WCO Council as binding.

2.8.2 Valuation for Customs Purposes

As previously explained, most customs duties are *ad valorem*. The customs administrations must therefore determine the value of the imported goods in order to be able to calculate the customs duty due. Unlike for customs classification, the WTO agreements provide for rules on customs valuation. These rules, which are crucial to ensure that the value of the tariff concessions is not nullified or undermined, are set out in: (1) Article VII of the GATT 1994, entitled 'Valuation for Customs Purposes'; (2) the Note *Ad* Article VII; and (3) the WTO *Agreement on the Implementation of Article VII of the GATT 1994*.[163] The latter agreement, commonly referred to as the *Customs Valuation Agreement*, elaborates the provisions of Article VII in order to provide greater uniformity and certainty in their implementation.

The core provision of Article VII on customs valuation is found in paragraph 2(a), which states:

> The value for customs purposes of imported merchandise should be based on the *actual value* of the imported merchandise on which duty is assessed, or of like merchandise, and should *not* be based on the value of merchandise of national origin or on arbitrary or fictitious values.[164]

Paragraph 2(b) of Article VII defines the concept of the 'actual value' of goods as the price at which such or like goods are sold or offered for sale in the ordinary course of trade under fully competitive conditions. Elaborating on and elucidating Article VII:2 of the GATT 1994, Article 1.1 of the *Customs Valuation Agreement* provides:

> The customs value of imported goods shall be the *transaction value*, that is the price actually paid or payable for the goods when sold for export to the country of importation adjusted in accordance with the provisions of Article 8.[165]

The primary basis for the customs value is thus the 'transaction value' of the imported goods, i.e. the price actually paid or payable for the goods. This price is normally shown in the invoice, contract or purchase order.[166] Article 1.1 is to be

163 The WTO *Agreement on the Implementation of Article VII of the GATT 1994* replaced the 1979 Tokyo Round *Agreement on the Implementation of Article VII of the GATT*, but is not significantly different from this 1979 Agreement.

164 Emphasis added.

165 Emphasis added. Note that, in the proviso to Article 1.1, a number of situations are identified in which the transaction value cannot be used to determine the customs value. This is, for example, the case when there are certain restrictions on the use or disposition of the goods. Furthermore, as a rule, the buyer and seller should not be related (within the meaning of Article 15) but, if they are, the use of the transaction value is still acceptable if this relationship did not influence the price (see Article 1.2(a)) or the transaction value closely approximates a test value (see Article 1.2(b)). See also Panel Report, *Thailand – Cigarettes (Philippines) (2011)*, paras. 7.143–7.173.

166 Pursuant to Article 17 of the *Customs Valuation Agreement*, customs authorities have the right to 'satisfy themselves as to the truth or accuracy of any statement, document or declaration'. In cases of doubt as to the truth or accuracy, customs authorities will first request the importer to provide further information and clarification. If reasonable doubt persists, the customs authorities will not determine the customs value on the basis of the transaction value but will apply a different method of valuation (see below, pp. 474–6).

read together with Article 8, which provides for *adjustments* to be made to the price actually paid or payable, as discussed below.[167]

Articles 2–7 of the *Customs Valuation Agreement* provide methods for determining the customs value whenever it cannot be determined under the provisions of Article 1. These methods to determine the customs value, other than the 'transaction value' method of Article 1, are, first, the 'transaction value of identical or similar goods' method set out in Articles 2 and 3; second, the deductive value method set out in Article 5; third, the computed value method set out in Article 6; and, fourth, the fallback method set out in Article 7. These methods to determine the customs value of imported goods are to be applied in the above order.[168]

Under the *deductive value method*, the customs authorities try to determine the customs value based on information provided by the importer concerning the price at which the imported goods are subsequently sold. This is done by determining the unit price at which the imported goods, or identical or similar imported goods, are sold at the greatest aggregate quantity to an unrelated buyer in the country of importation.[169] The greatest aggregate quantity is the greatest number of units sold at one price.[170] A number of elements are then 'deducted' (i.e. subtracted) from this price, including commissions paid to distributors in the importing country, the costs of transport and insurance in the country of importation, and customs duties and other internal taxes paid.

Under the *computed value method*, customs authorities try to 'compute' (i.e. reconstruct) the value of the good at the time of exportation based on information provided by the manufacturer, who is often located in the exporting country. The computed value is the sum of the production cost (i.e. the cost of materials and fabrication), profit and general expenses and other expenses (e.g. transport costs to the place or port of importation).[171]

167 Subparagraphs (a)–(d) of Article 1.1 of the *Customs Valuation Agreement* specify circumstances in which customs value need not be based on transaction value. This is the case when: (1) there are certain restrictions on the disposition or use of the goods by the buyer; (2) the sale or price is subject to some condition or consideration for which a value cannot be determined with respect to the goods being valued; (3) some part of the proceeds accrue to the seller; or (4) under certain circumstances, the buyer and seller are related.

168 See Article 4 and the General Note in Annex I to the *Customs Valuation Agreement*. Note, however, that, at the request of the importer, the order of application of the deductive method (Article 5) and the computed method (Article 6) may be reversed (*ibid.*).

169 Goods are 'identical' if they are the same in all respects, including physical characteristics, quality and reputation. 'Similar goods' means goods which, although not alike in all respects, have like characteristics and like component materials which enable them to perform the same functions and to be commercially interchangeable. In addition, goods shall not be regarded as 'similar' or 'identical' unless they are produced in the same country as the goods being valued. See Article 15.2 of the *Customs Valuation Agreement*.

170 See Article 5 and the Note to Article 5 in Annex I to the *Customs Valuation Agreement*. Since the deductive value method uses the sale price in the country of importation as a basis for the calculation of the customs value, a number of deductions (for profits, general expenses, transport, etc.) are necessary to reduce the sale price to the relevant customs value. See also Panel Report, *Thailand – Cigarettes (Philippines) (2011)*, paras. 7.345–7.362.

171 See Article 6 and the Note to Article 6 in Annex I to the *Customs Valuation Agreement*.

The *fallback method*, set out in Article 7.1, applies when the customs value cannot be determined under any of the other four methods. Under this method, the customs value shall be:

> determined using reasonable means consistent with the principles and general provisions of this Agreement and of Article VII of the GATT 1994 and on the basis of the data available in the country of importation.[172]

However, as explicitly stated in Article 7.2(a)–(g), the customs value of imported goods may never be determined on the basis of, for example: the selling price in the country of importation of goods produced in that country; the price of goods on the domestic market of the country of exportation; minimum customs values; or arbitrary or fictitious values.

In *Colombia – Ports of Entry (2009)*, one of the measures at issue was a Colombian regulation requiring customs authorities to use indicative prices for the customs valuation of imported products, unless the transaction value was higher than the indicative price. The panel found this regulation to be inconsistent with the obligation to conduct customs valuations of imported goods based on the sequential application of the methods established by Articles 1, 2, 3, 5 and 6 of the *Customs Valuation Agreement.*[173] Moreover, the panel found that Colombia's use of indicative prices did not constitute a 'reasonable means' of customs valuation within the meaning of Article 7.1 of the *Customs Valuation Agreement*, as it was inconsistent with Article 7.2(b) and (f) thereof.[174]

In *Colombia – Textiles (2016)*, the Appellate Body found that the existence of the alternative methods set out in Articles 2–7 of the *Customs Valuation Agreement* for determining the customs value when a declared value of a transaction is rejected because it is unduly low, confirms – as discussed above – that the underlying transaction remains subject to Article II:1 of the GATT 1994 and:

> further supports our understanding that the scope of Article II:1(a) and (b) of the GATT 1994 does not exclude what Colombia considers to be illicit trade.[175]

As mentioned above, the customs value of imported goods is – if possible (and, usually, this *is* possible) – determined on the basis of the transaction value of these goods. This transaction value must, however, be adjusted as provided for in Article 8 of the *Customs Valuation Agreement.* Pursuant to Article 8.1, the following costs and values, for example, must be added to the price actually paid or payable for the imported products: (1) commissions and brokerage;[176] (2) the cost of packing;[177] (3) royalties and licence fees related to the goods being valued

172 Paragraph 2 of the Note to Article 7 in Annex 1 to the *Customs Valuation Agreement* states: 'The methods of valuation to be employed under Article 7 should be those laid down in Articles 1 through 6 but a reasonable flexibility in the application of such methods would be in conformity with the aims and provisions of Article 7.'

173 See Panel Report, *Colombia – Ports of Entry (2009)*, para. 7.152.

174 See *ibid.*, para. 7.153.

175 Appellate Body Report, *Colombia – Textiles (2016)*, para. 5.39.

176 See Article 8.1(a)(i) of the *Customs Valuation Agreement.* 177 See *ibid.*, Article 8.1(a)(iii).

that the buyer must pay;[178] and (4) the value of any part of the proceeds of any subsequent resale that accrues to the seller.[179]

Pursuant to Article 8.2, each Member is free either to include or to exclude from the customs value of imported goods: (1) the cost of transport to the port or place of importation; (2) loading, unloading and handling charges associated with the transport to the port or place of importation; and (3) the cost of insurance. Note in this respect that most Members take the CIF price as the basis for determining the customs value, while Members such as the United States, Japan and Canada take the (lower) FOB price.[180]

To date, WTO Members have been found to have acted inconsistently with the obligations under Article VII of the GATT 1994 and the *Customs Valuation Agreement* in two disputes.[181]

2.8.3 Determination of Origin

In spite of the MFN treatment obligation, discussed in Chapter 4, the customs duties applied to imported goods may differ depending on the country from which the goods originate. For example, goods *from* developing-country Members commonly benefit from lower import duties in developed-country Members than do goods from other developed-country Members;[182] and no customs duties apply to goods *from* Members that are a party to the same free-trade agreement.[183] Moreover, only the goods *from* WTO Members benefit under WTO law from MFN treatment with respect to customs duties.[184] It is, therefore, important to determine the origin of imported goods, and this is not always an easy determination to make. As noted in Chapter 1, when discussing the global value chain, many industrial products, available on the market today, are produced with inputs and raw materials from more than one country.[185] For example, in the case of cotton shirts, it is possible that the cotton used in their production is manufactured in country A, the textile woven, dyed and printed in country B, the cloth cut and stitched in country C and the shirts packed for retail in country D before being exported to country E.[186]

The rules to determine the origin of imported goods differ from Member to Member, and many Members use different rules of origin depending on the

178 See *ibid.*, Article 8.1(c). 179 See *ibid.*, Article 8.1(d).

180 CIF (cost, insurance and freight) and FOB (free on board) are International Commercial terms (INCO terms). CIF means that the seller must pay the costs, insurance and freight involved in bringing the goods to the named port of destination. FOB means that the buyer has to bear all costs and risks of loss of, or damage to, the goods from the point that the goods pass the ship's rail at the named port of shipment.

181 See *Colombia – Ports of Entry (2009)*; and *Thailand – Cigarettes (Philippines) (2011)*.

182 On preferential customs duties for developing-country Members under the Enabling Clause of the GATT 1994, see above, pp. 321–5.

183 On customs duties in the context of customs unions and free-trade agreements pursuant to Article XXIV of the GATT 1994, see below, pp. 679–88.

184 Note that the determination of origin is also necessary for the imposition of antidumping duties and countervailing duties. See below, p. 709.

185 See below, pp. 11–14.

186 See *Business Guide to the World Trading System*, 2nd edn (International Trade Centre/Commonwealth Secretariat, 1999), 155.

purpose for which the origin is determined.[187] Generally speaking, the national rules of origin currently applied by Members use one or more of three methods to determine origin: (1) the method of 'value added'; (2) the method of 'change in tariff classification'; and (3) the method of 'qualifying processes'. Under national rules of origin using the method of 'value added', a good will be considered to have originated in country X if in that country a specified percentage (for example, 50 per cent) of the value of the good was added. Under national rules of origin using the method of 'change in tariff classification', a good will be considered to have originated in country X if, as a result of processing in that country, the tariff classification of the product changes. Finally, under national rules of origin using the method of 'qualifying processes', a good will be considered to have originated in country X if a particular technical manufacturing or processing operation relating to the good took place in that country.[188]

The GATT 1947 had no specific rules on the determination of the origin of imported goods, and the GATT 1994 still provides no specific rules on this matter. However, the negotiators during the Uruguay Round recognised the need for multilateral disciplines on rules of origin in order to prevent these rules from being a source of uncertainty and unpredictability in international trade. The consensus on the need for such disciplines resulted in the *Agreement on Rules of Origin*, which is part of Annex 1A to the WTO Agreement.

The *Agreement on Rules of Origin* makes a distinction between: (1) non-preferential rules of origin; and (2) preferential rules of origin. Non-preferential rules of origin are rules of origin used in non-preferential trade policy instruments (relating to, *inter alia*, MFN treatment, anti-dumping and countervailing duties, safeguard measures, origin marking or tariff quotas).[189] Most of the disciplines set out in the *Agreement on Rules of Origin* concern *non-preferential* rules of origin.[190] However, Annex II to the *Agreement on Rules of Origin* sets out some disciplines for *preferential* rules of origin. Preferential rules of origin are rules of origin applied by Members to determine whether goods qualify for preferential treatment under contractual or autonomous trade regimes (leading to the granting of tariff preferences going beyond the application of the MFN treatment obligation).[191] Note that 19 per cent of world trade is conducted on a preferential basis.[192]

With respect to *non-preferential* rules of origin, the *Agreement on Rules of Origin* provides for a work programme on the harmonisation of these rules.[193]

187 e.g. whether the origin of imported products is determined for the imposition of ordinary customs duties, anti-dumping or countervailing duties or the administration of country-specific tariff quota shares.
188 Members may also have a list of processes and operations, such as packaging, simple painting or dilution with water, that are considered insufficient to confer origin.
189 See Article 1.2 of the *Agreement on Rules of Origin*.
190 See *ibid.*, Article 1.1. 191 See *ibid.*, Article 1.1 and Annex II.2.
192 See below, p. 673.
193 See Article 9.1 of the *Agreement on Rules of Origin*. This work programme is to be undertaken in conjunction with the World Customs Organization.

Pursuant to Article 9.2 of the *Agreement on Rules of Origin*, this Harmonization Work Programme should have been completed by July 1998. However, the WTO Members failed to meet this deadline. In fact, work on the harmonisation of non-preferential rules of origin is still ongoing.[194]

The failure of WTO Members to agree, to date, on harmonised rules of origin does not, however, mean that no WTO disciplines apply to non-preferential rules of origin. Article 2 of the *Agreement on Rules of Origin* contains a rather extensive list of multilateral disciplines for rules of origin already applicable during the 'transition period', i.e. the period until the Harmonization Work Programme is completed. These multilateral disciplines applicable during the transitional period include: (1) a transparency requirement, namely, the rules of origin must clearly and precisely define the criteria they apply; (2) a prohibition on using rules of origin as instruments to pursue trade objectives; (3) a requirement that rules of origin shall not themselves create restrictive, distorting or disruptive effects on international trade; (4) a national treatment requirement, namely, that the rules of origin applied to imported products shall not be more stringent than the rules of origin applied to determine whether or not a good is domestic; (5) an MFN requirement, namely, that rules of origin shall not discriminate between other Members, irrespective of the affiliation of the manufacturers of the good concerned; (6) a requirement that rules of origin shall be administered in a consistent, uniform, impartial and reasonable manner; (7) a requirement that rules of origin state what confers origin (a positive standard) rather than state what does *not* confer origin (a negative standard); (8) a requirement to publish laws, regulations, judicial decisions, etc., relating to rules of origin; (9) requirements regarding the issuance of assessments of origin (no later than 150 days after the request) and the validity of the assessments (in principle, three years); (10) a prohibition on the retroactive application of new or amended rules of origin; (11) a requirement that any administrative action relating to the determination of origin is reviewable promptly by independent tribunals; and (12) a requirement to respect the confidentiality of information provided on a confidential basis.[195] Note that many of these disciplines are in fact the specific application of general GATT obligations (such as Articles I, III and X of the GATT 1994) to national non-preferential rules on the determination of origin.

To date, there has only been one dispute before a panel dealing with rules of origin. In *US – Textiles Rules of Origin (2003)*, India claimed that the United States applied rules of origin on textiles and certain other products that were inconsistent with several obligations under Article 2 of the *Agreement on Rules*

194 See WTO Secretariat, *Report (2015) of the Committee on Rules of Origin to the Council for Trade in Goods*, G/L/1127, dated 21 October 2015. The report refers to the issues discussed in detail in the earlier report of 2013 (G/L/1047) as the reason for little or no progress in harmonisation of the non-preferential rules of origin. Members hold divergent views with regard to the need to finalise the harmonisation work programme with some stating that conclusion of negotiations is no longer a political priority.

195 See Articles 2(a)–(k) of the *Agreement on Rules of Origin*.

of Origin. The panel in *US – Textiles Rules of Origin (2003)* noted that Article 2 does not provide what WTO Members must do, but rather what they should not do,[196] and that:

> [b]y setting out what Members cannot do, these provisions leave for Members themselves discretion to decide what, within those bounds, they can do. In this regard, it is common ground between the parties that Article 2 does not prevent Members from determining the criteria which confer origin, changing those criteria over time, or applying different criteria to different goods.[197]

Once the Harmonization Work Programme is completed, all Members will apply only one set of non-preferential rules of origin for all purposes.[198] As provided for in Article 3 of the *Agreement on Rules of Origin*, the disciplines set out in Article 2, already applicable, will continue to apply.[199] Moreover, Article 3 makes clear that, under the harmonised rules (still to be agreed on), Members will be required to determine as the country of origin of imported goods: (1) the country where the goods have been wholly obtained; or (2) the country where the last substantial transformation to the goods has been carried out.[200] However, to date, Members have been unsuccessful in reaching consensus either on detailed rules regarding the requirements for a good to be 'wholly obtained' in one country,[201] or on the criteria for a 'substantial transformation' (a change in tariff classification and/or a specific percentage of value added).[202]

The disciplines on rules of origin discussed above concern only non-preferential rules of origin. However, as already noted, Annex II to the *Agreement on Rules of Origin* provides – in the form of a 'Common Declaration' – for some disciplines applicable to preferential rules of conduct. Pursuant to Annex II, the general principles and requirements set out in the *Agreement on Rules of Origin* in respect of transparency, positive standards, administrative assessments, judicial review, non-retroactivity of changes and confidentiality apply also to *preferential* rules of origin. While, as discussed above, the Harmonization Work Programme has not yet resulted in an agreement on specific multilateral disciplines on non-preferential rules of origin, more progress has been achieved with respect to preferential rules of origin, at least with respect to preferential rules of origin applying to least-developed countries. Building on the *Decision on Measures in Favour of Least Developed Countries (LDCs)*, taken at the Hong Kong Ministerial

196 See Panel Report, *US – Textiles Rules of Origin (2003)*, para. 6.23.

197 *Ibid.*, para. 6.24. India argued that rules of origin applied by the United States on its textile imports were inconsistent with Articles 2(b)–(d) of the *Agreement on Rules of Origin*. The panel found with regard to all claims that India did not adduce sufficient evidence to make a *prima facie* case of inconsistency. See Panel Report, *US – Textiles Rules of Origin (2003)*, paras. 6.118; 6.190–6.191, 6.221 and 6.231; and 6.271–6.272.

198 See Article 3(a) of the *Agreement on Rules of Origin*.

199 See *ibid.*, Article 3(c)–(i) and Article 9(c)–(g). 200 See *ibid.*, Article 3(b).

201 The question of, for example, which minimal operations or processes can and cannot, by themselves, confer origin on a good is a matter of current debate.

202 Note, however, the agreement reached by the Nairobi Ministerial Conference in December 2016 on the requirements to be considered by developed- and developing-country Members to assess 'sufficient or substantial transformation' in the context of *preferential* rules of origin. See below, p. 461.

Conference in December 2005,[203] whereby developed- and developing-country Members committed to ensure transparent and simple application of preferential rules of origin to imports from least-developed countries, the Bali Ministerial Conference in December 2013 took a step further in this direction and agreed on guidelines providing elements to be considered by Members to determine the criteria to confer 'origin'.[204] Clarifying furthermore as to whether or not a product has originated from a least-developed country, the Nairobi Ministerial Conference in December 2015 set forth in detail the requirements to be considered by developed- and developing-country Members to assess '*sufficient or substantial transformation*'.[205] In order to ensure timely implementation, the Ministerial Decision mandates Members to inform the Committee on Rules of Origin on the efforts taken to implement the decision.[206]

Note that the United Nations 2030 Agenda for Sustainable Development expressly recognises the realisation of timely implementation of duty-free and quota-free access for all least-developed countries, including by ensuring transparency and simplicity of the preferential rules of origin applicable to imports from least-developed countries, as one of the goals to strengthen the means of implementation and revitalisation of the global partnership for sustainable development.[207]

To date, no WTO Member has been found in dispute settlement proceedings to have acted inconsistently with the obligations under the *Agreement on Rules of Origin*.[208]

3 OTHER DUTIES AND CHARGES ON IMPORTS

In addition to customs duties on imports, tariff barriers on imports can also take the form of 'other duties and charges'. This section deals in turn with: the definition and types of 'other duties and charges on imports'; the rule applicable to such measures; and the measures exempted from the scope of application of this rule.

203 See Hong Kong Ministerial Conference, *Ministerial Declaration of 18 December* (Annex F), WT/MIN(05)/DEC, dated 22 December 2005.

204 See Bali Ministerial Conference, *Decision of 7 December on Preferential Rules of Origin for Least Developed Countries*, WT/MIN(13)/42, dated 11 December 2013. The elements include other than for wholly obtained products, substantial or sufficient transformation, which can be defined in a number of ways including through: (a) *ad valorem* percentage criterion; (b) change of tariff classification; and (c) specific manufacturing or processing operation or a combination of any of the above.

205 See Nairobi Ministerial Conference, *Decision of 19 December 2015 on Preferential Rules of Origin for Least Developed Countries*, WT/MIN(15)/47, dated 21 December 2015.

206 See *ibid.*, para. 4.1.

207 See Goal 17.12, *Res 70/1* adopted by the General Assembly on 25 September 2015.

208 With regard to *US – Textiles Rules of Origin (2003)*, see above, p. 460, fn. 198.

3.1 Definition and Types

'Other duties and charges on imports' are financial charges or taxes, *other than* ordinary customs duties,[209] which are levied on imported products and are due because of their importation. In *India – Additional Import Duties (2008)*, the Appellate Body held that 'other duties and charges on imports', also referred to as 'ODC' on imports:

> are defined in relation to duties covered by the first sentence of Article II:1(b), such that ODCs encompass only duties and charges that are not [ordinary customs duties].[210]

'Other duties and charges on imports' form a *residual* category encompassing financial charges on imports that are not ordinary customs duties or customs duties *sensu stricto*.[211] The difference between ordinary customs duties and other duties and charges was at issue in *Chile – Price Band System (2002)*.[212] The panel in this case distinguished ordinary customs duties from other duties and charges by considering that customs duties:

> always relate to either the value of the imported goods, in the case of *ad valorem* duties, or the volume of the imported goods, in the case of specific duties. Such ordinary customs duties, however, do not appear to involve the consideration of any other, exogenous, factors, such as, for instance, fluctuating world market prices. We therefore consider that ... an 'ordinary' customs duty, that is, a customs duty *sensu stricto*, is to be understood as referring to a customs duty which is not applied on the basis of factors of an exogenous nature.[213]

On appeal, the Appellate Body disagreed with the panel that what distinguishes ordinary customs duties from other duties and charges is that the former are applied on the basis of the value or volume of the imported products, and not on the basis of factors of an exogenous nature.[214] The Appellate Body thus reversed the panel's finding but did not offer much further guidance on the distinction

209 The term '*ordinary* customs duties' (emphasis added) is used in Article II:1(b), first sentence, of the GATT 1994. The panel in *Chile – Price Band System (2002)* used the term 'customs duties *sensu stricto*'.

210 Appellate Body Report, *India – Additional Import Duties (2008)*, para. 151. The Appellate Body also noted that while both 'ordinary customs duties' and 'other duties and charges' relate to duties and charges applied 'on the importation', 'other duties and charges' also relate to duties and charges 'in connection with the importation'. See *ibid.*, para. 157.

211 See also Panel Report, *Peru – Agricultural Products (2015)*, para. 7.408; Panel Report, *Dominican Republic – Safeguard Measures (2012)*, paras. 7.79 and 7.85; and Panel Report, *Dominican Republic – Import and Sale of Cigarettes (2005)*, para. 7.113. The panel in the latter case also referred to the *travaux préparatoires* concerning the *Understanding on the Interpretation of Article II:1 (b) of the GATT 1994*, where it is stated that it would be impossible to draw up an exhaustive list of ODCs since it is always possible for governments to invent new charges. See *ibid.*, para. 7.114.

212 As discussed above, the Appellate Body in *China – Auto Parts (2009)* addressed the question whether the charges at issue in that dispute were a customs duty or an internal charge. The Appellate Body ruled in this respect that what is important in determining whether a charge is a border charge (such as a customs duty) or an internal charge is whether the obligation to pay that charge accrues due to the importation or to an internal event (such as the distribution, sale, use or transportation of the imported product). This usefully distinguishes border charges from internal charges, but is of little help in distinguishing, within the category of border charges, between customs duties *and* other duties and charges.

213 Panel Report, *Chile – Price Band System (2002)*, para. 7.52. See also *ibid.*, para. 7.104.

214 See Appellate Body Report, *Chile – Price Band System (2002)*, para. 278.

between ordinary customs duties and other duties and charges, except that an essential feature of ordinary customs duties is that 'any change in them is discontinuous and unrelated to an underlying scheme or formula'.[215]

In *Dominican Republic – Safeguard Measures (2012)*, the panel concluded that the safeguard measures imposed by Dominican Republic on imports of polypropylene bags and tubular fabric were 'other duties or charges' as they were neither 'ordinary customs duties',[216] nor any of the measures provided for in Article II: 2 of GATT. With regard to what is covered by an ordinary customs duty, the panel noted:

> All in all, using a meaning that seeks to reconcile the texts of the GATT 1994 in the various official languages, we could conclude that the expression 'ordinary customs duties' in Article II:1(b) of the GATT 1994 refers to duties collected at the border which constitute 'customs duties' in the strict sense of the term (stricto sensu) and that this expression does not cover possible extraordinary or exceptional duties collected in customs.[217]

Further, summarising the decision of the Appellate Body in *Chile – Price Band System* (2002), the panel noted:

> In its report in *Chile – Price Band System*, the Appellate Body made it clear that what determines whether 'a duty imposed on an import at the border' constitutes an ordinary customs duty is not the form which that duty takes. Nor is the fact that the duty is calculated on the basis of exogenous factors, such as the interests of consumers or of domestic producers ... a Member may periodically change the rate at which it applies an 'ordinary customs duty', provided it remains below the rate bound in the Member's schedule. This change in the applied rate of duty could be made, for example, through an act of the Member's legislature or executive at any time. However, one essential feature of 'ordinary customs duties' is that any change in them is discontinuous and unrelated to an underlying scheme or formula.[218]

In *Peru – Agricultural Products (2015)*, the panel concluded that 'a Member's measure which corresponds or is similar to any of the measures listed in footnote 1 to Article 4.2 of the Agreement on Agriculture may not correspond to the ordinary customs duty of the Member in question'.[219] Accordingly, it held that the additional duties resulting from Peru's price range system (PRS) being in the nature of variable import levies, or similar to variable import levies fell within the meaning of Article 4.2 of the Agreement on Agriculture, and were therefore not ordinary customs duties.[220]

The panel in *Colombia – Textiles (2016)* found that the compound tariff at issue was an ordinary customs duty, and not an 'other duty or charge' because the compound tariff was similar in nature to the tariff provided for in Colombia's Customs Tariff, and that there was 'no evidence whatsoever that the compound tariff forms part of possible extraordinary or exceptional duties collected in

215 *Ibid.*, para. 233.

216 The panel considered the design and structure of the impugned measures and concluded that the measures are 'extraordinary' or 'exceptional' and not 'ordinary' since they replace the ordinary tariff temporarily and only for imports originating in certain Members. See Panel Report, *Dominican Republic – Safeguard Measures (2012)*, para. 7.86.

217 *Ibid.*, para 7.85. 218 See *ibid.*, para. 7.84.

219 Panel Report, *Peru – Agricultural Products (2015)*, para. 7.423. 220 See *ibid.*

customs or that the compound tariff lacks the essential attributes or qualities of duties collected in customs'.[221]

Examples of 'other duties and charges on imports' identified in GATT/WTO case law are: (1) an import surcharge, i.e. a duty imposed on an imported product in addition to the ordinary customs duty;[222] (2) a security deposit to be made on the importation of goods;[223] (3) a statistical tax imposed to finance the collection of statistical information, with no maximum limit;[224] (4) a customs fee with no maximum limit;[225] (5) a transitional surcharge for economic stabilisation imposed on imported goods;[226] and (6) a foreign exchange fee imposed on imported goods.[227]

3.2 Rule Regarding Other Duties or Charges on Imports

To protect the tariff bindings set forth in the Schedules and to prevent 'circumvention' of the prohibition of Article II:1(b), first sentence, of the GATT 1994, to impose ordinary customs duties in excess of the bindings, WTO law provides for a rule on other duties and charges on imports. With regard to products subject to a tariff binding, Article II:1(b), second sentence, of the GATT 1994 requires that *no* other duties or charges be imposed *in excess of* those: (1) already imposed at the 'date of this Agreement'; or (2) provided for in mandatory legislation in force on that date. However, under the GATT 1947, there was considerable uncertainty and confusion regarding the 'date of this Agreement' and thus regarding the maximum level of other duties or charges on imports that could be imposed.[228] Therefore, the Uruguay Round negotiators agreed on the *Understanding on the Interpretation of Article II:1(b) of the GATT 1994*, commonly referred to as the *Understanding on Article II:1(b)*. This Understanding states, in relevant part:

> In order to ensure transparency of the legal rights and obligations deriving from paragraph 1(b) of Article II, the nature and level of any 'other duties or charges' levied on bound tariff items, as referred to in that provision, shall be recorded in the Schedules of Concessions annexed to GATT 1994 against the tariff item to which they apply.[229]

The Understanding thus requires Members to record in their Schedules all other duties or charges on imports imposed on products subject to a tariff binding.[230]

221 Panel Report, *Colombia – Textiles (2016)*, para. 7.141. See also Panel Report, *Dominican Republic – Safeguard Measures (2012)*, para. 7.85.

222 See e.g. *Korea – Beef (Australia) (1989)*.

223 See e.g. *EEC – Minimum Import Prices (1978)*; and *EEC – Animal Feed Proteins (1978)*.

224 See e.g. *Argentina – Textiles and Apparel (1998)*.

225 See e.g. *United States – Customs User Fee (1988)*. A customs fee is a financial charge imposed for the processing of imported goods by the customs authorities.

226 See e.g. *Dominican Republic – Import and Sale of Cigarettes (2005)*. 227 *Ibid.*

228 See *Analytical Index: Guide to GATT Law and Practice* (WTO, 1995), 84–5.

229 *Understanding on the Interpretation of Article II:1(b) of the GATT 1994* (hereinafter '*Understanding on Article II:1(b)*'), para. 1.

230 Members had to record other duties and charges in their Goods Schedule within six months of the date of the deposition of their Schedule. After six months, the right to record other duties and charges expired.

As noted above, the Uruguay Round Schedules have a special column for 'other duties or charges'.[231] The other duties or charges on imports must be recorded in the Schedules at the levels applying on 15 April 1994 or, for Members which acceded to the WTO, on the date of their accession.[232] The other duties or charges on imports are 'bound' at these levels.[233]

It follows from Article II:1(b), second sentence, and from the Understanding, that Members may: (1) impose only other duties and charges on imports that have been properly recorded in their Schedules; and (2) impose other duties and charges on imports only at a level that does not exceed the level recorded in their Schedules. Other duties and charges not recorded, or in excess of the recorded levels, are prohibited. Note, however, that the inclusion of an other duty or charge in a Member's Goods Schedule does not give rise to a presumption of consistency with other GATT provisions. Such duty or charge is not exempted from an examination of its consistency with other GATT provisions, such as e.g. Article VIII.[234]

In *Chile – Price Band System (2002)*, the panel, having found that the Chilean Price Band System (PBS) duties were not 'ordinary customs duties' but were 'other duties or charges', examined whether these duties were inconsistent with Article II:1(b), second sentence. The panel ruled:

> Pursuant to the Uruguay Round Understanding on the Interpretation of Article II:1(b), such other duties or charges had to be recorded in a newly created column 'other duties and charges' in the Members' Schedules ... Other duties or charges must not exceed the binding in this 'other duties and charges' column of the Schedule. If other duties or charges were not recorded but are nevertheless levied, they are inconsistent with the second sentence of Article II:1(b), in light of the Understanding on the Interpretation of Article II:1(b). We note that Chile did not record its PBS in the 'other duties and charges' column of its Schedule. We therefore find that the Chilean PBS duties are inconsistent with Article II:1(b) of GATT 1994.[235]

In *Dominican Republic – Import and Sale of Cigarettes (2005)*, the panel found that the two 'other duties or charges' at issue in this case, namely the transitional surcharge for economic stabilisation and the foreign exchange fee imposed on imported products, had not been recorded in a legally valid manner in the

231 See above, pp. 437–9.

232 See *Understanding on Article II:1(b)*, para. 2. Note, however, that paragraph 4 of the *Understanding on Article II:1(b)* states: 'Where a tariff item has previously been the subject of a concession, the level of "other duties or charges" recorded in the appropriate Schedule shall not be higher than the level obtaining at the time of the first incorporation of the concession in that Schedule.'

233 Note that paragraph 1 of the *Understanding on Article II:1(b)* states that the recording in the Schedules does not change the legal character of the 'other duties or charges' and that paragraphs 4 and 5 provide that – with certain restrictions in time – the Members can challenge the GATT consistency of recorded 'other duties or charges'. See Panel Report, *Argentina – Textiles and Apparel (1998)*, para. 6.81.

234 See *ibid.*, paras. 6.81–6.83.

235 Panel Report, *Chile – Price Band System (2002)*, paras. 7.105 and 7.107–7.108. On appeal, the Appellate Body found that the panel's finding on Article II:1(b), second sentence, related to a claim that had not been made, and this finding was therefore in violation of Article 11 of the DSU. As a result, the Appellate Body reversed the finding.

Schedule of Concessions of the Dominican Republic.[236] With regard to the transitional surcharge for economic stabilisation, the panel came to the following conclusion:

> For all legal and practical purposes, what was notified by the Dominican Republic in document G/SP/3 is equivalent to 'zero' in the Schedule. The Panel finds that the surcharge as an 'other duty or charge' measure is applied in excess of the level 'zero' pursuant to the Schedule. Therefore, the surcharge measure is inconsistent with Article II:1(b) of the GATT 1994.[237]

With regard to the foreign exchange fee, the panel came to the same conclusion.[238]

On the legal effects of the scheduling of other duties or charges on imports, note that, in *Argentina – Textiles and Apparel (1998)*, Argentina argued that, since its 3 per cent statistical tax was included in its Schedule of Concessions (Schedule LXIV), there was no violation of Article II:1(b) of the GATT 1994. The panel disagreed with Argentina, and noted that:

> [t]he provisions of the WTO Understanding on the Interpretation of Article II:1(b) of GATT 1994, dealing with 'other duties and charges', make clear that including a charge in a schedule of concessions in no way immunizes that charge from challenge as a violation of an applicable GATT rule.[239]

In *Peru – Agricultural Products (2015)*, the panel found that Peru did not record in its Schedule of Concessions any duty corresponding to 'other duties or charges' within the six months following the date on which the instrument was deposited. Having concluded that the additional duties resulting from Peru's price range system were 'other duties or charges ... imposed on or in connection with the importation' and based on evidence of application of such duties by Peru, the panel found that Peru acted inconsistently with its obligations under the second sentence of Article II:1(b) of the GATT 1994.[240]

To date, WTO Members have been found to have acted inconsistently with the obligations under Article II:1(b), second sentence of the GATT 1994 in three disputes.[241]

3.3 Measures Exempted from the Rule

There are a number of 'other duties and charges on imports' that are exempted from the rule that Members may not impose such duties or charges unless recorded and not in excess of the recorded level. Pursuant to Article II:2 of the

236 The panel ruled that the recording of the Selective Consumption Tax, i.e. an internal tax, could not be used as legal basis to justify the current transitional surcharge or the foreign exchange fee. See Panel Report, *Dominican Republic – Import and Sale of Cigarettes (2005)*, para. 7.86.

237 *Ibid.*, para. 7.89. 238 See *ibid.*, para. 7.121.

239 Panel Report, *Argentina – Textiles and Apparel (1998)*, para. 6.81. See also above, p. 446.

240 Panel Report, *Peru – Agricultural Products (2015)*, para. 7.432. On appeal, the finding of the panel that Peru acted inconsistently with its obligations under Article II:1(b), second sentence were upheld by the Appellate Body. See Appellate Body Report, *Peru – Agricultural Products (2015)*, para. 5.121.

241 See *Argentina – Textiles and Apparel (1998); Dominican Republic – Import and Sale of Cigarettes (2005)*; and *Peru – Agricultural Products (2015)*. With regard to *Chile – Price Band System (2002)*. With regard to *India – Additional Import Duties (2008)*, the Appellate Body found that the panel erred in its interpretation of Article II:1 (b), second sentence, and was unable to complete the legal analysis.

GATT 1994, Members may – despite their obligation under Article II:1(b), second sentence – impose on an imported product: (1) a financial charge equivalent to an internal tax on the like domestic product imposed consistently with Article III:2 of the GATT 1994 (border tax adjustment) (see Article II:2(a));[242] (2) WTO-consistent anti-dumping or countervailing duties (see Article II:2(b)); or (3) fees or other charges 'commensurate' with, i.e. matching, the cost of the services rendered (see Article II:2(c)).[243] In *India – Additional Import Duties (2008)*, the Appellate Body ruled with regard to Article II:2(a) that:

> Article II:2(a), subject to the conditions stated therein, *exempts* a charge from the coverage of Article II:1(b).[244]

In the same vein, but with regard to Article II:2(b), in *US – Zeroing (Japan) – (Article 21.5 – Japan) (2009)*, the Appellate Body upheld the panel's approach to Article II:2(b) as providing a *safe harbour* to Article II:1 to the extent that the anti-dumping duties concerned were applied in a WTO-consistent manner.[245]

Most case law on Article II:2 relates to Article II:2(c). The requirement set out in this provision, namely that the fees or other charges concerned must be commensurate with the cost of the services, is also reflected in Article VIII:1(a) of the GATT 1994. The latter provision requires that:

> All fees and charges of whatever character (other than import or export duties and other than taxes within the purview of Article III) imposed by [Members] on or in connection with importation or exportation shall be limited in amount to the approximate cost of services rendered and shall not represent an indirect protection to domestic products or a taxation of imports or exports for fiscal purposes.[246]

The fees and charges for services rendered within the meaning of Article II:2(c) and Article VIII:1(a) include, pursuant to Article VIII:4, fees and charges relating to: (1) consular transactions, such as consular invoices and certificates; (2) quantitative restrictions; (3) licensing; (4) exchange control; (5) statistical services; (6) documents, documentation and certification; (7) analysis and inspection; and (8) quarantine, sanitation and fumigation. With respect to the concept of 'services'

242 See Appellate Body Report, *India – Additional Import Duties (2008)*, paras. 170, 172 and 180. On the concept of 'border tax adjustment', see above, p. 384. On the requirements of Article III:2 of the GATT 1994, see above, pp. 351–76.

243 The three instances identified in Article II:2, in which the obligations set out in Article II:1 do not apply, constitute a closed, i.e. exhaustive, list. See Appellate Body Report, *Colombia – Textiles (2016)*, para. 5.36.

244 Appellate Body Report, *India – Additional Import Duties (2008)*, para. 153. Emphasis added. Note that the Appellate Body found that, where there is a reasonable basis to understand that the challenged measure may not result in a violation of Article II:1(b) because it satisfies the requirements of Article II:2(a), then the complaining party bears some burden of establishing that the conditions of Article II:2(a) are not met. See *ibid.*, para. 192.

245 See Appellate Body Report, *US – Zeroing (Japan) – (Article 21.5 – Japan) (2009)*, para. 209.

246 Note that there is a slight difference in wording between the two 'cost of services' limitations stated in Articles II:2(c) and VIII:1(a), i.e. 'commensurate with the cost of services rendered' and 'limited in amount to the approximate cost of services rendered'. However, the panel in *US – Customs User Fee (1988)*, after reviewing both the drafting history and the subsequent application of these provisions, concluded that no difference of meaning had been intended.

used in this context, the panel in *US – Customs User Fee (1988)* stated, not without wit:

> Granted that some government regulatory activities can be considered as 'services' in an economic sense when they endow goods with safety or quality characteristics deemed necessary for commerce, most of the activities that governments perform in connection with the importation process do not meet that definition. They are not desired by the importers who are subject to them. Nor do they add value to the goods in any commercial sense. Whatever governments may choose to call them, fees for such government regulatory activities are, in the Panel's view, simply taxes on imports. It must be presumed, therefore, that the drafters meant the term 'services' to be used in a more artful political sense, i.e. government activities closely enough connected to the processes of customs entry that they might, with no more than the customary artistic licence accorded to taxing authorities, be called a 'service' to the importer in question.[247]

In *US – Customs User Fee (1988)*, the financial charge at issue was a merchandise-processing fee, in the form of an *ad valorem* charge without upper limits. The complainants, the European Communities and Canada, challenged the GATT consistency of an *ad valorem* charge without upper limit. The panel in this case noted that the requirement of Article VIII:1(a) that a fee or charge be 'limited in amount to the approximate cost of services rendered' is in fact a dual requirement: (1) the fee or charge in question must first involve a 'service' rendered; and (2) the level of the charge must not exceed the approximate cost of that service.[248] With respect to the first element of this dual requirement, the panel in *Argentina – Textiles and Apparel (1998)* further clarified that the fee or charge in question must involve a 'service' rendered to the *individual* importer in question.[249] Services rendered to foreign trade operators in general and foreign trade as an activity *per se* would fail to meet this first element of the dual requirement.[250] With respect to the second element of the dual requirement, the panel in *US – Customs User Fee (1988)* stated that:

> the term 'cost of services rendered' in Articles II:2(c) and VIII:1(a) must be interpreted to refer to the cost of the customs processing for the individual entry in question and accordingly that the *ad valorem* structure of the United States merchandise processing fee was inconsistent with the obligations of Articles II:2(c) and VIII:1(a) to the extent that it caused fees to be levied in excess of such costs.[251]

In *Argentina – Textiles and Apparel (1998)*, the panel found that Argentina's 3 per cent *ad valorem* statistical tax on imports was inconsistent with Article VIII:1(a) of the GATT 1994 'to the extent it results in charges being levied in excess of the approximate costs of the services rendered'.[252] As the panel explained, an *ad valorem* charge with no maximum limit, as was the case with Argentina's statistical tax, by its very nature, is not 'limited in amount to the approximate

247 Panel Report, *US – Customs User Fee (1988)*, para. 77.

248 See *ibid.*, para. 69. See also Panel Report, *Argentina – Textiles and Apparel (1998)*, para. 6.74; and Panel Report, *US – Certain EC Products (2001)*, para. 6.69.

249 See Panel Report, *US – Customs User Fee (1988)*, para. 80.

250 See Panel Report, *Argentina – Textiles and Apparel (1998)*, para. 6.74.

251 Panel Report, *US – Customs User Fee (1988)*, para. 86. Underlining in the original deleted.

252 Panel Report, *Argentina – Textiles and Apparel (1998)*, para. 6.80.

cost of services rendered'. For example, high-price items necessarily will bear a much higher tax burden than low-price goods, yet the service accorded to both is essentially the same. An unlimited *ad valorem* charge on imported goods violates the provisions of Article VIII because such a charge cannot be related to the cost of the service rendered.[253]

Note that the panel in *Argentina – Textiles and Apparel (1998)* also found that the statistical tax was inconsistent with Article VIII:1(a) because this tax – according to Argentina's own admission – was imposed for 'fiscal purposes', which is explicitly prohibited under Article VIII:1(a).

In Article VIII:1(b) of the GATT 1994 Members explicitly 'recognize the need for reducing the number and diversity' of Article VIII:1(a) fees and charges.

Article 6 of the *Agreement on Trade Facilitation*, entitled 'Disciplines on Fees and Charges imposed on or in Connection with Importation and Exportation' also provides rules on other charges and duties. However, these rules add little, if anything, to the rules that already existed under the GATT 1994. Note that Article 6.1(2) of the *Agreement on Trade Facilitation* requires Members to publish information on fees and charges, including information on the amount of the fees and charges, the reason for such fees and charges, the responsible authority and when and how payment is to be made.[254] Also note that Article 6.2(ii) states that fees and charges for customs processing are not required to be linked to a specific import or export operation provided they are levied for services that are closely connected to the customs processing of goods. Article 6.3 provides for a few 'new' rules regarding 'penalties' for breach of a Member's customs rules. Most notable are: (1) the requirement to avoid conflicts of interest in the assessment and collection of penalties; and (2) the requirement to explain in writing the nature of the breach and the legal basis for the penalty imposed.

4 CUSTOMS DUTIES AND OTHER DUTIES AND CHARGES ON EXPORTS

As noted above, tariff barriers to trade in goods apply not only to imports. While much less common than customs duties and other duties and charges on imports, Members also impose customs duties and other duties and charges on exports, often in brief referred to as 'export duties'.[255] This section discusses in turn: (1) the definition and purpose of export duties; and (2) WTO rules applicable to export duties.

253 *Ibid.*, para. 6.75.

254 It could be argued that this obligation already exists under Article X:1 of the GATT 1994.

255 Unlike for customs duties and other duties and charges on imports, there is no need to distinguish between customs duties and other duties and charges on exports, since there is no difference in the rules that apply to customs duties on exports on the one hand and other duties and charges on exports on the other hand.

4.1 Definition and Purpose

Generally speaking, an export duty, be it a customs duty or another duty or charge on exports, is a financial charge or tax on exported products, due because of their exportation. Market exit of the products concerned is conditional upon the payment of the export duty. Like import duties, export duties have a long history, but, unlike the former, the latter largely fell into disuse in the mid-nineteenth century.[256] While there have always been some countries that applied export duties on some products, these 'sporadic' export duties were considered to be much less problematic to international trade than the 'omnipresent' import duties. As noted below, this was, and still is, clearly reflected in the GATT/WTO rules on export duties, or rather the paucity of these rules. Possibly because of this paucity of rules, there has, however, been a proliferation of the use of export duties in recent years. At present, export duties are most commonly imposed on raw materials and agricultural products, which are in short supply on the world market.

Like customs duties and other duties and charges on imports, export duties serve two main purposes. First, export duties are a source of revenue for governments. Some mineral-rich developing-country Members depend on export duties for much of their revenue. Second, export duties are used to protect and/or promote domestic industries. Some Members consider export duties to act as 'indirect subsidies' to domestic downstream industries.[257] By imposing export duties, exportation is commercially less attractive and goods are less likely to be exported, thus reserving them for use by domestic downstream industries. For example, by imposing an export duty on forest products, a Member will protect and/or promote the domestic milling, furniture and paper industries. An export duty will stem the exportation of forest products and ensure the availability of forest products for domestic downstream industries, often at prices lower than they would be if exportation were not impeded. In other words, export duties may give the domestic downstream industries a cost advantage in comparison with foreign downstream industries.[258] In some cases, export duties on agricultural products, in particular, may also be used to safeguard, in times of international scarcity, domestic supply of food products at affordable prices. In the context of its WTO accession negotiations, with regard to the purpose pursued by its export duties, Russia explained as follows:

> [I]n 1998 export duties had been imposed on raw materials and semi-finished goods, mainly for fiscal purposes, and now ranged from 3 to 50 per cent, with a few exceptions where

256 In the seventeenth century, England imposed export duty on more than 200 goods, but in 1842 all export duties were abolished. France abolished export duties in 1857 and Prussia in 1865. See www.britannica.com/EBchecked/topic/583535/tariff#ref592273.

257 *Report of the Working Party on the Accession of Russia*, WT/ACC/RUS/70, dated 17 November 2011, para. 629.

258 In situations in which a country produces a substantial share of the world output of a good (for example, a rare mineral), that country can, by imposing an export duty, push up the world price of that good. This would disadvantage foreign downstream industries in comparison to the domestic downstream industries, which would have access to this good at a lower price.

higher export duties were applied. In very few cases (oil seeds, raw hides and skins), export duties had been imposed to ensure greater availability of raw materials for the domestic industry. Export duties on non-ferrous and ferrous metals waste and scrap (and those in the guise of other products, e.g. used axle-boxes) had been imposed to address problems of environmental protection.[259]

4.2 Rules Applicable on Export Duties

Neither the GATT 1994 nor any of the other multilateral agreements on trade in goods prohibit or specifically regulate export duties, be it customs duties or other duties and charges on exports. While the WTO agreements do not *specifically* regulate export duties, there are some general GATT obligations which also apply to export duties. This is the case, for example, for Article I:1 of the GATT 1994, which sets out the MFN treatment obligation.[260] In short, if a Member imposes an export duty on a product exported to another Member, it must impose the same export duty on all like products exported to all other Members.

As discussed above, the GATT 1994 does not prohibit customs duties on imports but encourages negotiations on the lowering of these duties and protects the results of these negotiations. Pursuant to Articles II:1(a) and II:1(b), first sentence, of the GATT 1994, a Member is not allowed to impose customs duties on imports of a product above the relevant binding, i.e. the maximum level it has agreed on.[261] Some Members have agreed to bindings with regard to their export duties and have included these bindings in their Goods Schedule.[262] It is the subject of debate whether Article II:1(a) also applies to, and thus provides protection for, bindings regarding customs duties on exports. It has been observed that Article II:1(a) states:

> Each [Member] shall accord *to the commerce* of the other [Members] treatment no less favourable than that provided for in the appropriate Part of the appropriate Schedule annexed to this Agreement.[263]

It has been argued that the term 'commerce' in Article II:1(a) refers to both imports and exports. What is clear is that the obligation set out in Article II:1(b), first sentence, does not apply to customs duties on exports as it explicitly refers to the 'importation' of products. For the same reason, Article II:1(b), second sentence, which concerns other duties and charges, also does not apply to export duties.

259 *Report of the Working Party on the Accession of Russia*, WT/ACC/RUS/70, dated 17 November 2011, para. 626. See also *ibid.*, paras. 631–3. Russia also indicated that, over the last few years, the overall number of products subject to export duties had been reduced from 1,200 to 310 tariff lines. See *ibid.*, para. 627.

260 See above, p. 307. See also Articles VII, VIII and XVII of the GATT 1994.

261 See above, p. 443.

262 Part I, Section 2, of the Goods Schedule of Australia, for example, provides in the 'Notes' column with regard to eleven tariff lines that 'there shall be no export duty on this product'. See Schedule I, annexed to the *Marrakesh Protocol* of the GATT 1994, www.wto.org/english/tratop_e/schedules_e/goods_schedules_table_e.htm.

263 Emphasis added. Note also that Article XXVIII *bis* of the GATT 1994, which calls for negotiations on the reduction of customs duties, expressly refers to customs duties on imports *and* exports.

While the GATT 1994 or the other multilateral agreements on trade in goods do not prohibit or specifically regulate export duties, some WTO accession protocols do. The best-known example of such accession protocol is the 2001 *Protocol on the Accession of the People's Republic of China.*[264] Paragraph 11.3 of China's Accession Protocol contains specific obligations with respect to export duties, and provides that:

> China shall *eliminate* all taxes and charges applied to exports unless specifically provided for in Annex 6 of this Protocol or applied in conformity with the provisions of Article VIII of the GATT 1994.[265]

Annex 6 to China's Accession Protocol, entitled 'Products Subject to Export Duty', lists eighty-four different products, such as live eels fry, bones and horn-cores, yellow phosphorus, alloy pig iron, copper alloys and unwrought aluminium. The Note to Annex 6 states that:

> China confirmed that the tariff levels included in this Annex are *maximum levels* which will not be exceeded.[266]

In *China – Raw Materials (2012)*, the question arose whether China's export duties on bauxite, coke, fluorspar, magnesium, manganese, silicon metal, zinc and yellow phosphorus were inconsistent with paragraph 11.3 of China's Accession Protocol. The panel found that, with the exception of yellow phosphorus, none of these raw materials is listed in Annex 6 to China's Accession Protocol and that China therefore acted inconsistently with paragraph 11.3 of the Accession Protocol when it imposed export duties on these raw materials.[267] With regard to yellow phosphorus, which is included in the list of Annex 6, the complainants contended that China imposed a 'special' export duty of 50 per cent *ad valorem* on yellow phosphorus pursuant to the 2009 Tariff Implementation Program, while it had committed, pursuant to paragraph 11.3 of and Annex 6 to its Accession Protocol, not to exceed a maximum export duty of 20 per cent on yellow phosphorus. The panel, however, agreed with China that China had removed the 'special' export duty rate as of 1 July 2009, before the date of the panel's establishment and therefore did not make any finding on the WTO consistency of this measure.[268]

264 See WT/L/432, dated 23 November 2001.

265 Emphasis added.

266 Emphasis added. The Note to Annex 6 also states: 'China confirmed furthermore that it would not increase the presently applied rates, except under exceptional circumstances. If such circumstances occurred, China would consult with affected members prior to increasing applied tariffs with a view to finding a mutually acceptable solution.'

267 See Panel Reports, *China – Raw Materials (2012)*, para. 7.77 (for bauxite), para. 7.81 (for coke), para. 7.85 (for fluorspar), para. 7.89 (for magnesium), para. 7.93 (for manganese), para. 7.98 (for silicon metal) and para. 7.101 (for zinc). Note that China did not invoke Article VIII of the GATT 1994 in justification of the export duties at issue. However, with regard to most of the export duties, China did invoke Articles XX(b) or XX(g) of the GATT 1994 in justification of the inconsistency with paragraph 11.3 of its Accession Protocol. As discussed in Chapter 8, the panel found – as upheld by the Appellate Body – that Article XX did not apply in the case at hand.

268 See Panel Reports, *China – Raw Materials (2012)*, para. 7.71.

The issue whether export duties imposed by China were inconsistent with paragraph 11.3 of China's Accession Protocol, arose again in *China – Rare Earths (2014)*. This dispute concerned *inter alia* export duties on various forms of rare earths, tungsten and molybdenum. These metals are used in devices such as computer memory, mobile phones and rechargeable batteries, and global demand for them has grown exponentially in the last twenty years. In line with the ruling of the panel in *China – Raw Materials (2012)*, the panel in *China – Rare Earths (2014)* found that the China export duties at issue were inconsistent with paragraph 11.3 of China's Accession Protocol.[269]

China's Accession Protocol is not the only accession protocol, which provides for 'WTO-plus' obligations with regard to export duties.[270] As already noted, Russia imposed export duties on a significant number of goods, including minerals, petrochemicals, natural gas, raw hides and skins, wood, ferrous and non-ferrous metals and scrap.[271] The 2011 *Protocol on the Accession of the Russian Federation* and, in particular, the Schedule of Concessions and Commitments on Goods of the Russian Federation annexed to the Protocol, provides that the goods described in 'Part V' of that Schedule are, subject to the relevant terms, conditions or qualifications, *exempt from export duties in excess* of those set forth therein.[272] During its accession negotiations, Russia emphasised that export duties were permitted under WTO rules, and that many Members applied export duties as an instrument of trade policy.[273] However, as part of the deal on its accession to the WTO, Russia was required to agree on maximum levels for its export duties. Note that the obligation with regard to export duties undertaken by Russia is less far-reaching than the obligation undertaken by China.

In the context of the Doha Round negotiations, the European Union has advocated for specific WTO rules on export duties confirming and operationalising the basic GATT disciplines (and exceptions), while allowing flexibility to small developing-country Members and least-developed-country Members.[274] However, to date, it has been unsuccessful in garnering sufficient support for such rules on export duties.

269 See Panel Report, *China – Rare Earths (2014)*, para. 7.48. As in *China – Raw Materials (2012)*, China invoked Article XX(b) of the GATT 1994 in justification of the inconsistency with paragraph 11.3 of its Accession Protocol. As discussed in Chapter 8, the panel found – as upheld by the Appellate Body – that Article XX did not apply in the case at hand.

270 See with regard to Ukraine, Report of the Working Party on the Accession of Ukraine, WT/ACC/UKR/152, 25 January 2008, para. 240; with regard to Montenegro, Report of the Working Party on the Accession of Montenegro, WT/ACC/CGR/38, WT/MIN(11)/7, 5 December 2011, para. 132; with regard to Tajikistan, Report of the Working Party on the Accession of Tajikistan, WT/ACC/TJK/30, 6 November 2012, para. 169; with regard to Kazakhstan, Report of the Working Party on the Accession of Kazakhstan, WT/ACC/KAZ/93, 23 June 2015, para. 540.

271 For a complete list of the export duties applied by Russia, see *Report of the Working Party on the Accession of Russia*, WT/ACC/RUS/70, dated 17 November 2011, Table 32.

272 See Annex 1 to WT/L/839, dated 17 December 2011, which contains Russia's Goods Schedule, circulated as WT/ACC/RUS/70/Add.1.

273 *Report of the Working Party on the Accession of Russia*, WT/ACC/RUS/70, dated 17 November 2011, para. 635.

274 See Negotiating Group on Market Access, Communication from the European Communities, *Market Access for Non-Agricultural Products, Revised Submission on Export Taxes*, TN/MA/W/101, dated 17 January 2008.

5 SUMMARY

Market access for goods and services from other countries can be, and frequently is, impeded or restricted in various ways. There are two main categories of barriers to market access: (1) tariff barriers; and (2) non-tariff barriers. This chapter deals with tariff barriers. The category of tariff barriers includes: (1) customs duties on imports; (2) other duties and charges on imports; and (3) export duties (i.e. customs duties and other duties and charges on exports). Different rules apply to these different types of tariff barrier.

A customs duty or tariff on imports is a financial charge or tax on imported goods, due because of their importation. Market access for the goods concerned is conditional upon the payment of the customs duty. Customs duties are *ad valorem* specific, compound, mixed or otherwise. *Ad valorem* customs duties are by far the most common type of customs duties. The customs duties or tariffs, which are due on importation, are set out in a country's national customs tariff. Most national customs tariffs follow or reflect the structure set out in the Harmonized Commodity Description and Coding System, usually referred to as the 'Harmonized System' or 'HS'.

WTO law, and in particular the GATT 1994, does not prohibit the imposition of customs duties on imports. Customs duties, unlike quantitative restrictions discussed in Chapter 7, represent an instrument of protection against imports generally allowed by the GATT 1994. Article XXVIII *bis* of the GATT 1994 does, however, call upon WTO Members to negotiate the reduction of customs duties. The eight GATT Rounds of trade negotiations have been very successful in reducing customs duties. Nevertheless, customs duties remain a significant barrier in international trade, and further negotiations on the reduction of tariffs are therefore necessary. The basic principles and rules governing tariff negotiations are: (1) the principle of reciprocity and mutual advantage; and (2) the most-favoured-nation (MFN) treatment obligation. The principle of reciprocity does not apply in full to tariff negotiations between developed- and developing-country Members. Members can adopt different approaches, or modalities, to tariff negotiations, including the product-by-product approach, the formula approach (be it the linear reduction approach or the non-linear reduction approach), the sectoral approach, or a combination of these approaches.

The results of tariff negotiations are referred to as 'tariff concessions' or 'tariff bindings'. A tariff concession, or tariff binding, is a commitment not to raise the customs duty on a certain product above an agreed level. The tariff concessions or bindings made by a Member are set out in that Member's Schedule of Concessions (also referred to as a Goods Schedule). The Schedules of Concessions resulting from the Uruguay Round negotiations are all annexed to the *Marrakesh Protocol* to the GATT 1994 and are an integral part thereof. Therefore, the tariff schedules and tariff concessions must be interpreted in accordance with the rules of interpretation set out in Article 31 and 32 of the *Vienna Convention on the Law of Treaties*.

Article II:1(a) of the GATT 1994 provides that Members shall accord to products imported from other Members *treatment no less favourable* than that provided for in their Schedules. Article II:1(b), first sentence, of the GATT 1994 provides that products described in Part I of the Schedule of any Member shall, on importation, be *exempt from ordinary customs duties in excess of* those set out in the Schedule. This means that products may not be subjected to customs duties above the tariff concessions or bindings. Note, however, that Article XXVIII of the GATT 1994 provides a procedure for the modification or withdrawal of the agreed tariff concessions.

In addition to the rules to protect tariff concessions, WTO law also provides for some rules on the manner in which customs duties must be imposed. The imposition of customs duties may require three determinations to be made: (1) the determination of the proper classification of the imported good; (2) the determination of the customs value of the imported good; and (3) the determination of the origin of the imported good. The WTO agreements do not specifically address the issue of customs classification. However, in classifying products for customs purposes, Members have of course to consider their general obligations under the WTO agreements, such as the MFN treatment obligation. *Specific* rules on classification can be found in the *HS Convention*, to which most WTO Members are a party.

Unlike for customs classification, the *WTO Agreement* provides for rules on customs valuation. These rules are set out in: Article VII of the GATT 1994; the Note *Ad* Article VII; and the WTO *Customs Valuation Agreement*. The primary basis for the customs value is the 'transaction value' of the imported goods, i.e. the price actually paid or payable for the goods. This price is normally shown in the invoice, contract or purchase order, albeit that a number of adjustments usually have to be made. If the customs value cannot be established in this manner, it must be established pursuant to the alternative methods set out in the *Customs Valuation Agreement*.

The GATT 1994 provides no specific disciplines on rules of origin. However, the negotiators during the Uruguay Round recognised the need for multilateral disciplines on rules of origin in order to prevent these rules from being a source of uncertainty and unpredictability in international trade. The consensus on the need for such disciplines resulted in the WTO *Agreement on Rules of Origin*. With respect to *non-preferential* rules of origin, the *Agreement on Rules of Origin* provides for a work programme on the harmonisation of these rules. While the completion of the work programme is long overdue, Members have not yet been able to reach agreement on harmonised rules of origin. Until the successful completion of this work programme, Article 2 of the *Agreement on Rules of Origin* contains a list of multilateral disciplines on the application and administration of rules of origin applicable during the current 'transition period'. After harmonised rules of origin have been agreed on, these disciplines will continue to apply. With respect to *preferential* rules of origin, Annex 2 to the *Agreement on Rules of Origin* provides for a more modest list of multilateral disciplines on the application and administration of rules of origin.

In addition to 'ordinary' customs duties on imports, tariff barriers on imports can also take the form of other duties and charges on imports. 'Other duties and charges on imports' are financial charges or taxes, *other than* ordinary customs duties, which are levied on imported products and are due because of their importation. Pursuant to Article II:1(b), second sentence, of the GATT 1994 and the *Understanding on Article II:1(b)*, Members may: (1) impose only other duties and charges on imports that have been properly recorded in their Schedules; and (2) impose other duties and charges on imports only at a level that does not exceed the level recorded in their Schedules. There are, however, a number of 'other duties and charges on imports' that are *exempted* from the rule that Members may not impose such duties or charges unless recorded and not in excess of the recorded level. Pursuant to Article II:2 of the GATT 1994, Members may – in spite of their obligation under Article II:1(b), second sentence – impose on imported products: (1) a financial charge equivalent to an internal tax on the like domestic product imposed consistently with Article III:2 of the GATT 1994 (border tax adjustment); (2) WTO-consistent anti-dumping or countervailing duties; or (3) fees or other charges 'commensurate' with, i.e. matching, the cost of the services rendered.

Tariff barriers to trade in goods apply not only to imports. While much less common than customs duties and other duties and charges on imports, Members also impose export duties. An export duty, be it a customs duty or another duty or charge on exports, is a financial charge or tax on exported products, due because of their exportation. Market exit of the products concerned is conditional upon the payment of the export duty. Neither the GATT 1994 nor any of the other multilateral agreements on trade in goods prohibits or specifically regulates export duties. Note that some WTO accession protocols, including China's Accession Protocol (2001) and Russia's Accession Protocol (2011) do prohibit or specifically regulate export duties.

FURTHER READINGS

A. Tesafayesus, 'Liberalization Agreements in the GATT/WTO and the Terms-of-Trade Externality Theory: Evidence from Three Developing Countries', USPTO Economic Working Paper No. 2016-3, June 2016.

M. Daly, 'Is the WTO a World Tax Organization? A Primer on WTO Rules for Tax Policymakers', Fiscal Affairs Department, International Monetary Fund, March 2016.

D. Laborde and W. Martin, 'Formulas for Failure? Were the Doha Tariff Formulas Too Ambitious for Success?', *World Trade Review*, 2015, 14(1), 45–65.

A. Osnago, R. Piermartini and N. Rocha, 'Trade Policy Uncertainty as Barrier to Trade', WTO Working Paper ERSD-2015–05, WTO.

T. Cottier, O. Nartova and A. Shingal, 'The Potential of Tariff Policy for Climate Change Mitigation: Legal and Economic Analysis', *Journal of World Trade*, 2014, 48(5), 1007–37.

T. Yamaoka, 'Why Are Customs Classification Issues Adjudicated at the WTO?: Structural and Possible Solutions', *Global Trade and Customs Journal*, 2014, 9(5), 184–204.

S. Peng, 'Renegotiate the WTO "Schedules of Commitments"?: Technological Development and Treaty Interpretation', *Cornell International Law Journal*, 2012, 45(2), 403–30.

P. Klein-Bernard and J. A. Huerta-Goldman, 'The Cushioned Negotiation: The Case of WTO's Industrial Tariff Liberalization', *Journal of World Trade*, 2012, 46(4), 847–78.

O. Ralph, 'A "New Trade" Theory of GATT/WTO Negotiations', *Journal of Political Economy*, 2011, 119(1), 122–52.

L. Bartels and C. Häberli, 'Binding Tariff Preferences for Developing Countries under Article II GATT', *Journal of International Economic Law*, 2010, 13(4), 969–95.

J. Pauwelyn, '*Rien ne va plus?* Distinguishing Domestic Regulation from Market Access in GATT and GATS', *World Trade Review*, 2005, 4(2), 131–70.

Non-Tariff Barriers

CONTENTS

1 INTRODUCTION

As mentioned in Chapter 6, not only tariff barriers but also a wide range of non-tariff barriers restrict trade.[1] While tariff barriers were systematically reduced since the late 1940s as a result of successive rounds of tariff negotiations, non-tariff barriers have in recent decades gradually become an ever more prominent instrument of protection. The term 'non-tariff barrier' is not defined in WTO law, but this important residual category of barriers to trade can be understood to include all government imposed and sponsored actions or omissions that act as prohibitions or restrictions on trade, other than ordinary customs duties and other duties and charges on imports and exports.[2]

Unlike tariff barriers, non-tariff barriers not only affect trade in goods but also trade in services.[3]

This chapter deals in turn with: (1) quantitative restrictions on trade in goods; (2) 'other non-tariff barriers' on trade in goods; (3) market access barriers to trade in services; and (4) other barriers to trade in services. Note, however, that this chapter does not deal with two specific types of 'other non-tariff barriers' to trade in goods, namely, technical barriers to trade and sanitary and phytosanitary measures. Due to their importance and detailed nature, the rules on these 'other non-tariff barriers' are discussed, separately, in Chapters 13 and 14 respectively.[4] While non-tariff barriers have become a prominent instrument of protection, they often also serve important public policy objectives, such as public health, consumer safety and environmental protection. To the extent that they do so, their elimination or liberalisation may not be desirable at all. That is the case in particular, but not only, for the 'other non-tariff barriers' discussed in Chapters 13 and 14. WTO law regulates these other non-tariff barriers with a view to allowing their use but minimising discrimination and their adverse impact on trade.

1 In this book, the term 'non-tariff barrier' (NTB) encompasses the term 'non-tariff measure' (NTM), a term in vogue and referred to in the title of the WTO's World Trade Report 2012, *Trade and Public Policies: A Closer Look at Non-Tariff Measures in the 21st Century* (WTO, 2012). However, the term 'non-tariff barrier' is broader than the term 'non-tariff measure' as it also includes barriers to trade other than measures, such as the lack of transparency. See below, pp. 499–503.

2 See also Roy Santana and Lee Ann Jackson, 'Identifying Non-Tariff Barriers: Evolution of Multilateral Instruments and Evidence from the Disputes (1948–2011)', *World Trade Review*, 2012, 465.

3 On tariff barriers to trade in services, see above, p. 416. As discussed, tariff barriers to trade in services do not currently exist, but the debate, and the current WTO moratorium, on the 'bit tax', i.e. a tax imposed 'at the border' on electronic communications containing services outputs, shows that tariff barriers *can* exist for trade in services.

4 See below, pp. 893, 894 and 935–7. Note also that this chapter does not deal with non-tariff barriers to trade resulting from the lack of effective protection of intellectual property rights. The WTO rules addressing these barriers, i.e. the WTO rules ensuring a minimum level of protection and enforcement of intellectual property rights, are dealt with in Chapter 15. See below, p. 1042.

2 QUANTITATIVE RESTRICTIONS ON TRADE IN GOODS

The archetypical non-tariff barrier to trade is a quantitative restriction on trade in goods. This section discusses: (1) the definition and types of quantitative restriction on trade in goods; (2) the rules on quantitative restrictions; and (3) the administration of quantitative restrictions.[5]

2.1 Definition and Types

A quantitative restriction on trade in goods, also referred to as a 'QR', is a measure that *limits the quantity* of a product that may be imported or exported. A typical example of a quantitative restriction is a measure allowing the importation of a maximum of 1,000 tonnes of cocoa powder a year or a measure allowing the importation of a maximum of 450 tractors a year. While usually based on the number of units, weight or volume, quantitative restrictions may also be based on value, for example a limit on the importation of flowers to the value of €12 million per year.

There are different types of quantitative restriction: (1) a *prohibition*, or ban, on the importation or exportation of a product; such a prohibition may be absolute or conditional, i.e. only applicable when certain defined conditions are *not* fulfilled; (2) an import or export *quota*, i.e. a measure, as the examples given above, indicating the quantity that may be imported or exported; a quota can be a global quota, a global quota allocated among countries or a bilateral quota; (3) import or export *licensing*, as further discussed below;[6] and (4) *other* quantitative restrictions.[7] For an illustrative list of quantitative restrictions, refer to the 2012 WTO *Decision on Notification Procedures for Quantitative Restrictions*, also referred to as the 'QR Decision'.[8]

Confusingly perhaps, a tariff (rate) quota, or 'TRQ', is *not* a quota in the strict sense of the term; it is *not* a quantitative restriction.[9] A tariff quota is a quantity, which can be imported at a certain duty. The panel in *US – Line Pipe (2002)* stated that a tariff quota involves the 'application of a higher tariff rate to imported goods after a specific quantity of the item has entered the country at a lower prevailing rate'.[10] Any quantity above the quota is subject to a higher duty.[11]

5 This section concludes with a short note on special and differential treatment regarding quantitative restrictions on trade in goods.

6 See below, pp. 496–8.

7 On the scope of the subcategory of 'other quantitative restrictions', see below, pp. 498–517.

8 See Council for Trade in Goods, *Decision on Notification Procedures for Quantitative Restrictions*, adopted on 22 June 2012, G/L/59/Rev.1, dated 3 July 2012, Annex 2.

9 See Panel Report, *EEC – Bananas II (1994)*, paras. 138–9. Note that this GATT panel report was not adopted.

10 Panel Report, *US – Line Pipe (2002)*, para. 7.18.

11 To imports within the quota, the 'in quota duty' applies; to imports over and above the quota, the higher 'out of quota duty' applies.

For example, a Member may allow the importation of 5,000 tractors at 10 per cent *ad valorem* and any tractor imported above this quantity at 30 per cent *ad valorem*. Tariff quotas are not quantitative restrictions because rather than prohibit or restrict the quantity of imports, they subject the imports to varying duties. As discussed below, customs duties and other charges and duties are explicitly excluded from the scope of quantitative restrictions. Tariff quotas are widely used with regard to agricultural products, but are also used for non-agricultural products.[12]

The European Union's intricate import regime for bananas, at issue in *EC – Bananas III (1997)* and subsequent *EC – Bananas III* disputes, provided for tariff quotas. Under this regime, the European Union initially granted, for example, duty-free access to 90,000 tonnes of non-traditional ACP bananas; the out-of-quota tariff rate for these same bananas was 693 ECU per tonne. In *EC– Bananas III (Article 21.5– Ecuador II) / EC – Bananas III (Article 21.5 – US) (2008)*, the Appellate Body stated:

> In contrast to quantitative restrictions, tariff quotas do not fall under the prohibition in Article XI:1 and are in principle lawful under the GATT 1994, provided that quota tariff rates are applied consistently with Article I.[13]

WTO Members are required to notify the WTO Secretariat of any quantitative restrictions which they maintain, and of any changes to these restrictions, as and when they occur.[14] Such notifications must contain and/indicate: (1) a general description of the restriction; (2) the type of restriction; (3) the relevant tariff line code; (4) a detailed product description; (5) the WTO justification for the measure concerned; (6) the national legal basis for the restriction; and (7) information on the administration of the restriction and, where relevant, an explanation of the modification of a previously notified restriction.[15] With this information, the WTO Secretariat maintains a QR database, which its Members and the general public may consult.[16] As of 19 May 2015, only twenty-seven WTO Members had submitted notifications of all their quantitative restrictions in force. In total, 731 quantitative restrictions were notified.[17]

12 The frequent use of tariff quotas with regard to agricultural products is a result of the 'tariffication' exercise under which quantitative restrictions on trade in agricultural products were 'translated' into tariffs and in particular 'tariff quotas'. See below, p. 490.

13 Appellate Body Reports, *EC– Bananas III (Article 21.5 – Ecuador II) / EC – Bananas III (Article 21.5 – US) (2008)*, para. 335.

14 See Council for Trade in Goods, *Decision on Notification Procedures for Quantitative Restrictions*, G/L/59/Rev.1, dated 3 July 2012, para. 1.

15 See *ibid.*, para. 2. For an example of such notification, see a notification by Australia, G/MA/QR/N/AUS/2, dated 6 February 2015.

16 See www.wto.org/english/res_e/statis_e/statis_e.htm.

17 See Report by the Secretariat, *Quantitative Restrictions: Factual Information on Notifications Received*, Committee on Market Access, G/MA/W/114, dated 22 May 2015, paras. 3.2–3.3.

2.2 Rules on Quantitative Restrictions

The GATT 1994 and other multilateral agreements on trade in goods set out specific rules on quantitative restrictions. This subsection discusses in turn: (1) the general prohibition on quantitative restrictions set out in Article XI of the GATT 1994; (2) the rationale behind the marked difference in the GATT rules on customs duties and quantitative restrictions; (3) the rules on quantitative restrictions on specific products, in particular agricultural products and textiles; and (4) the rules on voluntary export restraints (VERs).

2.2.1 General Prohibition on Quantitative Restrictions

Article XI:1 of the GATT 1994, entitled 'General Elimination of Quantitative Restrictions', sets out a general prohibition on quantitative restrictions, whether on imports or exports. As the panel in *Turkey – Textiles (1999)* stated:

> The prohibition on the use of quantitative restrictions forms one of the cornerstones of the GATT system.[18]

Article XI:1 provides, in relevant part:

> No prohibitions or restrictions other than duties, taxes or other charges, whether made effective through quotas, import or export licences or other measures, shall be instituted or maintained by any [Member] on the importation of any product of the territory of any other [Member] or on the exportation or sale for export of any product destined for the territory of any other [Member].

The panel in *Japan – Semi-Conductors (1988)* noted that the wording of Article XI:1 is *comprehensive* as:

> it applied to *all measures* instituted or maintained by a contracting party *prohibiting or restricting* the importation, exportation or sale for export of products *other than* measures that take the form of duties, taxes or other charges.[19]

The broad scope of the prohibition on quantitative restrictions set out in Article XI:1 is clear from the text of Article XI:1 itself, which refers in addition to quotas and import licences, also to the undefined residual category of 'other measures'. As an illustration of the broad scope of the prohibition on quantitative restrictions, consider that Article XI was found to apply to: export quotas;[20] minimum import price requirements;[21] minimum export price requirements;[22] a discretionary and non-automatic licensing system;[23] trade balancing

18 Panel Report, *Turkey – Textiles (1999)*, para. 9.63.

19 Panel Report, *Japan – Semi-Conductors (1988)*, para. 104. Emphasis added. See also Panel Report, *India – Quantitative Restrictions (1999)*, para. 5.129. The panel in this case further noted that: 'the scope of the term "restriction" is also broad, as seen in its ordinary meaning, which is "a limitation on actions, a limiting condition or regulation"'.

20 See *China – Raw Materials (2012)*.

21 See *EEC – Minimum Import Prices (1978)*. Note that, in this case, the minimum import price requirement was enforced with an import certificate and a security lodgement measure.

22 See *Japan – Semi-Conductors (1988)*; and *China – Raw Materials (2012)*.

23 See *India – Quantitative Restrictions (1999)*; and *China – Raw Materials (2012)*.

requirements;[24] and restrictions on ports of entry.[25] However, note that the Appellate Body stated in *Argentina – Import Measures (2015)*, that the scope of the provision is 'not unfettered' and that the provision itself explicitly excludes 'duties, taxes and other charges' and 'does not extend to areas listed in Article XI:2, and other GATT provisions, such as Articles XII, XIV, XV, XVIII, XX, and XXI, which permit a Member, in certain specified circumstances, to be excused from its Article XI:1 obligations'.[26] Also measures that created uncertainty as to whether and under which conditions importation or exportation of products is allowed;[27] and measures that make importation prohibitively costly[28] have been found to be inconsistent with Article XI:1.

As the Appellate Body ruled in *China – Raw Materials (2012)*, the term 'restriction' refers generally to something that has a limiting effect, and the use of the term 'quantitative' in the title of Article XI suggests that the restriction within the meaning of Article XI:1 is a measure that has a limiting effect on the quantity or amount of a product being imported or exported.[29]

Unlike other GATT provisions, Article XI refers not to laws or regulations but more broadly to *measures*. A measure instituted or maintained by a Member, which restricts imports or exports, is covered by Article XI, *irrespective* of the legal status of the measure.[30] In *Japan – Semi-Conductors (1988)*, the panel thus ruled that *non-mandatory* measures of the Japanese Government, restricting the export of certain semi-conductors at below-cost price, were nevertheless 'restrictions' within the meaning of Article XI:1.[31]

Note that, in addition, quantitative restrictions which do *not actually* restrict or impede trade, such as quotas above current levels of trade, are nevertheless prohibited under Article XI:1 of the GATT 1994.[32] The panel in *EEC – Oilseeds I (1990)* ruled in this respect:

> [T]he Contracting Parties have consistently interpreted the basic provisions of the General Agreement on restrictive trade measures as provisions establishing conditions of competition. Thus they decided that an import quota constitutes an import restriction within the meaning of Article XI:1 whether or not it actually impeded imports.[33]

24 See *India – Autos (2002)*. 25 See *Colombia – Ports of Entry (2009)*.

26 See Appellate Body Reports, *Argentina – Import Measures (2015)*, para. 5.220. Note that in *Argentina – Financial Services (2016)*, the panel concluded that since the relevant measure at issue was 'fiscal in nature', it was thereby not covered by the disciplines of Article XI:1 of the GATT 1994. See Panel Report, *Argentina – Financial Services (2016)*, paras. 7.1067–7.1069.

27 See *China – Raw Materials (2012)*. 28 See *Brazil – Retreaded Tyres (2007)*.

29 See Appellate Body Report, *China – Raw Materials (2012)*, paras. 319–20.

30 See Panel Report, *Japan – Semi-Conductors (1988)*, para. 106.

31 *Ibid.*, paras. 104–17. The panel considered that, in order to determine whether the *non-mandatory* measures were measures falling within the scope of Article XI, it needed to be satisfied on two essential criteria: (1) there were reasonable grounds to believe that sufficient incentives or disincentives existed for non-mandatory measures to take effect; and (2) the operation of the measures was essentially dependent on government action or intervention. The panel considered that, if these two criteria were met, the measures would be operating in a manner equivalent to mandatory requirements such that the difference between the measures and mandatory requirements was only one of form and not one of substance.

32 Such non-binding quotas cause increased transaction costs and create uncertainties, which could affect investment plans. See Panel Report, *Japan – Leather (US II) (1984)*, para. 55.

33 Panel Report, *EEC – Oilseeds I (1990)*, para. 150.

On the other hand, the panel in *EEC – Minimum Import Prices* (1978) found that automatic import licensing does not constitute a restriction of the type meant to fall within the scope of application of Article XI:1.[34]

Article XI:1 of the GATT 1994 does not only prohibit *de jure* quantitative restrictions; restrictions of a *de facto* nature are also prohibited under Article XI:1. The scope of quantitative restrictions within the meaning of Article XI:1 is thus not limited to measures that set an explicit numerical ceiling. Rather, measures which have in fact that effect are also quantitative restrictions within the meaning of Article XI:1. In *Argentina – Hides and Leather (2001)*, the issue arose whether Argentina violated Article XI:1 by authorising the presence of domestic tanners' representatives in the customs inspection procedures for hides destined for export operations. According to the European Union, the complainant in this case, Argentina, imposed a *de facto* restriction on the exportation of hides inconsistent with Article XI:1. The panel ruled:

> There can be no doubt, in our view, that the disciplines of Article XI:1 extend to restrictions of a *de facto* nature.[35]

However, the panel concluded with respect to the Argentinian regulation providing for the presence of the domestic tanners' representatives in the customs inspection procedures that there was insufficient evidence that this regulation actually operated as an export restriction inconsistent with Article XI:1 of the GATT 1994.[36] According to the panel, there was 'no persuasive explanation of precisely how the measure at issue causes or contributes to the low level of exports'.[37] Taking a different approach, the panel in *Colombia – Ports of Entry (2009)* stated, however, that:

> to the extent Panama were able to demonstrate a violation of Article XI:1 based on the measure's design, structure, and architecture, the Panel is of the view that it would not be necessary to consider trade volumes or a causal link between the measure and its effects on trade volumes.[38]

The panel in *Colombia – Ports of Entry (2009)* found that the restriction to two ports of entry limited the *competitive opportunities* for the products at issue, and thus had a limiting effect on imports and therefore was inconsistent with Article XI:1.[39]

The broad scope of application of Article XI:1 was also confirmed by the panels in *India – Quantitative Restrictions (1999)* and *India – Autos (2002)*. The panel in the latter dispute explicitly addressed the question whether Article XI

34 See Panel Report, *EEC – Minimum Import Prices (1978)*, para. 4.1.

35 Panel Report, *Argentina – Hides and Leather (2001)*, para. 11.17. In support of this finding, the panel referred to the Panel Report in *Japan – Semi-Conductors (1988)*, paras. 105–9. For findings on *de facto* quantitative restrictions, see also Panel Reports, *Colombia – Ports of Entry (2009)*, *US – Poultry (China) (2010)* and *China – Raw Materials (2012)*.

36 See Panel Report, *Argentina – Hides and Leather (2001)*, para. 11.55. 37 *Ibid.*, para. 11.21.

38 Panel Reports, *Colombia – Ports of Entry (2009)*, para. 7.252. 39 See *ibid.*, para. 7.275.

also covered situations where products are technically allowed into the market without an express formal quantitative restriction, but yet subject to certain conditions which create a disincentive to import.[40] The panel responded to this question as follows:

On a plain reading, it is clear that a 'restriction' need not be a blanket prohibition or a precise numerical limit. Indeed, the term 'restriction' cannot mean merely 'prohibitions' on importation, since Article XI:1 expressly covers both 'prohibition or restriction'. Furthermore, the Panel considers that the expression 'limiting condition' used by the *India – Quantitative Restrictions* panel to define the term 'restriction' and which this Panel endorses, is helpful in identifying the scope of the notion in the context of the facts before it. That phrase suggests the need to identify not merely a condition placed on importation, but a condition that is limiting, i.e. that has a limiting effect. In the context of Article XI, that limiting effect must be on importation itself.[41]

The panel in *Dominican Republic – Import and Sale of Cigarettes (2005)* further clarified the scope of application of Article XI:1 of the GATT 1994 by stating:

Not every measure affecting the opportunities for entering the market would be covered by Article XI, but only those measures that constitute a prohibition or a restriction on the importation of products, i.e. those measures which affect the opportunities for importation itself.[42]

In *China – Raw Materials (2012)*, the panel found that the minimum export price requirement on exporters of bauxite, coke, fluorspar, magnesium, silicon carbide, yellow phosphorus and zinc was a quantitative restriction on exports, inconsistent with Article XI:1 of the GATT 1994.[43] The Appellate Body upheld this finding of inconsistency, considering *inter alia* that:

[t]he use of the word 'quantitative' in the title of Article XI of the GATT 1994 informs the interpretation of the words 'restriction' and 'prohibition' in Article XI:1, suggesting that the coverage of Article XI includes those prohibitions and restrictions that limit the quantity or amount of a product being imported or exported.[44]

In *Argentina – Import Measures (2015)*, the Appellate Body further clarified that Article XI does 'not cover simply *any* restriction or prohibition' but that it refers to prohibitions or restrictions 'on the importation ... or on the exportation or sale for export'.[45] The Appellate Body ruled that:

not every condition or burden placed on importation or exportation will be inconsistent with Article XI, but only those that are limiting, that is, those that limit the importation or exportation of products.[46]

The Appellate Body also noted that the words 'made effective through' in Article XI:1, which precede the words 'quotas, import or export licences or other

40 See Panel Report, *India – Autos (2002)*, para. 7.269. 41 *Ibid.*, para. 7.270.
42 Panel Report, *Dominican Republic – Import and Sale of Cigarettes (2005)*, para. 7.261.
43 See Panel Reports, *China – Raw Materials (2012)*, para. 8.20.
44 Appellate Body Reports, *China – Raw Materials (2012)*, para. 320.
45 See Appellate Body Reports, *Argentina – Import Measures (2015)*, para. 5.217. 46 *Ibid.*

measures', indicate that 'the scope of Article XI:1 covers measures through which a prohibition or restriction is produced or becomes operative'.[47]

As to the question of how the limitation of the importation or exportation is to be demonstrated, the Appellate Body ruled in *Argentina – Import Measures (2015)* that this limitation need not be demonstrated by quantifying the effects of the measure at issue.[48] In line with the panel's ruling in *Colombia – Ports of Entry (2010)*, referred to above, the Appellate Body stated that the limiting effects 'can be demonstrated through the design, architecture, and revealing structure of the measure at issue considered in its relevant context'.[49]

Finally, with regard to the controversial issue of whether Article XI:1 of the GATT 1994 covers only border measures or also measures concerning, for example, the sale, offering for sale, transportation, distribution and use of products after they have been imported, please refer to the discussion on the respective scopes of Articles III and XI of the GATT 1994 in Chapter 5.[50] Note that in *Brazil – Retreaded Tyres (2007)*, the European Communities claimed, *inter alia*, that the imposition of fines on the importation, marketing, transportation, storage, keeping and warehousing of imported retreaded tyres was inconsistent with Article XI:1 of the GATT 1994.[51] In addressing this claim, the panel considered whether these fines, imposed by Brazil as an enforcement measure of the import prohibition, constituted a restriction on importation within the meaning of Article XI:1. The panel reached the following conclusion:

> [W]hat is important in considering whether a measure falls within the types of measures covered by Article XI:1 is the nature of the measure. In the present case, we note that the fines as a whole, including that on marketing, have the effect of penalizing the act of 'importing' retreaded tyres by subjecting retreaded tyres already imported and existing in the Brazilian internal market to the prohibitively expensive rate of fines. To that extent, we consider that the fact that the fines are not administered at the border does not alter their nature as a restriction on importation within the meaning of Article XI:1.[52]

While it is explicitly referred to as a 'general prohibition', the prohibition on quantitative restrictions set out in Article XI:1 of the GATT 1994 is not without exceptions. The many and broad exceptions discussed in Chapters 8 and 9, as well as the special and differential treatment of developing-country Members referred to later in this chapter, are most important in this respect.[53] In addition, note that Article XI *exempts* certain measures from the scope of application of the prohibition on quantitative restrictions.[54] Note in particular Article XI:2(a) which allows for export prohibitions or restrictions temporarily applied

47 See *ibid.*, para. 5.218. 48 See *ibid.*, para. 5.217.

49 *Ibid.* 50 See above, p. 484.

51 See Panel Report, *Brazil – Retreaded Tyres (2007)*, para. 7.361. This finding was not appealed.

52 *Ibid.*, para. 7.372. The panel noted in addition that: 'the level of the fines – R$ 400 per unit, which significantly exceeds the average prices of domestically produced retreaded tyres for passenger cars (R$ 100–280) – is significant enough to have a restrictive effect on importation'. See *ibid.*

53 See below, pp. 544–623 and 630–68.

54 See Appellate Body Reports, *China – Raw Materials (2012)*, para. 334.

to prevent or relieve critical shortages of foodstuffs or other products essential to the exporting Member. In *China – Raw Materials (2012)* the Appellate Body clarified the meaning of the terms 'temporarily applied', 'essential products' and 'prevent or relieve critical shortages' as used in Article XI:2(a).[55]

In *Argentina – Import Measures (2015)*, Argentina argued that Article XI:1 did not apply to import and export formalities and requirements within the meaning of Article VIII of the GATT 1994. The Appellate Body conceded that Article VIII:1(c) could be read as implying that Members recognised that import formalities and requirements can have trade-restricting effects. The Appellate Body considered, however, that the general and hortatory language of Article VIII:1(c) did not suffice to establish a carve-out or derogation from Article XI:1 for formalities and requirements referred to in Article VIII of the GATT 1994.[56] The Appellate Body found that:

> formalities or requirements under Article VIII of the GATT 1994 are not excluded *per se* from the scope of application of Article XI:1 of the GATT 1994, and that their consistency could be assessed under either Article VIII or Article XI:1, or under both provisions. Thus, we reject Argentina's argument that Articles VIII and XI:1 have mutually exclusive spheres of application.[57]

As to the question of when formalities and requirements under Article VIII of the GATT 1994 are inconsistent with Article XI thereof, the Appellate Body noted in *Argentina – Import Measures (2015)*:

> Article XI:1 covers measures through which a prohibition or restriction is produced or becomes operative. If an import formality or requirement does not itself limit the importation of products independently of the limiting effects of another restriction, then such import formality or requirement cannot be said to produce the limiting effect and, thus, it will not amount to a 'restriction' captured by the prohibition in Article XI:1.[58]

To date, Members have been found to have acted inconsistently with the prohibition on quantitative restrictions of Article XI:1 of the GATT 1994 in fourteen disputes.[59] Most recently, the panel in *China – Rare Earths (2014)* found China's export quotas on rare earths, tungsten and molybdenum to be inconsistent with Article XI:1 of the GATT 1994,[60] and the panel in *Argentina – Import Measures (2015)* found, as upheld by the Appellate Body, that the Trade Related

55 See Appellate Body Reports, *China – Raw Materials (2012)*, paras. 318–28. The Appellate Body in this case upheld the finding of the panel that refractory-grade bauxite is 'essential' to China, but that China had not demonstrated that its export quota on refractory-grade bauxite is 'temporarily applied' within the meaning of Article XI:2(a) to either prevent or relieve a 'critical shortage'. See *ibid.*, para. 344.

56 Appellate Body Report, *Argentina – Import Measures (2015)*, paras. 5.233–5.235.

57 *Ibid.*, para. 5.237. 58 *Ibid.*, para. 5.244.

59 See *Canada – Periodicals (1997); US – Shrimp (1998); India – Quantitative Restrictions (1999); Turkey – Textiles (1999); Korea – Various Measures on Beef (2001); Argentina – Hides and Leather (2001); US – Shrimp (Article 21.5 – Malaysia) (2001); India – Autos (2002); Brazil – Retreaded Tyres (2007); Colombia – Ports of Entry (2009); US – Poultry (China) (2010); China – Raw Materials (2012); China – Rare Earths (2014); and Argentina – Import Measures (2015).*

60 See Panel Reports, *China – Rare Earths (2014)*, para. 7.200.

Requirements (TRRs) and Advance Sworn Import Declaration (DJAI) procedure were a restriction on importation inconsistent with Article XI:1.[61]

2.2.2 Quantitative Restrictions and Customs Duties

As already noted in Chapter 6, the WTO has a clear preference for customs duties over quantitative restrictions, and this preference is reflected in the relevant provisions of the GATT 1994.[62] In comparing customs duties with quantitative restrictions, the panel in *Turkey – Textiles (1999)* noted:

> A basic principle of the GATT system is that tariffs are the preferred and acceptable form of protection ... The prohibition against quantitative restrictions is a reflection that tariffs are GATT's border protection 'of choice'.[63]

The reasons for this preference are both economic and political in nature. First, customs duties are more transparent. The economic impact of customs duties on imported products, i.e. how much more expensive imported products are as a result of customs duties, is immediately clear. Quantitative restrictions also increase the price of the imported products. As supply of the imported product is limited, the price increases. However, it is not immediately clear by how much quantitative restrictions increase the price of imported products. As it is less obvious what the negative impact of quantitative restrictions is on prices (paid by consumers and companies using imports), those affected are less likely to mobilise against these measures, and special interest groups are more likely to be able to convince governments to adopt them.

Second, and related to the first reason, it is considered easier to negotiate, in successive rounds of negotiations, the gradual reduction of customs duties than it is to negotiate the elimination (or liberalisation) of quantitative restrictions.

Third, while the price increase resulting from customs duties goes to the government as revenue, the price increase resulting from quantitative restrictions ordinarily benefits the importers. The importers will be able to sell at higher prices because of the limits on the supply of the product. This 'extra profit' is commonly referred to as the 'quota rent', and, unless a quota is auctioned (which is seldom done), no part of this quota rent goes to the government.

Fourth, the administration of quantitative restrictions is more open to corruption than the administration of customs duties. This is because quantitative restrictions, and, in particular, quotas, are usually administered through an import-licensing system; import-licensing procedures are often not transparent, and decisions by government officials to award an import licence are not necessarily based on general interest.[64]

Finally, and arguably most importantly, quantitative restrictions impose absolute limits on imports, while customs duties do not. While customs duties are

61 See Panel Reports, *Argentina – Import Measures (2015)*, para. 6.265. 62 See above, p. 423.
63 Panel Report, *Turkey – Textiles (1999)*, para. 9.63.
64 On import-licensing procedures, see below, pp. 496–8.

surmountable (at least, if they are not set at prohibitively high levels), quantitative restrictions cannot be surmounted. If a foreign producer is sufficiently more efficient than a domestic producer, the customs duty will not prevent imported products from competing with domestic products. By contrast, once the limit of a quantitative restriction is reached, no more products can be imported. Even the most efficient foreign producer cannot 'overcome' the quantitative restriction. Above the quota, domestic products have no competition from imported products.[65]

2.2.3 Rules on Quantitative Restrictions on Specific Products

Under the GATT 1947, the prohibition against quantitative restrictions was often *not* respected. The panel in *Turkey – Textiles (1999)* noted:

> From early in the GATT, in sectors such as agriculture, quantitative restrictions were maintained and even increased ... In the sector of textiles and clothing, quantitative restrictions were maintained under the Multifibre Agreement [*sic*] ... Certain contracting parties were even of the view that quantitative restrictions had gradually been tolerated and accepted as negotiable and that Article XI could not be, and had never been considered to be, a provision prohibiting such restrictions irrespective of the circumstances specific to each case.[66]

However, the overall detrimental effect of these quantitative restrictions in the sectors of agriculture and textiles were generally recognised. Therefore, their elimination was high on the agenda of the Uruguay Round negotiations, and the *Agreement on Agriculture* and the *Agreement on Textiles and Clothing* (resulting from these negotiations) contain specific rules regarding the elimination of quantitative restrictions.

The *Agreement on Agriculture* provides that quantitative import restrictions and voluntary export restraints, *inter alia*, must be converted into tariffs and that no new restrictions of this kind can be adopted. Article 4.2 of the *Agreement on Agriculture* states:

> Members shall not maintain, resort to, or revert to any measures of the kind which have been required to be converted into ordinary customs duties, except as otherwise provided for in Article 5 and Annex 5.

In footnote 1 to this provision, the measures which had to be converted into tariffs (or tariff quotas) were identified as: quantitative import restrictions, variable import levies, minimum import prices, discretionary import licensing, non-tariff measures maintained through State trading enterprises, voluntary export restraints, and similar border measures other than ordinary customs duties.[67]

65 See also Panel Report, *Turkey – Textiles (1999)*, para. 9.63.

66 *Ibid.*, para. 9.64. Note that the argument of certain Contracting Parties that Article XI could not be a provision prohibiting quantitative restrictions irrespective of the circumstances in which they were imposed, in a specific case, was explicitly rejected by the panel in *EEC – Import Restrictions (1983)*.

67 Note that measures maintained under balance-of-payments provisions or under other general, non-agriculture-specific provisions of the GATT 1994 or of the other multilateral agreements on trade in goods did *not* need to be converted into tariffs.

The process of converting these non-tariff measures into tariffs is commonly referred to as the 'tariffication process'. As this process provided for the replacement of non-tariff measures with a tariff which afforded *an equivalent level of protection*, many of the tariffs resulting from the 'tariffication process' are very high.[68] However, by introducing a system of *tariff quotas*, it was possible to guarantee: (1) that the quantities imported before Article 4.2 of the *Agreement on Agriculture* took effect could continue to be imported; and (2) that some new quantities were subject to tariffs that were not prohibitive. Under this system of tariff quotas, lower tariffs applied to specified quantities (in-quota quantities), while higher (often prohibitive) tariffs applied to quantities that exceed the quota (over-quota quantities).[69]

At the Bali Ministerial Conference in December 2013, the WTO adopted an understanding on the administration of tariff quotas for agricultural products.[70] The Understanding stipulates that tariff quota administration shall be deemed to be an instance of import licensing to which the provisions of the *Agreement on Import Licensing Procedures* apply in full, subject to the *Agreement on Agriculture* and the more specific and additional obligations set out in the Understanding.[71] The Understanding addresses in particular the problem of under-filling the tariff quota.[72]

With respect to the relationship between Article 4.2 of the *Agreement on Agriculture* and Article XI of the GATT 1994, the panel in *Korea – Various Measures on Beef (2001)* stated that:

> when dealing with measures relating to agricultural products which should have been converted into tariffs or tariff-quotas, a violation of Article XI of GATT ... would necessarily constitute a violation of Article 4.2 of the *Agreement on Agriculture* and its footnote.[73]

As mentioned above, trade in textiles and clothing also largely 'escaped' from the GATT 1947 rules and disciplines, and in particular the prohibition of Article XI on quantitative restrictions. Under the *Multifibre Arrangement* (MFA), in effect from 1974, developed and developing countries, respectively importing and exporting textiles, entered into bilateral agreements requiring the exporting developing countries to limit their exports of certain categories of textiles and clothing. In 1995, the main importing countries had eighty-one such restraint agreements with exporting countries, comprising over a thousand individual quotas.[74]

68 The customs duties resulting from the 'tariffication process' concern, on average, one-fifth of the total number of agricultural tariff lines in the national customs tariffs of developed-country Members.

69 On the reduction of customs duties on agricultural products agreed on during the Uruguay Round negotiations, see above, pp. 434–5.

70 See *Understanding on Tariff Rate Quota Administration Provisions of Agricultural Products, as Defined in Article 2 of the Agreement on Agriculture*, Ministerial Decision of 7 December 2013, WT/MIN(13)/39 – WT/L/914, dated 11 December 2013.

71 See *ibid.*, para. 1. 72 See *ibid.*, paras. 6–15.

73 Panel Report, *Korea – Various Measures on Beef (2001)*, para. 7.62.

74 In addition, there were also a number of non-MFA agreements or unilateral measures restricting the imports of textiles and clothing. See *Business Guide to the World Trading System*, 2nd edn (International Trade Centre/Commonwealth Secretariat, 1999), 164.

The MFA, which was negotiated within the framework of the GATT, provided a 'legal cover' for the GATT inconsistency of these quotas.[75] The *Agreement on Textiles and Clothing* (ATC) negotiated during the Uruguay Round sought to address this situation and contained specific rules for quantitative restrictions on textiles and clothing.

The ten-year-long 'integration process', provided for in the ATC, was to be carried out in four stages, ending on 31 December 2004. At each stage, products amounting to a certain minimum percentage of the volume of a Member's 1990 imports of textiles and clothing were made fully subject to the disciplines of the GATT 1994, including the prohibition on quantitative restrictions of Article XI.[76] Moreover, the level of the remaining quantitative restrictions was to be increased annually.[77]

While the integration process of the ATC was successfully completed by the end of 2004 and quantitative restrictions on textiles terminated, the benefits of this return to GATT discipline have been unevenly spread. A number of smaller, textile-producing developing-country Members, such as Mauritius, Lesotho and Costa Rica, which before 2005 had enjoyed guaranteed quota access, encountered serious adjustment problems as their textile exports could not compete with the textile exports of the large textile-producing developing-country Members, such as Bangladesh, Brazil, India and especially China.[78] When it was suggested that the WTO should address the problems of small textile-producing developing-country Members adversely affected by the elimination of quotas, China, Brazil, India and Hong Kong objected to the inclusion of this issue on the agenda of the Council for Trade in Goods.[79]

2.2.4 Voluntary Export Restraints

Voluntary export restraints (VERs) are actions taken by exporting countries involving a *self-imposed* quantitative restriction of exports. VERs are taken either unilaterally or under the terms of an agreement or arrangement between two or more countries. As the term indicates, in theory, VERs are entered into on a *voluntary* basis, i.e. the exporting country voluntarily limits the volume of its

75 *Ibid.*, 165.

76 See Articles 2.6 and 2.7 of the ATC. Note, however, that this integration process applied to *all* textile products listed in the ATC, including products on which there were no quantitative restrictions. This allowed the United States and the European Communities, during the first stages, to 'integrate' mainly products on which there were *no* quantitative restrictions into the GATT 1994. To the discontent and disappointment of the textile-exporting Members, the two major importing Members, the European Union and the United States, could at least initially meet their obligations under the ATC without significantly removing quantitative restrictions. They removed most of their quantitative restrictions only in the fourth and last stage of the integration process, ending on 1 January 2005.

77 e.g. the quotas were increased by 25 per cent per year from 1998 to 2001. See Articles 2.13 and 2.14 of the ATC.

78 See F. Williams, 'China and India Gain from End of Quotas', *Financial Times*, 25 October 2005.

79 See *Bridges Weekly Trade News Digest*, 18 May 2005.

exports. However, in reality, the voluntary nature of VERs is usually a fiction. A 1983 GATT report observed:

> It appeared ... that exporting countries which accepted so-called 'grey-area' actions did so primarily because ... they felt that they had little choice and that the alternative was, or would have been, unilateral action in the form of quantitative restrictions, harassment by anti-dumping investigations, countervailing action ... involving greater harm to their exports in terms of quantity or price.[80]

Under the GATT 1947, the legality of voluntary export restraints was a much-debated issue. With the entry into force of the *WTO Agreement*, this issue has been definitively decided. The WTO *Agreement on Safeguards* specifically prohibits voluntary export restraints.[81] Article 11.1(b) of this Agreement provides:

> [A] Member shall not seek, take or maintain any voluntary export restraints, orderly marketing arrangements or any other similar measures on the export or the import side.[82]

Article 11.1(b) of the *Agreement on Safeguards* furthermore required that any such measure existing in 1995 had to be phased out (or brought into compliance with the *Agreement on Safeguards*) before the end of 1999.

2.3 Administration of Quantitative Restrictions

Article XI:1 of the GATT 1994 prohibits quantitative restrictions. There are, however, as noted above and discussed elsewhere in this book, many exceptions to this prohibition of Article XI:1.[83] Article XIII of the GATT 1994 bears testimony to this by setting out rules on the *administration* of quantitative restrictions. This subsection addresses: (1) the rule of non-discrimination; (2) the rules on the distribution of trade; and (3) the rules on import-licensing procedures.

While tariff quotas are not quantitative restrictions, pursuant to Article XIII:5 of the GATT 1994, the rules on the administration of quantitative restrictions set out in Article XIII, and discussed in this subsection, also apply to the administration of tariff quotas. In fact, many of the disputes on Article XIII are related to the administration of tariff quotas.[84] This subsection therefore includes some examples of tariff quotas applied by the European Union.

80 Report of the Chairman of the Safeguards Committee, BISD 30S/216, 218.

81 For a detailed discussion of the *Agreement on Safeguards*, see below, pp. 631–65. Also, Article 4.2, read together with fn. 1, of the *Agreement on Agriculture* contains a prohibition of voluntary export restraints.

82 Footnote 4 to this provision contains an illustrative list of 'similar measures', including export moderation, export-price or import-price monitoring systems, export or import surveillance, compulsory import cartels and discretionary export or import-licensing schemes, any of which afford protection.

83 See above, p. 484; and, *inter alia*, below, pp. 540–2.

84 See e.g. the controversial administration of the tariff quotas under the EC's import regime for bananas at issue in *EC – Bananas III (1997)*, or for poultry at issue in *EC – Poultry (1998)*. See also the tariff quotas at issue in *US – Line Pipe (2002)*.

2.3.1 Rule of Non-Discrimination

Article XIII:1 of the GATT 1994 provides that quantitative restrictions, when applied, should be administered in a non-discriminatory manner. Article XIII:1 states:

> No prohibition or restriction shall be applied by any [Member] on the importation of any product of the territory of any other [Member] or on the exportation of any product destined for the territory of any other [Member], unless the importation of the like product of all third countries or the exportation of the like product to all third countries is *similarly prohibited or restricted*.[85]

What Article XIII:1 requires is that, if a Member imposes a quantitative restriction on products to or from another Member, products to or from all other countries are 'similarly prohibited or restricted'. This requirement of Article XIII:1 is an MFN-like obligation. As the Appellate Body noted in *EC – Bananas III (1997)*, the essence of the non-discrimination obligations of Articles I:1 *and* XIII of the GATT 1994 is that:

> like products should be treated equally, irrespective of their origin.[86]

The GATT panel in *EEC – Apples (Chile I) (1980)* found that the European Communities had acted inconsistently with the non-discrimination obligation of Article XIII:1. The importation of apples from Argentina, Australia, New Zealand and South Africa into the European Communities had been restricted through voluntary restraint agreements negotiated and concluded with these countries. The European Communities tried to agree on a similar voluntary restraint agreement with Chile but the negotiations failed. The European Communities subsequently adopted measures restricting the importation of Chilean apples to approximately 42,000 tonnes a year. The panel in *EEC – Apples (Chile I) (1980)* found that the measure applied to apple imports from Chile were *not* a restriction *similar* to the voluntary restraint agreements negotiated with the other apple-exporting countries and therefore was inconsistent with Article XIII:1. The panel came to this conclusion primarily on the basis that: (1) there was a difference in transparency between the two types of action; (2) there was a difference in the administration of the restrictions, the one being an import restriction, the other an export restraint; and (3) the import restriction was unilateral and mandatory while the other was voluntary and negotiated.[87]

2.3.2 Rules on the Distribution of Trade

If quantitative restrictions, other than a prohibition or ban, are applied on the importation of a product, the question arises how the trade that is still allowed

85 Emphasis added.
86 Appellate Body Report, *EC – Bananas III (1997)*, para. 190.
87 See Panel Report, *EEC – Apples (Chile I) (1980)*, para. 4.11.

will be distributed among the different Members exporting that product. The chapeau of Article XIII:2 of the GATT 1994 provides in this respect:

> In applying import restrictions to any product, [Members] shall aim at a distribution of trade in such product approaching as closely as possible the shares which the various [Members] might be expected to obtain in the absence of such restrictions.[88]

In *EC – Bananas III (1997)*, the Appellate Body found the reallocation of non-utilised tariff quotas only among those countries that concluded the *Banana Framework Agreement* with the European Communities to be inconsistent with Article XIII:2, as the reallocation failed to approximate, in the administration of tariff quotas, the relative trade flows which would exist in the absence of the tariff quotas.[89] The panel in *US – Line Pipe* (2002) found:

> There is nothing in the record before the Panel to suggest that the line pipe measure was based in any way on historical trade patterns in line pipe, or that the United States otherwise 'aim[ed] at a distribution of trade ... approaching as closely as possible the shares which the various Members might be expected to obtain in the absence of' the line pipe measure. Instead, as noted by Korea, 'the in-quota import volume originating from Korea, the largest supplier historically to the US market, was reduced to the same level as the smallest – or even then non-existent – suppliers to the US market (9,000 short tons)'. For this reason, we find that the line pipe measure is inconsistent with the general rule contained in the chapeau of Article XIII:2.[90]

Furthermore, Article XIII:2 sets out a number of requirements to be met when imposing quantitative restrictions. Pursuant to Article XIII:2(a) and (b), when imposing a quantitative restriction, a quota – whether global or allocated among the supplying countries – is preferred to quantitative restrictions applied through import licences or permits without a quota. In cases in which a quota is allocated among supplying countries, Article XIII:2(d) provides:

> [T]he [Member] applying the restrictions may seek agreement with respect to the allocation of shares in the quota with all other [Members] having a substantial interest in supplying the product concerned.

However, when this method of allocating the shares in the quota 'is not reasonably practicable', i.e. when no agreement can be reached with *all* the Members having a substantial interest, the Member applying the quota:

> shall allot to [Members] having a substantial interest in supplying the product shares based upon the proportions, supplied by such [Members] during a previous representative period, of the total quantity or value of imports of the product, due account being taken of any special factors which may have affected or may be affecting the trade in the product.

In other words, if no agreement can be reached, the quota must be allocated among the Members having a substantial interest on the basis of their share of

88 Note that the panel in *US – Line Pipe (2002)* stated that the chapeau of Article XIII:2 contains 'a general rule, and not merely a statement of principle'. See Panel Report, *US – Line Pipe (2002)*, fn. 64.
89 See Appellate Body Report, *EC – Bananas III (1997)*, para. 163.
90 Panel Report, *US – Line Pipe (2002)*, para. 7.55.

the trade during a previous representative period. It is normal GATT practice to use a three-year period prior to the imposition of the quota as the 'representative period'.[91] Quotas allocated among supplying countries *must* be allocated among *all* Members having a *substantial interest* in supplying the product.[92] There is no additional obligation to allocate a part of the quota to Members *without* a substantial interest in supplying the product concerned. While the requirement of Article XIII:2(d) is not expressed as an exception to the basic non-discrimination requirement of Article XIII:1, it may be regarded, to the extent that its practical application is inconsistent with it, as a *lex specialis*.[93] It allows for the discrimination between Members with and Members without a substantial interest in supplying the product at issue.

In *EC – Bananas III (1997)*, the panel addressed the question of whether quota shares or tariff quota shares (as they were in this case) *can* also be allocated to Members that do not have a substantial interest in supplying the product at issue. According to the panel, quota shares and tariff quota shares *can* be allocated to Members with minor market shares. The panel ruled:

> [W]e note that the first sentence of Article XIII:2(d) refers to allocation of a quota 'among supplying countries'. This could be read to imply that an allocation may also be made to Members that do not have a substantial interest in supplying the product.[94]

However, if a Member wishes to allocate quota shares or tariff quota shares to some Members with minor market shares, then such shares must be allocated to *all* such Members. If not, imports from such Members would not be 'similarly restricted' as required by Article XIII:1 of the GATT 1994.[95] Moreover, the same method as was used to allocate the shares to the Members having a substantial interest in supplying the product would have to be used. Otherwise, again, the non-discrimination obligation of Article XIII:1 would not be met.[96] If a Member wishes to allocate a part of the quota or tariff quota to Members with minor market shares, then this is best done by providing – next to country-specific quota shares for Members with a substantial interest – for an 'others' category for all Members not having a substantial interest in supplying the product.[97] The use of an 'others' category is consistent with the object and purpose of Article XIII (as expressed in the chapeau of Article XIII:2) to achieve a distribution of trade as close as possible to that which would have been the distribution of trade in the

91 See Panel Report, *EEC – Apples (Chile I) (1980)*, para. 4.16; and Panel Report, *EEC – Dessert Apples (1989)*, para. 12.22.

92 As discussed above, a share of 10 per cent of the market of the Member applying the quota has generally been considered to be a 'significant share' of the market, required to claim a 'substantial interest'. See above, p. 448.

93 See Panel Reports, *EC – Bananas III (1997)*, para. 7.75. 94 *Ibid*., para. 7.73.

95 See above, p. 307. 96 See *ibid*.

97 The alternative is to allocate to all supplying countries, including Members with minor market shares, country-specific tariff quota shares. This method, however, is more likely to lead to a long-term freezing of market shares and a less competitive market. See also Panel Reports, *EC – Bananas III (1997)*, para. 7.76.

absence of the quantitative restriction.[98] The panel in *EC – Bananas III (1997)* noted:

> When a significant share of a tariff quota is assigned to 'others', the import market will evolve with a minimum amount of distortion. Members not having a substantial supplying interest will be able, if sufficiently competitive, to gain market share in the 'others' category and possibly achieve 'substantial supplying interest' status ... New entrants will be able to compete in the market, and likewise have an opportunity to gain 'substantial supplying interest' status.[99]

2.3.3 Import-Licensing Procedures

Quotas and tariff quotas are usually administered through import-licensing procedures. Article 1.1 of the *Agreement on Import Licensing Procedures*, commonly referred to as the *Import Licensing Agreement*, defines import-licensing procedures as:

> administrative procedures ... requiring the submission of an application or other documentation (other than that required for customs purposes) to the relevant administrative body as a prior condition for importation into the customs territory of the importing Member.[100]

A trader who wishes to import a product that is subject to a quota or tariff quota must apply for an import licence, i.e. a permit to import. Whether this import licence will be granted depends on whether the quota is already filled or not, and on whether the trader meets the requirements for an import licence.[101] Economists agree that a first-come, first-served distribution rule for import licences is the most economically efficient licensing method.[102] However, import-licensing rules and procedures are often much more complex, as was illustrated by the import-licensing system for bananas at issue in *EC – Bananas III (1997)*.[103]

One of the most important rules of the *Import Licensing Agreement* is set out in Article 1.3, which reads:

> The rules for import licensing procedures shall be neutral in application and administered in a fair and equitable manner.

As emphasised by the Appellate Body in *EC – Bananas III (1997)*, the requirements of Article 1.3 do not concern the licensing rules *per se*, but concern the *application* and *administration* of these rules.[104]

98 See *ibid.*, para. 7.76. 99 *Ibid.*, para. 7.76.

100 While Article 1.1 of the *Import Licensing Agreement* does not explicitly state that import-licensing procedures for tariff quotas are import-licensing procedures within the meaning of Article 1.1, the Appellate Body in *EC – Bananas III (1997)* ruled that a careful reading of that provision 'leads inescapably to that conclusion'. As the Appellate Body noted, import-licensing procedures for tariff quotas require 'the submission of an application' for import licences as 'a prior condition for importation' of a product at the lower in-quota tariff rate. See Appellate Body Report, *EC – Bananas III (1997)*, para. 193.

101 This would be an example of non-automatic import licensing. As discussed below, there is also automatic import licensing, but this would not occur with respect to the importation of a product that is subject to a quota or tariff quota. See below, p. 497.

102 See e.g. P. Lindert and T. Pugel, *International Economics*, 10th edn (McGraw Hill, 1996).

103 See Panel Reports, *EC – Bananas III (1997)*, paras. 7.142–7.273.

104 See Appellate Body Report, *EC – Bananas III (1997)*, paras. 197–8. See also Panel Report, *Korea – Various Measures on Beef (2001)*, paras. 784–5; and Panel Report, *EC – Poultry (1998)*, para. 254.

Moreover, Article 1.4 of the *Import Licensing Agreement* requires that the rules and all information concerning procedures for the submission of applications for import licences must be published in such a manner as to enable Members and traders to become acquainted with them.[105] In no event shall such a publication be later than the date on which the licence requirement becomes effective.[106] In *EC – Poultry (1998)*, Brazil argued that frequent changes to the EC licensing rules and procedures regarding the poultry tariff quota made it difficult for Members and traders to become familiar with the rules, contrary to the provisions of Article 1.4 and other provisions of the *Import Licensing Agreement*. The panel rejected this complaint as follows:

> We note that the transparency requirement under the cited provisions is limited to publication of rules and other information. While we have sympathy for Brazil regarding the difficulties caused by the frequent changes to the rules, we find that changes in rules *per se* do not constitute a violation of Articles 1.4, 3.3, 3.5(b), 3.5(c) or 3.5(d).[107]

Articles 1.7 and 1.8 of the *Import Licensing Agreement* require that, in the administration and application of licensing rules, minor documentation errors or minor variations in value should not matter. For example, an application for an import licence shall not be refused for minor documentation errors, which do not alter basic data contained therein.[108]

The *Import Licensing Agreement* distinguishes between automatic and non-automatic import licensing. *Automatic import licensing* is defined as import licensing where approval of the application is granted *in all cases*.[109] Automatic import licensing may be maintained to collect statistical and other information on imports. Article 2.2 of the *Import Licensing Agreement* requires that automatic import-licensing procedures shall not be administered in such a manner as to have 'restricting effects on imports subject to automatic licensing'.[110] *Non-automatic import licensing* is import licensing where approval is *not* granted in all cases. Import-licensing procedures for quotas and tariff quotas are by definition non-automatic import-licensing procedures. However, non-automatic import licences are also used by countries for many other reasons. Note, for example, that Saudi Arabia requires non-automatic import licences for certain 'distillation equipment' due to the fact that the latter has been used to produce alcoholic beverages in the past. Since alcohol is generally prohibited in Saudi Arabia, it has decided therefore to establish an import-licence requirement for

105 The rules and information concerned include rules and information on the eligibility of persons, firms and institutions to make such applications and the administrative body(ies) to be approached.

106 See *ibid.* Whenever practicable, the publication shall take place twenty-one days prior to the effective date. Note that any exceptions, derogations or changes in or from the rules concerning licensing procedures or the list of products subject to import licensing shall also be published in the same manner and within the same period. See *ibid.*

107 Panel Report, *EC – Poultry (1998)*, para. 246.

108 See Article 1.7 of the *Import Licensing Agreement*.

109 See *ibid.*, Article 2.1.

110 On situations in which automatic licensing procedures shall *be deemed* to have trade-restricting effects, see Article 2.2 of the *Import Licensing Agreement*.

certain distillation equipment.[111] With regard to non-automatic import licensing, Article 3.2 of the *Import Licensing Agreement* requires that:

> Non-automatic licensing shall not have trade-restrictive or distortive effects on imports additional to those caused by the imposition of the restriction.

Other requirements relating to non-automatic import licensing concern: (1) the non-discrimination among applicants for import licences;[112] (2) the obligation to give reasons for refusing an application;[113] (3) the right of appeal or review of the decisions on applications;[114] (4) time limits for processing applications;[115] (5) the validity of import licences;[116] and (6) the desirability of issuing licences for products in economic quantities.[117]

2.4 Special and Differential Treatment

The GATT 1994 provides for special and differential treatment of developing-country Members regarding the rules on quantitative restrictions discussed above. Article XVIII of the GATT 1994 allows developing-country Members to impose quantitative restrictions for balance-of-payments reasons under less demanding conditions than apply for developed-country Members under Article XII of the GATT 1994. For a discussion of this special and differential treatment, refer to Chapter 9.[118]

3 OTHER NON-TARIFF BARRIERS ON TRADE IN GOODS

In addition to customs duties and other duties and charges (i.e. tariff barriers), and quantitative restrictions (i.e. the first subcategory of non-tariff barriers), trade in goods may also be impeded by 'other non-tariff barriers'. As the term indicates, this is a *residual* category of measures, actions or omissions, which restrict, to various degrees and in different ways, market access for goods.[119] The category of 'other non-tariff barriers' includes, *inter alia*, technical barriers to trade, sanitary and phytosanitary measures, customs formalities and procedures, and government procurement laws and practices. Also, the unfair and arbitrary application of trade measures may constitute an important barrier to trade. However, not only action but also omission, and in particular the failure

111 See Working Party Report on the Accession of the Kingdom of Saudi Arabia to the WTO, WT/ACC/SAU/61, dated 1 November 2005, para. 149.
112 See Article 3.5(e) of the *Import Licensing Agreement*. 113 See *ibid.*
114 See *ibid.* 115 See *ibid.*, Article 3.5(f).
116 See *ibid.*, Article 3.5(g). 117 See *ibid.*, Article 3.5(j).
118 See below, pp. 659–68.
119 See e.g. *Table of Contents of the Inventory of Non-Tariff Measures*, Note by the Secretariat, TN/MA/S/5/Rev.1, dated 28 November 2003.

to inform about the applicable trade laws, regulations and procedures, promptly and accurately, may constitute a formidable barrier to trade.

This section addresses in turn the following 'other non-tariff barriers' to trade in goods: (1) lack of transparency; (2) unfair and arbitrary application of trade measures; (3) customs formalities and procedures; (4) government procurement laws and practices; and (5) other measures or actions, such as preshipment inspection, marks of origin and measures relating to transit shipments. As mentioned above, and due to their importance and detailed nature, the rules on technical barriers to trade and sanitary and phytosanitary measures are discussed, separately, in Chapters 13 and 14 respectively.[120]

3.1 Lack of Transparency

As discussed above, lack of information, uncertainty or confusion with respect to the trade laws, regulations and procedures applicable in actual or potential export markets is an important barrier to trade. Therefore, WTO law provides for rules and procedures to ensure a high level of transparency of its Members' trade laws, regulations and procedures. There are four kinds of relevant WTO rules and procedures: (1) the *publication* requirement; (2) the *notification* requirement; (3) the requirement to establish *enquiry points*; and (4) the trade policy *review* process.

Article X of the GATT 1994, entitled 'Publication and Administration of Trade Regulations', requires in its first paragraph that Members *publish* their laws, regulations, judicial decisions, administrative rulings of general application and international agreements relating to trade matters.[121] Article X:1 does not prescribe in any detail how these laws, regulations, etc. have to be published, but it does state that they have to be published: (1) 'promptly'; and (2) 'in such a manner as to enable governments and traders to become acquainted with them'.[122] The panel in *EC – IT Products (2010)* noted that:

> Article X:1 addresses the due process notion of notice by requiring publication that is prompt and that ensures those who need to be aware of certain laws, regulations, judicial

120 See below, pp. 883–932 and 935–90.

121 The many and diverse trade matters to which the laws, regulations, etc. may relate to include the classification or the valuation of products for customs purposes, rates of duties, taxes or other charges, and restrictions and prohibitions on imports and exports; and are set out in detail in Article X:1. Note that the term 'of general application' qualifies not just 'administrative rulings' but all types of measures referred to in Article X:1, first sentence. See Panel Report, *US – Countervailing and Anti-Dumping Measures (China) (2014)*, paras. 7.30–7.31. According to the Appellate Body in *US – Underwear (1997)* measures of 'general application' are those affecting 'an unidentified number of economic operators'. See Appellate Body Report, *US – Underwear (1997)*, 29. Therefore, licences issued to a specific company or applied to a specific shipment are not subject to the publication requirement of Article X:1. See Appellate Body Report, *EC – Poultry (1998)*, para. 113.

122 Note that Article X:1, unlike Article X:2, discussed below, does not require that the publication is in an official publication. See Panel Reports, *EC – IT Products (2010)*, para. 7.1082. Note also that the publication requirements set out in the first sentence of Article X:1 do not explicitly apply to the publication of the international agreements, but it may be assumed that they also apply in this context. Moreover, note that Article X:1 does not require Members to disclose confidential information which would impede law enforcement or otherwise be contrary to the public interest or which would prejudice the legitimate commercial interests of particular enterprises, public or private. See Article X:1, last sentence, of the GATT 1994. See also Panel Report, *Thailand – Cigarettes (Philippines) (2011)*, para. 7.819.

decisions and administrative rulings of general application can become acquainted with them.[123]

With regard to the 'promptness' requirement, the panel in *EC – IT Products (2010)* considered that:

> the meaning of prompt is not an absolute concept, i.e. a pre-set period of time applicable in all cases. Rather, an assessment of whether a measure has been published 'promptly', that is 'quickly' and 'without undue delay', necessarily requires a case-by-case assessment.[124]

In this case, the panel found that publication in the EU's *Official Journal* eight months after the measures were made effective was not 'prompt', i.e. 'quickly' or 'without undue delay'. However, the panel noted that the measures were posted on an EU website prior to the date that they were made effective. The panel found that the latter publication was 'prompt' but that it was not 'in such a manner as to enable governments and traders to become acquainted' with the measures at issue.[125]

With regard to the concept of 'administrative ruling of general application', note that, to the extent that an administrative ruling is addressed to a specific company or applied to a specific shipment, it cannot be qualified as an administrative ruling of general application. However, to the extent that an administrative ruling affects an unidentified number of economic operators, it can be qualified as a ruling of general application. The fact that a measure is country-specific does not preclude the possibility of it being an administrative ruling of general application.[126] In *EC – IT Products (2010)*, the question arose whether a CNEN (i.e. an explanatory note to the EU's Customs Nomenclature) could be considered to be a measure to which Article X:1 applied. The panel found that:

> the instruments covered by Article X:1 range from imperative rules of conduct to the exercise of influence or an authoritative pronouncement by certain authoritative bodies. Accordingly, we consider that the coverage of Article X:1 extends to instruments with a degree of authoritativeness issued by certain legislative, administrative or judicial bodies. This does not mean, however, that they have to be 'binding' under domestic law. Hence, the fact that CNENs are not legally binding under EC law does not preclude them from being contemplated by the terms 'laws, regulations, judicial decisions [or] administrative rulings' under Article X:1.[127]

The panel did emphasise, however, that for a measure to be a law, regulation, etc. within the meaning of Article X:1, it must have a 'degree of authoritativeness'

123 Panel Reports, *EC – IT Products (2010)*, para. 7.1015.

124 *Ibid.*, para. 7.1074. See also Panel Report, *US – Countervailing and Anti-Dumping Duties (2014)*, paras. 7.79–7.87.

125 See Panel Reports, *EC – IT Products (2010)*, para. 7.1088.

126 See Appellate Body Report, *US – Underwear (1997)*, 29. See also Appellate Body Report, *EC – Poultry (1998)*, paras. 111–13. Note that the panel in *Japan – Film (1998)* stated that: 'it stands to reason that inasmuch as the Article X:1 requirement applies to all administrative rulings of general application, it also should extend to administrative rulings in individual cases where such rulings establish or revise principles or criteria applicable in future cases'. See Panel Report, *Japan – Film (1998)*, para. 10.388.

127 Panel Reports, *EC – IT Products (2010)*, para. 7.1027.

and this will need to be established on a case-by-case basis considering the particular factual features of the measure at issue.[128]

The panel in *Thailand – Cigarettes (Philippines) (2011)* found that the explanation given by the Thai Excise Department of the methodology for calculating the maximum retail sales prices (MRSPs) for imported and domestic cigarettes applied 'prospectively and generally' to all potential sales of cigarettes. Therefore, the panel considered that this methodology for determining the MRSPs to be a measure of general application to which Article X:1 applied.[129]

The panel in *US – Countervailing and Anti-Dumping Measures (China) (2014)* found that a measure is of 'general application' when the 'measure applies to a class, or a set or category, of persons, entities, situations or cases that have some attributes in common'.[130] A measure that applies to named or otherwise specifically identified persons, entities, situations or cases would not be a measure of 'general application'.[131]

In addition to Article X:1, Article X:2 of the GATT 1994 also concerns the publication of trade measures of general application. Article X:2 provides:

> No measure of general application taken by any [Member] effecting an advance in a rate of duty or other charge on imports under an established and uniform practice, or imposing a new or more burdensome requirement, restriction or prohibition on imports, or on the transfer of payments therefor, shall be enforced before such measure has been officially published.

Pursuant to Article X:2, Members may not enforce, i.e. apply,[132] measures of general application, imposing new or higher barriers to trade, *before* they are officially published.[133] Such trade measures shall only take effect *after* official publication.[134] With respect to the rationale of Article X:2, the Appellate Body noted in *US – Underwear (1997)*:

> Article X:2, *General Agreement*, may be seen to embody a principle of fundamental importance – that of promoting full disclosure of governmental acts affecting Members and private persons and enterprises, whether of domestic or foreign nationality. The relevant policy principle is widely known as the principle of transparency and has obviously due

128 See *ibid.*, para. 7.1027. Whether a measure is a law, regulation, etc. within the meaning of Article X:1 must be based primarily on the content and substance of the instrument, and not merely on its form or nomenclature. See *ibid.*, para. 7.1023.

129 Panel Report, *Thailand – Cigarettes (Philippines) (2011)*, para. 7.773. Note that the panel in *China – Raw Materials (2012)* found that China's failure to set a quota amount was a measure to which Article XI:1 applied. See Panel Reports, *China – Raw Materials (2012)*, para. 7.803.

130 Panel Report, *US – Countervailing and Anti-Dumping Measures (China) (2014)*, para. 7.32.

131 See *ibid.*, para. 7.35.

132 See Panel Reports, *EC – IT Products (2010)*, para. 7.1129. See also Panel Report, *US – Countervailing and Anti-Dumping Measures (2014)*, para. 7.105.

133 The panel in *EC – IT Products (2011)* ruled that even a *single* instance of enforcement before the official publication could amount to a violation of Article X:2. See Panel Reports, *EC – IT Products (2011)*, para. 7.1131. Note that Article X:1 refers to 'publication', while Article X:2 refers to 'official publication'.

134 Note that, with respect to the issue of the retroactive effect of trade measures, the Appellate Body ruled in *US – Underwear (1997)* that Article X:2 does not speak to, and hence does not resolve, the permissibility of giving retroactive effect to trade-restrictive measures. Where no authority exists to give retroactive effect to a trade-restrictive measure, that deficiency is not cured by publishing the measure some time before its actual application. See Appellate Body Report, *US – Underwear (1997)*, 21.

process dimensions. The essential implication is that Members and other persons affected, or likely to be affected, by governmental measures imposing restraints, requirements and other burdens, should have a reasonable opportunity to acquire authentic information about such measures and accordingly to protect and adjust their activities or alternatively to seek modification of such measures.[135]

Article X:2 of the GATT 1994 concerns only two types of measures of general application: (1) measures of general application 'effecting an advance in a rate of duty or other charge on imports under an established and uniform practice';[136] and (2) measures of general application 'imposing a new or more burdensome requirement, restriction or prohibition on imports'. For neither type of measure, does Article X:2 explicitly specify the baseline of comparison to be used in order to determine whether there is an advance in a rate of duty or a new or more burdensome requirement.[137] However, the Appellate Body found in *US – Countervailing and Anti-Dumping Measures (China) (2014)* that:

the language in Article X:2 that refers to an *advance* in a rate of duty and a *new* or *more burdensome* requirement implies a comparison between the measure that is alleged to be increasing a rate of duty or imposing a new or more burdensome requirement and a relevant baseline, which is normally to be found in published measures of general application.[138]

The baseline of comparison for Article X:2 is thus the prior published measure of general application that was replaced or modified by the measure at issue,[139] as interpreted and applied by the relevant domestic authorities.[140] As already noted above, Article X:2 embodies the principles of transparency, due process and notice.[141] It follows therefrom that the relevant baseline of comparison should be reflected in norms that traders can rely upon and that accordingly create expectations among them, i.e. the prior published measures of general application.[142] As the Appellate Body stated:

Published measures create expectations among traders, and changes to such measures trigger the due process and notice obligations of Article X:2, which, for this reason, preclude the enforcement of those changes before publication.[143]

The Appellate Body recognised that there may be circumstances where there is no prior published measure of general application. It may be that: (1) the prior

135 *Ibid.* See also Appellate Body Report, *US – Countervailing and Anti-Dumping Measures (China) (2014)*, paras. 4.65–4.66.

136 'Effecting an advance in a rate of duty' may be understood to mean 'bringing about an increase in a rate of duty'. See Panel Report, *US – Countervailing and Anti-Dumping Measures (China) (2014)*, para. 7.145.

137 Note that the Appellate Body reversed the panel's finding that the phrase 'under an established and uniform practice' in Article X:2 served to define the appropriate baseline of comparison. See Appellate Body Report, *US – Countervailing and Anti-Dumping Measures (China) (2014)*, para. 4.93.

138 See *ibid.*, para. 4.96.

139 See *ibid.*, para. 4.105. While the Appellate Body agreed with the panel that the practices of government agencies are relevant in identifying the baseline of comparison under Article X:2 of the GATT 1994, it disagreed with the panel's use of the practice as the baseline of comparison without regard to other elements of municipal law. See *ibid.*, para. 4.92.

140 On the determination of the meaning of municipal law by panels and the Appellate Body, see above, p. 70.

141 See Appellate Body Report, *US – Underwear (1997)*, 29. See also above, p. 501.

142 See Appellate Body Report, *US Countervailing and Anti-Dumping Measures (China) (2014)*, para. 4.105.

143 *Ibid.*

measure of general application is unpublished; or (2) there is no measure at all. If the prior measure of general application is unpublished, this unpublished measure serves as the baseline of comparison.[144] If there is no prior measure at all, the absence of any rate of duty or any requirement will be the baseline of comparison.[145]

In *US – Countervailing and Anti-Dumping Measures (China) (2014)*, China, the complainant, argued that a measure that applies on a *retroactive* basis is, by definition, a measure that has been enforced prior to its publication and therefore in violation of Article X:2 of the GATT 1994. The panel in this case ruled that Article X:2 prohibits an administrative agency or court not only from enforcing a measure prior to its official publication, but also from enforcing or applying such measure in respect of *events or circumstances that occurred before it has been officially published*.[146] This finding was not appealed.

Note that the GATT 1994 and other WTO agreements also require Members to publish, or give public notice of, certain *specific* trade measures of general application.[147]

As noted above, WTO law also provides for a *notification* requirement. Almost all WTO agreements require Members to notify the WTO of measures or actions covered by these agreements. A typical example of such a notification requirement is found in Article 12.6 of the *Agreement on Safeguards*, which states:

> Members shall notify promptly the Committee on Safeguards of their laws, regulations and administrative procedures relating to safeguard measures as well as any modifications made to them.[148]

A number of WTO agreements also provide for the possibility for a Member to notify measures or actions of other Members, which the latter failed to notify.[149] The 1993 *Decision on Notification Procedures* lists in an annex the many measures and actions Members must notify to the WTO.[150] To improve the operation of the notification requirements under almost all WTO agreements, and thereby contribute to the transparency of Members' trade policies and measures, a *central registry of notifications* has been established under the responsibility of the WTO Secretariat. This central registry records the measures notified and the information provided by Members with respect to the purpose of the measure, its

144 See *ibid.*, para. 4.106. According to the Appellate Body, the content of such unpublished measure of general application should be ascertained based on its text, as well as other available elements of municipal law, such as practices of administrative agencies, court decisions and writings of recognised scholars. See *ibid.*

145 See *ibid.*

146 See Panel Report, *US – Countervailing and Anti-Dumping Measures (2014)*, para 7.118.

147 See e.g. Article XIII:3 of the GATT 1994 (concerning quotas and tariff quotas) and Article 2.11 of the *TBT Agreement* (concerning technical regulations).

148 See also below, p. 504.

149 See e.g. Article 12.8 of the *Agreement on Safeguards*. Such notifications are often referred to as 'cross notifications' or 'reverse notifications'.

150 *Decision on Notification Procedures*, adopted by the Trade Negotiations Committee on 15 December 1993 and annexed to the Final Act Embodying the Results of the Uruguay Round of Multilateral Trade Negotiations.

trade coverage and the requirement under which it has been notified. The central registry cross-references its records of notifications by Members and their obligations.[151] Information in the central registry regarding individual notifications is made available, on request, to any Member entitled to receive the notification concerned. The central registry informs each Member annually of the regular notification obligations to which that Member will be expected to respond in the course of the following year. It must be noted that many Members, and especially developing-country Members, fail to comply with one or more of their notification requirements. Often this failure is due to a lack of administrative capacity and WTO expertise within the relevant ministries of the Members concerned.[152]

In addition to a publication requirement and a notification requirement, some WTO agreements also require Members to establish national *enquiry points* where further information and relevant documents on certain trade laws and regulations can be obtained by other Members or interested parties. This is, for example, the case with regard to technical barriers to trade and SPS measures, as discussed in Chapters 13 and 14 respectively.[153]

Finally, the transparency of Members' trade policies, legislation and procedures is also advanced considerably by the periodic trade policy reviews under the *Trade Policy Review Mechanism*. This mechanism is discussed in detail in Chapter 2.[154]

Note that under its Accession Protocol, China is subject to a number of WTO-plus transparency obligations, such as: (a) the obligation to open its measures for pre-implementation public comments; (b) the obligation to publish its measures in the designated official journal; and (c) the obligation to make available the translation of its measures in one or more WTO languages.[155]

3.2 Unfair and Arbitrary Application of Trade Measures

It is clear that the unfair and arbitrary application of national trade measures, and the degree of uncertainty and unpredictability this generates for other Members and traders, constitutes a significant barrier to trade in the same way as the lack of transparency discussed above. To ensure minimum standards for transparency and procedural fairness in the administration of national trade measures,[156] Article X:3 of the GATT 1994 provides for: (1) a requirement of

151 See *ibid.*, 388.

152 On technical assistance in this respect to developing-country Members, see above, pp. 110–13. Note that the failure of Members to comply with their notification requirements may also be due to the lack of an incentive for doing so, or of a sanction for not doing so.

153 See below, pp. 883–932 and 935–90.

154 See above, p. 52.

155 See *Protocol on the Accession of the People's Republic of China*, WT/L/432, dated 23 November 2001.

156 See Appellate Body Report, *US – Shrimp (1998)*, para. 183.

uniform, impartial and reasonable administration of national trade measures; and (2) a requirement for procedures for the objective and impartial review of the administration of national customs rules.

The first of these two requirements is set out in Article X:3(a) of the GATT 1994, which provides:

> Each [Member] shall administer in a uniform, impartial and reasonable manner all its laws, regulations, decisions and rulings of the kind described in paragraph 1 of this Article.

The panel in *Thailand – Cigarettes (Philippines) (2011)* ruled that to establish a violation of Article X:3(a):

> a complaining party must therefore show that the responding Member *administers* the legal instruments of the kind described in Article X:1 in a manner that is *non-uniform, partial* and/or *unreasonable* ... The obligations of uniformity, impartiality and reasonableness are legally independent and the WTO Members are obliged to comply with all three requirements. This means that ... a violation of any of the three obligations will lead to a violation of the obligations under Article X:3(a).[157]

As the words of Article X:3(a) clearly indicate, the requirements of 'uniformity, impartiality and reasonableness' do not apply to the laws, regulations, decisions and rulings *themselves*, but rather to the *administration* of those laws, regulations, decisions and rulings.[158] To the extent that these measures themselves are discriminatory, they may be found inconsistent with, for example, Articles I:1, III:2 or III:4 of the GATT 1994.[159] However, as the Appellate Body clarified in *EC – Selected Customs Matters* (2006), it is possible to challenge under Article X:3(a) the substantive content of a legal instrument that regulates the administration of a law, regulation, decision or ruling falling under Article X:1.[160] The Appellate Body stated:

> Under Article X:3(a), a distinction must be made between the legal instrument being administered and the legal instrument that regulates the application or implementation of that instrument. While the substantive content of the legal instrument being administered is not challengeable under Article X:3(a), we see no reason why a legal instrument that regulates the application or implementation of that instrument cannot be examined under Article X:3(a) if it is alleged to lead to a lack of uniform, impartial, or reasonable administration of that legal instrument.[161]

Under Article X:3(a), one can thus challenge: (1) the manner in which legal instruments of the kind falling under Article X:1 are applied or implemented in particular cases; and (2) legal instruments that regulate such application or implementation. Note that also administrative processes leading to administrative

157 Panel Report, *Thailand – Cigarettes (Philippines) (2011)*, paras. 7.866–7.867.

158 See Appellate Body Report, *EC – Bananas III (1997)*, para. 200. See also Panel Report, *EC – Poultry (1998)*; and Panel Report, *US – Corrosion-Resistant Steel Sunset Review (2004)*.

159 See above, pp. 307–25, 351–76 and 376–99.

160 See Appellate Body Report, *EC – Selected Customs Matters (2006)*, para. 200. See also Panel Report, *Argentina – Hides and Leather (2001)*, paras. 11.71–11.72.

161 Appellate Body Report, *EC – Selected Customs Matters (2006)*, para. 200.

decisions have been found to fall within the scope of application of Article X:3(a).[162]

With regard to the requirement that national trade rules be applied in a uniform manner (the requirement of 'uniform administration'), the panel in *US – Stainless Steel (Korea) (2001)* stated:

> [T]he requirement of uniform administration of laws and regulations must be understood to mean uniformity of treatment in respect of persons similarly situated; it cannot be understood to require identical results where relevant facts differ.[163]

Furthermore, the Appellate Body ruled in *EC – Selected Customs Matters (2006)* that:

> Article X:3(a) of the GATT 1994 does not contemplate uniformity of administrative processes. In other words, non-uniformity or differences in administrative processes do not, by themselves, constitute a violation of Article X:3(a) ... [U]nder Article X:3(a), it is the application of a legal instrument ... that is required to be uniform, but not the processes leading to administrative decisions, or the tools that might be used in the exercise of administration.[164]

Note that, in *China – Raw Materials (2012)*, the panel found that a system under which export quotas were allocated by thirty-two local governmental entities which were not provided with any guidelines for the allocation of such export quotas, posed a very real risk to the interests of relevant parties such that this necessarily leads to 'non-uniform' administration inconsistent with Article X:3(a).[165]

The panel in *US – COOL (2012)* in considering whether the administration of the COOL measure at issue was 'non-uniform' noted:

> the interpretation of the term 'uniform' in Article X:3(a) does not necessarily entail *instantaneous* uniformity. Rather, uniformity must be attained within a period of time that is reasonable, and what is reasonable will depend on the form, nature and scale of the administration at issue, as well as on the complexity of the factual and legal issues raised by the act of administration that is being challenged.[166]

With respect to the requirement that national trade rules be applied in an impartial manner (the requirement of 'impartial administration'), the panel in *Thailand – Cigarettes (Philippines) (2011)* addressed the question whether the features of the administrative process at issue, namely, the fact that certain Thai government officials in charge of customs and tax determinations also serve on

162 See Panel Report, *Thailand – Cigarettes (Philippines) (2011)*, para. 7.873.

163 Panel Report, *US – Stainless Steel (Korea) (2001)*, para. 6.51.

164 Appellate Body Report, *EC – Selected Customs Matters (2006)*, para. 224.

165 See Panel Reports, *China – Raw Materials (2012)*, para. 7.752. Note, however, that the Appellate Body declared this finding moot and of no legal effect because the panel made this finding regarding a claim not properly identified in the panel request. See Appellate Body Reports, *China – Raw Materials (2012)*, para. 235. According to the panel in that case, 'reasonable' administration can be understood to be administration that is 'equitable', 'appropriate to the circumstances' and 'based on rationality'. See Panel Reports, *China – Raw Materials (2012)*, para. 7.696.

166 Panel Reports, *US – COOL (2012)*, para. 7.878. Emphasis added. Note that the findings of the panel in respect of Article X:3 of the GATT were not appealed.

the board of directors of the Thai Tobacco Monopoly to which these customs and tax determinations applied, leads to a lack of 'impartial administration'.[167] The panel started out by ruling that:

> [b]ased on the ordinary meaning ... *impartial* administration would appear to mean the application or implementation of the relevant laws and regulations in a fair, unbiased and unprejudiced manner.[168]

After considering in detail the evidence submitted by the complainant, the Philippines, the panel concluded that:

> unless it can be shown that these determinations are made because of the very presence of the government officials serving also as [Thai Tobacco Monopoly] directors, we are not in a position to find that the appointment of dual function officials led to a partial administration of customs and tax rules.[169]

With respect to the requirement that national trade rules be applied in a reasonable manner (the requirement of 'reasonable administration'), the panel in *Argentina – Hides and Leather (2001)* found that:

> a process aimed at assuring the proper classification of products, but which inherently contains the possibility of revealing confidential business information, is an unreasonable manner of administering the laws, regulations and rules identified in Article X:1 and therefore is inconsistent with Article X:3(a).[170]

The panel in *US – COOL (2012)* considered the term 'administer' in Article X:3(a) to refer to 'putting into practical effect or applying a legal instrument'.[171] Further, the panel considered that the act of providing guidance on the meaning of specific requirements of a measure amounts to an act of administering such measure within the meaning of Article X:3(a).[172]

Note that, in *Dominican Republic – Import and Sale of Cigarettes (2005)*, the panel found that the Dominican Republic had applied the provisions regarding

167 See Panel Report, *Thailand – Cigarettes (Philippines) (2011)*, para. 7.898. 168 *Ibid.*, para. 7.899.

169 *Ibid.*, para. 7.904. A similar situation arose in *Argentina – Hides and Leather (2001)*. At issue in that case was an Argentinian regulation providing for the participation of representatives of the domestic tanners' association, ADICMA, in the customs inspection procedures for hides destined for export operations. The representatives of ADICMA 'assisted' Argentina's customs authorities in the application and enforcement of the rules on customs classification, valuation and export duties. The panel in that case ruled that the Argentinian measure was inconsistent with the 'requirement of impartiality' of Article X:3(a). The panel noted that adequate safeguards could remedy this situation. However, such safeguards were, according to the panel, not in place. See Panel Report, *Argentina – Hides and Leather (2001)*, paras. 11.99–11.101. In *China – Raw Materials (2012)*, the panel examined the claim that the involvement of the China Chamber of Commerce of Metals, Minerals and Chemicals Importers and Exporters (CCCMC) in administering the export quotas on various raw materials constituted partial administration inconsistent with Article X:3(a). The panel concluded that, given the specific circumstances, it did not. See Panel Reports, *China – Raw Materials (2012)*, para. 7.787.

170 Panel Report, *Argentina – Hides and Leather (2001)*, para. 11.94.

171 Panel Reports, *US – COOL (2012)*, para. 7.821. The panel refers to Appellate Body Report, *EC – Selected Customs Matters (2006)*, para. 224 in this regard. The panel found that the contents of the 'Vilsack letter' and the circumstances surrounding its issuance 'indicate that the issuance ... of the letter to the US industry falls within the broad scope of administrative authority given to USDA regarding the application of the COOL measure, including any guidance on the specific requirements under the measure to be provided to the public'. See Panel Reports, *US – COOL (2012)*, para. 7.827.

172 *Ibid.*, para. 7.833.

the determination of the tax base for the imposition of tax on cigarettes in an unreasonable manner. According to the panel:

> [t]he fact that the Dominican Republic authorities did not support its decisions regarding the determination of the tax base for imported cigarettes by resorting to the rules in force at the time and that they decided to disregard retail selling prices of imported cigarettes, is not 'in accordance with reason', 'having sound judgement', 'sensible', 'within the limits of reason', nor 'articulate'.[173]

The panel in *Thailand – Cigarettes (Philippines) (2011)* examined whether the delays in appeals of customs valuation determinations constituted 'unreasonable administration' of the Thai customs laws. The panel found that, although the 'requirement of reasonable administration' of Article X:3(a) does not set a specific time limit for administrative review process, the delays at issue (the appeals process took over seven years) resulted in the administration of the Thai customs law in an unreasonable manner and were inconsistent with Article X:3(a).[174]

To conclude on Article X:3(a) of the GATT 1994, four more observations of a general nature must be made. First, the panel in *Argentina – Hides and Leather (2001)* clarified the nature of the obligation under Article X:3(a) by distinguishing between transparency between WTO Members and transparency with respect to individual traders. According to that panel, unlike for other rules under the GATT 1994, for Article X:3(a):

> the test generally will not be whether there has been discriminatory treatment in favour of exports to one Member relative to another. Indeed, the focus is on the treatment accorded by government authorities to the *traders* in question.[175]

Second, the same panel in *Argentina – Hides and Leather (2001)* ruled that, while a showing of trade damage is not required, Article X:3(a) requires an examination of the real effect that a measure might have on traders operating in the commercial world. The assessment of a violation of Article X:3(a) can therefore involve an examination of whether there is a possible impact on the competitive situation due to alleged partiality, unreasonableness or lack of uniformity in the application of a law, regulation, decision or ruling.[176]

Third, as the panel in *US – Hot-Rolled Steel (2001)* ruled, for a finding of violation of Article X:3(a), a Member's actions would have to have 'a significant impact on the overall administration of the law, and not simply on the outcome in the single case in question'.[177]

173 Panel Report, *Dominican Republic – Import and Sale of Cigarettes (2005)*, para. 7.388.
174 See Panel Report, *Thailand – Cigarettes (Philippines) (2011)*, para. 7.969.
175 See Panel Report, *Argentina – Hides and Leather (2001)*, para. 11.76. Emphasis added.
176 See *ibid.*, para. 11.77.
177 Panel Report, *US – Hot-Rolled Steel (2001)*, para. 7.268.

Fourth, the Appellate Body in *US – Oil Country Tubular Goods Sunset Reviews (2004)* cautioned WTO Members on bringing a case under Article X:3(a):

> We observe, first, that allegations that the conduct of a WTO Member is biased or unreasonable are serious under any circumstances. Such allegations should not be brought lightly, or in a subsidiary fashion.[178]

The requirements of uniform, impartial and reasonable administration of national trade measures are also reflected in WTO agreements other than the GATT 1994. Article 1.3 of the *Import Licensing Agreement*, for example, provides:

> The rules for import licensing procedures shall be neutral in application and administered in a fair and equitable manner.[179]

The Appellate Body ruled in *EC – Bananas III (1997)* that Article 1.3 of the *Import Licensing Agreement* and Article X:3(a) of the GATT 1994 have 'identical coverage'.[180] In disputes involving the administration of import-licensing procedures, Article 1.3 of the *Import Licensing Agreement* should be applied *first* since the *Import Licensing Agreement* deals specifically, and in detail, with the administration of import-licensing procedures.[181]

Apart from the requirements of Article X:3(a) that national trade measures be administered in a uniform, impartial and reasonable manner, Article X:3 contains – as noted above – a second rule to ensure transparency and procedural fairness in the administration of trade measures, namely the requirement of procedures for the *objective and impartial review*, and possible correction, of the administration of national customs rules. Article X:3(b) of the GATT 1994 provides:

> Each [Member] shall maintain, or institute as soon as practicable, judicial, arbitral or administrative tribunals or procedures for the purpose, *inter alia*, of the prompt review and correction of administrative action relating to customs matters.

In *EC – Selected Customs Matters (2006)*, the panel reflected on the function of Article X:3(b) as follows:

> [A] due process theme underlies Article X of the GATT 1994. In the Panel's view, this theme suggests that an aim of the review provided for under Article X:3(b) of the GATT 1994 is to ensure that a trader who has been adversely affected by a decision of an administrative agency has the ability to have that adverse decision reviewed by a tribunal or procedure that is independent from the agency that originally took the adverse decision.[182]

178 Appellate Body Report, *US – Oil Country Tubular Goods Sunset Reviews (2004)*, para. 217. See also Panel Report, *Thailand – Cigarettes (Philippines) (2011)*, para. 7.874.

179 See also above, pp. 496–8.

180 Appellate Body Report, *EC – Bananas III*, para. 203. The Appellate Body noted the difference in wording between Article 1.3 of the *Import Licensing Agreement* and Article X:3(a) of the GATT 1994, but considered that 'the two phrases are, for all practical purposes, interchangeable'.

181 See *ibid.*, para. 204.

182 Panel Report, *EC – Selected Customs Matters (2006)*, para. 7.536.

Article X:3(b) does not prescribe one particular type of review or correction. It refers very broadly to 'judicial, arbitral or administrative tribunals or procedures'. Members thus have a significant degree of discretion in complying with the obligation under Article X:3(b). However, Article X:3(b) does explicitly require that the 'tribunals or procedures' be *independent* of the agencies of which decisions are reviewed.[183] Furthermore, Article X:3(b) requires that the review or correction be 'prompt'. As discussed above, the panel in *Thailand – Cigarettes (Philippines) (2011)* was confronted with a situation in which there were excessive delays in the administrative appeals process; this process took over seven years and was the prerequisite step necessary to reach the Thai Tax Court. The panel ruled that Thailand had 'failed to maintain an independent tribunal for the *prompt* review of customs value determinations inconsistently with Article X:3(b)'.[184] Finally, Article X:3(b) requires that the decisions resulting from the review are implemented by, and govern the practice of, the agencies whose decisions are reviewed, unless an appeal is filed.[185]

Note that Article X:3(b) refers to 'administrative action relating to customs matters', i.e. the administration of *customs rules*, and *not* to the administration of the broader category of 'laws, regulations, decisions and rulings relating to trade matters' or, in short, the administration of *trade rules*.[186] However, in *Thailand – Cigarettes (Philippines) (2011)*, the Appellate Body agreed with the panel in that case that 'administrative action relating to customs matters' encompasses 'a *wide range of acts* applying legal instruments that have a rational relationship with customs matters'.[187]

Finally, in *US – Countervailing and Anti-Dumping Duties (2014)*, China, the complainant, argued that Article X:3(b) prevented WTO Members from changing legislation retroactively. According to China, the possibility of retroactive legislation would render judicial review under Article X:3(b) meaningless. The panel rejected China's argument.[188]

3.3 Customs Formalities and Procedures

Another important type of 'other non-tariff barrier' to trade in goods are customs formalities and procedures, i.e. administrative barriers to trade. The losses that traders suffer through delays at borders, complicated and/or unnecessary

183 Note, however, that pursuant Article X:3(c) of the GATT 1994, Members are not required to eliminate or replace procedures in place on the date of the GATT 1994 entered into force, which *in fact* provide for an objective and impartial review, even though these procedures are not fully or formally independent of the agencies of which decisions are being reviewed.

184 Panel Report, *Thailand – Cigarettes (Philippines) (2011)*, para. 7.1015.

185 This obligation does not, however, prohibit a Member from taking legislative action, which would retroactively change the law at issue. See Panel Report, *US – Countervailing and Anti-Dumping Measures (China) (2014)*, para. 7.291.

186 See in this respect the 'parallel' and broader obligation under Article VI:2 of the GATS, discussed below, p. 535.

187 Appellate Body Report, *Thailand – Cigarettes (Philippines) (2011)*, para. 202. Emphasis added.

188 See Panel Report, *US – Countervailing and Anti-Dumping Measures (China) (2014)*, para. 7.284.

documentation requirements and lack of automation of customs procedures are estimated to exceed, in many cases, the costs of customs duties. In a speech at the World Customs Organization in June 2011, the then WTO Director-General Pascal Lamy noted:

For OECD countries it currently takes on average about four separate documents and clearing the goods in an average of ten days at an average cost of about $1,100 per container. By contrast, in sub-Saharan Africa almost double the number of documents are required and goods take from 32 days (for exports) to 38 days (for imports) to clear at an average cost per container of between $2,000 (for exports) and $2,500 (for imports). The overall world champion at trade facilitation is Singapore, where four documents are required and goods are cleared in, at most, five days at an average cost of around $456 per container. At the other end of the scale are many of the low-income developing countries, in particular the landlocked developing countries, whose trade-processing costs can mushroom as a result of the effort required to move goods in transit by road or rail through their neighbours to their nearest international port. According to recent research, every extra day required to ready goods for import or export decreases trade by around 4%.[189]

Article VIII:1(c) of the GATT 1994 states:

The [Members] ... recognize the need for minimizing the incidence and complexity of import and export formalities and for decreasing and simplifying import and export documentation requirements.[190]

Article VIII:2 requires Members, in very general terms, to 'review' the operation of their laws and regulations in light of the acknowledged need for: (1) minimising the incidence and complexity of customs formalities; and (2) decreasing and simplifying documentation requirements. Article VIII:3 of the GATT 1994 furthermore requires penalties for breaches of customs regulations and procedural requirements to be *proportional*. Members may not impose substantial penalties for minor breaches of customs regulations or procedural requirements.

In view of the paucity of specific WTO rules with respect to customs formalities and procedures, the 1996 Singapore Ministerial Conference directed the Council for Trade in Goods 'to undertake exploratory and analytical work ... on the simplification of trade procedures in order to assess the scope for WTO rules in this area'.[191] The negotiations on simplification of trade procedures, commonly referred to as 'trade facilitation', were added to the agenda of the Doha Round negotiations in August 2004.[192] After almost a decade, it was at the Bali Ministerial Conference of December 2013, that the negotiations on rules to simplify customs formalities

189 Speech at the World Customs Organization in Brussels on 24 June 2011, www.wto.org/english/news_e/sppl_e/sppl197_e.htm.

190 The panel in *Argentina – Import Measures (2015)*, para. 6.432, considered that 'formalities' within the meaning of Article VIII:3 include 'all requirements that, although in appearance directed at mere observance of forms, must usually be observed in connection with the importation or exportation of goods'.

191 Ministerial Conference, *Singapore Ministerial Declaration*, adopted 13 December 1996, WT/MIN(96)/DEC, para. 21.

192 See Ministerial Conference, *Doha Ministerial Declaration*, adopted 14 November 2001, WT/MIN(01)/DEC/1, para. 27; and General Council, *Doha Work Programme*, Decision adopted on 1 August 2004, WT/L/579, dated 2 August 2004, para. 1(g). See also above, p. 93–9.

and procedures, were finally concluded resulting in a political agreement on an *Agreement on Trade Facilitation*.[193] In November 2014, the WTO Members adopted a *Protocol of Amendment* to insert this new Agreement into Annex 1A of the WTO Agreement. The *Agreement on Trade Facilitation* will enter into force once two-thirds of Members have completed their domestic ratification process.[194]

The *Agreement on Trade Facilitation* clarifies and improves relevant aspects of Articles V, VIII and X of the GATT 1994 with a view to further expediting the movement, release and clearance of goods, including goods in transit.[195] It further contains provisions for technical assistance and capacity building in this area. The *Agreement on Trade Facilitation* takes a unique approach towards special and differential treatment, in the form of provisions enabling developing and least-developed-country Members to self-designate the implementation periods of their commitments under the Agreement and identify their technical assistance needs.[196] It is estimated that full implementation of the *Agreement on Trade Facilitation* will bring down Members' trade costs by an average of 14.3 per cent; reduce time to import by over a day and a half (a 47 per cent reduction over the current average) and time to export by almost two days (a 91 per cent reduction over the current average); and add up to 2.7 per cent a year to world export growth and more than half a per cent a year to world GDP growth.[197]

3.4 Government Procurement Laws and Practices

National laws and/or practices relating to the procurement of goods by a government for its own use are often significant barriers to trade. Under such laws or practices, governments frequently buy domestic products rather than imported products. It is undisputed that a government can most effectively ensure 'best value for money' by purchasing goods (and services) through an open and non-discriminatory procurement process. However, governments often use public procurement to support the domestic industry or to promote employment. As discussed above, the national treatment obligation of Article III of the GATT 1994 does not apply to law, regulations and requirements governing government procurement.[198] As government procurement typically represents between 15 and 20 per cent of GDP,[199] it is clear that the absence of this and

193 See *Agreement on Trade Facilitation*, Ministerial Decision of 7 December 2013, WT/MIN(13)/36 – WT/L/911, dated 11 December 2013.

194 As of 1 October 2016, ninety-four WTO Members had submitted their instrument of ratification. See www.tfafacility.org/ratifications.

195 See Recital 3, *Agreement on Trade Facilitation*.

196 See Section II, *Agreement on Trade Facilitation*. See also above, p. 124.

197 See WTO, *World Trade Report 2015*, 7 and 8.

198 See Article III:8(a) of the GATT 1994; and above, pp. 347–50. Such measures governing government procurement must of course meet the requirements set out in Article III:8(a) of the GATT 1994.

199 The total size of the government procurement sector was estimated by the OECD to be in the range of 15–20 per cent of GDP across OECD and non-OECD economies. See R. Anderson, P. Pelletier, K. Osei-Lah and A. Müller, 'Assessing the Value of Future Accessions to the WTO Agreement on Government Procurement (GPA)', Staff Working Paper ERSD-2011-15 (WTO, 2011), 9.

other multilateral disciplines represents a significant gap in the multilateral trading system and leaves a considerable source of barriers to trade unaddressed.

The plurilateral WTO *Agreement on Government Procurement*, as revised, provides for some disciplines with respect to government procurement of goods as well as services.[200] However, it does so only for the forty-seven Members that are currently a party to this Agreement.[201] The *Agreement on Government Procurement* applies to the laws, regulations, procedures and practices regarding procurement by those government bodies which a party has listed in Appendix I to the Agreement[202] and which concern goods or services covered by the Agreement.[203] Furthermore, for the Agreement to apply, the government procurement contract must be worth more than a specified threshold value.[204] The key discipline provided for in the plurilateral *Agreement on Government Procurement* is non-discrimination. Article III:1(a) of the *Agreement on Government Procurement* sets out a national treatment obligation; Article III:1(b) sets out an MFN treatment obligation.[205] Furthermore, in order to ensure that these non-discrimination obligations are abided by, the Agreement also provides for rules to ensure that laws, regulations, procedures and practices regarding government procurement are transparent.[206] Compared to the original 1994 Agreement, the revised Agreement, which entered into force in 2014, makes the provisions of the Agreement more user-friendly and adapts them to recent developments in government procurement practices (such as the use of electronic tools in the procurement process). The revised Agreement also includes more explicit special and differential treatment provisions, so as to facilitate developing-country Members to become a party to the Agreement. Most importantly, however, the revised Agreement provides for a significantly extended coverage. The WTO Secretariat has estimated the gains in market access as a result of the extended coverage of the Agreement between US$80 and 100 billion annually.[207] These gains result from lower thresholds and additions of new entities and sectors to the parties' lists in Appendix I to the Agreement.

200 See Annex 4 of the *WTO Agreement* and the *Protocol Amending the Agreement on Government Procurement*, GPA/113, dated 2 April 2012. The revised *Agreement on Government Procurement* came into force on 6 April 2014.

201 See www.wto.org/english/tratop_e/gproc_e/memobs_e.htm. Note that these forty-seven Members include both the European Union and its twenty-eight Member States. The Agreement thus has only nineteen parties. Note also that another twenty-eight WTO Members participate in the GPA committee as observers, out of which eight are in the process of acceding to the Agreement.

202 See, in this respect, Panel Report, *Korea – Procurement (2000)*, in which the question arose whether the Korean Airport Construction Authority, the Korean Airports Authority and the Inchon International Airport Corporation were within the scope of Korea's list of 'central government entities' as specified in Korea's Schedule in Appendix I to the *Agreement on Government Procurement*.

203 The Agreement applies in principle to the procurement of all goods except those goods which a Member has explicitly excluded from the scope of application in its schedule (see annex 4 to a Member's schedule). For services, the Agreement only applies to those services Members have explicitly listed in their schedules (see annex 5 to a Member's schedule).

204 See Article I:4 of the *Agreement on Government Procurement*. In Appendix I to the Agreement, each party specifies relevant thresholds.

205 Note that these non-discrimination obligations *only apply* between the parties to the Agreement.

206 See Articles VII to XVI of the *Agreement on Government Procurement*.

207 See www.wto.org/english/tratop_e/gproc_e/negotiations_e.htm.

In the 2001 Doha Ministerial Declaration, Members expressly recognised the case for a *multilateral* agreement on transparency in government procurement.[208] However, in the years that followed, they failed to agree on the modalities of the negotiations on such a multilateral agreement, and transparency on government procurement was thus never included in the Doha Round agenda.[209] Many developing-country Members were concerned about their ability to engage 'successfully' in such negotiations and to implement the new international commitments resulting from these negotiations.

3.5 Other Measures and Actions

In addition to technical barriers to trade and SPS measures, the lack of transparency, unfair and arbitrary application of trade rules, customs formalities and procedures, and government procurement laws and practices, the category of 'other non-tariff barriers' to trade in goods also includes many other measures or actions, or the lack thereof. This section briefly addresses the following 'other non-tariff barriers': (1) preshipment inspection; (2) marks of origin; (3) measures relating to transit shipments; (4) operations of State trading enterprises; (5) trade-related investment measures; and (6) exchange controls or exchange restrictions.

Preshipment inspection is the practice of employing private companies to check the price, quantity, quality and/or the customs classification of goods *before* their shipment to the importing country.[210] Preshipment inspection is primarily used by developing-country Members to prevent commercial fraud and evasion of customs duties. Preshipment inspection is used to compensate for inadequacies in national customs administrations. While certainly beneficial, the problem with preshipment inspection is that it may give rise to unnecessary delays or unequal treatment, and thus constitute a barrier to trade. The WTO *Agreement on Preshipment Inspection* sets out obligations for both importing Members using preshipment inspection and the exporting Members on whose territory the inspection is carried out.

The importing Members using preshipment inspection must ensure, *inter alia*, that: (1) preshipment inspection activities are carried out in a non-discriminatory manner;[211] (2) preshipment inspection activities are carried out in a transparent manner;[212] (3) the companies carrying out the inspection respect the confidentiality of business information received in the course of the preshipment

208 Ministerial Conference, *Doha Ministerial Declaration*, adopted 14 November 2001, WT/MIN(01)/DEC/1, para. 26. A first step in this direction was taken at the 1996 Singapore Ministerial Conference. See Ministerial Conference, *Singapore Ministerial Declaration*, adopted 13 December 1996, WT/MIN(96)/DEC, para. 21.

209 See General Council, *Doha Work Programme*, Decision adopted on 1 August 2004, WT/L/579, dated 2 August 2004, para. 1(g).

210 See Article 1 of the *Agreement on Preshipment Inspection*.

211 See *ibid.*, Articles 2.1–2.2.

212 See *ibid.*, Articles 2.5–2.8.

inspection;[213] and (4) the companies carrying out the inspection avoid unreasonable delays in the inspection of shipments.[214]

The exporting Members on whose territory the preshipment inspection is carried out must ensure non-discrimination and transparency with regard to their laws and regulations relating to preshipment inspection activities.[215] The *Agreement on Preshipment Inspection* also provides for rules on procedures for independent review of disputes between the companies carrying out the inspection and the exporters.[216]

With respect to *marks of origin* 'attached' to imported goods, Article IX:2 of the GATT 1994 states:

> The [Members] recognize that, in adopting and enforcing laws and regulations relating to marks of origin, the difficulties and inconveniences which such measures may cause to the commerce and industry of exporting countries should be *reduced to a minimum*, due regard being had to the necessity of protecting consumers against fraudulent or misleading indications.[217]

Note that marking requirements are, of course, subject to all relevant WTO rules and disciplines, such as the MFN treatment obligation.[218]

With respect to measures concerning *traffic in transit*, Article V of the GATT 1994, entitled 'Freedom of Transit', sets out a number of obligations on Members not to impede this traffic. Traffic in transit is the traffic of goods from country A to country C, through the territory of country B. It is clear that any restriction or impediment that country B would impose on the transit of the goods concerned would constitute a barrier to trade. Article V:2 of the GATT 1994 provides:

> There shall be freedom of transit through the territory of each [Member], via the routes most convenient for international transit, for traffic in transit to or from the territory of other [Members]. No distinction shall be made which is based on the flag of vessels, the place of origin, departure, entry, exit or destination, or on any circumstances relating to the ownership of goods, of vessels or of other means of transport.

Traffic in transit shall not be subject to any unnecessary delays or restrictions and shall be exempt from customs duties and from all transit duties or other charges imposed in respect of transit, except charges for transportation or those commensurate with administrative expenses entailed by transit or with the cost of services rendered.[219] All charges, regulations and formalities in connection with transit shall be reasonable and be subject to the MFN treatment obligation.[220] The provisions of the recently concluded *Agreement on Trade Facilitation* are also pertinent in this regard.[221]

213 See *ibid.*, Articles 2.9–2.13. 214 See *ibid.*, Articles 2.15–2.19.

215 See *ibid.*, Articles 3.1–3.2. These Members must also provide to user Members, if requested, technical assistance directed towards the achievement of the objectives of this Agreement on mutually agreed terms. See *ibid.*, Article 3.3.

216 See *ibid.*, Article 4. 217 Emphasis added.

218 See Article IX:1 of the GATT 1994. 219 See Article V:3 of the GATT 1994.

220 See Article V:4 and 5 of the GATT 1994.

221 See Article 11 of the *Agreement on Trade Facilitation*.

Furthermore, the *operations of State trading enterprises* can be a significant barrier to trade in goods. State trading enterprises are:

[g]overnmental and non-governmental enterprises, including marketing boards, which have been granted exclusive or special rights or privileges, including statutory or constitutional powers, in the exercise of which they influence through their purchases or sales the level or direction of imports or exports.[222]

The WTO does not prohibit the establishment or maintenance of State trading enterprises. However, Article XVII of the GATT 1994 requires that: (1) State trading enterprises act in accordance with the MFN treatment obligation and other basic obligations under the GATT 1994;[223] and (2) only commercial considerations should guide their decisions on purchases and sales for import and export.[224] To increase transparency regarding the use of State trading, Members must notify their State trading enterprises to the WTO annually. Article XVII of the GATT 1994 is an anti-circumvention provision: a WTO Member may not, through state trading enterprises, 'engage in or facilitate conduct that would be condemned as discriminatory under the GATT 1994 if such conduct were undertaken directly by the Member itself'.[225]

Trade-related investment measures can also be barriers to trade when these measures take the form of direct or indirect quantitative restrictions on imports or exports. For example, a foreign car manufacturer may be allowed to establish a production plant in a country but only if it uses in the production of the cars steel produced in that country.[226] Article 2.1 of the *TRIMS Agreement* states in relevant part:

Without prejudice to other rights and obligations under GATT 1994, no Member shall apply any TRIM that is inconsistent with the provisions of ... Article XI of GATT 1994.

Finally, *exchange controls* or *exchange restrictions* may make it difficult, if not impossible, for an importer to pay for imports or for an exporter to be paid for exports. If so, these measures constitute a significant impediment to trade. Article XV:9 of the GATT 1994 stipulates in this regard that the GATT 1994 does not preclude Members to use exchange controls or exchange restrictions that are in accordance with: (1) the *Articles of Agreement* of the IMF; or (2) a Member's special exchange arrangement with the WTO. Nothing in the GATT 1994 precludes restrictions or controls on imports or exports the sole effect of which is to make effective such exchange controls or exchange restrictions.

222 *WTO Understanding on the Interpretation of Article XVII*, para. 1.

223 See Articles II:1 and XI of the GATT 1994, as discussed above, pp. 325 and 482.

224 See Appellate Body Report, *Canada – Wheat Exports and Grain Imports (2004)*, paras. 100–1 and 145.

225 *Ibid.*, para. 85.

226 For an illustrative list of trade-related investment measures in the form of quantitative restrictions, see *TRIMS Agreement*, Annex, para. 2.

4 MARKET ACCESS BARRIERS TO TRADE IN SERVICES

This chapter on non-tariff barriers to trade has dealt thus far with non-tariff barriers to trade in goods. The remainder of the chapter discusses non-tariff barriers to trade in services. As already discussed, the production and consumption of services are a principal economic activity in virtually all countries, developed and developing, alike. Financial, telecommunication and transport services are the backbone of a modern economy, and economic development and prosperity are dependent on the availability and efficiency of these and other services.[227] Services play a central role in the world economy. They represent 68.5 per cent of world GDP.[228] However, the importance of services in the world economy is *not* reflected (yet) in their share of world trade. In 2015, trade in services amounted to US$4.75 trillion, while trade in goods amounted to US$16.5 trillion.[229]

As discussed in Chapter 6 and in the introduction to this chapter, trade in services is, unlike trade in goods, not subject to tariff barriers.[230] Trade in services, however, faces many non-tariff barriers. The production and consumption of services are subject to a vast range of internal regulations. Barriers to trade in services are primarily the result of these internal regulations. Examples of such internal regulations that may constitute barriers to trade in services are: (1) a restriction on the number of drugstores allowed within a geographical area; (2) an obligation for all practising lawyers to be a member of the local bar association; (3) sanitation standards for restaurants; (4) technical safety requirements for oil-drilling companies; (5) a requirement that all professional services be offered in the national language; (6) professional qualification requirements for accountants; and (7) a prohibition for banks to sell life insurance.

WTO law, and the GATS in particular, provides for rules and disciplines on barriers to trade in services. Note, however, that, as explained below, most internal regulation of services does not constitute a GATS-inconsistent barrier to trade in services.[231] The production and consumption of services are often subject to internal regulation for good reason, including the protection of consumers and the protection of public health and safety. The Preamble to the GATS explicitly recognises:

> the right of Members to regulate, and to introduce new regulations on, the supply of services within their territories in order to meet national policy objectives.

It is important to stress that the objective of the GATS is *not* the *deregulation* of services. In fact, the liberalisation of some services sectors, such as

227 See WTO Secretariat, 'Market Access: Unfinished Business', Special Studies Series 6 (WTO, 2001), 98.
228 See World Bank, *Services, Etc., Value Added (% of GDP)*, http://data.worldbank.org/indicator/NV.SRV. TETC.ZS.
229 See above, p. 5.
230 See above, pp. 423 and 480. As discussed, tariff barriers to trade in services *currently* do not exist. However, such barriers *can* exist. See, for example, the 'bit tax'.
231 See below, pp. 518–20.

telecommunications, may require *increased* regulation in order to ensure quality of service or competition in the market.

With regard to non-tariff barriers to trade in services, the GATS distinguishes between, on the one hand, market access barriers, and, on the other hand, other barriers to trade in services. This section addresses the GATS rules on market access barriers and discusses in turn: (1) the definition and types of market access barriers; (2) rules on market access barriers; (3) negotiations on market access; (4) Schedules of Specific Commitments; and (5) modification and withdrawal of commitments. The next section in this chapter deals with the GATS rules on other barriers to trade in services.[232]

4.1 Definition and Types of Market Access Barriers

The GATS does not explicitly define the concept of 'market access barriers'. However, Article XVI:2(a)–(f) of the GATS provide an *exhaustive* list of such measures.[233] This list comprises six types of market access barriers. Five of the six types are quantitative restrictions on: (1) the number of service suppliers; (2) the value of the service transactions; (3) the number of service operations: (4) the number of natural persons employed by a service supplier; and (5) the amount of foreign capital invested in service suppliers.[234] One type of market access barrier is of a different nature. It is a limitation on the kind of legal entity or joint venture through which services may be supplied.[235]

These market access barriers can be discriminatory *or* non-discriminatory with respect to foreign services or service suppliers. For example, a restriction on the broadcasting time available for foreign movies is obviously a *discriminatory* market access barrier, while a licence for a fast food restaurant subject to an economic needs test based on population density is a *non-discriminatory* market access barrier.[236] Article XVI:2 of the GATS covers both discriminatory *and* non-discriminatory market access barriers.

232 Recall that Chapter 4 discusses the scope of application of the GATS. See above, pp. 325–7.
233 The panel in *US – Gambling (2005)* confirmed that the list of Article XVI:2 is exhaustive. It came to this conclusion based on the text of the provision, its context and the 1993 Scheduling Guidelines. See Panel Report, *US – Gambling (2005)*, paras. 6.293–6.298. Antigua appealed this finding. The Appellate Body, however, chose not to deal with this issue. See Appellate Body Report, *US – Gambling (2005)*, para. 256. The panel in *China – Publications and Audiovisual Products (2010)* reiterated that the list of Article XVI:2 is exhaustive. See also Panel Report, *China – Publications and Audiovisual Products (2010)*, para. 7.1353.
234 See Article XVI:2(a)–(d) and (f) of the GATS. As the Appellate Body noted in *US – Gambling (2005)*, the focus of Article XVI:2 is on quantitative restrictions. See Appellate Body Report, *US – Gambling (2005)*, para. 225.
235 See Article XVI:2(e) of the GATS.
236 See *Guidelines for the Scheduling of Specific Commitments under the General Agreement on Trade in Services (GATS)*, adopted by the Council for Trade in Services on 23 March 2001, S/L/92, dated 28 March 2001, para. 12. As stated in an explanatory note, these Guidelines were based on two documents which were produced and circulated during the Uruguay Round negotiations: MTN.GNS/W/164, *Scheduling of Initial Commitments in Trade in Services: Explanatory Note*, dated 3 September 1993; and MTN.GNS/W/164, Add.1, *Scheduling of Initial Commitments in Trade in Services: Explanatory Note, Addendum*, dated 30 November 1993. See *ibid.*, fn. 1.

Note that, when a market access barrier takes the form of a quantitative restriction referred to in subparagraphs (a)–(d), this restriction can be expressed numerically, *or* through the criteria specified in these provisions, such as an economic needs test. It is important to note, however, that these criteria do *not* relate to: (1) the quality of the service supplied; or (2) the ability of the supplier to supply the service (i.e. technical standards or qualification of the supplier).[237] A requirement, for example, that services be offered in the national language or a requirement for engineers to have specific professional qualifications may impede trade in services but is *not* a market access barrier within the meaning of Article XVI:2 of the GATS.

Note also that the quantitative restrictions specified in subparagraphs (a)–(d) refer to *maximum* limitations. Minimum requirements such as those common to licensing criteria (for example, minimum capital requirements for the establishment of a corporate entity) do not fall within the scope of Article XVI of the GATS.[238]

In *US – Gambling (2005)*, the panel found that, by maintaining measures that *prohibit* the supply of certain services, the United States effectively limited to zero the service suppliers and service operations relating to that service. According to the panel, such a zero quota constituted a limitation 'on the number of service suppliers ... in the form of numerical quotas' within the meaning of Article XVI:2(a) and a limitation 'on the total number of service operations ... in the form of quotas' within the meaning of Article XVI:2(c).[239] On appeal, the United States argued that the panel had ignored the fact that Article XVI:2(a) and (c) refer to measures in the *form* of numerical quotas and not to measures having the *effect* of numerical quotas. According to the United States, the measures concerned were not market access barriers within the meaning of Article XVI:2. The Appellate Body disagreed with the United States and upheld the relevant findings of the panel.[240] The Appellate Body noted that the words 'in the form of' must not be interpreted as 'prescribing a rigid mechanical formula'.[241] According to the Appellate Body, a measure equivalent to a zero quota is a market access barrier within the meaning of Article XVI:2.[242] An example of such limitation would be a nationality requirement for suppliers of services.[243]

The panel in *Mexico – Telecoms* (2004) noted that none of the six types of market access barrier of Article XVI:2 relates to *temporal* limitations on the supply of

237 *Guidelines for the Scheduling of Specific Commitments under the General Agreement on Trade in Services (GATS)*, S/L/92, dated 28 March 2001, para. 8.

238 See *ibid.*, para. 11.

239 See Panel Report, *US – Gambling (2005)*, paras. 6.330 and 6.347.

240 See Appellate Body Report, *US – Gambling (2005)*, paras. 239 and 252.

241 *Ibid.*, para. 231. It is the numerical or quantitative nature of the limitation that matters, not the form of the limitation.

242 See *ibid.*, paras. 238 and 251.

243 Note that the Appellate Body ruled in *US – Gambling (2005)* that 'it is neither necessary nor appropriate for us to draw, in the abstract, the line between quantitative and qualitative measures'. See Appellate Body Report, *US – Gambling (2005)*, para. 250.

a service. According to the panel, this suggests that temporal limitations cannot constitute market access barriers within the meaning of Article XVI:2.[244]

The panel in *Argentina – Financial Services (2016)* concluded that for a measure to be covered by Article XVI:2(a) of the GATS, the measure must regulate 'service suppliers' as such, that is, 'when the measure is aimed at persons in their capacity as service suppliers'.[245] Further, based on a combined reading of Article XXVIII(g) and Article XXVIII(j) of the GATS, it noted that 'Article XVI:2(a) covers measures whose purpose is to limit the number of persons, natural or legal, supplying a service'.[246]

4.2 Rules on Market Access Barriers

The GATS does not provide for a general prohibition on the market access barriers discussed in the above paragraphs. Whether a Member may maintain or adopt these market access barriers with regard to a specific service depends on whether, and if so to what extent, that Member has, in its Services Schedule, made market access commitments with regard to that service or the relevant services sector and the relevant mode of supply. This is commonly referred to as the 'positive list' or 'bottom-up' approach to the liberalisation of trade in services. Article XVI of the GATS, entitled 'Market Access', provides, in paragraph 1:

> With respect to market access through the modes of supply identified in Article I, each Member shall accord services and service suppliers of any other Member *treatment no less favourable* than that provided for under the terms, limitations and conditions agreed and specified in its Schedule.[247]

Furthermore, the chapeau of Article XVI:2 of the GATS states:

> In sectors where market-access commitments are undertaken, the measures which a Member shall not maintain or adopt either on the basis of a regional subdivision or on the basis of its entire territory, unless otherwise specified in its Schedule, are defined as ...

Paragraphs (a)–(f) of Article XVI:2 then provide for the list of market access barriers discussed above. In other words, when a Member has undertaken a market access commitment in respect of a services sector and a mode of supply, it

244 See Panel Report, *Mexico – Telecoms (2004)*, para. 7.358. For example, a measure that makes the supply of a service subject to a permit which would not be granted until the corresponding regulations are issued would not be a market access barrier within the meaning of Article XVI:2.

245 See Panel Report, *Argentina – Financial Services (2016)*, para. 7.424. The panel in this case found that the measure at issue regulated 'reinsurance operations' or 'individual risks', but did not specifically regulate any natural or legal person supplying reinsurance service. It therefore concluded that the measure is not covered by Article XVI(2)(a) of GATS because it does not regulate service suppliers within the meaning of that provision. Note that the panel's conclusion on this issue was not appealed.

246 See *ibid.*, para. 7.425.

247 Emphasis added. The panel in *China – Publications and Audiovisual Products (2010)* stated that, under Article XVI, a Member is free to maintain a market access regime less restrictive than that set out in its Schedule. See Panel Reports, *China – Publications and Audiovisual Products (2010)*, para. 7.1353.

may not maintain or adopt any of the listed market access barriers with regard to trade in services in that sector and that mode of supply, unless otherwise specified in its Services Schedule. A Member can specify in its Schedule that it maintains, or reserves the right to adopt, certain market access barriers.

When a Member makes a market access commitment, it *binds* the level of market access specified in its Schedule (see Article XVI:1) and agrees not to impose any market access barrier that would restrict access to the market beyond the level specified (see Article XVI:2).[248] In *US – Gambling (2005)*, the United States had inscribed the term 'none' in its Schedule with respect to market access limitations for 'other recreational services (excluding sporting)', which was interpreted to include gambling and betting services.[249] Both the panel and the Appellate Body confirmed that this means that the United States has committed itself to providing *full* market access in that services sector.[250]

To date, Members have been found to have acted inconsistently with the prohibition on market access barriers of Article XVI of the GATS in three disputes.[251]

4.3 Negotiations on Market Access for Services

Article XIX of the GATS, entitled 'Negotiation of Specific Commitments', states, in its first paragraph:

> In pursuance of the objectives of this Agreement, Members shall enter into successive rounds of negotiations ... with a view to achieving a progressively higher level of liberalization.

The GATS thus aims at achieving *progressively* higher levels of liberalisation of trade in services through *successive* rounds of negotiations. The Uruguay Round negotiations on the liberalisation of trade in services were only a first step in what will definitely be a long process of progressive liberalisation. The negotiations on 'specific commitments' under Article XIX concern not only market access commitments but also national treatment commitments, discussed in Chapter 6.[252] While the focus in this subsection is on the negotiations on market access, it must be kept in mind that the rules discussed in this subsection equally apply to the negotiations on national treatment. This subsection addresses in turn: (1) the basic rules governing Article XIX negotiations; and (2) the organisation of Article XIX negotiations.

248 On the relationship between Article XVI:1 and XVI:2, the panel in *China – Publications and Audiovisual Products (2010)* stated that Article XVI:2 was 'more specific' as it describes the measures that a Member must not adopt. See Panel Report, *China – Publications and Audiovisual Products (2010)*, para. 7.1353.

249 See below, pp. 527–8.

250 See Panel Report, *US – Gambling (2005)*, paras. 6.267–6.279; and Appellate Body Report, *US – Gambling (2005)*, paras. 214–15.

251 See *US – Gambling (2005)*; *China – Publications and Audiovisual Products (2009)*; and *China – Electronic Payment Services (2012)*.

252 See above, p. 400.

4.3.1 Basic Rules Governing Article XIX Negotiations

With regard to the negotiations on the progressive liberalisation of trade in services, Article XIX:1 of the GATS provides:

> Such negotiations shall be directed to the reduction or elimination of the adverse effects on trade in services of measures as a means of providing effective market access. This process shall take place with a view to promoting the interests of all participants on a mutually advantageous basis and to securing an overall balance of rights and obligations.

The objective of the negotiations is thus to provide effective *market access* for services. In Article XIX negotiations, Members strive for a 'mutually advantageous' outcome, i.e. 'reciprocity'. The main approach to negotiations on the liberalisation of services is a request-and-offer approach.[253] At the initial stage of negotiations, Members first make requests for the liberalisation of trade in specific services.[254] The exchange of requests, as a process, is mainly bilateral, but may also be plurilateral.[255] It is simply a process of letters being addressed from the requesting participants to their negotiating partners.[256] After Members participating in the negotiations have made requests, they submit offers.[257] A Member submits an offer in response to all the requests that it has received, but does not necessarily have to address each element contained in those requests in its offer.[258] Unlike a request, which is usually presented in the form of a letter, an offer is normally presented in the form of a draft schedule of commitments.[259] While requests are addressed bilaterally (or plurilaterally) to negotiating partners, offers are circulated multilaterally.[260] Offers are to be open to consultations and negotiation by all negotiating partners; not only to those who have made requests to the Member concerned but also any other participant in the negotiations.[261] In fact, offers are a signal of the real start of the advanced stage of bilateral negotiations, i.e. when negotiators come to Geneva to hold many

253 See *Guidelines and Procedures for the Negotiations on Trade in Services*, adopted by the Special Session of the Council for Trade in Services on 28 March 2001, S/L/93, dated 29 March 2001, para. 11. On approaches to tariff negotiations, see above, pp. 428–36.

254 There are possibly four types of content in a request, which are not mutually exclusive: (i) the addition of new services sectors; (ii) the removal of existing limitations or the introduction of bindings in modes which have so far been unbound; (iii) the undertaking of additional commitments under Article XVIII; and (iv) the termination of MFN exemptions. See *Technical Aspects of Requests and Offers*, Summary of Presentation by the WTO Secretariat at the WTO Seminar on the GATS, 20 February 2002, 1, www.wto.org/english/tratop_e/serv_e/requests_offers_approach_e.doc.

255 See *Guidelines and Procedures for the Negotiations on Trade in Services*, adopted by the Special Session of the Council for Trade in Services on 28 March 2001, S/L/93, dated 29 March 2001, para. 11; and Ministerial Conference, *Ministerial Declaration*, adopted on 18 December 2005, WT/MIN(05)/DEC, dated 22 December 2005, Annex C, para. 7.

256 See *ibid.*

257 In terms of content, offers normally address the same four types referred to in fn. 254 above.

258 See *Technical Aspects of Requests and Offers*, Summary of Presentation by the WTO Secretariat at the WTO Seminar on the GATS, 20 February 2002, 3, www.wto.org/english/tratop_e/serv_e/requests_offers_approach_e.doc.

259 See *ibid.*

260 See *ibid.* The multilateral circulation is useful not only from a transparency point of view but also from a functional point of view since, in an offer, a participant is actually responding to *all* the requests that it has received.

261 See *ibid.*

bilateral talks with various different delegations. The submission of offers may also trigger the submission of further requests and then the process continues and becomes a succession of requests and offers.[262]

Article XIX:2 of the GATS explicitly requires that the process of liberalisation of trade in services take place with due respect for: (1) national policy objectives; and (2) the level of development of individual Members, both overall and in individual sectors. Article XIX:2 further provides specifically with respect to the position of developing-country Members in the negotiations on the liberalisation of trade in services that:

> [t]here shall be appropriate flexibility for individual developing-country Members for opening fewer sectors, liberalizing fewer types of transactions, progressively extending market access in line with their development situation and, when making access to their markets available to foreign service suppliers, attaching to such access conditions aimed at achieving the objectives referred to in Article IV.

It is thus accepted that developing-country Members undertake fewer and more limited market access commitments than developed-country Members. 'Full reciprocity' is not required from developing-country Members. These Members are only expected to undertake market access commitments commensurate with their level of development.

4.3.2 Organisation of Article XIX Negotiations

As provided in Article XIX:3 of the GATS, for each round of multilateral negotiations on the liberalisation of trade in services, negotiating guidelines and procedures shall be established. For the current negotiations, initiated pursuant to Article XIX:1 of the GATS in January 2000 and now conducted in the context of the Doha Round negotiations,[263] the *Guidelines and Procedures for the Negotiations on Trade in Services* were adopted on 28 March 2001 by the Council for Trade in Services.[264]

Members have been exchanging bilateral initial requests since June 2002, and, as of the end of April 2011, WTO Members had submitted seventy-one initial offers and thirty-one revised offers.[265] However, from early on, there was – and there currently still is – widespread disappointment regarding the progress made in the negotiations. In its Decision of 1 August 2004 on the *Doha Work Programme*, the General Council reaffirmed the Members' commitment to make progress in the services negotiations;[266] and, in December 2005, the Ministerial

262 See *ibid.*

263 Ministerial Conference, *Doha Ministerial Declaration*, adopted 14 November 2001, WT/MIN(01)/DEC/1, dated 20 November 2001, para. 15.

264 Council for Trade in Services, *Guidelines and Procedures for the Negotiations on Trade in Services*, S/L/93, dated 29 March 2001. Note that, while the negotiations focus on market access, they also cover three other major areas, namely, internal regulation, GATS rules and the implementation of LDC modalities.

265 See www.wto.org/english/tratop_e/serv_e/market_access_negs_e.htm. On the request-and-offer approach to the negotiations on trade in services, see above, p. 522.

266 See General Council, *Doha Work Programme*, Decision adopted on 1 August 2004, WT/L/579, dated 2 August 2004, para. 1(e).

Conference, at its meeting in Hong Kong, called on Members to intensify the negotiations with a view to expanding coverage of commitments and improving their quality. The Ministerial Conference provided in Annex C to the Hong Kong Ministerial Declaration more detailed negotiating objectives to guide Members.[267] The Ministerial Conference also agreed that least-developed-country Members were not expected to undertake new services commitments. As provided for in Annex C to the Hong Kong Ministerial Declaration, Members tried out, as from March 2006, a new approach to the negotiations, namely, the plurilateral request approach. Under this approach, a group of Members requesting market access started negotiations with targeted Members on the basis of a *collective* request. However, this and other efforts to produce a breakthrough in the market access negotiations were to little avail. In short, the negotiations on market access for services are, as the Doha Round negotiations in general, deadlocked. On the one hand, there are Members, mainly developed-country Members, for which the market access offers currently on the table are insufficient. On the other hand, there are Members, primarily developing-country Members, for which the requests for market access go too far.[268] In its 2015 report to the Trade Negotiation Committee, the Chair of the Special Session of the Council for Trade in Services stated as follows:

> It is with considerable disappointment therefore that I must report that, despite our best efforts, it has not proved possible to agree on a work program in services. Although various interesting ideas have been put forward by Members in the course of our discussions, ultimately there has been no convergence toward any text containing a clearly-defined work program in services.[269]

Most recently, at an informal meeting of the Services Council in July 2016, WTO Members reportedly expressed strong interest in reviving service negotiations.[270]

As noted in Chapter 2, there are at present – outside the WTO – negotiations ongoing on an ambitious liberalisation of trade in services, building upon but going beyond the existing GATS.[271] These negotiations on a Trade in Services Agreement (TiSA), currently involve twenty-three developed- and developing-country Members, including the European Union and the United States, but not Brazil, China or India.[272] The latter Members have warned of the consequences for the multilateral trading system of adopting a plurilateral approach to negotiations on the liberalisation of trade in services.[273]

267 Ministerial Conference, *Ministerial Declaration*, adopted on 18 December 2005, WT/MIN(05)/DEC, dated 22 December 2005.

268 Note that some of these developing-country Members, and in particular Brazil, linked their willingness to accept far-reaching requests for market access to a successful conclusion of the negotiations on the liberalisation of trade in agricultural products.

269 Council for Trade in Services, Special Session, *Negotiations on Trade in Services*, Report by the Chairman, Ambassador Gabriel Duque, to the Trade Negotiations Committee, TN/S/39, dated 30 July 2015, 1.

270 See www.wto.org/english/news_e/news16_e/serv_04jul16_e.htm. 271 See above, p. 101.

272 See http://ec.europa.eu/trade/policy/in-focus/tisa/. Together, the WTO Members participating in the TiSA negotiations account for 70 per cent of world trade in services. See *ibid.*

273 See *Bridges Weekly Trade News Digest*, 4 April 2012, 11 July 2012 and 26 September 2012.

4.4 Schedules of Specific Commitments

The results of negotiations on market access for services are set out in Schedules of Specific Commitments, commonly referred to as 'Services Schedules'. This is what was done in 1994 with the results of the Uruguay Round negotiations on market access for services. This subsection discusses: (1) the contents and structure of Services Schedules; (2) the interpretation of Services Schedules; and (3) the market access commitments agreed to in the Uruguay Round Services Schedules.

4.4.1 Contents and Structure of Services Schedules

The Services Schedules set out the terms of market access for services agreed to in the context of market access negotiations. In addition to the terms of market access, Services Schedules also set out the terms of national treatment, discussed in Chapter 5, and the terms of additional commitments, discussed later in this chapter.[274] Each Member has a Services Schedule. In fact, each Member *must* have a Services Schedule, albeit that there is no minimum requirement as to the scope or depth of the commitments set out in that Schedule. All Services Schedules are annexed to the GATS and form an integral part thereof.[275] All Services Schedules are available on the WTO website.[276] The online WTO Services Database gives information on all commitments undertaken by all Members, and can be used to establish the commitments of a particular Member with regard to a specific services sector or subsector, or to compare services commitments across Members.[277]

Services Schedules have two parts: (1) a part containing the *horizontal commitments*; and (2) a part containing the *sectoral commitments*. Horizontal commitments apply to all sectors included in the Schedule. Schedules include horizontal commitments to *avoid repeating* in relation to each sector contained in the Schedule the same information regarding limitations, conditions or qualifications of commitments.[278] Horizontal commitment often concern two modes of supply in particular, namely, supply through commercial presence (mode 3) and supply through the presence of natural persons (mode 4).[279] For example,

274 See above, p. 400, and below, p. 536.

275 Article XX:3 of the GATS. 276 See www.wto.org/english/tratop_e/serv_e/serv_commitments_e.htm.

277 See http://tsdb.wto.org/wto/WTOHomepublic.htm. Be aware that the Consolidated Services Schedule of the European Union and its Member States (S/C/W/273, dated 9 October 2006), resulting from the enlargement of the European Union, is not included in the searchable database of commitments (as it had not yet entered into force at the time of establishing this database).

278 Horizontal commitments are found at the beginning of a schedule. The concept of 'horizontal commitments' may be misleading since 'horizontal commitments' are often, in fact, horizontal limitations, i.e. limitations applicable to all commitments. Only with regard to mode 4 supply of services, horizontal commitments are frequently positive undertakings.

279 On the four modes of supply of services (cross-border supply, consumption abroad, supply through commercial presence and supply through the presence of natural persons), see above, pp. 329–30.

with regard to mode 4 supply of all services scheduled, the Services Schedule of the European Union and its Member States stipulates:

> Unbound except for measures concerning the entry into and temporary stay within a Member State, without requiring compliance with an economic needs test, of the following categories of natural persons providing services ...[280]

Unlike horizontal commitments, sectoral commitments (or sector-specific commitments) are, as the term indicates, commitments made regarding specific services sectors or subsectors. For scheduling commitments, WTO Members distinguish twelve broad services sectors: business services; communication services; construction and related engineering services; distribution services; educational services; environmental services; financial services; health-related and social services; tourism and travel-related services; recreational, cultural and sporting services; transport services; and other services not included elsewhere. These twelve broad services sectors are further divided into more than 150 subsectors.[281] For example, the 'business services' sector includes: professional services (including, for example, legal services, accounting, architectural services, engineering services, and medical and dental services); computer and related services; research and development services; real estate services; rental/leasing services without operators; and other business services (including, for example, building cleaning services and publishing). The 'communication services' sector includes: postal services; courier services; telecommunications services (including, for example, voice telephone services, electronic mail, voice mail and electronic data interchange); and audiovisual services (including, for example, motion picture and video tape production and distribution services, radio and television services and sound recording). This WTO classification of services sectors, set out in the Services Sectoral Classification List of the WTO Secretariat, also referred to as 'document W/120',[282] is based on the provisional Central Product Classification (CPC) of the United Nations. In the Secretariat's List, each sector is identified by the corresponding CPC number. The CPC gives a detailed explanation of the services covered by each of the sectors and subsectors.[283] Note that a specific service cannot fall within two different sectors or subsectors. The sectors and subsectors are mutually exclusive.[284]

280 GATS/SC/31, dated 15 April 1994, 7–10.

281 Note that, if a market access commitment is given in a particular sector, that commitment applies to the whole of that sector, including all of its subsectors (unless of course a subsector is specifically excluded or a different regime is specified for it). See Panel Report, *US – Gambling (2005)*, para. 6.290.

282 See MTN.GNS/W/120, dated 10 July 1991.

283 A breakdown of the CPC, including explanatory notes for each subsector, is contained in the UN Provisional Central Product Classification, http://unstats.un.org/unsd/cr/registry/regcst.asp?Cl=16&Lg=1. To determine the coverage of the services sectors and subsectors of the WTO Services Sectoral Classification List, the detailed explanation of the CPC system can be used. Entries in Schedules often include CPC numbers.

284 See Appellate Body Report, *US – Gambling (2005)*, para. 180. See also Panel Report, *China – Electronic Payment Services (2012)*, para. 7.531.

In scheduling their commitments, most Members follow the WTO's Services Sectoral Classification List (W/120).[285] Thus, most Schedules have the same structure. A services sector or subsector is of course only included in a Member's Services Schedule if that Member undertakes commitments in that sector or subsector.

Services Schedules have four columns: (1) a first column identifying the services sector or subsector which is the subject of the commitment; (2) a second column containing the terms, limitations and conditions on market access; (3) a third column containing the conditions and qualifications on national treatment; and (4) a fourth column for undertakings relating to additional commitments. With regard to market access commitments, Members indicate, in the second column of their Schedule, the presence or absence of limitations on market access. They do so for each services sector scheduled and with regard to each of the four modes of supply: cross-border supply (mode 1); consumption abroad (mode 2); supply through commercial presence (mode 3); and supply through presence of natural persons (mode 4).

As set out in the 2001 Scheduling Guidelines,[286] for each market access commitment with respect to each mode of supply, four different situations can occur:

(1) First situation: *full commitment*, i.e. the situation in which a Member does not seek in any way to limit market access in a given sector and mode of supply through market access barriers within the meaning of Article XVI:2. A Member in this situation records in the second column of its Schedule the word 'none'.[287]

(2) Second situation: *commitment with limitations*, i.e. the situation in which a Member wants to limit market access in a given sector and mode of supply through market access barriers within the meaning of Article XVI:2. A Member in this situation describes in the second column of its Schedule the market access barrier(s) that is/are maintained.[288]

(3) Third situation: *no commitment*, i.e. the situation in which a Member wants to remain free in a given sector and mode of supply to introduce or maintain market access barriers within the meaning of Article XVI:2. A Member in this situation records in the second column of its Schedule the word 'unbound'.[289]

285 W/120 is therefore an important document for the interpretation of service commitments made by Members. The Appellate Body has considered and used W/120 as preparatory work within the meaning of Article 32 of the *Vienna Convention*. See Appellate Body Report, *US – Gambling (2005)*, paras. 196ff.

286 See Council for Trade in Services, *Guidelines for the Scheduling of Specific Commitments under the General Agreement on Trade in Services* (GATS), adopted on 23 March 2001, S/L/92, dated 28 March 2001, paras. 41–7.

287 Note, however, that any relevant limitation listed in the 'horizontal commitments' part of the Schedule also applies. See above, p. 526.

288 Two main possibilities can be envisaged in such a situation: the first is the binding of an existing situation ('standstill'); the second is the binding of a more liberal situation where some, but not all, of the access barriers inconsistent with Article XVI:2 will be removed ('rollback'). The Scheduling Guidelines state that: '[t]he entry should describe each measure concisely, indicating the elements which make it inconsistent with Articles XVI or XVII'. See Scheduling Guidelines 1993, para 25; and Scheduling Guidelines 2001, para. 44.

289 Note that this situation will only occur when a Member made a commitment in a sector with respect to at least one mode of supply. Where all modes of supply are 'unbound', and no additional commitments have been undertaken in the sector, the sector should not appear in the Schedule.

(4) Fourth situation: *no commitment technically feasible*, i.e. the situation in which a particular mode of supply is not technically possible, such as the cross-border supply of hair-dressing services. A Member in this situation records in the second column of its Schedule 'unbound*'.[290]

As discussed in Chapter 5, and as is evident from the excerpt from the Services Schedule of Brazil shown in Figure 7.1, national treatment commitments and limitations thereof are inscribed in the third column of the Schedules in the same way as market access commitments and limitations thereof are inscribed. It is possible that a measure is both a market access barrier prohibited under Article XVI:2 and a measure inconsistent with the national treatment obligation of Article XVII. For this type of situation, Article XX:2 of the GATS provides that:

[m]easures inconsistent with both Articles XVI and XVII shall be inscribed in the column relating to Article XVI. In this case the inscription will be considered to provide a condition or qualification to Article XVII as well.

In other words, any limitation to a market access commitment inscribed in the second column will also apply to the national treatment commitment made, even if that limitation is not inscribed in the third column (which deals with the national treatment commitments).

As the panel in *China – Publications and Audiovisual Products (2010)* stated:

If a limitation affects *both* market access and national treatment then, by a convention set out in Article XX:2 of the GATS (avoiding the need to repeat an inscription), it is to be inscribed *only* in the market access column.[291]

In *China – Electronic Payment Services (2012)*, China had with regard to mode 1 of the subsector at issue inscribed in the national treatment column of its Schedule 'None', while in the market access column it had inscribed 'Unbound'. The United States contended that China had made a full national treatment commitment with regard to mode 1 of the subsector at issue. China contested this, arguing that measures described in Article XVI:2 cannot simultaneously be subject to Article XVII. The panel in this case ruled:

By inscribing 'Unbound' under market access, China reserves the right to maintain any type of measure within the six categories falling under Article XVI:2, regardless of its inscription in the national treatment column.[292]

The panel added that its interpretation, however, also gave meaning to the term 'None' in the national treatment column, because:

[d]ue to the inscription of 'None', China must grant national treatment with respect to any of the measures at issue that are not inconsistent with Article XVI:2. China's national treatment commitment could thus have practical application should China, for example, choose

290 The asterisk refers to a footnote which states: 'Unbound due to lack of technical feasibility'.
291 Panel Report, *China – Publications and Audiovisual Products (2010)*, para. 7.921.
292 Panel Report, *China – Electronic Payment Services (2012)*, para. 7.663.

Modes of supply: 1) Cross-border supply 2) Consumption abroad 3) Commercial presence 4) Presence of natural persons

Sector or subsector	Limitations on market access	Limitations on national treatment	Additional commitments
e) Engineering Services			
Advisory and consultative engineering services (CPC 86721)	1) Unbound 2) Unbound 3) Same conditions as in Architectural services 4) Unbound except as indicated in the horizontal section	I) Unbound 2) Unbound 3) None 4) Unbound except as indicated in the horizontal section	
Industrial engineering (CPC 86725)	1) Unbound 2) Unbound 3) Same conditions as in Architectural services 4) Unbound except as indicated in the horizontal section	1) Unbound 2) Unbound 3) None 4) Unbound except as indicated in the horizontal section	
Engineering design (CPC 86722, CPC 86723, CPC 86724)	1) Unbound 2) Unbound 3) Same conditions as in Architectural services 4) Unbound except as indicated in the horizontal section	1) Unbound 2) Unbound 3) None 4) Unbound except as indicated in the horizontal section	
Other engineering services (CPC 86729)	1) Unbound 2) Unbound 3) Same conditions as in Architectural services 4) Unbound except as indicated in the horizontal section	1) Unbound 2) Unbound 3) None 4) Unbound except as indicated in the horizontal section	

Figure 7.1 Excerpt from the Schedule of Specific Commitments of Brazil

to allow in practice the supply of services from the territory of other WTO Members into its market, despite the fact that it has not undertaken any market access commitments in subsectors (a) to (f) of its Schedule.[293]

The panel in *China – Electronic Payment Services (2012)* emphasised that it did *not* find that either Article XVI or Article XVII is substantively subordinate to the other.[294] The panel stated:

> We find simply that Article XX:2 establishes a certain scheduling primacy for entries in the market access column, in that a WTO Member not wishing to make any commitment under Article XVI, discriminatory or non-discriminatory, may do so by inscribing the term 'Unbound' in the market access column of its schedule.[295]

4.4.2 Interpretation of Services Schedules

Just as Goods Schedules are an integral part of the GATT 1994, Services Schedules are an integral part of the GATS.[296] Article XX:3 of the GATS states:

> Schedules of specific commitments shall be annexed to this Agreement and shall form an integral part thereof.

293 *Ibid.*
294 See *ibid.*, para. 7.664. 295 *Ibid.*
296 On the interpretation of Goods Schedules, see above, pp. 440–2.

The issue of interpretation of Services Schedules arose in *US – Gambling (2005)*. In this case, the panel had to interpret the Services Schedule of the United States. The question was:

> whether the US Schedule includes specific commitments on gambling and betting services notwithstanding the fact that the words 'gambling and betting services' do not appear in the US Schedule.[297]

The United States had inscribed 'other recreational services (except sporting)' in its Schedule, and had recorded *no* limitations on market access in mode 1 (cross-border supply of services). It argued, however, that the term 'sporting' includes gambling and betting and that gambling and betting services were therefore excluded from its specific commitments. The panel in this case, however, first noted – referring to the Appellate Body's finding regarding tariff concessions in *EC – Computer Equipment (1998)* – that scheduled commitments 'are reciprocal and result from mutually advantageous negotiations between importing and exporting Members'.[298] The panel then noted:

> The United States has repeated several times in these proceedings that it did not intend to schedule a commitment for gambling and betting services. This may well be true, given that the legislation at issue in this dispute predates by decades, not only the GATS itself, but even the notion of 'trade in services' as embodied therein. We have, therefore, some sympathy with the United States' point in this regard. However, the scope of a specific commitment cannot depend upon what a Member intended or did not intend to do at the time of the negotiations.[299]

What matters, according to the panel, is the *common* intent of all negotiating parties. To determine this common intent with regard to the specific commitment at issue in this case, the panel applied – as did the Appellate Body in *EC – Computer Equipment (1998)* – the rules of interpretation set out in Articles 31 and 32 of the *Vienna Convention on the Law of Treaties*.[300] On appeal, the Appellate Body agreed with the panel's reliance on the rules of interpretation of the *Vienna Convention* to ascertain the meaning of the Services Schedule of the United States.[301] As the panel, the Appellate Body found that the United States' Services Schedule includes specific commitments on gambling and betting services.[302]

As the Appellate Body held in *US – Gambling (2005)*, other Members' Schedules could be relevant context for the interpretation of a particular Schedule, since all Schedules are an integral part of the GATS.[303] Furthermore, there are three specific

297 Panel Report, *US – Gambling (2005)*, para. 6.41.

298 Appellate Body Report, *EC – Computer Equipment (1998)*, para. 84.

299 Panel Report, *US – Gambling (2005)*, para. 6.136.

300 See Appellate Body Report, *EC – Computer Equipment (1998)*, para. 84.

301 See Appellate Body Report, *US – Gambling (2005)*, para. 160. See also Panel Report, *China – Publications and Audiovisual Products (2010)*, para. 7.922.

302 See Appellate Body Report, *US – Gambling (2005)*, para. 213. Although coming to the same conclusion as the panel, the Appellate Body applied the *Vienna Convention* rules of interpretation differently than the panel did. See Appellate Body Report, *US – Gambling (2005)*, para. 197.

303 See Appellate Body Report, *US – Gambling (2005)*, para. 182. As the Appellate Body noted, each Schedule has, however, 'its own intrinsic logic'. See *ibid*.

documents dealing with the classification of services that may be useful in assisting the interpretation of a Services Schedule, namely: (1) the 1991 UN *Provisional Central Product Classification* (CPC); (2) the GATT Secretariat's Services Sectoral Classification List (document W/120); and (3) the 1993 Guidelines for the Scheduling of Specific Commitments under the GATS.[304]

Finally, note that, in *China – Publication and Audiovisual Products (2009)*, China contended on appeal that the panel had erred in interpreting its Services Schedule entry 'Sound recording distribution services' according to the contemporary meaning of the words it contains, i.e. also covering the *electronic* distribution of sound recordings. According to China, the principle of progressive liberalisation does not allow for the expansion of the scope of the commitments of a WTO Member by interpreting the terms used in the Schedule based on the meaning of those terms at the time of interpretation.[305] Disagreeing with China, the Appellate Body ruled:

> we consider that the terms used in China's GATS Schedule ('sound recording' and 'distribution') are sufficiently generic that what they apply to may change over time.[306]

4.4.3 Market Access Commitments Agreed to in the Uruguay Round Services Schedules

The market access commitments agreed to during the Uruguay Round negotiations on the liberalisation of trade in services are, in general, modest. On average, WTO Members have only undertaken market access commitments on about twenty-five subsectors, i.e. 15 per cent of the total.[307] Only one-third of the Members have undertaken commitments on more than sixty-one subsectors.[308] Furthermore, the market access commitments rarely go beyond the *status quo*, i.e. they bind the degree of market access already existing. The value of these bindings, also referred to as 'standstill bindings', is that they give traders and investors a degree of security and predictability with respect to market access in the services sectors of interest to them.

In a number of important sectors, such as financial services, telecommunications and maritime transport, and with respect to the movement of natural persons, the Uruguay Round negotiators were unable to complete the market access negotiations, and the GATS made provision for further negotiations. These further negotiations led in 1997 to agreements providing for significant market

304 See Panel Report, *China – Publications and Audiovisual Products (2010)*, para. 7.923; and Appellate Body Report, *US – Gambling (2005)*, paras. 196–7. With regard to the 1993 Guidelines for the Scheduling and document W/120, the Appellate Body ruled in *US – Gambling (2005)*, that these instruments constituted 'supplementary means of interpretation' under Article 32 of the *Vienna Convention*. See *ibid.* On this point, the Appellate Body reversed the panel, which considered these instruments to be 'context' under Article 31.2 of the *Vienna Convention*. See also above, p. 194, fn. 166, and p. 198.

305 See Appellate Body Report, *China – Publications and Audiovisual Products (2009)*, para. 390.

306 *Ibid.*, para. 396.

307 See WTO Secretariat, *Market Access: Unfinished Business*, Special Studies Series 6 (WTO, 2001), 104.

308 See *ibid.*

access commitments in the sectors of basic telecommunications and financial services.[309] Further negotiations on market access for maritime transport failed, while further negotiations on the movement of natural persons were completed in July 1995 with very modest results. To the dissatisfaction of developing-country Members, the agreement reached on the movement of natural persons was largely confined to business visitors (to establish business contacts or negotiate contracts) and intra-corporate transfers of managers and technical staff.

Thus far, tourism has been the services sector in which most market access commitments have been made, followed by financial and business services. In the health and education sectors, Members have made the fewest market access commitments, but few commitments were also made in the sector of distribution services. On the whole, developed-country Members have made market access commitments with regard to nearly all sectors, except health and education. Note, however, that, for example, the European Union, Canada and Switzerland made no commitments with regard to audiovisual services.[310]

Market access commitments with respect to 'consumption abroad' (mode 2) are much less subject to limitations than market access commitments with respect to other modes of supply of services. Presumably, governments feel less of a need to restrict their nationals' consumption of services abroad or consider it impracticable to enforce such restrictions.[311] Market access commitments with respect to 'supply through the presence of natural persons' (mode 4), however, are usually subject to broad limitations.[312] Members, developed and developing alike, are clearly hesitant to undertake any commitments involving the entry of natural persons onto their territory. They are unwilling to expose their labour markets to competition from foreign workers.[313]

4.5 Modification or Withdrawal of Commitments

As is the case with tariff concessions for goods, market access commitments for services can also be modified or withdrawn.[314] According to Article XXI of the

309 See above, pp. 91–2.
310 See WTO Secretariat, *Market Access*, 104.
311 See WTO Secretariat, *Market Access*, 105.
312 Note also that the Annex on Movement of Natural Persons excludes from the scope of the GATS measures regarding citizenship and permanent residency, and visas.
313 In March 2016, India notified the WTO Secretariat of the initiation of dispute proceedings against the United States with respect to measures imposing increased fees on certain applicants for two categories of non-immigrant temporary working visas into the US, and measures relating to numerical commitments for some visas. See www.wto.org/english/news_e/news16_e/ds503rfc_04mar16_e.htm.
314 For the details of the relevant procedure, see *Procedures for the Implementation of Article XXI of the General Agreement on Trade in Services (GATS) (Modification of Schedules)*, adopted on 19 July 1999, S/L/80, dated 29 October 1999. On the modification or withdrawal of tariff concessions, see above, pp. 447–50. See also the 2000 *Procedures for the Certification of Rectifications or Improvements to Schedules of Specific Commitments*, regarding changes (changes through certification by the WTO Secretariat) that do not require the Article XXI procedure to be followed, unless another Member objects. Council for Trade in Services, *Procedures for the Certification of Rectifications or Improvements to Schedules of Specific Commitments*, S/L/84 (18 April 2000).

GATS, a Member may modify or withdraw any commitment in its Schedule, at any time after three years have elapsed from the date on which that commitment entered into force.[315] A Member wishing to 'unbind' a commitment must first notify its intention to do so to the Council for Trade in Services. Subsequently, it must – if so requested – enter into negotiations with a view to reaching agreement on any necessary compensatory adjustment. The purpose of these negotiations on compensatory adjustment is to maintain a general level of mutually advantageous commitments not less favourable to trade than that provided for in the Schedule. If no agreement on compensatory adjustment can be reached between the modifying Member and any affected Member, the affected Member(s) may refer the matter to arbitration.[316] Recall that this possibility to refer to arbitration is not specifically provided for in the context of the modification or withdrawal of tariff concessions.[317] If no arbitration is requested, the modifying Member is free to implement the intended modification or withdrawal.[318] If arbitration is requested, however, the modifying Member may not modify or withdraw its commitment until it has made compensatory adjustments in conformity with the findings of the arbitration.[319] In case the modifying Member does not comply with the findings of the arbitration, any affected Member that participated in the arbitration may modify or withdraw *substantially equivalent benefits* in conformity with those findings.[320] Note that any compensatory adjustment made by the Member 'unbinding' a commitment must be made on an MFN basis. However, the modification or withdrawal of substantially equivalent benefits by the affected Member(s) in case of non-compliance with the arbitration findings may be implemented solely with respect to the modifying Member.[321]

After an Article 21.5 panel had established in March 2007 that the United States had failed to comply with the recommendations and rulings of the DSB in *US – Gambling (2005)*,[322] the United States announced in May 2007 that it would not comply with these recommendations and rulings, but was modifying its market access commitments in the subsector of 'recreational services', the services subsector at issue in *US – Gambling (2005)*. Reportedly, seven other WTO

315 In certain exceptional circumstances, the period of three years is reduced to one year. See Article X of the GATS.

316 See Article XXI:3(a) of the GATS. Any affected Member that wishes to enforce a right that it may have to compensation must participate in the arbitration. See *ibid.*

317 See above, pp. 447–50. 318 See Article XXI:3(b) of the GATS.

319 See Article XXI:4(a) of the GATS. 320 See Article XXI:4(b) of the GATS.

321 See Article XXI:2(b) of the GATS (for the compensatory adjustment) and Article XXI:4(b) of the GATS (for the modification or withdrawal of substantially equivalent benefits).

322 See Panel Report, *US – Gambling (Article 21.5) (2007)*. Subsequently, in June 2007, Antigua requested the DSB to authorise the taking of retaliatory measures up to an amount of US$3.443 billion. See WT/DS285/22, dated 22 June 2007. On 21 December 2007, the Arbitrator under Article 22.6 of the DSU determined that the annual level of nullification or impairment of benefits accruing to Antigua is US$21 million. The Arbitrator also found that suspension of commitments or other obligations under the GATS was not practicable and effective for Antigua and that circumstances were serious enough to permit 'cross-retaliation' under various sections of the *TRIPS Agreement*. See WT/DS285/ARB, dated 21 December 2007. On 24 April 2012, Antigua informed the DSB that the United States was still not in compliance with the recommendations and rulings of the DSB, and that it had notified the United States of its wish to seek recourse to the good offices of the WTO Director-General in finding a mediated solution to this dispute. On 28 January 2013, the DSB granted Antigua authorisation to suspend commitments and other obligations including under the *TRIPS Agreement*.

Members joined Antigua in notifying their intent to seek compensation from the United States. The United States reached agreement on compensatory adjustment with Australia, Canada, the European Union and Japan, by making additional market access commitments in the subsectors of postal services, research and development services, technical testing services, and warehousing. However, with Antigua, no agreement on compensatory adjustment was reached. In early 2008, Antigua referred this matter to arbitration pursuant to Article XXI:3(a).

5 OTHER BARRIERS TO TRADE IN SERVICES

In addition to the market access barriers, discussed above, trade in services can also be impeded by a wide array of other barriers. With regard to a number of these other barriers, WTO law, and in particular the GATS, provides for specific rules. Some of these rules have general application.[323] Other rules apply only in services sectors with regard to which specific market access commitments were made.[324] This section discusses in turn the following other barriers to trade in services: (1) lack of transparency; (2) unfair or arbitrary application of measures affecting trade in services; (3) licensing and qualification requirements and technical standards; (4) lack of recognition of diplomas and professional certificates; (5) government procurement; and (6) other measures and actions.

Note that while the rules discussed below are rules that apply to measures that are not market access barriers within the meaning of Article XVI of the GATS, these rules, such as the rules on transparency, also apply to measures that are market access barriers.

5.1 Lack of Transparency

For trade in services, as much as for trade in goods discussed above, lack of information, uncertainty and confusion with respect to the relevant laws and regulations applicable in actual or potential foreign markets are formidable barriers to trade. Effective market access for services is impossible without transparency regarding the laws and regulations affecting the services concerned. Service suppliers must have accurate information concerning the rules with which they must comply.

As Article X of the GATT 1994 does with regard to trade in goods, Article III of the GATS requires with regard to trade in services that Members *publish* all

323 For example, the requirement that Members maintain or institute as soon as practicable judicial, arbitral or administrative tribunals for the prompt review of decisions affecting trade in services. See Article VI:2(a) of the GATS, and below, p. 535.

324 For example, the requirement to administer measures affecting trade in services in a reasonable, objective and impartial manner. See Article VI:1 of the GATS, and below, p. 535.

measures of general application affecting trade in services.[325] Publication must take place promptly, and at the latest by the time the measure enters into force.[326] Since the end of 1997, each Member has been required to establish one or more *enquiry points* to provide information on laws and regulations affecting trade in services.[327] Members have an obligation to respond promptly to all requests by any other Member for specific information on any of its measures of general application.[328] For the benefit of developing-country Members, developed-country Members have a special obligation to establish 'contact points' to facilitate the access of service suppliers from developing-country Members to information of special interest to them.[329] Article III of the GATS also requires a Member to *notify* the Council for Trade in Services of any new, or any changes to, laws, regulations or administrative guidelines which significantly affect trade in sectors where that Member has made specific commitments. Members must do so at least once a year.[330] Note that the transparency of Members' measures affecting trade in services is also advanced by the trade policy reviews under the *Trade Policy Review Mechanism*.[331]

5.2 Unfair and Arbitrary Application of Trade Measures

In sectors where specific commitments are undertaken, Article VI:1 of the GATS requires a Member to ensure:

> that all measures of general application affecting trade in services are administered in a reasonable, objective and impartial manner.

This obligation is the counterpart to Article X:3(a) of the GATT 1994, discussed above, for trade in services.[332]

In all services sectors, including those in which no specific commitments are undertaken, Article VI:2(a) of the GATS requires Members to maintain judicial, arbitral or administrative tribunals or procedures which allow service suppliers to challenge administrative decisions affecting them. The relevant procedures must not necessarily be independent of the agency entrusted with the administrative decision concerned, but must be objective and impartial.[333] Moreover, they must provide for prompt review and, where necessary, appropriate remedies.[334]

325 Where publication is not practicable, the information must be made otherwise publicly available (see Article III:2 of the GATS). The publication requirement exists also for measures affecting trade in services with regard to which a Member has not made specific commitments.

326 See Article III:1 of the GATS. This obligation can be waived in emergency situations. This publication obligation also applies to international agreements pertaining to or affecting trade in services to which a Member is a signatory.

327 See Article III:4 of the GATS. 328 See *ibid.*

329 See Article IV:2 of the GATS. Such information includes information on registration, recognition and obtaining of professional qualifications; and the availability of services technologies.

330 See Article III:3 of the GATS. Members are not required, however, to supply confidential information. See Article III *bis* of the GATS.

331 See above, pp. 102–4. 332 See above, p. 505.

333 See Article VI:2(a), second sentence of the GATS. 334 See Article VI:2(a), first sentence of the GATS.

Where authorisation is required for the supply of a service on which a commitment has been made, the competent authorities of a Member must, within a reasonable period of time, inform the applicant of the decision concerning the application.[335]

5.3 Licensing and Qualification Requirements and Technical Standards

As discussed above, trade in services is primarily impeded or restricted by internal regulations. For scheduled services, certain internal regulations may constitute market access barriers within the meaning of Article XVI:2 of the GATS and, as discussed above, are prohibited when, and, if so, to the extent, a market access commitment is made.[336] However, most internal regulations do not constitute market access barriers within the meaning of Article XVI:2.[337] Apart from the rules concerning transparency and the rules on unfair and arbitrary application, discussed above, the GATS currently only provides for a few other disciplines applicable to internal regulations which do not constitute market access barriers. The most important of these disciplines concerns licensing requirements, qualification requirements, and technical standards.[338] Article VI:5(a) of the GATS states:

> In sectors in which a Member has undertaken specific commitments ... the Member shall not apply licensing and qualification requirements and technical standards that nullify or impair such specific commitments in a manner which:
> i. does not comply with the criteria outlined in sub-paragraphs 4(a), (b) or (c); and
> ii. could not reasonably have been expected of that Member at the time the specific commitments in those sectors were made.

According to the criteria of Article VI:4(a)–(c) to which the above provision refers, licensing requirements, qualification requirements and technical standards relating to services sectors in which specific commitments are undertaken must: (1) be based on objective and transparent criteria such as competence and the ability to supply the service; (2) not be more burdensome than necessary to ensure the quality of the service; and (3) in the case of licensing procedures, not be, in themselves, a restriction on the supply of the service. If licensing requirements, qualification requirements or technical standards relating to services

335 See Article VI:3 of the GATS. 336 See above, pp. 520–1.

337 The panel in *US – Gambling (2005)* stated: 'Under Article VI and Article XVI, measures are either of the type covered by the disciplines of Article XVI or are internal regulations relating to qualification requirements and procedures, technical standards and licensing requirements subject to the specific provisions of Article VI. Thus, Articles VI:4 and VI:5 on the one hand and XVI on the other hand are mutually exclusive.' Panel Report, *US – Gambling (2005)*, para. 6.305.

338 Note that the scope of application of the different provisions of Article VI of the GATS, entitled 'Domestic regulation', differs. Articles VI:1–VI:3, discussed above, have a broad scope of application (e.g. 'measures of general application affecting trade in services' (Article VI:1) or 'administrative decisions affecting trade in services' (Article VI:2)), while the scope of application of Articles VI:4 and VI:5 is limited to technical standards and licensing and qualification requirements. See Panel Report, *Argentina – Financial Services (2016)*, paras. 7.837–7.838.

sectors, in which specific commitments are undertaken, do not meet these criteria *and*, furthermore, nullify or impair the specific commitments undertaken in a manner which could not reasonably have been expected at the time the commitments were made, the Member acts inconsistently with its obligations under Article VI:5(a) of the GATS.[339] The Member must then amend the licensing requirement, qualification requirement or technical standard at issue.

Note that Article VI:4 of the GATS gives the Council for Trade in Services a broad and ambitious mandate to develop the multilateral disciplines necessary to ensure that licensing requirements, qualification requirements and procedures and technical standards do not constitute *unnecessary barriers* to trade in services. However, rather than 'de-regulation', the aim of Article VI:4 is to promote *better regulation* based on objective and transparent criteria. To date, such disciplines have only been successfully developed with regard to accountancy.[340]

Note also that Article XVIII, entitled 'Additional Commitments', provides:

> Members may negotiate commitments with respect to measures affecting trade in services not subject to scheduling under Articles XVI or XVII, including those regarding qualifications, standards or licensing matters. Such commitments shall be inscribed in a Member's Schedule.

Members may therefore make commitments with respect to measures which are neither market access barriers (Article XVI) nor inconsistent with the national treatment obligation (Article XVII). These additional commitments are recorded in the fourth column of a Member's Schedule.[341] In practice, such commitments are uncommon in most services sectors. However, with regard to basic telecommunication services, many Members took additional commitments regarding transparency, licensing, competition and universal service in the telecommunication sector. They did so by inserting in the fourth column of their Schedule any or all of the provisions of the *Reference Paper on Basic Telecommunications* containing pro-competitive regulatory principles.[342]

5.4 Government Procurement Laws and Practices

As discussed above in the context of trade in goods, government procurement laws and practices often constitute significant barriers to trade as governments give preferences to domestic services or service suppliers over foreign services or

339 In determining whether a Member is in conformity with the obligation under Article VI:5(a), account shall be taken of international standards of relevant international organisations applied by that Member. See Article VII:5(b) of the GATS.

340 See Council for Trade in Services, *Disciplines on Domestic Regulation in the Accountancy Sector*, adopted on 14 December 1998, S/L/64, dated 17 December 1998. While adopted in 1998, these disciplines are not yet in force. There have been proposals for sector-specific domestic regulations disciplines for legal services, engineering and telecommunications sectors.

341 See above, p. 527.

342 Such additional commitments were at issue in *Mexico – Telecoms (2004)*.

service suppliers. The GATS, like the GATT 1994 with regard to government procurement of goods, does not set forth any multilateral disciplines on the procurement of services for governmental purposes. Article XIII:1 of the GATS provides:

> Articles II, XVI and XVII shall not apply to laws, regulations or requirements governing the procurement by governmental agencies of services purchased for governmental purposes and not with a view to commercial resale or with a view to use in the supply of services for commercial sale.

The general MFN treatment obligation (of Article II) and specific commitments on market access and national treatment (of Articles XVI and XVII respectively) do not, generally speaking, apply to laws, regulations or requirements governing government procurement of services. However, Article XIII:2 provides for multilateral negotiations on government procurement of services, which are currently taking place as part of the Doha Round of negotiations.[343]

Note that the plurilateral WTO *Agreement on Government Procurement*, discussed above, applies not only to government procurement of goods but also to government procurement of services. The plurilateral disciplines set forth in that Agreement also apply to laws and regulations on the government procurement of services.[344]

5.5 Other Measures and Actions

In addition to lack of transparency, unfair or arbitrary application of measures affecting trade in services, licensing and qualification requirements, technical standards and government procurement laws and practices, trade in services is impeded by a number of other measures and actions. This section briefly addresses the following: (1) lack of recognition of foreign diplomas and professional certificates; (2) monopolies and exclusive service providers; and (3) international payments and transfers.

Foreign service suppliers, such as doctors, engineers, nurses, lawyers or accountants, will usually have obtained their *diplomas and professional certificates* in their country of origin and will not have diplomas or professional certificates of other countries in which they may wish to be active. Members are required to provide for adequate procedures, in sectors where specific commitments regarding professional services are undertaken, to verify the competence of professionals from any other Member.[345] However, it is clear that, even with these procedures, having only a foreign diploma or professional certificate may constitute an important impediment for persons to supply services in other Members. While WTO law does not require that Members recognise foreign diplomas or professional certificates, it encourages and facilitates their recognition. As discussed in Chapter 4, the GATS does so by allowing Members

343 For an overview of the pace of negotiations, see WTO Working Paper, 'The Relationship between Services Trade and Government Procurement Commitments: Insights from Relevant WTO Agreements and Recent RTAs', ERSD-2014-21, Economics Research and Statistics Division, World Trade Organization, November 2014, para. 2.2.2.

344 See above, p. 513. 345 See Article VI:6 of the GATS.

to deviate, under certain conditions, from the basic MFN treatment obligation of Article II of the GATS.[346] Article VII:1 of the GATS provides in relevant part:

> [A] Member may recognize the education or experience obtained, requirements met, or licences or certifications granted in *a particular country*.[347]

Pursuant to Article VII:1, such recognition: (1) may be achieved through harmonisation *or* otherwise; and (2) may be based upon an agreement with the country concerned *or* may be accorded autonomously. However, the recognition must be based on objective criteria, and may not discriminate among Members where similar conditions prevail. As discussed in Chapter 4, Members who are parties to recognition agreements are required to afford adequate opportunity for other interested Members to negotiate their accession to such agreements or negotiate comparable agreements with them. If recognition is accorded on an autonomous basis, the Member concerned must give adequate opportunity for any other Member concerned to demonstrate that qualifications acquired in its territory should be recognised. Members must notify the Council for Trade in Services of all existing recognition measures.[348] In the long term, Members aim at adopting common standards for the recognition of diplomas and professional qualifications. A first effort in this respect has been the *Guidelines for Mutual Recognition Agreements or Arrangements in the Accountancy Sector*, agreed upon by the Council for Trade in Services in May 1997.[349]

While *monopolies* or *exclusive service suppliers* can obviously impede trade in services, WTO law does not prohibit them. It is common for governments to grant entities an exclusive right to supply certain services, such as rail transport, telecommunications, sanitation, etc. However, pursuant to Article VIII:1 of the GATS, a Member must ensure that:

> any monopoly supplier of a service in its territory does not, in the supply of the monopoly service in the relevant market, act in a manner inconsistent with that Member's obligations under Article II and specific commitments.

A Member must also ensure that, when a monopoly supplier competes in the supply of a service outside the scope of its monopoly rights, the supplier does not abuse its monopoly position inconsistent with its commitments regarding that service.[350] These obligations also apply with regard to exclusive service suppliers, subject to the conditions set out in Article VIII:5.[351] Business practices, other than monopolies, may also hinder competition and thereby restrict trade in services. Article IX of the GATS requires Members, at the request of

346 See above, pp. 325–38. 347 Emphasis added.

348 See Article VII:4 of the GATS. They must also inform the Council of the opening of negotiations on a recognition agreement in order to give any other Member the opportunity to indicate an interest in participating in the negotiations.

349 See S/L/38, dated 28 May 1997. Negotiations on these guidelines were conducted in the WTO Working Party on Professional Services. See S/WPPS/W/12/Rev.1, dated 20 May 1997.

350 See Article VIII:2 of the GATS.

351 The panel in *China – Electronic Payment Services (2012)* distinguished 'monopoly suppliers' from 'exclusive service suppliers'. See Panel Report, *China – Electronic Payment Services (2012)*, paras. 7.585–7.587.

any other Member, to enter into consultations with a view to eliminating such practices.

It is obvious that restrictions on *international transfers and payments for services* can constitute a barrier to trade in services. Article XI:1 of the GATS requires Members not to apply any restriction on international transfers and payments related to services covered by specific commitments. However, Article XI:2 allows the use of exchange controls or exchange restrictions in certain situations, such as serious balance-of-payments difficulties within the meaning of Article XII, or when such exchange actions are requested by the IMF.

6 SUMMARY

Market access for goods and services from other countries can be, and frequently is, impeded or restricted in various ways. There are two main categories of barriers to market access: tariff barriers, discussed in Chapter 6; and non-tariff barriers, the focus of this chapter. While tariff barriers have been systematically reduced since the late 1940s as a result of successive rounds of tariff negotiations, non-tariff barriers have in recent decades gradually become an ever more prominent instrument of protection. The non-tariff barriers discussed in this chapter include: (1) quantitative restrictions on trade in goods; (2) 'other non-tariff barriers' on trade in goods; (3) market access barriers to trade in services; and (4) other barriers to trade in services. Note, however, that this chapter does not deal with technical barriers to trade, and sanitary and phytosanitary measures. The rules on these 'other non-tariff barriers' are discussed in Chapters 13 and 14 respectively.

A quantitative restriction on trade in goods is a measure which *limits the quantity* of a product that may be imported or exported. Quantitative restrictions take many forms, including bans, quotas and import or export licences. Article XI:1 of the GATT 1994 sets out a general prohibition on quantitative restrictions, whether on imports or exports. Unlike other GATT provisions, Article XI refers not to laws or regulations but more broadly to measures. A measure instituted or maintained by a Member, which restricts imports or exports, is covered by Article XI, *irrespective* of the legal status of the measure. Furthermore, quantitative restrictions which do not *actually* impede trade are nevertheless prohibited under Article XI:1 of the GATT 1994. Note also that restrictions of a *de facto* nature are also prohibited under Article XI:1 of the GATT 1994.

While quantitative restrictions are, as a rule, prohibited, there are many exceptions to this prohibition. Article XIII of the GATT 1994 sets out rules on the *administration* of these GATT-consistent quantitative restrictions. Article XIII:1 of the GATT 1994 provides that quantitative restrictions, when applied, should be administered in a non-discriminatory manner. According to Article XIII:2 of the GATT 1994, the distribution of trade still allowed should be as close as possible to what would have been the distribution of trade in the absence of the quantitative restriction. Furthermore, Article XIII:2 sets out a number of requirements to be met when imposing quotas. Article XIII:2(d) provides that, if no agreement can be reached with all Members having a substantial interest in supplying the product concerned, the quota must be allocated among these Members on the basis of their share of the trade during a previous representative period. Note that the rules set out in Article XIII also apply to tariff rate quotas, even though the latter are not considered to be quantitative restrictions.

Quotas and tariff quotas are usually administered through import-licensing procedures. A trader who wishes to import a product that is subject to a quota or tariff quota must apply for an import licence, i.e. a permit to import. The *Import Licensing Agreement* sets out rules on import licensing. The most important of these rules, set out in Article 1.3, is that the rules for import-licensing procedures shall be neutral in application and administered in a fair and equitable manner.

Trade in goods is also impeded by 'other non-tariff barriers', including: lack of transparency; unfair and arbitrary application of trade laws and regulations; customs formalities and procedures; and government procurement laws and practices. Lack of information, uncertainty or confusion with respect to the trade laws, regulations and procedures applicable in actual or potential export markets is an important barrier to trade in goods. To ensure a high level of *transparency* of its Members' trade laws, regulations and procedures, WTO law requires their publication and notification, as well as the establishment of enquiry points. The *unfair and arbitrary application* of national trade measures, and the degree of uncertainty and unpredictability this generates for other Members and traders, also constitutes a significant barrier to trade in goods. Therefore, WTO law provides for: (1) a requirement of uniform, impartial and reasonable administration of national trade rules; and (2) a requirement of procedures for the objective and impartial review of the administration of national customs rules. The losses that traders suffer through delays at borders and complicated and/or unnecessary documentation requirements and other *customs procedures and formalities* are estimated to exceed the costs of tariffs in many cases. With the conclusion of the *Agreement on Trade Facilitation* (which is expected to enter into force soon), the WTO now has a significant body of rules on customs formalities and procedures aimed at mitigating their adverse impact on trade. National laws and/or practices relating to the procurement of goods by a government for its own use are often significant barriers to trade. Under such laws or practices, governments frequently buy domestic products rather than imported products. The plurilateral WTO *Agreement on Government Procurement* provides for some disciplines with respect to government procurement. However, it does so only for the forty-seven Members that are currently a party to this Agreement.

As with trade in goods, trade in services is also often subject to restrictions in the form of non-tariff barriers. The production and consumption of services are subject to a vast range of internal regulations. Barriers to trade in services primarily result from these internal regulations. WTO law, and the GATS in particular, provides for rules and disciplines on barriers to trade in services. A distinction must be made between: (1) market access barriers; and (2) other barriers to trade in services.

Article XVI:2 of the GATS contains an *exhaustive* list of *market access barriers*. This list comprises six types of market access barriers: five of these types are quantitative restrictions (subparagraphs (a)–(d) and (f)); and one type is a limitation on the kind of legal entity or joint venture through which services may be supplied (subparagraph (e)). These market access barriers can be discriminatory *or* non-discriminatory with regard to foreign services or service suppliers. Four of the five types of quantitative restrictions referred to in Article XVI:2 can be expressed numerically, or through the criteria specified in these provisions, such as an economic needs test. It is important, however, that these criteria do not relate to: (1) the quality of the service supplied; or (2) the ability of the supplier to supply the service (i.e. technical standards or qualification of the supplier). The GATS does not provide for a general prohibition of market access barriers. Whether a Member may maintain or adopt market access barriers with regard to a specific service depends on whether, and if so to what extent, that Member has made market access commitments with regard to the relevant services sector in its Schedule of Specific Commitments, i.e. its Services Schedule. When a Member makes a market access commitment, it binds the level of market access specified in its Services Schedule (see Article XVI:1) and agrees not to impose any market access barrier that would restrict access to the market beyond the level specified (see Article XVI:2).

To achieve *progressively* higher levels of liberalisation of trade in services, the GATS provides for *successive* rounds of negotiations on further market access and national treatment commitments. The approach to negotiations on the liberalisation of services is a request-and-offer approach. It is accepted that developing-country Members undertake fewer and more limited market access commitments than developed-country Members. The terms, limitations and conditions on *market access* agreed to in the negotiations are set out in the second column of the Services Schedules. Each Member has a Services Schedule, and these Schedules, all annexed to the GATS, form an integral part thereof, and are to be interpreted accordingly. Like tariff concessions for goods, market access commitments for services can also be modified or withdrawn. To do so, the procedure set out in Article XXI of the GATS must be followed.

In addition to market access barriers, trade in services can also be impeded by a wide array of other barriers. With regard to a number of these other barriers, WTO law, and in particular the GATS, provides for specific rules. The GATS requires the prompt *publication* of all measures of general application affecting trade in services. It also requires Members to establish *enquiry points* to provide information on laws and regulations affecting trade in services. Furthermore, the GATS requires Members to ensure that all measures of general application affecting trade in services with regard to which specific commitments were made are administered in a *reasonable, objective and impartial* manner. As noted above, trade in services is primarily impeded or restricted by internal regulation. Most internal regulations do not constitute market access barriers within the meaning of Article XVI:2. Apart from the rules concerning transparency and the rules on unfair and arbitrary application, the GATS currently only provides for a few other disciplines applicable to internal regulations, which do not constitute market access barriers. The most important of these disciplines concerns licensing requirements, qualification requirements, and technical standards. These requirements and standards must: (1) be based on objective and transparent criteria such as competence and the ability to supply the service; (2) not be more burdensome than necessary to ensure the quality of the service; and (3) in the case of licensing procedures, not be, in themselves, a restriction on the supply of the service. Finally, note that the GATS encourages and facilitates the recognition of diplomas and professional certificates of foreign service suppliers.

FURTHER READINGS

K. Dawar, 'Government Procurement in the WTO: A Case for Greater Integration', *World Trade Review*, 2016, 8, 1–26.

P. Kowalski and K. Perepechay, 'International Trade and Investment by State Enterprises', OECD Trade Policy Paper No. 184, 2015, Paris, OECD Publishing.

L. Chin, C. Rusli and A. Khusyairi, 'The Determinants of Non-Tariff Barriers: The Role of WTO Membership', *International Journal of Economics and Management*, 2015, 9(1), 155–75.

R. Zhang, 'Covered or Not Covered: That Is the Question – Services Classification and Its Implications for Specific Commitments under the GATS', WTO Working Paper ERSD-2015-11.

V. Thorstensen, C. Müller and D. Ramos, 'Exchange Rate Measures: Who Judges the Issue – IMF or WTO?', *Journal of International Economic Law*, 2015, 0, 1–20.

P. C. Mavroidis and R. Wolfe, 'From Sunshine to a Common Agent: The Evolving Understanding of Transparency in the WTO', RSCAS Policy Paper 2015/01, European University Institute.

B. Czapnik, 'The Unique Features of the Trade Facilitation Agreement: A Revolutionary New Approach to Multilateral Negotiations or the Exception Which Proves the Rule?', *Journal of International Economic Law*, 2015, 0, 1–22.

R. D. Anderson and C. Müller, 'Revised WTO Agreement on Government Procurement as an Emerging Pillar of the World Trading System: Recent Developments', *Trade Law and Development*, 2015, 7(1), 42–63.

H. P. Hestermeyer and L. Nielsen, 'The Legality of Local Content Measures Under WTO Law', *Journal of World Trade*, 2014, 48(3), 553–92.

N. Neufeld, 'The Long and Winding Road: How WTO Members Finally Reached a Trade Facilitation Agreement', Staff Working Paper ERSD-2014-06, WTO.

B. Fliess, 'Transparency of Export Restrictions: A Checklist Promoting Good Practice', OECD Trade Policy Papers, No. 164, 2014, Paris, OECD Publishing.

R. Adlung, P. Morrison, M. Roy and W. Zhang, 'Fog in GATS Commitments – Why WTO Members Should Care', *World Trade Review*, 2013, 12(1), 1–27.

B. Karapinar, 'Defining the Legal Boundaries of Export Restrictions: A Case Law Analysis', *Journal of International Economic Law*, 2012, 15(2), 443–79.

R. Santana and L.A. Jackson, 'Identifying Non-Tariff Barriers: Evolution of Multilateral Instruments and Evidence from the Disputes (1948–2011)', *World Trade Review*, 2012, 11(3), 462–78.

8 General and Security Exceptions

CONTENTS

1 INTRODUCTION

The promotion and protection of public health, consumer safety, the environment, employment, economic development and national security are *core* tasks of governments. Often, trade liberalisation and the resulting availability of better and cheaper products and services facilitate the promotion and protection of these and other societal values and interests. Through trade, environmentally friendly products or life-saving medicines, that would not be available otherwise, become available to consumers and patients respectively. At a more general level, trade generates the degree of economic activity and economic welfare that enables governments effectively to promote and protect the societal values and interests referred to above.

In order to protect and promote these societal values and interests, however, governments also adopt legislation or take other measures that, inadvertently or deliberately, constitute barriers to trade. Members may be, politically and/or economically, 'compelled' to adopt legislation or other measures, which are inconsistent with rules of WTO law and, in particular, with the rules on non-discrimination and the rules on market access, discussed in Chapters 4–7. Trade liberalisation, market access and non-discrimination rules may conflict with other important societal values and interests. WTO law recognises this and, therefore, provides for a set of rules to reconcile trade liberalisation, market access and non-discrimination rules with the need to protect and promote other societal values and interests. As the 2004 Sutherland Report noted:

> Neither the WTO nor the GATT was ever an unrestrained free trade charter. In fact, both were and are intended to provide a structured and functionally effective way to harness the value of open trade to principle and fairness. In so doing they offer the security and predictability of market access advantages that are sought by traders and investors. But the rules provide checks and balances including mechanisms that reflect political realism as well as free trade doctrine. It is not that the WTO disallows market protection, only that it sets some strict disciplines under which governments may choose to respond to special interests.[1]

This chapter and the next two chapters, Chapters 9 and 10, address the wide-ranging *exceptions* to the basic WTO rules, allowing Members to adopt trade-restrictive legislation or other measures that pursue the promotion and protection of other societal values and interests. This chapter deals with the 'general exceptions' as well as the 'security exceptions'. Chapter 9 deals with the 'economic emergency exceptions';[2] and Chapter 10 discusses the 'regional trade exceptions'.[3] These exceptions differ in scope and nature. Some allow deviation from all GATT or GATS obligations; others allow deviation from specific obligations only; some allow for measures of indefinite duration; others allow for temporary measures only. However, while different in scope and nature, all the exceptions have something in common: they allow Members, under specific conditions, to adopt and maintain legislation or other measures that promote or protect other important societal values and interests, even though this legislation or these measures are inconsistent with substantive disciplines imposed by the GATT 1994 or the GATS. These exceptions clearly allow Members, under specific conditions, to

1 The Sutherland Report, para. 39. Emphasis omitted. 2 See below, pp. 630–70.
3 As explained above, WTO law provisions providing for special and differential treatment of developing-country Members and least-developed-country Members are not discussed in a separate chapter of this book, but are discussed together with the rules from which they allow deviation. See below, pp. 671–95.

give *priority* to the protection or promotion of certain societal values and interests *over* trade liberalisation, market access and/or non-discrimination.

This chapter focuses on the most widely available of the exceptions, namely, the 'general exceptions' and the 'security exceptions'. It discusses in turn: (1) the 'general exceptions under the GATT 1994'; (2) the 'general exceptions under the GATS'; and (3) the 'security exceptions' under the GATT 1994 and the GATS.[4]

2 GENERAL EXCEPTIONS UNDER THE GATT 1994

Article XX of the GATT 1994, entitled 'General Exceptions', states:

> Subject to the requirement that such measures are not applied in a manner which would constitute a means of arbitrary or unjustifiable discrimination between countries where the same conditions prevail, or a disguised restriction on international trade, nothing in this Agreement shall be construed to prevent the adoption or enforcement by any [Member] of measures:
>
> (a) necessary to protect public morals;
> (b) necessary to protect human, animal or plant life or health;
> ...
> (d) necessary to secure compliance with laws or regulations which are not inconsistent with the provisions of this Agreement, including those relating to customs enforcement, the enforcement of monopolies operated under paragraph 4 of Article II and Article XVII, the protection of patents, trade marks and copyrights, and the prevention of deceptive practices;
> (e) relating to the products of prison labour;
> (f) imposed for the protection of national treasures of artistic, historic or archaeological value;
> (g) relating to the conservation of exhaustible natural resources if such measures are made effective in conjunction with restrictions on domestic production or consumption;
> ...
> (j) essential to the acquisition or distribution of products in general or local short supply;

Note that paragraphs (c), (h) and (i) of Article XX are not included in the quote above. These paragraphs relate to trade in gold and silver (see paragraph (c)); obligations under international commodities agreements (see paragraph (h)); and efforts to ensure essential quantities of materials to a domestic processing industry (see paragraph (i)). To date, these paragraphs have been of less importance in international trade law and practice and have not yet been invoked in WTO dispute settlement. Therefore, they are not discussed in this chapter.

4 Note that other agreements contain 'exceptions' or 'flexibilities' addressing the same concerns. They are discussed, together with those agreements, in other parts of this book. Consider, for example, the 'flexibility' in Article 2.1 of the *TBT Agreement* or the exceptions in Articles 8 and 31 of the *TRIPS Agreement*. See below, pp. 899, 997 and 1034, respectively.

2.1 Key Features of Article XX of the GATT 1994

This subsection discusses the key features of Article XX of the GATT 1994 and addresses first the nature and function of Article XX, and then its scope of application.

2.1.1 Nature and Function of Article XX

The panel in *US – Section 337 Tariff Act (1989)* noted with respect to the nature and function of Article XX:

> that Article XX is entitled 'General Exceptions' and that the central phrase in the introductory clause reads: 'nothing in this Agreement shall be construed to prevent the adoption or enforcement ... of measures ... '. Article XX(d) thus provides for a limited and conditional exception from obligations under other provisions. The Panel therefore concluded that Article XX(d) applies only to measures inconsistent with another provision of the General Agreement, and that, consequently, the application of Section 337 has to be examined first in the light of Article III:4. If any inconsistencies with Article III:4 were found, the Panel would then examine whether they could be justified under Article XX(d).[5]

Article XX is relevant, and will be invoked by a Member, *only* when a measure of that Member has been found to be inconsistent with another GATT provision. In such a case, Article XX will be invoked to justify the GATT-inconsistent measure. As the panel in *US – Section 337 Tariff Act (1989)* noted, the central phrase in the first sentence of Article XX is that 'nothing in this Agreement shall be construed to prevent the adoption or enforcement by any [Member] of measures ... '. Measures satisfying the conditions set out in Article XX are thus permitted, even if they are inconsistent with other provisions of the GATT 1994. As noted by the panel in *US – Section 337 Tariff Act (1989)*, Article XX provides, however, for *limited and conditional exceptions* from obligations under other GATT provisions. The exceptions are 'limited' as the list of exceptions in Article XX is exhaustive. The exceptions are 'conditional' in that Article XX only provides for justification of an otherwise GATT-inconsistent measure when the conditions set out in Article XX – and discussed in detail below – are fulfilled. While Article XX allows Members to adopt or maintain measures promoting or protecting other important societal values, it provides an exception to, or limitation of, affirmative commitments under the GATT 1994. In this light, it is not surprising that Article XX has played a prominent role in many GATT and WTO disputes.

It could be argued that it is an accepted principle of interpretation that exceptions are to be interpreted narrowly (*singularia non sunt extendenda*) and that Article XX should, therefore, be interpreted narrowly. However, the Appellate Body does not seem to have adopted this approach. Instead, it has followed in *US – Gasoline (1996)* and *US – Shrimp (1998)* an approach which seeks to

5 Panel Report, *US – Section 337 Tariff Act (1989)*, para. 5.9.

balance the affirmative commitments and the exceptions. It stated with regard to Article XX(g), the exception at issue in those cases, the following:

> The context of Article XX(g) includes the provisions of the rest of the *General Agreement*, including in particular Articles I, III and XI; conversely, the context of Articles I and III and XI includes Article XX. Accordingly, the phrase 'relating to the conservation of exhaustible natural resources' may not be read so expansively as seriously to subvert the purpose and object of Article III:4. Nor may Article III:4 be given so broad a reach as effectively to emasculate Article XX(g) and the policies and interests it embodies. The relationship between the affirmative commitments set out in, e.g. Articles I, III and XI, and the policies and interests embodied in the 'General Exceptions' listed in Article XX, can be given meaning within the framework of the *General Agreement* and its object and purpose by a treaty interpreter only on a case-to-case basis, by careful scrutiny of the factual and legal context in a given dispute, without disregarding the words actually used by the WTO Members themselves to express their intent and purpose.[6]

This does not reflect a restrictive interpretation by the Appellate Body of the exceptions of Article XX of the GATT 1994. Rather, the Appellate Body strikes a *balance* between, on the one hand, trade liberalisation, market access and non-discrimination rules and, on the other hand, other societal values and interests. Article XX is in essence a *balancing* provision. Therefore, a narrow interpretation of Article XX is as inappropriate as a broad interpretation.

Finally, with regard to the nature and function of Article XX, the Appellate Body stated in *Thailand – Cigarettes (Philippines) (2011)* stated that:

> [i]t is true that, in examining a specific measure, a panel may be called upon to analyze a substantive obligation and an affirmative defence, and to apply both to that measure. It is also true that such an exercise will require a panel to find and apply a 'line of equilibrium' between a substantive obligation and an exception. Yet this does not render that panel's analyses of the obligation and the exception a single and integrated one. On the contrary, an analysis of whether a measure infringes an obligation necessarily precedes, and is distinct from, the 'further and separate' assessment of whether such measure is otherwise justified.[7]

In that case, Thailand argued that the Appellate Body should also reverse its finding of inconsistency with Article III:4 of the GATT 1994 after, and because, it had found that the panel erred in its analysis of Thailand's Article XX(d) defence. The Appellate Body refused to do so because the Article III:4 analysis and the Article XX(d) analysis are distinct and separate.

2.1.2 Scope of Application of Article XX

As noted above, some exceptions discussed in this and the next chapters allow deviation from all GATT or GATS obligations, while other exceptions allow deviation from specific obligations only. Article XX allows, under specific conditions, deviation from *all* GATT obligations. In other words, Article XX may

6 Appellate Body Report, *US – Gasoline (1996)*, 18.

7 Appellate Body Report, *Thailand – Cigarettes (Philippines) (2011)*, para. 173.

justify inconsistency with *any* of the GATT obligations, be it Article I:1 (MFN treatment), Article II:1 (tariff concessions), Articles III:2 and III:4 (national treatment), Article XI:1 (quantitative restrictions) or any other obligation under the GATT 1994. As discussed above, Article XX states that '*nothing* in this Agreement shall be construed to prevent the adoption or enforcement by any [Member] of measures ...'.[8] In this sense, the scope of application of Article XX is broad.

The question has arisen whether Article XX may also justify inconsistency with obligations set out in WTO agreements other than the GATT 1994. In *China – Publications and Audiovisual Products (2010)*, China invoked Article XX(a) in order to justify measures that the panel found to be inconsistent with China's trading rights commitments under its Accession Protocol.[9] China invoked Article XX, relying upon the introductory clause of paragraph 5.1 of its Accession Protocol, which reads:

> Without prejudice to China's right to regulate trade in a manner consistent with the WTO Agreement ...

The panel in this case stated that:

> China's invocation of Article XX(a) presents complex legal issues. We observe in this respect that Article XX contains the phrase 'nothing in this Agreement', with the term 'Agreement' referring to the GATT 1994, not other agreements like the Accession Protocol. The issue therefore arises whether Article XX can be directly invoked as a defence to a breach of China's trading rights commitments under the Accession Protocol, which appears to be China's position, or whether Article XX could be invoked only as a defence to a breach of a GATT 1994 obligation.[10]

However, rather than resolving the issue whether China could invoke Article XX, the panel decided to proceed on the assumption that Article XX was available to China, and to examine first whether the measures found to be inconsistent with China's Accession Protocol satisfied the requirements of Article XX.[11] This examination led the panel to conclude that the measures concerned could not be justified under Article XX. The panel in *China – Publications and Audiovisual Products (2010)* thus never ruled on the availability of Article XX.[12] However, unlike the panel, the Appellate Body did address this issue.[13] According to the Appellate Body, the phrase 'China's right to regulate trade' in paragraph 5.1 of China's Accession Protocol is a reference to its power to subject international commerce to regulation. This power may not be impaired by China's obligation to grant the right to trade, *provided that* China regulates

8 Emphasis added.
9 Appellate Body Report, *China – Publications and Audiovisual Products (2010)*, para. 205.
10 Panel Report, *China – Publications and Audiovisual Products (2010)*, para. 7.743.
11 See *ibid.*, para. 7.745. 12 See *ibid.*, para. 8.2(a)(ii).
13 While recognising that reliance upon an assumption *arguendo* is a legal technique that an adjudicator may use in order to enhance simplicity and efficiency in decision-making, the Appellate Body criticised the panel's reliance on this technique with respect to the availability of Article XX of the GATT 1994 in this case. See Appellate Body Report, *China – Publications and Audiovisual Products (2010)*, para. 215.

trade 'in a manner consistent with the WTO Agreement'.[14] The Appellate Body observed that:

> the reference to China's power to regulate trade 'in a manner consistent with the WTO Agreement' seems to us to encompass both China's power to take regulatory action provided that its measures satisfy prescribed WTO disciplines and meet specified conditions (for example, an SPS measure that conforms to the *SPS Agreement*) and China's power to take regulatory action that derogates from WTO obligations that would otherwise constrain China's exercise of such power – that is, to relevant exceptions.[15]

The Appellate Body subsequently considered that the measures that China sought to justify have 'a clearly discernible, objective link to China's regulation of trade in the relevant products'.[16] In light of this relationship between, on the one hand, the measures that are inconsistent with China's trading rights commitments, and, on the other hand, China's regulation of trade in the relevant products, the Appellate Body found that China could rely upon the introductory clause of paragraph 5.1 of its Accession Protocol and that, therefore, in this particular case, Article XX was available to justify measures inconsistent with China's Accession Protocol, i.e. inconsistent with a WTO agreement other than the GATT 1994.[17]

The question of whether Article XX is available to justify measures inconsistent with WTO agreements other than the GATT 1994 arose again in *China – Raw Materials (2012)*, when China sought to justify under Article XX export duties found to be inconsistent with the obligations under paragraph 11.3 of its Accession Protocol.[18] Paragraph 11.3 requires China to eliminate export duties unless such duties are 'specifically provided for in Annex 6' to China's Accession Protocol. Annex 6 in turn provides for maximum export duty levels on eighty-four listed products. The Note to Annex 6 clarifies that the maximum rates set out in Annex 6 'will not be exceeded'. After careful examination of paragraph 11.3 of China's Accession Protocol and the context of that provision, the Appellate Body upheld the panel, which had concluded that paragraph 11.3 does not make available to China the exceptions under Article XX of the GATT 1994.[19] In coming to this conclusion, the Appellate Body noted, *inter alia*, that there is no language in paragraph 11.3 similar to that found in paragraph 5.1 of China's Accession Protocol, namely, 'without prejudice to China's right to regulate trade in a manner consistent with the WTO Agreement'.[20] As discussed above, it was the latter language which made the Appellate Body decide in *China – Publications and Audiovisual Products (2010)* that Article XX was available as a defence in that particular case.[21] Note, however, that the Appellate Body did not limit its analysis to the text of paragraph 11.3 alone, but additionally relied on the context

14 See *ibid.*, para. 221. 15 *Ibid.*, para. 228. See also *ibid.*, para. 223.
16 *Ibid.*, para. 233. 17 See *ibid.*
18 On the inconsistency of export duties with para. 11.3 of China's Accession Protocol, see above, p. 472.
19 See Appellate Body Reports, *China – Raw Materials (2012)*, para. 307.
20 See *ibid.*, para. 304. 21 See above, p. 550.

provided by Annex 6 of China's Accession Protocol, Article VIII of the GATT 1994, and the relevant structure of the Accession Protocol, including the specific exceptions to China's obligations to eliminate export duties.[22] On the basis of all these considerations, the Appellate Body upheld in *China – Raw Materials (2012)*, the panel's finding that, in the case at hand, Article XX was *not* available to justify measures inconsistent with China's Accession Protocol.[23]

The same question, namely whether Article XX of the GATT 1994 is available to justify a measure inconsistent with paragraph 11. 3 of China's Accession Protocol, arose again in *China – Rare Earths (2014)*. China presented three specific arguments in support of its position, namely that: (1) paragraph 11.3 of China's Accession Protocol has to be treated as an integral part of the GATT 1994; (2) the terms 'nothing in this Agreement' in the chapeau of Article XX of the GATT 1994 do not exclude the availability of Article XX to defend a violation of paragraph 11.3 of China's Accession Protocol; and (3) an appropriate holistic interpretation, taking due account, of the object and purpose of the *WTO Agreement*, confirms that China may justify export duties through recourse to Article XX of the GATT 1994.[24] The panel in *China – Rare Earths* considered that none of these arguments advanced by China constituted a cogent reason for departing from the Appellate Body's ruling in *China – Raw Materials (2012)* that Article XX was *not* available to justify measures inconsistent with paragraph 11.3 of China's Accession Protocol.[25] On appeal, China did not ask the Appellate Body to reconsider its ruling in *China – Raw Materials (2012)*. China's appeal was narrow in scope, and did not in fact involve any challenge to the panel's ultimate findings and conclusions regarding the WTO inconsistency of China's export duties.[26] As China stated, its appeal was intended to obtain clarification of the systemic relationship between specific provisions in China's Accession Protocol and other WTO agreements.[27] According to China, the panel should, on the basis of a 'holistic' interpretation of Article XII:1 of the *WTO Agreement* and the second sentence of paragraph 1.2 of China's Accession Protocol, have come to the conclusion that each provision of China's Accession Protocol is an integral part of the *WTO Agreement* or one of the Multilateral Trade Agreements to which the provision 'intrinsically relates'.[28] After a detailed interpretation of Article XII:1 of the *WTO Agreement* and paragraph 1.2 of China's Accession Protocol, the Appellate Body disagreed with China's argument that a *specific*

22 See Appellate Body Reports, *China – Raw Materials (2012)*, paras. 284–5, 290 and 300–6.

23 See Appellate Body Reports, *China – Raw Materials (2012)*, para. 307. Note, however, that Article XX of the GATT 1994 was available in *China – Raw Materials (2012)* with regard to the export restrictions, inconsistent with Article XI:1 of the GATT 1994, also at issue in that case. See above, p. 485.

24 See Panel Reports, *China – Rare Earths (2014)*, para. 7.62.

25 See *ibid.*, paras. 7.72, 7.99, 7.104, 7.114, 7.115. See, however, the dissenting opinion, paras. 7.118–7.138.

26 See Appellate Body Reports, *China – Rare Earths (2014)*, para. 5.2.

27 See *ibid.*, para. 2.10.

28 See *ibid.*, paras. 5.13–5.14. The second sentence of paragraph 1.2 of China's Accession Protocol provides that the Protocol 'shall be an integral part' of the *WTO Agreement*.

provision in China's Accession Protocol is an integral part of the *WTO Agreement* or one of the Multilateral Trade Agreements to which it intrinsically relates.[29] The Appellate Body concluded as follows:

> In our view, Paragraph 1.2 of China's Accession Protocol serves to build a bridge between the package of Protocol provisions and the package of existing rights and obligations under the WTO legal framework. Nonetheless, neither obligations nor rights may be automatically transposed from one part of this legal framework into another. The fact that Paragraph 1.2 builds such a bridge is only the starting point, and does not in itself answer the questions of whether there is an objective link between *an individual provision* in China's Accession Protocol and existing obligations under the Marrakesh Agreement and the Multilateral Trade Agreements, and whether China may rely on an exception provided for in those agreements to justify a breach of such Protocol provision.[30]

Whether there is an objective link between *an individual provision* of China's Accession Protocol and an obligation or right under any of the WTO agreements, such as the GATT 1994, and whether China may rely on an exception provided for in such WTO agreements, such as Article XX of the GATT 1994, are questions that according to the Appellate Body:

> must be answered through a thorough analysis of the relevant provisions on the basis of the customary rules of treaty interpretation and the circumstances of the dispute. The analysis must start with the text of the relevant provision in China's Accession Protocol and take into account its context, including that provided by the Protocol itself and by relevant provisions of the Accession Working Party Report, and by the agreements in the WTO legal framework. The analysis must also take into account the overall architecture of the WTO system as a single package of rights and obligations and any other relevant interpretative elements, and must be applied to the circumstances of each dispute, including the measure at issue and the nature of the alleged violation.[31]

In *China – Raw Materials (2012)*, the panel and the Appellate Body noted that WTO Members have, on occasion, incorporated, by cross-reference, the provisions of Article XX of the GATT 1994 into other covered agreements.[32] By way of example, they referred to Article 3 of the *TRIMs Agreement*, which states that '[a]ll exceptions under GATT 1994 shall apply, as appropriate, to the provisions of this Agreement'. In such instances in which Article XX is *explicitly* incorporated by reference, the availability of Article XX to justify measures inconsistent with obligations under WTO agreements other than the GATT 1994 is of course a non-issue.

Apart from the question whether Article XX may apply to measures inconsistent with WTO agreements other than the GATT 1994, also other questions regarding its scope of application have arisen. With regard to the *kind* of measure that can be justified under Article XX, the panel in *US – Shrimp (1998)* ruled that Article XX could not justify measures that 'undermine the WTO multilateral trading system'.[33] The measure at issue in *US – Shrimp (1998)* was a US measure,

29 See *ibid.*, para. 5.73. 30 See *ibid.*, para. 5.74.

31 See *ibid.*

32 See Appellate Body Reports, *China – Raw Materials (2012)*, para. 303. See also Panel Reports, *China – Raw Materials (2012)*, para. 7.153.

33 Panel Report, *US – Shrimp (1998)*, para. 7.44.

which required India, Pakistan, Thailand and Malaysia to harvest shrimp in the manner set out in US law if they wanted to export this shrimp into the United States. The panel found that a measure of a Member 'conditioning access to its market for a given product upon the adoption by the exporting Member of certain policies' would undermine the multilateral trading system.[34] On appeal, however, the Appellate Body categorically rejected this panel's finding on the scope of measures that Article XX can justify. The Appellate Body held that:

> conditioning access to a Member's domestic market on whether exporting Members comply with, or adopt, a policy or policies unilaterally prescribed by the importing Member may, to some degree, be a common aspect of measures falling within the scope of one or another of the exceptions (a) to (j) of Article XX. Paragraphs (a) to (j) comprise measures that are recognized as *exceptions to substantive obligations* established in the GATT 1994, because the domestic policies embodied in such measures have been recognized as important and legitimate in character. It is not necessary to assume that requiring from exporting countries compliance with, or adoption of, certain policies (although covered in principle by one or another of the exceptions) prescribed by the importing country, renders a measure *a priori* incapable of justification under Article XX. Such an interpretation renders most, if not all, of the specific exceptions of Article XX inutile, a result abhorrent to the principles of interpretation we are bound to apply.[35]

Measures requiring that exporting countries comply with, or adopt, certain policies prescribed by the importing country are, in fact, typical of the measures that Article XX *can* justify. They are definitely not *a priori* excluded from the scope of application of Article XX.

Another question relating to the scope of application of Article XX is whether it can also justify measures that protect, or purport to protect, a societal value or interest outside the territorial jurisdiction of the Member taking the measure – for example an import prohibition imposed by Richland on aluminium from Newland that is produced at very low cost but in a manner detrimental to the environment in Newland. To date, the Appellate Body has yet to rule whether such measures that protect, or purport to protect, a societal value or interest outside the territorial jurisdiction of the Member taking the measure, can be justified under Article XX. There is no *explicit* jurisdictional limitation in Article XX. However, is there an *implied* jurisdictional limitation, so that Article XX cannot be invoked to protect non-economic values *outside* the territorial jurisdiction of the Member concerned? In *US – Shrimp (1998)*, a case involving an import ban on shrimp harvested through methods resulting in the incidental killing of sea turtles, the Appellate Body noted that sea turtles migrate to or traverse waters subject to the jurisdiction of the United States, and subsequently stated:

> We do not pass upon the question of whether there is an implied jurisdictional limitation in Article XX(g), and if so, the nature or extent of that limitation. We note only that in the specific circumstances of the case before us, there is a sufficient nexus between the migratory and endangered marine populations involved and the United States for purposes of Article XX(g).[36]

34 *Ibid.*, para. 7.45. 35 Appellate Body Report, *US – Shrimp (1998)*, para. 121.
36 *Ibid.*, para. 133.

While the position of the Appellate Body on the question of the extra-territorial application of Article XX is still undetermined,[37] the panel in *EC – Tariff Preferences (2004)* found that:

> the policy reflected in the Drug Arrangements is not one designed for the purpose of protecting human life or health *in the European Communities* and, therefore, the Drug Arrangements are not a measure for the purpose of protecting human life or health under Article XX(b) of GATT 1994.[38]

Finally, note with regard to the scope of application of Article XX that the Appellate Body in *EC – Seal Products (2014)* held that the aspects of a measure to be justified under the paragraphs of Article XX are those aspects that gave rise to the finding of GATT inconsistency.[39]

2.1.3 Reliance on Article XX

As discussed below, Article XX of the GATT 1994 is often invoked by a respondent in WTO dispute settlement. However, WTO Members rely upon Article XX to justify otherwise GATT-inconsistent measures in many more instances than the cases that are subject to dispute settlement. For 593 quantitative restrictions, or 81 per cent of all quantitative restrictions notified to the WTO as of 19 May 2015, Members relied on Article XX to justify these otherwise GATT-consistent measures.[40] For 311 of these quantitative restrictions, Members relied on Article XX(b) regarding measures 'necessary to protect human, animal or plant life or health'.[41]

2.2 Two-Tier Test under Article XX of the GATT 1994

Article XX sets out a two-tier test for determining whether a measure, otherwise inconsistent with GATT obligations, can be justified. In *US – Gasoline (1996)*, the Appellate Body stated:

> In order that the justifying protection of Article XX may be extended to it, the measure at issue must not only come under one or another of the particular exceptions – paragraphs

37 In *EC – Seal Products (2014)*, the measure at issue, the EU Seal Regime, was designed to address seal hunting activities occurring 'within and outside' the European Union. The issue of whether there is implicit jurisdictional limitation in Article XX was, however, not addressed by the participants in their submissions on appeal. Therefore, the Appellate Body, while recognising the systemic importance of the issue, decided not to examine it. See Appellate Body Reports, *EC – Seal Products (2014)*, para. 5.173.

38 Panel Report, *EC – Tariff Preferences (2004)*, para. 7.210. Emphasis added. The panel in *US – Tuna (1994)* noted, in an unadopted report, that it could not be said that the GATT proscribed in an absolute manner measures that related to things or actions outside the territorial jurisdiction of the party taking the measure. See Panel Report, *US – Tuna (1994)*, para. 5.16.

39 Appellate Body Reports, *EC – Seal Products*, para. 5.185. In support of these findings, the Appellate Body referred to Appellate Body Report, *US – Gasoline (1996)*, pp. 12–13; and Appellate Body Report, *Thailand – Cigarettes (Philippines) (2012)*, para. 177.

40 See Report by the Secretariat, *Quantitative Restrictions: Factual Information on Notifications Received*, Committee on Market Access, G/MA/W/114, dated 22 May 2015, para. 3.11. For most of the quantitative restrictions with regard to which Members did not invoke, Article XX of the GATT 1994, they invoked Article XXI of the GATT 1994. See *ibid.*

41 See *ibid.*

(a) to (j) – listed under Article XX; it must also satisfy the requirements imposed by the opening clauses of Article XX. The analysis is, in other words, two-tiered: first, provisional justification by reason of characterization of the measure under Article XX(g); second, further appraisal of the same measure under the introductory clauses of Article XX.[42]

Thus, for a GATT-inconsistent measure to be justified under Article XX, it must meet: (1) the requirements of one of the exceptions listed in paragraphs (a)–(j) of Article XX; and (2) the requirements of the introductory clause, commonly referred to as the 'chapeau', of Article XX. The Appellate Body further clarified, in *US – Shrimp (1998)*, that, to determine whether a measure can be justified under Article XX, one must always examine, first, whether this measure can be provisionally justified under one of the paragraphs of Article XX; and, if so, whether the application of this measure meets the requirements of the chapeau of Article XX.[43] Hence, an analysis under Article XX first focuses on the measure at issue itself and then on the application of that measure.[44] This distinction between the two elements of the Article XX test is well illustrated by the panel in *Brazil – Retreaded Tyres (2007)*:

> [In its analysis under Article XX(b)] [t]he Panel will *not* ... examine ... the manner in which the measure is implemented *in practice*, including any elements extraneous to the measure itself that could affect its ability to perform its function ... or consider situations in which the ban does *not* apply ... These elements will, however, be relevant to later parts of the Panel's assessment, especially under the chapeau of Article XX, where the focus will be, by contrast, primarily on the manner in which the measure is applied.[45]

By its own terms, the chapeau of Article XX is concerned with the 'manner' in which a provisionally justified measure is 'applied'. However, as the Appellate Body noted in *Japan – Alcoholic Beverages II (1996)*, whether a measure is applied in a particular manner 'can most often be discerned from the design, the architecture, and the revealing structure of a measure'.[46] The examination of the 'manner' in which the measure at issue is 'applied' thus involves a consideration of 'both substantive and procedural requirements' under the measure at issue.[47]

42 Appellate Body Report, *US – Gasoline (1996)*, 22. See also Appellate Body Report, *Brazil – Retreaded Tyres (2007)*, para. 139; Appellate Body Reports, *EC – Seal Products (2014)*, para. 5.169; and Appellate Body Report, *Colombia – Textiles (2016)*, para. 6.20.

43 See Appellate Body Report, *US – Shrimp (1998)*, paras. 119–20.

44 As the Appellate Body observed in *US – Shrimp (1998)*, this order of analysis is not random, but rather reflects the fundamental structure and logic of Article XX of the GATT 1994. See *ibid.*, para. 119.

45 Panel Report, *Brazil – Retreaded Tyres (2007)*, para. 7.107. Emphasis added.

46 Appellate Body Report, *Japan – Alcoholic Beverages II (1996)*, 29; and Appellate Body Reports, *EC – Seal Products (2014)*, para. 5.302.

47 See Appellate Body Report, *US – Shrimp (1998)*, para. 160; and Appellate Body Reports, *EC – Seal Products (2014)*, para. 5.302.

To date, WTO Members have been successful only once in justifying otherwise GATT-inconsistent measures under Article XX of the GATT 1994.[48] It is important, however, to make two observations in this respect. First, many of the otherwise GATT-inconsistent measures adopted to promote or protect societal values, which were initially found non-justifiable under Article XX, were subsequently modified (rather than withdrawn) in accordance with the DSB recommendations and rulings, and were *not* further challenged. Second, Members adopt or maintain very many otherwise GATT-inconsistent measures to promote or protect societal values, which clearly meet the requirements of Article XX. These measures seldom go to WTO dispute settlement. Therefore, the limited success Members have had in invoking Article XX does *not* indicate that Article XX plays only a marginal role in allowing WTO Members to adopt or maintain otherwise GATT-inconsistent measures to promote or protect societal values. Rather, the opposite is true.

The following subsections will first discuss the specific exceptions and their requirements provided for in paragraphs (a)–(j) of Article XX, before analysing the requirements of the chapeau of Article XX.

2.3 Specific Exceptions under Article XX of the GATT 1994

Article XX sets out, in paragraphs (a)–(j), specific grounds of justification for measures, which are otherwise inconsistent with provisions of the GATT 1994. These grounds of justification, or policy objectives, relate to the protection of societal values such as human, animal or plant life or health, exhaustible natural resources, national treasures of artistic, historic or archaeological value, and public morals.[49] Comparing the terms used in the different paragraphs of Article XX, the Appellate Body stated in *US – Gasoline (1996)*:

> Article XX uses different terms in respect of different categories: 'necessary' – in paragraphs (a), (b) and (d); 'essential' – in paragraph (j); 'relating to' – in paragraphs (c), (e) and (g); 'for the protection of' – in paragraph (f); 'in pursuance of' – in paragraph (h); and 'involving' – in paragraph (i).

48 See *US – Shrimp (Article 21.5 – Malaysia) (2001)*. Article XX of the GATT 1994 was invoked, but 'unsuccessfully' or 'incorrectly' so, in *US – Gasoline (1996); US – Shrimp (1998); EC – Asbestos (2001); Argentina – Hides and Leather (2001); Canada – Wheat Exports and Grain Imports (2004); EC – Tariff Preferences (2004); Dominican Republic – Import and Sale of Cigarettes (2005); EC – Trademarks and Geographical Indications (Australia) (2005); EC – Trademarks and Geographical Indications (US) (2005); Mexico – Taxes on Soft Drinks (2006); Brazil – Retreaded Tyres (2007); US – Customs Bond Directive (2008); US – Shrimp (Thailand) (2008); China – Auto-Parts (2009); Colombia – Ports of Entry (2009); US – Poultry (China) (2010); China – Publications and Audiovisual Products (2010); Thailand – Cigarettes (Philippines) (2011); China – Raw Materials (2012); China – Rare Earths (2014); EC – Seal Products (2014); US – COOL (Article 21.5 – Canada and Mexico) (2015); US – Tuna II (Mexico) (Article 21.5) (2015); Argentina – Financial Services (2016); Colombia – Textiles (2016)*; and *India – Solar Cells (2016)*. Note with regard to *EC – Asbestos (2001)* that the Appellate Body found that there was *no* inconsistency with the GATT 1994 that needed to be justified under Article XX. See above, p. 377, fn. 187.

49 As noted above, the list of grounds of justification contained in Article XX of the GATT 1994 is exhaustive. See above, p. 546.

It does not seem reasonable to suppose that the WTO Members intended to require, in respect of each and every category, the same kind or degree of connection or relationship between the measure under appraisal and the state interest or policy sought to be promoted or realized.[50]

In *EC – Seal Products (2014)*, the Appellate Body explained that provisional justification under one of the paragraphs of Article XX requires that a challenged measure 'address the particular interest specified in that paragraph', and that 'there be a sufficient nexus between the measure and the interest protected'.[51] The paragraphs of Article XX contain different requirements regarding the relationship, or nexus, between the measure at issue and the societal interest or value pursued. Some measures need to be 'necessary' for the protection or promotion of the societal value they pursue (e.g. the protection of life and health of humans, animals and plants), while for other measures it suffices that they 'relate to' the societal value they pursue (e.g. the conservation of exhaustible natural resources). Therefore, the grounds of justification, and the accompanying requirements provided for in Article XX, will be examined separately. This subsection focuses first and foremost on those grounds of justification, or policy objectives, which have been most frequently invoked in GATT and WTO dispute settlement.

2.3.1 Article XX(b)

Article XX(b) concerns measures which are 'necessary to protect human, animal or plant life or health'. It sets out a two-tier legal standard to determine whether a measure is *provisionally* justified under this provision. A GATT-inconsistent measure is provisionally justified under Article XX(b) if: (1) the measure is *designed* to protect the life or health of humans, animals or plants; and (2) the measure is *necessary* to protect of the life or health of humans, animals or plants.[52]

The first element of the analysis under Article XX(b) is often relatively easy to apply and has not given rise to major interpretative problems.[53] To determine the policy objective pursued by a measure, panels and the Appellate Body have examined the design and structure of the measure. Overall, they have shown a significant degree of deference in accepting that the policy objective

50 Appellate Body Report, *US – Gasoline (1996)*, 17–18.

51 Appellate Body Reports, *EC – Seal Products (2014)*, para. 5.169, quoting Appellate Body Report, *US – Gambling*, para. 292.

52 See Panel Report, *US – Gasoline (1996)*, para. 6.20. For a more recent application of this legal standard, see Panel Report, *EC – Tariff Preferences (2004)*, paras. 7.179 and 7.199; Panel Report, *Brazil – Retreaded Tyres (2007)*, paras. 7.40–7.41; and Panel Reports, *China – Raw Materials (2012)*, paras. 7.479–7.480.

53 On the 'design' element of the Article XX analysis, see Appellate Body Report, *Colombia – Textiles (2016)*, paras. 5.68–5.70, 5.76–5.77 and 5.125–5.126 (regarding the 'design' element of the analysis under Article XX(a) and (d) of the GATT 1994; see below, pp. 579–80); and Appellate Body Report, *India – Solar Cells (2016)*, para. 5.58 (regarding the 'design' element of the analysis under Article XX(d) and Article XX(j) of the GATT 1994; see below, pp. 569 and 589).

of a measure is to protect the life or health of humans, animals or plants. The wide range of measures that has been considered to pursue this policy objective includes measures to reduce the smoking of cigarettes,[54] measures to reduce air pollution,[55] measures to reduce risks arising from the accumulation of waste tyres[56] and measures to protect dolphins.[57] In *Brazil – Retreaded Tyres (2007)*, for example, Brazil submitted with regard to its import ban on retreaded tyres that:

> the accumulation of waste tyres creates a risk of mosquito-borne diseases such as dengue and yellow fever ... because waste tyres create perfect breeding grounds for disease carrying mosquitoes and that these diseases are also spread through interstate transportation of waste tyres for disposal operations ... [The] accumulation of waste tyres [also] creates a risk of tyre fires and toxic leaching ...
>
> [M]osquito-borne diseases also pose health risks to animals. Numerous toxic chemicals and heavy metals contained in pyrolytic oil released from tyre fires harm animal and plant life and health, and hazardous substances contained in toxic plumes emitted from tyre fires harm not only humans but also animals.[58]

The panel accepted Brazil's arguments, and concluded that:

> Brazil's policy of reducing exposure to the risks to human, animal or plant life or health arising from the accumulation of waste tyres falls within the range of policies covered by Article XX(b).[59]

In *China – Raw Materials (2012)*, China submitted with regard to the export restrictions on certain raw materials at issue in this case that these export restrictions were:

> part of a comprehensive environmental protection framework whose objectives are pollution reduction for the protection of health of the Chinese population.[60]

However, the respondents in this case, the European Union, the United States and Mexico, argued that China's export restrictions were not designed to address the health risks associated with environmental pollution, and that China's invocation of environmental and health concerns was 'merely a post hoc rationalization developed solely for purposes of this dispute'.[61] The panel found that China was unable to substantiate that the export restrictions at issue 'were part of a comprehensive programme maintained in order to reduce pollution', and thus cast serious doubts over whether the policy objective pursued by the export

54 See *Thailand – Cigarettes (1990)*. 55 See *US – Gasoline (1996)*.

56 See *Brazil – Retreaded Tyres (2007)*.

57 See *US – Tuna II (Mexico) (Article 21.5) (2015)*. Note that before the panel in *EC – Seal Products (2014)*, the European Union invoked – without much argumentation – Article XX(b) to justify its EU Seal Regime. The European Union did not even assert that the protection of seal welfare as such was the objective of the EU Seal Regime. The panel found that the European Union had failed to establish a *prima facie* case for its defence under Article XX(b). See Panel Report, *EC – Seal Products (2014)*, para. 7.640. With regard to European Union's invocation of Article XX(a), see below, p. 579.

58 Panel Report, *Brazil – Retreaded Tyres (2007)*, paras. 7.53 and 7.84.

59 *Ibid.*, para. 7.102. This issue was not appealed.

60 Panel Reports, *China – Raw Materials (2012)*, para. 7.498. 61 *Ibid.*, para. 7.499.

restriction was the protection of life or health of humans, animals or plants.[62] As the Appellate Body held in *EC – Seal Products (2014)* relating to Article XX(a) and discussed below, a panel should take into account a Member's articulation of the objective pursued by the measure at issue, but is not bound by that articulation. To determine the objective pursued by the measure at issue, a panel must take account of all evidence put before it in this regard, including 'the texts of statutes, legislative history and other evidence regarding the structure and operation' of the measure at issue.[63]

As Article XX(b) covers measures designed for the protection of 'human, animal or plant life or health', it covers public health policy measures as well as environmental policy measures. However, as the panel noted in *Brazil – Retreaded Tyres (2007)*, a party invoking Article XX(b) with regard to environmental policy measures 'has to establish the existence not just of risks to "the environment" generally, but specifically of risks to animal or plant life or health'.[64] For this reason, not all environmental policy measures would fall within the scope of application of Article XX(b) of the GATT 1994.[65]

The second element of the analysis under Article XX(b), the 'necessity' requirement, is more complex than the first element. The interpretation and application of the 'necessity' requirement has evolved considerably over the years. It is not the ambition of this subsection to give a full account of this evolution.[66] Rather, this subsection focuses on those cases which best reflect the current interpretation and application of the 'necessity' requirement of Article XX(b). In fact, the current case law on the 'necessity' requirement was introduced by an Appellate Body report relating to the 'necessity' requirement, not in the context of Article XX(b), but in the context of Article XX(d), namely, the Appellate Body report in *Korea – Various Measures on Beef (2001)*, discussed in the next subsection.[67] The first case in which the Appellate Body applied this new approach to the 'necessity' requirement in the context of Article XX(b) was *Brazil – Retreaded Tyres (2007)*. In its report in this case, the Appellate Body summed up how the 'necessity' requirement of Article XX(b) is currently interpreted and applied, as follows:

> [I]n order to determine whether a measure is 'necessary' within the meaning of Article XX(b) of the GATT 1994, a panel must consider the relevant factors, particularly the importance

62 *Ibid.*, para. 7.516.

63 Appellate Body Reports, *EC – Seal Products (2014)*, para. 5.144.

64 Panel Report, *Brazil – Retreaded Tyres (2007)*, para. 7.46. Note that also when there is a risk to human life or health, Article XX(b) could be invoked to justify an environmental policy measure.

65 Note that Article XX(g) of the GATT 1994 is concerned with measures relating to the conservation of exhaustible natural resources. See below, section 2.3.3.

66 Unlike the current case law, the older case law and in particular the GATT case law focused in its necessity analysis on the question whether an alternative GATT-consistent, or less-GATT inconsistent measure existed. See e.g. GATT Panel Report, *Thailand – Cigarettes (1990)*, para. 75. As discussed below, the existence of alternative measures still plays a role in the examination of 'necessity' but is now only one aspect of this examination. See below, p. 563.

67 See below, pp. 564–5.

> of the interests or values at stake, the extent of the contribution to the achievement of the measure's objective, and its trade restrictiveness. If this analysis yields a preliminary conclusion that the measure is necessary, this result must be confirmed by comparing the measure with possible alternatives, which may be less trade restrictive while providing an equivalent contribution to the achievement of the objective. This comparison should be carried out in the light of the importance of the interests or values at stake. It is through this process that a panel determines whether a measure is necessary.[68]

The Appellate Body emphasised that the 'weighing and balancing' required to determine whether a measure is 'necessary' is 'a *holistic operation* that involves putting all the variables of the equation together and evaluating them in relation to each other after having examined them individually, in order to reach an overall judgement'.[69]

To understand the current case law on the 'necessity' requirement of Article XX(b), it is important, however, to consider the Appellate Body's findings in *EC – Asbestos (2001)* relating to Article XX(b). While the Appellate Body had found that the measure at issue in this case – a French ban on asbestos and asbestos products – was not inconsistent with Article III:4 of the GATT 1994 and the panel's findings relating to Article XX(b) were therefore moot, the Appellate Body nevertheless addressed *some* of the issues that arise when determining whether an otherwise GATT-inconsistent measure is justified under Article XX(b). The Appellate Body in *EC – Asbestos (2001)* made four findings in this respect which deserve to be mentioned as they are important in understanding the current state of the law as set out in *Brazil – Retreaded Tyres (2007)*.

First, according to the Appellate Body, the more important the societal value pursued by the measure at issue and the more this measure contributes to the protection or promotion of this value, the more easily the measure at issue may be considered to be 'necessary'.[70] In *EC – Asbestos (2001)*, the societal value pursued by the measure was the preservation of human life and health through the elimination, or reduction, of the well-known, and life-threatening, health risks posed by asbestos fibres. The Appellate Body observed with regard to this value that it is 'both vital and important in the highest degree'.[71] In *EC – Asbestos (2001)*, the Appellate Body did not explicitly refer to the third factor in the 'weighing and balancing' process now applied to determine whether an otherwise GATT-inconsistent measure is 'necessary', namely, the restrictive impact of the measure at issue on international trade. However, in *Brazil – Retreaded Tyres (2007)*, the Appellate Body clearly suggested with regard to this factor that the more restrictive the impact of the measure at issue is on international trade, the more difficult it is to consider that measure 'necessary'.[72]

68 Appellate Body Report, *Brazil – Retreaded Tyres (2007)*, para. 178. The Appellate Body referred in this regard to its report in *US – Gambling (2005)*, para. 307.

69 See *ibid.*, para. 182. Emphasis added. Note also that with regard to Article XIV(a) of the GATS, the Appellate Body held in *US – Gambling (2005)*, paras. 306–7, that the 'weighing and balancing' is not necessarily limited to the three factors referred to above. See below, p. 607.

70 Appellate Body Report, *EC – Asbestos (2001)*, para. 172. 71 *Ibid.*

72 See Appellate Body Report, *Brazil – Retreaded Tyres (2007)*, para. 150.

Second, with regard to the existence of less trade-restrictive alternative measures, Canada asserted before the Appellate Body in *EC – Asbestos (2001)* that the panel had erred in finding that 'controlled use' of asbestos and asbestos products is not a reasonably available alternative to the import ban on asbestos. According to Canada, an alternative measure is only excluded as a 'reasonably available' alternative if implementation of that measure is 'impossible'. The Appellate Body stated that, in determining whether a suggested alternative measure is 'reasonably available', several factors must be taken into account, *alongside* the difficulty of implementation. It subsequently referred to its earlier report in *Korea – Various Measures on Beef (2001)* (concerning the 'necessity' requirement under Article XX(d), discussed in the next section)[73] and noted with regard to the determination of 'necessity' under Article XX(b):

> We indicated in *Korea – Beef* that one aspect of the 'weighing and balancing process … comprehended in the determination of whether a WTO-consistent alternative measure' is reasonably available is the extent to which the alternative measure 'contributes to the realization of the end pursued'.[74]

Canada, the complainant in *EC – Asbestos (2001)*, had asserted that 'controlled use' of asbestos and asbestos products represented a 'reasonably available' measure that would serve the same end as the ban on asbestos and asbestos products. The issue for the Appellate Body was, therefore, whether France could reasonably be expected to employ 'controlled use' practices to achieve its chosen level of health protection – a halt in the spread of asbestos-related health risks. The Appellate Body concluded that this was not the case. It reasoned as follows:

> In our view, France could not reasonably be expected to employ *any* alternative measure if that measure would involve a continuation of the very risk that the Decree seeks to 'halt'. Such an alternative measure would, in effect, prevent France from achieving its chosen level of health protection. On the basis of the scientific evidence before it, the Panel found that, in general, the efficacy of 'controlled use' remains to be demonstrated. Moreover, even in cases where 'controlled use' practices are applied 'with greater certainty', the scientific evidence suggests that the level of exposure can, in some circumstances, still be high enough for there to be a 'significant residual risk of developing asbestos-related diseases' … 'Controlled use' would, thus, not be an alternative measure that would achieve the end sought by France.[75]

In *Brazil – Retreaded Tyres (2007)*, the Appellate Body confirmed that a Member cannot reasonably be expected to employ an alternative measure if that measure does not allow it to achieve its desired level of protection with respect to the policy objective pursued. The Appellate Body also recalled in *Brazil – Retreaded Tyres (2007)* its finding in *US – Gambling (2005)* (concerning the 'necessity' requirement under Article XIV(a) of the GATS, discussed later in this chapter)[76] that:

> [a]n alternative measure may be found not to be 'reasonably available' … where it is merely theoretical in nature, for instance, where the responding Member is not capable of taking it,

73 See below, 565. 74 Appellate Body Report, *EC – Asbestos (2001)*, para. 172.
75 *Ibid.*, para. 174. 76 See below, pp. 609–10.

or where the measure imposes an undue burden on that Member, such as prohibitive costs or substantial technical difficulties.[77]

Third, the Appellate Body ruled in *EC – Asbestos (2001)* that it is for WTO Members to determine the *level* of protection of health or the environment they consider appropriate.[78] Other Members cannot challenge the level of protection chosen; they can only argue that the measure at issue is not 'necessary' to achieve that level of protection.[79]

Fourth, quoting from its case law on the *SPS Agreement*, the Appellate Body in *EC – Asbestos (2001)* ruled that:

> responsible and representative governments may act in good faith on the basis of what, at a given time, may be a divergent opinion coming from qualified and respected sources. In justifying a measure under Article XX(b) of the GATT 1994, a Member may also rely, in good faith, on scientific sources which, at that time, may represent a divergent, but qualified and respected, opinion. A Member is not obliged, in setting health policy, automatically to follow what, at a given time, may constitute a majority scientific opinion. Therefore, a panel need not, necessarily, reach a decision under Article XX(b) of the GATT 1994 on the basis of the 'preponderant' weight of the evidence.[80]

With regard to the contribution to the achievement of the objective pursued, or, in short, the contribution to the objective pursued, the Appellate Body ruled in *Brazil – Retreaded Tyres (2007)* that a measure contributes to the achievement of the objective 'when there is a genuine relationship of ends and means between the objective pursued and the measure at issue'.[81] The Appellate Body furthermore held that a panel enjoys certain latitude in choosing its approach to analysing the contribution made; that such an analysis may be performed in qualitative or quantitative terms; and that it ultimately depends upon 'the nature of the risk, the objective pursued, and the level of protection sought' as well as on 'the nature, quantity, and quality of evidence existing at the time the analysis is made'.[82]

77 Appellate Body Report, *Brazil – Retreaded Tyres (2007)*, para. 156, citing Appellate Body Report, *US – Gambling (2005)*, para. 308. In *Brazil – Retreaded Tyres (2007)*, the Appellate Body found that the alternative measures proposed by the European Communities were either already part of the strategy implemented by Brazil to deal with waste tyres, did not achieve the level of protection chosen by Brazil, or were costly and required advanced technologies and know-how not readily available on a large scale. Therefore, they could not be regarded as 'reasonably available' alternatives to the import ban. See Appellate Body Report, *Brazil – Retreaded Tyres (2007)*, paras. 172–5.

78 See Appellate Body Report, *EC – Asbestos (2001)*, para. 168. This finding is in line with the case law under the *SPS Agreement*: see below, pp. 935–92. See also Panel Report, *Brazil – Retreaded Tyres (2007)*, para. 7.108.

79 As France did in *EC – Asbestos (2001)*, a WTO Member can choose a zero-risk level. This means that there will be few, if any, measures other than a full ban that will achieve this level of protection. Note also that the panel in *US – Gasoline (1996)* ruled that it is not the necessity of the policy objective but the necessity of the disputed measure to *achieve* that objective which is at issue. See Panel Report, *US – Gasoline (1996)*, para. 6.22.

80 Appellate Body Report, *EC – Asbestos (2001)*, para. 178, quoting from Appellate Body Report, *EC – Hormones (1999)*, para. 194, fn. 48. For a discussion of this SPS case law, see below, pp. 935–92.

81 Appellate Body Report, *Brazil – Retreaded Tyres (2007)*, para. 145. In this case, the Appellate Body rejected the European Communities' argument that the contribution of the measure at issue to the achievement of its objective must be quantified by a panel. It held instead that either a quantitative or a qualitative evaluation is permissible. What is required is 'a genuine relationship of ends and means between the objective pursued and the measure at issue'.

82 See *ibid.*, paras. 145–6.

The Appellate Body also held in *Brazil – Retreaded Tyres (2007)* that a measure must bring about a *material* contribution, and not merely a marginal or insignificant contribution, to the achievement of its objective; and that whether a measure brings about such a contribution can be demonstrated either by evidence that the measure: (1) has already resulted in a material contribution; or (2) is apt to produce a material contribution.[83] Note, however, that in *EC – Seal Products (2014)* (concerning the 'necessity' requirement under Article XX(a)) the Appellate Body clarified that in *Brazil – Retreaded Tyres (2007)* it did:

> *not* set out a generally applicable standard requiring the use of a pre-determined threshold of 'material' contribution in analysing the necessity of a measure under Article XX of the GATT 1994.[84]

As the Appellate Body explained, its approach in *Brazil – Retreaded Tyres (2007)* was tailored to the peculiar features of the measure at issue in that case.[85] According to the Appellate Body, whether a measure is 'necessary' cannot be determined by the level of contribution alone. Referring to its earlier case law discussed above, the Appellate Body recalled in *EC – Seal Products (2014)* that the determination of whether a measure is 'necessary' involves a *holistic* process of 'weighing and balancing' a series of factors, including the importance of the interests or values at stake, the contribution of the measure to the objective it pursues, and the trade-restrictiveness of the measure, following which a comparison with less trade-restrictive alternatives should in most cases be undertaken.[86] In the same vein, the Appellate Body noted in *Brazil – Retreaded Tyres (2007)* that an import ban is 'by design as trade-restrictive as can be', but nevertheless considered that 'there may be circumstances where such a measure can nevertheless be necessary, within the meaning of Article XX(b)'.[87]

On the question of which party bears the burden of proof with regard to the existence of a reasonably available alternative measure, the Appellate Body in *Brazil – Retreaded Tyres (2007)* recalled its finding in *US – Gambling (2005)* (concerning the 'necessity' requirement under Article XIV(a) of the GATS).[88] Applying the same allocation of the burden of proof as in the latter case, the Appellate Body stated:

> It rests upon the complaining Member to *identify* possible alternatives to the measure at issue that the responding Member could have taken. As the Appellate Body indicated in *US – Gambling*, while the responding Member must show that a measure is necessary, it

83 See *ibid.*, para. 151.
84 Appellate Body Reports, *EC – Seal Products (2014)*, para. 5.213. Emphasis added.
85 See *ibid.* As the Appellate Body explained, the measure at issue in *Brazil – Retreaded Tyres (2007)* formed part of a broader policy scheme, and was not yet having, or likely itself to produce, an immediately discernible impact on its objective. Accordingly, the Appellate Body sought in that dispute to determine whether the measure was 'apt to make a material contribution' to its objective.
86 See *ibid.*, para. 5.214.
87 Appellate Body Report, *Brazil – Retreaded Tyres (2007)*, para. 150.
88 See Appellate Body Report, *US – Gambling (2005)*, paras. 309–11.

does not have to 'show, in the first instance, that there are *no* reasonably available alternatives to achieve its objectives'.[89]

Finally, as discussed above, the Appellate Body held in *Brazil – Retreaded Tyres (2007)*, that when the 'weighing and balancing' analysis yields a preliminary conclusion of 'necessity', this conclusion needs to be confirmed by comparing the measure at issue with less trade-restrictive alternative measures. Note that in *EC – Seal Products (2014)* (concerning the 'necessity' requirement under Article XX(a)), the Appellate Body held that 'in most cases' a comparison between the challenged measure and possible alternatives should be undertaken. Referring to its report in *US – Tuna II (Mexico) (2012)* (concerning the 'necessity' requirement under Article 2.2 of the *TBT Agreement*), the Appellate Body suggested that a comparison with alternative measures would not be required *only* when, for instance, the measure at issue is not trade-restrictive or makes no contribution to the achievement of the objective pursued.[90] Note also that in *EC – Seal Products (2014)* the Appellate Body disagreed with the assertion that 'a preliminary determination of necessity is *required* before proceeding to compare the challenged measure with possible alternatives'.[91] As the Appellate Body held in *US – COOL (Article 21.5 – Canada and Mexico) (2015)* (concerning the 'necessity' requirement under Article XX(d) of the GATT 1994 and Article 2.2 of the *TBT Agreement*), the methodology to determine 'necessity' may be 'tailored to the specific claims, measures, and facts at issue in a given case'.[92]

2.3.2 Article XX(d)

As mentioned above, Article XX(d) concerns and can justify measures:

> necessary to secure compliance with laws or regulations which are not inconsistent with the provisions of this Agreement, including those relating to customs enforcement, the enforcement of monopolies operated under paragraph 4 of Article II and Article XVII, the protection of patents, trade marks and copyrights, and the prevention of deceptive practices.

The list of 'laws or regulations', introduced by the word 'including', is clearly not exhaustive. Article XX(d) also covers types of 'laws and regulations' not listed. It thus allows for the pursuit of a wide range of policy objectives not limited to the policy objectives explicitly referred to.

Article XX(d) sets out a two-tier legal standard for the provisional justification of otherwise GATT-inconsistent measures.[93] In *Korea – Various Measures on Beef (2001)*, a dispute concerning Korean regulation on retail sales of both domestic and imported beef products (the dual retail system), allegedly

89 Appellate Body Report, *Brazil – Retreaded Tyres (2007)*, para. 156. Emphasis added.
90 See Appellate Body Reports, *EC – Seal Products (2014)*, para. 5,169, referring to Appellate Body Report, *US – Tuna II (Mexico) (2012)*, para. 322 and fn. 647 to para. 322.
91 Appellate Body Reports, *EC – Seal Products (2014)*, fn. 1299 to para. 5.215. (emphasis added).
92 Appellate Body Reports, *US – COOL (Article 21.5 – Canada and Mexico) (2015)*, para. 5.205.
93 Note that the panel in *Canada – Wheat Exports and Grain Imports (2004)* applied a three-tier legal standard. See below, fn. 95.

designed to secure compliance with a consumer protection law, the Appellate Body ruled:

> For a measure, otherwise inconsistent with GATT 1994, to be justified provisionally under paragraph (d) of Article XX, two elements must be shown. First, the measure must be one designed to 'secure compliance' with laws or regulations that are not themselves inconsistent with some provision of the GATT 1994. Second, the measure must be 'necessary' to secure such compliance. A Member who invokes Article XX(d) as a justification has the burden of demonstrating that these two requirements are met.[94]

Thus, for a GATT-inconsistent measure to be provisionally justified under Article XX(d) the measure: (1) must be *designed* to secure compliance with laws and regulations, such as customs law or intellectual property law, which are not themselves GATT-inconsistent; and (2) must be *necessary* to secure such compliance.[95]

With respect to the first element of the Article XX(d) analysis, namely, that the measure must be 'designed' to secure compliance, the Appellate Body held in *Colombia – Textiles (2016)* that:

> a panel must examine the relationship between the measure and securing compliance with relevant provisions of laws or regulations that are not GATT-inconsistent.[96]

The Appellate Body considered that the terms 'to secure compliance' in Article XX(d) involve establishing the existence of such a relationship. The Appellate Body ruled that the relationship does not meet the requirements of the 'design' element of Article XX(d) analysis:

> [i]f the assessment of the design of the measure, including its content, structure, and expected operation, reveals that the measure is incapable of ... securing compliance with relevant provisions of laws or regulations that are not GATT-inconsistent ...[97]

It is clear that the examination of the 'design' of the measure is not a particularly demanding element of the Article XX(d) analysis. If the measure at issue is incapable of securing compliance, such that there is no relationship between the measure and securing compliance, further analysis with regard to whether this measure is 'necessary' would not be required. This is because there is no justification under Article XX(d) for a measure that is not 'designed' to secure compliance.[98] However, as the Appellate Body noted,

94 Appellate Body Report, *Korea – Various Measures on Beef (2001)*, para. 157. See also Panel Report, *US – Gasoline (1996)*, para. 6.31; and Appellate Body Report, *Colombia – Textiles (2016)*, para. 6.72.

95 As mentioned above, the panel in *Canada – Wheat Exports and Grain Imports (2004)* applied a *three*-tier legal standard. According to the panel, for a GATT-inconsistent measure to be provisionally justified under Article XX(d): (a) the measure for which justification is claimed must secure compliance with other laws or regulations; (b) those other laws or regulations must not be inconsistent with the provisions of the GATT 1994; and (c) the measure for which justification is claimed must be necessary to secure compliance with those other laws or regulations. See Panel Report, *Canada – Wheat Exports and Grain Imports (2004)*, para. 6.218.

96 Appellate Body Report, *Colombia – Textiles (2016)*, para. 6.67.

97 *Ibid.* See also Appellate Body Report, *India – Solar Cells (2016)*, para. 5.58.

98 See *ibid.*, referring to Appellate Body Report, *Argentina – Financial Services (2016)*, para. 6.203; and Appellate Body Report, *Mexico – Taxes on Soft Drinks (2006)*, para. 72.

> a panel must not ... structure its analysis of the [design element] in such a way as to lead it to truncate its analysis prematurely and thereby foreclose consideration of crucial aspects of the respondent's defence relating to the 'necessity' analysis.[99]

The panel in *Colombia – Textiles (2016)* had found that there was no relationship between the compound tariff, the measure at issue, and securing compliance with Colombia's anti-money laundering legislation. Therefore, the panel concluded that the measure at issue was not 'designed' to secure compliance with Colombia's anti-money laundering legislation, and ceased its Article XX(d) analysis. The Appellate Body reversed this finding. On the basis of the panel's own findings, the Appellate Body considered that the compound tariff is *not incapable* of securing compliance with Colombia's anti-money laundering legislation, such that there is a relationship between the measure and securing such compliance. The Appellate Body therefore concluded that the measure at issue is 'designed' to secure compliance with Colombia's anti-money laundering legislation. As the measure is 'designed' to secure compliance, the panel should not have ceased its Article XX(d) analysis at the 'design' element, but should have proceeded to the 'necessity' element of the analysis, so as not to foreclose crucial aspects of the respondent's defence relating to the 'necessity' of the measure at issue.[100]

In *EEC – Parts and Components (1990)* the question arose whether the phrase 'to secure compliance with laws or regulations' could be interpreted to mean to ensure the attainment of the objectives of the laws or regulations concerned. The panel in this case rejected this interpretation. It observed that Article XX(d) does *not* refer to the *objectives* of laws or regulations, but only to laws or regulations, and concluded this provision covers measures designed to secure compliance with laws or regulations as such and not with their objectives.[101] In the same vein, the panel in *Colombia – Ports of Entry (2009)*, and most recently the panel in *Colombia – Textiles (2016)*, held that 'to secure compliance' means to enforce obligations rather than to ensure the attainment of the objectives of laws and regulations.[102]

With regard to the meaning of the terms 'laws or regulation' in the context of the phrase 'to secure compliance with laws or regulations' in Article XX(d), the Appellate Body held in *India – Solar Cells (2016)* that the terms 'laws or regulations' refer to rules of conduct and principles governing behaviour or practice that form part of the domestic legal system of a Member.[103] With regard to the latter element (i.e. that form part of the domestic legal system), the Appellate

99 See *ibid.*, referring to Appellate Body Report, *Argentina – Financial Services*, para. 6.203.
100 See Appellate Body Report, *Colombia – Textiles (2016)*, paras. 6.81–6.85 and 6.89.
101 GATT Panel Report, *EEC – Parts and Components (1990)*, paras. 5.16–5.17.
102 See Panel Report, *Colombia – Ports of Entry (2009)*, para. 7.538; and Panel Report, in *Colombia – Textiles (2016)*, paras. 7.482–7.483.
103 See Appellate Body Report, *India – Solar Cells (2016)*, para. 5.106.

Body referred to its report in *Mexico – Taxes on Soft Drinks (2006)* in which it held that:

> [t]he terms 'laws or regulations' are generally used to refer to domestic laws or regulations. As Mexico and the United States note, previous GATT and WTO disputes in which Article XX(d) has been invoked as a defence have involved domestic measures. ... We agree with the United States that one does not immediately think about international law when confronted with the term 'laws' in the plural ... In our view, the terms 'laws or regulations' refer to rules that form part of the domestic legal system of a WTO Member.[104]

'Laws or regulations' within the meaning of Article XX(d) are thus 'rules that form part of the domestic legal system of a Member'. However, as the Appellate Body already explicitly recognised in *Mexico – Taxes on Soft Drinks (2006)* and confirmed in *India – Solar Cells (2016)*, the rules that form part of the domestic legal system of a Member include 'rules deriving from international agreements that have been incorporated into the domestic legal system of a WTO Member or have direct effect according to that WTO Member's legal system'.[105] In *India – Solar Cells (2016)*, the Appellate Body ruled that:

> An assessment of whether a given international instrument or rule forms part of the domestic legal system of a Member must be carried out on a case-by-case basis, in light of the nature of the instrument or rule and the subject matter of the law at issue, and taking into account the functioning of the domestic legal system of the Member in question.[106]

Note, however, that even if a particular international instrument can be said to form part of the domestic legal system of a Member, this does not, in and of itself, establish the existence of a rule, as a 'law or regulation' within the meaning of Article XX(d).[107]

With regard to the determination of whether a rule is a 'law or regulation' within the meaning of Article XX(d), the Appellate Body ruled in *India – Solar Cells (2016)* that:

> a panel should evaluate and give due consideration to all the characteristics of the relevant instrument(s) and should avoid focusing exclusively or unduly on any single characteristic. In particular, it may be relevant for a panel to consider, among others: (i) the degree of normativity of the instrument and the extent to which the instrument operates to set out a rule of conduct or course of action that is to be observed within the domestic legal system of a Member; (ii) the degree of specificity of the relevant rule; (iii) whether the rule is legally enforceable, including, e.g. before a court of law; (iv) whether the rule has been adopted or recognized by a competent authority possessing the necessary powers under the domestic legal system of a Member; (v) the form and title given to any instrument or instruments

104 See Appellate Body Report, *Mexico – Taxes on Soft Drinks (2006)*, para. 69. Note that Mexico had argued before the panel that the measures at issue in this case were necessary to secure compliance 'by the United States with the United States' obligations under the NAFTA. See Panel Report, *Mexico – Taxes on Soft Drinks (2006)*, para. 8.162.

105 Appellate Body Report, *Mexico – Taxes on Soft Drinks (2006)*, para. 79. See also Appellate Body Report, *India – Solar Cells (2016)*, para. 5.140. As the Appellate Body observed in *India – Solar Cells (2016)*, '[s]ubject to the domestic legal system of a Member, there may well be other ways in which international instruments or rules can become part of that domestic legal system'. *Ibid.*

106 Appellate Body Report, *India – Solar Cells (2016)*, para. 5.140.

107 See *ibid.*, para. 5.141.

containing the rule under the domestic legal system of a Member; and (vi) the penalties or sanctions that may accompany the relevant rule.[108]

As the Appellate Body explained, determining whether a rule is a 'law or regulation' within the meaning of Article XX(d) is relatively straightforward in case of a specific, legally enforceable rule under a single provision of a domestic legislative act.[109] However, in other cases such determination may be more complex. It is possible that a rule, which constitutes a 'law or regulation' within the meaning of Article XX(d), is not contained in a single instrument or a provision thereof, but that several elements of one or more instruments function together to set out a rule of conduct or course of action.[110] It is also possible that a rule, which cannot be enforced in a court of law, nevertheless sets out a rule of conduct or course of action, which constitutes a 'law or regulation'.[111] 'Laws or regulations' may:

in appropriate cases, include rules in respect of which a Member seeks to 'secure compliance', even when compliance is not coerced ...[112]

With regard to the meaning of the terms 'to secure compliance' in the context of the phrase 'to secure compliance with laws or regulations' in Article XX(d), the Appellate Body stated in *Mexico – Taxes on Soft Drinks (2006)* that these terms 'speak to the types of measures that a WTO Member can seek to justify under Article XX(d)' and 'relate to the design of the measures sought to be justified'.[113] The panel in that case had found that there was uncertainty regarding the effectiveness of the tax measures at issue, and that it was therefore not convinced that these measures were meant 'to secure compliance'. The Appellate Body, however, did not agree with this reasoning:

In our view, a measure can be said to be designed 'to secure compliance' even if the measure cannot be guaranteed to achieve its result with absolute certainty. Nor do we consider that the 'use of coercion' is a necessary component of a measure designed 'to secure compliance'. Rather, Article XX(d) requires that the design of the measure *contribute* 'to secur[ing]' compliance with laws or regulations which are not inconsistent with the provisions of the GATT 1994.[114]

The Appellate Body further clarified in *India – Solar Cells (2016)* that an otherwise GATT-inconsistent measure can be said 'to secure compliance' with laws or regulations:

when its design reveals that it secures compliance with *specific rules, obligations, or requirements* under such laws or regulations.[115]

108 *Ibid.*, para. 5.113.
109 See *ibid.*, para. 5.114.
110 See *ibid.* See also Appellate Body Report, *Argentina – Financial Services (2016)*, fn. 505 to para. 6.208 (with regard to Article XIV(c) of the GATS; see below, pp. 612–14).
111 See Appellate Body Report, *India – Solar Cells (2016)*, para. 5.109. 112 *Ibid.*
113 Appellate Body Report, *Mexico – Taxes on Soft Drinks (2006)*, para. 72.
114 *Ibid.*, para. 74. Emphasis added.
115 See Appellate Body Report, *India – Solar Cells (2016)*, para. 5.110, quoting from Appellate Body Report, *Argentina – Financial Services (2016)*, para. 6.203, which relates to Article XIV(c) of the GATS, discussed below, pp. 612–14.

As the Appellate Body explained, it is important, in this regard, to distinguish between the specific rules, obligations or requirements with respect to which a measure seeks to secure compliance, on the one hand, and the objectives of the relevant laws or regulations on the other hand.[116] As the Appellate Body stated in *India – Solar Cells (2016)*:

> The 'more precisely' a respondent is able to identify specific rules, obligations, or requirements contained in the relevant 'laws or regulations', the 'more likely' it will be able to elucidate how and why the inconsistent measure secures compliance with such 'laws or regulations'.[117]

With regard to the requirement that the 'laws or regulations' are not GATT-inconsistent, note that in *EC – Trademarks and Geographical Indications (2005)* the European Communities argued that the GATT-inconsistent measures at issue were employed to secure compliance with EU legislation, namely, EC Council Regulation (EEC) No. 2081/92 of 14 July 1992 on the protection of geographical indications and designations of origin for agricultural products and foodstuffs. The panel found, however, EC Council Regulation (EEC) No. 2081/92 to be inconsistent with the GATT 1994, and therefore not to qualify as a 'law or regulation' within the meaning of Article XX(d).[118] Similarly, in *Thailand – Cigarettes (Philippines) (2011)*, the panel rejected an Article XX(d) defence by Thailand that the measures at issue were necessary to secure compliance with Thai tax laws, because the panel had already found that these laws were GATT-inconsistent.[119]

Article XX(d) requires that the laws or regulations are 'not inconsistent'. It does not require that the laws or regulations are consistent. This is not without consequence for the burden of proof which rests on the respondent.[120] The use of the double negative ('not inconsistent') suggests that the respondent must not positively show the consistency of the relevant law or regulation, unless that consistency is explicitly challenged by the complainant. Note, as the panel in *Colombia – Textiles (2016)* recalled, that:

> the Appellate Body has made it clear that a responding Member's law should be treated as WTO-consistent until proven otherwise.[121]

116 *Ibid.* See also Appellate Body Report, *Argentina – Financial Services (2016)*, fn. 495 to para. 6.203. Note that the objectives may assist in elucidating the content of specific rules, obligations, or requirements of the laws or regulations.

117 Appellate Body Report, *India – Solar Cells (2016)*. See also Appellate Body Report, *Argentina – Financial Services (2016)*, para. 6.203.

118 See Panel Report, *EC – Trademarks and Geographical Indications (Australia) (2005)*, para. 7.332; and Panel Report, *EC – Trademarks and Geographical Indications (US) (2005)*, para. 7.297.

119 See Panel Report, *Thailand – Cigarettes (Philippines) (2011)*, para. 7.758. This latter finding was reversed on appeal but for a different reason. The Appellate Body was 'compelled' to reverse this panel finding because the panel made an obvious error in the relevant paragraph of its report by referring to the wrong Thai legislation. See Appellate Body Report, *Thailand – Cigarettes (Philippines) (2011)*, para. 171.

120 See Panel Report, *Colombia – Ports of Entry (2009)*, para. 7.529; and GATT Panel Report, *US – Malt Beverages (1992)*, para. 5.52.

121 Panel Report, *Colombia – Textiles (2016)*, para. 7.511, referring to Appellate Body Report, *US – Carbon Steel (2002)*, para. 157.

Finally, note that, as held by the panel in *Korea – Various Measures on Beef (2001)*, a measure need *not* be designed *exclusively* to secure compliance with the relevant law or regulation. It is sufficient that the measure was put in place, at least in part, in order to secure compliance with the law or regulation.[122]

With respect to the second element of the Article XX(d) analysis, namely the 'necessity' requirement, it was – as already noted above – in the context of a case involving Article XX(d) that the current approach to the interpretation and application of the 'necessity' requirement was introduced by the Appellate Body. The case in question was *Korea – Various Measures on Beef (2001)*. In its report in this case, the Appellate Body first noted that:

> [w]e believe that, as used in the context of Article XX(d), the reach of the word 'necessary' is not limited to that which is 'indispensable' or 'of absolute necessity' or 'inevitable'. Measures which are indispensable or of absolute necessity or inevitable to secure compliance certainly fulfil the requirements of Article XX(d). But other measures, too, may fall within the ambit of this exception. As used in Article XX(d), the term 'necessary' refers, in our view, to a range of degrees of necessity. At one end of this continuum lies 'necessary' understood as 'indispensable'; at the other end, is 'necessary' taken to mean as 'making a contribution to'. We consider that a 'necessary' measure is, in this continuum, located significantly closer to the pole of 'indispensable' than to the opposite pole of simply 'making a contribution to'.[123]

The Appellate Body subsequently stated:

> It seems to us that a treaty interpreter assessing a measure claimed to be necessary to secure compliance of a WTO-consistent law or regulation may, in appropriate cases, take into account the relative importance of the common interests or values that the law or regulation to be enforced is intended to protect. The more vital or important those common interests or values are, the easier it would be to accept as 'necessary' a measure designed as an enforcement instrument.
>
> There are other aspects of the enforcement measure to be considered in evaluating that measure as 'necessary'. One is the extent to which the measure contributes to the realization of the end pursued, the securing of compliance with the law or regulation at issue. The greater the contribution, the more easily a measure might be considered to be 'necessary'. Another aspect is the extent to which the compliance measure produces restrictive effects on international commerce, that is, in respect of a measure inconsistent with Article III:4, restrictive effects *on imported goods*. A measure with a relatively slight impact upon imported products might more easily be considered as 'necessary' than a measure with intense or broader restrictive effects.[124]

The Appellate Body thus came to the following conclusion in *Korea – Various Measures on Beef (2001)* concerning the 'necessity' requirement of Article XX(d):

> In sum, determination of whether a measure, which is not 'indispensable', may nevertheless be 'necessary' within the contemplation of Article XX(d), involves in every case a process of weighing and balancing a series of factors which prominently include the contribution

122 See Panel Report, *Korea – Various Measures on Beef (2001)*, para. 658.

123 Appellate Body Report, *Korea – Various Measures on Beef (2001)*, para. 161.

124 *Ibid.*, paras. 162–3; *ibid.*, para. 165, the Appellate Body cited Panel Report, *US – Section 337 Tariff Act (1989)*, para. 5.26.

made by the compliance measure to the enforcement of the law or regulation at issue, the importance of the common interests or values protected by that law or regulation, and the accompanying impact of the law or regulation on imports or exports.[125]

As noted by the Appellate Body in *Korea – Various Measures on Beef (2001)*, the process of weighing and balancing these factors:

> is comprehended in the determination of whether a WTO-consistent alternative measure which the Member concerned could 'reasonably be expected to employ' is available, or whether a less WTO-inconsistent measure is 'reasonably available'.[126]

Note that in case law relating to Article XX(a) of the GATT 1994, discussed below, and Article XX(b) of the GATT 1994, discussed above, the 'necessity' requirement under Article XX has been further clarified.[127]

As the Appellate Body first ruled in *US – Gambling (2005)* with regard to the 'necessity' requirement in Article XIV(a) of the GATS, it rests upon the complaining Member to *identify* possible alternative measures, after which it is for the responding Member to show that the proposed alternative measures are not reasonably available, are not less trade-restrictive or do not make an equivalent contribution to the objective pursued.[128]

With regard to the 'relative importance' of the interests or values protected (or intended to be protected) by the law or regulation with which compliance is to be secured, the Appellate Body held in *Korea – Various Measures on Beef (2001)*:

> Clearly, Article XX(d) is susceptible of application in respect of a wide variety of 'laws and regulations' to be enforced. It seems to us that a treaty interpreter assessing a measure claimed to be necessary to secure compliance of a WTO-consistent law or regulation may, *in appropriate cases*, take into account the relative importance of the common interests or values that the law or regulation to be enforced is intended to protect. The more vital or important those common interests or values are, the easier it would be to accept as 'necessary' a measure designed as an enforcement instrument.[129]

In *Colombia – Ports of Entry (2010)*, for example, the panel found that combating under-invoicing and money laundering associated with drug trafficking was 'a relatively more important reality for Colombia than for many other countries'.[130] In *Colombia – Textiles (2016)*, the panel found that 'the objective of securing compliance with the Colombian anti-money laundering legislation

125 *Ibid.*, para. 164. See also, for example, Appellate Body Report, *Colombia – Textiles (2016)*, para. 5.142.

126 *Ibid.*, para. 166. In *Canada – Wheat Exports and Grain Imports (2004)*, the panel stated, with reference to the Appellate Body reports in *EC – Asbestos (2001)* and *Korea – Various Measures on Beef (2001)*, that in order to establish whether an alternative measure was reasonably available the relevant factors to consider are: (1) the extent to which the alternative measure contributes to the achievement of the policy objective; (2) the difficulty of implementing the alternative measure; and (3) the impact of the alternative measure on international trade. See Panel Report, *Canada – Wheat Exports and Grain Imports (2004)*, para. 6.226.

127 See, for example, Appellate Body Report, *Brazil Retreaded Tyres (2007)*, para. 156; Appellate Body Reports, *EC – Seal Products (2014)*, para. 5,169; Appellate Body Report, *Colombia – Textiles (2016)*, para. 5.142.

128 See Appellate Body Report, *US – Gambling (2005)*, paras. 309ff.

129 Appellate Body Report, *Korea – Various Measures on Beef (2001)*, para. 162. Emphasis added.

130 Panel Report, *Colombia – Ports of Entry (2010)*, paras. 7.551–7.566.

reflects social interests that can be characterized as vital and important in the highest degree'.[131]

With regard to the 'contribution' of the measure to securing compliance with the law or regulation concerned, the panel in *Colombia – Textiles (2016)* noted that – as the Appellate Body ruled in *Brazil – Retreaded Tyres (2007)* with regard to Article XX(b) of the GATT 1994 – a measure contributes to the objective when there is a *genuine relationship* of ends and means between the objective pursued and the measure at issue.[132] Note that in the context of its analysis under Article XX(a), discussed below, the Appellate Body ruled in *Colombia – Textiles (2016)* that in assessing the contribution of the measure at issue to the objective it pursues:

> a panel's duty is to assess, in a qualitative or quantitative manner, the extent of the measure's contribution to the end pursued, rather than merely ascertaining whether or not the measure makes any contribution.[133]

As the Appellate Body explained, this is because, as it ruled previously, the greater the contribution of the measure at issue to the objective pursued, the more easily that measure might be considered to be 'necessary'.[134] The Appellate Body also recalled that:

> Since '[a] measure's contribution is ... only one component of the necessity calculus under Article XX', the assessment of whether a measure is 'necessary' cannot be determined by the degree of contribution alone, but will depend on the manner in which the other factors of the 'necessity' standard inform the analysis.[135]

Applying these considerations in the context of its analysis under Article XX(d) in *Colombia – Textiles (2016)*, the Appellate Body found that Colombia, the respondent, did not demonstrate with sufficient clarity the extent, i.e. the degree, of the contribution made by the compound tariff to secure compliance with Colombia's anti-money laundering legislation, and thus made it impossible to weigh and balance the contribution to the objective with the other factors in order to determine whether the measure at issue is 'necessary'.[136]

With regard to the 'trade-restrictiveness' of the measure at issue, the Appellate Body found in *Korea – Various Measures on Beef (2001)* that a measure with a relatively slight impact on imported products might more easily be considered as 'necessary' than a measure with an intense and broad trade-restrictive impact.[137]

131 Panel Report, *Colombia – Textiles (2016)*, para. 7.524.
132 See Panel Report, *Colombia – Textiles (2016)*, para. 7.492, referring to Appellate Body Report, *Brazil – Retreaded Tyres (2007)*, para. 145.
133 Appellate Body Report, *Colombia – Textiles (2016)*, para. 6.25. Note that the degree of a measure's contribution to its objective may be expressed in a qualitative or quantitative manner. See *ibid.*
134 See *ibid.*, discussed below, p. 585.
135 See *ibid.*, discussed below, p. 585.
136 See Appellate Body Report, *Colombia – Textiles (2016)*, paras. 6.94 and 6.97.
137 Appellate Body Report, *Korea – Various Measures on Beef (2001)*, para. 163. See also Panel Report, *Colombia – Textiles (2016)*, para. 7.494.

On the other hand, it would be difficult for a panel to find a measure with severe trade-restrictive effects to be 'necessary', unless – as the Appellate Body found in *Brazil – Retreaded Tyres (2007)* – that measure is apt to make a material contribution to the achievement of its objective.[138]

In the context of its analysis under Article XX(a), discussed below, the Appellate Body ruled in *Colombia – Textiles (2016)* that in assessing the trade-restrictiveness of the measure at issue:

> In assessing this factor, 'a panel must seek to assess the degree of a measure's trade restrictiveness, rather than merely ascertaining whether or not the measure involves some restriction on trade'.[139]

Similar to its finding on the contribution of the measure at issue to its objective, discussed above, the Appellate Body also found with regard to the trade-restrictiveness of the measure at issue that Colombia, the respondent, did not establish with sufficient clarity the degree of trade-restrictiveness of the measure, and thus made it impossible to weigh and balance this factor with the other factors in order to determine whether the measure at issue is necessary.[140]

Note that the panels in, for example, *Canada – Wheat Exports and Grain Imports (2004)*, *Colombia – Ports of Entry (2009)* and *Colombia – Textiles (2016)* have applied the 'necessity' requirement of Article XX(d) as interpreted and clarified by the Appellate Body in *Korea – Various Measures on Beef (2001)*.[141] Also note that the Appellate Body's ruling in this case on the 'necessity' element of Article XX(d) formed the basis of the Appellate Body's later rulings on the 'necessity' requirement of Article XIV(a) of the GATS (in *US – Gambling (2005)*), Article XX(b) of the GATT 1994 (in *Brazil – Retreaded Tyres (2007)*), Article XX(a) of the GATT 1994 (in *EC – Seal Products (2014)*) and Article XIV(c) of the GATS (in *Argentina – Financial Services (2016)*). However, this case law on the 'necessity' requirement did not cease to evolve.[142]

2.3.3 Article XX(g)

Article XX(g) concerns measures relating to the conservation of exhaustible natural resources. Like Article XX(b), it addresses measures that depart from core GATT rules for environmental protection purposes. Article XX(g) sets out a three-tier legal standard requiring that a measure: (1) relate to the 'conservation

138 See Appellate Body Report, *Brazil – Retreaded Tyres (2007)*, paras. 150–1. See also Panel Report, *Colombia – Textiles (2016)*, para. 7.494. Note that the Appellate Body in *EC – Seal Products (2014)* clarified that the Appellate Body in *Brazil – Retreaded Tyres (2007)* did not introduce a specific contribution threshold.

139 Appellate Body Report, *Colombia – Textiles (2016)*, para. 6.26, discussed below.

140 See *ibid.*, paras. 6.95 and 6.97.

141 See Panel Report, *Canada – Wheat Exports and Grain Imports (2004)*, paras. 6.222–6.248; Panel Report, *Colombia – Ports of Entry (2009)*, paras. 7.545–7.619; and Panel Report, *Colombia – Textiles (2016)*, para. 7.520–7.536.

142 With regard to Article XX(b) of the GATT 1994, see above, pp. 557–64. With regard to Article XX(a) of the GATT 1994 and Article XIV(a) and XIV(c) of the GATS, see below, pp. 578–89, 608–12 and 612–14.

of exhaustible natural resources'; (2) 'relate to' the conservation of exhaustible natural resources; and (3) be 'made effective in conjunction with' restrictions on domestic production or consumption.

With respect to the first element of the analysis under Article XX(g), namely, that the measure must relate to the 'conservation of exhaustible natural resources', the Appellate Body ruled in *China – Raw Materials (2012)* that the term 'conservation' means 'the preservation of the environment, especially of natural resources'.[143] Subsequently, the panel in *China – Rare Earths (2014)* recognised that, when interpreting the term 'conservation', the international law principles of sovereignty over natural resources and sustainable development should be taken into account.[144] Understood in the light of every State's permanent sovereignty over their own natural resources, the panel considered that the term 'conservation' in Article XX(g):

> does not simply mean placing a moratorium on the exploitation of natural resources, but includes also measures that regulate and control such exploitation in accordance with a Member's development and conservation objectives.[145]

Thus, the panel agreed with China that the term 'conservation' as used in Article XX(g) is not limited to mere 'preservation of natural resources'.[146] According to the panel, resource-endowed WTO Members are entitled under WTO law:

> to design conservation policies that meet their development needs, determine how much of a resource should be exploited today and how much should be preserved for the future, including for use by future generations, in a manner consistent with their sustainable development needs and their international obligations.[147]

As the panel emphasised, the right of WTO Members to adopt conservation programmes is, however, 'not a right to control the international markets in which extracted products are bought and sold'.[148] The right of WTO Members to adopt 'conservation programmes' does 'not permit the exercise of boundless discretion such that WTO Members may adopt GATT-inconsistent measures as they see fit'.[149] The panel in *China – Rare Earths (2014)* noted:

> In becoming a WTO Member, China has of course not forfeited permanent sovereignty over its natural resources, which it enjoys as a natural corollary of its statehood ... China has, however, agreed to exercise its rights in conformity with WTO rules, and to respect WTO provisions when developing and implementing policies to conserve exhaustible natural resources.[150]

143 Appellate Body Reports, *China – Raw Materials (2012)*, para. 355.

144 See Panel Reports, *China – Rare Earths (2014)*, paras. 7.262–7.263. The panel argued that these principles should be taken into account pursuant to Article 31.3(c) of the *Vienna Convention on the Law of Treaties*. Note that the panel in *China – Raw Materials (2012)* had held that the interpretation of Article XX(g) should 'take into account' the principle of sovereignty over natural resources. See Panel Reports, *China – Raw Materials (2012)*, para. 7.381.

145 Panel Reports, *China – Rare Earths (2014)*, para. 7.266.

146 See *ibid.* 147 *Ibid.*, para. 7.267.

148 *Ibid.*, para. 7.268. See also Appellate Body Report, *US – Softwood Lumber IV*.

149 Panel Reports, *China – Rare Earths (2014)*, para. 7.269.

150 *Ibid.*, para. 7.270. See also Panel Reports, *China – Raw Materials (2012)*, para. 7.382.

The meaning to be given to the term 'conservation' as used in Article XX(g) must strike an appropriate balance between trade liberalisation, sovereignty over natural resources and the right to sustainable development. To strike this balance, the panel in *China – Rare Earths (2014)*, as the panel in *China – Raw Materials (2012)*, gave 'a rather broad meaning' to the term 'conservation', broader than the Appellate Body did in *China – Raw Materials (2012)*.[151] The panel's interpretation of the term 'conservation' was not appealed but the Appellate Body nevertheless noted in *China – Rare Earths (2014)*:

> It seems to us that, for the purposes of Article XX(g), the precise contours of the word 'conservation' can only be fully understood in the context of the exhaustible natural resource at issue in a given dispute. For example, 'conservation' in the context of an exhaustible mineral resource may entail preservation through a reduction in the pace of its extraction, or by stopping its extraction altogether. In respect of the 'conservation' of a living natural resource, such as a species facing the threat of extinction, the word may encompass not only limiting or halting the activities creating the danger of extinction, but also facilitating the replenishment of that endangered species.[152]

With regard to the concept of 'exhaustible natural resources', the Appellate Body adopted in *US – Shrimp (1998)* a broad, 'evolutionary' interpretation. In this case, the complainants had taken the position that Article XX(g) was limited to the conservation of 'mineral' or 'non-living' natural resources. Their principal argument was rooted in the notion that 'living' natural resources are 'renewable' and therefore cannot be 'exhaustible' natural resources. The Appellate Body disagreed. It noted:

> We do not believe that 'exhaustible' natural resources and 'renewable' natural resources are mutually exclusive. One lesson that modern biological sciences teach us is that living species, though in principle, capable of reproduction and, in that sense, 'renewable', are in certain circumstances indeed susceptible of depletion, exhaustion and extinction, frequently because of human activities. Living resources are just as 'finite' as petroleum, iron ore and other non-living resources.[153]

The Appellate Body further noted with regard to the appropriate interpretation of the concept of 'exhaustible natural resources':

> The words of Article XX(g), 'exhaustible natural resources', were actually crafted more than 50 years ago. They must be read by a treaty interpreter in the light of contemporary concerns of the community of nations about the protection and conservation of the environment. While Article XX was not modified in the Uruguay Round, the preamble attached to the *WTO Agreement* shows that the signatories to that Agreement were, in 1994, fully aware of the importance and legitimacy of environmental protection as a goal of national and international policy. The preamble of the *WTO Agreement* – which informs not only the GATT 1994, but also the other covered agreements – explicitly acknowledges 'the objective of *sustainable development*'.

151 See Panel Reports, *China – Rare Earths (2014)*, para. 7.277. As discussed above, the Appellate Body ruled in *China – Raw Materials (2012)* that the term 'conservation' means 'the preservation of the environment, especially of natural resources'.

152 Appellate Body Reports, *China – Rare Earths (2014)*, para. 5.89.

153 Appellate Body Report, *US – Shrimp (1998)*, para. 128.

... From the perspective embodied in the preamble of the *WTO Agreement*, we note that the generic term of 'natural resources' in Article XX(g) is not 'static' in its content or reference but is rather 'by definition, evolutionary'. It is, therefore, pertinent to note that modern international conventions and declarations make frequent references to natural resources as embracing both living and non-living resources.[154]

The Appellate Body thus concluded on the scope of the concept of 'exhaustible natural resources' that 'measures to conserve exhaustible natural resources, whether *living* or *non-living*, may fall within Article XX(g)'.[155]

With respect to the second element of the analysis under Article XX(g), namely, that the measure must be a measure 'relating to' the conservation of exhaustible natural resources, the Appellate Body in *US – Shrimp (1998)*, Article XX(g) requires 'a close and real' relationship between the measure and the policy objective. The means employed, i.e. the measure, must be *reasonably* related to the end pursued, i.e. the conservation of an exhaustible natural resource. A measure may *not* be *disproportionately wide* in its scope or reach in relation to the policy objective pursued. In *China – Raw Materials (2012)*, the Appellate Body, referring to its report in *US – Shrimp (1998)* stated that:

[i]n order to fall within the ambit of [Article XX(g)], a measure must 'relat[e] to the conservation of exhaustible natural resources'. The term 'relat[e] to' is defined as 'hav[ing] some connection with, be[ing] connected to'. The Appellate Body has found that, for a measure to relate to conservation in the sense of Article XX(g), there must be 'a close and genuine relationship of ends and means'.[156]

In *China – Rare Earths (2014)*, the panel stated that the assessment of whether a measure 'relates to' conservation must focus on the design and structure of that measure and that the analysis under Article XX(g) does not require an evaluation of the actual effects of the concerned measure.[157] The Appellate Body found that the panel did not err in making these statements, but noted that a panel is 'not precluded from considering evidence relating to the actual operation or the impact of the measure at issue'.[158]

The third element of the analysis under Article XX(g), namely, that the measure at issue is 'made effective in conjunction with', has been interpreted and applied by the Appellate Body in *US – Gasoline (1996)* as follows:

[T]he clause 'if such measures are made effective in conjunction with restrictions on domestic product[ion] or consumption' is appropriately read as a requirement that the measures concerned impose restrictions, not just in respect of imported gasoline but also with respect to domestic gasoline. The clause is a requirement of *even-handedness* in the imposition of

154 *Ibid.*, paras. 129 and 130.

155 *Ibid.*, para. 131. Note that, in coming to this conclusion, the Appellate Body also referred to 'recent acknowledgement by the international community of the importance of concerted bilateral or multilateral action to protect living natural resources'. See *ibid.* The Appellate Body also noted that already the panels in *US – Canada Tuna (1982)*, at para. 4.9, and *Canada – Herring and Salmon (1988)*, at para. 4.4, had found fish to be an 'exhaustible' natural resource. See *ibid.*

156 Appellate Body Reports, *China – Raw Materials (2012)*, para. 355.

157 See Panel Reports, *China – Rare Earths (2014)*, paras. 7.290 and 7.379.

158 See Appellate Body Reports, *China – Rare Earths*, para. 5.114.

restrictions, in the name of conservation, upon the production or consumption of exhaustible natural resources.[159]

Basically, the third element of the Article XX(g) analysis is a requirement of 'even-handedness' in the imposition of restrictions on imported and domestic products. Article XX(g) does *not* require imported and domestic products to be treated identically; it merely requires that they are treated in an 'even-handed' manner. The Appellate Body in *US – Gasoline (1996)* stated in this respect:

There is, of course, no textual basis for requiring identical treatment of domestic and imported products. Indeed, where there is identity of treatment – constituting real, not merely formal, equality of treatment – it is difficult to see how inconsistency with Article III:4 would have arisen in the first place.[160]

Applying the 'even-handedness' requirement to the baseline establishment rules, the measure at issue in *US – Gasoline (1996)*, the Appellate Body found that 'restrictions on the consumption or depletion of clean air by regulating the domestic production of 'dirty' gasoline' were established 'jointly with corresponding restrictions with respect to imported gasoline'.[161] The baseline establishment rules at issue in *US – Gasoline (1996)* thus met the 'made effective in conjunction with' requirement.

In *US – Shrimp (1998)*, the Appellate Body confirmed its approach to the third element of the Article XX(g) analysis. It found in that case that the record reflected that the United States had – through earlier regulations[162] – taken measures applicable to US shrimp trawl vessels to prevent the incidental killing of sea turtles. Because of these regulations imposing 'restrictions on domestic production', the import ban at issue in this case met the 'even-handedness' requirement of the third element of the Article XX(g) analysis.[163]

In *China – Rare Earths (2014)*, China argued on appeal that the panel had considered the requirement of 'even-handedness' to be a separate requirement that must be fulfilled in addition to the conditions expressly set out in Article XX(g). The Appellate Body stated that:

[t]he term 'even-handedness' was used in *US – Gasoline* as a synonym or shorthand reference for the requirement in Article XX(g) that restrictions be imposed not only on international trade but also on domestic consumption or production. As we see it, 'even-handedness' is not a separate requirement to be fulfilled in addition to the conditions expressly set out in subparagraph (g). Rather, and in keeping with the Appellate Body report in *US – Gasoline*, the terms of Article XX(g) themselves embody a requirement of even-handedness in the imposition of restrictions.[164]

As the panel's position on the requirement of 'even-handedness' was not clear, the Appellate Body concluded that the panel erred *to the extent* that it found that

159 Appellate Body Report, *US – Gasoline (1996)*, 20–1.
160 *Ibid.*, 21. 161 *Ibid.*
162 i.e. regulations pursuant to the US *Endangered Species Act*, issued in 1987 and fully effective in 1990.
163 See Appellate Body Report, *US – Shrimp (1998)*, para. 144.
164 Appellate Body Reports, *China – Rare Earths (2014)*, para. 5.124.

'even-handedness' is a separate requirement that must be fulfilled in addition to the condition that a measure be 'made effective in conjunction with restrictions on domestic production or consumption'.[165]

The Appellate Body also considered in *China – Rare Earths (2014)* that the phrase 'made effective in conjunction with' requires that, when international trade is restricted, effective restrictions are also imposed on domestic production or consumption.[166] Referring to its reports in *US – Gasoline (1996)* and *US – Shrimp (1998)*, discussed above, the Appellate Body noted in *China – Rare Earths (2014)* that its prior case law did not suggest that Article XX(g) contains a requirement that the burden of conservation be *evenly distributed* between foreign consumers, on the one hand, and domestic producers or consumers, on the other hand.[167] According to the Appellate Body, the panel erred *to the extent* that it found that the burden of conservation must be evenly distributed.[168] The Appellate Body also noted, however, that:

> it would be difficult to conceive of a measure that would impose a significantly more onerous burden on foreign consumers or producers and that could still be shown to satisfy all of the requirements of Article XX(g).[169]

2.3.4 Article XX(a)

While Articles XX(b), (d) and (g) have frequently been invoked by respondents in GATT and WTO dispute settlement to justify otherwise GATT-inconsistent measures, Article XX(a), which concerns measures necessary for the protection of public morals, was virtually dormant until recently.[170] The panel in *China – Publications and Audiovisual Products (2010)* was the first panel to interpret and apply Article XX(a). The measures at issue in that case concerned restrictions on trading and distribution of publications and audiovisual products in China. These measures provided for a content–review mechanism and a system for the selection of importation entities which played an essential role in the content review of imported publications and audiovisual products. Only 'approved' importation entities were authorised to import publications and audiovisual products. China invoked Article XX(a) to justify certain of these otherwise GATT-inconsistent restrictions on trading and distribution of publications and audiovisual products. According to China, these restrictions could be justified under Article XX(a) because 'the system of selecting importation entities undertaking content review is, as a whole, necessary to protect public

165 *Ibid.*, para. 5.127.
166 See Appellate Body Reports, *China – Rare Earths (2014)*, paras. 5.132 and 5.136.
167 *Ibid.*, paras. 5.133–5.134 and 5.136.
168 See *ibid.*, para. 5.136. 169 *Ibid.*, para. 5.134.
170 Article XX(a) was referred to in *US – Tuna (Mexico) (1991)* and *US – Malt Beverages (1992)*, but in neither case did the panel examine the relevance of this provision. In *US – Tuna (Mexico) (1991)*, Australia, a third party in this case, suggested that the measure at issue could be justified, under Article XX(a) of the GATT 1947, as a measure against inhumane treatment of animals. See Panel Report, *US – Tuna (Mexico) (1991)*, para. 4.4.

morals'.[171] More recently, Article XX(a) was invoked by the European Union in *EC – Seal Products (2014)* and by Colombia in *Colombia – Textiles (2016)*. In *EC – Seal Products (2014)*, the European Union invoked Article XX(a) to justify the measures at issue, collectively referred to as the 'EU Seal Regime', which were found to be inconsistent with Articles I:1 and III:4 of the GATT 1994. The EU Seal Regime prohibited the importation and placing on the EU market of seal products except where they were: (1) derived from hunts conducted by Inuit or other indigenous communities (IC exception); (2) derived from hunts conducted for marine resource management purposes (MRM exception); or (3) imported for the personal use of travellers. The European Union contended that the EU Seal Regime was adopted to address EU public moral concerns regarding animal welfare and in particular the welfare of seals. The European Union sought to justify the EU Seal Regime under Article XX(a) on the grounds that it was 'necessary to protect public morals'. In *Colombia – Textiles (2016)*, Colombia invoked Article XX(a) to justify the compound tariff applied on imports of textiles, apparel and footwear, which had been found inconsistent with Articles II:1(a) and II:1(b), first sentence of the GATT 1994. Colombia contended that the compound tariff was an important instrument in the fight against money laundering linked with drug trafficking and other criminal activities and with Colombia's internal armed conflict. Colombia thus sought to justify the otherwise GATT-inconsistent compound tariff as necessary to protect public morals in Colombia.

In *Colombia – Textiles (2016)*, the Appellate Body ruled:

> In order to establish whether a measure is justified under Article XX(a), the analysis proceeds in two steps. First, the measure must be 'designed' to protect public morals. Second, the measure must be 'necessary' to protect such public morals.[172]

With regard to the first step, or element, of the Article XX(a) analysis, i.e. the examination of the 'design' of the measure at issue, the Appellate Body held in *Colombia – Textiles (2016)*:

> the phrase 'to protect public morals' calls for an initial, threshold examination in order to determine whether there is a relationship between an otherwise GATT-inconsistent measure and the protection of public morals. If this assessment reveals that the measure is incapable of protecting public morals, there is no relationship between the measure and the protection of public morals.[173]

If a measure is incapable of protecting public morals and is therefore not 'designed' to protect public morals, there is no need for a panel to engage in the second step, or element, of the Article XX(a) analysis, namely an examination

171 Panel Report, *China – Publications and Audiovisual Products (2010)*, para. 7.727.

172 Appellate Body Report, *Colombia – Textiles (2016)*, para. 6.20. Note that in *EC – Seal Products (2014)*, the Appellate Body stated that for a GATT-inconsistent measure to be provisionally justified under Article XX(a), the measure must be: (1) 'adopted or enforced' to protect public morals; and (2) 'necessary' to protect such public morals. See Appellate Body Reports, *EC – Seal Products (2014)*, para. 5.169.

173 Appellate Body Report, *Colombia – Textiles (2016)*, para. 6.21.

of whether the measure at issue is 'necessary' to protect public morals.[174] This is because there is no justification under Article XX(a) for a measure that is not 'designed' to protect public morals.[175] However, as the Appellate Body also noted in *Colombia – Textiles (2016)*:

> if the measure is not incapable of protecting public morals, this indicates the existence of a relationship between the measure and the protection of public morals. In this situation, further examination of whether the measure is 'necessary' is required under Article XX(a).[176]

It is clear that the examination of the 'design' of the measure is not a particularly demanding element of the Article XX(a) analysis.[177] A measure is considered to be 'designed' to protect public morals if it is *not incapable* of protecting public morals, such that there is *a* relationship between the measure and the objective of protecting public morals. By contrast and as discussed below, the examination of the 'necessity' of the measure at issue, i.e. the second element of the Article XX(a) analysis, 'entails a more in-depth, holistic analysis of the relationship between the inconsistent measure and the protection of public morals'.[178] As the Appellate Body noted in *Colombia – Textiles (2016)*:

> a panel must ... not structure its analysis of the [design element] in such a way as to lead it to truncate its analysis prematurely and thereby foreclose consideration of crucial aspects of the respondent's defence relating to the 'necessity' analysis.[179]

The panel in *Colombia – Textiles (2016)* had found that there was no relationship between the compound tariff, the measure at issue, and combating money laundering, one of the policies designed to protect public morals in Colombia. Therefore, the panel concluded that the measure at issue was not 'designed' to combat money laundering and therefore not 'designed' to protect public morals. The Appellate Body reversed this finding. On the basis of the panel's own findings, the Appellate Body considered that the compound tariff was *not incapable* of combating money laundering, such that there is a relationship between the measure at issue and the protection of public morals. The Appellate Body therefore concluded that the measure at issue is 'designed' to protect public morals. As the measure is 'designed' to protect public morals, the panel should not have

174 See *ibid.*

175 See *ibid.*, referring to Appellate Body Reports, *Argentina – Financial Services (2016)*, para. 6.203; and *Mexico – Taxes on Soft Drinks (2006)*, para. 72.

176 Appellate Body Report, *Colombia – Textiles (2016)*, paras. 6.21 and 6.30.

177 See *ibid.*, para. 6.23.

178 See *ibid.* As discussed below, the examination of the 'necessity' of the measure at issue involves a process of 'weighing and balancing' a series of factors, including the importance of the interests or values at stake, the contribution of the measure to the objective pursued, and the trade-restrictiveness of the measure. Moreover, in most cases, a comparison between the challenged measure and possible alternatives should subsequently be undertaken See below, p. 584.

179 See *ibid.*, para. 6.30, referring to Appellate Body Report, *Argentina – Financial Services*, para. 6.203. If a panel finds that the measure at issue makes some degree of contribution to the objective pursued, but ceases to analyse the other factors, namely the importance of the interests or values that are reflected in the objective of the measure at issue and the degree of trade-restrictiveness of the measure at issue, it would foreclose an assessment of whether the degree of the contribution, when weighed and balanced against the degree of trade-restrictiveness and the importance of the interests pursued, is sufficient to justify the measure under Article XX(a). See *ibid.*, para. 6.43.

ceased its Article XX(a) analysis at the 'design' element, but should have proceeded to the 'necessity' element of the analysis, so as not to foreclose crucial aspects of the respondent's defence relating to the 'necessity' of the measure at issue.[180]

With respect to the term 'public morals', the panels in *China – Publications and Audiovisual Products (2010), EC – Seal Products (2014)* and *Colombia – Textiles (2016)* all adopted the interpretation given to the term 'public morals' in the context of Article XIV(a) of the GATS by the panel in *US – Gambling (2005)*.[181] As discussed below, the panel in *US – Gambling (2005)* found, in brief, that: (1) the term 'public morals' denotes standards of right and wrong conduct maintained by or on behalf of a community or nation; (2) the content of the concept of 'public morals' can vary from Member to Member, depending upon a range of factors, including prevailing social, cultural, ethical and religious values; and (3) Members should be given some scope to define and apply for themselves the concept of 'public morals' in their respective territories, according to their own systems and scales of values.[182] In line with this deferential interpretation of the concept of 'public morals', the panel in *China – Publications and Audiovisual Products (2010)* proceeded with its analysis on the *assumption* that:

> each of the prohibited types of content listed in China's measures is such that, if it were brought into China as part of a physical product, it could have a negative impact on 'public morals' in China within the meaning of Article XX(a) of the GATT 1994.[183]

In *EC – Seal Products (2014)*, the panel found that EU public concerns regarding animal welfare, and in particular the welfare of seals, fell within the scope of the concept of 'public morals' under Article XX(a) of the GATT 1994.[184] In *Colombia – Textiles (2016)*, the panel found that Colombia had presented sufficient evidence to demonstrate the existence of a real and present concern in Colombia with regard to money laundering, as well as with regard to the way in which money laundering is linked with drug trafficking and other criminal activities and with Colombia's internal armed conflict. The panel therefore concluded that 'combating money laundering is one of the policies designed to protect public morals in Colombia'.[185]

To determine whether the policy objective pursued by the measure at issue is the protection of public morals, a panel has in the very first place to identify the policy objective of the measure. This is not always a straightforward exercise. A panel

180 See Appellate Body Report, *Colombia – Textiles (2016)*, paras. 6.42–6.45 and 6.51.
181 See Panel Report, *China – Publications and Audiovisual Products (2010)*, para. 7.759; Panel Report, *EC – Seal Products (2014)*, para. 7.380; and Panel Report, *Colombia – Textiles (2016)*, para. 7.334. The panel's interpretation of 'public morals' in *US – Gambling (2005)* was left undisturbed by the Appellate Body.
182 See below, pp. 578–89. See also e.g. Panel Report, *Colombia – Textiles (2016)*, para. 7.299.
183 Panel Report, *China – Publications and Audiovisual Products (2010)*, para. 7.763. Note that this finding by the panel was not appealed and that it was therefore not addressed by the Appellate Body.
184 See Panel Reports, *EC – Seal Products (2014)*, para. 7.410.
185 See Panel Report, *Colombia – Textiles (2016)*, paras. 7.338 and 7.339.

may well be confronted with conflicting arguments by the parties as to what is (or are) the objective(s) pursued by the measure at issue. In *EC – Seal Products (2014)*, Norway argued on appeal that the panel had erred in finding that the 'sole' objective of the EU Seal Regime was to address EU public moral concerns regarding seal welfare. According to Norway, the protection of the interests of Inuit communities (IC interests) and the promotion of the interests of marine resources management (MRM interests) were also policy objectives pursued by the EU Seal Regime. The European Union argued that the panel correctly found that the 'principal' or 'main' objective of the EU Seal Regime was to address EU public moral concerns with regard to the welfare of seals. The Appellate Body held that:

> A panel should take into account the Member's articulation of the objective or the objectives it pursues through its measure, but it is not bound by that Member's characterizations of such objective(s). Indeed, the panel must take account of all evidence put before it in this regard, including 'the texts of statutes, legislative history, and other evidence regarding the structure and operation' of the measure at issue.[186]

After a careful examination of the panel report, the Appellate Body disagreed with Norway that the panel had found that the 'sole' objective of the EU Seal Regime was to address EU public moral concerns regarding seal welfare. According to the Appellate Body the panel had found that the 'principal' objective of the EU Seal Regime was to address public concerns on seal welfare and that IC and other interests had been 'accommodated' in the EU Seal Regime so as to mitigate the impact of the Regime on those interests.[187]

In *Colombia – Textiles (2016)*, the Appellate Body held that in order to determine whether *a* relationship between the measure at issue and the objective of protecting public morals exists, or, in other words, whether the measure at issue is 'designed' to protect public morals:

> a panel must examine evidence regarding the design of the measure at issue, including its content, structure, and expected operation.[188]

The Appellate Body observed that the measure at issue may expressly mention an objective falling within the scope of 'public morals' in that society. However, such express reference may not, in and of itself, be sufficient to establish that the measure is 'designed' to protect public morals.[189] Conversely, the Appellate Body also observed:

> a measure that does not expressly refer to a 'public moral' may nevertheless be found to have such a relationship with public morals following an assessment of the design of the measure at issue, including its content, structure, and expected operation.[190]

186 Appellate Body Report, *EC – Seal Products (2014)*, para. 5.144, referring to Appellate Body Report, *US – Tuna II (Mexico) (2012)*, para. 314 and Appellate Body Report, *US – Gambling (2005)*, para. 304.
187 See Appellate Body Reports, *EC – Seal Products (2014)*, paras. 5.145–5.146.
188 Appellate Body Report, *Colombia – Textiles (2016)*, para. 6.22, referring to Appellate Body Report, *US – Shrimp (1998)*, paras. 135–42; Appellate Body Reports, *EC – Seal Products (2014)*, para. 5.144.
189 See Appellate Body Report, *Colombia – Textiles (2016)*, para. 6.22. 190 *Ibid.*

In *EC – Seal Products (2014)*, Canada, one of the complainants, claimed on appeal that the panel had erred in finding that the EU Seal Regime was 'designed *to protect* public morals' within the meaning of Article XX(a).[191] According to Canada, the phrase 'to protect' requires the identification of a risk to public morals against which the EU Seal Regime seeks to protect. Canada based its argument on the statement of the panel in *EC – Asbestos (2001)* that 'the notion of "protection" ... impl[ies] the existence of a health risk'.[192] The Appellate Body, however, observed that this statement was made in the context of Article XX(b) which focuses on the protection of human, animal or plant life or health and that the protection of human, animal, or plant life or health may well 'imply a particular focus on the protection from or against certain dangers or risks'.[193] According to the Appellate Body, the notion of risk in the context of Article XX(b) is, however, 'difficult to reconcile with the subject-matter of protection under Article XX(a), namely, public morals'.[194] Contrary to Canada, the Appellate Body therefore did *not* consider that:

> the term 'to protect', when used in relation to 'public morals' under Article XX(a), required the Panel ... to identify the existence of a risk to EU public moral concerns regarding seal welfare.[195]

In the same vein, the Appellate Body also had 'difficulty' accepting Canada's argument that 'a panel is required to *identify the exact content* of the public morals standard at issue'.[196] The Appellate Body recalled that, as the panel in *US – Gambling (2005)* had stated, that the content of public morals can be characterised by a degree of variation, and, for this reason, Members should be given some scope to define and apply for themselves the concept of public morals according to their own systems and scales of values.[197]

Finally, note that the Appellate Body, in *EC – Seal Products (2014)*, ruled that a Member has the right to determine the level of protection of public morals that it considers appropriate; and that Members may thus set different levels of protection even when responding to similar interests of moral concern.[198] The fact that the European Union sets different levels of protection with regard to animal welfare risks in seal hunts than with regard to animal welfare risks in EU slaughterhouses or terrestrial wildlife hunts is therefore irrelevant to whether the EU Seal Regime is a measure 'designed to protect public morals' within the meaning of Article XX(a).

191 Note that Canada did not directly challenge the panel's finding that there are public moral concerns in relation to animal welfare in the European Union.
192 Panel Report, *EC – Asbestos (2001)*, para. 8.170.
193 Appellate Body Reports, *EC – Seal Products (2014)*, para. 5.197.
194 See *ibid.*, para. 5.198. 195 *Ibid.*
196 *Ibid.*, para. 5.199. 197 See *ibid.*, referring to Panel Report, *US – Gambling (2005)*, para. 6.465.
198 See Appellate Body Reports, *EC – Seal Products (2014)*, para. 5.200. The Appellate Body referred to Panel Report, *US – Gambling (2005)*, para. 6.461, which itself referred to Appellate Body Report, *Korea – Various Measures on Beef (2001)*, para. 176; and Appellate Body Report, *EC – Asbestos (2001)*, para. 168.

With regard to the second element of the Article XX(a) analysis, namely the 'necessity' requirement, the panel in *China – Publications and Audiovisual Products (2010)* first recalled that it is the measures at issue (i.e. the restrictions on trading and distribution), and not the policy objective pursued (i.e. the content review and the protection of 'public morals'), that must be 'necessary'.[199] Subsequently, the panel engaged in the examination of the 'necessity' of the measures at issue. Very much in line with the case law on the 'necessity' requirement of Article XX(b) and (d) of the GATT 1994, the panel: (1) identified the importance of the interests or values at stake;[200] (2) identified, for each of the measures at issue, the contribution made to the achievement of the protection of 'public morals'; and (3) identified the restrictive impact on international trade of each of the measures at issue.[201] The panel then 'weighed and balanced' these three factors, and came to the conclusion with regard to some of the measures at issue that they were *not* necessary to protect public morals,[202] while with regard to other measures it concluded that – absent reasonably available, less trade-restrictive alternative measures – these measures could be characterised as 'necessary'.[203] For the latter measures, the panel subsequently analysed the alternative measures proposed by the United States and came to the conclusion that, because at least one less trade-restrictive alternative measure was available, the measures at issue were *not* 'necessary' to protect public morals.[204] On appeal, the Appellate Body upheld most of the panel's intermediate findings and upheld the panel's conclusion that the measures at issue were *not* 'necessary' to protect public morals.[205] The Appellate Body observed:

> The less restrictive the effects of the measure, the more likely it is to be characterized as 'necessary'. Consequently, if a Member chooses to adopt a very restrictive measure, it will have to ensure that the measure is carefully designed so that the other elements to be taken into account in weighing and balancing the factors relevant to an assessment of the 'necessity' of the measure will 'outweigh' such restrictive effect.[206]

Referring to and in line with its prior case law on the 'necessity' requirement, the Appellate Body held in *EC – Seal Products (2014)*:

> As the Appellate Body has explained, a necessity analysis involves a process of 'weighing and balancing' a series of factors, including the importance of the objective, the contribution of the measure to that objective, and the trade-restrictiveness of the measure. The

199 See Panel Report, *China – Publications and Audiovisual Products (2010)*, para. 7.789. The panel referred in this respect to the Appellate Body Report, *US – Gasoline (1996)*, 20.

200 The panel considered that the protection of 'public morals' ranks among the most important values or interests pursued by Members (see Panel Report, *China – Publications and Audiovisual Products (2010)*, para. 7.817), and that China has adopted a high level of protection of 'public morals' within its territory (see *ibid.*, para. 7.828).

201 The panel considered both the restrictive effect on imports and the restrictive effect on those wishing to engage in importing. See *ibid.*, para. 7.788.

202 See e.g. *ibid.*, paras. 7.848 and 7.868.

203 See e.g. *ibid.*, paras. 7.828 and 7.836.

204 See *ibid.*, para. 7.909. This alternative measure proposed by the United States was a measure under which the Chinese government would be given the sole responsibility for the conduct of the content review.

205 See Appellate Body Report, *China – Publications and Audiovisual Products (2010)*, paras. 336–7.

206 *Ibid.*, para. 310.

Appellate Body has further explained that, in most cases, a comparison between the challenged measure and possible alternatives should then be undertaken.[207]

The Appellate Body also noted in this regard that

> the very utility of examining the interaction between the various factors of the necessity analysis, and conducting a comparison with potential alternative measures, is that it provides a means of testing these factors as part of a holistic weighing and balancing exercise.[208]

In *Colombia – Textiles (2016)*, the Appellate Body furthermore, considered that:

> each of (the factors of the necessity analysis) must be demonstrated *with sufficient clarity* in order to conduct a proper weighing and balancing exercise that may yield a conclusion that the measure is 'necessary'.[209]

With respect to the importance of the interests or values at stake, the Appellate Body noted in *Colombia – Textiles (2016)*, referring to its Report in *Korea – Various Measures on Beef (2001)* discussed above:

> The more vital or important the interests or values that are reflected in the objective of the measure, the easier it would be to accept a measure as 'necessary'.[210]

The panel in *EC – Seal Products (2014)* considered the protection of public moral concerns regarding animal welfare to be 'an important value or interest'.[211] The panel in *Colombia – Textiles (2016)* found the objective of combating money laundering 'reflects social interests that can be described as vital and important in the highest degree'.[212] In neither case did the complainants dispute the importance of the social interests or values at stake.

With respect to the contribution of the measure to the objective it pursues, the panel in *EC – Seal Products (2014)* stated that the contribution made by the EU Seal Regime to its objective 'must be shown to be at least *material* given the extent of its trade-restrictiveness'.[213] The Appellate Body noted that in making this statement the panel relied on the Appellate Body's related ruling in *Brazil – Retreaded Tyres (2007)*. However, as already discussed above,[214] the Appellate Body clarified that in *Brazil – Retreaded Tyres (2007)* it did:

> *not* set out a generally applicable standard requiring the use of a pre-determined threshold of 'material' contribution in analysing the necessity of a measure under Article XX of the GATT 1994.[215]

207 Appellate Body Reports, *EC – Seal Products (2014)*, paras. 5.169 and 5.214, referring to Appellate Body Reports, *Korea – Various Measures on Beef (2001)*, paras. 164 and 166 (concerning the 'necessity' requirement under Article XX(d) of the GATT 1994); *US – Gambling (2005)*, paras. 306–7 (concerning the 'necessity' requirement in Article XIV(a) of the GATS); *Brazil – Retreaded Tyres (2007)*, para. 182 (concerning the 'necessity' requirement under Article XX(b) of the GATT 1994); and Appellate Body Report, *US – Tuna II (Mexico) (2012)*, para. 322 and fn. 647 to para. 322 (concerning the 'necessity' requirement under Article 22 of the *TBT Agreement*). See also Appellate Body Report, *Colombia – Textiles (2016)*, para. 6.23.

208 Appellate Body Reports, *EC – Seal Products*, para. 5.215. See also Appellate Body Report, *Colombia – Textiles (2016)*, para. 6.28. On the 'weighing and balancing' exercise as a holistic operation, see the Appellate Body in *Brazil – Retreaded Tyres (2007)*, para. 182, discussed above, pp. 557–64.

209 Appellate Body Report, *Colombia – Textiles (2016)*, para. 6.53. Emphasis added.

210 *Ibid.*, para. 6.24, referring to Appellate Body Report, *Korea – Various Measures on Beef (2001)*, para. 162.

211 See Panel Reports, *EC – Seal Products (2014)*, para. 7.632.

212 See Panel Report, *Colombia – Textiles (2016)*, para. 7.408.

213 Panel Reports, *EC – Seal Products (2014)*, para. 7.636.

214 See above, pp. 562–4.

215 Appellate Body Reports, *EC – Seal Products (2014)*, para. 5.213. Emphasis added.

According to the Appellate Body, the panel in *EC – Seal Products (2014)* erred *to the extent* that it applied a standard of 'materiality' as a generally applicable predetermined threshold in its contribution analysis.[216]

The panel in *EC – Seal Products (2014)* also found that the EU Seal Regime 'contributed *to a certain extent* to its objective of addressing the EU public moral concerns on seal welfare'.[217] On appeal Canada and Norway argued that the panel failed to make 'clear and precise' findings regarding the 'actual' contribution of the EU Seal Regime to the identified objective, and that 'such findings were required in order to establish the benchmark against which alternative measures could be compared'.[218] However, as already discussed above, the Appellate Body held in *Brazil – Retreaded Tyres (2007)* that a panel enjoys certain latitude in choosing its approach to analyse the contribution made; that such an analysis may be performed in qualitative or quantitative terms; and that it ultimately depends upon 'the nature of the risk, the objective pursued, and the level of protection sought' as well as on 'the nature, quantity, and quality of evidence existing at the time the analysis is made'.[219] In *EC – Seal Products (2014)*, the panel had opted for a qualitative 'contribution' analysis, which focused mainly on the design and expected operation of the EU Seal Regime.[220] Such 'contribution' analysis may by its nature not lead to 'clear and precise' findings regarding the 'actual' contribution of the EU Seal Regime to the objective of addressing the EU public moral concerns on seal welfare. The Appellate Body considered, however, that in the circumstances of this case and the information available to the panel such 'contribution' analysis was not improper.[221]

In *Colombia – Textiles (2016)*, the Appellate Body ruled that in assessing the contribution of the measure at issue to the objective it pursues:

> a panel's duty is to assess, in a qualitative or quantitative manner, the extent of the measure's contribution to the end pursued, rather than merely ascertaining whether or not the measure makes any contribution.[222]

As the Appellate Body explained, this is because, as it ruled previously, the greater the contribution of the measure at issue to the objective pursued, the more easily that measure might be considered to be 'necessary'.[223] The Appellate Body also recalled that:

> Since '[a] measure's contribution is ... only one component of the necessity calculus under Article XX', the assessment of whether a measure is 'necessary' cannot be determined by

216 See *ibid.*, para. 5.216. For more details, see above, pp. 562–4.
217 Panel Reports, *EC – Seal Products (2014)*, para. 7.638. Emphasis added.
218 Appellate Body Reports, *EC – Seal Products (2014)*, para. 5.219.
219 See Appellate Body Report, *Brazil – Retreaded Tyres (2007)*, paras. 145–6. See above, pp. 562–4.
220 See Appellate Body Reports, *EC – Seal Products (2014)*, para. 5.221.
221 See *ibid.*, paras. 5.222 and 5.224. See also the statement in para, 5.228 that 'it is not clear what greater clarity or precision the Panel could have achieved in the circumstances of this case'.
222 Appellate Body Report, *Colombia – Textiles (2016)*, para. 6.25, referring to Appellate Body Report, *Argentina – Financial Services (2016)*, para. 6.234, regarding Article XIV(c) of the GATS, discussed below, pp. 612–14.
223 *Ibid.*, referring to Appellate Body Report, *Korea – Various Measures on Beef (2001)*, para. 163, regarding Article XX(d) of the GATT 1994, discussed above, pp. 564–7.

the degree of contribution alone, but will depend on the manner in which the other factors of the 'necessity' standard inform the analysis.[224]

In *Colombia – Textiles (2016)*, the Appellate Body found that Colombia, the respondent, did not demonstrate with sufficient clarity the extent, i.e. the degree, of the contribution made by the compound tariff to the objective of combating money laundering, and thus made it impossible to weigh and balance the contribution to the objective with the other factors in order to determine whether the measure at issue is 'necessary'.[225]

With respect to the trade-restrictiveness of the measure at issue, the Appellate Body held in *Colombia – Textiles (2016)* that:

> In assessing this factor, 'a panel must seek to assess the degree of a measure's trade restrictiveness, rather than merely ascertaining whether or not the measure involves some restriction on trade'.[226]

Similar to its finding on the contribution of the measure at issue to its objective, discussed above, the Appellate Body also found with regard to the trade-restrictiveness of the measure at issue that Colombia, the respondent, did not establish with sufficient clarity the degree of trade-restrictiveness of the measure, and thus made it impossible to weigh and balance this factor with the other factors in order to determine whether the measure at issue is necessary.[227]

With respect to the existence of alternative measures that are less trade-restrictive than the measure at issue, the Appellate Body first recalled in *EC – Seal Products (2014)* its prior case law on 'alternative measures' under Article XX,[228] but then held that after the weighing and balancing exercise:

> *in most cases*, a comparison between the challenged measure and possible alternatives should then be undertaken.[229]

Referring to its report in *US – Tuna II (Mexico) (2012)* (concerning the 'necessity' requirement under Article 2.2 of the *TBT Agreement*), the Appellate Body suggested – as discussed above[230] – that a comparison with alternative measures would not be required *only* when, for instance, the measure at issue is not trade-restrictive or achieves the objective pursued.[231] Also note that in *EC – Seal*

224 See Appellate Body Report, *Colombia – Textiles (2016)*, para. 6.25, referring to Appellate Body Reports, *EC – Seal Products (2014)*, para. 5.213. The Appellate Body also recalled that in *EC – Seal Products (2014)* it had ruled that there is no 'generally applicable standard requiring the use of a predetermined threshold of contribution in analysing the necessity of a measure under Article XX of the GATT 1994'. See *ibid.*

225 See Appellate Body Report, *Colombia – Textiles (2016)*, paras. 6.61 and 6.67.

226 See *ibid.*, para. 6.26, referring to Appellate Body Report, *Argentina – Financial Services (2016)*, para. 6.234, regarding Article XIV(c) of the GATS, discussed below, pp. 612–14. As with the assessment of a measure's contribution to its objective, the examination of a measure's trade-restrictiveness may be done in a qualitative or quantitative manner. See *ibid.*

227 See Appellate Body Report, *Colombia – Textiles (2016)*, paras. 6.64 and 6.67.

228 See Appellate Body Reports, *EC – Seal Products (2014)*, paras. 5.214 and 5.261.

229 *Ibid.*, paras. 5.169 and 5.214. See also Appellate Body Report, *Colombia – Textiles (2016)*, para. 6.27.

230 See above, p. 564.

231 See Appellate Body Reports, *EC – Seal Products (2014)*, paras. 5.169 and 5.214, referring to Appellate Body Report, *US – Tuna II (Mexico) (2012)*, para. 322 and fn. 647 to para. 322.

Products (2014) the Appellate Body disagreed with the assertion that 'a preliminary determination of necessity is *required* before proceeding to compare the challenged measure with possible alternatives'.[232]

In *EC – Seal Products (2014)*, the complainants, Canada and Norway, proposed as an alternative measure for the EU Seal Regime market access for seal products that would be conditioned on compliance with animal welfare standards, and certification and labelling requirements. The panel concluded this alternative measure was not reasonably available.[233] On appeal, the Appellate Body upheld this conclusion. The Appellate Body considered that the panel had established that the alternative measures proposed by Canada and Norway would not allow the European Union to achieve its desired level of protection of the public moral concerns regarding seal welfare.[234] The panel was thus correct to conclude that the alternative measure was not reasonably available. Note that in this context of its review of the panel's assessment of the alternative measure proposed by Canada and Norway, the Appellate Body observed:

> As we see it, if there are reasons why the prospect of imposing an alternative measure faces significant, even prohibitive, obstacles, it may be that such a measure cannot be considered 'reasonably available'. We would not exclude *a priori* the possibility that an alternative measure may be deemed not reasonably available due to significant costs or difficulties faced by the affected industry.[235]

Thus, in assessing whether an alternative measure is reasonably available, the burden on the industry or industries concerned can potentially also be of relevance.[236]

In *Colombia – Textiles (2016)* the Appellate Body recalled that it had ruled in *US – Gambling (2005)* that an alternative measure may be found not to be 'reasonably available' where 'it is merely theoretical in nature, for instance, where the responding Member is not capable of taking it, or where the measure imposes an undue burden on that Member, such as prohibitive costs or substantial technical difficulties'.[237]

Finally, a comment regarding the relationship between the 'design' and 'necessity' elements of the analysis under Article XX(a). In *Colombia – Textiles (2016)*, the Appellate Body held that these two steps, or elements, are:

> conceptually distinct, yet related, aspects of the overall inquiry to be undertaken into whether a respondent has established that the measure at issue is 'necessary to protect

232 Appellate Body Reports, *EC – Seal Products (2014)*, fn. 1299 to para. 5.215 (emphasis added).
233 See Panel Reports, *EC – Seal Products (2014)*, para. 7.504.
234 See Appellate Body Reports, *EC – Seal Products (2014)*, para. 5.279. 235 *Ibid.*, para. 5.277.
236 See *ibid.*, referring to Appellate Body Report, *EC – Asbestos (2001)*, para. 174.
237 Appellate Body Report, *Colombia – Textiles (2016)*, para. 6.27, referring to Appellate Body Report, *US – Gambling*, para. 308, regarding Article XIV(a) of the GATS, discussed below, pp. 608–12. Note that, given the lack of sufficient clarity regarding the *degree* of the contribution of the measure to the objective and the *degree* of trade-restrictiveness of the measure, discussed above, the Appellate Body saw in *Colombia – Textiles (2016)* 'no basis to proceed with a comparison of the measure at issue with any possible alternative measures'. See Appellate Body Report, *Colombia – Textiles (2016)*, para. 6.66.

public morals'. As the assessment of these two steps is not entirely disjointed, there may, in fact, be some overlap in the sense that certain evidence and considerations may be relevant to both aspects of the defence under Article XX(a).[238]

While Article XX(a) has only been invoked three times in dispute settlement proceedings to date, it is frequently 'used' (explicitly or otherwise) by Members to impose import bans or restrictions on a wide array of products. Bangladesh, for example, invokes Article XX(a) to justify an import ban on horror comics, obscene and subversive literature and 'maps, charts and geographical globes which indicate the territory of Bangladesh but do not do so in accordance with the maps published by the Department of Survey, Government of the People's Republic of Bangladesh'.[239] From the Report of the Working Party on the Accession of Saudi Arabia, it appears that this Member, which acceded to the WTO in December 2005, invokes Article XX(a) of the GATT 1994 to ban the importation of the Holy Quran; alcoholic beverages and intoxicants of all kinds; all types of machines, equipment and tools for gambling or games of chance; live swine, meat, fat, hair, blood, guts, limbs and all other products of swine; dogs (other than hunting dogs, guard dogs or guide dogs for the blind); mummified animals; and all foodstuffs containing animal blood in their manufacturing.[240]

2.3.5 Article XX(j)

Article XX(j) of the GATT 1994 concerns, and allows for, measures 'essential to the acquisition or distribution of products in general or local short supply'.[241] This provision was invoked in dispute settlement for the first time in *India – Solar Cells (2016)*.[242] At issue in this case were Indian domestic content requirement (DCR) measures concerning solar cells and solar modules imposed on solar power producers selling electricity to government agencies. The panel found that these DCR measures were inconsistent with Article III:4 of the GATT 1994 and Article 2.1 of the *TRIMs Agreement*.[243] To justify this otherwise WTO-inconsistent measure, India invoked Article XX(j) of the GATT 1994.[244] India argued that the DCR measures were 'essential to the acquisition or distribution of products in short

238 Appellate Body Report, *Colombia – Textiles (2016)*, para. 6.29, referring to Appellate Body Report, *Argentina – Financial Services*, para. 6.205, regarding Article XIV(a) of the GATS, discussed below, pp. 608–12. In *Colombia – Textiles (2016)*, the Appellate Body noted that in the context of the 'design' step of the analysis, a panel is not precluded from taking into account evidence and considerations that may also be relevant to the assessment of the contribution of a measure in the context of the examination of 'necessity'. See *ibid.* and para. 6.33. See also Appellate Body Report, *India – Solar Cells (2016)*, para. 5.61, regarding Article XX(d) and Article XX(j) of the GATT 1994. See above, pp. 564–7 and below, pp. 589–92.

239 See Report by the Secretariat, *Trade Policy Review: Bangladesh*, WT/TPR/S/168, dated 9 August 2006, Appendix, Table AIII.3.

240 See Report of the Working Party on the Accession of the Kingdom of Saudi Arabia to the World Trade Organization, WT/ACC/SAU/61, dated 1 November 2005, Annex F, List of Banned Products.

241 Article XX(j) further states: '*Provided* that any such measures shall be consistent with the principle that all Members are entitled to an equitable share of the international supply of such products, and that any such measures, which are inconsistent with the other provisions of the Agreement shall be discontinued as soon as the conditions giving rise to them have ceased to exist.'

242 See Panel Report, *India – Solar Cells (2016)*, para. 7.202. 243 *Ibid.*, para. 7.73.

244 Note that India also invoked Article XX(d) of the GATT 1994. See above, pp. 564–7.

supply' within the meaning of Article XX(j). The objective of the DCR measures was, according to India, to ensure access of Indian solar power producers to a continuous and affordable supply of the solar cells and modules needed to generate solar power.

For an otherwise GATT-inconsistent measure to be provisionally justified under Article XX(j), a Member must establish that: (1) the measure is 'designed' to address the acquisition or distribution of products in general or local short supply; and (2) the measure is 'essential' to address the acquisition or distribution of such products.[245]

With regard to the concept of 'products in general or local short supply', the panel in *India – Solar Cells (2016)*, found that this concept refers to:

> a situation in which the quantity of available supply of a product, *from all sources*, does not meet demand in a relevant geographical area or market. They do not refer to products in respect of which there merely is a lack of domestic manufacturing capacity.[246]

As India had not argued that the quantity of solar cells and modules available *from all sources*, i.e. both international and domestic, is inadequate to meet the demand in India,[247] the panel concluded that solar cells and modules are not 'products in general or local short supply' in India, and that therefore the DCR measures cannot be justified under Article XX(j) of the GATT 1994.[248] India appealed the panel's interpretation and application of Article XX(j), and in particular the 'products in general or local short supply' requirement. India argued that the existence of a situation of 'short supply' within the meaning of Article XX(j) is to be determined exclusively by reference to whether there is 'sufficient' domestic manufacturing of a given product. The Appellate Body disagreed with India and upheld the panel's findings.[249] The Appellate Body ruled in *India – Solar Cells (2016)* that:

> Article XX(j) of the GATT 1994 reflects a balance of different considerations to be taken into account when assessing whether products are 'in general or local short supply'.[250]

In determining whether a product is in 'general or local short supply', a panel should examine:

> the extent to which a particular product is 'available' for purchase in a particular geographical area or market, and whether this is sufficient to meet demand in the relevant area or market. This analysis may, in appropriate cases, take into account not only the level of domestic production of a particular product and the nature of the products that are alleged to be 'in general or local short supply', but also such factors as the relevant product and geographical market, potential price fluctuations in the relevant market, the purchasing power of foreign and domestic consumers, and the role that foreign and domestic producers play in a particular market, including the extent to which domestic producers sell their production abroad.[251]

245 See Appellate Body Report, *India – Solar Cells (2016)*, para. 5.60.
246 Panel Report, *India – Solar Cells (2016)*, para. 7.236. Emphasis added.
247 See *ibid*. 248 See *ibid*., para. 7.265.
249 See Appellate Body Report, *India – Solar Cells (2016)*, para. 5.90.
250 *Ibid*., para. 5.89. 251 *Ibid*.

The Appellate Body emphasised in particular that:

> Due regard should be given to the total quantity of imports that may be '*available*' to meet demand in a particular geographical area or market. It may thus be relevant to consider the extent to which international supply of a product is stable and accessible, by examining factors such as the distance between a particular geographical area or market and production sites, as well as the reliability of local or transnational supply chains.[252]

The factors that are relevant in determining whether products are 'in general or local short supply' within the meaning of Article XX(j), will necessarily depend on the particularities of each case. In all cases, however, the respondent has the burden of demonstrating that the quantity of 'available' supply from both domestic and international sources in the relevant geographical market is insufficient to meet demand.[253]

In the light of its finding that the products at issue were not in 'general or local short supply' within the meaning of Article XX(j), it was unnecessary for the panel to make any further findings on whether the DCR measures are 'essential' to the acquisition of solar cells and modules for the purpose of Article XX(j). The panel therefore did not make such findings.[254] However, while leaving aside the question of whether the terms 'essential' and 'necessary' establish the same legal threshold, the panel in *India – Solar Cells (2016)* noted that:

> the parties agree that the threshold for establishing that a measure is 'essential' under XX(j) is at least as high as that for establishing that a measure is 'necessary' under Article XX(d). The parties further agree that the general analytical framework that would need to be applied to assess whether the DCR measures are 'essential' under Article XX(j) is similar to the two-step analysis of assessing whether a measure is 'necessary' to realize a given objective ... [A]ll of the third parties ... also seem to agree with the foregoing.[255]

On appeal, also the Appellate Body, after upholding the panel's finding that the products at issue were not in 'general or local short supply', saw no need to further examine whether the measures at issue were provisionally justified under Article XX(j). However, the Appellate Body noted that:

> [t]he analytical framework for the 'design' and 'necessity' elements of the analysis contemplated under Article XX(d) is relevant *mutatis mutandis* also under Article XX(j).[256]

With regard to the examination of whether a measure is 'essential' within the meaning of Article XX(j), the Appellate Body recalled that, as it had stated in its case law under Article XX(d), in a continuum ranging from 'indispensable' to 'making a contribution to', a 'necessary' measure is located significantly closer

252 *Ibid*. Emphasis added. The Appellate Body observed in this regard that the different levels of economic development of Members may, depending on the circumstances, impact the '*availability*' of supply of a product in a given market. Developing countries may be more vulnerable to disruptions in supply than developed countries. See *ibid*., para. 5.72.

253 *Ibid*., para. 5.89. 254 See Panel Report, *India – Solar Cells (2016)*, para. 7.382.

255 See *ibid*., para. 7.350.

256 Appellate Body Report, *India – Solar Cells (2016)*, para. 5.60. On the analytical framework for the 'design' and 'necessity' elements of the analysis under Article XX(d) and Article XX(a), see above, pp. 564–7 and 578–9.

to the pole of 'indispensable' than to the opposite pole of simply 'making a contribution to'.[257] The Appellate Body then noted that the word 'essential' is defined as '[a]bsolutely indispensable or necessary' and thus opined that:

> The word 'essential' in turn is defined as '[a]bsolutely indispensable or necessary'. The plain meaning of the term thus suggests that this word is located at least as close to the 'indispensable' end of the continuum as the word 'necessary'.[258]

2.3.6 Other Paragraphs of Article XX

In addition to Articles XX(a), (b), (d), (g) and (j) of the GATT 1994, also Articles XX(e) and (f) deserve to be mentioned, albeit briefly as there is no relevant case law on either provision.

Article XX(e) of the GATT 1994 concerns measures 'relating to' the products of prison labour. On the basis of Article XX(e), Members can, for example, ban the importation of goods that have been produced by prisoners. Article XX(e) is currently of little importance, and there is no case law under this paragraph to date. It has been suggested, however, that this could change if an evolutionary interpretation of the concept of 'products of prison labour' would allow this concept to include products produced in conditions of slave labour or conditions contrary to the most fundamental labour standards.[259]

Article XX(f) concerns measures 'imposed for' the protection of national treasures of artistic, historic or archaeological value. It allows Members to adopt or maintain otherwise GATT-inconsistent measures for the protection of national treasures. Note that Article XX(f) does not require that these measures are 'necessary' for, but merely that they are 'imposed for', the protection of national treasures. There is no case law on Article XX(f) to date. If the concept of 'national treasures of artistic value' could be given a broad meaning to include also 'endangered' cultural goods, Article XX(f) may be useful to justify import and export restrictions or bans imposed for the protection and promotion of cultural identity and/or diversity.

2.4 Chapeau of Article XX of the GATT 1994

As discussed above, Article XX sets out a two-tier test for determining whether a measure, otherwise inconsistent with GATT obligations, can be justified. First, a measure must meet the requirements of one of the particular exceptions listed in the paragraphs of Article XX. Second, the application of that measure must meet

257 See Appellate Body Report, *India – Solar Cells (2016)*, para. 5.62 (referring to Appellate Body Report, *Korea – Various Measures on Beef*, para. 161).
258 *Ibid.*
259 See Gabrielle Marceau, 'Trade and Labour', in D. Bethlehem, D. McRae, R. Neufeld and I. Van Damme, *International Trade Law* (Oxford University Press, 2009), 549–52. For an example of evolutionary interpretation, see the findings of the Appellate Body on the concept of 'exhaustible natural resources' in *US – Shrimp (1998)*, discussed above, p. 575.

the requirements of the chapeau of Article XX. The legal requirements imposed by the chapeau of Article XX of the GATT 1994 have been highly relevant in dispute settlement practice. Several of the most controversial decisions by panels and the Appellate Body have turned on these requirements. The chapeau of Article XX, with regard to measures provisionally justified under one of the paragraphs of Article XX, imposes:

> the requirement that such measures are not applied in a manner which would constitute a means of arbitrary or unjustifiable discrimination between countries where the same conditions prevail, or a disguised restriction on international trade.

Note that by its express terms, the chapeau of Article XX addresses not so much the measure at issue as such, but focuses on 'the *application* of a measure already found to be inconsistent with an obligation of the GATT 1994 but falling within one of the paragraphs of Article XX'.[260]

2.4.1 Object and Purpose of the Chapeau of Article XX

With respect to the object and purpose of the chapeau of Article XX, the Appellate Body ruled in *US – Gasoline (1996)*:

> The chapeau is animated by the principle that while the exceptions of Article XX may be invoked as a matter of legal right, they should not be so applied as to frustrate or defeat the legal obligations of the holder of the right under the substantive rules of the *General Agreement*. If those exceptions are not to be abused or misused, in other words, the measures falling within the particular exceptions must be applied reasonably, with due regard both to the legal duties of the party claiming the exception and the legal rights of the other parties concerned.[261]

Further, in *US – Shrimp (1998)*, the Appellate Body stated with regard to the chapeau:

> [W]e consider that it embodies the recognition on the part of WTO Members of the need to maintain a balance of rights and obligations between the right of a Member to invoke one or another of the exceptions of Article XX, specified in paragraphs (a) to (j), on the one hand, and the substantive rights of the other Members under the GATT 1994, on the other hand. Exercise by one Member of its right to invoke an exception, such as Article XX(g), if abused or misused, will, to that extent, erode or render naught the substantive treaty rights in, for example, Article XI:1, of other Members. Similarly, because the GATT 1994 itself makes available the exceptions of Article XX, in recognition of the legitimate nature of the policies and interests there embodied, the right to invoke one of those exceptions is not to be rendered illusory.[262]

In short, the object and purpose of the chapeau of Article XX is to avoid that provisionally justified measures are *applied* in such a way as would constitute a

260 Appellate Body Report, *Brazil – Retreaded Tyres (2007)*, para. 215. Emphasis added.
261 Appellate Body Report, *US – Gasoline (1996)*, 22. In a footnote, the Appellate Body referred to Panel Report, *US – Spring Assemblies (1983)*, para. 56.
262 Appellate Body Report, *US – Shrimp (1998)*, para. 156. In a footnote, to the following paragraph, the Appellate Body referred to Panel Report, *US – Section 337 Tariff Act (1989)*, para. 5.9.

misuse or an abuse of the exceptions of Article XX. According to the Appellate Body, a balance must be struck between the *right* of a Member to invoke an exception under Article XX and the substantive rights of the other Members under the GATT 1994. The chapeau was inserted at the head of the list of 'General Exceptions' in Article XX to ensure that this balance is struck and to prevent abuse.[263] The Appellate Body held in *US – Shrimp (1998)*:

> In our view, the language of the chapeau makes clear that each of the exceptions in paragraphs (a) to (j) of Article XX is a *limited and conditional* exception from the substantive obligations contained in the other provisions of the GATT 1994, that is to say, the ultimate availability of the exception is subject to the compliance by the invoking Member with the requirements of the chapeau.[264]

According to the Appellate Body, the chapeau of Article XX is an expression of the principle of good faith, a general principle of law as well as a general principle of international law, which controls the exercise of rights by States. As the Appellate Body held:

> One application of this general principle, the application widely known as the doctrine of *abus de droit*, prohibits the abusive exercise of a state's rights and enjoins that, whenever the assertion of a right 'impinges on the field covered by [a] treaty obligation, it must be exercised *bona fide*, that is to say, reasonably'. An abusive exercise by a Member of its own treaty right thus results in a breach of the treaty rights of the other Members, and, as well, a violation of the treaty obligation of the Member so acting.[265]

In light of the above, the Appellate Body came to the following conclusion in *US – Shrimp (1998)* with respect to the interpretation and application of the chapeau:

> The task of interpreting and applying the chapeau is, hence, essentially the delicate one of locating and marking out a line of equilibrium between the right of a Member to invoke an exception under Article XX and the rights of the other Members under varying substantive provisions (e.g. Article XI) of the GATT 1994, so that neither of the competing rights will cancel out the other and thereby distort and nullify or impair the balance of rights and obligations constructed by the Members themselves in that Agreement. The location of the line of equilibrium, as expressed in the chapeau, is not fixed and unchanging; the line moves as the kind and the shape of the measures at stake vary and as the facts making up specific cases differ.[266]

In short, the interpretation and application of the chapeau in a particular case is a search for the appropriate *line of equilibrium* between, on the one hand, the right of Members to adopt and maintain trade-restrictive legislation and measures that pursue certain legitimate societal values or interests and, on the other hand, the right of other Members to trade. The search for this line of equilibrium is guided by the requirements set out in the chapeau that the application of the

263 See also Appellate Body Reports, *EC – Seal Products (2014)*, para. 5.297.
264 Appellate Body Report, *US – Shrimp (1998)*, para. 157.
265 *Ibid.*, para. 158. See also Appellate Body Report, *Brazil – Retreaded Tyres (2007)*, paras. 215 and 224.
266 Appellate Body Report, *US – Shrimp (1998)*, para. 159. This was reiterated in Appellate Body Report, *Brazil – Retreaded Tyres (2007)*, para. 224.

trade-restrictive measure may not constitute: (1) 'a means of arbitrary or unjustifiable discrimination between countries where the same conditions prevail'; or (2) 'a disguised restriction on international trade'. The following subsections examine these requirements of the chapeau in more detail.[267]

2.4.2 Arbitrary or Unjustifiable Discrimination

For a measure to be justified under Article XX, the application of that measure, pursuant to the chapeau of Article XX, may *not* constitute 'a means of arbitrary or unjustifiable discrimination between countries where the same conditions prevail'. In *US – Gasoline (1996)*, the Appellate Body found that the 'discrimination' at issue in the chapeau of Article XX must necessarily be different from the discrimination addressed in other provisions of the GATT 1994, such as Articles I and III. The Appellate Body stated:

> The enterprise of applying Article XX would clearly be an unprofitable one if it involved no more than applying the standard used in finding that the [measure at issue] [was] inconsistent with Article III:4 ... The provisions of the chapeau cannot logically refer to the same standard(s) by which a violation of a substantive rule has been determined to have occurred.[268]

As the Appellate Body noted, the chapeau of Article XX does not prohibit discrimination *per se*, but rather *arbitrary* and *unjustifiable* discrimination.[269]

In *US – Shrimp (1998)*, the Appellate Body found that three elements must exist for 'arbitrary or unjustifiable discrimination' to be established: (1) the application of the measure at issue must result in *discrimination*; (2) this discrimination must be *arbitrary* or *unjustifiable* in character; and (3) this discrimination must occur *between countries where the same conditions prevail*.[270] The Appellate Body further elaborated on the concept of 'discrimination' within the meaning of the chapeau of Article XX, and stated:

> It may be quite acceptable for a government, in adopting and implementing a domestic policy, to adopt a single standard applicable to all its citizens throughout that country. However, it is not acceptable, in international trade relations, for one WTO Member to use an economic embargo to *require* other Members to adopt essentially the same comprehensive regulatory program, to achieve a certain policy goal, as that in force within that Member's territory, *without* taking into consideration different conditions which may occur in the territories of those other Members.

267 Note that while there are some similarities between the chapeau of Article XX of the GATT 1994 and Article 2.1 of the *TBT Agreement*, the Appellate Body ruled in *EC – Seal Products (2014)*, para. 5.313, that given the differences between the inquiries under the chapeau of Article XX of the GATT 1994 and Article 2.1 of the *TBT Agreement*, the panel 'erred in applying the same legal test to the chapeau of Article XX as it applied under Article 2.1 of the *TBT Agreement*, instead of conducting an independent analysis of the consistency of the EU Seal Regime with the specific terms and requirements of the chapeau'.

268 Appellate Body Report, *US – Gasoline (1996)*, 23. As the Appellate Body stated in its Report in *US – Shrimp (1998)*, para. 150, 'the nature and quality of this discrimination is different from the discrimination in the treatment of products which was already found to be inconsistent with one of the substantive obligations of the GATT 1994'. See also Appellate Body Reports, *EC – Seal Products (2014)*, para. 5.298.

269 See Appellate Body Report, *US – Gasoline (1996)*.

270 Appellate Body Report, *US – Shrimp (1998)*, para. 150. See also Panel Report, *EC – Tariff Preferences (2004)*, paras. 7.225–7.235; and Panel Report, *Brazil – Retreaded Tyres (2007)*, paras. 7.226–7.251.

We believe that discrimination results not only when countries in which the same conditions prevail are differently treated, but also when the application of the measure at issue does not allow for any inquiry into the appropriateness of the regulatory program for the conditions prevailing in those exporting countries.[271]

The Appellate Body came to the conclusion in *US – Shrimp (1998)* that the application of the measure at issue constituted '*arbitrary* discrimination' as follows:

Section 609, in its application, imposes a single, rigid and unbending requirement that countries applying for certification ... adopt a comprehensive regulatory program that is essentially the same as the United States' program, without inquiring into the appropriateness of that program for the conditions prevailing in the exporting countries. Furthermore, there is little or no flexibility in how officials make the determination for certification pursuant to these provisions. In our view, this rigidity and inflexibility also constitute 'arbitrary discrimination' within the meaning of the chapeau.[272]

The Appellate Body thus decided that discrimination may result when the same measure is applied to countries where different conditions prevail. When a measure is applied without any regard for the difference in conditions between countries and this measure is applied in a rigid and inflexible manner, the application of the measure may constitute 'arbitrary discrimination' within the meaning of the chapeau of Article XX.

To implement the recommendations and rulings in *US – Shrimp (1998)*, the United States modified the measure at issue in this case. Malaysia challenged the GATT consistency of the implementing measure in an Article 21.5 proceeding.[273] The panel in *US – Shrimp (Article 21.5 – Malaysia) (2001)* concluded that, unlike the original US measure, the implementing measure was justified under Article XX and thus GATT-consistent. On appeal the Appellate Body held:

In our view, there is an important difference between conditioning market access on the adoption of essentially the same programme, and conditioning market access on the adoption of a programme *comparable in effectiveness*. Authorizing an importing Member to condition market access on exporting Members putting in place regulatory programmes *comparable in effectiveness* to that of the importing Member gives sufficient latitude to the exporting Member with respect to the programme it may adopt to achieve the level of effectiveness required. It allows the exporting Member to adopt a regulatory programme that is suitable to the specific conditions prevailing in its territory. As we see it, the Panel correctly reasoned and concluded that conditioning market access on the adoption of a programme *comparable in effectiveness*, allows for sufficient flexibility in the application of the measure so as to avoid 'arbitrary or unjustifiable discrimination'.[274]

Note that the Appellate Body thus seemed to introduce into the chapeau of Article XX an 'embryonic' and 'soft' requirement on Members to recognise the

271 Appellate Body Report, *US – Shrimp (1998)*, paras. 164–5. 272 *Ibid.*, para. 177.
273 On proceedings under Article 21.5 of the DSU, see above, pp. 287–9.
274 Appellate Body Report, *US – Shrimp (Article 21.5 – Malaysia) (2001)*, para. 144.

equivalence of foreign measures comparable in effectiveness.[275] The Appellate Body found in *US – Shrimp (Article 21.5 – Malaysia) (2001)* that the revised US measure at issue in the implementation dispute was sufficiently flexible to meet the standards of the chapeau.[276] The Appellate Body added:

> [A] measure should be designed in such a manner that there is sufficient flexibility to take into account the specific conditions prevailing in *any* exporting Member, including, of course, Malaysia. Yet this is not the same as saying that there must be specific provisions in the measure aimed at addressing specifically the particular conditions prevailing in *every individual* exporting Member. Article XX of the GATT 1994 does not require a Member to anticipate and provide explicitly for the specific conditions prevailing and evolving in *every individual* Member.[277]

Pursuant to the chapeau of Article XX, the application of measures provisionally justified under one of the paragraphs of Article XX may not only not constitute 'arbitrary discrimination', it may also not constitute '*unjustifiable* discrimination'. As noted by the panel in *EU – Seal Products (2014)*, in many disputes the existence of arbitrary and unjustifiable discrimination are addressed together. This was the case, for example in *US – Shrimp (Article 21.5 – Malaysia) (2001)*, *US – Gambling (2005)*, and *Brazil – Retreaded Tyres (2007)*. Yet, these are distinct concepts.[278] In *US – Gasoline (1996)*, the Appellate Body concluded that the measure at issue constituted 'unjustifiable discrimination' for the following reasons:

> We have above located two omissions on the part of the United States: to explore adequately means, including in particular cooperation with the governments of Venezuela and Brazil, of mitigating the administrative problems relied on as justification by the United States for rejecting individual baselines for foreign refiners; and to count the costs for foreign refiners that would result from the imposition of statutory baselines. In our view, these two omissions go well beyond what was necessary for the Panel to determine that a violation of Article III:4 had occurred in the first place. The resulting discrimination must have been *foreseen*, and was *not merely inadvertent or unavoidable*. In the light of the foregoing, our conclusion is that the baseline establishment rules in the Gasoline Rule, in their application, constitute 'unjustifiable discrimination'.[279]

Note that the Appellate Body emphasised the *deliberate* nature of the discrimination, i.e. discrimination that is foreseen and not merely inadvertent or unavoidable. Likewise, the panel in *Argentina – Hides and Leather (2001)* found that the application of the measure at issue resulted in unjustifiable discrimination as several alternative measures were available, which rendered the measure *not unavoidable*.[280]

275 See also G. Marceau and J. Trachtmann, 'A Map of the World Trade Organization Law of Domestic Regulations of Goods', in G. A. Bermann and P. C. Mavroidis (eds.), *Trade and Human Health and Safety* (Cambridge University Press, 2006), 9 –76, at 42.
276 See Appellate Body Report, *US – Shrimp (Article 21.5 – Malaysia) (2001)*, paras. 145–8.
277 *Ibid.*, para. 149.
278 See Panel Report, *EU – Seal Products (2014)*, para. 7.645.
279 Appellate Body Report, *US – Gasoline (1996)*, 28–29. Emphasis added.
280 See Panel Report, *Argentina – Hides and Leather (2001)*, paras. 11.324–11.330.

The Appellate Body in *US – Shrimp (1998)* also addressed the question of whether the application of the measure at issue constituted an 'unjustifiable discrimination' within the meaning of the chapeau. The Appellate Body noted the following:

> Another aspect of the application of Section 609 that bears heavily in any appraisal of justifiable or unjustifiable discrimination is the failure of the United States to engage the appellees, as well as other Members exporting shrimp to the United States, in serious, across-the-board negotiations with the objective of concluding bilateral or multilateral agreements for the protection and conservation of sea turtles, before enforcing the import prohibition against the shrimp exports of those other Members.[281]

The Appellate Body made three observations in this respect.[282] First, the Congress of the United States expressly recognised in enacting Section 609 the importance of securing international agreements for the protection and conservation of the sea turtle species. Second, the protection and conservation of highly migratory species of sea turtle, i.e. the very policy objective of the measure, demands concerted and cooperative efforts on the part of the many countries whose waters are traversed in the course of recurrent sea turtle migrations. The need for, and the appropriateness of, such efforts are recognised in the WTO Agreement itself, as well as in a significant number of other international instruments and declarations. Third, the United States negotiated and concluded the *Inter-American Convention for the Protection and Conservation of Sea Turtles*. The existence of this regional agreement provided convincing demonstration that an alternative course of action was reasonably open to the United States for securing the legitimate policy goal of its measure, a course of action other than the unilateral and non-consensual procedures of the import prohibition under Section 609. However, the record did not show that serious efforts were made by the United States to negotiate similar agreements with any other country or group of countries.[283] The Appellate Body therefore concluded:

> Clearly, the United States negotiated seriously with some, but not with other Members (including the appellees), that export shrimp to the United States. The effect is plainly discriminatory and, in our view, unjustifiable. The unjustifiable nature of this discrimination emerges clearly when we consider the cumulative effects of the failure of the United States to pursue negotiations for establishing consensual means of protection and conservation of the living marine resources here involved.[284]

The extent to which a Member has to seek a multilateral solution to a problem before it may make use of unilateral measures was one of the main issues in

281 Appellate Body Report, *US – Shrimp (1998)*, para. 166.

282 See *ibid.*, paras. 167–9.

283 The record also did not show that the United States attempted to have recourse to such international mechanisms that exist to achieve cooperative efforts to protect and conserve sea turtles before imposing the import ban. The United States, for example, did not make any attempt to raise the issue of sea turtle mortality due to shrimp trawling in the CITES Standing Committee as a subject requiring concerted action by States.

284 Appellate Body Report, *US – Shrimp (1998)*, para. 172.

US – Shrimp (Article 21.5 – Malaysia) (2001). The Appellate Body made it clear that, in order to meet the requirement of the chapeau of Article XX, the Member needs to make serious efforts, in good faith, to negotiate a multilateral solution before resorting to unilateral measures.[285] Failure to make such efforts may lead to the conclusion that the discrimination is 'unjustifiable'.[286] Applying this standard in *US – Shrimp (Article 21.5 – Malaysia) (2001)* the Appellate Body upheld the findings of the panel that 'in view of the serious, good faith efforts made by the United States to negotiate an international agreement' with respect to actions on the protection of sea turtles, the US measure was 'applied in a manner that no longer constitutes a means of unjustifiable or arbitrary discrimination'.[287]

The panel in *Brazil – Retreaded Tyres (2007)* considered that the Appellate Body reports in *US – Gasoline (1996)*, *US – Shrimp (1998)* and *US – Shrimp (Article 21.5 – Malaysia) (2001)*, all discussed above, provided useful illustrations on what might render discrimination 'arbitrary' or 'unjustifiable' within the meaning of the chapeau of Article XX.[288] However, the panel continued:

> We do not assume ... that exactly the same elements will necessarily be determinative in every situation ... We recall in this regard the Appellate Body's observation, in its ruling in *US – Shrimp*, that the 'location of the line of equilibrium [between the right of a Member to invoke an exception under Article XX and the rights of the other Members under varying substantive provisions], as expressed in the chapeau, is not fixed and unchanging; the line moves as the kind and the shape of the measures at stake vary and as the facts making up specific cases differ'.[289]

In *Brazil – Retreaded Tyres (2007)*, the panel had determined that discrimination arose in the application of the measure at issue, an import ban on retreaded tyres, from two sources: discrimination arising from the exemption from the import ban of imports of remoulded tyres originating in MERCOSUR countries (the 'MERCOSUR exemption'); and discrimination arising from the importation of used tyres under court injunctions.[290]

With regard to the application of the import ban, in conjunction with imports of remoulded tyres under the MERCOSUR exemption, the panel found that this application constituted neither arbitrary nor unjustifiable discrimination,[291] as the MERCOSUR exemption was granted to MERCOSUR countries pursuant to a

285 See Appellate Body Report, *US – Shrimp (Article 21.5 – Malaysia) (2001)*, paras. 115–34.
286 In *US – Shrimp (1998)*, the Appellate Body also found that the application of the US measures resulted in differential treatment among various countries desiring certification: for example, by granting different countries different phasing-in periods to comply with the US requirements, and concluded that this differential treatment also constituted 'unjustifiable discrimination'. See Appellate Body Report, *US – Shrimp (1998)*, paras. 173–5.
287 Appellate Body Report, *US – Shrimp (Article 21.5 – Malaysia) (2001)*, para. 134.
288 See Panel Report, *Brazil – Retreaded Tyres (2007)*, para. 7.261.
289 *Ibid.*, para. 7.262. 290 See *ibid.*, para. 7.251.
291 See *ibid.*, para. 7.289.

ruling by the MERCOSUR Tribunal finding an import ban on remoulded tyres inconsistent with MERCOSUR rules.[292] The panel thus ruled that:

> the discrimination resulting from the MERCOSUR exemption cannot, in our view, be said to be 'capricious' or 'random'. To that extent, the measure at issue is not being applied in a manner that would constitute *arbitrary* discrimination.[293]

The panel considered that if imports of remoulded tyres under the MERCOSUR exemption were to take place in such amounts that the achievement of the objective of the import ban would be significantly undermined, the application of the import ban, in conjunction with the exemption, would constitute a means of *unjustifiable* discrimination.[294] The panel found, however, the levels of imports 'not to have been significant'[295] and thus concluded that the operation of the MERCOSUR exemption had not resulted in the measure being applied in a manner that would constitute *unjustifiable* discrimination.[296]

Similarly, with regard to the application of the import ban, in conjunction with imports of used tyres under court injunctions, the panel found that this application did not constitute *arbitrary* discrimination because the discrimination was not the result of 'capricious' or 'random' action (but the result of court injunctions).[297] However, the panel concluded that the application of the import ban, in conjunction with imports of used tyres under court injunctions, constituted *unjustifiable* discrimination because the imports of used tyres under court injunctions had taken place 'in significant amounts', undermining Brazil's stated policy objective.[298]

On appeal, the Appellate Body, referring to its analysis of whether the application of a measure results in arbitrary or unjustifiable discrimination in *US – Gasoline (1996)*, *US – Shrimp (1998)* and *US – Shrimp (Article 21.5 – Malaysia) (2001)*, noted that:

> [a]nalyzing whether discrimination is arbitrary or unjustifiable usually involves an analysis that relates primarily to *the cause or the rationale* of the discrimination.[299]

The Appellate Body thus rejected the panel's interpretation of the term 'unjustifiable' as it did not depend on the *cause* or *rationale* of the discrimination but, instead, 'focused exclusively on the assessment of the *effects* of the discrimination'.[300] According to the Appellate Body, an abuse of the Article XX

292 See *ibid.*, para. 7.270. As noted by both the panel and the Appellate Body, Brazil could have sought to justify before the MERCOSUR Tribunal the challenged Import Ban on the grounds of human, animal and plant health under Article 50(d) of the Treaty of Montevideo, but that Brazil, however, decided not to do so. See Appellate Body Report, *Brazil – Retreaded Tyres (2007)*, para. 234.
293 Panel Report, *Brazil – Retreaded Tyres (2007)*, para. 7.281.
294 See *ibid.*, para. 7.287. 295 *Ibid.*, para. 7.288.
296 See *ibid.*, para. 7.289. 297 See *ibid.*, para. 7.294.
298 See *ibid.*, paras. 7.303 and 7.306.
299 Appellate Body Report, *Brazil – Retreaded Tyres (2007)*, para. 225. Emphasis added.
300 *Ibid.*, para. 229.

exceptions – contrary to the purpose of the chapeau – exists when the reasons given for discrimination:

> bear no rational connection to the objective falling within the purview of a paragraph of Article XX, or would go against that objective.[301]

Therefore, whether discrimination is 'arbitrary or unjustifiable' should be assessed in light of the *objective* of the measure.[302]

The Appellate Body then had to assess whether the explanation provided by Brazil, namely, that it had introduced the MERCOSUR exemption to comply with a ruling issued by the MERCOSUR Tribunal, was 'acceptable as a justification for discrimination between MERCOSUR countries and non-MERCOSUR countries in relation to retreaded tyres'.[303] The Appellate Body stated:

> [W]e have difficulty understanding how discrimination might be viewed as complying with the chapeau of Article XX when the alleged rationale for discriminating does not relate to the pursuit of or would go against the objective that was provisionally found to justify a measure under a paragraph of Article XX.
>
> ... [T]he ruling issued by the MERCOSUR arbitral tribunal is not an acceptable rationale for the discrimination, because it bears no relationship to the legitimate objective pursued by the Import Ban that falls within the purview of Article XX(b), and even goes against this objective, to however small a degree. Accordingly, we are of the view that the MERCOSUR exemption has resulted in the Import Ban being applied in a manner that constitutes arbitrary or unjustifiable discrimination.[304]

While the Appellate Body agreed with the panel that Brazil's decision was not 'capricious' or 'random', since decisions to implement rulings of judicial or quasi-judicial bodies cannot be characterised as such, it noted that:

> discrimination can result from a rational decision or behaviour, and still be 'arbitrary or unjustifiable', because it is explained by a rationale that bears no relationship to the objective of a measure provisionally justified under one of the paragraphs of Article XX, or goes against that objective.[305]

The Appellate Body made a similar finding with regard to the imports of tyres under court injunctions.[306]

In brief, the application of a provisionally justified measure will constitute 'arbitrary or unjustifiable' discrimination when the *discrimination arising in the application* of the provisionally justified measure is explained by a rationale that bears no relation to the objective of the measure or even goes against that objective.

As the Appellate Body held in *Brazil – Retreaded Tyres (2007)*, whether discrimination is arbitrary or unjustifiable depends on the cause or rationale of the discrimination, *not* on the effects of the discrimination (as the panel had held).

301 *Ibid.*, para. 227. 302 See *ibid.*
303 *Ibid.* 304 *Ibid.*, paras. 227–8.
305 *Ibid.*, para. 232. 306 See *ibid.*, paras. 246–7.

The rationale of the discrimination must be assessed in light of the contribution of the discrimination to achieving the legitimate objective provisionally found to justify the measure at issue. In *EC – Seal Products (2014)* the Appellate Body held that *one of the most important* factors in the assessment of arbitrary or unjustifiable discrimination is:

> the question of whether the discrimination can be reconciled with, or is rationally related to, the policy objective with respect to which the measure has been provisionally justified under one of the subparagraphs of Article XX.[307]

In *EC – Seal Products (2014)*, the Appellate Body concluded that the measure at issue, the EU Seal Regime, which was provisionally justified under Article XX(a), was applied in a manner that constituted arbitrary or unjustifiable discrimination.[308] The Appellate Body advanced three main reasons for coming to this conclusion. First, the European Union did not show that the manner in which the EU Seal Regime treated seal products derived from IC hunts (i.e. hunts by Inuit and other indigenous communities) as compared to seal products derived from commercial hunts can be reconciled with the objective of addressing EU public moral concerns regarding seal welfare. Both IC hunts and commercial hunts seriously affected seal welfare. Second, given the considerable ambiguity in the 'subsistence' and 'partial use' criteria of the IC exception,[309] seal products derived from what should in fact be properly characterised as commercial hunts could potentially enter the EU market under the IC exception. The European Union did not sufficiently explain how such instances could be prevented in the application of the IC exception. Third, the Appellate Body was not persuaded that the European Union had made comparable efforts to facilitate the access of the Canadian Inuit to the IC exception as it did with respect to the Greenlandic Inuit.[310]

In *Colombia – Textiles (2016)*, the panel found that Colombia had failed to demonstrate that the measure at issue, the compound tariff, was justified under Article XX(a) or Article XX(d) of the GATT 1994.[311] The panel therefore considered that it was not necessary for it to analyse whether the compound tariff meets the requirements of the chapeau.[312] Nevertheless, the panel conducted its assessment of the chapeau by assuming, for the sake of argument, that Colombia had succeeded in showing that its measure is provisionally justified under Article XX(a) or Article XX(d) of the GATT 1994. The panel summarised the current case law on 'arbitrary and unjustifiable discrimination' as follows:

> With regard to the element of 'arbitrary or unjustifiable discrimination', the analysis relates primarily to the cause or the rationale of the discrimination, that is, whether the

307 Appellate Body Reports, *EC – Seal Products (2014)*, para. 5.306.
308 See *ibid.*, para. 5.338.
309 The Appellate Body also noted that broad discretion that the recognised EU bodies enjoyed in applying these ambiguous criteria.
310 See *ibid.* 311 See above, pp. 566 and 573.
312 See Panel Report, *Colombia – Textiles (2016)*, para. 7.550.

discrimination that results from the application of some measure has a legitimate cause or basis in the light of the guidelines laid down in the paragraphs of Article XX. In other words, there is arbitrary or unjustifiable discrimination 'when a Member seeks to justify the discrimination resulting from the application of its measure by a rationale that bears no relationship to the accomplishment of the objective that falls within the purview of one of the paragraphs of Article XX, or goes against this objective'.[313]

The panel in *Colombia – Textiles (2016)* thus concluded that the measure at issue, the compound tariff, was applied in a manner that constituted 'arbitrary or unjustifiable discrimination', because the various exclusions from the application of the measure did not bear any relationship with the measure's declared objective of combating money laundering.[314] On appeal, the Appellate Body upheld the panel's findings that Colombia had not demonstrated that the compound tariff was provisionally justified under Article XX(a) or Article XX(d) and did therefore not consider it necessary to review the panel's findings pertaining to the chapeau of Article XX.[315]

Finally, as noted above, the chapeau of Article XX of the GATT 1994 refers to arbitrary or unjustifiable discrimination *between countries where the same conditions prevail*. In *US – Shrimp (1998)* the Appellate Body had stated that the discrimination referred to in the chapeau of Article XX 'may occur not only between different exporting Members, but also between exporting Members and the importing Member concerned'.[316] More recently, in *EC – Seal Products (2014)*, the Appellate Body noted with regard to the 'conditions' that are relevant in this context the following:

the identification of the relevant 'conditions' under the chapeau should be understood by reference to the applicable subparagraph of Article XX under which the measure was provisionally justified and the substantive obligations under the GATT 1994 with which a violation has been found. If a respondent considers that the conditions prevailing in different countries are not 'the same' in relevant respects, it bears the burden of proving that claim.[317]

In *EC – Seal Products (2014)*, the Appellate Body found that the European Union, the respondent, had not shown that the 'conditions' with regard to seal welfare prevailing in Canada and Norway, on the one hand, and Greenland, on the other hand are relevantly different.[318] In the absence of a showing by the respondent that the conditions were 'relevantly different', the conditions were assumed to be the same.

313 *Ibid.*, para. 7.544.

314 See *ibid.*, para. 7.591. The exclusions from the application of the compound tariff related to: (1) imports originating in countries with which Colombia has trade agreements in force; (2) imports into Colombia's Special Customs Regime Zones; and (3) imports under the 'Plan Vallejo'.

315 See Appellate Body Report, *Colombia – Textiles (2016)*, paras. 5.152–5.153.

316 Appellate Body Report, *US – Shrimp (1998)*, para. 150.

317 Appellate Body Reports, *EC – Seal Products (2014)*, para. 5.301.

318 See *ibid.*, para. 5.317.

2.4.3 Disguised Restriction on International Trade

With respect to the requirement that the application of the measure at issue does not constitute a 'disguised restriction on international trade', the Appellate Body stated in *US – Gasoline (1996)*:

> 'Arbitrary discrimination', 'unjustifiable discrimination' and 'disguised restriction' on international trade may, accordingly, be read side-by-side; they impart meaning to one another. It is clear to us that 'disguised restriction' includes disguised *discrimination* in international trade. It is equally clear that *concealed or unannounced* restriction or discrimination in international trade does *not* exhaust the meaning of 'disguised restriction'. We consider that 'disguised restriction', whatever else it covers, may properly be read as embracing restrictions amounting to arbitrary or unjustifiable discrimination in international trade taken under the guise of a measure formally within the terms of an exception listed in Article XX.[319]

According to the Appellate Body in *US – Gasoline (1996)*:

> the kinds of considerations pertinent in deciding whether the application of a particular measure amounts to 'arbitrary or unjustifiable discrimination', may also be taken into account in determining the presence of a 'disguised restriction' on international trade. The fundamental theme is to be found in the purpose and object of avoiding abuse or illegitimate use of the exceptions to substantive rules available in Article XX.[320]

The panel in *EC – Asbestos (2001)* further clarified the requirement of the chapeau that the application of the measure at issue may not constitute a 'disguised restriction on international trade' as follows:

> [T]he key to understanding what is covered by 'disguised restriction on international trade' is not so much the word 'restriction', inasmuch as, in essence, any measure falling within Article XX is a restriction on international trade, but the word 'disguised'. In accordance with the approach defined in Article 31 of the Vienna Convention, we note that, as ordinarily understood, the verb 'to disguise' implies an intention. Thus, 'to disguise' (*déguiser*) means, in particular, 'conceal beneath deceptive appearances, counterfeit', 'alter so as to deceive', 'misrepresent', 'dissimulate'. Accordingly, a restriction which formally meets the requirements of Article XX(b) will constitute an abuse if such compliance is in fact only a disguise to conceal the pursuit of trade-restrictive objectives.[321]

2.5 Policy Space for Members to Protect Other Societal Values

In two prominent WTO disputes involving the protection of the environment, *US – Gasoline (1996)* and *US – Shrimp (1998)*, the measures at issue were found

319 Appellate Body Report, *US – Gasoline (1996)*, 25. On this basis, the panel in *China – Rare Earths (2014)* held that unjustifiable discrimination can constitute a disguised restriction on trade, but that a disguised restriction on trade may exist even if there is no discrimination. See Panel Report, *China – Rare Earths (2014)*, paras. 7.826 and 7.925.

320 *Ibid.* See also Panel Report, *Colombia – Textiles (2016)*, para. 7.549.

321 Panel Report, *EC – Asbestos (2001)*, para. 8.236. The panel noted that the aim of a measure may not be easily ascertained, but it recalled that the Appellate Body had suggested in *Japan – Alcoholic Beverages II (1996)* that the protective application of a measure can most often be discerned from its design, architecture and revealing structure. In a footnote, the panel noted that '[a]lthough this approach was developed in relation to Article III:4 of the GATT 1994, we see no reason why it should not be applicable in other circumstances where it is necessary to determine whether a measure is being applied for protective purposes'. *Ibid.*, fn. 199.

to be provisionally justified under Article XX(g), but the application of the measures failed to satisfy the requirements of the chapeau of Article XX. The public perception of the Appellate Body reports in these disputes has been negative and unsympathetic. In particular, there is a widely held view among environmental activists that the WTO undermines necessary environmental legislation. It is noteworthy that the Appellate Body (with foresight but only with relative success) added a paragraph to the end of both its report in *US – Gasoline (1996)* and its report in *US – Shrimp (1998)*. In these paragraphs, the Appellate Body explained in straightforward language the policy space for Members to enact environmental legislation and the limited nature of its rulings in both cases. In *US – Shrimp (1998)*, the Appellate Body concluded with the following observation:

> In reaching these conclusions, we wish to underscore what we have *not* decided in this appeal. We have *not* decided that the protection and preservation of the environment is of no significance to the Members of the WTO. Clearly, it is. We have *not* decided that the sovereign nations that are Members of the WTO cannot adopt effective measures to protect endangered species, such as sea turtles. Clearly, they can and should. And we have *not* decided that sovereign states should not act together bilaterally, plurilaterally or multilaterally, either within the WTO or in other international fora, to protect endangered species or to otherwise protect the environment. Clearly, they should and do.
>
> What we *have* decided in this appeal is simply this: although the measure of the United States in dispute in this appeal serves an environmental objective that is recognized as legitimate under paragraph (g) of Article XX of the GATT 1994, this measure has been applied by the United States in a manner which constitutes arbitrary and unjustifiable discrimination between Members of the WTO, contrary to the requirements of the chapeau of Article XX ... As we emphasized in *United States – Gasoline*, WTO Members are free to adopt their own policies aimed at protecting the environment as long as, in so doing, they fulfill their obligations and respect the rights of other Members under the *WTO Agreement*.[322]

3 GENERAL EXCEPTIONS UNDER THE GATS

Like the GATT 1994, the GATS also provides for a 'general exceptions' provision allowing Members to deviate, under certain conditions, from obligations and commitments under the GATS. Article XIV of the GATS provides, in relevant part:

> Subject to the requirement that such measures are not applied in a manner which would constitute a means of arbitrary or unjustifiable discrimination between countries where like conditions prevail, or a disguised restriction on trade in services, nothing in this Agreement shall be construed to prevent the adoption or enforcement by any Member of measures:
>
> (a) necessary to protect public morals or to maintain public order;
> (b) necessary to protect human, animal or plant life or health;

322 Appellate Body Report, *US – Shrimp (1998)*, paras. 185–6. For a similar statement, see Appellate Body Report, *US – Gasoline (1996)*, 29–30.

(c) necessary to secure compliance with laws or regulations which are not inconsistent with the provisions of this Agreement including those relating to:
   (i) the prevention of deceptive and fraudulent practices or to deal with the effects of a default on services contracts;
   (ii) the protection of the privacy of individuals in relation to the processing and dissemination of personal data and the protection of confidentiality of individual records and accounts;
   (iii) safety;
(d) inconsistent with Article XVII, provided that the difference in treatment is aimed at ensuring the equitable or effective imposition or collection of direct taxes in respect of services or service suppliers of other Members;
(e) inconsistent with Article II, provided that the difference in treatment is the result of an agreement on the avoidance of double taxation or provisions on the avoidance of double taxation in any other international agreement or arrangement by which the Member is bound.

The similarities between Article XX of the GATT 1994 and Article XIV of the GATS are striking. However, there are also differences. An obvious difference is that some of the justifications in Article XIV of the GATS, such as the maintenance of public order, the protection of safety and privacy, and the equitable and effective imposition or collection of direct taxes, do not appear (at least not explicitly) in Article XX of the GATT 1994. Likewise, some exceptions in Article XX of the GATT 1994, such as the protection of national treasures of artistic value, are not included in Article XIV of the GATS. Note also that while all the exceptions in Article XX of the GATT 1994 allow for deviation from all GATT obligations, the exceptions in Articles XIV(d) and (e) of the GATS only allow for deviation from the national treatment obligation and the MFN treatment obligation respectively. Nevertheless, because of the similarity in architecture and in core concepts, Article XX of the GATT and its jurisprudence provide us with a basis to interpret Article XIV of the GATS. In the first case that dealt with Article XIV of the GATS, *US – Gambling (2005)*, the Appellate Body stated:

> Article XIV of the GATS sets out the general exceptions from obligations under that Agreement in the same manner as does Article XX of the GATT 1994. Both of these provisions affirm the right of Members to pursue objectives identified in the paragraphs of these provisions even if, in doing so, Members act inconsistently with obligations set out in other provisions of the respective agreements, provided that all of the conditions set out therein are satisfied. Similar language is used in both provisions, notably the term 'necessary' and the requirements set out in their respective chapeaux. Accordingly, like the Panel, we find previous decisions under Article XX of the GATT 1994 relevant for our analysis under Article XIV of the GATS.[323]

3.1 Two-Tier Test under Article XIV of the GATS

As with Article XX of the GATT 1994, Article XIV of the GATS sets out a two-tier test for determining whether a measure, otherwise inconsistent with GATS

323 Appellate Body Report, *US – Gambling (2005)*, para. 291.

obligations, can be justified. As the Appellate Body in *US – Gambling (2005)* stated:

> Article XIV of the GATS, like Article XX of the GATT 1994, contemplates a 'two-tier analysis' of a measure that a Member seeks to justify under that provision. A panel should first determine whether the challenged measure falls within the scope of one of the paragraphs of Article XIV. This requires that the challenged measure address the particular interest specified in that paragraph and that there be a sufficient nexus between the measure and the interest protected. The required nexus – or 'degree of connection' – between the measure and the interest is specified in the language of the paragraphs themselves, through the use of terms such as 'relating to' and 'necessary to'. Where the challenged measure has been found to fall within one of the paragraphs of Article XIV, a panel should then consider whether that measure satisfies the requirements of the chapeau of Article XIV.[324]

Thus, to determine whether a measure can be justified under Article XIV of the GATS, it must be examined, first, whether this measure can provisionally be justified under one of the paragraphs of Article XIV; and, if so, second, whether the application of this measure meets the requirements of the chapeau of Article XIV.

To date, Article XIV of the GATS has been invoked in dispute settlement proceedings twice, and unsuccessfully, to justify a measure otherwise GATS-inconsistent.[325]

This subsection, first, discusses the specific exceptions provided for in Article XIV, and, second, analyses the requirements of the chapeau of Article XIV.

3.2 Specific Exceptions under Article XIV of the GATS

Article XIV of the GATS sets out, in paragraphs (a)–(e), specific grounds of justification for measures, which are otherwise inconsistent with the GATS. These grounds of justification relate, *inter alia*, to: (1) the protection of public morals; (2) the maintenance of public order; (3) the protection of human, animal or plant life or health; (4) the prevention of deceptive and fraudulent practices; (5) the protection of the privacy of individuals; (6) the protection of safety; (7) the equitable or effective imposition or collection of direct taxes; and (8) the avoidance of double taxation.[326]

As the Appellate Body noted in *US – Gambling (2005)*, the paragraphs of Article XIV of the GATS contain different requirements regarding the relationship between the measure at issue and the policy objective pursued. For a measure to be provisionally justified under the exceptions listed in paragraphs (a)–(c)

324 *Ibid.*, para. 292.

325 See *US – Gambling (2005)* and *Argentina – Financial Services (2016)*. Article XIV of the GATS was not invoked in *China – Publications and Audiovisual Products (2010)* or *China – Electronic Payment Services (2012)*.

326 Note that the grounds of justification in Article XIV of the GATS do not include a ground equivalent to Article XX(g) of the GATT 1994, relating to the conservation of exhaustible natural resources. See also above, pp. 573–8.

of Article XIV, that measure must be *necessary* to achieve the policy objective pursued. No such requirement of necessity exists under paragraphs (d) and (e). To date, there is case law only on the exceptions under paragraphs (a) and (c) of Article XIV.

3.2.1 Article XIV(a)

Article XIV(a) of the GATS deals with measures which are 'necessary to protect public morals or to maintain public order'. Article XIV(a) sets out a two-tier legal standard to determine whether a measure is *provisionally* justified under this provision. The Member invoking Article XIV(a) must establish that: (1) the measure at issue is *designed* to protect public morals or maintain public order; and (2) the measure is *necessary* to fulfil that policy objective.

With regard to the first element of the analysis under Article XIV(a), note that the panel in *US – Gambling (2005)* dealt extensively this element. Antigua and Barbuda challenged the GATS-consistency of a number of US federal and state laws, including the Wire Act, the Travel Act and the Illegal Gambling Business Act, which prohibit the remote supply of gambling and betting services, including Internet gambling.[327] The United States, *inter alia*, argued that the measures at issue could be justified under Article XIV(a) of the GATS, as necessary to protect public morals and maintain public order. With regard to the meaning of the concepts of 'public morals' and 'public order', the panel in *US – Gambling (2005)* found that it:

> can vary in time and space, depending upon a range of factors, including prevailing social, cultural, ethical and religious values. Further, the Appellate Body has stated on several occasions that Members, in applying similar societal concepts, have the right to determine the level of protection that they consider appropriate. Although these Appellate Body statements were made in the context of Article XX of the GATT 1994, it is our view that such statements are also valid with respect to the protection of public morals and public order under Article [XIV] of the GATS.[328]

According to the panel:

> Members should be given some scope to define and apply for themselves the concepts of 'public morals' and 'public order' in their respective territories, according to their own systems and scales of values.[329]

To determine the ordinary meanings of 'public morals' and 'public order', the panel in *US – Gambling (2005)* turned to the *Shorter Oxford English Dictionary*, and found that the term 'public' is defined therein as: 'Of or pertaining to the people as a whole; belonging to, affecting, or concerning the community or nation.' The panel thus considered that a measure that is sought to be justified under Article XIV(a) must be aimed at 'protecting the interests of the people within a community or a nation as a whole'.[330] The term 'morals' was defined by

327 Hereinafter referred to as 'Antigua'. 328 Panel Report, *US – Gambling (2005)*, para. 6.461.
329 *Ibid.* 330 *Ibid.*, para. 6.463.

the panel as: 'habits of life with regard to right and wrong conduct'. The panel therefore ruled that the term 'public morals' denotes:

> standards of right and wrong conduct maintained by or on behalf of a community or nation.[331]

With regard to the term 'order', the panel noted that the dictionary definition that appears to be relevant in the context of Article XIV(a) reads as follows:

> A condition in which the laws regulating the public conduct of members of a community are maintained and observed; the rule of law or constituted authority; absence of violence or violent crimes.[332]

The panel subsequently noted that footnote 5 to Article XIV(a) of the GATS states with regard to the 'public order' exception that it:

> may be invoked only where a genuine and sufficiently serious threat is posed to one of the fundamental interests of society.

The panel thus concluded that the dictionary definition of the term 'order', read together with footnote 5, suggests that 'public order' refers to:

> the preservation of the fundamental interests of a society, as reflected in public policy and law. These fundamental interests can relate, *inter alia*, to standards of law, security and morality.[333]

While 'public morals' and 'public order' are two different concepts, the panel in *US – Gambling (2005)* considered that overlap may nevertheless exist as those concepts 'seek to protect largely similar values'.[334] The Appellate Body left the panel's interpretation of the concepts of 'public morals' and 'public order', as well as the panel's application of the first element of the analysis under Article XIV(a), undisturbed.[335] The United States had argued that Internet gambling posed threats with regard to organised crime, money laundering and fraud; risks to children; and risks to health due to the possible development of an addiction to gambling.[336] The panel had no difficulty in finding that these concerns fell within the scope of 'public morals' and 'public order' as meant in Article XIV(a) and that the Wire Act, the Travel Act and the Illegal Gambling Business Act, the measures at issue, were measures to protect 'public morals or public order'.[337]

The second element of the analysis under Article XIV(a) of the GATS concerns the 'necessity' requirement. As both the panel and the Appellate Body in *US – Gambling (2005)* explicitly recognised, the extensive case law on the 'necessity' requirement of Article XX(b) and (d) of the GATT 1994 – discussed at length

331 *Ibid.*, para. 6.465. 332 *Ibid.*, para. 6.466.
333 *Ibid.*, para. 6.467. 334 *Ibid.*, para. 6.468.
335 See Appellate Body Report, *US – Gambling (2005)*, paras. 296–9. The Appellate Body merely clarified the function of fn. 5 to Article XIV(a). According to the Appellate Body, this footnote does *not* require a separate and explicit finding that its standard is met. See Appellate Body Report, *US – Gambling (2005)*, para. 298.
336 See Panel Report, *US – Gambling (2005)*, para. 6.479.
337 See *ibid.*, para. 6.487. The Appellate Body upheld the panel's findings, but did not discuss them substantively. See Appellate Body Report, *US – Gambling (2005)*, para. 299.

above – is very relevant for the interpretation and application of the 'necessity' requirement of Article XIV of the GATS.[338] On appeal, the Appellate Body in *US – Gambling (2005)* thus stated that the weighing and balancing process to determine whether a measure is 'necessary' to maintain public order or protect public morals within the meaning of Article XIV(a) of the GATS begins with:

> an assessment of the 'relative importance' of the interests or values furthered by the challenged measure. Having ascertained the importance of the particular interests at stake, a panel should then turn to the other factors that are to be 'weighed and balanced'. The Appellate Body has pointed to two factors that, in most cases, will be relevant to a panel's determination of the 'necessity' of a measure, although not necessarily exhaustive of factors that might be considered. One factor is the contribution of the measure to the realization of the ends pursued by it; the other factor is the restrictive impact of the measure on international commerce.[339]

Next, having assessed each of these factors:

> [a] comparison between the challenged measure and possible alternatives should then be undertaken, and the results of such comparison should be considered in the light of the importance of the interests at issue. It is on the basis of this 'weighing and balancing' and comparison of measures, taking into account the interests or values at stake, that a panel determines whether a measure is 'necessary' or, alternatively, whether another, WTO-consistent measure is 'reasonably available'.[340]

With respect to the availability and the nature of an 'alternative measure', the Appellate Body noted:

> An alternative measure may be found not to be 'reasonably available', however, where it is merely theoretical in nature, for instance, where the responding Member is not capable of taking it, or where the measure imposes an undue burden on that Member, such as prohibitive costs or substantial technical difficulties. Moreover, a 'reasonably available' alternative measure must be a measure that would preserve for the responding Member its right to achieve its desired level of protection with respect to the objective pursued under paragraph (a) of Article XIV.[341]

As to the question of who bears the burden of proof to establish the existence of a reasonably available 'alternative measure', the Appellate Body noted that:

> it is not the responding party's burden to show, in the first instance, that there are *no* reasonably available alternatives to achieve its objectives. In particular, a responding party need not identify the universe of less trade-restrictive alternative measures and then show that none of those measures achieves the desired objective. The WTO agreements do not contemplate such an impracticable and, indeed, often impossible burden.
>
> Rather, it is for a responding party to make a *prima facie* case that its measure is 'necessary' by putting forward evidence and arguments that enable a panel to assess the challenged measure in the light of the relevant factors to be 'weighed and balanced' in a given case. The responding party may, in so doing, point out why alternative measures would not achieve the same objectives as the challenged measure, but it is under no obligation to do so in order to establish, in the first instance, that its measure is 'necessary'.

338 See above, pp. 608–14.

339 Appellate Body Report, *US – Gambling (2005)*, para. 306. 340 *Ibid.*, para. 307.

341 *Ibid.*, para. 308.

If, however, the complaining party raises a WTO-consistent alternative measure that, in its view, the responding party should have taken, the responding party will be required to demonstrate why its challenged measure nevertheless remains 'necessary' in the light of that alternative or, in other words, why the proposed alternative is not, in fact, 'reasonably available'.[342]

The panel in *US – Gambling (2005)* had concluded that the United States had not established that its measures were 'necessary' because, in rejecting Antigua's invitation to engage in bilateral or multilateral consultations, it had failed to explore and exhaust reasonably available WTO-consistent alternatives to the measures at issue.[343] According to the Appellate Body, the panel's examination of 'necessity' was flawed because it did *not* focus on an alternative measure that was reasonably available to the United States to achieve the stated objectives.[344] Engaging in consultations with Antigua was not an appropriate alternative for the panel to consider because consultations are 'by definition a process, the results of which are uncertain and therefore not capable of comparison with the measures at issue in this case'.[345]

Having reversed the panel's conclusion on 'necessity', the Appellate Body then examined for itself whether the measures at issue, the Wire Act, the Travel Act and the Illegal Gambling Business Act, were 'necessary' within the meaning of Article XIV(a) of the GATS.[346] The Appellate Body agreed with the United States that the 'sole basis' for the panel's conclusion that the measures were not necessary was its finding relating to the requirement of consultations with Antigua.[347]

As the Appellate Body had found that the panel had erred in finding that consultations with Antigua constituted a measure reasonably available to the United States,[348] and as Antigua had raised no other 'alternative measure', the Appellate Body concluded as follows:

In our opinion, therefore, the record before us reveals no reasonably available alternative measure proposed by Antigua or examined by the Panel that would establish that the three federal statutes are not 'necessary' within the meaning of Article XIV(a). Because the United States made its *prima facie* case of 'necessity', and Antigua failed to identify a reasonably available alternative measure, we conclude that the United States demonstrated that its statutes are 'necessary', and therefore justified, under paragraph (a) of Article XIV.[349]

Thus, according to the Appellate Body, the measures at issue in *US – Gambling (2005)*, which prohibit the remote supply of gambling and betting services, including Internet gambling, are 'necessary' for the maintenance of public

342 *Ibid.*, paras. 309–11.
343 See Panel Report, *US – Gambling (2005)*, para. 6.531. For a summary by the Appellate Body of the key findings of the panel, see Appellate Body Report, *US – Gambling (2005)*, para. 315.
344 See Appellate Body Report, *US – Gambling (2005)*, para. 317.
345 *Ibid.* 346 See *ibid.*, paras. 322–7.
347 The Appellate Body noted that the panel had acknowledged that it would have found that the United States had made its *prima facie* case that its measures were 'necessary' if the United States had not refused to accept Antigua's invitation to consult. See *ibid.*, para. 325.
348 See *ibid.*, para. 317. 349 *Ibid.*, para. 326.

order and the protection of public morals within the meaning of Article XIV of the GATS.

3.2.2 Article XIV(c)

As mentioned above, Article XIV(c) can justify otherwise GATS-inconsistent measures which are necessary to secure compliance with laws or regulations which are not inconsistent with the provisions of the GATS. Article XIV(c) gives three broad *examples* of such laws or regulations, namely, those relating to: (1) the prevention of deceptive and fraudulent practices or the effects of a default on services contracts; (2) the protection of the privacy of individuals in relation to the processing and dissemination of personal data and the protection of confidentiality of individual records and accounts; and (3) safety. As the panel in *US – Gambling (2005)* and in *Argentina – Financial Services (2016)* noted, this list in Article XIV(c) of possible laws and regulations is not exhaustive.[350] Article XIV(c) also covers types of 'laws or regulations' not listed. As Article XX(d) of the GATT 1994, Article XIV(c) of the GATS thus allows for the pursuit of a wide range of policy objectives not limited to the policy objectives explicitly referred to.

Referring to the Appellate Body's ruling in *Korea – Various Measures on Beef (2001)* regarding Article XX(d) of the GATT 1994, the Appellate Body ruled in *Argentina – Financial Services (2016)* that for a measure to be provisionally justified under Article XIV(c) of the GATS, two elements must be shown: (1) the measure must be one designed to secure compliance with laws or regulations that are not themselves inconsistent with the GATS; and (2) the measure must be necessary to secure such compliance.[351]

With regard to the first element of the Article XIV(c) analysis, the Appellate Body ruled in *Argentina – Financial Services (2016)*, referring to its report in *Mexico – Taxes on Soft Drinks* regarding Article XX(d), that:

> a measure can be said 'to secure compliance' with laws or regulations when its design reveals that it secures compliance with specific rules, obligations, or requirements under such laws or regulations, even if the measure cannot be guaranteed to achieve such result with absolute certainty.[352]

However, the Appellate Body further ruled that:

> where the assessment of the design of the measure, including its content and expected operation, reveals that the measure is *incapable* of securing compliance with specific rules, obligations, or requirements under the relevant law or regulation, as identified by a respondent,

350 See Panel Report, *US – Gambling (2005)*, para. 6.540; and Panel Report, *Argentina – Financial Services (2016)*, para. 7.583.

351 See Appellate Body Report, *Argentina – Financial Services (2016)*, para. 6.202, referring to Appellate Body Report, *Korea – Various Measures on Beef (2001)*, para. 157. See also Panel Report, *US – Gambling (2005)*, paras. 6.536–6.537; and Panel Report, *Argentina – Financial Services (2016)*, para. 7.593.

352 Appellate Body Report, *Argentina – Financial Services (2016)*, para. 6.203, referring to Appellate Body Report, *Mexico – Taxes on Soft Drinks*, para. 74, discussed above, pp. 564–7, in the context of concerning Article XX(d) of the GATT 1994.

further analysis with regard to whether this measure is 'necessary' to secure such compliance may not be required.[353]

As the Appellate Body explained, this is so because a measure that is not 'designed' to secure compliance with a Member's laws or regulations cannot be justified under Article XIV(c).[354] The Appellate Body cautioned, however, panels not to structure the examination of the 'design' element of the analysis under Article XIV(c) 'in such a way as to lead it to truncate its analysis prematurely and thereby foreclose consideration of crucial aspects of the respondent's defence' relating to the 'necessity' element of the analysis.[355]

With regard to the second element of the Article XIV(c) analysis, the 'necessity' requirement, the Appellate Body observed in *Argentina – Financial Services (2016)* that this element:

entails a more in-depth, holistic analysis of the relationship between the inconsistent measure and the relevant laws or regulations. In particular, this element entails an assessment of whether, in the light of all relevant factors in the 'necessity' analysis, this relationship is sufficiently proximate, such that the measure can be deemed to be 'necessary' to secure compliance with such laws or regulations.[356]

In *US – Gambling (2005)*, the Appellate Body had ruled with regard to the second element of the Article XIV(c) analysis, that:

the standard of 'necessity' provided for in the general exceptions provision is an *objective* standard. To be sure, a Member's characterization of a measure's objectives and of the effectiveness of its regulatory approach – as evidenced, for example, by texts of statutes, legislative history, and pronouncements of government agencies or officials – will be relevant in determining whether the measure is, objectively, 'necessary'. A panel is not bound by these characterizations, however, and may also find guidance in the structure and operation of the measure and in contrary evidence proffered by the complaining party. In any event, a panel must, on the basis of the evidence in the record, independently and objectively assess the 'necessity' of the measure before it.[357]

The examination required to determine whether a measure is necessary under Article XIV(c) of the GATS is essentially the same as the examination required under Article XIV(a) of the GATS or Article XX(d) of the GATT 1994, discussed above.[358] In *US – Gambling (2005)* and *Argentina – Financial Services (2016)*, the Appellate Body applied this examination of 'necessity' in the context of Article XIV(c) of the GATS. As already discussed above in the context of Article XIV(a), the Appellate Body held in *US – Gambling (2005)* held:

The process begins with an assessment of the 'relative importance' of the interests or values furthered by the challenged measure. Having ascertained the importance of the particular interests at stake, a panel should then turn to the other factors that are to be 'weighed and balanced'. The Appellate Body has pointed to two factors that, in most cases, will be relevant

353 Appellate Body Report, *Argentina – Financial Services (2016)*, para. 6.203. Emphasis added.
354 See *ibid.* 355 See *ibid.*
356 Appellate Body Report, *Argentina – Financial Services (2016)*, para. 6.204.
357 Appellate Body Report, *US – Gambling (2005)*, para. 304.
358 See above, pp. 608–12 and 564–7.

to a panel's determination of the 'necessity' of a measure, although not necessarily exhaustive of factors that might be considered. One factor is the contribution of the measure to the realization of the ends pursued by it; the other factor is the restrictive impact of the measure on international commerce.

A comparison between the challenged measure and possible alternatives should then be undertaken, and the results of such comparison should be considered in the light of the importance of the interests at issue. It is on the basis of this 'weighing and balancing' and comparison of measures, taking into account the interests or values at stake, that a panel determines whether a measure is 'necessary' or, alternatively, whether another, WTO-consistent measure is 'reasonably available'.[359]

Note that the 'weighing and balancing' exercise is not necessarily limited to the three factors referred to above.[360]

Finally, note that that the Appellate Body in *Argentina – Financial Services (2016)* ruled with regard to the relationship between the 'design' element and the 'necessity' element of the analysis under Article XIV(c) that these two elements are 'conceptually distinct, yet related, aspects' of the same inquiry. According to the Appellate Body, the examination of the two elements 'may overlap in the sense that some considerations may be relevant to both elements of the Article XIV(c) defence'.[361] The Appellate Body observed that:

[t]he way in which a panel organizes its examination of these elements in scrutinizing a defence in any given dispute will be influenced by the measures and laws or regulations at issue, as well as by the way in which the parties present their respective arguments.[362]

3.2.3 Other Paragraphs of Article XIV

With regard to the remaining paragraphs of Article XIV of the GATS, a distinction must be drawn between paragraph (b), which requires that the measure be *necessary* to achieve the policy objective pursued, and paragraphs (d) and (e), which do not impose such a 'necessity' requirement.

Paragraph (b) relates to measures 'necessary to protect human, animal or plant life or health'. Hence, for an otherwise GATS-inconsistent measure to be *provisionally* justified under Article XIV(b): (1) the policy objective pursued by the measure must be the protection of life or health of humans, animals or plants; and (2) the measure must be necessary to fulfil that policy objective. To date, there has been no case law on the requirements set out by Article XIV(b). However, as regards the 'necessity' requirement, it may be assumed that the interpretation of this requirement under Article XIV(a) and (c) of the GATS and the extensive case law on the 'necessity' requirement of Article XX(a), (b) and (d) of the GATT 1994 are relevant.[363]

359 Appellate Body Report, *US – Gambling (2005)*, paras. 306–7, referring to Appellate Body Report, *Korea – Various Measures on Beef*, paras. 162, 164 and 166, which concerned Article XX(d) of the GATT 1994.

360 See Appellate Body Report, *US – Gambling (2005)*, paras. 306–7.

361 See Appellate Body Report, *Argentina – Financial Services (2016)*, para. 6.205

362 *Ibid.* 363 See above, pp. 578–89, 557–64 and 564–7 respectively.

With regard to Article XIV(d) and (e) of the GATS, it must be noted that the scope of these provisions is rather narrow. As already discussed above, the exceptions set out in these provisions *only* justify inconsistency with the national treatment obligation of Article XVII of the GATS *or* the MFN treatment obligation of Article II of the GATS.[364] With regard to measures relating to direct taxation, Article XIV(d) of the GATS allows Members to adopt or enforce measures which are inconsistent with the national treatment obligation of Article XVII:

> provided that the difference in treatment is aimed at ensuring the equitable or effective imposition or collection of direct taxes in respect of services or service suppliers of other Members.

Footnote 6 to Article XIV(d) contains a non-exhaustive list of measures that are aimed at ensuring the equitable or effective imposition or collection of direct taxes. This list includes measures taken by a Member under its taxation system which apply: (1) to non-residents in order to ensure the imposition or collection of taxes in the Member's territory; or (2) to non-residents or residents to prevent the avoidance or evasion of taxes.

Article XIV(e) of the GATS allows a Member to adopt or enforce measures which are inconsistent with the MFN treatment obligation of Article II:

> provided that the difference in treatment is the result of an agreement on the avoidance of double taxation or provisions on the avoidance of double taxation in any other international agreement or arrangement by which the Member is bound.

Note that Article XIV of the GATS does not contain a counterpart to Article XX(g) of the GATT relating to the conservation of natural resources. In this regard, the 1993 Uruguay Round *Decision on Trade in Services and the Environment* notes that, 'since measures necessary to protect the environment typically have as their objective the protection of human, animal or plant life or health, it is not clear that there is a need to provide for more than is contained' in Article XIV(b). The Decision contemplates that the Committee on Trade and Environment should examine and report 'whether any modification of Article XIV' is required to take into account the 'relationship between services trade and the environment, including sustainable development'. No such modification of Article XIV of the GATS has occurred.

3.3 Chapeau of Article XIV of the GATS

As discussed above, Article XIV of the GATS sets out a two-tier test for determining whether a measure, otherwise inconsistent with GATS obligations, can be justified. Under this test, once it has been established that the measure at issue meets the requirements of one of the paragraphs of Article XIV, it must be examined whether the measure meets the requirements of the chapeau of Article

364 See above, p. 606.

XIV. The chapeau of Article XIV requires that the *application* of the measure at issue does not constitute: (1) 'arbitrary or unjustifiable discrimination between countries where like conditions prevail';[365] or (2) 'a disguised restriction on trade in services'.

Note that the language of the chapeau of Article XIV of the GATS is quite similar to that of the chapeau of Article XX of the GATT 1994. Therefore, many lessons can be drawn from the extensive case law on the application of the chapeau of Article XX, discussed in detail above.[366] The panel in *US – Gambling (2005)* looked at this case law and concluded:

> To sum up these interpretive principles, the chapeau of Article XX of the GATT 1994 addresses not so much a challenged measure or its specific content, but rather the manner in which that measure is applied, with a view to ensuring that the exceptions of Article XX are not abused. In order to do so, the chapeau of Article XX identifies three standards which may be invoked in relation to the same facts: arbitrary discrimination, unjustifiable discrimination and disguised restriction on trade. In our view, these principles would also be applicable in relation to Article XIV of the GATS.[367]

Moreover, the panel stated that, in determining whether the application of the measures at issue constitutes 'arbitrary and unjustifiable discrimination' or a 'disguised restriction on trade':

> the *absence of consistency* in this regard may lead to a conclusion that the measures in question are applied in a manner that constitutes 'arbitrary and unjustifiable discrimination between countries where like conditions prevail' and/or a 'disguised restriction on trade'.[368]

In the course of its examination of the requirements of the chapeau of Article XIV of the GATS, the panel found that the United States had not prosecuted certain domestic remote suppliers of gambling services and that the US Interstate Horseracing Act was 'ambiguous' as to whether or not it permitted certain types of remote betting on horse racing within the United States.[369] On the basis of these two findings indicating a lack of consistency in the application of the prohibition on the remote supply of gambling and betting services, the panel in *US – Gambling (2005)* concluded that:

> the United States has not demonstrated that it does not apply its prohibition on the remote supply of wagering services for horse racing in a manner that [constitutes] 'arbitrary and unjustifiable discrimination between countries where like conditions prevail' and/or

365 Note that the chapeau of Article XX of the GATT 1994 refers to 'arbitrary or unjustifiable discrimination between countries where the *same* conditions prevail', whereas the chapeau of Article XIV of the GATS refers to 'arbitrary or unjustifiable discrimination between countries where *like* conditions prevail'. By referring to 'like conditions', Article XIV of the GATS arguably sets out a somewhat stricter requirement than Article XX of the GATT 1994.

366 See above, pp. 592–604.

367 Panel Report, *US – Gambling (2005)*, para. 6.581. The Appellate Body confirmed the importance of Article XX of the GATT 1994 for the interpretation of Article XIV of the GATS in *US – Gambling (2005)*, as explained above.

368 Panel Report, *US – Gambling (2005)*, para. 6.584. Emphasis added.

369 On the failure to prosecute certain domestic remote suppliers of gambling services, see Panel Report, *US – Gambling (2005)*, para. 6.588. On the US Interstate Horseracing Act, see Panel Report, *US – Gambling (2005)*, para. 6.599.

a 'disguised restriction on trade' in accordance with the requirements of the chapeau of Article XIV.[370]

On appeal, the United States argued that the 'consistency' standard applied by the panel is not adequate for a complete examination under the requirements of the chapeau of Article XIV.[371] The Appellate Body, however, dismissed this argument of the United States and upheld the panel's 'consistency' standard.[372]

The panel in *Argentina – Financial Services (2016)* also found that the provisionally justified measures were applied in a manner that constituted arbitrary and unjustifiable discrimination.[373] Referring to the Appellate Body Report in *Brazil – Retreaded Tyres (2007)* regarding Article XX(b) of the GATT 1994, discussed above,[374] the panel noted that Argentina was applying the measures at issue 'in a manner that is counterproductive with regard to the objective it has itself declared' in order to provisionally justify the measures at issue.[375]

3.4 The Prudential Exception under the GATS Annex on Financial Services

In addition to the general exceptions under the GATS, as set out in Article XIV thereof, the GATS, and in particular its Annex on Financial Services, provides for a specific exception regarding measures taken for prudential reasons. Paragraph 2(a) of the Annex on Financial Services states:

> Notwithstanding any other provisions of the Agreement, a Member shall not be prevented from taking measures for prudential reasons, including for the protection of investors, depositors, policy holders or persons to whom a fiduciary duty is owed by a financial service supplier, or to ensure the integrity and stability of the financial system. Where such measures do not conform with the provisions of the Agreement, they shall not be used as a means of avoiding the Member's commitments or obligations under the Agreement.

The panel in *Argentina – Financial Services (2016)* considered that to avail itself of the prudential exception of paragraph 2(a) of the Annex on Financial Services, a Member must demonstrate that the measure at issue: (1) is a measure affecting the supply of financial services; (2) is taken for prudential reasons;

370 Panel Report, *US – Gambling (2005)*, para. 6.608.

371 According to the United States, the panel assessed only whether the United States treats domestic service suppliers differently from foreign service suppliers. The United States considered such an assessment to be inadequate, because the chapeau of Article XIV of the GATS also requires a determination of whether differential treatment, or discrimination, is 'arbitrary' or 'unjustifiable'.

372 Appellate Body Report, *US – Gambling (2005)*, paras. 348–51. Note, however, that, while the Appellate Body agreed with the panel's approach to the examination of the chapeau of Article XIV of the GATS, it eventually upheld only the panel's finding of 'inconsistency' with regard to the Interstate Horseracing Act. The Appellate Body reversed the panel's finding of 'inconsistency' based on the alleged non-prosecution of certain domestic remote suppliers of gambling services (because the three Acts at issue, on their face, do *not* discriminate between US and foreign suppliers of remote gambling services *and* the evidence of the alleged non-enforcement of the three Acts was 'inconclusive'). See Appellate Body Report, *US – Gambling (2005)*, paras. 352–7, 358–66 and 368–9.

373 See Panel Report, *Argentina – Financial Services (2016)*, para. 7.762. This finding was not appealed.

374 See above, pp. 557–64.

375 See Panel Report, *Argentina – Financial Services (2016)*, para. 7.761.

and (3) is not being used as a means of avoiding the Member's commitments or obligations under the GATS.[376]

In *Argentina – Financial Services (2016)* the question arose whether the prudential exception of paragraph 2(a) of the Annex on Financial Services covers all measures affecting trade in financial services or, as argued by Panama, only domestic regulation and, even more narrowly, only technical standards and qualification and licensing requirements. Panama based its argument in particular on the title of paragraph 2, which reads 'Domestic Regulation'. The panel disagreed with Panama and ruled that paragraph 2(a) covers all types of measures affecting the supply of financial services. The panel expressed concern with respect to the 'serious systemic implications of the narrow interpretation proposed by Panama', which 'would dramatically reduce the scope of the prudential exception', and thus 'would go against the balance of rights and obligations of the Agreement'.[377] The Appellate Body upheld the panel's ruling on the scope of the prudential exception.[378]

While the panel found that the measures at issue in *Argentina – Financial Services (2016)* fell within the scope of application of the prudential exception as measures affecting trade in financial services, the panel found that these measures were not covered by the prudential exception because they were not 'measures for prudential reasons'.[379] This finding of the panel was not appealed.

4 SECURITY EXCEPTIONS UNDER THE GATT 1994 AND THE GATS

In addition to the 'general exceptions' contained in Article XX of the GATT 1994 and Article XIV of the GATS, WTO law also provides for exceptions relating to national and international security. This section discusses, first, the security exceptions of Article XXI of the GATT 1994 and, second, the security exceptions of Article XIV *bis* of the GATS.[380]

4.1 Article XXI of the GATT 1994

Article XXI of the GATT 1994, entitled 'Security Exceptions', states:

Nothing in this Agreement shall be construed

(a) to require any [Member] to furnish any information the disclosure of which it considers contrary to its essential security interests; or

376 See Panel Report, *Argentina – Financial Services (2016)*, paras. 7.818–7.825.
377 *Ibid.*, paras. 7.847–7.849.
378 See Appellate Body Report, *Argentina – Financial Services (2016)*, paras. 6.262 and 6.272.
379 See Panel Report, *Argentina – Financial Services (2016)*, paras. 7.947–7.948. The panel therefore did not go on to address the question of whether the measures were being used as a means to avoid GATS commitments or obligations.
380 Note that also other WTO agreements, such as the *TBT Agreement*, contain provisions relating to measures taken in the context of national security policies. See e.g. Article 2.2 of the *TBT Agreement*. See below, p. 912.

(b) to prevent any [Member] from taking any action which it considers necessary for the protection of its essential security interests
 (i) relating to fissionable materials or the materials from which they are derived;
 (ii) relating to the traffic in arms, ammunition and implements of war and to such traffic in other goods and materials as is carried on directly or indirectly for the purpose of supplying a military establishment;
 (iii) taken in time of war or other emergency in international relations; or
(c) to prevent any [Member] from taking any action in pursuance of its obligations under the United Nations Charter for the maintenance of international peace and security.

Unlike Article XX, Article XXI has, to date, not played a significant role in the practice of dispute settlement under the GATT 1947 or the WTO. Article XXI has been invoked in only a few disputes.[381] Nevertheless, this provision is not without importance. WTO Members do, on occasion, take trade-restrictive measures, either unilaterally or multilaterally, against other Members as a means to achieve national or international security. Members taking such measures will seek justification for these measures under Article XXI. As will be discussed, there are significant structural and interpretative differences between Article XX and Article XXI.

4.1.1 Article XXI(a) and (b)

Traditionally, in international relations, national security takes precedence over the benefits of trade. This may be the case in three types of situation. First, States may consider it necessary to restrict trade in order to protect strategic domestic production capabilities from import competition. The judgment as to which production capabilities deserve to be qualified as strategically important differs among countries and is, to a great extent, political. Some Members argue that industries equipping the military, industries producing staple foods and industries producing gasoline or other energy productions are of 'strategic' importance. Second, States may wish to use trade sanctions, as an instrument of foreign policy, against other States, which either violate international law or pursue policies considered to be unacceptable or undesirable. Third, States may want to prohibit the export of arms or other products of military use to countries with which they do not have friendly relations. Note that GATT provisions, other than Article XXI, may allow Members leeway, for example, to preserve national industries of strategic importance. WTO Members can, subject to limitations, provide protection through import tariffs, production subsidies and government procurement practices. In some situations, however, Article XXI can be useful to provide justification for otherwise GATT-inconsistent measures.

381 Article XXI of the GATT was of relevance in *US – Export Restrictions (Czechoslovakia) (1949)*, *US – Sugar Quota (1984)*, *US – Nicaraguan Trade (1986)* and *US – Cuban Liberty and Democratic Solidarity Act (Helms–Burton Act) (1996)*. Note also that, in December 1991, the European Communities notified the GATT Contracting Parties of the measures it took in respect of Yugoslavia, and indicated that such measures were taken under Article XXI of the GATT. See Communication from the European Communities, *Trade Measures Taken by the European Communities against the Socialist Federal Republic of Yugoslavia*, GATT Document L/6948, 2 December 1991.

Article XXI(a) allows a Member to withhold information that it would normally be required to supply when 'it considers' disclosure of that information 'contrary to its essential security interests'. Some Members have interpreted this provision broadly. In this regard, note the following statement by the United States from 1949:

> The United States does consider it contrary to its security interest – and to the security interest of other friendly countries – to reveal the names of the commodities that it considers to be most strategic.[382]

Article XXI(b) allows a Member to adopt or maintain certain measures which that Member considers necessary for the protection of its essential security interests. The categories of measure concerned are broadly defined in subparagraphs (i)–(iii) of Article XXI(b) as: (1) measures relating to fissionable materials; (2) measures relating to trade in arms or in other materials, directly or indirectly, for military use; and (3) measures taken in time of war or other emergency in international relations. In view of the wording of Article XXI(b), and in particular the use of the terms 'action which it *considers* necessary' (emphasis added), the question arises whether the exceptions of this paragraph are 'justiciable', i.e. whether the application of these exceptions can usefully be reviewed by panels and the Appellate Body. Indeed, Article XXI(b) gives a Member very broad discretion to take national security measures which it 'considers necessary' for the protection of its essential security interests. However, it is imperative that a certain degree of 'judicial review' be maintained; otherwise the provision would be prone to abuse without redress.[383] At a minimum, panels and the Appellate Body should conduct an examination as to whether the explanation provided by the Member concerned is reasonable or whether the measure constitutes an apparent abuse. With regard to avoiding abuse of the exceptions listed in Article XXI(b), and more generally the exceptions listed in Article XXI as a whole, it must be noted that, unlike Article XX of the GATT 1994, Article XXI does not have a chapeau to prevent misuse or abuse of the exceptions contained therein.[384]

The exceptions of Article XXI(b) have been invoked in a few GATT disputes and have been discussed on a few other occasions before the establishment of the WTO. For instance, in one of the very first panel reports, the panel report in *US – Export Restrictions (Czechoslovakia) (1949)*, it was stated that:

> every country must be the judge in the last resort on questions relating to its own security. On the other hand, every Contracting Party should be cautious not to take any step which might have the effect of undermining the General Agreement.[385]

382 GATT/CP.3/38, 9.

383 See the panel's statement in *US – Nicaraguan Trade (1986)*, in *GATT Activities 1986*, 58–9.

384 On the function of the chapeau of Article XX of the GATT 1994, see above, pp. 592–604.

385 Panel Report, *US – Export Restrictions (Czechoslovakia) (1949)*, GATT/CP.3/SR.22, Corr.1.

In 1982, in the context of the armed conflict between the United Kingdom and Argentina over the Falkland Islands/Islas Malvinas, the European Economic Community and its Member States as well as Canada and Australia applied trade restrictions against imports from Argentina. In a 'reaction' to these actions, the GATT Contracting Parties adopted a Ministerial Declaration, which stated that:

> the contracting parties undertake, individually and jointly ... to abstain from taking restrictive trade measures, for reasons of a non-economic character, *not consistent* with the General Agreement.[386]

At the time, the GATT Contracting Parties also adopted the following *Decision Concerning Article XXI of the General Agreement*:

> *Considering* that the exceptions envisaged in Article XXI of the General Agreement constitute an important element for safeguarding the rights of contracting parties when they consider that reasons of security are involved; *Noting* that recourse to Article XXI could constitute, in certain circumstances, an element of disruption and uncertainty for international trade and affect benefits accruing to contracting parties under the General Agreement; *Recognizing* that in taking action in terms of the exceptions provided in Article XXI of the General Agreement, contracting parties should take into consideration the interests of third parties which may be affected; That until such time as the Contracting Parties may decide to make a formal interpretation of Article XXI it is appropriate to set procedural guidelines for its application;
>
> The Contracting Parties *decide* that:
>
> 1. Subject to the exception in Article XXI:a, contracting parties should be informed to the fullest extent possible of trade measures taken under Article XXI.
> 2. When action is taken under Article XXI, all contracting parties affected by such action retain their full rights under the General Agreement.
> 3. The Council may be requested to give further consideration to this matter in due course.[387]

In 1985, the United States imposed a trade embargo on Nicaragua.[388] The United States was strongly opposed to the communist Sandinistas who were in power in Nicaragua at that time. Nicaragua argued that the trade embargo imposed by the United States was inconsistent with Articles I, II, V, XI and XIII and Part IV of the GATT and could not be justified – as the United States argued – under Article XXI. Nicaragua requested the establishment of a panel. According to the United States, however, Article XXI left it to each Contracting Party to judge what action it considered necessary for the protection of its essential security interests.[389] A panel was established in this case but the terms of reference of this

386 L/5424, adopted on 29 November 1982, 29S/9, 3. Emphasis added.

387 L/5426, adopted on 2 December 1982, 29S/23.

388 Note that, in 1983, Nicaragua's share of the total US sugar import quota was already substantially reduced. The United States stated before the panel examining this reduction that 'it was neither invoking any exceptions under the provisions of the General Agreement nor intending to defend its actions in GATT terms' (see Panel Report, *US – Sugar Quota (1984)*, para. 3.10). The panel found that the United States had acted inconsistently with Article XIII of the GATT 1947. See Panel Report, *US – Sugar Quota (1984)*.

389 See *Analytical Index: Guide to GATT Law and Practice* (WTO, 1995), 601, 603 and 604.

panel stated that the panel could not examine or judge the validity or motivation for the invocation of Article XXI by the United States. In its report, the panel therefore concluded that:

> as it was not authorized to examine the justification for the United States' invocation of [Article XXI], it could find the United States neither to be complying with its obligations under the General Agreement nor to be failing to carry out its obligations under that Agreement.[390]

To date, the exceptions of Article XXI have not been invoked in any case before a WTO panel or the Appellate Body. Note, however, that, in the *US – Cuban Liberty and Democratic Solidarity Act* dispute in 1996 between the European Communities and the United States, commonly referred to as *US – Helms–Burton Act* dispute, the United States informed the WTO that it would not participate in the panel proceedings since it was of the opinion that the Helms–Burton Act was not within the scope of application of WTO law and, therefore, not within the jurisdiction of the panel. The Helms–Burton Act permits US nationals to bring legal action in US courts against foreign companies that deal or traffic in US property confiscated by the Cuban government. The European Communities contended that this and other measures provided for under the Helms–Burton Act were inconsistent with the obligations of the United States under Articles I, III, V, XI and XIII of the GATT 1994.[391] According to the United States, however, this dispute concerned diplomatic and *security issues* and 'was not fundamentally a trade matter' and, therefore, not a WTO matter.[392] Few Members shared this opinion.[393]

Note that in 2015, the Russian Federation, referring to the 1982 *Decision Concerning Article XXI of the General Agreement*, quoted above, requested that WTO Members engage in negotiations on the scope of the rights and obligations under Article XXI of the GATT 1994 and Article XIV *bis* of the GATS, and adopt by June 2016 a General Council decision on the interpretation of these provisions. The WTO Members did not engage in negotiations on this issue.

4.1.2 Article XXI(c)

Article XXI(c) of the GATT 1994 allows WTO Members to take actions in pursuance of their obligations under the United Nations Charter for the maintenance of international peace and security. This means that Members may depart from their GATT obligations in order to implement economic sanctions imposed by

390 Panel Report, *US – Nicaraguan Trade (1986)*, L/6053, dated 13 October 1986, para. 5.3. This report was never adopted.

391 See Request for Consultations, *US – The Cuban Liberty and Democratic Solidarity Act (Helms–Burton Act)*, WT/DS38/1, dated 13 May 1996.

392 WT/DSB/M/24, dated 16 October 1996, 7. At the request of the European Communities, the panel proceedings were suspended to allow for further negotiations to reach a mutually agreed solution to this dispute. No such solution has ever been explicitly agreed on but the United States has never applied the most controversial aspects of the Helms–Burton Act.

393 See WT/DSB/M/24, dated 16 October 1996, 8–9. On the Helms–Burton Act dispute, see also above, p. 619.

the United Nations. Article 41 of the *UN Charter* empowers the Security Council to impose economic sanctions, once it has determined the existence of any threat to the peace, breach of the peace or act of aggression. Such Security Council decisions to apply economic sanctions are binding on UN Members according to Article 25 of the *UN Charter*. Hence, Article XXI(c) enables WTO Members to honour their commitments under the *UN Charter*.[394]

At first glance, the issue of 'justiciability', discussed above with regard to Article XXI(b), appears less problematic for the exception provided in Article XXI(c), given that this provision does not refer to what the Member invoking the exception 'considers' to be necessary. The basis for the departure from GATT obligations must be an obligation under the UN Charter, and a panel can assess the question of whether there is such an obligation.

4.2 Article XIV *bis* of the GATS

Article XIV *bis* of the GATS, entitled 'Security Exceptions', allows Members to adopt and enforce measures, in the interest of national or international security, otherwise inconsistent with GATS obligations. The language of this provision is virtually identical to Article XXI of the GATT 1994.[395] Like Article XXI of the GATT 1994, Article XIV *bis* of the GATS is not without importance. On occasion, WTO Members take unilateral or multilateral measures affecting the trade in services of other Members, as a means to achieve national or international security. Members taking such measures can seek justification for these measures under Article XIV *bis*. To date, Article XIV *bis* of the GATS has never been invoked in dispute settlement proceedings. However, in terms of 'justiciability' Article XIV *bis*, and in particular paragraph 2 thereof, is likely to be as problematic as Article XXI(b), discussed above.[396]

5 SUMMARY

Trade liberalisation, market access and non-discrimination rules may conflict with other important societal values and interests, such as the promotion and protection of public health, consumer safety, the environment, employment, economic development and national security. WTO law provides for rules to

394 Article XXI(c) of the GATT 1994 gives effect to the rule of conflict contained in Article 103 of the *UN Charter*, pursuant to which in the event of a conflict between obligations under the *UN Charter* and obligations under any other international agreement, the obligations under the *UN Charter* shall prevail.

395 Note that the second paragraph of Article XIV *bis* of the GATS provides for a requirement to inform the Council for Trade in Services, to the fullest extent possible, of measures taken under paragraphs 1(b) and (c) of Article XIV *bis*. Article XIV *bis*: 2 of the GATS reflects the *Decision Concerning Article XXI of the General Agreement* of the GATT Contracting Parties of 2 December 1982.

396 See above, pp. 620–2.

reconcile trade liberalisation, market access and non-discrimination rules, on the one hand, with these other important societal values and interests, on the other hand. These rules can take the form of wide-ranging *exceptions*, allowing Members, under specific conditions, to adopt or maintain legislation or other measures that protect other important societal values and interests, even though this legislation or these measures are in conflict with substantive disciplines imposed by the GATT 1994 or the GATS. These exceptions clearly allow Members, under specific conditions, to give *priority* to certain societal values and interests *over* trade liberalisation, market access and/or non-discrimination. This chapter discusses the 'general exceptions' and the 'security exceptions' under the GATT 1994 and the GATS.

The most widely available of the exceptions 'reconciling' trade liberalisation, market access and non-discrimination rules with other societal values and interests are the 'general exceptions' of Article XX of the GATT 1994 and Article XIV of the GATS.

Article XX of the GATT 1994 and Article XIV of the GATS allow, under specific conditions, for deviation from any GATT 1994 or GATS obligation, be it the MFN treatment, national treatment, market access or any other obligation under the GATT 1994 or GATS. Neither Article XX of the GATT 1994 nor Article XIV of the GATS are available to justify inconsistencies with any other WTO agreement unless they has been expressly or implicitly incorporated into such agreement. The *Agreement on Trade Related Investment Measures* is the only other WTO agreement, which expressly incorporates Article XX of the GATT 1994. Article XX can thus be invoked to justify inconsistencies with this Agreement. Certain provisions of China's Accession Protocol implicitly incorporate Article XX of the GATT 1994 and Article XX can therefore be invoked by China to justify a breach of the obligations under these provisions.

Article XX of the GATT 1994 and Article XIV of the GATS are in essence *balancing* provisions. Central to the interpretation and application of both provisions is the balance to be struck between trade liberalisation on the one hand and other societal values and interests on the other. Therefore, a narrow interpretation of these provisions is as inappropriate as a broad interpretation.

The Appellate Body has yet to rule on whether measures that aim to protect a societal value or interest *outside* the territorial jurisdiction of the Member taking the measure, can be justified under Article XX of the GATT 1994 or Article XIV GATS. There is no *explicit* jurisdictional limitation in Article XX or Article XIV, but it is an open question whether such a jurisdictional limitation can be implied.

In determining whether a measure which is otherwise GATT-inconsistent can be justified under Article XX of the GATT 1994, one must always examine: first, whether this measure can be *provisionally* justified under one of the paragraphs of Article XX; and, if so, second, whether the application of this measure meets the requirements of the chapeau of Article XX.

Article XX(b) concerns otherwise GATT-inconsistent measures allegedly adopted or maintained for the protection of public health or the environment. For such a measure to be provisionally justified under Article XX(b), a Member must establish that: (1) the measure is *designed* to protect the life or health of humans, animals or plants; and (2) the measure is *necessary* to fulfil that policy objective. In deciding whether a measure is necessary, the following factors must be 'weighed and balanced': (a) the *importance* of the societal value or interest at stake; (b) the *extent* to which the measure at issue contributes to the objective it pursues; and (c) the *impact* of the measure at issue on trade, i.e. its trade-restrictiveness. It is clear that the more important the societal value pursued by the measure at issue, the more this measure contributes to the protection or promotion of this value, and the less restrictive its impact is on international trade, the more easily the measure may be considered to be 'necessary'. If this 'weighing and balancing' exercise yields a preliminary conclusion that the measure is necessary, this result must be confirmed by comparing the measure at issue with possible alternative measures, which may be WTO-consistent or less trade-restrictive but provide an equivalent contribution to the achievement of the measure's objective. A measure can only be considered 'necessary' if there is no reasonably available alternative measure that achieves the policy objective of, and is WTO-consistent or less trade-restrictive than, the measure at issue. In most cases a comparison between the challenged measure and possible alternatives will have to be undertaken. A comparison with alternative measures would only not be required if, for example, the measure at issue is not trade-restrictive or makes no contribution to the objective pursued.

Article XX(d) concerns otherwise GATT-inconsistent measures allegedly adopted or maintained to secure compliance with national legislation. For such a measure to be provisionally justified under Article XX(d), a Member must establish that: (1) the measure is *designed* to secure compliance with national laws or regulations such as customs law, consumer protection law or intellectual property law, which are themselves not GATT-inconsistent; and (2) the measure must be *necessary* to secure such compliance. The 'design' requirement is not very demanding and has been found to be met when the measure at issue is not incapable of securing compliance. The 'necessity' requirement in Article XX(d) is interpreted and applied in the same way as in Article XX(b).

Article XX(g) concerns otherwise GATT-inconsistent measures allegedly adopted or maintained for the conservation of exhaustible natural resources. For such a measure to be provisionally justified under Article XX(g): (1) the measure must relate to the '*conservation of exhaustible natural resources*'; (2) the measure must '*relate to*' the conservation of exhaustible natural resources; and (3) the measure must be '*made effective in conjunction with*' restrictions on domestic production or consumption. The concept of 'exhaustible natural resources' has been interpreted in a broad, evolutionary manner to include also living resources and, in particular, endangered species. A measure 'relates to' the conservation of exhaustible natural resources when the relationship between the means, i.e. the measure, and the end, i.e. the conservation of exhaustible resources, is real and close, and the measure is not disproportionately wide in its scope or reach in relation to the policy objective pursued. Finally, the requirement that the measure must be 'made effective in conjunction with restrictions on domestic production or consumption' is, in essence, a requirement of 'even-handedness' in the imposition of restrictions on imported and domestic products.

Article XX(a) concerns otherwise GATT-inconsistent measures allegedly adopted or maintained to protect public morals. For such a measure to be provisionally justified under Article XX(a), a Member must establish that: (1) the measure is 'designed' to protect public morals; and (2) the measure is 'necessary' to protect such public morals. The concept of 'public morals' has been defined as 'standards of right and wrong conduct maintained by or on behalf of a community or nation'. The 'design' requirement is not very demanding and has been found to be met when the measure at issue is not incapable of protecting public morals. The 'necessity' requirement in Article XX(a) is interpreted and applied in the same way as in Article XX(b).

Article XX(j) of the GATT 1994 concerns otherwise GATT-inconsistent measures that are allegedly 'essential to the acquisition or distribution of products in general or local short supply'. For such a measure to be provisionally justified under Article XX(j), a Member must establish that: (1) the measure is 'designed' to address the acquisition or distribution of products in general or local short supply; and (2) the measure is 'essential' to address the acquisition or distribution of such products. To determine whether a product is in 'general or local short supply', a panel should examine the extent to which a particular product is 'available', from both domestic and international sources, in a particular geographical area or market, and whether this is sufficient to meet demand in the relevant area or market. With regard to the requirement that the measure at issue is 'essential' (rather than 'necessary', i.e. the requirement in Articles XX(a), (b) and (d)), the Appellate Body noted that the word 'essential' is defined as '[a]bsolutely indispensable or necessary' and is therefore at least as close to 'indispensable' as the term 'necessary'.

Measures provisionally justified under one of the paragraphs of Article XX must subsequently meet the requirements of the chapeau of Article XX. The object and purpose of the chapeau is to avoid the *application* of the measures provisionally justified to constitute a misuse or abuse of the exceptions of Article XX. The interpretation and application of the chapeau in a particular case is a search for the appropriate *line of equilibrium* between, on the one hand, the right of Members to adopt and maintain trade-restrictive measures that pursue certain legitimate policy objectives, and, on the other hand, the right of other Members to trade. The search for this line of equilibrium is guided by the requirements set out in the chapeau that the *application* of the trade-restrictive measure may not constitute: (1) *arbitrary* or *unjustifiable discrimination* between countries where the same conditions prevail; or (2) a *disguised restriction* on international trade.

Discrimination has been found to be 'arbitrary' when a measure is applied without any regard for the difference in conditions between countries and the measure is applied in a rigid and inflexible manner. Discrimination has been found to be 'unjustifiable' when the discrimination 'was not merely inadvertent or unavoidable'. Unjustifiable discrimination exists when a Member fails to make serious, good faith efforts to negotiate a multilateral solution before resorting to the unilateral, otherwise GATT-inconsistent measure for which justification is sought. Moreover, discrimination is arbitrary or unjustifiable when the reasons given for the discrimination bear no rational connection to the policy objective of the provisional measure or would go against that objective. A measure, which is provisionally justified under Article XX, will be considered to constitute a 'disguised restriction on international trade' if compliance with such measure is in fact only a disguise to conceal the pursuit of trade-restrictive objectives.

The Appellate Body has repeatedly emphasised that WTO Members are free to adopt their own policies and measures aimed at protecting or promoting other societal values, such as public health or the environment, as long as, in so doing, they fulfil their obligations, and respect the rights of other Members, under the *WTO Agreement*.

As is the case for Article XX of the GATT 1994, Article XIV of the GATS sets out a two-tier test for determining whether a measure affecting trade in services, otherwise inconsistent with GATS obligations and commitments, can be justified under that provision. To determine whether a measure can be justified under Article XIV of the GATS, one must always examine: first, whether this measure can be provisionally justified under one of the paragraphs of Article XIV; and, if so, second, whether the application of this measure meets the requirements of the chapeau of Article XIV. The similarities between Article XX of the GATT 1994 and Article XIV of the GATS are striking. However, there are also differences. The specific grounds of justification for measures which are otherwise inconsistent with provisions of the GATS are set out in Article XIV(a)–(e) of the GATS. In the case law to date, there has been particular attention given to Article XIV(a) and (c) of the GATS.

Article XIV(a) concerns otherwise GATS-inconsistent measures that are 'necessary to protect public morals or to maintain public order'. To provisionally justify a measure under Article XIV(a) of the GATS, a Member must establish that: (1) the measure is 'designed' to protect public morals or maintain public order; and (2) the measure is *necessary* to protect public morals or maintain public order. The concept of 'public morals' has been defined as stated above. The concept of 'public order' has been defined as 'the preservation of the fundamental interests of a society, as reflected in public policy and law'. The 'necessity' requirement in Article XIV(a) of the GATS is, *mutatis mutandis*, interpreted and applied in the same way as in Articles XX(a), (b) and (d) of the GATT 1994.

Article XIV(c) concerns otherwise GATS-inconsistent measures allegedly adopted or maintained to secure compliance with national laws or regulations. For such a measure to be provisionally justified under Article XIV(c) of the GATS, a Member must establish that: (1) the measure is *designed* to secure compliance with national laws or regulations which are themselves not GATS-inconsistent; and (2) the measure is *necessary* to secure such compliance. The 'design' requirement is not very demanding and has been found to be met when the measure at issue is not incapable of securing compliance. The 'necessity' requirement in Article XIV(c) is interpreted and applied in the same way as in Article XIV(a) of the GATS.

Just as with the chapeau of Article XX of the GATT 1994, the chapeau of Article XIV of the GATS requires that the *application* of the measure at issue does not constitute: (1) a means of *arbitrary or unjustifiable discrimination* between countries where the same conditions prevail; or (2) a *disguised restriction* on trade in services.

In addition to the 'general exceptions' contained in Article XX of the GATT 1994 and Article XIV of the GATS, the GATT 1994 and the GATS provide for exceptions relating to national and international security. WTO Members take, on occasion, either unilaterally or multilaterally, trade-restrictive measures against other Members as a means to achieve national or international security. Members taking such measures may seek justification for these measures under Article XXI of the GATT 1994 or Article XIV *bis* of the GATS. Article XXI(b) of the GATT 1994 allows a Member to adopt or maintain: (1) measures relating to fissionable materials; (2) measures relating to trade in arms or in other materials, directly or indirectly, for military use; and (3) measures taken in time of war or other emergency in international relations. A Member may take such measures if and when that Member *considers* these measures to be necessary for the protection of its essential security interests. Article XIV *bis* of the GATS is virtually identical to Article XXI(b) of the GATT 1994. The 'justiciability' of these exceptions is not clear. Article XXI(c) of the GATT 1994 and Article XIV *bis* (c) of the GATS are much less problematic in this respect as they allow WTO Members to take trade and economic sanctions in compliance with UN Security Council decisions related to the maintenance of international peace and security.

FURTHER READINGS

R. Howse, 'The World Trade Organization 20 Years on: Global Governance by Judiciary', *European Journal of International Law*, 2016, 27(1), 1–77.

J. Y. Yoo and D. Ahn, 'Security Exceptions in the WTO System: Bridge or Bottle-Neck for Trade and Security', *Journal of International Economic Law*, 2016, 0, 1–28.

G. M. Durán, 'Measures with Multiple Competing Purposes after EC – Seal Products: Avoiding a Conflict between GATT Article XX-Chapeau and Article 2.1 TBT Agreement', *Journal of International Economic Law*, 2016, 0, 1–29.

A. Herwig, 'Too much Zeal on Seals? Animal Welfare, Public Morals, and Consumer Ethics at the Bar of the WTO', *World Trade Review*, 2016, 15(1), 109–37.

P. Conconi and T. Voon, '*EC – Seal Products*: The Tension between Public Morals and International Trade Agreements', *World Trade Review*, 2016, 15, 211–34.

L. Bartels, 'The Chapeau of the General Exceptions in the WTO GATT and GATS Agreements: A Reconstruction', *American Journal of International Law*, 2015, 109, 95–125.

H. Andersen, 'Protection of Non-Trade Values in WTO Appellate Body Jurisprudence: Exceptions, Economic Arguments, and Eluding Questions', *Journal of International Economic Law*, 2015, 18, 383–405.

F. Sucker and G. Moon, 'The Case for a Public Interest Clause as a General Exception in Trade Agreements', UNSW Law Research Paper No. 201524, May 2015, available at SSRN http://dx.doi.org/10.2139/ssrn.2612292.

S. Peng, 'Cybersecurity Threats and the WTO National Security Exceptions', *Journal of International Economic Law*, 2015, 18, 449–78.

B. Gavin, 'Sustainable Development of China's Rare Earth Industry within and without the WTO', *Journal of World Trade*, 2015, 49(3), 495–515.

R. J. Neuwirth and A. Svetlicinii, 'The Economic Sanctions over the Ukraine Conflict and the WTO: "Catch-XXI" and the Revival of the Debate on Security Exceptions', *Journal of World Trade*, 2015, 49(5), 891–914.

G. Muller, 'The Necessity Test and Trade in Services: Unfinished Business?', *Journal of World Trade*, 2015, 49(6), 951–73.

B. Leycegui and I. Ramírez, 'Addressing Climate Change: A WTO Exception to Incorporate Climate Clubs', E15 Initiative, International Centre for Trade and Sustainable Development and World Economic Forum, May 2015.

C. M. Cantore, '"Shelter from the Storm": Exploring the Scope of Application and Legal Function of the GATS Prudential Carve-Out', *Journal of World Trade*, 2014, 48(6), 1223–46.

M. Chi, '"Exhaustible Natural Resource" in WTO Law: GATT Article XX(g) Disputes and Their Implications', *Journal of World Trade*, 2014, 48(5), 939–66.

K. Sykes, 'Sealing Animal Welfare into the GATT Exceptions: The International Dimension of Animal Welfare in WTO Disputes', *World Trade Review*, July 2014, 13(3), 471–98.

G. Marceau and J. Wyatt, 'The WTO's Efforts to Balance Economic Development and Environmental Protection: A Short Review of Appellate Body Jurisprudence', *Latin American Journal of International Trade Law*, 2013, 1(1), 291–314.

J. Pauwelyn, 'Carbon Leakage Measures and Border Tax Adjustments under WTO Law', in G. V. Calster and D. Prévost (eds.), *Research Handbook on Environment, Health and the WTO* (Edward Elgar, 2013), 448–506.

P. Conconi and J. Pauwelyn, 'Trading Cultures: Appellate Body Report on China – Audiovisuals (WT/DS363/AB/R, adopted 19 January 2010)', *World Trade Review*, 2011, 10, 95–118.

Economic Emergency Exceptions

CONTENTS

1 INTRODUCTION

As mentioned in Chapter 8, apart from the 'general exceptions' and the 'security exceptions', discussed in that chapter, WTO law also provides for 'economic emergency exceptions'. These exceptions allow Members to adopt two types of measures, otherwise WTO-inconsistent, namely, 'safeguard measures' and 'balance-of-payments measures'. This chapter deals in turn with: (1) safeguard measures under the GATT 1994 and the *Agreement on Safeguards*; (2) safeguard measures under other WTO agreements; and (3) balance-of-payments measures under the GATT 1994 and the GATS.

2 SAFEGUARD MEASURES UNDER THE GATT 1994 AND THE *AGREEMENT ON SAFEGUARDS*

The most important and most frequently used of the measures discussed in this chapter are the safeguard measures under the GATT 1994 and the *Agreement on Safeguards*. These safeguard measures may be adopted where a surge in imports causes, or threatens to cause, serious injury to the domestic industry. The possibility to restrict trade in such situations is a 'safety valve' which has always been, and still is, provided for in most trade agreements, including the *WTO Agreement*. It reflects the political reality that trade liberalisation may be difficult to sustain if and when it creates unexpected and severe economic hardship for certain sectors of a country's economy, especially import-competing industries. Safeguard measures temporarily restrict import competition to allow the domestic industry time to adjust to new economic realities. Their application does not depend upon 'unfair' trade actions, as is the case with anti-dumping or countervailing measures.[1] Safeguard measures are applied to 'fair trade', that is, trade occurring under normal competitive conditions and in accordance with WTO law. The Appellate Body therefore noted in *Argentina – Footwear (EC) (2000)* that:

> the import restrictions that are imposed on products of exporting Members when a safeguard action is taken must be seen ... as *extraordinary*. And, when construing the prerequisites for taking such actions, their extraordinary nature must be taken into account.[2]

In *US – Line Pipe (2002)*, the Appellate Body stated that 'part of the *raison d'être*' of safeguard measures is:

> unquestionably, that of giving a WTO Member the possibility, as trade is liberalized, of resorting to an effective remedy in an extraordinary emergency situation that, in the judgment of that Member, makes it necessary to protect a domestic industry temporarily.[3]

The Appellate Body further stated that there is:

> a natural tension between, on the one hand, defining the appropriate and legitimate scope of the right to apply safeguard measures and, on the other hand, ensuring that safeguard measures are not applied against 'fair trade' beyond what is necessary to provide extraordinary and temporary relief. A WTO Member seeking to apply a safeguard measure will argue, correctly, that the *right* to apply such measures must be respected in order to maintain the *domestic* momentum and motivation for ongoing trade liberalization. In turn, a

1 See below, pp. 696–767 and 769–881.
2 Appellate Body Report, *Argentina – Footwear (EC) (2000)*, para. 94. Emphasis added.
3 Appellate Body Report, *US – Line Pipe (2002)*, para. 82.

WTO Member whose trade is affected by a safeguard measure will argue, correctly, that the *application* of such measures must be limited in order to maintain the *multilateral* integrity of ongoing trade concessions. The balance struck by the WTO Members in reconciling this natural tension relating to safeguard measures is found in the provisions of the *Agreement on Safeguards*.[4]

Article XIX of the GATT 1994 and the provisions of the *Agreement on Safeguards* set out the rules according to which Members may take safeguard measures. Article XIX of the GATT 1994, entitled 'Emergency Action on Imports of Particular Products', provides, in paragraph 1(a):

> If, as a result of unforeseen developments and of the effect of the obligations incurred by a [Member] under this Agreement, including tariff concessions, any product is being imported into the territory of that [Member] in such increased quantities and under such conditions as to cause or threaten serious injury to domestic producers in that territory of like or directly competitive products, the [Member] shall be free ... to suspend the obligation in whole or in part or to withdraw or modify the concession.

Under Article XIX of the GATT 1947, which was, in all respects, identical to Article XIX of the GATT 1994, some 150 safeguard measures were officially notified to the Contracting Parties. However, Contracting Parties often resorted to measures other than safeguard measures to address situations in which imports caused particular economic hardship. These 'other' measures included voluntary export restraints (VERs), voluntary restraint arrangements (VRAs) and orderly marketing arrangements (OMAs), as discussed above.[5] Unlike safeguard measures, these other measures did not involve compensation, and were applied selectively to the main exporting countries.[6] This explained the 'popularity' of VERs, VRAs and OMAs. The *Agreement on Safeguards* was negotiated during the Uruguay Round because of the need to clarify and reinforce the disciplines of Article XIX of the GATT, re-establish multilateral control over safeguard measures and eliminate measures, such as VERs, VRAs and OMAs, that escaped such control. The *Agreement on Safeguards* now prohibits these 'other' measures and requires that all safeguard measures comply with Article XIX of the GATT 1994 and the detailed disciplines of the *Agreement on Safeguards* discussed below.

The *Agreement on Safeguards*, which is part of Annex 1A to the *WTO Agreement*, confirms and clarifies the provisions of Article XIX of the GATT 1994 but also provides for new rules. The *Agreement on Safeguards* sets out: (1) the substantive requirements that must be met in order to apply a safeguard measure (Articles 2 and 4); (2) the (national and international) procedural requirements that must be met by a Member applying a safeguard measure (Articles 3 and 12); and (3) the characteristics of, and conditions relating to, a safeguard measure (Articles 5 to 9).

4 *Ibid.*, para. 83. 5 See above, pp. 491–2.

6 For a discussion on the requirement of compensation and the difficulty of applying safeguard measures selectively, see below, pp. 649–51 and 847–8.

On the relationship between the provisions of the *Agreement on Safeguards* and Article XIX of the GATT 1994, the Appellate Body in *Korea – Dairy (2000)* ruled, on the basis of Articles 1 and 11.1(a) of the *Agreement on Safeguards*, that:

> any safeguard measure imposed after the entry into force of the *WTO Agreement* must comply with the provisions of *both* the *Agreement on Safeguards* and Article XIX of the GATT 1994.[7]

As the Appellate Body noted in *Argentina – Footwear (EC) (2000)*, nothing in the *WTO Agreement* suggests the intention by the Uruguay Round negotiators to subsume the requirements of Article XIX of the GATT 1994 *within* the *Agreement on Safeguards* and thus to render those requirements no longer applicable.[8] As discussed below, this is of particular importance for the requirement that the surge in imports be the result of 'unforeseen developments'.[9] This requirement is included in Article XIX of the GATT 1994 but not in the more detailed *Agreement on Safeguards*. Nevertheless, this requirement is in the Appellate Body's view fully applicable. Article XIX of the GATT 1994 and the *Agreement on Safeguards* apply *cumulatively*.[10]

Since the establishment of the WTO in 1995 until end of December 2015, 311 initiations of safeguard measure investigations were reported to the WTO. Approximately half of these investigations resulted in the actual imposition of safeguard measures. India has been the most frequent user of safeguard measures with a total of forty-one reported initiations since 1995. Indonesia follows with twenty-seven initiations, and then Turkey with twenty-one initiations. The United States has also been a significant user, with ten initiations since 1995.[11] Moreover, the 2002 US safeguard measures on steel were some of the largest ever imposed in terms of magnitude.[12] In contrast, the European Union has initiated only five investigations since 1995, thus appearing to avoid using safeguard measures if possible. Since the WTO's establishment, an average of approximately fifteen safeguard measure investigations have been initiated per year up to end of December 2015. New initiations peaked at thirty-three in 2002, with ten initiations in 2008, twenty-five initiations in 2009, twenty-four initiations in 2012, and seventeen initiations in 2015.[13]

7 Appellate Body Report, *Korea – Dairy (2000)*, para. 77.

8 See Appellate Body Report, *Argentina – Footwear (EC) (2000)*, para. 83. The Appellate Body therefore rejected the panel's finding that those requirements of Article XIX of the GATT 1994 which are not reflected in the *Agreement on Safeguards* were superseded by the requirements of the latter.

9 See below, pp. 638–9.

10 Note, however, that this does not prevent a panel or the Appellate Body from exercising judicial economy with respect to a claim of violation of Article XIX where it has found that the measure at issue is inconsistent with the *Agreement on Safeguards*. On the exercise of judicial economy, see above, pp. 225–8.

11 This number is based on the notifications of WTO Members under Article 12.1 of the *Agreement on Safeguards* from 1 January 1995 to 31 December 2015. See www.wto.org/english/tratop_e/safeg_e/SG-InitiationsByRepMember.pdf.

12 On 5 March 2002, the United States imposed safeguard measures on imports of a range of steel products in the form of additional duties ranging from 8, 13, 15 and up to 30 per cent as well as a tariff quota for a three-year period beginning on 20 March 2002.

13 See www.wto.org/english/tratop_e/safeg_e/SG-InitiationsByRepMember.pdf.

To date, 155 final safeguard measures have been imposed by Members.[14] The number of disputes relating to safeguard measures is not insignificant but overall still fairly moderate. To date, there have been forty-eight disputes relating to Article XIX of the GATT and the *Agreement on Safeguards*.[15] In ten of these disputes, panel proceedings were initiated and six of the resulting panel reports were subject to appellate review.[16] Issues related to specific safeguard mechanisms have also arisen in a few disputes related to safeguard mechanisms under the *Agreement on Textiles and Clothing*,[17] the *Agreement on Agriculture*,[18] and China's Protocol of Accession.[19]

To date, WTO Members have been found to have acted inconsistently with Article XIX of the GATT 1994 and/or the *Agreement on Safeguards* in ten disputes.[20]

2.1 Requirements for the Use of Safeguard Measures

Article 2.1 of the *Agreement on Safeguards* provides:

> A Member may apply a safeguard measure to a product only if that Member has determined, pursuant to the provisions set out below, that such product is being imported into its territory in such increased quantities, absolute or relative to domestic production, and under such conditions as to cause or threaten to cause serious injury to the domestic industry that produces like or directly competitive products.

Article XIX:1(a) of the GATT 1994, which – as explained above – applies together with the *Agreement on Safeguards*, provides for the same requirements for the application of safeguard measures as Article 2.1, but, in addition, requires – in its first clause – that the increase in imports occurs:

> as a result of unforeseen developments and of the effect of the obligations incurred by a [Member] under this Agreement ...

14 This number is based on the notifications of WTO Members under Article 12.1 of the *Agreement on Safeguards* from 1 January 1995 to 31 December 2015. See www.wto.org/english/tratop_e/safeg_e/SG-MeasuresByRepMember.pdf.

15 By October 2015, there had been forty-eight complaints under the *Agreement on Safeguards*. See http://worldtradelaw.net/databases/searchcomplaints.php.

16 See http://worldtradelaw.net/databases/wtopanels.php and http://worldtradelaw.net/databases/abreports.php. The latest panel report was Panel Report, *Ukraine – Passenger Cars (2015)*, which was not appealed. The Appellate Body Reports were Appellate Body Reports in *Korea – Dairy (2000)*; *Argentina – Footwear (EC) (2000)*; *US – Wheat Gluten (2001)*; *US – Lamb (2001)*; *US – Line Pipe (2002)*; and *US – Steel Safeguards (2003)*.

17 See Appellate Body Reports in *US – Underwear (1997)*; *US – Wool Shirts and Blouses (1997)*; and *US – Cotton Yarn (2001)*.

18 See Appellate Body Reports in *EC – Poultry (1998)*; *Chile – Price Band System (2002)*; *Chile – Price Band System (Article 21.5 – Argentina) (2007)*; and *Peru – Agricultural Products (2015)*.

19 For example, the dispute concerning a product-specific safeguard measure on *Certain Passenger Vehicle and Light Truck Tires from China* under Section 16 of the Protocol on the Accession of the People's Republic of China to the WTO (WT/L/432). Both the panel and the Appellate Body found the safeguard measures at issue to be consistent with Section 16 of China's Protocol of Accession.

20 These include: *Argentina – Footwear (EC) (2000)*; *Korea – Dairy (2000)*; *US – Wheat Gluten (2001)*; *US – Lamb (2001)*; *US – Line Pipe (2002)*; *Argentina – Preserved Peaches (2003)*; *US – Steel Safeguards (2003)*; *Dominican Republic – Safeguard Measures (2012)*; and *Ukraine – Passenger Cars (2015)*. In *Chile – Price Band System (2002)* and *Peru – Agricultural Products (2015)*, inconsistency with the *Agreement on Agriculture* was found; *China – Tyres (2011)* involved transitional safeguards under China's Protocol of Accession, but no finding of inconsistency was made.

In short, Members may apply safeguard measures only when three requirements are met. These requirements are: (1) the 'increased imports' requirement (including the 'unforeseen developments' requirement); (2) the 'serious injury' requirement; and (3) the 'causation' requirement. This section examines each of these requirements in turn.

2.1.1 'Increased Imports' Requirement

Article 2.1 of the *Agreement on Safeguards* explicitly states that the increase in imports can be: (1) an *absolute* increase (i.e. an increase by tonnes or units of the imported products) *or* (2) a *relative* increase (i.e. an increase of imports relative to domestic production, for example even if imports and domestic production decreased, imports decreased less than domestic production).[21] This, however, leaves unanswered the question as to how much, and over what time span, imports must have increased. In *Argentina – Footwear (EC) (2000)*, the Appellate Body clarified the 'increased imports' requirement as:

> [T]he increase in imports must have been recent enough, sudden enough, sharp enough, and significant enough, both quantitatively and qualitatively, to cause or threaten to cause 'serious injury'.[22]

In *US – Steel Safeguards (2003)*, the Appellate Body reaffirmed these parameters for the interpretation of the 'increased imports' requirement. According to the Appellate Body, the 'increased imports' requirement demands the presence of the following four elements: (1) recent increase; (2) sudden increase; (3) sharp increase; and (4) significant increase. However, the Appellate Body also held that there is no absolute standard as to *how* sudden, recent and significant the increase in imports must be.[23] Thus this test requires a *concrete* evaluation on a case-by-case basis.[24] The result of the test does not depend on the proof of the mere existence of the conditions, but on the extent and intensity of their manifestations.[25] That is why the Appellate Body held in *US – Steel Safeguards (2003)* that a demonstration of '*any* increase' in imports is not sufficient to establish 'increased imports' under the *Agreement on Safeguards*.[26] According to the Appellate Body:

> [t]he question whether 'such increased quantities' of imports will suffice as 'increased imports' to justify the application of a safeguard measure is a question that can be answered only in the light of 'such conditions' under which those imports occur. The relevant importance of these elements varies from case to case.[27]

If the increase in imports is not recent, sudden and sharp, there will be no economic *emergency* situation justifying the application of a safeguard measure.

21 See Appellate Body Report, *US – Steel Safeguards (2003)*, para. 390.
22 Appellate Body Report, *Argentina – Footwear (EC) (2000)*, para. 131.
23 See Appellate Body Report, *US – Steel Safeguards (2003)*, paras. 350, 358 and 360.
24 For a recent application of this test, see Panel Report, *Ukraine – Passenger Cars (2015)*, para. 7.191.
25 For a detailed discussion, see Appellate Body Report, *US – Steel Safeguards (2003)*, paras. 352–60.
26 See *ibid.*, para. 355. 27 *Ibid.*, para. 351.

Furthermore, the *rate* of the increase (e.g. an increase by 30 per cent) as well as the *amount* of the increase (e.g. an increase by 10,000 units) must be considered.[28] In addition, the import *trends* during the entire investigation period must be considered. It does not suffice to compare the level of imports at the beginning of the investigation period with the imports at the end and to conclude that there is an increase in imports within the meaning of the *Agreement on Safeguards*.[29] The analysis of the import trends during the investigation period must also show an increase in imports. However, recall that the increase in imports must be sudden and recent. Therefore, the investigation period should include the *recent past*. Thus, it is not appropriate to examine the import trends over an investigation period that ends some time before the safeguard determination is made.[30] Moreover, the period of investigation must, of course, be sufficiently long to allow appropriate conclusions to be drawn regarding the state of the domestic industry.[31]

Furthermore, while the competent authorities must consider the data for the entire investigation period,[32] more weight is to be given in the assessment to the data relating to the most recent past within the investigation period. In *US – Steel Safeguards (2003)*, the Appellate Body held that the United States made an error by failing to address the decrease in imports that had occurred at the very end of the investigation period.[33]

Consider the examples in Figures 9.1 and 9.2 concerning the imports of chocolate in Member A during the investigation period of 2014–16. In both examples, there is an increase in imports in the investigation period. The rate of increase as well as the amount of increase is quite significant. In both examples, imports increased from 30,000 tonnes to 140,000 tonnes, representing an increase of more than 460 per cent during the investigation period. However, a different picture emerges if one looks at the import trends. The example in Figure 9.1 is a clear case of a recent, sudden and sharp increase in imports within the meaning of the *Agreement on Safeguards*. It is doubtful whether that same conclusion can be reached with respect to the example in Figure 9.2.[34]

Pursuant to the first clause of Article XIX:1(a) of the GATT 1994, the increase in imports must occur as a result of 'unforeseen developments' and as a result of

28 See Article 4.2(a) of the *Agreement on Safeguards*.

29 See Appellate Body Report, *Argentina – Footwear (EC) (2000)*, para. 129.

30 See *ibid.*, para. 130. 31 See Appellate Body Report, *US – Lamb (2001)*, para. 138.

32 In *US – Lamb (2001)*, the Appellate Body noted that, 'in conducting their evaluation under Article 4.2(a), competent authorities cannot rely *exclusively* on data from the most recent past, but must assess that data in the context of the data for the entire investigative period'. See Appellate Body Report, *US – Lamb (2001)*, para. 138. See also Appellate Body Report, *Argentina – Footwear (EC) (2000)*, para. 129. The panel in *Argentina – Preserved Peaches (2003)* stated that, '[i]ndeed, detecting an increase in only part of the period is synonymous with isolating the data for that part from the data corresponding to the entire period'. See Panel Report, *Argentina – Preserved Peaches (2003)*, para. 7.67.

33 See Appellate Body Report, *US – Steel Safeguards (2003)*, para. 388.

34 It may also be possible to conclude that there is an increase in imports in the example in Figure 9.2, within the meaning of the *Agreement on Safeguards*, if it can be shown that the decline in 2016 was of a temporary and incidental nature.

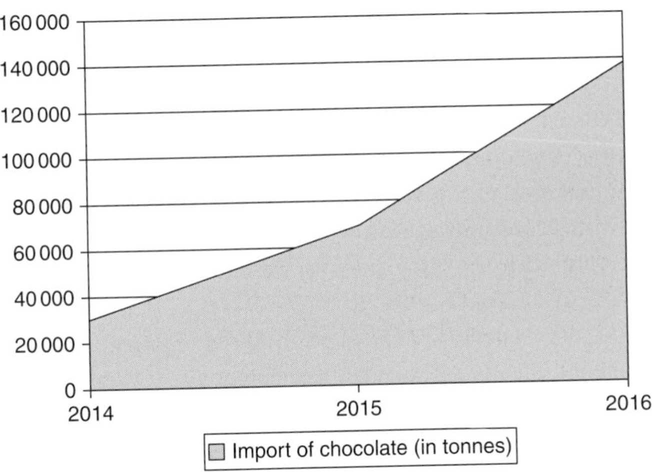

Figure 9.1 'Increased imports' requirement: example 1

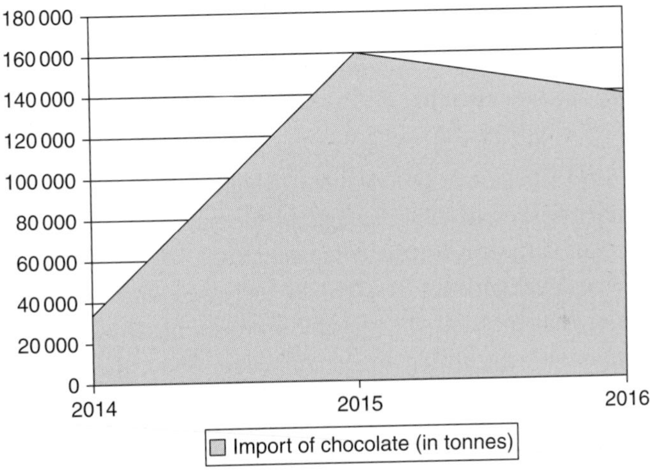

Figure 9.2 'Increased imports' requirement: example 2

the effect of obligations incurred under the GATT 1994, including tariff concessions. According to the Working Party in *US – Fur Felt Hats (1951)*, 'unforeseen developments' are:

> developments occurring after the negotiation of the relevant tariff concession which it would not be reasonable to expect that the negotiators of the country making the concession could and should have foreseen at the time when the concession was negotiated.[35]

In 1951, the Working Party held that the fact that hat styles had changed did not constitute an 'unforeseen development'. However, the degree to which the

35 Working Party Report, *US – Fur Felt Hats (1951)*, para. 9.

change in fashion affected the competitive situation could not, according to the Working Party, have reasonably been foreseen by the US authorities in 1947.

As discussed above, despite a challenge to the continuing existence of the 'unforeseen developments' requirement under the renovated multilateral safeguards framework of the WTO, this requirement is still 'alive'.[36] Therefore, 'any safeguard measure imposed after the entry into force of the WTO Agreement must comply with the provisions of *both* the *Agreement on Safeguards* and Article XIX of the GATT 1994'.[37]

In 2000, the Appellate Body ruled in *Korea – Dairy (2000)* that 'unforeseen developments' means unexpected developments.[38] Note that, before imposing a safeguard measure, the Member concerned must demonstrate, as a matter of fact, that the increase in imports is indeed the result of unforeseen, i.e. unexpected, developments.[39] The requirement to demonstrate the causal relationship between the measure taken and an 'unforeseen development' is independent of factual proof of increase in imports. As stated by the panel in *Argentina – Preserved Peaches (2003)*:

> [I]ncrease in imports and the unforeseen developments must be two distinct elements. A statement that the increase in imports, or the way in which they were being imported, was unforeseen, does not constitute a demonstration as a matter of fact of the existence of unforeseen *developments*.[40]

In *US – Steel Safeguards (2003)*, the Appellate Body held that, when an importing Member wishes to apply safeguard measures on imports of several products, it is not sufficient for the competent authority merely to demonstrate that 'unforeseen developments' resulted in increased imports of a *broad category of products* that includes the specific products on which the safeguard measure is imposed.[41] According to the Appellate Body, the competent authorities are required to demonstrate that the unforeseen developments have resulted in increased imports for the *specific products* that are subject to the safeguard measures.[42]

36 See above, p. 633. 37 Appellate Body Report, *Argentina – Footwear (EC) (2000)*, para. 84.
38 See Appellate Body Report, *Korea – Dairy (2000)*, para. 84.
39 See *ibid.*, para. 85. See also Appellate Body Report, *Argentina – Footwear (EC) (2000)*, para. 92; and Panel Report, *Ukraine – Passenger Cars (2015)*, para. 7.73.
40 Panel Report, *Argentina – Preserved Peaches (2003)*, para. 7.24. There seems to be a difference of opinion regarding the link between the 'unforeseen developments' and the 'increase in imports'. The panel in *Argentina – Preserved Peaches (2003)* expressly disagreed with the Appellate Body in *Argentina – Footwear (EC) (2000)* that the unforeseen development could itself be the increased quantities of imports. The contradiction appears to pertain to *what* may qualify as an unforeseen development – whether such development ought to be a factor *other than* the increased imports, though *necessarily resulting* in such increased imports, or whether the increased imports could have themselves been unforeseen (*ibid.*, para. 7.24). Note, however, that the Appellate Body itself interpreted the sentence in question, 'the increased quantities of imports should have been "unforeseen" or "unexpected"', appearing in *Argentina – Footwear (EC) (2000)*, para. 131, as 'referring to the fact that the increased imports must, under Article XIX:1(a), *result* from "unforeseen developments"'. See also Appellate Body Report, *US – Steel Safeguards (2003)*, para. 350.
41 See Appellate Body Report, *US – Steel Safeguards (2003)*, para. 319. 42 See *ibid.*

Also in *US – Steel Safeguards (2003)*, the Appellate Body held that the competent authority of the importing Member imposing a safeguard measure must demonstrate in its published report, *through a reasoned and adequate explanation* and a *reasoned conclusion*, that unforeseen developments resulted in increased imports.[43] The panel in *US – Steel Safeguards (2003)* ruled with respect to the determination of 'unforeseen circumstances':

> The nature of the facts, including their complexity, will dictate the extent to which the relationship between the unforeseen developments and increased imports causing injury needs to be explained. The timing of the explanation [relating to unforeseen developments], its extent and its quality are all factors that can affect whether [that] explanation is reasoned and adequate.[44]

On appeal, the Appellate Body upheld this finding.[45] The Appellate Body pointed out that, since a panel may not conduct a *de novo* review of the evidence before the competent authority, it is the *explanation* given by the competent authority for its determination that enables a panel to determine whether there has been compliance with the substantive requirements for the imposition of a safeguard measure.[46]

Referring to the Appellate Body case law discussed above, the panel in *Ukraine – Passenger Cars (2015)* considered that the two elements of the first clause of Article XIX:1(a) of the GATT 1994, namely 'as a result of unforeseen developments' and '[as the result] of the effect of the obligations incurred by a [Member] under [the GATT 1994]', are:

> *circumstances* that the competent authorities are legally required under Article XIX:1(a) to demonstrate as a matter of fact. They are not *conditions*. The conditions for the application of a safeguard measure are contained in the second clause of Article XIX:1(a) and Article 2 [of the *Agreement on Safeguards*]. Although different in legal nature, the relevant *conditions* and *circumstances* have in common that: (i) their satisfaction or existence must be demonstrated by the competent authorities, through reasoned and adequate explanations, (ii) in the published report, and (iii) before a safeguard measure is applied.[47]

2.1.2 'Serious Injury' Requirement

A second main substantive requirement for the application of a safeguard measure on imports of a product is the existence of serious injury or threat thereof to the domestic industry producing like or directly competitive products. Article 4.1(a)

43 See *ibid.*, paras. 273, 289–91 and 297. The panel in *Argentina – Preserved Peaches (2003)*, forcefully asserted that '[a] mere phrase in a conclusion, without supporting analysis of the existence of unforeseen developments, is not a substitute for a demonstration of fact'. See Panel Report, *Argentina – Preserved Peaches (2003)*, para. 7.33.

44 Panel Reports, *US – Steel Safeguards (2003)*, para. 10.115.

45 See Appellate Body Report, *US – Steel Safeguards (2003)*, paras. 293–6.

46 See *ibid.*, paras. 298–9 and 301–3. On the standard of review applicable under the *Agreement on Safeguards*, see also *US – Lamb (2001)*, paras. 103 and 106–7.

47 Panel Report, *Ukraine – Passenger Cars (2015)*, para. 7.57.

of the *Agreement on Safeguards* defines 'serious injury' as 'a significant overall impairment in the position of a domestic industry'. The Appellate Body has recognised the standard of 'serious injury' to be 'very high' and 'exacting'.[48] It is stricter than the standard of 'material injury' of the *Anti-Dumping Agreement* and the *SCM Agreement*.[49] Since safeguard measures, unlike anti-dumping and countervailing duties, are applied to 'fair' trade, it is not surprising that the threshold for applying these measures is higher.

Article 4.1(c) of the *Agreement on Safeguards* defines a 'domestic industry' as:

> the producers as a whole of the like or directly competitive products operating within the territory of a Member, or those whose collective output of the like or directly competitive products constitutes a major proportion of the total domestic production of those products.

Article 4.1(c) lays down two criteria to define the 'domestic industry' in a particular case. The first criterion relates to the products at issue; the second criterion relates to the number and the representative nature of the producers of these products.

As to the first criterion, note that the domestic industry is composed of producers making products that are 'like or directly competitive' to the imported products. As the Appellate Body noted in *US – Lamb (2001)*, the definition of 'domestic industry':

> focuses exclusively on the producers of a very specific group of products. Producers of products that are *not* 'like or directly competitive products' do not, according to the text of the treaty, form part of the domestic industry.[50]

Therefore, in order to determine what constitutes the 'domestic industry', in a particular case, one must first identify the domestic products which are 'like or directly competitive' to the imported products. The producers of those products will make up the 'domestic industry'. The concepts of 'like products' and 'directly competitive products' are not defined in the *Agreement on Safeguards*, and there is little relevant case law as of yet on the meaning of these concepts as used in the *Agreement on Safeguards*. However, there is a significant body of case law on the meaning of these concepts as used in the GATT 1994.[51] While the Appellate Body has ruled that the concept of 'like products' may have different meanings in the different contexts in which it is used, this case law – discussed in detail above – is definitely of relevance here. It follows from this case law that the determination of whether products are 'like products' or 'directly competitive products' is, fundamentally, a determination about the nature and extent of the competitive relationship between these products. The factors that must be considered in determining 'likeness' or 'direct competitiveness' include, among others, the following: (1) physical characteristics of the products; (2) end use; (3) consumer habits and preferences regarding the products; and (4) customs

48 See Appellate Body Report, *US – Lamb (2001)*, para. 124; and Appellate Body Report, *US – Wheat Gluten (2001)*, para. 149.

49 See below, pp. 723–33 and 813–17.

50 See Appellate Body Report, *US – Lamb (2001)*, para. 84.

51 See above, pp. 354–63 and 366–73.

classification of the products. In *US – Lamb (2001)*, one of the few safeguard cases in which the issue of 'like products' and 'directly competitive products' was addressed, the Appellate Body held that:

> if an input product and an end-product are not 'like or directly competitive', then it is irrelevant, under the *Agreement on Safeguards*, that there is a continuous line of production between an input product and an end-product.[52]

Consequently, production structures (for example, from lambs to lamb meat) are not relevant in determining whether products are 'like' or 'directly competitive' (and thus do not make lambs and meat products 'like products'). The Appellate Body explained in *US – Lamb (2001)* that the 'focus must, therefore, be on the identification of the *products*, and their "like or directly competitive" relationship, and not on the *processes* by which those products are produced'.[53]

As mentioned above, the second criterion to define the 'domestic industry' in a particular case relates to the number and the representative nature of the producers of the 'like or directly competitive' products. The 'domestic industry' for the purposes of the *Agreement on Safeguards* is: (1) the totality of the domestic producers; or (2) at least a major proportion thereof. There is no general explanation of what constitutes 'a major proportion' of the domestic producers. What is required to meet this condition will depend on the specific circumstances of a case and will most likely differ from case to case.[54]

Once the domestic industry has been identified, one can examine whether this domestic industry has suffered 'serious injury'. To this end, Article 4.2(a) of the *Agreement on Safeguards* requires an evaluation of 'all relevant factors of an objective and quantifiable nature having a bearing on the situation of that industry'. These so-called 'injury factors' include: (1) the rate and amount of the increase in imports, of the product concerned, in absolute and relative terms; (2) the share of the domestic market taken by increased imports; and (3) changes in the level of sales, production, productivity, capacity utilisation, profits and losses, and employment.[55] This list of injury factors is not exhaustive. *All* factors having a bearing on the situation of the domestic industry can and must be examined.[56] The examination of the factors expressly mentioned is, however, a minimum

52 See Appellate Body Report, *US – Lamb (2001)*, para. 90. According to the Appellate Body, '[w]hen input and end-product are not "like" or "directly competitive", then it is irrelevant ... that there is a continuous line of production between an input product and an end-product, that the input product represents a high proportion of the value of the end-product, that there is no use for the input product other than as an input for the particular end-product, or that there is a substantial coincidence of economic interests between the producers of these products'. *Ibid.*

53 See *ibid.*, para. 94.

54 This issue also arises in the context of anti-dumping measures and countervailing measures: see below, pp. 696–767 and 769–881.

55 See Article 4.2(a) of the *Agreement on Safeguards*.

56 See Appellate Body Report, *Argentina – Footwear (EC) (2000)*, para. 136; Appellate Body Report, *US – Wheat Gluten (2001)*, para. 55; and Appellate Body Report, *US – Lamb (2001)*, para. 103. Failure to consider a relevant factor, in full or in part, amounts to a violation of Article 4.2(a) of the *Agreement on Safeguards*.

requirement.[57] Domestic authorities do not have a duty to investigate *all* other possible injury factors. However, if the domestic authority considers a factor, other than a factor raised by one of the interested parties, to be relevant, it must be investigated.[58]

It is not sufficient for competent authorities applying safeguard measures to examine all relevant injury factors. The authorities are also required to give a reasoned and adequate explanation of how the facts support their conclusion that the domestic industry is suffering 'serious injury'.[59] As discussed above, the standard of 'serious injury' in Article 4.1(a) is 'very high' and 'exacting'.[60] To find 'serious injury', it is not necessary that all injury factors show that the domestic industry is under threat.[61] In a situation where employment and capacity utilisation in an industry are declining but profitability remains positive, it may nevertheless be possible to conclude that 'serious injury' exists provided that a reasoned and adequate explanation is given in the determination.

As noted above, a safeguard measure can be applied not only in case of 'serious injury' but also in case of a 'threat of serious injury'. A 'threat of serious injury' is defined as 'serious injury that is clearly imminent'.[62] The concept of 'clearly imminent' was clarified by the Appellate Body in *US – Lamb (2001)*. 'Imminent' implies that the anticipated 'serious injury' must be on the verge of occurring; 'clearly' indicates that there must be a very high degree of likelihood that the threat will materialise in the very near future.[63] In this regard, there is a duty to 'assess' the data from the most recent past against the overall trends during the entire investigating period in an injury analysis,[64] very similar to the duty in an 'increased imports' determination under Article 2.1 of the *Agreement*

57 These principles with regard to Article 4.2(a) now seem to be well established in dispute settlement practice. See Appellate Body Report, *US – Wheat Gluten (2001)*, para. 55.

58 See Appellate Body Report, *US – Wheat Gluten (2001)*, paras. 55–6.

59 See Appellate Body Report, *US – Lamb (2001)*, para. 103. This is usually referred to as the *substantive* aspect of the examination of the injury factors. See also Panel Report, *Argentina – Preserved Peaches (2003)*, paras. 7.102–7.117.

60 See above, p. 616; and Appellate Body Report, *US – Lamb (2001)*, para. 124; and Appellate Body Report, *US – Wheat Gluten (2001)*, para. 149.

61 See Appellate Body Report, *US – Lamb (2001)*, para. 144. However, competent authorities must have a *sufficient* factual basis to allow them to draw reasoned and adequate conclusions concerning the situation of the 'domestic industry'. The need for such a sufficient factual basis, in turn, implies that the data examined, concerning the relevant factors, must be *representative* of the 'domestic industry'. See Appellate Body Report, *US – Lamb (2001)*, para. 131.

62 Article 4.1(b) of the *Agreement on Safeguards*.

63 See Appellate Body Report, *US – Lamb (2001)*, para. 125. Note that an independent fact-based assessment of the 'high degree of likelihood' is necessary and that mere acknowledgment of possibility is not sufficient. See Panel Report, *Argentina – Preserved Peaches (2003)*, para. 7.122. For a recent finding of inconsistency with Article 4.2(a) of a determination of 'threat of serious injury', see Panel Report, *Ukraine – Passenger Cars (2015)*, para. 7.271.

64 See Appellate Body Report, *US – Lamb (2001)*, para. 138. Data relating to the most recent past will provide competent authorities 'with an essential, and, usually, the most reliable, basis for a determination of a threat of serious injury. The likely state of the domestic industry in the very near future can best be gauged from data from the most recent past.' However, 'although data from the most recent past has special importance, competent authorities should not consider such data in isolation from the data pertaining to the entire period of investigation. The real significance of the short-term trends in the most recent data, evident at the end of the period of investigation, may only emerge when those short-term trends are assessed in the light of the longer-term trends in the data for the whole period of investigation.' See Appellate Body Report, *US – Lamb (2001)*, paras. 137–8.

on Safeguards.[65] For a finding of 'threat of serious injury', Article 4.1(b) of the *Agreement on Safeguards* also requires that this determination must 'be based on facts and not merely on allegation, conjecture or remote possibility'.

The relationship between 'serious injury' and a 'threat of serious injury' was considered in *US – Line Pipe (2002)*. The question was whether a domestic authority could make an alternative finding of 'serious injury *or* [a] threat of serious injury', without a discrete finding as to which of these was, in fact, the reason for the imposition of the safeguard measure. Reversing the panel finding, the Appellate Body held:

> [A]s the right [to impose a safeguard] exists if there is a finding by the competent authorities of a 'threat of serious injury' or – something *beyond* – 'serious injury', then it seems to us that it is irrelevant, *in determining whether the right exists*, if there is 'serious injury' or only [a] 'threat of serious injury' – so long as there is a determination that there is *at least* a 'threat'.[66]

2.1.3 'Causation' Requirement

The third substantive requirement for the application of a safeguard measure to the imports of a product is the 'causation' requirement. Article 4.2(b) of the *Agreement on Safeguards* provides:

> The determination referred to in subparagraph (a) shall not be made unless this investigation demonstrates, on the basis of objective evidence, the existence of the causal link between increased imports of the product concerned and serious injury or a threat thereof. When factors other than increased imports are causing injury to the domestic industry at the same time, such injury shall not be attributed to increased imports.

The test for establishing causation is twofold: (1) a demonstration of the causal link between the 'increased imports' and the 'serious injury' or threat thereof (the 'causal link' element);[67] and (2) an identification of any injury caused by factors other than the increased imports and the non-attribution of this injury to these imports (the 'non-attribution' element).[68]

65 See Panel Report, *Chile – Price Band System (2002)*, fn. 714 to para. 7.153. In fact, the panel in that case affirmed this duty as applying *mutatis mutandis* to Article 2.1 and Article 4.1(b), read together with Article 4.2(a). The panel ruled that, where a pre-existing measure like a Price Band System is in place, leading to significantly increasing tariffs, it is not proper for a competent authority to argue *a contrario* in a safeguards investigation that the removal or reduction of such a measure would lead to lower net duties on the imported product, thereby causing injury. See *ibid*., para. 7.172.

66 Appellate Body Report, *US – Line Pipe (2002)*, para. 170. In the same report, the Appellate Body explained that, in 'terms of the rising continuum of an injurious condition of a domestic industry that ascends from a "threat of serious injury" up to "serious injury", we see "serious injury" – because it is something *beyond* a "threat" – as necessarily *including* the concept of a "threat" and *exceeding* the presence of a "threat"'. *Ibid.*

67 With respect to the phrase in Article 2.1, 'imported ... under such conditions', the panel in *US – Wheat Gluten (2001)* noted: 'We are of the view that the phrase "under such conditions" does not impose a separate analytical requirement in addition to the analysis of increased imports, serious injury and causation. Rather, this phrase refers to the *substance* of the causation analysis that must be performed under Article 4.2(a) and (b) SA.' See Panel Report, *US – Wheat Gluten (2001)*, para. 8.108.

68 See e.g. Appellate Body Report, *US – Line Pipe (2002)*, para. 215. For a recent application of this test, see Panel Report, *Ukraine – Passenger Cars (2015)*, para. 7.307 (regarding the 'causal link' element) and paras. 7.331–7.332 (regarding the 'non-attribution' element).

With respect to the 'causal link' element, a 'genuine and substantial relationship of cause and effect' has to exist between increased imports and serious injury to the domestic industry (or threat thereof).[69] The Appellate Body had ruled in *US – Wheat Gluten (2001)* that it is not necessary to show that increased imports *alone* must be capable of causing serious injury:

> [T]he need to distinguish between the facts caused by increased imports and the facts caused by other factors does *not* necessarily imply ... that increased imports *on their own* must be capable of causing serious injury nor that injury caused by other factors must be *excluded* from the determination of serious injury.[70]

To the contrary, the language of Article 4.2(b), as a whole, suggests that 'the causal link' between increased imports and serious injury may exist, even though other factors are also contributing, 'at the same time', to the situation of the domestic industry.[71]

With respect to the 'non-attribution' element, the Appellate Body found in *US – Wheat Gluten (2001)* that Article 4.2(b) presupposes, 'as a first step in the competent authorities' examination of causation', that the injurious effects caused to the domestic industry by increased imports 'are *distinguished from* the injurious effects caused by other factors'.[72] The competent authorities can then, as a second step in their examination, attribute to increased imports, on the one hand, and, by implication, to other relevant factors, on the other hand, 'injury' caused by all of these different factors, including increased imports. By virtue of this two-stage process, the competent authorities comply with Article 4.2(b) by ensuring that any injury to the domestic industry that was *actually* caused by factors other than increased imports is not 'attributed' to increased imports and is, therefore, not treated as if it were injury caused by increased imports, when it is not. In this way, the competent authorities can determine, as a final step, whether 'the causal link' exists between 'increased imports and serious injury, and whether this causal link involves a genuine and substantial relationship of cause and effect between these two elements, as required by the *Agreement on Safeguards*'.[73] When a number of Members raised questions about this ruling, the Appellate Body further explained in *US – Lamb (2001)*:

> In a situation where *several factors* are causing injury 'at the same time', a final determination about the injurious effects caused by *increased imports* can only be made if the injurious effects caused by all the different causal factors are distinguished and separated. Otherwise, any conclusion based exclusively on an assessment of only one of the causal factors – increased imports – rests on an uncertain foundation, because it *assumes* that the other causal factors are *not* causing the injury which has been ascribed to increased imports. The non-attribution language in Article 4.2(b) precludes such an assumption and, instead, requires that the competent authorities assess appropriately the injurious effects of the other

69 Appellate Body Report, *US – Wheat Gluten (2001)*, para. 69.

70 *Ibid.*, para. 70. The Appellate Body thus reversed the panel's finding that the imports, *in and of themselves*, must have caused the serious injury. See Panel Report, *US – Wheat Gluten (2001)*, paras. 8.90–8.154.

71 Appellate Body Report, *US – Wheat Gluten (2001)*, para. 67.

72 *Ibid.*, para. 69. 73 *Ibid.*

factors, so that those effects may be disentangled from the injurious effects of the increased imports. In this way, the final determination rests, properly, on the genuine and substantial relationship of cause and effect between increased imports and serious injury.[74]

Domestic authorities therefore have to separate and distinguish the injurious effects of 'other factors' from the injurious effects of the increased imports. They have to give a reasoned and adequate explanation of the nature and the extent of the injurious effects of the other factors, as distinguished from the injurious effects of the increased imports.[75]

Finally, it is clear that, when a competent authority's report neither demonstrates the threshold of 'increased imports' under Article 2.1, nor satisfies the requirement of the existence of 'serious injury' or 'threat thereof' under Article 4.2(b), *a fortiori*, no causal link between these two elements can exist.[76]

2.2 Domestic Procedures and Notification and Consultation Requirements

The *Agreement on Safeguards* sets out the procedural requirements that domestic authorities, wishing to impose safeguard measures, must meet.[77] Most importantly, Article 3 of the *Agreement on Safeguards* permits a Member to apply a safeguard measure only following an investigation by the competent authorities of that Member pursuant to procedures previously established and made public.[78] The competent domestic authorities must also publish a report setting forth their findings and reasoned conclusions reached on all pertinent issues of fact and law.[79] Failure to do so results in a formal defect in the safeguard measure. Moreover, if the report of the competent domestic authorities does not address the issues arising under Article 2 (increased imports) and/or Article 4 (serious injury), this absence amounts to a failure to show that the requirements

74 Appellate Body Report, *US – Lamb (2001)*, para. 179. See also Appellate Body Report, *US – Wheat Gluten (2001)*, paras. 67–9.

75 See Appellate Body Report, *US – Line Pipe (2002)*, paras. 213, 215 and 217. The mere assertion that injury caused by other factors has not been attributed to increased imports is definitely not sufficient to meet the requirement of Article 4.2(b) of the *Agreement on Safeguards*. As the Appellate Body noted in *US – Steel Safeguards (2003)*: 'In order to provide such a reasoned and adequate explanation, the competent authority *must explain how it ensured that it did not attribute* the injurious effects of factors other than included imports ... to the imports included in the measure' (emphasis added): Appellate Body Report, *US – Steel Safeguards (2003)*, para. 452. See also Appellate Body Report, *US – Hot-Rolled Steel (2001)*, paras. 226 and 230.

76 See Panel Report, *Chile – Price Band System (2002)*, para. 7.176, relying on Appellate Body Report, *Argentina – Footwear (EC) (2000)*, para. 145.

77 These procedural obligations are set out in Articles 3, 6 and 12 of the *Agreement on Safeguards*.

78 See Article 3.1 of the *Agreement on Safeguards*. Note that this investigation must include reasonable public notice to all interested parties and public hearings or other appropriate means by which importers, exporters and other interested parties could present evidence, and their views, *inter alia*, as to whether or not the application of a safeguard measure would be in the public interest. These procedural 'due process rights' of the parties to a safeguard investigation are set out in Article 3.1 of the *Agreement on Safeguards*. See Panel Report, *Ukraine – Passenger Cars (2015)*, para. 7.431.

79 See Article 3.1 of the *Agreement on Safeguards*. See also Appellate Body Report, *US – Lamb (2001)*, para. 76; and Appellate Body Report, *US – Steel Safeguards (2003)*, paras. 286–8. As to publication of confidential information, see Panel Report, *US – Wheat Gluten (2001)*, paras. 8.13–8.26. It is impermissible to adduce evidence of consideration of relevant information in a document that does not constitute a 'published' report; see Panel Report, *Chile – Price Band System (2002)*, para. 7.128.

of Articles 2 and 4 were met and results in a finding of breach of Article 2 and/or Article 4 of the *Agreement on Safeguards*.

The *Agreement on Safeguards* also imposes obligations on Members to notify the WTO Committee on Safeguards of matters relating to safeguard measures and to consult with other Members on such measures. Article 12.1 of the *Agreement on Safeguards* requires 'immediate' notification by Members to the WTO Committee on Safeguards whenever an investigation is initiated, a finding of serious injury or threat of serious injury caused by increased imports is made or where a decision is taken to apply or extend a safeguard measure.[80]

As to when a notification is necessary in the case of 'taking a decision to apply or extend a safeguard measure', the Appellate Body held in *US – Wheat Gluten (2001)* that notification needs to be given *only* after a decision has been taken and not when a decision is *proposed to be taken*.[81] However, it also noted that the meaning of the term '*immediate*' implies a 'degree of urgency'[82] and observed that the 'relevant triggering event' is the 'taking' of a decision. Article 12.1(c) is thus focused upon a 'decision' that 'has *occurred*, or has been taken', not on when that 'decision has been *given effect*'.[83]

Article 12.2 of the *Agreement on Safeguards* provides that a Member making a finding of serious injury or threat thereof, or taking a decision to apply or extend a safeguard, should provide 'all pertinent information' to the WTO Committee on Safeguards. The pertinent information to be provided includes a mandatory minimum list,[84] comprising: evidence of serious injury or threat thereof due to increased imports; precise description of the product involved and the proposed measure; proposed date of introduction; expected duration; and a timetable for progressive liberalisation. The 'evidence of serious injury' to be demonstrated is evidence that would satisfy the requirements of Article 4.2(a), and not merely what the applying Member considers sufficient.[85]

Under Article 12.3 of the *Agreement on Safeguards*, the Member applying or extending a measure shall provide *adequate opportunity* for prior consultations with Members affected by the measure, for the purpose of reviewing the information provided, exchanging views and, most importantly, to facilitate reaching

80 See Panel Report, *US – Wheat Gluten (2001)*, paras. 8.185–8.207. The use of the term 'immediately' indicates a certain degree of urgency of the notification. See Appellate Body Report, *US – Wheat Gluten (2001)*, para. 105. The panel in *Korea – Dairy (2000)* noted that the requirement to notify 'immediately' does not mean notifying 'as soon as practically possible'. See Panel Report, *Korea – Dairy (2000)*, para. 7.134. The degree of urgency that is required by the duty to notify immediately is assessed on a case-by-case basis. This degree of urgency will depend on administrative difficulties, the character of the information and the need to translate documents (if any). In any case, the time taken for notification should be kept to the bare minimum. See Appellate Body Report, *US – Wheat Gluten (2001)*, paras. 105–6. See also Panel Report, *Ukraine – Passenger Cars (2015)*, paras. 7.476, 7.494 and 7.502.

81 See Appellate Body Report, *US – Wheat Gluten (2001)*, paras. 119–25, reversing the panel's interpretation.

82 See *ibid.*, para. 105.

83 *Ibid.*, para. 120. See also Panel Report, *Ukraine – Passenger Cars (2015)*, fn. 538 to para. 7.507.

84 See Appellate Body Report, *Korea – Dairy (2000)*, para. 107. Additional information may be requested by the Council for Trade in Goods or the Committee on Safeguards in terms of Article 12.2 of the *Agreement on Safeguards*.

85 See Appellate Body Report, *Korea – Dairy (2000)*, para. 108, reversing the panel's interpretation.

an understanding on the substantially equivalent levels of concessions to be maintained under Article 8.1 of the *Agreement on Safeguards*. As the Appellate Body explained in *US – Wheat Gluten (2001)*, 'adequate opportunity' means that the exporting Member should be provided with sufficient *information* and *time* to allow a *meaningful exchange* on the issues identified.[86] In *US – Line Pipe (2002)*, the Appellate Body stated that the final measure applied ought to be one that is substantially the same as the proposed measure covered during the prior consultations:

> [W]here ... the proposed measure 'differed substantially' from the measure that was later applied, and not as a consequence of 'prior consultations', we fail to see how meaningful 'prior consultations' could have occurred, as required by Article 12.3.[87]

It is to be noted that a violation of Article 12.3 automatically triggers a violation of Article 8.1 of the *Agreement on Safeguards*. As the Appellate Body ruled in *US – Wheat Gluten (2001)*:

> In view of this explicit link between Articles 8.1 and 12.3 of the *Agreement on Safeguards*, a Member cannot ... 'endeavour to maintain' an adequate balance of concessions unless it has, as a first step, provided an adequate opportunity for prior consultations on a proposed measure.[88]

2.3 Characteristics of Safeguard Measures

Safeguard measures are measures, otherwise inconsistent with Articles II or XI of the GATT 1994, which are justified under the economic emergency exception provided for in Article XIX of the GATT 1994 and the *Agreement on Safeguards*. The purpose of a safeguard measure is to give 'breathing space' to a domestic industry to adapt itself to the new market situation by temporarily restricting imports. Safeguard measures therefore typically take the form of: (1) customs duties above the binding (inconsistent with Article II:1 of the GATT 1994); or (2) quantitative restrictions (inconsistent with Article XI of the GATT 1994).[89] Safeguard measures can also take other forms, because, unlike anti-dumping measures and countervailing measures, discussed above, safeguard measures are not limited to particular types of measures.[90] This does not mean, however, that safeguard measures are not subject to strict requirements. In general terms, Article 5.1, first sentence, of the *Agreement on Safeguards* provides:

> A Member shall apply safeguard measures only to the extent necessary to prevent or remedy serious injury or to facilitate adjustment ... Members should choose measures most suitable for the achievement of these objectives.[91]

86 See Appellate Body Report, *US – Wheat Gluten (2001)*, para. 136. See also Panel Report, *Ukraine – Passenger Cars (2015)*, para. 7.538.

87 Appellate Body Report, *US – Line Pipe (2002)*, para. 104. See also Appellate Body Report, *US – Wheat Gluten (2001)*, para. 137.

88 Appellate Body Report, *US – Wheat Gluten (2001)*, para. 146.

89 On customs duties above the binding and on quantitative restrictions, see above, pp. 471 and 488–9.

90 See below, pp. 699–700 and 773–4.

91 Also Article XIX:1 of the GATT 1994 states that Members 'shall be free' to take safeguard measures 'to the extent and for such time as may be necessary to prevent or remedy such injury'.

The *Agreement on Safeguards* sets out specific requirements with respect to: (1) the duration of safeguard measures; (2) the non-discriminatory application of safeguard measures; (3) the extent of safeguard measures; (4) the compensation of affected exporting Members; and (5) provisional safeguard measures. This section discusses each of these specific requirements regarding safeguard measures in turn.

2.3.1 Duration of Safeguard Measures

Safeguard measures are, by nature, *temporary* measures. Article 7.1 of the *Agreement on Safeguards* provides that safeguard measures may only be applied:

> for such period of time as may be necessary to prevent or remedy serious injury and to facilitate adjustment.[92]

In fact, the initial period of application of a definitive safeguard measure must not exceed four years.[93] Furthermore, a safeguard measure exceeding one year must be progressively liberalised,[94] and, if the measure exceeds three years, the Member applying the measure must carry out a mid-term review to establish whether the measure still meets the requirements discussed below.[95] Extension of a safeguard measure beyond four years is possible but only if: (1) the safeguard measure continues to be necessary to prevent or remedy serious injury to the domestic industry;[96] and (2) there is evidence that the domestic industry is adjusting.[97] In no case, however, may the duration of a safeguard measure exceed eight years.[98] Once the import of a product has been subjected to a safeguard measure, this product cannot be subjected to such a measure again for a period of time equal to the duration of the safeguard measure that was previously applied.[99] In other words, if a Member applies a safeguard measure on imports of trucks for a period of eight years, it cannot apply any safeguard measure on imports of these trucks during the eight years following the termination of the first measure. In this way, the *Agreement on Safeguards* prevents a situation where the temporary

92 Article 7.1, first sentence, of the *Agreement on Safeguards*.

93 See Article 7.1 of the *Agreement on Safeguards*. Pursuant to Article 6, the duration of a provisional safeguard measure, if applied, is included in this maximum period of four years.

94 See Article 7.4 of the *Agreement on Safeguards*. See Panel Report, *Ukraine – Passenger Cars (2015)*, para. 7.365.

95 See Article 7.4 of the *Agreement on Safeguards*. As a result of the review, the Member must, if appropriate, withdraw the safeguard measure or increase the rate of liberalisation of trade.

96 Note that, when the initial measure is itself not in compliance with Articles 2, 3, 4 or 5 of the *Agreement on Safeguards*, any extension of such measure by definition is tainted by inconsistency as well. See Panel Report, *Chile – Price Band System (2002)*, para. 7.198.

97 See Article 7.2 of the *Agreement on Safeguards*. A safeguard measure that is extended may never be more restrictive than it was at the end of the initial period. See Panel Report, *Argentina – Footwear (EC) (2000)*, paras. 8.303–8.304.

98 See Article 7.3 of the *Agreement on Safeguards*.

99 See Article 7.5 of the *Agreement on Safeguards*. However, the minimum period during which a safeguard measure cannot be applied again is two years. An exception to this rule, allowing for the application of safeguard measures of short duration (i.e. a maximum of 180 days), is provided for in Article 7.6 of the *Agreement on Safeguards*.

character of safeguards is circumvented by the repeated application of safeguard measures on the imports of the same product.

Note that Article 9.2 of the *Agreement on Safeguards* allows developing-country Members to apply a safeguard measure for up to ten years, instead of eight. Developing-country Members may also apply a *new* safeguard measure on the same product sooner than developed-country Members.[100]

2.3.2 Non-Discriminatory Application of Safeguard Measures

Article 2.2 of the *Agreement on Safeguards* provides:

> Safeguard measures shall be applied to a product being imported irrespective of its source.

Under the GATT 1947, there was much disagreement as to whether safeguard measures could be applied on a selective basis, that is, only against certain supplying countries and not against others. The *Agreement on Safeguards* has put an end to that debate by clearly requiring that safeguard measures be applied on an MFN basis, that is without discrimination between supplying Members. If the computer industry of Member A suffers serious injury as a result of a sudden surge of imports of laptops from Member B, Member A may be entitled to take a safeguard measure, for example, in the form of a quota on laptops, however, this measure will have to be applied to the importation of all 'like or directly competitive' laptops, whether from Member B or from other exporting countries. The 'selective' application of safeguard measures is, in principle, prohibited.

In a number of disputes, the question arose whether a Member can exclude products from Members that are its partners in a free-trade area or a customs union from the application of a safeguard measure. As also discussed in Chapter 10, in *Argentina – Footwear (EC) (2000)*, the Appellate Body ruled that, if a WTO Member has imposed a measure after conducting an investigation on imports from *all* sources, it is also required under Article 2.2 of the *Agreement on Safeguards* to apply such a measure to all sources, including partners in a free-trade area.[101] It reaffirmed in *US – Wheat Gluten (2001)* that, in 'the usual course', the imports included in the determinations made under Articles 2.1 and 4.2 of the *Agreement on Safeguards* should correspond to the imports included in the application of the measure, under Article 2.2 of the *Agreement on Safeguards*.[102] This has been referred to as the principle of 'parallelism'. In *US – Line Pipe (2002)* and in *US – Steel Safeguards (2002)*, the Appellate Body explained that the principle of 'parallelism' is derived from the parallel language used in the first and second paragraphs of Article 2 of the *Agreement on Safeguards*.[103]

100 See Article 9.2 of the *Agreement on Safeguards*.

101 See Appellate Body Report, *Argentina – Footwear (EC) (2000)*, para. 112; Appellate Body Report, *US – Wheat Gluten (2001)*, para. 96; Appellate Body Report, *US – Line Pipe (2002)*, para. 181; and Appellate Body Report, *US – Steel Safeguards (2003)*, para. 441. See also below, pp. 681–2.

102 Appellate Body Report, *US – Wheat Gluten (2001)*, para. 96.

103 For a further discussion of the concept of parallelism, see below, pp. 681–2.

The *Agreement on Safeguards* provides for two exceptions to the prohibition of 'selective' application of safeguard measures. These exceptions are set out in Article 5.2(b) and Article 9.1 of the *Agreement on Safeguards*. Article 5.2(b) allows the selective application of safeguard measures taken in the form of quotas allocated among supplying countries if, apart from other requirements:

> clear demonstration is provided to the Committee [on Safeguards] that ... imports from certain Members have increased in disproportionate percentage in relation to the total increase of imports of the product.[104]

Article 9.1 of the *Agreement on Safeguards* contains an exception from the prohibition of selective application for the benefit of developing-country Members. Article 9.1 states:

> Safeguard measures shall not be applied against a product originating in a developing country Member as long as its share of imports of the product concerned in the importing Member does not exceed 3 per cent, provided that developing country Members with less than 3 per cent import share collectively account for not more than 9 per cent of total imports of the product concerned.

The Appellate Body held in *US – Line Pipe (2002)* that Article 9.1 does not contain an obligation to provide a specific list of developing-country Members that are included or excluded from the safeguard measure.[105] In *US – Line Pipe (2002)*, the United States had set, for each country without any differentiation, a quantitative allocation of 9,000 tonnes for imports free from supplementary duties. These 9,000 tonnes represented 2.7 per cent of its overall imports. The United States argued that, since the safeguard measure would reduce the level of imports, it was 'expected' that any country which breached its quota-free import threshold of 9,000 tons would also breach the 3 per cent *de minimis* level set in Article 9.1 of the *Agreement on Safeguards*. The Appellate Body rejected this argument and held that the United States had not taken all reasonable steps to ensure that imports from developing-country Members above the US threshold level, but still below the *de minimis* level, would be excluded from the application of the safeguard measure.[106] Therefore, this mechanism was inconsistent with Article 9.1 of the *Agreement on Safeguards*.[107]

The panel in *Dominican Republic – Safeguard Measures (2012)* interpreted the obligation to exclude from the application of the safeguard those imports from developing-country Members that meet the requirements laid down in Article 9.1. The panel found that such developing-country imports must be excluded from application even when those imports were taken into account in the substantive injury and causation analysis of the investigation.[108] The panel found that the Dominican Republic did not act inconsistently with the *Agreement on*

104 For the other requirements, see Article 5.2(b) of the *Agreement on Safeguards*.
105 See Appellate Body Report, *US – Line Pipe (2002)*, para. 128.
106 See *ibid.*, paras. 120–33. 107 See *ibid.*, para. 133.
108 See Panel Report, *Dominican Republic – Safeguard Measures (2012)*, paras. 7.367–7.392.

Safeguards and the principle of 'parallelism' by not conducting a new analysis excluding imports from those developing countries that the Dominican Republic had excluded from the scope of application of the safeguard measure by virtue of Article 9.1, in order to determine the existence of an increase in imports, serious injury and causation in respect of imports from non-excluded countries only.[109]

2.3.3 Safeguard Measures Commensurate with the Extent of Necessity

As mentioned above, Article 5.1 of the *Agreement on Safeguards* provides that a safeguard shall apply only to the extent necessary to prevent or remedy serious injury and to facilitate adjustment. Article 5.1 also provides that, where the safeguard measure takes the form of a quantitative restriction and such a measure reduces the quantity of imports to a level less than the average imports in the last three representative years, a 'clear justification' to that effect is necessary.

A safeguard measure may not seek to address injury caused by factors other than *increased imports*. In *US – Line Pipe (2002)*, the Appellate Body held that, although the term 'serious injury' has the same meaning in Articles 4.2 and 5 of the *Agreement on Safeguards*,[110] safeguard measures may only be applied to the extent that they address the serious injury (or threat thereof) attributable to *increased imports*.[111] As the Appellate Body noted in *US – Line Pipe (2001)*, the object and purpose of both Article XIX of the GATT 1994 and the *Agreement on Safeguards* support the conclusion that safeguard measures should be applied so as to address only the consequences of *imports* and, therefore:

> the limited objective of Article 5.1, first sentence, is limited by the consequences of *imports*.[112]

Explaining the nature of the requirement in Article 5.1 of the *Agreement on Safeguards*, the Appellate Body in *Korea – Dairy (2000)* held that there is an '*obligation* on a Member applying a safeguard measure to ensure that the measure applied is commensurate with the goals of preventing or remedying serious injury or facilitating adjustment'.[113] This obligation applies regardless of the particular form a safeguard measure might take.[114] However, the Appellate Body disagreed with the panel in this case that Members are always required '*to explain* how they considered the facts before them and why they concluded, *at the time*

109 *Ibid.*

110 The US argued that, since the Appellate Body had held in *US – Wheat Gluten (2001)* that in the determination of 'serious injury' under Article 4.2 of the *Agreement on Safeguards*, injury caused by factors other than increased imports need not be excluded, safeguard measures may be applied to address the 'entirety' of serious injury. See Appellate Body Report, *US – Line Pipe (2002)*, paras. 242–3.

111 Appellate Body Report, *US – Line Pipe (2002)*, paras. 242–62.

112 *Ibid.*, para. 258.

113 Appellate Body Report, *Korea – Dairy (2000)*, para. 96. The panel in *Chile – Price Band System (2002)* held that the word 'ensure' means that there must be a 'rational connection' between the measure imposed and the objective of preventing or remedying serious injury or facilitating adjustment. See Panel Report, *Chile – Price Band System (2002)*, para. 7.183.

114 See Appellate Body Report, *Korea – Dairy (2000)*, para. 96.

of the decision, that the measure to be applied was necessary to remedy the serious injury and facilitate the adjustment of the industry'.[115] Instead, the Appellate Body held that Article 5.1, second sentence, requires 'clear justification' only for safeguard measures taking the form of a quantitative restriction that reduces the quantity of imports below the average of imports in the last three representative years for which statistics are available.[116] The Appellate Body reiterated this view in *US – Line Pipe (2002)*. It stated:

> Article 5.1 imposes a general substantive obligation, namely, to apply safeguard measures only to the permissible extent, and also a particular procedural obligation, namely, to provide a clear justification in the specific case of quantitative restrictions reducing the volume of imports below the average of imports in the last three representative years. Article 5.1 does not establish a general procedural obligation to demonstrate compliance with Article 5.1, first sentence, at the time a measure is applied.[117]

However, the Appellate Body clarified that this does not imply that, in cases not covered by Article 5.1, second sentence, 'the measure may be devoid of justification or that the multilateral verification of the consistency of the measure with the *Agreement on Safeguards* is impeded'.[118] Instead, several obligations in the *Agreement on Safeguards*, including those requiring Members to separate and distinguish the injurious effects of factors other than increased imports (Article 4.2(b)) and to include a detailed analysis in the report of their findings and reasoned conclusions (Articles 3.1 and 4.2(c)):

> should have the incidental effect of providing sufficient 'justification' for a measure and ... should also provide a benchmark against which the permissible extent of the measure should be determined.[119]

The Appellate Body found support for this interpretation in the non-attribution language found in the second sentence of Article 4.2(b),[120] which is 'a benchmark for ensuring that only an appropriate share of the overall injury is attributed to increased imports'.[121] This, in turn, 'informs the permissible extent to which the safeguard measure may be applied pursuant to Article 5.1, first sentence'.[122] For the Appellate Body it would be:

> illogical to require an investigating authority to ensure that the 'causal link' between increased imports and serious injury not be based on the share of injury attributed to factors other than increased imports while, at the same time, permitting a Member to apply a safeguard measure addressing injury caused by all factors.[123]

115 Panel Report, *Korea – Dairy (2000)*, para. 7.109.
116 See Appellate Body Report, *Korea – Dairy (2000)*, para. 98.
117 Appellate Body Report, *US – Line Pipe (2002)*, para. 234.
118 *Ibid.*, para. 236. 119 *Ibid.*
120 The Appellate Body recalled that the non-attribution requirement seeks, 'in situations where several factors cause injury at the same time, to prevent investigating authorities from inferring the required "causal link" between increased imports and serious injury or threat thereof on the basis of the injurious effects caused by factors other than increased imports'. See Appellate Body Report, *US – Line Pipe (2002)*, para. 252.
121 *Ibid.* 122 *Ibid.*
123 *Ibid.*

In cases where the safeguard measure takes the form of a quota allocated among supplying countries, Article 5.2(a) of the *Agreement on Safeguards* provides for rules on the allocation of the share of the quota. These rules are similar to the rules of Article XIII of the GATT 1994 on the 'non-discriminatory administration of quantitative restrictions', discussed above.[124]

2.3.4 Compensation of Affected Exporting Members

As noted above, a safeguard measure is a measure that restricts *fair* trade from other Members.[125] A safeguard measure disturbs the balance of rights and obligations to the detriment of the affected exporting Members. Therefore, the *Agreement on Safeguards* requires that a Member taking a safeguard measure agree with the affected exporting Members on appropriate *compensation* so as to restore the balance of rights and obligations. Article 8.1 of the *Agreement on Safeguards* provides:

> A Member proposing to apply a safeguard measure or seeking an extension of a safeguard measure shall endeavour to maintain a substantially equivalent level of concessions and other obligations ... between it and the exporting Members which would be affected by such a measure ... To achieve this objective, the Members concerned may agree on any adequate means of trade compensation for the adverse effects of the measure on their trade.[126]

The objective of appropriate compensation is to be achieved by following the consultation procedures established under Article 12.3 of the *Agreement on Safeguards*. When a Member fails to consult affected Members in accordance with Article 12.3, it also violates Article 8.1 of the *Agreement on Safeguards*.[127] If an agreement on compensation is not reached within thirty days, Article 8.2 of the *Agreement on Safeguards* provides that the affected exporting Members are free:

> to suspend ... the application of substantially equivalent concessions or other obligations under GATT 1994, to the trade of the Member applying the safeguard measure.[128]

However, affected exporting Members cannot always exercise this right of suspension. As set out in Article 8.3 of the *Agreement on Safeguards*, this right of suspension shall not be exercised during the first three years that a safeguard

124 See above, p. 494. Note, however, that Members may deviate from these rules as provided for in Article 5.2(b) of the *Agreement on Safeguards*, discussed above, p. 650. Note also that, unlike Article XIII of the GATT 1994, Article 5.1, second sentence, and Article 5.2(a) do not apply to tariff quotas. See Panel Report, *US – Line Pipe (2002)*, para. 7.75.

125 See above, pp. 630–4.

126 For a recent application of, and finding of inconsistency with, Article 8.1, see Panel Report, *Ukraine – Passenger Cars (2015)*, para. 7.553.

127 See Appellate Body Reports, *US – Wheat Gluten (2001)*, paras. 144–6; and *US – Line Pipe (2002)*, paras. 114–19. Both Articles 8.1 and 12.3 make an explicit reference to each other and are thus automatically linked.

128 The right of suspension of 'substantially equivalent concessions' is conditional upon the notification of the proposed suspension measure to the Council for Trade in Goods and the absence of disapproval by the Goods Council. As the Council for Trade in Goods takes decisions by consensus, disapproval is *de facto* excluded.

measure is in effect in cases where: (1) the safeguard measure has been taken as a result of an absolute increase in imports; and (2) the safeguard measure conforms to the provisions of the *Agreement on Safeguards*. In *US – Steel Safeguards (2003)*, the United States arguably did not provide an adequate opportunity for consultations on compensation prior to the imposition of its safeguard measures because it implemented the measures only fifteen days after its notification of the measures.[129] Although this issue was not raised before the panel, several affected Members, including the European Union, Japan, China, Switzerland and Norway notified, as required by Article 12.5 of the *Agreement on Safeguards*, their intention to suspend concessions of an equivalent amount against the United States.[130] In September 2002, the United States notified a reduction of the range of steel products subject to its safeguard measures.[131] After the adoption of the panel and Appellate Body reports that found its steel safeguards measures WTO-inconsistent, the United States withdrew these measures and the suspensions that other Members had threatened to impose were not implemented.[132]

2.3.5 Provisional Safeguard Measures

Article 6 of the *Agreement on Safeguards* allows Members to take provisional safeguard measures in 'critical circumstances'. Critical circumstances are defined as circumstances 'where delay would cause damage which it would be difficult to repair'. Before taking provisional safeguard measures, the competent domestic authorities must make a preliminary determination that there is clear evidence that the increased imports have caused or are threatening to cause serious injury.[133] Provisional measures may be applied only for a maximum of 200 days and can only take the form of tariff increases.[134] If the competent authorities conclude, after a fully-fledged investigation, that the conditions for imposing a safeguard measure are not fulfilled, the provisional measure shall lapse and duties collected must be refunded.[135]

129 Y. S. Lee, 'Test of Multilateralism in International Trade: US Steel Safeguards', bepress Legal Series Paper 253, 2004, 42.

130 See G/SG/43 and Suppl.1, G/SG/44 and Suppl.1, G/SG/45, G/SG/46, G/SG/47, all dated May 2002. For example, the European Communities notified the adoption of Council Regulation (EC) No. 1031/2002 of 13 June 2002 establishing additional customs duties on imports of certain products originating in the United States of America, OJ 2002, L157, 8. The regulation notes that the safeguard measure adopted by the US was not taken in response to an *absolute increase* in imports and therefore that a part of the Community's concessions corresponding to the safeguard measure that was not taken as a result of an absolute increase of imports and representing an amount of applicable duties of €379 million might be subject to additional duties as from 18 June 2002. However, the Community indicated that it would decide whether to apply additional duties in light of decisions by the United States on economically meaningful product exclusions and on the presentation of an acceptable offer on trade compensation. Similarly, Japan notified the adoption of the Cabinet Order concerning the Suspension of Concessions to Certain Steel Products Originating in the United States of America (Cabinet Order No. 212, proclaimed by publication in the Official Gazette on 17 June 2002) on 14 June 2002, which became effective on 18 June 2002, upon the expiration of thirty days from the day on which written notice of the suspension was received by the CTG.

131 G/SG/N/10/USA/6/Suppl.7, G/SG/N/11/USA/5/Suppl.7, dated September 2002.

132 G/SG/N/10/USA/6/Suppl.8, dated 12 December 2003.

133 On these requirements for the application of provisional safeguard measures, see above, pp. 639–43.

134 Extension is not possible and the duration of the provisional safeguard measure will be counted when calculating the duration of the definitive safeguard measure. See above, pp. 648–9.

135 See Article 6 of the *Agreement on Safeguards*.

In view of the maximum duration of provisional safeguard measures, the average length of WTO dispute settlement proceedings and the prospective nature of WTO remedies, it may be difficult to challenge such measures effectively in practice. In *Dominican Republic – Safeguard Measures (2012)*, the panel considered it unnecessary to make specific findings on the provisional measure which had expired and been replaced by the definitive measure at the time of the establishment of the panel, because the complainants' principal claims in respect of the expired provisional measure were the same claims made in respect of the definitive measure.[136]

3 SAFEGUARD MEASURES UNDER OTHER WTO AGREEMENTS

Next to safeguard measures under the GATT 1994 and the *Agreement on Safeguards*, WTO law also provides for safeguard measures under other WTO agreements. This section deals in turn with: (1) safeguard measures under the *Agreement on Agriculture*; and (2) safeguard measures under the *Protocol on the Accession of the People's Republic of China.*[137] This section also discusses the absence of safeguard measures under the GATS.

3.1 Safeguard Measures under the *Agreement on Agriculture*

The *Agreement on Agriculture* provides for 'special safeguards' that a Member may take in relation to the products that have been 'tariffied' (i.e. the conversion of non-tariff barriers into tariffs) and that have been designated in that Member's Schedule with the symbol 'SSG'.[138] As the Appellate Body explained in *Chile – Price Band System (Article 21.5 – Argentina) (2007)*, the provisions of Article 5 of the *Agreement on Agriculture* establish the conditions in which a Member may have recourse to such a special safeguard, set out rules on the form and duration of such safeguard measures, and establish certain transparency requirements that attach to their use. According to the Appellate Body in that case:

> One circumstance in which a qualifying Member may be authorized to adopt a special safeguard is when the price of imports of a relevant agricultural product falls below a specified trigger price. However, pursuant to Article 5, a special safeguard can be imposed only on those agricultural products for which measures within the meaning of footnote 1 were converted into ordinary customs duties and for which a Member has reserved in its Schedule of Concessions a right to resort to these safeguards.[139]

136 See Panel Report, *Dominican Republic – Safeguard Measures (2012)*, para. 7.22.

137 Note that the transitional textile safeguard measures under the *Agreement on Textiles and Clothing* are no longer available because that Agreement has expired. Safeguard measures under the now defunct *Agreement on Textiles and Clothing* were subject to WTO dispute settlement in *US – Underwear (Costa Rica) (1997)*; *US – Wool Shirts and Blouses from India (1997)*; and *US – Cotton Yarn (Pakistan) (2001)*.

138 On 'tariffication', see above, p. 490. 'SSG' stands for 'special safeguards'.

139 Appellate Body Report, *Chile – Price Band System (Article 21.5 – Argentina) (2007)*, para. 173.

Under Article 5 of the *Agreement on Agriculture*, a special safeguard can be imposed when the *volume* of imports of an agricultural product during any year *exceeds* a specific trigger level,[140] *or*, where the *import price* of such product, determined on the basis of its CIF import price, falls *below* a trigger price which is equal to the average 1986–8 reference price for the product.[141] With regard to special safeguards based on *prices*, the Appellate Body held in *EC – Poultry (1998)* that the import price to be considered against the trigger price is merely the CIF price and that it does not include ordinary customs duties that became payable on the imports.[142] Under Article 5.1(b), therefore, the price at which 'the product may enter the customs territory of the Member granting the concession, as determined on the basis of the CIF import price' is the CIF import price alone and not the CIF import price *plus* applicable duties. The method of calculation of these trigger levels and prices is specified in paragraphs 4 and 5 of Article 5, respectively. The amount of additional duty that may be imposed on a product is determined in accordance with these provisions. The Appellate Body held in *EC – Poultry (1998)* that, under Article 5.5 of the *Agreement on Agriculture*, the comparison of the CIF price with the trigger price can only be on a *shipment-by-shipment basis*. The practice of the European Communities to determine the import price on the basis of a fixed standard 'representative price' therefore was impermissible.[143] Note that, in order to impose special safeguards, there is no need to demonstrate injury to the domestic industry/agricultural sector. Note also that special safeguard measures can only take the form of additional duties on the products concerned.[144]

As discussed in Chapter 7, Article 4.2 of the *Agreement on Agriculture* states:

> Members shall not maintain, resort to, or revert to any measures of the kind which have been required to be converted into ordinary customs duties, except as otherwise provided for in Article 5 and Annex 5.[145]

The Appellate Body addressed the relationship between Articles 4.2 and 5 of the *Agreement on Agriculture* in *Chile – Price Band System (2002)*. The Appellate Body argued that:

> the existence of a market access exemption in the form of a special safeguard provision under Article 5 implies that Article 4.2 should *not* be interpreted in a way that permits

140 See Article 5.1(a) of the *Agreement on Agriculture*. The trigger level relates to existing market access opportunity as set out in Article 5.4. Note that, as a general rule, safeguards of this kind will expire by the end of the given year. See Article 5.4 of the *Agreement on Agriculture*.

141 See *ibid.*, Article 5.1(b) of *Agreement on Agriculture*. According to the footnote to the provision, this will in general be the average CIF per unit value of the product. Subparagraphs (a) and (b) of Article 5.1 cannot be applied concurrently.

142 See Appellate Body Report, *EC – Poultry (1998)*, paras. 144–6. Note that the panel's interpretation in this regard was reversed.

143 See *ibid.*, paras. 159–71.

144 On the relationship between the *Agreement on Agriculture*, on the one hand, and the *Agreement on Safeguards* and the GATT 1994, on the other hand, note Article 5.8 and Article 21.1 of the *Agreement on Agriculture*.

145 See above, pp. 489–91.

Members to maintain measures that a Member would not be permitted to maintain *but for* Article 5, and, much less, measures that are even more trade-distorting than special safeguards. In particular, if Article 4.2 were interpreted in a way that allowed Members to maintain measures that operate in a way similar to a special safeguard within the meaning of Article 5 – but without respecting the conditions set out in that provision for invoking such measures – it would be difficult to see how proper meaning and effect could be given to those conditions set forth in Article 5.[146]

According to the Appellate Body in Chile – *Price Band System (Article 21.5 – Argentina) (2007)*:

the existence of an exemption from the market access requirements in the form of a special safeguard under Article 5 suggests that this provision ... was the narrowly circumscribed vehicle to be used by those Members who reserved their rights to do so in order to derogate from the requirements of Article 4.2.[147]

During the Doha Round negotiations, the issue of a new Special Safeguard Mechanism (SSM) allowing developing countries to raise tariffs on agricultural products temporarily above bindings in response to import increases and price falls was much discussed.[148] However, Members have failed to reach agreement on several aspects of this new SSM, and in particular on the question of whether developing countries would be allowed to raise tariffs above the pre-Doha Round bindings.[149] It has been reported that it was the disagreement on this issue between the United States on the one hand and India and China on the other, that prevented Members in the summer of 2008 from realising a breakthrough in the Doha Round negotiations.[150] At the 2015 Nairobi Ministerial Conference, WTO Members declared that:

The developing country Members will have the right to have recourse to a special safeguard mechanism (SSM) ...[151]

and agreed to continue negotiations on such a SSM.[152]

3.2 Safeguard Measures under China's Accession Protocol

Section 16 of the *Protocol on the Accession of the People's Republic of China*, commonly referred to as China's Accession Protocol, provided for a *transitional product-specific safeguard mechanism.* Pursuant to paragraph 16.9 of China's Accession Protocol, this special safeguard mechanism expired at the end of

146 Appellate Body Report, *Chile – Price Band System (2002)*, para. 217.
147 Appellate Body Report, *Chile – Price Band System (Article 21.5 – Argentina) (2007)*, para. 174.
148 On tariff bindings, see above, p. 436.
149 See www.wto.org/english/tratop_e/agric_e/guide_agric_safeg_e.htm.
150 On the Doha Round negotiations, see above, pp. 93–9.
151 Ministerial Conference, *Ministerial Decision of 19 December 2015 on the Special Safeguard Mechanism (SSM) for Developing Countries*, WT/MIN(15)/43, dated 21 December 2015, para. 1.
152 See *ibid.*, para. 2.

2013. Under this mechanism, WTO Members were allowed a special safeguard measure:

> [i]n cases where products of Chinese origin are being imported into the territory of any WTO Member in such increased quantities or under such conditions as to cause or threaten to cause *market disruption* to the domestic producers of like or directly competitive products, the WTO Member so affected may request consultations with China with a view to seeking a mutually satisfactory solution.[153]

A core condition for the application of a product-specific transitional safeguard is 'market disruption'. Paragraph 16.4 of China's Accession Protocol provided that market disruption is deemed to exist whenever imports of a product, that is like or directly competitive with a product produced by the domestic industry, are increasing rapidly, either absolutely or relatively, so as to be a significant cause of material injury, or threat of material injury to the domestic industry.[154] The injury threshold provided for in paragraph 16.4 required a showing of 'material injury', rather than 'serious injury' (such as in Article 2.1 of the *Agreement on Safeguards* as discussed above). Generally speaking, the threshold for the application of special safeguard measures under China's Accession Protocol was significantly lower than that for general safeguard measures under the *Agreement on Safeguards*.[155]

3.3 Safeguard Measures under the GATS

Article X of the GATS calls for multilateral negotiations on the question of emergency safeguard measures relating to trade in services. After more than twenty years of negotiations, WTO Members still hold diverging views on the question of an emergency safeguard mechanism (ESM) under the GATS. Divergences remain on basic issues such as the structure, desirability, necessity and feasibility of such a services ESM.

Members who oppose or are sceptical about an ESM for trade in services (virtually all OECD countries and a few developing-country Members) are not convinced that an ESM is desirable, considering: (1) the flexibility that Members have in scheduling commitments under the GATS; and (2) the risk that an ESM might undermine the stability of existing commitments. Those Members also doubt how a services ESM would work in practice, and point to the scarcity of reliable trade and production data in many sectors and the technical complexities associated with the multi-modal structure of the GATS. For example, under mode 3 ('commercial presence') and mode 4 ('presence of natural persons'), how – and to what extent – would an ESM restrict service output of service suppliers of foreign origin that are established juridical persons (but

153 Paragraph 16.1 of China's Accession Protocol. Emphasis added.
154 See para. 16.4 of China's Accession Protocol.
155 Note that paragraph 16.4 of China's Accession Protocol also set out a distinct causation standard.

owned or controlled by another Member) or resident citizens of foreign origin in the Member that seeks to impose safeguard measures under such a mechanism?

Members who support the creation of a services ESM argue that the availability of safeguards in the event of unforeseeable market disruptions is necessary in order to convince domestic constituents to accept the undertaking of access commitments in services. These Members also argue that the availability of an ESM 'safety valve' would encourage Members to enter into more far-reaching commitments in services negotiations. In their view, abuse could be avoided through strict procedural disciplines, and data problems should not be exaggerated, given the existence of professional associations, regulators and licensing bodies that compile relevant information in many sectors.[156]

4 BALANCE-OF-PAYMENTS MEASURES UNDER THE GATT 1994 AND THE GATS

In addition to safeguard measures, the 'economic emergency exceptions' discussed in this chapter, also allow Members to adopt 'balance-of-payments measures', commonly referred to as 'BoP measures'. This section first addresses BoP measures under the GATT 1994, and then briefly refers to BoP measures under the GATS.

4.1 Balance-of-Payments Measures under the GATT 1994

The rules regarding BoP measures under the GATT 1994 are set out in Articles XII and XVIII:B of the GATT 1994. The BoP exception for trade in goods is further elaborated in the *Understanding on Balance of Payments Provisions of the GATT 1994* (the '*Understanding on BoP Provisions*'), which is part of the GATT 1994. The rules set out in these provisions allow Members to adopt measures, that would be otherwise GATT-inconsistent, to safeguard their external financial position and to protect their balance of payments. The outflow of money from a country can indeed be limited, in a fairly simple and effective manner, by imposing trade-restrictive measures on imports into the country. In the past, the BoP measures were quite frequent. In today's world of floating exchange rates, BoP problems may be resolved by other means than trade restrictions. Nevertheless, BoP measures are still of some importance. Developing-country Members, in particular, continue to use these measures. In times of rapid economic development, countries often experience severe pressure on their monetary reserves.

156 See Annual Report of the Working Party on GATS Rules to the Council for Trade in Services 2012, S/WPGR/23, dated 29 November 2012; and Annual Report of the Working Party on GATS Rules to the Council for Trade in Services 2011, S/WPGR/22, dated 10 November 2011.

However, important users in the 1980s and 1990s of trade restrictions for BoP purposes, such as India and Nigeria, no longer use such measures.[157] In 2015, Ukraine and Ecuador imposed trade restrictions for BoP purposes.[158]

On 20 January 2015 Ukraine notified the WTO that as from 25 February 2015 it would introduce a temporary import surcharge of 5 or 10 per cent on almost all imports.[159] Ukraine introduced this tariff surcharge to deal with 'exceptional conditions' affecting its balance of payments.[160] During several rounds of consultations in early 2015, Members were unable to reach consensus on the WTO consistency of the import surcharge applied by Ukraine.[161] At the meeting of the WTO Committee on Balance-of-Payments Restrictions on 17 February 2016, Ukraine announced that, in keeping with the time-schedule communicated in 2015, it had entirely dismantled its import surcharge.[162]

On 2 April 2015 Ecuador notified the WTO that on 11 March 2015 it had introduced a temporary tariff surcharge for a period of up to fifteen months.[163] Ecuador introduced this tariff surcharge 'in view of the highly unfavourable economic climate prevailing in the country and its impact on the balance of payments'.[164] The declared purpose of the tariff surcharge was to regulate the general level of imports and thereby resolve Ecuador's critical balance-of-payments problems.[165] The tariff surcharge of 5, 15, 25 or 45 per cent initially applied to 2,955 10-digit subheading and, in value terms, 31 per cent of the imports in 2014.[166] The highest tariff surcharge of 45 per cent was imposed on

157 On India, see Report by the Secretariat, *Trade Policy Review: India*, WT/TPR/S/182, dated 18 April 2007, para. 58. On Nigeria, see A. Oyejide, O. Ogunkola and A. Bankole, 'Nigeria: Import Prohibition as a Trade Policy', in P. Gallagher, P. Low and A. Stoler (eds.), *Managing the Challenges of WTO Participation: 45 Case Studies* (Cambridge University Press, 2005), 444–5.

158 Note that both Ukraine and Ecuador also applied trade restrictions for balance-of-payment purposes in 2009, which were withdrawn the same year and 2010 respectively. See Annual Report of the BoP Committee for 2009, WT/BOP/R/96, dated 30 October 2009; and Annual Report of the BoP Committee for 2010, WT/BOP/R/101, dated 2 November 2010.

159 Committee on Balance-of-Payments Restrictions, *Notification under Paragraph 9 of the Understanding on the Balance-of-Payments Provisions of the General Agreement on Tariffs and Trade 1994, Communication from Ukraine*, WT/BOP/N/78, dated 21 January 2015. See *ibid.* See also WT/BOP/N/78/Add.1, dated 31 March 2015. The surcharge 5 per cent on industrial products and 10 per cent on agricultural products.

160 The 'exceptional circumstances' referred to were increased barriers to Ukrainian export to traditional markets, unfavourable market prices for major export goods, anti-terrorist operation in eastern Ukraine and annexation of Crimea, dramatic devaluation of the national currency, destabilisation of the banking system and outflow of investments. See *ibid.*

161 Consensus was not reached because one Member considered Ukraine's import surcharges to be WTO-inconsistent. See www.wto.org/english/news_e/news16_e/bop_17feb16_e.htm.

162 See *ibid.*

163 Committee on Balance-of-Payments Restrictions, *Notification under Paragraph 9 of the Understanding on the Balance-of-Payments Provisions of the General Agreement on Tariffs and Trade 1994, Communication from Ecuador*, WT/BOP/N/79, dated 7 April 2015, para. 1.

164 *Ibid.* With regard to the unfavourable international environment, Ecuador referred *inter alia* to the fall in the international prices of oil and other commodities, the decline in remittances from Ecuadorian residents abroad, and the appreciation of the US dollar, which is legal tender in Ecuador. See *ibid.*, para. 3.

165 See *ibid.*, para. 2.

166 See *ibid.*, paras. 7–8. According to Ecuador the measure notified does not exceed what is necessary to address its balance-of-payments disequilibrium of between US$2 and 2.4 billion. See *ibid.*, para. 2.

final consumer goods.[167] In October 2015, Ecuador presented a time-schedule for gradual phasing out of the tariff surcharge by June 2016.[168] While several WTO Members expressed sympathy with Ecuador's balance-of-payments problems, Members were unable to reach consensus on whether the tariff surcharge applied is WTO consistent. In May 2016, Ecuador informed the WTO that in view of its 'unfavourable economic climate', which worsened following the devastating earthquake that hit the coastal areas of Ecuador in April 2016, the tariff surcharge will be extended for another year.[169] While all WTO Members expressed solidarity with the people of Ecuador who experienced the 'worst natural disaster in 70 years', several Members urged Ecuador to phase out its tariff surcharge as soon as possible and to adopt less trade-restrictive measures.[170]

Article XII of the GATT 1994, entitled 'Restrictions to Safeguard the Balance of Payments', states, in its first paragraph:

> Notwithstanding the provisions of paragraph 1 of Article XI, any [Member], in order to safeguard its external financial position and its balance of payments, may restrict the quantity or value of merchandise permitted to be imported, subject to the provisions of the following paragraphs of this Article.

Article XVIII of the GATT 1994, entitled 'Governmental Assistance to Economic Development', provides in paragraph 4(a) as follows:

> [A Member], the economy of which can only support low standards of living and is in the early stages of development, shall be free to deviate temporarily from the provisions of the other Articles of this Agreement, as provided in Sections A, B and C of this Article.

Section B of Article XVIII (i.e. paragraphs 8 to 12 of Article XVIII) provides for a special BoP exception for developing-country Members. Article XVIII:9 states, in relevant part:

> In order to safeguard its external financial position and to ensure a level of reserves adequate for the implementation of its programme of economic development, a [Member] coming within the scope of paragraph 4(*a*) of this Article may, subject to the provisions of paragraphs 10 to 12, control the general level of its imports by restricting the quantity or value of merchandise permitted to be imported; *Provided* that ...

Under Article XII, the purpose of a Member's BoP measure is 'to safeguard its external financial position and its balance of payments'. Under Article XVIII:B,

167 Products that are essential in the light of the country's policy of economic development, as well as those that meet the basic consumption needs of the Ecuadorian population, have been excluded from the tariff surcharge, for example: capital goods, inputs and raw materials essential to production, medicines and medical equipment. See *ibid.*, para. 6. On the surcharges imposed, see Committee on Balance-of-Payments Restrictions, *Notification under Paragraph 9 of the Understanding on the Balance-of-Payments Provisions of the General Agreement on Tariffs and Trade 1994, Communication from Ecuador, Addendum*, WT/BOP/N/79/Add. 1 and 2, dated 7 April 2015.

168 See www.wto.org/english/news_e/news15_e/bop_16oct15_e.htm.

169 The tariff surcharge will now be reduced by one-third by April 2017 and phased out by June 2017. See Committee on Balance-of-Payments Restrictions, *Notification under Paragraph 9 of the Understanding on the Balance-of-Payments Provisions of the General Agreement on Tariffs and Trade 1994, Communication from Ecuador, Addendum*, WT/BOP/N/82, dated 10 May 2016.

170 See www.wto.org/english/news_e/news16_e/bop_23jun16_e.htm.

the purpose of a BoP measure taken by a developing-country Member is also 'to safeguard its external financial position' but, in addition, 'to ensure a level of reserves adequate for the implementation of its programme of economic development'. This section examines: (1) the nature of measures that may be taken for BoP purposes; (2) the requirements for taking such measures; and (3) relevant procedural issues.

4.1.1 Nature of Balance-of-Payments Measures

Articles XII and XVIII:B of the GATT 1994 only allow quantitative restrictions to be used to address BoP problems.[171] However, it was common practice under the GATT 1947 for Contracting Parties to take BoP action in the form of tariff or tariff-like measures, such as import surcharges. In 1979, the use of such measures was formally authorised in the *Declaration on Trade Measures Taken for Balance of Payments Purposes* (the '*1979 Declaration*').[172] The 1994 *Understanding on BoP Provisions* goes much further and commits WTO Members to give preference to price-based BoP measures. Paragraph 2 of the *Understanding on BoP Provisions* states:

> Members confirm their commitment to give preference to those measures which have the least disruptive effect on trade. Such measures (referred to in this Understanding as 'price-based measures') shall be understood to include import surcharges, import deposit requirements or other equivalent trade measures with an impact on the price of imported goods. It is understood that, notwithstanding the provisions of Article II, price-based measures taken for balance-of-payments purposes may be applied by a Member in excess of the duties inscribed in the Schedule of that Member ...

If a Member decides to apply a price-based BoP measure, it must indicate the amount by which the price-based measure exceeds the bound duty clearly and separately.[173]

While, under Article XII, quantitative restrictions were initially the only form of BoP measures allowed, paragraph 3 of the *Understanding on BoP Provisions* now reads:

> Members shall seek to avoid the imposition of new quantitative restrictions for balance-of-payments purposes unless, because of a critical balance-of-payments situation, price-based measures cannot arrest a sharp deterioration in the external payments position.

If a Member applies a quantitative restriction as a BoP measure, it must provide justification as to the reasons why price-based measures are not an adequate instrument to deal with the BoP situation.[174] Pursuant to the *Understanding on*

171 Note that this rule is inconsistent with the general GATT preference for using tariffs instead of quantitative restrictions. See above, pp. 488–9.

172 Adopted on 28 November 1979, BISD 26S/205–9. Note that this Declaration is still applicable law.

173 See *Understanding on BoP Provisions*, para. 2. For this purpose, the notification procedure, discussed below, must be followed.

174 See *ibid.*, para. 3. Note that Members applying quantitative restrictions as BoP measures must also indicate in successive consultations the progress made in significantly reducing the incidence and restrictive effect of such measures (*ibid.*).

BoP Provisions, not more than one type of restrictive import measure, taken for BoP purposes, may be applied on the same product.[175] A combination of price-based measures and quantitative restrictions on the same product is therefore prohibited.

4.1.2 Requirements for the Use of Balance-of-Payments Measures

BoP measures, whether in the form of price-based measures or quantitative restrictions, are often inconsistent with the obligations under Articles II or XI of the GATT 1994. Therefore, they may only be applied when strict requirements are met.

First, BoP measures may *not exceed what is necessary* to address the BoP problem at hand. Article XII:2(a) of the GATT 1994 states that BoP measures adopted by a Member:

> shall not exceed those necessary: (i) to forestall the imminent threat of, or to stop, a serious decline in its monetary reserves, or (ii). in the case of a [Member] with very low monetary reserves, to achieve a reasonable rate of increase in its reserves.

Article XVIII:9 of the GATT 1994 requires that BoP measures adopted by a developing-country Member:

> shall not exceed those necessary: (a). to forestall the threat of, or to stop, a serious decline in its monetary reserves, or (b). in the case of a [Member] with inadequate monetary reserves, to achieve a reasonable rate of increase in its reserves.

Note that developing-country Members may adopt BoP measures to forestall a *threat* of a serious decline in monetary reserves, while other Members are only permitted to forestall an *imminent threat* of such decline. Also, developing-country Members with *inadequate* monetary reserves may also adopt BoP measures to achieve a reasonable rate of *increase* in their reserves while other Members may do so only when they have *very low* monetary reserves. In *India – Quantitative Restrictions (1999)*, the panel distinguished the requirements for taking BoP measures under Article XVIII from the requirements applicable under Article XII, and noted:

> These provisions reflect an acknowledgement of the specific needs of developing countries in relation to measures taken for balance-of-payments purposes.[176]

At the Doha Ministerial Conference in November 2001, the WTO Members explicitly affirmed that Article XVIII is a special and differential treatment provision for developing-country Members and that recourse to it should be *less onerous* than to Article XII.[177]

The determination of what constitutes a serious decline of monetary reserves or an (imminent) threat thereof, or the determination of what constitutes very

175 See *ibid*. 176 Panel Report, *India – Quantitative Restrictions (1999)*, para. 5.155.
177 See Ministerial Conference, *Ministerial Decision on Implementation-Related Issues and Concerns*, adopted on 14 November 2001, WT/MIN(01)/17, dated 20 November 2001, para. 1.1.

low or inadequate monetary reserves, is primarily left to the IMF. The WTO consults the IMF on these matters, and Article XV:2 of the GATT 1994 states, in relevant part:

> The [WTO] in reaching [its] final decision in cases involving the criteria set forth in paragraph 2(*a*) of Article XII or in paragraph 9 of Article XVIII, shall accept the determination of the [IMF] as to what constitutes a serious decline in the [Member's] monetary reserves, a very low level of its monetary reserves or a reasonable rate of increase in its monetary reserves, and as to the financial aspects of other matters covered in consultation in such cases.

Note that, in *India – Quantitative Restrictions (1999)*, the IMF reported that India's reserves as of 21 November 1997 were US$25.1 billion and that an adequate level of reserves at that date would have been US$16 billion. The IMF had also reported that India did not face a serious decline of its monetary reserves or a threat thereof.[178] To a large extent, the panel's conclusions in this case were based on these IMF findings.

Second, BoP measures must *avoid unnecessary damage* to the commercial and economic interests of other Members.[179] BoP measures may be discriminatory with respect to products (i.e. apply to some products and not to others), but *not* with respect to countries (i.e. apply to some countries and not to others). Note that the *Understanding on BoP Provisions* requires that Members administer BoP measures in a transparent manner. The authorities of the importing Member must therefore provide adequate justification as to the criteria used to determine which products are subject to the BoP measure.[180]

Third, BoP measures are *temporary measures*. Members applying BoP measures must announce publicly, as soon as possible, time-schedules for the removal of these measures.[181] Referring to the conditions for their adoption (such as 'a serious decline in monetary reserves' or 'inadequate monetary reserves'), Article XII:2(b) of the GATT 1994 states:

> [Members] applying restrictions under sub-paragraph (*a*) of this paragraph shall progressively relax them as such conditions improve, maintaining them only to the extent that the conditions specified in that sub-paragraph still justify their application. They shall eliminate the restrictions when conditions would no longer justify their institution or maintenance under that sub-paragraph.

As the external financial situation improves, the BoP measures must be relaxed; when the external financial situation has returned to 'normal', the BoP measures

178 See Panel Report, *India – Quantitative Restrictions (1999)*, paras. 5.174 and 5.177.
179 See Articles XII:3(c)(i) and XVIII:10 of the GATT 1994.
180 In the case of certain 'essential products', a Member may exclude or limit the application of surcharges applied across the board or other measures applied for BoP purposes. The concept of 'essential products' shall be understood to mean products which meet basic consumption needs or which contribute to the Member's effort to improve its BoP situation, such as capital goods or inputs needed for production. See Articles XII:3 and XVIII:10 of the GATT 1994; and *Understanding on BoP Provisions*, para. 4.
181 See *ibid.*, para. 1.

must be eliminated.[182] Article XVIII:11 of the GATT 1994 provides for similar obligations with respect to the elimination or relaxation of BoP measures adopted by developing-country Members. However, Article XVIII:11 adds the proviso:

> that no [Member] shall be required to withdraw or modify restrictions on the ground that a change in its development policy would render unnecessary the restrictions which it is applying under this Section.

In *India – Quantitative Restrictions (1999)*, the Appellate Body upheld the panel's finding that India could manage its BoP situation using macroeconomic policy instruments alone, without maintaining quantitative restrictions. India appealed this finding, arguing that the panel required India to change its development policy. The Appellate Body, however, ruled:

> [W]e are of the opinion that the use of macroeconomic policy instruments is not related to any particular development policy, but is resorted to by all Members regardless of the type of development policy they pursue.[183]

The Appellate Body clarified the meaning of the proviso of Article XVIII:11 by stating:

> We believe that structural measures are different from macroeconomic instruments with respect to their relationship to development policy. If India were asked to implement agricultural reform or to scale back reservations on certain products for small-scale units as indispensable policy changes in order to overcome its balance-of-payments difficulties, such a requirement would probably have involved a change in India's development policy.[184]

4.1.3 Procedural Issues

BoP measures are reviewed by the WTO to determine their consistency with the GATT 1994. This review is conducted by the Committee on Balance-of-Payments Restrictions (the 'BoP Committee'). The procedures applicable to this review are set out in the *Understanding on BoP Provisions.*[185] A Member shall notify the introduction of, or any changes in the application of, a BoP measure to the General Council.[186] A Member applying new restrictions or raising

182 For BoP measures of developing-country Members, however, note that, if the elimination or relaxation of the BoP measures would produce immediately or very quickly the conditions justifying the adoption or intensification of BoP measures, the BoP measures 'may be maintained'. See Note *Ad* Article XVIII; and Appellate Body Report, *India – Quantitative Restrictions (1999)*, paras. 117–20.

183 Appellate Body Report, *India – Quantitative Restrictions (1999)*, para. 126.

184 *Ibid.*, para. 128.

185 As *Understanding on BoP Provisions*, para. 5, states, the BoP Committee shall follow the procedures for consultations on BoP restrictions approved on 28 April 1970 (BISD18S/48–53) (the 'full consultation procedures'), subject to the provisions set out in the *Understanding.* Consultations may be held under the 'simplified consultation procedures' approved on 19 December 1972 (BISD 20S/47–9) in the case of least-developed-country Members or in the case of developing-country Members in certain situations. See *ibid.*, para. 8.

186 See *ibid.*, para. 9. Every year, each Member shall make available to the WTO Secretariat a consolidated notification on all aspects of the BoP measures applied. *Ibid.*

the general level of its existing restrictions must enter into consultation with the BoP Committee within four months of the adoption of such measures.[187] If the Member concerned fails to request a consultation, the Chair of the BoP Committee shall invite that Member to hold such a consultation. Any Member may request that notifications on BoP measures are reviewed by the BoP Committee.[188] Furthermore, all BoP measures are subject to *periodic* review by the BoP Committee.[189]

The BoP Committee reports on its consultations to the General Council. Pursuant to paragraph 13 of the *Understanding on BoP Provisions*, the BoP Committee shall endeavour to include in its conclusions 'proposals for recommendations aimed at promoting the implementation of Articles XII and XVIII:B, the 1979 Declaration and this Understanding'. In those cases in which a time-schedule has been presented for the removal of BoP measures, the General Council may recommend that, in adhering to such a time-schedule, a Member shall be deemed to be in compliance with its GATT 1994 obligations. Whenever the General Council has made specific recommendations, the rights and obligations of Members shall be assessed in light of such recommendations. In the absence of specific proposals for recommendations by the General Council, the Committee's conclusions should record the different views expressed in the Committee.[190]

Since its establishment in 1995, the BoP Committee has reviewed many BoP measures notified by Members. In most cases, the Members concerned made commitments to eliminate or relax the BoP measures under review and these commitments satisfied the BoP Committee. In other cases, Members were unable to agree within the BoP Committee on a time-schedule for the relaxation and/or elimination of the BoP measures under review.

In *India – Quantitative Restrictions (1999)*, India argued that it had the right to maintain BoP measures until the BoP Committee or the General Council ordered it to eliminate or relax these measures. The panel rejected this argument. It noted that the obligation of Article XVIII:11 to eliminate or relax BoP measures:

> is not conditioned on any BOP Committee or General Council decision. If we were to interpret Article XVIII:11 to be so conditioned, we would be adding terms to Article XVIII:11 that it does not contain.[191]

In *India – Quantitative Restrictions (1999)*, India also argued that WTO dispute settlement panels have no authority to examine Members' justifications of BoP

187 See *ibid.*, para. 6. Note that the Member adopting BoP measures may request that a consultation be held under Articles XII:4(a) or XVIII:12(a) of the GATT 1994 as appropriate. *Ibid.* On the course of the consultation process and the role of the WTO Secretariat, see *ibid.*, paras. 11 and 12.

188 See *ibid.*, para. 10.

189 See *ibid.*, para. 7, which refers in this respect to Articles XII:4(b) and XVIII:12(b) of the GATT 1994.

190 Note also the powers given to the Ministerial Conference in Articles XII:4(c), (d) and (f) and XVIII:12(c), (d) and (f) of the GATT 1994. These powers have never been used.

191 Panel Report, *India – Quantitative Restrictions (1999)*, para. 5.79.

measures.[192] India based its position on the second sentence of footnote 1 to the *Understanding on BoP Provisions*, which reads:

> The provisions of Articles XXII and XXIII of GATT 1994 as elaborated and applied by the Dispute Settlement Understanding may be invoked with respect to any matters arising from the application of restrictive import measures taken for balance-of-payments purposes.

India interpreted this footnote to mean that the WTO dispute settlement system may be invoked in respect of matters relating to the specific use or purpose of a BoP measure or to the manner in which a BoP measure is applied in a particular case, but not with respect to the question of the BoP *justification* of these measures. More generally, India argued for the existence of a 'principle of institutional balance' that requires panels to refrain from reviewing the justification of BoP restrictions under Article XVIII:B. Such review was entrusted to the BoP Committee and the General Council, the political organs of the WTO. Thus panels and the Appellate Body, the 'judicial' organs of the WTO, must refrain from such review. The Appellate Body rejected India's arguments and stated:

> Any doubts that may have existed in the past as to whether the dispute settlement procedures under Article XXIII were available for disputes relating to balance-of-payments restrictions have been removed by the second sentence of footnote 1 to the *BOP Understanding* ...
>
> [I]n light of footnote 1 to the *BOP Understanding*, a dispute relating to the justification of balance-of-payments restrictions is clearly within the scope of matters to which the dispute settlement provisions of Article XXIII of the GATT 1994, as elaborated and applied by the DSU, are applicable.[193]

The fact that panels are competent to review the justification of BoP measures does *not* make the competence of the BoP Committee and the General Council, discussed above, redundant. In *India – Quantitative Restrictions (1999)*, the Appellate Body ruled:

> We are cognisant of the competence of the BOP Committee and the General Council with respect to balance-of-payments restrictions under Article XVIII:12 of the GATT 1994 and the *BOP Understanding*. However, we see no conflict between that competence and the competence of panels. Moreover, we are convinced that, in considering the justification of balance-of-payments restrictions, panels should take into account the deliberations and conclusions of the BOP Committee, as did the panel in *Korea – Beef*.[194]

The Appellate Body agreed with the panel that the BoP Committee and panels have different functions, and that the BoP Committee procedures and the dispute settlement procedures differ in nature, scope, timing and type of outcome.[195]

In recent years, the use of BoP measures and notifications to the BoP Committee have become rare.[196]

192 See also above, p. 667.
193 Appellate Body Report, *India – Quantitative Restrictions (1999)*, paras. 87 and 95. 194 *Ibid.*, para. 104.
195 See *ibid.*, paras. 5.90 and 5.114. 196 With respect to recent use of BoP measures, see above, pp. 660–1.

4.2 Balance-of-Payments Measures under the GATS

Article XII:1 of the GATS, entitled 'Restrictions to Safeguard the Balance of Payments', provides, in its first sentence:

> In the event of serious balance-of-payments and external financial difficulties or threat thereof, a Member may adopt or maintain restrictions on trade in services on which it has undertaken specific commitments, including on payments or transfers for transactions related to such commitments.

Article XII:1, second sentence, of the GATS recognises that particular pressures on the balance-of-payments situation of a Member in the process of economic development or economic transition may necessitate the use of restrictions to maintain, *inter alia*, a level of financial reserves adequate for the implementation of its programme of economic development or economic transition.

In situations of *serious* BoP and external financial difficulties or a threat thereof, Members may adopt or maintain BoP measures that restrict trade in services in a GATS-inconsistent manner. However, as explicitly provided in Article XII:2 of the GATS, these BoP measures shall: (1) not discriminate among Members; (2) be consistent with the *Articles of Agreement of the IMF*; (3) avoid unnecessary damage to the commercial, economic and financial interests of any other Member; (4) not exceed those necessary to deal with the circumstances described in Article XII:1, quoted above; and (5) be temporary and phased out progressively as the situation described in Article XII:1 improves. Any BoP measure restricting trade in services, or any changes thereto, must be promptly notified to the General Council.[197] Members adopting or changing BoP measures must consult with the BoP Committee promptly.[198] Just as with BoP measures restricting trade in goods, BoP measures restricting trade in services are the subject of periodic consultations. The consultations with the BoP Committee shall address the compliance of BoP measures with the requirements of Article XII:2, in particular the progressive phasing out of restrictions.[199] The IMF also plays a central role with regard to BoP measures restricting trade in services in the consultations on the GATS-consistency of BoP measures.[200]

5 SUMMARY

WTO law provides for 'economic emergency exceptions'. These exceptions, set out primarily in Article XIX of the GATT 1994 and the *Agreement on*

197 See Article XII:4 of the GATS. 198 See Article XII:5(c) of the GATS.

199 See Article XII:5(d) of the GATS.

200 See Article XII:5(e) of the GATS. All findings of statistical and other facts presented by the IMF relating to foreign exchange, monetary reserves and balance of payments shall be accepted and the conclusions of the BoP Committee shall be based on the assessment by the IMF of the balance of payments and the external financial situation of the consulting Member.

Safeguards, allow Members to adopt measures that are otherwise WTO-inconsistent in situations where a surge in imports causes, or threatens to cause, serious injury to the domestic industry. The otherwise WTO-inconsistent measures taken in economic emergency situations are referred to as *safeguard measures*. Safeguard measures temporarily restrict imports to give the domestic industry concerned time for structural adjustment to new economic realities. Safeguard measures typically take the form of customs duties exceeding tariff bindings or quantitative restrictions. Safeguard measures must be limited in time and applied in a non-discriminatory manner to all sources of supply. Moreover, a Member applying a safeguard measure must seek to compensate other Members affected by the measure. Safeguard measures may only be applied when three requirements are met: (1) the 'increased imports' requirement; (2) the 'serious injury or threat thereof' requirement; and (3) the 'causation' requirement.

The 'increase in imports' must be recent, sudden, sharp and significant. 'Serious injury' exists when there is a significant overall impairment in the position of a domestic industry. A 'threat of serious injury' exists when serious injury is clearly imminent. The relevant domestic industry is the industry (or at least a major proportion of the domestic producers) producing like or directly competitive products. To determine whether there is, in fact, serious injury or a threat thereof to a domestic industry, all relevant factors of an objective and quantifiable nature having a bearing on the situation of that industry must be considered. The test for establishing 'causation' is twofold: (1) a demonstration of the causal link between the 'increased imports' and the 'serious injury or threat thereof' (the 'causal link' sub-requirement); and (2) an identification of any injury caused by factors other than the increased imports and the non-attribution of this injury to the increased imports (the 'non-attribution' sub-requirement).

WTO law also provides for 'balance-of-payments exceptions', set out in Articles XII and XVIII:B of the GATT 1994 (elaborated in the *Understanding on BoP Provisions*) and Article XII of the GATS. These exceptions allow Members to adopt measures, otherwise inconsistent with Articles II and XI of the GATT 1994 or Article XVI of the GATS, to safeguard their external financial position and to protect their balance of payments. BoP measures restricting trade in goods can take the form of quantitative restrictions *or* tariff-like, i.e. price-based, measures (such as import surcharges). The latter type of BoP measure is preferred. Generally speaking, BoP measures must not exceed what is necessary to safeguard the external financial situation (in terms of decline of its monetary reserves or the level of its monetary reserves). The requirements for BoP measures taken by developing-country Members (see Article XVIII:B) are less stringent than those for BoP measures taken by other Members (see Article XII).

FURTHER READINGS

J. Chaisse, D. Chakraborty and A. Kumar, 'Mastering a Two-Edged Sword: Lessons from the Rules and Litigation on Safeguards in the World Trade Organization', *Richmond Journal of Global Law and Business*, 2015, 13, 563.

C. P. Bown and M. Wu, 'Safeguards and the Perils of Preferential Trade Agreements: Dominican Republic – Safeguard Measures', *World Trade Review*, 2014, 13(2), 179–227.

J. Crawford, J. McKeagg and J. Tolstova, 'Mapping of Safeguard Provisions in Regional Trade Agreements', Staff Working Paper ERSD-2013-10, October 2013, World Trade Organization.

S. M. Higgins, 'The Special Safeguard Mechanism for Agriculture: The Use of Remedies Exceeding Pre-Doha Round Bound Tariff Commitments in the Most Concerned Developing Countries', *Manchester Journal of International Economic Law*, 2009, 6(3), 65–92.

R. Wolfe, 'The Special Safeguard Fiasco in the WTO: The Perils of Inadequate Analysis and Negotiation', *World Trade Review*, 2009, 8(4), 517–44.

M. Beshkar, 'Trade Skirmishes and Safeguards: A Theory of the WTO Dispute Settlement Process', WTO Staff Working Paper ERSD-2009-09, November 2009, World Trade Organization.

10 Regional Trade Exceptions

CONTENTS

1 INTRODUCTION

In addition to the 'general and security exceptions' and the 'economic emergency exceptions' discussed in Chapters 8 and 9 respectively, WTO law also provides for 'regional trade exceptions'. These exceptions allow Members to adopt measures that would otherwise be WTO-inconsistent, when they are in the pursuit of economic integration with other countries. While, in the past, the term 'regional trade exceptions' as well as the term 'regional trade agreements' (RTAs) described well the reality they referred to, in recent years these terms have given rise to some confusion. In the past, the term 'regional trade agreements' was used to refer to the economic integration efforts between adjacent countries or countries in the same region. Good examples of such *regional* economic integration efforts are the *North American Free Trade Agreement*, the *Southern Common Market (MERCOSUR) Agreement* and the *ASEAN Free Trade Area (AFTA) Agreement.*[1] To the extent that these and other *regional* economic integration efforts involved GATT 1994 or GATS-inconsistent measures, these measures could – under specific conditions – be justified under the *regional* trade exceptions of the GATT 1994 and the GATS. In recent years, however, the countries involved in economic integration efforts are often countries or groups of countries from *different regions*. Consider, for example, the *European Union–South Korea Free Trade Agreement*, the *United States–Colombia Trade Promotion Agreement* and the *India–MERCOSUR Preferential Trade Agreement.*[2] Instead of referring to these agreements as 'regional trade agreements', they are often referred to as 'preferential trade agreements' (PTAs). The WTO *World Trade Report 2011* stated:

> One half of the PTAs currently in force are not strictly 'regional'. The advent of cross-regional PTAs has been particularly pronounced in the last decade. The trend towards a broader geographical scope of PTAs is even more pronounced for those PTAs that are currently under negotiation or have recently been signed (but are not yet in force). Practically all of these are of the cross-regional type.[3]

However, as WTO Members and the WTO Secretariat continue to use the term 'regional trade agreements',[4] this book also continues to use this term, and discusses in this chapter the 'regional trade exceptions', even though the word 'regional' is almost a misnomer because such economic integration agreements often no longer have the traditional geographical connotation. The 'regional trade exceptions' are set out in Article XXIV and the Enabling Clause of the GATT 1994, and Article V of the GATS.[5] This chapter addresses: (1) the proliferation of regional trade agreements and their impact on the multilateral trading system; (2) regional trade exceptions under the GATT 1994; and (3) regional trade exceptions under the GATS.

1 For further details on these agreements, see below, pp. 673–9.

2 Also consider e.g. the *China–Costa Rica Free Trade Agreement*, the *Australia–Chile Free Trade Agreement*, the *Peru–Japan Economic Partnership Agreement*, the *Japan–Switzerland Free Trade and Economic Partnership Agreement* and the Economic Partnership Agreements (EPAs) between the European Union and groups of African, Caribbean and Pacific (ACP) States, such as the CARIFORUM States or the ECOWAS States.

3 World Trade Report 2011, *The WTO and Preferential Trade Agreements: From Co-existence to Coherence* (WTO, 2011), 6.

4 See e.g. www.wto.org/english/tratop_e/region_e/rta_pta_e.htm. Note also that the WTO Secretariat uses the term 'preferential trade *arrangements*' (PTAs) to refer to *unilateral* trade preferences. They include Generalised System of Preferences schemes (under which developed countries grant preferential tariffs to imports from developing countries). Information on PTAs notified to the WTO is available in the PTA Database, at http://ptadb.wto.org/?lang=1.

5 The economic integration exception for trade in goods is elaborated on further in the *Understanding on the Interpretation of Article XXIV of the GATT 1994* (the '*Understanding on Article XXIV*'), which forms part of the GATT 1994.

2 PROLIFERATION OF REGIONAL TRADE AGREEMENTS

Regional trade agreements have proliferated since the early 1990s, and have become an indelible feature of the international trading landscape. As of 1 October 2016, there were 268 regional trade agreements in force between WTO Members.[6] The share of world trade between parties to regional trade agreements has increased along with the proliferation of these agreements. It is estimated that, currently, half of world trade occurs among parties to regional trade agreements. However, it is important to note that only a portion of that trade actually takes place under the preferential conditions that in theory apply to the trade between parties to regional trade agreements.[7]

Well-known examples of regional trade agreements, establishing either a customs union or a free-trade area, are the European Union (EU),[8] the European Free Trade Association (EFTA),[9] the European Economic Area (EEA),[10] the North American Free Trade Agreement (NAFTA),[11] the ASEAN (Association of Southeast Asian Nations) Free Trade Area (AFTA),[12] the Southern Common Market (MERCOSUR),[13] the Andean Community,[14] the Common Market of the Caribbean (CARICOM),[15] the Australia–New Zealand Closer Economic Relations Agreement (ANZCERTA),[16] the Southern African Development Community (SADC),[17] the Economic Community of West African States (ECOWAS)[18] and the

6 See http://rtais.wto.org/UI/publicsummarytable.aspx. Note that this is the number of what the WTO refers to as 'physical' RTAs. For an RTA that includes both goods and services, the WTO database on RTAs counts two notifications (one for goods and the other services), even though it is physically one RTA. Up to 1 October 2016, the WTO received 426 notifications of RTAs. Note also that seventy-two 'physical' RTAs, which are currently in force, have not been notified to the WTO.

7 World Trade Report 2011, *WTO and Preferential Trade Agreements*, 72. Also see UNCTAD, *Key Statistics and Trends in Trade Policy 2015: Preferential Trade Agreements* (UN, 2015), 14.

8 The European Union comprises Austria, Belgium, Bulgaria, Cyprus, Czech Republic, Croatia, Denmark, Estonia, Finland, France, Germany, Greece, Hungary, Ireland, Italy, Latvia, Lithuania, Luxembourg, Malta, Netherlands, Poland, Portugal, Romania, Slovak Republic, Slovenia, Spain, Sweden and the United Kingdom. Note that United Kingdom voted in June 2016 to leave the European Union. However, the negotiations on the terms of the UK's exit from the European Union are yet to start. Note also that the European Union is of course more than a customs union, but at its core it is, *inter alia*, a customs union.

9 A free-trade agreement between Iceland, Liechtenstein, Norway and Switzerland.

10 A customs union and economic integration agreement between European Union and Iceland, Liechtenstein and Norway.

11 A free-trade agreement and economic integration agreement between Canada, Mexico and the United States.

12 A free-trade agreement between Brunei Darussalam, Cambodia, Indonesia, Laos, Malaysia, Myanmar, Philippines, Singapore, Thailand and Vietnam.

13 A customs union and economic integration agreement between Argentina, Brazil, Paraguay, Uruguay and Venezuela.

14 A customs union between Bolivia, Colombia, Ecuador and Peru.

15 A customs union and economic integration agreement between Antigua and Barbuda, Bahamas, Barbados, Belize, Dominica, Grenada, Guyana, Haiti, Jamaica, Montserrat, Saint Kitts and Nevis, Saint Lucia, Saint Vincent and the Grenadines, Suriname and Trinidad and Tobago.

16 A free-trade agreement and economic integration agreement between Australia and New Zealand.

17 A free-trade agreement between Angola, Botswana, the Democratic Republic of Congo, Lesotho, Madagascar, Malawi, Mauritius, Mozambique, Namibia, the Seychelles, South Africa, Swaziland, Tanzania, Zambia and Zimbabwe.

18 A customs union between Benin, Burkina Faso, Cape Verde, Côte d'Ivoire, Gambia, Ghana, Guinea, Guinea-Bissau, Liberia, Mali, Niger, Nigeria, Senegal, Sierra Leone and Togo.

Common Market of Eastern and Southern Africa (COMESA).[19] Negotiations on the Trans-Pacific Partnership (TPP) Agreement[20] were successfully concluded in October 2015 (but this agreement has not yet entered into force), while the negotiations on the Transatlantic Trade and Investment Partnership (TTIP)[21] are currently ongoing.

A WTO Member is, on average, a party to thirteen regional trade agreements.[22] There is no WTO Member that is not a party to a regional trade agreement.[23] The key characteristic of regional trade agreements is that the parties to such agreements offer each other more favourable treatment in trade matters than they offer other trading partners. To the extent that these other trading partners, which are denied the same treatment, are WTO Members, such discriminatory treatment is – as discussed in Chapter 4 – inconsistent with the MFN treatment obligation, one of the basic principles of WTO law. Yet, both the GATT 1994 and the GATS allow, under certain conditions, regional trade agreements establishing customs unions or free-trade areas. As is stated in Article XXIV:4 of the GATT 1994:

> The [Members] recognize the desirability of increasing freedom of trade by the development, through voluntary agreements, of closer integration between the economies of the countries parties to such agreements.

WTO law recognises the advantages of economic integration and trade liberalisation even when these efforts involve only some WTO Members. At a regional level, it may be possible to achieve a degree of trade liberalisation which may be out of reach at the global level. It has been argued that trade liberalisation will occur more quickly if it is pursued within regional trading blocs, and that trade liberalisation achieved at a regional level may serve as a *stepping stone* for trade liberalisation at the multilateral level at a later time. Also, regional trade liberalisation may create significant economic growth within the region concerned, which can, in turn, generate more trade with the rest of the world. It is not clear, however, whether regional trade agreements *divert* rather than *create* trade. In this connection, economic studies of customs unions and free-trade areas have revealed that the trade-creation effects may often be smaller than the trade-diversion effects as trade between the participants replaces trade between the participants and non-participants. The economic theory which, explains the

19 A customs union between Burundi, Comoros, the Democratic Republic of Congo, Djibouti, Egypt, Eritrea, Ethiopia, Kenya, Libya, Madagascar, Malawi, Mauritius, Rwanda, the Seychelles, Sudan, Swaziland, Uganda, Zambia and Zimbabwe.

20 A free-trade agreement between Australia, Brunei Darussalam, Chile, Canada, Japan, Malaysia, Mexico, New Zealand, Peru, Singapore, the United States and Vietnam.

21 The TTIP negotiations involve the European Union and the United States.

22 World Trade Report 2011, *WTO and Preferential Trade Agreements*, 72.

23 In recent years Mongolia was the only WTO Member that was not a party to an RTA. In 2016, however, Mongolia concluded an RTA with Japan.

potential dangers of regional trade agreements focuses on a trade creation/trade diversion dichotomy:

> [P]referential trade opening allows some domestic production to be replaced by imports from more efficient firms located in preference-receiving countries, leading to welfare gains (trade creation). At the same time [regional trade agreements] may reduce imports from more efficient non-member countries, implying a welfare loss (trade diversions). The net welfare effect of [regional trade agreements] depends on the relative magnitude of these opposing trends.[24]

On whether regional trade agreements may be stepping stones for later multilateral trade liberalisation, the 2004 Sutherland Report noted:

> There is ... real reason to doubt assertions that the pursuit of multiple PTAs will enhance, rather than undermine, the attractiveness of multilateral trade liberalization.[25]

However, apart from economic reasons, countries may also have political reasons to pursue deeper economic integration and trade liberalisation with some other countries. The example *par excellence* here is the European Union, which, through economic integration of, and trade liberalisation between, its Member States sought to create, and was successful in creating, 'an ever closer union' among the peoples of Europe to avoid the recurrence of war. The establishment of MERCOSUR, a customs union originally between Argentina, Brazil, Paraguay and Uruguay,[26] was motivated by the wish to buttress democracy in these countries. Furthermore, regional trade agreements can also serve to reinforce the participation of their member countries in the WTO, particularly in the case of the developing countries. A case study on the role of the COMESA and SADC membership of Zambia and Mauritius in supporting and facilitating the participation of these countries in the WTO revealed that:

> [while] RTA Membership had little *direct* impact so far on the preparation and conduct of the WTO negotiations ... regional groupings can play a much needed role in the WTO preparations through indirect means ... By raising awareness, by training, by providing a platform for the exchange of views and information, and by stimulating trade capacity building initiatives, COMESA and the SADC have contributed to a better preparation of their member countries on trade issues, which have had positive spillovers on their participation [in] the WTO.[27]

A 2015 report by the UNCTAD on key statistics and trends in international trade notes:

> it would be erroneous to simply gauge the success of PTAs exclusively by their effect on trade. PTAs can promote a number of noneconomic benefits, such as peace and security

24 World Trade Report 2011, *WTO and Preferential Trade Agreements*, 9.
25 Para. 85.
26 Note that Venezuela joined MERCOSUR as a full member on 31 July 2012.
27 S. Bilal and S. Szepesi, 'How Regional Economic Communities Can Facilitate Participation in the WTO: The Experience of Mauritius and Zambia', in Gallagher and Stoler (eds.), *Managing the Challenges of WTO Participation*, 389–90.

within members, and often result in more bargaining power for the members in further trade negotiations.[28]

WTO law should not stand in the way of such processes. However, a balance must be struck between the interests of countries pursuing closer economic integration among a select group of countries and the interests of countries excluded from that group. The *Understanding on Article XXIV of the GATT 1994* states in its Preamble:

> [T]he purpose of [regional trade] agreements should be to facilitate trade between the constituent territories and not to raise barriers to the trade of other Members with such territories ... [I]n their formation or enlargement the parties to them should to the greatest possible extent avoid creating adverse effects on the trade of other Members.

WTO rules on regional trade agreements are designed to ensure that these agreements create more trade than they divert. In the context of the Doha Round, Members have been engaged in negotiations with the aim of further clarifying and improving the current rules applying to regional trade agreements.[29] While these negotiations on the clarification and improvement of the substantive rules on regional trade agreements have not been successful, Members have been successful in agreeing in December 2006 on a new transparency mechanism, the Transparency Mechanism for Regional Trade Agreements (the 'RTA Transparency Mechanism'), established on a provisional basis.[30] This transparency mechanism provides for early announcement of negotiations towards a regional trade agreement, as well as of newly signed regional trade agreements. It sets out detailed notification requirements for parties to regional trade agreements, to allow Members to have a clearer picture of the rapidly growing 'spaghetti bowl' of overlapping regional trade agreements. The RTA Transparency Mechanism also establishes a procedure for the consideration of regional trade agreements on the basis of a factual presentation by the WTO Secretariat in either the WTO Committee on Regional Trade Agreements (CRTA) or the Committee on Trade and Development (CTD).[31] The RTA Transparency Mechanism also mandates the WTO Secretariat to maintain an updated electronic database on individual regional trade agreements.[32] This database, which can be accessed through the WTO's website, was launched in January 2009, and

28 UNCTAD, *Key Statistics and Trends in Trade Policy 2015: Preferential Trade Agreements* (UN, 2015), 3.

29 See Ministerial Conference, *Doha Ministerial Declaration*, adopted on 14 November 2001, WT/MIN(01)/DEC/1, dated 20 November 2001, para. 29.

30 General Council, *Transparency Mechanism for Regional Trade Agreements*, Decision adopted on 14 December 2006, WT/L/671, dated 18 December 2006. It must be noted that the new mechanism is implemented on a provisional basis, to be reviewed and replaced by a permanent mechanism as part of the overall results of the Doha Round. In 2015, one early announcement for a newly signed RTA was received from Members. See WT/REG/25, dated 17 November 2015.

31 The Committee on Regional Trade Agreements implements the transparency mechanism for RTAs falling under Article XXIV of the GATT 1994 and Article V of the GATS, and the Committee on Trade and Development does so for RTAs falling under para. 2(c) of the Enabling Clause. See *Decision on the Transparency Mechanism*, WT/L/671, para. 18.

32 See *Decision on the Transparency Mechanism*, WT/L/671, para. 21.

contains useful facts and figures on regional trade agreements which have been notified to the WTO.[33]

The 2015 Nairobi Ministerial Declaration called on Members to work towards the transformation of the provisional RTA Transparency Mechanism, to a permanent one without prejudice to questions related to the notification requirements.[34] In light of the proliferation of RTAs, the Nairobi Ministerial Declaration also instructed the CRTA to discuss systemic implications of RTAs for the multilateral trading system and their relationship to WTO rules.[35] Ten months later, on 27 September 2016, the Chair of the CRTA noted that 'WTO Members appear ready to start' these discussions.[36] He also noted that there was 'less clarity' on the type of discussions desired by Members.[37]

In times of no or slow progress in multilateral trade liberalisation in WTO negotiations, regional trade liberalisation has often been advocated as an alternative. Note, however, that such efforts may aggravate the lack of progress at the multilateral level. Moreover, such efforts are likely to leave out many of the world's poorest countries.[38] As Jagdish Bhagwati noted:

> Everyone loses out but the poor countries suffer the most because their companies are least prepared to deal with the confusion.[39]

Moreover, Bhagwati observed that:

> where a significant power such as the US or the European Union is involved in an agreement, it almost always sneaks in reverse preferences – and trade-unrelated issues such as patent protection and labour standards – that exact a heavy cost on developing countries.[40]

In an excerpt on the 'scope of RTAs' on the WTO website, a note of caution reads:

> The increase in RTAs, coupled with the preference shown for concluding bilateral free-trade agreements, has produced the phenomenon of overlapping membership. Because each RTA will tend to develop its own mini-trade regime, the coexistence in a single country of differing trade rules applying to different RTA partners has become a frequent feature. This can hamper trade flows merely by the costs involved for traders in meeting multiple sets of trade rules.[41]

Nonetheless, the debate on regionalism is gradually shifting away from a discussion of costs and benefits to a discussion on how to achieve coherence between multilateralism and regionalism. The WTO's *World Trade Report 2011* focused on the coherence between the regional and multilateral trade regimes. The

33 See the RTA Database, at http://rtais.wto.org/UI/PublicMaintainRTAHome.aspx.
34 Tenth WTO Ministerial Conference, *Nairobi Ministerial Declaration*, WT/MIN(15)/DEC dated 21 December 2015, para. 28.
35 *Ibid.* 36 See www.wto.org/english/news_e/news16_e/rta_05oct16_e.htm.
37 See *ibid.*
38 For a critical view on RTAs, see e.g. the Sutherland Report, paras. 75–87.
39 J. Bhagwati, 'A Costly Pursuit of Free Trade', *Financial Times*, 6 March 2001.
40 *Ibid.* 41 www.wto.org/english/tratop_e/region_e/scope_rta_e.htm.

report, *inter alia*, identified a number of different approaches, which have been proposed for improving coherence between regional trade agreements and the multilateral trading system. These include:

> accelerating multilateral trade opening; fixing the deficiencies in the WTO legal framework; adopting a softer approach as a complement to the existing legal framework; multilateralizing regionalism (extending preferential arrangements in a non-discriminatory manner to additional parties). These approaches are not mutually exclusive. They all aim at making sure that [regional trade agreements] contribute to trade co-operation and opening in a non-discriminatory manner.[42]

WTO Director-General Roberto Azevêdo at a 2014 WTO seminar on RTAs said that RTAs 'are important for the multilateral trading system – but they cannot substitute it'. He stated in particular:

> To start with, there are many big issues which can only be tackled in an efficient manner in the multilateral context through the WTO. Trade Facilitation was negotiated successfully in the WTO because it makes no economic sense to cut red tape or simplify trade procedures at the border for one or two countries ... Financial or telecoms regulations can't be efficiently liberalized for just one trade partner – so it is best to negotiate services trade-offs globally in the WTO. Nor can farming or fisheries subsidies be tackled in bilateral deals ... RTAs do not – and probably cannot – fully address the gains from trade that can be obtained through global value chains. Indeed, the strict, product specific rules of origin that often accompany RTAs may actually be detrimental to value chains and therefore exclusionary for some. The smaller the country, the smaller the company, the smaller the trader, the bigger the likelihood is that they will be excluded.[43]

Recent OECD findings throw light on the so-called 'multilateralising regionalism' agenda whereby 'deeper measures that are widely incorporated into RTAs could be diffused more widely and consistently across regional negotiations, and ultimately be multilateralised'.[44] The emphasis here is on leveraging the progress made in RTA negotiations on unresolved issues in the WTO. In terms of statistics, a 2014 WTO, OECD and World Bank study noted:

> In the case of RTAs notified to the WTO since 2000 for instance ... over half, 56%, contain provisions on goods and services, 54% on investment, 47% on intellectual property rights that go beyond WTO commitments, 59% on competition and 47% on government procurement provisions often involving both parties and non-parties of the WTO Government Procurement Agreement (GPA). A smaller but nevertheless significant number of RTAs also have provisions on electronic commerce (24%), environment (31%) and labour (22%).[45]

42 World Trade Report 2011, *WTO and Preferential Trade Agreements*, 15.

43 R. Azevêdo, speech at the WTO Seminar on 'Cross-Cutting Issues in Regional Trade Agreements (RTAs)', 25 September 2014, at www.wto.org/english/news_e/spra_e/spra33_e.htm. See also R. Azevêdo, speech at the Stockholm School of Economics in Riga, Latvia, 24 March 2015 at www.wto.org/english/news_e/spra_e/spra50_e.htm; R. Azevêdo, speech at the meeting of the Inter-Pacific Bar Association, Kuala Lumpur-Malaysia, 14 April 2016, at www.wto.org/english/news_e/spra_e/spra119_e.htm.

44 I. Lejárraga, *Deep Provisions in Regional Trade Agreements: How Multilateral-friendly?: An Overview of OECD Findings*, OECD Trade Policy Papers No. 168, 2014, 7.

45 WTO, OECD and the World Bank, *Regional Trade Agreements and the Multilateral Trading System*, Discussion Paper for the G-20 (WTO, 2015), 7.

In September 2016, WTO Director-General Roberto Azevêdo stated at the occasion of the presentation of the WTO study 'Regional Trade Agreements and the Multilateral Trading System'[46] that this study shows that:

in some areas RTAs are going further than multilateral rules and adding new layers of rules among the parties, while in others they tend not to change the existing WTO disciplines. Interestingly, in the areas where RTAs are introducing new rules, there appear to be common approaches taken by members. We can see this, for example, in services rules, dispute settlement, and intellectual property rights. This provides some reassurance to the recurring fear that RTAs represent a fragmentation of the global trading system.[47]

3 REGIONAL TRADE EXCEPTIONS UNDER THE GATT 1994

The chapeau of Article XXIV:5 of the GATT 1994 provides, in relevant part:

[T]he provisions of this Agreement shall not prevent, as between the territories of [Members], the formation of a customs union or of a free-trade area or the adoption of an interim agreement necessary for the formation of a customs union or of a free-trade area.

In examining this provision in *Turkey – Textiles (1999)*, the Appellate Body noted:

We read this to mean that the provisions of the GATT 1994 *shall not make impossible* the formation of a customs union. Thus, the chapeau makes it clear that Article XXIV may, under certain conditions, justify the adoption of a measure which is inconsistent with certain other GATT provisions, and may be invoked as a possible 'defence' to a finding of inconsistency.[48]

There are two conditions that must be met in order to justify under Article XXIV a measure which is otherwise GATT-inconsistent. As the Appellate Body stated in *Turkey – Textiles (1999)*:

First, the party claiming the benefit of this defence must demonstrate that the measure at issue is introduced upon the formation of a customs union that fully meets the requirements of sub-paragraphs 8(a) and 5(a) of Article XXIV. And, second, that party must demonstrate that the formation of that customs union would be prevented if it were not allowed to introduce the measure at issue.[49]

There is therefore a two-tier test to determine whether a measure, otherwise inconsistent with the GATT 1994, can be justified under Article XXIV.[50] Such

46 Rohini Acharya (ed.), *Regional Trade Agreements and the Multilateral Trading System* (WTO, 2016).
47 www.wto.org/english/news_e/spra_e/spra138_e.htm.
48 Appellate Body Report, *Turkey – Textiles (1999)*, para. 45.
49 *Ibid.*, para. 58. See also Appellate Body Report, *Argentina – Footwear (EC) (2000)*, para. 109.
50 Note that in *Canada – Autos (2000)*, the Appellate Body ruled that: 'Article XXIV clearly cannot justify a measure which grants WTO-inconsistent duty-free treatment to products originating in third countries not parties to a customs union or free trade agreement.' See Appellate Body Report, *Canada – Autos (2000)*, para. 10.55.

measure is justified: (1) if the measure is introduced upon the formation of a customs union, a free-trade area or an interim agreement that meets all the requirements set out in Article XXIV of the GATT 1994; and (2) if the formation of the customs union or free-trade area would be prevented, if the introduction of the measure concerned were not allowed.

This section discusses these conditions, first, with regard to a measure adopted in the context of a customs union, secondly, with regard to a measure adopted in the context of a free-trade area, and, finally, with regard to a measure adopted under an interim agreement. This section also discusses, *in fine*, special rules for developing-country Members' regional trade agreements as well as general procedural issues.

To date the regional trade exception under Article XXIV of the GATT 1994 has been invoked – albeit never successfully – four times in WTO dispute settlement to justify an otherwise GATT-inconsistent measure.[51] Also, to date, the consistency of a specific customs union, a free-trade area or an interim agreement with the requirements set out in Article XXIV of the GATT 1994, has never been examined by the Appellate Body and only once by a panel. In *US – Line Pipe (2002)*, the panel found:

> In our view, the information provided by the United States in these proceedings, the information submitted by the NAFTA parties to the Committee on Regional Trade Agreements ('CRTA') (which the United States has incorporated into its submissions to the Panel by reference), and the absence of effective refutation by Korea, establishes a prima facie case that NAFTA is in conformity with Article XXIV:5(b) and (c), and with Article XXIV:8(b).[52]

3.1 Exceptions Relating to Customs Unions

As noted above, a measure which is otherwise GATT-inconsistent is justified under Article XXIV of the GATT 1994: (1) if that measure is introduced upon the formation of a customs union that meets the requirements of Article XXIV:8(a) and Article XXIV:5(a); and (2) if the formation of that customs union would be prevented if the introduction of the measure concerned were not allowed. The Appellate Body noted in *Turkey – Textiles (1999)* that it is necessary to establish that both conditions are fulfilled and that it may not always be possible to determine whether the second condition is met 'without *first* determining whether there *is* a customs union'.[53] Therefore, this section explores the definition of a 'customs union' before addressing the conditions that need to be fulfilled to justify a measure that would otherwise be GATT-inconsistent.

51 See *Turkey – Textiles (1999)*; *Canada – Autos (2000)*; *US – Line Pipe (2002)*; and *Brazil – Retreaded Tyres (2007)*. In the latter case, the panel exercised judicial economy with regard to Brazil's invocation of Article XXIV. Note that in *Argentina – Footwear (EC) (2000)*; and *Peru – Agricultural Products (2015)*, Article XXIV of the GATT 1994 was much discussed but was not invoked as such to justify measure at issue.

52 Panel Report, *US – Line Pipe (2002)*, para. 7.144.

53 Appellate Body Report, *Turkey – Textiles (1999)*, para. 59. Emphasis on 'first' added.

3.1.1 Definition of a 'Customs Union'

A 'customs union' is defined in Article XXIV:8(a) of the GATT 1994 as follows:

> A customs union shall be understood to mean the substitution of a single customs territory for two or more customs territories so that
> i. duties and other restrictive regulations of commerce (except, where necessary, those permitted under Articles XI, XII, XIII, XIV, XV and XX) are eliminated with respect to *substantially all the trade* between the constituent territories of the union or at least with respect to substantially all the trade in products originating in such territories, and
> ii. ... *substantially the same* duties and other regulations of commerce are applied by each of the members of the union to the trade of territories not included in the union.[54]

To satisfy the definition of a 'customs union', Article XXIV:8(a) of the GATT 1994 establishes: (1) a standard for the *internal trade* between constituent members (under subparagraph (i)); and (2) a standard for the *trade* of constituent members *with third countries* (under subparagraph (ii)).

With respect to the first standard, i.e. the standard for the *internal trade* between the constituent members of a customs union, Article XXIV:8(a) requires that members of a customs union eliminate 'duties and other restrictive regulations of commerce' with respect to 'substantially all the trade' between them. As the Appellate Body noted in *Turkey – Textiles (1999)*, WTO Members have never reached an agreement on the interpretation of the term 'substantially all' in this provision.[55] According to the Appellate Body, it is clear that 'substantially all the trade' is not the same as *all* the trade, and also that 'substantially all the trade' is something considerably more than merely *some* of the trade.[56] It should also be noted that members of a customs union may maintain, where necessary, certain restrictive regulations of commerce in their internal trade that are permitted under Articles XI to XV and under Article XX of the GATT 1994.[57] The Appellate Body in *Turkey – Textiles (1999)* therefore agreed with the panel in that case that Article XXIV:8(a)(i), which sets out the standard for the *internal trade* between members of a customs union, offers 'some flexibility' to the constituent members of a customs union when liberalising their internal trade barriers. However, the Appellate Body cautioned that this degree of 'flexibility' is limited by the requirement that 'duties and other restrictive regulations of commerce' be 'eliminated with respect to substantially all' internal trade.[58]

As discussed in Chapter 9, in *Argentina – Footwear (EC) (2000)*, the question arose whether Article XXIV:8(a)(i) prohibited Argentina, as a member of MERCOSUR, from imposing safeguard measures on other MERCOSUR countries.[59] While imports from all sources had been taken into account in

54 Emphasis added.
55 See Appellate Body Report, *Turkey – Textiles (1999)*, para. 48. 56 See *ibid.*
57 See Article XXIV:8(a)(i) of the GATT 1994. For a discussion on Articles XI and XIII, see above, pp. 482–92 and 492–8; and Article XX, see above, pp. 546–604.
58 See Appellate Body Report, *Turkey – Textiles (1999)*, para. 48. 59 See above, p. 631.

the investigation at issue, Argentina imposed the safeguards measure at issue only on non-MERCOSUR countries. The Appellate Body considered that Article XXIV:8(a)(i) did not prohibit the imposition of safeguard measures on other MERCOSUR countries.[60] In light of the specific circumstances of this case, the Appellate Body even opined that Argentina *should* have applied the safeguard measures also to other MERCOSUR countries. The Appellate Body ruled:

> [W]e find that Argentina's investigation, which evaluated whether serious injury or the threat thereof was caused by imports from *all* sources, could only lead to the imposition of safeguard measures on imports from *all* sources. Therefore, we conclude that Argentina's investigation, in this case, cannot serve as a basis for excluding imports from other MERCOSUR member States from the application of the safeguard measures.[61]

The Appellate Body found again in *US – Wheat Gluten (2001)* that, in 'the usual course', the imports included in a safeguards investigation should correspond to the imports included in the application of the measure.[62] This has been referred to as the principle of 'parallelism'. In *US – Line Pipe (2002)* and in *US – Steel Safeguards (2003)*, the Appellate Body explained that the principle of 'parallelism' derives from the parallel language used in the first and second paragraphs of Article 2 of the *Agreement on Safeguards*.[63] In *US – Wheat Gluten (2001)* and *US – Line Pipe (2002)*, the competent US authorities took imports from all sources into consideration in the investigation, but excluded imports from other NAFTA countries from the application of the safeguards measure. In *US – Steel Safeguards (2003)*, the competent authority of the United States considered *all imports* in its injury investigation, but ultimately did not apply the safeguard measures to imports from Canada, Israel, Jordan and Mexico.[64]

With respect to the second standard, i.e. the standard for the trade of constituent members *with third countries*, Article XXIV:8(a)(ii) of the GATT 1994 requires that the constituent members of a customs union apply 'substantially the same' duties and other regulations of commerce to trade with third countries. The constituent members of a customs union are therefore required to apply a common external trade regime, relating to both duties and other regulations of commerce. As the Appellate Body noted in *Turkey – Textiles (1999)*, it is *not* required that each constituent member of a customs union applies the *same* duties and other regulations of commerce as other constituent members with respect to trade with third countries. Article XXIV:8(a)(ii) of the GATT 1994 requires that *substantially the same* duties and other regulations of commerce

60 Note that in *Argentina – Footwear (EC) (2000)*, Argentina did not argue before the panel that Article XXIV of the GATT 1994 justified the measures at issue. The Appellate Body therefore concluded that the panel erred in deciding that an examination of Article XXIV was relevant in this case. See Appellate Body Report, *Argentina – Footwear (EC) (2000)*, para. 110.

61 Appellate Body Report, *Argentina – Footwear (EC) (2000)*, para. 113.

62 Appellate Body Report, *US – Wheat Gluten (2001)*, para. 96.

63 For a further discussion of the concept of parallelism, see above, p. 649.

64 See Appellate Body Report, *US – Steel Safeguards (2003)*, paras. 440–4.

shall be applied.[65] Also, the phrase 'substantially the same' offers a certain degree of 'flexibility' to the constituent members of a customs union in 'the creation of a common commercial policy'. However, the Appellate Body cautioned that this 'flexibility' is limited. Something closely approximating 'sameness' is definitely required.[66]

A customs union under Article XXIV must, however, not only meet the requirements of Article XXIV:8(a). It must also meet the requirement of Article XXIV:5(a). This provision states:

> [W]ith respect to a customs union ... the duties and other regulations of commerce imposed at the institution of any such union ... in respect of trade with [Members] not parties to such union ... shall not on the whole be higher or more restrictive than the general incidence of the duties and regulations of commerce applicable in the constituent territories prior to the formation of such union ... as the case may be.

The precise meaning of the requirement that the duties and other regulations of commerce, applicable after the formation of the customs union, are, *on the whole*, not higher or more restrictive than the *general incidence* of the duties and other regulations of commerce applicable prior to the formation of the customs union, has been controversial. Paragraph 2 of the 1994 *Understanding on Article XXIV* has sought to clarify this requirement. With respect to duties, paragraph 2 requires that the evaluation under Article XXIV:5(a) of the *general incidence of the duties* applied before and after the formation of a customs union:

> shall ... be based upon an overall assessment of weighted average tariff rates and of customs duties collected.[67]

As noted by the Appellate Body in *Turkey – Textiles (1999)*, under the GATT 1947, the GATT Contracting Parties held divergent views as to whether in applying the test of Article XXIV:5(a), the *bound* rates of duty or the *applied* rates of duty should be considered. This issue has been resolved by paragraph 2 of the *Understanding on Article XXIV*, which clearly states that the *applied* rate of duty must be used.[68]

With respect to 'other regulations of commerce', paragraph 2 of the *Understanding on Article XXIV* recognises that it may be difficult to evaluate whether the general incidence of the 'other regulations of commerce' after the

65 See Appellate Body Report, *Turkey – Textiles (1999)*, para. 49. The Appellate Body agreed with the panel in *Turkey – Textiles (1999)* that the expression 'substantially the same duties and other regulations of commerce are applied by each of the Members of the [customs] union' would appear to encompass both quantitative and qualitative elements, the quantitative aspect being emphasised more in relation to duties. See Panel Report, *Turkey – Textiles (1999)*, para. 9.148.

66 Appellate Body Report, *Turkey – Textiles (1999)*, para. 50.

67 This assessment shall be based on import statistics for a previous representative period to be supplied by the customs union, on a tariff-line basis and in values and quantities, broken down by WTO country of origin. The WTO Secretariat shall compute the weighted average tariff rates and customs duties collected in accordance with the methodology used in the assessment of tariff offers in the Uruguay Round. For this purpose, the duties and charges to be taken into consideration shall be the applied rates of duty. See para. 2 of the *Understanding on Article XXIV*.

68 See Appellate Body Report, *Turkey – Textiles (1999)*, para. 53.

formation of the customs union is more restrictive than before its formation. Paragraph 2 recognises, in particular, that the quantification and aggregation of regulations of commerce other than duties may be difficult. Therefore, paragraph 2 of the *Understanding on Article XXIV* provides:

> [F]or the purpose of the overall assessment of the incidence of other regulations of commerce ... the examination of individual measures, regulations, products covered and trade flows affected may be required.

The test for assessing whether a specific customs union meets the requirements of Article XXIV:5(a) is, in essence, an *economic* test, i.e. a test of the extent of trade restriction before and after the formation of the customs union.[69]

If, in the formation of a customs union, a constituent member must increase a bound duty (because the duty of the customs union is higher than the bound duty of that Member applicable before the formation of the customs union), Article XXIV:6 of the GATT 1994 requires that the procedure for modification of schedules, set out in Article XXVIII of the GATT 1994, be applied.[70] This procedure for the withdrawal or modification of previously bound tariff concessions must be followed with a view to achieving mutually satisfactory compensatory adjustment.[71] Article XXIV:6 further stipulates, however, that:

> [i]n providing for compensatory adjustment, due account shall be taken of the compensation already afforded by the reduction brought about in the corresponding duty of the other constituents of the union.

If the reduction in the previously applicable bound duty of other constituent members of the customs union is not sufficient to provide the necessary compensatory adjustment, the customs union must offer compensation.[72] This compensation may take the form of reductions of duties on other tariff lines. If no agreement on compensatory adjustment can be reached, the customs union shall nevertheless be free to modify or withdraw the concessions at issue; and the affected WTO Members shall then be free to withdraw substantially equivalent concessions in accordance with Article XXVIII of the GATT 1994.[73]

3.1.2 Conditions for the Justification of GATT Inconsistency

As noted at the beginning of this section, a measure that would otherwise be GATT-inconsistent, can be justified under Article XXIV of the GATT 1994 when two conditions are fulfilled. The first condition – that the measure must be introduced upon the formation of a customs union that meets the requirements of Article XXIV:8(a) and Article XXIV:5(a) – is discussed in detail above. The second condition requires that, absent the introduction of the measure concerned, the formation of a customs union would be prevented.

69 See *ibid.*, para. 55. 70 See above, pp. 447–50. 71 See *Understanding on Article XXIV*, para. 5.
72 Note that the GATT 1994 does not require a WTO Member, benefiting from a reduction of duties upon the formation of a customs union, to provide compensatory adjustment. See *Understanding on Article XXIV*, para. 6.
73 See *Understanding on Article XXIV*, para. 5; and see above, pp. 447–50 (449 in particular).

In *Turkey – Textiles (1999)*, the measures at issue were quantitative restrictions on textiles and clothing from India. Turkey did not deny that these quantitative restrictions were inconsistent with its obligations under Articles XI and XIII of the GATT 1994 and Article 2.4 of the *Agreement on Textiles and Clothing*. However, according to Turkey, these quantitative restrictions were justified under Article XXIV of the GATT 1994. Turkey argued that, unless it was allowed to introduce quantitative restrictions on textiles and clothing from India, Turkey would be prevented from forming a customs union with the European Communities.[74] Turkey asserted that, had it not introduced the quantitative restrictions on textiles and clothing products from India that were at issue, the European Communities would have excluded these products from free trade within the EC–Turkey customs union. According to Turkey, the European Communities would have done so in order to prevent the circumvention of the EC's quantitative restrictions on textiles and clothing from India by importing them into the European Communities via Turkey. Turkey's exports of these products accounted for 40 per cent of Turkey's total exports to the European Communities. Therefore, Turkey expressed strong doubts as to whether the requirement of Article XXIV:8(a)(i) that duties and other restrictive regulations of commerce be eliminated with respect to 'substantially all trade' between Turkey and the European Communities could be met if 40 per cent of Turkey's total exports to the European Communities were excluded.[75] The Appellate Body rejected Turkey's argument that without the GATT-inconsistent quantitative restrictions on textiles and clothing from India, it would have been prevented from forming a customs union with the European Communities. It ruled:

> As the panel observed, there are other alternatives available to Turkey and the European Communities to prevent any possible diversion of trade, while at the same time meeting the requirements of sub-paragraph 8(a)(i). For example, Turkey could adopt rules of origin for textile and clothing products that would allow the European Communities to distinguish between those textile and clothing products originating in Turkey, which would enjoy free access to the European Communities under the terms of the customs union, *and* those textile and clothing products originating in third countries, including India.[76]

3.2 Exceptions Relating to Free-Trade Areas

As noted above, a measure which is otherwise GATT-inconsistent is justified under Article XXIV of the GATT 1994: (1) if that measure is introduced upon the formation of a free-trade area that meets the requirements of Article XXIV:8(b)

74 See Appellate Body Report, *Turkey – Textiles (1999)*, para. 61.
75 For this summary of Turkey's argument, see *ibid.*
76 *Ibid.*, para. 62. The Appellate Body also noted that Decision 1/95 of the EC–Turkey Association Council specifically provided for the possibility of applying a system of certificates of origin. Rather than making use of this possibility, Turkey had adopted quantitative restrictions on imports of textiles and clothing from India.

and Article XXIV:5(b); and (2) if the formation of that free-trade area would be made impossible if the introduction of the measure concerned were not allowed. This section explores, first, the definition of a 'free-trade area', before, secondly, addressing the conditions that need to be met in order to justify a measure that would otherwise be GATT-inconsistent.

3.2.1 Definition of a 'Free-Trade Area'

A 'free-trade area' is defined in Article XXIV:8(b) of the GATT 1994 as follows:

> A free-trade area shall be understood to mean a group of two or more customs territories in which the duties and other restrictive regulations of commerce (except, where necessary, those permitted under Articles XI, XII, XIII, XIV, XV and XX) are eliminated *on substantially all the trade* between the constituent territories in products originating in such territories.[77]

In contrast to the definition of a 'customs union', discussed above, the definition of a 'free-trade area' establishes only a standard for the *internal trade* between constituent members. There is no standard, i.e. there are no requirements, for the trade of constituent members *with third countries*. The standard for the *internal trade* between constituent members of a free-trade area – namely, the elimination of duties and other restrictive regulations of commerce on substantially all trade between constituent members – is identical to the standard for the internal trade between constituent members of a customs union. The case law discussed and observations made in the previous section on 'customs unions' are therefore also relevant for free-trade areas.

A free-trade area under Article XXIV of the GATT 1994, however, does not only have to meet the requirements of Article XXIV:8(b). It must also meet the requirement of Article XXIV:5(b). This provision states:

> [W]ith respect to a free-trade area ... the duties and other regulations of commerce maintained in each of the constituent territories and applicable at the formation of such free-trade area ... to the trade of [Members] not included in such area ... shall not be higher or more restrictive than the corresponding duties and other regulations of commerce existing in the same constituent territories prior to the formation of the free-trade area.

Article XXIV:5(b) therefore requires that the duties and other regulations of commerce applied by a member of a free-trade area to trade with third countries *after* the formation of the free-trade area must *not be higher or more restrictive* than the duties and other regulations of commerce applied by that member *before* the formation of the free-trade area. Establishing that this is indeed the case is much less problematic than establishing whether the requirements of Article XXIV:5(a) with respect to customs unions are met.[78]

3.2.2 Conditions for the Justification of GATT Inconsistency

As noted at the beginning of this section, for a measure, otherwise GATT-inconsistent, to be justified under Article XXIV of the GATT 1994 two conditions

77 Emphasis added. 78 See above, pp. 683–4.

must be fulfilled. The first condition – that the measure must be introduced upon the formation of a free-trade area that meets the requirements of Article XXIV:8(b) – is discussed above. The second condition requires that, absent the introduction of the measure concerned, the formation of the free-trade area would be prevented. There is no relevant WTO case law on this point as yet.

3.3 Interim Agreements

Measures that are otherwise GATT-inconsistent may be justified under Article XXIV of the GATT 1994 if they are taken in the context of interim agreements leading to the formation of customs unions and free-trade areas meeting the requirements discussed in the two previous sections.[79] This is a recognition of the fact that customs unions and free-trade areas will not, and cannot, be established overnight. Nevertheless, although most customs unions and free-trade areas have been – at least in part – implemented in stages, only a few have expressly been notified as 'interim agreements'.[80]

Article XXIV:5(c) of the GATT 1994 requires with respect to interim agreements:

> [A]ny interim agreement ... shall include a plan and schedule for the formation of such a customs union or of such a free-trade area within a reasonable length of time.

Not surprisingly, the vague requirement that the customs union or free-trade area be established 'within a reasonable length of time' was quite controversial under the GATT 1947. The 1994 *Understanding on Article XXIV* therefore provides that this reasonable period of time should not exceed ten years except in exceptional circumstances.[81] It remains an open question whether existing interim arrangements actually result in the formation of a free-trade area or customs union within this ten-year time limit.

3.4 Special and Differential Treatment of Developing-Country Members

The Decision of the GATT Contracting Parties of 28 November 1979 on *Differential and More Favourable Treatment, Reciprocity and Fuller Participation of Developing Countries*, commonly referred to as the 'Enabling Clause',[82] provides, in relevant part:

> 1. Notwithstanding the provisions of Article I of the General Agreement, [Members] may accord differential and more favourable treatment to developing countries, without according such treatment to other [Members].
> 2. The provisions of paragraph 1 apply to the following:
>
> [...]
>
> (c). Regional or global arrangements entered into amongst less-developed [Members] for the mutual reduction or elimination of tariffs and, in accordance with criteria or conditions

79 See above, p. 685.
80 See WT/REG/W/37, para. 47. Up to February 2013, only fourteen interim agreements had been notified to the WTO and were in force.
81 See *Understanding on Article XXIV*, para. 3.
82 On the Enabling Clause of the GATT 1994, see also above, pp. 321–5, and below, pp. 692–4.

which may be prescribed by the [Ministerial Conference], for the mutual reduction or elimination of non-tariff measures, on products imported from one another.[83]

The Enabling Clause is now part of the GATT 1994.[84] It allows preferential arrangements *among developing-country Members* in derogation from the MFN treatment obligation of Article I of the GATT 1994. The conditions that regional trade agreements under the Enabling Clause must meet are less demanding and less specific than those set out in Article XXIV of the GATT 1994. Thus, there are no substantive requirements under the Enabling Clause which approximate the substantive requirements – discussed above – of Article XXIV. In fact, paragraph 3 of the Enabling Clause 'merely' requires that:

[a]ny differential and more favourable treatment provided under this clause:
a. shall be designed to facilitate and promote the trade of developing countries and not to raise barriers to or create undue difficulties for the trade of any other [Members].
...

As of 1 October 2016, forty-two regional trade agreements had been notified to the WTO under the Enabling Clause.[85] These include: (1) the *Cartagena Agreement Establishing the Andean Community*; (2) *the Treaty Establishing the Common Market for Eastern and Southern Africa* (COMESA); (3) the *Treaty Establishing the Common Market of the South* (MERCOSUR); and (4) the *Common Effective Preferential Tariffs Scheme for the ASEAN Free Trade Area* (AFTA).

4 REGIONAL TRADE EXCEPTIONS UNDER THE GATS

Article V of the GATS, entitled 'Economic Integration', is the counterpart of Article XXIV of the GATT 1994 for trade in services. Article V:1 of the GATS provides:

This Agreement shall not prevent any of its Members from being a party to or entering into an agreement liberalizing trade in services between or among the parties to such an agreement, provided that such an agreement:

a. has substantial sectoral coverage,[86] and

83 See BISD 26S/203.
84 See paragraph 1(b)(iv) of the GATT 1994. See also above, pp. 692–40.
85 See http://rtais.wto.org/UI/publicsummarytable.aspx. As noted above, for an RTA that includes both goods and services, the WTO database on RTAs counts two notifications (one for goods and the other services), even though it is physically one RTA. Note also that the text of the Enabling Clause suggests that the parties to a preferential agreement that is notified under the Enabling Clause must be developing countries. This may seem obvious but this has given rise to some controversy due to the fact that in WTO law the concept of developing country is not defined and a Member 'self-selects' itself as a 'developing-country Member'. See above, pp. 321 (subsequently 322–5). For example, the Gulf Co-operation Council Agreement was initially notified under Article XXIV of the GATT 1994, but, before the CRTA could examine it, the parties rescinded the notification under Article XXIV and sought to notify the Gulf Co-operation Council Agreement under the Enabling Clause for review by the CTD. Other WTO Members questioned the change of course. The incentive to notify an RTA under the Enabling Clause rather than under Article XXIV of the GATT 1994 is that there are no substantive requirements for RTAs under the Enabling Clause that are similarly stringent as the requirements of Articles XXIV:8 and XXIV:5 of the GATT 1994.
86 The original fn. 1 in the quote reads: 'This condition is understood in terms of number of sectors, volume of trade affected and modes of supply. In order to meet this condition, agreements should not provide for the *a priori* exclusion of any mode of supply.'

b. provides for the absence or elimination of substantially all discrimination, in the sense of Article XVII, between or among the parties, in the sectors covered under subparagraph (a), through:
   i. elimination of existing discriminatory measures, and/or
   ii. prohibition of new or more discriminatory measures, either at the entry into force of that agreement or on the basis of a reasonable time-frame, except for measures permitted under Articles XI, XII, XIV and XIV*bis*.

Article V:4 of the GATS states:

Any agreement referred to in paragraph 1 shall be designed to facilitate trade between the parties to the agreement and shall not in respect of any member outside the agreement raise the overall level of barriers to trade in services within the respective sectors or subsectors compared to the level applicable prior to such an agreement.

To date the regional trade exception under Article V of the GATS has been invoked only once in the WTO dispute settlement.[87] Also, to date, the consistency of a specific economic integration agreement with the requirements set out in Article V of the GATS has never been examined by the Appellate Body or a panel.

4.1 Requirements for Economic Integration Agreements

The panel in *Canada – Autos (2000)* noted that:

Article V provides legal coverage for measures taken pursuant to economic integration agreements, which would otherwise be inconsistent with the MFN obligation in Article II.[88]

It follows from Article V:1 that a measure which is otherwise GATS-inconsistent can be justified under Article V of the GATS if: (1) the measure is introduced as part of an agreement liberalising trade in services that meets all the requirements set out in Article V:1(a) (the 'substantial sectoral coverage' requirement), Article V:1(b) (the 'substantially all discrimination' requirement) and Article V:4 (the 'level of barriers to trade' requirement); and (2) WTO Members would be prevented from entering into such an agreement liberalising trade in services, if the measure concerned were not allowed (see the chapeau of Article V:1). This section, further, discusses primarily the requirements that an economic integration agreement pursuant to Articles V:1(a), V:1(b) and V:4 of the GATS must meet.

4.1.1 'Substantial Sectoral Coverage' Requirement

Pursuant to Article V:1(a) of the GATS, an economic integration agreement must have 'substantial sectoral coverage' of the trade in services among the parties to the agreement. The footnote to the provision states that 'substantial sectoral coverage' should be 'understood in terms of the number of sectors, volume of trade affected and modes of supply'.[89] The footnote also provides that an economic

87 See *Canada – Autos (2000)*. As explained below this invocation was unsuccessful. See below, p. 691.
88 Panel Report, *Canada – Autos (2000)*, para. 10.271.
89 It is not clear whether the parameters to be examined in determining the conformity with an economic integration agreement with Article V of the GATS are limited to the parameters listed in the footnote, or whether other considerations may also be taken into account.

integration agreement may not *a priori* exclude any of the four modes of supply. In particular, no economic integration agreement should *a priori* exclude investment or labour mobility in the sense of modes 3 and 4. Members disagree on whether one or more services sectors can be excluded from an economic integration agreement, but the use of the wording 'number of sectors' in the footnote to paragraph 1(a) seems to indicate that not all sectors must be covered under an economic integration agreement to meet the 'substantial sectoral coverage' test. However, it is clear that the number of exclusions must be limited. As the panel in *Canada – Autos (2000)* stated:

> the purpose of Article V is to allow for ambitious liberalization to take place at a regional level, while at the same time guarding against undermining the MFN obligation by engaging in *minor preferential arrangements*.[90]

4.1.2 'Substantially All Discrimination' Requirement

Article V:1(b) of the GATS requires that an economic integration agreement should provide for 'the absence or elimination of substantially all discrimination'.[91] As Article V:1(b) of the GATS does not require the absence or elimination of *all* discrimination, but rather the absence or elimination of *substantially all* discrimination, the question arises as to what extent discriminatory measures should be allowed to exist in an economic integration agreement.[92] The scope of such permissible discriminatory measures is, of course, circumscribed by the scope of the list of exceptions in Article V:1(b) of the GATS. This list explicitly includes exceptions permitted under Articles XI, XII, XIV and XIV*bis* of the GATS, but it is unclear whether this list is exhaustive. The scope of permissible discriminatory measures is also affected by the meaning given to the 'and/or' wording in Article V:1(b) linking provisions (i) and (ii). Some Members are of the opinion that the 'or' allows the parties to an economic integration agreement to choose between provisions (i) and (ii), that is, the elimination of existing discriminatory measures, or, alternatively, the introduction of a standstill. A party could therefore choose only to refrain from adding new measures or from making existing measures more restrictive, rather than having to eliminate existing measures. Other Members have rejected this interpretation. They argue that, considering that Article V:1(b) aims to deal with 'substantially all discrimination', it would be appropriate to interpret the 'and/or' wording in such a way that both (i)

90 Panel Report, *Canada – Autos (2000)*, para. 10.271. Emphasis added.

91 Note that Article V:2 of the GATS states that the evaluation of an agreement's consistency with Article V:1(b) may also take into account its relationship with 'a wider process of economic integration or trade liberalization' among the parties to the agreement. A 'wider process of economic integration' refers to a process of economic integration involving the elimination of barriers to trade not only in services but also in goods.

92 Note that Article V:6 of the GATS provides that a third party supplier, legally recognised as a juridical person by a party to an economic integration agreement, is entitled to equivalent treatment granted within the economic integration area, provided that it engages in 'substantive business operations' in the territory of the parties to that agreement.

and (ii) are found to be applicable. Thus, it is argued that paragraphs (i) and (ii) are *options* to be judged as appropriate against the circumstances of the service sector being considered, *not* as *alternatives* to be freely chosen by the parties to the economic integration agreement.[93]

The panel in *Canada – Autos (2000)* noted with respect to the obligation under Article V:1(b) of the GATS:

> Although the requirement of Article V:1(b) is to provide non-discrimination in the sense of Article XVII (National Treatment), we consider that once it is fulfilled it would also ensure non-discrimination between all service suppliers of other parties to the economic integration agreement. It is our view that the object and purpose of this provision is to eliminate all discrimination among services and service suppliers of parties to an economic integration agreement, including discrimination between the suppliers of other parties to an economic integration agreement.[94]

According to the panel, it would be inconsistent with Article V:1(b) of the GATS if a party to an economic integration agreement were to extend more favourable treatment to the service suppliers of one party than it does to the service suppliers of another party to that agreement.[95] In other words, the obligation under Article V:1(b) of the GATS also has an MFN treatment dimension.

The concept of 'a reasonable time-frame' in Article V:1(b) is not defined or clarified in any way in the GATS. On the basis of Article XXIV:5(c) of the GATT 1994 and paragraph 3 of the *Understanding on Article XXIV* concerning the similar concept of 'a reasonable length of time', it would be reasonable to assume that, in defining the 'reasonable time-frame' of Article V:1(b) of the GATS, a ten-year limit would be used as a general starting point.

4.1.3 'Level of Barriers to Trade' Requirement

Article V:4 of the GATS requires that an economic integration agreement must be designed to facilitate trade between the parties to the agreement and must *not*, in respect of any WTO Member that is not a party to the agreement, *raise* the overall level of *barriers* to trade in services within the respective sectors or subsectors as compared to the level prior to such an agreement. The absence of detailed data on trade in services and differences in regulatory mechanisms between Members makes it difficult to evaluate the level of barriers in effect before the establishment of an economic integration agreement. A possible approach to the application of this 'level of barriers to trade' requirement would be to require that an economic integration agreement reduce neither the level, nor the growth, of trade in any sector or subsector below a historical trend.[96]

93 See Committee on Regional Trade Agreements, *Examination of the North American Free Trade Agreement*, Note on the Meeting of 24 February 1997, WT/REG4/M/4, dated 16 April 1997, para. 19.

94 Panel Report, *Canada – Autos (2000)*, para. 10.270. 95 *Ibid.*

96 Changes in the volume of trade could be judged by data on domestic economic activities if data on trade in services is unavailable.

4.2 Labour Markets Integration Agreements

Article V *bis* of the GATS entitled 'Labour Markets Integration Agreements', deals with a specific form of economic integration agreement which establishes full integration of labour markets between or among the parties to such an agreement. Such agreements give the nationals of the parties free access to each other's labour markets. Usually, these agreements also include provisions concerning conditions of pay, other conditions of employment and social benefits. Article V *bis* provides that the GATS shall not prevent any WTO Member from being a party to such an agreement provided that the agreement: (1) exempts citizens of parties to the agreement from requirements concerning residency and work permits; and (2) is notified to the Council for Trade in Services.

4.3 Special and Differential Treatment of Developing-Country Members

With regard to economic integration agreements to which developing countries are parties, Article V:3(a) of the GATS provides for flexibility regarding the conditions set out in Article V:1, quoted and discussed above. This flexibility is to be granted 'in accordance with the level of development of the countries concerned, both overall and in individual sectors and subsectors'. Article V:3(b) of the GATS provides that, in the case of an economic integration agreement involving only developing countries, 'more favourable treatment may be granted to juridical persons owned or controlled by natural persons of the parties to such an agreement'.[97]

5 INSTITUTIONAL AND PROCEDURAL MATTERS

Customs unions and free-trade areas, as well as interim agreements leading to the formation of such a union or area, are reviewed by the WTO to determine their consistency with the GATT 1994 (including the Enabling Clause). Economic integration agreements covering trade in services are also reviewed by the WTO to determine their consistency with the GATS. The final section of this chapter discusses the notification obligations of WTO members in respect of their regional trade agreements, as well as the WTO's institutional framework for the review of such agreements.

Article XXIV of the GATT, the Enabling Clause, and Article V of the GATS each require WTO Members to notify regional trade agreements to the WTO. Article XXIV:7(a) of the GATT and Article V:7(a) of the GATS require WTO Members to 'promptly' notify their participation in regional trade agreements

97 Article V:3(b) applies notwithstanding Article V:6 of the GATS, referred to above at p. 690, fn. 93.

concerning trade in goods, and trade in services, respectively. Moreover, paragraph 4(b) of the Enabling Clause calls for the notification of regional trade agreements in which developing countries are involved.

As discussed above, while Doha Round negotiations on the clarification and improvement of the substantive rules on regional trade agreements have not been successful, WTO Members have been successful in agreeing in December 2006 on the Transparency Mechanism for Regional Trade Agreements (the 'RTA Transparency Mechanism').[98] The RTA Transparency Mechanism clarifies and strengthens the notification obligations of WTO Members and introduces new procedures to enhance the transparency of regional trade agreements. The rationale for the introduction of the RTA Transparency Mechanism in relation to the notification of regional trade agreements has been explained as follows:

> The obligation for notification [had] not been complied with in a systematic manner by WTO Members: for instance, while the wording of GATT Article XXIV suggests that [a regional trade agreement] should be notified before the entry into force of the [regional trade agreement], notifications are generally received after the entry into force, in some cases months or even years after. There is no provision in WTO rules for counter-notification, i.e. for a third party to notify on behalf of other WTO Members. The [RTA Transparency Mechanism] tightens up existing provisions on notification by stipulating in paragraph 3 that notification is to take place 'as early as possible ... no later than directly following the parties' ratification of the [regional trade agreement] or any party's decision on application of the relevant part of an agreement, and before the application of preferential treatment between the parties'. By requiring notification to take place before the application of preferential treatment, WTO Members will be informed about new [regional trade agreements] before their implementation, thus promoting transparency.[99]

It is pertinent to note that the RTA Transparency Mechanism was established on a provisional basis. The Tenth Ministerial Conference at Nairobi called upon Members to work towards the transformation of the provisional RTA Transparency Mechanism, to a permanent one.[100] At the CRTA meeting of 27 September 2016, the CRTA Chair observed, however, that 'the appetite for negotiating a permanent transparency mechanism wasn't that strong'.[101] At the same meeting, the CRTA Chair also noted that seventy-two RTAs, which are currently in force, have not been notified to the WTO.[102]

WTO Members deciding to enter into a customs union, free-trade area or an interim agreement must notify this intention to the Council for Trade in Goods.[103] In contrast, WTO Members deciding to enter into an economic integration

98 See General Council, *Transparency Mechanism for Regional Trade Agreements*, Decision adopted on 14 December 2006, WT/L/671, dated 18 December 2006. See also above, p. 676.

99 J. Crawford, 'A New Transparency Mechanism for Regional Trade Agreements', *Singapore Yearbook of International Law*, 2007, 138.

100 Tenth WTO Ministerial Conference, *Nairobi Ministerial Declaration*, WT/MIN(15)/DEC dated 21 December 2015, para. 28.

101 See *ibid.* 102 See *ibid.*

103 See Article XXIV:7(a) of the GATT 1994. For example, on 27 September 2006, the European Communities notified the Treaty of Accession of Bulgaria and Romania to the European Union. See WT/REG220/N/1, dated 2 October 2006.

agreement, i.e. a regional trade agreement concerning trade in services, must notify this intention to the Council for Trade in Services.[104] Customs unions, free-trade areas, interim agreements and agreements between developing countries under the Enabling Clause are notified to the Council for Trade in Goods, while economic integration agreements in services are notified to the Council for Trade in Services. The Committee on Regional Trade Agreements (CRTA) considers regional trade agreements under Article XXIV of the GATT and Article V of the GATS, while the Committee on Trade and Development (CTD) considers regional trade agreements between developing countries under the Enabling Clause and Article V:3(a) of the GATS.[105] As stated by the panel in *Turkey – Textiles (1999)*, the examination of the WTO consistency of a RTA is 'a very complex undertaking' requiring consideration 'from the economic, legal and political perspectives of different Members, of the numerous facets of a regional trade agreement'.[106] Of the 426 notifications of RTAs received by the WTO up to 1 October 2016, only eighteen notifications resulted in a report from the relevant WTO Committee.[107]

It has been suggested that in view of the existence of the committee process of reviewing the GATT-consistency of customs unions, free-trade areas and interim agreements, WTO dispute settlement panels (and the Appellate Body) would not have jurisdiction to decide on the GATT-consistency of such unions, areas or agreements. In *Turkey – Textiles (1999)*, the Appellate Body effectively rejected this view.[108]

6 SUMMARY

Besides the 'general exceptions', the 'security exceptions' and the 'economic emergency exceptions', WTO law also provides for 'regional trade exceptions'. These exceptions allow Members to adopt measures which are otherwise GATT- or GATS-inconsistent but are taken in the context of (regional) economic integration. The regional trade exceptions are set out in Article XXIV of the GATT 1994 (elaborated in the *Understanding on Article XXIV*), in the Enabling Clause

104 See Article V:7 of the GATS.

105 On the terms of reference of the CRTA, see WT/L/127.

106 Panel Report, *Turkey – Textiles (1999)*, para. 9.52.

107 See http://rtais.wto.org/UI/publicsummarytable.aspx.

108 Appellate Body Report, *Turkey – Textiles (1999)*, para. 60. Although the Appellate Body was not called upon to address this issue, it explicitly referred to its conclusions on a 'similar' issue in *India – Quantitative Restrictions (1999)*, paras. 87 and 95. Furthermore, note para. 12 of the *Understanding on Article XXIV*, which states: 'The provisions of Articles XXII and XXIII of GATT 1994 as elaborated and applied by the Dispute Settlement Understanding may be invoked with respect to any matters arising from the application of those provisions of Article XXIV relating to customs unions, free-trade areas or interim agreements leading to the formation of a customs union or free-trade area.'

of the GATT 1994, and Article V of the GATS. WTO law recognises the advantages of economic integration and trade liberalisation even when these efforts involve only some of its Members. A measure which is otherwise inconsistent with the GATT 1994 can be justified under Article XXIV of the GATT 1994: (1) if the measure is introduced upon the formation of a customs union, a free-trade area or an interim agreement that meets all the requirements set out in Article XXIV:8 and Article XXIV:5 of the GATT 1994; and (2) if the formation of the customs union or free-trade area would be prevented if the introduction of the measure concerned were not allowed. A measure which is otherwise GATS-inconsistent can be justified under Article V of the GATS: (1) if the measure is introduced as part of an agreement liberalising trade in services that meets all the requirements set out in Article V:1(a), Article V:1(b) and Article V:4 of the GATS; and (2) if WTO Members would be prevented from being a party to an agreement liberalising trade in services if the measure concerned were not allowed. Regional trade agreements among developing-country Members are subject to less onerous requirements pursuant to the Enabling Clause of the GATT 1994 and Article V:3 of the GATS.

FURTHER READINGS

R. Baldwin, 'The World Trade Organization and the Future of Multilateralism', *Journal of Economic Perspectives*, 2016, 30(1), 95–116.

K. Suominen, 'Enhancing Coherence and Inclusiveness in the Global Trading System in the Era of Regionalism', E15 Expert Group on Regional Trade Agreements and Plurilateral Approaches – Policy Options Paper, International Centre for Trade and Sustainable Development and World Economic Forum, January 2016.

B. Hoekman and P. Mavroidis, 'WTO "à la carte" or "menu du jour"? Accessing the Case for More Plurilateral Agreements', *European Journal of International Law*, 2015, 26(2), 319–43.

F. Altemöller, 'A Future for Multilateralism?: New Regionalism, Counter-Multilateralism and Perspectives for the World Trade System after the Bali Ministerial Conference', *Global Trade and Customs Journal*, 2015, 10(1), 42–53.

WTO, OECD and the World Bank, 'Regional Trade Agreements and the Multilateral Trading System', Discussion Paper for the G-20, WTO, 2015.

G. Hufbauer and C. Cimino-Issacs, 'How Will TPP and TTIP Change the WTO System', *Journal of International Economic Law*, 2015, 18, 679–96.

I. Lejárraga, 'Deep Provisions in Regional Trade Agreements: How Multilateral-friendly?: An Overview of OECD Findings', OECD Trade Policy Papers No. 168, OECD, 2015.

K. Bagwell, C. P. Bown and R. W. Staiger, 'Is the WTO Passé?', Policy Research Working Paper 7304, World Bank Group, June 2015.

S. Yang, 'The Solution for Jurisdictional Conflicts between the WTO and the RTAs: The Forum Choice Clause', *Michigan State International Law Review*, 2015, 23(1), 107–52.

Global Agenda Council on Trade and Foreign Direct Investment, 'Mega Regional Trade Agreements: Game Changers or Costly Distractions for the World Trading System?', World Economic Forum, July 2014.

Note by Secretariat, *Synopsis of Systemic Issues Related to Regional Trade Agreements*, Committee on Regional Trade Agreements, WT/REG/W/37 dated 2 March 2000, WTO.

11 Dumping

CONTENTS

1 INTRODUCTION

While professing support for trade liberalisation, trade policy-makers often insist that international trade should be 'fair'. 'Unfair' trade comes in many forms and guises. Unfair trade practices may include cartel agreements, price fixing and the abuse of a dominant position on the market.[1] WTO law, at present, does not provide for rules on these and many other particular forms of unfair trade. This absence of rules partly reflects a lack of agreement on what are 'fair' and 'unfair' trade practices. WTO law provide for detailed rules with respect to dumping and certain types of subsidisation – two specific trade practices commonly considered to be 'unfair'. Members differ in opinion as to what extent these trade practices are truly 'unfair'. This difference in opinion among Members reflects differences in their societies in general and their economic systems in particular.

The basic idea underlying WTO rules on 'unfair' trade practices, such as dumping and subsidisation, is that the response of importing countries at least partially 'offsets' the negative effects of the unfair practices, and may even have punitive effects that inhibit such practices in the future. A commonly expressed goal of 'trade remedy' measures, such as anti-dumping or countervailing measures,[2] is to 'level the playing field', that is, international competition should occur based upon a set of rules agreed upon by all participants. In contrast, others consider 'price discrimination' (i.e. price differentiation) between the markets of the exporting and importing countries (as long as the sales price exceeds variable costs) as actually beneficial to national or global welfare. Another concern raised with regard to price discrimination is that large and economically powerful firms could use their market leverage to drive small firms out of business, thus reducing competition; in turn, these predatory firms can then raise their prices and reap monopoly profits.[3] Finally, it has also been argued that international dumping depends on import barriers of the exporting country that make reintroducing of the dumped product into the home market difficult, if not impossible, and thus unfair.

As noted by the Appellate Body in *US – Washing Machines (2016)*:

> Although the *Anti-Dumping Agreement* does not contain a preamble expressly setting out its object and purpose, it is apparent from the text of this Agreement that it deals with injurious dumping by allowing Members to take anti-dumping measures to counteract injurious dumping and imposing disciplines on the use of such anti-dumping measures.[4]

1 The concept of 'unfair trade' is also commonly used to refer to trade on terms and conditions which are disadvantageous for developing countries in general and small companies, workers and farmers in these countries in particular.

2 On the concept of 'trade remedies', see above, p. 41.

3 J. Jackson, *The World Trading System: Law and Policy of International Economic Relations*, 2nd edn (Cambridge, MA, MIT Press, 1997), 253–4. See also J. Viner, *Dumping: A Problem in International Trade* (1969), 120.

4 Appellate Body Report, *US – Washing Machines (2016)*, para. 5.52.

The next chapter, Chapter 12, deals with WTO rules on subsidies. This chapter examines WTO rules on dumping. It discusses the following topics: (1) basic elements of WTO law on dumping; (2) the determination of dumping; (3) the determination of injury to the domestic industry; (4) the determination of a causal link between the dumping and the injury; (5) the manner in which anti-dumping investigations must be conducted; (6) anti-dumping measures; (7) institutional and procedural provisions, including the standard of review applicable under the *Anti-Dumping Agreement*; and (8) special and differential treatment of developing-country Members.

2 BASIC ELEMENTS OF WTO LAW ON DUMPING

Before entering into a more detailed, and often technical, discussion of the rules on dumping and anti-dumping measures, this section first addresses the following in general terms: (1) the history of WTO law on dumping; (2) the concept of 'dumping' and its treatment in WTO law; and (3) current use of anti-dumping measures.

2.1 History of the Law on Dumping

WTO law on dumping and anti-dumping measures is set out in Article VI of the GATT 1994 and in the WTO *Agreement on Implementation of Article VI of the GATT 1994*, commonly referred to as the *Anti-Dumping Agreement*. When the GATT was negotiated in 1947, participants initially failed to agree on whether a provision allowing countries to impose anti-dumping measures in response to dumping should even be included.[5] However, largely at the insistence of the United States, Article VI was included to provide a basic framework as to how countries could respond to dumping.[6] In the following years, Article VI alone proved to be inadequate in addressing the anti-dumping measures. Its language was particularly vague and different WTO Members therefore interpreted and applied it in an incoherent manner.[7] Many GATT Contracting Parties felt that other Contracting Parties were applying anti-dumping laws in a manner that effectively raised new barriers to trade.[8] The inadequacies of Article VI required that it would have to be fleshed out in further agreements. This

5 The United Kingdom and others argued that national anti-dumping laws were a hindrance to free trade and that the GATT should actually prohibit the imposition of anti-dumping duties. See B. Blonigen and T. Prusa, 'Antidumping' (July 2001), NBER Working Paper No. W8398, http://papers.ssrn.com/sol3/papers.cfm?abstract_id=278031.

6 The United States was one of the few countries at this time with anti-dumping legislation in place.

7 See M. Trebilcock and R. Howse, *The Regulation of International Trade*, 3rd edn (Routledge, 2005), 233.

8 See Jackson, *World Trading System*, 2nd edn, 256.

was achieved in 1967 by the Kennedy Round *Anti-Dumping Code*, which was replaced by the Tokyo Round *Anti-Dumping Code* in 1979. Despite the clarification and elaboration of Article VI by the Tokyo Round *Anti-Dumping Code*, even more criticism of the anti-dumping regime emerged in the 1980s. At that time, anti-dumping action proliferated, with developed countries being the dominant users of the regime and developing countries being a significant target.[9] Not surprisingly, therefore, the anti-dumping regime was one of the most controversial issues placed on the agenda of the Uruguay Round negotiations. The positions taken by the participants in the negotiations varied greatly. Some participants wanted to facilitate the use of anti-dumping measures (i.e. the United States and the European Communities), while others wanted to impose stricter disciplines (i.e. Japan, Korea and Hong Kong, China). At the end of the Uruguay Round, a compromise was reached that was ultimately reflected in the WTO *Anti-Dumping Agreement* and which, together with Article VI of the GATT 1994, sets out the current rules on dumping and anti-dumping measures. As will be noted in this chapter, the conflicting, and sometimes even opposing, interests that existed in the negotiations resulted in provisions with ambiguous language. Some of these provisions have been 'clarified' by case law, while others still await clarification.

In the Doha Ministerial Declaration of November 2001, WTO Members agreed to place anti-dumping rules on the agenda of the Doha Round negotiations.[10]

From various negotiating texts, it is clear that the Membership is still deeply divided on what changes to the *Anti-Dumping Agreement* should be made, if any and to date, the WTO Members remain divided on this issue. The Chair of the Negotiating Group on Rules, in its December 2015 report to the Trade Negotiations Committee stated:

> Further, I am entirely conscious that the Group is far from achieving convergence even on any of the very significantly recalibrated proposals now before it. Indeed, the broader environment has not allowed us to really begin negotiations in earnest on these proposals.[11]

2.2 The Concept of 'Dumping' and Its Treatment in WTO Law

'Dumping' is a situation of *international price discrimination* involving the price and cost of a product in the exporting country in relation to its price in the

9 Between July 1980 and June 1988, nearly 1,200 anti-dumping actions were initiated. See Trebilcock and Howse, *Regulation of International Trade*, 2nd edn, 166.

10 The Doha Ministerial Declaration provides: 'In the light of experience and of the increasing application of these instruments by Members, we agree to negotiations aimed at clarifying and improving disciplines under the Agreements on Implementation of Article VI of the GATT 1994 and on Subsidies and Countervailing Measures, while preserving the basic concepts, principles and effectiveness of these Agreements and their instruments and objectives, and taking into account the needs of developing and least-developed participants.' See Ministerial Conference, *Doha Ministerial Declaration*, WT/MIN(01)/DEC/1, dated 20 November 2001, para. 28.

11 Negotiating Group on Rules, *Report by Chairman, H. E. Mr. Wayne McCook to the Trade Negotiations Committee*, TN/RL/27, dated 7 December 2015, 2.

importing country. Article VI of the GATT 1994 and Article 2.1 of the *Anti-Dumping Agreement* define dumping as the introduction of a product into the commerce of another country at less than its 'normal value'.[12] Thus, a product can be considered 'dumped' where the export price of that product is less than its normal value, that is, the comparable price, in the ordinary course of trade, for the 'like product' destined for consumption in the exporting country.[13]

WTO law does *not* prohibit dumping. In fact, since prices of products are ordinarily set by private companies, 'dumping' in and of itself is *not* regulated by WTO law. As discussed above, WTO law in general only imposes obligations on, and regulates the measures that may be taken and the actions of, WTO Members in response to dumping. It does not directly regulate the actions of private companies. However, as dumping may cause injury to the domestic industry of the importing country, Article VI of the GATT 1994 states, in relevant part, that:

> [t]he [Members] recognize that dumping ... is to be *condemned* if it causes or threatens material injury to an established industry in the territory of a [Member] or materially retards the establishment of a domestic industry.[14]

Consequently, Article VI of the GATT 1994 and the *Anti-Dumping Agreement* provide a framework of substantive and procedural rules governing how a Member may counteract or 'remedy' dumping, through the imposition of 'anti-dumping' measures.

WTO Members are not required to enact anti-dumping legislation or to have in place a system for conducting anti-dumping investigations and imposing anti-dumping measures. However, if a Member makes the policy choice to have recourse to the option of imposing anti-dumping measures, Article 1 of the *Anti-Dumping Agreement* specifies that:

> [a]n anti-dumping measure shall be applied only under the circumstances provided for in Article VI of GATT 1994 and pursuant to investigations initiated and conducted in accordance with the provisions of this Agreement. The following provisions govern the application of Article VI of GATT 1994 in so far as action is taken under anti-dumping legislation or regulations.

Pursuant to Article VI of the GATT 1994 and the *Anti-Dumping Agreement*, WTO Members are entitled to impose anti-dumping measures if, after an investigation initiated and conducted in accordance with the Agreement, on the basis of pre-existing legislation that has been properly notified to the WTO, a determination is made that: (1) there is dumping; (2) the domestic industry producing the like product in the importing country is suffering injury

12 Note that the Appellate Body in *US – Zeroing (Japan) (2007)* stated that Article 2.1 of the *Anti-Dumping Agreement* and Article VI:1 of the GATT 1994 are 'definitional provisions' and do not impose independent obligations. See Appellate Body Report, *US – Zeroing (Japan) (2007)*, para. 140.

13 See Article 2.1 of the *Anti-Dumping Agreement*. For a more detailed analysis of the concept of dumping, see below, pp. 703–5.

14 Emphasis added.

(or threat thereof); and (3) there is a causal link between the dumping and the injury. Later sections of this chapter discuss in detail the concepts of 'dumping', 'injury' and 'causal link'.[15]

In response to injurious dumping, Members may take anti-dumping measures. However, Article VI, and in particular Article VI:2, read in conjunction with the *Anti-Dumping Agreement*, limit the permissible responses to dumping to: (1) provisional measures; (2) price undertakings; and (3) definitive anti-dumping duties.[16] Article 18.1 of the *Anti-Dumping Agreement* provides:

> No specific action against dumping of exports from another Member can be taken except in accordance with the provisions of GATT 1994, as interpreted by this Agreement.[17]

In *US – 1916 Act (2000)*, the Appellate Body ruled that any 'specific action against dumping', i.e. action that is taken in response to situations presenting the constituent elements of 'dumping', can only take the form of the measures referred to in Article VI:2 of the GATT 1994.[18]

In *US – Offset Act (Byrd Amendment) (2003)*, the measure at issue, the United States Continued Dumping and Subsidy Offset Act of 2000 (CDSOA), provided, in relevant part, that United States Customs shall *distribute* duties assessed pursuant to an anti-dumping duty order to 'affected domestic producers' for 'qualifying expenditures'.[19] Recalling that Article VI:2, read in conjunction with the *Anti-Dumping Agreement*, limits the permissible responses to dumping to definitive anti-dumping duties, provisional measures and price undertakings,[20] the Appellate Body concluded in *US – Offset Act (Byrd Amendment) (2003)*:

> As CDSOA offset payments are not definitive anti-dumping duties, provisional measures or price undertakings, we conclude, in the light of our finding in *US – 1916 Act*, that the CDSOA is not 'in accordance with the provisions of the GATT 1994, as interpreted by' the *Anti-Dumping Agreement*.[21]

15 See below, pp. 703–5, 723 and 733–4, respectively.

16 See Appellate Body Report, *US – 1916 Act (2000)*, para. 137.

17 Footnote 24 to this provision reads: 'This is not intended to preclude action under other relevant provisions of GATT 1994, as appropriate.'

18 The US legislation at issue in *US – 1916 Act (2000)* provided for civil and criminal proceedings and penalties for conduct meeting the constituent elements of dumping. Since these civil and criminal actions are not among the permissible responses to dumping listed in Article VI:2, the Appellate Body and the panel in this case ruled that the 1916 Act is inconsistent with Article VI:2, as interpreted by the *Anti-Dumping Agreement*. See Appellate Body Report, *US – 1916 Act (2000)*, para. 137. On the concept of 'specific action against dumping', see Appellate Body Report, *US – 1916 Act (2000)*, para. 126. In *US – Offset Act (Byrd Amendment) (2003)*, the Appellate Body found that a measure is a 'specific action against dumping' when that measure is inextricably linked to, or has a strong correlation with, a determination of dumping. See Appellate Body, *US – Offset Act (Byrd Amendment) (2003)*, para. 239. See also Panel Report, *Mexico – Anti-Dumping Measures on Rice (2005)*, para. 7.278.

19 The CDSOA amends Title VII of the US Tariff Act of 1930 by adding a new Section 754 entitled 'Continued Dumping and Subsidy Offset' and is often referred to as the 'Byrd Amendment'. See Appellate Body Report, *US – Offset Act (Byrd Amendment) (2003)*, para. 12.

20 See below, pp. 749–50.

21 According to the Appellate Body, it follows that the CDSOA is inconsistent with Article 18.1 of that Agreement. See Appellate Body Report, *US – Offset Act (Byrd Amendment) (2003)*, para. 265. See also Panel Report, Mexico – *Anti-Dumping Measures on Rice (2005)*, para. 7.278.

2.3 Current Use of Anti-Dumping Measures

Anti-dumping law is one of the most controversial and politically sensitive areas of WTO law. WTO Members are often put under severe pressure by domestic producers to impose anti-dumping measures on particular products, and by foreign producers and domestic users of such products *not* to impose such measures.

During the period from 1 July 2015 to 30 June 2016, thirty-one Members initiated a total of 267 anti-dumping investigations.[22] This indicates that the number of investigations is on the rise, having already reached a high level in the preceding period from July 2014 to 30 June 2015, when twenty-five Members initiated 237 anti-dumping investigations.[23] In the period 1 July 2015 to 30 June 2016, twenty-five Members imposed a total of 151 new anti-dumping measures against exports from other countries or customs territories, whereas, in the period July 2014 to 30 June 2015, twenty-three Members imposed significantly higher number of new anti-dumping measures, totalling 197 in number.[24]

The overall use of anti-dumping measures fluctuates from year to year. In the period since the establishment of the WTO, the number of anti-dumping measures taken by Members has been on average 162 per year.[25] From January 1995 to December 2015, India was the most frequent user of the anti-dumping instrument, with a total of 572 measures. The United States was second, with 359 measures and the European Union was third with 309.[26] In the period from July 2015 to 30 June 2016, India imposed the most new measures (thirty-eight), followed by the United States (nineteen), Mexico (fourteen), the European Union (ten), Brazil (nine) and Turkey, China and Australia (eight each).[27] In the preceding year, the period from July 2014 to 30 June 2015, most anti-dumping measures were imposed by Brazil (fifty), followed by India (thirty-two), the United States (twenty-three), Australia (sixteen), Argentina (fourteen) and Canada (twelve).[28] These figures make clear that the days when anti-dumping measures were taken almost exclusively by developed-country Members have passed. Developing-country Members have 'discovered' this trade policy instrument and some have become avid users. In addition, some Members who acceded to the WTO in the last decade have begun using anti-dumping measures quite frequently.

Furthermore, contrary to a widespread misconception, anti-dumping measures are not only used against developing-country Members; indeed, they are used

22 See Annex C, *Report (2016) of the Committee on Anti-Dumping Practices*, G/L/1158, dated 1 November 2016.
23 See Annex C, *Report (2015) of the Committee on Anti-Dumping Practices*, G/L/1134, dated 30 October 2015.
24 See *ibid.* (the figure does not include number of price undertakings).
25 Note that, in the final years of the GATT, this number was considerably higher.
26 See www.wto.org/english/tratop_e/adp_e/AD_MeasuresByRepMem.pdf.
27 Annex C, *Report (2016) of the Committee on Anti-Dumping Practices*, G/L/1158, dated 1 November 2016.
28 Annex C, *Report (2015) of the Committee on Anti-Dumping Practices*, G/L/1134, dated 30 October 2015.

frequently against both developed Members and developing-country Members. China has been by far the biggest target of anti-dumping measures, with 820 such measures being taken between January 1995 and December 2015, followed by Republic of Korea (225) and Chinese Taipei being the target of 184 such measures.[29] In the period from July 2015 to 30 June 2016, most anti-dumping measures were imposed against China (fifty-six), Ukraine (twelve), the United States (ten) and Chinese Taipei (eight). In the preceding period from July 2014 to 30 June 2015, anti-dumping measures were imposed against mainly China (fifty-three), Korea (fourteen), Chinese Taipei (thirteen) and the United States (seven). Of the 3,240 anti-dumping measures imposed by Members since 1995, fifty were the subject of WTO dispute settlement.[30] To date, Members have been found to have acted inconsistently with their obligations under Article VI of the GATT 1994 and the *Anti-Dumping Agreement* in forty-three disputes.[31]

3 DETERMINATION OF DUMPING

As discussed above, Article VI:1 of the GATT 1994 and Article 2.1 of the *Anti-Dumping Agreement* define 'dumping' as the introduction of a product into the commerce of another country at less than its 'normal value'. In other words, 'dumping' exists where the 'normal value' of the product exceeds the 'export price'. This section explains: (1) how the 'normal value' of the product concerned is determined; (2) how the relevant 'export price' is determined; (3) how the existence of dumping is determined; and (4) how the 'dumping margin' is calculated.

Ordinarily, dumping is discerned through a price-to-price comparison of the 'normal value' with the 'export price'. However, the *Anti-Dumping Agreement* envisages circumstances in which such a straightforward price-to-price comparison may not be possible or appropriate, and, therefore, provides for alternative methods for determining the existence of dumping in such cases.

29 See www.wto.org/english/tratop_e/adp_e/AD_MeasuresByRepMem.pdf.

30 See www.worldtradelaw.net/databases/antidumping.php.

31 See *US – DRAMs (1999)*; *Guatemala – Cement II (2000)*; *Mexico – Corn Syrup (2000)*; *US – 1916 Act (2000)*; *Argentina – Ceramic Tiles (2001)*; *US – Hot-Rolled Steel (2001)*; *EC – Bed Linen (2001)*; *Thailand – H-Beams (2001)*; *US – Stainless Steel (Korea) (2001)*; *Egypt – Steel Rebar (2002)*; *US – Steel Plate (2002)*; *Argentina – Poultry Anti-Dumping Duties (2003)*; *US – Offset Act (Byrd Amendment) (2003)*; *EC – Tube or Pipe Fittings (2003)*; *EC – Bed Linen (Article 21.5 – India) (2003)*; *US – Softwood Lumber V (2004)*; *US – Softwood Lumber VI (2004)*; *US – Oil Country Tubular Goods Sunset Reviews (2004)*; *Korea – Certain Paper (2005)*; *Mexico – Anti-Dumping Measures on Rice (2005)*; *US – Anti-Dumping Measures on Oil Country Tubular Goods (2005)*; *US – Zeroing (EC) (2006)*; *US – Zeroing (Japan) (2007)*; *US – Shrimp (Ecuador) (2007)*; *Mexico – Steel Pipes and Tubes (2007)*; *EC – Salmon (Norway) (2008)*; *US – Shrimp (Thailand) (2008)*; *US – Customs Bond Directive (2008)*; *US – Stainless Steel (Mexico) (2008)*; *US – Continued Zeroing (2009)*; *US – Anti-Dumping Measures on PET Bags (2010)*; *US – Orange Juice (Brazil) (2011)*; *US – Shrimp (Viet Nam) (2011)*; *US – Zeroing (Korea) (2011)*; *EC – Fasteners (China) (2011)*; *US – Shrimp and Sawblades (2012)*; *EU – Footwear (China) (2012)*; *China – GOES (2012)*; *US – Shrimp II (Viet Nam) (2015)*; *China – High-Performance Stainless Steel Seamless Tubes (HP-SSST) (2015)*; *EC – Fasteners (Article 21.5 – China) (2016)*; *US – Washing Machines (2016)*; and *EU – Biodiesel (2016)*.

Before engaging in this discussion of how to determine the existence of dumping, it is important to recall that only dumping causing injury is to be condemned and potentially subject to anti-dumping measures under Article VI of the GATT 1994 and the *Anti-Dumping Agreement*. However, the injurious effect that 'dumping' may have on a Member's domestic industry is not relevant in determining whether there is 'dumping'. Injury to the domestic industry is not a constituent element of 'dumping'.[32] In addition, the intent of the persons engaging in 'dumping' is irrelevant in the determination of whether dumping exists.[33]

The Appellate Body has emphasised repeatedly that the definitions of the terms 'dumping', as well as 'dumped imports', have the same meaning in all provisions of the Agreement and for all types of anti-dumping proceedings, including original investigations, new shipper reviews, and periodic reviews.[34] In each case, they relate to a *product* because it is the product that is introduced into the commerce of another country at less than its normal value in that country.[35] Thus, the margin of dumping is also defined in relation to a 'product'. The Appellate Body noted in *US – Zeroing (Japan) (2007)*, *US – Stainless Steel (Mexico) (2008)*, and *US – Washing Machines (2016)* that: (1) the concepts of 'dumping' and 'margins of dumping' pertain to a 'product' and are related to an exporter or foreign producer;[36] (2) 'dumping' and 'dumping margins' must be determined for the products 'as a whole' and in respect of each known exporter or foreign producer examined.[37] The Appellate Body further clarified that a 'proper determination as to whether an exporter is dumping or not can only be made on the basis of an examination of the exporter's pricing behaviour as

32 See Appellate Body Report, *US – 1916 Act (2000)*, para. 107. 33 See *ibid*.

34 For a discussion on these various types of proceedings, see below, pp. 737–49 and 754–8. Note that 'periodic' reviews are also referred to as 'administrative' reviews. The Appellate Body noted that 'Article 2.1 of the *Anti-Dumping Agreement* and Article VI:1 of the GATT 1994 are definitional provisions' that 'set out a definition of "dumping" for the purposes of the *Anti-Dumping Agreement* and the GATT 1994'. See Appellate Body Reports, *US – Washing Machines (2016)*, para. 5.148, referring to Appellate Body Report, *US – Zeroing (Japan) (2007)*, para. 140.

35 See Appellate Body Report, *US – Zeroing (Japan) (2007)*, para. 109, referring to Article 2.1, regarding original investigations. See Appellate Body Report, *US – Stainless Steel (Mexico) (2008)*, para. 84, referring to Article 9.3, regarding periodic reviews; Appellate Body Report, *US – Corrosion-Resistant Steel Sunset Review (2004)*, para. 109, referring to Article 11.3, regarding sunset reviews. See also Appellate Body Report, *US – Continued Zeroing (2009)*, para. 280. The Appellate Body noted that the concepts of 'dumping', 'injury' and 'margin of dumping' are interlinked and, therefore, should be considered and interpreted in a coherent and consistent manner for all parts of the *Anti-Dumping Agreement*. Appellate Body Report, *US – Zeroing (Japan) (2007)*, para. 114; Appellate Body Report, *US – Stainless Steel (Mexico) (2008)*, para. 94; and *US – Washing Machines (2016)*, paras. 5.90–5.98.

36 According to the Appellate Body, '[d]umping arises from the pricing practices of exporters as both normal values and export prices reflect their pricing strategies in home and foreign markets. These margins of dumping have to be calculated on an exporter-wide rather than on a transaction-specific basis.' See Appellate Body Report, *US – Stainless Steel (Mexico) (2008)*, para. 95. For a more detailed discussion on 'zeroing', see below, pp. 714–20.

37 See Appellate Body Reports, *US – Washing Machines (2016)*, referring to *US – Softwood Lumber V (2004)*, para. 102. The Appellate Body also emphasised that anti-dumping duties can be levied only in an amount not exceeding the margin of dumping established for each exporter or foreign producer. See Appellate Body Report, *US – Zeroing (Japan) (2007)*, paras. 111–14; Appellate Body Report, *US – Stainless Steel (Mexico) (2008)*, para. 94; *US – Washing Machines (2016)*, paras. 5.90–5.98, 5.185–5.187; and *EU – Biodiesel (2016)*, para 6.96 (in respect of Article 9.3).

reflected in all its transactions over a period of time'.[38] However, as the Appellate Body recalled in *US – Washing Machines (2016)*, in case of 'targeted dumping' to certain purchasers, regions or in certain time periods, the applicable 'universe of export transactions' is more limited.[39]

3.1 'Normal Value'

Article 2.1 of the *Anti-Dumping Agreement* defines the 'normal value' of a product as:

> [t]he comparable price, in the ordinary course of trade, for the like product when destined for consumption in the exporting country.

In other words, the 'normal value' is the price of the like product in the home market of the exporter or producer. According to the Appellate Body in *US – Hot-Rolled Steel (2001)*, the text of Article 2.1 expressly imposes four conditions on domestic sales transactions so that they may be used to determine 'normal value': (1) the sale must be 'in the ordinary course of trade'; (2) the sale must be of the 'like product'; (3) the product must be 'destined for consumption in the exporting country'; and (4) the price must be 'comparable'.[40]

The first of the four conditions that sales transactions must fulfil so that they may be used to determine the 'normal value' is that the sale must be 'in the ordinary course of trade'. The decision as to whether sales in the domestic market of the exporting Member are made 'in the ordinary course of trade' can be a complex one. There are a number situations that *may* form a reason to determine that transactions were not made 'in the ordinary course of trade', such as sales to affiliated parties; [aberrationally high-priced sales, or abnormally low-priced sales;] or sales below cost.[41] Sales not made in the ordinary course of trade may be *disregarded* in determining normal value, which would then be determined on the basis of the remaining sales.[42] As the Appellate Body stated in *US – Hot-Rolled Steel (2001)*:

38 Appellate Body Report, *US – Stainless Steel (Mexico) (2008)*, para. 98. Note, however, the second sentence of Article 2.4.2, see *US – Washing Machines (2016)*, para. 5.91.

39 See Appellate Body Reports, *US – Washing Machines (2016)*, paras. 5.105–5.106 and 5.147, referring to Appellate Body Reports, *US – Zeroing (Japan) (2004)*, para. 135; *US – Softwood Lumber V (Article 21.5 – Canada) (2005)*, fn. 166 to para. 99.

40 See Appellate Body Report, *US – Hot-Rolled Steel (2001)*, para. 165. Other provisions in the *Anti-Dumping Agreement*, such as Article 2.4, discussed below, permit the domestic investigating authorities to take account of considerations that may not be expressly identified in Article 2.1, such as the identity of the seller in a particular sales transaction.

41 See Article 2.2.1 of the *Anti-Dumping Agreement*. Note that pricing below cost alone is not sufficient. Such sales must be made over an extended period of time, in substantial quantities, and at prices that do not provide for the recovery of costs within a reasonable period of time. With regard to the second of these criteria, see Panel Report, *EC – Salmon (Norway) (2008)*, paras. 7.231–7.279.

42 See Appellate Body Report, *US – Hot-Rolled Steel (2001)*, para. 139. However, where the exclusion of such below-cost sales results in a level of sales that is too low to permit a proper comparison with export price, an alternative method of calculation may be used.

Article 2.1 requires investigating authorities to exclude sales not made 'in the ordinary course of trade', from the calculation of normal value, precisely to ensure that normal value is, indeed, the 'normal' price of the like product, in the home market of the exporter.[43]

As the Appellate Body found in *US – Hot-Rolled Steel (2001)*, the *Anti-Dumping Agreement* affords WTO Members discretion to determine how to ensure that normal value is not distorted through the inclusion of sales that are not 'in the ordinary course of trade'. However, the Appellate Body noted at the same time that this discretion is not without limits.[44]

In *EU – Biodiesel (2016)*, the Appellate Body interpreted Article 2.2.1.1, which governs investigating authorities' determination of the costs of producing the relevant product.

Article 2.2.1.1, first sentence, provides that 'costs shall normally be calculated on the basis of records kept by the exporter or producer under investigation' if two conditions are met: first, such records are to be in accordance with the 'generally accepted accounting principles' of the exporting country and, second, they 'such records ... reasonably reflect the costs associated with the production and sale of the product under consideration'. The latter condition concerns whether the records kept by the exporter or producer under investigation 'suitably and sufficiently correspond to or reproduce those costs incurred by the investigated exporter or producer that have a genuine relationship with the production and sale of the specific product under consideration'.[45]

The Appellate Body upheld the Panel's finding that the European Union acted inconsistently with the first sentence of Article 2.2.1.1 by failing to calculate the cost of production of biodiesel on the basis of the records kept by the Argentine producers.[46]

The second of the four conditions under Article 2.1 that sales transactions have to meet so that they may be used to determine the 'normal value' is that the sale must be of the 'like product'. The determination of what constitutes a 'like product' involves, first examining the imported product or products that is or are alleged to be dumped and, secondly, establishing the product that is 'like'. Article 2.6 of the *Anti-Dumping Agreement* defines the 'like product' as:

[a] product which is identical, i.e. alike in all respects to the product under consideration, or in the absence of such a product, another product which, although not alike in all respects, has characteristics closely resembling those of the product under consideration.[47]

43 *Ibid.*, para. 140.

44 *Ibid.*, para. 148. The Appellate Body stated that the discretion must be exercised in an *even-handed* way that is fair to all parties affected by an anti-dumping investigation. If a Member elects to adopt general rules to prevent distortion of normal value through sales between affiliates, those rules must reflect, even-handedly, the fact that both high and low-priced sales between affiliates might not be 'in the ordinary course of trade' Appellate Body Report, *US – Hot-Rolled Steel (2001)*, para. 139.

45 Appellate Body Report, *EU – Biodiesel (2016)*, para. 6.26. The Appellate Body also agreed with the panel that the EU authorities' determination that domestic prices of soybeans in Argentina were 'artificially low' due to the Argentine differential export tax system was not, in itself, a sufficient basis for concluding that the producers' records did not reasonably reflect the costs of soybeans associated with the production and sale of biodiesel. Appellate Body Report, *EU – Biodiesel (2016)*, para. 6.55.

46 *Ibid.*, paras. 6.55–6.57.

47 Article 2.6 explicitly states that this definition applies 'throughout this Agreement', i.e. throughout the *Anti-Dumping Agreement*. See also Panel Report, *Korea – Certain Paper (2005)*, para. 7.272, as discussed below, p. 730.

A 'like product' is thus an identical product or a product with a close resemblance to the product under consideration.[48]

The third and fourth conditions provided for in Article 2.1 that sales transactions must meet, so that they may be used to determine the 'normal value', are that the product must be 'destined for consumption in the exporting country' *and* that the price must be 'comparable'. With respect to the latter condition, note that Article 2.4 of the *Anti-Dumping Agreement* requires that a 'fair comparison' be made between export price and normal value. In *EC – Fasteners (Article 21.5 – China) (2016)* and *EU – Biodiesel (2016)*, the Appellate Body recalled that Article 2.4 requires investigating authorities to make a fair comparison between the price of the exported product under investigation and the normal value, and to make due allowance for differences which affect price comparability.[49] This comparison 'shall be made at the same level of trade, normally at the ex-factory level'. As the Appellate Body stated in *US – Hot-Rolled Steel (2001)*, in making a 'fair comparison':

> Article 2.4 mandates that due account be taken of 'differences which affect price comparability', such as differences in the 'levels of trade' at which normal value and the export price are calculated.[50]

The last sentence of Article 2.4 of the *Anti-Dumping Agreement* requires investigating authorities to indicate to the parties in question, what information is required to ensure a fair comparison between export price and normal value. In this regard, the Appellate Body ruled in *EC – Fasteners (Article 21.5 – China) (2016)* that although exporters have to substantiate their requests for adjustments, the investigating authority must, first, inform the parties what information the authority will need in order to ensure a fair comparison.[51]

The *Anti-Dumping Agreement* acknowledges that in certain circumstances consideration of the domestic price in the exporting country does not produce an appropriate 'normal value' for the purposes of comparison with the export price. Such circumstances may arise when there are no sales of the like product in the 'ordinary course of trade' in the domestic market of the exporting country; or when, because of the low volume of sales in that market, such sales do not permit a proper comparison.[52] The *Anti-Dumping Agreement* also recognises

48 Compare with the concept of 'like products' as used in the GATT 1994 (see above, pp. 316–19 and 351–65) and in the *SCM Agreement*, especially Article 15.1 and fn. 46 to that Agreement (see below, pp. 813–17). See also Appellate Body Report, *EC and certain member States – Large Civil Aircraft (2011)*, para. 1118. See also Panel Report, *EC – Salmon (Norway) (2008)*, para. 7.52.

49 Appellate Body Report, *EC – Fasteners (Article 21.5 – China) (2016)*, para. 5.163; and Appellate Body Report *EU – Biodiesel (2016)*, para. 6.87.

50 Appellate Body Report, *US – Hot-Rolled Steel (2001)*, para. 167.

51 Appellate Body Reports, *EC – Fasteners (Article 21.5 – China) (2016)*, para. 5.172.

52 Footnote 2 to Article 2.2 of the *Anti-Dumping Agreement* provides that the volume of sales in the domestic market of the exporting country shall normally be considered 'sufficient' for the purposes of calculating normal value if such sales constitute 5 per cent or more of the sales of the like product under consideration to the importing Member.

that the domestic price in the exporting country market may not constitute an appropriate normal value for the purposes of comparison with the export price because of 'a particular market situation', but does not offer any criteria to assist domestic investigating authorities in determining whether such a particular market situation exists.[53] The second Supplementary Provision to Article VI:1 of the GATT 1994 (to which Article 2.7 of the *Anti-Dumping Agreement* also refers) acknowledges that a straightforward comparison with the home market price may not always be appropriate in the case of imports from a country which has a complete or substantially complete monopoly of its trade and where all domestic prices are fixed by the State, often referred to as a 'non-market economy'. Note in this respect the *EC – Fasteners (China) (2011)* investigation where the European Commission resorted to a so-called 'analogue country' methodology based on Section 15 of China's Accession Protocol. The Appellate Body found in *EC – Fasteners (Article 21.5 – China) (2016)* that an investigating authority has to take steps to achieve clarity as to the adjustment claimed, and determine whether, on its merits, the adjustment is warranted because it reflects a difference affecting price comparability or whether it would lead to adjusting back to costs or prices that were found to be distorted in the exporting country.[54] As noted above (i) when there are no sales of the like product in the ordinary course of trade in the domestic market of the exporting country, or (ii) when, because of the particular market situation or (iii) the low volume of the sales in the domestic market of the exporting country, the domestic price in the exporting country market may not represent an appropriate normal value for the purposes of comparison with the export price. In these scenarios, Article 2.2 of the *Anti-Dumping Agreement* provides that an importing Member may select one of two alternative methods for determining an appropriate normal value for comparison with the export price: (1) using a third country price as the normal value; or (2) constructing the normal value. No preference or hierarchy between these alternatives is expressed in the Agreement.

Pursuant to the first alternative method, Article 2.2 of the *Anti-Dumping Agreement* permits the determination of 'normal value' through consideration of the comparable price of the like product when exported to an 'appropriate' third country, provided that this price is representative. Note, however, that the Agreement does not define criteria for determining whether a third country is 'appropriate'.

Under the Second alternative method, Article 2.2 of the *Anti-Dumping Agreement* permits a Member to construct the normal value on the basis of:

> [t]he cost of production in the country of origin plus a reasonable amount for administrative, selling and general costs and for profits.

53 See Panel Report, *EEC – Cotton Yarn (1995)*, para. 479.
54 See Appellate Body Report, *EC – Fasteners (Article 21.5 – China) (2016)*, para. 5.207.

The amounts for administrative, selling and general costs and for profits shall be based on actual data pertaining to production and sales in the ordinary course of trade of the like product by the exporter or producer under investigation.[55]

In *EU – Biodiesel (2016)*, the Appellate Body while interpreting Article 2.2 of the *Anti-Dumping Agreement* and Article VI:1(b)(ii) of the GATT 1994 stated:

> An investigating authority will naturally look for information on the cost of production 'in the country of origin' from sources inside the country. At the same time, these provisions do not preclude the possibility that the authority may also need to look for such information from sources outside the country. The reference to 'in the country of origin', however, indicates that, whatever information or evidence is used to determine the 'cost of production', it must be apt to or capable of yielding a cost of production in the country of origin. This, in turn, suggests that information or evidence from outside the country of origin may need to be adapted in order to ensure that it is suitable to determine a 'cost of production' 'in the country of origin'.[56]

Further, the Appellate Body in *EU – Biodiesel (2016)* agreed with the panel that the surrogate price for soybeans used by the EU authorities to calculate the cost of production of biodiesel in Argentina did not represent the cost of soybeans in Argentina for producers or exporters of biodiesel.[57] The Appellate Body therefore found that the European Union acted inconsistently with Article 2.2 because the EU authorities did not use the cost of production in Argentina when constructing the normal value of biodiesel.[58]

3.2 'Export Price'

The export price is ordinarily based on the transaction price at which the producer in the exporting country sells the product to an importer in the importing country. However, the *Anti-Dumping Agreement* recognises that the transaction price may not be an appropriate export price. For example, there may be no export price where the transaction involves an internal transfer or barter. Additionally, an association or a compensatory arrangement between the exporter and the importer or a third party may affect the transaction price. Article 2.3 of the *Anti-Dumping Agreement* therefore provides for an alternative method to calculate, or 'construct', an appropriate export price. The 'constructed export price' is based on the price at which the product is first sold to an independent buyer. Where

55 See also Article 2.2.2 of the *Anti-Dumping Agreement*. If the amounts for administrative, selling and general costs and for profits cannot be determined in this way, they may be determined in one of the three ways discussed in Article 2.2.2(i)–(iii) of the *Anti-Dumping Agreement*. In *China – HP-SSST (EU) / China – HP-SSST (Japan) (2016)*, the Appellate Body found that China acted inconsistently with Article 2.2.2 by failing to determine selling, general and administrative (SG&A) costs for one of the EU companies investigated by MOFCOM, on the basis of actual data pertaining to production and sales in the ordinary course of trade of the like product. See Appellate Body Report, *China – HP-SSST (EU) / China – HP-SSST (Japan) (2016)*, para. 5.59. See Panel Report, *EC – Bed Linen (2001)*, paras. 6.59–6.562; and Appellate Body Report, *EC – Bed Linen (2001)*, paras. 74–83.

56 Appellate Body Report, *EU – Biodiesel (2016)*, para. 6.70.

57 *Ibid.*, paras. 6.81, 6.82.

58 *Ibid.*, para. 6.83.

it is not possible to construct the export price on this basis, the investigating authorities may determine a reasonable basis on which to calculate the export price.

3.3 Comparison of the 'Export Price' with the 'Normal Value'

To determine whether dumping, as defined above, exists, the export price is compared with the normal value. This section discusses in turn: (1) the 'fair comparison' requirement of Article 2.4 of the *Anti-Dumping Agreement*; and (2) the calculation of the dumping margin.

3.3.1 'Fair Comparison' Requirement

Article 2.4 of the *Anti-Dumping Agreement* provides in relevant part:

> A fair comparison shall be made between the export price and the normal value. This comparison shall be made at the same level of trade, normally at the ex-factory level, and in respect of sales made at as nearly as possible the same time.

In order to ensure a fair comparison between the export price and normal value, Article 2.4 of the *Anti-Dumping Agreement* requires that adjustments be made to the normal value, the export price, or both. Thus, Article 2.4 requires that:

> [d]ue allowance shall be made in each case, on its merits, for differences which affect price comparability, including differences in conditions and terms of sale, taxation, levels of trade, quantities, physical characteristics, and any other differences which are also demonstrated to affect price comparability.[59]

As the reference to 'any other differences' indicates, this provision does not exhaustively identify differences that may affect price comparability. What is identified in Article 2.4 is a difference 'in conditions and terms of sale', which refers to considerations such as, for example, transport costs or credit terms associated with particular transactions involving the product concerned. In *US – Stainless Steel (Korea) (2001)*, the question arose as to whether differences resulting from the unforeseen bankruptcy of a customer and consequent failure to pay for certain sales fell within 'differences in the conditions and terms of sale' for which due allowance is to be made. The panel in that case stated that:

> [t]he requirement to make due allowance for differences that affect price comparability is intended to neutralise differences in a transaction that an exporter could be expected to have reflected in his pricing.[60]

59 Footnote 7 to the *Anti-Dumping Agreement* notes that: 'It is understood that some of the above factors may overlap, and authorities shall ensure that they do not duplicate adjustments that have been already made under this provision.'

60 Panel Report, *US – Stainless Steel (Korea) (2001)*, para. 6.77. The panel therefore found that an unanticipated failure of a customer to pay for certain sales cannot be considered to be a 'difference in conditions and terms of sale', requiring adjustment to the export price, the normal value or both, to ensure price comparability.

In *US – Hot-Rolled Steel (2001)*, the United States used downstream sales prices to make a comparison without making any allowances. The Appellate Body ruled in this case that:

> Article 2.4 of the *Anti-Dumping Agreement* requires that appropriate 'allowances' be made to any downstream sales prices which are used to calculate normal value in order to ensure a 'fair comparison' between export price and normal value. If those proper 'allowances' were not, in fact, made in this case, the comparison made by [the US Department of Commerce] between export price and normal value was, by definition, not 'fair', and not consistent with Article 2.4 of the *Anti-Dumping Agreement*.[61]

The Appellate Body also recalled that Article 2.4 requires that allowances are made not only for the differences explicitly mentioned in that Article (i.e. differences in conditions and terms of sale, taxation, levels of trade, etc.) but for *any other differences* which are also demonstrated to affect price comparability.[62] The panel in *US – Softwood Lumber V (2004)*, agreeing with the panel in *EC – Tube or Pipe Fittings (2003)*, found that:

> [t]he requirement to make due allowance for such differences, in each case on its merits, means that the authority must *at least* evaluate identified differences – in this case, differences in dimension – with a view to determining whether or not an adjustment is required to ensure a fair comparison between normal value and export price under Article 2.4, and make an adjustment where it determines this to be necessary on the basis of its evaluation.[63]

In *US – Zeroing (EC) (2006)*, the Appellate Body stated that Article 2.4 also applies *a contrario*: it implies that allowances should not be made for differences that do not affect price comparability.[64]

In *EC Fasteners (Article 21.5 – China) (2016)*, the Appellate Body reiterated and emphasised that Article 2.4 requires investigating authorities to ensure a fair comparison between the export price and the normal value and, to this end, to make due allowance, or adjustments, for differences affecting price comparability. Whereas the obligation to ensure a fair comparison lies on the investigating authorities, 'exporters bear the burden of substantiating, "as constructively as possible", their requests for adjustments reflecting the "due allowance" within the meaning of Article 2.4'.[65] At the same time, the last sentence of Article 2.4 provides that the 'authorities shall indicate to the parties in question what information is necessary to ensure a fair comparison and shall

61 Appellate Body Report, *US – Hot-Rolled Steel (2001)*, para. 176.

62 *Ibid.*, para. 177.

63 Panel Report, *US – Softwood Lumber V (2004)*, para. 7.165. The panel considered that Article 2.4 does *not* require that an adjustment be made automatically in all cases where a difference is found to exist, but only where – based on the merits of the case – that difference is demonstrated to affect price comparability. *Ibid.* See also Panel Report, *EC – Tube or Pipe Fittings (2003)*, para. 7.157.

64 Appellate Body Report, *US – Zeroing (EC) (2006)*, para. 156.

65 Appellate Body Report, *EC – Fasteners (Article 21.5 – China) (2016)*, para. 5.204, referring to *EC – Fasteners (China) (2011)*, para. 488 and quoting Panel Report, *EC – Tube or Pipe Fittings (2003)*, para. 7.158.

not impose an unreasonable burden of proof on those parties'.[66] If the party requesting an adjustment fails to demonstrate to the investigating authorities that there is a difference affecting price comparability, there is no obligation to make an adjustment.[67] However, the authorities 'must take steps to achieve clarity as to the adjustment claimed and then determine whether and to what extent that adjustment is merited'.[68] In sum, the Appellate Body emphasised that the requirements of Article 2.4 of the *Anti-Dumping Agreement* apply in all investigations, irrespective of the methodology used to establish normal value.[69]

Special rules apply in a couple of circumstances. Where an Accession Protocol permits for recourse to prices of a surrogate country producer, adjustments are not required where such adjustments would reintroduce the price distortion that was the reason for recourse of the surrogate methodology in the first place.[70]

Where the export price is constructed, Article 2.4 of the *Anti-Dumping Agreement* contains special rules regarding adjustments. An allowance should be made for costs, including duties and taxes, incurred *between* the importation of the product and its resale to the first independent purchaser, as well as for profits.[71] Where the comparison of the 'normal value' with the export price requires conversion of currency, Article 2.4.1 of the *Anti-Dumping Agreement* provides specific rules governing that conversion.[72]

The question of making a *fair* comparison between the 'normal value' and the 'export price' is often one of the most contentious aspects of an anti-dumping investigation, as there will always be adjustments that arguably should be made. Frequently, the extent of the adjustments allowed will have an important impact on the outcome of the anti-dumping investigation.

In a considerable number of anti-dumping disputes, the question arose whether 'zeroing' is inconsistent with the fair comparison requirement in

66 Regarding the information to be provided pursuant to the procedural requirement in the last sentence of Article 2.4, see Appellate Body Reports, *EC – Fasteners (China) (2011)*, paras. 489–91; and *EC – Fasteners (Article 21.5 – China) (2016)*, paras. 5.164–5.167.

67 See Appellate Body Reports, *EC – Fasteners (Article 21.5 – China) (2016)*, paras. 5.163, 5.204, referring to *EC – Fasteners (China) (2011)*, para. 488 and Panel Report, *Korea – Certain Paper (2005)*, para. 7.147.

68 Appellate Body Reports, *EC – Fasteners (Article 21.5 – China) (2016)*, paras. 5.163, 5.204, referring to *EC – Fasteners (China) (2011)*, paras. 488 and 519 and quoting Panel Report, *EC – Tube or Pipe Fittings (2003)*, para. 7.158.

69 See Appellate Body Report, *EC – Fasteners (Article 21.5 – China) (2016)*, para. 5.205.

70 *Ibid.*, para. 5.207.

71 On the non-mandatory nature of these adjustments, see Panel Report, *US – Stainless Steel (Mexico) (2008)*, para. 6.93.

72 On the interpretation of this provision, see Panel Report, *US – Stainless Steel (Mexico) (2008)*, paras. 6.11–6.12. The panel in that case concluded that it was inconsistent with Article 2.4.1 of the *Anti-Dumping Agreement* to undertake currency conversions in instances where the prices being compared were in the same currency. On the currency conversion rules of Article 2.4.1 of the *Anti-Dumping Agreement*, see also Panel Report, *EC – Tube or Pipe Fittings (2003)*, paras. 7.198–7.199.

Article 2.4.[73] The Appellate Body found, first, that the 'fair comparison' language in the first sentence of Article 2.4 creates an independent obligation, and, second, that the scope of this obligation is not exhausted by the general subject matter expressly addressed by paragraph 4 (that is to say, price comparability). The Appellate Body concluded that it thus applies in original investigations (regardless of which comparison methodology is used), in periodic reviews and in sunset reviews as well.[74] The Appellate Body stated in *US – Softwood Lumber V (Article 21.5 – Canada) (2005)* that the subsequent paragraphs of that Article (e.g. Article 2.4.2 spelling out comparison methodologies for calculating margins of dumping are '[s]ubject to the provisions governing fair comparison') are expressly made subject to the requirements of Article 2.4.[75] It noted that the term 'fair' is generally understood to connote 'impartiality, even-handedness, or lack of bias', and that the use of zeroing was 'difficult to reconcile with the[se] notions'.[76] The Appellate Body found that:

> [t]he use of zeroing under the transaction-to-transaction comparison methodology artificially inflates the magnitude of dumping, resulting in higher margins of dumping and making a positive determination of dumping more likely. This way of calculating cannot be described as impartial, even-handed, or unbiased. For this reason, we do not consider that the calculation of 'margins of dumping', on the basis of a transaction-to-transaction comparison that uses zeroing, satisfies the 'fair comparison' requirement within the meaning of Article 2.4 of the *Anti-Dumping Agreement*.[77]

In *US – Washing Machines (2016)*, the question arose whether zeroing under the weighted-average normal value to individual export prices comparison methodology is foreseen in the second sentence of Article 2.4.2. According to the Appellate Body, given that it is the function of the second sentence of Article 2.4.2 to unmask and address 'targeted dumping' vis-à-vis specific purchasers, in specific regions or time periods, the 'fair comparison' requirement in Article 2.4

73 The concept of 'zeroing' relates to the determination of margins of dumping. When export prices and normal value are compared for purposes of calculating dumping margins (according to various methodologies such as weighted average to weighted average or transaction to transaction or weighted average normal value to individual export price transactions), the comparison results can be 'negative' or 'positive': i.e. when export prices are below normal value, the comparison result is 'positive'; when export price exceeds normal value, the comparison result is 'negative'. In calculating the dumping margin, some Members (including the European Communities and the United States) used to take into account only the positive comparison results (when export price was below normal value); however, it did not take into account negative comparison results (when export price exceeded normal value). Instead, it assigned these comparison results the value 'zero' (this practice was referred to as 'zeroing'); in other words, when the practice of zeroing is applied, positive comparison results are not 'offset' against negative comparison results between export price and normal value. For a further discussion of the concept of 'zeroing', see below, pp. 714–20.

74 Appellate Body Reports, *US – Zeroing (EC) (2006)*, para. 146; *US – Zeroing (Japan) (2006)*, para. 146; and *US – Washing Machines (2016)*, paras. 5.135–5.137, 5.177–5.179.

75 Appellate Body Report, *US – Softwood Lumber V (Article 21.5 – Canada) (2005)*, para. 132.

76 *Ibid.*, paras. 138–42, referring to the use of zeroing in the transaction-to-transaction comparison methodology. See also Appellate Body Reports, *US – Zeroing (Japan) (2007)*, para. 146; and *US – Washing Machines (2016)*, paras. 5.135–5.137, 5.177–5.179.

77 Appellate Body Report, *US – Softwood Lumber V (Article 21.5 – Canada) (2005)*, para. 142; Appellate Body Report, *US – Zeroing (Japan) (2007)*, para. 146.

applies only in relation to 'pattern transactions' that reflect targeted dumping.[78] The Appellate Body clarified in the same appeal that:

> the application of all three comparison methodologies (i.e. weighted-average normal value to weighted-average export price comparison methodology; the transaction to transaction comparison of export price and normal value; and the comparison methodology of weighted-average normal value with individual export prices) set out in the first and second sentences of Article 2.4.2 is expressly made subject to the 'fair comparison' requirement in Article 2.4.[79]

Further, the Appellate Body concluded that the use of zeroing when applying the W-T comparison methodology is inconsistent with Article 2.4 of the *Anti-Dumping Agreement.*[80]

The Appellate Body further ruled that the use of zeroing in periodic reviews (Article 9.3), new shipper reviews (Article 9.5) and the reliance in sunset reviews on 'zeroed' margins of dumping in likelihood-of-continuation or recurrence-of-dumping determinations are also inconsistent with the fair comparison requirement found in Article 2.4 of the *Anti-Dumping Agreement.*[81]

3.3.2 Calculation of the Margin of Dumping

The margin of dumping is the difference between the export price and the 'normal value'. This would appear simple enough. However, the methodology to be applied when calculating the difference between the export price and the 'normal value' may raise difficult and controversial issues.

As already noted above, the Appellate Body has clarified repeatedly that a number of provisions in the *Anti-Dumping Agreement* require a determination of dumping by reference to an exporter and to a 'product under consideration'.[82] This is because dumping arises from the pricing behaviour of individual exporters or foreign producers. The context found in various provisions of the *Anti-Dumping Agreement* confirms that dumping and margins of dumping are concepts that are exporter-specific and not importer-specific.[83] Margins are established accordingly for each exporter or foreign producer on the basis of a comparison between normal value and export prices, both of which relate to the pricing behaviour of that exporter or foreign producer. In order to assess properly the pricing behaviour of an individual exporter or foreign producer, and to determine whether the exporter or foreign producer is, in fact, dumping the

78 See Appellate Body Report, *US – Washing Machines (2016)*, paras. 5.177, 5.180–5.182.

79 *Ibid.*, para. 5.135.

80 See *ibid.*, para. 5.182.

81 See Appellate Body Report, *US – Zeroing (Japan) (2007)*, paras. 168–9; and Appellate Body Report, *US – Corrosion-Resistant Steel Sunset Review (2004)*, para. 127.

82 See Appellate Body Report, *US – Zeroing (Japan) (2007)*, para. 111; Appellate Body Report, *US – Stainless Steel (Mexico) (2008)*, para. 89; and Appellate Body Report, *US – Continued Zeroing (2009)*, para. 283.

83 See Appellate Body Report, *US – Stainless Steel (Mexico) (2008)*, para. 87. In this report, the Appellate Body relied upon the context found in Articles 2.1, 2.2, 2.3, 5.2(ii), 5.8, 6.1.1, 6.7, 6.10 and 9.5 of the *Anti-Dumping Agreement*. See Appellate Body Report, *US – Stainless Steel (Mexico) (2008)*, para. 89.

product under investigation and, if so, by which margin, it is necessary to take into account the prices of all the export transactions of that exporter or foreign producer.[84]

As provided in Article 2.4.2, first sentence, of the *Anti-Dumping Agreement*, the calculation of the dumping margin *normally* requires either the *comparison of the weighted average* 'normal value' to the weighted average of prices of all comparable export transactions (i.e. the W-W methodology); or a *transaction-to-transaction comparison* of 'normal value' and export price (i.e. the T-T methodology).[85] Article 2.4.2 requires investigating authorities using the weighted average-to-weighted average methodology to establish margins of dumping on the basis of the comparison of 'all comparable export transactions'. The Appellate Body considered that Article 2.4.2 requires a comparison of all models of the investigated producers that fall within the definition of like product.[86]

However, as provided in Article 2.4.2, second sentence, a normal value established on a weighted average basis may be compared to prices of individual export transactions (i.e. W-T methodology) if: (1) if the authorities find a pattern of export prices which differ significantly among different purchasers, regions or time periods ('targeted dumping'), and (2) if an explanation is provided as to why such differences cannot be taken into account appropriately by the use of a weighted average-to-weighted average or transaction-to-transaction comparison.[87]

Significant questions have arisen with regard to the calculation of margins of dumping under Article 2.4.2. Specifically, the practice of 'zeroing' has been challenged many times in anti-dumping disputes both in respect of 'model' and 'simple' zeroing. The practice of 'model' zeroing was explained by the Appellate Body in *EC – Bed Linen (2001)* as follows:

> [F]irst, the European Communities identified with respect to the product under investigation – cotton-type bed linen – a certain number of different 'models' or 'types' of that product. Next, the European Communities calculated, for each of these models, a *weighted average* normal value and a *weighted average* export price. Then, the European Communities compared the weighted average normal value with the weighted average export price for each model. For some models, normal value was *higher* than export price; by subtracting export price from normal value for these models, the European Communities established a '*positive* dumping margin' for each model. For other models, normal value was *lower*

84 According to the Appellate Body, other provisions of the *Anti-Dumping Agreement* also make it clear that 'dumping' and 'margins of dumping' relate to the exporter or foreign producer. See Appellate Body Report, *US – Zeroing (Japan) (2007)*, para. 112; Appellate Body Report, *US – Stainless Steel (Mexico) (2008)*, para. 89; and Appellate Body Report, *US – Continued Zeroing (2009)*, para. 283.

85 The first sentence of Article 2.4.2 provides that these two methodologies 'shall normally' be used by investigating authorities to establish margins of dumping.

86 However, non-matching models may be excluded from the dumping margin calculations when the W-W methodology is used. See Appellate Body Report, *EC – Fasteners (Article 21.5 – China) (2016)*, para. 5.282.

87 As the Appellate Body noted, the methodology in the second sentence of Article 2.4.2 is an exception. See Appellate Body Reports, *US – Softwood Lumber V (Article 21.5 – Canada) (2006)*, para. 97; and *US – Zeroing (Japan) (2007)*, para. 123.

than export price; by subtracting export price from normal value for these other models, the European Communities established a '*negative* dumping margin' for each model [...] Having made this calculation, the European Communities then added up the amounts it had calculated as 'dumping margins' for each model of the product in order to determine an *overall* dumping margin for the product *as a whole*. However, in doing so, the European Communities treated any 'negative dumping margin' as zero – hence the use of the word 'zeroing'. Then, finally, having added up the 'positive dumping margins' and the zeroes, the European Communities divided this sum by the cumulative total value of all the export transactions involving all types and models of that product. In this way, the European Communities obtained an overall margin of dumping for the product under investigation.[88]

The effect of zeroing, as the Appellate Body noted in *US – Corrosion-Resistant Steel Sunset Review (2004)*, is that, apart from artificially inflating the dumping margin for the product as a whole, it may turn a negative margin of dumping into a positive margin, introducing what the Appellate Body referred to as an 'inherent bias'.[89] The Appellate Body stated in *EC – Bed Linen (2001)*:

[w]hatever the method used to calculate the margins of dumping, in our view, these margins must be, and can only be, established for the *product* under investigation as a whole.[90]

Therefore, the practice where an investigating authority does not offset the difference between the export price and the normal value in cases where the export price is *above* the normal value, and treats the difference as 'zero', is incompatible with Article 2.4.2 of the *Anti-Dumping Agreement*. The *EC – Bed Linen (2001)* dispute focused on the first method for calculating the dumping margin set out in Article 2.4.2, first sentence, namely, the weighted-average-to-weighted-average comparison of normal value and export price, and thus related to so-called 'model zeroing'. The United States adopted a similar practice of margin determination, which was at issue in *US – Softwood Lumber V (2004)*. Again, the Appellate Body held that:

[i]f an investigating authority has chosen to undertake multiple comparisons, the investigating authority necessarily has to take into account the results of *all* those comparisons in order to establish margins of dumping for the product as a whole under Article 2.4.2.[91]

88 Appellate Body Report, *EC – Bed Linen (2001)*, para. 47.

89 See Appellate Body Report, *US – Corrosion-Resistant Steel Sunset Review (2004)*, para. 135. See also *ibid.*, paras. 127–8 and 130.

90 Appellate Body Report, *EC – Bed Linen (2001)*, para. 53.

91 Appellate Body Report, *US – Softwood Lumber V (2004)*, para. 98. The Appellate Body explained that zeroing 'means, *in effect*, that at least in the case of *some* export transactions, the export prices are treated as if they were less than what they actually are. Zeroing, therefore, does not take into account the *entirety* of the *prices* of *some* export transactions, namely, the prices of export transactions in those subgroups in which the weighted average normal value is less than the weighted average export price. Zeroing thus inflates the margin of dumping for the product as a whole.' See *ibid.*, para. 101. In *US – Softwood Lumber V (Article 21.5 – Canada) (2005)*, the Appellate Body again found nothing in the *Anti-Dumping Agreement* that would prohibit an investigating authority from dividing the product under investigation into product types or models of 'comparable' transactions. However, this did not permit zeroing in aggregating results of comparisons at the subgroup level by disregarding those where weighted average normal values are below weighted average export prices. See Appellate Body Report, *US – Softwood Lumber V (Article 21.5 – Canada) (2005)*, paras. 87–94.

The Appellate Body affirmed these rulings in *US – Zeroing (EC) (2006)*, *US – Zeroing (Japan) (2007)* and in *US – Stainless Steel (Mexico) (2008)* and emphasised that:

> there is no justification for 'taking into account the "results" of only some multiple comparisons in the process of calculating margins of dumping, while disregarding other "results"'.[92]

In addition, as noted in *US – Softwood Lumber V (Article 21.5 – Canada) (2005)*, an inflated margin of dumping, that violates Article 2.4.2, cannot qualify as being the result of a 'fair' comparison under Article 2.4.[93]

In *US – Softwood Lumber V (Article 21.5 – Canada) (2006)*, the Appellate Body ruled on the legality of 'simple' zeroing when the second methodology for calculating the dumping margin is used, as set out in Article 2.4.2, first sentence, that is, the transaction-to-transaction methodology. The Appellate Body found that 'simple' zeroing under the transaction-to-transaction methodology was also impermissible under Article 2.4.2 and Article 2.4 of the *Anti-Dumping Agreement*. This finding was reiterated in *US – Zeroing (Japan) (2007)*.[94]

Whereas the first sentence of Article 2.4.2 provides that investigating authorities 'shall normally' use the W-W or the T-T comparison methodology, the second sentence of Article 2.4.2 stipulates that a weighted average normal value 'may be compared' to prices of individual export transactions (W-T methodology), provided two conditions are met. Under the second sentence, a normal value established on a weighted average basis may be compared to prices of individual export transactions (1) if the authorities find a pattern of export prices which differ significantly among different purchasers, regions or time periods ('targeted dumping'); and (2) if an explanation is provided as to why such differences cannot be taken into account appropriately by the use of a weighted average-to-weighted average or transaction-to-transaction comparison.[95] The second sentence of Article

92 Appellate Body Report, *US – Zeroing (EC) (2006)*, para. 126, citing Appellate Body Report, *US – Softwood Lumber V (2004)*, para. 98. See also Appellate Body Report, *US – Zeroing (Japan) (2007)*, paras. 125–8. See also Panel Report, *US – Shrimp (Ecuador) (2007)*, para. 7.40.

93 Article 2.4.2 begins with the phrase '[s]ubject to the provisions governing fair comparison in paragraph 4'. Thus, the application of the comparison methodologies set out in Article 2.4.2 of the *Anti-Dumping Agreement*, including the transaction-to-transaction methodology is expressly made subject to the 'fair comparison' requirement set out in Article 2.4. Appellate Body Report, *US – Softwood Lumber V (Article 21.5 – Canada) (2006)*, para. 132. See also Appellate Body Report, *US – Zeroing (EC) (2006)*, para. 146, for a similar argument on the pervasiveness of the 'fair comparison' requirement in Article 2.4 and its role in the interpretation of Article 2.4.2.

94 Appellate Body Reports, *US – Softwood Lumber V (Article 21.5 – Canada) (2006)*, paras. 89 and 93; *US – Zeroing (Japan) (2007)*, paras. 129 and 138. In the latter report, the Appellate Body found that the zeroing prohibition also applies to subsequent stages of anti-dumping proceedings, such as periodic reviews and new shipper reviews under Articles 9.3 and 9.5.

95 See Appellate Body Reports, *US – Softwood Lumber V (Article 21.5 – Canada) (2006)*, para. 97; and *US – Zeroing (Japan) (2007)*, para. 123. The explanation requirement in the second sentence contemplates that there may be circumstances in which an investigating authority identifies a 'pattern of export prices which differ significantly among different purchasers, regions or time periods', but where 'such differences' could be taken into account appropriately by the W-W or T-T comparison methodology.

2.4.2 thus provides for an exceptional methodology for calculating the dumping margin.[96] The function of this method is to enable investigating authorities to 'unmask' and address 'targeted dumping'.[97]

While the Appellate Body had sought contextual guidance in the second sentence of Article 2.4.2 in *US – Softwood Lumber V (Article 21.5 – Canada) (2006)* and *US – Zeroing (Japan) (2007)*, the second sentence was squarely before the Appellate Body in *US – Washing Machines (2016)*. Regarding the first condition, the Appellate Body found that the relevant 'pattern' comprises prices that are significantly *lower* than other export prices.[98] It further clarified that some transactions that differ among purchasers, taken together with some transactions that differ among regions, and some transactions that differ among time periods, cannot form a single pattern. As such, a 'pattern' comprises *all* the export prices to one or more particular purchasers (or regions or time periods) which differ significantly from the export prices to the other purchasers (or regions or time periods) because they are significantly *lower* than those other prices.[99] The Appellate Body thus upheld the panel's findings regarding the relevant 'pattern'.[100]

Regarding the second condition in Article 2.4.2, second sentence, i.e. the requisite explanation, the Appellate Body reversed the panel. It found that an investigating authority has to explain why *both* of the W-W and the T-T comparison methodologies normally used to calculate the dumping margin under the first sentence, cannot take into account appropriately the identified differences in export prices before having recourse to the W-T methodology under the second sentence.[101]

The Appellate Body found that the second sentence of Article 2.4.2 allows an investigating authority to establish margins of dumping by applying the W-T

96 See Appellate Body Reports, *US – Washing Machines (2016)*, para. 5.18; *US – Zeroing (Japan) (2007)*, para. 131; *US – Softwood Lumber V (Article 21.5 – Canada) (2006)*, paras. 86 and 97. Investigating authorities may have recourse to the exceptional W-T methodology to establish margins of dumping under the second sentence of Article 2.4.2 (instead of the normally applicable W-W or T-T comparison methodologies set forth in the first sentence) provided that a number of conditions are met.

97 See Appellate Body Reports, *US – Washing Machines (2016)*, para. 5.17, see also, paras. 5.107–5.111; *US – Softwood Lumber V (Article 21.5 – Canada) (2006)*, para. 97; and *US – Zeroing (Japan) (2007)*, paras. 123, 135; *US – Stainless Steel (Mexico) (2008)*, paras. 122 and 127.

98 See Appellate Body Report, *US – Washing Machines (2016)*, paras. 5.29, 5.36.

99 See *ibid.*, paras. 5.33–5.36.

100 See *ibid.*, para. 5.37.

101 Therefore, the Appellate Body reversed the panel's findings that the United States did not act inconsistently with Article 2.4.2 by providing an explanation only in respect of the W-W comparison methodology. See *ibid.*, paras. 5.76–5.77. In addition, the Appellate Body found that the requirement to identify prices which differ *significantly* means that the investigating authority is required to assess in a quantitative and qualitative manner the price differences at issue. This may require the authority to consider certain objective market factors, such as circumstances regarding the nature of the product under consideration, the relevant industry, the market structure, or the intensity of competition in the markets at issue, depending on the case at hand. The Appellate Body agreed with the panel that an investigating authority is not required to consider the cause of (or reasons for) the price differences. However, the Appellate Body reversed the panel's findings to the extent that it found that a pattern of export prices which differ significantly can be established 'on the basis of purely quantitative criteria' (i.e. absent any qualitative analysis). See *ibid.*, para. 5.66.

comparison methodology only to transactions that constitute the 'pattern' of 'targeted prices' to the exclusion of 'non-pattern transactions' and by dividing the resulting amount by *all* the export sales of a given exporter or foreign producer.[102] The Appellate Body considered that the second sentence *neither* permits the combining of comparison methodologies (i.e. W-T and W-W or W-T and T-T) *nor* allows 'systemic disregarding', whereby an investigating authority conducts separate comparisons for transactions within the 'pattern', under the W-T comparison methodology, and for transactions outside the 'pattern', under the W-W or T-T comparison methodology, and disregards the latter when they yield an overall negative comparison result.[103]

Moreover, the Appellate Body upheld the Panel's findings that zeroing under the W-T comparison methodology is inconsistent with Article 2.4.2 and the 'fair comparison' requirement in Article 2.4.[104] The Appellate Body concluded that zeroing negative intermediate comparison results within the 'pattern' is not necessary to address 'targeted dumping' and that zeroing is inconsistent with the establishment of dumping and margins of dumping pertaining to the 'universe of export transactions' identified under the second sentence.[105]

The question of whether zeroing is permissible in periodic reviews arose in *US – Zeroing (EC) (2006), US – Zeroing (Japan) (2007), US – Stainless Steel (Mexico) (2008), US – Continued Zeroing (2009), and US – Washing Machines (2016).*[106] The Appellate Body determined that zeroing in periodic reviews is inconsistent with Article 9.3.[107] The Appellate Body concluded in *US – Continued Zeroing (2009)* as regards zeroing in periodic reviews:

We fail to see a textual or contextual basis in the GATT 1994 or the *Anti-Dumping Agreement* for treating transactions that occur above normal value as 'dumped', for purposes of determining the existence and magnitude of dumping in the original investigation, and as 'non-dumped', for purposes of assessing the final liability for payment of anti-dumping duties in a periodic review. If, as a consequence of zeroing, the results of certain comparisons are disregarded only for purposes of assessing final liability for payment of anti-dumping duties in a periodic review, a mismatch is created between the product considered 'dumped' in the original investigation and the product for which anti-dumping duties are collected. This is

102 *Ibid.*, paras. 5.55, 5.98, 5.111, 5.117.

103 *Ibid.*, paras. 5.55, 5.117, 5.124, 5.129–5.130.

104 *Ibid.*, paras. 5.152ff. The Appellate Body found that the exceptional W-T comparison methodology requires a comparison between a weighted average normal value and the entire 'universe of export transactions' that fall within the 'pattern' as properly identified under that provision, irrespective of whether the export price of individual 'pattern transactions' is above or below normal value. Appellate Body Report, *US – Washing Machines (2016)*, para. 5.160.

105 However, one Member of the Division expressed a separate opinion on the issue of zeroing.

106 On the concept of 'periodic review', also referred to as 'administrative review', see below, pp. 754–8.

107 Appellate Body Reports, *US – Zeroing (EC) (2006)*, para. 164; *US – Zeroing (Japan) (2007)*, para. 156. The Appellate Body reversed the findings of the panels in *US – Zeroing (EC) (2006)* and *US – Zeroing (Japan) (2007)* which had found that 'simple' zeroing was not in contravention of Article 2.4.2 and therefore also not inconsistent with Article 9.3. See also Appellate Body Report, *US – Stainless Steel (Mexico) (2008)*, para. 133.

not consonant with the need for consistent treatment of a product at the various stages of anti-dumping duty proceedings.[108]

In respect of sunset reviews, the Appellate Body noted in *US – Corrosion-Resistant Steel Sunset Review (2004)*:

> [W]e see no obligation under Article 11.3 for investigating authorities to calculate or rely on dumping margins in determining the likelihood of continuation or recurrence of dumping. However, should investigating authorities choose to rely upon dumping margins in making their likelihood determination, the calculation of these margins must conform to the disciplines of Article 2.4 ... If these margins were legally flawed because they were calculated in a manner inconsistent with Article 2.4, this could give rise to an inconsistency not only with Article 2.4, but also with Article 11.3 of the *Anti-Dumping Agreement*.[109]

In sum, the Appellate Body has ruled against zeroing in the context of original investigations (when the average-to-average, transaction-to-transaction, or average-to-transaction comparison methodologies within the meaning of Article 2.4.2 were used), periodic reviews (Article 9.3), new shipper reviews (Article 9.5) and sunset reviews (Article 11.3).

Thus, regardless of the methodology chosen for the calculation the dumping margin, the *entirety of the prices* and all comparison results for all comparable transactions involving the product that is the subject of the investigation must be included in the calculation of the dumping margin. The practice of zeroing has been rejected by the Appellate Body whenever it ruled on it.

4 DETERMINATION OF INJURY TO THE DOMESTIC INDUSTRY

As noted above, only dumping that causes, or threatens to cause, injury to the domestic industry is condemned and potentially subject to anti-dumping measures under Article VI of the GATT 1994 and the *Anti-Dumping Agreement*. Therefore, after having determined the existence of dumping, the competent authorities must establish: (1) the existence, or threat, of injury to the domestic industry; and (2) the causal link between dumping and injury. This section addresses the determination of injury to the domestic industry. It deals first with the concept of 'domestic industry', and then with the determination of injury.

108 See Appellate Body Report, *US – Continued Zeroing (2009)*, para. 285. Appellate Body Report, *US – Stainless Steel (Mexico) (2008)*, para. 106. In *US – Washing Machines (2016)*, Appellate Body found that, if margins of dumping are established inconsistently with the second sentence of Article 2.4.2 by using zeroing under the W-T comparison methodology, the corresponding antidumping duties that are levied will also be inconsistent with Article 9.3, as they will exceed the margin of dumping that should have been established under Article 2. See Appellate Body Report, *US – Washing Machines (2016)*, paras. 5.188–5.190.

109 Appellate Body Report, *US – Corrosion-Resistant Steel Sunset Review (2004)*, para. 127.

4.1 'Domestic Industry'

The concept of 'domestic industry' flows from the definition of the 'like product'. It establishes who may file a petition requesting the initiation of an anti-dumping investigation.[110] It also delineates the scope of the data to be taken into account in the injury determination, in that the domestic industry with respect to which injury is considered and determined must be the 'domestic industry' defined in accordance with Article 4.1 of the *Anti-Dumping Agreement*.[111] Article 4.1 provides that the term 'domestic industry' must be defined as referring to the 'domestic producers *as a whole* of the like product' or 'those of them whose collective output of the products constitutes *a major proportion* of the total domestic production', except in two specific circumstances.[112] Article 4.1 thus juxtaposes two methods for defining the term 'domestic industry'.[113] The Appellate Body noted in *EC – Fasteners (China) (2011)* that:

> [by] using the term 'a major proportion', the second method focuses on the question of *how much* production must be represented by those producers making up the domestic industry when the domestic industry is defined as less than the domestic producers as a whole. In answering this question, Article 4.1 does not stipulate a specific proportion for evaluating whether a certain percentage constitutes 'a major proportion'.[114]

With regard to the term 'a major proportion', the Appellate Body noted in *EC – Fasteners (China) (2011)* that it:

> [s]hould be properly understood as a relatively high proportion of the total domestic production ... Indeed, the lower the proportion, the more sensitive an investigating authority will have to be to ensure that the proportion used substantially reflects the total production of the producers as a whole.[115]

Thus, 'a major proportion of the total domestic production' should be determined so as to ensure that the domestic industry defined on this basis is capable of providing ample data that ensure an accurate injury analysis.[116] The Appellate Body recalled that Article 3.1:

> [r]equires that the domestic industry, and the effects of dumped imports, be investigated in an unbiased manner, without favouring the interests of any interested party, or group of interested parties, in the investigation ... In other words, to ensure the accuracy of an injury determination, an investigating authority must not act so as to give rise to a material risk

110 See below, pp. 712–23.

111 Appellate Body Report, *EC – Fasteners (Article 21.5 – China) (2016)*, para. 5.300.

112 Under Article 4.1(i), domestic producers that are related to the exporters or importers or are themselves importers of the allegedly dumped product may be excluded. Article 4.1(ii) further provides that the domestic industry may be limited to include only those producers within a particular geographic region, if certain criteria are met.

113 See Appellate Body Report, *EC – Fasteners (China) (2011)*, para. 411.

114 *Ibid.* The 25 per cent benchmark mentioned in Article 5.4 of the *Anti-Dumping Agreement* is not relevant for the determination of the domestic industry because Article 5.4 refers only to the initiation of an investigation.

115 Appellate Body Report, *EC – Fasteners (China) (2011)*, para. 412. 116 See *ibid.*, para. 413.

of distortion in defining the domestic industry, for example, by excluding a whole category of producers of the like product. The risk of introducing distortion will not arise when no producers are excluded and the domestic industry is defined as 'the domestic producers as a whole'. Where a domestic industry is defined as those producers whose collective output constitutes a major proportion of the total domestic production, it follows that the higher the proportion, the more producers will be included, and the less likely the injury determination conducted on this basis would be distorted.[117]

In *EC – Fasteners (Article 21.5 – China) (2016)*, the Appellate Body recalled that in the special case of a fragmented industry with numerous producers, such as the fasteners industry, what constitutes 'a major proportion' may be lower than what is ordinarily permissible. However, it emphasised that in such cases, the investigating authority will have to make a greater effort to ensure that the selected domestic producers are representative of the total domestic production by ascertaining that the process of the domestic industry definition, and ultimately the injury determination, does not give rise to a material risk of distortion.[118] The Appellate Body found that by relying on the original Notice of Initiation, which stated that only those producers willing to be included in the injury sample will be considered as cooperating and thus part of the domestic industry, the Commission introduced a material risk of distortion in the industry definition and in the injury determination. It therefore concluded that the European Union acted inconsistently with Article 4.1 of the *Anti-Dumping Agreement*.[119]

Further, the Appellate Body noted in *EC – Fasteners (Article 21.5 – China) (2016)* that a domestic industry definition based on such a self-selection process also has an impact on the injury determination under Article 3.1 because it 'introduces a material risk of distortion to the investigating authority's injury analysis would necessarily render the resulting injury determination inconsistent with the obligation to make an objective injury analysis based on positive evidence as laid down in Article 3.1 of the Anti-Dumping Agreement'.[120]

Finally, the domestic industry may presumably consist of one *or* multiple producers.[121] Article 4.1 of the *Anti-Dumping Agreement* recognises that it may not be appropriate to include *all* producers of the like product in the domestic industry when producers are 'related' to the exporters or importers or are themselves importers of the allegedly dumped product.[122] Related producers may not

117 *Ibid.*, para. 414. The Appellate Body explained that, in 'the special case of a fragmented industry with numerous producers, the practical constraints on an authority's ability to obtain information may mean that what constitutes "a major proportion" may be lower than what is ordinarily permissible in a less fragmented industry'. The Appellate Body, however, added as a cautionary note that 'a domestic industry defined on the basis of a proportion that is low, or defined through a process that involves active exclusion of certain domestic producers, is likely to be more susceptible to a finding of inconsistency under Article 4.1 of the *Anti-Dumping Agreement*'. See Appellate Body Report, *EC – Fasteners (China) (2011)*, para. 419. See also Appellate Body Report, *EC – Fasteners (Article 21.5 – China) (2016)*, para. 5.304.

118 Appellate Body Report, *EC – Fasteners (Article 21.5 – China) (2016)*, para. 5.319.

119 *Ibid.*, para. 5.325. 120 *Ibid.*, para. 5.325.

121 See Panel Report, *EC – Bed Linen (2001)*, para. 6.72.

122 See Article 4.1(i) of the *Anti-Dumping Agreement*.

entirely share the interests of purely domestic producers. A producer is deemed to be 'related' to exporters or importers only if: (1) one of them directly or indirectly controls the other; or both of them are directly or indirectly controlled by a third person; or together they directly or indirectly control a third person; and (2) there are grounds for believing or suspecting that the effect of the relationship is such as to cause the producer concerned to behave differently from non-related producers.[123]

The panel in *EC – Salmon (Norway) (2008)* made it clear that the text of Article 4.1 of the *Anti-Dumping Agreement* does not support the notion that there is any other circumstance in which the domestic industry can be interpreted, from the outset, as not including certain categories of producers of the like product, other than those set out in Article 4.1(i).[124] Note that, in limited circumstances, a *regional industry*, instead of the total domestic industry, may be defined as the basis for the injury analysis.[125]

4.2 'Injury'

An affirmative determination of injury to the domestic industry is a fundamental precondition for the imposition of anti-dumping measures, along with a determination of the causal link between the dumped imports and injury. The *Anti-Dumping Agreement* defines 'injury' to mean one of three things: (1) material injury to a domestic industry; (2) threat of material injury to a domestic industry; or (3) material retardation of the establishment of a domestic industry.[126] The following subsections will discuss in turn what 'material injury', 'threat of material injury' and 'material retardation' mean and how a domestic investigating authority establishes their existence.

However, before engaging in this discussion, it is appropriate to make a general observation on the architecture of Article 3 of the *Anti-Dumping Agreement*, entitled 'Determination of Injury'. As the title suggests, this Article deals with the determination of injury (or threat thereof), but it also deals with the requirement to demonstrate a causal link between the dumping and the injury, a requirement discussed in the next section of this chapter.[127]

As the Appellate Body noted in *Thailand – H-Beams (2001); China – GOES (2012)*; and most recently reiterated in *China – HP-SSST (EU)/China – HP-SSST*

123 See fn. 11 to the *Anti-Dumping Agreement*. Note that one is deemed to control another 'when the former is legally or operationally in a position to exercise restraint or direction over the latter'.

124 See Panel Report, *EC – Salmon (Norway) (2008)*, para. 7.112.

125 See Article 4.1(ii) of the *Anti-Dumping Agreement*. On the application of anti-dumping measures in that case, see Article 4.2 of the *Anti-Dumping Agreement*.

126 See fn. 9 to Article 3 of the *Anti-Dumping Agreement*. Note that the *Anti-Dumping Agreement*, like the *SCM Agreement*, requires *material* injury or threat thereof, rather than *serious* injury as required under the *Agreement on Safeguards*. See above, pp. 639–43. The Appellate Body in *US – Lamb (2001)* noted that the standard of 'serious injury' is higher than that of 'material injury'. See Appellate Body Report, *US – Lamb (2001)*, para. 124.

127 See below, pp. 733–7.

(Japan) (2015) and *EU – Biodiesel (2016)*, the first paragraph of Article 3 is an 'overarching provision' on the determination of injury and causation, while the subsequent paragraphs of Article 3 stipulate, in detail, an investigating authority's obligations in determining the injury to the domestic industry caused by dumping.[128] The Appellate Body stated in *China – GOES (2012)* that the paragraphs of Article 3, together, provide 'an investigating authority with the relevant framework and disciplines for conducting an injury and causation analysis'.[129] According to the Appellate Body, these provisions contemplate 'a logical progression of inquiry leading to an investigating authority's ultimate injury and causation determination'.[130]

4.2.1 Material Injury

Article 3.1 of the *Anti-Dumping Agreement* requires that a determination of injury to the domestic industry:

> [b]e based on positive evidence and involve an objective examination of both (*a*) the volume of dumped imports and the effect of the dumped imports on prices in the domestic market for like products, and (*b*) the consequent impact of these imports on domestic producers of such products.

As noted above, the Appellate Body referred to Article 3.1 as an 'overarching provision' that sets forth a Member's fundamental, substantive obligations with respect to the determination of injury.[131] Article 3.1 informs the more detailed obligations in succeeding paragraphs. These obligations concern: (1) the determination of the volume of dumped imports, and their effect on prices (Article 3.2); (2) investigations of imports from more than one country (Article 3.3); (3) the impact of dumped imports on the domestic industry (Article 3.4); (4) the causal link between dumped imports and injury (Article 3.5); (5) the assessment of the domestic production of the like product (Article 3.6); and (6) the determination of the threat of material injury (Articles 3.7 and 3.8). As the Appellate Body emphasised in *Thailand – H-Beams (2001)*, the focus of Article 3 is thus on *substantive* obligations that a Member must fulfil in making an injury determination.[132]

128 See Appellate Body Report, *Thailand – H-Beams (2001)*, para. 106; Appellate Body Report, *China – GOES (2012)*, para. 128; Appellate Body Report, *China – HP-SSST (EU)/China – HP-SSST (Japan) (2015)*, para. 5.137; and Appellate Body Report, *EU – Biodiesel (2016)*, para. 6.124.

129 Appellate Body Report, *China – GOES (2012)*, paras. 126–8.

130 See *Ibid*. See also Appellate Body Report, *China – HP-SSST (EU)/China – HP-SSST (Japan) (2015)*, para. 5.140. This inquiry entails a consideration of the volume of dumped imports and their price effects, and requires an examination of the impact of such imports on the domestic industry as revealed by a number of economic factors. These various elements are then linked through a causation analysis between dumped imports and the injury to the domestic industry, taking into account all factors that are being considered and evaluated.

131 Appellate Body Report, *Thailand – H-Beams (2001)*, para. 106; Appellate Body Report, *China – GOES (2012)*, para. 126; Appellate Body Report, *China – HP-SSST (EU)/China – HP-SSST (Japan) (2015)*, para. 5.137; and Appellate Body Report *EU – Biodiesel (2016)*, para. 6.124.

132 See Appellate Body Report, *Thailand – H-Beams (2001)*, para. 106.

In *US – Hot-Rolled Steel (2001)*, the Appellate Body held that the thrust of the investigating authorities' obligation under Article 3.1, lies in the requirement that they: (1) base their determination on 'positive evidence'; and (2) conduct an 'objective examination'. According to the Appellate Body, the concept of 'positive evidence' relates to the quality of the evidence that authorities may rely on in making a determination. It focuses on the facts underpinning and justifying the injury determination. The word 'positive' means that the evidence must be of an affirmative, objective and verifiable character, and that it must be credible.[133] The concept of 'objective examination' aims at a different aspect of the investigating authorities' determination. It is concerned with the investigation process itself. The word 'objective', which qualifies the word 'examination', indicates essentially that the 'examination' process must conform to the dictates of the basic principles of good faith and fundamental fairness.[134] In short, an 'objective examination' requires that the domestic industry, and the effects of dumped imports, be investigated in an unbiased manner, without favouring the interests of any interested party, or group of interested parties, in the investigation.[135] If an examination is to be 'objective', the identification, investigation and evaluation of the relevant factors must be *even-handed*. Thus, investigating authorities are not entitled to conduct their investigation in such a way that it becomes more likely that, because of the fact-finding or evaluation process, they will determine that the domestic industry is injured.[136] In *Mexico – Anti-Dumping Measures on Rice (2005)*, the Appellate Body stated that:

> [b]ecause the conditions to impose an anti-dumping duty are to be assessed with respect to the current situation, the determination of whether injury exists should be based on data that provide indications of the situation prevailing when the investigation takes place.[137]

The panel in *Mexico – Steel Pipes and Tubes (2007)* stated that the data considered by the investigating authority should include, to the extent practicable, the most recent information possible, 'taking into account the inevitable delay caused by the need for an investigation, as well as any practical problems of data collection in a particular case'.[138] As the Appellate Body stated in *Mexico – Anti-Dumping Measures on Rice (2005)*:

> Articles 3.1 and 3.2 do not prescribe a methodology that must be followed by an investigating authority in conducting an injury analysis. Consequently, an investigating authority enjoys a certain discretion in adopting a methodology to guide its injury analysis. Within the

133 See Appellate Body Report, *US – Hot-Rolled Steel (2001)*, para. 192; and Appellate Body Reports, *China – HP-SSST (EU)/China – HP-SSST (Japan) (2015)*, para. 5.138.

134 See *ibid.*, para. 193.

135 See *ibid.* See Appellate Body Reports, *China – HP-SSST (EU)/China – HP-SSST (Japan) (2015)*, para. 5.138.

136 See *ibid.*, para. 196. Note that the Appellate Body in *US – Hot-Rolled Steel (2001)* ruled that an examination of only certain parts of a domestic industry does not ensure a proper evaluation of the state of the domestic industry as a whole, and does not, therefore, satisfy the requirements of 'objectiv[ity]' in Article 3.1 of the *Anti-Dumping Agreement*. See Appellate Body Report, *US – Hot-Rolled Steel (2001)*, para. 206.

137 Appellate Body Report, *Mexico – Anti-Dumping Measures on Rice (2005)*, para. 165.

138 Panel Report, *Mexico – Steel Pipes and Tubes (2007)*, para. 7.228.

bounds of this discretion, it may be expected that an investigating authority might have to rely on reasonable assumptions or draw inferences. ... An investigating authority that uses a methodology premised on unsubstantiated assumptions does not conduct an examination based on positive evidence. An assumption is not properly substantiated when the investigating authority does not explain why it would be appropriate to use it in the analysis.[139]

As noted above, Article 3.1 requires that a determination of injury to the domestic market must involve an examination of both: (1) the volume of dumped imports and the effect of the dumped imports on prices in the domestic market for like products (first requirement); and (2) the consequent impact of these imports on domestic producers of such products (second requirement). With regard to the first requirement, the Appellate Body in *EC – Bed Linen (Article 21.5 – India) (2003)* emphasised that imports from those *exporters* who were not found to be dumping may *not* be included in the volume of dumped imports from a country:

It is clear from the text of Article 3.2 that investigating authorities must consider whether there has been a significant increase in *dumped* imports, and that they must examine the effect of *dumped* imports on prices resulting from price undercutting, price depression, or price suppression.[140]

Having considered also Article 3.5 of the *Anti-Dumping Agreement*, the Appellate Body concluded:

None of these provisions of the *Anti-Dumping Agreement* can be construed to suggest that Members may include in the volume of *dumped* imports the imports from producers that are *not* found to be dumping.[141]

With regard to the first requirement, that is, an examination of the volume of dumped imports and the effect of the dumped imports on prices in the domestic market for like products, note also that the injury inquiry focuses on developments in the domestic market of the importing Member. Article 3.2, first sentence, requires the investigating authorities:

[t]o *consider* whether there has been a *significant increase* in the dumped imports, either in absolute terms or relative to production or consumption, in the domestic market.[142]

Article 3.2, second sentence, requires the investigating authorities:

[t]o *consider* whether there has been *significant price undercutting* by the dumped imports as compared with the price of a like product of the importing Member, or whether the effect is otherwise to *depress prices to a significant degree* or *prevent price increases*, which would otherwise have occurred, to a significant degree.[143]

In *China – GOES (2012)*, China argued that Article 3.2 merely requires an investigating authority to *consider* whether the domestic prices are depressed

139 Appellate Body Report, *Mexico – Anti-Dumping Measures on Rice (2005)*, paras. 204–5.
140 Appellate Body Report, *EC – Bed Linen (Article 21.5 – India) (2003)*, para. 111.
141 *Ibid.*, para. 112. 142 *Ibid.* Emphasis added.
143 *Ibid.* Emphasis added. See also Panel Report, *EC – Tube or Pipe Fittings (2003)*, paras. 7.276 and 7.279.

or suppressed. Article 3.2 did not call for a consideration of the relationship between dumped imports and domestic prices. According to China, interpreting Article 3.2 as requiring a consideration of the relationship between dumped imports and domestic prices would result in *duplicating* the causation analysis under Article 3.5.[144]

The Appellate Body noted in *China – GOES (2012)* that the use of the word 'consider' in Article 3.2 obliges a decision-maker to 'take something into account' in reaching a decision. According to the Appellate Body, the word 'consider' does:

> [n]ot impose an obligation on an investigating authority to make *a definitive determination* on the volume of subject imports and the effect of such imports on domestic prices. Nonetheless, an authority's *consideration* of the volume of subject imports and their price effects ... is also subject to the overarching principles ... that it be based on positive evidence and involve an objective examination.[145]

With regard to the inquiry set out in Article 3.2, second sentence, the Appellate Body ruled in *China – GOES (2012)* that this provision postulates an inquiry as to the 'effect' of dumped imports on domestic prices, and each inquiry links the dumped imports with the prices of the like domestic products.[146] The Appellate Body noted that, with respect to significant price undercutting, Article 3.2, second sentence, expressly establishes 'a link between the price of [dumped] imports and that of like domestic products, by requiring that a comparison be made between the two'.[147]

In *China – HP-SSST (EU)/China – HP-SSST (Japan) (2015)*, the Appellate Body did not read Article 3.2 as suggesting that the 'effect' of price undercutting must either be price depression or price suppression, and agreed with the Panel that, while price undercutting by imports *may* lead to price depression or price suppression, there is *no requirement* in Article 3.2 to demonstrate the existence of these other phenomena when considering the existence of price undercutting.[148]

In addition, the Appellate Body found in *China – HP-SSST (EU)/China – HP-SSST (Japan) (2015)* that Article 3.2 requires a *dynamic assessment* of price developments and *trends* in the relationship between the prices of the dumped imports and those of domestic like products over the entire period of investigation, and that the investigating authority may not disregard evidence suggesting that the prices of dumped imports have no, or only a limited effect on domestic prices.[149] In order to assess whether the observed price undercutting is

144 On the causation analysis, see below, pp. 733–9.

145 Appellate Body Report, *China – GOES (2012)*, paras. 130–1, referring to, *inter alia*, Panel Report, *Thailand – H-Beams (2001)*, para. 7.161; and Panel Report, *Korea – Certain Paper (2005)*, para. 7.253. The Appellate Body in *China – GOES (2012)* finally stated that an investigating authority's *consideration* under Article 3.2 'must be reflected in relevant documentation, such as an authority's final determination, so as to allow an interested party to verify whether the authority indeed *considered* such factors'. See *ibid.*

146 Appellate Body Report, *China – GOES (2012)*, para. 135.

147 *Ibid.*, para. 136.

148 Appellate Body Reports, *China – HP-SSST (EU)/China – HP-SSST (Japan) (2015)*, para. 5.156.

149 See *Ibid.*, paras. 5.159–5.160. Emphasis added.

significant, an investigating authority may, depending on the case, rely on all positive evidence relating to the nature of the product or product types at issue, how long the price undercutting has been taking place and to what extent, and, as appropriate, the relative market shares of the product types with respect to which the authority has made a finding of price undercutting.[150] The Appellate Body added that while an examination of whether there is a price differential between imported and domestic products may be a useful starting point for an analysis of price undercutting, it does not provide a sufficient basis for an investigating authority to satisfy its obligation under Article 3.2.[151] With respect to price depression or price suppression,[152] the Appellate Body observed that Article 3.2, second sentence, expressly links also these market phenomena with dumped imports. Article 3.2 contemplates an inquiry into the relationship between two variables, namely, dumped imports and domestic prices.[153] Moreover, as the Appellate Body stated in *China – GOES (2012)*, given that Article 3.2 contemplates an inquiry into the relationship between dumped imports and domestic prices, it is *not* sufficient for an investigating authority to confine its consideration to what is happening to domestic prices for purposes of considering significant price depression or suppression. Rather, an investigating authority is required to examine domestic prices in conjunction with dumped imports in order to understand whether dumped imports have '*explanatory force for the occurrence of*' significant depression or suppression of domestic prices.[154] According to the Appellate Body, this interpretation is reinforced by the very concepts of price depression and price suppression. With regard to price depression, it explained that price depression refers to a situation in which prices are pushed down, or reduced, *by something*. An examination of price depression, by definition, calls for more than a simple observation of a price *decline*, and also encompasses an analysis of *what* is pushing down the prices. With regard to price suppression, the Appellate Body observed that Article 3.2 requires the investigating authority to consider 'whether the effect of' dumped imports is '[to] prevent price increases, *which otherwise would have occurred*, to a significant degree'. Accordingly, price suppression cannot be properly examined without a consideration of whether, in the absence of dumped imports, prices 'otherwise

150 See *Ibid.*, para. 5.161. Emphasis added.

151 See *Ibid.*, para. 5.163. The Appellate Body reversed the panel's finding that China had not acted inconsistently with Articles 3.1 and 3.2, and found instead that MOFCOM's assessment of whether there had been a significant price undercutting by Grade C imports, as compared with the price of the domestic Grade C, was inconsistent with Articles 3.1 and 3.2 of the Anti-Dumping Agreement. *Ibid.*, para. 5.164.

152 Article 3.2, second sentence, refers to 'prevent[ing] price increases, which would otherwise have occurred'. This market phenomenon is commonly referred to as 'price suppression'.

153 Appellate Body Report, *China – GOES (2012)*, para. 136. The inquiries set out in the second sentence of Article 3.2 are separated by the words 'or' and 'otherwise'. This indicates that the elements relevant to the consideration of significant price undercutting may differ from those relevant to the consideration of significant price depression and suppression. Thus, even if prices of dumped imports do not significantly undercut those of like domestic products, dumped imports could still have a price-depressing or price-suppressing effect on domestic prices. See *ibid.*, para. 137.

154 *Ibid.*, para. 138. Emphasis added.

would have' increased. The concepts of both price depression and price suppression thus implicate an analysis concerning the question of what brings about such price phenomena.[155] Interpreting Article 3.2 as requiring a consideration of the relationship between dumped imports and domestic prices does *not* result in a duplication of the causation analysis under Article 3.5. Rather, Article 3.5, on the one hand, and Article 3.2, on the other hand, posit different inquiries. The Appellate Body explained that:

> [t]he analysis pursuant to Article 3.5 ... concerns the causal relationship between [*dumped*] *imports* and *injury* to the domestic industry. In contrast, the analysis under Article 3.2 ... concerns the relationship between [dumped] imports and a different variable, that is, *domestic prices*. An understanding of the latter relationship serves as a basis for the injury and causation analysis under Article 3.5 ... In addition, Article 3.5 ... require[s] an investigating authority to demonstrate that [dumped] imports are causing injury 'through the effects of [dumping ...]', as set forth in Article 3.2 ... as well as in Article 3.4 ... Thus, the examination under Article 3.5 ... encompasses 'all relevant evidence' before the authority, including the volume of [dumped] imports and their price effects [listed under Article 3.2], as well as all relevant economic factors concerning the state of the domestic industry [listed in Article 3.4]. The examination under Article 3.5, by definition, covers a broader scope than the scope of the elements considered in relation to price depression and suppression under Article 3.2.[156]

As indicated in the quote above, apart from Article 3.2, also Article 3.4 of the *Anti-Dumping Agreement* plays an important role in setting out how an investigating authority must determine injury. Article 3.4 states:

> The examination of the impact of the dumped imports on the domestic industry concerned shall include an evaluation of all relevant economic factors and indices having a bearing on the state of the industry.

Article 3.4 then lists the following relevant economic factors or indicators that must be evaluated: (1) factors and indices having a bearing on the state of the industry (such as an actual or potential decline in sales, profits, output, market share, productivity, return on investments, or utilisation of capacity); (2) factors affecting the domestic prices; (3) the magnitude of the margin of dumping; and (4) actual or potential negative effects on cash flow, inventories, employment, wages, growth, ability to raise capital or investments. Article 3.4 explicitly states that this list is not exhaustive. It also stresses that one or more of these factors or indices, no matter how pronounced, will not necessarily give decisive guidance as to the existence of injury to the domestic industry or lack thereof.

While not exhaustive, it is widely accepted that the list of factors in Article 3.4 is a *mandatory* minimum, and that investigating authorities must therefore collect and analyse data relating to each of these individual enumerated factors.[157]

155 *Ibid.*, para. 141. 156 *Ibid.*, para. 147.

157 See Panel Report, *Thailand – H-Beams (2001)*, paras. 7.224–7.225, as upheld by Appellate Body Report, *Thailand – H-Beams (2001)*, para. 125. See also Panel Report, *Argentina – Poultry Anti-Dumping Duties (2003)*, para. 7.314.

In addition, investigating authorities must also collect and analyse data relating to *any other relevant factors* that may have a bearing on the state of a domestic industry in a particular case.[158] Clarifying what exactly is expected from an investigating authority, the panel in *Korea – Certain Paper (2005)* considered that:

the obligation to analyse the mandatory list of fifteen factors under Article 3.4 is not a mere 'checklist obligation' consisting of a mechanical exercise to make sure that each listed factor has somehow been addressed by the [investigating authority] [...] This analysis cannot be limited to a mere identification of the 'relevance or irrelevance' of each factor, but rather must be based on a thorough evaluation of the state of the industry. The analysis must explain in a satisfactory way why the evaluation of the injury factors set out under Article 3.4 lead[s] to the determination of material injury, including an explanation of why factors which would seem to lead in the other direction do not, overall, undermine the conclusion of material injury.[159]

In *China – GOES (2012)*, the Appellate Body emphasised that Article 3.4 requires an investigating authority to examine the *impact of dumped imports* on the domestic industry. According to the Appellate Body, Article 3.4 does not merely require an examination of the state of the domestic industry, but 'contemplate[s] that an investigating authority must derive an understanding of *the impact of* [dumped] imports on the basis of such an examination'.[160] In *China – HP-SSST (EU)/China – HP-SSST (Japan) (2015)*, the Appellate Body explained:

The evaluation of all relevant economic factors and indices having a bearing on the state of the industry, including market share and factors affecting domestic prices, must be such that it provides a 'meaningful basis' for an analysis of whether the dumped imports are, through the effects of dumping, as set forth in Articles 3.2 and 3.4, causing injury to the domestic industry. Depending on the particular circumstances of each case, an investigating authority may therefore be required to take into account, as appropriate, the relative market shares of product types with respect to which it has made a finding of price undercutting; and, for example, the duration and extent of price undercutting, price depression or price suppression, that it has found to exist.[161]

In *China – GOES (2012)*, the Appellate Body noted:

Consequently, Article 3.4 ... [is] concerned with the relationship between [dumped] imports and the state of the domestic industry, and this relationship is analytically akin to the type of link contemplated by the term 'the effect of' under Article 3.2 ... In other words, Article 3.4 ... require[s] an examination of the 'explanatory force of [dumped] imports for the state of the domestic industry' ... [S]uch an interpretation does not duplicate the relevant obligations in Article 3.5 ... [because] the inquiry set forth in Article 3.2 ... and the examination

158 See Panel Report, *Thailand – H-Beams (2001)*, para. 7.225; and Appellate Body Report, *US – Hot-Rolled Steel (2001)*, para. 195.

159 Panel Report, *Korea – Certain Paper (2005)*, para. 7.272. As the Appellate Body noted in *EC – Tube or Pipe Fittings (2003)*, 'the obligation of Article 3.4 to evaluate all listed factors is *distinct* from the manner in which the evaluation is to be set out in the published documents ... The provision simply requires Members to include an evaluation of all relevant economic factors in its examination of the impact of the dumped imports.' See Appellate Body Report, *EC – Tube or Pipe Fittings (2003)*, para. 131.

160 Appellate Body Report, *China – GOES (2012)*, para. 149.

161 Appellate Body Report, *China – HP-SSST (EU)/China – HP-SSST (Japan) (2015)*, para. 5.211. The Appellate Body reversed the panel's findings rejecting the complainants' claims that China acted inconsistently with Articles 3.1 and 3.4 because MOFCOM did not undertake a segmented analysis of the impact of the dumped imports on the state of the domestic industry. See *ibid.*, para. 5.212.

required under Article 3.4 ... are necessary in order to answer the ultimate question in Article 3.5 ... as to whether [dumped] imports are causing injury to the domestic industry.[162]

Finally, while an investigating authority is required under Article 3.4 to *examine* the impact of dumped imports on the domestic industry, it is *not* required under Article 3.4 to *demonstrate* that dumped imports are causing injury to the domestic industry, rather, the latter analysis is specifically mandated by Article 3.5.[163]

4.2.2 Threat of Material Injury

As discussed above, the term 'injury' in the *Anti-Dumping Agreement* refers not only to material injury but also to the threat of material injury. Article 3.7 of the *Anti-Dumping Agreement* relates to the determination of a threat of material injury. It provides:

> A determination of a threat of material injury shall be based on facts and not merely on allegation, conjecture or remote possibility. The change in circumstances which would create a situation in which the dumping would cause injury must be clearly foreseen and imminent.

Article 3.7 further provides that, in making a determination regarding the existence of a threat of material injury, the investigating authorities should consider, *inter alia*, factors such as: (1) a significant rate of increase of dumped imports into the domestic market indicating the likelihood of substantially increased importation; (2) sufficient freely disposable, or an imminent substantial increase in, capacity of the exporter indicating the likelihood of substantially increased dumped exports to the importing Member's market, taking into account the availability of other export markets to absorb any additional exports; (3) whether imports are entering at prices that will have a significant depressing or suppressing effect on domestic prices, and would be likely to increase demand for further imports; and (4) inventories of the product being investigated.[164] However, no one of these factors alone can necessarily give decisive guidance. The totality of the factors considered must lead to the conclusion that further dumped exports are imminent and that, unless protective action is taken, material injury would occur.[165] As the panel in *US – Softwood Lumber VI (2004)* concluded:

> What is critical, however, is that it be clear from the determination that the investigating authority has evaluated how the future will be different from the immediate past, such that the situation of no present material injury will change in the imminent future to a situation of material injury, in the absence of measures.[166]

162 *Ibid.* 163 See Appellate Body Report, *China – GOES (2012)*, para. 150. See below, pp. 733–9.

164 See Panel Report, *US – Softwood Lumber VI (2004)*, para. 7.67.

165 See Article 3.7 of the *Anti-Dumping Agreement*.

166 Panel Report, *US – Softwood Lumber VI (2004)*, para. 7.58. In *US – Softwood Lumber VI (Article 21.5 – Canada) (2006)*, the Appellate Body implied that a 'high standard ... applies to a threat of injury determination ... [T]he reasoning set out by an investigating authority making a determination of threat of injury must clearly disclose the assumptions and extrapolations that were made, on the basis of the record evidence, regarding future occurrences. Nor are the panel's statements inconsistent with the requirements that the reasoning of the investigating authority demonstrate that such assumptions and extrapolations were based on positive evidence and not merely on allegation, conjecture, or remote possibility; and show a high degree of likelihood that projected occurrences will occur.' See Appellate Body Report, *US – Softwood Lumber VI (Article 21.5 – Canada) (2006)*, para. 109.

The panel in *Mexico – Corn Syrup (2000)* stated that it is clear that, in making a determination regarding the threat of material injury, investigating authorities must conclude that *material injury would occur* in the absence of an anti-dumping measure. However, a determination that material injury would occur cannot be made solely on the basis of a consideration of the factors listed in Article 3.7. The panel in *Mexico – Corn Syrup (2000)* ruled that:

> [c]onsideration of the Article 3.4 factors in examining the consequent impact of imports is required in a case involving threat of injury in order to make a determination consistent with the requirements of Articles 3.1 and 3.7.[167]

The Appellate Body ruled in *Mexico – Corn Syrup (Article 21.5 – US) (2001)* that:

> In determining the existence of a *threat* of material injury, the investigating authorities will necessarily have to make assumptions relating to 'the occurrence of future events' since such *future* events 'can never be definitively proven by facts'. Notwithstanding this intrinsic uncertainty, a 'proper establishment' of facts in a determination of threat of material injury must be based on events that, although they have not yet occurred, must be 'clearly foreseen and imminent', in accordance with Article 3.7 of the *Anti-Dumping Agreement*.[168]

Not surprisingly, Article 3.8 of the *Anti-Dumping Agreement* requires that the application of anti-dumping measures shall be considered and decided with 'special care' where a determination of threat of material injury is involved. While Article 3.8 offers no further guidance as to the meaning of 'special care', it is clear that this provision cautions against the 'automatic' imposition of measures in such cases.[169]

4.2.3 Determination of Material Retardation

Beyond specifying that the term 'injury' as used in the *Anti-Dumping Agreement* also includes 'material retardation', the Agreement contains no further explicit language pertaining to this concept. Some guidance may perhaps be derived from the 1967 *Anti-Dumping Code*,[170] which refers to the retardation of the establishment of a new industry, and indicates that a finding must be based on 'convincing evidence' that such a new industry is actually forthcoming. Examples of such evidence include plans for an industry being at an advanced stage, a factory under construction or new capital equipment already having been ordered.

167 Panel Report, *Mexico – Corn Syrup (2000)*, para. 7.127. The panel in this case further stated that the language of Article 3.7 itself recognised that factors in addition to those set out in that provision would be relevant for a threat of injury determination. *Ibid.*, para. 7.124. See also Panel Report, *US – Softwood Lumber VI (2004)*, para. 7.105.

168 Appellate Body Report, *Mexico – Corn Syrup (Article 21.5 – US) (2001)*, para. 85.

169 See Panel Report, *US – Softwood Lumber VI (2004)*, para. 7.33. See also the concern of the Appellate Body regarding statements of the panel in *US – Softwood Lumber VI (Article 21.5 – Canada) (2006)*, which seemed to imply 'a greater likelihood of panels upholding a *threat* of injury determination, as compared to a determination of *current* material injury, when those determinations rest on the same level of evidence'. See Appellate Body Report, *US – Softwood Lumber VI (Article 21.5 – Canada) (2006)*, para. 110.

170 See above, pp. 698–9.

5 DEMONSTRATION OF A CAUSAL LINK

As already noted above, Article 3.5 of the *Anti-Dumping Agreement* requires the demonstration of a *causal link* between the dumped imports *and* the injury to the domestic industry. Article 3.5 also contains a *'non-attribution' requirement.* According to this requirement, investigating authorities must examine any known factors other than the dumped imports that are injuring the domestic industry at the same time *and* they must not attribute the injury caused by these other factors to the dumped imports. It is important to note that the *Anti-Dumping Agreement* does *not* require that the dumped imports are the *sole cause* of the injury to the domestic industry.[171] The *Anti-Dumping Agreement* requires that the dumped imports be a genuine and substantial cause of material injury and that other causes of injury not be attributed to the dumped imports.

In order to make a finding of causation of *present material injury* under Article 3.5, according to the Appellate Body in *China – HP-SSST (EU)/China – HP-SSST (Japan) (2015)*, the investigating authority must determine that the dumped imports (consisting of certain product models or grades) have the 'effect' of causing material injury to the domestic industry (producing mainly a different product model or grades). Such a finding cannot be made if the relevant imports are not substitutable for the domestic like products.[172]

5.1 Relevant Causation Factors and Non-Attribution

Article 3.5 of the *Anti-Dumping Agreement* identifies several factors which 'may be relevant' in demonstrating a causal link between dumped imports and injury *and* in ensuring non-attribution to the dumped imports of injury being caused by other factors. These factors include: (1) the volume and prices of imports not sold at dumping prices; (2) contraction in demand or changes in the patterns of consumption; (3) trade-restrictive practices of and competition between the foreign and domestic producers; (4) developments in technology; and (5) the export performance and productivity of the domestic industry. However, Article 3.5 does not *require* examination of any particular factors nor does it *give clear guidance* on the manner in which the investigating authorities should evaluate relevant evidence in order to establish the causal link *and* to ensure

171 Note that this was the requirement under Article 3 of the Kennedy Round *Anti-Dumping Code*, BISD 15S/74. As discussed above, the Kennedy Round *Anti-Dumping Code* was superseded by the Tokyo Round *Anti-Dumping Code* in which this requirement was already dropped.

172 See Appellate Body Report, *China – HP-SSST (EU)/China – HP-SSST (Japan) (2015)*, paras. 5.251, 5.256, 5.262. The Appellate Body found that China acted inconsistently with Articles 3.1 and 3.5 because MOFCOM improperly relied on the market share of dumped imports, and its flawed price effects and impact analyses, in determining a causal link between dumped imports and material injury to the domestic industry, and made *no finding of cross-grade price effects* whereby price undercutting by Grade B and C imports might be shown to affect the price of domestic Grade A HP-SSST. See *ibid.*, para. 5.277.

non-attribution to the dumped imports of injury being caused by other factors. As the Appellate Body ruled in *US – Hot-Rolled Steel (2001)*:

> [P]rovided that an investigating authority does not attribute the injuries of other causal factors to dumped imports, it is free to choose the methodology it will use in examining the 'causal relationship' between dumped imports and injury.[173]

The panel in *Thailand – H-Beams (2001)* made clear its view that, in contrast to the mandatory list of factors in Article 3.4, the list of factors in Article 3.5 was merely *illustrative*. Thus, while the listed factors in Article 3.5 might be relevant in many cases, and while the list contains useful guidance as to the kinds of factors other than imports that might cause injury to the domestic industry, the specific list in Article 3.5 is not itself mandatory.[174]

The Appellate Body in *US – Hot-Rolled Steel (2001)* clarified the 'non-attribution' requirement of Article 3.5 of the *Anti-Dumping Agreement* as follows:

> The non-attribution language in Article 3.5 of the *Anti-Dumping Agreement* applies solely in situations where dumped imports and other known factors are causing injury to the domestic industry *at the same time*. In order that investigating authorities, applying Article 3.5, are able to ensure that the injurious effects of the other known factors are not 'attributed' to dumped imports, they must appropriately assess the injurious effects of those other factors. Logically, such an assessment must involve separating and distinguishing the injurious effects of the other factors from the injurious effects of the dumped imports. If the injurious effects of the dumped imports are not appropriately separated and distinguished from the injurious effects of the other factors, the authorities will be unable to conclude that the injury they ascribe to dumped imports is actually caused by those imports, rather than by the other factors. Thus, in the absence of such separation and distinction of the different injurious effects, the investigating authorities would have no rational basis to conclude that the dumped imports are indeed causing the injury which, under the *Anti-Dumping Agreement*, justifies the imposition of anti-dumping duties.[175]

In brief, in order to comply with the 'non-attribution' requirement of Article 3.5, investigating authorities must make an appropriate *assessment* of the injury caused to the domestic industry by the other known factors, and they must *separate and distinguish* the injurious effects of the dumped imports from the injurious effects of those other factors.[176] In order for this obligation to be triggered, the Appellate Body noted in *EC – Tube or Pipe Fittings (2003)* that Article 3.5

173 Appellate Body Report, *US – Hot-Rolled Steel (2001)*, paras. 224 and 226. See also Appellate Body Report, *EC – Tube or Pipe Fittings (2003)*, para. 189.

174 See Panel Report, *Thailand – H-Beams (2001)*, para. 7.274.

175 Appellate Body Reports in: *US – Hot-Rolled Steel (2001)*, para. 223; *China – GOES (2012)*, para. 151; and *China – HP-SSST (EU)/China – HP-SSST (Japan) (2015)*, para. 5.283.

176 According to the Appellate Body, '[i]f the injurious effects of the dumped imports and the other known factors remain lumped together and indistinguishable, there is simply no means of knowing whether injury ascribed to dumped imports was, in reality, caused by other factors. Article 3.5, therefore, requires investigating authorities to undertake the process of assessing appropriately, and separating and distinguishing, the injurious effects of dumped imports from those of other known causal factors'. See Appellate Body Report, *US – Hot-Rolled Steel (2001)*, para. 228. The GATT 1947 and the Tokyo Round *Anti-Dumping Code* did not contain a provision akin to Article 3.5 of the WTO *Anti-Dumping Agreement*, which expressly requires that injury caused by any other known factors is not attributed to dumped imports.

requires that the factor at issue: (1) be 'known' to the investigating authority; (2) be a factor 'other than dumped imports'; and (3) be injuring the domestic industry at the same time as the dumped imports.[177] The *Anti-Dumping Agreement* does not expressly state how such factors should become 'known' to the investigating authority, or if and in what manner they must be raised by interested parties, in order to qualify as 'known'.[178]

In interpreting the 'non-attribution' requirement of Article 3.5, the Appellate Body in *US – Hot-Rolled Steel (2001)* recognised that the different causal factors operating on a domestic industry may interact, and their effects may well be interrelated, such that they produce a *combined* effect on the domestic industry.[179] Therefore, it may not be easy, as a practical matter, to separate and distinguish the injurious effects of different causal factors. However, although not easy, this is the function of the 'non-attribution' requirement.[180] In *China – HP-SSST (EU)/China – HP-SSST (Japan) (2015)*, the Appellate Body found that China acted inconsistently with Articles 3.1 and 3.5 because MOFCOM failed to ensure that the injury caused by other known factors was not attributed to the dumped imports, in particular because MOFCOM failed to ensure that the injury caused by the decrease in apparent consumption and the increase in domestic production capacity was not attributed to the dumped imports.[181]

5.2 Cumulation

A cumulative analysis is the consideration of the effects of dumped imports from more than one country in determining whether dumped imports are causing injury to the domestic industry. As such an analysis will necessarily increase the volume of imports whose impact is being considered, it will clearly augment the possibility of an affirmative injury determination. A controversial topic during the Uruguay Round negotiations, the conditions for cumulative analysis of the effects of imports from more than one country are now set forth in Article 3.3 of the *Anti-Dumping Agreement*. Cumulation is *not mandatory*

177 Appellate Body Report, *EC – Tube or Pipe Fittings (2003)*, para. 175. See Appellate Body Report, *US – Steel Safeguards (2003)*, para. 491.

178 See Appellate Body Report, *EC – Tube or Pipe Fittings (2003)*, para. 176. The Appellate Body added to this: 'In our view, a factor is either "known" to the investigating authority, or it is not "known"; it cannot be "known" in one stage of the investigation and unknown in a subsequent stage.' *Ibid.*, para. 178.

179 In *EU – Biodiesel (2016)*, the Appellate Body found that the panel did not err in interpreting Articles 3.1 and 3.5 because it did not articulate a legal standard pursuant to which it is relevant to examine whether the revised data played a significant role in the EU authorities' non-attribution analysis. See Appellate Body Report, *EU – Biodiesel (2016)*, paras. 6.131, 6.140. 6.148.

180 In *EC – Tube or Pipe Fittings (2003)*, the Appellate Body did not find that an examination of *collective* effects is necessarily required by the non-attribution language of the *Anti-Dumping Agreement*. The Appellate Body stated: 'In particular, we are of the view that Article 3.5 does not compel, *in every case*, an assessment of the *collective* effects of other causal factors, because such an assessment is not always necessary to conclude that injuries ascribed to dumped imports are actually caused by those imports and not by other factors.' See Appellate Body Report, *EC – Tube or Pipe Fittings (2003)*, para. 191. See also Appellate Body Report, *US – Softwood Lumber VI (Article 21.5 – Canada) (2006)*, para. 154.

181 Appellate Body Report, *China – HP-SSST (EU)/China – HP-SSST (Japan) (2015)*, para. 5.286.

under any circumstances but is *permitted*, be it only under the conditions set forth in Article 3.3.

Pursuant to Article 3.3 of the *Anti-Dumping Agreement*, an investigating authority may cumulatively assess the effects of imports if it determines that: (1) the margin of dumping established in relation to the imports from each country is more than *de minimis* (as defined in Article 5.8) and the volume of imports from each country is not negligible; and (2) a cumulative assessment of the effects of the imports is appropriate in light of the conditions of competition between the imported products and the conditions of competition between the imported products and the like domestic product.[182] In *EC – Tube or Pipe Fittings (2003)*, the Appellate Body stated that:

> The text of Article 3.3 expressly identifies three conditions that must be satisfied before an investigating authority is permitted under the *Anti-Dumping Agreement* to assess cumulatively the effects of imports from several countries ... By the terms of Article 3.3, it is 'only if' the above conditions are established that an investigating authority 'may' make a cumulative assessment of the effects of dumped imports from several countries.[183]

The Appellate Body further noted in *EC – Tube or Pipe Fittings (2003)*:

> A cumulative analysis logically is premised on a recognition that the domestic industry faces the impact of the 'dumped imports' as a whole and that it may be injured by the total impact of the dumped imports, even though those imports originate from various countries ... In our view, therefore, by expressly providing for cumulation in Article 3.3 of the *Anti-Dumping Agreement*, the negotiators appear to have recognized that a domestic industry confronted with dumped imports originating from several countries may be injured by the cumulated effects of those imports, and that those effects may not be adequately taken into account in a country-specific analysis of the injurious effects of dumped imports.[184]

In *US – Carbon Steel (India) (2014)*, the United States appealed the Panel's interpretation of Article 15.3 of the *SCM Agreement* that 'cross-cumulation' of the effects of subsidised imports with the effects of non-subsidised, dumped imports is inconsistent with this provision. The United States maintained that the fact that Article 15.3 does not specifically authorise an investigating authority to cumulate the effects of subsidised imports with those of dumped imports does not, in itself, indicate that such cross-cumulation is prohibited by the *SCM*

182 See Appellate Body Report, *EC – Bed Linen (Article 21.5 – India) (2003)*, para. 145; Appellate Body Report, *EC – Tube and Pipe Fittings (2003)*, para. 110; Appellate Body Report, *US – Oil Country Tubular Goods Sunset Reviews (2004)*, para. 300.

183 Appellate Body Report, *EC – Tube or Pipe Fittings (2003)*, para. 109. Note that, with regard to the third requirement, the Appellate Body ruled that: 'cumulation must be appropriate in the light of the conditions of competition: (i) between the imported products; and (ii) between the imported products and the like domestic product'. See *ibid.*

184 *Ibid.*, para. 116. According to the Appellate Body, '[i]f, for example, the dumped imports from some countries are low in volume or are declining, an exclusively country-specific analysis may not identify the causal relationship between the dumped imports from those countries and the injury suffered by the domestic industry. The outcome may then be that, because imports from such countries could not *individually* be identified as causing injury, the dumped imports from these countries would not be subject to anti-dumping duties, even though they are in fact causing injury.' See *ibid.*

Agreement. The United States further relied on the context provided by Article 3.3 of the *Anti-Dumping Agreement* and by Article VI:6(a) of the GATT 1994 in support of an interpretation of Article 15.3 permitting cross-cumulation of the effects of subsidised imports with the effects of dumped imports.[185] The Appellate Body agreed with the panel findings that Article 15.3 and Articles 15.1, 15.2, 15.4, and 15.5 of the *SCM Agreement* do not authorise investigating authorities to assess cumulatively the effects of (dumped) imports that are not subject to simultaneous countervailing duty investigations with the effects of imports that are subject to countervailing duty investigations.[186]

6 ANTI-DUMPING INVESTIGATION

The *Anti-Dumping Agreement* sets out, in considerable detail, how investigating authorities of WTO Members have to initiate and conduct an anti-dumping investigation. This section addresses in turn: (1) the initiation of an anti-dumping investigation; (2) the conduct of an investigation; and (3) public notice and judicial review.

6.1 Initiation of an Investigation

Article 5 of the *Anti-Dumping Agreement* contains numerous requirements concerning the initiation of an anti-dumping investigation. The domestic investigating authorities can instigate an investigation on their own initiative. However, the *Anti-Dumping Agreement* specifies that investigations must *generally* be initiated on the basis of a written application submitted 'by or on behalf of' a domestic industry as defined in Article 4 of the *Anti-Dumping Agreement*.[187] Sufficient support for the application must therefore exist among domestic producers to warrant initiation.[188] The *Anti-Dumping Agreement* contains guidance relating to the required contents of the initiation request, including: (1) evidence of dumping; (2) evidence of injury to the domestic industry; and (3) evidence of a causal link between the dumped imports and the injury to

185 See Appellate Body Report, *US – Carbon Steel (India) (2014)*, paras. 4.571, 4.591.

186 See *ibid.*, para. 4.600.

187 In *US – 1916 Act (Japan) (2000)*, the panel found a violation of Articles 4 and 5 of the *Anti-Dumping Agreement* because the 1916 Act did not require 'a minimum representation of a US industry in applications for the initiation of proceedings under the 1916 Act'. See Panel Report, *US – 1916 Act (Japan) (2000)*, paras. 6.255–6.261. See also Panel Report, *US – 1916 Act (EC) (2000)*, paras. 6.212–6.214.

188 An application is considered to have been made 'by or on behalf of the domestic industry' if it is supported by those domestic producers whose collective output makes up over 50 per cent of the total production of the like product produced by that portion of the domestic industry expressing support for or opposition to the application, *and* the domestic producers supporting the application account for at least 25 per cent of total domestic production of the like product. See Article 5.4 of the *Anti-Dumping Agreement*.

the domestic industry. As the panel in *Mexico – Corn Syrup (2000)* stated and the panel in *Thailand – H-Beams (2001)* affirmed:

Article 5.2 does not require an application to contain analysis, but rather to contain information, in the sense of evidence, in support of allegations.[189]

The application must contain information that is 'reasonably available' to the applicant in accordance with Article 5.2.[190] Simple assertion, unsubstantiated by relevant evidence, cannot be considered to meet the requirements of this provision.[191] In considering the nature and extent of the information that must be provided in an application pursuant to Article 5.2(iv), the panel in *Mexico – Corn Syrup (2000)* stated:

Obviously, the quantity and quality of the information provided by the applicant need not be such as would be required in order to make a preliminary or final determination of injury. Moreover, the applicant need only provide such information as is 'reasonably available' to it with respect to the relevant factors. Since information regarding the factors and indices set out in Article 3.4 concerns the state of the domestic industry and its operations, such information would generally be available to applicants. Nevertheless, we note that an application which is consistent with the requirements of Article 5.2 will not necessarily contain sufficient evidence to justify initiation under Article 5.3.[192]

Article 5.3 of the *Anti-Dumping Agreement* requires that the investigating authorities examine the accuracy and adequacy of the evidence provided in the application to determine whether there is sufficient evidence to justify the initiation of the investigation.[193] Statements and assertions unsubstantiated by any evidence cannot constitute sufficient evidence within the meaning of Article 5.3 of the *Anti-Dumping Agreement.*[194] However, in determining whether there is sufficient evidence to initiate an investigation, an investigating authority is not limited to the information contained in the application. The panel in *Guatemala – Cement II (2000)* noted:

We have expressed the view that Articles 5.2 and 5.3 contain different obligations. One of the consequences of this difference in obligations is that investigating authorities need not content themselves with the information provided in the application but may gather information on their own in order to meet the standard of sufficient evidence for initiation in Article 5.3.[195]

189 Panel Report, *Thailand – H-Beams (2001)*, para. 7.75, citing Panel Report, *Mexico – Corn Syrup (2000)*, para. 7.76.

190 As the panel in *US – Softwood Lumber V (2004)* found, this provision is not intended to require an applicant to submit *all* information that is reasonably available to it. The 'reasonably available' language is intended to avoid putting an undue burden on the applicant to submit information which is *not* reasonably available to it. See Panel Report, *US – Softwood Lumber V (2004)*, para. 7.54.

191 See Panel Report, *US – Softwood Lumber V (2004)*, para. 7.52.

192 Panel Report, *Mexico – Corn Syrup (2000)*, para. 7.74.

193 The panel in *Mexico – Steel Pipes and Tubes (2007)* found that, although there is no express reference to evidence of 'dumping' or 'injury' or 'causation' in Article 5.3 of the *Anti-Dumping Agreement*, reading Article 5.3 in the context of Article 5.2 makes clear that the evidence to which Article 5.3 refers is the evidence in the application concerning dumping, injury and causation. See Panel Report, *Mexico – Steel Pipes and Tubes (2007)*, para. 7.21.

194 See Panel Report, *Argentina – Poultry Anti-Dumping Duties (2003)*, para. 7.60. See also Panel Report, *US – Softwood Lumber V (2004)*, para. 7.79; and Panel Report, *Mexico – Steel Pipes and Tubes (2007)*, para. 7.24.

195 Panel Report, *Guatemala – Cement II (2000)*, para. 8.62. See also Panel Report, *US – Softwood Lumber V (2004)*, para. 7.75.

With respect to the nature and extent of the evidence required to initiate an anti-dumping investigation, the panel in *Guatemala – Cement II (2000)* ruled:

> We do not of course mean to suggest that an investigating authority must have before it at the time it initiates an investigation evidence of dumping within the meaning of Article 2 of the quantity and quality that would be necessary to support a preliminary or final determination. An anti-dumping investigation is a process where certainty on the existence of all the elements necessary in order to adopt a measure is reached gradually as the investigation moves forward. However, the evidence must be such that an unbiased and objective investigating authority could determine that there was sufficient evidence of dumping within the meaning of Article 2 to justify initiation of an investigation.[196]

The same is true for the evidence on injury to the domestic industry and the causal link between dumped imports and injury.[197]

Article 5.5 of the *Anti-Dumping Agreement* requires that the investigating authorities 'avoid, unless a decision has been made to initiate an investigation, any publicizing of the application for the initiation of an investigation'. However, 'after receipt of a properly documented application and before proceeding to initiate an investigation, the authorities shall notify the government of the exporting Member concerned'.[198] There are also public notice requirements concerning the initiation of an investigation in Article 12.1 of the *Anti-Dumping Agreement.*[199]

An application to initiate an anti-dumping investigation shall be rejected, and an investigation shall be terminated *promptly*, as soon as the investigating authorities are satisfied that there is not enough evidence either of dumping or of injury.[200] Moreover, in order to ensure that an unwarranted investigation is not continued, Article 5.8 provides for prompt termination of investigations in the event that: (1) the margin of dumping is *de minimis* (i.e. less than 2 per cent of the export price); and (2) the volume of imports from each country is *negligible* (i.e. normally less than 3 per cent of imports of the like product in the importing Member, unless countries accounting for less than 3 per cent *individually* account *collectively* for more than 7 per cent of imports of the like product in the importing Member).[201]

196 Panel Report, *Guatemala – Cement II (2000)*, para. 8.35. See also Panel Report, *US – Softwood Lumber V (2004)*, para. 7.84; and Panel Report, *Mexico – Steel Pipes and Tubes (2007)*, para. 7.22.

197 Where an investigation is self-initiated by the authorities, the authorities may proceed only if they have sufficient evidence of dumping, injury and a causal link to justify the initiation of the investigation. See Article 5.6 of the *Anti-Dumping Agreement.*

198 See Article 5.5 of the *Anti-Dumping Agreement.* Several panels (*Guatemala – Cement I (1998); Guatemala – Cement II (2000); US – 1916 Act (EC) (2000)*; and *Thailand – H-Beams (2001)*) have considered the nature and extent of the obligation imposed by Article 5.5. See also *Recommendation Concerning the Timing of the Notification under Article 5.5*, adopted by the Committee on Anti-Dumping Practices on 29 October 1998, G/ADP/5, dated 3 November 1998.

199 See below, pp. 746–9.

200 See Article 5.8 of the *Anti-Dumping Agreement.* See e.g. Panel Report, *Mexico – Steel Pipes and Tubes*, para. 7.61; Panel Report, *Mexico – Corn Syrup (2000)*, para. 7.99; Panel Report, *Guatemala – Cement II (2000)*, para. 8.75; Panel Report, *Argentina – Poultry Anti-Dumping Duties (2003)*, para. 7.112; and Appellate Body Report, *Mexico – Anti-Dumping Measures on Rice (2005)*, para. 208.

201 See Appellate Body Report, *Mexico – Anti-Dumping Measures on Rice (2005)*, paras. 217ff. and 305ff.

6.2 Conduct of the Investigation

Article 6 of the *Anti-Dumping Agreement* contains detailed rules concerning the process of the investigation, including evidentiary, informational and procedural elements. The Appellate Body in *EC – Tube or Pipe Fittings (2003)* stated:

> [W]e wish to underscore the importance of the obligations contained in Article 6 of the *Anti-Dumping Agreement*. This Article 'establishes a framework of procedural and due process obligations'. Its provisions 'set out evidentiary rules that apply *throughout* the course of the anti-dumping investigation, and provide also for due process rights that are enjoyed by "interested parties" *throughout* such an investigation'.[202]

Article 6.1 requires that all interested parties in an anti-dumping investigation be given *notice* of the information which the authorities require as well as ample *opportunity to present* in writing all evidence which parties consider relevant in respect of the investigation.[203] Domestic producers can control the timing of the submission of a request for initiation of an anti-dumping investigation as it is their complaint that triggers the authority's investigative process. The complaining producers therefore have an opportunity to gather the evidence necessary to support their complaint in advance. The responding parties, on the other hand, typically receive no notice until the initiation of the investigation. In practice, investigating authorities typically send interested parties 'questionnaires' in which they identify the information that they require in order to conduct the investigation.[204]

Article 6.1.1 protects exporters and foreign producers by requiring investigating authorities to provide them with at least thirty days to reply to 'questionnaires', and by allowing that extensions should be granted whenever practicable, upon cause shown.[205] This indicates that the specific due process interest of

202 Appellate Body Reports, *EC – Tube or Pipe Fittings (2003)*, para. 138; for an interpretation of Article 6.11 and 'interested parties', see *EC – Fasteners (Article 21.5 – China) (2016)*, paras. 5.148–5.151.

203 On the requirement to give notice, see Panel Report, *Egypt – Steel Rebar (2002)*, para. 7.96; and Appellate Body Report, *Mexico – Anti-Dumping Measures on Rice (2005)*, para. 251. On the requirement to give ample opportunity to present evidence, see Panel Report, *Guatemala – Cement II (2002)*, paras. 8.119, 8.178 and 8.237–8.239; Panel Report, *US – Corrosion-Resistant Steel Sunset Review (2004)*, paras. 6.257–6.263; Panel Report, *US – Oil Country Tubular Goods Sunset Reviews (2004)*, paras. 7.107–7.128; Appellate Body Report, *US – Oil Country Tubular Goods Sunset Reviews (2004)*, para. 241; and Panel Report, *US – Oil Country Tubular Goods Sunset Reviews (Article 21.5 – Argentina) (2007)*, paras. 7.109–7.120. In *US – Oil Country Tubular Goods Sunset Reviews (2004)*, the Appellate Body emphasised that 'disregarding a respondent's evidence ... is incompatible with the respondent's right, under Article 6.1, to present evidence that it considers relevant in respect of the sunset review'. See Appellate Body Report, *US – Oil Country Tubular Goods Sunset Reviews (2004)*, para. 246.

204 The 'questionnaires' referred to in Article 6.1.1 are a particular type of document containing substantial requests for information, distributed early in an investigation, and through which the investigating authority solicits a substantial amount of information relating to the key aspects of the investigation that is to be conducted by the authority (that is, on dumping, injury, and causation). Appellate Body Report, *EC – Fasteners (2011)*, paras. 612–13.

205 Article 6.1 sets 'flexible' thirty-day minimum time limits for submissions and responses to questionnaires from all interested parties. See Appellate Body Report, *US – Hot-Rolled Steel (2001)*, paras. 73–5, where the Appellate Body stated that pursuant to Article 6.1.1 investigating authorities may impose time limits for questionnaire responses, that these time limits are not necessarily absolute and immutable and that in appropriate circumstances these time limits must be extended.

exporters and foreign producers to be afforded an ample opportunity to respond has been expressly provided.[206] Article 6.1.2 requires that evidence presented in writing by one interested party be made available promptly to other interested parties participating in an investigation, subject to the requirement to protect confidential information.[207] Article 6.2 also requires that interested parties be given 'a full opportunity for the defence of [their] interests'.[208] Finally, the proper interpretation of Article 6.1.1 must also take into considerations the interests of investigating authorities in controlling the investigative process and bringing investigations to a close within a stipulated period of time.[209] All interested parties enjoy certain rights to participate in the proceedings and to make presentations.[210] To ensure the transparency of the anti-dumping investigation and proceedings, the investigating authorities must, according to Article 6.4 of the *Anti-Dumping Agreement*, provide timely opportunities for all interested parties to see all non-confidential information that is relevant to the presentation of *their* cases and used by the investigating authority.[211] Article 6.4 of the Anti-Dumping Agreement requires investigating authorities to provide 'timely opportunities' for interested parties to see information that is: (i) *relevant* to the presentation of their cases; (ii) *not confidential* as defined in Article 6.5; and (iii) *used* by the authorities in an anti-dumping investigation.[212] Article 6.4 applies to a broad range of information that is used by an investigating authority in carrying out a required step in an anti-dumping investigation.[213] One of the stated objectives of the disclosure of information under Article 6.4 is to allow

206 In *US – Oil Country Tubular Goods Sunset Reviews (2004)*, the Appellate Body stated: 'the "ample" and "full" opportunities guaranteed by Articles 6.1 and 6.2, respectively, cannot extend indefinitely and must, at some point, legitimately cease to exist ... Where the continued granting of opportunities to present evidence and attend hearings would impinge on an investigating authority's ability to "control the conduct" of its inquiry and to "carry out the multiple steps" required to reach a timely completion of the sunset review, a respondent will have reached the limit of the "ample" and "full" opportunities provided for in Articles 6.1 and 6.2.' See Appellate Body Report, *US – Oil Country Tubular Goods Sunset Reviews (2004)*, para. 242.

207 See Appellate Body Report, *EC – Fasteners (Article 21.5 – China) (2016)*, para. 5.153.

208 Appellate Body Report, *US – Oil Country Tubular Goods Sunset Reviews (2004)*, para. 246. In *EC – Fasteners (Article 21.5 – China) (2016)*, the Appellate Body further found that, as a consequence of acting inconsistently with Article 6.4, the European Union also acted inconsistently with Article 6.2 of the *Anti-Dumping Agreement* in the review investigation. See Appellate Body Report, *EC – Fasteners (Article 21.5 – China) (2016)*, paras. 5.124–5.125.

209 Appellate Body Report, *EC – Fasteners (2011)*, paras. 610–11.

210 Investigating authorities must provide opportunities for industrial users of the product under investigation and for representative consumer organisations, in cases where the product is commonly sold at the retail level, to provide information which is relevant to the investigation regarding dumping, injury and causation. See Article 6.12 of the *Anti-Dumping Agreement*. In *EC – Fasteners (Article 21.5 – China) (2016)*, the Appellate Body found that the analogue country producer was an 'interested party' in the review investigation within the meaning of Article 6.11. See Appellate Body Report, *EC – Fasteners (Article 21.5 – China) (2016)*, para. 5.154. Article 6.13 of the *Anti-Dumping Agreement* requires investigating authorities to take due account of the difficulties interested parties, in particular small companies, may experience in supplying information. Investigating authorities must provide interested parties with any assistance practicable.

211 Article 6.4 of the *Anti-Dumping Agreement* defines what information is 'relevant' for the purposes of this provision. See e.g. Appellate Body Report, *EC – Fasteners (2011)*, para. 480.

212 See Appellate Body Report, *EC – Fasteners (Article 21.5 – China) (2016)*, paras. 5.107–5.109.

213 Indeed, the broad range of information subject to the obligation under Article 6.4 may take various forms, including data submitted by the interested parties, and information that has been processed, organised, or summarised by the investigating authority. See Appellate Body Report, *EC – Fasteners (2011)*, para. 480.

interested parties 'to prepare presentations on the basis of this information'.[214] Note, however, that an investigating authority's reasoning or internal deliberation is not subject to the obligation under Article 6.4.[215]

In the same vein, the last sentence of Article 2.4 requires investigating authorities to indicate to the parties in question what information is required to ensure a fair comparison between export price and normal value and shall not impose an unreasonable burden of proof on those parties. In this regard, although exporters have to substantiate their requests for adjustments, the investigating authority must, first, inform the parties what information the authority will need in order to ensure a fair comparison.[216]

These disclosure obligations of the *Anti-Dumping Agreement* are counterbalanced by the confidentiality requirements that apply to sensitive business information. Article 6.5 requires that investigating authorities preserve the confidentiality of sensitive business information relating to the exporting firms and the domestic industry involved in the investigation.[217] The investigating authority must review whether a party requesting confidential treatment of information shows 'good cause' for such treatment.[218] As the Appellate Body stated in *EC – Fasteners (2011)* and *EC – Fasteners (Article 21.5 – China) (2016)*, the 'good cause' alleged must constitute a reason sufficient to justify the withholding of information both from the public and from the other parties interested in the investigation, who would otherwise have a right to view this information.[219]

214 See Appellate Body Report, *EC – Tube and Pipe Fittings (2003)*, para. 149. Article 6.2 confirms that access to all such information is important because, without such information, the interested parties may not have 'a full opportunity for the defence of their interests'. See *ibid.* As the Appellate Body explained in *EC – Fasteners (2011)*, the 'information' relevant to the presentation of an interested party's case can be a broader concept than the 'essential facts' within the meaning of Article 6.9 relied on by the authority, or they may overlap. See Appellate Body Report, *EC – Fasteners (2011)*, para. 483. While the disclosure obligations under Articles 2.4, 6.2 and 6.4 apply throughout the investigation, the Appellate Body stressed that disclosure under Article 6.9 takes place only at the end of the investigation. Appellate Body Report, *EC – Fasteners (Article 21.5 – China) (2016)*, para. 5.191.

215 See *ibid.*, para. 480.

216 Appellate Body Report, *EC – Fasteners (Article 21.5 – China) (2016)*, paras. 5.163–5.168, 5.172. More generally, Article 2.4 requires investigating authorities to make a fair comparison between the price of the exported product under investigation and the normal value, and to make due allowance for differences which affect price comparability.

217 Article 6.5 of the *Anti-Dumping Agreement* protects information which is by its nature confidential (i.e. information of which the disclosure would, for example, be of significant competitive advantage to a competitor or would have a significantly adverse effect upon a person supplying the information) or information which has been supplied on a confidential basis by the parties to the investigation. However, regardless of the type of confidential information, good cause must be shown in order to qualify for confidential treatment. See Appellate Body Reports, *EC – Fasteners (2011)*, para. 536; *EC – Fasteners (Article 21.5 – China) (2016)*, paras. 5.36–5.40.

218 See Panel Report, *Mexico – Steel Pipes and Tubes (2007)*, para. 7.382. As the Appellate Body stated in *EC – Fasteners (2011)*, the requirement to show 'good cause' for confidential treatment applies to both information that is 'by nature' confidential and that which is provided to the investigating authority 'on a confidential basis'. See Appellate Body Reports, *EC – Fasteners (2011)*, para. 536; *EC – Fasteners (Article 21.5 – China) (2016)*, paras. 5.36–5.40.

219 See Appellate Body Reports, *EC – Fasteners (2011)*, para. 538. A wide range of reasons could constitute 'good cause' justifying confidential treatment of information. For example, an advantage being bestowed on a competitor, or inflicting an adverse effect on the submitting party or the party from which it was acquired, may constitute 'good cause' which could justify the non-disclosure of confidential information. See *ibid.* Thus, 'the risk of a potential consequence [must be demonstrated], the avoidance of which is important enough to warrant the non-disclosure of the information'. Appellate Body Report, *EC – Fasteners (2011)*, paras. 537–40.

When investigating authorities grant confidential treatment, they shall require interested parties to furnish non-confidential summaries in sufficient detail to permit a reasonable understanding of the substance of the information submitted in confidence.[220]

In *China – HP-SSST (EU)/China – HP-SSST (Japan) (2015)*, the Appellate Body clarified that a WTO panel, tasked with reviewing whether an authority has objectively assessed 'good cause', is to do so on the basis of the investigating authority's published report and its related supporting documents, in the light of the nature of the information at issue, and the reasons given by the submitting party for its request for confidential treatment. In reviewing whether an authority has objectively assessed 'good cause', it is not for a panel to engage in a *de novo* review of the record of the investigation and determine for itself whether the existence of 'good cause' has been sufficiently substantiated by the submitting party;[221] nor can 'good cause' be determined merely based on the subjective concerns of the party submitting the information at issue.[222]

Pursuant to Article 6.6 of the *Anti-Dumping Agreement*, an investigating authority must *generally* satisfy itself as to the accuracy of the information supplied by interested parties upon which its determinations are based.[223] Article 6.7 grants Members a right 'to carry out investigations in the territory of other Members'.[224] The investigating authority will often verify the information supplied by on-site visits to review the records of the companies involved.[225] Article 6.6 includes the qualification '[e]xcept in circumstances provided for in paragraph 8' and thus it is not possible for investigating authorities to 'satisfy themselves as to the accuracy of the information' in circumstances where interested parties refuse access to, or otherwise do not provide, such information.[226] The panel in *US – DRAMs (1999)* stated the following in support of its position that the text of Article 6.6 does *not* explicitly *require* verification of all information relied upon:

> Article 6.6 simply requires Members to 'satisfy themselves as to the accuracy of the information'. In our view, Members could 'satisfy themselves as to the accuracy of the information'

220 See Article 6.5.1 of the *Anti-Dumping Agreement*. See also Appellate Body Report, *EC – Fasteners (2011)*, para. 542. In exceptional circumstances, parties may indicate that such information is not susceptible of summary. In such exceptional circumstances, a statement of the reasons why summarisation is not possible must be provided. See Appellate Body Report, *EC – Fasteners (2011)*, paras. 535 and 543–4. For the relationship between the disclosure obligation under Article 2.4 and the need to protect confidential information, see Appellate Body Report, *EC – Fasteners (Article 21.5 – China) (2016)*, para. 5.195.

221 Appellate Body Report, *China – HP-SSST (EU)/China – HP-SSST (Japan) (2015)*, para. 5.97; Appellate Body Report, *EC – Fasteners (Article 21.5 – China) (2016)*, para. 5.40.

222 *Ibid.*, para. 5.39 quoting *China – HP-SSST (EU)/China – HP-SSST (Japan) (2015)*, para. 5.95 and *EC – Fasteners (China) (2011)*, para. 537.

223 See Panel Report, *Guatemala – Cement II (2000)*, paras. 8.173–8.174.

224 Regarding the relationship between Article 6.7 and Annex I to the *Anti-Dumping Agreement*, the Appellate Body observed that, while Article 6.7 lays out the basic framework for verifications in the territory of another Member, Annex I, including paragraph 7, sets out further parameters for the conduct of such investigations. Appellate Body Report, *China – HP-SSST (EU)/China – HP-SSST (Japan) (2015)*, para. 5.70.

225 See Annex I to the *Anti-Dumping Agreement* on 'Procedures for on-the-spot investigations pursuant to paragraph 7 of Article 6'.

226 See Appellate Body Report, *China – HP-SSST (EU)/China – HP-SSST (Japan) (2015)*, paras. 5.70ff.

in a number of ways without proceeding to some type of formal verification, including for example reliance on the reputation of the original source of the information. Indeed, we consider that anti-dumping investigations would become totally unmanageable if investigating authorities were required to actually verify the accuracy of all information relied on.[227]

The Appellate Body noted in *China – HP-SSST (EU)/China – HP-SSST (Japan) (2015)* that Article 6.6 stipulates that investigating 'authorities shall during the course of an investigation satisfy themselves as to the accuracy of the information supplied by interested parties upon which their findings are based'.[228] This requirement does not mean, however, that investigating authorities are under an obligation to accept and use all information that is submitted to them. Rather, they have some degree of latitude in deciding whether to accept and use information submitted by an interested party during an on-the-spot investigation or thereafter. This latitude is limited, however, by the investigating authority's obligation under Article 6.6 to ensure that the information on which its findings are based is accurate, and by the legitimate due process interests of the parties to an investigation. The Appellate Body added that, throughout the investigation, an investigating authority must balance these due process interests with the need to control and expedite the investigating process, including during on-the-spot investigations.[229]

Hardly surprisingly, under the *Anti-Dumping Agreement* it is preferred that investigating authorities base their determinations on 'first-hand information'. The Agreement does not, however, allow any party to hold an investigating authority hostage by not providing the necessary information, and thus provides that 'second-best information' from secondary sources may be used in certain well-defined circumstances.[230] Article 6.8 of, and Annex II to, the *Anti-Dumping Agreement* identify the circumstances in which investigating authorities may overcome a lack of information, in the responses of the interested parties, by using 'facts' which are otherwise 'available' to the investigating authorities, i.e. the 'best information available'.[231] As the Appellate Body noted in *Mexico – Anti-Dumping Measures on Rice (2007)*:

[W]e understand that an investigating authority in an anti-dumping investigation may rely on the facts available to calculate margins for a respondent that failed to provide some or

227 Panel Report, *US – DRAMs (1999)*, para. 6.78. The panel in *US – DRAMs (1999)* questioned, for example, 'whether investigating authorities should be required to verify import statistics from a different government office' and 'whether investigating authorities should be required to verify "official" exchange rates obtained from a central bank'. See *ibid.*, para. 6.78, fn. 513.

228 Appellate Body Report, *China – HP-SSST (EU)/China – HP-SSST (Japan) (2015)*, para. 5.73.

229 *Ibid.*, para. 5.74. As to the factors that bear upon the latitude of an investigating authority to accept or reject information submitted during an on-the-spot investigation, the Appellate Body stated that these may include, for example, the timing of the presentation of new information; whether the acceptance of new information would cause undue difficulties in the conduct of the investigation; whether the interested party has submitted voluminous amounts of information or merely seeks to have an arithmetical or clerical error corrected; whether the information at issue relates to facts that are 'essential' within the meaning of Article 6.9; and whether the information supplied by an interested party relates to the information specifically requested by the investigating authority. See *Ibid.*, para. 5.75.

230 See Panel Report, *Mexico – Anti-Dumping Measures on Rice (2005)*, para. 7.238.

231 If the producer submits information meeting the requirements of Annex II, para. 3, no use may be made of 'best information available' under Article 6.8. See Panel Report, *EC – Salmon (Norway) (2008)*, paras. 7.371–7.372.

all of the necessary information requested by the agency. In so doing, however, the agency must first have made the respondent aware that it may be subject to a margin calculated on the basis of the facts available because of the respondent's failure to provide necessary information. Furthermore, assuming a respondent acted to the best of its ability, an agency must generally use, in the first instance, the information the respondent did provide, if any.[232]

Moreover, in *US – Hot-Rolled Steel (2001)*, the Appellate Body held:

According to Article 6.8, where the interested parties do not 'significantly impede' the investigation, recourse may be had to facts available only if an interested party fails to submit necessary information 'within a reasonable period'. Thus, if information is, in fact, supplied 'within a reasonable period', the investigating authorities cannot use facts available, but must use the information submitted by the interested party.[233]

In *EC – Fasteners (2011)*, the Appellate Body reaffirmed its ruling in *US – Hot-Rolled Steel (2001)*, and added that what is a reasonable period in one set of circumstances may prove to be less than reasonable in different circumstances. What is 'reasonable' must be defined on a case-by-case basis, in light of the specific circumstances of each investigation.[234]

Paragraph 7 of Annex II to the *Anti-Dumping Agreement* indicates that a lack of 'cooperation' by an interested party may, by virtue of the use made of facts available, lead to a result that is 'less favourable' to the interested party than would have been the case had that interested party cooperated. In *US – Hot-Rolled Steel (2001)*, the Appellate Body cautioned, however, that investigating authorities should not arrive at a 'less favourable' outcome simply because an interested party fails to furnish requested information if, in fact, the interested party has 'cooperated' with the investigating authorities. Parties may very well 'cooperate' to a high degree, even though the requested information is, ultimately, not obtained.[235] The Appellate Body noted:

In order to complete their investigations, investigating authorities are entitled to expect a very significant degree of effort – to the 'best of their abilities' – from investigated exporters. At the same time, however, the investigating authorities are not entitled to insist upon *absolute* standards or impose *unreasonable* burdens upon those exporters.[236]

232 Appellate Body Report, *Mexico – Anti-Dumping Measures on Rice (2005)*, para. 288.

233 Appellate Body Report, *US – Hot-Rolled Steel (2001)*, para. 77. See also Panel Report, *Guatemala – Cement II (2000)*, para. 8.255, in which the panel found that recourse to the 'best information available' was not warranted because the exporter had *not* impeded the investigation. See also Panel Report, *US – Steel Plate (2002)*, para. 7.55; Panel Report *Egypt – Steel Rebar (2002)*, para. 7.147; Panel Report, *Argentina – Poultry Anti-Dumping Duties (2003)*, para. 7.187; Panel Report, *Korea – Certain Paper (2005)*, para. 7.75; and Appellate Body Report *Mexico – Anti-Dumping Measures on Rice (2005)*, para. 259.

234 Appellate Body Report, *US – Hot-Rolled Steel (2001)*, para. 84. In considering whether information is submitted within a reasonable period of time, 'investigating authorities should consider, in the context of a particular case, factors such as: (i) the nature and quantity of the information submitted; (ii) the difficulties encountered by an investigated exporter in obtaining the information; (iii) the verifiability of the information and the ease with which it can be used by the investigating authorities in making their determination; (iv) whether other interested parties are likely to be prejudiced if the information is used; (v) whether acceptance of the information would compromise the ability of the investigating authorities to conduct the investigation expeditiously; and (vi) the numbers of days by which the investigated exporter missed the applicable time-limit.' See Appellate Body Report, *US – Hot-Rolled Steel (2001)*, para. 85.

235 See Appellate Body Report, *US – Hot-Rolled Steel (2001)*, para. 99.

236 *Ibid.*, para. 102.

It is the common practice of WTO Members to conduct an anti-dumping investigation using data from a fixed 'period of investigation' which precedes the date of initiation of an investigation. The *Anti-Dumping Agreement* refers to the concept of a 'period of investigation', and the use of such a period appears to be implicit in several provisions of the Agreement.[237]

The Appellate Body in *EC – Tube or Pipe Fittings (2003)* agreed with the panel in that case that:

> [d]iscretionary selection of data from a period of time within [a period of investigation] ... would defeat the objectives underlying investigating authorities' reliance on [such a period]. As the Panel correctly noted, the [period of investigation] 'form[s] the basis for an objective and unbiased determination by the investigating authority'.[238]

The Appellate Body further noted:

> [W]e understand a [period of investigation] to provide data collected over a sustained period of time, which period can allow the investigating authority to make a dumping determination that is less likely to be subject to market fluctuations or other vagaries that may distort a proper evaluation. We agree with the Panel that the standardized reliance on a [period of investigation], although not fixed in duration by the *Anti-Dumping Agreement*, assures the investigating authority and exporters of 'a consistent and reasonable methodology for determining present dumping', which anti-dumping duties are intended to offset.[239]

The WTO Committee on Anti-Dumping Practices has adopted a *Recommendation Concerning the Periods of Data Collection for Anti-Dumping Investigations*.[240] Pursuant to this Recommendation, the period of data collection for *dumping investigations* normally should not exceed twelve months and, in any case, be no less than six months, ending as close to the date of initiation as is practicable. Furthermore, the period of data collection for *injury investigations* normally should be at least three years, unless a party from whom data is being gathered has existed for a shorter period, and should include the entirety of the period of data collection for the dumping investigation.[241]

Finally, note with regard to the conduct of an anti-dumping investigation that Article 5.10 of the *Anti-Dumping Agreement* specifies that such investigation must be completed within one year, and in no case be more than eighteen months, after initiation.

6.3 Public Notice and Judicial Review

Article 6.9 and Article 12 of the *Anti-Dumping Agreement* both concern the transparency of the anti-dumping investigations and the conclusions reached.

237 For example, Articles 2.4.2 and 2.2.1 of the *Anti-Dumping Agreement*. See Panel Report, *Mexico – Anti-Dumping Measures on Rice (2005)*, para. 7.65

238 Appellate Body Report, *EC – Tube or Pipe Fittings (2003)*, para. 80. 239 *Ibid.*

240 G/ADP/6, adopted by the Committee on Anti-Dumping Practices on 5 May 2000.

241 While it reflects the common practice of Members, the Recommendation does not have binding effect. See E. Vermulst, *The WTO Anti-Dumping Agreement: A Commentary* (Oxford University Press, 2006), 82–3.

Both provisions require notice to be given to interested parties and/or the general public.

Article 6.9 requires investigating authorities, before a final determination is made, to inform all interested parties of the 'essential facts under consideration' which form the basis for the decision whether to apply definitive measures. Such disclosure should take place in sufficient time for the parties to defend their interests.[242] While Articles 6.4 and 2.4 apply throughout the domestic proceedings, Article 6.9 applies towards the end of the investigation when the authorities are in position to ascertain which facts will be essential for their determination. 'Essential facts' refer to those facts that are significant in the process of reaching a decision as to whether or not to apply definitive measures. Such facts are those that are salient for a decision to apply definitive measures, as well as those that are salient for a contrary outcome. An authority must disclose such facts, in a coherent way, so as to permit an interested party to understand the basis for the decision whether or not to apply definitive measures.[243] As the Appellate Body stated in *China – GOES (2012)*, disclosing the essential facts under consideration pursuant to Article 6.9 is paramount for ensuring the ability of the parties concerned to defend their interests and, therefore, such disclosure should take place in sufficient time for the parties to do so.[244]

In *China – HP-SSST (EU)/China – HP-SSST (Japan) (2015)*, the Appellate Body further clarified that whether a particular fact is essential or 'significant in the process of reaching a decision' depends on the nature and scope of the particular substantive obligations, the content of the particular findings needed to satisfy the substantive obligations at issue, and the factual circumstances of each case, including the arguments and evidence submitted by the interested parties.[245] The Appellate Body did not see how the mere fact that the investigating authority may be referring to data that are in the possession of an interested party would mean that it has disclosed the essential facts in a coherent way, so as to permit an interested party to understand the basis for each of the intermediate findings and conclusions reached by the authority and the decision whether or not to apply definitive measures such that it is able properly to defend its interests.[246]

242 As to the type of information that must be disclosed, Article 6.9 covers 'facts under consideration' in the course of such investigations 'before a final determination is made'. These are facts on the record that may be taken into account by an authority in reaching a decision as to whether or not to apply definitive anti-dumping duties. Article 6.9 does not require the disclosure of *all* the facts that are before an authority but, instead, those that are 'essential', i.e. facts that are significant, important, or salient. See Appellate Body Report, *China – GOES (2012)*, para. 240.

243 See *Ibid.* As discussed above, in order to apply definitive measures at the conclusion of an anti-dumping investigation, an investigating authority must find dumping, injury to the domestic industry and a causal link between dumping and injury. What constitutes an 'essential fact' must therefore be understood in light of the content of the findings needed to satisfy the substantive obligations with respect to the imposition of definitive measures under the *Anti-Dumping Agreement*, as well as the factual circumstances of each case.

244 See *ibid.*, para. 240.

245 Appellate Body Reports, *China – HP-SSST (EU)/China – HP-SSST (Japan) (2015)*, para. 5.130.

246 *Ibid.*, para. 5.131.

Article 12 of the *Anti-Dumping Agreement* contains detailed requirements for public notice by investigating authorities of: (1) the initiation of an investigation (see Article 12.1.1); (2) a preliminary determination (see Article 12.2.1); (3) a final determination (see Article 12.2.2); and (4) a price undertaking (see Article 12.2.2). While the disclosure of 'essential facts' under Article 6.9 must take place *before* a final determination is made, the obligation to give public notice of the conclusion of an investigation within the meaning of Article 12.2.2, for example, is triggered *once there is* an affirmative determination providing for the imposition of definitive duties.[247] The purpose of this public notice requirement set out in Article 12 is to increase the transparency of the determinations made by the investigating authorities and to encourage solid and thorough reasoning substantiating such determinations. The public notice of a final determination, for example, *must* set forth, or otherwise make available through a separate report, in sufficient detail, the findings and conclusions reached on all issues of fact and law considered material by the investigating authorities.[248] The Appellate Body explained in *China – GOES (2012)*, with regard to 'matters of fact', that Article 12.2.2 does not require authorities to disclose *all* the factual information that is before them, but rather those facts that allow an understanding of the factual basis that led to the imposition of final measures. The inclusion of this information should therefore give a reasoned account of the factual support for an authority's decision to impose final measures. Furthermore, the notice or report *must* set out the reasons for the acceptance or rejection of relevant legal arguments or claims made by the exporters and importers.[249] The consistency of notices or reports with the requirements of Article 12.2 of the *Anti-Dumping Agreement* at issue in many disputes.[250] In *EC – Tube or Pipe Fittings (2003)*, for example, the panel found that the European Communities acted inconsistently with Articles 12.2 and 12.2.2 of the *Anti-Dumping Agreement*:

> [i]n that it is not directly discernible from the published Provisional or Definitive Determination that the European Communities addressed or explained the lack of significance of certain listed Article 3.4 factors.[251]

247 See Article 12.2.2 in conjunction with Article 12.2.1 of the *Anti-Dumping Agreement*.

248 See Article 12.2.2 of the *Anti-Dumping Agreement*. Note, however, that Article 12.2.2 does require that due regard be paid to the requirement to protect confidential information. In particular, the notice or report *must* contain: (1) the names of the suppliers, or, when this is impracticable, the supplying countries involved; (2) a description of the product which is sufficient for customs purposes; (3) the margins of dumping established and a full explanation of the reasons for the methodology used in the establishment and comparison of the export price and the normal value under Article 2; (4) considerations relevant to the injury determination as set out in Article 3; and (5) the main reasons leading to the determination. See Article 12.2.2 in conjunction with Article 12.2.1 of the *Anti-Dumping Agreement*. As discussed above, the imposition of final anti-dumping duties requires that an authority finds dumping, injury to the domestic industry, and a causal link between dumping and injury. Therefore, what constitutes 'relevant information on the matters of fact' is to be understood in light of the content of the findings needed to satisfy the substantive requirements with respect to the imposition of final measures under the *Anti-Dumping Agreement*, as well as the factual circumstances of each case. See Appellate Body Report, *China – GOES (2012)*, paras. 256–7.

249 Article 12.2.2 of the *Anti-Dumping Agreement*.

250 See Panel Report, *EC – Tube or Pipe Fittings (2003)*, para. 7.435.

251 Appellate Body Report, *China – GOES (2012)*, para. 258. With respect to the form in which the relevant information must be disclosed, Article 12.2.2 allows authorities to decide whether to include the information in the public notice itself or otherwise make it available through a separate report. See also *ibid.*, para. 259.

In *China – GOES (2012)*, the Appellate Body took the view that Article 12.2.2 captures the principle that those parties whose interests are affected by the imposition of final anti-dumping duties are entitled to know, as a matter of fairness and due process, the facts, law and reasons that have led to the imposition of such duties. The Appellate Body stated in that case:

> The obligation of disclosure under Article 12.2.2 is framed by the requirement of 'relevance', which entails the disclosure of the matrix of facts, law and reasons that logically fit together to render the decision to impose final measures. By requiring the disclosure of 'all relevant information' regarding these categories of information, the provision seeks to guarantee that interested parties are able to pursue judicial review of a final determination as provided in Article 13 of the *Anti-Dumping Agreement*.[252]

As provided for in Article 13, entitled 'Judicial Review', each Member whose national legislation contains provisions on anti-dumping measures must maintain judicial, arbitral or administrative tribunals or procedures to ensure *inter alia*, the prompt review of administrative actions relating to final determinations and reviews of determinations. Such tribunals or procedures must be independent of the authorities responsible for the determination or review in question.[253]

7 ANTI-DUMPING MEASURES

The *Anti-Dumping Agreement* provides for three kinds of anti-dumping measures: (1) provisional measures; (2) price undertakings; and (3) definitive anti-dumping duties. This section discusses the rules on the imposition of each of these measures. It also addresses the issues of the duration, termination and review of definitive anti-dumping duties.

7.1 Imposition of Provisional Anti-Dumping Measures

Article 7 of the *Anti-Dumping Agreement* contains rules relating to the imposition of provisional measures. Before applying a provisional anti-dumping measure, investigating authorities must make a *preliminary* affirmative determination of dumping, injury and causation.[254] Furthermore, the investigating authorities must judge that such a measure is *necessary* to prevent injury being caused during the investigation. A provisional measure cannot be applied earlier than sixty days following the initiation of the investigation.[255] Provisional measures may take the form of a provisional duty or, preferably, a security, by cash deposit or bond, equal to the amount of the preliminarily determined margin of dumping.[256]

252 See Article 13 of the *Anti-Dumping Agreement*. 253 See *ibid.*, Article 7.1(ii).
254 See *ibid.*, Article 7.1(iii). 255 See *ibid.*, Article 7.3.
256 See *ibid.*, Article 7.2.

With regard to the time period for application of the provisional measure, Article 7.4 of the *Anti-Dumping Agreement* states that it:

> [s]hall be limited to as short a period as possible, not exceeding four months or, on decision of the authorities concerned, upon request by exporters representing a significant percentage of the trade involved, to a period not exceeding six months.

Where the Member applies the 'lesser duty rule' in its administration of anti-dumping duties, the period of provisional application is generally six months, with the possibility of extension to nine months upon request of the exporters.[257]

7.2 Price Undertakings

Article 8 of the *Anti-Dumping Agreement* provides for the option of offering and accepting price undertakings as an alternative to the imposition of anti-dumping duties. Undertakings to revise prices or cease exports at the dumped price may be entered into only after the investigating authorities have made an *affirmative preliminary determination* of dumping, injury and causation. Such undertakings are voluntary on the part of both exporters and investigating authorities.[258] An exporter may request that the investigation be continued after the acceptance of an undertaking. The undertaking would then automatically lapse in the event of a negative final determination of dumping, injury or causation.[259]

7.3 Imposition and Collection of Anti-Dumping Duties

Article 9 of the *Anti-Dumping Agreement* governs the imposition and collection of anti-dumping duties. This provision establishes the general principle that 'it is desirable' that, even where all the requirements for imposition of duties have been fulfilled, the imposition of anti-dumping duties remains *optional*. Article 9 also contains the so-called 'lesser duty rule', under which 'it is desirable' that the duty imposed be *less* than the margin of dumping *if* such lesser duty would be *adequate* to remove the injury to the domestic industry.[260]

Article 9.2 of the *Anti-Dumping Agreement* requires Members to collect anti-dumping duties on a *non-discriminatory* basis on imports from 'all sources' found to be dumped and causing injury.[261] The MFN treatment obligation thus

257 On the 'lesser duty rule', see below, p. 858. On the question of the allowable duration of a provisional measure, see Panel Report, *Mexico – Corn Syrup (2000)*, paras. 7.182–7.183.

258 Exporters and investigating authorities may enter into price undertakings over the opposition of the domestic industry. See Panel Report, *US – Offset Act (Byrd Amendment) (2003)*, paras. 7.79ff.

259 Article 8.6 of the *Anti-Dumping Agreement* sets out consequences of violation of an undertaking.

260 The European Union applies the 'lesser duty rule'; the United States usually does not. See P. F. J. Macrory, 'The Anti-Dumping Agreement', in P. Macrory, A. Appleton and M. Plummer (eds.), *The World Trade Organization: Legal, Economic and Political Analysis* (Springer, 2005), 519.

261 See Article 9.2 of the *Anti-Dumping Agreement*. Note, however, that the anti-dumping duty will not be applied to imports from sources in respect of which a price undertaking is in force.

applies to the collection of anti-dumping duties.[262] The competent national authorities should name the supplier or suppliers of the products affected by the anti-dumping duty. However, if several suppliers from the same country are involved, and it is impracticable to name all these suppliers, the authorities may just name the supplying country concerned. If several suppliers from more than one country are involved, the authorities may either name all the suppliers involved or, if this is impracticable, all the supplying countries involved.[263]

Pursuant to Article 9.3 of the *Anti-Dumping Agreement*, the anti-dumping duty collected *shall not exceed* the dumping margin as established under Article 2. As the Appellate Body stated in *US – Zeroing (Japan) (2007)*:

> Under any system of duty collection, the margin of dumping established in accordance with Article 2 operates as a ceiling for the amount of anti-dumping duties that could be collected in respect of the sales made by an exporter. To the extent that duties are paid by an importer, it is open to that importer to claim a refund if such a ceiling is exceeded. Similarly, under its retrospective system of duty collection, the United States is free to assess duty liability on a transaction-specific basis, but the total amount of anti-dumping duties that are levied must not exceed the exporters' or foreign producers' margins of dumping.[264]

In *EU – Biodiesel (2016)*, the Appellate Body upheld the panel's finding that the European Union acted inconsistently with Article 9.3 by imposing anti-dumping duties in excess of the margin of dumping that should have been established under Article 2. The Appellate Body agreed with the panel that the reference to 'margin of dumping' in Article 9.3 relates to a margin that is established consistently with Article 2.[265] However, the Appellate Body also stated that this interpretation does *not* mean that *any error* in the calculation of the dumping margin will *necessarily* lead to a violation of Article 9.3.[266] Since Article 9.3 is concerned with the maximum amount of anti-dumping duties that may be collected, the errors under Article 2 that matter for purposes of Article 9.3 are those that result in a *higher* dumping margin than the one that would have been calculated had the authority acted consistently with Article 2. Not all breaches of Article 2 will invariably or predictably entail such a result.[267] In the Appellate Body's view, the complainant must show that anti-dumping duties are imposed at a rate that is higher than the dumping margin that would have been established had the authority acted consistently with Article 2.[268]

262 See above, pp. 39 and 311–14. The Appellate Body noted in *EC – Fasteners (2011)* that the term 'all sources', as used in Article 9.2, 'refers to individual exporters or producers and not to the country as a whole'. See Appellate Body Report, *EC – Fasteners (2011)*, para. 338.

263 See Article 9.2 of the *Anti-Dumping Agreement*.

264 Appellate Body Report, *US – Zeroing (Japan) (2007)*, para. 162.

265 The Appellate Body concurred with the panel that, in light of the specific circumstances of this dispute, Argentina had made a *prima facie* case that the European Union acted inconsistently with Article 9.3 of the *Anti-Dumping Agreement*, which the European Union had failed to rebut. See Appellate Body Report, *EU – Biodiesel (2016)*, paras. 6.96–6.97, 6.104.

266 According to the Appellate Body, the application of the lesser duty rule provides one example of when this may not be the case.

267 In this respect, the Appellate Body shared the European Union's understanding that a complainant 'must show something more than a simple erroneous calculation of normal value' in order to succeed with a claim under Article 9.3. See Appellate Body Report, *EU – Biodiesel (2016)*, para. 6.104.

268 See *ibid*.

In sum, Article 9.3 lays down the 'margin of dumping' as the *ceiling* for collection of duties regardless of whether the duties are assessed 'retrospectively' or 'prospectively'.[269] In case the ceiling is exceeded, the Agreement provides for a refund obligation.[270]

When anti-dumping duties are imposed, pursuant to Article 6.10 of the *Anti-Dumping Agreement*, the investigating authorities must, 'as a rule', calculate a dumping margin for each known exporter or producer of the product under investigation. However, Article 6.10 recognises that this may not always be possible.[271] As set out in the second sentence of Article 6.10, it may not be possible to determine individual dumping margins in cases where the number of exporters, producers, importers or types of products is so large as to make such determinations impracticable. In such cases, the authorities may deviate from the obligation to determine individual anti-dumping margins for all known exporters or producers, and may limit their examination either: (1) to a reasonable number of interested parties or products by using samples, which are statistically valid; or (2) to the largest percentage of the volume of exports from the country in question that can reasonably be investigated. This limited examination is generally referred to as 'sampling'.[272] When 'sampling' is used, the anti-dumping duty imposed on exporters or producers not examined individually is calculated – in accordance with the first sentence of Article 9.4 of the *Anti-Dumping Agreement* – on the basis of the *weighted average dumping margin* actually established for individually investigated exporters or producers, commonly referred to as the 'all others' rate.[273] However, the investigating authorities: (1) must not include in this weighted average calculation any dumping margins that are *de minimis*, zero or based on the 'facts available'; and

269 See *ibid.*, para. 163. See also Appellate Body Report, *US – Stainless Steel (Mexico) (2008)*, paras. 102, 114 and 133; Appellate Body Report, *US – Zeroing (EC) (2006)*, para. 131; and Appellate Body Report, *US – Softwood Lumber V (Article 21.5 – Canada) (2006)*, para. 108. Which mechanism for duty assessment a Member opts to use will depend on whether the Member collects the anti-dumping duties on a prospective basis (i.e. where a Member collects the duty at the time of importation – as is the case for the European Union) or on a retrospective basis (i.e. where a Member calculates a specific amount of anti-dumping duty to be paid only after permitting importation and collecting an estimated duty – as the United States does). See further Articles 9.3.1 and 9.3.2 of the *Anti-Dumping Agreement*. As the Appellate Body has repeatedly ruled, the *Anti-Dumping Agreement* is neutral as between different systems for levy and collection of anti-dumping duties. See Appellate Body Report, *US – Zeroing (Japan) (2007)*, para. 156.

270 See Appellate Body Report, *US – Zeroing (Japan) (2007)*, para. 163.

271 This will be the case when the number of exporters, producers, importers or types of products concerned is considerable. The Appellate Body noted, in *EC – Fasteners (2011)*, that the obligation in Article 6.10 (see the use of the word 'shall') is qualified by the use of the term 'as a rule'. The use of this term indicates that the obligation in Article 6.10 is not absolute, and foreshadows the possibility of exceptions. The Appellate Body added, however, that, while the term 'as a rule' should be read as modifying the obligation to determine individual margins, it does not render it a mere preference. Otherwise, the use of 'shall' in the first sentence would be deprived of its ordinary meaning. See Appellate Body Report, *EC – Fasteners (2011)*, para. 317.

272 Even where a statistically valid sample is not used but the second alternative for limiting the examination is applied, such examination is commonly referred to as 'sampling'. See Appellate Body Report, *EC – Fasteners (2011)*, para. 318. 'Sampling' is the only exception to the determination of individual dumping margins that is expressly provided for in Article 6.10. See *ibid.*

273 Note, in this context, Panel Report, *Korea – Certain Paper (2005)*, para. 7.171.

(2) must calculate an individual margin for any exporter or producer who provides the necessary information during the course of the investigation.[274] With respect to the 'all others' rate applied to sources not examined individually, the Appellate Body stated in *US – Hot-Rolled Steel (2001)*:

> Article 9.4 does not prescribe any method that WTO Members must use to establish the 'all others' rate that is actually applied to exporters or producers that are not investigated. Rather, Article 9.4 simply identifies a maximum limit, or ceiling, which investigating authorities '*shall not exceed*' in establishing an 'all others' rate.[275]

With respect to the individual margin of dumping for producers or exporters who were not sources of imports considered during the period of investigation, commonly referred to as 'new shippers', Article 9.5 of the *Anti-Dumping Agreement* provides that:

> [t]he authorities shall promptly carry out a review for the purpose of determining individual margins of dumping.

The investigating authorities must therefore conduct an expedited review to determine a specific margin of dumping for exports from such 'new shippers'. No anti-dumping duties may be levied on imports from such exporters or producers while the review is being carried out.[276]

Article 10 of the *Anti-Dumping Agreement* establishes the general principle that both provisional and definitive duties may be applied only as of the date on which the preliminary or final determinations of dumping, injury and causation have been made.[277] *Retroactive application* of anti-dumping duties is thus, in principle, prohibited. However, Article 10 contains rules for the retroactive application of anti-dumping duties in specific circumstances. According to Article 10.2, where the imposition of the anti-dumping duty is based on a determination of material injury – as opposed to a threat thereof, or material retardation – the duties may be collected as of the date of imposition of the provisional measures.[278] If provisional duties were collected in an amount exceeding

274 See Article 9.4 of the *Anti-Dumping Agreement*. Also, when a dumping margin was calculated, even if only to a very limited extent, on the basis of 'facts available' pursuant to Article 6.8 of the *Anti-Dumping Agreement*, this dumping margin may not be used to calculate the 'all others' rate. See Appellate Body Report, *US – Hot-Rolled Steel (2001)*, paras. 122–3.

275 Appellate Body Report, *US – Hot-Rolled Steel (2011)*, para. 116. Article 9.4 of the *Anti-Dumping Agreement* seeks to prevent exporters who were not asked to cooperate in the investigation from being prejudiced by gaps or shortcomings in the information supplied by the investigated exporters. See *ibid.*, para. 123. The Appellate Body explained that this *lacuna* arises because, while Article 9.4 *prohibits* the use of certain margins in the calculation of the ceiling for the 'all others' rate, it does not expressly address the issue of *how* that ceiling should be calculated in the event that *all* margins are to be *excluded* from the calculation, under the prohibitions in Article 9.4. See Appellate Body Report, *US – Hot-Rolled Steel (2001)*, para. 126.

276 See Article 9.5 of the *Anti-Dumping Agreement*. The authorities may, however, withhold appraisal and/or request guarantees to ensure that, if necessary, anti-dumping duties can be levied retroactively to the date of the initiation of the review. See also Appellate Body Report, *Mexico – Anti-Dumping Measures on Rice (2005)*, paras. 323–4. Finally, the Appellate Body found zeroing in calculating dumping margins for new shippers to be inconsistent with Article 9.5 of the *Anti-Dumping Agreement*. See Appellate Body Report, *US – Zeroing (Japan) (2007)*, para. 165.

277 See Article 10.1 of the *Anti-Dumping Agreement*.

278 See Article 10.2 of the *Anti-Dumping Agreement*.

the amount of the final duty or if the imposition of duties is based on a finding of threat of material injury or of material retardation, a refund of provisional duties is necessary.[279] Article 10.6 also permits retroactive application of final anti-dumping duties in exceptional circumstances. These exceptional circumstances involve: (1) a history of dumping which caused injury; *or* a situation in which the importer was, or should have been, aware that the exporter practises injurious dumping; and (2) the injury is caused by massive dumped imports in a short time which is likely to undermine the remedial effect of the definitive anti-dumping duty (this may be the case because of a rapid and massive build-up of stocks of the imported product).[280] In these circumstances, Article 10.6 permits *retroactive application* of final duties to a date not earlier than ninety days prior to the application of provisional measures.[281]

7.4 Duration, Termination and Review of Anti-Dumping Duties

Responding to the concern of some Members that some countries were leaving anti-dumping duties in place indefinitely, Article 11 of the *Anti-Dumping Agreement* establishes rules governing the duration of anti-dumping duties and a requirement for the periodic review of any continuing necessity for the imposition of anti-dumping duties. With respect to the duration of anti-dumping duties, Article 11.1 of the *Anti-Dumping Agreement* provides:

> An anti-dumping duty shall remain in force only as long as and to the extent necessary to counteract dumping which is causing injury.[282]

The Appellate Body considered in *US – Anti-Dumping Measures on Oil Country Tubular Goods (2005)* that:

> Article 11.1 of the Agreement establishes an overarching principle for 'duration' and 'review' of anti-dumping duties in force ... This principle applies during the entire life of an anti-dumping duty. If, at any point in time, it is demonstrated that no injury is being caused to the domestic industry by the dumped imports, the rationale for the continuation of the duty would cease.[283]

With respect to the periodic review of anti-dumping duties applied, Article 11.2, first sentence, requires the investigating authorities to:

> review the need for the continued imposition of the duty, where warranted, on their own initiative or, provided that a reasonable period of time has elapsed since the imposition

279 See Article 10.3 of the *Anti-Dumping Agreement*. Note, however, that, if the final anti-dumping duty is higher than the provisional duty, the difference may *not* be collected.

280 See Article 10.6 of the *Anti-Dumping Agreement*.

281 Once the authorities have 'sufficient evidence' that the conditions of Article 10.6 are satisfied, they may take the conservatory or precautionary measures provided for in Article 10.7. On what constitutes 'sufficient evidence', and other issues relating to Articles 10.6 and 10.7, see Panel Report, *US – Hot-Rolled Steel (2001)*, paras. 7.143–7.144; and Panel Report, *Mexico – Corn Syrup (2000)*, paras. 7.190–7.191.

282 Article 11.2, last sentence, provides: 'If as a result of the review under [paragraph 2] the authorities determine that the anti-dumping duty is no longer warranted, it shall be terminated immediately.'

283 Appellate Body Report, *US – Anti-Dumping Measures on Oil Country Tubular Goods (2005)*, para. 115. See also Appellate Body Report, *US – Stainless Steel (Mexico) (2008)*, para. 93.

of the definitive anti-dumping duty, upon request by any interested party which submits positive information substantiating the need for a review.[284]

The Appellate Body in *Mexico – Anti-Dumping Measures on Rice (2005)* found that:

Article 11.2 *requires* an agency to conduct a review, *inter alia*, at the request of an interested party, and to terminate the anti-dumping duty where the agency determines that the duty 'is no longer warranted'. The interested party has the right to request the authority to examine whether the continued imposition of the duty is necessary to offset dumping, whether the injury would be likely to continue or recur if the duty were removed or varied, or both. Article 11.2 conditions this obligation on (i) the passage of a reasonable period of time since imposition of the definitive duty; and (ii) the submission by the interested party of 'positive information' substantiating the need for a review. As the Panel correctly observed, this latter condition may be satisfied in a particular case with information not related to export volumes. Where the conditions in Article 11.2 have been met, the plain words of the provision make it clear that the agency has no discretion to refuse to complete a review, including consideration of whether the duty should be terminated in the light of the results of the review.[285]

The second sentence of Article 11.2 requires investigating authorities to examine whether the 'continued imposition' of the duty is necessary to offset dumping. The panel in *US – DRAMs (1999)* interpreted the second sentence as follows:

The word 'continued' covers a temporal relationship between past and future. In our view, the word 'continued' would be redundant if the investigating authority were restricted to considering only whether the duty was necessary to offset *present* dumping. Thus, the inclusion of the word 'continued' signifies that the investigating authority is entitled to examine whether imposition of the duty may be applied henceforth to offset dumping.[286]

Furthermore, with regard to injury, Article 11.2, second sentence, provides for a review of 'whether the injury would be likely to continue or recur if the duty were removed or varied'. The panel in *US – DRAMs (1999)* stated in this respect that:

[i]n conducting an Article 11.2 injury review, an investigating authority may examine the causal link between injury and dumped imports. If, in the context of a review of such a causal link, the only injury under examination is injury that may recur following revocation (i.e. future rather than present injury), an investigating authority must necessarily be examining whether that future injury would be caused by dumping with a commensurately prospective timeframe. To do so, the investigating authority would first need to have established a status regarding the prospects of dumping. For these reasons, we do not agree that Article 11.2 precludes *a priori* the justification of continued imposition of anti-dumping duties when there is no present dumping.

284 The determination of whether or not good and sufficient grounds exist for the self-initiation of a review necessarily depends upon the factual situation in a given case and will vary from case to case. See Panel Report, *EC – Tube or Pipe Fittings (2003)*, para. 7.115. Where an interested party requests a review, the need for the continued imposition of the duty must be demonstrable on the basis of the evidence adduced. See Panel Report, *US – DRAMs (2007)*, para. 6.42.

285 Appellate Body Report, *Mexico – Anti-Dumping Measures on Rice (2005)*, para. 314.

286 Panel Report, *US – DRAMs (1999)*, para. 6.27.

In addition, we note that there is nothing in the text of Article 11.2 of the [Anti-Dumping] Agreement that explicitly limits a Member to a 'present' analysis, and forecloses a prospective analysis, when conducting an Article 11.2 review.[287]

In other words, Article 11.2 does not preclude *a priori* continued imposition of anti-dumping duties in the *absence* of present dumping. However, it may also be clear from the plain meaning of the text of Article 11.2 that the continued imposition must still satisfy the 'necessity' standard, even where the need for the continued imposition of an anti-dumping duty is tied to the *recurrence* of dumping.[288]

Pursuant to Article 11.3 (the so-called 'sunset clause'), any definitive anti-dumping duty shall be *terminated* on a date not later than *five years* from its imposition,[289] *unless* the authorities determine, in a review initiated before that date, that the expiry of the duty 'would be likely to lead to continuation or recurrence of dumping and injury'.[290] Such a review is commonly referred to as a 'sunset review'. It can be initiated: (1) at the initiative of the investigating authorities; or (2) upon a duly substantiated request made by or on behalf of the domestic industry.[291] Any such review shall be carried out expeditiously and shall normally be concluded within twelve months of the date of initiation of the review.[292] In *US – Oil Country Tubular Goods Sunset Reviews (2004)*, the Appellate Body noted:

[A] decision not to terminate an anti-dumping duty must be based on determinations of likelihood of continuation or recurrence of dumping and likelihood of continuation or recurrence of injury.[293]

In *US – Corrosion-Resistant Steel Sunset Review (2004)*, the Appellate Body explained the difference between original investigations and sunset reviews:

In an original anti-dumping investigation, investigating authorities must determine whether *dumping exists* during the period of investigation. In contrast, in a sunset review of an

287 See *ibid.*, paras. 6.28–6.29.

288 See *ibid.*, para. 6.43. Note also that the panel in *US – DRAMs (1999)* found that, with regard to injury, an absence of dumping during the preceding three years and six months is not in and of itself indicative of the likely state of the relevant domestic industry if the duty were removed or varied. Likewise, with regard to causality, an absence of dumping during the preceding three years and six months is not in and of itself indicative of causal factors other than the absence of dumping. See *ibid.*, para. 6.59.

289 Or, alternatively, from the date of the most recent review under Article 11.2, if that review has covered both dumping and injury, or the date of the most recent review under Article 11.3.

290 The duty may remain in force pending the outcome of such a review. See Article 11.3 of the *Anti-Dumping Agreement*.

291 See *ibid.*

292 See *ibid.*, Article 11.4. The provisions of Article 6 of the *Anti-Dumping Agreement* regarding evidence and procedure shall apply to any review carried out under Article 11.

293 Appellate Body Report, *US – Oil Country Tubular Goods Sunset Reviews (2004)*, para. 323. In *US – Corrosion-Resistant Steel Sunset Review (2004)*, the Appellate Body agreed with the panel that Article 11.3 does not expressly prescribe any specific methodology for investigating authorities to use in making a likelihood determination in a sunset review. Nor does Article 11.3 identify any particular factors that authorities must take into account in making such a determination. Thus, Article 11.3 neither explicitly requires authorities in a sunset review to calculate fresh dumping margins, nor explicitly prohibits them from relying on dumping margins calculated in the past. This silence in the text of Article 11.3 suggests that no obligation is imposed on investigating authorities to calculate or rely on dumping margins in a sunset review. See Appellate Body Report, *US – Corrosion-Resistant Steel Sunset Review (2004)*, para. 123.

anti-dumping duty, investigating authorities must determine whether the expiry of the duty that was imposed at the conclusion of an original investigation would be *likely to lead to continuation or recurrence of dumping.*[294]

In *US – Corrosion-Resistant Steel Sunset Review (2004)*, the Appellate Body furthermore explained the structure and content of the sunset review provisions:

Article 11.3 imposes a temporal limitation on the maintenance of anti-dumping duties. It lays down a mandatory rule with an exception. Specifically, Members are required to terminate an anti-dumping duty within five years of its imposition '*unless*' the following conditions are satisfied: first, that a review be initiated before the expiry of five years from the date of the imposition of the duty; second, that in the review the authorities determine that the expiry of the duty would be likely to lead to continuation or recurrence of *dumping*; and third, that in the review the authorities determine that the expiry of the duty would be likely to lead to continuation or recurrence of *injury*. If any one of these conditions is not satisfied, the duty must be terminated.[295]

The panel in *US – DRAMs (1999)* observed with regard to the termination of a definitive anti-dumping duty five years from its imposition that:

[s]uch termination is conditional. First, the terms of Article 11.3 itself lay down that this should occur unless the authorities determine that the expiry would be 'likely to lead to continuation or recurrence of dumping and injury'. Where there is a determination that both are likely, the duty may remain in force, and the five year clock is reset to start again from that point. Second, Article 11.3 provides also for another situation whereby this five year period can be otherwise effectively extended, viz in a situation where a review under paragraph 2 covering both dumping and injury has taken place. If, for instance, such a review took place at the four year point, it could effectively extend the sunset review until 9 years from the original determination. In the first case, we note that the provisions of Article 11.3 explicitly [condition] the prolongation of the five year period on a finding that there is *likelihood* of dumping and injury continuing or recurring. In the second case, where there is reference to review under Article 11.2, there is no such explicit reference.[296]

However, since both instances of review (i.e. review and sunset review) have the same practical effect of prolonging the application of anti-dumping duties beyond five years, the panel in *US – DRAMs (1999)* argued that the investigating authorities are entitled to apply the same test concerning the likelihood of recurrence or the continuation of dumping for both Article 11.2 and Article 11.3 reviews.

Moreover, in *US – Anti-Dumping Measures on Oil Country Tubular Goods (2005)*, the Appellate Body found in the context of sunset reviews that Article 11.3 does not require investigating authorities to establish the existence of a 'causal link' between likely dumping and likely injury, but that:

[i]nstead, by its terms, Article 11.3 requires investigating authorities to determine whether the *expiry of the duty* would be likely to lead to *continuation or recurrence of dumping and*

294 Appellate Body Report, *US – Corrosion-Resistant Steel Sunset Review (2004)*, para. 107.

295 *Ibid.*, para. 104; Appellate Body Report, *US – Oil Country Tubular Goods Sunset Reviews (Article 21.5 – Argentina) (2007)*, para. 163.

296 Panel Report, *US – DRAMs (1999)*, para. 6.48, fn. 494.

> *injury*. Thus, in order to continue the duty, there must be a nexus between the 'expiry of the duty', on the one hand, and 'continuation or recurrence of dumping and injury', on the other hand, such that the former 'would be likely to lead to' the latter. This nexus must be clearly demonstrated.[297]

Finally, the Appellate Body described the standard of review applicable in assessing sunset reviews in *US – Corrosion-Resistant Steel Sunset Review (2004)* as follows:

> This language in Article 11.3 makes clear that it envisages a process combining *both* investigatory and adjudicatory aspects. In other words, Article 11.3 assigns an active rather than a passive decision-making role to the authorities. The words 'review' and 'determine' in Article 11.3 suggest that authorities conducting a sunset review must act with an appropriate degree of diligence and arrive at a reasoned conclusion on the basis of information gathered as part of a process of reconsideration and examination. In view of the use of the word 'likely' in Article 11.3, an affirmative likelihood determination may be made only if the evidence demonstrates that dumping would be probable if the duty were terminated – and not simply if the evidence suggests that such a result might be possible or plausible.[298]

In addition, as the Appellate Body has explained, a sunset review determination must be made on the basis of a 'rigorous examination'[299] leading to 'reasoned and adequate conclusions',[300] and must be supported by 'positive evidence' and a 'sufficient factual basis'.[301]

7.5 Problem of Circumvention of Anti-Dumping Duties

As explained above, anti-dumping duties are typically levied on a specific product of a specific exporter or producer from a specific country. An exporter or producer may try to change the characteristics of the product concerned so that it no longer corresponds to the characteristics of the product subject to an anti-dumping duty. An exporter or producer also may move part of its assembly or manufacturing operations to the importing country or to a third country so that the product arguably no longer originates in the country an anti-dumping duty was imposed. In short, the exporter or producer may attempt to avoid or 'circumvent' the anti-dumping duties. Members have different ways of approaching this problem and the question as to what extent the 'new' products may continue to be subject to the existing anti-dumping duties.[302] The problem

297 Appellate Body Report, *US – Anti-Dumping Measures on Oil Country Tubular Goods (2005)*, para. 108.

298 Appellate Body Report, *US – Corrosion-Resistant Steel Sunset Review (2004)*, para. 111. Although the panel did not elaborate with respect to the meaning of 'likely', or expressly state that 'likely' means 'probable', the Appellate Body concluded that nothing in the Panel Report suggested that the panel was of the view that 'likely' does not mean 'probable', or that 'likely' means 'anything less than probable'. Appellate Body Report, *US – Oil Country Tubular Goods Sunset Reviews (2004)*, para. 309.

299 Appellate Body Report, *US – Corrosion-Resistant Steel Sunset Review (2004)*, para. 113.

300 *Ibid.*, para. 114 (quoting Panel Report, *US – Corrosion-Resistant Steel Sunset Review (2004)*, para. 7.271).

301 *Ibid.*

302 The rules of the European Communities on anti-circumvention were found inconsistent with Article III:2 of the GATT 1947 because they provided for an internal tax not applied to like products of EC origin and were found to be inconsistent with Article III:4 of the GATT 1947 because they made the grant of an advantage dependent on an undertaking to limit the use of Japanese parts or materials. See GATT Panel Report, *EEC – Parts and Components*, paras. 5.9 and 5.21.

of circumvention and anti-circumvention measures was on the agenda of the Uruguay Round but no agreement on specific rules was reached. The matter was referred to the WTO Committee on Anti-Dumping Practices for resolution.[303]

8 INSTITUTIONAL AND PROCEDURAL PROVISIONS OF THE *ANTI-DUMPING AGREEMENT*

As with most WTO agreements, the *Anti-Dumping Agreement* also contains a few institutional and procedural provisions. This section discusses in turn: (1) the Anti-Dumping Committee; and (2) dispute settlement regarding rights and obligations under the *Anti-Dumping Agreement.*

8.1 The Committee on Anti-Dumping Practices

The Committee on Anti-Dumping Practices, commonly referred to as the Anti-Dumping Committee, is composed of representatives of each Member. It met twice in 2016. According to Article 16.1, the Committee carries out the responsibilities assigned to it under the Agreement. It reviews Members' notifications of any changes of laws and regulations relevant to the Agreement and in the administration of such laws and regulations pursuant to Article 18.5. The Committee conducts an annual review of the implementation and operation of the Agreement as foreseen by Article 18.6 and informs the Council for Trade in Goods of developments. Article 16.4 requires Members to report all preliminary or definitive anti-dumping actions taken. They also have to submit, on a half-yearly basis, reports on any anti-dumping actions taken within the preceding six months. In accordance with Article 16.5, each Member has to notify the Committee which of its authorities are competent to initiate and conduct investigations and domestic procedures governing such investigations. Article 16.2 authorises the Anti-Dumping Committee to establish subsidiary bodies (such as the working groups on implementation and anti-circumvention). Pursuant to Article 16.3, the Committee and its subsidiary bodies may consult with and seek information from any source.

8.2 Dispute Settlement

As noted above, the rights and obligations under the *Anti-Dumping Agreement* have given rise to a significant number of disputes.[304] Pursuant to Article 17.1 of the *Anti-Dumping Agreement*, disputes between Members on the consistency of

303 See the Uruguay Round *Decision on Anti-Circumvention.* 304 See above, p. 702.

anti-dumping measures with the obligations under the Agreement are subject to the general rules on WTO dispute settlement contained in the Dispute Settlement Understanding (DSU), *except as otherwise provided.* This section discusses the special or additional dispute settlement rules and procedures provided for in Article 17 of the *Anti-Dumping Agreement.* This section addresses: (1) the standard of review under Article 17.6; and (2) other special or additional rules and procedures set out in Articles 17.4, 17.5 and 17.7.

8.2.1 Standard of Review

As discussed in Chapter 3, Article 11 of the DSU sets forth the appropriate standard of review for panels, the 'objective assessment' standard.[305] Article 17.6 of the *Anti-Dumping Agreement*, however, provides for two special rules with regard to the standard of review that applies to panels hearing disputes concerning anti-dumping measures.

The first of these special rules on the standard of review is found in Article 17.6(i) of the *Anti-Dumping Agreement*, which states:

> [I]n its assessment of the facts of the matter, the panel shall determine whether the authorities' establishment of the facts was proper and whether their evaluation of those facts was unbiased and objective. If the establishment of the facts was proper and the evaluation was unbiased and objective, even though the panel might have reached a different conclusion, the evaluation shall not be overturned.

In this context, the Appellate Body emphasised that it is 'important to bear in mind the different roles of panels and investigating authorities'.[306] Investigating authorities are charged with making factual determinations relevant to their overall determination of dumping and injury, while the 'task of panels is simply to review the investigating authorities' "establishment" and "evaluation" of the facts'.[307] The Appellate Body further explained that Article 17.6(i) requires a panel not to engage in a 'new and independent fact-finding exercise',[308] or to conduct a *de novo* review of the evidence before an investigating authority.[309] Rather, the mandate of the panel is confined to examining whether the evaluation of the evidence by the investigating authority was 'unbiased and objective'.[310] In doing so, a panel should consider all information, *both* confidential and non-confidential, that was *before* the investigating authority.[311] In *China – HP-SSST (EU)/ China – HP-SSST (Japan) (2015)*, the Appellate Body stated:

305 See above, pp. 220–5. 306 Appellate Body Report, *US – Hot-Rolled Steel (2001)*, para. 55.

307 *Ibid.*

308 Appellate Body Report, *Mexico – Corn Syrup (Article 21.5 – US) (2001)*, para. 84.

309 See Panel Report, *US – Steel Plate (2002)*, para. 7.6; and Panel Report, *Egypt – Steel Rebar (2002)*, paras. 7.8 and 7.14.

310 See Panel Report, *Mexico – Corn Syrup (2000)*, para. 7.94; Panel Report, *Guatemala – Cement II (2000)*, para. 8.19; Panel Report, *Thailand – H-Beams (2001)*, para. 7.51; Panel Report, *US – Stainless Steel (Mexico) (2008)*, para. 6.3; and Panel Report, *US – Hot-Rolled Steel (2001)*, para. 7.26.

311 See Appellate Body Report, *Thailand – H-Beams (2001)*, paras. 113–20. See also Panel Report, *EC – Tube or Pipe Fittings (2003)*, para. 7.45.

> We recall that the task of a WTO panel is to examine whether the investigating authority has adequately performed its investigative function, and has adequately explained how the evidence supports its conclusions. It follows from the requirement that the investigating authority provide a 'reasoned and adequate' explanation for its conclusions that the entire rationale for the investigating authority's decision must be set out in its report on the determination. This is not to say that the meaning of a determination cannot be explained or buttressed by referring to evidence on the record. Yet, in all instances, it is the explanation provided in the written report of the investigating authorities (and supporting documents) that is to be assessed in order to determine whether the determination was sufficiently explained and reasoned.[312]

Read together with Article 11 of the DSU, panels operating under the mandate of Article 17.6(i) of the *Anti-Dumping Agreement* should make an *objective* review of the investigating authority's establishment and evaluation of facts.[313] In interpreting Article 17.6(i), the Appellate Body largely assimilated the standard of review under that special provision to the general standard of review found in Article 11 of the DSU. In *US – Hot-Rolled Steel (2001)*, the Appellate Body noted that Article 17.6(i):

> [r]eflects closely the obligation imposed on panels under Article 11 of the DSU to make an '*objective assessment* of the *facts*'. [I]t is inconceivable that Article 17.6(i) should require anything other than that panels make an *objective* 'assessment of the facts of the matter'. In this respect, we see no 'conflict' between Article 17.6(i) of the *Anti-Dumping Agreement* and Article 11 of the DSU.[314]

The second special rule on the standard of review is set out in Article 17.6(ii) of the *Anti-Dumping Agreement*, which states:

> [T]he panel shall interpret the relevant provisions of the Agreement in accordance with customary rules of interpretation of public international law. Where the panel finds that a relevant provision of the Agreement admits of more than one permissible interpretation, the panel shall find the authorities' measure to be in conformity with the Agreement if it rests upon one of those permissible interpretations.[315]

Not surprisingly, the first sentence of Article 17.6(ii) requires panels to 'interpret the relevant provisions of the Agreement in accordance with customary rules of interpretation of public international law'. However, the second sentence of Article 17.6(ii) then continues with one of the most controversial rules of the *Anti-Dumping Agreement.*[316] According to the second sentence of Article 17.6(ii), '[w]here the panel finds that a relevant provision ... admits of more than one

312 Appellate Body Report, *China – HP-SSST (EU)/China – HP-SSST (Japan) (2015)*, para. 5.255.

313 See Appellate Body Report, *US – Hot-Rolled Steel (2001)*, paras. 55 and 62; Panel Report, *US – Steel Plate (2002)*, para. 7.5; Appellate Body Report, *Mexico – Corn Syrup (Article 21.5 – US) (2001)*, para. 130; and Panel Report, *Korea – Certain Paper (2005)*, paras. 6.1–6.3.

314 Appellate Body Report, *US – Hot-Rolled Steel (2001)*, para. 55.

315 See Article 17.6(ii) of the *Anti-Dumping Agreement*. See Appellate Body Report, *US – Softwood Lumber V (Article 21.5 – Canada) (2005)*, para. 123.

316 In several anti-dumping dispute settlement proceedings, the question arose whether, on the basis of the second sentence of Article 17.6(ii), zeroing in the calculation of dumping margins can be found to be one of the permissible interpretations of the relevant substantive provisions of the *Anti-Dumping Agreement*. See also separate opinion in *US – Washing Machines (2016)*, para. 5.202.

permissible interpretation, the panel shall find the authorities' measure to be in conformity with the Agreement if it rests upon one of the permissible interpretations'. The Appellate Body acknowledged in *US – Hot-Rolled Steel (2001)* that:

[t]he *second* sentence of Article 17.6(ii) *presupposes* that application of the rules of treaty interpretation in Articles 31 and 32 of the *Vienna Convention* could give rise to, at least, two interpretations of some provisions of the *Anti-Dumping Agreement*, which, under that Convention, would both be '*permissible* interpretations'.[317]

The Appellate Body subsequently observed in *US – Continued Zeroing (2009)*:

Article 17.6(ii) contemplates a sequential analysis. The first step requires a panel to apply the customary rules of interpretation to the treaty to see what is yielded by a conscientious application of such rules including those codified in the *Vienna Convention*. Only *after* engaging this exercise will a panel be able to determine whether the second sentence of Article 17.6(ii) applies. The structure and logic of Article 17.6(ii) therefore do not permit a panel to determine first whether an interpretation is permissible under the second sentence and then to seek validation of that permissibility by recourse to the first sentence.[318]

In the same case, the Appellate Body further stated that the second sentence of Article 17.6(ii):

[c]annot be interpreted in a way that would render it redundant, or that derogates from the customary rules of interpretation of public international law ... [T]he second sentence allows for the possibility that the application of the rules of the *Vienna Convention* may give rise to an interpretative range and, if it does, an interpretation falling within that range is permissible and must be given effect by holding the measure to be in conformity with the covered agreement.[319]

According to the Appellate Body, the rules and principles of the *Vienna Convention* cannot, however, contemplate interpretations with mutually contradictory results.[320] As the Appellate Body explained, the enterprise of interpretation is intended to ascertain the proper meaning of a provision – one that fits harmoniously with the terms, context and object and purpose of the treaty. The purpose of such an exercise is therefore to narrow the range of interpretations, not to generate conflicting, competing interpretations.[321] According to the Appellate Body, it would be a subversion of the interpretative disciplines of the *Vienna Convention* if application of those disciplines yielded contradiction instead of coherence and harmony among all relevant treaty provisions.[322] The Appellate Body then concluded by observing:

Moreover, a permissible interpretation for purposes of the second sentence of Article 17.6(ii) is not the result of an inquiry that asks whether a provision of domestic law is 'necessarily excluded' by the application of the *Vienna Convention*. Such an approach subverts the hierarchy between the treaty and municipal law. It is the proper interpretation of a covered agreement that is the enterprise with which Article 17.6(ii) is engaged, not whether the

317 Appellate Body Report, *US – Hot-Rolled Steel (2001)*, para. 59.
318 Appellate Body Report, *US – Continued Zeroing (2009)*, para. 271.
319 *Ibid.*, para. 272. 320 See *ibid.*, para. 273.
321 See *ibid.* 322 See *ibid.*

treaty can be interpreted consistently with a particular Member's municipal law or with municipal laws of Members as they existed at the time of the conclusion of the relevant treaty.[323]

In applying this interpretation of Article 17.6(ii) to the relevant provisions of the *Anti-Dumping Agreement*, the Appellate Body in *US – Continued Zeroing (2009)* ultimately found that the United States' practice of 'zeroing' did not rest upon a 'permissible interpretation' of any provision of the *Anti-Dumping Agreement*.[324]

8.2.2 Other Special or Additional Rules and Procedures

As noted above, further special and additional rules and procedures, set out in Articles 17.4, 17.5 and 17.7, apply to disputes under the *Anti-Dumping Agreement*. If consultations failed to achieve a mutually agreed solution and if final action has been taken by anti-dumping authorities, according to Article 17.4, the matter may be referred to the Dispute Settlement Body (DSB). When a provisional measure has a significant impact and is alleged to be contrary to the requirements relating to provisional measures under Article 7, such measure may also be referred to the DSB. At the request of the complaining party, the DSB shall, as provided for by Article 17.5, establish a panel to examine the matter, (i) based on a written statement indicating how a Member considers that a benefit accruing to it, directly or indirectly, under the Agreement has been nullified or impaired, and (ii) on the basis of the facts made available to the investigating authorities in conformity with appropriate domestic procedures. Article 17.7 requires that confidential information provided to the panel not be disclosed without formal authorisation from the person, body or authority providing such information. In the absence of such authorisation to disclose, a non-confidential summary shall be provided.

9 SPECIAL AND DIFFERENTIAL TREATMENT FOR DEVELOPING-COUNTRY MEMBERS

As with many other WTO agreements, the *Anti-Dumping Agreement* contains a provision relating to special and differential treatment for developing-country Members. Article 15 of the *Anti-Dumping Agreement* states:

> It is recognized that special regard must be given by developed country Members to the special situation of developing country Members when considering the application of anti-dumping measures under this Agreement. Possibilities of constructive remedies provided for by this Agreement shall be explored before applying anti-dumping duties where they would affect the essential interests of developing country Members.

323 *Ibid.* 324 See above, pp. 712–20.

The panel in *EC – Tube or Pipe Fittings (2003)* characterised Article 15 as follows:

> [T]here is no requirement for any specific outcome set out in the first sentence of Article 15. We are furthermore of the view that, even assuming that the first sentence of Article 15 imposes a general obligation on Members, it clearly contains no operational language delineating the precise extent or nature of that obligation or requiring a developed country Member to undertake any specific action. The second sentence serves to provide operational indications as to the nature of the specific action required. Fulfilment of the obligations in the second sentence of Article 15 would therefore necessarily, in our view, constitute fulfilment of any general obligation that might arguably be contained in the first sentence.[325]

While Article 15 clearly does not impose an obligation to actually provide or accept any constructive remedy that may be identified and/or offered, according to the panel in *EC – Bed Linen (2001)*, Article 15 does, however, impose an obligation to actively consider, with an open mind, the possibility of such a remedy prior to imposition of an anti-dumping measure that would affect the essential interests of a developing country.[326] For example, a developed-country Member that fails to acknowledge the willingness of a developing-country Member to enter into a price undertaking would fail to 'explore constructive remedies' and act inconsistently with Article 15.

With respect to the meaning of the phrase 'constructive remedies provided for by this Agreement' in the second sentence of Article 15, the panel in *EC – Bed Linen (2001)* rejected the argument that a 'constructive remedy' might be a decision not to impose anti-dumping duties at all. The panel stated that:

> Article 15 refers to 'remedies' in respect of injurious dumping. A decision not to impose an anti-dumping duty, while clearly within the authority of a Member under Article 9.1 of the [Anti-Dumping] Agreement, is not a 'remedy' of any type, constructive or otherwise.[327]

Addressing what the phrase 'constructive remedies provided for by this Agreement' might encompass, the panel in *EC – Bed Linen (2001)* stated:

> The Agreement provides for the imposition of anti-dumping duties, either in the full amount of the dumping margin, or desirably, in a lesser amount, or the acceptance of price undertakings, as a means of resolving an anti-dumping investigation resulting in a final affirmative determination of dumping, injury, and causal link. Thus, in our view, imposition of a lesser duty, or a price undertaking would constitute 'constructive remedies' within the meaning of Article 15. We come to no conclusions as to what other actions might in addition be considered to constitute 'constructive remedies' under Article 15, as none have been proposed to us.[328]

325 Panel Report, *EC – Tube or Pipe Fittings (2003)*, para. 7.68. On the meaning of the first sentence of Article 15, see also Panel Report, *US – Steel Plate (2002)*, para. 7.110.

326 See Panel Report, *EC – Bed Linen (2001)*, paras. 6.233 and 6.238. See also Panel Report, *EC – Tube or Pipe Fittings (2003)*, para. 7.72.

327 Panel Report, *EC – Bed Linen (2001)*, para. 6.228. The panel in *EC – Bed Linen (2001)* interpreted the term 'explore' as follows: 'while the exact parameters of the term are difficult to establish, the concept of "explore" clearly does not imply any particular outcome. We recall that Article 15 does not require that "constructive remedies" must be explored, but rather that the "possibilities" of such remedies must be explored, which further suggests that the exploration may conclude that no possibilities exist, or that no constructive remedies are possible, in the particular circumstances of a given case.' See Panel Report, *EC – Bed Linen (2001)*, para. 6.233.

328 *Ibid.*, para. 6.229. See also Panel Report, *EC – Tube or Pipe Fittings (2003)*, paras. 7.71–7.72.

The panel in *EC – Bed Linen (2001)* understood the phrase 'before applying anti-dumping duties' to mean before the application of definitive (as opposed to provisional) anti-dumping measures, at the end of the investigative process.[329]

10 SUMMARY

WTO law provides for detailed rules with respect to dumping and subsidisation – two specific practices commonly considered to be unfair trade practices. This chapter deals with dumping. 'Dumping' is the bringing of a product onto the market of another country at a price less than the normal value of that product. In WTO law, dumping is not prohibited. However, WTO Members are allowed to take measures to protect their domestic industry from the injurious effects of dumping. Pursuant to Article VI of the GATT 1994 and the *Anti-Dumping Agreement*, WTO Members are entitled to impose anti-dumping measures if three conditions are fulfilled.

The first condition for the imposition of an anti-dumping measure is that dumping exists. Dumping is generally determined through a price-to-price comparison of the 'normal value' with the 'export price'. The 'normal value' is the price of the like product in the domestic market of the exporter or producer. Where this price in the exporting country market is not an 'appropriate' normal value, an importing Member may determine the normal value by: (1) using the export price to an appropriate third country as the normal value; or (2) constructing the normal value. The export price is ordinarily based on the transaction price at which the producer in the exporting country sells the product to an importer in the importing country. Where the transaction price is not an 'appropriate' export price, the importing Member may calculate, or 'construct', an export price. In order to ensure a fair comparison between the export price and normal value, the *Anti-Dumping Agreement* requires that adjustments be made to either the normal value, the export price, or both. The dumping margin is the difference between the export price and the 'normal value'. The calculation of the dumping margin *generally* requires *either* a comparison of the weighted average 'normal value' to the weighted average of prices of all comparable export transactions; *or* a transaction-to-transaction comparison of 'normal value' and export price. However, in particular circumstances, a comparison of the weighted average normal value to export prices in individual transactions may be used.

The second condition for the imposition of an anti-dumping measure is that the domestic industry producing the like product in the importing country must be suffering injury. The *Anti-Dumping Agreement* defines 'injury' to mean one of

329 See Panel Report, *EC – Bed Linen (2001)*, paras. 6.231–6.232.

three things: (1) material injury to a domestic industry; (2) the threat of material injury to a domestic industry; or (3) material retardation of the establishment of a domestic industry. The *Anti-Dumping Agreement* defines the 'domestic industry' generally as 'the domestic producers as a whole of the like products or ... those of them whose collective output of the products constitutes a major proportion of the total domestic production of those products'. The *Anti-Dumping Agreement* requires that a determination of injury to the domestic industry be based on positive evidence and involve an objective examination of both: (1) the volume of dumped imports and the effect of the dumped imports on prices in the domestic market for like products; and (2) the consequent impact of these imports on domestic producers of such products. A determination of a threat of material injury shall be based on facts and not merely on allegation, conjecture or remote possibility. A threat of material injury exists when a change in circumstances, creating a situation in which the dumping would cause injury, is clearly foreseen and imminent.

The third and last condition for the imposition of an anti-dumping measure is that there is a causal link between the dumped imports *and* the injury to the domestic industry. According to the '*non-attribution' requirement*, investigating authorities must examine any known factors, other than the dumped imports, that are injuring the domestic industry at the same time and must not attribute the injury caused by these other factors to the dumped imports.

The *Anti-Dumping Agreement* contains detailed rules on the initiation of an anti-dumping investigation, the process of the investigation (including evidentiary issues) and requirements for public notice. The main objectives of these procedural rules are to ensure that: (1) the investigations are conducted in a transparent manner; (2) all interested parties have the opportunity to defend their interests; and (3) the investigating authorities adequately explain the basis for their determinations.

The *Anti-Dumping Agreement* provides for three kinds of anti-dumping measure: (1) provisional anti-dumping measures; (2) price undertakings; and (3) definitive anti-dumping duties. To apply a provisional anti-dumping measure, investigating authorities must make a *preliminary* affirmative determination of dumping, injury and causation. Furthermore, the investigating authorities must judge that such a measure is *necessary* to prevent injury being caused during the investigation. The *Anti-Dumping Agreement* provides for an alternative to the imposition of anti-dumping duties by affording exporters the possibility to offer, and investigating authorities the possibility to accept, price undertakings. These voluntary undertakings to revise prices or cease exports at the dumped price may be entered into only after the investigating authorities have made an affirmative preliminary determination of dumping, injury and causation. Where a definitive determination is made of the existence of dumping, injury and causation, a definitive anti-dumping duty may be imposed. The amount of the anti-dumping duty *may not exceed* the dumping margin, although it may be a lesser amount. Members are required to collect duties, on a *non-discriminatory* basis, on imports from each known exporter or producer found to be dumping and causing injury. When anti-dumping duties are imposed, the investigating authorities must, in principle, calculate a dumping margin for each exporter. However, the *Anti-Dumping Agreement* recognises that this may not always be possible. When it is not possible to calculate a dumping margin for each exporter, the investigating authorities may limit the number of exporters considered individually. The anti-dumping duty imposed on uninvestigated exporters is based on the weighted average dumping margin actually established for individually investigated exporters.

An anti-dumping duty shall remain in force only as long as and to the extent necessary to counteract dumping which is causing injury. The need for the continued imposition of an anti-dumping duty must be reviewed periodically by the competent authorities, where warranted, on their own initiative or upon a request by any interested party. In any case, any definitive anti-dumping duty shall be *terminated* at a date not later than *five years* from its imposition, *unless* the authorities determine – in the context of a sunset review – that the expiry of the duty 'would be likely to lead to continuation or recurrence of dumping and injury'. As with many other WTO agreements, the *Anti-Dumping Agreement* contains a provision relating to special and differential treatment for developing-country Members. Article 15 of the *Anti-Dumping Agreement* requires developed-country Members to explore 'possibilities of constructive remedies' provided for by the *Anti-Dumping Agreement* before applying anti-dumping duties, where such duties would affect the essential interests of developing-country Members.

Finally, the *Anti-Dumping Agreement* provides for two special rules with regard to the standard of review that applies to disputes concerning anti-dumping measures taken by national investigating authorities. The first rule relates to the objective, proper and unbiased assessment of the facts, and the second rule provides for the possibility that a provision of the Agreement may admit of more than one permissible interpretation.

FURTHER READINGS

M. Beshkar and A. S. Chilton, 'Revisiting Procedure and Precedent in the WTO: An Analysis of US – Countervailing and Anti-Dumping Measures (China)', *World Trade Review*, 2016, 15(2), 375–95.

A. D. Mitchell and T. J. Prusa, '*China – Autos*: Haven't We Danced This Dance before?', *World Trade Review*, 2016, 15(2), 303–25.

M. O. Moore and M. Wu, 'Antidumping and Strategic Industrial Policy: Tit-for-Tat Trade Remedies and the China–X-Ray Equipment Dispute', *World Trade Review*, 2015, 14(2), 239–86.

E. Vermulst, J. D. Sud and S. J. Evenett, 'Normal Value in Anti-Dumping Proceedings against China Post-2016: Are Some Animals Less Equal Than Others?', *Global Trade and Customs Journal*, 2016, 11(5), 212–28.

J. Chaisse and D. Chakraborty, 'Normative Obsolescence of the WTO Anti-Dumping Agreement – Topography of the Global Use and Misuse of Initiations and Measures', *Asian Journal of International Law*, 2016, 6(2), 233–63.

Y. Rovnov, 'The Relationship between the MFN Principle and Anti-Dumping Norms of the WTO Law Revisited', *Journal of World Trade*, 2015, 49(1), 173–97.

M. Wu, 'Antidumping in Asia's Emerging Giants', *Harvard International Law Journal*, 2012, 53(1).

J. Rey, 'Antidumping Regional Regimes and the Multilateral Trading System: Do Regional Antidumping Regimes Make a Difference', WTO Staff Working Paper ERSD-2012-22, October 2012, World Trade Organization.

12

Subsidies

CONTENTS

1 INTRODUCTION

In addition to rules on dumping and anti-dumping measures, WTO law also includes rules on another practice that may or may not be considered unfair, namely, subsidisation. Subsidies are a very sensitive matter in international trade relations. On the one hand, subsidies are evidently used by governments to pursue and promote important and fully legitimate objectives of economic and social policy. On the other hand, subsidies may have adverse effects on the interests of trading partners whose industry may suffer, in its domestic or export markets, from unfair competition with subsidised products. Disputes about subsidies, and in particular subsidies to 'strategic economic sectors', have been prominent on the GATT/WTO agenda. Most noteworthy are the long-running disputes initiated by the European Union and the United States in respect of subsidies to their respective civil aircraft industry.[1] Agricultural subsidies promoting production and export of commodities such as cotton or sugar have also triggered much WTO litigation.

As mentioned in Chapter 1, subsidies are subject to an intricate set of rules. Some subsidies, such as export and import substitution subsidies, are, as a rule, prohibited, while other subsidies are not prohibited but are 'actionable' (i.e. challengeable) and must be withdrawn (or their adverse effects removed) when they cause adverse effects to the interests of other Members. Furthermore, if a subsidy causes or threatens to cause material injury to the domestic industry of a Member, that Member is authorised to impose countervailing duties on the subsidised products to offset the subsidisation provided that the substantive and procedural requirements set out in WTO law and domestic regulation governing countervailing measures are observed.

1 More specifically, the original disputes in *EC and certain member States – Large Civil Aircraft (2011)* and *US – Large Civil Aircraft (2nd complaint) (2012)* and the compliance disputes in *EC and certain member States – Large Civil Aircraft (Article 21.5 – US)* and *US – Large Civil Aircraft (2nd complaint) (Article 21.5 – European Union)*.

This chapter examines the WTO rules on subsidies and subsidised trade. It discusses: (1) basic elements of WTO law on subsidies and subsidised trade; (2) subsidies covered by the *SCM Agreement*; (3) prohibited subsidies; (4) actionable subsidies; (5) countervailing investigation; (6) countervailing measures; (7) institutional and procedural provisions; (8) special and differential treatment for developing-country Members; and (9) special rules for agricultural subsidies.

2 BASIC ELEMENTS OF WTO LAW ON SUBSIDIES AND SUBSIDISED TRADE

Before entering into a more detailed, and often technical, discussion of the rules on subsidies and countervailing measures, this section addresses in general terms: (1) the history of the law on subsidies and subsidised trade; (2) the WTO concept of 'subsidies' and their treatment under WTO law; and (3) the current use of subsidies and countervailing duties.

2.1 History of the Law on Subsidies and Subsidised Trade

The WTO rules on subsidies and subsidised trade are set out in Articles VI and XVI of the GATT 1994 and, more importantly, in the WTO *Agreement on Subsidies and Countervailing Measures*, commonly referred to as the *SCM Agreement*. The GATT 1947 did not contain clear and comprehensive rules on subsidies. In fact, Article XVI of the GATT 1947, entitled 'Subsidies', did not even define the concept of 'subsidies'. Moreover, with regard to subsidies in general, Article XVI merely provided that Contracting Parties to the GATT should notify subsidies that have an effect on trade and should be prepared to discuss limiting such subsidies if they cause serious damage to the interests of other Contracting Parties.[2] With regard to export subsidies, Article XVI provided that Contracting Parties were to 'seek to avoid' using subsidies on exports of primary products.[3]

In 1962, Article XVI was amended to add a provision prohibiting Contracting Parties from granting export subsidies to non-primary products which would reduce the sales price on the export market below the sales price on the domestic market.[4] Note, however, that this amendment did not apply to developing countries. In addition, Article VI of the GATT 1947 dealt with measures taken to offset any subsidy granted to an imported product that causes, or threatens to cause, material injury to the domestic industry producing the like product

2 See Article XVI:1 of the GATT 1947.

3 See Article XVI:3, first sentence, of the GATT 1947. Contracting Parties 'should not' give a subsidy which results in the exporting country gaining 'more than an equitable share of world export trade in that product'. See Article XVI:3, second sentence, of the GATT 1947.

4 See Article XVI:4 of the GATT 1947, as amended.

(i.e. countervailing duties). However, Article VI did not provide for clear and comprehensive rules. In order to elaborate on the GATT rules on subsidies and countervailing duties and to provide greater uniformity and certainty in their implementation, the GATT Contracting Parties, during the Tokyo Round (1973–9), negotiated and concluded the *Agreement on Interpretation and Application of Articles VI, XVI and XXIII of the General Agreement*, commonly referred to as the Tokyo Round *Subsidies Code*.[5] No more than twenty-five Contracting Parties accepted this plurilateral agreement.[6] The *Subsidies Code* certainly did not bring the degree of clarification and elaboration of the rules on subsidies and countervailing duties sought by some of the Contracting Parties. During the 1980s, the lack of clear rules on subsidies and countervailing duties left many disputes between the GATT Contracting Parties unresolved. It was therefore not surprising that the 1986 Punta del Este Ministerial Declaration on the Uruguay Round instructed the negotiators to review Articles VI and XVI of the GATT 1947 as well as the Tokyo Round *Subsidies Code*:

> with the objective of improving GATT disciplines relating to all subsidies and countervailing measures that affect international trade.[7]

The Uruguay Round negotiations eventually resulted in the *SCM Agreement*, which forms part of Annex 1A to the *WTO Agreement*. The multilateral rules on subsidies and subsidised trade are now set out in Articles VI and XVI of the GATT 1994 and, most importantly, in the *SCM Agreement*.

The *SCM Agreement* does not contain a preamble or an explicit indication of its object and purpose. However, the Appellate Body recalled in *US – Anti-Dumping and Countervailing Duties (China) (2011)* that the object and purpose of the *SCM Agreement* is 'to increase and improve GATT disciplines relating to the use of both subsidies and countervailing measures'.[8] Furthermore, in *US – Softwood Lumber IV (2004)*, the Appellate Body noted that the object and purpose of the *SCM Agreement* is to 'strengthen and improve GATT disciplines relating to the use of both subsidies and countervailing measures, while, recognizing at the same time, the right of Members to impose such measures under certain conditions'. Finally, we note that, with respect to the object and purpose of the *SCM Agreement*, the Appellate Body stated in *US – Countervailing Duty Investigation on DRAMS (2005)* that the *SCM Agreement* 'reflects a delicate balance between the Members that sought to impose more disciplines on the use of subsidies and those that sought to impose more disciplines on the application of countervailing measures'.[9]

5 See BISD 26S/56.

6 Both the United States and the European Community accepted the Tokyo Round *Subsidies Code*.

7 BISD 33S/25.

8 Appellate Body Report, *US – Anti-Dumping and Countervailing Duties (China) (2011)*, para. 301 referring to Appellate Body Report, *US – Carbon Steel (2002)*, fn. 65 to para. 73.

9 Appellate Body Report, *US – Anti-Dumping and Countervailing Duties (China) (2011)*, para. 301 referring to Appellate Body Report, *US – Softwood Lumber IV (2004)*, para. 64 and Appellate Body Report, *US – Countervailing Duty Investigation on DRAMS (2005)*, para. 115.

2.2 The WTO Concept of 'Subsidies' and Their Treatment under WTO Law

The *SCM Agreement* contains, for the first time in the GATT/WTO context, a detailed and comprehensive definition of the concept of 'subsidy'. As the panel in *US – FSC (2000)* stated:

> the inclusion of this detailed and comprehensive definition of the term 'subsidy' is generally considered to represent one of the most important achievements of the Uruguay Round in the area of subsidy disciplines.[10]

Broadly speaking, Article 1.1 of the *SCM Agreement* defines a subsidy as a financial contribution by a government or public body, which confers a benefit.[11] Furthermore, Article 1.2 of the *SCM Agreement* provides that the WTO rules on subsidies and subsidised trade only apply to 'specific' subsidies, i.e. subsidies granted to an enterprise or industry, or a group of enterprises or industries. The concepts of 'subsidy' and 'specificity' are examined in detail below.[12]

As discussed in Chapter 11, dumping *per se* is not prohibited. However, WTO law permits the imposition of anti-dumping measures if dumping causes injury. The WTO law on subsidies is different. Article XVI of the GATT 1994 and Articles 3 to 9 of the *SCM Agreement* impose disciplines on the use of subsidies.[13] Certain subsidies are prohibited (e.g. export and import substitution subsidies). Many other subsidies, at least when they are *specific*, rather than generally available, may be challenged when they cause adverse effects to the interests of other Members.[14] The *SCM Agreement* distinguishes between prohibited subsidies and actionable subsidies. It also used to refer to non-actionable subsidies.[15] Each of these kinds of subsidies has its own substantive and procedural rules and remedies. Moreover, subsidies on agricultural products are subject to specific rules set out in the *Agreement on Agriculture.*

As discussed in Chapter 11, Members may respond to injurious dumping by imposing anti-dumping duties on dumped products. Similarly, Members may, pursuant to Article VI of the GATT 1994 and Articles 10–23 of the *SCM Agreement*, respond to subsidised trade which causes injury to the domestic industry producing the like product by imposing countervailing duties on subsidised imports. These countervailing duties are to offset the subsidisation. However, comparable to the anti-dumping duties discussed above, countervailing duties may only be imposed when the relevant investigating authority properly establishes that: (i)

10 Panel Report, *US – FSC (2000)*, para. 7.80.

11 On this definition and its constituent elements, see below, pp. 775–802.

12 See below, pp. 794–802.

13 On the relationship between Article XVI of the GATT 1994 and the provisions of the *SCM Agreement*, note that the obligations and procedures set out in Article XVI of the GATT 1994 must be read and applied together with the *SCM Agreement*. As the Appellate Body concluded in *Brazil – Desiccated Coconut (1997)*, Article XVI of the GATT 1994 cannot be invoked independently from the *SCM Agreement*. See Appellate Body Report, *Brazil – Desiccated Coconut (1997)*, 182–3.

14 See Part III on Actionable Subsidies and Part V on Countervailing Measures of the *SCM Agreement*.

15 Note, however, that, in accordance with Article 31 of the *SCM Agreement*, Part IV on 'Non-Actionable Subsidies' expired five years after the entry into force of the Agreement. See also below, p. 846.

there are subsidised imports; (ii) there is material injury to a domestic industry (or threat thereof); and (iii) there is a causal link between the subsidised imports and the injury. As with the conduct of anti-dumping investigations, the conduct of countervailing investigations is subject to detailed substantive and procedural requirements. Note that the substantive and procedural rules on the imposition and maintenance of countervailing measures are similar to (albeit somewhat less detailed than) the equivalent rules on anti-dumping measures.

2.3 Current Use of Subsidies and Countervailing Measures

With regard to the use of subsidies, note that Members have notified thousands of subsidy measures to the WTO Secretariat.[16] The number of notifications reflects the widespread use of subsidies by Members in pursuit of economic, social and other policy objectives. For example, consider the Indian fisheries subsidy schemes aiming to protect and secure the livelihood of traditional and poor fishing communities, notified in 2016;[17] the temporary import regime established by Honduras for strengthening its economy, boosting domestic production and exports, promoting employment and stimulating investment, notified in 2016;[18] the State programme of the Russian Federation for development of the aircraft industry for improving its competitiveness, notified in 2016;[19] the Climate Change Levy Scheme of the United Kingdom, aiming to encourage more usage of the combined heat and power technology, notified by the European Union in 2016;[20] and the US federal programmes such as the agricultural domestic support programmes to stabilise, support and protect farm income and prices; and energy conservation programmes to develop energy efficient technologies, notified in 2015.[21]

With regard to the use of countervailing measures, note that, in the period 1995–2015, Members imposed a total of 216 countervailing measures, while they initiated 410 countervailing investigations.[22] The most frequent users of this trade remedy instrument were the United States (ninety-five), the European Union (thirty-six) and Canada (twenty-six).[23] In terms of sources of imports, countervailing measures were primarily imposed on imports from China (sixty-six) and India (thirty-six); in terms of product categories, most countervailing measures were imposed on base metals and articles of base metal (101).[24] In the twelve-month period from 1 January 2015 to 31 December 2015, fifteen

16 On the notification of subsidies and countervailing measures, see below, pp. 864–6.
17 See G/SCM/N/284/IND, dated 27 October 2016, 2.
18 See G/SCM/N/284/HND, dated 26 July 2016, 1.
19 See G/SCM/N/284/RUS, dated 11 May 2016, 11.
20 See G/SCM/N/284/EU/Add.28, dated 10 May 2016, 5.
21 See G/SCM/N/284/USA, dated 18 November 2015, 6 and 14.
22 See www.wto.org/english/tratop_e/scm_e/scm_e.htm. The figures are as of 31 December 2015.
23 See *ibid.* In the period 1995–2015, Brazil imposed seven and Mexico eleven countervailing measures.
24 See *ibid.* Note that few countervailing measures were imposed on machinery and electrical equipment (sixteen), textiles and articles (eight) or vehicles, airplanes and vessels (two).

countervailing measures were notified: ten by the United States, two each by Canada and Australia, and one by the European Union. This was an increase over the previous three years, wherein eleven, thirteen and ten countervailing measures were notified in 2014, 2013 and 2012 respectively.[25] On 30 June 2015, a total of 112 countervailing measures (definitive duties and price undertakings) were in force, of which sixty were maintained by the United States, eighteen by Canada and fifteen by the European Union.[26] According to the 2016 Report of the SCM Committee, on 30 June 2016, a total of 126 notified countervailing measures were in force (definitive duties and price undertakings) of which seventy were maintained by the United States, twenty by Canada and fifteen by the European Union.[27]

3 SUBSIDIES COVERED BY THE *SCM AGREEMENT*

Article 1.1 of the *SCM Agreement* provides, in relevant part:

> For the purpose of this Agreement, a subsidy shall be deemed to exist if:
> (a)(1) there is a financial contribution by a government or any public body within the territory of a Member ... or
> (a)(2) there is any form of income or price support in the sense of Article XVI of GATT 1994; and
> (b) a benefit is thereby conferred.

Article 1.2 of the *SCM Agreement* further provides:

> A subsidy as defined in paragraph 1 shall be subject to the provisions of Part II or shall be subject to the provisions of Part III or V only if such a subsidy is specific in accordance with the provisions of Article 2.

Article 1.1 sets forth the general 'subsidy' definition 'for the purpose of this Agreement'. This definition, therefore, applies wherever the word 'subsidy' appears throughout the *SCM Agreement* and it conditions the application of its provisions regarding *prohibited* subsidies in Part II, *actionable* subsidies in Part III, *non-actionable* subsidies in Part IV (now defunct) and countervailing measures in Part V.[28]

The following sections examine the four constituent elements of the concept of 'subsidy': (1) a *financial contribution*; (2) a financial contribution *by a government or any public body*; (3) a financial contribution *conferring a benefit* (set out in the paragraph (3) of Article 1 of the *SCM Agreement*); and (4) the concept of 'specificity' (set forth in Article 2).

25 See *ibid*. Note that in 2000, twenty-one countervailing measures were notified, the highest for a year to date.
26 See WTO Secretariat, *WTO Annual Report 2016*, 66.
27 See Report (2016) of the Committee on Subsidies and Countervailing Duties (G/L/1157), dated 31 October 2016, Annex G, 17–18.
28 Appellate Body Report, *US – FSC (2000)*, para. 93.

3.1 Financial Contribution

For a measure to be a subsidy within the meaning of Article 1.1 of the *SCM Agreement*, that measure must constitute a 'financial contribution' *or* take the form of income or price support in the sense of Article XVI of the GATT 1994. Article 1.1 provides for an exhaustive list of types of financial contribution. This list includes: (1) direct transfers of funds, such as grants, loans and equity infusions;[29] (2) potential direct transfers of funds or liabilities, such as loan guarantees;[30] (3) government revenue, otherwise due, that is foregone or not collected;[31] (4) the provision by a government of goods or services other than general infrastructure;[32] (5) the purchase by a government of goods;[33] (6) government payments to a funding mechanism; or (7) through entrusting or directing a private body to make a financial contribution.[34] The Appellate Body thus found in *US – Softwood Lumber IV (2004)*:

> a wide range of transactions falls within the meaning of 'financial contribution' in Article 1.1(a) (1) ... [and] this range of government measures capable of providing subsidies is broadened still further by the concept of 'income or price support' in paragraph (2) of Article 1.1(a).[35]

While the list in Article 1.1 of types of financial contribution is *exhaustive*, the concept of 'financial contribution' is broad. As the Appellate Body noted in *Canada – Renewable Energy (2013)*, a transaction may fall under more than one type of financial contribution.[36] This section will discuss in turn the various types of financial contribution.

3.1.1 Direct Transfers of Funds

The Appellate Body observed in *Japan – DRAMs (Korea) (2007)* that the words 'grants, loans, and equity infusion' in Article 1.1(a)(1)(i) are preceded by the abbreviation 'e.g.', which indicates that grants, loans, and equity infusion are cited *examples* of transactions falling within the scope of Article 1.1(a)(1)(i). Therefore, transactions that are similar to those expressly listed, such as an interest rate reduction, debt forgiveness or the extension of a loan maturity, are also covered by the provision.[37] The Appellate Body noted in *Japan – DRAMs (Korea) (2007)* that:

> [t]he term 'funds' encompasses not only 'money' but also financial resources and other financial claims more generally. Thus direct transfers of funds are not confined to situations where there is an incremental flow of funds to the recipient that enhances the net worth of the recipient.[38]

29 See Article 1.1(a)(1)(i) of the *SCM Agreement*.
30 See *ibid*. 31 See Article 1.1(a)(1)(ii) of the *SCM Agreement*.
32 See Article 1.1(a)(1)(iii) of the *SCM Agreement*. 33 See *ibid*.
34 See Article 1.1(a)(1)(iv) of the *SCM Agreement*.
35 Appellate Body Report, *US – Softwood Lumber IV (2004)*, para. 52.
36 Appellate Body Report, *Canada – Renewable Energy (2013)*, para. 5.120.
37 See Appellate Body Report, *Japan – DRAMs (Korea) (2007)*, para. 251. As the Appellate Body noted: 'In all of these cases, the financial position of the borrower is improved and therefore there is a direct transfer of funds within the meaning of Article 1.1(a)(1)(i).' See *ibid*. See also e.g. Panel Report, *Korea – Commercial Vessels (2005)*, para. 7.31.
38 Appellate Body Report, *Japan – DRAMs (Korea) (2007)*, para. 250.

In *US – Large Civil Aircraft (2nd complaint) (2012)*, the Appellate Body further clarified that government practices involving 'a direct transfer of funds' within the meaning of Article 1.1(a)(1)(i) include:

action involving the conveyance of funds from the government to the recipient ... The direct transfer of funds ... therefore captures conduct on the part of the government by which money, financial resources, and/or financial claims are made available to a recipient.

Article 1.1(a)(1)(i) lists in brackets examples of direct transfers of funds ('e.g. grants, loans, and equity infusion') ... These examples, which are illustrative, do not exhaust the class of conduct captured by subparagraph (i). The inclusion of specific examples nevertheless provides an indication of the types of transactions intended to be covered by the more general reference to 'direct transfer of funds'. [I]t was 'clear from the[se] examples ... that a direct transfer of funds will normally involve financing by the government to the recipient. In some instances, as in the case of grants, the conveyance of funds will not involve a reciprocal obligation on the part of the recipient. In other cases, such as loans and equity infusions, the recipient assumes obligations to the government in exchange for the funds provided'.[39]

Thus, the Appellate Body concluded that the 'provision of funding may amount to a donation or may involve reciprocal rights and obligations'.[40]

In *US – Carbon Steel (India) (2014)*, the Appellate Body clarified the scope of *direct* transfer of funds. It did not consider that 'the fact that a government effects a transfer through an intermediary necessarily negates a finding of financial contribution under Article 1.1(a)(1)(i)' and noted that:

Indeed, it would seem that a conveyance of funds through an intermediary might still, depending on the circumstances relating to the nature and role of the intermediary, exhibit sufficient indicia of directness in order to establish that 'a government practice involves a direct transfer of funds' ... We again note that Article 1.1(a)(1)(i) relates to a 'government practice' that 'involves' a direct transfer of funds. Thus, while we would agree that a 'transfer' indicates that funds are moved from a transferor to a transferee, we do not consider that ... the resources must necessarily be drawn from government resources or result in a charge on the public account... [I]f there is a government practice that involves a transfer of financial resources exhibiting sufficient indicia of directness, we do not see that such a transfer must necessarily emanate from government title or possession over such resources. Indeed, there may be limited situations in which a government is able to exercise control over resources pooled from non-government contributors in such a manner that its decision to transfer those resources could qualify as a financial contribution under Article 1.1(a)(1)(i).[41]

A financial contribution exists not only when a direct transfer of funds or a potential direct transfer of funds has actually been effectuated. Pursuant to Article 1.1(a)(1)(i), it is sufficient that there is a 'government practice' involving the transfer of funds.[42]

39 See *ibid.*, para. 617. 40 *Ibid.*

41 Appellate Body Report, *US – Carbon Steel (India) (2014)*, paras. 4.94 and 4.96.

42 The panel in *Brazil – Aircraft (1999)* noted in this respect: 'If subsidies were deemed to exist only once a direct or potential direct transfer of funds had actually been effectuated, the Agreement would be rendered totally ineffective and even the typical WTO remedy (i.e. the cessation of the violation) would not be possible.' Panel Report, *Brazil – Aircraft (1999)*, para. 7.13.

3.1.2 Government Revenue, Otherwise Due, That Is Foregone

As provided in Article 1.1(a) (1) (ii), government revenue, otherwise due, that is foregone or not collected is also a financial contribution within the meaning of Article 1.1. In *US – FSC (2000)*, the Appellate Body held:

> In our view, the '*foregoing*' of revenue '*otherwise* due' implies that less revenue has been raised by the government than would have been raised in a different situation, or, that is, 'otherwise'. Moreover, the word 'foregone' suggests that the government has given up an entitlement to raise revenue that it could 'otherwise' have raised. This cannot, however, be an entitlement in the abstract, because governments, in theory, could tax *all* revenues. There must, therefore, be some defined, normative benchmark against which a comparison can be made between the revenue actually raised and the revenue that would have been raised 'otherwise'. We, therefore, agree with the Panel that the term 'otherwise due' implies some kind of comparison between the revenues due under the contested measure and revenues that would be due in some other situation. We also agree with the Panel that the basis of comparison must be the tax rules applied by the Member in question ... A Member, in principle, has the sovereign authority to tax any particular categories of revenue it wishes. It is also free *not* to tax any particular categories of revenues. But, in both instances, the Member must respect its WTO obligations. What is 'otherwise due', therefore, depends on the rules of taxation that each Member, by its own choice, establishes for itself.[43]

The term 'otherwise due' refers to a normative benchmark as established by the tax rules applied by the Member concerned.[44] The panel in *US – FSC (2000)* explained that the term 'otherwise due' refers to the situation that would prevail *but for* the measure at issue.[45] In *US – Large Civil Aircraft (2nd complaint) (2012)*, the Appellate Body addressed the question of whether the reduction in the Washington State business-and-occupation tax rate applicable to commercial aircraft and component manufacturers constitutes the foregoing of revenue *otherwise due* within the meaning of Article 1.1(a) (1) (ii).[46] The Appellate Body explained that:

> [a] panel must be aware of the limitations inherent in identifying and comparing a general rule of taxation, and an exception from that rule. For instance, we noted that it could be misleading to identify a benchmark within a domestic tax regime solely by reference to historical tax rates. By that measure, the fact that commercial aircraft and component manufacturers were *previously* subject to higher tax rates would not in itself be determinative of what the benchmark is at the time of the challenge ...
>
> We have also noted that it could be misleading to compare rates applicable to a general category of income with rates applicable to a subcategory of that income, without

43 Appellate Body Report, *US – FSC (2000)*, para. 90.

44 The Appellate Body in *US – FSC (Article 21.5 – EC) (2002)* clarified that Article 1.1(a)(1)(ii) does not require panels to identify a general rule of taxation and exceptions to that general rule, but rather they should compare the domestic fiscal treatment of 'legitimately' comparable income 'to determine whether the contested measure involves the foregoing of revenue that is "otherwise due"'. See Appellate Body Report, *US – FSC (Article 21.5 – EC) (2002)*, para. 91.

45 See Panel Report, *US – FSC (2000)*, para. 7.45. Note, however, that the Appellate Body stated that, although the panel's 'but for' test works in this case, it may not work in other cases. The Appellate Body had 'certain abiding reservations' about applying any legal standard, such as this 'but for' test, in place of the actual treaty language. See Appellate Body Report, *US – FSC (2000)*, para. 91.

46 Appellate Body Report, *US – Large Civil Aircraft (2nd complaint) (2012)*, paras. 801–31.

considering whether the scope of the 'exceptions' undermines the existence of a 'general rule' ... This reflects consideration by the Panel as to the relative tax treatment of other taxpayers engaged in the same broad category of business activities as commercial aircraft manufacturers.[47]

The Appellate Body concluded in *US – Large Civil Aircraft (2nd complaint) (2012)* that it was satisfied the panel had a proper basis for selecting as the benchmark the tax treatment generally applicable in Washington State to businesses engaged in manufacturing, wholesaling, and retailing activities. In addition, the Appellate Body considered that the panel properly concluded that a comparison of these general tax rates to the lower tax rate that was applied to the gross income of commercial aircraft and component manufacturers indicated the foregoing of government revenue otherwise due within the meaning of Article 1.1(a) (1) (ii) of the *SCM Agreement*.[48]

3.1.3 Provision or Purchase by a Government

Article 1.1(a) (1) (iii) covers financial contributions where 'a government provides goods or services other than general infrastructure, or purchases goods'. According to the Appellate Body in *US – Softwood Lumber IV (2004)*, subparagraph (iii) contemplates two distinct types of transaction:

The first is where a government provides goods or services other than general infrastructure. Such transactions have the potential to lower artificially the cost of producing a product by providing, to an enterprise, inputs having a financial value. The second type of transaction falling within [subparagraph (iii)] is where a government purchases goods from an enterprise. This type of transaction has the potential to increase artificially the revenues gained from selling the product.[49]

With regard to the 'provision of goods' within the meaning of Article 1.1(a) (1) (iii), first subclause, the Appellate Body stated in *US – Softwood Lumber IV (2004)* and *US – Carbon Steel (India) (2014)* that:

[t]he concept of 'making available' or 'putting at the disposal of' ... requires there to be a reasonably proximate relationship between the action of the government providing the good or service on the one hand, and the use or enjoyment of the good or service by the recipient on the other. Indeed, a government must have some control over the *availability* of a specific thing being 'made available'.[50]

The *US – Softwood Lumber IV (2004)* dispute involved the examination of so-called 'stumpage arrangements', which gave private entities a right to enter onto government lands, cut standing timber, and enjoy exclusive rights over the timber that is harvested.[51] Canada contended on appeal that these stumpage arrangements only provide 'an intangible right to harvest'. If the term 'provides' were understood as to 'make available', Canada argued, it would capture 'any

47 *Ibid.*, paras. 823–4. 48 See *ibid.*, para. 825.
49 Appellate Body Report, *US – Softwood Lumber IV (2004)*, para. 53.
50 *Ibid.*, para. 71; and Appellate Body Report, *US – Carbon Steel (India) (2014)*, para. 4.68.
51 Appellate Body Report, *US – Softwood Lumber IV (2004)*, para. 75.

circumstance in which a government action makes possible a later receipt of services and ... every property law in a jurisdiction'.[52] The Appellate Body disagreed and did not see how such general governmental acts would necessarily fall within the scope of Article 1.1(a) (1) (iii).[53] Ultimately, the Appellate Body upheld the panel that the stumpage arrangements amount to a financial contribution through the provision of goods.

In *US – Carbon Steel (India) (2014)*, the Appellate Body reiterated that not every governmental act, even if it could be argued to make available a particular good or service, or to put a particular good or service at the disposal of a beneficiary, will necessarily constitute a provision of that good or service.[54] The Appellate Body recalled that 'such actions would be too remote from the concept of "making available" or "putting at the disposal of", which requires there to be a reasonably proximate relationship between the action of the government providing the good or service on the one hand, and the use or enjoyment of the good or service by the recipient on the other'.[55] The Appellate Body concluded that there is a reasonably proximate relationship between the Indian government's grant of mining rights and the final goods consisting of extracted iron ore and coal.[56] Indeed, rights over extracted iron ore and coal follow as a natural and inevitable consequence of the steel companies' exercise of their mining rights, which suggests that making available iron ore and coal is the *raison d'être* of the mining rights.[57] For the Appellate Body this supported the panel's conclusion that the government's grant of mining rights is reasonably proximate to the use or enjoyment of the minerals by the beneficiaries of those rights.[58]

With regard to the 'purchase of goods' within the meaning of Article 1.1(a) (1) (iii), second subclause, the Appellate Body stated in *US – Large Civil Aircraft (2nd complaint) (2012)* that:

> the goods are provided *to* the government by the recipient, in contrast to the first sub-clause of that paragraph, where the goods are provided *by* the government.[59]

As to the difference between the first and second subclauses of Article 1.1(a) (1) (iii), the Appellate Body noted that: (1) the second subclause uses the term 'purchase', which is usually understood to mean that the person or entity providing the goods will receive some consideration in return; (2) in contrast to the first

52 *Ibid.*, para. 70. 53 *Ibid.*

54 Appellate Body Report, *US – Carbon Steel (India) (2014)*, para. 4.68 referring to *US – Softwood Lumber IV, (2004)*, para. 70.

55 Appellate Body Report, *US – Carbon Steel (India) (2014)*, paras. 4.68–4.69, referring to *US – Softwood Lumber IV (2004)*, para. 71. The panel in *US – Softwood Lumber IV (2004)* found that, 'in certain circumstances, a government might properly be determined to have provided goods by making them available through the grant of extraction rights'. Panel Report, *US – Softwood Lumber IV, (2004)*, paras. 7.235–7.240.

56 Appellate Body Report, *US – Carbon Steel (India) (2014)*, paras. 4.72–4.73.

57 *Ibid.*, paras. 4.73–4.74. 58 *Ibid.*

59 Appellate Body Report, *US – Large Civil Aircraft (2nd complaint) (2012)*, para. 619. The meaning of 'purchase of goods' has been elaborated upon by the panel in *Canada – Renewable Energy (2013)*, paras. 7.226ff.

subclause that addresses the provision of goods *and services*, the second subclause refers only to purchases of 'goods', and not of 'services'.[60] While government purchase of services is excluded from the scope of subparagraph (iii), the question has arisen whether such 'purchase' or 'measures' could fall within the scope of subparagraph (i), discussed above. According to the panel in *US – Large Civil Aircraft (2nd complaint) (2012)*, the omission of the term 'services' from the second subclause of subparagraph (iii) is an indication that the drafters of the *SCM Agreement* did not intend measures constituting government purchases of services to be covered as financial contributions under subparagraph (i). The Appellate Body did not rule on this interpretative issue, as it was not relevant for purposes of resolving the dispute before it.[61] The Appellate Body found instead that the payments and access to facilities, equipment and employees provided to Boeing pursuant to the NASA procurement contracts and Department of Defense assistance instruments at issue constituted 'direct transfers of funds' and the 'provision of goods or services', and were therefore financial contributions covered by Article 1.1(a) (1) (i) and (iii) of the *SCM Agreement*.[62]

As noted above, Article 1.1(a) (1) (iii) covers financial contributions through the government provision of goods or services, *other than general infrastructure*. Excluded from the scope of subparagraph (iii) is therefore the provision of general infrastructure. The term 'general infrastructure' has been defined by the panel in *EC and certain member States – Large Civil Aircraft (2011)* as:

> [i]nfrastructure that is not provided to or for the advantage of only a single entity or limited group of entities, but rather is available to all or nearly all entities.[63]

The provision of infrastructure that is not 'general' falls within the scope of subparagraph (iii). With regard to this infrastructure, the Appellate Body noted in *EC and certain member States – Large Civil Aircraft (2011)* that the panel erred in its interpretation and application of subparagraph (iii) by failing to recognise that the relevant transaction for purposes of its analysis under subparagraph

60 See *ibid.*

61 The Appellate Body declared the panel's interpretation in *US – Large Civil Aircraft (2nd complaint) (2012)* that 'transactions properly characterized as purchases of services are excluded from the scope of Article 1.1(a)(1)(i) of the SCM Agreement' to be moot and of no legal effect. *Ibid.*, paras. 619–20.

62 *Ibid.*, paras. 550–625. The Appellate Body found that the NASA procurement contracts and Department of Defense assistance instruments at issue 'are most appropriately characterized as being akin to a species of joint venture and that these joint venture arrangements between NASA/[Department of Defense] and Boeing have characteristics analogous to equity infusions, one of the examples of financial contribution included in Article 1.1(a)(1)(i) of the *SCM Agreement*'. 'These payments constitute a direct transfer of funds within the meaning of Article 1.1(a)(1)(i). In addition, Boeing was given access to NASA facilities, equipment, and employees and to [Department of Defense] facilities, which constitute the provision of goods or services within the meaning of Article 1.1(a)(1)(iii) of the *SCM Agreement*.' See *ibid.*, para. 624.

63 Panel Report, *EC and certain member States – Large Civil Aircraft (2011)*, para. 7.1063. For the panel, 'the existence of limitations on access to or use of infrastructure, whether *de jure* or *de facto*, is highly relevant in determining whether that infrastructure is "general infrastructure"'. See Panel Report, *EC and certain member States – Large Civil Aircraft (2011)*, paras. 7.1037 and 7.1039.

(iii) was the *provision* of goods or services in the form of infrastructure to Airbus, not the *creation* of that infrastructure.[64] The Appellate Body emphasised that, 'when a good or service has not been *provided* by a government, there cannot be a financial contribution cognizable under Article 1.1(a) (1) (iii)'.[65]

3.1.4 Payments to a Funding Mechanism or Financial Contributions through a Private Body

Article 1.1(a) (1) (iv) refers to financial contributions where a 'government makes payments to a funding mechanism, or entrusts or directs a private body to carry out one or more of the type of functions' illustrated in subparagraphs (i)–(iii), which would normally be vested in the government and the practice, in no real sense, differs from practices normally followed by governments. In defining government payments in a funding mechanism or entrustment or direction of a private body within the meaning of subparagraph (iv) of Article 1.1(a) (1), the Appellate Body recalled in *US – Countervailing Duty Investigation on DRAMs (2005)* that the *SCM Agreement* reflects a 'delicate balance between the Members that sought to impose more disciplines on the use of subsidies and those that sought to impose more disciplines on the application of countervailing measures'.[66] It noted that this balance must be borne in mind in interpreting subparagraph (iv):

> [w]hich allows Members to apply countervailing measures to products in situations where a government uses a private body as a proxy to provide a financial contribution ... At the same time, the interpretation of paragraph (iv) cannot be so broad so as to allow Members to apply countervailing measures to products whenever a government is merely exercising its general regulatory powers.[67]

According to the Appellate Body, subparagraph (iv) is, in essence, an anti-circumvention provision.[68] In *US – Countervailing Duty Investigation on DRAMs (2005)*, the Appellate Body ruled:

> [P]ursuant to paragraph (iv), 'entrustment' occurs where a government gives responsibility to a private body, and 'direction' refers to situations where the government exercises its authority over a private body. In both instances, the government uses a private body as proxy to effectuate one of the types of financial contributions listed in [sub]paragraphs (i) through (iii).[69]

The Appellate Body recognised that it may be difficult to identify precisely, in the abstract, the types of government actions that constitute entrustment or direction and those that do not. The terms 'entrusts' and 'directs' are not limited to acts of 'delegation' and 'command'. The particular label used to describe the governmental action is not necessarily dispositive. Indeed, in some circumstances, 'guidance' by a government can constitute direction. However, in most

64 See Appellate Body Report, *EC and certain member States – Large Civil Aircraft (2011)*, para. 966.
65 See *ibid.*, para. 964.
66 Appellate Body Report, *US – Countervailing Duty Investigation on DRAMs (2005)*, para. 115.
67 *Ibid.* 68 See *ibid.*, para. 113. 69 See *ibid.*, para. 116.

cases, one would expect entrustment or direction of a private body to 'involve some form of *threat* or *inducement*, which could, in turn, serve as evidence of entrustment or direction'.[70]

3.1.5 Income and Price Support

Article 1.1(a) (2) refers to 'any form of income or price support in the sense of Article XVI of GATT 1994', which may also qualify as a subsidy if it confers a benefit to a specific enterprise or industry. The panel in *China – GOES (2012)* addressed the meaning of 'any form of ... price support', and observed that the phrase is broad and, on its face, could be read to include any government measure that has the effect of raising prices within a market. However, reading the term 'price support' in context, the panel found that this term only captures government measures that set or target a given price; it does not capture every government measure that has an incidental and random effect on price.[71] This more narrow interpretation is appropriate because, under Article 1.1(a) (1) (i)–(iv), the existence of each of the four types of financial contribution is determined by reference to the action of the government concerned, rather than by reference to the effects of the measure on a market.[72] Reading the term 'price support' in this context, the panel concluded that:

> [i]t does not include all government intervention that may have an effect on prices, such as tariffs and quantitative restrictions. In particular, it is not clear that Article 1.1(a) (2) was intended to capture all manner of government measures that do not otherwise constitute a financial contribution, but may have an indirect effect on a market, including on prices. The concept of 'price support' also acts as a gateway to the SCM Agreement, and it is our view that its focus is on the nature of government action, rather than upon the effects of such action. Consequently, the concept of 'price support' has a more narrow meaning than suggested by the applicants, and includes direct government intervention in the market with the design to fix the price of a good at a particular level, for example, through purchase of surplus production when price is set above equilibrium.[73]

3.2 Financial Contribution by a Government or a Public Body

For a financial contribution to be a subsidy within the meaning of Article 1.1 of the *SCM Agreement*, the financial contribution must be made by a government or a public body, including regional and local authorities as well as State-owned companies. The Appellate Body interpreted the meaning of the term 'public body' in Article 1.1(a) (1) in *US – Anti-Dumping and Countervailing Duties (China) (2011)*. It reversed the panel's finding in that case that the term means 'any entity controlled by a government' and found instead that the term 'public body' in the context of Article 1.1(a) (1) covers only those entities that possess,

70 *Ibid.* Emphasis added. 71 See Panel Report, *China – GOES (2012)*, para. 7.84.
72 See *ibid.*, para. 7.85. 73 *Ibid.*

exercise or are vested with governmental authority.[74] The Appellate Body started its interpretation of the term 'public body' by pointing out that:

> [t]he dictionary definitions suggest a rather broad range of potential meanings of the term 'public body', which encompasses a variety of entities, including both entities that are vested with or exercise governmental authority and entities belonging to the community or nation.[75]

The Appellate Body subsequently noted that the term 'government' is used twice in the chapeau of Article 1.1(a) (1). It appears, first, within the phrase 'a government or any public body' (i.e. government in the narrow sense), and, secondly, it appears within a parenthetical phrase specifying that, for purposes of the *SCM Agreement*, this word refers collectively to 'a government or any public body' (i.e. government in the collective sense).[76] The Appellate Body then turned to the question of what essential characteristics an entity must share with government in the narrow sense in order to be a public body and, thus, part of government in the collective sense. In *Canada – Dairy (1999)*, the Appellate Body found that the essence of government is that it enjoys the effective power to regulate, control or supervise individuals, or otherwise restrain their conduct, through the exercise of lawful authority.[77] The Appellate Body further found that this meaning is derived, in part, from the functions performed by a government and, in part, from the government having the powers and authority to perform those functions.[78] From this, the Appellate Body concluded in *US – Anti-Dumping and Countervailing Duties (China) (2011)* that:

> [t]he performance of governmental functions, or the fact of being vested with, and exercising, the authority to perform such functions are core commonalities between government and public body.[79]

The Appellate Body found contextual support for its interpretation of 'public body' in Article 1.1(a) (1) (iv), discussed above. The Appellate Body noted that:

> [p]ursuant to subparagraph (iv), a public body may exercise its authority in order to compel or command a private body, or govern a private body's actions (direction), and may be responsibility for certain tasks to a private body (entrustment). As we see it, for a public body to be able to exercise its authority over a private body (direction), a public body must itself possess such authority, or ability to compel or command. Similarly, in order to be able to give responsibility to a private body (entrustment), it must itself be vested with such responsibility. If a public body did not itself dispose of the relevant authority or responsibility, it could not effectively control or govern the actions of a private body or delegate such responsibility to a private body. This, in turn, suggests that the requisite attributes to be able to entrust or direct a private body, namely, authority in the case of direction and responsibility in the case of entrustment, are common characteristics of both government in the narrow sense and a public body.[80]

74 See Appellate Body Report, *US – Anti-Dumping and Countervailing Duties (2011)*, paras. 290 and 322.
75 *Ibid.*, para. 285. 76 See *ibid.*, para. 286.
77 See Appellate Body Report, *Canada – Dairy (1999)*, para. 97. 78 See *ibid.*
79 Appellate Body Report, *US – Anti-Dumping and Countervailing Duties (China) (2011)*, para. 290.
80 *Ibid.*, para. 294.

The Appellate Body recognised that, while a public body within the meaning of Article 1.1(a) (1) must be an entity that possesses, exercises or is vested with governmental authority, the precise contours and characteristics of a public body are bound to differ from entity to entity, State to State, and case to case.[81] The Appellate Body considered that:

> [p]anels or investigating authorities confronted with the question of whether conduct falling within the scope of Article 1.1(a) (1) is that of a public body will be in a position to answer that question only by conducting a proper evaluation of the core features of the entity concerned, and its relationship with government in the narrow sense.[82]

As the Appellate Body noted, in some cases, 'such as when a statute or other legal instrument expressly vests authority in the entity concerned, determining that such entity is a public body may be a straightforward exercise'.[83] However, in others, the picture may be more mixed, and the challenge more complex. The same entity may possess certain features suggesting it is a public body, and others that suggest that it is a private body.[84] According to the Appellate Body, the absence of an express statutory delegation of authority does not necessarily preclude a determination that a particular entity is a public body.[85] As the Appellate Body stated:

> What matters is *whether* an entity is vested with authority to exercise governmental functions, rather than *how* that is achieved. There are many different ways in which government in the narrow sense could provide entities with authority. Accordingly, different types of evidence may be relevant to showing that such authority has been bestowed on a particular entity. Evidence that an entity is, in fact, exercising governmental functions may serve as evidence that it possesses or has been vested with governmental authority, particularly where such evidence points to a sustained and systematic practice.[86]

Evidence that a government exercises *meaningful control* over an entity and its conduct *may serve*, in certain circumstances, *as evidence* that the relevant entity possesses governmental authority and exercises such authority in the performance of governmental functions.[87] The Appellate Body emphasised that:

> [t]he mere fact that a government is the majority shareholder of an entity does not demonstrate that the government exercises meaningful control over the conduct of that entity, much less that the government has bestowed it with governmental authority. In some instances, however, where the evidence shows that the formal indicia of government control are manifold, and there is also evidence that such control has been exercised in a meaningful way, then such evidence may permit an inference that the entity concerned is exercising governmental authority.[88]

81 See *ibid.*, para. 317.
82 *Ibid.* 83 *Ibid.*, para. 318.
84 See *ibid.* In this context, the Appellate Body referred to comments by the panel in *US – Countervailing Duty Investigation on DRAMs (2005)*. See Panel Report, *US – Countervailing Duty Investigation on DRAMs (2005)*, fn. 29 to para. 7.8.
85 See Appellate Body Report, *US – Anti-Dumping and Countervailing Duties (China) (2011)*, para. 318.
86 *Ibid.* 87 See *ibid.*
88 *Ibid.*

In *US – Carbon Steel (India) (2014)*, the Appellate Body recalled its findings in *US – Anti-Dumping and Countervailing Duties (China) (2011)* that the term 'public body' means 'an entity that possesses, exercises or is vested with governmental authority' and that, in determining whether an entity is a public body, it may be relevant to consider 'whether the functions or conduct are of a kind that are ordinarily classified as governmental in the legal order of the relevant Member', as well as the classification and functions of entities within WTO Members generally.[89] The Appellate Body clarified in this case that:

> consistent with the Appellate Body's interpretation, a government's exercise of 'meaningful control' over an entity and its conduct, including control such that the government can use the entity's resources as its own, may certainly be relevant evidence for purposes of determining whether a particular entity constitutes a public body. Similarly, government ownership of an entity, while not a decisive criterion, may serve, in conjunction with other elements, as evidence. Significantly, however, in its consideration of evidence, an investigating authority must 'avoid focusing exclusively or unduly on any single characteristic without affording due consideration to others that may be relevant'.[90]

In sum, whether the conduct of an entity is that of a public body must in each case be determined on its own merits, with due regard being had to the core characteristics and functions of the relevant entity, its relationship with the government, and the legal and economic environment prevailing in the country in which the investigated entity operates.[91] For example, evidence regarding the scope and content of government policies relating to the sector in which the investigated entity operates may inform the question of whether the conduct of an entity is that of a public body. The absence of an express statutory delegation of governmental authority does not necessarily preclude a determination that a particular entity is a public body.[92] Instead, there are different ways in which a government could be understood to vest an entity with 'governmental authority', and therefore different types of evidence may be relevant in this regard.[93] In order to properly characterise an entity as a public body in a particular case, it may be relevant to consider 'whether the functions or conduct [of the entity] are of a kind that are ordinarily classified as governmental in the legal order of the relevant Member', and the classification and functions of entities within WTO Members generally.[94] In the same way that 'no two governments are exactly

89 Appellate Body Reports, *US – Carbon Steel (India) (2014)*, para. 4.29; *US – Anti-Dumping and Countervailing Duties (China) (2011)*, para. 317.

90 Appellate Body Report, *US – Carbon Steel (India) (2014)*, paras. 4.20, 4.29 and 4.42–4.43.

91 *Ibid.*, para. 4.20.

92 *Ibid.*, para. 4.29. As the Appellate Body observed, '[w]hat matters is *whether* an entity is vested with authority to exercise governmental functions, rather than *how* that is achieved'. See Appellate Body Report, *US – Anti-Dumping and Countervailing Duties (China) (2011)*, para. 318.

93 For instance, '[e]vidence that an entity is, in fact, exercising governmental functions may serve as evidence that it possesses or has been vested with governmental authority'. Appellate Body Report, *US – Anti-Dumping and Countervailing Duties (China) (2011)*, para. 318.

94 Appellate Body Reports, *US – Carbon Steel (India) (2014)*, para. 4.29; *US – Anti-Dumping and Countervailing Duties (China) (2011)*, para. 297.

alike, the precise contours and characteristics of a public body are bound to differ from entity to entity, State to State, and case to case'.[95]

Turning to the panel's assessment in *US – Carbon Steel (India) (2014)*, the Appellate Body considered that, 'while the panel reviewed some indicia of control by the Government of India (such as shareholding and the Government's involvement in the selection of directors), it did not address the question of whether there was evidence that the entity at issue was performing governmental functions on behalf of the Government of India'. Moreover, the Appellate Body found that the panel failed to evaluate whether the investigating authority had properly considered the relationship between the entity at issue and the government of India within the Indian legal order, or the extent to which the government of India in fact 'exercised' meaningful control over that entity and over its *conduct*.[96]

3.3 Financial Contribution Conferring a Benefit

A financial contribution by a government or a public body is a subsidy within the meaning of Article 1.1 of the *SCM Agreement* only if the financial contribution *confers a benefit*. If a government gives a sum of money to a company, it seems clear that this financial contribution would generally confer a benefit. However, it may be less clear whether a government loan to that same company, the purchase of goods by the government from the company or an equity infusion by the government in the company confer a benefit. In *Canada – Aircraft (1999)*, Canada argued that 'cost to government' is one way of conceiving of 'benefit'. The Appellate Body rejected this argumentation as follows:

> A 'benefit' does not exist in the abstract, but must be received and enjoyed by a beneficiary or a recipient. Logically, a 'benefit' can be said to arise only if a person, natural or legal, or a group of persons, has in fact received something. The term 'benefit', therefore, implies that there must be a recipient. This provides textual support for the view that the focus of the inquiry under Article 1.1(b) of the *SCM Agreement* should be on the recipient and not on the granting authority. The ordinary meaning of the word 'confer', as used in Article 1.1(b), bears this out. 'Confer' means, *inter alia*, 'give', 'grant' or 'bestow'. The use of the past participle 'conferred' in the passive form, in conjunction with the word 'thereby', naturally calls for an inquiry into *what was conferred on the recipient*.[97]

This reading of the term 'benefit' is confirmed by Article 14 of the *SCM Agreement*, which sets forth guidelines for calculating the amount of a subsidy in terms of 'the benefit *to the recipient*'.[98] The guidelines set forth in Article 14

95 Appellate Body Reports, *US – Carbon Steel (India) (2014)*, para. 4.29; *US – Anti-Dumping and Countervailing Duties (China) (2011)*, para. 317.

96 Appellate Body Report, *US – Carbon Steel (India) (2014)*, paras. 4.42–4.43.

97 Appellate Body Report, *Canada – Aircraft (1999)*, para. 154.

98 See *ibid.*, para. 155. The reference to 'benefit to the recipient' in Article 14 also implies that the word 'benefit', as used in Article 1.1, is concerned with the 'benefit to the recipient' and not with the 'cost to government'. Although Article 14 explicitly states that its guidelines apply '[f]or the purposes of Part V' of the *SCM Agreement*, which relates to 'countervailing measures', the Appellate Body was of the opinion that Article 14, nonetheless, constitutes relevant context for the interpretation of 'benefit' in Article 1.1(b).

apply to the calculation of the 'benefit *to the recipient* conferred pursuant to paragraph 1 of Article 1'.[99] In *Canada – Aircraft (1999)*, the Appellate Body further held with regard to the term 'benefit' that:

> [t]he word 'benefit', as used in Article 1.1(b), implies some kind of comparison. This must be so, for there can be no 'benefit' to the recipient unless the 'financial contribution' makes the recipient 'better off' than it would otherwise have been, absent that contribution. In our view, the marketplace provides an appropriate basis for comparison in determining whether a 'benefit' has been 'conferred', because the trade-distorting potential of a 'financial contribution' can be identified by determining whether the recipient has received a 'financial contribution' on terms more favourable than those available to the recipient in the market.[100]

The Appellate Body confirmed its interpretation of 'benefit' in *US – Large Civil Aircraft (2nd complaint) (2012), US – Carbon Steel (India) (2014)* and *US – Countervailing Duties (China) (2014)*, that:

> [t]he determination of 'benefit' under Article 1.1(b) of the *SCM Agreement* seeks to identify whether the financial contribution has made 'the recipient "better off" than it would otherwise have been, absent that contribution'.[101]

This interpretation of 'benefit' within the meaning of Article 1.1(b) is supported by Article 14 of the *SCM Agreement*. The title of Article 14 – 'Calculation of the Amount of a Subsidy in Terms of the Benefit to the Recipient' – also suggests that the adequacy of the 'remuneration' paid, for example, in exchange for goods or services under Article 14(d) is to be examined from the perspective of the recipient, rather than the government provider. Such remuneration is to be determined in relation to prevailing market conditions in the country of provision. In *Canada – Aircraft (1999)* and *US – Carbon Steel (India) (2014)*, the Appellate Body held that a benefit arises under *each* of the paragraphs of Article 14 if the recipient has received a 'financial contribution' on terms more favourable than those that are available to the recipient in the market. In the latter case, the Appellate Body agreed with the panel that '[o]nce it is established that the price paid to the government provider is less than the price that would be required by the market', the government price in question is inadequate, and a benefit is thereby conferred.[102]

On the relationship between Articles 1.1(b) and 14, the Appellate Body stated in *US – Carbon Steel (India) (2014)*:

> The term 'benefit' appears in Article 1.1(b), as well as Article 14, of the SCM Agreement. While the former provision is concerned with the existence of a 'benefit', the latter provision is, in the context of Part V of the SCM Agreement, concerned with the calculation of its amount. The determination of the mere existence, as opposed to the amount, of benefit conferred by a financial contribution does not, however, call for different interpretations of the

99 See *ibid.* 100 *Ibid.*, para. 157.

101 Appellate Body Report, *Canada – Aircraft (1999)*, para. 157; Appellate Body Report, *US – Large Civil Aircraft (2nd complaint) (2012)*, para. 662; Appellate Body Report, *US – Carbon Steel (India) (2014)*, para. 4.123; and Appellate Body Report, *US – Countervailing Duties (China) (2014)*, para. 4.44.

102 Appellate Body Report, *US – Carbon Steel (India) (2014)*, para. 4.128.

term 'benefit'. Indeed, the explicit textual reference to Article 1.1 in the chapeau of Article 14 indicates that 'benefit' is used in the same sense in Article 14 as it is in Article 1.1.[103]

Pursuant to Article 14(a), a government provision of equity capital shall not be considered as conferring a benefit when the investment decision can be regarded as consistent with the usual investment practice of private investors. Pursuant to Article 14(b), governmental loans shall not be considered as conferring a benefit, unless (and to the extent that) there is a difference between the amount that the firm receiving the loan pays on the government loan and the amount the firm would pay on a comparable commercial loan which the firm could actually obtain on the market. Pursuant to Article 14(c), the same benchmark applies for loan guarantees. Pursuant to Article 14(d), the provision of goods or services or the purchase of goods by a government shall not be considered as conferring a benefit unless the provision is made for less than adequate remuneration, or the purchase is made for more than adequate remuneration. As Article 14(d) states, the adequacy of the remuneration shall be determined in relation to prevailing market conditions for the good or service in question in the country of provision or purchase (including price, quality, availability, marketability, transportation and other conditions of purchase or sale).

Article 14(a) states that *equity capital* provided by a government shall not be considered to confer a benefit unless it is inconsistent with what is termed the 'usual investment practice' of private investors in the territory of that Member. In *EC – Large Civil Aircraft (2011)*, the Appellate Body understood the term 'usual practice' to describe common or customary conduct of private investors in respect of equity investment. It also observed that Article 14(a) focuses the inquiry on the 'investment decision'. This reflects an *ex ante* approach to assessing the equity investment by comparing the decision, based on the costs and expected returns of the transaction, to the usual investment practice of private investors *at the moment the decision to invest is undertaken*. The focus in Article 14(a) on the 'investment decision' is thus critical because it identifies *what* is to be compared to a market benchmark, and *when* that comparison is to be situated.[104]

In determining whether a *government loan* confers a benefit, Article 14(b) calls for a comparison of the 'amount that the firm receiving the loan pays on the government loan' with 'the amount the firm would pay on a comparable commercial loan which the firm could actually obtain on in the market'. This suggests that the comparison is to be performed as though the loans were obtained at the same time. In other words, the comparable commercial loan is one that would have been available to the recipient firm at the time it received the government loan.[105] The Appellate Body held that a panel relying on Article 14(b) would thus have to

103 Appellate Body Report, *US – Carbon Steel (India) (2014)*, para. 4.122. See also paras. 4.124 and 4.126.
104 Appellate Body Report, *EC and certain member States – Large Civil Aircraft (2011)*, para. 999.
105 *Ibid.*, para. 835.

examine whether there is a difference between the amount that the recipient pays on the government loan and the amount the recipient would pay on a comparable commercial loan, which the recipient could have actually obtained on the market. There is a benefit – and therefore a subsidy – where the amount that the recipient pays on the government loan is less than what the recipient would have paid on a comparable commercial loan that the recipient could have obtained on the market. There is no benefit – and therefore no subsidy – if what the recipient pays on the government loan is equal to or higher than what it would have paid on a comparable commercial loan. The amount the recipient would have paid on a commercial loan is a function of the size of the loan, the interest rate, the duration and other relevant terms of the transaction.[106]

If there is no undistorted market benchmark, a proxy may be constructed to serve as a substitute market benchmark for the determination of benefit. The benefit issues, appealed in *EC – Large Civil Aircraft (2011)* largely focused on the components of such a proxy benefit benchmark, for example the rates of return that a market lender would have required to provide launch aid/member State financing to Airbus. Both the United States and the European Communities had sought to develop a proxy that, in their view, most accurately reflected the rate of return that would have been demanded by a market lender. Such proxy and particularly one of its components (the project-specific risk premia), was at the heart of the European Union's appeal of the panel's findings that launch aid/ member State financing conferred a benefit.[107]

The second sentence of Article 14(d) prescribes that the adequacy of remuneration for a government-provided good or service 'shall be determined in relation to prevailing market conditions for the good or service in question in the country of provision or purchase'. In *US – Carbon Steel (India) (2014)*, the Appellate Body stated that 'prevailing market conditions in the country of provision' are the standard for assessing the adequacy of remuneration. These terms describe generally accepted characteristics of an area of economic activity in which the forces of supply and demand interact to determine market prices.[108] Since the assessment of the adequacy of remuneration must be made in relation to *prevailing market conditions in the country of provision*, any benchmark for conducting such an assessment must consist of market-determined prices for the same or similar goods that relate or refer to, or are connected with, the prevailing market conditions for the good in question in the country of provision.

106 *Ibid.*, para. 834.

107 *Ibid.*, paras. 856–64.

108 Appellate Body Report, *US – Carbon Steel (India) (2014)*, para. 4.243. An assessment of 'prevailing market conditions', within the meaning of Article 14(d), necessarily involves an analysis of the market generally, rather than isolated transactions in that market. It is only through such an analysis that a conclusion can be drawn as to the conditions that are 'prevailing' in the market in the country of provision. Moreover, 'prevailing market conditions' cannot be assessed solely from the perspective of the providers of the relevant good in question. This would be in tension with the proposition that a government-provided financial contribution confers a benefit if the '"financial contribution" makes the *recipient* "better off" than it would otherwise have been, absent that contribution'. *Ibid.*, paras. 4.245ff.

Proper benchmark prices would normally emanate from the market for the good in question in the country of provision because, to the extent that such in-country prices are market determined, they would necessarily have the requisite connection with the prevailing market conditions in the country of provision. Such in-country prices could emanate from a variety of potential sources, including private or government-related entities. Investigating authorities bear the responsibility to conduct the necessary analysis in order to determine, on the basis of information supplied by petitioners and respondents in a countervailing duty investigation, whether proposed benchmark prices are market determined such that they can be used to determine a benchmark.[109]

The Appellate Body recognised in *US – Carbon Steel (India) (2014)* that some types of prices may, from an evidentiary standpoint, be more easily found to constitute market-determined prices in the country of provision. This does not suggest, however, that there is, in the abstract, a hierarchy between different types of in-country prices that can be relied upon in arriving at a proper benchmark. Whether a price may be relied upon for benchmarking purposes under Article 14(d) is not a function of its source but, rather, whether it is a market-determined price reflective of prevailing market conditions in the country of provision. While the prices at which the same or similar goods are sold by private suppliers in the country of provision may serve as a starting point of analysis, prices of government-related entities (other than the entity providing the financial contribution at issue) also need to be considered in order to assess whether they are market determined and can therefore form part of a proper benchmark. The Appellate Body held in *US – Carbon Steel (India) (2014)* that Article 14(d) establishes no legal presumption that in-country prices from any particular source can be discarded in a benchmark analysis.[110] Thus, in the Appellate Body's view, private prices and government-related prices can both reflect prevailing market conditions in the country of provision.

In *US – Softwood Lumber IV (2004)* and *US – Anti-Dumping and Countervailing Duties (China) (2011)*, the Appellate Body established that out-of-country prices may be used to determine a benefit benchmark when in-country prices are distorted by government predominance in the market.[111] In such a case, the ability of a government provider to have such an influence on in-country private prices presupposes that it has sufficient market power to do so.[112] When the government's role in providing the financial contribution may be so predominant that it effectively determines the price at which private suppliers sell the same or similar goods, the comparison contemplated by Article 14 would become circular.[113]

109 Appellate Body Report, *US – Carbon Steel (India) (2014)*, paras. 4.151–4.152. 110 *Ibid.*, para. 4.154.

111 *Ibid.*, para. 4.156, referring to Appellate Body Report, *US – Anti-Dumping and Countervailing Duties (China) (2011)*, paras. 453, 443–6; and Appellate Body Report *US – Softwood Lumber IV (2004)*, para. 102.

112 Appellate Body Report, *US – Carbon Steel (India) (2014)*, para. 4.155; Appellate Body Report, *US – Softwood Lumber IV (2004)*, paras. 100–2.

113 Appellate Body Report, *US – Carbon Steel (India) (2014)*, para. 4.155 (quoting from *US – Softwood Lumber IV (2004)*, para. 93).

In *US – Carbon Steel (India) (2014)*, the Appellate Body addressed the question whether Article 14(d) permits the use of *out-of-country benchmarks* also in other situations. The Appellate Body considered that the rationale underpinning its earlier findings implies that Article 14(d) permits recourse to alternative benchmarks also where in-country prices are distorted as a result of governmental intervention in the market.[114] Therefore, the Appellate Body agreed with the panel in *US – Carbon Steel (India) (2014)* that Article 14(d) permits the use of out-of-country benchmarks in situations other than where the government is a predominant provider of the good in question.[115]

While the Appellate Body agreed in *US – Countervailing Measures (China) (2015)* that there is a single definition of the term 'government' for purposes of the entire *SCM Agreement*, it did not follow that, in determining the appropriate benefit benchmark under Article 14(d), investigating authorities are required to limit their analysis to an examination of the role played in the market by government-related entities that have been properly found to be government (in the narrow sense) or public bodies within the meaning of Article 1.1.(a) (1). The Appellate Body considered that the pricing behaviour of entities operating in the market, including government-related entities that have not been found to be public bodies, may be relevant to examine whether the government acts through such government-related entities so as to exert market power and distort in-country prices.[116]

Therefore, the Appellate Body reiterated in *US – Countervailing Measures (China) (2015)* that the selection of a benchmark for the purposes of Article 14(d) cannot, at the outset, exclude consideration of in-country prices from any particular source, including government-related prices other than the financial contribution at issue. This is because the issue of 'whether a price may be relied upon for benchmarking purposes under Article 14(d) is not a function of its source, but rather, whether it is a market-determined price reflective of prevailing market conditions in the country of provision'. As a consequence, prices of government-related entities other than those of the entity providing the financial contribution at issue need to be examined to determine whether they are market determined and can therefore form part of a proper benchmark.[117]

In brief, a 'benefit' arises if the recipient has received a 'financial contribution' on terms more favourable than those available to any recipient in the market.[118] However, the Appellate Body recognised in *Japan – DRAMs (Korea) (2007)* that it may be difficult to find a proper *undistorted* market benchmark. It noted:

> The terms of a financial transaction must be assessed against the terms that would result from unconstrained exchange in the relevant market. The relevant market may be more or

114 The Appellate Body in *US – Carbon Steel (India) (2014)* gave the example of information pertaining to in-country prices that cannot be verified so as to determine whether they are market determined in accordance with the second sentence of Article 14(d). Appellate Body Report, *US – Carbon Steel (India) (2014)*, para. 4.155.

115 *Ibid.*, para. 4.156.

116 Appellate Body Report, *US – Countervailing Measures (China) (2015)*, para. 4.63.

117 *Ibid.*, para. 4.64 (quoting from Appellate Body Report, *US – Carbon Steel (India) (2014)*, para. 4.154).

118 Appellate Body Report, *Canada – Aircraft (1999)*, para. 157.

less developed; it may be made up of many or few participants ... In some instances, the market may be more rudimentary. In other instances, it may be difficult to establish the relevant market and its results. But these informational constraints do not alter the basic framework from which the analysis should proceed ... There is but one standard – the market standard – according to which rational investors act.[119]

In *US – Large Civil Aircraft (2nd complaint) (2012)*, the Appellate Body had difficulties with the panel's reasoning regarding the market benchmark with respect to both the NASA procurement contracts and the Department of Defense assistance instruments:

[T]he Panel stated its view that 'no commercial entity, i.e. no private entity acting pursuant to commercial considerations, would provide payments (and access to its facilities and personnel) to another commercial entity on the condition that the other entity perform R&D activities principally for the benefit and use of that other entity' ... The Panel's finding as to the behaviour of a market actor was based exclusively on the Panel's own view of how a commercial actor would behave and its inferences as to what a rational investor would do.

It is possible that the Panel believed that its view represented common sense, or its own conception of economic rationality ... We do not believe that panels can base determinations as to what would occur in the marketplace only on their own intuition of what rational economic actors would do ... More importantly, we are of the view that a panel should test its intuitions empirically, especially where the parties have submitted evidence as to how market actors behave.[120]

Similarly, in its benefit analysis in *Canada – Renewable Energy (2013)*, the Appellate Body considered that the panel erred in determining whether the financial contribution conferred a benefit because it defined the relevant market for the benefit benchmark comparison as the market for electricity generated from all sources of energy, without considering relevant demand and supply-side factors.[121] As the Appellate Body further noted in *Canada – Renewable Energy (2013)*:

in view of the fact that the government's definition of the energy supply-mix for electricity generation does not *in and of itself* constitute a subsidy, we believe that benefit benchmarks for wind- and solar PV-generated electricity should be found in the markets for wind- and solar PV-generated electricity that result from the supply-mix definition.[122]

With regard to 'benefit' within the meaning of Article 1.1(b) of the *SCM Agreement*, some other issues that have arisen in case law deserve special attention: (1) the issue of 'pass-through' of benefit; and (2) the issue of 'extinction' of benefit. With regard to the issue of 'pass-through' of benefit, the Appellate Body explained in *US – Softwood Lumber IV (2005)* that:

[w]here a subsidy is conferred on input products, and the countervailing duty is imposed on processed products, the initial recipient of the subsidy and the producer of the eventually countervailed product, may not be the same. In such a case, there is a direct recipient of the benefit – the producer of the input product. When the input is subsequently processed, the

119 Appellate Body Report, *Japan – DRAMs (Korea) (2007)*, para. 172.
120 Appellate Body Report, *US – Large Civil Aircraft (2nd complaint) (2012)*, paras. 642–3.
121 Appellate Body Report, *Canada – Renewable Energy (2013)*, para. 5.178. 122 *Ibid.*, para. 5.190.

producer of the processed product is an indirect recipient of the benefit – provided it can be established that the benefit flowing from the input subsidy is passed through, at least in part, to the processed product. Where the input producers and producers of the processed products operate at arm's length, the pass-through of input subsidy benefits from the direct recipients to the indirect recipients downstream cannot simply be presumed; it must be established by the investigating authority.[123]

With regard to the issue of 'extinction' of benefit, the Appellate Body found in *US – Lead and Bismuth (2000)* and *US – Countervailing Measures on Certain EC Products (2003)* that benefits provided to the State-owned firm, which was subsequently *privatised* through transactions conducted *at arm's length* and *for fair market value*, could be treated as having been 'extinguished', and therefore not passed to the new private owners.[124] In *US – Countervailing Measures on Certain EC Products (2003)*, the Appellate Body specifically stated that '[p]rivatizations at arm's length and for fair market value *may* result in extinguishing the benefit' and that 'there is a *rebuttable* presumption that a benefit ceases to exist after such a privatization'.[125] As the Appellate Body emphasised, it depends, however, on the facts of each case whether a 'benefit' derived from pre-privatisation financial contributions is extinguished following privatisation at arm's length and for fair market value.[126] The issue of 'extinction' of benefit also arose in *EC and certain member States – Large Civil Aircraft (2011)*, albeit that the sales transactions in that case did not amount to a full privatisation of a previously State-owned company. In *EC and certain member States – Large Civil Aircraft (2011)*, the issue was whether sales of shares between private entities, and sales conducted in the context of partial privatisations, eliminate all or part of past subsidies, when these sales are at arm's length and for fair market value.[127] The Appellate Body discussed this issue at length, but 'no common view emerged'.[128] Eventually, the Appellate Body reversed the panel's reasoning and findings concerning this issue, because the panel had failed to assess: (1) whether each of the sales was on arm's-length terms and for fair market value; and (2) to what extent the sales involved a transfer in ownership and control to new owners.[129]

3.4 Requirement of 'Specificity' of the Subsidy

The WTO rules on subsidies do not apply to all financial contributions by a government that confer a benefit. In other words, these rules do not apply

123 Appellate Body Report, *US – Softwood Lumber IV (2004)*, para. 143; in *EC and certain member States – Large Civil Aircraft (2011)*, however, the Appellate Body found that a 'pass-through' analysis between different companies and components of the Airbus conglomerate companies was not required. Appellate Body Report, *EC and certain member States – Large Civil Aircraft (2011)*, paras. 774–5.

124 See Appellate Body Report, *US – Lead and Bismuth (2000)*, para. 68; and Appellate Body Report, *US – Countervailing Measures on Certain EC Products (2003)*, para. 127.

125 *Ibid.* Emphasis added. 126 See *ibid.*

127 See Appellate Body Report, *EC and certain member States – Large Civil Aircraft (2011)*, para. 724.

128 See *ibid.*, para. 725. As set out in the report, each Member of the Division took a different view. See *ibid.*

129 See *ibid.*, para. 733.

to all subsidies. They apply only to *specific* subsidies. Article 1.2 of the *SCM Agreement*, quoted above, states:

> A subsidy as defined in paragraph 1 shall be subject to the provisions of Part II or shall be subject to the provisions of Part III or V only if such a subsidy is specific in accordance with the provisions of Article 2.

Article 2 of the *SCM Agreement* distinguishes between different types of specificity: (1) *enterprise or industry specificity*, i.e. a situation in which a government targets a particular company or industry or group of companies or a group of industries for subsidisation;[130] (2) *regional specificity*, i.e. a situation in which a government targets producers in specified parts of its territory for subsidisation;[131] and (3) the *specificity of prohibited subsidies*, i.e. a situation in which a government targets export goods or goods using domestic inputs for subsidisation.[132] For a subsidy to be subject to the disciplines of the *SCM Agreement*, it has to be *specific* in one of the above-mentioned ways. A subsidy that is widely available within an economy is presumed not to distort the allocation of resources within that economy and, therefore, does not fall within the scope of the *SCM Agreement*.

The Appellate Body interpreted Article 2 of the *SCM Agreement* in *US – Anti-Dumping and Countervailing Duties (China) (2011); EC and certain member States – Large Civil Aircraft (2011); US – Large Civil Aircraft (2nd complaint) (2012); US – Carbon Steel (India) (2014)*; and *US – Countervailing Measures (China) (2015)*. The Appellate Body noted in *US – Anti-Dumping and Countervailing Duties (China) (2011)* that the chapeau of Article 2.1 frames the central inquiry as to whether a subsidy is specific to 'certain enterprises'. In such an examination, the 'principles' set out in subparagraphs (a)–(c) of Article 2.1 'shall apply'. The use of the term 'principles' – instead of, for instance, 'rules' – suggests that the subparagraphs:

> [a]re to be considered within an analytical framework that recognizes and accords appropriate weight to each principle. Consequently, the application of one of the subparagraphs of Article 2.1 may not by itself be determinative in arriving at a conclusion that a particular subsidy is or is not specific.[133]

The chapeau of Article 2.1 establishes that the term 'certain enterprises' refers to 'an enterprise or industry or group of enterprises or industries'. Turning to the nouns qualified by 'certain' and 'group', the Appellate Body considered that 'enterprise' may be defined as '[a] business firm, a company', whereas 'industry' signifies '[a] particular form or branch of productive labour; a trade, a manufacture'.[134] In *US – Anti-Dumping and Countervailing Duties (China) (2011)*, the

130 See Article 2.1 of the *SCM Agreement*. See below, pp. 795–802.
131 See Article 2.2 of the *SCM Agreement*. See below, pp. 801–2.
132 See Article 2.3 of the *SCM Agreement*. See below, p. 802.
133 Appellate Body Report, *US – Anti-Dumping and Countervailing Duties (China) (2011)*, para. 366.
134 *Ibid.*, para. 373.

Appellate Body noted with approval the statement by the panel in *US – Upland Cotton (2004)* that: (1) an industry, or group of 'industries', may be generally referred to by the type of products they produce; (2) the concept of an 'industry' relates to producers of certain products; and (3) the breadth of this concept of 'industry' may depend on several factors in a given case.[135]

According to the Appellate Body in *US – Anti-Dumping and Countervailing Duties (China) (2011)*, the term 'certain enterprises': (1) refers to a single enterprise or industry or a class of enterprises or industries that are known and particularised; and (2) this concept involves 'a certain amount of indeterminacy at the edges', such that any determination of whether a number of enterprises or industries constitute 'certain enterprises' can only be made on a case-by-case basis.[136]

As mentioned above, Article 2.1 of the *SCM Agreement* sets out in subparagraphs (a)–(c) 'principles' to determine specificity. The Appellate Body stated in *US – Anti-Dumping and Countervailing Duties (China) (2011)* that:

> [a] proper understanding of specificity under Article 2.1 must allow for the *concurrent application* of these principles to the various legal and factual aspects of a subsidy in any given case.[137]

As already noted, the application of one of the principles 'may not by itself be determinative in arriving at a conclusion that a particular subsidy is or is not specific'.[138] This section further discusses in turn the three principles to determine specificity.

With regard to Article 2.1(a) of the *SCM Agreement*, the Appellate Body held in *US – Anti-Dumping and Countervailing Duties (China) (2011)* that:

> Article 2.1(a) establishes that a subsidy is specific if the granting authority, or the legislation pursuant to which the granting authority operates, *explicitly* limits access to that subsidy to eligible enterprises or industries.[139]

The word 'explicitly' qualifies the phrase 'limits access to a subsidy to certain enterprises'. The Appellate Body, therefore, considered that:

> [a] subsidy is specific under Article 2.1(a) if the limitation on access to the subsidy to certain enterprises is express, unambiguous, or clear from the content of the relevant instrument, and not merely 'implied' or 'suggested'.[140]

135 See Panel Report, *US – Upland Cotton (2004)*, para. 7.1142. The same panel explained that: '[a]t some point that is not made precise in the text of the agreement, and which may modulate according to the particular circumstances of a given case, a subsidy would cease to be specific because it is sufficiently broadly available throughout an economy as not to benefit a particular limited group of producers of certain products. The plain words of Article 2.1 indicate that specificity is a general concept, and the breadth or narrowness of specificity is not susceptible to rigid quantitative definition. Whether a subsidy is specific can only be assessed on a case-by-case basis.' *Ibid.*

136 See Appellate Body Report, *US – Anti-Dumping and Countervailing Duties (China) (2011)*, para. 373, referring to Panel Report, *US – Upland Cotton (2004)*, para. 7.1142.

137 Appellate Body Report, *US – Anti-Dumping and Countervailing Duties (China) (2011)*, para. 371.

138 *Ibid.*, para. 366. 139 *Ibid.*, para. 372.

140 *Ibid.*

In *Japan – DRAMs (Korea) (2007)*, the panel addressed the concern that, if an investigating authority were to focus on *individual payments* made under a subsidy programme, rather than on the *programme per se*, it would always find 'specificity'.[141] In *US – Large Civil Aircraft (2nd complaint) (2012)*, the Appellate Body noted that:

> Article 2.1(a) refers to limitations on access to 'a subsidy'. Although the use of this term in the singular might suggest a limited conception, we note that, if construed too narrowly, any individual subsidy transaction would be, by definition, specific to the recipient. Other context in Article 2.1 suggests a potentially broader framework within which to examine specificity.[142]

The Appellate Body considered that, although the subsidy is the starting point of the specificity inquiry under Article 2.1(a), the scope of this inquiry is broader in the sense that it must examine the legislation pursuant to which the granting authority operates, or the express acts of the granting authority.[143] As the Appellate Body noted in *US – Large Civil Aircraft (2nd complaint) (2012)*:

> Members may design the legal framework for the distribution of subsidies in many ways. However, the choice of the legal framework by the respondent cannot predetermine the outcome of the specificity analysis.[144]

According to the Appellate Body, determining whether multiple subsidies are part of the same 'subsidy' is not always a clear-cut exercise and may require careful scrutiny of the relevant legislation (set out in one *or* several instruments) or of the pronouncements of the granting authority(ies).[145] Another factor that may be considered is whether there is an 'overarching purpose behind the subsidies', albeit that this overarching purpose must be something more concrete than a vague policy of providing assistance or promoting economic growth.[146] As the Appellate Body explained:

> Once the proper subsidy scheme is identified, then the question is whether that subsidy is explicitly limited to 'certain enterprises', defined in the chapeau of Article 2.1 as 'an enterprise or industry or group of enterprises or industries'. To be clear, such examination must seek to discern from the legislation and/or the express acts of the granting authority(ies) which enterprises are eligible to receive the subsidy and which are not. This inquiry focuses

141 The panel noted that: '[i]f an investigating authority were to focus on an individual transaction, and that transaction flowed from a generally available support programme whose normal operation would generally result in financial contributions on pre-determined terms (that are therefore not tailored to the recipient company), that individual transaction would not, in our view, become "specific" in the meaning of Article 2.1 simply because it was provided to a specific company. An individual transaction would be "specific", though, if it resulted from a framework programme whose normal operation (1) does not generally result in financial contributions, and (2) does not pre-determine the terms on which any resultant financial contributions might be provided, but rather requires (a) conscious decisions as to whether or not to provide the financial contribution (to one applicant or another), and (b) conscious decisions as to how the terms of the financial contribution should be tailored to the needs of the recipient company.' See Panel Report, *Japan – DRAMs (Korea) (2007)*, para. 7.374.

142 Appellate Body Report, *US – Large Civil Aircraft (2nd complaint) (2012)*, para. 749.

143 See *ibid.*, para. 750. 144 *Ibid.*

145 See *ibid.*, para. 752. 146 See *ibid.*

> not only on whether the subsidy was provided to the particular recipients identified in the complaint, but focuses also on all enterprises or industries eligible to receive that same subsidy. Thus, even where a complaining Member has focused its complaint on the grant of a subsidy to one or more enterprises or industries, the inquiry may have to extend beyond the complaint to determine what other enterprises or industries also have access to that same subsidy under that subsidy scheme.[147]

Article 2.1 refers to subsidies that are specific to 'certain enterprises' *within the jurisdiction of the granting authority*. The Appellate Body held in *US – Countervailing Measures (China) (2015)* that the identification of the 'jurisdiction of the granting authority' involves a holistic analysis and does not focus on the identity of the 'granting authority' independently from its 'jurisdiction'. The Appellate Body therefore disagreed with China that identification of the jurisdiction must necessarily be preceded by identification of the granting authority. Noting that the notion of jurisdiction is linked to, and does not exist in isolation from, the granting authority, the Appellate Body observed that a proper identification of 'the jurisdiction of the granting authority' will require an analysis of both the 'granting authority' and its 'jurisdiction' in a conjunctive manner.[148]

While Article 2.1(a) sets out when 'specificity' exists, Article 2.1(b) of the *SCM Agreement* sets out that 'specificity' shall *not* exist if the granting authority, or the legislation pursuant to which the granting authority operates, establishes *objective* criteria or conditions governing the eligibility for, and the amount of, the subsidy, provided that: (1) eligibility is automatic; (2) such criteria or conditions are strictly adhered to; and (3) the criteria or conditions are clearly spelt out in an official document so as to be capable of verification.[149] In the footnote to Article 2.1(b), 'objective criteria and conditions' are defined as:

> [c]riteria or conditions which are neutral, which do not favour certain enterprises over others, and which are economic in nature and horizontal in application.

While Article 2.1(a) describes limitations on eligibility that favour certain enterprises, Article 2.1(b) describes criteria or conditions that guard against selective eligibility. A critical common feature of these provisions, however, is that they both situate the analysis for assessing any limitations on *eligibility* in the particular legal instrument or government conduct effecting such limitations. In *US – Anti-Dumping and Countervailing Duties (China) (2011)*, the Appellate Body noted that:

> Article 2.1(a) thus focuses not on whether a subsidy has been granted to certain enterprises, but on whether *access* to that subsidy has been explicitly limited. This suggests that the focus of the inquiry is on whether certain enterprises are eligible for the subsidy, not on whether they in fact receive it. Similarly, Article 2.1(b) points the inquiry towards 'objective criteria or conditions governing the eligibility for, and the amount of, a subsidy'.[150]

147 *Ibid.*, para. 753. 148 Appellate Body Report, *US – Countervailing Measures (China) (2015)*, para. 4.168.
149 Appellate Body Report, *US – Anti-Dumping and Countervailing Duties (China) (2011)*, para. 367.
150 *Ibid.*, para. 368. Emphasis added.

According to the Appellate Body in *US – Anti-Dumping and Countervailing Duties (China) (2011)*, where the eligibility requirements of a measure present some indications pointing to subparagraph (a) and certain others pointing to subparagraph (b), the specificity analysis must accord appropriate consideration to both principles.[151]

A third principle for determining specificity is set out in Article 2.1(c) of the *SCM Agreement*. The introductory sentence of Article 2.1(c) establishes that, 'notwithstanding any appearance of non-specificity' resulting from the application of Article 2.1(a) and (b), a subsidy may nevertheless be found to be *de facto* specific. The reference in Article 2.1(c) to 'any appearance of non-specificity' resulting from the application of Article 2.1(a) and (b) suggests that the conduct or instruments of a granting authority may not clearly satisfy the eligibility requirements of Article 2.1(a) or (b), but may nevertheless give rise to specificity 'in fact'. In such circumstances, the consideration of 'other factors', namely, those listed in Article 2.1(c), is warranted in order to determine whether the subsidy at issue is *de facto* specific. In other words, 'while *de jure* and *de facto* analyses are both focused on whether a subsidy is specific, they do so from somewhat different perspectives. While a *de jure* analysis examines concrete evidence relating to *explicit limitations on access*, a *de facto* analysis focuses on *indicia* of the allocation or use of a subsidy that support a finding of specificity.'[152]

Whereas the specificity analysis under each subparagraph of Article 2.1 should 'ordinarily' proceed in a certain sequence, the Appellate Body did not exclude the possibility that, in certain circumstances, an investigating authority could properly conduct the specificity analysis without examining the subparagraphs of Article 2.1 in a strict sequential order. The Appellate Body found in *US – Countervailing Measures (China) (2015)*, that the application of the principles laid down in subparagraphs (a) and (b) does not necessarily constitute a *condition* that must be met in order to consider the factors listed under subparagraph (c). It recalled that:

> there may be instances in which the evidence under consideration unequivocally indicates specificity or non-specificity by reason of law, or by reason of fact, under one of the subparagraphs, and that *in such circumstances further consideration* under the other subparagraphs of Article 2.1 *may be unnecessary*.[153]

The Appellate Body found that the United States did not act inconsistently with Article 2.1 by analysing specificity exclusively under Article 2.1(c), without further determining that 2.1(a) and (b) did not apply.[154] According to the Appellate Body, Article 2.1 does not call for a strict sequential analysis of its three subparagraphs in each and every case.[155]

151 *Ibid.*, para. 369.

152 Appellate Body Report, *US – Carbon Steel (India) (2014)*, para. 4.373.

153 Appellate Body Report, *US – Countervailing Measures (China) (2015)*, para. 4.123 (quoting Appellate Body Report, *US – Anti-Dumping and Countervailing Duties (China) (2011)*, para. 371).

154 *Ibid.*, para. 4.130. 155 *Ibid.*, para. 4.130.

The factors listed in Article 2.1(c) as relevant for determining whether a subsidy is *de facto* specific are: (1) the use of a subsidy programme by a limited number of certain enterprises; (2) the predominant use of a subsidy programme by certain enterprises; (3) the granting of disproportionately large subsidies to certain enterprises; and (4) the manner in which discretion has been exercised by the granting authority in the decision to grant a subsidy. With regard to this latter factor, the frequency with which applications for a subsidy are refused or approved and the reasons for such decisions are of particular relevance.[156] In determining whether a subsidy is *de facto* specific, account shall be taken of: (1) the extent of diversification of economic activities within the jurisdiction of the granting authority: and (2) the length of time during which the subsidy programme has been in operation.[157]

In *US – Large Civil Aircraft (2nd complaint) (2012)*, the Appellate Body addressed the meaning of 'the granting of disproportionately large amounts of subsidy to certain enterprises' in Article 2.1(c). It noted that:

> Article 2.1(c) does not offer clear guidance as to how to measure whether certain enterprises are 'grant[ed] disproportionately large amounts of subsidy'. The language ... indicates that the first task is to identify the 'amounts of subsidy' granted. Second, an assessment must be made as to whether the amounts of subsidy are 'disproportionately large'. This term suggests that disproportionality is a relational concept that requires an assessment as to whether the amounts of subsidy are out of proportion, or relatively too large. When viewed against the analytical framework set out above regarding Article 2.1(c), this factor requires a panel to determine whether the actual allocation of the 'amounts of subsidy' to certain enterprises is too large relative to what the allocation would have been if the subsidy were administered in accordance with the conditions for eligibility for that subsidy as assessed under Article 2.1(a) and (b). In our view, where the granting of the subsidy indicates a disparity between the expected distribution of that subsidy, as determined by the conditions of eligibility, and its actual distribution, a panel will be required to examine the reasons for that disparity so as ultimately to determine whether there has been a granting of disproportionately large amounts of subsidy to certain enterprises.[158]

The Appellate Body addressed the first factor listed in Article 2.1(c), that is, use of a subsidy programme by a limited number of certain enterprises in *US – Carbon Steel (India) (2014)*. It noted that this factor is focused on a quantitative assessment of the entities that *actually use* a subsidy programme and, in particular, on whether such *use* is shared by a 'limited number of certain enterprises'.[159] A limited quantity of enterprises or industries qualifying as 'certain enterprises' must

156 See Article 2.1(c) of, and fn. 3 to, the *SCM Agreement*. See Panel Report, *EC – Countervailing Measures on DRAM Chips (2005)*, para. 7.226. See also Panel Report, *US – Softwood Lumber IV (2005)*, para. 7.123, on the fact that there is no obligation on the investigating authorities to examine the 'other factors' referred to in Article 2.1(c) of the *SCM Agreement*. Article 2.1(c) states that these factors 'may' be considered.

157 See Article 2.1(c) of the *SCM Agreement*. See Panel Report, *US – Softwood Lumber IV (2004)*, para. 7.124.

158 Appellate Body Report, *US – Large Civil Aircraft (2nd complaint) (2012)*, para. 879.

159 Appellate Body Report, *US – Carbon Steel (India) (2014)*, para. 4.374.

be found to have used the subsidy programme, without requiring that the limited quantity represent a subset of some larger grouping of 'certain enterprises'.[160]

In assessing the third factor, that is, 'the granting of disproportionately large amounts of subsidies to certain enterprises', the Appellate Body stated that it is not necessary to establish specificity on the basis of discrimination in favour of 'certain enterprises' against a broader category of other, similarly situated entities.[161] Moreover, if the inherent characteristics of the subsidised good limit the possible use of the subsidy to a certain industry, it is not necessary, in establishing specificity, that the subsidy be limited to a subset of this industry.[162]

As mentioned above, the *SCM Agreement* distinguishes between several types of specificity: enterprise specificity, industry specificity, regional specificity and the specificity of prohibited subsidies. Article 2.1 of the *SCM Agreement*, discussed at length in this section, concerns specificity with respect to specific enterprises, industries or groups thereof. Regional specificity is dealt with in Article 2.2 of the *SCM Agreement*, which provides that:

> [a] subsidy which is limited to certain enterprises located within a designated geographical region within the jurisdiction of the granting authority shall be specific.

The panel in *EC and certain member States – Large Civil Aircraft (2011)* addressed the question whether a subsidy granted by a regional authority must, to be specific within the meaning of Article 2.2, not only be limited to a designated region within the territory of the granting authority, but must in addition be limited to only a subset of enterprises within that region. The panel concluded that Article 2.2 is properly understood to provide that a subsidy available in a designated region within the territory of the granting authority is specific, even if it is available to all enterprises in that designated region.[163]

In *US – Washing Machines (2016)*, the Appellate Body noted that: (i) the term 'certain enterprises' in Article 2.2 is not limited to entities with legal personality, but also encompasses subunits or constituent parts of a company – including, but not limited to, its branch offices and the facilities in which it conducts manufacturing operations – that may or may not have distinct legal personality; (ii) the 'designation' of a region for the purposes of Article 2.2 need not be affirmative or explicit, but may also be carried out by exclusion or implication, provided that the region in question is clearly discernible from the text, design, structure, and operation of the subsidy at issue; and (iii) the concept of

160 *Ibid.*, para. 4.378.

161 *Ibid.*, para. 4.390. 162 *Ibid.*, para. 4.398.

163 Panel Report, *EC and certain member States – Large Civil Aircraft (2011)*, para. 7.1223. The panel in *US – Anti-Dumping and Countervailing Duties (China) (2011)* reached the same conclusion. This panel stated that the term 'certain enterprises' in Article 2.2 'refers to those enterprises located within, as opposed to outside, the designated geographical region in question, with no further limitation within the region being required'. See Panel Report, *US – Anti-Dumping and Countervailing Duties (China) (2010)*, para. 9.135.

'geographical region' in Article 2.2 does not depend on the territorial size of the area covered by a subsidy.[164]

Finally, pursuant to Article 2.3 of the *SCM Agreement*, any *de jure* or *de facto* export-contingent subsidies or import substitution subsidies falling under the provisions of Article 3, i.e. any prohibited subsidy, shall be deemed to be specific.[165]

4 PROHIBITED SUBSIDIES

The *SCM Agreement* distinguishes between prohibited subsidies, actionable subsidies and non-actionable subsidies.[166] This section will discuss the rules relating to prohibited subsidies. Article 3 of the *SCM Agreement*, entitled 'Prohibition', states, in its first paragraph:

> Except as provided in the Agreement on Agriculture, the following subsidies, within the meaning of Article 1, shall be prohibited:
> a. subsidies contingent, in law or in fact, whether solely or as one of several conditions, upon export performance, including those illustrated in Annex I;
> b. subsidies contingent, whether solely or as one of several other conditions, upon the use of domestic over imported products.

In short, WTO Members may not grant or maintain: (1) export subsidies; or (2) import substitution subsidies.[167] These subsidies, which are often referred to as 'red light' subsidies, are prohibited because they aim to affect trade and are most likely to cause adverse effects to other Members.

4.1 Export Subsidies

As defined in Article 3.1(a) of the *SCM Agreement*, quoted above, export subsidies are subsidies contingent upon export performance. Annex I to the *SCM Agreement* contains an 'Illustrative List of Export Subsidies'. This non-exhaustive list includes eleven types of export subsidy, including, *inter alia*: (1) direct export subsidies; (2) export retention schemes which involve a bonus on exports; (3) export-related exemption, remission or deferral of direct taxes and social welfare charges; (4) excess exemption or remission, in respect of the production

164 Appellate Body Report, *US – Washing Machines (2016)*, para. 5.240. In this case, the subsidy targeted the entire territory except for the Seoul overcrowding area (which represents 2 per cent of Korea's landmass). The Appellate Body explained that the function of Article 2.2 is to address subsidy schemes by which Members direct resources to certain geographical regions within their jurisdictions, thereby interfering with the market's allocation of resources. The Appellate Body further explained that a subsidy programme that excludes from its coverage an area that, albeit territorially small, is nevertheless important from an economic standpoint, could in fact limit eligibility in a significant way. In this respect, it noted the United States' argument that, although the Seoul overcrowding area only occupies 2 per cent of Korea's landmass, such area accounts for a large proportion of the country's population and concentrates a substantial portion of its economy. See Appellate Body Report, *US – Washing Machines (2016)*, paras. 5.236ff.

165 On prohibited subsidies, see below, pp. 802–11.

166 Note, however, that, since 1 January 2000, the category of 'non-actionable subsidies' only contains non-specific subsidies, to which the *SCM Agreement* does not apply. See above, p. 773, fn. 15, and below, p. 846.

167 See Article 3.2 of the *SCM Agreement*.

and distribution of exported products, of indirect taxes in excess of those levied in respect of the production and distribution of like products when sold domestically; (5) provision of goods or services for use in the production of exported goods on terms more favourable than those for the production of goods for domestic consumption; and (6) provision of certain forms of export financing extended at rates below those which the government actually had to pay for the funds (subject to certain considerations).

Article 3.1(a) of the *SCM Agreement* prohibits subsidies *contingent* upon export performance. The meaning of 'contingent' in this provision is 'conditional' or 'dependent for its existence on something else'.[168] Thus, for a subsidy to be an export subsidy, the Appellate Body ruled in *US – FSC (Article 21.5 – EC) (2002)* that 'the grant of the subsidy must be conditional or dependent upon export performance'.[169] In *US – Upland Cotton (2005)*, the Appellate Body emphasised that:

> [a] relationship of conditionality or dependence', namely that the granting of a subsidy should be 'tied to' the export performance, lies at the 'very heart' of the legal standard in Article 3.1(a) of the *SCM Agreement*.[170]

Article 3.1(a) prohibits both subsidies that are contingent *de jure* and subsidies that are contingent *de facto* on export performance. In *Canada – Aircraft (1999)*, the Appellate Body stated:

> The Uruguay Round negotiators have, through the prohibition against export subsidies that are contingent *in fact* upon export performance, sought to prevent circumvention of the prohibition against subsidies contingent *in law* upon export performance.[171]

Pursuant to footnote 4 to the *SCM Agreement*, a subsidy is contingent *de facto* upon export performance:

> [w]hen the facts demonstrate that the granting of a subsidy, without having been made legally contingent upon export performance, is in fact tied to actual or anticipated exportation or export earnings. The mere fact that a subsidy is granted to enterprises which export shall not for that reason alone be considered to be an export subsidy within the meaning of this provision.

While the legal standard expressed by the term 'contingent' is the same for both *de jure* and *de facto* contingency, there is an important difference in what evidence may be employed to demonstrate that a subsidy is export contingent.[172] *De jure* export contingency can be demonstrated on the basis of the words of the relevant legislation, regulation or other legal instrument.[173] In *Canada – Autos (2000)*, the Appellate Body held:

> The simplest, and hence, perhaps, the uncommon, case is one in which the condition of exportation is set out expressly, in so many words, on the face of the law, regulation or other legal instrument. We believe, however, that a subsidy is also properly held to be *de*

168 See Appellate Body Report, *Canada – Aircraft (1999)*, para. 166. See also Panel Report, *Australia – Automotive Leather II (1999)*, para. 9.55.

169 Appellate Body Report, *US – FSC (Article 21.5 – EC) (2002)*, para. 111.

170 Appellate Body Report, *US – Upland Cotton (2005)*, para. 572.

171 Appellate Body Report, *Canada – Aircraft (1999)*, para. 167.

172 See *ibid*.

173 See e.g. Appellate Body Report, *Canada – Autos (2000)*, para. 100; and Appellate Body Report, *US – Upland Cotton (2005)*, para. 572.

jure export contingent where the condition to export is clearly, though implicitly, in the instrument comprising the measure.[174]

According to the Appellate Body, for a subsidy to be *de jure* export contingent, the underlying law, regulation or other legal instrument does *not* have to provide *expressis verbis* that the subsidy is available only upon the fulfilment of the condition of export performance.[175] The *de jure* export contingency can also 'be derived by necessary implication from the words actually used in the measure'.[176]

With respect to *de facto* export contingency, footnote 4 to the *SCM Agreement* states that the standard of 'in fact' contingency is met if the facts demonstrate that the subsidy is 'in fact tied to actual or anticipated exportation or export earnings'.[177] *De facto* export contingency is much more difficult to demonstrate than *de jure* export contingency. The Appellate Body stated in *Canada – Aircraft (1999)* that satisfaction of the standard for determining *de facto* export contingency set out in footnote 4 requires proof of three different substantive elements: (1) the '*granting* of a subsidy'; (2) 'is ... *tied to* ... '; and (3) 'actual or anticipated exportation or export earnings'.[178] According to the Appellate Body in *Canada – Aircraft (1999), de facto* export contingency must be inferred from the *total* configuration of the facts constituting and surrounding the granting of the subsidy.[179] None of these facts on its own is likely to be decisive. In combination, however, they may lead to the conclusion that there is *de facto* export contingency in a given case.

The panel in *Australia – Automotive Leather II (1999)* considered that, in certain circumstances, a Member's awareness that its domestic market is too small to absorb domestic production of a subsidised product may indicate that the subsidy is granted on the condition that it be exported.[180] However, a subsidy to an export-oriented company is not *per se* an export subsidy. The second sentence of footnote 4 precludes a panel from making a finding of *de facto* export contingency for the sole reason that the subsidy is 'granted to enterprises which export'.[181] The export orientation of a recipient may be taken into account but it will be only one among several facts which are considered and cannot be the only fact supporting a finding of *de facto* export contingency.[182] The Appellate Body further cautioned in *Canada – Aircraft (1999)* that the term 'tied to' should not be equated with a 'but for' test, in the sense of simply examining whether the subsidy would have been granted 'but for' the anticipated exportation or export earnings.[183]

174 Appellate Body Report, *Canada – Autos (2000)*, para. 100. See also Appellate Body Report, *US – FSC (Article 21.5 – EC) (2002)*, para. 117.

175 See *ibid.* 176 *Ibid.*

177 Panel Report, *Australia – Automotive Leather II (1999)*, para. 9.55. The panel in this case noted that the ordinary meaning of 'tied to' is 'restrain or constrain to or from an action; limit or restrict as to behaviour, location, conditions, etc.'. See *ibid.* For a further discussion of the term 'tied to', see Appellate Body Report, *Canada – Aircraft (1999)*, para. 171.

178 See Appellate Body Report, *Canada – Aircraft (1999)*, para. 169. 179 See *ibid.*

180 See Panel Report, *Australia – Automotive Leather II (1999)*, para. 9.67.

181 Appellate Body Report, *Canada – Aircraft (1999)*, para. 173.

182 Appellate Body Report, *Canada – Aircraft (Article 21.5 – Brazil) (2000)*, paras. 48 and 51. See fn. 4, second sentence, to the *SCM Agreement*; and Panel Report, *Australia – Automotive Leather II (1999)*, paras. 9.56 and 9.66. The panel also noted that 'consideration of the level of a particular company's exports' is not precluded. See Panel Report, *Australia – Automotive Leather II (1999)*, para. 9.57.

183 Appellate Body Report, *Canada – Aircraft (1999)*, para. 171.

The Appellate Body clarified the test for determining whether a subsidy is *de facto* contingent upon export performance in *EC and certain member States – Large Civil Aircraft (2011)*. It emphasised that the existence of *de facto* export contingency 'must be *inferred* from the total configuration of the facts constituting and surrounding the granting of the subsidy',[184] which may include the following factors: (1) the design and structure of the measure granting the subsidy; (2) the modalities of operation set out in such a measure; and (3) the relevant factual circumstances surrounding the granting of the subsidy that provide the context for understanding the measure's design, structure, and modalities of operation. It further explained:

> [W]here relevant evidence exists, the assessment could be based on a comparison between, on the one hand, the ratio of *anticipated* export and domestic sales of the subsidized product that would come about in consequence of the granting of the subsidy, and, on the other hand, the situation in the absence of the subsidy. The situation in the absence of the subsidy may be understood on the basis of historical sales of the same product by the recipient in the domestic and export markets before the subsidy was granted. In the event that there are no historical data untainted by the subsidy, or the subsidized product is a new product for which no historical data exists, the comparison could be made with the performance that a profit-maximizing firm would hypothetically be expected to achieve in the export and domestic markets in the absence of the subsidy. Where the evidence shows, all other things being equal, that the granting of the subsidy provides an incentive to skew anticipated sales towards exports, in comparison with the historical performance of the recipient or the hypothetical performance of a profit-maximizing firm in the absence of the subsidy, this would be an indication that the granting of the subsidy is in fact tied to anticipated exportation within the meaning of Article 3.1(a) and footnote 4 of the *SCM Agreement*.[185]

The Appellate Body ruled in *EC and certain member States – Large Civil Aircraft (2011)* that the standard for determining whether the granting of a subsidy is 'in fact tied to ... anticipated exportation' within the meaning of Article 3.1(a) and footnote 4 is an objective standard:

> [t]o be established on the basis of the total configuration of facts constituting and surrounding the granting of the subsidy, including the design, structure, and modalities of operation of the measure granting the subsidy. Indeed, the conditional relationship between the granting of the subsidy and export performance must be objectively observable on the basis of such evidence in order for the subsidy to be geared to induce the promotion of future export performance by the recipient.[186]

184 Appellate Body Report, *EC and certain member States – Large Civil Aircraft (2011)*, para. 1046.

185 *Ibid.*, para. 1047. It gave the following numerical example to illustrate when the granting of a subsidy may, or may not, be geared to induce promotion of future export performance by a recipient: 'Assume that a subsidy is designed to allow a recipient to increase its future production by five units. Assume further that the existing ratio of the recipient's export sales to domestic sales, at the time the subsidy is granted, is 2:3. The granting of the subsidy will *not* be tied to anticipated exportation if, all other things being equal, the anticipated ratio of export sales to domestic sales is not greater than the existing ratio. In other words, if, under the measure granting the subsidy, the recipient would not be expected to export more than two of the additional five units to be produced, then this is indicative of the absence of a tie. By contrast, the granting of the subsidy would be tied to anticipated exportation if, all other things being equal, the recipient is expected to export at least three of the five additional units to be produced. In other words, the subsidy is designed in such a way that it is expected to skew the recipient's future sales in favour of export sales, even though the recipient may also be expected to increase its domestic sales.' See Appellate Body Report, *EC and certain member States – Large Civil Aircraft (2011)*, para. 1048.

186 *Ibid.*, para. 1051.

Given that the standard for *de facto* export contingency is an *objective* standard, this standard cannot be satisfied by relying on the subjective motivation of the granting government to promote the future export performance of the recipient. However, as noted by the Appellate Body, 'objectively reviewable expressions of a government's policy objectives for granting a subsidy' may constitute relevant evidence in an inquiry into whether a subsidy is geared to induce the promotion of future export performance by the recipient.[187] Similarly, for the Appellate Body, the standard for *de facto* export contingency does not require a panel to ascertain a government's reason(s) for granting a subsidy:

> The government's reason for granting a subsidy only explains *why* the subsidy is granted. It does not necessarily answer the question as to *what* the government did, in terms of the design, structure, and modalities of operation of the subsidy, in order to induce the promotion of future export performance by the recipient. Indeed, whether the granting of a subsidy is conditional on future export performance must be determined by assessing *the subsidy itself*, in the light of the relevant factual circumstances, rather than by reference to the granting authority's reasons for the measure. This is not to say, however, that evidence regarding the policy reasons of a subsidy is necessarily excluded from the inquiry into whether a subsidy is geared to induce the promotion of future export performance by the recipient.[188]

The Appellate Body summarised in *EC and certain member States – Large Civil Aircraft (2011)* its test for *de facto* export contingency as follows:

> We find that the [*de facto*] conditionality between the granting of a subsidy and anticipated exportation can be established where the granting of the subsidy is geared to induce the promotion of future export performance of the recipient. The standard for *de facto* export contingency under Article 3.1(a) and footnote 4 of the SCM Agreement would be met when the subsidy is granted so as to provide an incentive to the recipient to export in a way that is not simply reflective of the conditions of supply and demand in the domestic and export markets undistorted by the granting of the subsidy.[189]

To illustrate the scope of the prohibition on export subsidies, note that panels and/or the Appellate Body found *inter alia* the following measures to be prohibited export subsidies: (1) payments by the government of Brazil, related to the export of regional aircraft, which cover, at most, the difference between the interest charges contracted with the buyer and the cost to the financing party of raising the required funds; these payments were made under the interest rate equalisation component of the 'PROEX', an export financing programme (see *Brazil – Aircraft (1999)*); (2) grants for a total of A$30 million and a loan of A$25 million (on 'non-commercial' terms) provided by the Australian government to Howe, the only producer and exporter of automotive leather in Australia (see *Australia – Automotive Leather II (1999)*); and (3) the exemption from US income tax of a portion of export-related income of 'foreign sales corporations' (FSCs), i.e. foreign corporations in charge of specific activities with respect to the

187 *Ibid.*

188 *Ibid.*, para. 1052. 189 *Ibid.*, para. 1102.

sale or lease of goods produced in the United States for export outside the United States (see *US – FSC (2000)*). Note that the Appellate Body was unable to come to a conclusion in *EC and certain member States – Large Civil Aircraft (2011)* as to whether – under its newly clarified test of *de facto* export contingency discussed above – the 'Launch Aid/Member State Financing' subsidies at issue amounted to prohibited export subsidies, because the panel's factual findings and undisputed facts on the record did not provide a sufficient basis to do so.

4.2 Import Substitution Subsidies

In addition to export subsidies, the category of prohibited subsidies also includes import substitution subsidies. As defined in Article 3.1(b) of the *SCM Agreement*, quoted above, import substitution subsidies are subsidies contingent upon the use of domestic over imported goods.[190] The Appellate Body in *Canada – Autos (2000)* noted that the phrase 'contingent ... upon the use of domestic over imported goods' is unclear as to whether Article 3.1(b) covers both subsidies contingent 'in law' and subsidies contingent 'in fact' upon the use of domestic over imported goods.[191] Unlike in Article 3.1(a), the words 'in law or in fact' are absent from Article 3.1(b). However, according to the Appellate Body, this does not necessarily mean that Article 3.1(b) extends to *de jure* contingency only.[192] The Appellate Body held:

> [W]e believe that a finding that Article 3.1(b) extends only to contingency 'in law' upon the use of domestic over imported goods would be contrary to the object and purpose of the *SCM Agreement* because it would make circumvention of obligations by Members too easy.[193]

In *US – Upland Cotton (2005)*, the panel (and the Appellate Body on appeal) concluded that the subsidies at issue in that case, namely, payments to domestic users of US upland cotton, were subsidies contingent upon the use of domestic over imported goods and were, therefore, inconsistent with Article 3.1(b) of the *SCM Agreement*.[194]

In *Canada – Renewable Energy (2013)*, the Appellate Body examined whether it could complete the analysis and determine if the challenged measures conferred a benefit within the meaning of Article 1.1(b) and whether they constituted prohibited subsidies, inconsistent with Articles 3.1(b) and 3.2 of the

190 'Import substitution subsidies' are also referred to as 'local content subsidies'.

191 See Appellate Body Report, *Canada – Autos (2000)*, para. 139.

192 See *ibid.*, para. 141. 193 *Ibid.*, para. 142.

194 See Panel Report, *US – Upland Cotton (2005)*, paras. 7.1088 and 7.1097–7.1098; and Appellate Body Report, *US – Upland Cotton (2005)*, para. 552. In the same case, the Appellate Body recalled 'that the introductory language of Article 3.1 of the *SCM Agreement* clarifies that this provision applies "[e]xcept as provided in the Agreement on Agriculture"', but also held that import substitution subsidies on agricultural products are not exempt from the prohibition in Article 3.1(b) of the *SCM Agreement* by virtue of Article 6.3 of, or Annex 3, paragraph 7, to, the *Agreement on Agriculture*. Appellate Body Report, *US – Upland Cotton (2005)*, paras. 541, 545–6 and 550.

SCM Agreement.[195] The Appellate Body considered that in principle a comparison between prices for wind-power contracts under FIT with prices of wind-power contracts under a previous feed-in tariff programme, which were awarded through competitive bidding, could be made to determine the existence of benefit. The Appellate Body, however, was unable to complete the analysis due to insufficiency of factual findings by the panel or undisputed facts on the panel record that would have allowed it to do so. Moreover, the Appellate Body considered that the application of a benefit benchmarks based on the government of Ontario's definition of the energy supply mix had not sufficiently been explored before the panel and on appeal, also raising due process concerns, in completing the legal analysis. As a result, the Appellate Body made no finding as to whether the measures at issue conferred a benefit and, consequently, whether they were prohibited subsidies within the meaning of Articles 3.1(b) and 3.2 of the *SCM Agreement*.[196]

4.3 Multilateral Remedies for Prohibited Subsidies

The multilateral remedies for prohibited subsidies, be they export subsidies or import substitution subsidies, are set out in Article 4 of the *SCM Agreement*. Pursuant to Article 4.1, consultations may be requested with any Member believed to be granting or maintaining a prohibited subsidy. Such a request for consultations shall include a 'statement of available evidence with regard to the existence and nature of the subsidy in question'.[197] If such consultations fail to resolve the dispute, the dispute may be referred to a dispute settlement panel, and then to the Appellate Body, for adjudication.[198] Article 4 of the *SCM Agreement* sets out a number of 'special or additional rules and procedures', which prevail over the DSU rules in cases of conflict.[199] The most notable difference between the rules and procedures of Article 4 of the *SCM Agreement* and the DSU rules and procedures relate to time frames. The time frames under Article 4 are half as long as the time frames provided for under the DSU.[200] For example, the time frame for 'ordinary' panel proceedings is six months from the date of composition of the panel;[201] under Article 4 of the *SCM Agreement*, the time limit for panel proceedings concerning prohibited subsidies is three months.

195 Appellate Body Report, *Canada – Renewable Energy (2013)*, paras. 5.223ff. 196 *Ibid.*, para. 5.246.

197 Article 4.2 of the *SCM Agreement*. On the interpretation of Article 4.2, see Panel Report, *Canada – Aircraft (1999)*; Panel Report, *Australia – Automotive Leather II (1999)*; Panel Report, *US – FSC (2000)* and Appellate Body Report, *US – FSC (2000)*; Panel Report, *US – Upland Cotton (2004)* and Appellate Body Report, *US – Upland Cotton (2005)*; see also Annex V on 'Procedures for Developing Information Concerning Serious Prejudice'.

198 The rules applicable to consultations and adjudication are primarily those of the DSU, discussed in detail in Chapter 3. See above, pp. 266–85.

199 See below, pp. 808–11.

200 Note, however, that parties can, and commonly do, agree on an extension of these special timeframes. See Article 4.12 of the *SCM Agreement*. Also, when a complainant brings claims under both the *SCM Agreement* and other WTO agreements, the shorter timeframes under the *SCM Agreement* do not apply.

201 See Article 12.8 of the DSU. See also above, pp. 248–51.

Note also that a panel established for a 'prohibited subsidy' dispute may ask a Permanent Group of Experts (PGE) whether the measure at issue is a prohibited subsidy.[202] The determination of the PGE is binding on the panel. To date, panels have not yet made use of this possibility.

If a panel finds a measure to be a prohibited subsidy, Article 4.7 of the *SCM Agreement* states that:

> the panel shall recommend that the subsidizing Member withdraw the subsidy without delay. In this regard, the panel shall specify in its recommendation the time-period within which the measure must be withdrawn.

On several occasions, panels and the Appellate Body have emphasised that prohibited subsidies must therefore be withdrawn *without delay*, and the time period within which the subsidy must be withdrawn is to be specified by the panel.[203] As the Appellate Body clarified in *Brazil – Aircraft (Article 21.5 – Canada) (2000)*, withdrawal of the prohibited subsidy involves the removal of the subsidy.[204] The panel in *Australia – Automotive Leather II (Article 21.5 – US) (2000)* concluded that the obligation to withdraw the prohibited subsidy, in that case, could only be met by repayment of the subsidy received. As discussed in Chapter 3, in general, remedies for breaches of WTO law are only prospective, but, according to the panel in *Australia – Automotive Leather II (Article 21.5 – US) (2000)*, the obligation under Article 4.7 to withdraw the prohibited subsidy requires the company that received a non-recurrent prohibited subsidy to repay that subsidy to the subsidising Member.[205] The panel in *Australia – Automotive Leather II (Article 21.5 – US) (2000)* reasoned as follows:

> We believe it is incumbent upon us to interpret 'withdraw the subsidy' so as to give it effective meaning. A finding that the term 'withdraw the subsidy' may not encompass repayment would give rise to serious questions regarding the efficacy of the remedy in prohibited subsidy cases involving one-time subsidies paid in the past whose retention is not contingent upon future export performance.[206]

This ruling of that panel was heavily criticised by WTO Members because of its retroactive character.[207] To date, no other panel has made a similar ruling.[208]

Panels in 'prohibited subsidy' disputes specify the time period within which the prohibited subsidy must be withdrawn, i.e. they specify what is meant by

202 See Article 4.5 of the *SCM Agreement*. See also above, p 139.
203 See Appellate Body Report, *US – FSC (Article 21.5 – EC II) (2006)*, para. 82.
204 See Appellate Body Report, *Brazil – Aircraft (Article 21.5 – Canada) (2000)*, para. 45.
205 See also above, pp. 207–9.
206 Panel Report, *Australia – Automotive Leather II (Article 21.5 – US) (2000)*, para. 6.35.
207 See Dispute Settlement Body, *Minutes of the DSB Meeting of 11 February 2000*, WT/DSB/M/75. See also above, p. 208, fn. 251. Note that the United States, the original complainant in this dispute, had *not* requested the repayment of the export subsidy at issue.
208 Note that the panels in *Canada – Aircraft (Article 21.5 – Brazil) (2000)* and *Brazil – Aircraft (Article 21.5 – Canada) (2000)* did not rule on the repayment of subsidies because repayment had not been requested by the complainants and the panels considered that their findings should be restricted to the scope of the disagreement between the parties. See Panel Report, *Canada – Aircraft (Article 21.5 – Brazil) (2000)*, para. 5.48; and Panel Report, *Brazil – Aircraft (Article 21.5 – Canada) (2000)*, fn. 17.

'withdraw without delay' as required by Article 4.7 of the *SCM Agreement*.[209] Note by way of example the conclusion reached by the panel in *Korea – Commercial Vessels (2005)*:

> Taking into account the procedures that may be required to implement our recommendation on the one hand, and the requirement that Korea withdraw its subsidies 'without delay' on the other, we recommend that Korea withdraw the individual APRG and PSL subsidies within 90 days.[210]

To date, several panels have specified a period of three months for the withdrawal of a prohibited subsidy. In *US – FSC (2000)*, however, the panel specified a period of more than a year to allow the United States to adopt the necessary fiscal legislation.[211] In *Brazil – Aircraft (Article 21.5 – Canada) (2000)*, the Appellate Body stated that 'the obligation to withdraw prohibited subsidies "without delay" is unaffected by contractual obligations that a Member itself may have assumed under municipal law'.[212] Similarly, in *US – FSC (Article 21.5 – EC) (2002)*, the Appellate Body clarified that there is 'no basis' for extending the time period prescribed in Article 4.7 for withdrawal: (1) to protect the contractual interests of private parties; or (2) to ensure an orderly transition to the regime of the new measure.[213]

If in an Article 21.5 proceeding the measure taken to comply with the Article 4.7 recommendation in the original proceedings is found not to achieve full withdrawal of the prohibited subsidy – either because it leaves the entirety or part of the original prohibited subsidy in place, or because it replaces that subsidy with another prohibited subsidy – the implementing Member continues to be under the obligation to achieve full withdrawal of the subsidy.[214]

If a recommendation to withdraw a prohibited subsidy is not followed within the time period set by the panel, the DSB must, upon the request of the original complainant(s) and by reverse consensus, authorise 'appropriate countermeasures' pursuant to Article 4.10 of the *SCM Agreement*. In 'prohibited subsidies' disputes, these 'appropriate countermeasures' replace the suspension of concessions or other obligations, i.e. retaliation measures, available under the DSU in case of non-implementation in WTO disputes under covered agreements other than the *SCM Agreement*.[215] 'Appropriate countermeasures' and 'retaliation measures' may differ in that the level of 'appropriate countermeasures' could be the amount of the prohibited subsidy

209 On the general rules of Article 21.3 of the DSU concerning the 'reasonable period of time for implementation', see above, pp. 199–204.
210 Panel Report, *Korea – Commercial Vessels (2005)*, para. 8.5.
211 See Panel Report, *US – FSC (2000)*, para. 8.8.
212 Appellate Body Report, *Brazil – Aircraft (Article 21.5 – Canada) (2000)*, paras. 45–6.
213 See Appellate Body Report, *US – FSC (Article 21.5 – EC) (2002)*, paras. 229–30.
214 Appellate Body Report, *US – FSC (Article 21.5 – EC II) (2006)*, para. 82.
215 See above, pp. 808–11.

rather than the level of any trade effects or the nullification or impairment that has been caused.[216]

5 ACTIONABLE SUBSIDIES

Unlike export subsidies and import substitution subsidies, most subsidies are not prohibited but are 'actionable', i.e. they are subject to challenge in the event that they cause adverse effects on the interests of another Member. To the extent that these subsidies do not cause adverse effects, or the adverse effects are removed, they cannot, or can no longer, be challenged successfully. The chapeau of Article 5 of the *SCM Agreement* provides:

> No Member should cause, through the use of any subsidy referred to in paragraphs 1 and 2 of Article 1, adverse effects to the interests of other Members.

Paragraphs (a)–(c) of Article 5 distinguish between three types of 'adverse effects' on the interests of other Members: (1) *injury* to the domestic industry of another Member (Article 5(a)); (2) *nullification or impairment* of benefits accruing directly or indirectly to other Members under the GATT 1994 (Article 5(b)); and (3) *serious prejudice*, including a threat thereof, to the interests of another Member (Article 5(c)). This section discusses in turn these three types of 'adverse effects'.

5.1 Subsidies Causing Injury

Subsidies have adverse effects on the interests of other Members within the meaning of Article 5(a) of the *SCM Agreement* – and are therefore 'actionable' – when

216 The arbitrators in *Brazil – Aircraft (Article 22.6 – Brazil) (2000)* accepted the view of the parties that the term 'countermeasures', as used in these provisions, includes suspension of concessions or other obligations. Furthermore, the arbitrators concluded that, when dealing with a prohibited export subsidy, an amount of countermeasures that corresponds to the total amount of the subsidy is appropriate. See Decision by the Arbitrator, *Brazil – Aircraft (Article 22.6 – Brazil) (2000)*, paras. 3.28, 3.29 and 3.33–3.40 and 3.44. According to the arbitrators in *US – FSC (Article 22.6 – US) (2002)*, it would be 'consistent with the reading of the plain meaning of the concept of countermeasure to say that it can be directed either at countering the measure at issue (in this case, at effectively neutralizing the export subsidy with respect to all countries affected by it) or at counteracting its effects on the affected party, or both'. See Decision by the Arbitrators, *US – FSC (Article 22.6 – US) (2002)*, para. 5.6. See however, the Decision by the Arbitrator, *US – Upland Cotton (Article 22.6 – Brazil) (2009)*. The arbitrators in that arbitration noted the difference between the use of the term 'countermeasures' in Article 4.10 of the *SCM Agreement* and the terms of Article 22 of the DSU, which refers to the 'suspension of concessions or other obligations'. However, they understood the term 'countermeasures' not to designate anything other than a temporary suspension of certain obligations. The arbitrators were not convinced that the use of the term 'countermeasures' necessarily connotes, in and of itself, an intention to refer to retaliatory action that 'goes beyond the mere rebalancing of trade interests' between the parties to the dispute. See Decision by the Arbitrator, *US – Upland Cotton (Article 22.6 – Brazil) (2009)*, paras. 4.34–4.43. In *US – Large Civil Aircraft (2nd complaint) (2012)*, although the European Union requested authorisation to take countermeasures and the matter was referred to arbitration, the arbitration proceedings were suspended until completion of the Article 21.5 compliance proceedings between the United States and the European Union.

the subsidised imports cause injury to the domestic industry producing the like product.[217] This subsection examines, in turn, the concepts of (1) 'like product', (2) 'domestic industry', (3) 'injury' and (4) 'causation' as they apply in Part III of the *SCM Agreement* on actionable subsidies.[218]

5.1.1 Like Product

The concept of 'like product' is defined in footnote 46 to the *SCM Agreement* as:

> a product which is identical, i.e. alike in all respects to the product under consideration, or in the absence of such a product, another product which, although not alike in all respects, has characteristics closely resembling those of the product under consideration.[219]

When compared to the definitions of 'like products' resulting from the case law on Articles I and III of the GATT 1994 or the definition of 'like products' in the *Agreement on Safeguards*, the definition in the *SCM Agreement* seems narrower in scope. The approach to establishing 'likeness' under the *SCM Agreement* is, however, in fact similar to the approach under the GATT 1994.[220] In *Indonesia – Autos (1998)*, the panel found:

> Although we are required in this dispute to interpret the term 'like product' in conformity with the specific definition provided in the SCM Agreement, we believe that useful guidance can nevertheless be derived from prior analysis of 'like product' issues under other provisions of the WTO Agreement.[221]

The provisions of the *WTO Agreement* referred to are, of course, Articles I:1, III:2 and III:4 of the GATT 1994. In establishing 'likeness', the same elements (physical characteristics as well as end uses, consumer habits and preferences and tariff classification) will be of importance. As the panel in *Indonesia – Autos (1998)* ruled, the term 'characteristics closely resembling' includes but is not limited to physical characteristics; the *SCM Agreement* does not preclude looking at criteria other than physical characteristics, where relevant to the like product analysis.[222]

217 In *EC and certain member States – Large Civil Aircraft (2011)*, the panel explained that it would interpret 'injury to the domestic industry' in Article 5(a) harmoniously with the provisions of Article 15 governing countervailing duty investigations. Since, in an 'adverse effects' case, it was essentially fulfilling the role of an investigating authority in a countervailing or anti-dumping duty investigation, the panel decided to base its examination and determination of the various injury elements as required by the more specific provisions of Article 15. See Panel Report, *EC and certain member States – Large Civil Aircraft (2011)*, paras. 7.2068 and 7.2080.

218 Note that fn. 11 to the *SCM Agreement* stipulates that the term 'injury to the domestic industry' is used in Article 5(a) in the same sense as it is used in Part V of that Agreement. They are addressed here together, although it may be important to note that considerations may differ under certain provisions of Part III and Part V of the Agreement. See below, pp. 834–7.

219 Note that this definition applies throughout the *SCM Agreement* and not merely in the context of the determination of material injury. It also applies, for example, in the context of the serious prejudice determination of Article 6 of the *SCM Agreement*. See below, pp. 818–19.

220 For the determination of 'likeness' under Articles I:1, III:2 and III:4 of the GATT 1994, see above, pp. 316–19, 354–73 and 381–90.

221 Panel Report, *Indonesia – Autos (1998)*, para. 14.174. 222 See *ibid.*, para. 14.173.

5.1.2 Domestic Industry

The definition of 'domestic industry' in the *SCM Agreement* is quite similar to the definition of that concept in the *Anti-Dumping Agreement*.[223] Article 16.1 of the *SCM Agreement* defines the 'domestic industry' as:

> [t]he domestic producers as a whole of the like products or ... those of them whose collective output of the products constitutes a major proportion of the total domestic production of those products.

There are two exceptions to this definition of 'domestic industry'. First, domestic *producers that are related* to exporters or importers or which themselves import the subsidised products may be excluded from the relevant 'domestic industry'.[224] Second, in exceptional circumstances, the territory of a Member may be divided into *two or more competitive markets* and the producers within each market may be regarded as a separate industry. A regional industry then constitutes the relevant 'domestic industry'.[225]

5.1.3 Injury

The concept of 'injury' to a domestic industry in the *SCM Agreement* covers: (1) material injury to a domestic industry;[226] (2) a threat of material injury to a domestic industry; and (3) material retardation of the establishment of a domestic industry.[227]

The determination of 'injury' to the domestic industry must, pursuant to Article 15.1 of the *SCM Agreement*, be based on positive evidence and involve an objective examination of, *first*, the volume of the subsidised imports and the effect of the subsidised imports on prices in the domestic market for like products, and, *second*, the consequent impact of these imports on the domestic producers of such products.[228] With regard to the *first* element of the examination under Article 15.1 of the *SCM Agreement*, Article 15.2 thereof provides that, with respect to the volume of the subsidised imports, it must be examined whether there has been a *significant increase* of the subsidised imports.[229] With respect to the effect of the subsidised imports on prices, it must be examined

223 See above, pp. 720–3. With regard to the definition of 'domestic industry' under the *Anti-Dumping Agreement*, consider, in particular, the Appellate Body's interpretation of that term in *EC – Fasteners (China) (2011)*. See Appellate Body Report, *EC – Fasteners (China) (2011)*, para. 411.

224 See Article 16.1 of the *SCM Agreement*.

225 See Article 16.2 of the *SCM Agreement*.

226 Note that the *SCM Agreement*, like the *Anti-Dumping Agreement*, requires *material* injury, or a threat thereof, rather than *serious* injury as required under the *Agreement on Safeguards*. As already mentioned, the Appellate Body in *US – Lamb (2001)* noted that the standard of 'serious injury' is higher than that of 'material injury'. See above, pp. 640–3.

227 See fn. 45 to the *SCM Agreement*.

228 Note in this regard that the panel in *US – Softwood Lumber VI (2004)* recalled the definitions of the Appellate Body with respect to 'positive evidence' and 'objective examination' under the *Anti-Dumping Agreement* (as in *US – Hot-Rolled Steel (2001)*). See Panel Report, *US – Softwood Lumber VI (2004)*, para. 7.28, referring to Appellate Body Report, *US – Hot-Rolled Steel (2001)*, paras. 192–3.

229 This increase may be an increase in absolute terms or relative to production or consumption in the importing country.

whether there has been a *significant price undercutting* by the subsidised imports, or whether these imports otherwise *depress or suppress prices to a significant degree.*[230] As discussed in Chapter 11, the Appellate Body interpreted in *China – GOES (2012)* the requirements of Article 15.2 of the *SCM Agreement* and the identical requirements of Article 3.2 of the *Anti-Dumping Agreement.* According to the Appellate Body, Article 15.2 contemplates an inquiry into the relationship between two variables, namely, subsidised imports and domestic prices. More specifically, an investigating authority is required to consider whether a first variable – that is, dumped imports – has *explanatory force for the occurrence of* significant depression or suppression of a second variable – that is, domestic prices.[231] For a further discussion on the requirements of Article 15.2 of the *SCM Agreement*, please refer to the discussion of the *Anti-Dumping Agreement* in Chapter 11.[232]

With regard to the *second* element of the examination under Article 15.1 of the *SCM Agreement*, Article 15.4 thereof requires that the examination of the consequent impact of the subsidised imports on the domestic industry must include an evaluation of all *relevant economic factors and indices* having a bearing on the state of the industry. Article 15.4 lists the following specific factors: (1) an actual and potential decline in the output, sales, market share, profits, productivity, return on investments or utilisation of capacity; (2) factors affecting domestic prices; and (3) actual and potential negative effects on cash flow, inventories, employment, wages, growth or the ability to raise capital or investments. The examination of all factors on this list is mandatory in each case.[233] However, this list is not exhaustive and *other* relevant factors must also be considered. Furthermore, note that no single factor, or combination of factors, listed in Article 15.4 necessarily gives decisive guidance.[234] In *China – GOES (2012)*, the Appellate Body emphasised that Article 15.4 also requires an examination of the *impact of subsidised imports* on the domestic industry. In other words, Article 15.4 does not merely require an examination of the state of the domestic industry, but contemplates that an understanding of *the impact* of subsidised imports be derived on the basis of such an examination.[235]

As indicated above, the concept of 'injury' to a domestic industry in the *SCM Agreement* covers not only 'material injury' but also 'threat of material injury'.

230 Note that to 'suppress' prices is to prevent price increases that would otherwise occur.
231 Appellate Body Report, *China – GOES (2012)*, paras. 136–7.
232 See above, pp. 724–31.
233 The existence of an obligation to examine all the factors of the Article 15.4 list can be established by analogy to panel and Appellate Body reports interpreting similar provisions in the *Anti-Dumping Agreement* and the *Agreement on Safeguards*. See above, pp. 729–31 (AD Agreement), 641–3 (Safeguards Agreement).
234 See Article 15.4, last sentence, of the *SCM Agreement*.
235 Appellate Body Report, *China – GOES (2012)*, para. 149.

The determination of a 'threat of material injury' must be based on facts and not merely on allegations, conjecture or remote possibility.[236] For there to be a 'threat of material injury', the change in circumstances which would create a situation in which the subsidy would cause injury must be clearly foreseen and imminent.[237] Article 15.7 lists a number of factors to be considered in making a determination regarding the existence of a 'threat of material injury'. This non-exhaustive list of factors includes, *inter alia*: (1) the nature of the subsidy and the trade effects likely to arise from it; (2) a significant rate of increase of subsidised imports; and (3) whether imports are entering at prices that will have a significant depressing or suppressing effect on domestic prices.[238] Article 15.7 does not prescribe a specific methodology for determining the rate of increase in imports or for the examination of the price effects of dumped/subsidised imports.[239] The factors listed in Article 15.7 must all be considered.[240] Moreover, any other relevant factor must also be considered in order to establish whether further subsidised imports are imminent and whether, unless protective action is taken, material injury would occur.[241] In addition, as in the case of dumping, Article 15.8 requires 'special care' when considering and deciding on situations of 'threat of material injury'.[242] Therefore, there is definitely no *lower* standard of care and explanation on the grounds that a determination of 'threat of injury' rather than a determination of current material injury is to be made. To the contrary, the reasoning underlying a determination of 'threat of injury' must clearly disclose the assumptions and extrapolations that were made, on the basis of the positive record evidence, regarding future occurrences and not merely on allegation, conjecture or remote possibility; and show a high degree of likelihood that projected occurrences will materialise.[243]

Pursuant to Article 15.3 of the *SCM Agreement*, when the subsidised imports originate in several countries and several countries are therefore subject to the

236 See Article 15.7 of the *SCM Agreement*. 237 Article 15.7, second sentence, of the *SCM Agreement*.

238 See the factors mentioned in Article 15.7(i), (ii) and (iv) of the *SCM Agreement*.

239 Regardless of the methodology followed, the Appellate Body clarified that what must be examined is: (i) the trends in the prices at which 'imports are entering'; (ii) the 'effect' of those prices on 'domestic prices'; and (iii) the 'demand for further imports'. Discerning the 'effect' of prices of imports on domestic prices necessarily calls for an analysis of the interaction between the two. Otherwise, the links between the prices of imports and the depressing or suppressing effect on domestic prices, and the consequent likelihood of a 'demand for further imports', may not be properly established. See Appellate Body Report, *US – Softwood Lumber VI (Article 21.5 – Canada) (2006)*, para. 151.

240 See, by analogy, Panel Report, *Mexico – Corn Syrup (2000)*, para. 7.133, which concerned an identical provision in the *Anti-Dumping Agreement*. See above, p. 732.

241 See Article 15.7, last sentence, of the *SCM Agreement*. Note that the panel in *US – Softwood Lumber VI (2004)* stated that a threat of injury determination is made against the background of an evaluation of the condition of the industry in light of the Article 15.4 factors. Once such an analysis has been carried out in the context of an investigation of material injury, however, the panel found that none of the relevant provisions of Article 15 require a second analysis of the injury factors in cases involving a threat of material injury. See Panel Report, *US – Softwood Lumber VI (2004)*, paras. 7.97–7.112.

242 See Panel Report, *US – Softwood Lumber VI (2004)*, para. 7.33.

243 Appellate Body Report, *US – Softwood Lumber VI (Article 21.5 – Canada) (2006)*, paras. 107 and 109.

anti-subsidy investigations, the effects of the subsidised imports may be assessed *cumulatively* for the purpose of establishing injury to the domestic industry. It is quite common for WTO Members to make a cumulative assessment of the effects of subsidised imports. However, pursuant to Article 15.3 of the *SCM Agreement*, such cumulative assessment is allowed only when: (1) the amount of subsidisation is more than *de minimis* (i.e. more than or equal to 1 per cent *ad valorem*);[244] (2) the volume of the imports of each country is not negligible; and (3) the cumulative assessment of the effects of the imports is appropriate in light of the conditions of competition between products imported from different countries and the conditions of competition between the imported products and the like domestic products.

In *US – Carbon Steel (India) (2014)*, the United States appealed the panel finding that Articles 15.3 and Articles 15.1, 15.2, 15.4 and 15.5 of the *SCM Agreement* do not authorise investigating authorities to assess cumulatively the effects of imports that are not subject to countervailing duty investigations ('non-subsidized imports') with the effects of imports that are subject to such investigations ('subsidized imports'). The Appellate Body agreed with the panel that 'being subject to countervailing duty investigations is a prerequisite for the cumulative assessment of the effects of imports under Article 15.3'.[245] Regarding cross-cumulation of anti-dumping duties and countervailing duties, the Appellate Body noted:

> In sum, the reference in Article 15.3 to 'products ... simultaneously subject to countervailing duty investigations' indicates that investigating authorities must examine the volume, price effect, and consequent impact of imports that are subsidized, and must exclude from their assessment the volume, price effect, and consequent impact of imports that are *not* subsidized. The overarching requirement under Article 15.1 that an injury determination be based on positive evidence and involve an objective examination of the volume and the effect of subsidized imports [on prices] and the impact of such imports on domestic producers confirms this interpretation. Furthermore, the references to 'subsidized imports' in Articles 15.2, 15.4, and 15.5, as well as various references to 'subsidized imports' in other provisions of Part V of the SCM Agreement, further confirm that the imposition of a countervailing duty is consistent with the SCM Agreement only if adopted to counteract injury caused by subsidized imports.[246]

Accordingly, the Appellate Body considered that Article 15.3 and Articles 15.1, 15.2, 15.4 and 15.5 of the *SCM Agreement* require that the injury analysis in the context of a countervailing duty determination be limited to consideration of the effects of subsidised imports.[247] The Appellate Body upheld the panel's finding in *US – Carbon Steel (India) (2014)* that these provisions do not authorise

244 See Article 11.9 of the *SCM Agreement*. The amount of the subsidy is considered *de minimis* if the subsidy is less than 1 per cent of the value of the subsidised product.

245 Appellate Body Report, *US – Carbon Steel (India) (2014)*, para. 4.579.

246 *Ibid.*, para. 4.586.

247 *Ibid.*, para. 4.586. It is worth noting that the Appellate Body used Article 3.1 of the *Anti-Dumping Agreement* as contextual guidance. See *ibid.*, para. 4.582.

investigating authorities to assess cumulatively the effects of subsidised imports with the effects of non-subsidised, but dumped imports.

5.1.4 Causation

Finally, Article 15.5 of the *SCM Agreement* spells out the requirement to establish the existence of a *causal link* between subsidised imports and injury to the domestic industry. The first sentence of Article 15.5 requires that 'the subsidized imports are, through the effects of subsidies, causing injury' to the domestic industry. The second sentence emphasises that the demonstration of the causal relationship between the subsidised imports and the injury shall be based on all relevant evidence. In both sentences, the subject to which the phrase 'are causing injury' applies, or in respect of which 'a causal relationship' is to be established, is 'the subsidized imports'.[248]

The injury suffered by the domestic industry may be caused not only by the subsidised imports. Other factors may also cause injury to the domestic industry, including: (1) the volumes and prices of non-subsidised imports of the product in question; (2) a contraction in demand or changes in the patterns of consumption; (3) trade-restrictive practices of, and competition between, the foreign and domestic producers; (4) developments in technology; and (5) the export performance and productivity of the domestic industry. As set out in Article 15.5, third sentence, the injury caused by these other factors may *not be attributed* to the subsidised imports.[249]

In sum, the demonstration of the causal relationship envisaged in the first two sentences of Article 15.5 is to be carried out by following the analysis set forth in Articles 15.2 and 15.4 for examining the 'effects' of the subsidised imports. Accordingly, such an examination will comprise the following elements: (1) whether there has been a significant increase in subsidised imports; (2) the effect of the subsidised imports on prices; and (3) the consequent impact of the subsidised imports on the domestic industry.[250] The Appellate Body found that the phrase 'the subsidized imports are, through the effects of subsidies, causing injury' in Article 15.5 does not impose an additional requirement to make two distinct types of examinations into (1) the 'effects of the subsidies' as distinguished from (2) the effects of 'the subsidised imports' on a case-by-case basis.[251] The 'non-attribution' requirement contained in the third sentence of Article 15.5 is concerned with ensuring that the injurious effects of any known factors *other than subsidised imports* are not attributed to the subsidised imports.[252]

248 Appellate Body Report, *Japan – DRAMs (Korea) (2007)*, para. 262. 249 *Ibid.*, para. 267.
250 See *ibid.*, para. 263. 251 See *ibid.*, paras. 264 and 277.
252 See *ibid.*, para. 267.

5.2 Subsidies Causing Nullification or Impairment

Subsidies have adverse effects on the interests of other Members within the meaning of Article 5(b) of the *SCM Agreement* – and are therefore 'actionable' – when the subsidised imports cause the nullification or impairment of benefits accruing directly or indirectly to other Members under the GATT 1994. This may be the case, in particular, with respect to the benefits from tariff concessions bound under Article II:1 of the GATT 1994. Subsidisation may undercut improved market access resulting from a tariff concession.[253]

5.3 Subsidies Causing Serious Prejudice

Subsidies have adverse effects on the interests of other Members within the meaning of Article 5(c) of the *SCM Agreement* – and are therefore 'actionable' – when the subsidised imports cause serious prejudice to the interests of another Member. Pursuant to Article 6.3 of the *SCM Agreement*, 'serious prejudice' *may* arise where a subsidy has one or more of the following effects: (1) the subsidy displaces or impedes imports of a like product of another Member into the market of the subsidising Member (Article 6.3(a)); (2) the subsidy displaces or impedes the export of a like product of another Member from a third country market (Article 6.3(b)); (3) the subsidy results in a significant price undercutting by the subsidised product in comparison to the like product of another Member in the same market, or significant price suppression, price depression or lost sales in the same market (Article 6.3(c)); or (4) the subsidy leads to an increase in the world market share of the subsidising Member in a particular primary product or commodity in comparison to the average share it had during the previous period of three years (Article 6.3(d)).[254] If a complaining Member can show that a subsidy has any of these effects, then 'serious prejudice' may be found to exist. On the other hand, if the subsidising Member can show that subsidies do not result in any of these effects, these subsidies will *not* be found to cause serious prejudice.[255]

The concepts of 'serious prejudice' and 'injury' to a particular domestic industry are different and distinct concepts. The panel in *Korea – Commercial Vessels*

253 The existence of nullification or impairment is established in accordance with the practice of the application of Article XXIII of the GATT 1994. See fn. 12 of the *SCM Agreement*. However, in *US – Offset Act (Byrd Amendment) (2003)*, Mexico, one of the complainants, had argued that, since the panel had already found that the CDSOA was inconsistent with, *inter alia*, Articles 11.4 and 32.1, there was, pursuant to Article 3.8 of the DSU, a presumption of nullification or impairment. According to Mexico, this nullification or impairment was sufficient to demonstrate nullification or impairment for the purpose of Article 5(b) of the *SCM Agreement*. The panel rejected this argument and stated that, for the purpose of Article 5(b) of the *SCM Agreement*, Mexico must show that the *use* of the subsidy caused nullification or impairment. See Panel Report, *US – Offset Act (Byrd Amendment) (2003)*, para. 7.119.

254 Note that Article 6.1 of the *SCM Agreement* listed several situations in which subsidies are *deemed* to cause 'serious prejudice'. However, this provision lapsed on 31 December 1999. See Article 31 of the *SCM Agreement*.

255 Article 6.2 of the *SCM Agreement*.

(2005) explained that the concept of serious prejudice is concerned with negative effects on a Member's trade interests in respect of a product, such as lost import or export volume or market share, or adverse price effects, or a combination thereof, in various product and geographic markets.[256]

Both Article 5(c) and Article 6.3 of the *SCM Agreement* refer to 'serious prejudice'. In *US – Upland Cotton (2005)*, the question arose whether a finding of 'significant price suppression' under Article 6.3(c) is conclusive in establishing 'serious prejudice' under Article 5(c). The panel concluded that a detrimental impact on a complaining Member's production of, and/or trade in, the product concerned under Article 6.3 may fall within the concept of 'prejudice' in Article 5(c) of the *SCM Agreement*. In the particular facts and circumstances of *US – Upland Cotton (2005)*, the panel arrived at the conclusion that 'significant price suppression' under Article 6.3 amounted to 'serious prejudice' within the meaning of Article 5(c) of the *SCM Agreement*.[257] To assess whether there is 'serious prejudice' within the meaning of Articles 5(c) and 6 of the *SCM Agreement*, it is necessary to determine: (1) what the relevant 'geographical market' and 'product market' is; (2) whether there is 'displacement' or 'impedance' of imports or exports; (3) whether there is 'price undercutting', 'price suppression', 'price depression' or 'lost sales'; (4) whether the price undercutting, price suppression, price depression or lost sales are 'significant'; (5) whether there is an 'increase in world market share'; (6) whether there is 'threat of serious prejudice'; and/or (7) whether the market phenomena referred to above are 'the effect of' the challenged subsidies (i.e. causal link and non-attribution). This section deals with each of these issues in turn. In conclusion, this section also addresses a number of other issues relevant to the analysis of the effects on subsidies, including: (1) the temporal scope of Articles 5 and 6 of the *SCM Agreement*; (2) the pass-through of subsidies; (3) the effect of subsidies over time; (4) the collective analysis of the effects of subsidies; and (5) Annex V on Procedures for Developing Information Concerning Serious Prejudice.

5.3.1 The Relevant Geographic and Product Market

Article 6.3(c) of the *SCM Agreement* addresses the situation *inter alia* where 'the effect of the subsidy is ... significant price suppression ... in the same *market*'. Aside from the qualification that it must be 'the same' market, Article 6.3(c) imposes no explicit *geographical* limitation on the scope of the relevant market. The question of the relevant geographic and product market for the assessment of serious prejudice claims under Article 6.3 arose in *US – Upland Cotton (2005)*, *US – Upland*

256 Panel Report, *Korea – Commercial Vessels (2005)*, para. 7.578.

257 Panel Report, *US – Upland Cotton (2004)*, paras. 7.1392–7.1395. See also Panel Report, *Indonesia – Autos (1998)*, paras. 14.254–14.255. The panel in *US – Upland Cotton (Article 21.5 – Brazil) (2008)* concurred that, once the conditions set forth in Article 6.3(a)–(d) are fulfilled, there is a sufficient basis for a finding of serious prejudice within the meaning of Article 5(c). Panel Report, *US – Upland Cotton (Article 21.5 – Brazil) (2008)*, para. 10.255.

Cotton (Article 21.5 – Brazil) (2008), EC and certain member States – Large Civil Aircraft (2011) and *US – Large Civil Aircraft (2nd complaint) (2012)*. According to the Appellate Body in *US – Upland Cotton (2005)* Article 6.3(c):

> contrasts with the other paragraphs of Article 6.3: paragraph (a) restricts the relevant market to 'the market of the subsidizing Member'; paragraph (b) restricts the relevant market to 'a third country market'; and paragraph (d) refers specifically to the 'world market share' ... [T]his difference may indicate that the drafters did not intend to confine, *a priori*, the market examined under Article 6.3(c) to any particular area. Thus, the ordinary meaning of the word 'market' in Article 6.3(c), when read in the context of the other paragraphs of Article 6.3, neither requires nor excludes the possibility of a national market or a world market.[258]

The phrase 'in the same market' in Article 6.3(c) 'applies to all four situations covered in that provision, namely, "significant price undercutting", "significant price suppression, price depression [and] lost sales"'.[259] In *US – Upland Cotton (2005)*, the term 'market' was defined as 'a place ... with a demand for a commodity or service'; 'a geographical area of demand for commodities or services'; 'the area of economic activity in which buyers and sellers come together and the forces of supply and demand affect prices'.[260] The Appellate Body noted, however, that this 'does not, of itself, impose any limitation on the "geographical area" that makes up any given market. Nor does it indicate that a "world market" cannot exist for a given product'. The 'degree to which a market is limited by geography will depend on the product itself and its ability to be traded across distances'.[261] The Appellate Body concluded that:

> [t]wo products would be in the same market if they were engaged in actual or potential competition in that market. Thus, two products may be 'in the same market' even if they are not necessarily sold at the same time and in the same place or country ... The scope of the 'market', for determining the area of competition between two products, may depend on several factors such as the nature of the product, the homogeneity of the conditions of competition, and transport costs. This market for a particular product could well be a 'world market'.[262]

With regard to the relevant 'market price' for making a finding on the price phenomena listed in Article 6.3(c), in *US – Upland Cotton (2005)*, the question arose whether it was sufficient for the panel to analyse the price of upland cotton in general in the world market or whether an analysis of the price of Brazilian

258 Appellate Body Report, *US – Upland Cotton (2005)*, para. 406.

259 In *US – Upland Cotton (2005)*, the Appellate Body was of the view that the phrase 'in the same market' suggests that the subsidised product in question (US upland cotton in this case) and the relevant product of the complaining Member (Brazilian upland cotton) must be 'in the same market'. See Appellate Body Report, *US – Upland Cotton (2005)*, para. 407.

260 Panel Report, *US – Upland Cotton (2004)*, para. 7.1236.

261 Appellate Body Report, *US – Upland Cotton (2005)*, para. 405. See also Panel Report, *Korea – Commercial Vessels (2005)*, paras. 7.562–7.566.

262 See Appellate Body Report, *US – Upland Cotton (2005)*, para. 408. The Appellate Body agreed with the panel that 'the fact that a world market exists for one product does not necessarily mean that such a market exists for every product'. See *ibid.* Thus the determination of the relevant market under Article 6.3(c) of the *SCM Agreement* depends on the subsidised product in question. If a world market exists for the product in question, Article 6.3(c) does not exclude the possibility of this 'world market' being the 'same market' for the purposes of a significant price suppression analysis under that Article. See *ibid.*

upland cotton in the world market was required in order to make a finding of significant price suppression with respect to that price. The Appellate Body agreed with the panel that:

> '[d]evelopments in the world upland cotton price would inevitably affect prices' wherever Brazilian and United States upland cotton compete, 'due to the nature of the world prices in question and the nature of the world upland cotton market, and the relative proportion of that market enjoyed by the United States and Brazil'. It was not necessary, in these circumstances, for the Panel to proceed to a separate analysis of the prices of Brazilian upland cotton in the world market.[263]

In contrast to the words 'same market' that appear in Article 6.3(c), Article 6.3(a) refers to the 'market of the subsidizing Member', and Article 6.3(b) refers to a 'third country market'. Despite this wording, the Appellate Body found in *EC and certain member States – Large Civil Aircraft (2011)* that under Articles 6.3(a) and (b) an assessment of the competitive relationship between products in the market is nevertheless required in order to determine 'whether such products form part of the same market' and 'whether and to what extent one product may displace another'.[264] Thus, while the Appellate Body accepted that 'a complaining Member may identify a subsidized product and the like product by reference to footnote 46, the products thereby identified must be analysed under the discipline of the *product market* so as to be able to determine whether displacement is occurring'.[265] Ordinarily, the subsidised product and the like product will form part of a larger product market. But it may be the case that a complainant chooses to define the subsidised and like products so broadly that it is necessary to analyse these products in different product markets. This will be necessary so as to analyse further the real competitive interactions that are taking place, and thereby determine whether displacement is occurring.[266]

In making these observations in *EC and certain member States – Large Civil Aircraft (2011)*, the Appellate Body relied on the fundamental economic proposition that:

> [a] market comprises only those products that exercise competitive constraint on each other. This is the case when the relevant products are substitutable.

Although physical characteristics, end uses and consumer preferences may assist in deciding whether two products are in the same market, the Appellate Body cautioned that these likeness criteria should *not* be treated as exclusive factors in deciding whether those products are sufficiently substitutable so as to create competitive constraints on each other.[267] The Appellate Body explained that:

> [d]emand-side substitutability – that is, when two products are considered substitutable by consumers – is an indispensable, but not the only relevant, criterion to consider when

263 Appellate Body Report, *US – Upland Cotton (2005)*, para. 417.
264 Appellate Body Report, *EC and certain member States – Large Civil Aircraft (2011)*, para. 1119.
265 *Ibid.* 266 *Ibid.*
267 See *ibid.*, para. 1120.

assessing whether two products are in a single market. Rather, a consideration of substitutability on the supply side may also be required. For example, evidence on whether a supplier can switch its production at limited or prohibitive cost from one product to another in a short period of time may also inform the question of whether two products are in a single market.[268]

In respect of the relevant product market to be examined for the purposes of displacement and impedance under Article 6.3(a) and (b), the Appellate Body concluded in *EC and certain member States – Large Civil Aircraft (2011)* that it is likely to vary from case to case depending upon the particular factual circumstances, including the nature of the products at issue, as well as demand-side and supply-side factors. The Appellate Body noted:

In some cases, the entire product range offered by the complainant may compete with the range of products of the respondent that is allegedly subsidized. In other cases, an assessment ... may reveal the existence of multiple product markets in which particular products of the complaining Member compete with particular subsidized products of the respondent. However, it is important to note that whether or not a broad or narrow range of products benefit from subsidization says little about whether all these products compete in the same market. Indeed, products benefiting from subsidies may compete in very different markets.[269]

On the basis of these considerations, the Appellate Body observed in *EC and certain member States – Large Civil Aircraft (2011)* that there is 'both a geographic and product market component to the assessment of displacement'[270] and, by implication, impedance.[271] In principle, the manner in which the geographic dimension of a market is determined will depend on a number of factors. As explained by the Appellate Body in *EC and certain member States – Large Civil Aircraft (2011)* and *US – Large Civil Aircraft (2nd complaint) (2012)*:

[I]n some cases, the geographic market may extend to cover the entire country concerned; in others, an analysis of the conditions of competition for sales of the product in question may provide an appropriate foundation for a finding that a geographic market exists *within* that area, for example, a region. There may also be cases where the geographic dimension of a particular market exceeds national boundaries or could be the world market.[272]

A plain reading of Article 6.3(b), however, reveals that a finding of displacement or impedance under that provision is to be limited to the territory of the third country at issue. The Appellate Body recognised that findings of displacement and impedance under Article 6.3(b) are to be made only with respect to the territory of the third country involved, even though, from an economic perspective, the geographic market may not be national in scope. The Appellate Body concluded that:

[e]ven in cases where the geographic dimension of a particular market exceeds national boundaries or is worldwide, a panel faced with a claim under Article 6.3(b) should 'focus

268 *Ibid.*, para. 1121.
269 *Ibid.*, para. 1123. 270 *Ibid.*, para. 1168.
271 See *ibid.*, fn. 2466 to para. 1119.
272 *Ibid.*, para. 1117; and Appellate Body Report, *US – Large Civil Aircraft (2nd complaint) (2012)*, para. 1076. Where the geographical size of the market is smaller in scope than the entire territory of the third country Member concerned, the wording of Article 6.3(b) suggests that a panel will nonetheless have to ensure that any finding reached relates to that territory as a whole, and explain why this is so. *Ibid.*

the analysis of displacement and impedance on the territory of the ... third countries involved'.[273]

5.3.2 Displacement or Impedance of Imports or Exports

As noted above, pursuant to Article 6.3(a) and (b) of the *SCM Agreement*, 'serious prejudice' may arise where a subsidy results in the 'displacement' or 'impedance' of imports or exports of like products of another Member. The Appellate Body interpreted the concepts of 'displacement' and 'impedance' in *EC and certain member States – Large Civil Aircraft (2011)* and in *US – Large Civil Aircraft (2nd complaint) (2012)*. Displacement refers to an 'economic mechanism in which exports of a like product are replaced by the sales of the subsidized product'.[274] The concept connotes 'a substitution effect between the subsidised product and the like product of the complaining Member'. In the context of Article 6.3(a), this means that the effect of the subsidy is that imports of a like product of the complaining Member are substituted by the subsidised product. Under Article 6.3(b), displacement arises where exports of the like product of the complaining Member are substituted in a third country market by exports of the subsidised product.[275] According to the Appellate Body:

> The existence of displacement depends upon there being a competitive relationship between these two sets of products in that market and, when this is the case, certain behaviour such as '[a]ggressive pricing' may 'lead to displacement of exports ... in [that] particular market'.[276]

An analysis of displacement should assess whether this phenomenon is discernible by examining trends in data relating to export volumes and market shares over an appropriately representative period.[277]

With regard to 'impedance', the Appellate Body considered in *US – Large Civil Aircraft (2nd complaint)* that this concept:

> [m]ay involve a broader range of situations than displacement and arises both in 'situations where the exports or imports of the like product of the complaining Member would have expanded had they not been "obstructed" or "hindered" by the subsidized product', as well as when such exports or imports 'did not materialize at all because production was held back by the subsidized product'.[278]

While there may be some overlap between the concepts, 'displacement' and 'impedance' are therefore not interchangeable concepts.[279]

273 Appellate Body Report, *US – Large Civil Aircraft (2nd complaint) (2012)*, para. 1076. See also Appellate Body Report, *EC and certain member States – Large Civil Aircraft (2011)*, para. 1117.

274 *Ibid.*, para. 1071; and *ibid.*, para. 1119.

275 See *ibid.*, para. 1160.

276 Appellate Body Report, *US – Large Civil Aircraft (2nd complaint) (2012)*, para. 1071. See also Appellate Body Report, *EC and certain member States – Large Civil Aircraft (2011)*, para. 1119.

277 See Appellate Body Report, *EC and certain member States – Large Civil Aircraft (2011)*, paras. 1165, 1166 and 1170; and Appellate Body Report, *US – Large Civil Aircraft (2nd complaint) (2012)*, para. 1071.

278 Appellate Body Report, *US – Large Civil Aircraft (2nd complaint) (2012)*, para. 1071. See also Appellate Body Report, *EC and certain member States – Large Civil Aircraft (2011)*, para. 1161. While the Appellate Body was not required to consider the meaning of impedance in that appeal, it nevertheless considered that this concept (which is found within the same provision of the *SCM Agreement*) serves as relevant context for a better understanding of displacement.

279 Appellate Body Report, *US – Large Civil Aircraft (2nd complaint) (2012)*, para. 1071.

5.3.3 Price Undercutting, Price Suppression, Price Depression and Lost Sales

Article 6.3(c) of the *SCM Agreement* states that serious prejudice may arise where a subsidy results in a significant price undercutting by the subsidised product in comparison to the like product of another Member in the same market, or significant price suppression, price depression or lost sales in the same market. This section discusses in turn the 'market phenomena' referred to in Article 6.3(c), and in particular price suppression, price depression and lost sales.

'Price suppression' refers to the situation where prices either are prevented or inhibited from rising (i.e. they do not increase when they otherwise would have) or they do actually increase, but the increase is less than it otherwise would have been. 'Price depression' refers to the situation where prices are pressed down, or reduced.[280] The Appellate Body, however, recognised in *US – Upland Cotton (2005)* that the situation where prices are prevented or inhibited from rising (i.e. 'price suppression') and the situation where prices are pressed down, or reduced (i.e. 'price depression') may overlap.[281] There are nevertheless important differences between these two market phenomena. As the Appellate Body observed in *US – Upland Cotton (Article 21.5 – Brazil) (2008)*, while 'price depression' is a directly observable phenomenon, 'price suppression' is not. 'Price suppression' exists where prices are less than they would otherwise have been, as a result of the subsidies.[282] The Appellate Body explained:

> The identification of price suppression, therefore, presupposes a comparison of an observable factual situation (prices) with a counterfactual situation (what prices would have been) where one has to determine whether, in the absence of the subsidies (or some other controlling phenomenon), prices would have increased or would have increased more than they actually did.[283]

Thus, the Appellate Body considered in *US – Upland Cotton (Article 21.5 – Brazil) (2008)* that a counterfactual analysis is an 'inescapable part' of analysing the effect of a subsidy under Article 6.3(c) of the *SCM Agreement*.[284] It recalled in *US – Large Civil Aircraft (2nd complaint) (2012)* that price suppression is concerned with 'whether prices are less than they would otherwise have been in consequence of ... the subsidies' and that, for this reason, 'a counterfactual analysis is likely to be of particular utility for panels faced with claims that subsidies have caused price suppression'.[285]

280 Panel Report, *US – Upland Cotton (2005)*, para. 7.1277; and Appellate Body Report, *US – Upland Cotton (2005)*, para. 423. The Panel described the assessment of 'price suppression' under Article 6.3(c) as an examination of 'whether these prices were suppressed, that is, lower than they would have been without the United States subsidies in respect of upland cotton'. See Panel Report, *US – Upland Cotton (2005)*, para. 7.1288. See also Appellate Body Report, *US – Large Civil Aircraft (2nd complaint) (2012)*, paras. 1091–2. The Appellate Body interpreted the concepts of 'price suppression' and 'price depression' in *US – Upland Cotton (2005), US – Upland Cotton (Article 21.5 – Brazil) (2008), EC and certain member States – Large Civil Aircraft (2011)* and *US – Large Civil Aircraft (2nd complaint) (2012)*.

281 Appellate Body Report, *US – Upland Cotton (2005)*, para. 424.

282 Appellate Body Report, *US – Upland Cotton (Article 21.5 – Brazil) (2008)*, para. 351.

283 *Ibid.* 284 *Ibid.*

285 Appellate Body Report, *US – Large Civil Aircraft (2nd complaint) (2012)*, paras. 1091–2.

With regard to the market phenomenon of 'lost sales', the Appellate Body stated in *EC and certain member States – Large Civil Aircraft (2011)* that a 'lost sale' is one that a supplier 'failed to obtain'.[286] The concept of 'lost sales' was understood in *EC and certain member States – Large Civil Aircraft (2011)* and *US – Large Civil Aircraft (2nd complaint) (2012)* as 'relational', entailing consideration of 'the behaviour of both the subsidized firm(s), which must have won the sales, and the competing firm(s), which allegedly lost the sales', due to the effect of the subsidy.[287] Sales can be lost 'in the same market', within the meaning of Article 6.3(c), only if the subsidised product and the like product compete in the same product market. The Appellate Body noted in *EC and certain member States – Large Civil Aircraft (2011)* that:

> [it] will sometimes be necessary to look beyond individual sales campaigns fully to understand the competitive dynamics that are at play in a particular market. Thus, an approach in which sales are aggregated by supplier or by customer, or on a country-wide or global basis, rather than examined individually, is also permissible.[288]

Understood in this way, the Appellate Body recognised that there may be some overlap between the concepts of displacement, impedance and lost sales.[289]

5.3.4 The Meaning of 'Significant'

When price undercutting, price depression, price suppression or lost sales occurs, it must reach the degree or level of 'significance' contemplated by Article 6.3(c). In *US – Washing Machines (2016)*, the Appellate Body found that the word 'significant' means 'important, notable or consequential'.[290] As the Appellate Body explained in *US – Upland Cotton (Article 21.5 – Brazil) (2008)*, the fact that the price suppression must be 'significant' does not mean, however, that a panel examining various factors that support a finding of significant price suppression:

> [m]ust make a determination precisely quantifying the effects of each factor. A factor that itself is not 'significant' may, together with other factors (whether individually shown to be of a significant degree or not), establish 'significant price suppression'. What needs to be significant is the degree of price suppression, not necessarily the degree of each factor used as an indicator for establishing its existence. Nor does each factor necessarily have to be capable of demonstrating, to the same extent, significant price suppression.[291]

The Appellate Body concluded that the panel in *US – Upland Cotton (2008) (Article 21.5 – Brazil)* did not have to determine 'the precise degree of market insulation, which is but one factor in the Panel's overall analysis'.[292] The panel in *US – Upland Cotton (2005)* had based its conclusion not only on a 'given

286 Appellate Body Report, *EC and certain member States – Large Civil Aircraft (2011)*, para. 1214.
287 *Ibid.* 288 *Ibid.*, para. 1217.
289 See *ibid.*, para. 1218.
290 Appellate Body Report, *US – Washing Machines (2016)*, para. 5.62; see also Panel Report, *US – Upland Cotton (2005)*, para. 7.1325; and Appellate Body Report, *US – Upland Cotton (2005)*, para. 426.
291 Appellate Body Report, *US – Upland Cotton (Article 21.5 – Brazil) (2008)*, para. 416.
292 *Ibid.*, paras. 416–18.

level of numerical significance', it also relied on the structure, design, and operation of the payments at issue as well as market structure and product homogeneity.[293] The text of Article 6.3(c) does not set forth any specific guidance or methodology for establishing the existence of *significant* price suppression. The Appellate Body considered in *US – Upland Cotton (2005)* that there 'may well be different ways to make this determination'.[294] In *US – Upland Cotton (2005)*, the panel examined the following factors in determining whether *significant* price suppression occurred: (1) the relative magnitude of US production and exports in the world upland cotton market; (2) general price trends; and (3) the nature of the subsidies at issue, and in particular whether or not the nature of these subsidies is such as to have discernible price-suppressive effects.[295] The panel in *US – Upland Cotton (2005)* also noted that:

> [w]hat may be significant in a market for upland cotton would [not] necessarily also be applicable or relevant to a market for a very different product ... [F]or a basic and widely traded commodity, such as upland cotton, a relatively small decrease or suppression of prices could be significant because, for example, profit margins may ordinarily be narrow, product homogeneity means that sales are price sensitive or because of the sheer size of the market in terms of the amount of revenue involved in large volumes traded on the markets experiencing the price suppression.[296]

In the absence of explicit guidance in the text of Article 6.3(c), the Appellate Body found in *US – Upland Cotton (2005)*:

> [n]o reason to reject the relevance of these factors for the Panel's assessment in the present case. An assessment of 'general price trends' is clearly relevant to significant price suppression (although, as the Panel itself recognized, price trends alone are not conclusive). The two other factors – the nature of the subsidies and the relative magnitude of the United States' production and exports of upland cotton – are also relevant for this assessment.[297]

An assessment of whether subsidy amounts are significant should not necessarily be limited to a mere inquiry into *what* those amounts are, either in absolute or per-unit terms:

> Rather, such an analysis may be situated within a larger inquiry that could, for instance, entail viewing these amounts against considerations such as the size of the market as a whole, the size of the subsidy recipient, the per-unit price of the subsidized product, the price elasticity of demand, and, depending on the market structure, the extent to which a subsidy recipient is able to set its own prices in the market, and the extent to which rivals are able or prompted to react to each other's pricing within that market structure.[298]

In sum, it is not only the *absolute* amounts of subsidies that may be of relevance; also, the *relative* significance of subsidies and, in particular, whether the

293 Panel Report, *US – Upland Cotton (2005)*, paras. 7.1329–7.1330.

294 Appellate Body Report, *US – Upland Cotton (2005)*, para. 427.

295 See Panel Report, *US – Upland Cotton (2005)*, para. 7.1332. 296 *Ibid.*, para. 7.1330.

297 Appellate Body Report, *US – Upland Cotton (2005)*, para. 434.

298 Appellate Body Report, *US – Large Civil Aircraft (2nd complaint) (2012)*, para. 1193; Appellate Body Report, *US – Upland Cotton (2005)*, para. 468; and Appellate Body Report, *US – Upland Cotton (Article 21.5 – Brazil) (2008)*, para. 362.

challenged subsidies were of a size that, when considered in relation to product values or prices, could produce market effects amounting to serious prejudice may have to be taken into account.

With regard to 'price undercutting', the panel in *Indonesia – Autos (1998)* stated that the inclusion of the qualifier 'significant' in Article 6.3(c) 'presumably was intended to ensure that margins of undercutting so small that they could not meaningfully affect suppliers of the imported product whose price was being undercut are not considered to give rise to serious prejudice'.[299] The Appellate Body noted in *US – Washing Machines (2016)* that, just as when it is used to qualify 'price suppression' and 'price depression', 'significant means "important, notable or consequential", and has both quantitative and qualitative dimensions'.[300]

5.3.5 Increase in World Market Share

Article 6.3(d) of the *SCM Agreement* states that serious prejudice may arise where a subsidy leads to an increase in the world market share of the subsidising Member in a particular primary product or commodity in comparison to the average share it had during the previous period of three years.[301] The panel in *US – Upland Cotton (2005)* found that 'world market share' did not refer to either a Member's share of the world market for *exports* as argued by Brazil, nor did it refer to all *consumption* by a Member as contended by the United States; rather, the panel found that the phrase referred to the 'share of the world market supplied by the subsidizing member of the product concerned'.[302] Because Brazil had failed to establish a *prima facie* case due to its erroneous legal interpretation of the phrase at issue,[303] and because its appeal was conditional, the Appellate Body considered it 'unnecessary' to develop an interpretation of the term 'world market share' in Article 6.3(d) for purposes of resolving the dispute.[304]

5.3.6 Threat of Serious Prejudice

Footnote 13 to Article 5(c) clarifies that:

> [t]he term 'serious prejudice to the interests of another Member' is used in [the SCM] Agreement in the same sense as it is used in paragraph 1 of Article XVI of [the] GATT 1994, and *includes threat of serious prejudice*.[305]

299 Panel Report, *Indonesia – Autos (1998)*, para. 14.254.

300 Appellate Body Report, *US – Large Civil Aircraft (2nd complaint) (2012)*, para. 1052; Appellate Body Report, *EC and certain member States – Large Civil Aircraft (2011)*, para. 1218. See also Appellate Body Report, *US – Upland Cotton (2005)*, para. 426, referring to Panel Report, *US – Upland Cotton (2005)*, para. 7.1326. Albeit in the different context of Article 2.4.2 of the *Anti-Dumping Agreement*, the Appellate Body explained in *US – Washing Machines (2016)* that the term 'significant' has both quantitative and qualitative dimensions. See Appellate Body Report, *US – Washing Machines (2016)* , para. 5.63.

301 Note that Article 6.3(d) refers to 'world *market* share', whereas Article XVI of the GATT 1994 refers to subsidies resulting in a more than equitable share of world *export trade* in the product in question.

302 Panel Report, *US – Upland Cotton (2005)*, para. 7.1464.

303 See *ibid.*, para. 7.1465.

304 See Appellate Body Report, *US – Upland Cotton (2005)*, paras. 505–7 and 511.

305 Emphasis added.

A claim of present serious prejudice may relate to a different situation than a claim of *threat* of serious prejudice. The Appellate Body explained in *US – Upland Cotton (Article 21.5 – Brazil) (2008)* that 'a claim of *present* serious prejudice relates to the existence of prejudice in the past, and present, and that may continue in the future. By contrast, a claim of *threat* of serious prejudice relates to prejudice that does not yet exist, but is imminent such that it will materialise in the near future. Therefore, a threat of serious prejudice claim does not necessarily capture and provide a remedy with respect to the same scenario as a claim of present serious prejudice.'[306]

In *EC and certain member States – Large Civil Aircraft (2011)*, the Appellate Body noted that neither subparagraph (a) nor (b) of Article 6.3 expressly refer to 'threat of displacement'.[307] Nevertheless, the introductory paragraph of Article 6.3 states that '[s]erious prejudice in the sense of paragraph (c) of Article 5 may arise' where there is one of the market phenomena described in the subparagraphs, including (a) and (b). Footnote 13 in turn clarifies that serious prejudice 'includes threat of serious prejudice'. The Appellate Body found relevant guidance for the interpretation of that concept in Article 15.7 even though the latter concerns 'threat of *material injury*'.[308] Thus, it considered it reasonable to require that the determination of threat of serious prejudice 'be based on facts and not merely on allegation, conjecture or remote possibility' and that '[t]he change in circumstances' that would create a situation in which the subsidy would cause displacement 'must be clearly foreseen and imminent'.[309]

5.3.7 Causation and Non-Attribution

As Article 6.3 of the *SCM Agreement* states, serious prejudice may arise where *the effect of the subsidy* is one or more of the market phenomena, listed in paragraphs (a)–(d) of Article 6.3 and discussed above. The Appellate Body noted in *US – Upland Cotton (2005)* that the ordinary meaning of the noun 'effect' is '[s]omething ... caused or produced; a result, a consequence'.[310] It agreed therefore with the panel that:

> [t]he text of the treaty requires the establishment of a causal link between the subsidy and the significant price suppression.[311]

306 Appellate Body Report, *US – Upland Cotton (Article 21.5 – Brazil) (2008)*, para. 244. The Appellate Body further noted that a 'distinction between injury and threat of injury also exists in the context of countervailing duty measures. Once a determination of present material injury is made, a Member may impose countervailing duties on future imports without any obligation to demonstrate a threat of material injury.' See *ibid.*

307 Appellate Body Report, *EC and certain member States – Large Civil Aircraft (2011)*, para. 1171.

308 *Ibid.* 309 See Article 15.7 of the *SCM Agreement*.

310 Appellate Body Report, *US – Upland Cotton (2005)*, para. 435.

311 *Ibid.*, quoting Panel Report, *US – Upland Cotton (2005)*, para. 7.1341.

In *US – Upland Cotton (Article 21.5 – Brazil) (2008)*, the Appellate Body observed that:

> [w]hile the term 'cause' focuses on the factors that may trigger a certain event, the term 'effect of' focuses on the results of that event. The effect – price suppression – must result from a chain of causation that is linked to the impugned subsidy.[312]

Thus, in respect of all forms of serious prejudice under Part III of the *SCM Agreement*, the complainant must demonstrate not only the existence of the relevant subsidies and of the adverse effects to its interests, but also that the subsidies at issue have *caused* such effects.[313] In all serious prejudice cases under Articles 5(c) and 6.3, the Appellate Body has consistently described the causal link required as 'a genuine and substantial relationship of cause and effect'. While it gave its guidance concerning the assessment of causation in the cotton disputes in the context of significant price suppression under Article 6.3(c), the Appellate Body noted in *EC and certain member States – Large Civil Aircraft (2011)* that the language of Article 6.3(a) and (b) expresses the causation requirement in very similar terms to those used in Article 6.3(c). The Appellate Body therefore saw no reason why the standard for causation and non-attribution should be different under Article 6.3(a) and (b) than under Article 6.3(c).[314] The Appellate Body further explained in *US – Large Civil Aircraft (2nd complaint) (2012)* that, in order to find that the subsidy is a genuine and substantial cause, a panel need not determine it to be the *sole* cause of that effect, or even that it is the *only* substantial cause of that effect.[315]

Questions related to the causal link between challenged subsidies and the market phenomena listed in Article 6.3 of the *SCM Agreement* have been at the centre of all disputes under Part III of the *SCM Agreement*. In *US – Upland Cotton (2005), US – Upland Cotton (Article 21.5 – Brazil) (2008), EC and certain member States – Large Civil Aircraft (2011)* and *US – Large Civil Aircraft (2nd complaint) (2012)*, the Appellate Body has discussed issues such as: (1) the order of analysis; (2) the methodologies and elements relevant for establishing causation; (3) the role of counterfactual analysis; and (4) the non-attribution of effects of other factors.

First, with regard to the *order of analysis*, the question that arises is whether the examination of the effect of the subsidy – i.e. whether the effect of the subsidy is one or more of the market phenomena of Article 6.3(a)–(d) – that can, or perhaps even should, take a 'two-step approach' or a 'unitary approach'. Under the 'two-step approach', one would examine, first, whether one of the

312 Appellate Body Report, *US – Upland Cotton (Article 21.5 – Brazil) (2008)*, para. 372.
313 See Appellate Body Report, *US – Large Civil Aircraft (2nd complaint) (2012)*, para. 913.
314 See Appellate Body Report, *EC and certain member States – Large Civil Aircraft (2011)*, para. 1232.
315 See Appellate Body Report, *US – Large Civil Aircraft (2nd complaint) (2012)*, para. 914.

market phenomena exists, i.e. whether there is displacement, impedance, significant price undercutting, significant price suppression, significant price depression or significant lost sales; second, whether the market phenomena are the 'effect' of challenged subsidies, i.e. whether a causal relationship exists between the subsidies and the market phenomena. Under the 'unitary approach', one would address these questions together and conduct *one* all-encompassing examination.

Article 6.3(c) is silent as to which approach is to be followed in assessing whether the effect of a subsidy is serious prejudice. In *US – Upland Cotton (2005)*, the Appellate Body considered that the provision does not 'preclude the approach taken by the Panel to examine first whether significant price suppression exists and then, if it is found to exist, to proceed further to examine whether the significant price suppression is the effect of the subsidy'.[316] The Appellate Body saw no legal error in this two-step approach,[317] but stated that one might contend that, 'having decided to separate its analysis of significant price suppression from its analysis of the effects of the challenged subsidies, the Panel's price suppression analysis should have addressed prices without reference to the subsidies and their effects'.[318] That would be the logic of a two-step approach. However, according to the Appellate Body, an analysis of price suppression without reference to the subsidies and their effect may be problematic. The Appellate Body noted that:

> [t]he ordinary meaning of the transitive verb 'suppress' implies the existence of a subject (the challenged subsidies) and an object (in this case, prices in the world market for upland cotton). This suggests that it would be difficult to make a judgment on significant price *suppression* without taking into account the effect of the subsidies. The Panel's definition of price suppression ... reflects this problem; it includes the notion that prices 'do not increase when they *otherwise* would have' or 'they do actually increase, but the increase is less than it *otherwise* would have been'. The word 'otherwise' in this context refers to the hypothetical situation in which the challenged subsidies are absent. Therefore, the fact that the Panel may have addressed some of the same or similar factors in its reasoning as to significant price suppression and its reasoning as to 'effects' is not necessarily wrong.[319]

In *US – Upland Cotton (Article 21.5 – Brazil) (2008)*, the panel adopted a 'unitary approach' and decided not to separate the analytical steps of whether there was price suppression in the world market for upland cotton, whether this price suppression was significant, and whether a causal relationship existed between this significant price suppression and the subsidies. On appeal, the Appellate Body, referring to its observations in *US – Upland Cotton (2005)*, quoted above, stated that:

> [t]he Panel's 'unitary analysis', at least in respect of identifying price suppression and its causes, has a sound conceptual foundation.[320]

316 Appellate Body Report, *US – Upland Cotton (2005)*, para. 431. 317 See *ibid.*
318 *Ibid.*, para. 432. 319 *Ibid.*, para. 433.
320 Appellate Body Report, *US – Upland Cotton (Article 21.5 – Brazil) (2008)*, para. 354.

The Appellate Body consequently endorsed a 'unitary approach' to analysing whether significant price suppression was the effect of the challenged subsidies. The Appellate Body noted that

> [i]n undertaking a unitary analysis, the Panel considered both quantitative and qualitative elements in its assessment. It made a quantitative assessment of significance by evaluating the magnitude of the subsidies, the gap between United States upland cotton producers' revenues and costs of production, the United States' share of world production and exports, and the economic simulations; and it made a qualitative assessment by evaluating the structure, design, and operation of the subsidies.[321]

Note, however, that the Appellate Body cautioned that the adoption of a unitary approach did 'not absolve the Panel from clearly explaining its position on the question of "significance"'.[322]

Second, with regard to the *methodologies and elements* relevant for establishing whether market phenomena listed in Article 6.3 are the effect of the challenged subsidies, it is important to bear in mind that, in an Article 6.3 analysis, a panel is the *first trier of facts*, and not a reviewer of factual determinations made by a domestic investigating authority.[323] It is therefore the panel's responsibility to gather and analyse relevant factual data and information in assessing claims under Article 6.3(c) in order to arrive at reasoned conclusions.[324] Panels and the Appellate Body have recognised the relevance of a number of factors for an assessment of serious prejudice, such as: (1) the nature of the subsidy; (2) the way in which the subsidy operates; (3) the extent to which the subsidy is provided in respect of a particular product or products; (4) conditions in the market; and (5) the conceptual distance between the activities of the subsidy recipient and the products in respect of which price suppression/price depression is alleged.[325] With regard to the correlation between the subsidies and suppressed prices, the Appellate Body noted in *US – Upland Cotton (2005)* that:

> [o]ne would normally expect a discernible correlation between significantly suppressed prices and the challenged subsidies if the effect of these subsidies is significant price suppression.[326]

While correlation is an important factor, the Appellate Body cautioned that 'mere correlation' between payment of subsidies and significantly suppressed prices would be 'insufficient, without more, to prove that the effect of the subsidies is significant price suppression'.[327] Note, however, that, in *US – Upland Cotton (Article 21.5 – Brazil) (2008)*, the Appellate Body found that the difficulty in discerning a temporal coincidence between the US subsidies, the increase in US exports, and the drop in market prices did not necessarily undermine the panel's

321 *Ibid.*, para. 361. 322 *Ibid.*
323 See Appellate Body Report, *US – Upland Cotton (2005)*, para. 458. 324 See *ibid.*, para. 458.
325 See Panel Report, *Korea – Commercial Vessels (2005)*, para. 7.560.
326 Appellate Body Report, *US – Upland Cotton (2005)*, para. 451. 327 *Ibid.*

finding on market insulation.[328] With regard to the magnitude of subsidies and benefit, the text of Article 6.3(c) does not state explicitly that a panel needs to quantify the amount of the challenged subsidy. However, in *US – Upland Cotton (2005)*, the Appellate Body found the magnitude of the subsidy to be an important factor in assessing whether 'the effect of the subsidy is ... significant price suppression', and ultimately serious prejudice.[329] Still, the magnitude of a subsidy is 'only one of the factors that may be relevant to the determination of the effects of a challenged subsidy'.[330] A panel needs to assess the effect of the subsidy 'taking into account all relevant factors'.[331] In the same case, the Appellate Body considered that 'the definitions of a specific subsidy in Articles 1 and 2 do not expressly require the quantification of the "benefit" conferred by the subsidy on any particular product'.[332] The Appellate Body summed up in *US – Upland Cotton (2005)* that Article 6.3(c), read in its context, suggests that:

> [a] panel should have regard to the magnitude of the challenged subsidy and its relationship to prices of the product in the relevant market when analyzing whether the effect of a subsidy is significant price suppression. In many cases, it may be difficult to decide this question in the absence of such an assessment. Nevertheless, this does not mean that Article 6.3(c) imposes an obligation on panels to quantify precisely the amount of a subsidy benefiting the product at issue in every case. A precise, definitive quantification of the subsidy is not required.[333]

In addition, the Appellate Body recalled in *US – Upland Cotton (Article 21.5 – Brazil) (2008)* that the panel had 'linked the probative value of the magnitude of the subsidies, for purposes of the analysis of significant price suppression, to its findings on the structure, design, and operation of the subsidies and on the gap between costs of production and market revenues of United States upland cotton producers'.[334]

The Appellate Body explained in *US – Upland Cotton (Article 21.5 – Brazil) (2008)* that the analysis should focus on the effects of the subsidies on production levels by examining whether there was more production than there otherwise would have been as a result of the payments. For the Appellate Body, 'it is the marginal production attributable to the payments that matters'.[335] It stated that, 'given the focus on production and price effects, an analysis of price

328 While the share of US production and exports was not increasing, this did not undermine the panel's finding (i.e. that the subsidies shielded US cotton producers from world market price fluctuations), which was based also on market insulation factors, such as their mandatory and price-contingent nature and their revenue-stabilising effect. See Appellate Body Report, *US – Upland Cotton (Article 21.5 – Brazil) (2008)*, para. 414.

329 Appellate Body Report, *US – Upland Cotton (2005)*, para. 461. 330 *Ibid.*

331 *Ibid.* 332 *Ibid.*, para. 462.

333 *Ibid.*, para. 467. 334 *Ibid.*, para. 443.

335 *Ibid.*, para. 355. According to the Appellate Body, if there were to be increased upland cotton production, the analysis would then focus on whether that increase in supply had effects on prices in the world market. All else being equal, the marginal production attributable to the subsidy would be expected to have an effect on world prices, particularly if the subsidy is provided in a country with a meaningful share of world output. See *ibid.*

suppression would normally include a quantitative component. There is some inherent difficulty in quantifying the effects of subsidies', because the increase in prices, absent the subsidies, cannot be directly observed. The Appellate Body suggested that '[o]ne way to undertake the analysis is to use economic modelling or other quantitative techniques. These techniques can be used to estimate whether there are higher levels of production resulting from the subsidies and, in turn, the price effects of that production. Economic modelling and other quantitative techniques provide a framework to analyse the relationship between subsidies, other factors, and price movements.'[336]

Third, with regard to the role of counterfactual analysis, panels and the Appellate Body have emphasised repeatedly the relevance and importance of counterfactual analysis in determining whether market phenomena, such as price suppression, are the effect of the challenged subsidies. Already in *Korea – Commercial Vessels (2005)*, the panel stated that establishing a causal relationship between the *subsidy* and the significant price suppression or price depression implies looking at a *counterfactual situation*, i.e. 'trying to determine what prices would have been in the absence of the subsidy'. In the case of alleged price depression, 'whether in the absence of the subsidies prices for ships would not have declined, or would have declined by less than was in fact the case'. For price suppression, the question would be whether, 'in the absence of the subsidies, ship prices would have increased, or would have increased by more than was in fact the case'.[337]

The Appellate Body noted in *US – Upland Cotton (2005)* that Part III of the *SCM Agreement* leaves panels with 'a certain degree of discretion in selecting an appropriate methodology for determining whether the "effect" of a subsidy is significant price suppression under Article 6.3(c)'.[338] In *US – Upland Cotton (Article 21.5 – Brazil) (2008)*, the Appellate Body recalled that a price-suppression analysis is *counterfactual* in nature. This required consideration of what prices would have been absent the subsidies, and thus a counterfactual analysis is an 'inescapable part' of analysing the effect of a subsidy under Article 6.3(c).[339] In consequence, it was for the panel to determine whether the world price of upland cotton would have been higher in the absence of the subsidies (that is, *but for* the subsidies).[340] In some circumstances, a determination that the market

336 *Ibid.*, para. 356. 337 Panel Report, *Korea – Commercial Vessels (2005)*, paras. 7.604 and 7.612–7.615.

338 Appellate Body Report, *US – Upland Cotton (2005)*, para. 436.

339 The Appellate Body explained that the identification of price suppression presupposes a comparison of an observable factual situation (prices) with a counterfactual situation (what prices would have been) where one has to determine whether, in the absence of the subsidies (or some other controlling phenomenon), prices would have increased or would have increased more than they actually did. Price depression, by contrast, can be directly observed, in that falling prices are observable. The determination of whether such falling prices are the effect of the subsidies will require consideration of what prices would have been absent the subsidies. See Appellate Body Report, *US – Upland Cotton (Article 21.5 – Brazil) (2008)*, para. 351. See also above, pp. 824–37.

340 See *ibid.*, para. 370.

phenomena captured by Article 6.3 would not have occurred 'but for' the challenged subsidies will suffice to establish causation:

> This is because, in some circumstances, the 'but for' analysis will show that the subsidy is both a necessary cause of the market phenomenon *and* a substantial cause. It is not required that the 'but for' analysis establish that the challenged subsidies are a sufficient cause of the market phenomenon provided that it shows a genuine and substantial relationship of cause and effect. However, there are circumstances in which a 'but for' approach does not suffice. For example, where a necessary cause is too remote and other intervening causes substantially account for the market phenomenon.[341]

In *EC and certain member States – Large Civil Aircraft (2011)*, the Appellate Body explained that counterfactual analysis provides an adjudicator with a useful analytical framework to isolate and properly identify the effects of the challenged subsidies:

> In general terms, the counterfactual analysis entails comparing the actual market situation that is before the adjudicator with the market situation that would have existed in the absence of the challenged subsidies. This requires the adjudicator to undertake a modelling exercise as to what the market would look like in the absence of the subsidies. Such an exercise is a necessary part of the counterfactual approach. As with other factual assessments, panels clearly have a margin of discretion in conducting the counterfactual analysis.[342]

The Appellate Body reiterated in *US – Large Civil Aircraft (2nd complaint) (2012)* that 'a counterfactual analysis is likely to be of particular utility for panels faced with claims that subsidies have caused price suppression'.[343] As with the other market phenomena in Article 6.3, the 'lost sales must be the "effect" of the challenged subsidy', and counterfactual analysis is a useful and appropriate approach to assessing whether this is so. According to the Appellate Body in *EC and certain member States – Large Civil Aircraft (2011)*:

> [t]his would involve a comparison of the sales actually made by the competing firm(s) of the complaining Member with a counterfactual scenario in which the firm(s) of the respondent Member would not have received the challenged subsidies. There would be lost sales where the counterfactual scenario shows that sales won by the subsidized firm(s) of the respondent Member would have been made instead by the competing firm(s) of the complaining Member, thus revealing the effect of the challenged subsidies.[344]

Fourth, with regard to the non-attribution of effects of other factors, note that Articles 5 and 6.3 of the *SCM Agreement* do not contain the more elaborate and precise causation and non-attribution language found in Part V of the *SCM Agreement*, which relates to the imposition of countervailing duties, and requires, *inter alia*, an examination of 'any known factors other than the

341 Appellate Body Report, *EC and certain member States – Large Civil Aircraft (2011)*, para. 1233. According to the Appellate Body, this example underscored the importance of carrying out a proper non-attribution analysis. See *ibid.*

342 *Ibid.*, para. 1110. See Appellate Body Report, *US – Upland Cotton (Article 21.5 – Brazil) (2008)*, para. 357.

343 See Appellate Body Report, *US – Large Civil Aircraft (2nd complaint) (2012)*, paras. 1091–2.

344 Appellate Body Report, *EC and certain member States – Large Civil Aircraft (2011)*, para. 1216.

subsidized imports which at the same time are injuring the domestic industry'.[345] The Appellate Body noted in *US – Upland Cotton (2005)* that the absence of such express non-attribution requirements in Part III suggests that:

> [a] panel has a certain degree of discretion in selecting an appropriate methodology for determining whether the 'effect' of a subsidy is significant price suppression under Article 6.3(c).[346]

Nevertheless, it is necessary to ensure that the effects of other factors on prices are not improperly attributed to the challenged subsidies.[347] Therefore, the Appellate Body did:

> [n]ot find fault with the Panel's approach of 'examin[ing] whether or not "the effect of the subsidy" is the significant price suppression which [it had] found to exist in the same world market' and separately 'consider[ing] the role of other alleged causal factors in the record before [it] which may affect [the] analysis of the causal link between the United States subsidies and the significant price suppression'.[348]

At the same time, the Appellate Body cautioned in *US – Upland Cotton (2005)* that its interpretations of the provisions relating to causation and non-attribution of the *Agreement on Safeguards* and the *Anti-Dumping Agreement*, as well as the provisions of Part V of the *SCM Agreement*:

> [r]elate to a determination of 'injury' rather than 'serious prejudice', and they apply in different contexts and with different purposes. Therefore, they must not be automatically transposed into Part III of the *SCM Agreement*. Nevertheless, they may suggest ways of assessing whether the effect of a subsidy is significant price suppression rather than it being the effect of other factors.[349]

In *US – Upland Cotton (Article 21.5 – Brazil) (2008)*, the Appellate Body noted that the compliance panel had taken a different approach to causation and non-attribution than that taken by the original panel. In the original proceedings, the panel examined whether or not 'the effect of the subsidy' is significant price suppression which it had found to exist 'in the same world market'. The original panel then separately considered the role of other alleged causal factors in the record before it, which may have affected the analysis of the causal link between the US subsidies and the significant price suppression. The Article 21.5 'compliance' panel adopted a 'but for' approach to the question of whether the effect of the challenged subsidies to upland cotton producers is significant price suppression within the meaning of Article 6.3(c). In the view of the compliance panel, having adopted a 'but for' approach, it was not necessary to undertake 'a

345 Article 15.5 of the *SCM Agreement*. See above, p. 817.

346 Appellate Body Report, *US – Upland Cotton (2005)*, para. 436.

347 See *ibid.*, para. 437. The Appellate Body reasoned that, pursuant to 'Article 6.3(c) of the *SCM Agreement*, "[s]erious prejudice in the sense of paragraph (c) of Article 5 may arise" when "the effect of *the subsidy* is ... significant price suppression" ... If the significant price suppression found in the world market for upland cotton were caused by factors other than the challenged subsidies, then that price suppression would not be "the effect of" the challenged subsidies in the sense of Article 6.3(c).' See *ibid.*

348 *Ibid.* 349 *Ibid.*, para. 438.

comprehensive evaluation of factors affecting the world market price for upland cotton'.[350] The Appellate Body recalled in *US – Upland Cotton (Article 21.5 – Brazil) (2008)* that 'a panel has a certain degree of discretion in selecting an appropriate methodology' and 'Articles 5(c) and 6.3(c) of the *SCM Agreement* do not exclude, therefore, that a panel could examine causation based on a "but for" approach'. The panel's choice, in *US – Upland Cotton (Article 21.5 – Brazil) (2008)*, 'of a "but for" approach reflects [that] a price suppression analysis is counterfactual in nature'[351] and 'is consistent with the definition of price suppression endorsed by the Appellate Body in the original proceedings, insofar as the counterfactual determination of whether price suppression exists cannot be separated from the analysis of the effects of the subsidies'.[352] However, the Appellate Body chided the Article 21.5 compliance panel for not clearly articulating the standard implicated in its 'but for' approach. It stated that:

> [a] subsidy may be necessary, but not sufficient, to bring about price suppression. Understood in this way, the 'but for' test may be too undemanding. By contrast, the 'but for' test would be too rigorous if it required the subsidy to be the only cause of the price suppression. Instead, the 'but for' test should determine that price suppression is the effect of the subsidy and that there is a 'genuine and substantial relationship of cause and effect'.[353]

While the panel was required 'to have ensured that the effects of other factors on prices did not dilute the "genuine and substantial" link between the subsidies and the price suppression', in view of the discretion enjoyed by panels in choosing the methodology used for its Article 6.3 analysis:

> [i]t would not have been improper for the Panel to have assessed the effect of other factors as part of its counterfactual analysis, rather than conducting a separate analysis of non-attribution.[354]

On the basis of that understanding, the Appellate Body found the panel's 'but for' standard 'permissible under Article 6.3(c) of the *SCM Agreement*, and consistent with the panel's counterfactual analysis of price suppression'.[355]

The Appellate Body recognised the need for a non-attribution analysis also in *US – Large Civil Aircraft (2nd complaint) (2012)*. It noted that a panel will often be confronted with multiple factors that may have contributed, to varying degrees, to the adverse effect. In some circumstances, factors other than the subsidy at issue have caused a particular market effect. Yet the mere presence of other causes that contribute to a particular market effect does not, in itself, preclude the subsidy from being found to be a 'genuine and substantial' cause

350 Appellate Body Report, *US – Upland Cotton (Article 21.5 – Brazil) (2008)*, para. 369.
351 *Ibid.*, para. 370. In consequence, the panel had to determine whether the world price of upland cotton would have been higher in the absence of the subsidies (that is, *but for* the subsidies). See *ibid.*
352 *Ibid.*, para. 371. 353 *Ibid.*, para. 374.
354 *Ibid.*, para. 375. 355 See *ibid.*

of that effect. Thus, the Appellate Body explained in *US – Large Civil Aircraft (2nd complaint) (2012)* that:

> [a]s part of its assessment of the causal nexus between the subsidy at issue and the effect(s) that it is alleged to have had, a panel must seek to understand the interactions between the subsidy at issue and the various other causal factors, and make an assessment of their connections to, as well as the relative importance of the subsidy and of the other factors in bringing about, the relevant effects ... A panel must, however, take care to ensure that it does not attribute the effects of those other causal factors to the subsidies at issue, and that the other causal factors do not dilute the causal link between those subsidies and the alleged adverse effects such that it is not possible to characterize that link as a genuine and substantial relationship of cause and effect.[356]

Thus, the subsidy at issue may be found to exhibit the requisite causal link notwithstanding the existence of other causes that contribute to producing the relevant market phenomena if, having given proper consideration to all other relevant contributing factors and their effects, the panel is satisfied that the contribution of the subsidy has been demonstrated to rise to that of a *genuine and substantial cause*.[357]

5.3.8 Other Issues Relevant to the Analysis of the Effects of Subsidies

In addition to the issues relating to 'serious prejudice' discussed so far in this section, there are a number of other issues relevant to the analysis of the effects of subsidies that deserve to be discussed, including: (1) the temporal scope of Article 5 of the *SCM Agreement*; (2) the pass-through of subsidies; (3) the effect of subsidies over time; (4) the collective analysis of the effects of subsidies; and (5) Annex V on Procedures for Developing Information Concerning Serious Prejudice.

First, with regard to the *temporal scope* of Article 5 of the *SCM Agreement*, the Appellate Body rejected in *EC and certain member States – Large Civil Aircraft (2011)* the European Communities' request to exclude from the temporal scope of the dispute subsidies granted prior to 1 January 1995, when the *SCM Agreement* entered into force. The Appellate Body found that Article 5 addresses:

> [a] 'situation' that consists of causing, through the use of any subsidy, adverse effects to the interests of another Member.[358]

According to the Appellate Body, it is this 'situation' which 'is to be construed consistently with the non-retroactivity principle reflected in Article 28 of the

356 Appellate Body Report, *US – Large Civil Aircraft (2nd complaint) (2012)*, para. 914. See also Appellate Body Report, *US – Upland Cotton (2005)*, para. 437; Appellate Body Report, *US – Upland Cotton (Article 21.5 – Brazil) (2008)*, para. 375; Appellate Body Report, *EC and certain member States – Large Civil Aircraft (2011)*, paras. 1232 and 1376.

357 Appellate Body Report, *US – Large Civil Aircraft (2nd complaint) (2012)*, para. 914.

358 Appellate Body Report, *EC and certain member States – Large Civil Aircraft (2011)*, para. 686.

Vienna Convention'.[359] The relevant question for purposes of determining the temporal scope of Article 5 is whether the causing of adverse effects has 'ceased to exist' or continues as a 'situation'.[360] The Appellate Body consequently disagreed with the proposition that, by virtue of Article 28 of the *Vienna Convention*, no obligation arising from Article 5 of the *SCM Agreement* is to be imposed on a Member in respect of subsidies granted or brought into existence prior to 1 January 1995.[361] A pre-1995 subsidy may fall within the scope of Article 5 of the *SCM Agreement* because of its possible nexus to the continuing situation of causing, through the use of this subsidy, adverse effects to which Article 5 applies.[362]

Second, with regard to the *pass-through of subsidies*, recall the discussion earlier in this chapter on 'pass-through' in the context of the determination of 'benefit', an essential element of any subsidy.[363] As noted there, the Appellate Body found in *US – Softwood Lumber IV (2004)* that 'it cannot be presumed that a "subsidy" ... provided to a producer of an input "passes through" to the producer of the processed product'.[364] However, in *US – Upland Cotton (2005)*, the Appellate Body observed that its reasoning regarding pass-through in *US – Softwood Lumber IV (2004)* did not focus on the requirements for establishing serious prejudice under Articles 5(c) and 6.3(c) of Part III, but rather on the existence of a subsidy and the conduct of countervailing duty investigations pursuant to Part V of the *SCM Agreement*.[365] Specifically with regard to the establishment of serious prejudice, the Appellate Body ruled in *US – Upland Cotton (2005)* that the need for a 'pass-through' analysis under Part V is 'not critical' for an assessment of significant price suppression under Article 6.3(c) in Part III.[366] Nevertheless, the Appellate Body acknowledged that:

> [t]he 'subsidized product' must be properly identified for purposes of significant price suppression under Article 6.3(c) of the *SCM Agreement*. And if the challenged payments do not, in fact, subsidize that product, this may undermine the conclusion that the effect of the subsidy is significant suppression of prices of that product in the relevant market.[367]

The Appellate Body found that the facts in *EC and certain member States – Large Civil Aircraft (2011)* did not give rise to a requirement to conduct an analysis of whether the benefit of subsidies provided to the Airbus Industrie consortium *passed through* to Airbus SAS. First, there was no suggestion that 'subsidies were provided to a different "input product" that was separate or distinct from a downstream "subsidized product", as was the case in *US – Softwood Lumber IV*'.[368] Second, although it did not exclude that there may be other circumstances,

359 *Ibid.* 360 See *ibid.*

361 See *ibid.*

362 See *ibid.* Note, however, that, in reaching this conclusion, the Appellate Body was '*not* saying that the causing of adverse effects, through the use of pre-1995 subsidies, can necessarily be characterized as a "continuing" situation ... [R]ather ... [it found] that a challenge to pre-1995 subsidies is not *precluded* under the terms of the *SCM Agreement*'. See *ibid.*

363 See above, pp. 788–94. 364 Appellate Body Report, *US – Softwood Lumber IV (2004)*, paras. 140–2.

365 See Appellate Body Report, *US – Upland Cotton (2005)*, para. 471. 366 See *ibid.*

367 *Ibid.* 368 Appellate Body Report, *EC and certain member States – Large Civil Aircraft (2011)*, para. 775.

including ones involving the restructuring of companies in which the receipt of a subsidy by a predecessor company may not mean that it is enjoyed by a successor company, it recalled the panel's finding that, 'despite the changes to their "legal organization", the "economic realities" of production of Airbus LCA [large civil aircraft] demonstrated that the Airbus Industrie consortium ... and Airbus SAS were the "same producer" of LCA'.[369] Finally, the Appellate Body concluded, therefore, that it was 'not faced with a situation where predecessor and successor companies are unrelated and operate at arm's length and where a "pass-through" analysis might therefore be required'.[370]

Third, with regard to the *effect of subsidies over time*, the question that arises is whether the effect of a subsidy may continue beyond the year in which it is paid. In *US – Upland Cotton (2005)*, the parties disagreed on whether the effect of a 'recurring' subsidy may continue beyond the year in which it was paid. The Appellate Body noted that there is:

> [n]othing in the text of Article 6.3(c) that excludes *a priori* the possibility that the effect of a 'recurring' subsidy may continue after the year in which it is paid.[371]

The Appellate Body further observed that also the context of Article 6.3(c), and in particular Article 6.2 and 6.4, did *not* support the view that 'the effect of a subsidy is immediate, short-lived, or limited to one year, regardless of whether or not it is paid every year'.[372] To the contrary, the Appellate Body considered that one might expect a time lag between the provision of the subsidy and the resulting effect.[373] Consequently, the Appellate Body found that the 'proposition that, if subsidies are paid annually, their effects are also necessarily extinguished annually' cannot stand.[374]

In *EC and certain member States – Large Civil Aircraft (2011)*, the Appellate Body found that Articles 5 and 6 do not require that a complainant demonstrate that a benefit 'continues' or is 'present' during the reference period for purposes of an adverse effects analysis.[375] The Appellate Body emphasised, however, in *EC and certain member States – Large Civil Aircraft (2011)*, that:

> [e]ffects of a subsidy will ordinarily dissipate over time and will end at some point after the subsidy has expired. Indeed, as with a subsidy that has a finite life and materializes over time, so too do the effects of a subsidy accrue and diminish over time.[376]

369 *Ibid.* The Appellate Body referred to Panel Report, *EC and certain member States – Large Civil Aircraft (2011)*, para. 7.199.

370 Appellate Body Report, *EC and certain member States – Large Civil Aircraft (2011)*, para. 776. The Appellate Body did not consider that 'the relationship between the predecessor companies and Airbus SAS is one that can be characterized as a relationship between unrelated companies operating at "arm's length". Instead, the companies and Airbus SAS were related, at least to some extent, through common ownership.' See *ibid.*

371 Appellate Body Report, *US – Upland Cotton (2005)*, para. 476.

372 *Ibid.*, para. 477. The Appellate Body refers to Article 6.2 of the *SCM Agreement* in para. 477, and to Article 6.4 in para. 478.

373 See *ibid.*, para. 477. 374 *Ibid.*, para. 482.

375 See Appellate Body Report, *EC and certain member States – Large Civil Aircraft (2011)*, para. 715.

376 *Ibid.*, para. 713.

Therefore, a panel is required to consider whether the 'life of a subsidy' has ended, for example, by reason of the 'amortization of the subsidy over the relevant period or because the subsidy was removed from the recipient'.[377] Moreover, the Appellate Body emphasised that 'the effects of a subsidy will generally diminish and come to an end with the passage of time'.[378]

Fourth, with regard to the *collective analysis of the effects of subsidies*, it should be noted that a 'serious prejudice' analysis of multiple subsidies may be integrated to the extent appropriate in the light of the facts and circumstances of a given case. As the panel in *US – Upland Cotton (2005)* found, while due attention must be paid to each subsidy at issue as it relates to the subsidised product, the reference in Article 6.3 to 'the effect of the subsidy' in the singular does not mean that price suppression analysis 'must clinically isolate each individual subsidy and its effects'.[379] Accordingly, Article 6.3 permits an *integrated* examination of the effects of any subsidies when these subsidies have a sufficient nexus with the subsidised product and the particular effects-related variable under examination. The panel in *US – Upland Cotton (2005)* concluded that:

> [t]o the extent a sufficient nexus with [the subsidised product and the particular effects-related variable under examination] exists among the subsidies at issue so that their effects manifest themselves collectively, we believe that we may legitimately treat them as a 'subsidy' and group them and their effects together.[380]

In *EC and certain member States – Large Civil Aircraft (2011)*, the panel undertook what it called an *aggregated* analysis of the effects of the subsidies. It first examined the effects of Launch Aid/Member State Financing subsidies (LA/MSF) on Airbus' ability to launch particular models of large civil aircraft, and then sought to determine whether other non-LA/MSF subsidies had similar effects.[381] On the basis of a separate and quite limited assessment of the collective effect of measures comprised under each group of non-LA/MSF subsidies, the panel concluded that the effect of LA/MSF was 'complemented and supplemented' by the effects of other specific non-LA/MSF subsidies it found to exist in this dispute.[382] The Appellate Body was of the view that the panel had *not* conducted an 'aggregated' effects analysis, but had rather examined whether the effects of these non-LA/MSF subsidies 'complemented and supplemented' the effects of LA/MSF subsidies. According to the Appellate Body, the panel had established a 'genuine and substantial relationship of cause and effect' between the LA/MSF measures, the launch and marketing of each of Airbus models of LCA,

377 *Ibid.*, para. 1236.
378 *Ibid.* See also *ibid.*, para. 714.
379 Panel Report, *US – Upland Cotton (2005)*, para. 7.1192.
380 *Ibid.*
381 The non-LA/MSF subsidies comprised three groups: (1) equity infusions; (2) infrastructure measures; and (3) research & technology development subsidies.
382 Panel Report, *EC and certain member States – Large Civil Aircraft (2011)*, para. 7.1956.

and the displacement and lost sales of Boeing LCA during the reference period. According to the Appellate Body, the panel had further concluded that, 'insofar as the three sets of non-LA/MSF subsidies "complemented and supplemented" the "product effect" of LA/MSF, these subsidies "had the same effect on Airbus' ability to launch the LCA it launched at the time that it did"'.[383] The Appellate Body ruled that the panel's approach 'is permissible under Article 6.3 ... provided that a *genuine* causal link between the non-LA/MSF subsidies and the market phenomena alleged under Article 6.3 is established'.[384] The Appellate Body furthermore ruled that:

> [o]nce the Panel determined that LA/MSF subsidies were a substantial cause of the observed displacement and lost sales, it was not necessary to establish that non-LA/MSF subsidies were also substantial causes of the same phenomena ... Rather, it was conceivable that non-LA/MSF subsidies complemented or supplemented the effects of LA/MSF subsidies.[385]

The Appellate Body thus concluded in *EC and certain member States – Large Civil Aircraft (2011)* that Articles 5(c) and 6.3 do not preclude an affirmative finding that non-LA/MSF subsidies cause adverse effects where they 'complement and supplement' the effects of LA/MSF subsidies that have been found to be a substantial and genuine cause of adverse effects.[386] Finally, note that, in *US – Large Civil Aircraft (2nd complaint) (2012)*, the Appellate Body observed that two distinct means of undertaking a *collective* assessment of the effects of multiple subsidies have been used, namely, 'aggregation' and 'cumulation'. First, *aggregation* referred to an *ex ante* decision taken by a panel to undertake a single analysis of the effects of multiple subsidies whose structure, design and operation are similar and thereby to assess in an integrated causation analysis the collective effects of such subsidy measures (this was the approach employed by the panel in *US – Upland Cotton (2005)*).[387] Second, *cumulation* referred to an examination undertaken by a panel *after* it has found that at least one subsidy has caused adverse effects as to whether the effects of other subsidies complement

383 Appellate Body Report, *EC and certain member States – Large Civil Aircraft (2011)*, para. 1377.
384 *Ibid.*, para. 1378. Emphasis added. 385 *Ibid.* 340.
386 *Ibid.*
387 According to the Appellate Body, a panel may group together subsidy measures that are sufficiently similar in their design, structure and operation in order to ascertain their aggregated effects in an integrated causation analysis and determine whether there is a genuine and substantial causal relationship between these multiple subsidies, taken together, and the relevant market phenomena identified in Article 6.3. In such circumstances, the panel is not required to find that each subsidy measure is, individually, a genuine and substantial cause of the relevant phenomenon. Nor is it required to assess the relative contribution of each subsidy within the group to the resulting effects. When such an analysis is appropriate in light of the design, structure and operation of multiple subsidies, a panel may also add together the *amounts* of the subsidies as part of its analysis of the collective effects of that group of subsidies. Whether such an analysis is appropriate will depend upon the particular features of the subsidies at issue and the case presented by the complainant. The causal mechanism through which a subsidy produces effects is one criterion that will be relevant to the issue of whether aggregation is appropriate in any given instance. See Appellate Body Report, *US – Large Civil Aircraft (2nd complaint) (2012)*, para. 1285.

and supplement those adverse effects (this was the approach employed by the panel in *EC and certain member States – Large Civil Aircraft (2011)*).[388]

In sum, Articles 5(c) and 6.3 do not require that a serious prejudice analysis 'clinically isolate each individual subsidy and its effects'.[389] The way in which a panel structures its evaluation of a claim that multiple subsidies have caused serious prejudice will necessarily vary from case to case. Relevant circumstances that will bear upon the appropriateness of a panel's approach include the design, structure and operation of the subsidies at issue, the alleged market phenomena, and the extent to which the subsidies are provided in relation to a particular product or products.[390] A panel must also take account of the manner in which the claimant presents its case, and the extent to which it claims that multiple subsidies have similar effects on the same product, or that the effects of multiple subsidies manifest themselves collectively in the relevant market. A panel enjoys a 'degree of methodological latitude' in selecting its approach to analysing the collective effects of multiple subsidies for purposes of assessing causation. However, the Appellate Body emphasised in *US – Large Civil Aircraft (2nd complaint) (2012)* that 'a panel is never absolved from having to establish a "genuine and substantial relationship of cause and effect"[391] between the impugned subsidies and the alleged market phenomena under Article 6.3, or from assessing whether such causal link is diluted by the effects of other factors'.[392] Moreover, a panel must take care not to segment unduly its analysis such that, when confronted with multiple subsidy measures, it considers the effects of each on an individual basis only, and, as a result of such an atomised approach, finds that no subsidy alone is a substantial cause of the relevant adverse effects.[393]

388 The Appellate Body noted in *US – Large Civil Aircraft (2nd complaint) (2012)* that, in the alternative, a panel may begin by analysing the effects of a *single* subsidy, or an *aggregated* group of subsidies, in order to determine whether it constitutes a genuine and substantial cause of adverse effects. Having reached that conclusion, a panel may then assess whether *other* subsidies – either individually or in aggregated groups – have a *genuine* causal connection to the same effects, and complement and supplement the effects of the *first* subsidy (or group of subsidies) that was found, alone, to be a *genuine* and *substantial* cause of the alleged market phenomena. The other subsidies have to be a 'genuine' cause, but they need not, in themselves, amount to a 'substantial' cause in order for their effects to be combined with those of the first subsidy or group of subsidies that, alone, has been found to be a genuine and substantial cause of the adverse effects. See Appellate Body Report, *US – Large Civil Aircraft (2nd complaint) (2012)*, para. 1287.

389 Panel Report, *US – Upland Cotton (2005)*, para. 7.1192. See also Panel Report, *Indonesia – Autos (1998)*, para. 14.206; and Panel Report, *Korea – Commercial Vessels (2005)*, para. 7.616.

390 Appellate Body Report, *EC and certain member States – Large Civil Aircraft (2011)*, para. 1376 referring to Panel Report, *US – Upland Cotton (2005)*, para. 7.1194; and Panel Report, *Korea – Commercial Vessels (2005)*, para. 7.560.

391 Appellate Body Report, *US – Large Civil Aircraft (2nd complaint) (2012)*, para. 1284 referring to Appellate Body Report, *US – Upland Cotton (Article 21.5 – Brazil) (2008)*, para. 368 (quoting Appellate Body Report, *US – Upland Cotton (2005)*, para. 438).

392 Appellate Body Report, *US – Large Civil Aircraft (2nd complaint) (2012)*, para. 1284 referring to Appellate Body Report, *US – Upland Cotton (Article 21.5 – Brazil) (2008)*, para. 375.

393 Appellate Body Report, *US – Large Civil Aircraft (2nd complaint) (2012)*, para. 1284.

Fifth, the existence of serious prejudice must be determined on the basis of the information submitted to, or obtained by, the panel. If a Member fails to cooperate in the information-gathering process, the panel may rely on the 'best information available', and it may draw adverse inferences from the lack of cooperation.[394] Specific procedures for developing information on serious prejudice are set out in Annex V to the *SCM Agreement* on the *Procedures for Developing Information Concerning Serious Prejudice.* The Appellate Body ruled in *US – Large Civil Aircraft (2nd complaint) (2012)* that the initiation of an Annex V procedure occurs *automatically* when there is a request for initiation of such a procedure at the time that the DSB establishes a panel, even if the respondent or another Member would object in the DSB.[395] The Appellate Body reasoned that:

> the first sentence of paragraph 2 of Annex V, along with other provisions of Annex V, refers directly to the establishment of a panel pursuant to Article 7.4 of the *SCM Agreement.* Provided that a request for initiation of an Annex V procedure has been made, the DSB's initiation of such a procedure is a procedural incident of the establishment of a panel in serious prejudice cases. The function assigned to the DSB under paragraph 2 of Annex V is executory in nature, and is automatically discharged by it once the two specified conditions precedent are satisfied.[396]

The Appellate Body said that an interpretation of Annex V:2 that 'would enable a single WTO Member to frustrate the important role that an information-gathering procedure plays in serious prejudice disputes by preventing the DSB from initiating such a procedure would be at odds with WTO Members' clear intention to promote the early and targeted collection of information pertinent to the parties' subsequent presentation of their cases to the panel'.[397] As the Appellate Body explained:

> The initiation and conduct of Annex V procedures have important consequences for the ability of parties to a dispute to present their case, and for panels and the Appellate Body to fulfil their respective roles in complex serious prejudice disputes under the *SCM Agreement.* Annex V procedures are key to affording parties early access to critical information, which may in turn serve as the foundation upon which those parties will construct their arguments and seek to satisfy their evidentiary burden. Moreover, the initiation and conduct of such procedures are key to the ability of panels to make findings of fact that have a sufficient evidentiary basis or to draw negative inferences from instances of non-cooperation.[398]

394 See Annex V, paras. 6 and 7, to the *SCM Agreement.*

395 Appellate Body Report, *US – Large Civil Aircraft (2nd complaint) (2012)*, paras. 480–549. The Appellate Body considered that the panel had erred in rejecting various requests made by the European Communities regarding the information-gathering procedure under Annex V to the *SCM Agreement.*

396 Appellate Body Report, *US – Large Civil Aircraft (2nd complaint) (2012)*, para. 532.

397 *Ibid.*, para. 533. It would also be contrary to the obligation to cooperate in the collection of information in serious prejudice disputes imposed on all Members under Annex V:1 to and Article 6.6 of the *SCM Agreement.* See *ibid.*

398 See *ibid.*

5.4 Multilateral Remedies for Actionable Subsidies

The multilateral remedies for actionable subsidies are set out in Article 7 of the *SCM Agreement*. Like the remedies for prohibited subsidies, the remedies for actionable subsidies also differ from the remedies generally provided for in the DSU. Compared with the remedies against prohibited subsidies, however, the time frames are longer and the Permanent Group of Experts is not involved.[399] If a panel concludes that a subsidy causes adverse effects to the interests of another Member (be it injury, nullification or impairment, or serious prejudice), the subsidising Member must:

> [t]ake appropriate steps to remove the adverse effect or ... withdraw the subsidy.[400]

In *US – Upland Cotton (2005)*, the Appellate Body noted that Article 7.8 provides that:

> [w]here it has been determined that 'any subsidy has *resulted* in adverse effects to the interests of another Member', the subsidizing Member must 'take appropriate steps *to remove the adverse effects* or ... withdraw the subsidy'. The use of the word 'resulted' suggests that there could be a time-lag between the payment of a subsidy and any consequential adverse effects. If expired measures underlying past payments could not be challenged in WTO dispute settlement proceedings, it would be difficult to seek a remedy for such adverse effects. Further – in contrast to Articles 3.7 and 19.1 of the DSU – the remedies under Article 7.8 of the *SCM Agreement* for adverse effects of a subsidy are (i) the withdrawal of the subsidy *or* (ii) the removal of adverse effects. Removal of adverse effects through actions other than the withdrawal of a subsidy could not occur if the expiration of a measure would automatically exclude it from a panel's terms of reference.[401]

Further elaborating on the implementing Member's obligation to withdraw the subsidy or remove adverse effects under Article 7.8, the Appellate Body ruled in *US – Upland Cotton (Article 21.5 – Brazil) (2008)*:

> Article 7.8 is one of the 'special or additional rules and procedures on dispute settlement contained in the covered agreements' ... which prevail over the general DSU rules and procedures to the extent that there is a difference between them. As we see it, Article 7.8 specifies the actions that the respondent Member must take when a subsidy granted or maintained by that Member is found to have resulted in adverse effects to the interests of another Member ... Pursuant to Article 7.8, the implementing Member has two options to come into compliance. The implementing Member: (i) shall take appropriate steps to remove the adverse effects; or (ii) shall withdraw the subsidy. The use of the terms 'shall take' and 'shall withdraw' indicate that compliance with Article 7.8 of the SCM Agreement will usually involve some action by the respondent Member. This affirmative action would be directed at effecting the withdrawal of the subsidy or the removal of its adverse effects. A Member would normally not be able to abstain from taking any action on the assumption that the subsidy will expire or that the adverse effects of the subsidy will dissipate on their own.[402]

399 Several of the timeframes provided for under Article 7 are, however, still shorter than the 'ordinary' time frames provided for in the DSU. For example, the time frame for the panel proceedings is four months. See Article 7.5 of the *SCM Agreement*. For the 'normal' timeframes, see above, pp. 808–11.

400 Article 7.8 of the *SCM Agreement*.

401 Appellate Body Report, *US – Upland Cotton (2005)*, para. 273. Emphasis added.

402 Appellate Body Report, *US – Upland Cotton (Article 21.5 – Brazil) (2008)*, paras. 235–6. A Member would not comply with the obligation in Article 7.8 to withdraw the subsidy 'if it leaves an actionable subsidy in place, either entirely or partially, or replaces that subsidy with another actionable subsidy'. Appellate Body Report, *US – Upland Cotton (Article 21.5 – Brazil) (2008)*, para. 238.

As to the question in relation to which subsidies the implementing Member must take steps to remove the adverse effects or withdraw the subsidy, the Appellate Body ruled in *US – Upland Cotton (Article 21.5 – Brazil) (2008)* that it did:

> [n]ot see the obligation in Article 7.8 as being limited to subsidies granted in the past. Article 7.8 expressly refers to a Member 'granting or maintaining such subsidy'.[403]

According to the Appellate Body, this means that, in the case of recurring annual payments, the obligation in Article 7.8 would extend to payments 'maintained' by the respondent Member beyond the time period examined by the panel for purposes of determining the existence of serious prejudice, as long as those payments continue to have adverse effects.[404]

As noted, an implementing Member has under Article 7.8 of the *SCM Agreement* the choice between: (1) removing the adverse effects; or (2) withdrawing the subsidy. In *US – Upland Cotton (Article 21.5 – Brazil) (2008)*, the Appellate Body noted that the availability of this choice is 'arguably a consequence of the fact that actionable subsidies are not prohibited *per se*; rather, they are actionable to the extent they cause adverse effects'. The Appellate Body emphasised, however, that the fact that the implementing Member may choose to remove the adverse effects, rather than withdraw the subsidy:

> [c]annot be read as allowing a Member to continue to cause adverse effects by maintaining the subsidies that were found to have resulted in adverse effects.[405]

The subsidising Member must withdraw the subsidy or remove adverse effects within six months from the adoption of the report by the DSB.[406] Instead of withdrawing the subsidy at issue or removing its adverse effects, the subsidising Member may also agree with the complaining Member on compensation.[407] If an Article 21.5 'compliance' proceeding results in a finding that the subsidy has not been withdrawn, or its adverse effects have not been removed, within six months from the adoption of the report, or no agreement on compensation is reached, the DSB must, at the request of the complaining Member and by reverse consensus, grant authorisation to the complaining Member to take countermeasures. These countermeasures must be commensurate with the degree and nature of the adverse effects of the subsidies granted.[408]

403 *Ibid.*, para. 237.

404 See *ibid.* Otherwise, the adverse effects of subsequent payments would simply replace the adverse effects that the implementing Member was under an obligation to remove. See *ibid.*

405 *Ibid.*, para. 238.

406 See Article 7.9 of the *SCM Agreement.*

407 See *ibid.* Note that, in this specific context, compensation is a permanent alternative for bringing the measure into consistency with WTO law. This is not the case under the DSU. See above, p. 204.

408 Article 7.9 of the *SCM Agreement.* The contrast between 'appropriate countermeasures' in Article 4.10 and 'countermeasures ... commensurate with the degree and nature of the adverse effects' was emphasised in Decision by the Arbitrators in *Brazil – Aircraft (Article 22.6 – Brazil) (2000)*, para. 3.49, and Decision by the Arbitrators in *US – FSC (Article 22.6 – US) (2002)*, paras. 4.24–4.26.

5.5 Non-Actionable Subsidies

As already mentioned, in addition to prohibited subsidies and actionable subsidies, the *SCM Agreement* identifies a third category of subsidies: non-actionable subsidies.[409] This group of subsidies now only includes non-specific subsidies, to which, as discussed above, the disciplines of the *SCM Agreement* do not apply.[410] Until 31 December 1999, this category of non-actionable subsidies also included certain types of specific subsidies listed in Article 8.2 of the *SCM Agreement*, such as certain narrowly defined regional subsidies, environmental subsidies and research and development subsidies. At present, these subsidies, provided that they are specific and cause adverse effects, are actionable.[411]

6 COUNTERVAILING MEASURES

Prohibited subsidies and actionable subsidies which cause injury to the domestic industry can be challenged directly in WTO dispute settlement, or, in the alternative, they can be offset by the application of a countervailing measure.[412] A Member whose domestic industry is injured by subsidised imports has the choice between: (1) challenging the subsidy concerned *multilaterally*, pursuant to Article 4 or 7 of the *SCM Agreement*, as discussed in detail above;[413] or (2) *unilaterally* imposing countervailing duties on the subsidised imports, following an investigation procedure before a domestic investigating authority conducted pursuant to the procedural requirements set out in Part V of the *SCM Agreement*. A countervailing duty is defined in Article VI of the GATT 1994 and footnote 36 to the *SCM Agreement*. Article VI of the GATT provides that:

> a special duty levied for the purpose of offsetting ... any subsidy bestowed, directly, or indirectly, upon the manufacture, production or export of any merchandise.

Article 10 of the *SCM Agreement* provides with respect to countervailing duties:

> Members shall take all necessary steps to ensure that the imposition of a countervailing duty on any product of the territory of any Member imported into the territory of another Member is in accordance with the provisions of Article VI of GATT 1994 and the terms of this Agreement. Countervailing duties may only be imposed pursuant to investigations initiated and conducted in accordance with the provisions of this Agreement and the Agreement on Agriculture.

This section examines: (1) under what conditions countervailing duties may be imposed on subsidised imports; (2) how the investigations leading up to the

409 See above, p. 846. 410 See above, p. 802, fn. 166.
411 See Article 31 of the *SCM Agreement*.
412 A countervailing measure is also sometimes referred to as an 'anti-subsidy measure'.
413 See above, pp. 808–11 (multilateral remedies for prohibited subsidies) 844–5 (multilateral remedies for actionable subsidies).

imposition of countervailing duties should be conducted; and (3) how countervailing duties must be applied.

6.1 Conditions for the Imposition of Countervailing Duties

It follows from Article VI of the GATT 1994 and Articles 10 and 32.1 of the *SCM Agreement* that WTO Members may impose countervailing duties when three conditions are fulfilled, namely: (1) there are *subsidised imports*, i.e. imports of products from producers who benefited or benefit from specific subsidies within the meaning of Articles 1, 2 and 14 of the *SCM Agreement*; (2) there is *injury* to the domestic industry of the like products within the meaning of Articles 15 and 16 of the *SCM Agreement*; and (3) there is a *causal link* between the subsidised imports and the injury to the domestic industry *and* injury caused by other factors is *not attributed* to the subsidised imports. The discussion in the previous sections of this chapter on 'specific subsidies', 'injury' and 'causal link and non-attribution' is, *mutatis mutandis*, also relevant for the three conditions for the imposition of countervailing duties.[414] On each of these conditions, please refer to the discussion above.

6.2 Conduct of Countervailing Investigations

The *SCM Agreement* provides for detailed procedural requirements regarding the initiation and conduct of a countervailing investigation by the competent authorities of the Member imposing the countervailing duties on the subsidised imports. These requirements are set out in Articles 11 to 13 of the *SCM Agreement*. The main objectives of these requirements are to ensure that: (1) the investigations are conducted in a transparent manner; (2) all interested parties have the opportunity to defend their interests; and (3) the investigating authorities adequately explain the basis for their determinations.

Some of the procedural requirements for countervailing investigations set out in the *SCM Agreement* are very similar to the procedural requirements for anti-dumping investigations set out in the *Anti-Dumping Agreement* and discussed in Chapter 11.

6.2.1 Initiation of an Investigation

A countervailing investigation normally starts with the submission of a so-called application, i.e. a written complaint that injurious subsidisation is taking place. This application is submitted by, or on behalf of, the domestic industry allegedly injured by the subsidised imports.[415] Pursuant to Article 11.2 of the *SCM*

414 On 'specific subsidies', see above, pp. 794–802; on 'injury', see above, pp. 813–17; and on 'causal link and non-attribution', see above, p. 817.

415 See Article 11.1 of the *SCM Agreement*.

Agreement, the application must contain sufficient evidence of the existence of: (1) a subsidy and, if possible, its amount; (2) injury to the domestic industry; and (3) a causal link between the subsidised imports and the alleged injury.[416] Simple assertion, unsubstantiated by relevant evidence, is not considered to meet the requirement of 'sufficient evidence' under Article 11.2 of the *SCM Agreement*. Pursuant to Article 11.3 of the *SCM Agreement*, an investigating authority has an obligation to determine whether there is 'sufficient evidence' to justify initiation of an investigation. Part of this determination must involve an assessment of the accuracy and adequacy of the evidence furnished.[417] Although definitive proof of the existence and nature of a subsidy, injury and a causal link is not necessary for the purposes of justifying initiation under Article 11.3, adequate evidence, providing a sufficient indication of the existence of these elements, is required.[418] The panel in *China – GOES (2012)* stated that, in making the determination of whether there is sufficient evidence for initiation:

> [t]he investigating authority is balancing two competing interests, namely the interest of the domestic industry 'in securing the initiation of an investigation' and the interest of respondents in ensuring that 'investigations are not initiated on the basis of frivolous or unfounded suits'.[419]

As mentioned above, the application for the initiation of a countervailing investigation is submitted by, or on behalf of, the domestic industry allegedly injured by the subsidised imports. As is set out in Article 11.4 of the *SCM Agreement*, the application shall be considered to have been made 'by or on behalf of the domestic industry' if it is supported by those domestic producers whose collective output constitutes more than 50 per cent of the total production of the like product produced by that portion of the domestic industry expressing either support for *or* opposition to the application. However, no investigation shall be initiated when domestic producers expressly supporting the application account for less than 25 per cent of total production of the like product produced by the domestic industry. Article 11.4 does not provide that an investigating authority examine the motives of domestic producers that elect to support an investigation. As the Appellate Body explained in *US – Offset Act (Byrd Amendment) (2003)*:

> The use of the terms 'expressing support' and 'expressly supporting' clarify that Article ... 11.4 require[s] only that authorities 'determine' that support has been 'expressed' by a sufficient number of domestic producers. Thus ... 'examination' of the 'degree' of support, and

416 Article 11.2 of the *SCM Agreement* sets out in significant detail the information the application must contain.

417 See Article 11.3 of the *SCM Agreement*. Note, however, that Article 11.3 of the *SCM Agreement* does not specify how this examination is to be carried out. Note also that 'sufficient evidence' is, of course, not the same as 'full proof'; it is clearly a lower standard.

418 See Panel Report, *China – GOES (2012)*, para. 7.55.

419 *Ibid.*, para. 7.54. See also Panel Report, *US – Offset Act (Byrd Amendment) (2003)*, para. 7.61. For the interpretation of Article 5.3 of the *Anti-Dumping Agreement* which provides for largely similar obligations, see Panel Report, *Guatemala – Cement I (1998)*, para. 7.52.

not the 'nature' of support is required. In other words, it is the 'quantity', rather than the 'quality', of support that is the issue.[420]

In special circumstances, investigating authorities may also decide to initiate countervailing investigations of their own accord.[421] However, they may only do so when they have sufficient evidence of the existence of a subsidy, injury and causal link to justify the initiation of an investigation.

If the investigating authorities concerned find that there is not sufficient evidence of either subsidisation or injury to justify proceeding with the case, they must reject the application for the initiation of an investigation, or, if the investigation has already been initiated, promptly terminate that investigation.[422] There shall be immediate termination in cases where the amount of a subsidy is *de minimis* (i.e. less than 1 per cent *ad valorem*), or where the volume of subsidised imports, actual or potential, or the injury, is negligible.[423] The nature of the *de minimis* rule set forth in Article 11.9 was explored by the Appellate Body in *US – Carbon Steel (2002)*. The Appellate Body clarified:

> To us, there is nothing in Article 11.9 to suggest that its *de minimis* standard was intended to create a special category of '*non-injurious*' subsidization, or that it reflects a concept that subsidization at less than a *de minimis* threshold *can never* cause injury. For us, the *de minimis* standard in Article 11.9 does no more than lay down an agreed rule that if *de minimis* subsidization is found to exist in an original investigation, authorities are obliged to terminate their investigation, with the result that no countervailing duty can be imposed in such cases.[424]

In *Mexico – Anti-Dumping Measures on Rice (2005)*, the Appellate Body further ruled that, when a company has been found not to have received countervailable subsidies above *de minimis* levels during the original period of investigation, it necessarily follows from Article 11.9 of the *SCM Agreement* that such companies can no longer be made subject to administrative and changed circumstances reviews.[425]

6.2.2 Conduct of the Investigation

When the investigating authorities decide to initiate an investigation, be it at the request of the domestic industry or of their own accord, several procedural obligations must be respected in order to provide adequate protection for those potentially affected by such an investigation. First, a public notice of the initiation must be issued,[426] and, as soon as the investigation is initiated,[427] the application for the initiation of an investigation must be made available to the known

420 Appellate Body Report, *US – Offset Act (Byrd Amendment) (2003)*, para. 283.
421 See Article 11.6 of the *SCM Agreement*. 422 See Article 11.9 of the *SCM Agreement*.
423 See *ibid*. 424 Appellate Body Report, *US – Carbon Steel (2002)*, para. 83.
425 Appellate Body Report, *Mexico – Anti-Dumping Measures on Rice (2005)*, para. 305.
426 See Article 22.1 of the *SCM Agreement*. Article 22.2 sets out the information which this public notice must contain. The Appellate Body clarified that the requirements of Article 22 apply to both investigations under Article 11 and reviews under Article 21 of the *SCM Agreement*. See Appellate Body Report, *US – Carbon Steel (India) (2014)*, para. 4.534.
427 Note that, before the investigation is actually initiated, the investigating authorities must invite the subsidising Member for consultations. Such consultations will continue throughout the investigation. See Articles 13.1 and 13.2 of the *SCM Agreement*.

exporters of the subsidised products and the exporting Member.[428] Second, interested Members and all interested parties in the investigation, including, of course, the exporter(s) of the subsidised products and the domestic producer(s) of the like product,[429] must be given: (1) notice of the information which the authorities require; and (2) ample opportunity to present in writing all evidence which they consider relevant.[430] Third, Members and interested parties must then be given at least thirty days to reply to the questionnaire they receive from the investigating authorities.[431] In *Mexico – Anti-Dumping Measures on Rice (2005)*, the Appellate Body made clear that the thirty-day period must be accorded to *all* exporters and foreign producers receiving a questionnaire, to be counted from the date of receipt of the questionnaire.[432] The Appellate Body furthermore made clear that it interprets the thirty-day period strictly: a period of twenty-eight working days following the date of publication of the initiating resolution does not suffice.[433] Fourth, the investigating authorities must provide opportunities for industrial users of the product under investigation, and for representative consumer organisations in cases where the product is commonly sold at the retail level, to provide information.[434] Fifth, all interested parties must be invited to participate in the hearings held by the investigating authorities.[435] Sixth, the investigating authorities are obliged to make all information that is not confidential available to all interested Members and interested parties.[436] However, any information the disclosure of which would be of significant competitive advantage to a competitor or would have significant adverse effects on those supplying the information (i.e. any confidential information or other information which is provided on a confidential basis) must, where good cause is shown, be treated as confidential by the investigating authorities.[437] Such confidential information may only be disclosed with the specific permission of the party submitting it.[438] Finally, throughout an investigation, the investigating authorities must satisfy themselves as to the

428 See Article 12.1.3 of the *SCM Agreement*. The application shall also be made available, upon request, to other interested parties involved.

429 For a definition of 'interested parties', see Article 12.9 of the *SCM Agreement*. Note that domestic or foreign parties other than those mentioned above may also be considered to be 'interested parties'.

430 See Article 12.1 of the *SCM Agreement*.

431 See Article 12.1.1 of the *SCM Agreement*. Where cause is shown, a thirty-day extension period should be granted whenever practicable.

432 See Appellate Body Report, *Mexico – Anti-Dumping Measures on Rice (2005)*, para. 280.

433 See *ibid.*, para. 283.

434 See Article 12.10 of the *SCM Agreement*.

435 See Article 12.2 of the *SCM Agreement*. Note, however, that any decision of the investigating authorities can only be based on such information and arguments as were on the written record of these authorities. Therefore, information provided orally must also be submitted in writing.

436 See Article 12.3 of the *SCM Agreement*.

437 See Article 12.4 of the *SCM Agreement*.

438 See *ibid*. Investigating authorities may, however, be asked to provide non-confidential summaries in sufficient detail to provide a reasonable understanding of the substance of the information submitted in confidence. See Article 12.4.1 of the *SCM Agreement*. See also Appellate Body Report, *EC – Fasteners (2011)*, paras. 535–44 and 549; and Panel Report, *US – Oil Country Tubular Goods Sunset Reviews (Article 21.5 – Argentina) (2007)*, para. 7.135 for the interpretation of Article 6.5 of the *Anti-Dumping Agreement* which provides for largely similar obligations in respect of the protection of confidential information and the provision of non-confidential summaries.

accuracy of the information supplied by interested Members or interested parties upon which their findings are based.[439]

When investigating authorities, in spite of their best efforts, fail to obtain all relevant information, they may take decisions on the basis of the 'best information available'. Article 12.7 of the *SCM Agreement* provides:

> In cases in which any interested Member or interested party refuses access to, or otherwise does not provide, necessary information within a reasonable period or significantly impedes the investigation, preliminary and final determinations, affirmative or negative, may be made on the basis of the facts available.

According to the Appellate Body in *Mexico – Anti-Dumping Measures on Rice (2005)*, Article 12.7 is intended to ensure that the failure of an interested party to provide necessary information does not hinder an agency's investigation. Thus, the provision permits the use of facts on record solely for the purpose of replacing information that may be missing, in order to arrive at an accurate subsidisation or injury determination.[440] In the same appeal, the Appellate Body drew a comparison with Article 6.8 of the *Anti-Dumping Agreement*, which also 'permits an investigating authority, under certain circumstances, to fill in gaps in the information necessary to arrive at a conclusion, as to dumping and injury'.[441] While the Appellate Body recognised that Article 6.8 of the *Anti-Dumping Agreement* contains far more detailed rules as regards the use of 'facts available' by an investigating authority, it considered that:

> it would be anomalous if Article 12.7 of the *SCM Agreement* were to permit the use of 'facts available' in countervailing duty investigations in a manner markedly different from that in anti-dumping investigations.[442]

Hence, according to the Appellate Body in *Mexico – Anti-Dumping Measures on Rice (2005)*, similar limitations apply under Article 12.7 of the *SCM Agreement* (as apply under Article 6.8 of the *Anti-Dumping Agreement*). It held that:

> recourse to facts available does not permit an investigating authority to use any information in whatever way it chooses. First, such recourse is not a licence to rely on only part of the evidence provided. To the extent possible, an investigating authority using the 'facts available' in a countervailing duty investigation must take into account all the substantiated facts provided by an interested party, even if those facts may not constitute the complete information requested of that party. Second, the 'facts available' to the agency are generally limited to those that may reasonably replace the information that an interested party failed to provide. In certain circumstances, this may include information from secondary sources.[443]

439 Article 12.5 of the *SCM Agreement*.

440 See Appellate Body Report, *Mexico – Anti-Dumping Measures on Rice (2005)*, para. 293. See also the Appellate Body in its reports in *US – Carbon Steel (India) (2014)*, para. 4.416 and in *US – Countervailing Measures (China) (2014)*, para. 4.178.

441 Appellate Body Report, *Mexico – Anti-Dumping Measures on Rice (2005)*, para. 291.

442 *Ibid.*, para. 295. 443 *Ibid.*, para. 294.

The Appellate Body further clarified the parameters for recourse to 'facts available' in *US – Carbon Steel (India) (2014)*. It held that the process of identifying the 'facts available' should be limited to identifying replacements for the 'necessary information' that is missing from the record.[444] In turn, it noted that the 'facts available' are those facts that are in the possession of the investigating authority and on its written record, which may include, for instance, facts contained in the application of the domestic industry that led to the initiation of the investigation, or facts contained in information requested by, and submitted to, the investigating authority by other interested parties or interested Members.[445] As part of the process of reasoning and evaluating which 'facts available' reasonably replace the missing information, all substantiated facts on the record must be taken into account.[446] The extent of the evaluation of the 'facts available' that is required, and the form it may take, depends on the particular circumstances of a given case, including the nature, quality, and amount of the evidence on the record, and the particular determinations to be made in the course of an investigation.[447] Finally, the manner or procedural circumstances in which information is missing can be relevant to an investigating authority's use of 'facts available'.[448]

To the extent that the Panel Report in *US – Carbon Steel (India) (2014)* can be read to exclude, in all instances, a comparative evaluation of all available evidence with a view to selecting the best information from the legal standard for Article 12.7, the Appellate Body modified the panel's finding and found that Article 12.7 requires an investigating authority to use 'facts available' that reasonably replace the missing 'necessary information', with a view to arriving at an accurate determination, which calls for a process of evaluation of available evidence, the extent and nature of which depends on the particular circumstances of a given case.[449]

While the possibility for investigating authorities to use 'facts available' is important to avoid investigations being frustrated and deadlocked because of the lack of cooperation from an interested party holding the relevant information, this possibility may evidently also potentially give rise to abuse on the part of investigating authorities. To ensure due process in the countervailing investigation, Article 12.8 of the *SCM Agreement* requires that:

> [t]he authorities shall, before a final determination is made, inform all interested Members and interested parties of the essential facts under consideration which form the basis for the decision whether to apply definitive measures. Such disclosure should take place in sufficient time for the parties to defend their interests.

As to the type of information that must be disclosed, the provision covers 'those facts on the record that may be taken into account by an authority in reaching

444 Appellate Body Report, *US – Carbon Steel (India) (2014)*, para. 4.416. 445 *Ibid.*, para. 4.417.
446 *Ibid.*, para. 4.419. 447 *Ibid.*, para. 4.421.
448 *Ibid.*, para. 4.422. 449 *Ibid.*, para. 4.435.

a decision as to whether or not to apply' definitive countervailing duties.[450] Unlike Article 22.5, which governs the disclosure of matters of fact and law and reasons at the conclusion of the countervailing duty investigations, Article 12.8 concerns the disclosure of 'facts' in the course of such investigations 'before a final determination is made'. According to the Appellate Body in *China – GOES (2012)*, Article 12.8:

> [d]oes not require the disclosure of *all* the facts that are before an authority but, instead, those that are 'essential'; a word that carries a connotation of significant, important, or salient. In considering which facts are 'essential' ... such facts are, first, those that 'form the basis for the decision whether to apply definitive measures' and, second, those that ensure the ability of interested parties to defend their interests.[451]

As the Appellate Body also found in *China – GOES (2012)*, an investigating authority must 'disclose such facts, *in a coherent way*, so as to permit an interested party to understand the basis for the decision whether or not to apply definitive measures' because disclosing the essential facts under consideration pursuant to Article 12.8 is 'paramount for ensuring the ability of the parties concerned to defend their interests'.[452]

Note that Articles 12.7 and 12.8 of the *SCM Agreement* refer to 'interested parties'. Article 12.9 of the *SCM Agreement* provides in this respect:

> For the purposes of this Agreement, 'interested parties' shall include:
> (i) an exporter or foreign producer or the importer of a product subject to investigation, or a trade or business association a majority of the members of which are producers, exporters or importers of such product; and
> (ii) a producer of the like product in the importing Member or a trade and business association a majority of the members of which produce the like product in the territory of the importing Member.
>
> This list shall not preclude Members from allowing domestic or foreign parties other than those mentioned above to be included as interested parties.

In *Japan – DRAMs (Korea) (2007)*, the panel and the Appellate Body addressed the question whether the inclusion of a party as an 'interested party' in an investigation requires a prior determination that that party has an interest in the outcome of an investigation.[453] Korea had argued that such a requirement was implied in the language of Article 12.9.[454] The panel disagreed and found that Article 12.9 does not provide an exhaustive list as to which parties 'can be taken to be "interested parties"'.[455] The Appellate Body in *Japan – DRAMs (Korea) (2007)* stated that, while it agreed with Korea that:

> [t]he entities specified in subparagraphs (i) and (ii) – which are all involved in the production, export, or import of the product under investigation, or in the production of the like product in the importing country – are likely to 'have an interest in the outcome of

450 Appellate Body Report, *China – GOES (2012)*, para. 240. 451 *Ibid.*
452 *Ibid.* 453 See Appellate Body Report, *Japan – DRAMs (Korea) (2007)*, para. 237.
454 See *ibid.*, para. 238. 455 See Panel Report, *Japan – DRAMs (Korea) (2007)*, para. 7.388.

> the proceeding', but [it found] nothing in Article 12.9 to suggest that interested parties are restricted to entities of this kind under the residual clause of Article 12.9. Although the term 'interested party' by definition suggests that the party must have an interest related to the investigation, the mere fact that the lists in subparagraphs (i) and (ii) comprise entities that may be directly interested in the outcome of the investigation does not imply that parties that may have other forms of interest pertinent to the investigation are excluded.[456]

The last sentence of Article 12.9 provides that Members are not precluded from *allowing* domestic or foreign parties other than those listed in subparagraphs (i) and (ii) to be included as interested parties. This does not mean, however, that investigating authorities enjoy an unfettered discretion in designating entities as interested parties regardless of the relevance of such entities to the conduct of an objective investigation. At the same time, an investigating authority needs to have some discretion to include as interested parties entities that are relevant for conducting an objective investigation and for obtaining information or evidence relevant to the investigation at hand. Nonetheless, the Appellate Body stressed that, in designating entities as interested parties, an investigating authority must be mindful of the burden that such designation may entail for other interested parties.[457]

Investigations must normally be concluded within one year,[458] and in no case should an investigation take longer than eighteen months.[459]

6.2.3 Public Notice and Judicial Review

In order to increase the transparency of decisions taken by investigating authorities and to encourage solid and thorough reasoning supporting such decisions, Article 22 of the *SCM Agreement* contains detailed requirements for public notice by investigating authorities of decisions on the initiation of an investigation, provisional countervailing measures, voluntary undertakings or definitive countervailing duties. For example, under Article 22.5 of the *SCM Agreement*, the public notice issued when the investigating authorities decide to impose a definitive countervailing duty *must* set forth, or otherwise make available through a separate report, all relevant information on the matters of fact and law and reasons which have led to the imposition of the countervailing duty.[460] In particular, the notice or report *must* contain: (1) the names of the suppliers or, when this is impracticable, the supplying countries involved; (2) a description of the product which is sufficient for customs purposes; (3) the amount of subsidy established and the basis on which the existence of a subsidy has been determined; (4) considerations relevant to the injury determination as set out in

456 Appellate Body Report, *Japan – DRAMs (Korea) (2007)*, paras. 238–9.

457 See *ibid.*, para. 242; regarding the interpretation of 'interested parties' within the meaning of Article 6.9 of the *Anti-Dumping Agreement* see, Appellate Body Report, *EC – Fasteners (China) (21.5)*, paras. 5.148ff.

458 See Article 11.11 of the *SCM Agreement*. 459 See *ibid.*

460 See Article 22.5 of the *SCM Agreement*. Note, however, that Article 22.5 requires that due regard be paid to the requirement for the protection of confidential information.

Article 15; and (5) the main reasons leading to the determination.[461] Furthermore, the notice or report *must* set out the reasons for the acceptance or rejection of relevant arguments or claims made by interested Members and by the exporters and importers.[462] In *China – GOES (2012)*, the Appellate Body found with regard to the requirement to disclose 'relevant information on the matters of fact' that Article 22.5 does not require authorities to disclose *all* the factual information that is before them, but rather those facts that allow an understanding of the factual basis that led to the imposition of final measures.[463] According to the Appellate Body, what constitutes 'relevant information on the matters of fact' is to be understood in light of the content of the findings needed to satisfy the substantive requirements for the imposition of definitive measures under the *SCM Agreement*, as well as the factual circumstances of each case.[464] The Appellate Body in *China – GOES (2012)* stated with regard to the 'public notice' requirement under Article 22.5 of the *SCM Agreement* that:

> [Article 22.5] capture[s] the principle that those parties whose interests are affected by the imposition of final ... countervailing duties are entitled to know, as a matter of fairness and due process, the facts, law and reasons that have led to the imposition of such duties. The obligation of disclosure under [Article 22.5] is framed by the requirement of 'relevance', which entails the disclosure of the matrix of facts, law and reasons that logically fit together to render the decision to impose final measures ... [Article 22.5] seeks to guarantee that interested parties are able to pursue judicial review of a final determination as provided in ... Article 23.[465]

As provided for in Article 23 of the *SCM Agreement*, entitled 'Judicial Review', each Member whose national legislation contains provisions on countervailing measures must maintain judicial, arbitral or administrative tribunals or procedures for the purpose of, *inter alia*, the prompt review of administrative actions relating to definitive determinations and reviews of determinations. Such tribunals or procedures must be independent from the authorities responsible for the determination or review in question, and must provide all interested parties who participated in the administrative proceeding, and are affected directly and individually by the administrative actions, with access to review.[466]

6.3 Application of Countervailing Measures

The *SCM Agreement* provides for three types of countervailing measure: (1) provisional countervailing measures; (2) voluntary undertakings; and (3) definitive

461 *Ibid.*, referring to Article 22.4 thereof. 462 See Article 22.5 of the *SCM Agreement*.

463 See Appellate Body Report, *China – GOES (2012)*, para. 256. The inclusion of this information should therefore give a reasoned account of the factual support for an authority's decision to impose definitive measures. See *ibid.*

464 The imposition of final countervailing duties requires that an investigating authority finds subsidisation, injury to the domestic industry, and a causal link between subsidisation and injury. See Appellate Body Report, *China – GOES (2012)*, para. 257.

465 *Ibid.*, para. 258. 466 See Article 23 of the *SCM Agreement*.

countervailing duties. This section discusses in turn these three types of countervailing measure.

6.3.1 Imposition of Provisional Countervailing Measures

After making a preliminary determination that a subsidy is causing or threatening to cause injury to a domestic industry, an importing Member can impose *provisional countervailing measures* on the subsidised imports if the authorities judge such measures necessary to prevent injury being caused during the investigation.[467] Provisional countervailing measures may take the form of provisional countervailing duties guaranteed by cash deposits or bonds equal to the amount of the provisionally calculated amount of subsidisation.[468] However, such provisional countervailing measures cannot be applied earlier than sixty days from the date of initiation of the investigation. Furthermore, their application must be limited to as short a period as possible and in no case may they be applied for more than four months.[469] In *US – Softwood Lumber III (2002)*, the panel found that the United States had violated Articles 17.3 and 17.4 of the *SCM Agreement* because it had imposed provisional countervailing measures on imports of softwood lumber prior to the lapse of the sixty-day period after the date of initiation and had exceeded the four-month maximum length by three months.[470]

6.3.2 Voluntary Undertakings

Investigations may be suspended or terminated without the imposition of provisional measures or countervailing duties upon receipt of satisfactory *voluntary undertakings* under which: (1) the government of the exporting Member agrees to eliminate or limit the subsidy or to take other measures concerning its effects; or (2) the exporter agrees to revise its prices so that the investigating authorities are satisfied that the injurious effect of the subsidy is eliminated.[471] Note that, pursuant to Article 18.2 of the *SCM Agreement*, undertakings may not be sought or accepted unless the investigating authorities have made a preliminary affirmative determination of subsidisation and injury caused by such subsidisation. In case of undertakings from exporters, the consent of the exporting Member must be obtained. Article 18.4 of the *SCM Agreement* provides that, if an undertaking is accepted, the investigation of subsidisation and injury shall nevertheless be completed if the exporting Member so desires or the importing Member so decides.[472]

467 See Article 17 of the *SCM Agreement*. 468 See Article 17.2 of the *SCM Agreement*.
469 See Articles 17.3 and 17.4 of the *SCM Agreement*.
470 See Panel Report, *US – Softwood Lumber III (2002)*, para. 7.101.
471 See Article 18.1 of the *SCM Agreement*.
472 Article 18.6 of the *SCM Agreement* sets out the consequences of a violation of an undertaking.

6.3.3 Imposition and Collection of Countervailing Duties

Members may impose *definitive countervailing duties* only after making a final determination that: (1) a countervailable subsidy exists; and (2) the subsidised imports cause, or threaten to cause, injury to the domestic industry.[473] Note that Article 32.1 of the *SCM Agreement* states:

> No specific action against a subsidy of another Member can be taken except in accordance with the provisions of GATT 1994, as interpreted by this Agreement.[474]

In *US – Offset Act (Byrd Amendment) (2003)*, the Appellate Body ruled that it follows from this provision that the response to a countervailable subsidy must be in one of the *four* forms provided for in provisions of the GATT 1994 or the *SCM Agreement*.[475] As discussed above, the GATT 1994 and the *SCM Agreement* provide several responses to a countervailable subsidy: definitive countervailing duties; provisional measures; price undertakings; and multilaterally sanctioned countermeasures under the dispute settlement system. This is not to say that the *SCM Agreement* excludes challenging a prohibited or actionable subsidy in dispute settlement proceedings as a permissible response in itself. No other response to subsidisation is permitted. In *US – Offset Act (Byrd Amendment) (2003)*, the measure at issue was the US Continued Dumping and Subsidy Offset Act of 2000 (CDSOA).[476] This Act provided, in relevant part, that the United States Customs shall *distribute* duties assessed pursuant to a countervailing duty order to 'affected domestic producers' for 'qualifying expenditures'.[477] According to the Appellate Body, in applying Article 32.1 of the *SCM Agreement* to the measure at issue in this case, it was necessary:

> [t]o assess whether the design and structure of a measure is such that the measure is 'opposed to', has an adverse bearing on, or, more specifically, has the effect of dissuading ... the practice of subsidization, or creates an incentive to terminate such practice.[478]

In the Appellate Body's view, the CDSOA has exactly those effects because of its design and structure.[479] However, a measure cannot 'be against' a subsidy simply

473 See Article 19.1 of the *SCM Agreement*.

474 The Appellate Body established in *US – Offset Act (Byrd Amendment) (2003)* the following test to determine whether a measure constitutes 'a specific action': '[A] measure that may be taken only when the constituent elements of ... a subsidy are present, is a "specific action" in response to ... subsidization within the meaning of Article 32.1 of the *SCM Agreement*. In other words, the measure must be inextricably linked to, or have a strong correlation with, the constituent elements of dumping or of a subsidy. Such link or correlation may ... be derived from the text of the measure itself.' See Appellate Body Report, *US – Offset Act (Byrd Amendment) (2003)*, para. 239.

475 *Ibid.*, para. 269. 476 See *ibid.*, paras. 11–14.

477 See *ibid.*, para. 14. 478 *Ibid.*, para. 254.

479 See *ibid.*, para. 254. The Appellate Body further explained that 'in order to determine whether the CDSOA is "against" ... subsidization, it was not necessary, nor relevant, for the Panel to examine the conditions of competition under which domestic products and ... subsidized imports compete, and to assess the impact of the measure on the competitive relationship between them'. See *ibid.*, para. 257.

because it facilitates or induces the exercise of rights that are WTO-consistent.[480] The Appellate Body concluded:

> As the CDSOA does not correspond to any of the responses to subsidization envisaged by the GATT 1994 and the *SCM Agreement*, we conclude that it is not in accordance with the provisions of the GATT 1994, as interpreted by the *SCM Agreement*, and that, therefore, the CDSOA is inconsistent with Article 32.1 of the *SCM Agreement*.[481]

The panel in *Mexico – Anti-Dumping Measures on Rice (2005)* held that the provision in a Mexican regulation imposing fines on importers importing products subject to countervailing duty investigations was a form of 'specific action' against a subsidy, that fines were not provided for in the GATT 1994 or the *SCM Agreement*, and that the fines at issue were thus inconsistent with Article 32.1 of the *SCM Agreement*.[482] However, the panel in *EC – Commercial Vessels (2005)* ruled that a European regulation on shipbuilding constituted a form of 'specific action', but as it was not directed 'against' a subsidy, Article 32.1 of the *SCM Agreement* was not violated.[483]

With respect to the amount of the countervailing duty imposed on subsidised imports, Article 19.4 of the *SCM Agreement* provides:

> No countervailing duty shall be levied on any imported product in excess of the amount of the subsidy found to exist, calculated in terms of subsidization per unit of the subsidized and exported product.

Thus, Article 19.4 'places a quantitative ceiling on the amount of a countervailing duty which may not exceed the amount of subsidization'.[484] Moreover, if the amount of the injury caused is less than the amount of the subsidy, the definitive countervailing duty should *preferably* be limited to the amount necessary to counteract the injury caused.[485] This is commonly referred to as the 'lesser duty' rule.[486] As discussed above, Members have a margin of discretion in deciding on the method used to calculate the amount of the subsidy.[487] The Appellate Body's reference in *US – Softwood Lumber IV (2004)* to calculation of countervailing duty rates on a per unit basis under Article 19.4 supports the interpretation that an investigating authority is permitted to calculate the total amount and the rate of subsidisation on an aggregate basis.[488]

In *Japan – DRAMs (Korea) (2007)*, the issue was raised whether subsidisation must be 'found to exist' – as is stated in Article 19.4 of the *SCM Agreement* – at the time of imposition of the countervailing duty, or whether a determination

480 *Ibid.*, para. 258. 481 *Ibid.*, para. 273.
482 See Panel Report, *Mexico – Anti-Dumping Measures on Rice (2005)*, para. 7.278.
483 See Panel Report, *EC – Commercial Vessels (2005)*, para. 7.143.
484 Appellate Body Report, *US – Anti-Dumping and Countervailing Duties (China) (2011)*, para. 554.
485 See Article 19.2 of the *SCM Agreement*. Moreover, a Member may even decide to abstain from imposing countervailing duties altogether. See also Article 19.2 of the *SCM Agreement*.
486 See above, p. 750. 487 See Article 14 of the *SCM Agreement*, explained in detail above.
488 Appellate Body Report, *US – Softwood Lumber IV (2004)*, para. 153.

that a subsidy was 'found to exist' during some prior period suffices.[489] The panel found that 'countervailing duties may only be imposed if there is present subsidization at the time of duty imposition'.[490] According to the panel, this does not, however, exclude the possibility that an investigating authority may rely on previous data.[491] As the panel observed, the situation during the period of investigation may serve as a proxy for the situation prevailing at the time of imposition. However, in the case of non-recurring subsidies, if the review of the period of investigation indicates that the subsidy will no longer exist at the time of imposition, the fact that subsidisation existed during the period of investigation will not be sufficient to demonstrate 'current' subsidisation at the time of imposition.[492] On appeal, the Appellate Body noted in this regard that, by its terms, Article 19.4 refers to a subsidy 'found to exist',[493] and that it saw:

> [n]o requirement in Article 19.4 for an investigating authority to conduct a new investigation or to 'update' the determination at the time of imposition of a countervailing duty in order to confirm the continued existence of the subsidy. However, in the case of a non-recurring subsidy, a countervailing duty cannot be imposed if the investigating authority has made a finding in the course of its investigation as to the duration of the subsidy and, according to that finding, the subsidy is no longer in existence at the time that the Member makes a final determination to impose a countervailing duty.[494]

This is because, in such a situation, the countervailing duty, if imposed, would be in excess of the amount of subsidy found to exist, contrary to the provisions of Article 19.4.

As noted above, pursuant to Articles 19.4 of the *SCM Agreement* and Article VI:3 of the GATT 1994, an investigating authority may not impose a countervailing duty in excess of the amount of subsidy found to have been granted on the subsidised product. This is why an investigating authority will conduct 'tying analysis' in order to determine whether a subsidy can be considered to be bestowed on a particular product under investigation. The Appellate Body stated that a subsidy is 'tied' to a particular product if the bestowal of that subsidy is connected to, or conditioned upon, the production or sale of the product concerned. An assessment of whether this connection or conditional relationship exists will inevitably depend on the specific circumstances of each case. In conducting such an assessment, an investigating authority must examine the design, structure, and operation of the measure granting the subsidy at issue and take into account all the relevant facts surrounding the granting of that subsidy. The Appellate Body concluded in *US – Washing Machines (2016)* that the panel improperly endorsed a flawed tying test applied by the USDOC in the Washers countervailing duty investigation, whereby a subsidy is considered to

489 See Panel Report, *Japan – DRAMs (Korea) (2007)*, para. 7.351. 490 *Ibid.*, para. 7.355.
491 See Panel Report, *Japan – DRAMs (Korea) (2007)*, para. 7.356.
492 See *ibid.*, para. 7.357. 493 See Appellate Body Report, *Japan – DRAMs (Korea) (2007)*, para. 210.
494 *Ibid.* 495 Appellate Body Report, *US – Washing Machines (2016)*, para. 5.274.

be tied to a specific product only when the intended use of the subsidy is known to the granting authority and so acknowledged prior to or concurrent with the bestowal of the subsidy.[495] In *US – Washing Machines (2016)*, the Appellate Body also stated that in its review of the 'tying' findings of the domestic authority, the panel erroneously conflated the concept of 'recipient of the benefit' under Article 1.1(b) of the *SCM Agreement* with the concept of 'subsidized product' under Article 19.4 of the *SCM Agreement* and Article VI:3 of the GATT 1994.[496]

Countervailing duties must be collected on a non-discriminatory basis. Article 19.3 of the *SCM Agreement* states:

> When a countervailing duty is imposed in respect of any product, such countervailing duty shall be levied, in the appropriate amounts in each case, on a non-discriminatory basis on imports of such product from all sources found to be subsidized and causing injury.[497]

Thus, the provision contains: (1) a requirement that countervailing duties be levied in the appropriate amounts in each case; and (2) a requirement that these duties be levied on a non-discriminatory basis on imports of such product from all sources found to be subsidised and causing injury, except for imports from sources that have renounced the relevant subsidies or from which undertakings have been accepted.[498] While a Member imposing countervailing duties has to levy such duties 'on a non-discriminatory basis', this does not mean that the 'appropriate' amount of the countervailing duty imposed will necessarily be the same for each individual exporter. An exporter or producer who was examined individually and has cooperated in the investigation will normally be levied an individual countervailing duty. Note that any exporter whose exports are subject to a definitive countervailing duty but who was not actually investigated is entitled to an expedited review so that the investigating authorities can promptly establish an individual countervailing duty rate for that exporter.[499] Moreover, the Appellate Body stressed that:

> [c]ountry-wide or company-specific countervailing duty rates may be imposed under Part V of the *SCM Agreement* only *after* the investigating authority has determined the existence of subsidization, injury to the domestic industry, and a causal link between them. In other words, the fact that Article 19 permits the imposition of countervailing duties on imports from producers or exporters not investigated individually, does not exonerate a Member from the obligation to determine the total amount of subsidy and the countervailing duty rate consistently with the provisions of the *SCM Agreement* and Article VI of the GATT 1994.[500]

496 *Ibid.*, para. 5.305.

497 As discussed above, the MFN treatment obligation applies to countervailing duties. See above, p. 313. The MFN treatment obligation also applies to anti-dumping duties. See above, pp. 750–1. Note that countervailing duties shall not be applied to imports from sources which have renounced any subsidies in question or sources from which undertakings have been accepted. See Article 19.3 of the *SCM Agreement*.

498 See Appellate Body Report, *US – Anti-Dumping and Countervailing Duties (China) (2011)*, para. 552.

499 See Article 19.3 of the *SCM Agreement*. This does not apply to exporters for whom no individual countervailing duty was established due to their refusal to cooperate with the investigating authorities. See also Appellate Body Report, *US – Anti-Dumping and Countervailing Duties (China) (2011)*, para. 553.

500 Appellate Body Report, *US – Softwood Lumber IV (2004)*, para. 154.

A final comment regarding Article 19.3 of the *SCM Agreement* concerns the issue of 'double-counting' or 'double-remedies', i.e. a situation in which duties are imposed against the same imports from non-market economies – and allegedly for the same injury – under both the *Anti-Dumping Agreement* and the *SCM Agreement*. In *US – Anti-Dumping and Countervailing Duties (China) (2011)*, the Appellate Body found that Article 19.3 is of relevance to this issue. The Appellate Body held that, under Article 19.3:

> [t]he appropriateness of the amount of countervailing duties cannot be determined without having regard to anti-dumping duties imposed on the same product to offset the same subsidization. The amount of a countervailing duty cannot be 'appropriate' in situations where that duty represents the full amount of the subsidy and where anti-dumping duties, calculated at least to some extent on the basis of the same subsidization, are imposed concurrently to remove the same injury to the domestic industry. Dumping margins calculated based on an NME [non-market economy] methodology are, for the reasons explained above, likely to include some component that is attributable to subsidization.[501]

The Appellate Body concluded that the imposition of double remedies, that is, offsetting the same subsidisation twice by the concurrent imposition of anti-dumping duties calculated on the basis of a non-market economy methodology and countervailing duties, is inconsistent with Article 19.3 of the *SCM Agreement*.[502]

Pursuant to Article 20.1 of the *SCM Agreement*, countervailing duties, in principle, may not be applied retroactively, i.e. they may only be applied to products imported after the decision to impose countervailing duties entered into force.[503] As set out in Article 20.5 of the *SCM Agreement*, where a final determination is negative, any cash deposit made during the period of the application of provisional measures shall be refunded and any bonds released in an expeditious manner.[504]

6.3.4 Duration, Termination and Review of Countervailing Duties

With respect to the period of imposition of countervailing duties, Article 21.1 of the *SCM Agreement* states as a rule:

> A countervailing duty shall remain in force only as long as and to the extent necessary to counteract subsidization which is causing injury.

501 Appellate Body Report, *US – Anti-Dumping and Countervailing Duties (China) (2011)*, para. 582. On why dumping margins calculated based on an NME methodology are likely to include some component that is attributable to subsidisation, see *ibid.*, paras. 542–3. In the same report, the Appellate Body noted that 'Article 19.4 makes clear that the amount that could be "appropriate" cannot be more than the amount of the subsidy'. It also noted that Article 19.2 'states that it is "desirable" that "duty should be less than the total amount of the subsidy if such lesser duty would be adequate to remove the injury"'. See *ibid.*, paras. 556–7.

502 Appellate Body Report, *US – Anti-Dumping and Countervailing Duties (China) (2011)*, para. 583.

503 Note, however, that the retroactive application of countervailing duties is permitted in specific circumstances. See Articles 20.2 and 20.6 of the *SCM Agreement*.

504 However, if the definitive countervailing duty is higher than the amount guaranteed by the cash deposit or bond, the difference shall not be collected. See Article 20.3 of the *SCM Agreement*.

The Appellate Body held in *US – Carbon Steel (2002)* that it considered Article 21.1 of the *SCM Agreement* to be:

[a] general rule that, after the imposition of a countervailing duty, the continued application of that duty is subject to certain disciplines. These disciplines relate to the *duration* of the countervailing duty ('only as long as ... necessary'), its *magnitude* ('only ... to the extent necessary'), and its *purpose* ('to counteract subsidization which is causing injury'). Thus, the general rule of Article 21.1 underlines the requirement for periodic review of countervailing duties and highlights the factors that must inform such reviews.[505]

Upon a request from an interested party or upon their own initiative where warranted, the investigating authorities shall review the need for the continued application of the duty.[506] Interested parties may request such review once a reasonable period has elapsed since the imposition of the definitive countervailing duty. The interested parties requesting a review must submit positive information substantiating the need for a review.[507] During the review, the investigating authorities examine at the request of the interested party: (1) whether the continued imposition of the duty is necessary to offset subsidisation; and/or (2) whether injury would be likely to continue or recur if the duty were removed or varied.[508] The Appellate Body in *Mexico – Anti-Dumping Measures on Rice (2005)* found that Members are not allowed to condition the right of interested parties to a review upon requirements other than those set out in Article 21.2 of the *SCM Agreement*.[509]

In *US – Lead and Bismuth II (2000)*, the Appellate Body noted with regard to the determination an investigating authority must make in an Article 21.2 review:

On the basis of its assessment of the information presented to it by interested parties, as well as of other evidence before it relating to the period of review, the investigating authority must determine whether there is a continuing need for the application of countervailing duties. The investigating authority is not free to ignore such information. If it were free to ignore this information, the review mechanism under Article 21.2 would have no purpose.[510]

As to the question of whether the existence of a 'benefit' in an Article 21.2 review, the Appellate Body held in *US – Lead and Bismuth II (2000)*:

We do not agree with the Panel's implied view that, in the context of an administrative review under Article 21.2, an investigating authority must *always* establish the existence of

505 Appellate Body Report, *US – Carbon Steel (2002)*, para. 70.

506 See Article 21.2 of the *SCM Agreement*. Such periodic reviews can be initiated upon the initiative of the investigating authorities or, provided that a reasonable period of time has elapsed since the imposition of the definitive countervailing duty, upon request by any interested party which submits positive information substantiating the need for such a review. Interested parties have the right to request the authorities to examine whether the continued imposition of the duty is necessary to offset subsidisation, whether the injury would be likely to continue or recur if the duty were removed or varied, or both. See also Appellate Body Report, *US – Lead and Bismuth II (2000)*, para. 53. See also Panel Report, *US – Softwood Lumber III (2002)*, para. 7.151.

507 See Article 21.2 of the *SCM Agreement*.

508 See *ibid*. The review must be conducted pursuant to the same procedural rules as those that applied to the original investigation. See Article 21.4 of the *SCM Agreement*.

509 See Appellate Body Report, *Mexico – Anti-Dumping Measures on Rice (2005)*, para. 314.

510 Appellate Body Report, *US – Lead and Bismuth II (2000)*, para. 61. 511 *Ibid*., paras. 62–3.

> a 'benefit' during the period of review *in the same way as* an investigating authority must establish a 'benefit' in an original investigation ... In an original investigation, the investigating authority must establish that *all* conditions set out in the *SCM Agreement* for the imposition of countervailing duties are fulfilled. In an administrative review, however, the investigating authority must address those issues which have been raised before it by the interested parties or, in the case of an investigation conducted on its own initiative, those issues which warranted the examination.[511]

The Appellate Body hence draws a distinction between the original investigation which is concerned with the initial imposition of a countervailing duty *and* the review procedure of Article 21.2.[512]

If the investigating authorities, upon such a review, reach the conclusion that continued imposition of the countervailing duty is no longer necessary it shall be terminated immediately.[513] Should the investigating authorities conclude that the countervailing duty remains warranted, it will continue to apply, albeit possibly at a reduced level.

Article 21.3 of the *SCM Agreement* provides for a so-called 'sunset' clause according to which all definitive countervailing duties must be terminated, at the latest, five years after their imposition or latest review. However, where the investigating authorities determine that the lapse of the countervailing duty would be likely to lead to continuation or recurrence of subsidisation and injury, the duty will not be terminated.[514] Investigating authorities make that determination in the context of a review that is commonly referred to as a 'sunset review'. A sunset review may be initiated by the investigating authorities at their own initiative *or* upon a duly substantiated request made by, or on behalf of, the domestic industry.[515] The Appellate Body explained in *US – Carbon Steel (2002)* that Article 21.3 differs from Article 21.2, discussed above, in that the latter identifies certain circumstances in which investigating authorities are under an *obligation* to review ('shall review') whether the continued imposition of the countervailing duty is necessary. In contrast, the principal obligation in Article 21.3 is not, *per se*, to conduct a review, but rather to *terminate* a countervailing duty *unless* a specific determination is made in a review that the continued imposition is necessary.[516]

512 The extent of the obligations of the investigating authorities in the context of a review procedure was clarified by the Appellate Body in *US – Countervailing Measures on Certain EC Products (2003)*. See Appellate Body Report, *US – Countervailing Measures on Certain EC Products (2003)*, para. 146.

513 See Article 21.2 of the *SCM Agreement*.

514 See Article 21.3 of the *SCM Agreement*.

515 See Article 21 of the *SCM Agreement*. Note that a request for a sunset review must be made within a reasonable period of time prior to the expiry of the countervailing duties and that investigating authorities must initiate the review before that expiration date. Note also that Article 21.3, unlike Article 11.9, does not impose a *de minimis* standard for the initiation of a sunset review. The Appellate Body held in *US – Carbon Steel (2002)* that the *de minimis* requirement of Article 11.9 is also *not implied* in Article 21.3. See Appellate Body Report, *US – Carbon Steel (2002)*, para. 92. See also above, p. 863. With regard to sunset reviews initiated by investigating authorities on their own initiative, the Appellate Body held in *US – Carbon Steel (2002)* that there are no evidentiary standards for self-initiation of sunset reviews. See Appellate Body Report, *US – Carbon Steel (2002)*, para. 112.

516 See Appellate Body Report, *US – Carbon Steel (2002)*, para. 108.

The provisions of Article 12 of the *SCM Agreement*, setting out rules on the collection of evidence, transparency, due process and procedure with regard to original investigations, also apply to sunset reviews.[517] Sunset reviews shall be carried out expeditiously and shall normally be concluded within twelve months of their initiation.[518]

6.4 Countervailing Duties or Countermeasures

Note that the provisions relating to prohibited and actionable subsidies, discussed above, may be invoked, and relied upon, *in parallel with* the provisions relating to countervailing duties. However, with regard to the effects of a particular subsidy, only *one* form of remedy (either a countervailing duty *or* a countermeasure) may be applied.[519]

7 INSTITUTIONAL AND PROCEDURAL PROVISIONS

Like most other WTO agreements, the *SCM Agreement* contains a few institutional and procedural provisions. This section discusses, in particular, Article 24, which establishes the WTO Subsidies Committee, and Article 25, which provides for transparency and notification requirements. This section also refers to Articles 4 and 7, which deal with dispute settlement regarding prohibited and actionable subsidies, as discussed above.

7.1 Transparency and Notification Requirements

Transparency is essential for the effective operation of the *SCM Agreement*. Article 25 requires that Members notify all specific subsidies by 30 June of each year.

As of October 2016, thirty-three Members[520] had submitted their 2015 new and full notifications indicating that they provided specific subsidies within the meaning of the *SCM Agreement*. Fifteen Members had notified that they provided no notifiable specific subsidies.[521]

The transparency requirements under the *SCM Agreement* are complemented by the general transparency provisions of the GATT 1994. According to the

517 See Article 21.4 of the *SCM Agreement*.

518 See *ibid*. During a sunset review, the countervailing duties may remain in force. See Article 21.3 of the *SCM Agreement*.

519 See fn. 35 to the *SCM Agreement*.

520 For this purpose, the European Union was counted as one Member.

521 See document series G/SCM/N/284. See also *Report (2016) of the Committee on Subsidies and Countervailing Measures*, G/L/1157, G/SCM/148 dated 31 October 2016, 2.

Appellate Body in *US – Countervailing and Anti-Dumping Measures (China) (2014)*, Article X:2 embodies the principle of transparency, which has due process dimensions.[522] A baseline of comparison is used to determine whether a measure of general application effects an advance in a rate of duty or imposes a new or more burdensome requirement. The proper baseline of comparison under Article X:2 should thus reflect traders' expectations about the applicable measure, considering that Article X:2 is meant to ensure that traders 'have a reasonable opportunity to acquire authentic information about [the new] measures and accordingly to protect and adjust their activities or alternatively to seek modification of such measures'.[523] The baseline of comparison under Article X:2 to determine whether a measure 'effects an advance in a rate of duty' is not the practice of the administrative agency as such, but rather the prior published measure of general application as interpreted and applied by the relevant domestic authorities.[524]

7.2 Subsidies Committee

The Committee on Subsidies and Countervailing Measures, commonly referred to as the Subsidies Committee, is composed of representatives from each WTO Member. Pursuant to Article 24.1 of the *SCM Agreement*, the Committee shall meet not less than twice a year. It carries out the responsibilities assigned to it under the *SCM Agreement*. It shall afford Members the opportunity to consult on any matter relating to the operation of the agreement or the furtherance of its objectives. Article 25.9 of the *SCM Agreement* entitles a Member that considers that requested information has not been provided at all or not with sufficient detail, to bring the matter before the Committee. The same may occur under Article 25.10 if a measure having the effects of a subsidy has not been properly notified by a Member. Article 25.11 provides that Members shall report without delay to the Subsidies Committee all preliminary or final actions taken with respect to countervailing duties as well as submit semi-annual reports on any countervailing duty actions taken within the preceding six months. Pursuant to Article 26 of the *SCM Agreement*, such notifications and reports shall be kept under surveillance at meetings of the Subsidies Committee. Finally, Article 25.12 requires each Member to notify the Committee which of its authorities are competent to initiate and conduct countervailing investigations and its domestic procedures governing the initiation and conduct of such investigations.

According to Articles 24.2 and 24.3 of the *SCM Agreement*, the Subsidies Committee may set up subsidiary bodies, including the Permanent Group of Experts (PGE), which is composed of five independent persons highly qualified

522 Appellate Body Report, *US – Countervailing and Anti-Dumping Measures (China) (2014)*, para. 4.66.
523 *Ibid.*, para. 4.67. 524 *Ibid.*, paras. 4.110 and 4.114.

in the fields of subsidies and trade relations. The PGE may be requested to assist panels, in accordance with Article 24.3, or may be consulted by any Member and may give confidential advisory opinions on the existence and nature of any subsidy pursuant to Article 24.4. The Subsidies Committee or its advisory bodies may, as foreseen in Article 24.5, consult with and seek information from any source.[525]

7.3 Dispute Settlement

The provisions of the DSU apply also to consultations and the settlement of disputes relating to subsidies and countervailing measures. As explained above, accelerated procedures and specific remedies apply to prohibited and actionable subsidies in accordance with Articles 4 and 7 of the *SCM Agreement*, respectively.[526] For example, a number of the time periods provided for in the DSU for particular procedural steps or compliance are halved for prohibited subsidies and shortened for actionable subsidies that have been found to cause adverse effects such as injury or serious prejudice.

8 SPECIAL AND DIFFERENTIAL TREATMENT FOR DEVELOPING-COUNTRY MEMBERS

Subsidies can play an important role in the economic development programmes of developing-country Members. Article 27 of the *SCM Agreement* recognises this and provides for some rules and disciplines for developing-country Members that are less strict than the general rules and disciplines. Pursuant to Article 27, the prohibition on export subsidies under Article 3 of the *SCM Agreement* does not apply to least-developed countries and to countries with a per capita annual income of less than US$1,000.[527] The remedies available against these export subsidies are those available against actionable subsidies as set out in Article

525 On the Permanent Group of Experts (PGE), see also above, pp. 130–40, 808–9.

526 See above, pp. 808–9.

527 See Article 27.2 of the *SCM Agreement*. Note that, until 2003, the prohibition of export subsidies also did not apply to other developing-country Members even though these Members had to phase out export subsidies progressively. Their export subsidies could not be increased and had to be phased out even before 2003 if their use was inconsistent with their development needs. See Article 27.4 of the *SCM Agreement* and the panel and Appellate Body reports in *Brazil – Aircraft (1999)*. The Subsidies Committee was authorised to extend the period of non-application of the prohibition of export subsidies in Article 3 under certain conditions and/or in certain countries beyond 2003. Accordingly, in 2002, the Subsidies Committee granted extensions of the transition period for exemption from the prohibition of export subsidies with respect to a number of programmes of twenty-one developing-country Members. These extensions were time-bound and programme-specific. They were granted on the basis of Article 27.4, in most cases in conjunction with procedures (G/SCM/39) adopted by Ministers at the Doha Ministerial Conference and/or paragraph 10.6 of the *Doha Decision on Implementation Issues* (WT/MIN(01)/17). The Subsidies Committee authorised some further extensions in 2003. Note that the prohibition of import substitution subsidies applies to least-developed-country Members since 2003 and to other developing-country Members since 2000. See Article 27.3 of the *SCM Agreement*.

7 of the *SCM Agreement*.[528] Furthermore, certain subsidies which are normally actionable are not actionable when granted by developing-country Members in the context of privatisation programmes. This is the case, for example, for direct forgiveness of debts and subsidies to cover social costs.[529]

With respect to countervailing duties, Article 27.2 of the *SCM Agreement* provides that any countervailing investigation of a product originating in a developing-country Member must be terminated as soon as the investigating authorities determine that: (1) the overall level of subsidies granted to the product in question does not exceed 2 per cent *ad valorem*; or (2) the volume of the subsidised imports represents less than 4 per cent of the total imports of the like product of the importing Member. Note, however, that the latter rule does not apply when the imports from developing-country Members whose individual shares of total imports represent less than 4 per cent, collectively account for more than 9 per cent of the total imports of the like product of the importing Member.[530]

9 AGRICULTURAL SUBSIDIES UNDER THE *AGREEMENT ON AGRICULTURE*

Agricultural subsidies have traditionally been, and continue to be, a very contentious issue in international trade. Agricultural subsidies were a central issue during the Uruguay Round and were one of the major stumbling blocks in the Doha Development Round.[531] Agricultural export subsidies and domestic agricultural support measures are indispensable instruments of agricultural policies of a number of developed-country Members. At the same time, the trade interests and the economic development of many other Members are severely affected by these agricultural subsidies. Developing countries in particular are seriously harmed by the effects of agricultural subsidies of developed countries.

The subsidies paid by the US government to cotton farmers were successfully challenged by Brazil in several WTO dispute settlement proceedings. When the United States was found to have failed to comply fully with the DSB's rulings, Brazil obtained authorisation from the DSB to take retaliatory measures against imports of US goods and US intellectual property rights up to amount determined by an arbitrator.[532] In order to avoid this retaliation, the

528 See above, pp. 844–5.
529 See Article 27.13 of the *SCM Agreement*. Note also the limitation in Article 27.9 of the *SCM Agreement* on remedies for actionable subsidies granted by developing countries.
530 See Article 27.10 of the *SCM Agreement*.
531 On the negotiations on agricultural trade in the context of the Doha Round, see above, p. 86, fn. 26 and 94–5.
532 On retaliation, see above, pp. 204–7.

United States negotiated a compensatory settlement with Brazil. A commentator polemicised:

What could be more outrageous than the hefty subsidies the US government lavishes on rich American cotton farmers? How about the hefty subsidies the US government is about to start lavishing on rich Brazilian cotton farmers? If that sounds implausible or insane, well, welcome to US agricultural policy, where the implausible and the insane are the routine. Our perplexing $147.3 million-a-year handout to Brazilian agribusiness, part of a last-minute deal to head off an arcane trade dispute, barely even qualified as news ... If you're perplexed, here's the short explanation: We're shoveling our taxpayer dollars to Brazilian farmers to make sure we can keep shoveling our taxpayer dollars to American farmers – which is, after all, the overriding purpose of US agricultural policy. Basically, we're paying off foreigners to let us maintain our ludicrous *status quo*.

By encouraging Americans to plant cotton even when prices are low, [US cotton subsidies] promote overproduction and further depress prices. An Oxfam study found that removing them entirely would boost world prices about 10%, which would be especially helpful to the 20,000 subsistence cotton growers in Africa.[533]

However, the current US cotton subsidy regime, introduced with the 2014 bill only does little to alleviate the situation.[534]

The particular sensitivities of agricultural subsidies explain why the disciplines of the *SCM Agreement* do not apply *in full* to agricultural subsidies. The *Agreement on Agriculture* provides for special rules on agricultural subsidies and, in case of conflict, these special rules prevail over the rules of the *SCM Agreement*. Article 21.1 of the *Agreement on Agriculture* states in this respect:

The provisions of GATT 1994 and of other Multilateral Trade Agreements in Annex 1A to the WTO Agreement shall apply subject to the provisions of this Agreement.

In *US – Upland Cotton (2005)*, the Appellate Body has interpreted Article 21.1 to mean that the provisions of the GATT 1994 and of other Multilateral Trade Agreements in Annex 1A apply, 'except to the extent that the *Agreement on Agriculture* contains specific provisions dealing specifically with the same matter'.[535]

533 M. Grunwald, 'Why the US Is Also Giving Brazilians Farm Subsidies', *Time*, 9 April 2010. See http://content.time.com/time/nation/article/0,8599,1978963,00.html.

534 For more information, see Africa Bridges, *How Could the 2014 US Farm Bill Affect the World Market for Cotton?*, October 2014, 4(8).

535 See Appellate Body Report, *US – Upland Cotton (2005)*, para. 532, referring to Appellate Body Report, *EC – Bananas III (1997)*, para. 155; and Appellate Body Report, *Chile – Price Band System (2002)*, para. 186. The Appellate Body agreed with the panel in *US – Upland Cotton (2005)* that Article 21.1 could apply in the three situations, namely: (1) where, for example, the domestic support provisions of the *Agreement on Agriculture* would prevail in the event that an explicit carve-out or exemption from the prohibition of import substitution subsidies in Article 3.1(b) of the *SCM Agreement* existed in the *text* of the *Agreement on Agriculture*; (2) where it would be impossible for a Member to comply with its domestic support obligations under the *Agreement on Agriculture* and the Article 3.1(b) prohibition simultaneously; or (3) where the text of the *Agreement on Agriculture* explicitly authorises a measure that, in the absence of such authorisation, would be prohibited by Article 3.1(b) of the *SCM Agreement*. According to the Appellate Body, there could, however, be situations other than those identified by the panel where Article 21.1 of the *Agreement on Agriculture* may be applicable. See Appellate Body Report, *US – Upland Cotton (2005)*, para. 532.

This section briefly discusses the special rules of the *Agreement on Agriculture* regarding: (1) agricultural export subsidies; and (2) domestic agricultural support measures.[536]

9.1 Agricultural Export Subsidies

The prohibition on export subsidies, provided for in Article 3 of the *SCM Agreement* and discussed in detail above, applies to agricultural export subsidies *except* as provided otherwise in the *Agreement on Agriculture*. The relationship between the *SCM Agreement* and the *Agreement on Agriculture* is defined, in part, by Article 3.1 of the *SCM Agreement*, which states that export subsidies and import substitution subsidies are prohibited '[e]*xcept* as provided in the Agreement on Agriculture'.[537] This clause indicates that the WTO consistency of an export subsidy for agricultural products has to be examined, in the first place, under the *Agreement on Agriculture*.[538]

In *US – FSC (2000)*, the Appellate Body found that the *Agreement on Agriculture* and the *SCM Agreement* use exactly the same words to define 'export subsidies' and that, although there are differences between the disciplines established under the two agreements, those differences do not, according to the Appellate Body, 'affect the common substantive requirements relating to export contingency'.[539] The Appellate Body thus concluded that it is appropriate to apply the interpretation of export contingency adopted under the *SCM Agreement* to the interpretation of export contingency under the *Agreement on Agriculture*.[540]

While export subsidies on non-agricultural products are prohibited, with respect to export subsidies on agricultural products a distinction must be made between export subsidies on: (1) agricultural products that are specified in Section II of Part IV of a Member's GATT Schedule of Concessions; and (2) agricultural products that are not specified in that section.[541] With respect to agricultural products *not* specified in the relevant section of their Schedule, Members shall not provide any export subsidies.[542] With respect to the agricultural products specified in the

536 The third pillar of the *Agreement on Agriculture* relating to WTO Members' market access commitments is discussed in Chapter 6 (on tariff barriers) and Chapter 7 (on non-tariff barriers). See above, pp. 436–7 and 520–9.

537 Emphasis added.

538 See Appellate Body Report, *Canada – Dairy (Article 21.5 – New Zealand and US) (2001)*, paras. 123–4.

539 Appellate Body Report, *US – FSC (2000)*, para. 141. See also Panel Report, *US – Upland Cotton (2005)*, para. 7.754.

540 See Appellate Body Report, *US – FSC (2000)*, para. 141. See also Appellate Body Report, *US – Upland Cotton (2005)*, para. 571.

541 Note that the term 'export subsidy commitments' covers commitments and obligations relating to *both* scheduled and unscheduled agricultural products.

542 See Article 3.3 of the *Agreement on Agriculture*. Under the second clause of Article 3.3, Members have committed *not* to provide *any* export subsidies, listed in Article 9.1, with respect to *unscheduled* agricultural products. This clause clearly also involves 'export subsidy commitments' within the meaning of Article 10.1. See Appellate Body Report, *US – FSC (2000)*, para. 146.

relevant section of their Schedule, Members have agreed – pursuant to Article 9 of the *Agreement on Agriculture* – to subject all export subsidies, defined in paragraphs (a)–(f) of Article 9.1, to reduction commitments.[543] Article 9.1 sets forth a list of practices that, by definition, involve export subsidies: (1) direct export subsidies (including payments-in-kind) by governments or their agencies contingent on export performance (Article 9.1(a));[544] (2) sales of non-commercial stocks of agricultural products for export at prices lower than comparable prices for such goods on the domestic market (Article 9.1(b)); (3) payments on agricultural exports financed by virtue of governmental action, whether or not a charge on the public account is involved (Article 9.1(c));[545] (4) cost reduction measures such as subsidies to reduce the cost of marketing goods for export (Article 9.1(d));[546] (5) internal transport subsidies applying to exports only, provided or mandated by the government, on terms more favourable than for domestic shipments (Article 9.1(e)); and (6) subsidies on agricultural products contingent on their incorporation into exported products (Article 9.1(f)).

543 See Article 3.3 of the *Agreement on Agriculture*. Under the first clause of Article 3.3, Members have made a commitment that 'they will not "provide export subsidies listed in paragraph 1 of Article 9 in respect of the agricultural products or groups of products specified in Section II of Part IV of its Schedule in excess of the budgetary outlay and quantity commitments levels specified therein"'. See Appellate Body Report, *US – FSC (2000)*, para. 145.

544 See Appellate Body Report, *US – Upland Cotton (2005)*, para. 582. On the term 'payments' in the term 'payments-in-kind', and the distinction between the economic transfer effected and the analysis of the benefit thereby conferred, see Appellate Body Report, *Canada – Dairy (1999)*, para. 87. On the meaning of the terms 'government' and 'government agency', as well as the relevance of 'functions performed by the government', the 'power and authority' to perform those functions 'vested in an agency' and the 'degree of discretion in the exercise of such functions', see Appellate Body Report, *Canada – Dairy (1999)*, para. 97. The Appellate Body discussed the appropriate benchmark for 'payments-in-kind' in Appellate Body Report, *Canada – Dairy (Article 21.5 – New Zealand and US) (2001)*, paras. 73–6. The benchmarks discussed by the Appellate Body included the world market price versus domestic prices or also total cost of production. See Appellate Body Report, *Canada – Dairy (Article 21.5 – New Zealand and US) (2001)*, paras. 83–8.

545 Note that Article 9.1(c) describes an unusual form of export subsidy in that 'payments' can be made and funded by private parties, and not just by the government. The Appellate Body further noted that '"payments" need not be funded from government resources, provided they are "financed by virtue of governmental action". Article 9.1(c), therefore, contemplates that "payments" may be made and funded by private parties, without the type of governmental involvement ordinarily associated with a subsidy.' See Appellate Body Report, *Canada – Dairy (Article 21.5 – New Zealand and US II) (2003)*, para. 87. The Appellate Body in *EC – Export Subsidies on Sugar (2005)* stated that: '[A] "payment", within the meaning of Article 9.1(c) certainly occurs when one entity transfers economic resources to another entity ... This, however, does not imply that the term "payment" necessarily requires, in each and every case, the presence of two distinct entities.' See Appellate Body Report, *EC – Export Subsidies on Sugar (2005)*, paras. 263–4. Regarding the meaning of the term 'financed', payments do not have to be funded from government resources because Article 9.1(c) contemplates that payments can be financed by virtue of governmental action *whether or not* a charge on the public account is involved. See Appellate Body Report, *Canada – Dairy (Article 21.5 – New Zealand and US) (2001)*, para. 114. The words 'by virtue of' indicate the need to demonstrate a 'link' or 'nexus' between the 'governmental action' at issue and the 'financing of the payments' as a result of that action. Where a government does not fund the payment itself, it must play a sufficiently important part in the process through which a private party funds payments, such that the requisite nexus exists between governmental action and financing. See Appellate Body Report, *Canada – Dairy (Article 21.5 – New Zealand and US II) (2003)*, paras. 131–3; and Appellate Body Report, *EC – Export Subsidies on Sugar (2005)*, para. 237. The Appellate Body ruled in *Canada – Dairy (Article 21.5 – New Zealand and US) (2001)* 'that "payments" will be an export subsidy "only when they are financed by virtue of governmental action"'. See Appellate Body Report, *Canada – Dairy (Article 21.5 – New Zealand and US) (2001)*, paras. 97 and 112.

546 This can include upgrading and handling costs and the costs of international freight. See Appellate Body Report, *US – FSC (2000)*, paras. 130–1.

As the Appellate Body found in *EC – Export Subsidies on Sugar (2005)*, a measure falling within the list in Article 9.1:

> is deemed to be an export subsidy within the meaning of Article 1(e) of the *Agreement on Agriculture* ... Article 9.1(c) requires no independent enquiry into the existence of a 'benefit'.[547]

Note also that Article 1(e) defines 'export subsidies' as:

> [s]ubsidies contingent upon export performance, including the export subsidies listed in Article 9 of this Agreement.

The use of the word 'including' suggests that the term 'export subsidies' should be interpreted broadly and that the list of export subsidies in Article 9 is not exhaustive.[548]

Export subsidy commitments in a Member's Schedule must be expressed in terms of both budgetary outlay *and* quantity commitment levels.[549] The drafters of the *Agreement on Agriculture* recognised the need to limit both budgetary outlays and quantities in order to restrain subsidised exports. The Appellate Body explained in *EC – Export Subsidies on Sugar (2005)* that:

> [a] commitment on budgetary outlay alone provides little predictability on export quantities, while a commitment on quantity alone could lead to subsidized exports taking place that would otherwise have not taken place but for the budgetary support.[550]

This is especially so given that the *Agreement on Agriculture* has initiated a reform process in an environment of high levels of export subsidies taking the form of budgetary outlays and quantities. As set out in the relevant section of their Schedule, developed-country Members agreed to reduce the export subsidies on these products by an average of 36 per cent by value (budgetary outlay) and 21 per cent by volume (subsidised quantities). Developing-country Members agreed to reduce the export subsidies by an average of 24 per cent by value and 14 per cent by volume. Members may *not* provide listed export subsidies *in excess of* the budgetary outlay and quantitative commitment levels specified in their Schedules.[551] As the Appellate Body ruled in *EC – Export Subsidies on Sugar (2005)*, Article 3.1 thus requires with regard to export subsidies:

> [a] Member to limit its subsidization to the budgetary outlay and quantity reduction commitments specified in its Schedule in accordance with the provisions of the *Agreement on Agriculture*.[552]

547 Appellate Body Report, *EC – Export Subsidies on Sugar (2005)*, para. 269.

548 See Appellate Body Report, *US – Upland Cotton (2005)*, para. 615.

549 See Article 3.3 (as well as Article 9.2).

550 Appellate Body Report, *EC – Export Subsidies on Sugar (2005)*, para. 197.

551 See *ibid.* See also Article 8 of the *Agreement on Agriculture*, which states that a Member must undertake not to provide export subsidies otherwise than in conformity with the Agreement and with commitments as specified in that Member's Schedule. See also Appellate Body Report, *EC – Export Subsidies on Sugar (2005)*, paras. 209 and 216.

552 *Ibid.*, para. 209. 553 See Appellate Body Report, *US – FSC (2000)*, para. 152.

In other words, as the Appellate Body already noted in *US – FSC (2000)*, as regards *scheduled* products, when the specific reduction commitment levels have been reached, the *limited authorisation* to provide export subsidies as listed in Article 9.1 is transformed, effectively, into a *prohibition* against the provision of further subsidies.[553] A finding of inconsistency with Article 3.3 of the *Agreement on Agriculture* cannot be made unless the Member concerned has provided export subsidies *listed in Article 9.1*.[554]

Pursuant to Article 10.1 of the *Agreement on Agriculture*, Members shall *not* apply export subsidies that are not listed in Article 9.1 of the *Agreement on Agriculture* in a manner that results in or threatens to lead to circumvention of export subsidy commitments.[555] This effectively prohibits any other export subsidies.

The 2015 Nairobi Ministerial Conference marked a significant progress in the reform of agricultural trade by securing a historic decision to fully eliminate any form of agricultural export subsidies, aiming to ensure that countries do not resort to trade-distorting export subsidies and thereby create a level playing field for agriculture exporters.[556] Under the Ministerial Decision on Export Competition, developed countries will immediately remove export subsidies, except for a handful of agriculture products, and developing countries will do so by 2018, with a longer time frame in some limited cases.

With regard to international food aid, the Appellate Body stated in *US – Upland Cotton (2005)* that such aid is covered by the second clause of Article 10.1 to the extent that it is a 'non-commercial transaction', which should 'not be used to circumvent' a Member's export subsidy commitments. Article 10.4 provides specific disciplines that may be relied on to determine whether international food aid is being 'used to circumvent' a WTO Member's export subsidy commitments. Therefore, WTO Members are free to grant as much food aid as they wish, provided that they do so consistently with Articles 10.1 and 10.4 of the *Agreement on Agriculture*.[557]

With regard to export credit guarantees, export credits and insurance programmes, the Appellate Body noted in *US – Upland Cotton (2005)* that:

> [a]lthough Article 10.2 commits WTO Members to work toward the development of internationally agreed disciplines on export credit guarantees, export credits and insurance

554 See *ibid.*, para. 132.

555 Thus it is not necessary to show actual circumvention: a threat or likelihood of circumvention is also prohibited. See Appellate Body Report, *US – Upland Cotton (2005)*, paras. 616 and 704. See also Appellate Body Report, *US – FSC (2000)*, para. 148. According to the Appellate Body, '[it] is clear from the opening clause of Article 10.1 that this provision is residual in character to Article 9.1 ... If a measure is an export subsidy listed in Article 9.1, it cannot simultaneously be an export subsidy under Article 10.1'. See Appellate Body Report, *Canada – Dairy (Article 21.5 – New Zealand and US) (2001)*, para. 121.

556 See Nairobi Ministerial Conference, *Ministerial Decision on Export Competition* (WT/MIN(15)/45), dated 21 December 2015.

557 See Appellate Body Report, *US – Upland Cotton (2005)*, para. 619.

programs, it is in Article 10.1 that [it found] the disciplines that currently apply to export subsidies not listed in Article 9.1.[558]

Even though an export credit guarantee may not necessarily include a subsidy component, there is nothing inherent about export credit guarantees that precludes such measures from falling within the definition of a subsidy. The Appellate Body did not believe that Article 10.2 of the *Agreement on Agriculture* exempts export credit guarantees, export credits and insurance programmes from the export subsidy disciplines in the *Agreement on Agriculture.*[559] However, the Appellate Body cautioned that this does not mean that export credit guarantees, export credits and insurance programmes will necessarily constitute export subsidies for purposes of the *Agreement on Agriculture.* Export credit guarantees are subject to the export subsidy disciplines only to the extent that such measures include an export subsidy component.[560]

Article 10.3 of the *Agreement on Agriculture* pursues the aim of preventing circumvention of export subsidy commitments by providing special rules on the reversal of burden of proof where a Member exports an agricultural product in quantities that exceed its reduction commitment level; in such a situation, a WTO Member is treated as if it has granted WTO-*inconsistent* export subsidies for the excess quantities, unless the Member presents adequate evidence to 'establish' the contrary.[561] This special rule for proof of export subsidies applies in certain disputes under Articles 3, 8, 9 and 10 of the *Agreement on Agriculture.*[562] By contrast, as discussed in Chapter 3, under the usual allocation of the burden of proof, a responding Member's measure will be considered to be WTO-consistent, until the complaining Member has presented sufficient evidence to prove the contrary.[563]

558 *Ibid.*, para. 615. The Appellate Body explained that, under 'Article 10.2, WTO Members have taken on two distinct commitments in respect of these three types of measures: (i) to work toward the development of internationally agreed disciplines to govern their provision; and (ii) after agreement on such disciplines, to provide them only in conformity therewith ... This means that "after" international disciplines have been agreed upon, Members shall provide export credit guarantees, export credits and insurance programs only in conformity with those agreed disciplines.' See *ibid.*, para. 607.

559 *Ibid.* Note that one Appellate Body member dissented from that interpretation, explaining in a separate opinion that neither Article 9 nor 10 covered and prohibited export credit guarantees. *Ibid.*, paras. 631–41. For the majority, such an interpretation would have led to a situation where 'WTO Members are free to "circumvent" their export subsidy commitments through the use of export credit guarantees, export credits and insurance programs until internationally agreed disciplines are developed, whenever that may be ... Indeed, such an interpretation would *undermine* the objective of preventing circumvention of export subsidy commitments, which is central to the *Agreement on Agriculture*.' See *ibid.*, para. 617.

560 See *ibid.*, para. 626. 561 See *ibid.*, para. 616.

562 The Appellate Body held in *US – Upland Cotton (2005)* that this reversal of the burden of proof does not apply to *unscheduled* products (for which no export subsidies at all may be maintained) because this would in effect mean that 'any export of unscheduled products is presumed to be subsidized'. See Appellate Body Report, *US – Upland Cotton (2005)*, para. 652.

563 See above, pp. 257–61. See also Appellate Body Report, *Canada – Dairy (Article 21.5 – New Zealand and US II) (2003)*, paras. 66 and 68. The Appellate Body clarified in *Canada – Dairy (Article 21.5 – New Zealand and US II) (2003)* that there are *two* separate parts to a claim alleging illegal agricultural export subsidies in respect of products for which reduction commitments have been scheduled. 'First, the responding Member must have exported an agricultural product in quantities exceeding its quantity commitment level ... The second part of the claim is ... that the responding Member must have granted export subsidies with respect to quantities exceeding the quantity commitment level. There is, in other words, a *quantitative* aspect and an *export subsidization* aspect to the claim.' See Appellate Body Report, *Canada – Dairy (Article 21.5 – New Zealand and US II) (2003)*, para. 70.

The Nairobi Ministerial Decision on Export Competition contains rules to minimise the possible distorting impact of export policies, such as on export finance, international food aid and operations of agricultural exporting state trading enterprises on international trade.[564] These include maximum repayment terms for export financing programmes for agriculture exporters supported by the government, provisions on state trading enterprises engaging in agriculture trade, and disciplines to ensure that food aid does not displace trade and does not cause adverse effects on domestic production.

In *Canada – Dairy (Article 21.5 – New Zealand and US) (2001)*, the Appellate Body noted that it is possible that the economic effects of WTO-consistent domestic support in favour of producers may 'spill over' to provide certain benefits to export production.[565] In this respect, it considered:

> [i]t would erode the distinction between the domestic support and export subsidies disciplines of the *Agreement on Agriculture* if WTO-consistent domestic support measures were automatically characterized as export subsidies because they produced spill-over economic benefits for export production.[566]

However, the Appellate Body also considered that this distinction 'would also be eroded if a WTO Member were entitled to use domestic support, without limit, to provide support for exports of agricultural products'.[567] Consequently, if domestic support could be used, without limit, to provide support for exports, it would undermine the benefits intended to accrue through a WTO Member's export subsidy commitments.[568]

9.2 Domestic Agricultural Support Measures

Unresolved issues on agricultural domestic support and market access are likely to remain high on the WTO agenda. Meanwhile, the progress at the Nairobi Ministerial Conference on export competition could mean that this topic receives less attention in the years ahead. Some negotiators suggested that an outcome on domestic support should be a target for WTO's next ministerial conference, scheduled to be held in late 2017. Negotiators said that the United States remains unlikely to accept any cap on its own farm subsidies unless China did so too, while Beijing has been unwilling to accept more onerous commitments than those outlined in the 2008 draft Doha deal.[569]

Turning to the interpretation of the existing WTO law provisions relating to domestic agricultural support measures, Members have agreed – pursuant

564 See Nairobi Ministerial Conference, *Ministerial Decision on Export Competition* (WT/MIN(15)/45), dated 21 December 2015.
565 See Appellate Body Report, *Canada – Dairy (Article 21.5 – New Zealand and US) (2001)*, paras. 89–90.
566 *Ibid.* 567 *Ibid.*, para. 91.
568 See *ibid.* 569 See Africa Bridges, 18 February 2016.

to Article 6 of the *Agreement on Agriculture* – to reduce the level of support. Developed-country Members agreed to reduce between 1995 and 2000 their 'aggregate measurement of support', or 'AMS', by 20 per cent.[570] Developing-country Members agreed to reduce their AMS by 13.3 per cent in the period 1995–2004.[571] The commitments of Members on the reduction of domestic agricultural support measures are set out in Part IV of their GATT Schedule of Concessions. Pursuant to Article 6.3 of the *Agreement on Agriculture*, Members may *not* provide domestic support *in excess* of the commitment levels specified in their Schedules. As the Appellate Body noted in *US – Upland Cotton (2005)*, Article 6.3:

> [e]stablishes only a *quantitative* limitation on the amount of domestic support that a WTO Member can provide in a given year. The quantitative limitation in Article 6.3 applies generally to all domestic support measures that are included in a WTO Member's AMS.[572]

Recall that, under Article 3.1(b) of the *SCM Agreement*, 'subsidies contingent ... upon the use of domestic over imported goods' are prohibited.[573] This raises the question as to the WTO consistency of *agricultural* import substitution subsidies. In *US – Upland Cotton (2005)*, the Appellate Body answered this question as follows:

> Article 6.3 does not authorize subsidies that are contingent on the use of domestic over imported goods. It only provides that a WTO Member shall be considered to be in compliance with its domestic support *reduction commitments* if its Current Total AMS does not exceed that Member's annual or final bound commitment level specified in its Schedule. It does not say that compliance with Article 6.3 of the *Agreement on Agriculture* insulates the subsidy from the prohibition in Article 3.1(b).[574]

Domestic agricultural support measures that do not have the effect of providing price support to producers are, under certain conditions, exempt from the reduction commitments. These exempted domestic support measures are commonly referred to as 'green box' and 'blue box' measures.[575] 'Green box' measures

570 On the calculation of the AMS, see Annex 3 to the *Agreement on Agriculture*.

571 See Article 15.2 of the *Agreement on Agriculture*. Least-developed-country Members are not required to undertake reduction commitments. See *ibid*.

572 Appellate Body Report, *US – Upland Cotton (2005)*, para. 544. 573 See above, pp. 807–8.

574 Appellate Body Report, *US – Upland Cotton (2005)*, para. 545. In the same case, the Appellate Body recalled 'that the introductory language of Article 3.1 of the *SCM Agreement* clarifies that this provision applies "[e]xcept as provided in the Agreement on Agriculture"'. Nevertheless, the Appellate Body concluded that import substitution subsidies on agricultural products are not exempt from the prohibition in Article 3.1(b) of the *SCM Agreement* by virtue of Annex 3, paragraph 7, as 'measures directed at agricultural processors that shall be included in the aggregate measurement of support calculation'. Nor does Article 6.3 (which provides that a WTO Member shall be considered in compliance with its domestic support commitment level specified in its Schedule) 'insulate a subsidy from the prohibition in Article 3.1(b) of the *SCM Agreement*'. Thus, in providing domestic support that is consistent with the *Agreement on Agriculture*, WTO Members 'must be mindful of the prohibition in Article 3.1(b) of the *SCM Agreement* on the provision of subsidies that are contingent on the use of domestic over imported goods'. Appellate Body Report, *US – Upland Cotton (2005)*, paras. 541, 545–6 and 550.

575 Note that domestic support measures that are subject to reduction commitments are commonly referred to as 'amber box' subsidies.

include support for agricultural research and infrastructure, training and advisory services, domestic food aid and environmental programmes.[576] 'Blue box' subsidies include certain developing-country subsidies designed to encourage agricultural production, certain *de minimis* subsidies, and certain direct payments aimed at limiting agricultural production.[577] The conditions which these subsidies must fulfil to be exempted from the reduction commitments are set out in the *Agreement on Agriculture* in Annex 2 (for 'green box' subsidies) and in Articles 6.2, 6.4 and 6.5 (for 'blue box' subsidies). With regard to 'green box' subsidies, Annex 2, entitled 'Domestic Support: The Basis for Exemption from the Reduction Commitments', lays down in paragraph 1 a 'fundamental requirement' for 'green box' measures. 'Green box' subsidies must have 'no, or at most minimal, trade-distorting effects or effects on production'. Accordingly, 'green box' measures must conform to the basic criteria stated in that provision, *plus* the 'policy-specific criteria and conditions' set out in the remaining paragraphs of Annex 2, including those in paragraph 6. The specific paragraphs of Annex 2 deal with: (1) payments for general services; (2) public stockholding for food security purposes; (3) domestic food aid; (4) direct payments to producers; (5) decoupled income support; (6) governmental financial participation in income insurance and income safety-net programmes; (7) payments for relief in natural disasters; (8) structural adjustment assistance provided through producer or resource retirement programmes, or through investment aids; (9) payments under environmental programmes; and (10) payments under regional assistance programmes.

In *US – Upland Cotton (2005)*, the Appellate Body interpreted 'decoupled income support' within the meaning of paragraph 6 of Annex 2.[578] The paragraph applies to one type of 'direct payments' to producers that may benefit from exemption from reduction commitments.[579] The Appellate Body found that '[d]ecoupling of payments from production under paragraph 6(b) can only be ensured if the payments are not related to, or based upon, either a positive requirement to produce certain crops or a negative requirement not to produce certain crops or a combination of both positive and negative requirements on production of crops'. The Appellate Body concluded that the measures at issue

576 See Annex 2 to the *Agreement on Agriculture*. Article 7 provides that Members must ensure that any 'green box' subsidies are maintained in conformity with the criteria set out in Annex 2, which justify their exemption from reduction commitments.

577 See Article 6 of the *Agreement on Agriculture*.

578 See Appellate Body Report, *US – Upland Cotton (2005)*, paras. 321–5.

579 Paragraph 6(a) sets forth that eligibility for payments under a decoupled income support program must be determined by reference to certain 'clearly defined criteria' in a 'defined and fixed base period'. Paragraph 6(b) requires the severing of any link between the *amount of payments* under such a program and the *type or volume of production* undertaken by recipients of payments under that program in any year after the base period. Paragraphs 6(c) and 6(d) serve to require that payments are also decoupled from *prices* and *factors of production employed* after the base period. Paragraph 6(e) makes it clear that '[n]o production shall be required in order to receive ... payments' under a decoupled income support program. See Appellate Body Report, *US – Upland Cotton (2005)*, para. 321.

(production flexibility contract payments and direct payments)[580] did not qualify for the 'green box' exemption from the domestic support disciplines under the *Agreement on Agriculture*.[581]

9.3 The 'Peace' Clause

Until the end of the nine-year implementation period,[582] agricultural export subsidies that conformed fully to the requirements of the *Agreement on Agriculture*, and domestic agricultural support that was within commitment levels and fulfilled certain other conditions, benefited from the 'due restraint' or 'peace' clause of Article 13 of the *Agreement on Agriculture*.[583] Pursuant to Article 13, the consistency of many agricultural subsidies with the *SCM Agreement* could not be challenged. Furthermore, 'green box' subsidies could not be offset by countervailing duties.[584] Since 2004, when the implementation period expired, however, the 'peace' clause no longer applies. The consistency of agricultural subsidies with the *SCM Agreement* can be challenged and countervailing duties be imposed on 'green box' subsidies. As mentioned above, in case of conflict between the rules of the *SCM Agreement* and those of the *Agreement on Agriculture*, the rules of the *Agreement on Agriculture* prevail.

10 SUMMARY

WTO law provides for detailed rules with respect to subsidies as well as countervailing measures, i.e. measures taken against injurious subsidisation. The *SCM Agreement* defines a subsidy as a financial contribution by a government or public body which confers a benefit. Both the *SCM Agreement* and the case

580 Production flexibility contract payments and direct payments do 'not concern a measure *requiring* producers to grow certain crops in order to receive payments; it also does not concern a measure with complete planting *flexibility* that provides payments without regard whatsoever to the crops that are grown. Indeed, it does not concern a measure that requires the production of any crop at all; nor does it involve a measure that totally *prohibits* the growing of any crops as a condition for payments.' See Appellate Body Report, *US – Upland Cotton (2005)*, para. 322.

581 See *ibid.*, para. 342.

582 This period began in 1995. By virtue of Article 1(i) of the *Agreement on Agriculture*, the term 'year' refers to the calendar, financial or marketing year specified in the Schedule relating to that Member.

583 With respect to the requirements to be fulfilled for agricultural export subsidies, see Articles 9, 10 and 11 of the *Agreement on Agriculture*; for 'amber box' subsidies, see Article 7 (not in excess of the reduction commitments); for 'green box' subsidies, see Annex 2; and for 'blue box' subsidies, see Article 6.

584 In *US – Upland Cotton (2005)*, Brazil challenged US domestic subsidies on cotton during the implementation period in which Article 13 applied. The Appellate Body upheld the panel's finding that those measures were not entitled to the exemption provided by the peace clause from actions under Article XVI:1 of the GATT 1994 and Articles 5 and 6 of the *SCM Agreement*. This was due to the fact that the US subsidies did not meet the requirement in Article 13(b)(ii) that non-green box domestic support measures must not 'grant support to a specific commodity in excess of that decided during the 1992 marketing year', if such measures are to enjoy exemption. See Appellate Body Report, *US – Upland Cotton (2005)*, paras. 391–4.

law work out and clarify each element of this definition. Furthermore, the *SCM Agreement* provides that the WTO rules on subsidies and countervailing measures only apply to 'specific' subsidies. Article XVI of the GATT 1994 and Parts II, III and IV of the *SCM Agreement* deal with the WTO treatment of subsidies. The WTO treatment of subsidies is different from the treatment of dumping. Under WTO law, certain subsidies are prohibited, and many other subsidies may be challenged as WTO-inconsistent when they cause adverse effects to the interests of other Members. Article VI of the GATT 1994 and Part V of the *SCM Agreement* concern the manner in which WTO Members may respond to subsidised trade which causes injury to the domestic industry. Members may, in these situations, impose countervailing duties on the subsidised imports to offset the subsidisation.

The *SCM Agreement* distinguishes between prohibited subsidies and actionable subsidies. The prohibited subsidies are: (1) export subsidies; and (2) import substitution subsidies. Export subsidies are subsidies contingent upon export performance. Annex I of the *SCM Agreement* contains an 'Illustrative List of Export Subsidies'. Import substitution subsidies are subsidies contingent upon the use of domestic over imported goods. Both export subsidies and import substitution subsidies are prohibited regardless of whether the subsidy is contingent *de jure* or *de facto* upon exportation or the use of domestic over imported goods. The rules applicable to consultations and adjudication concerning allegedly prohibited subsidies are primarily those of the DSU. However, the time frames under Article 4 of the *SCM Agreement* are half as long as the time frames provided for under the DSU. Moreover, if a panel finds a measure to be a prohibited subsidy, that subsidy must be withdrawn, i.e. removed, without delay. If a compliance panel finds that a recommendation for withdrawal has not been followed within the time period set by the panel in original proceedings, the DSB must, upon the request of the original complainant(s) and by reverse consensus, authorise 'appropriate countermeasures'.

Unlike export subsidies and import substitution subsidies, most subsidies are not prohibited but are 'actionable', i.e. they are subject to challenge in the event that they cause adverse effects to the interests of another Member. There are three main types of 'adverse effects' to the interests of other Members: (1) *injury* to the domestic industry of another Member; (2) *nullification or impairment* of benefits accruing directly or indirectly to other Members under the GATT 1994; and (3) *serious prejudice*, including a threat thereof, to the interests of another Member.

The concept of 'injury' to a domestic industry covers: material injury, i.e. genuine injury, to a domestic industry; a threat of material injury to a domestic industry; and material retardation of the establishment of a domestic industry. The definition of 'domestic industry' in the *SCM Agreement* is quite similar to the definition of this concept in the *Anti-Dumping Agreement*. There is also a high degree of similarity between the concepts of 'material injury' and the 'threat of material injury' in the *Anti-Dumping Agreement* and the *SCM Agreement.* Note that it must be demonstrated that the subsidised imports are causing injury to the domestic industry (the 'causal link' requirement) and that injury caused by other factors may not be attributed to the subsidised imports (the 'non-attribution' requirement).

The adverse effects of subsidies on the interests of other Members can also take the form of 'serious prejudice'. 'Serious prejudice' *may arise* where a subsidy has one or more of the effects described in the *SCM Agreement*, including the displacement or impedance of imports of another Member into the market of the subsidising Member or third country markets. Other forms of serious prejudice are significant price undercutting by the subsidised product as compared to the like product of another Member in the same market, significant price suppression, significant price depression or significant lost sales in the same market (provided that the relevant product and geographic markets have been determined properly). Finally, serious prejudice may also arise where subsidisation has the effect of a disproportionate increase in the world market share of the subsidising Member. A demonstration that these volume or price phenomena are the 'effect' of the challenged subsidies must include establishing the existence of a causal link between the subsidy and the serious prejudice phenomena as well as ensuring that effects caused by other factors are not attributed to the subsidised imports. Members and panels enjoy a margin of discretion in structuring the analysis of serious prejudice phenomena, in choosing appropriate methodologies, parameters and tools for analysing causation/non-attribution. If a complaining Member can show that a subsidy has any of the effects listed in the *SCM Agreement*, serious prejudice may be found to exist. Note that the concept of 'serious prejudice' includes a 'threat of serious prejudice', i.e. a situation in which the serious prejudice is clearly foreseen and imminent.

As is the case with multilateral remedies for prohibited subsidies, the multilateral remedies for actionable subsidies are principally, but not entirely, the remedies for breach of WTO law provided for in the DSU. If a panel concludes that a subsidy causes adverse effects to the interests of another Member (be it injury, nullification or impairment, or serious prejudice), the subsidising Member must take appropriate steps to remove the adverse effect or withdraw the subsidy. The subsidising Member must do so within six months from the adoption of the report by the DSB. Instead of withdrawing the subsidy at issue or removing its adverse effects, the subsidising Member can also agree with the complaining Member on compensation. If a compliance panel concludes that, within six months from the adoption of the report, the subsidy has not been withdrawn, its adverse effects have not been removed or no agreement on compensation is reached, the DSB shall, at the request of the complaining Member and by reverse consensus, grant authorisation to that Member to take countermeasures commensurate with the degree and nature of the adverse effects of the subsidy.

Prohibited and actionable subsidies which cause injury to the domestic industry can, apart from being challenged multilaterally, also be offset by the application of a countervailing duty. WTO Members may impose countervailing duties when three conditions are fulfilled: (1) there are *subsidised imports*, i.e. imports of products from producers who benefited from specific subsidies; (2) there is *injury* to the domestic industry; and (3) there is a *causal* link between the subsidised imports and the injury to the domestic industry *and* injury caused by other factors is *not attributed* to the subsidised imports. The *SCM Agreement* provides for detailed procedural requirements regarding the initiation and conduct of a countervailing investigation by the competent authorities of the Member imposing the countervailing duties on the subsidised imports. Note that the procedural requirements for countervailing investigations set out in the *SCM Agreement* are largely the same as the procedural requirements for anti-dumping investigations set out in the *Anti-Dumping Agreement*. The main objectives of these requirements are also the same. The *SCM Agreement* provides for three types of countervailing measures: (1) provisional countervailing measures; (2) voluntary undertakings; and (3) definitive countervailing duties.

After making a preliminary determination that a subsidy is causing or threatening to cause injury to a domestic industry, an importing Member can impose *provisional countervailing measures* on the subsidised imports. Investigations may be suspended or terminated without the imposition of provisional measures or countervailing duties upon receipt of satisfactory *voluntary undertakings* under which: (1) the government of the exporting Member agrees to eliminate or limit the subsidy or take other measures concerning its effects; or (2) the exporter agrees to revise its prices so that the investigating authorities are satisfied that the injurious effect of the subsidy is eliminated.

Members may impose *definitive countervailing duties* only after they have made a final determination that a countervailable subsidy exists; and that the subsidy causes, or threatens to cause, injury to the domestic industry. The amount of a countervailing duty must never exceed the amount of the subsidy. Moreover, if the amount of the injury caused is less than the amount of the subsidy, the definitive countervailing duty should preferably be limited to the amount necessary to counteract the injury caused. Countervailing duties must be collected on a non-discriminatory basis. Note that any exporter whose exports are subject to a definitive countervailing duty but who was not investigated individually is entitled to an expedited review so that the investigating authorities promptly establish an individual countervailing duty rate for that exporter. Countervailing duties may not be applied retroactively, except in certain specific circumstances. A countervailing duty shall remain in force only as long as and to the extent necessary to counteract subsidisation which is causing injury. Upon their own initiative or upon a request from an interested party, the investigating authorities shall review the need for the continued imposition of the duty.

All definitive countervailing duties must be terminated, at the latest, five years after their imposition or the latest review. However, where the investigating authorities determine – in the context of a sunset review – that the expiry of the countervailing duty would be likely to lead to a continuation or recurrence of subsidisation and injury, the duty will not be terminated. Note that countervailing duties and countermeasures cannot be applied simultaneously with regard to the same instance of subsidisation.

The *Agreement on Agriculture* provides for special rules on agricultural export subsidies and domestic agricultural support measures. In case of conflict, these special rules prevail over the rules of the *SCM Agreement*. Export subsidies on agricultural products not specified in Section II of Part IV of a Member's GATT Schedule of Concessions are prohibited under the terms of the *Agreement on Agriculture*. Export subsidies on agricultural products specified in Section II of Part IV of a Member's GATT Schedule of Concessions and listed in Article 9.1 of the *Agreement on Agriculture* are not prohibited but are subject to reduction commitments. Members may *not* provide these export subsidies *in excess of* the budgetary outlay and quantitative commitment levels specified in the Schedules. Also with respect to domestic agricultural support measures, Members have agreed to reduce the level of support. Members may *not* provide domestic support *in excess of* the commitment levels specified in their Schedules. However, domestic agricultural support measures that do not have the effect of providing price support to producers (i.e. 'green box' and 'blue box' subsidies) are exempt from the reduction commitments.

The 2015 Nairobi Ministerial Conference secured a historic decision to fully eliminate any form of agricultural export subsidies.

FURTHER READINGS

L. Bartels, 'The Relationship between the WTO Agreement on Agriculture and the SCM Agreement: An Analysis of Hierarchy Rules in the WTO Legal System', *Journal of World Trade*, 2016, 50(1), 7–20.

H. Jung and J. Suh, 'Preventing Systematic Circumvention of the SCM Agreement: Beyond the Mandatory/Discretionary Distinction', *World Trade Review*, 2016, 15(3), 475–93.

J. Lee, 'SCM Agreement Revisited: Climate Change, Renewable Energy and the SCM Agreement', *World Trade Review*, 2016, 15(4), 613–44.

Hyo-young Lee, 'Remedying the Remedy System for Prohibited Subsidies in the WTO: Reconsidering Its Retrospective Aspect', *Asian Journal of WTO & International Health Law & Policy*, 2015, 10, 423.

H. B. Asmelash, 'Energy Subsidies and WTO Dispute Settlement: Why Only Renewable Energy Subsidies Are Challenged', *Journal of International Economic Law*, 2015, 18, 261–85.

B. Hoekman, 'Subsidies and Spillovers in a Value Chain World: New Rules Required? E15Initiative', International Centre for Trade and Sustainable Development and World Economic Forum, 2015.

I. Espa and S. E. Rolland, 'Subsidies, Clean Energy and Climate Change', E15Initiative, International Centre for Trade and Sustainable Development and World Economic Forum, 2015

A. Cosbey and P. C. Mavroidis, 'A Turquoise Mess: Green Subsidies, Blue Industrial Policy and Renewable Energy: The Case for Redrafting the Subsidies Agreement of the WTO', *Journal of International Economic Law*, 2014, 17, 11–47.

G. N. Horlick, 'Trade Remedies and Development of Renewable Energy', E15Initiative, International Centre for Trade and Sustainable Development and World Economic Forum, 2014.

R. Howse, 'Securing Policy Space for Clean Energy under the SCM Agreement: Alternative Approaches', E15Initiative, International Centre for Trade and Sustainable Development and World Economic Forum, 2014.

S. Guan, 'WTO Retaliation Rules in Subsidy-Related Cases: What Can We Learn from the US – Upland Cotton Arbitration?', *Journal of World Trade*, 2014, 48(4), 815–42.

L. Rubini, '"The Good, the Bad, and the Ugly". Lessons on Methodology in Legal Analysis from the Recent WTO Litigation on Renewable Energy Subsidies', *Journal of World Trade*, 2014, 48(5), 895–938.

A. Matthews, 'Food Security and WTO Domestic Support Disciplines post-Bali', ICTSD Programme on Agricultural Trade and Sustainable Development; 2014, Issue Paper No. 53; International Centre for Trade and Sustainable Development, Geneva.

S. Charnovitz, 'Green Subsidies and the WTO', Policy Research Working Paper 7060, World Bank Group, October 2014.

D. Coppens, 'How Special is the Special and Differential Treatment under the SCM Agreement? A Legal and Normative Analysis of WTO Subsidy Disciplines on Developing Countries', *World Trade Review*, 2013, 12(1), 79–109.

J. Miranda, 'Causal Link and Non-attribution as Interpreted in WTO Trade Remedy Disputes', *Journal of World Trade*, 2010, 44(4), 729–62.

13

Technical Barriers to Trade

CONTENTS

1 INTRODUCTION

As discussed in Chapters 6 and 7, the importance of tariffs and quantitative restrictions as barriers to trade in goods has gradually decreased over time. While continued vigilance and further liberalisation efforts regarding these traditional barriers to trade are certainly called for, *regulatory measures* affecting trade in goods raise now a more pressing challenge for the multilateral trading system.[1] As discussed in Chapter 7, such regulatory measures can take the form of technical barriers to trade. The current chapter deals with the WTO rules applicable to technical barriers to trade (TBT). The next chapter, Chapter 14, will deal with the different WTO rules applicable to sanitary and phytosanitary (SPS) measures, which pose challenges to international trade similar to technical barriers to trade.

The WTO rules applicable to technical barriers to trade and those applicable to SPS measures have in common that they go *beyond* the general rules applicable to non-tariff barriers, as set out in the GATT 1994. As discussed in Chapters 4, 5 and 7, these general rules focus on eliminating the negative trade effects of non-tariff measures, primarily by prohibiting them (as is the case for quantitative restrictions) or by ensuring their non-discriminatory application (as is the case for internal tax and regulatory measures).[2] However, the rules applicable to technical barriers to trade, as set out in the *TBT Agreement*, and the rules applicable to SPS measures, as set out in the *SPS Agreement*, go *further* in addressing non-tariff barriers to trade by *also* promoting regulatory harmonisation.[3] The relevant rules of the *TBT Agreement* and the *SPS Agreement* encourage Members to harmonise their national TBT and SPS measures around standards set by the relevant international standard-setting bodies.

Technical barriers to trade, the subject matter of this chapter, are omnipresent in modern society. Television sets, toys, cosmetics, medical equipment, fertilisers, meat and cheese are all subject to requirements relating to their (intrinsic and extrinsic) characteristics and the manner in which they are produced. The objective of these requirements may be – and often is – the protection of life or health, the protection of the environment, the protection of consumers, the prevention of deceptive practices, or the protection or promotion of many other legitimate societal values or interests. These requirements may be mandatory, set and enforced by governments. More often, however, these requirements are rules laid down by national standardising bodies, which are not mandatory but are nevertheless generally applied in business transactions in a given country. In both cases, these requirements may constitute formidable barriers to trade, even where they are not applied in a discriminatory manner. This is so because the divergence in the regulatory requirements imposed in different countries increases the cost and difficulty of gaining market access for exporters. Television sets and cheese made according to the requirements of Newland

1 For a general discussion, see World Trade Report 2012, *Trade and Public Policies*, 34–223, available at www.wto.org/english/res_e/publications_e/wtr12_e.htm.

2 See above, pp. 307–38 (MFN treatment), 351–76 (internal tax), 376–99 (regulatory measures) and 480–98 (quantitative restrictions).

3 As discussed in Chapter 15, the rules set out in the *TRIPS Agreement* also promote regulatory harmonisation around international standards. However, unlike the *TBT Agreement* and the *SPS Agreement*, the *TRIPS Agreement* lays down mandatory *minimum standards* of intellectual property protection and enforcement. See below, pp. 1013 (fn. 90) and in particular pages 1043–6.

may be banned from, or difficult to market in, Richland when the requirements of Richland relating to the product characteristics or the manner of production are different. Furthermore, procedures used to verify whether a product meets certain mandatory or voluntary requirements may also obstruct trade.

It is beyond dispute that technical barriers to trade play an important role in fulfilling multiple societal needs, such as those mentioned above. However, technical barriers to trade can also be a means of hidden protectionism. To date, WTO Members have been found to have acted inconsistently with their obligations under the *TBT Agreement* in six disputes.[4]

This chapter consecutively addresses: (1) the scope of application of the *TBT Agreement*; (2) the substantive provisions of the *TBT Agreement*; and (3) the institutional and procedural provisions of the *TBT Agreement*.

2 SCOPE OF APPLICATION OF THE *TBT AGREEMENT*

With respect to the scope of application of the *TBT Agreement*, this section distinguishes between: (1) the measures to which the *TBT Agreement* applies; (2) the entities covered by the Agreement: and (3) the *temporal* scope of application of the Agreement. This section also addresses the relationship between the *TBT Agreement* and other agreements on trade in goods, such as the *SPS Agreement*, the *Agreement on Government Procurement* and the GATT 1994.

2.1 Measures to Which the *TBT Agreement* Applies

The rules of the *TBT Agreement* apply to: (1) technical regulations; (2) standards; and (3) conformity assessment procedures. As the Appellate Body stated in *EC – Asbestos (2001)*, the *TBT Agreement* thus applies to a 'limited class of measures'.[5] The three types of measures to which the *TBT Agreement* applies are defined in Annex 1 of the *TBT Agreement*.

In Annex 1.1, a *technical regulation* is defined as a:

> [d]ocument which lays down product characteristics or their related processes and production methods, including the applicable administrative provisions, with which compliance is mandatory. It may also include or deal exclusively with terminology, symbols, packaging, marking or labelling requirements as they apply to a product, process or production method.

For example, a law requiring that batteries be rechargeable or a law requiring that wine be sold in green glass bottles is a technical regulation within the

4 See *EC – Sardines (2002)*; *US – Clove Cigarettes (2012)*; *US – Tuna II (Mexico) (2012)*; and *US – COOL (2012)*; *US – Tuna II (Mexico) (Article 21.5)*; and *US – COOL (Article 21.5 – Canada and Mexico) (2015)*. With regard to *EC – Asbestos (2001)*, see below, pp. 889–90. See also *EC – Seal Products (2014)*.

5 Appellate Body Report, *EC – Asbestos (2001)*, para. 80.

meaning of the *TBT Agreement*. The rules specifically applicable to technical regulations are set out in Articles 2 and 3 of the *TBT Agreement*.

Annex 1.2 of the *TBT Agreement* defines a *standard* as a:

> [d]ocument approved by a recognized body, that provides, for common and repeated use, rules, guidelines or characteristics for products or related processes and production methods, with which compliance is not mandatory. It may also include or deal exclusively with terminology, symbols, packaging, marking or labelling requirements as they apply to a product, process or production method.

Contrary to technical regulations, standards are of a voluntary nature, meaning that compliance is not mandatory. The voluntary standards set by, for example, SAC (the Standardization Administration of the People's Republic of China) or CEN (the European Committee for Standardization),[6] such as standards for building materials, mobile phones or electric toothbrushes, are 'standards' within the meaning of the *TBT Agreement*. While only products complying with the standards would be eligible to be certified by the relevant body and/or bear its mark or logo, compliance with these standards is not mandatory. Companies comply with these voluntary standards for various reasons, ranging from the wish to be responsive to consumer concerns to practical considerations of compatibility of products. However, often companies have little choice but to comply with these voluntary standards as non-adherence would *in practice* make it much more difficult (if not impossible) to sell their products. It is therefore important that these voluntary standards are also subject to international disciplines under the *TBT Agreement*. As discussed below, the distinction between a mandatory 'technical regulation' and a non-mandatory 'standard' is not always clear-cut.[7] The rules specifically applicable to standards are set out in Article 4 of and Annex 3 to the *TBT Agreement*. Annex 3 contains the Code of Good Practice for the Preparation, Adoption and Application of Standards.

Note that the definition of both a 'technical regulation' and a 'standard' refers to 'a document'. As a 'document' is defined quite broadly as 'something written, inscribed, etc., which furnishes evidence or information upon any subject', the Appellate Body stated in *US – Tuna II (Mexico) (2012)* that 'the use of the term "document" could therefore cover a broad range of instruments or apply to a variety of measures'.[8] However, in *EC – Seal Products (2014)*, the Appellate Body noted with regard to 'technical regulations' that, the scope of Annex 1.1 appears to be limited 'to those documents that establish or prescribe something and thus have a certain *normative content*'.[9]

6 Note that the SAC is a central government body, while the CEN is a non-governmental body. On the application of the *TBT Agreement* on standards set by non-governmental bodies, see below, pp. 931–2.

7 See below, pp. 892–3.

8 Appellate Body Report, *US – Tuna II (Mexico) (2012)*, para. 185. See also Appellate Body Report, *EC – Seal Products (2014)*, para. 5.9.

9 Appellate Body Report, *EC – Seal Products (2014)*, para. 5.10. Emphasis added.

In addition to technical regulations and standards, conformity assessment procedures also fall within the scope of application of the *TBT Agreement*. Conformity assessment procedures are defined in Annex 1.3 to the *TBT Agreement* as:

> [a]ny procedure used, directly or indirectly, to determine that relevant requirements in technical regulations or standards are fulfilled.

Examples of conformity assessment procedures include procedures for sampling, testing and inspection. The rules specifically applicable to conformity assessment procedures are set out in Articles 5–9 of the *TBT Agreement*.

The *TBT Agreement* applies to technical regulations, standards and conformity assessment procedures relating to: (1) products (including industrial and agricultural products); and (2) processes and production methods (PPMs).[10] It is the subject of much debate, however, whether the processes and production methods to which the *TBT Agreement* applies include so-called *non-product-related processes and production methods* (NPR–PPMs). This term is commonly used to refer to processes and production methods that do not affect the physical characteristics of the final product put on the market. An example of a technical regulation relating to an NPR–PPM would be the prohibition of the use of environmentally unfriendly sources of energy, or the use of child labour, in the production of a product. During the negotiations on the *TBT Agreement*, there was much discussion on whether technical regulations, standards or conformity assessment procedures relating to NPR–PPMs should be included in the scope of the Agreement. However, the negotiators seem to have failed to reach agreement on this issue.[11] The definitions in Annex 1, quoted above, could be read to indicate that technical regulations, standards and conformity assessment procedures relating to NPR–PPMs do *not* fall within the scope of application of the *TBT Agreement*. The definition of 'technical regulation' in Annex 1.1 of the *TBT Agreement* refers in its first sentence to 'product characteristics or their *related* processes and production methods'; and the definition of 'standard' in Annex 1.2 of the *TBT Agreement* refers in its first sentence to 'characteristics for products or *related* processes and production methods'.[12] However, note that the explanatory note to Annex 1.2 states that the *TBT Agreement* deals with 'technical regulations, standards and conformity assessment procedures related to products or processes and production methods'. There is thus debate about

10 See Article 1.3 and the explanatory note to Annex 1, para. 2, of the *TBT Agreement*. Note that the *TBT Agreement* does not apply to technical regulations, standards and conformity assessment procedures that deal with services.

11 See Committee on Technical Barriers to Trade, *Negotiating History of the Coverage of the Agreement on Technical Barriers to Trade with regard to Labelling Requirements, Voluntary Standards and Processes and Production Methods Unrelated to Product Characteristics*, Note by the Secretariat, G/TBT/W/11, dated 29 August 1995. See also Committee on Trade and Environment, *Report (1996) of the Committee on Trade and Environment*, WT/CTE/1, dated 12 November 1996, paras. 55–81.

12 Emphasis added.

whether technical regulations, standards or conformity assessment procedures relating to NPR–PPMs fall within the scope of application of the *TBT Agreement*. In *EC – Seal Products (2014)*, the Appellate Body noted that:

> the use here of the disjunctive 'or' indicates that 'related [PPMs]' may play an additional or alternative role vis-à-vis 'product characteristics' under Annex 1.1.[13]

According to the Appellate Body, a plain reading of the clause 'product characteristics or their related processes and production methods' suggests that:

> a 'related' PPM is one that is 'connected' or 'has a relation' to the characteristics of a product. The word 'their', which immediately precedes the words 'related processes and production methods', refers back to 'product characteristics'. Thus, in the context of the first sentence of Annex 1.1, we understand the reference to 'or their related processes and production methods' to indicate that the subject matter of a technical regulation may consist of a process or production method that is related to product characteristics.[14]

To determine whether a measure lays down '*related* PPMs', a panel will, according to the Appellate Body in *EC – Seal Products (2014)*, have to examine whether the PPMs prescribed by the measure at issue have 'a sufficient nexus to the characteristics of a product in order to be considered *related* to those characteristics'.[15] Note, however, that the Appellate Body stated that drawing the line between PPMs that fall, and those that do not fall, within the scope of the *TBT Agreement* raises 'important systemic issues' and did not further address the issue in *EC – Seal Products (2014)*.[16]

With regard to some types of measures, the definitions of Annexes 1.1 and 1.2 give more guidance as to whether technical regulations, standards or conformity assessment procedures relating to PPMs fall within the scope of application of the *TBT Agreement*. According to the last sentence of both definitions, technical regulations and standards include measures that are concerned with 'terminology, symbols, packaging, marking or labelling requirements *as they apply to a product, process or production method*'.[17] Note the absence of the adjective 'related'. It could therefore be argued that, for example, labelling requirements relating to NPR–PPMs are technical barriers to trade within the meaning of Annex 1 to the *TBT Agreement*, and thus fall within the scope of application of the *TBT Agreement*. The measures at issue in *US – Tuna II (Mexico) (2012)*, *US – Tuna II (Mexico) (Article 21.5) (2015)*, *US – COOL (2012)* and *US – COOL (Article 21.5 – Canada and Mexico) (2015)* were labelling requirements relating

13 Appellate Body Report, *EC – Seal Products (2014)*, para. 5.12. 14 *Ibid.*

15 *Ibid.* Emphasis added.

16 *Ibid.*, para. 5.69. These 'important systemic issues' were one of the reasons why the Appellate Body declined to complete the legal analysis on the question whether the EU Seal Regime was a 'technical regulation' within the meaning of Annex 1.1.

17 Emphasis added.

to NPR–PPMs. In none of these cases did the respondent, the United States, argue that these measures fall outside the scope of application of the *TBT Agreement.*[18]

The definition of 'technical regulation' in Annex 1.1 does not only refer to 'product characteristics and their related processes and production methods' but also to 'applicable administrative provisions'. In *EC – Seal Products (2014)*, the Appellate Body stated in this regard:

> we understand the appositive clause 'including the applicable administrative provisions' to refer to provisions to be applied by virtue of a governmental mandate in relation to either product characteristics or their related processes and production methods.[19]

There have been a number of disputes to date in which panels and/or the Appellate Body have had occasion to examine whether the measure at issue was a 'technical regulation'.

In *EC – Asbestos (2001)*, the measure at issue consisted of, on the one hand, a general ban on asbestos and asbestos-containing products and, on the other hand, some exceptions referring to situations in which asbestos-containing products would be allowed. The panel concluded that the ban itself was *not* a technical regulation, whereas the exceptions to the ban *were*.[20] On appeal, the Appellate Body first firmly rejected the panel's approach of considering separately the ban and the exceptions to the ban. According to the Appellate Body, the 'proper legal character' of the measure cannot be determined unless the measure is looked at as a whole, including both the prohibitive and the permissive elements that are part of it.[21] The Appellate Body then examined whether the measure at issue, considered as a whole, was a technical regulation within the meaning of the *TBT Agreement*. On the basis of the definition of a 'technical regulation' in Annex 1.1 of the *TBT Agreement*, quoted above, the Appellate Body set out a number of considerations for determining whether a measure is a technical regulation.

First, for a measure to be a 'technical regulation', it must 'lay down' – i.e. set forth, stipulate or provide – 'product characteristics'. With respect to the term 'characteristics', the Appellate Body noted:

> [T]he 'characteristics' of a product include, in our view, any objectively definable 'features', 'qualities', 'attributes', or other 'distinguishing mark' of a product. Such 'characteristics' might relate, *inter alia*, to a product's composition, size, shape, colour, texture, hardness, tensile strength, flammability, conductivity, density, or viscosity.[22]

18 Note also that the panel in *EC – Trademarks and Geographical Indications (Australia) (2005)* stated that '[t]he issue is not whether the content of the label refers to a product characteristic; the label on a product *is* a product characteristic'. See Panel Report, *EC – Trademarks and Geographical Indications (Australia) (2005)*, para. 7.449.

19 Appellate Body Report, *EC – Seal Products (2014)*, para. 5.13. In *EC – Asbestos (2001)*, para. 67, the Appellate Body already noted that: 'according to the definition in Annex 1.1 of the TBT Agreement, a "technical regulation" may set forth the "applicable administrative provisions" for products which have certain "characteristics"'.

20 See Panel Report, *EC – Asbestos (2001)*, paras. 8.71–8.72.

21 See Appellate Body Report, *EC – Asbestos (2001)*, para. 64.

22 *Ibid.*, para. 67. See also Appellate Body Report, *EC – Seal Products (2014)*, para 5.11.

The Appellate Body further noted that, in the second sentence of the definition of a 'technical regulation' in Annex 1.1, the *TBT Agreement* itself gives certain examples of 'product characteristics', namely: 'terminology, symbols, packaging, marking or labelling requirements'.[23] These examples, according to the Appellate Body, indicate that:

> 'product characteristics' include, not only features and qualities *intrinsic* to the product itself, but also related *extrinsic* 'characteristics', such as the means of identification, the presentation and the appearance of a product.[24]

The Appellate Body also noted that pursuant to the definition in Annex 1.1, a 'technical regulation' may be confined to laying down *only* one or a few product characteristics.[25] In other words, it is not required that a 'technical regulation' lays down the characteristics of a product in a comprehensive manner.

Second, a 'technical regulation' lays down product characteristics or their related PPMs 'with which compliance is mandatory'. According to the Appellate Body in *EC – Asbestos (2001)*, it follows that:

> with respect to products, a 'technical regulation' has the effect of *prescribing* or *imposing* one or more 'characteristics' – 'features', 'qualities', 'attributes', or other 'distinguishing mark'.[26]

The Appellate Body further noted that product characteristics may be prescribed or imposed in either a *positive* or a *negative* form. For example, the regulation may provide, positively, that products *must possess* certain characteristics, or the regulation may require, negatively, that products *must not possess* certain characteristics.[27] In both cases, the result is the same: the regulation lays down certain 'characteristics' with which compliance is mandatory.[28]

Third, the Appellate Body in *EC – Asbestos (2001)* held that a 'technical regulation' must 'be applicable to an *identifiable* product, or group of products'.[29] Unlike the panel, the Appellate Body did not consider that a 'technical regulation' must apply to 'given' products, which are actually named, identified or specified in the regulation. Nothing in the text of the *TBT Agreement* suggests that the products concerned need be named or otherwise *expressly* identified in a 'technical regulation'. The Appellate Body noted that:

> there may be perfectly sound administrative reasons for formulating a 'technical regulation' in a way that does *not* expressly identify products by name, but simply makes them identifiable – for instance, through the 'characteristic' that is the subject of regulation.[30]

23 Note that according to the Appellate Body in *EC – Seal Products (2014)*, para. 5.14, the use of the words 'also include' and 'deal exclusively with' indicates that the second sentence includes elements that are *additional to*, and may be *distinct from*, those covered by the first sentence of Annex 1.1.

24 Appellate Body Report, *EC – Asbestos (2001)*, para. 67. Emphasis added. See also Appellate Body Report, *EC – Seal Products (2014)*, para. 5.11.

25 See Appellate Body Report, *EC – Asbestos (2001)*, para. 67. See also Appellate Body Report, *EC – Seal Products (2014)*, para. 5.11.

26 Appellate Body Report, *EC – Asbestos (2001)*, para. 68.

27 See *ibid.*, para. 69. The prohibition of all asbestos-containing products at issue in *EC – Asbestos (2001)* was a measure which effectively prescribed – albeit negatively – certain objective characteristics for all products.

28 See *ibid.* 29 *Ibid.*, para. 70.

30 *Ibid.*, para. 70. In *EC – Asbestos (2001)* the Appellate Body considered that while the products to which the prohibition applied could not be determined from the terms of the measure at issue itself, the products covered by the measure are *identifiable*: all products must be asbestos-free; any products containing asbestos are prohibited. See *ibid.*, para. 72. It is often the product characteristics set out in the measure at issue that make the product 'identifiable'. See *ibid.*, para. 70.

On the basis of the above three considerations, the Appellate Body concluded that the measure at issue in *EC – Asbestos (2001)* constituted a 'technical regulation' under the *TBT Agreement.*[31]

Confirming its ruling in *EC – Asbestos (2001)*, the Appellate Body in *EC – Sardines (2002)* established a three-tier test for determining whether a measure is a 'technical regulation' under the *TBT Agreement*: (1) the measure must apply to an *identifiable* product or group of products; (2) the measure must lay down *product characteristics*; and (3) compliance with the product characteristics laid down in the measure must be *mandatory.*[32]

Applying this test in *EC – Sardines (2002)*, the Appellate Body further clarified its reasoning in *EC – Asbestos (2001)*. The measure at issue in *EC – Sardines (2002)* was an EC regulation setting out a number of prescriptions for the sale of 'preserved sardines', including a requirement that a product sold under the name 'preserved sardines' contained only one species of sardines (namely, the *Sardina pilchardus Walbaum*), to the exclusion of other species (such as the *Sardinops sagax*). With regard to the first element of its three-tier test, the Appellate Body held that a measure, which does not expressly identify the products to which it applies, could still be applicable to identifiable products (as required by the first element of the test).[33] The tool that the Appellate Body used to determine whether, in this case, *Sardinops sagax* was an identifiable product was an examination of the way the EC Regulation was enforced. As the enforcement of the EC Regulation had led to a prohibition against labelling *Sardinops sagax* as 'preserved sardines', this product was considered to be 'identifiable'.[34]

With regard to the second element of the three-tier test, the question arose as to whether a 'naming' rule, such as the rule that only *Sardina pilchardus* could be named 'preserved sardines', laid down product characteristics. The Appellate Body held in this respect that product characteristics include means of identification and that, therefore, the naming rule at issue definitely met the requirement of the second element of the test.[35] As the European Communities did not contest that compliance with the Regulation at issue was mandatory, the Appellate Body found that the third element of the three-tier test was also met, and the measure was therefore a 'technical regulation' for purposes of the *TBT Agreement.*[36]

31 *Ibid.*, para. 75. Note that the Appellate Body observed that, if this measure consisted *only* of a prohibition on *asbestos in its pure form*, it might not constitute a 'technical regulation'. The prohibition of asbestos as such does not constitute a technical regulation, because it 'does not, in itself, prescribe or impose any "characteristics" on asbestos fibres, but simply bans them in their natural state'. See *ibid.*, para. 71. However, the Appellate Body considered that 'an integral and essential aspect of the measure' is the regulation of *products containing asbestos fibres*. In effect, the measure provides that *all* products must *not* contain asbestos fibres. See *ibid.*, para. 72. Moreover, the Appellate Body noted that, through the exceptions to the prohibition, the measure at issue set out the 'applicable administrative provisions, with which compliance is mandatory' for products with certain objective 'characteristics'. See *ibid.*, para. 74. Note that the Appellate Body in *EC – Seal Products (2014)*, paras. 5.35–6 and 5.58, found that to the extent that the EU Seal Regime regulates the placing on the EU market of *pure seal products*, it did not prescribe or impose any 'characteristics' on the products themselves. According to the Appellate Body, the panel should have assessed the relevance of this aspect of the measure in order to determine whether it was a part of the integral and essential aspects of the measure and, if so, what weight it should ascribe to it in determining whether the EU Seal Regime, as a whole, lays down product characteristics.

32 *See* Appellate Body Report, *EC – Sardines (2002)*, para. 176. 33 See *ibid.*, para. 180.

34 See *ibid.*, para. 184. 35 See *ibid.*, paras. 190–1.

36 See *ibid.*, paras. 194–5.

In *EC – Trademarks and Geographical Indications (Australia) (2005)*, the panel applied the Appellate Body's three-tier test in order to assess whether (1) a requirement that the country of origin must be indicated clearly on the product label, and (2) inspection structures for the registration of individual geographical indications (GIs), qualified as technical regulations. First, with regard to the labelling requirement, the panel concluded that this requirement was a 'technical regulation' within the meaning of Annex 1.1 to the *TBT Agreement*.[37] The panel noted that '[t]he issue is not whether the content of the label refers to a product characteristic; the label on a product *is* a product characteristic'.[38] Second, with regard to the inspection structures, Australia had argued that these inspection structures qualified as a 'technical regulation'. The panel disagreed. The panel appeared to consider that the inspection structures were 'conformity assessment procedures', and, since they were 'conformity assessment procedures', they could not be 'technical regulations' at the same time.[39]

In *US – Clove Cigarettes (2012)*, which concerned a US ban on clove cigarettes and other flavoured cigarettes, with the exception of menthol cigarettes, and in *US – COOL (2012)*, which concerned a US measure imposing a requirement on retailers selling beef and pork to label those products with their country of origin,[40] the question of whether the core measures at issue were 'technical regulations' was not disputed between the parties.[41] However, in *US – Tuna II (Mexico) (2012)*, which concerned a measure establishing the conditions for use of a 'dolphin-safe' label on tuna products, the correct characterisation of the measure at issue was a central element of the dispute.[42] According to the respondent, the United States, the measure at issue was a 'standard' and not a 'technical regulation'. The panel disagreed. According to the panel, the measure at issue

37 Panel Report, *EC – Trademarks and Geographical Indications (Australia) (2005)*, para. 7.449.

38 See *ibid*. The panel furthermore held that the labelling requirement at issue was a mandatory requirement because products with a geographical indication identical to a Community-protected name that do not satisfy this labelling requirement must *not* be marketed in the European Communities using that geographical indication. See *ibid*., para. 7.456. Compare with *US – Tuna II (Mexico) (2012)* below, pp. 829–33.

39 See Panel Report, *EC – Trademarks and Geographical Indications (Australia) (2005)*, para. 7.514. The panel noted that the terms 'technical regulations' and 'standards' are themselves part of the definition of the term 'conformity assessment procedures'. According to the panel, this suggests that 'technical regulations' and 'conformity assessment procedures' are not only distinct from one another, but mutually exclusive. As the panel argued, '[w]hilst a single measure can combine both a technical regulation and a procedure to assess conformity with that technical regulation, it would be an odd result if a conformity assessment procedure could fall within the definition of a technical regulation as well'. *Ibid*., para. 7.512.

40 Note that, under the US measure at issue, the 'country of origin' of beef or pork is defined not as a function of the country in which the last substantial transformation to the beef or pork took place, but as a function of the country or countries in which the production steps (birth, raising and slaughter), involving the animals from which the beef and pork is derived, took place.

41 In *US – COOL (2012)*, the United States did argue that a second measure at issue, the Vilsack letter, was not a 'technical regulation'. The panel agreed with the United States after finding that the Vilsack letter was not 'mandatory within the meaning of Annex 1.1'. See Panel Reports, *US – COOL (2012)*, paras. 7.194–7.196.

42 Eligibility for a 'dolphin-safe' label depended upon certain documentary evidence that varied depending on the area where the tuna contained in the tuna product was harvested and the type of vessel and fishing method by which it was harvested.

was a 'technical regulation'.[43] On appeal, the United States did not challenge the panel's findings regarding the first and second element of the test set out above. However, it did challenge the panel's finding regarding the third element of the test, namely, that compliance with the measure at issue was mandatory. In challenging this finding, the United States argued, in particular, that compliance with a labelling requirement is 'mandatory' within the meaning of Annex 1.1 only 'if there is also a requirement to use the label in order to place the product for sale on the market'.[44] Since tuna products could be sold on the US market with *or* without a 'dolphin-safe' label, the labelling requirement was, according to the United States, not 'mandatory'. The Appellate Body disagreed. The Appellate Body pointed out that a labelling requirement, i.e. a provision that sets out conditions to be fulfilled in order to use a particular label, can be a 'technical regulation' *or* a 'standard'.[45] According to the Appellate Body, the mere fact that a labelling requirement does not require the use of a particular label in order to place a product for sale on the market, does not preclude that this labelling requirement is a 'technical regulation'.[46] The Appellate Body considered that a determination of whether a particular measure constitutes a 'technical regulation' or a 'standard' must be made in light of the features of the measure and the circumstances of the case.[47] Such exercise may involve considering: (1) whether the measure consists of a law or a regulation enacted by a WTO Member; (2) whether it prescribes or prohibits particular conduct; (3) whether it sets out specific requirements that constitute the sole means of addressing a particular matter; and (4) the nature of the matter addressed by the measure.[48] After careful examination of the measure at issue in *US – Tuna II (Mexico) (2012)*, the Appellate Body concluded:

> In this case, we note that the US measure is composed of legislative and regulatory acts of the US federal authorities and includes administrative provisions. In addition, the measure at issue sets out a single and legally mandated definition of a 'dolphin-safe' tuna product and disallows the use of other labels on tuna products that do not satisfy this definition. In doing so, the US measure prescribes in a broad and exhaustive manner the conditions that apply for making any assertion on a tuna product as to its 'dolphin-safety', regardless of the manner in which that statement is made. As a consequence, the US measure covers the entire field of what 'dolphin-safe' means in relation to tuna products. For these reasons, we *find* that the Panel did not err in characterizing the measure at issue as a 'technical regulation' within the meaning of Annex 1.1 to the *TBT Agreement*.[49]

43 Note, however, the separate opinion of one of the panellists, see Panel Report, *US – Tuna II (Mexico) (2012)*, paras. 7.146–7.188. The dissenting panellist was of the opinion that the measure at issue, the 'dolphin-safe' labelling scheme, was not a technical regulation because it was not a mandatory scheme as the tuna could be put on the market without the label. See *ibid.*

44 United States' appellant's submission, para. 32 (as referred to in Appellate Body Report, *US – Tuna II (Mexico) (2012)*, para. 196).

45 See *ibid.*, para. 187. 46 See *ibid.*, para. 196.

47 See *ibid.*, para. 190. 48 See *ibid.*, para. 188.

49 *Ibid.*, para. 199. Note that, having found that the measure at issue constituted a 'technical regulation', Mexico's alternative argument that the US measure is *de facto* mandatory did not need to be addressed by the Appellate Body.

In *EC – Seal Products (2014)*, the measures at issue, collectively referred to as the 'EU Seal Regime', prohibited the importation and placing on the EU market of seal products except where they were: (1) derived from hunts conducted by Inuit or other indigenous communities (IC exception); (2) derived from hunts conducted for marine resource management purposes (MRM exception); or (3) imported into the EU for the personal use of travellers. The panel in this case found that the EU Seal Regime laid down product characteristics, including the applicable administrative provisions, and was thus a 'technical regulation' within the meaning of Annex 1.1 to the *TBT Agreement*. The Appellate Body disagreed. The panel had reached its conclusion that the EU Seal Regime was a technical regulation on the basis of an examination of one aspect of the Regime alone, namely the aspect that sets out a 'prohibition on seal-containing products'.[50] According to the Appellate Body, the panel should have examined the design and operation of the EU Seal Regime and analysed the weight and relevance of the essential and integral elements of the Regime as an integrated whole.[51] When the prohibitive aspects of the EU Seal Regime (the prohibition on seal-containing products) are considered in the light of the permissive aspects (the IC and MRM exceptions), the Appellate Body found that the EU Seal Regime did not prohibit seal-containing products merely on the basis that such products contained seal as an input. The prohibition was imposed based on criteria relating to the *identity of the hunter* or the *type or purpose of the hunt* from which the product was derived. That being its main feature, the Appellate Body thus concluded that the EU Seal Regime did not lay down 'product characteristics' and therefore reversed the panel's finding that the EU Seal Regime was a 'technical regulation' within the meaning of Annex 1.1.[52] The Appellate Body subsequently declined to complete the legal analysis on whether the EU Seal Regime was a 'technical regulation' because the panel and the participants had not sufficiently explored the question of whether the Regime laid down 'related PPMs', a question that raised 'important systemic issues'.[53]

As was the case in, for example, *EC – Asbestos (2001)*, *US – Tuna II (Mexico) (2012)* and *US – Tuna II (Mexico) (Article 21.5) (2015)*, the technical regulations at issue in disputes under the *TBT Agreement* are often measures with multiple constituent parts. In *US – Tuna II (Mexico) (Article 21.5) (2015)*, the Appellate Body observed that analysing such measures 'in a segmented manner may raise concerns when the constituent parts of the measure are interrelated and operate in an integrated way'.[54] According to

50 See Appellate Body Report, *EC – Seal Products (2014)*, para. 5.29. 51 See *ibid.*

52 See *ibid.* As the Appellate Body found, this is not changed by the fact that the *administrative provisions* under the EU Seal Regime may 'apply' to products containing seal. This aspect of the measure is ancillary, and does not render the measure a 'technical regulation'. See *ibid.*, paras. 5.52–5.58.

53 See Appellate Body Report, *EC – Seal Products (2014)*, para. 5.69.

54 Appellate Body Report, *US – Tuna II (Mexico) (Article 21.5) (2015)*, para. 7.13. See also Appellate Body Report, *EC – Asbestos (2001)*, para. 64; Appellate Body Reports, *EC – Seal Products (2014)*, para. 5.20.

the Appellate Body, the panel in *US – Tuna II (Mexico) (Article 21.5) (2015)* conducted:

> a segmented analysis that isolated consideration of each element of the measure without accounting for the manner in which the elements are interrelated, and without aggregating or synthesizing its analyses or findings relating to those elements before reaching its ultimate conclusions as to the consistency or inconsistency of the amended tuna measure.[55]

The Appellate Body found that this segmented analysis by the panel amounted to, or led it to commit, legal error in its assessment of the TBT-consistency (and GATT-consistency) of the measure at issue.[56]

To conclude, while the concept of 'technical regulation' in Annex 1.1 has already been clarified by the case law, the concept of 'standard' has – except in *US – Tuna II (Mexico) (2012)*, discussed above – received little attention so far. Note, however, that, as the definition of a 'standard' in Annex 1.2, quoted above, makes clear, a standard is 'approved by a recognized body', while a technical regulation is typically adopted by a government body. A 'recognized body' within the meaning of Annex 1.2, can be either governmental or non-governmental.[57] Also, a 'standard' sets out, for common and repeated use, not only 'characteristics' but also 'rules' and 'guidelines' for products or related PPMs. The definition of a 'technical regulation' does not refer to 'rules' or 'guidelines'.

2.2 Entities Covered by the *TBT Agreement*

The *TBT Agreement* is mainly addressed to *central government* bodies. However, it explicitly aims to extend its application to other bodies involved in the preparation, adoption and application of technical regulations, standards and/or conformity assessment procedures. These other bodies covered by the *TBT Agreement* are local government bodies and non-governmental bodies.[58] *Local government* bodies are all bodies of government other than central government, such as provinces or municipalities. They include any organ subject to the 'control of such a government in respect of the activity in question'.[59] *Non-governmental* bodies in the context of the *TBT Agreement* are very broadly defined as bodies other than central government or local government bodies.[60] These non-governmental bodies include, for example, ABNT (the Associação Brasileira de Normas Técnicas), ANSI (the American National Standards Institute) and CEN (the European Committee for Standardization).[61]

55 Appellate Body Report, *US – Tuna II (Mexico) (Article 21.5) (2015)*, para. 7.21.

56 See e.g. *ibid.*, paras. 7.159 and 7.280. 57 See examples given above, p. 886, fn. 6.

58 The *TBT Agreement* also covers 'regional bodies' or 'regional systems' See Annex 1.5 to the *TBT Agreement*. The TBT rules applicable to regional bodies or regional systems are those set out in Article 4 and Annex 3.B (with regard to standards) and Article 9 (with regard to conformity assessment). Note, however, that the TBT rules applicable to the European Union are the rules applicable to central government bodies, and thus also include those set out in Article 2 of the *TBT Agreement*. See Explanatory Note to Annex 1.6 to the *TBT Agreement*.

59 Annex 1.7 to the *TBT Agreement*. 60 See Annex 1.8 to the *TBT Agreement*.

61 Note that CEN, together with ETSI (the European Telecommunications Standards Institute) and CENELEC (the European Committee for Electrotechnical Standardisation) are officially recognised by the European Union as a European standardising body.

Pursuant to Article 3 (with regard to technical regulations), Article 4 and Annex 3.B (with regard to standards) and Articles 7 and 8 (with regard to conformity assessment procedures), the *TBT Agreement* extends its application to local government and non-governmental bodies, by imposing, on WTO Members, the obligation: (1) to take 'such reasonable measures as may be available to them' to ensure compliance with the *TBT Agreement* by local government and non-governmental bodies; and (2) to refrain from taking measures that could encourage actions by these bodies that are inconsistent with the provisions of the *TBT Agreement*. Article 3.5 of the *TBT Agreement* further provides that:

> Members shall formulate and implement positive measures and mechanisms in support of the observance of the provisions of Article 2 by other than central government bodies.

The obligation set out in Article 4 and Annex 3.B (with regard to standards) may be of particular importance in light of the increasing impact on international trade of 'private sector standards', i.e. standards adopted by NGOs such as the Forest Stewardship Council (FSC) (which sets standards for sustainable forest management),[62] or standards adopted by commercial enterprises such as Tesco, the multinational grocery and general merchandise retailer (which sets and applies, *inter alia*, minimum labour standards to its suppliers in China, India and Bangladesh). The proliferation of these 'private sector standards' is of significant concern to producers in developing-country Members.[63] As noted above, 'non-governmental bodies' are very broadly defined in Annex 1.8, as bodies other than central government or local government bodies. There is, however, much debate on whether NGOs and commercial enterprises are 'non-governmental standardizing bodies' within the meaning of Article 4 Annex 3.B of the *TBT Agreement*.

2.3 Temporal Scope of Application of the *TBT Agreement*

In *EC – Sardines (2002)*, the issue arose whether the *TBT Agreement* applies to technical regulations which were already in force on 1 January 1995, i.e. the date on which the *TBT Agreement* entered into force. In deciding this issue, the panel and Appellate Body referred to Article 28 of the *Vienna Convention on the Law of Treaties*, which states that:

> [u]nless a different intention appears from the treaty or is otherwise established, its provisions do not bind a party in relation to any act or fact which took place or any situation which ceased to exist before the date of the entry into force of the treaty with respect to that party.

Applying this basic provision of treaty law, both the panel and the Appellate Body held that the EC regulation at issue, although adopted prior to 1 January

62 Other examples of such NGOs adopting 'private sector standards' are GlobalGAP (which sets standards for production processes of agricultural products trade), and the Fairtrade Foundation (which sets standards for socially responsible production and trade).

63 For a further discussion on 'private sector standards' in the context of the *SPS Agreement*, see below, p. 942.

1995, was still in force and thus could not be considered as a 'situation which has ceased to exist'.[64] Therefore, it can be concluded that the *TBT Agreement* applies to technical regulations, which, although adopted prior to 1995, are still in force.

2.4 Relationship with Other WTO Agreements

This section examines, first, the relationship of the *TBT Agreement* with the *SPS Agreement* and the *Agreement on Government Procurement*, and then its relationship with the GATT 1994.

2.4.1 The *SPS Agreement* and the *Agreement on Government Procurement*

As mentioned above, the scope of application of the *TBT Agreement* is determined by the type of measure. The *TBT Agreement* applies, in principle, to technical regulations, standards and conformity assessment procedures as defined in Annex 1 thereof. However, to avoid overlap with other WTO agreements, the scope of application of the *TBT Agreement* has been limited in favour of two other WTO agreements: the *SPS Agreement* and the *Agreement on Government Procurement*. Generally speaking, the applicability of either of these agreements to a measure excludes the applicability of the *TBT Agreement*. However, in specific cases, the situation may not be so clear-cut.

Pursuant to Article 1.4 of the *TBT Agreement*, purchasing specifications related to the production or consumption of governmental bodies do not fall within the scope of application of the *TBT Agreement* as they are dealt with in the *Agreement on Government Procurement*. Note, however, that the *Agreement on Government Procurement* is a plurilateral agreement; the disciplines set out in this agreement do not apply to most WTO Members.[65]

Pursuant to Article 1.5 of the *TBT Agreement*, sanitary and phytosanitary measures are excluded from the scope of application of the *TBT Agreement*, even if they take the form of technical regulations, standards or conformity assessment procedures. Sanitary and phytosanitary measures are subject to the distinct disciplines of the *SPS Agreement*, discussed in Chapter 14.[66] It is the *purpose* of the measure that qualifies it as a sanitary or phytosanitary measure. In *EC – Hormones (1998)*, the United States and Canada claimed, *inter alia*, that the measures at issue were inconsistent with the *TBT Agreement*. Referring to Article 1.5 of the *TBT Agreement*, the panel found, however, that, since these measures were SPS measures, the *TBT Agreement* did not apply in the *EC – Hormones (1998)* dispute.[67] However, note that the panel in *EC – Approval and*

64 See Panel Report, *EC – Sardines (2002)*, para. 7.60; and Appellate Body Report, *EC – Sardines (2002)*, para. 216.

65 See above, pp. 512–14. 66 See below, pp. 937–41.

67 See Panel Report, *EC – Hormones (US) (1998)*, para. 8.29; and Panel Report, *EC – Hormones (Canada) (1998)*, para. 8.32.

Marketing of Biotech Products (2006) recognised that a single measure can have more than one purpose: one that falls within the definition of an SPS measure *and* one that does not. The panel thus held that, assuming that the measure at issue falls within the definition of a technical regulation, to the extent that the measure is applied for a non-SPS purpose, it is a measure to which the disciplines of the *TBT Agreement* apply.[68]

2.4.2 The GATT 1994

The relationship between the GATT 1994 and the *TBT Agreement* is of a different nature and is not characterised by mutual exclusivity. In *US – Clove Cigarettes (2012)* the Appellate Body stated that the *TBT Agreement* expands on the pre-existing GATT disciplines and emphasises that the two agreements should be interpreted in a coherent and consistent manner.[69] The panel in *EC – Asbestos (2001)* held that, in a case where both the GATT 1994 and the *TBT Agreement* appear to apply to a given measure, a panel must first examine whether the measure at issue is consistent with the *TBT Agreement* since this agreement deals 'specifically and in detail' with technical barriers to trade.[70] However, should a panel find a measure to be consistent with the *TBT Agreement*, it must still examine whether the measure is also consistent with the GATT 1994.[71] Under the *TBT, Agreement* there is – unlike under the *SPS Agreement* – no presumption of GATT-consistency when a technical barrier to trade is found to be consistent with the *TBT Agreement*.[72] Note that in *US – Tuna II (Mexico) (2012)*, the Appellate Body reversed the panel's decision to exercise judicial economy regarding the complainant's claim of inconsistency with Article III:4 of the GATT 1994 after it had found that the measure at issue was not inconsistent with Article 2.1 of the *TBT Agreement*.[73] The Appellate Body observed that the Panel's decision to exercise judicial economy rested upon the assumption that the non-discrimination obligations under the *TBT Agreement* and the GATT 1994 are substantially the same.[74] As discussed below, the assumption was incorrect.[75] Therefore, after finding that the measure at issue was not inconsistent with Article 2.1 of the *TBT Agreement*, the panel should have addressed the complainant's claims under the GATT 1994.[76]

68 See Panel Reports, *EC – Approval and Marketing of Biotech Products (2006)*, para. 7.167.

69 See Appellate Body Report, *US – Clove Cigarettes (2012)*, para. 96.

70 See Panel Report, *EC – Asbestos (2001)*, para. 8.16. See on this point more generally, Appellate Body Report, *EC – Bananas III (1997)*, para. 204. See also Panel Report, *EC – Sardines (2002)*, paras. 7.14–7.19.

71 It is understood that, if a panel should find that a measure is inconsistent with the *TBT Agreement*, it may exercise judicial economy with regard to a claim that this measure is also inconsistent with the GATT 1994. On the exercise of judicial economy, see above, pp. 225–7.

72 On the presumption of GATT-consistency under Article 2.4 of the *SPS Agreement*, see below, p. 944.

73 See Appellate Body Report, *US – Tuna II (Mexico) (2012)*, para. 405.

74 See *ibid*. 75 See below, pp. 906–12.

76 On appeal, the Appellate Body found the measure at issue to be inconsistent with Article 2.1 of the *TBT Agreement*. Since the complainant, Mexico, had explicitly stated that it did not request the Appellate Body to complete the legal analysis regarding its claims under the GATT 1994 in case the Appellate Body would find inconsistency with Article 2.1 of the *TBT Agreement*, the Appellate Body made no findings regarding Mexico's claims under the GATT 1994. See Appellate Body Report, *US – Tuna II (Mexico) (2012)*, para. 406.

In *US – COOL (2012)*, *US – COOL (Article 21.5 – Canada and Mexico) (2015)* and *US – Tuna II (Mexico) (Article 21.5) (2015)*, the technical regulations at issue were found to be inconsistent with obligations under the *TBT Agreement* as well as the GATT 1994.

Note, in general, that the relationship between the GATT 1994 and the other multilateral agreements on trade in goods (including the *TBT Agreement*) is governed by the *General Interpretative Note to Annex 1A* of the *WTO Agreement*. This Note provides that, in case of conflict between a provision of the GATT 1994 and a provision of another multilateral agreement on trade in goods, the latter will prevail to the extent of the conflict.[77]

3 SUBSTANTIVE PROVISIONS OF THE *TBT AGREEMENT*

The substantive provisions of the *TBT Agreement* contain several obligations that are also found in the GATT 1994, such as: the most-favoured-nation (MFN) treatment obligation, the national treatment obligation and the obligation to refrain from creating unnecessary obstacles to international trade. In *EC – Asbestos (2001)*, the Appellate Body observed that the *TBT Agreement* intends to further the objectives of the GATT 1994. However, it immediately noted that the *TBT Agreement* does so through a specialised legal regime, containing *different* and *additional* obligations to those emanating from the GATT 1994.[78] This section will address the following obligations under the *TBT Agreement*: (1) the MFN treatment and national treatment obligations; (2) the obligation to refrain from creating unnecessary obstacles to international trade; (3) the obligation to base technical barriers to trade on international standards; and (4) other obligations, including obligations relating to mutual recognition and transparency.

3.1 MFN Treatment and National Treatment Obligations

With respect to technical regulations, Article 2.1 of the *TBT Agreement* provides that:

> Members shall ensure that in respect of technical regulations, products imported from the territory of any Member shall be accorded treatment no less favourable than that accorded to like products of national origin and to like products originating in any other country.

77 For a discussion on the relationship between the GATT 1994 and other multilateral agreements on trade in goods, see above, pp. 46–8.

78 See Appellate Body Report, *EC – Asbestos (2001)*, para. 80. Therefore, caution needs to be used when transposing the interpretation given to these obligations under the GATT 1994 to the similar provisions in the *TBT Agreement*. See also below, pp. 899–912.

Technical regulations are thus subject to a national treatment obligation and the MFN treatment obligation. Pursuant to Annex 3.D to and Article 5.1.1 of the *TBT Agreement*, these obligations also apply to standards and conformity assessment procedures respectively. Thus, a requirement that furniture from Brazil must be made from sustainable wood (i.e. wood from sustainably managed forests), while there is no such requirement for furniture from African countries, would constitute a violation of the MFN treatment obligation set out in Article 2.1 of the *TBT Agreement*. Requiring accurate testing for the presence of GMOs in corn imported from the United States, while such verification is not required for corn from Australia, would constitute a violation of the MFN treatment obligation set out in Article 5.1.1 of the *TBT Agreement*. A requirement that imported furniture is fire-resistant, while no such requirement exists for domestically produced furniture, would constitute a violation of the national treatment obligation set out in Article 2.1 of the *TBT Agreement*.

The Appellate Body first interpreted the national treatment obligation of Article 2.1 of the *TBT Agreement* in *US – Clove Cigarettes (2012)* and further clarified this obligation in *US – Tuna II (Mexico) (2012)* and *US – COOL (2012)*. In *US – Tuna II (Mexico) (2012)*, the Appellate Body also addressed the MFN treatment obligation of Article 2.1.

In *US – Clove Cigarettes (2012)*, the Appellate Body ruled that:

> [f]or a violation of the national treatment obligation in Article 2.1 to be established, three elements must be satisfied: (i) the measure at issue must be a technical regulation; (ii) the imported and domestic products at issue must be like products; and (iii) the treatment accorded to imported products must be less favourable than that accorded to like domestic products.[79]

Article 2.1 of the *TBT Agreement* thus sets out a three-tier test of consistency with the national treatment obligation. This test of consistency requires the examination of: (1) whether the measure at issue is a '*technical regulation*' within the meaning of Annex 1.1; (2) whether the imported and domestic products at issue are '*like products*'; and (3) whether the imported products are accorded '*treatment no less favourable*' than like domestic products.

As the Appellate Body found in *US – Tuna II (Mexico) (2012)*, Article 2.1 of the *TBT Agreement* sets out a largely similar test of consistency with the MFN treatment obligation. Under the third element of the test, however, instead of examining whether the imported products are accorded 'treatment no less favourable' than like domestic products, a panel must examine whether products imported from one WTO Member are accorded 'treatment no less favourable' than like products originating in any other country.[80] As noted above, standards and conformity assessment procedures are also subject to the MFN treatment and the national treatment obligation under the *TBT Agreement*.[81] It

79 Appellate Body Report, *US – Clove Cigarettes (2012)*, para. 87.
80 See Appellate Body Report, *US – Tuna II (Mexico) (2012)*, para. 202. 81 See above, pp. 899–900.

is reasonable to expect that, *mutatis mutandis*, a similar test of consistency with the MFN treatment obligation and the national treatment obligation will apply with regard to standards and conformity assessment procedures.

Below, each element of the three-tier test of consistency with the national treatment and MFN treatment obligations under Article 2.1 of the *TBT Agreement* will be discussed in turn.[82] Before engaging in this discussion, it is useful to note the following. For a proper understanding of this test of consistency, and in particular the third element of the test ('treatment no less favourable'), it is important to keep in mind that the *TBT Agreement* does not contain a provision, such as Article XX of the GATT 1994, which could justify measures found to be inconsistent with the MFN-treatment obligation or the national treatment obligation of Article 2.1.[83]

To date, WTO Members have been found to have acted inconsistently with the national treatment obligation of Article 2.1 of the *TBT Agreement* in five disputes.[84] In two disputes, a WTO Member was found to have acted inconsistently with the MFN treatment obligation of Article 2.1.[85]

3.1.1 'Technical Regulations'

With regard to this first element of the test of consistency with the non-discrimination obligations of Article 2.1 of the *TBT Agreement*, namely, whether the measure at issue is a 'technical regulation', refer to the discussion above on the scope of application of the *TBT Agreement*.[86]

3.1.2 'Like Products'

The second element of the test of consistency with the non-discrimination obligations of Article 2.1 of the *TBT Agreement* relates to the question of whether the imported and domestic products concerned (for the national treatment obligation) or the imported products originating in different countries concerned (for the MFN treatment obligation) are 'like'. As the non-discrimination obligations under the GATT 1994 discussed in Chapters 4 and 5, the non-discrimination obligations of Article 2.1 only apply to 'like products'. Therefore, for the application of these non-discrimination obligations, it is also important to be able to determine whether, for example, a sports utility vehicle (SUV) is 'like' a family car; orange juice is 'like' tomato juice; a laptop is 'like' a tablet computer; pork is 'like' beef; or whisky is 'like' brandy.

82 See below, pp. 901–12. 83 See below, section 3.1.3.

84 See *US – Clove Cigarettes (2012)*; *US – Tuna II (Mexico) (2012)*; *US – COOL (2012)*; *US – Tuna II (Mexico) (Article 21.5) (2015)*; and *US – COOL (Article 21.5 – Canada and Mexico) (2015)*.

85 See *US – Tuna II (Mexico) (2012)* and *US – Tuna II (Mexico) (Article 21.5) (2015)*. With regard to *EC – Seal Products (2014)*, note that after reversing the panel's finding that the EU Seal Regime is a 'technical regulation', the Appellate Body declared the panel's conclusions under Article 2.1 of the *TBT Agreement* moot and of no legal effect. See Appellate Body Report, *EC – Seal Products (2014)*, para. 5.70.

86 See above, pp. 885–95. 87 See Panel Report, *US – Clove Cigarettes (2012)*, para. 7.119.

As discussed above in Chapter 5, the determination of 'likeness' under Article III of the GATT 1994 is a determination about the nature and extent of a competitive relationship between and among products. The panel in *US – Clove Cigarettes (2012)* held that the text and context of the *TBT Agreement* supported an interpretation of the concept of 'likeness' in Article 2.1 of the *TBT Agreement* that focused on the objectives and purposes of the technical regulation, rather than on the competitive relationship between and among the products. The panel adopted a purpose-based approach to the determination of 'likeness', rather than a competition-based approach. The panel found that, in the circumstances of this case, in the determination of 'likeness' under Article 2.1 the weighing of the evidence relating to the 'likeness' criteria (physical characteristics, end-uses, consumers' tastes and habits, and customs classification) should be influenced by the fact that the measure at issue was a technical regulation having the immediate purpose of regulating flavoured cigarettes for public health reasons.[87] The Appellate Body rejected the panel's purpose-based approach to the determination of 'likeness' under Article 2.1.[88] The Appellate Body considered in *US – Clove Cigarettes (2012)* that:

> the concept of 'like products' serves to define the scope of products that should be compared to establish whether less favourable treatment is being accorded to imported products. If products that are in a sufficiently strong competitive relationship to be considered like are excluded from the group of like products on the basis of a measure's regulatory purposes, such products would not be compared in order to ascertain whether less favourable treatment has been accorded to imported products. This would inevitably distort the less favourable treatment comparison, as it would refer to a 'marketplace' that would include some like products, but not others.[89]

While it rejected the panel's purpose-based approach to the determination of 'likeness', the Appellate Body noted, however, that:

> regulatory concerns underlying a measure, such as the health risks associated with a given product, may be relevant to an analysis of the 'likeness' criteria under Article III:4 of the GATT 1994, as well as under Article 2.1 of the *TBT Agreement*, to the extent they have an impact on the competitive relationship between and among the products concerned.[90]

The Appellate Body in *US – Clove Cigarettes (2012)* unmistakably opted for a competition-based approach to the determination of 'likeness' under Article 2.1.

88 See Appellate Body Report, *US – Clove Cigarettes (2012)*, para. 112. The Appellate Body noted in this context that measures often pursue a multiplicity of objectives, which are not always easily discernible. The Appellate Body also noted that the panel's purpose-based approach to the determination of 'likeness' does not, necessarily, leave more regulatory autonomy for Members, because it almost invariably puts panels into the position of having to determine which of the various objectives purportedly pursued by Members are more important, or which of these objectives should prevail in determining 'likeness' in the event of conflicting objectives. See Appellate Body Report, *US – Clove Cigarettes (2012)*, paras. 113–15.

89 *Ibid.*, para. 116.

90 *Ibid.*, para. 119. See also *ibid.*, paras. 120 and 156. The Appellate Body explicitly referred to its approach to the determination of 'likeness' in *EC – Hormones (1998)*.

It stated that the determination of 'likeness' under Article 2.1 of the *TBT Agreement* is, as under Article III:4 of the GATT 1994:

> a determination about the nature and extent of a competitive relationship between and among the products at issue.[91]

As noted above, the panel considered in its determination of 'likeness' the 'likeness' criteria already discussed in Chapters 4 and 5 in the context of the non-discrimination obligations of the GATT 1994. The United States did not appeal the panel's findings regarding 'physical characteristics' or 'customs classification'. It did appeal the panel's findings regarding 'end-uses' and 'consumers' tastes and habits'. While the Appellate Body disagreed with certain aspects of the panel's analysis, it did agree with the panel that the 'likeness' criteria it examined supported its overall conclusion that clove cigarettes and menthol cigarettes are 'like' products within the meaning of Article 2.1 of the *TBT Agreement*.[92]

In *US – Clove Cigarettes (2012)*, the Appellate Body also noted that, while the products identified by the complainant are the starting point of a panel's 'likeness' analysis, a panel is not limited to those products specifically identified by the complainant when it determines the scope of like imported and domestic products. The Appellate Body held that:

> Article 2.1 requires panels to assess objectively, on the basis of the nature and extent of the competitive relationship between the products in the market of the regulating Member, the universe of domestic products that are like the products imported from the complaining Member.[93]

3.1.3 'Treatment No Less Favourable'

The third and last element of the test of consistency with the non-discrimination obligations of Article 2.1 of the *TBT Agreement* relates to the question of whether the measure at issue accords 'treatment no less favourable'. As discussed below, the fact that a measure distinguishes between 'like products' does not suffice to conclude that this measure is inconsistent with Article 2.1.[94] To establish inconsistency with Article 2.1, a panel must examine whether or not imported products are accorded 'treatment no less favourable' than like products imported from other countries (the MFN treatment obligation) or like domestic products (national treatment obligation).

As discussed in Chapter 5 in the context of national treatment under the GATT 1994, there is well-established case law on the term 'treatment no less

91 Appellate Body Report, *US – Clove Cigarettes (2012)*, para. 120. See also *ibid.*, para. 156. For the relevant case law under Article III:4 of the GATT 1994, see above, pp. 376–99.

92 *Ibid.*, para. 160.

93 See *ibid.*, para. 192. Note, however, that this does not absolve the complainant from making a *prima facie* case of violation of Article 2.1. See *ibid.*

94 See below, pp. 905–7.

favourable' in Article III:4 of the GATT 1994. Recall that the Appellate Body ruled in *Korea – Various Measures on Beef (2001)* that:

> [w]hether or not imported products are treated 'less favourably' than like domestic products should be assessed ... by examining whether a measure modifies the *conditions of competition* in the relevant market to the detriment of imported products.[95]

According to this case law regarding Article III:4, the term 'treatment no less favourable' prohibits WTO Members from modifying the conditions of competition in the marketplace to the detriment of the group of imported products vis-à-vis the group of domestic like products.[96] According to this same case law, Article III:4 prohibits both *de jure* and *de facto* less favourable treatment.[97] While the Appellate Body was mindful that the term 'treatment no less favourable' in Article 2.1 of the *TBT Agreement* is to be interpreted in the light of the specific context provided by the *TBT Agreement*, the Appellate Body nonetheless considered in *US – Clove Cigarettes (2012)* the case law on the term 'treatment no less favourable' in Article III:4 of the GATT 1994 to be 'instructive' in assessing the meaning of the term 'treatment no less favourable' in Article 2.1.[98] Inspired by the case law regarding Article III:4, the Appellate Body ruled in *US – Clove Cigarettes (2012)* that the 'treatment no less favourable' requirement of Article 2.1 prohibited both *de jure* and *de facto* discrimination against imported products, and that:

> a panel examining a claim of violation under Article 2.1 should seek to ascertain whether the technical regulation at issue modifies the conditions of competition in the market of the regulating Member to the detriment of the group of imported products *vis-à-vis* the group of like domestic products.[99]

However, while a detrimental impact on the competitive conditions in the relevant market may be sufficient to establish a violation of Article III:4 of the GATT 1994, the Appellate Body unequivocally stated in *US – Clove Cigarettes (2012)* that the existence of such detrimental impact is *not sufficient* to establish a violation of Article 2.1 of the *TBT Agreement*. The Appellate Body ruled that:

> where the technical regulation at issue does not *de jure* discriminate against imports, the existence of a detrimental impact on competitive opportunities for the group of imported *vis-à-vis* the group of domestic like products is not dispositive of less favourable treatment under Article 2.1.[100]

95 Appellate Body Report, *Korea – Various Measures on Beef (2001)*, para. 137.
96 See above, pp. 395–9. 97 See above, pp. 395–9.
98 See Appellate Body Report, *US – Clove Cigarettes (2012)*, para. 180. More generally, the Appellate Body found that '[t]he very similar formulation of the provisions, and the overlap in their scope of application in respect of technical regulations, confirm that Article III:4 of the GATT 1994 is relevant context for the interpretation of the national treatment obligation of Article 2.1 of the TBT Agreement'. See *ibid.*, para. 100.
99 Appellate Body Report, *US – Clove Cigarettes (2012)*, para. 180.
100 *Ibid.*, para. 182. See also *ibid.*, para. 215.

According to the Appellate Body, a panel must in such cases of *de facto* discrimination:

further analyze whether the detrimental impact on imports stems exclusively from a legitimate regulatory distinction rather than reflecting discrimination against the group of imported products.[101]

To determine whether the detrimental impact stems exclusively from a legitimate regulatory distinction rather than reflecting discrimination, a panel must:

carefully scrutinize the particular circumstances of the case, that is, the design, architecture, revealing structure, operation, and application of the technical regulation at issue, and, in particular, whether that technical regulation is even-handed, in order to determine whether it discriminates against the group of imported products.[102]

The Appellate Body came to this understanding of the meaning of the term 'treatment no less favourable' in Article 2.1 of the *TBT Agreement* on the basis of its context and the object and purpose of the *TBT Agreement*. With regard to the context of the term 'treatment no less favourable', the Appellate Body referred to Annex 1.1,[103] Article 2.2[104] and the sixth recital of the Preamble[105] to the *TBT Agreement*. The Appellate Body emphasised, in particular, that, while the *TBT Agreement* does not contain a general exceptions clause similar to Article XX of the GATT 1994,[106] the WTO Members recognise in the sixth recital of the Preamble to the *TBT Agreement* that 'no country should be prevented from taking measures necessary' to pursue policy objectives such as the protection of public health, the protection of the environment and the protection of the consumer. As the sixth recital of the Preamble states, countries should not be prevented from taking such measures 'subject to the requirement that [these measures] are not applied in a manner which would constitute a means of arbitrary or unjustifiable discrimination between countries where the same conditions prevail or a disguised restriction on international trade, and are otherwise in accordance with the provisions of this Agreement'. With regard to the object and purpose of the *TBT Agreement*, the Appellate Body noted that the object and purpose of the *TBT Agreement* is to strike a balance between, on the one hand, the objective of trade liberalisation and, on the other hand, a Member's right to regulate.[107] Thus, the Appellate Body interpreted the 'treatment no less favourable' requirement of Article 2.1 as:

prohibiting both *de jure* and *de facto* discrimination against imported products, while at the same time permitting detrimental impact on competitive opportunities for imports that stems exclusively from legitimate regulatory distinctions.[108]

101 *Ibid.*, para. 182. See also *ibid.*, para. 215. Note that the measure at issue may draw many regulatory distinctions. The only regulatory distinction which matters here is the regulatory distinction that accounts for the detrimental impact on the conditions of competition. See Appellate Body Report, *US – Tuna II (Mexico) (2012)*, para. 286.

102 Appellate Body Report, *US – Clove Cigarettes (2012)*, para. 182.

103 See *ibid.*, para. 169. 104 See *ibid.*, paras. 170–1.

105 See *ibid.*, paras. 172–3. 106 See *ibid.*, para. 101.

107 See *ibid.*, para. 174. See also *ibid.*, paras. 94 and 95. 108 *Ibid.*, para. 175.

As discussed in Chapter 5, the national treatment obligation of Article III:4 of the GATT 1994 does not require Members to accord no less favourable treatment to *each and every* imported product as compared to *each and every* domestic like product. Recall that regulatory distinctions between like products are not inconsistent with the national treatment obligation of Article III:4 as long as the treatment accorded to the *group* of imported products is no less favourable than the treatment accorded to the *group* of like domestic products.[109] In *US – Clove Cigarettes (2012)*, the Appellate Body ruled that the same is true for the national treatment obligation of Article 2.1 of the *TBT Agreement*.[110] The Appellate Body also stated that when examining a claim of *de facto* discrimination a panel must base its determination of detrimental impact on the conditions of competition:

> on the totality of facts and circumstances before it, including the design, architecture, revealing structure, operation, and application of the technical regulation at issue.[111]

In *US – Clove Cigarettes (2012)*, the Appellate Body held that the design, architecture, revealing structure, operation and application of the measure at issue (a US ban on clove cigarettes and other flavoured cigarettes, with the exception of menthol cigarettes) strongly suggested that the detrimental impact on competitive opportunities for clove cigarettes reflects discrimination against the group of like products imported from Indonesia. Note that the 'vast majority' of clove cigarettes consumed in the United States came from Indonesia, while almost all menthol cigarettes consumed in the United States were produced in the United States.[112] Moreover, the Appellate Body was not persuaded that the detrimental impact of the measure at issue on competitive opportunities for imported clove cigarettes stemmed from a legitimate regulatory distinction.[113] The Appellate Body ultimately upheld, albeit for different reasons, the panel's finding that, by exempting menthol cigarettes from the ban on flavoured cigarettes, the measure at issue accorded to clove cigarettes imported from Indonesia less favourable treatment than that accorded to domestic like products, and was, therefore, inconsistent with the national treatment obligation of Article 2.1 of the *TBT Agreement*.[114]

In *US – Tuna II (Mexico) (2012)*, *US – COOL (2012)*, *US – Tuna II (Mexico) (Article 21.5) (2015)*, and *US – COOL (Article 21.5 – Canada and Mexico) (2015)*, the Appellate Body built on, and further clarified, the two-step analysis, set out in *US – Clove Cigarettes (2012)*, to determine whether a technical

109 See above, p. 396. 110 See Appellate Body Report, *US – Clove Cigarettes (2012)*, para. 193.

111 Appellate Body Reports, *US – Clove Cigarettes (2012)*, para. 206.

112 See *ibid.*, para. 224. 113 See *ibid.*, para. 225.

114 Note that the Appellate Body expressly stated that it was not saying that a Member cannot adopt measures to pursue legitimate health objectives such as curbing and preventing youth smoking. The Appellate Body stated: 'In particular, we are not saying that the United States cannot ban clove cigarettes: however, if it chooses to do so, this has to be done consistently with the TBT Agreement.' See *ibid.*, para. 236.

regulation accords 'treatment no less favourable' within the meaning of Article 2.1 of the *TBT Agreement.*

With regard to the first step of this analysis, namely the question whether the measure at issue distorts the conditions of competition to the detriment of imported products, the Appellate Body noted in *US – Tuna II (Mexico) (2012)* that there must be a *genuine relationship* between the measure at issue and the detrimental impact on competitive opportunities for imported products for the measure at issue to be found to modify the conditions of competition to the detriment of imported products.[115]

In *US – COOL (2012)*, the Appellate Body held that:

> Such an examination must take account of all the relevant features of the market, which may include the particular characteristics of the industry at issue, the relative market shares in a given industry, consumer preferences, and historical trade patterns. That is, a panel must examine the operation of the particular technical regulation at issue in the particular market in which it is applied.[116]

The Appellate Body also held in *US – COOL (2012)* that a panel is not required to ground its findings on the detrimental impact of the measure at issue on evidence of the actual trade effects of that measure.[117] Rather a panel may reach its findings on the detrimental impact on the basis of evidence and arguments discernible from the 'design, structure, and expected operation of the measure'.[118] Furthermore, in *US – COOL (Article 21.5 – Canada and Mexico) (2015)*, the Appellate Body held that a panel, in analysing the detrimental impact of the measure at issue, is not limited to scenarios that are representative of *current* patterns of trade.[119] However, a panel's analysis must be grounded on scenarios under which competitive opportunities *may* arise.[120]

As discussed above, the second step of the 'treatment no less favourable' analysis under Article 2.1 of the *TBT Agreement*, as set out by the Appellate Body in *US – Clove Cigarettes (2012)*, concerns the question of whether the detrimental impact stems exclusively from a legitimate regulatory distinction. In *US – Tuna II (Mexico) (2012)*, the Appellate Body held that the detrimental impact of the measure at issue (a measure establishing the conditions for use of a 'dolphin-safe' label on tuna products) did not stem exclusively from a legitimate regulatory distinction because of the *lack of even-handedness* of the measure in addressing the risks to dolphins.[121] The United States had argued that the difference in labelling conditions was 'calibrated' to the risks to dolphins arising

115 See Appellate Body Report, *US – Tuna II (Mexico) (2012)*, fn. 457 to para. 214. See also Appellate Body Reports, *US – COOL (2012)*, para. 270. See also above, pp. 390–9, with regard the 'no less favourable treatment' requirement under Article III:4 of the GATT 1994.

116 Appellate Body Reports, *US – COOL (2012)*, para. 269. 117 *Ibid.*, para. 325.

118 *Ibid.*, para. 269, referring to Appellate Body Report, *Thailand – Cigarettes (Philippines) (2011)*, para. 130.

119 Appellate Body Reports, *US – COOL (Article 21.5 – Canada and Mexico) (2015)*, para. 5.15.

120 *Ibid.*, para. 5.16. 121 Appellate Body Report, *US – Tuna II (Mexico) (2012)*, para. 298.

from different fishing methods in different areas of the oceans. The Appellate Body considered that the United States had not demonstrated that this was the case.[122] The Appellate Body noted, in particular, that:

> the US measure *fully* addresses the adverse effects on dolphins resulting from setting on dolphins [i.e. a fishing method particularly used by Mexican tuna fishers] in the ETP [Eastern Tropical Pacific where Mexican tuna fishers were primarily active], whereas it does 'not address mortality (observed or unobserved) arising from fishing methods other than setting on dolphins outside the ETP'. In these circumstances, we are not persuaded that the United States has demonstrated that the measure is even-handed in the relevant respects, even accepting that the fishing technique of setting on dolphins is particularly harmful to dolphins.[123]

In *US – COOL (2012)*, the Appellate Body ruled that to determine whether the detrimental impact of the measure at issue stems exclusively from a legitimate regulatory distinction, one must examine whether the measure at issue:

> is designed and applied in an even-handed manner, or whether it lacks even-handedness, for example, because it is designed or applied in a manner that constitutes a means of arbitrary or unjustifiable discrimination, and thus reflects discrimination in violation of Article 2.1 of the *TBT Agreement*.[124]

The Appellate Body also ruled that:

> the regulatory distinctions drawn by the [measures at issue] are designed or applied in a manner that constitutes arbitrary or unjustifiable discrimination, those distinctions cannot be considered 'legitimate'.[125]

In order to make that determination, one must scrutinise the particular circumstances of the case, including the design, architecture, revealing structure, operation and application of the measure at issue.[126]

In *US – COOL (2012)*, the Appellate Body held that informational requirements imposed on upstream producers and processors by the measure at issue (a US measure imposing a requirement on retailers selling beef and pork to label those products with their country of origin) were *disproportionate* as compared to the level of information communicated to consumers through the retail labels. The detailed information on origin required to be tracked and transmitted by upstream producers and processors was not necessarily conveyed to consumers through the labels prescribed under the COOL measure. This was because the prescribed labels did not expressly identify specific production steps and contained confusing or inaccurate origin information, as well as because

122 *Ibid.*, para. 297. In isolation, this finding by the Appellate Body may be incorrectly read as suggesting that the burden was on the United States to demonstrate that the measure at issue was *not* inconsistent with Article 2.1. This is not so. The burden of proof is on the complainant, *in casu* Mexico. Mexico had, however, made a *prima facie* case that the measure at issue was inconsistent with Article 2.1, and the Appellate Body noted that the United States failed to rebut this *prima facie* case. See *ibid.*, para. 216. See also Appellate Body Reports, *US – COOL (2012)*, para. 272.

123 Appellate Body Report, *US – Tuna II (Mexico) (2012)*, para. 297.

124 Appellate Body Reports, *US – COOL (2012)*, para. 340. See also, para. 271.

125 *Ibid.* See also para. 271.

126 See *ibid.* See also para. 271.

much beef and pork were exempted from the labelling requirements. According to the Appellate Body, nothing in the panel's findings or on the panel record explained or supplied a rational basis for the 'disconnect' between the informational requirements imposed on upstream producers and processors and the level of information communicated to consumers.[127] The Appellate Body, therefore, considered that the manner in which the measure at issue sought to provide information on origin to consumers was arbitrary, and that the disproportionate burden on upstream producers and processors was unjustifiable.[128] The Appellate Body thus came to the conclusion that the regulatory distinctions imposed by the COOL measure amounted to arbitrary and unjustifiable discrimination against imported livestock, such that they could not be said to be applied in an even-handed manner. The detrimental impact of the COOL measure did therefore not exclusively stem from legitimate regulatory distinctions and the COOL measure was thus inconsistent with Article 2.1 of the *TBT Agreement*.[129]

In *US – COOL (Article 21.5 – Canada and Mexico) (2015)*, the Appellate Body stated:

> if a panel finds that a technical regulation has a *de facto* detrimental impact on competitive opportunities for like imported products, the focus of the inquiry shifts to whether such detrimental impact stems exclusively from legitimate regulatory distinctions. This inquiry probes the legitimacy of regulatory distinctions through careful scrutiny of whether they are designed and applied in an even-handed manner such that they may be considered 'legitimate' for the purposes of Article 2.1.[130]

The Appellate Body also held in *US – COOL (Article 21.5 – Canada and Mexico) (2015)* that the assessment of even-handedness *focuses* on the regulatory distinction(s) causing the detrimental impact on imported products.[131] However, for that assessment, other elements of the technical regulation are *relevant* to the extent that they are probative of whether such detrimental impact stems exclusively from legitimate regulatory distinctions.[132]

Referring to its report in *US – COOL (2012)*, the Appellate Body in *US – COOL (Article 21.5 – Canada and Mexico) (2015)* recalled that regulatory distinctions are not designed and applied in an even-handed manner and are thus not 'legitimate, "when they are applied" in a manner that constitutes arbitrary or unjustifiable discrimination'.[133] With regard to the amended COOL measure, i.e. the measure adopted by the United States to comply with the recommendations and rulings in *US – COOL (2012)*, the panel in *US – COOL (Article 21.5 – Canada and Mexico) (2015)* found that this measure did address and correct a number of deficiencies of the original COOL measure. However, the panel also found that

127 See *ibid.*, para. 347. 128 See *ibid.*, paras. 347–9. 129 See *ibid.*, para. 349.
130 Appellate Body Reports, *US – COOL (Article 21.5 – Canada and Mexico) (2015)*, para. 5.92.
131 Appellate Body Report, *US – Tuna II (Mexico) (Article 21.5)*, para. 5.93, referring to Appellate Body Report, *US – Tuna II (Mexico) (2012)*, para. 286.
132 Appellate Body Reports, *US – COOL (Article 21.5 – Canada and Mexico) (2015)*, para. 5.93.
133 *Ibid.*, paras. 5.91–5.92, referring to Appellate Body Reports, *US – COOL*, para. 271.

the amended COOL measure entailed an increased recordkeeping burden and a potential for label inaccuracy, as well as continued to exempt a large proportion of beef and pork from the coverage of the measure.[134] For these reasons, the Article 21.5 panel found, as the Appellate Body had done in *US – COOL (2012)*, that the manner in which the amended COOL measure sought to provide information on origin to consumers was arbitrary and the disproportionate (recordkeeping and verification) burden imposed on upstream producers and processors was unjustifiable. The Article 21.5 panel therefore concluded that, under the particular circumstances of the case, the detrimental impact caused by the amended COOL measure did not stem exclusively from legitimate regulatory distinctions, and that the amended COOL measure was inconsistent with Article 2.1 of the *TBT Agreement*.[135] On appeal, the Appellate Body upheld the panel's conclusion regarding the inconsistency of the amended COOL measure with Article 2.1 of the *TBT Agreement*.[136]

Referring to the Appellate Body's case law on the chapeau on Article XX of the GATT 1994, the panel in *US – Tuna II (Mexico) (Article 21.5) (2015)* stated that, in determining whether the detrimental impact stems exclusively from a legitimate regulatory distinction, it could consider whether the detrimental treatment can be reconciled with, or is rationally related to, the policy pursued by the measure at issue.[137] On appeal the United States argued that this was an 'erroneous articulation' of the 'treatment no less favourable' requirement under Article 2.1 of the *TBT Agreement*. The Appellate Body held that:

> a panel does not err by assessing whether the detrimental impact can be reconciled with, or is rationally related to, the policy pursued by the measure at issue, so long as, in doing so, it does not preclude consideration of other factors that may also be relevant to the analysis.[138]

In *US – Tuna II (Mexico) (Article 21.5) (2015)*, the Appellate Body also noted that:

> the fact that a measure is designed in a manner that constitutes a means of arbitrary or unjustifiable discrimination is *not* the only way in which a measure may lack even-handedness, such that the detrimental impact cannot be said to stem exclusively from legitimate regulatory distinctions.[139]

The Appellate Body further clarified that:

> as the term itself implies, 'even-handedness' is a relational concept, and must be tested through a comparative analysis.[140]

The Appellate Body explained that regulatory distinctions by definition treat groups of products differently, and that is therefore only through examining

134 See Panel Reports, *US – COOL (Article 21.5 – Canada and Mexico) (2015)*, para. 7.282.
135 See *ibid.*, paras. 7.283–7.284.
136 Appellate Body Reports, *US – COOL (Article 21.5 – Canada and Mexico) (2015)*, para. 6.2.
137 Panel Report, *US – Tuna II (Mexico) (Article 21.5) (2015)*, para. 7.91.
138 Appellate Body Report, *US – Tuna II (Mexico) (Article 21.5) (2015)*, para. 7.95.
139 *Ibid.*, para. 7.31. 140 *Ibid.*, para. 7.125.

the treatment accorded to all the groups that are being compared that a proper assessment of 'even-handedness' can be made.[141] With direct reference to the case at hand, the Appellate Body explained:

> Whether a regulatory distinction that involves a denial of access to the dolphin-safe label in respect of setting on dolphins is even-handed depends not only on how the risks associated with this method of fishing are addressed, but also on whether the risks associated with other fishing methods in other fisheries are addressed, commensurately with their respective risk profiles, in the labelling conditions that apply in respect of tuna caught in such other fisheries.[142]

The amended tuna measure, i.e. the measure adopted by the United States to comply with the recommendations and rulings in *US – Tuna II (Mexico) (2012)*, modified the original tuna measure in a way that affected the treatment of only one of the two groups of tuna products, namely the tuna products containing tuna caught by setting on dolphins in the Eastern Tropical Pacific (ETP). According to the Appellate Body, the legal significance of the changed treatment afforded to this group of tuna products could not properly be understood by examining that group in isolation.[143] It is only through an examination of the treatment accorded to both the groups of tuna products, i.e. the tuna products containing tuna caught by setting on dolphins in the ETP, on the one hand, and the tuna products containing tuna caught by other fishing methods outside the ETP, on the other hand, that a proper assessment of the even-handedness of the measure at issue could be made.[144] The Appellate Body found the panel in *US – Tuna II (Mexico) (Article 21.5) (2015)* failed to engage in such an examination, and therefore reversed the panel's findings of inconsistency with Article 2.1.[145] However, the panel's limited evaluation of the relative risks for dolphins associated with different fishing methods in different areas of the oceans significantly constrained the Appellate Body's ability to complete the legal analysis on the even-handedness of the amended tuna measure. Only one feature of this measure, namely the 'determination provisions', was not dependent on an evaluation of the relative risks associated with different fishing methods in different areas of the oceans.[146] With regard to these 'determination provisions', the Appellate Body observed that they did 'not provide for the substantive conditions of access to the dolphin-safe label to be reinforced by observer certification in all circumstances of comparably high risks'.[147] The Appellate Body therefore held that it had not been demonstrated that the differences in the dolphin-safe labelling conditions under the amended tuna measure were 'calibrated' to the risks to dolphins

141 See *ibid.* 142 *Ibid.*, para. 7.126.
143 See *ibid.*, para. 7.127. 144 See *ibid.*, para. 7.129.
145 See *ibid.*, para. 7.130.
146 The 'determination provisions' are those provisions in the amended tuna measure that authorise the Assistant Administrator of the US National Marine Fisheries Service (NMFS) to impose observer certification in any such other fishery upon determining that the risks to dolphins in that fishery are similar to those arising in the ETP large purse-seine fishery.
147 See Appellate Body Report, *US – Tuna II (Mexico) (Article 21.5) (2015)*, para. 7.266.

arising from different fishing methods in different areas of the oceans.[148] The detrimental impact of the amended tuna measure could thus not be said to stem exclusively from a legitimate regulatory distinction. The Appellate Body concluded that the amended tuna measure was inconsistent with the 'treatment no less favourable' obligation of Article 2.1 of the *TBT Agreement*.[149]

3.2 Obligation to Refrain from Creating Unnecessary Obstacles to International Trade

The first sentence of Article 2.2 of the *TBT Agreement* provides that, with respect to technical regulations:

> Members shall ensure that technical regulations are not prepared, adopted or applied with a view to or with the effect of creating unnecessary obstacles to international trade.

With respect to standards and conformity assessment procedures, Annex 3.E and Article 5.1.2 of the *TBT Agreement* provide for the same obligation that such measures shall not be 'prepared, adopted or applied with the view to, or the effect of, creating unnecessary obstacles to trade'.[150]

The first sentence of Article 2.2 is followed by a second sentence, which reads:

> For this purpose, technical regulations shall not be more trade-restrictive than necessary to fulfil a legitimate objective, taking account of the risks non-fulfilment would create.[151]

With regard to the relationship between the first and second sentences of Article 2.2, the Appellate Body observed that both the first and second sentences of Article 2.2 reflect the notion of 'necessity'. In the first sentence, this is through the reference to '*unnecessary* obstacles to international trade'; in the second sentence through the reference to 'not ... more trade restrictive than *necessary*'.[152] The Appellate Body also observed that these sentences are linked by the term '[f]or this purpose' and it found that this suggests that the second sentence qualifies the terms of the first sentence and elaborates on the scope and the meaning of the obligation contained in the first sentence.[153]

The third sentence of Article 2.2 enumerates several of the 'legitimate objectives' to which the second sentence refers. This list of legitimate objectives includes: (1) national security; (2) the prevention of deceptive practices; (3) the protection of human health and safety, animal or plant life or health; and (4) the protection of the environment.

148 See *ibid.* 149 See *ibid.*

150 Annex 3.E to the *TBT Agreement*. With respect to conformity assessment procedures, the implementation of this obligation is further specified in Articles 5.2.2, 5.2.3, 5.2.6 and 5.2.7 of the *TBT Agreement*.

151 For conformity assessment procedures, a similar provision is contained in Article 5.1.2, second sentence, of the *TBT Agreement*.

152 See Appellate Body Report, *US – Tuna II (Mexico) (2012)*, para. 318. See also Appellate Body Reports, *US – COOL (2012)*, para. 374.

153 See Appellate Body Report, *US – Tuna II (Mexico) (2012)*, para. 318.

Finally, the fourth sentence of Article 2.2 refers back to the final clause of the second sentence, namely, 'taking account of the risks non-fulfilment would create'. The fourth sentence states that, in assessing such risks, it is relevant to consider, *inter alia*: (1) available scientific information; (2) related processing technology; or (3) intended end uses of products.

Article 2.2 sets out a four-tier test of consistency. There are four main questions which must be answered to determine whether or not a measure is consistent with Article 2.2, namely: (1) whether the measure at issue is a 'technical regulation' within the meaning of Annex 1.1; (2) whether the measure at issue is '*trade-restrictive*'; (3) whether the measure at issue *fulfils a legitimate objective*; and (4) whether the measure at issue is '*not more trade-restrictive than necessary*' to fulfil a legitimate objective, taking account of the risks non-fulfilment would create.

Below, each element of this four-tier test of consistency will be discussed in turn.

To date, no WTO Member has been found to have acted inconsistently with Article 2.2 of the *TBT Agreement*.[154]

3.2.1 'Technical Regulations'

With regard to this first element of the test of consistency with Article 2.2 of the *TBT Agreement*, namely, whether the measure at issue is a 'technical regulation' within the meaning of Annex 1.1, refer to the discussion above on the scope of application of the *TBT Agreement*.[155]

3.2.2 'Trade-Restrictive'

The second element of the test of consistency with Article 2.2 of the *TBT Agreement* relates to the question of whether the measure at issue is 'trade-restrictive'. In *US – Tuna II (Mexico) (2012)*, the Appellate Body defined 'trade-restrictive' to mean 'having a limiting effect on trade'.[156] It is clear that the mere fact that a measure is 'trade-restrictive' does not make that measure inconsistent with Article 2.2. In fact, the reference in the first sentence of Article 2.2 to 'unnecessary obstacles to international trade' implies that *some* trade-restrictiveness is allowed.[157] It is, however, equally clear from the text of Article 2.2 that measures that are not trade-restrictive cannot be inconsistent with Article 2.2. A measure that is *not* trade-restrictive can never be *more* trade-restrictive than necessary. In this

154 The panel in *US – COOL (2012)* had found that the United States acted inconsistently with Article 2.2. The Appellate Body, however, found that the panel had erred in its interpretation and application of Article 2.2 and thus reversed the panel's finding of inconsistency, but was unable to complete the legal analysis. With regard to *EC – Seal Products (2014)*, note that after reversing the panel's finding that the EU Seal Regime is a 'technical regulation', the Appellate Body declared the panel's conclusions under Article 2.2 of the *TBT Agreement* moot and of no legal effect. See Appellate Body Reports, *EC – Seal Products (2014)*, para. 5.70.

155 See above, pp. 885–99.

156 See Appellate Body Report, *US – Tuna II (Mexico) (2012)*, para. 319.

157 See *ibid*. What is prohibited under Article 2.2 are restrictions on international trade which exceed what is necessary to fulfil a legitimate objective. See below, pp. 903–4.

sense, the trade-restrictiveness of the measure at issue is a threshold issue. It is unlikely that there will be many disputes in which the trade-restrictiveness *as such* of the measure at issue is contested between the parties. It is more likely that disagreement relating to the trade-restrictiveness relates to the *degree* of trade-restrictiveness. The degree of trade-restrictiveness is important in both the 'relational analysis' and the 'comparative analysis' under the fourth element of the test of consistency discussed below.[158]

3.2.3 Fulfilling a Legitimate Objective

The third element of the test of consistency with Article 2.2 of the *TBT Agreement* relates to the question of whether the measure at issue fulfils a legitimate objective. This question raises a number of intermediate questions, such as: (1) how to establish the objective pursued by the measure at issue; (2) which objectives are 'legitimate objectives' within the meaning of Article 2.2; (3) when a measure 'fulfil[s]' a legitimate objective; and (4) how to establish whether, and if so, to what extent, the measure at issue fulfils the legitimate objective pursued. Below, each of these intermediate questions will be addressed in turn.

With regard to the first intermediate question, namely, how to establish the objective pursued by the measure at issue, the Appellate Body ruled in *US – Tuna II (Mexico) (2012)* – referring to its ruling in *US – Gambling (2005)* relating to Article XIV of the GATS[159] – that a panel is *not* bound by a Member's characterisation of the objectives it pursues through the measure. While a panel may well take a Member's characterisation of the objectives as a starting point, it must independently and objectively assess the objective or objectives pursued. In doing so, a panel may take into account the text of statutes, the legislative history and other evidence regarding the structure and operation of the measure.[160]

With regard to the second intermediate question, namely, which objectives are 'legitimate objectives' within the meaning of Article 2.2 of the *TBT Agreement*, the Appellate Body observed in *US – Tuna II (Mexico) (2012)* that the dictionary meaning of the term 'legitimate objective' is an aim or target that is lawful, justifiable or proper.[161] As already noted above, the third sentence of Article 2.2 lists specific examples of such 'legitimate objectives', namely: (1) national security; (2) the prevention of deceptive practices; (3) the protection of human health and safety, animal or plant life or health; and (4) the protection of the environment.[162] However, as indicated by the words '*inter alia*' at the beginning of the list, this is *not* an exhaustive list of legitimate policy objectives.[163] It is an open question which other policy objectives may be considered to be legitimate

158 See below, pp. 903–405. 159 See above, pp. 608–11.
160 See Appellate Body Report, *US – Tuna II (Mexico) (2012)*, para. 314. See also Appellate Body Reports, *US – COOL (2012)*, para. 395.
161 See Appellate Body Report, *US – Tuna II (Mexico) (2012)*, para. 313. 162 See above, p. 913.
163 Recall that the list of legitimate policy objectives of Article XX of the GATT 1994 is an *exhaustive* list. See above, p. 546.

within the meaning of Article 2.2 of the *TBT Agreement*. Are animal welfare or fair labour practices '*legitimate* objectives' within the meaning of Article 2.2? As the Appellate Body stated in *US – Tuna II (Mexico) (2012)*, the objectives expressly listed provide an illustration and reference point for other objectives that may be considered 'legitimate'.[164] Also, the objectives recognised in the sixth and seventh recitals of the Preamble to the *TBT Agreement* as well as objectives reflected in the provisions of other WTO agreements may provide guidance for, or may inform, the analysis of what might be considered to be a legitimate objective under Article 2.2.[165] In *US – COOL (2012)*, the Appellate Body considered the provision of information to consumers on origin to be a 'legitimate objective'. The Appellate Body reasoned that this objective bears some relationship to the objective of the prevention of deceptive practices reflected in both Article 2.2 itself and Article XX(d) of the GATT 1994, and that the objective of providing information to consumers on origin is also found in Article IX of the GATT 1994.[166] Whether objectives not reflected in the WTO agreements may nevertheless be 'legitimate objectives' for the purpose of Article 2.2 is a question which is likely to give rise to some debate. It is, however, important to note in this regard that it is for the complainant to prove that an objective is *not* legitimate within the meaning of Article 2.2. The respondent does not have to prove that an objective is legitimate.[167]

With regard to the third intermediate question, namely, when does a measure 'fulfil' a legitimate objective, or, in other words, what does 'fulfil' mean in this context, the Appellate Body observed in *US – Tuna II (Mexico) (2012)* that the word 'fulfil' is defined in the dictionary as 'provide *fully* with what is wished for'.[168] The Appellate Body recognised that, read in isolation, the word 'fulfil' appears to describe complete achievement of something. However, the Appellate Body considered that, in Article 2.2 of the *TBT Agreement*, the word 'fulfil' is used in the phrase 'to fulfil a legitimate objective', and that it is inherent in the notion of an 'objective' that it may be pursued and achieved to a greater or lesser degree.[169] The Appellate Body thus ruled that:

> we consider that the question of whether a technical regulation 'fulfils' an objective is concerned with the *degree of contribution* that the technical regulation makes toward the achievement of the legitimate objective.[170]

That degree of contribution towards the achievement of the legitimate objective is of significant importance in both the 'relational analysis' and the

164 See Appellate Body Report, *US – Tuna II (Mexico) (2012)*, para. 313. See also Appellate Body Reports, *US – COOL (2012)*, para. 444.

165 See Appellate Body Report, *US – Tuna II (Mexico) (2012)*, para. 313.

166 See Appellate Body Reports, *US – COOL (2012)*, para. 445.

167 See *ibid*., para. 449.

168 Appellate Body Report, *US – Tuna II (Mexico) (2012)*, para. 315. Emphasis added.

169 See *ibid*. Note that the panel in *US – COOL (2012)* wrongly considered it necessary for the measure at issue to have 'fulfilled' the objective completely (or at least to have satisfied some minimum level of fulfilment) to be consistent with Article 2.2.

170 Appellate Body Report, *US – Tuna II (Mexico) (2012)*, para. 315. Emphasis added.

'comparative analysis' under the fourth element of the test of consistency discussed below.[171]

With regard to the fourth and last intermediate question, namely, how to establish whether, and, if so, to what extent, the measure at issue fulfils the legitimate objective pursued, the Appellate Body noted in *US – Tuna II (Mexico) (2012)* that the degree of fulfilment of the objective pursued, i.e. the degree of contribution towards the achievement of the objective, may be discerned from the design, structure and operation of the technical regulation, *as well as* from evidence relating to the application of the measure.[172] As in the context of Article XX of the GATT 1994 and Article XIV of the GATS,[173] a panel must also in the context of Article 2.2 of the *TBT Agreement* assess the contribution to the legitimate objective *actually achieved* by the measure at issue, not the contribution that is intended to be achieved.[174]

3.2.4 'Not More Trade-Restrictive Than Necessary'

The fourth and last element of the test of consistency with Article 2.2 of the *TBT Agreement* relates to the question of whether the measure at issue is '*not more trade-restrictive than necessary*' to fulfil a legitimate objective, taking account of the risks non-fulfilment would create. As discussed in Chapter 8, in the context of Article XX of the GATT 1994 and Article XIV of the GATS, it is the measure at issue, which is assessed for 'necessity'.[175] As is clear from the text of Article 2.2, in the context of this provision, it is not the measure but the *trade-restrictiveness* of the measure, which is assessed for 'necessity'.[176] In *US – Tuna II (Mexico) (2012)*, the Appellate Body found that in the assessment of whether a technical regulation is 'not more trade-restrictive than necessary' within the meaning of Article 2.2 of the *TBT Agreement*:

> a panel should begin by considering factors that include: (i) the degree of contribution made by the measure to the legitimate objective at issue; (ii) the trade-restrictiveness of the measure; and (iii) the nature of the risks at issue and the gravity of consequences that would arise from non-fulfilment of the objective(s) pursued by the Member through the measure.[177]

171 See below, p. 917. 172 See Appellate Body Report, *US – Tuna II (Mexico) (2012)*, para. 317.
173 See above, p. 911.
174 See Appellate Body Report, *US – Tuna II (Mexico) (2012)*, para. 317. See also Appellate Body Reports, *US – COOL (2012)*, paras. 373 and 390.
175 See e.g. Panel Report, *China – Audiovisual Products (2010)*, para. 7.789, referring to Appellate Body Report, *US – Gasoline (1996)*.
176 See Appellate Body Report, *US – Tuna II (Mexico) (2012)*, para. 319.
177 *Ibid.*, para. 322. See also Appellate Body Reports, *US – COOL (2012)*, para. 471; and Appellate Body Reports, *US – COOL (Article 21.5 – Canada and Mexico) (2015)*, para. 5.197. While, as discussed in Chapter 8, in the context of the necessity analysis under Article XX of the GATT 1994 and Article XIV of the GATS, the relative importance of the objective pursued is a separate factor to be considered, the relative importance of the objective pursued is not relevant in the context of the necessity analysis under Article 2.2 of the *TBT Agreement*. Instead, a panel is to address the 'risk nonfulfilment of the objective would create', which has been specifically identified by the Appellate Body as a factor of the Article 2.2 legal test. However, the importance of the objective to the Member pursuing the technical regulation at issue could inform the analysis under Article 2.2 in some capacity, such as to the extent it is reflected in the level considered appropriate by the Member at which to pursue the relevant objective, or the actual degree of contribution made by the technical regulation to its objective.

The Appellate Body referred to this analysis as a 'relational analysis' of the factors referred to above.[178] The Appellate Body immediately added, however, that, *in most cases*:

> a comparison of the challenged measure and possible alternative measures should be undertaken.[179]

In other words, in addition to a 'relational analysis', *in most cases* also a 'comparative analysis' should be undertaken to establish whether a technical regulation is 'more trade-restrictive than necessary'.[180] In the context of such 'comparative analysis', it may be relevant to consider in particular: (1) whether the proposed alternative measure is less trade-restrictive; (2) whether it would make an equivalent contribution to the relevant legitimate objective, taking account of the risks non-fulfilment would create; and (3) whether it is reasonably available.[181]

As the Appellate Body stated in *US – Tuna II (Mexico) (2012)*, the assessment of whether a technical regulation is more trade restrictive than necessary under Article 2.2 of the *TBT Agreement* involves the *holistic weighing and balancing* of the factors set out above.[182] This weighing and balancing of factors called for under Article 2.2 is similar to the 'weighing and balancing' to establish 'necessity' in the context of Article XX of the GATT 1994 and Article XIV of the GATS, discussed in Chapter 8.[183]

In *US – COOL (Article 21.5 – Canada and Mexico) (2015)*, the Appellate Body held that Article 2.2 of the *TBT Agreement* does not explicitly prescribe, in

178 See Appellate Body Report, *US – Tuna II (Mexico) (2012)*, para. 318.

179 *Ibid.*, para. 322. Appellate Body Reports, *US – COOL*, para. 471 and fn. 950; and Appellate Body Reports, *US – COOL (Article 21.5 – Canada and Mexico) (2015)*, para. 5.197. The Appellate Body identified two instances where a comparison of the challenged measure and possible alternative measures may not be required, namely: (1) when the measure at issue is not trade-restrictive; and (2) when the measure makes *no* contribution to the achievement of the legitimate objective. See Appellate Body Report, *US – Tuna II (Mexico) (2012)*, fn. 647 to para. 322. See also Appellate Body Reports, *US – COOL (2012)*, fn. 748 to para. 376. Note that the Appellate Body stated in *US – COOL (Article 21.5 – Canada and Mexico) (2015)* that: 'given that an alternative measure proposed by a complainant functions as a "conceptual tool" to illustrate that a technical regulation is more trade restrictive than necessary, once an alternative measure has been proposed by the complainant, it should be considered by a panel in the overall weighing and balancing under Article 2.2'. See Appellate Body Reports, *US – COOL (Article 21.5 – Canada and Mexico) (2015)*, para. 5.213.

180 Appellate Body Report, *US – Tuna II (Mexico) (2012)*, para. 320. As the Appellate Body noted in *US – COOL (Article 21.5 – Canada and Mexico) (2015)*, the comparative character of Article 2.2 of the *TBT Agreement* is 'confirmed by the context afforded by Article 2.3 of the TBT Agreement, which provides that "[t]echnical regulations shall not be maintained if the circumstances or objectives giving rise to their adoption no longer exist or if the changed circumstances or objectives can be addressed *in a less trade-restrictive manner*"'. See Appellate Body Reports, *US – COOL (Article 21.5 – Canada and Mexico) (2015)*, para. 5.199.

181 See Appellate Body Report, *US – Tuna II (Mexico) (2012)*, para. 322. As the Appellate Body stated *ibid.*, para. 323, a complainant may, to make a *prima facie* case, have to 'identify a possible alternative measure that is less trade restrictive, makes an equivalent contribution to the relevant objective, and is reasonably available'. See also Appellate Body Reports, *US – COOL (Article 21.5 – Canada and Mexico) (2015)*, para. 5.213.

182 See Appellate Body Reports, *US – Tuna II (Mexico) (2012)*, fn. 643 to para. 318, referring to Appellate Body Report, *Brazil – Retreaded Tyres (2007)*, para. 178; and Appellate Body Report, *US – Gambling (2005)*, paras. 306–8.

183 See Appellate Body Report, *US – Tuna II (Mexico) (2012)*, fn. 645 to para. 320. See Appellate Body Reports, *US – COOL (2012)*, fn. 745 to para. 374 and fn. 750 to para. 376; and *US – Tuna II (Mexico) (2012)*, fn. 643 to para. 318 and fn. 645 to para. 320. For the discussion of 'weighing and balancing' to establish 'necessity' in the context of Article XX of the GATT 1994 and Article XIV of the GATS, see above, pp. 560–4 and 610–14.

rigid terms, the sequence and order of analysis in conducting the weighing and balancing under Article 2.2.[184] The particular manner of sequencing the steps of this analysis is adaptable, and may be tailored to the specific claims, measures, facts, and arguments at issue in a given case.[185] However, the degree of latitude to tailor the sequence and order of analysis is not boundless.[186]

With regard to the different factors that need to be weighed and balanced under Article 2.2 of the *TBT Agreement*, the Appellate Body recognised in *US – COOL (Article 21.5 – Canada and Mexico) (2015)* that 'it will not always be possible to quantify a particular factor, or to do so with precision'.[187] This is, however, not a reason for not proceeding with the weighing and balancing under Article 2.2. Referring to its case law regarding Article XX of the GATT 1994, the Appellate Body found that:

> [t]he weighing and balancing of the relevant factors both in respect of the challenged technical regulation and in the comparison with proposed alternative measures involves a holistic analysis in order to reach an overall conclusion on claims under Article 2.2. A panel should proceed with this weighing and balancing even if a particular factor under Article 2.2 ... cannot be quantified with precision or can only be assessed in qualitative terms.[188]

With respect to the requirement that the alternative measure makes an equivalent contribution to the relevant legitimate objective, the Appellate Body explained in *US – COOL (2012)* that this requirement stems from, *inter alia*, the principle, set out in the Preamble of the *TBT Agreement*, that a Member shall not be prevented from pursuing a legitimate objective 'at the levels it considers appropriate'.[189] In *US – COOL (Article 21.5 – Canada and Mexico) (2015)*, the Appellate Body clarified that the requirement that an alternative measure makes an *equivalent* contribution to the relevant legitimate objective, does not require a complainant to demonstrate that its proposed alternative measure achieves a degree of contribution *identical* to that achieved by the measure at issue.[190] According to the Appellate Body, there is:

> a margin of appreciation in the assessment of whether a proposed alternative measure achieves an equivalent degree of contribution, the contours of which may vary from case to case.[191]

184 See Appellate Body Reports, *US – COOL (Article 21.5 – Canada and Mexico) (2015)*, paras. 5.202–5.204 (referring to Appellate Body Report, *US – Tuna II (Mexico) (2012)*, fn. 643 to para. 318; Appellate Body Reports, *Brazil – Retreaded Tyres (2007)*, paras. 155 and 178; *US – Gambling (2005)*, paras. 306–7; and Appellate Body Report, *China – Publications and Audiovisual Products (2010)*, para. 242).

185 See Appellate Body Reports, *US – COOL (Article 21.5 – Canada and Mexico) (2015)*, para. 5.205.

186 See *ibid.*, para. 5.206. Note also that a certain sequence and order of analysis may flow logically from the nature of the examination under Article 2.2. See *ibid.*, para. 5.202. See also *ibid.*, paras. 5.235–5.236.

187 *Ibid.*, para. 5.208.

188 *Ibid.*, para. 5.211. The panel in this case failed to proceed with the weighing and balancing of the relevant factors. The Appellate Body referred to its reports in *Brazil – Retreaded Tyres (2007)* and *EC – Seal Products (2014)*.

189 Appellate Body Reports, *US – COOL (2012)*, para. 373. See also Appellate Body Reports, *US – COOL (Article 21.5 – Canada and Mexico) (2015)*, para. 5.214.

190 See Appellate Body Reports, *US – COOL (Article 21.5 – Canada and Mexico) (2015)*, para. 5.215.

191 *Ibid.*

The Appellate Body emphasised in this regard that a proposed alternative measure may 'achieve an equivalent degree of contribution in ways different from' the measure at issue.[192] The Appellate Body also noted that there may be instances in which it is difficult to assess with any precision whether there is equivalence in the contribution made.[193] Some imprecision in assessing the equivalence of the contribution made may be inevitable in certain circumstances.[194] Reaffirming a more general ruling referred to above,[195] the Appellate Body stated, however, that:

> such imprecision should not, in and of itself, relieve a panel from its duty to assess the equivalence of the respective degrees of contribution. In spite of such imprecision, a panel should proceed with the overall weighing and balancing under Article 2.2.[196]

As stated above, in assessing whether an alternative measure would make an equivalent contribution to the relevant legitimate objective, a panel must take account of the risks non-fulfilment would create. In *US – Tuna II (Mexico) (2012)*, the Appellate Body considered that this suggests that the comparison of the challenged measure with a possible alternative measure should be made:

> in the light of the nature of the risks at issue and the gravity of the consequences that would arise from non-fulfilment of the legitimate objective.[197]

It is clear that, for example, the risks created by non-fulfilment of the objective of preventing deceptive practices are less grave than the risks created by non-fulfilment of the objective of protecting human health.[198] In *US – COOL (Article 21.5 – Canada and Mexico) (2015)*, the Appellate Body noted that Article 2.2 of the *TBT Agreement* does not prescribe a particular methodology for assessing 'the risks non-fulfilment would create' or define how they should be 'tak[en] account of'. However, referring to its case law under Article XX of the GATT 1994, the Appellate Body ruled that 'risks may be assessed in either qualitative or quantitative terms', and that:

> in some contexts, it might be possible and appropriate to seek to determine separately the nature of the risks, on the one hand, and to quantify the gravity of the consequences that would arise from non-fulfilment, on the other hand. In other contexts, however, it might be difficult, in practice, to determine or quantify those elements separately with precision. In such contexts, it may be more appropriate to conduct a conjunctive analysis of both the

192 *Ibid.* Note that in *US – COOL (Article 21.5 – Canada and Mexico) (2015)* the Appellate Body found that the panel in that case did not err in contemplating that an alternative measure that would provide less or less accurate information but have significantly wider product coverage could qualify as making an 'equivalent' degree of contribution as compared to the measure at issue. See *ibid.*, para. 5.270.

193 See *ibid.*, para. 5.216.

194 See *ibid.*

195 See above, p. 918.

196 Appellate Body Reports, *US – COOL (Article 21.5 – Canada and Mexico) (2015)*, para. 5.216.

197 Appellate Body Report, *US – Tuna II (Mexico)*, para. 321. See also Appellate Body Reports, *US – COOL (Article 21.5 – Canada and Mexico) (2015)*, para. 5.217.

198 As mentioned above, the fourth sentence of Article 2.2 states that, in assessing the risks non-fulfilment would create, it is relevant to consider, *inter alia*: (1) available scientific information; (2) related processing technology; or (3) intended end uses of products. See above, p. 913.

> nature of the risks and the gravity of the consequences of non-fulfilment, in which 'the risks non-fulfilment would create' are assessed in qualitative terms.[199]

The Appellate Body ruled that Article 2.2 of the *TBT Agreement* requires in the weighing and balancing:

> an active and meaningful consideration of 'the risks non-fulfilment would create', even where there is imprecision as to the nature and magnitude of such risks.[200]

With regard to the requirement that alternative measures are 'reasonably available', the Appellate Body stated in *US – Tuna II (Mexico) (2012)* and again in *US – COOL (Article 21.5 – Canada and Mexico) (2015)* that:

> it is important to keep in mind that such 'reasonable availability' pertains to proposed alternative measures that function as 'conceptual tool[s]' to assist in assessing whether a technical regulation is more trade restrictive than necessary. Such alternative measures are of a hypothetical nature in the context of the analysis under Article 2.2 because they do not yet exist in the Member in question, or at least not in the particular form proposed by the complainant.[201]

According to the Appellate Body, these considerations should inform the nature and degree of evidence that the complainant must present to establish the 'reasonable availability' of proposed alternative measures in making a *prima facie* case of inconsistency of the measure at issue with Article 2.2. of the *TBT Agreement*.[202] Since the alternative measures are of a hypothetical nature the complainants cannot be expected 'to provide complete and exhaustive descriptions of the alternative measures they propose'.[203] As the Appellate Body stated:

> It would appear incongruous to expect a complainant, under Article 2.2 of the TBT Agreement, to provide detailed information on how a proposed alternative would be implemented by the respondent in practice, and precise and comprehensive estimates of the cost that such implementation would entail.[204]

In other words, a panel should not put too high a burden on a complainant for establishing *prima facie* that a proposed alternative measure is reasonably available. It would be more appropriate, for the respondent, once the complainant made a *prima facie* case, to establish that a proposed alternative measure is *not* reasonably available.[205] As discussed above in the context of Article XX of the GATT 1994, whether an alternative measure is reasonably available depends on the costs and technical difficulties associated with the implementation of this measure.[206]

199 See Appellate Body Reports, *US – COOL (Article 21.5 – Canada and Mexico) (2015)*, para. 5.128 (referring to Appellate Body Report, *EC – Asbestos (2001)*, para. 167).

200 *Ibid.*

201 *Ibid.*, para. 5.328. See also Appellate Body Report, *US – Tuna II (Mexico) (2012)*, para. 320.

202 See Appellate Body Reports, *US – COOL (Article 21.5 – Canada and Mexico) (2015)*, para. 5.328.

203 *Ibid.*, para. 5.334.

204 *Ibid.*, para. 5.338.

205 See *ibid.*, para. 5.339.

206 See above, p. 562. See also Appellate Body Reports, *US – COOL (Article 21.5 – Canada and Mexico) (2015)*, para. 5.339.

A technical regulation, which is found to be not more trade-restrictive than necessary within the meaning of Article 2.2 of the *TBT Agreement*, will not necessarily remain so in the future. Article 2.3 of the *TBT Agreement* provides that:

> Technical regulations shall not be maintained if the circumstances or objectives giving rise to their adoption no longer exist or if the changed circumstances or objectives can be addressed in a less trade-restrictive manner.

WTO Members must therefore continually assess whether their technical regulations are not more trade-restrictive than necessary.[207]

3.3 Obligation to Base Technical Barriers to Trade on International Standards

The harmonisation of national technical regulations, standards and conformity assessment procedures around international standards greatly facilitates the conduct of international trade. Harmonisation around international standards diminishes the trade-restrictive effect of technical barriers to trade by minimising the variety of requirements that exporters have to meet in their different export markets.

Thus, the *TBT Agreement* requires Members to base their technical regulations, standards and conformity assessment procedures on international standards. Article 2.4 of the *TBT Agreement* provides in relevant part:

> Where technical regulations are required and relevant international standards exist or their completion is imminent, Members shall use them, or the relevant parts of them, as a basis for their technical regulations.

However, Article 2.4 of the *TBT Agreement* further provides that Members do not have to use international standards as a basis when:

> such international standards or relevant parts would be an ineffective or inappropriate means for the fulfilment of the legitimate objectives pursued, for instance because of fundamental climatic or geographical factors or fundamental technological problems.

With respect to standards and conformity assessment procedures, Annex 3.F and Article 5.4 of the *TBT Agreement* respectively provide for the same or a similar obligation that such measures shall use international standards or international guides or recommendations as a basis.

Article 2.4 of the *TBT Agreement* sets out a three-tier test of consistency. There are three main questions, which must be answered to determine whether or not a technical regulation is consistent with Article 2.4, namely: (1) whether there exists a *relevant international standard*; (2) whether the relevant international standard is '*used as a basis*' for the technical regulation at issue; and (3) whether the relevant international standard is an *effective and appropriate*

207 With regard to conformity assessment procedures, see Article 5.2.7 of the *TBT Agreement*.

means for the fulfilment of the legitimate objectives pursued. Below, each element of this three-tier test of consistency will be discussed in turn. To date, WTO Members have been found to have acted inconsistently with Article 2.4 of the *TBT Agreement* in one dispute.[208]

3.3.1 Relevant International Standard

The first element of the test of consistency with Article 2.4 of the *TBT Agreement* relates to the question of whether there exists a 'relevant international standard' or its completion is imminent. This question raises a number of intermediate questions, such as: (1) when is a standard an 'international' standard? (2) what is an international standardising body? (3) when is an international standard a 'relevant' international standard? (4) how must an international standard be adopted? Below, each of these intermediate questions will be addressed in turn.

With regard to the first intermediate question, namely, when is a standard an *'international' standard*, the Appellate Body found in *US – Tuna II (Mexico) (2012)* that it is primarily the characteristics of the entity approving a standard that makes a standard an 'international' standard.[209] The subject matter of a standard is not material to the determination of whether a standard is 'international'. A standard is an international standard if it is approved by an international standardising body.[210]

This brings us to the second intermediate question, namely, what is an *'international standardising body'*. First, note that a 'body' is a broader concept than an 'organisation'. As the Appellate Body found in *US – Tuna II (Mexico) (2012)*, a 'body' is a 'legal or administrative entity that has specific tasks and composition', whereas an 'organisation' is a 'body that is based on the membership of other bodies or individuals and has an established constitution and its own administration'.[211] It follows that international standardising bodies may be, but need not necessarily be, international organisations.[212] Second, pursuant to a TBT Committee decision of November 2000, for a standardising body to be an 'international standardising body' within the meaning of Article 2.4 of the *TBT Agreement*, its membership 'should be open on a non-discriminatory basis to relevant bodies of at least all WTO Members'.[213] In *US – Tuna II (Mexico) (2012)*, the Appellate Body ruled that provisions for accession that *de jure* or *de facto* disadvantage some WTO Members or their relevant bodies as compared to other Members or their bodies 'would tend to indicate that a body is not an "international" standardising body'.[214] The Appellate Body further held that it is not sufficient for the body to be open, or have been open, at a particular point in time; the body must be 'open at every

208 See *EC – Sardines (2002)*. 209 See *Appellate Body Report, US – Tuna II (Mexico) (2012)*, para. 353.
210 See *ibid.*, para. 356. 211 *Ibid.*, para. 355.
212 See *ibid.*, para. 356.
213 TBT Committee Decision on *Principles for the Development of International Standards, Guides and Recommendations with Relation to Articles 2, 5, and Annex 3 to the Agreement*, in WTO document G/TBT/1/Rev.10, dated 9 June 2011, pp. 46–8, para. 6.
214 See Appellate Body Report, *US – Tuna II (Mexico) (2012)*, para. 375.

stage of standards development'.[215] As to the question whether a body is 'open' if WTO Members, or their relevant bodies, can only accede pursuant to an invitation, the Appellate Body replied that such a body could be considered 'open' if the invitation 'occurred automatically once a Member or its relevant body has expressed interest in joining' the body concerned.[216]

For an international body to be an 'international standardising body', such body must have 'recognized activities in standardization'. According to the Appellate Body in *US – Tuna II (Mexico) (2012)*, 'evidence of recognition by WTO Members as well as evidence of recognition by national standardizing bodies would be relevant' in this respect.[217] Moreover, the Appellate Body found that, for an international body to be an 'international standardising body', such body does not need to be, or have been, involved in the development of more than one standard.[218] Also, an 'international standardising body' does not need to have 'standardisation as its principal function'.[219] However, at a minimum, WTO Members must be aware, or have reason to expect, that the international body is engaged in standardising activities.[220]

With regard to the third intermediate question, namely, *when is an international standard a 'relevant' international standard*, the panel in *EC – Sardines (2002)* found that the international standard 'Codex Stan 94', developed by an international food-standard-setting body, the Codex Alimentarius Commission, and the EC's technical regulation at issue both covered the same product (*Sardina pilchardus*). They both also included similar types of requirements as regards this product, such as those relating to labelling, presentation and packing medium. The panel, therefore, concluded that the Codex Stan 94 was a *relevant* international standard for the EC's technical regulation at issue.[221]

With regard to the fourth and last intermediate question, namely, *how must an international standard be adopted*, the Appellate Body ruled in *EC – Sardines (2002)* that it is not required that an international standard within the meaning of Article 2.4 of the *TBT Agreement* is adopted *by consensus* in the relevant international standardising body.[222] Note, however, that the Appellate Body stated in *US – Tuna II (Mexico) (2012)*:

> Since the United States' appeal is limited to the characteristics of the entity approving an 'international' standard, we do not need to address in this appeal the question of whether in order to constitute an 'international standard', a standard must also be 'based on consensus'.[223]

215 See *ibid.*, para. 374. 216 *Ibid.*, para. 386.

217 *Ibid.*, para. 363. Also, to the extent that a standardising body complies with the principles and procedures of the TBT Decision of November 2000, referred to above in fn. 214, it would be easier to find that the body has 'recognized activities in standardization'. See *ibid.*, para. 376.

218 See *ibid.*, para. 360. 219 *Ibid.*, para. 362.

220 See *ibid.*

221 See Panel Report, *EC – Sardines (2002)*, paras. 7.69–7.70. The finding was upheld by the Appellate Body. See Appellate Body Report, *EC – Sardines (2002)*, para. 233.

222 See Appellate Body Report, *EC – Sardines (2002)*, paras. 222–3. The Appellate Body came to this conclusion because the Explanatory Note to Annex 1.2 to the *TBT Agreement* states that the *TBT Agreement* covers also documents that are *not* based on consensus. See, however, paras. 8 and 9 of the TBT Committee Decision of November 2000, referred to above in fn. 214.

223 Appellate Body Report, *US – Tuna II (Mexico) (2012)*, para. 353.

3.3.2 'Used as a Basis'

The second element of the test of consistency with Article 2.4 of the *TBT Agreement* relates to the question of whether the relevant international standard is '*used as a basis*' for the technical regulation at issue. In line with the case law on the meaning of the term 'based on' in Article 3.2 of the *SPS Agreement*, discussed in Chapter 14,[224] the panel in *EC – Sardines (2002)* concluded that the requirement to 'use as a basis' imposes the obligation to 'employ or apply' the international standard as 'the principal constituent or fundamental principle for the purpose of enacting the technical regulation'.[225] According to the Appellate Body in *EC – Sardines (2002)*, this comes down to an analysis of 'whether there is a contradiction between Codex Stan 94 and the EC regulation'.[226]

3.3.3 Ineffective or Inappropriate Means

The third and last element of the test of consistency with Article 2.4 of the *TBT Agreement* relates to the question of whether the relevant international standard is an *ineffective or inappropriate means* for the fulfilment of the legitimate objectives pursued. As indicated above, the relevant international standard must not be used as a basis for the technical regulation at issue *when* that standard constitutes an inappropriate or ineffective means to achieve the legitimate objective pursued. The question to be answered here raises a number of intermediate questions, such as: (1) whether a legitimate objective is pursued; (2) how to assess the ineffectiveness and inappropriateness of the international standard; and (3) who has the burden of proof with regard to the ineffectiveness or inappropriateness of the relevant international standard. Below, each of these intermediate questions will be addressed in turn.

With regard to the first intermediate question, namely, *whether a legitimate objective is pursued*, please refer to the discussion in the context of Article 2.2 of the *TBT Agreement* on the determination of the objective(s) pursued by a technical regulation, and on the concept of 'legitimate objective'.[227]

With regard to the second intermediate question, namely, *how to assess the ineffectiveness and inappropriateness of the international standard*, the panel observed in *EC – Sardines (2002)* that the difference between effectiveness and appropriateness is that:

> [t]he question of effectiveness bears upon the *results* of the means employed, whereas the question of appropriateness relates more to the *nature* of the means employed.[228]

224 See below, pp. 951–5 (953 in particular).

225 Panel Report, *EC – Sardines (2002)*, para. 7.110. On the meaning of 'based on' in the *SPS Agreement*, see below, pp. 951–5.

226 Appellate Body Report, *EC – Sardines (2002)*, para. 249. The Appellate Body thus concluded in *EC – Sardines (2002)* that the EC technical regulation at issue was not based on Codex Stan 94 because the former contradicted the latter.

227 See above, p. 914. 228 Panel Report, *EC – Sardines (2002)*, para. 7.116.

In other words, the international standard is *effective* if it has the capacity to accomplish the objective(s) pursued, and it is *appropriate* if it is suitable for the fulfilment thereof.[229] Note that the panel in *US – COOL (2012)* found that Codex Stan 1–1985 did not have the capacity of accomplishing the objective of providing information about the countries in which an animal was born, raised and slaughtered, because this international standard conferred origin exclusively on the country of slaughter or another substantial transformation (such as processing). The panel concluded that Codex Stan 1–1985 was neither an effective nor an appropriate means to fulfil the legitimate objective of the technical regulation at issue.[230] Recall that Article 2.4 of the *TBT Agreement* itself states that an international standard may be ineffective or inappropriate because of 'fundamental climatic or geographical factors or fundamental technological problems'. Note in this respect also Article 12.2 of the *TBT Agreement*, which provides for relevant special and differential treatment for developing-country Members, and which is discussed below.[231]

With regard to the third and last intermediate question, namely, who has the burden of proof with regard to the ineffectiveness or inappropriateness of the relevant international standard, the Appellate Body in *EC – Sardines (2002)* ruled that it is for the complainant to demonstrate that the international standard in question is both an effective and an appropriate means to fulfil the legitimate objective.[232]

Finally, note that – as provided for in Article 2.5 of the *TBT Agreement* – a technical regulation which is adopted with a view to achieving a legitimate objective explicitly enumerated in Article 2.2 of the *TBT Agreement* and is in accordance with a relevant international standard, shall be *presumed* not to create an unnecessary obstacle to trade. Such technical regulation shall thus be presumed to be consistent with Article 2.2.[233]

3.4 Other Substantive Provisions

Apart from the substantive provisions discussed in the previous subsections, the *TBT Agreement* also contains a number of other substantive provisions, which deserve to be mentioned. This subsection briefly examines the substantive provisions of the *TBT Agreement* relating to: (1) equivalence and mutual

229 See Appellate Body Report, *EC – Sardines (2002)*, para. 288.
230 See Panel Reports, *US – COOL (2012)*, para. 7.735. 231 See below, pp. 928–9.
232 See Appellate Body Report, *EC – Sardines (2002)*, paras. 274–5 and 287. Given the conceptual similarities between Articles 3.1 and 3.3 of the *SPS Agreement*, and Article 2.4 of the *TBT Agreement*, the Appellate Body held that its findings in *EC – Hormones (1998)* regarding the burden of proof under the former provisions were 'equally apposite' for the case at hand. It accordingly found that, 'as with Articles 3.1 and 3.3 of the SPS Agreement, there is no "general rule–exception" relationship between the first and the second parts of Article 2.4'. See *ibid.*, paras. 274–5.
233 See above, pp. 912–21.

recognition; (2) product requirements in terms of performance; (3) transparency and notification; and (4) special and differential treatment for developing-country Members.

3.4.1 Equivalence and Mutual Recognition

Article 2.7 of the *TBT Agreement* provides:

> Members shall give positive consideration to accepting as equivalent technical regulations of other Members, even if these regulations differ from their own, provided they are satisfied that these regulations adequately fulfil the objectives of their own regulations.

The *TBT Agreement* thus requires WTO Members to *consider* accepting, as equivalent, the technical regulations of other Members. However, they must do so only if the foreign technical regulations *adequately* fulfil the legitimate objectives pursued by their own technical regulations.

With regard to conformity assessment procedures, Article 6.1 of the *TBT Agreement* requires Members to ensure, whenever possible, that results of such procedures by other Members, are accepted even if their conformity assessment procedures differ, as long as they provide an assurance of conformity with the domestic technical regulations or standards.

3.4.2 Product Requirements in Terms of Performance

With respect to technical regulations, Article 2.8 of the *TBT Agreement* provides:

> Wherever appropriate, Members shall specify technical regulations based on product requirements in terms of performance rather than design or descriptive characteristics.

The *TBT Agreement* thus prefers Members to adopt technical regulations on the basis of product requirements in terms of performance. With regard to standards, Annex 3.I to the *TBT Agreement* provides for the same preference for standards based on product requirements in terms of performance. Performance-based requirements are typically less prescriptive than requirements based on product characteristics. Note, however, that the obligation of Article 2.8 of the *TBT Agreement* applies only when 'appropriate'.

3.4.3 Transparency and Notification

When no relevant international standard exists or when a proposed technical regulation is not in accordance with a relevant international standard and the proposed technical regulation may have a significant effect on trade of other Members, Article 2.9 of the *TBT Agreement* imposes on WTO Members detailed transparency and notification requirements. Members are, *inter alia*, required to notify other Members through the WTO Secretariat of the proposed technical regulation.[234] Such notification must be done at an early stage of the process,

234 Article 2.9.2 of the *TBT Agreement*.

when amendments to the proposed technical regulation can still be made and comments can be taken into account.

When a technical regulation is adopted to address an *urgent* problem of safety, health, environmental protection or national security, a Member may set aside the notification (and consultation) requirements set out in Article 2.9 of the *TBT Agreement*. However, in such instances, Members are subject to certain notification (and consultation) obligations *after* the adoption of the technical regulation.[235]

Article 2.11 of the *TBT Agreement* requires that all adopted technical regulations are published promptly or otherwise made available in such a manner as to enable interested parties in other Members to become acquainted with them. Except when a technical regulation addresses an *urgent* problem, technical regulations may not enter into force immediately after publication. Article 2.12 of the *TBT Agreement* provides in relevant part:

> Members shall allow a reasonable interval between the publication of technical regulations and their entry into force in order to allow time for producers in exporting Members to adapt their products or methods of production to the requirements of the importing Member.

Such a reasonable interval between the publication and the entry into force of a technical regulation is particularly important for producers in exporting developing-country Members. This interest is reflected in paragraph 5.2 of the Doha Ministerial Decision on *Implementation-Related Issues and Concerns* of 14 November 2001, which provides:

> Subject to the conditions specified in paragraph 12 of Article 2 of the Agreement on Technical Barriers to Trade, the phrase 'reasonable interval' shall be understood to mean normally a period of not less than 6 months, except when this would be ineffective in fulfilling the legitimate objectives pursued.[236]

In *US – Clove Cigarettes (2012)*, the Appellate Body ruled that Article 2.12 of the *TBT Agreement*, as clarified by paragraph 5.2 of the Doha Ministerial Decision, imposes an obligation on importing Members to provide a 'reasonable interval' of not less than six months between the publication and entry into force of a technical regulation. However, an importing Member may depart from this obligation if this interval 'would be ineffective to fulfil the legitimate objectives pursued' by the technical regulation.[237] In *US – Clove Cigarettes (2012)*, the interval between the publication of the technical regulation at issue and its entry into force was three months. The Appellate Body found that Indonesia, the complainant, had made a *prima facie* case of inconsistency by establishing that there was no interval of at least six months between the publication and

235 See Article 2.10 of the *TBT Agreement*.

236 Ministerial Conference, Decision of 14 November 2001 on *Implementation-Related Issues and Concerns*, WT/MIN(01)/17, dated 20 November 2001, para. 5.2. On the legal status of this decision, see above, p. 194.

237 See Appellate Body Report, *US – Clove Cigarettes (2012)*, para. 275.

the entry into force of the technical regulation at issue;[238] and that the United States, the respondent, failed to rebut this *prima facie* case of inconsistency, since it did not show that allowing a period of not less than six months would have been ineffective to fulfil the legitimate objective of the technical regulation at issue.[239] The Appellate Body thus concluded that the United States had acted inconsistently with Article 2.12 of the *TBT Agreement*.[240]

The *TBT Agreement* contains similar transparency and notification provisions with regard to standards and conformity assessment procedures.[241] As an additional requirement for standards, the Code of Good Practice of the *TBT Agreement* requires standardising bodies to publish, at least every six months, their work programme and report on the progress regarding the preparation and adoption of standards.[242]

Furthermore, Article 10 of the *TBT Agreement* requires each Member to establish an enquiry point which will answer inquiries of other Members and which will provide relevant documentation related to adopted technical regulations, standards and conformity assessment procedures.[243]

The WTO Secretariat maintains a publicly available database of all information provided by WTO Members in relation to technical regulations, standards and conformity assessment procedures. This database, the *Technical Barriers to Trade Information Management System* (TBT IMS), greatly enhances the implementation of the transparency provisions of the *TBT Agreement*.[244] As of 1 October 2016, this database contained almost 22,000 regular notifications relating to technical barriers to trade.

3.4.4 Special and Differential Treatment

The *TBT Agreement* explicitly recognises the difficulties that developing-country Members may face in implementing their obligations under the *TBT Agreement*. Therefore, Members shall, pursuant to Article 12.1 of the *TBT Agreement*, 'provide differential and more favourable treatment' to developing-country Members, and shall, pursuant to Articles 12.2 and 12.3, 'take into account [their] special development, financial and trade needs' in the implementation of the *TBT Agreement* as well as in the preparation and application of technical regulations, standards and conformity assessment procedures. In accordance with Article 12.8 of the *TBT Agreement*, the TBT Committee may grant, upon request, time-limited exceptions, in whole or in part, from obligations under the *TBT*

238 See *ibid.*, para. 291. 239 See *ibid.*, para. 295.
240 See *ibid.*, para. 297.
241 See Annex 3.L, M, N and O to the *TBT Agreement* (for standards) and Articles 5.6, 5.7, 5.8 and 5.9 of the *TBT Agreement* (for conformity assessment procedures).
242 See Annex 3.J to the *TBT Agreement*.
243 A full list of national enquiry points is contained in Committee on Technical Barriers to Trade, *Note by the Secretariat on National Enquiry Points*, G/TBT/ENQ/38/Rev.1, dated 8 July 2011.
244 See http://tbtims.wto.org.

Agreement. In addition, pursuant to Article 12.4 of the *TBT Agreement*, developing-country Members do not have to base their technical regulations, standards or conformity assessment procedures on international standards, if the international standards are not appropriate to their development or financial and trade needs. Finally, Article 12.6 of the *TBT Agreement* requires that Members shall take 'such reasonable measures as available to them' to ensure that the international standardising bodies, upon the request of developing-country Members, examine the possibility of developing international standards concerning products of special interest to developing-country Members.

In *US – Clove Cigarettes (2012)* and *US – COOL (2012)*, the developing-country complainants, Indonesia and Mexico respectively, argued that the respondent, the United States, had acted inconsistently with its obligation under Article 12.3 of the *TBT Agreement* by failing to take into account the complainant's special development, financial and trade needs when preparing and applying the measures at issue. With respect to the obligation set out in Article 12.3, both panels referred to, and agreed with, the findings of the panel in *EC – Approval and Marketing of Biotech Products (2006)*, which concerned a very similar provision in the *SPS Agreement*, namely, Article 10.1 thereof.[245] The panel in *US – COOL (2012)* noted:

> [W]e do not consider that the United States had an explicit obligation, enforceable in WTO dispute settlement, to reach out and collect Mexico's views during the preparation and application of the COOL measure. The United States is merely required under Article 12.3 to 'take account of [Mexico's] special development, financial and trade needs' 'in the preparation and application of [the COOL measure]'. This means giving active and meaningful consideration to such needs.[246]

According to the panel, Mexico had not demonstrated that the United States failed to do this.[247] The panel in *US – Clove Cigarettes (2012)* came to the same conclusion with regard to Indonesia's claim.[248] These findings by the panels in *US – Clove Cigarettes (2012)* and *US – COOL (2012)* illustrate well the limited 'value' which at least some of the special and differential treatment provisions of Article 12 of the *TBT Agreement* have for developing-country Members.

4 INSTITUTIONAL AND PROCEDURAL PROVISIONS OF THE *TBT AGREEMENT*

In addition to the substantive provisions discussed above, the *TBT Agreement* also contains a number of institutional and procedural provisions. This section

245 See below, pp. 981–3.
246 Panel Reports, *US – COOL (2012)*, para. 7.790. 247 See *ibid*., paras. 7.791–7.799.
248 See Panel Report, *US – Clove Cigarettes*, paras. 7.634–7.648.

deals briefly with the provisions on: (1) the TBT Committee; (2) dispute settlement; and (3) technical assistance to developing-country Members.

4.1 TBT Committee

The *TBT Agreement* establishes a Committee on Technical Barriers to Trade, commonly referred to as the 'TBT Committee'.[249] This Committee is composed of representatives of all WTO Members and meets when necessary.[250] In 2015, the TBT Committee held three regular meetings.[251] The function of the TBT Committee is to provide Members with a forum for consultations regarding any matters pertaining to the operation or objectives of the *TBT Agreement*. In particular, the TBT Committee has functioned as a forum to discuss so-called 'specific trade concerns' with regard to proposed draft measures notified to the TBT Committee or the implementation of existing measures. At the TBT Committee meeting of 9–10 March 2016, for example, Members discussed eleven new and forty-nine previously raised trade concerns. The new specific trade concerns discussed at this meeting included, for example: (1) amendments by South Africa to its regulation on health messages on labels for alcoholic beverages, requiring the use of seven different health warning labels during a twelve-month cycle (concern raised by the EU and Canada); (2) India's new compositional requirements and alcohol content limits for beer, wine and spirits (concerns raised by Australia, Canada, Chile, the EU, Guatemala, Japan, the US and New Zealand); (3) Thailand's draft act on marketing and promotion of food for infants and young children to ensure that marketing of infant formula did not negatively impact breastfeeding (concerns raised by the US); and (4) the United Arab Emirates' control scheme to restrict the use of hazardous materials in electronic and electrical devices (concern raised by the EU).[252] At this TBT Committee meeting, WTO Members raised the 500th specific trade concern. WTO Director-General Azevêdo described at this occasion the work of the TBT Committee as 'essential to avoid concerns escalating into disputes and to keep trade flowing'.[253] The WTO Secretariat compiles information about the status of specific trade concerns raised by Members in the TBT Committee.[254]

The TBT Committee also undertakes an annual review of the implementation and operation of the *TBT Agreement* (annual review).[255] Moreover, at the end of

249 See Article 13.1 of the *TBT Agreement*.

250 Pursuant to Article 13.1 of the *TBT Agreement*, the TBT Committee has to meet *at least* once a year.

251 See Committee on Technical Barriers to Trade, *Twenty-First Annual Review of the Implementation and Operation of the TBT Agreement, Revision*, Note by the Secretariat G/TBT/38/Rev.1, dated 24 March 2016, para. 2.2.

252 See Committee on Technical Barriers to Trade – Minutes of the meeting of 9–10 March 2016, G/TBT/M/68.

253 See www.wto.org/english/news_e/news16_e/tbt_11mar16_e.htm. In 2015, eighty-six specific trade concerns were discussed in the TBT Committee, the second highest number since 1995. See Committee on Technical Barriers to Trade, *Twenty-First Annual Review of the Implementation and Operation of the TBT Agreement, Revision*, Note by the Secretariat G/TBT/38/Rev.1, dated 24 March 2016.

254 The G/TBT/GEN/74/ – series of documents contain an overview of the specific trade concerns raised since 1995. Alternatively, one can consult the Technical Barriers to Trade Information Management System (TBT IMS) at http://tbtims.wto.org.

255 See Article 15.3 of the *TBT Agreement*.

every three-year period, the TBT Committee undertakes an in-depth review of the operation of the Agreement (triennial review), at which time it may recommend amendments to the *TBT Agreement* if this is considered necessary 'to ensure mutual economic advantage and balance of rights and obligations'.[256]

While not as 'productive' as the SPS Committee, discussed in Chapter 14, the TBT Committee has adopted a number of decisions and recommendations. These decisions and recommendations include, for example, the 2000 Decision on *Principles for the Development of International Standards, Guides and Recommendations with relation to Articles 2, 5 and Annex 3 of the Agreement.*[257] As discussed above, the Appellate Body ruled in *US – Tuna II (Mexico) (2012)* with regard to this TBT Committee Decision that:

> [it] can be considered as a 'subsequent agreement' within the meaning of Article 31(3) (a) of the *Vienna Convention*. The extent to which this Decision will inform the interpretation and application of a term or provision of the *TBT Agreement* in a specific case, however, will depend on the degree to which it 'bears specifically' on the interpretation and application of the respective term or provision.[258]

4.2 Dispute Settlement

Consultations and the settlement of disputes with respect to any matter affecting the operation of the *TBT Agreement* shall follow the provisions of Articles XXII and XXIII of the GATT 1994 as elaborated on and applied by the DSU.[259] The *TBT Agreement* contains a few 'special or additional rules and procedures' set out in Articles 14.2, 14.3, 14.4 of and Annex 2 to the *TBT Agreement.*[260] Pursuant to Article 14.2 of the *TBT Agreement*, a panel, charged with the settlement of a dispute under the *TBT Agreement*, may establish, at the request of one of the parties to the dispute or at its own initiative, a *technical expert group* to assist the panel in questions of a technical nature.[261] Note, however, that, in *EC – Asbestos (2001)*, the panel decided to consult experts on an individual basis, rather than establishing a technical expert group.[262]

256 See Article 15.4 of the *TBT Agreement*. For the report on 7th triennial review, completed in 2015, see Committee on Technical Barriers to Trade, *Seventh Triennial Review of the Operation and Implementation of the Agreement on Technical Barriers to Trade under Article 15.4*, G/TBT/37, dated 3 December 2015.

257 See G/TBT/9, 13 November 2000, para. 20 and Annex 4. The most recent compilation of the decisions and recommendations adopted by the TBT Committee can be found in G/TBT/1/Rev.12, dated 21 January 2015.

258 Appellate Body Report, *US – Tuna II (Mexico) (2012)*, para. 372.

259 See Article 14.1 of the *TBT Agreement*. For a discussion of the WTO dispute settlement system, see above, pp. 164–296.

260 See Appendix 2 to the DSU.

261 As stated in Article 14.3, a technical expert group is governed by the procedures set out in Annex 2 to the *TBT Agreement*. The panel in question shall define the composition, terms of reference and working procedures of the expert group it has established. The members of a technical expert group shall be persons of professional standing and of relevant experience and shall not include citizens or government officials of a Member that is party to the dispute.

262 See Panel Report, *EC – Asbestos (2001)*, paras. 8.10–8.11.

As mentioned above, not only central government bodies but also local government and non-governmental entities may adopt and apply technical regulations, standards and conformity assessment procedures. Articles 3, 4, 7, 8 and 9 of the *TBT Agreement* impose certain obligations on Members with regard to the conduct of these local government and non-governmental entities.[263] Article 14.4 of the *TBT Agreement* provides:

> The dispute settlement provisions set out above can be invoked in cases where a Member considers that another Member has not achieved satisfactory results under Articles 3, 4, 7, 8 and 9 and its trade interests are significantly affected. In this respect, such results shall be equivalent to those as if the body in question were a Member.

4.3 Technical Assistance

Pursuant to Article 11 of the *TBT Agreement*, Members shall, upon request, advise or provide technical assistance to requesting Members, in particular to developing-country Members. The advice and technical assistance referred to in Article 11 primarily concern assistance in establishing institutions or legal frameworks dealing with the preparation of technical regulations and standards and the development of conformity assessment procedures. In addition, requested Members shall, *inter alia*, assist the requesting Member to meet technical regulations of the requested Members; and assist the requesting Member to participate in the work of international standardisation bodies. In the provision of advice or technical assistance under Article 11, priority must be given to the needs of least-developed-country Members.[264]

5 SUMMARY

While continued vigilance and further liberalisation efforts regarding traditional barriers to trade (customs duties and quantitative restrictions) are certainly called for, *regulatory measures* for trade in goods now raise a more pressing challenge for the multilateral trading system. As discussed in Chapter 7, many such regulatory measures are 'technical barriers to trade'. This chapter deals with the WTO rules applicable to these measures. The next chapter, Chapter 14, will deal with the different WTO rules applicable to sanitary and phytosanitary (SPS) measures, which poses to international trade challenges similar to technical barriers to trade.

The WTO rules applicable to technical barriers to trade, as set out in the *TBT Agreement*, go *beyond* the general rules applicable to non-tariff barriers, as set

263 See above, p. 895.
264 See Article 11.8 of the *TBT Agreement*.

out in the GATT 1994. They go *further* in addressing non-tariff barriers to trade by *also* promoting regulatory harmonisation around international standards.

The rules of the *TBT Agreement* apply to technical regulations, standards and conformity assessment procedures relating to products and (related) processes and production methods (PPMs). A measure is a 'technical regulation' within the meaning of the *TBT Agreement* if: (1) the measure applies to an identifiable product or group of products; (2) the measure lays down product characteristics; and (3) compliance with the product characteristics laid down in the measure is mandatory. A standard differs from a technical requirement in that compliance with a standard is not mandatory.

Although the *TBT Agreement* is mainly addressed to central government bodies, it extends its application also to local government and non-governmental standardising bodies. WTO Members must: (1) take 'such reasonable measures as may be available to them' in order to ensure compliance with the *TBT Agreement* by local government and non-governmental standardising bodies; and (2) refrain from taking measures that could encourage actions by these bodies that are inconsistent with the provisions of the *TBT Agreement.*

With regard to the relationship between the *TBT Agreement* and other WTO agreements, note that, generally speaking, the applicability of the *SPS Agreement* or the *Agreement on Government Procurement* to a specific measure excludes the applicability of the *TBT Agreement* to that measure. However, the *TBT Agreement* and the GATT 1994 can both be applicable to a specific measure.

The *TBT Agreement* requires that, in respect of technical barriers to trade, Members accord national treatment and MFN treatment to imported products. With regard to technical regulations, Article 2.1 of the *TBT Agreement* sets out a three-tier test of consistency with the national treatment obligation and the MFN treatment obligation. This test of consistency requires the examination of: (1) whether the measure at issue is a '*technical regulation*' within the meaning of Annex 1.1; (2) whether the imported and domestic products (for the national treatment obligation) or the imported products originating in different countries (for the MFN treatment obligation) are '*like products*'; and (3) whether the imported products at issue are accorded '*treatment no less favourable*' than like domestic products or than like imported products originating in other countries.

The *TBT Agreement* also requires that technical barriers to trade do not create unnecessary obstacles to international trade. With regard to technical regulations, Article 2.2 of the *TBT Agreement* sets out a four-tier test of consistency. This test of consistency requires the examination of: (1) whether the measure at issue is a '*technical regulation*' within the meaning of Annex 1.1; (2) whether the technical regulation at issue is '*trade-restrictive*'; (3) whether the technical regulation at issue *fulfils a legitimate objective*; and (4) whether the technical regulation at issue is '*not more trade-restrictive than necessary*' to fulfil a legitimate objective, taking account of the risks non-fulfilment would create.

The *TBT Agreement* requires that, in principle, Members use international standards as a basis for their technical barriers to trade. With regard to technical regulations, Article 2.4 of the *TBT Agreement* sets out a *three-tier test of consistency*. This test of consistency requires the examination of: (1) whether there exists a *relevant international standard*; (2) whether the relevant international standard is '*used as a basis*' for the technical regulation at issue; and (3) whether the relevant international standard is an *effective or appropriate means* for the fulfilment of the legitimate objectives pursued.

In addition to these core, substantive obligations, the *TBT Agreement* furthermore requires WTO Members *to consider* accepting, as equivalent, the technical regulations of other Members if they are satisfied that the foreign technical regulations *adequately* fulfil the legitimate objectives pursued by their own technical regulations. The *TBT Agreement* also subjects Members to a number of detailed transparency and notification obligations and provides for special and differential treatment for developing-country Members.

FURTHER READINGS

D. McDaniels and M. Karttunen, 'Trade, Testing and Toasters: Conformity Assessment Procedures and the TBT Committee', WTO Staff Working Paper ERSD-2016-09, July 2016, World Trade Organization.

S. Ayral, 'TBT and Trade Facilitation Agreements: Leveraging Linkages to Reduce Trade Costs', WTO Staff Working Paper ERSD-201602, June 2016, World Trade Organization.

G. Marín Durán, 'Measures with Multiple Competing Purposes after *EC – Seal Products*: Avoiding a Conflict between GATT Article XX-Chapeau and Article 2.1 TBT Agreement', *Journal of International Economic Law*, 2016, 19, 467–95.

A. C. Molina and V. Khoroshavina, 'TBT Provisions in Regional Trade Agreements: To What Extent Do They Go Beyond the WTO TBT Agreement?', WTO Staff Working Paper ERSD-2015-09, December 2015, World Trade Organization.

T. Voon, 'Exploring the Meaning of Trade-Restrictiveness in the WTO', *World Trade Review*, July 2015, 14(3), 451–77.

T. Broude and P. I. Levy, 'Do You Mind If I Don't Smoke? Products, Purpose and Indeterminacy in *US – Measures Affecting the Production and Sale of Clove Cigarettes*', *World Trade Review*, 2014, 13(2), 357–92.

E. R. Lowe, 'Technical Regulations to Prevent Deceptive Practices: Can WTO Members Protect Consumers from [un] Fair-Trade Coffee and [Less-Than] Free-Range Chicken?', *Journal of World Trade*, 2014, 48(3), 593–628.

G. Marceau and J. P. Trachtman, 'A Map of the World Trade Organization Law of Domestic Regulation of Goods: The Technical Barriers to Trade Agreement, the Sanitary and Phytosanitary Measures Agreement, and the General Agreement on Tariffs and Trade', *Journal of World Trade*, 2014, 48(2), 351–432.

S. Lester and W. Stemberg, 'The GATT Origins of TBT Agreement Articles 2.1 and 2.2', *Journal of International Economic Law*, 2014, 17(1), 215–32.

A. Davies, 'Technical Regulations and Standards under the WTO Agreement on Technical Barriers to Trade', *Legal Issues of Economic Integration*, 2014, 41(1), 37–63.

E. Wijkström and D. McDaniels, 'International Standards and the WTO TBT Agreement: Improving Governance for Regulatory Alignment', WTO Staff Working Paper ERSD-2013-06, April 2013, World Trade Organization.

F. Fontanelli, 'ISO and CODEX Standards and International Trade Law: What Gets Said Is Not What's Heard', *International and Comparative Law Quarterly*, 2011, 60, 895–932.

14 Sanitary and Phytosanitary Measures

CONTENTS

1 INTRODUCTION

This chapter deals with the WTO rules applicable to sanitary and phytosanitary measures, commonly referred to as 'SPS measures'. Generally speaking, SPS measures are measures aimed at the protection of human, animal or plant life or health from certain specified risks. As mentioned in Chapter 13, SPS measures often take the form of technical barriers to trade but are subject to a different set of WTO rules.[1] The negotiators of the WTO agreements considered that these measures merited special attention for two reasons: first, because the preservation of domestic regulatory autonomy was, and still is, considered of particular importance where health risks are at issue; and, second, because of the close link between SPS measures and agricultural trade, a sector that is notoriously difficult to liberalise. As a result, SPS measures are dealt with in a separate agreement, the *Agreement on the Application of Sanitary and Phytosanitary Measures*, commonly referred to as the *SPS Agreement*. This Agreement provides for rights and obligations, which, although broadly similar, differ in certain key respects from those provided in the GATT 1994 and the *TBT Agreement*.[2]

WTO Members frequently adopt SPS measures to protect humans and animals from food safety risks, or to protect humans, animals and plants from risks arising from pests and diseases. However, countries exporting food and agricultural products, as well as international organisations, have observed that SPS measures are increasingly used as instruments of 'trade protectionism'. W. Barnes reported in the *Financial Times* in April 2006:

> Stringent, often excessively strict, hygiene standards are increasingly being used by rich countries to block food imports from developing economies, according to researchers in Thailand, India and Australia ... The recent bird flu scare was manna for Western safety officials, said a trade negotiator at the Thai commerce ministry. 'The rich food importers are getting better and better at manufacturing safety hazards – real and imagined', the official said ... A World Bank study found that trade in cereals and nuts would increase by $12bn if all 15 importing countries [referring to the fifteen EU Member States at the time of the study] adopted the international Codex standards for aflatoxin contamination, which is produced by a cancer-linked mould, than if they all abided by tougher EU requirements. Some safety measures appear exotic. Australia demands that imported chicken flesh be heated to 70 degrees Celsius for 143 minutes, creating 'poultry soup' according to one exporter.[3]

Similarly, the following report by A. Beattie in the *Financial Times* in July 2007 illustrates well the tension between regulations to address health concerns and trade in food and agricultural products:

> The spat between the US and China over contaminated food exports highlights a rapidly spreading battle line in the world economy: the use of product standards to regulate, and some would say stifle, international trade. Such 'non-tariff barriers', particularly food standards, are frequently both more important and harder to eliminate than simple tariffs. Arguments frequently descend into a mire of competing scientific claims about safety and risk in which trade negotiators – let alone ministers and the general public – risk drowning in complexity. And while consumers' patriotic desire to protect domestic farmers or

1 See above, p. 883.

2 As explained further below, while the GATT 1994 may also apply to SPS measures, Article 1.5 of the *TBT Agreement* expressly provides that the provisions of that Agreement do not apply to sanitary and phytosanitary measures as defined in the *SPS Agreement*. See above, pp. 897–9 and below, 943.

3 W. Barnes, 'Food Safety Fears "Used as Excuse to Ban Imports"', *Financial Times*, 6 April 2006.

> manufacturers requires some degree of altruism, given the higher prices this entails, fears of being poisoned by foreign food appeal directly to their self-interest ... As the global trade in processed and perishable food grows faster than that for traditional commodities, there appears every likelihood that standards rather than tariffs will be the greater barrier to such goods' unimpeded journey around the world economy.[4]

The rules contained in the *SPS Agreement* reflect an attempt to balance the sometimes conflicting interests of the protection of health against SPS risks and the liberalisation of trade in food and agricultural products. To date, WTO Members have been found to have acted inconsistently with their obligations under the *SPS Agreement* in eleven disputes.[5]

This chapter deals with: (1) the scope of application of the *SPS Agreement*; (2) the substantive provisions of the *SPS Agreement*; and (3) the institutional and procedural provisions of the *SPS Agreement*.

2 SCOPE OF APPLICATION OF THE *SPS AGREEMENT*

With regard to the scope of application of the *SPS Agreement*, this section distinguishes between: (1) the measures to which the *SPS Agreement* applies; (2) the entities covered by the Agreement; and (3) the temporal scope of application of the Agreement. This section will also address the relationship between the *SPS Agreement* and other agreements on trade in goods, such as the *TBT Agreement* and the GATT 1994.

2.1 Measures to Which the *SPS Agreement* Applies

The disciplines of the *SPS Agreement* do not cover all measures for the protection of human, plant or animal life or health but, rather, apply to an explicitly circumscribed set of measures. The substantive scope of application of the *SPS Agreement* is set out in Article 1.1, which provides, in relevant part:

> This Agreement applies to all sanitary and phytosanitary measures which may, directly or indirectly, affect international trade.

Thus, for a measure to be subject to the *SPS Agreement*, it must be: (1) a sanitary or phytosanitary measure; and (2) a measure that may affect international trade.

4 A. Beattie, 'Food Safety Clash Tells of Trade Battles Ahead', *Financial Times*, 31 July 2007.

5 See *EC – Hormones (1998); Australia – Salmon (1998); Japan – Agricultural Products II (1999); Australia – Salmon (Article 21.5 – Canada) (2000); Japan – Apples (2003); Japan – Apples (Article 21.5 – US) (2005); EC – Approval and Marketing of Biotech Products (2006); US – Poultry (China) (2010); Australia – Apples (2010); India – Agricultural Products (2015); and US – Animals (2015)*. Note that, in *US/Canada – Continued Suspension (2008)*, the Appellate Body reversed the panel's findings of inconsistency with the *SPS Agreement* and was unable to complete the legal analysis.

A sanitary or phytosanitary measure, or 'SPS measure', is defined in paragraph 1 of Annex A to the *SPS Agreement* as:

Any measure applied:

(a) to protect animal or plant life or health within the territory of the Member from risks arising from the entry, establishment or spread of pests, diseases, disease-carrying organisms or disease-causing organisms;
(b) to protect human or animal life or health within the territory of the Member from risks arising from additives, contaminants, toxins or disease-causing organisms in foods, beverages or feedstuffs;
(c) to protect human life or health within the territory of the Member from risks arising from diseases carried by animals, plants or products thereof, or from the entry, establishment or spread of pests; or
(d) to prevent or limit other damage within the territory of the Member from the entry, establishment or spread of pests.

Sanitary or phytosanitary measures include all relevant laws, decrees, regulations, requirements and procedures including, *inter alia*, end product criteria; processes and production methods; testing, inspection, certification and approval procedures; quarantine treatments including relevant requirements associated with the transport of animals or plants, or with the materials necessary for their survival during transport; provisions on relevant statistical methods, sampling procedures and methods of risk assessment; and packaging and labelling requirements directly related to food safety.

As pointed out by the Appellate Body in *Australia – Apples (2010)*, the fundamental element of this definition relates to the *purpose* or *intention* of the measure, which 'is to be ascertained on the basis of objective considerations'.[6] The Appellate Body held that the purpose of a measure:

must be ascertained not only from the objectives of the measure as expressed by the responding party, but also from the text and structure of the relevant measure, its surrounding regulatory context, and the way in which it is designed and applied.[7]

In broad terms, an 'SPS measure' is one that: (1) *aims at* the protection of human or animal life or health from food-borne risks; or (2) *aims at* the protection of human, animal or plant life or health from risks from pests or diseases; or (3) *aims at* the prevention or limitation of other damage from risks from pests.[8]

In *EC – Approval and Marketing of Biotech Products (2006)*, involving a complaint by the United States, Canada and Argentina against the European Communities with respect to measures relating to biotech products (i.e. genetically modified organisms or GMOs), the panel had to determine whether the contested measures, namely: (1) the *de facto* moratorium on new approvals of biotech products by the European Communities; (2) certain measures of the European

6 Appellate Body Report, *Australia – Apples (2010)*, para. 172. 7 *Ibid.*, para. 173.
8 A measure aimed at protecting humans, animals or plants from health-related risks other than food-borne risks, or risks from pests or diseases, such as e.g. health risks from lead-based paint (as used in children's toys) or asbestos fibres (as used in building materials), are not SPS measures.

Communities affecting the approval of specific biotech products, including the EC Regulation on novel foods; and (3) the bans on biotech products in place in six EU Member States, were 'SPS measures' within the meaning of Annex A(1) of the *SPS Agreement*, quoted above.[9] The panel interpreted the purposes enumerated in subparagraphs (a)–(d) of Annex A(1) very broadly and found that almost all the objectives of the challenged European approval legislation, as well as those of the EU Member States' bans, fell within the scope of Annex A(1)(a)–(d). Only with regard to the EC Regulation on novel foods did the panel find that two of the three purposes of that Regulation were outside the scope of subparagraphs (a)–(d).[10] To the extent that the Regulation pursued those two purposes, it was held not to be an SPS measure. To the extent that the Regulation sought to ensure that novel foods did not present health risks to consumers, however, the panel considered it to be an SPS measure falling within Annex A(1)(b).

It is interesting to note that the panel in *EC – Approval and Marketing of Biotech Products (2006)* disagreed with the European Communities' argument that the *SPS Agreement* was not intended to cover risks to the environment in general. Instead, the panel interpreted 'other damage' in subparagraph (d) to include not only economic damage or damage to property, but also damage to the environment (other than to the life or health of plants or animals) encompassing adverse effects on biodiversity, population dynamics of species or biogeochemical cycles.[11] The residual category of 'other damage' referred to in subparagraph (d) is potentially broad, be it that the damage concerned is limited to damage caused by pests.

In *Australia – Apples (2010)*, the Appellate Body found that, as indicated by the words 'include' and 'all relevant', the first part of the last sentence of Annex A(1), quoted above, provides an 'illustrative and expansive'[12] list of instruments which may be SPS measures. According to the Appellate Body, the word 'relevant' refers back to the 'list of specific purposes that are the defining characteristic of every SPS measure',[13] and is key to a proper understanding of what an SPS measure within the meaning of Annex A(1) is.[14] Similarly, use of the words 'including,

9 Note that the bans on biotech products in place in six EU Member States related to varieties of biotech products that had already been approved at the European level. These bans are also referred to as 'safeguard measures'.

10 According to the panel, to the extent that the Regulation seeks to achieve the second and the third of its three purposes, namely, to ensure that novel foods do not mislead the consumer, and that they are not nutritionally disadvantageous for the consumer, it is not a measure applied for one of the purposes mentioned in Annex A(1) and is therefore not an SPS measure (and could be a measure falling within the scope of application of the *TBT Agreement*). See Panel Reports, *EC – Approval and Marketing of Biotech Products (2006)*, paras. 7.415–7.416.

11 See *ibid.*, paras. 7.197–7.211.

12 Appellate Body Report, *Australia – Apples (2010)*, para. 175. Note that it is the list of instruments in the final paragraph of Annex A(1) that is 'illustrative and expansive', *not* the list of purposes in Annex A(1)(a)–(d).

13 Appellate Body Report, *Australia – Apples (2010)*, para. 175.

14 The Appellate Body found in *Australia – Apples (2010)*: 'measures of a type not expressly listed may nevertheless constitute SPS measures when they are "relevant", that is, when they are "applied" for a purpose that corresponds to one of those listed in subparagraphs (a) through (d). Conversely, the fact that an instrument is of a type listed in the last sentence of Annex A(1) is not, in itself, sufficient to bring such an instrument within the ambit of the *SPS Agreement*.' *Ibid.*

inter alia' in the second part of that sentence to introduce the list of instruments 'emphasizes that the list is only indicative'.[15] The Appellate Body held:

> The list thus serves to illustrate, through a set of concrete examples, the different types of measures that, when they exhibit the appropriate nexus to one of the specified purposes, will constitute SPS measures and, accordingly, be subject to the disciplines set out in the SPS Agreement.[16]

The broad range of possible types of measures that may fall within the definition of a 'SPS measure' once they have one of the purposes listed in Annex A(1) (a)–(d) is illustrated by the *US – Poultry (China) (2010)* dispute, where the measure at issue was a provision in a US appropriations bill that prohibited the use of funds under the relevant bill to establish or implement a rule allowing Chinese poultry products to be imported into the US. This restriction was imposed due to concerns arising from serious incidents of food contamination and the high incidence of the H5N1 virus in China together with the weakness of its government controls which undermined confidence that poultry imports from China would be H5N1-free. Thus, despite the fact that the measure, an appropriations restriction, was not of a nature normally associated with SPS measures, the fact that it aimed to protect human and animal life and health from risks posed by contaminated poultry products from China and was of a type described in the last sentence of Annex A(1) (a law), led the panel to conclude that it fell within the definition of an 'SPS measure'.[17]

Thus, once a measure is objectively determined to aim at one of the purposes listed in Annex A(1) (a)–(d) of the *SPS Agreement*, and is of a type covered by the open, illustrative list in the final paragraph of Annex A(1), it falls within the definition of an 'SPS measure'.

Note that the definitions in Annex A(1) refer specifically to the protection of human, animal or plant life or health or the prevention of other damage 'within the territory of the Member', thus excluding measures aimed at extraterritorial health protection from the scope of application of the *SPS Agreement*.

15 *Ibid.*, para. 176.

16 *Ibid.*, para. 176. Note that the panel in *EC – Approval and Marketing of Biotech Products (2006)* had a fundamentally different interpretation of the definition of 'SPS measures'. The panel in that case held on the basis of a textual analysis of the second sentence of Annex A(1), quoted above, that the definition of 'SPS measures' had three separate elements: (1) the *purpose* of the measure, as enumerated in subparagraphs (a)–(d); (2) the *form* of the measure, namely, 'laws, decrees [and] regulations'; and (3) the *nature* of the measure, namely, 'requirements and procedures'. See Panel Reports, *EC – Approval and Marketing of Biotech Products (2006)*, para. 7.149. The panel found that (1) the *de facto* moratorium on new approvals of biotech products by the European Communities; and (2) certain of the measures of the European Communities affecting the approval of specific biotech products, did not have the 'nature' of SPS measures as they were neither 'requirements' nor 'procedures' and thus fell outside the scope of the *SPS Agreement.* See Panel Reports, *EC – Approval and Marketing of Biotech Products (2006)*, paras. 7.1338–7.1378, 7.1690–7.1697, 7.1701–7.1704 and 7.1711–7.1712. However, first the panel in *Australia – Apples (2010)* and then the panel in *US – Poultry (China) (2010)* both rejected this interpretation of the definition of 'SPS measures' for having no clear basis in the text of Annex A(1). See Panel Report, *Australia – Apples (2010)*, para. 7.153; and Panel Report, *US – Poultry (China) (2010)*, paras. 7.100–7.101. The Appellate Body in *Australia – Apples (2010)* made no reference to the interpretation of the definition of 'SPS measures' in the panel reports in *EC – Approval and Marketing of Biotech Products (2006)*, and clearly interpreted this definition differently.

17 Panel Report, *US – Poultry (China) (2010)*, paras. 7.119–7.120.

As noted above, a further requirement for the application of the *SPS Agreement* according to Article 1.1 is that the measure at issue must be a measure that 'may directly or indirectly affect international trade'. This requirement is easy to fulfil, as any measure that applies to imports can be said to affect international trade. Moreover, as pointed out by the panel in *EC – Approval and Marketing of Biotech Products (2006)*, Article 1.1 only requires that the measure *may* affect international trade. Thus, 'it is not necessary to demonstrate that an SPS measure has an actual effect on trade'.[18] Hygiene requirements for street vendors of home-made food are arguably an example of a SPS measure that does not fall within the scope of application of the *SPS Agreement* because such a measure does not – actually or potentially – affect international trade.

When a measure is a SPS measure *and* affects international trade, actually or potentially, that measure falls within the substantive scope of application of the *SPS Agreement*.[19]

2.2 Entities Covered by the *SPS Agreement*

SPS measures are often measures adopted and implemented by the central government bodies of a WTO Member. Members are fully responsible for the observance of the *SPS Agreement* by their central government bodies. However, the adoption and implementation of SPS measures are not only in the hands of central government bodies. They may also be in the hands of other bodies, such as regulatory agencies, regional bodies, subfederal governments and nongovernmental entities.[20] With regard to these other bodies, Article 13 of the *SPS Agreement* provides:

> Members shall formulate and implement positive measures and mechanisms in support of the observance of the provisions of this Agreement by other than central government bodies. Members shall take such reasonable measures as may be available to them to ensure that non-governmental entities within their territories, as well as regional bodies in which relevant entities within their territories are members, comply with the relevant provisions of this Agreement. In addition, Members shall not take measures which have the effect of, directly or indirectly, requiring or encouraging such regional or non-governmental entities, or local governmental bodies, to act in a manner inconsistent with the provisions of this Agreement.

Moreover, Article 13 of the *SPS Agreement* states that WTO Members may not rely on non-governmental bodies to implement their SPS measures *unless* these bodies comply with the *SPS Agreement*.

18 Panel Reports, *EC – Approval and Marketing of Biotech Products (2006)*, para. 7.435.

19 As the panel in *EC – Hormones (1998)* noted, there are no additional requirements for the applicability of the *SPS Agreement*. In particular, and contrary to what the European Communities argued in that case, the *SPS Agreement* contains no requirement of a prior violation of a provision of the GATT 1994. See Panel Report, *EC – Hormones (Canada) (1998)*, para. 8.39; and Panel Report, *EC – Hormones (US) (1998)*, para. 8.36.

20 Note that, in *Australia – Salmon (Article 21.5 – Canada) (2000)*, the measures at issue were measures taken by the Government of Tasmania, an Australian state. See Panel Report, *Australia – Salmon (Article 21.5 – Canada) (2000)*, para. 7.13.

In recent years, the obligations enshrined in Article 13 of the *SPS Agreement* have become of particular significance with regard to SPS-related private sector standards.[21] While these standards have the potential to boost international trade, they can also be – and increasingly are – burdensome for small suppliers. Since 2005, when St Vincent and the Grenadines first raised concerns regarding the impact of EurepGAP standards imposed by supermarket chains on banana exports to the UK, this issue of private sector standards has been a regular item on the agenda of SPS Committee meetings.[22] It remains a much-debated question to what extent WTO Members should and/or could take responsibility for the WTO-compatibility of standards adopted by NGOs such as GlobalGAP (the successor of EurepGAP), standards adopted by trade associations, such as the British Retail Consortium, or standards adopted by commercial enterprises such as McDonald's, the world's largest chain of fast food restaurants.[23]

2.3 Temporal Scope of Application of the *SPS Agreement*

In *EC – Hormones (1998)*, the European Communities, the respondent in that case, raised the question whether the *SPS Agreement* is applicable to SPS measures adopted and/or applied before the Agreement entered into force. The Appellate Body answered this question as follows:

> If the negotiators had wanted to exempt the very large group of SPS measures in existence on 1 January 1995 from the disciplines of provisions as important as Articles 5.1 and 5.5, it appears reasonable to us to expect that they would have said so explicitly. Articles 5.1 and 5.5 do not distinguish between SPS measures adopted before 1 January 1995 and measures adopted since; the relevant implication is that they are intended to be applicable to both.[24]

Thus, the *SPS Agreement* applies pre-1995 SPS measures, to the extent of course that these measures are still in force.

21 For a definition of 'private sector standards', see the draft definition proposed by the WTO Secretariat on the basis of discussions in the SPS Committee. See G/SPS/W/265/Rev.1, 26 June 2012. According to this draft definition, 'SPS-related private standards are market requirements which are [developed and/or] applied by [private] [non-governmental] entities, which may directly or indirectly affect international trade, and which relate to' one of the objectives set out in subparagraphs (a)–(d) of Annex A(1) to the *SPS Agreement* (square brackets in the original). A non-governmental entity is any entity that does not possess, exercise, or is not vested with governmental authority. Non-governmental entities are private entities, including private sector bodies, companies, industrial organisations, and private standard-setting bodies. To date, Members have been unable to agree on a definition of 'private sector standards'.

22 An *ad hoc* working group was established in 2008 to consider the issue, and to date five actions have been adopted. See Committee on Sanitary and Phytosanitary Measures, *Decision of the Committee on Actions regarding SPS-Related Private Standards*, G/SPS/55, dated 6 April 2011. In March 2015, WTO Members agreed on a 'time-out' in the efforts of this working group to agree on a definition of 'private sector standards'. See www.wto.org/english/news_e/news15_e/sps_26mar15_e.htm.

23 This question also arises in the context of the *TBT Agreement*. For a discussion of the applicability of the *TBT Agreement* on private sector standards, see above, p. 895.

24 Appellate Body Report, *EC – Hormones (1998)*, para. 128.

2.4 Relationship with Other WTO Agreements

The *SPS Agreement* is not the only WTO agreement of relevance to measures for the protection of human, animal or plant life or health. The GATT 1994 and the *TBT Agreement* obviously also contain rules applicable to such measures. Within their respective spheres of application, all three agreements are relevant in determining the WTO consistency of health measures. It is therefore necessary to examine the relationship between the *SPS Agreement* and the other relevant WTO agreements.

2.4.1 The *TBT Agreement*

The *TBT Agreement*, as discussed in Chapter 13, applies to technical regulations, standards and conformity assessment procedures in general. Clearly, SPS measures often take the form of technical regulations, standards or conformity assessment procedures. However, as already discussed above and as explicitly set out in Article 1.5 of the *TBT Agreement*, the *TBT Agreement* does not apply to SPS measures.[25] When a measure is an 'SPS measure', as defined in Annex A(1) to the *SPS Agreement*, the *SPS Agreement* applies to the exclusion of the *TBT Agreement*, even if the measure would otherwise be considered a 'technical regulation, standard or conformity assessment procedure' for purposes of the *TBT Agreement*. The relationship between the *SPS Agreement* and the *TBT Agreement* can thus be described as one of mutual exclusivity. However, as discussed above,[26] the panel in *EC – Approval and Marketing of Biotech Products (2006)* noted that a single measure or requirement may be imposed for a purpose that falls within the definition of an SPS measure as well as for a purpose not covered by this definition. It held that:

> to the extent the requirement in the consolidated law is applied for one of the purposes enumerated in Annex A(1), it may be properly viewed as a measure which falls to be assessed under the *SPS Agreement*; to the extent it is applied for a purpose which is not covered by Annex A(1), it may be viewed as a separate measure which falls to be assessed under a WTO agreement other than the *SPS Agreement*. It is important to stress, however, that our view is premised on the circumstance that the requirement at issue could be split up into two separate requirements which would be identical to the requirement at issue, and which would have an autonomous *raison d'être*, i.e., a different purpose which would provide an independent basis for imposing the requirement.[27]

According to the panel, such a requirement would simultaneously be an SPS measure and a 'non-SPS measure'. As Article 1.5 of the *TBT Agreement* does not apply to non-SPS measures, if the requirement falls within the definition of a 'technical regulation' as defined in Annex 1.1 of the *TBT Agreement*, it is

25 See above, p. 898. 26 See *ibid.*
27 Panel Reports, *EC – Approval and Marketing of Biotech Products (2006)*, para. 7.165.

to be assessed under the *TBT Agreement* 'to the extent it embodies a non-SPS measure'.[28]

2.4.2 The GATT 1994

Contrary to the situation with respect to the *TBT Agreement*, no relationship of mutual exclusivity exists between the *SPS Agreement* and the GATT 1994. It is therefore possible for a measure to be subject to the GATT disciplines as well as those of the *SPS Agreement*.[29] However, Article 2.4 of the *SPS Agreement* states:

> Sanitary or phytosanitary measures which conform to the relevant provisions of this Agreement shall be presumed to be in accordance with the obligations of the Members under the provisions of GATT 1994 which relate to the use of sanitary or phytosanitary measures, in particular the provisions of Article XX(b).

Article 2.4 thus provides for a (rebuttable) presumption of GATT 1994 consistency of all measures that are in conformity with the *SPS Agreement*. The opposite is not the case. Measures that are in conformity with the GATT 1994 cannot be presumed to be consistent with the *SPS Agreement*, as the latter Agreement also provides for obligations that clearly do not exist under the GATT 1994.[30]

3 SUBSTANTIVE PROVISIONS OF THE *SPS AGREEMENT*

This section deals with the substantive provisions of the *SPS Agreement*. It first discusses the basic principles of the *SPS Agreement* provided for in Article 2 of the *SPS Agreement*. Subsequently, this section discusses the goal of harmonisation; the obligations relating to risk assessment; the obligations relating to risk management; and provisional SPS measures and the precautionary principle. This section concludes with a brief discussion of some other substantive provisions, such as the provisions relating to the recognition of equivalence, adaptation to regional conditions, transparency, and special and differential treatment of developing-country Members.

28 *Ibid*., para. 7.167. Although the Regulation on novel foods was found to be both an SPS measure and a non-SPS measure, the panel exercised judicial economy with regard to the claims of Canada and Argentina under the *TBT Agreement*. See *ibid*., paras. 7.2524 and 7.2527, and paras. 7.3412–7.3413.

29 While panels may be expected to exercise judicial economy with respect to claims of inconsistency with obligations under the GATT 1994, after having found that the measure at issue is inconsistent with obligations under the more specific *SPS Agreement*, note that the panel in *US – Poultry (China) (2010)* found that the measure at issue was inconsistent with Articles I and XI of the GATT 1994 after having found that this measure was inconsistent with Articles 2.2, 2.3, 5.1, 5.2, 5.5 and 8 of the *SPS Agreement*. See Panel Report, *US – Poultry (China) (2010)*, paras. 7.399 and 7.455.

30 e.g. the obligations set out in Articles 5.1 and 5.5 of the *SPS Agreement*. See below, pp. 956–60.

3.1 Basic Principles

The basic principles of the *SPS Agreement* are set out in Article 2, entitled 'Basic rights and obligations'.[31] These basic principles reflect the underlying aim of balancing the need to increase market access for food and agricultural products, on the one hand, with the recognition of the sovereign right of governments to take measures to protect human, animal and plant life and health in their territories, on the other.

This section discusses the following basic principles of the *SPS Agreement*: (1) the sovereign right of WTO Members to take SPS measures; (2) the obligation to take or maintain only SPS measures *necessary* to protect human, animal or plant life or health (the 'necessity requirement'); (3) the obligation to take or maintain only SPS measures based on scientific principles and on sufficient scientific evidence (the 'scientific disciplines'); and (4) the obligation not to adopt or maintain SPS measures that arbitrarily or unjustifiably discriminate or constitute a disguised restriction on trade (the 'non-discrimination' requirement).

3.1.1 Right to Take SPS Measures

It is significant that the *SPS Agreement*, in Article 2.1, expressly recognises the *right* of Members to take SPS measures necessary for the protection of human, animal or plant life or health. This differs from the position of health measures under GATT rules, where discriminatory measures or quantitative restrictions for health protection purposes are in principle prohibited; justification for such measures must be found under Article XX(b) of the GATT 1994. This difference has important implications for the burden of proof in dispute settlement proceedings.[32] Under the GATT 1994, a Member imposing a discriminatory health measure or one that constitutes a quantitative restriction bears the burden of proving that it complies with the requirements of the Article XX(b) exception. In contrast, under the *SPS Agreement*, the complaining Member must show that the measure is inconsistent with the rules of the *SPS Agreement*.

The right to take SPS measures is, however, not unlimited but is subject to the disciplines contained in the rest of the *SPS Agreement*. The basic disciplines are set out in Articles 2.2 and 2.3, and are further elaborated upon in other provisions of the *SPS Agreement*. These provisions incorporate the existing GATT rules applicable to health measures *and* introduce new requirements for the use of SPS measures.

31 The panel in *US – Poultry (China) (2010)* noted that the title of Article 2 leads to the conclusion that the provisions of this Article inform all of the *SPS Agreement*. See Panel Report, *US – Poultry (China) (2010)*, para. 7.142.

32 See above, pp. 256–9.

3.1.2 'Only to the Extent Necessary'

As set forth in Article 2.2 of the *SPS Agreement*, the sovereign right of Members to take SPS measures is, first of all, limited by the requirement that:

> any sanitary or phytosanitary measure [be] applied only to the extent necessary to protect human, animal or plant life and health.

Although this general necessity requirement in Article 2.2 has not yet been subject to interpretation in dispute settlement, the related, and more specific, requirement set forth in Article 5.6 has been interpreted, as explained below.[33] As the Appellate Body has suggested, a violation of Article 5.6 may also imply a violation of Article 2.2.[34]

3.1.3 Scientific Basis for SPS Measures

Article 2.2 of the *SPS Agreement* also sets out new scientific disciplines for the use and maintenance of SPS measures. It requires that:

> any sanitary or phytosanitary measure ... [be] based on scientific principles and ... not [be] maintained without sufficient scientific evidence, except as provided for in paragraph 7 of Article 5.

These requirements introduce science as the touchstone against which SPS measures will be judged. These requirements are further elaborated on in Article 5.1, which provides that SPS measures must be based on a risk assessment.[35] With regard to these requirements under Articles 2.2 and 5.1, the Appellate Body held in *EC – Hormones (1998)*:

> The requirements of a risk assessment under Article 5.1, as well as of 'sufficient scientific evidence' under Article 2.2, are essential for the maintenance of the delicate and carefully negotiated balance in the *SPS Agreement* between the shared, but sometimes competing, interests of promoting international trade and of protecting the life and health of human beings.[36]

The panel in *Japan – Apples (2003)* was the first to consider the meaning of the terms 'scientific' and 'evidence' in Article 2.2.[37] It held that for evidence to be 'scientific' it must be gathered through scientific methods[38] and it favoured relying on scientifically produced evidence rather than purely circumstantial evidence.[39] With regard to the term 'evidence', the panel held:

> Negotiators could have used the term 'information', as in Article 5.7, if they considered that any material could be used. By using the term 'scientific evidence', Article 2.2 excludes in essence not only insufficiently substantiated information, but also such things as a non-demonstrated hypothesis.[40]

33 See below, pp. 964–7.

34 See Appellate Body Report, *Australia – Salmon (1998)*, fn. 166 to para. 213; and Appellate Body Report, *Australia – Apples (2010)*, paras. 340 and 346–7. The panel in *India – Agricultural Products (2015)* found that the SPS measures at issue were inconsistent with Article 5.6 of the *SPS Agreement*, and that these measures were *consequentially* also inconsistent with Article 2.2 of the *SPS Agreement* because they were applied beyond the extent necessary to protect human and animal life or health. See Panel Report, *India – Agricultural Products (2015)*, paras. 7.614–7.615.

35 See below, pp. 955–61. 36 Appellate Body Report, *EC – Hormones (1998)*, para. 177.

37 See Panel Report, *Japan – Apples (2003)*, paras. 8.91–8.98. 38 *Ibid.*, para. 8.92.

39 *Ibid.*, para. 8.95. 40 *Ibid.*, para. 8.93.

The panel noted that it would consider both direct and indirect scientific evidence, although their probative value would differ.[41]

The issue of what is meant by '*sufficient* scientific evidence' was addressed for the first time in *Japan – Agricultural Products II (1999)*. In that case, the Appellate Body held that this requires a *rational relationship* between the SPS measure and the scientific evidence. The Appellate Body ruled as follows:

> [W]e agree with the Panel that the obligation in Article 2.2 that an SPS measure not be maintained without sufficient scientific evidence requires that there be a rational or objective relationship between the SPS measure and the scientific evidence. Whether there is a rational relationship between an SPS measure and the scientific evidence is to be determined on a case-by-case basis and will depend upon the particular circumstances of the case, including the characteristics of the measure at issue and the quality and quantity of the scientific evidence.[42]

It is thus clear that panels have some discretion in determining whether a 'rational relationship' between the measure and the scientific evidence exists, in light of the particular circumstances of each case. It would seem that where reputable scientific support for a measure exists, the requirement of 'sufficient scientific evidence' would be met. Moreover, in *EC – Hormones (1998)*, the Appellate Body noted that, in determining whether sufficient scientific evidence exists, panels should:

> bear in mind that responsible, representative governments commonly act from perspectives of prudence and precaution where risks of irreversible, e.g. life-terminating, damage to human health are concerned.[43]

It therefore seems that the more serious the risks to life or health, the less demanding the requirement of 'sufficient scientific evidence'. The panel in *Japan – Apples (2003)* further elaborated on the 'rational relationship' test by introducing a proportionality criterion into Article 2.2 of the *SPS Agreement*. It found, based on the evidence before it, that the risk of transmission of fire blight through the importation of apple fruit was negligible,[44] and contrasted this with the rigorous requirements of the measure at issue. It found the measure at issue to be clearly disproportionate to the risk and thus a violation of Article 2.2.[45] The Appellate Body did not take issue with this proportionality test.[46] More recently, the panel in *US – Poultry (China) (2010)* found that, for the SPS measure at issue to be maintained with sufficient scientific evidence:

> the scientific evidence must bear a rational relationship to the measure, be sufficient to demonstrate the existence of the risk which the measure is supposed to address, and be of the kind necessary for a risk assessment.[47]

41 See *ibid.*, para. 8.98. 42 Appellate Body Report, *Japan – Agricultural Products II (1999)*, para. 84.
43 Appellate Body Report, *EC – Hormones (1998)*, para. 124.
44 See Panel Report, *Japan – Apples (2003)*, para. 8.169. 45 See *ibid.*, para. 8.198.
46 Appellate Body Report, *Japan – Apples (2003)*, para. 163. The panel also found that, in order to be sufficient, the scientific evidence must confirm the existence of the risk that the measure is supposed to address. *Ibid.*, para. 8.104. See also Panel Report, *Japan – Apples (Article 21.5 – US) (2005)*, paras. 8.45 and 8.71.
47 Panel Report, *US – Poultry (China) (2010)*, para. 7.200.

Pursuant to Article 2.2 of the *SPS Agreement*, SPS measures must not be maintained without sufficient scientific evidence, *except* as provided for under Article 5.7. This provision, discussed in more detail below, deals with a situation in which scientific evidence is lacking.[48] Governments are sometimes faced with situations where they need to act to prevent a possible risk despite insufficient scientific data regarding the existence and likelihood of the risk. Article 2.2 takes account of this fact by expressly referring to Article 5.7, which allows for provisional SPS measures to be taken. The relationship between Articles 2.2 and 5.7 was set out by the Appellate Body in *Japan – Agricultural Products II (1999)* as follows:

> [I]t is clear that Article 5.7 of the *SPS Agreement*, to which Article 2.2 explicitly refers, is part of the context of the latter provision and should be considered in the interpretation of the obligation not to maintain an SPS measure without sufficient scientific evidence. Article 5.7 allows Members to adopt provisional SPS measures '[i]n cases where relevant scientific evidence is insufficient' and certain other requirements are fulfilled. Article 5.7 operates as a *qualified* exemption from the obligation under Article 2.2 not to maintain SPS measures without sufficient scientific evidence.[49]

As the Appellate Body recognised in that dispute, the existence of Article 5.7 thus is an argument against an 'overly broad and flexible interpretation' of the requirement in Article 2.2 that SPS measures not be maintained without sufficient scientific evidence.[50] In *EC – Approval and Marketing of Biotech Products (2006)*, the relationship between Article 5.7 and the scientific obligations contained in Article 2.2 (and Article 5.1) was again at issue. The European Communities argued that 'Article 5.7 is not an exception to Article 2.2 in the sense that it could be invoked as an affirmative defence to a claim of violation under Article 2.2'.[51] Rather, it averred that 'Article 5.7 establishes an autonomous right of the importing Member'.[52] The panel agreed with the European Communities in this regard,[53] and therefore considered that a measure falling under Article 5.7 is excluded from the scope of application of the scientific disciplines in Article 2.2.[54] In *US/Canada – Continued Suspension (2008)*, the Appellate Body confirmed this interpretation of the relationship between Articles 2.2 and 5.7.[55]

48 See below pp. 968–73.

49 Appellate Body Report, *Japan – Agricultural Products II (1999)*, para. 80.

50 See *ibid.*

51 Panel Reports, *EC – Approval and Marketing of Biotech Products (2006)*, para. 7.2962.

52 *Ibid.* The argument of the European Communities was based on an analogy with the relationship between Articles 3.1 and 3.3 of the *SPS Agreement*, as set out by the Appellate Body in *EC – Hormones (1998)*, para. 104. See *ibid.*

53 See Panel Reports, *EC – Approval and Marketing of Biotech Products (2006)*, paras. 7.2969 and 7.2976. Note that the panel refers not only to the scientific obligations set out in Article 2.2 but also those set out in Article 5.1 of the SPS Agreement, discussed below at section 3.3.1. While this is contrary to the finding of the panel in *Japan – Apples (2003)*, which held that the burden of proof under Article 5.7 is on the respondent, the panel in *EC – Approval and Marketing of Biotech Products (2006)* understood the Appellate Body in the former case as implicitly expressing its reservations with regard to this allocation of the burden of proof. In coming to its interpretation of the relationship between Articles 2.2 and 5.7, the panel relied on the test used by the Appellate Body in *EC – Tariff Preferences (2004)*. See Panel Reports, *EC – Approval and Marketing of Biotech Products (2006)*, para. 7.2985, citing Appellate Body Report, *EC – Tariff Preferences (2004)*, para. 88.

54 See Panel Reports, *EC – Approval and Marketing of Biotech Products (2006)*, para. 7.2969.

55 See Appellate Body Reports, *US/Canada – Continued Suspension (2008)*, para. 674.

The practical implication of this interpretation is that the complaining party bears the burden of proof with respect to Article 5.7. In other words, to be successful in claiming that an SPS measure is inconsistent with Article 2.2, a complainant may also have to show that the measure does *not* fall under Article 5.7.[56]

It should also be borne in mind that – as mentioned above – the basic scientific disciplines contained in Article 2.2 are further elaborated in Article 5.1 of the *SPS Agreement*, which requires – as discussed below – that SPS measures be based on a risk assessment, taking into account certain factors.[57] Article 5.1 may be viewed as a specific application of the basic obligations contained in Article 2.2 of the *SPS Agreement*.[58] A panel's task under Article 5.1 is linked to, and is informed by, the requirements of Article 2.2, in particular as such task encompasses a scrutiny of the scientific basis underlying a risk assessment and, ultimately, the SPS measure at issue.[59] As it noted in *India – Agricultural Products (2015)*, the Appellate Body has consistently held that a SPS measure found to be inconsistent with Articles 5.1 and 5.2 can be presumed, more generally, to be inconsistent with Article 2.2.[60] However, the terms used in Article 2.2 and Articles 5.1 and 5.2 are not identical and the respective scope of these two provisions may not be entirely coextensive.[61] Therefore, the Appellate Body observed in *India – Agricultural Products (2015)* that:

> although it may give rise to a presumption of inconsistency with Article 2.2, a finding of a violation of Articles 5.1 and 5.2 might not invariably lead to a finding of inconsistency with Article 2.2.[62]

Thus, the Appellate Body emphasised that the presumption of inconsistency with Article 2.2 of an SPS measure that violates Articles 5.1 and 5.2 is rebuttable. However, it noted that:

> establishing that there exists a rational or objective relationship between the SPS measure and the scientific evidence for purposes of Article 2.2 would, in most cases, be difficult

56 For a detailed discussion of these requirements of Article 5.7 of the *SPS Agreement*, see below, pp. 967–73.

57 See below, pp. 955–61; and Appellate Body Report, *EC – Hormones (1998)*, para. 180. Note that the requirement in Article 5.1 is itself elaborated in Articles 5.2 and 5.3 of the *SPS Agreement*. As the panel in *Australia – Salmon (1998)* noted, Articles 5.2 and 5.3 qualify the way in which a risk assessment has to be carried out; they do not qualify the substantive obligation set out in Article 5.1. See Panel Report, *Australia – Salmon (1998)*, para. 8.57.

58 Appellate Body Reports, *EC – Hormones (1998)*, para. 180; and *Australia – Apples (2010)*, para. 209.

59 Appellate Body Reports, *US/Canada – Continued Suspension (2008)*, para. 591; Appellate Body Report, *Australia – Apples (2010)*, para. 215.

60 See Appellate Body Report, *India – Agricultural Products (2015)*, para. 5.23. The Appellate Body referred to Appellate Body Report, *Australia – Apples (2010)*, para. 340 and Appellate Body Report, *Australia – Salmon (1998)*, para. 138. Note the opposite is *not* true.

61 See *ibid.*, para. 5.24.

62 *Ibid.* As the Appellate Body explained, it cannot be excluded that there may be circumstances in which an SPS measure that violates Articles 5.1 and 5.2 will not be inconsistent with Article 2.2. The Appellate Body referred in this regard to the textual differences between Article 2.2 and Articles 5.1 and 5.2, together with the general, as opposed to the specific, nature of the obligations set out in Article 2.2 as compared to the obligations in Articles 5.1 and 5.2

without a Member demonstrating that such a measure is based on an assessment of the risks, as appropriate to the circumstances.[63]

Hence, in most cases, a measure that violates Articles 5.1 and 5.2 will also be inconsistent with Article 2.2. In *India – Agricultural Products (2015)*, the Appellate Body found that the panel had erred in its application of Article 2.2 because it had failed to consider whether the presumption of inconsistency had been rebutted by the arguments and evidence presented by India.[64] Finally, note that a measure that is inconsistent with Article 2.2 is not necessarily inconsistent with Articles 5.1 and 5.2 as the scope of Article 2.2 is broader than that of Articles 5.1 and 5.2.

3.1.4 No Arbitrary or Unjustifiable Discrimination ...

A third basic limitation on a Member's right to impose SPS measures can be found in Article 2.3 of the *SPS Agreement*. Article 2.3 reflects the basic GATT non-discrimination obligations of national treatment and most-favoured-nation treatment, and its language replicates part of the chapeau of Article XX of the GATT 1994.[65] Article 2.3 provides:

> Members shall ensure that their sanitary and phytosanitary measures do not arbitrarily or unjustifiably discriminate between Members where identical or similar conditions prevail, including between their own territory and that of other Members. Sanitary and phytosanitary measures shall not be applied in a manner which would constitute a disguised restriction on international trade.

Article 2.3 was at issue in *Australia – Salmon (Article 21.5 – Canada) (2000)*, where Canada claimed that Australia violated this provision by imposing import requirements on particular types of fish (salmonids) imported from Canada but providing no internal control measures on the movement of dead fish within Australia. The panel identified three cumulative requirements that must be met for a violation of Article 2.3 of the *SPS Agreement* to be established, namely, that: (1) the measure discriminates between the territories of Members other than the Member imposing the measure, or between the territory of the Member imposing the measure and another Member; (2) the discrimination is arbitrary or unjustifiable; and (3) identical or similar conditions prevail in the territory of the Members compared.[66]

Further, the panel in *Australia – Salmon (Article 21.5 – Canada) (2000)* noted that discrimination in the sense of the first element of Article 2.3 includes discrimination between *different* products (in this case, salmonids from Canada and Australian fish including non-salmonids).[67] This differs significantly from

63 *Ibid.*, para. 5.29. 64 See *ibid.*, para. 5.40.

65 See *ibid.*, para. 251. For a detailed discussion of Articles I and III of the GATT 1994, see above, pp. 307–21 and 342–99; for a discussion of the chapeau of Article XX of the GATT 1994, see above, pp. 592–604.

66 See Panel Report, *Australia – Salmon (Article 21.5 – Canada) (2000)*, para. 7.111.

67 *Ibid.*, para. 7.112.

the non-discrimination rules of the GATT (and the *TBT Agreement*) that apply only to 'like' or 'directly competitive or substitutable' products.[68] Article 2.3 recognises that it is the similarity of the risks, rather than the similarity of the products, that matters. Thus, when dissimilar products pose the same or similar health risks, they should be treated in the same way. For example, different animals may be carriers of foot-and-mouth disease and should thus be subject to similar measures where this risk is present. This broad prohibition on discriminatory treatment is tempered by the other two elements that must be established before a violation of Article 2.3 can be found. Thus, if the discriminatory treatment is not arbitrary or unjustifiable, or if conditions in the Members compared are not similar or identical, Article 2.3 is not violated. In this regard, the panel in *Australia – Salmon (Article 21.5 – Canada) (2000)* was not convinced that 'identical or similar' conditions prevailed in Australia and Canada, as there was a substantial difference in the disease status of these two Members.[69]

The basic discipline in Article 2.3 finds reflection in the more specific prohibition in Article 5.5 on arbitrary or unjustifiable distinctions in the levels of protection chosen by a Member in different situations, where these distinctions lead to discrimination or disguised restrictions on trade.[70] A measure violating Article 5.5 may be presumed to be inconsistent with Article 2.3, but the opposite is not true as the scope of Article 2.3 is broader than that of Article 5.5.[71]

3.2 Goal of Harmonisation

Due to the different factors that regulators take into account when enacting SPS measures (national consumer preferences, industry interests, geographic and climatic conditions, etc.), there are large differences in SPS measures from one country to another. The resulting wide variety of SPS measures that producers face in their different export markets has a negative impact on market access for their products, as they may have to adjust products to many different SPS measures.[72] The *SPS Agreement* addresses this problem in Article 3 by encouraging, but not obliging, Members to harmonise their SPS measures around international standards.[73] In *US/Canada – Continued Suspension (2008)*, the Appellate Body noted:

As the preamble of the *SPS Agreement* recognizes, one of the primary objectives of the *SPS Agreement* is to 'further the use of harmonized sanitary and phytosanitary measures

68 See above, pp. 307–21 (for Article I of the GATT 1994); pp. 342–99 (for Article III of the GATT 1994); and pp. 899–912 (for Article 2.1 of the *TBT Agreement*).
69 See Panel Report, *Australia – Salmon (Article 21.5 – Canada) (2000)*, para. 7.113.
70 See below, pp. 961–70.
71 See in this regard the ruling of the Appellate Body in *India – Agricultural Products (2015)* on the relationship between Article 2.2 and Articles 5.1 and 5.2 of the *SPS Agreement*.
72 See also above, pp. 973–8.
73 Article 3 refers to 'international standards, guidelines or recommendations'. For reasons of convenience, the term 'international standards' will be used in this chapter to refer to 'international standards, guidelines or recommendations'.

between Members, on the basis of international standards, guidelines and recommendations developed by the relevant international organizations'. This objective finds reflection in Article 3 of the *SPS Agreement*, which encourages the harmonization of SPS measures on the basis of international standards, while at the same time recognizing the WTO Members' right to determine their appropriate level of protection.[74]

Under Article 3 of the *SPS Agreement*, Members have three *autonomous options* with regard to international standards, each with its own consequences. Members may choose to: (1) *base* their SPS measures on international standards according to Article 3.1; (2) *conform* their SPS measures to international standards under Article 3.2; or (3) impose SPS measures resulting in a *higher level* of protection than would be achieved by the relevant international standard in terms of Article 3.3.

As the Appellate Body already made clear in *EC – Hormones (1998)*, these options are equally available options and there is no rule–exception relationship between them.[75] Thus a Member is not penalised for choosing the Article 3.3 alternative. The three options will now be examined in more detail.

The first option is set out in Article 3.1 of the *SPS Agreement*. Article 3.1 obliges Members to base their SPS measures on international standards where they exist, except as provided for in Article 3.3. The 'international standards' to which Article 3.1 refers are standards set by international organisations, such as the Codex Alimentarius Commission with respect to food safety, the World Organisation for Animal Health (formerly called the International Office of Epizootics (OIE)) for animal health, and the Secretariat of the International Plant Protection Convention (IPPC) with respect to plant health.[76]

Where a relevant international standard exists, Members must – according to Article 3.1 – base their SPS measures thereon. With respect to this requirement, the Appellate Body made the following observations in *EC – Hormones (1998)*:

To read Article 3.1 as requiring Members to harmonize their SPS measures *by conforming those measures with international standards*, guidelines and recommendations, *in the here and now*, is, in effect, to vest such international standards, guidelines and recommendations (which are by the terms of the Codex *recommendatory* in form and nature) with *obligatory* force and effect. The Panel's interpretation of Article 3.1 would, in other words, transform those standards, guidelines and recommendations into binding *norms*. But, as already noted, the *SPS Agreement* itself sets out no indication of any intent on the part of the Members to do so. We cannot lightly assume that sovereign states intended to impose upon themselves

74 Appellate Body Reports, *US/Canada – Continued Suspension (2008)*, para. 692.

75 See Appellate Body Report, *EC – Hormones (1998)*, para. 104.

76 See Annex A, para. 3(a)–(c) of the *SPS Agreement*. For matters not covered by the three organisations mentioned, see Annex A, para. 3(d) of the *SPS Agreement*. Note that the panel in *EC – Hormones (1998)* found that it only needs to establish whether an international standard exists; there is no need to establish for example whether these standards were adopted by consensus or by a wide or narrow majority, or whether they were adopted before or after the entry into force of the *SPS Agreement*. See Panel Report, *EC – Hormones (Canada) (1998)*, para. 8.72; and Panel Report, *EC – Hormones (US) (1998)*, para. 8.69. Pursuant to Article 3.4 of the *SPS Agreement*, Members have an obligation to participate in the work of the Codex Alimentarius Commission and the other organisations to the extent that their resources permit and to promote the development and periodic review of international standards.

the more onerous, rather than the less burdensome, obligation by mandating *conformity* or *compliance with* such standards, guidelines and recommendations. To sustain such an assumption and to warrant such a far-reaching interpretation, treaty language far more specific and compelling than that found in Article 3 of the *SPS Agreement* would be necessary.[77]

Thus, the non-binding standards set by the international standard-setting organisations do not become binding by virtue of the *SPS Agreement.* According to the Appellate Body in *EC – Hormones (1998)*, a measure that is 'based on' an international standard is one that 'stands' or 'is founded' on, or 'built' upon or 'supported' by, the international standard. To be 'based on' an international standard, an SPS measure need not incorporate all of the elements of that standard.[78] It suffices that some of the elements of the standard are adopted and that the measure does not contradict the standard. In *India – Agricultural Products (2015)*, the SPS measures at issue prohibited the importation of mainly poultry and poultry products from countries that had reported the occurrence of avian influenza (AI, commonly known as 'bird flu') and did not allow importation from AI-free zones within such countries. The panel considered whether these measures were 'based on' the relevant international standard set out in the Terrestrial Code of the World Organisation for Animal Health (OIE). On examining the OIE Code, the panel found that it does not envisage, either explicitly or implicitly, the imposition of import prohibitions, but rather envisages that SPS measures relating to AI allow for the possibility of importing from AI-free zones within countries.[79] The panel thus concluded that India's SPS measures amounted to a 'fundamental departure' from, and contradicted, the OIE Code and were therefore not 'based on' the relevant international standard under Article 3.1.[80]

When a WTO Member maintains that its SPS measure is 'based on' an international standard, another WTO Member challenging such measure under Article 3.1 will bear the burden of proving that this is not the case.[81]

The *second* option available to Members under Article 3.2 of the *SPS Agreement* is to 'conform' their SPS measures to the relevant international standard. To 'conform to' is more demanding than to 'base on'. In *EC – Hormones (1998)*, the Appellate Body interpreted this requirement as follows:

Such a measure would embody the international standard completely and, for practical purposes, converts it into a municipal standard.[82]

77 Appellate Body Report, *EC – Hormones (1998)*, para. 165.

78 *Ibid.*, para. 163. As discussed below, if a SPS measure incorporates all the elements of the international standard, it 'conforms to' the standard within the meaning of Article 3.2 of the *SPS Agreement.*

79 See Panel Report, *India – Agricultural Products (2015)*, paras. 7.253 and 7.263.

80 See *ibid.*, paras. 7.271–7.274. In *US – Animals (2015)* the panel concluded that contrary to the United States arguments the US measures contradict the OIE Terrestrial Code in that 'a measure that prohibits trade cannot be said to be based on a measure that allows trade under certain conditions' and is therefore inconsistent with Article 3.1 of the *SPS Agreement.* See Panel Report *US – Animals (2015)*, paras. 7.233–7.240.

81 Appellate Body Report, *EC – Hormones (1998)*, para. 171. As discussed below with regard to Article 3.2 of the *SPS Agreement*, an SPS measure benefits from a presumption of consistency when it *conforms* to the international standard. See below, pp. 912–13. However, a measure which is *based on* an international standard under Article 3.1 does not benefit from any presumption of consistency.

82 *Ibid.*, para. 170.

Article 3.2 provides that SPS measures, which 'conform to' international standards, are presumed to be consistent with the *SPS Agreement* and the GATT 1994. This presumption of consistency is rebuttable.[83] However, the presumption of consistency is designed to create an *incentive* for Members to conform their SPS measures to international standards, rather than to base them on those standards.[84] Clearly, the burden of proof lies on the complaining party to demonstrate a violation of the *SPS Agreement*, under both the Article 3.1 option and the Article 3.2 option. However, the burden is heavier in the latter case as the complaining party has to overcome the presumption of consistency. Members conforming their SPS measures to international standards make these measures less vulnerable to challenges under the *SPS Agreement* and the GATT. Hence, there is an *incentive* for Members to opt for conforming their SPS measures to international standards. As the Appellate Body noted in *US/Canada – Continued Suspension (2008)*:

> International standards are given a prominent role under the *SPS Agreement*, particularly in furthering the objective of promoting the harmonization of sanitary and phytosanitary standards between WTO Members. This is to be achieved by encouraging WTO Members to base their SPS measures on international standards, guidelines or recommendations, where they exist. There is a rebuttable presumption that SPS measures that conform to international standards, guidelines or recommendations are 'necessary to protect human, animal or plant life or health, and ... [are] consistent with the relevant provisions of this Agreement and of GATT 1994'.[85]

The third option that Members may choose, with respect to international standards, is to differ from the relevant international standard by choosing a measure resulting in a higher level of protection than that achieved by the international standard. This option, provided for in Article 3.3 of the *SPS Agreement*, is important as it reflects the recognition of the right of Members to choose the level of protection they deem appropriate in their territories. In respect of this option, the Appellate Body in *EC – Hormones (1998)* held that:

> [t]his right of a Member to establish its own level of sanitary protection under Article 3.3 of the *SPS Agreement* is an autonomous right and *not* an 'exception' from a 'general obligation' under Article 3.1.[86]

This right to choose measures that deviate from international standards is not an 'absolute or unqualified right', as confirmed by the Appellate Body in *EC – Hormones (1998)*.[87] Two *alternative* conditions are laid down in Article 3.3, namely, that: (1) either there must be a scientific justification for the SPS measure (defined in a footnote as a scientific examination and evaluation in accordance

83 See *ibid.* See also Appellate Body Reports, *US/Canada – Continued Suspension (2008)*, para. 532.
84 See Appellate Body Report, *EC – Hormones (1998)*, para. 102.
85 Appellate Body Reports, *US/Canada – Continued Suspension (2008)*, para. 532.
86 *Ibid.*, para. 172.
87 See Appellate Body Report, *EC – Hormones (1998)*, para. 173.

with the rules of the *SPS Agreement*); or (2) the measure must be a result of the level of protection chosen by the Member in accordance with Articles 5.1–5.8. The difference between these two conditions is not clear and the Appellate Body noted, in *EC – Hormones (1998)*, that 'Article 3.3 is evidently not a model of clarity in drafting and communication'.[88] What is clear, however, is that under both alternative conditions a risk assessment in terms of Article 5.1 is required.[89] Therefore, the Appellate Body held *in EC – Hormones (1998)* that, given that the European Communities had established for itself a level of protection higher than that implied in the relevant Codex standards, it was bound to comply with the requirements established in Article 5.1.[90] In *US/Canada – Continued Suspension (2008)*, the Appellate Body stated that where a Member exercises its right under Article 3.3 to adopt an SPS measure that results in a higher level of protection, that right 'is qualified in that the SPS measure must comply with the other requirements of the *SPS Agreement*, including the requirement to perform a risk assessment'.[91]

Note that the Appellate Body found in *EC – Hormones (1998)*, and confirmed in *US/Canada – Continued Suspension (2008)*, that the adoption of an SPS measure that does not conform to an international standard and results in a higher level of protection does not give rise to a more exacting burden of proof under the *SPS Agreement*.[92]

3.3 Obligations Relating to Risk Assessment

The national regulatory process by means of which SPS measures are imposed typically involves *risk analysis*. For the purposes of the *SPS Agreement*, two elements of risk analysis are relevant, namely, risk assessment and risk management. The term 'risk assessment' refers to the scientific process of identifying the existence of a risk and establishing the likelihood that the risk may actually materialise according to the measures that could be applied to address the risk. 'Risk management', by contrast, is the policy-based process of determining the level of protection a country wants to ensure in its territory and choosing the measure that will be used to achieve that level of protection. Risk management decision-making takes into account not only the scientific results of the risk assessment, but also considerations relating to societal values such as consumer preferences, industry interests, relative costs, etc. The distinction between these two elements of the risk analysis process is not absolute. Non-scientific considerations do play some part in risk assessment, and scientific considerations

88 *Ibid.*, para. 175.
89 *Ibid.* 90 *Ibid.*, para. 176.
91 Appellate Body Reports, *US/Canada – Continued Suspension (2008)*, para. 532.
92 See Appellate Body Report, *EC – Hormones (1998)*, para. 102; and Appellate Body Reports, *US/Canada – Continued Suspension (2008)*, para. 532.

inform risk management. However, the distinction is a useful tool in understanding the regulatory process.

The risk assessment/risk management distinction is *implicitly* taken into account in those disciplines of the *SPS Agreement* that relate to the risk analysis process contained in Article 5.[93] Articles 5.1 and 5.2 establish disciplines for the risk assessments on which SPS measures must be based, whereas a Member's choice of the appropriate level of protection – an aspect of risk management – is regulated by Articles 5.4 and 5.5. The selection of a measure to achieve this level of protection – another aspect of risk management – is subject to Article 5.6.

3.3.1 Risk Assessment

Article 5.1 of the *SPS Agreement* states:

> Members shall ensure that their sanitary or phytosanitary measures are based on an assessment, as appropriate to the circumstances, of the risks to human, animal or plant life or health, taking into account risk assessment techniques developed by the relevant international organizations.

Article 5.1 thus obliges Members to base their SPS measures on a risk assessment, as appropriate to the circumstances. As noted by the panel in *EC – Approval and Marketing of Biotech Products (2006)*, two distinct issues must be addressed to determine whether there is a violation of Article 5.1: (1) whether there is a 'risk assessment' within the meaning of the *SPS Agreement*; and (2) whether the SPS measure at issue is 'based on' this risk assessment.[94]

A 'risk assessment' is defined in paragraph 4 of Annex A to the *SPS Agreement* as follows:

> The evaluation of the likelihood of entry, establishment or spread of a pest or disease, within the territory of an importing Member according to the sanitary or phytosanitary measures which might be applied, and of the associated potential biological and economic consequences; *or* the evaluation of the potential for adverse effects on human or animal health arising from the presence of additives, contaminants, toxins or disease-causing organisms in food, beverages or feedstuffs.[95]

Thus, there are *two* types of risk assessment, each with different requirements. The type of risk assessment required in a given case will depend on the objective of the SPS measure at issue. The first type of risk assessment is applicable to SPS measures aimed at risks from pests or diseases; the second to SPS measures aimed at food-borne risks.

93 In *EC – Hormones (1998)*, the Appellate Body noted that the *SPS Agreement* does not expressly use the term 'risk management', and it rejected the rigid distinction drawn by the panel between 'risk assessment' and 'risk management' for 'having no textual basis'. See *ibid*., para. 181. In *US/Canada – Continued Suspension (2008)*, the Appellate Body found that the panel in that case made the same error of drawing a rigid distinction between 'risk assessment' and 'risk management'. See Appellate Body Reports, *US/Canada – Continued Suspension (2008)*, paras. 541–2. This does not mean, however, that it would be incorrect to use the term 'risk management'. It is undeniable that the *SPS Agreement* deals in different ways with the obligations of Members with regard to risk assessment and their obligations applicable to what is commonly referred to as risk management.

94 See Panel Reports, *EC – Approval and Marketing of Biotech Products (2006)*, para. 7.3019.

95 Emphasis added.

The first type of risk assessment involves not only an assessment of the risk of entry, establishment or spread of a pest or disease, but also an assessment of the risk of the associated potential biological and economic consequences.[96] Such a risk assessment must: (1) *identify the pests or diseases* whose entry, establishment or spread a Member wants to prevent, as well as the *potential biological and economic consequences* associated with the entry, establishment or spread of such pests/diseases; (2) *evaluate the likelihood* of entry, establishment or spread of these pests or diseases and the associated biological and economic consequences; and (3) evaluate the likelihood of entry, establishment or spread of these pests or diseases *according to the SPS measures that might be applied.*[97]

The second type of risk assessment, which applies to food-borne risks, must: (1) *identify the adverse effects* on human or animal health (if any) arising from the additive, contaminant, toxin or disease-causing organism in food/beverages/feedstuffs; and (2) if such adverse health effects exist, *evaluate the potential* for such adverse effects to occur.[98]

There are three important differences between these two types of risk assessment. First, the requirements for the second type of risk assessment do not include an evaluation of associated biological and economic consequences. Second, while the first type of risk assessment requires an evaluation of the 'likelihood' that the risk might materialise, the second type requires only an evaluation of the 'potential' for adverse effects. The word 'likelihood' used with regard to the first type of risk assessment was held to imply a higher degree of potentiality than the word 'potential' used with regard to the second type.[99] Third, a risk assessment of the first type must evaluate likelihood according to the SPS measures 'which might be applied'. A risk assessment of this type may not be limited to an examination of the measure already in place but other possible alternatives must also be evaluated.[100]

It would appear that the differences between the two types of risk assessment are intended to set less strict requirements for those risk assessments where risks to human health are more likely to be at issue, namely, when dealing with food safety issues rather than when the risk relates to animal or plant pests or diseases.

Furthermore, nine general observations can be made with respect to the requirements for risk assessments, as identified by the Appellate Body in its case law. First, a risk assessment must show proof of an actual risk, not just

96 See Panel Report, *Australia – Salmon (1998)*, para. 8.72.

97 This three-pronged test was first set out by the panel, and endorsed by the Appellate Body, in *Australia – Salmon (1998)*. See Appellate Body Report, *Australia – Salmon (1998)*, para. 121.

98 This two-pronged test can be deduced from Panel Report, *EC – Hormones (Canada)*, para. 8.101; and Panel Report, *EC – Hormones (US) (1998)*, para. 8.98, as modified by the Appellate Body (Appellate Body Report, *EC – Hormones (1998)*, paras. 184–6).

99 See Appellate Body Report, *Australia – Salmon (1998)*, para. 123 (with regard to the first type of risk assessment); Appellate Body Report, *EC – Hormones (1998)*, para. 184; and Appellate Body Reports, *US/Canada – Continued Suspension (2008)*, para. 569 (with regard to the second type of risk assessment).

100 See Panel Report, *Japan – Apples (2003)*, para. 8.283. As the Appellate Body noted in this case, 'a risk assessment should not be distorted by preconceived views on the nature and the content of the measure to be taken; nor should it develop into an exercise tailored to and carried out for the purpose of justifying decisions *ex post facto*'. See Appellate Body Report, *Japan – Apples (2003)*, para. 208.

a theoretical uncertainty.[101] Second, a risk assessment does not require the risk assessed to be quantified (i.e. expressed numerically). The risk may be expressed either quantitatively or qualitatively.[102] Third, a risk assessment may go beyond controlled laboratory conditions and take account of the actual potential for adverse effects in the 'real world where people live and work and die'.[103] Fourth, the risk assessment must be specific to the particular type of risk at issue in the case and not merely show a general risk of harm.[104] Fifth, Article 5.1 does not oblige Members to carry out their own risk assessments. Instead, they may rely on risk assessments carried out by other Members or an international organisation.[105] Sixth, as discussed in more detail below, a risk assessment need not embody the mainstream scientific opinion. It may also reflect a divergent or minority view from a *qualified and respected source*.[106] Seventh, the phrase 'as appropriate to the circumstances' in Article 5.1 does *not alleviate* the obligation of Members to base their SPS measures on a risk assessment, but relates to the way such risk assessment is carried out.[107] Eighth, the phrase 'taking into account risk assessment techniques developed by the relevant international organisations' in Article 5.1 does not mean that a risk assessment must be based on or conform to such techniques, nor does it mean that compliance with such techniques alone suffices to show that the risk assessment is consistent with the requirements under the *SPS Agreement*.[108] However, reference by the risk assessor to such techniques 'is useful ... should a dispute arise in relation to the risk assessment'.[109] Ninth, since Article 5.1 is to be read together with Article 2.2, which requires that SPS measures not be 'maintained' without sufficient scientific evidence, the evolution of the scientific evidence since the completion of the risk assessment must also be considered as 'this may be an indication that the risk assessment should be reviewed or a new assessment undertaken'.[110]

101 See Appellate Body Report, *EC – Hormones (1998)*, para. 186. See also Appellate Body Reports, *US/Canada – Continued Suspension (2008)*, para. 569.

102 See Appellate Body Report, *EC – Hormones (1998)*, para. 186; Appellate Body Report, *Australia – Salmon (1998)*, paras. 124–5; and Appellate Body Reports, *US/Canada – Continued Suspension (2008)*, para. 569. Note, however, that the panel in *Australia – Apples (2010)* observed that a quantitative method should only be used when reliable specific numeric data are available. In the absence of such data, a quantitative method may be misleading. See Panel Report, *Australia – Apples (2010)*, para. 7.441.

103 See Appellate Body Report, *EC – Hormones (1998)*, para. 187. See also below, p. 959.

104 See Appellate Body Report, *EC – Hormones (1998)*, para. 200. In *Japan – Apples (2003)*, the Appellate Body agreed with the panel that a risk assessment must be specific not only to the harm at issue but also to the agent that causes the harm (in that case, the product that transmitted the disease). See Appellate Body Report, *Japan – Apples (2003)*, para. 204.

105 See Appellate Body Report, *EC – Hormones (1998)*, para. 190. 106 See *ibid.*, para. 194.

107 See Panel Report, *Australia – Salmon (1998)*, para. 8.57. See also Appellate Body Reports, *US/Canada – Continued Suspension (2008)*, para. 562; and Appellate Body Report, *Australia – Apples (2010)*, paras. 237 and 244.

108 See Appellate Body Report, *Australia – Apples (2010)*, para. 246. 109 *Ibid.*

110 Panel Report, *Japan – Apples (2003)*, para. 7.12. In a similar vein, in *EC – Approval and Marketing of Biotech Products (2006)*, the panel held that, as circumstances may change (for example, new scientific evidence may affect the relevance or validity of a risk assessment on which a measure is based), a panel must determine whether, on the date of its establishment, the measure at issue was based on an assessment of risks which was appropriate to the circumstances existing *at that time*. See Panel Reports, *EC – Approval and Marketing of Biotech Products (2006)*, paras. 7.3033–7.3034.

Although the *SPS Agreement* does not lay down any methodology of risk assessment to be followed by Members, other than to require them to take account of risk assessment techniques developed by international organisations, it does specify certain factors that Members must take into account in their risk assessments. Article 5.2 of the *SPS Agreement* lists certain scientific and technical factors that Members must consider when assessing risks. These are:

> [A]vailable scientific evidence; relevant processes and production methods; relevant inspection, sampling and testing methods; prevalence of specific diseases or pests; existence of pest- or disease-free areas; relevant ecological and environmental conditions; and quarantine or other treatment.

In *Australia – Apples (2010)*, the Appellate Body ruled:

> Article 5.2 requires a risk assessor to take into account the available scientific evidence, together with other factors. Whether a risk assessor has taken into account the available scientific evidence in accordance with Article 5.2 of the SPS Agreement and whether its risk assessment is a proper risk assessment within the meaning of Article 5.1 and Annex A(4) must be determined by assessing the relationship between the conclusions of the risk assessor and the relevant available scientific evidence.[111]

As already observed, a risk assessment for the purposes of the *SPS Agreement* is *not* purely scientific (in the sense of laboratory science) but includes a consideration of real-world factors that affect risk, such as climatic conditions, control mechanisms, etc. The Appellate Body in *EC – Hormones (1998)* rejected the panel's finding that the risks relating to control and detection of failure to observe good veterinary practices must be excluded from risk assessments as they are non-scientific and thus outside the scope of Article 5.2.[112] In *US/Canada – Continued Suspension (2008)*, the Appellate Body confirmed the relevance of such risks.[113] While the Appellate Body has not provided a clear demarcation of the factors that may be considered in a 'risk assessment', the Appellate Body held in *EC – Hormones (1998)*, and reaffirmed in *US/Canada – Continued Suspension (2008)*, that the list of factors provided in Article 5.2 is not a closed list and, in particular, that the risks arising from the abuse or misuse and difficulties of control in the administration of hormones may be considered in the context of a risk assessment.[114] The Appellate Body added in *US/Canada – Continued Suspension (2008)* that:

> Where a WTO Member has taken such risks into account, they must be considered by a panel reviewing that Member's risk assessment. Any suggestion that such risks cannot form part of a risk assessment would constitute legal error.[115]

111 Appellate Body Report, *Australia – Apples (2010)*, para. 208.

112 Appellate Body Report, *EC – Hormones (1998)*, para. 187. However, the Appellate Body qualified its finding by noting that it does not imply that risks related to problems of control *always* need to be evaluated in a risk assessment. The necessity to evaluate such risks depends on the circumstances of each case. See *ibid.*, para. 206.

113 Appellate Body Reports, *US/Canada – Continued Suspension (2008)*, para. 535.

114 See Appellate Body Report, *EC – Hormones (1998)*, paras. 187 and 206; and Appellate Body Reports, *US/Canada – Continued Suspension (2008)*, para. 535.

115 Appellate Body Reports, *US/Canada – Continued Suspension (2008)*, para. 545.

Moreover, the Appellate Body has made certain observations about the relationship between the risk assessment and the 'appropriate level of protection', a concept discussed below.[116] In *US/Canada – Continued Suspension (2008)*, the Appellate Body stated:

> The risk assessment cannot be entirely isolated from the appropriate level of protection. There may be circumstances in which the appropriate level of protection chosen by a Member affects the scope or method of the risk assessment. This may be the case where a WTO Member decides not to adopt an SPS measure based on an international standard because it seeks to achieve a higher level of protection. In such a situation, the fact that the WTO Member has chosen to set a higher level of protection may require it to perform certain research as part of its risk assessment that is different from the parameters considered and the research carried out in the risk assessment underlying the international standard.[117]

Finally, with regard to risk assessments concerning animal or plant life or health, Article 5.3 of the *SPS Agreement* requires Members to take into account the following relevant economic factors: (1) the potential damage in terms of loss of production or sales; (2) the costs of control or eradication in the territory of the importing Member; and (3) the relative cost-effectiveness of alternative approaches to limiting risks.[118] There is no requirement to take such economic factors into account in risk assessments concerning human life or health.

3.3.2 Based on a Risk Assessment

As noted above, Article 5.1 of the *SPS Agreement* requires that SPS measures be 'based on' a risk assessment. The meaning of 'based on' was clarified in *EC – Hormones (1998)*. The Appellate Body in that case rejected the panel's finding that the risk assessment must be shown to have been 'taken into account' by the Member in imposing the SPS measure and that the SPS measure must 'conform' to the risk assessment.[119] Instead, the Appellate Body held that, for an SPS measure to be 'based on' a risk assessment, there must be a 'rational relationship' between the measure and the risk assessment, and the risk assessment must 'reasonably support' the measure.[120]

The Appellate Body has also ruled that it is permissible for an SPS measure to be based on a divergent or minority view rather than mainstream scientific opinion. In *EC – Hormones (1998)*, it stated:

> The risk assessment could set out both the prevailing view representing the 'mainstream' of scientific opinion, as well as the opinions of scientists taking a divergent view. Article 5.1

116 See below, pp. 961–4.

117 Appellate Body Reports, *US/Canada – Continued Suspension (2008)*, para. 534.

118 Note that Article 5.3 of the *SPS Agreement* also requires that these economic factors are taken into account in the choice of SPS measures for the protection of the life and health of animals and plants.

119 See Appellate Body Report, *EC – Hormones (1998)*, paras. 189–94.

120 *Ibid.*, para. 193. In *EC – Approval and Marketing of Biotech Products (2006)*, the panel held that there existed no apparent rational relationship between the bans on biotech products imposed by six EU Member States, and the relevant risk assessments, which found no evidence that the biotech products concerned present any greater risk to human health or the environment than their conventional (non-biotech) counterparts. See e.g. Panel Reports, *EC – Approval and Marketing of Biotech Products (2006)*, paras. 7.3085–7.3089 (with regard to Austria's ban on T25 maize).

> does not require that the risk assessment must necessarily embody only the view of a majority of the relevant scientific community ... In most cases, responsible and representative governments tend to base their legislative and administrative measures on 'mainstream' scientific opinion. In other cases, equally responsible and representative governments may act in good faith on the basis of what, at a given time, may be a divergent opinion coming from *qualified and respected sources*. By itself, this does not necessarily signal the absence of a reasonable relationship between the SPS measure and the risk assessment, especially where the risk involved is life-threatening in character and is perceived to constitute a clear and imminent threat to public health and safety. Determination of the presence or absence of that relationship can only be done on a case-to-case basis, after account is taken of all considerations rationally bearing upon the issue of potential adverse health effects.[121]

The Appellate Body confirmed in *US/Canada – Continued Suspension (2008)* that the 'scientific basis need not reflect the majority view within the scientific community but may reflect divergent or minority views', and clarified the nature of the divergent or minority view on which an SPS measure can be based as follows:

> Having identified the scientific basis underlying the SPS measure, the panel must then verify that the scientific basis comes from a respected and qualified source. Although the scientific basis need not represent the majority view within the scientific community, it must nevertheless have the necessary scientific and methodological rigour to be considered reputable science. In other words, while the correctness of the views need not have been accepted by the broader scientific community, the views must be considered to be legitimate science according to the standards of the relevant scientific community.[122]

3.4 Obligations Relating to Risk Management

Risk management, as explained above, entails policy decision-making regarding: (1) the level of protection that a country wants to secure in its territory; and (2) the measure it will use to achieve this level of protection. These choices are 'based on' both scientific evidence and societal value judgments. The *SPS Agreement* gives national regulators substantial latitude in making risk management decisions, but there are certain non-scientific disciplines in place to ensure that the adverse trade effects of these decisions are limited as much as possible.

3.4.1 Appropriate Level of Protection

Risk management involves, in the first place, a decision on the 'appropriate level of protection', defined in paragraph 5 of Annex A to the *SPS Agreement* as:

> The level of protection *deemed appropriate by the Member* establishing a sanitary or phytosanitary measure to protect human, animal or plant life or health within its territory.[123]

121 Appellate Body Report, *EC – Hormones (1998)*, para. 194. Emphasis added.
122 Appellate Body Reports, *US/Canada – Continued Suspension (2008)*, para. 591.
123 Emphasis added. In *Australia – Apples (2010)*, the Appellate Body referred to the 'appropriate level of protection' also as the 'acceptable level of risk'. See Appellate Body Report, *Australia – Apples (2010)*, para. 405.

Thus, there is a clear recognition that it is the *prerogative* of the Member imposing the SPS measure to choose the level of protection of human, animal or plant life or health it will ensure in its territory.[124] Once the existence of a risk has been established by means of a risk assessment, a Member is free to choose even a zero-risk level of protection.[125]

Two provisions in the *SPS Agreement* deal with the choice of an appropriate level of protection. First, Article 5.4 provides that 'Members should ... take into account the objective of minimising negative trade effects' when choosing their level of protection. The word 'should' suggests that this provision is merely hortative. Indeed, obliging Members to choose the least trade-restrictive level of protection would seem to go against the underlying principle of the *SPS Agreement* that it is the prerogative of each Member to determine the level of protection it deems appropriate in its territory. The Appellate Body has, nonetheless, stated that Article 5.4 is one of the disciplines that a WTO Member *must respect* when it sets its appropriate level of protection with regard to a particular risk.[126] Note, however, that the obligation under Article 5.4 is not to '[minimise] negative trade effects', but to 'take into account the objective of minimising negative trade effects'.

The second discipline with regard to the appropriate level of protection is contained in Article 5.5, which provides in relevant part:

> With the objective of achieving consistency in the application of the concept of appropriate level of sanitary or phytosanitary protection against risks to human life or health, or to animal and plant life or health, each Member shall avoid arbitrary or unjustifiable distinctions in the levels it considers to be appropriate in different situations, if such distinctions result in discrimination or a disguised restriction on international trade.

The Article 5.5 discipline consists of two elements, namely: (1) the *goal* of achieving consistency in the application of the concept of appropriate level of sanitary or phytosanitary protection;[127] and (2) the *legal obligation* to avoid arbitrary or unjustifiable distinctions in the levels of protection deemed appropriate in different situations, *if* these distinctions lead to discrimination or disguised restrictions on trade.

In *EC – Hormones (1998)*, the Appellate Body recognised that countries establish their levels of protection *ad hoc* as risks arise. Absolute consistency in levels of protection is neither realistic nor required by Article 5.5 of the

124 See Appellate Body Report, *Australia – Salmon (1998)*, para. 199; and Appellate Body Reports, *US/Canada – Continued Suspension (2008)*, para. 523.

125 See Appellate Body Report, *Australia – Salmon (1998)*, para. 125.

126 See Appellate Body Reports, *US/Canada – Continued Suspension (2008)*, fn. 1088.

127 In *EC – Hormones (1998)*, the Appellate Body agreed with the panel that no legal obligation of consistency in levels of protection exists, but that consistency in levels of protection is only a goal for the future. See Appellate Body Report, *EC – Hormones (1998)*, para. 213.

SPS Agreement.[128] To establish whether an SPS measure is inconsistent with Article 5.5, three questions need to be answered:

- whether the Member concerned has set *different levels of protection* in different situations;
- whether these different levels of protection show *arbitrary or unjustifiable differences* in their treatment of different situations; and
- whether these arbitrary or unjustifiable differences lead to *discrimination or disguised restrictions* on trade.[129]

With regard to the *first element* of this three-tier test, it is obvious that not all risks can be treated the same. Thus, according to the Appellate Body in *EC – Hormones (1998)*, the 'different situations' referred to in Article 5.5 of the *SPS Agreement* must be *comparable* situations, that is, they must have some common element or elements.[130] For example, a common element would be the fact that the spread of the same disease is at issue, or that identical biological or economic consequences could result.[131] A difference in the levels of protection applied in the comparable situations must then be shown. With regard to the *second element* of the test of consistency with Article 5.5, it is necessary to examine whether reasons exist to justify the differences in levels of protection in order to determine whether these differences are 'arbitrary or unjustifiable'.[132] In *Australia – Salmon (1998)*, the Appellate Body found that distinctions in the level of protection can be said to be arbitrary or unjustifiable where the risk is at least equally high between the different situations at issue.[133] With regard to the *third element* of the Article 5.5 test, the Appellate Body stated in *EC – Hormones (1998)* that this is the most important of the elements of this three-tier test.[134] Whether the arbitrary or unjustifiable distinctions in levels of protection lead to 'discrimination or disguised restrictions on trade' can be determined by means of three 'warning signals' identified in the case law. Such 'warning signals' are not conclusive in their own right but, taken together and with other factors, they may support a finding that arbitrary or unjustifiable distinctions in levels of protection lead to 'discrimination or disguised restrictions on trade'.[135] The

128 *Ibid.*
129 See *ibid.*, para. 214, reiterated in Appellate Body Report, *Australia – Salmon (1998)*, para. 140. Note, however, that the panel in *Australia – Apples (2010)*, due to the 'specific circumstances' of the case, departed from a strict application of this three-tier test. See Panel Report, *Australia – Apples (2010)*, para. 7.985.
130 Appellate Body Report, *EC – Hormones (1998)*, para. 217.
131 See Appellate Body Report, *Australia – Salmon (1998)*, para. 146.
132 For a discussion of the meaning of the terms 'unjustifiable' and 'arbitrary' as used in the chapeau of Article XX of the GATT 1994 and Article XIV of the GATS, see above, pp. 592–604 and 615–17. See also Panel Report, *US – Poultry (2010)*, paras. 7.260–7.261.
133 See Appellate Body Report, *Australia – Salmon (1998)*, para. 158.
134 See Appellate Body Report, *EC – Hormones (1998)*, para. 240.
135 See Panel Report, *Australia – Salmon (1998)*, paras. 8.149–8.151, as approved by the Appellate Body. See Appellate Body Report, *Australia – Salmon (1998)*, paras. 162, 164 and 166. The first two warning signals were also relied upon in Appellate Body Report, *EC – Hormones (1998)*, paras. 215 and 240.

'warning signals' that may indicate that the measure is a disguised restriction on trade are: (1) the arbitrary character of the differences in the levels of protection; (2) the existence of substantial differences in the levels of protection; and (3) the absence of scientific justification for the differences.[136]

In June 2000, the SPS Committee drew up guidelines for the implementation of Article 5.5.[137] The guidelines, resulting from a series of consultations in the SPS Committee, reflect the clarifications emerging from the case law on Article 5.5, including the use of the three 'warning signals'.

3.4.2 'Not More Trade-Restrictive than Required'

In addition to the disciplines regarding the choice of an appropriate level of protection, the *SPS Agreement* contains rules regarding the choice of a SPS measure to achieve the chosen level of protection.

The first such rule is Article 5.3 of the *SPS Agreement*, which lists certain economic criteria, such as damage in terms of loss of production or sales that Members must consider in their choice of SPS measures.[138] This rule, however, only applies to SPS measures for the protection of the life and health of animals and plants.[139]

The second and much more important rule on the choice of measure is contained in Article 5.6 of the *SPS Agreement*, which provides:

> Without prejudice to paragraph 2 of Article 3, when establishing or maintaining sanitary or phytosanitary measures to achieve the appropriate level of sanitary or phytosanitary protection, Members shall ensure that such measures are not more trade-restrictive than required to achieve their appropriate level of sanitary or phytosanitary protection, taking into account technical and economic feasibility.

In a footnote to Article 5.6, it is stated:

> For purposes of paragraph 6 of Article 5, a measure is not more trade-restrictive than required unless there is another measure, reasonably available taking into account technical and economic feasibility, that achieves the appropriate level of sanitary or phytosanitary protection and is significantly less restrictive to trade.

On the basis of this footnote, the panel in *Australia – Salmon (1998)* identified a three-tier test, which was later upheld by the Appellate Body. Pursuant to this test, an SPS measure is more trade-restrictive than required (and thus inconsistent with Article 5.6) *only* if there is an alternative SPS measure which: (1) is reasonably available, taking into account technical and economic feasibility; (2) achieves the Member's appropriate level of protection; and (3) is significantly

136 See *ibid*. The absence of scientific justification can be clear from earlier findings of a violation of Articles 2.2 and 5.1.

137 These guidelines are contained in Committee on Sanitary and Phytosanitary Measures, *Guidelines to Further the Practical Implementation of Article 5.5*, G/SPS/15, dated 18 June 2000.

138 Note that Article 5.3 of the *SPS Agreement* also requires that these economic factors are taken into account in the assessment of risks to the life and health of animals and plants. See above, p. 964.

139 See also above, p. 960, fn. 118.

less trade-restrictive than the contested measure.[140] Only when all three of these cumulative requirements are satisfied will an SPS measure be inconsistent with Article 5.6.[141]

In *Australia – Apples (2010)*, the Appellate Body identified the general function of Article 5.6 as follows:

> The function of Article 5.6 is to ensure that SPS measures are not more trade restrictive than necessary to achieve a Member's appropriate level of protection. Compliance with this requirement is tested through a comparison of the measure at issue to possible alternative measures. Such alternatives, however, are mere conceptual tools for the purpose of the Article 5.6 analysis. A demonstration that an alternative measure meets the relevant Member's appropriate level of protection, is reasonably available, and is significantly less trade restrictive than the existing measure suffices to prove that the measure at issue is more trade restrictive than necessary. Yet this does not imply that the importing Member must adopt that alternative measure or that the alternative measure is the only option that would achieve the desired level of protection.[142]

To determine whether the first element of the test under Article 5.6 of the *SPS Agreement* is met, namely, *whether an alternative measure is reasonably available*, a panel will look at the facts of the case, including the characteristics of the SPS measure actually applied, as well as the alternative measures considered in the risk assessment, in order to determine which of the latter measures is a feasible alternative.[143] It is important to emphasise that it is the complainant, and not the panel or the panel's scientific experts, which must identify the alternative measure or measures, which is or are reasonably available.[144] In assessing whether an alternative measure is reasonably available, one must take into account the technical and economic feasibility of this measure.[145]

To determine whether the second element of this test is met, namely, *whether an alternative measure achieves the importing Member's appropriate level of protection*, it is necessary: (1) to identify the importing Member's appropriate level of protection; (2) to determine the level of protection that would be achieved by the complainant's proposed alternative measure; and (3) to determine whether the level of protection that would be achieved by the alternative measure would satisfy the importing Member's appropriate level of protection.[146]

140 See Panel Report, *Australia – Salmon (1998)*, para. 8.167; and Appellate Body Report, *Australia – Salmon (1998)*, para. 194. Note also that the Appellate Body ruled in *Australia – Apples (2010)* that the obligations set out in Article 5.1 and Article 5.6 are distinct and legally independent of each other and that a complainant is free to challenge the consistency of a measure with Article 5.6 without, at the same time, alleging a violation of Article 5.1. See Appellate Body Report, *Australia – Apples (2010)*, para. 354.

141 See Appellate Body Report, *Australia – Salmon (1998)*, para. 194, reiterated in Appellate Body Report, *Japan – Agricultural Products II (1999)*, para. 95.

142 Appellate Body Report, *Australia – Apples (2010)*, para. 363.

143 See Panel Report, *Australia – Salmon (1998)*, para. 8.171; and Panel Report, *Australia – Salmon (Article 21.5 – Canada) (2000)*, paras. 7.146–7.149.

144 See *Japan – Agricultural Products II (1999)*, paras. 124–5.

145 See Article 5.6 of the *SPS Agreement*.

146 Appellate Body Report, *Australia – Apples (2010)*, para. 368.

In *Australia – Salmon (1998)*, the Appellate Body reversed the panel's finding that the appropriate level of protection can be implied from the level of protection that is afforded by the SPS measure imposed. The Appellate Body emphasised that the choice of a level of protection is the prerogative of the Member concerned.[147] Further, it held:

> The 'appropriate level of protection' established by a Member and the 'SPS measure' have to be clearly distinguished. They are not one and the same thing. The first is an *objective*, the second is an *instrument* chosen to attain or implement that objective.
>
> It can be deduced from the provisions of the *SPS Agreement* that the determination by a Member of the 'appropriate level of protection' logically precedes the establishment or decision on maintenance of an 'SPS measure'.[148]

There are, however, cases where Members do not expressly determine their appropriate level of protection, or do so with insufficient clarity so that it becomes impossible to apply Article 5.6.[149] The Appellate Body in *Australia – Salmon (1998)* recognised this, and thus read into paragraph 3 of Annex B and Articles 4.1, 5.4 and 5.6 an implicit obligation on Members to determine their appropriate levels of protection.[150] This was further explained as follows in *Australia – Apples (2010)*:

> While there is no obligation to set the appropriate level of protection in quantitative terms, a Member is not free to establish its level with such vagueness or equivocation as to render impossible the application of the relevant disciplines of the *SPS Agreement*, including the obligation set out in Article 5.6.[151]

The Appellate Body has also explained, in *Australia – Salmon (1998)*, that, when a Member does not comply with its obligation to identify its appropriate level of protection, that level may be deduced from the SPS measure actually applied:

> [I]n cases where a Member does not determine its appropriate level of protection, or does so with insufficient precision, the appropriate level of protection may be established by panels on the basis of the level of protection reflected in the SPS measure actually applied. Otherwise, a Member's failure to comply with the implicit obligation to determine its appropriate level of protection – with sufficient precision – would allow it to escape from its obligations under this Agreement and, in particular, its obligations under Articles 5.5 and 5.6.[152]

In *India – Agricultural Products (2015)*, the Appellate Body reiterated that the specification of the appropriate level of protection is 'both a prerogative and an obligation of the responding Member'.[153] The Appellate Body also stated that:

> in the context of WTO dispute settlement proceedings, a responding Member is generally better placed than the complainant to know what objective it has set in terms of the level

147 Appellate Body Report, *Australia – Salmon (1998)*, para. 199; and Appellate Body Reports, *US/Canada – Continued Suspension (2008)*, para. 523.
148 Appellate Body Report, *Australia – Salmon (1998)*, paras. 200–1.
149 The same problem may arise under Article 5.5 of the *SPS Agreement*.
150 See Appellate Body Report, *Australia – Salmon (1998)*, paras. 205–7.
151 Appellate Body Report, *Australia – Apples (2010)*, para. 343.
152 Appellate Body Report, *Australia – Salmon (1998)*, para. 207.
153 Appellate Body Report, *India – Agricultural Products (2015)*, para. 5.221.

> of SPS protection it wishes to achieve. For these reasons, typically a panel adjudicating a claim under Article 5.6 of the SPS Agreement would be expected to accord weight to the respondent's articulation of its appropriate level of protection.[154]

However, the Appellate Body emphasised that this does not mean that a panel must defer completely to a respondent's characterisation of its own appropriate level of protection.[155] As the Appellate Body stated:

> Rather, in examining a claim under Article 5.6 of the SPS Agreement, a panel is required to ascertain the respondent's appropriate level of protection on the basis of *the totality of the arguments and evidence on the record.*[156]

The third and last element of the test under Article 5.6 of the *SPS Agreement*, namely, that *the alternative measure is significantly less trade-restrictive*, was examined by both the original panel and the Article 21.5 panel in *Australia – Salmon (1998)* and by the panel in *Japan – Agricultural Products II (1999).*[157] It appears from these cases that the issue relates to whether market access would be substantially improved if an alternative measure were imposed.

3.5 Provisional Measures and the Precautionary Principle

While the *SPS Agreement* requires that SPS measures be 'based on' science and uses science as the touchstone against which SPS measures will be judged, it is obvious that science does not have clear and unambiguous answers to all regulatory questions. Situations may arise where there is, in fact, insufficient scientific evidence regarding the existence and extent of the relevant risk but where governments consider they need to act promptly and take measures to avoid possible harm. Thus, governments act with precaution without waiting for the collection of sufficient scientific information to assess the risks conclusively. This is commonly referred to as acting in accordance with the 'precautionary principle', or the 'precautionary approach'. Considerable difference of opinion exists between Members regarding the role that precaution should play in the regulatory process, and the European Union and the United States often find themselves on opposite sides in this debate. It is indisputable that precaution is an inherent part of risk regulation, particularly in the area of health and environment. What is disputed, however, is whether precaution should be taken into account in risk assessment or whether it only comes into play in risk

154 *Ibid.* Note that the burden of proof to show that the SPS measure at issue is inconsistent with Article 5.6 of the *SPS Agreement* is on the complainant. However, as the Appellate Body observed, there is a distinction between that burden of proof, on the one hand, and the analysis that must be undertaken by a panel in assessing the claim of inconsistency with Article 5.6, on the other hand. The panel assessing such claim is charged with, *inter alia*, identifying the level of protection of the Member whose SPS measure is challenged. See *ibid.*, para. 5.220.

155 See *ibid.*, para. 5.221. 156 *Ibid.* Emphasis added.

157 See Panel Report, *Australia – Salmon (1998)*, para. 8.182; Panel Report, *Australia – Salmon (Article 21.5 – Canada) (2000)*, paras. 7.150–7.153; Panel Report, *Japan – Agricultural Products II (1999)*, paras. 8.79, 8.89, 8.95–8.96 and 8.103–8.104.

management decisions.[158] It is therefore important to establish to what extent the *SPS Agreement* allows for precaution to play a role in Members' SPS regulation.

Article 5.7 of the *SPS Agreement* provides for the possibility to take – under certain conditions – provisional SPS measures where scientific evidence is insufficient. As already discussed above, the Appellate Body stated in *Japan – Agricultural Products II (1999)* that:

> Article 5.7 operates as a *qualified* exemption from the obligation under Article 2.2 not to maintain SPS measures without sufficient scientific evidence.[159]

Article 5.7 could thus be regarded as a particular formulation of the precautionary principle. As held by the Appellate Body in *US/Canada – Continued Suspension (2008)*, Article 5.7 provides: [a] temporary 'safety valve' in situations where some evidence of risk exists but not enough to complete a full risk assessment, thus making it impossible to meet the rigorous standards set by Articles 2.2 and 5.1.[160] As stated by the Appellate Body in *Japan – Agricultural Products II (1999)*, Article 5.7 limits the scope of application of Articles 2.2 and 5.1. It embodies an *autonomous right* of WTO Members, rather than a justification for violation of other relevant provisions of the *SPS Agreement.*[161]

Article 5.7 provides:

> In cases where relevant scientific evidence is insufficient, a Member may provisionally adopt sanitary or phytosanitary measures on the basis of available pertinent information, including that from the relevant international organizations as well as from sanitary or phytosanitary measures applied by other Members. In such circumstances, Members shall seek to obtain the additional information necessary for a more objective assessment of risk and review the sanitary or phytosanitary measure accordingly within a reasonable period of time.

From this provision, four cumulative requirements for provisional measures were identified by the panel, and confirmed by the Appellate Body, in *Japan – Agricultural Products II (1999)* and *US/Canada – Continued Suspension (2008)*, namely, that the measure must: (1) be imposed in respect of a situation where relevant scientific evidence is insufficient; (2) be adopted on the basis of available pertinent information; (3) not be maintained unless the Member seeks to obtain the additional information necessary for a more objective assessment of risk; and (4) be reviewed accordingly within a reasonable period of time.[162]

158 There is also a difference of opinion as to whether precaution has emerged as a 'principle' in international law, or whether it is a mere 'approach' followed by countries.

159 Appellate Body Report, *Japan – Agricultural Products II (1999)*, para. 80.

160 Appellate Body Reports, *US/Canada – Continued Suspension (2008)*, para. 678.

161 See Panel Report, *EC – Approval and Marketing of Biotech Products (2006)*, paras. 7.3000–7.3002.

162 See Panel Report, *Japan – Agricultural Products II (1999)*, para. 8.54; Appellate Body Report, *Japan – Agricultural Products II (1999)*, para. 89; and Appellate Body Reports, *US/Canada – Continued Suspension (2008)*, para. 676.

According to the Appellate Body in *US/Canada – Continued Suspension (2008)*, the four conditions set out above must be interpreted keeping in mind that the precautionary principle finds reflection in Article 5.7.[163] In *Japan – Apples (2003)*, the panel addressed the *first* requirement. It held that the existence of a situation where 'relevant scientific evidence is insufficient' cannot merely be implied from a finding that the measure is maintained 'without sufficient scientific evidence' under Article 2.2.[164] It held:

> Article 5.7 refers to 'relevant scientific evidence' which implies that the body of material that might be considered includes not only evidence supporting Japan's position, but also evidence supporting other views.[165]

Since a wealth of scientific evidence was submitted in that case by both the parties and the panel experts, the panel found that it was indisputable that a large amount of relevant scientific evidence was available. It held:

> The current 'situation', where scientific studies as well as practical experience have accumulated for the past 200 years, is clearly not the type of situation Article 5.7 was intended to address. Article 5.7 was obviously designed to be invoked in situations where little, or no, reliable evidence was available on the subject-matter at issue.[166]

On appeal, Japan challenged the panel's finding that Article 5.7 is intended only to address situations where little, or no, reliable evidence was available on the subject matter at issue. According to Japan, Article 5.7 covers not only situations of 'new uncertainty' (where a new risk is identified) but also 'unresolved uncertainty' (where considerable scientific evidence exists on the risk but uncertainty still remains). The Appellate Body, however, upheld the panel's finding, pointing out that Article 5.7:

> is triggered not by the existence of scientific uncertainty, but rather by the insufficiency of scientific evidence.[167]

Thus the concept of *insufficiency* of scientific evidence and the concept of scientific *uncertainty* are not interchangeable. Further, the Appellate Body identified a contextual link between the first requirement of Article 5.7 and the obligation to perform a risk assessment in Article 5.1. Thus, relevant scientific evidence will be 'insufficient' within the meaning of Article 5.7 if it:

> does not allow, in qualitative or quantitative terms, the performance of an adequate assessment of risks as required under Article 5.1.[168]

163 Appellate Body Reports, *US/Canada – Continued Suspension (2008)*, para. 680.
164 Panel Report, *Japan – Apples (2003)*, para. 8.215. 165 *Ibid.*, para. 8.216.
166 *Ibid.*, para. 8.219.
167 Appellate Body Report, *Japan – Apples (2003)*, para. 184. Moreover, it noted that the panel's finding referred to the availability of *reliable* evidence, and thus did not exclude cases 'where the available evidence is more than minimal in quantity, but has not led to reliable or conclusive results'. *Ibid.*, para. 185.
168 *Ibid.*, para. 179.

According to the Appellate Body in *Japan – Apples (2003)*, the factual findings of the panel showed that the scientific evidence available *did* permit the performance of a risk assessment under Article 5.1 and the relevant scientific evidence was thus not insufficient within the meaning of Article 5.7. This analysis of the first requirement of Article 5.7 in *Japan – Apples (2003)* is important. It clarifies the role of Article 5.7, establishing that it is there to address situations where there is a true lack of sufficient scientific evidence regarding the risk at issue, either due to the small amount of evidence on new risks, or due to the fact that accumulated evidence is inconclusive or unreliable. In either case, the insufficiency of the evidence must be such as to make the performance of an adequate risk assessment impossible. Thus, Article 5.7 cannot be used to justify measures that are adopted in disregard of reliable scientific evidence.[169]

The first requirement of Article 5.7 of the *SPS Agreement* was again at issue in *EC – Approval and Marketing of Biotech Products (2006)*. The European Communities argued that, because the bans on biotech products imposed by certain of its Member States are by nature provisional, it is by reference to the rules in Article 5.7, not the rules in Article 5.1, that these bans must be assessed.[170] The panel examined this argument in light of the first sentence of Article 5.7. It found:

> The first sentence follows a classic 'if–then' logic: if a certain condition is met (*in casu*, insufficiency of relevant scientific evidence), a particular right is conferred (*in casu*, the right provisionally to adopt an SPS measure based on available pertinent information). Thus, it is clear that Article 5.7 is applicable whenever the relevant condition is met, that is to say, in every case where relevant scientific evidence is insufficient. The provisional adoption of an SPS measure is not a condition for the applicability of Article 5.7. Rather, the provisional adoption of an SPS measure is permitted by the first sentence of Article 5.7.[171]

Therefore, the trigger for applicability of Article 5.7 is the insufficiency of the scientific evidence, not the provisional nature of the measure at issue.[172]

In *US/Canada – Continued Suspension (2008)*, the Appellate Body further clarified that 'the existence of scientific controversy in itself is not enough to conclude that the relevant scientific evidence is "insufficient"',[173] since Article 5.1 allows Members to base their SPS measures on divergent or minority views from a qualified and respected source. In such cases, it is possible to perform a risk assessment that meets the requirements of Article 5.1. Instead, the Appellate Body emphasised that:

> Article 5.7 is concerned with situations where deficiencies in the body of scientific evidence do not allow a WTO Member to arrive at a sufficiently objective conclusion in relation to risk.[174]

169 When an international standard (presumably based on a risk assessment) exists, a complainant may argue that the existence of such standard indicates that there is not insufficient evidence to conduct a risk assessment and that therefore recourse to Article 5.7 is not possible. However, the existence of an international standard is not dispositive as to the question of the sufficiency of the scientific evidence. See Appellate Body Reports, *US/Canada – Continued Suspension (2008)*, para. 696.

170 See Panel Reports, *EC – Approval and Marketing of Biotech Products (2006)*, paras. 7.2930–7.2933.

171 *Ibid.*, para. 7.2939.

172 Further, the panel pointed out that the insufficiency of the evidence must be determined by reference to the time the relevant provisional SPS measure was adopted. See *ibid.*, para. 7.3253.

173 Appellate Body Reports, *US/Canada – Continued Suspension (2008)*, para. 677.

174 *Ibid.*

In *US/Canada – Continued Suspension (2008)*, the Appellate Body made two further observations on the 'insufficiency' of scientific evidence, namely, that: (1) the possibility of conducting further scientific investigation (which is in fact always possible) does not, by itself, mean that the relevant scientific evidence is or becomes 'insufficient' within the meaning of Article 5.7;[175] and (2) for existing scientific evidence to become 'insufficient' within the meaning of Article 5.7, no paradigmatic shift in the scientific knowledge is required; it is enough that 'new scientific developments call into question whether the body of scientific evidence still permits of a sufficiently objective assessment of risk'.[176] The Appellate Body noted that 'science continuously evolves', and considered it was:

> useful to think of the degree of change as a spectrum. On one extreme of this spectrum lies the incremental advance of science. Where these scientific advances are at the margins, they would not support the conclusion that previously sufficient evidence has become insufficient. At the other extreme lie the more radical scientific changes that lead to a paradigm shift. Such radical change is not frequent. Limiting the application of Article 5.7 to situations where scientific advances lead to a paradigm shift would be too inflexible an approach. WTO Members should be permitted to take a provisional measure where new evidence from a qualified and respected source puts into question the relationship between the pre-existing body of scientific evidence and the conclusions regarding the risks.[177]

Accordingly, the Appellate Body rejected the panel's notion that 'there must be a *critical mass* of new evidence and/or information that calls into question the fundamental precepts of previous knowledge and evidence so as to make relevant, previously sufficient, evidence now insufficient' because this could be understood as requiring that the new scientific evidence lead to a paradigm shift, an approach that the Appellate Body found too inflexible.[178]

Finally, note with regard to the insufficiency of the scientific evidence that the Appellate Body disagreed with the European Communities' argument in *US/ Canada – Continued Suspension (2008)* that SPS measures either are 'based on' a risk assessment under Article 5.1, or otherwise the relevant scientific evidence will be 'insufficient' within the meaning of Article 5.7, so that provisional SPS measures may be justified. The Appellate Body explained:

> There may be situations where the relevant scientific evidence is sufficient to perform a risk assessment, a WTO Member performs such a risk assessment, but does not adopt an SPS measure either because the risk assessment did not confirm the risk, or the risk identified did not exceed that Member's chosen level of protection. Also, there may be situations where there is no pertinent scientific information available indicating a risk such that an SPS measure would be unwarranted even on a provisional basis.[179]

The second requirement of Article 5.7 of the *SPS Agreement*, namely, that provisional measures must be adopted on the basis of available pertinent information,

175 See *ibid.*, para. 702. 176 *Ibid.*, para. 725.

177 *Ibid.*, para. 703.

178 *Ibid.*, para. 705, referring to Panel Report, *US – Continued Suspension (2008)*, para. 7.648; and Panel Report, *Canada – Continued Suspension (2008)*, para. 7.626. See also Appellate Body Reports, *US/Canada – Continued Suspension (2008)*, para. 725.

179 Appellate Body Reports, *US/Canada – Continued Suspension (2008)*, para. 681.

was addressed for the first time in the *US/Canada – Continued Suspension (2008)* cases. The Appellate Body held that this refers to situations where 'there is some evidentiary basis indicating the possible existence of a risk, but not enough to permit the performance of a risk assessment'.[180] It further held that a 'rational and objective relationship' between the information concerning a risk and the provisional SPS measure is required.[181]

As the Appellate Body found in *US/Canada – Continued Suspension (2008)*, the third and fourth requirements of Article 5.7 of the *SPS Agreement* relate to the *maintenance* of SPS measures taken under Article 5.7 and highlight their provisional nature.[182]

The third requirement of Article 5.7 of the *SPS Agreement* obliges Members to seek to obtain the additional information necessary for a more objective risk assessment. This requirement was clarified by the Appellate Body in *Japan – Agricultural Products II (1999)* and *US/Canada – Continued Suspension (2008)* in three respects, namely: (1) the insufficiency of scientific evidence 'is not a perennial state, but a transitory one'; as of the adoption of the provisional measure, a WTO Member 'must make best efforts to remedy the insufficiency'; (2) Article 5.7 does not specify what actual results must be achieved; the obligation is to 'seek to obtain' additional information; and (3) the information sought must be germane to conducting a risk assessment within the meaning of Article 5.1.[183]

The fourth requirement of Article 5.7 of the *SPS Agreement*, namely, to review the provisional SPS measure within a reasonable period of time, is another reflection of the time-limited nature of such measures under the *SPS Agreement*. However, as a situation of insufficiency of scientific evidence may persist for an extended period of time, artificially linking the requirement of review to a fixed time limit was avoided in the *SPS Agreement*. Instead, Article 5.7 refers to a 'reasonable period of time'. As the Appellate Body stated in *Japan – Agricultural Products II (1999)*, what constitutes a 'reasonable period of time' depends on the specific circumstances of each case, including the difficulty of obtaining the additional information necessary for the review *and* the characteristics of the provisional SPS measure.[184]

Finally, the question has arisen whether Article 5.7 of the *SPS Agreement* exhausts the relevance of the precautionary principle for purposes of the *SPS Agreement*. In *EC – Hormones (1998)*, the European Communities relied on the precautionary principle as a rule of customary international law, or at least a general principle of law, applicable to the interpretation of the scientific disciplines in the *SPS Agreement*. The Appellate Body expressed doubts as to whether

180 *Ibid.*, para. 678.
181 *Ibid.*
182 See *ibid.*, para. 679. See also already Appellate Body Report, *Japan – Apples (2003)*, fn. 318 to para. 176.
183 See Appellate Body Report, *Japan – Agricultural Products II (1999)*, para. 92; and Appellate Body Reports, *US/Canada – Continued Suspension (2008)*, para. 679.
184 See Appellate Body Report, *Japan – Agricultural Products II (1999)*, para. 93.

the precautionary principle had developed into a principle of general or customary international law, but considered that it was 'unnecessary, and probably imprudent', to take a position on this important, but abstract, question.[185] The Appellate Body did postulate, however, that Article 5.7 does not exhaust the relevance of the precautionary principle in the *SPS Agreement*. This principle is also reflected in the sixth paragraph of the Preamble and Article 3.3 of the *SPS Agreement*. Both these provisions deal with the right of Members to set their own level of protection, even if this level is higher than that reflected in international standards.[186] Note, however, that the Appellate Body held in *EC – Hormones (1998)* that the precautionary principle (presumably regardless of its status under international law) cannot override the explicit requirements of the *SPS Agreement*, and in particular Articles 5.1 and 5.2 thereof.[187] The practical effect of this ruling is to limit the relevance of the precautionary principle under the *SPS Agreement* to the situation covered by Article 5.7. The precautionary principle can thus *not* be relied upon to add flexibility to the scientific disciplines in Articles 2.2 and 5.1 of the *SPS Agreement*. However, as the Appellate Body held in *US/Canada – Continued Suspension (2008)* and as discussed above, Article 5.7 'must be interpreted keeping in mind that the precautionary principle finds reflection in this provision'.[188]

3.6 Other Substantive Provisions

In addition to the basic substantive provisions discussed in the previous sections, the *SPS Agreement* also contains a number of other substantive provisions, which deserve to be mentioned. This section briefly examines the substantive provisions of the *SPS Agreement* relating to: (1) recognition of equivalence; (2) adaptation to regional conditions; (3) control, inspection and approval procedures; (4) transparency and notification; and (5) special and differential treatment for developing-country Members.

3.6.1 Recognition of Equivalence

Due to differences between Members with regard to local climatic and geographical conditions, consumer preferences and technical and financial resources, it may sometimes be difficult, or even undesirable, to harmonise SPS measures. In such cases, the resulting variety of SPS measures can substantially hinder trade. Such negative effects can be limited if importing Members recognise that it is possible for different measures to achieve the same level of protection (i.e. be equally effective in reducing risk) and are willing to allow imports of products

185 See Appellate Body Report, *EC – Hormones (1998)*, para. 123. On this question, see also Panel Reports, *EC – Approval and Marketing of Biotech Products (2006)*, paras. 7.88–7.89.

186 See above, pp. 951–5.

187 See Appellate Body Report, *EC – Hormones (1998)*, para. 124.

188 Appellate Body Reports, *US/Canada – Continued Suspension (2008)*, para. 680.

that comply with different, but equally effective, SPS measures. For this reason, Article 4 of the *SPS Agreement* sets out certain obligations for Members with regard to the recognition of equivalence.

Article 4.1 of the *SPS Agreement* obliges Members to accept different SPS measures as equivalent if the exporting Member objectively demonstrates to the importing Member that its measures achieve the latter's appropriate level of protection. The exporting Member is to provide appropriate science-based and technical information to the importing Member, as well as reasonable access, upon request, to the importing Member for inspection, testing and other relevant procedures for the recognition of equivalence.[189] In addition, Article 4.2 obliges Members, when requested, to enter into consultations with the aim of concluding agreements on the recognition of equivalence.

Problems with the implementation of Article 4 of the *SPS Agreement* led the SPS Committee to engage in discussions on equivalence. These discussions resulted in the adoption, in October 2001, of the 'Decision on Equivalence'.[190] This Decision sets out binding guidelines for any Member requesting the recognition of equivalence and for the importing Member to whom such request is addressed.[191] After the adoption of the Decision on Equivalence, the SPS Committee undertook a work programme to clarify and further elaborate certain provisions of that Decision. This led, in July 2004, to the adoption of the current version of the Decision.[192]

3.6.2 Adaptation to Regional Conditions

Although traditionally an importing country applies its SPS measures to an exporting country as a whole, differences in sanitary and phytosanitary conditions *within* exporting countries often exist. In particular, pest and disease prevalence is independent of national boundaries and can differ within a specific country, due to variations in climate, environment, geographic conditions and regulatory systems in place to control or eradicate pests or diseases. The adaptation of SPS measures to the conditions prevailing in the region of origin of the product may thus be highly desirable. Failure to adapt SPS measures to regional conditions may lead to excessively trade-restrictive SPS measures.

For this reason, Article 6 of the *SPS Agreement* establishes, in three interconnected paragraphs, a number of obligations regarding the adaptation of

189 See Committee on Sanitary and Phytosanitary Measures, *Decision on the Implementation of Article 4 of the Agreement on the Application of Sanitary and Phytosanitary Measures. Revision*, G/SPS/19/Rev.2, dated 23 July 2004, para. 4.

190 See Committee on Sanitary and Phytosanitary Measures, *Decision on the Implementation of Article 4 of the Agreement on the Application of Sanitary and Phytosanitary Measures*, G/SPS/19, dated 24 October 2001.

191 While the Decision on Equivalence sets out binding guidelines, these guidelines cannot be enforced through recourse to WTO dispute settlement. See above, pp. 983–5.

192 See Committee on Sanitary and Phytosanitary Measures, *Decision on the Implementation of Article 4 of the Agreement on the Application of Sanitary and Phytosanitary Measures. Revision*, G/SPS/19/Rev.2, dated 23 July 2004.

SPS measures to regional conditions. Article 6.1 of the *SPS Agreement* obliges Members to ensure that their SPS measures are adapted to the sanitary and phytosanitary *characteristics* of the region of origin and destination of the product. These characteristics must be determined with reference to, *inter alia*: (1) the level of pest or disease prevalence; (2) the existence of eradication or control programmes; and (3) guidelines developed by international organisations. Article 6.2 of the *SPS Agreement* obliges Members, in particular, to recognise the concepts of pest- or disease-free areas and areas of low pest or disease prevalence. The Appellate Body noted in *India – Agricultural Products (2015)* that Article 6.2 is 'one particular way through which a Member can ensure that its SPS measures are "adapted", as required by Article 6.1'.[193] According to the Appellate Body, Members enjoy a 'degree of latitude' in determining how to ensure the adaptation of its SPS measures to regional conditions as required under Article 6.1 or how to recognise the concepts of pest- or disease-free areas and areas of low pest or disease prevalence, as required under Article 6.2.[194] The Appellate Body noted, however, that:

> it is nevertheless clear that compliance with the obligations in Articles 6.1 and 6.2 will be facilitated in circumstances where WTO Members put in place a regulatory scheme or structure that accommodates adaptation of SPS measures on an ongoing basis.[195]

The Appellate Body also noted that it agreed with the panel's observation that:

> SPS measures or regulatory schemes that explicitly foreclose the possibility of recognition of the concepts of pest- or disease-free areas and areas of low pest or disease prevalence cannot, when these concepts are relevant with respect to the diseases addressed by such SPS measures, be found to be consistent with Article 6.2.[196]

With regard to Article 6.3 of the *SPS Agreement*, the Appellate Body noted that this last paragraph of Article 6 relates to the specific situation of an exporting Member claiming that an area within its territory is a pest- or disease-free area or an area of low pest or disease prevalence.[197]

In *India – Agricultural Products (2015)*, India argued on appeal that a Member adopting or maintaining an SPS measure can *only* be found to have breached the obligation under Article 6.1 after an exporting Member has made the objective demonstration provided for in Article 6.3. The Appellate Body disagreed with India.[198] As the Appellate Body explained:

> even in the absence of such objective demonstration by an exporting Member, a Member may still be found to have failed to ensure that an SPS measure is adapted to regional conditions within the meaning of Article 6.1 in a situation where, for example, the concepts of pest- and disease-free areas are relevant, but such Member's regulatory regime precludes the recognition of such concept.[199]

193 Appellate Body Report, *India – Agricultural Products (2015)*, para. 5.133. 194 See *ibid.*, para. 5.137.
195 *Ibid.*, para. 5.138. 196 *Ibid.*
197 See *ibid.*, para. 5.140. 198 See *ibid.*, para. 5.157.
199 *Ibid.*

In May 2008, the SPS Committee adopted a decision on non-binding guidelines for implementing Article 6 of the *SPS Agreement*, commonly referred to as the Regionalisation Decision.[200]

3.6.3 Control, Inspection and Approval Procedures

In order to ensure that their SPS requirements are complied with, countries usually have control, inspection and approval procedures in place.[201] If these procedures are complex, lengthy or costly, they may restrict market access. To avoid this, Article 8 of the *SPS Agreement* obliges Members to comply with the disciplines contained in Annex C as well as other provisions of the *SPS Agreement* in the operation of their control, inspection and approval procedures. The disciplines in Annex C aim to ensure that procedures are not more lengthy and burdensome than is reasonable and necessary and do not discriminate against imports.

Paragraph 1 of Annex C provides, *inter alia*:

> Members shall ensure, with respect to any procedure to check and ensure the fulfilment of sanitary or phytosanitary measures, that:
>
> (a) such procedures are undertaken and completed without undue delay and in no less favourable manner for imported products than for like domestic products;
>
> ...
>
> (c) information requirements are limited to what is necessary for appropriate control, inspection and approval procedures, including for approval of the use of additives or for the establishment of tolerances for contaminants in food, beverages or feedstuffs;

The panel in *US – Animals (2015)* concluded that Article 8 and Annex C of the *SPS Agreement* cover a broad array of procedures and rejected the United States' argument that the covered procedures are limited to those addressing products, and exclude procedures aiming at determinations of the disease status of certain geographic regions.[202] The panel emphasised that not only the immediate object, but also the ultimate effect of the completion of procedures must be considered. The panel noted:

> In our view, focusing solely on the immediate object of an importing Member's procedures, while losing sight of the ultimate effect of the completion of such procedures, might enable Members to avoid the application of Article 8 and Annex C by simply parsing their regulatory processes between regional determinations and approvals to import.[203]

With regard to the word 'complete', panels and the Appellate Body have stated that it indicates that 'approval procedures are not only to be undertaken, but are also to be finished, or concluded'.[204]

200 See Committee on Sanitary and Phytosanitary Measures, *Guidelines to Further the Practical Implementation of Article 6 of the Agreement on the Application of Sanitary and Phytosanitary Measures*, G/SPS/48, dated 16 May 2008.

201 Note that, in the context of the *TBT Agreement* these measures are referred to as 'conformity assessment procedures'. See above, p. 887.

202 See Panel Report, *US – Animals (2015)*, paras. 7.68 and 7.69. 203 *Ibid.*, para. 7.70.

204 *Ibid.*, para. 7.11. The panel in *US –Animals (2015)* referred to Panel Report, *EC – Approval and Marketing of Biotech Products (2006)*, para. 7.1494; Panel Reports, *US – Poultry (China) (2010)*, para. 7.383; *EC – Seal Products (2014)*, para. 7.562; and Appellate Body Report, *Australia– Apples (2010)*, para. 438.

With regard to the 'without undue delay' requirement of Annex C(1) (a), the Appellate Body ruled in *Australia – Apples (2010)*:

Annex C(1) (a) requires Members to ensure that relevant procedures are undertaken and completed with appropriate dispatch, that is, that they do not involve periods of time that are unwarranted, or otherwise excessive, disproportionate or unjustifiable. Whether a relevant procedure has been unduly delayed is, therefore, not an assessment that can be done in the abstract, but one which requires a case-by-case analysis as to the reasons for the alleged failure to act with appropriate dispatch, and whether such reasons are justifiable.[205]

The panel in *US – Animals (2015)* interpreted the term 'undertaken and completed without undue delay' to include not only undue delay in the commencement of the procedure and its completion, but also in the intervening process that leads from commencement to completion.[206]

In the context of 'without undue delay', the panel in *US – Animals (2015)* noted that the normal course of a procedure requires competent authorities to actively engage with the applicant Member on the substance of its application.[207] It noted:

Thus, inaction or an inability to proceed on the substance of the application would constitute something outside the normal course of the procedure and should be considered a delay within the meaning of Article 8 and Annex C(1) (a).[208]

The panel further noted that a determination of whether a delay exists should be made in light of the nature and complexity of the procedure to be undertaken and completed.[209]

With regard to assessment of the reasons or justification for the delay, the panel in *EC – Approval and Marketing of Biotech Products (2006)* examined and rejected the European Communities' arguments that the delays were justified by the perceived inadequacy of its existing legislation and the prudent and precautionary approach it applied due to the fact that the relevant science was evolving and in a state of flux.[210]

The panel in *US – Animals (2015)* disagreed with the United States that the need to 're-confirm and update' pre-existing information constitutes, in and of itself, a justification for the delay in the completion of a control, inspection or approval procedure.[211] The panel noted that accepting such an argument would seriously undermine the obligations in Annex C(1) (a), as it would allow a WTO

205 Appellate Body Report, *Australia – Apples (2010)*, para. 437.

206 See Panel Report, *US – Animals (2015)*, para. 7.112. 207 See *ibid.*, para. 7.113.

208 *Ibid.*

209 *Ibid.*, para. 7.114. The panel pointed out that 'in making an assessment of whether delays occurred with respect to Argentina's applications, the Panel cannot simply compare the time taken to review Argentina's applications to a standard processing time. Instead, the Panel must examine each of the time periods identified by Argentina as delays to determine whether they were periods when the procedure did not move forward because of inaction or inability to proceed.'

210 See Panel Reports, *EC – Approval and Marketing of Biotech Products (2006)*, paras. 7.1509–7.1530. The panel pointed out that the core obligation of Annex C(1)(a) is for Members to come to a substantive decision. This decision need not give 'a straight yes or no answer to applicants'. Instead, a Member, for example, may reject an application subject to later review, or give a time-limited approval.

211 See Panel Report, *US – Animals (2015)*, para. 7.143.

Member to indefinitely postpone the completion of a procedure by invoking the need to reconfirm information that had become outdated by virtue of its own inaction, creating a dangerous loophole and rewarding behaviour opposite to the diligence called for by Annex C(1).[212]

With regard to the 'in no less favourable manner' requirement of Annex C(1) (a), the panel in *EC – Approval and Marketing of Biotech Products (2006)* found that, in order to establish a violation of this requirement of Annex C(1) (a), it is necessary to establish:

> (i) that imported products have been treated in a 'less favourable manner' than domestic products in respect of the undertaking and completion of approval procedures, and (ii) that the imported products which are alleged to have been treated less favourably are 'like' the domestic products which are alleged to have been treated more favourably.[213]

On the first element of this test, the panel noted that it clearly lays down a national treatment obligation, and it therefore considered it useful to look to case law on Article III:4 of the GATT 1994 for appropriate interpretative guidance.[214]

3.6.4 Transparency and Notification

Lack of transparency with regard to SPS measures may constitute a significant barrier to market access since it increases the cost and difficulty for exporters in determining what requirements their products must comply with in their export markets.[215] This issue is addressed in Article 7 of the *SPS Agreement*, which obliges Members to notify changes in their SPS measures and to provide information on their SPS measures according to Annex B to the *SPS Agreement*. Annex B contains multiple, detailed rules on: (1) the publication of adopted SPS measures; (2) national enquiry points; and (3) the prior notification of proposed SPS measures that differ from international standards, to allow time for comments from other Members.

With regard to the 'publication' requirement of Annex B(1), the Appellate Body in *Japan – Agricultural Products II (1999)* found that the object and purpose of Annex B(1) is:

> 'to enable interested Members to become acquainted with' the sanitary and phytosanitary regulations adopted or maintained by other Members and thus to enhance transparency regarding these measures. In our opinion, the scope of application of the publication requirement of paragraph 1 of Annex B should be interpreted in the light of the object and purpose of this provision.[216]

In *Japan – Agricultural Products II (1999)*, the Appellate Body upheld the panel's finding that Japan had violated the 'publication' requirement of Annex B(1)

212 *Ibid.*
213 Panel Reports, *EC – Approval and Marketing of Biotech Products (2006)*, para. 7.2400.
214 See *ibid.*, para. 7.2401. On the case law on Article III:4 of the GATT 1994, see above, pp. 376–99.
215 For a general discussion of the lack of transparency as a trade barrier, see above, pp. 534–5.
216 Appellate Body Report, *Japan – Agricultural Products II (1999)*, para. 106.

and Article 7 of the *SPS Agreement*. It was undisputed that Japan's varietal testing requirement was generally applicable, and that it had not been published. The Appellate Body agreed with the panel that the actual impact of the varietal testing requirement on exporting countries was such that it had 'a character similar to laws, decrees and ordinances', i.e. the instruments with regard to which Annex B(1) explicitly imposes a 'publication' requirement.[217]

With regard to the 'prior notification' requirements of Annex B(5) and (7), the panel in *Japan – Apples (2003)* had to determine whether the relevant changes to the SPS measure at issue constituted changes which were subject to the 'prior notification' requirement because they 'may have a significant effect on trade of other Members', as the chapeau to Annex B(5) states. The panel considered that:

> the most important factor in this regard is whether the change affects the conditions of market access for the product concerned, that is, would the exported product (apple fruit from the United States in this case) still be permitted to enter Japan if they complied with the prescription contained in the previous regulations. If this is not the case, then we must consider whether the change could be considered to potentially have a *significant* effect on trade of other Members. In this regard, it would be relevant to consider whether the change has resulted in any increase in production, packaging and sales costs, such as more onerous treatment requirements or more time-consuming administrative formalities.[218]

As the United States, the complainant in that case, had not presented arguments regarding in what respects the SPS measure at issue departed from the previous one, the panel found that the United States had failed to make a *prima facie* case and accordingly rejected the US claim.[219]

In order to promote the implementation of the transparency obligations, the SPS Committee in 2002 adopted recommended notification procedures, which were revised in 2008.[220] As of 1 October 2015, 119 WTO Members had submitted at least one notification to the WTO.[221] While the number of notifications circulated by Members has increased significantly in recent years and the share of notifications by developing-country Members stood at 72 per cent in 2015,[222] the failure to notify (or notify correctly) new, or changes to, SPS measures is still a frequently raised concern at meetings of the SPS Committee.[223] In response, in 2011, the WTO Secretariat launched a new online SPS Notification Submission System. On 1 October 2015, the total number of notifications since the entry into force of the *SPS Agreement* in 1995 amounted to 19,138.[224] To

217 See *ibid.*, paras. 107–8. Footnote 5 to Annex B(1) of the *SPS Agreement* refers to 'laws, decrees and ordinances'.

218 Panel Report, *Japan – Apples (2003)*, para. 8.314.

219 *Ibid.*, paras. 8.324 and 8.327.

220 See Committee on Sanitary and Phytosanitary Measures, *Recommended Procedures for Implementing the Transparency Obligations of the SPS Agreement (Article 7), Revision*, G/SPS/7/Rev.3, dated 20 June 2008.

221 See Committee on Sanitary and Phytosanitary Measures, *Report (2015) on the Activities of the Committee on Sanitary and Phytosanitary Measures*, G/L/1129, dated 28 October 2015, para. 1.10.

222 See *ibid.*

223 See Committee on Sanitary and Phytosanitary Measures, Note by the Secretariat, *Specific Trade Concerns*, G/SPS/GEN/204/Rev.12, dated 2 March 2012.

224 See Committee on Sanitary and Phytosanitary Measures, *Report (2015) on the Activities of the Committee on Sanitary and Phytosanitary Measures*, G/L/1129, dated 28 October 2015, para. 1.10.

assist Members in the formidable task of managing the flow of information regarding notified SPS measures, the WTO Secretariat launched in 2007 the SPS Information Management System, which has since remained available on a dedicated website.[225]

In addition to the 'publication' and 'prior notification' requirements discussed above, Annex B also provides for an 'enquiry point' requirement. Annex B(3) and (4) of the *SPS Agreement* oblige WTO Members to create the necessary infrastructure to carry out their transparency obligations by establishing a National Notification Authority, responsible for the implementation of notification procedures, and an 'Enquiry Point', responsible for answering all reasonable questions and providing relevant documents upon request.[226]

Finally, note that Article 5.8 of the *SPS Agreement* also contains an important obligation for the promotion of transparency. It obliges Members to provide information, upon request, regarding the reasons for their SPS measures where such measures are not 'based on' international standards or no relevant international standards exist. A Member, which has reason to believe that such an SPS measure does or could potentially restrain its exports, may request information under Article 5.8 of the *SPS Agreement* from the Member adopting or maintaining the SPS measure.

Note that the panel in *India – Agricultural Products (2015)* found that India acted inconsistently with its transparency and notification obligations under: (1) Annex B(2) because it failed to allow a reasonable interval between the publication and the entry into force of one of the two SPS measures at issue, namely S.O. 1663(E); (2) Annex B(5) (a) because it failed to publish a notice 'at an early stage' about the 'proposed' S.O. 1663(E); (3) Annex B(5) (b) because it failed to notify other Members through the WTO Secretariat, 'at an early stage', of the 'proposed' S.O. 1663(E); and (4) Annex B(5) (d) because it had not allowed a 'reasonable time' for other Members to make comments on the 'proposed' S.O. 1663(E).[227]

3.6.5 Special and Differential Treatment

The *SPS Agreement* provides for special and differential treatment of developing-country Members, both by other Members and by the SPS Committee, in order to take account of the difficulties they face in implementing the *SPS Agreement* and complying with SPS measures on their export markets. These provisions aim to give additional flexibility to developing-country Members.

225 See http://spsims.wto.org. The SPS Information Management System also contains information on national notification authorities and enquiry points.

226 The WTO Secretariat regularly updates and circulates lists of these authorities, under official document numbers G/SPS/NNA/– and G/SPS/ENQ/–.

227 See Panel Report, *India – Agricultural Products (2015)*, paras. 7.759, 7.765, 7.790 and 7.796. 'S.O.' stands for Statutory Order.

Article 10.1 of the *SPS Agreement* provides:

> In the preparation and application of sanitary or phytosanitary measures, Members shall take account of the special needs of developing country Members, and in particular of the least-developed country Members.

This provision was relied upon for the first time by Argentina in *EC – Approval and Marketing of Biotech Products (2006)*. Argentina claimed that the general *de facto* moratorium on the approval of biotech products maintained by the European Communities had important implications for Argentina's economic development, due to its strong dependence on agricultural exports and its position as the world's second-largest producer, and leading developing-country producer, of biotech products. It further pointed to its great interest in the integrated European market. Therefore, Argentina argued that the European Communities was obliged, under Article 10.1 of the *SPS Agreement*, to take into account Argentina's special needs in the preparation and application of its SPS measure. Argentina emphasised the mandatory nature of Article 10.1 and claimed that it requires more than mere attention to developing-country problems. Instead, Article 10.1 requires 'positive action', in this case 'preferential market access' for developing-country products or implementation of the Member's obligations in a manner that is 'beneficial, or less detrimental, to the interests of developing country Members'.[228] According to Argentina, the European Communities had failed to comply with this obligation. The panel in this case interpreted Article 10.1 in keeping with previous case law on special and differential treatment provisions in other WTO agreements.[229] It held that the obligation to 'take account' of developing-country needs merely requires Members 'to consider' the needs of developing countries. This obligation, according to the panel, does not prescribe a particular result to be achieved, and notably does not provide that the importing Member must invariably accord special and differential treatment where a measure may lead to a decrease, or slower increase, in developing-country exports.[230] Indeed, the panel considered it conceivable that the European Communities did take account of Argentina's needs, but at the same time took account of other legitimate interests (such as those of its consumers and environment) and gave priority to the latter.[231] After examining the arguments made by Argentina in this regard, the panel found that Argentina had not met its burden of proof for showing a violation of Article 10.1.[232]

The panel in *US – Animals (2015)* rejected the submission of the European Union, that Article 10.1 was too general and vague to be the subject of dispute

228 See *ibid.*, para. 7.1607. 229 See above, pp. 763–5, 866–7 and below, 1051–4.

230 See Panel Reports, *EC – Approval and Marketing of Biotech Products (2006)*, para. 7.1620.

231 See *ibid.*, para. 7.1621.

232 See *ibid.*, paras. 7.1623–7.1625. Note, however, that the panel explicitly stated that, in coming to this conclusion, it was *not* suggesting that there is a duty on developing countries specifically to request that their needs as developing countries be considered. See *ibid.*, para. 7.1625.

settlement and held that Article 10.1 imposes a positive obligation that is subject to dispute settlement.[233] Further, the panel interpreted the phrase 'special needs of developing country Members' broadly so as to encompass both the needs of developing-country Members generally, and the needs of a particular developing-country Member.[234] It noted with regard to the requirement to take account of special needs that the use of the word 'shall' indicates a mandatory obligation.[235]

The panel in *US – Animals (2015)* noted that the burden of proof in Article 10.1 begins with a determination of whether a specific special need of a developing-country Member has been identified.[236] The panel was further of the view that:

> there are multiple ways in which a special need could be brought to the attention of the importing Member. It could be that the developing country knows of a need that it needs to remedy and should make that known to the importing country, this would make sense from a practical viewpoint as the developing country Member would be identifying its own special needs. Conversely, the importing country could identify a special need, for example while conducting its risk assessment, and convey that to the developing country Member.[237]

Article 10.2 of the *SPS Agreement* provides:

> Where the appropriate level of sanitary or phytosanitary protection allows scope for the phased introduction of new sanitary or phytosanitary measures, longer time-frames for compliance should be accorded on products of interest to developing country Members so as to maintain opportunities for their exports.

This provision encourages, but does not oblige, Members to grant developing countries a longer period for compliance with new SPS measures. In the 2001 Doha Ministerial Decision on *Implementation-Related Issues and Concerns*, this longer period was specified as normally not less than six months.[238] The Doha Decision further provides that, if longer periods for compliance are not possible and a Member identifies specific problems with the measure, the importing Member must enter into consultations with a view to reaching a mutually satisfactory solution that continues to achieve its appropriate level of protection.[239]

Article 10.3 of the *SPS Agreement* allows the SPS Committee to grant developing-country Members, upon request, specified, time-limited 'exceptions' from some or all of their obligations, taking account of their financial, trade and development needs. These 'exceptions' are – as is explicitly stated in Article 10.3 – aimed at 'ensuring that developing country Members are able to comply with the provisions of this Agreement'.

Finally, Article 10.4 of the *SPS Agreement* provides that Members should encourage and facilitate the participation of developing countries in the relevant

233 See Panel Report, *US – Animals (2015)*, paras. 7.689–7.691.
234 See *ibid.*, para. 7.692. 235 See *ibid.*, para. 7.694.
236 See *ibid.*, para. 7.698. 237 *Ibid.*, para. 7.699.
238 See Ministerial Conference, Doha Decision on *Implementation-Related Issues and Concerns*, WT/MIN(01)/17, dated 14 November 2001, para. 3.1.
239 See *ibid.*

international organisations. This provision does not contain any binding obligation but is purely hortatory.

As discussed above, the Doha Ministerial Declaration mandates, as part of the Doha Round negotiations, a review of the special and differential treatment provisions in the WTO agreements, in order to make them more precise, effective and operational.[240] The proposals concerning Articles 9 and 10 of the *SPS Agreement* made in this context are still under consideration.[241] Note, however, that, in October 2009, the SPS Committee adopted a procedure to enhance the transparency of special and differential treatment of developing-country Members.[242]

4 INSTITUTIONAL AND PROCEDURAL PROVISIONS OF THE *SPS AGREEMENT*

In addition to the substantive provisions discussed above, the *SPS Agreement* also contains a number of institutional and procedural provisions. This section deals with the provisions on: (1) the SPS Committee; (2) dispute settlement; and (3) technical assistance to developing-country Members.

4.1 SPS Committee

The Committee on Sanitary and Phytosanitary Measures, commonly referred to as the 'SPS Committee', is established under Article 12.1 of the *SPS Agreement* with a mandate to carry out the functions necessary for the implementation of the *SPS Agreement* and the furtherance of its objectives. The SPS Committee is composed of representatives of all WTO Members and takes decisions by consensus. In 2015, it held three regular two-day meetings.[243]

The SPS Committee has three main tasks. First, pursuant to Article 12.2 of the *SPS Agreement*, it is a forum for consultations and must encourage and facilitate consultations or negotiations between Members on SPS issues. Often SPS disputes can be resolved through such consultations without resort to dispute settlement. At each meeting of the SPS Committee, Members raise and discuss specific trade concerns with regard to the SPS measures of other Members. By

240 Ministerial Conference, *Doha Ministerial Declaration*, WT/MIN(01)/DEC/1, dated 20 November 2001, para. 44.

241 For the relevant proposals, see Committee on Sanitary and Phytosanitary Measures, *Report on Proposals for Special and Differential Treatment*, G/SPS/35, dated 7 July 2005, para. 41. This report noted that some Members are concerned that modification of Articles 9 or 10 could change the balance of rights and obligations established by the *SPS Agreement*.

242 See Committee on Sanitary and Phytosanitary Measures, Decision by the Committee on *Procedure to Enhance Transparency of Special and Differential Treatment in Favour of Developing Country Members*, G/SPS/33/Rev.1, dated 18 December 2009.

243 See Committee on Sanitary and Phytosanitary Measures, *Report (2015) on the Activities of the Committee on Sanitary and Phytosanitary Measures*, G/L/1129, dated 28 October 2015, para. 1.1. See *ibid.*, para. 1.2.

the end of 2015, 403 specific trade concerns had been raised, of which 230 were raised by developing-country Members and five by least-developed-country Members.[244] In all but one year since 2008, developing-country Members raised significantly more concerns than developed-country Members.[245] Of the 403 specific trade concerns raised in the SPS Committee by the end of 2015, 146 trade concerns have been reported resolved and 31 partially resolved.[246] In 2015, twenty-three new specific trade concerns were raised and many previously raised concerns were discussed again.[247] The specific trade concerns discussed in the SPS Committee in 2015 related to *inter alia* China's measures on bovine meat (concern raised by India); Mexico's measures on imports of hibiscus flowers (concern raised by Nigeria); Costa Rica's temporary suspension of the issuing of phytosanitary import certificates for avocados (concerns raised by Guatemala and Mexico); and several Members raised concerns regarding GMO-related policies proposed by the European Union and China.[248] In addition to specific trade concerns, the SPS Committee also discusses general issues relating to the implementation of the *SPS Agreement*. More than any other WTO committee, the SPS Committee has been successful in translating such discussions into decisions. In this respect, note in particular the Decision on Equivalence of 2001, as last revised in 2004, and the Decision on Mediation of 2014.[249]

Second, pursuant to Article 12.2 of the *SPS Agreement*, the SPS Committee must encourage the use of international standards by Members. In this respect, the SPS Committee is obliged, pursuant to Article 12.3 of the *SPS Agreement*, to maintain close contact with the international standard-setting organisations, and must, pursuant to Article 12.4 of the *SPS Agreement*, develop a procedure for monitoring the process of international harmonisation.[250]

244 The WTO Secretariat maintains an annually updated list, summarising specific trade concerns brought to the Committee's attention since 1995. See e.g. Committee on Sanitary and Phytosanitary Measures, *Specific Trade Concerns*, Note by the Secretariat, G/SPS/GEN/204/Rev.16, dated 23 February 2016. For the number of concerns raised, see para. 1.4.

245 See *ibid.*, para. 1.3, Chart 1.3b.

246 See *ibid.*, para. 1.4. Note that other trade concerns may have been resolved without the SPS Committee being informed of this.

247 Committee on Sanitary and Phytosanitary Measures, *Report (2015) on the Activities of the Committee on Sanitary and Phytosanitary Measures*, G/L/1129, dated 28 October 2015, para. 1.7.

248 See *ibid.*

249 See Decision on the *Implementation of Article 4 of the Agreement on the Application of Sanitary and Phytosanitary Measures*, of 2001 and revised in 2004, G/SPS/19, dated 24 October 2001; and Decision on the *Implementation of Article 4 of the Agreement on the Application of Sanitary and Phytosanitary Measures. Revision*, G/SPS/19/Rev.2, dated 23 July 2004, para. 4. For a discussion on the Decision on Equivalence, see above, p. 974. Other decisions by the SPS Committee include: *Guidelines to Further the Practical Implementation of Article 6 of the Agreement on the Application of Sanitary and Phytosanitary Measures*, G/SPS/48, dated 16 May 2008 (see above, p. 976); *Decision on a Procedure to Enhance Transparency of Special and Differential Treatment in Favour of Developing Country Members*, G/SPS/33/Rev.1, dated 18 December 2009 (see above, p. 983); *Decision on Actions regarding SPS-Related Private Standards*, G/SPS/55, dated 6 April 2011 (see above, p. 942, fn. 21); and *Decision on a Procedure to Encourage and Facilitate the Resolution of Specific Sanitary or Phytosanitary Issues Among Members*, G/SPS/61, dated 8 September 2014 (see below, p. 983).

250 Such a procedure was developed in 1997 (see G/SPS/11) on a provisional basis, in terms of which the SPS Committee draws up annual reports regarding the use of existing standards, the need for new standards and work on the adoption of such standards. This provisional procedure was revised in October 2004 (see G/SPS/GEN/11/Rev.1) and extended indefinitely in 2006 (see G/SPS/40).

Third, pursuant to Article 12.7 of the *SPS Agreement*, the SPS Committee is obliged to undertake a review of the operation and implementation of the *SPS Agreement* three years after its entry into force and as necessary thereafter. Where appropriate, it may propose amendments to the *SPS Agreement* to the Council for Trade in Goods. The first review was completed in 1999 and no amendments were proposed. In the 2001 Doha Ministerial Decision on *Implementation-Related Issues and Concerns*, the SPS Committee was instructed to conduct subsequent reviews at least once every four years.[251] The Fourth Review was completed in 2014. This review resulted in a number of proposals currently under discussion, including a proposal on developing a catalogue of instruments available for Members to manage SPS issues, and a proposal to improve the quality and completeness of notifications.[252]

4.2 Dispute Settlement

Pursuant to Article 11.1 of the *SPS Agreement*, the provisions of Articles XXII and XXIII of the GATT 1994 as elaborated by the DSU apply to consultations and the settlement of disputes under the *SPS Agreement*, except as otherwise provided. To date, two specific issues relating to the settlement of SPS disputes have generated much debate: (1) the issue of the selection and the role of scientific experts consulted by panels; and (2) the issue of the standard of review to be applied by panels when reviewing the SPS-consistency of SPS measures.

Note that in September 2014 the SPS Committee adopted a new voluntary 'consultation' procedure, also referred to as a 'mediation' procedure, which is intended to encourage and facilitate the resolution of specific SPS issues between Members.[253] When the responding Member accepts the consultation request, the consulting Members will agree on a Facilitator. The Chair of the SPS Committee will normally serve as the Facilitator, unless the consulting Members decide otherwise.[254] All communications and documents relating to the consultations, including the Facilitator's final report, shall be confidential, unless otherwise agreed by the consulting Members.[255] The consultation process should not exceed 180 days, unless a different time frame is agreed on.[256] This procedure is without prejudice to the rights and obligations of Members under the *SPS Agreement* or any other WTO agreement and shall *not* constitute a legally binding agreement.[257]

251 Ministerial Conference, *Doha Decision on Implementation-Related Issues and Concerns*, WT/MIN(01)/17, dated 14 November 2001.

252 Committee on Sanitary and Phytosanitary Measures, *Report (2014) on the Activities of the Committee on Sanitary and Phytosanitary Measures*, G/L/1086, dated 6 November 2014, para. 1.4.

253 Committee on Sanitary and Phytosanitary Measures, *Decision of the Committee on a Procedure to Encourage and Facilitate the Resolution of Specific Sanitary or Phytosanitary Issues Among Members*, G/SPS/61, dated 8 September 2014, para. 1.1.

254 See *ibid.*, para. 2.8.

255 See *ibid.*, paras. 2.12 and 2.14. However, the Chair of the SPS Committee will report the general outcome of the consultations to the SPS Committee. See *ibid.*, para. 2.15.

256 See *ibid.*, para. 2.13. 257 See *ibid.*, para. 1.2.

4.2.1 Scientific Experts

As discussed in Chapter 3, Article 13 of the DSU generally authorises panels to seek information and technical advice from any individual or body, and to seek information from any source, consult experts or request advisory reports. This provision also applies to disputes under the *SPS Agreement*.[258] However, the *SPS Agreement* sets out a special and additional rule regarding the consultation of experts. Article 11.2 of the *SPS Agreement* provides:

> In a dispute under this Agreement involving scientific or technical issues, a panel should seek advice from experts chosen by the panel in consultation with the parties to the dispute. To this end, the panel may, when it deems it appropriate, establish an advisory technical experts group, or consult the relevant international organizations, at the request of either party to the dispute or on its own initiative.

In *Japan – Agricultural Products II (1999)*, the Appellate Body ruled that Article 11.2 'explicitly instructs' panels in SPS disputes involving scientific and technical issues to seek advice from experts.[259] In all SPS disputes to date, panels have consulted individual experts to help them to understand the complex issues of scientific fact that arose in these disputes. Experts are to act as an 'interface' between the often very technical and intricate scientific evidence and the panel, to allow the latter to perform its task as the trier of fact. The selection and the use made of experts was controversial in *US/Canada – Continued Suspension (2008)*. In that case, the Appellate Body noted the central role that scientific experts, and their opinions, may play in a panel's review of the SPS measure at issue, especially in cases involving highly complex scientific issues.[260] Experts consulted by a panel can have a decisive role in such cases.[261] The independence and impartiality of these scientific experts consulted by a panel is therefore of great importance. The Appellate Body recognised that panels are often faced with practical difficulties in selecting experts who have the required level of expertise and to whose selection the parties do not object.[262] However, as the Appellate Body observed, the practical difficulties that a panel may encounter in selecting experts cannot displace the need to ensure their independence and impartiality and thus to guarantee that the consultations with the experts respect the parties' due process rights.[263]

With regard to the use of scientific experts by panels, recall that the Appellate Body in *Japan – Agricultural Products II (1999)* found that, while a panel has broad authority to consult experts to help it to understand and evaluate the evidence submitted and the arguments made by the parties, a panel may not – with the help of its experts – make the case for one or the other party.[264] Similarly, in *Australia – Apples (2010)*, the Appellate Body cautioned that:

> whether or not an alternative measure's level of risk achieves a Member's appropriate level of protection is a question of legal characterization, the answer to which will determine the

258 See above, p. 228. 259 See Appellate Body Report, *Japan – Agricultural Products II (1999)*, para. 128.
260 See Appellate Body Reports, *US/Canada – Continued Suspension (2008)*, para. 436.
261 See *ibid.*, para. 480. 262 See *ibid.* 263 See *ibid.*
264 See Appellate Body Report, *Japan – Agricultural Products II (1999)*, para. 129. See above, p. 230.

consistency or inconsistency of a Member's measure with its obligation under Article 5.6. Answering this question is not a task that can be delegated to scientific experts.[265]

In *India – Agricultural Products (2015)*, India challenged on appeal the panel's seeking of, and reliance upon, advice from the World Organisation for Animal Health (OIE) with respect to the meaning of certain recommendations of the OIE Terrestrial Code. India did not consider the meaning of recommendations of the OIE Code to be a scientific or technical issue on which a panel could seek the advice of experts. The Appellate Body noted in this regard that:

> although Article 11.2 indicates the reason a panel 'should seek advice from experts' is because the dispute 'involve[s] scientific or technical issues', we consider this to be a reference to the types of issues common to SPS disputes, and not to suggest a limitation as to the scope or nature of questioning that would be permitted in such disputes.[266]

According to the Appellate Body, the advice sought from experts is therefore not limited to scientific and technical issues.[267]

4.2.2 Standard of Review

The second issue relating to the settlement of SPS disputes that has generated much debate is the issue of the standard of review to be applied by panels when reviewing the SPS consistency of SPS measures.[268] In *US/Canada – Continued Suspension (2008)*, the Appellate Body held with regard to the standard of review to be applied by a panel when it assesses under Article 5.1 of the *SPS Agreement* whether an SPS measure is 'based on' a risk assessment:

> It is the WTO Member's task to perform the risk assessment. The panel's task is to review that risk assessment. Where a panel goes beyond this limited mandate and acts as a risk assessor, it would be substituting its own scientific judgement for that of the risk assessor and making a *de novo* review and, consequently, would exceed its functions under Article 11 of the DSU.[269]

According to the Appellate Body, the review power of a panel is not to determine whether the risk assessment undertaken by a WTO Member is correct, but rather to determine whether that risk assessment 'is supported by coherent reasoning and respectable scientific evidence and is, in this sense, objectively justifiable'.[270] A panel reviewing the consistency of an SPS measure with Article 5.1 of the *SPS Agreement* must: (1) identify the scientific basis upon which the SPS measure was adopted; (2) verify that the scientific basis comes from a respected and qualified source; (3) review whether the particular conclusions drawn by the Member assessing the risk find sufficient support in the scientific evidence relied upon, or, in other words, assess whether the reasoning articulated on the basis of the scientific evidence is objective and coherent; and (4) determine whether the results of the risk assessment 'sufficiently warrant' the

265 Appellate Body Report, *Australia – Apples (2010)*, para. 384.
266 Appellate Body Report, *India – Agricultural Products (2015)*, para. 5.89. 267 See *ibid.*
268 For a general discussion on the standard of review of panels, see above, pp. 222–5.
269 Appellate Body Reports, *US/Canada – Continued Suspension (2008)*, para. 590. 270 *Ibid.*

SPS measure at issue.[271] It is important in this context to keep in mind that the scientific basis cited as warranting the SPS measure at issue need not reflect the majority view of the scientific community. As discussed above, SPS measures can be based on a divergent or minority view rather than mainstream scientific opinion, provided that it 'comes from a qualified and respected source', and has 'the necessary scientific and methodological rigour to be considered reputable science'.[272]

In *Australia – Apples (2010)*, the Appellate Body further clarified the standard of review applicable under Article 5.1 of the *SPS Agreement*. The Appellate Body distinguished two aspects of a panel's scrutiny of a risk assessment: (1) scrutiny of the underlying scientific basis; and (2) scrutiny of the reasoning of the risk assessor based upon such underlying science. With respect to the first aspect, the Appellate Body saw the panel's role as limited to reviewing whether the scientific basis constitutes 'legitimate science according to the standards of the relevant scientific community'.[273] However, the Appellate Body considered that the second aspect of a panel's review was somewhat less deferential and that it involved an 'assessment of whether the reasoning of the risk assessor is objective and coherent, that is, whether the conclusions find sufficient support in the scientific evidence relied upon'.[274] The Appellate Body disagreed with the view that 'a panel should assess the reasoning and conclusions reached by a risk assessor and the scientific evidence relied upon in the same way', and pointed out that:

> a distinction should be drawn between, on the one hand, the scientific evidence relied upon by the risk assessor and, on the other hand, the reasoning employed and the conclusions reached by the risk assessor on the basis of that scientific evidence.[275]

The Appellate Body stated in *Australia – Apples (2010)* that the more deferential standard of review applicable to the underlying scientific evidence was explained by the fact that 'a panel is not well suited to conduct scientific research and assessments itself'. In contrast, the Appellate Body affirmed that, without substituting its judgment for that of the risk assessor, a panel must be able to review the reasoning of the risk assessor, because this reasoning plays an important role in revealing whether or not the requisite rational or objective relationship between the reasoning and scientific evidence exists.[276]

In *Australia – Apples (2010)*, the Appellate Body also made clear that the standard of review to be applied by a panel assessing a claim under Article 5.6

271 See *ibid.*, para. 591.

272 See *ibid.* Note that, in *Australia – Apples (2010)*, the Appellate Body stated that: 'in *US/Canada – Continued Suspension*, [it] did not set out a series of steps that a panel must *mechanically* follow in the evaluation of a risk assessment under Article 5.1 of the *SPS Agreement*'. See Appellate Body Report, *Australia – Apples (2010)*, para. 219. Emphasis added.

273 See Appellate Body Report, *Australia – Apples (2010)*, para. 215 (referring to Appellate Body Reports, *US/Canada – Continued Suspension (2008)*, para. 591).

274 Appellate Body Report, *Australia – Apples (2010)*, para. 215.

275 *Ibid.*, para. 224. 276 *Ibid.*, para. 225.

of the *SPS Agreement* differs from, and is less deferential than, the standard of review to be employed when assessing a claim under Article 5.1:

> Caution not to conduct a *de novo* review is appropriate where a panel reviews a risk assessment conducted by the importing Member's authorities in the context of Article 5.1. However, the situation is different in the context of an Article 5.6 claim. The legal question under Article 5.6 is not whether the authorities of the importing Member have, in conducting the risk assessment, acted in accordance with the obligations of the *SPS Agreement.* Rather, the legal question is whether the importing Member could have adopted a less trade-restrictive measure. This requires the panel itself to objectively assess, *inter alia,* whether the alternative measure proposed by the complainant would achieve the importing Member's appropriate level of protection.[277]

4.3 Technical Assistance

Due to the financial and human resource constraints encountered by developing-country Members, they are often in need of technical assistance in various areas of relevance to the *SPS Agreement.* Technical assistance encompasses not only information and training to enhance understanding of the disciplines of the *SPS Agreement,* but also the provision of soft infrastructure (training of technical and scientific personnel and the development of national regulatory frameworks) as well as hard infrastructure (laboratories, equipment, veterinary services and the establishment of pest- or disease-free areas).[278]

Technical assistance is dealt with in Article 9 of the *SPS Agreement.*[279] In terms of Article 9.1, Members 'agree to facilitate' the provision of technical assistance to other Members, especially developing countries, either bilaterally or through international organisations. Such technical assistance may take various forms and may aim, *inter alia,* at helping developing countries to comply with SPS measures on their export markets. Article 9.2 deals with the situation where a Member's SPS measure requires substantial investments from an exporting developing-country Member and obliges the importing Member to 'consider providing' technical assistance to allow the developing country to maintain or increase its market opportunities for the relevant product. These provisions are in the nature of 'best-endeavour' obligations and are thus difficult to enforce. The 2001 Doha Ministerial Decision on *Implementation-Related Issues and Concerns* urges Members to provide 'to the extent possible' technical and financial assistance to least-developed-country Members to help them respond to SPS measures that may affect their trade and to assist them to implement the *SPS Agreement.*[280]

277 *Ibid.*, para. 356.

278 This typology of technical assistance was drawn up by the WTO Secretariat. See Committee on Sanitary and Phytosanitary Measures, *Technical Assistance Typology,* Note by the Secretariat, G/SPS/GEN/206, dated 18 October 2000. Note that between 1995 and 2015, over 13,000 people, primarily government officials from developing-country Members, received WTO SPS training. See G/SPS/GEN/521/Rev.11.

279 For a discussion on trade-related technical assistance in general, see above, pp. 110–13.

280 See Ministerial Conference, *Doha Decision on Implementation-Related Issues and Concerns,* WT/MIN(01)/17, dated 14 November 2001, para. 3.6.

As a result of an initiative taken at the 2001 Doha Ministerial Conference, the WTO together with the World Bank, the Food and Agricultural Organization (FAO), the World Health Organization (WHO) and the World Organisation for Animal Health (OIE), established in 2004, the Standards and Trade Development Facility (STDF). The STDF acts as a coordinating and financing mechanism and aims to assist developing countries to establish and implement SPS standards, in order to improve their human, animal and plant health status and their ability to gain or maintain access to markets. The STDF trust fund, which is financed through voluntary contributions from donors and has an annual funding target of US$5million, is administered by the WTO.[281]

5 SUMMARY

The *SPS Agreement* applies to SPS measures that may affect international trade. Whether a measure is a 'SPS measure' depends on its purpose or aim. In broad terms, a 'SPS measure' is a measure that: (1) aims at the protection of human or animal life or health from food-borne risks; or (2) aims at the protection of human, animal or plant life or health from risks from pests or diseases. The adoption and implementation of SPS measures is sometimes in the hands of bodies other than the central government, such as regulatory agencies, regional bodies, subfederal governments and non-governmental entities. The *SPS Agreement* takes this into account by providing that Members must enact and implement positive measures to ensure the observance of its rules by bodies other than central government bodies. With regard to the relationship between the *SPS Agreement* and other WTO agreements, note that, to the extent a measure is a 'SPS measure' as defined in Annex A to the *SPS Agreement*, the *SPS Agreement* applies to the exclusion of the *TBT Agreement*. No such relationship of mutual exclusivity exists between the *SPS Agreement* and the GATT 1994. However, the *SPS Agreement* contains a presumption of consistency with the relevant provisions of the GATT 1994 for all measures that are in conformity with the *SPS Agreement*.

The *SPS Agreement* explicitly acknowledges the sovereign right of WTO Members to take SPS measures (Article 2.1). At the same time, however, the *SPS Agreement* subjects Members to a number of obligations regarding their SPS measures. These obligations include: (1) the obligation to take or maintain only SPS measures *necessary* to protect human, animal or plant life or health (Article 2.2); (2) the obligation to take or maintain only SPS measures 'based on' scientific principles and on sufficient scientific evidence (Article 2.2); and (3) the obligation not to adopt or maintain SPS measures that arbitrarily or

281 See www.standardsfacility.org.

unjustifiably discriminate or constitute a disguised restriction on trade (Article 2.3). Moreover, the *SPS Agreement* encourages the harmonisation of SPS measures around international standards (Article 3). Members have three *autonomous options* with regard to international standards, each with its own consequences. Members may choose to: (1) *base* their SPS measures on international standards (Article 3.1); (2) *conform* their SPS measures to international standards (Article 3.2); or (3) impose SPS measures resulting in a *higher level* of protection than would be achieved by the relevant international standard (Article 3.3). These options are equally available options and there is no rule–exception relationship between them.

The obligations set out in Articles 2.2 and 2.3 of the *SPS Agreement* are further specified and elaborated on in a number of other provisions containing substantive obligations relating to risk assessment *and* risk management. With regard to risk assessment, the *SPS Agreement* primarily requires that SPS measures be 'based on' a risk assessment (Article 5.1), as defined in Annex A(4). The latter provides for two types of risk assessment: one for risks from pests and diseases; and one for risks from food and feed. With regard to risk management, the *SPS Agreement* primarily requires Members to: (1) avoid arbitrary or unjustifiable distinctions in the levels of protection deemed appropriate in different situations, if these distinctions lead to discrimination or disguised restrictions on trade (Article 5.5); and (2) ensure that SPS measures are not more trade-restrictive than required to achieve their appropriate level of protection (Article 5.6). Where scientific evidence is insufficient for the conduct of a risk assessment, the *SPS Agreement* allows Members to take – under certain conditions – provisional SPS measures which are not based on a risk assessment (Article 5.7). The *SPS Agreement* thus contains a specific formulation of what is often referred to as the precautionary principle. The *SPS Agreement* also provides for substantive provisions relating to: (1) the recognition of equivalence of SPS measures of other Members (Article 4); (2) the obligation to adapt SPS measures to regional conditions in other Members (Article 6); (3) SPS-related control, inspection and approval procedures (Article 8 and Annex C); (4) transparency and notification obligations regarding SPS measures (Article 7 and Annex B); and (5) special and differential treatment of developing-country Members (Article 10).

Members consult regarding any matters pertaining to the operation or objectives of the *SPS Agreement* in the SPS Committee. This Committee is composed of all WTO Members and meets several times a year. The WTO dispute settlement rules and procedures, discussed in Chapter 3, apply to disputes concerning the *SPS Agreement*. However, in the context of SPS disputes, specific questions have arisen regarding the standard of review to be applied by panels as well as the appointment and use made of scientific experts by panels. Acknowledging the difficulties developing-country Members may face in implementing the obligations under the *SPS Agreement*, Members have agreed 'to facilitate' the provision of technical assistance to Members in need.

FURTHER READINGS

N. Park and M. Chung, 'Analysis of a New Mediation Procedure under the WTO SPS Agreement', *Journal of World Trade*, 2016, 50(1), 93–116.

C. Downes, 'Worth Shopping Around? Defending Regulatory Autonomy under the SPS and TBT Agreements', *World Trade Review*, 2015, 14(4), 553–78.

V. Thorstensen, R. Weissinger and X. Sun, 'Private Standards – Implications for Trade, Development and Governance', E15Initiative, International Centre for Trade and Sustainable Development and World Economic Forum, 2015.

M. Murina and A. Nicita, 'Trading with Conditions: The Effect of Sanitary and Phytosanitary Measures on the Agricultural Exports from Low-income Countries', Policy Issues in International Trade and Commodities, Research Study Series No. 68, United Nations, 2014.

B. Rigod, 'The Purpose of the WTO Agreement on the Application of Sanitary and Phytosanitary Measures (SPS)', *European Journal of International Law*, 2013, 24(2), 503–32.

L. Gruszczynski, 'Standard of Review of Health and Environmental Regulations by WTO Panels', in G. V. Calster and D. Prévost (eds.), *Research Handbook on Environment, Health and the WTO* (Edward Elgar, 2013).

C. Downes, 'The Impact of WTO Transparency Rules: Is the 10,000th SPS Notification a Cause for Celebration? – A Case Study of EU Practice', *Journal of International Economic Law*, 2012, 15(2), 503–24.

E. Reid, 'Risk Assessment, Science and Deliberation: Managing Regulatory Diversity under the SPS Agreement', *European Journal of Risk Regulation*, 2012, 3(4), 535–44.

E. Vecchione, 'Is it Possible to Provide Evidence of Insufficient Evidence? The Precautionary Principle at the WTO', *Chicago Journal of International Law*, 2012, 13(1), Article 7.

J. Wouters and D. Geraets, 'Private Food Standards and the World Trade Organization: Some Legal Considerations', *World Trade Review*, 2012, 11(3), 479–89.

J. Peel, 'Of Apples and Oranges (And Hormones in Beef): Science and the Standard of Review in WTO Disputes under the SPS Agreement', *International and Comparative Law Quarterly*, 2012, 61(2), 427–58.

C. E. Foster, 'Public Opinion and the Interpretation of the World Trade Organization's Agreement on Sanitary and Phytosanitary Measures', *Journal of International Economic Law*, 2008, 11(2), 427–58.

15

Intellectual Property Rights

CONTENTS

1 INTRODUCTION

The *Agreement on Trade-Related Aspects of Intellectual Property Rights* (the '*TRIPS Agreement*') is arguably the most innovative of the WTO agreements. While references to intellectual property (IP) rights were included in the GATT 1947,[1] the *TRIPS Agreement*, for the first time, establishes and imposes a positive regulatory obligation on Members to ensure a minimum level of protection and enforcement of IP rights in their territories.

Part I of the *TRIPS Agreement* contains general provisions and basic principles that apply to all the IP rights falling within its coverage. Part II is subdivided into eight sections, each dealing with a different area of IP protection. Part III sets out the obligations of Members with regard to enforcement of IP rights. The remainder of the *TRIPS Agreement* addresses issues relating to the acquisition and maintenance of IP rights, and contains institutional and procedural provisions.

This chapter provides an overview of the *TRIPS Agreement* and focuses on: (1) origins and objectives; (2) scope of application; (3) basic principles; (4) substantive protection provided to selected IP rights; (5) rules on enforcement of IP rights; (6) rules on acquisition of IP rights; (7) institutional and procedural provisions; and (8) rules providing for special and differential treatment of developing-country Members.

2 THE ORIGINS AND OBJECTIVES OF THE *TRIPS AGREEMENT*

Intellectual property, broadly speaking, refers to the legal rights that result from intellectual activity in the artistic, literary, scientific or industrial fields.[2] When this intellectual activity leads to the creation of something new and innovative, many countries recognise and protect the right of the author or inventor in his or her creation, in order to reward and stimulate creative endeavour. Many countries have rules in place for the protection and enforcement of IP rights. IP rights, it should be noted, confer *negative* rights, i.e. the right to exclude others from the use of the protected subject matter for a particular period of time. They

1 Articles XX(d), IX, XII:3(c)(iii) and XVIII:10 of the GATT refer to intellectual property rights. In addition, other GATT provisions lay down general rules that are also applicable to trade-related aspects of intellectual property rights, for example the national treatment and most-favoured-nation obligations and the prohibition on quantitative restrictions. See Negotiating Group on Trade-Related Aspects of Intellectual Property Rights, Including Trade in Counterfeit Goods, Note by the Secretariat, *GATT Provisions Bearing on Trade-Related Aspects of Intellectual Property Rights*, MTN.GNG/NG11/W/6, dated 22 May 1987, para. 2. On the relationship between the GATT 1994 and the *TRIPS Agreement*, see the General Interpretative Note to Annex 1A of the *WTO Agreement*, discussed above, at pp. 46–8.

2 See *WIPO Intellectual Property Handbook: Policy, Law and Use* (WIPO, 2004), 3, available at www.wipo.int/about-ip/en/iprm/index.html.

do not confer positive rights, such as the right to produce or market the product embodying the IP right.

Trade and intellectual property protection are closely connected. The achievements in trade liberalisation through WTO disciplines on and removal of trade barriers, discussed in previous chapters, can be greatly undermined if IP rights related to the traded goods or services are not respected in the export market or in the country of origin of imports. The possibility that traded products incorporating patents, copyrights or industrial designs will be copied, or that brand names or services marks will be used, by competitors without the consent of the creator/author creates a strong disincentive for innovation, investment and trade. This section discusses (1) the origins of the *TRIPS Agreement*, and (2) the objectives and principles of this Agreement.

2.1 Origins of the *TRIPS Agreement*

International agreements to strengthen and harmonise protection in the field of IP law exist since the late nineteenth century. However, they were plagued by deficiencies. In particular, they were fragmented in their coverage of IP rights; they lacked effective enforcement standards and systems for the settlement of disputes; and they often had very limited membership, with non-members being notorious violators of IP rights.[3] At the outset of the Uruguay Round negotiations in 1986, some participants noted that:

> trade distortions and impediments were resulting from, among other things: the displacement of exports of legitimate goods by unauthorized copies, or of domestic sales by imports of unauthorized copies; the disincentive effect that inadequate protection of intellectual property rights had on inventors and creators to engage in research and development and in trade and investment; the deliberate use in some instances of intellectual property right protection to discourage imports and encourage local production, often of an inefficient and small-scale nature; and the inhibiting effect on international trade of disparities in the protection accorded under different legislations.[4]

3 See e.g. the *Paris Convention for the Protection of Industrial Property (1967)*, the *Berne Convention for the Protection of Literary and Artistic Works (1971), the International Convention for the Protection of Performers, Producers of Phonograms and Broadcasting Organizations (1961) (the 'Rome Convention') and the Treaty on Intellectual Property in Respect of Integrated Circuits (1989).*

4 Negotiating Group on Trade-Related Aspects of Intellectual Property Rights, Including Trade in Counterfeit Goods, Note by the Secretariat, MTN.GNG/NG11/1, dated 10 April 1987, para. 4. Reference was also made to trade problems arising from restrictive business practices linked to intellectual property rights. See *ibid.* On the pre-Uruguay Round 'history' of the *TRIPS Agreement*, Taubman, Wager and Watal noted: 'In the Tokyo Round, there was a proposal to negotiate rules on trade in counterfeit goods resulting in a draft agreement on Measures to Discourage the Importation of Counterfeit Goods. However, negotiators did not reach agreement. In 1982, pursuant to a work programme agreed by trade ministers, a revised version of a draft agreement on trade in counterfeit goods was submitted. This draft was referred to a group of experts in 1984, which submitted its report a year later ... It produced a report on Trade in Counterfeit Goods that recommended that joint action was probably needed, but could not decide on the appropriate forum. It left it to the GATT Council to make a decision.' See A. Taubman, H. Wager and J. Watal (eds.), *A Handbook on the WTO TRIPS Agreement* (Cambridge University Press, 2012), 5–6.

Hence, the *TRIPS Agreement* was negotiated to address these problems. Developed countries in general, and the United States in particular, were the driving force behind these negotiations. Although developing countries initially objected to the inclusion of negotiations on IP protection on the Uruguay Round agenda and never truly embraced these negotiations, they came to realise that they were better off with multilateral disciplines than being subject to bilateral pressure to improve IP protection.[5]

2.2 Objectives and Principles of the *TRIPS Agreement*

The objectives of the *TRIPS Agreement* clearly reflect the concerns of negotiators, mentioned above. The Preamble identifies as the main objectives of the *TRIPS Agreement*:

> to reduce distortions and impediments to international trade ... taking into account the need to promote effective and adequate protection of intellectual property rights, and to ensure that measures and procedures to enforce intellectual property rights do not themselves become barriers to legitimate trade.

The various objectives of the *TRIPS Agreement* are sometimes in conflict with each other. As aptly noted by Thomas Cottier:

> Lack of, or insufficient protection [of intellectual property rights] amounts to *de facto* restrictions on market access, as exported products will be replaced by both generic and copied products that free ride on research and development, investment in creative activities and in quality control and product differentiation undertaken elsewhere. On the other hand, lack of appropriate limitations on rights may unduly hamper the flow of goods and services. *The real issue is one of balancing different policy goals.*[6]

The *TRIPS Agreement* reflects the effort to achieve this balance. According to Carlos Correa:

> The TRIPS Agreement must be viewed as a means for the realization of public policy objectives via the 'inducement to innovation' *and* the access to the results thereof by those who need them. In other words the objectives of the patent system would not be fulfilled if it only served to induce innovations to the benefit of those who control them.[7]

Article 7 of the *TRIPS Agreement*, entitled 'Objectives', reflects the rationale of the *TRIPS Agreement* to create a balance between these competing goals. It states:

> The protection and enforcement of intellectual property rights should contribute to the promotion of technological innovation and the transfer and dissemination of technology,

5 See P. Drahos, 'Developing Countries and International Intellectual Property Standard-Setting', *Journal of World Intellectual Property*, 2002, 774.

6 T. Cottier, 'The Agreement on Trade-Related Aspects of Intellectual Property Rights', in Macrory, Appleton and Plummer (eds.), *World Trade Organization*, 1054. Emphasis added.

7 C. M. Correa, *Trade-Related Aspects of Intellectual Property Rights: A Commentary on the TRIPS Agreement* (Oxford University Press, 2007), 94.

to the *mutual advantage* of producers and users of technological knowledge and in a manner conducive to *social and economic welfare*, and to a *balance* of rights and obligations.[8]

The objective of creating an equilibrium between rewarding creators of IP and protecting the public interest in disseminating IP is also present in Article 8 of the *TRIPS Agreement*, entitled 'Principles'. Paragraph 1 of Article 8 recognises that Members may adopt measures 'necessary to protect public health and nutrition' and to 'promote the public interest in sectors of vital importance to their socio-economic and technological development'. Paragraph 2 of Article 8 suggests that Members take appropriate measures to counteract abuse of IP rights by right holders, or anti-competitive practices.[9] The types of measures that could fall within the scope of Article 8 are in some respects similar to those falling within the scope of Article XX of the GATT 1994, however, whereas Article XX provides for a general exception for measures that are otherwise GATT-inconsistent, the relevance of Article 8 is limited by the requirement that measures referred to therein be *consistent* with the provisions of the *TRIPS Agreement*.[10] Thus, rather than creating an exception from *TRIPS* disciplines for measures serving public policy objectives, Article 8 is best seen as enunciating a fundamental principle of the *TRIPS Agreement*, to be taken into account, along with Article 7, when interpreting and applying its remaining provisions.

In *Canada – Pharmaceutical Patents (2000)*, the European Communities challenged provisions of Canada's patent law that allowed producers of generic medicines, before the expiry of the patent term, to stockpile generic products and use patented products to prepare their submissions for marketing authorisation of a generic version. While Canada conceded that these provisions violated Article 28.1 of the *TRIPS Agreement*, which grants exclusive rights to patent holders, it relied on the exception in Article 30 to justify its measures, and argued that the objectives and principles of Articles 7 and 8 of the *TRIPS Agreement* should inform the interpretation of Article 30. The panel in *Canada – Pharmaceutical Patents (2000)* held that:

> Article 30's very existence amounts to a recognition that the definition of patent rights contained in Article 28 would need certain adjustments. On the other hand, the three limiting conditions attached to Article 30 testify strongly that the negotiators of the Agreement did not intend Article 30 to bring about what would be equivalent to a renegotiation of the basic balance of the Agreement. Obviously, the exact scope of Article 30's authority will depend

8 Emphasis added. While couched in hortatory language ('should' instead of 'shall'), the fact that this provision is placed in the operative part of the agreement rather than in its Preamble highlights its importance in informing the interpretation of the *TRIPS Agreement*. See D. Gervais, *The TRIPS Agreement: Drafting History and Analysis*, 2nd edn (Sweet & Maxwell, 2003), 116.

9 Specifically, Article 8.2 refers to appropriate measures needed to prevent 'the resort to practices which unreasonably restrain trade or adversely affect the international transfer of technology'.

10 See also Panel Report, *EC – Trademarks and Geographical Indications (Australia) (2005)*, paras. 7.245–7.246; and Panel Report, *EC – Trademarks and Geographical Indications (US) (2005)*, paras. 7.209–7.210.

on the specific meaning given to its limiting conditions. The words of those conditions must be examined with particular care on this point. Both the goals and the limitations stated in Articles 7 and 8.1 must obviously be borne in mind when doing so as well as those of other provisions of the TRIPS Agreement which indicate its object and purposes.[11]

As an important further development since *Canada – Pharmaceutical Patents (2000), the Doha Declaration on the TRIPS Agreement and Public Health* reaffirms the right of WTO Members to use fully the provisions in the *TRIPS Agreement*, which provide flexibilities for Members in order to protect public health.[12] It states:

Accordingly ... while maintaining our commitments in the TRIPS Agreement, we recognize that these flexibilities include:

(a) In applying the customary rules of interpretation of public international law, *each provision* of the TRIPS Agreement shall be read in the light of the object and purpose of the Agreement *as expressed, in particular, in its objectives and principles.*[13]

3 SCOPE OF APPLICATION OF THE *TRIPS AGREEMENT*

This section discusses both the substantive and temporal scope of application of the *TRIPS Agreement.*

3.1 Substantive Scope of Application

Article 1.3 of the *TRIPS Agreement* requires Members to accord the treatment provided for in this Agreement to 'nationals' of other Members.[14] 'Nationals' of other Members are understood as:

those natural or legal persons that would meet the criteria for eligibility for protection provided for in the Paris Convention (1967), the Berne Convention (1971), the Rome Convention and the Treaty on Intellectual Property in Respect of Integrated Circuits, were all Members of the WTO members of those conventions.

11 Panel Report, *Canada – Pharmaceutical Patents (2000)*, para. 7.26.

12 See Ministerial Conference, *Doha Declaration on the TRIPS Agreement and Public Health*, WT/MIN(01)/DEC/2, dated 20 November 2001, para. 4. On the legal status of this Declaration, see above, pp. 93–101.

13 Ministerial Conference, *Doha Declaration on the TRIPS Agreement and Public Health*, WT/MIN(01)/DEC/2, dated 20 November 2001, para. 5. Emphasis added.

14 Given that the *TRIPS Agreement* confers IP protection on the 'nationals' of WTO Members, but separate customs territories (that may be WTO Members) do not confer nationality, a supplementary definition was required for 'nationals' in the case of separate customs territories that are WTO Members. These nationals are defined in fn. 1 to the *TRIPS Agreement* as 'persons, natural or legal, who are domiciled or who have a real and effective industrial or commercial establishment in that customs territory'. Note that the panel in *EC – Trademarks and Geographical Indications (US) (2005)* stated that the European Communities is not a 'separate customs territory Member' of the WTO and its nationals are therefore not defined by the terms of this footnote. See Panel Report, *EC – Trademarks and Geographical Indications (US) (2005)*, paras. 7.141–7.171; see also Panel Report, *EC – Trademarks and Geographical Indications (Australia) (2005)*, paras. 7.191–7.205.

The *TRIPS Agreement* does not define the concept of intellectual property. Instead it specifies which categories of IP rights are covered by its provisions. Article 1.2 provides:

For the purposes of this Agreement, the term 'intellectual property' refers to all categories of intellectual property that are the subject of Sections 1 through 7 of Part II.

Thus, clearly the *TRIPS Agreement* does *not* cover every form of IP right. Sections 1–7 of Part II of the *TRIPS Agreement* cover: (1) copyright and related rights; (2) trademarks; (3) geographical indications; (4) industrial design; (5) patents; (6) layout designs of integrated circuits; and (7) protection of undisclosed information. It should be borne in mind, however, that the categories of IP rights covered by the *TRIPS Agreement* are not always clearly delineated, and are not limited to those explicitly mentioned in the titles of Sections 1–7. In *US – Section 211 Appropriations Act (2002)*, the panel had to interpret Article 2.1 of the *TRIPS Agreement* in relation to 'trade names', which, although not explicitly mentioned in the *TRIPS Agreement*, are referred to in Article 1.2 of the *Paris Convention (1967)*. The panel read the references in Article 1.2 of the *TRIPS Agreement* to 'all categories' as an indication that this Article contains an exhaustive list.[15] The Appellate Body disagreed with this analysis. It stated:

[T]he subject of Sections 1 through 7 of Part II deals not only with the categories of intellectual property indicated in each section *title*, but with other *subjects* as well. For example, in Section 5 of Part II, entitled 'Patents', Article 27(3)(b) provides that Members have the option of protecting inventions of plant varieties by *sui generis* rights (such as breeder's rights) instead of through patents. Under the Panel's theory, such *sui generis* rights would not be covered by the *TRIPS Agreement*. The option provided by Article 27(3)(b) would be read out of the *TRIPS Agreement*.[16]

With regard to 'trade names', the Appellate Body ruled that WTO Members have an obligation under the *TRIPS Agreement* to provide protection to trade names, since Article 2.1 of the *TRIPS Agreement* explicitly incorporates Article 8 of the *Paris Convention (1967)* into the *TRIPS Agreement*. The latter provision covers only the protection of trade names and has no other subject.[17] In general, the categories of IP rights covered by the *TRIPS Agreement* are those expressly mentioned in Sections 1–7 of Part II *as well as* those in the incorporated conventions that are the '*subject*' of these Sections.

The *TRIPS Agreement* does not cover every *aspect of IP protection* for the covered categories of IP rights. For example, it expressly excludes the issue of exhaustion of IP rights from its coverage.[18] Other aspects of the protection of IP rights that are not mentioned in the *TRIPS Agreement* or in the incorporated

15 See Panel Report, *US – Section 211 Appropriations Act (2002)*, para. 8.26.

16 Appellate Body Report, *US – Section 211 Appropriations Act (2002)*, para. 335.

17 *Ibid.*, paras. 336–8 and 341.

18 See below, pp. 1011–13. Note that Members are nevertheless required to respect the non-discrimination principles in respect of exhaustion of rights.

provisions of the World Intellectual Property Organization (WIPO) conventions are also excluded from the disciplines of the agreement.[19]

3.2 Temporal Scope of Application

Article 70 of the *TRIPS Agreement* deals with the protection of existing subject matter, i.e. the temporal scope of application of the *TRIPS Agreement*. Article 70.1 specifies certain acts which do *not* give rise to obligations under the *TRIPS Agreement*. It states:

> This Agreement does not give rise to obligations *in respect of acts which occurred* before the date of application of the Agreement for the Member in question.[20]

In other words, the *TRIPS Agreement* does not apply retroactively to acts that occurred before its 'date of application' for a Member.[21] In contrast, Article 70.2 of the *TRIPS Agreement* provides that the Agreement does create obligations in respect of subject matter that existed at the date of application. It provides, in relevant part:

> Except as otherwise provided for in this Agreement, this Agreement gives rise to obligations *in respect of all subject-matter existing* at the date of application of this Agreement for the Member in question, and which is *protected* in that Member on the said date, or which meets or comes subsequently to meet the criteria for protection under the terms of this Agreement ...[22]

In *Canada – Patent Term (2000)*, Canada relied on Article 70.1 to justify that its (Old) Patent Act, which granted a patent protection term of seventeen years, did not confer the twenty-year term of protection required by Article 33 of the *TRIPS Agreement*. The Appellate Body interpreted the phrase 'acts which occurred before the date of application' as encompassing acts of public authorities as well as acts of private or third parties.[23] Where such acts 'occurred' (were done, carried out or completed) before the date of application of the *TRIPS Agreement* for a Member, Article 70.1 provides that the *TRIPS Agreement* does not give rise to obligations in respect of those '*acts*'.[24] However, the Appellate Body noted the fundamental importance of distinguishing in respect of IP rights between 'acts' and the 'rights' created by those acts.[25] For example, the grant of a patent is an 'act' conferring various substantive rights, such as national

19 See e.g. Panel Report, *Indonesia – Autos (1998)*, para. 14.275. With regard to these aspects of IP rights, Members do not have to ensure a minimum level of protection and to provide non-discriminatory treatment (under the *TRIPS Agreement*).
20 Emphasis added.
21 The 'date of application' refers to the dates at which different transitional periods for developed, developing and least-developed countries expire, as discussed below. See below, pp. 1051–2.
22 Emphasis added.
23 See Appellate Body Report, *Canada – Patent Term (2000)*, para. 54. 24 See *ibid.*, para. 55.
25 *Ibid.*, para. 56.

treatment, MFN treatment, and term of protection. The Appellate Body then identified the key question before it in *Canada – Patent Term (2000)* as follows:

> if patents created by 'acts' of public authorities under the Old Act continue to be in force on the date of application of the *TRIPS Agreement* for Canada (that is, on 1 January 1996), can Article 70.1 operate to exclude those patents from the scope of the *TRIPS Agreement*, on the ground that they were created by 'acts which occurred' before that date?[26]

The Appellate Body answered this question in the negative. It acknowledged that an 'act' is something that is 'done', and that the use of the phrase 'acts which occurred' suggests that what was done is now complete or ended.[27] However, it pointed out that this 'excludes situations, including existing rights and obligations, that have *not* ended'.[28] It noted that, if 'acts which occurred' would be interpreted to cover all continuing situations involving patents granted before the date of application of the *TRIPS Agreement*, then:

> Article 70.1 would preclude the application of virtually the whole of the *TRIPS* Agreement to rights conferred by the patents arising from such 'acts'.[29]

4 GENERAL PROVISIONS AND BASIC PRINCIPLES OF THE *TRIPS AGREEMENT*

Part I of the *TRIPS Agreement* contains the general provisions and basic principles that apply to all covered areas of IP. Article 1.1 of the *TRIPS Agreement* obliges Members to 'give effect' to its provisions. However, it expressly states that Members are 'free to determine the appropriate method' of implementing their obligations under the Agreement within their own legal systems and practice.[30] In addition, Article 1.1 provides that Members are free, but not obliged, to implement more extensive protection than that required by the *TRIPS Agreement*. This firmly establishes the nature of the *TRIPS Agreement* as setting a *minimum level* of IP protection. The flexibility available to Members with regard to *how* they give effect to their *TRIPS* obligations is an important tool in balancing the competing policy goals mentioned above.[31] However, the flexibility available to

26 *Ibid.*, para. 57.

27 See *ibid.*, para. 58. 28 *Ibid.*

29 *Ibid.*, para. 59.

30 Note that, in *EC – Trademarks and Geographical Indications (US) (2005)*, the United States argued that the EC's inspection structure requirements for the protection of geographical indications conditioned the protection on the adoption by other Members of structures that the EC unilaterally determines to be equivalent to its own. The panel disagreed, holding that the evidence before it did not establish that these inspection structures concerned the systems of protection of *other* WTO Members; rather, they only ensured compliance with product specifications, which are a feature of the EC's system of protection. See Panel Report, *EC – Trademarks and Geographical Indications (US) (2005)*, paras. 7.762–7.766.

31 See, for example, the flexibility in determining domestic limitations and exceptions to copyright under the 'three-step test' and other relevant provisions, discussed below, pp. 1018–20.

Members is obviously not without limits. When, in *India – Patents (US) (1998)*, in interpreting India's obligation under Article 70.8(a) of the *TRIPS Agreement*,[32] the Appellate Body recalled the 'important general rule' of Article 1.1, and noted:

> Members, therefore, are free to determine how best to meet their obligations under the *TRIPS Agreement* within the context of their own legal systems. And, as a Member, India is 'free to determine the appropriate method of implementing' its obligations under the *TRIPS Agreement* within the context of its own legal system.[33]

However, in this case, the Appellate Body, like the panel, was not persuaded that the 'administrative instructions' given by India to its patent office to accept 'mailbox' applications as required under Article 70.8(a) would prevail over the conflicting and mandatory provisions of the Indian Patents Act.[34] Therefore, despite the flexibility provided in Article 1.1, India was found to have failed to properly implement its obligations under Article 70.8(a) of the *TRIPS Agreement.*[35]

This section discusses the basic principles laid down in Part I of the *TRIPS Agreement.* More specifically, it addresses: (1) the relationship between the *TRIPS Agreement* and WIPO conventions; (2) the national treatment obligation; (3) the most-favoured-nation treatment obligation; and (4) the issue of exhaustion of IP rights.

4.1 Relationship between the *TRIPS Agreement* and WIPO Conventions

The *TRIPS Agreement* builds upon the standards of IP protection enshrined in the IP conventions administered by the World Intellectual Property Organization (WIPO). It does so by incorporating by reference specific provisions of the relevant conventions, namely, the *Paris Convention for the Protection of Industrial Property of 1883*, as revised in the Stockholm Act of 1967 (the *Paris Convention (1967)*), the *Berne Convention for the Protection of Literary and Artistic Works of 1886*, as revised in the Paris Act of 1971 (*the Berne Convention (1971)*), the *International Convention for the Protection of Performers, Producers of Phonograms and Broadcasting Organizations of 1961 (the Rome Convention)* and the *Treaty on Intellectual Property in Respect of Integrated Circuits of 1989* (the *IPIC Treaty*). The obligations of the *TRIPS Agreement* must therefore be read together with the relevant WIPO conventions.

However, the *TRIPS Agreement* does more than simply incorporate the substantive provisions of these conventions. Developed-country negotiators of

32 This provision allows Members availing themselves of transitional arrangements under Part VI of the *TRIPS Agreement* to delay patent protection for pharmaceutical and agricultural chemical products subject to the requirement that they provide a 'means' by which patent applications in those fields can be filed. These applications are often referred to as 'mailbox applications' and Article 70.8 is called the 'mailbox provision'.

33 Appellate Body Report, *India – Patents (US) (1998)*, para. 59.

34 See *ibid.*, paras. 69–70.

35 See *ibid.*, para. 71. See also Panel Report, *Canada – Patent Term (2000)*, para. 6.94, where the panel noted that: 'Article 1.1 gives Members the freedom to determine the appropriate method of implementing [the two requirements at issue], but not to ignore either requirement'.

the *TRIPS Agreement* viewed the existing WIPO conventions as 'inadequate to address the needs of their business sectors in the "post-industrial era" or "information age"'.[36] Therefore, the *TRIPS Agreement* supplements and innovates the rules of the relevant WIPO conventions, as well as expressly provides additional protection in some areas. In addition, it creates an obligation under municipal law for Members to have a system in place to ensure the enforcement of the protected IP rights, and links them to the effective and binding dispute settlement system of the WTO.[37]

The relationship between the WIPO conventions and the *TRIPS Agreement* is set out in Article 2 of the *TRIPS Agreement.* Article 2.1 of the *TRIPS Agreement* explicitly obliges Members to comply with Articles 1 to 12 and 19 of the *Paris Convention (1967)* in respect of Parts II, III and IV of the *TRIPS Agreement.* Therefore, even WTO Members that are not Parties to the *Paris Convention (1967)* must comply with these provisions.[38] Article 2.2 of the *TRIPS Agreement* provides that nothing in Parts I to IV of the *TRIPS Agreement* shall derogate from Members' obligations under the *Paris Convention (1967)*, the *Berne Convention (1971)*, the *Rome Convention* or the *IPIC Treaty.* This non-derogation clause does not create new obligations but seeks to ensure that Members do not apply their *TRIPS* obligations in a manner that results in a violation of their obligations under the above-mentioned WIPO conventions. In addition, various provisions in Part II of the *TRIPS Agreement* dealing with different categories of IP rights incorporate certain provisions of the relevant WIPO conventions. With regard to the *Berne Convention (1971)*, the *Paris Convention (1967)* and the *IPIC Treaty*, these incorporation clauses oblige all WTO Members to comply with the incorporated articles of the WIPO conventions, and make them binding even on those WTO Members that are not Parties to WIPO conventions.[39]

4.2 The National Treatment Obligation

The principles of national treatment and MFN treatment, familiar from the discussion of the non-discrimination obligations under the GATT 1994 and the GATS in Chapters 4 and 5, apply also in the context of the *TRIPS Agreement.*[40] However, there are some differences in their formulation in the *TRIPS Agreement* in order to take into account the intangible nature of IP rights.

36 *Course on Dispute Settlement in International Trade, Investment and Intellectual Property – Module 3.14. WTO: TRIPS*, UNCTAD Document EDM/Misc.232/Add.18 (2003), 11.

37 See D. Matthews, *Globalising Intellectual Property Rights: The TRIPs Agreement* (Routledge, 2002), 46. These enforcement obligations are discussed below, pp. 1042–8.

38 See Appellate Body Report, *US – Section 211 Appropriations Act (2002)*, para. 125.

39 See, for example, Article 9.1 of the *TRIPS Agreement*, which obliges Members to comply with Articles 1–21, and the Appendix to the *Berne Convention (1971)* and Article 35 of the *TRIPS Agreement*, which obliges Members to provide protection to layout designs of integrated circuits in accordance with Articles 2–7 (except Article 6.3), 12 and 16.3 of the *IPIC Treaty*. Note that no similar provision exists with regard to the *Rome Convention*, which continues to bind only its Contracting Parties.

40 See above, pp. 306 and 342.

The national treatment obligation of the *TRIPS Agreement*, in Article 3.1, requires each Member to accord to nationals of other Members treatment 'no less favourable' than it accords to its own nationals in respect of IP protection.[41] As discussed above, Article 1.2 of the *TRIPS Agreement* defines the term 'intellectual property'.[42] Footnote 3 to Article 3.1 in turn defines the meaning of the term 'protection' of IP for purposes of Articles 3 and 4, and provides that it:

> shall include matters affecting the availability, acquisition, scope, maintenance and enforcement of intellectual property rights as well as those matters affecting the use of intellectual property rights *specifically addressed in this Agreement.*[43]

The national treatment obligation of Article 3 thus applies only to the categories of IP rights covered by the *TRIPS Agreement*. While 'protection' of those rights includes 'matters affecting the availability, acquisition, scope, maintenance and enforcement', 'matters affecting the use' of those rights are included only to the extent covered by the Agreement.[44] Unlike Article III of the GATT 1994 and Article XVII of the GATS, the national treatment obligation in Article 3 of the *TRIPS Agreement* applies to 'nationals' as defined in Article 1.3, rather than to 'like products' or 'like services and service suppliers'. This is because IP rights are intangible, and attach to an IP right holder, rather than to the product or service in which these rights are embodied.

The Appellate Body addressed the national treatment obligation in the *TRIPS Agreement* for the first time in *US – Section 211 Appropriations Act (2002)*. In this case, the Appellate Body observed the 'fundamental significance of the obligation of national treatment ... in the *TRIPS Agreement*',[45] and noted that:

> [i]ndeed, the significance of the national treatment obligation can hardly be overstated. Not only has the national treatment obligation long been a cornerstone of the Paris Convention and other international intellectual property conventions. So, too, has the national treatment obligation long been a cornerstone of the world trading system that is served by the WTO.[46]

The Appellate Body stated that the national treatment obligation is 'a fundamental principle underlying the *TRIPS Agreement*, just as it has been in what is now the GATT 1994'.[47] It agreed with the panel that, because the language of Article 3.1 of the *TRIPS Agreement* is similar to that of Article III:4 of the GATT

41 Note that the *TRIPS Agreement* incorporates, in addition, three national treatment obligations of pre-existing IP conventions, namely: Article 2 of the *Paris Convention (1967)* (incorporated by Article 2.1 of the *TRIPS Agreement*); Article 5 of the *Berne Convention (1971)* (incorporated by Article 9.1 of the *TRIPS Agreement*); and Article 5 of the *IPIC Treaty* (incorporated by Article 35 of the *TRIPS Agreement*). See e.g. Panel Report, *EC – Trademarks and Geographical Indications (US) (2005)*, fn. 166 to para. 7.131.

42 See above, p. 999.

43 Emphasis added. On the 'limited' scope of application of the national treatment obligation of Article 3 of the *TRIPS Agreement*, see Panel Report, *Indonesia – Autos (1998)*, para. 14.275.

44 See Correa, *Trade-Related Aspects of Intellectual Property Rights*, 62.

45 Appellate Body Report, *US – Section 211 Appropriations Act (2002)*, para. 240.

46 *Ibid.*, para. 241. 47 *Ibid.*, para. 242.

1994, the case law concerning Article III:4 of the GATT 1994 'may be useful in interpreting the national treatment obligation in the *TRIPS Agreement*'.[48]

In applying the national treatment obligation of Article 3.1 in *US – Section 211 Appropriations Act (2002)*, the Appellate Body pointed out that Section 211(a) (2) of the US Appropriations Act, on its face, imposed an 'extra hurdle' on successors-in-interest to the confiscated trademark who were not US nationals, and that hurdle did not apply to successors-in-interest that were US nationals. More importantly, non-nationals faced the additional problem that under the terms of Section 211(a) of the Appropriations Act, their trademark would not be recognised, validated or enforced by US courts. Although it was not very likely that in practice foreign nationals would actually have to overcome both 'hurdles', according to the Appellate Body 'even the *possibility* that non-United States successors-in-interest face two hurdles is *inherently less favourable* than the undisputed fact that United States successors-in-interest face only one'.[49] Therefore, the Appellate Body found that the United States had violated the national treatment obligation in Article 3.1 of the *TRIPS Agreement*.[50]

The panel in *EC – Trademarks and Geographical Indications (2005)* also discussed the national treatment obligation of Article 3.1 of the *TRIPS Agreement*. The measure at issue in that case was an EC regulation with two sets of detailed procedures for the registration of geographical indications (GIs) for agricultural products and foodstuffs. The first procedure (Articles 5–7) applied to the names of geographical areas located in the European Communities. The second procedure (Articles 12a and 12b) applied to the names of geographical areas located in third countries outside the European Communities. Furthermore additional conditions (Article 12.1) required that a third country must provide reciprocal and equivalent protection for GIs to those available in the European Communities (known as the 'reciprocity and equivalence conditions').[51] The complainants (the United States and Australia) claimed that the EC regulation at issue was inconsistent with the national treatment obligation in Article 3.1 of the *TRIPS Agreement*, because it imposed conditions of reciprocity and equivalence on the availability of protection.[52] The panel identified two elements for establishing an inconsistency with the national treatment obligation of Article 3.1 of the *TRIPS Agreement*: (1) the measure at issue must relate to the protection of intellectual property; and (2) the nationals of other Members must be accorded 'less favourable' treatment than the nationals of the Member whose measure

48 *Ibid.* 49 *Ibid.*, para. 265.
50 See *ibid.*, para. 268. The Appellate Body also found that the United States acted inconsistently with Article 2.1 of the *Paris Convention (1967)*. See *ibid.*
51 See Panel Report, *EC – Trademarks and Geographical Indications (US) (2005)*, paras. 7.57–7.75 and 7.102; and Panel Report, *EC – Trademarks and Geographical Indications (Australia) (2005)*, para. 7.109–7.125 and 7.152.
52 See Panel Report, *EC – Trademarks and Geographical Indications (US) (2005)*, para. 7.104; Panel Report, *EC – Trademarks and Geographical Indications (Australia) (2005)*, para. 7.154. Note that the United States and Australia also claimed that the EC regulation was inconsistent with the national treatment obligation of Article 2.1 of the *Paris Convention (1967)*, as incorporated by Article 2.1 of the *TRIPS Agreement*.

is challenged.[53] In examining the *first* element of this two-tier test, the panel pointed out that it was undisputed that 'designations of origin' and 'geographical indications', as defined in the EC regulation at issue, fell within the category of 'geographical indications', i.e. the subject matter of Section 3 of Part II of the *TRIPS Agreement*, and were therefore part of a category of intellectual property within the meaning of the *TRIPS Agreement*.[54] The panel concluded that:

> this claim concerns the 'protection' of intellectual property, as clarified in footnote 3 to the TRIPS Agreement, within the scope of the national treatment obligation in Article 3 of that Agreement.[55]

Turning to the *second* element of the two-tier test under Article 3.1 of the *TRIPS Agreement*, that is, whether 'less favourable treatment' is accorded to nationals of other Members, the panel noted:

> It is useful to recall that Article 3.1 of the TRIPS Agreement combines elements of national treatment both from pre-existing intellectual property agreements and GATT 1994. Like the pre-existing intellectual property conventions, Article 3.1 applies to 'nationals', not products. Like GATT 1994, Article 3.1 refers to 'no less favourable' treatment, not the advantages or rights that laws now grant or may hereafter grant, but it does not refer to likeness.[56]

The panel pointed out that Article 3 of the *TRIPS Agreement* prohibits not only measures, which *on their face* discriminate between the nationals of a Member and foreign nationals, but also *de facto* discriminatory measures. The panel referred to the case law regarding less favourable treatment under Article III:4 of the GATT 1994, which has been interpreted as including situations where the application of formally identical legal provisions would in practice accord less favourable treatment.[57] The panel held:

> We consider that this reasoning applies with equal force to the no less favourable treatment standard in Article 3.1 of the TRIPS Agreement. In our view, even if the provisions of the Regulation are formally identical in the treatment that they accord to the nationals of other Members and to the European Communities' own nationals, this is not sufficient to demonstrate that there is no violation of Article 3.1 of the TRIPS Agreement.[58]

The panel recalled that the panel and Appellate Body in *US – Section 211 Appropriations Act (2002)*[59] found that the appropriate standard for 'no less

53 See Panel Report, *EC – Trademarks and Geographical Indications (US) (2005)*, para. 7.125; Panel Report, *EC – Trademarks and Geographical Indications (Australia) (2005)*, para. 7.175.

54 See Panel Report, *EC – Trademarks and Geographical Indications (US) (2005)*, para. 7.128; and Panel Report, *EC – Trademarks and Geographical Indications (Australia) (2005)*, para. 7.178.

55 Panel Report, *EC – Trademarks and Geographical Indications (US) (2005)*, para. 7.129; and Panel Report, *EC – Trademarks and Geographical Indications (Australia) (2005)*, para. 7.179.

56 Panel Report, *EC – Trademarks and Geographical Indications (US) (2005)*, para. 7.131; and Panel Report, *EC – Trademarks and Geographical Indications (Australia) (2005)*, para. 7.181.

57 See Panel Report, *EC – Trademarks and Geographical Indications (US) (2005)*, para. 7.173; and Panel Report, *EC – Trademarks and Geographical Indications (Australia) (2005)*, para. 7.207.

58 Panel Report, *EC – Trademarks and Geographical Indications (US) (2005)*, para. 7.176; and Panel Report, *EC – Trademarks and Geographical Indications (Australia) (2005)*, para. 7.210.

59 See Panel Report, *US – Section 211 Appropriations Act (2002)*, paras. 8.130–8.131; and Appellate Body Report, *US – Section 211 Appropriations Act (2002)*, para. 258.

favourable treatment' under Article 3 of the *TRIPS Agreement* is that developed by the GATT panel in *US – Section 337 Tariff Act (1989)* under Article III of the GATT.[60] The panel in *EC – Trademarks and Geographical Indications (2005)* thus proceeded to examine whether the difference in treatment affected the 'effective equality of opportunities' between the nationals of other Members and the European Communities' nationals with regard to the protection of IP rights, to the detriment of nationals of other Members.[61] The equivalence and reciprocity conditions of the EC regulation at issue were held by the panel to modify the effective equality of opportunities to obtain protection of intellectual property.[62] Those conditions, according to the panel, constituted a significant 'extra hurdle'[63] to obtaining GI protection that did not apply to geographic areas located within the European Communities. The panel concluded:

> [T]he equivalence and reciprocity conditions modify the effective equality of opportunities with respect to the availability of protection to persons who wish to obtain GI protection under the Regulation, to the detriment of those who wish to obtain protection in respect of geographical areas located in third countries, including WTO Members. This is less favourable treatment.[64]

The EC regulation at issue referred to the location of geographical indications, whereas the national treatment obligation in Article 3.1 of the *TRIPS Agreement* refers to treatment accorded to 'nationals'. Therefore the panel had to determine how less favourable treatment accorded under the EC regulation with respect to the *availability of protection* affects the treatment accorded to the *nationals* of other Members and that accorded to the European Communities' *nationals* for the purposes of Article 3.1 of the *TRIPS Agreement.*[65] The fact that the EC regulation, on its face, provided formally identical treatment to the nationals of other Members and to the European Communities' nationals was not considered to be sufficient to demonstrate that there was no violation of Article 3.1 of the *TRIPS Agreement.* The panel then proceeded to examine whether the 'fundamental thrust and effect' of the regulation at issue was such that it affected the 'effective equality of opportunities' with regard to the protection of IP rights. Regarding the question of which nationals to compare for the purposes of establishing whether less favourable treatment was conferred, the panel held that:

> the nationals that are relevant to an examination under Article 3.1 of the TRIPS Agreement should be those who seek opportunities with respect to the same type of intellectual property

60 See Panel Report, *US – Section 337 Tariff Act (1989)*, para. 5.11.

61 See Panel Report, *EC – Trademarks and Geographical Indications (US) (2005)*, para. 7.134; Panel Report, *EC – Trademarks and Geographical Indications (Australia) (2005)*, para. 7.184.

62 See Panel Report, *EC – Trademarks and Geographical Indications (US) (2005)*, para. 7.139; and Panel Report, *EC – Trademarks and Geographical Indications (Australia) (2005)*, para. 7.189.

63 Here the panel referred to the approach of the Appellate Body in US – *Section 211 Appropriations Act (2002)* to an 'extra hurdle' imposed only on foreign nationals. See Appellate Body Report, *US – Section 211 Appropriations Act (2002)*, para. 268.

64 Panel Report, *EC – Trademarks and Geographical Indications (US) (2005)*, para. 7.140; and Panel Report, *EC – Trademarks and Geographical Indications (Australia) (2005)*, para. 7.190.

65 See Panel Report, *EC – Trademarks and Geographical Indications (US) (2005)*, para. 7.141; and Panel Report, *EC – Trademarks and Geographical Indications (Australia) (2005)*, para. 7.191.

in comparable situations. On the one hand, this excludes a comparison of opportunities for nationals with respect to different categories of intellectual property, such as GIs and copyright. On the other hand, no reason has been advanced as to why the equality of opportunities should be limited *a priori* to rights with a territorial link to a particular Member.[66]

Therefore, the panel did not have to make a factual assumption that 'every person who wishes to obtain protection for a GI in a particular Member is a national of that Member'.[67] Having examined the provisions of the EC regulation at issue, the panel found that:

the distinction made by the Regulation on the basis of the location of a GI will operate in practice to discriminate between the group of nationals of other Members who wish to obtain GI protection, and the group of the European Communities' own nationals who wish to obtain GI protection, to the detriment of the nationals of other Members. This will not occur as a random outcome in a particular case but as a feature of the *design and structure of the system*. This design is evident in the Regulation's objective characteristics, in particular, the definitions of 'designation of origin' and 'geographical indication' and the requirements of the product specifications. The structure is evident in the different registration procedures.[68]

The panel noted that the *TRIPS Agreement* itself recognises that discrimination based on residence and establishment will be a 'close substitute for nationality'.[69] In its view, the object and purpose of the *TRIPS Agreement*:

would be severely undermined if a Member could avoid its obligations by simply according treatment to its own nationals on the basis of close substitute criteria, such as place of production, or establishment, and denying treatment to the nationals of other WTO Members who produce or are established in their own countries.[70]

Therefore, the panel found that the reciprocity and equivalence conditions in the EC regulation with respect to the availability of GI protection, violate Article 3.1 because the treatment accorded to the group of nationals of other Members was different from, and less favourable than, that accorded to the European Communities' nationals.[71]

66 Panel Report, *EC – Trademarks and Geographical Indications (US) (2005)*, para. 7.181; and Panel Report, *EC – Trademarks and Geographical Indications (Australia) (2005)*, para. 7.217 (footnotes omitted).

67 Panel Report, *EC – Trademarks and Geographical Indications (US) (2005)*, para. 7.182; and Panel Report, *EC – Trademarks and Geographical Indications (Australia) (2005)*, para. 7.218.

68 Panel Report, *EC – Trademarks and Geographical Indications (US) (2005)*, para. 7.194; and Panel Report, *EC – Trademarks and Geographical Indications (Australia) (2005)*, para. 7.230. Emphasis added.

69 Panel Report, *EC – Trademarks and Geographical Indications (US) (2005)*, para. 7.198; and Panel Report, *EC – Trademarks and Geographical Indications (Australia) (2005)*, para. 7.234. Here the panel highlighted the criteria set out in fn. 1 to the *TRIPS Agreement* which it stated 'are clearly intended to provide close substitute criteria to determine nationality where criteria to determine nationality as such are not available in a Member's domestic law. These criteria are "domicile" and "real and effective industrial or commercial establishment"'.

70 Panel Report, *EC – Trademarks and Geographical Indications (US) (2005)*, para. 7.199; and Panel Report, *EC – Trademarks and Geographical Indications (Australia) (2005)*, para. 7.235.

71 See Panel Report, *EC – Trademarks and Geographical Indications (US) (2005)*, paras. 7.204 and 7.213; and Panel Report, *EC – Trademarks and Geographical Indications (Australia) (2005)*, paras. 7.240 and 7.249.

The national treatment obligation in Article 3.1 of the *TRIPS Agreement* has exceptions. As noted by the panel in *EC – Trademarks and Geographical Indications (2005)*:

> [t]he scope of the national treatment obligation in Article 3.1 of the TRIPS Agreement also differs from that of the national treatment obligation in Article III:4 of GATT 1994, as it is subject to certain exceptions in Articles 3.1, 3.2 and 5, one of which is inspired by the language of Article XX of GATT 1994.[72]

Article 3.1 exempts from the national treatment obligation the exceptions already provided for in the *Paris Convention (1967)*, the *Berne Convention (1971)*, the *Rome Convention* or the *IPIC Treaty*.[73] This exemption reflects the fact that IP treaties sometimes require reciprocity. Furthermore, the national treatment obligation applies to performers, producers of phonograms and broadcasting organisations only with respect to the rights provided for in the *TRIPS Agreement*.[74] Therefore, the obligation does not cover other rights that holders of related rights may have under domestic laws or other international agreements. This avoids, for example, that Members who are not parties to the *Rome Convention* obtain 'through the back door',[75] any such other rights protected under this convention without committing to provide such protection themselves. In addition, Article 5 of the *TRIPS Agreement* provides that the national treatment obligation of Article 3 does not apply to procedures for the acquisition of IP rights provided in multilateral agreements negotiated under the auspices of the WIPO.[76]

4.3 The Most-Favoured-Nation Treatment Obligation

Article 4 contains the MFN obligation of the *TRIPS Agreement*. It requires that any advantage, favour, privilege or immunity with regard to IP protection granted by a Member to the nationals of any other country be accorded immediately and unconditionally to the nationals of all other Members. We recall that Article 1.2 of the *TRIPS Agreement* defines the term 'intellectual property', and footnote 3 to Article 3.1 in turn defines the meaning of the term 'protection' of IP for purposes of Articles 3 and 4.[77] Members are required to provide MFN treatment only with respect to categories of IP rights covered by the *TRIPS Agreement*.

72 *Ibid.*, paras. 7.211 and 7.247.

73 Note that Article 3.1 of the *TRIPS Agreement* provides that, in the case of two of these exceptions, those under Article 6 of the *Berne Convention (1971)* and Article 16.1(b) of the *Rome Convention*, notification to the Council for TRIPS is required if a Member intends to avail itself of them.

74 Article 3.2 of the *TRIPS Agreement* provides that the exceptions of Article 3.1 that relate to judicial and administrative procedures apply only to the extent necessary to secure compliance with laws and regulations that are not inconsistent with the *TRIPS Agreement* and where they are not applied in a way that constitutes a disguised restriction on trade. Compare this to Article XX(d) of the GATT 1994, discussed above, pp. 564–73.

75 Correa, *Trade-Related Aspects of Intellectual Property Rights*, 63.

76 Note that the Article 5 exception applies also to the MFN obligation of Article 4 of the *TRIPS Agreement*.

77 This footnote is quoted above, pp. 1003–4.

While 'protection' of those rights includes 'matters affecting the availability, acquisition, scope, maintenance and enforcement', 'matters affecting the use' of those rights are included only to the extent covered by the *TRIPS Agreement.*[78]

Unlike the MFN treatment obligations of Article I:1 of the GATT 1994 and Article II:1 of the GATS, Article 4 of the *TRIPS Agreement* applies to 'nationals' as defined in Article 1.3, rather than to 'like products' or 'like services and service suppliers'. As noted above, this is because IP rights are intangible, and attach to an IP right holder, rather than to the product or service in which they are embodied. Interestingly, none of the pre-existing IP conventions contains an MFN treatment obligation. Thus, the *TRIPS Agreement* introduced such an obligation for the first time in the area of IP protection. In *US – Section 211 Appropriations Act (2002)*, the Appellate Body emphasised the importance of MFN treatment, which is key to the multilateral trading system, and that the *TRIPS Agreement* extends to IP right holders. It noted:

> [T]he obligation to provide most-favoured-nation treatment has long been one of the cornerstones of the world trading system. For more than fifty years, the obligation to provide most-favoured-nation treatment in Article I of the GATT 1994 has been both central and essential to assuring the success of a global rules-based system for trade in goods. Unlike the national treatment principle, there is no provision in the Paris Convention (1967) that establishes a most-favoured-nation obligation with respect to rights in trademarks or other industrial property. However, the framers of the *TRIPS Agreement* decided to extend the most-favoured-nation obligation to the protection of intellectual property rights covered by that Agreement. As a cornerstone of the world trading system, the most-favoured-nation obligation must be accorded the same significance with respect to intellectual property rights under the *TRIPS Agreement* that it has long been accorded with respect to trade in goods under the GATT. It is, in a word, fundamental.[79]

Article 4 of the *TRIPS Agreement* is subject to exceptions. Advantages granted by a Member that drives from international agreements on judicial assistance or law enforcement need not be granted to all Members.[80] Further, the advantages granted in the *Rome Convention* and the *Berne Convention (1971)* on condition of reciprocity are excluded from the coverage of the MFN obligation of the

78 Note that Cottier considers that the MFN treatment obligation extends to all categories of IP protection covered by the *TRIPS Agreement*, and as a consequence Members that extend TRIPS-plus protection to certain countries are obliged by Article 4 to extend such protection to all WTO Members. Note that the *TRIPS Agreement* does not contain an exception to the MFN treatment obligation for regional trade agreements, similar to Article XXIV of the GATT 1994 and Article V of the GATS. See T. Cottier, 'The Agreement on Trade-Related Aspects of Intellectual Property Rights', in Macrory, Appleton and Plummer (eds.), *World Trade Organization*, 1068 and 1069. See contra Correa, *Trade-Related Aspects of Intellectual Property Rights*, 66–7. Correa believes that fn. 3 limits the MFN principle to the rights specifically addressed in the *TRIPS Agreement* and incorporated IP conventions. Therefore, according to Correa, Members providing higher levels of IP protection, beyond that required by the *TRIPS Agreement*, under bilateral agreements (so-called 'TRIPS-plus' protection) need not extend that same protection to all WTO Members.

79 Appellate Body Report, *US – Section 211 Appropriations Act (2002)*, para. 297. As the arguments advanced by both parties in relation to the alleged violation of MFN treatment were basically the same as those they relied upon in respect of the alleged violation of national treatment, discussed above, the Appellate Body held, for the same reasons *mutatis mutandis*, that a violation of Article 4 had been established. See *ibid.*, paras. 305–19. See also above, p. 1004.

80 See Article 4(a) of the *TRIPS Agreement*. Note that the agreements referred to are 'of a general nature and not particularly confined to the protection of intellectual property'.

TRIPS Agreement.[81] Members are also not required to provide on an MFN basis rights that performers, phonogram producers and broadcasting organisations may have under domestic laws or other international agreements but which are not protected under the *TRIPS Agreement*.[82] The most important exception in Article 4(d) relates to advantages that derive from international agreements 'related to the protection of intellectual property', which predate the entry into force of the *WTO Agreement*.[83] Such advantages need not be granted to all WTO Members on an MFN basis, provided that the relevant agreements have been notified to the Council for TRIPS, and they 'do not constitute an arbitrary or unjustifiable discrimination against nationals of other Members'.[84] In addition, Article 5 of the *TRIPS Agreement* provides that Article 4 does not apply to procedures for the acquisition of IP rights that are protected under multilateral agreements negotiated under the auspices of WIPO.[85]

4.4 Exhaustion of Intellectual Property Rights

Intellectual property rights are often embodied in a product (for example, a book, compact disc or medicine). However, the rights exist independently of the products in which they may be embodied. Theoretically therefore, IP rights can 'follow' products indefinitely, even after they have been legitimately sold, allowing the IP right holder to control their resale. In order to balance the rights of the IP right holder with the interests of others, the doctrine of exhaustion of rights determines when the IP right holder's right to control the product in which the IP right is embodied ends. Note that exhaustion applies only to the right to control distribution (such as resale) of the product after it has been put on the market by or with the consent of the right holder.[86] It does not affect the essence

81 See Article 4(b) of the *TRIPS Agreement*.

82 This is in line with the exception to the national treatment obligation in respect of rights of performers, phonogram producers and broadcasting organisations in the second sentence of Article 3.1 of the *TRIPS Agreement*. See above, p. 1009.

83 Members have interpreted this exemption broadly. They have made clear in respective communications that future acts based on such agreements would also be exempted from the MFN treatment obligation. See the Notification under Article 4(d) of the Agreement: European Communities and its Member States, IP/N/4/EEC/1, dated 29 January 1996; ANDEAN Pact – the Notification under Article 4(d) of the Agreement: Bolivia, Colombia, Ecuador, Peru, Venezuela, IP/N/4/BOL/1, IP/N/4/COL/1, IP/N/4/ECU/1, IP/N/4/PER/1, IP/N/4/VEN/1, dated 19 August 1997; and MERCOSUR – Notification of Argentina, Brazil, Paraguay, Uruguay, IP/N/4/ARG/1, IP/N/4/BRA/1, IP/N/4/PRY/1, IP/N/4/URY/1, dated 14 July 1998.

84 Correa notes that this exception seems to imply that parties to agreements related to IP protection (such as free-trade agreements with chapters on IP protection) that post-date the entry into force of the *WTO Agreement* are obliged to extend the advantages contained therein to all WTO Members. This would be the case despite the fact that WTO Members that are not parties to these agreements are not obliged to extend reciprocal advantages to such parties, which Correa regards as a 'troublesome implication' of this provision. See Correa, *Trade-Related Aspects of Intellectual Property Rights*, 69.

85 Note that, as stated above, the Article 5 exception applies also to the national treatment obligation of Article 3 of the *TRIPS Agreement*. See below, p. 1057.

86 See T. Cottier, 'The Agreement on Trade-Related Aspects of Intellectual Property Rights', in Macrory, Appleton and Plummer (eds.), *World Trade Organization*, 1069. See, however, Correa, *Trade-Related Aspects of Intellectual Property Rights*, 82, who argues that Article 6 of the *TRIPS Agreement* refers to 'IP rights' without qualification, and states that, therefore, the question arises whether exhaustion may be applied to all exclusive rights or only a subset thereof.

of an IP right, namely, the right to exclude others from exploiting the IP right without the consent of the right holder (for example, by making pirated copies of a compact disc or copying a patented medicine).[87]

There are three possible approaches to the exhaustion of IP rights: (1) *national* exhaustion of rights, meaning that the first sale of a product exhausts IP rights to control the resale of the product only on the national market; the IP right holder retains these rights in other countries; (2) *regional* exhaustion of rights, meaning that the first sale of a product in a country that is a party to a regional agreement exhausts IP rights to control further distribution in other parties to the regional agreement; and (3) *international* exhaustion of rights, meaning that, once a product is sold by or with the consent of the right holder, whether on the domestic market or on a foreign market, the IP rights to control the further distribution of the product are exhausted both domestically and internationally.

International exhaustion makes it possible to allow the parallel importation of products that are subject to IP rights. This means that it is permitted to import and resell legally a product without the consent of the IP right holder, if that product was put on the market of the exporting country by or with the consent of the right holder. This is of great importance to developing countries, as it enables their importers to buy products that are subject to IP rights, such as patented medicines, wherever they are cheapest and to resell them on their domestic markets.

As negotiators were deeply divided on the issue of exhaustion, the *TRIPS Agreement* does not mandate a particular approach to the exhaustion of IP rights. Article 6 of the *TRIPS Agreement* expressly provides that nothing in this Agreement, leaving aside the obligations of national treatment and MFN treatment, shall be used to address the subject matter of exhaustion of IP rights. Thus Members are free to choose their own approach to this matter. To alleviate concerns regarding the interpretation of Article 6 of the *TRIPS Agreement*, the *Doha Declaration on the TRIPS Agreement and Public Health* made clear that:

> [t]he effect of the provisions in the TRIPS Agreement that are relevant to the exhaustion of intellectual property rights is to leave each Member free to establish its own regime for such exhaustion without challenge, subject to the MFN and national treatment provisions of Articles 3 and 4.[88]

While this statement does not add anything to the *TRIPS Agreement*, it does clarify that Members cannot be challenged in WTO dispute settlement under the

87 See T. Cottier, 'The Agreement on Trade-Related Aspects of Intellectual Property Rights', in Macrory, Appleton and Plummer (eds.), *World Trade Organization*, 1069.

88 Doha Ministerial Conference, *Declaration on the TRIPS Agreement and Public Health*, WT/MIN(01)/DEC/2, dated 20 November 2001, para. 5(d).

TRIPS Agreement for allowing the international exhaustion of IP rights, and therefore permitting parallel importation.[89]

5 SUBSTANTIVE PROTECTION OF INTELLECTUAL PROPERTY RIGHTS

Part II of the *TRIPS Agreement* contains the mandatory minimum standards of IP protection that Members are required to guarantee in their territories. These standards concern, more specifically, the availability, scope and use of those IP rights covered by the *TRIPS Agreement*. As noted above, the *TRIPS Agreement* does not cover every category of IP, but only deals with those seven categories specified in sections 1–7 of Part II of the Agreement.[90]

This section limits itself to an examination of four categories of the IP rights covered by the *TRIPS Agreement*, namely: (1) copyright and related rights; (2) trademarks; (3) geographical indications (GIs); and (4) patents. These four categories of IP rights have already been the subject of WTO dispute settlement.

5.1 Copyright and Related Rights

Section 1 of Part II of the *TRIPS Agreement* deals with copyright and related rights. It incorporates and supplements the relevant provisions of the *Berne Convention (1971)*.[91] Article 9.1 of the *TRIPS Agreement* expressly incorporates

89 One of the main incentives for this clarification in the *Doha Declaration on the TRIPS Agreement and Public Health* was the fact that a large number of pharmaceutical firms challenged the South African Ministry of Health's authorisation of parallel importation of medicines under Section 15C of the South African Medicines and Related Substances Control Amendment Act, No. 90 of 1997. The challenge was withdrawn in 2001. As discussed in detail below, at p. 1057, under the General Council Decision waiving the obligations of Article 31(f) of the *TRIPS Agreement*, Members are required to take reasonable measures to prevent re-exportation of essential medicines imported under the compulsory licence regime provided under the waiver. See Decision of the General Council of 30 August 2003, *Implementation of Paragraph 6 of the Doha Declaration on the TRIPS Agreement and Public Health*, WT/L/540 and Corr.1, dated 2 September 2003. See also the subsequent Decision of the General Council on the Amendment of the TRIPS Agreement of 29 July 2005, para. 4 of the Annex to the *TRIPS Agreement*.

90 See Panel Report, *EC – Trademarks and Geographical Indications (US) (2005)*, para. 7.598; and Panel Report, *EC – Trademarks and Geographical Indications (Australia) (2005)*, para. 7.598.

91 Note that the panel in *US – Section 110(5) Copyright Act (2000)* held: 'In the area of copyright, the Berne Convention and the TRIPS Agreement form the overall framework for multilateral protection. Most WTO Members are also parties to the Berne Convention. We recall that it is a general principle of interpretation to adopt the meaning that reconciles the texts of different treaties and avoids a conflict between them. Accordingly, one should avoid interpreting the TRIPS Agreement to mean something different than the Berne Convention except where this is explicitly provided for. This principle is in conformity with the public international law presumption against conflicts, which has been applied by WTO panels and the Appellate Body in a number of cases.' See Panel Report, *US – Section 110(5) Copyright Act (2000)*, para. 6.66.

Articles 1–21 and the Appendix to the *Berne Convention (1971)*.[92] In Article 2, the *Berne Convention (1971)* contains a non-exhaustive list of protected works, which covers 'every production in the literary, scientific and artistic domain'.[93] Pursuant to Article 2.8 of the *Berne Convention (1971)*, news of the day or mere items of press information are clearly excluded from copyright protection. The protection of some other categories of works is optional; thus every Party may decide to what extent it wishes to protect works of applied art (Article 2.7), and political speeches (Article 2*bis*.1), and to what extent lectures, addresses and other oral works may be reproduced by the press, broadcast and communicated to the public.[94] Parties to the *Berne Convention (1971)* also have the possibility to limit the protection of works to their being fixed in some material form.[95] For example, the protection of performances of a theatre play may be dependent on their being fixed in some form.

These provisions of the *Berne Convention (1971)* are supplemented by the provisions of the *TRIPS Agreement*. Article 10 of the *TRIPS Agreement* confirms that copyright protection covers two new types of works, namely, computer programs and compilations of data, and clarifies how protection is to be applied to them.

Under both the *Berne Convention (1971)* and the *TRIPS Agreement*, every Party is free to determine the *level* of originality or artistic creativity required for the work to be subject to copyright protection. The scope of copyright protection under the *TRIPS Agreement* is clarified in Article 9.2 as follows:

> Copyright protection shall extend to expressions and not to ideas, procedures, methods of operation or mathematical concepts as such.

Thus, copyright protection is only granted to the 'expression' of an idea, not the idea itself, because ideas are seen as common goods that should be shared with all, whereas the expression thereof may be subject to property rights. Frederick Abbott illustrated the idea – expression dichotomy with the following example:

> [T]he idea of writing a book about wizards and witches probably is as old as book writing itself ... [A]n author has earned a great deal of money by writing a popular series ... concerning a young man's coming of age in a school for wizards and witches. The author of this series cannot through copyright protection of her books prevent other authors from writing new books about wizards and witches. That would represent an attempt to control the use of an idea. What the author may be able to prevent is the use by others of a particular way of expressing an idea, such as describing specific individuals or the details in a storyline.[96]

92 Note, however, that the rights under Article 6 *bis* of the *Berne Convention (1971)* have been expressly excluded. These relate to the 'moral rights' of authors, which refer to the inherent and inalienable rights of authors, aside from economic rights, such as the right to prevent distortion or modification of the author's work in a way that would negatively affect his or her reputation or honour. Under the *TRIPS Agreement*, Members are not obliged to extend protection to these 'moral rights'.

93 Article 2.1 of the *Berne Convention (1971)*.

94 See *ibid.*, Article 2 *bis*(2). 95 See *ibid.*, Article 2.2.

96 *Course on Dispute Settlement in International Trade, Investment and Intellectual Property – Module 3.14. WTO: TRIPS*, UNCTAD Document EDM/Misc.232/Add.18 (2003), 12–13.

Article 9.1 of the *TRIPS Agreement* expressly incorporates Articles 1 to 21 and the Appendix of the *Berne Convention (1971)*.[97] In Article 2, the *Berne Convention (1971)* contains a non-exhaustive list of 'copyrightable' works, which covers 'every production in the literary, scientific and artistic domain'.[98] The copyright provisions of the *Berne Convention (1971)* are supplemented by the recognition in the *TRIPS Agreement* of new rights regarding the protection of computer programs and compilations of data and related rights of performers and broadcasters. However, under both the *Berne Convention (1971)* and the *TRIPS Agreement*, every Party is free to determine the *level* of originality or artistic creativity required for the work to be subject to copyright protection.

In Article 5.1, the *Berne Convention (1971)* provides for two overlapping sets of rights, namely: (1) rights which the respective laws of the parties to the *Berne Convention (1971)* other than the country of origin grant (or may hereafter grant) to their nationals; and (2) rights specially granted by the *Berne Convention (1971)*. In *China – Intellectual Property Rights (2009)*, no party disputed that the 'works' which Chinese law denied copyright protection because they failed content review, included works falling within the definition of 'literary and artistic works' in Article 2.1 of the *Berne Convention (1971)*.[99] The panel in *China – Intellectual Property Rights (2009)* found:

> [a] government's right to permit, to control, or to prohibit the circulation, presentation, or exhibition of a work may interfere with the exercise of certain rights with respect to a protected work by the copyright owner or a third party authorized by the copyright owner. However, there is no reason to suppose that censorship will eliminate those rights entirely with respect to a particular work.[100]

The *Berne Convention (1971)* provides that authors of literary and artistic works shall have the exclusive rights to make and authorise the translation[101] and the reproduction of their works in any form, which includes any sound or visual recording.[102] Authors of dramatic, dramatico-musical and musical works enjoy the right to authorise the public performance of their works, as well as any communication to the public thereof, including translations.[103] The broadcasting or the communication to the public, by wire, rebroadcasting, loudspeaker or any other analogous instrument is also regarded as an exclusive right of authors of literary and artistic works.[104] In 1998, the United States requested consultations with Greece because a significant number of television stations in Greece regularly broadcasted motion pictures and television programmes without the

97 Note, however, that the rights under Article 6 *bis* of the *Berne Convention (1971)* have been expressly excluded. These relate to the 'moral rights' of authors, which refer to the inherent and inalienable rights of authors, aside from economic rights, such as the right to prevent distortion or modification of the author's work in a way that would negatively affect his or her reputation or honour. Under the *TRIPS Agreement*, Members are not obliged to extend protection to these 'moral rights'.

98 Article 2.1 of the *Berne Convention (1971)*.

99 See Panel Report, *China – Intellectual Property Rights (2009)*, para. 7.116. 100 *Ibid.*, para. 7.132.

101 See Article 8 of the *Berne Convention (1971)*. 102 See *ibid.*, Article 9.1 and 9.3.

103 See *ibid.*, Article 11. 104 See *ibid.*, Article 11 *bis*.

authorisation of copyright owners and there appeared to be no effective provision or enforcement of remedies against copyright infringement in Greece.[105] The matter was resolved through consultations, as notified to the WTO in 2003.[106] Further, authors of literary works enjoy the exclusive right of authorising the public recitation of their works by any means or process and any communication thereof to the public.[107] In addition, the *Berne Convention (1971)* grants authors of literary or artistic works the right to authorise adaptations, arrangements and other alterations of their works,[108] as well as the cinematographic adaptation, the reproduction of these works, the public performance thereof and the communication to the public.[109] The author of a book, for example, would have to be asked before a producer of movies could adapt the story of the book into a screenplay.

With regard to authors of original works of art and original manuscripts, Parties to the *Berne Convention (1971)* have the option, but no obligation, to grant them the right to an interest in any sale of the work subsequent to the first transfer by the author of the work, referred to as 'droit de suite'.[110] In contrast, Article 11 of the *TRIPS Agreement*, dealing with 'rental rights', contains a significant innovation – it requires the recognition of 'rental rights' in some cases. Specifically, Members to the *TRIPS Agreement* are required to provide authors (and their successors) of computer programs and cinematographic works the right to authorise or to prohibit commercial rental to the public of originals or copies of their copyright works.[111] However, Article 11 exempts Members from this obligation in respect of cinematographic works unless such rental has led to widespread copying of the copyrighted works, which materially impairs the right of reproduction of the author. This implies that, a Member that avails itself of this 'impairment test' in its domestic law, the right of authors of cinematographic works to authorise or prohibit the commercial rental of their works can be limited to situations where authors can prove that the copying of their works will lead to loss of considerable revenue. In respect of computer programs, this obligation does not apply to rentals where the program itself is not the essential object of the rental. Here, one can think of the example of global positioning software included in rental cars.

Copyright protection is not granted indefinitely, but is limited to a particular term of protection. According to Article 7.1 of the *Berne Convention (1971)*, incorporated by reference in the *TRIPS Agreement*, the minimum term

105 See Request for Consultations by the United States, *Greece – Enforcement of Intellectual Property Rights for Motion Pictures and Television Programmes*, WT/DS125/1, dated 7 May 1998.

106 See Notification of Mutually Agreed Solution, *Greece – Enforcement of Intellectual Property Rights for Motion Pictures and Television Programmes*, WT/DS125/2, dated 26 March 2001.

107 See Article 11 *ter* of *the Berne Convention (1971)*.

108 See *ibid.*, Article 12. 109 See *ibid.*, Article 14.

110 See *ibid.*, Article 14 *ter*.

111 Note that this is limited to 'commercial rental', and therefore not-for-profit rentals are not covered by this obligation.

of protection is the life of the author plus fifty years after his or her death. With regard to the duration of the protection of copyright when it is calculated on a basis other than the life of a natural person, Article 12 of the *TRIPS Agreement* provides:

> Whenever the term of protection of a work, other than photographic work or a work of applied art, is calculated on a basis other than the life of a natural person, such term shall be *no less than* 50 years from the end of the calendar year of authorized publication, or, failing such authorized publication within 50 years from the making of the work, 50 years from the end of the calendar year of making.[112]

There are, however, exceptions to this basic rule in Article 7.1 of the *Berne Convention.* In the case of cinematographic works, the minimum term of protection, required by the *Berne Convention (1971)*, is fifty years after the work has been made available to the public with the author's consent, or, failing such an event, fifty years after the making.[113] Less than fifty years of protection are required for three categories of works. Article 7.4 of the *Berne Convention (1971)* specifies that photographic works and works of applied art shall be protected for at least twenty-five years from the making of such a work.

Both the *Berne Convention (1971)* and the *TRIPS Agreement* provide limitations and exceptions to the strict application of the rules regarding exclusive rights. In other words, both agreements provide for the possibility of using protected works in particular cases without having to obtain the authorisation of the owner of the copyright. Some of the limitations require that the author be compensated, while others allow for the free use of copyrighted works in special cases. The way in which countries make use of these, in part, optional free uses of works is a matter of economic and social circumstances as well as cultural preferences and differs from country to country. These exceptions are then included in national law and therefore apply to individuals directly. The relevant provision in the *TRIPS Agreement* is Article 13, which is entitled 'Limitations and Exceptions' and states:

> Members shall confine limitations or exceptions to exclusive rights to certain special cases which do not conflict with a normal exploitation of the work and do not unreasonably prejudice the legitimate interests of the right holder.

Article 13 of the *TRIPS Agreement* constitutes a binding guideline for WTO Members. It lays down the requirements that exceptions and limitations to exclusive rights provided for in national IP law have to meet. The limitations contained in the *Berne Convention (1971)* and the *TRIPS Agreement* will be dealt with in turn.

112 Emphasis added. This provision solves the problem that arose under the *Berne Convention (1971)* with regard to the term of protection in countries which do not recognise legal persons as 'authors'. It provides for the term of protection where this is calculated 'on a basis other than the life of a natural person'.

113 See Article 7.2 of the *Berne Convention (1971)*.

The *Berne Convention (1971)* permits the free reproduction of protected works in certain special cases (Article 9.2); allows quotations and the use of works for teaching purposes (Article 10); permits the reproduction of newspaper or similar articles for the purpose of reporting current events (Article 10*bis*); and allows ephemeral (i.e. brief and temporary) recordings (Article 11*bis*. 3). Consequently, if a Party to the *Berne Convention (1971)* has permitted the reproduction of articles already published in newspapers or periodicals on current topics, a broadcaster established in that country can use these articles in its broadcastings.

The rationale behind Article 13 of the *TRIPS Agreement*, quoted above, is the search for the 'appropriate balance between the rights of creators and the public interest in access to copyrighted works'.[114] Too many limitations could reduce the economic rewards to right holders; however, certain exceptions are desired in order to advance the public good. While Article 13 undisputedly applies to the newly created rights set out in the *TRIPS Agreement*, the question arises whether it also creates a new exception to the existing rights in the *Berne Convention (1971)*. In *US – Section 110(5) Copyright Act (2000)*, the European Communities argued that Article 13 of the *TRIPS Agreement* applies only to those rights that were added to the *TRIPS Agreement*, and, therefore, not to those provisions of the *Berne Convention (1971)* that were incorporated into the *TRIPS Agreement* by reference.[115] The panel in this case addressed the scope of application of Article 13 of the TRIPS Agreement as follows:

> In our view, neither the express wording nor the context of Article 13 or any other provision of the TRIPS Agreement supports the interpretation that the scope of application of Article 13 is limited to the exclusive rights newly introduced under the TRIPS Agreement.[116]

According to the panel in *US – Section 110(5) Copyright Act (2000)*, Article 13 of the *TRIPS Agreement* sets out three cumulative requirements for limitations and exceptions to exclusive rights. They must: (1) be confined to certain special cases; (2) not conflict with a normal exploitation of the work; and (3) not unreasonably prejudice the legitimate interests of the right holder.[117] The panel emphasised from the outset that:

> Article 13 cannot have more than a narrow or limited operation. Its tenor, consistent as it is with the provisions of Article 9(2) of the Berne Convention (1971), discloses that it was not intended to provide for exceptions or limitations except for those of a limited nature.[118]

With regard to the *first requirement*, the panel in *US – Section 110(5) Copyright Act (2000)* found that the concept of 'certain special cases' prohibits broad exceptions of general application. Limitations under Article 13 'should be clearly defined and should be narrow in scope and reach'.[119] Note that the *Berne*

114 UNCTAD–ICTSD, *Resource Book on TRIPS and Development: An Authoritative and Practical Guide to the TRIPS Agreement* (Cambridge University Press, 2005), 186.

115 See Panel Report, *US – Section 110(5) Copyright Act (2000)*, para. 6.75.

116 *Ibid.*, para. 6.80. 117 See *ibid.*, para. 6.97.

118 *Ibid.* 119 See *ibid.*, para. 6.112.

Convention (1971) provides for special exceptions that allow the unauthorised use of copyrighted material, as explained above.[120] These exceptions can be invoked and relied upon regardless of Article 13 of the *TRIPS Agreement.*[121]

Whether a limitation or an exception conflicts with a normal exploitation of a work must be judged for each exclusive right individually.[122] In *US – Section 110(5) Copyright Act (2000)*, the panel referred in that regard to the empirical and normative component that has to be evaluated. According to the panel, the commercial use of a work is not necessarily in conflict with the normal exploitation. Such a conflict would exist, however, if the use of a work 'enter[ed] into economic competition with the ways that right holders normally extract economic value from that right'.[123] For example, there might be a conflict if copies of copyrighted works were sold on the market and thus reduced sales opportunities for the copyright holder. If copies of copyrighted work would be used for research only, this would most likely not interfere with the normal exploitation of the copyright by the right holder.

Finally, the *third requirement* of Article 13 demands that an exception shall not 'unreasonably prejudice the legitimate interests of the right holder'. The panel in *US – Section 110(5) Copyright Act (2000)* ruled that 'legitimate interests' constitute both normative *and* legal positivist advantages of the right holder.[124] The normative concern for protecting interests could arguably refer to public policy interests such as free speech objectives, given that it is one of the objectives that underlie the protection of copyright. An 'unreasonable loss' to the copyright owner occurs if a limitation 'causes or has the potential to cause an unreasonable loss of income to the copyright owner'.[125] This is most likely not the case if the exception is limited to teaching or research purposes and applies to materials, such as fiction or news articles, that are not specifically produced for that purpose. A heavily commercial use, however, would probably not pass this test.

In *US – Section 110(5) Copyright Act (2000)*, the European Communities complained about the so-called 'business exemption' and 'homestyle exemption' of Section 110(5) of the US Copyright Act. These exemptions permitted the playing of radio and television music in public places such as bars, shops and restaurants, without paying a royalty fee. The United States argued that both exemptions met the conditions of Article 13 of the *TRIPS Agreement.* The panel found that the 'business exemption', which allowed the non-payment of royalties if the size of the establishment was limited to a certain square footage, did not comply with the requirements of Article 13. The panel stated that, in fact, the substantial majority of the eating and drinking establishments were covered by the 'business exemption' and therefore did not constitute a 'certain special

120 See above, p. 1017. 121 In *US – Section 110(5) Copyright Act (2000)*, para. 6.80.
122 See *ibid.*, para. 6.173. 123 *Ibid.*, para. 6.183.
124 See *ibid.*, para. 6.224. 125 *Ibid.*, para. 6.229.

case' to which Article 13 of the *TRIPS Agreement* refers.[126] With regard to the 'homestyle exemption', allowing small restaurants and retail outlets to amplify music broadcasts by the use of 'homestyle equipment' (i.e. equipment of a kind commonly used in private homes) only, the panel found that the conditions of Article 13 were fulfilled and that this exemption was therefore lawful.[127]

Under Article 14 of the *TRIPS Agreement*, special rights apply to performers, producers of phonograms and broadcasting organisations. According to Article 14.1, performers have the exclusive right to authorise the fixation, i.e. recording or taping, of their unfixed performances, the reproduction of such fixation and/or the broadcasting/communication to the public of their live performance. For example, a music band performing in a concert has the right to authorise or prohibit the recording of its performance. Furthermore, producers of phonograms enjoy the right to authorise or prohibit the reproduction of their sound recordings.[128] In this respect, note that, in 1997, the United States filed a complaint alleging that Ireland did not grant sufficient protection to producers and performers of sound recordings.[129] Ireland eventually amended its copyright law on various points to remedy this lack of protection.[130] According to Article 14.3 of the *TRIPS Agreement*, broadcasting organisations have the right to prohibit the re-fixation or rebroadcasting of broadcasts.

The term of protection for performers and producers of phonograms shall last at least fifty years from the end of the year in which the fixation was made or the performance took place.[131] Article 14.5, second sentence, of the *TRIPS Agreement* requires that broadcasting organisations be granted a minimum term of protection of twenty years from the year in which the broadcast took place.

With regard to the duration of protection for performers and producers of sound recordings, in 1996 the United States and the European Communities filed a complaint against Japan at the WTO. According to the complainants, Japanese law only granted protection to foreign sound recordings produced on or after 1 January 1971, the date on which Japan first provided specialised protection for sound recordings under its copyright law.[132] After consultations, this issue was resolved one year later by amendments to the Japanese copyright law providing for protection to recordings produced between 1946 and 1971.[133]

126 See *ibid.*, para. 6.133. 127 See *ibid.*, para. 6.159.

128 See Article 14.2 of the *TRIPS Agreement.*

129 See A. B. Zampetti, 'WTO Rules in the Audio-Visual Sector', *HWWA* Hamburg Report 229, 24.

130 See *Request for Consultations by the United States, Ireland – Measures Affecting the Grant of Copyright and Neighbouring Rights*, WT/DS82/1, dated 22 May 1997; *Request for Consultations by the United States, European Communities – Measures Affecting the Grant of Copyright and Neighbouring Rights*, WT/DS115/1, dated 12 January 1998; and *Notification of Mutually Agreed Solution*, WT/DS82/3, DS115/3, dated 13 September 2002.

131 Article 14.5, first sentence, of the *TRIPS Agreement.*

132 *Complaint by the United States and the European Communities, Japan – Measures Concerning Sound Recordings*, WT/DS28/1 and WT/DS42/1, dated 14 February 1996 and 4 June 1996.

133 See *Notification of a Mutually-Agreed Solution, Japan – Measures Concerning Sound Recordings*, WT/DS42/4, dated 17 November 1997; and *Notification of Mutually Agreed Solution, Japan – Measures Concerning Sound Recordings*, WT/DS28/4, dated 5 February 1997.

5.2 Trademarks

Section 2 of Part II of the *TRIPS Agreement* deals with trademarks. Trademarks are signs that aim to distinguish goods or services by communicating information about their source. These marks have economic value, as they can build up a reputation (for example, with regard to quality or reliability) and generate goodwill. Section 2 incorporates the rights of trademark owners set out in the *Paris Convention (1967)* into the *TRIPS Agreement* and strengthens them.[134]

Article 15.1 of the *TRIPS Agreement* defines the protectable subject matter, i.e. what is capable of constituting a trademark and therefore eligible for registration as such, as follows:

> Any sign, or any combination of signs, capable of distinguishing the goods or services of one undertaking from those of other undertakings, *shall be capable of constituting a trademark*. Such signs, in particular words including personal names, letters, numerals, figurative elements and combinations of colours as well as any combination of such signs, *shall be eligible for registration as trademarks*. Where signs are not inherently capable of distinguishing the relevant goods or services, Members may make registrability depend on distinctiveness acquired through use. Members may require, as a condition of registration, that signs be visually perceptible.[135]

This provision covers both trademarks for goods and trademarks for services (otherwise known as 'service marks').[136] In principle, *distinctiveness* is required – whether inherent in the sign itself or acquired through use. As held by the Appellate Body in *US – Section 211 Appropriations Act (2002)*:

> If such signs are capable of distinguishing the goods or services of one undertaking from those of other undertakings, then they become *eligible for* registration as trademarks. To us, the title of Article 15.1 – 'Protectable Subject-Matter' – indicates that Article 15.1 embodies a *definition* of what can constitute a trademark. WTO Members are obliged under Article 15.1 to ensure that those signs or combinations of signs that meet the distinctiveness criteria set forth in Article 15.1 – and are, thus, *capable of constituting a trademark* – are *eligible for registration* as trademarks within their domestic legislation.[137]

In *US – Section 211 Appropriations Act (2002)*, the European Communities argued that, because Section 211(a) (1) of the US Appropriations Act prohibits registration of trademarks that are 'protectable', it is contrary to Article 15.1 of the *TRIPS Agreement*, as this provision obliges Members to register trademarks that meet the requirements of Article 15.1.[138] As emphasised by the Appellate Body in this case, the fact that a sign falls under the definition of Article 15.1

134 For example, the protection of well-known trademarks in the *Paris Convention (1967)* is expanded.

135 Emphasis added.

136 While the *Paris Convention (1967)* obliges parties to protect service marks, it does not require them to provide for the registration of such marks. In this sense, the *TRIPS Agreement* increases the protection of the *Paris Convention (1967)*.

137 Appellate Body Report, *US – Section 211 Appropriations Act (2002)*, para. 154 (footnote omitted, emphasis original).

138 See *ibid.*, para. 149.

means only that it is *capable of registration*, not that Members are *obliged to register it*. The Appellate Body stated:

> [I]n our view, the European Communities sees an obligation in Article 15.1 that is not there. Identifying certain signs that are *capable of* registration and imposing on WTO Members an obligation to make those signs *eligible for* registration in their domestic legislation is not the same as imposing on those Members an obligation to register *automatically* each and every sign or combination of signs that are *capable of* and *eligible for* registration under Article 15.1. This Article describes which trademarks are 'capable of' registration. It does not say that all trademarks that are capable of registration 'shall be registered'. This Article states that such signs or combinations of signs 'shall be *eligible* for registration' as trademarks. It does not say that they 'shall be registered'.[139]

Therefore, according to the Appellate Body, Members are free under Article 15.1 to stipulate in their national legislation, conditions for the registration of trademarks that do *not* address the definition of either 'protectable subject-matter' or what constitutes a trademark.[140] In particular, Article 15.2 provides that Members are permitted to deny trademark registration on 'other grounds' provided that they do not derogate from the *Paris Convention (1967)*. Such 'other grounds' are, as noted by the Appellate Body in *US – Section 211 Appropriations Act (2002)*, 'grounds *different from* those already mentioned in Article 15.1, such as lack of inherent distinctiveness of signs, lack of distinctiveness acquired through use, or lack of visual perceptibility'.[141] The Appellate Body stated in *US – Section 211 Appropriations Act (2002)*:

> The right of Members under Article 15.2 to deny registration of trademarks on grounds other than the failure to meet the distinctiveness requirements set forth in Article 15.1 implies that Members are not obliged to register any and every sign or combination of signs that meet those distinctiveness requirements.[142]

As stated above, Article 15.2 requires that the other grounds for denial of trademark registration 'do not derogate from the provisions of the Paris Convention (1967)'. The question thus arises as to what extent, if at all, 'Members are permitted to deny trademark registration on grounds *other than those expressly provided for* in the *TRIPS Agreement* and the Paris Convention (1967)'.[143] The Appellate Body in *US – Section 211 Appropriations Act (2002)* pointed out in this regard that Article 6.1 of the *Paris Convention (1967)* allows each party to

139 *Ibid.*, para. 155 (emphasis original).

140 See *ibid.*, para. 156. The Appellate Body further pointed out that Article 6.1 of the *Paris Convention (1967)* allows parties to determine the conditions for filing and registration of trademarks in their national legislation. In the Appellate Body's view, Article 15.1 of the *TRIPS Agreement* limits the right of Members to determine the conditions for filing and registration of trademarks under their domestic legislation pursuant to Article 6.1 *only* as it relates to the distinctiveness requirements enunciated in Article 15.1. See *ibid.*, para. 165.

141 *Ibid.*, para. 158 (emphasis original).

142 *Ibid.*, para. 159. One of such 'other grounds' mentioned in Article 15.2 is, as pointed out by the Appellate Body in *US – Section 211 Appropriations Act (2002)*, made explicit in Article 15.3, first sentence, which permits Members to condition registration of a trademark on use. See *ibid.*, para. 164. See further below, p. 1023 and fn. 178 on p. 1029.

143 *Ibid.*, para. 174.

determine conditions for the filing and registration of trademarks in its domestic legislation, provided that this is done consistently with the provisions of the *Paris Convention (1967).*[144] These provisions set out internationally agreed grounds for denying registration,[145] as well as internationally agreed grounds for *not* denying registration.[146] Therefore, implicitly, Members have the right to refuse trademark registration under Article 6.1 of the *Paris Convention (1967)* on grounds other than those explicitly set out in the convention.[147] Thus, the Appellate Body found that:

> 'other grounds' for the denial of registration within the meaning of Article 15.2 of the *TRIPS Agreement* are not limited to grounds expressly provided for in the exceptions contained in the Paris Convention (1967) or the *TRIPS Agreement.*[148]

Therefore, Members are free to define in their own legislation the 'other grounds' for denying trademark registration, provided that they are not among those explicitly prohibited by the *Paris Convention (1967).*[149]

A controversial issue in the negotiation of the *TRIPS Agreement* was whether *use* could be required as a condition for the registration of a trademark.[150] Article 15.3 of the *TRIPS Agreement* reflects the compromise reached: Members may make registrability, but not the filing of an application for registration, dependent on use.[151] Pursuant to Article 15.4 of the *TRIPS Agreement*, the nature of the goods and services to which a trademark is applied may not be used as a ground to deny registration of the trademark.

In order to promote transparency, Article 15.5 of the *TRIPS Agreement* requires a Member to publish each trademark either before, or promptly after, it is registered. Members must provide an opportunity for petitions to cancel registration and *may* provide an opportunity for the registration of a trademark to be opposed.

144 See *ibid.*, para. 175.

145 For example, Article 6 *bis* of the *Paris Convention (1967)* requires the refusal of the registration of a well-known trademark by a third party, and Article 6 *ter* covers prohibitions on the registration of State emblems, official hallmarks and emblems of international organisations. While Article 6 *quinquies* (A) contains a general rule that every trademark duly registered in the country of origin shall be accepted for filing and protected as it is in other parties, Article 6 *quinquies* (B) permits the denial of registration of such trademarks if they are devoid of distinctive character or have become customary, that are contrary to morality or public order, or infringe rights acquired by third parties.

146 See Appellate Body Report, *US – Section 211 Appropriations Act (2002)*, paras. 175–6. An example of a ground upon which registration may not be refused, mentioned by the Appellate Body, is that contained in Article 6.2 of the *Paris Convention (1967)*, which limits the legislative discretion of parties by providing that an application for registration by a national of a country of the Paris Union may not be refused on the ground that the national has not filed for registration or renewal in its country of origin. See *ibid.*, fn. 111 to para. 176.

147 See *ibid.*, para. 176.

148 *Ibid.*, para. 178. See also Panel Report, *US – Section 211 Appropriations Act (2002)*, paras. 8.53 and 8.70.

149 Appellate Body Report, *US – Section 211 Appropriations Act (2002)*, para. 177.

150 In Anglo-American legal systems, trademark rights can be created through use of the trademark without registration, and actual use is traditionally required as a condition for trademark registration. In civil law systems, trademarks are acquired through registration. See C. M. Correa, 'The TRIPS Agreement and Developing Countries', in Macrory, Appleton and Plummer (eds.), *World Trade Organization*, 181.

151 In addition, a Member may not refuse to register a trademark *solely* on the ground that the intended use has not taken place within three years of the filing of the application.

Article 16 of the *TRIPS Agreement* sets out the exclusive rights conferred on trademark owners. It provides in paragraph 1 thereof:

> The owner of a registered trademark shall have the exclusive right to prevent all third parties not having the owner's consent from using in the course of trade identical or similar signs for goods or services which are identical or similar to those in respect of which the trademark is registered where such use would result in a likelihood of confusion. In case of the use of an identical sign for identical goods or services, a likelihood of confusion shall be presumed. The rights described above shall not prejudice any existing prior rights, nor shall they affect the possibility of Members making rights available on the basis of use.

Therefore, a Member may decide for itself whether it will not only provide these exclusive rights to owners of registered trademarks, but also confer these rights on the basis of use. In *US – Section 211 Appropriations Act (2002)*, the European Communities challenged Section 211 of the US Omnibus Appropriations Act, which effectively prohibits registration and renewal – without the consent of the original owner or *bona fide* successor-in-interest – of trademarks and trade names used in connection with a business or assets that were confiscated without compensation by the Cuban government after the revolution. Under this provision, the trademark 'Havana Club' that had been confiscated by the Cuban government without compensation from its Cuban owners could not be registered or enforced in the United States. The trademark was later in the hands of a French–Cuban joint venture. The European Communities claimed that Section 211 of the Appropriations Act violated the rules of the *Paris Convention (1967)* on trademark registration and was inconsistent with the national treatment and MFN treatment obligations of the *TRIPS Agreement*. On appeal, the Appellate Body agreed with the panel that: neither Article 16.1 of the *TRIPS Agreement*, nor any other provision of either the *TRIPS Agreement* [or] the Paris Convention (1967), determines who owns or who does not own a trademark. Article 16.1 does not, in express terms, define how ownership of a registered trademark is to be determined. Article 16.1 confers exclusive rights on the 'owner', but Article 16.1 does not tell us who the 'owner' *is*. As used in this treaty provision, the ordinary meaning of 'owner' can be defined as the proprietor or person who holds the title or dominion of the property constituted by the trademark.[152]

The European Communities' argument that, under the *TRIPS Agreement*, the 'undertaking' that uses the trademark to distinguish its goods or services must be regarded as the owner of the trademark was rejected by the Appellate Body as having no basis in the text of the *TRIPS Agreement*.[153]

A few elements of the rights conferred under Article 16.1 of the *TRIPS Agreement* deserve attention. Note that the exclusive right is limited to the right to use the trademark 'in the course of trade'. Non-commercial use of trademarks is therefore not covered. Also, the owner is only granted the right to prevent

152 Appellate Body Report, *US – Section 211 Appropriations Act (2002)*, paras. 187 and 195.
153 See *ibid.*, para. 194.

the use of 'identical or similar signs' for goods or services that are 'identical or similar' to those in respect of which the trademark is registered. There is no definition of how similarity is to be determined, and this is left to Members to determine in their own legal systems. Note further that the exclusive right to prevent use of a trademark is only granted 'where such use would result in a likelihood of confusion'.[154]

In *EC – Trademarks and Geographical Indications (2005)*, the complainants alleged a violation of Article 16.1 of the *TRIPS Agreement* by the EC regulation on the protection of geographical indications (GIs) and designations of origin for agricultural products and foodstuffs. This regulation allowed for so-called 'coexistence', i.e. a legal regime under which a GI and a trademark can be used concurrently to some extent even though the use of one or both of them would otherwise infringe the rights conferred by the other. The complainants argued that the EC regulation did not ensure that an owner of a trademark was able to prevent uses of GIs, which would result in a 'likelihood of confusion' with a prior trademark.[155] The panel examined whether Article 16.1 of the *TRIPS Agreement* requires Members to make available to trademark owners the right to prevent confusing uses of signs, even where the signs are used as GIs. It noted:

> Although each of the Sections in Part II provides for a different category of intellectual property, at times they refer to one another, as certain subject-matter may be eligible for protection by more than one category of intellectual property. This is particularly apparent in the case of trademarks and GIs, both of which are, in general terms, forms of distinctive signs. The potential for overlap is expressly confirmed by Articles 22.3 and 23.2, which provide for the refusal or invalidation of the registration of a trademark which contains or consists of a GI.[156]

Examining the text of Article 16.1, the panel noted that it contains no express or implied limitation with respect to GIs.[157] It held:

> The text of Article 16.1 stipulates that the right for which it provides is an 'exclusive' right. This must signify more than the fact that it is a right to 'exclude' others, since that notion is already captured in the use of the word 'prevent'. Rather, it indicates that this right belongs to the owner of the registered trademark alone, who may exercise it to prevent certain uses by 'all third parties' not having the owner's consent. The last sentence provides for an exception to that right, which is that it shall not prejudice any existing prior rights. Otherwise, the text of Article 16.1 is unqualified.[158]

154 See C. M. Correa, 'The TRIPS Agreement and Developing Countries', in Macrory, Appleton and Plummer (eds.), *World Trade Organization*, 186. Correa points out that Article 15.1 informs the meaning of 'confusion', i.e. confusion should be understood in relation to the capacity of the trademark to distinguish the similar/identical goods or services of one undertaking from those of another.

155 See Panel Report, *EC – Trademarks and Geographical Indications (US) (2005)*, para. 7.512; and Panel Report, *EC – Trademarks and Geographical Indications (Australia) (2005)*, para. 7.516.

156 Panel Report, *EC – Trademarks and Geographical Indications (US) (2005)*, para. 7.599; and Panel Report, *EC – Trademarks and Geographical Indications (Australia) (2005)*, para. 7.599.

157 See Panel Report, *EC – Trademarks and Geographical Indications (US) (2005)*, paras. 7.601 and 7.603; and Panel Report, *EC – Trademarks and Geographical Indications (Australia) (2005)*, paras. 7.601 and 7.603.

158 Panel Report, *EC – Trademarks and Geographical Indications (US) (2005)*, para. 7.602; and Panel Report, *EC – Trademarks and Geographical Indications (Australia) (2005)*, para. 7.602.

Therefore, the trademark owner has the exclusive right to prevent use of the trademark by all third parties, also GI holders, without the owner's consent.

Articles 16.2 and 16.3 of the *TRIPS Agreement* extend the protection of Article 6*bis* of the *Paris Convention (1967)* in respect of 'well-known' trademarks on identical or similar goods to include, respectively: (1) 'well-known' trademarks on identical or similar *services*; and (2) 'well-known' trademarks on goods or services that are *not similar* to those in respect of which a trademark is registered. To determine whether a trademark is 'well known', Members must take account of the knowledge of the trademark in the relevant sector of the public, including that resulting from the promotion of the trademark.[159] Note that the knowledge need not be present in the public at large, but it is sufficient if it is present in the 'relevant sector' (for example, software users in the banking sector). However, the level of knowledge required for a mark to be 'well known' is left to Members to determine for themselves within their own legal systems. The extension of protection to 'well known' trademarks on goods or services that are not similar to those in respect of which the trademark is registered is limited to situations where the use of the trademark in relation to those goods or services would 'indicate a connection' between them and the trademark owner and thereby damage the latter's interests.[160] This aims to prevent 'dilution' of a trademark, i.e. where the value of the trademark is diminished by being associated with products that are, for example, of lesser quality.

The possibility to provide exceptions to trademark rights is contained in Article 17 of the *TRIPS Agreement*, which states:

> Members may provide limited exceptions to the rights conferred by a trademark, such as fair use of descriptive terms, provided that such exceptions take account of the legitimate interests of the owner of the trademark and of third parties.

Note that this provision does not create an exception itself – it only allows Members to do so. The possibility to make such exceptions is, however, explicitly subject to two requirements, as identified by the panel in *EC – Trademarks and Geographical Indications (2005)*, namely: (1) the exception must be limited; and (2) the exception must satisfy the proviso that 'such exceptions take account of the legitimate interests of the owner of the trademark and of third parties'.[161]

With regard to the first requirement of Article 17 of the *TRIPS Agreement*, the panel agreed with the interpretation, made by the panel in *Canada – Pharmaceutical Patents (2000)*, of the identical term of 'limited exceptions' in Article 30 of the *TRIPS Agreement*, that '[t]he word "exception" by itself connotes a limited derogation, one that does not undercut the body of rules from

159 See Article 16.2 of the *TRIPS Agreement*. 160 See Article 16.3 of the *TRIPS Agreement*.

161 See *EC – Trademarks and Geographical Indications (US) (2005)*, para. 7.648; and Panel Report, *EC – Trademarks and Geographical Indications (Australia) (2005)*, para. 7.648.

which it is made'.[162] The panel in *EC – Trademarks and Geographical Indications (2005)* held:

The addition of the word 'limited' emphasizes that the exception must be narrow and permit only a small diminution of rights. The limited exceptions apply 'to the rights conferred by a trademark'. They do not apply to the set of all trademarks or all trademark owners.[163]

Accordingly, the fact that it may affect only few trademarks or few trademark owners is irrelevant to the question whether an exception is limited. The issue is whether the exception to the *rights conferred by a trademark* is narrow.

Finding that only one right, namely, the exclusive right to prevent certain uses of a sign provided in Article 16.1, was conferred by the trademark at issue in this dispute, the panel in *EC – Trademarks and Geographical Indications (2005)* found it necessary to examine the exception of Article 17 'on an individual "per right" basis'.[164] According to the panel:

[t]his is a legal assessment of the extent to which the exception curtails that right. There is no indication in the text of Article 17 that this involves an economic assessment, although economic impact can be taken into account in the proviso. In this regard, we note the absence of any reference to a 'normal exploitation' of the trademark in Article 17, and the absence of any reference in Section 2, to which Article 17 permits exceptions, to rights to exclude legitimate competition. Rather, they confer, *inter alia*, the right to prevent uses that would result in a likelihood of confusion, which can lead to the removal of products from sale where they are marketed using particular signs, but without otherwise restraining the manufacture, sale or importation of competing goods or services.[165]

The panel held that the EC regulation at issue curtailed the trademark owner's right: (1) 'in respect of certain goods but not all goods identical or similar to those in respect of which the trademark is registered';[166] (2) 'against certain third parties, but not "all third parties"';[167] and (3) 'in respect of certain signs but not all signs identical or similar to the one protected as a trademark'.[168] Therefore, the panel found that the EC regulation at issue created a 'limited exception' within the meaning of Article 17 of the *TRIPS Agreement*.[169]

With regard to the second requirement of Article 17 of the *TRIPS Agreement*, namely, that the limited exceptions must satisfy the proviso that 'such exceptions take account of the legitimate interests of the owner of the trademark and of third parties', the panel in *EC – Trademarks and Geographical Indications (2005)* agreed with the interpretation of the panel in *Canada – Pharmaceutical Patents (2000)* of the term 'legitimate interests' of a patent owner and third parties in the context of Article 30 of the *TRIPS Agreement*.[170]

162 Panel Report, *Canada – Pharmaceutical Patents (2000)*, para. 7.30.

163 Panel Report, *EC – Trademarks and Geographical Indications (US) (2005)*, para. 7.650; and Panel Report, *EC – Trademarks and Geographical Indications (Australia) (2005)*, para. 7.650.

164 *Ibid.*, para. 7.651; and *ibid.*, para. 7.651.

165 *Ibid.*; and *ibid.*

166 *Ibid.*, para. 7.655; and *ibid.*, para. 7.655.

167 *Ibid.*, para. 7.656; and *ibid.*, para. 7.656.

168 *Ibid.*, para. 7.657; and *ibid.*, para. 7.657.

169 See *ibid.*, para. 7.661; and *ibid.*, para. 7.661.

170 *Ibid.*, para. 7.663; and *ibid.*, para. 7.663.

The panel in *Canada – Pharmaceutical Patents (2000)* held that the term must be defined as:

a normative claim calling for protection of interests that are 'justifiable' in the sense that they are supported by relevant public policies or other social norms.[171]

With respect to the 'legitimate interests' of the trademark owner and third parties in the context of Article 17 of the *TRIPS Agreement*, the panel in *EC – Trademarks and Geographical Indications (2005)* held:

The function of trademarks can be understood by reference to Article 15.1 as distinguishing goods and services of undertakings in the course of trade. Every trademark owner has a legitimate interest in preserving the distinctiveness, or capacity to distinguish, of its trademark so that it can perform that function. This includes its interest in using its own trademark in connection with the relevant goods and services of its own and authorized undertakings. Taking account of that legitimate interest will also take account of the trademark owner's interest in the economic value of its mark arising from the reputation that it enjoys and the quality that it denotes.[172]

The panel found that the EC regulation at issue took account of the trademark owner's rights in preserving the distinctiveness of its trademark in various ways. The panel emphasised that the proviso to Article 17 requires only that exceptions 'take account' of the legitimate interests of the owner of the trademark.[173] The panel subsequently examined whether the EC regulation took account of the legitimate interests of third parties. The panel identified as relevant third parties consumers and GI users,[174] and determined that the interests of these third parties were taken into account in the EC regulation at issue.[175] Therefore, the panel found the EC regulation at issue to be justified by Article 17 of the *TRIPS Agreement*.[176]

Unlike copyright, trademarks can be protected for an unlimited period. Article 18 of the *TRIPS Agreement* provides that trademarks 'shall be renewable indefinitely'. Although Members may require that trademark registrations be renewed, this may not be more often than once every seven years. However, a trademark registration may be cancelled if a Member requires use to maintain a registration, as permitted by Article 19 of the *TRIPS Agreement*. Such a requirement may lead to the cancellation of the trademark registration only after an uninterrupted

171 Panel Report, *Canada – Pharmaceutical Patents (2000)*, para. 7.69.

172 Panel Report, *EC – Trademarks and Geographical Indications (US) (2005)*, para. 7.664; and Panel Report, *EC – Trademarks and Geographical Indications (Australia) (2005)*, para. 7.664.

173 There is no reference to 'unreasonabl[e] prejudice' to those interests, unlike the provisos in Articles 13, 26.2 and 30 of the *TRIPS Agreement* and Article 9.2 of the *Berne Convention (1971)* as incorporated by Article 9.1 of the *TRIPS Agreement*, suggesting that a lesser standard of regard for the legitimate interests of the owner of the trademark is required. See Panel Report, *EC – Trademarks and Geographical Indications (US) (2005)*, para. 7.671; and Panel Report, *EC – Trademarks and Geographical Indications (Australia) (2005)*, para. 7.671.

174 See Panel Report, *EC – Trademarks and Geographical Indications (US) (2005)*, paras. 7.676, 7.680 and 7.681; and Panel Report, *EC – Trademarks and Geographical Indications (Australia) (2005)*, paras. 7.675 and 7.679.

175 See *ibid.*, para. 7.686; and *ibid.*, para. 7.684.

176 See *ibid.*, para. 7.688; and *ibid.*, para. 7.686.

period of at least three years, and not if the non-use was for valid reasons due to obstacles to such use.[177] Valid reasons include, for example, import restrictions or other government requirements for goods or services protected by the trademark.[178]

Article 20 prohibits unjustifiable encumbrances on trademarks by means of 'special requirements' such as use with another trademark or in a special form or manner that is detrimental to its capability to distinguish the goods or services of one undertaking from those of another. In *Indonesia – Autos (1998)*, the United States claimed that the Indonesian National Car Programme was inconsistent with Article 20. The panel disagreed, holding in this regard that:

> if a foreign company enters into an arrangement with [an Indonesian] Pioneer company it does so voluntarily and in the knowledge of any consequent implications for its ability to use any pre-existing trademark. In these circumstances, we do not consider the provisions of the National Car Programme as they relate to trademarks can be construed as 'requirements', in the sense of Article 20.[179]

Finally, note that, under Article 21 of the *TRIPS Agreement*, Members are free to determine conditions on the licensing and assignment of trademarks. The only limitations on this freedom, also contained in Article 21, are: (1) the prohibition on compulsory licensing of trademarks;[180] and (2) the requirement that Members allow the transfer of a trademark with or without the transfer of the business to which it belongs.

5.3 Geographical Indications

The quality, characteristics or reputation of a product are sometimes determined by where it comes from, i.e. its geographical origin. Geographical indications (such as 'Champagne', 'Parma' ham, 'Bohemian' crystal, 'Orkney' beef, 'Tequila', 'Gorgonzola' cheese and 'Darjeeling' tea)[181] are place names that are used to identify the products that originate in these places and have the characteristics associated with that place. The provision of protection to geographical indications was a contentious issue in the Uruguay Round negotiations. Section 3 of Part II of the *TRIPS Agreement* reflects the compromise reached.

177 Article 5C (1) of the *Paris Convention (1967)* also allows the cancellation of a trademark for non-use after a reasonable period if the trademark holder does not justify his inaction. However, the reasonable period is not specified. In this regard the *TRIPS Agreement* supplements the *Paris Convention (1967)*.

178 Note that the use of a trademark by someone other than the owner will be recognised as 'use' of the trademark for purposes of maintaining the registration if such use is subject to the control of the trademark owner. See Article 19.2 of the *TRIPS Agreement*.

179 Panel Report, *Indonesia – Autos (1998)*, para. 14.277.

180 Correa notes that compulsory licences have rarely been granted in the field of trademarks, so Article 21 is merely preventative of an unlikely future event. See C. M. Correa, 'The TRIPS Agreement and Developing Countries', in Macrory, Appleton and Plummer (eds.), *World Trade Organization*, 202.

181 These are frequently given examples of geographical indications. However, inclusion in this illustrative list should not be read as an affirmation that these names are 'geographical indications' within the meaning of Article 22.1 of the *TRIPS Agreement*.

Geographical indications (GIs) are defined in Article 22.1 of the *TRIPS Agreement* as:

> indications which identify a good as originating in the territory of a Member, or a region or locality in that territory, where a given quality, reputation or other characteristic of the good is *essentially attributable to its geographical origin.*[182]

In terms of this definition, it is clear that, in order to qualify for GI protection, it is not necessary to show that the product from that geographical area is *in fact* better or different from a similar product that originates elsewhere. It may also be established that a particular reputation or goodwill has been built in a particular place with regard to that product.[183] The 'indication' used does not have to be the place name itself, but may also be a name or symbol that is understood by the public as identifying a specific geographical origin (for example, 'Basmati' rice).[184] Note that a geographical indication is *not* the same as an indication of origin, such as 'Made in India', which only specifies the place where the product was produced, without indicating any associated product attributes. A geographical indication is also different from a trademark. A trademark identifies the *undertaking* offering the product or service on the market, whereas a GI indicates only the *place* where the product is produced. Several undertakings may use the same GI.[185]

The protection of GIs required under the *TRIPS Agreement* is specified in two provisions: (1) Article 22.2 of the *TRIPS Agreement*, which sets out the standard level of protection to be accorded to *all* products; this protection focuses on preventing misuse of GIs so as to mislead the public or constitute unfair competition; and (2) Article 23 of the *TRIPS Agreement*, which provides a higher or enhanced level of protection for *wines and spirits*; this protection must be provided even if misuse would not mislead the public. These two levels of protection will now be discussed in more detail.

Pursuant to Article 22.2 of the *TRIPS Agreement*, Members must protect GIs for all products by providing interested parties with the 'legal means' to prevent: (1) use of any means in the designation or presentation of the good that misleads the public as to the geographical origin of the good; and (2) use that constitutes unfair competition under Article 10*bis* of the *Paris Convention (1967)*. The form

182 Emphasis added.

183 It may be harder to prove that a particular reputation is essentially attributable to a geographical location, than that a product characteristic or the product quality are so attributable. It will be up to the Member in which GI protection is sought to determine whether the conditions for acquiring a GI are met, within the limits set by Article 22.1. See Correa, *Trade-Related Aspects of Intellectual Property Rights*, 220.

184 For example, 'Ouzo' is associated with Greece and 'Grappa' with Italy, and symbols such as the Eiffel Tower and the Matterhorn are widely associated with France and Switzerland respectively. See Correa, *Trade-Related Aspects of Intellectual Property Rights*, 212, fn. 12 and 13.

185 As several undertakings may be producing the relevant product in the identified geographical location, the GI may be combined with a trademark in order to identify a particular producer within the geographical area. Correa, *Trade-Related Aspects of Intellectual Property Rights*, 210.

that these 'legal means' take is left up to the Member involved.[186] Pursuant to Article 22.4 of the *TRIPS Agreement*, the protection against use of a GI that 'misleads the public' is extended to the use of 'homonymous' GIs. This prevents the use of a GI that is literally true as to the origin of the product, but falsely represents to the public that the product originates in another place with the same name. To avoid the use of a GI that 'misleads the public', producers may use additions such as 'imitation', 'like' or 'type' (for example, 'Roquefort-type' cheese or 'Delft-style' pottery). It is for the authorities in the Member where GI protection is provided to determine if public confusion is effectively avoided in this way.[187]

The enhanced GI protection for wines and spirits provided in Article 23 of the *TRIPS Agreement* requires Members to provide interested parties with legal means to prevent the use of a GI identifying a wine or a spirit for a wine or a spirit not originating in the place indicated by the GI in question. This is the case even if use of these GIs would *not* cause the public to be misled nor lead to unfair competition. According to Article 23.1 of the *TRIPS Agreement*, a Member must make it possible for the holder of a GI to prevent the use of the GI on the non-originating product even if confusion is prevented by an indication of the true origin of the product, the translation of the GI or the use of terms such as 'like' or 'type' (for example, 'Champagne-like' or 'Bordeaux-type') to distinguish products originating outside the place attributed to the GI.[188] Article 23.3 of the *TRIPS Agreement* deals with the use of homonymous GIs for wines (not for spirits) whose use is not misleading under Article 22.4.[189] It provides that both GIs shall be protected and the Member concerned must determine the practical conditions under which the homonymous GIs will be differentiated from each other. Such conditions must ensure that the producers concerned are treated equitably and that consumers are not misled.

Under Article 24.1 of the *TRIPS Agreement*, Members agree to negotiate with a view to increasing the protection of individual GIs under Article 23.

The expansion of coverage of the higher level of protection of Article 23 of the *TRIPS Agreement* beyond GIs for wines and spirits to other products is being discussed under the Doha Work Programme as a so-called outstanding implementation issue.[190] Members are deeply divided on this issue. Some Members advocate the extension of the higher level of protection of Article 23 to other

186 Note that Members are obliged, under Article 22.3 of the *TRIPS Agreement*, to refuse or to invalidate trademark registration where the trademark is a GI with respect to goods not originating in the indicated territory, if the use of the GI in the trademark is of such a nature as to mislead the public as to the true place of origin of the product.

187 See Correa, *Trade-Related Aspects of Intellectual Property Rights*, 231.

188 With regard to fn. 4 dealing with the enforcement of the protection, see below, p. 1044.

189 For example, 'Rioja' wine is produced in both Spain and Argentina. See Gervais, *The TRIPS Agreement*, 197, fn. 60.

190 See Ministerial Conference, Doha Ministerial Declaration, WT/MIN(01)/DEC/1, dated 20 November 2001, paras. 12 and 18.

products as a way to differentiate their products more effectively from those of their competitors, and to prevent other Members from 'usurping' their GIs. Others see the protection reflected in Article 22 as sufficient and are concerned that added protection would restrict legitimate marketing practices. They also point out that since a number of Members have received many immigrants who have brought with them their cultural traditions, including names and terms, it would be culturally insensitive for Members, predominantly those from which these people had migrated, to try to claim back terms that had been used for decades without being contested.[191]

Article 23.4 of the *TRIPS Agreement* provides for negotiations in the Council for TRIPS to establish a multilateral system of notification and registration of geographical indications for wines in those Members participating in the system, in order to facilitate the protection of GIs for wines. Although this provision refers only to wines, paragraph 18 of the Doha Ministerial Declaration provides for negotiations on the establishment of a multilateral system of notification and registration of geographical indications for wines and spirits, with a view to completing the work started in the Council for TRIPS on the implementation of Article 23.4.[192] These negotiations were to be completed in 2003, but, due to the strongly diverging positions of Members, no agreement has been reached on such a system to date.[193] Key issues on which disagreement exists are: what legal effect, if any, registration of a GI in such a 'multilateral register' should Members be required to accord; to what extent, if at all, should this effect apply to Members that choose not to participate in the system; and whether the administrative and financial costs of implementing such a system for individual governments would outweigh the possible benefits.[194]

In order to prevent the provisions on GI protection in the *TRIPS Agreement* to result in a reduction in the protection already provided for by some Members, Article 24.3 of the *TRIPS Agreement* contains an 'anti-rollback' provision, which states:

> In implementing this Section, a Member shall not diminish the protection of geographical indications that existed in that Member immediately prior to the date of entry into force of the WTO Agreement.

191 On the positions taken by Members in these negotiations, see Trade Negotiations Committee, Note by the Secretariat, *Issues Related to the Extension of the Protection of Geographical Indications Provided for in Article 23 of the TRIPS Agreement to Products Other Than Wines and Spirits: Compilation of Issues Raised and Views Expressed*, TN/C/W/25, WT/GC/W/546, dated 18 May 2005, para. 14.

192 See Ministerial Conference, *Doha Ministerial Declaration*, WT/MIN(01)/DEC/1, dated 20 November 2001, para. 18.

193 See also Council for TRIPS, *Multilateral System of Notification and Registration of Geographical Indications for Wines and Spirits*, Report by the Chairman, Ambassador Dacio Castillo, TN/IP/23, dated 3 December 2015.

194 The WTO Secretariat has made a useful compilation of the proposals and comments received on this issue. See Council for TRIPS, Special Session, Note by the Secretariat, *Side-by-Side Presentation of Proposals*, TN/IP/W/12, dated 14 September 2005. See also Report by the Director-General, *Issues Related to the Extension of the Protection of Geographical Indications Provided for in Article 3 of the TRIPS Agreement to Products other than Wines and Spirits and Those Related to the Relationship between the TRIPS Agreement and the Convention on Biological Diversity*, TN/C/W/61, WT/GC/W/633, dated 21 April 2011, highlighting the divergence of views among Members.

The above obligation applies indefinitely and prohibits any reduction in the level of protection for GIs, even if the protection remains above the standards mandated by the *TRIPS Agreement*.[195]

The *TRIPS Agreement* sets out a number of permissible exceptions to GI protection in paragraphs 4 to 9 of Article 24 of the *TRIPS Agreement*. Note, for example, that Article 24.5 of the *TRIPS Agreement* provides that the protection of GIs shall not prejudice prior trademark rights that were acquired in good faith. Under this exception, the fact that a trademark is identical with or similar to a GI shall not prejudice the eligibility for or validity of the registration of the trademark if it has been applied for, registered or acquired through use, in good faith, either: (1) before the provisions of Section 3 of Part II became applicable in the Member concerned; or (2) before the GI was protected in its country of origin.[196] Article 24.4 of the *TRIPS Agreement* contains an exception of GI protection to wines and spirits, allowing under specific conditions continued and similar use of a geographical indication of another Member when that GI has been used continuously and with respect to the same goods or services. As a final example of an exception to GI protection, consider Article 24.6 of the *TRIPS Agreement*. Pursuant to Article 24.6, a Member is not obliged to provide protection to a GI of another Member that is identical with a term that is customary in common language as the common name for goods or services in its territory. This takes account of the fact that some GIs have become common terms for particular products.[197]

5.4 Patents

Minimum requirements for patent protection are set out in Section 5 of Part II of the *TRIPS Agreement*. Article 27.1 of the *TRIPS Agreement* defines the patentable subject matter as follows:

> Subject to the provisions of paragraphs 2 and 3, patents shall be available for any inventions, whether products or processes, in all fields of technology, provided that they are new, involve an inventive step and are capable of industrial application.

Thus, when requested, patent protection must be granted to any invention in any field, provided three requirements are met: (1) the invention is new; (2) it involves an inventive step; and (3) it is capable of industrial application. Furthermore, Article 27.1 of the *TRIPS Agreement* provides:

> Subject to paragraph 4 of Article 65, paragraph 8 of Article 70 and paragraph 3 of this Article, patents shall be available and patent rights enjoyable without discrimination as to

195 Note the difference with Article 65 of the *TRIPS Agreement*, discussed below. See below, p. 1051.

196 For an analysis of the scope and nature of Article 24.5 of the *TRIPS Agreement* as well as possible conflicts between the protection of GIs and trademarks, see Panel Report, *EC – Trademarks and Geographical Indications (US) (2005)*, paras. 7.604–7.625; Panel Report, *EC – Trademarks and Geographical Indications (Australia) (2005)*, paras. 7.604–7.625.

197 Note that Members availing themselves of the use of the exceptions provided for in Article 24 of the *TRIPS Agreement* must be willing to enter into negotiations under Article 24.1 about their continued application to individual geographical indications.

the place of invention, the field of technology and whether products are imported or locally produced.

In addition to the general non-discrimination obligations set out in Articles 3 and 4 of the *TRIPS Agreement* discussed above, with regard to patents, Article 27.1 thus prohibits discrimination regarding the availability and enjoyment of patent rights based on: (1) the place of invention; (2) the field of technology; and (3) whether products are imported or locally produced.[198]

Articles 27.2 and 27.3 of the *TRIPS Agreement* allow Members to exclude certain inventions from patentability. Article 27.2 provides that:

Members may exclude from patentability inventions, the prevention within their territory of the commercial exploitation of which is necessary to protect *ordre public* or morality, including to protect human, animal or plant life or health or to avoid serious prejudice to the environment, provided that such exclusion is not made merely because the exploitation is prohibited by their domestic law.

It is likely that, in line with case law on the concept of public order and public morality under the GATS, this exception will take into account national perceptions that differ across Members.[199] Note that health and the environment are illustrative examples only, as indicated by the word 'including'. The link between the use of the exception and the prevention of commercial exploitation of the invention in the territory of the Member aims to ensure that this exception is not used to deny patent protection to an invention on public order or morality grounds, while the invention itself is in fact exploited commercially in the Member. Article 27.3 of the *TRIPS Agreement* allows the exclusion from patentability of: (1) diagnostic, therapeutic and surgical methods for the treatment of humans or animals; and (2) plants and animals other than micro-organisms, and essentially biological processes for the production of plants or animals other than non-biological and microbiological processes.[200]

The exclusive rights conferred on patent owners are set out in Article 28 of the *TRIPS Agreement*. Article 28.1 of the *TRIPS Agreement* provides:

A patent shall confer on its owner the following exclusive rights:

(a) where the subject-matter of a patent is a product, to prevent third parties not having the owner's consent from the acts of: making, using, offering for sale, selling, or importing[201] for these purposes that product;

198 For a dispute involving alleged discrimination based on the field of technology, see Panel Report, *Canada – Pharmaceutical Patents (2000)*, para. 7.105.

199 See above, pp. 608–12.

200 Note in respect of this exclusion that Members are, however, required to provide for the protection of plant *varieties* either by patents or by an 'effective *sui generis* system', or by any combination thereof. See Article 27.3(b), second sentence, of the *TRIPS Agreement*.

201 Footnote 6 to the *TRIPS Agreement* notes that '[t]his right, like all other rights conferred under this Agreement in respect of the use, sale, importation or other distribution of goods, is subject to the provisions of Article 6'. Article 6 provides that nothing in the *TRIPS Agreement* shall be used to address the issue of exhaustion of IP rights: see above, pp. 1011–12.

(b) where the subject-matter of a patent is a process, to prevent third parties not having the owner's consent from the act of using the process, and from the acts of: using, offering for sale, selling, or importing for these purposes at least the product obtained directly by that process.

Article 28.2 of the *TRIPS Agreement* gives patent owners the additional right to assign, or transfer by succession, the patent and to conclude licensing contracts.

The filing of patent applications is usually subject to conditions. In terms of Article 29.1 of the *TRIPS Agreement*, Members must require patent applicants to disclose the invention 'in a manner sufficiently clear and complete' for a person skilled in the art to be able to carry out the invention. Members may also require the applicant to disclose the best way of carrying out the invention known to the inventor. In addition, Members may require the applicant to provide information about his or her foreign applications for or grants of patents.[202]

There are two provisions in the *TRIPS Agreement* allowing for exceptions to the exclusive rights conferred by a patent: (1) the 'limited exceptions' provision of Article 30 of the *TRIPS Agreement*; and (2) the 'compulsory licences' provision of Article 31 of the *TRIPS Agreement*. Article 30 of the *TRIPS Agreement* states:

> Members may provide limited exceptions to the exclusive rights conferred by a patent, provided that such exceptions do not unreasonably conflict with a normal exploitation of the patent and do not unreasonably prejudice the legitimate interests of the patent owner, taking account of the legitimate interests of third parties.

In *Canada – Pharmaceutical Patents (2000)*, the European Communities challenged the regulatory review and stockpiling exceptions in Canada's patent law. Canada conceded that these provisions were inconsistent with Article 28.1 of the *TRIPS Agreement*, which grants exclusive rights to patent holders.[203] However, it relied on the exception of Article 30 of the *TRIPS Agreement* to justify its measures, and argued that the objectives and principles of Articles 7 and 8 of the *TRIPS Agreement* should inform the interpretation of Article 30.[204] The panel in *Canada – Pharmaceutical Patents (2000)* identified *three* cumulative requirements that must be met to qualify for an exception under Article 30: (1) the exception must be 'limited'; (2) the exception must not 'unreasonably conflict with a normal exploitation of the patent'; and (3) the exception must not 'unreasonably prejudice the legitimate interests of the patent owner, taking account of the legitimate interests of third parties'.[205] Turning to the first requirement, the panel chose a narrow interpretation, holding that such interpretation is more appropriate:

> when the word 'limited' is used as part of the phrase 'limited exception'. The word 'exception' by itself connotes a limited derogation, one that does not undercut the body of rules from which it is made. When a treaty uses the term 'limited exception', the word 'limited'

202 See Article 29.2 of the *TRIPS Agreement*.
203 See Panel Report, *Canada – Pharmaceutical Patents (2000)*, para. 7.12.
204 On Articles 7 and 8 of the *TRIPS Agreement*, see above, pp. 996–8.
205 See Panel Report, *Canada – Pharmaceutical Patents (2000)*, para. 7.20.

must be given a meaning separate from the limitation implicit in the word 'exception' itself. The term 'limited exception' must therefore be read to connote a narrow exception – one which makes only a *small diminution of the rights in question.*[206]

On a literal reading of the text, the panel focused on the extent to which rights have been curtailed, rather than on the economic impact, to determine whether the exception was 'limited'. The panel supported this conclusion by referring to the fact that the other two requirements of Article 30 'ask more particularly about the economic impact of the exception, and provide two sets of standards by which such impact may be judged'.[207] In examining the extent to which the stockpiling exception curtailed the patent owner's rights to exclude 'making' and 'using' the patented product, the panel noted that this exception sets no limitation at all on the quantity of the product that could be produced and stockpiled pending expiry of the patent.[208] The panel thus found that the stockpiling exception constituted a *substantial* curtailment of the exclusive rights to be granted to patent owners under Article 28.1 and was thus not a 'limited' exception.[209] With regard to the regulatory review exception, however, the panel found that it was a 'limited' exception as required by Article 30. It held:

It is 'limited' because of the narrow scope of its curtailment of Article 28.1 rights. As long as the exception is confined to conduct needed to comply with the requirements of the regulatory approval process, the extent of the acts unauthorized by the right holder that are permitted by it will be small and narrowly bounded.[210]

With regard to the second requirement of Article 30 of the *TRIPS Agreement*, namely, that the exception must not 'unreasonably conflict with a normal exploitation of the patent', the panel in *Canada – Pharmaceutical Patents (2000)* held that 'exploitation' refers to 'the commercial activity by which patent owners employ their exclusive patent rights to extract economic value from their patent'.[211] As to the meaning of 'normal', the panel noted that this word 'defines the kind of commercial activity Article 30 seeks to protect' and that it has both an empirical content (what is 'common' within a community) and a normative content (a standard of entitlement).[212] The panel agreed with Canada that the additional period of market exclusivity arising from using patent rights to prevent submissions for regulatory authorisation could not be seen as 'normal' exploitation.[213] Consequently, the panel held that the regulatory review exception did not conflict with the 'normal exploitation' of patents, under the second requirement of Article 30.

Finally, with regard to the third requirement of Article 30 of the *TRIPS Agreement*, namely, that the exception must not 'unreasonably prejudice the legitimate interests of the patent owner, taking account of the legitimate interests

206 *Ibid.*, para. 7.30. Emphasis added. 207 *Ibid.*, paras. 7.31 and 7.49.
208 See *ibid.*, para. 7.34. 209 See *ibid.*, para. 7.36.
210 *Ibid.*, para. 7.45. 211 *Ibid.*, para. 7.54.
212 See *ibid.* 213 See *ibid.*, para. 7.57.

of third parties', the panel in *Canada – Pharmaceutical Patents (2000)* noted that similar considerations arose as under the second requirement.[214] In the case of the third requirement, the issue was:

> whether patent owners could claim a 'legitimate interest' in the economic benefits that could be derived from such an additional period of *de facto* market exclusivity and, if so, whether the regulatory review exception 'unreasonably prejudiced' that interest.[215]

The European Communities claimed that 'legitimate' should be equated with 'lawful', implying that full respect for the legal interests reflected in Article 28.1 is necessary. The panel disagreed. It held:

> To make sense of the term 'legitimate interests' in this context, that term must be defined in the way that it is often used in legal discourse – as a normative claim calling for protection of interests that are 'justifiable' in the sense that they are supported by relevant public policies or other social norms.[216]

Therefore, the panel held that the argument of the European Communities, which was based only on the legal rights of the patent owner under Article 28.1, 'without reference to any more particular normative claims of interest' did not show non-compliance with the third requirement of Article 30.[217] The European Communities raised a second argument with regard to the 'legitimate interests' requirement. It pointed out that, as patent owners are required to obtain marketing approval for their innovative products, they suffer delays that prevent them from marketing their products for a large part of the patent term, thereby reducing their period of market exclusivity. They should therefore be entitled to impose the same type of delay in connection with corresponding regulatory requirements for the market entry of competing products.[218] According to the panel, the 'primary issue was whether the normative basis of that claim rested on a widely recognized policy norm'.[219] Examining the approaches of various governments to this issue, the panel noted that governments are still divided in this regard. It then stated:

> Article 30's 'legitimate interests' concept should not be used to decide, through adjudication, a normative policy issue that is still obviously a matter of unresolved political debate.[220]

Consequently, the panel held that Canada's regulatory review exception fell within the exception under Article 30 of the *TRIPS Agreement* and was thus not inconsistent with Article 28.1 thereof.[221]

Leaving aside Article 30 of the *TRIPS Agreement*, the other provision in the *TRIPS Agreement* allowing for exceptions to the exclusive rights conferred by a

214 The key issue was again the fact that the exception would remove the additional period of *de facto* market exclusivity enjoyed by patent owners if they were permitted to employ their rights to exclude 'making', 'using' and 'selling' the patented product during the term of the patent to prevent potential competitors from preparing and/or applying for regulatory approval during the term of the patent.

215 Panel Report, *Canada – Pharmaceutical Patents (2000)*, para. 7.61.

216 *Ibid.*, para. 7.69. 217 *Ibid.*, para. 7.73.

218 See *ibid.*, para. 7.74. 219 *Ibid.*, para. 7.77.

220 *Ibid.*, para. 7.82. 221 See *ibid.*, para. 7.84.

patent is Article 31. Article 31 relates to the exception for 'other use' of a patent without authorisation of the right holder. 'Other use' is defined as use other than that allowed under Article 30.[222] This 'other use' of a patent without the authorisation of the right holder is commonly known as *compulsory licensing*, although this term is not used in Article 31. Article 31 refers to the situation where:

> the law of a Member allows for other use of the subject-matter of a patent without the authorization of the right holder, including use by the government or third parties authorized by the government.[223]

Article 31 of the *TRIPS Agreement* contains a detailed list of requirements for the grant of compulsory licences.[224] However, it does not limit the grounds on which compulsory licences may be granted.[225] It only mentions some possible grounds, such as: (1) public non-commercial use;[226] (2) national emergency;[227] (3) remedying of anti-competitive practices;[228] and (4) dependent patents (i.e. patents on improvements to an earlier patent-protected invention).[229] Due to concerns regarding the interpretation of this provision, the *Doha Declaration on the TRIPS Agreement and Public Health* confirms that:

> [e]ach member has the *right* to grant compulsory licences and the *freedom to determine the grounds* upon which such licences are granted.[230]

However, Article 31 of the *TRIPS Agreement* lays down conditions for and limitations on an application for a compulsory licence for any particular use be considered on its individual merits. Therefore, compulsory licences cannot be granted with regard to broad categories of patents. Under Article 31(b) of the *TRIPS Agreement*, an attempt must have been made prior to applying for a compulsory licence to obtain authorisation from the patent holder to use the patent on reasonable commercial terms and conditions. Only if that attempt was unsuccessful within a reasonable period, can the compulsory licence be granted. However, there are three exceptions to this requirement: (1) cases of national emergency or other circumstances of extreme urgency; (2) cases of public non-commercial use; and (3) cases where the use is permitted to remedy an anticompetitive practice.[231]

222 See fn. 7 to Article 31 of the *TRIPS Agreement*. 223 Chapeau of Article 31 of the *TRIPS Agreement*.

224 See the conditions set out in paragraphs (a) to (l) of Article 31 of the *TRIPS Agreement*.

225 An exception to this is in the case of semiconductor technology, which may only be subject to compulsory licence for public non-commercial use and to remedy anti-competitive practices determined as such through a judicial or administrative process. See Article 31(c) of the *TRIPS Agreement*.

226 See Article 31(b) of the *TRIPS Agreement*. 227 See *ibid*.

228 See Article 31(k) of the *TRIPS Agreement*. 229 See Article 31(l) of the *TRIPS Agreement*.

230 Ministerial Conference, *Doha Declaration on the TRIPS Agreement and Public Health*, WT/MIN(01)/DEC/2, dated 20 November 2001, para. 5(b). Emphasis added.

231 Note that, while the exceptions of national emergency and public non-commercial use are contained in Article 31(b), that of remedying an anti-competitive practice is reflected in Article 31(k) of the *TRIPS Agreement*. In the first case, the right holder must be notified as soon as is reasonably practicable, and in the second case as soon as there are demonstrable grounds to know that the patent will be used by or for the government.

The use of compulsory licences in cases of 'national emergency' could, for example, relate to the need to ensure affordable access to essential medicines to deal with public health crises. Compulsory licences may be used to authorise producers of generic medicines to copy a patented drug, without the consent of the right holder. The *Doha Declaration on the TRIPS Agreement and Public Health* recognises explicitly that, as part of the 'flexibilities' provided in the *TRIPS Agreement*:

> [e]ach member has the right to determine what constitutes a national emergency or other circumstances of extreme urgency, it being understood that public health crises, including those relating to HIV/AIDS, tuberculosis, malaria and other epidemics, can represent a national emergency or other circumstances of extreme urgency.[232]

By including epidemics such as HIV/AIDS and malaria within the scope of the concept of 'national emergency or other situations of extreme urgency', the Doha Declaration clarified that situations of 'national emergency' or of 'extreme urgency' are not limited to short-term crises. In addition, by leaving Members the right to determine what is an emergency, it has been argued that the burden of proof shifts to the complaining party to show that an emergency does *not* in fact exist.[233]

Further requirements for the granting of compulsory licences, set out in subsequent paragraphs of Article 31 of the *TRIPS Agreement*, are: (1) that the scope and duration of the use of the patent shall be limited to the purpose for which it was authorised (paragraph (c)); (2) that such use shall be non-exclusive (paragraph (d)); (3) that such use shall be non-assignable except with that part of the enterprise or goodwill which enjoys such use (paragraph (e)); (4) that any such use shall be authorised predominantly for the supply of the domestic market of the authorising Member (paragraph (f));[234] (5) that authorisation of such use is liable to be terminated when the circumstances that led to it cease to exist (paragraph (g));[235] (6) that the right holder be paid adequate remuneration in the circumstances of each case (paragraph (h));[236] and (7) that the decision to authorise such use and the decision relating to

232 Ministerial Conference, *Doha Declaration on the TRIPS Agreement and Public Health*, WT/MIN(01)/DEC/2, dated 20 November 2001, para. 5(c).

233 See C. M. Correa, 'The TRIPS Agreement and Developing Countries', in Macrory, Appleton and Plummer (eds.), *World Trade Organization*, 441.

234 This requirement does not apply in cases of compulsory licences granted to remedy anti-competitive practices. See Article 31(k) of the *TRIPS Agreement*.

235 Under this paragraph, the competent authority is required to have the authority to review whether such circumstances continue to exist upon motivated request where compulsory licences were granted to remedy anti-competitive practices, competent authorities may refuse to terminate the authorisation if the anticompetitive practices are likely to recur. See Article 31(k) of the *TRIPS Agreement*.

236 The economic value of the authorisation must be taken into account in calculating the remuneration, under Article 31(h) of the *TRIPS Agreement*. In cases of compulsory licences to remedy anti-competitive practices, the need to correct such practices may be taken into account in determining the remuneration in terms of Article 31(k) of the *TRIPS Agreement*.

the remuneration be subject to review by a court or other independent higher authority (paragraphs (i) and (j)).[237]

An important problem in complying with the requirement of Article 31(f) of the *TRIPS Agreement* arose with respect to the use of compulsory licences to ensure access to essential medicines in developing countries. Article 31(f), as set out above, requires that compulsory licences be provided 'predominantly for the supply of the domestic market'. However, some countries lack sufficient manufacturing capacity in pharmaceuticals to produce the necessary generic medicines themselves for their domestic market. Article 31(f) prevents other Members from granting compulsory licences to produce generic medicines predominantly for export. This constraint was expected to become more important in 2005 when some developing countries with significant generic industries and export capacities (such as India) became obliged to provide patent protection for pharmaceutical products pursuant to the special transition arrangement in Article 65.4 of the *TRIPS Agreement*.[238] The concern was raised that this would undermine the ability of developing countries, and in particular least-developed countries, with insufficient manufacturing capacity, to ensure access to affordable essential medicines. A first step towards resolving this serious problem was made in the *Doha Declaration on the TRIPS Agreement and Public Health*, which, in paragraph 6, instructed the Council for TRIPS to 'find an expeditious *solution* to this problem and to report to the General Council before the end of 2002'.[239] The General Council adopted, on 30 August 2003, a decision whereby the obligations of Article 31(f) were waived in order to allow Members to export medicines produced under compulsory licence to Members with insufficient manufacturing capacity.[240] On 6 December 2005, the General Council took an important further step by adopting the decision to amend the *TRIPS Agreement* in order to resolve the conflict with Article 31(f) in a permanent manner.[241] When the amendment takes effect, a new Article 31*bis* as well as a new Annex will be added to the *TRIPS Agreement*, clarifying that the obligations of Article 31(f) do not apply with respect to the grant by a Member of

237 With respect to compulsory licences to permit the exploitation of a dependent patent (a patent that cannot be exploited without infringing another prior patent), three additional conditions apply: (1) the invention in the second patent must involve an important technical advance of considerable economic significance in relation to the first patent; (2) the owner of the first patent must be entitled to a cross-licence on reasonable terms to use the second patent; and (3) the use shall be non-assignable except with the assignment of the second patent. See Article 31(l) of the *TRIPS Agreement*.

238 See Taubman, Wager and Watal (eds.), *Handbook on the WTO TRIPS Agreement*, 184.

239 Ministerial Conference, *Doha Declaration on the TRIPS Agreement and Public Health*, WT/MIN(01)/DEC/2, dated 20 November 2001, para. 6. Emphasis added.

240 On waivers, see above, pp. 125–8. Recall that waivers adopted under Article IX of the *WTO Agreement*, as was the waiver at issue here, are *temporary* in nature. Note that the obligations under Article 31(h) of the *TRIPS Agreement* were also waived in the Decision of the General Council of 30 August 2003.

241 See General Council, *Amendment of the TRIPS Agreement: Decision of the General Council of 6 December 2005*, WT/L/641, dated 8 December 2005. Note that this is the first and thus far only decision to amend a WTO agreement. See above, p. 150.

a compulsory licence necessary for the production of a pharmaceutical product and its export to an 'eligible' importing Member in accordance with the terms set out in paragraph 2 of the new Annex to the *TRIPS Agreement*.[242] As discussed in Chapter 2, as of October 2016, 105 Members had notified their acceptance of the amendment.[243] Therefore, this amendment, agreed in December 2005, has yet to take effect.

To date, Rwanda and Canada are the only Members that have used the possibility provided under the waiver decision of 30 August 2003. Apotex, a Canadian pharmaceutical firm, exports to Rwanda TriAvir, a generic HIV medicine produced under a compulsory licence granted by Canada.[244] As the patent holders, GlaxoSmithKline and Boehringer Ingelheim, could indeed not come to an agreement with Apotex on a voluntary licence, Canada granted Apotex a compulsory licence to produce TriAvir for export to Rwanda.[245]

In May 2010, India and Brazil requested consultations with the European Union and the Netherlands regarding alleged repeated seizures on patent infringement grounds of generic drugs originating in India and other third countries when transiting through ports and airports in the Netherlands to Brazil and other third country destinations.[246] These seizures were made by applying the so-called 'manufacturing fiction' under which generic drugs actually manufactured in India and in transit to third countries were treated as if they had been manufactured in the Netherlands. India claimed violation of Article 31 of the *TRIPS Agreement*, read together with the provisions of the 2003 waiver decision, discussed above, because the measures at issue, *inter alia*, authorise interference with the freedom of transit of drugs that may be produced in, and exported from, India to WTO Members with insufficient or no capacity in the pharmaceutical sector that seek to obtain supplies of such products needed to address their public health problems. Reportedly, the consultations in this dispute resulted in a mutually agreed solution.[247] However, this solution has not been notified to the WTO.

242 Annex 2, paragraph 2, defines an 'eligible' importing Member as any least-developed-country Member; and any other Member that has notified the Council for TRIPS of its intention to use the Article 31 *bis* system as an importer. Note that the notification does *not* need to be approved by any WTO body before the Article 31 *bis* system may be used.

243 See above, pp. 126 and 150. See also www.wto.org/english/tratop_e/trips_e/amendment_e.htm. Note that the European Union notified its acceptance and did so also on behalf of the twenty-seven EU Member States.

244 On 4 October 2007, Canada notified the Council for TRIPS of its granting of a compulsory licence to Apotex. *See Notification under Paragraph 2(c) of the Decision of 30 August 2003 on the Implementation of Paragraph 6 of the Doha Declaration on the TRIPS Agreement and Public Health – Canada*, IP/N/10/CAN/1, dated 8 October 2007. There is a dedicated page on the WTO website for notifications of this kind, available at www.wto.org/english/tratop_e/trips_e/public_health_e.htm.

245 *Bridges Weekly Trade News Digest*, 25 July 2007.

246 See Request for Consultations by India, *European Union and a Member State – Seizure of Generic Drugs in Transit*, WT/DS408/1, dated 19 May 2010; and Request for Consultations by Brazil, *European Union and a Member State – Seizure of Generic Drugs in Transit*, WT/DS409/1, dated 19 May 2010.

247 See http://pib.nic.in/newsite/erelease.aspx?relid=73554.

The duration of patent protection is addressed in Article 33 of the *TRIPS Agreement*. It provides:

> The term of protection available shall not end before the expiration of a period of twenty years counted from the filing date.[248]

Article 33 was at issue in *Canada – Patent Term (2000)* involving a challenge by the United States to Canada's patent legislation, which granted patent protection for only seventeen years for patents filed before 1 October 1989. Examining the terms of Article 33, the Appellate Body held:

> In our view, the words used in Article 33 present very little interpretative difficulty. The 'filing date' is the date of filing of the patent application. The term of protection 'shall not end' before twenty years counted from the date of filing of the patent application.[249]

The Appellate Body rejected Canada's argument that a twenty-year period was in fact available under its regulatory practices and procedures, as every patent applicant has statutory and other means to delay the procedure so as to extend the period of patent protection to at least twenty years.[250] According to the Appellate Body, not only 'those who are somehow able to meander successfully through a maze of administrative procedures'[251] must have the opportunity to obtain the twenty-year patent term, but this opportunity:

> must be a readily discernible and specific right, and it must be clearly seen as such by the patent applicant when a patent application is filed. The grant of the patent must be sufficient *in itself* to obtain the minimum term mandated by Article 33.[252]

Finally, note that Article 32 of the *TRIPS Agreement* requires that any decision to revoke or forfeit a patent be subject to an opportunity for judicial review.

6 ENFORCEMENT OF INTELLECTUAL PROPERTY RIGHTS

The protection of IP depends not only on substantive norms providing minimum standards of protection, but also on procedural rules that allow right holders to effectively enforce them. Therefore, the *TRIPS Agreement* includes rules on the enforcement of IP rights. The Preamble to the *TRIPS Agreement* reflects the recognition that new rules and disciplines were needed concerning 'the provision of effective and appropriate means for the enforcement of trade-related intellectual

248 Footnote 8 to this provision clarifies that Members that do not have a system of original grant may provide that the term of protection shall be calculated from the filing date in the system of original grant.
249 Appellate Body Report, *Canada – Patent Term (2000)*, para. 85.
250 See *ibid.*, para. 91. 251 *Ibid.*, para. 92.
252 *Ibid.* The Appellate Body pointed out that the text of Article 33 of the *TRIPS Agreement* does not support the notion of an 'effective' term of protection as distinguished from a 'nominal' term of protection. See *ibid.*, para. 95.

property rights, taking into account differences in national legal systems'. These rules on enforcement are contained in Part III of the *TRIPS Agreement*, entitled 'Enforcement of Intellectual Property Rights'. With regard to the coverage of Part III, the Appellate Body held in *US – Section 211 Appropriations Act (2002)* that this Part:

> applies to all intellectual property rights covered by the *TRIPS Agreement*. According to Article 1.2 of the *TRIPS Agreement*, the term 'intellectual property' refers to 'all categories of intellectual property that are the subject of Sections 1 through 7 of Part II' of that Agreement.[253]

The panel report in *China – Intellectual Property Rights (2009)* noted that the concept of 'enforcement procedures', as used in Part III of the *TRIPS Agreement*, is an 'extensive' concept.[254] Part III deals with: civil and administrative procedures and remedies (Section 2); provisional measures (Section 3); special requirements related to border measures (Section 4); and criminal procedures (Section 5). Before dealing with these specific enforcement procedures, however, Part III first sets out a number of general obligations with regard to the enforcement of IP rights.

6.1 General Obligations

The general obligations with regard to enforcement of IP rights are contained in Article 41 of the *TRIPS Agreement*. Article 41.1 requires Members to ensure that the enforcement procedures specified in Part III are available under their law 'so as to permit effective action' against infringement of IP rights protected in the *TRIPS Agreement*. This is specified as including expeditious remedies to *prevent* infringements and remedies to *deter* further infringements. As the panel in *China – Intellectual Property Rights (2009)* noted:

> Where a Member chooses to make available other procedures – for enforcement of intellectual property rights or for enforcement of other policies with respect to certain subject-matter – that policy choice does not diminish the Member's obligation under Article 41.1 of the TRIPS Agreement to ensure that enforcement procedures as specified in Part III are available.[255]

Article 41.1 of the *TRIPS Agreement* further requires that enforcement procedures must be applied in a way that avoids creating barriers to legitimate trade and to provide safeguards against their abuse. A number of provisions supplement this general obligation. For example, Article 48 of the *TRIPS Agreement* provides for compensation of a party that has suffered injury due to abuse of

253 Appellate Body Report, *US – Section 211 Appropriations Act (2002)*, para. 205.

254 See Panel Report, *China – Intellectual Property Rights (2009)*, para. 7.179. According to the panel, this is clear, among other things, from the text of Article 41.1 of the *TRIPS Agreement*, which specifies that these procedures include 'remedies'. See *ibid*. For example, Articles 44–6 and 50 of the *TRIPS Agreement* specify that the judicial authorities shall have the authority to make certain orders, such as injunctions, orders to pay damages, orders for the disposal or destruction of infringing goods, and provisional measures. See *ibid*.

255 Panel Report, *China – Intellectual Property Rights (2009)*, para. 7.180.

enforcement procedures. Article 41.2–41.4 of the *TRIPS Agreement* sets out normal due process requirements. These paragraphs require that: (1) enforcement procedures be fair and equitable, and not unnecessarily costly, complicated or lengthy (Article 41.2); (2) decisions on the merits of a case be reasoned and preferably in writing, and be based on evidence on which the parties had an opportunity to be heard (Article 41.3); and (3) parties to a proceeding have the opportunity for judicial review of administrative decisions and of at least the legal aspects of judicial decisions (with the exclusion of acquittals in criminal cases) (Article 41.4). Article 41.5 of the *TRIPS Agreement* clarifies that Part III does not oblige Members to create a separate judicial system for the enforcement of IP rights, or create any obligation regarding the distribution of resources between enforcement of IP rights and other law enforcement. It clarifies that the enforcement of IP rights can take place through the existing law-enforcement system of a country, provided that the required level of enforcement specified in Part III is achieved.

6.2 Civil and Administrative Procedures and Remedies

The usual way of enforcing IP rights is through civil procedures initiated only at the request of or by the right holder but not *ex officio* by the Member State.[256] Article 42 of the *TRIPS Agreement* specifies that Members are required to make available to right holders civil *judicial* procedures for the enforcement of any IP right covered by the *TRIPS Agreement*. This means that the provision of only *administrative* enforcement procedures is insufficient.[257] Article 42 requires that civil judicial procedures are 'fair and equitable'.[258] These requirements reflect normal due process rules applicable in civil proceedings.

Article 42 of the *TRIPS Agreement* was at issue in *US – Section 211 Appropriations Act (2002)*. The European Communities claimed that Sections 211(a) (2) and (b) of the US Appropriations Act violated Article 42 of the *TRIPS Agreement* as they expressly denied the availability of United States courts to enforce the rights targeted by Section 211.[259] The panel found that Section 211(a) (2) was inconsistent with Article 42.[260] It noted:

> While Section 211(a) (2) would not appear to prevent a right holder from initiating civil judicial procedures, its wording indicates that the right holder is not entitled to effective procedures as the court is *ab initio* not permitted to recognize its assertion of rights if the

256 See *ibid.*, para. 7.247.

257 An exception is made for the enforcement of the enhanced protection for GIs on wine and spirits, which may take place through administrative action rather than judicial proceedings. See fn. 4 to Article 23.1 of the *TRIPS Agreement*.

258 See Appellate Body Report, *US – Section 211 Appropriations Act (2002)*, para. 207.

259 See *ibid.*, para. 208.

260 With regard to Section 211(b), the panel held that the European Communities had failed to explain the provisions referred to in the Section and had therefore not proved its case. See Panel Report, *US – Section 211 Appropriations Act (2002)*, para. 8.162.

conditions of Section 211(a) (2) are met. In other words, the right holder is effectively prevented from having a chance to substantiate its claim, a chance to which a right holder is clearly entitled under Article 42, because effective civil judicial procedures mean procedures with the possibility of an outcome which is not pre-empted *a priori* by legislation.[261]

On appeal, the Appellate Body agreed with the panel that:

the ordinary meaning of the term 'make available' suggests that 'right holders' are entitled under Article 42 to have *access* to civil judicial procedures that are effective in bringing about the enforcement of their rights covered by the Agreement ... The term 'right holders' ... also includes persons who claim to have legal standing to assert rights.[262]

The Appellate Body also noted that, as the term 'civil judicial procedures' is not defined in Article 42 of the *TRIPS Agreement*:

[t]he *TRIPS Agreement* thus reserves, subject to the procedural minimum standards set out in that Agreement, a degree of discretion to Members on this, taking into account 'differences in national legal systems'.[263]

The Appellate Body then turned to the fourth sentence of Article 42 of the *TRIPS Agreement*, which requires that '[a]ll parties to such procedures shall be duly entitled to substantiate their claims and present all relevant evidence'. It noted that right holders are entitled thereby to choose how many and which claims to bring, to provide grounds for their claims and to bring all relevant evidence.[264] The Appellate Body stated:

we understand that the rights which Article 42 obliges Members to make available to right holders are *procedural* in nature. These *procedural* rights guarantee an international minimum standard for nationals of other Members within the meaning of Article 1.3 of the *TRIPS Agreement*.[265]

The Appellate Body then noted that Sections 211(a) (2) and (b) deal with the *substantive* requirements of ownership of trademarks in particular cases.[266] Further, it pointed out that the European Communities agreed with the United States that US Federal Rules of Civil Procedure apply to cases under Section 211 and guarantee 'fair and equitable ... civil judicial procedures'.[267] Referring to the argument of the European Communities that Sections 211(a) (2) and (b) limit the discretion of the courts by directing the courts to examine certain substantive requirements before, and to the exclusion of, other substantive requirements, the Appellate Body held:

In our view, a conclusion by a court on the basis of Section 211, after applying the Federal Rules of Civil Procedure and the Federal Rules of Evidence, that an enforcement proceeding has failed to establish ownership – a requirement of substantive law – with the result that it

261 *Ibid.*, para. 8.100.

262 Appellate Body Report, *US – Section 211 Appropriations Act (2002)*, paras. 215 and 217, referring to para. 8.95 of the Panel Report, *US – Section 211 Appropriations Act (2002)*.

263 Appellate Body Report, *US – Section 211 Appropriations Act (2002)*, para. 216.

264 See *ibid.*, paras. 219–20. 265 *Ibid.*, para. 221.

266 See *ibid.*, para. 222. 267 See *ibid.*, para. 223.

> is impossible for the court to rule in favour of that claimant's or that defendant's claim to a trademark right, does not constitute a violation of Article 42. There is nothing in the *procedural* obligations of Article 42 that prevents a Member, in such a situation, from legislating whether or not its courts must examine *each and every* requirement of substantive law at issue before making a ruling.[268]

Consequently, the Appellate Body found that Sections 211(a) (2) and (b) of the Appropriations Act were not, on their face, inconsistent with Article 42.[269]

The other provisions of the *TRIPS Agreement* relating to 'Civil and Administrative Procedures and Remedies' set out the powers that the judicial authorities involved are required to have in enforcement proceedings, such as: (1) the authority to require, in specific cases, the production of evidence by a party in whose control the evidence is (Article 43); (2) the authority to order a party to desist from an infringement, including to prevent the entry of infringing imports into channels of commerce in their jurisdiction after clearing customs (Article 44); and (3) the authority to order the infringer to pay damages and costs in certain cases (Article 45).[270]

6.3 Provisional Measures and Border Measures

Article 50 and Articles 51 to 60 of the *TRIPS Agreement* contain rules with regard to provisional measures and border measures, respectively, aiming at the prevention of IP infringements. Article 50 of the *TRIPS Agreement* requires judicial authorities to have the power to order 'prompt and effective provisional measures':

> (a) to prevent an infringement of any intellectual property right from occurring, and in particular to prevent the entry into the channels of commerce in their jurisdiction of goods, including imported goods immediately after customs clearance;
> (b) to preserve relevant evidence in regard to the alleged infringement. Article 50 aims to deal with infringements that are taking place or are imminent.[271]

It requires judicial authorities to have the authority to adopt provisional measures without hearing the other party (*inaudita altera parte*) where appropriate, in particular: (1) where any delay is likely to cause irreparable harm to the right holder, or (2) where there is a demonstrable risk of evidence being destroyed. Article 51 of the *TRIPS Agreement* deals with measures applied *at the border* (i.e. applied to imports) in order to prevent IP infringements. Such measures can be applied when a right holder has valid grounds for suspecting that importation of counterfeit trademark or pirated copyright goods may take place.[272] While Article

268 *Ibid.*, para. 226. 269 See *ibid.*, para. 231.

270 Other remedies aimed at creating an effective *deterrent* to infringement of IP rights (e.g. by ordering the destruction of infringing goods without compensation) are provided for in Article 46 of the *TRIPS Agreement.*

271 See Article 50.3 of the *TRIPS Agreement*. On this point, see Correa, *Trade-Related Aspects of Intellectual Property Rights*, 433–8.

272 For a definition of 'counterfeit trademark goods' and 'pirated copyright goods', see fn. 14 to Article 51 of the *TRIPS Agreement.*

50 of the *TRIPS Agreement* aims to prevent the introduction of the infringing product into commerce *after* it has cleared customs, Article 51 of the *TRIPS Agreement* addresses measures applied at the border *before* the release of the infringing product into free circulation by the customs authority. It provides for procedures to apply for the suspension by customs authorities of the release of the goods. While these border measures are required only for counterfeit trademark or pirated copyright goods, they *may* be extended to goods that involve infringements of other IP rights. Articles 52 to 60 of the *TRIPS Agreement* provide rules on the application of these border measures.

6.4 Criminal Procedures

Article 61 of the *TRIPS Agreement* deals with criminal procedures and penalties for infringement. It requires criminal procedures and penalties to be provided at least in cases of wilful trademark counterfeiting or copyright piracy on a commercial scale.[273] It requires the remedies of 'imprisonment and/or monetary fines sufficient to provide a deterrent, consistently with the level of penalties applied for crimes of a corresponding gravity'. In appropriate cases, the remedies must also include 'the seizure, forfeiture and destruction of the infringing goods and of any materials and implements the predominant use of which has been in the commission of the offence'.[274]

6.5 Acquisition and Maintenance of Intellectual Property Rights

Part IV of the *TRIPS Agreement* deals with the procedural aspects of the acquisition and maintenance of IP rights. For practical reasons, formalities and procedures apply to the acquisition of IP rights (for example, through the registration of a trademark or filing of a patent) and to their maintenance. Article 62.1 acknowledges that Members may require compliance with reasonable procedures and formalities as a condition for the acquisition or maintenance of the IP rights provided for in the *TRIPS Agreement*, except copyright and undisclosed information.[275] The *TRIPS Agreement* cautions that the effective protection of IP rights can be undermined if these procedural requirements are used to unfairly

273 Members may, but are not obliged to, extend the application of criminal procedures and penalties to other cases of IP infringement, in particular where they are committed wilfully and on a commercial scale. The panel in *China – Intellectual Property Rights (2009)* did not endorse thresholds applied by China, but concluded that the factual evidence presented by the United States was inadequate to show whether or not the cases excluded from criminal liability met the TRIPS standard of 'commercial scale' when that standard is applied to China's marketplace. See Panel Report, *China – Intellectual Property Rights (2009)*, para. 7.614.

274 Taubman, Wager and Watal (eds.), *Handbook on the WTO TRIPS Agreement*, 152.

275 This is because, under Article 5.2 of the *Berne Convention (1971)*, copyrights cannot be subject to these types of formalities, and undisclosed information is by the very nature of the protected subject matter not subject to registration. See Correa, *Trade-Related Aspects of Intellectual Property Rights*, 467.

restrict the access to, and exercise of, these rights. Therefore, Article 62 of the *TRIPS Agreement* sets out the procedures and formalities for the acquisition and maintenance of IP rights. For example, Article 62.2 obliges Members to prevent unreasonable delays in procedures for the acquisition of IP rights, and Article 62.5 requires that decisions on the acquisition or maintenance of IP rights be subject to judicial or quasi-judicial review.

7 INSTITUTIONAL AND PROCEDURAL PROVISIONS OF THE *TRIPS AGREEMENT*

Parts V and VII of the *TRIPS Agreement* contain the provisions dealing with institutional and procedural arrangements. These provisions relate to: (1) the Council for TRIPS (Articles 68 and 71); (2) the transparency requirements (Article 63); (3) the rules on dispute settlement under the *TRIPS Agreement* (Article 64); (4) international cooperation between Members to prevent trade in goods that infringe IP rights (Article 69); and (5) the prohibition on reservations to the provisions of the *TRIPS Agreement* without the consent of other Members (Article 72). The most important of these provisions are briefly discussed in this section.

7.1 Council for TRIPS

Article 68 of the *TRIPS Agreement* provides for a 'Council for TRIPS' (also referred to as the 'TRIPS Council'), in which all WTO Members are represented.[276] Pursuant to Article 68, the tasks of the Council for TRIPS are: (1) to monitor the operation of the *TRIPS Agreement*, and, in particular, Members' compliance with their obligations thereunder; (2) to provide the possibility for Members to consult on matters relating to the trade-related aspects of IP rights; and (3) to carry out any other responsibilities assigned to it by the Members, and provide any assistance requested by them in the context of dispute settlement procedures.[277] In 2015, the TRIPS Council met three times. The TRIPS Council reports annually on its activities and developments regarding IP protection in the context of the WTO.[278] In carrying out its functions, the TRIPS Council may consult with or seek information from any source it deems appropriate. Within a year of its first meeting, the TRIPS Council was required to seek to establish appropriate arrangements for cooperation with WIPO. A cooperation agreement

276 See also above, pp. 134–6

277 Additional tasks of the TRIPS Council are, for example, set out in Articles 23.4 and 24.2 of the *TRIPS Agreement* (with regard to GIs) and Article 66.1 of the *TRIPS Agreement* (with regard to the extension of the transitional period for least-developed countries).

278 See e.g. Council for TRIPS, *Annual Report (2015)*, IP/C/71, dated 29 October 2015.

was concluded between the WTO and WIPO in 1995, and came into force on 1 January 1996.[279]

7.2 Transparency

Interestingly, the transparency provisions of the *TRIPS Agreement* are contained in Part V, entitled 'Dispute Settlement and Prevention'. This indicates that transparency with regard to IP protection is regarded as a way of preventing disputes between Members. Article 63 of the *TRIPS Agreement* lays down transparency obligations on Members. Under Article 63.1, Members are required, with regard not only to laws and regulations, but also to judicial decisions and administrative rulings of general application pertaining to the subject matter of the *TRIPS Agreement*, to publish them or, if this is impracticable, to make them publicly available in a manner that enables governments and IP right holders to become acquainted with them.[280] Article 63.2 requires Members to notify the TRIPS Council of any laws and regulations referred to in Article 63.1, to facilitate the Council's review of the operation of the *TRIPS Agreement*. Article 63.3 requires Members to supply information of the sort referred to in Article 63.1 or with regard to specific judicial decisions or administrative rulings in response to a written request by another Member.[281]

In *India – Patents (US) (1998)*, the panel found a violation by India of the transparency obligation in Article 63.1 due to the fact that an administrative ruling regarding the mechanism for the implementation of the 'mailbox' system for patent applications under Article 70.8(a) of the *TRIPS Agreement* had not been published or made publicly available.[282] India's argument that the existence of the mailbox system was recognised in a written answer by the government to a question in Parliament was rejected by the panel, which pointed out that such a way of conveying information could not be regarded as a sufficient means of publicity under Article 63.1 of the *TRIPS Agreement*.[283]

7.3 Dispute Settlement

One of the great achievements of the *TRIPS Agreement* is that it brings disputes regarding IP protection under the effective and enforceable mechanism for dispute settlement contained in the Dispute Settlement Understanding (DSU).

279 See www.wto.org/english/thewto_e/coher_e/wto_wipo_e.htm.

280 The subject matter of the *TRIPS Agreement* is defined as 'the availability, scope, acquisition, enforcement and prevention of the abuse of IP rights'. Article 63.1 further requires that agreements between Members or their governmental agencies concerning the subject matter of the *TRIPS Agreement* also be published.

281 See Article 63.4 of the *TRIPS Agreement*. Note that 'confidential information' is exempted from this obligation.

282 This finding was reversed by the Appellate Body on procedural grounds, as the terms of reference of the panel did not include Article 63 of the *TRIPS Agreement*. See Appellate Body Report, *India – Patents (US) (1998)*, paras. 85–6.

283 See Panel Report, *India – Patents (US) (1998)*, para. 7.48.

Article 64.1 of the *TRIPS Agreement* provides that the rules of Articles XXII and XXIII of the GATT 1994, as elaborated and applied by the DSU, apply to the settlement of disputes under that agreement, except as otherwise specifically provided therein. As noted by the Appellate Body in *India – Patents (US) (1998)*:

> As one of the covered agreements under the DSU, the *TRIPS Agreement* is subject to the dispute settlement rules and procedures of that Understanding.[284]

To date, thirty-three disputes have been initiated involving complaints under the *TRIPS Agreement*.[285] Of these, ten have resulted in panel reports and three eventually in Appellate Body reports.[286] Members have been found to have acted inconsistently with their obligations under the *TRIPS Agreement* in ten disputes.[287]

The *TRIPS Agreement* contains a specific provision deviating from the normal WTO dispute settlement rules. As discussed in Chapter 3, under normal dispute settlement rules, Members can bring three types of complaints: violation complaints, non-violation complaints and situation complaints.[288] There was strong resistance from developing countries during the Uruguay Round negotiations against inclusion of non-violation and situation complaints as a cause of action under the *TRIPS Agreement*, as they were concerned that this would create the possibility to extend the protection of the *TRIPS Agreement* beyond that specified in its provisions.[289] For this reason, Article 64.2 of the *TRIPS Agreement* provided that, for a period of five years from the entry into force of the *WTO Agreement*, no non-violation or situation complaints could be brought under the *TRIPS Agreement*. The moratorium under Article 64.2 of the *TRIPS Agreement* expired on 1 January 2000.[290] Under Article 64.3, the Council for TRIPS was directed to examine the scope and modalities for non-violation and situation complaints and make recommendations to the Ministerial Conference for approval. Any decision of the Ministerial Conference to adopt such recommendations or to extend the moratorium must be made by consensus.[291] The moratorium has been extended a number of times, under which Members have

284 Appellate Body Report, *India – Patents (US) (1998)*, para. 29.

285 See www.worldtradelaw.net/databases/agreementcount.php.

286 See www.worldtradelaw.net/dsc/database/trips.asp.

287 See *India – Patents (US) (1997); Indonesia – Autos (1998); India – Patents (EC) (1998); Canada – Pharmaceutical Patents (2000); US – Section 110(5) Copyright Act (2000); Canada – Patent Term (2000); US – Section 211 Appropriation Act (2002); EC – Trademarks and Geographical Indications (Australia) (2005); EC – Trademarks and Geographical Indications (US) (2005); and China – Intellectual Property Rights (2009)*.

288 See above, pp. 179–83.

289 Abbott notes two specific concerns of developing countries, namely, that developed countries would: (1) claim that the TRIPS provisions are intended to provide IP right holders with market access, not just protection of their IP rights; and (2) try to use the non-violation cause of action to 'expand the literal language of the TRIPS Agreement in light of whatever their "expectations" might have been about its effects'. F. M. Abbott, 'TRIPS in Seattle: The Not-So-Surprising Failure and the Future of the TRIPS Agenda', *Berkeley Journal of International Law*, 2000, 172.

290 With regard to Article 64.2 of the *TRIPS Agreement*, see Appellate Body Report, *India – Patents (US) (1998)*, paras. 36–42.

291 See Article 64.3 of the *TRIPS Agreement*.

agreed not to initiate non-violation or situation complaints under the *TRIPS Agreement* and to continue the examination of modalities for such complaints.[292] To date, no agreement has been reached on such modalities.

8 SPECIAL AND DIFFERENTIAL TREATMENT OF DEVELOPING-COUNTRY MEMBERS

The implementation of the obligations under the *TRIPS Agreement* requires regulatory capacity and an infrastructure for enforcement. This may create problems for developing-country Members in particular. The *TRIPS Agreement* thus provided, and to some extent still provides, for transitional periods for implementation of the obligations, and provides for technical cooperation.

8.1 Transitional Periods

Article 65.1 of the *TRIPS Agreement* provided a *one-year* implementation period for *all* Members from the entry into force of the *WTO Agreement.* Pursuant to Article 65.2 of the *TRIPS Agreement*, developing-country Members, and certain Members with economies in transition,[293] could delay implementation of the provisions of the *TRIPS Agreement* (other than Articles 3, 4 and 5) for a further four years, until 1 January 2000.[294] An additional five-year implementation period was added to this initial period by Article 65.4 of the *TRIPS Agreement* in respect of product patent protection for those developing-country Members which did not provide such protection to particular areas of technology at the time when the *TRIPS Agreement* became applicable to them under Article 65.2 of the *TRIPS Agreement.*[295] These transitional periods have now all come to an end. Only least-developed-country Members still 'benefit' from a transitional period. In view of their 'special needs and requirements', their 'economic financial and administrative constraints', and their need for 'flexibility to create a viable

292 This agreement was last renewed at the 2015 Nairobi Ministerial Conference. See Tenth WTO Ministerial Conference, Ministerial Decision on *TRIPS Non-Violation and Situation Complaints*, WT/L/976, dated 19 December 2015.

293 Note that only Members in transition from a centrally planned economy to a free-market economy that were undertaking structural reform of their IP systems and facing 'special problems' in preparing and implementing IP laws could make use of this additional transitional period. See Article 65.3 of the *TRIPS Agreement*.

294 Note that the transitional periods of Article 65 of the *TRIPS Agreement* do not apply to Article 70.8 (known as the 'mailbox' provision). See Panel Report, *India – Patents (US) (1998)*, para. 7.27. On Members' obligations under the 'mailbox' provision, see Appellate Body Report, *India – Patents (US) (1998)*, para. 58.

295 Note that Article 65.5 of the *TRIPS Agreement* contains an 'anti-rollback' obligation, i.e. an obligation that, during the implementation period, no changes could be made to national legislation that resulted in a lesser degree of consistency with the *TRIPS Agreement.* On Article 65.5 of the *TRIPS Agreement*, see also Panel Report, *Indonesia – Autos (1998)*, para. 14.282.

technological base', least-developed-country Members were given, in Article 66 of the *TRIPS Agreement*, a transitional period of eleven years, starting from the date of the entry into force of the *WTO Agreement*. The transitional period was thus due to expire on 1 January 2006. However, the TRIPS Council decided to further extend the transitional period first until 1 July 2013 and then again until 1 July 2021 or until the date on which the Member involved graduates from least-developed-country status, whichever date is the earlier.[296]

Paragraph 7 of the *Doha Declaration on the TRIPS Agreement and Public Health* states that least-developed-country Members will not be obliged, with respect to pharmaceutical products, to implement the obligations of the *TRIPS Agreement* regarding patents and the protection of undisclosed information or to enforce these IP rights until 1 January 2016. The TRIPS Council was directed to take the necessary action to give effect to this, pursuant to Article 66.1 of the *TRIPS Agreement*. In accordance with this direction, on 27 June 2002, the TRIPS Council approved a decision extending until 2016 the implementation period for least-developed-country Members with regard to *certain* obligations with respect to *pharmaceutical products*.[297] The TRIPS Council, on 6 November 2015, further extended the implementation period until 1 January 2033, or until the date on which the Member ceases to be a least-developed country, whichever date is earlier.[298] In addition, on 8 July 2002, the General Council approved a waiver exempting least-developed countries from the obligation under Article 70.9 of the *TRIPS Agreement* to provide exclusive marketing rights for any new drugs in the period when they do not provide patent protection.[299] The General Council further extended the waiver granted to least-developed countries from their obligations under Article 70.8 and 70.9 of the *TRIPS Agreement* until 1 January 2033, or until such a date on which the Member ceases to be a least-developed country, whichever date is earlier.[300]

296 See Council for TRIPS, Decision of 29 November 2005, *Extension of the Transition Period under Article 66.1 for the Least-Developed Country Members*, IP/C/40, dated 30 November 2005. On a further extension of the transitional period, see Council for TRIPS, *Request for an Extension of the Transitional Period under Article 66.1 of the TRIPS Agreement*, Communication from Haiti on behalf of the LDC Group, IP/C/W/583, dated 5 November 2012; and Council for TRIPS, *Extension of the Transitional Period under Article 66.1 of the TRIPS Agreement, Decision of the Council for TRIPS of 11 June 2013*, IP/C/64, dated 12 June 2013.

297 Council for TRIPS, *Extension of the Transition Period under Article 66.1 of the TRIPS Agreement for Least-Developed Country Members for Certain Obligations with Respect to Pharmaceutical Products, Decision of the Council for TRIPS of 27 June 2002*, IP/C/25, dated 1 July 2002.

298 Council for TRIPS, *Extension of the Transition Period under Article 66.1 of the TRIPS Agreement for Least-Developed Country Members for Certain Obligations with Respect to Pharmaceutical Products, Decision of the Council for TRIPS of 6 November 2015*, IP/C/73, dated 6 November 2015.

299 See General Council, *Least-Developed Country Members – Obligations under Article 70.9 of the TRIPS Agreement with Respect to Pharmaceutical Products. Decision of 8 July 2002*, WT/L/478, dated 12 July 2002.

300 General Council, *Least-Developed Country Members – Obligations under Article 70.8 and Article 70.9 of the TRIPS Agreement with Respect to Pharmaceutical Products. Decision of 30 November 2015*, WT/L/971, dated 2 December 2015.

8.2 Technical Assistance and Transfer of Technology

Article 67 of the *TRIPS Agreement* obliges developed-country Members to provide technical and financial assistance to developing- and least-developed-country Members, upon request and on mutually agreed terms and conditions. Such assistance includes helping with the preparation of legislation for the protection and enforcement of IP rights and the prevention of their abuse, and support for the establishment and maintenance of the relevant national offices and agencies, including training their staff. To make information on available technical assistance accessible and to facilitate the monitoring of compliance with the obligation of Article 67, developed-country Members have agreed to submit descriptions of their technical and financial cooperation programmes annually. Intergovernmental organisations have also presented, on the invitation of the TRIPS Council, information on their activities in order to promote transparency.[301] The Decision of the TRIPS Council of 29 November 2005 provided for further commitments on technical assistance for least-developed-country Members to help them prepare to implement the Agreement.[302]

Developed-country Members are also obliged, under Article 66.2 of the *TRIPS Agreement*, to provide incentives to their enterprises and institutions to promote the transfer of technology to least-developed-country Members so that they can create a 'sound and viable technological base'. In order to establish a mechanism for ensuring the monitoring and full implementation of the obligations in Article 66.2, as instructed in the Doha Decision on Implementation-Related Issues and Concerns,[303] the TRIPS Council adopted a decision on 19 February 2003.[304] In terms of this decision, developed-country Members must submit annual reports on actions taken or planned in pursuance of their commitments under Article 66.2.[305] The TRIPS Council must review these submissions at its end-of-year meeting each year, and Members shall have an opportunity to pose questions, request additional information and 'discuss the effectiveness of the incentives provided in promoting and encouraging technology transfer to least-developed-country Members in order to enable them to create a sound and viable technological base'.[306]

301 See www.wto.org/english/tratop_e/trips_e/intel9_e.htm. The information from developed-country Members, intergovernmental organisations and the WTO Secretariat on their technical cooperation activities with regard to the *TRIPS Agreement* is circulated in documents in the IP/C/W/series.

302 See Council for TRIPS, Decision of 29 November 2005, *Extension of the Transitional Period under Article 66.1 for Least-Developed-Country Members*, IP/C/40, dated 30 November 2005.

303 See Ministerial Conference, *Doha Decision on Implementation-Related Issues and Concerns*, WT/MIN(01)/17, dated 20 November 2001, para. 11.2.

304 See Council for TRIPS, Decision of 19 February 2003, *Implementation of Article 66.2 of the TRIPS Agreement*, IP/C/28, dated 20 February 2003.

305 Members must provide new detailed reports every third year and, in the intervening years, provide updates to their most recent reports. These reports must be submitted prior to the last Council meeting scheduled for the year in question. See *ibid.*, para. 1.

306 *Ibid.*, para. 2. Paragraph 3 of this decision sets out the information which must be provided in these annual submissions.

9 SUMMARY

The *Agreement on Trade-Related Aspects of Intellectual Property Rights* (the '*TRIPS Agreement*') reflects the recognition that trade and intellectual property protection are closely connected. The achievements in liberalisation of trade through disciplines on trade barriers can be greatly undermined if the IP rights related to the traded goods or services are not respected. The *TRIPS Agreement* is arguably the most innovative of the WTO agreements. It was the first trade agreement to establish positive regulatory obligations for Members to ensure a minimum level of protection and enforcement of IP rights in their territories. The need to balance the competing interests of holders of IP rights on the one hand and the public interest on the other forms the basic rationale underlying the rights and obligations laid down in the *TRIPS Agreement*. The *Doha Declaration on the TRIPS Agreement and Public Health* reaffirms the right of WTO Members to use, to the full, the provisions in the *TRIPS Agreement*, providing flexibilities for Members in order to protect public health.

The *TRIPS Agreement* builds upon the standards of IP protection enshrined in pre-existing IP conventions administered by the World Intellectual Property Organization (WIPO). It does so by incorporating by reference specific provisions of the relevant conventions, namely, the *Paris Convention (1967)*, the *Berne Convention (1971)*, the *Rome Convention* and the *IPIC Treaty*. The obligations of the *TRIPS Agreement* must, therefore, be read together with the relevant WIPO conventions. However, the *TRIPS Agreement* does more than simply incorporate the substantive provisions of these conventions. It supplements and updates the rules of the relevant WIPO conventions, as well as expressly provides new rules in some areas. In addition, it creates an obligation on Members to have a system in place for the enforcement of the protected IP rights, and links them to the effective and enforceable dispute settlement system of the WTO.

The *TRIPS Agreement* does *not* cover every form of IP right, but only those expressly mentioned in Sections 1–7 of Part II *as well as* those in the incorporated conventions that are the 'subject matter' of these Sections. These Sections address: (1) copyright and related rights; (2) trademarks; (3) geographical indications; (4) industrial design; (5) patents; (6) layout designs of integrated circuits; and (7) protection of undisclosed information. The *TRIPS Agreement* does not apply retroactively to *acts* that occurred before its 'date of application' for a Member. In contrast, the *TRIPS Agreement* does create obligations in respect of *subject matter* that existed at the date of application of the *TRIPS Agreement*.

The *TRIPS Agreement* obliges Members to 'give effect' to its provisions, but leaves Members 'free to determine the appropriate method' of implementing their obligations under the *TRIPS Agreement* within their own legal systems and practice. In addition, Members may, but are not obliged to, implement more extensive protection than that laid down in the *TRIPS Agreement*. The *TRIPS Agreement* therefore lays down a *minimum level* of harmonised IP protection.

The non-discrimination obligations of national treatment and MFN treatment apply also in the context of the *TRIPS Agreement*. However, there are some differences in their formulation compared to the national treatment and MFN treatment obligations of the GATT 1994 and the GATS, in order to take into account the intangible nature of IP rights. These obligations apply only to the IP rights covered by the *TRIPS Agreement* (including in the incorporated conventions) and apply to 'nationals' as defined in Article 1.3 of the *TRIPS Agreement*, rather than to 'like products' or 'like services or service providers' as is the case in the GATT 1994 and GATS respectively. Both the national treatment and the MFN treatment obligations in the *TRIPS Agreement* are subject to specific exceptions.

The *TRIPS Agreement* does not mandate a particular approach to the exhaustion of IP rights. Members are free to choose their own approach to this matter, provided that they apply their chosen approach in a non-discriminatory manner.

Part II of the *TRIPS Agreement* contains the mandatory minimum standards of IP protection that Members are obliged to provide in their territories to nationals of other Members. Sections 1–7 of Part II contain standards relating to various categories of IP rights (including copyright, trademarks, geographical indications and patents) and set out, as a minimum, the *subject matter* which is eligible for protection, the scope of the *rights conferred* by the relevant category of intellectual property and permitted *exceptions* to those rights.

The protection of IP depends not only on substantive norms providing minimum standards of protection, but also on procedural rules providing effective means to enforce them. Part III of the *TRIPS Agreement* therefore contains rules on enforcement of IP rights. This constitutes a significant innovation by which the *TRIPS Agreement* supplements the existing WIPO conventions and strengthens the protection of IP rights. Members are required to ensure that the enforcement procedures specified in Part III are available under their law 'so as to permit effective action' against infringement of IP rights protected in the *TRIPS Agreement*, including by providing expeditious remedies to *prevent* infringements and remedies to *deter* further infringements. In general, Members are required to have civil *judicial* procedures available for the enforcement of any IP right covered by the *TRIPS Agreement*. Criminal procedures and penalties must be provided at least in cases of wilful trademark counterfeiting or copyright piracy on a commercial scale.

Part IV of the *TRIPS Agreement* deals with the procedural aspects of the acquisition and maintenance of IP rights. It allows Members to require compliance with procedures and formalities as a condition for the acquisition or maintenance of IP rights (except copyright and undisclosed information), but limits these to what is 'reasonable'.

Part V of the *TRIPS Agreement* sets out rules with regard to transparency and dispute settlement. Members are required to publish not only laws and regulations, but also judicial decisions and administrative rulings of general application pertaining to the subject matter of the *TRIPS Agreement*. If this is impracticable, Members must make them publicly available in a manner that enables governments and IP right holders to become acquainted with them. The WTO dispute settlement rules and procedures, discussed in Chapter 3, apply to disputes under the *TRIPS Agreement*. The *TRIPS Agreement* contains one special dispute settlement rule, with regard to the possible causes of action. For a period of five years from the entry into force of the *WTO Agreement*, no non-violation or situation complaints could be brought under the *TRIPS Agreement*. This moratorium has been extended a number of times, but no agreement has yet been reached on modalities for such complaints.

Members consult on all matters pertaining to the *TRIPS Agreement* in the TRIPS Council, which comprises all WTO Members.

Finally, the *TRIPS Agreement* acknowledges the difficulties developing-country Members may face in implementing their obligations under that Agreement. It thus provided, and still continues to provide, for least-developed-country Members, for transition periods for implementation of the obligations, and contains commitments on technical cooperation and incentives for transfer of technology.

FURTHER READINGS

N. Kuei-Jung, 'Legal Aspects (Barriers) of Granting Compulsory Licenses for Clean Technologies in Light of WTO/TRIPS Rules: Promise or Mirage?', *World Trade Review*, June 2015, 1–19.

T. Cottier, S. Lalani and M. Temmerman, 'Use It or Lose It: Assessing the Compatibility of the Paris Convention and TRIPS Agreement with Respect to Local Working Requirements', *Journal of International Economic Law*, 2014, 17(2), 437–71.

P. Zapatero Miguel, 'Trade in Generics v. World-Scale Market Segmentation: Market-Driven Solutions to the "Paragraph 6" Issue', *Journal of World Trade*, 2014, 48(1), 81–110.

C. Wadlow, 'The Beneficiaries of TRIPs: Some Questions of Rights, Ressortissants and International Locus Standi', *European Journal of International Law*, 2014, 25(1), 59–82.

Kil Won Lee, 'Suspending TRIPS Obligations as a Viable Option for Developing Countries to Enforce WTO Rulings', *Asian Journal of WTO and International Health Law and Policy*, 2014, 9, 217.

A. Slade, 'Good Faith and the TRIPS Agreement: Putting Flesh on the Bones of the TRIPS "Objectives"', *International and Comparative Law Quarterly*, 2014, 63(2), 353–83.

T. Cottier and M. Foltea, 'Global Governance in Intellectual Property Protection: Does the Decision-making Forum Matter?', *WIPO Journal*, 2012, 3(2), 139.

B. Mercurio, '"Seizing" Pharmaceuticals in Transit: Analysing the WTO Dispute That Wasn't', *International and Comparative Law Quarterly*, 2012, 61(2), 389–426.

R. K. Rai and S. Jagannathan, 'Parallel Imports and Unparallel Laws: Does the WTO Need to Harmonize the Parallel Import Law?', *Journal of World Trade*, 2012, 46(3), 657–94.

R. Valdés and R. Tavengwa, 'Intellectual Property Provisions in Regional Trade Agreements', Staff Working Paper ERSD-2012-21, October 2012, WTO.

J. Pauwelyn, 'The Dog That Barked But Didn't Bite: 15 Years of Intellectual Property Disputes at the WTO', *Journal of International Dispute Settlement*, 2010, 1(2), 389–42.

S. Frankel, 'Challenging TRIPS-Plus Agreements: The Potential Utility of Non-Violation Disputes', *Journal of International Economic Law*, 2009, 12(4), 1023–65.

A. D. Mitchell and T. Voon, 'Patents and Public Health in the WTO, FTAs and Beyond: Tension and Conflict in International Law', *Journal of World Trade*, 2009, 43(3), 571–601.

INDEX